Philosophy: The Classic Readings

PHILOSOPHY:
THE CLASSIC READINGS

Edited by

David E. Cooper

and

Peter S. Fosl

WILEY-BLACKWELL

A John Wiley & Sons, Ltd., Publication

Library of Congress Cataloging-in-Publication Data
Philosophy : the classic readings / edited by David E. Cooper and Peter S. Fosl.
    p. cm.
   Includes bibliographical references and index.
   ISBN 978-1-4051-4585-5 (hardcover : alk. paper) – ISBN 978-1-4051-4586-2 (pbk. : alk. paper)
   1. Philosophy.   I. Cooper, David E. (David Edward)   II. Fosl, Peter S.
   B72.P485 2010
   100–dc22
                                                              2009007106
A catalogue record for this book is available from the British Library.

Set in 9.5/11pt Minion by Graphicraft Limited, Hong Kong
Printed and bound in Singapore by Fabulous Printers Pte Ltd

1   2010

For Guy Montag and all those who fight the firemen.

Contents

Acknowledgments

The editors wish to acknowledge the generous support of Transylvania University, Bellarmine University, and the University of Durham in making this volume possible. Ann Cranfill in particular performed heroic work preparing primary texts. We wish to thank Anthony Cerulli, Ellen Cox, and Jack Furlong with advice on the introductions and with the selection of entries for the volume. The editorial work of Liz Cremona and Nick Bellorini at Wiley-Blackwell has proven invaluable, and we also thank Sarah M. Hall for her copy-editing. For seeing the book through its final stages, we express our thanks to Kathy Auger, Project Manager for Graphicraft Ltd. Thanks, too, to Ellen Cox, Simona Fojtova, Jack Furlong, Melissa Fortner, Melissa McEuen, Greg Partain, Veronica Dean-Thacker, Kremena Todorova and Meg Upchurch for their assistance with proof-reading. We are also extremely grateful for the patient support of our families in bringing this text to its realization.

Source Acknowledgments

The editor and publisher gratefully acknowledge the permission granted to reproduce the copyright material in this book:

Part I

I.1
From Plato, *Gorgias*, trans. Benjamin Jowett, Harmondsworth: Penguin, 1960.

I.2
Aristotle, *Nicomachean Ethics*, Book I, from *Aristotle's Ethics*, ed. J. L. Ackrill and trans. W. D. Ross (with amendments by J. L. Ackrill), London: Faber & Faber, 1973, pp. 41–60. © 1973 by Oxford University Press. Reprinted with permission from Oxford University Press.

I.3
Epicurus, "Letter to Menoeceus" and "Leading Doctrines," from Epicurus, *The Philosophy of Epicurus*, trans. G. K. Strodach, Evanston, IL: Northwestern University Press, 1963, pp. 178–85, 196–203. © 1963 by Northwestern University Press.

I.4
Mencius, "Human Nature Is Good," from Mencius, *The Works of Mencius*, trans. James Legge, London: Trübner, 1861, pp. 270–97.

Hsun Tzu, "Man's Nature Is Evil," from *Basic Writings of Mo Tzu, Hsun Tzu and Han Fei Tzu*, trans. Burton Watson, New York: Columbia University Press, 1967, pp. 157–71. © 1967 by Columbia University Press. Reprinted with permission from Columbia University Press.

I.5
Chapters 9, 13, and 14 from *The Book of Chuang Tzu*, trans. Martin Palmer with Elizabeth Breuilly, Chang Wai Ming and Jay Ramsay, Harmondsworth: Penguin, 1996, pp. 72–4, 106–14, 118, 122–7. © 1996 by ICOREC. Reproduced by permission of Penguin Books Ltd.

I.6
Chapters 1–5 from *The Bhagavad Gita*, trans. W. J. Johnson, Oxford: Oxford University Press, 1994, pp. 4–24. © 1994 by W. J. Johnson. Reprinted with permission from Oxford University Press.

I.7
Cicero, *De finibus* and *De officiis* from *Cicero: Volume XXI*, Loeb Classical Library Volume 30, trans. Walter Miller, Cambridge, MA: Harvard University Press, 1913, pp. 3–47, and *Cicero: Volume XVII*, Loeb Classical Library Volume 40, trans. H. Rackham, Cambridge, MA: Harvard University Press, 1914, pp. 217–55, 281–97. The Loeb Classical Library® is a registered trademark of the President and Fellows of Harvard College. Reprinted by permission of the publishers and the Trustees of the Loeb Classical Library.

I.8
Marcus Aurelius, *The Meditations*, trans. G. M. A. Grube, Indianapolis, IN: Hackett, 1983, pp. 19–48,

86–8. © 1983 by Hackett Publishing. Reprinted by permission of Hackett Publishing Company, Inc. All rights reserved.

I.9
Śāntideva, Chapter 8 (verses 89–140), from *The Bodhicaryāvatāra*, trans. K. Crosby and A. Skilton, Oxford: Oxford University Press, 1996, pp. 96–100. © 1995 by Kate Crosby and Andrew Skilton. Reprinted with permission from Oxford University Press.

Tsongkapa and Pabongka Rinpoche, "The Second Path," from *The Principle Teachings of Buddhism*, with a commentary by Pabongka Rinpoche, trans. L. Tharchin and M. Roach, Howell, NJ: Mahayana Sutra and Tantra Press, 1988, pp. 93–104. © 1988. Reprinted with permission from the publisher, Mahayana Sutra and Tantra Press, 112 West 2nd Street, Howell, NJ 07731.

I.10
Plotinus, *Enneads* (selection), from *The Essential Plotinus*, 2nd edn, ed. and trans. E. O'Brien, Indianapolis, IN: Hackett, 1986, pp. 65–70. © 1964 by Elmer O'Brien, S.J. Reprinted by permission of Hackett Publishing Company, Inc. All rights reserved.

I.11
St Thomas Aquinas, *Summa theologica*, I–II, Questions 55, 58, 61–3, from St Thomas Aquinas, *Aquinas Ethicus: or, The Moral Teaching of St Thomas*, vol. 1, trans. J. Rickaby, London: Burns & Oates, 1896, pp. 155, 167–74, 179–87.

I.12
Giovanni Pico della Mirandola, "Oration on the Dignity of Man," trans. E. Livermore Forbes, from *The Renaissance Philosophy of Man*, ed. E. Cassirer, P. O. Kristeller, and J. H. Randall, Jr, Chicago: University of Chicago Press, 1948, pp. 223–54. © 1948 by University of Chicago. Reprinted with permission from University of Chicago Press.

I.13
Benedict de Spinoza, *Ethics*, Book V, from Benedict de Spinoza, *On the Improvement of Understanding: The Ethics Correspondence*, trans. R. H. M. Elwes, New York: Dover, 1955, pp. 244–71.

I.14
David Hume, Book III, Part I (sections 1–2), from David Hume, *A Treatise of Human Nature*, ed. L. A. Selby-Bigge, Oxford: Clarendon Press, 1902, pp. 455–76.

I.15
Immanuel Kant, Preface and Section 1, from Immanuel Kant, *Fundamental Principles of the Metaphysics of Morals*, trans. T. K. Abbott, Buffalo, NY: Prometheus, 1987, pp. 9–13, 17–33.

I.16
John Stuart Mill, *Utilitarianism*, Chapter 2, from John Stuart Mill, *The Ethics of John Stuart Mill*, ed. C. Douglas, Edinburgh: Blackwood & Sons, 1897, pp. 89–127.

I.17
Søren Kierkegaard, *Fear and Trembling*, Problema I, from Søren Kierkegaard, *Fear and Trembling*, trans. A. Hannay, Harmondsworth: Penguin, 1985, pp. 83–95. © 1985 by Alastair Hannay. Reproduced by permission of Penguin Books Ltd.

I.18
Friedrich Nietzsche, *On the Genealogy of Morals*, First Essay, Sections 2–14, 16, from Friedrich Nietzsche, *The Basic Writings of Nietzsche*, trans. and ed. Walter Kaufmann, New York: The Modern Library, 1968. © 1967 by Walter Kaufmann. Copyright renewed © 1994 by Mrs Hazel Kaufmann. Used by permission of Random House, Inc.

I.19
G. E. Moore, *Principia Ethica*, Chapter 1, sections 1–2, 5–15, from G. E. Moore, *Principia Ethica*, Cambridge: Cambridge University Press, 1960, pp. 1–3, 5–21. © 1960 by Cambridge University Press. Reprinted with permission of the author's estate and Cambridge University Press.

I.20
W. D. Ross, *The Right and the Good*, Chapter 2, from W. D. Ross, *The Right and the Good*, Oxford: Clarendon Press, 1930, pp. 16–24, 28–37. © 1930 by Oxford University Press. Reprinted with permission from Oxford University Press.

I.21
Tanabe Hajime, Preface, from Tanabe Hajime, *Philosophy as Metanoetics*, trans. T. Yoshinori, Berkeley: University of California Press, 1986, pp. il–lxii. © 1986 by The Regents of the University of California. Reprinted by permission of The University of California Press.

I.22
Charles L. Stevenson, "The Emotive Meaning of Ethical Terms," from Charles L. Stevenson, *Facts and Values: Studies in Ethical Analysis*, New Haven, CT: Yale University Press, 1963, pp. 10–31. © 1963 by Charles L. Stevenson. Reprinted with permission from Yale University Press.

I.23
Jean-Paul Sartre, "Existentialism Is a Humanism," trans Philip Mairet, from *Existentialism from Dostoevsky to Sartre*, ed. W. Kaufmann, New York: Meridian Books, 1975, pp. 345–69. Originally a 1946 lecture in French entitled "L'Existentialisme est un Humanisme." © 1996 by Editions Gallimard. The English translation is original to Jean-Paul Sartre, *Existentialism and Humanism*, trans. Philip Mairet, London: Methuen Publishing Ltd (new edn 2007). Reprinted by permission of Methuen Publishing Ltd and Georges Borchardt, Inc., for Editions Gallimard.

I.24
Simone de Beauvoir, "Myth and Reality" and "Conclusion," from Simone de Beauvoir, *The Second Sex*, trans. and ed. H. M. Parshley, New York: Alfred A. Knopf, 1978, pp. 253–63, 724–26, 730–32. © 1952 and renewed 1980 by Alfred A. Knopf, a division of Random House, Inc. © 1953 by Jonathan Cape. Used by permission of Alfred A. Knopf, a division of Random House, Inc., and The Random House Group Limited. A new English translation is due to be published in 2009 by Jonathan Cape (London) and Knopf (New York).

Part II

II.1
Plato, 475e–480a, 506d–518c from Plato, *Republic*, trans. Robin Waterfield, Oxford: Oxford University Press, 1993, pp. 196–202, 233–45. © 1993 by Robin Waterfield. Reprinted with permission from Oxford University Press.

II.2
Aristotle, *Posterior Analytics*, Book I, 1–4, 31 and Book III, 19, from *The Oxford Translation of Aristotle*, ed. W. D. Ross, vol. I, trans. G. R. G. Mure. Oxford: Oxford University Press, 1928. © 1928 by Oxford University Press. Reprinted with permission from Oxford University Press.

II.3
Chapter 2 from *The Book of Chuang Tzu*, trans. Martin Palmer with Elizabeth Breuilly, Chang Wai Ming and Jay Ramsay, Harmondsworth: Penguin, 1996, pp. 8–20. © 1996 by ICOREC. Reproduced by permission of Penguin Books Ltd.

II.4
Sextus Empiricus, *Outlines of Pyrrhonism*, Book I, Sections 1–16, 18–27, from Sextus Empiricus, *The Skeptic Way: Sextus Empiricus's Outlines of Pyrrhonism*, trans. Benson Mates, Oxford: Oxford University Press, 1996, pp. 89–94, 110–17. © 1996 by Benson Mates. Reprinted with permission from Oxford University Press.

II.5
Nyāya-Sūtras, Book I, Chapter 1 and Book II, Chapter 1, with Vātsyāyana's Commentary from *The Nyāya-Sūtras of Gotama*, ed. N. Sinha and trans. S. C. Vidyabhusana, Delhi: Motilal Banarsidass, 1981, pp. 1–6, 32, 34–7, 48–9, 232–7, 248–51, 255–6. © 1981. Reprinted with permission from Motilal Banarsidass, Delhi.

II.6
Thomas Aquinas, *De veritate*, Question One, Articles I–III and VIII–IX, from St Thomas Aquinas, *Truth*, vol. I, trans. Robert W. Mulligan, Indianapolis, IN: Hackett, 1994, pp. 3–14, 36–42; Question Ten, Articles I, IV–VI, XI–XII, from St Thomas Aquinas, *Truth*, vol. II, trans. James V. McGlynn, Indianapolis, IN: Hackett, 1994, pp. 3–8, 18–30, 58–71. © 1994 by Hackett. Reprinted by permission of Hackett Publishing Company, Inc. All rights reserved.

II.7
Francis Bacon, *Novum Organum* I: selected *Aphorisms*, from Francis Bacon, *Advancement of Learning and Novum Organum*, ed. J. E. Creighton, New York: Wiley Book Co., 1944, pp. 315–31, 349–53.

II.8
René Descartes, *Meditations on First Philosophy*, I–III, and "Objections and Replies" (selections), from *Descartes: Meditations of First Philosophy (with Selections from the Objections and Replies)*, 2nd edn, trans. J. Cottingham, Cambridge: Cambridge University Press, 1996, pp. 12–25, 63–70. © 1996 by Cambridge University Press. Reprinted with permission from the translator and Cambridge University Press.

II.9
John Locke, Book I, Chapter 2, Sections 1–24, from John Locke, *An Essay Concerning Human Understanding*, ed. John W. Yolton, vol. 1, London: Dent, 1961, pp. 9–22.

G. W. Leibniz, *New Essays on the Human Understanding*, Preface, from Gottfried Wilhelm Leibniz, *Philosophical Writings*, ed. G. Parkinson, London: J. M. Dent, 1973, pp. 150–4. © 1973. Reprinted by permission of Everyman's Library, an imprint of Alfred A. Knopf.

II.10
Giambattista Vico, "Poetic Wisdom," from Giambattista Vico, *The New Science of Giambattista Vico*, ed. T. G. Bergen and M. H. Fisch, New York: Anchor Books, 1961, pp. 69–87. Reprinted from Giambattista Vico, *The New Science of Giambattista Vico: Unabridged Translation of the Third Edition (1744) with the addition of "Practice of the New Science*," trans. Thomas Goddard Bergin and Max Harold Fisch. © 1948 by Cornell University. Rev. and abr. edn © 1961 by Thomas Goddard Bergin and Max Harold Fisch. Rev. and unabr. edn © 1968 by Cornell University. Used by permission of the publisher, Cornell University Press.

David Hume, "Of the Idea of Necessary Connexion" and "Of the Academical or Sceptical Philosophy," from David Hume, *Enquiries Concerning the Human Understanding and Concerning the Principles of Morals*, 2nd edn, ed. L. A. Selby-Bigge, Oxford: Clarendon Press, 1902, pp. 60–79, 148–65.

II.11
Thomas Reid, Essay 6, Chapter 5, from Thomas Reid, *Essays on the Intellectual Powers of Man*, ed. A. D. Woozley, London: Macmillan, 1941, pp. 372–91.

II.12
Immanuel Kant, Introduction, Sections I–VI, from Immanuel Kant, *Critique of Pure Reason*, 2nd edn, trans. Werner S. Pluhar, Indianapolis, IN: Hackett, 1996, pp. 43–63. © 1996 by Hackett Publishing Company, Inc. Reprinted by permission of Hackett Publishing Company, Inc. All rights reserved.

II.13
G. W. F. Hegel, Sections 73–103, from G. W. F. Hegel, *Phenomenology of Spirit*, trans. A.V. Miller, Oxford: Oxford University Press, 1977, pp. 46–62. © 1977 by Oxford University Press. Reprinted with permission from Oxford University Press.

II.14
John Stuart Mill, Book II, Chapters V–VII (selections), from John Stuart Mill, *A System of Logic: Ratiocinative and Inductive*, London: Longmans, Green & Co., 1886, pp. 147–9, 151–3, 164–70, 183–4.

II.15
Arthur Schopenhauer, "On the Possibility of Knowing the Thing-in-Itself," Chapter 18 from Arthur Schopenhauer, *The World as Will and Representation*, vol. II., trans. E. F. J. Payne, New York: Dover Publications, Inc., 1958, pp. 191–200. © 1958 by The Falcon's Wing Press. Reprinted with permission from Dover Publications, Inc.

II.16
Søren Kierkegaard, "Truth Is Subjectivity," from Søren Kierkegaard, *Kierkegaard's Concluding Unscientific Postscript*, trans. D. F. Swenson and W. Lowrie, Princeton, NJ: Princeton University Press, 1941, pp. 169–83. © 1941 by Princeton University Press, renewed 1969. Reprinted by permission of Princeton University Press.

II.17
Friedrich Nietzsche, "On Truth and Lies in a Nonmoral Sense," from Friedrich Nietzsche, *Philosophy and Truth: Selections from Nietzsche's Notebooks of the Early 1870s*, ed. and trans. Daniel Breazeale, Amherst, NY: Humanity Books, 1979, pp. 79–91, 93–4, 97. © 1979 by Daniel Breazeale. All rights reserved. Reprinted with permission from the publisher, Humanity Books.

II.18
Charles S. Peirce, "Some Consequences of Four Incapacities" (excerpt) and "The Fixation of Belief," from Charles S. Peirce, *Selected Writings*, ed. P. Wiener. New York: Dover, 1966, pp. 39–41, 92–112.

II.19
Edmund Husserl, Lectures 1–2, from Edmund Husserl, *The Idea of Phenomenology*, trans. W. P. Alston, The Hague: Nijhoff, 1964, pp. 13–32. © 1964 by W. P. Alston. Reprinted with kind permission from Springer Science and Business Media.

II.20
Bertrand Russell, "Knowledge by Acquaintance and Knowledge by Description," from Bertrand Russell, *The Problems of Philosophy*, Oxford: Oxford University Press, 1959, pp. 46–59. © 1959 by Bertrand Russell. Reprinted with permission from Oxford University Press.

II.21
Moritz Schlick, "On the Foundation of Knowledge," from Moritz Schlick, *Philosophical Papers, Volume II (1925–1936)*, ed. H. L. Mulder and B. van de Velde-Schlick, Dordrecht: D. Reidel, 1979. © 1980 by Albert M. Schlick and Barbara F. B. van de Velde-Schlick. Reprinted with kind permission from Springer Science and Business Media.

Karl R. Popper, Chapter 10 and Addendum from Karl R. Popper, *The Logic of Scientific Discovery*, New York: Basic Books, 1959, pp. 251–81. © Karl Raimund Popper, 1959. Reprinted with permission from the Karl-Popper-Sammlung, Universitätsbibliothek Klagenfurt. The "Addendum" to Chapter 10 of *The Logic of Scientific Discovery* does not appear in the 1959 edition by Basic Books, but is printed in later editions, for example Hutchinson (8th impr., London: 1975) and Routlege (London and New York: 2002). Permission to reprint the Addendum is kindly granted by the Karl-Popper-Sammlung, Universitätsbibliothek Klagenfurt.

II.22
Martin Heidegger, "*Dasein*, Disclosedness, and Truth," from Martin Heidegger, *Being and Time*, ed. J. Macquarrie and E. Robinson, San Francisco: Harper & Row, 1962, pp. 256–69. Translation © 1962 by Blackwell Publishing Ltd. Reprinted by permission of HarperCollins Publishers and Blackwell Publishing Ltd.

II.23
Ludwig Wittgenstein, Sections 60–81, 112–16, 269–75, from Ludwig Wittgenstein, *Philosophical Investigations*, 3rd edn, trans. G. E. M. Anscombe, Oxford: Blackwell Publishing, 2001, pp. e25–e33, e47–e41, e80–e81. © 1953, 1958, 2001 by Blackwell Publishing Ltd. Reproduced with permission of Blackwell Publishing Ltd.

II.24
Maurice Merleau-Ponty, Preface, from Maurice Merleau-Ponty, *The Phenomenology of Perception*, trans. C. Smith, New York: The Humanities Press, 1962, pp. vii–xxi. © 1962 by Brill Academic Publishers. Reproduced with permission from Brill Academic Publishers in the format Textbook via Copyright Clearance Center.

II.25
W. V. O. Quine, "Two Dogmas of Empiricism," from W. V. O. Quine, *From a Logical Point of View: Logico-Philosophical Essays*, 2nd edn, New York: Harper & Row, 1961. pp. 20–46. © 1953, 1961, 1980 by the President and Fellows of Harvard College, renewed 1989 by W. V. O. Quine. Reprinted by permission of Harvard University Press.

Part III

III.1
Tao Te Ching (selected chapters), from *A Source Book in Chinese Philosophy*, trans. Wing-Tsit Chan, Princeton, NJ: Princeton University Press, 1969, pp. 139–50, 152–54, 156–64, 166, 172. © 1963 by Princeton University Press, 1991 renewed PUP. Reprinted by permission of Princeton University Press.

III.2
Heraclitus of Ephesus, selected fragments from *Heraclitus: The Cosmic Fragments*, ed. G. S. Kirk, Cambridge: Cambridge University Press, 1970, pp. 48, 57, 65, 97, 105, 113, 116, 135, 155, 168, 180, 184, 203, 238, 245, 250, 258, 284, 307, 325, 339, 345, 349, 362, 367, 381, 386, 392. © 1970 by Cambridge University Press. Reprinted with permission from Cambridge University Press.

Parmenides of Elea, "The Way of Truth" (fr. 344–55), from *The Presocratic Philosophers*, ed. G. S. Kirk and J. E. Raven, Cambridge: Cambridge University Press, 1957, pp. 269–81. © 1957 by Cambridge University Press. Reprinted with permission from Cambridge University Press.

III.3
Plato, *Phaedrus*, 245–50, from Plato, *The Dialogues of Plato*, vol. 1, trans. B. Jowett, New York: Macmillan & Co., 1892, pp. 451–7.

III.4
Aristotle, *Metaphysica* Books I.1–2, VI, VII, XII.1–10; Books "Alpha" (Chapters 1 and 2) and "Lambda," from *The Oxford Translation of Aristotle*, ed. W. D. Ross, Oxford: Oxford University Press, 1971. © 1971 by Oxford University

Press. Reprinted with permission from Oxford University Press.

III.5
Gotama (the Buddha), Sayings on "Conditional Genesis," and *Lalitavistara*, XIII, 95–117, from *Buddhist Texts Through the Ages*, trans. and ed. Edward Conze, Boston, MA: Shambhala, 1990, pp. 65–70, 91–4, 158–61. © 1990 by Edward Conze, Reprinted with permission from Oneworld Publications.

Nāgārjuna, *Madhyamaka-Kārikā*, Dedication and Chapter XXV from Theodore Stcherbatsky, *The Conception of Buddhist Nirvana*, Delhi: Motilal Banarsidass, 1977, pp. 77, 81–4. © 1977. Reprinted with permission from Motilal Banarsidass, Delhi.

III.6
Plotinus, Sections 1–7 and 10, from *Plotinus, The Enneads*, trans. S. MacKenna, abr. John Dillon, London: Penguin, 1991, pp. 347–56, 358–60. © 1991 by John Dillon. Reproduced by permission of Penguin Books Ltd.

III.7
Śaṁkara, *Brahmasūtrabhāṣya* (selections), from *A Source Book of Advaita Vedānta*, ed. Eliot Deutsch and J. A. B. van Buitenen, trans. George Thibaut, Honolulu: University Press of Hawaii, 1971. pp. 151–6, 158–60, 162–5, 173–85, 189–90, 196–8. © 1971 by University of Hawai'i Press. Reprinted with permission from University of Hawai'i Press.

III.8
Ibn Sina (Avicenna), *Kitab al-Shifa*, Book I, Chapters Six and Seven, Book II, Chapters Two and Three, from Avicenna, *The Metaphysics of The Healing*, ed. and trans. M. E. Marmura, Provo, UT: Brigham Young University Press, 2005, pp. 29–38, 48–63. © 2005 by Brigham Young University Press. Reprinted by permission of Brigham Young University.

III.9
Chu Hsi, *Recorded Sayings* (selections), from *Wing-Tsit Chan, A Source Book in Chinese Philosophy*, Princeton, NJ: Princeton University Press, 1963, pp. 623–43. © 1963 by Princeton University Press, 1991 renewed PUP. Reprinted by permission of Princeton University Press.

III.10
Thomas Aquinas, Introduction and Chapters I–II, IV–V, from Thomas Aquinas, *On Being and Essence*, trans. A. Maurer, Toronto: The Pontifical Institute of Mediaeval Studies, 1949, pp. 25–59. © 1949 by The Pontifical Institute of Mediaeval Studies. Reprinted with the permission of The Pontifical Institute of Medieval Studies.

III.11
Duns Scotus, *Ordinatio* (or Oxford Commentary on the Sentences of Peter Lombard) I.1–5, from Duns Scotus, *Philosophical Writings*, ed. A. Wolter, Edinburgh: Thomas Nelson and Sons Ltd, 1962, pp. 2–12. © 1962 by Allan Wolter.

III.12
René Descartes, *Principles of Philosophy*, Part I, from *Descartes: Selected Philosophical Writings*, trans. J. Cottingham, R. Stoothoff and D. Murdoch, Cambridge: Cambridge University Press, 1988, pp. 160–66, 169–70, 172–75, 188.

Princess Elisabeth, selections from her correspondence with Descartes, from *Women Philosophers of the Early Modern Period*, ed. Margaret Atherton, Indianapolis, IN: Hackett, 1994, pp. 11–21. This material was originally published in *Descartes: His Moral Philosophy and Psychology*, trans. John J. Blom, New York: New York University Press, 1978, pp. 105–16. © 1978 by John J. Blom.

III.13
Benedict de Spinoza, Part I, from Benedict de Spinoza, *Ethics*, ed. and trans. E. Curley. Harmondsworth: Penguin, 1996. pp. 1–10, 13–23, 25. This material originally appeared in Edwin Curley, *A Spinoza Reader*. © 1994 Princeton University Press. Reprinted by permission of Princeton University Press.

III.14
John Locke, Book II, Chapters VIII (sections 7–26) and XXIII (sections 1–11), from John Locke, *An Essay Concerning Human Understanding*, vol. I, ed. J. W. Yolton, London: J. M. Dent & Sons, 1961, pp. 103–11, 244–50.

III.15
G. W. Leibniz, *Monadology* from Gottfried Wilhelm Leibniz, *Philosophical Writings*, ed. G. H. R. Parkinson, trans. M. Morris and G. H. R. Parkinson. London: J. M. Dent & Sons, 1973. pp. 179–94. © 1973. Reprinted by permission of Everyman's Library, an imprint of Alfred A. Knopf.

III.16
George Berkeley, *Of the Principles of Human Knowledge*, Part I (sections 1–37), from George

Berkeley, *Philosophical Works*, ed. M. R. Ayers, London: J. M. Dent & Sons, 1995. pp. 77–87.

III.17
Immanuel Kant, "Transcendental Aesthetic," Sections 1–3, 8, from Immanuel Kant, *Critique of Pure Reason*, 2nd edn, trans. Werner S. Pluhar, Indianapolis, IN: Hackett, 1996, pp. 71–84, 94–104. © 1996 by Hackett Publishing Company, Inc. Reprinted by permission of Hackett Publishing Company, Inc. All rights reserved.

III.18
G. W. F. Hegel, Preface, from G. W. F. Hegel, *Hegel's Phenomenology of Spirit*, trans. A. V. Miller, Oxford: Oxford University Press, 1977, pp. 3–6, 7–13, 14, 15–17, 18–22. © 1977 by Oxford University Press. Reprinted with permission from Oxford University Press.

III.19
John Stuart Mill, Chapter 11, from John Stuart Mill, *An Examination of Sir William Hamilton's Philosophy and of the Principal Philosophical Questions Discussed in His Writings*, ed. J. M. Robson, Toronto: University of Toronto Press, 1979, pp. 177–87.

III.20
F. H. Bradley, Chapters 13 and 14, from F. H. Bradley, *Appearance and Reality: A Metaphysical Essay*, 9th impr., Oxford: Clarendon Press, 1930, pp. 119–30, 140–2.

III.21
William James, "The One and the Many," from William James, *The Writings of William James*, ed. John J. McDermott, Chicago: University of Chicago Press, 1977, pp. 258–70.

III.22
Henri Bergson, *An Introduction to Metaphysics*, Second Part, from Henri Bergson, *An Introduction to Metaphysics*, trans. T. E. Hulme, New York: Liberal Arts Press, 1949, pp. 48–61.

III.23
Bertrand Russell, *The Philosophy of Logical Atomism*, Lecture VIII, from Bertrand Russell, *Logic and Knowledge: Essays 1901–1950*, ed. R. C. Marsh, London: George Allen & Unwin, 1956, pp. 269–81. © 1956 by Bertrand Russell. Reprinted with permission of the Bertrand Russell Peace Foundation.

III.24
Martin Heidegger, Sections 14, 15, 19, and 21 from Martin Heidegger, *Being and Time*, trans. J. Macquarrie and E. Robinson. Oxford: Blackwell, 1962, pp. 91–102, 122–3, 128–34. Translation © 1962 by Blackwell Publishing Ltd. Reprinted by permission of HarperCollins Publishers and Blackwell Publishing Ltd.

III.25
A. N. Whitehead, *Process and Reality*, Part I, Chapters I and II (selected sections), from A. N. Whitehead, *Alfred North Whitehead: An Anthology*, ed. F. S. C. Northrop and M. W. Gross, Cambridge: Cambridge University Press, 1953, pp. 567–72, 576–87. © 1953 by Cambridge University Press. Reprinted with permission from Cambridge University Press.

III.26
W. V. O. Quine, "Ontological Relativity," from W. V. O. Quine, *Ontological Relativity and Other Essays*, New York: Columbia University Press, 1969, pp. 26–68. © 1969 by W. V. O. Quine. Reprinted with permission of Columbia University Press.

Part IV

IV.1
Plato, *Euthyphro*, from Plato, *The Trial and Death of Socrates*, trans. G. M. A. Grube, Indianapolis, IN: Hackett, 1975, pp. 4–20. © 1975 by Hackett Publishing Company, Inc. Reprinted by permission of Hackett Publishing Company, Inc. All rights reserved.

Plato, "Ladder of Loves" (201c–212c), from Plato, *Symposium and Phaedrus*, trans. B. Jowett, New York: Dover Publications, Inc., 1993, pp. 23–34.

IV.2
Mānavadharmaśastra, Chapters 1, 6 (abridged), and 12, from *The Laws of Manu*, trans. W. Doniger & B. K. Smith, London: Penguin Books, 1991, pp. 3–16, 124–7, 278–90. © 1991 by Wendy Doniger and Brian K. Smith. Reproduced by permission of Penguin Books Ltd.

IV.3
Augustine of Hippo, *Confessions*, Book Eight and Book Nine, Chapters 8–10, from St Augustine, *Confessions*, trans. V. J. Bourke, New York: Fathers of the Church, Inc., 1953, pp. 195–226, 243–53. © 1953 by Fathers of the Church, Inc. Used with permission from The Catholic University of America Press, Washington, DC.

IV.4
Boethius, Book IV, Sections I and V–VII, from Boethius, *The Consolation of Philosophy*, trans. V. E. Watts, London: Penguin, 1969, pp. 116–17, 132–44. © 1969 by V. E. Watts. Reproduced by permission of Penguin Books Ltd.

IV.5
Anselm of Canterbury, The Ontological Argument, *Proslogion*, Chapters I–V, from *St Anselm's Proslogion: with A Reply on Behalf of the Fool by Gaunilo and the Author's Reply to Gaunilo*, ed. and trans. M. J. Charlesworth, Oxford: Oxford University Press, 1965, pp. 111–21. © 1965 by Oxford University Press. Reprinted with permission from Oxford University Press.

IV.6
Al-Ghazālī, "On Causality and Miracles," from Al-Ghazālī, *The Incoherence of the Philosophers*, trans. Michael E. Marmura, Provo, UT: Brigham Young University Press, 2000, pp. 166–77. © 2000 by Brigham Young University Press. Reprinted by permission of Brigham Young University.

IV.7
Ibn Rushd (Averroës), "That Philosophy and Logic are Obligatory," "That Demonstration Accords with the Law," and "On What Is Intended by the Law and Its Methods" (selection), from Averroës, *The Book of the Decisive Treatise Determining the Connection between the Law and Wisdom*, trans. C. E. Butterworth, Provo, UT: Brigham Young University Press, 2001, pp. 1–23. © 2001 by Brigham Young University Press. Reprinted by permission of Brigham Young University.

IV.8
Moses ben Maimon (Maimonides), "On Negative Theology," from Maimonides, *The Guide for the Perplexed*, trans. M. Friedlander, 2nd edn, New York: Dover Publications, 1956, pp. 68–91. © 1956 by Dover Publications. Reprinted with permission from Dover Publications, Inc.

IV.9
Thomas Aquinas, *Summa theologica*, Part I, Questions II and XIII, from Thomas Aquinas, *Basic Writings of Saint Thomas Aquinas*, vol. 1, ed. Anton C. Pegis, Indianapolis, IN: Hackett, 1997, pp. 18–24, pp. 114–16, 118–21. © 1945 by Random House, Inc. Copyright renewed 1973 by Random House, Inc. Reprinted by permission of Hackett Publishing Company, Inc. All rights reserved.

IV.10
Duns Scotus, *Ordinatio* I and IV (selections), from Duns Scotus, *Duns Scotus on the Will and Morality*, trans. A. B. Wolter, ed. W. A. Frank, Washington, DC: The Catholic University of America Press, 1997, pp. 183–94. © 1986, 1997 The Catholic University of America Press. Used with permission from The Catholic University of America Press, Washington, DC.

IV.11
Nicolas Cusanus, *De docta ignorantia* (selections), from Nicolas of Cusa, *Of Learned Ignorance*, trans. G. Heron, London: Routledge & Kegan Paul, 1954, pp. 7–17, 59–61, 83–6. © 1954 by Routledge & Kegan Paul. Reproduced by permission of Taylor & Francis Books UK.

IV.12
Blaise Pascal, "The Wager," from Blaise Pascal, *Pensées and Other Writings*, trans. Honor Levi, Oxford: Oxford University Press, 1995, pp. 153–6. © 1995 by Honor Levi. Reprinted with permission from Oxford University Press.

IV.13
G. W. Leibniz, "Principles of Nature and Grace, Founded on Reason," from Gottfried Wilhelm Leibniz, *Philosophical Writings*, ed. G. Parkinson, London: J. M. Dent, 1973, pp. 195–204. © 1973. Reprinted by permission of Everyman's Library, an imprint of Alfred A. Knopf.

IV.14
Matthew Tindal, Chapters I, II, and VI, from *Christianity as Old as the Creation*, London: Routledge/Thoemmes Press, 1999, pp. 1–18, 49–58. © 1999 by Thoemmes Press. Reproduced with permission of Thoemmes Press in the format Textbook via Copyright Clearance Center.

IV.15
David Hume, "Of Miracles," from David Hume, *Enquiries Concerning Human Understanding and Concerning the Principles of Morals*, 2nd edn, ed. L.A. Selby-Bigge, Oxford: Oxford University Press, 1902, pp. 109–31.

IV.16
Immanuel Kant, "The Transcendental Dialectic," "The Impossibility of an Ontological Proof of the Existence of God," and "The Impossibility of a Cosmological Proof of the Existence of God,"

from Immanuel Kant, *Critique of Pure Reason*, trans. N. Kemp Smith, London: Macmillan, 1968, pp. 500–18. Translation © The Estate of Norman Kemp Smith 1929, 1933, 2003. Reprinted by permission of Palgrave Macmillan.

IV.17
William Paley, "The Argument from Design," from William Paley, Nat*ural Theology: Selections*, ed. F. Ferré, Indianapolis, IN: The Bobbs-Merrill, 1963, pp. 3–12, 32–3, 45–9.

IV.18
Søren Kierkegaard, *Fear and Trembling*, Problema II, from Søren Kierkegaard, *Fear and Trembling: Dialectical Lyric*, trans. A. Hannay, Harmondsworth: Penguin, 1985, pp. 96–108. © 1985 by Alastair Hannay. Reproduced by permission of Penguin Books Ltd.

IV.19
William James, "Mysticism," from William James, *The Varieties of Religious Experience, Lectures XVI–XVII*, New York and London: Longmans, Green & Co., 1923, pp. 379–82, 415–16, 422–8.

IV.20
Bertrand Russell, "A Free Man's Worship," from Bertrand Russell, *Mysticism and Logic: and Other Essays*, London: Allen & Unwin, 1963, pp. 40–7. © 1963 by Bertrand Russell. Reprinted with permission from the Bertrand Russell Peace Foundation.

IV.21
Martin Buber, Part III (selections), from Martin Buber, *I and Thou*, trans. R. Gregor Smith, Edinburgh: T. & T. Clark, 1937, pp. 75–81, 95–112. © 1937 by T. & T. Clark International. Reproduced with permission of T. & T. Clark International in the format of Textbook via Copyright Clearance Center.

IV.22
Sarvepalli Radhakrishnan, "Conflict of Religions: The Hindu Attitude," from Sarvepalli Radhakrishnan, *The Hindu View of Life*, London: George Allen & Unwin, 1927, pp. 26–44. © 1927 by Sarvepalli Radhakrishnan. Reprinted with permission from HarperCollins Publishers Ltd.

IV.23
Reinhold Niebuhr, "The Christian Attitude to Government," chapter 9 from Reinhold Niebuhr, *The Nature and Destiny of Man: A Christian Interpretation II*, New York: Charles Scribner's Sons, 1951, pp. 269–284. © 1996 by Westminster John Knox Press. Used by permission of Westminster John Knox Press.

IV.24
Paul Tillich, "Courage and Transcendence" (selections), chapter 6 from Paul Tillich, *The Courage To Be*, New Haven, CT and London: Yale University Press, 2000, pp. 155–67, 171–8. © 1952 by Yale University Press. Copyright renewed © 1980 by Hannah Tillich. Reprinted with permission from Yale University Press.

Part V

V.1
Tao Te Ching (selected chapters), from Wang Keping, *The Classic of the Dao: A New Investigation*, Beijing: Foreign Languages Press, 1998, pp. 221–2, 225, 227–30, 232–4, 236–7, 240–1, 243–7, 250–1, 253–6. © 1998 by Wang Keping. Reprinted with kind permission from the translator.

V.2
Gotama (The Buddha), selected sayings on kingship, from *The Long Discourses of the Buddha: A Translation of the Dīgha Nikāya*, 2nd edn, trans. M. Walshe, Boston, MA: Wisdom Publications, 1995, pp. 135–6, 395–403, 413. © 1995 by Maurice Walshe. Reprinted with permission from Wisdom Publications, 199 Elm Street, Somerville, MA 02144, USA. www.wisdompubs.org.

V.3
Confucius, selections from *The Analects*, trans. D. C. Lau, Harmondsworth: Penguin, 1979, pp. 59, 63, 65–6, 73–4, 85, 94, 109, 112–16, 118–23, 131, 135. © 1979 by D. C. Lau. Reproduced by permission of Penguin Books Ltd.

V.4
Plato, *Republic*, V, 451c–462e, 471c–480a, from Plato, *The Republic of Plato*, 2nd edn, trans. A. Bloom, New York: Basic Books, 1991, pp. 129–42, 151–61. © 1968 by Allan Bloom. Reprinted by permission of Basic Books, a member of Perseus Books Group.

V.5
Aristotle, I:1–13, II:1–6, VII:14–15, from Aristotle, *Politics*, trans. B. Jowett, Oxford: Oxford

University Press, 1938, in *The Basic Works of Aristotle*, ed. R. McKeon, New York: Random House, 1941, pp. 1127–58, 1296–1301. © 1938 by Oxford University Press. Reprinted with permission from Oxford University Press.

V.6
Cicero, "The Dream of Scipio," in *Cicero: Volume XVI*, Loeb Classical Library Volume 213, trans. Clinton W. Keyes, Cambridge, MA: Harvard University Press, 1928, pp. 261–86. © 1928 by the President and Fellows of Harvard College. The Loeb Classical Library® is a registered trademark of the President and Fellows of Harvard College. Reprinted by permission of the publishers and the Trustees of the Loeb Classical Library.

V.7
Ibn Tufayl, *The Story of Hayy Ibn Yaqzan* (extracts), from *Two Andalusian Philosophers: The Story of Hayy Ibn Yaqzan by Abu Bakr Muhammad ibn Tufayl & The Definitive Statement by Abu'l Walid Muhammad ibn Rushd*, trans. Jim Colville, London and NY: Kegan Paul International, 1999, pp. 57–65.

V.8
Marsilius of Padua, *Defensor pacis*, Discourse One, Chapters X and XII; Discourse Two, Chapters VII and VIII, from Marsilius of Padua, *Defender of the Peace*, vol. 2, ed. A. Gewirth, New York: Columbia University Press, 1956, pp. 34–7, 44–9, 152–63. © 1956, Columbia University Press. Reprinted with permission from Columbia University Press.

V.9
Niccolò Machiavelli, Chapter Fifteen to Eighteen and Twenty-five, from Niccolò Machiavelli, *The Prince*, trans. W. K. Marriott, London: Dent, 1908, pp. 83–100, 139–43.

V.10
Thomas Hobbes, Chapters XIII–XV, XVII, XVIII (selections), from Thomas Hobbes, *Leviathan Or the Matter, Form and Power of a Commonwealth Ecclesiastical and Civil*, Oxford: Blackwell, 1960, pp. 80–8, 89–92, 103–5, 109–18. © 1960 by Blackwell Publishing. Reprinted with permission from Blackwell Publishing Ltd.

V.11
John Locke, "Of Property," from John Locke, *Two Treatises of Government*, ed. Peter Laslett, New York: New American Library, 1965, pp. 327–44.

V.12
Jean-Jacques Rousseau, Books I and II (selections), from Jean-Jacques Rousseau, *The Social Contract*, trans. Maurice Cranston, London: Penguin, 2004, pp. 1–9, 12–21, 26–37. Selections from *The Social Contract* by Jean-Jacques Rousseau, trans. Maurice Cranston (© Maurice Cranston 1968) is reproduced by permission of PFD (www.pfd.co.uk) on behalf of the Estate of Maurice Cranston.

V.13
David Hume, "Of Justice," "Enquiry Concerning Human Understanding, Section III, Part I," from David Hume, *Enquiries Concerning Human Understanding and Concerning the Principles of Morals*, 2nd edn, ed. L. A. Selby-Bigge, Oxford: Clarendon Press, 1902, pp. 183–204. "Of the Origin of Government," "Of the Original Contract" from David Hume, *Essays Moral, Political, and Literary from Hume's Moral and Political Philosophy*, ed. Henry D. Aiken, New York: Hafner Publishing Co., 1948, pp. 311–14, 356–72.

V.14
Immanuel Kant, *Perpetual Peace: A Philosophical Sketch* (selections), from *Kant: Political Writings*, ed. Hans Reiss and trans. H. B. Nisbet, Cambridge: Cambridge University Press, 1991, pp. 93–109, 112–14. © 1991 by Cambridge University Press, Reprinted with permission from the translator, the editor and Cambridge University Press.

V.15
Edmund Burke, selections from *Reflections on the Revolution in France*, ed. W. B. Todd, New York: Holt, Rinehart, and Winston, 1959, pp. 64–75, 91–6.

V.16
Thomas Paine, *The Rights of Man* (selections), from Thomas Paine, *The Life and Works of Thomas Paine*, ed. W. V. van der Weyde, New Rochelle, NY: Thomas Paine National Historical Association, 1925, pp. 91–4, 255–9, 263–74.

Mary Wollstonecraft, Chapters 6 and 9 from Mary Wollstonecraft, *A Vindication of the Rights of Woman*, and John Stuart Mill, *The Subjection of Women*, ed. M. Warnock, London: Charles E. Tuttle Co., Inc., pp. 58–85, 154–65.

V.17

G. W. F. Hegel, *Philosophy of Right*, Part III, Section iii, from G. W. F. Hegel, *Hegel: Selections*, ed. and trans. J. Loewenberg, New York: Charles Scribner's Sons, 1929, pp. 443–68.

V.18

John Stuart Mill, *On Liberty*, Chapter 1, from John Stuart Mill, *Three Essays*, Oxford: Oxford University Press, 1975, pp. 5–20.

V.19

Karl Marx, *Manifesto of the Communist Party* (1848) (Sections I and II), from Karl Marx, *The Portable Karl Marx*, ed. Eugene Kamenka, London: Penguin, 1983, pp. 203–23, 224–8. © 1983 by Viking Penguin Inc. Used by permission of Viking Penguin, a division of Penguin Group (USA) Inc. "Theses on Feuerbach" from Karl Marx, *Karl Marx: Selected Writings*, ed. Lawrence H. Simon, Indianapolis, IN: Hackett, 1994, pp. 99–101. © 1975 by Hackett Publishing Company, Inc. Reprinted by permission of Hackett Publishing Company, Inc. All rights reserved.

Vladimir Ilich Lenin, selections from *State and Revolution*, New York: International Publishers, 1943, pp. 7–20, 29–31, 35–9.

V.20

M. K. Gandhi, *Satyagraha* (selections), from Mahatma Gandhi, *Selected Political Writings*, ed. D. Dalton, Indianapolis, IN: Hackett, 1996, pp. 50–7, 60–4, 81–3. © 1996 by Hackett Publishing Company, Inc. Reprinted by permission of the Navajivan Trust.

V.21

Max Horkheimer and Theodor W. Adorno, "The Concept of Enlightenment" from Max Horkheimer and Theodor W. Adorno, *Dialectic of Enlightenment: Philosophical Fragments*, trans. Edmund Jephcott, Stanford, CA: Stanford University Press, 2002, pp. 1–12. © 1944 by Social Studies Association, NY. New edition © S. Fischer Verlag GmbH, Frankfurt am Main, 1969; English trans. © 2002 by Board of Trustees of Leland Stanford Jr University. All rights reserved. Used with permission of Stanford University Press, www.sup.org.

V.22

Michael Oakeshott, "Political Education," from Michael Oakeshott, *Rationalism in Politics and Other Essays*, London: Methuen, 1962, pp. 112–30, 133. © 1962 by Michael Oakeshott. Reprinted by kind permission of Oliver Letwin.

V.23

John Rawls, Chapter I, Sections 1–4, from John Rawls, *A Theory of Justice*, Oxford: Oxford University Press, 1971, pp. 3–22. "Justice as Fairness" reprinted by permission of the publisher from *A Theory of Justice* by John Rawls, Cambridge, MA: The Belknap Press of Harvard University Press, pp. 3–22. © 1971, 1999 by the President and Fellows of Harvard College.

Editors' Introduction

The very large volume that you are holding in your hands as you read these words is indeed the largest treasury of essential philosophical texts that has ever been published. *Philosophy: The Classic Readings* contains 133 substantial texts drawn from all periods of the history of philosophy up until modern times, from many geographical regions, and from a wide variety of cultural traditions.

The broad scope of the volume reflects two convictions on our – the Editors' – part. First, we entirely welcome the growing appreciation, among philosophers in the English-language world, of the importance of the history of their discipline. The mood that prevailed during the period after World War II, especially among the "ordinary language" philosophers at Oxford, to the effect that philosophy could safely ignore its history – rather as the natural sciences tend to ignore theirs – has almost entirely disappeared. It has disappeared, in part, because of a sharper recognition that philosophy, as pursued at any given time, *is* to a significant degree an engagement or conversation with earlier philosophers, many of whom still have something significant to contribute to even the most contemporary, state-of-the-art discussions. One thinks, for example, of the way in which ancient views on the virtues have in recent years been invoked by those challenging the hegemony of a style of moral philosophy that focused myopically on rights, duties, and principles. Or, to take another example, of the way that equally ancient claims

about the essential "oneness" and "wholeness" of reality have come to inform recent debates in Metaphysics and the Philosophy of Science.

The atrophy of that "Oxford" hostility towards the history of philosophy is also due, however, to another welcome development that is characteristic, some would say, of "post-modernity." Here we have in mind the maturing of a kind of modesty or humility among philosophers, specifically an increased perception on their part that the credentials of the positions philosophers currently embrace are problematic. How is one to tell that their embrace is not "fashion," a product of current tastes rather than of sound or at least durable reasoning? For example, can "physicalists" – for whom there exists nothing other than the physical – be confident that their conviction is more than a symptom of the scientific (or scientistic) mood of our times? Or, can "liberals" – with their emphasis on the sanctity of individual choice – be sure that their position does not simply reflect the easy-going, hedonistic, "do-your-own-thing" climate of the day? An important way, surely, in which to reflect on the standing of our beliefs – beliefs that can seem so very natural to us – is to read philosophers from earlier times, and different cultures, who would have found these very same beliefs incredible. Understanding the strengths and weaknesses of what today passes for "true" and "good" requires considering how earlier thinkers reached contrary conclusions using arguments that may remain germane and challenging. In addition, and perhaps more importantly, by comparing and testing current philosophical thought against that of the past, we can not only discern the pre-suppositions and prejudices of earlier eras. We can also expose similar presuppositions and prejudices that may be shaping beliefs and commitments today. After all, those who come later than us will be able to scrutinize our beliefs and commitments in the same more perspicuous way in which we can look back on earlier times.

A second conviction, shared by the Editors, which also inspires the wide scope of the volume, is again one that has been growing among the philosophical community in recent years. This is the recognition that philosophy itself is wider in its scope and more diverse in its content than many recent publications and curricula have acknowledged. Re-examining the Western tradi-tions themselves, philosophers have come to see that the reigning self-understanding of those traditions is incomplete. In part, philosophers have come to see that the Western traditions include much more within themselves than had been commonly acknowledged, especially with regard to medieval, Renaissance, and humanistic thought, as well as the philosophical work pro-duced by women. And while for far too long there was some truth in the observation that one could not swim the English Channel philo-sophically, European-Continental and Anglo-American philosophers have resumed not only acknowledging one another's existence but also actually reading one another's work. Philo-sophers have in addition come to acknowledge how very blurry and artificial the boundaries erected to separate and distinguish "Western" from "non-Western" philosophical traditions have been. Not only have serious questions been raised about the extent to which the earliest Greek philosophers were influenced by the thought of India and Africa; scholars have also come to see the remarkably omnivorous quality of the read-ing and study of philosophers straight through philosophical history. Italy's and France's Thomas Aquinas was, indeed, influenced by Germany's Albert the Great – but also by Persia's Ibn Sina. Schopenhauer scoured the work of Plato and Kant – but also the Upanishads. Since Augustine was African and influenced by a religion whose origins lay east of Constantinople, should he be regarded as non-Western? If not, then why not consider the Córdoban Aristotelian, Ibn Rushd,

a Western philosopher? And, anyway, where should one say the East begins? Istanbul? Per-sepolis? With the shores of the Indus River? Typically, the application of the terms "East" and "West" are highly context-dependent. Often, how-ever, in the contexts of philosophy, because they can be misleading one is better off without them. Accordingly, each Part of *Philosophy: The Classic Readings* contains several seminal texts by thinkers of non-European provenance like India, China, and Japan, as well as entries by Islamic philosophers.

Then, of course, there is simply the question of continuing relevance. The kind of European hubris expressed by G. W. F. Hegel early in the nineteenth century, when he dismissed the think-ing of India as "childlike" and merely "dreamy," has long since disappeared. But it is still not sufficiently appreciated how directly relevant the rich work of, say, ancient Indian philosophers remains to epistemological and metaphysical debates that some people might wrongly imagine to be the preserve of Western philosophy. (One unfortunate sign of this is that works by Chinese and Indian philosophers are still more likely to be found in the "Occult" or "Spirituality" sec-tion of bookshops than among the philosophy volumes.) A sense of justice alone, one might think, should deter us from giving sole credit to European writers for conceptions of knowledge or causality that were respectively articulated many centuries earlier by the Nyāya school in northern India and by al-Ghazālī in Baghdad. But the main reason, once again, for introducing and restoring "non-Western" thought to the stand-ing of philosophical "classic" is the insight that doing so affords into the contexts, presupposi-tions and "mindsets" that encourage or obstruct philosophical thinking. To many modern "Westerners," certain positions just seem incred-ible: they are simply "off the menu," as it were. It is then salutary, surely, to acquaint readers with contexts of thought and sensibility within which those apparently strange positions struck men and women as not only credible but also com-pelling – no less compelling than the contempor-ary *idées fixes* of our own intellectual culture.

It would be wrong, however, to give the impression that the only reasons for students of philosophy to acquaint themselves with the authors of the past, and with traditions thought to be different from their own, are of a "pragmatic" kind. To the extent that this acquaintance opens the doors to important and perhaps neglected contributions to contemporary debates, and also helps to expose the prejudices that may inform our own views, it is of course to be encouraged. But the story of philosophy, from its earliest days to the present, and from China through India, Greece, and Persia to Africa, the Middle East, Europe, and the Americas, is one of the great stories of humankind – or, better, it is itself a collection of great stories, rather than a single narrative. For Hegel – this time saying something we can endorse – philosophy, alongside religion and art, were the three primary expressions of "spirit." In acquainting themselves with the classic philosophical texts included in this volume, readers should not simply be seeking some "payoff" in the form of relevant contributions to the philosophical problems on which they are writing essays or taking tests. For readers are also being inducted into one of the great conversations of humankind: they are becoming participants in traditions that embody some of the deepest spiritual aspirations and the most illuminating intellectual achievements of the world's men and women. Inheriting and participating in this conversation and these traditions is, in and by itself, no small reward. Indeed, it is a privilege.

Large as the book you are holding certainly is, it does not pretend to be comprehensive in its coverage. Total comprehensiveness would, of course, be a futile ambition, even for a set of several books of the same size. This is because there could be no unanimous agreement on which philosophical texts deserve the label "classic." The Editors have had to make some hard decisions – on which texts to include and on which areas or branches of philosophy to cover. Many texts, to be sure, were self-selecting. Plato's discussion of the Forms in his *Republic*, Thomas Aquinas's proofs of the existence of God, and the verses of the *Tao Te Ching* on the wise ruler – these are texts whose omission from the classics of Metaphysics, Philosophy of Religion, and Political Philosophy respectively is hard to imagine. But in many other cases, the Editors – with the help of colleagues who are expert in the areas covered by the book – have been thrown back on their own judgment. There will be readers, no doubt, who are disappointed by the absence of

some texts they admire, and others will probably raise an eyebrow at some of the texts we have selected for inclusion. But we hope that most users of the volume will agree that the great majority of the texts included are of sufficient importance, interest, and influence to deserve their place.

One general policy adopted by the Editors was, with certain exceptions, not to include texts that were first published after the middle of the twentieth century. Among the reasons behind this policy are the ready availability of anthologies of important articles that have appeared since then and, more significantly, the difficulty of deciding which recent writings are likely to withstand the test of time. Many philosophy teachers, recalling their days as students, will dimly remember articles that were prescribed reading on their courses, but which today remain largely unread. And they can probably name other articles, unnoticed at the time, which are recognized today as seminal contributions to a field. Our editorial policy in this connection, however, has not been rigid, and we have selected a handful of texts that were published after 1950 because of their exceptional impact on the direction of philosophical thought in some area. These are texts whose status as "classic" may safely be predicted. A good example is the chapter in Part V (Political Philosophy) from John Rawls's book *A Theory of Justice*. This work did not appear until 1971, but it made an immediate impact upon political philosophy, in effect giving it a whole new impetus and rescuing it from what many commentators judged to be the stagnant, even moribund condition into which it had fallen some decades earlier.

A further tough decision to be made by the Editors, in consultation with their publisher and with advisers, concerned the areas of philosophy to be covered in *Philosophy: The Classic Readings*. Given the policy just mentioned of a cut-off date around the middle of the twentieth century, it was natural enough not to devote sections of the volume to those more fledgling areas of philosophy – such as Philosophy of Language – where the bulk of the most important literature has appeared after that date. Nor would it have been sensible to include texts in areas like Logic which are not, except on highly specialist courses, taught and studied in a historically orientated way. In the end, we opted for five areas of our discipline – Ethics, Epistemology, Metaphysics, Philosophy of Religion, and Political Philosophy. It was our and our advisors' judgment that, to begin with, these are central areas of philosophy in nearly all cultural traditions. Second, they are all areas that repay and indeed demand engagement with historical texts. Finally, they are areas that are almost certain to figure on the curricula of university philosophy programs. One area of the discipline with a strong claim for inclusion was Aesthetics. We decided not to include it primarily for reasons of space (and weight), but also because it is an area that is already and perhaps surprisingly well provided with historically slanted anthologies, including *Aesthetics: The Classic Readings* (edited by David E. Cooper, Oxford: Blackwell 1997).

The order in which the five Parts of this volume occur should not be taken to reflect any particular commitment by the Editors to a hierarchy of importance or centrality among the five corresponding areas of philosophy. There are philosophers, certainly, for whom Metaphysics – "the queen of the sciences," as Immanuel Kant called it – should take pride of place. Philosophy, as they see it, is primarily the attempt to uncover the fundamental structure of reality, to discover – at the most general level possible – what there is. Others would regard Epistemology as the most central form of philosophical enquiry. The main task of the discipline, in their view, is to determine – to borrow the title of a book by Bertrand Russell – "the scope and limits of human knowledge" and, in connection with this, to distinguish between reason and unreason, objectivity and subjectivity, warranted belief and superstition, or evidence and prejudice. Yet others would argue that philosophy was in its earliest days and throughout much of its history inspired by an essentially *practical* ambition – to determine how human beings ought to act, treat each other, feel and live. For such philosophers, this is still the driving inspiration, so that it is Ethics and not any other branch of the subject that, in their opinion, grounds or fuels the larger enterprise of philosophy.

None of these is a silly attitude to adopt, and each has had its worthy champions. But, to repeat, the structure of this volume – in particular, the order of its five Parts – is not to be taken as an implicit endorsement or rejection of any of them. Perhaps it is best to regard each of these attitudes as elevating to a unique status a component of the discipline that, crucial though it is, depends for its final importance on its integration with other components. Philosophy is not first and foremost the delineation of reality, or an enquiry into the nature of knowledge, or a pursuit of the good life – as if these were separate, discrete activities. Instead, it is that endeavor of the human spirit whereby men and women strive to lead the sorts of lives and to become the sorts of beings that are informed and guided by disciplined thinking about the ways of things. So characterized, it is not difficult to see why Philosophy of Religion and Political Philosophy – to which Parts IV and V are devoted – should be so closely integrated into this wider endeavor. There is, many would say, no vision of the ways of things that has done more – whether for good or ill – to guide people's conception of how they should live than the vision, or cluster of visions, variously found in the world's religions. And there is, arguably, no dimension of human life that is more relevant to people's aspiration for that life to be well lived than the relationships they have to one another in political and social communities.

Once it was decided which areas of philosophy should be covered in this volume, and which texts to include, there still remained a problem of organization for the Editors. This is a difficulty of a kind they share with librarians, cataloguers, publishers, and teachers responsible for the design and naming of courses on their institution's philosophy curriculum. The problem here is that of allocating texts to the most appropriate of the designated areas, such as Metaphysics or Philosophy of Religion. In the case of many texts, to be sure, this is no real difficulty. Aristotle's discussion of "substance" and Sarvepalli Radhakrishnan's account of the Hindu attitude towards religious conflict clearly belong, respectively, to the two areas just mentioned – just as René Descartes's rehearsal and rebuttal of radical skepticism belongs under the title of "Epistemology." But in the case of other texts, matters are less obvious. This is primarily because the names of the traditional areas of philosophy, including our five, do not refer to hived off fields of enquiry, between which there is little or no traffic. Indeed, given that philosophy endeavors to make it possible for people to lead lives informed by a proper understanding of the ways of things, one would surely expect many philosophical classics to combine moral, metaphysical, epistemological, religious, and social observations.

Readers of, say, the Ethics texts in Part I may therefore wonder why some of them – ones which, like David Hume's, discuss knowledge and rationality, or, like Mencius's, speculate about human nature – were not allocated to Epistemology and Metaphysics respectively. And why, they may ask, are some of the texts that address issues that are both moral and religious found under "Ethics," while others are placed under "Philosophy of Religion"? They will have noticed, for instance, and perhaps been puzzled, that one chapter from Søren Kierkegaard's book, *Fear and Trembling*, is included in Part I, and another in Part IV. Similar puzzlement, of course, could arise with respect to the texts found, or not found, in the other Parts. And this could give rise to a view that is not at all unknown among contemporary professional philosophers, to the effect that the traditional divisions of philosophy – into Metaphysics, Ethics, and so on – are conventional and largely arbitrary. We continue with these divisions, they charge, only because of a conservative reluctance to change the names of philosophy courses and the sub-categories used by librarians when distributing new philosophy holdings among the shelves. It would be more sensible, they sometimes go on to propose, to divide philosophical enquiries and writings according to the main concepts with which they deal. If that were done, the resulting areas would have titles like the Philosophy of Meaning, the Philosophy of Value, and the Philosophy of Nature.

This is a position with which it is reasonable to hold some sympathy. At any rate, it can be conceded that convention and habit no doubt do play their part in the allocation of texts and topics to the familiar categories. But the accusation of sheer arbitrariness is exaggerated. It is surely not arbitrary to distinguish questions that concern, first and foremost, how reality is, how and whether we can know what is the case, and how we should live. "First and foremost," since, as we have already emphasized, any of these types of questions can then come to involve ones of the other types. As for the suggestion that, in place of the traditional categories, one should use different titles like the Philosophy of Value or Philosophy of Meaning, this immediately confronts two difficulties. First, it is hard to see how doing so would reduce the alleged arbitrariness of the divisions. It is easy to think of classic texts – those by Charles Stevenson and Jean-Paul Sartre in Part I, for example – which concern both meaning and value. So to which of the new categories would they be allocated? Second, the proposed categories just do not correspond to the prevailing way in which the philosophy curriculum is currently divided up on philosophy programs. Even if, for the sake of argument, it is granted that the persistence of this division owes to mere conservatism and inertia, a volume that is designed to be maximally useful to students on philosophy programs must be structured in a way that makes it as helpful as possible. And in this case this means, in contrast to what we have argued about "Western" and "Non-Western" philosophy, appropriating the categories used to organize today's philosophy curricula.

Two guidelines we have followed when allocating texts to Parts serve, moreover, to reduce the degree of arbitrariness with which such allocations get accused. First, we follow the well-established practice of allocating to such relatively circumscribed categories as Philosophy of Religion those texts that, while addressing metaphysical and epistemological matters as well, do so with particular reference to a restricted range of enquiry, like religious belief. Roughly speaking, the texts included in the Metaphysics and Epistemology sections address highly general issues concerning reality, substance, causality, truth, belief, knowledge, reason, or evidence. Where the questions addressed concern, for example, the nature of moral truth in particular, or of divine causality, or of rationality in the specific realm of politics, the relevant texts are instead allocated to Ethics, Philosophy of Religion, and Political Philosophy respectively. A similar remark applies to texts concerning moral questions. Where these address general issues about, say, the nature of obligation or virtue, they will be found in Part I; where, more narrowly, they address questions about political obligation or the virtues of political rulers, they will be found in Part V.

Second, we have asked the question, in the case of each text whose appropriate allocation is not obvious, to which area it makes the most significant and original contribution. A good example is provided by the case we mentioned earlier, the two texts selected from Kierkegaard's *Fear and Trembling*, a work in which moral and religious questions are discussed in close proximity. One of those texts addresses the issue of whether moral concerns can ever be subordinated to other concerns; the second asks if there is a special "absolute" duty towards God. In our judgment, despite the interweaving of the ethical and the religious in both texts, the former makes its primary and most contentious contribution to Ethics, the latter a similar contribution to the Philosophy of Religion. Not every reader, perhaps, would concur in all the judgments we have made on this kind of basis: but he or she can at least be assured that judgment, rather than coin-tossing, has been responsible for the allocation of texts in problematic cases.

Philosophy: The Classic Readings contains 133 primary texts, divided into five Parts. Each text is preceded by an introduction written by one or other of the two Editors of the volume. These introductions serve to place the texts in their context, to relate them to other relevant texts, and where necessary to explain difficult points that are being made in the texts. The Editors also provide explanatory endnotes to many of the texts. Where they have been retained, asterisked footnotes are the original editor's except where stated otherwise.

The introductions and notes to the texts help to make the volume entirely suitable for use on a range of philosophy courses, as well as for general readers in philosophy. First-year students taking introductory courses in, say, Ethics or Theory of Knowledge, may find that all the historical materials they are required to consult are contained within this volume. Students enrolled on courses dedicated to the history of philosophy will, of course, find many of the texts that they need to study included in the volume. Because of the inclusion of many non-Western texts, the volume is also suitable for students taking courses in comparative or "world" philosophy. The size and scope of the book also makes this a useful sourcebook for more advanced courses. We like to think that students who benefited from using the book when studying Ethics, say, in their First year, may continue to benefit in their Second, Third, or (in the US, anyway) Fourth years when taking a course on, for instance, Philosophy of Religion or Metaphysics. We like to think, as well, that *Philosophy: The Classic Readings* is a valuable as well as vast collection that people will retain and consult long after their student days are over.

We are encouraged in these hopes and thoughts by the critical success of a number of books in a "Classics Readings" series published by Blackwell in the 1990s. The present volume includes nearly all of the texts – in the areas of Ethics, Epistemology, and Metaphysics – which were anthologized in three of those earlier books. A substantial number of further texts have been added in each of those areas, and two Parts of the new volume – Philosophy of Religion and Political Philosophy – are new anthologies of texts selected specifically for this volume.

Note that cross-referencing within the introductions to each entry will cite first, with a Roman numeral, the relevant general Part of this volume, followed by an Arabic numeral indicating the specific entry to which we wish to refer in that Part. So, for example, "III.2" refers to the second entry of Part III of the present volume – the Part on Metaphysics, the entry on Heraclitus and Parmenides.

David E. Cooper
Peter S. Fosl

A Philosophical Chronology

- Big Bang (13.7 billion years BP, before the present)
- Formation of the Earth (4.5 billion BP)
- Abiogenesis (generation of life) (4.4–2.7 billion BP)
- Earliest hominids (5 million BP)
- Earliest known artwork (500,000–300,000 BP) (Venus of Tan-Tan)
- Appearance of homo sapiens (250,000 BP)
- Hunting/gathering gives way to agriculture (c. 10,000 BP)
- Sumerian Cuneiform (c. 3,500 BCE)
- *Gilgamesh* (extant c. 700 BCE; developed c. 3000 BCE)
- Egyptian *Book of the Dead* (earliest portions 5th Dynasty, from c. 2400 BCE)
- *Rigveda* (c. 1500–1000; revised c. 500 BCE)
- Law of Minos in Crete and Theseus in Athens (c. 1250 BCE)
- Zoroaster and the *Gathas* (Zarathustra, Zartosht; 10th or 11th century BCE)
- Jawhwist portions of Pentateuch (c. 1000–850 BCE)
- Emigration of Ionians to Asia Minor (c. 950 BCE)

- Formation of Greek City States (c. 850 BCE)
- *Iliad* and *Odyssey* in current form (c. 800 BCE)
- *Theogony* and *Works and Days* by Hesiod (late 8th century BCE)
- Rome founded by Romulus (21 April 753 BCE, Period of Kings)

- Law of Lykurgus (early 7th century BCE)

- Thales of Miletus (624–546 BCE)
- Anaximander of Miletus (611–547/6 BCE)
- Bias of Priene (fl. early 6th century BCE)

- Vardhamana (Mahavira) (599–527 BCE) (Jainism)
- Lao Tzu (Lao Zi; probably legend, possibly 6th–4th centuries BCE)
- Anaximenes of Miletus (586/8–526/4 BCE)
- Pythagoras of Samos (581/2–497 BCE)
- *Leviticus* (c. 570–400 BCE)
- Epimenides of Knossos (possibly 6th century BCE)
- Hippasus of Metapontium (6th century BCE)
- Xenophanes of Colophon (c. 570–475 BCE)
- Siddhattha Gotama (The Buddha) (c. 563–483 BCE)
- Simonides of Ceos (c. 556–468 BCE)
- Confucius (Kong Fuzi) (551–479 BCE)
- *Deuteronomy* (mid 6th century BCE)
- Oldest *Upanishads* (mid first millennium BCE)
- Heraclitus of Ephesus (c. 535–after 480 BCE)
- Foundation of the Pythagorean Order (532 BCE)
- Alcmaeon of Croton (fl. early 5th century BCE) (pupil of Pythagoras)
- Ameinias (6th century BCE, teacher of Parmenides)
- Aeschylus (525–456 BCE) (tragedian)
- Epicharmus of Kos (c. 540–c. 450 BCE)
- Pindar of Thebes (c. 522–443 BCE) (poet)
- Parmenides of Elea (b. c. 515 BCE)
- Beginning of the Roman Republic (510 BCE)

- Anaxagoras of Clazomenae (c. 500–428 BCE)
- Metrodorus of Lampsacus (b. c. 500 BCE) (pupil of Anaxagoras)

- Sophocles (497–406 BCE) (tragedian)
- Empedocles of Acragas (c. 490–c. 433 BCE)
- Battle of Marathon (490 BCE)
- Zeno of Elea (c. 490–430 BCE)
- Herodotus of Halicarnasus (c. 485–c. 425 BCE)
- Archelaus of Athens (pupil of Anaxagoras, teacher of Socrates)
- Protagoras of Abdera (c. 490–c. 420 BCE) (sophist)
- Gorgias of Leontini (c. 487–c. 376 BCE) (sophist)
- Euripides (c. 480–405 BCE) (tragedian)
- Battles of Thermopylae and of Salamis (480 BCE); Battle of Plataea (479 BCE)
- Antiphon of Athens (c. 479–c. 411 BCE)
- Aspasia (c. 470–c. 400 BCE)
- Melissus of Samos (b. c. 470 BCE)
- Leucippus of Miletus (fl. c. 450 BCE)
- Diogenes of Apollonia (b. c. 460 BCE)
- Socrates (c. 470–399 BCE)
- Hippocrates of Cos (c. 460–c. 370 BCE)
- Hippias of Elis (b. c. 460 BCE)
- So-called First Peloponnesian War (461–451 BCE)
- Thrasymachus (c. 459–c. 395 BCE)
- Mo Tzu (Mozi) (c. 470–c. 390 BCE)
- Democritus of Abdera (c. 460–c. 370 BCE)
- Thucydides (c. 460–400 BCE)
- Prodicus of Ceos (c. 460–c. 395 BCE)
- Philolaus of Croton (mid 5th century BCE)
- Timaeus of Locri (fl. c. 400 BCE) (Pythagorean)
- Diagoras of Melos (5th century BCE) (sophist)
- Lycophron (5th century BCE) (sophist)
- Aristophanes (445–385 BCE) (Old Comedy)
- Antisthenes (c. 445/50–c. 360 BCE) (Cycnicism) (pupil of Socrates)
- Isocrates (436–338 BCE)
- Cratylus of Athens (late 5th century BCE)
- Eurytus of Croton (late 5th century BCE) (pupil of Philolaus)
- Alcidamus of Elaea (late 5th century BCE) (pupil of Gorgias)
- Aristippus of Cyrene (c. 435–c. 360 BCE) (Cyrenaics) (pupil of Socrates)
- Euclides of Megara (c. 435–c. 365 BCE) (Megarians) (pupil of Socrates)

- Xenophon (431–355 BCE)
- Peloponnesian War (431–404 BCE)
- Plato (c. 428–c. 347 BCE) (founds Academy 387 BCE)
- Archytas of Tarentum (428–347 BCE)
- Aeschines Socraticus (c. 425–c. 350 BCE)
- Theaetetus of Athens (c. 417–c. 369 BCE)
- Eudoxus of Cnidus (c. 410–c. 355 BCE)
- Speusippus (c. 407–339 BCE) (Plato's nephew, inherits the Academy)
- Menedemus of Pyrrha (contemporary of Speusippus)
- Philip of Opus (pupil of Plato, editor of the *Laws*)
- Diogenes of Sinope (c. 400–c. 325 BCE) (Cynicism)
- Metrodorus of Chios (Democritus's student)

- Xenocrates of Chalcedon (396–c. 314 BCE) (second scholarch of the Academy)
- Heraclides Ponticus (c. 387–312 BCE)
- Demosthenes (384–322 BCE)
- Aristotle of Stagira (384–322 BCE) (arrives at Academy 366 BCE, Lyceum founded 334/5 BCE)
- Theophrastus of Eressos (371–287 BCE) (successor to Aristotle)
- Eudemus of Rhodes (c. 370–c. 300 BCE)
- Chuang Tzu (Zhuang Zi) (369–286 BCE)
- Ecphantus of Syracuse (possibly 4th century BCE)
- Crates of Thebes (fl. 325 BCE) (Cynicism; spouse of Hipparchia)
- Stilpo of Megara (Timon's teacher)
- Hipparchia (b. c. 350 BCE) (Cynicism; spouse of Crates)
- Anaxarchus (fl. 340 BCE; Democritean, teacher of Pyrrho)
- Aristoxenus of Tarentum (ob. c. 300 BCE)
- Mencius (Meng Zi; Meng Tzu) (372–289 BCE)
- Crantor of Soli (fl. early 2nd century BCE)
- Theophrastus of Eressos (371–c. 287 BCE) (successor to Aristotle as head of Lyceum)
- Diodorus of Cronus (ob. 284 BCE) (Megarian)
- Polemo of Athens (ob. c. 276 BCE) (third scholarch of the Academy)
- Pyrrho of Elis (c. 360–c. 270 BCE) (Scepticism)
- Euclid (fl. c. 300 BCE)
- Clearchus of Soli (fl. c. 300 BCE)
- Epicurus of Samos (341–271 BCE) (arrives in Athens, 307 BCE)

- Crates of Athens (ob. c. 265 BCE) (fourth scholarch of the Academy)
- Herophilos (335–280 BCE)
- Strato of Lampsacus (c. 335–269 BCE) (third head of the Lyceum)
- Zeno of Citium (c. 334–262 BCE) (arrives in Athens, c. 310 BCE) (Old Stoa)
- Metrodorus of Lampsacus (the younger) (331–278 BCE)
- Cleanthes of Assos (c. 330–c. 232 BCE) (succeeds Zeno as scholarch of the Stoa)
- Timon of Phlius (c. 320–c. 230 BCE) (skeptic)
- Arcesilaus of Pitane (c. 315–241 BCE) (succeeds Crates, founds Middle Academy 264 BCE)
- Hieronymus of Rhodes (contemporary of Arcesilaus)
- Persaeus of Citium (306–243 BCE, student of Zeno)
- Erasistratus of Chias (304–250 BCE)
- Aristarchus of Samos (fl. c. 275 BCE)
- Philo the Dialectician (c. 300 BCE)

- Lycon of Troas (c. 299–225 BCE) (succeeded Strato as head of Lyceum)
- Ariston of Chios (fl. c. 260 BCE) (Old Stoa colleague of Zeno of Citium)
- Author of Ecclesiastes (fl. c. 250 BCE)
- Sphaerus of the Bosphorus (c. 285–210 BCE)
- Chrysippus of Soli (c. 280–207 BCE) (third leader of the Stoa)
- *Bhagavad Gita* (c. 3rd century BCE)
- Ariston of Keos (fl. 225 BCE)
- Eratosthenes of Cyrene (fl. c. 225 BCE)
- Archimedes of Syracuse (c. 287–212 BCE)
- Lacydes of Cyrene (ob. 205 BCE) (succeeds Arcesilaus as scholarch of Middle Academy)
- Telecles (ob. c. 166 BCE) (succeeds Lacydes as scholarch of Middle Academy)
- Zeno of Tarsus (in 207 BCE succeeds Chrysippus as scholarch of Stoa)
- Euander of Phocis (jointly leads and succeeds Telecles as scholarch of Middle Academy)
- Appolonius of Perge (fl. c. 200 BCE)
- Hegesinus of Pergamon (succeeds Euander as scholarch of Middle Academy)
- Diogenes of Babylon (c. 230–c. 150 BCE) (succeeded Zeno of Tarsus as scholarch of Stoa)
- Carneades of Cyrene (c. 214–129 BCE) (skeptic; succeeds Hegesinus and establishes New Academy)
- Antipater of Tarsus (c. 200–129 BCE)

- Aksapāda Gautama (fl. 2nd century BCE) (author of Nyāya Sūtras)
- Clitomachus (187–109 BCE) (pupil of Carneades)
- Metrodorus of Stratonicea (pupil of Carneades)
- Hipparchus of Nicaea (fl. 135 BCE)
- Panaetius of Rhodes (185–110 BCE) (Middle Stoa)
- Philo of Larissa (c. 159–84 BCE) (succeeded Clitomachus as scholarch of New Academy)
- Poseidonius of Apameia (c. 135–51 BCE) (Middle Stoa)
- Antiochus of Ascalon (c. 130–68 BCE) (Ecclecticism)
- Antipater of Tyre (ob. c. 45 BCE)
- Philodemus of Gadara (110–c. 40 BCE)
- Titus Pomponius Atticus (109–32 BCE)
- Aenesidemus (fl. c. 90 BCE) (Skepticism)
- Cicero (Marcus Tullius Cicero) (106–43 BCE)
- Diodotus the Stoic (friend of Cicero)

- Lucretius (Titus Lucretius Carus) (99/94–55/51 BCE) (Epicureanism)
- Cato the Younger (95–46 BCE)
- Lyceum sacked by Lucius Cornelius Sulla (86 BCE)
- Andronicus of Rhodes (fl. 1st century BCE)
- Sallust (Gaius Sallustius Crispus) (86–34 BCE)
- Julius Caesar consolidates power (45; assassinated 15 March 44 BCE)
- Ovid (Publius Ovidius Naso) (43 BCE–17 CE)
- Philo of Alexandria (c. 20 BCE–c. 40 CE)
- Jesus of Nazareth (5 BCE–29 CE)
- Seneca (Lucius Annaeus Seneca) (4 BCE–65 CE) (New Stoa)

- Paul of Tarsus (ob. 64)
- Ammonius the Peripatetic (fl. 1st century, teacher of Plutarch)
- Agrippa the Skeptic (fl. end of 1st century)
- Pliny the Elder (c. 23–79)
- Plutarch of Chaeronea (46–c. 125)
- Moderatus of Gades (c. 50–100)
- Apollonius of Tyana (fl. c. 100)
- Zeusippus (follower of Agrippa)
- Zeuxis (follower of Agrippa)
- Antiochus (follower of Agrippa)
- Epictetus (60–117) (New Stoa)
- Aeschines of Neapolis (fl. 109)
- Ptolemy (Claudius Ptolemaeus) (c. 90–168)

- Albinus (fl. 152)
- Numenius (Neo-Pythagorean, fl. 160)
- Herodotus of Tarsus (Sextus's predecessor)
- Theodas (Sextus's predecessor)
- Menodotus of Nicomedia (teacher of Sextus)
- Marcus Aurelius (121–180) (ruled 161–180) (New Stoa)
- Lucian (c. 125–200)
- Lucius Apuleius (fl. 2nd century)
- Galen (Claudios Galenos) (130–200)
- Sosigenes (teacher of Alexander of Aphrodisias)
- Irenaeus (130–202)
- Sextus Empiricus (ob. 210) (Later Skepticism)
- Alexander of Aphrodisias (fl. 200) ("the expositor" and head of Lyceum)
- Tertullian (c. 160–c. 230)
- Clement of Alexandria (c. 150–216)
- Nāgārjuna (2nd–3rd centuries)
- Ammonius Saccas (175–242)
- Origen of Alexandria (185–254)

- Diogenes Laertius (fl. 3rd century)
- Paul of Samosata (fl. 260–272)
- Plotinus (204–270) (Neo-Platonism)
- Manes (Mani) (215–276) (Manicheanism)
- Porphyry of Tyre (Malchus) (c. 232–304)
- Iamblichus of Chalcis (c. 245–c. 330) (Neo-Platonist)
- Lactantius (Lucius Caelius Firmianus) (c. 260–340)
- Donatus of Casa Nigrae (fl. 313) (Donatism)

- Arius (c. 250–336) (Arianism)
- Constantine I (c. 288–337); Seat of power moved to Constantinople (330)
- Donatus Magnus (c. 311–355) (Donatism)
- Aëtius of Antioch (ob. 367)
- Themistius (320–390)
- Council of Nicea (Doctrine of the Trinity) (325)
- Gregory of Nyssa (c. 330–c. 394)
- Julian the Apostate (c. 331–363)
- Ambrose of Milan (c. 340–397)
- Nemesius of Emesa (fl. 390) (Neo-Platonist)
- Sallustius (fl. mid 4th century)
- Jerome (347–420)
- Plutarch of Athens (c. 350–433)
- Hierocles (pupil of Plutarch)
- Augustine of Hippo (Aurelius Augustinus) (354–430)
- Hypatia of Alexandria (c. 360–415)

- Pelagius (360–420) (Pelagianism)
- Nestorius (c. 386–c. 451) (Nestorianism)
- Olympiodorus the Elder (teacher of Proclus)
- Synesius (c. 373–414)
- Bodhidharma (fl. early 5th century)
- Roman empire divided permanently after death of Theodosius I (395)

- Claudianus Mamertus (ob. c. 474)
- Proclus (c. 412–485) ("The Successor"; Neo-Platonist)
- Aeneas of Gaza (ob. c. 518) (Neo-Platonist)
- Ammonius Hermiae (c. 440–c. 520) (Neo-Platonist)
- Marinus of Neapolis (succeeds Proclus as head of Neo-Platonic school of Athens)
- Fan Zhen (c. 450–515)
- Damascius (458–538) (Neo-Platonist)
- Isidore of Alexandria (succeeds Marinus as head of Neo-Platonic school of Athens)
- Emperor Romulus Augustus deposed by Odoacer (476) (End of Western Roman Empire)
- Anicius Manlius Torquatus Severinus Boethius (c. 480–524)
- Pseudo-Dionysius (Dionysius the psuedo-Areopagite) (fl. c. 500)
- Benedict of Nursia (c. 480–543) (Monastic)
- Cassiodorus (Flavius Magnus Aurelius Cassiodorus) (c. 480–575)
- Simplicius of Cilicia (490–560) (Neo-Platonist)
- Asclepius of Tralles (ob. c. 565) (Neo-Platontist)
- Priscian of Lydia (fl. early 6th century) (Neo-Platonist)
- John Philoponus (c. 490–c. 570)
- Olympiodorus the Younger (c. 495–570) (Neo-Platonist)

- Udyotakara (fl. 6th century)
- Bodhiruci (fl. 6th century)
- Closing of the Schools of Athens (529)
- Zhiyi (Chih-k'ai or Chih-i) (531–597)
- Jizang (549–623) (Buddhist)
- Muhammed (c. 570–632)
- Isidore of Seville (c. 560–c. 636)
- Hsuan Tsang (Zuanzang) (fl. early 7th century)
- Stephen of Alexandria (fl. early 7th century)

- Bhartrihari (fl. mid 7th century)
- Prabhākara (fl. mid 7th century)

- Augustine Eriugena (Augustinus Hibernicus) (fl. 655)
- Shan-tao (612–681)
- Jacob of Edessa (640–708)
- I-Tsing (fl. late 7th century)
- Kumārila Bhatta (fl. early 8th century) (Mimamsa Hindu philosophy)
- Gyogi of Korea (668–749)
- Venerable Bede (672–735)
- John of Damascus (676–749)

- Mandana Miśra (fl. 8th century) (Mimamsa and Advaita Hindu philosophy)
- Gaudapada (fl. 8th century) (Advaita Vendanta Hindu philosophy)
- Padmapadacharya (fl. 8th century) (Vivarana Hindu philosophy)
- Śālikanātha (fl. 8th century) (Mimamsa Hindu philosophy)
- Wasil ibn Ata (700–748)
- Geber (Abu Musa Jābir ibn Hayyān) (721–815)
- Alcuin of York (Albinus) (c. 735–804)
- Sureśvara (b. c. 750) (follower of Śaṁkara)
- Li Ao (772–841)
- Han Yü (768–824)
- Albumasar (al-Falaki) (787–886)
- Śaṁkara (Adi Shankara) (c. 788–820) (Advaita Vendanta Hindu philosophy)
- Fridugisus of Tours (ob. c. 834)
- Radbertus Paschasius (c. 790–865)
- Linji (ob. 866) (Chán Buddhism)
- Candidus of Fulda (fl. 9th century)

- Al-Kindi (Alkindus) (c. 801–873)
- Johannes Scotus Erigena (c. 815–c. 877)
- Photius I (c. 820–893)
- Rhazes (al-Razi; 856–925)
- Al-Fārābi (Abunasser) (c. 872–c. 950)
- Jacob ben Nissim (fl. early 10th century)
- Saadia Gaon (Sa'adiah ben Yosef Gaon) (892–942)

- The Brethren of Purity (fl. 10th century)
- Vācaspati Miśra (900–980) (Bhāmatī Hindu philosophy)
- Abu Yaqub Sijista (ob. c. 973)
- Al-'Amiri (Abu'l Hasan Muhammad Ibn Yusuf al-'Amiri) (ob. 992)
- Gerbert of Aurillac (c. 946–1003)
- Alhacen (Ibn al-Haytham) (965–1039)
- Avicenna (Ibn Sina, Abn' Ali al-Husayn) (980–1037)

- Berengar of Tours (c. 1000–1088)
- Lanfranc of Bec (1005–1089)
- Peter Damian (c. 1007–1072)
- Shao Yong (1011–1077)
- Zhou Dunyi (1017–1073)
- Michael Psellus (c. 1018–1079)
- Avicebron (Ibn Gabirol) (1021–1070)
- Cheng Hao (older brother of Cheng Yi)
- Anselm of Canterbury (1033–1109)
- Cheng Yi (1033–1107)
- Rocelin of Compiegne (1050–1125)
- Al-Ghazālī (Algazel) (1058–1111)
- William of Champeaux (1070–1121)
- Bernard of Chartres (ob. after 1124)
- Ibn Bajjah (Avempace; ob. 1138)
- Hugh of St Victor (1078–1141)
- Yehudah (Judah) Hallevi (1075–1141)
- Gilbert of Poitiers (c. 1076–1154)
- Peter Abelard (1079–1142)
- Adelard of Bath (c. 1080–1152)
- Bernard of Clairvaux (1090–1153)
- Hildegard von Bingen (1098–1178)

- Peter the Lombard (1100–1160)
- Richard of St Victor (ob. 1173)
- Abu'l-Barakat ibn-Malka (ob. 1174/5)
- Adam de Lille (c. 1128–1202)
- Walter of St. Victor (ob. 1180)
- John of Salisbury (1115–1180)
- Ibn Rushd (Averroës) (1126–1198)
- Maimonides (Moses ben Maimon) (1135–1204)
- Thomas Gallus (c. 1170–1226)
- Edmund of Abingdon (1170–1240)
- John Blund (ob. 1248)
- Robert Grosseteste (1168–1253)
- Dominic (Dominic Guzman) (c. 1170–1221)
- Alexander of Hales (c. 1183–1245)
- John de la Rochelle (c. 1190–1245)
- Albertus Magnus (Albert the Great) (1193/1206–c. 1280)
- Moses Nahmanides (1194–1270)

- Peter of Spain (c. 1210–1277)
- Robert Kilwardby (c. 1215–1279)
- Roger Bacon (1214–c. 1292)
- William of Moerbeke (1215–1286)
- Bonaventure of Bagnoregio (c. 1221–1274)
- Thomas Aquinas (c. 1224/5–1274)
- John Pecham (c. 1225–1292)
- Boetius of Dacia (b. early 13th century)
- Henry of Ghent (c. 1217–1293)

- Siger of Brabant (c. 1235–c. 1281)
- Richard of Middleton (c. 1249–c. 1300)
- Arnaldus de Villanova (c. 1235–1311)
- Raymond Lully (1235–1315)
- Matthew of Aquasparta (c. 1240–1302)
- Theodoric of Freiberg (?–1310)
- Giles of Rome (1247–1316)
- Peter Olivi (1248/9–1298)
- Roger Marston (c. 1250–1303)
- Johannes (Meister) Eckhart (1260–1327)
- Dante Alighieri (1265–1321)
- John Duns Scotus (1266–1308)
- Henry of Harclay (1270–1317)
- Durand de Saint Pourcain (1275–1334)
- Peter Aureol (Peter Oriole) (c. 1275–1322)
- Marsilius of Padua (c. 1275–c. 1342)
- Gersonides (Levi ben Gershom) (Ralbag) (1288–1344)
- William of Ockham (1290–1349)
- Thomas Bradwardine (c. 1290–1349)
- Heinrich Suso (c. 1295–1366)

- Jean Buridan (c. 1300–1358)
- Adam de Wodeham (c. 1300–1358)
- Nicholas of Autrecourt (fl. 1347)
- Gregory of Rimini (c. 1300–1358)
- Petrarch (Francesco Petrarca) (1304–1374)
- John Wyclyf (Wycliffe) (c. 1320–1384)
- Albert of Saxony (1320–1390)
- Nicholas Oresme (c. 1325–1382)
- Albert of Saxony (c. 1325–1390)
- Marsilius of Inghen (?–1396)
- Coluccio Salutati (1331–1406)
- Hasdai ben Abraham Crescas (1340–1410)
- Geoffrey Chaucer (c. 1343–1400)
- Catherine of Siena (1347–1380)
- Tsongkapa (1357–1419)
- Jean de Gerson (1363–1429)
- Gorgius Gemistus (fl. early 15th century)
- Jan Hus (1369–1415)
- John Capreolous (1380–1444)
- Joseph Albo (1380–1444)
- Thomas à Kempis (1380–1471)
- Gianozzo Manetti (1396–1459)

- Nicholas of Cusa (Kryfts; Krebs; Nicolaus Cusanus) (1401–1464)
- Leon Battista Alberti (1404–1472)
- Lorenzo Valla (c. 1407–1457)
- Cristoforo Landino (1424–1498)
- Julius Pomponius Laetus (1425–1498)
- Marsilio Ficino (1433–1499)

- Isaac Abranel (1437–1508)
- Schism between Eastern and Western Churches formalized (1439)
- Leonardo da Vinci (1452–1519)
- Girolamo Savonarola (1452–1498)
- Fall of Constantinople (1453)
- Jacques Lefevre d'Etaples (c. 1453–1536)
- Politian (Poliziano) (1454–1494)
- Johannes Reuchlin (1457–1522)
- Leone Ebreo (1460–c. 1521)
- Judah Abrabanel (1460–1530)
- Pietro Pomponazzi (1462–1525)
- Pico della Mirandola (1463–1494)
- John Colet (1466/7–1519)
- Desiderius Erasmus (1466–1536)
- Niccolò Machiavelli (1469–1527)
- Thomas de Vio Cajetan (1469–1534)
- John Fisher (1469–1535)
- Nicolaus Copernicus (1473–1543)
- Thomas More (1478–1535)
- Guilio Camillo (c. 1480–1544)
- Martin Luther (1483–1546) (Ninety-Five Theses, 1517)
- Agrippa von Nettesheim (1486–1535)
- Giovanni Francesco Pico della Mirandola (1469–1533)
- Ulrich von Hutten (1488–1523)
- Mario Nizolio (1488–1567)
- Ignatius of Loyola (1491–1556)
- Juan Luis Vives (1492–1540)
- Menno Simons (1492–1559)
- Paracelsus (Theophrastus Phillippus Aureolus Bombastus von Hohenheim) (1493–1541)

- Girolamo Cardano (1501–1564)
- John Calvin (Jean Cauvin) (1509–1564)
- Bernardino Telesio (1509–1588)
- Roger Ascham (1515–1568)
- Peter Ramus (1515–1572)
- Moses Cordovero (1522–1570)
- Jean Bodin (1530–1596)
- Jacobi Zabarella (1532–1589)
- Michel de Montaigne (c. 1533–1592)
- Luis de Molina (1535–1600)
- Pierre Charron (1541–1603)
- John of the Cross (1542–1591)
- Torquato Tasso (1544–1595)
- Justus Lipsius (1547–1606)
- Giordano Bruno (1548–1600)
- Francisco Suarez (1548–1617)
- Francisco Sanches (c. 1550–1623)
- Alberico Gentile (1551–1611)

- Richard Hooker (1553–1600)
- Guillaume du Vair (1556–1621)
- Francis Bacon (1561–1626)
- William Shakespeare (1564–1616)
- Galileo Galilei (1564–1642)
- Tommaso Campanella (1568–1639)
- Johannes Kepler (1571–1630)
- Mulla Sadra (1571–1640)
- Robert Fludd (1574–1673)
- Jacob Boehme (Jakob Bohme) (1575–1621)
- Hugo Grotius (Huig de Groot) (1583–1645)
- Herbert of Cherbury (1583–1648)
- Hayashi Razan (1583–1657)
- Marin Mersenne (1588–1648)
- Francois de la Mothe le Vayer (1588–1672)
- Thomas Hobbes (1588–1679)
- Pierre Gassendi (1592–1655)
- René Descartes (1596–1650)

- Gerard du Cordemoy (c. 1605–1684)
- Anna Maria van Schurmann (1607–1678)
- Lord Brooke (Robert Greville) (1608–1643)
- John Milton (1608–1674)
- Gerrard Winstanley (c. 1609–c. 1660)
- Benjamin Whichcote (1609–1683)
- Antoine Arnauld (1612–1694)
- Henry More (1614–1687)
- Ralph Cudworth (1617–1688)
- Nathaniel Culverwel (1619-51)
- Blaise Pascal (1623–1662)
- Margaret Cavendish (1623–73)
- Arnold Geulincx (1624–1669)
- Pierre Nicole (1625–1655)
- Shabbetai Zevi (1626–1676)
- Robert Boyle (1627–1691)
- Jacques Beuigne Bossuet (1627–1704)
- Pierre-Daniel Huet (1630–1721)
- Anne Viscountess Conway (1631–1678)
- Benedictus Spinoza (1632–1677)
- Samuel von Pufendorf (1632–1694)
- John Locke (1632–1704)
- Robert Hooke (1635–1703)
- Joseph Glanvill (1636–1680)
- Nicolas Malebranche (1638–1715)
- Aphra Behn (1640–1689)
- Isaac Newton (1642–1727)
- Leibniz (Gottfried Wilhelm, Baron von Leibniz) (1646–1716)
- Pierre Bayle (1647–1706)
- Sor Juana (c. 1651–1695)
- Christian Thomasius (1655–1728)
- John Norris (1657–1711)

- Matthew Tindal (1657–1733)
- Fontenelle (1657–1757)
- William Wollaston (1660–1724)
- Mary Astell (c. 1666–1731)
- Giambattista Vico (1668–1744)
- John Gay (1669–1745)
- John Toland (1670–1722)
- Bernard Mandeville (1670–1733)
- Shaftesbury (Anthony Ashley Cooper, Earl of Shaftesbury) (1671–1713)
- Andreas Rüdiger (1673–1731)
- Samuel Clarke (1675–1729)
- Anthony Collins (1676–1723)
- Catherine Trotter Cockburn (1679–1749)
- Christian Wolff (1679–1754)
- George Berkeley (1685–1753)
- Johann Sebastian Bach (1685–1750)
- Alexander Pope (1688–1744)
- Emmanuel Swedenborg (1688–1772)
- Montesquieu (Charles de Secondat, Baron de Montesquieu) (1689–1755)
- Joseph Butler (1692–1752)
- Francis Hutcheson (1694–1747)
- Francois Quesnay (1694–1774)
- Voltaire (François-Marie Arouet) (1694–1778)
- Henry Home, Lord Kames (1696–1782)
- Philip Thummig (1697–1728)
- Pierre Louis de Maupertuis (1698–1758)
- Ba'al Shem Tov (1698–1760)

- Nikolaus von Zinzendorf (1700–1760)
- Thomas Bayes (1702–1761)
- Anton Wilhelm Amo (1703–c. 1759)
- Jonathan Edwards (1703–1758)
- David Hartley (1705–1757)
- Émilie du Châtelet (1706–1749)
- Benjamin Franklin (1706–1790)
- Leonhard Euler (1707–1783)
- Georges-Louis de Buffon (1707–1788)
- Julien Offroy de La Mettrie (1709–1751)
- Thomas Reid (1710–1796)
- David Hume (1711–1776)
- Jean-Jacques Rousseau (1712–1778)
- Martin Knutzen (1713–1751)
- Frederick the Great (1712–1786)
- Denis Diderot (1713–1784)
- Alexander G. Baumgarten (1714–1762)
- Nicolas de Béguelin (1714–1789)
- Claude-Adrien Helvetius (1715–1771)
- Christian August Cruisius (1715–1775)
- Étienne Bonnot de Condillac (1715–1780)
- Gottfried Plouquet (1716–1790)

- Jean le Rond d'Alembert (1717–1783)
- Georg Sulzer (1720–1779)
- William Robertson (1721–1793)
- d'Holbach (Paul Heinrich Dietrich, Baron d'Holbach) (1723–1789)
- Adam Smith (1723–1790)
- Richard Price (1723–1791)
- Adam Ferguson (1723–1816)
- Franz Aepinus (1724–1802)
- Immanuel Kant (1724–1804)
- Peter Eberhard (1727–1779)
- Anne Robert Jacques Turgot (1727–1781)
- Johan Heinrich Lambert (1728–1777)
- Moses Mendelssohn (1729–1786)
- José Antonio Alzate (1729–1790)
- Edmund Burke (1729–1797)
- Gotthold Ephraim Lessing (1729–1781)
- Johann Georg Hamman (1730–1788)
- Joseph Priestly (1773–1804)
- James Beattie (1735–1803)
- Thomas Paine (1737–1809)
- Cesare Beccaria (1738–1794)
- Sade (Donatien Alphonse Francois, comte de Sade) (1740–1814)
- Condorcet (Marie Jean Antoine Nicolas de Caritat, marquis de Condorcet) (1743–1794)
- Johann Christian Lossius (1743–1779)
- Friedrich Heinrich Jacobi (1743–1819)
- Thomas Jefferson (1743–1826)
- Johann Gottfried von Herder (1744–1803)
- Benito Diaz de Gamarra (1745–1783)
- A. Guevara y Basoazábal (1748–1801)
- Jeremy Bentham (1748–1832)
- Johann Wolfgang von Goethe (1749–1832)
- Claude-Adrien Helvetius (1751–1771)
- Dugald Stewart (1753–1828)
- Antoine comte de Tracy (Antoine Louis Claude Destutt) (1754–1836)
- William Godwin (1756–1836)
- Pierre Laromiguière (1756–1837)
- William Blake (1757–1827)
- Mary Wollstonecraft (1759–1797)
- J. C. F. Schiller (1759–1805)
- Christoph Gottfried Bardili (1761–1808)
- Gottlob Ernst Schulze (1761–1833)
- Johann Gottlieb Fichte (1762–1814)
- Madame de Staël (1766–1817)
- Maine de Biran (1766–1824)
- Karl Wilhelm von Humboldt (1767–1835)
- F. D. E. Schleiermacher (1768–1834)
- Ludwig van Beethoven (1770–1827)
- George Wilhelm Friedrich Hegel (1770–1831)

- Friedrich C. Forberg (1770–1848)
- José Agustin Caballero (1771–1835)
- Robert Owen (1771–1858)
- Novalis (Friedrich Leopold, Baron von Hardenberg) (1772–1801)
- David Ricardo (1772–1823)
- Friedrich von Schlegel (1772–1829)
- Samuel Taylor Coleridge (1772–1834)
- James Mill (1773–1836)
- Jakob Friedrich Fries (1773–1843)
- F. W. J. Schelling (1775–1854)
- Johann Friedrich Herbart (1776–1841)
- Karl Friedrich Gauss (1777–1855)
- Karl C. F. Krause (1781–1832)
- Bernard Bolzano (1781–1848)
- Andrés Bello (1781–1865)
- José Joaqín de Mora (1783–1864)
- Nachman Knochmal (1785–1840)
- Alexander Bryan Johnson (1786–1867)
- William Hamilton (1788–1856)
- Arthur Schopenhauer (1788–1860)
- S. L. Steinheim (1789–1866)
- Carl Gustav Carus (1789–1869)
- John Austin (1790–1859)
- Victor Cousin (1792–1867)
- Leopold Zunz (1794–1886)
- Antonio Rosmini (1797–1855)
- Thomas Carlyle (1795–1881)
- Giacomo Leopardi (1798–1835)
- Auguste Comte (1798–1857)
- Jules Michelet (1798–1874)

- José Cipriano de la Luz y Caballero (1800–1862)
- Vincenzo Gioberti (1801–1852)
- Gustav Theodor Fechner (1801–1887)
- Friedrich A. Trendelenburg (1802–1872)
- Orestes Augustus Brownson (1803–1876)
- Ralph Waldo Emerson (1803–1882)
- Ludwig Feuerbach (1804–1872)
- Alexis de Tocqueville (1805–1859)
- Max Stirner (1806–1856)
- Augustus De Morgan (1806–1871)
- John Stuart Mill (1806–1873)
- David Friedrich Strauss (1808–1874)
- Pierre-Joseph Proudhon (1809–1865)
- Charles Robert Darwin (1809–1882)
- Aleksandr Ivanovich Herzen (1812–1870)
- Moses Hess (1812–1877)
- Søren Kierkegaard (1813–1855)
- Nikolai Stakevich (1813–1883)
- Mikail A. Bakunin (1814–1876)

- Eduard Zeller (1814–1908)
- George Boole (1815–1864)
- Charles Bernard Renouvier (1815–1903)
- Henry David Thoreau (1817–1862)
- Rudolf Hermann Lotze (1817–1881)
- Francesco De Santis (1817–1883)
- Karl Marx (1818–1883)
- Friedrich Engels (1820–1895)
- Herbert Spencer (1820–1903)
- Fyodor M. Dostoievski (1821–1881)
- Hermann von Helmholtz (1821–1894)
- Moritz Lazarus (1824–1903)
- Friedrich Albert Lange (1828–1875)
- Hippolyte Taine (1828–1893)
- Chauncy Wright (1830–1875)
- Christoph Sigwart (1830–1904)
- Wilhelm Wundt (1832–1920)
- Johannes Brahms (1833–1897)
- Wilhelm Dilthey (1833–1911)
- Mark Twain (1835–1910)
- Thomas Hill Green (1836–1882)
- Henry Sidgwick (1838–1900)
- Ernst Mach (1838–1916)
- Franz Brentano (1838–1917)
- Henry George (1839–1897)
- Charles Sanders Peirce (1839–1914)
- Otto Liebmann (1840–1912)
- Stephane Mallarmé (1842–1898)
- Eduard von Hartmann (1842–1906)
- William James (1842–1910)
- Hermann Cohen (1842–1918)
- Peter Kropotkin (1842–1921)
- Richard Avenarius (1843–1896)
- Friedrich Wilhelm Nietzsche (1844–1900)
- Ludwig Boltzmann (1844–1906)
- Alois Riehl (1844–1924)
- Gaston Bachelard (1844–1926)
- Georg Cantor (1845–1918)
- Francis Herbert Bradley (1846–1924)
- Georges Sorel (1847–1922)
- Wilhelm Windelband (1848–1915)
- Bernard Bosanquet (1848–1923)
- Vilfredo Pareto (1848–1923)
- Gottlob Frege (1848–1925)
- Enrique José Varona (1849–1933)
- Alejandro Deústua (Peruvian) (1849–1945)
- Hans Vaihinger (1852–1933)
- Alexius Meinong (1853–1921)
- Jules Henri Poincaré (1854–1912)
- Paul Natorp (1854–1924)
- Josiah Royce (1855–1916)
- H. Ginsberg (Ahad Ha'am) (1856–1927)
- Sigmund Freud (1856–1939)
- George Bernard Shaw (1856–1950)
- Ferdinand de Saussure (1857–1913)
- Thornstein Bunde Veblen (1857–1929)
- Émile Durkheim (1858–1917)
- Georg Simmel (1858–1918)
- Samuel Alexander (1859–1938)
- Edmund G. A. Husserl (1859–1938)
- Henri Bergson (1859–1941)
- John Dewey (1859–1952)
- Alejandro Korn (1860–1936)
- Rudolf Steiner (1861–1925)
- Rabindranath Tagore (1861–1941)
- Alfred North Whitehead (1861–1947)
- Maurice Blondel (1861–1949)
- Farias Brito (1862–1917)
- George H. Mead (1863–1931)
- Heinrich Rickert (1863–1936)
- George Santayana (1863–1952)
- Max Weber (1864–1920)
- Miguel de Unamuno y Jugo (1864–1936)
- F. C. S. Schiller (1864–1937)
- William Butler Yeats (1865–1939)
- John McTaggart (1866–1925)
- Benedetto Croce (1866–1952)
- W. E. B. DuBois (1868–1963)
- Rudolph Otto (1869–1937)
- Emma Goldman (1869–1940)
- Leon Brunschvicg (1869–1944)
- Rosa Luxemburg (c. 1870–1919)
- Nikolai Lenin (1870–1924)
- Kitaro Nishida (1870–1945)
- Joseph Hilaire Pierre Belloc (1870–1953)
- Federigo Euriquez (1871–1946)
- Alexandria M. Kollontai (1872–1952)
- Sri Aurobindo Ghose (1872–1950)
- Bertrand A. W. Russell (1872–1970)
- Leo Baeck (1873–1956)
- George Edward Moore (1873–1958)
- Arthur Oncken Lovejoy (1873–1962)
- Gilbert Keith Chesterton (1874–1936)
- Nicholai Berdyaev (1874–1948)
- Max Scheler (1874–1928)
- Ernst Cassirer (1874–1945)
- Emil Lask (1875–1915)
- Giovanni Gentile (1875–1944)
- Carl Gustav Jung (1875–1961)
- Peter Maurin (1877–1949)
- Pabongka Rinpoche (1878–1941)
- Peter D. Ouspensky (1878–1947)
- Martin Buber (1878–1965)
- Georg Misch (1878–1965)

- Joseph Marechal (1878–1944)
- Albert Einstein (1879–1955)
- Oswald Spengler (1880–1936)
- Pierre Teilhard de Chardin (1881–1955)
- Giovanni Papini (1881–1956)
- Karl Barth (1881–1968)
- Moritz Schlick (1882–1936)
- Otto Elis (1882–1945)
- Nicolai Hartmann (1882–1950)
- Jacques Maritain (1882–1973)
- Adolf Reinach (1883–1917)
- John Maynard Keynes (1883–1946)
- Jose Ortega y Gasset (1883–1955)
- Karl Theodor Jaspers (1883–1969)
- Clarence Irving Lewis (1883–1964)
- Étienne Gilson (1884–1978)
- Rudolf Bultmann (1884–1976)
- Tanabe Hajime (1885–1962)
- Gyorgy Lukacs (1885–1971)
- Ernst Bloch (1885–1977)
- Franz Rosenzweig (1886–1929)
- Antonio Banfi (1886–1957)
- Karl Polanyi (1886–1964)
- Paul Johannes Tillich (1886–1965)
- Carlo Michelstaedter (1887–1910)
- Charlie Dunbar Broad (1887–1971)
- Erwin Schrödinger (1887–1961)
- Werner Wilhelm Jaeger (1888–1961)
- Thomas Stearns Eliot (1888–1965)
- Carl Schmitt (1888–1985)
- Sarvepalli Radhakrishnan (1888–1972)
- Robin George Collingwood (1889–1943)
- Ludwig Wittgenstein (1889–1951)
- Gabriel Marcel (1889–1973)
- Arnold Joseph Toynbee (1889–1975)
- Martin Heidegger (1889–1976)
- Antonio Gramsci (1891–1937)
- Hans Reichenbach (1891–1953)
- Rudolf Carnap (1891–1970)
- Walter Benjamin (1892–1940)
- Alexandre Koyre (1892–1964)
- Reinhold Niebuhr (1892–1964)
- Karl Mannheim (1893–1947)
- Aldous Leonard Huxley (1894–1963)
- Helmut Richard Niebuhr (1894–1971)
- Fung Yu-Lan (1895–1990)
- Galvano Della Volpe (1895–1968)
- Susanne Knauth Langer (1895–1985)
- Max Horkheimer (1895–1973)
- John William Miller (1895–1978)
- Antonin Artaud (1896–1948)
- Friedrich Waismann (1896–1959)
- Georges Bataille (1897–1962)
- Dorothy Day (1897–1980)
- Leo Strauss (1898–1973)
- O. K. Bouwsma (1898–1978)
- Herbert Marcuse (1898–1979)
- Alfred Schutz (1899–1959)
- John Herman Randall (1899–1980)

- Gilbert Ryle (1900–1976)
- Leroy Earl Loemker (1900–1985)
- Keiji Nishitani (1900–1990)
- Hans-Georg Gadamer (1900–2002)
- Werner Heisenberg (1901–1976)
- Jacques Lacan (1901–1981)
- Ernest Nagel (1901–1985)
- Michael Oakeshott (1901–1992)
- Eric Voeglin (1901–1985)
- Alexandre Kojeve (1902–1968)
- Alfred Tarski (1902–1983)
- Ernesto Grassi (1902–1991)
- Karl Raimund Popper (1902–1994)
- Sidney Hook (1902–1989)
- Ludwig Landgrebe (1902–1991)
- Frank Plumpton Ramsey (1903–1930)
- John von Neumann (1903–1957)
- Theodor W. Adorno (1903–1969)
- Otto Friedrich Bollnow (1903–91)
- Rudolph Arnheim (1904–2007)
- Arnold Gehlen (1904–1976)
- J. Robert Oppenheimer (1904–1967)
- Burrhus Fredric Skinner (1904–1990)
- John Wisdom (1904–1993)
- Jean-Paul Sartre (1905–1980)
- Raymond Aron (1905–1983)
- Rush Rhees (1905–1989)
- Carl Gustav Hempel (1905–1997)
- Paul Oskar Kristeller (1905–1999)
- Emmanuel Lévinas (1905–1995)
- Hannah Arendt (1906–1975)
- Kurt Gödel (1906–1978)
- Gustav Bergmann (1906–1987)
- Nelson Goodman (1906–1998)
- Maurice Blanchot (1907–2003)
- Maurice Merleau-Ponty (1908–1961)
- Charles L. Stevenson (1908–1979)
- Simone de Beauvoir (1908–1986)
- Claude Lévi-Strauss (b. 1908)
- Willard Van Orman Quine (1908–2000)
- Simone Weil (1909–1943)
- Isaiah Berlin (1909–1997)
- Max Black (1909–1988)
- Alfred Jules Ayer (1910–1989)

- John Langshaw Austin (1911–1960)
- Norman Malcolm (1911–1999)
- Alan Turing (1912–1954)
- Herman Northrop Frye (1912–1991)
- Alan Gewirth (1912–2004)
- Arne Naess (1912–2009)
- Wilfrid Stalker Sellars (1912–1989)
- Albert Camus (1913–1960)
- H. Paul Grice (1913–1988)
- Paul Ricoeur (1913–2005)
- Stuart Newton Hampshire (1914–2004)
- Thomas Merton (1915–1968)
- Roland Barthes (1915–1980)
- Ivor Leclerc (1915–1999)
- J. O. Urmson (b. 1915)
- Georg Henrik von Wright (1916–2003)
- Robert Denoon Cumming (1916–2004)
- Peter Thomas Geach (b. 1916)
- Donald Davidson (1917–2003)
- Louis Althusser (1918–1990)
- G. Elizabeth M. Anscombe (1919–2001)
- P. F. Strawson (1919–2006)
- Richard Mervyn Hare (1919–2002)
- Mary Midgley (b. 1919)
- Iris Murdoch (1919–1999)
- William P. Alston (b. 1921)
- John Rawls (1921–2002)
- Karl-Otto Apel (b. 1922)
- Richard Wollheim (1923–2003)
- Frantz Fanon (1925–1961)
- Michael A. E. Dummett (b. 1925)
- Michel Foucault (1926–1984)
- Peter G. Winch (1926–1997)
- David M. Armstrong (b. 1926)
- Stanley Cavell (b. 1926)
- Joel Feinberg (1926–2004)
- Hilary Whitehall Putnam (b. 1926)
- Avram Noam Chomsky (b. 1928)
- Hayden V. White (b. 1928)
- Hubert L. Dreyfus (b. 1929)
- Harry G. Frankfurt (b. 1929)
- Alasdair Chalmers MacIntyre (b. 1929)

- Jürgen Habermas (b. 1929)
- Jaakko Hintikka (b. 1929)
- Bernard Williams (1929–2003)
- Jacques Derrida (1930–2004)
- Derrick A. Bell (b. 1930)
- Ronald M. Dworkin (1931)
- Anthony Kenny (b. 1931)
- Richard Rorty (1931–2007)
- Charles Taylor (b. 1931)
- Timothy L. S. Sprigge (1932–2007)
- Luce Irigaray (b. 1932)
- Alvin Plantinga (b. 1932)
- Holmes Rolston III (b. 1932)
- John R. Searle (b. 1932)
- Ted Honderich (b. 1933)
- Antonio Negri (b. 1933)
- Amartya Kumar Sen (b. 1933)
- D. Z. Phillips (1934–2006)
- Jerry A. Fodor (b. 1935)
- Bimal Krishna Matilal (1935–1991)
- Monique Wittig (b. 1935)
- Thomas Nagel (b. 1937)
- Robert Nozick (1938–2002)
- Saul Kripke (b. 1940)
- David Lewis (1941–2001)
- Julia Kristeva (b. 1941)
- Daniel Dennett (b. 1942)
- John McDowell (b. 1942)
- Derek Parfit (b. 1942)
- Crispin Wright (b. 1942)
- Roger Scruton (b. 1944)
- Peter Singer (b. 1946)
- Martha C. Nussbaum (b. 1947)
- Slavoj Žižek (b. 1949)
- Robert Brandom (b. 1950)
- Colin McGinn (b. 1950)
- Christine Korsgaard (b. 1952)
- Cornel West (b. 1953)
- Kwame Anthony Appiah (b. 1954)
- Timothy Willamson (b. 1955)
- Judith Butler (b. 1956)

Suggested Additional Reading
in the History of Philosophy

- (Various editors) *Routledge History of Philosophy*, London: Routledge, 1993–9.
- (Various authors) *A History of Western Philosophy*, 8 vols, Oxford: Oxford University Press, 1989–98.
- Peter Adamson and Richard C. Taylor, eds, *The Cambridge Companion to Arabic Philosophy*, Cambridge: Cambridge University Press, 2005.
- Robert Arrington, ed., *A Companion to the Philosophers*, Oxford: Blackwell, 1988.
- Nicholas Bunnin and E. Tsui-James, eds, *The Blackwell Companion to Philosophy*, Oxford: Blackwell, 2002.
- Brian Carr and Indira Mahalingam, eds, *Companion Encyclopedia of Asian Philosophy*, London: Routledge, 1997.
- David E. Cooper, *World Philosophies: An Historical Introduction*, 2nd edn, Oxford: Blackwell, 2003.
- Fredrick Copleston, *A History of Philosophy* (1946), 8 vols, New York: Image, 1993.
- Edward Craig, ed., *The Routledge Encyclopedia of Philosophy*, 10 vols, London: Routledge, 1998.
- Simon Critchley and William Schroeder, eds, *A Companion to Continental Philosophy*, Oxford: Blackwell, 1999.
- Surendranath Dasgupta, *A History of Indian Philosophy*, 5 vols, Delhi: Motilal Banarsidass, 1975 (1922).
- Hubert Dreyfus and Mark Wrathall, eds, *A Companion to Phenomenology and Existentialism*, Oxford: Blackwell, 2006.
- Gavin Flood, *The Blackwell Companion to Hinduism*, Oxford: Blackwell, 2005.
- Dan Frank and Oliver Leaman, eds, *The Cambridge Companion to Medieval Jewish Philosophy*, Cambridge: Cambridge University Press, 2003.
- Fung Yu-Lan, *A History of Chinese Philosophy*, 2 vols, trans. D. Bodde, Princeton, NJ: Princeton University Press, 1952.
- Mary Louise Gill and Pierre Pellegrin, *A Companion to Ancient Philosophy* Oxford: Blackwell, 2006.
- Étienne Gilson, *A History of Christian Philosophy in the Middle Ages*, London: Sheed & Ward, 1955.
- Jorge J. E. Gracia and Timothy Noone, eds, *A Companion to Philosophy in the Middle Ages*, Oxford: Blackwell, 2003.
- G. W. F. Hegel, *Lectures on the History of Philosophy*, 2nd edn, 3 vols (1840); Atlantic Highlands, NJ: Humanities Press, 1983.
- Anthony Kenny, *A New History of Philosophy*, 4 Vols, Oxford: Oxford University Press, 2004–7.
- Fredrick Lange, *History of Materialism: And Criticism of Its Importance* (1879), 2nd edn, 3 vols; Edinburgh: Balantyne, Hanson, & Co.; 3rd edn, New York: Routledge & Kegan Paul, 1950.
- Oliver Leaman, *A History of Jewish Philosophy*, London: Taylor & Francis, 2007.
- Oliver Leaman, *Encyclopedia of Asian Philosophy*, London: Routledge, 2001.

- JeeLoo Liu, *An Introduction to Chinese Philosophy: From Ancient Philosophy to Chinese Buddhism*, Oxford: Blackwell, 2006.
- Alasdair MacIntyre, *A Short History of Ethics*, New York: Macmillan, 1966.
- A. S. McGrade, ed., *The Cambridge Companion to Medieval Philosophy*, Cambridge: Cambridge University Press, 2003.
- Steven Nadler, ed., *A Companion to Early Modern Philosophy*, Oxford: Blackwell, 2007.
- Seyyed Hossein Nasr and Oliver Leaman, eds, *History of Islamic Philosophy*, 2 vols, London: Routledge, 1996.
- John Passmore, *A Hundred Years of Philosophy*, London: Penguin, 1968.
- Chakravarthi Ram-Prasad, *Eastern Philosophy*, London: Weidenfeld & Nicolson, 2005.
- Sarvepalli Radhakrishnan, *Indian Philosophy* (1923), 2 vols, Delhi: Oxford University Press, 1989.
- Bertrand Russell, *A History of Western Philosophy* (1945), New York: Simon & Schuster, 1972.
- John Shook and Joseph Margolis, eds, *A Companion to Pragmatism*, Oxford: Blackwell, 2006.
- Ninian Smart, *World Philosophies*, London: Routledge, 2000.
- Tom Sorell, ed., *The Rise of Modern Philosophy*, Oxford: Clarendon Press, 1993.
- Wilhelm Windelband, *A History of Philosophy*, 2nd edn, 2 vols (1901); New York: Elibron Classics, 2006.
- John Yolton, Roy Porter, Barbara Stafford, and Pat Rogers, eds, *A Companion to the Enlightenment*, Oxford: Blackwell, 1991.

I
Ethics

1

Plato, *Gorgias*, 482–4, 488–500

Introduction

The *Gorgias* of the great Athenian philosopher, Plato (c. 427–347 BCE), is one of his early dialogues, free as yet of his mature metaphysical doctrines, notably the theory of the "Forms" (*eidē*). Dark intimations of the fate of Socrates, the main character in the dialogue, and unusually bitter animosity toward Socrates' opponents, suggest that it may have been written by Plato not long after his teacher's trial and death in 399 BCE. As such, the *Gorgias* is one of the very first sustained discussions of morality to have come down to us from the Greeks – and one of the most influential, for it announces themes that have continued to occupy philosophers ever since, such as the relation between goodness and pleasure. Above all, in the person of Callicles, the dialogue introduces a stark prototype of a "might is right" amoralism which, ever since, has had its advocates in Western thought, right down to the apologists of Realpolitik and Fascism.

Callicles, like many of Socrates' adversaries, was a Sophist, one of those teachers of the skills – notably in oratory – deemed essential to success in Athenian public life. Like today's PR men, advertising executives and "spin doctors," the Sophists had a not disadvantageous reputation

From The Dialogues of Plato, Vol. II, trans. B. Jowett. New York: Macmillan and Co., 1892, pp. 369–71, 375–90 (notes and some passages omitted).

for nonchalance toward accepted morality. For the go-ahead Athenian orator or litigant, it might be useful to wear "the appearance of goodness," but of no particular benefit to worry about its substance. And by the more philosophically minded Sophists, like Protagoras and Thrasymachus, the very prospect of rational, objective moral norms is rejected. "[T]he just and the unjust . . . are in truth to each state such as it thinks they are . . . in these matters no citizen or state is wiser than another," said Protagoras, the "father" of moral relativism; while, for Thrasymachus – anticipating Marx's views (V.19) – justice is simply "the interest of the stronger" and morality only a system of rules furthering that interest.[1]

Callicles' position, while equally dismissive of conventional morality itself and of people's usual understanding of it, is rather different. That morality varies from society to society is not the relevant point; nor is it that conventional morality is a tool exploited by the strong. Rather, the point is the more Nietzschean one (I.18) that conventional morality is a crutch used by inferior, weaker people, and something to despise in comparison with the "natural" morality of the unbridled strong man. (Callicles thereby stands behind another long tradition in Western thought, the opposition – in Rousseau (V.12), for instance – between the "natural" and "social" characteristics of human beings)?

Callicles introduces this point at the stage where our extract from the *Gorgias* begins, after he has impatiently listened to the reasons Socrates has given for denying both that oratory is a beneficial art and that it confers the power to get what one wants. Socrates, he exclaims, cannot be in earnest in holding that "it is better to suffer wrong than to do wrong" and that the wrongdoer is "more miserable than the man who is wronged" (479). For Callicles, Socrates' previous interlocutors, Gorgias and Polus, have conceded too much to familiar concepts of good and justice. What is needed is a blunt equation of "better" and "stronger," a radical rejection of familiar moral understanding.

This very bluntness and radicalism, however, lays him open to Socrates' objections. What, after all, can Callicles mean by terms like "better" if he has broken completely with ordinary conceptions? Callicles is soon forced to qualify his initial equation and to shift toward a notion of good in terms of a lusty pursuit of pleasure, a move that is brought to a halt by Socrates' forcing of the concession that pleasures, too, can be appraised as good and bad. Not all of Socrates' arguments are good ones, notably the one which relies on the example of thirst and its quenching to show that pleasure and pain, unlike good and evil, can be found combined (494ff.). But much of the argumentation is exemplary for subsequent attempts (G. E. Moore's, for example; I.19) to stop the radical moral revisionist or amoralist in his tracks. By appealing to how terms in the moral lexicon are actually employed, Socrates endeavors to show that the radical debars himself from saying what he wants to: for by loosing terms like "good" and "just" from their moorings, the radical is precluded from using them to approve the courses of action, or ways of life, which he urges. Readers will need to look at some of the other texts in this volume to decide whether that endeavor was necessarily a decisive one.

Note

1   For Protagoras, see Plato's *Theaetetus*, 172; for Thrasymachus, see Plato's *Republic*, Book I.

Plato, *Gorgias*

Cal. [. . .] For the truth is, Socrates, that you, who pretend to be engaged in the pursuit of truth, are appealing now to the popular and vulgar notions of right, which are not natural, but only conventional. Convention and nature are generally at variance with one another: and hence, if 483 a person is too modest to say what he thinks, he is compelled to contradict himself; and you, in your ingenuity perceiving the advantage to be thereby gained, slyly ask of him who is arguing conventionally a question which is to be determined by the rule of nature; and if he is talking of the rule of nature, you slip away to custom: as, for instance, you did in this very discussion about doing and suffering injustice. When Polus was speaking of the conventionally dishonourable, you assailed him from the point of view of nature; for by the rule of nature, to suffer injustice is the greater disgrace because the greater evil; but conventionally, to do evil is the more disgraceful. For the suffering of injustice is not the part of a man, but of a slave, who indeed had better die than live; since when he is wronged and trampled upon, he is unable to help himself, or any other about whom he cares. The reason, as I conceive, is that the makers of laws are the majority who are weak ; and they make laws and distribute praises and censures with a view to themselves and to their own interests; and they terrify the stronger sort of men, and those who are able to get the better of them, in order that they may not get the better of them; and they say, that dishonesty is shameful and unjust; meaning, by the word injustice, the desire of a man to have more than his neighbours; for knowing their own inferiority, I suspect that they are too glad of equality. And therefore the endeavour to have more than the many, is conventionally said to be shameful and unjust, and is called injustice, whereas nature herself intimates that it is just for the better to have more than the worse, the more powerful than the weaker; and in many ways she shows, among men as well as among animals, and indeed among whole cities and races, that justice consists in the superior ruling over and having more than the inferior. For on what principle of justice did Xerxes invade Hellas, or his father the

Scythians? (not to speak of numberless other examples). Nay, but these are the men who act according to nature; yes, by Heaven, and according to the law of nature: not, perhaps, according to that artificial law, which we invent and impose upon our fellows, of whom we take the best and strongest from their youth upwards, and tame
484 them like young lions, – charming them with the sound of the voice, and saying to them, that with equality they must be content, and that the equal is the honourable and the just. But if there were a man who had sufficient force, he would shake off and break through, and escape from all this; he would trample under foot all our formulas and spells and charms, and all our laws which are against nature: the slave would rise in rebellion and be lord over us, and the light of natural justice would shine forth. And this I take to be the sentiment of Pindar, when he says in his poem, that

> Law is the king of all, of mortals as well as of immortals;

this, as he says,

> Makes might to be right, doing violence with highest hand; as I infer from the deeds of Heracles, for without buying them –

I do not remember the exact words, but the meaning is, that without buying them, and without their being given to him, he carried off the oxen of Geryon, according to the law of natural right, and that the oxen and other possessions of the weaker and inferior properly belong to the stronger and superior. And this is true, as you may ascertain, if you will leave philosophy and go on to higher things: for philosophy, Socrates, if pursued in moderation and at the proper age, is an elegant accomplishment, but too much philosophy is the ruin of human life.

[. . .]

488   *Soc.* Once more, then, tell me what you and Pindar mean by natural justice: Do you not mean that the superior should take the property of the inferior by force; that the better should rule the worse, the noble have more than the mean? Am I not right in my recollection?

Cal. Yes; that is what I was saying, and so I still aver.

Soc. And do you mean by the better the same as the superior? for I could not make out what you were saying at the time – whether you meant by the superior the stronger, and that the weaker must obey the stronger, as you seemed to imply when you said that great cities attack small ones in accordance with natural right, because they are superior and stronger, as though the superior and stronger and better were the same; or whether the better may be also the inferior and weaker, and the superior the worse, or whether better is to be defined in the same way as superior: – this is the point which I want to have cleared up. Are the superior and better and stronger the same or different?

Cal. I say unequivocally that they are the same.

Soc. Then the many are by nature superior to the one, against whom, as you were saying, they make the laws?

Cal. Certainly.

Soc. Then the laws of the many are the laws of the superior?

Cal. Very true.

Soc. Then they are the laws of the better; for the superior class are far better, as you were saying?

Cal. Yes.

Soc. And since they are superior, the laws which are made by them are by nature good?

Cal. Yes.

Soc. And are not the many of opinion, as you were lately saying, that justice is equality, and that 489 to do is more disgraceful than to suffer injustice? – is that so or not? Answer, Callicles, and let no modesty be found to come in the way; do the many think, or do they not think thus? – I must beg of you to answer, in order that if you agree with me I may fortify myself by the assent of so competent an authority.

Cal. Yes; the opinion of the many is what you say.

Soc. Then not only custom but nature also affirms that to do is more disgraceful than to suffer injustice, and that justice is equality; so that you seem to have been wrong in your former assertion, when accusing me you said that nature and custom are opposed, and that I, knowing this, was dishonestly playing between them, appealing to custom when the argument is about nature, and to nature when the argument is about custom?

Cal. This man will never cease talking nonsense. At your age, Socrates, are you not ashamed to be catching at words and chuckling over some verbal slip? do you not see – have I not told you already, that by superior I mean better: do you imagine me to say, that if a rabble of slaves and nondescripts, who are of no use except perhaps for their physical strength, get together, their ipsissima verba are laws?

Soc. Ho! my philosopher, is that your line?

Cal. Certainly.

Soc. I was thinking, Callicles, that something of the kind must have been in your mind, and that is why I repeated the question, – What is the superior? I wanted to know clearly what you meant; for you surely do not think that two men are better than one, or that your slaves are better than you because they are stronger? Then please to begin again, and tell me who the better are, if they are not the stronger; and I will ask you, great Sir, to be a little milder in your instructions, or I shall have to run away from you.

Cal. You are ironical.

Soc. No, by the hero Zethus, Callicles, by whose aid you were just now saying (486 A) many ironical things against me, I am not: – tell me, then, whom you mean by the better?

Cal. I mean the more excellent.

Soc. Do you not see that you are yourself using words which have no meaning and that you are explaining nothing? – will you tell me whether you mean by the better and superior the wiser, or if not, whom?

490   *Cal.* Most assuredly, I do mean the wiser.

Soc. Then according to you, one wise man may often be superior to ten thousand fools, and he ought to rule them, and they ought to be his subjects, and he ought to have more than they should. This is what I believe that you mean (and you must not suppose that I am word-catching), if you allow that the one is superior to the ten thousand ?

Cal. Yes; that is what I mean, and that is what I conceive to be natural justice – that the better and wiser should rule and have more than the inferior.

Soc. Stop there, and let me ask you what you would say in this case: Let us suppose that we are all together as we are now; there are several of us, and we have a large common store of meats and drinks, and there are all sorts of persons in our company having various degrees of strength and weakness, and one of us, being a physician, is wiser in the matter of food than all the rest, and he is probably stronger than some and not so strong as others of us – will he not, being wiser, be also better than we are, and our superior in this matter of food?

Cal. Certainly.

Soc. Either, then, he will have a larger share of the meats and drinks, because he is better, or he will have the distribution of all of them by reason of his authority, but he will not expend or make use of a larger share of them on his own person, or if he does, he will be punished; – his share will exceed that of some, and be less than that of others, and if he be the weakest of all, he being the best of all will have the smallest share of all, Callicles: – am I not right, my friend?

Cal. You talk about meats and drinks and physicians and other nonsense; I am not speaking of them.

Soc. Well, but do you admit that the wiser is the better? Answer 'Yes' or 'No.'

Cal. Yes.

Soc. And ought not the better to have a larger share?

Cal. Not of meats and drinks.

Soc. I understand: then, perhaps, of coats – the skilfullest weaver ought to have the largest coat, and the greatest number of them, and go about clothed in the best and finest of them?

Cal. Fudge about coats!

Soc. Then the skilfullest and best in making shoes ought to have the advantage in shoes; the shoemaker, clearly, should walk about in the largest shoes, and have the greatest number of them?

Cal. Fudge about shoes! What nonsense are you talking?

Soc. Or, if this is not your meaning, perhaps you would say that the wise and good and true husbandman should actually have a larger share of seeds, and have as much seed as possible for his own land?

Cal. How you go on, always talking in the same way, Socrates!

Soc. Yes, Callicles, and also about the same   491 things.

Cal. Yes, by the Gods, you are literally always talking of cobblers and fullers and cooks and doctors, as if this had to do with our argument.

Soc. But why will you not tell me in what a man must be superior and wiser in order to claim a larger share; will you neither accept a suggestion, nor offer one?

Cal. I have already told you. In the first place, I mean by superiors not cobblers or cooks, but wise politicians who understand the administration of a state, and who are not only wise, but also valiant and able to carry out their designs, and not the men to faint from want of soul.

Soc. See now, most excellent Callicles, how different my charge against you is from that which you bring against me, for you reproach me with always saying the same; but I reproach you with never saying the same about the same things, for at one time you were defining the better and the superior to be the stronger, then again as the wiser, and now you bring forward a new notion; the superior and the better are now declared by you to be the more courageous: I wish, my good friend, that you would tell me, once for all, whom you affirm to be the better and superior, and in what they are better?

Cal. I have already told you that I mean those who are wise and courageous in the administration of a state – they ought to be the rulers of their states, and justice consists in their having more than their subjects.

Soc. But whether rulers or subjects will they or will they not have more than themselves, my friend?

Cal. What do you mean?

Soc. I mean that every man is his own ruler; but perhaps you think that there is no necessity for him to rule himself; he is only required to rule others?

Cal. What do you mean by his 'ruling over himself'?

Soc. A simple thing enough; just what is commonly said, that a man should be temperate and master of himself, and ruler of his own pleasures and passions.

Cal. What innocence! you mean those fools, – the temperate?

Soc. Certainly: – any one may know that to be my meaning.

Cal. Quite so, Socrates; and they are really fools, for how can a man be happy who is the servant of anything? On the contrary, I plainly assert, that he who would truly live ought to allow his desires to wax to the uttermost, and not to chastise them; but when they have grown to 492 their greatest he should have courage and intelligence to minister to them and to satisfy all his longings. And this I affirm to be natural justice and nobility. To this however the many cannot attain; and they blame the strong man because they are ashamed of their own weakness, which they desire to conceal, and hence they say that intemperance is base. As I have remarked already, they enslave the nobler natures, and being unable to satisfy their pleasures, they praise temperance and justice out of their own cowardice. For if a man had been originally the son of a king, or had a nature capable of acquiring an empire or a tyranny or sovereignty, what could be more truly base or evil than temperance – to a man like him, I say, who might freely be enjoying every good, and has no one to stand in his way, and yet has admitted custom and reason and the opinion of other men to be lords over him? – must not he be in a miserable plight whom the reputation of justice and temperance hinders from giving more to his friends than to his enemies, even though he be a ruler in his city? Nay, Socrates, for you profess to be a votary of the truth, and the truth is this: – that luxury and intemperance and licence, if they be provided with means, are virtue and happiness – all the rest is a mere bauble, agreements contrary to nature, foolish talk of men, nothing worth.

Soc. There is a noble freedom, Callicles, in your way of approaching the argument; for what you say is what the rest of the world think, but do not like to say. And I must beg of you to persevere, that the true rule of human life may become manifest. Tell me, then: – you say, do you not, that in the rightly-developed man the passions ought not to be controlled, but that we should let them grow to the utmost and somehow or other satisfy them, and that this is virtue?

Cal. Yes; I do.

Soc. Then those who want nothing are not truly said to be happy?

Cal. No indeed, for then stones and dead men would be the happiest of all.

Soc. But surely life according to your view is an awful thing; and indeed I think that Euripides may have been right in saying,

Who knows if life be not death and death life;

and that we are very likely dead; I have heard 493 a philosopher say that at this moment we are actually dead, and that the body is our tomb, and that the part of the soul, which is the seat of the desires is liable to be tossed about by words and blown up and down; and some ingenious person, probably a Sicilian or an Italian, playing with the word, invented a tale in which he called the soul – because of its believing and make-believe nature – a vessel,[1] and the ignorant he called the uninitiated or leaky, and the place in the souls of the uninitiated in which the desires are seated, being the intemperate and incontinent part, he compared to a vessel full of holes, because it can never be satisfied. He is not of your way of thinking, Callicles, for he declares, that of all the souls in Hades, meaning the invisible world, these uninitiated or leaky persons are the most miserable, and that they pour water into a vessel which is full of holes out of a colander which is similarly perforated. The colander, as my informer assures me, is the soul, and the soul which he compares to a colander is the soul of the ignorant, which is likewise full of holes, and therefore incontinent, owing to a bad memory and want of faith. These notions are strange enough, but they show the principle which, if I can, I would fain prove to you; that you should change your mind, and, instead of the intemperate and insatiate life, choose that which is orderly and sufficient and has a due provision for daily needs. Do I make any impression on you, and are you coming over to the opinion that the orderly are happier than the intemperate? Or do I fail to persuade you, and, however many tales I rehearse to you, do you continue of the same opinion still?

Cal. The latter, Socrates, is more like the truth.

Soc. Well, I will tell you another image, which comes out of the same school: – Let me request you to consider how far you would accept this as an account of the two lives of the temperate and intemperate in a figure: – There are two men, both of whom have a number of casks; the one man has his casks sound and full, one of wine, another of honey, and a third of milk, besides others filled with other liquids, and the streams which fill them are few and scanty, and he can only obtain them with a great deal of toil and difficulty; but when his casks are once filled he has no need to feed them any more, and has no further trouble with them or care about them. The other, in like manner, can procure streams, though not without difficulty; but his vessels are leaky and unsound, and night and day he is compelled to be filling them, and if he pauses for a moment, he is in an agony of pain. Such are their respective lives: – And now would you say that the life of the intemperate is happier than that of the temperate? Do I not convince you that the opposite is the truth? 494

Cal. You do not convince me, Socrates, for the one who has filled himself has no longer any pleasure left; and this, as I was just now saying, is the life of a stone: he has neither joy nor sorrow after he is once filled; but the pleasure depends on the superabundance of the influx.

Soc. But the more you pour in, the greater the waste; and the holes must be large for the liquid to escape.

Cal. Certainly.

Soc. The life which you are now depicting is not that of a dead man, or of a stone, but of a cormorant; you mean that he is to be hungering and eating?

Cal. Yes.

Soc. And he is to be thirsting and drinking?

Cal. Yes, that is what I mean; he is to have all his desires about him, and to be able to live happily in the gratification of them.

Soc. Capital, excellent; go on as you have begun, and have no shame; I, too, must disencumber myself of shame: and first, will you tell me whether you include itching and scratching, provided you have enough of them and pass your life in scratching, in your notion of happiness?

Cal. What a strange being you are, Socrates! a regular mob-orator.

Soc. That was the reason, Callicles, why I scared Polus and Gorgias, until they were too modest to say what they thought; but you will not be too modest and will not be scared, for you are a brave man. And now, answer my question.

Cal. I answer, that even the scratcher would live pleasantly.

Soc. And if pleasantly, then also happily?

Cal. To be sure.

Soc. But what if the itching is not confined to the head? Shall I pursue the question? And here, Callicles, I would have you consider how you would reply if consequences are pressed upon you, especially if in the last resort you are asked, whether the life of a catamite is not terrible, foul, miserable? Or would you venture to say, that they too are happy, if they only get enough of what they want?

Cal. Are you not ashamed, Socrates, of introducing such topics into the argument?

Soc. Well, my fine friend, but am I the introducer of these topics, or he who says without any qualification that all who feel pleasure in whatever manner are happy, and who admits of no distinction between good and bad pleasures? And I would still ask, whether you say that pleasure and good are the same, or whether there is some pleasure which is not a good?

Cal. Well, then, for the sake of consistency, I will say that they are the same.

Soc. You are breaking the original agreement, Callicles, and will no longer be a satisfactory companion in the search after truth, if you say what is contrary to your real opinion.

Cal. Why, that is what you are doing too, Socrates.

Soc. Then we are both doing wrong. Still, my dear friend, I would ask you to consider whether pleasure, from whatever source derived, is the good; for, if this be true, then the disagreeable consequences which have been darkly intimated must follow, and many others.

Cal. That, Socrates, is only your opinion.

Soc. And do you, Callicles, seriously maintain what you are saying?

Cal. Indeed I do.

Soc. Then, as you are in earnest, shall we proceed with the argument?

Cal. By all means.

Soc. Well, if you are willing to proceed, determine this question for me: – There is something, I presume, which you would call knowledge?

Cal. There is.

Soc. And were you not saying just now, that some courage implied knowledge?

Cal. I was.

Soc. And you were speaking of courage and knowledge as two things different from one another?

Cal. Certainly I was.

Soc. And would you say that pleasure and knowledge are the same, or not the same?

Cal. Not the same, O man of wisdom.

Soc. And would you say that courage differed from pleasure?

Cal. Certainly.

Soc. Well, then, let us remember that Callicles, the Acharnian, says that pleasure and good are the same; but that knowledge and courage are not the same, either with one another, or with the good.

Cal. And what does our friend Socrates, of Foxton, say – does he assent to this, or not?

Soc. He does not assent; neither will Callicles, when he sees himself truly. You will admit, I suppose, that good and evil fortune are opposed to each other?

Cal. Yes.

Soc. And if they are opposed to each other, then, like health and disease, they exclude one another; a man cannot have them both, or be without them both, at the same time?

Cal. What do you mean?

Soc. Take the case of any bodily affection: – a man may have the complaint in his eyes which is called ophthalmia?

Cal. To be sure.

Soc. But he surely cannot have the same eyes well and sound at the same time?

Cal. Certainly not.

Soc. And when he has got rid of his ophthalmia, has he got rid of the health of his eyes too? Is the final result, that he gets rid of them both together?

Cal. Certainly not.

Soc. That would surely be marvellous and absurd?

Cal. Very.

Soc. I suppose that he is affected by them, and gets rid of them in turns?

Cal. Yes.

Soc. And he may have strength and weakness in the same way, by fits?

Cal. Yes.

Soc. Or swiftness and slowness?

Cal. Certainly.

Soc. And does he have and not have good and happiness, and their opposites, evil and misery, in a similar alternation?

Cal. Certainly he has.

Soc. If then there be anything which a man has and has not at the same time, clearly that cannot be good and evil – do we agree? Please not to answer without consideration.

Cal. I entirely agree.

Soc. Go back now to our former admissions. – Did you say that to hunger, I mean the mere state of hunger, was pleasant or painful?

Cal. I said painful, but that to eat when you are hungry is pleasant.

Soc. I know; but still the actual hunger is painful: am I not right?

Cal. Yes.

Soc. And thirst, too, is painful?

Cal. Yes, very.

Soc. Need I adduce any more instances, or would you agree that all wants or desires are painful?

Cal. I agree, and therefore you need not adduce any more instances.

Soc. Very good. And you would admit that to drink, when you are thirsty, is pleasant?

Cal. Yes.

Soc. And in the sentence which you have just uttered, the word 'thirsty' implies pain?

Cal. Yes.

Soc. And the word 'drinking' is expressive of pleasure, and of the satisfaction of the want?

Cal. Yes.

Soc. There is pleasure in drinking?

Cal. Certainly.

Soc. When you are thirsty?

Cal. Yes.

Soc. And in pain?

Cal. Yes.

Soc. Do you see the inference: – that pleasure and pain are simultaneous, when you say that being thirsty, you drink? For are they not simultaneous, and do they not affect at the same time the same part, whether of the soul or the body? – which of them is affected cannot be supposed to be of any consequence: Is not this true?

Cal. It is.

Soc. You said also, that no man could have good and evil fortune at the same time?

Cal. Yes, I did.

Soc. But you admitted, that when in pain a man
497 might also have pleasure?

Cal. Clearly.

Soc. Then pleasure is not the same as good fortune, or pain the same as evil fortune, and therefore the good is not the same as the pleasant?

Cal. I wish I knew, Socrates, what your quibbling means.

Soc. You know, Callicles, but you affect not to know.

Cal. Well, get on, and don't keep fooling: then you will know what a wiseacre you are in your admonition of me.

Soc. Does not a man cease from his thirst and from his pleasure in drinking at the same time?

Cal. I do not understand what you are saying.

Gor. Nay, Callicles, answer, if only for our sakes; – we should like to hear the argument out.

Cal. Yes, Gorgias, but I must complain of the habitual trifling of Socrates; he is always arguing about little and unworthy questions.

Gor. What matter? Your reputation, Callicles, is not at stake. Let Socrates argue in his own fashion.

Cal. Well, then, Socrates, you shall ask these little peddling questions, since Gorgias wishes to have them.

Soc. I envy you, Callicles, for having been initiated into the great mysteries before you were initiated into the lesser. I thought that this was not allowable. But to return to our argument: – Does not a man cease from thirsting and from the pleasure of drinking at the same moment?

Cal. True.

Soc. And if he is hungry, or has any other desire, does he not cease from the desire and the pleasure at the same moment?

Cal. Very true.

Soc. Then he ceases from pain and pleasure at the same moment?

Cal. Yes.

Soc. But he does not cease from good and evil at the same moment, as you have admitted: – do you still adhere to what you said?

Cal. Yes, I do; but what is the inference?

Soc. Why, my friend, the inference is that the good is not the same as the pleasant, or the evil the same as the painful; there is a cessation of pleasure and pain at the same moment; but not of good and evil, for they are different. How then can pleasure be the same as good, or pain as evil? And I would have you look at the matter in another light, which could hardly, I think, have been considered by you when you identified them: Are not the good good because they have good present with them, as the beautiful are those who have beauty present with them?

Cal. Yes.

Soc. And do you call the fools and cowards good men? For you were saying just now that the courageous and the wise are the good – would you not say so?

Cal. Certainly.

Soc. And did you never see a foolish child rejoicing?

Cal. Yes, I have.

Soc. And a foolish man too?   498

Cal. Yes, certainly; but what is your drift?

Soc. Nothing particular, if you will only answer.

Cal. Yes, I have.

Soc. And did you ever see a sensible man rejoicing or sorrowing?

Cal. Yes.

Soc. Which rejoice and sorrow most – the wise or the foolish?

Cal. They are much upon a par, I think, in that respect.

Soc. Enough: And did you ever see a coward in battle?

Cal. To be sure.

Soc. And which rejoiced most at the departure of the enemy, the coward or the brave?

Cal. I should say 'most' of both; or at any rate, they rejoiced about equally.

Soc. No matter; then the cowards, and not only the brave, rejoice?

Cal. Greatly.

Soc. And the foolish; so it would seem?

Cal. Yes.

Soc. And are only the cowards pained at the approach of their enemies, or are the brave also pained?

Cal. Both are pained.

Soc. And are they equally pained?

Cal. I should imagine that the cowards are more pained.

Soc. And are they not better pleased at the enemy's departure?

Cal. I dare say.

Soc. Then are the foolish and the wise and the cowards and the brave all pleased and pained, as you were saying, in nearly equal degree; but are the cowards more pleased and pained than the brave?

Cal. Yes.

Soc. But surely the wise and brave are the good, and the foolish and the cowardly are the bad?

Cal. Yes.

Soc. Then the good and the bad are pleased and pained in a nearly equal degree?

Cal. Yes.

Soc. Then are the good and bad good and bad in a nearly equal degree, or have the bad the advantage both in good and evil? [i.e. in having more pleasure and more pain.]

Cal. I really do not know what you mean.

Soc. Why, do you not remember saying that the good were good because good was present with them, and the evil because evil; and that pleasures were goods and pains evils?

Cal. Yes, I remember.

Soc. And are not these pleasures or goods present to those who rejoice – if they do rejoice?

Cal. Certainly.

Soc. Then those who rejoice are good when goods are present with them?

Cal. Yes.

Soc. And those who are in pain have evil or sorrow present with them?

Cal. Yes.

Soc. And would you still say that the evil are evil by reason of the presence of evil?

Cal. I should.

Soc. Then those who rejoice are good, and those who are in pain evil?

Cal. Yes.

Soc. The degrees of good and evil vary with the degrees of pleasure and of pain?

Cal. Yes.

Soc. Have the wise man and the fool, the brave and the coward, joy and pain in nearly equal degrees? or would you say that the coward has more?

Cal. I should say that he has.

Soc. Help me then to draw out the conclusion which follows from our admissions; for it is good to repeat and review what is good twice and 499 thrice over, as they say. Both the wise man and the brave man we allow to be good?

Cal. Yes.

Soc. And the foolish man and the coward to be evil?

Cal. Certainly.

Soc. And he who has joy is good?

Cal. Yes.

Soc. And he who is in pain is evil?

Cal. Certainly.

Sec. The good and evil both have joy and pain, but, perhaps, the evil has more of them?

Cal. Yes.

Soc. Then must we not infer, that the bad man is as good and bad as the good, or, perhaps, even better? – is not this a further inference which follows equally with the preceding from the assertion that the good and the pleasant are the same: – can this be denied, Callicles?

Cal. I have been listening and making admissions to you, Socrates; and I remark that if a person grants you anything in play, you, like a child, want to keep hold and will not give it back. But do you really suppose that I or any other human being denies that some pleasures are good and others bad?[2]

Soc. Alas, Callicles, how unfair you are! you certainly treat me as if I were a child, sometimes saying one thing, and then another, as if you were meaning to deceive me. And yet I thought at first that you were my friend, and would not have deceived me if you could have helped. But I see that I was mistaken; and now I suppose that I must make the best of a bad business, as they said of old, and take what I can get out of you. – Well, then, as I understand you to say, I may assume that some pleasures are good and others evil?

Cal. Yes.

Soc. The beneficial are good, and the hurtful are evil?

Cal. To be sure.

Soc. And the beneficial are those which do some good, and the hurtful are those which do some evil?

Cal. Yes.

Soc. Take, for example, the bodily pleasures of eating and drinking, which we were just now mentioning – you mean to say that those which promote health, or any other bodily excellence, are good, and their opposites evil?

Cal. Certainly.

Soc. And in the same way there are good pains and there are evil pains?

Cal. To be sure.

Soc. And ought we not to choose and use the good pleasures and pains?

Cal. Certainly.

Soc. But not the evil?

Cal. Clearly.

Soc. Because, if you remember, Polus and I have agreed that all our actions are to be done for the sake of the good; – and will you agree with us in saying, that the good is the end of all our actions, and that alil our actions are to be done for the sake of the good, and not the good for the sake of them? – will you add a third vote to our two?

Cal. I will.   500

Soc. Then pleasure, like everything else, is to be sought for the sake of that which is good, and not that which is good for the sake of pleasure?

Cal. To be sure. . . .

Notes

1 The translator points out that an untranslatable pun is here being played on the Greek word for "vessel" or "pitcher." The Sicilian and Italian referred to are probably Empedocles and Pythagoras. And it is the latter's doctrine of the soul entombed in the body which was referred to a few lines earlier.

2 Callicles, rather typically, is incapable of appreciating that the distinction he now concedes has fatal implications, soon exposed by Socrates, for his earlier equation of pleasure and goodness.

Aristotle, *Nicomachean Ethics*, Book I

Introduction

The *Nicomachean Ethics*, the second of three works which Plato's student Aristotle (384–322 BCE) devoted to ethics, is the most influential of all writings in Western moral philosophy. Indeed, it is the work which virtually defined this branch of philosophy, and Aristotle's discussions of its main topics – the human "function," justice, the golden "mean," responsibility and the will, the nature of practical reason, etc. – have shaped nearly all later treatments. Moreover, one would have to go back to the Islamic and medieval Christian scholars, for whom Aristotle was "The Philosopher," to find a time when his ethics was as live a subject of interest as it is today. One main reason for this is that for many contemporary philosophers Aristotle's conception of the moral life as the rational exercise of virtues within a socio-political context is the only sensible alternative to the "universalism" of Enlightenment thought and the stark "individualism" of Kierkegaard and other critics of Enlightenment – to, that is, dreams of the betterment of humankind or of securing universal human rights, on the one hand, and to ideals of an inner personal authenticity, on the other.[1]

In Book I, Aristotle sets out the conception of ethics that provides the framework for his ensuing discussions. His is not, he explains, a disinterested enquiry into the nature and vocabulary of ethics, but the practical endeavor to show people, in broad terms, how they might best achieve the good at which all of them aim – flourishing or "happiness" (*eudaimonia*). (In this Aristotle differs from the Socrates of Plato's early dialogues, who typically restricts himself to exposing his opponents' confusions.) Since this is the good life of humans, it must be one that accords with distinctively human "function" (*ergon*), namely "activity of the soul implying a rational principle." Since this activity must be "excellently" or "virtuously" conducted, the human good turns out to be "activity of the soul in accordance with virtue" (1098a). And since it is no less part of the distinctive human essence to be a "political animal," the requisite virtues – justice, magnanimity, friendship, and others – are those needed for effective conduct in the public life of one's community.

For all its influence, Aristotle's ethics has attracted many critics. Do human beings as such have a "function" and single "end"? Are all of Aristotle's virtues really moral ones? Does he not exaggerate the centrality of politics? Did he not, unforgivably, exclude women and slaves from the compass of ethical life? Some, at least, of such objections can be defused by careful attention, avoiding anachronism, to Aristotle's key terms.[2] A person's *ergon* is not a "function" in the sense of a pre-set objective, but the dimension of his or her existence which best explains characteristically

From *Aristotle's Ethics*, ed. J. L. Ackrill, trans. W. D. Ross (with amendments by J. L. Ackrill). London: Faber & Faber, 1973, pp. 41–60.

human behavior. *Eudaimonia* is not a psychological state of "happiness" which virtuous activities produce, not an "end" to which they are "means," but the flourishing, fully realized life of which they are constituents.[3] The *ethikai aretai* are not necessarily "moral virtues" as these are usually understood today, but the "excellences of character" conducive to flourishing within the *polis*. And that is what "political" life is – responsible, public activity within one's *polis* or community, not the electioneering, wheeler-dealing, and the like which the term "political" today conjures up. Women and natural slaves are excluded from ethical life, not because they are immoral or just don't count, but because, Aristotle believed for antiquated reasons, they do not possess the qualifications for rational participation in the affairs of the *polis*.

Readers of the *Ethics* should be warned of a surprise in store in the final Book X. Despite an early reference in Book I (1103a) to the "intellectual" virtues, the work will have given the impression that the best life is the ethical-social one. Yet, in Book X, we are told that philosophical contemplation, the paramount exercise of the intellectual virtues, is "the highest form of activity" (1177a). Any attempt to reconcile this claim with the general thrust of the work, it has been said, is bound to be "broken-backed"? Perhaps Aristotle is indeed inconsistent here, but then he was not the first or last of those – including the author(s) of *The Bhagavad Gita* (see I.6) – who have struggled, successfully or otherwise, to reconcile the ideal of contemplative truth with the importance of ethical conduct.

Notes

1 Cf. A. MacIntyre, *After Virtue: A Study in Moral Theory*, London: Duckworth, 1982.
2 For a clear account of these terms, see J. Barnes, *Aristotle*, Oxford: Oxford University Press, 1986, pp. 77ff.
3 J. L. Ackrill, "Aristotle on Eudaimonia," in A. Rorty (ed.), *Essays on Aristotle's Ethics*, Berkeley: University of California Press, 1980, p. 33.

Aristotle, *Nicomachean Ethics*

Book I

Chapter 1

Every art and every inquiry, and similarly every action and pursuit, is thought to aim at some good; and for this reason the good has rightly been declared to be that at which all things aim. But a certain difference is found among ends; some are activities, others are products apart from the activities that produce them. Where there are ends apart from the actions, it is the nature of the products to be better than the activities. Now, as there are many actions, arts and sciences, their ends also are many; the end of the medical art is health, that of shipbuilding a vessel, that of strategy victory, that of economics wealth. But where such arts fall under a single capacity – as bridle-making and the other arts concerned with the equipment of horses fall under the art of riding, and this and every military action under strategy, in the same way other arts fall under yet others – in all of these the ends of the master arts are to be preferred to all the subordinate ends; for it is for the sake of the former that the latter are pursued. It makes no difference whether the activities themselves are the ends of the actions, or something else apart from the activities, as in the case of the sciences just mentioned.

Chapter 2

If, then, there is some end of the things we do, which we desire for its own sake (everything else being desired for the sake of this), and if we do not choose everything for the sake of something else (for at that rate the process would go on to infinity, so that our desire would be empty and vain), clearly this must be the good and the chief good. Will not the knowledge of it, then, have a great influence on life? Shall we not, like archers who have a mark to aim at, be more likely to hit upon what is right? If so, we must try, in outline at least, to determine what it is, and of which of the sciences or capacities it is the object. It would seem to belong to the most authoritative art and that which is most truly the master art. And politics appears to be of this nature; for it is this that

1094a

ordains which of the sciences should be studied
in a state, and which each class of citizens should
learn and up to what point they should learn them;
and we see even the most highly esteemed of capacities to fall under this, e.g. strategy, economics,
rhetoric; now, since politics uses the rest of the
sciences, and since, again, it legislates as to what
we are to do and what we are to abstain from,
the end of this science must include those of
the others, so that this end must be the good for
man. For even if the end is the same for a single
man and for a state, that of the state seems at
all events something greater and more complete
whether to attain or to preserve; though it is
worth while to attain the end merely for one
man, it is finer and more godlike to attain it for
a nation or for city-states. These, then, are the ends
at which our inquiry aims, since it is political science, in one sense of that term.

Chapter 3

Our discussion will be adequate if it has as much
clearness as the subject-matter admits of, for
precision is not to be sought for alike in all discussions, any more than in all the products of the
crafts. Now fine and just actions, which political
science investigates, exhibit much variety and
fluctuation of opinion, so that they may be
thought to exist only by convention, and not by
nature. And goods also exhibit a similar fluctuation because they bring harm to many people;
for before now men have been undone by reason
of their wealth, and others by reason of their
courage. We must be content, then, in speaking
of such subjects and with such premises to indicate the truth roughly and in outline, and in
speaking about things which are only for the
most part true and with premises of the same kind
to reach conclusions that are no better. In the same
spirit, therefore, should each type of statement be
received; for it is the mark of an educated man to
look for precision in each class of things just so
far as the nature of the subject admits; it is evidently equally foolish to accept probable reasoning from a mathematician and to demand from
a rhetorician demonstrative proofs.

Now each man judges well the things he
knows, and of these he is a good judge. And so
the man who has been educated in a subject is a
good judge of that subject, and the man who has
received an all-round education is a good judge
in general. Hence a young man is not a proper

hearer of lectures on political science; for he is inexperienced in the actions that occur in life, but
its discussions start from these and are about
these; and, further, since he tends to follow his
passions, his study will be vain and unprofitable,
because the end aimed at is not knowledge but
action. And it makes no difference whether he
is young in years or youthful in character; the
defect does not depend on time, but on his
living, and pursuing each successive object, as
passion directs. For to such persons, as to the
incontinent, knowledge brings no profit; but to
those who desire and act in accordance with a
rational principle knowledge about such matters
will be of great benefit.

These remarks about the student, the sort of
treatment to be expected, and the purpose of the
inquiry, may be taken as our preface.

Chapter 4

Let us resume our inquiry and state, in view of
the fact that all knowledge and every pursuit
aims at some good, what it is that we say political science aims at and what is the highest of all
goods achievable by action. Verbally there is very
general agreement; for both the general run of men
and people of superior refinement say that it is
happiness, and identify living well and doing
well with being happy; but with regard to what
happiness is they differ, and the many do not give
the same account as the wise. For the former think
it is some plain and obvious thing, like pleasure,
wealth or honour; they differ, however, from one
another – and often even the same man identifies
it with different things, with health when he is ill,
with wealth when he is poor; but, conscious of
their ignorance, they admire those who proclaim
some great thing that is above their comprehension. Now some thought that apart from these
many goods there is another which is good in itself
and causes the goodness of all these as well.
To examine all the opinions that have been held
were perhaps somewhat fruitless; enough to
examine those that are most prevalent or that seem
to be arguable.

Let us not fail to notice, however, that there is
a difference between arguments from and those
to the first principles. For Plato, too, was right
in raising this question and asking, as he used to
do, 'are we on the way from or to the first
principles?' There is a difference, as there is in a
racecourse between the course from the judges to

the turning-point and the way back. For, while 1095b we must begin with what is known, things are objects of knowledge in two senses – some to us, some without qualification. Presumably, then, *we* must begin with things known to *us*. Hence any one who is to listen intelligently to lectures about what is noble and just and, generally, about the subjects of political science must have been brought up in good habits. For the fact is a starting-point, and if this is sufficiently plain to him, he will not need the reason as well; and the man who has been well brought up has or can easily get starting-points. And as for him who neither has nor can get them, let him hear the words of Hesiod:

Far best is he who knows all things himself;
Good, he that hearkens when men counsel right;
But he who neither knows, nor lays to heart
Another's wisdom, is a useless wight.

Chapter 5

Let us, however, resume our discussion from the point at which we digressed. To judge from the lives that men lead, most men, and men of the most vulgar type, seem (not without some ground) to identify the good, or happiness, with pleasure; which is the reason why they love the life of enjoyment. For there are, we may say, three prominent types of life – that just mentioned, the political, and thirdly the contemplative life. Now the mass of mankind are evidently quite slavish in their tastes, preferring a life suitable to beasts, but they get some ground for their view from the fact that many of those in high places share the tastes of Sardanapallus. A consideration of the prominent types of life shows that people of superior refinement and of active disposition identify happiness with honour; for this is, roughly speaking, the end of the political life. But it seems too superficial to be what we are looking for, since it is thought to depend on those who bestow honour rather than on him who receives it, but the good we divine to be something proper to a man and not easily taken from him. Further, men seem to pursue honour in order that they may be assured of their goodness; at least it is by men of practical wisdom that they seek to be honoured, and among those who know them, and on the ground of their virtue; clearly, then, according to them, at any rate, virtue is better. And perhaps one might even suppose this to be,

rather than honour, the end of the political life. But even this appears somewhat incomplete; for possession of virtue seems actually compatible with being asleep, or with lifelong inactivity, and, further, with the greatest sufferings and 1096a misfortunes; but a man who was living so no one would call happy, unless he were maintaining a thesis at all costs. But enough of this; for the subject has been sufficiently treated even in the current discussions. Third comes the contemplative life, which we shall consider later.

The life of money-making is one undertaken under compulsion, and wealth is evidently not the good we are seeking; for it is merely useful and for the sake of something else. And so one might rather take the aforenamed objects to be ends; for they are loved for themselves. But it is evident that not even these are ends; yet many arguments have been thrown away in support of them. Let us leave this subject, then.

Chapter 6

We had perhaps better consider the universal good and discuss thoroughly what is meant by it, although such an inquiry is made an uphill one by the fact that the Forms have been introduced by friends of our own.[1] Yet it would perhaps be thought to be better, indeed to be our duty, for the sake of maintaining the truth even to destroy what touches us closely, especially as we are philosophers or lovers of wisdom; for, while both are dear, piety requires us to honour truth above our friends.

The men who introduced this doctrine did not posit Ideas of classes within which they recognized priority and posteriority (which is the reason why they did not maintain the existence of an Idea embracing all numbers); but the term 'good' is used both in the category of substance and in that of quality and in that of relation, and that which is *per se*, i.e. substance, is prior in nature to the relative (for the latter is like an offshoot and accident of being); so that there could not be a common Idea set over all these goods. Further, since 'good' has as many senses as 'being' (for it is predicated both in the category of substance, as of God and of reason, and in quality, i.e. of the virtues, and in quantity, i.e. of that which is moderate, and in relation, i.e. of the useful, and in time, i.e. of the right opportunity, and in place, i.e. of the right locality and the like), clearly it cannot be something universally present in all cases and single; for then it could not have been predicated in all the categories but in one only. Further, since of the things answering to one Idea there is one science, there would have been one science of all the goods; but as it is there are many sciences even of the things that fall under one category, e.g. of opportunity, for opportunity in war is studied by strategics and in disease by medicine, and the moderate in food is studied by medicine and in exercise by the science of gymnastics. And one might ask the question, what in the world they *mean* by 'a thing itself', if (as is the case) in 'man himself' and in a particular man the account of man is one and the same. For 1096b in so far as they are man, they will in no respect differ; and if this is so, neither will 'good itself' and particular goods, in so far as they are good. But again it will not be good any the more for being eternal, since that which lasts long is no whiter than that which perishes in a day. The Pythagoreans seem to give a more plausible account of the good, when they place the one in the column of goods; and it is they that Speusippus seems to have followed.

But let us discuss these matters elsewhere; an objection to what we have said, however, may be discerned in the fact that the Platonists have not been speaking about *all* goods, and that the goods that are pursued and loved for themselves are called good by reference to a single Form, while those which tend to produce or to preserve these somehow or to prevent their contraries are called so by reason of these, and in a different way. Clearly, then, goods must be spoken of in two ways, and some must be good in themselves, the others by reason of these. Let us separate, then, things good in themselves from things useful, and consider whether the former are called good by reference to a single Idea. What sort of goods would one call good in themselves? Is it those that are pursued even when isolated from others, such as intelligence, sight, and certain pleasures and honours? Certainly, if we pursue these also for the sake of something else, yet one would place them among things good in themselves. Or is nothing other than the Idea of good good in itself? In that case the Form will be empty. But if the things we have named are also things good in themselves, the account of the good will have to appear as something identical in them all, as that of whiteness is identical in snow and in white lead. But of honour, wisdom and pleasure,

just in respect of their goodness, the accounts are distinct and diverse. The good, therefore, is not something common answering to one Idea.

But what then do we mean by the good? It is surely not like the things that only chance to have the same name. Are goods one, then, by being derived from one good or by all contributing to one good, or are they rather one by analogy? Certainly as sight is in the body, so is reason in the soul, and so on in other cases. But perhaps these subjects had better be dismissed for the present; for perfect precision about them would be more appropriate to another branch of philosophy. And similarly with regard to the Idea; even if there is some one good which is universally predicable of goods or is capable of separate and independent existence, clearly it could not be achieved or attained by man; but we are now seeking something attainable. Perhaps, however, some one might think it worth while to recognize this with a view to the goods that *are* attainable 1097a and achievable; for having this as a sort of pattern we shall know better the goods that are good for us, and if we know them shall attain them. This argument has some plausibility, but seems to clash with the procedure of the sciences; for all of these, though they aim at some good and seek to supply the deficiency of it, leave on one side the knowledge of *the* good. Yet that all the exponents of the arts should be ignorant of, and should not even seek, so great an aid is not probable. It is hard, too, to see how a weaver or a carpenter will be benefited in regard to his own craft by knowing this 'good itself', or how the man who has viewed the Idea itself will be a better doctor or general thereby. For a doctor seems not even to study health in this way, but the health of man, or perhaps rather the health of a particular man; it is individuals that he is healing. But enough of these topics.

Chapter 7

Let us again return to the good we are seeking, and ask what it can be. It seems different in different actions and arts; it is different in medicine, in strategy, and in the other arts likewise. What then is the good of each? Surely that for whose sake everything else is done. In medicine this is health, in strategy victory, in architecture a house, in any other sphere something else, and in every action and pursuit the end; for it is for the sake of this that all men do whatever else they do. Therefore, if there is an end for all that we do, this will be the good achievable by action, and if there are more than one, these will be the goods achievable by action.

So the argument has by a different course reached the same point; but we must try to state this even more clearly. Since there are evidently more than one end, and we choose some of these (e.g. wealth, flutes, and in general instruments) for the sake of something else, clearly not all ends are final ends; but the chief good is evidently something final. Therefore, if there is only one final end, this will be what we are seeking, and if there are more than one, the most final of these will be what we are seeking. Now we call that which is in itself worthy of pursuit more final than that which is worthy of pursuit for the sake of something else, and that which is never desirable for the sake of something else more final than the things that are desirable both in themselves and for the sake of that other thing, and therefore we call final without qualification that which is always desirable in itself and never for the sake of something else.

Now such a thing happiness, above all else, is held to be; for this we choose always for itself and never for the sake of something else, but honour, pleasure, reason and every virtue we choose indeed for themselves (for if nothing resulted from them we should still choose each of them), but we choose them also for the sake of happiness, judging that through them we shall be happy. Happiness, on the other hand, no one chooses for the sake of these, nor, in general, for anything other than itself.

From the point of view of self-sufficiency the same result seems to follow; for the final good is thought to be self-sufficient. Now by self-sufficient we do not mean that which is sufficient for a man by himself, for one who lives a solitary life, but also for parents, children, wife, and in general for his friends and fellow citizens, since man is born for citizenship. But some limit must be set to this; for if we extend our requirement to ancestors and descendants and friends' friends we are in for an infinite series. Let us examine this question, however, on another occasion; the self-sufficient we now define as that which when isolated makes life desirable and lacking in nothing; and such we think happiness to be; and further we think it most desirable of all things, without being counted as one

1097b

good thing among others – if it were so counted it would clearly be made more desirable by the addition of even the least of goods; for that which is added becomes an excess of goods, and of goods the greater is always more desirable. Happiness, then, is something final and self-sufficient, and is the end of action.

Presumably, however, to say that happiness is the chief good seems a platitude, and a clearer account of what it is is still desired. This might perhaps be given, if we could first ascertain the function of man. For just as for a flute-player, a sculptor, or any artist, and, in general, for all things that have a function or activity, the good and the 'well' is thought to reside in the function, so would it seem to be for man, if he has a function. Have the carpenter, then, and the tanner certain functions or activities, and has man none? Is he born without a function? Or as eye, hand, foot, and in general each of the parts evidently has a function, may one lay it down that man similarly has a function apart from all these? What then can this be? Life seems to be common even to plants, but we are seeking what is peculiar to man. Let us exclude, therefore, the life of nutrition and growth. Next there would be a life of perception, but *it* also seems to be common even to the horse, the ox and every animal. There remains, then, an active life of the element that has a rational principle; of this, one part has such a principle in the sense of being obedient to one, the other in the sense of possessing one and exercising thought. And, as 'life of the rational element' also has two meanings, we must state that life in the sense of activity is what we mean; for this seems to be the more proper sense of the term. Now if the function of man is an activity of soul which follows or implies a rational principle, and if we say 'a so-and-so' and 'a good so-and-so' have a function which is the same in kind, e.g. a lyre-player and a good lyre-player, and so without qualification in all cases, eminence in respect of goodness being added to the name of the function (for the function of a lyre-player is to play the lyre, and that of a good lyre-player is to do so well): if this is the case, [and we state the function of man to be a certain kind of life, and this to be an activity or actions of the soul implying a rational principle, and the function of a good man to be the good and noble performance of these, and if any action is well performed when it is performed in accordance with the

1098a

appropriate excellence: if this is the case,] human good turns out to be activity of the soul in accordance with virtue, and if there are more than one virtue, in accordance with the best and most complete.

But we must add 'in a complete life'. For one swallow does not make a summer, nor does one day; and so too one day, or a short time, does not make a man blessed and happy.

Let this serve as an outline of the good; for we must presumably first sketch it roughly, and then later fill in the details. But it would seem that any one is capable of carrying on and articulating what has once been well outlined, and that time is a good discoverer or partner in such a work; to which facts the advances of the arts are due; for any one can add what is lacking. And we must also remember what has been said before, and not look for precision in all things alike, but in each class of things such precision as accords with the subject-matter, and so much as is appropriate to the inquiry. For a carpenter and a geometer investigate the right angle in different ways; the former does so in so far as the right angle is useful for his work, while the latter inquires what it is or what sort of thing it is; for he is a spectator of the truth. We must act in the same way, then, in all other matters as well, that our main task may not be subordinated to minor questions. Nor must we demand the cause in all matters alike; it is enough in some cases that the *fact* be well established, as in the case of the first principles; the fact is a primary thing or first principle. Now of first principles we see some by induction, some by perception, some by a certain habituation, and others too in other ways. But each set of principles we must try to investigate in the natural way, and we must take pains to determine them correctly, since they have a great influence on what follows. For the beginning is thought to be more than half of the whole, and many of the questions we ask are cleared up by it.

1098b

Chapter 8

We must consider it, however, in the light not only of our conclusion and our premises, but also of what is commonly said about it; for with a true view all the data harmonize, but with a false one the facts soon clash. Now goods have been divided into three classes, and some are described as external, others as relating to soul or to body; we call those that relate to soul most

properly and truly goods, and psychical actions and activities we class as relating to soul. Therefore our account must be sound, at least according to this view, which is an old one and agreed on by philosophers. It is correct also in that we identify the end with certain actions and activities; for thus it falls among goods of the soul and not among external goods. Another belief which harmonizes with our account is that the happy man lives well and does well; for we have practically defined happiness as a sort of good life and good action. The characteristics that are looked for in happiness seem also, all of them, to belong to what we have defined happiness as being. For some identify happiness with virtue, some with practical wisdom, others with a kind of philosophic wisdom, others with these, or one of these, accompanied by pleasure or not without pleasure; while others include also external prosperity. Now some of these views have been held by many men and men of old, others by a few eminent persons; and it is not probable that either of these should be entirely mistaken, but rather that they should be right in at least some one respect or even in most respects.

With those who identify happiness with virtue or some one virtue our account is in harmony; for to virtue belongs virtuous activity. But it makes, perhaps, no small difference whether we place the chief good in possession or in use, in state of mind or in activity. For the state of mind may exist without producing any good result, as in a man who is asleep or in some other way quite inactive, but the activity cannot; for one who has the activity will of necessity be acting, and acting well. And as in the Olympic Games it is not the most beautiful and the strongest that are crowned but those who compete (for it is some of these that are victorious), so those who act win, and rightly win, the noble and good things in life.

1099a

Their life is also in itself pleasant. For pleasure is a state of *soul*, and to each man that which he is said to be a lover of is pleasant; e.g. not only is a horse pleasant to the lover of horses, and a spectacle to the lover of sights, but also in the same way just acts are pleasant to the lover of justice and in general virtuous acts to the lover of virtue. Now for most men their pleasures are in conflict with one another because these are not by nature pleasant, but the lovers of what is noble find pleasant the things that are by nature pleasant; and virtuous actions are such, so that these are pleasant for such men as well as in their own nature. Their life, therefore, has no further need of pleasure as a sort of adventitious charm, but has its pleasure in itself. For, besides what we have said, the man who does not rejoice in noble actions is not even good; since no one would call a man just who did not enjoy acting justly, nor any man liberal who did not enjoy liberal actions; and similarly in all other cases. If this is so, virtuous actions must be in themselves pleasant. But they are also *good* and *noble*, and have each of these attributes in the highest degree, since the good man judges well about these attributes; his judgement is such as we have described. Happiness then is the best, noblest and most pleasant thing in the world, and these attributes are not severed as in the inscription at Delos –

> Most noble is that which is justest, and best is
> health;
> But pleasantest is it to win what we love.

For all these properties belong to the best activities; and these, or one – the best – of these, we identify with happiness.

Yet evidently, as we said, it needs the external 1099b goods as well; for it is impossible, or not easy, to do noble acts without the proper equipment. In many actions we use friends and riches and political power as instruments; and there are some things the lack of which takes the lustre from happiness, as good birth, goodly children, beauty; for the man who is very ugly in appearance or ill-born or solitary and childless is not very likely to be happy, and perhaps a man would be still less likely if he had thoroughly bad children or friends or had lost good children or friends by death. As we said, then, happiness seems to need this sort of prosperity in addition; for which reason some identify happiness with good fortune, though others identify it with virtue.

Chapter 9

For this reason also the question is asked, whether happiness is to be acquired by learning or by habituation or some other sort of training, or comes in virtue of some divine providence or again by chance. Now if there is *any* gift of the gods to men, it is reasonable that happiness should be god-given, and most surely god-given

of all human things inasmuch as it is the best. But this question would perhaps be more appropriate to another inquiry; happiness seems, however, even if it is not god-sent but comes as a result of virtue and some process of learning or training, to be among the most godlike things; for that which is the prize and end of virtue seems to be the best thing in the world, and something godlike and blessed.

It will also on this view be very generally shared; for all who are not maimed as regards their potentiality for virtue may win it by a certain kind of study and care. But if it is better to be happy thus than by chance, it is reasonable that the facts should be so, since everything that depends on the action of nature is by nature as good as it can be, and similarly everything that depends on art or any rational cause, and especially if it depends on the best of all causes. To entrust to chance what is greatest and most noble would be a very defective arrangement.

The answer to the question we are asking is plain also from the definition of happiness; for it has been said to be a virtuous activity of soul, of a certain kind. Of the remaining goods, some must necessarily pre-exist as conditions of happiness, and others are naturally co-operative and useful as instruments. And this will be found to agree with what we said at the outset; for we stated the end of political science to be the best end, and political science spends most of its pains on making the citizens to be of a certain character, viz. good and capable of noble acts.

It is natural, then, that we call neither ox nor horse nor any other of the animals happy; for none of them is capable of sharing in such activity.[2] For 1100a this reason also a boy is not happy; for he is not yet capable of such acts, owing to his age; and boys who are called happy are being congratulated by reason of the hopes we have for them. For there is required, as we said, not only complete virtue but also a complete life, since many changes occur in life, and all manner of chances, and the most prosperous may fall into great misfortunes in old age, as is told of Priam in the Trojan Cycle; and one who has experienced such chances and has ended wretchedly no one calls happy.

Chapter 10

Must no one at all, then, be called happy while he lives; must we, as Solon says, see the end? Even if we are to lay down this doctrine, is it also the case that a man *is* happy when he is *dead?* Or is not this quite absurd, especially for us who say that happiness is an activity? But if we do not call the dead man happy, and if Solon does not mean this, but that one can then safely *call* a man blessed as being at last beyond evils and misfortunes, this also affords matter for discussion; for both evil and good are thought to exist for a dead man, as much as for one who is alive but not aware of them; e.g. honours and dishonours and the good or bad fortunes of children and in general of descendants. And this also presents a problem; for though a man has lived happily up to old age and has had a death worthy of his life, many reverses may befall his descendants – some of them may be good and attain the life they deserve, while with others the opposite may be the case; and clearly too the degrees of relationship between them and their ancestors may vary indefinitely. It would be odd, then, if the dead man were to share in these changes and become at one time happy, at another wretched; while it would also be odd if the fortunes of the descendants did not for *some* time have *some* effect on the happiness of their ancestors.

But we must return to our first difficulty; for perhaps by a consideration of it our present problem might be solved. Now if we must see the end and only then call a man happy, not as being happy but as having been so before, surely this is a paradox, that when he is happy the attribute that 1100b belongs to him is not to be truly predicated of him because we do not wish to call living men happy, on account of the changes that may befall them, and because we have assumed happiness to be something permanent and by no means easily changed, while a single man may suffer many turns of fortune's wheel. For clearly if we were to follow his fortunes, we should often call the same man happy and again wretched, making the happy man out to be a 'chameleon and insecurely based'. Or is this following his fortunes quite wrong? Success or failure in life does not depend on these, but human life, as we said, needs these as well, while virtuous activities or their opposites are what determine happiness or the reverse.

The question we have now discussed confirms our definition. For no function of man has so much permanence as virtuous activities (these are thought to be more durable even than knowledge of the sciences), and of these themselves the most valuable are more durable because those who are happy spend their life most readily and most continuously in these; for this seems to be the reason why we do not forget them. The attribute in question, then, will belong to the happy man, and he will be happy throughout his life; for always, or by preference to everything else, he will be engaged in virtuous action and contemplation, and he will bear the chances of life most nobly and altogether decorously, if he is 'truly good' and 'foursquare beyond reproach'.

Now many events happen by chance, and events differing in importance; small pieces of good fortune or of its opposite clearly do not weight down the scales of life one way or the other, but a multitude of great events if they turn out well will make life happier (for not only are they themselves such as to add beauty to life, but the way a man deals with them may be noble and good), while if they turn out ill they crush and maim happiness; for they both bring pain with them and hinder many activities. Yet even in these nobility shines through, when a man bears with resignation many great misfortunes, not through insensibility to pain but through nobility and greatness of soul.

If activities are, as we said, what determine the character of life, no happy man can become miserable; for he will never do the acts that are hateful and mean. For the man who is truly good 1101a and wise, we think, bears all the chances of life becomingly and always makes the best of circumstances, as a good general makes the best military use of the army at his command and a good shoemaker makes the best shoes out of the hides that are given him; and so with all other craftsmen. And if this is the case, the happy man can never become miserable – though he will not reach *blessedness*, if he meet with fortunes like those of Priam.

Nor, again, is he many-coloured and changeable; for neither will he be moved from his happy state easily or by any ordinary misadventures, but only by many great ones, nor, if he has had many great misadventures, will he recover his happiness in a short time, but if at all, only in a long and complete one in which he has attained many splendid successes.

Why then should we not say that he is happy who is active in accordance with complete virtue and is sufficiently equipped with external goods, not for some chance period but throughout a complete life? Or must we add 'and who is destined to live thus and die as befits his life'? Certainly the future is obscure to us, while happiness, we claim, is an end and something in every way final. If so, we shall call happy those among living men in whom these conditions are, and are to be, fulfilled – but happy *men*. So much for these questions.

Chapter 11

That the fortunes of descendants and of all a man's friends should not affect his happiness at all seems a very unfriendly doctrine, and one opposed to the opinions men hold; but since the events that happen are numerous and admit of all sorts of difference, and some come more near to us and others less so, it seems a long – nay, an infinite – task to discuss each in detail; a general outline will perhaps suffice. If, then, as some of a man's own misadventures have a certain weight and influence on life while others are, as it were, lighter, so too there are differences among the misadventures of our friends taken as a whole, and it makes a difference whether the various sufferings befall the living or the dead (much more even than whether lawless and terrible deeds are presupposed in a tragedy or done on the stage), this difference also must be taken into account; or rather, perhaps, the fact that doubt is felt whether the dead share in any good or evil. For it seems, from these considerations, 1101b that even if anything whether good or evil penetrates to them, it must be something weak and negligible, either in itself or for them, or if not, at least it must be such in degree and kind as not to make happy those who are not happy nor to take away their blessedness from those who are. The good or bad fortunes of friends, then, seem to have some effects on the dead, but effects of such a kind and degree as neither to make the happy unhappy nor to produce any other change of the kind.

Chapter 12

These questions having been definitely answered, let us consider whether happiness is among the things that are praised or rather among the things that are prized; for clearly it is not to be placed among *potentialities*. Everything that is praised seems to be praised because it is of a certain kind and is related somehow to something else; for we praise the just or brave man and in general both the good man and virtue itself because of the actions and functions involved, and we praise the strong man, the good runner, and so on, because he is of a certain kind and is related in a certain way to something good and important. This is clear also from the praises of the gods; for it seems absurd that the gods should be referred to our standard, but this *is* done because praise involves a reference, as we said, to something else. But if praise is for things such as we have described, clearly what applies to the best things is not praise, but something greater and better, as is indeed obvious; for what we do to the gods and the most godlike of men is to call them blessed and happy. And so too with good *things*; no one praises happiness as he does justice, but rather calls it blessed, as being something more divine and better.

Eudoxus also seems to have been right in his method of advocating the supremacy of pleasure; he thought that the fact that, though a good, it is not praised indicated it to be better than the things that are praised, and that this is what God and the good are; for by reference to these all other things are judged. *Praise* is appropriate to virtue, for as a result of virtue men tend to do noble deeds; but *encomia* [or panegyrics – Ed.] are bestowed on acts, whether of the body or of the soul. But perhaps nicety in these matters is more proper to those who have made a study of encomia; to us it is clear from what has been said 1102a that happiness is among the things that are prized and perfect. It seems to be so also from the fact that it is a first principle; for it is for the sake of this that we all do everything else, and the first principle and cause of goods is, we claim, something prized and divine.

Chapter 13

Since happiness is an activity of soul in accordance with perfect virtue, we must consider the nature of virtue; for perhaps we shall thus see better the nature of happiness. The true student of politics, too, is thought to have studied virtue above all things; for he wishes to make his fellow citizens good and obedient to the laws. As an example of this we have the lawgivers of the Cretans and the Spartans, and any others of the kind that there may have been. And if this inquiry belongs to political science, clearly the pursuit of it will be in accordance with our original plan. But, clearly the virtue we must study is human virtue;

for the good we were seeking was human good and the happiness human happiness. By human virtue we mean not that of the body but that of the soul; and happiness also we call an activity of soul. But if this is so, clearly the student of politics must know somehow the facts about soul, as the man who is to heal the eyes must know about the whole body also; and all the more since politics is more prized and better than medicine; but even among doctors the best educated spend much labour on acquiring knowledge of the body. The student of politics, then, must study the soul, and must study it with these objects in view, and do so just to the extent which is sufficient for the questions we are discussing; for further precision is perhaps something more laborious than our purposes require.

Some things are said about it, adequately enough, even in the discussions outside our school, and we must use these; e.g. that one element in the soul is irrational and one has a rational principle. Whether these are separated as the parts of the body or of anything divisible are, or are distinct by definition but by nature inseparable, like convex and concave in the circumference of a circle, does not affect the present question.

Of the irrational element one division seems to be widely distributed, and vegetative in its nature, I mean that which causes nutrition and growth; for it is this kind of power of the soul that 1102b one must assign to all nurslings and to embryos, and this same power to full-grown creatures; this is more reasonable than to assign some different power to them. Now the excellence of this seems to be common to all species and not specifically human; for this part or faculty seems to function most in sleep, while goodness and badness are least manifest in sleep (whence comes the saying that the happy are no better off than the wretched for half their lives; and this happens naturally enough, since sleep is an inactivity of the soul in that respect in which it is called good or bad), unless perhaps to a small extent some of the movements actually penetrate to the soul, and in this respect the dreams of good men are better than those of ordinary people. Enough of this subject, however; let us leave the nutritive faculty alone, since it has by its nature no share in human excellence.

There seems to be also another irrational element in the soul – one which in a sense, however, shares in a rational principle. For we praise the rational principle of the continent man and of the incontinent, and the part of their soul that has such a principle, since it urges them aright and towards the best objects; but there is naturally found in them also another element beside the rational principle, which fights against and resists that principle. For exactly as paralysed limbs when we intend to move them to the right turn on the contrary to the left, so is it with the soul; the impulses of incontinent people move in contrary directions. But while in the body we see that which moves astray, in the soul we do not. No doubt, however, we must none the less suppose that in the soul too there is something beside the rational principle, resisting and opposing it. In what sense it is distinct from the other elements does not concern us. Now even this seems to have a share in a rational principle, as we said; at any rate in the continent man it obeys the rational principle – and presumably in the temperate and brave man it is still more obedient; for in him it speaks, on all matters, with the same voice as the rational principle.

Therefore the irrational element also appears to be twofold. For the vegetative element in no way shares in a rational principle, but the appetitive and in general the desiring element in a sense shares in it, in so far as it listens to and obeys it; this is the sense in which we speak of 'taking account' of one's father or one's friends, not that in which we speak of 'accounting' for a mathematical property. That the irrational element is in some sense persuaded by a rational principle is indicated also by the giving of advice and by 1103a all reproof and exhortation. And if this element also must be said to have a rational principle, that which has a rational principle (as well as that which has not) will be twofold, one subdivision having it in the strict sense and in itself, and the other having a tendency to obey as one does one's father.

Virtue too is distinguished into kinds in accordance with this difference; for we say that some of the virtues are intellectual and others moral, philosophic wisdom and understanding and practical wisdom being intellectual, liberality and temperance moral. For in speaking about a man's character we do not say that he is wise or has understanding but that he is good-tempered or temperate; yet we praise the wise man also with respect to his state of mind [or disposition

– Ed.]; and of states of mind we call those which merit praise virtues.

Notes

1 In this difficult chapter, Aristotle is preparing to distinguish his own view that there is a single end, *eudaimonia*, at which all our activities finally aim from the Platonists' – our "friends" – idea that there is a single Form of the Good by reference to which justice, happiness, and so on are deemed good. Readers not acquainted with the debate between Plato and Aristotle over the Forms are advised to proceed to Chapter 7.

2 This denial that children can enjoy *eudaimonia* is, of course, an excellent reason for questioning the translation of that term by "happiness."

3

Epicurus, "Letter to Menoeceus" and "Leading Doctrines"

Introduction

It comes as a surprise to modern readers to learn that during the centuries of the "Hellenistic Age" following Aristotle's death it was not he and Plato who exerted the greatest influence upon the thought and practice of Greeks and Romans; it was instead some slightly later schools of philosophy, notably the Stoics and Epicureans. The man who gave his name to the latter was born in Samos in 341 and died in 271 BCE near Athens, where he had founded his famous "Garden," a kind of ashram of which he was the *guru*. Today's connotations of "epicurean" and "epicure" might suggest that the Garden was a place of sybaritic indulgence. In fact, it was a community of people living, if not Spartan, then simple and austere lives. For Epicurus himself, "barley bread and water" could "yield the peak of pleasure," and "a little pot of cheese" was a true luxury.

This indicates that care is needed with the usual labeling of Epicurus as a "hedonist." For while he indeed declares that "pleasure is the goal of living," he has something different in mind from the "epicure." Still, the claim that pleasure is the goal of life, and that the virtues are simply means – albeit necessary ones – to that goal, is sufficient to put Epicurus importantly at odds

From The Philosophy of Epicurus, trans. G. K. Strodach. Evanston, IL: Northwestern University Press, 1963, pp. 178–85, 196–203.

with Plato, Aristotle, and his rivals, the Stoics. For Plato, we saw in I.1, pleasure cannot be identified with happiness and the good, and for each of these other thinkers virtue is not a means to the good, but constitutive of it. (Aristotle's exercise of the virtues, for example, is part of *eudaimonia*.) In contemporary parlance, Epicurus is more accurately characterized as a "consequentialist": something is morally good because of the results – pleasure or whatever – it yields. Unjust acts, for example, are not bad in themselves; they are bad because of the unpleasant fear of punishment that follows in their wake (*Leading Doctrines* 34).

Epicurus's ethics emerges from his view of nature. Human beings are purely material creatures (souls being composed of special physical "atoms") and like everything else are "naturally" in a state of equilibrium. This means, in the words of Epicurus's most famous disciple, Lucretius, that "nature is clamouring for . . . a body free from pain, a mind released from worry and fear."[1] And this gives the clue to the master's understanding of pleasure. Even in the case of activities that produce positive or "kinetic" pleasures, like drinking fine wine, the pleasure that counts is the "static" one of being free from desire and its discomforts.[2] More generally, the pleasure which is the goal of life is "freedom from pain and . . . fear" (*ataraxia*). Wine, women, and song do very badly by this test: for not only do they cause subsequent remorse and suffering, they also belong to a way of life ill-designed to achieve peace of mind.

Epicurus, then, is an early representative of that tradition – familiar among Indian thinkers, but popular too among French Enlightenment writers – which condemns the indulgent life, not out of Puritanism, but for reasons of self-interest. Epicurus is no utilitarian, however: a person is equipped by nature, he argues, only to aim at his or her own pleasure, and there can be no compelling reason to think that this requires maximizing of the general happiness. Indeed, Epicurus – here at odds once more with Aristotle – is scornful of political, public life, which he describes as a "prison house" we must escape (*Vatican Sayings* 58). Friendship, though, is a different matter, for it is only through the succor which close friends afford one another that peace of mind and freedom from anxiety are achievable.

Unfortunately, thinks Epicurus, few people appreciate that these achievements constitute the goal of pleasure. And a main reason for this failure, he famously argues, is due to the fear of death, something which prompts everything from a "make hay while the sun shines" abandon to excessive asceticism performed in order to escape eternal punishment. Whether or not his argument for saying that death should "mean nothing to us" is "about as absurd as any I have seen,"[3] readers must judge. But they should perhaps ask themselves whether such a reaction does not depend on commitments and attitudes that are indeed central to a certain way of life – our usual way – but which, if Epicurus is right, we should surely try to put aside or overcome.

Notes

1 *On the Nature of the Universe*, trans. R. Latham, Harmondsworth: Penguin, 1986, p. 60.

2 See A. A. Long's excellent *Hellenistic Philosophy: Stoics, Epicureans, Sceptics*, London: Duckworth, 1986, pp. 64ff.

3 S. Luper, *Invulnerability: On Securing Happiness*, Chicago: Open Court, 1996, p. 109.

Epicurus, "Letter to Menoeceus"

No one should postpone the study of philosophy when he is young, nor should he weary of it when he becomes mature, because the search for mental health is never untimely or out of season. To say that the time to study philosophy has not yet arrived or that it is past is like saying that the time for happiness is not yet at hand or is no longer present. Thus both the young and the mature should pursue philosophy, the latter in order to be rejuvenated as they age by the blessings that accrue from pleasurable past experience, and the youthful in order to become mature immediately through having no fear of the future. Hence we should make a practice of the things that make for happiness, for assuredly when we have this we have everything, and we do everything we can to get it when we don't have it.

The Preconditions of Happiness

(I) You should do and practise all the things I constantly recommended to you, with the knowledge that they are the fundamentals of the good life.

(a) First of all, you should think of deity as imperishable and blessed being (as delineated in the universal conception of it common to all men), and you should not attribute to it anything foreign to its immortality or inconsistent with its blessedness. On the contrary, you should hold every doctrine that is capable of safeguarding its blessedness in common with its imperishability. The gods do indeed exist, since our knowledge of them is a matter of clear and distinct perception; but they are not like what the masses suppose them to be, because most people do not maintain the pure conception of the gods. The irreligious man is not the person who destroys the gods of the masses but the person who imposes the ideas of the masses on the gods. The opinions held by most people about the gods are not true conceptions of them but fallacious notions, according to which awful penalties are meted out to the evil and the greatest of blessings to the good. The masses, by assimilating the gods in every respect to their own moral qualities, accept deities similar to themselves and regard anything not of this sort as alien.

(b) Second, you should accustom yourself to believing that death means nothing to us, since every good and every evil lies in sensation; but death is the privation of sensation. Hence a correct comprehension of the fact that death means nothing to us makes the mortal aspect of life pleasurable, not by conferring on us a boundless period of time but by removing the yearning for deathlessness. There is nothing fearful in living for the person who has really laid hold of the fact that there is nothing fearful in not living. So it is silly for a person to say that he dreads death – not because it will be painful when it arrives but because it pains him now as a future certainty; for that which makes no trouble for us when it arrives is a meaningless pain when we await it. This, the most horrifying of evils, means nothing to us, then, because so long as we are existent death is not present and whenever it is present we are nonexistent. Thus it is of no concern either to the living or to those who have completed their lives. For the former it is nonexistent, and the latter are themselves nonexistent.

Most people, however, recoil from death as though it were the greatest of evils; at other times they welcome it as the end-all of life's ills. The sophisticated person, on the other hand, neither begs off from living nor dreads not living. Life is not a stumbling block to him, nor does he regard not being alive as any sort of evil. As in the case of food he prefers the most savoury dish to merely the larger portion, so in the case of time he garners to himself the most agreeable moments rather than the longest span.

Anyone who urges the youth to lead a good life but counsels the older man to end his life in good style is silly, not merely because of the welcome character of life but because of the fact that living well and dying well are one and the same discipline. Much worse off, however, is the person who says it were well not to have been born 'but once born to pass Hades' portals as swiftly as may be'. Now if he says such a thing from inner persuasion why does he not withdraw from life? Everything is in readiness for him once he has firmly resolved on this course. But if he speaks facetiously he is a trifler standing in the midst of men who do not welcome him.

It should be borne in mind, then, that the time to come is neither ours nor altogether not ours. In this way we shall neither expect the future outright as something destined to be nor despair of it as something absolutely not destined to be.

The Good Life

(II) It should be recognized that within the category of desire certain desires are natural, cer-

tain others unnecessary and trivial; that in the case of the natural desires certain ones are necessary, certain others merely natural; and that in the case of necessary desires certain ones are necessary for happiness, others to promote freedom from bodily discomfort, others for the maintenance of life itself. A steady view of these matters shows us how to refer all moral choice and aversion to bodily health and imperturbability of mind, these being the twin goals of happy living. It is on this account that we do everything we do – to achieve freedom from pain and freedom from fear. When once we come by this, the tumult in the soul is calmed and the human being does not have to go about looking for something that is lacking or to search for something additional with which to supplement the welfare of soul and body. Accordingly we have need of pleasure only when we feel pain because of the absence of pleasure, but whenever we do not feel pain we no longer stand in need of pleasure. And so we speak of pleasure as the starting point and the goal of the happy life because we realize that it is our primary native good, because every act of choice and aversion originates with it, and because we come back to it when we judge every good by using the pleasure feeling as our criterion.

Because of the very fact that pleasure is our primary and congenital good we do not select every pleasure; there are times when we forgo certain pleasures, particularly when they are followed by too much unpleasantness. Furthermore, we regard certain states of pain as preferable to pleasures, particularly when greater satisfaction results from our having submitted to discomforts for a long period of time. Thus every pleasure is a good by reason of its having a nature akin to our own, but not every pleasure is desirable. In like manner every state of pain is an evil, but not all pains are uniformly to be rejected. At any rate, it is our duty to judge all such cases by measuring pleasures against pains, with a view to their respective assets and liabilities, inasmuch as we do experience the good as being bad at times and, contrariwise, the bad as being good.

In addition, we consider limitation of the appetites a major good, and we recommend this practice not for the purpose of enjoying just a few things and no more but rather for the purpose of enjoying those few in case we do not have much. We are firmly convinced that those who need expensive fare least are the ones who relish it most keenly and that a natural way of life is easily procured, while trivialities are hard to come by. Plain foods afford pleasure equivalent to that of a sumptuous diet, provided that the pains of penury are wholly eliminated. Barley bread and water yield the peak of pleasure whenever a person who needs them sets them in front of himself. Hence becoming habituated to a simple rather than a lavish way of life provides us with the full complement of health; it makes a person ready for the necessary business of life; it puts us in a position of advantage when we happen upon sumptuous fare at intervals and prepares us to be fearless in facing fortune.

Thus when I say that pleasure is the goal of living I do not mean the pleasures of libertines or the pleasures inherent in positive enjoyment, as is supposed by certain persons who are ignorant of our doctrine or who are not in agreement with it or who interpret it perversely. I mean, on the contrary, the pleasure that consists in freedom from bodily pain and mental agitation. The pleasant life is not the product of one drinking party after another or of sexual intercourse with women and boys or of the sea food and other delicacies afforded by a luxurious table. On the contrary, it is the result of sober thinking – namely, investigation of the reasons for every act of choice and aversion and elimination of those false ideas about the gods and death which are the chief source of mental disturbances.

The starting point of this whole scheme and the most important of its values is good judgement, which consequently is more highly esteemed even than philosophy.[1] All the other virtues stem from sound judgement, which shows us that it is impossible to live the pleasant Epicurean life without also living sensibly, nobly and justly and, vice versa, that it is impossible to live sensibly, nobly and justly without living pleasantly. The traditional virtues grow up together with the pleasant life; they are indivisible. Can you think of anyone more moral than the person who has devout beliefs about the gods, who is consistently without fears about death, and who has pondered man's natural end? Or who realizes that the goal of the good life is easily gained and achieved and that the term of evil is brief, both in extent of time and duration of pain? Or the man who laughs at the 'decrees of Fate', a deity whom some people have set up as sovereign of all? * * * * [A lacuna in the MSS here – Ed.]

The good Epicurean believes that certain events occur deterministically, that others are chance events, and that still others are in our own hands. He sees also that necessity cannot be held morally responsible and that chance is an unpredictable thing, but that what is in our own hands, since it has no master, is naturally associated with blameworthiness and the opposite. (Actually it would be better to subscribe to the popular mythology than to become a slave by accepting the determinism of the natural philosophers, because popular religion underwrites the hope of supplicating the gods by offerings but determinism contains an element of necessity, which is inexorable.) As for chance, the Epicurean does not assume that it is a deity (as in popular belief)[2] because a god does nothing irregular; nor does he regard it as an unpredictable cause of all events. It is his belief that good and evil are not the chance contributions of a deity, donated to mankind for the happy life, but rather that the initial circumstances for great good and evil are sometimes provided by chance. He thinks it preferable to have bad luck rationally than good luck irrationally. In other words, in human action it is better for a rational choice to be unsuccessful than for an irrational choice to succeed through the agency of chance.

Think about these and related matters day and night, by yourself and in company with someone like yourself. If you do, you will never experience anxiety, waking or sleeping, but you will live like a god among men. For a human being who lives in the midst of immortal blessings is in no way like mortal man!

Epicurus, "Leading Doctrines"

1–5: Five Fundamental Teachings Bearing on the Good Life

(1)   The blessed and indestructible being of the divine has no concerns of its own, nor does it make trouble for others. It is not affected by feelings of anger or benevolence, because these are found where there is lack of strength.

(2)   Death means nothing to us, because that which has been broken down into atoms has no sensation and that which has no sensation is no concern of ours.

(3) The quantitative limit of pleasure is the elimination of all feelings of pain. Wherever the pleasurable state exists, there is neither bodily pain nor mental pain nor both together, so long as the state continues.

(4) Bodily pain does not last continuously. The peak is present for a very brief period, and pains that barely exceed the state of bodily pleasure do not continue for many days. On the other hand, protracted illnesses show a balance of bodily pleasure over pain.

(5) It is impossible to live the pleasant life without also living sensibly, nobly and justly, and conversely it is impossible to live sensibly, nobly and justly without living pleasantly. A person who does not have a pleasant life is not living sensibly, nobly and justly, and conversely the person who does not have these virtues cannot live pleasantly.

6–7: Personal Security and the Good Life

(6) Any means by which it is possible to procure freedom from fearing other men is a natural good.

(7) Some men have desired to gain reputation and to be well regarded, thinking in this way to gain protection from other people. If the lives of such men are secure, they have acquired a natural blessing; but if they are not, they do not possess what they originally reached for by natural instinct.

8–9: How to Choose Pleasures

(8) No pleasure is bad in itself. But the things that make for pleasure in certain cases entail disturbances many times greater than the pleasures themselves.

(9) If all pleasures could be compressed in time and intensity, and were characteristic of the whole man or his more important aspects, the various pleasures would not differ from each other.

10–13: The Good Life is Dependent on Science*

(10) If the things that produce the debauchee's pleasures dissolved the mind's fears regarding

* I.e. knowledge.

the heavenly bodies, death and pain and also told us how to limit our desires, we would never have any reason to find fault with such people, because they would be glutting themselves with every sort of pleasure and never suffer physical or mental pain, which is the real evil.

(11) We would have no need for natural science unless we were worried by apprehensiveness regarding the heavenly bodies, by anxiety about the meaning of death, and also by our failure to understand the limitations of pain and desire.

(12) It is impossible to get rid of our anxieties about essentials if we do not understand the nature of the universe and are apprehensive about some of the theological accounts. Hence it is impossible to enjoy our pleasures unadulterated without natural science.

(13) There is no advantage in gaining security with regard to other people if phenomena occurring above and beneath the earth – in a word, everything in the infinite universe – are objects of anxiety.

14: Withdrawal into Obscurity is the Best Form of Security

(14) The simplest means of procuring protection from other men (which is gained to a certain extent by deterrent force) is the security of quiet solitude and withdrawal from the mass of people.

15: Wealth, Natural and Unnatural

(15) Nature's wealth is restricted and easily won, while that of empty convention runs on to infinity.

16: Luck Versus Reason in the Good Life

(16) Bad luck strikes the sophisticated man in a few cases, but reason has directed the big, essential things, and for the duration of life it is and will be the guide.

17: Justice and Mental Health

(17) The just man is the least disturbed by passion, the unjust man the most highly disturbed.

18–21: The Limits of True Pleasure

(18)   Bodily pleasure is not enlarged once the pains brought on by need have been done away with; it is only diversified. And the limit of mental pleasure is established by rational reflection on pleasures themselves and those kindred emotions that once instilled extreme fear in human minds.

(19)   Infinite time contains no greater pleasure than does finite time, if one determines the limits of pleasure rationally.

(20)   The body takes the limits of pleasure to be infinite, and infinite time would provide such pleasure. But the mind has provided us with the complete life by a rational examination of the body's goal and limitations and by dispelling our fears about a life after death; and so we no longer need unlimited time. On the other hand, it does not avoid pleasure, nor, when conditions occasion our departure from life, does it come to the end in a manner that would suggest that it had fallen short in any way of the best possible existence.

(21)   One who understands the limits of the good life knows that what eliminates the pains brought on by need and what makes the whole of life perfect is easily obtained, so that there is no need for enterprises that entail the struggle for success.

22–25: Empirical Considerations

(22)   It is necessary to take into account both the actual goal of life and the whole body of clear and distinct percepts to which we refer our judgements. If we fail to do this, everything will be in disorder and confusion.

(23)   If you reject all sensations, you will not have any point of reference by which to judge even the ones you claim are false.

(24)   If you summarily rule out any single sensation and do not make a distinction between the element of belief that is superimposed on a percept that awaits verification and what is actually present in sensation or in the feelings or some percept of the mind itself, you will cast doubt on all other sensations by your unfounded interpretation and consequently abandon all the criteria of truth. On the other hand, in cases of interpreted data, if you accept as true those that

need verification as well as those that do not, you will still be in error, since the whole question at issue in every judgement of what is true or not true will be left intact.

(25)   If at any time you fail to refer each of your acts to nature's standard, and turn off instead in some other direction when making a choice to avoid or pursue, your actions will not be consistent with your creed.

26, 29, 30: Classification of Human Desires

(29)   Some desires are (1) natural and necessary, others (2) natural but not necessary, still others (3) neither natural nor necessary but generated by senseless whims.

(26)   All desires that do not lead to physical pain if not satisfied are unnecessary, and involve cravings that are easily resolved when they appear to entail harm or when the object of desire is hard to get.

(30)   If interest is intense in the case of those natural desires that do not lead to physical pain when they are not satisfied, then such desires are generated by idle fancy, and it is not because of their own nature that they are not dissipated but because of the person's own senseless whims.

27–28: Friendship

(27)   Of all the things that wisdom provides for the happiness of the whole man, by far the most important is the acquisition of friendship.

(28)   It is the same judgement that has made us feel confident that nothing fearful is of long duration or everlasting, and that has seen personal security during our limited span of life most nearly perfected by friendship.

31–38: Justice and Injustice

(31)   The justice that seeks nature's goal is a utilitarian pledge of men not to harm each other or be harmed.[3]

(32)   Nothing is either just or unjust in the eyes of those animals that have been unable to make agreements not to harm each other or be harmed. The same is true of those peoples who

are unable or unwilling to make covenants not to harm or be harmed.

(33) Justice was never an entity in itself. It is a kind of agreement not to harm or be harmed, made when men associate with each other at any time and in communities of any size whatsoever.

(34) Injustice is not an evil in itself. Its evil lies in the anxious fear that you will not elude those who have authority to punish such misdeeds.

(35) It is impossible for a person who underhandedly breaks the agreement not to harm or be harmed to feel sure that he will escape punishment, even though he manages to do so time after time; for up to the very end of his life he cannot be sure that he will actually escape.

(36) In its general meaning, justice is the same for all because of its utility in the relations of men to each other, but in its specific application to countries and various other circumstances it does not follow that the same thing is just for all.

(37) In the case of actions that are legally regarded as just, those that are of tested utility in meeting the needs of human society have the hallmark of justice, whether they turn out to be equally just in all cases or not. On the other hand, if somebody lays down a law and it does not prove to be of advantage in human relations, then such a law no longer has the true character of justice. And even if the element of utility should undergo a change after harmonizing for a time with the conception of justice, the law was still just during that period, in the judgement of those who are not confused by meaningless words but who look at the actualities.

(38) In cases where the surrounding conditions are not new and where laws regarded as just have been shown to be inconsistent with the conception of justice in their actual workings, such laws are unjust. Again, in cases where the circumstances are new and where the same laws, once deemed to be just, are no longer serviceable, the laws in this case were just as long as they were useful to the community of citizens, but later when they were no longer useful they became unjust.

39–40: The Sectarian Spirit and Life

(39) The person who is the most successful in controlling the disturbing elements that come from the outside world has assimilated to himself what he could, and what he could not assimilate he has at least not alienated. Where he could not do even this, he has dissociated himself or eliminated all that it was expedient to treat in this way.

(40) All who have the capacity to gain security, especially from those who live around them, live a most agreeable life together, since they have the firm assurance of friendship; and after enjoying their comradeship to the full they do not bewail the early demise of a departed friend as if it were a pitiable thing.

Notes

1 The targets here are Plato and Aristotle, who elevated the "intellectual virtues" of contemplative philosophy over prudence or "practical wisdom".

2 The reference here is to the Greek cults of gods or goddesses of "Fate" and "Fortune".

3 Notice, however, that Epicurus's position is not that of later "social contract" theorists, who think we ought to act justly *because* we have pledged to do so. For Epicurus, my own peace of mind is the reason for acting justly.

4

(A) Mencius, "Human Nature Is Good"
(B) Hsun Tzu, "Man's Nature Is Evil"

Introduction

Historically, moral philosophy has been intimately related to moral psychology and the study of human nature. Even when the proponents of ethical systems have not tried to justify them by appeal to human nature, they have been keen to show that their proposals are not vitiated by any innate recalcitrance of human beings. In the absence of an account of human nature, moreover, it is hard to envisage the shape that moral and political education should take. It was unsurprising, therefore, to find the Greek thinkers represented in the opening three chapters of Part I of this volume devoting attention to people's nature and motivation. No less attention was paid further east, in China, where philosophical interest was almost exclusively "centered in human needs, in the improvement of government, [and] in morals."[1]

The most abiding ethical system of China – and indeed of anywhere else – was Confucianism. The primary emphases of Confucian ethics were altruistic benevolence (*jen*) and "righteousness" (*yi*) the latter largely understood as the correct performance

of "rites" (*li*), pre-eminently those of "filial piety" toward relatives and ancestors. The defense of this system offered by Confucius (Kǒng Fūzǐ; 6th–5th century BCE; see V.3) himself was primarily by way of appeal to ancient tradition, but he hints as well that benevolence and righteousness are in accordance with both human nature and "the way of Heaven." Unfortunately, these were two topics, so a disciple tells us, on which it was impossible to persuade the master to elaborate.[2] Elaboration had to await Confucius's best-known followers, Mencius (Mengzi, Master Meng, c. 372–289 BCE) and Hsun Tzu (Xunzi, Master Hsun, c. 298–238 BCE). Their articulations of the Confucian tradition could, however, hardly have been more different – on the surface at least. The two selections that follow are from Book 6, Part 1, of Mencius's works and from the critical rejoinder to this in §23 of Hsun Tzu's writings.

Mencius develops Confucius's hint that morality accords with human nature, asserting that "human nature is good." Just as water will flow downwards and grains ripen unless obstacles are placed in the way, so human beings will behave rightly unless circumstances are adverse. A variety of evidence is cited in favor of this claim – the fact that people prefer to die than to do something utterly shameful, for example, or the "gut" sympathy people feel when seeing a child drown or an animal suffer. These are not things we learn to do or to feel, and the difference between the "sage" and the ordinary person is that the former has not lost something – his natural "heart-mind" (*hsin*)

(A) *From The Works of Mencius*, trans. James Legge. London: Trübner, 1861, pp. 270–97. (B) *From Basic Writings of Mo Tzu, Hsun Tzu and Han Fei Tzu*, trans. Burton Watson. New York: Columbia University Press, 1967, pp. 157–71 (some passages omitted and some Chinese names given standard spellings).

– which, in the case of the latter, has atrophied as a result of adverse circumstances and lack of diligence. Morality, for Mencius, belongs to human nature in the further sense that it, and the "heart-mind" which predisposes toward it, distinguish human beings from all other creatures.

Since the view that the "good heart" is innate was held by most Confucians,[3] Hsun Tzu is maverick in arguing, against Mencius, that "man's nature is evil," though few Confucians were more zealous than he in defense of the performance of "rites."[4] In Hsun Tzu's view, what is natural to human beings is desire, and desire inevitably leads to conflict: since conflict is an evil, so is the nature in which it is rooted. Even if the young child possesses innate benevolence, it is no less natural for this to disappear; and it is absurd, Hsun Tzu holds, to suppose that something as obviously acquired and requiring training as moral behavior is natural in the way sight is natural to the eye. Far from the "sage" being a person who has not lost some innate endowment, he is someone who has fought much harder than the rest of us to acquire the virtues. Performance of "rites" is not something that flows from our inner being, but instead something that must be instilled in us in order to prevent social conflict.

The distance between the two philosophers may, however, be rather less than it appears. Mencius does not deny that most human beings behave badly most of the time, no more than Hsun Tzu denies that they have a capacity to act out of altruistic motives. (He is not a philosophical egoist.) Mencius's claim that a capacity for morality is what distinguishes human from animal nature is not contradicted by Hsun Tzu's insistence that the exercise of this capacity is the result of training, environment and the disciplining of natural desires. Yes, it is clear that at various points they mean different things by "natural." But arguably the most interesting difference between the two philosophers is that for Mencius the precepts of Confucian "righteousness" are ones to which the uncorrupted "sage" will intuitively assent, while for Hsun Tzu their only warrant is their success over the centuries in effectively controlling social conflict and in lending order (the primary imperative of "Heaven") to the affairs of humanity.[5]

Although Mencius's position was to become Confucian orthodoxy, the debate between him and Hsun Tzu was to be replayed many times within Chinese philosophy, right down to recent arguments over the malleability of human nature that Marxism seems to presuppose. Similar debates, of course, were to be conducted by philosophers in the West – by, for example, the eighteenth-century advocates of "moral sentiment" and their critics (see David Hume's discussion in I.14 below).

Notes

1 A. C. Graham, "The Place of Reason in the Chinese Philosophical Tradition," in R. Dawson (ed.), *The Legacy of China*, Oxford: Clarendon Press, 1964, p. 54.

2 Confucius, *The Analects*, Harmondsworth: Penguin, 1979, V, 13.

3 See Xinzhong Yao, *Confucianism and Christianity: A Comparative Study of Jen and Agape*, Brighton: Sussex Academic Press, 1996, pp. 132ff.

4 In D. E. Cooper, ed., *Aesthetics: The Classic Readings*, Malden, MA: Blackwell Publishing, 1997, Chapter 3, one may find Hsun Tzu's robust defense (in §20 of his works) of musical and artistic "rites" against Mo Tzu's attack.

5 See C. Hansen, *A Daoist Theory of Chinese Thought*, New York: Oxford University Press, 1992, cf. 195 and 132.

(A) Mencius, "Human Nature Is Good"

Chapter 1

(1) The philosopher Kao Tzu said, 'Man's nature is like the *ch'i* willow, and righteousness is like a cup or a bowl. The fashioning benevolence and righteousness out of man's nature is like the making cups and bowls from the *ch'i* willow.'

(2) Mencius replied, 'Can you, leaving untouched the nature of the willow, make with it cups and bowls? You must do violence and injury to the willow, before you can make cups

and bowls with it. If you must do violence and injury to the willow in order to make cups and bowls with it, on your principles you must in the same way do violence and injury to humanity in order to fashion from it benevolence and righteousness! Your words, alas! would certainly lead all men on to reckon benevolence and righteousness to be calamities.'

Chapter 2

(1) The philosopher Kao said, 'Man's nature is like water whirling round in a corner. Open a passage for it to the east, and it will flow to the east; open a passage for it to the west, and it will flow to the west. Man's nature is indifferent to good and evil, just as the water is indifferent to the east and west.'

(2) Mencius replied, 'Water indeed will flow indifferently to the east or west, but will it flow indifferently up or down? The tendency of man's nature to good is like the tendency of water to flow downwards. There are none but have this tendency to good, just as all water flows downwards.

(3) 'Now by striking water and causing it to leap up, you may make it go over your forehead, and, by damming and leading it, you may force it up a hill – but are such movements according to the nature of water? It is the force applied which causes them. When men are made to do what is not good, their nature is dealt with in this way.'

Chapter 3

(1) The philosopher Kao said, 'Life is what is to be understood by nature.'

(2) Mencius asked him, 'Do you say that by nature you mean life, just as you say that white is white?' 'Yes, I do,' was the reply. Mencius added, 'Is the whiteness of a white feather like that of white snow, and the whiteness of white snow like that of a white gem?' Kao again said 'Yes.'

(3) 'Very well,' pursued Mencius. 'Is the nature of a dog like the nature of an ox, and the nature of an ox like the nature of a man?'

Chapter 4

(1) The philosopher Kao said, 'To enjoy food and delight in colours[1] is nature. Benevolence is

internal and not external; righteousness is external and not internal.'

(2) Mencius asked him, 'What is the ground of your saying that benevolence is internal and righteousness external?' He replied, 'There is a man older than I, and I give honour to his age. It is not that there is first in me a principle of such reverence to age. It is just as when there is a white man, and I consider him white – according as he is so externally to me. On this account, I pronounce of righteousness that it is external.'

(3) Mencius said, 'There is no difference between our pronouncing of a white horse to be white and our pronouncing a white man to be white. But is there no difference between the regard with which we acknowledge the age of an old horse and that with which we acknowledge the age of an old man? And what is it which is called righteousness? – the fact of a man's being old? or the fact of our giving honour to his age?'

(4) Kao said, 'There is my younger brother – I love him. But the younger brother of a man of Ch'in I do not love: that is, the feeling is determined by myself, and therefore I say that benevolence is internal. On the other hand, I give honour to an old man of Ch'u and I also give honour to an old man of my own people: that is, the feeling is determined by the age, and therefore I say that righteousness is external.'

(5) Mencius answered him, 'Our enjoyment of meat roasted by a man of Ch'in does not differ from our enjoyment of meat roasted by ourselves. Thus, what you insist on takes place also in the case of such things, and will you say likewise that our enjoyment of a roast is external?'

Chapter 5

(1) The disciple Meng Chi-Tzu asked Kung-tu Tzu [another disciple of Mencius – Ed.] saying, 'On what ground is it said that righteousness is internal?'

(2) Kung-tu Tzu replied, 'We therein act out our feeling of respect, and therefore it is said to be internal.'

(3) The other objected, 'Suppose the case of a villager older than your elder brother by one year, to which of them would you show the greater respect?' 'To my brother,' was the reply. 'But for which of them would you first pour out wine at a feast?' 'For the villager.' Meng Chi-Tzu argued,

'Now your feeling of reverence rests on the one, and now the honour due to age is rendered to the other – this is certainly determined by what is without, and does not proceed from within.'

(4)   Kung-tu Tzu was unable to reply, and told the conversation to Mencius. Mencius said, 'You should ask him, "Which do you respect most, your uncle, or your younger brother?" He will answer, "My uncle." Ask him again, "If your younger brother be personating a dead ancestor, to which do you show the greater respect, to him or to your uncle?" He will say, "To my younger brother." You can go on, "But where is the respect due, as you said, to your uncle?" He will reply to this, "I show the respect to my younger brother, because of the position which he occupies," and you can likewise say, "So my respect to the villager is because of the position which he occupies. Ordinarily, my respect is rendered to my elder brother; for a brief season, on occasion, it is rendered to the villager."'

(5)   Meng chi-Tzu heard this and observed, 'When respect is due to my uncle, I respect him, and when respect is due to my younger brother, I respect him; the thing is certainly determined by what is without, and does not proceed from within.' Kung-tu Tzu replied, 'In winter we drink things hot, in summer we drink things cold; and so, on your principle, eating and drinking also depend on what is external!'

Chapter 6

(1)   The disciple Kung-tu Tzu said, 'The philosopher Kao says "Man's nature is neither good nor bad."

(2)   'Some say, "Man's nature may be made to practise good, and it may be made to practise evil, and accordingly, under [Kings] Wen and Wu the people loved what was good, while under [Kings] Yu and Li they loved what was cruel." . . .

(4)   'And now you say, "The nature is good." Then are all those wrong?'

(5)   Mencius said, 'From the feelings proper to it, it is constituted for the practice of what is good. This is what I mean in saying that the nature is good.

(6)   'If men do what is not good, the blame cannot be imputed to their natural powers.

(7)   'The feeling of commiseration belongs to all men; so does that of shame and dislike;

and that of reverence and respect; and that of approving and disapproving. The feeling of commiseration implies the principle of benevolence; that of shame and dislike, the principle of righteousness; that of reverence and respect, the principle of propriety; and that of approving and disapproving, the principle of knowledge. Benevolence, righteousness, propriety and knowledge are not infused into us from without. We are certainly furnished with them. And a different view is simply from want of reflection. Hence it is said "Seek and you will find them. Neglect and you will lose them." Men differ from one another in regard to them; some as much again as others, some five times as much, and some to an incalculable amount – it is because they cannot carry out fully their natural powers.

(8)   'It is said in the *Book of Poetry* [or *Book of Odes* – Ed.],

Heaven in producing mankind,
Gave them their various faculties and relations
  with *their specific* laws.
These are the invariable rules of nature for all
  to hold,
And *all* love this admirable virtue.

Confucius said, "The maker of this ode knew indeed the principle of our nature!" We may thus see that every faculty and relation must have its law, and since there are invariable rules for all to hold, they consequently love this admirable virtue.'

Chapter 7

(1)   Mencius said, 'In good years the children of the people are most of them good, while in bad years the most of them abandon themselves to evil. It is not owing to their natural powers conferred by Heaven that they are thus different. The abandonment is owing to the circumstances through which they allow their minds to be ensnared and drowned in evil.

(2)   'There now is barley. Let it be sown and covered up; the ground being the same, and the time of sowing likewise the same, it grows rapidly up, and when the full time is come, it is all found to be ripe. Although there may be inequalities of produce, that is owing to the difference of the soil, as rich or poor, to the unequal nourishment afforded by the rains and dews, and to the

different ways in which man has performed his business in reference to it.

(3) 'Thus all things which are the same in kind are like to one another; why should we doubt in regard to man, as if he were a solitary exception to this? The sage and we are the same in kind.

(4) 'In accordance with this the scholar Lung said, "If a man make hempen sandals without knowing the size of people's feet, yet I know that he will not make them like baskets." Sandals are all like one another, because all men's feet are like one another.

(5) 'So with the mouth and flavours; all mouths have the same relishes. Yi-ya [a famous chef – Ed.] only apprehended before me what my mouth relishes. Suppose that his mouth in its relish for flavours differed from that of other men, as is the case with dogs or horses which are not the same in kind with us, why should all men be found following Yi-ya in their relishes? In the matter of tastes the whole empire models itself after Yi-ya; that is, the mouths of all men are like one another.

(6) 'And so also it is with the ear. In the matter of sounds, the whole empire models itself after the music-master K'uang; that is, the ears of all men are like one another.

(7) 'And so also it is with the eye. In the case of Tzu-tu, there is no man but would recognize that he was beautiful. Any one who would not recognize the beauty of Tzu-tu must have no eyes.

(8) 'Therefore I say, men's mouths agree in having the same relishes; their ears agree in enjoying the same sounds; their eyes agree in recognizing the same beauty – shall their minds alone be without that which they similarly approve? What is it then of which they similarly approve? It is, I say, the principles of our nature, and the determinations of righteousness. The sages only apprehended before me that of which my mind approves along with other men. Therefore the principles of our nature and the determinations of righteousness are agreeable to my mind, just as the flesh of grass and grain-fed animals is agreeable to my mouth.'

Chapter 8

(1) Mencius said, 'The trees of the New mountain were once beautiful. Being situated,

however, in the borders of a large State, they were hewn down with axes and billhooks; and could they retain their beauty? Still through the activity of the vegetative life day and night, and the nourishing influence of the rain and dew, they were not without buds and sprouts springing forth, but then came the cattle and goats and browsed upon them. To these things is owing the bare and stripped appearance of the mountain, which when people see, they think it was never finely wooded. But is this the nature of the mountain?

(2) 'And so also of what properly belongs to man – shall it be said that the mind of any man was without benevolence and righteousness? The way in which a man loses his proper goodness of mind is like the way in which the trees are denuded by axes and billhooks. Hewn down day after day, can it – the mind – retain its beauty? But there is a development of its life day and night, and in the calm air of the morning, just between night and day, the mind feels in a degree those desires and aversions which are proper to humanity, but the feeling is not strong, and it is fettered and destroyed by what takes place during the day. This fettering taking place again and again, the restorative influence of the night is not sufficient to preserve the proper goodness of the mind; and when this proves insufficient for that purpose, the nature becomes not much different from that of the irrational animals, which when people see, they think it never had those powers which I assert. But does this condition represent the feelings proper to humanity?

(3) 'Therefore, if it receive its proper nourishment, there is nothing which will not grow. If it lose its proper nourishment, there is nothing which will not decay away.

(4) 'Confucius said, "Hold it fast, and it remains with you. Let it go, and you lose it. Its outgoing and incoming cannot be defined as to time or place." It is the mind of which this is said!'

Chapter 9

(1) Mencius said, 'It is not to be wondered at that the king is not wise!

(2) 'Suppose the case of the most easily growing thing in the world – if you let it have one day's genial heat, and then expose it for ten days to cold, it will not be able to grow. It is but

seldom that I have an audience of the king, and when I retire, there come all those who act upon him like the cold. Though I succeed in bringing out some buds of goodness, of what avail is it!

(3) 'Now chess-playing is but a small art,[2] but without his whole mind being given, and his will bent to it, a man cannot succeed at it. Yi Ch'iu is the best chess-player in all the kingdom. Suppose that he is teaching two men to play. The one gives to the subject his whole mind and bends to it all his will, doing nothing but listening to Yi Ch'iu. The other, although he seems to be listening to him, has his whole mind running on a swan which he thinks is approaching, and wishes to bend his bow, adjust the string to the arrow, and shoot it. Although he is learning along with the other, he does not come up to him. Why? Because his intelligence is not equal? Not so.'

Chapter 10

(1) Mencius said, 'I like fish and I also like bear's palm. If I cannot have the two together, I will let the fish go, and take the bear's palm. So, I like life, and I also like righteousness. If I cannot keep the two together, I will let life go and choose righteousness.

(2) 'I like life indeed, but there is that which I like more than life, and therefore, I will not seek to possess it by any improper ways. I dislike death indeed, but there is that which I dislike more than death, and therefore there are occasions when I will not avoid danger.

(3) 'If among the things which man likes there were nothing which he liked more than life, why should he not use every means by which he could preserve it? If among the things which man dislikes there were nothing which he disliked more than death, why should he not do every thing by which he could avoid danger?

(4) 'There are cases when men by a certain course might preserve life, and they do not employ it; when by certain things they might avoid danger, and they will not do them.

(5) 'Therefore, men have that which they like more than life, and that which they dislike more than death. They are not men of distinguished talents and virtue only who have this mental nature. All men have it; what belongs to such men is simply that they do not lose it.' . . .

Chapter 11

(1) Mencius said, 'Benevolence is man's mind, and righteousness is man's path.

(2) 'How lamentable is it to neglect the path and not pursue it, to lose this mind and not know to seek it again!

(3) 'When men's fowls and dogs are lost, they know to seek for them again, but they lose their mind, and do not know to seek for it.

(4) 'The great end of learning is nothing else but to seek for the lost mind.' . . .

Chapter 15

(1) The disciple Kung-tu Tzu said, 'All are equally men, but some are great men, and some are little men – how is this?' Mencius replied, 'Those who follow that part of themselves which is great are great men; those who follow that part which is little are little men.'

(2) Kung-tu Tzu pursued, 'All are equally men, but some follow that part of themselves which is great, and some follow that part which is little – how is this?' Mencius answered, 'The senses of hearing and seeing do not think, and are obscured by external things. When one thing comes into contact with another, as a matter of course it leads it away. To the mind belongs the office of thinking. By thinking, it gets the right view of things; by neglecting to think, it fails to do this. These – the senses and the mind – are what Heaven has given to us. Let a man first stand fast in the supremacy of the nobler part of his constitution, and the inferior part will not be able to take it from him. It is simply this which makes the great man.'

Chapter 16

(1) Mencius said, 'There is a nobility of Heaven, and there is a nobility of man. Benevolence, righteousness, self-consecration and fidelity, with unwearied joy in these virtues – these constitute the nobility of Heaven. . . .

(2) 'The men of antiquity cultivated their nobility of Heaven, and the nobility of man came to them in its train.

(3) 'The men of the present day cultivate their nobility of Heaven in order to seek for the

nobility of man, and when they have obtained that, they throw away the other – their delusion is extreme. The issue is simply this that they must lose that nobility of man as well.'

Chapter 17

(1) Mencius said, 'To desire to be honoured is the common mind of men. And all men have in themselves that which is truly honourable. Only they do not think of it.

(2) 'The honour which men confer is not good honour. Those whom Chaou the Great ennobles he can make mean again.

(3) 'It is said in the *Book of Poetry* [or *Book of Odes* – Ed.],

He has filled us with his wine,
He has satiated us with his goodness.

"Satiated us with his goodness", that is, satiated us with benevolence and righteousness, and he who is so, consequently, does not wish for the fat meat and fine millet of men. A good reputation and far-reaching praise fall to him, and he does not desire the elegant embroidered garments of men.'

Chapter 18

(1) Mencius said, 'Benevolence subdues its opposite just as water subdues fire. Those, however, who nowadays practise benevolence do it as if with one cup of water they could save a whole waggon-load of fuel which was on fire, and when the flames were not extinguished, were to say that water cannot subdue fire. This conduct, moreover, greatly encourages those who are not benevolent.

(2) 'The final issue will simply be this – the loss of that small amount of benevolence.'

Chapter 19

Mencius said, 'Of all seeds the best are the five kinds of grain, yet if they be not ripe, they are not equal to the *t'e* or the *pae*. So, the value of benevolence depends entirely on its being brought to maturity.'

Chapter 20

(1) Mencius said, 'Yi, in teaching men to shoot, made it a rule to draw the bow to the full, and his pupils also did the same.

(2) 'A master workman, in teaching others, uses the compass and square, and his pupils do the same.'

Notes

1 More recent translators suggest 'the appetitite for sex' rather than 'delight in colours'.
2 Mencius's reference here is probably to the game of *go* rather than chess.

(B)   Hsun Tzu, "Man's Nature Is Evil"

Man's nature is evil; goodness is the result of conscious activity. The nature of man is such that he is born with a fondness for profit. If he indulges this fondness, it will lead him into wrangling and strife, and all sense of courtesy and humility will disappear. He is born with feelings of envy and hate, and if he indulges these, they will lead him into violence and crime, and all sense of loyalty and good faith will disappear. Man is born with the desires of the eyes and ears, with a fondness for beautiful sights and sounds. If he indulges these, they will lead him into licence and wantonness, and all ritual principles and correct forms will be lost. Hence, any man who follows his nature and indulges his emotions will inevitably become involved in wrangling and strife, will violate the forms and rules of society, and will end as a criminal. Therefore, man must first be transformed by the instructions of a teacher and guided by ritual principles, and only then will he be able to observe the dictates of courtesy and humility, obey the forms and rules of society, and achieve order. It is obvious from this, then, that man's nature is evil, and that his goodness is the result of conscious activity.

A warped piece of wood must wait until it has been laid against the straightening board, steamed and forced into shape before it can become straight; a piece of blunt metal must wait until it has been whetted on a grindstone before it can become sharp. Similarly, since man's nature is evil, it must wait for the instructions of a teacher before it can become upright, and for the guidance of ritual principles before it can become orderly. If men have no teachers to instruct them, they will be inclined towards evil and not upright; and if they have no ritual principles to guide them, they will be perverse and violent and lack order. In ancient times the sage kings realized that man's nature is evil, and that therefore he inclines toward evil and violence and is not upright or orderly. Accordingly they created ritual principles and laid down certain regulations in order to reform man's emotional nature and make it upright, in order to train and transform it and guide it in the proper channels. In this way they caused all men to become orderly and to conform to the Way. Hence, today any man who takes to heart the instructions of his teacher, applies himself to his studies, and abides by ritual principles may become a gentleman, but anyone who gives free rein to his emotional nature, is content to indulge his passions, and disregards ritual principles becomes a petty man. It is obvious from this, therefore, that man's nature is evil, and that his goodness is the result of conscious activity.

Mencius states that man is capable of learning because his nature is good, but I say that this is wrong. It indicates that he has not really understood man's nature nor distinguished properly between the basic nature and conscious activity. The nature is that which is given by Heaven; you cannot learn it, you cannot acquire it by effort. Ritual principles, on the other hand, are created by sages; you can learn to apply them, you can work to bring them to completion. That part of man which cannot be learned or acquired by effort is called the nature; that part of him which can be acquired by learning and brought to completion by effort is called conscious activity. This is the difference between nature and conscious activity.

It is a part of man's nature that his eyes can see and his ears can hear. But the faculty of clear sight can never exist separately from the eye, nor can the faculty of keen hearing exist separately from the ear. It is obvious, then, that you cannot acquire clear sight and keen hearing by study. Mencius states that man's nature is good, and that all evil arises because he loses his original nature. Such a view, I believe, is erroneous. It is the way with man's nature that as soon as he is born he begins to depart from his original naïveté and simplicity, and therefore he must inevitably lose what Mencius regards as his original nature. It is obvious from this, then, that the nature of man is evil.

Those who maintain that the nature is good praise and approve whatever has not departed from the original simplicity and naïveté of the child. That is, they consider that beauty belongs to the original simplicity and naïveté and goodness to the original mind in the same way that clear sight is inseparable from the eye and keen hearing from the ear. Hence, they maintain that [the nature possesses goodness] in the same way that the eye possesses clear vision or the ear keenness of hearing. Now it is the nature of man that when he is hungry he will desire satisfaction, when he is cold he will desire warmth, and when he is weary he will desire rest. This is his emotional nature. And yet a man, although he is hungry, will not dare to be the first to eat if he is in the presence of his elders, because he knows that he should yield to them, and although he is weary, he will not dare to demand rest because he knows that he should relieve others of the burden of labour. For a son to yield to his father or a younger brother to yield to his elder brother, for a son to relieve his father of work or a younger brother to relieve his elder brother – acts such as these are all contrary to man's nature and run counter to his emotions. And yet they represent the way of filial piety and the proper forms enjoined by ritual principles. Hence, if men follow their emotional nature, there will be no courtesy or humility; courtesy and humility in fact run counter to man's emotional nature. From this it is obvious, then, that man's nature is evil, and that his goodness is the result of conscious activity.

Someone may ask: if man's nature is evil, then where do ritual principles come from? I would reply: all ritual principles are produced by the conscious activity of the sages; essentially they are not products of man's nature. A potter moulds clay and makes a vessel, but the vessel is the product of the conscious activity of the potter, not essentially a product of his human nature. A carpenter carves a piece of wood and makes a utensil, but the utensil is the product of the conscious activity of the carpenter, not essentially a product of his human nature. The sage gathers together his thoughts and ideas, experiments with various forms of conscious activity, and so produces ritual principles and sets forth laws and regulations. Hence, these ritual principles and laws are the products of the conscious activity of the sage, not essentially products of his human nature.

Phenomena such as the eye's fondness for beautiful forms, the ear's fondness for beautiful sounds, the mouth's fondness for delicious flavours, the mind's fondness for profit, or the body's fondness for pleasure and ease – these are all products of the emotional nature of man. They are instinctive and spontaneous; man does not have to do anything to produce them. But that which does not come into being instinctively but must wait for some activity to bring it into being is called the product of conscious activity. These are the products of the nature and of conscious activity respectively, and the proof that they are not the same. Therefore, the sage transforms his nature and initiates conscious activity; from this conscious activity he produces ritual principles, and when they have been produced he sets up rules and regulations. Hence, ritual principles and rules are produced by the sage. In respect to human nature the sage is the same as all other men and does not surpass them; it is only in his conscious activity that he differs from and surpasses other men.

It is man's emotional nature to love profit and desire gain. Suppose now that a man has some wealth to be divided. If he indulges his emotional nature, loving profit and desiring gain, then he will quarrel and wrangle even with his own brothers over the division. But if he has been transformed by the proper forms of ritual principle, then he will be capable of yielding even to a complete stranger. Hence, to indulge the emotional nature leads to the quarrelling of brothers, but to be transformed by ritual principles makes a man capable of yielding to strangers.

Every man who desires to do good does so precisely because his nature is evil. A man whose accomplishments are meagre longs for greatness; an ugly man longs for beauty; a man in cramped quarters longs for spaciousness; a poor man longs for wealth; a humble man longs for eminence. Whatever a man lacks in himself he will seek outside. But if a man is already rich, he will not long for wealth, and if he is already eminent, he will not long for greater power. What a man already possesses in himself he will not bother to look for

outside. From this we can see that men desire to do good precisely because their nature is evil. Ritual principles are certainly not a part of man's original nature. Therefore, he forces himself to study and to seek to possess them. An understanding of ritual principles is not a part of man's original nature, and therefore he ponders and plans and thereby seeks to understand them. Hence, man in the state in which he is born neither possesses nor understands ritual principles. If he does not possess ritual principles, his behaviour will be chaotic, and if he does not understand them, he will be wild and irresponsible. In fact, therefore, man in the state in which he is born possesses this tendency towards chaos and irresponsibility. From this it is obvious, then, that man's nature is evil, and that his goodness is the result of conscious activity.

Mencius states that man's nature is good, but I say that this view is wrong. All men in the world, past and present, agree in defining goodness as that which is upright, reasonable and orderly, and evil as that which is prejudiced, irresponsible and chaotic. This is the distinction between good and evil. Now suppose that man's nature was in fact intrinsically upright, reasonable and orderly – then what need would there be for sage kings and ritual principles? The existence of sage kings and ritual principles could certainly add nothing to the situation. But because man's nature is in fact evil, this is not so. Therefore, in ancient times the sages, realizing that man's nature is evil, that it is prejudiced and not upright, irresponsible and lacking in order, for this reason established the authority of the ruler to control it, elucidated ritual principles to transform it, set up laws and standards to correct it, and meted out strict punishments to restrain it. As a result, all the world achieved order and conformed to goodness. Such is the orderly government of the sage kings and the transforming power of ritual principles. Now let someone try doing away with the authority of the ruler, ignoring the transforming power of ritual principles, rejecting the order that comes from laws and standards, and dispensing with the restrictive power of punishments, and then watch and see how the people of the world treat each other. He will find that the powerful impose upon the weak and rob them, the many terrorize the few and extort from them, and in no time the whole world will be given up to chaos and mutual destruction. It is obvious from this, then, that man's nature is evil, and that his goodness is the result of conscious activity.

Those who are good at discussing antiquity must demonstrate the validity of what they say in terms of modern times; those who are good at discussing Heaven must show proofs from the human world. In discussions of all kinds, men value what is in accord with the facts and what can be proved to be valid. Hence if a man sits on his mat propounding some theory, he should be able to stand right up and put it into practice, and show that it can be extended over a wide area with equal validity. Now Mencius states that man's nature is good, but this is neither in accord with the facts, nor can it be proved to be valid. One may sit down and propound such a theory, but he cannot stand up and put it into practice, nor can he extend it over a wide area with any success at all. How, then, could it be anything but erroneous?

If the nature of man were good, we could dispense with sage kings and forget about ritual principles. But if it is evil, then we must go along with the sage kings and honour ritual principles. The straightening board is made because of the warped wood; the plumb line is employed because things are crooked; rulers are set up and ritual principles elucidated because the nature of man is evil. From this it is obvious, then, that man's nature is evil, and that his goodness is the result of conscious activity. A straight piece of wood does not have to wait for the straightening board to become straight; it is straight by nature. But a warped piece of wood must wait until it has been laid against the straightening board, steamed and forced into shape before it can become straight, because by nature it is warped. Similarly, since man's nature is evil, he must wait for the ordering power of the sage kings and the transforming power of ritual principles; only then can he achieve order and conform to goodness. From this it is obvious, then, that man's nature is evil, and that his goodness is the result of conscious activity.

Someone may ask whether ritual principles and concerted conscious activity are not themselves a part of man's nature, so that for that reason the sage is capable of producing them. But I would answer that this is not so. A potter may mould clay and produce an earthen pot, but surely moulding pots out of clay is not a part of the potter's human nature. A carpenter may carve wood and produce a utensil, but surely carving utensils out of wood is not a part of the carpenter's human nature. The sage stands in the same relation to ritual principles as the potter to the things he moulds and produces. How, then, could ritual principles and concerted conscious activity be a part of man's basic human nature? . . .

The man in the street can become a Yu. What does this mean? What made the sage emperor Yu a Yu, I would reply, was the fact that he practised benevolence and righteousness and abided by the proper rules and standards. If this is so, then benevolence, righteousness and proper standards must be based upon principles which can be known and practised. Any man in the street has the essential faculties needed to understand benevolence, righteousness and proper standards, and the potential ability to put them into practice. Therefore it is clear that he can become a Yu.

Would you maintain that benevolence, righteousness and proper standards are not based upon any principles that can be known and practised? If so, then even a Yu could not have understood or practised them. Or would you maintain that the man in the street does not have the essential faculties needed to understand them or the potential ability to put them into practice? If so, then you are saying that the man in the street in his family life cannot understand the duties required of a father or a son and in public life cannot comprehend the correct relationship between ruler and subject. But in fact this is not true. Any man in the street *can* understand the duties required of a father or a son and *can* comprehend the correct relationship between ruler and subject. Therefore, it is obvious that the essential faculties needed to understand such ethical principles and the potential ability to put them into practice must be a part of his make-up. Now if he takes these faculties and abilities and applies them to the principles of benevolence and righteousness, which we have already shown to be knowable and practicable, then it is obvious that he can become a Yu. If the man in the street applies himself to training and study, concentrates his mind and will, and considers and examines things carefully, continuing his efforts over a long period of time and accumulating good acts without stop, then he can achieve a godlike understanding and form a triad with Heaven and earth. The sage is a man who has arrived where he has through the accumulation of good acts.

You have said, someone may object, that the sage has arrived where he has through the accumulation of good acts. Why is it, then, that everyone is not able to accumulate good acts in the same way? I would reply: everyone is capable of doing so, but not everyone can be made to do so. The petty man is capable of becoming a gentleman, yet he is not willing to do so; the gentleman is capable of becoming a petty man but he is not willing to do so. The petty man and the gentleman are perfectly capable of changing places; the fact that they do not actually do so is what I mean when I say that they are capable of doing so but they cannot be made to do so. Hence, it is correct to say that the man in the street is *capable* of becoming a Yu but it is not necessarily correct to say that he will in fact find it possible to

do so. But although he does not find it possible to do so does not prove that he is incapable of doing so.

A person with two feet is theoretically capable of walking to every corner of the earth, although in fact no one has ever found it possible to do so. Similarly, the artisan, the carpenter, the farmer and the merchant are theoretically capable of exchanging professions, although in actual practice they find it impossible to do so. From this we can see that, although someone may be theoretically capable of becoming something, he may not in practice find it possible to do so. But although he does not find it possible to do so, this does not prove that he is not capable of doing so. To find it practically possible or impossible to do something and to be capable or incapable of doing something are two entirely different things. It is perfectly clear, then, that a man is theoretically capable of becoming something else. . . .

The Book of Chuang Tzu, Chapters 9, 13–14

Introduction

After the *Tao Te Ching, The Book of Chuang Tzu is* the most famous text of classical Taoism. Unlike the "author" of the *Tao Te Ching*, Lao Tzu (Laozi, "Old Master"), Chuang Tzu (or Zhuangzi, "Master Chuang") seems to have been an actual historical figure, an official in the Lacquer Garden at Meng who lived from around 369 to 286 BCE. Which parts of his book he himself penned, however, is unclear, and the chapters from which we have drawn are quite probably later accretions – so that when we refer to "Chuang Tzu" from now on, it may not be the man from Meng himself whose views are presented.

Taoism is traditionally thought of as the great rival to Confucian ethics. But this can be misleading. One should recall that the division of Chinese philosophy into various "schools" and "-isms" was made several centuries after Confucius, Mencius, Chuang Tzu and other leading thinkers flourished. One should also keep in mind that in Taoist texts – though not in the chapters chosen here – Confucius is often portrayed in a favourable light. Moreover, in later centuries, Confucianism and Taoism were often perceived "not as rival systems," but as "complementary doctrines, an ethical and political system for the conduct of

From The Book of Chuang Tzu, trans. M. Palmer. Harmondsworth: Penguin, 1996, pp. 72–4, 106–14, 118, 122–7 (some passages omitted).

public and family life, and a mystical philosophy for the spiritual nourishment of the individual," respectively.[1] Still, the fact that the "systems" had to operate in distinct walks of life suggests that there are important differences between them, and in the following pages of *The Book of Chuang Tzu* Confucian ethics, while not ridiculed, are subjected to serious criticisms.

Chuang Tzu is often represented as a vitriolic critic of "artifice" and "conventions," including the "rites" on which Confucians placed such a premium. But there is a sense in which for Chuang Tzu convention and artifice are unavoidable. He was a relativist for whom all beliefs and distinctions, including ethical ones, are the product of people's "perspectives" and the languages they have forged (see II.3 of this volume for Chuang's relativism). Indeed, his animating complaint is against those who fail to appreciate relativism, who "reify" our perspectival distinctions and treat them – as Confucians do in their principles of benevolence (*jen*) and righteousness (*yi*) – as if they were naturally woven into the order of things (see I.4 above). To this complaint are added the conviction, shared by the *Tao Te Ching*,[2] that people's obsession with moral principles is already a sign that their lives and society are awry, and the insistence that, while some reliance on "convention" is unavoidable, any dogged clinging to artifice is destructive of authentic human existence (rather as horse-training is to authentic equine existence – Chapter 9).

For Chuang Tzu, the "true man," by refusing to cling to conventional principles and distinctions, thereby "follows the Way" (*tao* or *dao*). It is notoriously difficult to know what is meant by *tao*, which is anyway said to be "almost indescribable," to have "no name" (Chapter 22). Suffice it to say that, as the "source" and "sustainer" of everything in Heaven and Earth, it is not dependent upon anything and has nothing against which to act or contend. In these respects, it can be described as "free," and the "true man" will emulate this freedom. In particular, his (and perhaps her) life will be one of "actionless action" (*wu wei*): by acting without specific purpose, relatively unconstrained by particular conventions, and refusing to contend against circumstance and other men, he emulates the "freedom" of the *tao* itself. Only such a person is capable of appreciating the role, limited though it is, which principles of benevolence and righteousness may play. The Taoist hero is not the busy Confucian official endeavouring to beef up the moral fibre of the body politic, but the retiring, contemplative sage who disdains the latest fashionable "perspective," or the artisan (like the wheelwright in Chapter 13) who responds smoothly and naturally to the demands of his materials, without the mediation of precepts and formulas. Each in his own way "lets things be" and, in doing so, "follows the Way." (Chuang Tzu is said to have turned down offers of government office and, spurning Confucian principles, cheerfully practised his drumming after his wife's death.)

Taoism, unsurprisingly, did not enjoy the state sponsorship that Confucian ethics did for nearly two millennia. But Chinese painting and fiction testify to the enduring appeal of Taoism, one which in recent years has spread to the West, not least because of the feeling that, in Taoist calls to "follow Nature," there is inspiration for an "environmental ethic."[3] Not that the West has itself lacked a tradition of ethical thought which, in its essentials, corresponds to that of Taoism. From Democritus to Heidegger, there have always been those who have located the proper life for human beings not in adherence to what they see as the artifice of a moral system, but instead in obedience to something mysterious and indescribable.

Notes

1 B. Watson, Introduction to his translation of *The Complete Works of Chuang Tzu*, New York: Columbia University Press, 1968, p. 10.
2 Harmondsworth: Penguin, 1985. See especially Chapter 38, according to which benevolence, rectitude and rites emerged only "when the Way was lost."
3 See N. J. Girardot, J. Miller and L. Xiaogan, eds, *Daoism and Ecology: Ways within a Cosmic Landscape*, Cambridge, MA: Harvard University Press, 2001.

The Book of Chuang Tzu

Chapter 9: Horses' Hooves

Horses have hooves so that their feet can grip on frost and snow and hair so that they can withstand the wind and cold. They eat grass and drink water, they buck and gallop, for this is the innate nature of horses. Even if they had great towers and magnificent halls, they would not be interested in them. However, when [the horse-trainer] Po Lo came on the scene, he said, 'I know how to train horses.' He branded them, cut their hair and their hooves, put halters on their heads, bridled them, hobbled them and shut them up in stables. Out of ten horses at least two or three die. Then he makes them hungry and thirsty, gallops them, races them, parades them, runs them together. He

keeps before them the fear of the bit and ropes, behind them the fear of the whip and crop. Now more than half the horses are dead.

The potter said, 'I know how to use clay, how to mould it into rounds like the compass and into squares as though I had used a T-square.' The carpenter said, 'I know how to use wood: to make it bend, I use the template; to make it straight, I use the plumb line.' However, is it really the innate nature of clay and wood to be moulded by compass and T-square, template and plumb line? It is true, nevertheless, that generation after generation has said, 'Po Lo is good at controlling horses, and indeed the potter and carpenter are good with clay and wood.' And the same nonsense is spouted by those who rule the world.

I think that someone who truly knows how to rule the world would not be like this. The people have a true nature, they weave their cloth, they farm to produce food. This is their basic Virtue.[1] They are all one in this, not separated, and it is from Heaven.[2] Thus, in an age of perfect Virtue the people walk slowly and solemnly. They see straight and true. In times such as these the mountains have neither paths nor tunnels, on the lakes there are neither boats nor bridges; all life lives with its own kind, living close together. The birds and beasts multiply in their flocks and herds, the grass and trees grow tall. It is true that at such a time the birds and beasts can be led around without ropes, and birds' nests can be seen with ease.

In this time of perfect Virtue, people live side by side with the birds and beasts, sharing the world in common with all life. No one knows of distinctions such as nobles and the peasantry! Totally without wisdom but with virtue which does not disappear; totally without desire they are known as truly simple. If people are truly simple, they can follow their true nature. Then the perfect sage comes,[3] going on about benevolence, straining for self-righteousness, and suddenly everyone begins to have doubts. They start to fuss over the music, cutting and trimming the rituals, and thus the whole world is disturbed. If the pure essence had not been so cut about, how could they have otherwise ended up with sacrificial bowls? If the raw jade was not broken apart, how could the symbols of power be made? If the Tao and Te – Way and Virtue – had not been ignored, how could benevolence and righteousness have been preferred? If innate nature had not been left behind, how could rituals and music have been invented? If the five colours had not been confused, how could patterns and designs have occurred? If the five notes had not been confused, how could they have been supplanted by the six tones? The abuse of the true elements to make artefacts was the crime of the craftsman. The abuse of the Tao and Te – Way and Virtue – to make benevolence and righteousness, this was the error of the sage.

Horses, when they live wild, eat grass and drink water; when they are content, they entwine their necks and rub each other. When angry, they turn their backs on each other and kick out. This is what horses know. But if harnessed together and lined up under constraints, they know to look sideways and to arch their necks, to career around and try to spit out the bit and rid themselves of the reins. The knowledge thus gained by the horse, and its wicked behaviour, is in fact the fault of Po Lo.

At the time of [Emperor] Ho Hsu, people stayed where they were, not knowing anything else; they walked but did not know where they were going; filled themselves with food and were happy slapping their bellies to show their contentment. This was what the people had. Then came the sage. He brought the cringing and grovelling of the rituals and music and infected all under Heaven with his offer of benevolence and righteousness, which he said would comfort the hearts of all.

As a result the people desired and longed for knowledge, and warred against each other to gain the advantage. Nothing could stop them. All this was the fault of the sage.

Chapter 13: Heaven's Tao

It is Heaven's Tao to journey and to gather no
moss,
thus all the forms of life are brought to
perfection.
It is the Emperor's Tao to journey and to gather
no moss,
which is why the whole world comes to his feet.
It is the sages' Tao to journey and to gather no
moss,
thus all that lies within the oceans venerates
them.
To understand Heaven clearly,
to comprehend the sages,
to journey through the entire cosmos
following the Virtue of the Emperors and the
kings
but also to be spontaneous themselves;
this is the nature of those who comprehend,
seeming not to know
but being centred in stillness.

The sages are quiescent, not because of any value in being quiescent, they simply are still. Not even the multitude of beings can disturb them, so they are calm. Water, when it is still, reflects back even your eyebrows and beard. It is perfectly level and from this the carpenter takes his level. If water stilled offers such clarity, imagine what pure spirit offers! The sage's heart is stilled! Heaven and Earth are reflected in it, the mirror of all life. Empty, still, calm, plain, quiet, silent, non-active, this is the centredness of Heaven and Earth and of the Tao and of Virtue. The Emperor, king and sages rest there. Resting, they are empty; empty, they can be full; fullness is fulfilment. From the empty comes stillness; in stillness they can travel; in travelling they achieve. In stillness they take actionless action. Through actionless action they expect results from those with responsibilities. Through actionless action they are happy, very happy; being so happy they are not afflicted by cares and worries, for these have no place, and their years of life are prolonged. Empty, still, calm, plain, quiet, silent, actionless action is the foundation of all life. If you are clear on this and facing south, it means you are a noble like [Emperor] Yao; if you are clear on this and facing north, you will become a minister like Shun.

Looking up to them, you observe the Virtue of Emperors, kings and the Sons of Heaven. Looking down on them, you observe the Tao of the dark sages and the uncrowned king. If you retire as they did, amongst the hermits of the rivers and oceans, mountains and forests, you will be considered like them as true scholars. Coming forward and offering help to this generation brings great fame and merit and the whole world becomes one. The sage is still; the king travels. Actionless action brings honour. The beauty radiated, since it arises from simplicity, outshines the rest of the world. Clarity is the Virtue of Heaven and Earth: this is the great Origin, the great Beginning. To have it is to be in harmony with Heaven, to bring equality with everything below Heaven and to be in harmony with all people. To be in harmony with all people is called human happiness; to be in harmony with Heaven, this is called Heavenly happiness.

Chuang Tzu said,

My Master Teacher! My Master Teacher!
He judges all life but does not feel he is
    being judgemental;
he is generous to multitudes of generations
but does not think this benevolent;
he is older than the oldest
but does not think himself old;
he overarches Heaven and sustains Earth,
shaping and creating endless bodies
but he does not think himself skilful.
This is what is known as Heavenly happiness.

'There is a saying: "If you know the happiness of Heaven, then you know that life is from Heaven and death is the transformation of things. In their stillness they are yin and in their journeying they are yang."[4] To know Heavenly happiness means that you do not upset Heaven, nor go against others. You are not reliant on material things, you are not rebuked by the ghosts. There is a saying: "He moves with Heaven and rests with Earth, his heart is one, he is the king of the whole world; the ghosts do not worry him and his soul is not wearied, his heart is one with all living beings." This means his emptiness and stillness enter all beings in Heaven and Earth, travelling alongside all beings. This is known as the Heavenly happiness. Heavenly happiness is the heart of the sage; this is how he cares for all under Heaven.'

The Virtue of Emperors and kings considers Heaven and Earth as its parents, the Tao and Virtue as its master and actionless action as its core. Through actionless action they can make the whole world do as they will and yet not be wearied. Through action they cannot even begin to fulfil what the world requires. This is why the ancient ones valued actionless action. When both the leaders and those below them are in actionless action, then both the leaders and the underlings have the same Virtue. If those below and those above share the same Virtue, then none of them is in the position of a minister. If those below act and those above act also, then those above and those below share the same Tao. If those above and those below share the same Tao, then there is no one to be the lord. However, those above tend to care for the world by actionless action, while those below care for the world by action. This has always been the case. Thus the ancient kings of the world, who knew everything about Heaven and Earth, had no designs; even though they understood the whole of life, they did not speak out; though their skills were greater than any in the lands bounded by oceans, they did nothing.

Heaven produces nothing,
yet all life is transformed;
Earth does not support,
yet all life is sustained;
the Emperor and the king take actionless action,
yet the whole world is served.
There is a saying that there is
nothing as spiritual as Heaven,
nothing as rich as Earth,
nothing as great as Emperors and kings.

It is also said that the Virtue of Emperors and kings finds its match in that of Heaven and Earth. Thus can one ascend with Heaven and Earth, gallop with all life and harness all people to the Tao.

The beginning lies with those above, the out-working with those below; the important lies with the ruler, the details with the minister.

The three armies and five types of weapons* are the irrelevant aspects of Virtue.

Handing down rewards and punishments, advantage and loss and the inflicting of the five types of sentence,† these are the irrelevant aspects of teaching.

Rituals and laws, weights and measures and all the attention to self and name are the irrelevant aspects of governing.

The sound of bells and drums, the attention to feathers and hangings, these are the irrelevant aspects of music.

The attributes of official mourning are the irrelevant aspects of grief.

These five unimportant aspects await the movement of the spirit and the liveliness of the heart's skills before they can be of service.

The ancient ones were aware of all these aspects but did not give them any importance.

> The ruler precedes and the minister follows;
> the father precedes and the son follows;
> the elder brother precedes and the younger
>   brother follows;
> the senior one precedes and the junior follows;
> the man precedes and the woman follows;
> the husband precedes and the wife follows.

This progression of the greater followed by the lesser mirrors that of Heaven and Earth. The sages take their example from this. Heaven is elevated, Earth lowly, and this reflects their spiritual illumination. Spring and summer precede and autumn and winter follow: this is the pattern of the four seasons. In the growth of all life, their roots and buds have their appointed place and distinct shape, and from this comes maturation and then decay, the constant stream of transformation

and change. If Heaven and Earth, the most perfect in spirit, have their hierarchy of precedence and sequence, then how much more should this be so with the people!

> In the ancestor shrine it is kinship which brings
>   honour;
> in the court it is nobility;
> in the local areas it is age;
> in the governing of things it is wisdom.

This is the pattern of the great Tao. To speak about the Tao but not about its pattern of sequence goes against the Tao itself. If we speak about the Tao that has no Tao, then there is no Tao to guide!

Thus it was that the ancient ones clearly grasped the great Tao, seeking first the meaning of Heaven and then the meaning of its Tao and Virtue.

> When they clearly understood the Tao and
>   Virtue,
> they then understood benevolence and
>   righteousness.
> When they clearly grasped benevolence and
>   righteousness,
> they could see how to perform their duties.
> When they grasped how to perform their duties,
> they came to understand form and fame.
> When they comprehended form and fame,
> they were able to make appointments.
> When they had made appointments,
> they went on to examining people and their
>   efforts.
> When they had examined people's efforts,
> they moved to judgements of good or bad.
> When they had made judgements of good and
>   bad,
> they went on to punishments and rewards.

Following this, the foolish and the wise knew what they should do and the elevated and the lowly went to their appropriate places. The good and the worthy as well as those below them found in their own selves that all had assignments adapted to their skills, appropriate to their rank. Thus did they serve those above them and encourage those below; external matters were governed and their own selves developed. Knowledge and plotting were never used and they relied upon Heaven.

This is known as the great peace and perfect government.

---

* The three armies are the standard subdivisions of a feudal state, and the five weapons are the spear, halberd, axe, shield and bow.
† The five sentences are branding or tattooing, cutting off the nose, cutting off the feet, castration and execution.

The Book says, 'There is form and there is title.' Form and title were known to the ancient ones, but they gave it no importance. In the olden days, when they talked of the great Tao, they spoke of the five steps which brought them to 'form and fame', or they went to nine steps and debated 'rewards and punishments'. If they had just gone straight to discussing 'form and fame' they would have shown up their ignorance of the origin; or if they had plunged straight into 'rewards and punishments' they would have shown their ignorance of the correct beginning. Those who turn the Tao upside down before talking of it, who in fact oppose the Tao before speaking of it, will be governed by other people, for they could not rule others! Those who plunge straight in, gabbling on about 'form and fame' or 'rewards and punishments', may have some understanding of the means of governing but do not understand the Tao of governing. They may be of use to the world, but they cannot use the world. They are typical pompous scholars, just stuck in their little corner. Rituals, laws, weights and measures, all the pointscoring of correct forms and titles: the ancient ones had all this, but they were the tools of those below to serve those above. Those above did not use this to rule those below.

In days gone by Shun spoke to Yao, saying, 'Being Heaven's king, how do you use your heart?'

'I do not abuse those who are defenceless,' said Yao, 'nor do I ignore the poor. I mourn for those who die, caring for the orphaned child and for the widow. This is how I use my heart.'

'Righteous as far as righteousness goes, but not that great,' commented Shun.

'What ought I to do, then?' said Yao.

'When Heaven's Virtue is found, the hills rejoice, the sun and moon shine and the four seasons are in line. The regular pattern of each day and night follows properly and the rain clouds are moved accordingly.'

Yao said, 'So all I've really been doing is getting worked up and bothered! You seek compliance with Heaven, whereas I have sought compliance with humanity.'

Since earliest times Heaven and Earth have been known as great. The Yellow Emperor, Yao and Shun have all praised them. The ancient kings who ruled all under Heaven, did they need to act? Heaven and Earth were sufficient for them.

Confucius travelled west to place his books in the archives of Chou. Tzu Lu offered advice, saying, 'I have heard that the official in charge of the Royal Archives is Lao Tzu. But he has resigned and lives at home. Sir, if you want to place your books there, go and see him and ask his assistance.'

'Splendid,' said Confucius. So off he went to see Lao Tzu,[5] but Lao Tzu refused to help. So Confucius took out his Twelve Classics, and started to preach.

When he was halfway through, Lao Tzu said, 'This is too much. Put it briefly.'

Confucius said, 'In essence, it is benevolence and righteousness.'

'May I ask,' said Lao Tzu, 'are benevolence and righteousness of the very essence of humanity?'

'Certainly,' said Confucius. 'If the nobleman is without benevolence, he has no purpose; if without righteousness, he has no life. Benevolence and righteousness, these are truly of the innate nature of humanity. How else could it be?'

'May I ask, what are benevolence and righteousness?'

'To be at one, centred in one's heart, in love with all, without selfishness, this is what benevolence and righteousness are,' replied Confucius.

'Really! Your words reveal misunderstanding,' said Lao Tzu. '"Love of all", that's both vague and an exaggeration! "Without selfishness", isn't that rather selfish? Sir, if you want people to remain simple, shouldn't you look to the ways of Heaven and Earth?

'Heaven and Earth have their boundaries which
　　are constant;
the sun and moon hold their courses in their
　　brightness;
the stars and planets proceed in the boundaries
　　of their order;
the birds and creatures find their confines
　　within their herds and flocks.
Think of the trees which stand within their own
　　boundaries in order.

'So Sir, walk with Virtue and travel with the Tao, and you will reach the perfect end. Why bother with all this benevolence and righteousness, prancing along as if you were beating a drum and looking for a lost child? Sir, you will just confuse people's true nature!'

Shih Cheng Chi came to see Lao Tzu and asked him, 'I have heard tell that you, Sir, are a sage, so I came to see you, regardless of the length of the journey. Over the hundred nights of the journey my feet became blistered, but I did not stop nor rest. Now I find, Sir, that you are not a sage. Even though you were wealthy enough for even the rat holes of your house to be full of left-over rice, you nevertheless kicked your poor little sister out of the house. What an unkind action! When your food is placed before you, even if you cannot eat it all, you hoard it, whether it is raw or cooked.'

Lao Tzu showed no emotion and made no reply. The next day Shih Cheng Chi came to see him again and said, 'Yesterday I was rude to you, Sir. Today I have no heart for it. Why is this?'

Lao Tzu said, 'I think I have freed myself from knowledge, from the spiritual and from being a sage. If you had called me an ox yesterday, Sir, then I would have said I was an ox. If you had called me a horse, I would have said I was a horse. If people name a reality, but someone won't have it, then he just makes life more problematic. I am always like this, I don't just put it on for certain occasions.'

Shih Cheng Chi shrank back so as not to be even near Lao Tzu's shadow, then he came forward once more in a humble way and asked how he could cultivate himself. Lao Tzu said, 'Your face is unpleasant; your eyes glare; your forehead is broad; your mouth hangs open; your style is pompous; you are like a tethered horse waiting to bolt, ready to go like an arrow from a crossbow; you examine everything in too much detail; you are cunning in your use of knowledge, yet you lounge around. All this makes me distrust you. Out on the frontier someone like you would be called a bandit.'

The Master said,

'The Tao does not hesitate before that which is vast,
nor does it abandon the small.
Thus it is that all life is enlivened by it.
So immense, so immense there is nothing which is not held by it;
so deep, so unfathomable beyond any reckoning.
The form of its Virtue is in benevolence and righteousness,
though this is a minor aspect of its spirit.
Who but the perfect man could comprehend all this?
The perfect man has charge of this age,
a somewhat daunting task!

However, this does not fool him or trap him.
He holds the reins of power over the whole world
but it is of little consequence to him.
His discernment unearths all falsehood
but he gives no thought to personal gain.
He gets to the heart of issues and knows how to protect the foundation of truth.
Thus Heaven and Earth are outside him,
he ignores all life and his spirit is never wearied.
He travels with the Tao,
is in agreement with Virtue,
bids farewell to benevolence and righteousness
and ignores ritual and music,
because the perfect man has set his heart upon what is right.'

This generation believes that the value of the Tao is to be found in books. But books are nothing more than words, and words have value but only in terms of their meaning. Meaning is constantly seeking to express what cannot be said in words and thus passed on. This generation values words and puts them into books, yet what it values is perhaps mistaken, because what it values is not really all that valuable. So we look at things and see things, but it is only an outward form and colour, and what can be heard is just the name and sound. How sad that this generation imagines that the form, colour, name and sound are enough to capture the essence of something! The form, colour, name and sound are in no way sufficient to capture or convey the truth, which is why it is said that the knowledgeable do not speak and those who speak are not knowledgeable. But how can this generation understand this?

Duke Huan was sitting up in his hall reading a book. The wheelwright Pien was down below in the courtyard making a wheel. He put down his chisel and hammer, went up to the hall and asked Duke Huan, 'May I ask you, Sir, what words you are reading?'

Duke Huan replied, 'The words of the sages.'

'Are these sages still living?'

'They are long dead,' said Duke Huan.

'Then, Sir, what you are reading is nothing but rubbish left over from these ancient men!'

'How dare you, a wheelwright, comment on what I read! If you can explain this, fine, if not you shall die!' thundered Duke Huan.

The wheelwright Pien replied, 'Your Lordship's servant looks at it from the perspective of his own work. When I work on a wheel, if I hit too softly, pleasant as this is, it doesn't make for a good wheel. If I hit furiously, I get tired and the thing doesn't work! So, not too soft, not too vigorous, I grasp it in my hand and hold it in my heart. I cannot express this by word of mouth, I just know it. I cannot teach this to my son, nor can my son learn it from me. So for seventy years I have gone along this path and here I am still making wheels. The ancient ones, when they died, took their words with them. Which is why I can state that what Your Lordship is reading is nothing more than rubbish left over from these ancient ones!'

Chapter 14: Does Heaven Move?

... Tang, the Prime Minister of Shang, asked Chuang Tzu about benevolence. Chuang Tzu said, 'Tigers and wolves are benevolent.'

'What do you mean?'

'The father cares for his children,' said Chuang Tzu. 'Is this not benevolence?'

'But it is perfect benevolence that I am interested in.'

'Perfect benevolence has nothing to do with affection,' said Chuang Tzu.

But the Prime Minister replied, 'I have heard that where there is no affection, there is no love; where there is no love, there is no filial piety. Do you mean to say that perfect benevolence is without filial piety?'

'Certainly not. Perfect benevolence is of the highest order, and words such as "filial piety" cannot describe it. What you want to say is not that filial piety is surpassed, but that nothing even comes close to it. When a traveller goes south and then turns to face north when he has reached Ying, he cannot see Ming mountain. Why is this? Because it is far away. There is the saying: filial piety arising from respect is easy, filial piety arising from love is hard. If filial piety from love is easy, then to forget your parents is hard. It is easy to forget your parents, but it is hard to make my parents forget me. It is easy to make my parents forget me, but it is hard to make me forget the whole world. It is easy to forget the whole world, but it is hard for the whole world to forget me.

'Virtue ignores Yao and Shun and dwells in actionless action. Its benefits embrace every generation, though no one in the world understands this. Despite your protestations, how can you talk of benevolence and filial piety? Filial piety, mutual respect, benevolence, righteousness, loyalty, integrity, resoluteness and purity, all of these can be of service to Virtue. But they are not worthy in themselves. So it is said,

> "'Perfect nobility disregards the honours
> of state;
> Perfect richness ignores the wealth of the
> country;
> Perfect fulfilment ignores fame and glory.
> Alone of all, the Tao never alters."'...

... Confucius had pottered along for fifty-one years and had never heard anyone speak of the Tao until he went south to Pei and went to see Lao Tzu.

Lao Tzu said, 'So you've come then, Sir? I have heard of you, that you are the wise man of the north. Have you, Sir, followed the Tao?'

'I have not yet followed it,' replied Confucius.

'Well, Sir, where have you looked?'

'I looked for it in what can be measured and regulated, but even after five years I still haven't been able to find it.'

'So, Sir, what did you do then?' asked Lao Tzu.

'I looked for it in yin and yang, but ten, twelve years went by and I still couldn't find it.'

'Obviously!' said Lao Tzu. 'If the Tao could be served up, everyone would serve it up to their lords. If the Tao could be offered, there is no one who would not offer it to their parents. If the Tao could be spoken of, there is no one who would not speak of it to their brothers and sisters. If the Tao could be passed on, there is no one who would not pass it on to their heirs. However, it obviously cannot be so and the reason is as follows.

> 'If there is no true centre within to receive it,
> it cannot remain;
> if there is no true direction outside to guide it,
> it cannot be received.
> If the true centre is not brought out
> it cannot receive on the outside.
> The sage cannot draw it forth.
> If what comes in from the outside is not
> welcomed by the true centre,
> then the sage cannot let it go.
> Fame is something sought by all,
> but don't go for too much of it.
> Benevolence and righteousness are as the houses
> of the former kings,
> useful for one night's shelter,
> but don't stay there too long.
> To stay long causes considerable adverse
> comment.

'The perfect man of old walked the Tao of benevolence, a path which he took on loan; he used righteousness as a place to lodge for a night. So it was that he ambled through the void and uncontrolled places; found food in the open fields and enjoyed the gardens which were not his. To be in such freedom, you must take actionless action. The open fields make living easy. He gives nothing and requires nothing. The ancient ones knew this as the wandering of the Truth Gatherer.

'Someone who believes wealth is the most important thing cannot give up their income; someone who seeks pre-eminence cannot give up the hunt for fame; those who love power cannot hand it over to others.

'Those who cling to things like these are usually fearful. Letting them go just once causes such agony that they will not consider even once doing so, although it would show them the folly of their ways. These are people bearing the punishment of Heaven. Hatred and kindness, taking and giving, correction and instruction, life and death, these eight things are tools of reform. However, only the one who abides by the great change and who does not stand in its way can use them. So it is said, to correct is to reform. If the heart cannot accept this, then the gate of Heaven is not opened.'

Confucius went to see Lao Tzu and talked with him about benevolence and righteousness. Lao Tzu said, 'If you get grit in your eye from winnowing chaff, then Heaven and Earth and the four directions get mixed up. A mosquito or gadfly which stings you can keep you awake all night. And benevolence and righteousness, when forced upon us, disturb your heart and produce great distress. You, Sir, if you want to stop everything below Heaven losing its original simplicity, you must travel with the wind and stand firm in Virtue. Why do you exert yourself so much, banging a big drum and hunting for a lost child? The snow goose doesn't need a daily bath to stay white, nor does the crow need to be stained every day to stay black. Black and white comes from natural simplicity, not from argument. Fame and fortune, though sought after, do not make people greater than they actually are. When the waters dry up and the fish are stranded on the dry land, they huddle together and try to keep each other moist by spitting and wetting each other. But wouldn't it be even better if they could just forget each other, safe in their lakes and rivers?'

After seeing Lao Tzu, Confucius went home and for three days he said nothing.

. . . Confucius said to Lao Tzu, 'I have mastered the *Poems*, the *Histories*, the *Rites*, the *Music*, the *I Ching* and the *Spring and Autumn* – all of the Six Classics. I know them inside out. However, I have discussed them with seventy-two rulers, telling them of the Tao of the first kinds and the illumination of the path trodden by Chou and Shao, but not one king has been interested. They've done nothing! It is so difficult to preach to such people! How can I make the Tao clear to them?'

Lao Tzu said, 'It is very lucky, Sir, that you did not discover a ruler who would try to govern this generation in such a way! The Six Classics are the tired footpaths of the first kings, not the actual feet that trod those paths! Now, Sir, what you are going on about is just these worn footpaths. But footpaths are created by the feet that first walked them. They are not the feet themselves! The white herons only have to look into each other's eyes without blinking for impregnation to happen. A male insect buzzes above and the female replies from below and impregnation takes place, borne upon the air. The creature called Lei contains both male and female and so impregnates itself. Innate nature does not change; fate is unalterable; time cannot be stopped and the Tao cannot be halted. Hold fast to the Tao and there is nothing it cannot do; lose it and there is nothing that can be done.'

Confucius did not go out for three months, then he went to see Lao Tzu and said, 'I've grasped it! The raven hatches its young; the fish spew forth their eggs; the slim-waisted wasp transforms, and when a younger brother comes along the elder brother weeps. For too long I have not been able to work in harmony with these changes. So, given that I did not play my part in harmony with others, how could I expect to change people?'

Lao Tzu replied, 'Well done. So now you've grasped it.'

Notes

1   "Virtue" (*te*) sometimes refers, as here, to something like people's nature or dispositions. Elsewhere it has more of the ethical connotation that we associate with the word.

2 "Heaven" (*tsien*) seems to have no "supernatural" meaning for Chuang Tzu. Often it seems to mean no more than "Nature."

3 Here, but not always, "the perfect sage" is used ironically, to refer to the sage as portrayed by Confucians.

4 *Yin* and *Yang* in ancient Chinese cosmology are the two opposed, yet mutually dependent, principles – "dark," "feminine," and "hidden" *versus* "bright," "masculine," and "open" – whose interaction produces balance in the universe.

5 The references to Lao Tzu should not be taken as evidence that the author(s) regard him as an actual person. Many of the figures in whose mouths words are put are clearly fictitious.

6

The Bhagavad Gita, Chapters 1–5

Introduction

For hundreds of millions of people over the centuries, the *Bhagavad Gita* ("*The Song of the Lord*") has been the most important text ever composed. Its canonical status among many Hindus, especially the devotees of Vishnu, is primarily due to the later chapters' articulation – for the first time in Indian literature – of a theistic, devotional religion. But the *Gita* begins with and is structured by a concrete moral dilemma and the account of moral action within which that dilemma is resolved has, despite its ambiguities, been inspirational for countless later writers, not least Mahatma Gandhi (V.20), for whom it was an "infallible guide," a "dictionary of daily reference."[1]

The *Gita*, probably composed around the third century BCE, is a short philosophical interlude within the massive epic, the *Mahabharata*, which tells of the rivalry between two branches of a royal clan that eventually leads to war. Just before the decisive battle, the leading hero of one branch, Arjuna, is assailed by doubt. Although it is his duty as a member of the *kshatriya* (nobleman warrior) caste to fight, and although justice is on the side

From The Bhagavad Gita, trans. W. J. Johnson. Oxford: Oxford University Press, 1994, pp. 4–24 (first part of Chapter 1 and last part of Chapter 5 omitted; asterisked notes are the translator's).

of his branch of the family, ought he really to kill his kinsmen in what is bound to be a devastating war from which he can expect no peace or happiness? The *Gita* records the attempt of Arjuna's charioteer – who, it turns out, is Krishna, the embodiment or avatar of the god Vishnu – to dispel the hero's doubts and urge him to fight. (It seems clear that, while Arjuna's predicament may be sharpened by his caste allegiance, the kind of dilemma he faces is one that people outside of any caste system might face – a modern-day soldier, for example, embroiled in a civil war.)

Krishna's strategy of argument, wisely enough, is not simply to remind Arjuna of a code of duties and the dishonor that disobedience will bring – for of course it is precisely the validity of this code which Arjuna is questioning. The strategy, rather, is to impart a philosophical understanding of the cosmos; and of the individual's place within it, which will enable the reluctant hero to see that fighting is his proper course. Krishna's emphasis on understanding and knowledge – on seeing, for example, that only *bodies* can be killed, not the selves or souls of their owners (2.18) – soon prompts Arjuna to wonder, however, why *action*, including the performance of soldierly duties, should matter at all. In wondering this, he gives voice to the central problem in traditional Hindu or Brahminical thought. According to that scheme of thought, the true human goal is that of freedom or release (*moksha*) from the round of rebirth with the apparent implication that morality is, as the philosopher Śaṃkara was to say, a mere

"preliminary" – useful but inessential training, perhaps, for the acquisition of that knowledge of
Brahman (the underlying principle of reality
which enables release.[2] It is remarks like this that
prompted Western commentators like Albert
Schweitzer to deny that Indian thought was genuinely ethical.[3]

In replying to Arjuna's question, Krishna offers
a retort to this downgrading of ethics and rejects
the idea that it is through renunciation and navel-
gazing contemplation that freedom and release are
to be obtained. Human beings, he insists, cannot
avoid acting (3.5): even the contemplative yogi
must beg and eat. The real issue, therefore, is to
ascertain which actions are without those karmic
consequences that bind a person to the cycle of
rebirth. For Krishna, these are actions performed
without "attachment" – without desires, interests
and future consequences in mind (3.7ff). (Readers
will note a parallel with the Taoist ideal of "actionless action" see V.1 of this volume.) Arjuna
is encouraged to adopt this detached stance
toward his action by reflecting that, strictly
speaking, it is never the *self* which acts, for the
self is something separate from the physical processes of the world which owe to the operation of
underlying material constituents. Provided Arjuna
does his duty purely for its own sake, and hence
without attachment, he will obtain release. There
is, therefore, no conflict between the two "disciplines" (*yogas*) of action and knowledge: for
proper action is what is conducted with true understanding of one's self and reality at large. Through
a true "vision of cosmic reality," Arjuna is "in a
position to act from the motive of duty alone."[4]

There are anticipations, here, of the *dharmas*
articulated by the *Laws of Manu* (IV.2) and the
conception of duty developed by Immanuel Kant,
though it needs to be stressed that the duty

Arjuna is exhorted to perform is that of his "station in life," not one which, as duties are for Kant,
is binding on all rational beings as such (I.15).
Certainly, however, the ethical position urged in
the *Gita* has been subjected to the same criticism
as Kant's: that of preaching an unacceptable
"coldness" in our affective relations with one
another. (In gaudier editions of the *Gita*, pictures
of Arjuna and Krishna, serene and smiling as they
scythe their way through the enemy, can indeed
be chilling.[5]) Nobody, however, can gainsay the
seriousness of the *Gita's* attempt to seek for a
resolution of moral dilemmas and an articulation
of a moral stance within the framework of a
metaphysical system.

Several Indian names occur in the chapters
selected. "Sanjaya," the narrator, is court bard
to "Dhritarashtra," King of Arjuna's enemies.
Most of the other names, such as "Govinda" and
"Bharata," are alternative names or titles of
either Krishna or Arjuna. Some other names are
explained in the notes.

Notes

1   *The Sayings of Mahatma Gandhi*, Singapore:
    Brash, 1984, p. 78.
2   A. J. Alston, *A Śaṁkara Source-Book*, vol. 5,
    London: Shanti Sadan, 1989, p. 107.
3   See S. Radhakrishnan, *Eastern Religions and
    Western Thought*, Oxford: Clarendon Press,
    1939, Chapter 3.
4   M. M. Agrawal, "Arjuna's moral predica-
    ment," in B. K. Motilal, ed., *Moral Dilemmas
    in the Mahabharata*, M. Banarsidass: Delhi,
    1989, p. 140.
5   See A. Danto, *Mysticism and Morality*,
    Harmondsworth: Penguin, 1976, p. 99.

The Bhagavad Gita

Chapter 1

[. . .]

26 There Arjuna saw, standing their ground,
    fathers, grandfathers, teachers, maternal
    uncles, brothers, sons, grandsons, friends,

27 Fathers-in-law, and companions in both
    armies. And looking at all these kinsmen so
    arrayed, Arjuna, the son of Kunti,

28 Was overcome by deep compassion; and in
    despair he said: 'Krishna, when I see these
    my own people eager to fight, on the brink,

29 'My limbs grow heavy, and my mouth is
    parched, my body trembles and my hair
    bristles,

30 'My bow, Gandiva, falls from my hand, my skin's on fire, I can no longer stand – my mind is reeling,

31 'I see evil omens, Krishna: nothing good can come from slaughtering one's own family in battle – I foresee it!

32 'I have no desire for victory, Krishna, or kingship, or pleasures. What should we do with kingship, Govinda? What are pleasures to us? What is life?

33 'The men for whose sake we desire kingship, enjoyment and pleasures are precisely those drawn up for this battle, having abandoned their lives and riches.

34 'Teachers, fathers, sons, as well as grand-fathers, maternal uncles, fathers-in-law, grandsons, brothers-in-law, and kinsmen –

35 'I have no desire to kill them, Madhusudana, though they are killers themselves – no, not for the lordship of the three worlds,* let alone the earth!

36 'Where is the joy for us, Janardana, in destroying Dhritarashtra's people? Having killed these murderers, evil would attach itself to us.

37 'It follows, therefore, that we are not required to kill the sons of Dhritarashtra – they are our own kinsmen, and having killed our own people, how could we be happy, Madhava?

38 'And even if, because their minds are over-whelmed by greed, *they* cannot see the evil incurred by destroying one's own family, and the degradation involved in the betrayal of a friend,

39 'How can *we* be so ignorant as not to recoil from this wrong? The evil incurred by destroying one's own family is plain to see, Janardana.

40 'With the destruction of family the eternal family laws are lost; when the law is des-troyed, lawlessness overpowers the entire family.

41 'Krishna, because of overpowering law-lessness, the women of the family are corrupted; when women are corrupted, Varshneya, there is intermingling of the four estates.[1]

42 'And intermingling leads to hell for the family-destroyers *and* the family, for their ancestors, robbed of their rice-ball and water offerings, fall back.

43 'Through these evils of the family-destroyers, which cause intermingling of the four estates, caste laws and the eternal family laws are obliterated.

44 'For men whose family laws have been obliterated we have heard that a place in hell is certain, Janardana.

45 'Oh, ignominy! We are about to perpetrate a great evil – out of sheer greed for kingdoms and pleasures, we are prepared to kill our own people.

46 'It would be better for me if Dhritarashtra's armed men were to kill me in battle, un-resisting and unarmed.'

47 Having spoken this on the field of conflict, Arjuna sank down into the chariot, letting slip his bow and arrow, his mind distracted with grief.

Chapter 2

Sanjaya said:

1 Then, Krishna, the destroyer of the demon Madhu, spoke these words to the dejected Arjuna, who, eyes blurred and brimming with tears, was so overcome by pity:

The Lord said:

2 Arjuna, where do you get this weakness from at a moment of crisis? A noble should not experience this. It does not lead to heaven, it leads to disgrace.

3 No impotence, Partha, it does not become you. Abandon this base, inner weakness. Get up, Incinerator of the Foe!

Arjuna said:

4 Destroyer of Madhu, destroyer of the enemy, how can I shoot arrows at Bhishma and Drona in battle when they should be honoured?

5 Better to eat begged food among common people than to kill such worthy teachers. For having killed my teachers, who desire legitimate worldly ends, I should be con-suming food smeared with blood.

6 And we do not know which is better for us – that we should overcome Dhritarashtra's men, standing there before us, or that they should overcome us. For if we were to kill them, we should have no desire to go on living.

---

* Heaven, earth, and the atmosphere or sometimes the lower regions.

7   My inner being is disabled by that vice of dejection. My mind is bewildered as to what is right. I ask you, which would be better? Tell me for certain. I am your student, I have come to you for help. Instruct me!

8   Though I were to obtain a prosperous, unrivalled kingdom on earth, and even mastery over the gods, I cannot imagine what could dispel my grief, which withers the senses.

Sanjaya said:

9   And having spoken thus to Krishna, to Govinda, having said 'I will not fight!' Arjuna, the Incinerator of the Foe, fell silent.

10   O Dhritarashtra, between the two armies, Krishna, with the shadow of a smile, spoke these words to that dejected man:

The Lord said:

11   You utter wise *words*, yet you have been mourning those who should not be mourned; the truly wise do not grieve for the living or the dead.

12   There never was a time when I was not, or you, or these rulers of men. Nor will there ever be a time when we shall cease to be, all of us hereafter.

13   Just as within this body the embodied self passes through childhood, youth and old age, so it passes to another body. The wise man is not bewildered by this.

14   But contacts with matter, Son of Kunti, give rise to cold and heat, pleasure and pain. They come and go, Bharata; they are impermanent and you should endure them.

15   For these things, Bull among men, do not perturb that wise man for whom pleasure and pain are the same; he is ready for immortality.

16   For the non-existent there is no coming into existence, for the existent there is no lapsing into non-existence; the division between them is observed by those who see the underlying nature of things.

17   But know that that on which all this is stretched is indestructible. No one can destroy this imperishable one.

18   It is just these *bodies* of the indestructible, immeasurable, and eternal embodied self that are characterized as coming to an end – therefore fight, Bharata!

19   Anyone who believes this a killer, and anyone who thinks this killed, they do not understand: it does not kill, it is not killed

20   It is not born, it never dies; being, it will never again cease to be. It is unborn, invariable, eternal, primeval. It is not killed when the body is killed.

21   Partha, how can that man who knows it to be indestructible, invariable, unborn and imperishable bring about the death of anyone? Whom does he kill?

22   Just as a man casting off worn-out clothes takes up others that are new, so the embodied self, casting off its worn-out bodies, goes to other, new ones.

23   Blades do not pierce it, fire does not burn it, waters do not wet it, and the wind does not parch it.

24   It cannot be pierced, it cannot be burned, it cannot be wetted, it cannot be parched. It is invariable, everywhere, fixed, immovable, eternal.

25   It is said to be imperceptible, unthinkable and immutable; knowing it to be so, you should not therefore grieve.

26   And even if you believe that it is regularly born and regularly dead, you should not grieve for it, Great Arm.

27   Death is inevitable for those who are born; for those who are dead birth is just as certain. Therefore you must not grieve for what is ineluctable.

28   Bharata, beings have imperceptible beginnings; the interim is clear; their ends are again indistinct. What is there to lament in this?

29   Quite exceptionally does anyone see it, and quite exceptionally does anyone speak of it; it is quite exceptional for anyone to hear of it, but even when they have heard of it, no one in fact knows it.

30   Bharata, this embodied self in the body of everyone is eternally unkillable. Therefore you must not grieve for any beings at all.

31   Recognizing your inherent duty, you must not shrink from it. For there is nothing better for a warrior than a duty-bound war.

32   It is a door to heaven, opened fortuitously. Fortunate are the warriors, Partha, who are presented with such a war.

33   But if, careless of your inherent duty and renown, you will not undertake this duty-bound conflict, you shall transgress.

34   Moreover, people will recount your limitless disgrace – and disgrace is worse than death for the man who has once been honoured.

35 The great warriors will suppose that you withdrew from the battle out of fear. And you will fade from their high regard into insignificance.

36 Then your enemies will say many things that would be better unsaid, slighting your strength – and what could be more painful than that?

37 You will either be killed and attain heaven, or conquer and enjoy the earth. So rise, Son of Kunti, determined to fight.

38 Making yourself indifferent to pleasure and pain, gain and loss, victory and defeat, commit yourself to battle. And in that way you shall not transgress.

39 You have received this intelligence according to Sankhya theory,[2] now hear it as it applies to practice. Disciplined with such intelligence, Partha, you shall throw off the bondage of action.

40 In this there is no wasted effort, no reverse; just a little of this truth saves from great danger.

41 Son of the Kurus, in this the resolute intelligence is one, the intellects of the irresolute are without limit and many-branched.

42 Partha, that florid speech the uninspired utter, addicted to the words of the Veda,* claiming that there is nothing else.

43 Their nature desire, their aim heaven – that speech which produces rebirth as the fruit of action, and which is dense with specific ritual acts aimed at the attainment of enjoyment and power,

44 Robs those addicted to enjoyment and power of their minds. For them no resolute intelligence is established in concentration.

45 The Vedas' sphere of activity is the three constituents of material nature. Arjuna, be free from the three constituents, free from duality, forever grounded in purity, beyond getting and keeping, possessed of the self.

46 For the brahmin who knows, there is no more purpose in all the Vedas than in a water-tank surrounded by a flood.

47 You are qualified simply with regard to action, never with regard to its results. You must be neither motivated by the results of action nor attached to inaction.

48 Grounded in yogic discipline, and having abandoned attachment, undertake actions, Dhananjaya, evenly disposed as to their success or failure. Yoga is defined as evenness of mind.

49 For action in itself is inferior by far to the discipline of intelligence, Dhananjaya. You must seek refuge in intelligence. Those motivated by results are wretched.

50 The man disciplined in intelligence renounces in this world the results of both good and evil actions. Therefore commit yourself to yogic discipline; yogic discipline is skill in actions.

51 For, having abandoned the result produced from action, those who understand, who are disciplined in intelligence, are freed from the bondage of rebirth and achieve a state without disease.

52 When your intelligence emerges from the thicket of delusion, then you will become disenchanted with what is to be heard and has been heard in the Veda.

53 When, turned away from the Veda, your intelligence stands motionless, immovable in concentration, then you will attain yogic discipline.

Arjuna said:

54 O Keshava, how do you describe that man whose mentality is stable, whose concentration is fixed? What should the man whose thought is settled say? How should he sit? How should he walk?

The Lord said:

55 Partha, when he abandons every desire lodged in the mind, by himself content within the self, then he is called a man of stable mentality.

56 He is called a holy man, settled in thought, whose mind is not disturbed in the midst of sorrows, who has lost the desire for pleasures, whose passion, fear and anger have disappeared.

57 His mentality is stabilized who feels no desire for anything, for getting this or that good or evil, and who neither rejoices in nor loathes anything.

58 When this man, like a tortoise retracting its limbs, entirely withdraws his senses from the objects of sense, his mentality is stabilized.

59 For the embodied being who does not feed on them the objects of sense disappear,

---

* The revealed texts of Brahminical religion and mainstream Hinduism.

except flavour; flavour fades too for the one who has seen the highest.

60 Son of Kunti, even for the man of discernment who strives, the harassing senses forcibly seize the mind.

61 Restraining all the senses, one should sit, yogically disciplined, focused on me; for if one's senses are under control one's mentality is grounded.

62 When a man meditates on the objects of sense he becomes attached to them; from attachment desire is born, from desire anger.

63 Out of anger confusion arises, through confusion memory wanders, from loss of memory the intelligence is destroyed; from the destruction of intelligence a man is lost.

64 But engaging the objects of sense with his senses separated from desire and loathing, and subject to the will of the self, a man who is self-controlled attains calmness.

65 In calm all his miseries are ended, for the intelligence of the man whose mind is calm is immediately stabilized.

66 The undisciplined man has no intelligence, and no capacity to produce anything, and one who has no capacity is without serenity. And how can there be happiness for the man who lacks serenity?

67 For a mind conforming to the wandering senses carries away one's insight, as the wind a ship on the water.

68 Therefore, Great Arm, whoever has entirely withheld the senses from the objects of sense has stabilized his insight.

69 When it is night for all creatures, the man who restrains himself is awake; when creatures are awake, it is night for the perceptive seer.

70 Just as waters enter the sea, which is forever being filled although its depths are unmoving, so the man whom all desires enter in the same way attains peace – but not the desirer of desires.

71 The man who, having abandoned all desires, lives free from longing, unpossessive and unegoistical, approaches peace.

72 This, Partha, is the Brahman state; having attained it, one is not deluded; fixed in it, even at the moment of death one reaches the nirvana of Brahman.³

Chapter 3

Arjuna said:

1 Krishna, if it is your belief that the way of intelligence is superior to action, then why do you enjoin me, Keshava, to this terrible undertaking?

2 With such equivocal words you seem to confuse my intelligence. Describe clearly an unambiguous way through which I may attain what is best.

The Lord said:

3 Blameless one, I have taught of old that in this world two ways are open: the discipline of knowledge for Sankhya theorists, and the discipline of action for yogins.

4 A man does not attain freedom from the results of action by abstaining from actions, and he does not approach perfection simply by renunciation.

5 For no one ever, even for a moment, exists without acting; everyone, regardless of their will, is made to perform actions by the constituents which originate from material nature.

6 The man who, having restrained his action organs, then sits with his mind preoccupied with sense objects, is called a self-deluding hypocrite.

7 But the man who, controlling his senses with his mind, undertakes through his action organs the discipline of action without attachment, distinguishes himself, Arjuna.

8 You should perform enjoined action, for action is better than nonaction; even the minimum of bodily subsistence would be impossible without action.

9 The entire world is bound by actions; the only exception is action undertaken for sacrificial purposes. Therefore, Son of Kunti, free from attachment, you should perform that kind of action.

10 When he created creatures in the beginning, along with the sacrifice, Prajapati* said: 'May you be fruitful by this sacrifice, let this be the cow which produces all you desire.

11 'You should nourish the gods with this so that the gods may nourish you; nourishing each other, you shall achieve the highest good.

* The 'Lord of Creatures' . . . protector of life and procreation.

12 'For nourished by the sacrifice, the gods will give you the pleasures you desire. The man who enjoys these gifts without repaying them is no more than a thief.'

13 The virtuous who eat the remainder of the sacrifice are released from all faults; the wicked who cook for the sake of themselves consume impurity.

14 Beings exist through food, the origin of food is rain, rain comes from sacrifice, sacrifice derives from action.

15 Know that action originates from Brahman – Brahman whose source is the imperishable. Therefore all-pervading Brahman is eternally established in the sacrifice.

16 Whoever in this world does not turn the wheel thus set in motion, Partha, lives in vain, making a pleasure garden of his senses, intent upon evil.

17 But it is clear that, for the man who delights in the self, and is satisfied with the self, and fulfilled only in the self, there is nothing that has to be done.[4]

18 For him there is no significance whatsoever in what has been done or has not been done in this world, and he has no kind of dependence at all on any being.

19 Therefore, without attachment, always do whatever action has to be done; for it is through acting without attachment that a man attains the highest.

20 Indeed, it was by action alone that King Janaka and others attained perfection. Looking only to what maintains the world, you too must act.

21 Whatever the superior man does, so do the rest; whatever standard he sets, the world follows it.

22 Partha, as for me there is nothing whatever that has to be done in the three worlds; there is nothing unaccomplished to be accomplished. Yet I still engage in action.

23 For were I not to engage tirelessly in action, humans everywhere would follow in my wake, Partha.

24 If I did not engage in action, these worlds would fall into ruin; I should be the instrument of anarchy; I should destroy these creatures.

25 Just as the ignorant act out of attachment to action, Bharata, so the wise should also act, but without attachment, intent upon maintaining the world.

26 The wise man should not disturb the minds of those ignorant people who are attached to action; acting in a disciplined manner himself, he should encourage involvement in all actions.

27 In every case, actions are performed by the constituents of material nature; although the man who is deluded by egotism thinks to himself, '*I* am the actor.'

28 But he who knows the principle underlying the division of constituents and actions, understanding that it is constituents that are acting on constituents, is not attached, Great Arm.

29 The person whose knowledge is comprehensive should not agitate those dullards whose knowledge is not so great – those who are deluded by the constituents of material nature and attached to the actions of the constituents.

30 Giving up all actions to me, with your mind on what relates to the self, desireless and not possessive, fight! Your fever is past.

31 Faithful, uncontentious men, who constantly practise this doctrine of mine, are also released from the results of action.

32 But you should know that those who object to this, who do not follow my doctrine, and who are blind to all knowledge, are mindless and lost.

33 Even the one who knows acts in accordance with his own material nature. Creatures conform to material nature – what good will repression do?

34 In the case of a sense, desire and aversion adhere to the object of that sense; you should not fall into the power of those two, for they will block your path.

35 It is better to practise your own inherent duty deficiently than another's duty well. It is better to die conforming to your own duty; the duty of others invites danger.

Arjuna said:

36 So what is it that impels a man to do evil, Varshneya, even unwillingly, as though compelled to it by force?

The Lord said:

37 It is desire, it is anger, produced from the constituent of passion, all-consuming, all-injuring; know that that is the enemy here.

38   As a fire is covered by smoke and a mirror by dust; as an embryo is covered by a sac, this world is enveloped by that.

39   By this perpetual enemy of the wise, by this insatiable fire in the form of desire, knowledge is obscured, Son of Kunti.

40   It is said that the senses, the mind and the intelligence are its locality; having obscured a man's knowledge with these, it deludes the embodied self.

41   Therefore, having first restrained the senses, Bull of the Bharatas, strike down this evil thing, the destroyer of insight and knowledge.

42   They say that the senses are great; the mind is greater than the senses. Yet greater than the mind is the intelligence; but he [i.e. the true self – Ed.] is that which is still greater than the intelligence.

43   So, Great Arm, having learned what is higher than the intelligence, and having strengthened yourself through the self, kill that enemy in the shape of desire, so difficult to pin down.

Chapter 4

The Lord said:

1   I taught this eternal way to Vivasvat; Vivasvat showed it to Manu; Manu told it to Ikshvaku.*

2   And it was this way, passed on from teacher to teacher in an unbroken line, that the royal seers knew. Over a long period of time here on earth that track was obliterated, Incinerator of the Foe.

3   It is this very same ancient way that I have shown you now, for you are devoted, and my friend, and this is the most secret teaching.

Arjuna said:

4   You were born recently, Vivasvat was born a long time ago, so what should I understand by the saying that you taught it in the beginning?

The Lord said:

5   I have passed through many births, and so have you, Arjuna. I know them all, you do not, Incinerator of the Foe.

6   Although I am unborn and have a self that is eternal, although I am lord of beings, by controlling my own material nature I come into being by means of my own incomprehensible power.

7   Whenever there is a falling away from the true law and an upsurge of unlawfulness, then, Bharata, I emit myself.

8   I come into being age after age, to protect the virtuous and to destroy evil-doers, to establish a firm basis for the true law.

9   Whoever knows my divine birth and action as they really are is not born again on leaving the body. He comes to me, Arjuna.

10   There are many, free of passion, fear and anger, at one with me, taking refuge in me, who, refined in the heat of knowledge, have come to my state of being.

11   I favour them according to the manner in which they approach me. Men, Partha, universally follow my path.

12   Desiring the attainment that comes from ritual acts, men here sacrifice to the gods; for in the human world the attainment born of sacrificial action comes quickly.

13   The four estates were created by me, divided according to constituents and actions. Although I alone am the one who did this, know that I am an eternal non-actor.

14   Actions do not taint me. I have no desire for the results of action. Whoever understands that I am like this is not bound by actions.

15   Men of old who desired release knew this and acted. Therefore you should act as they once acted.

16   What is action, what is non-action? Even inspired seers are confused about this. Such action I shall explain to you, and understanding it you shall be freed from evil.

17   You should know what constitutes action, wrong action, and non-action. The way of action runs deep.

18   He who sees action in non-action, non-action in action, is wise among men; performing all actions he is disciplined.

19   The wise call him a man of learning whose every activity is free from desire and specific intention; his actions are consumed in the fire of knowledge.

20   That man who depends upon nothing, who has given up attachment to the results of action, is perpetually satisfied, and even

---

* Vivasvat [is] a sun god and the father of the original ancestor of the human race, Manu. Ikshvaku is one of Manu's sons.

though engaged in action he does nothing whatsoever.

21 Acting for the body alone, without expectation, having abandoned possessions, restrained in thought and self, he incurs no defilement.

22 Content with what comes by chance, having gone beyond dualities, free from envy, the same in success and in failure, even when he has acted he is not bound.

23 For the man who is rid of attachment, who has attained release, whose thought is anchored in knowledge, action is sacrificial and melts entirely away.

24 The offering is Brahman, the oblation is Brahman, poured by Brahman into the fire that is Brahman. Brahman is to be attained by that man who concentrates intensely on the action that is Brahman.[5]

25 Some skilled performers concentrate on sacrifice to one of the deities; some offer sacrifice through the sacrifice itself into the fire of Brahman;

26 Others offer the senses (such as hearing) into the fires of restraint; others again offer the objects of the senses (such as sound) into the fires of the senses;

27 Some offer all actions of sense and breath into the fire of the discipline of self-restraint, kindled by knowledge.

28 Similarly there are others, sacrificers with material substance, with bodily mortification, with spiritual exercise, with Vedic study and knowledge – ascetics with uncompromising vows.

29 And again, those whose object is breath-control offer the inhaled into the exhaled breath, and the exhaled into the inhaled, restricting their passage.

30 Others, who have put limits on their consumption of food, offer their inhalation into their inhalation. All these, who know what sacrifice is, have their imperfections obliterated by sacrifice.

31 Those who eat the immortality-conferring remnants of the sacrifice go to primeval Brahman. Best of Gurus, this world, let alone the other, is not for non-sacrificers.

32 Thus many kinds of sacrifice are stretched out in the mouth of Brahman. Remember that they are all born of action; knowing that, you will be liberated.

33 Incinerator of the Foe, the sacrifice of knowledge is better than the sacrifice of material substance. There is no action whatsoever, Partha, which is not concluded in knowledge.

34 Know this: through your submission, through the questions you ask, through your service, those who have knowledge, who see things as they are, will teach you knowledge.

35 And having it, you will never be bewildered in such a way again, Pandava. Through it you shall see all creatures in yourself, and then in me.

36 Even if you are the very worst of all transgressors, with the boat of knowledge you shall plot a safe course through all crookedness.

37 As a lighted fire reduces kindling to ash, in the same way, Arjuna, the fire of knowledge incinerates all actions.

38 Nothing on earth has the purificatory power of knowledge; eventually, the man who has perfected his disciplined practice discovers it in himself.

39 Restraining his senses, the man of faith who is devoted to knowledge attains it. And having attained knowledge, he rapidly achieves supreme peace.

40 The faithless and ignorant man, whose nature it is to doubt, perishes. Not this world, nor the one beyond, nor happiness exists for the doubter.

41 But the self-possessed man, Dhananjaya, who has renounced action through discipline, and cut through doubt with knowledge, is not bound by actions.

42 Therefore, having severed with the blade of knowledge this doubt of yours, which stems from ignorance and is fixed in the heart, act with discipline, Bharata – arise!

Chapter 5

Arjuna said:

1 Krishna, you approve the renunciation of actions, and then again the practice of yogic discipline. Tell me unambiguously, which is the better of these two? The Lord said:

2 Both renunciation and the practice of yogic action lead to ultimate bliss, but, of the two,

the practice of yogic action is superior to the renunciation of action.

3 Great Arm, the man who neither desires nor hates is considered a perpetual renouncer; free from duality, he is easily liberated.

4 Fools hold that the way of Sankhya and the practice of yogic action are different, but not those who know. Through either one of them, carried out properly, one attains the reward of both.

5 The state achieved by Sankhyas is also achieved by yogic actors; whoever sees the ways of Sankhya and yogic action as one truly sees.

6 But renunciation, Great Arm, is hard to attain without yogic practice; the sage disciplined in yogic practice swiftly reaches Brahman.

7 Even when he is acting, the man who is disciplined in yogic practice, whose self is pure, whose self and senses are controlled, whose self is the self of all beings, is not defiled.

8–9 The disciplined man, who knows the underlying principle of reality, thinks: 'I really don't do anything at all,' certain that whether seeing, hearing, touching, smelling, eating, walking, sleeping, breathing, talking, excreting, grasping, opening or shutting the eyes, it is merely the senses acting on the objects of sense.

10 The man who acts, having rendered his actions to Brahman and abandoned attachment, is untainted by evil, in the same way that a lotus leaf is unstained by water.

11 Having abandoned attachment, yogins undertake action with the body, mind and intelligence, even with the senses alone, for the sake of self-purification.

12 The disciplined man, having abandoned the result of action, attains complete peace; the undisciplined man, whose action is impelled by desire, and who is attached to the result, is bound.

13 Having renounced all actions with the mind, the embodied self sits easily, ruler in its nine-gated city,* neither acting nor causing action.

14 The lord of the body does not create agency or actions for the world, or the connection of action and result; rather it is inherent nature that accomplishes this. . . .

Notes

1 I.e. the four castes of Indian society: priests (*brahmins*), warrior-nobles, merchants, and laborers.

2 The two main tenets of the Sankhya school of philosophy to which the *Gita* appeals are (a) the separation of the true self or soul from the natural world, and (b) the explanation of the natural world in terms of three material constituents (*gunas*).

3 The *Gita* is an eclectic work. Sankhyan and Yogic thought figures large, and in this verse we find a reference to the Buddhist notion *of nirvana* and the Vedantic concept of *Brahman*.

4 The reference here is clearly to the "pure" or "true" self, to be distinguished from the empirical ego, the psychological subject of desires, motives, etc.

5 *Brahman* came to be the name of absolute or underlying reality in Hindu thought; but earlier the word had referred, first, to prayers and invocations used in sacrificial rituals and then to the power supposedly invoked in such rituals.

* I.e. the body.

Cicero, *De finibus*, Book III,
Chapters I–X and XIX–XXII;
De officiis, Book I, Chapters I–XIII

Introduction

His name derives from the Latin word for "chick-pea" (*cicer*), but Marcus Tullius Cicero (106–43 BCE) was no trivial thinker. His rise to power in the Roman Republic was meteoric, traversing a career from lawyer, through a string of public offices, to the Senate and Consulship. Cicero's life spans the period during which the Republic reached its bloody end (just as he would). Laboring to save something of the Republic, or at least something of its moral fibre, Cicero writes with a pointed political as well as a philosophical purpose.

Cicero was an eclectic thinker, his work exhibiting the strong influence of the Academic Skeptics and the Stoics. Excerpted here from *De finibus* (*On Ends*) is an explication of Stoic ethics. The passage orbits around reflections on the chief "end" (from the Greek, *telos*) of human life and argues for the superiority of the stoic position over those of competing philosophical movements.

To achieve real moral worth, according to this conception, one begins by following our "primary impulses" to self-preservation and to knowing the

From Cicero, *De finibus bonorum et malorum*, trans. H. Rackham, Loeb Classical Library, Cambridge: Harvard University Press, 1914, pp. 217–55, 281–97 odd numbered pages only); and Cicero, *De officiis*, trans. W. Miller, Loeb Classical Library XXI, Cambridge: Harvard University Press, 1968, pp. 3–47 (odd numbered pages only). (Some notes omitted.)

truth. After learning how to employ our natural powers of reasoning and how to act upon "conceptions" rather than blind impulses, one becomes able to choose among various possibilities of conduct. For the Stoics, those choices that best "accord with nature" and serve as means to achieving a life of virtue are "preferred" choices. Once the ability to exercise reason and to choose what is preferred becomes perfected and habitual, one's conduct will be composed of "right action," and one will be truly happy. Tersely put, "the final aim is to live in agreement and harmony with nature." The stoic standard of goodness, therefore, is fixed and does not change with the contingencies of convention or fashion.

Stoic happiness, curiously, has nothing to do with "pleasure" or the "absence of pain," as Epicureans such as Cicero's contemporary, Lucretius (99–55 BCE), maintained (I.3). Contrary to the Aristotelians, who hold that there are many goods subordinate to the chief end (for example, wealth, health, and friends), the Stoics hold that nothing besides virtue is good, at all – even those primary impulses and those preferred things that make it possible achieve virtue. To the Stoics, everything besides the chief end is "indifferent." This position differs from that of the Skeptics, however (at least as Cicero's character, Cato, portrays them), who even treat virtue with indifference. For the Stoics some indifferent things are still to be preferred, but there is nothing indifferent about real virtue or harmony with nature and nature's law.

De officiis (*On Duties*) is the last text Cicero wrote. Addressed to his son, Marcus, who was then studying philosophy in Athens, and presumably to Roman citizens generally, the work expands the conceptions of virtue developed by the Stoics, especially Panaetius of Rhodes (185–110 BCE), as well as by the line of thinkers associated with Plato.[1] The selection here begins with the recommendation that the terms of various apparently different pairs – Greek/Latin, Athens/Rome, philosophy/oratory – ought to be seen as complementary and, in fact, better when combined. This synthetic-eclectic advice sets the scene for the philosophical task of linking individual virtue to civic virtue, to our duties to the public good, and to our duties to the state itself.

When Plato explicated what have come to be known as the four cardinal virtues (courage, moderation, wisdom, justice) in *Republic* IV, he defined them in a decidedly asocial way, describing each virtue as a condition of the individual soul – even justice. As a metaphor of the polity, Plato's rendering considers things from the point of view of the ruler, looking at the polity as a whole.

Cicero, by contrast, advocates in *De officiis* a socially engaged concept of virtue with regard to citizens as well as rulers. While Plato's philosopher kings (and perhaps queens) must be compelled to turn away from contemplating transcendent truth in order to take up the mundane business of ruling subjects of which we learn little, Cicero insists that "the whole glory of virtue is in [social-political] activity." For human beings are not only born to serve their personal desires and interests (cf. Hobbes, V.10), or even to find their place in a harmonious, natural cosmos. Human beings, maintains Cicero, "are born for the sake of other human beings, that they may be able to mutually help one another."

Notes

1   For more on the background and context of *De officiis*, see A. R. Dyck, *A Commentary on Cicero, De Officiis*, Ann Arbor: University of Michigan Press, 1996.

Cicero, *De finibus*

Book III, Chapters I–X

1   I. MY DEAR BRUTUS. – Were Pleasure to speak for herself, in default of such redoubtable advocates as she now has to defend her, my belief is that she would own defeat. Vanquished by the arguments of our preceding Book, she would yield the victory to true Worth. Indeed she would be lost to shame if she persisted any longer in the battle against Virtue, and rated what is pleasant above what is morally good, or maintained that bodily enjoyment or the mental gratification which springs from it is of higher value than firmness and dignity of character. Let us then give Pleasure her dismissal, and bid her keep within her own domains, lest her charms and blandishments put snares in the way of strict philosoph-

2   ical debate. The question before us is, where is that Chief Good, which is the object of our inquiry, to be found? Pleasure we have eliminated; the doctrine that the End of Goods consists in freedom from pain is open to almost identical objections; and in fact no Chief Good can be accepted that is without the element of Virtue, the most excellent thing that can exist.

Hence although in our debate with Torquatus we did not spare our strength, nevertheless a keener struggle now awaits us with the Stoics. For pleasure is a topic that does not lend itself to very subtle or profound discussion; its champions are little skilled in dialectic, and their adversaries have no difficult case to refute. In fact Epicurus 3 himself declares that there is no occasion to argue about pleasure at all: its criterion resides in the senses, so that proof is entirely superfluous; a reminder of the facts is all that is needed. Therefore our preceding debate consisted of a simple statement of the case on either side. There was nothing abstruse or intricate in the discourse of Torquatus, and my own exposition was, I believe, as clear as daylight. But the Stoics, as you are aware, affect an exceedingly subtle or rather crabbed style of argument; and if the Greeks find it so, still more must we, who have actually to create a vocabulary, and to invent new terms to convey new ideas. This necessity will cause no surprise to anyone of moderate learning, when he reflects that in every branch of science lying outside the range of common everyday practice there must always be a large degree of novelty in the vocabulary, when it comes to fixing a terminology to denote the

4 conceptions with which the science in question deals. Thus Logic and Natural Philosophy alike make use of terms unfamiliar even to Greece; Geometry, Music, Grammar also, have an idiom of their own. Even the manuals of Rhetoric, which belong entirely to the practical sphere and to the life of the world, nevertheless employ for purposes of instruction a sort of private arid peculiar phraseology.

II.   And to leave out of account these liberal arts and accomplishments, even artisans would be unable to preserve the tradition of their crafts if they did not make use of words unknown to us though familiar to themselves. Nay, agriculture itself, a subject entirely unsusceptible of literary refinement, has yet had to coin technical terms to denote the things with which it is occupied. All the more is the philosopher compelled to do likewise; for philosophy is the Science of Life, and

5 cannot be discussed in language taken at random from the street. Still of all the philosophers the Stoics have been the greatest innovators in this respect, and Zeno their founder was rather an inventor of new terms than a discoverer of new ideas. But if men so learned, using a language generally supposed to be more copious than our own, were allowed in handling recondite subjects to employ unfamiliar terms, how much more right have we to claim this licence who are venturing now to approach these topics for the first time? Moreover we have often declared, and this under some protest not from Greeks only but also from persons who would rather be considered Greeks than Romans, that in fullness of vocabulary we are not merely not surpassed by the Greeks but are actually their superiors. We are therefore bound to do our utmost to make good this claim not in our native arts only but also in those that belong to the Greeks themselves. However, words which the practice of past generations permits us to employ as Latin, e.g. the term 'philosophy' itself, or 'rhetoric,' 'logic,' 'grammar,' 'geometry,' 'music' we may consider as being our own; the ideas might it is true have been translated into Latin, but the Greek terms have been naturalized by use. So much for terminology.

As regards my subject, I often fear, Brutus, that 6 I shall meet with censure for writing upon this topic to you, who are yourself so great an adept in philosophy, and in the highest branch of philosophy. Did I assume the attitude of an instructor, such censure would be deserved. But nothing could be farther from me. I dedicate my work to you, not to teach you what you know extremely well already, but because your name gives me a very comforting sense of support, and because I find in you a most impartial judge and critic of the studies which I share with yourself. You will therefore grant me, as always, your closest attention, and act as umpire of the debate which I held with that remarkable man of genius, your uncle.

I was down at my place at Tusculum, and 7 wanted to consult some books from the library of the young Lucullus; so I went to his country-house, as I was in the habit of doing, to help myself to the volumes I needed. On my arrival, seated in the library I found Marcus Cato; I had not known he was there. He was surrounded by piles of books on Stoicism; for he possessed, as you are aware, a voracious appetite for reading, and could never have enough of it; indeed it was often his practice actually to brave the idle censure of the mob by reading in the senate-house itself, while waiting for the senate to assemble, – he did not steal any attention from public business. So it may well be believed that when I found him taking a complete holiday, with a vast supply of books at command, he had the air of indulging in a literary debauch, if the term may be applied to so honourable an occupation. Upon 8 this chance encounter, each of us being equally surprised to see the other, he at once rose, and we began to exchange the usual greetings. "What brings you here?" cried he; "You are from your country-seat, I suppose. Had I known you were there," he continued, "I should have anticipated you with a visit." "Yes," I answered, "the games began yesterday, so I came out of town, and arrived late in the afternoon. My reason for coming on here was to get some books from the library. By the way, Cato, it will soon be time for our friend Lucullus to make acquaintance with this fine collection; for I hope he will take more pleasure in his library than in all the other appointments of his country-house. I am extremely anxious (though of course the responsibility belongs especially to you) that he should have the kind of education that will turn him out after the same pattern as his father and our dear Caepio, and also yourself, to whom he is so closely related. And I have every motive for my interest in him. I cherish the memory of his grandfather (and you are aware how highly I esteemed Caepio, who in my belief would to-day be in the front rank, were he still alive). And also Lucullus is always present to my mind; he was a man of surpassing eminence, united to me in

9   sentiment and opinion as well as by friendship." "I commend you," rejoined Cato, "for your loyalty to the memory of men who both bequeathed their children to your care, as well as for your affectionate interest in the lad. My own responsibility, as you call it, I by no means disown, but I enlist you to share it with me. Moreover I may say that the youth already seems to me to show many signs both of modesty and talent; but you know how young he is." "I do," said I, "but all the same it is time for him to be dipping into studies which, if allowed to soak in at this impressionable age, will render him better equipped when he comes to the business of life." "True, and we will discuss this matter again several times more fully and take common action. But let us be seated," he said, "if agreeable to you." So we sat down.

10   III.   Cato then resumed: "But what pray are the books that you must come here for, when you have so large a library of your own?" "I have come to fetch some commentaries on Aristotle," I replied, "which I knew were here. I wanted to read them during my holiday; I do not often get any leisure." "How I wish," said he, "that you had thrown in your lot with the Stoics! You of all men might have been expected to reckon virtue as the only good." "Perhaps *you* might rather have been expected," I answered, "to refrain from adopting a new terminology, when in substance you think as I do. Our principles agree; it is our language that is at variance." "Indeed," he rejoined, "they do not agree in the least. Once pronounce anything to be desirable, once reckon anything as a good, other than Moral Worth, and you have extinguished the very light of vir-

11 tue, Moral Worth itself, and overthrown virtue entirely." "That all sounds very fine, Cato," I replied, "but are you aware that you share your lofty pretensions with Pyrrho and with Aristo, who make all things equal in value? I should like to know what your opinion is of them." "My opinion?" he said. "You ask what my opinion is?

That those good, brave, just and temperate men, of whom we have heard as having lived in our state, or whom we have ourselves seen, who under the guidance of Nature herself, without the aid of any learning, did many glorious deeds, – that these men were better educated by nature than they could possibly have been by philosophy had they accepted any other system of philosophy than the one that counts Moral Worth the only good and Moral Baseness the only evil. All other philosophical systems – in varying degrees no doubt, but still all, – which reckon anything of which virtue is not an element either as a good or an evil, do not merely, as I hold, give us no assistance or support towards becoming better men, but are actually corrupting to the character. Either this point must be firmly maintained, that Moral Worth is the sole good, or it is absolutely impossible to prove that virtue constitutes happiness. And in that case I do not see why we should trouble to study philosophy. For if a Wise Man could be miserable, I should not set much value on your vaunted and belauded virtue."

IV.   "What you have said so far, Cato," I   12
answered, "might equally well be said by a follower of Pyrrho or of Aristo. They, as you are aware, think as you do, that this Moral Worth you speak of is not merely the chief but the only Good; and from this of necessity follows the proposition that I notice you maintain, namely, that the Wise are always happy. Do you then," I asked, "commend these philosophers, and think that we ought to adopt this view of theirs ?" "I certainly would not have you adopt *their* view," he said; "for it is of the essence of virtue to exercise choice among the things in accordance with nature; so that philosophers who make all things absolutely equal, rendering them indistinguishable either as better or worse, and leaving no room for selection among them, have abolished virtue   13
itself." "Excellently put," I rejoined; "but pray are not you committed to the same position, if you say that only what is right and moral is good, and abolish all distinction between everything else?" "Quite so," said he, "if I did abolish all distinction, but I do not." "How so?" I said, "If only   14
virtue, only that one thing which you call moral, right, praiseworthy, becoming (for its nature will be better understood if it is denoted by a number of synonyms), if then, I say, this is the sole good, what other object of pursuit will you have

beside it? or, if there be nothing bad but what is base, dishonourable, disgraceful, evil, sinful, foul (to make this clear also by using a variety of terms), what else will you pronounce worthy to be avoided?" "You know quite well," he retorted, "what I am going to say; but I suspect you want to catch up something in my answer if I put it shortly. So I won't answer you point by point. Instead of that, as we are at leisure, I will expound, unless you think it out of place, the whole system of Zeno and the Stoics." "Out of place?" I cried. "By no means. Your exposition will be of great assistance towards solving the 15 questions we are asking." "Then let us make the attempt," said he, "albeit there is a considerable element of difficulty and obscurity in this Stoic system. For at one time even the terms employed in Greek for its novel conceptions seemed unendurable, when they were novel, though now daily use has made them familiar; what then do you think will be the case in Latin?" "Do not feel the least difficulty on that score," said I. "If when Zeno invented some novel idea he was permitted to denote it by an equally unheard-of word, why should not Cato be permitted to do so too? Though all the same it need not be a hard and fast rule that every word shall be represented by its exact counterpart, when there is a more familiar word conveying the same meaning. That is the way of a clumsy translator. Indeed my own practice is to use several words to give what is expressed in Greek by one, if I cannot convey the sense otherwise. And at the same time I hold that we may fairly claim the licence to employ a Greek word when no Latin word is readily forthcoming. Why should this licence be granted to *ephippia* (saddles) and *acratophora* (jars for neat wine) more than to *proēgmena* and *apoproēgmena*? These latter however it is true may be 16 correctly translated 'preferred' and 'rejected.'" "Thanks for your assistance," he said. "I certainly shall use for choice the Latin equivalents you have just given; and in other cases you shall come to my aid if you see me in difficulties." "I'll do my best," I replied. "But fortune favours the bold; so pray make the venture. What sublimer occupation could we find?"

V. He began: "It is the view of those whose system I adopt, that immediately upon birth (for that is the proper point to start from) a living creature feels an attachment for itself, and an impulse to preserve itself and to feel affection for its own constitution and for those things which tend to preserve that constitution; while on the other hand it conceives an antipathy to destruction and to those things which appear to threaten destruction. In proof of this opinion they urge that infants desire things conducive to their health and reject things that are the opposite before they have ever felt pleasure or pain; this would not be the case, unless they felt an affection for their own constitution and were afraid of destruction. But it would be impossible that they should feel desire at all unless they possessed self-consciousness, and consequently felt affection for themselves. This leads to the conclusion that it is love of self which supplies the primary impulse to action. Pleasure on the 17 contrary, according to most Stoics, is not to be reckoned among the primary objects of natural impulse; and I very strongly agree with them, for fear lest many immoral consequences would follow if we held that nature has placed pleasure among the earliest objects of desire. But the fact of our affection for the objects first adopted at nature's prompting seems to require no further proof than this, that there is no one who, given the choice, would not prefer to have all the parts of his body sound and whole, rather than maimed or distorted although equally serviceable.

"Again, acts of cognition (which we may term comprehensions or perceptions, or, if these words are distasteful or obscure, *katalēpseis*), – these we consider meet to be adopted for their own sake, because they possess an element that so to speak embraces and contains the truth. This can be seen in the case of children, whom we may observe to take pleasure in finding something out for themselves by the use of reason, even though they gain nothing by it. The sciences 18 also, we consider, are things to be chosen for their own sake, partly because there is in them something worthy of choice, partly because they consist of acts of cognition and contain an element of fact established by methodical reasoning. The mental assent to what is false, as the Stoics believe, is more repugnant to us than all the other things that are contrary to nature.

"(Again, of the members or parts of the body, some appear to have been bestowed on us by nature for the sake of their use, for example the hands, legs, feet, and the internal organs, as to the degree of whose utility even physicians are not agreed; while others serve no useful purpose, but

appear to be intended for ornament: for instance the peacock's tail, the plumage of the dove with its shifting colours, and the breasts and beard
19 of the male human being.) All this is perhaps somewhat baldly expressed; for it deals with what may be called the primary elements of nature, to which any embellishment of style can scarcely be applied, nor am I for my part concerned to attempt it. On the other hand, when one is treating of more majestic topics the style instinctively rises with the subject, and the brilliance of the language increases with the dignity of the theme." "True," I rejoined; "but to my mind, any clear statement of an important topic possesses excellence of style. It would be childish to desire an ornate style in subjects of the kind with which you are dealing. A man of sense and education will be content to be able to express his meaning plainly and clearly."

20   VI.   "To proceed then," he continued, "for we have been digressing from the primary impulses of nature; and with these the later stages must be in harmony. The next step is the following fundamental classification: That which is in itself in accordance with nature, or which produces something else that is so, and which therefore is deserving of choice as possessing a certain amount of positive value – *axia* as the Stoics call it – this they pronounce to be 'valuable' (for so I suppose we may translate it); and on the other hand that which is the contrary of the former they term 'valueless.' The initial principle being thus established that things in accordance with nature are 'things to be taken' for their own sake, and their opposites similarly 'things to be rejected,' the first 'appropriate act' (for so I render the Greek *kathēkon*) is to preserve oneself in one's natural constitution; the next is to retain those things which are in accordance with nature and to repel those that are the contrary; then when this principle of choice and also of rejection has been discovered, there follows next in order choice conditioned by 'appropriate action'; then, such choice become a fixed habit; and finally, choice fully rationalized and in harmony with nature. It is at this final stage that the Good properly so called first emerges and comes to be understood in its
21 true nature. Man's first attraction is towards the things in accordance with nature; but as soon as he has attained to understanding, or rather to conscious intelligence – in Stoic phraseology *ennoia* – and has discerned the order and so to speak

harmony that should govern conduct, he then esteems this harmony far more highly than all the things for which he originally felt an affection, and by exercise of intelligence and reason infers the conclusion that in this order resides the Chief Good of man, the thing that is praiseworthy and desirable for its own sake; and that inasmuch as this consists in what the Stoics term *homologia* and we with your approval may call 'conformity'* – inasmuch I say as in this resides that Good which is the End to which all else is a means, moral conduct and Moral Worth itself, which alone is counted as a good, although of subsequent development, is nevertheless the sole thing that is for its own efficacy and value desirable, whereas none of the primary objects of nature is desirable for its own sake. But since those 22 actions which I have termed 'appropriate acts' are based on the primary natural objects, it follows that the former are means to the latter. Hence it may correctly be said that all 'appropriate acts' are means to the end of attaining the primary needs of nature. Yet it must not be inferred that their attainment is the ultimate Good, inasmuch as moral action is not one of the primary natural attractions, but is an outgrowth of these, a later development, as I have said. At the same time moral action is in accordance with nature, and stimulates our desire far more strongly than all the objects that attracted us earlier. But at this point a caution is necessary at the outset. It will be an error to infer that this view implies *two* Ultimate Goods. For though if a man were to make it his purpose to take a true aim with a spear or arrow at some mark, his ultimate end, corresponding to the ultimate good as we pronounce it, would be to do all he could to aim straight: the man in this illustration would have to do everything to aim straight, and yet, although he did everything to attain his purpose, his 'ultimate End,' so to speak, would be what corresponded to what we call the Chief Good in the conduct of life, whereas the actual hitting of the mark would be in our phrase 'to be chosen' but not 'to be desired.'

VII.   "Again, as all 'appropriate acts' are based 23 on the primary impulses of nature, it follows

---

* 'To live conformably,' ὁμολογουμένως ζῆν, was Zeno's formula for the End; it was interpreted as meaning 'to live on one harmonious plan.' Cleanthes added, τῇ φύσει, 'to live in conformity with nature.'

that Wisdom itself is based on them also. But as it often happens that a man who is introduced to another values this new friend more highly than he does the person who gave him the introduction, so in like manner it is by no means surprising that though we are first introduced to Wisdom by the primary natural instincts, afterwards Wisdom itself becomes dearer to us than are the instincts from which we came to her. And just as our limbs are so fashioned that it is clear that they were bestowed upon us with a view to a certain mode of life, so our faculty of appetition, in Greek *hormē*, was obviously designed not for any kind of life one may choose, but for a particular mode of living: and the same is true of

24 Reason and of perfected Reason. For just as an actor or dancer has assigned to him not any but a certain particular part or dance, so life has to be conducted in a certain fixed way, and not in any way we like. This fixed way we speak of as 'conformable' and suitable. In fact we do not consider Wisdom to be like seamanship or medicine, but rather like the arts of acting and of dancing just mentioned; its End, being the actual exercise of the art, is contained within the art itself, and is not something extraneous to it. At the same time there is also another point which marks a dissimilarity between Wisdom and these same arts. In the latter a movement perfectly executed nevertheless does not involve all the various motions which together constitute the subject matter of the art; whereas in the sphere of conduct, what we may call, if you approve, 'right actions,' or 'rightly performed actions,' in Stoic phraseology *katorthōmata*, contain all the categories of virtue. For Wisdom alone is entirely self-

25 contained, which is not the case with the other arts. It is erroneous, however, to place the End of medicine or of navigation exactly on a par with the End of Wisdom. For Wisdom includes also magnanimity and justice and a sense of superiority to all the accidents of man's estate, but this is not the case with the other arts. Again, even the very virtues I have just mentioned cannot be attained by anyone unless he has realized that all things are indifferent and indistinguishable except moral worth and baseness.

26 "We may now observe how strikingly the principles I have established support the following corollaries. Inasmuch as the final aim – (and you have observed, no doubt, that I have all along been translating the Greek term *telos* either by 'final' or 'ultimate aim,' or 'chief Good,' and for 'final or ultimate aim' we may also substitute 'End') – inasmuch then as the final aim is to live in agreement and harmony with nature, it necessarily follows that all wise men at all times enjoy a happy, perfect and fortunate life, free from all hindrance, interference or want. The essential principle not merely of the system of philosophy I am discussing but also of our life and fortunes is, that we should believe Moral Worth to be the only good. This principle might be amplified and elaborated in the rhetorical manner, with great length and fullness and with all the resources of choice diction and impressive argument; but for my own part I like the terse and pointed syllogisms of the Stoics.

VIII. "They put their arguments in the fol- 27 lowing syllogistic form: Whatever is good is praiseworthy: but whatever is praiseworthy is morally honourable: therefore that which is good is morally honourable. Do you think this is a valid deduction? Undoubtedly it is so: you can see that the conclusion rests on an inference logically drawn from the two premises. The usual line of reply is to deny the major premise, and say that not everything good is praiseworthy; for there is no denying that what is praiseworthy is morally honourable. But it would be paradoxical to maintain that there is something good which is not desirable; or desirable that is not pleasing; or if pleasing, not also esteemed; and therefore approved as well; and so also praiseworthy. But the praiseworthy is the morally honourable. Hence it follows that what is good is also morally honourable.

"Next I ask, who can be proud of a life that is 28 miserable or not happy? It follows that one can only be proud of one's lot when it is a happy one. This proves that the happy life is a thing that deserves, so to speak, that one should be proud of it; and this cannot rightly be said of any life but one morally honourable. Therefore the moral life is the happy life. And the man who deserves and wins praise has exceptional cause for pride and self-satisfaction; but these things count for so much that he can justly be pronounced happy; therefore the life of such a man can with full correctness be described as happy also. Thus if Moral Worth is the criterion of happiness, Moral Worth must be deemed the only Good.

"Once more; could it be denied that it is im- 29 possible for there ever to exist a man of steadfast, firm and lofty mind, such a one as we call a brave man, unless it be established that pain is not an evil? For just as it is impossible for one who counts death as an evil not to fear death, so in no case can a man disregard and despise a thing that he decides to be evil. This being laid down as generally admitted, we take as our minor premise that the brave and high-minded man despises and holds of no account all the accidents to which mankind is liable. The conclusion follows that nothing is evil that is not base. Also, your lofty, distinguished, magnanimous and truly brave man, who thinks all human vicissitudes beneath him, I mean, the character we desire to produce, our ideal man, must unquestionably have faith in himself and in his own career both past and future, and think well of himself, holding that no ill can befall the wise man. Here then is another proof of the same position, that Moral Worth alone is good, and that to live honourably, that is virtuously, is to live happily.

30 IX. "I am well aware, it is true, that varieties of opinion have existed among philosophers, I mean among those of them who have placed the Chief Good, the ultimate aim as I call it, in the mind. In following out these various views some of them fell into errors; but nevertheless I rank all those, of whatever type, who have placed the Chief Good in the mind and in virtue, not merely above the three philosophers who dissociated the Chief Good from virtue altogether and identified it either with pleasure or freedom from pain or the primary impulses of nature, but also above the other three, who held that virtue would be incomplete without some enhancement, and therefore added to it one or other respectively of the three things I have just enumerated. But still those thinkers are quite beside the mark who pronounced the ultimate Good to be a life devoted to knowledge; and those who declared that all things are indifferent, and that the Wise Man will secure happiness by not preferring any one thing in the least degree to any other; and those again who said, as some members of the Academy are said to have maintained, that the final Good and supreme duty of the Wise Man is to resist appearances and resolutely withhold his assent to the reality of sense-impressions. It is customary to take these doctrines severally and reply to them at length. But there is really no need to labour what is self-evident; and what could be more obvious than that, if we can exercise no choice as between things consonant with and things contrary to nature, no scope is left at all for the much-prized and belauded virtue of Prudence? Eliminating therefore the views just enumerated and any others that resemble them, we are left with the conclusion that the Chief Good consists in applying to the conduct of life a knowledge of the working of natural causes, choosing what is in accordance with nature and rejecting what is contrary to it; in other words, the Chief Good is to live in agreement and in harmony with nature.

"But in the other arts when we speak of an 32 'artistic' performance, this quality must be considered as in a sense subsequent to and a result of the action; it is what the Stoics term *epigennēmatikon* (in the nature of an after-growth). Whereas in conduct, when we speak of an act as 'wise,' the term is applied with full correctness from the first inception of the act. For every action that the Wise Man initiates must necessarily be complete forthwith in all its parts; since the thing desirable, as we term it, consists in his activity. As it is a sin to betray one's country, to use violence to one's parents, to rob a temple, where the offence lies in the result of the act, so the passions of fear, grief and lust are sins, even when no extraneous result ensues. The latter are sins not in their subsequent effects, but immediately upon their inception; similarly, actions springing from virtue are to be judged right from their first inception, and not in their successful completion.

X. "Again, the term 'Good,' which has 33 been employed so frequently in this discourse, is also explained by definition. The Stoic definitions do indeed differ from one another in a very minute degree, but they all point in the same direction. Personally I agree with Diogenes in defining the Good as that which is by nature perfect. In consonance with this he pronounced the 'beneficial' (for so let us render the Greek *ōphelēma*) to be a motion or state in accordance with that which is by nature perfect. Now notions of things are produced in the mind when something has become known either by experience or by combination of ideas or by likeness or by analogy. The fourth and last method in this list is the one that has given us the conception of the Good. The mind ascends by analogy from the things in accordance with nature till finally it arrives at the notion of Good. At the same time Goodness is absolute, and is not a question of degree; the Good is recognized and pronounced to be good from its own inherent properties and not by comparison with other things. Just as honey, though extremely sweet, is yet perceived to be sweet by its own peculiar kind of flavour and not by being compared with something else, so this Good which we are discussing is superlatively valuable, yet the value in its case depends on kind and not on quantity. Value, in Greek *axiā*, is not counted as a Good nor yet as an Evil; so that however much you increase it in amount, it will still remain the same in kind. The value of Virtue is therefore peculiar and distinct; it depends on kind and not on degree.

35 "Moreover the emotions of the mind, which harass and embitter the life of the foolish (the Greek term for these is *pathos*, and I might have rendered this literally and styled them 'diseases,' but the word 'disease' would not suit all instances; for example, no one speaks of pity, nor yet anger, as a disease, though the Greeks term these *pathos*. Let us then accept the term 'emotion,' the very sound of which seems to denote something vicious, and these emotions are not excited by any natural influence. The list of the emotions is divided into four classes, with numerous subdivisions, namely sorrow, fear, lust, and that mental emotion which the Stoics call by a name that also denotes a bodily feeling, *hēdonē* 'pleasure,' but which I prefer to style 'delight,' meaning the sensuous elation of the mind when in a state of exultation), these emotions, I say, are not excited by any influence of nature; they are all of them mere fancies and frivolous opinions. Therefore the Wise Man will always be free from them.

[. . .]

Book III, Chapters XIX–XXII

62 XIX. "Again, it is held by the Stoics to be important to understand that nature creates in parents an affection for their children; and parental affection is the germ of that social community of the human race to which we afterwards attain. This cannot but be clear in the first place from the conformation of the body and its members, which by themselves are enough to show that nature's scheme included the procreation of offspring. Yet it could not be consistent that nature

should at once intend offspring to be born and make no provision for that offspring when born to be loved and cherished. Even in the lower animals nature's operation can be clearly discerned; when we observe the labour that they spend on bearing and rearing their young, we seem to be listening to the actual voice of nature. Hence as it is manifest that it is natural for us to shrink from pain, so it is clear that we derive from nature herself the impulse to love those to whom we have given birth. From this impulse is devel- 63 oped the sense of mutual attraction which unites human beings as such; this also is bestowed by nature. The mere fact of their common humanity requires that one man should feel another man to be akin to him. For just as some of the parts of the body, such as the eyes and the ears, are created as it were for their own sakes, while others like the legs or the hands also subserve the utility of the rest of the members, so some very large animals are born for themselves alone; whereas the sea-pen, as it is called, in its roomy shell, and the creature named the 'pinoteres' because it keeps watch over the sea-pen, which swims out of the sea-pen's shell, then retires back into it and is shut up inside, thus appearing to have warned its host to be on its guard – these creatures, and also the ant, the bee, the stork, do certain actions for the sake of others besides themselves. With human beings this bond of mutual aid is far more intimate. It follows that we are by nature fitted to form unions, societies and states.

"Again, they hold that the universe is gov- 64 erned by divine will; it is a city or state of which both men and gods are members, and each one of us is a part of this universe; from which it is a natural consequence that we should prefer the common advantage to our own. For just as the laws set the safety of all above the safety of individuals, so a good, wise and law-abiding man, conscious of his duty to the state, studies the advantage of all more than that of himself or of any single individual. The traitor to his country does not deserve greater reprobation than the man who betrays the common advantage or security for the sake of his own advantage or security. This explains why praise is owed to one who dies for the commonwealth, because it becomes us to love our country more than ourselves. And as we feel it wicked and inhuman for men to declare (the saying is usually expressed in a familiar Greek line) that they care not if, when they themselves are dead, the universal conflagration ensues, it is undoubtedly true that we are bound to study the interest of posterity also for its own sake.

65   XX. "This is the feeling that has given rise to the practice of making a will and appointing guardians for one's children when one is dying. And the fact that no one would care to pass his life alone in a desert, even though supplied with pleasures in unbounded profusion, readily shows that we are born for society and intercourse, and for a natural partnership with our fellow men. Moreover nature inspires us with the desire to benefit as many people as we can, and especially by imparting information and the

66   principles of wisdom. Hence it would be hard to discover anyone who will not impart to another any knowledge that he may himself possess; so strong is our propensity not only to learn but also to teach. And just as bulls have a natural instinct to fight with all their strength and force in defending their calves against lions, so men of exceptional gifts and capacity for service, like Hercules and Liber in the legends, feel a natural impulse to be the protectors of the human race. Also when we confer upon Jove the titles of Most Good and Most Great, of Saviour, Lord of Guests, Rallier of Battles, what we mean to imply is that the safety of mankind lies in his keeping. But how inconsistent it would be for us to expect the immortal gods to love and cherish us, when we ourselves despise and neglect one another! Therefore just as we actually use our limbs before we have learnt for what particular useful purpose they were bestowed upon us, so we are by nature united and allied in the common society of the state. Were this not so, there would be no room either for justice or benevolence.

67   "But just as they hold that man is united with man by the bonds of right, so they consider that no right exists as between man and beast. For Chrysippus well said, that all other things were created for the sake of men and gods, but that these exist for their own mutual fellowship and society, so that men can make use of beasts for their own purposes without injustice. And the nature of man, he said, is such, that as it were a code of law subsists between the individual and the human race, so that he who upholds this code will be just and he who departs from it, unjust. But just as though the theatre is a public place it is yet correct to say that the particular seat a man

has taken belongs to him, so in the state or in the universe, though these are common to all, no principle of justice militates against the possession of private property. Again, since we see that man is 68 designed by nature to safeguard and protect his fellows, it follows from this natural disposition, that the Wise Man should desire to engage in politics and government, and also to live in accordance with nature by taking to himself a wife and desiring to have children by her. Even the passion of love when pure is not thought incompatible with the character of the Stoic Sage. As for the principles and habits of the Cynics, some say that these befit the Wise Man, if circumstances should happen to indicate this course of action; but other Stoics reject the Cynic rule unconditionally.

XXI. "To safeguard the universal alliance, 69 solidarity and affection that subsist between all mankind, the Stoics held that both 'benefits' and 'injuries' (in their terminology, *ōphelēmata* and *blammata*) are common, the former doing good and the latter harm; and they pronounced them to be not only 'common' but also 'equal.' 'Disadvantages' and 'advantages' (for so I render *euchrēstēmata* and *duschrēstēmata*) they held to be 'common' but not 'equal.' For things 'beneficial' and 'injurious' are goods and evils respectively, and these must needs be equal; but 'advantages' and 'disadvantages' belong to the class we speak of as 'preferred' and 'rejected,' and these may differ in degree. But whereas 'benefits' and 'injuries' are pronounced to be 'common,' righteous and sinful acts are not considered 'common.'

"They recommend the cultivation of friendship, 70 classing it among 'things beneficial.' In friendship some profess that the Wise Man will hold his friends' interests as dear as his own, while others say that a man's own interests must necessarily be dearer to him; at the same time the latter admit that to enrich oneself by another's loss is an action repugnant to that justice towards which we seem to possess a natural propensity. But the school I am discussing emphatically rejects the view that we adopt or approve either justice or friendship for the sake of their utility. For if it were so, the same claims of utility would be able to undermine and overthrow them. In fact the very existence of both justice and friendship will be impossible if they are not desired for their 71 own sake. Right moreover, properly so styled and entitled, exists (they aver) by nature; and it is foreign to the nature of the Wise Man not only to wrong but even to hurt anyone. Nor again is it righteous to enter into a partnership in wrong-doing with one's friends or benefactors; and it is most truly and cogently maintained that honesty is always the best policy, and that whatever is fair and just is also honourable, and conversely whatever is honourable will also be just and fair.

72   "To the virtues we have discussed they also add Dialectic and Natural Philosophy. Both of these they entitle by the name of virtue; the for-mer because it conveys a method that guards us from giving assent to any falsehood or ever being deceived by specious probability, and enables us to retain and to defend the truths that we have learned about good and evil; for without the art of Dialectic they hold that any man may be seduced from truth into error. If therefore rash-ness and ignorance are in all matters fraught with mischief, the art which removes them is correctly entitled a virtue.

73   XXII.   "The same honour is also bestowed with good reason upon Natural Philosophy, because he who is to live in accordance with nature must base his principles upon the system and govern-ment of the entire world. Nor again can anyone judge truly of things good and evil, save by a knowledge of the whole plan of nature and also of the life of the gods, and of the answer to the question whether the nature of man is or is not in harmony with that of the universe. And no one without Natural Philosophy can discern the value (and their value is very great) of the ancient maxims and precepts of the Wise Men, such as to 'obey occasion,' 'follow God,' 'know thyself,' and 'moderation in all things.' Also this science alone can impart a conception of the power of nature in fostering justice and main-taining friendship and the rest of the affections; nor again without unfolding nature's secrets can we understand the sentiment of piety towards the gods or the degree of gratitude that we owe to them.

74   "However I begin to perceive that I have let myself be carried beyond the requirements of the plan that I set before me. The fact is that I have been led on by the marvellous structure of the Stoic system and the miraculous sequence of its topics; pray tell me seriously, does it not fill you with admiration? Nothing is more finished, more nicely ordered, than nature; but what has nature, what have the products of handicraft to

show that is so well constructed, so firmly jointed and welded into one? Where do you find a conclusion inconsistent with its premise, or a discrepancy between an earlier and a later state-ment ? Where is lacking such close interconnex-ion of the parts that, if you alter a single letter, you shake the whole structure? Though indeed there is nothing that it would be possible to alter.

"Then, how dignified, how lofty, how consist-   75
ent is the character of the Wise Man as they depict it! Since reason has proved that moral worth is the sole good, it follows that he must always be happy, and that all those titles which the ignorant are so fond of deriding do in very truth belong to him. For he will have a better claim to the title of King than Tarquin, who could not rule either himself or his subjects; a better right to the name of 'Master of the People' (for that is what a dictator is) than Sulla, who was a master of three pestilential vices, licentiousness, avarice and cruelty; a better claim to be called rich than Crassus, who had he needed nothing would never have been induced to cross the Euphrates for any military reason. Rightly will he be said to own all things, who alone knows how to use all things; rightly also will he be styled beautiful, for the beauty of the soul is fairer than that of the body; rightly the one and only free man, as subject to no man's authority, and slave of no appetite; rightly unconquerable, for though his body be thrown into fetters, no bondage can   76
enchain his soul. Nor does he wait for any period of time that the decision whether he has been happy or not may be finally pronounced only when he has rounded off his life's last day in death, – the famous warning so unwisely given to Croesus by old Solon, one of the seven Wise Men; for had Croesus ever been happy, he would have carried his happiness uninterrupted to the pyre raised for him by Cyrus. If then it be true that all the good and none but the good are happy, what possession is more precious than philosophy, what more divine than virtue ?"

Cicero, *De officiis*

Book I, Chapters I–XIII

I.   My dear son Marcus, you have now been   *1*
studying a full year under Cratippus, and that too

in Athens, and you should be fully equipped with the practical precepts and the principles of philosophy; so much at least one might expect from the pre-eminence not only of your teacher but also of the city; the former is able to enrich you with learning, the latter to supply you with models. Nevertheless, just as I for my own improvement have always combined Greek and Latin studies – and I have done this not only in the study of philosophy but also in the practice of oratory – so I recommend that you should do the same, so that you may have equal command of both languages. And it is in this very direction that I have, if I mistake not, rendered a great service to our countrymen, so that not only those who are unacquainted with Greek literature but even the cultured consider that they have gained much both in oratorical power and in mental training.

2   You will, therefore, learn from the foremost of present-day philosophers, and you will go on learning as long as you wish; and your wish ought to continue as long as you are not dissatisfied with the progress you are making. For all that, if you will read my philosophical books, you will be helped; my philosophy is not very different from that of the Peripatetics (for both they and I claim to be followers of Socrates and Plato). As to the conclusions you may reach, I leave that to your own judgment (for I would put no hindrance in your way), but by reading my philosophical writings you will be sure to render your mastery of the Latin language more complete. But I would by no means have you think that this is said boastfully. For there are many to whom I yield precedence in knowledge of philosophy; but if I lay claim to the orator's peculiar ability to speak with propriety, clearness, elegance, I think my claim is in a measure justified, for I have spent my life in that profession.

3   And therefore, my dear Cicero, I cordially recommend you to read carefully not only my orations but also these books of mine on philosophy, which are now about as extensive. For while the orations exhibit a more vigorous style, yet the unimpassioned, restrained style of my philosophical productions is also worth cultivating. Moreover, for the same man to succeed in both departments, both in the forensic style and in that of calm philosophic discussion has not, I observe, been the good fortune of any one of the Greeks so far, unless, perhaps, Demetrius of Phalerum can

be reckoned in that number – a clever reasoner, indeed, and, though rather a spiritless orator, he is yet charming, so that you can recognize in him the disciple of Theophrastus. But let others judge how much I have accomplished in each pursuit; I have at least attempted both.

I believe, of course, that if Plato had been 4 willing to devote himself to forensic oratory, he could have spoken with the greatest eloquence and power; and that if Demosthenes had continued the studies he pursued with Plato and had wished to expound his views, he could have done so with elegance and brilliancy. I feel the same way about Aristotle and Isocrates, each of whom, engrossed in his own profession, undervalued that of the other.

II.   But since I have decided to write you a little now (and a great deal by and by), I wish, if possible, to begin with a matter most suited at once to your years and to my position. Although philosophy offers many problems, both important and useful, that have been fully and carefully discussed by philosophers, those teachings which have been handed down on the subject of moral duties seem to have the widest practical application. For no phase of life, whether public or private, whether in business or in the home, whether one is working on what concerns oneself alone or dealing with another, can be without its moral duty; on the discharge of such duties depends all that is morally right, and on their neglect all that is morally wrong in life.

Moreover, the subject of this inquiry is the 5 common property of all philosophers; for who would presume to call himself a philosopher, if he did not inculcate any lessons of duty? But there are some schools that distort all notions of duty by the theories they propose touching the supreme good and the supreme evil. For he who posits the supreme good as having no connection with virtue and measures it not by a moral standard but by his own interests – if he should be consistent and not rather at times over-ruled by his better nature, he could value neither friendship nor justice nor generosity; and brave he surely cannot possibly be that counts pain the supreme evil, nor temperate he that holds pleasure to be the supreme good.

Although these truths are so self-evident that 6 the subject does not call for discussion, still I have discussed it in another connection. If, therefore, these schools should claim to be consistent, they could not say anything about duty; and no fixed, invariable, natural rules of duty can be posited except by those who say that moral goodness is worth seeking solely or chiefly for its own sake. Accordingly, the teaching of ethics is the peculiar right of the Stoics, the Academicians, and the Peripatetics; for the theories of Aristo, Pyrrho, and Erillus have been long since rejected; and yet they would have the right to discuss duty if they had left us any power of choosing between things, so that there might be a way of finding out what duty is. I shall, therefore, at this time and in this investigation follow chiefly the Stoics, not as a translator, but, as is my custom, I shall at my own option and discretion draw from those sources in such measure and in such manner as shall suit my purpose.

7   Since, therefore, the whole discussion is to be on the subject of duty, I should like at the outset to define what duty is, as, to my surprise, Panaetius has failed to do. For every systematic development of any subject ought to begin with a definition, so that everyone may understand what the discussion is about.

III. Every treatise on duty has two parts: one, dealing with the doctrine of the supreme good; the other, with the practical rules by which daily life in all its bearings may be regulated. The following questions are illustrative of the first part: whether all duties are absolute; whether one duty is more important than another; and so on. But as regards special duties for which positive rules are laid down, though they are affected by the doctrine of the supreme good, still the fact is not so obvious, because they seem rather to look to the regulation of everyday life; and it is these special duties that I propose to treat at length in the following books.

8   And yet there is still another classification of duties: we distinguish between "mean" duty, so-called, and "absolute" duty. Absolute duty we may, I presume, call "right," for the Greeks call it κατόρθωμα, while the ordinary duty they call καθῆκον. And the meaning of those terms they fix thus: whatever is right they define as "absolute" duty, but "mean" duty, they say, is duty for the performance of which an adequate reason may be rendered.

9   The consideration necessary to determine conduct is, therefore, as Panaetius thinks, a three-fold one: first, people question whether the contemplated act is morally right or morally wrong; and in such deliberation their minds are often led to widely divergent conclusions. And then they examine and consider the question whether the action contemplated is or is not conducive to comfort and happiness in life, to the command of means and wealth, to influence, and to power, by which they may be able to help themselves and their friends; this whole matter turns upon a question of expediency. The third type of question arises when that which seems to be expedient seems to conflict with that which is morally right; for when expediency seems to be pulling one way, while moral right seems to be calling back in the opposite direction, the result is that the mind is distracted in its inquiry and brings to it the irresolution that is born of deliberation.

Although omission is a most serious defect in   10 classification, two points have been overlooked in the foregoing: for we usually consider not only whether an action is morally right or morally wrong, but also, when a choice of two morally right courses is offered, which one is morally better; and likewise, when a choice of two expedients is offered, which one is more expedient. Thus the question which Panaetius thought threefold ought, we find, to be divided into five parts. First, therefore, we must discuss the moral – and that, under two sub-heads; secondly, in the same manner, the expedient; and finally, the cases where they must be weighed against each other.

IV. First of all, Nature has endowed every   11 species of living creature with the instinct of self-preservation, of avoiding what seems likely to cause injury to life or limb, and of procuring and providing everything needful for life – food, shelter, and the like. A common property of all creatures is also the reproductive instinct (the purpose of which is the propagation of the species) and also a certain amount of concern for their offspring. But the most marked difference between man and beast is this: the beast, just as far as it is moved by the senses and with very little perception of past or future, adapts itself to that alone which is present at the moment; while man – because he is endowed with reason, by which he comprehends the chain of consequences, perceives the causes of things, understands the relation of cause to effect and of effect to cause, draws analogies, and connects and associates the present and the future – easily surveys the course of his whole life and makes the necessary preparations for its conduct.

12   Nature likewise by the power of reason associates man with man in the common bonds of speech and life; she implants in him above all, I may say, a strangely tender love for his offspring. She also prompts men to meet in companies, to form public assemblies and to take part in them themselves; and she further dictates, as a consequence of this, the effort on man's part to provide a store of things that minister to his comforts and wants – and not for himself alone, but for his wife and children and the others whom he holds dear and for whom he ought to provide; and this responsibility also stimulates his courage and makes it stronger for the active duties of life.

13   Above all, the search after truth and its eager pursuit are peculiar to man. And so, when we have leisure from the demands of business cares, we are eager to see, to hear, to learn something new, and we esteem a desire to know the secrets or wonders of creation as indispensable to a happy life. Thus we come to understand that what is true, simple, and genuine appeals most strongly to a man's nature. To this passion for discovering truth there is added a hungering, as it were, for independence, so that a mind well-moulded by Nature is unwilling to be subject to anybody save one who gives rules of conduct or is a teacher of truth or who, for the general good, rules according to justice and law. From this attitude come greatness of soul and a sense of superiority to worldly conditions.

14   And it is no mean manifestation of Nature and Reason that man is the only animal that has a feeling for order, for propriety, for moderation in word and deed. And so no other animal has a sense of beauty, loveliness, harmony in the visible world; and Nature and Reason, extending the analogy of this from the world of sense to the world of spirit, find that beauty, consistency, order are far more to be maintained in thought and deed, and the same Nature and Reason are careful to do nothing in an improper or unmanly fashion, and in every thought and deed to do or think nothing capriciously.

It is from these elements that is forged and fashioned that moral goodness which is the subject of this inquiry – something that, even though it be not generally ennobled, is still worthy of all honour; and by its own nature, we correctly maintain, it merits praise, even though it be praised by none.

V. You see here, Marcus, my son, the very form 15
and as it were the face of Moral Goodness; "and if," as Plato says, "it could be seen with the physical eye, it would awaken a marvellous love of wisdom." But all that is morally right rises from some one of four sources: it is concerned either (1) with the full perception and intelligent development of the true; or (2) with the conservation of organized society, with rendering to every man his due, and with the faithful discharge of obligations assumed; or (3) with the greatness and strength of a noble and invincible spirit; or (4) with the orderliness and moderation of everything that is said and done, wherein consist temperance and self-control.

Although these four are connected and interwoven, still it is in each one considered singly that certain definite kinds of moral duties have their origin: in that category, for instance, which was designated first in our division and in which we place wisdom and prudence, belong the search after truth and its discovery; and this is the pecu- 16
liar province of that virtue, For the more clearly anyone observes the most essential truth in any given case and the more quickly and accurately he can see and explain the reasons for it, the more understanding and wise he is generally esteemed, and justly so. So, then, it is truth that is, as it were, the stuff with which this virtue has to deal and on which it employs itself.

Before the three remaining virtues, on the other 17
hand, is set the task of providing and maintaining those things on which the practical business of life depends, so that the relations of man to man in human society may be conserved, and that largeness and nobility of soul may be revealed not only in increasing one's resources and acquiring advantages for one's self and one's family but far more in rising superior to these very things. But orderly behaviour and consistency of demeanour and self-control and the like have their sphere in that department of things in which a certain amount of physical exertion, and not mental activity merely, is required. For if we bring a certain amount of propriety and order into the transactions of daily life, we shall be conserving moral rectitude and moral dignity.

VI. Now, of the four divisions which we have 18
made of the essential idea of moral goodness, the first, consisting in the knowledge of truth, touches human nature most closely. For we are all attracted and drawn to a zeal for learning

and knowing; and we think it glorious to excel therein, while we count it base and immoral to fall into error, to wander from the truth, to be ignorant, to be led astray. In this pursuit, which is both natural and morally right, two errors are to be avoided: first, we must not treat the unknown as known and too readily accept it; and he who wishes to avoid this error (as all should do) will devote both time and attention

19 to the weighing of evidence. The other error is that some people devote too much industry and too deep study to matters that are obscure and difficult and useless as well.

If these errors are successfully avoided, all the labour and pains expended upon problems that are morally right and worth the solving will be fully rewarded. Such a worker in the field of astronomy, for example, was Gaius Sulpicius, of whom we have heard; in mathematics, Sextus Pompey, whom I have known personally; in dialectics, many; in civil law, still more. All these professions are occupied with the search after truth; but to be drawn by study away from active life is contrary to moral duty. For the whole glory of virtue is in activity; activity, however, may often be interrupted, and many opportunities for returning to study are opened. Besides, the working of the mind, which is never at rest, can keep us busy in the pursuit of knowledge even without conscious effort on our part. Moreover, all our thought and mental activity will be devoted either to planning for things that are morally right and that conduce to a good and happy life, or to the pursuits of science and learning.

With this we close the discussion of the first source of duty.

20 VII. Of the three remaining divisions, the most extensive in its application is the principle by which society and what we may call its "common bonds" are maintained. Of this again there are two divisions – justice, in which is the crowning glory of the virtues and on the basis of which men are called "good men"; and, close akin to justice, charity, which may also be called kindness or generosity.

The first office of justice is to keep one man from doing harm to another, unless provoked by wrong; and the next is to lead men to use common possessions for the common interests, private property for their own.

21 There is, however, no such thing as private ownership established by nature, but property becomes private either through long occupancy (as in the case of those who long ago settled in unoccupied territory) or through conquest (as in the case of those who took it in war) or by due process of law, bargain, or purchase, or by allotment. On this principle the lands of Arpinum are said to belong to the Arpinates, the Tusculan lands to the Tusculans; and similar is the assignment of private property. Therefore, inasmuch as in each case some of those things which by nature had been common property became the property of individuals, each one should retain possession of that which has fallen to his lot; and if anyone appropriates to himself anything beyond that, he will be violating the laws of human society.

But since, as Plato has admirably expressed 22 it, we are not born for ourselves alone, but our country claims a share of our being, and our friends a share; and since, as the Stoics hold, everything that the earth produces is created for man's use; and as men, too, are born for the sake of men, that they may be able mutually to help one another; in this direction we ought to follow Nature as our guide, to contribute to the general good by an interchange of acts of kindness, by giving and receiving, and thus by our skill, our industry, and our talents to cement human society more closely together, man to man.

The foundation of justice, moreover, is good 23 faith – that is, truth and fidelity to promises and agreements. And therefore we may follow the Stoics, who diligently investigate the etymology of words; and we may accept their statement that "good faith" is so called because what is promised is "made good," although some may find this derivation rather far-fetched.

There are, on the other hand, two kinds of injustice – the one, on the part of those who inflict wrong, the other on the part of those who, when they can, do not shield from wrong those upon whom it is being inflicted. For he who, under the influence of anger or some other passion, wrongfully assaults another seems, as it were, to be laying violent hands upon a comrade; but he who does not prevent or oppose wrong, if he can, is just as guilty of wrong as if he deserted his parents or his friends or his country. Then, too, 24 those very wrongs which people try to inflict on purpose to injure are often the result of fear: that is, he who premeditates injuring another is afraid that, if he does not do so, he may himself be made to suffer some hurt. But, for the most part, people are led to wrong-doing in order to secure some personal end; in this vice, avarice is generally the controlling motive.

25   VIII.   Again, men seek riches partly to supply the needs of life, partly to secure the enjoyment of pleasure. With those who cherish higher ambitions, the desire for wealth is entertained with a view to power and influence and the means of bestowing favours; Marcus Crassus, for example, not long since declared that no amount of wealth was enough for the man who aspired to be the foremost citizen of the state, unless with the income from it he could maintain an army. Fine establishments and the comforts of life in elegance and abundance also afford pleasure, and the desire to secure it gives rise to the insatiable thirst for wealth. Still, I do not mean to find fault with the accumulation of property, provided it hurts nobody, but unjust acquisition of it is always to be avoided.

26   The great majority of people, however, when they fall a prey to ambition for either military or civil authority, are carried away by it so completely that they quite lose sight of the claims of justice. For Ennius says:

"There is no fellowship inviolate,

No faith is kept, when kingship is concerned;"
and the truth of his words has an uncommonly wide application. For whenever a situation is of such a nature that not more than one can hold pre-eminence in it, competition for it usually becomes so keen that it is an extremely difficult matter to maintain a "fellowship inviolate." We saw this proved but now in the effrontery of Gaius Caesar, who, to gain that sovereign power which by a depraved imagination he had conceived in his fancy, trod underfoot all laws of gods and men. But the trouble about this matter is that it is in the greatest souls and in the most brilliant geniuses that we usually find ambitions for civil and military authority, for power, and for glory, springing up; and therefore we must be the more heedful not to go wrong in that direction.

27   But in any case of injustice it makes a vast deal of difference whether the wrong is done as a result of some impulse of passion, which is usually brief and transient, or whether it is committed wilfully and with premeditation; for offences that come through some sudden impulse are less culpable than those committed designedly and with malice aforethought.

But enough has been said on the subject of inflicting injury.

IX.   The motives for failure to prevent injury   28 and so for slighting duty are likely to be various: people either are reluctant to incur enmity or trouble or expense; or through indifference, indolence, or incompetence, or through some preoccupation or self-interest they are so absorbed that they suffer those to be neglected whom it is their duty to protect. And so there is reason to fear that what Plato declared of the philosophers may be inadequate, when he says that they are just because they are busied with the pursuit of truth and because they despise and count as naught that which most men eagerly seek and for which they are prone to do battle against each other to the death. For they secure one sort of justice, to be sure, in that they do no positive wrong to anyone, but they fall into the opposite injustice; for hampered by their pursuit of learning they leave to their fate those whom they ought to defend. And so, Plato thinks, they will not even assume their civic duties except under compulsion. But in fact it were better that they should assume them of their own accord; for an action intrinsically right is just only on condition that it is voluntary.

There are some also who, either from zeal in   29 attending to their own business or through some sort of aversion to their fellow-men, claim that they are occupied solely with their own affairs, without seeming to themselves to be doing anyone any injury, But while they steer clear of the one kind of injustice, they fall into the other: they are traitors to social life, for they contribute to it none of their interest, none of their effort, none of their means.

Now since we have set forth the two kinds of injustice and assigned the motives that lead to each, and since we have previously established the principles by which justice is constituted, we shall be in a position easily to decide what our duty on each occasion is, unless we are extremely self-centred; for indeed it is not an   30 easy matter to be really concerned with other people's affairs; and yet in Terence's play, we know, Chremes "thinks that nothing that concerns man is foreign to him." Nevertheless, when things turn out for our own good or ill, we realize it more fully and feel it more deeply than when the same things happen to others and we see them only, as it were, in the far distance; and for this reason we judge their case differently from our own. It is, therefore, an excellent rule that they give who bid us not to do a thing, when there is a doubt whether it be right or wrong; for righteousness shines with a brilliance of its own, but doubt is a sign that we are thinking of a possible wrong.

31 X. But occasions often arise, when those duties which seem most becoming to the just man and to the "good man," as we call him, undergo a change and take on a contrary aspect. It may, for example, not be a duty to restore a trust or to fulfil a promise, and it may become right and proper sometimes to evade and not to observe what truth and honour would usually demand. For we may well be guided by those fundamental principles of justice which I laid down at the outset: first, that no harm be done to anyone; second, that the common interests be conserved. When these are modified under changed circumstances, moral duty also undergoes a change, 32 and it does not always remain the same. For a given promise or agreement may turn out in such a way that its performance will prove detrimental either to the one to whom the promise has been made or to the one who has made it. If, for example, Neptune, in the drama, had not carried out his promise to Theseus, Theseus would not have lost his son Hippolytus; for, as the story runs, of the three wishes that Neptune had promised to grant him the third was this: in a fit of anger he prayed for the death of Hippolytus, and the granting of this prayer plunged him into unspeakable grief. Promises are, therefore, not to be kept, if the keeping of them is to prove harmful to those to whom you have made them; and, if the fulfilment of a promise should do more harm to you than good to him to whom you have made it, it is no violation of moral duty to give the greater good precedence over the lesser good. For example, if you have made an appointment with anyone to appear as his advocate in court, and if in the meantime your son should fall dangerously ill, it would be no breach of your moral duty to fail in what you agreed to do; nay, rather, he to whom your promise was given would have a false conception of duty, if he should complain that he had been deserted in his time of need. Further than this, who fails to see that those promises are not binding which are extorted by intimidation or which we make when misled by false pretences? Such obligations are annulled in most cases by the praetor's edict in equity, in some cases by the laws.

Injustice often arises also through chicanery, 33 that is, through an over-subtle and even fraudulent construction of the law. This it is that gave rise to the now familiar saw, "More law, less justice." Through such interpretation also a great deal of wrong is committed in transactions between state and state; thus, when a truce had been made with the enemy for thirty days, a famous general went to ravaging their fields by night, because, he said, the truce stipulated "days," not nights. Not even our own countryman's action is to be commended, if what is told of Quintus Fabius Labeo is true – or whoever it was (for I have no authority but hearsay): appointed by the Senate to arbitrate a boundary dispute between Nola and Naples, he took up the case and interviewed both parties separately, asking them not to proceed in a covetous or grasping spirit, but to make some concession rather than claim some accession. When each party had agreed to this, there was a considerable strip of territory left between them. And so he set the boundary of each city as each had severally agreed; and the tract in between he awarded to the Roman People. Now that is swindling, not arbitration. And therefore such sharp practice is under all circumstances to be avoided.

XI. Again, there are certain duties that we owe even to those who have wronged us. For there is a limit to retribution and to punishment; or rather, I am inclined to think, it is sufficient that the aggressor should be brought to repent of his wrong-doing, in order that he may not repeat the offence and that others may be deterred from doing wrong.

Then, too, in the case of a state in its external 34 relations, the rights of war must be strictly observed. For since there are two ways of settling a dispute: first, by discussion; second, by physical force; and since the former is characteristic of man, the latter of the brute, we must resort to force only in case we may not avail ourselves 35 of discussion. The only excuse, therefore, for going to war is that we may live in peace unharmed; and when the victory is won, we should spare those who have not been blood-thirsty and barbarous in their warfare. For instance, our forefathers actually admitted to full rights of citizenship the Tusculans, Aequians, Volscians, Sabines, and Hernicians, but they razed Carthage and Numantia to the ground. I wish they had not destroyed Corinth; but I believe they had some special reason for what they did – its convenient situation, probably – and feared that its very location might some day furnish a temptation to renew the war. In my opinion, at least, we should always strive to secure a peace that shall not admit of guile. And if my advice had been heeded on this point, we should still have at least some sort of constitutional government, if not the best in the world, whereas, as it is, we have none at all.

Not only must we show consideration for those whom we have conquered by force of arms but we must also ensure protection to those who lay down their arms and throw themselves upon the mercy of our generals, even though the battering-ram has hammered at their walls. And among our countrymen justice has been observed so conscientiously in this direction, that those who have given promise of protection to states or nations subdued in war become, after the custom of our forefathers, the patrons of those states.

36   As for war, humane laws touching it are drawn up in the fetial code of the Roman People under all the guarantees of religion; and from this it may be gathered that no war is just, unless it is entered upon after an official demand for satisfaction has been submitted or warning has been given and a formal declaration made. Popilius was general in command of a province. In his army Cato's son was serving on his first campaign. When Popilius decided to disband one of his legions, he discharged also young Cato, who was serving in that same legion. But when the young man out of love for the service stayed on in the field, his father wrote to Popilius to say that if he let him stay in the army, he should swear him into service with a new oath of allegiance, for in view of the voidance of his former oath he could not legally fight the foe. So extremely scrupulous was the observance of the

37   laws in regard to the conduct of war. There is extant, too, a letter of the elder Marcus Cato to his son Marcus, in which he writes that he has heard that the youth has been discharged by the consul, when he was serving in Macedonia in the war with Perseus. He warns him, therefore, to be careful not to go into battle; for, he says, the man who is not legally a soldier has no right to be fighting the foe.

XII.   This also I observe – that he who would properly have been called "a fighting enemy" (*perduellis*) was called "a guest" (*hostis*), thus relieving the ugliness of the fact by a softened expression; for "enemy" (*hostis*) meant to our ancestors what we now call "stranger" (*peregrinus*). This is proved by the usage in the Twelve Tables: "Or a day fixed for trial with a stranger" (*hostis*). And again: "Right of ownership is inalienable for ever in dealings with a stranger" (*hostis*). What can exceed such charity, when he with whom one is at war is called by so gentle a name? And yet long lapse of time has given that word a harsher meaning: for it has lost its signification of "stranger" and has taken on the technical connotation of "an enemy under arms."

But when a war is fought out for suprem-   38 acy and when glory is the object of war, it must still not fail to start from the same motives which I said a moment ago were the only righteous grounds for going to war. But those wars which have glory for their end must be carried on with less bitterness. For we contend, for example, with a fellow-citizen in one way, if he is a personal enemy, in another, if he is a rival: with the rival it is a struggle for office and position, with the enemy for life and honour. So with the Celtiberians and the Cimbrians we fought as with deadly enemies, not to determine which should be supreme, but which should survive; but with the Latins, Sabines, Samnites, Carthaginians, and Pyrrhus we fought for supremacy. The Carthaginians violated treaties; Hannibal was cruel; the others were more merciful. From Pyrrhus we have this famous speech on the exchange of prisoners:

"Gold will I none, nor price shall ye give; for I
    ask none;
Come, let us not be chaff'rers of war, but
    warriors embattled.
Nay; let us venture our lives, and the sword, not
    gold, weigh the outcome.
Make we the trial by valour in arms and see if
    Dame Fortune
Wills it that ye shall prevail or I, or what be her
    judgment.
Hear thou, too, this word, good Fabricius:
    whose valour soever
Spared hath been by the fortune of war – their
    freedom I grant them.
Such my resolve. I give and present them to
    you, my brave Romans;

Take them back to their homes; the great gods'
   blessings attend you."

A right kingly sentiment this and worthy a scion
of the Aeacidae.

39   XIII.   Again, if under stress of circumstances
individuals have made any promise to the enemy,
they are bound to keep their word even then. For
instance, in the First Punic War, when Regulus
was taken prisoner by the Carthaginians, he was
sent to Rome on parole to negotiate an exchange
of prisoners; he came and, in the first place, it
was he that made the motion in the Senate that
the prisoners should not be restored; and in the
second place, when his relatives and friends
would have kept him back, he chose to return to
a death by torture rather than prove false to his
promise, though given to an enemy.

40   And again in the Second Punic War, after the
Battle of Cannae, Hannibal sent to Rome ten
Roman captives bound by an oath to return
to him, if they did not succeed in ransoming his
prisoners; and as long as any one of them lived,
the censors kept them all degraded and disfran-
chised, because they were guilty of perjury in not
returning. And they punished in like manner the
one who had incurred guilt by an evasion of his
oath: with Hannibal's permission this man left
the camp and returned a little later on the pretext that he had forgotten something or other; and
then, when he left the camp the second time, he
claimed that he was released from the obligation

of his oath; and so he was, according to the letter of it, but not according to the spirit. In the
matter of a promise one must always consider the
meaning and not the mere words.

Our forefathers have given us another striking
example of justice toward an enemy: when a
deserter from Pyrrhus promised the Senate to
administer poison to the king and thus work his
death, the Senate and Gaius Fabricius delivered
the deserter up to Pyrrhus. Thus they stamped with
their disapproval the treacherous murder even
of an enemy who was at once powerful, un-
provoked, aggressive, and successful.

With this I will close my discussion of the 41
duties connected with war.

But let us remember that we must have regard
for justice even towards the humblest. Now the
humblest station and the poorest fortune are
those of slaves; and they give us no bad rule who
bid us treat our slaves as we should our employ-
ees: they must be required to work; they must be
given their dues.

While wrong may be done, then, in either of
two ways, that is, by force or by fraud, both are
bestial: fraud seems to belong to the cunning
fox, force to the lion; both are wholly unworthy
of man, but fraud is the more contemptible. But
of all forms of injustice, none is more flagrant than
that of the hypocrite who, at the very moment
when he is most false, makes it his business to
appear virtuous.

This must conclude our discussion of justice.

8

Marcus Aurelius,
The Meditations (selections)

Introduction

Marcus Aurelius (121–180) was the adopted son of Antoninus Pius, whom he reluctantly succeeded as Roman Emperor in 161 CE. This reluctance was due to a desire to spend a peaceful life immersed in books and philosophy and a fear that the life of an emperor would frustrate that desire. His fears were well founded, for most of his 20-year reign was spent leading his armies in the defense against invaders launching attacks across the northeastern borders of the empire. It was, in fact, during such a military expedition in the Danube region that Marcus died.

Inevitably, Marcus Aurelius has been described as a – or even *the* – real-life "philosopher-king." Certainly he was both a ruler and a philosopher, but the label is nevertheless misleading. As Marcus himself wrote, "Do not expect Plato's ideal republic; be satisfied with the smallest step forward" (9.29). It was never his ambition to devise a new constitution or an ideological blueprint for the Roman Empire; and if he ruled "philosophically" this was only in the sense of resigning himself, in the manner of the Stoic he was, to the conscientious execution of his duties as emperor and general. In those "Exhortations to Myself," which have come to be called "The Meditations,"

From Marcus Aurelius, *The Meditations*, trans. G. M. A. Grube, Indianapolis, IN: Hackett Publishing Co., 1983, pp. 19–48, 86–7 (notes omitted).

we encounter an often world-weary and overworked man in intimate conversation with himself. There is not, incidentally, any strong reason to think that Marcus's thoughts, dark as some of them are, were written down under the influence of opium, or were the splenetic products of an ulcer condition, as some imaginative commentators have suggested. In effect, as Pierre Hadot explains, Marcus's meditations were "spiritual exercises," devices for the encouragement of a properly philosophical life, in which action, judgment, desire, and emotion are all under rational control.[1] For example, the rather brutal definitions offered of sex and other enjoyments (e.g. 6.13) are to be taken as devices to discourage over-attachment to such pleasures.

Marcus was the third great Stoic thinker, after the wealthy patrician Seneca (4–65) and the freed slave Epictetus (c. 55–c. 135), of the Roman imperial epoch, and in *The Meditations* one encounters all the main doctrines of Stoicism originally articulated by the Hellenist thinkers, Zeno of Citium (c. 334–262 BCE) and Chrysippus (c. 280–c. 270 BCE), 400 years earlier. According to all these philosophers, the universe is a rational material whole, ordered by the *logos* for the maximum good of that whole. As such, everything that occurs in the universe is fated to occur, since it is a necessary ingredient in the overall rational good. Like his Roman predecessors, Marcus is less concerned to elaborate on this Stoic cosmology than to identify and to encourage the appropriate response to these cosmological truths by human beings. The response of the Stoic sage is to treat as matters of "indifference" (*adiaphora*) whatever is not under his or her autonomous control. This, given the doctrine of fate, will be everything other than one's inner mental states. Pleasure and pain, health and illness, living and dying – these are all "indifferent," since they are under the sovereign control of the individual (see 9.1). The sage's focus, then, will be on the cultivation of appropriate inner states – warranted beliefs, for example, and reasonable emotions. In the sphere of moral action, the Stoic position anticipates Immanuel Kant's notion of "the good will" (I.15). The sole morally admirable feature of an action is the sense of duty out of which it is performed. The consequences of the action are morally irrelevant.

Marcus differs from some earlier Stoics in the emphasis he places on obligations to try to promote the good of one's community or society – ones which, on the surface, might seem to conflict with the obligation to cultivate one's inner states. In a spirit more Aristotelian, perhaps, than Stoic,

Marcus's thought is that no one can achieve his or her own good – a proper set of virtuous inner states – except as a member of a community. "The good of a rational creature lies in a community . . . [for] we are born for association in a community" (5.16).

Marcus's meditations or exhortations were probably written down solely for his own edification, and do not have the structure and system one might expect from a book written for the instruction of others. Each of the 12 Books consists of relatively unconnected remarks on a range of topics. The passages we have selected, mostly from Books 3–5, provide a representative sample of Marcus's main reflections.

Note

1   P. Hadot, *Philosophy as a Way of Life*, trans. M. Chase, Oxford: Blackwell, 1995, Chapter 6.

Marcus Aurelius, *The Meditations*

Book III

[. . .]

4.   Do not waste what remains of your life thinking about other people, if these thoughts bear no relation to some common good. Why deprive yourself of some other task in order to do this: to imagine what so-and-so is doing and why, what he is saying, thinking or contriving, and other such things as keep you from observing your own directing reason. The sequence of your thoughts should avoid vain and random fancies, interference and malice above all. You must accustom yourself to think only such thoughts as would enable you, when asked what you are thinking, frankly to answer "this" or "that." Your answer would make clear that all your thoughts were simple and kind, as becomes a social being who is not concerned with pleasures or any sensuous delights of the imagination, or with rivalry, slander, suspicion, or anything else which you would blush to reveal that you had in mind.

Such a man no longer puts off joining the company of the best; he is priest and servant to the gods, he has the right relationship with the spirit established within him, which makes him a man uncorrupted by pleasure, unwounded by pain, untouched by violence, immune to evil and a contender for the greatest prize, which is: not to be overcome by any passion, to be deeply steeped in justice; to welcome one's lot and portion with one's whole soul; rarely, and then only when the common good makes it imperative, to imagine what another may be saying, doing, or thinking.

It is only with what is part of himself that a man can act, and only his own fate, assigned to him from the whole of Nature, which he can at all times reflect upon; his actions he makes beautiful; his fate, he is convinced, is good, for every man carries his appointed fate with him, and it carries him along. He also keeps in mind that all that is endowed with Reason is akin, and that while it is in accordance with man's nature to care for all men, he must not be swayed by the opinion of all men, but only by that of those who live in agreement with nature. As for those who do not live in such agreement, he will have it in mind always what kind of men they are at home and abroad, by night and by day, and what tainted company they keep. Praise from such men he will think of no account, for they are not content even with themselves.

[. . .]

6. If you find in human life something better than justice, truth, self-control, courage, something better, in a word, than that your mind should be contented with itself when it makes you act according to the rule of Reason and contented with your destiny in what is allotted to you without any choice – if, I say, you see something better than this, then turn to it with all your soul and enjoy this best which you have found. But if nothing is shown to be better than the divine spirit itself which is established within you, the spirit which brings your private impulses under its dominion, scrutinizes your impressions and, as Socrates said, withdraws itself from the emotions of sense; a spirit which subordinates itself to the service of the gods and takes thought for men; if then you find all other things unimportant and paltry in comparison, then give no place to anything else in your thoughts, for if you incline and lean toward anything else you will no longer be able without distraction to give the place of honor to that good which is peculiarly your own.

It is not lawful for anything different – be it the praise of men, offices of power, wealth, or the enjoyment of pleasures – to stand in the way of what is reasonable and for the common good. All these things, even if for a while they seem to accord with the good life, suddenly overwhelm one and lead one astray. Do you, I say, in freedom and simplicity choose the better part and cling to it. "But the better is the advantageous." If you mean to your advantage as a reasonable being, give heed to it, but if you mean to your advantage as an animal creature, say so, and keep to your decision without vanity. Only see to it that your examination of the question be without danger to yourself.

[. . .]

10. Discard all else; cling to these few things only. Remember, moreover, that each man lives only this present moment; as for the rest, either it has been lived in the past or it is but an uncertain future. Small is the moment which each man lives, small too the corner of the earth which he inhabits; even the greatest posthumous fame is small, and it too depends upon a succession of short-lived men who will die very soon, who do not know even themselves, let alone one who died long ago.

11. To the above advice one thing must yet be added: always to define or describe to oneself the object of our perceptions so that we can grasp its essential nature unadorned, a separate and distinct whole, to tell oneself its particular name as well as the names of the elements from which it was made and into which it will be dissolved.

Nothing is more conducive to high-mindedness than the capacity to examine methodically and with truth everything that one meets in life, and to observe it in such a manner as to understand the nature of the universe, the usefulness of each thing within it, and the value of each in relation to the Whole and in relation to man as a citizen of that Whole, the greatest city of which other cities are but households. What is this which now makes an impression on me? What elements went into its making? How long is it meant to last? And again, what virtue can be employed in dealing with it – be it gentleness or courage, or truthfulness, loyalty, simplicity, self-sufficiency and the rest?

Therefore one must say in each case: This comes from the gods, or this is in accordance with the pattern of the fates' weaving or with the structure of events and chance; that other comes from a man of the same tribe and kin and community as I, but one who does not know what, for him, is according to nature, whereas I do know. Therefore I deal with him in accordance with the law of our common nature, kindly and justly, but at the same time I aim at his true deserts in the dispensing of things in themselves neither good nor evil.

[. . .]

16. Body, soul, mind. Sense perceptions are of the body, desires of the soul, doctrines of the mind. To receive sense impressions belongs also to cattle; the jerks on the leading strings of desires are felt also by wild beasts, by male prostitutes, by a Phalaris or a Nero; the direction of the mind in what they believe to be their duty is accepted by unbelievers, traitors, and those

who commit any crime behind closed doors. If then all else is shared by those mentioned, there remains as characteristic of the good man that he loves and welcomes whatever happens to him and whatever his fate may bring, that he does not pollute the spirit established within his breast or confuse it with a mass of impressions and imaginings, but preserves it blameless, modestly following the divine, saying nothing but what is true, doing nothing but what is just.

If all men refuse to believe that he lives a simple, self-respecting and cheerful life, he will feel no resentment against anyone, nor will he be diverted from the path which leads him to the end of life; and to this he must come pure, calm, ready for release, and attuned without compulsion to his fate.

Book IV

[. . .]

2.   Let no action be done at random, or in any other way than in accordance with the principle which perfects the art.

3.   Men seek retreats for themselves in country places, on beaches and mountains, and you yourself are wont to long for such retreats, but that is altogether unenlightened when it is possible at any hour you please to find a retreat within yourself. For nowhere can a man withdraw to a more untroubled quietude than in his own soul, especially a man who has within him things of which the contemplation will at once put him perfectly at ease, and by ease I mean nothing other than orderly conduct. Grant yourself this withdrawal continually, and refresh yourself. Let these be brief and elemental doctrines which when present will suffice to overwhelm all sorrows and to send you back no longer resentful of the things to which you return.

For what is it you resent? The wickedness of men? Reflect on the conclusion that rational beings are born for the sake of each other, that tolerance is a part of righteousness, and that men do not sin on purpose. Consider how many men have been hostile and suspicious, have hated and waged war, and then been laid out for burial or reduced to ashes. Desist then. Do you resent the portions received from the whole? Consider the alternatives afresh, namely "Provid-

ence or atoms,"[1] and how many proofs there are that the universe is like a city community. Are you still affected by the things of the body? Reflect that the mind, once it has freed itself and come to know its own capacities, is no longer involved in the movements of animal life, whether these be smooth or tumultuous. For the rest, recall all you have heard about pain and pleasure, to which you have given assent.

Does paltry fame disturb you? Look how swift is the forgetting of all things in the chaos of infinite time before and after, how empty is noisy applause, how liable to change and uncritical are those who seem to speak well of us, how narrow the boundaries within which fame is confined. The whole earth is but a point in the universe, and how small a part of the earth is the corner in which you live. And how many are those who there will praise you, and what sort of men are they?

From now on keep in mind the retreat into this little territory within yourself. Avoid spasms and tensions above all; be free and look at your troubles like a man, a citizen and a mortal creature. Among the foremost things which you will look into are these two: first, that external matters do not affect the soul but stand quietly outside it, while true disturbances come from the inner judgment; second, that everything you see has all but changed already and is no more. Keep constantly in mind in how many things you yourself have witnessed changes already. The universe is change, life is understanding.

4.   If we have intelligence in common, so we have reason which makes us reasoning beings, and that practical reason which orders what we must or must not do; then the law too is common to us and, if so, we are citizens; if so, we share a common government; if so, the universe is, as it were, a city – for what other common government could one say is shared by all mankind?

From this, the common city, we derive our intelligence, our reason and our law – from what else? Just as the dry earth-element in me has been portioned off from earth somewhere, and the water in me from the other element, the air or breath from some other source and the dry and fiery from a source of its own (for nothing comes from what does not exist or returns to it), so also then the intelligence comes from somewhere.

5.   Death, like birth, is a mystery of nature. The one is a joining together of the same elements into which the other is a dissolving. In any case, it is

nothing of which one should be ashamed, for it is not incompatible with the nature of a rational being or the logic of its composition.

6. Their nature inevitably required that they behave in this way. He who wants this not to be wants a fig tree not to produce its acrid juice. In any case remember this: within a very short time both you and he will have died, and soon not even your name will survive.

7. Discard the thought of injury, and the words "I have been injured" are gone; discard the words "I have been injured," and the injury is gone.

8. What does not make a man worse does not make his life worse, and does him no injury, external or internal.

9. The nature of the universally beneficial has inevitably brought this about.

10. "Everything which happens, is right." Examine this saying carefully and you will find it so. I do not mean right merely in the sense that it fits the pattern of events, but in the sense of just, as if someone were giving each his due. Examine this then as you have begun to do, and, whatever you do, do it as a good man should, as the word good is properly understood. Safeguard this goodness in your every action.

[. . .]

14. You exist but as a part of the Whole. You will disappear into the Whole which created you, or rather you will be taken up into the creative Reason when the change comes.

[. . .]

19. The man who thrills at the thought of later fame fails to realize that every one of those who remember him will very shortly die, as well as himself. So will their successors, until all memory of him is quenched as it travels through the minds of men, the flame of whose life is lit and then put out. But suppose those who will remember you to be immortal and the memory of you everlasting; even so, what is it to you? And I do not mean that praise is nothing to you when dead, but what is it to you while you live, except insofar as it affects your management of affairs? For now you inopportunely neglect nature's gift of virtue while you cling to some other concern.

[. . .]

23. Everything which is in tune with you, O Universe, is in tune with me. Nothing which happens at the right time for you is early or late for me. Everything, O Nature, which your seasons produce is fruit to me. All things come from you, exist in you, and will return to you.

[. . .]

26. You have seen those things; look also at these: do not disturb yourself, achieve simplicity in yourself. Someone does wrong? The wrong is to himself. Something has happened to you? It is well. From the beginning all that happens has been ordained and fated for you as your part of the Whole. In a word, life is short; we must therefore derive benefit from the present circumstances with prudence and with justice. Be sober and relaxed.

[. . .]

33. [. . .]

What is it which should earnestly concern us? This only: a just mind, actions for the common good, speech which never lies, and a disposition which welcomes all that happens as necessary and comprehensible, as flowing from a like origin and source.

[. . .]

36. Observe continually all that is born through change, and accustom yourself to reflect that the nature of the Whole loves nothing so much as to change existing things and to make similar new things. All that exists is in a sense the seed of what will be born from it, but you regard as seeds only those which are cast into the earth or the womb. But that is too unenlightened.

[. . .]

39. Whether a thing is bad for you does not depend upon another man's directing mind, nor upon any turn or change in your environment. Upon what then? Upon that part of you which judges what is bad. Let it make no such judgment and all is well. Even when that which is closest to it, your body, is cut, burnt, suppurating or festering, let the judging part of you keep calm.

That is, let it judge that anything which happens equally to a bad and a good man cannot be either bad or good; for that which happens both to the man who lives in disaccord with nature and to the man who lives in accord with it cannot itself be either in accord with nature or contrary to it.

40. One should continually think of the universe as one living being, with one substance and one soul – how all it contains falls under its one unitary perception, how all its actions derive from one impulse, how all things together cause all that happens, and the nature of the resulting web and pattern of events.

41. You are a little soul carrying a corpse, as Epictetus says.

42. There is no evil in things in process of change, nor any good in things resulting from change.

43. Time is a river of things that become, with a strong current. No sooner is a thing seen than it has been swept away, and something else is being carried past, and still another thing will follow.

44. Everything that happens is as customary and understandable as the rose in springtime or the fruit in summer. The same is true of disease, death, slander and conspiracy, and all the things which delight or pain foolish men.

45. What happens next is always intimately related to what went before. It is not a question of merely adding up disparate things connected by inevitable succession, but events are logically interdependent. Just as the realities are established in tune with one another, so, in the world of sense, phenomena do not occur merely in succession, but they display an amazing affinity with one another.

[. . .]

48. [. . .]

Go over in your mind the dead whom you have known, one after the other: one paid the last rites to a friend and was himself laid out for burial by a third, who also died; and all in a short time. Altogether, human affairs must be regarded as ephemeral, and of little worth: yesterday sperm, tomorrow a mummy or ashes. Journey then through this moment of time in accord with nature, and graciously depart, as a ripened olive might fall, praising the earth which produced it, grateful to the tree that made it grow.

49. Be like a rock against which the waves of the sea break unceasingly. It stands unmoved, and the feverish waters around it are stilled.

"I am unfortunate because this has happened to me." No indeed, but I am fortunate because I endure what has happened without grief, neither shaken by the present nor afraid of the future.

[. . .]

Remember in the future, when something happens which tends to make you grieve, to cling to this doctrine: this is no misfortune, but to endure it nobly is good fortune.

[. . .]

Book V

1. When, in the early morning, you are reluctant to get up, have this thought in mind: "I rise to do a man's work. Am I still resentful as I go to do the task for which I was born and for the sake of which I was brought into the world? Was I made to warm myself under the blankets?" "But this is more pleasant." Were you born for pleasure, to feel things, and not to do them? Do you not see plants, sparrows, ants, spiders and bees perform their proper task and contribute, as far as in them lies, to the order of the universe? Yet you refuse to perform man's task and you do not hasten to do what your nature demands. "But one must also rest." Certainly, I agree. Nature, however, has set a limit to rest, as it has to eating and drinking, and you go on resting beyond that limit, beyond what is sufficient. Not so with your actions, which remain well within the limits of what you could do.

You do not love yourself. If you did, you would certainly love your own nature and its purpose. Other men love their own craft and wear themselves out in the performance of it without bath or food. You love your own nature less than the metalworker loves the art of working metals, the dancer the art of dancing, the money-lover his money or the lover of glory his precious reputation. They, in their passionate eagerness, sacrifice food and sleep to promote the objects of their passion, whereas you believe public affairs to be less important and less deserving of devotion.

[...]

5.   Men cannot admire you for cleverness. Very well, but there are many other qualities of which you cannot say: "I have not the natural gift." Display then those virtues which are entirely within your power: sincerity, dignity, endurance of pain, indifference to pleasure, contentment, self-sufficiency, kindliness, freedom, simplicity, common sense, and magnanimity. Do you not see how many virtues can be yours which do not admit the excuse of lack of inborn talent or of inaptitude? And yet you are still willing to be inferior in them. Does any lack of natural talent compel you to grumble, to be grasping, to toady, to denounce your poor body, to curry favor, to be vulgarly complacent, or to be always undecided in your mind? No, by the gods. You could have rid yourself of all these faults long ago and only been convicted, if such is indeed the case, of being a somewhat dull and slow learner. And even a man's mind must be trained, unless he is satisfied to encourage his slowness of wit and to take pleasure in it.

[...]

8.   Just as we say that Asclepius prescribed horseback riding for someone, or cold baths, or walking barefoot, so we say that the nature of the Whole has prescribed disease for someone, or lameness, or loss of limb, or anything else of the same kind. In the first statement the word "prescribed" is used with much the same meaning as in the second. Asclepius orders something as contributing to health, and what happens to every individual is somehow ordered for him as contributing to his destiny. We say these things "happen" to us as builders say that square stones "happen" to fit into walls and pyramids when in a certain position. For there is one universal harmony, and, as out of all bodies the universe is composed into one harmonious body, so out of all the causes the one harmonious fated cause is perfected. Even the quite unenlightened grasp my meaning for they say: "This was his lot." Thus this was allotted to him and ordered for him. Let us then accept these happings as we accept

those prescriptions of Asclepius, for some of them too are harsh, but we welcome them, hoping for health.

You must consider the doing and perfecting of what the universal Nature decrees in the same light as your health, and welcome all that happens, even if it seems harsh, because it leads to the health of the universe, the welfare and well-being of Zeus. For he would not have allotted this to anyone if it were not beneficial to the Whole. No sort of nature brings anything to pass which does not contribute to that which it governs. You must therefore welcome with love what happens to you, for two reasons: first, because it happens to you, is prescribed for you, is related to you, a fate spun for you from above by the most venerable of causes; second, because whatever comes to an individual is a cause of the well-being and the welfare, indeed of the permanence, of that which governs the Whole. For the whole universe is maimed if you sever anything whatever from the coalescing continuity of its parts, and the same is true of its causes. Yet you do sever something, insofar as it is in your power to do so, whenever you are discontented, and in a way you destroy that continuity.

[...]

10.   The truth of things is, we might say, so wrapped in obscurity that not a few philosophers, and those not the least, have thought it altogether beyond understanding, while the Stoics themselves think it hard to grasp. Every judgment we make is fallible, for where is there an infallible man? Next, consider the things themselves, how short-lived they are, how unimportant, how they can be acquired by a male prostitute, a whore, or a thief. After this, consider the characters of your associates, of which even the most charming is hard to tolerate, not to mention that a man finds it hard to tolerate his own character. In such darkness and dirt, in such a changing stream of existence, time, movement, and moving things, I do not see what there is to be honored or even to be seriously pursued at all. On the contrary, one should exhort oneself to await natural dissolution, not to chafe at delay but to find refreshment in these reflections only: first, "Nothing will happen to me which is not in accord with the nature of the Whole," and second, "It is possible for me to do nothing contrary to the god and the spirit within

me, for there is no one who can compel me to do so."

[...]

15. A man should give no heed to those things which do not belong to man's portion as a human being. They are not demanded of man, the nature of man does not proclaim them, nor do they make his nature more complete. Man does not find his end in them, nor the means to that end, which is the good. Moreover, if any of these things were proper to man, then neither contempt for them nor neglect of them could be proper to him; we would not praise one who shows he does not need them; nor could one who is not at his best in dealing with one or other of them be a good man, if these things were good. As it is, the more a man does without them or allows himself to be deprived of them, the better man he is.

16. The kind of thoughts you frequently have will make your mind of the same kind, for your mind is dyed by your thoughts. Color your mind therefore with a succession of thoughts like these, for example: Where it is possible to live, it is also possible to live the good life; it is possible to live in a palace, therefore it is also possible to live the good life in a palace. Or again: each thing is made with that in view for the sake of which it was made; it is drawn towards that for which it was made; its end is found in that to which it is drawn; and where its end is, there too the advantage and the good of each is to be found. Now the good of a rational creature lies in a community, and it has long ago been shown that we are born for association in a community. For surely it is clear that the inferior exist for the sake of the better, and the better for the sake of each other. Now what is endowed with life is better than what is lifeless, and what is endowed with Reason is better than the merely alive.

[...]

19. Things cannot in themselves touch the soul at all; they have no entrance to it, cannot deflect or move it; it is the soul alone which deflects or moves itself, and it fashions external events to depend upon the judgment which it deems itself worthy to make about them.

20. In one way man is very close to us, insofar as we must do good to him and tolerate him,

but insofar as some men stand in the way of my proper duties, man is among things indifferent to me, no less than the sun, the wind or a wild beast. These can hinder some action, but they can be no obstacle to our desire or our state of mind because of our power of remaining uncommitted and of adaptation. The mind adapts any obstacle and turns it into a means toward its preferred aim, so that what hinders a particular action becomes a means to action, and an obstacle on a particular path becomes a help.

21. Honor that which is the best of all things in the universe [ie. Reason – Ed.]; it makes use of all and governs all. Similarly, of things within you, honor that which is the best, and it is that which is akin to that other, for in your case too it is that which uses all else, and your life is directed by it.

22. What brings no harm to the community does not harm its members. Whenever you think you have been injured, apply this rule: if the community is not hurt by it, then neither have I been hurt. If, on the other hand, the community has been hurt, you should not be angry, but point out to him who hurt it what he has overlooked.

23. Reflect frequently on the swiftness with which things that are, or come to be, flow past and are carried away, for existence is like a river in perpetual flow; activities change continually; causes vary in innumerable ways; even that which is close to you hardly endures at all. The infinity of past and future time is a chasm in which all things vanish. Surely it is foolish for a man to be puffed up in the midst of this, to be excited or distressed as if his surroundings endured or his troubles were lasting.

24. Think of existence as a whole, in which you have a very small share; think of eternity, of which a brief and momentary portion has been allotted to you; think of destiny and how small a part of it is yours.

[...]

26. Your directing mind, the ruler of your soul, must remain unaffected by the activity of your flesh, whether painful or pleasurable. It must not mingle with it but stay within its own frontiers and confine the affections of the body to their own sphere. When, however, these affections reach the mind through the other channel of common

feeling, since both exist in a body organically one, then we should not resist this perception of them, since it is natural; but the directing mind should not add to this any judgment of its own as to whether the bodily affections are good or bad.

[. . .]

30. The intelligence of the Whole has the common good in view. Therefore it has fashioned the inferior for the sake of the higher, and brought the higher into harmony with each other. You see how it has put some below, others beside one another, and given each his due, and brought the ruling ones together to be of one mind.

[. . .]

33. We shall very soon be only ashes or dry bones, merely a name or not even a name, while a name in any case is only a noise and an echo. The things much honored in life are vain, corruptible, and of no import. The living are like puppies who bite, or quarrelsome children who laugh and then immediately weep. [. . .] What is it which holds us here, if indeed the objects of sense are ever changing and last not, the senses themselves are blurred and variable as wax, our soul is but an exhalation from the blood, and good repute among such is vain? What holds us? To await death with good grace, whether it be extinction or a going elsewhere. And until the time for it comes, what suffices? What else but to honor the gods and praise them, to do good to men, bear with them and forbear. As for all that lies within the limits of mere flesh and mere life, remember that none of it belongs to you or is within your power.

[. . .]

36. Do not be entirely swept along by the thought of another's grief. Help him as far as you can and as the case deserves, even if he is overwhelmed by the loss of indifferent things. Do not, however, imagine that he is suffering a real injury, for to develop that habit is a vice. Rather be like the old man who went off to beg for his foster child's top, fully aware that it was only a top; so must you do likewise. Well, then, when you are seen weeping on the rostrum, my good

man, have you forgotten what these things are worth? "Yes, but these men do long for them." Is that any reason for you also to be foolish?

[. . .]

Book IX

1. Wrongdoing is impious, for the nature of the Whole has fashioned rational creatures for each other's sake, so that they should benefit each other as they deserve but never injure one another. The man who transgresses its intent is clearly guilty of impiety toward the oldest of divinities, for the universal nature is the nature of ultimate realities, and these are closely related to all that now exists.

The man who speaks untruth is impious toward the same goddess, for her name is Truth and she is the first cause of all that is true. The deliberate liar is therefore impious insofar as he wrongs people by deceiving them, and the involuntary liar is also impious insofar as he is out of tune with the nature of the Whole and brings disorder as he struggles against the nature of the orderly universe. He who on his own initiative is carried towards the opposite of what is true does struggle against this. He received his original impulses from nature, and it is through neglecting them that he is no longer able to distinguish the false from the true.

And indeed the man who pursues pleasure as good, and avoids pain as evil, is impious also. He must needs reproach the common nature frequently for distributing something unfairly between inferior and good men, since inferior men often enjoy pleasures and possess the means to attain them, while good men are often involved in pain and in things that produce pain.

Then again, the man who is afraid of pain will at times be afraid of something that is to happen in the world, and this is already impious. Further, the pleasure seeker will not refrain from wrongdoing, which is obviously impious.

With regard to those things toward which the common nature is indifferent (for she would not create both pains and pleasures if she were not indifferent to both), those who would follow nature and be of like mind with her must also be indifferent. Whoever is not himself indifferent to pain and pleasure or to life and death, or to reputation and the lack of it – things which the nature of the Whole uses indifferently – is clearly impious.

When I say that the common nature uses these things indifferently, I mean that they happen in due sequence and without difference to those who now are living, and to their posterity, and are caused by some long past impulse of Providence. In accordance with this impulse and from a first principle Providence started the process which culminated in the present orderliness of the universe; for Providence had grasped certain rational, creative principles of what was to be, and marked out certain powers generative of substances, changes, and things of the same kind to succeed them.

[...]

3.   Do not despise death, but find satisfaction in it, since it is one of the things which nature intends. As are youth and age, adolescence and maturity, growing teeth and beard and gray hairs, begetting, gestation, and giving birth, and the other natural activities of the different seasons of life, such too is dissolution. This then is the thoughtful human attitude to death: not exaggerated or violent or arrogant, but to await it as one of nature's activities, as now you wait for the time when the embryo will leave your wife's womb. Welcome in the same way the time when your soul will leave its present shell.

[...]

Note

1   The alternatives referred to here are the Stoic conception of the universe as governed by Reason or Providence and the Epicurean view – most fully expounded by Lucretius (first century BCE) in *On the Nature of the Universe* – that it is a chance conglomeration of atoms.

(A)   Śāntideva, *The Bodhicaryāvatāra*, Chapter 8, verses 89–140
(B)   Tsongkapa and Pabongka Rinpoche, "The Second Path: The Wish to Achieve Enlightenment for Every Living Being"

Introduction

In recent years, Buddhism has won many converts in the West. It appears to offer a perspective that is at once religious and free from the theistic notion, unacceptable to many modern minds, of a personal creator-God. But its attraction owes, as well, to a moral doctrine of universal compassion that knows no boundaries of nation, class, sex or even species. The exhortation, "whatever living beings there be: feeble or strong . . . seen or unseen . . . far or near . . . may all beings be happy!"[1] seems more congenial to the modern sensibility than the Gita's call (I.6) to the performance of duties, military ones included, for their own sake.

The importance of compassion and "loving-kindness" seems to be implied by the first of the "four noble truths" announced by Gotama, the Buddha, in the fifth century BCE – that life is "suffering," "sorrow," "dis-ease," "unsatisfactoriness" (just some of the suggested translations of the Pali word *dukkha*). But other Buddhist

doctrines make it problematic as to why and how moral concern should have a central role. The other noble truths suggest that it is essentially through understanding and wisdom that "suffering" is to be overcome – through, above all, recognizing that the desires or "cravings" which are responsible for "suffering" are due to a mistaken "clinging" to a nonexistent "self." Morality, it can seem, is at most a useful preparation for that "renunciation" of self-centered desire which is a prerequisite for entry into the enlightened condition of *nirvana* ("extinction").[2] Moreover, one is bound to ask, if this "extinction," this release from the round of rebirth, is the proper goal, why should one care too much about improving conditions for creatures still caught up in this process? Anyway, if a person is "not-self," but perhaps merely a bundle of passing mental states without any center of identity, to whom exactly are compassion and loving-kindness directed?

It is unsurprising, therefore, that some commentators, such as Max Weber and Albert Schweitzer, have regarded Buddhism as a "cold," amoral religion – and certainly in the Theravada tradition of Buddhism, the emphasis, it is alleged by critics, has tended to be upon renunciation and asceticism rather than moral action.[3] But in the Mahayana ("Great Vehicle") tradition which arose in opposition to the earlier one, a central tenet is that of universal compassion, understood as a loving commitment to help all creatures escape from "suffering." The pledge of the

(A) *From* Śāntideva, *The Bodhicaryāvatāra*, trans. K. Crosby and A. Skilton. Oxford: Oxford University Press, 1996, pp. 96–100. (B) *From* Tsongkapa, *The Principal Teachings of Buddhism*, with a commentary by Pabongka Rinpoche, trans. I. Tharchin and M. Roach. Howell, NJ: Mahayana Sutra and Tantra Press, 1988, pp. 93–104 (some passages omitted).

bodhisattva ("the being of enlightenment") who postpones his or her attainment of *nirvana*, is this: "However numerous are the sentient beings that exist, I vow to save them all!"[4]

While there are many moral "manuals" in the Buddhist literature, edifying precepts enjoining temperance, charity, friendship and so on, there is a dearth of sustained discussion attempting to reconcile the importance of morality with the doctrines mentioned above. In our two selections – both from the Mahayana tradition – one discerns, however, arguments for universal compassion compatible with, or even grounded in, those doctrines. In his commentary on the poem, *Three Principal Paths* by the most famous Buddhist philosopher of Tibet, Tsongkapa (1357–1419), the monk and university teacher Pabongka Rinpoche (1878–1941) mentions two methods of "training one's mind" for aiming at "saving" all creatures – (a) the "seven-part, cause-and-effect instruction" and (b) "exchanging self and others." It is the former which he adumbrates, the latter being the main theme in the selection from the eighth-century CE Indian monk Śāntideva's "Guide to the Buddhist Path to Awakening," "one of the great spiritual poems of mankind" and a text especially influential in Tibetan Buddhism.[5] Although both authors speak of "methods" for inducing a compassionate attitude, we might instead think of these as arguments for why one *ought to* adopt such an attitude.

The two "methods" or arguments are, we think, fairly self-explanatory: both aim to cultivate a "selfless" or "neutral" attitude toward others and ourselves. In the Tibetan text, the argument is based on our relationships with other people in past and future lives. This raises the question of the relevance of such arguments to those non-Buddhists who are unable to accept the doctrine of rebirth. Readers are invited to try amending the arguments, to treat them as grounded in reflections not on how we *actually* were and will be related to other people in past and future lives, but on how we *might* have been related to them in this one. Instead, for example, of reflecting, like Tsongkapa, that this woman, whom I may be treating badly, was my mother in a previous life, reflect on the facts that she *might* have been my mother in this one and that she probably is the mother of someone who *might* have been my best friend.

A residual worry may be that, for all the talk of selfless compassion, the motive for it remains a selfish one – ensuring *nirvana* for oneself. But, as a great commentator pointed out, "if a Buddhist undergoes the discipline that leads to *nirvana* ... it is in order to diminish by one the number of living and suffering beings."[6] In other words, someone with a selfless or neutral attitude will regard his or her own future lives as just one more series of "bundles of suffering," no more, but no less, deserving of compassion than any other. Moreover, as Śāntideva reminds us (e.g. verse 98), the doctrine of "not-self" entails that these future lives are not in any substantial sense "mine," but only loosely continuous with "my" present one, so that aiming to forestall them (by achieving *nirvana*) is no more egocentric than it is altruistic.[7]

Notes

1 *The Sutta-Nipata*, London: Curzon Press, 1985, I.8.4–5.
2 Compare with the neo-Platonic transcendence of the self (I.10).
3 In the authoritative Theravada treatise, Buddhaghosa's *The Path of Purification*, Kandy: Buddhist Publication Society, 1991, "virtue" is only the first stage, before "concentration" and "understanding," on this path. But see Steven Collins, *Selfless Persons*, Cambridge: Cambridge University Press, pp. 194ff. on not exaggerating the difference between the two traditions.
4 Quoted in H. Dumoulin, *Understanding Buddhism*, New York: Weatherhill, 1994, p. 76.
5 P. Williams, *Mayahana Buddhism: The Doctrinal Foundations*, London: Routledge, 1989, p. 198.
6 Louis de la Vallée Poussin, quoted in Collins, *Selfless Persons, op. cit*, p. 193.
7 For an interesting attempt by a modern Western philosopher to explore the implications of something like the Buddhist "not-self" doctrine, see Derek Parfit, *Reasons and Persons*, Oxford: Clarendon Press, 1984.

(A) Śāntideva, *The Bodhicaryāvatāra*

Chapter 8

[. . .]

89 By developing the virtues of solitude . . . , distracted thoughts being calmed, one should now develop the Awakening Mind.[1]

90 At first one should meditate intently on the equality of oneself and others as follows: 'All equally experience suffering and happiness. I should look after them as I do myself.'

91 Just as the body, with its many parts from division into hands and other limbs, should be protected as a single entity, so too should this entire world which is divided, but undivided in its nature to suffer and be happy.

92 Even though suffering in me does not cause distress in the bodies of others, I should nevertheless find their suffering intolerable because of the affection I have for myself,

93 In the same way that, though I cannot experience another's suffering in myself, his suffering is hard for him to bear because of his affection for himself.

94 I should dispel the suffering of others because it is suffering like my own suffering. I should help others too because of their nature as beings, which is like my own being.

95 When happiness is liked by me and others equally, what is so special about me that I strive after happiness only for myself?

96 When fear and suffering are disliked by me and others equally, what is so special about me that I protect myself and not the other?

97 If I give them no protection because their suffering does not afflict me, why do I protect my body against future suffering when it does not afflict me?

98 The notion 'it is the same me even then' is a false construction, since it is one person who dies, quite another who is born.

99 If you think that it is for the person who has the pain to guard against it, a pain in the foot is not of the hand, so why is the one protected by the other?

100 If you argue that, even though this conduct is inappropriate, it proceeds from the sense of self-identity, [our response is that] one should avoid what is inappropriate in respect of self and others as far as one can.

101 The continuum of consciousnesses, like a queue, and the combination of constituents, like an army, are not real. The person who experiences suffering does not exist. To whom will that suffering belong?

102 Without exception, no sufferings belong to anyone. They must be warded off simply because they are suffering. Why is any limitation put on this?[2]

103 If one asks why suffering should be prevented, no one disputes that! If it must be prevented, then all of it must be. If not, then this goes for oneself as for everyone.

104 You may argue: compassion causes us so much suffering, why force it to arise? Yet when one sees how much the world suffers, how can this suffering from compassion be considered great?

105 If the suffering of one ends the suffering of many, then one who has compassion for others and himself must cause that suffering to arise.

106 That is why [the monk] Supuṣpacandra, though undergoing torture at the hands of the king, did nothing to prevent his own suffering out of sacrifice for many sufferers.

107 Those who have developed the continuum of their mind in this way, to whom the suffering of others is as important as the things they themselves hold dear, plunge down into the Avīci hell as geese into a cluster of lotus blossoms.[3]

108 Those who become oceans of sympathetic joy when living beings are released, surely it is they who achieve fulfilment. What would be the point in a liberation without sweetness?

109 In fact, though acting for the good of others, there is neither intoxication nor dismay, nor desire for the resulting reward, with a thirst solely for the well-being of others.

110 Therefore, just as I protect myself to the last against criticism, let me develop in this way an attitude of protectiveness and of generosity towards others as well.

111 Through habituation there is the understanding of 'I' regarding the drops of sperm

and blood of two other people, even though there is in fact no such thing.[4]

112 Why can I not also accept another's body as my self in the same way, since the otherness of my own body has been settled and is not hard to accept?

113 One should acknowledge oneself as having faults and others as oceans of virtues. Then one should meditate on renouncing one's own self-identity and accepting other people.

114 In the same way that the hands and other limbs are loved because they form part of the body, why are embodied creatures not likewise loved because they form part of the universe?

115 In the same way that, with practice, the idea of a self arose towards this, one's own body, though it is without a self, with practice will not the same idea of a self develop towards others too?

116 Though acting like this for the good of others, there is neither intoxication nor dismay. Even after giving oneself as food, there arises no hope for reward.

117 Therefore, in the same way that one desires to protect oneself from affliction, grief and the like, so an attitude of protectiveness and of compassion should be practised towards the world.

118 That is why the Protector, Avalokita, empowered even his own name to drive away even such fear as the shyness people have in front of an audience.[5]

119 One should not turn away from difficulty, because by the power of practice the very thing one once feared to hear becomes something without which one has no delight.

120 Whoever longs to rescue quickly both himself and others should practise the supreme mystery: exchange of self and other.

121 If even slight danger causes fear because of overfondness for oneself, who would not detest that self like a fear-inspiring enemy?

122 One who, wishing to fend off hunger, thirst and weakness, kills birds, fish and animals, or lurks in wait on the highway,

123 One who, motivated by possessions and honour, would even kill his parents, or would take the property of the Three Jewels, who would thereby become fuel in the Avīci hell,

124 What wise person would want such a self, protect it, worship it, and not see it as an enemy? Who would treat it with regard?

125 'If I give, what shall I enjoy?' Such concern for one's own welfare is fiendish. 'If I enjoy, what shall I give?' Such concern for the welfare of others is divine.

126 By oppressing another for one's own sake, one is roasted in hells, but by oppressing oneself for the sake of another, one meets with success in everything.

127 A bad rebirth, inferiority and stupidity result from the mere desire for self-advancement. By transferring that same desire to others, one achieves a good rebirth, honour and intelligence.

128 By commanding another to one's own end one attains positions of servitude, whereas by commanding oneself to the benefit of others one attains positions of power.

129 All those who suffer in the world do so because of their desire for their own happiness. All those happy in the world are so because of their desire for the happiness of others.

130 Why say more? Observe this distinction: between the fool who longs for his own advantage and the sage who acts for the advantage of others.

131 For one who fails to exchange his own happiness for the suffering of others, Buddhahood is certainly impossible – how could there even be happiness in cyclic existence?

132 Never mind the next life! Even right here and now the objective of a servant who does not work or of a master who does not pay the wages cannot be achieved.

133 Having forsaken the promotion of one another's happiness, the fountain of happiness now and in the future, by causing mutual distress, the deluded seize upon gruesome suffering.

134 The calamities which happen in the world, the sufferings and fears, many as they are, they all result from clinging on to the notion of self, so what good is this clinging of mine?

135   If one does not let go of self one cannot let go of suffering, as one who does not let go of fire cannot let go of burning.

136   Therefore, in order to allay my own suffering and to allay the suffering of others, I devote myself to others and accept them as myself.

137   Hey Mind, make the resolve, 'I am bound to others'! From now on you must have no other concern than the welfare of all beings.

138   It is not right to look to one's own good with others' eyes and other senses. It is not right to set in motion one's own good with others' hands and other limbs.

139   So having become devoted to others, remove from this body everything you see in it, and use that to benefit others.

140   Creating a sense of self in respect of inferiors and others, and a sense of other in oneself, imagine envy and pride with a mind free from false notions!

Notes

1   I.e. "the Mind resolved on Awakening" or enlightenment, as Śāntideva explains in Chapter 1, verses 15–16.

2   This is Śāntideva's reply to the familiar charge that Buddhism is "impersonal." That states of suffering are not those of any self is morally irrelevant, for what matters is, simply, that they are states of *suffering*, and hence ones which should inspire compassion.

3   The meaning here is that the "awakened" person is willing to suffer for the sake of others. The Avīci hell is the most gruesome of the hells portrayed in some Mahayana texts.

4   "According to ancient Indian physiology, the sperm of the father and the blood of the mother give rise to the individual who, in Buddhist terms, then mistakenly perceives the product as his self" [Trans.].

5   Avalokita (or Avalokitesvara) is the Buddha of compassion, whose name means something like "The Lord who looks down [to see the suffering of the world]" [Trans.].

(B)   Tsongkapa and Pabongka Rinpoche, "The Second Path"

11: Why You Need the Wish for Enlightenment

We have now reached the second of the four parts in the actual body of the text [i.e. the poem *Three Principal Paths* – Ed.]. This is an explanation of the wish to achieve enlightenment for the sake of every living being. This explanation itself will include three sections: why you need the wish for enlightenment, how to go about developing this wish, and how to know when you've finally developed it. The next verse of the root text tells us why we need this great wish:

(6)
Renunciation though can never bring
The total bliss of matchless Buddhahood
Unless it's bound by the purest wish; and so,
The wise seek the high wish for enlightenment.

You may be able to gain some fierce feelings of renunciation ..., any good deeds you do under their influence though can only bring you an ordinary nirvana – they alone can never serve to bring you to omniscient enlightenment. We can see this from the fact that even practitioners of lower paths – people we call 'listeners' and 'self-made victors' – can possess true renunciation.

For full enlightenment then a person needs to develop within his mind all three of the principal paths – and more specifically, he must have gained the second path: the wish to achieve enlightenment for every living being. You may possess extra-sensory powers, you may be able to perform miracles, you may have any number of fantastic qualities – but unless you have this precious jewel in your heart, you will never enter that select group of people who practise the greater way. Without this highest wish, none of your qualities will ever bring you total bliss – none of them, none of them at all, will bring you Buddhahood: the ability to free each and every living being from all the troubles of cyclic life, and from those of a lower escape from cyclic life.

Those great practitioners of the lower paths – 'enemy destroyers' of the 'listener' or 'self-made' type – possess fine qualities like a huge mountain made of pure gold; even such qualities as the ability to perceive emptiness directly. But these paths never bring them to Buddhahood. Why? Because they lack the wish to achieve enlightenment for every living being.

If you do gain this great wish, you become a person who truly deserves to have the entire world – with all its different kinds of beings up to humans and gods – bow down at your feet, just as holy books like *The Bodhisattva's Life*, and *Entering the Middle Way*, and *The Rare Stack* describe it.[1] You find yourself in a different class of being, and then you completely outshine listeners and self-made victors – practitioners of the lower paths. Every virtuous act you do, even down to throwing a scrap of food to some wild bird, becomes a practice of the greater way; becomes a cause for your future Buddhahood; becomes the way of life of a bodhisattva.

If a person possesses this holy wish to achieve enlightenment for the sake of every living being, then all the countless Buddhas in all the ten directions of space look upon him as their son. And all the great bodhisattvas look upon him as their brother.

But that's not all; the whole question of whether you have reached the greater way, and the whole question of whether you will be able to achieve Buddhahood in this one short life, depend on whether you have truly gained this wish. . . .

12: How to Develop the Wish for Enlightenment

The second section in our explanation of the wish to achieve enlightenment for every living being describes how to develop this wish. As the next two verses say,

(7, 8)
They're swept along on four fierce river currents,
Chained up tight in past deeds, hard to undo,
Stuffed in a steel cage of grasping 'self',
Smothered in the pitch-black ignorance.

In a limitless round they're born, and in their births
Are tortured by three sufferings without a break;
Think how your mothers feel, think of what's happening
To them: try to develop this highest wish.

We may begin with another pair of verses, from *The Bodhisattva's Life*:

Even just wishing you could stop
A headache another person has
Can bring you merit without measure
Because of the helpful intent you feel.

What need then to mention the wish
That you could stop the immeasurable pain
Of every being, and put every one
In a state of measureless happiness?

The *Sutra that Viradatta Requested* says as well,

Were the merit of the wish for enlightenment
To take on some kind of physical form
It would fill the reaches of space itself
And then spill over farther still.

The benefits of this wish to achieve enlightenment for all living beings are thus described, in these and other texts, as limitless. And so here are the mass of living beings, all of them our mothers, *swept along* the flow of *four river currents*, all *fierce suffering*. From one viewpoint, while they are acting as causes, these four are the torrent of desire, the torrent of views, the torrent of the ripe force of deeds, and the torrent of ignorance. Later, when they serve as results, they are the four torrents of birth, and aging, and illness, and death.

And these mother beings are not just hurtling along in these four great rivers; it's just as if their hands and feet too were bound fast – they are *chained up tight*, they are snared, *in* their own *past deeds, hard to undo*.

But that's not all; the bonds which hold them tight are no regular ties, like our twined ropes of yak-skin or hair. It's more like our mothers are clasped in fetters of iron, ever so hard to sever, ever so hard to unshackle – for while they are swept along they are *stuffed in a steel cage of grasping* to some non-existent '*self*'.

And there's more. If there were some daylight, these mother beings would have some glimmer of hope – they could at least cry out, and try to get some help. But it is night, and the darkest hour of the night, and in pitch-black dark they are swept downstream the mighty river: they are *smothered* completely *in pitch-black ignorance*.

In a limitless round, in an endless round, *they are born* into the ocean of life, *and in these births* they *are tortured by three* different kinds of *suffering*: the suffering of suffering, the suffering of change, and the all-pervading suffering. And their torture comes to them *without a break* – it is always there.

This is *what's happening to them*, to our mother beings, this is their situation: unbearable pain. There's nothing they can do like this to help themselves; the son though has a chance at hand to pull his mother free. He must find a way, and find it now, to grasp her hand and draw her out. And the way he must *try* is *to develop this* jewel *wish* for enlightenment: he must do so first by *thinking how* his *mothers feel*, tortured by pain; then by deciding to take personal responsibility, the duty of freeing them, upon himself; and so on, all in the proper stages.

To actually gain the wish for enlightenment he must first contemplate it. To contemplate it, he must first learn about it from another. 'Loving-kindness' is an almost obsessive desire that each and every living being find happiness. 'Compassion' is an almost obsessive desire that they be free of any pain. Think of how a mother feels when her one and only and most beloved son is in the throes of a serious illness. Wherever she goes, whatever she does, she is always thinking how wonderful it would be if she could find some way of freeing him quickly from his sickness. These thoughts come to her mind in a steady stream, without a break, and all of their own, automatically. They become an obsession with her. When we feel this way towards every living being, and only then, we can say we have gained what they call 'great compassion'.

Here in the teachings of the Buddha there are two methods given for training one's mind in this precious jewel, the wish for enlightenment. The first is known as the 'seven-part, cause-and-effect instruction'. The second we call 'exchanging self and others'. No matter which of the two you use to train your mind, you can definitely gain the wish for enlightenment. The way to train oneself in the wish, the way which is complete and which never errs, the way unmatched by any other here upon this earth, is the instruction of the Steps of the path to Buddhahood, the very essence of all the teachings of our gentle protector, the great Tsongkapa. Thus you should train your mind in the wish for enlightenment by using this very instruction.

Here we'll give just a brief summary of how one trains himself in the wish to achieve enlightenment for every living being. The start-off is to practise feelings of neutrality towards all beings; after that, one begins meditation on each of the steps from 'mother recognition' on up. The first

three steps are to recognize all beings as one's mothers, to feel gratitude for their kindness, and to wish to repay that kindness. These three act as a cause for what we call 'beautiful' loving-kindness. This type of loving-kindness is itself the fourth step; it is both an effect brought about by the first three, and a cause for the fifth: great compassion.

[. . .]

Once you develop great compassion, then you can develop the extraordinary form of personal responsibility, where you take upon yourself the load of working for others' benefit. And the wish to achieve enlightenment for every living being comes from this.

The meditation on neutrality goes like this. First you put your thoughts in an even state, free of feelings of like and dislike, by thinking about someone who is for you a neutral figure: neither your enemy nor your friend. Then you imagine that two people are sitting before you: one of your best-loved friends, and one of your ugliest enemies. Next you think very carefully about how the friend has, in many of your previous lives, taken birth as your enemy and hurt you. You think too about how the enemy has, in so many of your past lives, taken birth as your friend and helped you. This puts your mind in the even state, free of feelings of like and dislike.

You go on then to think about how all living beings are equal in that, from his own point of view, each one of them wants to be happy. They are equal too in not wanting pain. And they are equal in that every one has acted as both my enemy and my friend, many many times. So who am I supposed to like? And who am I supposed to dislike? You have to keep on practising this way until, one day, you gain neutral feelings towards all sentient beings, as vast in extent as space itself.

The next step is the meditation where you recognize that every living being is your mother. Gaining this recognition is much easier if you apply the line of reasoning mentioned in the *Commentary on Valid Perception* [by Dharmakirti, seventh century CE] for demonstrating the infinite regression of one's awareness. We'll present this reasoning here, in brief.

Your awareness of today is a mental continuation of the awareness you had yesterday. This year's awareness is a mental continuation of the awareness you had the year before. Just so, your awareness over this entire life is a mental continuation of the awareness you had in your former life. The awareness you had in your former life was, in turn, a mental continuation of the awareness you had in the life before that. You can continue back in a regression like this and absolutely never reach some point where you can say, 'Prior to this, I had no awareness.' This then proves the infinite regression of one's awareness.

My own circle of life then must also be beginningless, and the births I have taken as well can have no starting point. There exists no place where I have never taken birth. I have taken birth in every single place, countless times. There exists no creature whose body I have not worn. I have worn every kind of body, countless times. Just the lives I have taken as a dog are themselves beyond any number to count. And the same is true for every living being.

Therefore there exists no being who has never been my mother. Absolutely every single one of them has been my mother a countless number of times. Even the number of times that each has been my mother in just my births as a human is past all counting too.

Do this meditation over and over until you gain a deep-felt certainty that each and every living being has been your mother, over and over, countless times.

Developing a sense of gratitude is the next step, and you can start by taking your mother in this present life. She began her hardships for me while I was still in her womb, gladly taking it upon herself to avoid anything she felt might hurt me – even down to the food she ate – treating herself with care, as though she were sick. For nine months and ten days she carried me in her womb, looking at her own body as though it belonged to someone else, someone very ill, and hesitating even to take big steps.

As she gave me birth, my mother was torn with violent suffering, excruciating pain, and yet still felt an overwhelming joy, as though she had discovered some precious gem that would grant her any wish.

Right then I knew absolutely nothing more than to cry and wave my arms around somehow. I was totally helpless. Totally stupid. Incapacitated. Nothing more than some baby chick with a red-rubber beak still yet to harden. But she swayed me on her fingertips, and pressed me to her body's warmth, and greeted me with a smile of love.

With joyful eyes she gazed on me, and wiped the snot from my face with her lips, and cleaned my filthy shit with her hands. Sometimes she chewed my food for me, and fed me things like milky porridge straight from her mouth to mine. She did her best to protect me from any hurt. She did her best to get me any good.

In those days I had to look to her for everything; good or bad, happy or sad, all the hope I could have lay in one person: mother. But for her kindness, I wouldn't have lasted an hour; they could have set me out in the open right then and some birds or a dog would have come and made a meal of me – I'd have no hope of coming out alive. Every single day she protected me from harms that could have taken my life, no less than a hundred times. Such was her kindness.

And while I was growing up she gathered together whatever I needed, avoiding no bad deed, and no suffering, and caring nothing for what other people might say of her. All the money and things she had she handed over to me, hesitating to use anything for herself.

For those of us who are fortunate enough to be practising the monastic life, it was Mother who put forth all the necessary expenses, giving without reservation, to arrange our admission into the monastery. And from that time on she supported us here, from whatever resources she had. Thus the kindness she has shown us is truly without measure.

And this is not the only life in which my present mother has given this kindness to me. She has showered me with this kindness, great kindness, over and over, countless times, in my many lives before. And she is not the only one; every single living being has been my mother in my past lives, and during those lives cared for me no less than my present mother does – it is only my transitions from death to birth that prevent me from recognizing all these mothers now.

Look now . . . at the way any common animal – a dog or bird, even the tiny sparrow – shows affection for its young, and cares for it well. From watching this we can imagine what kindness we were given too.

The next step in gaining the wish for enlightenment is to develop a wish to repay this great kindness. So every living being is my mother, and has given me her loving care over and over endlessly, for time with no beginning. And we know from what was described above that they are being swept along by four great currents, out to sea – to the vast expanse of the ocean of cyclic life. They are tormented, without a break, by the three types of suffering, and all the other pains. Their situation is desperate.

And here am I, their child. Right now I have a chance to rescue them from this ocean of cyclic life. Suppose I simply sit and bide my time, and give no thought to them. This is the lowest a person could stoop – base and absolutely shameless.

Right now I could give them things that they would be happy to get – food, or clothes, or beds to sleep on, whatever. But these are only some temporary happiness within the circle of life. The very highest way of repaying their kindness would be to put them into the state of ultimate happiness. So let me decide within myself that every living being must come to have every happiness. And every one should be freed as well from every form of pain.

Right now it's absurd to say that these beings have any kind of pure happiness – they don't even have any of the impure kinds. Every single thing they think is happiness is, in its essence, nothing more than pain. They want wantables but don't want to know about doing the good deeds that bring happiness. They want no unwantables but don't want to know about giving up the bad deeds that bring pain. They act ass backwards: they do what they shouldn't and don't what they should. And so my dear aged mothers, these living beings, are made to suffer.

> How good it would be if they could all find
> every happiness, and every cause of
> happiness. I wish they could. I'll see that
> they do.
> How good it would be if they could all be free
> of every pain, and every cause of pain. I wish
> they could. I'll see that they do.

Let these two trains of thought run through your mind; meditate on them over and over again. Then you will come to feel the very strongest loving-kindness and compassion.

Some people might come up with the idea that 'Why should I take upon myself this great load, of every living being? There are plenty of Buddhas and bodhisattvas around to guide them on their way.' This kind of thought though is absolutely improper. It's base. It's shameless. It's

as if your mother in this life was hungry, and parched, and you expected someone else's child to go and give her food and drink. But it's you for whom she has cared, and the responsibility of paying her back has fallen only to you.

It's the same with all these living beings, who for beginningless time have served as my mother so many times, and who in each of these times cared for me in every way with the kindness of this present mother. Returning their kindness is no business of anyone else at all, not for some Buddha or bodhisattva – it is my responsibility, and only mine.

So someone is going to do it – to make sure every sentient being has every happiness, and never a single pain. It is going to be myself; I'll rely on no one else. I by myself will see to it that every single being comes to have every single happiness. And I by myself will see to it that every single being gets free of every single pain. I will by myself put them into . . . the state of Buddhahood. Meditate strongly on these thoughts; they are the step we call the 'extraordinary form of personal responsibility'.

I may be able to develop this noble intention, but the fact is that I'm completely incapable of leading a single being to Buddhahood – much less every one of them. Who then has the capacity? This power is had by a fully enlightened Buddha – only by him, and by no one else at all. If I can reach the same state, I will by definition have brought both mine and others' benefit to its perfection. And then every single ray of light that emanates from me, whether it be an action of my body, or my speech, or my thoughts, will have the power to accomplish the ends of countless sentient beings.

And so, for the sake of every living being, I will do anything I can to achieve this one great goal – the state of a Buddha – with every speed. Think this way to yourself, and do anything you can to develop the genuine wish to reach enlightenment for every living being.

[. . .]

Note

1 The first of the works mentioned here is Śāntideva's *The Bodhicaryāvatāra*, which is then quoted a few lines later.

10

Plotinus, *Enneads* from IV.8 [6], Sections 4–8

Introduction

Among the most influential ethical streams flowing from the ancient world is that of neo-Platonism or, emphasizing the continuity with Plato's own work, simply Platonism. This stream finds its roots not just in Plato's texts but also in the tradition of which Plotinus (c. 205–270) and later Proclus "The Successor" (c. 411–485) were among the most prominent figures. Plotinus seems to have been born in the Nile delta city of Lycopolis in Egypt. At the age of 27 he began to study philosophy and set out to find a suitable teacher. He settled upon the neo-Platonist, Ammonius Saccas (175–242), in the important philosophical center of Alexandria – exploring in addition the thought of Stocism, the Aristotelianism of Alexander of Aphrodisias (fl. late 2nd century) and the neo-Pythagorianism of Numenius of Apamea (fl. late 2nd century). Around his 38th year, he acquired an interest in Persian and Indian thought, and joined the army of Gordian III on its march into the east. At about the age of 40 Plotinus finally settled in Rome, where he attracted a large following of students, including a number of senators, leading physicians, and Porphyry (c. 232–304), whose work Boethius

From Plotinus, *The Essential Plotinus*, 2nd edition, ed. and trans. E. O'Brien, Indianapolis, IN: Hackett Publishing Co., Inc., 1984, pp. 65–70 (notes omitted).

studied and who edited Plotinus's magnum opus, the *Enneads*.[1] Notably, Plotinus's students included Arabic thinkers and women such as Gemina, with whom he lived while in Rome, and Amphiclea, wife of Iamblichus's son Ariston. Plotinus had gained the admiration of the Emperor Gallienus and his wife, Salonia, and he sought, with what seemed some promise, grants from the couple to establish a "City of Philosophers" in the southern Italian province of Campania. The Philosophical City was to be governed by a constitution consistent with the principles set out in Plato's dialogue, *The Laws*; but the project never, however, materialized. Plotinus himself retired to an estate in Campania bequeathed to him by his Arab student Zethos, where he died, reportedly after pronouncing in his final words, "Strive to give back the Divine in yourselves to the Divine in All." A snake is said to have slipped through a hole in the wall under Plotinus's bed at the moment of his death.

Reams of Plotinus's notes and essays were collected, edited, and perhaps altered by Porphyry into a compilation of nine books called the *Enneads*. The ethical import of these texts largely comprises accounts of the soul's liberation from matter and its reunion with the divine, not by a transcendence that moves outward beyond oneself but, rather, by an ecstatic turning into the interior depths of the common divinity within us all. In the *Enneads*, Plotinus recounts a narrative of the soul's initial descent or falling away from the utterly transcendent "One," from which it had *emanated*, via first the divine "Intelligence" and then the world

"Soul," into its individual entanglement with matter. "When a soul remains for long in this withdrawal and estrangement from the whole, with never a glance toward the intelligible, it becomes a thing fragmented, isolated, and weak." Evil or vice, on this account, is not some force or state of being opposed to goodness but is, rather, the lack of goodness, the lack of unity with all things, and the degradation of being. Ethical practice, accordingly, involves activities which make it possible for the soul to detach or disentangle itself from the fragmentation and ignorance of the body, its sensual pleasures, and the temporal-material world together in order to turn back into the intelligible world and the eternal "One."

Characteristic of this moral project is conflict within oneself as the soul alternatively follows (a) the intellectual desire to reunite with the One and (b) the sensual desires of bodily existence.[2] Plotinus largely follows the Platonic prescriptions of achieving transcendence through the disciplining of sensation and bodily pleasure to be found in, say, *Phaedrus* (III.3) and *Phaedo* as well as, crucially, by the rational acquisition of knowledge of the intelligible bases of the world found in *Republic* (II.1) and *Timaeus*. But, importantly, Plotinus also (as Augustine would after him) radicalizes the erotic vision of Plato's *Symposium* (IV.1) to emphasize how the last stage of the soul's return to the One is not the result of discursive or dialectical reason but instead happens in the midst of an erotic but non-bodily ecstasy (*nous eron*) in which the individual self is annihilated. Like a drop of rainwater as it finally touches the surface of an infinite ocean, the soul's individuality is obliterated in an instantaneous moment of reunification with the One.[3]

Much of this narrative of emanation or fall followed by re-union through detachment, intellection, and erotic ecstasy was later adopted by Christian and Islamic philosophers – personified best, perhaps, by Giovanni Bernini's 1652 sculpture, the "Ecstasy of St Teresa." Islamic philosophers like al-Kindi (c. 801–873) and al-Farabi (c. 872–950) were keen to deploy the emanationist theory in theorizing about God and the soul's relation to God. But Christians from the pseudo-Dionysius (fl. 500) to Marsilio Ficino struggled with the problem of figuring a way of employing the neo-Platonic model while somehow also preserving the individuality demanded by Christian soteriology.[4] Among the most influential of Christian neo-Platonic thinkers were Augustine (IV.3) and Boethius (IV.4). Augustine, of course, like the Calvinists who followed him, is well known for his stern repudiation of bodily pleasure and desire – for instance, arguing that all sexual desire, even among married couples, is sinful. Boethius, though less austere, argues in Book III of his *Consolation of Philosophy* that happiness must be unitary, whole, self-sufficient and cannot be achieved through material acquisition or worldly status: "sufficiency cannot come through wealth, nor power through kingdoms, nor veneration through office, nor renown through glory seeking, nor joy through bodily pleasures." In fact, the highest good, the good that all people by nature desire is God: "God is nothing other than the Good itself." To be happy, then one must become God-like: "Since men become happy by attaining happiness," writes Boethius, "and happiness is identical with divinity, it is plain that they become happy by attaining divinity." Drawing on the Platonic term for the way individual entities each share in the "Forms" and rejecting the idea of individual annihilation, Boethius maintains that to be happy individual people must actually "participate" in divinity: "Every happy man, then, is God-like; but, while there is nothing to prevent as many men as possible from being God-like, only One is God by nature: men are God-like by participation."[5]

Notes

1 The *Enneads* first became available to modern Europe through the 1492 Latin translation executed by Renaissance neo-Platonist Marsilio Ficino (1433–99) of Florence.

2 L. P. Gerson, *Plotinus*, London: Routledge, 1994, pp. 185–202.

3 Neo-Platonic annihilation of individuality may usefully be contrasted with the Buddhist idea of *nirvana* or "extinction" (I.9). Spinoza's ethics (I.13) also bears interesting comparisons with neo-Platonism.

4 Dionysius the Areopagite was thought to be a neo-Platonic Greek converted to Christianity by St Paul's speech to the Athenians from the rocky outcropping, the Areopagus, just below the Acropolis. Works of neo-Platonic philosophy

attributed to him were among the most influential of the western tradition. Scholars, later, however, determined that he or she must have actually lived in the sixth century.

5 See Plato's *Theaetetus* 176a–b: "That is why we should make all speed to take flight from this world to the other, and that means becoming like the divine so far as we can."

Plotinus, *Enneads*

Book IV, Chapter 8 [6]

4. Thus individual souls are possessed by a desire for the intelligible that would have them return there whence they came, and they possess, too, a power over the realm of sense much in the way that sunshine, although attached to the sun above, does not deny its rays to what is below. If the souls remain in the intelligible realm with The Soul, they are beyond harm and share in The Soul's governance. They are like kings who live with the high king and govern with him and, like him, do not come down from the palace.

Thus far all are in the one same place.

But there comes a point at which they come down from this state, cosmic in its dimensions, to one of individuality. They wish to be independent. They are tired, you might say, of living with someone else. Each steps down into its own individuality.

When a soul remains for long in this withdrawal and estrangement from the whole, with never a glance towards the intelligible, it becomes a thing fragmented, isolated, and weak. Activity lacks concentration. Attention is tied to particulars. Severed from the whole, the soul clings to the part; to this one sole thing, buffeted about by a whole worldful of things, has it turned and given itself. Adrift now from the whole, it manages even this particular thing with difficulty, its care of it compelling attention to externals, presence to the body, the deep penetration of the body.

Thus comes about what is called "loss of wings" or the "chaining" of the soul. Its [i.e. the soul's] no longer are the ways of innocence in which, with The Soul, it presided over the higher realms. Life above was better by far than this. A thing fallen, chained, at first barred off from intelligence and living only by sensation, the soul is, as they say, in tomb or cavern pent.

Yet its higher part remains. Let the soul, taking its lead from memory, merely "think on essential being" and its shackles are loosed and it soars.

Souls of necessity lead a double life, partly in the intelligible realm and partly in that of sense, the higher life dominant in those able to commune more continuously with The Intelligence, the lower dominant where character or circumstance are the less favorable. This is pretty much what Plato indicates in distinguishing those of the second mixing bowl: after they have been divided in this way they must, he says, be born. When he speaks of divinity "sowing" souls, he is to be understood as when he has divinity giving orations and speeches; he describes the things contained in the universe as begotten and created and presents as successive what in truth exist in an eternal state of becoming or of being.

5. There is no contradiction between the sowing to birth and the willing descent for the perfection of the whole, between justice and the cave, between necessity and free choice (necessity includes free choice), being in the body being an evil; nor, in the teaching of Empedocles: the flight from God and the wandering and the sin that is justly punished; nor, in that of Heracleitus: the repose that is flight; in general, willing descent that is also unwilling. Everything that becomes worse does so unwillingly, yet when it becomes so through inherent tendency, that submission to the lower can be regarded as a penalty. Then, too, these experiences and acts are determined by an eternal law of nature, so that it may be said, without being either inconsistent or untruthful, that a soul that descends from the world above to some lower being is sent by the divinity; for final effects, however far removed by intermediate effects, are always to be referred back to the starting point.

There are two wrongs the soul commits. The first is its descent; the second, the evil done after arrival here below. The first is punished by the very conditions of its descent. Punishment for the second is passage once more into other bodies, there to remain at greater or less length according to the judgment of its deserts. (The word "judgment" indicates that this takes place as a result of divine law.) If, however, its perversity goes beyond all measure, the soul incurs an even more severe penalty administered by avenging daimons.

Thus, too, The Soul enters body – although its nature is divine and its realm the intelligible. A lesser divinity, it is impelled by the stress of its powers and the attraction of governing the next below it. By voluntary inclination it plunges into this sphere. If it returns quickly, it will have suffered no harm in thus learning of evil and of what sin is, in bringing its powers into manifest play, in exhibiting activities and achievements that, remaining merely potentialities in the intelligible realm, might as well never have been if they were never meant to be actualized: The Soul itself would never really know these suppressed, inhibited potencies. Potencies are revealed by acts, for potencies in themselves are hidden and undetectable and, for all practical purposes, nonexistent. As it is, all now marvel at the inner greatness of The Soul exteriorly revealed in the richness of its acts.

6. The One must not be solely the solitary. If it were, reality would remain buried and shapeless since in The One there is no differentiation of forms. No beings would exist if The One remained shut up in itself. More than that, the multiplicity of beings issued from The One would not exist as they do if there did not issue from The One those beings that are in the rank of souls. Likewise, souls must not play the solitaries, their issue stifled. Every nature must produce its next, for each thing must unfold, seedlike, from indivisible principle into a visible effect. Principle continues unaltered in its proper place; what unfolds from it is the product of the inexpressible power that resides in it. It must not stay this power and, as though jealous, limit its effects. It must proceed continuously until all things, to the very last, have within the limits of possibility come forth. All is the result of this immense power giving its gifts to the universe, unable to let any part remain without its share.

Nothing hinders anything from sharing in the Good to the extent it is able. That statement holds true even for matter. If, on the one hand, matter is assumed to have existed from all eternity, it is impossible that, having existence, it should not have a share in that which, in accord with each receptivity, communicates the Good to all. If, on the other hand, matter is held to be the necessary consequence of anterior causes, it will not be separated from this principle either as though, having graciously given it existence, it was powerless to reach it.

The excellence, the power, and the goodness of the intelligible realm is revealed in what is most excellent in the realm of sense, for the realms are linked together. From the one, self-existent, the other eternally draws its existence by participation and, to the extent it reproduces the intelligible; by imitation.

7. As there are these two realms, the intelligible and that of sense, it is better for the soul to dwell in the intelligible. But, such is its nature, it is necessary that it live also in the realm of sense. Accordingly it occupies only an intermediate rank. Yet there is no cause for complaint that it is not in all respects the highest. By nature divine, it is located at the nethermost limit of the intelligible realm, bordering on the realm of sense, and there gives to the realm of sense something of its own. In turn it is itself affected when, instead of controlling the body without endangering its own security, it lets itself be carried away by an excessive zeal and plunges deep into the body and ceases to be wholly united to The Soul. Yet the soul can rise above this condition again and, turning to account the experience of what it has seen and suffered here below, can better appreciate the life that is above and can know more clearly what is the better by contrast with its opposite. Indeed, knowledge of good is sharpened by experience of evil in those incapable of any sure knowledge of evil unless they have experienced it.

For The Intelligence, to reason discursively is to descend to its lowest level rather than to rise to the level of the existence beyond. But it cannot remain within itself. Of necessity it produces. Of necessity, then, by the very law of its nature, it proceeds to the level of The Soul. It goes no further. Entrusting the later stages of being to The Soul, it returns once more to the intelligible realm.

For The Soul it is much the same. Its lowest act is the realm of sense; its highest, contemplation of the supernal beings.

For individual souls this contemplation is fragmentary and divided by time, so their conversion begins on a lower level. But The Soul never becomes involved in the activities of the lower world. Immune to evil, it comprehends intellectually what is below while always cleaving to what is above it. Therefore is it able, at one and the same time, to be debtor to what is above and, since as soul it cannot escape touching this sphere, benefactor to what is below.

8. This, now, goes counter to current belief. But let us take our courage in our hands and say it: No soul, not even our own, enters into the body completely. Soul always remains united by its higher part to the intelligible realm. But if the part that is in the realm of sense dominates, or rather becomes dominated and disturbed, it keeps us unaware of what the higher part of the soul contemplates. Indeed we are aware of what the soul contemplates only if the content descends to the level of sensation. We do not know what happens in any part of the soul until it becomes present to the entire soul. (For instance, an appetite does not become known to us as long as it remains in the faculty of desire. We detect it only when we perceive it by interior sense or by the act of judgment, or by both.)

Every soul has a lower part directed towards the bodily and a higher part directed towards the intelligible. The Soul, effortlessly, manages the universe by that part directed towards the bodily. For The Soul governs the bodily not by discursive reasoning, as we do, but by intuition (much as is done in the arts). Individual souls, each of which manages a part of the universe, also have a higher phase. But they are preoccupied with sensation and its impressions. Much they perceive is contrary to nature and troubles and confuses them. This is so because the body in their care is deficient, hedged about with alien influences, filled with desires, deceived in its very pleasures. Yet there is a part of the soul insensitive to the lure of these passing pleasures, whose living is correspondent to its reality.

11

Thomas Aquinas, *Summa theologica,* I–II Questions 55, 58, 61–3

Introduction

During the Middle Ages, in both the Islamic and Christian worlds, a battle was fought between "the philosophers" and "the theologians" over the respective authority of unaided reason and of revelation and faith. In Islam, it was al-Ghazālī (IV.6) and other theologians who were victorious, with the result that ever since philosophy has been at best a suspect enterprise in Muslim countries, Persia excepted. That a similar fate did not befall philosophy in Christendom was largely due to the genius of a Dominican friar, Thomas Aquinas (1225–74). Ironically, it was Aquinas's debt to the Aristotelianism of Muslim *falasifah* such as Ibn Rushd (Averroës; IV.7) that enabled his own compromise between reason and faith, not least in the domain of ethics.

So much the "official" philosopher of Roman Catholicism has Aquinas become that it surprises people to learn that several of his doctrines were officially condemned by the Church three years after his death – though in a rapid ecclesiastical volteface, sainthood was bestowed fifty years later. Certainly Aquinas's ethical position ran strongly counter to prevailing orthodoxy. According to the view inherited from Augustine, Bernard and

others, human beings are "fallen," sinful creatures, quite incapable of true understanding and moral virtue without the help of God. Moral life is an uphill struggle of the soul against man's corrupt nature, "imprisoned" as it is "in th[e] body . . . sunk in its mire."[1] Without knowledge of God, indeed, there could be no genuine moral understanding and virtue, for what is morality if not rooted in God's goodness and God's commands?

Doubtless the label of "Aristotle baptized" sometimes attached to Thomism is rather too cute, but Thomas's discussion of virtue – in the first division of the second part of the gigantic *Summa theologica*, from which the following "Questions" are selected – is a fine example of his judicious use of the Greek philosopher in combating the orthodox view and of Aquinas's conviction that "Grace does not destroy nature, but completes it" (*ST* 1.1.8). Prior to that discussion, Aquinas presents an amended version of Aristotle's notion of *eudaimonia* as the final end of all our "appetites" and hence the good; and he adds to Aristotle's catalogue of "moral" and "intellectual" virtue a third category, "theological virtue." As a devout Christian, Aquinas substitutes for Aristotelian "happiness" that "final happiness" which comes with direct, visionary knowledge of God.

The virtues are then understood as the "habits" or dispositions that, as reason shows us, equip us to realize beatitude. Since it natural to us to seek this super-natural end, the virtues are not merely "acquired," nor are they exercised in conflict

From Aquinas Ethicus: or, The Moral Teaching of St Thomas, Vol. 1, trans. J. Rickaby. London: Burns & Oates, 1896, pp. 155, 167–74, 179–87.

with our other natural tendencies. The rational "man should be attracted by the good," performing for example "acts of kindness with pleasure [rather] than . . . with set teeth, as it were."[2] Indeed, the "continent" and "persevering" person who does need to set his teeth is, for that reason, not fully virtuous (*ST* 1–11.68.3). (Compare Kant's account of "the good will" in I.15.)

Aquinas, of course, does not subscribe to the whole list of Aristotelian virtues, geared as they were to the *eudaimonia* of the Athenian citizen. More importantly, that God has revealed Himself and that it is beatitude rather than "happiness" in the here and now which is our final end mean that there are some virtues which would have been foreign to even the most rational and reflective Greek. These are the "theological virtues" of "faith" (*fides*), "hope" (*spes*) and, above all, "charity" (love; *caritas*), this last to be understood, not as alms-giving, but as loving God "with thy whole soul" and "thy neighbour as thyself."

But even in the case of these "theological virtues," we can rationally grasp why they are required of us given our understanding of God.

Moral principles are never simply the arbitrary commandments of God, as they were for Thomas's fourteenth-century critic William of Ockham (1290–1349). God does, to be sure, command us to follow them, as Aquinas indicates in his famous definition of "natural law" as "participation in the eternal law by rational creatures" (*ST* 1–11.91.2). But as that definition also makes clear, such principles are never arbitrary: for given our nature, conferred on us by God in His own image, there are only certain ways in which human beings can fulfil their, and God's, purpose. It is to Aquinas's formulation of this position that the tradition of rational Christian ethics owes its primary debt.

Notes

1 Bernard of Clairvaux (1090–1153), quoted in E. Gilson, *The Mystical Theology of Saint Bernard*, London: Sheed & Ward, 1940, p. 133.
2 F. C. Copleston, *Aquinas*, Harmondsworth: Penguin, 1982, p. 214.

Aquinas, *Summa theologica*

Question 55: Of Virtues in Their Essence

Article 1: Is Human Virtue a Habit? R. Virtue denotes some perfection of a power. The perfection of everything is estimated chiefly in regard to its end: now the end of power is action: hence a power is said to be perfect inasmuch as it is determined to its act. Now there are powers which are determined of themselves to their acts, as the active powers of physical nature. But the rational powers, which are proper to man, are not determined to one line of action, but are open indeterminately to many, and are determined to acts by habits. And therefore human virtues are habits [or dispositions – Ed.].

§3. We are said to merit by a thing in two ways: in one way as by the merit itself, in the same way that we are said to run by running; and in this way we merit by acts. In another way we are said to merit by a thing as by a principle of merit, as we are said to run by motive power; and thus we are said to merit by virtues and habits.

Question 58: Of the Distinction of Moral Virtues from Intellectual

Article 1: Is All Virtue Moral? R. We must consider what the (Latin) word *mos* means; for so we shall be able to know what *moral* virtue is. *Mos* has two meanings: sometimes it means *custom*; sometimes it means a sort of *natural* or *quasi-natural inclination* to do a thing. These two meanings are distinguished in Greek, ἔθος, ἦθος. *Moral* virtue is so called from *mos*, inasmuch as the word signifies a certain *natural* or *quasi-natural inclination* to do a thing. And to this meaning the other meaning of *custom* is allied: for custom in a manner turns into nature, and makes an inclination like to that which is natural. But it is manifest that the inclination to act is properly to be attributed to the appetitive faculty, the function whereof is to move the other powers to action. And therefore not every virtue is called *moral*, but that only which is in the appetitive faculty.

Article 2: Is Moral Virtue Distinct from Intellectual? R. Reason is the first principle of all human acts: all other principles obey reason, though in different degrees. Some obey reason's every beck without any contradiction, as do the limbs of the body if they are in their normal state. Hence the Philosopher [i.e. Aristotle – Ed.] says that 'the soul rules the body with a despotic command,' as the master rules the slave, who has no right to contradict. Some authorities have laid it down that all the active principles in man stand in this way subordinate to reason. If that were true, it would suffice for well-doing to have the reason perfect. Hence as virtue is a habit whereby we are perfected towards well-doing, it would follow that virtue was in reason alone; and thus there would be no virtue but that which is intellectual. Such was the opinion of Socrates, who said that all virtues were modes of prudence. Hence he laid it down that man, while knowledge was present in him, could not sin, but that whoever sinned, sinned through ignorance. This argumentation, however, goes on a false supposition: for the appetitive part is obedient to reason, not to every beck, but with some contradiction. Hence the Philosopher says that 'reason commands appetite with a constitutional command', like to that authority which a parent has over his children, who have in some respects the right of contradiction. Hence Augustine says, 'sometimes understanding goes before, and tardy or none the affection that follows after': inasmuch as, owing to passions or habits in the appetitive faculty, the use of reason on some particular point is impeded. And to this extent it is in some sort true what Socrates said that 'in the presence of knowledge sin is not', provided that the knowledge here spoken of be taken to include the use of reason on the particular point that is matter of choice. Thus then for well-doing it is required that not only reason be well disposed by the habit of intellectual virtue, but also that the appetitive power be well disposed by the habit of moral virtue. As then appetite is distinct from reason, so is moral virtue distinct from intellectual. Hence as appetite is a principle of human action by being in a manner partaker of

reason, so a moral habit has the character of a human virtue by being conformable to reason.

Article 3: Is the Division of Virtues into Moral and Intellectual an Exhaustive Division? R. Human virtue is a habit perfecting man unto well-doing. Now the principle of human acts in man is only twofold, namely, intellect or reason, and appetite. Hence every human virtue must be perfective of one or other of these two principles. If it is perfective of the speculative or practical intellect towards a good human act, it will be intellectual virtue: if it is perfective of the appetitive part, it will be moral virtue.

§1.   Prudence in its essence is an intellectual virtue: but in its subject-matter it falls in with the moral virtues, being *a right method of conduct*; and in this respect it is counted among the moral virtues.

§2.   Continence and perseverance are not perfections of the sensitive appetite, as is evident from this, that in the continent and in the persevering man there are inordinate passions to excess, which would not be the case if the sensitive appetite were perfected by any habit conforming it to reason. But continence, or perseverance, is a perfection of the rational faculty, holding out against passion so as not to be carried away. Nevertheless it falls short of the character and rank of virtue; because that intellectual virtue which makes the reason stand well in moral matters supposes the appetitive faculty to be rightly bent upon the end, which is not the case with the continent and with the persevering man. For no operation proceeding from two powers can be perfect, unless each of the two powers be perfected by the due habit: as there does not follow a perfect action on the part of one acting through an instrument, if the instrument be not well disposed, however perfect be the principal agent. Hence, if the sensitive appetite, which the rational faculty moves, be not perfect, however perfect be the rational faculty itself, still the action ensuing will not be perfect: hence the principle of action will not be a virtue. And therefore continence from pleasures and perseverance in the midst of sorrows are not virtues, but something less than virtue, as the Philosopher says.[1]

§3.   Faith, hope and charity are above human virtues; for they are the virtues of man as he is made partaker of divine grace.

Article 4: Can There Be Moral Virtue Without Intellectual? R. Moral virtue may be without some intellectual virtues, as without wisdom, science and art, but it cannot be without intuition [or intellect – Ed.] and prudence. Moral virtue cannot be without prudence, because moral virtue is an *elective habit*, making a good election. Now to the goodness of an election two things are requisite: first, a due intention of the end – and that is secured by moral virtue, which inclines the appetitive powers to good in accordance with reason, which is the due end; secondly, it is required that the person make a right application of means to the end, and this cannot be except by the aid of reason, rightly counselling, judging and prescribing: all which offices belong to prudence and the virtues annexed thereto. Hence moral virtue cannot be without prudence, and consequently not without intuition either: for by the aid of intuition principles are apprehended, such principles as are naturally knowable, both in speculative and in practical matters. Hence as right reason in matters of speculation, proceeding on principles naturally known, presupposes the intuition of principles, so also does prudence, being right reason applied to conduct, presuppose the same intuition or insight.

§2. In a virtuous person it is not necessary for the use of reason to be vigorous on all points, but only in those things that are to be done according to virtue, and to this extent the use of reason is vigorous in all virtuous persons. Hence even they who seem to be simple, and to lack worldly wisdom, may be prudent persons for all that, according to the text: 'Be ye wise as serpents and simple as doves' [Matthew x.16].

§3. A natural inclination to the good that is in virtue is a beginning of virtue, but it is not perfect virtue. For the more perfect such inclination is, the more dangerous may it prove, unless right reason be conjoined with it, to make a right election of proper means to a due end. Thus a blind horse runs amuck; and the higher its speed, the more it hurts itself.

Article 5: Can There Be Intellectual Virtue Without Moral? R. Other intellectual virtues can be without moral virtue, but prudence cannot. The reason is because prudence is right reason applied to conduct, and that not only in general, but also in particular, as actions are particular. But right reason demands pre-established principles, and on them it proceeds. Now in particular matters reason must proceed not only on general but also on particular principles. As for general principles of conduct, man is kept right on these points by his natural insight into principles, whereby he knows that no evil is to be done, or again by some piece of practical knowledge. But this is not sufficient for reasoning aright in particular cases. For it happens sometimes that a general principle of this sort, ascertained by intuition or by science, is set aside in a particular case by some passion. Thus when desire gets the better of a man, that seems good which he desires, though it be against the general judgement of reason. And therefore as man is disposed by natural insight, or by a habit of science, to hold himself aright in respect of general principles, so, to keep right in respect of particular principles of conduct, which are ends of action, he must be perfected by certain habits that make it in a manner connatural to him to judge rightly of the end. And this is done by moral virtue: for the virtuous man judges rightly of the end that virtue should aim at, because 'as each one is, so does the end appear to him.' And therefore for prudence, or the application of right reason to conduct, it is requisite for man to have moral virtue.

Question 61: Of the Cardinal Virtues

Article 2: Are There Four Cardinal Virtues? R. The formal principle of virtue is rational good; and that may be considered in two ways – in one way as consisting in the mere consideration of reason; and in that way there will be one principal virtue, which is called *prudence*: in another way according as a rational order is established in some matter, and that, either in the matter of actions, and so there is *justice*; or in the matter of passions, and so there must be two virtues. For rational order must be established in the matter of the passions with regard to their repugnance to reason. Now this repugnance may be in two ways: in one way by passion impelling to something contrary to reason; and for that, passion must be *tempered*, or repressed: hence *temperance* takes its name; in another way by passion holding back from that which reason dictates; and for that, man must put his foot down there where reason places him, not to budge from thence: and so *fortitude* gets its name. And in like manner according to subjects the same number is found. For we observe a fourfold subject of this virtue whereof we speak: to wit, the part *rational by essence*, which prudence perfects; and the part *rational by participation*, which is divided into three, namely, the *will*, the subject of justice; the *concupiscible* faculty, the subject of temperance; and the *irascible* faculty, the subject of fortitude.

Article 4: Do the Four Cardinal Virtues Differ One from Another? R. The four virtues above-mentioned are differently understood by different authors. Some take them as meaning certain general conditions of the human mind which are found in all virtues, so that *prudence* is nothing else than a certain correctness of discernment in any acts or matters whatsoever, *justice* is a certain rectitude of mind whereby a man does what he ought to do in any matter; *temperance* is a disposition of mind, which sets bounds to all manner of passions or actions, that they may not exceed; while *fortitude* is a disposition of the soul whereby it is strengthened in what is according to reason against all manner of assaults of passion or toil of active labours. This fourfold distinction does not involve any difference of virtuous habits so far as justice, temperance and fortitude are concerned. For to every virtue by the fact of its being a *habit* there attaches a certain firmness, so that it may not be moved by any impulse to the contrary; and this has been said to be a point of *fortitude*. Also from the fact of its being a *virtue* it has a direction towards good, wherein is involved the notion of something right and due, which was said to be a point of *justice*. Again, by the fact of its being a *moral* virtue partaking in reason, it has that which makes it observe the bounds of reason in all things, and not go beyond, which was said to be a point of *temperance*. Only the having of discretion, which was attributed to *prudence*, seems to be distinguished from the other three points, inasmuch as this belongs to reason essentially so called, whereas the other three involve only a certain participation in reason by way of application thereof to passions or acts. Thus then on the foregoing reckoning, prudence would be a virtue distinct from the other three; but the other three would not be virtues distinct from one another. For it is manifest that one and the same virtue is at once a *habit*, and a *virtue*, and is *moral*.

Others better understand these four virtues as being determined to special matters, each of them to one matter, so that every virtue which produces that goodness which lies in the consideration of reason, is called *prudence*; and every virtue which produces that goodness which consists in what is due and right in action, is called *justice*; and every virtue which restrains and represses the passions, is called *temperance*; and every virtue which produces a firmness of soul against all manner of sufferings, is called *fortitude*. On this arrangement it is manifest that the aforesaid virtues are different habits, distinct according to the diversity of their objects.

Question 62: Of the Theological Virtues

Article 1: Are There Any Theological Virtues? R. By virtue man is perfected unto the acts whereby he is set in the way to happiness. Now there is a twofold happiness of man: one proportionate to human nature, whereunto man can arrive by the principles of his own nature. Another happiness there is exceeding the nature of man, whereunto man can arrive only by a divine virtue involving a certain participation in the Deity, according as it is said that by Christ we are made 'partakers of the divine nature' [Peter i. 4]. And because this manner of happiness exceeds the capacities of human nature, the natural principles of human action, on which man proceeds to such well-doing as is in proportion with himself, suffice not to direct man unto the aforesaid happiness. Hence there must be superadded to man by the gift of God certain principles, whereby he may be put on the way to supernatural happiness, even as he is directed to his connatural end by natural principles, yet not without the divine aid. Such principles are called *theological virtues*: both because they have God for their object, inasmuch as by them we are directed aright to God; as also because it is only by divine revelation in Holy Scripture that such virtues are taught.

Article 2: Are Theological Virtues Distinct from Virtues Intellectual and Moral? R. Habits are specifically distinct according to the formal difference of their objects. But the object of the theological virtues is God Himself, the last end of all things, as He transcends the knowledge of our reason: whereas the object of the intellectual and moral virtues is something that can be comprehended by human reason. Hence theological virtues are specifically distinct from virtues moral and intellectual.

§1. The intellectual and moral virtues perfect the intellect and appetite of man according to the capacity of human nature, but the theological virtues supernaturally.

Article 3: Are Faith, Hope and Charity Fitly Assigned as the Theological Virtues? R. The theological virtues set man in the way of supernatural happiness, as he is directed to his connatural end by a natural inclination. This latter direction is worked out in two ways: first, by way of the reason or intellect, as that power holds in its knowledge the general principles of rational procedure, theoretical and practical, known by the light of nature: secondly, by the rectitude of the will naturally tending to rational good. But both these agencies fall short of the order of supernatural good. Hence for both of them some supernatural addition was necessary to man, to direct him to a supernatural end. On the side of the intellect man receives the addition of certain supernatural principles, which are perceived by divine light; and these are the objects of belief, with which *faith* is conversant. Secondly, there is the will, which is directed to the supernatural end, both by way of an affective movement directed thereto as to a point possible to gain, and this movement belongs to *hope*; and by way of a certain spiritual union, whereby the will is in a manner transformed into that end, which union and transformation is wrought by *charity*. For the appetite of every being has a natural motion and tendency towards an end connatural to itself; and that movement arises from some sort of conformity of the thing to its end.

§2. Faith and hope denote a certain imperfection: because faith is of the things that are seen not, and hope of the things that are possessed not. Hence to have faith in and hope of the things that are amenable to human power, is a falling short of the character of virtue. But to have faith in and hope of the things that are beyond the ability of human nature, transcends all virtue proportionate to man, according to the text: 'The weakness of God is stronger than men' [I Corinthians i. 25].

Question 63: Of the Cause of Virtues

Article 1: Is Virtue in Us by Nature? R. As regards sciences and virtues some have laid it down that they are totally from within, meaning that all virtues and sciences naturally pre-exist in the soul, and that discipline and exercise do no more than remove the obstacles to virtue and science, which arise in the soul from the lumpishness of the body, as when iron is polished by filing; and this was the opinion of the Platonists. Others, on the contrary, have said that they are totally from without. Others again have said that in aptitude the sciences and virtues are in us by nature, but not in perfection. So says the Philosopher, and this is the more correct thing to say. In evidence whereof we must consider that a thing is said to be natural to man in two ways: in one way according to the nature of the species, in another way according to the nature of the individual. And because everything has its species according to its form, and is individualized according to its matter: and man's form is his rational soul, and his matter his body; therefore that which belongs to man by virtue of his rational soul is natural to him in point of his species; while that which is natural to him by his having a given complexion of body is natural to him according to his nature as an individual. Now in both these ways a rudimentary phase of virtue is natural to man. First, as regards his specific nature, in this way, that there are by nature in the reason of man certain naturally known principles, theoretical and practical, which are seminal principles of virtues intellectual and moral; and again inasmuch as there is in the will a natural craving after the good that is according to reason. Secondly, as regards his individual nature, inasmuch as by conformation of body some are better and some worse disposed to certain virtues: the explanation being this, that the sensitive powers are energies of corresponding parts of the body; and according to the disposition of those parts the said powers are helped or hindered in their operations; and consequently the rational powers also, which these sensitive powers serve, are helped or hindered in like manner. Thus one man has a natural aptitude for knowledge, another for fortitude, another for temperance. And in these ways the virtues, as well intellectual as moral, are in us by nature to the extent of a certain rudimentary aptitude, but not in their perfect completeness: the reason being that nature is limited to one fixed course of action, whereas the perfection of the said virtues does not lead to one fixed course of action, but is varied according to the diversity of matters wherein the virtues operate, and the diversity of circumstances. It appears then that virtues are in us by nature, in aptitude, and in a rudimentary phase, but not in their perfection – except the theological virtues, which are wholly from without.[2]

Article 2 §2. Virtue divinely infused, considered in its perfection, is incompatible with any mortal sin. But virtue humanly acquired is compatible with an act even of mortal sin, because the use of a habit in us is subject to our will. Nor is a habit of acquired virtue destroyed by one act of sin: for the direct contrary of a habit is not an act, but another habit. And therefore, though without grace a man cannot avoid mortal sin so as never to sin mortally, still there is nothing to hinder him from acquiring a habit of virtue,

enough to keep him from evil acts for the most part, and especially from those that are very much opposed to reason. There are, however, some mortal sins that man can nowise avoid without grace, to wit, the sins that are directly contrary to the theological virtues which are in us by the gift of grace.

Notes

1 The point Aquinas and Aristotle (*Nicomachean Ethics*, Book VII) are making is that, while continence, self-discipline, perseverance, and the like are to be admired, the truly virtuous person would not require them, since he or she would not be subject to the temptations that they are required to overcome. For such a person, acting virtuously has become, as we might say, "second nature."

2 It may seem odd to say that the theological virtues, being "infused" in us by God, can in any sense be "in us by nature." But "natural" here contrasts, not with "supernatural," but with "acquired." A gift of Grace is not an acquisition of mine.

Giovanni Pico della Mirandola, "Oration on the Dignity of Man"

Introduction

Pico della Mirandola (1463–94) lived a short life but one that burned brightly. Born the youngest of three sons to a noble family in the small Duchy of Modena in northern Italy, the extraordinary qualities of Pico's mind, especially his formidable memory, were recognized early. First studying canon law at the University of Bologna as part of the initial steps of an ecclesiastical career, Pico soon found his interest turning to philosophy and theology. His voracious intellectual appetite carried him through various universities and centers of learning in Italy and France, including the Universities of Padua and Paris. Along the way, he acquired an understanding not only of the various strains of scholastic, mystical, and hermetic philosophy but also facility with Greek, Latin, Hebrew, Aramaic, and Arabic. In 1484 Pico traveled to Florence where he met two men who would be crucial not only to the course of his own life but also to the development of the Renaissance itself: the neo-Platonist and leader of the Florentine Academy, Marsilio Ficino, who would become Pico's teacher; and the great patron Lorenzo the Magnificent (1433–99), who would come to be one of Pico's most stalwart sup-

From Giovanni Pico della Mirandola, *Oration on the Dignity of Man*, trans. E. Livermore Forbes, in *The Renaissance Philosophy of Man*, ed. E. Cassirer, P. O. Kristeller and J. H. Randall, Jr, Chicago: University of Chicago Press, 1948, pp. 223–54 (some notes omitted).

porters, providing him with backing and protection throughout the rest of his life.

Pico's work exhibits both the feverish eclecticism and the self-assured audacity that came to be associated with the Renaissance. In 1486 he went to Rome and proposed a public disputation open to anyone on 900 of his theses concerning a vast expanse of topics in philosophy and theology, offering even to pay the transport costs of those who wished to challenge him. Despite Pico's concerted efforts, however, the disputation was never permitted, and he was forced to flee to France where he was briefly arrested and imprisoned at Vincennes, before returning to Perugia and finally Florence. Despite this setback, Pico's subsequent efforts show little diminishment in either vigor or scope. His syncretistic work drew upon Greek, Christian, Jewish, Muslim, neo-Platonic, and hermetic thought to explore the Creation, to argue for the unity and sameness of the divinity addressed by different religions, to defend Christianity, and to advance trenchant criticisms of astrology.

We present here Pico's famous essay, which has come to be known as the *Oration on the Dignity of Man*. It was originally composed as the introduction he planned to deliver before the Roman assembly in defense of his 900 theses. The text is relevant to ethics not so much as an articulation of a general ethical theory or as a statement of method in tackling some ethical problem. Instead, the oration presents what might be called a philosophical anthropology – that is, a philosophical description of human being – with ethical implications.

Pico's oration advances the startling claim that the dignity of humankind is rooted precisely in the fact that humans have no definite nature of their own but that through the exercise of their own free choice they are able to transform themselves and acquire the natures of various beings up and down the great chain of being. In this human dignity surpasses even that of the angels. Pico tells a tale in which God creates the world and the great chain of beings that compose it but still desires to produce another creature, a creature with the intellectual capacity to contemplate and appreciate the wonders of the universe – in short, a creature with the capacity for philosophy. Rather than installing this creature in a specific location in the great chain, God implanted the seeds of all beings within it, giving it a kind of connection with all things above and below. Human beings are in this way a microcosm of the larger macrocosm.

According to prevalent metaphysics of the day, all things have "natures" or "essences" (*essentia*, as Aquinas called them) that define those beings, including human beings, as what they are. The project of ethics, from this point of view, is then largely the project of realizing those natures in their most perfect and excellent ways. But natures or essences of this kind are fixed and unique to each creature. Pico's radical departure from this position portrays instead a human being without any fixed being, a plastic being with countless possibilities for being. Indeed, for Pico humans don't simply possess the possibility of different ways of being, they possess the capacity to make those possibilities actual.

Certainly, the idea that human beings are free beings possessing free wills extends back at least to Augustine. But here we see the establishment of a more extensive conception of freedom, an idea

that would become pervasive in modern Western philosophy, namely the idea that humans are in a very real way free to re-create themselves with perhaps little help from the divine beyond the gift of freedom itself (see I.23 and I.24 below). This heady vision of humanity suggests that the good life entails not only the ancient ends of perfecting oneself, contemplating truth, and returning to God. In Pico's vision, the most excellent life is one where human beings re-create themselves in elevated and wondrous ways, as works of art in an image and extension of divine creation. Among Renaissance thinkers, Pico's vision contrasts sharply against those of Michel de Montaigne (1533–92) and Desiderius Erasmus (1466–1536) for whom the moral project is not to re-create oneself but rather to understand, accept, and refine what it is to be a finite, historical, and natural being.[1]

Notes

1   Montaigne's moral vision is woven through his *Essais* (1580). In "Of Experience," for example, Montaigne writes: "They want to get out of themselves and escape from the man. That is madness: instead of changing into angels, they change into beasts; instead of raising themselves, they lower themselves. These transcendental humors frighten me. . . . There is nothing so beautiful and legitimate as to play the man well and properly, no knowledge so hard to acquire as the knowledge of how to live this life well and naturally; and the most barbarous of our maladies is to despise our being." *The Complete Works of Montaigne*, ed. and trans. Donald M. Frame, Stanford, CA: Stanford University Press, 1958, p. 856.

Pico, "Oration on the Dignity of Man"

A speech by Giovanni Pico della Mirandola, Prince of Concord

I have read in the records of the Arabians, reverend Fathers, that Abdala the Saracen,* when

---

* Abdala, that is, Abd Allah, probably the cousin of Mohammed.

questioned as to what on this stage of the world, as it were, could be seen most worthy of wonder, replied: "There is nothing to be seen more wonderful than man." In agreement with this opinion is the saying of Hermes Trismegistus: "A great miracle, Asclepius, is man." But when I weighed the reason for these maxims, the many grounds for the excellence of human nature reported by many men failed to satisfy me – that man is the intermediary between creatures, the intimate of the gods, the king of the lower beings, by the acuteness of his senses, by the discernment of his reason, and by the light of his intelligence the interpreter of nature, the interval between fixed eternity and fleeting time, and (as the Persians say) the bond, nay, rather, the marriage song of the world, on David's testimony but little lower than the angels.* Admittedly great though these reasons be, they are not the principal grounds, that is, those which may rightfully claim for themselves the privilege of the highest admiration. For why should we not admire more the angels themselves and the blessed choirs of heaven? At last it seems to me I have come to understand why man is the most fortunate of creatures and consequently worthy of all admiration and what precisely is that rank which is his lot in the universal chain of Being – a rank to be envied not only by brutes but even by the stars and by minds beyond this world. It is a matter past faith and a wondrous one. Why should it not be? For it is on this very account that man is rightly called and judged a great miracle and a wonderful creature indeed.

2. But hear, Fathers, exactly what this rank is and, as friendly auditors, conformably to your kindness, do me this favor. God the Father, the supreme Architect, had already built this cosmic home we behold, the most sacred temple of His godhead, by the laws of His mysterious wisdom. The region above the heavens He had adorned with Intelligences, the heavenly spheres He had quickened with eternal souls, and the excrementary and filthy parts of the lower world He had filled with a multitude of animals of every kind. But, when the work was finished, the Craftsman kept wishing that there were someone to ponder the plan of so great a work, to love its beauty, and to wonder at its vastness. Therefore, when everything was done (as Moses and Timaeus bear witness), He finally took thought concerning the creation of man. But there was not among His archetypes that from which He could fashion a new offspring, nor was there in His treasure-houses anything which He might bestow on His new son as an inheritance, nor was there in the seats of all the world a place where the latter might sit to contemplate the universe. All was now complete; all things had been assigned to the highest, the middle, and the lowest orders.† But

in its final creation it was not the part of the Father's power to fail as though exhausted. It was not the part of His wisdom to waver in a needful matter through poverty of counsel. It was not the part of His kindly love that he who was to praise God's divine generosity in regard to others should be compelled to condemn it in regard to himself.

3. At last the best of artisans ordained that that creature to whom He had been able to give nothing proper to himself should have joint possession of whatever had been peculiar to each of the different kinds of being. He therefore took man as a creature of indeterminate nature and, assigning him a place in the middle of the world, addressed him thus: "Neither a fixed abode nor a form that is thine alone nor any function peculiar to thyself have we given thee, Adam, to the end that according to thy longing and according to thy judgment thou mayest have and possess what abode, what form, and what functions thou thyself shalt desire. The nature of all other beings is limited and constrained within the bounds of laws prescribed by Us. Thou, constrained by no limits, in accordance with thine own free will, in whose hand We have placed thee, shalt ordain for thyself the limits of thy nature. We have set thee at the world's center that thou mayest from thence more easily observe whatever is in the world. We have made thee neither of heaven nor of earth, neither mortal nor immortal, so that with freedom of choice and with honor, as though the maker and molder of thyself, thou mayest fashion thyself in whatever shape thou shalt prefer. Thou shalt have the power to degenerate into the lower forms of life, which are brutish. Thou shalt have the power, out of thy soul's judgment, to be reborn into the higher forms, which are divine."

4. O supreme generosity of God the Father, O highest and most marvelous felicity of man! To him it is granted to have whatever he chooses, to be whatever he wills. Beasts as soon as they are born (so says Lucilius) bring with them from their mother's womb all they will ever possess. Spiritual beings, either from the beginning or soon thereafter, become what they are to be for ever and ever. On man when he came into life the Father conferred the seeds of all kinds and the germs of every way of life. Whatever seeds each man cultivates will grow to maturity and bear in him their own fruit. If they be vegetative, he will be like a plant. If sensitive, he will become brutish. If rational, he will grow into a

* Psalms 8:5
† Cf. Plato *Protagoras* 321c ff.

heavenly being. If intellectual, he will be an angel and the son of God.* And if, happy in the lot of no created thing, he withdraws into the center of his own unity, his spirit, made one with God, in the solitary darkness of God, who is set above all things, shall surpass them all. Who would not admire this our chameleon? Or who could more greatly admire aught else whatever? It is man who Asclepius of Athens, arguing from his mutability of character and from his self-transforming nature, on just grounds says was symbolized by Proteus in the mysteries. Hence those metamorphoses renowned among the Hebrews and the Pythagoreans.

5. For the occult theology of the Hebrews sometimes transforms the holy Enoch into an angel of divinity whom they call "Mal'akh Adonay Shebaoth," and sometimes transforms others into other divinities. The Pythagoreans degrade impious men into brutes and, if one is to believe Empedocles, even into plants. Mohammed, in imitation, often had this saying on his tongue: "They who have deviated from divine law become beasts," and surely he spoke justly. For it is not the bark that makes the plant but its senseless and insentient nature; neither is it the hide that makes the beast of burden but its irrational, sensitive soul; neither is it the orbed form that makes the heavens but their undeviating order; nor is it the sundering from body but his spiritual intelligence that makes the angel. For if you see one abandoned to his appetites crawling on the ground, it is a plant and not a man you see; if you see one blinded by the vain illusions of imagery, as it were of Calypso, and, softened by their gnawing allurement, delivered over to his senses, it is a beast and not a man you see. If you see a philosopher determining all things by means of right reason, him you shall reverence: he is a heavenly being and not of this earth. If you see a pure contemplator, one unaware of the body and confined to the inner reaches of the mind, he is neither an earthly nor a heavenly being; he is a more reverend divinity vested with human flesh.

6. Are there any who would not admire man, who is, in the sacred writings of Moses and the Christians, not without reason described sometimes by the name of "all flesh," sometimes

by that of "every creature," inasmuch as he himself molds, fashions, and changes himself into the form of all flesh and into the character of every creature? For this reason the Persian Euanthes, in describing the Chaldaean theology, writes that man has no semblance that is inborn and his very own but many that are external and foreign to him; whence this saying of the Chaldaeans: "Hanorish tharah sharinas," that is, "Man is a being of varied, manifold, and inconstant nature." But why do we emphasize this? To the end that after we have been born to this condition – that we can become what we will – we should understand that we ought to have especial care to this, that it should never be said against us that, although born to a privileged position, we failed to recognize it and became like unto wild animals and senseless beasts of burden, but that rather the saying of Asaph the prophet should apply: "Ye are all angels and sons of the Most High," and that we may not, by abusing the most indulgent generosity of the Father, make for ourselves that freedom of choice He has given into something harmful instead of salutary. Let a certain holy ambition invade our souls, so that, not content with the mediocre, we shall pant after the highest and (since we may if we wish) toil with all our strength to obtain it.

7. Let us disdain earthly things, despise heavenly things, and, finally, esteeming less whatever is of the world, hasten to that court which is beyond the world and nearest to the Godhead. There, as the sacred mysteries relate, Seraphim, Cherubim, and Thrones hold the first places; let us, incapable of yielding to them, and intolerant of a lower place, emulate their dignity and their glory. If we have willed it, we shall be second to them in nothing.

8. But how shall we go about it, and what in the end shall we do? Let us consider what they do, what sort of life they lead. If we also come to lead that life (for we have the power), we shall then equal their good fortune. The Seraph burns with the fire of love. The Cherub glows with the splendor of intelligence. The Throne stands by the steadfastness of judgment. Therefore if, in giving ourselves over to the active life, we have after due consideration undertaken the care of the lower beings, we shall be strengthened with the firm stability of Thrones. If, unoccupied by deeds, we pass our time in the leisure of contemplation, considering the Creator in the creature and the

* Cf. Ficino *Theologia Platonica* xiv. 3.

creature in the Creator, we shall be all ablaze with Cherubic light. If we long with love for the Creator himself alone, we shall speedily flame up with His consuming fire into a Seraphic likeness. Above the Throne, that is, above the just judge, God sits as Judge of the ages. Above the Cherub, that is, above him who contemplates, God flies, and cherishes him, as it were, in watching over him. For the spirit of the Lord moves upon the waters, the waters, I say, which are above the firmament and which in Job praise the Lord with hymns before dawn. Whoso is a Seraph, that is, a lover, is in God and God in him, nay, rather, God and himself are one. Great is the power of Thrones, which we attain in using judgment, and most high the exaltation of Seraphs, which we attain in loving.

9. But by what means is one able either to judge or to love things unknown? Moses loved a God whom he saw and, as judge, administered among the people what he had first beheld in contemplation upon the mountain. Therefore, the Cherub as intermediary by his own light makes us ready for the Seraphic fire and equally lights the way to the judgment of the Thrones. This is the bond of the first minds, the Palladian order, the chief of contemplative philosophy. This is the one for us first to emulate, to court, and to understand; the one from whence we may be rapt to the heights of love and descend, well taught and well prepared, to the functions of active life. But truly it is worth while, if our life is to be modeled on the example of the Cherubic life, to have before our eyes and clearly understood both its nature and its quality and those things which are the deeds and the labor of Cherubs. But since it is not permitted us to attain this through our own efforts, we who are but flesh and know of the things of earth, let us go to the ancient fathers who, inasmuch as they were familiar and conversant with these matters, can give sure and altogether trustworthy testimony. Let us consult the Apostle Paul, the chosen vessel, as to what he saw the hosts of Cherubim doing when he was himself exalted to the third heaven. He will answer, according to the interpretation of Dionysius,* that he saw them being purified,

then being illuminated, and at last being made perfect. Let us also, therefore, by emulating the Cherubic way of life on earth, by taming the impulses of our passions with moral science, by dispelling the darkness of reason with dialectic, and by, so to speak, washing away the filth of ignorance and vice, cleanse our soul, so that her passions may not rave at random nor her reason through heedlessness ever be deranged.

10. Then let us fill our well-prepared and purified soul with the light of natural philosophy, so that we may at last perfect her in the knowledge of things divine. And lest we be satisfied with those of our faith, let us consult the patriarch Jacob, whose form gleams carved on the throne of glory. Sleeping in the lower world but keeping watch in the upper, the wisest of fathers will advise us. But he will advise us through a figure (in this way everything was wont to come to those men) that there is a ladder extending from the lowest earth to the highest heaven, divided in a series of many steps, with the Lord seated at the top, and angels in contemplation ascending and descending over them alternately by turns.

11. If this is what we must practice in our aspiration to the angelic way of life, I ask: "Who will touch the ladder of the Lord either with fouled foot or with unclean hands?" As the sacred mysteries have it, it is impious for the impure to touch the pure. But what are these feet? What these hands? Surely the foot of the soul is that most contemptible part by which the soul rests on matter as on the soil of the earth, I mean the nourishing and feeding power, the tinder of lust, and the teacher of pleasurable weakness. Why should we not call the hands of the soul its irascible power, which struggles on its behalf as the champion of desire and as plunderer seizes in the dust and sun what desire will devour slumbering in the shade? These hands, these feet, that is, all the sentient part whereon resides the attraction of the body which, as they say, by wrenching the neck holds the soul in check, lest we be hurled down from the ladder as impious and unclean, let us bathe in moral philosophy as if in a living river. Yet this will not be enough if we wish to be companions of the angels going up and down on Jacob's ladder, unless we have first been well fitted and instructed to be promoted duly from step to step, to stray nowhere from the stairway, and to engage in the alternate comings and goings. Once we have achieved this by the art of discourse

* Dionysius the Areopagite. The writings current under that name, composed by an unknown author probably about 500, were long attributed to Dionysius, the disciple of Paul, and hence enjoyed an enormous authority.

or reasoning, then, inspired by the Cherubic spirit, using philosophy through the steps of the ladder, that is, of nature, and penetrating all things from center to center, we shall sometimes descend, with titanic force rending the unity like Osiris into many parts, and we shall sometimes ascend, with the force of Phoebus collecting the parts like the limbs of Osiris into a unity, until, resting at last in the bosom of the Father who is above the ladder, we shall be made perfect with the felicity of theology.

12.   Let us also inquire of the just Job, who entered into a life-covenant with God before he himself was brought forth into life, what the most high God requires above all in those tens of hundreds of thousands who attend him. He will answer that it is peace, in accord with what we read in him: "He maketh peace in his high places." And since the middle order expounds to the lower orders the counsel of the highest order, let Empedocles the philosopher expound to us the words of Job the theologian. He indicates to us a twofold nature present in our souls, by one side of which we are raised on high to the heavenly regions, and by the other side plunged downward into the lower, through strife and friendship or through war and peace, as he witnesses in the verses in which he makes complaint that he is being driven into the sea, himself goaded by strife and discord into the semblance of a madman and a fugitive from the gods.

13.   Surely, Fathers, there is in us a discord many times as great; we have at hand wars grievous and more than civil, wars of the spirit which, if we dislike them, if we aspire to that peace which may so raise us to the sublime that we shall be established among the exalted of the Lord, only philosophy will entirely allay and subdue in us. In the first place, if our man but ask a truce of his enemies, moral philosophy will check the unbridled inroads of the many-sided beast and the leonine passions of wrath and violence. If we then take wiser counsel with ourselves and learn to desire the security of everlasting peace, it will be at hand and will generously fulfil our prayers. After both beasts are felled like a sacrificed sow, it will confirm an inviolable compact of holiest peace between flesh and spirit. Dialectic will appease the tumults of reason made confused and anxious by inconsistencies of statement and sophisms of syllogisms. Natural philosophy will allay the strife and differences of opinion which

vex, distract, and wound the spirit from all sides. But she will so assuage them as to compel us to remember that, according to Heraclitus, nature was begotten from war, that it was on this account repeatedly called "strife" by Homer, and that it is not, therefore, in the power of natural philosophy to give us in nature a true quiet and unshaken peace but that this is the function and privilege of her mistress, that is, of holiest theology. She will show us the way and as comrade lead us to her who, seeing us hastening from afar, will exclaim "Come to me, ye who have labored. Come and I will restore you. Come to me, and I will give you peace, which the world and nature cannot give you."

14.   When we have been so soothingly called, so kindly urged, we shall fly up with winged feet, like earthly Mercuries, to the embraces of our blessed mother and enjoy that wished-for peace, most holy peace, indivisible bond, of one accord in the friendship through which all rational souls not only shall come into harmony in the one mind which is above all minds but shall in some ineffable way become altogether one. This is that friendship which the Pythagoreans say is the end of all philosophy. This is that peace which God creates in his heavens, which the angels descending to earth proclaimed to men of good will, that through it men might ascend to heaven and become angels. Let us wish this peace for our friends, for our century. Let us wish it for every home into which we go; let us wish it for our own soul, that through it she shall herself be made the house of God, and to the end that as soon as she has cast out her uncleanness through moral philosophy and dialectic, adorned herself with manifold philosophy as with the splendor of a courtier, and crowned the pediments of her doors with the garlands of theology, the King of Glory may descend and, coming with his Father, make his stay with her. If she show herself worthy of so great a guest, she shall, by the boundless mercy which is his, in golden raiment like a wedding gown, and surrounded by a varied throng of sciences, receive her beautiful guest not merely as a guest but as a spouse from whom she will never be parted. She will desire rather to be parted from her own people and, forgetting her father's house and herself, will desire to die in herself in order to live in her spouse, in whose sight surely the death of his saints is precious – death, I say, if we must call death that fulness of

life, the consideration of which wise men have asserted to be the aim of philosophy.*

15. Let us also cite Moses himself, but little removed from the springing abundance of the holy and unspeakable wisdom by whose nectar the angels are made drunk. Let us hearken to the venerable judge in these words proclaiming laws to us who are dwellers in the desert loneliness of this body: "Let those who, as yet unclean, still need moral philosophy, live with the people outside the tabernacle under the sky, meanwhile purifying themselves like the priests of Thessaly. Let those who have already ordered their conduct be received into the sanctuary but not quite yet touch the holy vessels; let them first like zealous Levites in the service of dialectic minister to the holy things of philosophy. Then when they have been admitted even to these, let them now behold the many-colored robe of the higher palace of the Lord, that is to say, the stars; let them now behold the heavenly candlestick divided into seven lights; let them now behold the fur tent, that is, the elements, in the priesthood of philosophy, so that when they are in the end, through the favor of theological sublimity, granted entrance into the inner part of the temple, they may rejoice in the glory of the Godhead with no veil before his image." This of a surety Moses commands us and, in commanding, summons, urges, and encourages us by means of philosophy to prepare ourselves a way, while we can, to the heavenly glory to come.

16. But indeed not only the Mosaic and Christian mysteries but also the theology of the ancients show us the benefits and value of the liberal arts, the discussion of which I am about to undertake. For what else did the degrees of the initiates observed in the mysteries of the Greeks mean? For they arrived at a perception of the mysteries when they had first been purified through those expiatory sciences, as it were, moral philosophy and dialectic. What else can that perception possibly be than an interpretation of occult nature by means of philosophy? Then at length to those who were so disposed came that ΕΠΟΠΤΕΙΑ, that is to say, the observation of things divine by the light of theology. Who would not long to be initiated into such sacred rites? Who would not desire, by neglecting all human concerns, by despising the goods of

fortune, and by disregarding those of the body, to become the guest of the gods while yet living on earth, and, made drunk by the nectar of eternity, to be endowed with the gifts of immortality though still a mortal being? Who would not wish to be so inflamed with those Socratic frenzies sung by Plato in the *Phaedrus*,† that, by the oarage of feet and wings escaping speedily from hence, that is, from a world set on evil, he might be borne on the fastest of courses to the heavenly Jerusalem? Let us be driven, Fathers, let us be driven by the frenzies of Socrates, that they may so throw us into ecstasy as to put our mind and ourselves in God. Let us be driven by them, if we have first done what is in our power. For if through moral philosophy the forces of our passions have by a fitting agreement become so intent on harmony that they can sing together in undisturbed concord, and if through dialectic our reason has moved progressively in a rhythmical measure, then we shall be stirred by the frenzy of the Muses and drink the heavenly harmony with our inmost hearing. Thereupon Bacchus, the leader of the Muses, by showing in his mysteries, that is, in the visible signs of nature, the invisible things of God to us who study philosophy, will intoxicate us with the fulness of God's house, in which, if we prove faithful, like Moses, hallowed theology shall come and inspire us with a doubled frenzy. For, exalted to her lofty height, we shall measure therefrom all things that are and shall be and have been in indivisible eternity; and, admiring their original beauty, like the seers of Phoebus, we shall become her own winged lovers. And at last, roused by ineffable love as by a sting, like burning Seraphim rapt from ourselves, full of divine power we shall no longer be ourselves but shall become He Himself Who made us.

17. If anyone investigates the holy names of Apollo, their meanings and hidden mysteries, these amply show that that god is no less a philosopher than a seer; but, since Ammonius has sufficiently examined this subject, there is no reason why I should now treat it otherwise. But, Fathers, three Delphic precepts may suggest themselves to your minds, which are very necessary to those who are to go into the most sacred and revered temple, not of the false but of the true

---

* Cf. Plato *Phaedo* 81a.   † 245b ff.

Apollo, who lights every soul as it enters this world. You will see that they give us no other advice than that we should with all our strength embrace this threefold philosophy which is the concern of our present debate. For the saying μηδὲν ἄγαν, that is, "Nothing too much," prescribes a standard and rule for all the virtues through the doctrine of the Mean, with which moral philosophy duly deals. Then the saying γνῶθι σεαυτόν, that is, "Know thyself," urges and encourages us to the investigation of all nature, of which the nature of man is both the connecting link and, so to speak, the "mixed bowl." For he who knows himself in himself knows all things, as Zoroaster first wrote, and then Plato in his *Alcibiades.** When we are finally lighted in this knowledge by natural philosophy, and nearest to God are uttering the theological greeting, εἶ, that is, "Thou art," we shall likewise in bliss be addressing the true Apollo on intimate terms.

18.   Let us also consult the wise Pythagoras, especially wise in that he never deemed himself worthy the name of a wise man. He will first enjoin us not to sit on a bushel, that is, not by unoccupied sloth to lose our rational faculty, by which the soul measures, judges, and considers all things; but we must direct and stimulate it unremittingly by the discipline and rule of dialectic. Then he will point out to us two things particularly to beware of: that we should not make water facing the sun or cut our nails while offering sacrifice. But after we have, through the agency of moral philosophy, both voided the lax desires of our too abundant pleasures and pared away like nail-cuttings the sharp corners of anger and the stings of wrath, only then may we begin to take part in the holy rites, that is, the mysteries of Bacchus we have mentioned, and to be free for our contemplation, whose father and leader the Sun is rightly named. Finally, Pythagoras will enjoin us to feed the cock, that is, to feast the divine part of our soul on the knowledge of things divine as if on substantial food and heavenly ambrosia. This is the cock at whose sight the lion, that is, all earthly power, trembles and is filled with awe. This is that cock to whom, we read in Job, intelligence was given. When this cock crows, erring man comes to his senses. This cock in the twilight of morning daily sings with

the morning stars as they praise God. The dying Socrates, when he hoped to join the divinity of his spirit with the divinity of a greater world, said that he owed this cock to Aesculapius, that is, to the physician of souls, now that he had passed beyond all danger of illness.†

19.   Let us review also the records of the Chaldeans, and we shall see (if they are to be trusted) the road to felicity laid open to mortals through the same sciences. His Chaldaean interpreters write that it was a saying of Zoroaster that the soul is winged and that, when the wings drop off, she falls headlong into the body; and then, after her wings have grown again sufficiently, she flies back to heaven. When his followers asked him in what manner they could obtain souls winged with well-feathered wings, he replied: "Refresh ye your wings in the waters of life." Again when they asked where they should seek those waters, he answered them thus by a parable (as was the custom of the man): "God's paradise is laved and watered by four rivers, from whose same source ye may draw the waters of your salvation. The name of that in the north is Pischon, which meaneth the right. The name of that in the west is Dichon, which signifieth expiation. The name of that in the east is Chiddikel, which expresseth light, and of that in the south, Perath, which we may interpret as piety."

20.   Turn your attention, Fathers, to the diligent consideration of what these doctrines of Zoroaster mean. Surely nothing else than that we should wash away the uncleanness from our eyes by moral science as if by the western waves; that we should align their keen vision toward the right by the rule of dialectic as if by the northern line; that we should then accustom them to endure in the contemplation of nature the still feeble light of truth as if it were the first rays of the rising sun, so that at last, through the agency of theological piety and the most holy worship of God, we may like heavenly eagles boldly endure the most brilliant splendor of the meridian sun. These are, perhaps, those ideas proper to morning, midday, and evening first sung by David and given a broader interpretation by Augustine. This is that noonday light which incites the Seraphs to their goal and equally sheds light on the Cherubs. This is that country toward which

---

* 133c ff.

† Cf. *Phaedo* 118a.

Abraham, our father of old, was ever journeying. This is that place where, as the doctrines of Cabalists and Moors have handed down to posterity, there is no room for unclean spirits. And, if it is right to bring into the open anything at all of the occult mysteries, even in the guise of a riddle, since a sudden fall from heaven has condemned the head of man to dizziness, and, in the words of Jeremiah, death has come in through our windows and smitten our vitals and our heart, let us summon Raphael, celestial physician, that he may set us free by moral philosophy and by dialectic as though by wholesome drugs. Then, when we are restored to health, Gabriel, "the strength of God," shall abide in us, leading us through the miracles of nature and showing us on every side the merit and the might of God. He will at last consign us to the high priest Michael, who will distinguish those who have completed their term in the service of philosophy with the holy office of theology as if with a crown of precious stones.

21. These, reverend Fathers, are the considerations that have not only inspired but compelled me to the study of philosophy. I should certainly not set them forth were I not answering those who are wont to condemn the study of philosophy, especially among men of rank or even of a mediocre station in life. For this whole study of philosophy has now (and it is the misfortune of our age) come to despise and contumely rather than to honor and glory. Thus this deadly and monstrous conviction has come to pervade the minds of well-nigh all – that philosophy either must be studied not at all or by few persons, as if it were absolutely nothing to have clearly ascertained, before our eyes and before our hands, the causes of things, the ways of nature, the plan of the universe, the purposes of God, and the mysteries of heaven and earth; unless one may obtain some favor, or make money for one's self. Rather, it has come to the point where none is now deemed wise, alas, save those who make the study of wisdom a mercenary profession, and where it is possible to see the chaste Pallas, who was sent among men as the gift of the gods, hooted, hissed, and whistled off the stage; and not having anyone to love or to befriend her, unless by selling herself, as it were, she repays into the treasury of her "lover" even the ill-gained money received as the poor price of her tarnished virginity.

22. I speak all these accusations (not without the deepest grief and indignation) not against the princes of this time but against the philosophers, who both believe and openly declare that there should be no study of philosophy for the reason that no fee and no compensation have been fixed for philosophers, just as if they did not show by this one sign that they are no philosophers, that since their whole life is set either on profit or on ambition they do not embrace the very discovery of truth for its own sake. I shall grant myself this and blush not at all to praise myself to this extent that I have never studied philosophy for any other reason than that I might be a philosopher; and that I have neither hoped for any pay from my studies, from my labors by lamplight, nor sought any other reward than the cultivation of my mind and the knowledge of the truth I have ever longed for above all things. I have always been so desirous, so enamored of this, that I have relinquished all interest in affairs private and public and given myself over entirely to leisure for contemplation, from which no disparagements of those who hate me, no curses of the enemies of wisdom, have been able in the past or will be able in the future to discourage me. Philosophy herself has taught me to rely on my own conscience rather than on the opinions of others, and always to take thought not so much that people may speak no evil of me, as, rather, that I myself may neither say nor do aught that is evil.

23. For my part, reverend Fathers, I was not unaware that this very disputation of mine would be as grateful and pleasing to you who favor all good sciences, and have been willing to honor it with your most august presence, as it would be offensive and annoying to many others. And I know there is no lack of those who have heretofore condemned my project, and who condemn it at present on a number of grounds. Enterprises that are well and conscientiously directed toward virtue have been wont to find no fewer – not to say more – detractors than those that are wickedly and falsely directed toward vice. There are, indeed, those who do not approve of this whole method of disputation and of this institution of publicly debating on learning, maintaining that it tends rather to the parade of talent and the display of erudition than to the increase of learning. There are those who do not indeed disapprove this kind of practice, but who in no wise

approve it in me because I, born I admit but twenty-four years ago, should have dared at my age to offer a disputation concerning the lofty mysteries of Christian theology, the highest topics of philosophy and unfamiliar branches of knowledge, in so famous a city, before so great an assembly of very learned men, in the presence of the apostolic senate. Others, who give me leave to offer this disputation, are unwilling to allow me to debate nine hundred theses, and misrepresent it as being a work as unnecessary and as ostentatious as it is beyond my powers. I would have yielded to their objections and given in immediately if the philosophy I profess had so instructed me; and I should not now be answering them, even with philosophy as my preceptress, if I believed that this debate between us had been undertaken for the purpose of quarreling and scolding. Therefore, let the whole intention to disparage and to exasperate depart from our minds, and malice also, which Plato writes is ever absent from the heavenly choir.* Let us in friendly wise try both questions: whether I am to debate and whether I am to debate about this great number of theses.

24.   First, as to those who revile this custom of debating in public I shall certainly not say a great deal, since this crime, if it is held a crime, is shared with me not only by all of you, excellent doctors, who have rather frequently engaged in this office not without the highest praise and glory, but also by Plato, also by Aristotle, and also by the most worthy philosophers of every age. For them it was certain that, for the attainment of the knowledge of truth they were always seeking for themselves, nothing is better than to attend as often as possible the exercise of debate. For just as bodily energy is strengthened by gymnastic exercise, so beyond doubt in this wrestling-place of letters, as it were, energy of mind becomes far stronger and more vigorous. And I could not believe, either that the poets, by the arms of Pallas which they sang, or that the Hebrews, when they called the sword the symbol of wise men, were indicating to us anything else than that such honorable contests are surely a necessary way of attaining wisdom. For this reason it is, perchance, that the Chaldaeans desired in the horoscope of one who was to be a philosopher that Mars should be to Mercury in the trinal aspect,

as much as to say, "If these assemblies, these disputations, should be given up, all philosophy would become sluggish and drowsy."

25.   But truly with those who say I am unequal to this commission, my method of defense is more difficult. For if I say that I am equal to it, it seems that I shall take on myself the reproach of being immodest and of thinking too well of myself, and, if I admit that I am not equal to it, the reproach of being imprudent and thoughtless. See into what straits I have fallen, in what a position I am placed, since I cannot without blame promise about myself what I cannot then fail to fulfil without blame. Perhaps I could refer to that saying of Job: "The spirit is in all men," and be told with Timothy, "Let no man despise thy youth." But out of my own conscience I shall with more truth say this: that there is nothing either great or extraordinary about me. I do not deny that I am, if you will, studious and eager for the good sciences, but nevertheless I neither assume nor arrogate to myself the title of learned. However great the burden I may have taken on my shoulders, therefore, it was not because I was not perfectly aware of my own want of strength but because I knew that it is a distinction of contests of this kind, that is, literary ones, that there is a profit in being defeated. Whence it is that even the most feeble are by right able and bound not only not to decline but even more to court them, seeing that he who yields receives no injury but a benefit from the victor, in that through him he returns home even richer, that is, wiser and better equipped for future contests. Inspired by this hope, I, who am but a feeble soldier, have feared not at all to wage so burdensome a war with the strongest and most vigorous men of all. Whether this action be ill considered or not may be judged from the outcome of the battle and not from my age.

26.   It remains in the third place to answer those who take offense at the great number of my propositions, as if the weight of these lay on their shoulders, and as if the burden, such as it is, were not rather to be borne by me alone. It is surely unbecoming and beyond measure captious to wish to set bounds to another's effort and, as Cicero says, to desire moderation in a matter which is the better as it is on a larger scale.† In

---

* Phaedrus 247a.

† De finibus i. 1.

so great a venture it was necessary for me either to give complete satisfaction or to fail utterly. Should I succeed, I do not see why what is laudable to do in an affair of ten theses should be deemed culpable to have done also in an affair of nine hundred. Should I fail, they will have the wherewithal to accuse me if they hate me and to forgive me if they love me. For the failure of a young man with but slender talent and little learning in so grave and so great a matter will be more deserving of pardon than of blame. Nay, according to the poet: "If strength fails, there shall surely be praise for daring; and to have wished for great things is enough." And if many in our time, in imitation of Gorgias of Leontini, have been wont, not without praise, to propose debates not concerning nine hundred questions only, but also concerning all questions in all branches of knowledge, why should I not be allowed, and that without criticism, to discuss questions admittedly numerous but at least fixed and limited? Yet they say it is unnecessary and ostentatious. I contend that this enterprise of mine is in no way superfluous but necessary indeed; and if they will ponder with me the purpose of studying philosophy, they must, even against their wills, admit that it is plainly needful. Those who have devoted themselves to any one of the schools of philosophy, favoring, for instance, Thomas or Scotus, who are now most in fashion, are, to be sure, quite capable of making trial of their particular doctrines in the discussion of but a few questions. I, on the other hand, have so prepared myself that, pledged to the doctrines of no man, I have ranged through all the masters of philosophy, investigated all books, and come to know all schools. Therefore, since I had to speak of them all in order that, as champion of the beliefs of one, I might not seem fettered to it and appear to place less value on the rest, even while proposing a few theses concerning individual schools I could not help proposing a great number concerning all the schools together. And let no man condemn me for coming as a friend whithersoever the tempest bear me. For it was a custom observed by all the ancients in studying every kind of writer to pass over none of the learned works they were able to read, and especially by Aristotle, who for this reason was called by Plato ἀναγνώστης, that is, "reader." And surely it is the part of a narrow mind to have confined itself within a single Porch or Academy. Nor can one rightly choose what suits one's self from all of them who has not first come to be familiar with them all. Consider, in addition, that there is in each school something distinctive that is not common to the others.

27. And now, to begin with the men of our faith, to whom philosophy came last: There is in John Scotus something lively and subtle; in Thomas, sound and consistent; in Aegidius, terse and exact; in Francis, acute and penetrating; in Albert, venerable, copious, and grand; in Henry, as it always seems to me, something sublime and to be revered. Among the Arabs, there is in Averroes something stable and unshaken; in Avempace [...]; in Alfarabi, serious and thoughtful; in Avicenna, divine and Platonic. Among the Greeks philosophy as a whole is certainly brilliant and above all chaste. With Simplicius it is rich and abundant; with Themistius, graceful and compendious; with Alexander, harmonious and learned; with Theophrastus, weightily worked out; with Ammonius, smooth and agreeable. And if you turn your attention to the Platonists, to examine a few: in Porphyry you will rejoice in the abundance of his material and in the complexity of his religion; in Jamblichus you will revere an occult philosophy and the mysteries of the East. In Plotinus there is no isolated aspect you will admire; he shows himself admirable on every side. The toiling Platonists themselves scarcely understand him when he speaks divinely of things divine and, with learned obliquity of speech, far more than humanly of human things. I prefer to pass over the later Platonists: Proclus abounding in Asiatic richness, and those stemming from him, Hermias, Damascius, Olympiodorus, and several others, in all of whom there ever gleams that τὸ θεῖον. that is, "the Divine," which is the distinctive mark of the Platonists.*

28. Add to this that any sect which assails the truer doctrines, and makes game of good

---

* This catalogue is a brief survey of the philosophers utilized in Pico's nine hundred theses. John Scotus is Duns Scotus (d. 1308), Thomas is Thomas Aquinas (d. 1274), Aegidius is Giles of Rome (d. 1316), Francis is Franciscus de Mayronis (d. 1325), Albert is Albertus Magnus (d. 1280), and Henry is Henry of Ghent (d. 1293), Averroes (d. 1198), Avempace (d. 1138), Alfarabi (d. 950), Simplicius (fl. ca. 530), Themistius (fl. ca. 350), and Alexander of Aphrodisias (fl. ca. A.D. 200). Most of the remaining thinkers are Neo-Platonists.

causes by clever slander, strengthens rather than weakens the truth and, like flames stirred by agitation, fans rather than extinguishes it. This has been my reason for wishing to bring before the public the opinions not of a single school alone (which satisfied some I could name) but rather of every school, to the end that that light of truth Plato mentions in his *Epistles** through this comparison of several sects and this discussion of manifold philosophies might dawn more brightly on our minds, like the sun rising from the deep. What were the gain if only the philosophy of the Latins were investigated, that is, that of Albert, Thomas, Scotus, Aegidius, Francis, and Henry, if the Greek and Arabian philosophers were left out – since all wisdom has flowed from the East to the Greeks and from the Greeks to us? In their way of philosophizing, our Latins have always found it sufficient to stand on the discoveries of foreigners and to perfect the work of others. Of what use were it to treat with the Peripatetics on natural philosophy, unless the Platonic Academy were also invited? Their teaching in regard to divinity besides has always (as Augustine witnesses) been thought most hallowed of all philosophies;† and now for the first time, so far as I know (may no one grudge me the word), it has after many centuries been brought by me to the test of public disputation. What were it to have dealt with the opinions of others, no matter how many, if we are come to a gathering of wise men with no contribution of our own and are supplying nothing from our own store, brought forth and worked out by our own genius? It is surely an ignoble part to be wise only from a notebook (as Seneca says)‡ and, as if the discoveries of our predecessors had closed the way to our own industry and the power of nature were exhausted in us, to produce from ourselves nothing which, if it does not actually demonstrate the truth, at least intimates it from afar. For if a tiller of the soil hates sterility in his field, and a husband in his wife, surely the Divine mind joined to and associated with an infertile soul will hate it the more in that a far nobler offspring is desired.

29.   For this reason I have not been content to add to the tenets held in common many teachings taken from the ancient theology of Hermes Trismegistus, many from the doctrines of the Chaldaeans and of Pythagoras, and many from the occult mysteries of the Hebrews. I have proposed also as subjects for discussion several theses in natural philosophy and in divinity, discovered and studied by me. I have proposed, first of all, a harmony between Plato and Aristotle, believed to exist by many ere this but adequately proved by no one. Boethius among the Latins promised that he would do it, but there is no trace of his having done what he always wished to do. Among the Greeks, Simplicius made the same declaration, and would that he had been as good as his word! Augustine also writes, in the *Contra Academicos*, that there were not lacking several who tried with their keenest arguments to prove the same thing, that the philosophies of Plato and Aristotle are identical.§ John the Grammarian** likewise, although he did say that Plato differs from Aristotle only in the minds of those who do not understand Plato's words, nevertheless left it to posterity to prove. I have, moreover, brought to bear several passages in which I maintain that the opinions of Scotus and Thomas, and several in which I hold that those of Averroes and Avicenna, which are considered to be contradictory, are in agreement.

30.   In the second place, I have next arranged the fruit of my thinking on both the Platonic and the Aristotelian philosophy, and then seventy-two new physical and metaphysical theses by means of which whoever holds them will be able (unless I am mistaken – which will soon be made manifest to me) to answer any question whatever proposed in natural philosophy or divinity, by a system far other than we are taught in that philosophy which is studied in the schools and practised by the doctors of this age. Nor ought anyone, Fathers, to be so amazed that I, in my first years, at my tender age, at which it was hardly legitimate for me (as some have taunted) to read the books of others, should wish to introduce a new philosophy; but rather one should praise it if it is sustained or condemn it if it does not find favor, and finally, when these my discoveries and my scholarship come to be judged, number not their author's years so much as their own merits or faults.

---

* Cf. *Epistle* vii. 341c–d.
† Cf. *City of God* ix. 1 and many other passages.
‡ *Epistles* xxxiii. 7.

§ *Contra academicos* iii. 42.
** Joannes Philoponus.

31. There is, furthermore, still another method of philosophizing through numbers, which I have introduced as new, but which is in fact old, and was observed by the earliest theologians, principally by Pythagoras, by Aglaophamos, Philolaus, and Plato, and by the first Platonists, but which in this present era, like many other illustrious things, has perished through the carelessness of posterity, so that hardly any traces of it can be found. Plato writes in the *Epinomis* that, of all the liberal arts and theoretical sciences, the science of computation is the chief and the most divine.* Likewise, inquiring, "Why is man the wisest of animals?" he concludes, "Because he knows how to count," an opinion which Aristotle also mentions in his *Problems.*† Abumasar writes that it was a saying of Avenzoar of Babylon that he knows all things who knows how to count. These statements cannot possibly be true if by the science of computation they mean that science in which, at present, merchants in particular are most skilled. To this also Plato bears witness, warning us with raised voice not to think that this divine arithmetic is the arithmetic of traders.‡ I therefore promised, when I seemed after much nocturnal labor to have discovered that arithmetic which is so highly extolled, that I myself would (in order to make trial of this matter) reply in public through the art of number to seventy-four questions considered of chief importance in physics and metaphysics.

32. I have also proposed theorems dealing with magic, in which I have indicated that magic has two forms, one of which depends entirely on the work and authority of demons, a thing to be abhorred, so help me the God of truth, and a monstrous thing. The other, when it is rightly pursued, is nothing else than the utter perfection of natural philosophy. While the Greeks make mention of both of them, they call the former γοητεία, in no wise honoring it with the name of magic; the latter they call by the characteristic and fitting name of μαγεία, as if it were a perfect and most high wisdom. For, as Porphyry says, in the Persian tongue *magus* expresses the same idea as "interpreter" and "worshiper of the divine" with us. Moreover, Fathers, the disparity and unlikeness

between these arts is great, nay, rather, the greatest possible. The former not only the Christian religion but all religions and every well-constituted state condemn and abhor. The latter all wise men, all peoples devoted to the study of heavenly and divine things, approve and embrace. The former is the most deceitful of arts; the latter a higher and more holy philosophy. The former is vain and empty; the latter, sure, trustworthy, and sound. Whoso has cherished the former has ever dissembled, because it is a shame and a reproach to an author; but from the latter the highest renown and glory of letters was derived in ancient days, and almost always has been. No man who was a philosopher and eager to study the good arts has ever been a student of the former; but Pythagoras, Empedocles, Democritus, and Plato all traveled to study the latter, taught it when they returned, and esteemed it before all others in their mysteries. As the former is approved by no reasonable arguments, so is it not by established authors; the latter, honored by the most celebrated fathers, as it were, has in particular two authors: Zamolxis, whom Abaris the Hyperborean copied, and Zoroaster, not him of whom perhaps you are thinking but him who is the son of Oromasius.

33. If we ask Plato what the magic of both these men was, he will reply, in his *Alcibiades*,§ that the magic of Zoroaster was none other than the science of the Divine in which the kings of the Persians instructed their sons, to the end that they might be taught to rule their own commonwealth by the example of the commonwealth of the world. He will answer, in the *Charmides*,** that the magic of Zamolxis was that medicine of the soul through which temperance is brought to the soul as through temperance health is brought to the body. In their footsteps Charondas, Damigeron, Apollonius, Osthanes, and Dardanus thereafter persevered. Homer persevered, whom I shall sometime prove, in my *Poetic Theology*, to have concealed this philosophy beneath the wanderings of his Ulysses, just as he has concealed all others. Eudoxus and Hermippus persevered. Almost all who have searched through the Pythagorean and Platonic mysteries have persevered. Furthermore, from among the later philosophers I find three who have

* 976c ff.
† xxxi. 6. 956 *a* 11 ff.
‡ *Republic* 525b ff.

§ 122a.
** 156e–157a.

scented it out – the Arabian al-Kindi, Roger Bacon, and William of Paris. Plotinus also mentions it when he demonstrates that a *magus* is the servant of nature and not a contriver. This very wise man approves and maintains this magic, so hating the other that, when he was summoned to the rites of evil spirits, he said that they should come to him rather than that he should go to them; and surely he was right. For even as the former makes man the bound slave; of wicked powers, so does the latter make him their ruler and their lord. In conclusion, the former can claim for itself the name of neither art nor science, while the latter, abounding in the loftiest mysteries, embraces the deepest contemplation of the most secret things, and at last the knowledge of all nature. The latter, in calling forth into the light as if from their hiding-places the powers scattered and sown in the world by the loving-kindness of God, does not so much work wonders as diligently serve a wonder-working nature. The latter, having more searchingly examined into the harmony of the universe, which the Greeks with greater significance call συμπάθεια, and having clearly perceived the reciprocal affinity of natures, and applying to each single thing the suitable and peculiar inducements (which are called the ἴυγγες of the magicians) brings forth into the open the miracles concealed in the recesses of the world, in the depths of nature, and in the storehouses and mysteries of God, just as if she herself were their maker; and, as the farmer weds his elms to vines, even so does the *magus* wed earth to heaven, that is, he weds lower things to the endowments and powers of higher things. Whence it comes about that the latter is as divine and as salutary as the former is unnatural and harmful; for this reason especially, that in subjecting man to the enemies of God, the former calls him away from God, but the latter rouses him to the admiration of God's works which is the most certain condition of a willing faith, hope, and love. For nothing moves one to religion and to the worship of God more than the diligent contemplation of the wonders of God; if we have thoroughly examined them by this natural magic we are considering, we shall be compelled to sing, more ardently inspired to the worship and love of the Creator: "The heavens and all the earth are full of the majesty of thy glory." And this is enough about magic. I have said these things about it, for I know there are many

who, just as dogs always bark at strangers, in the same way often condemn and hate what they do not understand.

34. I come now to the things I have elicited from the ancient mysteries of the Hebrews and have cited for the confirmation of the inviolable Catholic faith. Lest perchance they should be deemed fabrications, trifles, or the tales of jugglers by those to whom they are unfamiliar, I wish all to understand what they are and of what sort, whence they come, by what and by how illustrious authors supported, and how mysterious, how divine, and how necessary they are to the men of our faith for defending our religion against the grievous misrepresentations of the Hebrews. Not only the famous doctors of the Hebrews, but also from among men of our opinion Esdras, Hilary, and Origen write that Moses on the mount received from God not only the Law, which he left to posterity written down in five books, but also a true and more occult explanation of the Law. It was, moreover, commanded him of God by all means to proclaim the Law to the people but not to commit the interpretation of the Law to writing or to make it a matter of common knowledge. He himself should reveal it only to Iesu Nave, who in his turn should unveil it to the other high priests to come after him, under a strict obligation of silence. It was enough through guileless story to recognize now the power of God, now his wrath against the wicked, his mercy to the righteous, his justice to all; and through divine and beneficial precepts to be brought to a good and happy way of life and the worship of true religion. But to make public the occult mysteries, the secrets of the supreme Godhead hidden beneath the shell of the Law and under a clumsy show of words – what else were this than to give a holy thing to dogs and to cast pearls before swine? Therefore to keep hidden from the people the things to be shared by the initiate, among whom alone, Paul says, he spoke wisdom, was not the part of human deliberation but of divine command. This custom the ancient philosophers most reverently observed, for Pythagoras wrote nothing except a few trifles, which he intrusted on his deathbed to his daughter Dama. The Sphinxes carved on the temples of the Egyptians reminded them that mystic doctrines should be kept inviolable from the common herd by means of the knots of riddles. Plato, writing certain things to Dion

concerning the highest substances, said: "It must be stated in riddles, lest the letter should fall by chance into the hands of others and what I am writing to you should be apprehended by others.* Aristotle used to say that his books of *Metaphysics*, in which he treated of things divine, were both published and not published. What further? Origen asserts that Jesus Christ, the Teacher of life, made many revelations to his disciples, which they were unwilling to write down lest they should become commonplaces to the rabble. This is in the highest degree confirmed by Dionysius the Areopagite, who says that the occult mysteries were conveyed by the founders of our religion ἐκ νοῦ εἰς νοῦν διὰ μέσον λόγου, from mind to mind, without writing, through the medium of speech.

35. In exactly the same way, when the true interpretation of the Law according to the command of God, divinely handed down to Moses, was revealed, it was called the Cabala, a word which is the same among the Hebrews as "reception" among ourselves; for this reason, of course, that one man from another, by a sort of hereditary right, received that doctrine not through written records but through a regular succession of revelations. But after the Hebrews were restored by Cyrus from the Babylonian captivity, and after the temple had been established anew under Zorobabel, they brought their attention to the restoration of the Law. Esdras, then the head of the church, after the book of Moses had been amended, when he plainly recognized that, because of the exiles, the massacres, the flights, and the captivity of the children of Israel, the custom instituted by their forefathers of transmitting the doctrine from mouth to mouth could not be preserved, and that it would come to pass that the mysteries of the heavenly teachings divinely bestowed on them would be lost, since the memory of them could not long endure without the aid of written records, decided that those of the elders then surviving should be called together and that each one should impart to the gathering whatever he possessed by personal recollection concerning the mysteries of the Law and that scribes should be employed to collect them into seventy volumes (about the number of elders in the Sanhedrin). That you may not have to rely on me alone in this matter, Fathers, hear Esdras himself speak thus: "And it came to pass, when the forty days were fulfilled, that the Most High spake unto me, saying, The first that thou hast written publish openly, and let the worthy and the unworthy read it: but keep the seventy last books, that thou mayst deliver them to such as be wise among thy people: for in them is the spring of understanding, the fountain of wisdom, and the stream of knowledge. And I did so." And these are the words of Esdras to the letter. These are the books of cabalistic lore. In these books principally resides, as Esdras with a clear voice justly declared, the spring of understanding, that is, the ineffable theology of the supersubstantial deity; the fountain of wisdom, that is, the exact metaphysic of the intellectual and angelic forms; and the stream of knowledge, that is, the most steadfast philosophy of natural things. Pope Sixtus the Fourth who last preceded the pope under whom we are now fortunate to be living, Innocent the Eighth, took the greatest pains and interest in seeing that these books should be translated into the Latin tongue for a public service to our faith, and, when he died, three of them had been done into Latin. Among the Hebrews of the present day these books are cherished with such devotion that it is permitted no man to touch them unless he be forty years of age.

36. When I had purchased these books at no small cost to myself, when I had read them through with the greatest diligence and with unwearying toil, I saw in them (as God is my witness) not so much the Mosaic as the Christian religion. There is the mystery of the Trinity, there the Incarnation of the Word, there the divinity of the Messiah; there I have read about original sin, its expiation through Christ, the heavenly Jerusalem, the fall of the devils, the orders of the angels, purgatory, and the punishments of hell, the same things we read daily in Paul and Dionysius, in Jerome and Augustine. But in those parts which concern philosophy you really seem to hear Pythagoras and Plato, whose principles are so closely related to the Christian faith that our Augustine gives immeasurable thanks to God that the books of the Platonists have come into his hands.† Taken altogether, there is absolutely no controversy between ourselves and the Hebrews on any matter, with regard to

---

* *Epistle* ii. 321*d*.

† Cf. *Confessions* viii. 2.

which they cannot be refuted and gainsaid out of the cabalistic books, so that there will not be even a corner left in which they may hide themselves. I have as a most weighty witness of this fact that very learned man Antonius Chronicus who, when I was with him at a banquet, with his own ears heard Dactylus, a Hebrew trained in this lore, with all his heart agree entirely to the Christian idea of the Trinity.

37. But let me return to surveying the chapters of my disputation. I have introduced also my own idea of the interpretation of the prophetic verses of Orpheus and Zoroaster. Orpheus is read among the Greeks in a nearly complete text, Zoroaster only in part, though, among the Chaldaeans, in a more complete text, and both are believed to be the fathers and authors of ancient wisdom. Now, to pass over Zoroaster, the frequent mention of whom among the Platonists is never without the greatest respect, Jamblichus of Chalcis writes that Pythagoras followed the Orphic theology as the model on which he fashioned and built his own philosophy. Nay, furthermore, they say that the maxims of Pythagoras are alone called holy, because he proceeded from the principles of Orpheus; and that the secret doctrine of numbers and whatever Greek philosophy has of the great or the sublime has flowed from thence as its first font. But as was the practice of the ancient theologians, even so did Orpheus protect the mysteries of his dogmas with the coverings of fables, and conceal them with a poetic veil, so that whoever should read his hymns would suppose there was nothing beneath them beyond idle tales and perfectly unadulterated trifles. I have wished to say this so that it might be known what a task it was for me, how difficult it was to draw out the hidden meaning of the secrets of philosophy from the intentional tangles of riddles and from the obscurity of fables, especially since I have been aided, in a matter so serious, so abstruse, and so little known, by no toil, no application on the part of other interpreters. And yet like dogs they have barked that I have made a kind of heap of inconsequential nothings for a vain display of mere quantity, as if these were not all questions in the highest degree disputed and controversial, in which the main schools are at swords' points, and as if I had not contributed many things utterly unknown and untried to these very men who are even now tearing at my reputation and who consider that they are the leaders in philosophy. Nay, I am so far from this fault that I have taken great pains to reduce my argument to as few chapters as I could. If I myself had (after the wont of others) wished to divide it into parts and to cut it to pieces, it would undoubtedly have grown to a countless number.

38. And, to hold my peace about the rest, who is there who does not know that a single proposition of the nine hundred, the one that treats of reconciling the philosophies of Plato and Aristotle, I could have developed, beyond all suspicion of my having wooed mere quantity, into six hundred, nay, more chapters, by enumerating one after the other all those points in which others consider those philosophers to differ and I, to agree? But I must certainly speak (for I shall speak, albeit neither modestly nor in conformity with my own character), since my enviers and detractors compel me to: I have wished to give assurance by this contest of mine, not so much that I know many things, as that I know things of which many are ignorant. And now, in order that this, reverend Fathers, may become manifest to you by the facts and that my oration may no longer stand in the way of your desire, excellent doctors, whom I perceive to be prepared and girded up in the expectation of the dispute, not without great delight: let us now – and may the outcome be fortunate and favorable – join battle as to the sound of a trumpet of war.

13

Benedict Spinoza, *Ethics*, Book V

Introduction

Born in Amsterdam (1632), the only son of his father's second wife, Benedict (Baruch) Spinoza was raised by a Jewish family that, like so many others, had fled the oppression of Spain-Portugal for the more open and tolerant Netherlands. Spinoza's grandfather had been a leader in the Sephardic community in Amsterdam, and the young philosopher received a rigorous education, studying almost certainly Hebrew, Scripture, Talmud, and Jewish philosophers like Hasdai Crescas (1340–c. 1412), Levi ben Gerson (Gersonides; 1288–1344), and the great Cordoban, Moses ben Maimon (Maimonides; IV.8). It was reading Descartes (II.8, III.12), however, that would transform Spinoza; and the subsequent unorthodox course of his intellectual development brought him in early adulthood into intractable conflict with the Jewish authorities. In 1656 he was excommunicated.

Adopting the Latin version of his Hebrew name, Spinoza settled into a relatively solitary and independent life, pursuing philosophical study and supporting himself as a lens grinder by producing the optical devices used in newly advanced scien-

From Baruch Spinoza, *The Ethics and Selected Letters*, ed. S. Feldman, trans. S. Shirley, Indianapolis, IN: Hackett Publishing Co., 1982, pp. 203–25 (notes omitted).

tific instruments, like the telescope and microscope. Spinoza's writings brought him widespread admiration, and in 1673 he was offered a professorship at the University of Heidelberg, one of Europe's leading academic institutions. He turned it down, however, explaining that he wished to remain unhindered in his thought. While he published two other books during his lifetime, Spinoza's magnum opus was the posthumous *Ethica* (1677, the year of his death). At first blush the *Ethics* has seemed to many to be an odd, difficult, and overwhelmingly metaphysical text. That's because Spinoza's ethical vision is so deeply bound up with his view of reason and his view of reality.

Reality for Spinoza comprises a great rational system, following in its movement a geometric and necessary order. For this reason, the *Ethics* itself is written, like Euclid's *Elements*, as a system of geometric proofs, deriving "propositions" from "axioms" and elaborating upon them in various "scholia." Our selection here is taken from Part V, the last part – the ultimate part – of Spinoza's *Ethics*. Here Spinoza argues that the *summum bonum* or "highest good" for human beings is not pleasure, not the cultivation of excellent habits of character and emotion, not the proper exercise of will or free choice, and of course not the acquisition of wealth, honor, or social power. Instead, the highest good entails achieving a special kind of understanding, what he calls the *amor Dei intellectualis*, the "intellectual love of God" (*Ethics*, V.20, V.32–33).

The idea that humanity's supreme good comprises an intellectual grasp of the divine certainly isn't new to philosophy. In *Phaedrus* (III.3), in *Republic* (II.1), and elsewhere, Plato describes the achievement of human excellence as bound up with an intellectual grasp of eternal, hyperuranian (supra-heavenly) "forms" (*eidē*). Aristotle, in Book X of the *Nicomachean Ethics* roots the highest good of human beings in the "contemplation" (*theoria*) of eternal truth (I.2). Aquinas argues that the ultimate good of human beings in the afterlife is the apprehension of God by the intellect (I.11). The divinity, however, toward which Spinoza directs the intellect, is something rather different from that of his predecessors. "*Deus sive natura*" ("God or nature") in Spinoza's famous turn of phrase, names the ultimate object of the intellect; for according to Spinoza, God is nature, and nature is God. More precisely, God is in one sense (as what he calls "*natura naturans*") the very "substance" of the universe. The two dimensions of this substance we experience, "thought" and "extension," are however simply "attributes" of God. And there are many more attributes of God we don't experience, in fact there must an infinite number of them, since God is an infinite being. Individual human beings are just modifications or "modes" of those attributes of the world's substance. We are all, then, in a way connected, part of the great, rational system of reality, part of God (as "*natura naturata*"). Romantics of the nineteenth century drank deeply from Spinoza's well.

The thing is, for the most part, people do not realize that they are part of this vast order, much less how they fit into it. We are for the most part, as Spinoza put it in his letter to Oldenburg (Letter #32), like tiny worms living in the bloodstream of some much larger animal. The worms do not understand that they are living in a larger being, nor do they understand what happens to them – driven, as they are, through various vessels and channels by forces beyond their control as well as beyond their comprehension. Of course, that's just where human beings depart from worms. Humans possess the capacity to enlarge their understanding of the world through the exercise of reason. First grasping the world through observation and sensation, we subsequently (secondly), through the development of scientific and philosophical theories, are able to discern the general laws and "common notions" that govern

the course of nature. In what Spinoza calls an even higher or "third" kind of knowledge (*scientia intuitive*, or intuitive knowledge) knowers both grasp the fundamental principles or "axioms" of all things and come to see how those principles manifest themselves in particulars. As it did for the neo-Platonist Plotinus (204–70), the path of ethics, then, comprises an ever-deeper grasp of the basis of reality (I.10). While for the neo-Platonists, however, the final stage of this path is a moment of supra-intellectual ecstasy, for Spinoza the journey to the highest good marks simply and ever-clearer and ever more "adequate" understanding of things.

Like the Stoics – Marcus Aurelius, for example (I.8) – and Descartes before him, Spinoza portrays the achievement of human perfection in terms of silencing and controlling emotion and desire. While this is accomplished for the Stoics through the exercise of something like will on the basis of reason, for Spinoza it is strictly an affair of understanding. For Spinoza, moral perfection does not entail the repression of emotion under the dictates of understanding (a model common in Plato; I.1); rather understanding itself *is* the silencing of the passions. As the mind comes to think more adequate thoughts, accordingly to Spinoza, emotions like anger, fear, hatred, and desire simply recede (*Ethics*, V.20). The mind abandons the illusory idea that it is compelled by external causes to feel certain ways (*Ethics*, V.2). In place of the turbulence of passive emotions, a clearer and clearer understanding of the order of nature and the order of God brings with it a distinctive and superlative kind of "contentment," happiness, and "joy" (*Ethics*, V.10, V.27). In this way, it is possible for human beings to become more "active" and gain a kind of "freedom," even a kind of "salvation," from the passive, painful, and narrow life to which most are subject as they are blown this way and that by unstable and turbulent emotions (*Ethics*, V.35). As one's thoughts become increasingly God's thoughts one sees things not as a particular individual but rather "under the aspect of eternity" (*sub species aeternitatis*). Truth is, after all, according to Spinoza, universal.

In Spinoza's synthesis, then, the seemingly divergent goals of self-knowledge, understanding nature, and understanding God actually coincide. Through this extraordinary, synthetic understanding, human beings may even acquire a peculiar kind of "immortality" (*Ethics*, V.21ff.). The "blessedness" of this condition is not the separate, consequent "reward of virtue but virtue itself" (*Ethics*, V.42). Achieving it is not easy; but as Spinoza famously put it, "All things excellent are as difficult as they are rare."

Spinoza, *Ethics*, Book V

Of the Power of the Understanding, or of Human Freedom

Preface At length I pass to the remaining portion of my Ethics, which is concerned with the way leading to freedom. I shall therefore treat therein of the power of the reason, showing how far the reason can control the emotions, and what is the nature of Mental Freedom or Blessedness; we shall then be able to see, how much more powerful the wise man is than the ignorant. It is no part of my design to point out the method and means whereby the understanding may be perfected, nor to show the skill whereby the body may be so tended, as to be capable of the due performance of its functions. The latter question lies in the province of Medicine, the former in the province of Logic. Here, therefore, I repeat, I shall treat only of the power of the mind, or of reason; and I shall mainly show the extent and nature of its dominion over the emotions, for their control and moderation. That we do not possess absolute dominion over them, I have already shown. Yet the Stoics have thought, that the emotions depended absolutely on our will, and that we could absolutely govern them. But these philosophers were compelled, by the protest of experience, not from their own principles, to confess, that no slight practice and zeal is needed to control and moderate them: and this someone endeavoured to illustrate by the example (if I remember rightly) of two dogs, the one a house-dog and the other a hunting-dog. For by long training it could be brought about, that the house-dog should become accustomed to hunt, and the hunting-dog to cease from running after hares. To this opinion Descartes not a little inclines. For he maintained, that the soul or mind is specially united to a particular part of the brain, namely, to that part called the pineal gland, by the aid of which the mind is enabled to feel all the movements which are set going in the body, and also external objects, and which the mind by a simple act of volition can put in motion in various ways. He asserted, that this gland is so suspended in the midst of the brain, that it could be moved by the slightest motion of the animal spirits: further, that this gland is suspended in the midst of the brain in as many different manners, as the animal spirits can impinge thereon; and, again, that as many different marks are impressed on the said gland, as there are different external objects which impel the animal spirits towards it; whence it follows, that if the will of the soul suspends the gland in a position, wherein it has already been suspended once before by the animal spirits driven in one way or another, the gland in its turn reacts on the said spirits, driving and determining them to the condition wherein they were, when repulsed before by a similar position of the gland. He further asserted, that every act of mental volition is united in nature to a certain given motion of the gland. For instance, whenever anyone desires to look at a remote object, the act of volition causes the pupil of the eye to dilate, whereas, if the person in question had only thought of the dilatation of the pupil, the mere wish to dilate it would not have brought about the result, inasmuch as the motion of the gland, which serves to impel the animal spirits towards the optic nerve in a way which would dilate or contract the pupil, is not associated in nature with the wish to dilate or contract the pupil, but with the wish to look at remote or very near objects. Lastly, he maintained that, although every motion of the aforesaid gland seems to have been united by nature to one particular thought out of the whole number of our thoughts from the very beginning of our life, yet it can nevertheless become through habituation associated with other thoughts; this he endeavours to prove in the *Passions de l'âme*, I. 50. He thence concludes, that there is no soul so weak, that it cannot, under proper direction, acquire absolute power over its passions. For passions as defined by him are "perceptions, or feelings, or disturbances of the soul, which are referred to the soul as species, and which (mark the expression) are produced, preserved, and strengthened through some movement of the spirits." (*Passions de l'âme*, I. 27.) But, seeing that we can join any motion of the gland, or consequently of the spirits, to any volition, the determination of the will depends entirely on our own powers; if, therefore, we determine our will with sure and firm decisions in the direction to which we wish our actions to tend, and associate the motions of the passions which we wish to acquire with the said decisions, we shall acquire an absolute dominion over our passions. Such is the doctrine of this illustrious philosopher (in so far as I gather it from his own words); it is one which, had it been less ingenious, I could hardly believe to have proceeded from so great a man. Indeed, I am lost in wonder, that a philosopher, who had stoutly asserted, that he would draw no conclusions which do not follow from self-evident premises, and would affirm nothing which he did not clearly and distinctly perceive, and who had so often taken to task the scholastics for wishing to explain obscurities through occult qualities, could maintain a hypothesis, beside which occult qualities are commonplace. What does he understand, I ask, by the union of the mind and the body? What clear and distinct conception has he got of thought in most intimate union with a certain particle of extended matter? Truly I should like him to explain this union through its proximate cause. But he had so distinct a conception of mind being distinct from body, that he could not assign any particular cause of the union between the two, or of the mind itself, but was obliged to have recourse to the cause of the whole universe, that is to God. Further, I should much like to know, what degree of motion the mind can impart to this pineal gland, and with what force can it hold it suspended? For I am in ignorance, whether this gland can be agitated more slowly or more quickly by the mind than by the animal spirits, and whether the motions of the passions, which we have closely united with firm decisions, cannot be again disjoined therefrom by physical causes; in which case it would follow that, although the mind firmly intended to face a given danger, and had united to this decision the motions of boldness, yet at the sight of the danger the gland might become suspended in a way, which would preclude the mind thinking of anything except running away. In truth, as there is no common standard of volition and motion,

so is there no comparison possible between the powers of the mind and the power or strength of the body; consequently the strength of one cannot in any wise be determined by the strength of the other. We may also add, that there is no gland discoverable in the midst of the brain, so placed that it can thus easily be set in motion in so many ways, and also that all the nerves are not prolonged so far as the cavities of the brain. Lastly, I omit all the assertions which he makes concerning the will and its freedom, inasmuch as I have abundantly proved that his premises are false. Therefore, since the power of the mind, as I have shown above, is defined by the understanding only, we shall determine solely by the knowledge of the mind the remedies against the emotions, which I believe all have had experience of, but do not accurately observe or distinctly see, and from the same basis we shall deduce all those conclusions, which have regard to the mind's blessedness.

Axioms   I.   If two contrary actions be started in the same subject, a change must necessarily take place, either in both, or in one of the two, and continue until they cease to be contrary.

II.   The power of an effect is defined by the power of its cause, in so far as its essence is explained or defined by the essence of its cause.

(This axiom is evident from III. vii.)

PROP. I. *Even as thoughts and the ideas of things are arranged and associated in the mind, so are the modifications of body on the images of things precisely in the same way arranged and associated in the body.*

Proof. – The order and connection of ideas is the same (II. vii.) as the order and connection of things, and *vice versā* the order and connection of things is the same (II. vi. Coroll. and vii.) as the order and connection of ideas. Wherefore, even as the order and connection of ideas in the mind takes place according to the order and association of modifications of the body (II. xviii.), so *vice versā* (III. ii.) the order and connection of modifications of the body takes place in accordance with the manner, in which thoughts and the ideas of things are arranged and associated in the mind.   *Q.E.D.*

PROP. II. *If we remove a disturbance of the spirit, or emotion, from the thought of an external cause, and unite it to other thoughts, then will the love or hatred towards that external cause, and also the vacillations of spirit which arise from these emotions, be destroyed.*

Proof. – That, which constitutes the reality of love or hatred, is pleasure or pain, accompanied by the idea of an external cause (Def. of the Emotions, vi. vii.); wherefore, when this cause is removed, the reality of love or hatred is removed with it; therefore these emotions and those which arise therefrom are destroyed.   *Q.E.D.*

Prop. III. *An emotion, which is a passion, ceases to be a passion, as soon as we form a clear and distinct idea thereof.*

Proof. – An emotion, which is a passion, is a confused idea (by the general Def. of the Emotions). If, therefore, we form a clear and distinct idea of a given emotion, that idea will only be distinguished from the emotion, in so far as it is referred to the mind only, by reason (II. xxi. and note); therefore (III. iii.), the emotion will cease to be a passion.   *Q.E.D.*

Corollary. – An emotion therefore becomes more under our control, and the mind is less passive in respect to it, in proportion as it is more known to us.

Prop. IV. *There is no modification of the body, whereof we cannot form some clear and distinct conception.*

Proof. – Properties which are common to all things can only be conceived adequately (II. xxxviii.); therefore (II. xii. and Lemma ii. after II. xiii.) there is no modification of the body, whereof we cannot form some clear and distinct conception.   *Q.E.D.*

Corollary. – Hence it follows that there is no emotion, whereof we cannot form some clear and distinct conception. For an emotion is the idea of a modification of the body (by the general Def. of the Emotions), and must therefore (by the preceding Prop.) involve some clear and distinct conception.

Note. – Seeing that there is nothing which is not followed by an effect (I. xxxvi.), and that we clearly and distinctly understand whatever follows from an idea, which in us is adequate (II. xl.), it follows that everyone has the power of clearly and distinctly understanding himself and his emotions, if not absolutely, at any rate in part, and consequently of bringing it about, that he should become less subject to them. To attain this result, therefore, we must chiefly direct our efforts to acquiring, as far as possible, a clear and distinct knowledge of every emotion, in order that

the mind may thus, through emotion, be determined to think of those things which it clearly and distinctly perceives, and wherein it fully acquiesces: and thus that the emotion itself may be separated from the thought of an external cause, and may be associated with true thoughts; whence it will come to pass, not only that love, hatred, &c. will be destroyed (V. ii.), but also that the appetites or desires, which are wont to arise from such emotion, will become incapable of being excessive (IV. lxi.). For it must be especially remarked, that the appetite through which a man is said to be active, and that through which he is said to be passive is one and the same. For instance, we have shown that human nature is so constituted, that everyone desires his fellow-men to live after his own fashion (III. xxxi. note); in a man, who is not guided by reason, this appetite is a passion which is called ambition, and does not greatly differ from pride; whereas in a man, who lives by the dictates of reason, it is an activity or virtue which is called piety (IV. xxxvii. note i. and second proof.). In like manner all appetites or desires are only passions, in so far as they spring from inadequate ideas; the same results are accredited to virtue, when they are aroused or generated by adequate ideas. For all desires, whereby we are determined to any given action, may arise as much from adequate as from inadequate ideas (IV. lix.). Than this remedy for the emotions (to return to the point from which I started), which consists in a true knowledge thereof, nothing more excellent, being within our power, can be devised. For the mind has no other power save that of thinking and of forming adequate ideas, as we have shown above (III. iii.).

Prop. V. *An emotion towards a thing, which we conceive simply, and not as necessary, or as contingent, or as possible, is, other conditions being equal, greater than any other emotion.*

Proof. – An emotion towards a thing, which we conceive to be free, is greater than one towards what we conceive to be necessary (III. xlix.), and, consequently, still greater than one towards what we conceive as possible, or contingent (IV. xi.). But to conceive a thing as free can be nothing else than to conceive it simply, while we are in ignorance of the causes whereby it has been determined to action (II. xxxv. note); therefore, an emotion towards a thing which we conceive simply is, other conditions being equal, greater than one, which we feel towards what is necessary, possible, or contingent, and, consequently, it is the greatest of all. *Q.E.D.*

Prop. VI. *The mind has greater power over the emotions and is less subject thereto, in so far as it understands all things as necessary.*

Proof. – The mind understands all things to be necessary (I. xxix.) and to be determined to existence and operation by an infinite chain of causes; therefore (by the foregoing Proposition), it thus far brings it about, that it is less subject to the emotions arising therefrom, and (III. xlviii.) feels less emotion towards the things themselves. *Q.E.D.*

Note. – The more this knowledge, that things are necessary, is applied to particular things, which we conceive more distinctly and vividly, the greater is the power of the mind over the emotions, as experience also testifies. For we see, that the pain arising from the loss of any good is mitigated, as soon as the man who has lost it perceives, that it could not by any means have been preserved. So also we see that no one pities an infant, because it cannot speak, walk, or reason, or lastly, because it passes so many years, as it were, in unconsciousness. Whereas, if most people were born full-grown and only one here and there as an infant, everyone would pity the infants; because infancy would not then be looked on as a state natural and necessary, but as a fault or delinquency in Nature; and we may note several other instances of the same sort.

Prop. VII. *Emotions which are aroused or spring from reason, if we take account of time, are stronger than those, which are attributable to particular objects that we regard as absent.*

Proof. – We do not regard a thing as absent, by reason of the emotion wherewith we conceive it, but by reason of the body being affected by another emotion excluding the existence of the said thing (II. xvii.). Wherefore, the emotion, which is referred to the thing which we regard as absent, is not of a nature to overcome the rest of a man's activities and power (IV. vi.), but is, on the contrary, of a nature to be in some sort controlled by the emotions, which exclude the existence of its external cause (IV. ix.). But an emotion which springs from reason is necessarily referred to the common properties of things (see the def. of reason in II. xl. note ii.), which we always regard as present (for there can be nothing to exclude their present existence), and which we always conceive in the same manner (II.

xxxviii.). Wherefore an emotion of this kind always remains the same; and consequently (V. Ax. i.) emotions, which are contrary thereto and are not kept going by their external causes, will be obliged to adapt themselves to it more and more, until they are no longer contrary to it; to this extent the emotion which springs from reason is more powerful. *Q.E.D.*

Prop. VIII. *An emotion is stronger in proportion to the number of simultaneous concurrent causes whereby it is aroused.*

Proof. – Many simultaneous causes are more powerful than a few (III. vii.): therefore (IV. v.), in proportion to the increased number of simultaneous causes whereby it is aroused, an emotion becomes stronger. *Q.E.D.*

Note. – This proposition is also evident from V. Ax. ii.

Prop. IX. *An emotion, which is attributable to many and diverse causes which the mind regards as simultaneous with the emotion itself, is less hurtful, and we are less subject thereto and less affected towards each of its causes, than if it were a different and equally powerful emotion attributable to fewer causes or to a single cause.*

Proof. – An emotion is only bad or hurtful, in so far as it hinders the mind from being able to think (IV. xxvi. xxvii.); therefore, an emotion, whereby the mind is determined to the contemplation of several things at once, is less hurtful than another equally powerful emotion, which so engrosses the mind in the single contemplation of a few objects or of one, that it is unable to think of anything else; this was our first point. Again, as the mind's essence, in other words, its power (III. vii.), consists solely in thought (II. xi.), the mind is less passive in respect to an emotion, which causes it to think of several things at once, than in regard to an equally strong emotion, which keeps it engrossed in the contemplation of a few or of a single object: this was our second point. Lastly, this emotion (III. xlviii.), in so far as it is attributable to several causes, is less powerful in regard to each of them. *Q.E.D.*

Prop. X. *So long as we are not assailed by emotions contrary to our nature, we have the power of arranging and associating the modifications of our body according to the intellectual order.*

Proof. – The emotions, which are contrary to our nature, that is (IV. xxx.), which are bad, are bad in so far as they impede the mind from understanding (IV. xxvii.). So long, therefore, as we are not assailed by emotions contrary to our nature, the mind's power, whereby it endeavours to understand things (IV. xxvi.), is not impeded, and therefore it is able to form clear and distinct ideas and to deduce them one from another (II. xl. note ii. and xlvii. note); consequently we have in such cases the power of arranging and associating the modifications of the body according to the intellectual order.   *Q.E.D.*

Note. – By this power of rightly arranging and associating the bodily modifications we can guard ourselves from being easily affected by evil emotions. For (V. vii.) a greater force is needed for controlling the emotions, when they are arranged and associated according to the intellectual order, than when they are uncertain and unsettled. The best we can do, therefore, so long as we do not possess a perfect knowledge of our emotions, is to frame a system of right conduct, or fixed practical precepts, to commit it to memory, and to apply it forthwith to the particular circumstances which now and again meet us in life, so that our imagination may become fully imbued therewith, and that it may be always ready to our hand. For instance, we have laid down among the rules of life (IV. xlvi. and note), that hatred should be overcome with love or high-mindedness, and not requited with hatred in return. Now, that this precept of reason may be always ready to our hand in time of need, we should often think over and reflect upon the wrongs generally committed by men, and in what manner and way they may be best warded off by high-mindedness: we shall thus associate the idea of wrong with the idea of this precept, which accordingly will always be ready for use when a wrong is done to us (II. xviii.) If we keep also in readiness the notion of our true advantage, and of the good which follows from mutual friendships, and common fellowships; further, if we remember that complete acquiescence is the result of the right way of life (IV. lii.), and that men, no less than everything else, act by the necessity of their nature: in such case I say the wrong, or the hatred, which commonly arises therefrom, will engross a very small part of our imagination and will be easily overcome; or, if the anger which springs from a grievous wrong be not overcome easily, it will nevertheless be overcome, though not without a spiritual conflict, far sooner than if we had not thus reflected on the

subject beforehand. As is indeed evident from V. vi. vii. viii. We should, in the same way, reflect on courage as a means of overcoming fear; the ordinary dangers of life should frequently be brought to mind and imagined, together with the means whereby through readiness of resource and strength of mind we can avoid and overcome them. But we must note, that in arranging our thoughts and conceptions we should always bear in mind that which is good in every individual thing (IV. lxiii. Coroll. and III. lix.), in order that we may always be determined to action by an emotion of pleasure. For instance, if a man sees that he is too keen in the pursuit of honour, let him think over its right use, the end for which it should be pursued, and the means whereby he may attain it. Let him not think of its misuse, and its emptiness, and the fickleness of mankind, and the like, whereof no man thinks except through a morbidness of disposition; with thoughts like these do the most ambitious most torment themselves, when they despair of gaining the distinctions they hanker after, and in thus giving vent to their anger would fain appear wise. Wherefore it is certain that those, who cry out the loudest against the misuse of honour and the vanity of the world, are those who most greedily covet it. This is not peculiar to the ambitious, but is common to all who are ill-used by fortune, and who are infirm in spirit. For a poor man also, who is miserly, will talk incessantly of the misuse of wealth and of the vices of the rich; whereby he merely torments himself, and shows the world that he is intolerant, not only of his own poverty, but also of other people's riches. So, again, those who have been ill received by a woman they love think of nothing but the inconstancy, treachery, and other stock faults of the fair sex; all of which they consign to oblivion, directly they are again taken into favour by their sweetheart. Thus he who would govern his emotions and appetite solely by the love of freedom strives, as far as he can, to gain a knowledge of the virtues and their causes, and to fill his spirit with the joy which arises from the true knowledge of them: he will in no wise desire to dwell on men's faults, or to carp at his fellows, or to revel in a false show of freedom. Whosoever will diligently observe and practise these precepts (which indeed are not difficult) will verily, in a short space of time, be able, for the most part, to direct his actions according to the commandments of reason.

PROP. XI. *In proportion as a mental image is referred to more objects, so is it more frequent, or more often vivid, and occupies the mind more.*

Proof. – In proportion as a mental image or an emotion is referred to more objects, so are there more causes whereby it can be aroused and fostered, all of which (by hypothesis) the mind contemplates simultaneously in association with the given emotion; therefore the emotion is more frequent, or is more often in full vigour, and (V. viii.) occupies the mind more. *Q.E.D.*

PROP. XII. *The mental images of things are more easily associated with the images referred to things which we clearly and distinctly understand, than with others.*

Proof. – Things, which we clearly and distinctly understand, are either the common properties of things or deductions therefrom (see definition of Reason, II. xl. note ii.), and are consequently (by the last Prop.) more often aroused in us. Wherefore it may more readily happen, that we should contemplate other things in conjunction with these than in conjunction with something else, and consequently (II. xviii.) that the images of the said things should be more often associated with the images of these than with the images of something else. *Q.E.D.*

PROP. XIII. *A mental image is more often vivid, in proportion as it is associated with a greater number of other images.*

Proof. – In proportion as an image is associated with a greater number of other images, so (II. xviii.) are there more causes whereby it can be aroused. *Q.E.D.*

PROP. XIV. *The mind can bring it about, that all bodily modifications or images of things may be referred to the idea of God.*

Proof. – There is no modification of the body, whereof the mind may not form some clear and distinct conception (V. iv.); wherefore it can bring it about, that they should all be referred to the idea of God (I. xv.). *Q.E.D.*

PROP. XV. *He who clearly and distinctly understands himself and his emotions loves God, and so much the more in proportion as he more understands himself and his emotions.*

Proof. – He who clearly and distinctly understands himself and his emotions feels pleasure (III. liii.), and this pleasure is (by the last Prop.) accompanied by the idea of God; therefore (Def. of the Emotions, vi.) such an one loves God, and (for the same reason) so much the more in pro-portion as he more understands himself and his emotions. *Q.E.D.*

PROP. XVI. *This love towards God must hold the chief place in the mind.*

Proof. – For this love is associated with all the modifications of the body (V. xiv.) and is fostered by them all (V. xv.); therefore (V. xi.), it must hold the chief place in the mind. *Q.E.D.*

PROP. XVII. *God is without passions, neither is he affected by any emotion of pleasure or pain.*

Proof. – All ideas, in so far as they are referred to God, are true (II. xxxii.), that is (II. Def. iv.) adequate; and therefore (by the general Def. of the Emotions) God is without passions. Again, God cannot pass either to a greater or to a lesser per-fection (I. xx. Coroll. ii.); therefore (by Def. of the Emotions, ii. iii.) he is not affected by any emo-tion of pleasure or pain.

Corollary. – Strictly speaking, God does not love or hate anyone. For God (by the foregoing Prop.) is not affected by any emotion of pleasure or pain, consequently (Def. of the Emotions, vi. vii.) he does not love or hate anyone.

PROP. XVIII. *No one can hate God.*

Proof. – The idea of God which is in us is ade-quate and perfect (II. xlvi. xlvii.); wherefore, in so far as we contemplate God, we are active (III. iii.); consequently (III. lix.) there can be no pain accompanied by the idea of God, in other words (Def. of the Emotions, vii.), no one can hate God. *Q.E.D.*

Corollary. – Love towards God cannot be turned into hate.

Note. – It may be objected that, as we under-stand God as the cause of all things, we by that very fact regard God as the cause of pain. But I make answer, that, in so far as we understand the causes of pain, it to that extent (V. iii.) ceases to be a passion, that is, it ceases to be pain (III. lix.); therefore, in so far as we understand God to be the cause of pain, we to that extent feel pleasure.

PROP. XIX. *He, who loves God, cannot endeav-our that God should love him in return.*

Proof. – For, if a man should so endeavour, he would desire (V. xvii. Coroll.) that God, whom he loves, should not be God, and consequently he would desire to feel pain (III. xix.); which is absurd (III. xxviii.). Therefore, he who loves God, &c. *Q.E.D.*

PROP. XX. *This love towards God cannot be stained by the emotion of envy or jealousy: con-trariwise, it is the more fostered, in proportion as we conceive a greater number of men to be joined to God by the same bond of love.*

Proof. – This love towards God is the highest good which we can seek for under the guidance of reason (IV. xxviii.), it is common to all men (IV. xxxvi.), and we desire that all should rejoice therein (TV. xxxvii.); therefore (Def. of the Emotions, xxiii.), it cannot be stained by the emotion of envy, nor by the emotion of jealousy (V. xviii. see definition of Jealousy, III. xxxv. note); but, contrariwise, it must needs be the more fostered, in proportion as we conceive a greater number of men to rejoice therein.   *Q.E.D.*

Note. – We can in the same way show, that there is no emotion directly contrary to this love, whereby this love can be destroyed; therefore we may conclude, that this love towards God is the most constant of all the emotions, and that, in so far as it is referred to the body, it cannot be destroyed, unless the body be destroyed also. As to its nature, in so far as it is referred to the mind only, we shall presently inquire.

I have now gone through all the remedies against the emotions, or all that the mind, considered in itself alone, can do against them. Whence it appears that the mind's power over the emotions consists:–

I.   In the actual knowledge of the emotions (V. iv. note).

II.   In the fact that it separates the emotions from the thought of an external cause, which we conceive confusedly (V. ii. and iv. note).

III.   In the fact, that, in respect to time, the emotions referred to things, which we distinctly understand, surpass those referred to what we conceive in a confused and fragmentary manner (V. vii.).

IV.   In the number of causes whereby those modifications are fostered, which have regard to the common properties of things or to God (V. ix. xi.).

V.   Lastly, in the order wherein the mind can arrange and associate, one with another, its own emotions (V. x. note and xii. xiii. xiv.).

But, in order that this power of the mind over the emotions may be better understood, it should be specially observed that the emotions are called by us strong, when we compare the emotion of one man with the emotion of another, and see that one man is more troubled than another by the same emotion; or when we are comparing the various emotions of the same man one with

another, and find that he is more affected or stirred by one emotion than by another. For the strength of every emotion is defined by a comparison of our own power with the power of an external cause. Now the power of the mind is defined by knowledge only, and its infirmity or passion is defined by the privation of knowledge only: it therefore follows, that that mind is most passive, whose greatest part is made up of inadequate ideas, so that it may be characterized more readily by its passive states than by its activities: on the other hand, that mind is most active, whose greatest part is made up of adequate ideas, so that, although it may contain as many inadequate ideas as the former mind, it may yet be more easily characterized by ideas attributable to human virtue, than by ideas which tell of human infirmity. Again, it must be observed, that spiritual unhealthiness and misfortunes can generally be traced to excessive love for something which is subject to many variations, and which we can never become masters of. For no one is solicitous or anxious about anything, unless he loves it; neither do wrongs, suspicions, enmities, &c. arise, except in regard to things whereof no one can be really master.

We may thus readily conceive the power which clear and distinct knowledge, and especially that third kind of knowledge (II. xlvii. note), founded on the actual knowledge of God, possesses over the emotions: if it does not absolutely destroy them, in so far as they are passions (V. iii. and iv. note); at any rate, it causes them to occupy a very small part of the mind (V. xiv.). Further, it begets a love towards a thing immutable and eternal (V. xv.), whereof we may really enter into possession (II. xlv.); neither can it be defiled with those faults which are inherent in ordinary love; but it may grow from strength to strength, and may engross the greater part of the mind, and deeply penetrate it.

And now I have finished with all that concerns this present life: for, as I said in the beginning of this note, I have briefly described all the remedies against the emotions. And this everyone may readily have seen for himself, if he has attended to what is advanced in the present note, and also to the definitions of the mind and its emotions, and, lastly, to Propositions i. and iii. of Part III. It is now, therefore, time to pass on to those matters, which appertain to the duration of the mind, without relation to the body.

PROP. XXI. *The mind can only imagine anything, or remember what is past, while the body endures.*

Proof. – The mind does not express the actual existence of its body, nor does it imagine the modifications of the body as actual, except while the body endures (II. viii. Coroll.); and, consequently (II. xxvi.), it does not imagine any body as actually existing, except while its own body endures. Thus it cannot imagine anything (for definition of Imagination, see II. xvii. note), or remember things past, except while the body endures (see definition of Memory, II. xviii. note). *Q.E.D.*

PROP. XXII. *Nevertheless in God there is necessarily an idea, which expresses the essence of this or that human body under the form of eternity.*

Proof. – God is the cause, not only of the existence of this or that human body, but also of its essence (I. xxv.). This essence, therefore, must necessarily be conceived through the very essence of God (I. Ax. iv.), and be thus conceived by a certain eternal necessity (I. xvi.); and this conception must necessarily exist in God (II. iii.). *Q.E.D.*

PROP. XXIII. *The human mind cannot be absolutely destroyed with the body, but there remains of it something which is eternal.*

Proof. – There is necessarily in God a concept or idea, which expresses the essence of the human body (last Prop.), which, therefore, is necessarily something appertaining to the essence of the human mind (II. xiii.). But we have not assigned to the human mind any duration, definable by time, except in so far as it expresses the actual existence of the body, which is explained through duration, and may be defined by time – that is (II. viii. Coroll.), we do not assign to it duration, except while the body endures. Yet, as there is something, notwithstanding, which is conceived by a certain eternal necessity through the very essence of God (last Prop.); this something, which appertains to the essence of the mind, will necessarily be eternal. *Q.E.D.*

Note. – This idea, which expresses the essence of the body under the form of eternity, is, as we have said, a certain mode of thinking, which belongs to the essence of the mind, and is necessarily eternal. Yet it is not possible that we should remember that we existed before our body, for our body can bear no trace of such existence, neither can eternity be defined in terms of time, or have any relation to time. But, notwith-

standing, we feel and know that we are eternal. For the mind feels those things that it conceives by understanding, no less than those things that it remembers. For the eyes of the mind, whereby it sees and observes things, are none other than proofs. Thus, although we do not remember that we existed before the body, yet we feel that our mind, in so far as it involves the essence of the body, under the form of eternity, is eternal, and that thus its existence cannot be defined in terms of time, or explained through duration. Thus our mind can only be said to endure, and its existence can only be defined by a fixed time, in so far as it involves the actual existence of the body. Thus far only has it the power of determining the existence of things by time, and conceiving them under the category of duration.

PROP. XXIV. *The more we understand particular things, the more do we understand God.*

Proof. – This is evident from I. xxv. Coroll.

PROP. XXV. *The highest endeavour of the mind, and the highest virtue is to understand things by the third kind of knowledge.*

Proof. – The third kind of knowledge proceeds from an adequate idea of certain attributes of God to an adequate knowledge of the essence of things (see its definition II. xl. note ii.); and, in proportion as we understand things more in this way, we better understand God (by the last Prop.); therefore (IV. xxviii.) the highest virtue of the mind, that is (IV. Def. viii.) the power, or nature, or (III. vii.) highest endeavour of the mind, is to understand things by the third kind of knowledge. *Q.E.D.*

PROP. XXVI. *In proportion as the mind is more capable of understanding things by the third kind of knowledge, it desires more to understand things by that kind.*

Proof. – This is evident. For, in so far as we conceive the mind to be capable of conceiving things by this kind of knowledge, we, to that extent, conceive it as determined thus to conceive things; and consequently (Def. of the Emotions, i.), the mind desires so to do, in proportion as it is more capable thereof. *Q.E.D.*

PROP. XXVII. *From this third kind of knowledge arises the highest possible mental acquiescence.*

Proof. – The highest virtue of the mind is to know God (IV. xxviii.), or to understand things by the third kind of knowledge (V. xxv.), and this virtue is greater in proportion as the mind knows things more by the said kind of knowledge

(V. xxiv.): consequently, he who knows things by this kind of knowledge passes to the summit of human perfection, and is therefore (Def. of the Emotions, ii.) affected by the highest pleasure, such pleasure being accompanied by the idea of himself and his own virtue; thus (Def. of the Emotions, xxv.), from this kind of knowledge arises the highest possible acquiescence. *Q.E.D.*

PROP. XXVIII. *The endeavour or desire to know things by the third kind of knowledge cannot arise from the first, but from the second kind of knowledge.*

Proof. – This proposition is self-evident. For whatsoever we understand clearly and distinctly, we understand either through itself, or through that which is conceived through itself; that is, ideas which are clear and distinct in us, or which are referred to the third kind of knowledge (II. xl. note ii.) cannot follow from ideas that are fragmentary and confused, and are referred to knowledge of the first kind, but must follow from adequate ideas, or ideas of the second and third kind of knowledge; therefore (Def. of the Emotions, i.), the desire of knowing things by the third kind of knowledge cannot arise from the first, but from the second kind. *Q.E.D.*

PROP. XXIX. *Whatsoever the mind understands under the form of eternity, it does not understand by virtue of conceiving the present actual existence of the body, but by virtue of conceiving the essence of the body under the form of eternity.*

Proof. – In so far as the mind conceives the present existence of its body, it to that extent conceives duration which can be determined by time, and to that extent only has it the power of conceiving things in relation to time (V. xxi. II. xxvi.). But eternity cannot be explained in terms of duration (I. Def. viii. and explanation). Therefore to this extent the mind has not the power of conceiving things under the form of eternity, but it possesses such power, because it is of the nature of reason to conceive things under the form of eternity (II xliv. Coroll. ii.), and also because it is of the nature of the mind to conceive the essence of the body under the form of eternity (V. xxiii.), for besides these two there is nothing which belongs to the essence of mind (II. xiii.). Therefore this power of conceiving things under the form of eternity only belongs to the mind in virtue of the mind's conceiving the essence of the body under the form of eternity. *Q.E.D.*

Note. – Things are conceived by us as actual in two ways; either as existing in relation to a given time and place, or as contained in God and following from the necessity of the divine nature. Whatsoever we conceive in this second way as true or real, we conceive under the form of eternity, and their ideas involve the eternal and infinite essence of God, as we showed in II. xlv. and note, which see.

PROP. XXX. *Our mind, in so far as it knows itself and the body under the form of eternity, has to that extent necessarily a knowledge of God, and knows that it is in God, and is conceived through God.*

Proof. – Eternity is the very essence of God, in so far as this involves necessary existence (I. Def. viii.). Therefore to conceive things under the form of eternity, is to conceive things in so far as they are conceived through the essence of God as real entities, or in so far as they involve existence through the essence of God; wherefore our mind, in so far as it conceives itself and the body under the form of eternity, has to that extent necessarily a knowledge of God, and knows, &c. *Q.E.D.*

PROP. XXXI. *The third kind of knowledge depends on the mind, as its formal cause, in so far as the mind itself is eternal.*

Proof. – The mind does not conceive anything under the form of eternity, except in so far as it conceives its own body under the form of eternity (V. xxix.); that is, except in so far as it is eternal (V. xxi. xxiii.); therefore (by the last Prop.), in so far as it is eternal, it possesses the knowledge of God, which knowledge is necessarily adequate (II. xlvi.); hence the mind, in so far as it is eternal, is capable of knowing everything which can follow from this given knowledge of God (II. xl.), in other words, of knowing things by the third kind of knowledge (see Def. in II. xl. note ii.), whereof accordingly the mind (III. Def. i.), in so far as it is eternal, is the adequate or formal cause of such knowledge. *Q.E.D.*

Note. – In proportion, therefore, as a man is more potent in this kind of knowledge, he will be more completely conscious of himself and of God; in other words, he will be more perfect and blessed, as will appear more clearly in the sequel. But we must here observe that, although we are already certain that the mind is eternal, in so far as it conceives things under the form of eternity, yet, in order that what we wish to show may be more readily explained and better understood, we will consider the mind itself, as though it had just begun to exist and to understand things under the form of eternity, as indeed we have done hitherto; this we may do without any danger of error, so long as we are careful not to draw any conclusion, unless our premises are plain.

PROP. XXXII. *Whatsoever we understand by the third kind of knowledge, we take delight in, and our delight is accompanied by the idea of God as cause.*

Proof. – From this kind of knowledge arises the highest possible mental acquiescence, that is (Def. of the Emotions, xxv.), pleasure, and this acquiescence is accompanied by the idea of the mind itself (V. xxvii.), and consequently (V. xxx.) the idea also of God as cause. *Q.E.D.*

Corollary. – From the third kind of knowledge necessarily arises the intellectual love of God. From this kind of knowledge arises pleasure accompanied by the idea of God as cause, that is (Def. of the Emotions, vi.), the love of God ; not in so far as we imagine him as present (V. xxix.), but in so far as we understand him to be eternal; this is what I call the intellectual love of God.

PROP. XXXIII. *The intellectual love of God, which arises from the third kind of knowledge, is eternal.*

Proof. – The third kind of knowledge is eternal (V. xxxi. I. Ax. iii.); therefore (by the same Axiom) the love which arises therefrom is also necessarily eternal. *Q.E.D.*

Note. – Although this love towards God has (by the foregoing Prop.) no beginning, it yet possesses all the perfections of love, just as though it had arisen as we feigned in the Coroll. of the last Prop. Nor is there here any difference, except that the mind possesses as eternal those same perfections which we feigned to accrue to it, and they are accompanied by the idea of God as eternal cause. If pleasure consists in the transition to a greater perfection, assuredly blessedness must consist in the mind being endowed with perfection itself.

PROP. XXXIV. *The mind is, only while the body endures, subject to those emotions which are attributable to passions.*

Proof. – Imagination is the idea wherewith the mind contemplates a thing as present (II. xvii. note); yet this idea indicates rather the present disposition of the human body than the nature of the external thing (II. xvi. Coroll. ii.). Therefore emotion (see general Def. of Emotions) is imagination, in so far as it indicates the present

disposition of the body; therefore (V. xxi.) the mind is, only while the body endures, subject to emotions which are attributable to passions. *Q.E.D.*

Corollary. – Hence it follows that no love save intellectual love is eternal.

Note. – If we look to men's general opinion, we shall see that they are indeed conscious of the eternity of their mind, but that they confuse eternity with duration, and ascribe it to the imagination or the memory which they believe to remain after death.

PROP. XXXV. *God loves himself with an infinite intellectual love.*

Proof. – God is absolutely infinite (I. Def. vi.), that is (II. Def. vi.), the nature of God rejoices in infinite perfection; and such rejoicing is (II. iii.) accompanied by the idea of himself, that is (I. xi. and Def. i.), the idea of his own cause: now this is what we have (in V. xxxii. Coroll.) described as intellectual love.

PROP. XXXVI. *The intellectual love of the mind towards God is that very love of God whereby God loves himself, not in so far as he is infinite, but in so far as he can be explained through the essence of the human mind regarded under the form of eternity; in other words, the intellectual love of the mind towards God is part of the infinite love wherewith God loves himself.*

Proof. – This love of the mind must be referred to the activities of the mind (V. xxxii. Coroll. and III. iii.); it is itself, indeed, an activity whereby the mind regards itself accompanied by the idea of God as cause (V. xxxii. and Coroll.); that is (I. xxv. Coroll. and II. xi. Coroll.), an activity whereby God, in so far as he can be explained through the human mind, regards himself accompanied by the idea of himself; therefore (by the last Prop.), this love of the mind is part of the infinite love wherewith God loves himself. *Q.E.D.*

Corollary. – Hence it follows that God, in so far as he loves himself, loves man, and, consequently, that the love of God towards men, and the intellectual love of the mind towards God are identical.

Note. – From what has been said we clearly understand, wherein our salvation, or blessedness, or freedom, consists: namely, in the constant and eternal love towards God, or in God's love towards men. This love or blessedness is, in the Bible, called Glory, and not undeservedly. For whether this love be referred to God or to the mind, it may rightly be called acquiescence of spirit, which (Def. of the Emotions, xxv. xxx.) is not really distinguished from glory. In so far as it is referred to God, it is (V. xxxv.) pleasure, if we may still use that term, accompanied by the idea of itself, and, in so far as it is referred to the mind, it is the same (V. xxvii.).

Again, since the essence of our mind consists solely in knowledge, whereof the beginning and the foundation is God (I. xv. and II. xlvii. note), it becomes clear to us, in what manner and way our mind, as to its essence and existence, follows from the divine nature and constantly depends on God. I have thought it worth while here to call attention to this, in order to show by this example how the knowledge of particular things, which I have called intuitive or of the third kind (II. xl. note ii.), is potent, and more powerful than the universal knowledge, which I have styled knowledge of the second kind. For, although in Part I. I showed in general terms, that all things (and consequently, also, the human mind) depend as to their essence and existence on God, yet that demonstration, though legitimate and placed beyond the chances of doubt, does not affect our mind so much, as when the same conclusion is derived from the actual essence of some particular thing, which we say depends on God.

Prop. XXXVII. *There is nothing in nature, which is contrary to this intellectual love, or which can take it away.*

Proof. – This intellectual love follows necessarily from the nature of the mind, in so far as the latter is regarded through the nature of God as an eternal truth (V. xxxiii. and xxix.). If, therefore, there should be anything which would be contrary to this love, that thing would be contrary to that which is true; consequently, that, which should be able to take away this love, would cause that which is true to be false; an obvious absurdity. Therefore there is nothing in nature which, &c. *Q.E.D.*

Note. – The Axiom of Part IV. has reference to particular things, in so far as they are regarded in relation to a given time and place: of this, I think, no one can doubt.

Prop. XXXVIII. *In proportion as the mind understands more things by the second and third kind of knowledge, it is less subject to those emotions which are evil, and stands in less fear of death.*

Proof. – The mind's essence consists in knowledge (II. xi.); therefore, in proportion as the mind understands more things by the second and third kinds of knowledge, the greater will be the part of it that endures (V. xxix. and xxiii.), and, consequently (by the last Prop.), the greater will be the part that is not touched by the emotions, which are contrary to our nature, or in other words, evil (IV. xxx.). Thus, in proportion as the mind understands more things by the second and third kinds of knowledge, the greater will be the part of it, that remains unimpaired, and, consequently, less subject to emotions, &c. *Q.E.D.*

Note. – Hence we understand that point which I touched on in IV. xxxix. note, and which I promised to explain in this Part; namely, that death becomes less hurtful, in proportion as the mind's clear and distinct knowledge is greater, and, consequently, in proportion as the mind loves God more. Again, since from the third kind of knowledge arises the highest possible acquiescence (V. xxvii.), it follows that the human mind can attain to being of such a nature, that the part thereof which we have shown to perish with the body (V. xxi.) should be of little importance when compared with the part which endures. But I will soon treat of the subject at greater length.

Prop. XXXIX. *He, who possesses a body capable of the greatest number of activities, possesses a mind whereof the greatest part is eternal.*

Proof. – He, who possesses a body capable of the greatest number of activities, is least agitated by those emotions which are evil (IV. xxxviii.) – that is (IV. xxx.), by those emotions which are contrary to our nature; therefore (V. x.), he possesses the power of arranging and associating the modifications of the body according to the intellectual order, and, consequently, of bringing it about, that all the modifications of the body should be referred to the idea of God; whence it will come to pass that (V. xv.) he will be affected with love towards God, which (V. xvi.) must occupy or constitute the chief part of the mind; therefore (V. xxxiii.), such a man will possess a mind whereof the chief part is eternal. *Q.E.D.*

Note. – Since human bodies are capable of the greatest number of activities, there is no doubt but that they may be of such a nature, that they may be referred to minds possessing a great knowledge of themselves and of God, and whereof the greatest or chief part is eternal, and, therefore, that they should scarcely fear death. But, in order that this may be understood more clearly, we must here call to mind, that we live in a state of perpetual variation, and, according as we are changed for the better or the worse, we are called happy or unhappy.

For he, who, from being an infant or a child, becomes a corpse, is called unhappy; whereas it is set down to happiness, if we have been able to live through the whole period of life with a sound mind in a sound body. And, in reality, he, who, as in the case of an infant or a child, has a body capable of very few activities, and depending, for the most part, on external causes, has a mind which, considered in itself alone, is scarcely conscious of itself, or of God, or of things; whereas, he, who has a body capable of very many activities, has a mind which, considered in itself alone, is highly conscious of itself, of God, and of things. In this life, therefore, we primarily endeavour to bring it about, that the body of a child, in so far as its nature allows and conduces thereto, may be changed into something else capable of very many activities, and referable to a mind which is highly conscious of itself, of God, and of things; and we desire so to change it, that what is referred to its imagination and memory may become insignificant, in comparison with its intellect, as I have already said in the note to the last Proposition.

PROP. XL. *In proportion as each thing possesses more of perfection, so is it more active, and less passive; and, vice versā, in proportion as it is more active, so is it more perfect.*

Proof. – In proportion as each thing is more perfect, it possesses more of reality (II. Def. vi.), and, consequently (III. iii. and note), it is to that extent more active and less passive. This demonstration may be reversed, and thus prove that, in proportion as a thing is more active, so is it more perfect.   Q.E.D.

Corollary. – Hence it follows that the part of the mind which endures, be it great or small, is more perfect than the rest. For the eternal part of the mind (V. xxiii. xxix.) is the understanding, through which alone we are said to act (III. iii.); the part which we have shown to perish is the imagination (V. xxi.), through which only we are said to be passive (III. iii. and general Def. of the Emotions); therefore, the former, be it great or small, is more perfect than the latter.   Q.E.D.

Note. – Such are the doctrines which I had purposed to set forth concerning the mind, in so far as it is regarded without relation to the body; whence, as also from I. xxi. and other places, it is plain that our mind, in so far as it understands, is an eternal mode of thinking, which is determined by another eternal mode of thinking, and this other by a third, and so on to infinity; so that all taken together at once constitute the eternal and infinite intellect of God.

PROP. XLI. *Even if we did not know that our mind is eternal, we should still consider as of primary importance piety and religion, and generally all things which, in Part IV., we showed to be attributable to courage and high-mindedness.*

Proof. – The first and only foundation of virtue, or the rule of right living is (IV. xxii. Coroll. and xxiv.) seeking one's own true interest. Now, while we determined what reason prescribes as useful, we took no account of the mind's eternity, which has only become known to us in this Fifth Part. Although we were ignorant at that time that the mind is eternal, we nevertheless stated that the qualities attributable to courage and high-mindedness are of primary importance. Therefore, even if we were still ignorant of this doctrine, we should yet put the aforesaid precepts of reason in the first place. Q.E.D.

Note. – The general belief of the multitude seems to be different. Most people seem to believe that they are free, in so far as they may obey their lusts, and that they cede their rights, in so far as they are bound to live according to the commandments of the divine law. They therefore believe that piety, religion, and, generally, all things attributable to firmness of mind, are burdens, which, after death, they hope to lay aside, and to receive the reward for their bondage, that is, for their piety and religion; it is not only by this hope, but also, and chiefly, by the fear of being horribly punished after death, that they are induced to live according to the divine commandments, so far as their feeble and infirm spirit will carry them.

If men had not this hope and this fear, but believed that the mind perishes with the body, and that no hope of prolonged life remains for the wretches who are broken down with the burden of piety, they would return to their own inclinations, controlling everything in accordance with their lusts, and desiring to obey fortune rather than themselves. Such a course appears to me not less absurd than if a man, because he does not believe that he can by wholesome food sustain his body for ever, should wish to cram himself with poisons and deadly fare; or if, because he sees that the mind is not eternal or immortal, he should prefer to be out of his mind altogether, and to live without the use of reason; these ideas are so absurd as to be scarcely worth refuting.

PROP. XLII. *Blessedness is not the reward of virtue, but virtue itself; neither do we rejoice therein, because we control our lusts, but, contrariwise, because we rejoice therein, we are able to control our lusts.*

Proof. – Blessedness consists in love towards God (V. xxxvi. and note), which love springs from the third kind of knowledge (V. xxxii. Coroll.); therefore this love (III. iii. lix.) must be referred to the mind, in so far as the latter is active; therefore (IV. Def. viii.) it is virtue itself. This was our first point. Again, in proportion as the mind rejoices more in this divine love or blessedness, so does it the more understand (V. xxxii.); that is (V. iii. Coroll.), so much the more power has it over the emotions, and (V. xxxviii.) so much the less is it subject to those emotions which are evil; therefore, in proportion as the mind rejoices in this divine love or blessedness, so has it the power of controlling lusts. And, since human power in controlling the emotions con-sists solely in the understanding, it follows that no one rejoices in blessedness, because he has controlled his lusts, but, contrariwise, his power of controlling his lusts arises from this blessedness itself. *Q.E.D.*

Note. – I have thus completed all I wished to set forth touching the mind's power over the emotions and the mind's freedom. Whence it appears, how potent is the wise man, and how much he surpasses the ignorant man, who is driven only by his lusts. For the ignorant man is not only distracted in various ways by external causes without ever gaining the true acquiescence of his spirit, but moreover lives, as it were unwitting of himself, and of God, and of things, and as soon as he ceases to suffer, ceases also to be.

Whereas the wise man, in so far as he is regarded as such, is scarcely at all disturbed in spirit, but, being conscious of himself, and of God, and of things, by a certain eternal necessity, never ceases to be, but always possesses true acquiescence of his spirit.

If the way which I have pointed out as leading to this result seems exceedingly hard, it may nevertheless be discovered. Needs must it be hard, since it is so seldom found. How would it be possible, if salvation were ready to our hand, and could without great labour be found, that it should be by almost all men neglected? But all things excellent are as difficult as they are rare.

David Hume, *A Treatise of Human Nature,* Book III, Part I (Sections 1–2)

Introduction

There were many significant "English moralists" of the seventeenth and eighteenth centuries, such as Bishop Joseph Butler and the Earl of Shaftesbury, but the accolade of "the greatest of all English moralists, were he not a Scotsman" usually goes to the Edinburgh philosopher David Hume (1711–76).[1] Certainly Hume's moral philosophy had an immense impact, immediately upon the *philosophes* of the French Enlightenment and, in the twentieth century, upon analytic philosophers seeking precursors of their own theories of moral discourse.

Hume shared the concern of Butler, to whose Sermon "Upon the Love of Our Neighbour" he acknowledged a debt, to counter the fashionable egoism of his day. Beyond self-love, he insists, there is a common human "sentiment" which is "no other than a feeling for the happiness of mankind, and a resentment of their misery," the two ends which "virtue and vice" respectively promote.[2] Even rules of justice, which may not immediately arouse this "sentiment," are approved of because they contribute to a system of behavior that does promote general happiness. But in the famous text we

From David Hume, *A Treatise of Human Nature,* ed. L. A. Selby-Bigge. Oxford: Clarendon Press, 1960, pp. 455–76 (asterisked notes are Hume's own; some notes omitted).

have selected from his *A Treatise of Human Nature* (1739–40), Hume's main target is at an opposite extreme from egoism. It might be called "ethical rationalism." Among both followers of Descartes and the English Neo-Platonists, it was held that moral truths were discoverable in the same manner as those of mathematics or science, either by unaided reason or by reason in conjunction with empirical enquiry into the objective order of the world. For example, it was held by the theologian William Wollaston (1660–1724), whom Hume demolishes in a long footnote (omitted), that all bad actions are a species of falsehood – the adulterer, for instance, representing another's wife as his own. Others imagined that moral principles were innately implanted in us just as, allegedly, were the truths of logic.

It is views such as these that Hume rejects in claiming that "moral distinctions [are] not deriv'd from reason." Care is needed, however, over his use of "reason." He is no irrationalist denying, say, the role of rational enquiry in ascertaining which rules of justice best contribute to a society's well being. Nor, when he famously remarks that "'tis not contrary to reason to prefer the destruction of the whole world to the scratching of my finger" (*Treatise,* II.3.3), is he embracing moral nihilism. Reason, he explains, enables us to establish only "relations of ideas" and "matters of fact": its scope, in modern parlance, is the truths of logic and the truths ascertainable by empirical investigation. The point of the scratched finger example, then, is that no amount of logical and scientific enquiry – excluding as it does considerations of "sentiment" or emotion, can by itself show why mass destruction is worse than a minor wound.

Hume advances several arguments against the rationalists, of which the most enduring is presaged in his earlier remark that "reason is, and ought only to be the slave of the passions" (II.3.3). This is not a wild romantic manifesto, enjoining submission of the head to the heart, but the insistence that reason *per se* is incapable of moving people to action. Since our moral convictions necessarily do move us to action, and to praise and blame, it follows that these convictions involve the "passions" and cannot therefore merely be judgments of logic or empirical fact.

So, one conclusion Hume draws is clear enough: "since vice and virtue are not discoverable merely by reason, . . . it must be by means of . . . sentiment . . . that we are able to mark the difference" (III.1.2). But does he want to draw a stronger conclusion? Focusing on the notorious final paragraph of Section 1, many commentators attribute to Hume the view that no "ought" can be derived from an "is," that moral and evaluative judgments can never be inferred from statements of fact. This interpretation is then supported by citing lines where Hume seems to suggest that, in calling something "good," one is simply expressing a favorable feeling toward it. Against this, other commentators hold that Hume is claiming only this: "oughts" cannot be derived from factual statements that "say nothing about human sentiments."[3] Once we take into account the *fact* that a certain kind of action has a tendency to arouse general approval, Hume would have no objection, they argue, to concluding that the action is a good one. These latter commentators also draw attention to the passages, in Hume's aesthetic as well as his ethical writings, where he compares evaluative properties to "secondary qualities," like color. Nothing is colored except in relation to our impressions, but it remains an empirical fact that a thing has the color it does. Why should it be any different with its moral and aesthetic properties? It is fair to say that the jury is still out on the exact meaning of Hume's ambiguous remarks, as indeed it is on the issue of the relation between moral and empirical discourse which those remarks have done so much to place at the center of modern philosophical ethics.

Notes

1   A. MacIntyre, A Short History *of Ethics*, London: Macmillan, 1966, p. 168.
2   D. Hume, *An Inquiry Concerning the Principles of Morals* (1751), Indianapolis, IN: Bobbs-Merrill, 1957, p. 105.
3   G. Hunter, "A Reply to Professor Flew," in W. D. Hudson, ed., *The Is/Ought* Question, London: Macmillan, 1969, p. 71. The first six articles of this book are devoted to Hume.

Hume, *A Treatise of Human Nature*, Book III, Part I

Section 1: Moral Distinctions not Deriv'd from Reason

There is an inconvenience which attends all abstruse reasoning, that it may silence, without convincing an antagonist, and requires the same intense study to make us sensible of its force, that was at first requisite for its invention. When we leave our closet, and engage in the common affairs of life, its conclusions seem to vanish, like the phantoms of the night on the appearance of the morning; and 'tis difficult for us to retain even that conviction, which we had attain'd with difficulty. This is still more conspicuous in a long chain of reasoning, where we must preserve to the end the evidence of the first propositions, and where we often lose sight of all the most receiv'd maxims, either of philosophy or common life. I am not, however, without hopes that the present system of philosophy will acquire new force as it advances; and that our reasonings concerning *morals* will corroborate whatever has been said concerning the *understanding* and the *passions*. Morality is a subject that interests us above all others: we fancy the peace of society to be at stake in every decision concerning it: and 'tis evident, that this concern must make our speculations appear more real and solid than where the subject is, in a great measure, indifferent to us. What affects us, we conclude can never be a chimera; and as our passion is engag'd on the one side or the other, we naturally think that the question lies within human comprehension; which, in other cases of this nature, we are apt to entertain some doubt of. Without this advantage I never should have ventur'd upon a third volume of such abstruse philosophy, in an age wherein the greatest part of men seem agreed to convert reading into an amusement, and to reject every thing that requires any considerable degree of attention to be comprehended.

It has been observ'd that nothing is ever present to the mind but its perceptions; and that all the actions of seeing, hearing, judging, loving, hating and thinking fall under this denomination. The mind can never exert itself in any action, which we may not comprehend under the term of *perception*; and consequently that term is no less applicable to those judgments, by which we distinguish moral good and evil, than to every other operation of the mind. To approve of one character, to condemn another, are only so many different perceptions.

Now as perceptions resolve themselves into two kinds, viz. *impressions* and *ideas*, this distinction gives rise to a question, with which we shall open up our present enquiry concerning morals, *Whether 'tis by means of our* ideas *or impressions we distinguish betwixt vice and virtue, and pronounce an action blameable or praiseworthy?*[1] This will immediately cut off all loose discourses and declamations, and reduce us to something precise and exact on the present subject.

Those who affirm that virtue is nothing but a conformity to reason; that there are eternal fitnesses and unfitnesses of things, which are the same to every rational being that considers them; that the immutable measures of right and wrong impose an obligation, not only on human creatures, but also on the Deity himself: all these systems concur in the opinion, that morality, like truth, is discern'd merely by ideas, and by their juxtaposition and comparison. In order, therefore, to judge of these systems, we need only consider, whether it be possible, from reason alone, to distinguish betwixt moral good and evil, or whether there must concur some other principles to enable us to make that distinction.

If morality had naturally no influence on human passions and actions, 'twere in vain to take such pains to inculcate it; and nothing would be more fruitless than that multitude of rules and precepts, with which all moralists abound. Philosophy is commonly divided into *speculative* and *practical*; and as morality is always comprehended under the latter division, 'tis supposed to influence our passions and actions, and to go beyond the calm and indolent judgments of the understanding. And this is confirm'd by common experience, which informs us that men are often govern'd by their duties, and are deter'd from some actions by the opinion of injustice, and impell'd to others by that of obligation.

Since morals, therefore, have an influence on the actions and affections, it follows that they cannot be deriv'd from reason; and that because reason alone, as we have already prov'd, can never have any such influence. Morals excite passions, and produce or prevent actions. Reason of itself is utterly impotent in this particular. The rules of morality, therefore, are not conclusions of our reason.

No one, I believe, will deny the justness of this inference; nor is there any other means of evading it, than by denying that principle on which it is founded. As long as it is allow'd that reason has no influence on our passions and actions, 'tis in vain to pretend that morality is discover'd only by a deduction of reason. An active principle can never be founded on an inactive; and if reason be inactive in itself, it must remain so in all its shapes and appearances, whether it exerts itself in natural or moral subjects, whether it considers the powers of external bodies, or the actions of rational beings.

It would be tedious to repeat all the arguments, by which I have prov'd [Book II, Part III, Section 3], that reason is perfectly inert, and can never either prevent or produce any action or affection. 'Twill be easy to recollect what has been said upon that subject. I shall only recall on this occasion one of these arguments, which I shall endeavour to render still more conclusive, and more applicable to the present subject.

Reason is the discovery of truth or falshood. Truth or falshood consists in an agreement or disagreement either to the *real* relations of ideas, or to *real* existence and matter of fact. Whatever, therefore, is not susceptible of this agreement or disagreement, is incapable of being true or false, and can never be an object of our reason. Now 'tis evident our passions, volitions and actions are not susceptible of any such agreement or disagreement; being original facts and realities, compleat in themselves, and implying no reference to other passions, volitions and actions. 'Tis impossible, therefore, they can be pronounced either true or false, and be either contrary or conformable to reason.

This argument is of double advantage to our present purpose. For it proves *directly*, that actions do not derive their merit from a conformity to reason, nor their blame from a contrariety to it; and it proves the same truth more *indirectly*, by shewing us, that as reason can never immediately prevent or produce any action by contradicting or approving of it, it cannot be the source of moral good and evil, which are found to have that influence. Actions may be laudable or blameable; but they cannot be reasonable or unreasonable: laudable or blameable, therefore, are not the same with reasonable or unreasonable. The merit and demerit of actions frequently contradict, and sometimes control our natural propensities. But reason has no such influence. Moral distinctions, therefore, are not the offspring of reason. Reason is wholly inactive, and can never be the source of so active a principle as conscience, or a sense of morals.

But perhaps it may be said that tho' no will or action can be immediately contradictory to reason, yet we may find such a contradiction in some of the attendants of the action, that is, in its causes or effects. The action may cause a judgment, or may be *obliquely* caus'd by one, when the judgment concurs with a passion; and by an abusive way of speaking, which philosophy will scarce allow of, the same contrariety may, upon that account, be ascrib'd to the action. How far this truth or falshood may be the source of morals, 'twill now be proper to consider.

It has been observ'd that reason, in a strict and philosophical sense, can have an influence on our conduct only after two ways: either when it excites a passion by informing us of the existence of something which is a proper object of it; or when it discovers the connexion of causes and effects, so as to afford us means of exerting any

passion. These are the only kinds of judgment, which can accompany our actions, or can be said to produce them in any manner; and it must be allow'd, that these judgments may often be false and erroneous. A person may be affected with passion by supposing a pain or pleasure to lie in an object, which has no tendency to produce either of these sensations, or which produces the contrary to what is imagin'd. A person may also take false measures for the attaining his end, and may retard, by his foolish conduct, instead of forwarding the execution of any project. These false judgments may be thought to affect the passions and actions, which are connected with them, and may be said to render them unreasonable, in a figurative and improper way of speaking. But tho' this be acknowledg'd, 'tis easy to observe, that these errors are so far from being the source of all immorality, that they are commonly very innocent, and draw no manner of guilt upon the person who is so unfortunate as to fall into them. They extend not beyond a mistake of *fact*, which moralists have not generally suppos'd criminal, as being perfectly involuntary. I am more to be lamented than blam'd, if I am mistaken with regard to the influence of objects in producing pain or pleasure, or if I know not the proper means of satisfying my desires. No one can ever regard such errors as a defect in my moral character. A fruit, for instance, that is really disagreeable appears to me at a distance, and thro' mistake I fancy it to be pleasant and delicious. Here is one error. I choose certain means of reaching this fruit, which are not proper for my end. Here is a second error; nor is there any third one which can ever possibly enter into our reasonings concerning actions. I ask, therefore, if a man, in this situation and guilty of these two errors, is to be regarded as vicious and criminal, however unavoidable they might have been? Or if it be possible to imagine that such errors are the sources of all immorality?

And here it may be proper to observe, that if moral distinctions be deriv'd from the truth or falshood of those judgments, they must take place wherever we form the judgments; nor will there be any difference, whether the question be concerning an apple or a kingdom, or whether the error be avoidable or unavoidable. For as the very essence of morality is suppos'd to consist in an agreement or disagreement to reason, the other circumstances are entirely arbitrary, and can never either bestow on any action the character of virtuous or vicious, or deprive it of that character. To which we may add, that this agreement or disagreement, not admitting of degrees, all virtues and vices would of course be equal.

Should it be pretended, that tho' a mistake of *fact* be not criminal, yet a mistake of *right* often is; and that this may be the source of immorality: I would answer, that 'tis impossible such a mistake can ever be the original source of immorality, since it supposes a real right and wrong; that is, a real distinction in morals, independent of these judgments. A mistake, therefore, of right may become a species of immorality; but 'tis only a secondary one, and is founded on some other, antecedent to it.

As to those judgments which are the *effects* of our actions, and which, when false, give occasion to pronounce the actions contrary to truth and reason; we may observe, that our actions never cause any judgment, either true or false, in ourselves, and that 'tis only on others they have such an influence. 'Tis certain that an action, on many occasions, may give rise to false conclusions in others; and that a person, who thro' a window sees any lewd behaviour of mine with my neighbour's wife, may be so simple as to imagine she is certainly my own. In this respect my action resembles somewhat a lye or falshood; only with this difference, which is material, that I perform not the action with any intention of giving rise to a false judgment in another, but merely to satisfy my lust and passion. It causes, however, a mistake and false judgment by accident; and the falshood of its effects may be ascribed, by some odd figurative way of speaking, to the action itself. But still I can see no pretext of reason for asserting that the tendency to cause such an error is the first spring or original source of all immorality.[2]

Thus upon the whole, 'tis impossible that the distinction betwixt moral good and evil can be made by reason; since that distinction has an influence upon our actions, of which reason alone is incapable. Reason and judgment may, indeed, be the mediate cause of an action, by prompting, or by directing a passion: but it is not pretended that a judgment of this kind, either in its truth or falshood, is attended with virtue or vice. And as to the judgments, which are caused by our judgments, they can still less bestow those

moral qualities on the actions, which are their causes.

But to be more particular, and to shew that those eternal immutable fitnesses and unfitnesses of things cannot be defended by sound philosophy, we may weigh the following considerations.

If the thought and understanding were alone capable of fixing the boundaries of right and wrong, the character of virtuous and vicious either must lie in some relations of objects, or must be a matter of fact, which is discovered by our reasoning. This consequence is evident. As the operations of human understanding divide themselves into two kinds, the comparing of ideas, and the inferring of matter of fact; were virtue discover'd by the understanding; it must be an object of one of these operations, nor is there any third operation of the understanding which can discover it. There has been an opinion very industriously propagated by certain philosophers, that morality is susceptible of demonstration; and tho' no one has ever been able to advance a single step in those demonstrations; yet 'tis taken for granted, that this science may be brought to an equal certainty with geometry or algebra. Upon this supposition, vice and virtue must consist in some relations; since 'tis allow'd on all hands that no matter of fact is capable of being demonstrated. Let us, therefore, begin with examining this hypothesis, and endeavour, if possible, to fix those moral qualities, which have been so long the objects of our fruitless researches. Point out distinctly the relations, which constitute morality or obligation, that we may know wherein they consist, and after what manner we must judge of them.

If you assert that vice and virtue consist in relations susceptible of certainty and demonstration, you must confine yourself to those *four* relations, which alone admit of that degree of evidence; and in that case you run into absurdities, from which you will never be able to extricate yourself. For as you make the very essence of morality to lie in the relations, and as there is no one of these relations but what is applicable, not only to an irrational, but also to an inanimate object, it follows that even such objects must be susceptible of merit or demerit. *Resemblance, contrariety, degrees in quality*, and *proportions in quantity and number*, all these relations belong as properly to matter as to our actions, passions, and volitions. 'Tis unquestionable, therefore, that morality lies not in any of these relations, nor the sense of it in their discovery.*

Should it be asserted that the sense of morality consists in the discovery of some relation, distinct from these, and that our enumeration was not compleat, when we comprehended all demonstrable relations under four general heads: to this I know not what to reply, till some one be so good as to point out to me this new relation. 'Tis impossible to refute a system which has never yet been explain'd. In such a manner of fighting in the dark, a man loses his blows in the air, and often places them where the enemy is not present.

I must, therefore, on this occasion, rest contented with requiring the two following conditions of any one that would undertake to clear up this system. *First*, as moral good and evil belong only to the actions of the mind, and are deriv'd from our situation with regard to external objects, the relations, from which these moral distinctions arise, must lie only betwixt internal actions and external objects, and must not be applicable either to internal actions, compared among themselves, or to external objects, when placed in opposition to other external objects. For as morality is supposed to attend certain relations, if these relations could belong to internal actions consider'd singly, it would follow, that we might be guilty of crimes in ourselves, and independent of our situation, with respect to the universe: and in like manner, if these moral relations

could be apply'd to external objects, it would follow that even inanimate beings would be susceptible of moral beauty and deformity. Now it seems difficult to imagine that any relation can be discover'd betwixt our passions, volitions and actions, compared to external objects, which relation might not belong either to these passions and volitions, or to these external objects, compar'd among *themselves*.

But it will be still more difficult to fulfil the *second* condition, requisite to justify this system. According to the principles of those who maintain an abstract rational difference betwixt moral good and evil, and a natural fitness and unfitness of things, 'tis not only suppos'd, that these relations, being eternal and immutable, are the same, when consider'd by every rational creature, but their *effects* are also suppos'd to be necessarily the same; and 'tis concluded they have no less, or rather a greater, influence in directing the will of the deity, than in governing the rational and virtuous of our own species. These two particulars are evidently distinct. 'Tis one thing to know virtue, and another to conform the will to it. In order, therefore, to prove that the measures of right and wrong are eternal laws, *obligatory* on every rational mind, 'tis not sufficient to shew the relations upon which they are founded: we must also point out the connexion betwixt the relation and the will; and must prove that this connexion is so necessary, that in every well-disposed mind it must take place and have its influence; tho' the difference betwixt these minds be in other respects immense and infinite. Now besides what I have already prov'd, that even in human nature no relation can ever alone produce any action; besides this, I say, it has been shewn, in treating of the understanding, that there is no connexion of cause and effect, such as this is suppos'd to be, which is discoverable otherwise than by experience, and of which we can pretend to have any security by the simple consideration of the objects. All beings in the universe, consider'd in themselves, appear entirely loose and independent of each other. 'Tis only by experience we learn their influence and connexion; and this influence we ought never to extend beyond experience.

Thus it will be impossible to fulfil the *first* condition required to the system of eternal rational measures of right and wrong; because it is impossible to shew those relations, upon which such a distinction may be founded: and 'tis as

* As a proof, how confus'd our way of thinking on this subject commonly is, we may observe, that those who assert that morality is demonstrable, do not say that morality lies in the relations, and that the relations are distinguishable by reason. They only say that reason can discover such an action, in such relations, to be virtuous, and such another vicious. It seems they thought it sufficient, if they could bring the word, relation, into the proposition, without troubling themselves whether it was to the purpose or not. But here, I think, is plain argument. Demonstrative reason discovers only relations. But that reason, according to this hypothesis, discovers also vice and virtue. These moral qualities, therefore, must be relations. When we blame any action, in any situation, the whole complicated object, of action and situation, must form certain relations, wherein the essence of vice consists. This hypothesis is not otherwise intelligible. For what does reason discover, when it pronounces any action vicious? Does it discover a relation or a matter of fact? These questions are decisive, and must not be eluded.

impossible to fulfil the *second* condition; because we cannot prove *a priori*, that these relations, if they really existed and were perceiv'd, would be universally forcible and obligatory.

But to make these general reflexions more clear and convincing, we may illustrate them by some particular instances, wherein this character of moral good or evil is the most universally acknowledged. Of all crimes that human creatures are capable of committing, the most horrid and unnatural is ingratitude, especially when it is committed against parents, and appears in the more flagrant instances of wounds and death. This is acknowledg'd by all mankind, philosophers as well as the people; the question only arises among philosophers, whether the guilt or moral deformity of this action be discover'd by demonstrative reasoning, or be felt by an internal sense, and by means of some sentiment, which the reflecting on such an action naturally occasions. This question will soon be decided against the former opinion if we can shew the same relations in other objects, without the notion of any guilt or iniquity attending them. Reason or science is nothing but the comparing of ideas, and the discovery of their relations; and if the same relations have different characters, it must evidently follow that those characters are not discover'd merely by reason. To put the affair, therefore, to this trial, let us chuse any inanimate object, such as an oak or elm; and let us suppose that by the dropping of its seed it produces a sapling below it, which springing up by degrees, at last overtops and destroys the parent tree: I ask, if in this instance there be wanting any relation, which is discoverable in parricide or ingratitude? Is not the one tree the cause of the other's existence, and the latter the cause of the destruction of the former, in the same manner as when a child murders his parent? 'Tis not sufficient to reply, that a choice or will is wanting. For in the case of parricide, a will does not give rise to any *different* relations, but is only the cause from which the action is deriv'd; and consequently produces the *same* relations, that in the oak or elm arise from some other principles. 'Tis a will or choice that determines a man to kill his parent; and they are the laws of matter and motion that determine a sapling to destroy the oak, from which it sprung. Here then the same relations have different causes; but still the relations are the same: and as their discovery is not in both cases attended

with a notion of immorality, it follows that that notion does not arise from such a discovery.

But to chuse an instance, still more resembling; I would fain ask anyone why incest in the human species is criminal, and why the very same action and the same relations in animals have not the smallest moral turpitude and deformity? If it be answer'd that this action is innocent in animals, because they have not reason sufficient to discover its turpitude; but that man, being endow'd with that faculty which *ought* to restrain him to his duty, the same action instantly becomes criminal to him; should this be said, I would reply that this is evidently arguing in a circle. For before reason can perceive this turpitude, the turpitude must exist; and consequently is independent of the decisions of our reason, and is their object more properly than their effect. According to this system, then, every animal that has sense, and appetite, and will; that is, every animal must be susceptible of all the same virtues and vices, for which we ascribe praise and blame to human creatures. All the difference is that our superior reason may serve to discover the vice or virtue, and by that means may augment the blame or praise: but still this discovery supposes a separate being in these moral distinctions, and a being which depends only on the will and appetite, and which, both in thought and reality, may be distinguish'd from the reason. Animals are susceptible of the same relations, with respect to each other, as the human species, and therefore would also be susceptible of the same morality, if the essence of morality consisted in these relations. Their want of a sufficient degree of reason may hinder them from perceiving the duties and obligations of morality, but can never hinder these duties from existing; since they must antecedently exist in order to their being perceiv'd. Reason must find them, and can never produce them. This argument deserves to be weigh'd as being, in my opinion, entirely decisive.

Nor does this reasoning only prove, that morality consists not in any relations, that are the objects of science; but if examin'd, will prove with equal certainty, that it consists not in any *matter of fact*, which can be discover'd by the understanding. This is the *second* part of our argument; and if it can be made evident, we may conclude that morality is not an object of reason. But can there be any difficulty in proving that vice and virtue are not matters of fact, whose existence we can infer by reason? Take any action allow'd to be vicious: wilful murder, for instance. Examine it in all lights, and see if you can find that matter of fact, or real existence, which you call *vice*. In whichever way you take it, you find only certain passions, motives, volitions and thoughts. There is no other matter of fact in the case. The vice entirely escapes you, as long as you consider the object. You never can find it till you turn your reflexion into your own breast, and find a sentiment of disapprobation, which arises in you, towards this action. Here is a matter of fact; but 'tis the object of feeling, not of reason. It lies in yourself, not in the object. So that when you pronounce any action or character to be vicious, you mean nothing but that from the constitution of your nature you have a feeling or sentiment of blame from the contemplation of it. Vice and virtue, therefore, may be compar'd to sounds, colours, heat and cold, which, according to modern philosophy, are not qualities in objects, but perceptions in the mind: and this discovery in morals, like that other in physics, is to be regarded as a considerable advancement of the speculative sciences; tho', like that too, it has little or no influence on practice. Nothing can be more real, or concern us more, than our own sentiments of pleasure and uneasiness; and if these be favourable to virtue and unfavourable to vice, no more can be requisite to the regulation of our conduct and behaviour.

I cannot forbear adding to these reasonings an observation which may, perhaps, be found of some importance. In every system of morality which I have hitherto met with, I have always remark'd that the author proceeds for some time in the ordinary way of reasoning, and establishes the being of a God, or makes observations concerning human affairs; when of a sudden I am surpriz'd to find that instead of the usual copulations of propositions, *is* and *is not*, I meet with no proposition that is not connected with an *ought* or an *ought not*. This change is imperceptible; but is, however, of the last consequence. For as this *ought*, or *ought not*, expresses some new relation or affirmation, 'tis necessary that it should be observ'd and explain'd; and at the same time that a reason should be given for what seems altogether inconceivable, how this new relation can be a deduction from others, which are entirely different from it. But as authors do not commonly use this precaution, I shall presume to recommend it to the readers; and am persuaded that this small attention would subvert all the vulgar systems of morality, and let us see that the distinction of vice and virtue is not founded merely on the relations of objects, nor is perceiv'd by reason.

Section 2: Moral Distinctions Deriv'd from a Moral Sense

Thus the course of the argument leads us to conclude that since vice and virtue are not discoverable merely by reason, or the comparison of ideas, it must be by means of some impression or sentiment they occasion, that we are able to mark the difference betwixt them. Our decisions concerning moral rectitude and depravity are evidently perceptions; and as all perceptions are either impressions or ideas, the exclusion of the one is a convincing argument for the other. Morality, therefore, is more properly felt than judg'd of; tho' this feeling or sentiment is commonly so soft and gentle that we are apt to confound it with an idea, according to our common custom of taking all things for the same, which have any near resemblance to each other.

The next question is, of what nature are these impressions, and after what manner do they operate upon us? Here we cannot remain long in suspense, but must pronounce the impression arising from virtue to be agreeable, and that proceeding from vice to be uneasy. Every moment's experience must convince us of this. There is no spectacle so fair and beautiful as a noble and generous action; nor any which gives us more abhorrence than one that is cruel and treacherous. No enjoyment equals the satisfaction we receive from the company of those we love and esteem; as the greatest of all punishments is to be oblig'd to pass our lives with those we hate or contemn. A very play or romance may afford us instances of this pleasure, which virtue conveys to us; and pain, which arises from vice.

Now since the distinguishing impressions, by which moral good or evil is known, are nothing but *particular* pains or pleasures; it follows, that in all enquiries concerning these moral distinctions, it will be sufficient to shew the principles, which make us feel a satisfaction or uneasiness from the survey of any character, in order to satisfy us why the character is laudable or blameable.

An action, or sentiment, or character is virtuous or vicious; why? Because its view causes a pleasure or uneasiness of a particular kind. In giving a reason, therefore, for the pleasure or uneasiness, we sufficiently explain the vice or virtue. To have the sense of virtue is nothing but to *feel* a satisfaction of a particular kind from the contemplation of a character. The very *feeling* constitutes our praise or admiration. We go no farther; nor do we enquire into the cause of the satisfaction. We do not infer a character to be virtuous, because it pleases: but in feeling that it pleases after such a particular manner, we in effect feel that it is virtuous. The case is the same as in our judgments concerning all kinds of beauty, and tastes and sensations. Our approbation is imply'd in the immediate pleasure they convey to us.

I have objected to the system, which establishes eternal rational measures of right and wrong, that 'tis impossible to shew, in the actions of reasonable creatures, any relations which are not found in external objects; and therefore, if morality always attended these relations, 'twere possible for inanimate matter to become virtuous or vicious. Now it may, in like manner, be objected to the present system, that if virtue and vice be determin'd by pleasure and pain, these qualities must, in every case, arise from the sensations; and consequently any object, whether animate or inanimate, rational or irrational, might become morally good or evil, provided it can excite a satisfaction or uneasiness. But tho' this objection seems to be the very same, it has by no means the same force in the one case as in the other. For, *first*, 'tis evident that under the term *pleasure*, we comprehend sensations which are very different from each other, and which have only such a distant resemblance, as is requisite to make them be express'd by the same abstract term. A good composition of music and a bottle of good wine equally produce pleasure; and what is more, their goodness is determin'd merely by the pleasure. But shall we say upon that account that the wine is harmonious, or the music of a good flavour? In like manner an inanimate object, and the character or sentiments of any person may, both of them, give satisfaction; but as the satisfaction is different, this keeps our sentiments concerning them from being confounded, and makes us ascribe virtue to the one, and not to the other. Nor is every sentiment of pleasure or pain, which arises from characters and actions, of that *peculiar* kind which makes us praise or condemn. The good qualities of an enemy are hurtful to us, but may still command our esteem and respect. 'Tis only when a character is considered in general, without reference to our particular interest, that it causes such a feeling or sentiment, as denominates it morally good or evil. 'Tis true, those sentiments, from interest and morals, are apt to be confounded, and naturally run into one another. It seldom happens that we do not think an enemy vicious, and can distinguish betwixt his opposition to our interest and real villainy or baseness. But this hinders not, but that the sentiments are, in themselves, distinct; and a man of temper and judgment may preserve himself from these illusions. In like manner, tho' 'tis certain a musical voice is nothing but one that naturally gives a *particular* kind of pleasure; yet 'tis difficult for a man to be sensible, that the voice of an enemy is agreeable, or to allow it to be musical. But a person of a fine ear, who has the command of himself, can separate these feelings, and give praise to what deserves it.

Secondly, we may call to remembrance the preceding system of the passions, in order to remark a still more considerable difference among our pains and pleasures. Pride and humility, love and hatred are excited, when there is any thing presented to us that both bears a relation to the object of the passion, and produces a separate sensation related to the sensation of the passions. Now virtue and vice are attended with these circumstances. They must necessarily be plac'd either in ourselves or others, and excite either pleasure or uneasiness; and therefore must give rise to one of these four passions, which clearly distinguishes them from the pleasure and pain arising from inanimate objects, that often bear no relation to us: and this is, perhaps, the most considerable effect that virtue and vice have upon the human mind.

It may now be ask'd *in general*, concerning this pain or pleasure, that distinguishes moral good and evil, *From what principles is it derived, and whence does it arise in the human mind?* To this I reply, *first*, that 'tis absurd to imagine, that in every particular instance, these sentiments are produc'd by an *original* quality and *primary* constitution. For as the number of our duties is, in a manner, infinite, 'tis impossible that our original instincts should extend to each of them, and from our very first infancy impress on the human mind all that multitude of precepts, which are contain'd in the compleatest system of ethics. Such a method of proceeding is not conformable to the usual maxims, by which nature is conducted, where a few principles produce all that variety we observe in the universe, and every thing is carry'd on in the easiest and most simple manner. 'Tis necessary, therefore, to abridge these primary impulses, and find some more general principles, upon which all our notions of morals are founded.

But in the *second* place, should it be ask'd whether we ought to search for these principles in *nature*, or whether we must look for them in some other origin? I would reply, that our answer to this question depends upon the definition of the word, Nature, than which there is none more ambiguous and equivocal. If *nature* be oppos'd to miracles, not only the distinction betwixt vice and virtue is natural, but also every event which has ever happen'd in the world, *excepting those miracles on which our religion is founded*. In saying, then, that the sentiments of vice and virtue are natural in this sense, we make no very extraordinary discovery.

But *nature* may also be opposed to rare and unusual; and in this sense of the word, which is the common one, there may often arise disputes concerning what is natural or unnatural; and one may in general affirm that we are not possess'd of any very precise standard by which these disputes can be decided. Frequent and rare depend upon the number of examples we have observ'd; and as this number may gradually encrease or diminish, 'twill be impossible to fix any exact boundaries betwixt them. We may only affirm on this head, that if ever there was any thing, which could be call'd natural in this sense, the sentiments of morality certainly may; since there never was any nation of the world, nor any single person in any nation, who was utterly depriv'd of them, and who never, in any instance, shew'd the least approbation or dislike of manners. These sentiments are so rooted in our constitution and temper, that without entirely confounding the human mind by disease or madness, 'tis impossible to extirpate and destroy them.

But *nature* may also be opposed to artifice, as well as to what is rare and unusual; and in this sense it may be disputed, whether the notions of virtue be natural or not. We readily forget that the designs, and projects, and views of men are principles as necessary in their operation as heat and cold, moist and dry: but taking them to be free and entirely our own, 'tis usual for us to set them in opposition to the other principles of nature. Should it, therefore, be demanded whether the sense of virtue be natural or artificial, I am of opinion that 'tis impossible for me at present to give any precise answer to this question. Perhaps it will appear afterwards that our sense of some virtues is artificial, and that of others natural. The discussion of this question will be more proper, when we enter upon an exact detail of each particular vice and virtue [Book III, Parts II–III].

Meanwhile it may not be amiss to observe from these definitions of *natural* and *unnatural*, that nothing can be more unphilosophical than those systems which assert that virtue is the same with what is natural, and vice with what is unnatural. For in the first sense of the word, nature, as opposed to miracles, both vice and virtue are equally natural; and in the second sense, as oppos'd to what is unusual, perhaps virtue will be found to be the most unnatural. At least it must be own'd, that heroic virtue, being as unusual, is as little natural as the most brutal barbarity. As to the third sense of the word, 'tis certain, that both vice and virtue are equally artificial, and out of nature. For however it may be disputed, whether the notion of a merit or demerit in certain actions be natural or artificial, 'tis evident that the actions themselves are artificial, and are perform'd with a certain design and intention; otherwise they could never be rank'd under any of these denominations. 'Tis impossible, therefore, that the character of natural and unnatural can ever, in any sense, mark the boundaries of vice and virtue.

Thus we are still brought back to our first position, that virtue is distinguished by the pleasure, and vice by the pain, that any action, sentiment or character gives us by the mere view and contemplation. This decision is very commodious; because it reduces us to this simple question, *why any action or sentiment upon the general view or survey, gives a certain satisfaction or uneasiness,* in order to shew the origin of its moral rectitude or depravity, without looking for any incomprehensible relations and qualities, which never did exist in nature nor even in our imagination by any clear and distinct conception. I flatter myself I have executed a great part of my present design by a state of the question, which appears to me so free from ambiguity and obscurity.

Notes

1 Hume is referring here to his distinction made in Book I, Part I, between the "impressions" which we experience through the senses or when our "passions" are affected and the "ideas" which are before the mind when we think and reflect. In the present context, his point is that moral distinctions cannot be drawn merely through reflection since they are functions of the different "passions" actuated in us.

2 There follows the long footnote, which I have omitted, on Wollaston's construal of moral wrong as a species of falsehood. Hume argues that if what makes my adultery wrong is the false message it conveys that another's wife is my own, I could avoid the wrong by taking "the precaution of shutting the windows, while I indulg'd myself." Nobody then gets any message, true or false.

Immanuel Kant, *Fundamental Principles of the Metaphysic of Morals,* Preface and Section 1

Introduction

In moral philosophy, as in other branches of the subject, the man most responsible for setting the modern agenda was the German philosopher Immanuel Kant (1724–1804). Anyone now wanting to defend the *idées fixes* of the eighteenth-century Enlightenment – though their pedigree goes back to Aristotle or Epicurus – must do so against Kant's critique. There were at least three such dominant ideas, apparent in Hume's writings (see I.14 above), for example. First, the "teleological" or "consequentialist" assumption that actions are right only if they tend to produce a certain result, such as, according to utilitarians, the general happiness. Second, the conviction that a result or goal is good if it is *natural*, in the sense of being one that people would, according to their human nature, aim at unless blinded by ignorance, indoctrination or whatever. Third, and related, the view that a good person is one motivated by such natural dispositions – benevolence, sympathy, enlightened self-love and the like.

In the remarkably rich few pages that follow, Kant challenges each of these claims. Driving his criticisms, one feels, is a nightmare scenario that he envisaged. What results our actions tend to pro-

From Immanuel Kant, *Fundamental Principles of the Metaphysic of Morals,* trans. T. K. Abbott. Buffalo, NY: Prometheus, 1987, pp. 9–13, 17–33 (some passages from Preface omitted; asterisked notes are Kant's own).

duce, as well as our currently "natural" make-up and aspirations, are contingent matters, in which case conformity to morality must itself be a "very contingent and uncertain" thing if it is based on such considerations (Preface). But morality must have a more secure foundation if the possibility of moral collapse is to be excluded. Moreover, he argues, the untenability of the *idées fixes* is surely attested to by ordinary intuitions, by our "common rational knowledge of morality." Is it not apparent, first, that the moral worth of an action is totally independent of its results, in which luck plays such a part? Is it not clear, second, that the moral law cannot be determined by reference to human nature, since it is binding on *all* rational beings, whether or not they share our nature? And, finally, how can a person deserve *moral* praise if, by a mere "gift of nature," he or she happens to prefer acting violently to acting selfishly?

It is, Kant proceeds, only "a Good Will," the resolve to act for the sake of duty, out of respect for the moral law, and independently of any other motives, which has moral worth. What this entails is that the "maxims" or principles on which alone I should act are those which conform to "law in general" – that is, are binding on all rational creatures. Hence, in Section 1, we find Kant formulating, without as yet using the actual expression, his famous categorical imperative: never to act upon a maxim unless I can "will that my maxim should become a universal law." It would be wrong, for example, to act on the principle that promises may be broken when it is personally advantageous to do so. Such a principle could not become a universal law, and it could not become one for logical reasons, since the very practice of promising would itself be undermined if people never kept their promises. Kant goes on, in Section 2, to argue that this imperative is equivalent to the demand to treat people as ends in themselves, "never as means only": for to treat someone simply as a means is to act on a maxim which he or she could never rationally accept as a general law. Respect for persons and respect for the moral law are, therefore, two sides of the same coin.

In his own day and ever since, Kant's position has provoked many criticisms. One, pressed by the poet Friedrich Schiller (1759–1805), is that there is something chilling in the idea, which contradicts the whole Aristotelian tradition, that a natural inclination to virtuous behavior is without moral worth.[1] Another, anticipated by Kant himself when he admitted the "incomprehensible" mystery involved, is how mere knowledge of one's duty, unaccompanied by any other "spring" to action, can serve to motivate one's behavior. Wasn't Hume right to insist that reason without "passion" is idle? Perhaps the key to answering these criticisms resides in the notion of "respect." Without becoming overtaxed about the meaning of the word "moral," it might be admitted that a distinct kind of worth, overlooked since the Stoics, attaches to the person who acts against his inclinations, purely out of rational recognition of duty – a worth that elicits a special respect. And perhaps this special respect owed to rational beings, including oneself, for their capacity so to act is explanation enough of how a person can be moved to behave morally. Is it really such a mystery, once the leading ideas of Enlightenment moral psychology are unfixed, that I can be moved to act by a view of myself which, as Kant puts it elsewhere, "infinitely elevates my worth, as an *intelligence,* through my personality, in which the moral law reveals to me a life independent of animality."[2]

Notes

1 See the articles by O. O'Neill and J. B. Schneewind in P. Guyer, ed., *The Cambridge Companion to Kant*, Cambridge: Cambridge University Press, 1992.

2 I. Kant, *Critique of Practical Reason*, Indianapolis, IN: Bobbs-Merrill, 1976, pp. 161–2.

Kant, *Fundamental Principles of the Metaphysics of Morals*

Preface

Ancient Greek philosophy was divided into three sciences: physics, ethics and logic. This division is perfectly suitable to the nature of the thing, and the only improvement that can be made in it is to add the principle on which it is based, so that we may both satisfy ourselves of its completeness, and also be able to determine correctly the necessary subdivisions.

All rational knowledge is either *material* or *formal*: the former considers some object, the latter is concerned only with the form of the understanding and of the reason itself, and with the universal laws of thought in general without distinction of its objects. Formal philosophy is called logic. Material philosophy, however, which has to do with determinate objects and the laws to which they are subject, is again twofold; for these laws are either laws of *nature* or of *freedom*. The science of the former is physics, that of the latter, ethics; they are also called *natural philosophy* and *moral philosophy* respectively.

Logic cannot have any empirical part; that is, a part in which the universal and necessary laws of thought should rest on grounds taken from experience; otherwise it would not be logic, i.e. a canon for the understanding or the reason, valid for all thought, and capable of demonstration. Natural and moral philosophy, on the contrary, can each have their empirical part, since the former has to determine the laws of nature as an object of experience; the latter the laws of the human will, so far as it is affected by nature: the former, however, being laws according to which everything does happen; the latter, laws according to which everything ought to happen. Ethics, however, must also consider the conditions under which what ought to happen frequently does not.

We may call all philosophy *empirical*, so far as it is based on grounds of experience: on the other hand, that which delivers its doctrines from a priori principles alone we may call *pure* philosophy. When the latter is merely formal it is *logic*; if it is restricted to definite objects of the understanding it is *metaphysic*.

In this way there arises the idea of a twofold metaphysic – a *metaphysic of nature* and a *metaphysic of morals*. Physics will thus have an empirical and also a rational part. It is the same with ethics; but here the empirical part might have the special name of *practical anthropology*, the name *morality* being appropriated to the rational part. . . .

As my concern here is with moral philosophy, I limit the question . . . to this: Whether it is not of the utmost necessity to construct a pure moral philosophy, perfectly cleared of everything which is only empirical, and which belongs to anthropology? for that such a philosophy must be possible is evident from the common idea of duty and of the moral laws. Every one must admit that if a law is to have moral force, i.e. to be the basis of an obligation, it must carry with it absolute necessity; that, for example, the precept, 'Thou shalt not lie,' is not valid for men alone, as if other rational beings had no need to observe it; and so with all the other moral laws properly so called; that, therefore, the basis of obligation must not be sought in the nature of man, or in the circumstances in the world in which he is placed, but a priori simply in the conceptions of pure reason; and although any other precept which is founded on principles of mere experience may be in certain respects universal, yet in as far as it rests even in the least degree on an empirical basis, perhaps only as to a motive, such a precept, while it may be a practical rule, can never be called a moral law.

Thus not only are moral laws with their principles essentially distinguished from every other kind of practical knowledge in which there is anything empirical, but all moral philosophy rests wholly on its pure part. When applied to man, it does not borrow the least thing from the knowledge of man himself (anthropology), but gives laws a priori to him as a rational being. No doubt these laws require a judgement sharpened by experience, in order on the one hand to distinguish in what cases they are applicable, and on the other to procure for them access to the will

of the man, and effectual influence on conduct; since man is acted on by so many inclinations that, though capable of the idea of a practical pure reason, he is not so easily able to make it effective *in concreto* in his life.

A metaphysic of morals is therefore indispensably necessary, not merely for speculative reasons, in order to investigate the sources of the practical principles which are to be found a priori in our reason, but also because morals themselves are liable to all sorts of corruption, as long as we are without that clue and supreme canon by which to estimate them correctly. For in order that an action should be morally good, it is not enough that it *conform* to the moral law, but it must also be done *for the sake of the law*, otherwise that conformity is only very contingent and uncertain; since a principle which is not moral, although it may now and then produce actions conformable to the law, will also often produce actions which contradict it. Now it is only in a pure philosophy that we can look for the moral law in its purity and genuineness (and, in a practical matter, this is of the utmost consequence): we must, therefore, begin with pure philosophy (metaphysic), and without it there cannot be any moral philosophy at all. That which mingles these pure principles with the empirical does not deserve the name of philosophy (for what distinguishes philosophy from common rational knowledge is that it treats in separate sciences what the latter only comprehends confusedly); much less does it deserve that of moral philosophy, since by this confusion it even spoils the purity of morals themselves, and counteracts its own end.

[. . .]

Section 1: Transition from the Common Rational Knowledge of Morality to the Philosophical

Nothing can possibly be conceived in the world, or even out of it, which can be called good without qualification, except a Good Will. Intelligence, wit, judgement, and the other *talents* of the mind, however they may be named, or courage, resolution, perseverance, as qualities of temperament, are undoubtedly good and desirable in many respects; but these gifts of nature may also become extremely bad and mischievous if the will which is to make use of them, and which, therefore, constitutes what is called *character*, is not good. It is the same with the *gifts of fortune*. Power, riches, honour, even health, and the general well-being and contentment with one's condition which is called *happiness*, inspire pride, and often presumption, if there is not a good will to correct the influence of these on the mind, and with this also to rectify the whole principle of acting, and adapt it to its end. The sight of a being who is not adorned with a single feature of a pure and good will, enjoying unbroken prosperity, can never give pleasure to an impartial rational spectator. Thus a good will appears to constitute the indispensable condition even of being worthy of happiness.

There are even some qualities which are of service to this good will itself, and may facilitate its action, yet which have no intrinsic unconditional value, but always presuppose a good will, and this qualifies the esteem that we justly have for them, and does not permit us to regard them as absolutely good. Moderation in the affections and passions, self-control and calm deliberation are not only good in many respects, but even seem to constitute part of the intrinsic worth of the person; but they are far from deserving to be called good without qualification, although they have been so unconditionally praised by the ancients. For without the principles of a good will, they may become extremely bad, and the coolness of a villain not only makes him far more dangerous, but also directly makes him more abominable in our eyes than he would have been without it.

A good will is good not because of what it performs or effects, not by its aptness for the attainment of some proposed end, but simply by virtue of the volition, that is, it is good in itself, and considered by itself is to be esteemed much higher than all that can be brought about by it in favour of any inclination, nay, even of the sum total of all inclinations. Even if it should happen that, owing to special disfavour of fortune, or the niggardly provision of a stepmotherly nature, this will should wholly lack power to accomplish its purpose, if with its greatest efforts it should yet achieve nothing, and there should remain only the good will (not, to be sure, a mere wish, but the summoning of all means in our power), then, like a jewel, it would still shine by its own light, as a thing which has its own value in itself. Its usefulness or fruitfulness can neither add to nor take away anything from this value. It would

be, as it were, only the setting to enable us to handle it the more conveniently in common commerce, or to attract to it the attention of those who are not yet connoisseurs, but not to recommend it to true connoisseurs, or to determine its value.

There is, however, something so strange in this idea of the absolute value of the mere will, in which no account is taken of its utility, that notwithstanding the thorough assent of even common reason to the idea, yet a suspicion must arise that it may perhaps really be the product of mere high-flown fancy, and that we may have misunderstood the purpose of nature in assigning reason as the governor of our will. Therefore we will examine this idea from this point of view.

In the physical constitution of an organized being, that is, a being adapted suitably to the purposes of life, we assume it as a fundamental principle that no organ for any purpose will be found but what is also the fittest and best adapted for that purpose. Now in a being which has reason and a will, if the proper object of nature were its *conservation*, its *welfare*, in a word, its *happiness*, then nature would have hit upon a very bad arrangement in selecting the reason of the creature to carry out this purpose. For all the actions which the creature has to perform with a view to this purpose, and the whole rule of its conduct, would be far more surely prescribed to it by instinct, and that end would have been attained thereby much more certainly than it ever can be by reason. Should reason have been communicated to this favoured creature over and above, it must only have served it to contemplate the happy constitution of its nature, to admire it, to congratulate itself thereon, and to feel thankful for it to the beneficent cause, but not that it should subject its desires to that weak and delusive guidance, and meddle bunglingly with the purpose of nature. In a word, nature would have taken care that reason should not break forth into *practical exercise*, nor have the presumption, with its weak insight, to think out for itself the plan of happiness, and of the means of attaining it. Nature would not only have taken on herself the choice of the ends, but also of the means, and with wise foresight would have entrusted both to instinct.

And, in fact, we find that the more a cultivated reason applies itself with deliberate purpose to the enjoyment of life and happiness, so much the more does the man fail of true satisfaction. And from this circumstance there arises in many, if they are candid enough to confess it, a certain degree of *misology*, that is, hatred of reason, especially in the case of those who are most experienced in the use of it, because after calculating all the advantages they derive, I do not say from the invention of all the arts of common luxury, but even from the sciences (which seem to them to be after all only a luxury of the understanding), they find that they have, in fact, only brought more trouble on their shoulders, rather than gained in happiness; and they end by envying, rather than despising, the more common stamp of men who keep closer to the guidance of mere instinct, and do not allow their reason much influence on their conduct. And this we must admit, that the judgement of those who would very much lower the lofty eulogies of the advantages which reason gives us in regard to the happiness and satisfaction of life, or who would even reduce them below zero, is by no means morose or ungrateful to the goodness with which the world is governed, but that there lies at the root of these judgements the idea that our existence has a different and far nobler end, for which, and not for happiness, reason is properly intended, and which must, therefore, be regarded as the supreme condition to which the private ends of man must, for the most part, be postponed.

For as reason is not competent to guide the will with certainty in regard to its objects and the satisfaction of all our wants (which it to some extent even multiplies), this being an end to which an implanted instinct would have led with much greater certainty; and since, nevertheless, reason is imparted to us as a practical faculty, i.e. as one which is to have influence on the *will*, therefore, admitting that nature generally in the distribution of her capacities has adapted the means to the end, its true destination must be to produce a *will*, not merely good as a *means* to something else, but *good in itself*, for which reason was absolutely necessary. This will then, though not indeed the sole and complete good, must be the supreme good and the condition of every other, even of the desire of happiness. Under these circumstances, there is nothing inconsistent with the wisdom of nature in the fact that the cultivation of the reason, which is requisite for the first and unconditional purpose, does in many ways interfere, at least in this life, with the attainment of the second, which is always conditional, namely, happiness. Nay, it may even reduce it to

nothing, without nature thereby failing of her purpose. For reason recognizes the establishment of a good will as its highest practical destination, and in attaining this purpose is capable only of a satisfaction of its own proper kind, namely, that from the attainment of an end, which end again is determined by reason only, notwithstanding that this may involve many a disappointment to the ends of inclination.

We have then to develop the notion of a will which deserves to be highly esteemed for itself, and is good without a view to anything further, a notion which exists already in the sound natural understanding, requiring rather to be cleared up than to be taught, and which in estimating the value of our actions always takes the first place, and constitutes the condition of all the rest. In order to do this we will take the notion of duty, which includes that of a good will, although implying certain subjective restrictions and hindrances. These, however, far from concealing it, or rendering it unrecognizable, rather bring it out by contrast, and make it shine forth so much the brighter.

I omit here all actions which are already recognized as inconsistent with duty, although they may be useful for this or that purpose, for with these the question whether they are done *from duty* cannot arise at all, since they even conflict with it. I also set aside those actions which really conform to duty, but to which men have *no* direct *inclination*, performing them because they are impelled thereto by some other inclination. For in this case we can readily distinguish whether the action which agrees with duty is done *from duty*, or from a selfish view. It is much harder to make this distinction when the action accords with duty, and the subject has besides a *direct* inclination to it. For example, it is always a matter of duty that a dealer should not overcharge an inexperienced purchaser, and wherever there is much commerce the prudent tradesman does not overcharge, but keeps a fixed price for everyone, so that a child buys of him as well as any other. Men are thus *honestly* served; but this is not enough to make us believe that the tradesman has so acted from duty and from principles of honesty: his own advantage required it; it is out of the question in this case to suppose that he might besides have a direct inclination in favour of the buyers, so that, as it were, from love he should give no advantage to one over another. Accordingly the action was done neither from duty nor from direct inclination, but merely with a selfish view.

On the other hand, it is a duty to maintain one's life; and, in addition, everyone has also a direct inclination to do so. But on this account the often anxious care which most men take for it has no intrinsic worth, and their maxim has no moral import. They preserve their life *as duty requires*, no doubt, but not *because duty requires*. On the other hand, if adversity and hopeless sorrow have completely taken away the relish for life; if the unfortunate one, strong in mind, indignant at his fate rather than desponding or dejected, wishes for death, and yet preserves his life without loving it – not from inclination or fear, but from duty – then his maxim has a moral worth.

To be beneficent when we can is a duty; and besides this, there are many minds so sympathetically constituted that, without any other motive of vanity or self-interest, they find a pleasure in spreading joy around them and can take delight in the satisfaction of others so far as it is their own work. But I maintain that in such a case an action of this kind, however proper, however amiable it may be, has nevertheless no true moral worth, but is on a level with other inclinations, e.g. the inclination to honour, which, if it is happily directed to that which is in fact of public utility and accordant with duty, and consequently honourable, deserves praise and encouragement, but not esteem. For the maxim lacks the moral import, namely, that such actions be done *from duty*, not from inclination. Put the case that the mind of that philanthropist were clouded by sorrow of his own, extinguishing all sympathy with the lot of others, and that while he still has the power to benefit others in distress, he is not touched by their trouble because he is absorbed with his own; and now suppose that he tears himself out of this dead insensibility, and performs the action without any inclination to it, but simply from duty, then first has his action its genuine moral worth. Further still; if nature has put little sympathy in the heart of this or that man; if he, supposed to be an upright man, is by temperament cold and indifferent to the sufferings of others, perhaps because in respect of his own he is provided with the special gift of patience and fortitude, and supposes, or even requires, that others should have the same – and such a man would certainly not be the meanest product of nature – but if nature had not specially framed him for a philanthropist, would he not still find

in himself a source from whence to give himself a far higher worth than that of a good-natured temperament could be? Unquestionably. It is just in this that the moral worth of the character is brought out which is incomparably the highest of all, namely, that he is beneficent, not from inclination, but from duty.

To secure one's own happiness is a duty, at least indirectly; for discontent with one's condition, under a pressure of many anxieties and amidst unsatisfied wants, might easily become a great *temptation to transgression of duty*. But here again, without looking to duty, all men have already the strongest and most intimate inclination to happiness, because it is just in this idea that all inclinations are combined in one total. But the precept of happiness is often of such a sort that it greatly interferes with some inclinations, and yet a man cannot form any definite and certain conception of the sum of satisfaction of all of them which is called happiness. It is not then to be wondered at that a single inclination, definite both as to what it promises and as to the time within which it can be gratified, is often able to overcome such a fluctuating idea, and that a gouty patient, for instance, can choose to enjoy what he likes, and to suffer what he may, since, according his calculation, on this occasion at least, he has [only] not sacrificed the enjoyment of the present moment to a possibly mistaken expectation of a happiness which is supposed to be found in health. But even in this case, if the general desire for happiness did not influence his will, and supposing that in his particular case health was not a necessary element in this calculation, there yet remains in this, as in all other cases, this law, namely, that he should promote his happiness not from inclination but from duty, and by this would his conduct first acquire true moral worth.

It is in this manner, undoubtedly, that we are to understand those passages of Scripture also in which we are commanded to love our neighbour, even our enemy. For love, as an affection, cannot be commanded, but beneficence for duty's sake may; even though we are not impelled to it by any inclination – nay, are even repelled by a natural and unconquerable aversion. This is *practical* love, and not *pathological* – a love which is seated in the will, and not in the propensions of sense – in principles of action and not of tender sympathy; and it is this love alone which can be commanded.

The second[1] proposition is: That an action done from duty derives its moral worth, *not from the purpose* which is to be attained by it, but from the maxim by which it is determined, and therefore does not depend on the realization of the object of the action, but merely on the *principle of volition* by which the action has taken place, without regard to any object of desire. It is clear from what precedes that the purposes which we may have in view in our actions or their effects regarded as ends and springs of the will, cannot give to actions any unconditional or moral worth. In what, then, can their worth lie, if it is not to consist in the will and in reference to its expected effect? It cannot lie anywhere but in the *principle of the will* without regard to the ends which can be attained by the action. For the will stands between its *a priori* principle, which is formal, and its *a posteriori* spring, which is material, as between two roads, and as it must be determined by something, it follows that it must be determined by the formal principle of volition when an action is done from duty, in which case every material principle has been withdrawn from it.

The third proposition, which is a consequence of the two preceding, I would express thus: *Duty is the necessity of acting from respect for the law.* I may have *inclination* for an object as the effect of my proposed action, but I cannot have *respect* for it, just for this reason, that it is an effect and not an energy of will. Similarly, I cannot have respect for inclination, whether my own or another's; I can at most, if my own, approve it; if another's sometimes even love it; i.e. look on it as favourable to my own interest. It is only what is connected with my will as a principle, by no means as an effect – what does not subserve my inclination, but overpowers it, or at least in case of choice excludes it from its calculation – in other words, simply the law of itself, which can be an object of respect, and hence a command. Now an action done from duty must wholly exclude the influence of inclination, and with it every object of the will, so that nothing remains which can determine the will except objectively the *law*, and subjectively *pure respect* for this practical law, and consequently the maxim* that I should

* A *maxim* is the subjective principle of volition. The objective principle (i.e. that which would also serve subjectively as a practical principle to all rational beings if reason had full power over the faculty of desire) is the practical *law*.

follow this law even to the thwarting of all my inclinations.[2]

Thus the moral worth of an action does not lie in the effect expected from it, nor in any principle of action which requires to borrow its motive from this expected effect. For all these effects – agreeableness of one's condition, and even the promotion of the happiness of others – could have been also brought about by other causes, so that for this there would have been no need of the will of a rational being; whereas it is in this alone that the supreme and unconditional good can be found. The pre-eminent good which we call moral can therefore consist in nothing else than *the conception of law* in itself, *which certainly is only possible in a rational being*, in so far as this conception, and not the expected effect, determines the will. This is a good which is already present in the person who acts accordingly, and we have not to wait for it to appear first in the result.†

But what sort of law can that be, the conception of which must determine the will, even

† It might be here objected to me that I take refuge behind the word *respect* in an obscure feeling, instead of giving a distinct solution of the question by a concept of the reason. But although respect is a feeling, it is not a feeling *received* through influence, but is *self-wrought* by a rational concept, and, therefore, is specifically distinct from all feelings of the former kind, which may be referred either to inclination or fear. What I recognize immediately as a law for me, I recognize with respect. This merely signifies the consciousness that my will is *subordinate* to a law, without the intervention of other influences on my sense. The immediate determination of the will by the law, and the consciousness of this is called *respect*, so that this is regarded as an *effect* of the law on the subject, and not as the *cause* of it. Respect is properly the conception of a worth which thwarts my self-love. Accordingly it is something which is considered neither as an object of inclination nor of fear, although it has something analogous to both. The *object* of respect is the *law* only, and that, the law which we impose on *ourselves*, and yet recognize as necessary in itself. As a law, we are subjected to it without consulting self-love; as imposed by us on ourselves, it is a result of our will. In the former respect it has an analogy to fear, in the latter to inclination. Respect for a person is properly only respect for the law (of honesty, etc.), of which he gives us an example. Since we also look on the improvement of our talents as a duty, we consider that we see in a person of talents, as it were, the *example of a law* (viz. to become like him in this by exercise), and this constitutes our respect. All so-called moral *interest* consists simply in *respect* for the law.

without paying any regard to the effect expected from it, in order that this will may be called good absolutely and without qualification? As I have deprived the will of every impulse which could arise to it from obedience to any law, there remains nothing but the universal conformity of its actions to law in general, which alone is to serve the will as a principle, i.e. I am never to act otherwise than so *that I could also will that my maxim should become a universal law.* Here now, it is the simple conformity to law in general, without assuming any particular law applicable to certain actions, that serves the will as its principle, and must so serve it, if duty is not to be a vain delusion and a chimerical notion. The common reason of men in its practical judgements perfectly coincides with this, and always has in view the principle here suggested. Let the question be, for example: May I when in distress make a promise with the intention not to keep it? I readily distinguish here between the two significations which the question may have. Whether it is prudent, or whether it is right, to make a false promise. The former may undoubtedly often be the case. I see clearly indeed that it is not enough to extricate myself from a present difficulty by means of this subterfuge, but it must be well considered whether there may not hereafter spring from this lie much greater inconvenience than that from which I now free myself, and as, with all my supposed *cunning*, the consequences cannot be so easily foreseen but that credit once lost may be much more injurious to me than any mischief which I seek to avoid at present, it should be considered whether it would not be more *prudent* to act herein according to a universal maxim, and to make it a habit to promise nothing except with the intention of keeping it. But it is soon clear to me that such a maxim will still only be based on the fear of consequences. Now it is a wholly different thing to be truthful from duty, and to be so from apprehension of injurious consequences. In the first case, the very notion of the action already implies a law for me; in the second case, I must first look about elsewhere to see what results may often be combined with it which would affect myself. For to deviate from the principle of duty is beyond all doubt wicked; but to be unfaithful to my maxim of prudence may often be very advantageous to me although to abide by it is certainly safer. The shortest way, however, and an unerring one, to discover the

answer to this question whether a lying promise is consistent with duty, is to ask myself, Should I be content that my maxim (to extricate myself from difficulty by a false promise) should hold good as a universal law, for myself as well as for others? and should I be able to say to myself, 'Every one may make a deceitful promise when he finds himself in a difficulty from which he cannot otherwise extricate himself'? Then I presently become aware that while I can will the lie, I can by no means will that lying should be a universal law. For with such a law there would be no promises at all, since it would be in vain to allege my intention in regard to my future actions to those who would not believe this allegation, or if they overhastily did so, would pay me back in my own coin. Hence my maxim, as soon as it should be made a universal law, would necessarily destroy itself.

I do not, therefore, need any far-reaching penetration to discern what I have to do in order that my will may be morally good. Inexperienced in the course of the world, incapable of being prepared for all its contingencies, I only ask myself: Canst thou also will that thy maxim should be a universal law? If not, then it must be rejected, and that not because of a disadvantage accruing from it to myself or even to others, but because it cannot enter as a principle into a possible universal legislation, and reason extorts from me immediate respect for such legislation. I do not indeed as yet *discern* on what this respect is based (this the philosopher may inquire), but at least I understand this, that it is an estimation of the worth which far outweighs all worth of what is recommended by inclination, and that the necessity of acting from *pure* respect for the practical law is what constitutes duty, to which every other motive must give place, because it is the condition of a will being good *in itself*, and the worth of such a will is above everything.

Thus, then, without quitting the moral knowledge of common human reason, we have arrived at its principle. And although, no doubt, common men do not conceive it in such an abstract and universal form, yet they always have it really before their eyes, and use it as the standard of their decision. Here it would be easy to show how, with this compass in hand, men are well able to distinguish, in every case that occurs, what is good, what bad, conformably to duty or inconsistent with it, if, without in the least teaching them anything new, we only, like Socrates, direct their attention to the principle they themselves employ; and that therefore we do not need science and philosophy to know what we should do to be honest and good, yea, even wise and virtuous. Indeed we might well have conjectured beforehand that the knowledge of what every man is bound to do, and therefore also to know, would be within the reach of every man, even the commonest. Here we cannot forbear admiration when we see how great an advantage the practical judgement has over the theoretical in the common understanding of men. In the latter, if common reason ventures to depart from the laws of experience and from the perceptions of the senses it falls into mere inconceivabilities and self-contradictions, at least into chaos of uncertainty, obscurity, and instability. But in the practical sphere it is just when the common understanding excludes all sensible springs from practical laws that its power of judgement begins to show itself to advantage. It then becomes even subtle, whether it be that it chicanes with its own conscience or with other claims respecting what is to be called right, or whether it desires for its own instruction to determine honestly the worth of actions; and, in the latter case, it may even have as good a hope of hitting the mark as any philosopher whatever can promise himself. Nay, it is almost more sure of doing so, because the philosopher cannot have any other principle, while he may easily perplex his judgement by a multitude of considerations foreign to the matter, and so turn aside from the right way. Would it not therefore be wiser in moral concerns to acquiesce in the judgement of common reason or at most only to call in philosophy for the purpose of rendering the system of morals more complete and intelligible, and its rules more convenient for use (especially for disputation), but not so as to draw off the common understanding from its happy simplicity, or to bring it by means of philosophy into a new path of inquiry and instruction?

Innocence is indeed a glorious thing, only, on the other hand, it is very sad that it cannot well maintain itself, and is easily seduced. On this account even wisdom – which otherwise consists more in conduct than in knowledge – yet has need of science, not in order to learn from it, but to secure for its precepts admission and permanence. Against all the commands of duty which reason represents to man as so deserving of respect, he feels in himself a powerful counterpoise in his wants and inclinations, the entire satisfaction of which he sums under the name of happiness. Now reason issues its commands unyieldingly, without promising anything to the inclinations, and, as it were, with disregard and contempt for these claims, which are so impetuous, and at the same time so plausible, and which will not allow themselves to be suppressed by any command. Hence there arises a natural *dialectic*, i.e. a disposition, to argue against these strict laws of duty and to question their validity, or at least their purity and strictness; and, if possible, to make them more accordant with our wishes and inclinations, that is to say, to corrupt them at their very source, and entirely to destroy their worth – a thing which even common practical reason cannot ultimately call good.

Thus is the *common reason of man* compelled to go out of its sphere, and to take a step into the field of a *practical philosophy*, not to satisfy any speculative want (which never occurs to it as long as it is content to be mere sound reason), but even on practical grounds, in order to attain in it information and clear instruction respecting the source of its principle, and the correct determination of it in opposition to the maxims which are based on wants and inclinations, so that it may escape from the perplexity of opposite claims, and not run the risk of losing all genuine moral principles through the equivocation into which it easily falls. Thus, when practical reason cultivates itself, there insensibly arises in it a dialectic which forces it to seek aid in philosophy, just as happens to it in its theoretic use; and in this case, therefore, as well as in the other, it will find rest nowhere but in a thorough critical examination of our reason.

Notes

1　The first proposition, which Kant did not explicitly state as such, was that only actions done from duty have moral worth.

2　It is worth noting that some commentators prefer "reverence" to "respect" as a translation of Kant's term *Achtung*.

16

John Stuart Mill, *Utilitarianism,* Chapter 2

Introduction

Textbooks on Chinese philosophy report that "the first utilitarian" was Mo Tzu (Mo Zi) in the fifth century BCE. Europe had to wait 2,300 years, however, for the famous "Principle of Utility" or "Greatest Happiness Principle" to be proclaimed – by Jeremy Bentham (1748–1832) in England and Claude-Adrien Helvétius (1715–71) in France – as the sole principle for judging the moral value of actions. Utilitarianism became the characteristic moral doctrine of radical eighteenth-century Enlightenment thought, its seemingly "no nonsense" approach rooted in the predominant view of human nature "under the governance," as Bentham put it, "of two sovereign masters, *pain* and *pleasure.*[1] If human beings *cannot* desire anything but happiness or pleasure, any religion or morality that tells them they ought to aim elsewhere must be so much pie-in-the-sky.

Despite the influence of utilitarianism on public policy in the early nineteenth century, its philosophical basis had come under fierce attack – from Immanuel Kant (I.15), from Romantics like Samuel Taylor Coleridge (1772–1834), and from the pulpit – by the time Bentham's godson and the most important British philosopher of the century, John Stuart Mill (1806–73), wrote his famous

From *The Ethics of John Stuart Mill*, ed. C. Douglas. Edinburgh: Blackwood & Sons, 1897, pp. 89–127 (notes and two paragraphs omitted).

book *Utilitarianism* in 1861. Chapter 2 of this work is intended as a rebuttal of "the stock arguments against utilitarianism," which Mill characterizes as "the creed which . . . holds that actions are right in proportion as they tend to promote happiness." These "stock" objections ranged from the Kantian insistence that an action's consequences have no relevance to its moral worth to the accusation of "swinishness" in regarding happiness and pleasure as our sole ends; and from the impracticability of guiding our behavior by so grand a goal as "the greatest happiness of the greatest number" to affirmation of the value "for their own sake" of virtuous conduct and the performance of duty.

To these and other objections, Mill offers replies – whether by way of rebuttal, as when he accuses the Kantian objection of confusing the worth of actions with that of their agents; or by showing that the objectors misconstrue utilitarianism, wrongly imagining, for example, that the criterion of right action (the "greatest happiness") should always be our explicit motive; or by amending Benthamite doctrine in order to pre-empt an objection, as when he makes his famous distinction between "higher" and "lower" pleasures in response to the accusation of "swinishness."

There is little doubt that Mill articulates a more plausible moral philosophy than those of his utilitarian predecessors, not least through providing a more convincing moral psychology.[2] Although happiness or pleasure is our sole end, this should not be thought of as some "hedonic state,"

susceptible to measurement by a "felicific calculus," which we are constantly trying to produce.
Rather as for Aristotle, happiness is something we
find in and through our actions. This enables Mill
to lend sense to the idea of virtuous behavior being
good in itself: for when I help a friend in need,
this is not a means to producing a state of pleasurable satisfaction, but something which does – or
should – carry with it its own satisfaction.

Those looking for a decisive defense of utilitarianism, however, are liable to be disappointed.
No more than Bentham does Mill genuinely argue
for the Greatest Happiness Principle, both men
leaving it obscure how a person is to move from
valuing his or her own happiness to regard for the
general happiness. On certain crucial issues, moreover, Mill is hard to pin down. Thus, while he is
surely right to insist that any workable moral
code must employ "subordinate principles," such
as "Don't steal!," and not simply the "ultimate"
principle of the greatest happiness, he leaves the
connection between the two opaque. What if I am
convinced that, on this occasion, stealing will
promote the general happiness? Should I steal? If,
as Mill hints, I should not, is his position any longer
one that deserves to be called utilitarian? This is
a worry to which other of his remarks also give
rise, notably the "higher" versus "lower" pleasures
distinction. How, by reference to pleasure alone,
can we make such an evaluative distinction among
pleasures?[3]

Whether it mounts a successful defense of
utilitarianism or not, Mill's *Utilitarianism* was
responsible for securing a central place for that
doctrine in subsequent moral philosophy. Within
a few years of its publication, British ethicists
were divided between those, like Henry Sidgwick,
who continued to refine the utilitarian tradition
and those, like F. H. Bradley, to whom that whole
tradition was anathema. As every First Year student of ethics today knows, the issues at the heart
of such divisions show no sign of evaporating.[4]

Notes

1 *A Fragment of Government and An Introduction to the Principles of Morals and Legislation*, Oxford: Blackwell, 1960, p. 125.
2 See J. Skorupski, *John Stuart Mill*, London:
   Routledge, 1989.
3 For doubts as to whether Mill really *was* a
   utilitarian, see Isaiah Berlin's essay on Mill in
   his *Four Essays on Liberty*, Oxford: Oxford
   University Press, 1969.
4 H. Sidgwick, *Methods of Ethics*, London: Macmillan, 1962; F. H. Bradley, *Ethical Studies*,
   Oxford: Oxford University Press, 1962; and for
   more recent debates, see J. J. C. Smart and
   B. A. O. Williams, eds, *Utilitarianism: For and
   Against*, Cambridge: Cambridge University
   Press, 1973.

Mill, *Utilitarianism*

Chapter 2: What Utilitarianism Is

A passing remark is all that needs be given to
the ignorant blunder of supposing that those
who stand up for utility as the test of right and
wrong, use the term in that restricted and merely
colloquial sense in which utility is opposed to
pleasure. An apology is due to the philosophical opponents of utilitarianism, for even the
momentary appearance of confounding them
with any one capable of so absurd a misconception; which is the more extraordinary, inasmuch
as the contrary accusation, of referring everything to pleasure, and that too in its grossest
form, is another of the common charges against

utilitarianism: and, as has been pointedly
remarked by an able writer, the same sort of persons, and often the very same persons, denounce
the theory 'as impractically dry when the word
utility precedes the word pleasure, and as too
practically voluptuous when the word pleasure
precedes the word utility'. Those who know anything about the matter are aware that every writer,
from Epicurus to Bentham, who maintained the
theory of utility, meant by it, not something to
be contradistinguished from pleasure, but pleasure itself, together with exemption from pain; and
instead of opposing the useful to the agreeable or
the ornamental, have always declared that the
useful means these, among other things. Yet the
common herd, including the herd of writers, not
only in newspapers and periodicals, but in books

of weight and pretension, are perpetually falling into this shallow mistake. Having caught up the word utilitarian, while knowing nothing whatever about it but its sound, they habitually express by it the rejection, or the neglect, of pleasure in some of its forms – of beauty, of ornament, or of amusement. Nor is the term thus ignorantly misapplied solely in disparagement, but occasionally in compliment; as though it implied superiority to frivolity and the mere pleasures of the moment. And this perverted use is the only one in which the word is popularly known, and the one from which the new generation are acquiring their sole notion of its meaning. Those who introduced the word, but who had for many years discontinued it as a distinctive appellation, may well feel themselves called upon to resume it, if by doing so they can hope to contribute anything towards rescuing it from this utter degradation.

The creed which accepts as the foundation of morals, Utility, or the Greatest Happiness Principle, holds that actions are right in proportion as they tend to promote happiness, wrong as they tend to produce the reverse of happiness. By happiness is intended pleasure, and the absence of pain; by unhappiness, pain, and the privation of pleasure. To give a clear view of the moral standard set up by the theory, much more requires to be said: in particular, what things it includes in the ideas of pain and pleasure; and to what extent this is left an open question. But these supplementary explanations do not affect the theory of life on which this theory of morality is grounded – namely, that pleasure, and freedom from pain, are the only things desirable as ends; and that all desirable things (which are as numerous in the utilitarian as in any other scheme) are desirable either for the pleasure inherent in themselves, or as means to the promotion of pleasure and the prevention of pain.

Now, such a theory of life excites in many minds, and among them in some of the most estimable in feeling and purpose, inveterate dislike. To suppose that life has (as they express it) no higher end than pleasure – no better and nobler object of desire and pursuit – they designate as utterly mean and grovelling; as a doctrine worthy only of swine, to whom the followers of Epicurus were, at a very early period, contemptuously likened; and modern holders of the doctrine are occasionally made the subject of

equally polite comparisons by its German, French and English assailants.

When thus attacked, the Epicureans have always answered that it is not they, but their accusers, who represent human nature in a degrading light; since the accusation supposes human beings to be capable of no pleasures except those of which swine are capable. If this supposition were true, the charge could not be gainsaid, but would then be no longer an imputation: for if the sources of pleasure were precisely the same to human beings and to swine, the rule of life which is good enough for the one would be good enough for the other. The comparison of the Epicurean life to that of beasts is felt as degrading, precisely because a beast's pleasures do not satisfy a human being's conceptions of happiness. Human beings have faculties more elevated than the animal appetites, and when once made conscious of them, do not regard anything as happiness which does not include their gratification. I do not, indeed, consider the Epicureans to have been by any means faultless in drawing out their scheme of consequences from the utilitarian principle. To do this in any sufficient manner, many Stoic as well as Christian elements require to be included. But there is no known Epicurean theory of life which does not assign to the pleasures of the intellect, of the feelings and imagination, and of the moral sentiments, a much higher value as pleasures than to those of mere sensation. It must be admitted, however, that utilitarian writers in general have placed the superiority of mental over bodily pleasures chiefly in the greater permanency, safety, uncostliness, &c., of the former – that is, in their circumstantial advantages rather than in their intrinsic nature. And on all these points utilitarians have fully proved their case; but they might have taken the other, and, as it may be called, higher ground, with entire consistency. It is quite compatible with the principle of utility to recognize the fact, that some *kinds* of pleasure are more desirable and more valuable than others. It would be absurd that while, in estimating all other things, quality is considered as well as quantity, the estimation of pleasures should be supposed to depend on quantity alone.

If I am asked what I mean by difference of quality in pleasures, or what makes one pleasure more valuable than another, merely as a pleasure, except its being greater in amount, there is but one possible answer. Of two pleasures, if there be one to which all or almost all who have experience of both give a decided preference, irrespective of any feeling of moral obligation to prefer it, that is the more desirable pleasure. If one of the two is, by those who are competently acquainted with both, placed so far above the other that they prefer it, even though knowing it to be attended with a greater amount of discontent, and would not resign it for any quantity of the other pleasure which their nature is capable of, we are justified in ascribing to the preferred enjoyment a superiority in quality, so far outweighing quantity as to render it, in comparison, of small account.

Now it is an unquestionable fact that those who are equally acquainted with, and equally capable of appreciating and enjoying, both, do give a most marked preference to the manner of existence which employs their higher faculties. Few human creatures would consent to be changed into any of the lower animals, for a promise of the fullest allowance of a beast's pleasures; no intelligent human being would consent to be a fool, no instructed person would be an ignoramus, no person of feeling and conscience would be selfish and base, even though they should be persuaded that the fool, the dunce or the rascal is better satisfied with his lot than they are with theirs. They would not resign what they possess more than he, for the most complete satisfaction of all the desires which they have in common with him. If they ever fancy they would, it is only in cases of unhappiness so extreme, that to escape from it they would exchange their lot for almost any other, however undesirable in their own eyes. A being of higher faculties requires more to make him happy, is capable probably of more acute suffering, and is certainly accessible to it at more points, than one of an inferior type; but in spite of these liabilities, he can never really wish to sink into what he feels to be a lower grade of existence. We may give what explanation we please of this unwillingness: we may attribute it to pride, a name which is given indiscriminately to some of the most and to some of the least estimable feelings of which mankind are capable; we may refer it to the love of liberty and personal independence, an appeal to which was with the Stoics one of the most effective means for the inculcation of it; to the love of power, or to the love of excitement, both of which do really enter into and contri-

bute to it. But its most appropriate appellation is a sense of dignity, which all human beings possess in one form or other, and in some, though by no means in exact, proportion to their higher faculties, and which is so essential a part of the happiness of those in whom it is strong, that nothing which conflicts with it could be, otherwise than momentarily, an object of desire to them. Whoever supposes that this preference takes place at a sacrifice of happiness – that the superior being, in anything like equal circumstances, is not happier than the inferior – confounds the two very different ideas, of happiness and content. It is indisputable that the being whose capacities of enjoyment are low, has the greatest chance of having them fully satisfied; and a highly endowed being will always feel that any happiness which he can look for, as the world is constituted, is imperfect. But he can learn to bear its imperfections, if they are at all bearable; and they will not make him envy the being who is indeed unconscious of the imperfections, but only because he feels not at all the good which those imperfections qualify. It is better to be a human being dissatisfied than a pig satisfied; better to be Socrates dissatisfied than a fool satisfied. And if the fool, or the pig, is of a different opinion, it is because they only know their own side of the question. The other party to the comparison knows both sides.

It may be objected that many who are capable of the higher pleasures, occasionally, under the influence of temptation, postpone them to the lower. But this is quite compatible with a full appreciation of the intrinsic superiority of the higher. Men often, from infirmity of character, make their election for the nearer good, though they know it to be the less valuable; and this no less when the choice is between two bodily pleasures, than when it is between bodily and mental. They pursue sensual indulgences to the injury of health, though perfectly aware that health is the greater good. It may be further objected that many who begin with youthful enthusiasm for everything noble, as they advance in years sink into indolence and selfishness. But I do not believe that those who undergo this very common change, voluntarily choose the lower description of pleasures in preference to the higher. I believe that before they devote themselves exclusively to the one, they have already become incapable of the other. Capacity for the nobler feelings is in most natures a very tender plant, easily killed, not only by hostile influences, but by mere want of sustenance; and in the majority of young persons it speedily dies away if the occupations to which their position in life has devoted them, and the society into which it has thrown them, are not favourable to keeping that higher capacity in exercise. Men lose their high aspirations as they lose their intellectual tastes, because they have not time or opportunity for indulging them; and they addict themselves to inferior pleasures, not because they deliberately prefer them, but because they are either the only ones to which they have access, or the only ones which they are any longer capable of enjoying. It may be questioned whether any one who has remained equally susceptible to both classes of pleasures, ever knowingly and calmly preferred the lower; though many, in all ages, have broken down in an ineffectual attempt to combine both.

From this verdict of the only competent judges, I apprehend there can be no appeal. On a question which is the better worth having of two pleasures, or which of two modes of existence is the more grateful to the feelings, apart from its moral attributes and from its consequences, the judgement of those who are qualified by knowledge of both, or, if they differ, that of the majority among them, must be admitted as final. And there needs be the less hesitation to accept this judgement respecting the quality of pleasures, since there is no other tribunal to be referred to even on the question of quantity. What means are there of determining which is the acuter of two pains, or the intenser of two pleasurable sensations, except the general suffrage of those who are familiar with both? Neither pains nor pleasures are homogeneous, and pain is always heterogeneous with pleasure. What is there to decide whether a particular pleasure is worth purchasing at the cost of a particular pain, except the feelings and judgement of the experienced? When, therefore, those feelings and judgement declare the pleasures derived from the higher faculties to be preferable *in kind*, apart from the question of intensity, to those of which the animal nature, disjoined from the higher faculties, is susceptible, they are entitled on this subject to the same regard.

I have dwelt on this point, as being a necessary part of a perfectly just conception of Utility or Happiness, considered as the directive rule of human conduct. But it is by no means an indispensable condition to the acceptance of the utilitarian standard, for that standard is not the agent's own greatest happiness, but the greatest amount of happiness altogether; and if it may possibly be doubted whether a noble character is always the happier for its nobleness, there can be no doubt that it makes other people happier, and that the world in general is immensely a gainer by it. Utilitarianism, therefore, could only attain its end by the general cultivation of nobleness of character, even if each individual were only benefited by the nobleness of others, and his own, so far as happiness is concerned, were a sheer deduction from the benefit. But the bare enunciation of such an absurdity as this last renders refutation superfluous.

According to the Greatest Happiness Principle, as above explained, the ultimate end, with reference to and for the sake of which all other things are desirable (whether we are considering our own good or that of other people), is an existence exempt as far as possible from pain, and as rich as possible in enjoyments, both in point of quantity and quality; the test of quality, and the rule for measuring it against quantity, being the preference felt by those who, in their opportunities of experience, to which must be added their habits of self-consciousness and self-observation, are best furnished with the means of comparison. This, being, according to the utilitarian opinion, the end of human action, is necessarily also the standard of morality; which may accordingly be defined, the rules and precepts for human conduct, by the observance of which an existence such as has been described might be, to the greatest extent possible, secured to all mankind; and not to them only, but, so far as the nature of things admits, to the whole sentient creation.

Against this doctrine, however, rises another class of objectors, who say that happiness, in any form, cannot be the rational purpose of human life and action; because, in the first place, it is unattainable: and they contemptuously ask, What right hast thou to be happy? a question which Mr [Thomas] Carlyle clenches by the addition, What right, a short time ago, hadst thou even *to be*? Next, they say, that men can do *without* happiness; that all noble human beings have felt this, and could not have become noble but by learning the lesson of Entsagen, or renunciation; which lesson, thoroughly learnt and submitted to, they affirm to be the beginning and necessary condition of all virtue.

The first of these objections would go to the root of the matter were it well founded; for if no happiness is to be had at all by human beings, the attainment of it cannot be the end of morality, or of any rational conduct. Though, even in that case, something might still be said for the utilitarian theory, since utility includes not solely the pursuit of happiness, but the prevention or mitigation of unhappiness; and if the former aim be chimerical, there will be all the greater scope and more imperative need for the latter, so long at least as mankind think fit to live, and do not take refuge in the simultaneous act of suicide recommended under certain conditions by Novalis [pseudonym of Friedrich von Hardenberg (1772–1801) – Ed.]. When, however, it is thus positively asserted to be impossible that human life should be happy, the assertion, if not something like a verbal quibble, is at least an exaggeration. If by happiness be meant a continuity of highly pleasurable excitement, it is evident enough that this is impossible. A state of exalted pleasure lasts only moments, or in some cases, and with some intermissions, hours or days, and is the occasional brilliant flash of enjoyment, not its permanent and steady flame. Of this the philosophers who have taught that happiness is the end of life were as fully aware as those who taunt them. The happiness which they meant was not a life of rapture; but moments of such, in an existence made up of few and transitory pains, many and various pleasures, with a decided predominance of the active over the passive, and having, as the foundation of the whole, not to expect more from life than it is capable of bestowing. A life thus composed, to those who have been fortunate enough to obtain it, has always appeared worthy of the name of happiness. And such an existence is even now the lot of many, during some considerable portion of their lives. The present wretched education, and wretched social arrangements, are the only real hindrance to its being attainable by almost all.

The objectors perhaps may doubt whether human beings, if taught to consider happiness as the end of life, would be satisfied with such a moderate share of it. But great numbers of mankind have been satisfied with much less. The main constituents of a satisfied life appear to be two, either of which by itself is often found sufficient for the purpose – tranquillity, and excitement.[1] With much tranquillity, many find that they can be content with very little pleasure: with much excitement, many can reconcile themselves to a considerable quantity of pain. There is assuredly no inherent impossibility in enabling even the mass of mankind to unite both; since the two are so far from being incompatible that they are in natural alliance, the prolongation of either being a preparation for, and exciting a wish for, the other. It is only those in whom indolence amounts to a vice, that do not desire excitement after an interval of repose; it is only those in whom the need of excitement is a disease, that feel the tranquillity which follows excitement dull and insipid, instead of pleasurable in direct proportion to the excitement which preceded it. When people who are tolerably fortunate in their outward lot do not find in life sufficient enjoyment to make it valuable to them, the cause generally is, caring for nobody but themselves. To those who have neither public nor private affections, the excitements of life are much curtailed, and in any case dwindle in value as the time approaches when all selfish interests must be terminated by death: while those who leave after them objects of personal affection, and especially those who have also cultivated a fellow-feeling with the collective interests of mankind, retain as lively an interest in life on the eve of death as in the vigour of youth and health. Next to selfishness, the principal cause which makes life unsatisfactory is want of mental cultivation. A cultivated mind – I do not mean that of a philosopher, but any mind to which the fountains of knowledge have been opened, and which has been taught, in any tolerable degree, to exercise its faculties – finds sources of inexhaustible interest in all that surrounds it: in the objects of nature, the achievements of art, the imaginations of poetry, the incidents of history, the ways of mankind past and present, and their prospects in the future. It is possible, indeed, to become indifferent to all this, and that too without having exhausted a thousandth part of it; but only when one has had from the beginning no moral or human interest in these things, and has sought in them only the gratification of curiosity.

Now there is absolutely no reason in the nature of things why an amount of mental culture sufficient to give an intelligent interest in these objects of contemplation, should not be the inheritance of every one born in a civilized country. As little is there an inherent necessity that any human being should be a selfish egotist, devoid of every feeling or care but those which centre in his own miserable individuality. Something far superior to this is sufficiently common even now, to give ample earnest of what the human species may be made. Genuine private affections, and a sincere interest in the public good, are possible, though in unequal degrees, to every rightly brought up human being. In a world in which there is so much to interest, so much to enjoy, and so much also to correct and improve, every one who has this moderate amount of moral and intellectual requisites is capable of an existence which may be called enviable; and unless such a person, through bad laws, or subjection to the will of others, is denied the liberty to use the sources of happiness within his reach, he will not fail to find this enviable existence, if he escape the positive evils of life, the great sources of physical and mental suffering – such as indigence, disease and the unkindness, worthlessness or premature loss of objects of affection. The main stress of the problem lies, therefore, in the contest with these calamities, from which it is a rare good fortune entirely to escape; which, as things now are, cannot be obviated, and often cannot be in any material degree mitigated. Yet no one whose opinion deserves a moment's consideration can doubt that most of the great positive evils of the world are in themselves removable, and will, if human affairs continue to improve, be in the end reduced within narrow limits. Poverty, in any sense implying suffering, may be completely extinguished by the wisdom of society, combined with the good sense and providence of individuals. Even that most intractable of enemies, disease, may be indefinitely reduced in dimensions by good physical and moral education, and proper control of noxious influences; while the progress of science holds out a promise for the future of still more direct conquests over this detestable foe. And every advance in that direction relieves us from some, not only of the chances which cut short our own lives, but, what concerns us still more, which deprive us of those in whom our happiness is wrapt up. As for vicissitudes of fortune, and other disappointments connected with worldly circumstances, these are principally the effect either of gross imprudence, of ill-regulated desires, or of bad or imperfect social institutions. All the grand sources, in short, of human suffering are in a great degree, many of them almost entirely, conquerable by human care and effort; and though their removal is grievously slow – though a long succession of generations will perish in the breach before the conquest is completed, and this world becomes all that, if will and knowledge were not wanting, it might easily be made – yet every mind sufficiently intelligent and generous to bear a part, however small and unconspicuous, in the endeavour, will draw a noble enjoyment from the contest itself, which he would not for any bribe in the form of selfish indulgence consent to be without.

And this leads to the true estimation of what is said by the objectors concerning the possibility, and the obligation, of learning to do without happiness. Unquestionably it is possible to do without happiness: it is done involuntarily by nineteen-twentieths of mankind, even in those parts of our present world which are least deep in barbarism; and it often has to be done voluntarily by the hero or the martyr, for the sake of something which he prizes more than his individual happiness. But this something, what is it, unless the happiness of others, or some of the requisites of happiness? It is noble to be capable of resigning entirely one's own portion of happiness, or chances of it: but, after all, this self-sacrifice must be for some end; it is not its own end; and if we are told that its end is not happiness, but virtue, which is better than happiness, I ask, would the sacrifice be made if the hero or martyr did not believe that it would earn for others immunity from similar sacrifices? Would it be made, if he thought that his renunciation of happiness for himself would produce no fruit for any of his fellow-creatures, but to make their lot like his, and place them also in the condition of persons who have renounced happiness? All honour to those who can abnegate for themselves the personal enjoyment of life, when by such renunciation they contribute worthily to increase the amount of happiness in the world; but he who does it, or professes to do it, for any other purpose, is no more deserving of admiration than the ascetic mounted on his pillar. He may be an inspiriting proof of what men *can* do, but assuredly not an example of what they *should*.

Though it is only in a very imperfect state of the world's arrangements that any one can best serve the happiness of others by the absolute sacrifice of his own, yet so long as the world is in that imperfect state, I fully acknowledge that the readiness to make such a sacrifice is the highest virtue which can be found in man. I will add, that in this condition of the world, paradoxical as the assertion may be, the conscious ability to do without happiness gives the best prospect of realizing such happiness as is attainable.[2] For nothing except that consciousness can raise a person above the chances of life, by making him feel that, let fate and fortune do their worst, they have not power to subdue him: which, once felt, frees him from excess of anxiety concerning the evils of life, and enables him, like many a Stoic in the worst times of the Roman empire, to cultivate in tranquillity the sources of satisfaction accessible to him, without concerning himself about the uncertainty of their duration, any more than about their inevitable end.

Meanwhile, let utilitarians never cease to claim the morality of self-devotion as a possession which belongs by as good a right to them, as either to the Stoic or to the Transcendentalist. The utilitarian morality does recognize in human beings the power of sacrificing their own greatest good for the good of others. It only refuses to admit that the sacrifice is itself a good. A sacrifice which does not increase, or tend to increase, the sum total of happiness, it considers as wasted. The only self-renunciation which it applauds is devotion to the happiness, or to some of the means of happiness, of others; either of mankind collectively, or of individuals within the limits imposed by the collective interests of mankind.

I must again repeat, what the assailants of utilitarianism seldom have the justice to acknowledge, that the happiness which forms the utilitarian standard of what is right in conduct is not the agent's own happiness, but that of all concerned. As between his own happiness and that of others, utilitarianism requires him to be as strictly impartial as a disinterested and benevolent spectator. In the golden rule of Jesus of Nazareth, we read the complete spirit of the ethics of utility. To do as one would be done by, and to love one's neighbour as oneself, constitute the ideal perfection of utilitarian morality. As the means of making the nearest approach to this ideal, utility would enjoin, first, that laws and social arrangements should place the happiness, or (as speaking practically it may be called) the interest, of every individual, as nearly as possible in harmony with the interest of the whole; and secondly, that education and opinion, which have so vast a power over human character, should so use that power as to establish in the mind of every individual an indissoluble association between his own happiness and the good of the whole; especially between his own happiness and the practice of such modes of conduct, negative and positive, as regard for the universal happiness prescribes: so that not only he may be unable to conceive the possibility of happiness to himself, consistently with conduct opposed to the general good, but also that a direct impulse to promote the general good may be in every individual one of the habitual motives of action, and the sentiments connected therewith may fill a large and prominent place in every human being's sentient existence. If the impugners of the utilitarian morality represented it to their own minds in this its true character, I know not what recommendation possessed by any other morality they could possibly affirm to be wanting to it; what more beautiful or more exalted developments of human nature any other ethical system can be supposed to foster, or what springs of action, not accessible to the utilitarian, such systems rely on for giving effect to their mandates.

The objectors to utilitarianism cannot always be charged with representing it in a discreditable light. On the contrary, those among them who entertain anything like a just idea of its disinterested character, sometimes find fault with its standard as being too high for humanity. They say it is exacting too much to require that people shall always act from the inducement of promoting the general interests of society. But this is to mistake the very meaning of a standard of morals, and to confound the rule of action with the motive of it. It is the business of ethics to tell us what are our duties, or by what test we may know them; but no system of ethics requires that the sole motive of all we do shall be a feeling of duty: on the contrary, ninety-nine hundredths of all our actions are done from other motives, and rightly so done, if the rule of duty does not condemn them. It is the more unjust to utilitarianism that this particular misapprehension should be made a ground of objection to it, inasmuch as utilitarian moralists have gone beyond almost all others in affirming that the motive has nothing to do with the morality of the action, though much with the worth of the agent. He who saves a fellow-creature from drowning does what is morally right, whether his motive be duty, or the hope of being paid for his trouble: he who betrays the friend that trusts him is guilty of a crime, even if his object be to serve another friend to whom he is under greater obligations. But to speak only of actions done from the motive of duty, and in direct obedience to principle: it is a misapprehension of the utilitarian mode of thought, to conceive it as implying that people should fix their minds upon so wide a generality as the world, or society at large. The great majority of good actions are intended, not for the benefit of the world, but for that of individuals, of which the good of the world is made up; and the thoughts of the most virtuous man need not on these occasions travel beyond the particular persons concerned, except so far as is necessary to assure himself that in benefiting them he is not violating the rights – that is, the legitimate and authorized expectations – of any one else. The multiplication of happiness is, according to the utilitarian ethics, the object of virtue: the occasions on which any person (except one in a thousand) has it in his power to do this on an extended scale, in other words, to be a public benefactor, are but exceptional; and on these occasions alone is he called on to consider public utility; in every other case, private utility, the interest or happiness of some few persons, is all he has to attend to. Those alone the influence of whose actions extends to society in general, need concern themselves habitually about so large an object. In the case of abstinences indeed – of things which people forbear to do, from moral considerations, though the consequences in the particular case might be beneficial – it would be unworthy of an intelligent agent not to be consciously aware that the action is of a class which, if practised generally, would be generally injurious, and that this is the ground of the obligation to abstain from it. The amount of regard for the public interest implied in this recognition is no greater than is demanded by every system of morals, for they all enjoin to abstain from whatever is manifestly pernicious to society.

The same considerations dispose of another reproach against the doctrine of utility, founded on a still grosser misconception of the purpose of a standard of morality, and of the very meaning of the words right and wrong. It is often affirmed that utilitarianism renders men cold and unsympathizing; that it chills their moral feelings towards individuals; that it makes them regard only the dry and hard consideration of the consequences of actions, not taking into their moral estimate the qualities from which those actions emanate. If the assertion means that they do not allow their judgement respecting the rightness or wrongness of an action to be influenced by their opinion of the qualities of the person who does it, this is a complaint not against utilitarianism, but against having any standard of morality at all; for certainly no known ethical standard decides an action to be good or bad because it is done by a good or a bad man, still less because done by an amiable, a brave, or a benevolent man, or the contrary. These considerations are relevant, not to the estimation of actions, but of persons; and there is nothing in the utilitarian theory inconsistent with the fact that there are other things which interest us in persons besides the rightness and wrongness of their actions. The Stoics, indeed, with the paradoxical misuse of language which was part of their system, and by which they strove to raise themselves above all concern about anything but virtue, were fond of saying that he who has that has everything; that he, and only he, is rich, is beautiful, is a king. But no claim of this description is made for the virtuous man by the utilitarian doctrine. Utilitarians are quite aware that there are other desirable possessions and qualities besides virtue, and are perfectly willing to allow to all of them their full worth. They are also aware that a right action does not necessarily indicate a virtuous character, and that actions which are blameable often proceed from qualities entitled to praise. When this is apparent in any particular case, it modifies their estimation, not certainly of the act, but of the agent. I grant that they are, notwithstanding, of opinion, that in the long-run the best proof of a good character is good actions; and resolutely refuse to consider any mental disposition as good, of which the predominant tendency is to produce bad conduct. This makes them unpopular with many people; but it is an unpopularity which they must share with every one who regards the distinction between right and wrong in a serious light, and the reproach is not one which a conscientious utilitarian need be anxious to repel.

If no more be meant by the objection than that many utilitarians look on the morality of actions, as measured by the utilitarian standard, with too exclusive a regard, and do not lay sufficient stress upon the other beauties of character which go towards making a human being loveable or admirable, this may be admitted. Utilitarians who have cultivated their moral feelings, but not their sympathies nor their artistic perceptions, do fall into this mistake; and so do all other moralists under the same conditions. What can be said in excuse for other moralists is equally available for them, namely, that if there is to be any error, it is better that it should be on that side. As a matter of fact, we may affirm that among utilitarians, as among adherents of other systems, there is every imaginable degree of rigidity and of laxity in the application of their standard: some are even puritanically rigorous, while others are as indulgent as can possibly be desired by sinner or by sentimentalist. But, on the whole, a doctrine which brings prominently forward the interest that mankind have in the repression and prevention of conduct which violates the moral law is likely to be inferior to no other in turning the sanctions of opinion against such violations. It is true, the question, What does violate the moral law? is one on which those who recognize different standards of morality are likely now and then to differ. But difference of opinion on moral questions was not first introduced into the world by utilitarianism, while that doctrine does supply, if not always an easy, at all events a tangible and intelligible, mode of deciding such differences. [. . .]

Again, defenders of utility often find themselves called upon to reply to such objections as this – that there is not time, previous to action, for calculating and weighing the effects of any line of conduct on the general happiness. This is exactly as if any one were to say that it is impossible to guide our conduct by Christianity, because there is not time, on every occasion on which anything has to be done, to read through the Old and New Testaments. The answer to the objection is, that there has been ample time, namely, the whole past duration of the human species. During all that time mankind have been learning by experience the tendencies of actions; on which experience all the prudence, as well as all the morality, of life, is dependent. People talk as if the commencement of this course of experience had hitherto been put off, and as if, at the moment when some man feels tempted to meddle with the property or life of another, he had to begin considering for the first time whether murder and theft are injurious to human happiness. Even then I do not think that he would find the question very puzzling; but, at all events, the matter is now done to his hand. It is truly a whimsical supposition, that if mankind were agreed in considering utility to be the test of morality, they would remain without any agreement as to what *is* useful, and would take no measures for having their notions on the subject taught to the young, and enforced by law and opinion. There is no difficulty in proving any ethical standard whatever to work ill, if we suppose universal idiocy to be conjoined with it, but on any hypothesis short of that, mankind must by this time have acquired positive beliefs as to the effects of some actions on their happiness; and the beliefs which have thus come down are the rules of morality for the multitude, and for the philosopher until he has succeeded in finding better. That philosophers might easily do this, even now, on many subjects; that the received code of ethics is by no means of divine right; and that mankind have still much to learn as to the effects of actions on the general happiness, I admit, or rather, earnestly maintain. The corollaries from the principle of utility, like the precepts of every practical art, admit of indefinite improvement, and, in a progressive state of the human mind, their improvement is perpetually going on. But to consider the rules of morality as improvable, is one thing; to pass over the intermediate generalizations entirely, and endeavour to test each individual action directly by the first principle, is another. It is a strange notion that the acknowledgement of a first principle is inconsistent with the admission of secondary ones. To inform a traveller respecting the place of his ultimate destination, is not to forbid the use of landmarks and direction-posts on the way. The proposition that happiness is the end and aim of morality, does not mean that no road ought to be laid down to that goal, or that persons going thither should not be advised to take one direction rather than another. Men really ought to leave off talking a kind of nonsense on this subject, which they would neither talk nor listen to on other matters of practical concernment. Nobody argues that the art of navigation is not founded on astronomy, because sailors cannot wait to calculate the Nautical Almanack. Being rational creatures, they go to sea with it ready calculated; and all rational creatures go out upon the sea of life with their minds made up on the common questions of right and wrong, as well as on many of the far more difficult questions of wise and foolish. And this, as long as foresight is a human quality, it is to be presumed they will continue to do. Whatever we adopt as the fundamental principle of morality, we require subordinate principles to apply it by: the impossibility of doing without them, being common to all systems, can afford no argument against any one in particular. But gravely to argue as if no such secondary principles could be had, and as if mankind had remained till now, and always must remain, without drawing any general conclusions from the experience of human life, is as high a pitch, I think, as absurdity has ever reached in philosophical controversy.

The remainder of the stock arguments against utilitarianism mostly consist in laying to its charge the common infirmities of human nature, and the general difficulties which embarrass conscientious persons in shaping their course through life. We are told that an utilitarian will be apt to make his own particular case an exception to moral rules, and, when under temptation, will see an utility in the breach of a rule, greater than he will see in its observance. But is utility the only creed which is able to furnish us with excuses for evil-doing, and means of cheating our own conscience? They are afforded in abundance by all doctrines which recognize as a fact in morals the existence of conflicting considerations; which all doctrines do, that have been believed by sane persons. It is not the fault of any creed, but of the complicated nature of human affairs, that rules of conduct cannot be so framed as to require no exceptions, and that hardly any kind of action can safely be laid down as either always obligatory or always condemnable. There is no ethical creed which does not temper the rigidity of its laws, by giving a certain latitude, under the moral responsibility of the agent, for accommodation to peculiarities of circumstances; and under every creed, at the opening thus made, self-deception and dishonest casuistry get in. There exists no moral system under which there do not arise unequivocal cases of conflicting obligation. These are the real difficulties, the knotty points both in the theory of ethics and in the conscientious guidance of personal conduct. They are overcome practically with greater or with less success according to the intellect and virtue of the individual; but it can hardly be pretended that any one will be the less qualified for dealing with them, from possessing an ultimate standard to which conflicting rights and duties can be referred. If utility is the ultimate source of moral obligations, utility may be invoked to decide between them when their demands are incompatible. Though the application of the standard may be difficult, it is better than none at all: while in other systems, the moral laws all claiming independent authority, there is no common umpire entitled to interfere between them; their claims to precedence one over another rest on little better than sophistry, and unless determined, as they generally are, by the unacknowledged influence of considerations of utility, afford a free scope for the action of personal desires and partialities. We must remember that only in these cases of conflict between secondary principles is it requisite that first principles should be appealed to. There is no case of moral obligation in which some secondary principle is not involved; and if only one, there can seldom be any real doubt which one it is, in the mind of any person by whom the principle itself is recognized.

Notes

1   This paragraph might almost be a reply to Arthur Schopenhauer's "pessimism." According to him, it is the oscillation between the frenzied excitement of desire and the boredom of satiation that helps to make life so wretched. See, e.g., chapter 46 of volume 2 of *The World as Will and Representation*, New York: Dover, 1966.

2   This important point is frequently urged by Mill, e.g. in his *Autobiography*, Harmondsworth: Penguin, 1989, p. 118, where he writes, "Ask yourself whether you are happy, and you cease to be so. The only chance is to treat, not happiness, but some end external to it, as the purpose of life."

Søren Kierkegaard, *Fear and Trembling,* Problema I

Introduction

For Kant, we saw (I.15), the moral person acts on principles universally binding on rational beings. One criticism soon levelled, notably by G. W. F. Hegel (1770–1831), was that such principles, even if there were any, would be too abstract and empty to constitute a substantial ethical code by which anyone could live. For Hegel, an ethical system (*Sittlichkeit*) is "universal" in the more restricted sense of comprising the laws and rules of the particular state or society by which its members are bound (see V.17). Despite this important difference, Kant and most of his German successors were agreed on a number of crucial points. Ethical demands are, in some sense of the term, "universal" and reason requires willing submission to them, at the expense, if need be, of a person's individuality. Or better, it is through such submission that human beings achieve their true individuality and dignity as rational beings. Moreover, such demands are sovereign: having no purpose or *telos* beyond them, there is nothing that could justify "suspension of the ethical."

That final expression belongs to the Danish philosopher, Søren Kierkegaard (1813–55), who in the famous first "Problema" of *Fear and*

From Søren Kierkegaard, *Fear and Trembling,* trans. A. Hannay. Harmondsworth: Penguin, 1985, pp. 83–95 (note omitted).

Trembling raises the question, "Is there a teleological suspension of the ethical?" Are there, that is, any circumstances in which a person is to be condoned, admired even, for overriding ethical imperatives? His answer – or rather, that of the pseudonymous "author," Johannes de Silentio – is affirmative. Kierkegaard's strategy is to focus on an implication that may be drawn from the positions of Kant and Hegel. If we are always bound to act ethically but also have a constant duty to God, this can only be because God is understood – by definition, as it were – as the endorser of the moral law, as "a powerful moral lawgiver," to cite Kant.[1] This means, in turn, that a "conscientious" person who imagines that God is calling on him to act unethically should conclude that he is mistaken – a point that Kant illustrates with the story of Abraham's (mistaken) readiness to sacrifice his son in apparent accordance with God's command.

It is this story, which Kierkegaard takes to relate a genuine command of God, that is the centerpiece of *Fear and Trembling.* Kierkegaard's point is that, on Kantian and Hegelian premisses, Abraham should indeed be simply condemned as a would-be murderer – something however that Hegel, inconsistently, fails to do. That failure is instructive: it suggests that Hegel, like many other people, cannot but admire Abraham. But admiring conduct like this, of course, calls into question the whole insistence on the sovereignty of ethical demands. To show this, Kierkegaard needs to show that Abraham's sacrifice of Isaac would in no sense have been ethically justified. Thus we must distinguish Abraham's predicament from that of the so-called "tragic hero," like Agamemnon, who is forced to choose between competing ethical demands – those of fatherhood and kingship. Nor is it that Abraham is acting on some general principle like "If God tells you to do X, then do it!," for he "feels no vain desire to show others the way." Nor, finally, is there anything rational in Abraham's willingness to sacrifice: on the contrary, he is a "knight of faith" acting "on the strength of the absurd" conviction that Isaac, though killed, will somehow be "returned." "Faith begins precisely where thinking leaves off."

Unlike an ethical action, Abraham's is a purely "private" and "personal" one that he feels he must perform in virtue of his particular relation to God. Perhaps the main implication for moral philosophy (as distinct from theology) of Problema I is not that God, *pace* Kant and Hegel, may order us to defy the moral law, but that some "private" and "personal" convictions, religious or otherwise, may go so deep with an individual that he or she is justified in acting upon them despite their contradicting the requirements of ethical rules and principles. The "single individual," as Kierkegaard puts it, is "higher than the universal."

Despite the importance of always considering the demands of ethics, and despite the "terrible solitude" of stepping "outside the universal," the integrity of the individual is secured, not by identification with the ethical life of one's society, but by remaining "true to oneself."[2] What matters, Kierkegaard wrote in his Journals, is not to find a truth which "can work upon men" in general, but one that is "true for me . . . for *which I can live and die*" (1 August 1835).

In the end, perhaps, it is not important whether Kierkegaard is described as elevating certain demands *over* those of morality or as proposing a new and individualized conception of morality. Either way, his message was a revolutionary one: an early manifesto of that personal "authenticity" which was to loom so large in the writings of later existentialist writers, such as Sartre (I.23)[3], and which, moreover, was to enter the bloodstream of countless twentieth-century men and women disenchanted with, or "alienated" by, the pretensions of universal prescriptions for the conduct of their lives.

Notes

1 *Religion Within the Limits of Reason Alone*, San Francisco: Harper, 1960, p. 5.
2 See A. Hannay, *Kierkegaard*, London: Routledge, 1982, *circa* p. 80.
3 See, e.g., K. Jaspers, *Philosophy*, Chicago: University of Chicago Press, 1969–71, on the "boundary situations" where I am "on my own," without guidance from general principles, thereby confirming that "I am not a result of social configurations . . . I retain my own original potential" (vol. 2, p. 30).

Kierkegaard, *Fear and Trembling*

Problema I. Is There a Teleological Suspension of the Ethical?

The ethical as such is the universal, and as the universal it applies to everyone, which can be put from another point of view by saying that it applies at every moment. It rests immanently in itself, has nothing outside itself that is its *telos* [end, purpose] but is itself the *telos* for everything outside, and when that is taken up into it, it has no further to go. Seen as an immediate, no more than sensate and psychic, being, the single individual is the particular that has its *telos* in the universal, and the individual's ethical task is always to express himself in this, to abrogate his particularity so as to become the universal. As soon as the single individual wants to assert himself in his particularity, in direct opposition to the universal, he sins, and only by recognizing this can he again reconcile himself with the universal. Whenever, having entered the universal, the single individual feels an urge to assert his particularity, he is in a state of temptation, from which he can extricate himself only by surrendering his particularity to the universal in repentance. If that is the highest that can be said of man and his existence, then the ethical and a person's eternal blessedness, which is his *telos* in all eternity and at every moment, are identical; for in that case it would be a contradiction to say that one surrendered that *telos* (i.e. suspended it *teleologically*) since by suspending the *telos* one would be forfeiting it, while what is said to be suspended in this sense is not forfeited but preserved in something higher, the latter being precisely its *telos*.

If that is the case, then Hegel is right in his 'Good and Conscience' where he discusses man seen merely as the single individual and regards this way of seeing him as a 'moral form of evil' to be annulled in the teleology of the ethical life,[1] so that the individual who stays at this stage is either in sin or in a state of temptation. Where Hegel goes wrong, on the other hand, is in talking about faith, in not protesting loudly and clearly against the honour and glory enjoyed by Abraham as the father of faith when he should really be remitted to some lower court for trial and exposed as a murderer.

For faith is just this paradox, that the single individual is higher than the universal, though in such a way, be it noted, that the movement is repeated, that is, that, having been in the universal, the single individual now sets himself apart as the particular above the universal. If that is not faith, then Abraham is done for and faith has never existed in the world, just because it has always existed. For if the ethical life is the highest and nothing incommensurable is left over in man, except in the sense of what is evil, i.e. the single individual who is to be expressed in the universal, then one needs no other categories than those of the Greek philosophers, or whatever can be logically deduced from them. This is something Hegel, who has after all made some study of the Greeks, ought not to have kept quiet about.

One not infrequently hears people who prefer to lose themselves in clichés rather than studies say that light shines over the Christian world, while paganism is shrouded in darkness. This kind of talk has always struck me as strange, since any reasonably deep thinker, any reasonably serious artist will still seek rejuvenation in the eternal youth of the Greeks. The explanation may be that they know not what to say, only that they have to say something. There is nothing wrong with saying that paganism did not have faith, but if this is to mean anything one must be a little clearer what one means by faith, otherwise one falls back into those clichés. It is easy to explain the whole of existence, faith included, and he is not the worst

reckoner in life who counts on being admired for having such an explanation; for it is as Boileau says: '*un sot trouve toujours un plus sot, qui l'admire*' ['a fool can always find a greater fool who admires him'].

Faith is just this paradox, that the single individual as the particular is higher than the universal, is justified before the latter, not as subordinate but superior, though in such a way, be it noted, that it is the single individual who, having been subordinate to the universal as the particular, now by means of the universal becomes that individual who, as the particular, stands in an absolute relation to the absolute. This position cannot be mediated, for all mediation occurs precisely by virtue of the universal; it is and remains in all eternity a paradox, inaccessible to thought.[2] And yet faith *is* this paradox. Or else (these are implications which I would ask the reader always to bear in mind, though it would be too complicated for me to spell them out each time) – or else faith has never existed just because it has always existed. And Abraham is done for.

That the individual can easily take this paradox for a temptation is true enough. But one should not keep it quiet on that account. True enough, too, that many people may have a natural aversion to the paradox, but that is no reason for making faith into something else so that they too can have it; while those who do have faith should be prepared to offer some criterion for distinguishing the paradox from a temptation.

Now the story of Abraham contains just such a teleological suspension of the ethical. There has been no want of sharp intellects and sound scholars who have found analogies to it. Their wisdom amounts to the splendid principle that basically everything is the same. If one looks a little closer I doubt very much whether one will find in the whole world a single analogy, except a later one that proves nothing, for the fact remains that Abraham represents faith, and that faith finds its proper expression in him whose life is not only the most paradoxical conceivable, but so paradoxical that it simply cannot be thought. He acts on the strength of the absurd; for it is precisely the absurd that as the single individual he is higher than the universal. This paradox cannot be mediated; for as soon as he tries Abraham will have to admit that he is in a state of temptation, and in that case he will never sacrifice Isaac, or if he has done so he must return repentantly to the universal. On the strength of the absurd he got Isaac back. Abraham is therefore at no instant the tragic hero, but something quite different, either a murderer or a man of faith. The middle-term that saves the tragic hero is something Abraham lacks. That is why I can understand a tragic hero, but not Abraham, even though in a certain lunatic sense I admire him more than all others.

Abraham's relation to Isaac, ethically speaking, is quite simply this, that the father should love the son more than himself. Yet within its own compass the ethical has several rankings; let us see whether this story contains any such higher expression of the ethical which might explain his behaviour ethically, justify him ethically for suspending the ethical duty to the son, yet without thereby exceeding the ethical's own teleology.

When an enterprise involving a whole nation is prevented, when such an enterprise is brought to a halt by heaven's disfavour, when divine wrath sends a dead calm which mocks every effort, when the soothsayer performs his sad task and proclaims that the deity demands a young girl as a sacrifice – then it is with heroism that the father has to make that sacrifice.[3] Nobly will he hide his grief though he could wish he were 'the lowly man who dares to weep' and not the king who must bear himself as befits a king. And however solitarily the pain enters his breast, for he has only three confidants among his people, soon the entire population will be privy to his pain, but also to his deed, to the fact that for the well-being of the whole he was willing to offer that girl, his daughter, this lovely young maiden. Oh, what bosom! What fair cheeks! What flaxen hair! And the daughter will touch him with her tears, and the father avert his face, but the hero will raise the knife. And when the news of this reaches the ancestral home all the beauteous maidens of Greece will blush with animation, and were the daughter a bride the betrothed would not be angered but proud to have been party to the father's deed, because the maiden belonged to him more tenderly than to the father.

When that bold judge, who saved Israel in the hour of need binds God and himself in one breath with the same promise, then it is with heroism that he is to transform the young girl's jubilation, the beloved daughter's joy, to sorrow, and all Israel will grieve with her maidenly youth; but every free-born man will understand Jephthah, every stout-hearted woman admire

him, and every maiden in Israel will want to do as his daughter; for what good would it be for Jephthah to triumph by making his promise but fail to keep it? Would the victory not be taken once more from the people?

When a son forgets his duty, when the State entrusts the father with the sword of judgement, when the laws demand punishment at the father's hand, then it is with heroism that the father must forget that the guilty one is his son. Nobly will he hide his pain, but in the nation there will be not one, not even the son, who fails to admire the father, and every time the laws of Rome are interpreted it will be recalled that many interpreted them more learnedly but none more gloriously than Brutus.

On the other hand, if it had been while his fleet was being borne by wind under full sail to its destination that Agamemnon had sent that messenger who brought Iphigenia to the sacrifice; if unbound by any promise that would decide the fate of his people Jephthah had said to his daughter: 'Sorrow now for two months henceforth over the short day of your youth, for I shall sacrifice you': if Brutus had had a righteous son and still called upon the lictors to execute him – who would understand them? If to the question, why did you do it?, these three had replied: 'It is a trial in which we are being tested', would one then have understood them better?

When at the decisive moment Agamemnon, Jephthah and Brutus heroically overcome their pain, have heroically given up the loved one, and have only the outward deed to perform, then never a noble soul in the world will there be but sheds tears of sympathy for their pain, tears of admiration for their deed. But if at that decisive moment these three men had added to the heroism with which they bore their pain the little words 'It won't happen', who then would understand them? If in explanation they added: 'We believe it on the strength of the absurd', who then would understand them better? For who would not readily understand that it was absurd? But who would understand that for that reason one could believe it?

The difference between the tragic hero and Abraham is obvious enough. The tragic hero stays within the ethical. He lets an expression of the ethical have its *telos* in a higher expression of the ethical; he reduces the ethical relation between father and son, or daughter and father, to a sentiment that has its dialectic in its relation to the idea of the ethical life. Here, then, there can be no question of a teleological suspension of the ethical itself.

With Abraham it is different. In his action he overstepped the ethical altogether, and had a higher *telos* outside it, in relation to which he suspended it. For how could one ever bring Abraham's action into relationship with the universal? How could any point of contact ever be discovered between what Abraham did and the universal other than that Abraham overstepped it? It is not to save a nation, not to uphold the idea of the State, that Abraham did it, not to appease angry gods. If there was any question of the deity's being angry, it could only have been Abraham he was angry with, and Abraham's whole action stands in no relation to the universal, it is a purely private undertaking. While, then, the tragic hero is great through his deed's being an expression of the ethical life, Abraham is great through an act of purely personal virtue. There is no higher expression of the ethical in Abraham's life than that the father shall love the son. The ethical in the sense of the ethical life is quite out of the question. In so far as the universal was there at all it was latent in Isaac, concealed as it were in his loins, and it would have to cry out with Isaac's mouth: 'Don't do it, you are destroying everything.'[4]

Then why does Abraham do it? For God's sake, and what is exactly the same, for his own. He does it for the sake of God because God demands this proof of his faith; he does it for his own sake in order to be able to produce the proof. The unity here is quite properly expressed in the saying in which this relationship has always been described: it is a trial, a temptation. A temptation, but what does that mean? What we usually call a temptation is something that keeps a person from carrying out a duty, but here the temptation is the ethical itself which would keep him from doing God's will. But then what is the duty? For the duty is precisely the expression of God's will.

Here we see the need for a new category for understanding Abraham. Such a relationship to the divine is unknown to paganism. The tragic hero enters into no private relationship with God, but the ethical is the divine and therefore the paradox in the divine can be mediated in the universal.

Abraham cannot be mediated, which can also be put by saying he cannot speak. The moment I speak I express the universal, and when I do not no one can understand me. So the moment Abraham wants to express himself in the universal, he has to say that his situation is one of temptation, for he has no higher expression of the universal that overrides the universal he transgresses.

Thus while Abraham arouses my admiration, he also appals me. The person who denies himself and sacrifices himself for duty gives up the finite in order to grasp on to the infinite; he is secure enough. The tragic hero gives up what is certain for what is still more certain, and the eye of the beholder rests confidently upon him. But the person who gives up the universal to grasp something still higher that is not the universal, what does he do? Can this be anything but temptation? And if it were something else but the individual were mistaken, what salvation is there for him? He suffers all the pain of the tragic hero, he brings all his joy in the world to nothing, he abandons everything, and perhaps the same instant debars himself from that exalted joy so precious to him that he would buy it at any price. That person the beholder cannot at all understand, nor let his eye rest upon him with confidence. Perhaps what the believer intends just cannot be done, after all it is unthinkable. Or if it could be done and the individual had misunderstood the deity, what salvation would there be for him? The tragic hero, he needs tears and he claims them; yes, where was that envious eye so barren as not to weep with Agamemnon, but where was he whose soul was so confused as to presume to weep for Abraham? The tragic hero has done with his deed at a definite moment in time, but in the course of time he achieves something no less important, he seeks out the one whose soul is beset with sorrow, whose breast cannot draw air for its stifled sighs, whose thoughts, weighed down with tears, hang heavy upon him; he appears before him, he breaks the spell of grief, loosens the corset, coaxes forth the tear by making the sufferer forget his own suffering in his. Abraham one cannot weep over. One approaches him with a *horror religiosus* [holy terror] like that in which Israel approached Mount Sinai. What if the lonely man who climbs the mountain in Moriah, whose peak soars heaven-high over the plains of Aulis, is not a sleepwalker who treads surefootedly over the abyss, while someone standing at the foot of the mountain, seeing him there, trembles with anxiety and out of respect and fear dares not even shout to him – what if he should be distracted, what if he has made a mistake? – Thanks! And thanks again, to whoever holds out to one who has been assaulted and left naked by life's sorrows, holds out to him the leaf of the word with which to hide his misery. Thanks to you, great Shakespeare!, you who can say everything, everything, everything exactly as it is – and yet why was this torment one you never gave voice to? Was it perhaps that you kept it to yourself, like the beloved whose name one still cannot bear the world to mention? For a poet buys this power of words to utter all the grim secrets of others at the cost of a little secret he himself cannot utter, and a poet is not an apostle, he casts devils out only by the power of the devil.

But now when the ethical is thus teleologically suspended, how does the single individual in whom it is suspended exist? He exists as the particular in opposition to the universal. Does this mean he sins? For this is the form of sin looked at ideally, just as the fact that the child does not sin because it is not conscious of its own existence as such does not mean that, looked at ideally, its existence is not that of sin or that the ethical does not make its demands of the child at every moment. If this form cannot be said to repeat itself in a way other than that of sin, then judgement has been delivered upon Abraham. Then how did Abraham exist? He had faith. That is the paradox that keeps him at the extremity and which he cannot make clear to anyone else, for the paradox is that he puts himself as the single individual in an absolute relation to the absolute. Is he justified? His justification is, once again, the paradox; for if he is the paradox it is not by virtue of being anything universal, but of being the particular.

How does the single individual assure himself that he is justified? It is a simple enough matter to level the whole of existence down to the idea of the State or to a concept of society. If one does that one can no doubt also mediate; for in this way one does not come to the paradox at all, to the single individual's as such being higher than the universal, which I can also put pointedly in a proposition of Pythagoras's, that the odd numbers are more perfect than the even. Should one happen to catch word of an answer in the direction of the paradox in our time, it will no doubt

go like this: 'That's to be judged by the outcome.' A hero who has become the scandal of his generation, aware that he is a paradox that cannot be understood, cries undaunted to his contemporaries: 'The future will show I was right!' This cry is heard less frequently nowadays, for as our age to its detriment produces no heroes, so it has the advantage that it also produces few caricatures. Whenever nowadays we hear the words 'That's to be judged by the outcome' we know immediately with whom we have the honour of conversing. Those who speak thus are a populous tribe which, to give them a common name, I shall call the 'lecturers'. They live in their thoughts, secure in life, they have a *permanent* position and *sure* prospects in a well-organized State; they are separated by centuries, even millennia, from the convulsions of existence; they have no fear that such things could happen again; what would the police and the newspapers say? Their lifework is to judge the great, to judge them according to the outcome. Such conduct in respect of greatness betrays a strange mixture of arrogance and pitifulness, arrogance because they feel called to pass judgement, pitifulness because they feel their lives unrelated in even the remotest manner to those of the great. Surely anyone with a speck of *erectior ingenii* [nobility of mind] cannot become so completely the cold and clammy mollusc as to lose sight altogether, in approaching the great, of the fact that ever since the Creation it has been accepted practice for the outcome to come last, and that if one is really to learn something from the great it is precisely the beginning one must attend to. If anyone on the verge of action should judge himself according to the outcome, he would never begin. Even though the result may gladden the whole world, that cannot help the hero; for he knows the result only when the whole thing is over, and that is not how he becomes a hero, but by virtue of the fact that he began.

But in any case the outcome in its dialectic (in so far as it is finitude's answer to the infinite question) is totally incompatible with the existence of the hero. Or are we to take it that Abraham was justified in relating himself as the single individual to the universal by the fact that he got Isaac by a *marvel*? Had Abraham actually sacrificed Isaac, would that have meant he was less justified?

But it is the outcome that arouses our curiosity, as with the conclusion of a book; one wants nothing of the fear, the distress, the paradox. One flirts with the outcome aesthetically; it comes as unexpectedly and yet as effortlessly as a prize in the lottery; and having heard the outcome one is improved. And yet no robber of temples hard-labouring in chains is so base a criminal as he who plunders the holy in this way, and not even Judas, who sold his master for thirty pieces of silver, is more contemptible than the person who would thus offer greatness for sale.

It goes against my nature to speak inhumanity of greatness, to let its grandeur fade into an indistinct outline at an immense distance, or represent it as great without the human element in it coming to the fore – whence it ceases to be the great; for it is not what happens to me that makes me great, but what I do, and there is surely no one who thinks that anyone became great by winning the big lottery prize. Even of a person born in humble circumstances I ask that he should not be so inhuman towards himself as to be unable to think of the king's castle except at a distance and by dreaming of its grandeur indistinctly, wanting to exalt it and simultaneously destroying its grandeur by exalting it in such a debasing way. I ask that he be human enough to approach and bear himself with confidence and dignity there too. He should not be so inhuman as shamelessly to want to violate every rule of respect by storming into the king's salon straight from the street – he loses more by doing that than the king; on the contrary he should find pleasure in observing every rule of decorum with a glad and confident enthusiasm, which is just what will make him frank and open-hearted. This is only an analogy, for the difference here is only a very imperfect expression of the spiritual distance. I ask everyone not to think so inhumanly of himself as to dare not set foot in those palaces where not just the memory of the chosen lives on but the chosen themselves. He should not push himself shamelessly forward and thrust upon them his kinship with them, he should feel happy every time he bows before them, but be frank and confident and always something more than a cleaning woman; for unless he wants to be more than that he will never come in there. And what will help him are exactly the fear and distress in which the great are tried, for otherwise, at least if there is a drop of red blood in him, they will merely arouse his righteous envy. And whatever can only be great at a distance, whatever people want

to exalt with empty and hollow phrases, that they themselves reduce to nothing.

Was there ever in the world anyone as great as that blessed woman, the mother of God, the Virgin Mary? And yet how do people speak of her? To say she was favoured among women doesn't make her great, and if it were not for the odd fact that those who listen can think as inhumanly as those who speak, surely every young girl would ask, why am I not favoured too? And had I nothing more to say I should by no means dismiss such a question as stupid; for as regards favours, abstractly considered, everyone is equally entitled. What is left out is the distress, the fear, the paradox. My thought is as pure as the next man's and surely the thought of anyone able to think in this way will be pure; if not, something dreadful is in store; for a person who has once called these images to mind cannot be rid of them again, and if he sins against them, then in their quiet wrath, more terrifying than the clamour of ten voracious critics, they will wreak their awful vengeance on him. No doubt Mary bore the child miraculously, but it went with Mary 'after the manner of women', and such a time is one of fear, distress and paradox. No doubt the angel was a ministering spirit, but he was not an obliging one who went round to all the other young girls in Israel and said: 'Do not despise Mary, something out of the ordinary is happening to her.' The angel came only to Mary, and no one could understand her. Yet what woman was done greater indignity than Mary, and isn't it true here too that those whom God blesses he damns in the same breath? This is the spirit's understanding of Mary, and she is not at all – as it offends me to say, though even more so that people have mindlessly and irresponsibly thought of her thus – she is not at all the fine lady sitting in her finery and playing with a divine child. Yet for saying notwithstanding, 'Behold the handmaid of the Lord' [Luke i.38 – Ed.], she is great, and it seems to me that it should not be difficult to explain why she became the mother of God. She needs no worldly admiration, as little as Abraham needs our tears, for she was no heroine and he no hero, but both of them became greater than that, not by any means by being relieved of the distress, the agony and the paradox, but because of these.

Great indeed it is when the poet presents his tragic hero for popular admiration and dares to say: 'Weep for him, for he deserves it'; for there is greatness in meriting the tears of those who deserve to shed them; great indeed for the poet to dare hold the crowd in check, dare discipline people into testing their own worthiness to weep for the hero, for the waste-water of snivellers is a degradation of the holy. But greater than all these is that the knight of faith dares to say even to the noble person who would weep for him: 'Do not weep for me, but weep for yourself.'

One is stirred, one harks back to those beautiful times, sweet tender longings lead one to the goal of one's desire, to see Christ walking about in the promised land. One forgets the fear, the distress, the paradox. Was it so easy a matter not to be mistaken? Was it not a fearful thought that this man who walked among the others was God? Was it not terrifying to sit down to eat with him? Was it so easy a matter to become an apostle? But the outcome, eighteen centuries, that helps; it helps that shabby deception wherein one deceives oneself and others. I do not feel brave enough to wish to be contemporary with such events, but for that reason I do not judge harshly of those who were mistaken, nor think meanly of those who saw the truth.

But now I return to Abraham. In the time before the outcome either Abraham was a murderer every minute or we stay with the paradox which is higher than all mediation.

So Abraham's story contains a teleological suspension of the ethical. He has, as the single individual, become higher than the universal. This is the paradox which cannot be mediated. How he got into it is just as inexplicable as how he stayed in it. If this is not how it is with Abraham, then he is not even a tragic hero but a murderer. To want to go on calling him the father of faith, to talk of this to those who are only concerned with words, is thoughtless. A tragic hero can become a human being by his own strength, but not the knight of faith. When a person sets out on the tragic hero's admittedly hard path there are many who could lend him advice; but he who walks the narrow path of faith no one can advise, no one understand. Faith is a marvel, and yet no human being is excluded from it; for that in which all human life is united is passion, and faith is a passion.

Notes

1   See Hegel's *Philosophy of Right*, Part 2, Section 3, Oxford: Clarendon Press, 1942, where he argues that "morality (*Moralität*)," the "subjective" sphere of individual conscience, must give way to "the ethical life (*Sittlichkeit*)," the "objective," "universal" sphere of public duty.

2   "Mediation" is Hegel-speak for the resolving of contradictions or paradoxes.

3   In this and the following two paragraphs, Kierkegaard discusses three "tragic heroes": Agamemnon, who must sacrifice his daughter Iphigenia in order to ensure a wind to take his fleet to Troy (the lines quoted are from Euripides' *Iphigenia in Aulis*); Jephthah, who finds he must sacrifice his daughter as a burnt offering in gratitude for Jehovah's military assistance (Judges 11); and L. Junius Brutus, a Roman consul who executed his own sons for treason.

4   This alludes to the important point that, in killing Isaac, Abraham would not only be killing his son but the future leader of the nation. Unlike those of the tragic heroes, therefore, Abraham's deed would violate *both* paternal *and* patriotic duty.

18

Friedrich Nietzsche, *On the Genealogy of Morals*, First Essay, Sections 2–14, 16

Introduction

Whether or not he was "the greatest moral philosopher of the past century,"[1] the German writer Friedrich Wilhelm Nietzsche (1844–1900) was surely that century's most powerful critic of morality – morality itself, that is, "the moral point of view," and not simply the precepts and practices of his contemporaries. Nietzsche's ambition was a "revaluation of all values," and the values of the future – those incarnate in the "over-man" (*Übermensch*) – are to be "moraline-free," "immoral."

Since the Renaissance, at least, morality has come to be identified, Nietzsche argues, with "Judaeo-Christian" morality and its various offshoots, such as Enlightenment utilitarianism (I.14 and I.16) and Kant's ethics of duty (I.15). The main critical strategy Nietzsche deploys is what he calls "genealogy," the "unmasking" of beliefs by examining their forgotten historical origins and psychological motivations. He is aware, of course, that merely by uncovering the "seedy" origin of a belief, one does not automatically invalidate it – an error known to logicians as the "genetic fallacy." Nietzsche agrees that the "question of the origin of our evaluations . . .

From *Basic Writings of Nietzsche*, trans. and ed. Walter Kaufmann. New York: The Modern Library, 1968 (some passages omitted).

is not at all equivalent to their critique."[2] Nevertheless, by demonstrating that people subscribe to moral values like charity and justice for reasons much less elevated than they imagine, any confidence that these values have a genuine grounding is dispelled. Moreover, it is Nietzsche's view that "there are no moral facts,"[3] only moral "interpretations," and that interpretations necessarily reflect the needs and interests of interpreters. Hence if it can be shown that the needs and interests to which moral values cater are despicable, a genealogy of morality will in effect serve to discredit those values.

In *On the Genealogy of Morals* (1887), Nietzsche attempts to "unmask" the credentials of a welter of moral concepts, including – in the First Essay – the notion of moral goodness itself. Against the "English psychologists," such as Hume, Nietzsche argues that this notion does not reflect an original sympathetic concern for others. It arose, rather, as part of a defensive reaction, on the part of the "weak" or the "herd," against the proto-morality of the "warrior-nobles," "masters," and "natural aristocrats" of earlier ages such as Homeric Greece. Suffering from a sense of powerlessness and inferiority, the "herd" successfully deployed a morality of putative compassion, justice, and other Judaeo-Christian virtues in order to emasculate and control the unbooted behavior of the "aristocrats." In the mouth of the "herd," Nietzsche argues, the words "good" and "bad" come to mean almost the precise opposite of what they meant for the nobles.[4]

Implicit here is a challenge to one of the most central tenets of "the moral point of view," apparent for example in Kant's ethics – that moral principles and duties are incumbent on all human beings. We encountered a limited challenge to this tenet in Kierkegaard (I.17) for whom, in special circumstances, an individual may have to obey a higher calling than morality. Nietzsche's challenge is more radical. There is a "rank order" among human beings, and moral values – which are suited for governing the behavior of one type of person (the "weak," the "botched and bungled") – serve only to "diminish" and "choke" the lives of a higher, more exuberant type. The "leveling" effect of moral universalism is, says Nietzsche, "our greatest danger." It is important to note, however, that elsewhere Nietzsche is not insensitive to the "civilizing" effects of the emergence of morality and that he does not deny the genuine benefits it has afforded the mass of men and women. It would be wrong, moreover, to suppose – as some Nazi ideologues did – that the "warrior-nobles" and "blond beasts of prey" he describes constitute Nietzsche's ideal type. They lack, for example, both the intelligence and self-discipline that Nietzsche's ideal requires.

In the famous and brilliant §13, we encounter a different aspect of Nietzschean genealogy. Here Nietzsche reverses the usual assumption that morality presupposes various beliefs about human beings, such as that they are responsible "subjects" possessed of free will. For Nietzsche, metaphysical notions like freedom of the will are motivated by the same "resentment" against the "strong" as "herd" values themselves are; and they function as devices to buttress those values. Rather than honestly admit that they are simply incapable of acting with the strength of the "nobles," the "weak" pretend that they simply choose not to act in such ways – a ploy that enables the weak to congratulate themselves at the same time they blame their enemies.

Alongside Marx and Freud, Nietzsche is one of the great "masters of the hermeneutics of suspicion," to cite Paul Ricoeur's phrase, and it would be hard to exaggerate the impact of his writings upon twentieth-century moral debate.[5] More than any other philosopher, it is Nietzsche who has destroyed an older, unreflective confidence in the integrity of moral thought and talk. As many recent writers have remarked, Nietzsche is the man to wrestle with if any such confidence is to be restored.[6]

Notes

1 B. Williams, "Nietzsche's Centaur," *London Review of Books*, 3 October 1981, p. 17.
2 *The Will to Power*, New York: Vintage, 1968, §284.
3 *The Twilight of the Idols*, in *The Portable Nietzsche*, New York: Viking, 1954, §6.1.
4 For more on *On the Genealogy of Morals*, see the articles by A. C. Danto and F. Bergmann in *Reading Nietzsche*, ed. R. C. Solomon and K. M. Higgins, Oxford: Oxford University Press 1988.
5 According to Ricoeur, a "hermeneutics of suspicion" is "a method of interpretation which assumes that the literal or surface-level meaning of a text is an effort to conceal the political interests which are served by the text. The purpose of interpretation is to strip off the concealment, unmasking those interests"; *Freud and Philosophy: An Essay on Interpretation*, New Haven, CT: Yale University Press, 1970, p. 33.
6 See, e.g., A. Bloom's *The Closing of the American Mind*, New York: Simon & Schuster, 1987.

 ## Nietzsche, *On the Genealogy of Morals*

First Essay: "Good and Evil," "Good and Bad"

2 [. . .] As is the hallowed custom with philosophers, the thinking of all of them is *by nature* unhistorical; there is no doubt about that. The way they have bungled their moral genealogy comes to light at the very beginning, where the task is to investigate the origin of the concept and judgement 'good'. 'Originally' – so they decree – 'one approved unegoistic actions and called them good from the point of view of those to whom they were done, that is to say, those to whom they were *useful*; later one *forgot* how this approval

originated and, simply because unegoistic actions were always *habitually* praised as good, one also felt them to be good – as if they were something good in themselves.' One sees straightaway that this primary derivation already contains all the typical traits of the idiosyncrasy of the English psychologists – we have 'utility', 'forgetting', 'habit', and finally 'error', all as the basis of an evaluation of which the higher man has hitherto been proud as though it were a kind of prerogative of man as such. This pride *has* to be humbled, this evaluation disvalued: has that end been achieved?

Now it is plain to me, first of all, that in this theory the source of the concept 'good' has been sought and established in the wrong place: the judgement 'good' did *not* originate with those to whom 'goodness' was shown! Rather it was 'the good' themselves, that is to say, the noble, powerful, high-stationed and high-minded, who felt and established themselves and their actions as good, that is, of the first rank, in contradistinction to all the low, low-minded, common and plebeian. It was out of this *pathos of distance* that they first seized the right to create values and to coin names for values: what had they to do with utility! The viewpoint of utility is as remote and inappropriate as it possibly could be in face of such a burning eruption of the highest rank-ordering, rank-defining value judgements: for here feeling has attained the antithesis of that low degree of warmth which any calculating prudence, any calculus of utility, presupposes – and not for once only, not for an exceptional hour, but for good. The pathos of nobility and distance, as aforesaid, the protracted and domineering fundamental total feeling on the part of a higher ruling order in relation to a lower order to a 'below' – *that* is the origin of the antithesis 'good' and 'bad'. (The lordly right of giving names extends so far that one should allow oneself to conceive the origin of language itself as an expression of power on the part of the rulers: they say 'this *is* this and this', they seal every thing and event with a sound and, as it were, take possession of it.) It follows from this origin that the word 'good' was definitely *not* linked from the first and by necessity to 'unegoistic' actions, as the superstition of these genealogists of morality would have it. Rather it was only when aristocratic value judgements *declined* that the whole antithesis 'egoistic' 'unegoistic' obtruded itself more and more on the human conscience – it is, to speak in my own language, the *herd instinct* that through this antithesis at last gets its word (and its *words*) in. And even then it was a long time before that instinct attained such dominion that moral evaluation was actually stuck and halted at this antithesis (as, for example, is the case in contemporary Europe: the prejudice that takes 'moral', 'unegoistic', '*désintéressé*' as concepts of equivalent value already rules today with the force of a 'fixed idea' and brain-sickness).

3 In the second place, however: quite apart from the historical untenability of this hypothesis regarding the origin of the value judgement 'good', it suffers from an inherent psychological absurdity. The utility of the unegoistic action is supposed to be the source of the approval accorded it, and this source is supposed to have been *forgotten* – but how is this forgetting *possible*? Has the utility of such actions come to an end at some time or other? The opposite is the case: this utility has rather been an everyday experience at all times, therefore something that has been underlined again and again: consequently, instead of fading from consciousness, instead of becoming easily forgotten, it must have been impressed on the consciousness more and more clearly. How much more reasonable is that opposing theory (it is not for that reason more true –) which Herbert Spencer [1820–1903], for example, espoused: that the concept 'good' is essentially identical with the concept 'useful', 'practical', so that in the judgements 'good' and 'bad' mankind has summed up and sanctioned precisely its *unforgotten* and *unforgettable* experiences regarding what is useful-practical and what is harmful-impractical. According to this theory, that which has always proved itself useful is good: therefore it may claim to be 'valuable in the highest degree', 'valuable in itself'. This road to an explanation is, as aforesaid, also a wrong one, but at least the explanation is in itself reasonable and psychologically tenable.

4 The signpost to the *right* road was for me the question: what was the real etymological significance of the designations for 'good' coined in the various languages? I found they all led back to the *same conceptual transformation* – that everywhere 'noble', 'aristocratic' in the social sense, is the basic concept from which 'good' in the sense of 'with aristocratic soul', 'noble', 'with a soul of a high

order', 'with a privileged soul', necessarily developed: a development which always runs parallel with that other in which 'common', 'plebeian', 'low' are finally transformed into the concept 'bad'. The most convincing example of the latter is the German word *schlecht* [bad] itself: which is identical with *schlicht* [plain, simple] – compare *schlechtweg* [plainly], *schlechterdings* [simply] – and originally designated the plain, the common man, as yet with no inculpatory implication and simply in contradistinction to the nobility. About the time of the Thirty Years' War, late enough therefore, this meaning changed into the one now customary.

With regard to a moral genealogy this seems to me a *fundamental* insight; that it has been arrived at so late is the fault of the retarding influence exercised by the democratic prejudice in the modern world toward all questions of origin. And this is so even in the apparently quite objective domain of natural science and physiology, as I shall merely hint here. But what mischief this prejudice is capable of doing, especially to morality and history, once it has been unbridled to the point of hatred is shown by the notorious case of [Henry Thomas] Buckle [1821–62] here the *plebeianism* of the modern spirit, which is of English origin, erupted once again on its native soil, as violently as a mud volcano and with that salty, noisy, vulgar eloquence with which all volcanos have spoken hitherto.

5   With regard to *our* problem, which may on good grounds be called a *quiet* problem and one which fastidiously directs itself to few ears, it is of no small interest to ascertain that through those words and roots which designate 'good' there frequently still shines the most important nuance by virtue of which the noble felt themselves to be men of a higher rank. Granted that, in the majority of cases, they designate themselves simply by their superiority in power (as 'the powerful', 'the masters', 'the commanders') or by the most clearly visible signs of this superiority, for example, as 'the rich', 'the possessors' (this is the meaning of *arya*; and of corresponding words in Iranian and Slavic). But they also do it by a *typical character trait*: and this is the case that concerns us here. They call themselves, for instance, 'the truthful'; this is so above all of the Greek nobility, whose mouthpiece is the Megarian poet Theognis [6th century BCE]. The

root of the word coined for this, *esthlos*, signifies one who *is*, who possesses reality, who is actual, who is true; then, with a subjective turn, the true as the truthful: in this phase of conceptual transformation it becomes a slogan and catchword of the nobility and passes over entirely into the sense of 'noble', as distinct from the *lying* common man, which is what Theognis takes him to be and how he describes him – until finally, after the decline of the nobility, the word is left to designate nobility of soul and becomes as it were ripe and sweet.

[. . .] I believe I may venture to interpret the Latin *bonus* as 'the warrior', provided I am right in tracing *bonus* back to an earlier *duonus* (compare *bellum* = *duellum* = *duen-lum*, which seems to me to contain *duonus*). Therefore *bonus* as the man of strife, of dissention (*duo*), as the man of war: one sees what constituted the 'goodness' of a man in ancient Rome. Our German *gut* [good] even: does it not signify 'the godlike', the man of 'godlike race'? And is it not identical with the popular (originally noble) name of the Goths? The grounds for this conjecture cannot be dealt with here.

6   To this rule that a concept denoting political superiority always resolves itself into a concept denoting superiority of soul it is not necessarily an exception (although it provides occasions for exceptions) when the highest caste is at the same time the *priestly* caste and therefore emphasizes in its total description of itself a predicate that calls to mind its priestly function. It is then, for example, that 'pure' and 'impure' confront one another for the first time as designations of station; and here too there evolves a 'good' and a 'bad' in a sense no longer referring to station. One should be warned, moreover, against taking these concepts 'pure' and 'impure' too ponderously or broadly, not to say symbolically: all the concepts of ancient man were rather at first incredibly uncouth, coarse, external, narrow, straightforward and altogether *unsymbolical* in meaning to a degree that we can scarcely conceive. The 'pure one' is from the beginning merely a man who washes himself, who forbids himself certain foods that produce skin ailments, who does not sleep with the dirty women of the lower strata, who has an aversion to blood – no more, hardly more! On the other hand, to be sure, it is clear from the whole nature of an essentially priestly

aristocracy why antithetical valuations could in precisely this instance soon become dangerously deepened, sharpened and internalized; and indeed they finally tore chasms between man and man that a very Achilles of a free spirit would not venture to leap without a shudder. There is from the first something *unhealthy* in such priestly aristocracies and in the habits ruling in them which turn them away from action and alternate between brooding and emotional explosions, habits which seem to have as their almost invariable consequence that intestinal morbidity and neurasthenia which has afflicted priests at all times; but as to that which they themselves devised as a remedy for this morbidity – must one not assert that it has ultimately proved itself a hundred times more dangerous in its effects than the sickness it was supposed to cure? Mankind itself is still ill with the effects of this priestly naïveté in medicine! Think, for example, of certain forms of diet (abstinence from meat), of fasting, of sexual continence, of flight 'into the wilderness' [...]: add to these the entire antisensualistic metaphysic of the priests that makes men indolent and overrefined, their autohypnosis in the manner of fakirs and Brahmins – Brahma used in the shape of a glass knob and a fixed idea – and finally the only-too-comprehensible satiety with all this, together with the radical cure for it, *nothingness* (or God – the desire for a *unio mystica* with God is the desire of the Buddhist for nothingness, Nirvāṇa – and no more!). For with the priests *everything* becomes more dangerous, not only cures and remedies, but also arrogance, revenge, acuteness, profligacy, love, lust to rule, virtue, disease – but it is only fair to add that it was on the soil of this *essentially dangerous* form of human existence, the priestly form, that man first became *an interesting animal*, that only here did the human soul in a higher sense acquire *depth* and become *evil* – and these are the two basic respects in which man has hitherto been superior to other beasts!

7   One will have divined already how easily the priestly mode of valuation can branch off from the knightly-aristocratic and then develop into its opposite; this is particularly likely when the priestly caste and the warrior caste are in jealous opposition to one another and are unwilling to come to terms. The knightly-aristocratic value judgements presupposed a powerful physicality, a flourishing, abundant, even overflowing health, together with that which serves to preserve it: war, adventure, hunting, dancing, war games, and in general all that involves vigorous, free, joyful activity. The priestly-noble mode of valuation presupposes, as we have seen, other things: it is disadvantageous for it when it comes to war! As is well known, the priests are the *most evil enemies* – but why? Because they are the most impotent. It is because of their impotence that in them hatred grows to monstrous and uncanny proportions, to the most spiritual and poisonous kind of hatred. The truly great haters in world history have always been priests; likewise the most ingenious haters: other kinds of spirit hardly come into consideration when compared with the spirit of priestly vengefulness. Human history would be altogether too stupid a thing without the spirit that the impotent have introduced into it – let us take at once the most notable example. All that has been done on earth against 'the noble', 'the powerful', 'the masters', 'the rulers', fades into nothing compared with what the *Jews* have done against them; the Jews, that priestly people, who in opposing their enemies and conquerors were ultimately satisfied with nothing less than a radical revaluation of their enemies' values, that is to say, an act of the *most spiritual revenge*. For this alone was appropriate to a priestly people, the people embodying the most deeply repressed priestly vengefulness. It was the Jews who, with awe-inspiring consistency, dared to invert the aristocratic value-equation (good = noble = powerful = beautiful = happy = beloved of God) and to hang on to this inversion with their teeth, the teeth of the most abysmal hatred (the hatred of impotence), saying 'the wretched alone are the good; the poor, impotent, lowly alone are the good; the suffering, deprived, sick, ugly alone are pious, alone are blessed by God, blessedness is for them alone – and you, the powerful and noble, are on the contrary the evil, the cruel, the lustful, the insatiable, the godless to all eternity; and you shall be in all eternity the unblessed, accursed, and damned!' [...] One knows *who* inherited this Jewish revaluation [i.e., Christians – Ed.]. In connection with the tremendous and immeasurably fateful initiative provided by the Jews through this most fundamental of all declarations of war, I recall the proposition I arrived at on a previous occasion (*Beyond Good and Evil*, section 195) – that with the Jews there begins *the slave*

revolt in morality: that revolt which has a history of two thousand years behind it and which we no longer see because it – has been victorious.

8 But you do not comprehend this? You are incapable of seeing something that required two thousand years to achieve victory? – There is nothing to wonder at in that: all *protracted* things are hard to see, to see whole. *That*, however, is what has happened: from the trunk of that tree of vengefulness and hatred, Jewish hatred – the profoundest and sublimest kind of hatred, capable of creating ideals and reversing values, the like of which has never existed on earth before – there grew something equally incomparable, a *new love*, the profoundest and sublimest kind of love – and from what other trunk could it have grown?

One should not imagine it grew up as the denial of that thirst for revenge, as the opposite of Jewish hatred! No, the reverse is true! That love grew out of it as its crown, as its triumphant crown spreading itself farther and farther into the purest brightness and sunlight, driven as it were into the domain of light and the heights in pursuit of the goals of that hatred – victory, spoil and seduction – by the same impulse that drove the roots of that hatred deeper and deeper and more and more covetously into all that was profound and evil. This Jesus of Nazareth, the incarnate gospel of love, this 'Redeemer' who brought blessedness and victory to the poor, the sick and the sinners – was he not this seduction in its most uncanny and irresistible form, a seduction and bypath to precisely those *Jewish* values and new ideals? Did Israel not attain the ultimate goal of its sublime vengefulness precisely through the bypath of this 'Redeemer', this ostensible opponent and disintegrator of Israel? Was it not part of the secret black art of truly *grand* politics of revenge, of a farseeing, subterranean, slowly advancing and premeditated revenge, that Israel must itself deny the real instrument of its revenge before all the world as a mortal enemy and nail it to the cross, so that 'all the world', namely all the opponents of Israel, could unhesitatingly swallow just this bait? And could spiritual subtlety imagine any *more dangerous* bait than this? Anything to equal the enticing, intoxicating, overwhelming and undermining power of that symbol of the 'holy cross', that ghastly paradox of a 'God on the cross', that

mystery of an unimaginable ultimate cruelty and self-crucifixion of God *for the salvation of man*?

What is certain, at least, is that [under this sign] Israel, with its vengefulness and revaluation of all values, has hitherto triumphed again and again over all other ideals, over all *nobler* ideals.

9 'But why are you talking about *nobler* ideals! Let us stick to the facts: the people have won – or "the slaves" or "the mob" or "the herd" or whatever you like to call them – if this has happened through the Jews, very well! in that case no people ever had a more world-historic mission. "The masters" have been disposed of; the morality of the common man has won. One may conceive of this victory as at the same time a blood-poisoning (it has mixed the races together) – I shan't contradict; but this in-toxication has undoubtedly been *successful*. The "redemption" of the human race (from "the masters", that is) is going forward; everything is visibly becoming Judaized, Christianized, mob-ized (what do the words matter!). The progress of this poison through the entire body of mankind seems irresistible, its pace and tempo may from now on even grow slower, subtler, less audible, more cautious – there is plenty of time. [. . .]'

This is the epilogue of a 'free spirit' to my speech; an honest animal, as he has abundantly revealed, and a democrat, moreover; he had been listening to me till then and could not endure to listen to my silence. For at this point I have much to be silent about.

10 The slave revolt in morality begins when *ressentiment* [resentment] itself becomes creative and gives birth to values: the *ressentiment* of natures that are denied the true reaction, that of deeds, and compensate themselves with an imaginary revenge. While every noble morality develops from a triumphant affirmation of itself, slave morality from the outset says No to what is 'outside', what is 'different', what is 'not itself'; and *this* No is its creative deed. This inversion of the value-positing eye – this *need* to direct one's view outward instead of back to oneself – is of the essence of *ressentiment*: in order to exist, slave morality always first needs a hostile external world; it needs, physiologically speaking, external stimuli in order to act at all – its action is fundamentally reaction.

The reverse is the case with the noble mode of valuation: it acts and grows spontaneously, it seeks its opposite only so as to affirm itself more gratefully and triumphantly – its negative concept 'low', 'common', 'bad' is only a subsequently-invented pale, contrasting image in relation to its positive basic concept – filled with life and passion through and through – 'we noble ones, we good, beautiful, happy ones!' When the noble mode of valuation blunders and sins against reality, it does so in respect to the sphere with which it is *not* sufficiently familiar, against a real knowledge of which it has indeed inflexibly guarded itself: in some circumstances it misunderstands the sphere it despises, that of the common man, of the lower orders; on the other hand, one should remember that, even supposing that the affect of contempt, of looking down from a superior height, *falsifies* the image of that which it despises, it will at any rate still be a much less serious falsification than that perpetrated on its opponent – *in effigie* of course – by the submerged hatred, the vengefulness of the impotent. There is indeed too much carelessness, too much taking lightly, too much looking away and impatience involved in contempt, even too much joyfulness, for it to be able to transform its object into a real caricature and monster.

One should not overlook the almost benevolent nuances that the Greek nobility, for example, bestows on all the words it employs to distinguish the lower orders from itself; how they are continuously mingled and sweetened with a kind of pity, consideration and forbearance, so that finally almost all the words referring to the common man have remained as expressions signifying 'unhappy', 'pitiable' [. . .] – and how on the other hand 'bad', 'low', 'unhappy' have never ceased to sound to the Greek ear as one note with a tone-colour in which 'unhappy' preponderates: this as an inheritance from the ancient nobler aristocratic mode of evaluation, which does not belie itself even in its contempt. [. . .] The 'well-born' *felt* themselves to be the 'happy'; they did not have to establish their happiness artificially by examining their enemies, or to persuade themselves, *deceive* themselves, that they were happy (as all men of *ressentiment* are in the habit of doing); and they likewise knew, as rounded men replete with energy and therefore *necessarily* active, that happiness should not be sundered from action – being active was with them necessarily a

part of happiness [. . .] all very much the opposite of 'happiness' at the level of the impotent, the oppressed, and those in whom poisonous and inimical feelings are festering, with whom it appears as essentially narcotic, drug, rest, peace, 'sabbath', slackening of tension and relaxing of limbs, in short *passively*.

While the noble man lives in trust and openness with himself (*gennaios* 'of noble descent' underlines the nuance 'upright' and probably also 'naïve'), the man of *ressentiment* is neither upright nor naïve nor honest and straightforward with himself. His soul *squints*; his spirit loves hiding places, secret paths and back doors, everything covert entices him as *his* world, *his* security, *his* refreshment; he understands how to keep silent, how not to forget, how to wait, how to be provisionally self-deprecating and humble. A race of such men of *ressentiment* is bound to become eventually *cleverer* than any noble race; it will also honour cleverness to a far greater degree: namely, as a condition of existence of the first importance; while with noble men cleverness can easily acquire a subtle flavour of luxury and subtlety – for here it is far less essential than the perfect functioning of the regulating *unconscious* instincts or even than a certain imprudence, perhaps a bold recklessness whether in the face of danger or of the enemy, or that enthusiastic impulsiveness in anger, love, reverence, gratitude and revenge by which noble souls have at all times recognized one another. *Ressentiment* itself, if it should appear in the noble man, consummates and exhausts itself in an immediate reaction, and therefore does not *poison*: on the other hand, it fails to appear at all on countless occasions on which it inevitably appears in the weak and impotent.

To be incapable of taking one's enemies, one's accidents, even one's misdeeds seriously for very long – that is the sign of strong, full natures in whom there is an excess of the power to form, to mould, to recuperate and to forget (a good example of this in modern times is [the Comte de] Mirabeau [1749–91], who had no memory for insults and vile actions done him and was unable to forgive simply because he – forgot). Such a man shakes off with a *single* shrug many vermin that eat deep into others; here alone genuine 'love of one's enemies' is possible – supposing it to be possible at all on earth. How much reverence has a noble man for his enemies! – and such reverence is a bridge to love. – For he desires his enemy for himself, as his mark of distinction; he can endure no other enemy than one in whom there is nothing to despise and *very much* to honour! In contrast to this, picture 'the enemy' as the man of *ressentiment* conceives him – and here precisely is his deed, his creation: he has conceived 'the evil enemy', '*the Evil One*', and this in fact is his basic concept, from which he then evolves, as an afterthought and pendant, a 'good one' – himself!

11 This, then, is quite the contrary of what the noble man does, who conceives the basic concept 'good' in advance and spontaneously out of himself and only then creates for himself an idea of 'bad'! This 'bad' of noble origin and that 'evil' out of the cauldron of unsatisfied hatred – the former an after-production, a side issue, a contrasting shade, the latter on the contrary the original thing, the beginning, the distinctive *deed* in the conception of a slave morality – how different these words 'bad' and 'evil' are, although they are both apparently the opposite of the same concept 'good'. But it is *not* the same concept 'good': one should ask rather precisely *who* is 'evil' in the sense of the morality of *ressentiment*. The answer, in all strictness, is: *precisely* the 'good man' of the other morality, precisely the noble, powerful man, the ruler, but dyed in another colour, interpreted in another fashion, seen in another way by the venomous eye of *ressentiment*.

Here there is one thing we shall be the last to deny: he who knows these 'good men' only as enemies knows only *evil enemies*, and the same men who are held so sternly in check *inter pares* [among equals] by custom, respect, usage, gratitude, and even more by mutual suspicion and jealousy, and who on the other hand in their relations with one another show themselves so resourceful in consideration, self-control delicacy, loyalty, pride and friendship – once they go outside, where the strange, the *stranger* is found, they are not much better than uncaged beasts of prey. There they savour a freedom from all social constraints, they compensate themselves in the wilderness for the tension engendered by protracted confinement and enclosure within the peace of society, they go *back* to the innocent conscience of the beast of prey, as triumphant monsters who perhaps emerge from a disgusting procession of murder, arson, rape and torture,

exhilarated and undisturbed of soul, as if it were no more than a students' prank, convinced they have provided the poets with a lot more material for song and praise. One cannot fail to see at the bottom of all these noble races the beast of prey, the splendid *blond beast*[1] prowling about avidly in search of spoil and victory; this hidden core needs to erupt from time to time, the animal has to get out again and go back to the wilderness: the Roman, Arabian, Germanic, Japanese nobility, the Homeric heroes, the Scandinavian Vikings – they all shared this need. [. . .]

Supposing that what is at any rate believed to be the 'truth' really is true, and the *meaning of all culture* is the reduction of the beast of prey 'man' to a tame and civilized animal, a *domestic animal*, then one would undoubtedly have to regard all those instincts of reaction and *ressentiment* through whose aid the noble races and their ideals were finally confounded and overthrown as the actual *instruments of culture*; which is not to say that the *bearers* of these instincts themselves represent culture. Rather is the reverse not merely probable – no! today it is *palpable*! These bearers of the oppressive instincts that thirst for reprisal, the descendants of every kind of European and non-European slavery, and especially of the entire pre-Aryan populace – they represent the *regression* of mankind! These 'instruments of culture' are a disgrace to man and rather an accusation and counterargument against 'culture' in general! One may be quite justified in continuing to fear the blond beast at the core of all noble races and in being on one's guard against it: but who would not a hundred times sooner fear where one can also admire than *not* fear but be permanently condemned to the repellent sight of the ill-constituted, dwarfed, atrophied and poisoned? And is that not *our* fate? What today constitutes *our* antipathy to 'man'? – for we *suffer* from man, beyond doubt.

Not fear; rather that we no longer have anything left to fear in man; that the maggot 'man' is swarming in the foreground; that the 'tame man', the hopelessly mediocre and insipid man, has already learned to feel himself as the goal and zenith, as the meaning of history, as 'higher man' – that he has indeed a certain right to feel thus, in so far as he feels himself elevated above the surfeit of ill-constituted, sickly, weary and exhausted people of which Europe is beginning to stink today, as something at least relatively well-constituted, at least still capable of living, at least affirming life.

12   At this point I cannot suppress a sigh and a last hope. What is it that I especially find utterly unendurable? That I cannot cope with, that makes me choke and faint? Bad air! Bad air! The approach of some ill-constituted thing; that I have to smell the entrails of some ill-constituted soul!

How much one is able to endure: distress, want, bad weather, sickness, toil, solitude. Fundamentally one can cope with everything else, born as one is to a subterranean life of struggle; one emerges again and again into the light, one experiences again and again one's golden hour of victory – and then one stands forth as one was born, unbreakable, tensed, ready for new, even harder, remoter things, like a bow that distress only serves to draw tauter.

But grant me from time to time – if there are divine goddesses in the realm beyond good and evil – grant me the sight, but *one* glance of something perfect, wholly achieved, happy, mighty, triumphant, something still capable of arousing fear! Of a man who justifies *man*, of a complementary and redeeming lucky hit on the part of man for the sake of which one may still *believe in man*!

For this is how things are: the diminution and levelling of European man constitutes *our* greatest danger, for the sight of him makes us weary. – We can see nothing today that wants to grow greater, we suspect that things will continue to go down, down, to become thinner, more good-natured, more prudent, more comfortable, more mediocre, more indifferent, more Chinese, more Christian – there is no doubt that man is getting 'better' all the time.

Here precisely is what has become a fatality for Europe – together with the fear of man we have also lost our love of him, our reverence for him, our hopes for him, even the will to him. The sight of man now makes us weary – what is nihilism today if it is not *that*? – We are weary *of man*.

13   But let us return: the problem of the *other* origin of the 'good', of the good as conceived by the man of *ressentiment*, demands its solution.

That lambs dislike great birds of prey does not seem strange: only it gives no ground for reproaching these birds of prey for bearing off little lambs. And if the lambs say among themselves: 'these birds of prey are evil; and whoever is least like a bird of prey, but rather its opposite, a lamb – would he not be good?' there is no reason to find fault with this institution of an ideal, except perhaps that the birds of prey might view it a little ironically and say: '*we* don't dislike them at all, these good little lambs; we even love them: nothing is more tasty than a tender lamb.'

To demand of strength that it should *not* express itself as strength, that it should *not* be a desire to overcome, a desire to throw down, a desire to become master, a thirst for enemies and resistances and triumphs, is just as absurd as to demand of weakness that it should express itself as strength. A quantum of force is equivalent to a quantum of drive, will, effect – more, it is nothing other than precisely this very driving, willing, effecting, and only owing to the seduction of language (and of the fundamental errors of reason that are petrified in it) which conceives and misconceives all effects as conditioned by something that causes effects, by a 'subject', can it appear otherwise. For just as the popular mind separates the lightning from its flash and takes the latter for an *action*, for the operation of a subject called lightning, so popular morality also separates strength from expressions of strength, as if there were a neutral substratum behind the strong man, which was *free* to express strength or not to do so. But there is no such substratum; there is no 'being' behind doing, effecting, becoming; 'the doer' is merely a fiction added to the deed – the deed is everything. The popular mind in fact doubles the deed; when it sees the lightning flash, it is the deed of a deed: it posits the same event first as cause and then a second time as its effect. Scientists do no better when they say 'force moves', 'force causes', and the like – all its coolness, its freedom from emotion notwithstanding, our entire science still lies under the misleading influence of language and has not disposed of that little changeling, the 'subject' (the atom, for example, is such a changeling, as is the Kantian 'thing-in-itself'); no wonder if the submerged, darkly glowering emotions of vengefulness and hatred exploit this belief for their own ends and in fact maintain no belief more ardently than the belief that *the strong man is free* to be weak and the bird of prey to be a lamb – for thus they gain the right to make the bird of prey *accountable* for being a bird of prey.

When the oppressed, downtrodden, outraged exhort one another with the vengeful cunning of impotence: 'let us be different from the evil, namely good! And he is good who does not outrage, who harms nobody, who does not attack, who does not requite, who leaves revenge to God, who keeps himself hidden as we do, who avoids evil and desires little from life, like us, the patient, humble, and just' – this, listened to calmly and without previous bias, really amounts to no more than: 'we weak ones are, after all, weak; it would be good if we did nothing *for which we are not strong enough*'; but this dry matter of fact, this prudence of the lowest order which even insects possess (posing as dead, when in great danger, so as not to do 'too much'), has, thanks to the counterfeit and self-deception of impotence, clad itself in the ostentatious garb of the virtue of quiet, calm resignation, just as if the weakness of the weak – that is to say, their *essence*, their effects, their sole ineluctable, irremovable reality – were a voluntary achievement, willed, chosen, a *deed*, a *meritorious* act. This type of man *needs* to believe in a neutral independent 'subject', prompted by an instinct for self-preservation and self-affirmation in which every lie is sanctified. The subject (or, to use a more popular expression, the *soul*) has perhaps been believed in hitherto more firmly than anything else on earth because it makes possible to the majority of mortals, the weak and oppressed of every kind, the sublime self-deception that interprets weakness as freedom, and their being thus-and-thus as a *merit*.

14 Would anyone like to take a look into the secret of how *ideals are made* on earth? Who has the courage? – Very well! Here is a point we can see through into this dark workshop. But wait a moment or two, Mr Rash and Curious: your eyes must first get used to this false iridescent light. – All right! Now speak! What is going on down there? Say what you see, man of the most perilous kind of inquisitiveness – now I am the one who is listening.

– 'I see nothing, but I hear the more. There is a soft, wary, malignant muttering and whispering coming from all the corners and nooks. It seems to me one is lying; a saccharine sweetness clings to every sound. Weakness is being lied into something *meritorious*, no doubt of it – so it is just as you said'

– Go on!

– 'and impotence which does not requite into "goodness of heart"; anxious lowliness into "humility"; subjection to those one hates into "obedience" (that is, to one of whom they say he commands this subjection – they call him God). The inoffensiveness of the weak man, even the cowardice of which he has so much, his lingering at the door, his being ineluctably compelled to wait, here acquire flattering names, such as "patience", and are even called virtue itself; his inability for revenge is called unwillingness to revenge, perhaps even forgiveness ("for *they* know not what they do – we alone know what *they* do!"). They also speak of "loving one's enemies" – and sweat as they do so.'

– Go on!

– 'They are miserable, no doubt of it, all these mutterers and nook counterfeiters, although they crouch warmly together – but they tell me their misery is a sign of being chosen by God; one beats the dogs one likes best; perhaps this misery is also a preparation, a testing, a schooling, perhaps it is even more – something that will one day be made good and recompensed with interest, with huge payments of gold, no! of happiness. This they call "bliss",'

– Go on!

– 'Now they give me to understand that they are not merely better than the mighty, the lords of the earth whose spittle they have to lick (*not* from fear, not at all from fear! but because God has commanded them to obey the authorities) – that they are not merely better but are also "better off", or at least will be better off someday. [Allusion to Romans 13:1–2 – Ed.] But enough! enough! I can't take any more. Bad air! Bad air! This workshop where *ideals are manufactured* – it seems to me it stinks of so many lies.'

– No! Wait a moment! You have said nothing yet of the masterpiece of these black magicians, who make whiteness, milk and innocence of every blackness – haven't you noticed their perfection of refinement, their boldest, subtlest, most ingenious, most mendacious artistic stroke? Attend to them! These cellar rodents full of vengefulness and hatred – what have they made of revenge and hatred? Have you heard these words uttered? If you trusted simply to their words, would you suspect you were among men of *ressentiment*? . . .

– 'I understand; I'll open my ears again (oh! oh! oh! and *close* my nose). Now I can really hear what they have been saying all along: "We good men – *we are the just*" – what they desire they call, not retaliation, but "the triumph of *justice*"; what they hate is not their enemy, no! they hate "injustice", they hate "godlessness"; what they believe in and hope for is not the hope of revenge, the intoxication of sweet revenge ("sweeter than honey" Homer called it), but the victory of God, of the *just* God, over the godless; what there is left for them to love on earth is not their brothers in hatred but their "brothers in love", as they put it, all the good and just on earth.'

– And what do they call that which serves to console them for all the suffering of life – their phantasmagoria of anticipated future bliss?

– 'What? Do I hear aright? They call that "the Last Judgement", the coming of *their* kingdom, of the "Kingdom of God" – meanwhile, however, they live "in faith", "in love", "in hope".'

– Enough! Enough!

16 Let us conclude. The two *opposing* values 'good and bad', 'good and evil' have been engaged in a fearful struggle on earth for thousands of years; and though the latter value has certainly been on top for a long time, there are still places where the struggle is as yet undecided. One might even say that it has risen ever higher and thus become more and more profound and spiritual: so that today there is perhaps no more decisive mark of a '*higher nature*', a more spiritual nature, than that of being divided in this sense and a genuine battleground of these opposed values. [. . .]

Note

1 That the "blond beast" is found in Arabia and Japan is sufficient to show that, by this expression, Nietzsche does not intend "Aryan man." According to the translator, the reference is to the lion, a metaphor for the "warrior-noble."

G. E. Moore, *Principia Ethica*, Chapter 1, sections 1–2, 5–15

Introduction

Friedrich Nietzsche (I.18), self-proclaimed "amor-alist" and thinker of "dynamite" thoughts, would not have been surprised at his role in engendering the irrationalist and iconoclastic views of moral-ity which have prospered in twentieth-century continental Europe. The mild-mannered and soft-spoken Cambridge philosopher G. E. Moore (1873–1958), however, would have been (indeed, was) perturbed at the way his 1903 book, *Principia Ethica*, helped to spawn a whole shoal of not so very different views in the English-language world – "subjectivism," "emotivism," "non-cognitivism," etc. As he himself noted, his answer to the question "What is good?" – namely, that "good is good, and that is the end of the matter" – hardly sounds one to quicken the blood.

Moore was less vexed, presumably, by the dithyrambic welcome given by the Bloomsbury group to the final chapter of the book, with its proclamation of "personal affections and aes-thetic enjoyments [as] . . . by *far* the greatest goods," which prompted J. M. Keynes to speak of the book as "the beginning of a renaissance, the opening of a new heaven on earth."[1] But among professional philosophers, for whom this personal

From G. E. Moore, *Principia Ethica*. Cambridge: Cam-bridge University Press, 1960, pp. 1–3, 5–21.

credo rather contradicted Moore's own perception of the proper "analytical" role of moral philo-sophy, it was not Chapter 5 but Chapter 1 that heralded a true renaissance. This is the chapter in which Moore launches his famous attack on the "naturalistic fallacy."

Three remarks on this expression, so much part of the contemporary ethical lexicon, are in order. First, it was a misnomer; for what Moore was attacking was the attempt to define "good" by equating good with *any* other property, natural or otherwise. The "fallacy" is as much committed by someone who equates "good" with "commanded by God" as by someone who identifies it with "plea-surable." Thus it is perfectly possible to join in Moore's attack while remaining a "naturalist" in the "broad, useful" sense of adhering to an "ethical view that stems from the general attitude that man is part of nature."[2] Second, it is not clear that many earlier philosophers ever committed the "fallacy" in the crass form that Moore char-acterizes it. Certainly it was unjust of him to accuse Mill of an "artless use of the naturalistic fallacy," or of simply *equating* the "desirable" and the "desired" by stipulative definition. But this, perhaps, matters less than it might seem. Moore's main objection to the "fallacy" (§13) is that someone who defines "good" as, say, "pleasurable" reduces what is intended as a substantive moral claim, "Pleasure alone is good," to the tautology "Pleasure alone is pleasurable," and illegitim-ately precludes even raising the question "Is plea-sure good?" Suitably amended, this objection would also be effective against philosophers who, without bluntly identifying good and pleasure, nevertheless insist that we could not really understand moral concepts except in terms of pleasure. And that is a kind of insistence very familiar in the history of ethics. Bentham, for example, denied that "the word *right* can have any meaning without reference to utility."

The third remark is that, if it was questionable to foist on Hume (I.14) the thesis that "ought" cannot be derived from "is" – that evaluative judgments cannot be deduced from factual premises – it is certainly wrong to suppose that this was Moore's thesis in rejecting "the naturalistic fallacy." (Unfortunately, the expression is often taken these days to refer to *any* attempt to derive an "ought" from an "is.") For Moore, "good" is indefinable because it refers to an absolutely simple, "non-natural" property. That certain things, such as friendship, have this property is a fact which we are able to "see" or intuit, and one from which obligations can be deduced – for what a person ought to do, says Moore, is to produce good. As we will see in I.22, in connection with C. L. Stevenson's article, it is only when this "intuitionist" thesis is rejected – as it was by the Logical Positivists in the 1920s – that dismissal of the "naturalistic fallacy" can yield any general thesis about the impossibility of moving from statements of facts to the making of moral judgments.

In the short term, however, Moore's main impact was not upon iconoclastic thinkers, such as the "emotivists" (whose doctrine he strongly opposed), but upon highly conservative philosophers standing in the "moral sense" tradition of British ethics, such as W. D. Ross (see I.20).[3] Nevertheless, the time-bomb planted by Moore was ticking away, timed to go off during the era after the First World War when any confidence in a universally shared intuitive faculty capable of giving moral guidance to our lives had itself, and for obvious reasons, exploded.

Notes

1 From his *Two Memoirs*, quoted in J. Skorupski, *English-Language Philosophy 1750–1945*, Oxford: Oxford University Press, 1993, p. 152.

2 B. Williams, *Ethics and the Limits of Philosophy*, London: Fontana, 1985, p. 121.

3 For Moore's rejection of "emotivism," see his "Replies" in P. A. Schilpp, ed., The *Philosophy of G. E. Moore*, Evanston, IL: Northwestern University Press, 1942.

Moore, *Principia Ethica*

Chapter 1: The Subject-matter of Ethics

(1) It is very easy to point out some among our everyday judgements, with the truth of which ethics is undoubtedly concerned. Whenever we say, 'So and so is a good man,' or 'That fellow is a villain'; whenever we ask, 'What ought I to do?' or 'Is it wrong for me to do like this?'; whenever we hazard such remarks as 'Temperance is a virtue and drunkenness a vice' – it is undoubtedly the business of ethics to discuss such questions and such statements; to argue what is the true answer when we ask what it is right to do, and to give reasons for thinking that our statements about the character of persons or the morality of actions are true or false. In the vast majority of cases, where we make statements involving any of the terms 'virtue', 'vice', 'duty', 'right', 'ought', 'good', 'bad', we are making ethical judgements; and if we wish to discuss their truth, we shall be discussing a point of ethics.

So much as this is not disputed; but it falls very far short of defining the province of ethics. That province may indeed be defined as the whole truth about that which is at the same time common to all such judgements and peculiar to them. But we have still to ask the question: what is it that is thus common and peculiar? And this is a question to which very different answers have been given by ethical philosophers of acknowledged reputation, and none of them, perhaps, completely satisfactory.

(2) If we take such examples as those given above, we shall not be far wrong in saying that they are all of them concerned with the question of 'conduct' – with the question, what, in the conduct of us, human beings, is good, and what is

bad, what is right, and what is wrong. For when we say that a man is good, we commonly mean that he acts rightly; when we say that drunkenness is a vice, we commonly mean that to get drunk is a wrong or wicked action. And this discussion of human conduct is, in fact, that with which the name 'ethics' is most intimately associated. It is so associated by derivation; and conduct is undoubtedly by far the commonest and most generally interesting object of ethical judgements.

Accordingly we find that many ethical philosophers are disposed to accept as an adequate definition of 'ethics' the statement that it deals with the question what is good or bad in human conduct. They hold that its enquiries are properly confined to 'conduct' or to 'practice'; they hold that the name 'practical philosophy' covers all the matter with which it has to do. Now, without discussing the proper meaning of the word (for verbal questions are properly left to the writers of dictionaries and other persons interested in literature; philosophy, as we shall see, has no concern with them), I may say that I intend to use 'ethics' to cover more than this – a usage, for which there is, I think, quite sufficient authority. I am using it to cover an enquiry for which, at all events, there is no other word: the general enquiry into what is good.

Ethics is undoubtedly concerned with the question what good conduct is; but, being concerned with this, it obviously does not start at the beginning, unless it is prepared to tell us what is good as well as what is conduct. For 'good conduct' is a complex notion: all conduct is not good, for some is certainly bad and some may be indifferent. And on the other hand, other things beside conduct may be good; and if they are so, then 'good' denotes some property that is common to them and conduct; and if we examine good conduct alone of all good things, then we shall be in danger of mistaking for this property, some property which is not shared by those other things: and thus we shall have made a mistake about ethics even in this limited sense; for we shall not know what good conduct really is. This is a mistake which many writers have actually made, from limiting their enquiry to conduct. And hence I shall try to avoid it by considering first what is good in general; hoping, that if we can arrive at any certainty about this, it will be much easier to settle the question of good conduct: for we all know pretty well what 'conduct' is. This,

then, is our first question: What is good? and What is bad? and to the discussion of this question (or these questions) I give the name of ethics, since that science must, at all events, include it. . . .

(5)   But our question 'What is good?' may have still another meaning. We may, in the third place, mean to ask, not what thing or things are good, but how 'good' is to be defined. This is an enquiry which belongs only to ethics . . . and this is the enquiry which will occupy us first.

It is an enquiry to which most special attention should be directed; since this question, how 'good' is to be defined, is the most fundamental question in all ethics. That which is meant by 'good' is, in fact, except its converse 'bad,' the *only* simple object of thought which is peculiar to ethics. Its definition is, therefore, the most essential point in the definition of ethics; and moreover a mistake with regard to it entails a far larger number of erroneous ethical judgements than any other. Unless this first question be fully understood, and its true answer clearly recognized, the rest of ethics is as good as useless from the point of view of systematic knowledge. True ethical judgements . . . may indeed be made by those who do not know the answer to this question as well as by those who do; and it goes without saying that the two classes of people may lead equally good lives. But it is extremely unlikely that the *most general* ethical judgements will be equally valid, in the absence of a true answer to this question: I shall presently try to shew that the gravest errors have been largely due to beliefs in a false answer. And, in any case, it is impossible that, till the answer to this question be known, any one should know *what is the evidence* for any ethical judgement whatsoever. But the main object of ethics, as a systematic science, is to give correct *reasons* for thinking that this or that is good; and, unless this question be answered, such reasons cannot be given. Even, therefore, apart from the fact that a false answer leads to false conclusions, the present enquiry is a most necessary and important part of the science of ethics.

(6)   What, then, is good? How is good to be defined? Now, it may be thought that this is a verbal question. A definition does indeed often mean the expressing of one word's meaning in other words. But this is not the sort of definition I am asking for. Such a definition can never be of ultimate importance in any study except lexicography. If I wanted that kind of definition

I should have to consider in the first place how people generally used the word 'good'; but my business is not with its proper usage, as established by custom. I should, indeed, be foolish, if I tried to use it for something which it did not usually denote: if, for instance, I were to announce that, whenever I used the word 'good', I must be understood to be thinking of that object which is usually denoted by the word 'table'. I shall, therefore, use the word in the sense in which I think it is ordinarily used; but at the same time I am not anxious to discuss whether I am right in thinking that it is so used. My business is solely with that object or idea, which I hold, rightly or wrongly, that the word is generally used to stand for. What I want to discover is the nature of that object or idea, and about this I am extremely anxious to arrive at an agreement.

But if we understand the question in this sense, my answer to it may seem a very disappointing one. If I am asked 'What is good?' my answer is that good is good, and that is the end of the matter. Or if I am asked 'How is good to be defined?' my answer is that it cannot be defined, and that is all I have to say about it. But disappointing as these answers may appear, they are of the very last importance. To readers who are familiar with philosophic terminology, I can express their importance by saying that they amount to this: that propositions about the good are all of them synthetic and never analytic; and that is plainly no trivial matter. And the same thing may be expressed more popularly by saying that, if I am right, then nobody can foist upon us such an axiom as that 'Pleasure is the only good' or that 'The good is the desired' on the pretence that this is 'the very meaning of the word'.

(7)   Let us, then, consider this position. My point is that 'good' is a simple notion, just as 'yellow' is a simple notion; that just as you cannot, by any manner of means, explain to anyone who does not already know it, what yellow is, so you cannot explain what good is. Definitions of the kind that I was asking for, definitions which describe the real nature of the object or notion denoted by a word, and which do not merely tell us what the word is used to mean, are only possible when the object or notion in question is something complex. You can give a definition of a horse, because a horse has many different properties and qualities, all of which you can enumerate. But when you have enumerated them all, when you have reduced a horse to his simplest terms, then you can no longer define those terms. They are simply something which you think of or perceive, and to any one who cannot think of or perceive them, you can never, by any definition, make their nature known. It may perhaps be objected to this that we are able to describe to others objects which they have never seen or thought of. We can, for instance, make a man understand what a chimaera is, although he has never heard of one or seen one. You can tell him that it is an animal with a lioness's head and body, with a goat's head growing from the middle of its back, and with a snake in place of a tail. But here the object which you are describing is a complex object; it is entirely composed of parts with which we are all perfectly familiar – a snake, a goat, a lioness; and we know, too, the manner in which those parts are to be put together, because we know what is meant by the middle of a lioness's back, and where her tail is wont to grow. And so it is with all objects, not previously known, which we are able to define: they are all complex; all composed of parts, which may themselves, in the first instance, be capable of similar definition, but which must in the end be reducible to simplest parts, which can no longer be defined. But yellow and good, we say, are not complex: they are notions of that simple kind, out of which definitions are composed and with which the power of further defining ceases.

(8)   When we say, as Webster says, 'The definition of horse is "A hoofed quadruped of the genus *Equus*",' we may, in fact, mean three different things, (*a*) We may mean merely: 'When I say "horse", you are to understand that I am talking about a hoofed quadruped of the genus *Equus*.' This might be called the arbitrary verbal definition: and I do not mean that good is indefinable in that sense. (*b*) We may mean, as Webster ought to mean: 'When most English people say "horse", they mean a hoofed quadruped of the genus *Equus*.' This may be called the verbal definition proper, and I do not say that good is indefinable in this sense either; for it is certainly possible to discover how people use a word: otherwise, we could never have known that 'good' may be translated by *gut* in German and by *bon* in French. But (*c*) we may, when we define horse, mean something much more important. We may mean that a certain object, which we all of us know, is composed in a certain manner: that

it has four legs, a head, a heart, a liver, etc., etc., all of them arranged in definite relations to one another. It is in this sense that I deny good to be definable. I say that it is not composed of any parts, which we can substitute for it in our minds when we are thinking of it. We might think just as clearly and correctly about a horse if we thought of all its parts and their arrangement instead of thinking of the whole: we could, I say, think how a horse differed from a donkey just as well, just as truly, in this way as now we do, only not so easily; but there is nothing whatsoever which we could so substitute for good; and that is what I mean, when I say that good is indefinable.

(9) But I am afraid I have still not removed the chief difficulty which may prevent acceptance of the proposition that good is indefinable. I do not mean to say that *the* good, that which is good, is thus indefinable; if I did think so, I should not be writing on ethics, for my main object is to help towards discovering that definition. It is just because I think there will be less risk of error in our search for a definition of 'the good', that I am now insisting that *good* is indefinable. I must try to explain the difference between these two. I suppose it may be granted that 'good' is an adjective. Well 'the good', 'that which is good', must therefore be the substantive to which the adjective 'good' will apply: it must be the whole of that to which the adjective will apply, and the adjective must *always* truly apply to it. But if it is that to which the adjective will apply, it must be something different from that adjective itself; and the whole of that something different, whatever it is, will be our definition of *the* good. Now it may be that this something will have other adjectives beside 'good' that will apply to it. It may be full of pleasure, for example; it may be intelligent: and if these two adjectives are really part of its definition, then it will certainly be true that pleasure and intelligence are good. And many people appear to think that if we say 'Pleasure and intelligence are good,' or if we say 'Only pleasure and intelligence are good,' we are defining 'good'. Well, I cannot deny that propositions of this nature may sometimes be called definitions; I do not know well enough how the word is generally used to decide upon this point. I only wish it to be understood that that is not what I mean when I say there is no possible definition of good, and that I shall not mean this if I use the word again.

I do most fully believe that some true proposition of the form 'Intelligence is good and intelligence alone is good' can be found; if none could be found, our definition of *the* good would be impossible. As it is, I believe *the* good to be definable; and yet I still say that good itself is indefinable.

(10) 'Good', then, if we mean by it that quality which we assert to belong to a thing, when we say that the thing is good, is incapable of any definition, in the most important sense of that word. The most important sense of 'definition' is that in which a definition states what are the parts which invariably compose a certain whole; and in this sense 'good' has no definition because it is simple and has no parts. It is one of those innumerable objects of thought which are themselves incapable of definition, because they are the ultimate terms by reference to which whatever *is* capable of definition must be defined. That there must be an indefinite number of such terms is obvious, on reflection; since we cannot define anything except by an analysis, which, when carried as far as it will go, refers us to something which is simply different from anything else, and which by that ultimate difference explains the peculiarity of the whole which we are defining: for every whole contains some parts which are common to other wholes also. There is, therefore, no intrinsic difficulty in the contention that 'good' denotes a simple and indefinable quality. There are many other instances of such qualities.

Consider yellow, for example. We may try to define it, by describing its physical equivalent; we may state what kind of light-vibrations must stimulate the normal eye in order that we may perceive it. But a moment's reflection is sufficient to shew that those light-vibrations are not themselves what we mean by yellow. *They* are not what we perceive. Indeed we should never have been able to discover their existence unless we had first been struck by the patent difference of quality between the different colours. The most we can be entitled to say of those vibrations is that they are what corresponds in space to the yellow which we actually perceive.

Yet a mistake of this simple kind has commonly been made about 'good'. It may be true that all things which are good are *also* something else, just as it is true that all things which are yellow produce a certain kind of vibration in the light. And it is a fact that ethics aims at discovering what are those other properties belonging to all things which are good. But far too many philosophers have thought that when they named those other properties they were actually defining good; that these properties, in fact, were simply not 'other', but absolutely and entirely the same with goodness. This view I propose to call the 'naturalistic fallacy' and of it I shall now endeavour to dispose.

(11) Let us consider what it is such philosophers say. And first it is to be noticed that they do not agree among themselves. They not only say that they are right as to what good is, but they endeavour to prove that other people who say that it is something else, are wrong. One, for instance, will affirm that good is pleasure; another, perhaps, that good is that which is desired; and each of these will argue eagerly to prove that the other is wrong. But how is that possible? One of them says that good is nothing but the object of desire, and at the same time tries to prove that it is not pleasure. But from his first assertion, that good just means the object of desire, one of two things must follow as regards his proof:

(*a*) He may be trying to prove that the object of desire is not pleasure. But, if this be all, where is his ethics? The position he is maintaining is merely a psychological one. Desire is something which occurs in our minds, and pleasure is something else which so occurs; and our would-be ethical philosopher is merely holding that the latter is not the object of the former. But what has that to do with the question in dispute? His opponent held the ethical proposition that pleasure was the good, and although he should prove a million times over the psychological proposition that pleasure is not the object of desire, he is no nearer proving his opponent to be wrong. The position is like this. One man says a triangle is a circle: another replies 'A triangle is a straight line, and I will prove to you that I am right: *for*' (this is the only argument) 'a straight line is not a circle.' 'That is quite true,' the other may reply; 'but nevertheless a triangle is a circle, and you have said nothing whatever to prove the contrary. What is proved is that one of us is wrong, for we agree that a triangle cannot be both a straight line and a circle: but which is wrong, there can be no earthly means of proving, since you define triangle as straight line and I define it as circle.' – Well, that is one alternative which any naturalistic ethics has to face; if good is *defined*

as something else, it is then impossible either to prove that any other definition is wrong or even to deny such definition.

(*b*) The other alternative will scarcely be more welcome. It is that the discussion is after all a verbal one. When A says 'Good means pleasant' and B says 'Good means desired,' they may merely wish to assert that most people have used the word for what is pleasant and for what is desired respectively. And this is quite an interesting subject for discussion: only it is not a whit more an ethical discussion than the last was. Nor do I think that any exponent of naturalistic ethics would be willing to allow that this was all he meant. They are all so anxious to persuade us that what they call the good is what we really ought to do. 'Do, pray, act so, because the word "good" is generally used to denote actions of this nature': such, on this view, would be the substance of their teaching. And in so far as they tell us how we ought to act, their teaching is truly ethical, as they mean it to be. But how perfectly absurd is the reason they would give for it! 'You are to do this, because most people use a certain word to denote conduct such as this.' 'You are to say the thing which is not, because most people call it lying.' That is an argument just as good! – My dear sirs, what we want to know from you as ethical teachers, is not how people use a word; it is not even, what kind of actions they approve, which the use of this word 'good' may certainly imply: what we want to know is simply what *is* good. We may indeed agree that what most people do think good, is actually so; we shall at all events be glad to know their opinions: but when we say their opinions about what *is* good, we do mean what we say; we do not care whether they call that thing which they mean 'horse' or 'table' or 'chair,' *gut* or *bon* or ἀγαθός; we want to know what it is that they so call. When they say 'Pleasure is good,' we cannot believe that they merely mean 'Pleasure is pleasure' and nothing more than that.

(12) Suppose a man says 'I am pleased'; and suppose that is not a lie or a mistake but the truth. Well, if it is true, what does that mean? It means that his mind, a certain definite mind, distinguished by certain definite marks from all others, has at this moment a certain definite feeling called pleasure. 'Pleased' *means* nothing but having pleasure, and though we may be more pleased or less pleased, and even, we may

admit for the present, have one or another kind of pleasure; yet in so far as it is pleasure we have, whether there be more or less of it, and whether it be of one kind or another, what we have is one definite thing, absolutely indefinable, some one thing that is the same in all the various degrees and in all the various kinds of it that there may be. We may be able to say how it is related to other things: that, for example, it is in the mind, that it causes desire, that we are conscious of it, etc., etc. We can, I say, describe its relations to other things, but define it we can *not*. And if anybody tried to define pleasure for us as being any other natural object; if anybody were to say, for instance, that pleasure *means* the sensation of red, and were to proceed to deduce from that that pleasure is a colour, we should be entitled to laugh at him and to distrust his future statements about pleasure. Well, that would be the same fallacy which I have called the naturalistic fallacy. That 'pleased' does not mean 'having the sensation of red', or anything else whatever, does not prevent us from understanding what it does mean. It is enough for us to know that 'pleased' does mean 'having the sensation of pleasure', and though pleasure is absolutely indefinable, though pleasure is pleasure and nothing else whatever, yet we feel no difficulty in saying that we are pleased. The reason is, of course, that when I say 'I am pleased,' I do *not* mean that 'I' am the same thing as 'having pleasure'. And similarly no difficulty need be found in my saying that 'pleasure is good' and yet not meaning that 'pleasure' is the same thing as 'good', that pleasure *means* good, and that good *means* pleasure. If I were to imagine that when I said 'I am pleased,' I meant that I was exactly the same thing as 'pleased', I should not indeed call that a naturalistic fallacy, although it would be the same fallacy as I have called naturalistic with reference to ethics. The reason of this is obvious enough. When a man confuses two natural objects with one another, defining the one by the other, if for instance, he confuses himself, who is one natural object, with 'pleased' or with 'pleasure' which are others, then there is no reason to call the fallacy naturalistic. But if he confuses 'good', which is not in the same sense a natural object, with any natural object whatever, then there is a reason for calling that a naturalistic fallacy; its being made with regard to 'good' marks it as something quite specific, and this specific mistake deserves a name because it is so common. As for the reasons why good is not to be considered a natural object, they may be reserved for discussion in another place. But, for the present, it is sufficient to notice this: Even if it were a natural object, that would not alter the nature of the fallacy nor diminish its importance one whit. All that I have said about it would remain quite equally true: only the name which I have called it would not be so appropriate as I think it is. And I do not care about the name: what I do care about is the fallacy. It does not matter what we call it, provided we recognize it when we meet with it. It is to be met with in almost every book on ethics; and yet it is not recognized: and that is why it is necessary to multiply illustrations of it, and convenient to give it a name. It is a very simple fallacy indeed. When we say that an orange is yellow, we do not think our statement binds us to hold that 'orange' means nothing else than 'yellow', or that nothing can be yellow but an orange. Supposing the orange is also sweet! Does that bind us to say that 'sweet' is exactly the same thing as 'yellow', that 'sweet' must be defined as 'yellow'? And supposing it be recognized that 'yellow' just means 'yellow' and nothing else whatever, does that make it any more difficult to hold that oranges are yellow? Most certainly it does not: on the contrary, it would be absolutely meaningless to say that oranges were yellow, unless yellow did in the end mean just 'yellow' and nothing else whatever – unless it was absolutely indefinable. We should not get any very clear notion about things, which are yellow – we should not get very far with our science, if we were bound to hold that everything which was yellow, *meant* exactly the same thing as yellow. We should find we had to hold that an orange was exactly the same thing as a stool, a piece of paper, a lemon, anything you like. We could prove any number of absurdities; but should we be the nearer to the truth? Why, then, should it be different with 'good'? Why, if good is good and indefinable, should I be held to deny that pleasure is good? Is there any difficulty in holding both to be true at once? On the contrary, there is no meaning in saying that pleasure is good, unless good is something different from pleasure. It is absolutely useless, so far as ethics is concerned, to prove, as Mr [Herbert] Spencer tries to do, that increase of pleasure coincides with increase of life, unless good *means* something different from either life or pleasure. He might just as well try to prove that an orange is yellow by shewing that it always is wrapped up in paper.

(13) In fact, if it is not the case that 'good' denotes something simple and indefinable, only two alternatives are possible: either it is a complex, a given whole, about the correct analysis of which there may be disagreement; or else it means nothing at all, and there is no such subject as ethics. In general, however, ethical philosophers have attempted to define good, without recognizing what such an attempt must mean. They actually use arguments which involve one or both of the absurdities considered in §11. We are, therefore, justified in concluding that the attempt to define good is chiefly due to want of clearness as to the possible nature of definition. There are, in fact, only two serious alternatives to be considered, in order to establish the conclusion that 'good' does denote a simple and indefinable notion. It might possibly denote a complex, as 'horse' does; or it might have no meaning at all. Neither of these possibilities has, however, been clearly conceived and seriously maintained, as such, by those who presume to define good; and both may be dismissed by a simple appeal to facts.

(a) The hypothesis that disagreement about the meaning of good is disagreement with regard to the correct analysis of a given whole, may be most plainly seen to be incorrect by consideration of the fact that, whatever definition be offered, it may be always asked, with significance, of the complex so defined, whether it is itself good. To take, for instance, one of the more plausible, because one of the more complicated, of such proposed definitions, it may easily be thought, at first sight, that to be good may mean to be that which we desire to desire. Thus if we apply this definition to a particular instance and say 'When we think that A is good, we are thinking that A is one of the things which we desire to desire,' our proposition may seem quite plausible. But, if we carry the investigation further, and ask ourselves 'Is it good to desire to desire A?' it is apparent, on a little reflection, that this question is itself as intelligible, as the original question 'Is A good?' – that we are, in fact, now asking for exactly the same information about the desire to desire A, for which we formerly asked with regard to A itself. But it is also apparent that the meaning of this second question cannot be correctly analysed into 'Is the desire to desire A one

of the things which we desire to desire?': we have not before our minds anything so complicated as the question 'Do we desire to desire to desire to desire A?' Moreover any one can easily convince himself by inspection that the predicate of this proposition – 'good' – is positively different from the notion of 'desiring to desire' which enters into its subject: 'That we should desire to desire A is good' is *not* merely equivalent to 'That A should be good is good.' It may indeed be true that what we desire to desire is always also good; perhaps even the converse may be true: but it is very doubtful whether this is the case, and the mere fact that we understand very well what is meant by doubting it, shews clearly that we have two different notions before our minds.

(b) And the same consideration is sufficient to dismiss the hypothesis that 'good' has no meaning whatsoever. It is very natural to make the mistake of supposing that what is universally true is of such a nature that its negation would be self-contradictory: the importance which has been assigned to analytic propositions in the history of philosophy shews how easy such a mistake is. And thus it is very easy to conclude that what seems to be a universal ethical principle is in fact an identical proposition; that, if, for example, whatever is called 'good' seems to be pleasant, the proposition 'Pleasure is the good' does not assert a connection between two different notions, but involves only one, that of pleasure, which is easily recognized as a distinct entity. But whoever will attentively consider with himself what is actually before his mind when he asks the question 'Is pleasure (or whatever it may be) after all good?' can easily satisfy himself that he is not merely wondering whether pleasure is pleasant. And if he will try this experiment with each suggested definition in succession, he may become expert enough to recognize that in every case he has before his mind a unique object, with regard to the connection of which with any other object, a distinct question may be asked. Every one does in fact understand the question 'Is this good?' When he thinks of it, his state of mind is different from what it would be, were he asked 'Is this pleasant, or desired, or approved?' It has a distinct meaning for him, even though he may not recognize in what respect it is distinct. Whenever he thinks of 'intrinsic value', or 'intrinsic worth', or says that a thing 'ought to exist', he has before his mind the unique object

– the unique property of things – which I mean by 'good'. Everybody is constantly aware of this notion, although he may never become aware at all that it is different from other notions of which he is also aware. But, for correct ethical reasoning, it is extremely important that he should become aware of this fact; and, as soon as the nature of the problem is clearly understood, there should be little difficulty in advancing so far in analysis.

(14) 'Good', then, is indefinable; and yet, so far as I know, there is only one ethical writer, Professor Henry Sidgwick, who has clearly recognized and stated this fact. We shall see, indeed, how far many of the most reputed ethical systems fall short of drawing the conclusions which follow from such a recognition. At present I will only quote one instance, which will serve to illustrate the meaning and importance of this principle that 'good' is indefinable, or, as Professor Sidgwick says, an 'unanalysable notion'. It is an instance to which Professor Sidgwick himself refers in a note on the passage, in which he argues that 'ought' is unanalysable.[1]

'Bentham,' says Sidgwick, 'explains that his fundamental principle "states the greatest happiness of all those whose interest is in question as being the right and proper end of human action"'; and yet 'his language in other passages of the same chapter would seem to imply' that he *means* by the word 'right' 'conducive to the general happiness'. Professor Sidgwick sees that, if you take these two statements together, you get the absurd result that 'greatest happiness is the end of human action, which is conducive to the general happiness'; and so absurd does it seem to him to call this result, as Bentham calls it, 'the fundamental principle of a moral system', that he suggests that Bentham cannot have meant it. Yet Professor Sidgwick himself states elsewhere that Psychological Hedonism is 'not seldom confounded with Egoistic Hedonism',[2] and that confusion, as we shall see, rests chiefly on that same fallacy, the naturalistic fallacy, which is implied in Bentham's statements. Professor Sidgwick admits therefore that this fallacy is sometimes committed, absurd as it is; and I am inclined to think that Bentham may really have been one of those who committed it. Mill, as we shall see, certainly did commit it. In any case, whether Bentham committed it or not, his doctrine, as above quoted, will serve as a very good illustration of

this fallacy, and of the importance of the contrary proposition that good is indefinable.

Let us consider this doctrine. Bentham seems to imply, so Professor Sidgwick says, that the word 'right' *means* 'conducive to general happiness'. Now this, by itself, need not necessarily involve the naturalistic fallacy. For the word 'right' is very commonly appropriated to actions which lead to the attainment of what is good; which are regarded as *means* to the ideal and not as ends-in-themselves. This use of 'right', as denoting what is good as a means, whether or not it be also good as an end, is indeed the use to which I shall confine the word. Had Bentham been using 'right' in this sense, it might be perfectly consistent for him to *define* right as 'conducive to the general happiness', *provided only* (and notice this proviso) he had already proved, or laid down as an axiom, that general happiness was *the* good, or (what is equivalent to this) that general happiness alone was good. For in that case he would have already defined *the* good as general happiness (a position perfectly consistent, as we have seen, with the contention that 'good' is indefinable), and, since right was to be defined as 'conducive to *the* good', it would actually *mean* 'conducive to general happiness'. But this method of escape from the charge of having committed the naturalistic fallacy has been closed by Bentham himself. For his fundamental principle is, we see, that the greatest happiness of all concerned is the *right* and proper *end* of human action. He applies the word 'right', therefore, to the end, as such, not only to the means which are conducive to it; and, that being so, right can no longer be defined as 'conducive to the general happiness', without involving the fallacy in question. For now it is obvious that the definition of right as conducive to general happiness can be used by him in support of the fundamental principle that general happiness is the right end; instead of being itself derived from that principle. If right, by definition, means conducive to general happiness, then it is obvious that general happiness is the right end. It is not necessary now first to prove or assert that general happiness is the right end, before right is defined as conducive to general happiness – a perfectly valid procedure; but on the contrary the definition of right as conducive to general happiness proves general happiness to be the right end – a perfectly invalid procedure, since in this case the statement that 'general happiness is the right end of human action' is not an ethical principle at all, but either, as we have seen, a proposition about the meaning of words, or else a proposition about the *nature* of general happiness, not about its rightness or goodness.

Now, I do not wish the importance I assign to this fallacy to be misunderstood. The discovery of it does not at all refute Bentham's contention that greatest happiness is the proper end of human action, if that be understood as an ethical proposition, as he undoubtedly intended it. That principle may be true all the same; we shall consider whether it is so in succeeding chapters. Bentham might have maintained it, as Professor Sidgwick does, even if the fallacy had been pointed out to him. What I am maintaining is that the *reasons* which he actually gives for his ethical proposition are fallacious ones so far as they consist in a definition of right. What I suggest is that he did not perceive them to be fallacious; that, if he had done so, he would have been led to seek for other reasons in support of his Utilitarianism; and that, had he sought for other reasons, he *might* have found none which he thought to be sufficient. In that case he would have changed his whole system – a most important consequence. It is undoubtedly also possible that he would have thought other reasons to be sufficient, and in that case his ethical system, in its main results, would still have stood. But, even in this latter case, his use of the fallacy would be a serious objection to him as an ethical philosopher. For it is the business of ethics, I must insist, not only to obtain true results, but also to find valid reasons for them. The direct object of ethics is knowledge and not practice; and any one who uses the naturalistic fallacy has certainly not fulfilled this first object, however correct his practical principles may be.

My objections to Naturalism are then, in the first place, that it offers no reason at all, far less any valid reason, for any ethical principle whatever; and in this it already fails to satisfy the requirements of ethics, as a scientific study. But in the second place I contend that, though it gives a reason for no ethical principle, it is a *cause* of the acceptance of false principles – it deludes the mind into accepting ethical principles, which are false; and in this it is contrary to every aim of ethics. It is easy to see that if we start with

a definition of right conduct as conduct conducive to general happiness; then, knowing that right conduct is universally conduct conducive to the good, we very easily arrive at the result that the good is general happiness. If, on the other hand, we once recognize that we must start our ethics without a definition, we shall be much more apt to look about us, before we adopt any ethical principle whatever; and the more we look about us, the less likely are we to adopt a false one. It may be replied to this: Yes, but we shall look about us just as much, before we settle on our definition, and are therefore just as likely to be right. But I will try to shew that this is not the case. If we start with the conviction that a definition of good can be found, we start with the conviction that good *can mean* nothing else than some one property of things; and our only business will then be to discover what that property is. But if we recognize that, so far as the meaning of good goes, anything whatever may be good, we start with a much more open mind. Moreover, apart from the fact that, when we think we have a definition, we cannot logically defend our ethical principles in any way whatever, we shall also be much less apt to defend them well, even if illogically. For we shall start with the conviction that good must mean so and so, and shall therefore be inclined either to misunderstand our opponent's arguments or to cut them short with the reply, 'This is not an open question: the very meaning of the word decides it; no one can think otherwise except through confusion.'

(15) Our first conclusion as to the subject-matter of ethics is, then, that there is a simple, indefinable, unanalysable object of thought by reference to which it must be defined. By what name we call this unique object is a matter of indifference, so long as we clearly recognize what it is and that it does differ from other objects. The words which are commonly taken as the signs of ethical judgements all do refer to it; and they are expressions of ethical judgements solely because they do so refer. [. . .]

Notes

1   *Methods of Ethics*, London: Macmillan, 1962, book I, chapter iii, §1.
2   Ibid., book I, chapter iv, §1.

20

W. D. Ross, *The Right and the Good,* Chapter 2

Introduction

In the preamble to the previous chapter (I.19), it was noted that G. E. Moore's immediate influence was upon some philosophically conservative moral philosophers, who were, in effect, rehabilitating the ethical intuitionism of such eighteenth-century writers as Richard Price (1723–91), author of *A Review of the Principal Questions in Morals* (1757).[1] The most prominent of these later intuitionists were the Oxford philosophers H. A. Prichard (1871–1947) and W. D. (later Sir David) Ross (1877–1971). A more precise label for them would be "deontological intuitionists": for while they agreed with Moore that good was an intuitable property, they rejected his view that deontological (from the Greek word meaning "what is binding") concepts, such as "right," "duty," and "obligation," could be reduced to, or understood in terms of, the notion of good. For both men, the right or obligatory is itself intuited or "apprehended" – and independently of good that right action might produce. Consciously aping Moore's claim that "good is good, and that is the end of the matter," Prichard held that no reasons can be given for why some action is right or obligatory, since its rightness is "apprehended

From W. D. Ross, *The Right and the Good.* Oxford: Clarendon Press, 1930, pp. 16–24, 28–37 (some notes and passages omitted).

directly by an act of moral thinking." Moral philosophy, if its aim is to search for such reasons, simply "rests on a mistake."[2]

Ross has been described as a "less fanatical" intuitionist than Prichard, and this is because of a crucial amendment in the direction of common sense that he makes, in Chapter 2 of *The Right and the Good* (1930), to his predecessor's position. An obvious objection to Prichard is that we do *not* at all generally just "see" what our duty in some situation is. If we did, we would hardly confront the moral dilemmas we often face. Ross accommodates this objection by claiming that what a person directly apprehends is not that a certain action is actually a duty, but that performing it is a "prima facie" duty in virtue, say, of its being the repayment of a debt. That this action is prima facie obligatory is perfectly compatible with its also being prima facie non-obligatory: for it may at the same time be an action which involves breaking a promise or causing harm to an undeserving victim. A prima facie duty is explained as one that *would* be an actual duty, a "duty sans phrase," in the absence of competing considerations. Whereas our prima facie duties can be known for certain, verdicts as to our actual duties, where prima facie considerations collide, can only be a matter of "probable judgement."

Despite Ross's important concession to common sense, he has come in for many criticisms. Some of these miss their mark. It is not, for example, Ross's view that one has only to hear a moral principle stated to "see" its truth. For him, what we apprehend, in the first instance, is not the truth of principles, but the prima facie obligatory quality of particular actions. Another criticism, levelled against the whole idea of objective moral properties, will occupy us in a later chapter (I.22). A third criticism, predictable in the present climate, is that even the prima facie obligatoriness of actions is hardly the self-evident matter Ross assumes. It might be argued, for instance, that the duty to repay debts only exists in debt-incurring societies whose moral basis is questionable. More harshly, some have held that Ross's ethics breathes a complacent, ivory tower confidence in a universal moral sense that already seemed antediluvian by 1930.

Despite such criticisms, Ross is today enjoying renewed attention, partly because of his sharp arguments – several of which occur in the following pages – against utilitarian and teleological conceptions of right and duty. But his notion of prima facie duties is also frequently invoked as an antidote to the "universalizability thesis," associated with R. M. Hare (1919–2002) and Immanuel Kant (I.15), that an action is right if and only if it falls under some exceptionless moral principle. This has not prevented the so-called

"particularist" critics of Hare from arguing that Ross is also too much of a "generalist." Not only, they argue, are there no features – such as those characteristic of keeping a promise – that always make an action actually right; there are no features that always make it prima facie right. In some circumstances – those of a parlor-game in which breaking one's word is a crucial ingredient, say – the failure to keep one's word may be either morally irrelevant or even morally required.[3] Ross's views will surely continue to be discussed as long as this unresolved dispute between "particularists" and "generalists" continues.

Notes

1 Oxford: Oxford University Press, 1948.
2 See Prichard's "Does Moral Philosophy Rest on a Mistake?" (1912), in his *Moral Obligation*, Oxford: Oxford University Press, 1949.
3 For R. M. Hare, see his *Freedom and Reason*, Oxford: Oxford University Press, 1963. For the "particularist" criticism, see Jonathan Dancy, *Moral Reasons*, Oxford: Blackwell, 1993, Chapters 5–6.

Ross, *The Right and the Good*

Chapter 2: What Makes Right Acts Right?

The real point at issue between hedonism and utilitarianism on the one hand and their opponents on the other is not whether 'right' means 'productive of so and so'; for it cannot with any plausibility be maintained that it does. The point at issue is that to which we now pass, viz. whether there is any general character which makes right acts right, and if so, what it is. Among the main historical attempts to state a single characteristic of all right actions which is the foundation of their rightness are those made by egoism and utilitarianism. But I do not propose to discuss these, not because the subject is unimportant, but because it has been dealt with so often and so well already, and because there has come to be so much agreement among moral philosophers that neither of these theories is satisfactory. A much more attractive theory

has been put forward by Professor Moore: that what makes actions right is that they are productive of more *good* than could have been produced by any other action open to the agent.[1]

This theory is in fact the culmination of all the attempts to base rightness on productivity of some sort of result. The first form this attempt takes is the attempt to base rightness on conduciveness to the advantage or pleasure of the agent. This theory comes to grief over the fact, which stares us in the face, that a great part of duty consists in an observance of the rights and a furtherance of the interests of others, whatever the cost to ourselves may be. Plato and others may be right in holding that a regard for the rights of others never in the long run involves a loss of happiness for the agent, that 'the just life profits a man'. But this, even if true, is irrelevant to the rightness of the act. As soon as a man does an action *because* he thinks he will promote his own interests thereby, he is acting not from a sense of its rightness but from self-interest.

To the egoistic theory hedonistic utilitarianism supplies a much-needed amendment. It points out correctly that the fact that a certain pleasure will be enjoyed by the agent is no reason why he *ought* to bring it into being rather than an equal or greater pleasure to be enjoyed by another, though, human nature being what it is, it makes it not unlikely that he *will* try to bring it into being. But hedonistic utilitarianism in its turn needs a correction. On reflection it seems clear that pleasure is not the only thing in life that we think good in itself, that for instance we think the possession of a good character, or an intelligent understanding of the world, as good or better. A great advance is made by the substitution of 'productive of the greatest good' for 'productive of the greatest pleasure'.

Not only is this theory more attractive than hedonistic utilitarianism, but its logical relation to that theory is such that the latter could not be true unless *it* were true, while it might be true though hedonistic utilitarianism were not. It is in fact one of the logical bases of hedonistic utilitarianism. For the view that what produces the maximum pleasure is right has for its bases the views (1) that what produces the maximum good is right, and (2) that pleasure is the only thing good in itself. If they were not assuming that what produces the maximum *good* is right, the utilitarians' attempt to show that pleasure is the only thing good in itself, which is in fact the point they take most pains to establish, would have been quite irrelevant to their attempt to prove that only what produces the maximum *pleasure* is right. If, therefore, it can be shown that productivity of the maximum good is not what makes all right actions right, we shall *a fortiori* have refuted hedonistic utilitarianism.

When a plain man fulfils a promise because he thinks he ought to do so, it seems clear that he does so with no thought of its total consequences, still less with any opinion that these are likely to be the best possible. He thinks in fact much more of the past than of the future. What makes him think it right to act in a certain way is the fact that he has promised to do so – that and, usually, nothing more. That his act will produce the best possible consequences is not his reason for calling it right. What lends colour to the theory we are examining, then, is not the actions (which form probably a great majority of our actions) in which some such reflection as 'I

have promised' is the only reason we give ourselves for thinking a certain action right, but the exceptional cases in which the consequences of fulfilling a promise (for instance) would be so disastrous to others that we judge it right not to do so. It must of course be admitted that such cases exist. If I have promised to meet a friend at a particular time for some trivial purpose, I should certainly think myself justified in breaking my engagement if by doing so I could prevent a serious accident or bring relief to the victims of one. And the supporters of the view we are examining hold that my thinking so is due to my thinking that I shall bring more good into existence by the one action than by the other. A different account may, however, be given of the matter, an account which will, I believe, show itself to be the true one. It may be said that besides the duty of fulfilling promises I have and recognize a duty of relieving distress, and that when I think it right to do the latter at the cost of not doing the former, it is not because I think I shall produce more good thereby but because I think it the duty which is in the circumstances more of a duty. This account surely corresponds much more closely with what we really think in such a situation. If, so far as I can see, I could bring equal amounts of good into being by fulfilling my promise and by helping some one to whom I had made no promise, I should not hesitate to regard the former as my duty. Yet on the view that what is right is right because it is productive of the most good I should not so regard it.

There are two theories, each in its way simple, that offer a solution of such cases of conscience. One is the view of Kant, that there are certain duties of perfect obligation, such as those of fulfilling promises, of paying debts, of telling the truth, which admit of no exception whatever in favour of duties of imperfect obligation, such as that of relieving distress. The other is the view of, for instance, Professor Moore and Dr [Hastings] Rashdall, that there is only the duty of producing good, and that all 'conflicts of duties' should be resolved by asking 'by which action will most good be produced?' But it is more important that our theory fit the facts than that it be simple, and the account we have given above corresponds (it seems to me) better than either of the simpler theories with what we really think, viz. that normally promise-keeping, for example, should come before benevolence, but that when and only when the good to be produced by the benevolent act is very great and the promise comparatively trivial, the act of benevolence becomes our duty.

In fact the theory of 'ideal utilitarianism',[2] if I may for brevity refer so to the theory of Professor Moore, seems to simplify unduly our relations to our fellows. It says, in effect, that the only morally significant relation in which my neighbours stand to me is that of being possible beneficiaries by my action.* They do stand in this relation to me, and this relation is morally significant. But they may also stand to me in the relation of promisee to promiser, of creditor to debtor, of wife to husband, of child to parent, of friend to friend, of fellow countryman to fellow countryman, and the like; and each of these relations is the foundation of a prima facie duty, which is more or less incumbent on me according to the circumstances of the case. When I am in a situation, as perhaps I always am, in which more than one of these prima facie duties is incumbent on me, what I have to do is to study the situation as fully as I can until I form the considered opinion (it is never more) that in the circumstances one of them is more incumbent than any other; then I am bound to think that to do this prima facie duty is my duty *sans phrase* in the situation.

I suggest 'prima facie duty' or 'conditional duty' as a brief way of referring to the characteristic (quite distinct from that of being a duty proper) which an act has, in virtue of being of a certain kind (e.g. the keeping of a promise), of being an act which would be a duty proper if it were not at the same time of another kind which is morally significant. Whether an act is a duty proper or actual duty depends on *all* the morally significant kinds it is an instance of. The phrase 'prima facie duty' must be apologized for, since (1) it suggests that what we are speaking of is a certain kind of duty, whereas it is in fact not a duty, but something related in a special way to duty. Strictly speaking, we want not a phrase in which duty is qualified by an adjective, but a separate noun. (2) 'Prima' facie suggests that one is speaking only of an appearance which a moral

situation presents at first sight, and which may turn out to be illusory; whereas what I am speaking of is an objective fact involved in the nature of the situation, or more strictly in an element of its nature, though not, as duty proper does, arising from its *whole* nature. I can, however, think of no term which fully meets the case. [. . .]

There is nothing arbitrary about these prima facie duties. Each rests on a definite circumstance which cannot seriously be held to be without moral significance. Of prima facie duties I suggest, without claiming completeness or finality for it, the following division.†

(1) Some duties rest on previous acts of my own. These duties seem to include two kinds, (*a*) those resting on a promise or what may fairly be called an implicit promise, such as the implicit undertaking not to tell lies which seems to be implied in the act of entering into conversation (at any rate by civilized men), or of writing books that purport to be history and not fiction. These may be called the duties of fidelity. (*b*) Those resting on a previous wrongful act. These may be called the duties of reparation. (2) Some rest on previous acts of other men, i.e. services done by them to me. These may be loosely described as the duties of gratitude. (3) Some rest on the fact or possibility of a distribution of pleasure or happiness (or of the means thereto) which is not in accordance with the merit of the persons concerned; in such cases there arises a duty to upset or prevent such a distribution. These are the duties of justice. (4) Some rest on the mere fact

---

* Some will think it, apart from other considerations, a sufficient refutation of this view to point out that I also stand in that relation to myself, so that for this view the distinction of oneself from others is morally insignificant.

† I should make it plain at this stage that I am *assuming* the correctness of some of our main convictions as to prima facie duties, or, more strictly, am claiming that we *know* them to be true. To me it seems as self-evident as anything could be, that to make a promise, for instance, is to create a moral claim on us in someone else. Many readers will perhaps say that they do *not* know this to be true. If so, I certainly cannot prove it to them; I can only ask them to reflect again, in the hope that they will ultimately agree that they also know it to be true. The main moral convictions of the plain man seem to me to be, not opinions which it is for philosophy to prove or disprove, but knowledge from the start; and in my own case I seem to find little difficulty in distinguishing these essential convictions from other moral convictions which I also have, which are merely fallible opinions based on an imperfect study of the working for good or evil of certain institutions or types of action.

that there are other beings in the world whose condition we can make better in respect of virtue, or of intelligence, or of pleasure. These are the duties of beneficence. (5) Some rest on the fact that we can improve our own condition in respect of virtue or of intelligence. These are the duties of self-improvement. (6) I think that we should distinguish from (4) the duties that may be summed up under the title of 'not injuring others'. No doubt to injure others is incidentally to fail to do them good; but it seems to me clear that non-maleficence is apprehended as a duty distinct from that of beneficence, and as a duty of a more stringent character. It will be noticed that this alone among the types of duty has been stated in a negative way. An attempt might no doubt be made to state this duty, like the others, in a positive way. It might be said that it is really the duty to prevent ourselves from acting either from an inclination to harm others or from an inclination to seek our own pleasure, in doing which we should incidentally harm them. But on reflection it seems clear that the primary duty here is the duty not to harm others, this being a duty whether or not we have an inclination that if followed would lead to our harming them; and that when we have such an inclination the primary duty not to harm others gives rise to a consequential duty to resist the inclination. The recognition of this duty of non-maleficence is the first step on the way to the recognition of the duty of beneficence; and that accounts for the prominence of the commands 'thou shalt not kill', 'thou shalt not commit adultery', 'thou shalt not steal', 'thou shalt not bear false witness', in so early a code as the Decalogue. But even when we have come to recognize the duty of beneficence, it appears to me that the duty of non-maleficence is recognized as a distinct one, and as prima facie more binding. We should not in general consider it justifiable to kill one person in order to keep another alive, or to steal from one in order to give alms to another.

The essential defect of the 'ideal utilitarian' theory is that it ignores, or at least does not do full justice to, the highly personal character of duty. If the only duty is to produce the maximum of good, the question who is to have the good – whether it is myself, or my benefactor, or a person to whom I have made a promise to confer that good on him, or a mere fellow man to whom I stand in no such special relation –

should make no difference to my having a duty to produce that good. But we are all in fact sure that it makes a vast difference.

One or two other comments must be made on this provisional list of the divisions of duty. (1) The nomenclature is not strictly correct. For by 'fidelity' or 'gratitude' we mean, strictly, certain states of motivation; and, as I have urged, it is not our duty to have certain motives, but to do certain acts. By 'fidelity', for instance, is meant, strictly, the disposition to fulfil promises and implicit promises *because we have made them*. We have no general word to cover the actual fulfilment of promises and implicit promises *irrespective of motive;* and I use 'fidelity', loosely but perhaps conveniently, to fill this gap. So too I use 'gratitude' for the returning of services, irrespective of motive. The term 'justice' is not so much confined, in ordinary usage, to a certain state of motivation, for we should often talk of a man as acting justly even when we did not think his motive was the wish to do what was just simply for the sake of doing so. Less apology is therefore needed for our use of 'justice' in this sense. And I have used the word 'beneficence' rather than 'benevolence', in order to emphasize the fact that it is our duty to do certain things, and not to do them from certain motives.

(2) If the objection be made, that this catalogue of the main types of duty is an unsystematic one resting on no logical principle, it may be replied, first, that it makes no claim to being ultimate. It is a prima facie classification of the duties which reflection on our moral convictions seems actually to reveal. And if these convictions are, as I would claim that they are, of the nature of knowledge, and if I have not misstated them, the list will be a list of authentic conditional duties, correct as far as it goes though not necessarily complete. The list of *goods* put forward by the rival theory is reached by exactly the same method – the only sound one in the circumstances – viz. that of direct reflection on what we really think. Loyalty to the facts is worth more than a symmetrical architectonic or a hastily reached simplicity. If further reflection discovers a perfect logical basis for this or for a better classification, so much the better.

(3) It may, again, be objected that our theory that there are these various and often conflicting types of prima facie duty leaves us with no principle upon which to discern what is our

actual duty in particular circumstances. But this objection is not one which the rival theory is in a position to bring forward. For when we have to choose between the production of two heterogeneous goods, say knowledge and pleasure, the 'ideal utilitarian' theory can only fall back on an opinion, for which no logical basis can be offered, that one of the goods is the greater; and this is no better than a similar opinion that one of two duties is the more urgent. And again, when we consider the infinite variety of the effects of our actions in the way of pleasure, it must surely be admitted that the claim which *hedonism* sometimes makes, that it offers a readily applicable criterion of right conduct, is quite illusory.

I am unwilling, however, to content myself with an *argumentum ad hominem*, and I would contend that in principle there is no reason to anticipate that every act that is our duty is so for one and the same reason. Why should two sets of circumstances, or one set of circumstances, *not* possess different characteristics, any one of which makes a certain act our prima facie duty? When I ask what it is that makes me in certain cases sure that I have a prima facie duty to do so and so, I find that it lies in the fact that I have made a promise; when I ask the same question in another case, I find the answer lies in the fact that I have done a wrong. And if on reflection I find (as I think I do) that neither of these reasons is reducible to the other, I must not on any a priori ground assume that such a reduction is possible. [. . .]

It is necessary to say something by way of clearing up the relation between prima facie duties and the actual or absolute duty to do one particular act in particular circumstances. If, as almost all moralists except Kant are agreed, and as most plain men think, it is sometimes right to tell a lie or to break a promise, it must be maintained that there is a difference between prima facie duty and actual or absolute duty. When we think ourselves justified in breaking, and indeed morally obliged to break, a promise in order to relieve someone's distress, we do not for a moment cease to recognize a prima facie duty to keep our promise, and this leads us to feel, not indeed shame or repentance, but certainly compunction, for behaving as we do; we recognize, further, that it is our duty to make up somehow to the promisee for the breaking of the promise. We have to distinguish from the characteristic of being our duty that of tending to be our duty. Any act that we do contains various elements in virtue of which it falls under various categories. In virtue of being the breaking of a promise, for instance, it tends to be wrong; in virtue of being an instance of relieving distress it tends to be right. Tendency to be one's duty may be called a parti-resultant attribute, i.e. one which belongs to an act in virtue of some one component in its nature. *Being* one's duty is a toti-resultant attribute, one which belongs to an act in virtue of its whole nature and of nothing less than this.

Another instance of the same distinction may be found in the operation of natural laws. *Qua* subject to the force of gravitation towards some other body, each body tends to move in a particular direction with a particular velocity; but its actual movement depends on *all* the forces to which it is subject. It is only by recognizing this distinction that we can preserve the absoluteness of laws of nature, and only by recognizing a corresponding distinction that we can preserve the absoluteness of the general principles of morality. But an important difference between the two cases must be pointed out. When we say that in virtue of gravitation a body tends to move in a certain way, we are referring to a causal influence actually exercised on it by another body or other bodies. When we say that in virtue of being deliberately untrue a certain remark tends to be wrong, we are referring to no causal relation, to no relation that involves succession in time, but to such a relation as connects the various attributes of a mathematical figure. And if the word 'tendency' is thought to suggest too much a causal relation, it is better to talk of certain types of act as being prima facie right or wrong (or of different persons as having different and possibly conflicting claims upon us), than of their tending to be right or wrong.

Something should be said of the relation between our apprehension of the prima facie rightness of certain types of act and our mental attitude towards particular acts. It is proper to use the word 'apprehension' in the former case and not in the latter. That an act, *qua* fulfilling a promise, or *qua* effecting a just distribution of good, or *qua* returning services rendered, or *qua* promoting the good of others, or *qua* promoting the virtue or insight of the agent, is prima facie right, is self-evident; not in the sense that it is evident from the beginning of our lives, or as soon as we attend to the proposition for the first time, but in the sense that when we have reached sufficient mental maturity and have given sufficient attention to the proposition it is evident without any need of proof, or of evidence beyond itself. It is self-evident just as a mathematical axiom, or the validity of a form of inference, is evident. The moral order expressed in these propositions is just as much part of the fundamental nature of the universe (and, we may add, of any possible universe in which there were moral agents at all) as is the spatial or numerical structure expressed in the axioms of geometry or arithmetic. In our confidence that these propositions are true there is involved the same trust in our reason that is involved in our confidence in mathematics; and we should have no justification for trusting it in the latter sphere and distrusting it in the former. In both cases we are dealing with propositions that cannot be proved, but that just as certainly need no proof.

Some of these general principles of prima facie duty may appear to be open to criticism. It may be thought, for example, that the principle of returning good for good is a falling off from the Christian principle, generally and rightly recognized as expressing the highest morality, of returning good for evil. To this it may be replied that I do not suggest that there is a principle commanding us to return good for good and forbidding us to return good for evil, and that I do suggest that there is a positive duty to seek the good of all men. What I maintain is that an act in which good is returned for good is recognized as *specially* binding on us just because it is of that character, and that *ceteris paribus* any one would think it his duty to help his benefactors rather than his enemies, if he could not do both; just as it is generally recognized that *ceteris paribus* we should pay our debts rather than give our money in charity, when we cannot do both. A benefactor is not only a man, calling for our effort on his behalf on that ground, but also our benefactor, calling for our *special* effort on *that* ground.

Our judgements about our actual duty in concrete situations have none of the certainty that attaches to our recognition of the general principles of duty. A statement is certain, i.e. is an expression of knowledge, only in one or other of two cases: when it is either self-evident, or a valid conclusion from self-evident premises. And our judgements about our particular duties

have neither of these characters. (1) They are not self-evident. Where a possible act is seen to have two characteristics, in virtue of one of which it is prima facie right, and in virtue of the other prima facie wrong, we are (I think) well aware that we are not certain whether we ought or ought not to do it; that whether we do it or not, we are taking a moral risk. We come in the long run, after consideration, to think one duty more pressing than the other, but we do not feel certain that it is so. And though we do not always recognize that a possible act has two such characteristics, and though there *may* be cases in which it has not, we are never certain that any particular possible act has not, and therefore never certain that it is right, nor certain that it is wrong. For, to go no further in the analysis, it is enough to point out that any particular act will in all probability in the course of time contribute to the bringing about of good or of evil for many human beings, and thus have a prima facie rightness or wrongness of which we know nothing. (2) Again, our judgements about our particular duties are not logical conclusions from self-evident premises. The only possible premises would be the general principles stating their prima facie rightness or wrongness *qua* having the different characteristics they do have; and even if we could (as we cannot) apprehend the extent to which an act will tend on the one hand, for example, to bring about advantages for our benefactors, and on the other hand to bring about disadvantages for fellow men who are not our benefactors, there is no principle by which we can draw the conclusion that it is on the whole right or on the whole wrong. In this respect the judgement as to the rightness of a particular act is just like the judgement as to the beauty of a particular natural object or work of art. A poem is, for instance, in respect of certain qualities beautiful and in respect of certain others not beautiful; and our judgement as to the degree of beauty it possesses on the whole is never reached by logical reasoning from the apprehension of its particular beauties or particular defects. Both in this and in the moral case we have more or less probable opinions which are not logically justified conclusions from the general principles that are recognized as self-evident.

There is therefore much truth in the description of the right act as a fortunate act. If we cannot be certain that it is right, it is our good fortune if the act we do is the right act. This consideration does not, however, make the doing of our duty a mere matter of chance. There is a parallel here between the doing of duty and the doing of what will be to our personal advantage. We never *know* what act will in the long run be to our advantage. Yet it is certain that we are more likely in general to secure our advantage if we estimate to the best of our ability the probable tendencies of our actions in this respect, than if we act on caprice. And similarly we are more likely to do our duty if we reflect to the best of our ability on the prima facie rightness or wrongness of various possible acts in virtue of the characteristics we perceive them to have, than if we act without reflection. With this greater likelihood we must be content.

Many people would be inclined to say that the right act for me is not that whose general nature I have been describing, viz. that which if I were omniscient I should see to be my duty, but that which on all the evidence available to me I should think to be my duty. But suppose that from the state of partial knowledge in which I think act *A* to be my duty, I could pass to a state of perfect knowledge in which I saw act *B* to be my duty, should I not say 'act *B* was the right act for me to do'? I should no doubt add 'though I am not to be blamed for doing act *A*'. But in adding this, am I not passing from the question 'what is right' to the question 'what is morally good'? At the same time I am not making the *full* passage from the one notion to the other; for in order that the act should be morally good, or an act I am not to be blamed for doing, it must not merely be the act which it is reasonable for me to think my duty; it must also be done for that reason, or from some other morally good motive. Thus the conception of the right act as the act which it is reasonable for me to think my duty is an unsatisfactory compromise between the true notion of the right act and the notion of the morally good action.

The general principles of duty are obviously not self-evident from the beginning of our lives. How do they come to be so? The answer is, that they come to be self-evident to us just as mathematical axioms do. We find by experience that this couple of matches and that couple make four matches, that this couple of balls on a wire and that couple make four balls: and by reflection on these and similar discoveries we come to see that it is of the nature of two and two to make four. In a precisely similar way, we see the prima facie rightness of an act which would be the fulfilment of a particular promise, and of another which would be the fulfilment of another promise, and when we have reached sufficient maturity to think in general terms, we apprehend prima facie rightness to belong to the nature of any fulfilment of promise. What comes first in time is the apprehension of the self-evident prima facie rightness of an individual act of a particular type. From this we come by reflection to apprehend the self-evident general principle of prima facie duty. From this, too, perhaps along with the apprehension of the self-evident prima facie rightness of the same act in virtue of its having another characteristic as well, and perhaps in spite of the apprehension of its prima facie wrongness in virtue of its having some third characteristic, we come to believe something not self-evident at all, but an object of probable opinion, viz. that this particular act is (not prima facie but) actually right.

In this respect there is an important difference between rightness and mathematical properties. A triangle which is isosceles necessarily has two of its angles equal, whatever other characteristics the triangle may have – whatever, for instance, be its area, or the size of its third angle. The equality of the two angles is a parti-resultant attribute. And the same is true of all mathematical attributes. It is true, I may add, of prima facie rightness. But no act is ever, in virtue of falling under some general description, necessarily actually right; its rightness depends on its whole nature and not on any element in it. The reason is that no mathematical object (no figure, for instance, or angle) ever has two characteristics that tend to give it opposite resultant characteristics, while moral acts often (as every one knows) and indeed always (as on reflection we must admit) have different characteristics that tend to make them at the same time prima facie right and prima facie wrong; there is probably no act, for instance, which does good to any one without doing harm to some one else, and vice versa.

Supposing it to be agreed, as I think on reflection it must, that no one *means* by 'right' just 'productive of the best possible consequences', or 'optimific', the attributes 'right' and 'optimific' might stand in either of two kinds of relation to each other. (1) They might be so related that we could apprehend a priori, either immediately or deductively, that any act that is optimific is right and any act that is right is optimific, as we can apprehend that any triangle that is equilateral is equiangular and vice versa. Professor Moore's view is, I think, that the co-extensiveness of 'right' and 'optimific' is apprehended immediately. He rejects the possibility of any proof of it. Or (2) the two attributes might be such that the question whether they are invariably connected had to be answered by means of an inductive inquiry. Now at first sight it might seem as if the constant connection of the two attributes could be immediately apprehended. It might seem absurd to suggest that it could be right for any one to do an act which would produce consequences less good than those which would be produced by some other act in his power. Yet a little thought will convince us that this is not absurd. The type of case in which it is easiest to see that this is so is, perhaps, that in which one has made a promise. In such a case we all think that prima facie it is our duty to fulfil the promise irrespective of the precise goodness of the total consequences. And though we do not think it is necessarily our actual or absolute duty to do so, we are far from thinking that any, even the slightest, gain in the value of the total consequences will necessarily justify us in doing something else instead. Suppose, to simplify the case by abstraction, that the fulfilment of a promise to A would produce 1,000 units of good for him, but that by doing some other act I could produce 1,001 units of good for B, to whom I have made no promise, the other consequences of the two acts being of equal value; should we really think it self-evident that it was our duty to do the second act and not the first? I think not. We should, I fancy, hold that only a much greater disparity of value between the total consequences would justify us in failing to discharge our prima facie duty to A. After all, a promise is a promise, and is not to be treated so lightly as the theory we are examining would imply. What, exactly, a promise is, is not so easy to determine, but we are surely agreed that it constitutes a serious moral limitation to our freedom of action. To produce the 1,001 units of good for B rather than fulfil our promise to A would be to take, not perhaps our duty as philanthropists too seriously, but certainly our duty as makers of promises too lightly.

Or consider another phase of the same problem. If I have promised to confer on A a particular benefit containing 1,000 units of good, is it self-evident that if by doing some different act I could produce 1,001 units of good for A himself (the other consequences of the two acts being supposed equal in value), it would be right for me to do so? Again, I think not. Apart from my general prima facie duty to do A what good I can, I have another prima facie duty to do him the particular service I have promised to do him, and this is not to be set aside in consequence of a disparity of good of the order of 1,001 to 1,000, though a much greater disparity might justify me in so doing.

Or again, suppose that A is a very good and B a very bad man, should I then, even when I have made no promise, think it self-evidently right to produce 1,001 units of good for B rather than 1,000 for A? Surely not. I should be sensible of a prima facie duty of justice, i.e. of producing a distribution of goods in proportion to merit, which is not outweighed by such a slight disparity in the total goods to be produced.

Such instances – and they might easily be added to – make it clear that there is no self-evident connection between the attributes 'right' and 'optimific'. The theory we are examining has a certain attractiveness when applied to our decision that a particular act is our duty (though I have tried to show that it does not agree with our actual moral judgements even here). But it is not even plausible when applied to our recognition of prima facie duty. For if it were self-evident that the right coincides with the optimific, it should be self-evident that what is prima facie right is prima facie optimific. But whereas we are certain that keeping a promise is prima facie right, we are not certain that it is prima facie optimific (though we are perhaps certain that it is prima facie bonific). Our certainty that it is prima facie right depends not on its consequences but on its being the fulfilment of a promise. The theory we are examining involves too much difference between the evident ground of our conviction about prima facie duty and the alleged ground of our conviction about actual duty.

The coextensiveness of the right and the optimific is, then, not self-evident. And I can see no way of proving it deductively; nor, so far as I know, has any one tried to do so. There remains the question whether it can be established inductively. Such an inquiry, to be conclusive, would have to be very thorough and extensive. We should have to take a large variety of the acts which we, to the best of our ability, judge to be right. We should have to trace as far as possible their consequences, not only for the persons directly affected but also for those indirectly affected, and to these no limit can be set. To make our inquiry thoroughly conclusive, we should have to do what we cannot do, viz. trace these consequences into an unending future. And even to make it reasonably conclusive, we should have to trace them far into the future. It is clear that the most we could possibly say is that a large variety of typical acts that are judged right appear, so far as we can trace their consequences, to produce more good than any other acts possible to the agents in the circumstances. And such a result falls far short of proving the constant connection of the two attributes. But it is surely clear that no inductive inquiry justifying even this result has ever been carried through. The advocates of utilitarian systems have been so much persuaded either of the identity or of the self-evident connection of the attributes 'right' and 'optimific' (or 'felicific') that they have not attempted even such an inductive inquiry as is possible. And in view of the enormous complexity of the task and the inevitable inconclusiveness of the result, it is worth no one's while to make the attempt. What, after all, would be gained by it? If, as I have tried to show, for an act to be right and to be optimific are not the same thing, and an act's being optimific is not even the ground of its being right, then if we could ask ourselves (though the question is really unmeaning) which we ought to do, right acts because they are right or optimific acts because they are optimific, our answer must be 'the former'. If they are optimific as well as right, that is interesting but not morally important; if not, we still ought to do them (which is only another way of saying that they *are* the right acts), and the question whether they are optimific has no importance for moral theory. [. . .]

Notes

1   The views of Moore on which Ross focuses are less those of *Principia Ethica* than the later (1912) *Ethics*, London: Oxford University Press, 1966.
2   The point of this term – which, despite being liable to mislead, has caught on – is that Moore's position shares with utilitarianism the idea that actions are right only in so far as they contribute to some good, while differing from classical utilitarianism in conceiving this good, not in terms of pleasure, but of certain "ideals," like beauty.

21

Tanabe Hajime, *Philosophy as Metanoetics*, "Preface"

Introduction

Like Jean-Paul Sartre's lecture, "Existentialism Is a Humanism" (I.23), *Philosophy as Metanoetics* – the magnum opus of the Japanese philosopher, Tanabe Hajime (1885–1962), a leading figure in the Kyoto School, which flourished in the first half of the twentieth century – was written at the end of World War II.[1] Like Sartre's lecture, the Preface to this immense work explicitly engages moral issues made urgent by the war, including that of the individual's responsibility for events that might seem beyond his or her control. But the responses to these issues of the two men, set as they are in very different metaphysical contexts, are strikingly divergent. Sartre's response to a student's dilemma – whether to look after his mother or go off to fight – was to remind him of his inalienable freedom and responsibility to make an authentic, autonomous choice. Tanabe's response to his own wartime dilemma – whether to criticize his government or "patriotically" remain silent – was an "astonishing" recognition of his total inability and "lack of freedom" as a philosopher to resolve such a dilemma, and of the need to "surrender" himself to an "Other-power" that might "think through" him.

From Tanabe Hajime, *Philosophy as Metanoetics*, trans. T. Yoshinori. Berkeley: University of California Press, 1986, pp. il–lxii (footnote is the translator's).

The English term "surrender," however, does not fully capture what Tanabe means by the New Testament Greek notion of *metanoia*, which invokes the idea of repentant conversion and spiritual transformation as well as the idea of self-abandonment to something "Other" – pointedly expressed in St Paul's words, "It is not I who live, but Christ who lives in me" (Galatians 2:19–20). In Tanabe's hands, however, metanoeisis (or *zange*, in Japanese) is conceived in distinctly Buddhist terms. The salvific "Other-power" to which one surrenders is not a god, but "absolute nothingness" – Tanabe's term for what, in Mahayana Buddhist tradition, is called "emptiness" (*sunyata*), the ineffable "source" of all things and all human thought and action. For Tanabe, this prospect of "salvation by Other-power" is given especially profound, figurative expression in the "Pure Land" or Shin sect's emphasis on total devotion to, and dependence on, Amida, the "Buddha of Compassion."

Whatever else this vision of "Other-power" amounts to, it constitutes a radical rejection of the self-sufficiency of human reason. "We arrive at metanoetics by way of a critique of reason . . . in both its theoretical and practical aspects" (p. lvi). The word "practical" (in the sense of "moral") needs stressing, for as one commentator puts it, appreciation of the insufficiency of reason is "triggered by the recognition of failure and human limitation," so that the metanoetic "consciousness is already an ethical one . . . intimated in the midst of action by the experience of remorse."[2] There is a further respect in which, for Tanabe, metanoesis is a moral manoeuvre. For, as another commentator explains, the manoeuvre is really a double one – "abandonment to the saving power" of Amida Buddha, followed by a "returning to the world . . . to work for the salvation of others."[3] As Tanabe puts it, the "Great Nay" spoken to everything merely "relative," including human moral conventions, generates a "Great Compassion." This is because, in humble experience of one's helplessness and limits, a person also recognizes that his or her suffering counts for no more than anyone else's. There occurs, Tanabe says, a "conversion of the self-affirming ego into no-self" (lxii).

The continuity of Tanabe's position with Buddhist moral thought – with, for example, the views articulated by Śāntideva and Tsongkapa (I.9) – is clear. But it bears comparison, as well, with those of several western thinkers – including Kierkegaard (I.17) and Wittgenstein – for whom moral reflection is not, primarily, a matter of identifying moral principles to govern our behavior in everyday situations. Such reflection belongs, rather, to an effort to transform ourselves and our stance toward the world in the face of the extreme dilemmas with which war, for example, confronts us – an effort, albeit, in which we cannot succeed without the help of "grace," of "Other-power."

Notes

1 Other important philosophers of the Kyoto School include Nishida Kitaro (1870–1945), D. T. Suzuki (1870–1966), Nishitani Keiji (1900–90), Takeuchi Yoshinori (1913–2002), and Abe Masao (1915–2006).

2 M. McGhee, *Transformations of Mind: Philosophy as Spiritual Practice*, Cambridge: Cambridge University Press, 2000, p. 12.

3 J. W. Heisig, *Philosophers of Nothingness: An Essay on the Kyoto School*, Honolulu: University of Hawaii Press, 2001, p. 164. This book contains a long discussion of Tanabe's life and philosophy.

Tanabe, *Philosophy as Metanoetics*, Preface

Last summer, when the fortunes of war had turned against Japan and the nation was under the increasing threat of direct raids and attacks, the government found itself at a loss as to how to handle the situation, and in the stalemate that ensued, it showed itself completely incapable of undertaking the reforms necessary to stem the raging tide of history. Instead, government officials tried to keep the actual course of events secret from the people in order to conceal their own responsibility. Criticism of any kind became impossible. All public opinion, except for propaganda in favor of the government's policy, was suppressed. Freedom of thought was severely restricted, and the only ideas given official recognition were those of the extreme rightists. In the midst of economic distress and tensions, and an ever deepening anxiety, our people were greatly concerned about their nation's future but did not know where to turn or to whom to appeal.

I myself shared in all these sufferings of my fellow Japanese, but as a philosopher I experienced yet another kind of distress. On the one hand, I was haunted by the thought that as a student of philosophy I ought to be bringing the best of my thought to the service of my nation, to be addressing the government frankly with regard to its policies toward academic thought and demanding a reexamination, even if this should incur the displeasure of those currently in power. In such a critical situation, where there was no time for delay, would it not be disloyal to my country to keep silent and fail to express whatever ideas I had on reform? On the other hand, there seemed something traitorous about expressing in time of war ideas that, while perfectly proper in time of peace, might end up causing divisions and conflicts among our people that would only further expose them to their enemies.

Caught between these alternatives, I was unable to make up my mind and was tormented by my own indecision. In the impasse I even wondered whether I should go on teaching philosophy or give it up altogether, since I had no adequate solution to a dilemma that philosophically did not appear all that difficult. My own indecision, it seemed to me, disqualified me as a philosopher and university professor. I spent my days wrestling with questions and doubts like this from within and without, until I had been quite driven to the point of exhaustion and in my despair concluded that I was not fit to engage in the sublime task of philosophy.

At that moment something astonishing happened. In the midst of my distress I let go and surrendered myself humbly to my own inability. I was suddenly brought to new insight! My penitent confession – metanoesis (*zange*) – unexpectedly threw me back on my own interiority and away from things external. There was no longer any question of my teaching and correcting others under the circumstances – I who could not deliver myself to do the correct thing. The only thing for me to do in the situation was to resign myself honestly to my weakness, to examine my own inner self with humility, and to explore the depths of my powerlessness and lack of freedom. Would not this mean a new task to take the place of the philosophical task that had previously engaged me? Little matter whether it be called "philosophy" or not: I had already come to realize my own incompetence as a philosopher. What mattered was that I was being confronted at the moment with an intellectual task and ought to do my best to pursue it.

The decision was reached, as I have said, through metanoia, or the way of *zange*, and led to *a philosophy that is not a philosophy*: philosophy seen as the self-realization of *metanoetic consciousness*. It is no longer I who pursue philosophy, but rather *zange* that thinks through me. In my practice of metanoesis, it is metanoesis itself that is seeking its own realization. Such is the nonphilosophical philosophy that is reborn out of the denial of philosophy as I had previously understood it. I call it a philosophy that is not a philosophy because, on the one hand, it has arisen from the vestiges of a philosophy I had cast away in despair, and on the other, it maintains the purpose of functioning as a reflection on what is ultimate and as a radical self-awareness, which are the goals proper to philosophy.

To be sure, this is not a philosophy to be undertaken on my own power (*jiriki*). That power has already been abandoned in despair. It is rather a philosophy to be practiced by Other-power (*tariki*), which has turned me in a completely new direction through metanoesis, and has induced me to make a fresh start from the realization of my utter helplessness. Metanoesis (*zange*) signifies repentance for the wrongs I had done, with the accompanying torment of knowing that there is no way to expiate my sins. It also signifies shame for the powerlessness and inability that have driven me to despair and self-surrender. Yet insofar as this entails an act of self-denial, it points to a paradox: even though it is my own act, it cannot be my own act. It has been prompted by a Power outside of myself. This Other-power brings about a conversion in me that heads me in a new direction along a path hitherto unknown to me.

Zange thus represents for me an experience of Other-power acting in and through *zange* to urge me to a new advance in philosophy. I entrust my entire being to Other-power (*tariki*), and by practicing *zange* and maintaining faith in this Power I confirm the truth of my own conversion-and-resurrection experience. In this way the practice-faith-witness (*gyō-shin-shō*) of my *zange* becomes the philosophy of my regenerated existence. This is what I am calling "metanoetics," the philosophy of Other-power. I have died to philosophy and been resurrected by *zange*. It is not a question of simply carrying on the same philosophy I had abandoned in my despair, as if resuming a journey after a temporary interruption. It cannot be a mere repetition without negation and change. In the life of the spirit, "repetition" must mean self-transcendence; "resurrection" must mean regeneration to a new life. I no longer live of myself, but live because life has been granted to me from the transcendent realm of the absolute which is neither life nor death. Since this absolute is the negation and transformation – that is, conversion – of everything relative, it may be defined as absolute nothingness. I experience this absolute nothingness through which I am reborn to new life as nothingness-*qua*-love. One might also say that it is an experience of the truth of absolute negation: the confirmation of the Great Nay as the Great Compassion. The truth of my conversion and resurrection in dependence on *tariki* (Other-power) is confirmed in the practice and faith (*gyō-shin*) of *zange*.

While I have no doubt that metanoetics is the way to a new philosophy of Other-power as the "action-faith-witness" of *zange*, I am but a finite and imperfect being whose *zange* may not be fully pure and true. It may sometimes happen that my *zange* is not accompanied by a resurrection, or that even after a resurrection experience, I may fall away from *zange* into reliance on self-power. I may grow complacent with my accomplishments and in my arrogance imagine myself a wise man. In that case I should inevitably be driven back to my former despair, since anything I achieve apart from true *zange* can only be immediately contradicted by reality itself. Only through continual *zange* can we achieve the faith and witness (*shin-shō*) of continuous resurrection. By acting in and witnessing to the circular process of death-and-resurrection that characterizes *zange* and indeed accords with the unfolding of reality itself, the infinity and eternity of *zange* are revealed to us and the dialectical unity of absolute and relative affirmed. This is in fact the basic principle that shapes history. In terms of its concrete content, metanoetics is a radical historicism in that the continuous repetition of *zange* provides basic principles for the circular development of history.

My experience of conversion – that is, of transformation and resurrection – in metanoesis corresponds to the experience that led Shinran (1173–1262) to establish the doctrine of the Pure Land Shin sect (*Jōdo Shin-shū*). Quite by accident I was led along the same path that Shinran followed in Buddhist discipline, although in my case it occurred in the philosophical realm. Reflection on this parallel led me to an interpretation of Shinran's *Kyōgyōshinshō* from a metanoetical point of view. I had, of course, been interested in Shinran before that time. In particular I found his *Tanni-shō* and one of the hymns from his *Shōzōmatsu Wasan* entitled "Confession and Lamentation" deeply moving for their treatment and tone of metanoesis.

Shinran's doctrine of salvation through the praise and recitation of the name of Amida Buddha, as an expression of faith in Amida Buddha alone, has often been mistaken for a kind of spiritual laxity, especially seen in conjunction with his advocacy of the "easy way" of salvation (*igyōdō*). This is due to the common error of confusing the realm of the transcendent – where we must speak of people being saved "just as they are," without any merit on their part, as a result of the conversion and transformation brought about by absolute compassion – with the realm of the relative – normal, everyday life. Thus his doctrine of the salvation of people "just as they are" led to the error of disregarding morality, and at times even served the evil purpose of providing excuses for wrongdoings.

In contrast with these abuses of his teaching, Shinran's own faith was based on the bitter experience of metanoesis. This had been my firm conviction from the outset in reading Shinran's works. But I had no idea at the time that his *Kyōgyōshinshō* was in its very essence nothing other than metanoetics. The oversight was a natural one in that metanoesis does not appear as one of the central ideas of the work, even though Shinran mentions and explains the "three kinds of metanoesis" developed by the Chinese priest Shan'tao (Jap., *Zendō*, 613–681) in one of his doctrinal discourses, and in his hymns in praise of Amida Buddha we find strong elements of metanoesis at various places. Among contemporary scholar-priests of the Shin sect, Soga Ryōjin (1875–1971) should be mentioned for his appreciation of and deep insight into the basic notion of metanoesis, as well as for his recognition of its significance for understanding Shinran's faith. I have found his interpretation and doctrinal analysis most enlightening, and owe him a great debt of gratitude in this regard.

Understanding the *Kyōgyōshinshō* as the metanoetical development of Buddhism has not received general approval as a correct interpretation. I myself had long been reluctant to accept such a viewpoint. My innate attraction for the idealistic doctrine of self-power made me more sympathetic to the Zen sect than to sects that taught "salvation by Other-power." Although I had never undergone discipline in a Zen monastery, I had long been familiar with the discourses of Chinese and Japanese Zen masters. I was ashamed that I still remained an outsider to Zen and could not enter into the depths of its holy truth, and yet I felt closer to Zen than to Shin doctrine. This was why I had taken little notice of the *Kyōgyōshinshō* up until that time.

One of my students, Takeuchi Yoshinori (1913–), had published a book under the title *The Philosophy of the "Kyōgyōshinshō"* (1941). Drawing on the intellectual acumen he had developed through reading Hegel under me, he was able to produce an outstanding interpretation of the work. While I learned much from reading this study, it was impossible for me at the time to develop a philosophy of my own based on the thought of the *Kyōgyōshinshō*. It was only when I set out to develop a new philosophy, a philosophy of metanoetics based on Other-power, that I returned to reread the *Kyōgyōshinshō* carefully and was able to find a way to understand it. I regard Shinran with gratitude, love, and respect as a great teacher from the past. As I shall demonstrate in chapters 6 and 7, his idea of the three stages of religious transformation and his interpretation of the "Three Minds" (*sanshin*) is unique in the history of the philosophy of religion as an explanation of the structure of salvation. I cannot but feel thankful for the grace of Other-power that led me to metanoetics and to reliance on the guidance of Shinran.

I was also surprised to find that once I had arrived at belief in Other-power, I found myself feeling still closer to the spirit of Zen, whose emphasis on self-power is generally considered opposed to Pure Land doctrine. Nor was this the last of my surprises. A key to solving a problem in mathematical philosophy, which would at first glance seem to be rather far removed from religious concerns, also emerged at this time. I refer to the puzzle of infinite-set theory, over which I had cudgeled my brains for many years in vain. Moreover, it became clear that a philosophy of history could be based on metanoetics, inasmuch as the content of metanoetics itself consists in a "radical historicism." In this way I grew confident of the range of applicability of metanoetics with its broad and ample perspective, although I must admit that at first I had no idea it was capable of such scope.

Some may contend that metanoesis is so extraordinary a phenomenon in one's spiritual life that it is hardly possible to develop a universal philosophy out of it. But I have been convinced from the start that metanoetics involves social solidarity inasmuch as we are always obliged to practice metanoesis so long as we are aware of our collective responsibility for every event that takes place in our society. In my case, metanoesis was aroused because I had been driven to the limits of my philosophical position as I confronted the desperate straits into which my country had fallen. My distress resulted not only from my own personal inability to execute my responsibilities as a philosopher at the time but also from my feeling the responsibility that each of my

fellow Japanese had to assume in his or her particular situation. Naturally I was indignant at the militarists and the government authorities for having duped the people and suppressed criticism among them, for having had the audacity to pursue the most irrational of policies in violation of international law, causing our nation to be stripped of its honor before the rest of the world. But in the strict sense we Japanese are all responsible for the failure and disgrace since we were unable to restrain the reckless ways of the government and the militarists. After those who are directly to be blamed for the disasters that befell Japan, the leaders in the world of social and political thought are most responsible. There is no excusing the standpoint of the innocent bystander so often adopted by members of the intelligentsia.

I am deeply convinced of the fact that, in the last analysis, everyone is responsible, collectively, for social affairs. Once one assumes this standpoint of social responsibility, there can be no doubt that metanoetics is indispensable for each person at each moment. Therefore metanoetics, like morality, can provide the way to a universal philosophy. Furthermore, when metanoetics is viewed in relation to the *Kyōgyōshinshō* of Shinran, our guide in metanoetical thinking, his profound idea of "returning to this world from the Pure Land" (*gensō-ekō*) suggests a distinctive theory of religious society established on the ideal of "fraternity" – an ideal of equality within the social order which at the same time recognizes the ranks of elder and younger in the religious sense. This is somewhat different from the equality that emerges from love of neighbor in Christianity. There is no disputing the fact that freedom based on democracy has led to forms of socialism that run counter to the ideal of freedom. The unity of freedom and equality is not a selfevident fact but a project difficult to achieve. In order to achieve this goal of unity, is it not necessary that the idea of fraternity, restored to its original meaning, mediate in the concrete the conflict between freedom and equality? The idea of "returning to this world" in the Shin sect thus offers a concrete suggestion for a basic principle of social structure, and opens broad vistas in the philosophy of history insofar as it represents the ideal of the compassionate way of the bodhisattva in Mahāyāna Buddhism. We may therefore conclude that metanoetics is more than a mere exercise carried out in the realms of abstract thought.

During the fall of last year I devoted myself assiduously to developing metanoetics into a form of philosophy. From the point of its very inception, metanoetics needs to be developed metanoetically. That is, it should not be a "philosophy of metanoesis" in the sense that it treats an object called metanoesis. Neither should it be a phenomenological or *lebensphilosophisch* interpretation that applies its own established methodology to the investigation of metanoesis. Metanoetics is a philosophy that has to be erected at the very point that all prior philosophical standpoints and methods have been negated in their entirety. It is a philosophical method of "destruction" more radical than even the methodical skepticism of Descartes. It cannot be treated on the same level as philosophy up to the present inasmuch as it is a philosophy achieved through a death-and-resurrection process of transformation. Only one awakened to Other-power who practices metanoetics in "action-witness" (*gyō-shō*) can witness its truth in self-consciousness. In this sense I gain personal conviction of the truth of metanoetics by means of my own action-witness, and thereby deepen my metanoetic self-consciousness.

In the course of my reflections, I discovered a logic that functions throughout metanoetical thinking, which I call "absolute criticism." Philosophy based on reason can with good cause be described as a philosophy of self-power: the reason it presupposes as its basis is bound to fall into antinomies in the encounter with actual reality. Kant's remedy, as laid out in the *Critique of Pure Reason*, was to narrow the scope of reason to make room for faith. The solution is clearly incomplete. In the radical self-consciousness of being driven to the extreme, reason can only be torn to shreds in absolute disruption, after which such self-affirming reason is no longer of any use to us. Absolute criticism means that reason, faced with the absolute crisis of its dilemma, surrenders itself of its own accord. In the course of this critical task, the subject that is undertaking the critique of pure reason cannot remain a mere bystander at a safe remove from the criticism. The subject of the critique cannot avoid getting tangled in its own web and exposing itself to self-criticism. It cannot avoid dismemberment by the absolute dilemma of its own thought. Yet in the very midst of this absolute disruption and contradiction, the power of contradiction is itself negated: the absolute contradiction contradicts itself. At this point an absolute conversion takes place and philosophy is restored, through the power of the transcendent, as a "philosophy that is not a philosophy."

Thus metanoetics includes within itself the logic of absolute criticism. We arrive at metanoetics by way of the critique of reason – reason in both its theoretical and practical aspects – if the critique is pursued radically. This is in fact how the Kantian criticism of the *Critique of Pure Reason* developed into the Hegelian critique of the *Phenomenology of Mind*. The transcendental dialectic of the former was transformed into the true dialectic of the latter. Still, Hegel maintained that the absolute disruption and contradiction in reason could be overcome by the unity of reason, and that the state of reason prior to the antinomies could be recovered in its simple self-identity, because reason is able to embrace in self-consciousness its own death and resurrection by means of infinite thought in the form of the concept (*Begriff*). This led him to neglect the important fact that the resurrected life of reason is not the same as the former state of reason prior to negation, but comes about only through the activity of absolute transformation – that is, through the activity of absolute nothingness, which is neither life nor death. In the resurrection into new life, self-consciousness is only a temporary axis of transformation posited as a subjective center accessible only through action-faith-witness. But Hegel thought that the identity of absolute contradictories could be grasped in the form of the concept quite apart from any such temporary subjective center, that infinite thinking provided the unity of an infinite circle that could embrace the whole within itself.

Here we see why Hegel's concept of reason was unable to break through the constraints of the Aristotelian logic of identity completely. His failure is itself a negation of the dialectic in that the practical transformation of the self is uprooted at the core under the sway of the objective concept. And since the nonobjectifiable and nonmaterializable subjective self ceases to exist, concept turns into substance and absolute idealism into materialism. We are left with a nonexistentialism that denies the practical transformation of the self any mediating role. Not surprisingly, instead of self-consciousness in absolute nothingness we have only substance as being. As a result, Hegel's thought, which shows an affinity here with the thought of Spinoza, could evolve into Marxism.

In contrast, metanoetics remains grounded entirely on a standpoint of practical transformation and thereby open to the Great Nay–*qua*–Great Compassion. It is a standpoint on which the transformative unity of the death-and-resurrection of the self is practiced and witnessed by means of a radical criticism leading to transformation by Other-power, which I would argue is the final culmination of the Kantian critique of reason. The dialectic of absolute mediation that Hegel aimed for but was unable to attain is carried out in practice-faith in a way that was closed to Hegel's contemplation of reason. Here metanoetics is akin to Schelling's theory of freedom which, in opposition to Hegelian reason, probed deeply into Kant's notion of absolute evil. There is also a similarity here to Heidegger's existential philosophy, which, under the influence of Kierkegaard's opposition to Hegel's intellectual philosophy, strove to maintain the authentic self as the center of practical transformation. At the same time, metanoetics is critical of Schelling's speculative philosophy of "construction" insofar as it claims a standpoint of self-consciousness in absolute mediation. It likewise stands opposed to the existentialism of Heidegger which, by diverging from Kierkegaard's "existentialism of faith" to assert the freedom of the self, has affinities with the atheistic thought of Nietzsche. In contrast with these positions, metanoesis seeks throughout to maintain a standpoint of action-faith through Other-power, and thereby to insist on a relationship of reciprocal mediatory transformation between the absolute and the self. Moreover, the redeeming truth that the absolute can function only as the power of absolute mediation can reach self-consciousness by way of reciprocal mediatory activity between relative selves. In this sense, the transformation through vertical mediation between the absolute and the self (Thou and I) must also be realized in horizontal social relationships between my self and other selves (I and thou). Thus metanoetics is able to overcome the deficiencies of individualism common to both Schelling's doctrine of freedom and Heidegger's existential philosophy, and to make the abstract truth of each more concrete through the realization of responsibility

in "social solidarity." Shinran's idea of "returning to the world" (*gensō*) referred to earlier recommends such a doctrine of social solidarity. It gives the idea of a "logic of species" (*shu no ronri*), which I have long advocated as a theory of social existence, a new and deeper basis.

In light of the above considerations, I was confident that metanoetics, as a philosophical principle, would provide sufficient grounds for a new philosophy. This is why I was able to return to philosophy with peace of mind. With this idea of a renewed philosophy in mind, I ascended the platform to deliver my final series of lectures at Kyoto Imperial University. Although a new Cabinet had been formed at the time, in accord with the long-suppressed wish of the Japanese people, it proved no less ineffective in improving the situation. Fears and anxieties grew stronger by the day, as the destitution and disaster continued to spread. While I shared in the deepening pessimism of the people of Japan, I had at least one source of consolation and encouragement. And thus, with a sense of gratitude to Other-power, I presented my lectures, which began in October of 1944 and ended in December, under the title "Metanoetics." During this period I also offered an outline of my lectures in the form of a public lecture with the same title sponsored by the Kyoto Philosophical Society. Such is the history of how my philosophy of metanoetics came to be.

In preparing this last lecture, I developed the logic of "absolute criticism," and through the "destruction" of the Western philosophy in which I had been trained for many years, I attempted a reconstruction from a metanoetical point of view. It was for me a great joy to discover in the course of reconsidering the thought of such figures as Meister Eckhart, Pascal, and Nietzsche that problems I had never been able to penetrate deeply now grew clear to me – at least as far as my limited abilities would allow. Naturally, I concentrated my energies in the main on a metanoetical reading of the *Kyōgyōshinshō*, the results of which filled several notebooks. In order to make a coherent whole of my lectures, I was able to work only on the essentials. A single three-month term was too short; if I had had a year to lecture, it still would have been too short. At any rate, I was approaching the retirement age set for university professors, and on top of that, weak of constitution as I am, I fell ill in November. But so ardent was my desire to complete the lectures at all costs that I left my sickbed just long enough to deliver them. It was with a great sigh of relief that I completed the final lecture in December, after which I spent the rest of the winter in bed. I have no words to express my gratitude for the kindness shown me by my students and colleagues at that time. Since February of this year I have been legally retired from the university professorship. Looking back over my career of twenty-five years at Kyoto Imperial University, I felt regret for the personal inadequacies that inhibited the performance of my duties, but at the same time I was full of thanks to Heaven and to all those whose help enabled me to see my academic career to its end despite my poor health.

But once I had turned my attention away from my private life to focus on the destiny of our nation, my regret and sadness were without bounds. Even after a second change of Cabinet, there was still no improvement. The mainland of Japan was under attack, and the ravages of war were beyond description. Notwithstanding these calamities and even though the situation was considerably worse than before, I was no longer sunk in despair but endeavored to concentrate on the problems that lay before me. In this I could feel the power of metanoetics. Far from relinquishing myself to despair, I was transformed, converted, by the absolute and elevated to a spirit of detachment. This confirmed my conviction that metanoetics is as strong as we are weak. After a thoroughgoing and humble assessment of my own powerlessness, I experienced the grace of resurrection through the compassion of Other-power.

Toward the end of July I decided to move out of Kyoto and into a rural area, the increasing severity of the air raids having made it impossible for me to remain in a large city. It was entirely through the kind assistance of my close friends that I was able to make the transition in safety. Living here in these quiet surroundings refreshed me in mind and body, though I remained quite as weak as before. My spirits rose during the following two months as I began to order my notes into a longer study, the results of which are contained in this book. At first I had no clear idea of how to pursue its publication, though I did consider serializing it in the pages of the *Journal of Philosophical Studies* (*Tetsugaku kenkyū*) as I had done before with other works.

Then, in mid-August, Japan met with the unhappy fate of unconditional surrender, plunging the entire nation – myself included – into deep sorrow. We the Japanese people have to perform metanoesis when we reflect on how this catastrophe came to be. Looking back, I have come to realize that my own metanoesis of a year earlier was destined to prepare the future for my country. The thought of this coincidence brought me great sorrow and pain. Of course, I despise the shamelessness of the leaders primarily responsible for the defeat who are now urging the entire nation to repentance only in order to conceal their own complicity. Metanoesis is not something to be urged on others before one has performed it for oneself. Still, it is clear that we the nation of Japan, having fallen into these tragic and appalling circumstances, should practice metanoesis (*zange*) together as a people. Since I am one of those who believe in the collective responsibility of a nation, I am convinced that all of us should engage in collective metanoesis (*sō-zange*) in the literal sense of the term. I feel compelled to conclude that metanoetics is not only my own private philosophy but a philosophical path the entire nation should follow.

Since metanoesis implies remorse and sorrow, it is necessarily accompanied by feelings of shame and disgrace. This is true both in the way that Shinran used the word and in the connotation of the Latin word *paenitentia*, which originally carried a sense of "pang."* There can be no *paenitentia*, no *zange*, without pain. But the heart of metanoesis is the experience of conversion or transformation: sorrow and lament are turned into joy, shame and disgrace into gratitude. Hence when I say that our nation has no way to walk but the way of *zange* (metanoetics), I do not mean that we should sink into despair and stop there, but that we can hope to be transformed through resurrection and regeneration. It is true that metanoesis is the activity of conversion and transformation performed by Other-power (*tariki*) – I can personally attest to the truth of this through my own "faith-witness" (*shin-shō*) – and I cannot but recommend it to all our people. It is as an act of gratitude that I offer metanoetics (*zangedō*) as a philosophy that belongs

---

* Tanabe's etymology is misinformed. The root word *poena* has to do with punishment or indemnity.

rightly not only to me but to all of you. With this thought in mind, I felt I ought to publish this work as quickly as possible. Of course, in making this recommendation I have no intention of forcing others to accept this philosophy. Nonetheless, it is my sincere desire to offer metanoetics to those of the Japanese people who seek a philosophy at the present time.

In spite of the suffering that goes along with defeat, the suppression of thought that we had to endure for many years has now come to an end through the intervention of foreign powers, and freedom of thought is being extolled as an ideal to which we can all aspire. As is evident to all of us, emancipation from state control has led the people of Japan to rally behind the development of culture as the sole means of rebuilding our nation. I find it a rather curious phenomenon that intellectuals in a country that has just suffered defeat should be stimulated by their freedom of activity to embrace belief in culture. So heavy was the oppression we endured for so many years, at first I am tempted to join them. But can a nation compelled to surrender, with liberalism being forced upon it from without and the development of culture urged from within, be expected to come up with the spiritual resources needed to create a new culture simply because the oppressive controls of the past have been removed? True freedom is not something one receives from another; one has to acquire it for oneself. Even should there be a flowering of new culture in such circumstances as ours, it would be like blossoms on a hothouse plant: beautiful to the eye but too weak and shallow of root to survive in the open air.

Here we see the paradox that true and living culture is not something that can be made by culture worshipers; if anything, their "culturism" is a symptom of the decadence of culture. In general, I have always been critical of abstract ideals like culturism and culture-worship, and I am especially reluctant to approve of the present stress on "culture" since I place no faith in its future. It must be said that the very ones now optimistically espousing the cause of culture are mere onlookers who have no sense of social responsibility to the nation. A moment's glance at some of the current social problems – the hunger and poverty of the vast majority of the people in sharp contrast with the luxury enjoyed by a very few owing to the maldistribution of food and goods, the stagnation and paralysis of industry despite the large number of soldiers returning to the ranks of the unemployed – shows how difficult it will be to rebuild our war-devastated nation. One step in the wrong direction, even one day's delay, may be enough to spell the total ruin of our land. Unless we all undertake the new way of *zange*, free ourselves from the evil institutions of the past, and collaborate in carrying out whatever changes are necessary in the social system, there is no possibility of reconstruction. The only course open to us at present is metanoetics, not culturism. Does not the Old Testament prophet Jeremiah show us the way?

Speaking frankly, I would say that the occupying powers themselves have yet to achieve a harmony between democracy and socialism, and that this will remain a difficult problem for them in the foreseeable future. But so long as that problem is not resolved, it is inevitable that these nations will be beset by a host of difficulties both internal and external. All nations, be they democratic or socialist, have their own need to perform metanoesis. If there is any vocation of significance for world history in the reconstruction of our nation, it lies in the search for a middle path between these two ideologies, a middle path that is neither democracy nor socialism but moves freely between the two systems to make use of the strengths of both. And if this is so, then metanoetics must become the philosophy not only of Japan but of all humanity.

Will not the true meaning of humanity be found when people enter into absolute peace with one another, helping one another in a spirit of reconciliation and cooperation, seeking mutual emancipation and salvation in the conversion of the self-affirming ego into no-self through the mediatory activity of absolute nothingness? For it is the self-affirming ego that is the cause of all conflict among people, while in the life of absolute peace all contribute their best efforts to deepen the joy of fraternal love. For this reason, all people everywhere need to perform *zange* collectively. I do not think I am arguing from a self-centered point of view in making the claim that world history has reached a turning point at the present moment in which all philosophy of any significance should be grounded in metanoetics. Naturally, I have no intention of offering myself as a guide for the world; that would run counter to the very spirit of metanoetics. "Shinran had not a single disciple," wrote Shinran in the *Tanni-shō*. His idea of a horizontal fellowship, not of a vertical or authoritarian teacher–disciple relationship, laid the foundations for an "equality" in which no one enjoyed any special privilege. What Shinran said of invoking the name of Amida – "It is a matter of your decision whether you accept *nembutsu* or reject it" – I should also say of metanoetics.[1] And this, too, confirms my belief

that metanoetics, carried out in this spirit of freedom and equality, can become a philosophy for all people.

Note

1 *Nembutsu* is the practice of invoking the name of Amida Buddha.

22

Charles L. Stevenson, "The Emotive Meaning of Ethical Terms"

Introduction

Both in English-language and "continental" circles, the salient feature of twentieth-century moral philosophy since around 1930 has been the dominance of "non-cognitivist" theories. Whatever it is that moral judgments do – express emotions, register commitments or prescribe actions – they do not, on these theories, state beliefs about reality. In the case of "continental" trends, such as Existentialism, inspiration came from Kierkegaard (I.17) and Nietzsche (I.18), with their emphases on the primacy of the will and the seedy genealogy of conventional moral norms. In English-language philosophy, "non-cognitivism" owed to a combination of G. E. Moore's exposure of the "naturalistic fallacy" (I.19) and later reflections, by thinkers far removed from Moore, on the nature of meaning. The dry character of much of the writing should not disguise the radical nature of the message. Time will doubtless tell whether, as one recent author sees it, the "non-cognitivist" "den[ial] that anything is really worth struggling for, in the sense of 'really' in which two and two really make four," poses one of those "risks" which may hasten "the end of the

world."[1] But that such views of twentieth-century ethics can be seriously held is itself testimony to its dominant and disturbing tone.

The Logical Positivists and others in the 1920s and 1930s agreed with Moore and Ross (I.20) that moral judgments are not empirical statements, about what contributes to happiness, say. For them, however, the "non-natural" properties to which Moore took moral terms to refer belong to metaphysical mythology. Indeed, if, as the Positivists held, the only meaningful statements are those which are empirically verifiable or the "analytic" ones of logic, it followed that moral judgments are either meaningless or that they are not statements at all. The best-known product of this line of thought was the "emotivist" – or "Hurrah-Boo" – view of moral judgments. According to one Positivist, "stealing is bad," say, is "merely an expression of a certain wish"; while another writes that it is "purely 'emotive' . . . used to express feeling about certain objects."[2]

The Positivists' remarks on ethics read as rather casual codas to what really interested them – the theory of meaning. And the same is true of other writers on language, such as Ogden and Richards, who were exploring the "dynamic" roles that words can play over and above their informative and descriptive ones. It was left to the American philosopher, Charles L. Stevenson (1908–79), to articulate carefully a plausible version of the "emotive," "dynamic" meaning of moral language, one sensitive to the various constraints on a proper account of moral meaning.

From Charles L. Stevenson, *Facts and Values: Studies in Ethical Analysis.* New Haven, CT: Yale University Press, 1963, pp. 10–31 (asterisked notes are Stevenson's; some notes omitted or shortened).

Two of the constraints on which he particularly dwells – ones which, he believes, earlier views have failed to honor – are that such an account must be able to accommodate the fact of genuine moral disagreement, and must do justice to the "magnetic," action-influencing force of moral terms. His 1937 paper, which we have selected here, is a paradigmatic example of much twentieth-century moral philosophizing in the "analytical" vein. The philosopher's job is not the "first order" one of proposing moral values, but the "metaethical" one of analyzing moral language – something Stevenson does in terms, not primarily of the personal feelings expressed by "good," "right," etc., but of the "persuasive" effect of such words on audiences. Subscribing to Moore's rejection of "naturalism," yet able to "find no indefinable property" of goodness, Stevenson is of course following the prevailing "non-cognitivist" line.

A quarter of a century on, Stevenson wrote that "no one, I suppose, continues to hold this [emotivist] view just as it stands" (*Facts and Values*, p. 79), but the long list he gives of philosophers who subsequently qualified and elaborated it bears witness to the remarkable grip exerted by the wider conviction that moral discourse belongs in a quite different category from that of informative or descriptive discourse.[3] Perhaps, though, this conviction is not so remarkable. For it cannot, of course, be denied how well "emotivism" and its successors chime with the predilections – born of recent history rather than of the writings of philosophers – of a larger modern culture where it is apparently held, by many people, that morality is a "personal" matter, one of "opinion" or "conviction" and certainly not, at any rate, a matter to be settled in the manner of "2 + 2 = 4."

Notes

1 J. Leslie, *The End of the World: The Sciences and Ethics of Human Extinction*, London: Routledge, 1996, p. 11.

2 R. Carnap, *Philosophy and Logical Syntax*, London: Kegan Paul, 1935, p. 24; A. J. *Ayer, Language, Truth and Logic*, London: Gollancz, 1967, p. 108.

3 For a detailed discussion of Stevenson, his precursors, and successors, see W. D. Hudson, *Modern Moral Philosophy*, London: Macmillan, 1983.

Stevenson, "The Emotive Meaning of Ethical Terms"

1

Ethical questions first arise in the form 'is so and so good?' or 'is this alternative better than that?' These questions are difficult partly because we don't quite know what we are seeking. We are asking, 'is there a needle in the haystack?' without even knowing just what a needle is. So the first thing to do is to examine the questions themselves. We must try to make them clearer, either by defining the terms in which they are expressed or by any other method that is available.

The present essay is concerned wholly with this preliminary step of making ethical questions clear. In order to help answer the question 'is *X* good?' we must *substitute* for it a question that is free from ambiguity and confusion.

It is obvious that in substituting a clearer question we must not introduce some utterly different kind of question. It won't do (to take an extreme instance of a prevalent fallacy) to substitute for 'is *X* good?' the question 'is *X* pink with yellow trimmings?' and then point out how easy the question really is. This would beg the original question, not help answer it. On the other hand, we must not expect the substituted question to be strictly 'identical' with the original one. The original question may embody hypostatization, anthropomorphism, vagueness, and all the other ills to which our ordinary discourse is subject. If our substituted question is to be clearer it must remove these ills. The questions will be identical only in the sense that a child is identical with the man he later becomes. Hence we must not demand that the substitution strike us, on immediate introspection, as making no change in meaning.

Just how, then, must the substituted question be related to the original? Let us assume (inaccurately) that it must result from replacing 'good' by some set of terms that define it. The question then resolves itself to this: How must the defined meaning of 'good' be related to its original meaning?

I answer that it must be *relevant*. A defined meaning will be called 'relevant' to the original meaning under these circumstances: Those who have understood the definition must be able to say all that they then want to say by using the term in the defined way. They must never have occasion to use the term in the old, unclear sense. (If a person did have to go on using the word in the old sense, then to this extent his meaning would not be clarified and the philosophical task would not be completed.) It frequently happens that a word is used so confusedly and ambiguously that we must give it *several* defined meanings, rather than one. In this case only the whole set of defined meanings will be called 'relevant', and any one of them will be called 'partially relevant'. This is not a rigorous treatment of *relevance*, by any means, but it will serve for the present purposes.

Let us now turn to our particular task – that of giving a relevant definition of 'good'. Let us first examine some of the ways in which others have attempted to do this.

The word 'good' has often been defined in terms of *approval*, or similar psychological attitudes. We may take as typical examples: 'good' means *desired by me* (Hobbes); and 'good' means *approved by most people* (Hume, in effect).* It will be convenient to refer to definitions of this sort as 'interest theories', following R. B. Perry, although neither 'interest' nor 'theory' is used in the most usual way.

Are definitions of this sort relevant?

It is idle to deny their *partial relevance*. The most superficial inquiry will reveal that 'good' is exceedingly ambiguous. To maintain that 'good' is *never* used in Hobbes' sense, and never in Hume's, is only to manifest an insensitivity to the complexities of language. We must recognize, perhaps, not only these senses, but a variety of

similar ones, differing both with regard to the kind of interest in question and with regard to the people who are said to have the interest.

But that is a minor matter. The essential question is not whether interest theories are *partially* relevant, but whether they are *wholly* relevant. This is the only point for intelligent dispute. Briefly: Granted that some senses of 'good' may relevantly be defined in terms of interest, is there some *other* sense which is *not* relevantly so defined? We must give this question careful attention. For it is quite possible that when philosophers (and many others) have found the question 'is X good?' so difficult, they have been grasping for this *other* sense of 'good' and not any sense relevantly defined in terms of interest. If we insist on defining 'good' in terms of interest, and answer the question when thus interpreted, we may be begging *their* question entirely. Of course this *other* sense of 'good' may not exist, or it may be a complete confusion; but that is what we must discover.

Now many have maintained that interest theories are *far* from being completely relevant. They have argued that such theories neglect the very sense of 'good' that is most typical of ethics. And certainly, their arguments are not without plausibility.

Only – what *is* this typical sense of 'good'? The answers have been so vague and so beset with difficulties that one can scarcely determine.

There are certain requirements, however, with which the typical sense has been expected to comply – requirements which appeal strongly to our common sense. It will be helpful to summarize these, showing how they exclude the interest theories:

In the first place, we must be able sensibly to *disagree* about whether something is 'good'. This condition rules out Hobbes' definition. For consider the following argument: 'This is good.' 'That isn't so; it's not good.' As translated by Hobbes, this becomes: 'I desire this.' 'That isn't so, for I don't.' The speakers are not contradicting one another, and think they are only because of an elementary confusion in the use of pronouns. The definition, 'good' means *desired by my community*, is also excluded, for how could people from different communities disagree?

In the second place, 'goodness' must have, so to speak, a magnetism. A person who recognizes X to be 'good' must *ipso facto* acquire a stronger

---

* The definition ascribed to Hume is oversimplified, but not, I think, in a way that weakens the force of the observations that I am about to make. Perhaps the same should be said of Hobbes.

tendency to act in its favour than he otherwise would have had. This rules out the Humian type of definition. For according to Hume, to recognize that something is 'good' is simply to recognize that the majority approve of it. Clearly a man may see that the majority approve of X without having, himself, a stronger tendency to favour it. This requirement excludes any attempt to define 'good' in terms of the interest of people *other* than the speaker.

In the third place, the 'goodness' of anything must not be verifiable solely by use of the scientific method. 'Ethics must not be psychology.' This restriction rules out all of the traditional interest theories without exception. It is so sweeping a restriction that we must examine its plausibility. What are the methodological implications of interest theories which are here rejected?

According to Hobbes' definition a person can prove his ethical judgements with finality by showing that he is not making an introspective error about his desires. According to Hume's definition one may prove ethical judgements (roughly speaking) by taking a vote. *This* use of the empirical method, at any rate, seems highly remote from what we usually accept as proof and reflects on the complete relevance of the definitions that imply it.

But are there not more complicated interest theories that are immune from such methodological implications? No, for the same factors appear; they are only put off for a while. Consider, for example, the definition: 'X is good' means *most people would approve of 'X' if they knew its nature and consequences*. How, according to this definition, could we prove that a certain X was good? We should first have to find out, empirically, just what X was like and what its consequences would be. To this extent the empirical method as required by the definition seems beyond intelligent objection. But what remains? We should next have to discover whether most people would approve of the sort of thing we had discovered X to be. This could not be determined by popular vote – but only because it would be too difficult to explain to the voters, beforehand, what the nature and consequences of X really were. Apart from this, voting would be a pertinent method. We are again reduced to counting noses as a *perfectly final* appeal.

Now we need not scorn voting entirely. A man who rejected interest theories as irrelevant

might readily make the following statement: 'If I believed that X would be approved by the majority, when they knew all about it, I should be strongly *led* to say that X was good.' But he would continue: '*Need* I say that X was good, under the circumstances? Wouldn't my acceptance of the alleged "final proof" result simply from my being democratic? What about the more aristocratic people? They would simply say that the approval of most people, even when they knew all about the object of their approval, simply had nothing to do with the goodness of anything, and they would probably add a few remarks about the low state of people's interests.' It would indeed seem, from these considerations, that the definition we have been considering has presupposed democratic ideals from the start; it has dressed up democratic propaganda in the guise of a definition.

The omnipotence of the empirical method, as implied by interest theories and others, may be shown unacceptable in a somewhat different way. G. E. Moore's familiar objection about the open question is chiefly pertinent in this regard.[1] No matter what set of scientifically knowable properties a thing may have (says Moore, in effect), you will find, on careful introspection, that it is an open question to ask whether anything having these properties is *good*. It is difficult to believe that this recurrent question is a totally confused one, or that it seems open only because of the ambiguity of 'good'. Rather, we must be using some sense of 'good' which is not definable, relevantly, in terms of anything scientifically knowable. That is, the scientific method is not sufficient for ethics.

These, then, are the requirements with which the 'typical' sense of 'good' is expected to comply: (1) goodness must be a topic for intelligent disagreement; (2) it must be 'magnetic'; and (3) it must not be discoverable solely through the scientific method.

2

I can now turn to my proposed analysis of ethical judgements. First let me present my position dogmatically, showing to what extent I vary from tradition.

I believe that the three requirements given above are perfectly sensible, that there is some *one* sense of 'good' which satisfies all three requirements, and that no traditional interest theory satisfies them all. But this does not imply that 'good' must be explained in terms of a Platonic Idea, or of a categorical imperative, or of a unique, unanalysable property. On the contrary, the three requirements can be met by a *kind* of interest theory. *But we must give up a presupposition that all the traditional interest theories have made.*

Traditional interest theories hold that ethical statements are *descriptive* of the existing state of interests – that they simply *give information* about interests. (More accurately, ethical judgements are said to describe what the state of interests is, was, or will be, or to indicate what the state of interests *would* be under specified circumstances.) It is this emphasis on description, on information, which leads to their incomplete relevance. Doubtless there is always *some* element of description in ethical judgements, but this is by no means all. Their major use is not to indicate facts but to *create an influence*. Instead of merely describing people's interests they *change* or *intensify* them. They *recommend* an interest in an object, rather than state that the interest already exists.

For instance: When you tell a man that he ought not to steal, your object is not merely to let him know that people disapprove of stealing. You are attempting, rather, to get *him* to disapprove of it. Your ethical judgement has a quasi-imperative force which, operating through suggestion and intensified by your tone of voice, readily permits you to begin to *influence*, to *modify*, his interests. If in the end you do not succeed in getting *him* to disapprove of stealing, you will feel that you have failed to convince him that stealing is wrong. You will continue to feel this, even though he fully acknowledges that you disapprove of it and that almost everyone else does. When you point out to him the consequences of his actions – consequences which you suspect he already disapproves of – these *reasons* which support your ethical judgement are simply a means of facilitating your influence. If you think you can change his interests by making vivid to him how others will disapprove of him, you will do so, otherwise not. So the consideration about other people's interest is just an additional means you may employ in order to move him and is not a part of the ethical judgement itself. Your

ethical judgement does not merely describe interests to him, it directs his very interests. The difference between the traditional interest theories and my view is like the difference between describing a desert and irrigating it.

Another example: A munitions maker declares that war is a good thing. If he merely meant that he approved of it, he would not have to insist so strongly nor grow so excited in his argument. People would be quite easily convinced that he approved of it. If he merely meant that most people approved of war, or that most people would approve of it if they knew the consequences, he would have to yield his point if it were proved that this was not so. But he would not do this, nor does consistency require it. He is not *describing* the state of people's approval; he is trying to *change* it by his influence. If he found that few people approved of war, he might insist all the more strongly that it was good, for there would be more changing to be done.

This example illustrates how 'good' may be used for what most of us would call bad purposes. Such cases are as pertinent as any others. I am not indicating the *good* way of using 'good'. I am not influencing people but am describing the way this influence sometimes goes on. If the reader wishes to say that the munitions maker's influence is bad – that is, if the reader wishes to awaken people's disapproval of the man, and to make him disapprove of his own actions – I should at another time be willing to join in this undertaking. But this is not the present concern. I am not using ethical terms but am indicating how they *are* used. The munitions maker, in his use of 'good', illustrates the persuasive character of the word just as well as does the unselfish man who, eager to encourage in each of us a desire for the happiness of all, contends that the supreme good is peace.

Thus ethical terms are *instruments* used in the complicated interplay and readjustment of human interests. This can be seen plainly from more general observations. People from widely separated communities have different moral attitudes. Why? To a great extent because they have been subject to different social influences. Now clearly this influence does not operate through sticks and stones alone; words play a great part. People praise one another to encourage certain inclinations and blame one another to discourage others. Those of forceful personalities issue commands which weaker people, for complicated instinctive reasons, find it difficult to disobey, quite apart from fears of consequences. Further influence is brought to bear by writers and orators. Thus social influence is exerted, to an enormous extent, by means that have nothing to do with physical force or material reward. The ethical terms facilitate such influence. Being suited for use in *suggestion*, they are a means by which men's attitudes may be led this way or that. The reason, then, that we find a greater similarity in the moral attitudes of one community than in those of different communities is largely this: ethical judgements propagate themselves. One man says 'this is good'; this may influence the approval of another person, who then makes the same ethical judgement, which in turn influences another person, and so on. In the end, by a process of mutual influence, people take up more or less the same attitudes. Between people of widely separated communities, of course, the influence is less strong; hence different communities have different attitudes.

These remarks will serve to give a general idea of my point of view. We must now go into more detail. There are several questions which must be answered: How does an ethical sentence acquire its power of influencing people – why is it suited to suggestion? Again, what has this influence to do with the *meaning* of ethical terms? And finally, do these considerations really lead us to a sense of 'good' which meets the requirements mentioned in the preceding section?

Let us deal first with the question about *meaning*. This is far from an easy question, so we must enter into a preliminary inquiry about meaning in general. Although a seeming digression this will prove indispensable.

3

Broadly speaking, there are two different *purposes* which lead us to use language. On the one hand we use words (as in science) to record, clarify and communicate *beliefs*. On the other hand we use words to give vent to our feelings (interjections), or to create moods (poetry), or to incite people to actions or attitudes (oratory).

The first use of words I shall call 'descriptive', the second, 'dynamic'. Note that the distinction depends solely upon the *purpose* of the *speaker*.

When a person says 'hydrogen is the lightest known gas,' his purpose *may* be simply to lead the hearer to believe this, or to believe that the speaker believes it. In that case the words are used descriptively. When a person cuts himself and says 'damn', his purpose is not ordinarily to record, clarify or communicate any belief. The word is used dynamically. The two ways of using words, however, are by no means mutually exclusive. This is obvious from the fact that our purposes are often complex. Thus when one says 'I want you to close the door', part of his purpose, ordinarily, is to lead the hearer to believe that he has this want. To that extent the words are used descriptively. But the major part of one's purpose is to lead the hearer to *satisfy* the want. To that extent the words are used dynamically.

It very frequently happens that the same sentence may have a dynamic use on one occasion and not on another, and that it may have different dynamic uses on different occasions. For instance: A man says to a visiting neighbour, 'I am loaded down with work.' His purpose may be to let the neighbour know how life is going with him. This would *not* be a dynamic use of words. He may make the remark, however, in order to drop a hint. This *would* be dynamic usage (as well as descriptive). Again, he may make the remark to arouse the neighbour's sympathy. This would be a *different* dynamic usage from that of hinting.

Or again, when we say to a man, 'of course you won't make those mistakes any more,' we *may* simply be making a prediction. But we are more likely to be using 'suggestion', in order to encourage him and hence *keep* him from making mistakes. The first use would be descriptive, the second, mainly dynamic.

From these examples it will be clear that we can not determine whether words are used dynamically or not merely by reading the dictionary – even assuming that everyone is faithful to dictionary meanings. Indeed, to know whether a person is using a word dynamically we must note his tone of voice, his gestures, the general circumstances under which he is speaking, and so on.

We must now proceed to an important question: What has the dynamic use of words to do with their *meaning*? One thing is clear – we must not define 'meaning' in a way that would make meaning vary with dynamic usage. If we did, we should have no use for the term. All that we could say about such 'meaning' would be that it is very complicated and subject to constant change. So we must certainly distinguish between the dynamic use of words and their meaning.

It does not follow, however, that we must define 'meaning' in some non-psychological fashion. We must simply restrict the psychological field. Instead of identifying meaning with *all* the psychological causes and effects that attend a word's utterance, we must identify it with those that it has a *tendency* (causal property, dispositional property) to be connected with. The tendency must be of a particular kind, moreover. It must exist for all who speak the language; it must be persistent and must be realizable more or less independently of determinate circumstances attending the word's utterance. There will be further restrictions dealing with the interrelations of word in different contexts. Moreover, we must include, under the psychological responses which the words tend to produce, not only immediately introspectable experiences but *dispositions* to react in a given way with appropriate stimuli. I hope to go into these matters in a subsequent essay. Suffice it now to say that I think 'meaning' may be thus defined in a way to include 'propositional' meaning as an important kind.

The definition will readily permit a distinction between meaning and dynamic use. For when words are accompanied by dynamic purposes, it does not follow that they *tend* to be accompanied by them in the way mentioned above. E.g. there need be no tendency realizable more or less independently of the determinate circumstances under which the words are uttered.

There will be a kind of meaning, however, in the sense above defined, which has an intimate relation to dynamic usage. I refer to 'emotive' meaning (in a sense roughly like that employed by Ogden and Richards).[2] The emotive meaning of a word is a tendency of a word, arising through the history of its usage, to produce (result from) *affective* responses in people. It is the immediate aura of feeling which hovers about a word. Such tendencies to produce affective responses cling to words very tenaciously. It would be difficult, for instance, to express merriment by using the interjection 'alas'. Because

of the persistence of such affective tendencies (among other reasons) it becomes feasible to classify them as 'meanings'.

Just *what* is the relation between emotive meaning and the dynamic use of words? Let us take an example. Suppose that a man tells his hostess, at the end of a party, that he thoroughly enjoyed himself, and suppose that he was in fact bored. If we consider his remark an innocent one, are we likely to remind him, later, that he 'lied' to his hostess? Obviously not, or at least, not without a broad smile; for although he told her something that he believed to be false, and with the intent of making her believe that it was true – those being the ordinary earmarks of a lie – the expression, 'you lied to her', would be emotively too strong for our purposes. It would seem to be a reproach, even if we intended it not to be a reproach. So it will be evident that such words as 'lied' (and many parallel examples could be cited) become suited, on account of their emotive meaning, to a certain kind of dynamic use – so well suited, in fact, that the hearer is likely to be misled when we use them in any other way. The more pronounced a word's emotive meaning is, the less likely people are to use it purely descriptively. Some words are suited to encourage people, some to discourage them, some to quiet them, and so on.

Even in these cases, of course, the dynamic purposes are not to be identified with any sort of meaning; for the emotive meaning accompanies a word much more persistently than do the dynamic purposes. But there is an important contingent relation between emotive meaning and dynamic purpose: the former assists the latter. Hence if we define emotively laden terms in a way that neglects their emotive meaning, we become seriously confused. *We lead people to think that the terms defined are used dynamically less often than they are.*

4

Let us now apply these remarks in defining 'good'. This word may be used morally or nonmorally. I shall deal with the non-moral usage almost entirely, but only because it is simpler. The main points of the analysis will apply equally well to either usage.

As a preliminary definition let us take an inaccurate approximation. It may be more misleading than helpful but will do to begin with. Roughly, then, the sentence '*X* is good' means *we like '*X*'* ('We' includes the hearer or hearers.)

At first glance this definition sounds absurd. If used, we should expect to find the following sort of conversation: A: 'This is good.' B: 'But I *don't* like it. What led you to believe that I did?' The unnaturalness of B's reply, judged by ordinary word usage, would seem to cast doubt on the relevance of my definition.

B's unnaturalness, however, lies simply in this: he is assuming that 'we like it' (as would occur implicitly in the use of 'good') is being used descriptively. This will not do. When 'we like it' is to take the place of 'this is good,' the former sentence must be used not purely descriptively, but dynamically. More specifically, it must be used to promote a very subtle (and for the non-moral sense in question, a very easily resisted) kind of *suggestion*. To the extent that 'we' refers to the hearer it must have the dynamic use, essential to suggestion, of leading the hearer to *make* true what is said, rather than merely to believe it. And to the extent that 'we' refers to the speaker, the sentence must have not only the descriptive use of indicating belief about the speaker's interest, but the quasi-interjectory, dynamic function of giving direct expression to the interest. (This immediate expression of feelings assists in the process of suggestion. It is difficult to disapprove in the face of another's enthusiasm.)

For an example of a case where 'we like this' is used in the dynamic way that 'this is good' is used, consider the case of a mother who says to her several children, 'one thing is certain, *we all like to be neat.*' If she really believed this, she would not bother to say so. But she is not using the words descriptively. She is *encouraging* the children to like neatness. By telling them that they like neatness, she will lead them to *make* her statement true, so to speak. If, instead of saying 'we all like to be neat' in this way, she had said 'it's a good thing to be neat', the effect would have been approximately the same.

But these remarks are still misleading. Even when 'we like it' is used for suggestion, it is not quite like 'this is good'. The latter is more subtle. With such a sentence as 'this is a good book', for example, it would be practically impossible to use instead 'we like this book'. When the latter is used it must be accompanied by so exaggerated an intonation, to prevent its becoming confused with a descriptive statement, that the force of suggestion becomes stronger and ludicrously more overt than when 'good' is used.

The definition is inadequate, further, in that the definiens has been restricted to dynamic usage. Having said that dynamic usage was different from meaning, I should not have to mention it in giving the *meaning* of 'good'.

It is in connection with this last point that we must return to emotive meaning. The word 'good' has a laudatory emotive meaning that fits it for the dynamic use of suggesting favourable interest. But the sentence 'we like it' has no such emotive meaning. Hence my definition has neglected emotive meaning entirely. Now to neglect emotive meaning serves to foster serious confusions, as I have previously intimated; so I have sought to make up for the inadequacy of the definition by letting the restriction about dynamic usage take the place of emotive meaning. What I should do, of course, is to find a definiens whose emotive meaning, like that of 'good', simply does *lead* to dynamic usage.

Why did I not do this? I answer that it is not possible if the definition is to afford us increased clarity. No two words, in the first place, have quite the same emotive meaning. The most we can hope for is a rough approximation. But if we seek for such an approximation for 'good', we shall find nothing more than synonyms, such as 'desirable' or 'valuable'; and these are profitless because they do not clear up the connection between 'good' and favourable interest. If we reject such synonyms, in favour of non-ethical terms, we shall be highly misleading. For instance 'this is good' has something like the meaning of 'I *do* like this; do so as well.' But this is certainly not accurate. For the imperative makes an appeal to the conscious efforts of the hearer. Of course he cannot like something just by trying. He must be led to like it through suggestion. Hence an ethical sentence differs from an imperative in that it enables one to make changes in a much more subtle, less fully conscious way. Note that the ethical sentence centres the hearer's attention not on his interests but on the object of interest, and thereby facilitates suggestion. Because of its subtlety, moreover, an ethical sentence readily permits counter-suggestion and leads to the give and take situation that is so characteristic of arguments about values.

Strictly speaking, then, it is impossible to define 'good' in terms of favourable interest if emotive meaning is not to be distorted. Yet it is possible to say that 'this is good' is *about* the favourable interest of the speaker and the hearer or hearers, and that it has a laudatory emotive meaning which fits the words for use in suggestion. This is a rough description of meaning, not a definition. But it serves the same clarifying function that a definition ordinarily does, and that, after all, is enough.

A word must be added about the moral use of 'good'. This differs from the above in that it is about a different kind of interest. Instead of being about what the hearer and speaker *like*, it is about a stronger sort of approval. When a person *likes* something, he is pleased when it prospers and disappointed when it does not. When a person *morally approves* of something he experiences a rich feeling of security when it prospers and is indignant or 'shocked' when it does not. These are rough and inaccurate examples of the many factors which one would have to mention in distinguishing the two kinds of interest. In the moral usage, as well as in the non-moral, 'good' has an emotive meaning which adapts it to suggestion.

And now, are these considerations of any importance? Why do I stress emotive meanings in this fashion? Does the omission of them really lead people into errors? I think, indeed, that the errors resulting from such omissions are enormous. In order to see this, however, we must return to the restrictions, mentioned in section 1, with which the typical sense of 'good' has been expected to comply.

5

The first restriction, it will be remembered, had to do with disagreement. Now there is clearly some sense in which people disagree on ethical points, but we must not rashly assume that all disagreement is modelled after the sort that occurs in the natural sciences. We must distinguish between 'disagreement in belief (typical of the sciences) and 'disagreement in interest'. Disagreement in belief occurs when A believes *p* and B disbelieves it.

Disagreement in interest occurs when A has a favourable interest in *X* and when B has an unfavourable one in it. (For a full-bodied disagreement, neither party is content with the discrepancy.)

Let me give an example of disagreement in interest. A: 'Let's go to a cinema tonight.' B: 'I don't want to do that. Let's go to the symphony.' A continues to insist on the cinema, B on the symphony. This is disagreement in a perfectly conventional sense. They cannot agree on where they want to go, and each is trying to redirect the other's interest. (Note that imperatives are used in the example.)

It is disagreement in *interest* which takes places in ethics. When C says 'this is good,' and D says 'no, it's bad,' we have a case of suggestion and counter-suggestion. Each man is trying to redirect the other's interest. There obviously need be no domineering, since each may be willing to give ear to the other's influence; but each is trying to move the other none the less. It is in this sense that they disagree. Those who argue that certain interest theories make no provision for disagreement have been misled, I believe, simply because the traditional theories, in leaving out emotive meaning, give the impression that ethical judgements are used descriptively only; and of course when judgements are used purely descriptively, the only disagreement that can arise is disagreement *in belief*. Such disagreement may be disagreement in belief *about* interests, but this is not the same as disagreement *in* interest. My definition does not provide for disagreement in belief about interests any more than does Hobbes'; but that is no matter, for there is no reason to believe, at least on common sense grounds, that this kind of disagreement exists. There is only disagreement *in* interest. (We shall see in a moment that disagreement in interest does not remove ethics from sober argument – that this kind of disagreement may often be resolved through empirical means.)

The second restriction, about 'magnetism', or the connection between goodness and actions, requires only a word. This rules out only those interest theories that do *not* include the interest of the speaker in defining 'good'. My account does include the speaker's interest, hence is immune.

The third restriction, about the empirical method, may be met in a way that springs naturally from the above account of disagreement.

Let us put the question in this way: When two people disagree over an ethical matter, can they completely resolve the disagreement through empirical considerations, assuming that each applies the empirical method exhaustively, consistently, and without error?

I answer that sometimes they can and sometimes they cannot, and that at any rate, even when they can, the relation between empirical knowledge and ethical judgements is quite different from the one that traditional interest theories seem to imply.

This can best be seen from an analogy. Let us return to the example where A and B could not agree on a cinema or a symphony. The example differed from an ethical argument in that imperatives were used, rather than ethical judgements, but was analogous to the extent that each person was endeavouring to modify the other's interest. Now how would these people argue the case, assuming that they were too intelligent just to shout at one another?

Clearly, they would give 'reasons' to support their imperatives. A might say, 'but you know, Garbo is at the Bijou.' His hope is that B, who admires Garbo, will acquire a desire to go to the cinema when he knows what film will be there. B may counter, 'but Toscanini is guest conductor tonight, in an all-Beethoven programme'. And so on. Each supports his imperative ('let's do so and so') by reasons which may be empirically established.

To generalize from this: disagreement in interest may be rooted in disagreement in belief. That is to say, people who disagree in interest would often cease to do so if they knew the precise nature and consequences of the object of their interest. To this extent disagreement in interest may be resolved by securing agreement in belief, which in turn may be secured empirically.

This generalization holds for ethics. If A and B, instead of using imperatives, had said, respectively, 'it would be *better* to go to the cinema,' and 'it would be better to go to the symphony,' the reasons which they would advance would be roughly the same. They would each give a more thorough account of the object of interest, with the purpose of completing the redirection of interest which was begun by the suggestive force of the ethical sentence. On the whole, of course, the suggestive force of the ethical statement merely exerts enough pressure to start such

trains of reasons, since the reasons are much more essential in resolving disagreement in interest than the persuasive effect of the ethical judgement itself.

Thus the empirical method is relevant to ethics simply because our knowledge of the world is a determining factor to our interests. But note that empirical facts are not inductive grounds from which the ethical judgement problematically follows. (This is what traditional interest theories imply.) If someone said 'close the door,' and added the reason 'we'll catch cold,' the latter would scarcely be called an inductive ground of the former. Now imperatives are related to the reasons which support them in the same way that ethical judgements are related to reasons.

Is the empirical method *sufficient* for attaining ethical agreement? Clearly not. For empirical knowledge resolves disagreement in interest only to the extent that such disagreement is rooted in disagreement in belief. Not all disagreement in interest is of this sort. For instance: A is of a sympathetic nature and B is not. They are arguing about whether a public dole would be good. Suppose that they discovered all the consequences of the dole. Is it not possible, even so, that A will say that it is good and B that it is bad? The disagreement in interest may arise not from limited factual knowledge but simply from A's sympathy and B's coldness. Or again, suppose in the above argument that A was poor and unemployed and that B was rich. Here again the disagreement might not be due to different factual knowledge. It would be due to the different social positions of the men, together with their predominant self-interest.

When ethical disagreement is not rooted in disagreement in belief, is there *any* method by which it may be settled? If one means by 'method' a *rational* method, then there is no method. But in any case there is a 'way'. Let us consider the above example again, where disagreement was due to A's sympathy and B's coldness. Must they end by saying, 'well, it's just a matter of our having different temperaments'? Not necessarily. A, for instance, may try to *change* the temperament of his opponent. He may pour out his enthusiasms in such a moving way – present the sufferings of the poor with such appeal – that he will lead his opponent to see life through different eyes. He may build up by the contagion of his feelings an influence which will modify B's temperament and create in him a sympathy for the poor which did not previously exist. This is often the only way to obtain ethical agreement, if there is any way at all. It is persuasive, not empirical or rational; but that is no reason for neglecting it. There is no reason to scorn it, either, for it is only by such means that our personalities are able to grow, through our contact with others.

The point I wish to stress, however, is simply that the empirical method is instrumental to ethical agreement only to the extent that disagreement in interest is rooted in disagreement in belief. There is little reason to believe that all disagreement is of this sort. Hence the empirical method is not sufficient for ethics. In any case, ethics is not psychology, since psychology does not endeavour to *direct* our interests; it discovers facts about the ways in which interests are or can be directed, but that is quite another matter.

To summarize this section: my analysis of ethical judgements meets the three requirements for the typical sense of 'good' that were mentioned in section 1. The traditional interest theories fail to meet these requirements simply because they neglect emotive meaning. This neglect leads them to neglect dynamic usage, and the sort of disagreement that results from such usage, together with the method of resolving the disagreement. I may add that my analysis answers Moore's objection about the open question. Whatever scientifically knowable properties a thing may have, it *is* always open to question whether a thing having these (enumerated) qualities is good. For to ask whether it is good is to ask for *influence*. And whatever I may know about an object, I can still ask, quite pertinently, to be influenced with regard to my interest in it.

6

And now, have I really pointed out the 'typical' sense of 'good'?

I suppose that many will still say 'no', claiming that I have simply failed to set down *enough* requirements that this sense must meet, and that my analysis, like all others given in terms of interest, is a way of begging the issue. They will say: 'When we ask "is X good?" we don't want mere influence, mere advice. We decidedly don't want to be influenced through persuasion, nor are we fully content when the influence is supported by a wide scientific knowledge of X. The answer to our question will, of course, modify our interests. But this is only because a unique sort of truth will be revealed to us – a truth that must be apprehended a priori. We want our interests to be guided by this truth and by nothing else. To substitute for this special truth mere emotive meaning and mere factual truth is to conceal from us the very object of our search.'

I can only answer that I do not understand. What is this truth to be *about*? For I recollect no Platonic Idea, nor do I know what to *try* to recollect. I find no indefinable property nor do I know what to look for. And the 'self-evident' deliverances of reason, which so many philosophers have mentioned, seem on examination to be deliverances of their respective reasons only (if of anyone's) and not of mine.

I strongly suspect, indeed, that any sense of 'good' which is expected both to unite itself in synthetic a priori fashion with other concepts and to influence interests as well, is really a great confusion. I extract from this meaning the power of influence alone, which I find the only intelligible part. If the rest is confusion, however, then it certainly deserves more than the shrug of one's shoulders. What I should like to do is to *account* for the confusion – to examine the psychological needs which have given rise to it and show how these needs may be satisfied in another way. This is *the* problem, if confusion is to be stopped at its source. But it is an enormous problem and my reflections on it, which are at present worked out only roughly, must be reserved until some later time.

I may add that if 'X is good' has the meaning that I ascribe to it, then it is not a judgement that professional philosophers and only professional philosophers are qualified to make. To the extent that ethics predicates the ethical terms of anything, rather than explains their meaning, it becomes more than a purely intellectual study. Ethical judgements are social instruments. They are used in a cooperative enterprise that leads to a mutual readjustment of human interests. Philosophers have a part in this; but so too do all men.

Notes

1   See §13 of Chapter 1 of Moore's *Principia Ethica* in this volume (I.19).

2 In their *The Meaning of Meaning*, London: Kegan Paul, 1923, p. 125, C. K. Ogden and I. A. Richards in effect sketched the position that Stevenson elaborates and defends in the present article. They wrote: "T[he] peculiar ethical use of 'good' is, we suggest, a purely emotive one ... it serves only as an emotive sign expressing our attitude ... and perhaps evoking similar attitudes in other persons, or inciting them to actions ...".

23

Jean-Paul Sartre, "Existentialism Is a Humanism"

Introduction

Winner of the 1964 Nobel Prize for Literature but who for political reasons declined the award, Jean-Paul Sartre (1905–80) was born in Paris and educated at the prestigious École Normale Supèrieure, taking a doctorate in 1929 and becoming a teacher of philosophy in 1931. His mother was cousin to humanitarian Albert Schweitzer, his father a naval officer who died when Sartre was fifteen months old. In 1932 Sartre traveled to Berlin, where he studied the thought of Martin Heidegger (II.22 and III.24) and Edmund Husserl (II.19); the latter was especially influential in the development of Sartre's thought.[1]

Drafted into the French army with the start of World War II, Sartre was captured by invading Nazi troops in 1940 at Padoux. After spending nine months as a prisoner-of-war, Sartre was released for health reasons. He resumed his work as a teacher, taking up a position that was vacated by a Jewish instructor who had been banned from teaching by Vichy law. Sartre became a founding member of the underground political group *Socialisme et liberté* and contributed to Albert Camus's resistance newspaper, *Combat*. In 1943 Sartre published his magnum opus, *Being and Nothingness* (*L'être et le néant*), a book that pulls together elements of Hegelian and phenomeno-

From W. Kaufmann, ed., *Existentialism from Dostoevsky to Sartre*, trans. W. Kaufmann. New York: Meridian Books, 1975, pp. 345–69.

logical thought to construct an expansive philosophy of free consciousness.

For Sartre, reality is composed of two fundamental factors: being (or, using Sartre's Hegelian terminology, being "in itself," *en-soi*) and nothingness (being "for itself," *pour-soi*). Being *pour-soi* is consciousness and absolute freedom. Through an activity of continuous negation, the *pour-soi* differentiates each thing from every other thing as well as from the *pour-soi* itself.[2] Consciousness as absolute, negating freedom is free from the determinations of any causal order. It is literally no-thing and not part of the natural causal order where effects follow causes in a necessary and regular way. Moreover, at every instant consciousness utterly transcends itself so that, in fact, no conscious human being can be a definite thing.[3] Consciousness, therefore, has no abiding nature or essence, and no one is determined by the "situation" or limitations of circumstance, history, and environment. There simply is no human nature.

This means that in a strict sense no one "is" a human being, an animal, a criminal, a homosexual, a European, or a coward. At each instant, everyone is free to choose to become something other than what he or she has been. But, perhaps paradoxically, no one is free to become something fixed and permanent either. Because of this, each of us is absolutely responsible for every choice we make. Indeed, in Sartre's extraordinarily demanding regard, no one can be compelled, even under torture, to do anything beyond one's choice. In short, no one is free to become un-free. Humans have been irrevocably "abandoned" to their freedom.

Facing up to absolute freedom, total responsibility, and the irreducible role freedom plays in the world can be a dizzying, even nauseating affair. Sartre set out to describe this strange experience in his 1938 novel, *Nausée*. Because of the anxiety or "anguish" embracing human freedom can produce, people tend to deny it, fleeing into rationalizing explanations of themselves and their conduct that shift responsibility for their choices to something besides themselves – to nature, to society, to their genetic endowments, to their upbringing, to God. But because awareness of fundamental freedom is inescapable and the reality of this freedom is on some level understood by everyone, these attempts to avoid it are always made in "bad faith" (*mauvaise foi*); and living in "bad faith" means living "inauthentically."

The selection that follows has been drawn from an essay that Sartre wrote in 1946 to explain and defend his philosophy of being and nothingness. Sartre calls his philosophy Existentialism, and in particular atheistic Existentialism, because it is centered on the assertion that for humans "existence precedes essence." That is, unlike natural objects, human beings appear in the world as pure freedom without the constraints that would be entailed by being instances of a type or "form" or "idea." The human being, in short, is "a being which exists before it can be defined by any conception of it." For Sartre each of us "first of all exists, encounters himself, surges up in the world – and defines himself afterwards." In a sense, therefore, each of us is a sort of self-created work of art: "Man is nothing else but that which he makes of himself." It is a view that in remarkable ways repeats the doctrine set out by Pico della Mirandola (I.12). Because human beings are the absolute source of themselves and the meanings of the world, including their moral principles, Existentialism is therefore a humanism: "There is no other universe except the human universe, the universe of human subjectivity."[4]

There is, in addition, a sense for Sartre in which this doctrine supports a universalism in ethics. For one thing, all ethical choices are accessible to every consciousness: "In every purpose there is a universality, in this sense that every purpose is comprehensible to every man." Moreover, echoing Kant (I.15), Sartre maintains that in making any particular moral choice, free consciousness makes it as though it were the choice everyone ought to make in such a circumstance: "For in effect, of all the actions a man may take in order to create himself as he wills to be, there is not one which is not creative, at the same time, of an image of man such as he believes he ought to be." Finally, to embrace and support one's own freedom requires willing that all should enjoy the political liberty necessary to exercise their freedom. It is incoherent, according to Sartre, to promote one's own liberty while at the same time thwarting the liberty of others: "I cannot make liberty my aim unless I make that of others equally my aim."

Notes

1 One year after Husserl's death as a sort of *homage*, Sartre published, "Une idée fondamentale de la phénoménologie de Husserl: l'intentionnalité," *La nouvelle revue française* 304 (January 1939): 129–31.
2 This idea of a fundamental difference and otherness would later influence deconstructionist Jacques Derrida.
3 Jean-Paul Sartre, *Transcendence of the Ego* (1936–7): "La transcendance de l'ego: Esquisse d'une description phénoménologique," *Recherches philosophiques* 6 (1936–7): 85–123.
4 It was in opposition to this doctrine – that humanity is the source of meaning – that Heidegger composed his "Letter on 'Humanism'" ("Brief über den 'Humanismus'") in 1946.

Sartre, "Existentialism Is a Humanism"

My purpose here is to offer a defence of existentialism against several reproaches that have been laid against it.

First, it has been reproached as an invitation to people to dwell in quietism of despair. For if every way to a solution is barred, one would have to regard any action in this world as entirely ineffective, and one would arrive finally at a contemplative philosophy. Moreover, since contemplation is a luxury, this would be only another bourgeois philosophy. This is, especially, the reproach made by the Communists.

From another quarter we are reproached for having underlined all that is ignominious in the human situation, for depicting what is mean, sordid or base to the neglect of certain things that possess charm and beauty and belong to the brighter side of human nature: for example, according to the Catholic critic, Mlle. Mercier, we forget how an infant smiles. Both from this side and from the other we are also reproached for leaving out of account the solidarity of mankind and considering man in isolation. And this, say the Communists, is because we base our doctrine upon pure subjectivity – upon the Cartesian "I think": which is the moment in which solitary man attains to himself; a position from which it is impossible to regain solidarity with other men who exist outside of the self. The *ego* cannot reach them through the *cogito*.

From the Christian side, we are reproached as people who deny the reality and seriousness of human affairs. For since we ignore the commandments of God and all values prescribed as eternal, nothing remains but what is strictly voluntary. Everyone can do what he likes, and will be incapable, from such a point of view, of condemning either the point of view or the action of anyone else.

It is to these various reproaches that I shall endeavor to reply today; that is why I have entitled this brief exposition "Existentialism is a Humanism." Many may be surprised at the mention of humanism in this connection, but we shall try to see in what sense we understand it. In any case, we can begin by saying that existentialism, in our sense of the word, is a doctrine that does render human life possible; a doctrine, also, which affirms that every truth and every action imply both an environment and a human subjectivity.

[. . .]

The question is only complicated because there are two kinds of existentialists. There are, on the one hand, the Christians, amongst whom I shall name Jaspers and Gabriel Marcel, both professed Catholics; and on the other the existential atheists, amongst whom we must place Heidegger as well as the French existentialists and myself. What they have in common is simply the fact that they believe that *existence* comes before *essence* – or, if you will, that we must begin from the subjective. What exactly do we mean by that?

If one considers an article of manufacture – as, for example, a book or a paper-knife – one sees that it has been made by an artisan who had a conception of it; and he has paid attention, equally, to the conception of a paper-knife and to the pre-existent technique of production which is a part of that conception and is, at bottom, a formula. Thus the paper-knife is at the same time an article producible in a certain manner and one which, on the other hand, serves a definite purpose, for one cannot suppose that a man would produce a paper-knife without knowing what it was for. Let us say, then, of the paper-knife that its essence – that is to say the sum of the formulae and the qualities which made its production and its definition possible – precedes its existence. The presence of such-and-such a paper-knife or book is thus determined before my eyes. Here, then, we are viewing the world from a technical standpoint, and we can say that production precedes existence.

When we think of God as the creator, we are thinking of him, most of the time, as a supernal artisan. Whatever doctrine we may be considering, whether it be a doctrine like that of Descartes, or of Leibnitz himself, we always imply that the will follows, more or less, from the understanding or at least accompanies it, so that when God creates he knows precisely what he is creating. Thus, the conception of man in the mind of God is comparable to that of the paper-knife in the mind of the artisan: God makes man according to a procedure and a conception, exactly as the artisan manufactures a paper-knife, following a definition and a formula. Thus each individual man is the realization of a certain conception which dwells in the divine understanding. In the philosophic atheism of the eighteenth century, the notion of God is suppressed, but not, for all that, the idea that essence is prior to existence; something of that idea we still find everywhere, in Diderot, in Voltaire and even in Kant. Man possesses a human nature; that "human nature," which is the conception of human being, is found in every man; which means that each man is a particular example of a universal conception, the conception of Man. In Kant, this universality goes so far that the wild man of the woods, man in the state of nature and the bourgeois are all contained in the same definition and have the same fundamental qualities. Here again, the essence of man precedes that historic existence which we confront in experience.

Atheistic existentialism, of which I am a representative, declares with greater consistency that if God does not exist there is at least one being whose existence comes before its essence, a being which exists before it can be defined by any conception of it. That being is man or, as Heidegger has it, the human reality. What do we mean by saying that existence precedes essence? We mean that man first of all exists, encounters himself, surges up in the world – and defines himself afterwards. If man as the existentialist sees him is not definable, it is because to begin with he is nothing. He will not be anything until later, and then he will be what he makes of himself. Thus, there is no human nature, because there is no God to have a conception of it. Man simply is. Not that he is simply what he conceives himself to be, but he is what he wills, and as he conceives himself after already existing – as he wills to be after that leap towards existence. Man is nothing else but that which he makes of himself. That is the first principle of existentialism. And this is what people call its "subjectivity," using the word as a reproach against us. But what do we mean to say by this, but that man is of a greater dignity than a stone or a table? For we mean to say that man primarily exists – that man is, before all else, something which propels itself towards a future and is aware that it is doing so. Man is, indeed, a project which possesses a subjective life, instead of being a kind of moss, or a fungus or a cauliflower. Before that projection of the self nothing exists; not even in the heaven of intelligence: man will only attain existence when he is what he purposes to be. Not, however, what he may wish to be. For what we usually understand by wishing or willing is a conscious decision taken – much more often than not – after we have made ourselves what we are. I may wish to join a party, to write a book or to marry – but in such a case what is usually called my will is probably a manifestation of a prior and more spontaneous decision. If, however, it is true that existence is prior to essence, man is responsible for what he is. Thus, the first effect of existentialism is that it puts every man in possession of himself as he is, and places the entire responsibility for his existence squarely upon his own shoulders. And,

when we say that man is responsible for himself, we do not mean that he is responsible only for his own individuality, but that he is responsible for all men. The word "subjectivism" is to be understood in two senses, and our adversaries play upon only one of them. Subjectivism means, on the one hand, the freedom of the individual subject and, on the other, that man cannot pass beyond human subjectivity. It is the latter which is the deeper meaning of existentialism. When we say that man chooses himself, we do mean that every one of us must choose himself; but by that we also mean that in choosing for himself he chooses for all men. For in effect, of all the actions a man may take in order to create himself as he wills to be, there is not one which is not creative, at the same time, of an image of man such as he believes he ought to be. To choose between this or that is at the same time to affirm the value of that which is chosen; for we are unable ever to choose the worse. What we choose is always the better; and nothing can be better for us unless it is better for all. If, moreover, existence precedes essence and we will to exist at the same time as we fashion our image, that image is valid for all and for the entire epoch in which we find ourselves. Our responsibility is thus much greater than we had supposed, for it concerns mankind as a whole. If I am a worker, for instance, I may choose to join a Christian rather than a Communist trade union. And if, by that membership, I choose to signify that resignation is, after all, the attitude that best becomes a man, that man's kingdom is not upon this earth, I do not commit myself alone to that view. Resignation is my will for everyone, and my action is, in consequence, a commitment on behalf of all mankind. Or if, to take a more personal case, I decide to marry and to have children, even though this decision proceeds simply from my situation, from my passion or my desire, I am thereby committing not only myself, but humanity as a whole, to the practice of monogamy. I am thus responsible for myself and for all men, and I am creating a certain image of man as I would have him to be. In fashioning myself I fashion man.

This may enable us to understand what is meant by such terms – perhaps a little grandiloquent – as anguish, abandonment and despair. As you will soon see, it is very simple. First, what do we mean by anguish? The existentialist frankly states that man is in anguish. His meaning is as

follows – When a man commits himself to anything, fully realizing that he is not only choosing
what he will be, but is thereby at the same time
a legislator deciding for the whole of mankind –
in such a moment a man cannot escape from the
sense of complete and profound responsibility.
There are many, indeed, who show no such
anxiety. But we affirm that they are merely disguising their anguish or are in flight from it.
Certainly, many people think that in what they
are doing they commit no one but themselves to
anything: and if you ask them, "What would
happen if everyone did so?" they shrug their
shoulders and reply, "Everyone does not do so."
But in truth, one ought always to ask oneself
what would happen if everyone did as one is
doing; nor can one escape from that disturbing
thought except by a kind of self-deception. The
man who lies in self-excuse, by saying "Everyone will not do it" must be ill at ease in his
conscience, for the act of lying implies the universal value which it denies. By its very disguise
his anguish reveals itself. This is the anguish that
Kierkegaard called "the anguish of Abraham."
You know the story: An angel commanded
Abraham to sacrifice his son: and obedience was
obligatory, if it really was an angel who had appeared and said, "Thou, Abraham, shalt sacrifice
thy son." But anyone in such a case would
wonder, first, whether it was indeed an angel and
secondly, whether I am really Abraham. Where
are the proofs? A certain mad woman who suffered from hallucinations said that people were
telephoning to her, and giving her orders. The
doctor asked, "But who is it that speaks to you?"
She replied: "He says it is God." And what,
indeed, could prove to her that it was God? If an
angel appears to me, what is the proof that it is
an angel; or, if I hear voices, who can prove that
they proceed from heaven and not from hell, or
from my own subconsciousness or some pathological condition? Who can prove that they are
really addressed to me?

Who, then, can prove that I am the proper person to impose, by my own choice, my conception of man upon mankind? I shall never find any
proof whatever; there will be no sign to convince
me of it. If a voice speaks to me, it is still I myself
who must decide whether the voice is or is not
that of an angel. If I regard a certain course
of action as good, it is only I who choose to say
that it is good and not bad. There is nothing

to show that I am Abraham: nevertheless I also
am obliged at every instant to perform actions
which are examples. Everything happens to
every man as though the whole human race had
its eyes fixed upon what he is doing and regulated
its conduct accordingly. So every man ought to
say, "Am I really a man who has the right to act
in such a manner that humanity regulates itself
by what I do?" If a man does not say that, he is
dissembling his anguish. Clearly, the anguish
with which we are concerned here is not one that
could lead to quietism or inaction. It is anguish
pure and simple, of the kind well known to all
those who have borne responsibilities. When, for
instance, a military leader takes upon himself the
responsibility for an attack and sends a number
of men to their death, he chooses to do it and
at bottom he alone chooses. No doubt he acts
under a higher command, but its orders, which
are more general, require interpretation by him
and upon that interpretation depends the life
of ten, fourteen or twenty men. In making the
decision, he cannot but feel a certain anguish.
All leaders know that anguish. It does not prevent
their acting, on the contrary it is the very condition of their action, for the action presupposes that
there is a plurality of possibilities, and in choosing one of these, they realize that it has value only
because it is chosen. Now it is anguish of that kind
which existentialism describes, and moreover,
as we shall see, makes explicit through direct
responsibility towards other men who are concerned. Far from being a screen which could
separate us from action, it is a condition of
action itself.

And when we speak of "abandonment" – a
favorite word of Heidegger – we only mean to say
that God does not exist, and that it is necessary
to draw the consequences of his absence right to
the end. The existentialist is strongly opposed
to a certain type of secular moralism which seeks
to suppress God at the least possible expense.
Towards 1880, when the French professors endeavored to formulate a secular morality, they
said something like this: – God is a useless and
costly hypothesis, so we will do without it.
However, if we are to have morality, a society and
a law-abiding world, it is essential that certain
values should be taken seriously; they must have
an *a priori* existence ascribed to them. It must be
considered obligatory *a priori* to be honest, not
to lie, not to beat one's wife, to bring up children

and so forth; so we are going to do a little work on this subject, which will enable us to show that these values exist all the same, inscribed in an intelligible heaven although, of course, there is no God. In other words – and this is, I believe, the purport of all that we in France call radicalism – nothing will be changed if God does not exist; we shall rediscover the same norms of honesty, progress and humanity, and we shall have disposed of God as an out-of-date hypothesis which will die away quietly of itself. The existentialist, on the contrary, finds it extremely embarrassing that God does not exist, for there disappears with Him all possibility of finding values in an intelligible heaven. There can no longer be any good *a priori*, since there is no infinite and perfect consciousness to think it. It is nowhere written that "the good" exists, that one must be honest or must not lie, since we are now upon the plane where there are only men. Dostoevsky once wrote "If God did not exist, everything would be permitted"; and that, for existentialism, is the starting point. Everything is indeed permitted if God does not exist, and man is in consequence forlorn, for he cannot find anything to depend upon either within or outside himself. He discovers forthwith, that he is without excuse. For if indeed existence precedes essence, one will never be able to explain one's action by reference to a given and specific human nature; in other words, there is no determinism – man is free, man *is* freedom. Nor, on the other hand, if God does not exist, are we provided with any values or commands that could legitimize our behavior. Thus we have neither behind us, nor before us in a luminous realm of values, any means of justification or excuse. We are left alone, without excuse. That is what I mean when I say that man is condemned to be free. Condemned, because he did not create himself, yet is nevertheless at liberty, and from the moment that he is thrown into this world he is responsible for everything he does. The existentialist does not believe in the power of passion. He will never regard a grand passion as a destructive torrent upon which a man is swept into certain actions as by fate, and which, therefore, is an excuse for them. He thinks that man is responsible for his passion. Neither will an existentialist think that a man can find help through some sign being vouchsafed upon earth for his orientation: for he thinks that the man himself interprets the sign as he chooses. He

thinks that every man, without any support or help whatever, is condemned at every instant to invent man. As Ponge has written in a very fine article, "Man is the future of man." That is exactly true. Only, if one took this to mean that the future is laid up in Heaven, that God knows what it is, it would be false, for then it would no longer even be a future. If, however, it means that, whatever man may now appear to be, there is a future to be fashioned, a virgin future that awaits him – then it is a true saying. But in the present one is forsaken.

As an example by which you may the better understand this state of abandonment, I will refer to the case of a pupil of mine, who sought me out in the following circumstances. His father was quarrelling with his mother and was also inclined to be a "collaborator"; his elder brother had been killed in the German offensive of 1940 and this young man, with a sentiment somewhat primitive but generous, burned to avenge him. His mother was living alone with him, deeply afflicted by the semi-treason of his father and by the death of her eldest son, and her one consolation was in this young man. But he, at this moment, had the choice between going to England to join the Free French Forces or of staying near his mother and helping her to live. He fully realized that this woman lived only for him and that his disappearance – or perhaps his death – would plunge her into despair. He also realized that, concretely and in fact, every action he performed on his mother's behalf would be sure of effect in the sense of aiding her to live, whereas anything he did in order to go and fight would be an ambiguous action which might vanish like water into sand and serve no purpose. For instance, to set out for England he would have to wait indefinitely in a Spanish camp on the way through Spain; or, on arriving in England or in Algiers he might be put into an office to fill up forms. Consequently, he found himself confronted by two very different modes of action; the one concrete, immediate, but directed towards only one individual; and the other an action addressed to an end infinitely greater, a national collectivity, but for that very reason ambiguous – and it might be frustrated on the way. At the same time, he was hesitating between two kinds of morality; on the one side the morality of sympathy, of personal devotion and, on the other side, a morality of wider scope but of more debatable validity. He had to choose between those two. What could help him to choose? Could the Christian doctrine? No. Christian doctrine says: Act with charity, love your neighbour, deny yourself for others, choose the way which is hardest, and so forth. But which is the harder road? To whom does one owe the more brotherly love, the patriot or the mother? Which is the more useful aim, the general one of fighting in and for the whole community, or the precise aim of helping one particular person to live? Who can give an answer to that *a priori*? No one. Nor is it given in any ethical scripture. The Kantian ethic says, Never regard another as a means, but always as an end. Very well; if I remain with my mother, I shall be regarding her as the end and not as a means: but by the same token I am in danger of treating as means those who are fighting on my behalf; and the converse is also true, that if I go to the aid of the combatants I shall be treating them as the end at the risk of treating my mother as a means.

If values are uncertain, if they are still too abstract to determine the particular, concrete case under consideration, nothing remains but to trust in our instincts. That is what this young man tried to do; and when I saw him he said, "In the end, it is feeling that counts; the direction in which it is really pushing me is the one I ought to choose. If I feel that I love my mother enough to sacrifice everything else for her – my will to be avenged, all my longings for action and adventure – then I stay with her. If, on the contrary, I feel that my love for her is not enough, I go." But how does one estimate the strength of a feeling? The value of his feeling for his mother was determined precisely by the fact that he was standing by her. I may say that I love a certain friend enough to sacrifice such or such a sum of money for him, but I cannot prove that unless I have done it. I may say, "I love my mother enough to remain with her," if actually I have remained with her. I can only estimate the strength of this affection if I have performed an action by which it is defined and ratified. But if I then appeal to this affection to justify my action, I find myself drawn into a vicious circle.

[. . .]

Upon this level therefore, what we are considering is an ethic of action and self-commitment.

However, we are still reproached, upon these few data, for confining man within his individual subjectivity. There again people badly misunderstand us.

Our point of departure is, indeed, the subjectivity of the individual, and that for strictly philosophic reasons. It is not because we are bourgeois, but because we seek to base our teaching upon the truth, and not upon a collection of fine theories, full of hope but lacking real foundations. And at the point of departure there cannot be any other truth than this, *I think, therefore I am*, which is the absolute truth of consciousness as it attains to itself. Every theory which begins with man, outside of this moment of self-attainment, is a theory which thereby suppresses the truth, for outside of the Cartesian *cogito*, all objects are no more than probable, and any doctrine of probabilities which is not attached to a truth will crumble into nothing. In order to define the probable one must possess the true. Before there can be any truth whatever, then, there must be an absolute truth, and there is such a truth which is simple, easily attained and within the reach of everybody; it consists in one's immediate sense of one's self.

In the second place, this theory alone is compatible with the dignity of man, it is the only one which does not make man into an object. All kinds of materialism lead one to treat every man including oneself as an object – that is, as a set of pre-determined reactions, in no way different from the patterns of qualities and phenomena which constitute a table, or a chair or a stone. Our aim is precisely to establish the human kingdom as a pattern of values in distinction from the material world. But the subjectivity which we thus postulate as the standard of truth is no narrowly individual subjectivism, for as we have demonstrated, it is not only one's own self that one discovers in the *cogito*, but those of others too. Contrary to the philosophy of Descartes, contrary to that of Kant, when we say "I think" we are attaining to ourselves in the presence of the other, and we are just as certain of the other as we are of ourselves. Thus the man who discovers himself directly in the *cogito* also discovers all the others, and discovers them as the condition of his own existence. He recognizes that he cannot be anything (in the sense in which one says one is spiritual, or that one is wicked or jealous) unless others recognize him as such. I cannot obtain any truth whatsoever about myself, except through the mediation of another. The other is indispensable to my existence, and equally so to any knowledge I can have of myself. Under these conditions, the intimate discovery of myself is at the same time the revelation of the other as a freedom which confronts mine, and which cannot think or will without doing so either for or against me. Thus, at once, we find ourselves in a world which is, let us say, that of "inter-subjectivity." It is in this world that man has to decide what he is and what others are.

Furthermore, although it is impossible to find in each and every man a universal essence that can be called human nature, there is nevertheless a human universality of *condition*. It is not by chance that the thinkers of today are so much more ready to speak of the condition than of the nature of man. By his condition they understand, with more or less clarity, all the *limitations* which *a priori* define man's fundamental situation in the universe. His historical situations are variable: man may be born a slave in a pagan society, or may be a feudal baron, or a proletarian. But what never vary are the necessities of being in the world, of having to labor and to die there. These limitations are neither subjective nor objective, or rather there is both a subjective and an objective aspect of them. Objective, because we meet with them everywhere and they are everywhere recognizable: and subjective because they are *lived* and are nothing if man does not live them – if, that is to say, he does not freely determine himself and his existence in relation to them. And, diverse though man's purposes may be, at least none of them is wholly foreign to me, since every human purpose presents itself as an attempt either to surpass these limitations, or to widen them, or else to deny or to accommodate oneself to them. Consequently every purpose, however individual it may be, is of universal value. Every purpose, even that of a Chinese, an Indian or a Negro, can be understood by a European. To say it can be understood, means that the European of 1945 may be striving out of a certain situation towards the same limitations in the same way, and that he may reconceive in himself the purpose of the Chinese, of the Indian or the African. In every purpose there is universality, in this sense that every purpose is comprehensible to every man. Not that this or that purpose defines man for ever, but that it may be

entertained again and again. There is always some way of understanding an idiot, a child, a primitive man or a foreigner if one has sufficient information. In this sense we may say that there is a human universality, but it is not something given; it is being perpetually made. I make this universality in choosing myself; I also make it by understanding the purpose of any other man, of whatever epoch. This absoluteness of the act of choice does not alter the relativity of each epoch.

What is at the very heart and center of existentialism, is the absolute character of the free commitment, by which every man realizes himself in realizing a type of humanity – a commitment always understandable, to no matter whom in no matter what epoch – and its bearing upon the relativity of the cultural pattern which may result from such absolute commitment. One must observe equally the relativity of Cartesianism and the absolute character of the Cartesian commitment. In this sense you may say, if you like, that every one of us makes the absolute by breathing, by eating, by sleeping or by behaving in any fashion whatsoever. There is no difference between free being – being as self-committal, as existence choosing its essence – and absolute being. And there is no difference whatever between being as an absolute, temporarily localized – that is, localized in history – and universally intelligible being.

This does not completely refute the charge of subjectivism. Indeed that objection appears in several other forms, of which the first is as follows. People say to us, "Then it does not matter what you do," and they say this in various ways. First they tax us with anarchy; then they say, "You cannot judge others, for there is no reason for preferring one purpose to another"; finally, they may say, "Everything being merely voluntary in this choice of yours, you give away with one hand what you pretend to gain with the other." These three are not very serious objections. As to the first, to say that it does not matter what you choose is not correct. In one sense choice is possible, but what is not possible is not to choose. I can always choose, but I must know that if I do not choose, that is still a choice. This, although it may appear merely formal, is of great importance as a limit to fantasy and caprice. For, when I confront a real situation – for example, that I am a sexual being, able to have relations with a being of the other sex and able to have children

– I am obliged to choose my attitude to it, and in every respect I bear the responsibility of the choice which, in committing myself, also commits the whole of humanity. Even if my choice is determined by no *a priori* value whatever, it can have nothing to do with caprice: and if anyone thinks that this is only Gide's theory of the *acte gratuit* over again, he has failed to see the enormous difference between this theory and that of Gide. Gide does not know what a situation is, his "act" is one of pure caprice. In our view, on the contrary, man finds himself in an organized situation in which he is himself involved: his choice involves mankind in its entirety, and he cannot avoid choosing. Either he must remain single, or he must marry without having children, or he must marry and have children. In any case, and whichever he may choose, it is impossible for him, in respect of this situation, not to take complete responsibility. Doubtless he chooses without reference to any pre-established values, but it is unjust to tax him with caprice. Rather let us say that the moral choice is comparable to the construction of a work of art.

[. . .]

In the second place, people say to us, "You are unable to judge others." This is true in one sense and false in another. It is true in this sense, that whenever a man chooses his purpose and his commitment in all clearness and in all sincerity, whatever that purpose may be, it is impossible for him to prefer another. It is true in the sense that we do not believe in progress. Progress implies amelioration; but man is always the same, facing a situation which is always changing, and choice remains always a choice in the situation. The moral problem has not changed since the time when it was a choice between slavery and anti-slavery – from the time of the war of Secession, for example, until the present moment when one chooses between the M.R.P. [*Mouvement Rèpublicain Populaire*] and the Communists.

We can judge, nevertheless, for, as I have said, one chooses in view of others, and in view of others one chooses himself. One can judge, first – and perhaps this is not a judgment of value, but it is a logical judgment – that in certain cases choice is founded upon an error, and in others upon the truth. One can judge a man by saying that he deceives himself. Since we have defined the situation of man as one of free choice, without excuse and without help, any man who takes refuge behind the excuse of his passions, or by inventing some deterministic doctrine, is a self-deceiver. One may object: "But why should he not choose to deceive himself?" I reply that it is not for me to judge him morally, but I define his self-deception as an error. Here one cannot avoid pronouncing a judgment of truth. The self-deception is evidently a falsehood, because it is a dissimulation of man's complete liberty of commitment. Upon this same level, I say that it is also a self-deception if I choose to declare that certain values are incumbent upon me; I am in contradiction with myself if I will these values and at the same time say that they impose themselves upon me. If anyone says to me, "And what if I wish to deceive myself?" I answer, "There is no reason why you should not, but I declare that you are doing so, and that the attitude of strict consistency alone is that of good faith." Furthermore, I can pronounce a moral judgment. For I declare that freedom, in respect of concrete circumstances, can have no other end and aim but itself; and when once a man has seen that values depend upon himself, in that state of forsakenness he can will only one thing, and that is freedom as the foundation of all values. That does not mean that he wills it in the abstract: it simply means that the actions of men of good faith have, as their ultimate significance, the quest of freedom itself as such. A man who belongs to some communist or revolutionary society wills certain concrete ends, which imply the will to freedom, but that freedom is willed in community. We will freedom for freedom's sake, in and through particular circumstances. And in thus willing freedom, we discover that it depends entirely upon the freedom of others and that the freedom of others depends upon our own. Obviously, freedom as the definition of a man does not depend upon others, but as soon as there is a commitment, I am obliged to will the liberty of others at the same time as my own. I cannot make liberty my aim unless I make that of others equally my aim. Consequently, when I recognize, as entirely authentic, that man is a being whose existence precedes his essence, and that he is a free being who cannot, in any circumstances, but will his freedom, at the same time I realize that I cannot not will the freedom of others. Thus, in the name of that will to freedom which is implied in freedom itself, I can form judgments upon those who seek to hide from themselves the wholly voluntary nature of their existence and its complete freedom. Those who hide from this total freedom, in a guise of solemnity or with deterministic excuses, I shall call cowards. Others, who try to show that their existence is necessary, when it is merely an accident of the appearance of the human race on earth – I shall call scum. But neither cowards nor scum can be identified except upon the plane of strict authenticity. Thus, although the content of morality is variable, a certain form of this morality is universal. Kant declared that freedom is a will both to itself and to the freedom of others. Agreed: but he thinks that the formal and the universal suffice for the constitution of a morality. We think, on the contrary, that principles that are too abstract break down when we come to defining action. To take once again the case of that student; by what authority, in the name of what golden rule of morality, do you think he could have decided, in perfect peace of mind, either to abandon his mother or to remain with her? There are no means of judging. The content is always concrete, and therefore unpredictable; it has always to be invented. The one thing that counts, is to know whether the invention is made in the name of freedom.

[. . .]

The third objection, stated by saying, "You take with one hand what you give with the other," means, at bottom, "your values are not serious, since you choose them yourselves." To that I can only say that I am very sorry that it should be so; but if I have excluded God the Father, there must be somebody to invent values. We have to take things as they are. And moreover, to say that we invent values means neither more nor less than this; that there is no sense in life *a priori*. Life is nothing until it is lived; but it is yours to make sense of, and the value of it is nothing else but the sense that you choose. Therefore, you can see that there is a possibility of creating a human community. I have been reproached for suggesting that existentialism is a form of humanism: people have said to me, "But you have written in your *Nausée* that the humanists are wrong, you have even ridiculed a certain type of humanism, why do you now go back upon that?" In reality, the

word humanism has two very different meanings. One may understand by humanism a theory which upholds man as the end-in-itself and as the supreme value. Humanism in this sense appears, for instance, in Cocteau's story *Round the World in 80 Hours,* in which one of the characters declares, because he is flying over mountains in an airplane, "Man is magnificent!" This signifies that although I, personally, have not built airplanes I have the benefit of those particular inventions and that I personally, being a man, can consider myself responsible for, and honored by, achievements that are peculiar to some men. It is to assume that we can ascribe value to man according to the most distinguished deeds of certain men. That kind of humanism is absurd, for only the dog or the horse would be in a position to pronounce a general judgment upon man and declare that he is magnificent, which they have never been such fools as to do – at least, not as far as I know. But neither is it admissible that a man should pronounce judgment upon Man. Existentialism dispenses with any judgment of this sort: an existentialist will never take man as the end, since man is still to be determined. And we have no right to believe that humanity is something to which we could set up a cult, after the manner of Auguste Comte. The cult of humanity ends in Comtian humanism, shut-in upon itself, and – this must be said – in Fascism. We do not want a humanism like that.

But there is another sense of the word, of which the fundamental meaning is this: Man is all the time outside of himself: it is in projecting and losing himself beyond himself that he makes man to exist; and, on the other hand, it is by pursuing transcendent aims that he himself is able to exist. Since man is thus self-surpassing, and can grasp objects only in relation to his self-surpassing, he is himself the heart and center of his transcendence. There is no other universe except the human universe, the universe of human subjectivity. This relation of transcendence as constitutive of man (not in the sense that God is transcendent, but in the sense of self-surpassing) with subjectivity (in such a sense that man is not shut up in himself but forever present in a human universe) – it is this that we call existential humanism. This is humanism, because we remind man that there is no legislator but himself; that he himself, thus abandoned, must decide for himself; also because we show that it is not by turning back upon himself, but always by seeking, beyond himself, an aim which is one of liberation or of some particular realization, that man can realize himself as truly human.

You can see from these few reflections that nothing could be more unjust than the objections people raise against us. Existentialism is nothing else but an attempt to draw the full conclusions from a consistently atheistic position. Its intention is not in the least that of plunging men into despair. And if by despair one means – as the Christians do – any attitude of unbelief, the despair of the existentialists is something different. Existentialism is not atheist in the sense that it would exhaust itself in demonstrations of the non-existence of God. It declares, rather, that even if God existed that would make no difference from its point of view. Not that we believe God does exist, but we think that the real problem is not that of His existence; what man needs is to find himself again and to understand that nothing can save him from himself, not even a valid proof of the existence of God. In this sense existentialism is optimistic. It is a doctrine of action, and it is only by self-deception, by confusing their own despair with ours that Christians can describe us as without hope.

Simone de Beauvoir, *The Second Sex,* I.3.XI, "Myth and Reality," and "Conclusion" (abridged)

Introduction

Born in Paris, Simone de Beauvoir (1908–80) went on to become a leading Existentialist philosopher and one of the foundational figures of twentieth-century feminist philosophy. Educated at the Institut Catholique, the Institut Saint-Marie, and at the Sorbonne, Beauvoir became in 1929, at age 21, the youngest person to have sat for the *agrégation* in philosophy. In 1943, in the midst of World War II, Beauvoir published what she called a "metaphysical novel," *She Came to Stay*. It was followed in 1944 by an essay *Pyrrhus et Cinéas*. Both works take up and explore a theme that would occupy her for the rest of her life – what it means to be a free consciousness. Many of the ideas she advanced on this topic she generated in partnership with Jean-Paul Sartre (I.23).

Beauvoir developed her philosophical positions in her 1947 *The Ethics of Ambiguity*, exploring what it means to be a free consciousness that is "embodied" and "situated." Possessing a body and being situated in a world of other free consciousnesses, in history, nature and in culture, the human condition is irreducibly ambiguous. We find ourselves natural yet free of nature, individual yet intertwined with others, acting apparently for one reason but doing so in bad faith, rebelling

From Simone de Beauvoir, *The Second Sex*, trans. and ed. H. M. Parshley, New York: Alfred A. Knopf, 1978, pp. 253–63, 724–6, 730–2 (some notes omitted).

against our oppression and complicit in it, free agents who mystify ourselves into passivity. From these investigations springs Beauvoir's moral imperative: the necessity of liberating human freedom by freeing it from the cultural forces that inhibit its realization and its exercise in the world. *The Second Sex* (1949), from which the following selection is taken, may be read as an attempt to apply these theoretical ideas to the concrete case of women situated in western European society.

Beauvoir holds the Existentialist doctrine that human beings have no intrinsic nature but must be self-creating – "essence does not precede existence: in pure subjectivity, the human being is *not anything*." This is, of course, true of women no less than men. Hence, in her now famous phrase, "One is not born but rather becomes a woman." Or, as Beauvoir puts it in what follows: "it must be repeated once more that in human society nothing is natural and that woman, like much else, is a product elaborated by civilization. The intervention of others in her destiny is fundamental."

Women, according to Beauvoir, are particularly constrained by being rendered "Other" to men. Drawing on Hegel's "master–slave dialectic,"[1] Beauvoir develops an analysis showing how women are understood not as their own beings but as "not-men," as deviations from the male norm. Humanity is thought of as "man," masculine virtue is thought of as true virtue, male occupations are thought of as real work, and male thinking is what counts as authentic philosophy. While both women and men exist in an ambiguous play of immanence (being a passive thing upon which the world acts) and transcendence (being a consciousness with agency acting freely in the world), men are privileged in their transcendence, while women are relegated to positions of stultifying immanence. Men in our patriarchal society are made the Absolute Subjects while women are made the Objects of male subjectivity. In other words, women are objectified, made the objects of the male gaze, the things looked at, the instruments of male pleasure. Women, in this society, become marginalized, elided, substandard, or invisible, even to themselves. In fact, ambiguously, women become both resistant and complicit in their own oppression by internalizing the male view of themselves and by accepting the privileges of womanhood together with the subordination that is their price while simultaneously bridling against them.

More particularly, women are subordinated and effaced by myths of the "Eternal Feminine" and feminine "mystery." The Eternal Feminine comprises a set of paired but opposing types into which women are made to fit, even if under pain of contradiction: "The saintly mother has for correlative the cruel stepmother, the angelic young girl has the perverse virgin: thus it will be said sometimes that Mother equals Life, sometimes that Mother equals Death, that every virgin is pure spirit or flesh dedicated to the devil." To become authentic human beings and achieve equal standing, reciprocal acknowledgment among transcending subjects, among men and women, is necessary. To achieve this reciprocal recognition, however, requires deconstructing the myths and mysteries of the feminine. Woman must "shed her old skin and cut her own new clothes." In short, in order to "gain the supreme victory, it is necessary for one thing, that by and through their natural differentiation men and women unequivocally affirm their brotherhood."

Note

1   G. W. F. Hegel (1770–1831), *Phenomenology of Spirit*, trans. A. V. Miller, Oxford: Oxford University Press, 1977. B.IV.a, "Independence and Dependence of Self-Consciousness: Lordship and Bondage ["*Herrschaft und Knechtschaft*"], pp. 111–19.

Beauvoir, *The Second Sex*

"Myth and Reality"

The myth of woman plays a considerable part in literature; but what is its importance in daily life? To what extent does it affect the customs and conduct of individuals? In replying to this question it will be necessary to state precisely the relations this myth bears to reality.

There are different kinds of myths. This one, the myth of woman, sublimating an immutable aspect of the human condition – namely, the "division" of humanity into two classes of individuals – is a static myth. It projects into the realm of Platonic ideas a reality that is directly experienced or is conceptualized on a basis of experience; in place of fact, value, significance, knowledge, empirical law, it substitutes a transcendental Idea, timeless, unchangeable, necessary. This idea is indisputable because it is beyond the given: it is endowed with absolute truth.

Thus, as against the dispersed, contingent, and multiple existences of actual women, mythical thought opposes the Eternal Feminine, unique and changeless. If the definition provided for this concept is contradicted by the behavior of flesh-and-blood women, it is the latter who are wrong: we are told not that Femininity is a false entity, but that the women concerned are not feminine. The contrary facts of experience are impotent against the myth. In a way, however, its source is in experience. Thus it is quite true that woman is other than man, and this alterity is directly felt in desire, the embrace, love; but the real relation is one of reciprocity; as such it gives rise to authentic drama. Through eroticism, love, friendship, and their alternatives, deception, hate, rivalry, the relation is a struggle between conscious beings each of whom wishes to be essential, it is the mutual recognition of free beings who confirm one another's freedom, it is the vague transition from aversion to participation. To pose Woman is to pose the absolute Other, without reciprocity, denying against all experience that she is a subject, a fellow human being.

In actuality, of course, women appear under various aspects; but each of the myths built up around the subject of woman is intended to sum her up *in toto*; each aspires to be unique. In consequence, a number of incompatible myths exist, and men tarry musing before the strange incoherencies manifested by the idea of Femininity. As every woman has a share in a majority of these archetypes – each of which lays claim to containing the sole Truth of woman – men of today also are moved again in the presence of their female companions to an astonishment like that of the old sophists who failed to understand how man could be blond and dark at the same time! Transition toward the absolute was indicated long ago in social phenomena: relations are easily congealed in classes, functions in types, just as relations, to the childish mentality, are fixed in things. Patriarchal society, for example, being centered upon the conservation of the patrimony, implies necessarily, along with those who own and transmit wealth, the existence of men and women who take property away from its owners and put it into circulation. The men – adventurers, swindlers, thieves, speculators – are generally repudiated by the group; the women, employing their erotic attraction, can induce young men and even fathers of families to scatter their patrimonies, without ceasing to be within the law. Some of these women appropriate their victims' fortunes or obtain legacies by using undue influence; this role being regarded as evil, those who play it are called "bad women." But the fact is that quite to the contrary they are able to appear in some other setting – at home with their fathers, brothers, husbands, or lovers – as guardian angels; and the courtesan who "plucks" rich financiers is, for painters and writers, a generous patroness. It is easy to understand in actual experience the ambiguous personality of Aspasia or Mme de Pompadour. But if woman is depicted as the Praying Mantis, the Mandrake, the Demon, then it is most confusing to find in woman also the Muse, the Goddess Mother, Beatrice.

As group symbols and social types are generally defined by means of antonyms in pairs, ambivalence will seem to be an intrinsic quality of the Eternal Feminine. The saintly mother has for correlative the cruel stepmother, the angelic young girl has the perverse virgin: thus it will be said sometimes that Mother equals Life, sometimes that Mother equals Death, that every virgin is pure spirit or flesh dedicated to the devil.

Evidently it is not reality that dictates to society or to individuals their choice between the two opposed basic categories; in every period, in each case, society and the individual decide in accordance with their needs. Very often they project into the myth adopted the institutions and values to which they adhere. Thus the paternalism that claims woman for hearth and home defines her as sentiment, inwardness, immanence. In fact every existent is at once immanence and transcendence; when one offers the existent no aim, or prevents him from attaining any, or robs him of his victory, then his transcendence falls vainly into the past – that is to say, falls back into immanence. This is the lot assigned to woman in the patriarchate; but it is in no way a vocation, any more than slavery is the vocation of the slave. The development of this mythology is to be clearly seen in Auguste Comte. To identify Woman with Altruism is to guarantee to man absolute rights in her devotion, it is to impose on women a categorical imperative.

The myth must not be confused with the recognition of significance; significance is immanent in the object; it is revealed to the mind through a living experience; whereas the myth is a transcendent Idea that escapes the mental grasp entirely. When in *L'Age d'homme* Michel Leiris describes his vision of the feminine organs, he tells us things of significance and elaborates no myth. Wonder at the feminine body, dislike for menstrual blood, come from perceptions of a concrete reality. There is nothing mythical in the experience that reveals the voluptuous qualities of feminine flesh, and it is not an excursion into myth if one attempts to describe them through comparisons with flowers or pebbles. But to say that Woman is Flesh, to say that the Flesh is Night and Death, or that it is the splendor of the Cosmos, is to abandon terrestrial truth and soar into an empty sky. For man also is flesh for woman; and woman is not merely a carnal object; and the flesh is clothed in special significance for each person and in each experience. And likewise it is quite true that woman – like man – is a being rooted in nature; she is more enslaved to the species than is the male, her animality is more manifest; but in her as in him the given traits are taken on through the fact of existence, she belongs also to the human realm. To assimilate her to Nature is simply to act from prejudice.

Few myths have been more advantageous to the ruling caste than the myth of woman: it justifies all privileges and even authorizes their abuse. Men need not bother themselves with alleviating the pains and the burdens that physiologically are women's lot, since these are "intended by Nature"; men use them as a pretext for increasing the misery of the feminine lot still further, for instance by refusing to grant to woman any right to sexual pleasure, by making her work like a beast of burden.

Of all these myths, none is more firmly anchored in masculine hearts than that of the feminine "mystery." It has numerous advantages. And first of all it permits an easy explanation of all that appears inexplicable; the man who "does not understand" a woman is happy to substitute an objective resistance for a subjective deficiency of mind; instead of admitting his ignorance, he perceives the presence of a "mystery" outside himself: an alibi, indeed, that flatters laziness and vanity at once. A heart smitten with love thus avoids many disappointments: if the loved one's behavior is capricious, her remarks stupid, then the mystery serves to excuse it all. And finally, thanks again to the mystery, that negative relation is perpetuated which seemed to Kierkegaard infinitely preferable to positive possession; in the company of a living enigma man remains alone – alone with his dreams, his hopes, his fears, his love, his vanity. This subjective game, which can go all the way from vice to mystical ecstasy, is for many a more attractive experience than an authentic relation with a human being. What foundations exist for such a profitable illusion?

Surely woman is, in a sense, mysterious, "mysterious as is all the world," according to Maeterlinck. Each is *subject* only for himself; each can grasp in immanence only himself, alone: from this point of view the *other* is always a mystery. To men's eyes the opacity of the self-knowing self, of the *pour-soi*, is denser in the *other* who is feminine; men are unable to penetrate her special experience through any working of sympathy: they are condemned to ignorance of the quality of woman's erotic pleasure, the discomfort of menstruation, and the pains of childbirth. The truth is that there is mystery on both sides: as the *other* who is of masculine sex, every

man, also, has within him a presence, an inner self impenetrable to woman; she in turn is in ignorance of the male's erotic feeling. But in accordance with the universal rule I have stated, the categories in which men think of the world are established *from their point of view, as absolute*: they misconceive reciprocity, here as everywhere. A mystery for man, woman is considered to be mysterious in essence.

To tell the truth, her situation makes woman very liable to such a view. Her physiological nature is very complex; she herself submits to it as to some rigmarole from outside; her body does not seem to her to be a clear expression of herself; within it she feels herself a stranger. Indeed, the bond that in every individual connects the physiological life and the psychic life – or better the relation existing between the contingence of an individual and the free spirit that assumes it – is the deepest enigma implied in the condition of being human, and this enigma is presented in its most disturbing form in woman.

But what is commonly referred to as the mystery is not the subjective solitude of the conscious self, nor the secret organic life. It is on the level of communication that the word has its true meaning: it is not a reduction to pure silence, to darkness, to absence; it implies a stammering presence that fails to make itself manifest and clear. To say that woman is mystery is to say, not that she is silent, but that her language is not understood; she is there, but hidden behind veils; she exists beyond these uncertain appearances. What is she? Angel, demon, one inspired, an actress? It may be supposed either that there are answers to these questions which are impossible to discover, or, rather, that no answer is adequate because a fundamental ambiguity marks the feminine being; and perhaps in her heart she is even for herself quite indefinable: a sphinx.

The fact is that she would be quite embarrassed to decide *what* she *is*; but this not because the hidden truth is too vague to be discerned: it is because in this domain there is no truth. An existent *is* nothing other than what he does; the possible does not extend beyond the real, essence does not precede existence: in pure subjectivity, the human being *is not anything*. He is to be measured by his acts. Of a peasant woman one can say that she is a good or a bad worker, of an actress that she has or does not have talent; but if one considers a woman in her immanent presence, her inward self, one can say absolutely nothing about her, she falls short of having any qualifications. Now, in amorous or conjugal relations, in all relations where the woman is the vassal, the other, she is being dealt with in her immanence. It is noteworthy that the feminine comrade, colleague, and associate are without mystery; on the other hand, if the vassal is male, if, in the eyes of a man or a woman who is older, or richer, a young fellow, for example, plays the role of the inessential object, then he too becomes shrouded in mystery. And this uncovers for us a substructure under the feminine mystery which is economic in nature.

A sentiment cannot be supposed to *be* anything. "In the domain of sentiments," writes Gide, "the real is not distinguished from the imaginary. And if to imagine one loves is enough to be in love, then also to tell oneself that one imagines oneself to be in love when one is in love is enough to make one forthwith love a little less." Discrimination between the imaginary and the real can be made only through behavior. Since man occupies a privileged situation in this world, he is in a position to show his love actively; very often he supports the woman or at least helps her; in marrying her he gives her social standing; he makes her presents; his independent economic and social position allows him to take the initiative and think up contrivances: it was M. de Norpois who, when separated from Mme de Villeparisis, made twenty-four-hour trips to visit her. Very often the man is busy, the woman idle: he *gives* her the time he passes with her; she takes it: is it with pleasure, passionately, or only for amusement? Does she accept these benefits through love or through self-interest? Does she love her husband or her marriage? Of course, even the man's evidence is ambiguous: is such and such a gift granted through love or out of pity? But while normally a woman finds numerous advantages in her relations with a man, his relations with a woman are profitable to a man only in so far as he loves her. And so one can almost judge the degree of his affection by the total picture of his attitude.

But a woman hardly has means for sounding her own heart; according to her moods she will view her own sentiments in different lights, and as she submits to them passively, one interpretation will be no truer than another. In those rare instances in which she holds the position of economic and social privilege, the mystery is reversed, showing that it does not pertain to *one* sex rather than the other, but to the situation. For a great many women the roads to transcendence are blocked: because they *do* nothing, they fail to *make themselves* anything. They wonder indefinitely what they *could have* become, which sets them to asking about what they *are*. It is a vain question. If man fails to discover that secret essence of femininity, it is simply because it does not exist. Kept on the fringe of the world, woman cannot be objectively defined through this world, and her mystery conceals nothing but emptiness.

Furthermore, like all the oppressed, woman deliberately dissembles her objective actuality; the slave, the servant, the indigent, all who depend upon the caprices of a master, have learned to turn toward him a changeless smile or an enigmatic impassivity; their real sentiments, their actual behavior, are carefully hidden. And moreover woman is taught from adolescence to lie to men, to scheme, to be wily. In speaking to them she wears an artificial expression on her face; she is cautious, hypocritical, play-acting.

But the Feminine Mystery as recognized in mythical thought is a more profound matter. In fact, it is immediately implied in the mythology of the absolute Other. If it be admitted that the inessential conscious being, too, is a clear subjectivity, capable of performing the *Cogito*, then it is also admitted that this being is in truth sovereign and returns to being essential; in order that all reciprocity may appear quite impossible, it is necessary for the Other to be for itself an other, for its very subjectivity to be affected by its otherness; this consciousness which would be alienated as a consciousness, in its pure immanent presence, would evidently be Mystery. It would be Mystery in itself from the fact that it would be Mystery for itself; it would be absolute Mystery.

In the same way it is true that, beyond the secrecy created by their dissembling, there is mystery in the Black, the Yellow, in so far as they are considered absolutely as the inessential Other. It should be noted that the American citizen, who profoundly baffles the average European, is not, however, considered as being "mysterious": one states more modestly that one does not understand him. And similarly woman does not always "understand" man; but there is no such thing as a masculine mystery. The point is that rich America, and the male, are on the Master side and that Mystery belongs to the slave.

To be sure, we can only muse in the twilight byways of bad faith upon the positive reality of the Mystery; like certain marginal hallucinations, it dissolves under the attempt to view it fixedly. Literature always fails in attempting to portray "mysterious" women; they can appear only at the beginning of a novel as strange, enigmatic figures; but unless the story remains unfinished they give up their secret in the end and they are then simply consistent and transparent persons. The heroes in Peter Cheyney's books, for example, never cease to be astonished at the unpredictable caprices of women: no one can ever guess how they will act, they upset all calculations. The fact is that once the springs of their action are revealed to the reader, they are seen to be very simple mechanisms: this woman was a spy, that one a thief; however clever the plot, there is always a key; and it could not be otherwise, had the author all the talent and imagination in the world. Mystery is never more than a mirage that vanishes as we draw near to look at it.

We can see now that the myth is in large part explained by its usefulness to man. The myth of woman is a luxury. It can appear only if man escapes from the urgent demands of his needs; the more relationships are concretely lived, the less they are idealized. The fellah of ancient Egypt, the Bedouin peasant, the artisan of the Middle Ages, the worker of today has in the requirements of work and poverty relations with his particular woman companion which are too definite for her to be embellished with an aura either auspicious or inauspicious. The epochs and the social classes that have been marked by the leisure to dream have been the ones to set up the images, black and white, of femininity. But along with luxury there was utility; these dreams were irresistibly guided by interests. Surely most of the myths had roots in the spontaneous attitude of man toward his own existence and toward the world around him. But going beyond experience toward the transcendent Idea was deliberately used by patriarchal society for purposes of self-justification; through the myths this society imposed its laws and customs upon individuals in a picturesque, effective manner; it is under a mythical form that the group-imperative is indoctrinated into each conscience. Through such intermediaries as religions, traditions, language, tales, songs, movies, the myths penetrate even into such existences as are most harshly enslaved to material realities. Here everyone can find sublimation of his drab experiences: deceived by the woman he loves, one declares that she is a Crazy Womb; another, obsessed by his impotence, calls her a Praying Mantis; still another enjoys his wife's company: behold, she is Harmony, Rest, the Good Earth! The taste for eternity at a bargain, for a pocket-sized absolute, which is shared by a majority of men, is satisfied by myths. The smallest emotion, a slight annoyance, becomes the reflection of a timeless Idea – an illusion agreeably flattering to the vanity.

The myth is one of those snares of false objectivity into which the man who depends on ready-made valuations rushes headlong. Here again we have to do with the substitution of a set idol for actual experience and the free judgments it requires. For an authentic relation with an autonomous existent, the myth of Woman substitutes the fixed contemplation of a mirage. "Mirage! Mirage!" cries Laforgue. "We should kill them since we cannot comprehend them; or better tranquilize them, instruct them, make them give up their taste for jewels, make them our genuinely equal comrades, our intimate friends, real associates here below, dress them differently, cut their hair short, say anything and everything to them." Man would have nothing to lose, quite the contrary, if he gave up disguising woman as a symbol. When dreams are official community affairs, clichés, they are poor and monotonous indeed beside the living reality; for the true dreamer, for the poet, woman is a more generous fount than is any down-at-heel marvel. The times that have most sincerely treasured women are not the period of feudal chivalry nor yet the gallant nineteenth century. They are the times – like the eighteenth century – when men have regarded women as fellow creatures; then it is that women seem truly romantic, as the reading of *Liaisons dangereuses*, *Le Rouge et le noir*, *Farewell to Arms*, is sufficient to show. The heroines of Laclos, Stendhal, Hemingway are without mystery, and they are not the less engaging for that. To recognize in woman a human being is not to impoverish man's experience: this would lose none of its diversity, its richness, or its intensity if it were to occur between two subjectivities. To discard the myths is not to destroy all dramatic relation between the sexes, it is not to deny the significance authentically revealed to man through feminine reality; it is not to do away with poetry, love, adventure, happiness, dreaming. It is simply to ask that behavior, sentiment, passion be founded upon the truth.

"Woman is lost. Where are the women? The women of today are not women at all!" We have seen what these mysterious slogans mean. In men's eyes – and for the legion of women who see through men's eyes – it is not enough to have a woman's body nor to assume the female function as mistress or mother in order to be a "true woman." In sexuality and maternity woman as subject can claim autonomy; but to be a "true woman" she must accept herself as the Other. The men of today show a certain duplicity of attitude which is painfully lacerating to women; they are willing on the whole to accept woman as a fellow being, an equal; but they still require her to remain the inessential. For her these two destinies are incompatible; she hesitates between one and the other without being exactly adapted to either, and from this comes her lack of equilibrium. With man there is no break between public and private life: the more he confirms his grasp on the world in action and in work, the more virile he seems to be; human and vital values are combined in him. Whereas woman's independent successes are in contradiction with her femininity, since the "true woman" is required to make herself object, to be the Other.

It is quite possible that in this matter man's sensibility and sexuality are being modified. A new æsthetics has already been born. If the fashion of flat chests and narrow hips – the boyish form – has had its brief season, at least the overopulent ideal of past centuries has not returned. The feminine body is asked to be flesh, but with discretion; it is to be slender and not loaded with fat; muscular, supple, strong, it is bound to suggest transcendence; it must not be pale like a too shaded hothouse plant, but preferably tanned like a workman's torso from being bared to the open sun. Woman's dress in becoming practical need not make her appear sexless: on the contrary, short skirts made the most of legs and thighs as never before. There is no reason why working should take away woman's sex appeal. It may be disturbing to contemplate woman as at once a social personage and carnal prey: in a recent series of drawings by Peynet (1948), we see a young man break his engagement because he was seduced by the pretty mayoress who was getting ready to officiate at his marriage. For a woman to hold some "man's position" and be desirable at the same time has long been a subject for more or less ribald joking; but gradually the impropriety and the irony have become blunted, and it would seem that a new form of eroticism is coming into being – perhaps it will give rise to new myths.

What is certain is that today it is very difficult for women to accept at the same time their status as autonomous individuals and their womanly destiny; this is the source of the blundering and restlessness which sometimes cause them to be considered a "lost sex." And no doubt it is more comfortable to submit to a blind enslavement than to work for liberation: the dead, for that matter, are better adapted to the earth than are the living. In all respects a return to the past is no more possible than it is desirable. What must be hoped for is that the men for their part will unreservedly accept the situation that is coming into existence; only then will women be able to live in that situation without anguish. Then Laforgue's prayer will be answered: "Ah, young women, when will you be our brothers, our brothers in intimacy without ulterior thought of exploitation? When shall we clasp hands truly?" Then Breton's "Mélusine, no longer under the weight of the calamity let loose upon her by man alone, Mélusine set free . . ." will regain "her place in humanity." Then she will be a full human being, "when," to quote a letter of Rimbaud, "the infinite bondage of woman is broken, when she will live in and for herself, man – hitherto detestable – having let her go free."

"Conclusion" (abridged)

A world where men and women would be equal is easy to visualize, for that precisely is what the Soviet Revolution *promised*: women raised and trained exactly like men were to work under the same conditions* and for the same wages. Erotic liberty was to be recognized by custom, but the

* That certain too laborious occupations were to be closed to women is not in contradiction to this project. Even among men there is an increasing effort to obtain adaptation to profession; their varying physical and mental capacities limit their possibilities of choice; what is asked is that, in any case, no line of sex or caste be drawn.

sexual act was not to be considered a "service" to be paid for; woman was to be *obliged* to provide herself with other ways of earning a living; marriage was to be based on a free agreement that the spouses could break at will; maternity was to be voluntary, which meant that contraception and abortion were to be authorized and that, on the other hand, all mothers and their children were to have exactly the same rights, in or out of marriage; pregnancy leaves were to be paid for by the State, which would assume charge of the children, signifying not that they would be *taken away* from their parents, but that they would not be *abandoned* to them.

But is it enough to change laws, institutions, customs, public opinion, and the whole social context, for men and women to become truly equal? "Women will always be women," say the skeptics. Other seers prophesy that in casting off their femininity they will not succeed in changing themselves into men and they will become monsters. This would be to admit that the woman of today is a creation of nature; it must be repeated once more that in human society nothing is natural and that woman, like much else, is a product elaborated by civilization. The intervention of others in her destiny is fundamental: if this action took a different direction, it would produce a quite different result. Woman is determined not by her hormones or by mysterious instincts, but by the manner in which her body and her relation to the world are modified through the action of others than herself. The abyss that separates the adolescent boy and girl has been deliberately opened out between them since earliest childhood; later on, woman could not be other than what she *was made*, and that past was bound to shadow her for life. If we appreciate its influence, we see clearly that her destiny is not predetermined for all eternity.

We must not believe, certainly, that a change in woman's economic condition alone is enough to transform her, though this factor has been and remains the basic factor in her evolution; but until it has brought about the moral, social, cultural, and other consequences that it promises and requires, the new woman cannot appear. At this moment they have been realized nowhere, in Russia no more than in France or the United States; and this explains why the woman of today is torn between the past and the future. She appears most often as a "true woman" disguised

as a man, and she feels herself as ill at ease in her flesh as in her masculine garb. She must shed her old skin and cut her own new clothes. This she could do only through a social evolution. No single educator could fashion a *female human being* today who would be the exact homologue of the *male human being*; if she is raised like a boy, the young girl feels she is an oddity and thereby she is given a new kind of sex specification. Stendhal understood this when he said: "The forest must be planted all at once." But if we imagine, on the contrary, a society in which the equality of the sexes would be concretely realized, this equality would find new expression in each individual.

[. . .]

Let us not forget that our lack of imagination always depopulates the future; for us it is only an abstraction; each one of us secretly deplores the absence there of the one who was himself. But the humanity of tomorrow will be living in its flesh and in its conscious liberty; that time will be its present and it will in turn prefer it. New relations of flesh and sentiment of which we have no conception will arise between the sexes; already, indeed, there have appeared between men and women friendships, rivalries, complicities, comradeships – chaste or sensual – which past centuries could not have conceived. To mention one point, nothing could seem to me more debatable than the opinion that dooms the new world to uniformity and hence to boredom. I fail to see that this present world is free from boredom or that liberty ever creates uniformity.

To begin with, there will always be certain differences between man and woman; her eroticism, and therefore her sexual world, have a special form of their own and therefore cannot fail to engender a sensuality, a sensitivity, of a special nature. This means that her relations to her own body, to that of the male, to the child, will never be identical with those the male bears to his own body, to that of the female, and to the child; those who make much of "equality in difference" could not with good grace refuse to grant me the possible existence of differences in equality. Then again, it is institutions that create uniformity. Young and pretty, the slaves of the harem are always the same in the sultan's embrace; Christianity gave eroticism its savor of sin and legend when it endowed the human female with a soul; if society restores her sovereign individuality to woman, it will not thereby destroy the power of love's embrace to move the heart.

It is nonsense to assert that revelry, vice, ecstasy, passion, would become impossible if man and woman were equal in concrete matters; the contradictions that put the flesh in opposition to the spirit, the instant to time, the swoon of immanence to the challenge of transcendence, the absolute of pleasure to the nothingness of forgetting, will never be resolved; in sexuality will always be materialized the tension, the anguish, the joy, the frustration, and the triumph of existence. To emancipate woman is to refuse to confine her to the relations she bears to man, not to deny them to her; let her have her independent existence and she will continue none the less to exist for him *also*: mutually recognizing each other as subject, each will yet remain for the other an *other*. The reciprocity of their relations will not do away with the miracles – desire, possession, love, dream, adventure – worked by the division of human beings into two separate categories; and the words that move us – giving, conquering, uniting – will not lose their meaning. On the contrary, when we abolish the slavery of half of humanity, together with the whole system of hypocrisy that it implies, then the "division" of humanity will reveal its genuine significance and the human couple will find its true form. "The direct, natural, necessary relation of human creatures is the *relation of man to woman*," Marx has said. "The nature of this relation determines to what point man himself is to be considered as a *generic being*, as mankind; the relation of man to woman is the most natural relation of human being to human being. By it is shown, therefore, to what point the *natural* behavior of man has become *human* or to what point the *human* being has become his *natural* being, to what point his *human nature* has become his *nature*."

The case could not be better stated. It is for man to establish the reign of liberty in the midst of the world of the given. To gain the supreme victory, it is necessary, for one thing, that by and through their natural differentiation men and women unequivocally affirm their brotherhood.

II
Epistemology

1

Plato, *Republic*, 475e–480a, and 506d–518c

Introduction

Part II of this volume begins with selections from the most famous of all philosophical works. Plato (c. 427–347 BCE) was not the first Greek to have raised questions about the nature of knowledge, but he was the first to provide extended and seminal treatment of a range of epistemological issues that have since so occupied philosophers. For example, in his early dialogue, *Meno*, he addresses the problem of how, seemingly, one can know things, like geometrical truths, without having to learn them, while in *Theaetetus* he attacks the view that knowledge and truth are necessarily relative to individuals. But, in epistemology as in other areas, it is in *Republic* that his most influential ideas are found.

In Book 5 (475e–480a), Plato's teacher Socrates is represented as distinguishing knowledge from belief and ignorance, while in Books 6–7 (506d–518c), Socrates presents three analogies to illuminate his contention that knowledge presupposes an acquaintance with "goodness." In what has come to be known as the "Sun" analogy, the relation between visual perception and the sun is compared to that between knowledge and the source of intellectual "light" – goodness. In

From Plato, *Republic*, trans. R. Waterfield. Oxford: Oxford University Press, 1993, pp. 196–202 and 233–45 (translator's commentary and some short passages omitted).

the "Line," Plato draws an analogy contrasting two relations: (a) the relation between *perceiving* "*likenesses*" (or copies) and *perceiving* "*things*" *of which they are likenesses* and (b) the relation between *mathematical understanding* of physical things and *pure understanding* of the "Forms" (*ēide*, "patterns" or, as in the present translation, "types"), including that crucial "Form of Forms" – "the Good." In the "Cave" allegory, the prisoners' ascent through and out of the cave into the sunlight is compared to "the mind's ascent to the intelligible realm" from the everyday world of sense-experience.

Both sections are difficult and have accordingly generated many competing interpretations. It has been said of the three analogies that "more has probably been written on them than on any other specific part of Plato's work."[1] It helps, in any case, to understand the following pages if they are taken in the wider context of *Republic*. Plato is trying to show that "communities [should] have philosophers as kings" and queens (473c), or put less royally, as ruling "guardians." The main reasons for this are that philosophers possess knowledge that others lack and that they stand in a special relation to knowledge and goodness. Naturally enough, Socrates' interlocutors request him to spell out what he means by knowledge and how it relates to good.

Bearing this context in mind helps us appreciate, first, that Plato's main interest, unlike that of most recent philosophers, is not in knowledge in the sense of someone's knowing that such-and-such is the case

– of knowing that a *proposition* is true. Philosophers are not distinguished from other people by knowing lots more facts. So much is obvious, indeed, from Plato's contention that knowledge, in the relevant sense, is not "introduced into a mind" by teaching, but is the result of a certain "orientation" of the mind. One gets closer to what Plato intends if one thinks of expressions like "a person of great historical knowledge" or "knowing a country well," which suggest a notion of knowledge consisting, not of possession of lots of facts, but of a capacity to understand and explain, to fit things together and into the wider picture. The context also helps us to understand the allegedly intimate connection between knowledge and goodness, which would be unintelligible if the former were simply knowledge of the facts. It is not similarly unintelligible to suppose that someone with a deep understanding of some field possesses that understanding in virtue of models or exemplars which guide his or her enquiries and with which the messier actual world can be compared and contrasted. Ideal models or exemplars are at least part of what Plato means by Forms or "types," and it is because of the philosopher's acquaintance with these that he or she possesses knowledge.

It is with this latter claim that Plato's main legacy to epistemology is to be found. On what was once the "orthodox" or "two-worlds" interpretation, Plato holds that only the realm of abstract, immaterial Forms can underwrite "knowledge," so that the everyday world of material objects, actions and so on is one about which only mere "belief" is possible. More recently, however, commentators have challenged this interpretation, pointing out how it conflicts with Plato's overriding objective of justifying the rule of philosopher kings and queens – precisely because they do know what worldly actions are just, say, or what worldly things are ugly.[2] And this seems so whether one takes Plato's discussion of philosopher-rulers literally or merely as an allegory for the ruling parts of the human mind.

Nothing, it seems, in the Book 5 sections or in the first two analogies, explicitly rules out the possibility of someone having knowledge of the everyday, empirical world. What is excluded is the possibility of knowledge without acquaintance with the Forms – at any rate with such "polar" oppositions of Forms as "the Just" *versus* "the Unjust" or "the Beautiful" *versus* "the Ugly." In the "Cave" allegory, to be sure, Plato leaves us in no doubt as to the superiority of a purely contemplative wisdom whose domain is the Forms alone. But it is a matter of continuing debate whether the philosopher who can be persuaded to descend from the enlightened world back into the cave of everyday life is thereby abandoning the realm of knowledge for that of mere opinion, or whether, equipped with what has been learned in that higher realm, the philosopher brings back a capacity to know how things are "down here" in ways that the rest of us, who have not yet made the ascent, lack.

The Book 5 extract begins just as Glaucon ("he") has asked Socrates ("I") to clarify matters after Glaucon misunderstands Socrates' account of the true philosopher. Socrates has just described the genuine philosopher as one who "desires the whole of knowledge"; but Glaucon wrongly takes that to mean that philosophers, like "sightseers," simply desire to amass information. The second extract from *Republic* 5 begins with Socrates converting Glaucon's question about the nature of goodness into one about the nature of knowledge or intelligence, "the child of goodness."

Notes

1 R. C. Cross and A. D. Woozley, *Plato's Republic: A Philosophical Commentary*, London: Macmillan, 1964, p. 201.
2 See especially J. Annas, *An Introduction to Plato's Republic*, Oxford: Clarendon Press, 1981.

Plato, *Republic*

[...]

'Who are the true philosophers you have in mind?' he asked.

'Sightseers of the truth,' I answered.   475e

'That must be right, but what exactly does it mean?' he asked.

'It wouldn't be easy to explain to anyone else,' I said. 'But you'll grant me this, surely.'

'What?'

'Since beautiful is the opposite of ugly, they are two things.'

476a 'Of course.'

'In so far as they are two, each of them is single?'

'Yes.'

'And the same principle applies to moral and immoral, good and bad, and everything of any type [or Form]; in itself, each of them is single, but each of them has a plurality of manifestations because they appear all over the place, as they become associated with actions and bodies and one another.'

'You're right,' he said.

'Well,' I continued, 'this is what enables me to distinguish the sightseers (to borrow your term) and the ones who want to acquire some expertise or other and the men of action from the

b people in question, the ones who are philosophers in the true sense of the term.'

'What do you mean?' he asked.

'Theatre-goers and sightseers are devoted to beautiful sounds and colours and shapes, and to works of art which consist of these elements, but their minds are constitutionally incapable of seeing and devoting themselves to beauty itself.'

'Yes, that's certainly right,' he said.

'However, people with the ability to approach beauty itself and see beauty as it actually is are bound to be few and far between, aren't they?'

c 'Definitely.'

'So does someone whose horizon is limited to beautiful things, with no conception of beauty itself, and who is incapable of following guidance as to how to gain knowledge of beauty itself, strike you as living in a dream-world or in the real world? Look at it this way. Isn't dreaming precisely the state, whether one is asleep or awake, of taking something to be the real thing, when it is actually only a likeness?'

'Yes, that's what I'd say dreaming is,' he said.

'And what about someone who does the opposite – who does think that there is such a thing

d as beauty itself, and has the ability to see it as well as the things which partake in it, and never gets them muddled up? Do you think he's living in the real world or in a dream-world?'

'Definitely in the real world,' he said.

'So wouldn't we be right to describe the difference between their mental states by saying that while this person has knowledge, the other one has beliefs?'

'Yes.'

'Now, suppose this other person – the one we're saying has beliefs, not knowledge – were to get cross with us and query the truth of our assertions. Will we be able to calm him down and gently convince him of our point of view, while e keeping him in the dark about the poor state of his health?'

'We really ought to,' he said.

'All right, but what shall we say to him, do you think? Perhaps this is what we should ask him. We'll tell him that we don't resent any knowledge he might have – indeed, we'd be delighted to see that he does know something – and then we'll say, "But can you tell us, please, whether someone with knowledge knows something or nothing?" You'd better answer my questions for him.'

'My answer will be that he knows something,' he said.

'Something real or something unreal?'

'Real. How could something unreal be known?' 477a

'We could look at the matter from more angles, but we're happy enough with the idea that something completely real is completely accessible to knowledge, and something utterly unreal is entirely inaccessible to knowledge. Yes?'

'Perfectly happy.'

'All right. But if something is in a state of both reality and unreality, then it falls between that which is perfectly real and that which is utterly unreal, doesn't it?'[1]

'Yes.'

'So since the field of knowledge is reality, and since it must be incomprehension whose field is unreality, then we need to find out if there is in fact something which falls between incomprehension and knowledge, whose field is this inter- b mediate, don't we?'

'Yes.'

'Now, we acknowledge the existence of belief, don't we?'

'Of course.'

'Is it a different faculty from knowledge, or is it the same?'

'Different.'

'Every faculty has its own distinctive abilities, so belief and knowledge must have different domains.'

'Yes.'

'Now, since the natural field of knowledge is reality – its function is to know reality as reality … Actually, I think there's something else we need to get clear about first.'

'What?'

c   'Shall we count as a distinct class of things the
faculties which give human beings and all other
creatures their abilities? By "faculties" I mean
things like sight and hearing. Do you understand
the type of thing I have in mind?'

'Yes, I do,' he said.

'Let me tell you something that strikes me
about them. I can't distinguish one faculty from
another the way I commonly distinguish other
things, by looking at their colours or shapes or
anything like that, because faculties don't have any
of those sorts of qualities for me to look at. The
only aspect of a faculty I can look at is its field,
d   its effect. This is what enables me to identify
each of them as a particular faculty. Where I find
a single domain and a single effect, I say there is
a single faculty; and I distinguish faculties which
have different fields and different effects. What
about you? What do you do?'

'The same as you,' he said.

'Let's go back to where we were before, then,
Glaucon,' I said. 'Do you think that knowledge
is a faculty, or does it belong in your opinion to
some other class?'

'I think it belongs to that class,' he said, 'and
is the most powerful of all the faculties.'

e   'And shall we classify belief as a faculty, or
what?'

'As a faculty,' he said. 'Belief is precisely that
which enables us to entertain beliefs.'

'Not long ago, however, you agreed that
knowledge and belief were different.'

'Of course,' he said. 'One is infallible and the
other is fallible, so anyone with any sense would
keep them separate.'

'Good,' I said. 'There can be no doubt of our
478a   position: knowledge and belief are different.'

'Yes.'

'Since they're different faculties, then, they
have different natural fields, don't they?'[2]

'Necessarily.'

'The field of knowledge is reality, isn't it? Its
function is to know the reality of anything real?'

'Yes.'

'And the function of belief, we're saying, is to
entertain beliefs?'

'Yes.'

'Does it entertain beliefs about the same thing
which knowledge knows? Will what is accessible
to knowledge and what is accessible to belief be
identical? Or is that out of the question?'

'It's ruled out by what we've already agreed,'
he said. 'If different faculties naturally have different fields, and if both knowledge and belief
are faculties, and different faculties too, as we said,   b
then it follows that it is impossible for what is
accessible to knowledge and what is accessible to
belief to be identical.'

'So if it is reality that is accessible to knowledge,
then it is something else, not reality, that is
accessible to belief, isn't it?'

'Yes.'

'Does it entertain beliefs about what is unreal?
Or is it also impossible for that to happen? Think
about this: isn't it the case that someone who
is entertaining a belief is bringing his believing
mind to bear on something? I mean, is it possible to have a belief, and to be believing nothing?'

'That's impossible.'

'In fact, someone who has a belief has some
single thing in mind, doesn't he?'

'Yes.'

'But the most accurate way to refer to something unreal would be to say that it is nothing,   c
not that it is a single thing, wouldn't it?'

'Yes.'

'Didn't we find ourselves forced to relate
incomprehension to unreality and knowledge to
reality?'

'That's right,' he said.

'So the field of belief is neither reality nor
unreality?'

'No.'

'Belief can't be incomprehension or knowledge, then?'

'So it seems.'

'Well, does it lie beyond their limits? Does it shed
more light than knowledge or spread more
obscurity than incomprehension?'

'It does neither.'

'Alternatively, does belief strike you as more
opaque than knowledge and more lucid than
incomprehension?'

'Considerably more,' he said.

'It lies within their limits?'   d

'Yes.'

'Then belief must fall between them.'

'Absolutely.'

'Now, didn't we say earlier that something
which is simultaneously real and unreal (were
such a thing to be shown to exist) would fall
between the perfectly real and the wholly unreal,
and wouldn't be the field of either knowledge or

incomprehension, but of an intermediate (again, if such a thing were shown to exist) between incomprehension and knowledge?'

'Right.'

'And now we've found that what we call belief is such an intermediate, haven't we?'

'We have.'

e 'So the only thing left for us to discover, apparently, is whether there's anything which partakes of both reality and unreality, and cannot be said to be perfectly real or perfectly unreal. If we were to come across such a thing, we'd be fully justified in describing it as the field of belief, on the principle that extremes belong together, and so do intermediates. Do you agree?'

'Yes.'

479a 'Let's return, on this basis, to the give and take of conversation with that fine fellow who doesn't acknowledge the existence of beauty itself or think that beauty itself has any permanent and unvarying character, but takes the plurality of beautiful things as his norm – that sightseer who can't under any circumstances abide the notion that beauty, morality, and so on are each a single entity. What we'll say to him is, "My friend, is there one beautiful thing, in this welter of beautiful things, which won't turn out to be ugly? Is there one moral deed which won't turn out to be immoral? Is there one just act which won't turn out to be unjust?"'

b 'No, there isn't,' he said. 'It's inevitable for these things to turn out to be both beautiful and ugly, in a sense, and the same goes for all the other qualities you mentioned in your question.'

'And there are doubles galore – but they turn out to be halves just as much as doubles, don't they?'

'Yes.'

'And do things which are large, small, light, and heavy deserve these attributes any more than they deserve the opposite attributes?'

'No, each of them is bound to have both qualities,' he said.

So isn't it the case, then, that any member of a plurality no more *is* whatever it is said to be than it *is not* whatever it is said to be?'

c '. . . it is impossible to form a stable conception of any of them as either being what it is, or not being what it is, or being both, or being neither,'

'How are you going to cope with them, then?' I asked. 'Can you find a better place to locate them than between real being and unreality? I mean, they can't turn out to be more opaque and unreal than unreality, or more lucid and real d than reality.'

'True,' he said.

'So there we are. We've discovered that the welter of things which the masses conventionally regard as beautiful and so on mill around somewhere between unreality and perfect reality.'

'Yes, we have.'

'But we have a prior agreement that were such a thing to turn up, we'd have to call it the field of belief, not of knowledge, since the realm which occupies some uncertain intermediate point must be accessible to the intermediate faculty.'

'Yes, we do.'

'What shall we say about those spectators, e then, who can see a plurality of beautiful things, but not beauty itself, and who are incapable of following if someone else tries to lead them to it, and who can see many moral actions, but not morality itself, and so on? That they only ever entertain beliefs, and do not *know* any of the things they believe?'

'That's what we have to say,' he said.

'As for those who can see each of these things in itself, in its permanent and unvarying nature, we'll say they have knowledge and are not merely entertaining beliefs, won't we?'

'Again, we have to.'

'And won't our position be that they're 480a devoted to and love the domain of knowledge, as opposed to the others, who are devoted to and love the domain of belief? I mean, surely we haven't forgotten our claim that these others love and are spectators of beautiful sounds and colours and so on, but can't abide the idea that there is such a thing as beauty itself?'

'No, we haven't forgotten.'

'They won't think us nasty if we refer to them as "lovers of belief" rather than as philosophers, who love knowledge, will they? Are they going to get very cross with us if we say that now?'

'Not if they listen to me,' he replied. 'It's not right to get angry at the truth.'

'But the term "believers" is inappropriate for those who are devoted to everything that is real: they should be called philosophers, shouldn't they?'

'Absolutely.' [. . .]

[. . .] 'Socrates,' said Glaucon, '[. . .] We'd be 506d happy with the kind of description of goodness that you gave of morality, self-discipline, and so on.'

'So would I, Glaucon,' I said, 'very happy. But I'm afraid it'll be more than I can manage, and that my malformed efforts will make me ridiculous. What I suggest, my friends, is that we forget about trying to define goodness itself for
e the time being. You see, I don't at the moment think that our current impulse is enough to take us to where I'd like to see us go. However, I am prepared to talk about something which seems to me to be the child of goodness and to bear a very strong resemblance to it. Would you like me to do that? If not, we can just forget it.'

'Please do,' he said. 'You can settle your account by discussing the father another time.' [. . .]
507a   'First I want to make sure that we're not at cross purposes,' I said, 'and to remind you of something that came up earlier, though you've often heard it on other occasions as well.'
b   'What?' he asked.

'As we talk,' I said, 'we mention and differentiate between a lot of beautiful things and a lot of good things and so on.'

'Yes, we do.'

'And we also talk about beauty itself, goodness itself and so on. All the things we refer to as a plurality on those occasions we also conversely count as belonging to a single class by virtue of the fact that they have a single particular character, and we say that the *x* itself is "what really is".'

'True.'

'And we say that the first lot is visible rather than intelligible, whereas characters are intelligible rather than visible.'

'Absolutely.'
c   'With what aspect of ourselves do we see the things we see?'

'With our sight,' he replied.

'And we use hearing for the things we hear, and so on for all the other senses and the things we perceive. Yes?'

'Of course.'

'Well, have you ever stopped to consider', I asked, 'how generous the creator of the senses was when he created the domain of seeing and being seen?'

'No, not really,' he said.

'Look at it this way. Are hearing and sound
d deficient? Do they need an extra something to make the one hear and the other be heard – some third thing without which hearing won't hear and sound won't be heard?'

'No,' he answered.

'And in my opinion', I went on, 'the same goes for many other domains, if not all: they don't need anything like this. Or can you point to one that does?'

'*I* can't,' he said.

'But do you realize that sight and the visible realm *are* deficient?'

'How?'

'Even if a person's eyes are capable of sight, and he's trying to use it, and what he's trying to look at is coloured, the sight will see nothing and the colours will remain unseen, surely, unless there e is also present an extra third thing which is made specifically for this purpose.'

'What is this thing you're getting at?' he asked.

'It's what we call light,' I said.

'You're right,' he said.

'So if light has value, then because it links the sense of sight and the ability to be seen, it is far 508a and away the most valuable link there is.'

'Well, it certainly does have value,' he said.

'Which of the heavenly gods would you say is responsible for this? Whose light makes it possible for our sight to see and for the things we see to be seen?'

'My reply will be no different from what yours or anyone else's would be,' he said. 'I mean, you're obviously expecting the answer, "the sun".'

'Now, there are certain conclusions to be drawn from comparing sight to this god.'

'What?'

'Sight and the sun aren't to be identified: neither the sense itself nor its location – which b we call the eye – is the same as the sun.'

'True.'

'Nevertheless, there's no sense-organ which more closely resembles the sun, in my opinion, than the eye.'[3]

'The resemblance is striking.'

'Moreover, the eye's ability to see has been bestowed upon it and channelled into it, as it were, by the sun.'

'Yes.'

'So the sun is not to be identified with sight, but is responsible for sight and is itself within the visible realm. Right?'

'Yes,' he said.

'The sun is the child of goodness I was talking about, then,' I said. 'It is a counterpart to its father, goodness. As goodness stands in the intelligible realm to intelligence and the things we know, so c in the visible realm the sun stands to sight and the things we see.'

'I don't understand,' he said. 'I need more detail, please.'

'As you know,' I explained, 'when our eyes are directed towards things whose colours are no longer bathed in daylight, but in artificial light instead, then they're less effective and seem to be virtually blind, as if they didn't even have the potential for seeing clearly.'

'Certainly,' he said.

d 'But when they're directed towards things which are lit up by the sun, then they see clearly and obviously do have that potential.'

'Of course.'

'Well, here's how you can think about the mind as well. When its object is something which is lit up by truth and reality, then it has – and obviously has – intelligent awareness and knowledge. However, when its object is permeated with darkness (that is, when its object is something which is subject to generation and decay), then it has beliefs and is less effective, because its beliefs chop and change, and under these circumstances it comes across as devoid of intelligence.'

'Yes, it does.'

e 'Well, what I'm saying is that it's goodness which gives the things we know their truth and makes it possible for people to have knowledge. It is responsible for knowledge and truth, and you should think of it as being within the intelligible realm, but you shouldn't identify it with knowledge and truth, otherwise you'll be wrong: for all their value, it is even more valuable. In the other

509a realm, it is right to regard light and sight as resembling the sun, but not to identify either of them with the sun; so in this realm it is right to regard knowledge and truth as resembling goodness, but not to identify either of them with goodness, which should be rated even more highly.'

'You're talking about something of inestimable value,' he said, 'if it's not only the source of knowledge and truth, but is also more valuable than them. I mean, you certainly don't seem to be identifying it with pleasure!'

'How could you even think it?' I exclaimed. 'But we can take our analogy even further.'

'How?' b

'I think you'll agree that the ability to be seen is not the only gift the sun gives to the things we see. It is also the source of their generation, growth, and nourishment, although it isn't actually the process of generation.'

'Of course it isn't.'

'And it isn't only the known-ness of the things we know which is conferred upon them by goodness, but also their reality and their being, although goodness isn't actually the state of being, but surpasses being in majesty and might.'

'It's way beyond human comprehension, all c right,' was Glaucon's quite amusing comment.

'It's your fault for forcing me to express my views on the subject,' I replied.

'Yes, and please don't stop,' he said. 'If you've left anything out of your explanation of the simile of the sun, then the least you could do is continue with it.'

'There are plenty of omissions, in fact,' I said.

'Don't leave any gaps,' he said, 'however small.'

'I think I'll have to leave a lot out,' I said, 'but I'll try to make it as complete as I can at the moment.'

'All right,' he said.

'So bear in mind the two things we've been d talking about,' I said, 'one of which rules over the intelligible realm and its inhabitants, while the other rules over the visible realm. . . . Anyway, do you understand this distinction between visible things and intelligible things?'

'Yes.'

'Well, picture them as a line [Figure 1] cut into two unequal sections and, following the same proportion, subdivide both the section of the visible realm and that of the intelligible realm.

Now you can compare the sections in terms of e clarity and unclarity. The first section [A] in the visible realm consists of likenesses, by which I mean a number of things: shadows, reflections (on 510a the surface of water or on anything else which is inherently compact, smooth, and bright), and so on. Do you see what I'm getting at?'

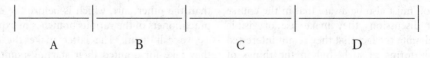

Figure 1

'I do.'

'And you should count the other section [B] of the visible realm as consisting of the things whose likenesses are found in the first section: all the flora and fauna there are in the world, and every kind of artefact too.'

'All right.'

'I wonder whether you'd agree,' I said, 'that truth and lack of truth have been the criteria for distinguishing these sections, and that the image stands to the original as the realm of beliefs stands to the realm of knowledge?'

b   'Yes,' he said, 'I certainly agree.'

'Now have a look at how to subdivide the section which belongs to the intelligible realm.'

'How?'

'Like this. If the mind wants to explore the first subdivision [C] it can do so only by using those former originals as likenesses and by taking things for granted on its journey, which leads it to an end-point, rather than to a starting-point. If it wants to explore the second subdivision [D], however, it takes things for granted in order to travel to a starting-point where nothing needs to be taken for granted, and it has no involvement with likenesses, as before, but makes its approach by means of types [or Forms] alone, in and of themselves.'

'I don't quite understand what you're saying,' he said.

c   'You will if I repeat it,' I said, 'because this preamble will make it easier to understand. I'm sure you're aware that practitioners of geometry, arithmetic, and so on take for granted things like numerical oddness and evenness, the geometrical figures, the three kinds of angle, and any other things of that sort which are relevant to a given subject. They act as if they know about these things, treat them as basic, and don't feel any further need to explain them either to themselves or to anyone else, on the grounds that there is

d nothing unclear about them. They make them the starting-points for their subsequent investigations, which end after a coherent chain of reasoning at the point they'd set out to reach in their research.'

'Yes, I'm certainly well aware of this,' he said.

'So you must also be aware that in the course of their discussions they make use of visible forms, despite the fact that they're not interested in visible forms as such, but in the things of which the visible forms are likenesses: that is, their

discussions are concerned with what it is to be a square, and with what it is to be a diagonal (and so on), rather than with the diagonal (and so on) e which occurs in their diagrams. They treat their models and diagrams as likenesses, when these things have likenesses themselves, in fact (that is, shadows and reflections on water); but they're actually trying to see squares and so on in themselves, which only thought can see.'[4]   511a

'You're right,' he said.

'So it was objects of this type that I was describing as belonging to the intelligible realm, with the rider that the mind can explore them only by taking things for granted, and that its goal is not a starting-point, because it is incapable of changing direction and rising above the things it is taking for granted. And I went on to say that it used as likenesses those very things which are themselves the originals of a lower order of likenesses, and that relative to the likenesses, the originals command respect and admiration for their distinctness.'

'I see,' he said. 'You're talking about the objects b of geometry and related occupations.'

'Now, can you see what I mean by the second subdivision [D] of the intelligible realm? It is what reason grasps by itself, thanks to its ability to practise dialectic. When it takes things for granted, it doesn't treat them as starting-points, but as basic in the strict sense – as platforms and rungs, for example. These serve it until it reaches a point where nothing needs to be taken for granted, and which is the starting-point for everything. Once it has grasped this starting-point, it turns around and by a process of depending on the things which depend from the starting-point, it descends to an end-point. It makes absolutely no use of anything perceptible by the senses: it aims for types by means of c types alone, in and of themselves, and it ends its journey with types.'

'I don't quite understand,' he said. 'I mean, you're talking about crucial matters here, I think. I do understand, however, that you want to mark off that part of the real and intelligible realm which is before the eyes of anyone who knows how to practise dialectic as more clear than the other part, which is before the eyes of practitioners of the various branches of expertise, as we call them. The latter make the things they take for granted their starting-points, and although they inevitably use thought, not the senses, to observe what they observe, yet because of their failure to ascend to a starting-point –

d because their enquiries rely on taking things for granted – you're saying that they don't understand these things, even though they are intelligible, when related to a starting-point. I take you to be describing what geometers and so on do as thinking rather than knowing, on the grounds that thinking is the intermediate state between believing and knowing.'

'There's nothing wrong with your understanding,' I said. 'And you should appreciate that there are four states of mind, one for each of the four sections. There's knowledge for the highest section and thought for the second one; and you'd better assign confidence to the third one

e and conjecture to the final one.[5] You can make an orderly progression out of them, and you should regard them as possessing as much clarity as their objects possess truth.'

'I see,' he said. 'That's fine with me: I'll order them in the way you suggest.'

514a 'Next,' I said, 'here's a situation which you can use as an analogy for the human condition – for our education or lack of it. Imagine people living in a cavernous cell down under the ground; at the far end of the cave, a long way off, there's an entrance open to the outside world. They've been there since childhood, with their legs

b and necks tied up in a way which keeps them in one place and allows them to look only straight ahead, but not to turn their heads. There's firelight burning a long way further up the cave behind them, and up the slope between the fire and the prisoners there's a road, beside which you should imagine a low wall has been built – like the partition which conjurors place between themselves and their audience and above which they show their tricks.'

'All right,' he said.

'Imagine also that there are people on the other side of this wall who are carrying all sorts of artefacts. These artefacts, human statuettes, and animal models carved in stone and wood and

c all kinds of materials stick out over the wall; and

515a as you'd expect, some of the people talk as they carry these objects along, while others are silent.'

'This is a strange picture you're painting,' he said, 'with strange prisoners.'

'They're no different from us,' I said. 'I mean, in the first place, do you think they'd see anything of themselves and one another except the shad-

ows cast by the fire on to the cave wall directly opposite them?'

'Of course not,' he said. 'They're forced to spend their lives without moving their heads.' b

'And what about the objects which were being carried along? Won't they only see their shadows as well?'

'Naturally.'

'Now, suppose they were able to talk to one another: don't you think they'd assume that their words applied to what they saw passing by in front of them?'

'They couldn't think otherwise.'

'And what if sound echoed off the prison wall opposite them? When any of the passers-by spoke, don't you think they'd be bound to assume that the sound came from a passing shadow?'

'I'm absolutely certain of it,' he said.

'All in all, then,' I said, 'the shadows of arte- c facts would constitute the only reality people in this situation would recognize.'

'That's absolutely inevitable,' he agreed.

'What do you think would happen, then,' I asked, 'if they were set free from their bonds and cured of their inanity? What would it be like if they found that happening to them? Imagine that one of them has been set free and is suddenly made to stand up, to turn his head and walk, and to look towards the firelight. It hurts him to do all this and he's too dazzled to be capable of making out the objects whose shadows he'd formerly been looking at. And suppose someone d tells him that what he's been seeing all this time has no substance, and that he's now closer to reality and is seeing more accurately, because of the greater reality of the things in front of his eyes – what do you imagine his reaction would be? And what do you think he'd say if he were shown any of the passing objects and had to respond to being asked what it was? Don't you think he'd be bewildered and would think that there was more reality in what he'd been seeing before than in what he was being shown now?'

'Far more,' he said.

'And if he were forced to look at the actual e firelight, don't you think it would hurt his eyes? Don't you think he'd turn away and run back to the things he could make out, and would take the truth of the matter to be that these things are clearer than what he was being shown?'

'Yes,' he agreed.

'And imagine him being dragged forcibly away from there up the rough, steep slope,' I went on, 'without being released until he's been 516a pulled out into the sunlight. Wouldn't this treatment cause him pain and distress? And once he's reached the sunlight, he wouldn't be able to see a single one of the things which are currently taken to be real, would he, because his eyes would be overwhelmed by the sun's beams?'

'No, he wouldn't,' he answered, 'not straight away.'

'He wouldn't be able to see things up on the surface of the earth, I suppose, until he'd got used to his situation. At first, it would be shadows that he could most easily make out, then he'd move on to the reflections of people and so on in water, and later he'd be able to see the actual things themselves. Next, he'd feast his eyes on the heav-
b enly bodies and the heavens themselves, which would be easier at night: he'd look at the light of the stars and the moon, rather than at the sun and sunlight during the daytime.'

'Of course.'

'And at last, I imagine, he'd be able to discern and feast his eyes on the sun – not the displaced image of the sun in water or elsewhere, but the sun on its own, in its proper place.'

'Yes, he'd inevitably come to that,' he said.

'After that, he'd start to think about the sun and he'd deduce that it is the source of the seasons and the yearly cycle, that the whole of the
c visible realm is its domain, and that in a sense everything which he and his peers used to see is its responsibility.'

'Yes, that would obviously be the next point he'd come to,' he agreed.

'Now, if he recalled the cell where he'd originally lived and what passed for knowledge there and his former fellow prisoners, don't you think he'd feel happy about his own altered circumstances, and sorry for them?'

'Definitely.'

'Suppose that the prisoners used to assign prestige and credit to one another, in the sense that they rewarded speed at recognizing the shadows as they passed, and the ability to remember which ones normally come earlier and later and at the same time as which other ones, and exper-
d tise at using this as a basis for guessing which ones would arrive next. Do you think our former prisoner would covet these honours and would envy the people who had status and power there, or would he much prefer, as Homer describes it, "being a slave labouring for someone else – someone without property" [*Odyssey*. II.489], and would put up with anything at all, in fact, rather than share their beliefs and their life?'

'Yes, I think he'd go through anything rather e than live that way,' he said.

'Here's something else I'd like your opinion about,' I said. 'If he went back underground and sat down again in the same spot, wouldn't the sudden transition from the sunlight mean that his eyes would be overwhelmed by darkness?'

'Certainly,' he replied.

'Now, the process of adjustment would be quite long this time, and suppose that before his eyes had settled down and while he wasn't seeing well, he had once again to compete against those 517a same old prisoners at identifying those shadows. Wouldn't he make a fool of himself? Wouldn't they say that he'd come back from his upward journey with his eyes ruined, and that it wasn't even worth trying to go up there? And wouldn't they – if they could – grab hold of anyone who tried to set them free and take them up there and kill him?'

'They certainly would,' he said.

'Well, my dear Glaucon,' I said, 'you should apply this allegory, as a whole, to what we were b talking about before. The region which is accessible to sight should be equated with the prison cell, and the firelight there with the light of the sun. And if you think of the upward journey and the sight of things up on the surface of the earth as the mind's ascent to the intelligible realm, you won't be wrong – at least, *I* don't think you'd be wrong, and it's my impression that you want to hear. Only God knows if it's actually true, however. Anyway, it's my opinion that the last thing to be seen – and it isn't easy to see either – in the c realm of knowledge is goodness; and the sight of the character of goodness leads one to deduce that it is responsible for everything that is right and fine, whatever the circumstances, and that in the visible realm it is the progenitor of light and of the source of light, and in the intelligible realm it is the source and provider of truth and knowledge. And I also think that the sight of it is a prerequisite for intelligent conduct either of one's own private affairs or of public business.'

'I couldn't agree more,' he said.

'All right, then,' I said. 'I wonder if you also agree with me in not finding it strange that people who've travelled there don't want to engage in human business: there's nowhere else their d minds would ever rather be than in the upper region – which is hardly surprising, if our allegory has got this aspect right as well.'

'No, it's not surprising,' he agreed.

'Well, what about this?' I asked. 'Imagine someone returning to the human world and all its misery after contemplating the divine realm. Do you think it's surprising if he seems awkward and ridiculous while he's still not seeing well, before he's had time to adjust to the darkness of his situation, and he's forced into a contest (in a lawcourt or wherever) about the shadows of morality or the statuettes which cast the shadows, e and into a competition whose terms are the conceptions of morality held by people who have never seen morality itself?'

'No, that's not surprising in the slightest,' he said.

518a 'In fact anyone with any sense,' I said, 'would remember that the eyes can become confused in two different ways, as a result of two different sets of circumstances: it can happen in the transition from light to darkness, and also in the transition from darkness to light. If he took the same facts into consideration when he also noticed someone's mind in such a state of confusion that it was incapable of making anything out, his reaction wouldn't be unthinking ridicule. Instead, he'd try to find out whether this person's mind was returning from a mode of existence which involves greater lucidity and had been blinded by the unfamiliar darkness, or whether it was moving from relative ignorance to relative lucidity and had been overwhelmed and dazzled by the increased brightness. Once he'd distinguished between the two conditions and modes of existence, he'd congratulate anyone he found in the b second state, and feel sorry for anyone in the first state. If he did choose to laugh at someone in the second state, his amusement would be less absurd than when laughter is directed at someone returning from the light above.'

c 'Yes,' he said, 'you're making a lot of sense.'

'Now, if this is true,' I said, 'we must bear in mind that education is not capable of doing what some people promise. They claim to introduce knowledge into a mind which doesn't have it, as if they were introducing sight into eyes which are blind.'

'Yes, they do,' he said.

'An implication of what we're saying at the moment, however,' I pointed out, 'is that the capacity for knowledge is present in everyone's mind. If you can imagine an eye that can turn from darkness to brightness only if the body as a whole turns, then our organ of understanding is like that. Its orientation has to be accompanied by turning the mind as a whole away from the world of becoming, until it becomes capable of bearing the sight of real being and reality at its most bright, which we're saying is goodness. Yes?' d

'Yes.'

Notes

1 The meaning seems to be that beauty, say, is not something that a person either "perfectly" ("unqualifiably") has or "perfectly" ("unqualifiably") lacks, since not only do people change but attributions of such qualities presuppose comparisons. Helen is more beautiful than her grandfather, but less so than some goddess.

2 The translator prefers "fields" to "objects," on the grounds that fields – of expertise, for instance – can overlap. Hence it is not excluded that something can be both known and believed.

3 The translator notes that, among the Greeks, "the eye was commonly regarded as containing a good proportion of fire – it flashes and twinkles" (*Republic*, trans. Waterfield, p. 420).

4 Since a diagram can be viewed as a mere physical object, but also serve as a tool for mathematical thinking, this shows that B and C on the line do not represent different objects (nor indeed do A and D) but, as Plato puts it, different degrees of "clarity" or "unclarity" with which things may be considered.

5 The four Greek words here translated as "knowledge," "thought," "confidence," and "conjecture" are *noesis, dianoia, pistis,* and *eikasia.* The best rendition of the last three is a disputed matter. "Reflective belief," "unreflective belief," and "illusion" respectively have sometimes been suggested.

2

Aristotle, *Posterior Analytics*, Book I.1–4 and 31, and Book II.19

Introduction

"All men by nature desire to know" is the famous beginning of Aristotle's (384–322 BCE) greatest work, *Metaphysics*.[1] Given that, in his view, it is this desire which best distinguishes humans from all other creatures, it is perhaps surprising that Aristotle devoted relatively little attention to the notion of knowledge. But, like his teacher Plato and unlike later Greek philosophers, he was not unduly vexed either by the threat of general skepticism or by any alleged opacity in the meaning of "A knows that p." With an important caveat, to which we will return, the interesting issues, for Aristotle, surround the things we know, not our knowledge of them.

Having articulated, however, in *Prior Analytics* his theory of "pure" logic and the syllogism, Aristotle turns in *Posterior Analytics*, to discussing the nature of a peculiarly important form of knowledge, *episteme* – what we might today call "scientific knowledge" or "scientific understanding." The work belongs, therefore, as much to the philosophies of science and mathematics (lumped together by Aristotle) as to epistemology. Indeed, in one well-known general commentary on

From *The Oxford Translation of Aristotle*, Vol. 1, ed. W. D. Ross, trans. G. R. G. Mure, Oxford: Oxford University Press, 1928 (most notes and part of Chapter 4 omitted; asterisked note is the translator's).

Aristotle, the *Posterior Analytics* is discussed not under the heading of "The theory of knowledge," but of "The logic of science."[2]

Crucially, unlike the "accidental" knowledge that the non-scientist may have acquired of triangles, cows or whatever, scientific knowledge of them must be "demonstrable" – incorporating an understanding of the reasons why they must be as they are.[3] Scientific knowledge must be deducible from "basic premisses" or principles that are "true, primary, immediate, better known than and prior to the conclusion," which is related to the premisses as "effect to cause" (71b). These basic premisses include the axioms of a science as well as "definitions," which in Aristotelian terms are formulations of what things in their "essence" are.

In order to avoid a vicious circle or a regress (Ch. 3), Aristotle must hold that these basic premisses, while indisputably true, need not and cannot themselves be demonstrated – though the question of how, in that case, they are known gets postponed until the final chapter of the work. The result is, therefore, that Aristotle is perhaps the first to have unequivocally advanced what philosophers now call a "foundationalist" view of knowledge – however much his view differs from later foundationalist theories where, typically, it is instead something general like immediate sense-experience or universal logical truths, and not immediately-evident axioms or definitions peculiar to a science, that is foundational.[4] The distance between Aristotelian foundationalism and later, empiricist foundationalisms is clearly discernible in Aristotle's insistence that knowledge "is not possible through the act of perception" (87b). In effect, this is a tautology given his definition of *episteme*: for scientific knowledge involves an ability to explain and to recognize as characteristic of knowledge a kind of necessity that unaided perception could never confer.

Earlier, we qualified our remark that Aristotle sees no general problem with the nature of knowledge. Our caveat concerned the issue of how knowledge arises in the first place, and this is one that Aristotle addresses, in rather different guises, in the opening and closing chapters of the work. In the former, he considers the issue of "innate" knowledge, raised by Plato in his *Meno*. To the question, "How do we ever learn anything?" Plato answers this way: If we already know something, we can't learn it anew; and if we don't already know it, we can't possibly recognize it as the right answer to an enquiry. So, since in every case of possible knowledge we either already know it or don't already know it, we must already know all that we can know. But for Aristotle the more urgent issue is how we acquire knowledge of "basic premisses" (Book II.19). He resolves the issue – with Plato looking over his shoulder – in a manner that was to provide some, but not total, satisfaction to both empiricists and rationalists of later times. While knowledge of basic premisses presupposes a process of perception, memory, and inductive generalization, it requires as well a capacity for intellectual "intuition" (*nôus*) that does not itself belong to any such developmental process. The implication, found paradoxical by some, is that scientific knowledge rests on a kind of knowledge of a quite different order.

Aristotle's *De anima* (or *On the Soul*) goes some distance in explicating the way in which Aristotle argues the mind-soul (*psyche*) must be constructed and ordered to make it possible for the

intellect to apprehend basic premises and other objects of knowledge.[5] In particular, Aristotle is keen to explore the relationship between the mind and body, the relationship between the intellect and sensation, and the way imagination plays into the acquisition of knowledge.

There exist more literal translations of *Posterior Analytics* than the one we have chosen,[6] but while those translations may be better suited to classical scholars, their very fidelity to Aristotle's tortuous style renders his views barely intelligible to the more general reader in the absence of a whole battery of explanatory notes.[7]

Notes

1 The familiar names of the Aristotelian texts were, notably, not Aristotle's own; rather, they were given to the texts by later editors.

2 W. D. Ross, *Aristotle*, London: Methuen, 1949, pp. 43ff.

3 A similar claim is made by Plato in *Theaetetus*.

4 See T. Irwin, "Aristotle," in A *Companion to Epistemology*, ed. J. Dancy and E. Sosa, Oxford: Blackwell, 1992, p. 28.

5 Readers may find it useful to compare Thomas Aquinas's understanding of the acquisition of knowledge by the intellect, as his model is in many ways rooted in Aristotle's (II.6).

6 See, especially, J. Barnes, trans., *Aristotle's Posterior Analytics*, Oxford: Clarendon Press, 1975. Barnes does provide the required battery of extremely helpful notes.

7 Indeed, there is some reason to believe that many of the Aristotelian texts extant today are not finished, polished text but, rather, something more like research or lecture notes – an hypothesis which helps to explain their difficult organization and presentation.

Aristotle, *Posterior Analytics*

Book I

71a **1** All instruction given or received by way of argument proceeds from pre-existent knowledge. This becomes evident upon a survey of all

the species of such instruction. The mathematical sciences and all other speculative disciplines are acquired in this way, and so are the two forms of dialectical reasoning, syllogistic and inductive; for each of these latter makes use of old knowledge to impart new, the syllogism assuming an audience that accepts its premisses, induction exhibiting the universal as implicit in the clearly known particular. Again, the persuasion exerted by rhetorical arguments is in principle the same, since they use either example, a kind of induction, or enthymeme [deduction in a rhetorical context], a form of syllogism.

The pre-existent knowledge required is of two kinds. In some cases admission of the fact must be assumed, in others comprehension of the meaning of the term used, and sometimes both assumptions are essential.[1] Thus, we assume that every predicate can be either truly affirmed or truly denied of any subject, and that 'triangle' means so and so; as regards 'unit' we have to make the double assumption of the meaning of the word and the existence of the thing. The reason is that these several objects are not equally obvious to us. Recognition of a truth may in some cases contain as factors both previous knowledge and also knowledge acquired simultaneously with that recognition – knowledge, this latter, of the particulars actually falling under the universal and therein already virtually known. For example, the student knew beforehand that the angles of every triangle are equal to two right angles; but it was only at the actual moment at which he was being led on to recognize this as true in the instance before him that he came to know 'this figure inscribed in the semicircle' to be a triangle. For some things (viz. the singulars finally reached which are not predicable of anything else as subject) are only learnt in this way, i.e. there is here no recognition through a middle of a minor term as subject to a major. Before he was led on to recognition or before he actually drew a conclusion, we should perhaps say that in a manner he knew, in a manner not.

If he did not in an unqualified sense of the term *know* the existence of this triangle, how could he *know* without qualification that its angles were equal to two right angles? No: clearly he *knows* not without qualification but only in the sense that he *knows* universally. If this distinction is not drawn, we are faced with the dilemma in [Plato's] *Meno*: either a man will learn nothing or what he already knows; for we cannot accept the solution which some people offer. A man is asked, 'Do you, or do you not, know that every pair is even?' He says he does know it. The questioner then produces a particular pair, of the existence, and so *a fortiori* of the evenness, of which he was unaware. The solution which some peo-

ple offer is to assert that they do not know that every pair is even, but only that everything which they know to be a pair is even: yet what **71b** they know to be even is that of which they have demonstrated evenness, i.e. what they made the subject of their premiss, viz. not merely every triangle or number which they know to be such, but any and every number or triangle without reservation. For no premiss is ever couched in the form 'every number which you know to be such', or 'every rectilinear figure which you know to be such': the predicate is always construed as applicable to any and every instance of the thing. On the other hand, I imagine there is nothing to prevent a man in one sense knowing what he is learning, in another not knowing it. The strange thing would be, not if in some sense he knew what he was learning, but if he were to know it in that precise sense and manner in which he was learning it.

2   We suppose ourselves to possess unqualified scientific knowledge of a thing, as opposed to knowing it in the accidental way in which the sophist knows, when we think that we know the cause on which the fact depends, as the cause of that fact and of no other, and, further, that the fact could not be other than it is. Now that scientific knowing is something of this sort is evident – witness both those who falsely claim it and those who actually possess it, since the former merely imagine themselves to be, while the latter are also actually, in the condition described. Consequently the proper object of unqualified scientific knowledge is something which cannot be other than it is.

There may be another manner of knowing as well – that will be discussed later. What I now assert is that at all events we do know by demonstration. By demonstration I mean a syllogism productive of scientific knowledge, a syllogism, that is, the grasp of which is *eo ipso* such knowledge. Assuming then that my thesis as to the nature of scientific knowing is correct, the premisses of demonstrated knowledge must be true, primary, immediate, better known than and prior to the conclusion, which is further related to them as effect to cause. Unless these conditions are satisfied, the basic truths will not be 'appropriate' to the conclusion. Syllogism there may indeed be without these conditions, but such syllogism, not being productive of scientific knowledge, will not be demonstration. The premisses must be true: for that which is non-existent cannot be known – we cannot know, e.g., that the diagonal of a square is commensurate with its side. The premisses must be primary and indemonstrable; otherwise they will require demonstration in order to be known, since to have knowledge, if it be not accidental knowledge, of things which are demonstrable, means precisely to have a demonstration of them. The premisses must be the causes of the conclusion, better known than it, and prior to it; its causes, since we possess scientific knowledge of a thing only when we know its cause; prior, in order to be causes; antecedently known, this antecedent knowledge being not our mere understanding of the meaning, but knowledge of the fact as well. Now 'prior' and 'better known' are ambiguous terms, for there is a difference between what is prior and better known in the order of being and what is prior and better

72a known to man. I mean that objects nearer to sense are prior and better known to man; objects without qualification prior and better known are those further from sense. Now the most universal causes are furthest from sense and particular causes are nearest to sense, and they are thus exactly opposed to one another. In saying that the premisses of demonstrated knowledge must be primary, I mean that they must be the 'appropriate' basic truths, for I identify primary premiss and basic truth. A 'basic truth' in a demonstration is an immediate proposition. An immediate proposition is one which has no other proposition prior to it. A proposition is either part of an enunciation, i.e. it predicates a single attribute of a single subject. If a proposition is dialectical, it assumes either part indifferently; if it is demonstrative, it lays down one part to the definite exclusion of the other because that part is true. The term 'enunciation' denotes either part of a contradiction indifferently. A contradiction is an opposition which of its own nature excludes a middle. The part of a contradiction which conjoins a predicate with a subject is an affirmation; the part disjoining them is a negation. I call an immediate basic truth of syllogism a 'thesis' [or 'posit'] when, though it is not susceptible of proof by the teacher, yet ignorance of it does not constitute a total bar to progress on the part of the pupil: one which the pupil must know if he is to learn anything whatever is an axiom. I call it an axiom because there are such truths and we

give them the name of axioms *par excellence.* If a thesis assumes one part or the other of an enunciation, i.e. asserts either the existence or the non-existence of a subject, it is a hypothesis;* if it does not so assert, it is a definition. Definition *is* a 'thesis' or a 'laying something down', since the arithmetician lays it down that to be a unit is to be quantitatively indivisible; but it is not a hypothesis, for to define what a unit is is not the same as to affirm its existence.

Now since the required ground of our knowledge – i.e. of our conviction – of a fact is the possession of such a syllogism as we call demonstration, and the ground of the syllogism is the facts constituting its premisses, we must not only know the primary premisses – some if not all of them – beforehand, but know them better than the conclusion: for the cause of an attribute's inherence in a subject always itself inheres in the subject more firmly than that attribute; e.g. the cause of our loving anything is dearer to us than the object of our love. So since the primary premisses are the cause of our knowledge – i.e. of our conviction – it follows that we know them better – that is, are more convinced of them – than their consequences, precisely because our knowledge of the latter is the effect of our knowledge of the premisses. Now a man cannot believe in anything more than in the things he knows, unless he has either actual knowledge of it or something better than actual knowledge. But we are faced with this paradox if a student whose belief rests on demonstration has not prior knowledge; a man must believe in some, if not in all, of the basic truths more than in the conclusion. Moreover, if a man sets out to acquire the scientific knowledge that comes through demonstration, he must not only have a better knowledge of the basic truths and a firmer conviction of them than of the connexion which is being demonstrated: more than **72b** this, nothing must be more certain or better known to him than these basic truths in their character as contradicting the fundamental premisses which lead to the opposed and erroneous conclusion. For indeed the conviction of pure science must be unshakable.

* 'Hypothesis' to Aristotle and Plato means an assumption not calling for proof within the sphere of the special science in which it functions, not a 'working hypothesis'.

3   Some hold that, owing to the necessity of knowing the primary premises, there is no scientific knowledge. Others think there is, but that all truths are demonstrable. Neither doctrine is either true or a necessary deduction from the premises. The first school, assuming that there is no way of knowing other than by demonstration, maintain that an infinite regress is involved, on the ground that if behind the prior stands no primary, we could not know the posterior through the prior (wherein they are right, for one cannot traverse an infinite series): if on the other hand – they say – the series terminates and there are primary premises, yet these are unknowable because incapable of demonstration, which according to them is the only form of knowledge. And since thus one cannot know the primary premises, knowledge of the conclusions which follow from them is not pure scientific knowledge nor properly knowing at all, but rests on the mere supposition that the premises are true. The other party agree with them as regards knowing, holding that it is only possible by demonstration, but they see no difficulty in holding that all truths are demonstrated, on the ground that demonstration may be circular and reciprocal.

Our own doctrine is that not all knowledge is demonstrative: on the contrary, knowledge of the immediate premises is independent of demonstration. (The necessity of this is obvious; for since we must know the prior premises from which the demonstration is drawn, and since the regress must end in immediate truths, those truths must be indemonstrable.) Such, then, is our doctrine, and in addition we maintain that besides scientific knowledge there is its originative source which enables us to recognize the definitions.

Now demonstration must be based on premises prior to and better known than the conclusion; and the same things cannot simultaneously be both prior and posterior to one another: so circular demonstration is clearly not possible in the unqualified sense of 'demonstration', but only possible if 'demonstration' be extended to include that other method of argument which rests on a distinction between truths prior to us and truths without qualification prior, i.e. the method by which induction produces knowledge. But if we accept this extension of its meaning, our definition of unqualified knowledge will prove faulty; for there seem to be two kinds of it.

Perhaps, however, the second form of demonstration, that which proceeds from truths better known to us, is not demonstration in the unqualified sense of the term.

The advocates of circular demonstration are not only faced with the difficulty we have just stated: in addition their theory reduces to the mere statement that if a thing exists, then it does exist – an easy way of proving anything. That this is so can be clearly shown by taking three terms, for to constitute the circle it makes no difference whether many terms or few or even only two are taken. Thus by direct proof, if A is, B must be; if B is, C must be; therefore if A is, C must be. Since then – by the circular proof – if A is, B must be, and if B is, A must be, A may be substituted for C above. Then 'if B is, A must be' = 'if B is, C must be', which above gave the conclusion 'if A is, C must be': but C and A have been identified. Consequently the upholders of circular demonstration are in the position of saying that if A is, A must be – a simple way of proving anything. Moreover, even such circular demonstration is impossible except in the case of attributes that imply one another, viz. 'peculiar' properties.

Now, it has been shown that the positing of one thing – be it one term or one premiss – never involves a necessary consequent: two premises constitute the first and smallest foundation for drawing a conclusion at all and therefore *a fortiori* for the demonstrative syllogism of science. If, then, A is implied in B and C, and B and C are reciprocally implied in one another and in A, it is possible, as has been shown in my writings on the syllogism [*Prior Analytics*], to prove all the assumptions on which the original conclusion rested, by circular demonstration in the first figure. But it has also been shown that in the other figures either no conclusion is possible, or at least none which proves both the original premisses. Propositions the terms of which are not convertible cannot be circularly demonstrated at all, and since convertible terms occur rarely in actual demonstrations, it is clearly frivolous and impossible to say that demonstration is reciprocal and that therefore everything can be demonstrated.

4   Since the object of pure scientific knowledge cannot be other than it is, the truth obtained by demonstrative knowledge will be necessary. And since demonstrative knowledge is only

present when we have a demonstration, it follows that demonstration is an inference from necessary premisses. So we must consider what are the premisses of demonstration – i.e. what is their character: and as a preliminary, let us define what we mean by an attribute 'true in every instance of its subject', an 'essential' attribute, and a 'commensurate and universal' attribute. I call 'true in every instance' what is truly predicable of all instances – not of one to the exclusion of others – and at all times, not at this or that time only; e.g. if animal is truly predicable of every instance of man, then if it be true to say 'this is a man', 'this is an animal' is also true, and if the one be true now the other is true now. A corresponding account holds if point is in every instance predicable as contained in line. There is evidence for this in the fact that the objection we raise against a proposition put to us as true in every instance is either an instance in which, or an occasion on which, it is not true. Essential attributes are (1) such as belong to their subject as elements in its essential nature (e.g. line thus belongs to triangle, point to line; for the very being or 'substance' of triangle and line is composed of these elements, which are contained in the formulae defining triangle and line): (2) such that, while they belong to certain subjects, the subjects to which they belong are contained in the attribute's own defining formula. Thus straight and curved belong to line, odd and even, prime and compound, square and oblong, to number;

73b and also the formula defining any one of these attributes contains its subject – e.g. line or number as the case may be.

Extending this classification to all other attributes, I distinguish those that answer the above description as belonging essentially to their respective subjects; whereas attributes related in neither of these two ways to their subjects I call accidents or 'coincidents'; e.g. musical or white is a 'coincident' of animal. [. . .]

87b 31   Scientific knowledge is not possible through the act of perception. Even if perception as a faculty is of 'the such [and such]', and not merely of a 'this somewhat', yet one must at any rate actually perceive a 'this somewhat', and at a definite present place and time: but that which is commensurately universal and true in all cases one cannot perceive, since it is not 'this' and it is not 'now'; if it were, it would not be commensurately

universal – the term, we apply to what is always and everywhere. Seeing, therefore, that demonstrations are commensurately universal and universals imperceptible, we clearly cannot obtain scientific knowledge by the act of perception: nay, it is obvious that even if it were possible to perceive that a triangle has its angles equal to two right angles, we should still be looking for a demonstration – we should not (as some say) possess knowledge of it; for perception must be of a particular, whereas scientific knowledge involves the recognition of the commensurate universal. So if we were on the moon, and saw the earth shutting out the sun's light, we should not know the cause of the eclipse: we should perceive the pre-   **88a** sent fact of the eclipse, but not the reasoned fact at all, since the act of perception is not of the commensurate universal. I do not, of course, deny that by watching the frequent recurrence of this event we might, after tracking the commensurate universal, possess a demonstration, for the commensurate universal is elicited from the several groups of singulars.

The commensurate universal is precious because it makes clear the cause; so that in the case of facts like these which have a cause other than themselves universal knowledge is more precious than sense-perceptions and than intuition. (As regards primary truths there is of course a different account to be given [see Book II, ch. 19].) Hence it is clear that knowledge of things demonstrable cannot be acquired by perception, unless the term perception is applied to the possession of scientific knowledge through demonstration. Nevertheless certain points do arise with regard to connexions to be proved which are referred for their explanation to a failure in sense-perception: there are cases when an act of vision would terminate our inquiry, not because in seeing we should be knowing, but because we should have elicited the universal from seeing; if, for example, we saw the pores in the glass and the light passing through, the reason of the kindling would be clear to us because we should at the same time see it in each instance and intuit that it must be so in all instances.

Book II

19   [. . .] As regards syllogism and demonstration,   **99b** the definition of, and the conditions required

to produce each of them, are now clear, and with that also the definition of, and the conditions required to produce, demonstrative knowledge, since it is the same as demonstration. As to the basic premisses, how they become known and what is the developed state of knowledge of them is made clear by raising some preliminary problems.

We have already said that scientific knowledge through demonstration is impossible unless a man knows the primary immediate premisses. But there are questions which might be raised in respect of the apprehension of these immediate premisses: one might not only ask whether it is of the same kind as the apprehension of the conclusions, but also whether there is or is not scientific knowledge of both; or scientific knowledge of the latter, and of the former a different kind of knowledge; and, further, whether the developed states of knowledge are not innate but come to be in us, or are innate but at first unnoticed. Now it is strange if we possess them from birth; for it means that we possess apprehensions more accurate than demonstration and fail to notice them. If on the other hand we acquire them and do not previously possess them, how could we apprehend and learn without a basis of pre-existent knowledge? For that is impossible, as we used to find [Book I, ch. 1], in the case of demonstration. So it emerges that neither can we possess them from birth, nor can they come to be in us if we are without knowledge of them to the extent of having no such developed state at all. Therefore we must possess a capacity of some sort, but not such as to rank higher in accuracy than these developed states. And this at least is an obvious characteristic of all animals, for they possess a congenital discriminative capacity which is called sense-perception. But though sense-perception is innate in all animals, in some the sense-impression comes to persist, in others it does not. So animals in which this persistence does not come to be have either no knowledge at all outside the act of perceiving, or no knowledge of objects of which no impression persists; animals in which it does come into being have perception and can continue to retain the sense-impression in the soul: and when such persistence is frequently repeated a further distinction at once arises between those which out of the persistence of such sense-impressions develop a power of systematizing them and those which

100a

do not. So out of sense-perception comes to be what we call memory, and out of frequently repeated memories of the same thing develops experience; for a number of memories constitute a single experience. From experience again – i.e. from the universal now stabilized in its entirety within the soul, the one beside the many which is a single identity within them all – originate the skill of the craftsman and the knowledge of the man of science, skill in the sphere of coming to be and science in the sphere of being.

We conclude that these states of knowledge are neither innate in a determinate form, nor developed from other higher states of knowledge, but from sense-perception. It is like a rout in battle stopped by first one man making a stand and then another, until the original formation has been restored. The soul is so constituted as to be capable of this process.

Let us now restate the account given already, though with insufficient clearness. When one of a number of logically indiscriminable particulars has made a stand, the earliest universal is present in the soul: for though the act of sense-perception **100b** is of the particular, its content is universal – is man, for example, not the man Callias. A fresh stand is made among these rudimentary universals, and the process does not cease until the indivisible concepts, the true universals, are established: e.g. such and such a species of animal is a step towards the genus animal, which by the same process is a step towards a further generalization.

Thus it is clear that we must get to know the primary premisses by induction; for the method by which even sense-perception implants the universal is inductive. Now of the thinking states by which we grasp truth, some are unfailingly true, others admit of error – opinion, for instance, and calculation, whereas scientific knowing and intuition are always true: further, no other kind of thought except intuition is more accurate than scientific knowledge, whereas primary premisses are more knowable than demonstrations, and all scientific knowledge is discursive. From these considerations it follows that there will be no scientific knowledge of the primary premisses, and since except intuition nothing can be truer than scientific knowledge, it will be intuition that apprehends the primary premisses – a result which also follows from the fact that demonstration cannot be the originative source of demonstration, nor, consequently, scientific knowledge of scientific knowledge. If, therefore, it is the only other kind of true thinking except scientific knowing, intuition will be the originative source of scientific knowledge. And the originative source of science grasps the original basic premiss, while science as a whole is similarly related as originative source to the whole body of fact.

Note

1 Aristotle can hardly mean that we only *sometimes* require "comprehension of the meaning of the term[s] used" in statements. His point, presumably, is that we are often entitled to take their meaning for granted, so that only sometimes – in the case of ambiguous words, say – do we need *explicitly* to assume that a term means such-and-such.

3

The Book of Chuang Tzu, Chapter 2

Introduction

In the following chapter (II.4) we will see that, for the Greek skeptic Pyrrho and his followers, "the skeptical way" was attractive primarily because it secured a good and tranquil life. In the Chinese tradition, where practical philosophy was always the main interest, questions about knowledge and its limits were similarly set within a broadly ethical context. Indeed, it is difficult to identify, within that tradition, a single sustained discussion of epistemological matters that is not tied to reflections on the good life. Certainly this ethical context sets what is, perhaps, the most famous Chinese discussion of the limits of knowledge, Chapter 2 of *The Book of Chuang Tzu*, its "most philosophically acute and challenging" chapter.[1] (For further extracts from this Book, see I.5.)

Chuang Tzu (or Zhuangzi, c. 369–286 BCE) was the foremost architect of that tendency of thought we now know as Taoism (or Daoism). (Lao Tzu or Laozi, "author" of the best-known Taoist text, the *Tao Te Ching* (III.1, V.1), though often dated between the 6th and 4th centuries BCE, was probably a legendary figure.) A central aspect of that tendency was rejection of the Confucian insistence on obedience to "conventional" morality. In I.5 of the present volume, the selections from

From *The Book of Chuang Tzu*, trans. M. Palmer. Harmondsworth: Penguin, 1996, pp. 8–20 (notes omitted).

Chuang Tzu exhibited his Cynic-like hostility to convention and artifice which, he held, militated against "the true person" and "natural" life – that is, life led in harmony with the *tao* (Way), the "source" and "sustainer" of the world. Chuang Tzu practiced what he preached. Offered a position at court, he turned it down with the remark that he preferred to enjoy himself in the mud rather than serve a ruler of a kingdom (Chapter 32).[2]

It is in Chapter 2 of his Book that Chuang Tzu makes the epistemological preparations for his attack on convention and artifice and, in so doing, "substantially contributed to China's long tradition of scepticism."[3] Unfortunately, his unsystematic, anecdotal style precludes confident interpretation of his overall position. There is, however, general agreement that he is denying that any of our everyday judgments amount to knowledge of, or even warranted, rational belief about, reality – though in the Pyrrhonian manner, he is hesitant about the denial itself. "Then does nothing know anything?" – "How could I know that?"

It is not obvious, however, that Chuang Tzu should be classed as a skeptic. Two other possibilities are these: first, that he was a "mystic," for whom there can be genuine knowledge of reality (the *tao*), but only of an ineffable kind; and second, that he was a "relativist," one who is not so much questioning whether our judgments "fit" reality as denying sense to the notion of a reality beyond our merely conventional "perspectives."[4]

Be that as it may, Chuang Tzu certainly marshals a number of considerations designed to show that our everyday judgments do not constitute knowledge of reality (if such there be). Like Sextus Empiricus (II.4) and Michel de Montaigne (c. 1533–92), he likes to assemble examples of seemingly irresolvable disagreements in judgment and taste, arguing that attempts to resolve them always presuppose some prior prejudice. He also deploys a somewhat strange version of "the argument from dreaming": "I . . . dreamt that I was a butterfly. . . . But I could not tell, had I been Chuang Tzu dreaming I was a butterfly, or a butterfly dreaming I was now Chuang Tzu?"

But his most original and interesting argument revolves around the role of language and is prescient of both Nietzsche's "perspectivism" and what, in our century, has been called "linguistic relativism." For Chuang Tzu, it seems, the languages we speak are simply convenient artifices, whose utility for purposes of communication need not and should not be taken to imply any correspondence between our statements and an independent reality. The distinctions we make among things are merely conventional and these things are what they are in virtue of how they are called. Unfortunately, we take these distinctions to be real ones and hence too seriously, like the monkeys in the anecdote told in the following text. True sages, recognizing that "the great *tao* is not named" and is something seamless, will confine themselves to speaking for simple, practical purposes, eschewing "speech which enables argument" by purporting to express knowledge of how things are.

Notes

1 E. Y. Chinn, "Zhuangzi and Relativistic Scepticism," *Asian Philosophy* 7 (1997): 207.

2 Diogenes of Sinope (c. 400–c. 325 BCE), also known as Diogenes the Cynic, is also well known for having rejected convention for the dictates of nature. He is reputed to have gone about wearing only a barrel and, like an animal, exercising the natural functions of his body in public places.

3 Wing-Tsit Chan, *A Source Book in Chinese Philosophy*, Princeton, NJ: Princeton University Press, 1963, p. 188.

4 See E. Y. Chinn, "Zhuangzi and Relativistic Scepticism," and also C. Hansen, *A Daoist Theory of Chinese Thought*, Oxford: Oxford University Press, 1992.

The Book of Chuang Tzu

Chapter 2: Working Everything Out Evenly

Master Chi of the Southern District sat leaning forward on his chair, staring up at Heaven and breathing steadily, as if in a trance, forgetful of all around him. Master Yen Cheng Yu stood beside him and said, 'What is it? Is it true that you can make the body like a shrivelled tree, the heart like cold, dead ashes? Surely the man here now is not the same as the one who was here yesterday.'

Master Chi said, 'Yen, this is a good point to make, but do you really understand?

'I have lost myself, do you understand?
You hear the pipes of the people, but not the pipes of earth.
Even if you hear the pipes of earth, you don't hear the pipes of Heaven!'

'Please explain this,' said Master Yu.
Master Chi replied,

'The vast breath of the universe, this is called Wind.
Sometimes it is unmoving;
when it moves it makes the ten thousand openings resound dramatically.
Have you not heard it,
like a terrifying gale?
Mountains and forests are stormed by it,
great trees, a hundred spans round with dips and hollows,
are like noses, like mouths, like ears, like sockets,
like cups, like mortars, like pools, like gulleys;
sounding like a crashing wave, a whistling arrow, a screech; sucking, shouting, barking, wailing, moaning,
the winds ahead howling *yeeh*,
those behind crying *yooh*,
light breezes making gentle sounds,
while the typhoon creates a great din.
When the typhoon has passed, all goes quiet again.
Have you not witnessed this disturbance settle down again?'

Master Yu said, 'What you've just described are the notes of the earth, while the notes of humanity come from wind instruments, but you have said nothing about the notes of Heaven.'

'The role of these forces on all forms of living things is not the same,' said Master Chi. 'For each is different, using what they need to be, not influenced by any other force!'

* * *

True depth of understanding is wide and steady,
Shallow understanding is lazy and wandering,
Words of wisdom are precise and clear,
Foolish words are petty and mean.

When we sleep, our spirits roam the earth,
when awake our bodies are alert,
whatever we encounter captures us,
day by day our hearts are struggling.

Often simple,
often deep,
often intimate.

Minor troubles make them unsettled, anxious,
Major troubles are plain and simple.

They fly off like an arrow,
convinced that they know right from wrong;
it is like one who makes a sacred promise,
standing sure and true and on their way to
    victory.
They give way, like autumn and winter,
decaying away with the ebb and flow of each
    day;
it is like a stream of water, it cannot be brought
    back;
they stagnate, because they are like old blocked
    drains,
brought on by old age,
which makes their minds closed as if near death,
and there is nothing which can draw their
    hearts into the power of the yang[1] –
the life-giving light.

Joy and anger,
sadness and delight,
hope and disappointment;
faithlessness and certainty,
forcefulness and sloth,
eagerness and reticence,
like notes from an empty reed,
or mushrooms growing in dampness,
day and night follow each other before our very
    eyes and we have no idea why.
Enough, enough!
Morning and night exist,

we cannot know more about the Origin than
    this!

Without them, we don't exist,
Without us, they have no purpose.
This is close to our meaning,
but we cannot know what creates things to be
    thus.
It is as if they have a Supreme Guidance, but
    there is no way of grasping such a One.
He can certainly act, of that there is no doubt,
but I cannot see his body.
He has desires, but no body.
A hundred parts and nine orifices and six
    organs,
are parts that go to make up myself,
but is any part more noble than another?.
You say I should treat all parts as equally noble:
But shouldn't I also treat some as better than
    other?
Don't they all serve me as well as each others?
If they are all servants, then aren't they all as
    bad as each other?
Or are there rulers amongst these servants?
There must be some Supreme Ruler who is over
    them all.
Though it is doubtful that you can find his true
    form,
and even if it were possible,
is it not meaningless to his true nature?
When someone is born in this body, doesn't life
    continue until death?
Either in conflict with others or in harmony
    with them,
we go through life like a runaway horse, unable
    to stop.
Working hard until the end of his life,
unable to appreciate any achievement,
worn out and incapable of resting,
isn't he a pathetic sight?
He may say, 'I'm still alive,' but so what?
When the body rots, so does the mind – is this
    not tragic?
Is this not ridiculous, or is it just me that is
    ridiculous and everyone else is sane?
If you allow your mind to guide you,
who then can be seen as being without a
    teacher?
Why is it thought that only the one who
    understands change and whose heart
    approves this can be the teacher?
Surely the fool is just the same.
But if you ignore your mind but insist you
    know right from wrong, you are like the
    saying,
'Today I set off for Yueh and arrived yesterday.'
This is to claim that what is not, is;

That what is not, does exist –
why, even the holy sage [emperor] Yu cannot
  understand this,
let alone poor old me!

* * *

Our words are not just hot air. Words work because they say something, but the problem is that, if we cannot define a word's meaning, it doesn't really say anything. Is it possible that there really is something here? Or does it really mean nothing? Is it possible to make a proper case for it being any different from the chirruping of chicks? How is it that we have the Tao so obscured that we have to distinguish between true and false? What has clouded our words so that we can have both what is and what is not? How can it be that the Tao goes off and is no longer? How can it be that words are found but are not understood? When the Tao is obscured by pettiness and the words are obscured by elaboration, then we end up having the 'this is, this is not' of the Confucians and Mohists, with what one of them calls reality being denied by the other, and what the other calls real disputed by the first. If we want to confound what they call right and confirm what they call wrong, we need to shed light on both of them.

Nothing exists which is not 'that', nothing exists which is not 'this'. I cannot look at something through someone else's eyes, I can only truly know something which I know. Therefore 'that' comes out of 'this' and 'this' arises from 'that'. That is why we say that 'that' and 'this' are born from each other, most definitely.

Compare birth with death, compare death with life; compare what is possible with what is not possible and compare what is not possible with what is possible; because there is, there is not, and because there is not, there is.

Thus it is that the sage does not go down this way, but sheds the light of Heaven upon such issues. This is also that and that is also this. The 'that' is on the one hand also 'this', and 'this' is on the other hand also 'that'. Does this mean he still has a this and that? Does this mean he does not have a this and that?

When 'this' and 'that' do not stand against each other, this is called the pivot of the Tao. This pivot provides the centre of the circle, which is without end, for it can react equally to that which is

and to that which is not. This is why it is best to shed light on such issues. To use a finger to show that a finger is not a finger, is not really as good as using something that is not a finger to show that a finger is not a finger; to use a horse to show a horse is not a horse is not as good as using something other than a horse to show that a horse is not a horse. Heaven and Earth are as one as a finger is, and all of creation is as one as a horse is.

What is, is, what is not, is not.
The Tao is made because we walk it,
things become what they are called.
Why is this so? Surely because this is [called] so.
Why is this not so? Surely because this is not
  [called] so.
Everything has what is innate,
everything has what is necessary.
Nothing is not something,
nothing is not so.
Therefore, take a stalk of wheat and a pillar,
a leper or a beauty like Hsi-shih,
the great and the insecure,
the cunning and the odd:
all these are alike to the Tao.
In their difference is their completeness;
in their completeness is their difference.

Through the Tao they are all seen as one, regardless of their completeness or difference, by those who are capable of such extended vision. Such a person has no need for distinctions but follows the ordinary view. The ordinary view is firmly set on the ground of usefulness. The usefulness of something defines its use; the use is its flexibility; its flexibility is its essence and from this it comes to a stop. We stop but do not know why we stop, and this is called Tao.

To tax our spirits and our intellect in this way without realizing that everything is the same is called 'Three in the Morning'. And what is 'Three in the Morning'? A monkey trainer was giving out acorns and he said, 'In the morning I will give you each three acorns and in the evening you will get four.' The monkeys were very upset at this and so he said, 'All right, in the morning you will get four and in the evening, three.' This pleased the monkeys no end. His two statements were essentially the same, but got different reactions from the monkeys. He gained what he wanted by his skill. So it is with the sage, who manages to harmonize right and wrong and is content to abide by the Natural Equality of Heaven. This is called walking two roads.

* * *

The men of old understood a great deal. How much?

In the beginning they did not know that anything existed; this is virtually perfect knowledge, for nothing can be added. Later, they knew that some things existed but they did not distinguish between them. Next came those who distinguished between things, but did not judge things as 'being' or 'not being'. It was when judgements were made that the Tao was damaged, and because the Tao was damaged, love became complete. Is anything complete or damaged? Is anything not complete or damaged? There is completion and damage, just as Chao Wen played the lute. There is nothing which is complete or damaged, just as Chao Wen did not play the lute.

> Chao Wen played the lute,
> Shih Kuang conducted,
> Hui Tzu debated.

The understanding of these three was almost perfect and they followed it to the end of their years. They cared about this because it was different, and they wanted to teach others about it. But it was not possible to make things clear, though they tried to make things simple. They ended up instead with the folly of the 'hard' and the 'white'.[2]

Wen's son ended up continuing to play Wen's lute and achieved nothing for himself. If someone like this is called complete, then am I not also? And if someone like this is called incomplete, then surely neither I nor anyone else has ever been complete. Also, by the light shining out of chaos, the sage is guided; he does not make use of distinctions but is led on by the light.

* * *

Now, however, I have something to say. Do I know whether this is in the same sort of category as what is said by others? I don't know. At one level, what I say is not the same. At another level, it most definitely is, and there is no difference between what I say and what others say. Whatever the case, let me try and tell you what I mean.

There is the beginning; there is not as yet any beginning of the beginning; there is not as yet beginning not to be a beginning of the beginning. There is what is, and there is what is not, and it is not easy to say whether what is not, is not; or whether what is, is.

I have just made a statement, yet I do not know whether what I said has been real in what I said or not really said.

Under Heaven there is nothing greater than the tip of a hair, but Mount Tai is smaller; there is no one older than a dead child, yet Peng Tsu [who supposedly lived for centuries] died young.

Heaven and Earth and I were born at the same time, and all life and I are one.

As all life is one, what need is there for words? Yet I have just said all life is one, so I have already spoken, haven't I? One plus one equals two, two plus one equals three. To go on from here would take us beyond the understanding of even a skilled accountant, let alone the ordinary people. If going from 'no-thing' to 'some-thing' we get to three, just think how much further we would have to go if we went from 'some-thing' to something!

Don't even start, let's just stay put.

The great Tao has no beginning, and words have changed their meaning from the beginning, but because of the idea of a 'this is' there came to be limitations. I want to say something about these limitations. There is right and left, relationships and their consequences, divisions and disagreements, emulations and contentions. These are known as the eight Virtues.

The sage will not speak of what is beyond the boundaries of the universe – though he will not deny it either. What is within the universe, he says something about but does not pronounce upon. Concerning the record of the past actions of the kings in the *Spring and Autumn Annals*, the sage discusses but does not judge. When something is divided, something is not divided; when there is disagreement there are things not disagreed about.

You ask, what does this mean? The sage encompasses everything, while ordinary people just argue about things. This is why I say that disagreement means you do not understand at all.

> The great Way is not named,
> the great disagreement is unspoken,
> great benevolence is not benevolent,

great modesty is not humble,
great courage is not violent.
The Tao that is clear is not the Tao,
speech which enables argument is not worthy,
benevolence which is ever present does not
    achieve its goal,
modesty if flouted, fails,
courage that is violent is pointless.

These five are fine: they are, as it were,
rounded. But if they lose this they can become
awkward. This is why the one who knows how
to stop at what he knows is best. Who knows the
argument that needs no words, and the Tao that
cannot be named? To those who do, this is called
the Treasury of Heaven. Pour into it and it is never
full; empty it and it is never empty. We do not
know where it comes from originally, and this is
called our Guiding Light.

* * *

In the olden days Yao said to Shun [two em-
perors], 'I want to attack Tsung, Kuai and
Hsu Ao. I have wanted to do this since I became
king. What do you think?'

Shun replied, 'These three rulers are just
primitives living in the backwoods – why can't you
just forget them? In ancient times, ten suns rose
and all life was illuminated. But how much more
does Virtue illuminate life than even these suns!'

* * * *

Yeh Chueh said to Wang Ni, 'Do you know,
Master, what everything agrees upon?'

'How can I possibly know?' said Wang Ni.

'Do you know, Master, what you do not
know?'

'How can I know?' he replied.

'Then does nothing know anything?'

'How could I know that?' said Wang Ni.
'Nevertheless, I want to try and say something.
How can I know that what I say I know is not
actually what I don't know? Likewise, how can I
know that what I think I don't know is not really
what I do know? I want to put some questions
to you:

'If someone sleeps in a damp place, he will ache
all over and he will be half paralysed, but is it
the same for an eel? If someone climbs a tree, he
will be frightened and shaking, but is it so for a
monkey? Out of these three, which is wisest
about where to live?

'Humans eat meat, deer consume grass, centi-
pedes devour snakes and owls and crows enjoy
mice. Of these four, which has the best taste?

'Monkeys mate with each other, deer go with
deer. People said that Mao Chiang and Li Chi were
the most beautiful women in the world, but fish
seeing them dived away, birds took off into the
air and deer ran off. Of these four, who really
knows true beauty? As I see it, benevolence and
righteousness, also the ways of right and wrong,
are completely interwoven. I do not think I can
know the difference between them!'

Yeh Chueh said: 'Master, if you do not know
the difference between that which is good and that
which is harmful, does this mean the perfect
man is also without such knowledge?'

'The perfect man is pure spirit,' replied Wang
Ni. 'He does not feel the heat of the burning
deserts nor the cold of the vast waters. He is not
frightened by the lightning which can split open
mountains, nor by the storms that can whip up
the seas. Such a person rides the clouds and
mounts upon the sun and moon, and wanders
across and beyond the four seas. Neither death nor
life concern him, nor is he interested in what is
good or bad!'

* * *

Chu Chiao Tzu asked Chang Wu Tzu,

'I have heard from the Master [Confucius]
    that the sage does not labour at anything,
    does not look for advantage,
    does not act benevolently,
    does not harm,
    does not pursue the Tao;
    He speaks without speaking,
    and does not speak when he speaks,
    and looks beyond the confines of this
        dusty world.

'The Master sees all this as an endless stream
of words, but to me they are like the words of the
mysterious Tao. Master, what do you think?'

Chang Wu Tzu said, 'Such a saying as this
would have confused even the Yellow Emperor
[a legendary sage], so how could Confucius be able
to understand them! However, you are getting
ahead of yourself, counting your chickens before

your eggs are hatched and looking at the bowl, imagining, the roasted fowl. I will try to speak to you in a random way, so you listen to me likewise. How can the wise one sit beside the sun and moon and embrace the universe? Because he brings all things together in harmony, he rejects difference and confusion and ignores status and power. While ordinary people rush busily around, the sage seems stupid and ignorant, but to him all life is one and united. All life is simply what it is and all appear to him to be doing what they rightly should.

'How do I know that the love of life is not a delusion? Or that the fear of death is not like a young person running away from home and unable to find his way back? The Lady Li Chi was the daughter of a border warden, Ai. When the state of Chin captured her, she wept until she had drenched her robes; then she came to the King's palace, shared the King's bed, ate his food, and repented of her tears. How do I know whether the dead now repent for their former clinging to life?

'Come the morning, those who dream of the drunken feast may weep and moan; when the morning comes, those who dream of weeping and moaning go hunting in the fields. When they dream, they don't know it is a dream. Indeed, in their dreams they may think they are interpreting dreams, only when they awake do they know it was a dream. Eventually there comes the day of reckoning and awakening, and then we shall know that it was all a great dream. Only fools think that they are now awake and that they really know what is going on, playing the prince and then playing the servant. What fools! The Master and you are both living in a dream. When I say a dream, I am also dreaming. This very saying is a deception. If after ten thousand years we could once meet a truly great sage, one who understands, it would seem as if it had only been a morning.

'Imagine that you and I have a disagreement, and you get the better of me, rather than me getting the better of you, does this mean that you are automatically right and I am automatically wrong? Suppose I get the better of you, does it follow that I am automatically right and you are therefore wrong? Is it really that one of us is right and the other wrong? Or are we both right and both wrong? Neither you nor I can really know and other people are even more in the dark. So who can we ask to give us the right answer? Should you ask someone who thinks you are right? But how then can that person give a fair answer? Should we ask someone who thinks I am right? But then if he agrees with me, how can he make a fair judgement? Then again, should we ask someone who agrees with both of us? But again, if he agrees with both of us, how can he make a true judgement? Should we ask someone who disagrees with both of us? But here again, if he disagrees with both of us, how can he make an honest judgement? It is clear that neither you, I nor anyone else can make decisions like this amongst ourselves. So should we wait for someone else to turn up?

'To wait for one voice to bring it all together is as pointless as waiting for no one. Bring all things together under the Equality of Heaven, allow their process of change to go on unimpeded, and learn to grow old. What do I mean by bringing everything together under the Equality of Heaven? With regard to what is right and wrong, I say not being is being and being is not being. But let us not get caught up in discussing this. Forget about life, forget about worrying about right and wrong. Plunge into the unknown and the endless and find your place there!'

* * *

The Outline said to the Shadow, 'First you are on the move, then you are standing still; you sit down and then you stand up. Why can't you make up your mind?'

Shadow replied, 'Do I have to look to something else to be what I am? Does this something else itself not have to rely upon yet another something? Do I have to depend upon the scales of a snake or the wings of a cicada? How can I tell how things are? How can I tell how things are not?'

Once upon a time, I, Chuang Tzu, dreamt that I was a butterfly, flitting around and enjoying myself. I had no idea I was Chuang Tzu. Then suddenly I woke up and was Chuang Tzu again. But I could not tell, had I been Chuang Tzu dreaming I was a butterfly, or a butterfly dreaming I was now Chuang Tzu? However, there must be some sort of difference between Chuang Tzu and a butterfly! We call this the transformation of things.

Notes

1 One of the famous polarity of *yin* and *yang*, two opposed, but interdependent, principles – "dark," "feminine," "hidden" *versus* "bright," "masculine," "open" – whose balance sustains the universe.

2 A reference to Chuang Tzu's friend and intellectual sparring partner, Hui Tzu's, penchant for discussing abstract issues about the existence and identity of universals, such as "hardness" and "whiteness."

4

Sextus Empiricus, *Outlines of Pyrrhonism*, Book I, Sections 1–16, 18–27

Introduction

Greek philosophy did not grind to a halt after Aristotle, and in recent years there has been a welcome revival of interest, subdued since Renaissance times, in thinkers of the Hellenistic period that followed the death of Alexander the Great in 323 BCE and of Aristotle a year later. These three centuries were lively ones during which battle on many issues, including epistemological ones, was joined by warring schools – most famously, the Stoics, Epicureans, and Skeptics. Common to these schools, however, was an ideal of tranquility or "freedom from disturbance" (*ataraxia*), of what is now popularly called a "philosophical attitude to life." For the Stoics and Epicureans (see I.3, I.7 and I.8), this was to be achieved through arriving at a true and satisfying account of reality, but for the skeptical followers of Pyrrho of Elis tranquility comes with "suspension of judgement" (*epochē*) and keeping silent (*aphasia*) about philosophical dogmatics – a gentle refusal to attach oneself to any dogmatic beliefs whatsoever about how things *really are*, as distinct from acknowledging how they may *seem* to be.

From Benson Mates, *The Skeptic Way: Sextus Empiricus's Outlines of Pyrrhonism*, trans. B. Mates. Oxford: Oxford University Press, Inc., 1996, pp. 89–94, 110–17 (most of Section 14 omitted).

Pyrrho, whose dates (c. 365–270 BCE) situate this entry, maintained that "nothing is honourable or base, or just or unjust, and that . . . nothing exists in truth": allegedly, according to Diogenes Laertius's probably caricatured account, Pyrrho followed his principles by "taking no precautions, facing everything that came, wagons, precipices, dogs," trusting nothing.[1] Pyrrho it seems, like Timon of Philus (c. 320–c. 230 BCE), was more intent on advocating this skeptical lifestyle than on providing reasons for "suspension of judgement,"[2] this latter task being taken up by later skeptics like Aenesidemus (first century BCE), who is credited with formulating the famous "tropes" (*tropoi*) or "modes" of skeptical argument. It is the views of later skeptics, and their opponents, that were chronicled with clarity and detail by a second-century physician, Sextus Empiricus, an otherwise obscure figure.

We have omitted most of §14 where all ten "tropes" are described, since some of them – like their supporting examples – are too silly to take seriously; the more plausible of the arguments are distilled in §§ 15–16. Suffice it to say that they "include practically all the ingredients of what nowadays is called 'the argument from illusion',"[3] and that their thrust is to show that there is "equipollence" between conflicting beliefs about reality, that there is never reason to adopt one such belief in preference to a rival one. An intriguing feature of Pyrrhonian skepticism was its resolutely self-referential nature. Sextus says many times that he himself is not committed to the arguments and evidence marshalled in favor of the skeptical stance. They merely seem to him to be plausible and therefore result in it seeming to him that no belief deserves credence. The point of such remarks, of course, is to divert the familiar objection that the skeptic refutes himself when employing reason and evidence in order to discredit their authority.

The skeptic, as portrayed by Sextus, does not end up with a skeptical dogma: rather, the skeptic suspends his faculty of dogmatic belief and judgment, emulating, one might say, the condition of an animal or young child who acts naturally and without the mediation of beliefs.[4] (Students of Taoism will recognize similarities with the position of Chuang Tzu, II.3.) More theoretically, one might say that the skeptic – like Socrates, who is said to have accepted that he was wisest because he admitted he knew nothing – separates wisdom from knowledge.[5] Rather than requiring knowledge as a necessary condition for wisdom, the Skeptic actually takes the pursuit of knowledge as well as claims to having achieved it to characterize the absence of wisdom. Instead of knowledge, Skeptics undogmatically aspire to what Sextus calls, perhaps ironically, the "criterion" of skepticism or the skeptical "fourfold": (1) the guidance of nature; (2) the constraint of the passions; (3) deference to custom and tradition; and (4) employment of the technical arts.[6] Sextus seems to relate this instruction to adhering to "appearances" (*phainomena*) and to "common life" (*ho bios ho koinos*).[7]

Sextus's writings were an important discovery for Renaissance scholars, and they served as one of the two major conduits of skeptical ideas to the modern world – Cicero's *Academica* was the other (I.7). The *Outlines* influenced such philosophers as Michel de Montaigne (1533–92) and, through them, the founder of modern skepticism, René Descartes (II.8). In contrast to the "Academic" skepticism developed by those who inherited Plato's Academy Pyrrhonism has been commonly regarded as more radical – this largely because the Academics seemed to have accepted probabilistic criteria of truth, while the Pyrrhonians refused epistemic criteria altogether.[8] Pyrrhonism, indeed, is at once more and less radical than Cartesian skepticism: more radical, first, because the skeptical position is not for the Pyrrhonians merely a tactical, methodological one to be provisionally adopted but then overcome and, second, because the Pyrrhonian urges something stronger than the dubitability of our beliefs. It is not doubt but rather *aporia* – bafflement as to the very sense of making objective claims – that the tropes or modes of Pyrrhonism are intended to induce. Pyrrhonism is less radical, however, than Cartesian doubt – though some commentators would contest this – in that Sextus does not call into question the very existence of an external world. The point, rather, is that we should (undogmatically, of course) suspend all judgment as to what that world beyond our "feelings" (*pathē*) is like.

Notes

1 Diogenes Laertius, quoted in A. A. Long and D. N. Sedley, *The Hellenistic Philosophers*, vol. 1, Cambridge: Cambridge University Press, 1987, p. 13.
2 Timon's skeptical remarks were collected under the title, *Silloi*.
3 B. Mates, *The Skeptic Way*, Oxford: Oxford University Press, 1996, p. 57.
4 See W. Jordan, *Ancient Concepts of Philosophy*, London: Routledge, 1992, pp. 162ff.
5 See Plato's account of Socrates' self-characterization in *Apology*.
6 *Outlines of Pyrrhonism* I: 23–4.
7 *Outlines of Pyrrhonism* I: 237.
8 Recent scholars, however, have come to think that the Academics advanced their probabilistic criteria (the *eulogon* and the *pithanon*) in ironic ways or simply as argumentative gambits used against their principal adversaries, the Stoics.

Sextus Empiricus, *Outlines of Pyrrhonism*, Book I

1. The Main Difference between the Philosophies

When people search for something, the likely outcome is that either they find it or, not finding it, they accept that it cannot be found, or they continue to search. So also in the case of what is sought in philosophy, I think, some people have claimed to have found the truth, others have asserted that it cannot be apprehended, and others are still searching. Those who think that they have found it are the Dogmatists, properly so called – for example, the followers of Aristotle and Epicurus, the Stoics, and certain others. The followers of Cleitomachus and Carneades, as well as other Academics, have asserted that it cannot be apprehended. The Skeptics continue to search. Hence it is with reason that the main types of philosophy are thought to be three in number: the Dogmatic, the Academic, and the Skeptic. Concerning the first two it will best become others to speak; but concerning the Skeptic Way we shall now give an outline account, stating in advance that as regards none of the things that we are about to say do we firmly maintain that matters are absolutely as stated, but in each instance we are simply reporting, like a chronicler, what now appears to us to be the case.

2. The Accounts of Skepticism

One account of the Skeptic philosophy is called "general"; the other, "specific." In the general account we set forth the characteristic traits of Skepticism, stating its basic idea, its origins, arguments, criterion and goal, as well as the modes of *epochē* [suspension of judgment], and how we take the Skeptic statements, and the distinction between Skepticism and the competing philosophies. In the specific account we state objections to each part of so-called "philosophy." Let us, then, first take up the general account, beginning the exposition with the various terms for the Skeptic Way.

3. The Nomenclature of the Skeptic Way

The Skeptic Way is called Zetetic ["questioning"] from its activity in questioning and inquiring, Ephectic ["suspensive"] from the *pathos* that arises concerning the subject of inquiry, Aporetic ["inclined to *aporiai*"] either, as some say, from its being puzzled and questioning about everything or from its being at a loss as to whether to assent or dissent, and Pyrrhonean because it appears to us that Pyrrho applied himself to Skepticism more vigorously and conspicuously than his predecessors did.

4. What Skepticism Is

The Skeptic Way is a disposition to oppose phenomena and noumena to one another in any way whatever,[1] with the result that, owing to the equipollence among the things and statements thus opposed, we are brought first to *epochē* and then to *ataraxia*. We do not apply the term "disposition" in any subtle sense, but simply as cognate with "to be disposed." At this point we are taking as phenomena the objects of sense perception, thus contrasting them with the noumena. The phrase "in any way whatever" can modify both the word "disposition" (so as to make us take that word in a plain sense, as we said) and the phrase "to oppose phenomena and noumena"; for since we oppose these in various ways – phenomena to phenomena, noumena to noumena, or *alternando* phenomena to noumena, we say "in any way whatever" in order to include all such oppositions. Or we can apply "in any way whatever" to "phenomena and noumena," in order that we may not have to inquire how the phenomena appear or the noumena are thought, but may take these terms in their plain senses. By "opposed" statements we simply mean inconsistent ones, not necessarily affirmative and negative. By "equipollence" we mean equality as regards credibility and the lack of it, that is, that no one of the inconsistent statements takes precedence over any other as being more credible. *Epochē* is a state of the intellect on account of which we neither deny nor affirm anything. *Ataraxia* is an untroubled and tranquil condition of the soul. In our remarks on the goal of Skepticism we shall come back to the question of how *ataraxia* enters the soul along with *epochē*.

5.   The Skeptic

The definition of the Pyrrhonean philosopher is implicitly contained in that of the Skeptic Way: he is the person who has the aforementioned disposition.

6.   The Origins of Skepticism

We say that the causal origin of the Skeptic Way is the hope of attaining *ataraxia*. Certain talented people, upset by anomaly in "the facts" and at a loss as to which of these "facts" deserve assent, endeavored to discover what is true in them and what is false, expecting that by settling this they would achieve *ataraxia*. But the main origin of Skepticism is the practice of opposing to each statement an equal statement; it seems to us that doing this brings an end to dogmatizing.

7.   Does the Skeptic Dogmatize?

When we say that the Skeptic does not dogmatize we are not using the term "dogma" as some do, in its more common meaning, "something that one merely agrees to", for the Skeptic does give assent to the *pathē* [feelings, affects] that are forced upon him by a *phantasia* [impression]: for example, when feeling hot (or cold) he would not say "I seem not to be hot (or cold)." But when we assert that he does not dogmatize, we use "dogma" in the sense, which others give it, of assent to one of the non-evident matters investigated by the sciences. For the Pyrrhonist assents to nothing that is non-evident. Not even in putting forward the Skeptic slogans about non-evident things does he dogmatize – slogans like "Nothing more" or "I determine nothing" or any of the others of which we shall speak later. For the dogmatizer propounds as certainty the things about which he is said to be dogmatizing, but the Skeptic does not put forward these slogans as holding absolutely. He considers that, just as the "All things are false" slogan says that together with the other things it is itself false, as does the slogan "Nothing is true," so also the "Nothing more" slogan says that it itself is no more the case than its opposite, and thus it applies to itself along with the rest. We say the same of the other Skeptic slogans. So that since the dogmatizer is one who posits the content of his dogmas as

being true, while the Skeptic presents his skeptical slogans as implicitly self-applicable, the Skeptic should not be said to dogmatize thereby. But the most important point is that in putting forward these slogans he is saying what seems to him to be the case and is reporting his *pathos* without belief, not firmly maintaining anything concerning what exists externally.

8.   Does the Skeptic Have a System?

We proceed in the same way when asked whether the Skeptic has a system. If one defines a system as an attachment to a number of dogmas that agree with one another and with appearances, and defines a dogma as an assent to something non-evident, we shall say that the Skeptic does not have a system. But if one says that a system is a way of life that, in accordance with appearances, follows a certain rationale, where that rationale shows how it is possible to seem to live rightly ("rightly" being taken, not as referring only to virtue, but in a more ordinary sense) and tends to produce the disposition to suspend judgment, then we say that he does have a system. For we do follow a certain rationale that, in accord with appearances, points us toward a life in conformity with the customs of our country and its laws and institutions, and with our own particular *pathē*.

9.   Does the Skeptic Theorize about Nature?

We reply in the same vein if asked whether the Skeptic needs to theorize about nature. On the one hand, if there is a question of making an assertion with firm confidence about any of the matters dogmatically treated in physical theory, we do not theorize; but, on the other hand, in the course of opposing to every statement an equal statement, and in connection with *ataraxia*, we do touch upon physical theory. This, too, is the way we approach the logical and ethical parts of so-called "philosophy."

10.   Do the Skeptics Deny Appearances?

Those who claim that the Skeptics deny appearances seem to me not to have heard what we say. For, as we stated above, we do not reject the things that lead us involuntarily to assent in accord with a passively received *phantasia*, and these are appearances. And when we question whether the external object is such as it appears, we grant that it does appear, and we are not raising a question about the appearance but rather about what is said about the appearance; this is different from raising a question about the appearance itself. For example, the honey appears to us to be sweet. This we grant, for we sense the sweetness. But whether it *is* sweet we question insofar as this has to do with the [philosophical] theory, for that theory is not the appearance, but something said about the appearance. And even when we do present arguments in opposition to the appearances, we do not put these forward with the intention of denying the appearances but by way of pointing out the precipitancy of the Dogmatists; for if the theory is so deceptive as to all but snatch away the appearances from under our very eyes, should we not distrust it in regard to the non-evident, and thus avoid being led by it into precipitate judgments?

11.   The Criterion of the Skeptic Way

That we hold to the appearances is obvious from what we say about the criterion of the Skeptic Way. The word "criterion" is used in two ways: first, for the criterion that is assumed in connection with belief about existence or nonexistence, and that we shall discuss in our objections; and second, for the criterion of action, by attention to which in the conduct of daily life we do some things and not others; it is of the latter that we are now speaking. Accordingly, we say that the criterion of the Skeptic Way is the appearance – in effect using that term here for the *phantasia* – for since this appearance lies in feeling and involuntary *pathos* it is not open to question. Thus nobody, I think, disputes about whether the external object appears this way or that, but rather about whether it is such as it appears to be.

Holding to the appearances, then, we live without beliefs but in accord with the ordinary regimen of life, since we cannot be wholly inactive. And this ordinary regimen of life seems to be fourfold: one part has to do with the guidance of nature, another with the compulsion of the *pathē*, another with the handing down of laws and customs, and a fourth with instruction in arts and crafts. Nature's guidance is that by which we are naturally capable of sensation and thought; compulsion of the *pathē* is that by which hunger drives us to food and thirst makes us drink; the handing down of customs and laws is that by which we accept that piety in the conduct of life is good and impiety bad; and instruction in arts and crafts is that by which we are not inactive in whichever of these we acquire. And we say all these things without belief.

12.   What Is the Goal of Skepticism?

After these remarks, our next task is to explain the goal of the Skeptic Way. Now the goal or end is that for the sake of which everything is done or considered, while it, in turn, is not done or considered for the sake of anything else; or, it is the ultimate object of the desires. We always say that as regards belief the Skeptic's goal is *ataraxia*, and that as regards things that are unavoidable it is having moderate *pathē*. For when the Skeptic set out to philosophize with the aim of assessing his *phantasiai* – that is, of determining which are true and which are false so as to achieve *ataraxia* – he landed in a controversy between positions of equal strength, and, being unable to resolve it, he suspended judgment. But while he was thus suspending judgment there followed by chance the sought-after *ataraxia* as regards belief. For the person who believes that something is by nature good or bad is constantly upset; when he does not possess the things that seem to be good, he thinks he is being tormented by things that are by nature bad, and he chases after the things he supposes to be good; then, when he gets these, he falls into still more torments because of irrational and immoderate exultation, and, fearing any change, he does absolutely everything in order not to lose the things that seem to him good. But the person who takes no position as to what is by nature good or bad neither avoids nor pursues intensely. As a result, he achieves *ataraxia*.[2]

Indeed, what happened to the Skeptic is just like what is told of Apelles the painter. For it is said that once upon a time, when he was painting a horse and wished to depict the horse's froth, he failed so completely that he gave up and threw his sponge at the picture – the sponge on which he used to wipe the paints from his brush – and that in striking the picture the sponge produced the desired effect. So, too, the Skeptics were hoping to achieve *ataraxia* by resolving the anomaly of phenomena and noumena, and, being unable to do this, they suspended judgment. But then, by chance as it were, when they were suspending judgment the *ataraxia* followed, as a shadow follows the body. We do not suppose, of course, that the Skeptic is wholly untroubled, but we do say that he is troubled only by things unavoidable. For we agree that sometimes he is cold and thirsty and has various feelings like those. But even in such cases, whereas ordinary people are affected by two circumstances – namely by the *pathē* themselves and not less by its seeming that these conditions are by nature bad – the Skeptic, by eliminating the additional belief that all these things are naturally bad, gets off more moderately here as well. Because of this we say that as regards belief the Skeptic's goal is *ataraxia*, but in regard to things unavoidable it is having moderate *pathē*. But some notable Skeptics have added "suspension of judgment during investigations" to these.

13. The General Modes of *Epochē*

Since we have been saying that *ataraxia* follows on suspending judgment about everything, the next thing would be to explain how we reach this suspension. Roughly speaking, one may say that it comes about through the opposition of things. We oppose phenomena to phenomena or noumena to noumena, or *alternando*. For instance, we oppose phenomena to phenomena when we say that the same tower appears round from a distance but square from close up; and noumena to noumena when, in reply to one who infers the existence of divine providence from the order of the heavenly bodies, we oppose the fact that often the good fare ill and the bad fare well, and deduce from this that divine providence does not exist; and noumena to phenomena, as when Anaxagoras argued, in opposition to snow's being white, that snow is frozen water and water is dark in color, and therefore snow is dark in color. Or, with a different concept of opposition, we sometimes oppose present things to present things, as in the foregoing examples, and sometimes present things to things past or to things future; for example, when somebody brings up an argument that we are not able to refute, we say to him:

"Just as before the birth of the person who introduced the system which you follow, the argument supporting that system did not yet appear sound although it really was, so also it is possible that the opposite of the argument you now advance is really sound despite its not yet appearing so to us, and hence we should not yet assent to this argument that now seems so strong."

But in order that we may more accurately understand these oppositions, I shall set down the modes or arguments by means of which suspension of judgment is brought about, without, however, maintaining anything about their number or their force. For they may well be unsound, and there may be more than the ones I shall mention.

14. The Ten Modes

The older Skeptics, according to the usual, account, have handed down some modes, ten in number, through which it seems that suspension of judgment is brought about, and which they also synonymously call 'arguments' or 'points.' And these modes are as follows: first, there is the one based on the variety of animals; second, the one based on the differences among human beings; third, that based on the differences in constitution of the sense organs; fourth, on the circumstances; fifth, on positions, distances and locations; sixth, on admixtures; seventh, on the quantity and constitution of the external objects; eighth, on relativity; ninth, on the frequency or infrequency of occurrence; and tenth, on ways of life, customs and laws, mythic beliefs and dogmatic opinions [. . .]

15. The Five Modes

The more recent Skeptics hand down the following five modes of *epochē*: the first is the mode based on disagreement; the second is that based on infinite regress; the third, that based on relativity; the fourth, on hypothesis; and the fifth is the circularity mode. The one based on disagreement is that according to which we find that, both in ordinary life and among philosophers, with regard to a given topic there has been reached an unresolvable impasse on account of which we are unable to reach a verdict one way or the other, and we end up with suspension of judgment. The one based on infinite regress is that in which we say that what is offered as support for believing a given proposition is itself in need of such support, and that support is in need of other support, and so on ad infinitum, so that, since we have no place from which to begin to establish anything, suspension of judgment follows. The one based on relativity is, as we said before, that in which the external object appears this way or that way in relation to the judging subject and the things observed at the same lime, but we suspend judgment as to how it is in its nature. And the one based on hypothesis comes into play when the Dogmatists, involved in an infinite regress, begin with something that they do not establish but that they deem worthy of acceptance as agreed upon without question or demonstration. And the circularity mode occurs when what ought to make the case for the matter in question has need of support from that very matter; whence, being unable to assume either in order to establish the other, we suspend judgment about both.

That every matter of inquiry can be brought under these modes we shall show in brief as follows. Anything proposed for consideration is either a sense object or a thought object, but whichever it is, there is a disagreement concerning it. For some people say that only the sense objects are true, others that only the thought objects, and still others that some of each. Now, will they say that the disagreement can be decided or that it cannot? If it cannot, we have the conclusion that one must suspend judgment, for concerning disagreements that are not decidable one cannot make an assertion. On the other hand, if it is decidable, then we want to know how it is to be decided. Shall we decide about a sense object, for example (for first we shall base the argument on this case) by a sense object or a thought object? If by a sense object, then, since the sense objects are what our inquiry is about, this object too will need something else as support. And if that also is a sense object, it again will need support from another one, and so on ad infinitum. But if we are to decide about the sense object by a thought object, then, since there is a disagreement about the thought objects, too, and this is a thought object, it also will be in need of decision and support. But by what will it be supported? If by a thought object, it will similarly involve an infinite regress; but if by a sense object, then, since a thought object was used as support for a sense object and a sense object for a thought object, the circularity mode of *epochē* comes in.

But if, to avoid these points, our interlocutor should think to assume something, by consent and without demonstration, as a basis for demonstrating what follows, the hypothesis mode comes into play and allows no way out. For if the hypothesizer is worthy of credence, we shall be no less worthy of credence whenever we hypothesize the opposite. And if what the hypothesizer hypothesizes is true, he makes it suspect by taking it as a hypothesis instead of establishing it; but if it is false, the underpinnings of the things being established will be rotten. Further, if hypothesizing contributes something to credibility, we might as well hypothesize what is in question and not something else from which the hypothesizer is going to establish the point at issue; and if it is absurd to hypothesize what is in question, it will also be absurd to hypothesize a proposition superordinate to this.

That all sense objects are relative is evident, for they are relative to whoever does the sensing. It is therefore plain that any sense object that is proposed to us is easily brought under the five modes. And we reason in the same way about thought objects. For if it is said that the dispute is not decidable, the necessity of suspending judgment about it will be granted us. And if the dispute is going to be decided, then if by means of a thought object, we shall produce an infinite regress, while if by means of a sense object, a circular inference. For when the dispute is about the sense object and cannot be decided by means of a sense object because of an infinite regress, there will be need of a thought object, just as for the thought object there will be need of a sense object. For these reasons, again, anyone who assumes something as a hypothesis will be acting absurdly. Furthermore, the thought objects, too, are relative; for they are so named with respect to the people who think them, and if they were in nature as they are said to be, there would be no dispute about them. Hence the thought objects, too, are brought under the five modes, so that in all cases it is necessary for us to suspend judgment about any matter proposed for consideration.

Such, then, are the five modes handed down by the later Skeptics; they are not put forward by way of throwing out the ten modes, but in order to combat the precipitancy of the Dogmatists in greater detail by means of both together.

16. The Two Modes

They also hand down two other modes of *epochē*. For since everything that is apprehended is either apprehended through itself or through something else, by pointing out that what is apprehended is apprehended neither through itself nor through anything else they produce *aporiai*, as they suppose, about everything. That nothing is apprehended through itself is apparent, they say, from the dispute among the physical scientists concerning not only all sense objects but also, I think, all thought objects – a dispute that is not decidable since we cannot use either a sense object or a thought object as a criterion, for anything we take will be in dispute and hence not credible. And the following is the reason why they do not agree that something can be apprehended through something else. If that through which something is apprehended must in every case be apprehended through something else, they encounter the circularity or infinite regress modes of *epochē*. But if somebody should wish to take as apprehended through itself something through which something else is apprehended, he runs up against the fact that for the aforementioned reasons nothing is apprehended through itself. So we are at a loss as to how the thing in question could be apprehended either on the basis of itself or on that of something else, since there is no apparent criterion of truth or of apprehension and since signs, even apart from proof, are eliminated, as we shall show later.

It will suffice for the present to have said thus much about the modes leading to suspension of judgment.

[...]

18. The Skeptic Slogans

Since, in using each of these modes and those leading to suspension of judgment, we utter certain slogans expressive of the Skeptic temper of mind and of our *pathē* – for example, "not more," "nothing is to be determined," and the like – it

would be reasonable to take up these next. Let us begin with "not more."

19. The "Not More" Slogan

We say this sometimes in the form I have just mentioned, but sometimes in the form "nothing more"; for we do not, as some people suppose, employ the "not more" in specific investigations and the "nothing more" in general ones; rather, we say either "not more" or "nothing more" indifferently, and now we shall discuss them as though they were identical. This slogan, then, is elliptical. Just as when we say "a duplex" we are saying in effect "a duplex house," and when we say "a wide [*plateia*, a square]" we are saying in effect "a wide street," so also when we say "not more" we are saying in effect "not more this than that, up than down." Some of the Skeptics, however, in place of the "not" adopt "what" – "what more this than that" – taking the "what" to refer to the cause, so that the meaning is "because of what [i.e., why] this more than that?" For it is common practice to use questions instead of assertions, as in the line

What mortal doesn't know the bride of Zeus?
Euripides, *Hercules* 1

and assertions instead of questions, such as "I want to know where Dion lives" and "I ask why one should marvel at a poetic person." Also, the use of "what" instead of "why" [i.e., "because of what"] is found in Menander:

[Because of] what was I left behind?
Frag. 900 Kock

And the slogan "not more this than that" also makes evident our *pathos* with respect to which we reach equilibrium through the equipollence of the opposed things – where we use the term "equipollence" for equality as regards what appears persuasive to us, and "opposed things" in the everyday sense of things that conflict, and "equilibrium" for the absence of assent to either alternative.

Even if the slogan "nothing more" exhibits the character of assent or denial, we do not use it in that way, but rather we take it in an imprecise and not strictly correct sense, either in place of a question or instead of saying "I don't know to which of these I ought to assent and to which I ought not to assent." For our goal is to make evident what appears to us, and we do not care with what expression we do it. And this also should be noticed: that in uttering the "nothing more" slogan we are not maintaining that it is entirely true and firm, but in its case, too, we are speaking in accord with what appears to us.

20.   "Non-assertion" (*Aphasia*)

Concerning non-assertion we say the following. The term "assertion" has two senses, a wider and a narrower. In the wider sense an assertion is an expression indicating affirmation or denial, such as "It is day," "It is not day"; whereas in the narrower sense it is an expression indicating affirmation only; in this sense people do not call negative statements "assertions." Non-assertion, then, is the avoidance of assertion in the wider sense, in which we say that both affirmation and negation are covered; so that non-assertion is a *pathos* of ours in view of which we say that we do not affirm or deny anything. From this it is evident that we adopt the "non-assertion" slogan, too, not on the assumption that things are in their nature such as to produce non-assertion in every case, but simply as making evident that we, now, when we are uttering it, and in the case of the particular matters in question, are experiencing this *pathos*. And this, too, must be kept in mind: it is dogmatic statements about the non-evident that we say we neither affirm nor deny; we grant the things that stir our *pathē* and drive us by force to assent.

21.   "Perhaps," "It Is Possible," "Maybe"

The slogans "perhaps" and "perhaps not," and "possibly" and "possibly not," and "maybe" and "maybe not" we take in place of "perhaps it is the case" and "perhaps it is not the case," and "possibly it is the case" and "possibly it is not the case," and "maybe it is the case" and "maybe it is not the case" – for brevity's sake using "possibly not" for "possibly it is not the case" and "maybe not" for "maybe it is not the case," and "perhaps not" for "perhaps it is not the case." But here again we do not fight over words, nor are we raising the

issue of whether the slogans make evident the nature of these matters; rather, as I said before, we employ them imprecisely. Nevertheless, I think, it is evident that these slogans are expressive of non-assertion. Certainly the person who says "perhaps it is the case," by not firmly maintaining that it is the case, is in effect also asserting the seemingly inconsistent "perhaps it is not the case", similarly for the remaining slogans.

22.   "I Withhold Assent"

We use "I withhold assent" as short for "I am unable to say which of the alternatives proposed I ought to believe and which I ought not believe," indicating that the matters appear equal to us as regards credibility and incredibility. As to whether they are equal, we maintain no firm opinion, but we do state what appears to us to be the case about them when that appearance affects us. And withholding assent [*epochē*] is so called from the intellect's being held back [*epechesthai*] in such a way as neither to assert nor deny, because of the equipollence of the matters in question.

23.   "I Determine Nothing"

Concerning "I determine nothing" we say the following. We think that "determining" is not simply saying something but rather is putting forward and assenting to something non-evident. Thus, I suppose, the Skeptic will be found not to be determining anything, not even the slogan "I determine nothing" itself. For that slogan is not a dogmatic opinion, that is, an assent to the non-evident, but rather it makes evident our *pathos*. Whenever the Skeptic says "I determine nothing," he is saying this: "I am now in such a state of mind as neither dogmatically to affirm nor deny any of the matters in question." And this he says, reporting what appears to him concerning the matters at hand, not dogmatically and confidently, but just as a description of his state of mind, his *pathos*.

24.   "Everything Is Indeterminate"

Indeterminateness is a *pathos* of the intellect in accord with which we take neither a negative nor an affirmative position on the matters of dogmatic inquiry, that is, the non-evident. Whenever the Skeptic says "Everything is indeterminate," he uses "is" in place of "appears to me to be," and with "everything" he does not refer simply to all there is, but rather to the Dogmatists' non-evident objects that are under his consideration; and by "indeterminate" he means "not standing out as superior, as regards credibility and incredibility, among the things that are opposite or mutually inconsistent." And just as the person who says "I'm walking around" is in effect saying "I am walking around," so, according to us, the one who is saying "Everything is indeterminate" means also "as relates to me" or "as appears to me"; consequently, what is said comes down to this: "all the matters of dogmatic inquiry that I have considered appear to me to be such that not one of them seems to me superior, as regards credibility and incredibility, to anything inconsistent with it."

25. "Everything Is Non-apprehensible"

And we adopt a similar stance, too, when we say "Everything is non-apprehensible." For we explain "everything" in the same way, and we add "to me," so that what is said amounts to this: "All of the non-evident matters of dogmatic inquiry that I have considered appear to me to be non-apprehensible." This is not the assertion of one who is firmly maintaining that the things investigated by the Dogmatists are of such a nature as to be non-apprehensible, but rather of one who is reporting his own *pathos*, in accord with which he says: "I take it that up to now, because of the equipollence of the opposites, I have apprehended none of them; and consequently everything that is brought forward by way of refutation seems to me to be irrelevant to what we are reporting."

26. "I Am Non-apprehensive" and "I Do Not Apprehend"

Both of the slogans "I am non-apprehensive" and "I do not apprehend" express a personal *pathos*, in accord with which the Skeptic declines for the present to take an affirmative or negative position on any of the non-evident matters of inquiry, as is evident from what we have previously said about the other slogans.

27. "To Every Argument an Equal Argument Is Opposed"

When we say "To every argument an equal argument is opposed," by "every argument" we mean "every argument that has been considered by us," and we use "argument" not in its ordinary sense but for that which establishes something dogmatically, that is to say, concerning the non-evident, and which establishes it in any way at all, not necessarily by means of premises and conclusion. We say "equal" as regards credibility and the lack of it, and we use "opposed" in its common meaning of "conflicting"; and we tacitly supply "as appears to me." Thus, when I say "To every argument an equal argument is opposed," I say in effect this: "for every argument that I have examined and that establishes something dogmatically, there appears to me to be opposed another argument that establishes something dogmatically and is equal to it as regards credibility and lack of credibility," so that the utterance of the statement is not dogmatic but is just a report of a human *pathos*, which is apparent to the person experiencing it.

But also some people state the slogan thus: "To every argument an equal argument is to be opposed," intending to give this admonition: "To every argument establishing something dogmatically let us oppose some conflicting argument that proceeds dogmatically and is equal to it as regards credibility and lack of credibility"; they are addressing the statement to the Skeptic, although they use the infinitive "to be opposed" in place of the imperative "let us oppose." And they address this admonition to the Skeptic lest he be tricked somehow by the Dogmatist into ceasing to raise questions about the arguments and through precipitancy should miss out on the *ataraxia* that appears to them and that they, as we mentioned before, think follows on suspension of judgment about everything.

Notes

1   Phenomena and noumena are, roughly, the objects of sense-experience and of thought respectively.

2   The capacity of the skeptic way to engender *ataraxia* is, of course, questionable. Some people, one might think, would end up in a state of neurotic uncertainty. One might wonder, too, if the goal of *ataraxia* is compatible with Sextus's insistence, in §1, that the skeptic is someone who continues to search for truth. For discussion of these and related issues, see M. F. Burnyeat, "Can the Sceptic Live His Scepticism?," in *Doubt and Dogmatism*, ed. M. Schofield et al., Oxford: Clarendon Press, 1980.

(A) *The Nyāya-Sūtras*, from Book I, Chapter 1 and Book II, Chapter 1, with Vātsyāyana's Commentary
(B) Nāgārjuna, *Vigrahavyāvartanī*, Verses 5–6, 30–51

Introduction

In contrast to the Chinese philosophical tradition, epistemological issues represented a central concern of Indian thought. During a remarkably fertile period from around 500 BCE to 1000 CE, thinkers belonging to the many Indian "schools" (*darśanas*) formulated and debated competing positions on almost every epistemological question familiar in modern Western philosophy. Several of those positions, indeed, almost exactly prefigure ones later adopted by Western epistemologists. In the theory of perception, for example, positions closely akin to Berkeley's idealism (III.16), phenomenalism, and direct and indirect realism all had their champions and critics.

As the opening sections of the *Nyāya-Sūtras* ("logical sayings," roughly) indicate, however, this epistemological focus was closely related to a practical purpose, albeit one of a very different kind from that which informed the much scantier Chinese discussions of knowledge. Common to

(A) *From The Nyāya-Sūtras of Gotama*, trans. S. C. Vidyabhusana, ed. N. Sinha. Motilal Banarsidass, Delhi, 1981, pp. 1–6, 32, 34–7, 48–9, 232–7, 248–51, 255–6 (notes and some passages omitted; bracketed commentary is the editor's). (B) *From The Dialectical Method of Nāgārjuna: Vigrahavyāvartanī*, trans. Kamaleswar Bhattacharya. Delhi: Motilal Banarsidass, 1978, pp. 99–100, 114–24 (notes omitted).

all the Indian Schools – whether "orthodox" (in virtue of accepting the authority of Vedic scripture) or "unorthodox" – was a soteriological purpose intrinsically bound up with gaining knowledge, and hence bound up with articulating an understanding of what truly counts as knowledge. The purpose was "release" from a cycle of rebirth, from a world of "suffering," through dispelling the ignorance (*avidyā*), which binds men and women to it. Western epistemologists who do not share such soteriological concerns should not be put off, however; for, as the bulk of the *Nyāya-Sūtras* demonstrates, these concerns barely intrude once the discussions of knowledge, reason, doubt, evidence etc. are underway. Anyway, one should recall that soteriological concerns also inspired the epistemological interests of important figures in the Western tradition, including Augustine, Aquinas, and Descartes.

The primary topic of Indian epistemological debate was the *pramāṇas*. Usually translated as "'means of knowledge' (or of cognition)," the term is triply ambiguous, referring at once to the causally effective instruments for acquiring knowledge, the ways of proving things and (most importantly) the authoritative grounds on which to make knowledge-claims.[1] Two main questions were raised about the *pramāṇas*. First, assuming that there are such "means of knowledge," what are they? Answers varied widely, but perhaps the most enduring is the one offered by the Nyāya School, according to which there are four irreducible "means": perception, inference, comparison (or analogy), and "word" (or verbal testimony). These last two deserve comment. The relevant claims here seem to be: (1) that a capacity for recognizing similarities is required for knowledge gained through perception and for inductive inference to be extended to novel cases; and (2) that the reliability of some people, and so their testimony, is a *sui generis* source of knowledge, irreducible to inductive warrant. This second thought is especially important for a school like the Nyāya, which as "orthodox" accepts the "word" of the Vedic scriptures. It is perhaps the Indian attention to "word" (*śábda*) that most distinguishes that tradition from a Western one in which, until very recently, the epistemic role of testimony has been strangely neglected.[2]

The second main question about the *pramāṇas* was how they might be validated as legitimate grounds for knowledge-claims. In Book II, Chapter 1, §§17ff., the author of the Sūtras considers an objection to the effect that any attempt to validate them must either be circular or involve an infinite regress. In fact, just such an objection, as we will see in II.5 (B) below, was raised by the Buddhist philosopher, Nāgārjuna. Whether or not the reply to this criticism, in terms of the "self-illuminating" character of the *pramāṇas*, is satisfying, readers must judge for themselves.

The Nyāya School is of great antiquity. As a result, the life of the supposed author of the *Nyāya-Sūtras*, Akṣapāda Gotama, is cloudy. He has been placed anywhere between 400 BCE and 100 CE. The most important commentator on the Sūtras, Vātsyāyana, can be located rather more definitely, around 300 CE. His main commentary, the *Nyāyabhāṣya*, is not simply exegesis and interpretation of the Sūtras since, at crucial places, it presents different messages from the original – for example, on the question of the "self-illuminating" character of the *pramāṇas*.

Our selection includes the general statement of the *pramāṇas* theory from Book I of the Sūtras and the attempt, in Book II, to respond to various objections to that theory. We have also included some of the editor's explanatory comments and following the selections from Books I and II are the corresponding sections from Vātsyāyana's commentary.[3] This commentary was, in part, a response to the main critic of Nyāya epistemology.

Nāgārjuna, a second-century CE Buddhist monk from southern India and the most renowned exponent of the Mādhyamaka ("middle way") tendency within Mahāyana ("great vehicle") Buddhism. In his best-known work, the Mādhyamakakarikā, he advances the apparently startling view that everything is "empty" or "void" (or lacking in "own-being") on the basis of the central Buddhist doctrines of "not-self" and "conditioned co-origination." Extracts from that work are included in III.5 of this volume; so here we simply note an implication that Nāgārjuna draws from his discussion of "emptiness." This is that none of our claims about objects, persons, or whatever can possess more than relative truth, and therefore register genuinely objective knowledge.

In his *Vigrahavyāvartanī* ("End to Discussions") Nāgārjuna is concerned to rebut various objections to the "emptiness" view – in particular the objection that he himself has relied upon various "means of knowledge" (*pramāṇas*) in order even to identify the objects he then pronounces "empty," and so cannot consistently deny all objective knowledge. Nāgārjuna bluntly replies that he has not relied on these "means" and then proceeds to launch a "brilliant criticism of the *pramāṇas*" and of the philosophers, especially those of the Nyāya School, who defend the existence of these "means of knowledge."[4] Nāgārjuna's main charge against his opponent is that of circularity. If, he argues, all objects of knowledge (*prameyas*) are ascertained through the "means of knowledge," then, since these latter must themselves be objects of knowledge (why else rely on them?), some objects of knowledge are ascertained on the basis of themselves – which is circular. The alternative is an infinite regress, with each *pramāṇa* being validated on the basis of a further one, which in turn is validated by another, and so on (verse 32).

Beginning at verse 40, Nāgārjuna detects a further circularity in *pramāṇa* theory. Advocates of that theory, like the Nyāya School, typically define the *pramāṇas* in terms of their enabling us to ascertain *prameyas*, objects of knowledge such as physical bodies, colors, souls, etc. But the existence of such objects is then asserted solely on the evidence of the *pramāṇas*. The *pramāṇa* theorist, concludes Nāgārjuna, is caught in a circle: "neither the *prameyas* nor the *pramāṇas* are [independently] established" (verse 46).

Both of Nāgārjuna's circularity charges raise issues familiar in contemporary epistemological debate.[5] These include: (1) is there any alleged "means of knowledge" or epistemic ground – sense-perception, say – which it would be incoherent to challenge?; and (2) is it viciously circular to invoke "means of knowledge" in one another's support? Might it not be, instead, that the mutual support these "means" offer is good reason to trust our general epistemic apparatus?

The second charge will remind readers of such issues as those of the relationship between theory and data, and of the impossibility, alleged by Richard Rorty (1931–2007) and others, of jumping "out of our skins" so as to compare an objective domain of objects with our ways of thinking and talking.[6] It is one mark of Nāgārjuna's brilliance that he was, arguably, the first philosopher to have raised, in an acute and precise manner, doubts as to the very sense of a correspondence between two supposedly independent terms, thought and the world – doubts, of course, which have come to shape much modern epistemological debate.

Notes

1 See Bimal Krishna Matilal, *Perception: An Essay on Classical Indian Theories of Knowledge*, Oxford: Clarendon Press, 1991, pp. 35ff.

2 J. N. Mohanty, "Indian Epistemology," in *A Companion to Epistemology*, ed. J. Dancy and E. Sosa, Oxford: Blackwell, 1992. See also Ernest Sosa, "Testimony," in the same volume.

3 Detailed accounts of Nyāya epistemology may be found in Matilal, *Perception*, J. N. Mohanty, *Reason and Tradition in Indian Thought*, Oxford: Clarendon Press, 1992, and S. Radhakrishnan, *Indian Philosophy*, Vol. 2, Delhi: Oxford University Press, 1989.

4 Kamaleswar Bhattacharya, Introduction to *The Dialectical Method of Nagarjuna*, p. 89.

5 See Bimal Krishna Matilal, *Perception*, pp. 49ff. See also the article on Nagarjuna in *Encyclopedia of Asian Philosophy*, ed. B. Carr and I. Mahalingam, London: Routledge, 1997.

6 Richard Rorty, *Philosophy and the Mirror of Nature*, Princeton, NJ: Princeton University Press, 1980.

(A)   *The Nyāya-Sūtras*

Book I, Chapter 1

1. **Supreme felicity** is attained by the knowledge about the true nature of the sixteen categories, [such as] means of right knowledge (pramāṇa), object of right knowledge (prameya), doubt (saṃśaya), and purpose (prayojana). [. . .]

Knowledge about the true nature of the sixteen categories means true knowledge by the 'enunciation,' 'definition' and 'critical examination' of the categories. . . . The attainment of supreme felicity is preceded by the knowledge of four things, *viz.*, (1) that which is fit to be abandoned (*viz.*, pain), (2) that which produces what is fit to be abandoned (*viz.*, misapprehension, etc.), (3) complete destruction of what is fit to be abandoned and (4) the means of destroying what is fit to be abandoned (*viz.*, true knowledge).

2.   Pain, birth, activity, faults and misapprehension – on the successive annihilation of these in the reverse order, there follows **release**.

Misapprehension, faults, activity, birth and pain – these in their uninterrupted course constitute the "world." Release, which consists in the soul's getting rid of the world, is the condition of supreme felicity marked by perfect tranquillity and not tainted by any defilement. A person, by the true knowledge of the sixteen categories, is able to remove his misapprehensions. When this is done, his faults, *viz.*, affection, aversion and stupidity, disappear. He is then no longer subject to any activity and is consequently freed from transmigration and pains. This is the way in which his release is effected and supreme felicity secured.

3.   Perception, inference, comparison and word (verbal testimony – these are the **means of right knowledge**. [. . .]

4.   **Perception** is that knowledge which arises from the contact of a sense with its object, and which is determinate, unnameable and non-erratic.

Determinate – This epithet distinguishes perception from indeterminate knowledge; as, for instance, a man looking from a distance cannot ascertain whether there is smoke or dust.

Unnameable – Signifies that the knowledge of a thing derived through perception has no connection with the name which the thing bears.[1]

Non-erratic – In summer the sun's rays coming in contact with earthly heat quiver and appear to the eyes of men as water. The knowledge of water derived in this way is not perception. To eliminate such cases the epithet non-erratic has been used. [. . .]

5.   **Inference** is knowledge which is preceded by perception, and is of three kinds, *viz.*, a priori, a posteriori and 'commonly seen.'

A priori is the knowledge of effect derived from the perception of its cause, *e.g.*, one seeing clouds infers that there will be rain.

A posteriori is the knowledge of cause derived from the perception of its effects, *e.g.*, one seeing a river swollen infers that there was rain.

'*Commonly seen*' is the knowledge of one thing derived from the perception of another thing with which it is commonly seen, *e.g.*, one seeing a beast possessing horns, infers that it possesses also a tail, or one seeing smoke on a hill infers that there is fire on it.

6.   **Comparison** is the knowledge of a thing through its similarity to another thing previously well known.

A man, hearing from a forester that a *bos gavaeus* is like a cow, resorts to a forest where he sees an animal like a cow. Having recollected what he heard he institutes a comparison, by which he arrives at the conviction that the animal which he sees is *bos gavaeus*. This is knowledge derived through comparison. Some hold that comparison is not a separate means of knowledge, for when one notices the likeness of a cow in a strange animal one really performs an act of perception. In reply, it is urged that we cannot deny comparison as a separate means of knowledge, for how does otherwise the name *bos gavaeus* signify the general notion of the animal called *bos gavaeus*? That the name *bos gavaeus* signifies one and all members of the *bos gavaeus* class is not a result of perception, but the consequence of a distinct knowledge, called comparison.

7.   **Word** (**verbal testimony**) is the instructive assertion of a reliable person.

A reliable person is one [. . .] who as an expert in a certain matter is willing to communicate his experiences of it.

[Suppose a young man coming to the side of a river cannot ascertain whether the river is fordable or not, and immediately an old experienced man of the locality, who has no enmity against him, comes and tells him that the river is easily fordable: the word of the old man is to be accepted as a means of right knowledge, called verbal testimony].

8.   It is of two kinds, *viz.*, that which refers to *matter which is seen*, and that which refers to *matter which is not seen*.

The first kind involves matter which can be actually verified. Though we are incapable of verifying the matter involved in the second kind, we can somehow ascertain it by means of inference.

[*Matter which is seen*, *e.g.*, a physician's assertion that physical strength is gained by taking butter].

[*Matter which is not seen*, *e.g.*, a religious teacher's assertion that one conquers heaven by performing horse-sacrifices].

9.   Soul, body, senses, objects of sense, intellect, mind, activity, fault, transmigration, fruit, pain and release – are the **objects of right knowledge** [. . .][2]

Vātsyāyana's Commentary on Book I, Chapter 1

[. . .] False knowledge, faults, activity, birth and pain, ever following without interruption, constitute saṃsāra or the wheel of life. Knowledge of truth removes false knowledge. On the removal of false knowledge faults disappear. On the disappearance of faults activity ceases. On the cessation of activity birth does not take place. In the absence of birth there is no pain. In the absence of pain absolute success, *i.e.* release, which is the supreme good, is attained.

Knowledge of truth is the opposite of the false notions mentioned above. And therefore just as food mixed with honey and poison is unacceptable so is also pleasure tainted with pain.

The method of the Nyāya-Sūtras is threefold: enumeration, definition and examination. First is given the division of the subject enumerated, and then the definition of each division. Next is given the subdivision of the subject enumerated and defined.

The subdivisions of Pramāṇa are Pratyakṣa (perception), Anumāna (inference), Upamāna (comparison) and Śabda (word).

Pratyakṣa is the vṛitti (modification) of each sense according to each object appropriate to it. Vṛitti is proximity or knowledge. Whenever there is proximity there is knowledge of reality. The consequence of knowledge is the idea of avoidance or acquisition or indifference.

Anumāna is the knowledge of the object after the observation of the previously known mark.

Upamāna is the knowledge of an object by means of its resemblance to a known object.

Śabda is that by which an object is designated, *i.e.*, made known as such and such.

The four pramāṇas sometimes operate conjointly and sometimes individually according to the nature of the prameya. Thus: the existence of the soul is known from testimony, by inference, and by perception through a particular conjunction of the internal organ with the soul brought about by the power of meditation of a Yogī. In the case of heaven there can be neither the observation of a mark nor perception. When the rumbling of a cloud is heard, the cloud is not an object of perception or of testimony, but of inference from the sound. In the case of one's own hand there is neither inference nor testimony.

Pramiti, knowledge, which is thus the result of the pramāṇas, ultimately rests on perception. The object of enquiry which is obtained from testimony, is sought to be known by means of the observation of the mark; that which is inferred from the observation of the mark, is sought to be seen by perception; and when the object is realised in perception the enquiry ceases.

Definition of Pramāṇas: Sūtras 3–8 Gotama now proceeds to give the definition of each of the four pramāṇas.

Perception is the knowledge which is produced from the contact of the sense with the object. The contact of the soul with the mind and of the mind with the sense is not mentioned, because it is common to cognitions produced by all the pramāṇas. The definition only gives the specific cause of perceptual knowledge. The knowledge of the object produced from the contact of the sense with the object takes the form of "colour," "taste," etc. The words, colour, taste, etc. are the names of the viṣayas or contents of the knowledge. But the name-words have no operation at the time of the production of the knowledge of the object; they operate only when use has to be made of the knowledge. Hence the knowledge of the object produced from the contact of the sense with the object is independent of words. Again, mirage is also produced from the contact of the sense with the object. But it is not perception, because it is erratic, unreal. Perceptual knowledge must be unerring, real. For the same reason doubt or uncertain knowledge, *e.g.* be that a post or a man, a cloud of smoke or of dust, is not perceptual knowledge. Moreover, the latter must be discrete, specific, particular, and not general such as is produced from the contact of the soul with the mind alone.

The soul, etc. as well as pleasure, etc. are also objects of perception. But their perception is not produced from the contact of the sense with the object.

Manas, the mind, is a sense, but it has been separately mentioned because of its distinctive character. The senses are constituted by the elements, are restricted each to its own province, and possess attributes. The mind, on the other hand, is not constituted by the elements, and is all-extensive and without attribute. Hence it is said that perceptual knowledge of the soul, etc., which is produced from a particular conjunction of the soul and the mind, is not produced from the contact of the sense with the object. [. . .]

Inference is the knowledge the antecedents of which are the observation of the connection between the mark and the thing marked, and the observation of the mark (liṅga, sign). Recollection of the mark follows from the observation of the mark and the thing marked as connected. By means of recollection and the observation of the mark an unperceived object is inferred.

Inference of succession is of three kinds: (1) from cause to effect, (2) from effect to cause, and (3) from change of position, as, *e.g.*, the inference of the movement of the sun from its change of position in the sky. Inference of co-existence is as of the fire by smoke; that is, when two objects have been previously known as co-existent, the presence of one, though not perceived, is inferred from the presence of the other. Inference also takes place by the method of exhaustion or residue. Again, where the connection of the mark and the thing marked is not an object of perception, inference of the thing marked which is unperceived, may yet take place through the resemblance

of the mark to some other object *e.g.*, the inference of the soul by means of desire, etc.; desire,
etc. are attributes, attributes reside in substances,
the substance in which desire, etc. reside, is the
soul.

The sphere of perception is the present; that of
inference is the present, past and future.

Comparison makes an object known through
its resemblance to a known object, *e.g.* as the cow
so the *bos gavaeus*. Comparison subserves perception. It enables one to know an object designated by a particular name.

Testimony is the direction of an Āpta, *i.e.* of
one, be he a seer or a man of culture or a savage,
who possesses true knowledge and is truthful. The
object of testimony may be of this world or of the
other world. The testimony of common people
is confined to the things of this world; the testimony of seers embraces things of the other
world also. Both kinds of testimony are pramāṇa: the former is based on actual experience;
the latter, on inference.

It is by means of these four pramāṇas and not
otherwise, that the affairs of gods, men and
lower animals are conducted.

Definition of Prameya (knowable): Sūtra 9 The
pramāṇas make known the soul, the body, the
senses, object, cognition, the mind, activity,
faults, re-birth, the fruit, pain and release. The soul
is the seer of all, the experience of all, the all-
knower, the all-reacher. The body is the field of
its experience. The senses are the instruments of
its experience. The objects of the senses are the
things to be experienced. The experience is cognition. The senses do not extend to all objects. That
which embraces all objects is the inner sense, the
mind. Activity and faults are the causes which
accomplish the soul's experiences of the body, the
senses, the objects, cognition and pleasure. This
body is neither its first nor its last. There is no
beginning of its past bodies. Its future bodies
will end only when release is attained. This is rebirth. The fruit is the action of pleasure and pain
with their causes on the soul. Pain is a constant
companion of pleasure and enters as an element
in its experience. For this reason, and not to
ignore the experience of pleasure as an agreeable
feeling, pleasure has not been separately mentioned. Release is the negation of all possibility of
births and deaths, the total annihilation of all pain.
It is the final fruit of a process of self-culture of

which the successive stages are withdrawal from
the world and concentration upon the self, meditation, thoughtfulness and dispassion.

There are innumerable prameyas such as substance, attribute, action, genus, species, combination and their varieties. In the Nyāya-Sūtras
twelve prameyas have been specially taught,
because knowledge of the truth about them leads
to release, while false knowledge about them
leads to the stream of births and deaths. [. . .]

Book II, Chapter 1

[. . .]

69.   Perception and other means of knowledge,
says an objector, are invalid, as they are impossible at all the three times. – 8.

According to the objector, perception is impossible at the present, past and future times, or, in
other words, perception can neither be prior to,
nor posterior to, nor simultaneous with, the
objects of sense.[3]

[. . .]

73.   In reply, it is stated that if perception
and other means of right knowledge are impossible, the denial of them is also impossible. – 12.

Owing to absence of the matter to be denied, the
denial is inoperative.

74.   Moreover, the denial itself cannot be
established, if you deny all means of right
knowledge. – 13.

If you are to establish anything (*e.g.*, denial), you
can do so only by one or more of the means of
right knowledge, *viz.*, perception, inference, comparison, etc. If you deny them, there will be left
nothing which will lead you to the establishment
of the thing. Hence you will not be able to establish the denial itself.[4]

75.   If you say that your denial is based on a
certain means of right knowledge, you do there
by acknowledge the validity of the means. – 14.

Suppose you deny a thing, because it is not perceived.
You do thereby acknowledge that perception is a

means of right knowledge. Similarly, inference, etc., are also to be acknowledged as means of right knowledge.

76. The means of right knowledge cannot, therefore, be denied. They are established in the manner that a drum is proved by its sound. – 15. [. . .]

77. The character of an object of right knowledge resembles that of a balance by which a thing is weighed. – 16.

Just as a balance is an instrument for measuring weight, but is a measured object when it is itself weighed in another balance, so the senses, etc., are said to be instruments of right knowledge from one point of view, and objects of right knowledge from another point of view. The eye, for instance, is an instrument of perception as well as an object of perception. So also the means of right knowledge may, if occasion arises, be also regarded as objects of right knowledge.

78. If an object of right knowledge, continues the objector, is to be established by a means of right knowledge, this latter needs also to be established by another means of right knowledge. – 17.

The objection stands thus: –
You say that an object of right knowledge is to be established by a means of right knowledge. I admit this, and ask how you establish the means of right knowledge itself. Since a means of right knowledge may also be regarded as an object of right knowledge, you are required to establish the so-called means of right knowledge by another means of right knowledge, and so on.

79. Or, he continues, if a means of right knowledge does not require another means of right knowledge for its establishment, let an object of right knowledge be also established without any means of right knowledge. – 18.

A means of right knowledge stands in the same category as an object of right knowledge, if you are to establish either of them. If the means of right knowledge is accepted as self-established, the object of right knowledge must also, according to the objector, be accepted as self-established. In such a contingency perception, inference, etc., will be superfluous.

80. It is not so: the means of right knowledge are established like the illumination of a lamp. – 19.

A lamp illumines a jar and our eye illumines the lamp. Though it is sometimes the lamp, and sometimes the eye, that illumines, you are bound to admit a general notion of illuminator. Similarly, you must admit a general notion of the means of right knowledge as distinguished from that of the objects of right knowledge. The means will not, of course, be regarded as such when included under the category of an object.

[The aphorism is also interpreted as follows; – Just as a lamp illumines itself and the other objects, the means of right knowledge establish themselves and the objects of right knowledge. Hence perception establishes itself and the objects of sense]. [. . .]

[. . .]

110. **Verbal testimony,** say some, is inference, because the object revealed by it is not perceived but inferred. – 49.

Inference gives us the knowledge of an unperceived object, through the knowledge of an object which is perceived. Similarly, verbal testimony enables us to acquire the knowledge of an unperceived object, through the knowledge of a word which is perceived. The verbal testimony is, therefore, supposed by some to be inference, as the object revealed by both is unperceived.

111. In respect of perceptibility the two cases are not, continues the objector, different. – 50.

In inference as well as in verbal testimony we pass to an unperceived object through an object which is perceived. In respect of perceptibility of the object through which we pass, the inference does not, continues the objector, differ from the verbal testimony.

112. There is, moreover, adds the objector, the same connection. – 51.

Just as in inference there is a certain connection between a sign (e.g. smoke) and the thing signified by it (e.g., fire), so in verbal testimony there is connection between a word and the object signified by it. So inference, says the objector, is not different from verbal testimony.

113.   In reply, we say that there is reliance on the matter signified by a word, because the word has been used by a reliable person. – 52.

In reference to the objections raised in aphorisms 49 and 50, we say that we rely on unseen matter, not simply because it is signified by words, but because they are spoken by a reliable person. There are, some say, paradise, nymphs, [. . .] seven islands, ocean human settlements, etc. We accept them as realities, not because they are known through words, but because they are spoken of by persons who are reliable. Hence verbal testimony is not inference. The two agree in conveying knowledge of an object through its sign, but the sign in one is different from the sign in the other. In the case of verbal testimony, the special point is to decide whether the sign (word) comes from a reliable person. [. . .]

Vātsyāyana's Commentary on Book II, Chapter 1

The Pramāṇas in General: Sūtras 8, 12–19
Some thinkers maintain that Perception, Inference, Comparison and Word are not pramāṇas (sources of knowledge) because it cannot be shown that they exist before, after, or along with, the prameyas (objects of knowledge). If Perception, *e.g.* cognition of smell, etc. by the senses, exists as a pramāṇa before the existence of the smell, etc., then the definition of Perception as cognition produced from the contact of the senses and objects does not hold good. On the other hand, if Perception as a pramāṇa comes after the cognition of the prameya, then it is useless as the prameya has already been otherwise cognised. Lastly, if the pramāṇas co-exist with the prameyas then there would-be simultaneity of several cognitions and the inference of the mind by the non-simultaneity of cognitions would be demolished.

To the above objection, we reply as follows:
The fallacy of the objector's reasoning lies in this that he has distributed the pramāṇas, and has compounded the prameyas, in respect of time. The prameyas (like the pramāṇas) do come some before, some after, and some along with, the pramāṇas. Thus, the sun's rays appear before their effect, the blooming of the lotus; a lamp which illumines an object in a dark room comes after the object; where the existence of fire is

inferred by the existence of the smoke the cause and object of cognition appear at the same time. There is therefore no hard and fast rule as to the relative position of the pramāṇas and the prameyas in time. Moreover, pramāṇa and prameya are correlative terms as the cause and the object of cognition. Where the pramāṇa follows the prameya the correlation still exists, as a "cook" is always a cook even when he is not actually cooking.

Then, what does the objection establish? Is it the negation of the existence of the pramāṇas or the knowledge of their non-existence? It cannot be the former because when you proceed to negate their existence you thereby admit their existence, for what is non-existent cannot be negated. It cannot be the latter, because your very argument becomes a pramāṇa as it makes known the non-existence of the pramāṇas, Perception, etc.

The reason advanced by the objector again can be turned equally against himself. The reason is "non-existence in the past, future and present." The negation cannot precede the thing to be negated, *i.e.* the pramāṇas, because there is then nothing to be negated. If it follows, then in the absence of the negation, the pramāṇas cannot be called the thing to be negated. If it co-exists with the pramāṇas, then the existence of the thing to be negated being admitted the negation becomes useless.

Again, the opponent's reasoning is invalid if he cannot cite a familiar instance in support of the reason. If he cites a familiar instance then this being an object of perception, Perception as a pramāṇa is admitted by him and his negation of all pramāṇas falls to the ground. The reason thus becomes what is known as the fallacy of the contradictory reason.

Further, we have already shown that in the reasoning of five members all the pramāṇas are combined. The opponent cannot say that the pramāṇas are valid in his reasoning and not in the reasoning of others.

The reason, "non-existence in the past, future and present," advanced by the opponent, does not also stand scrutiny. For pramāṇas do operate subsequently as when the existence of a flute is inferred by its tune.

The pramāṇas are thus established. Pramāṇa and prameya are, however, correlative terms. Whatever is the cause of cognition is pramāṇa; whatever is the object of cognition is prameya.

When the nature, character and strength of a pramāṇa is under examination it is a prameya, just as scales and weights by which things are measured may themselves be objects of measurement. Thus the soul, being the object of cognition, is a prameya (knowable); as it is an independent agent in the act of cognition, it is the knower. Cognition, being the cause of apprehension, is pramāṇa; as an object of apprehension, it is a prameya. Where it is neither pramāṇa nor a prameya it is pramiti (knowledge).

Now, admitting all this, asks the opponent, are the pramāṇas, Perception, etc., established by other pramāṇas or are they independent of any pramāṇa? Our answer is that to admit the need of other pramāṇas would entail infinite regression which is illogical, while to say that the pramāṇas do not stand in need of establishment would imply that the soul and other prameyas also do not require to be established and that the pramāṇas themselves are futile. Our reply therefore is that just as a lamp which is a cause of perception is itself made known by the contact of the eye which is also a cause of perception, in other words, just as Perception is the pramāṇa of Perception, so the pramāṇas, Perception, etc., are established by themselves mutually. It is not necessary that pramāṇa and prameya should belong to different classes of objects. It is seen that the soul knows itself by itself in such cases as "I feel pleasure, I feel pain." So also is the mind inferred by the mind, non-simultaneity of heterogeneous cognitions being the mark of its inference. Moreover, nothing is known to exist which cannot be cognised by the four pramāṇas. There is therefore no reason to assume other pramāṇas.

Some are of opinion that just as a lamp reveals itself as well an object without the aid of another lamp so the pramāṇas reveal themselves as well as their objects and do not require the aid of other pramāṇas. This view cannot be accepted.[5] For there are objects such as a pot which do not reveal themselves but require pramāṇas. Is there any special reason to account for the difference in the two cases? If there is no such reason, the example cited leads to no conclusion but stands by itself. If there is such a reason then the example presents a special case and does not establish a general rule.

Of the Word in General: Sūtras 49–52 The opponent says that Testimony is not different from Inference, because (1) the meaning which is not known and which is not an object of perception is known by means of the word which is known, as in Inference the unknown is known by means of the known, (2) cognition from Testimony does not, as does cognition from Comparison, differ from cognition from Inference, and (3) there is universal concomitance of the word and its meaning. To this we reply that in Testimony the word by itself is not competent to produce cognition of truth, and that it derives the force to produce such a cognition only from its being spoken by an āpta or truth-knowing benevolent person, as in the case of "heaven," "seven islands and seven oceans," and so on. Inference is not so dependent upon an āpta. This also constitutes the difference of cognition from Testimony to cognition from Inference. Again, the relation of the word and the meaning is that of the signifier and the significate, and is not natural (dependent on and following from a law of nature). Natural concomitance exists between two objects when both are perceptible to the senses, as in the case of fire and smoke. But objects denoted by words are not perceived by Hearing, and there are objects denoted by words which are not perceptible by any sense. Therefore the supposed natural connection of the word aud meaning cannot be established by any means. It cannot be said that the meaning always accompanies the word, for in that case whenever the words food, fire, and sword are uttered the mouth should be filled with food, burnt with fire and cut with sword. Neither can it be said that the word always accompanies the meaning, for in that case the vocal apparatus should be found near the pot and other objects. It is true there is a uniformity in the relation of the word and the meaning. But this uniformity is due to convention created by the will of man and handed down from generation to generation. This is clear from the fact that the same word conveys different meanings among different races of mankind.

Notes

1 The point, as Vātsyāyana explains, is that, contrary to the opinion of some recent philosophers, one can have perceptual knowledge of something without that thing being conceptualized or linguistically represented.

2 "Fruit" here refers to the karmic effects of actions.
3 See Vātsyāyana's commentary for an explanation of this point about "the three times." A point the objector seems to assume is that cognitions always come singly and in succession and cannot, therefore, correspond in any obvious way to the objects of cognition, which can occur simultaneously.
4 The reply being made in this and the following Sūtras is of just the kind that Nāgārjuna in turn responds to in chapter 6.
5 Here Vātsyāyana appears to distance himself from the position of the *Nyāya-Sūtras* themselves. His view is that the *pramāṇas* are not "self-illuminating": rather, they serve to support one another so as, together, to constitute a coherent epistemic system.

(B) Nāgārjuna, *Vigrahavyāvartanī*

V. Now, if [you (Nāgārjuna) say that] you deny the things after having apprehended them through perception, [we reply:] that perception through which the things are apprehended does not exist.

You cannot say that you deny all things in the statement 'All things are void', after having apprehended them through perception. – Why? – Because even perception, an instrument of true cognition (*pramāṇa*), is void, being included in all things. The person who apprehends the things is also void. Thus, there is no such thing as apprehension through perception, an instrument of true cognition; and a negation of that which is not apprehended is a logical impossibility. In these circumstances, your statement that all things are void is not valid.

You think, perhaps, that you deny all things after having apprehended them through inference, verbal testimony and comparison.

To this we [i.e. the objectors] reply:

VI. In our refutation of perception, we have [already] refuted inference, verbal testimony and comparison, as well as the objects to be established by inference, verbal testimony and example.

We have [already] refuted inference, comparison and verbal testimony, in our refutation of the 'instrument of true cognition' (*pramāṇa*), perception. Just as perception, an 'instrument of true cognition', is void because all things are void, so also are inference, comparison and ver-

bal testimony void because all things are void. Those objects which are to be established by inference, verbal testimony and comparison are also void because all things are void. The person who apprehends the things through inference, comparison and verbal testimony, is also void. Thus, there is no apprehension of things, and a negation of the intrinsic nature of things that are not apprehended is a logical impossibility. In these circumstances, your [Nāgārjuna's] statement that all things are void is not valid.

[. . . Refutation of the third objection; see vv. V, VI above].[1]

XXX. If I apprehended something with the help of perception, etc., then I would either affirm or deny. [But] since that thing does not exist, I am not to blame.

If I apprehended something with the help of the four *pramāṇas*, viz., perception, inference, comparison and verbal testimony, or with the help of one of these, then only would I either affirm or deny. [But] since I do not even apprehend an object of any kind, I neither affirm nor deny. In these circumstances, your criticism: 'If [you say that] you deny the things after having apprehended them through one of the *pramāṇas*, viz., perception, etc., [we reply:] those *pramāṇas* do not exist, nor do exist the objects to be apprehended through them', does not concern me at all.

Furthermore:

XXXI. If such and such objects are established for you through the *pramāṇas*, tell me how those *pramāṇas* are established for you.

If you think that such and such 'objects of true cognition' are established through the 'instruments of true cognition' (*pramāṇa*), just as the things to be measured (*meya*) are established through the measuring instruments (*māna*), [we ask:] How are those 'instruments of true cognition', viz., perception, inference, comparison and verbal testimony, established? If [you say that] the *pramāṇas* are established without the help of *pramāṇas*, then [your] proposition that [all] objects are established through *pramāṇas* is abandoned.

XXXII a–b. If the *pramāṇas* are established through other *pramāṇas*, then there is an infinite series.

If you think that the 'objects of true cognition' (*prameya*) are established through the 'means of true cognition' (*pramāṇa*) and that those 'means of true cognition' are established through other 'means of true cognition', then there follows an infinite series. – What harm is there if there is an infinite series? –

XXXII c–d. Neither the beginning nor the middle nor the end can then be established.

If there is an infinite series, the beginning cannot be established. – Why? – Because those *pramāṇas* are established through other *pramāṇas*, and those others again through other *pramāṇas*. Thus there is no beginning. [And] if there is no beginning, how can there be a middle? how can there be an end?

Consequently, the statement that those *pramāṇas* are established through other *pramāṇas* is not valid.

XXXIII. Now, if [you think that] those *pramāṇas* are established without *pramāṇas*, then your philosophic position is abandoned. There is a discordance, and you should state the special reason for that.

Now, if you think: those *pramāṇas* are established without *pramāṇas*; the objects to be cognized, however, are established through the *pramāṇas*, then your position that [all] objects are established through *pramāṇas* is abandoned. There is, moreover, a discordance, namely that some objects are established through *pramāṇas*, while some others are not. And you should state the special reason why some objects are established through *pramāṇas*, while some others are not. But you have not stated that. Thus this assumption, too, is not valid.

The opponent replies: The *pramāṇas* establish themselves as well as other things. As it is said:

'Fire illuminates itself as well as other things. Likewise, the *pramāṇas* establish themselves as well as other things'.[2]

Here we observe:

XXXIV. This is a defective proposition. Fire does not illuminate itself, for its non-perception is not seen to be comparable to that of a pot in darkness.

Your proposition that the *pramāṇas* establish themselves as well as other things like fire [that illuminates itself as well as other things] is defective. For fire does not illuminate itself. A pot, not illuminated by fire, is first not perceived in darkness. Then, being illuminated by fire, it is perceived. If, in the same manner, fire, not being illuminated, first existed in darkness and then were illuminated, it would be possible to say: it illuminates itself. This, however, is not the case. Thus this assumption, too, is not valid.

Furthermore:

XXXV. If, as you say, fire illuminates itself as it illuminates other things, then it will also burn itself.

If, as you say, fire illuminates itself just as it illuminates other things, then it will also burn itself just as it burns other things. This, however, is not the case. In these circumstances, your statement that fire illuminates itself as it illuminates other things, is not valid.

Besides:

XXXVI. If, as you say, fire illuminates both other things and itself, then darkness will cover both other things and itself.

If in your opinion fire illuminates both other things and itself, then its opposite, darkness, too, would cover both other things and itself. This, however, is not seen. In these circumstances, your statement that fire illuminates both other things and itself is not valid.

And again:

XXXVII. There is no darkness in fire nor in something else in which fire stands. How can it [then] illuminate? For illumination is destruction of darkness.

Here, in fire, there is no darkness. Nor is there any darkness where fire is. Now, illumination is obstruction caused to darkness. But since there is no darkness in fire nor where fire is, what is that darkness which is obstructed by fire, and by virtue of whose obstruction it illuminates both other things and itself?

The opponent replies: But is it not true that fire illuminates both other things and itself, for this very reason that there is no darkness in fire nor where fire is? For, in the very process of its origination, fire obstructs darkness. If there is no darkness in fire nor where fire is, it is because in the very process of its origination fire illuminates both other things and itself.

Here we observe:

XXXVIII. It is wrong to say that fire illuminates in the very process of its origination. For, in the very process of its origination, fire does not come in contact with darkness.

The opinion that fire, in the very process of its origination, illuminates both other things and itself, is not tenable. – Why? – Because, in the very process of its origination, fire does not come in contact with darkness; since it does not come in contact with it, it does not destroy it; and since darkness is not destroyed, there is no illumination.

XXXIX. Or, if fire destroyed darkness even without coming in contact with it, then this fire, standing here, would destroy darkness in all the worlds.

Or, if you think that fire destroys darkness even without coming in contact with it, then this fire, standing here at this moment, will equally destroy the darkness existing in all the worlds, without coming in contact with it. This, however, is not seen to be the case. Thus, your opinion that fire destroys darkness even without coming in contact with it, is not valid.

Furthermore:

XL. If the *pramāṇas* are self-established, then the 'means of true cognition' are established for you independently of the 'objects of true cognition'. For self-establishment does not require another thing.

The opponent replies: What defect will ensue if the means of true cognition do not require the objects to be cognized?

Here we observe:

XLI. If you think that the 'means of true cognition' (*pramāṇa*) are established independently of the 'objects of true cognition', then those *pramāṇas* are [*pramāṇas*] of nothing.

If [you think that] the 'means of true cognition' are established independently of the 'objects of true cognition', then those *pramāṇas* are *pramāṇas* of nothing. Thus there is a defect.

If, however, the *pramāṇas* are *pramāṇas* of something, they do not then become 'means of true cognition' independently of the 'objects of true cognition'.

XLII. [The opponent may reply:] If it is admitted that they are established in relation [to the objects to be cognized], what defect is there? – [The defect is that] what is [already] established is established [again]. For something that is not established does not require something else.[3]

If it is admitted that the 'means of true cognition' are established in relation to the 'objects of true cognition', then the four 'means of true cognition', which are [already] established, are established [anew]. – Why? – Because an object that is not established does not require [something else]. For instance, Devadatta, who is not [yet] established, does not require anything whatever. But it is not admissible that something that is [already] established be established [anew]. One does not do something that is [already] done.

Besides:

XLIII. If the *pramāṇas* are at all events established in relation to the *prameyas*, the *prameyas* are not established in relation to the *pramāṇas*.

If the *pramāṇas* are established in relation to the *prameyas*, then the *prameyas* are not established in relation to the *pramāṇas*. – Why? – Because the object to be established does not establish the instrument by which it is established. The *pramāṇas*, however, it is said, are the instruments by which the *prameyas* are established.

XLIV. And if the *prameyas* are established even independently of the *pramāṇas*, what do you gain by establishing the *pramāṇas*? That whose purpose they serve is [already] established.

XLV. Besides, if you establish the *pramāṇas* in relation to the *prameyas*, then there is certainly an interchange of *pramāṇas* and *prameyas*.

Moreover, if you think, in order to avoid the defect stated before [XLI], that the 'means of true cognition' exist only in relation to the 'objects of true cognition', then there is an interchange of *pramāṇas* and *prameyas*. Your *pramāṇas* become *prameyas*, because they are established by the *prameyas*. And the *prameyas* become *pramāṇas*, because they establish the *pramāṇas*.

XLVI. Now, if you think that through the establishment of the *pramāṇas* are established the *prameyas*, and that through the establishment of the *prameyas* are established the *pramāṇas*, then neither the *prameyas* nor the *pramāṇas* are established for you.

Now, if you think that through the establishment of the *pramāṇas* are established the *prameyas* – because the *prameyas* require the *pramāṇas* – and that through the establishment of the *prameyas* are established the *pramāṇas* – because the *pramāṇas* require the *prameyas* – then neither the *prameyas* nor the *pramāṇas* are established – Why? –

XLVII. Because, if the *prameyas* owe their establishment to the *pramāṇas*, and if those *pramāṇas* are to be established by the very *prameyas*, how will the *pramāṇas* establish [the *prameyas*]?

Because, if the *prameyas* owe their establishment to the *pramāṇas*, and if those *pramāṇas* are to be established by those very *prameyas*, [we encounter the following difficulty:] the *prameyas* not having been established, the *pramāṇas* are not established, for their cause is not established.[4] How, then, will the *pramāṇas* establish the *prameyas*?

XLVIII. And if the *pramāṇas* owe their establishment to the *prameyas*, and if those *prameyas* are to be established by those very *pramāṇas*, how will the *prameyas* establish [the *pramāṇas*]?

And if the *pramāṇas* owe their establishment to the *prameyas*, and if those *prameyas* are to be established by those very *pramāṇas*, [we encounter the following difficulty:] the *pramāṇas* not having been established, the *prameyas* are not established, for their cause is not established. How, then, will the *prameyas* establish the *pramāṇas*?

XLIX. If the son is to be produced by the father, and if that father is to be produced by that very son, tell me which of these produces which other.

Supposing somebody said: the son is to be produced by the father, and that father is to be produced by that very son, tell me who is to be produced by whom. In exactly the same manner you say: the *prameyas* are to be established by the *pramāṇas*, and those very *pramāṇas* in turn are to be established by those very *prameyas*. Now, which of these are to be established for you by which others?

L. Tell me which of these is the father, and which other the son. Both of them bear, indeed, the mark of a father and that of a son, wherefore we have a doubt here.

Of that father and that son, mentioned before, which is the son, and which other the father? Both of them, as producers, bear the mark of a father, and, as produced, the mark of a son. We have a doubt here: which of these is the father, and which other the son? In just the same manner, of these *pramāṇas* and *prameyas* of yours, which are the *pramāṇas*, and which others the *prameyas*? For both of these, as those which establish, are *pramāṇas*, and as those which are to be established, *prameyas*. We have a doubt here as to which of these are the *pramāṇas*, and which others the *prameyas*.

LI. The *pramāṇas* are not established by themselves or by one another or by other *pramāṇas*. Nor are they established by the *prameyas*, or accidentally.

Perception is not established by that very perception, inference is not established by that very inference, comparison is not established by that very comparison, and testimony is not established by that very testimony. Nor are they established by one another, i.e., perception by inference, comparison and testimony, inference by perception, comparison and testimony, comparison by perception, inference and testimony, and testimony by perception, inference and comparison. Nor are perception, inference, comparison and testimony established, respectively, by another perception, another inference, another comparison, and another testimony. Nor are the *pramāṇas* established by the *prameyas*, taken collectively or severally, included in their own field or in those of the other *pramāṇas* as well. Nor are they established accidentally. Nor again are they established by a combination of the causes mentioned before whatever their number ... – In these circumstances, your statement: 'Because the things to be cognized are to be apprehended through the means of true cognition, those things to be cognized exist as well as those means of true cognition through which those things to be cognized are apprehended', is not valid.

Notes

1   From this verse on, Nāgārjuna is speaking in his own voice and "you" refers to his opponents. In verse XXX, we get a hint of Nāgārjuna's seemingly paradoxical insistence, developed elsewhere in the book, that he is not making assertions at all, not even when saying that all things are "void." One

might compare this maneuver with that of the Pyrrhonian skceptic (see II.3 above).

2   See the *Nyāya-Sūtras*, Book II, ch. 1, §19. Nāgārjuna will argue that the comparison of the *pramāṇas* with a self-illuminating fire is unhelpful since, in fact, fire does not illuminate itself at all.

3   The obscurely put point is, perhaps, this: if the reliability of the *pramāṇas* does not require justification in terms of anything independent of them, but is a matter, say, of the internal coherence among the claims they warrant, then it is incoherent to try to justify ("establish") them on the basis of a reality independent of them.

4   "Ground" or "basis" might be better than "cause" in this and the following verses.

6

Thomas Aquinas, *De veritate*:
Question One, Articles I–III and VIII–IX;
Question Ten, Articles I, IV–VI, XI–XII

Introduction

A number of important medieval epistemological controversies flowed from Aristotle's division of the mind-soul (*psychē*) into three parts (vegetative, sensitive-appetitive, and intellectual) together with the Platonic-Aristotelian doctrine that acquiring knowledge means the apprehending immaterial "Forms" (*eidē*) (see II.1 and II.2 in this volume). Platonic metaphysics had described the forms as existing in a transcendent realm, distinct and separate from the perceptible objects that are dependent upon them for their being. Epistemologically, the intellect's grasp of the forms is, according to Platonists, similarly distinct and separate from the perception of sensible things. Aquinas, however, like Aristotle, takes a different view. The senses, says Aquinas, are the vehicle that transmits Forms by means of "images" or "phantasms" from external objects to the intellect (Aristotle, *De anima* 8.3; 432a6). For this reason Aquinas has often been called an empiricist and associated with the principle "nothing is in the intellect without first being in the senses" (*nihil est in intellectu quod non prius fuerit in sensu*) (QX.a4). Of course, it's just this idea that acquiring knowledge means becoming in-formed (taking

From Thomas Aquinas, *Truth*, trans. R. W. Mulligan, Chicago: Regnery, 1952, Vol. I, pp. 3–14, 36–42; Vol. II, pp. 3–8, 18–30, 58–71.

in immaterial forms) that separates modern from medieval empiricism. With the elimination of immaterial, substantial forms from modern metaphysics, the content modern empiricists credit to empirical perception is decidedly leaner.

Also like Aristotle, Aquinas maintains that the soul is the form of the living body, but he adds to Aristotle's account what has come to be known as a "faculty psychology," arguing that the mind (*mens*) is not the essence of the soul but is, rather, one of its inseparable "powers" or "faculties" (QI.a1). Here Aquinas engages a longstanding dispute concerning the nature of the intellect and its relationship to the rest of the mind. According to Aristotle, a division within the intellect is discernible. What he calls the "possible intellect" or "passive intellect" (*nous pathetikos*) is receptive; like matter it receives the forms of things, but unlike matter it does so in an immaterial, mental way. When paper receives the form "red" it physically turns red. When the soul receives the form "red" it perceives and understands redness. The possible intellect, however, only receives forms as they are embedded in the phantasms of sensation and imagination. In order to elevate what the senses have acquired to the level of knowledge, the mind must abstract or actualize forms so that they become objects of intellectual apprehension. Doing this is the job of the "active intellect" or "agent intellect" (*nous poietikos*). In this work the active intellect is the "light" of the mind: "Thus," says Aquinas, "in a certain sense, we can say that the phantasm acts on the possible intellect in virtue of the light of the agent intellect, just as colour can act on sight in virtue of bodily light" (QX.a7).[1]

Philosophers like Siger of Brabant, Ibn Rushd (Averroës; IV.7), and Ibn Sina (Avicenna; III.8) had followed a provocative passage in Aristotle (*De anima* 430a17–25) that seems to describe the active intellect as a distinct entity, separable from the rest of the human being and, unlike other parts of the mind, able to survive death.[2] Because according to these thinkers, however, the agent intellect is not individual, individual immortality is impossible.[3] Motivated perhaps in part by a desire to secure the Christian doctrine of individual immortality, Aquinas challenged this view, arguing that even on Aristotle's own grounds, the agent intellect must remain an inseparable power of a unified soul. It may be the case, Aquinas concedes to the Averroists, that the agent intellect is universal and impersonal in its operations; for while errors and sensations may be individual, there's nothing distinctly personal in 2 + 2 = 4 or "All dogs are mammals." But, according to Aquinas it does not follow that the agent intellect can exist independently.[4]

Truth itself, for Aquinas, is universal but a matter of the individual intellect. The term, "truth," however, may be understood in four ways, each one representing a variant of what philosophers have come to call a "correspondence theory of truth." Truth may, says Aquinas, be either: (1) the mind's grasp of the "essence" of something; or (2) the mind's joining ideas of subjects and predicates in theory in a way that reflects the manner substances, properties, accidents, and their differences are joined in independent reality. This conformity may be either human or (3) divine (QI.a3). In addition to the conformity of ideas-to-things, the conformity characteristic of truth may be (4) the conformity of words-to-things. True thoughts and ideas of any of these types, for Aquinas, apply only to being, not to non-being.

Aquinas holds that neither the existence, nor the nature of God is self-evident to the human mind,

as the mind naturally can only apprehend sensible objects (QX.11, reply). The human mind, however, does possess through its natural capacities the ability to develop chains of reasoning that will prove God's existence. Aquinas's "Five Ways" are often taken to be just such proofs (IV.9; *Summa theologica* I.Q2.a1–3). God's "essence" cannot, however, be fully apprehended by the human mind or human language; and so, for Aquinas, Anselm's ontological argument (IV.5) cannot succeed (QX.12). The very terms of human thought and language cannot apply in the same way (predicate "univocally") to God and other beings. But neither is it true to say that the terms of human language apply in an utterly different way (predicate "equivocally") to God (cp. III.10). Aquinas holds that through terms like "wise" and "good" human thought and language can express something of God's essence, albeit in a metaphorical or "analogical" way (*Summa theologica* I.Q13).[5]

Notes

1 T. Aquinas, *Summa Theologica*, I.Q79.a2.

2 See Siger of Brabant (c. 1235–81), *De anima intellectiva* (1270); Ibn Rushd (1126–98), *Tahafut Al-Tahafut* (c. 1180), or *Incoherence of the Incoherence* (a refutation of al-Ghazālī's *Incoherence of the Philosophers*); al-Fārābi (870–950), *The Intellect and the Intelligible*; Ibn Sina (980–1037) held that the possible intellect survives, too, *The Cure* (1027) and *Compendium on the Soul* (c. 1110).

3 H. A. Davidson, *Alfarabi, Avicenna, and Averroes on Intellect: Their Cosmologies, Theories of the Active Intellect, and Theories of Human Intellect*, Oxford: Oxford University Press, 1992.

4 T. Aquinas, *On the Unity of the Intellect Against the Averroists*, c. 1268.

5 R. McInerny, *Aquinas and Analogy*, Washington, DC: Catholic University of America Press, 1996.

Question one: Truth

Article I: The Problem under Discussion Is Truth, and in the First Article We Ask: What Is Truth?

Difficulties:

It seems that the true is exactly the same as being, for

1. Augustine says: "The true is that which is." But that which is, is simply being. The true, therefore, means exactly the same as being.

2. It was said in reply that the true and being are the same materially but differ formally. On the contrary the nature of a thing is signified by its definition, and the definition of the true, according to Augustine, is "that which is." He rejects all other definitions. Now, since the true and being are materially the same, it seems that they are also formally the same.

3. Things that differ conceptually are so related to each other that one of them can be understood without the other. For this reason, Boethius says that the existence of God can be understood if for a moment we mentally separate His goodness from His existence. Being, however, can in no way be understood apart from the true, for being is known only in so far as it is true. Therefore, the true and being do not differ conceptually.

4. If the true is not the same as being, it must be a state of being. But it cannot be a state of being. It is not a state that entirely corrupts – otherwise, this would follow: "It is true. Therefore, it is non-being" – as it follows when we say: "This man is dead. Therefore, this is not a man."

Similarly, the true is not a state that limits. If it were, one could not say: "It is true. Therefore it is." For one cannot say that a thing is white, simply because it has white teeth. Finally, the true is not a state which contracts or specifies being, for it is convertible with being. It follows, therefore, that the true and being are entirely the same.

5. Things in the same state are the same. But the true and being are in the same state. Therefore, they are the same. For Aristotle writes: "The state of a thing in its act of existence is the same as its state in truth."* Therefore, the true and being are entirely the same.

6. Things not the same differ in some respect. But the true and being differ in no respect. They do not differ essentially, for every being is true by its very essence. And they do not differ in any other ways, for they must belong to some common genus. Therefore, they are entirely the same.

7. If they were not entirely the same, the true would add something to being. But the true adds nothing to being, even though it has greater extension than being. This is borne out by the statement of the Philosopher that we define the true as: "That which affirms the existence of what is, and denies the existence of what is not."† Consequently, the true includes both being and nonbeing; since it does not add anything to being, it seems to be entirely the same as being.

To the Contrary:

1'. Useless repetition of the same thing is meaningless; so, if the true were the same as being, it would be meaningless to say: "Being is true." This, however, is hardly correct. Therefore, they are not the same.

2'. Being and the good are convertible. The true and the good, however, are not interchangeable, for some things, such as fornication, are true but not good. The true, therefore, and being are not interchangeable. And so they are not the same.

3'. In all creatures, as Boethius has pointed out, "to be is other than that which is." Now, the true signifies the existence of things. Consequently, in creatures it is different from that which is. But that which is, is the same as being. Therefore, in creatures the true is different from being.

4'. Things related as before and after must differ. But the true and being are related in the aforesaid manner; for, as is said in *The Causes*: "The first of all created things is the act of existence." In a study of this work, a commentator writes as follows: "Everything else is predicated as a specification of being." Consequently, everything else comes after being. Therefore, the true and being are not the same.

5'. What are predicated of a cause and of the effects of the cause are more united in the cause than in its effects and more so in God than in creatures. But in God four predicates – being, the one, the true, and the good – are appropriated

---

* Aristotle, *Metaphysica* A, I (993b27).

† Aristotle *Metaphysica* Γ, 7 (1011b27).

as follows: being, to the essence; the one, to the Father; the true, to the Son; and the good, to the Holy Spirit. Since the divine Persons are really and not merely conceptually distinct, these notions cannot be predicated of each other; if really distinct when verified of the divine Persons, the four notions in question are much more so when verified of creatures.

Reply:
When investigating the nature of anything, one should make the same kind of analysis as he makes when he reduces a proposition to certain self-evident principles. Otherwise, both types of knowledge will become involved in an infinite regress, and science and our knowledge of things will perish.

Now, as Avicenna says, that which the intellect first conceives as, in a way, the most evident, and to which it reduces all its concepts, is being.* Consequently, all the other conceptions of the intellect are had by additions to being. But nothing can be added to being as though it were something not included in being – in the way that a difference is added to a genus or an accident to a subject – for every reality is essentially a being. The Philosopher has shown this by proving that being cannot be a genus.† Yet, in this sense, some predicates may be said to add to being inasmuch as they express a mode of being not expressed by the term *being*. This happens in two ways.

First, the mode expressed is a certain special manner of being; for there are different grades of being according to which we speak when we speak of different levels of existence, and according to these grades different things are classified. Consequently, *substance* does not add a difference to being by signifying some reality added to it, but *substance* simply expresses a special manner of existing, namely, as a being in itself. The same is true of the other classes of existents.

Second, some are said to add to being because the mode they express is one that is common, and consequent upon every being. This mode can be taken in two ways: first, in so far as it follows upon every being considered absolutely; second, in so far as it follows upon every being considered in relation to another. In the first, the term

is used in two ways, because it expresses something in the being either affirmatively or negatively. We can, however, find nothing that can be predicated of every being affirmatively and, at the same time, absolutely, with the exception of its essence by which the being is said to be. To express this, the term *thing is* used; for, according to Avicenna, thing differs from being because being gets its name from to be, but thing expresses the quiddity or essence of the being.‡ There is, however, a negation consequent upon every being considered absolutely: its undividedness, and this is expressed by *one*. For the *one is* simply undivided being.

If the mode of being is taken in the second way – according to the relation of one being to another – we find a twofold use. The first is based on the distinction of one being from another, and this distinctness is expressed by the word *something*, which implies, as it were, *some other thing*. For, just as a being is said to be *one* in so far as it is without division in itself, so it is said to be *something* in so far as it is divided from others. The second division is based on the correspondence one being has with another. This is possible only if there is something which is such that it agrees with every being. Such a being is the soul, which, as is said in *The Soul*, "in some way is all things."§ The soul, however, has both knowing and appetitive powers. *Good* expresses the correspondence of being to the appetitive power, for, and so we note in the *Ethics*, the good is "that which all desire."** *True* expresses the correspondence of being to the knowing power, for all knowing is produced by an assimilation of the knower to the thing known, so that assimilation is said to be the cause of knowledge. Similarly, the sense of sight knows a color by being informed with a species of the color.

The first reference of being to the intellect, therefore, consists in its agreement with the intellect. This agreement is called "the conformity, of thing and intellect." In this conformity is fulfilled the formal constituent of the true, and this is what *the true* adds to being, namely, the conformity or equation of thing and intellect. As we said, the knowledge of a thing is a consequence of this conformity; therefore, it is an effect of truth,

---

* Avicenna [Ibn Sina] *Metaphysica* I, 6 (72rb); I, 4 (71vb); I, 6 (73ra).
† Aristotle, *Metaphysica* B, 3 (993b23).

‡ Avicenna, *Metaphysica* I, 6 (72va).
§ Aristotle, *De anima* III, 8 (431b21).
** Aristotle, *Ethica Nicomachea* I, 1 (1094a2).

even though the fact that the thing is a being is prior to its truth.

Consequently, truth or the true has been defined in three ways. First of all, it is defined according to that which precedes truth and is the basis of truth. This is why Augustine writes: "The true is that which is"; and Avicenna: "The truth of each thing is a property of the act of being which has been established for it."* Still others say: "The true is the undividedness of the act of existence from that which is."

Truth is also defined in another way – according to that in which its intelligible determination is formally completed. Thus, Isaac writes: "Truth is the conformity of thing and intellect"; and Anselm: "Truth is a rectitude perceptible only by the mind." This rectitude, of course, is said to be based on some conformity. The Philosopher says that in defining truth we say that truth is had when one affirms that "to be which is, and that not to be which is not."†

The third way of defining truth is according to the effect following upon it. Thus, Hilary says that the true is that which manifests and proclaims existence. And Augustine says: "Truth is that by which that which is, is shown"; and also: "Truth is that according to which we judge about inferior things."

Answers to Difficulties:

1. That definition of Augustine is given for the true as it has its foundation in reality and not as its formal nature is given complete expression by conformity of thing and intellect. An alternative answer would be that in the statement, "The true is that which is," the word *is* is not here understood as referring to the act of existing, but rather as the mark of the intellectual act of judging, signifying, that is, the affirmation of a proposition. The meaning would then be this: "The true is that which is – it is had when the existence of what is, is affirmed." If this is its meaning, then Augustine's definition agrees with that of the Philosopher mentioned above.

2. The answer is clear from what has been said.

3. "Something can be understood without another" can be taken in two ways. It can mean that something can be known while another remains unknown. Taken in this way, it is true

that things that differ conceptually are such that one can be understood without the other. But there is another way that a thing can be understood without another: when it is known even though the other does not exist. Taken in this sense, being cannot be known without the true, for it cannot be known unless it agrees with or conforms to intellect. It is not necessary, however, that everyone who understands the formal notion of being should also understand the formal notion of the true – just as not everyone who understands being understands the agent intellect, even though nothing can be known without the agent intellect.

4. The true is a state of being even though it does not add any reality to being or express any special mode of existence. It is rather something that is generally found in every being, although it is not expressed by the word *being.* Consequently, it is not a state that corrupts, limits, or contracts.

5. In this objection, *condition* should not be understood as belonging to the genus of quality. It implies, rather, a certain order; for those which are the cause of the existence of other things are themselves beings most completely, and those which are the cause of the truth of other things are themselves true most completely. It is for this reason that the Philosopher concludes that the rank of a thing in its existence corresponds to its rank in truth, so that when one finds that which is most fully being, he finds there also that which is most fully true.‡ But this does not mean that being and the true are the same in concept. It means simply that in the degree in which a thing has being, in that degree it is capable of being proportioned to intellect. Consequently, the true is dependent upon the formal character of being.

6. There is a conceptual difference between the true and being since there is something in the notion of the true that is not in the concept of the existing – not in such a way, however, that there is something in the concept of being which is not in the concept of the true. They do not differ essentially nor are they distinguished from one another by opposing differences.

7. The true does not have a wider extension than being. Being is, in some way, predicated of non-being in so far as non-being is apprehended

---

* Avicenna, *Metaphysica* VIII, 6 (100r).

† Aristotle, *Metaphysica* Γ, 7 (1011b27).

‡ Aristotle, *Metaphysica* A, 1 (993b27–30).

by the intellect. For, as the Philosopher says, the negation or the privation of being may, in a sense, be called being.* Avicenna supports this by pointing out that one can form propositions only of beings, for that about which a proposition is formed must be apprehended by the intellect.† Consequently, it is clear that everything true is being in some way.

Answers to Contrary Difficulties:

1′. The reason why it is not tautological to call a being true is that something is expressed by the word *true* that is not expressed by the word *being*, and not that the two differ in reality.

2′. Although fornication is evil, it possesses some being and can conform to intellect. Accordingly, the formal character of the true is found here. So it is clear that *true is* coextensive with *being*.

3′. In the statement, "To be is other than that which is," the act of being is distinguished from that to which that act belongs. But the name of being is taken from the act of existence, not from that whose act it is. Hence, the argument does not follow.

4′. The true comes after being in this respect, that the notion of the true differs from that of being in the manner we have described.

5′. This argument has three flaws. First, although the Persons are really distinct, the things appropriated to each Person are only conceptually, and not really, distinct. Secondly, although the Persons are really distinct from each other, they are not really distinct from the essence; so, truth appropriated to the Person of the Son is not distinct from the act of existence He possesses through the divine essence. Thirdly, although being, the true, the one, and the good are more united in God than they are in created things, it does not follow from the fact that they are conceptually distinct in God that they are really distinct in created beings. This line of argument is valid only when it is applied to things which are not by their very nature one in reality, as wisdom and power, which, although one in God, are distinct in creatures. But being, the true, the one, and the good are such that by their very nature they are one in reality. Therefore, no matter where they

are found, they are really one. Their unity in God, however, is more perfect than their unity in creatures.

Article II: In the Second Article We Ask: Is Truth Found Principally in the Intellect or in Things?

Difficulties:

It seems that it is found principally in things, for

1. It was pointed out that the true is convertible with being. But being is found more principally in things than in the soul. The true, therefore, is principally outside the soul.

2. Things are not in the soul through their essences but, as pointed out by the Philosopher, through species. If, therefore, truth is found principally in the soul, truth will not be the essence of a thing, but merely its likeness or species; and the true will be the species of a being existing outside the soul. But the species of a thing existing in the soul is not predicated of a thing outside the soul and is not convertible with it; for, if this were so, the true could not be converted with being – which is false.

3. That which is in something is based upon that in which it is. If truth, then, is principally in the soul, judgments about truth will have as their criterion the soul's estimation. This would revive that error of the ancient philosophers who said that any opinion a person has in his intellect is true and that two contradictories can be true at the same time.‡ This, of course, is absurd.

4. If truth is principally in the intellect, anything which pertains to the intellect should be included in the definition of truth. Augustine, however, sharply criticizes such definitions, as, for example, "The true is that which is as it is seen."§ For, according to this definition, something would not be true if it were not seen. This is clearly false of rocks hidden deep in the earth. Augustine similarly criticizes the following definition: "The true is that which is as it appears to the knower, provided he is willing and able to know." For, according to this definition, something would not be true unless the knower wished and were able to know. The same criticism can

---

* Aristotle, *Metaphysica* Γ, 2 (1004a16); *Physica* II, 1 (193b20).
† Avicenna, *Metaphysica* I, 6 (72rb).

‡ Aristotle, *De anima* III, 8 (431b29).
§ Democritus and Protagoras, according to Aristotle, *De anima* I, 2 (404a28); *Metaphysica* Γ, 5 (1009a8).

be leveled against other definitions that include any reference to intellect. Truth, therefore, is not principally in the intellect.

To the Contrary:

1′. The Philosopher says: "The true and the false are not in things but in the mind."

2′. Truth is "the conformity of thing and intellect." But since this conformity can be only in the intellect, truth is only in the intellect.

Reply:

When a predicate is used primarily and secondarily of many things, it is not necessary that that which is the cause of the others receive the primary predication of the common term, but rather that in which the meaning of the common term is first fully verified. For example, *healthy is* primarily predicated of an animal, for it is in an animal that the nature of health is first found in its fullest sense. But inasmuch as medicine causes health, it is also said to be healthy. Therefore, since truth is predicated of many things in a primary and a secondary sense, it ought to be primarily predicated of that in which its full meaning is primarily found.

Now, the fulfillment of any motion is found in the term of the motion; and, since the term of the motion of a cognitive power is the soul, the known must be in the knower after the manner of the knower. But the motion of an appetitive power terminates in things. For this reason the Philosopher speaks of a sort of circle formed by the acts of the soul: for a thing outside the soul moves the intellect, and the thing known moves the appetite, which tends to reach the things from which the motion originally started.* Since good, as mentioned previously,† expresses a relation to appetite, and true, a relation to the intellect, the Philosopher says that good and evil are in things, but true and false are in the mind. A thing is not called true, however, unless it conforms to an intellect. The true, therefore, is found secondarily in things and primarily in intellect.

Note, however, that a thing is referred differently to the practical intellect than it is to the speculative intellect. Since the practical intellect causes things, it is a measure of what it causes.

But, since the speculative intellect is receptive in regard to things, it is, in a certain sense, involved by things and consequently measured by them. It is clear, therefore, that, as is said in the *Metaphysics*, natural things from which our intellect gets its scientific knowledge measure our intellect.‡ Yet these things are themselves measured by the divine intellect, in which are all created things – just as all works of art find their origin in the intellect of an artist. The divine intellect, therefore, measures and is not measured; a natural thing both measures and is measured, but our intellect is measured, and measures only artifacts, not natural things.

A natural thing, therefore, being placed between two intellects is called *true* in so far as it conforms to either. It is said to be true with respect to its conformity with the divine intellect in so far as it fulfills the end to which it was ordained by the divine intellect. This is clear from the writings of Anselm and Augustine, as well as from the definition of Avicenna, previously cited: "The truth of anything is a property of the act of being, which has been established for it."§ With respect to its conformity with a human intellect, a thing is said to be true in so far as it is such as to cause a true estimate about itself and a thing is said to be false if, as Aristotle says, "by nature it is such that it seems to be what it is not, or seems to possess qualities which it does not possess."**

In a natural thing, truth is found especially in the first, rather than in the second, sense; for its reference to the divine intellect comes before its reference to a human intellect. Even if there were no human intellects, things could be said to be true because of their relation to the divine intellect. But if, by an impossible supposition, intellect did not exist and things did continue to exist, then the essentials of truth would in no way remain.

Answers to Difficulties:

1. As is clear from the discussion, *true* is predicated primarily of a true intellect and secondarily of a thing conformed with intellect. *True* taken in either sense, however, is interchangeable with being, but in different ways. Used of things, it can

---

* Aristotle, *Metaphysica* E, 4 (1027b26).
† Aristotle, *De anima* III, 10 (433b21–30).
‡ Aristotle, *Metaphysica* E, 4 (1027b26).
§ Avicenna, *Metaphysica* VIII, 6 (100r).
** Aristotle, *Metaphysica* Δ, 29 (1024b22–24).

be interchanged with being through a judgment asserting merely material identity, for every being is conformed with the divine intellect and can be conformed with a human intellect. The converse of this is also true.

But if *true* is understood as used of the intellect, then it can be converted with being outside the soul – not as denominating the same subject, but as expressing conformity. For every true act of understanding is referred to a being, and every being corresponds to a true act of understanding.

2. The solution of the second argument is clear from the solution of the first.

3. What is in another does not depend on that other unless it is caused by the principles of that other. For example, even though light is in the air, it is caused by something extrinsic, the sun; and it is based on the motion of the sun rather than on air. In the same way, truth that is in the soul but caused by things does not depend on what one thinks but on the existence of things. For from the fact that a thing is or is not, a statement or an intellect is said to be true or false.

4. Augustine is speaking of a thing's being seen by the human intellect. Truth, of course, does not depend on this, for many things exist that are not known by our intellects. There is nothing, however, that the divine intellect does not actually know, and nothing that the human intellect does not know potentially, for the agent intellect is said to be that "by which we make all things knowable," and the possible intellect, as that "by which we become all things."[*] For this reason, one can place in the definition of a true thing its actually being seen by the divine intellect, but not its being seen by a human intellect – except potentially, as is clear from our earlier discussion.

Article III: In the Third Article We Ask: Is Truth Only in the Intellect Joining and Separating?

Difficulties:

It seems not, for

1. The true is predicated from the relation of being to intellect. But the first operation by which an intellect is related to things is that in which the intellect forms the quiddities of things by conceiving their definitions. Truth, therefore,

is principally and more properly found in that operation of the intellect.

2. The true is a "conformity of thing and intellect." Now, although the intellect, in joining and separating, can be conformed with things, it can also be conformed with things in understanding their quiddities. Truth, therefore, is not merely in the intellect joining and separating.

To the Contrary:

1'. In the *Metaphysics* we read: "The true and the false are not in things but in the mind. In regard to simple natures and quiddities, however, it is not in the mind."[†]

2'. In *The Soul* the statement is made that the true and the false are not to be found in simple apprehension.[‡]

Reply:

Just as the true is found primarily in the intellect rather than in things, so also is it found primarily in an act of the intellect joining and separating, rather than in an act by which it forms the quiddities of things. For the nature of the true consists in a conformity of thing and intellect. Nothing becomes conformed with itself, but conformity requires distinct terms. Consequently, the nature of truth is first found in the intellect when the intellect begins to possess something proper to itself, not possessed by the thing outside the soul, yet corresponding to it, so that between the two – intellect and thing – a conformity may be found. In forming the quiddities of things, the intellect merely has a likeness of a thing existing outside the soul, as a sense has a likeness when it receives the species of a sensible thing. But when the intellect begins to judge about the thing it has apprehended, then its judgment is something proper to itself – not something found outside in the thing. And the judgment is said to be true when it conforms to the external reality. Moreover, the intellect judges about the thing it has apprehended at the moment when it says that something is or is not. This is the role of "the intellect composing and dividing."

For these reasons, the Philosopher says that composition and division are in the intellect, and not in things.[§] Moreover, this is why truth is

---

[*] Aristotle, *De anima* III, 5 (430a14).

[†] Aristotle, *Metaphysica*, E, 4 (1027b28).

[‡] Aristotle, *De anima* III, 6 (430a26).

[§] Aristotle, *Metaphysica* E, 4 (1027b26).

found primarily in the joining and separating by the intellect, and only secondarily in its formation of the quiddities of things or definitions, for a definition is called true or false because of a true or false combination. For it may happen that a definition will be applied to something to which it does not belong, as when the definition of a circle is assigned to a triangle. Sometimes, too, the parts of a definition cannot be reconciled, as happens when one defines a thing as "an animal entirely without the power of sensing." The judgment implied in such a definition – "some animal is incapable of sensing" – is false. Consequently, a definition is said to be true or false only because of its relation to a judgment, as a thing is said to be true because of its relation to intellect.

From our discussion, then, it is clear that the true is predicated, first of all, of joining and separating by the intellect; second, of the definitions of things in so far as they imply a true or a false judgment. Third, the true may be predicated of things in so far as they are conformed with the divine intellect or in so far as, by their very nature, they can be conformed with human intellects. Fourth, true or false may be predicated of man in so far as he chooses to express truth, or in so far as he gives a true or false impression of himself or of others by his words and actions; for truth can be predicated of words in the same way as it can be predicated of the ideas which they convey.

Answers to Difficulties:
1. Although the formation of a quiddity is the first operation of the intellect, by it the intellect does not yet possess anything that, properly speaking, is its own and can be conformed to the thing. Truth, accordingly, is not found in it.
2. From this the solution of the second difficulty is clear.

[. . .]

Article VIII: In the Eighth Article We Ask: Is Every Other Truth from the First Truth?

Difficulties:
It seems not, for
1. Fornication is a true thing; yet it is not from the first truth. Therefore, not every truth is from the first truth.

2. The answer was given that fornication is said to be true by reason of the truth of the sign or concept, and this is from God. Its truth as a thing, however, is not from God. – On the contrary, besides the first truth, there is not only the truth of the sign or of the concept, but also the truth of the thing. Therefore, if its truth as a thing is not from God, then there is a truth of a thing not from God, and our proposition that not every truth other than the first is from God will have to be granted.
3. From "He fornicates," it follows that "fornication is true." Therefore, a transition can be made from the truth of a proposition to the truth of what is said, which in turn expresses the truth of the thing. Consequently, the truth mentioned consists in this: that that act is joined to that subject. But the truth of what is said would not arise from the conjunction of such an act with a subject unless the conjunction of the act, which has the deformity, were understood. Therefore, the truth of the thing regards not only the very essence of an act but also its deformity. But an act considered as having a deformity is by no means from God. Not all truth of things, therefore, is from God.
4. Anselm says that a thing is called true if it is as it ought to be. Among the ways in which a thing can be said to be what it ought to be he mentions one, namely, that it happens with God's permission. Now, God's permission extends even to the deformity in an act. Therefore, the truth of the thing reaches as far as that deformity. But deformity is in no way from God. Therefore, not every truth is from God.
5. It was said, however, that just as a deformity or privation cannot be called a being without qualification, but only a being in a certain respect, so also a deformity or privation cannot be said to have truth without qualification, but only in a certain respect. Such a restricted truth is not from God. – On the contrary, to being, the true adds a reference to intellect. Now, although privation or deformity in itself is not being absolutely, it is apprehended absolutely by the intellect. Therefore, even though it does not have entity absolutely, it does have truth absolutely.
6. Everything qualified is reduced to something unqualified. For example, "An Ethiopian is white with respect to teeth" is reduced to this: "The teeth of an Ethiopian are white without qualification." Consequently, if some limited truth is not

from God, then not every unqualified truth will be from God – which is absurd.

7. What is not the cause of the cause is not the cause of the effect. For example, God is not the cause of the deformity of sin, for He is not the cause of the defect in a free choice from which the deformity of sin arises. Now, just as the act of existing is the cause of the truth of affirmative propositions, so non-existing is the cause of negative propositions. Now, as Augustine says, since God is not the cause of this non-existing, it follows that He is not the cause of negative propositions. Hence, not every truth is from God.

8. Augustine says: "The true is that which is as it appears." Now, an evil thing is as it appears. Therefore, something evil is true. But no evil is from God. Therefore, not every true thing is from God.

9. But it was said that evil is not seen through the species of evil but through the species of a good. – On the contrary, the species of a good never makes anything appear but that good. Consequently, if evil is seen only through the species of a good, evil will appear only as a good. But this is false.

To the Contrary:

1'. Commenting on the text, "And no man can say the Lord Jesus . . ." (I Corinthians 12:3), Ambrose says: "Every true thing, no matter who says it, is from the Holy Spirit."

2'. All created goodness is from the first uncreated goodness, God. For the same reason, all other truth is from the first truth, God

3'. The formal character of truth finds its completion in the intellect. But every intellect is from God. Hence, every truth is from God,

4'. Augustine says: "The true is that which is." But every act of existing is from God. Therefore, every truth is from Him.

5'. Just as the one is interchangeable with being, so is the true, and conversely. But all unity is from the first unity, as Augustine says. Therefore, every truth also is from the first truth.

Reply:

As is clear from what has been said, among created things truth is found both in things and in intellect. In the intellect it is found according to the conformity that the intellect has with the things whose notions it has. In things it is found

according as they imitate the divine intellect, which is their measure – as art is the measure of all products of art – and also in another way, according as they can by their very nature bring about a true apprehension of themselves in the human intellect, which, as is said in the *Metaphysics, is* measured by things.* By its form a thing existing outside the soul imitates the art of the divine intellect; and, by the same form, it is such that it can bring about a true apprehension in the human intellect. Through this form, moreover, each and every thing has its act of existing. Consequently, the truth of existing things includes their entity in its intelligible character, adding to this a relation of conformity to the human or divine intellect. But negations or privations existing outside the soul do not have any form by which they can imitate the model of divine art or introduce a knowledge of themselves into the human intellect. The fact that they are conformed to intellect is due to the intellect, which apprehends their intelligible notes.

It is clear, therefore, that when a stone and blindness are said to be true, truth is not related to both in the same way; for truth predicated of the stone includes in its notion the entity of the stone, adding a reference to intellect, which is also caused by the thing itself since it has something by which it can be referred to intellect. As predicated of blindness, however, truth does not include in itself that privation which is blindness, but only the relation of blindness to intellect. This relation, moreover, is not supported by anything in the blindness itself, since blindness is not conformed to intellect by virtue of anything that it has in itself.

Hence, it is clear that the truth found in created things can include nothing more than the entity of a thing and conformity of the thing to intellect or conformity of intellect to things or to the privations of things. All this is entirely from God, because both the very form of a thing, through which it is conformed, is from God, and the truth itself in so far as it is the good of the intellect, as is said in the *Ethics*; for the good of any thing whatsoever consists in its perfect operation.† But since the perfect operation of the

---

* Aristotle, *Metaphysica* I, 1 (1053a31).
† Aristotle, *Ethica Nicomachean* VI, 2 (1139a28; 1139b12).

intellect consists in its knowing the true, that is its good in the sense just mentioned. Hence, since every good and every form is from God, one must say, without any qualification, that every truth is from God.

Answers to Difficulties:

1. The argument – "Every true thing is from God. But to fornicate is true. Therefore . . . " – falls into the fallacy of accident. For, as is evident from our discussion above, when we say that fornicating is true, we do not imply that the defect involved in the act of fornication is included in the notion of truth. *True* predicates merely the conformity of that act to an intellect. Hence, one cannot conclude that fornicating is from God, but merely that its truth is from God.

2. As is clear from our reply just above, deformities and other defects do not possess truth in the same way that other things do. Consequently, even though the truth of defects is from God, it does not follow that the deformity is from God.

3. According to the Philosopher, truth does not consist in the composition found in things but in that made by the soul.* Hence, truth does not consist in this, that the act with its deformity inheres in a subject (for this is proper, rather, to the character of good and evil). It consists in the conformity of the act, inherent in its subject, to the soul's apprehension.

4. The good, the due, the right, and all other things of this sort are related in one way to the divine permission, and in another, to other manifestations of the divine will. In the latter, there is a reference to the object of the will act, as well as to the will act itself. For example, when God commands that parents be honored, both the honor to be given parents and the act of commanding are goods. But in a divine permission there is a reference only to the subjective act of permitting, and not to the object of the permission. Hence, it is right that God should permit deformities, but it does not follow from this that the deformity itself has some rectitude.

5. [The solution to the fifth difficulty is not given.]

6. The qualified truth that belongs to negations and defects is reducible to that unqualified

truth which is in the intellect and from God. Consequently, the truth of defects is from God, although the defects themselves are not from Him.

7. Non-existing is not the cause of the truth of negative propositions in the sense that it causes them to exist in the intellect. The soul itself does this by conforming itself to a non-being outside the soul. Hence, this non-existing outside the soul is not the efficient cause of truth in the soul but, as it were, its exemplary cause. The difficulty is based upon the efficient cause.

8. Although evil is not from God, that evil is seen to be what it is, is from God. Hence, the truth by which it is true that there is evil is from God.

9. Although evil does not act on the soul except through the species of good, nevertheless, since evil is a deficient good, the soul grasps the intelligible character of the defect, and so conceives the character of evil. Accordingly, evil is seen as evil.

Article IX: In the Ninth Article We Ask: Is Truth in Sense?

Difficulties:

It seems that it is not, for

1. Anselm says: "Truth is a correctness perceivable only by the mind." But sense does not have the same nature as the mind. Hence, truth is not in sense.

2. Augustine proves that truth is not known by the bodily senses, and his reasons were set down above." Hence, truth is not in sense.

To the Contrary:

Augustine says: "Truth manifests that which is." But that which is, is manifested not only to the intellect, but also to sense. Therefore.

Reply:

Truth is both in intellect and in sense, but not in the same way. It is in intellect as a consequence of the act of the intellect and as known by the intellect. Truth follows the operation of the intellect inasmuch as it belongs to the intellect to judge about a thing as it is. And truth is known by the intellect in view of the fact that the intellect reflects upon its own act – not merely as knowing its own act, but as knowing the proportion

* Aristotle, *Metaphysica* E, 4 (1027b26).

of its act to the thing. Now, this proportion cannot be known without knowing the nature of the act; and the nature of the act cannot be known without knowing the nature of the active principle, that is, the intellect itself, to whose nature it belongs to be conformed to things. Consequently, it is because the intellect reflects upon itself that it knows truth.

Truth is in sense also as a consequence of its act, for sense judges of things as they are. Truth is not in sense, however, as something known by sense; for, although sense judges truly about things, it does not know the truth by which it truly judges. Although sense knows that it senses, it does not know its own nature; consequently, it knows neither the nature of its act nor the proportion of this act to things. As a result, it does not know its truth.

The reason for this is that the most perfect beings, such as, for example, intellectual substances, return to their essence with a complete return: knowing something external to themselves, in a certain sense they go outside of themselves; but by knowing that they know, they are already beginning to return to themselves, because the act of cognition mediates between the knower and the thing known. That return is completed inasmuch as they know their own essences. Hence, it is said in *The Causes:* "A being which is such as to know its own essence returns to it by a complete return."

Since sense is closer to an intellectual substance than other things are, it begins to return to its essence; it not only knows the sensible, but it also knows that it senses. Its return, however, is not complete, since it does not know its own essence. Avicenna has given the reason for this by pointing out that the sense knows nothing except through a bodily organ, and a bodily organ cannot be a medium between a sensing power and itself.* But powers without any ability to sense cannot return to themselves in any way, for they do not know that they are acting. For example, fire does not know that it is heating.

From this discussion the solutions to the difficulties are clear.

Question ten: The Mind

Article I: This Question Treats of the Mind, Which Contains the Image of the Trinity, and in the First Article We Ask: Is the Mind, as Containing within Itself the Image of the Trinity, the Essence of the Soul, or One of Its Powers?

Difficulties:
It seems that it is the essence of the soul, for

1.   Augustine says: "The terms *mind* and *spirit* are not taken relatively," but denote the essence, and nothing but the essence, of the soul. Therefore, the mind is the essence of the soul.

2.   Different classes of powers of the soul are found only in its essence. But the appetitive and intellective are different classes of powers of the soul. For *The Soul* gives five most general classes of powers of the soul: vegetative, sensitive, appetitive, locomotive, and intellective.† But the mind includes within it appetitive and intellective powers, for Augustine puts understanding and will in the mind. It seems, then, that the mind is not a power, but the very essence of the soul.

3.   Augustine says: "We are in the image of God by the fact that we exist, that we know that we exist, and that we love this knowledge and this existence." He also bases the attribution of the likeness of God in us upon knowledge, mind, and love. Since, then, loving is the act of love, and knowing is the act of knowledge, it seems that existence is the act of the mind. But existence is the act of essence. Therefore, the mind is the very essence of the soul.

4.   Mind has the same nature in angels and in us. But the very essence of an angel is its mind. For this reason Dionysius frequently calls angels divine or intellectual minds. Therefore, our mind, also, is the very essence of our soul.

5.   Augustine says: "Memory, understanding, and will are one mind, one essence, one life." Therefore, as life belongs to the essence of the soul, so does mind.

6.   An accident cannot be the source of a substantial distinction. But, by his possession of mind, man is substantially distinguished from brute animals. So, mind is not an accident. But a power of the soul is a property of the soul, according to Avicenna, and so it belongs to the

---

* Avicenna, *De anima* V, 7 (27r); II, 2 (7v); V, 6 (26r).   † Aristotle, *De anima* II, 3 (414a31).

class of accident.* Therefore, mind is not a power, but the very essence of the soul.

7. Acts specifically different do not come from one power. But, as is clear from Augustine, acts specifically different – namely: remembering, understanding, and willing – come from the mind. Therefore, mind is not a power of the soul, but its very essence.

8. One power is not the subject of another power. But mind is the subject of the image of the Trinity, which is constituted by the three powers. Therefore, mind is not a power, but the essence of the soul.

9. No power contains in itself other powers. But the mind includes understanding and will. Therefore, it is not a power, but the essence.

To the Contrary:

1′. Powers of the soul are its only parts. But mind is the higher part of the soul, as Augustine says. Therefore, mind is a power of the soul.

2′. The essence of the soul is common to all the powers, because all are rooted in it. But mind is not common to all the powers, because it is distinguished from sense. Therefore, mind is not the essence of the soul.

3′. We cannot speak of highest and lowest in the essence of the soul. But there are highest and lowest in mind. For Augustine divides mind into higher and lower reason. Therefore, mind is a power of the soul and not its essence.

4′. The essence of the soul is the principle of life. But mind is not the principle of life, but of understanding. Therefore, mind is not the essence of the soul, but one of its powers.

5′. A subject is not predicated of an accident. But mind is predicated of memory, understanding, and will, which are in the soul as in a subject. Therefore, mind is not the essence of the soul.

6′. According to Augustine, the relation of the soul to the image does not arise from the whole soul, but only from part of it, namely, the mind. Therefore, the mind does not denote the whole soul, but a part of it.

7′. The name *mind* (*mens*) seems to have been attributed [to the soul] from the fact that it remembers (*memini*). But memory refers to a power of the soul. Therefore, mind also denotes a power and not the essence.

Reply:

The term *mind* (*mens*) *is* taken from the verb *measure* (*mensurare*). For a thing of any genus is measured by that which is least and first in its genus, as is clear from the *Metaphysics*.† So, the word *mind* is applied to the soul in the same way as *understanding* is. For understanding knows about things only by measuring them, as it were, according to its own principles. But, since it signifies reference to act, understanding designates a faculty of the soul. But a power or faculty lies between essence and activity, as Dionysius says.

Since, however, the essences of things are not known to us, and their powers reveal themselves to us through their acts, we often use the names of the faculties and powers to denote the essences. But, since knowledge of a thing comes only from that which is proper to it, when an essence takes its name from one of its powers, it must be named according to a power proper to it. It is commonly true of powers that that which can do more can do less, but not conversely. So, a man who can carry a thousand pounds can carry a hundred, as is said in *Heaven and Earth*. Hence, if a thing is to be classified by its power, it must be classified according to the utmost of its power.

Now, among souls, the soul in plants has only the lowest level of power, and so is classified according to this when it is called nutritive or vegetative. The soul of a brute animal, however, reaches a higher level, that of sense, and so its soul is called sensitive, or, sometimes, even simply sense. But the human soul reaches the highest level which there is among powers of soul and takes its name from this, being called intellective or, sometimes, also understanding and mind, inasmuch as from the intellective soul such power naturally arises, as is proper to the human soul above other souls.

It is clear, then, that in us mind designates the highest power of our soul. And since the image of God is in us according to that which is highest in us, that image will belong to the essence of the soul only in so far as mind is its highest power. Thus, mind, as containing the image of God, designates a power of the soul and not its essence. Or, if we take mind to mean essence, it means it only inasmuch as such a power flows from the essence.

---

* Avicenna, *De anima* V, 6 (26r).

† Aristotle, *Metaphysica* I, 1 (1052b24, 34).

Answers to Difficulties:

1. Mind is not taken to mean essence, as essence is contrasted with power, but as absolute essence is distinguished from that which is relatively so called. Thus, mind is distinguished from knowledge of itself in this, that through knowledge mind is referred to itself, but mind itself is an absolute term. Or we can say that mind is taken by Augustine to mean the essence of the soul along with this power.

2. There are two ways of classifying powers of the soul: first, according to their objects, and second, according to their subjects, or, what comes to the same thing, according to their manner of acting. If we classify them according to their objects, we have the five classes of powers of the soul mentioned above. However, if we classify them according to their subjects or manner of acting, there are three classes of powers of the soul: vegetative, sensitive, and intellective. For the activity of the soul can be related to matter in three ways.

In the first of these, the relation is such that the activity is performed as a natural activity. The source of this kind of activity is the nutritive power, and the exercise of the acts of this power takes place through active and passive qualities, just as other material activity does. In the second way, the relation is such that the activity of the soul does not reach matter itself, but only the conditions of matter, as in the activity of the sensitive power. For, in sense, the species is received without matter, but with the conditions of matter. In the third way, the relation is such that the activity of the soul is beyond both matter and the conditions of matter. The intellective part of the soul acts in this way.

According to these different divisions of powers of the soul, two powers of the soul can belong to the same or different classes when compared with each other. For, if sensible appetite and intellectual appetite, which is will, are considered with reference to their object, both belong to the same class, because the good is the object of both.

But, if we view them with reference to their manner of acting, they belong to different classes, for we classify the lower appetite as sensitive, and the higher as intellective. For, just as the sense grasps its object under the material conditions it has here and now, so, too, the sense appetite tends toward its object in the same way, and thus to a particular good. But the higher appetite is directed to its object after the manner in which the understanding perceives. So, with reference to manner of acting, will belongs to the intellective class.

The manner of acting follows the state of the agent, for, as the agent is more perfect, so its activity is more perfect. Therefore, if we consider powers of this kind as they issue from the essence of the soul, which is, as it were, their subject, we find that will is on an equal footing with understanding, whereas the lower appetite, which is divided into the concupiscible and irascible, is not. Therefore, mind can include both understanding and will without thereby being the essence of the soul. Thus, mind denotes a certain class of powers of the soul, the group in which we include all the powers that withdraw entirely from matter and the conditions of matter in their activity.

3. According to Augustine and other saints, the image of the Trinity is attributed to man under diverse formulae, and there is no need that the members of one formula correspond to those of another. This is clearly the case when Augustine makes the image of the Trinity follow mind, cognition, and love, and also memory, understanding, and will. Now, although will and love are parallel, as are understanding and cognition, it is not necessary that mind parallel memory, for mind includes all three which are given in the other way of attributing this likeness. Similarly, the attribution of Augustine referred to in the objection differs from the two we have just mentioned. So, there is no need for existence to relate as proper act to mind, in so far as it is mind, although loving so relates to love and knowing so relates to knowledge.

4. Angels are called minds not because the mind or understanding of an angel, in so far as it designates a power, is its essence, but because they have no other powers of the soul except those that are included in the mind, and, so, are completely mind. Our soul, however, since it is the act of the body, has other powers that are not included in the mind, namely, sensitive and nutritive powers. So, soul cannot be called mind as an angel can.

5. Living adds something to existing, and understanding something to living. But, for something to have the image of God in it, it must reach the highest kind of perfection to which a creature can aspire. So, if a thing has existence only, as

stones, or existence and life, as plants and beasts, these are not enough to preserve the character of image. To have the complete character of image, the creature must exist, live, and understand. For in this it has most perfectly the generic likeness to the essential attributes.

Therefore, since in applying the image mind takes the place of the divine essence, and memory, intellect, and will take the place of the three Persons, Augustine attributes to mind those things which are needed for the image in creatures when he says: "Memory, understanding, and will are one life, one mind, and one essence." Still, it is not necessary to conclude from this that in the soul mind and life mean the same as essence, for to be, to live, and to understand are not the same thing in us as they are in God. Nevertheless, these three are called one essence since they flow from the one essence of the mind, one life because they belong to one kind of life, and one mind because they are included in one mind as parts in the whole, just as sight and hearing are included in the sensitive part of the soul.

6. Since, according, to the Philosopher, we do not know the substantial differences of things, those who make definitions sometimes use accidental differences because they indicate or afford knowledge of the essence as the proper effects afford knowledge of a cause.* Therefore, when *sensible is* given as the constitutive difference of animal, it is not derived from the sense power, but the essence of the soul from which that power comes. The same is true of rational, or of that which has mind.

7. Just as we do not understand that the sensitive part of the soul is a single power over and above the particular powers contained in it, but, rather, a kind of potential whole, including all those powers as parts, so, too, mind is not a single power over and above memory, understanding, and will, but a kind of potential whole including these three. In the same way, we see that the power of house building embraces those of cutting the stones and building the wall. The same holds true for the other powers.

8. Mind, when taken for the power itself, is not related to understanding and will as subject, but as whole to parts. But, if it is taken for the essence of the soul, in so far as such a power

naturally flows from it, mind does denote the subject of the powers.

9. A single particular power does not contain many powers, but there is nothing to prevent a general power from embracing many powers as parts, just as one part of the body includes many organic parts, as the hand includes the fingers.

[...]

Article IV: In the Fourth Article We Ask: Does the Mind Know Material Things?

Difficulties:
It seems that it does not, for

1. The mind knows things only by intellectual cognition. But, according to the Gloss: "Intellectual sight is that which embraces those things which have no likenesses which are not identical with themselves." Since, then, material things cannot exist in the soul of themselves, but only through representations similar to them, yet really different from them, it seems that the mind does not know material things.

2. Augustine says: "Through the mind we know things which are neither bodies nor likenesses of bodies." But material things are bodies and have bodily likenesses. Therefore, they are not known by the mind.

3. The mind, or intellect, is capable of knowing the quiddity of things because the object of the intellect is what a thing is, as is said in *The Soul*.† But the quiddity of material things is not corporeity; otherwise, it would be necessary for all things that have quiddities to be corporeal. Therefore, the mind does not know material things.

4. Mental cognition follows upon form, which is the principle of knowing. But the intelligible forms in the mind are altogether immaterial. So, through them, the mind is not able to know material things.

5. All cognition takes place through assimilation. But there is no assimilation possible between the mind and material things, because likeness depends on sameness of quality. However, the qualities of material things are bodily accidents

---

* Aristotle, *Metaphysica* H, 2 (1043a11).

† Aristotle, *De anima* III, 4 (429b20).

that cannot exist in the mind. Therefore, the mind cannot know material things.

6. The mind knows nothing except by abstracting from matter and the conditions of matter. But material things, as physical beings, cannot be separated from matter even in the mind, because matter is part of their definition. Therefore, the mind cannot know material things.

To the Contrary:

1'. Objects of natural science are known by the mind. But natural science is concerned with material things. Therefore, the mind knows material things.

2'. Each person is a good judge – in fact, as Aristotle says, the best judge – of those things of which he has knowledge.* But, as Augustine notes, it is by the mind that these less perfect beings are judged. Therefore, these less perfect beings, which are material, are understood by the mind.

3'. Through sense we know only material beings. But mental cognition is derived from sense. Therefore, the mind also knows material things.

Reply:

All cognition follows some form, which is the principle of cognition in the knower. Such a form can be considered under two aspects: either with relation to the being it has in the knower, or in the reference it has to the thing it represents. Under the first aspect, it causes the knower actually to know. Under the second, it limits the cognition to some definite knowable object. Therefore, the manner of knowing a thing conforms to the state of the knower, which receives the form in its own way. It is not necessary that the thing known exist in the manner of the knower or in the manner in which the form which is the principle of knowing exists in the knower. From this it follows that nothing prevents us from knowing material things through forms that exist immaterially in our minds.

There is a difference on this point between the human mind, which derives forms from things, and the divine or angelic minds, which do not draw their cognition from things. In the mind, which depends on things for knowledge, the

forms exist because of a certain action of things on the soul. But, since all action is through form, the forms in our minds first and mainly refer to things that exist outside our soul according to their forms. These forms are of two kinds. Some forms involve no determined matter, as line, surface, and so forth. Others do involve a special matter, as all natural forms.

Therefore, knowledge of forms implying no matter does not give knowledge of matter, but the knowledge of natural forms gives some knowledge of matter, in so far as it is correlative to form. For this reason, the Philosopher says that first matter is knowable through analogy, and that the material thing itself is known through the likeness of its form, just as, by the very fact of knowing snubness, snub nose is known.† But in the divine mind there are forms of things from which the existence of things flows.

And this existence is common to form and matter. So, those forms are directly related to matter and form without the mediation of one to the other. So, too, angelic intellect has forms similar to the forms of the divine mind, although in angels the forms are not the causes of things. Therefore, our mind has immaterial knowledge of material things, whereas the divine and angelic minds have knowledge of the same material things in a way at once more immaterial and yet more perfect.

Answers to Difficulties:

1. The text cited in the first objection can be explained in two ways. In the first place, it can be taken to refer to intellectual sight with reference to all that is included in its scope. Taken in this way, intellectual sight is taken to refer only to those things that have no likenesses that are not identical with themselves. This is not to be understood of the likenesses by which we see things in intellectual sight, for these are a kind of means of knowing. What is known by intellectual sight is the things themselves, not their representations. This differs from bodily (sensitive) vision and spiritual (imaginative) vision. For the objects of imagination and sense are certain accidents from which the shape or image of a thing is made up. But the object of the intellect is the very essence of the thing, although the intellect

---

* Aristotle, *Ethica Nicomachean* I, 13 (1094b28 ff.).

† Aristotle, *Metaphysica* Z, 10 (1036a9).

knows the essence of the thing through its like-ness, as through a cognoscitive medium, and not through an object which is known first.

A second explanation would be that the text cited refers to intellectual sight in so far as it surpasses the imaginative and sensitive powers. Following this line of thought, Augustine, from whose words the comment in the *Gloss* is taken, wishes to differentiate three types of sight, desig-nating the higher by that in which it surpasses the lower. Thus it is said that spiritual sight takes place when through certain likenesses we know things that are absent. Spiritual (imaginative) sight can nevertheless relate to things seen as present. But imagination outstrips sense, inasmuch as it can also see things absent. Hence, this is attributed to it as a sort of property. Similarly, intellectual sight surpasses imagination and sense because it can reach things that are essentially intelligible through their essence. So, Augustine makes this a sort of property of intellectual vision, although it can also know material things which are know-able by means of their likenesses. For this reason Augustine says: "Through the mind judgment is passed even upon those lower types of being, and those things which are not bodies and do not have forms of a bodily kind are known."

2. The answer to the second difficulty is clear from the first response.

3. If corporeity is taken of body in so far as it is in the category of quantity, it is not the quiddity of a physical thing, but an accident of it; namely, triple dimension. But, if it is taken of body in so far as it is in the category of substance, then corporeity designates the essence of a phys-ical thing. Nevertheless, it will not follow from this that every quiddity is corporeity, unless one would say that quiddity, by its very nature as quid-dity, has the same meaning as corporeity.

4. Although in the mind there are only im-material forms, these can be likenesses of mater-ial things. For it is not necessary that the likeness and that of which it is the likeness have the same manner of existing, but only that they agree in intelligible character, just as the form of man in a golden statue need not have the same kind of existence as the form of man in bones and flesh.

5. Although bodily qualities cannot exist in the mind, their representations can, and through these the mind is made like bodily things.

6. Intellect knows by abstracting from par-ticular matter and its conditions, as from this flesh

and these bones. It does not have to abstract from common matter. Hence, it can study the physical form in flesh and bones, although not in this flesh and these bones.

Article V: In the Fifth Question
We Ask: Can Our Mind Know Material
Things in Their Singularity?

Difficulties:
It seems that it can, for

1. Since the singular has existence through matter, things are called physical which have matter in their definition. But the mind, even though it is immaterial, can know physical things. For the same reason it can know singular things.

2. No one can correctly decide about things and use them properly unless he knows them. But the wise man through his mind decides correctly about singular things and uses them properly, for example, his family and his posses-sions. Therefore, we know singular things with our mind.

3. No one knows a composition unless he knows the components. But the mind makes this conjunction: "Socrates is man." No sense would be able to do so, since it does not perceive man in general. Therefore, the mind knows singular things.

4. No one can command any act without knowing the object of that act. But the mind, or reason, commands acts of the concupiscible power and the irascible power, as is clear in the *Ethics.** Therefore, since the objects of these are singular things, the mind can know singular things.

5. According to Boethius, a higher power can do anything the lower power can.† But the sen-sitive powers, which are lower than the mind, know singulars. Therefore, the mind can know sin-gulars much more fully.

6. The higher a mind is, the more general is its knowledge, as is clear from Dionysius. But the angelic mind, though higher than the human mind, knows singulars. So, the human mind knows them much more fully.

---

* Aristotle, *Ethica Nicomachean* I, 13 (1102b23).
† Boethius, *De consolatione philosophiae* V, prosa 4.

To the Contrary:

We understand the universal, but sense the singular, as Boethius says.

Reply:

As is clear from what has been said, human and angelic minds know material things in different ways. For the cognition of the human mind is directed, first, to material things according to their form, and, second, to matter in so far as it is correlative to form. However, just as every form is of itself universal, so correlation to form makes us know matter only by universal knowledge. Matter thus considered is not the principle of individuation. Designated matter, existing under definite dimensions and considered as singular, is, rather, that principle because form receives its individuation from such matter. For this reason, the Philosopher says: "The parts of man are matter and form taken generally, whereas the parts of Socrates are this form and this matter."*

From this it is clear that our mind is not able directly to know singulars, for we know singulars directly through our sensitive powers which receive forms from things into a bodily organ. In this way, our senses receive them under determined dimensions and as a source of knowledge of the material singular. For, just as a universal form leads to the knowledge of matter in general, so an individual form leads to the knowledge of designated matter, which is the principle of individuation.

Nevertheless, the mind has contact with singulars by reason of something else in so far as it has continuity with the sensitive powers, which have particulars for their object. This conjunction comes about in two ways. First, the movement of the sensitive part terminates in the mind, as happens in the movement that goes from things to the soul. Thus, the mind knows singulars through a certain kind of reflection, as when the mind, in knowing its object, which is some universal nature, returns to knowledge of its own act, then to the species which is the principle of its act, and, finally, to the phantasm from which it has abstracted the species. In this way, it attains to some knowledge about singulars.

In the other way, this conjunction is found in the movement from the soul to things, which

begins from the mind and moves forward to the sensitive part in the mind's control over the lower powers. Here, the mind has contact with singulars through the mediation of particular reason, a power of the sensitive part, which joins and divides individual intentional likenesses, which is also known as the cogitative power, and which has a definite bodily organ, a cell in the center of the head. The mind's universal judgment about things to be done cannot be applied to a particular act except through the mediation of some intermediate power which perceives the singular. In this way, there is framed a kind of syllogism whose major premise is universal, the decision of the mind, and whose minor premise is singular, a perception of the particular reason. The conclusion is the choice of the singular work, as is clear in *The Soul.*†

The angelic mind, since it knows material things through forms that immediately refer to matter as well as to form, knows by direct vision not only matter in general, but also matter as singular. So, also, does the divine mind.

Answers to Difficulties:

1. The operation by which we know matter through the analogy that it has to form is sufficient for knowledge of physical reality, but not for knowledge of the singular thing, as is clear from what has been said.

2. The wise man arranges singulars by the mind only through the mediation of the cogitative power whose function it is to know particular intentions, as is clear from what has been said.

3. The intellect makes a proposition of a singular and a universal term since it knows the singular through a certain reflection, as was said.

4. The intellect or reason knows universally the end to which it directs the act of the concupiscible power and the act of the irascible power when it commands them. It applies this universal knowledge to singulars through the mediation of the cogitative power, as has been said.

5. The higher power can do what the lower power can, but not always in the same way. Sometimes it acts in a higher way. Thus, intellect can know what sense knows, but in a way that is superior. For sense knows these things according to their material dispositions and external

---

* Aristotle, *Metaphysica* Z, 8 (1034a5); Z, 10 (1035b28); Z, 11 (1037a5).

† Aristotle, *De anima* III, 11 (434a16).

accidents, but intellect penetrates to the intimate nature of the species that is in these individuals.

6. Cognition of the angelic mind is more universal than cognition of the human mind, because, by the use of fewer media, it reaches more things. Nevertheless, it is more effective than the human mind for knowing singulars, as is clear from what has been said.

Article VI: In the Sixth Article We Ask: Does the Human Mind Receive Knowledge from Sensible Things?

Difficulties:
It seems that it does not, for

1. Action and passion cannot take place between things unless both are material, as is clear from Boethius, and also from the Philosopher.* But our mind does not share in matter with sensible things. Therefore, sensible things cannot act on our mind to imprint knowledge on it.

2. What a thing is, is the object of intellect, as is said in *The Soul*.† But the quiddity of a thing is not perceived by any sense. Therefore, mental cognition is not received from sense.

3. When speaking of the way in which we acquire cognition of intelligible things, Augustine says: "They were there" that is, intelligibles in our mind, "before I learned them, but they were not in my memory."‡ Therefore, it seems that intelligible species are not received in the mind from the senses.

4. Augustine proves that the soul can love only what it knows. But one loves a science before he learns it, as is clear from the eagerness with which he seeks this knowledge. Therefore, before he learns such a science, he has some acquaintance with it. So, it seems that the mind does not receive knowledge from sensible things.

5. Augustine says: "The body does not make the image of the body in the spirit. Rather, the spirit itself with a wonderful swiftness which is ineffably far from the slowness of the body makes in itself the image of the body." Therefore, it seems that the mind does not receive intelligible species from sensible things but constructs them in itself.

6. Augustine says that our mind judges about bodily things through non-bodily and eternal principles. But principles received from the senses are not of this kind. Therefore, it seems that the human mind does not receive knowledge from sensible things.

7. If the mind receives knowledge from sensible things, it must do so because the species received from sensible things set the possible intellect in motion. But such species cannot influence the possible intellect. For, when they are in the imagination, they are not intelligible actually, but only potentially, and so cannot set the possible intellect in motion. The intellect, however, is moved only by something actually intelligible, just as the power of sight is moved only by something actually visible. Similarly, something existing in the agent intellect cannot move the possible intellect, because the agent intellect does not receive species. If it did, it would not differ from the possible intellect. Again, these representations do not actuate the possible intellect by existing in it, for a form already adhering in a subject does not set the subject in motion, but is, as it were, at rest in it. Finally, they do not cause movement in the possible intellect by existing of themselves, for intelligible species are not substances, but belong to the class of accidents, as Avicenna says.§ Therefore, in no way can our mind receive knowledge from sensible things.

8. The agent is more noble than the patient, as is clear from Augustine and from the Philosopher.** But the receiver is related to that which it receives, as a patient is related to the agent. Since, therefore, the mind is much more noble than sensible things and the senses themselves, it cannot receive knowledge from them.

9. The Philosopher says that the soul comes to acquire knowledge and prudence by coming to rest.†† But the soul cannot receive knowledge from sensible things unless it be somehow set in motion by them. Therefore, the soul does not receive knowledge from sensible things.

To the Contrary:
1′. As the Philosopher says, and as experience proves, one who lacks a sense is deprived of one kind of knowledge, as the blind have no

---

* Aristotle, *De generatione* I, 10 (327b19).
† Aristotle, *De anima* III, 4 (429b20).
‡ Augustine, *Confessiones* X, 10.

§ Avicenna, *Metaphysica* III, 8 (82r).
** Aristotle, *De anima* III, 5 (430a18).
†† Aristotle, *Physica* VII, 3 (247b12, 17).

knowledge of colors.* This would not happen if the soul received knowledge from a source other than the senses. Therefore, the soul receives knowledge from sensible objects through the senses.

2′. At first, all our cognition consists in the knowledge of first undeducible principles. But the cognition of these arises in us from sense, as is clear from the *Posterior Analytics*.† Therefore, all our knowledge arises from sense.

3′. Nature does nothing to no purpose and does not fail in necessary matters. But senses would have been given to the soul to no purpose unless the soul received cognition from things through them. Therefore, our mind receives knowledge from sensible things.

Reply:

The views of the ancients on this question are manifold. Some held that our knowledge derived completely from an external cause separated from matter. There are two explanations of this position.

Some, as the Platonists, held that the forms of sensible things existed apart from matter and so were actually intelligible.‡ According to them, real individuals come about through the participation by sensible matter in these forms, and the human mind has knowledge by sharing in them. Thus, these forms are the principle of generation and knowledge, as the Philosopher says.§ But the Philosopher has adequately confuted this position by showing that sensible forms must exist in sensible matter, and that sensible matter in general is necessary for the understanding of physical forms, just as there is no snub without nose.**

For this reason, others, bypassing separated forms of sensible things, demanded only intelligences, which we call angels, and made separated substances of this sort the sole source of our knowledge.†† Accordingly, Avicenna holds that just as sensible forms are not received into sensible matter except through the influence of the agent intelligence, so, too, intelligible forms are not imprinted on human minds except by the agent intelligence, which for him is not a part of the soul, but a separated substance.‡‡ However, the soul needs the senses to prepare the way and stimulate it to knowledge, just as the lower agents prepare matter to receive form from the agent intelligence.

But this opinion does not seem reasonable, because, according to it, there is no necessary interdependence of the human mind and the sensitive powers. The opposite seems quite clear both from the fact that, when a given sense is missing, we have no knowledge of its sensible objects, and from the fact that our mind cannot actually consider even those things which it knows habitually unless it forms some phantasms. Thus, an injury to the organ of imagination hinders consideration. Furthermore, the explanation just given does away with the proximate principles of things, inasmuch as all lower things would derive their intelligible and sensible forms immediately from a separated substance.

A second explanation has been given by those who make an inferior cause the complete source of our knowledge. There are also two explanations of this position. Some held that human souls had within themselves knowledge of all things, but that this cognition was darkened by union with the body.§§ Therefore, they said that we need assiduous use of the senses to remove the hindrance to knowledge. Learning, they said, is nothing but remembering, as is abundantly clear from the way in which those things which we have seen and heard make us remember what we formerly knew. But this position does not seem reasonable. For, if the union of soul and body is natural, it cannot wholly hinder natural knowledge. And if this opinion were true, we would not be subject to the complete ignorance of those objects that demand a sense faculty of which one is deprived. This opinion would fit in with the theory that holds that souls were created before bodies and later united to them.*** Then,

---

* Aristotle, *Analytica posteriora* I, 18 (81a38).

† Aristotle, *Analytica posteriora* II, 19 (100a10).

‡ Plato, *Phaedo* 100d.

§ Aristotle, *Metaphysica* A, 6 (987b4 ff.); A, 9 (9991b4).

** Aristotle, *Metaphysica* A, 6 (987b ff.).

†† Avicenna, *De anima* V, 6 (26r); *Metaphysica* VII, 2 (96r).

‡‡ Avicenna, *Metaphysica* IX, 4–5 (105r).

§§ E.g. Plato, *Meno* 181a-d; *Phaedo* 65a, 91e–92e; *Timaeus* 44b.

*** Plato, *Gorgias* 525e–526; *Phaedo* 92a; *Republic* X, 614e–625a; *Timaeus* 42b).

the conjunction of body and soul would not be natural, but only an accidental accretion to the soul. This opinion must be rejected on the score both of faith and philosophic tenets.

Other proponents of this second opinion said that the soul is the cause of its own knowledge.* For it does not receive knowledge from sensible things as if likenesses of things somehow reached the soul because of the activity of sensible things, but the soul itself, in the presence of sensible things, constructs in itself the likenesses of sensible things. But this statement does not seem altogether reasonable. For no agent acts except in so far as it is in act. Thus, if the soul formed the likenesses of all things in itself, it would be necessary for the soul to have those likenesses of things actually within itself. This would be a return to the previous opinion which held that the knowledge of all things is naturally present in the human soul.

Therefore, the opinion of the Philosopher is more reasonable than any of the foregoing positions. He attributes the knowledge of our mind partly to intrinsic, partly to extrinsic, influence.† Not only things separated from matter, but also sensible things themselves, play their part. For, when our mind is considered in relation to sensible things outside the soul, it is found to be related to them in a twofold manner. In one way, it is related as act to potency, to the extent that things outside the mind are only potentially intelligible. The mind itself, however, is intelligible in act, and it is on this basis that the agent intellect, which makes potentially intelligible things actually intelligible, is held to be included in the soul. In another way, it is related to things as potency to act, inasmuch as determined forms of things are only potentially in our mind, but actually in things outside the soul. In this respect our soul includes the possible intellect, whose function it is to receive forms abstracted from sensible things and made actually intelligible through the light of the agent intellect. This light of the agent intellect comes to the soul from the separated substances and especially from God as from its first source.

Accordingly, it is true that our mind receives knowledge from sensible things; nevertheless, the soul itself forms in itself likenesses of things, inasmuch as through the light of the agent intellect the forms abstracted from sensible things are made actually intelligible so that they may be received in the possible intellect. And in this way all knowledge is in a certain sense implanted in us from the beginning (since we have the light of the agent intellect) through the medium of universal conceptions that are immediately known by the light of the agent intellect. These serve as universal principles through which we judge about other things, and in which we foreknow these others. In this respect, that opinion is true which holds that we previously had in our knowledge those things that we learn.

Answers to Difficulties:

1. Sensible forms, those, namely, which are abstracted from sensible things, cannot act on our mind unless they are rendered immaterial through the light of the agent intellect, and thus in some way are made homogeneous with the possible intellect on which they must act.

2. A higher and a lower power do not operate in the same way even in respect to the same thing, but the higher power acts more nobly. Thus, when sense knows a thing through a form received from things, it does not know it so effectively as the intellect. Sense is led through it to a knowledge of the external accidents; the intellect reaches to the bare quiddity of the thing, distinguishing it from all material dispositions. Thus, when the mental knowing is said to take its origin from sense, this does not mean that sense apprehends all that the mind knows, but that, from those things which sense apprehends, the mind is led on to something more, just as the intellectual knowledge of sensible things leads to knowledge of divine things.

3. The statement from Augustine refers to that precognition by which we know particulars in universal principles. In this sense it is true that what we learn is already in our soul.

4. One can love scientific knowledge before he acquires it in so far as he has some general acquaintance with it by sight, or by knowing its usefulness, or in some other way.

5. The soul is to be understood to fashion itself in this sense, that the forms which arise from the activity of the agent intellect determine the possible intellect, as has been said. And in this sense, too, the imaginative power can fashion the forms

---

* Plotinus, IV, iii, 23.
† Aristotle, *De anima* III, 7 (432a6 ff.).

of different sensible objects, as especially appears when we imagine things that we have never perceived by sense.

6. The first principles of which we have innate cognition are certain likenesses of uncreated truth. When we judge about other things through these likenesses, we are said to judge about things through unchangeable principles or through uncreated truth. Nevertheless, we should refer this statement of Augustine to higher reason, which confines itself to the contemplation of eternal truths. Although this higher reason is first in dignity, its operation is subsequent in time: "For the invisible things of him [God] . . . are clearly seen, being understood by the things that are made" (Romans 1: 20).

7. In the reception through which the possible intellect receives species from phantasms, the phantasms act as instrumental and secondary agents. The agent intellect acts as the principal and first agent. Therefore, the effect of the action is received in the possible intellect according to the condition of both, and not according to the condition of either one alone. Therefore, the possible intellect receives forms whose actual intelligibility is due to the power of the agent intellect, but whose determinate likeness to things is due to cognition of the phantasms. These actually intelligible forms do not, of themselves, exist either in the imagination or the agent intellect, but only in the possible intellect.

8. Although the possible intellect is simply more noble than the phantasm, nothing prevents the phantasm from being more noble in a certain respect, namely, that it is actually the likeness of such a thing, whereas this likeness belongs to the possible intellect only potentially. Thus, in a certain sense, we can say that the phantasm acts on the possible intellect in virtue of the light of the agent intellect, just as color can act on sight in virtue of bodily light.

9. The rest in which knowledge is achieved eliminates the movement of material passions. It does not eliminate movement and passion in a general sense, inasmuch as all receiving is called passion and movement. In accord with this, the Philosopher says in *The Soul*: "Intellection is a kind of passion."*

[. . .]

---

* Aristotle, *De anima* III, 4 (429a14, 429b23).

Article XI: In the Eleventh Article We Ask: Can the Mind in This Life See God through His Essence?

Difficulties:
It seems that it can, for

1. In Numbers (12:8) it is said of Moses: "For I speak to him mouth to mouth: and plainly and not by riddles doth he see the Lord." But to see God without riddles is to see Him through His essence. Therefore, since Moses was still a wayfarer, it seems that someone in this life can see God through His essence.

2. Gregory's gloss on Exodus (33:20), "For man shall not see me and live," says: "The glory of God everlasting can be seen with the keenness of contemplation by some living in this flesh but growing in priceless virtue." But the glory of God is His essence, as is said in the same gloss. Therefore, one living in this mortal flesh can see God through His essence.

3. Christ's understanding was of the same nature as ours. But the conditions of this life did not prevent His understanding from seeing God through His essence. Therefore, we, too, can see God in this life through His essence.

4. In this life God is known by means of intellectual sight. Hence, Romans (1:20) says: "For the invisible things of him . . . are clearly seen, being understood by the things that are made." But the sight of understanding is that through which things are seen in themselves, as Augustine says. Therefore, our mind can see God in this life through His essence.

5. The Philosopher says: "Our soul in a certain sense is all things,"† because sense is all sensible things and understanding is all intelligible things. But the divine essence is most intelligible. Therefore, our understanding even according to the conditions of this life, about which the Philosopher is speaking, can see God through His essence, just as our sense can perceive all sensible things.

6. As there is boundless goodness in God, so, too, there is boundless truth. But the divine goodness, even though it is boundless, can be loved in itself by us in this life. Therefore, the truth of His essence can be seen in itself in this life.

7. Our understanding has been made to see God. If it cannot see God in this life, this is only

---

† Aristotle, *De anima* III, 8 (431b26).

because of some veil. This is twofold, a veil of guilt and of creaturehood. The veil of guilt did not exist in the state of innocence, and even now is taken away from the saints. The second Epistle to the Corinthians (3:18) says: "But we all beholding the glory of the Lord with open face. . . ." Now, the veil of creaturehood, as it seems, cannot keep us from seeing the divine essence, because God is deeper within our mind than any creature. Therefore, in this life our mind sees God through His essence.

8. Everything that is in another is there according to the mode of the one receiving. But God is in our mind through His essence. Since, therefore, intelligibility itself is the mode of our mind, it seems that the divine essence is in our mind as intelligible. So, our mind understands God through His essence in this life.

9. Cassiodorus says: "The soundness of the human mind understands that unapproachable glory." But our mind is made sound through grace. Therefore, the divine essence, which is unapproachable glory, can be seen in this life by one who has grace.

10. As the being which is predicated of all things stands first in universality, so the being by which all things are caused, that is to say, God, stands first in causality. But the being which is first in universality is the first concept of our understanding even in this life. Therefore, in this life we can immediately know through His essence the being which is first in causality.

11. For sight there must be one who sees, something seen, and an intention. But we have these three in our mind with reference to the divine essence. For our mind itself is naturally capable of seeing the divine essence, since it was made for this. And the divine essence is present in our mind. Nor is an intention lacking, for, whenever our mind turns to a creature, it also turns to God, since in the creature there is a likeness of God. Therefore, our mind can see God through His essence in this life.

12. Augustine says: "If we both see that what you say is true, and if we both see that what I say is true, where, I ask, do we see this? Surely, I do not see it in you, nor you in me, but we both see it in the unchangeable truth which is above our minds."* But the unchangeable truth is the divine essence, in which nothing can be seen unless it itself is seen. Therefore, we see the divine essence in this life, and we see all truth in it.

13. Truth, as such, is knowable. Therefore, the highest truth is most knowable. But this is the divine essence. Therefore, even in the conditions of this life we can know the divine essence as most knowable.

14. Genesis (32:30) says: "I have seen the Lord face to face." And, as the *Gloss* comments: "The face of God is the form in which the Son did not consider it robbery to be equal to God." But the form is the divine essence. Therefore, Jacob saw God through His essence in this life.

To the Contrary:

1′. In the first Epistle to Timothy (6:16) we read: "Who inhabiteth light inaccessible, whom no man hath seen nor can see."

2′. On Exodus (33:20), "For a man will not see me and live," the gloss of Gregory says: "God could be seen by those living in this flesh through limited images; He could not be seen through the unlimited light of eternity." But this light is the divine essence. Therefore, no one living in this life can see God through His essence.

3′. Bernard says that, although God can be entirely loved in this life, He cannot be entirely understood. But, if He were seen through His essence, He would be entirely understood. Therefore, He is not seen through His essence in this life.

4′. As the Philosopher says,† our intellect understands in space and time. But the divine essence transcends all space and time. Therefore, our intellect cannot see God through His essence in this life.

5′. The divine essence is farther away from the gift of it than first act from second act. But, sometimes, when one sees God in contemplation through the gift of understanding or wisdom, the soul is separated from the body with reference to sense activities, which are second acts. Therefore, if the soul would see God through His essence, it must be separated from the body, even in so far as it is the first act of the body. But this does not happen as long as man is in this life. Therefore, in this life no one can see God through His essence.

---

* Augustine, *Confessiones* XII, 25 (*PL* 32: 840).

† Aristotle, *De anima* III, 6 (430a30).

Reply:

An action can belong to someone in two ways. In one way it is such that the principle of that action is in the doer, as we see in all natural actions. In the other way it is such that the principle of that activity or movement is from an extrinsic principle, as happens in forcibly imposed movements, and also in miraculous works, such as giving sight to the blind, resuscitation of the dead, and things of this sort which take place only through divine power.

In this life, the vision of God through His essence cannot belong to our mind in the first way. For, in natural knowledge, our mind looks to phantasms as objects from which it receives intelligible species, as is said in *The Soul*.* Hence, everything it understands in the present life, it understands through species of this sort abstracted from phantasms. But no species of this sort is sufficient to represent the divine essence or that of any other separated essence. For the quiddities of sensible things, of which intelligible species abstracted from phantasms are likenesses, are essentially different from the essences of even created immaterial substances, and much more from the divine essence. Hence, by means of the natural knowledge, which we experience in this life, our mind cannot see either God or angels through their essence. Nevertheless, angels can be seen through their essence by means of intelligible species different from their essence, but the divine essence cannot, for it transcends every genus and is outside every genus. As a result, it is impossible to find any created species which is adequate to represent it.

Thus, if God is to be seen through His essence, He must be seen through no created species, but His very essence must become the intelligible form of the understanding which sees Him. This cannot take place unless the created intellect is disposed for it through the light of glory. And in thus seeing God through His essence by reason of the disposition of infused light, the mind reaches the end of its course, which is glory, and so is not in this life.

Moreover, just as bodies are subject to the divine omnipotence, so, too, are minds. Hence, just as it can cause some bodies to produce effects, the dispositions for which they do not have within themselves, as it made Peter walk on

water without giving him the gift of agility, so it can bring it about that the mind be united to the divine essence in the present life in the way in which it is united to it in heaven without being bathed in the light of glory.

When, however, this takes place, the mind must leave off that mode of knowing in which it abstracts from phantasms in the same way that a corruptible body is not actually heavy at the same time that it is miraculously given that act of agility. Therefore, those to whom it is given to see God through His essence in this way are withdrawn completely from activity of the senses, so that the whole soul is concentrated on seeing the divine essence. Hence, they are said to be in a state of rapture, as if by virtue of a higher power they were separated from that which naturally belongs to them.

Therefore, in the ordinary course of events, no one sees God through His essence in this life. And if it is miraculously granted to some to see God through His essence before the soul is completely separated from mortal flesh, such are, nevertheless, not altogether in this life, for they are without the activity of the senses, which we use in the state of mortal existence.

Answers to Difficulties:

1. According to Augustine, from those words Moses is shown to have seen God through His essence in a rapture, as we are told of Paul in the second Epistle to the Corinthians (12:2), in order that the lawgiver of the Jews and the teacher of the Gentiles might be equal in this respect.

2. Gregory is speaking about men who grow in keenness of contemplation to the point that they see the divine essence in rapture. Hence, he adds: "He who sees the wisdom which is God entirely dies to this life."

3. It was unique in Christ that at the same time He was a wayfarer and a possessor [of the beatific vision]. This belonged to Him because He was God and man. As a result, everything which related to human nature was under His control, so that each power of soul and body was affected in the way in which He determined. Hence, bodily pain did not hinder contemplation of the mind, nor did delight of the mind lessen bodily pain. Thus, His understanding, which was illumined by the light of glory, saw God through His essence in such a way that the glory did not affect the lower parts. In this way He was at once

---

* Aristotle, *De anima* III, 7 (431a14).

a wayfarer and a possessor of the beatific vision. This cannot be said of others, in whom there is some necessary diffusion from the higher powers to the lower, and in whom the higher powers are drawn down by the strong passions of the lower powers.

4. In this life God is known by means of intellectual sight, yet not with the result that we know what He is, but only what He is not. To this extent we know His essence, understanding that it stands above everything. Such cognition, however, takes place through certain likenesses. The statement from Augustine should be taken as referring to that which is known and not to that by which it is known, as is clear from what has been said.

5. Even in this life our understanding can in a certain manner know the divine essence, not that it knows what it is, but only what it is not.

6. We can love God directly without having loved anything else first, although sometimes we are drawn to invisible things through love of other things which can be seen. In this life, however, we cannot know God directly without first knowing something else. The reason for this is that the activity of affection begins where the activity of understanding ends, since affection follows understanding. But the understanding, going from effects to causes, finally arrives at some sort of knowledge of God, by knowing what He is not. Hence, affection is directed to that which is presented to it through the understanding, without having to go back through all the intermediate things through which the understanding passed.

7. Although our understanding has been made to see God, it cannot see God by its own natural power, but through the light of glory infused into it. Therefore, even though every veil is taken away, it is still not necessary to see God through His essence if the soul is not enlightened with the light of glory. For this lack of glory will be an obstacle to seeing God.

8. Along with intelligibility, which it has as a property, our mind also has existence in common with other things. Hence, although God is in it, it is not necessary that He be there always as an intelligible form, but as giving existence, just as He is in other creatures. Moreover, although He gives existence to all creatures alike, He gives each creature its own mode of existence. Furthermore, in the sense that He is in all of them through essence, presence, and power, He is seen to exist differently in different things, and in each one according to its own mode.

9. Soundness of mind is twofold. There is one by which the mind is healed from sin through the grace of faith. This soundness makes the mind see that unapproachable glory in a mirror and obscurely. The other, which will come through glory, is a remedy for all sin, punishment, and distress. This soundness makes the mind see God face to face. These two kinds of sight are distinguished in the first Epistle to the Corinthians (13:12): "We see now through a glass in a dark manner; but then face to face."

10. The being which is most extensive in universality does not exceed the proportion of anything, since it is essentially identified with everything. Therefore, it is perceived in the knowledge of anything whatsoever. But the being which is first in causality exceeds all other things and has no proportion to them. Hence, it cannot be known adequately through knowledge of any other thing. Therefore, in this life, in which we understand through species abstracted from things, we have adequate knowledge of being in general, but not of uncreated being.

11. Although the divine essence is present to our understanding, still, as long as our understanding is not made perfect by the light of glory, it is not joined to it as an intelligible form which it can understand. For the mind itself does not have the faculty of seeing God through His essence before it is illumined with the aforesaid light. Thus, the faculty of seeing and the presence of what is seen are lacking. Again, the intention is not always present, for, although some likeness of the Creator is found in creatures, still, whenever we look at a creature, we do not consider it as a likeness of the Creator. Hence, it is not necessary that our intention always reach God.

12. As the *Gloss* on Psalms (11:2) says: "Truths are decayed. . . . Many truths are imprinted on human minds," by the one uncreated truth, "just as from one face many faces appear in different mirrors," or in one broken mirror. According to this, we are said to see something in uncreated truth when we judge about something through the likeness of uncreated truth reflected in our mind, as when we judge of conclusions through self-evident principles. Hence, it is not necessary that we see uncreated truth through its essence.

13.   The highest truth, in so far as it exists in itself, is most knowable. But in our regard it happens to be less knowable to us, as is clear from the Philosopher.*

14.   This citation is explained in two ways in the *Gloss*. In one way it is taken to refer to the sight of imagination. Thus, the interlinear *Gloss* says: "I have seen the Lord face to face. This does not mean that God can be seen, but that he saw the form in which God spoke to him." It is explained differently in Gregory's gloss, as referring to intellectual sight, by which saints have seen divine truth in contemplation, not, indeed, knowing what it is, but what it is not. Hence, Gregory says: "He saw by perceiving the truth, for he does not see how great the truth itself is, since the closer he approaches to it, the farther he thinks he is from it. For, unless he saw the truth in some way, he would not perceive that he was not able to see it." And he adds: "This sight, which comes through contemplation, is not firm and permanent, but, as a kind of imitation of sight, is called the face of God. For, since we recognize a person by his face, we call knowledge of God the face of God."

Article XII: In the Twelfth Article We Ask: Is God's Existence Self-Evident to the Human Mind, Just as First Principles of Demonstration, Which Cannot Be Thought Not to Exist?

Difficulties:
It seems that it is, for

1.   Those things which it is given us to know naturally are self-evident. But "knowledge of God's existence is naturally given to everybody," as Damascene says. Therefore, it is self-evident that God exists.

2.   "God is that than which nothing greater can be thought," as Anselm says.† But that which cannot be thought not to exist is greater than that which can be thought not to exist. Therefore, God cannot be thought not to exist.

3.   God is truth itself. But no one can think that truth does not exist, because, if it is declared not to exist, it follows that it exists. For, if truth

does not exist, it is true that truth does not exist. Therefore, no one can think that God does not exist.

4.   God is His own existence. But it is impossible to think that a thing is not predicated of itself, for example, that man is not man. Therefore, it is impossible to think that God does not exist.

5.   All things desire the highest good, as Boethius says.‡ But only God is the highest good. Therefore, all things desire God. But what is not known cannot be desired. Therefore, that God exists is a notion common to all. Therefore, He cannot be thought not to exist.

6.   First truth surpasses all created truth. But some created truth is so evident that it is impossible to think that it does not exist, as for instance, the truth of the proposition that affirmation and denial cannot both be true at the same time. Therefore, much less can it be thought that uncreated truth, which is God, does not exist.

7.   God has existence more truly than the human soul has. But the soul cannot think that it does not exist. Therefore, much less can it think that God does not exist.

8.   Before anything existed it was true that it would exist. But truth exists. Therefore, before it existed it was true that it would exist. But this is true only because of truth. Therefore, it is impossible to think that truth did not always exist. But God is truth. Therefore, it cannot be thought that God does not exist or has not always existed.

9.   It was said that there is a fallacy in this argument, with an equivocation on "simply" and "in some respect." For that truth would exist before it did exist does not state a truth simply, but only in some respect. Thus, we cannot conclude that truth exists simply. – On the contrary, there is the fact that everything which is true in some respect is reduced to something which is true simply, just as every imperfect thing is reduced to something perfect. Therefore, if the fact that truth would exist was true in some respect, something had to be true simply. Thus, it was simply true to say that truth existed.

10.   God's proper name is HE WHO IS, as is clear from Exodus (3:14). But it is impossible to think that being is not. Therefore, it is also impossible to think that God is not.

---

* Aristotle, *Metaphysica* A, 1 (993b8).
† St Anselm of Canterbury, *Proslogium* II (*PL* 158:227).

‡ Boethius, *De consolatione philosophiae* III, prosa 2 (*PL* 63:724:25).

To the Contrary:

1'.   The Psalmist says (Ps. 13:1): "The fool hath said in his heart, 'There is no God.'"

2'.   It was said that the fact that God exists is self-evident habitually to the mind, but it is possible actually to think that He does not exist. – On the contrary, in our inner reason we cannot hold the opposite about those things which we know by a natural habit, such as first principles of demonstration. If, therefore, the contrary of the proposition, God exists, could actually be held, that God does exist would not be habitually self-evident.

3'.   Those things which are self-evident are known without passing from things which are caused to their causes. For they are known as soon as the terms are known, as is said in the *Posterior Analytics.** But we know God only by looking at what He has made, according to Romans (1:20): "For the invisible things of him, . . . by the things that are made. . . ." Therefore, that God exists is not self-evident.

4'.   We cannot know the existence of a thing without knowing what it is. But in this life we cannot know what God is. Therefore, that He exists is not evident to us, much less self-evident.

5'.   That God exists is an article of faith. But an article of faith is something that faith supplies and reason contradicts. But things which reason contradicts are not self-evident. Therefore, that God exists is not self-evident.

6'.   There is nothing more certain for a man than his faith, as Augustine says. But doubt can arise in us about matters of faith and, so, about anything else. Thus, it can be thought that God does not exist.

7'.   Knowledge of God belongs to wisdom. But not everybody has wisdom. Therefore, it is not evident to everybody that God exists. Therefore, it is not self-evident.

8'.   Augustine says: "The highest good is discerned only by the most purified minds." But not everybody has a most purified mind. Therefore, all do not know the highest good, namely, that God exists.

9'.   It is possible to think of one of the things between which reason distinguishes without the other. Thus, we can think that God exists without thinking that He is good, as is clear from Boethius. But, in God, existence and essence

differ in reason. Therefore, we can think of His essence without thinking of His existence. We conclude as before.

10'.   It is the same thing for God to be God and to be just. But some are of the opinion that God is not just and say that evil pleases God. Therefore, some can think that God does not exist. Thus, that God exists is not self-evident.

Reply:

There are three opinions on this question. Some have said, as Rabbi Moses relates,† that the fact that God exists is not self-evident, nor reached through demonstration, but only accepted on faith. The weakness of the reasons which many advance to prove that God exists prompted them to assert this.

Others, as Avicenna,‡ say that the fact that God exists is not self-evident, but is known through demonstration. Still others, as Anselm,§ are of the opinion that the fact that God exists is self-evident to this extent, that no one in his inner thoughts can think that God does not exist, although exteriorly he can express it and interiorly think the words with which he expresses it.

The first opinion is obviously false. For we find that the existence of God has been proved by the philosophers with unimpeachable proofs, although trivial reasons have also been brought forth by some to show this.

Each of the two following opinions has some truth. For something is immediately evident in two ways: in itself and to us. That God exists, therefore, is immediately evident in itself, but not to us. Therefore, to know this it is necessary in our case to have demonstrations proceeding from effects. This is clear from what follows.

For a thing to be immediately evident in itself, all that is needed is that the predicate pertain to the nature of the subject. For then the subject cannot be considered without it appearing that the predicate is contained in it. But for something to be immediately evident with reference to us, we have to know the meaning of the subject in which the predicate is included. Hence it is that some things are immediately evident to everybody,

---

* Aristotle, *Analytica posteriora* I, 2 (72a27).

† Moses Maimonides, *The Guide for the Perplexed* I, 75 (FR 141).

‡ Aricenna, *Metaphysica* I, 1 (70r).

§ St Anselm of Canterbury, *Proslogium* I (*PL* 158:227) [remainder of note omitted].

as, for instance, when propositions of this sort have subjects which are such that their meaning is evident to everybody, as every whole is greater than its part. For anyone knows what a whole is and what a part is. Some things, however, are immediately evident only to those with trained minds, who know the meaning of the terms, whereas ordinary people do not know them.

It is in this sense that Boethius says: "There are two types of common notions. One is common to everybody, for example, if you take equal parts from things that are equal. . . . The other is found only in the more educated, for example, that non-bodily things are not in a place. Ordinary people cannot see the truth of this, but the educated can." For the thought of ordinary people is unable to go beyond imagination to reach the nature of incorporeal things.

Now, existence is not included perfectly in the essential nature of any creature, for the act of existence of every creature is something other than its quiddity. Hence, it cannot be said of any creature that its existence is immediately evident even in itself. But, in God, His existence is included in the nature of His quiddity, for in God *essence* and *existence* are the same, as Boethius says. And *that He is* and *what He is* are the same, as Avicenna says.* Therefore, it is immediately evident in itself.

But, since the essence of God is not evident to us, the fact of God's existence is not evident to us, but has to be demonstrated. In heaven, however, where we shall see His essence, the fact of God's existence will be immediately evident to us much more fully than the fact that affirmation and denial cannot both be true at the same time is immediately evident to us now. Since, therefore, each part of the question is true to some extent, we must answer both sides.

Answers to Difficulties:
1. Knowledge of God's existence is said naturally to be implanted in everybody, because in everyone there is naturally implanted something from which he can arrive at knowledge of the fact of God's existence.

2. The reasoning would follow if God were not self-evident because of something connected with Himself. The possibility, however, of thinking that He does not exist is now due to something in us, who are incapable of knowing those things which are most evident in themselves. Hence, the fact that God can be thought of as not existing does not prevent Him from being that than which nothing greater can be thought.

3. Truth is based on being. Hence, as it is self-evident that being exists in general, so it is also self-evident that truth exists. However, that there is a first being which is the cause of every being is not immediately evident to us until it is accepted on faith or proved by a demonstration. Consequently, neither is it self-evident that the truth of all things derives from some first truth. Hence, it does not follow that God's existence is self-evident.

4. If it were immediately evident to us that the divine nature is God's existence, the argument would follow. However, at present it is not immediately evident to us, since we do not see God through His essence, but need a demonstration or faith to hold this truth.

5. The highest good is desired in two ways. In one, it is desired in its essence, a way in which not everything desires highest good. In the other way, it is desired in its likeness, in which manner all things desire the highest good, for nothing is desirable except in so far as some likeness of the highest good is seen in it. Hence, we cannot conclude from this that God's existence, which is essentially the highest good, is self-evident.

6. Although uncreated truth surpasses every created truth, nothing prevents created truth from being more evident to us than uncreated truth. For those things which are less evident in themselves are more evident to us, according to the Philosopher.†

7. To think that something does not exist can be taken in two ways. In one, it is taken to mean that these two things are grasped at the same time. In this sense, there is nothing to prevent one from thinking that he does not exist, just as he thinks that at one time he did not exist. However, in this sense, we cannot at the same time conceive that something is a whole and that it is less than a part of itself, for one of these excludes the other.

In the other way, it is taken to mean that assent is given to what is thus conceived. In this sense, no one can assent to the thought that he does not exist. For, in thinking something, he perceives that he exists.

---

* Aricenna, *Metaphysica* VIII, 1 (97v).

† Aristotle, *Physica* I, 1 (184a19).

8. Before present things existed, it had to be true that they would exist only on the supposition that something existed at the time when it was said that this would exist. But, if we lay down the impossible condition that at one time nothing existed, then, on the basis of such an hypothesis, nothing is true except only materially. For not only existence but also nonexistence is the subject matter of truth, for we can speak truth about being or non-being. Thus it follows that there will be truth at that time only materially and so in some respect.

9. It is necessary to reduce that which is true in some respect to that which is true or truth simply if it is presupposed that truth exists, but not otherwise.

10. Although the name of God is HE WHO IS, this is not immediately evident to us. Hence, the argument does not follow.

Answers to Contrary Difficulties:

1′. According to Anselm,* that the fool said in his heart: "There is no God," means that he thought these words, and not that he could think this in his inner reason.

2′. That God exists is self-evident and not self-evident in the same way with reference to habit and to act.

3′. That we can know God only from what He has made is due to the inadequacy of our knowledge. Hence, this does not keep Him from being immediately evident in Himself.

4′. To know that a thing exists, it is not necessary to know what it is by definition, but only what is meant by the name.

5′. That God exists is not an article of faith but the preamble to an article of faith, unless we understand something else along with God's existence, for example, that He has unity of essence with trinity of Persons, and other things such as this.

6′. Matters of faith are known with greatest certainty in so far as certainty means firmness of adherence. For the believer clings to nothing more firmly than those things which he holds by faith. But they are not known with greatest certainty in so far as certainty implies repose of understanding in the thing known. For the believer's assent to what he believes does not come from the fact that his understanding concludes to the things believed by virtue of any principles, but from the will, which influences the understanding to assent to what is believed. Hence it is that in matters of faith, movements of doubt can arise in one who believes.

7′. Wisdom consists not only in knowing that God exists, but in attaining to a knowledge of what He is. But in this life we can know this only in so far as we know what He is not. For one who knows something in so far as it differs from all other things approaches the knowledge by which one knows what it is. It is to this knowledge, too, that the citation from Augustine which follows is taken to refer.

8′. The answer to the eighth difficulty is clear from the seventh response.

9′. Those things which have been distinguished by reason cannot always be thought of as separated from each other, although they can be considered separately. For, although it is possible to think of God without considering His goodness, it is impossible to think that God exists and is not good. Hence, although in God that which exists and existence are distinguished in reason, it does not follow that it is possible to think that He does not exist.

10′. God is known not only in the works which proceed from His justice, but also in His other works. Hence, granted that someone does not know Him as just, it does not follow that he does not know Him at all. Nor is it possible for anyone to know none of His works, since being in general, which cannot be unknown, is His work.

* St Anselm of Canterbury, *Proslogium* II, III, IV (*PL* 158:227 ff.).

Francis Bacon, *Novum Organum* I: Selected *Aphorisms*

Introduction

This article presents a selection from one of the most important philosophical documents in the development of modern science. Francis Bacon's *Novum Organum* (1620) or *New Organon* self-consciously set out to displace what had by that time become known as the *Organon* (tool or instrument) of Aristotle – that is, Aristotle's texts on logic and scientific method (the *Categories, Prior Analytics, Posterior Analytics, On Interpretation, Topics*, and *Sophistical Refutations*). Bacon's new tool, however, was part of a much larger intellectual project of even grander scope. Calling it in the preface to the second part of the *Novum organum*, the *Great Renewal* (*Instauratio magna*), Bacon aimed at nothing less than a radical reconceptualization and methodological reform of the practices of scientific discovery and justification. In many ways, his aspirations have been realized.[1]

Born the son of the Keeper of the Great Seal under Elizabeth I, Bacon (1561–1626) was educated at Trinity College, Cambridge. His meteoric career carried him to important achievements as a legal-political scholar, to a seat in the House of Commons, to appointment as Lord Chancellor, to the titles of Baron Verulam and Viscount St Albans, and finally to a tragic fall from power on

From Francis Bacon, *Advancement of Learning and Novum Organum*, ed. J. E. Creighton, New York: Willey Book Co., 1944, pp. 315–31, 349–53.

what were probably trumped-up charges. Critics have excoriated Bacon for prosecuting and sending to the gallows his close friend and patron, the Earl of Essex, and for torturing state prisoners. An almost certainly apocryphal story tells how Bacon died of an illness acquired in the course of an experiment in the refrigeration of meat.

Bacon's project of scientific renewal includes both constructive and destructive dimensions. From the destructive side, the shallow ornament of Renaissance humanism, the trivial sophistry of legal and Biblical philology, and the confused entanglements of philosophical-theology and metaphysics all receive upbraiding. His error theory, laid out in *Novum Organum*, describes how human beings fall prey to four kinds of "idols" prejudices or illusions. The "Idols of the Tribe" (*idola tribus*) represent features of human nature that lead us astray (e.g. through errors of perception, memory, and the effects of passions). "Idols of the Den" or Cave (*idola specus*), calling to mind Plato's Cave, pertain to limitations and distortions related to our individual shortcomings. 'Idols of the Marketplace' or Forum (*idola fori*) are rooted in the misleading tendencies of language generally and different local forms of discourses specifically (for example, theological discourse). In this way, Bacon anticipates Ludwig Wittgenstein's later attention to the capacity of language to "bewitch" us (II.23). The "Idols of the Theater" (*idola theatri*) derive from the confusing and misleading effects of abstract theory and ideology upon our minds.

In *The Advancement of Learning* I.3.b (1605), Bacon compares some thinkers to ants (*Aphorism* 95). They are diligent and accumulate a great deal; but, lacking systematic method, they merely pile up scattered bits and pieces of knowledge without really understanding them. Other thinkers, says Bacon, are like spiders. Solitary and aloof, they spin theoretical webs that entrap the unsuspecting but produce nothing; they sap the intellectual talents of those they ensnare. The best thinkers, however, the sort Bacon aims to engender, would be like bees, working together in an organized and orderly fashion, they would transform what they collect into the sweetest and most nourishing of products. The Royal Society (est. 1660) founded itself on just this vision, a vision Bacon cultivates in his allegorical story of Solomon's House in the *New Atlantis* (1626).

This last theme, that science must be useful, runs through the whole of Bacon's work and points to its constructive aspirations. Bacon admired the argumentative skill of scholastic thought, but he found the paucity of real benefits it brought to human life disappointing. In Bacon's famous claim that "knowledge is power" (*Aphorism* 111), he means in the first place the power to control nature through the manipulation of causes and effects to the benefit of humankind. Science, he says, must be fruitful – a *scientia operativa*, a productive science. In this Bacon's objective includes overcoming, in part, the consequences attributed to the fall from Eden, not least of all by extending life (*De vijs mortis*, c. 1618), an idea that would also animate Descartes.[2]

Although he hardly makes a systematic presentation of it, Bacon's method is often called "inductive," and he does use the term "induction" to describe the way sound science should proceed. But the term, as Bacon deployed it, means something rather different from the idea as logicians define it today. Today logicians define "induction" as a form of reasoning from which a conclusion follows only with a degree of probability, not with certainty or by necessity. For Bacon, by contrast, induction points to a method of careful, methodical observation through which one generates general principles – principles that may then be used to deduce testable hypotheses. "There are and can be only two ways of searching into and discovering truth. The one flies from the senses and particulars to the most general axioms, and from these principles, the truth of which it takes for

settled and immovable, proceeds to judgment and to the discovery of middle axioms. And this way is now in fashion. The other derives axioms from the senses and particulars, rising by a gradual and unbroken ascent, so that it arrives at the most general axioms last of all. This is the true way, but as yet untried" (*Aphorism* 19).

It's not, then, simply that Bacon insists on empirical observation (*Aphorism* 36), as is so often said. Much of medieval science employed observation. Rather, for Bacon observation must be guided and disciplined by method, especially in laboratory conditions where, again control can be exerted over nature. Indeed, this concern with *method* becomes one of the hallmarks of modern philosophy of science. For Bacon, mere observation, undisciplined by a proper method yields only "anticipations of nature." Observation disciplined by method, by contrast, produces what he calls "interpretations of nature," something today that might be called justified scientific "fact" (*Aphorisms* 24, 32). One of the benefits of systematic method, according to Bacon, is that it will make it possible to overcome skepticism (*Aphorisms* 37, 68).

Bacon's method departs from the dominant forms of then-contemporary and precedent science in a number of ways. In addition to issues of technological power, Bacon's dispute with Renaissance, medieval, and ancient science is in large measure a dispute about starting points. Many among his contemporaries, no less than medievals and ancients, held that the starting points or axioms of science are acquired through either intuition or authority – either through authoritative philosophical and religions traditions or through the direct seeing of the intellect (*nôus, noesis*) that emerges in "dialectic" or through "collecting and separating" ideas (cf. Plato, *Symposium* 210e, *Sophist*, and *Phaedrus* 265d; Aristotle, *Metaphysics* E, 1027b217). Instead, for Bacon methodical observation should generate and discipline first principles.

Bacon also rejects, in what would become characteristic of modern science, the Aristotelian method of explanation by four causes (*aitia*; *Metaphysics* A.3, 983a24): (1) the "material" cause (or matter of a thing); (2) the "efficient" or moving cause (the immediately proximate event that leads to an effect); (3) the "formal" cause (the "form" or "essence" of a thing); and (4) the "final" cause (the thing's purpose or end). Like the modern scientists who would follow him, Bacon eliminates the last two of these, reducing scientific explanation to a description of matter and motion (retaining the language of "form" to denote something much more like natural law than immaterial substance or essence). Through this reduction, Bacon also helped liberate natural science from religion, though the precise nature of their relationship would remain a contested one (*Valerius terminus* [*Authoritative Limit*], 1603). In Bacon's insistence that in order to acquire knowledge scientists must exclude falsehoods (e.g. his "tables of exclusion") and not just verify

truth, he anticipates the influential scientific logic of falsification developed in the twentieth century by Karl Popper (II.21).

Notes

1   L. Jardine and A. Stewart, *Hostage to Fortune: The Troubled Life of Francis Bacon*, New York: Hill & Wang, 1999.
2   R. Davies, "Francis Bacon" in P. Dematteis and P. Fosl, eds, *The Dictionary of Literary Biography*, Detroit, MI: Gale Research, 2002, p. 28.

Bacon, *Novum Organum* I: selected *Aphorisms*

On the Interpretation of Nature and the Empire of Man

1.   Man, as the minister and interpreter of nature, does and understands as much as his observations on the order of nature, either with regard to things or the mind, permit him, and neither knows nor is capable of more.

2.   The unassisted hand and the understanding left to itself possess but little power. Effects are produced by the means of instruments and helps, which the understanding requires no less than the hand; and as instruments either promote or regulate the motion of the hand, so those that are applied to the mind prompt or protect the understanding.

3.   Knowledge and human power are synonymous, since the ignorance of the cause frustrates the effect; for nature is only subdued by submission, and that which in contemplative philosophy corresponds with the cause in practical science becomes the rule.

4.   Man whilst operating can only apply or withdraw natural bodies; nature internally performs the rest.

5.   Those who become practically versed in nature are, the mechanic, the mathematician, the physician, the alchemist, and the magician, but all (as matters now stand) with faint efforts and meagre success.

6.   It would be madness and inconsistency to suppose that things which have never yet been

performed can be performed without employing some hitherto untried means.

7.   The creations of the mind and hand appear very numerous, if we judge by books and manufactures; but all that variety consists of an excessive refinement, and of deductions from a few well-known matters – not of a number of axioms.

8.   Even the effects already discovered are due to chance and experiment, rather than to the sciences; for our present sciences are nothing more than peculiar arrangements of matters already discovered, and not methods for discovery or plans for new operations.

9.   The sole cause and root of almost every defect in the sciences is this, that while we falsely admire and extol the powers of the human mind, we do not search for its real helps.

10.   The subtilty of nature is far beyond that of sense or of the understanding; so that the specious meditations, speculations, and theories of mankind are but a kind of insanity, only there is no one to stand by and observe it.

11.   As the present sciences are useless for the discovery of effects, so the present system of logic is useless for the discovery of the sciences.

12.   The present system of logic rather assists in confirming and rendering inveterate the errors founded on vulgar notions than in searching after truth, and is therefore more hurtful than useful.

13.   The syllogism is not applied to the principles of the sciences, and is of no avail in intermediate axioms, as being very unequal to the subtilty of nature. It forces assent, therefore, and not things.

14. The syllogism consists of propositions, propositions of words; words are the signs of notions. If, therefore, the notions (which form the basis of the whole) be confused and carelessly abstracted from things, there is no solidity in the superstructure. Our only hope, then, is in genuine induction.

15. We have no sound notions either in logic or physics; substance, quality, action, passion, and existence are not clear notions; much less weight, levity, density, tenuity, moisture, dryness, generation, corruption, attraction, repulsion, element, matter, form, and the like. They are all fantastical and ill-defined.

16. The notions of less abstract natures, as man, dog, dove, and the immediate perceptions of sense, as heat, cold, white, black, do not deceive us materially, yet even these are sometimes confused by the mutability of matter and the intermixture of things. All the rest which men have hitherto employed are errors, and improperly abstracted and deduced from things.

17. There is the same degree of licentiousness and error in forming axioms as in abstracting notions, and that in the first principles, which depend on common induction; still more is this the case in axioms and inferior propositions derived from syllogisms.

18. The present discoveries in science are such as lie immediately beneath the surface of common notions. It is necessary, however, to penetrate the more secret and remote parts of nature, in order to abstract both notions and axioms from things by a more certain and guarded method.

19. There are and can exist but two ways of investigating and discovering truth. The one hurries on rapidly from the senses and particulars to the most general axioms, and from them, as principles and their supposed indisputable truth, derives and discovers the intermediate axioms. This is the way now in use. The other constructs its axioms from the senses and particulars, by ascending continually and gradually, till it finally arrives at the most general axioms, which is the true but unattempted way.

20. The understanding when left to itself proceeds by the same way as that which it would have adopted under the guidance of logic, namely, the first; for the mind is fond of starting off to generalities, that it may avoid labor, and after dwelling a little on a subject is fatigued by experiment. But those evils are augmented by logic, for the sake of the ostentation of dispute.

21. The understanding, when left to itself in a man of a steady, patient, and reflecting disposition (especially when unimpeded by received doctrines), makes some attempt in the right way, but with little effect, since the understanding, undirected and unassisted, is unequal to and unfit for the task of vanquishing the obscurity of things.

22. Each of these two ways begins from the senses and particulars, and ends in the greatest generalities. But they are immeasurably different; for the one merely touches cursorily the limits of experiment and particulars, whilst the other runs duly and regularly through them – the one from the very outset lays down some abstract and useless generalities, the other gradually rises to those principles which are really the most common in nature.

23. There is no small difference between the idols of the human mind and the ideas of the Divine mind – that is to say, between certain idle dogmas and the real stamp and impression of created objects, as they are found in nature.

24. Axioms determined upon in argument can never assist in the discovery of new effects; for the subtilty of nature is vastly superior to that of argument. But axioms properly and regularly abstracted from particulars easily point out and define new particulars, and therefore impart activity to the sciences.

25. The axioms now in use are derived from a scanty handful, as it were, of experience, and a few particulars of frequent occurrence, whence they are of much the same dimensions or extent as their origin. And if any neglected or unknown instance occurs, the axiom is saved by some frivolous distinction, when it would be more consistent with truth to amend it.

26. We are wont, for the sake of distinction, to call that human reasoning which we apply to nature the anticipation of nature (as being rash and premature), and that which is properly deduced from things the interpretation of nature.

27. Anticipations are sufficiently powerful in producing unanimity, for if men were all to become even uniformly mad, they might agree tolerably well with each other.

28. Anticipations, again, will be assented to much more readily than interpretations, because

being deduced from a few instances, and these principally of familiar occurrence, they immediately hit the understanding and satisfy the imagination; whilst on the contrary interpretations, being deduced from various subjects, and these widely dispersed, cannot suddenly strike the understanding, so that in common estimation they must appear difficult and discordant, and almost like the mysteries of faith.

29. In sciences founded on opinions and dogmas, it is right to make use of anticipations and logic if you wish to force assent rather than things.

30. If all the capacities of all ages should unite and combine and transmit their labors, no great progress will be made in learning by anticipations, because the radical errors, and those which occur in the first process of the mind, are not cured by the excellence of subsequent means and remedies.

31. It is in vain to expect any great progress in the sciences by the superinducing or engrafting new matters upon old. An instauration must be made from the very foundations, if we do not wish to revolve forever in a circle, making only some slight and contemptible progress.

32. The ancient authors and all others are left in undisputed possession of their honors; for we enter into no comparison of capacity or talent, but of method, and assume the part of a guide rather than of a critic.

33. To speak plainly, no correct judgment can be formed either of our method or its discoveries by those anticipations which are now in common use; for it is not to be required of us to submit ourselves to the judgment of the very method we ourselves arraign.

34. Nor is it an easy matter to deliver and explain our sentiments; for those things which are in themselves new can yet be only understood from some analogy to what is old.

35. Alexander Borgia said of the expedition of the French into Italy that they came with chalk in their hands to mark up their lodgings, and not with weapons to force their passage. Even so do we wish our philosophy to make its way quietly into those minds that are fit for it, and of good capacity; for we have no need of contention where we differ in first principles, and in our very notions, and even in our forms of demonstration.

36. We have but one simple method of delivering our sentiments, namely, we must bring men to particulars and their regular series and order, and they must for a while renounce their notions, and begin to form an acquaintance with things.

37. Our method and that of the sceptics agree in some respects at first setting out, but differ most widely, and are completely opposed to each other in their conclusion; for they roundly assert that nothing can be known; we, that but a small part of nature can be known, by the present method; their next step, however, is to destroy the authority of the senses and understanding, whilst we invent and supply them with assistance.

38. The idols and false notions which have already preoccupied the human understanding, and are deeply rooted in it, not only so beset men's minds that they become difficult of access, but even when access is obtained will again meet and trouble us in the instauration of the sciences, unless mankind when forewarned guard themselves with all possible care against them.

39. Four species of idols beset the human mind, to which (for distinction's sake) we have assigned names, calling the first Idols of the Tribe, the second Idols of the Den, the third Idols of the Market, the fourth Idols of the Theatre.

40. The formation of notions and axioms on the foundation of true induction is the only fitting remedy by which we can ward off and expel these idols. It is, however, of great service to point them out; for the doctrine of idols bears the same relation to the interpretation of nature as that of the confutation of sophisms does to common logic.

41. The idols of the tribe are inherent in human nature and the very tribe or race of man; for man's sense is falsely asserted to be the standard of things; on the contrary, all the perceptions both of the senses and the mind bear reference to man and not to the universe, and the human mind resembles those uneven mirrors which impart thir own properties to different objects, from which rays are emitted and distort and disfigure them.

42. The idols of the den are those of each individual; for everybody (in addition to the errors common to the race of man) has his own individual den or cavern, which intercepts and corrupts the light of nature, either from his own peculiar and singular disposition, or from his education and intercourse with others, or from

his reading, and the authority acquired by those whom he reverences and admires, or from the different impressions produced on the mind, as it happens to be preoccupied and predisposed, or equable and tranquil, and the like; so that the spirit of man (according to its several dispositions), is variable, confused, and, as it were, actuated by chance; and Heraclitus said well that men search for knowledge in lesser worlds, and not in the greater or common world.

43.   There are also idols formed by the reciprocal intercourse and society of man with man which we call idols of the market, from the commerce and association of men with each other; for men converse by means of language, but words are formed at the will of the generality, and there arises from a bad and unapt formation of words a wonderful obstruction to the mind. Nor can the definitions and explanations with which learned men are wont to guard and protect themselves in some instances afford a complete remedy – words still manifestly force the understanding, throw everything into confusion, and lead mankind into vain and innumerable controversies and fallacies.

44.   Lastly, there are idols which have crept into men's minds from the various dogmas of peculiar systems of philosophy, and also from the perverted rules of demonstration, and these we denominate idols of the theatre: for we regard all the systems of philosophy hitherto received or imagined, as so many plays brought out and performed, creating fictitious and theatrical worlds. Nor do we speak only of the present systems, or of the philosophy and sects of the ancients, since numerous other plays of a similar nature can be still composed and made to agree with each other, the causes of the most opposite errors being generally the same. Nor, again, do we allude merely to general systems, but also to many elements and axioms of sciences which have become inveterate by tradition, implicit credence, and neglect. We must, however, discuss each species of idols more fully and distinctly in order to guard the human understanding against them.

45.   The human understanding, from its peculiar nature, easily supposes a greater degree of order and equality in things than it really finds; and although many things in nature be sui generis and most irregular, will yet invent parallels and conjugates and relatives, where no

such thing is. Hence the fiction, that all celestial bodies move in perfect circles, thus rejecting entirely spiral and serpentine lines (except as explanatory terms). Hence also the element of fire is introduced with its peculiar orbit, to keep square with those other three which are objects of our senses. The relative rarity of the elements (as they are called) is arbitrarily made to vary in tenfold progression, with many other dreams of the like nature. Nor is this folly confined to theories, but it is to be met with even in simple notions.

46.   The human understanding, when any proposition has been once laid down (either from general admission and belief, or from the pleasure it affords), forces everything else to add fresh support and confirmation; and although most cogent and abundant instances may exist to the contrary, yet either does not observe or despises them, or gets rid of and rejects them by some distinction, with violent and injurious prejudice, rather than sacrifice the authority of its first conclusions. It was well answered by him who has shown in a temple the votive tablets suspended by such as had escaped the peril of shipwreck, and was pressed as to whether he would then recognize the power of the gods, by an inquiry. But where are the portraits of those who have perished in spite of their vows? All superstition is much the same, whether it be that of astrology, dreams, omens, retributive judgment, or the like, in all of which the deluded believers observe events which are fulfilled, but neglect and pass over their failure, though it be much more common. But this evil insinuates itself still more craftily in philosophy and the sciences, in which a settled maxim vitiates and governs every other circumstance, though the latter be much more worthy of confidence. Besides, even in the absence of that eagerness and want of thought (which we have mentioned), it is the peculiar and perpetual error of the human understanding to be more moved and excited by affirmatives than negatives, whereas it ought duly and regularly to be impartial; nay, in establishing any true axiom the negative instance is the most powerful.

47.   The human understanding is most excited by that which strikes and enters the mind at once and suddenly, and by which the imagination is immediately filled and inflated. It then begins almost imperceptibly to conceive and suppose that everything is similar to the few objects

which have taken possession of the mind, whilst it is very slow and unfit for the transition to the remote and heterogeneous instances by which axioms are tried as by fire, unless the office be imposed upon it by severe regulations and a powerful authority.

48. The human understanding is active and cannot halt or rest, but even, though without effect, still presses forward. Thus we cannot conceive of any end or external boundary of the world, and it seems necessarily to occur to us that there must be something beyond. Nor can we imagine how eternity has flowed on down to the present day, since the usually received distinction of an infinity, a parte ante and a parte post cannot hold good; for it would thence follow that one infinity is greater than another, and also that infinity is wasting away and tending to an end. There is the same difficulty in considering the infinite divisibility of lines arising from the weakness of our minds, which weakness interferes to still greater disadvantage with the discovery of causes; for although the greatest generalities in nature must be positive, just as they are found, and in fact not causable, yet the human understanding, incapable of resting, seeks for something more intelligible. Thus, however, whilst aiming at further progress, it falls back to what is actually less advanced, namely, final causes; for they are clearly more allied to man's own nature, than the system of the universe, and from this source they have wonderfully corrupted philosophy. But he would be an unskilful and shallow philosopher who should seek for causes in the greatest generalities, and not be anxious to discover them in subordinate objects.

49. The human understanding resembles not a dry light, but admits a tincture of the will and passions, which generate their own system accordingly; for man always believes more readily that which he prefers. He, therefore, rejects difficulties for want of patience in investigation; sobriety, because it limits his hope; the depths of nature, from superstition; the light of experiment, from arrogance and pride, lest his mind should appear to be occupied with common and varying objects; paradoxes, from a fear of the opinion of the vulgar; in short, his feelings imbue and corrupt his understanding in innumerable and sometimes imperceptible ways.

50. But by far the greatest impediment and aberration of the human understanding proceeds from the dulness, incompetency, and errors of the senses; since whatever strikes the senses preponderates over everything, however superior, which does not immediately strike them. Hence contemplation mostly ceases with sight, and a very scanty, or perhaps no regard is paid to invisible objects. The entire operation, therefore, of spirits enclosed in tangible bodies is concealed, and escapes us. All that more delicate change of formation in the parts of coarser substances (vulgarly called alteration, but in fact a change of position in the smallest particles) is equally unknown; and yet, unless the two matters we have mentioned be explored and brought to light, no great effect can be produced in nature. Again, the very nature of common air, and all bodies of less density (of which there are many) is almost unknown ; for the senses are weak and erring, nor can instruments be of great use in extending their sphere or acuteness – all the better interpretations of nature are worked out by instances, and fit and apt experiments, where the senses only judge of the experiment, the experiment of nature and the thing itself.

51. The human understanding is, by its own nature, prone to abstraction, and supposes that which is fluctuating to be fixed. But it is better to dissect than abstract nature; such was the method employed by the school of Democritus, which made greater progress in penetrating nature than the rest. It is best to consider matter, its conformation, and the changes of that conformation, its own action, and the law of this action or motion; for forms are a mere fiction of the human mind, unless you will call the laws of action by that name.

52. Such are the idols of the tribe, which arise either from the uniformity of the constitution of man's spirit, or its prejudices, or its limited faculties or restless agitation, or from the interference of the passions, or the incompetency of the senses, or the mode of their impressions.

53. The idols of the den derive their origin from the peculiar nature of each individual's mind and body, and also from education, habit, and accident; and although they be various and manifold, yet we will treat of some that require the greatest caution, and exert the greatest power in polluting the understanding.

54. Some men become attached to particular sciences and contemplations, either from supposing themselves the authors and inventors

of them, or from having bestowed the greatest pains upon such subjects, and thus become most habituated to them. If men of this description apply themselves to philosophy and contemplations of a universal nature, they wrest and corrupt them by their preconceived fancies, of which Aristotle affords us a signal instance, who made his natural philosophy completely subservient to his logic, and thus rendered it little more than useless and disputatious. The chemists, again, have formed a fanciful philosophy with the most confined views, from a few experiments of the furnace. Gilbert, too, having employed himself most assiduously in the consideration of the magnet, immediately established a system of philosophy to coincide with his favorite pursuit.

55. The greatest and, perhaps, radical distinction between different men's dispositions for philosophy and the sciences is this, that some are more vigorous and active in observing the differences of things, others in observing their resemblances; for a steady and acute disposition can fix its thoughts, and dwell upon and adhere to a point, through all the refinements of differences, but those that are sublime and discursive recognize and compare even the most delicate and general resemblances; each of them readily falls into excess, by catching either at nice distinctions or shadows of resemblance.

56. Some dispositions evince an unbounded admiration of antiquity, others eagerly embrace novelty, and but few can preserve the just medium, so as neither to tear up what the ancients have correctly laid down, nor to despise the just innovations of the moderns. But this is very prejudicial to the sciences and philosophy, and instead of a correct judgment we have but the factions of the ancients and moderns. Truth is not to be sought in the good fortune of any particular conjuncture of time, which is uncertain, but in the light of nature and experience, which is eternal. Such factions, therefore, are to be abjured, and the understanding must not allow them to hurry it on to assent.

57. The contemplation of nature and of bodies in their individual form distracts and weakens the understanding; but the contemplation of nature and of bodies in their general composition and formation stupefies and relaxes it. We have a good instance of this in the school of Leucippus and Democritus compared with others, for they applied themselves so much to particulars as almost to neglect the general structure of things, whilst the others were so astounded whilst gazing on the structure that they did not penetrate the simplicity of nature. These two species of contemplation must, therefore, be interchanged, and each employed in its turn, in order to render the understanding at once penetrating and capacious, and to avoid the inconveniences we have mentioned, and the idols that result from them.

58. Let such, therefore, be our precautions in contemplation, that we may ward off and expel the idols of the den, which mostly owe their birth either to some predominant pursuit, or, secondly, to an excess in synthesis and analysis, or, thirdly, to a party zeal in favor of certain ages, or, fourthly, to the extent or narrowness of the subject. In general, he who contemplates nature should suspect whatever particularly takes and fixes his understanding, and should use so much the more caution to preserve it equable and unprejudiced.

59. The idols of the market are the most troublesome of all, those namely which have entwined themselves round the understanding from the associations of words and names. For men imagine that their reason governs words, whilst, in fact, words react upon the understanding; and this has rendered philosophy and the sciences sophistical and inactive. Words are generally formed in a popular sense, and define things by those broad lines which are most obvious to the vulgar mind; but when a more acute understanding, or more diligent observation is anxious to vary those lines, and to adapt them more accurately to nature, words oppose it. Hence the great and solemn disputes of learned men often terminate in controversies about words and names, in regard to which it would be better (imitating the caution of mathematicians) to proceed more advisedly in the first instance, and to bring such disputes to a regular issue by definitions. Such definitions, however, cannot remedy the evil in natural and material objects, because they consist themselves of words, and these words produce others; so that we must necessarily have recourse to particular instances, and their regular series and arrangement, as we shall mention when we come to the mode and scheme of determining notions and axioms.

60. The idols imposed upon the understanding by words are of two kinds. They are either

the names of things which have no existence (for as some objects are from inattention left without a name, so names are formed by fanciful imaginations which are without an object), or they are the names of actual objects, but confused, badly defined, and hastily and irregularly abstracted from things. Fortune, the primum mobile, the planetary orbits, the element of fire, and the like fictions, which owe their birth to futile and false theories, are instances of the first kind. And this species of idols is removed with greater facility, because it can be exterminated by the constant refutation or the desuetude of the theories themselves. The others, which are created by vicious and unskilful abstraction, are intricate and deeply rooted. Take some word for instance, as moist, and let us examine how far the different significations of this word are consistent. It will be found that the word moist is nothing but a confused sign of different actions admitted of no settled and defined uniformity. For it means that which easily diffuses itself over another body; that which is indeterminable and cannot be brought to a consistency; that which yields easily in every direction; that which is easily divided and dispersed; that which is easily united and collected; that which easily flows and is put in motion; that which easily adheres to, and wets another body; that which is easily reduced to a liquid state though previously solid. When, therefore, you come to predicate or impose this name, in one sense flame is moist, in another air is not moist, in another fine powder is moist, in another glass is moist; so that it is quite clear that this notion is hastily abstracted from water only, and common ordinary liquors, without any due verification of it.

There are, however, different degrees of distortion and mistake in words. One of the least faulty classes is that of the names of substances, particularly of the less abstract and more defined species (those then of chalk and mud are good, of earth bad); words signifying actions are more faulty, as to generate, to corrupt, to change; but the most faulty are those denoting qualities (except the immediate objects of sense), as heavy, light, rare, dense. Yet in all of these there must be some notions a little better than others, in proportion as a greater or less number of things come before the senses.

61.   The idols of the theatre are not innate, nor do they introduce themselves secretly into the understanding, but they are manifestly instilled and cherished by the fictions of theories and depraved rules of demonstration. To attempt, however, or undertake their confutation would not be consistent with our declarations. For since we neither agree in our principles nor our demonstrations, all argument is out of the question. And it is fortunate that the ancients are left in possession of their honors. We detract nothing from them, seeing our whole doctrine relates only to the path to be pursued. The lame (as they say) in the path outstrip the swift who wander from it, and it is clear that the very skill and swiftness of him who runs not in the right direction must increase his aberration.

Our method of discovering the sciences is such as to leave little to the acuteness and strength of wit, and indeed rather to level wit and intellect. For as in the drawing of a straight line, or accurate circle by the hand, much depends on its steadiness and practice, but if a ruler or compass be employed there is little occasion for either; so it is with our method. Although, however, we enter into no individual confutations, yet a little must be said, first, of the sects and general divisions of these species of theories; secondly, something further to show that there are external signs of their weakness; and, lastly, we must consider the causes of so great a misfortune, and so long and general a unanimity in error, that we may thus render the access to truth less difficult, and that the human understanding may the more readily be purified, and brought to dismiss its idols.

62.   The idols of the theatre, or of theories, are numerous, and may, and perhaps will, be still more so. For unless men's minds had been now occupied for many ages in religious and theological considerations, and civil governments (especially monarchies), had been averse to novelties of that nature even in theory (so that men must apply to them with some risk and injury to their own fortunes, and not only without reward, but subject to contumely and envy), there is no doubt that many other sects of philosophers and theorists would have been introduced, like those which formerly flourished in such diversified abundance amongst the Greeks. For as many imaginary theories of the heavens can be deduced from the phenomena of the sky, so it is even more easy to found many dogmas upon the phenomena of philosophy – and the plot of this our theatre resembles those of the poetical, where the plots

which are invented for the stage are more consistent, elegant, and pleasurable than those taken from real history.

In general, men take for the groundwork of their philosophy either too much from a few topics, or too little from many; in either case their philosophy is founded on too narrow a basis of experiment and natural history, and decides on too scanty grounds. For the theoretic philosopher seizes various common circumstances by experiment, without reducing them to certainty or examining and frequently considering them, and relies for the rest upon meditation and the activity of his wit.

There are other philosophers who have diligently and accurately attended to a few experiments, and have thence presumed to deduce and invent systems of philosophy, forming everything to conformity with them.

A third set, from their faith and religious veneration, introduce theology and traditions; the absurdity of some among them having proceeded so far as to seek and derive the sciences from spirits and genii. There are, therefore, three sources of error and three species of false philosophy; the sophistic, empiric, and superstitious.

63. Aristotle affords the most eminent instance of the first; for he corrupted natural philosophy by logic – thus he formed the world of categories, assigned to the human soul, the noblest of substances, a genus determined by words of secondary operation, treated of density and rarity (by which bodies occupy a greater or lesser space), by the frigid distinctions of action and power, asserted that there was a peculiar and proper motion in all bodies, and that if they shared in any other motion, it was owing to an external moving cause, and imposed innumerable arbitrary distinctions upon the nature of things; being everywhere more anxious as to definitions in teaching and the accuracy of the wording of his propositions, than the internal truth of things. And this is best shown by a comparison of his philosophy with the others of greatest repute among the Greeks. For the similar parts of Anaxagoras, the atoms of Leucippus and Democritus, the heaven and earth of Parmenides, the discord and concord of Empedocles, the resolution of bodies into the common nature of fire, and their condensation according to Heraclitus, exhibit some sprinkling of natural philosophy, the nature of things, and experiment; whilst Aristotle's

physics are mere logical terms, and he remodelled the same subject in his metaphysics under a more imposing title, and more as a realist than a nominalist. Nor is much stress to be laid on his frequent recourse to experiment in his books on animals, his problems, and other treatises; for he had already decided, without having properly consulted experience as the basis of his decisions and axioms, and after having so decided, he drags experiment along as a captive constrained to accommodate herself to his decisions; so that he is even more to be blamed than his modern followers (of the scholastic school) who have deserted her altogether.

64. The empiric school produces dogmas of a more deformed and monstrous nature than the sophistic or theoretic school; not being founded in the light of common notions (which, however poor and superstitious, is yet in a manner universal, and of a general tendency), but in the confined obscurity of a few experiments. Hence this species of philosophy appears probable, and almost certain to those who are daily practised in such experiments, and have thus corrupted their imagination, but incredible and futile to others. We have a strong instance of this in the alchemists and their dogmas; it would be difficult to find another in this age, unless perhaps in the philosophy of Gilbert. We could not, however, neglect to caution others against this school, because we already foresee and argue, that if men be hereafter induced by our exhortations to apply seriously to experiments (bidding farewell to the sophistic doctrines), there will then be imminent danger from empirics, owing to the premature and forward haste of the understanding, and its jumping or flying to generalities and the principles of things. We ought, therefore, already to meet the evil.

65. The corruption of philosophy by the mixing of it up with superstition and theology, is of a much wider extent, and is most injurious to it both as a whole and in parts. For the human understanding is no less exposed to the impressions of fancy, than to those of vulgar notions. The disputatious and sophistic school entraps the understanding, whilst the fanciful, bombastic, and, as it were, poetical school, rather flatters it. There is a clear example of this among the Greeks, especially in Pythagoras, where, however, the superstition is coarse and overcharged, but it is more dangerous and refined in Plato and

his school. This evil is found also in some branches of other systems of philosophy, where it introduces abstracted forms, final and first causes, omitting frequently the intermediate and the like. Against it we must use the greatest caution; for the apotheosis of error is the greatest evil of all, and when folly is worshipped, it is, as it were, a plague spot upon the understanding. Yet some of the moderns have indulged this folly with such consummate inconsiderateness, that they have endeavored to build a system of natural philosophy on the first chapter of Genesis, the book of Job, and other parts of Scripture; seeking thus the dead amongst the living. And this folly is the more to be prevented and restrained, because not only fantastical philosophy, but heretical religion spring from the absurd mixture of matters divine and human. It is therefore most wise soberly to render unto faith the things that are faith's.

66. Having spoken of the vicious authority of the systems founded either on vulgar notions, or on a few experiments, or on superstition, we must now consider the faulty subjects for contemplation, especially in natural philosophy. The human understanding is perverted by observing the power of mechanical arts, in which bodies are very materially changed by composition or separation, and is induced to suppose that something similar takes place in the universal nature of things. Hence the fiction of elements, and their co-operation in forming natural bodies. Again, when man reflects upon the entire liberty of nature, he meets with particular species of things, as animals, plants, minerals, and is thence easily led to imagine that there exist in nature certain primary forms which she strives to produce, and that all variation from them arises from some impediment or error which she is exposed to in completing her work, or from the collision or metamorphosis of different species. The first hypothesis has produced the doctrine of elementary properties, the second that of occult properties and specific powers; and both lead to trifling courses of reflection, in which the mind acquiesces, and is thus diverted from more important subjects. But physicians exercise a much more useful labor in the consideration of the secondary qualities of things, and the operations of attraction, repulsion, attenuation, inspissation, dilation, astringency, separation, maturation, and the like; and would do still more if they would not corrupt these proper observations by the two systems I have alluded to, of elementary qualities and specific powers, by which they either reduce the secondary to first qualities, and their subtile and immeasurable composition, or at any rate neglect to advance by greater and more diligent observation to the third and fourth qualities, thus terminating their contemplation prematurely. Nor are these powers (or the like) to be investigated only among the medicines for the human body, but also in all changes of other natural bodies.

A greater evil arises from the contemplation and investigation rather of the stationary principles of things from which, than of the active by which things themselves are created. For the former only serve for discussion, the latter for practice. Nor is any value to be set on those common differences of motion which are observed in the received system of natural philosophy, as generation, corruption, augmentation, diminution, alteration, and translation. For this is their meaning: if a body, unchanged in other respects, is moved from its place, this is translation; if the places and species be given, but the quantity changed, it is alteration; but, if from such a change, the mass and quantity of the body do not continue the same, this is the motion of augmentation and diminution; if the change be continued so as to vary the species and substance, and transfuse them to others, this is generation and corruption. All this is merely popular, and by no means penetrates into nature; and these are but the measures and bounds of motion, and not different species of it; they merely suggest how far, and not how or whence. For they exhibit neither the affections of bodies nor the process of their parts, but merely establish a division of that motion, which coarsely exhibits to the senses matter in its varied form. Even when they wish to point out something relative to the causes of motion, and to establish a division of them, they most absurdly introduce natural and violent motion, which is also a popular notion, since every violent motion is also in fact natural, that is to say, the external efficient puts nature in action in a different manner to that which she had previously employed.

But if, neglecting these, any one were for instance to observe that there is in bodies a tendency of adhesion, so as not to suffer the unity of nature to be completely separated or broken, and a vacuum to be formed, or that they have a tendency to return to their natural dimensions or tension, so that, if compressed or extended within or beyond it, they immediately strive to recover themselves, and resume their former volume and extent; or that they have a tendency to congregate into masses with similar bodies – the dense, for instance, towards the circumference of the earth, the thin and rare towards that of the heavens. These and the like are true physical genera of motions, but the others are clearly logical and scholastic, as appears plainly from a comparison of the two.

Another considerable evil is, that men in their systems and contemplations bestow their labor upon the investigation and discussion of the principles of things and the extreme limits of nature, although all utility and means of action consist in the intermediate objects. Hence men cease not to abstract nature till they arrive at potential and shapeless matter, and still persist in their dissection, till they arrive at atoms; and yet were all this true, it would be of little use to advance man's estate.

67. The understanding must also be cautioned against the intemperance of systems, so far as regards its giving or withholding its assent; for such intemperance appears to fix and perpetuate idols, so as to leave no means of removing them.

These excesses are of two kinds. The first is seen in those who decide hastily, and render the sciences positive and dictatorial. The other in those who have introduced scepticism, and vague unbounded inquiry. The former subdues, the latter enervates the understanding. The Aristotelian philosophy, after destroying other systems (as the Ottomans do their brethren) by its disputatious confutations, decided upon everything, and Aristotle himself then raises up questions at will, in order to settle them; so that everything should be certain and decided, a method now in use among his successors.

The school of Plato introduced scepticism, first, as it were in joke and irony, from their dislike to Protagoras, Hippias, and others, who were ashamed of appearing not to doubt upon any subject. But the new academy dogmatized in their scepticism, and held it as their tenet. Although this method be more honest than arbitrary decision (for its followers allege that they by no means confound all inquiry, like Pyrrho and his disciples, but hold doctrines which they can

follow as probable, though they cannot maintain them to be true), yet when the human mind has once despaired of discovering truth, everything begins to languish. Hence men turn aside into pleasant controversies and discussions, and into a sort of wandering over subjects rather than sustain any rigorous investigation. But as we observed at first, we are not to deny the authority of the human senses and understanding, although weak, but rather to furnish them with assistance.

68. We have now treated of each kind of idols, and their qualities, all of which must be abjured and renounced with firm and solemn resolution, and the understanding must be completely freed and cleared of them, so that the access to the kingdom of man, which is founded on the sciences, may resemble that to the kingdom of heaven, where no admission is conceded except to children.

[...]

94. We will next give a most potent reason for hope deduced from the errors of the past, and the ways still unattempted; for well was an ill-governed state thus reproved, "That which is worst with regard to the past should appear most consolatory for the future; for if you had done all that your duty commanded, and your affairs proceeded no better, you could not even hope for their improvement; but since their present unhappy situation is not owing to the force of circumstances, but to your own errors, you have reason to hope that by banishing or correcting the latter you can produce a great change for the better in the former." So if men had, during the many years that have elapsed, adhered to the right way of discovering and cultivating the sciences without being able to advance, it would be assuredly bold and presumptuous to imagine it possible to improve; but if they have mistaken the way and wasted their labor on improper objects, it follows that the difficulty does not arise from things themselves, which are not in our power, but from the human understanding, its practice and application, which is susceptible of remedy and correction. Our best plan, therefore, is to expose these errors; for in proportion as they impeded the past, so do they afford reason to hope for the future. And although we have touched upon them above, yet we think it right to give a brief,

bare, and simple enumeration of them in this place.

95.   Those who have treated of the sciences have been either empirics or dogmatical. The former like ants only heap up and use their store, the latter like spiders spin out their own webs. The bee, a mean between both, extracts matter from the flowers of the garden and the field, but works and fashions it by its own efforts. The true labor of philosophy resembles hers, for it neither relies entirely nor principally on the powers of the mind, nor yet lays up in the memory the matter afforded by the experiments of natural history and mechanics in its raw state, but changes and works it in the understanding. We have good reason, therefore, to derive hope from a closer and purer alliance of these faculties (the experimental and rational) than has yet been attempted.

96.   Natural philosophy is not yet to be found unadulterated, but is impure and corrupted – by logic in the school of Aristotle, by natural theology in that of Plato, by mathematics in the second school of Plato (that of Proclus and others) which ought rather to terminate natural philosophy than to generate or create it. We may, therefore, hope for better results from pure and unmixed natural philosophy.

97.   No one has yet been found possessed of sufficient firmness and severity to resolve upon and undertake the task of entirely abolishing common theories and notions, and applying the mind afresh, when thus cleared and leveled, to particular researches; hence our human reasoning is a mere farrago and crude mass made up of a great deal of credulity and accident, and the puerile notions it originally contracted.

But if a man of mature age, unprejudiced senses, and clear mind, would betake himself anew to experience and particulars, we might hope much more from such a one; in which respect we promise ourselves the fortune of Alexander the Great, and let none accuse us of vanity till they have heard the tale, which is intended to check vanity.

For Æschines spoke thus of Alexander and his exploits: "We live not the life of mortals, but are born at such a period that posterity will relate and declare our prodigies;" as if he considered the exploits of Alexander to be miraculous.

But in succeeding ages Livy took a better view of the fact, and has made some such observation as this upon Alexander: "That he did no more than dare to despise insignificance." So in our opinion posterity will judge of us, that we have achieved no great matters, but only set less account upon what is considered important; for the mean time (as we have before observed) our only hope is in the regeneration of the sciences, by regularly raising them on the foundation of experience and building them anew, which I think none can venture to affirm to have been already done or even thought of.

98.   The foundations of experience (our sole resource) have hitherto failed completely or have been very weak; nor has a store and collection of particular facts, capable of informing the mind or in any way satisfactory, been either sought after or amassed. On the contrary, learned, but idle and indolent, men have received some mere reports of experience, traditions as it were of dreams, as establishing or confirming their philosophy, and have not hesitated to allow them the weight of legitimate evidence. So that a system has been pursued in philosophy with regard to experience resembling that of a kingdom or state which would direct its councils and affairs according to the gossip of city and street politicians, instead of the letters and reports of ambassadors and messengers worthy of credit. Nothing is rightly inquired into, or verified, noted, weighed, or measured, in natural history; indefinite and vague observation produces fallacious and uncertain information. If this appear strange, or our complaint somewhat too unjust (because Aristotle himself, so distinguished a man and supported by the wealth of so great a king, has completed an accurate history of animals, to which others with greater diligence but less noise have made considerable additions, and others again have composed copious histories and notices of plants, metals, and fossils), it will arise from a want of sufficiently attending to and comprehending our present observations; for a natural history compiled on its own account, and one collected for the mind's information as a foundation for philosophy, are two different things. They differ in several respects, but principally in this – the former contains only the varieties of natural species without the experiments of mechanical arts; for as in ordinary life every person's disposition, and the concealed feelings of the mind and passions are most drawn out when they are disturbed – so the secrets of nature betray themselves more

readily when tormented by art than when left to their own course. We must begin, therefore, to entertain hopes of natural philosophy then only, when we have a better compilation of natural history, its real basis and support.

99. Again, even in the abundance of mechanical experiments, there is a very great scarcity of those which best inform and assist the understanding. For the mechanic, little solicitous about the investigation of truth, neither directs his attention, nor applies his hand to anything that is not of service to his business. But our hope of further progress in the sciences will then only be well founded, when numerous experiments shall be received and collected into natural history, which, though of no use in themselves, assist materially in the discovery of causes and axioms; which experiments we have termed enlightening, to distinguish them from those which are profitable. They possess this wonderful property and nature, that they never deceive or fail you; for being used only to discover the natural cause of some object, whatever be the result, they equally satisfy your aim by deciding the question.

100. We must not only search for, and procure a greater number of experiments, but also introduce a completely different method, order, and progress of continuing and promoting experience. For vague and arbitrary experience is (as we have observed), mere groping in the dark, and rather astonishes than instructs. But when experience shall proceed regularly and uninterruptedly by a determined rule, we may entertain better hopes of the sciences.

101. But after having collected and prepared an abundance and store of natural history, and of the experience required for the operations of the understanding or philosophy, still the understanding is as incapable of acting on such materials of itself, with the aid of memory alone, as any person would be of retaining and achieving, by memory, the computation of an almanac. Yet meditation has hitherto done more for discovery than writing, and no experiments have been committed to paper. We cannot, however, approve of any mode of discovery without writing, and when that comes into more general use, we may have further hopes.

102. Besides this, there is such a multitude and host, as it were, of particular objects, and lying so widely dispersed, as to distract and confuse the understanding; and we can, therefore, hope for no advantage from its skirmishing, and quick movements and incursions, unless we put its forces in due order and array, by means of proper and well arranged, and, as it were, living tables of discovery of these matters, which are the subject of investigation, and the mind then apply itself to the ready prepared and digested aid which such tables afford.

103. When we have thus properly and regularly placed before the eyes a collection of particulars, we must not immediately proceed to the investigation and discovery of new particulars or effects, or, at least, if we do so, must not rest satisfied therewith. For, though we do not deny that by transferring the experiments from one art to another (when all the experiments of each have been collected and arranged, and have been acquired by the knowledge, and subjected to the judgment of a single individual), many new experiments may be discovered tending to benefit society and mankind, by what we term literate experience; yet comparatively insignificant results are to be expected thence, whilst the more important are to be derived from the new light of axioms, deduced by certain method and rule from the above particulars, and pointing out and defining new particulars in their turn. Our road is not a long plain, but rises and falls, ascending to axioms, and descending to effects.

104. Nor can we suffer the understanding to jump and fly from particulars to remote and most general axioms (such as are termed the principles of arts and things), and thus prove and make out their intermediate axioms according to the supposed unshaken truth of the former. This, however, has always been done to the present time from the natural bent of the understanding, educated too, and accustomed to this very method, by the syllogistic mode of demonstration. But we can then only augur well for the sciences, when the ascent shall proceed by a true scale and successive steps, without interruption or breach, from particulars to the lesser axioms, thence to the intermediate (rising one above the other), and lastly, to the most general. For the lowest axioms differ but little from bare experiments; the highest and most general (as they are esteemed at present), are notional, abstract, and of no real weight. The intermediate are true, solid, full of life, and upon them depend the business and fortune of mankind; beyond these

are the really general, but not abstract, axioms, which are truly limited by the intermediate.

We must not then add wings, but rather lead and ballast to the understanding, to prevent its jumping or flying, which has not yet been done; but whenever this takes place, we may entertain greater hopes of the sciences.

105.   In forming axioms, we must invent a different form of induction from that hitherto in use; not only for the proof and discovery of principles (as they are called), but also of minor, intermediate, and, in short, every kind of axioms. The induction which proceeds by simple enumeration is puerile, leads to uncertain conclusions, and is exposed to danger from one contradictory instance, deciding generally from too small a number of facts, and those only the most obvious. But a really useful induction for the discovery and demonstration of the arts and sciences, should separate nature by proper rejections and exclusions, and then conclude for the affirmative, after collecting a sufficient number of negatives. Now this has not been done, nor even attempted, except perhaps by Plato, who certainly uses this form of induction in some

measure, to sift definitions and ideas. But much of what has never yet entered the thoughts of man must necessarily be employed, in order to exhibit a good and legitimate mode of induction or demonstration, so as even to render it essential for us to bestow more pains upon it than have hitherto been bestowed on syllogisms. The assistance of induction is to serve us not only in the discovery of axioms, but also in defining our notions. Much indeed is to be hoped from such an induction as has been described.

106.   In forming our axioms from induction, we must examine and try whether the axiom we derive be only fitted and calculated for the particular instances from which it is deduced, or whether it be more extensive and general. If it be the latter, we must observe, whether it confirm its own extent and generality by giving surety, as it were, in pointing out new particulars, so that we may neither stop at actual discoveries, nor with a careless grasp catch at shadows and abstract forms, instead of substances of a determinate nature: and as soon as we act thus, well authorized hope may with reason, be said to beam upon us.

René Descartes, *Meditations on First Philosophy*, I–III, and "Objections and Replies" (selections)

Introduction

Renaissance philosophy received its stimulus from the rediscovery, accelerated by the fall of Constantinople in 1453, of long-lost Greek texts, most famously many of Plato's dialogues. But of equal importance for future developments was the re-emergence of works, like Sextus Empiricus's (see II.4 above), chronicling Greek skeptical thought: for, as one historian puts it, with only slight exaggeration, "*modern* philosophy from Descartes to Kant can be seen as [so many] attempts to answer the challenge of modern scepticism, or to live with it."[1] Pre-eminent among those thinkers who wished to answer skepticism was the French philosopher René Descartes (1596–1650), "the father of modern philosophy."

For Descartes, it was imperative to scotch the skeptical temper of his times for at least two reasons. Skepticism, of course, had proven awesomely powerful in its capacity to undermine the scholastic and hermetic thought from which early moderns wished to distinguish their own projects. But once unleashed the beast threatened to turn about and subvert the new philosophies and sci-

From Descartes, *Meditations on First Philosophy (With Selections from the Objections and Replies)*, trans. J. Cottingham, Cambridge: Cambridge University Press, rev. edn 1996, pp. 12–25, 63–70 (notes and latter part of Meditation III omitted).

ences of modernity, as well. Moreover, secondly, not only did skepticism present a threat to acceptance of the fledgling cosmology and physics being developed by Galileo et al.; worse, for Christians, it threatened belief in God and personal immortality. Indeed, skepticism is a formidable adversary, and it is one of the great ironies in the history of ideas that Descartes's strategy for refuting skepticism should have served only to make its challenge seem all the more powerful. In *Meditation* I, he articulates with great clarity and force a radically skeptical stance toward virtually all our received beliefs – in the existence of an external world, in the truths of mathematics, and so on. By general consensus, however, his attempts in Meditation III and elsewhere to recover much of the ground conceded to the skeptic for purely "methodological" reasons are a failure.

The following extract from *Meditations* ends at the point where Descartes stands poised to prove the existence of a non-deceiving God, a proof that is designed to enable us once again to accept many of the beliefs previously surrendered to the skeptic. That proof, however, belongs more in the annals of the philosophy of religion than of epistemology. Appended to our extract from the *Meditations* are some of Descartes's replies to some sharp objections raised against that work by a number of leading philosophers of the day, among others Thomas Hobbes (V.10).

Even in this extract, Descartes's contribution to epistemology is not exhausted by his rehearsal of the skeptics' position and by the famous *cogito* argument, establishing the certainty of his own existence as "a thinking thing" and hence placing a limit on skeptical doubt. For in the discussion in Meditation II of the piece of wax, one finds an important and typically "rationalist" case made out for holding that it is through the intellect, not the senses, that the existence of substances is recognized. More generally, the criterion of knowledge laid down (in Meditation III), though left unelaborated, by Descartes, in terms of the "clearness and distinctness" of our ideas was to become a distinctive tenet of "rationalist" thought.

There has been much debate in recent years about the originality or otherwise of Descartes's position. Certainly he relies, especially in his attempt to prove God's existence, on well-worn (and dubious) principles of scholastic philosophy (such as "what is more perfect cannot be produced by what is less perfect"). Nor is his proof of the existence of the mind as something distinct from anything bodily an original one. A very similar argument known as "the flying (or suspended or floating) man argument" – was produced by the Persian philosopher Ibn Sina (Avicenna, see III.8) in the eleventh century.[2] Nor, to readers of Vedantic thought, is there anything new in the idea that, provisionally at least, we can think of the external

world as a dream or illusion (see III.7). Perhaps, however, Descartes was the first who, for good or ill, articulated in detail and rendered plausible the idea of the mind as something logically self-contained, as an inner arena of thoughts and experiences which can at least be imagined to take place in the absence of an objective order to which, ordinarily, we take them to be related.[3] This "methodological solipsism," with its accompanying problem of how anyone breaks out of his or her private mental enclosure so as to gain knowledge of anything external, was to set the stamp upon philosophical enquiry during the centuries which followed, as several further chapters in this volume will confirm.

Notes

1   R. H. Popkin, "Scepticism and Modernity," in *The Rise of Modern Philosophy*, ed. T. Sorell, Oxford: Clarendon Press, 1993, p. 15.

2   See L. E. Goodman, *Avicenna*, London: Routledge, 1992, pp. 155ff.

3   See John McDowell, "Singular Thought and the Extent of Inner Space," in *Subject Thought and Context*, ed. P. Pettit and J. McDowell, Oxford: Clarendon Press, 1986.

Descartes, *Meditations on First Philosophy*

In which are demonstrated the existence of God and the distinction between the human soul and the body

FIRST MEDITATION: What can be called into doubt Some years ago I was struck by the large number of falsehoods that I had accepted as true in my childhood, and by the highly doubtful nature of the whole edifice that I had subsequently based on them. I realized that it was necessary, once in the course of my life, to demolish everything completely and start again right from the foundations if I wanted to establish anything at all in the sciences that was stable and likely to last. But the task looked an enormous one, and I began to wait until I should reach a

mature enough age to ensure that no subsequent time of life would be more suitable for tackling such inquiries. This led me to put the project off for so long that I would now be to blame if by pondering over it any further I wasted the time still left for carrying it out. So today I have expressly rid my mind of all worries and 18 arranged for myself a clear stretch of free time. I am here quite alone, and at last I will devote myself sincerely and without reservation to the general demolition of my opinions.

But to accomplish this, it will not be necessary for me to show that all my opinions are false, which is something I could perhaps never manage. Reason now leads me to think that I should hold back my assent from opinions which are not completely certain and indubitable just as carefully as I do from those which are patently false. So, for the purpose of rejecting all my opinions, it will be enough if I find in each of them at least some reason for doubt. And to do this I will not need to run through them all individually, which would be an endless task. Once the foundations of a building are undermined, anything built on them collapses of its own accord; so I will go straight for the basic principles on which all my former beliefs rested.

Whatever I have up till now accepted as most true I have acquired either from the senses or through the senses. But from time to time I have found that the senses deceive, and it is prudent never to trust completely those who have deceived us even once.

Yet although the senses occasionally deceive us with respect to objects which are very small or in the distance, there are many other beliefs about which doubt is quite impossible, even though they are derived from the senses – for example, that I am here, sitting by the fire, wearing a winter dressing-gown, holding this piece of paper in my hands, and so on. Again, how could it be denied that these hands or this whole body are 19 mine? Unless perhaps I were to liken myself to madmen, whose brains are so damaged by the persistent vapours of melancholia that they firmly maintain they are kings when they are paupers, or say they are dressed in purple when they are naked, or that their heads are made of earthenware, or that they are pumpkins, or made of glass. But such people are insane, and I would be thought equally mad if I took anything from them as a model for myself.

A brilliant piece of reasoning! As if I were not a man who sleeps at night, and regularly has all the same experiences while asleep as madmen do when awake – indeed sometimes even more improbable ones. How often, asleep at night, am I convinced of just such familiar events – that I am here in my dressing-gown, sitting by the fire – when in fact I am lying undressed in bed! Yet at the moment my eyes are certainly wide awake when I look at this piece of paper; I shake my head and it is not asleep; as I stretch out and feel my hand I do so deliberately, and I know what I am doing. All this would not happen with such distinctness to someone asleep. Indeed! As if I did not remember other occasions when I have been tricked by exactly similar thoughts while asleep! As I think about this more carefully, I see plainly that there are never any sure signs by means of which being awake can be distinguished from being asleep. The result is that I begin to feel dazed,

and this very feeling only reinforces the notion that I may be asleep.

Suppose then that I am dreaming, and that these particulars – that my eyes are open, that I am moving my head and stretching out my hands – are not true. Perhaps, indeed, I do not even have such hands or such a body at all. Nonetheless, it must surely be admitted that the visions which come in sleep are like paintings, which must have been fashioned in the likeness of things that are real, and hence that at least these general kinds of things – eyes, head, hands and the body 20 as a whole – are things which are not imaginary but are real and exist. For even when painters try to create sirens and satyrs with the most extraordinary bodies, they cannot give them natures which are new in all respects; they simply jumble up the limbs of different animals. Or if perhaps they manage to think up something so new that nothing remotely similar has ever been seen before – something which is therefore completely fictitious and unreal – at least the colours used in the composition must be real. By similar reasoning, although these general kinds of things – eyes, head, hands and so on – could be imaginary, it must at least be admitted that certain other even simpler and more universal things are real. These are as it were the real colours from which we form all the images of things, whether true or false, that occur in our thought.

This class appears to include corporeal nature in general, and its extension; the shape of extended things; the quantity, or size and number of these things; the place in which they may exist, the time through which they may endure, and so on.

So a reasonable conclusion from this might be that physics, astronomy, medicine, and all other disciplines which depend on the study of composite things, are doubtful; while arithmetic, geometry and other subjects of this kind, which deal only with the simplest and most general things, regardless of whether they really exist in nature or not, contain something certain and indubitable. For whether I am awake or asleep, two and three added together are five, and a square has no more than four sides. It seems impossible that such transparent truths should incur any suspicion of being false.

And yet firmly rooted in my mind is the long- 21 standing opinion that there is an omnipotent God who made me the kind of creature that I am. How do I know that he has not brought it about that there is no earth, no sky, no extended thing, no shape, no size, no place, while at the same time ensuring that all these things appear to me to exist just as they do now? What is more, just as I consider that others sometimes go astray in cases where they think they have the most perfect knowledge, how do I know that God has not brought it about that I too go wrong every time I add two and three or count the sides of a square, or in some even simpler matter, if that is imaginable? But perhaps God would not have allowed me to be deceived in this way, since he is said to be supremely good. But if it were inconsistent with his goodness to have created me such that I am deceived all the time, it would seem equally foreign to his goodness to allow me to be deceived even occasionally; yet this last assertion cannot be made.

Perhaps there may be some who would prefer to deny the existence of so powerful a God rather than believe that everything else is uncertain. Let us not argue with them, but grant them that everything said about God is a fiction. According to their supposition, then, I have arrived at my present state by fate or chance or a continuous chain of events, or by some other means; yet since deception and error seem to be imperfections, the less powerful they make my original cause, the more likely it is that I am so imperfect as to be deceived all the time. I have no answer to these arguments, but am finally compelled to admit that there is not one of my former beliefs about which a doubt may not properly be raised; and this is not a flippant or ill-considered 22 conclusion, but is based on powerful and well thought-out reasons. So in future I must withhold my assent from these former beliefs just as carefully as I would from obvious falsehoods, if I want to discover any certainty.

But it is not enough merely to have noticed this; I must make an effort to remember it. My habitual opinions keep coming back, and, despite my wishes, they capture my belief, which is as it were bound over to them as a result of long occupation and the law of custom. I shall never get out of the habit of confidently assenting to these opinions, so long as I suppose them to be what in fact they are, namely highly probable opinions – opinions which, despite the fact that they are in a sense doubtful, as has just been shown, it is still much more reasonable to believe than to deny. In view of this, I think it will be a good plan to

turn my will in completely the opposite direction and deceive myself, by pretending for a time that these former opinions are utterly false and imaginary. I shall do this until the weight of pre-conceived opinion is counter-balanced and the distorting influence of habit no longer prevents my judgement from perceiving things correctly. In the meantime, I know that no danger or error will result from my plan, and that I cannot possibly go too far in my distrustful attitude. This is because the task now in hand does not involve action but merely the acquisition of knowledge.

I will suppose therefore that not God, who is supremely good and the source of truth, but rather some malicious demon of the utmost power and cunning has employed all his energies in order to deceive me. I shall think that the sky, the air, the earth, colours, shapes, sounds and all external things are merely the delusions of dreams which he has devised to ensnare my judgement. I shall 23 consider myself as not having hands or eyes, or flesh, or blood or senses, but as falsely believing that I have all these things. I shall stubbornly and firmly persist in this meditation; and, even if it is not in my power to know any truth, I shall at least do what is in my power, that is, resolutely guard against assenting to any falsehoods, so that the deceiver, however powerful and cunning he may be, will be unable to impose on me in the slightest degree. But this is an arduous undertaking, and a kind of laziness brings me back to normal life. I am like a prisoner who is enjoying an imaginary freedom while asleep; as he begins to suspect that he is asleep, he dreads being woken up, and goes along with the pleasant illusion as long as he can. In the same way, I happily slide back into my old opinions and dread being shaken out of them, for fear that my peaceful sleep may be followed by hard labour when I wake, and that I shall have to toil not in the light, but amid the inextricable darkness of the problems I have now raised.

SECOND MEDITATION: The nature of the human mind, and how it is better known than the body So serious are the doubts into which I have been thrown as a result of yesterday's meditation that I can neither put them out of my mind nor see any way of resolving them. It 24 feels as if I have fallen unexpectedly into a deep whirlpool which tumbles me around so that I can neither stand on the bottom nor swim up to the top. Nevertheless I will make an effort and once more attempt the same path which I started on yesterday. Anything which admits of the slightest doubt I will set aside just as if I had found it to be wholly false; and I will proceed in this way until I recognize something certain, or, if nothing else, until I at least recognize for certain that there is no certainty. Archimedes used to demand just one firm and immovable point in order to shift the entire earth; so I too can hope for great things if I manage to find just one thing, however slight, that is certain and unshakeable.

I will suppose then, that everything I see is spurious. I will believe that my memory tells me lies, and that none of the things that it reports ever happened. I have no senses. Body, shape, extension, movement and place are chimeras. So what remains true? Perhaps just the one fact that nothing is certain.

Yet apart from, everything I have just listed, how do I know that there is not something else which does not allow even the slightest occasion for doubt? Is there not a God, or whatever I may call him, who puts into me the thoughts I am now having? But why do I think this, since I myself may perhaps be the author of these thoughts? In that case am not I, at least, something? But I have just said that I have no senses and no body. This 25 is the sticking point: what follows from this? Am I not so bound up with a body and with senses that I cannot exist without them? But I have convinced myself that there is absolutely nothing in the world, no sky, no earth, no minds, no bodies. Does it now follow that I too do not exist? No: if I convinced myself of something then I certainly existed. But there is a deceiver of supreme power and cunning who is deliberately and constantly deceiving me. In that case I too undoubtedly exist, if he is deceiving me; and let him deceive me as much as he can, he will never bring it about that I am nothing so long as I think that I am something. So after considering everything very thoroughly, I must finally conclude that this proposition, *I am, I exist,* is necessarily true whenever it is put forward by me or conceived in my mind.[1]

But I do not yet have a sufficient understanding of what this 'I' is, that now necessarily exists. So I must be on my guard against carelessly taking something else to be this 'I', and so making a mistake in the very item of knowledge that I maintain is the most certain and evident of all. I will therefore go back and meditate on what I originally believed myself to be, before I embarked on this present train of thought. I will then subtract anything capable of being weakened, even minimally, by the arguments now introduced, so that what is left at the end may be exactly and only what is certain and unshakeable.

What then did I formerly think I was? A man. But what is a man? Shall I say 'a rational animal'? No; for then I should have to inquire what an animal is, what rationality is, and in this way one question would lead me down the slope to other harder ones, and I do not now have the time to waste on subtleties of this kind. Instead I propose to concentrate on what came into my thoughts spontaneously and quite naturally whenever 26 I used to consider what I was. Well, the first thought to come to mind was that I had a face, hands, arms and the whole mechanical structure of limbs which can be seen in a corpse, and which I called the body. The next thought was that I was nourished, that I moved about, and that I engaged in sense-perception and thinking; and these actions I attributed to the soul. But as to the nature of this soul, either I did not think about this or else I imagined it to be something tenuous, like a wind or fire or ether, which permeated my more solid parts. As to the body, however, I had no doubts about it, but thought I knew its nature distinctly. If I had tried to describe the mental conception I had of it, I would have expressed it as follows: by a body I understand whatever has a determinable shape and a definable location and can occupy a space in such a way as to exclude any other body; it can be perceived by touch, sight, hearing, taste or smell, and can be moved in various ways, not by itself but by whatever else comes into contact with it. For, according to my judgement, the power of self-movement, like the power of sensation or of thought, was quite foreign to the nature of a body; indeed, it was a source of wonder to me that certain bodies were found to contain faculties of this kind.

But what shall I now say that I am, when I am supposing that there is some supremely powerful and, if it is permissible to say so, malicious deceiver, who is deliberately trying to trick me in every way he can? Can I now assert that I possess even the most insignificant of all the attributes which I have just said belong to the nature of a 27 body? I scrutinize them, think about them, go over them again, but nothing suggests itself; it is tiresome and pointless to go through the list once more. But what about the attributes I assigned to the soul? Nutrition or movement? Since now I do not have a body, these are mere fabrications. Sense-perception? This surely does not occur without a body, and besides, when asleep I have appeared to perceive through the senses many things which I afterwards realized I did not perceive through the senses at all. Thinking? At last I have discovered it – thought; this alone is inseparable from me. I am, I exist – that is certain. But for how long? For as long as I am thinking. For it could be that were I totally to cease from thinking, I should totally cease to exist. At present I am not admitting anything except what is necessarily true. I am, then, in the strict sense only a thing that thinks; that is, I am a mind, or intelligence, or intellect, or reason – words whose meaning I have been ignorant of until now. But for all that I am a thing which is real and which truly exists. But what kind of a thing? As I have just said – a thinking thing.

What else am I? I will use my imagination. I am not that structure of limbs which is called a human body. I am not even some thin vapour which permeates the limbs – a wind, fire, air, breath, or whatever I depict in my imagination; for these are things which I have supposed to be nothing. Let this supposition stand; for all that I am still something. And yet may it not perhaps be the case that these very things which I am supposing to be nothing, because they are unknown to me, are in reality identical with the 'I' of which I am aware? I do not know, and for the moment I shall not argue the point, since I can make judgements only about things which are known to me. I know that I exist; the question is, what is this 'I' that I know? If the 'I' is understood strictly as we have been taking it, then it is quite certain that knowledge of it does not depend on things of whose existence I am as yet unaware; so it cannot depend on any of the things which I invent in my imagination. And this very word 'invent' shows me my mistake. It would indeed be a case of fictitious invention if I used my imagination to establish that I was something or other; for imagining is simply contemplating the shape or image of a corporeal thing. Yet now I know for certain both that I exist and at the same time that all such images and, in general, everything relating to the nature of body, could be mere dreams <and chimeras>. Once this point has been grasped, to say 'I will use my imagination to get to know more distinctly what I am' would seem to be as silly as saying 'I am now awake, and see some truth; but since my vision is not yet clear enough, I will deliberately fall asleep so that my dreams may provide a truer and clearer representation.' I thus realize that none of the things that the imagination enables me to grasp is at all relevant to this knowledge of myself which I possess, and that the mind must therefore be most carefully diverted from such things if it is to perceive its own nature as distinctly as possible.

But what then am I? A thing that thinks. What is that? A thing that doubts, understands, affirms, denies, is willing, is unwilling, and also imagines and has sensory perceptions.

This is a considerable list, if everything on it belongs to me. But does it? Is it not one and the same 'I' who is now doubting almost everything, who nonetheless understands some things, who affirms that this one thing is true, denies everything else, desires to know more, is unwilling to be deceived, imagines many things even involuntarily, and is aware of many things which apparently come from the senses? Are not all these things just as true as the fact that I exist, even if I am asleep all the time, and even if he who created me is doing all he can to deceive me? Which of all these activities is distinct from my thinking? Which of them can be said to be separate from myself? The fact that it is I who am doubting and understanding and willing is so evident that I see no way of making it any clearer. But it is also the case that the 'I' who imagines is the same 'I'. For even if, as I have supposed, none of the objects of imagination are real, the power of imagination is something which really exists and is part of my thinking. Lastly, it is also the same 'I' who has sensory perceptions, or is aware of bodily things as it were through the senses. For example, I am now seeing light, hearing a noise, feeling heat. But I am asleep, so all this is false. Yet I certainly *seem* to see, to hear, and to be warmed. This cannot be false; what is called 'having a sensory perception' is strictly just this, and in this restricted sense of the term it is simply thinking.

From all this I am beginning to have a rather better understanding of what I am. But it still appears – and I cannot stop thinking this – that the corporeal things of which images are formed in my thought, and which the senses investigate, are known with much more distinctness than this puzzling 'I' which cannot be pictured in the imagination. And yet it is surely surprising that I should have a more distinct grasp of things which I realize are doubtful, unknown and foreign to me, than I have of that which is true and known – my own self. But I see what it is: my mind enjoys wandering off and will not yet submit to being restrained within the bounds of truth. Very well then; just this once let us give it a completely free rein, so that after a while, when it is time to tighten the reins, it may more readily submit to being curbed.

Let us consider the things which people commonly think they understand most distinctly of all; that is, the bodies which we touch and see. I do not mean bodies in general – for general perceptions are apt to be somewhat more confused – but one particular body. Let us take, for example, this piece of wax. It has just been taken from the honeycomb; it has not yet quite lost the taste of the honey; it retains some of the scent of the flowers from which it was gathered; its colour, shape and size are plain to see; it is hard, cold and can be handled without difficulty; if you rap it with your knuckle it makes a sound. In short, it has everything which appears necessary to enable a body to be known as distinctly as possible. But even as I speak, I put the wax by the fire, and look: the residual taste is eliminated, the smell goes away, the colour changes, the shape is lost, the size increases; it becomes liquid and hot; you can hardly touch it, and if you strike it, it no longer makes a sound. But does the same wax remain? It must be admitted that it does; no one denies it, no one thinks otherwise. So what was it in the wax that I understood with such distinctness? Evidently none of the features which I arrived at by means of the senses; for whatever came under taste, smell, sight, touch or hearing has now altered – yet the wax remains.

Perhaps the answer lies in the thought which now comes to my mind; namely, the wax was not after all the sweetness of the honey, or the fragrance of the flowers, or the whiteness, or the shape, or the sound, but was rather a body which presented itself to me in these various forms a little while ago, but which now exhibits different ones. But what exactly is it that I am now imagining? Let us concentrate, take away everything which does not belong to the wax, and see what is left: merely something extended, flexible and changeable. But what is meant here by 'flexible' and 'changeable'? Is it what I picture in my imagination: that this piece of wax is capable of changing from a round shape to a square shape, or from a square shape to a triangular shape? Not at all; for I can grasp that the wax is capable of countless changes of this kind, yet I am unable to run through this immeasurable number of changes in my imagination, from which it follows that it is not the faculty of imagination that gives me my grasp of the wax as flexible and changeable. And what is meant by 'extended'? Is the extension of the wax also unknown? For it increases if the wax melts, increases again if it boils, and is greater still if the heat is increased. I would not be making a correct judgement about the nature of wax unless I believed it capable of being extended in many more different ways than I will ever encompass in my imagination. I must therefore admit that the nature of this piece of wax is in no way revealed by my imagination, but is perceived by the mind alone. (I am speaking of this particular piece of wax; the point is even clearer with regard to wax in general.) But what is this wax which is perceived by the mind alone? It is of course the same wax which I see, which I touch, which I picture in my imagination, in short the same wax which I thought it to be from the start. And yet, and here is the point, the perception I have of it is a case not of vision or touch or imagination – nor has it ever been, despite previous appearances – but of purely mental scrutiny; and this can be imperfect and confused, as it was before, or clear and distinct as it is now, depending on how carefully I concentrate on what the wax consists in.

But as I reach this conclusion I am amazed at how <weak and> prone to error my mind is. For although I am thinking about these matters within myself, silently and without speaking, nonetheless the actual words bring me up short, and I am almost tricked by ordinary ways of talking. We say that we see the wax itself, if it is there before us, not that we judge it to be there from its colour or shape; and this might lead me to conclude without more ado that knowledge of the wax comes from what the eye sees, and not from the scrutiny of the mind alone. But then if I look out of the window and see men crossing the square, as I just happen to have done, I normally say that I see the men themselves, just as I say that I see the wax. Yet do I see any more than hats and coats which could conceal automatons? I *judge* that they are men. And so something which I thought I was seeing with my eyes is in fact grasped solely by the faculty of judgement which is in my mind.

However, one who wants to achieve knowledge above the ordinary level should feel ashamed at having taken ordinary ways of talking as a basis for doubt. So let us proceed, and consider on which occasion my perception of the nature of the wax was more perfect and evident. Was it when I first looked at it, and believed I knew it by my external senses, or at least by what they call the 'common' sense – that is, the power of imagination? Or is my knowledge more perfect now, after a more careful investigation of the nature of the wax and of the means by which it is known? Any doubt on this issue would clearly be foolish; for what distinctness was there in my earlier perception? Was there anything in it which an animal could not possess? But when I distinguish the wax from its outward forms – take the clothes off, as it were, and consider it naked – then although my judgement may still contain errors, at least my perception now requires a human mind.

33   But what am I to say about this mind, or about myself? (So far, remember, I am not admitting that there is anything else in me except a mind.) What, I ask, is this 'I' which seems to perceive the wax so distinctly? Surely my awareness of my own self is not merely much truer and more certain than my awareness of the wax, but also much more distinct and evident. For if I judge that the wax exists from the fact that I see it, clearly this same fact entails much more evidently that I myself also exist. It is possible that what I see is not really the wax; it is possible that I do not even have eyes with which to see anything. But when I see, or think I see (I am not here distinguishing the two), it is simply not possible that I who am now thinking am not something. By the same token, if I judge that the wax exists from the fact that I touch it, the same result follows, namely that I exist. If I judge that it exists from the fact that I imagine it, or for any other reason, exactly the same thing follows. And the result that I have grasped in the case of the wax may be applied to everything else located outside me.

Moreover, if my perception of the wax seemed more distinct after it was established not just by sight or touch but by many other considerations, it must be admitted that I now know myself even more distinctly. This is because every consideration whatsoever which contributes to my perception of the wax, or of any other body, cannot but establish even more effectively the nature of my own mind. But besides this, there is so much else in the mind itself which can serve to make my knowledge of it more distinct, that it scarcely seems worth going through the contributions made by considering bodily things.

I see that without any effort I have now finally   34 got back to where I wanted. I now know that even bodies are not strictly perceived by the senses or the faculty of imagination but by the intellect alone, and that this perception derives not from their being touched or seen but from their being understood; and in view of this I know plainly that I can achieve an easier and more evident perception of my own mind than of anything else. But since the habit of holding on to old opinions cannot be set aside so quickly, I should like to stop here and meditate for some time on this new knowledge I have gained, so as to fix it more deeply in my memory.

THIRD MEDITATION: The existence of God   I will now shut my eyes, stop my ears, and withdraw all my senses. I will eliminate from my thoughts all images of bodily things, or rather, since this is hardly possible, I will regard all such images as vacuous, false and worthless. I will converse with myself and scrutinize myself more deeply; and in this way I will attempt to achieve, little by little, a more intimate knowledge of myself. I am a thing that thinks: that is, a thing that doubts, affirms, denies, understands a few things, is ignorant of many things, is willing, is unwilling, and also which imagines and has sensory perceptions; for as I have noted before, even though the objects of my sensory experience and imagination may have no existence outside me, nonetheless the modes of thinking which I refer to as cases of sensory perception and imagination, in so far as   35 they are simply modes of thinking, do exist within me – of that I am certain.

In this brief list I have gone through everything I truly know, or at least everything I have so far discovered that I know. Now I will cast around more carefully to see whether there may be other things within me which I have not yet noticed. I am certain that I am a thinking thing. Do I not therefore also know what is required for my being certain about anything? In this first item of knowledge there is simply a clear and distinct perception of what I am asserting; this would not be enough to make me certain of the truth of the matter if it could ever turn out that something which I perceived with such clarity and distinctness was false. So I now seem to be able to lay it down as a general rule that whatever I perceive very clearly and distinctly is true.

Yet I previously accepted as wholly certain and evident many things which I afterwards realized were doubtful. What were these? The earth, sky, stars, and everything else that I apprehended with the senses. But what was it about them that I perceived clearly? Just that the ideas, or thoughts, of such things appeared before my mind. Yet even now I am not denying that these ideas occur within me. But there was something else which I used to assert, and which through habitual belief I thought I perceived clearly, although I did not in fact do so. This was that there were things outside me which were the sources of my ideas and which resembled them in all respects. Here was my mistake; or at any rate, if my judgement was true, it was not thanks to the strength of my perception.

36 But what about when I was considering something very simple and straightforward in arithmetic or geometry, for example that two and three added together make five, and so on? Did I not see at least these things clearly enough to affirm their truth? Indeed, the only reason for my later judgement that they were open to doubt was that it occurred to me that perhaps some God could have given me a nature such that I was deceived even in matters which seemed most evident. But whenever my preconceived belief in the supreme power of God comes to mind, I cannot but admit that it would be easy for him, if he so desired, to bring it about that I go wrong even in those matters which I think I see utterly clearly with my mind's eye. Yet when I turn to the things themselves which I think I perceive very clearly, I am so convinced by them that I spontaneously declare: let whoever can do so deceive me, he will never bring it about that I am nothing, so long as I continue to think I am something; or make it true at some future time that I have never existed, since it is now true that I exist; or

bring it about that two and three added together are more or less than five, or anything of this kind in which I see a manifest contradiction. And since I have no cause to think that there is a deceiving God, and I do not yet even know for sure whether there is a God at all, any reason for doubt which depends simply on this supposition is a very slight and, so to speak, metaphysical one. But in order to remove even this slight reason for doubt, as soon as the opportunity arises I must examine whether there is a God, and, if there is, whether he can be a deceiver. For if I do not know this, it seems that I can never be quite certain about anything else.[2]

Descartes, "Objections and Replies" [Selections]

[On Meditation One]

[The rejection of previous beliefs] Here I shall employ an everyday example to explain to my critic 481 the rationale for my procedure, so as to prevent him misunderstanding it, or having the gall to pretend he does not understand it, in future. Suppose he had a basket full of apples and, being worried that some of the apples were rotten, wanted to take out the rotten ones to prevent the rot spreading. How would he proceed? Would he not begin by tipping the whole lot out of the basket? And would not the next step be to cast his eye over each apple in turn, and pick up and put back in the basket only those he saw to be sound, leaving the others? In just the same way, those who have never philosophized correctly have various opinions in their minds which they have begun to store up since childhood, and which they therefore have reason to believe may in many cases be false. They then attempt to separate the false beliefs from the others, so as to prevent their contaminating the rest and making the whole lot uncertain. Now the best way they can accomplish this is to reject all their beliefs together in one go, as if they were all uncertain and false. They can then go over each belief in turn and re-adopt only those which they recognize to be true and indubitable. Thus I was right to begin by rejecting all my beliefs.

[Seventh Replies]

[The reliability of the senses] Although there is deception or falsity, it is not to be found in the senses; for the senses are quite passive and report only appearances, which must appear in the way they do owing to their causes. The error or falsity is in the judgement or the mind, which is not circumspect enough and does not notice that things at a distance will for one reason or another appear smaller and more blurred than when they are nearby, and so on. Nevertheless, when deception occurs, we must not deny that it exists; the only difficulty is whether it occurs all the time, thus making it impossible for us ever to be sure of the truth of anything which we perceive by the senses.

333   It is quite unnecessary to look for obvious examples here. With regard to the cases you mention, or rather put forward as presenting a problem, I will simply say that it seems to be quite uncontroversial that when we look at a tower from nearby, and touch it, we are sure that it is square, even though when we were further off we had occasion to judge it to be round, or at any rate to doubt whether it was square or round or some other shape.

Similarly the feeling of pain which still appears to occur in the foot or hand after these limbs have been amputated may sometimes give rise to deception, because the spirits responsible for sensation have been accustomed to pass into the limbs and produced a sensation in them. But such deception occurs, of course, in people who have suffered amputation; those whose bodies are intact are so certain that they feel pain in the foot or hand when they see it is pricked, that they cannot be in doubt.

Again, since during our lives we are alternately awake or dreaming, a dream may give rise to deception because things may appear to be present when they are not in fact present. But we do not dream all the time, and for as long as we are really awake we cannot doubt whether we are awake or dreaming.   *[Fifth Objections]*

Here you show quite clearly that you are relying entirely on a preconceived opinion which you have never got rid of. You maintain that we never suspect any falsity in situations where we have never detected it, and hence that when we look at a tower from nearby and touch it we are sure that it is square, if it appears square. You also main-

386 tain that when we are really awake, we cannot

doubt whether we are awake or asleep, and so on. But you have no reason to think that you have previously noticed all the circumstances in which error can occur; moreover, it is easy to prove that you are from time to time mistaken in matters which you accept as certain.

[Fifth Replies]

* * *

Our *ninth* and most worrying difficulty is your (418) assertion that we ought to mistrust the operations of the senses and that the reliability of the intellect is much greater than that of the senses. But how can the intellect enjoy any certainty unless it has previously derived it from the senses when they are working as they should? How can it correct a mistake made by one of the senses unless some other sense first corrects the mistake? Owing to refraction, a stick which is in fact straight appears bent in water. What corrects the error? The intellect? Not at all; it is the sense of touch. And the same sort of thing must be taken to occur in other cases. Hence if you have recourse to all your senses when they are in good working order, and they all give the same report, you will achieve the greatest certainty of which man is naturally capable. But you will often fail to achieve it if you trust the operations of the mind; for the mind often goes astray in just those areas where it had previously supposed doubt to be impossible.   *[Sixth Objections]*

When people say that a stick in water 'appears bent because of refraction', this is the same as saying that it appears to us in a way which would lead a child to judge that it was bent – and which may even lead us to make the same judgement, 439 following the preconceived opinions which we have become accustomed to accept from our earliest years. But I cannot grant my critics' further comment that this error is corrected 'not by the intellect but by the sense of touch'. As a result of touching it, we may judge that the stick is straight, and the kind of judgement involved may be the kind we have been accustomed to make since childhood, and which is therefore referred to as the 'sense' of touch. But the sense alone does not suffice to correct the visual error: in addition we need to have some degree of reason which tells us that in this case we should believe the judgement based on touch rather than that elicited by vision. And since we did not have this power of reasoning in our infancy, it must be attributed not to the senses but to the intellect. Thus even in the very example my critics produce, it is the intellect alone which corrects the error of the senses; and it is not possible to produce any case in which error results from our trusting the operation of the mind more than the senses.

[*Sixth Replies*]

[*Certainty in dreams*]   Has it never happened to you, as it has to many people, that things seemed clear and certain to you while you were dreaming, but that afterwards you discovered that they were doubtful or false? It is indeed 'prudent
457 never to trust completely those who have deceived you even once'. 'But', you reply, 'matters of the utmost certainty are quite different. They are such that they cannot appear doubtful even to those who are dreaming or mad.' But are you really serious in what you say? Can you pretend that matters of the utmost certainty cannot appear doubtful even to dreamers or madmen? What are these utterly certain matters? If things which are ridiculous or absurd sometimes appear certain, even utterly certain, to people who are asleep or insane, then why should not things which are certain, even utterly certain, appear false and doubtful? I know a man who once, when falling asleep, heard the clock strike four, and counted the strokes as 'one, one, one, one'. It then seemed to him that there was something absurd about this, and he shouted out: 'That clock must be going mad; it has struck one o'clock four times!' Is there really anything so absurd or irrational that it could not come into the mind of someone who is asleep or raving? There are no limits to what a dreamer may not 'prove' or believe, and indeed congratulate himself on, as if he had managed to invent some splendid thought.

[*Seventh Objections*]

Everything that anyone clearly and distinctly perceives is true, although the person in question may from time to time doubt whether he is dreaming or awake, and may even, if you like, be dreaming or mad. For no matter who the perceived is, nothing can be clearly and distinctly perceived without its being just as we perceive it to be, i.e. without being true. But because it requires some care to make a proper distinction between what is clearly and distinctly perceived and what

merely seems or appears to be, I am not surprised that my worthy critic should here mistake the one for the other.					[*Seventh Replies*]

[ON MEDITATION TWO]

[*Cogito ergo sum ('I am thinking, therefore I exist')*]   You conclude that this proposition, *I am, I exist,* is true whenever it is put forward by you or conceived in your mind. But I do not see that 259 you needed all this apparatus, when on other grounds you were certain, and it was true, that you existed. You could have made the same inference from any one of your other actions, since it is known by the natural light that whatever acts exists.

[*Fifth Objections*]

When you say that I 'could have made the same (352) inference from any one of my other actions' you are far from the truth, since I am not wholly certain of any of my actions, with the sole exception of thought (in using the word 'certain' I am referring to metaphysical certainty, which is the sole issue at this point). I may not, for example, make the inference 'I am walking, therefore I exist', except in so far as the awareness of walking is a thought. The inference is certain only if applied to this awareness, and not to the movement of the body which sometimes – in the case of dreams – is not occurring at all, despite the fact that I seem to myself to be walking. Hence from the fact that I think I am walking I can very well infer the existence of a mind which has this thought, but not the existence of a body that walks. And the same applies in other cases.

[*Fifth Replies*]

*   *   *

When someone says 'I am thinking, therefore I am, or I exist', he does not deduce existence from thought by means of a syllogism, but recognizes it as something self-evident by a simple intuition of the mind. This is clear from the fact that if he were deducing it by means of a syllogism, he would have to have had previous knowledge of the major premiss 'Everything which thinks is, or exists'; yet in fact he learns it from experiencing in his own case that it is impossible that he 141 should think without existing.[3] It is in the nature of our mind to construct general propositions on the basis of our knowledge of particular ones.   [*Second Replies*]

* * *

413 From the fact that we are thinking it does not seem to be entirely certain that we exist. For in order to be certain that you are thinking you must know what thought or thinking is, and what your existence is; but since you do not yet know what these things are, how can you know that you are thinking or that you exist? Thus neither when you say 'I am thinking' nor when you add 'therefore, I exist' do you really know what you are saying. Indeed, you do not even know that you are saying or thinking anything, since this seems to require that you should know that you know what you are saying; and this in turn requires that you be aware of knowing that you know what you are saying, and so on *ad infinitum*. Hence it is clear that you cannot know whether you exist or even whether you are thinking.   [*Sixth Objections*]

(422) It is true that no one can be certain that he is thinking or that he exists unless he knows what thought is and what existence is. But this does not require reflective knowledge, or the kind of knowledge that is acquired by means of demonstrations; still less does it require knowledge of reflective knowledge, i.e. knowing that we know, and knowing that we know that we know, and so on *ad infinitum*. This kind of knowledge cannot possibly be obtained about anything. It is quite sufficient that we should know it by that internal awareness which always precedes reflective knowledge. This inner awareness of one's thought and existence is so innate in all men that, although we may pretend that we do not have it if we are overwhelmed by preconceived opinions and pay more attention to words than to their meanings, we cannot in fact fail to have it. Thus when anyone notices that he is thinking and that it follows from this that he exists, even though he may never before have asked what thought is or what existence is, he still cannot fail to have sufficient knowledge of them both to satisfy himself in this regard.   [*Sixth Replies*]

[Sum res cogitans ('I am a thinking thing')]
Correct. For from the fact that I think, or have an image (whether I am awake or dreaming), it can be inferred that I am thinking; for 'I think'

and 'I am thinking' mean the same thing. And from the fact that I am thinking it follows that I exist, since that which thinks is not nothing. But when the author adds 'that is, I am a mind, or intelligence, or intellect or reason', a doubt arises. It does not seem to be a valid argument to say 'I am thinking, therefore I am thought' or 'I am using my intellect, hence I am an intellect.' I might just as well say 'I am walking, therefore I am a walk.' M. Descartes is identifying the thing which understands with intellection, which is an act of that which understands. Or at least he is identifying the thing which understands with the intellect, which is a power of that which understands. Yet all philosophers make a distinction between a subject and its faculties and acts, i.e. between a 173 subject and its properties and its essences: an entity is one thing, its essence is another. Hence it may be that the thing that thinks is the subject to which mind, reason or intellect belong; and this subject may thus be something corporeal. The contrary is assumed, not proved. Yet this inference is the basis of the conclusion which M. Descartes seems to want to establish.[4] [*Third Objections*]

When I said 'that is, I am a mind, or intelligence, (174) or intellect or reason', what I meant by these terms was not mere faculties, but things endowed with the faculty of thought. This is what the first two terms are commonly taken to mean by everyone; and the second two are often understood in this sense. I stated this point so explicitly, and in so many places, that it seems to me there was no room for doubt.

There is no comparison here between 'a walk' and 'thought'. 'A walk' is usually taken to refer simply to the act of walking, whereas 'thought' is sometimes taken to refer to the act, sometimes to the faculty, and sometimes to the thing which possesses the faculty.

I do not say that the thing which understands is the same as intellection. Nor, indeed, do I identify the thing which understands with the intellect, if 'the intellect' is taken to refer to a faculty; they are identical only if 'the intellect' is taken to refer to the thing which understands. Now I freely admit that I used the most abstract terms I could in order to refer to the thing or substance in question, because I wanted to strip away from it everything that did not belong to it. This philosopher, by contrast, uses absolutely concrete words, namely 'subject', 'matter' and 'body', to refer to this thinking thing, because he wants to prevent its being separated from the body.

[*Third Replies*]

Notes

1 Or "*cogito ergo sum*" – "I am thinking, therefore I exist" – as Descartes more famously put it in his *Principles of Philosophy* I.7.

2 The previous paragraphs may give the impression that Descartes intends, having established God's existence, to reinstate nearly all our familiar conceptions. In fact, Descartes never fully reverts to "common sense." Notably, he follows Galileo in denying that our perception of colors and other "secondary qualities" resembles anything in the objective world.

3 This important reply shows that "*cogito ergo sum*" is not to be read as a standard inference. How the *cogito* argument should be interpreted remains a matter of dispute.

4 This crucial objection challenges Descartes's move from "I am a thing that thinks" to the conclusion that the "I" is distinct from the body. Readers may feel that Descartes's reply evades the challenge.

9

(A) John Locke, *An Essay Concerning Human Understanding*, Book I, Chapter II, Sections 1–24
(B) Gottfried Wilhelm von Leibniz, *New Essays on the Human Understanding*, "Preface"

Introduction

Descartes's argument for the existence of God requires the premiss that our idea of God is not an acquired one, but innate – an idea, in fact, that God Himself must have implanted in our minds. In appealing to what we innately know, Descartes was recalling a tradition that goes back to Plato who, in his *Meno*, argued that a boy's recognition of geometrical truths presupposes a pre-natal knowledge of mathematical principles. (Aristotle, we saw in II.2 above, also allows that we know things innately, at least in one sense.) By the time John Locke (1632–1704) launched his famous attack on innate ideas, Cartesians, the Cambridge Platonists and others were busily postulating any number of innate principles – moral and religious ones, as well as those of logic and mathematics.[1] Because of this, it was this part of Locke's *Essay* that quickly became the work's most notorious section.

For good or ill, the issue of innate knowledge came to be seen as the pivotal one joined by the empiricists and their rationalist rivals. Certainly it looks to be pivotal when empiricism is characterized, in Locke's words, as the view that "all

(A) *From* John Locke, *An Essay Concerning Human Understanding*, ed. J. W. Yolton, Vol. 1, London: Dent, 1961, pp. 9–22. (B) *From* Gottfried Wilhelm Leibniz, *Philosophical Writings*, ed. G. Parkinson, London: Dent, 1973, pp. 150–4 (some passages omitted).

our knowledge is founded" in, and "ultimately derives from," experience (Book II, Ch. I). It might be argued, however, that a characterization of empiricism in terms of a psychological thesis about the origin of knowledge, rather than of an epistemological claim about the justification of knowledge-claims, is an unhappy one. Be that as it may, the question of innate knowledge is important, quite apart from its connection with seventeenth- and eighteenth-century rivalries.

It is misleading to write that "Locke plainly treats the question . . . as an empirical one, to be settled by evidence" about children and "savage nations."[2] More important than his denial that children and savages have the knowledge that Cartesians regard as universally innate are Locke's attempts to identify a version of the innateness doctrine that is neither blatantly false nor a misleading way of stating the obvious (e.g. that we have the capacity to come to know mathematical truths). It is his conclusion that no such version can be found, together with his attempted demonstration in the *Essay* as a whole that experience does suffice to explain our ideas and knowledge, which constitute his real case against his opponents.

When Leibniz (1646–1716) wrote his critique of Locke's *Essay*, it was that conclusion and demonstration that he challenged, arguing for example that experience cannot explain our recognition of the necessity of mathematical truths. (The criticism of Locke contained in the "Preface" to Leibniz's *New Essays* is continued at greater leisure in Book I of the work.)

There is a certain irony in Locke's objection to the innateness doctrine, which appeals to the need to have learned a language in order to articulate, and so come to know, any principles. For, in recent years, that doctrine has been revitalized by Noam Chomsky's claim that it is precisely linguistic knowledge, of the principles of "universal grammar," that must be innate.[3] It is a moot question, however, whether his claim is significantly similar to the seventeenth-century doctrine, and indeed whether his point is best expressed as one about innate knowledge at all.

In paying rather scant attention to the notion of knowledge, Chomsky is, unfortunately, emulating those involved in the older debate. Neither Locke nor Leibniz makes clear what he means by "knowledge" when they respectively deny and affirm the existence of innate knowledge. Surely, though, it does make a difference to the plausibility of the innateness doctrine which concept of knowledge is being employed. If knowing a principle to be true requires an ability to justify and defend one's claim to know the principle, then it will indeed sound absurd to attribute knowledge to neonates. On a more relaxed understanding of knowledge, that attribution might sound a good deal more acceptable.

Notes

1　See J. Yolton, *John Locke and the Way of Ideas*, Oxford: Oxford University Press, 1956.

2　J. L. Mackie, *Problems From Locke*, Oxford: Clarendon Press, 1976, p. 215.

3　See N. Chomsky, *Cartesian Linguistics*, New York: Harper & Row, 1966, and, for critical discussions of Chomsky, ed. S. P. Stich, *Innate Ideas*, Berkeley: University of California Press, 1975, and D. E. Cooper, "Innateness: Old and New," *Philosophical Review*, 81 (1972).

(A)　Locke, *An Essay Concerning Human Understanding*

Book I, Chapter II: No Innate Principles in the Mind

1.　It is an established opinion amongst some men that there are in the *understanding* certain *innate principles*, some primary notions, κοιναὶ ἔννοιαι, characters, as it were, stamped upon the mind of man, which the soul receives in its very first being and brings into the world with it. It would be sufficient to convince unprejudiced readers of the falseness of this supposition, if I should only show (as I hope I shall in the following parts of this discourse) how men, barely by the use of their natural faculties, may attain to all the knowledge they have, without the help of any innate impressions, and may arrive at certainty without any such original notions or principles. For I imagine anyone will easily grant that it would be impertinent to suppose the *ideas* of colours innate in a creature to whom God has given sight, and a power to receive them by the eyes, from external objects; and no less unreasonable would it be to attribute several truths to the impressions of nature and innate characters, when we may observe in ourselves faculties, fit to attain as easy and certain knowledge of them, as if they were originally imprinted on the mind.

But because a man is not permitted without censure to follow his own thoughts in the search of truth, when they lead him ever so little out of the common road, I shall set down the reasons that made me doubt of the truth of that opinion, as an excuse for my mistake, if I be in one; which I leave to be considered by those who, with me, dispose themselves to embrace truth, wherever they find it.

2.　There is nothing more commonly taken for granted than that there are certain principles, both *speculative* and *practical* (for they speak of both), universally agreed upon by all mankind: which therefore, they argue, must needs be constant impressions which the souls of men receive in their first beings, and which they bring into the world with them, as necessarily and really as they do any of their inherent faculties.

3.　This argument, drawn from *universal consent*, has this misfortune in it, that if it were true in matter of fact that there were certain truths wherein all mankind agreed, it would not prove them innate, if there can be any other way shown how men may come to that universal agreement, in the things they do consent in, which I presume may be done.

4. But, which is worse, this argument of universal consent, which is made use of to prove innate principles, seems to me a demonstration that there are none such: because there are none to which all mankind give an universal assent. I shall begin with the speculative, and instance in those magnified principles of demonstration, *Whatsoever is, is* and *It is impossible for the same thing to be and not to be*, which of all others I think have the most allowed title to innate. These have so settled a reputation of maxims universally received that it will, no doubt, be thought strange if anyone should seem to question it. But yet I take liberty to say that these propositions are so far from having an universal assent, that there are a great part of mankind to whom they are not so much as known.

5. For, first, it is evident that all *children* and *idiots* have not the least apprehension or thought of them. And the want of that is enough to destroy that universal assent which must needs be the necessary concomitant of all innate truths: it seeming to me near a contradiction to say that there are truths imprinted on the soul which it perceives or understands not: imprinting, if it signify anything, being nothing else but the making certain truths to be perceived. But to imprint anything on the mind, without the mind's perceiving it, seems to me hardly intelligible. If therefore *children* and *idiots* have souls, have minds, with those impressions upon them, they must unavoidably perceive them, and necessarily know and assent to these truths; which since they do not, it is evident that there are no such impressions. For if they are not notions naturally imprinted, how can they be innate? And if they are notions imprinted, how can they be unknown? To say a notion is imprinted on the mind, and yet at the same time to say that the mind is ignorant of it, and never yet took notice of it, is to make this impression nothing. No proposition can be said to be in the mind, which it never yet knew, which it was never yet conscious of. For if any one may, then by the same reason all propositions that are true and the mind is capable ever of assenting to, may be said to be in the mind and to be imprinted: since, if any one can be said to be in the mind which it never yet knew, it must be only because it is capable of

knowing it; and so the mind is of all truths it ever shall know. Nay, thus truths may be imprinted on the mind which it never did nor ever shall know; for a man may live long, and die at last in ignorance of many truths which his mind was capable of knowing, and that with certainty. So that if the capacity of knowing be the natural impression contended for, all the truths a man ever comes to know will, by this account, be every one of them innate; and this great point will amount to no more, but only to a very improper way of speaking; which, whilst it pretends to assert the contrary, says nothing different from those who deny innate principles. For nobody, I think, ever denied that the mind was capable of knowing several truths. The capacity they say is innate, the knowledge acquired. But then to what end such contest for certain innate maxims? If truths can be imprinted on the understanding without being perceived, I can see no difference there can be between any truths the mind is capable of knowing, in respect of their original: they must all be innate, or all adventitious. In vain shall a man go about to distinguish them. He therefore that talks of innate notions in the understanding, cannot (if he intend thereby any distinct sort of truths) mean such truths to be in the understanding as it never perceived, and is yet wholly ignorant of. For if these words (*to be in the understanding*) have any propriety, they signify to be understood. So that to be in the understanding and not to be understood, to be in the mind and never to be perceived, is all one as to say: anything is and is not in the mind or understanding. If therefore these two propositions, *Whatsoever is, is* and *It is impossible for the same thing to be and not to be*, are by nature imprinted, children cannot be ignorant of them; infants, and all that have souls, must necessarily have them in their understandings, know the truth of them, and assent to it.

6. To avoid this, it is usually answered that all men know and *assent* to them, *when they come to the use of reason*; and this is enough to prove them innate. I answer:

7. Doubtful expressions, that have scarce any signification, go for clear reasons to those who, being prepossessed, take not the pains to examine even what they themselves say. For, to apply this answer with any tolerable sense to our present purpose, it must signify one of these two things: either, that as soon as men come to the

use of reason these supposed native inscriptions come to be known and observed by them; or else, that the use and exercise of men's reason assists them in the discovery of these principles, and certainly makes them known to them.

8.   If they mean that by the *use of reason* men may discover these principles, and that this is sufficient to prove them innate, their way of arguing will stand thus: viz. that whatever truths reason can certainly discover to us and make us firmly assent to, those are all naturally imprinted on the mind, since that universal assent, which is made the mark of them, amounts to no more but this: that by the use of reason we are capable to come to a certain knowledge of and assent to them; and, by this means, there will be no difference between the maxims of the mathematicians and theorems they deduce from them: all must be equally allowed innate, they being all discoveries made by the use of reason, and truths that a rational creature may certainly come to know, if he apply his thoughts rightly that way.

9.   But how can these men think the *use of reason* necessary to discover principles that are supposed innate, when reason (if we may believe them) is nothing else but the faculty of deducing unknown truths from principles or propositions that are already known? That certainly can never be thought innate which we have need of reason to discover, unless, as I have said, we will have all the certain truths that reason ever teaches us to be innate. We may as well think the use of reason necessary to make our eyes discover visible objects, as that there should be need of reason, or the exercise thereof, to make the understanding see what is originally engraven in it, and cannot be in the understanding before it be perceived by it. So that to make reason discover those truths thus imprinted is to say that the use of reason discovers to a man what he knew before; and if men have those innate, impressed truths originally, and before the use of reason, and yet are always ignorant of them till they come to the use of reason, it is in effect to say that men know and know them not at the same time.

10.   It will perhaps be said that mathematical demonstrations and other truths that are not innate, are not assented to as soon as proposed, wherein they are distinguished from these maxims and other innate truths. I shall have occasion to speak of assent upon the first proposing, more particularly by and by. I shall here only, and that

very readily, allow that these maxims and mathematical demonstrations are in this different: that the one have need of reason, using of proofs, to make them out and to gain our assent; but the other, as soon as understood, are, without any the least reasoning, embraced and assented to. But I withal beg leave to observe that it lays open the weakness of this subterfuge which requires the *use of reason* for the discovery of these general truths, since it must be confessed that in their discovery there is no use made of reasoning at all. And I think those who give this answer will not be forward to affirm that the knowledge of this maxim, *That it is impossible for the same thing to be, and not to be,* is a deduction of our reason. For this would be to destroy that bounty of nature they seem so fond of, whilst they make the knowledge of those principles to depend on the labour of our thoughts. For all reasoning is search and casting about and requires pains and application. And how can it with any tolerable sense be supposed that what was imprinted by nature, as the foundation and guide of our reason, should need the use of reason to discover it?

11.   Those who will take the pains to reflect with a little attention on the operations of the understanding will find that this ready assent of the mind to some truths depends not either on native inscription or the *use of reason*, but on a faculty of the mind quite distinct from both of them, as we shall see hereafter. Reason, therefore, having nothing to do in procuring our assent to these maxims, if by saying that *men know and assent to them when they come to the use of reason* be meant that the use of reason assists us in the knowledge of these maxims, it is utterly false; and were it true, would prove them not to be innate.

12.   If by knowing and assenting to them *when we come to the use of reason* be meant that this is the time when they come to be taken notice of by the mind; and that as soon as children come to the use of reason, they come also to know and assent to these maxims: this also is false and frivolous. *First,* it is false. Because it is evident these maxims are not in the mind so early as the use of reason; and therefore the coming to the use of reason is falsely assigned as the time of their discovery. How many instances of the use of reason may we observe in children a long time before they have any knowledge of

this maxim, *That it is impossible for the same thing to be, and not to be*? And a great part of illiterate people and savages pass many years, even of their rational age, without ever thinking on this, and the like general propositions. I grant men come not to the knowledge of these general and more abstract truths, which are thought innate, till they come to the use of reason; and I add, nor then neither. Which is so, because, till after they come to the use of reason, those general abstract *ideas* are not framed in the mind, about which those general maxims are which are mistaken for innate principles, but are indeed discoveries made and verities introduced and brought into the mind by the same way and discovered by the same steps as several other propositions, which nobody was ever so extravagant as to suppose innate. This I hope to make plain in the sequel of this discourse. I allow therefore a necessity that men should come to the use of reason before they get the knowledge of those general truths, but deny that men's coming to the use of reason is the time of their discovery.

13. In the meantime, it is observable that this saying, that men know and assent to these maxims *when they come to the use of reason*, amounts in reality of fact to no more but this, that they are never known nor taken notice of before the use of reason, but may possibly be assented to sometime after, during a man's life; but when, is uncertain. And so may all other knowable truths, as well as these which therefore have no advantage nor distinction from others, by this note of being known when we come to the use of reason; nor are thereby proved to be innate, but quite the contrary.

14. But, *secondly*, were it true that the precise time of their being known and assented to were when men come to the *use of reason*, neither would that prove them innate. This way of arguing is so frivolous as the supposition of itself is false. For, by what kind of logic will it appear that any notion is originally by nature imprinted in the mind in its first constitution, because it comes first to be observed and assented to when a faculty of the mind, which has quite a distinct province, begins to exert itself? And therefore the coming to the use of speech, if it were supposed the time that these maxims are first assented to (which it may be with as much truth as the time when men come to the use of reason), would be as good a proof that they were innate, as to say they are

innate because men assent to them when they come to the use of reason. I agree then with these men of innate principles that there is no knowledge of these general and self-evident maxims in the mind till it comes to the exercise of reason; but I deny that the coming to the use of reason is the precise time when they are first taken notice of; and if that were the precise time, I deny that it would prove them innate. All that can with any truth be meant by this proposition, that men *assent to them when they come to the use of reason*, is no more but this: that the making of general abstract *ideas* and the understanding of general names being a concomitant of the rational faculty and growing up with it, children commonly get not those general *ideas* nor learn the names that stand for them, till having for a good while exercised their reason about familiar and more particular *ideas*, they are by their ordinary discourse and actions with others acknowledged to be capable of rational conversation. If assenting to these maxims, when men come to the use of reason, can be true in any other sense, I desire it may be shown; or at least, how in this or any other sense it proves them innate.

15. The senses at first let in particular *ideas* and furnish the yet empty cabinet; and the mind by degrees growing familiar with some of them, they are lodged in the memory, and names got to them. Afterwards the mind, proceeding further, abstracts them, and by degrees learns the use of general names. In this manner the mind comes to be furnished with *ideas* and language, the materials about which to exercise its discursive faculty. And the use of reason becomes daily more visible, as these materials that give it employment increase. But though the having of general *ideas* and the use of general words and reason usually grow together, yet I see not how this any way proves them innate. The knowledge of some truths, I confess, is very early in the mind, but in a way that shows them not to be innate. For, if we will observe, we shall find it still to be about *ideas*, not innate, but acquired: it being about those first which are imprinted by external things, with which infants have earliest to do, which make the most frequent impressions on their senses. In *ideas* thus got, the mind discovers that some agree and others differ, probably as soon as it has any use of memory, as soon as it is able to retain and receive distinct *ideas*. But whether it be then or no, this is certain: it does so long before it

has the use of words, or comes to that which we commonly call the *use of reason*. For a child knows as certainly, before it can speak, the difference between the *ideas* of sweet and bitter (i.e. that sweet is not bitter) as it knows afterwards (when it comes to speak) that wormwood and sugar-plums are not the same thing.

16.   A child knows not that three and four are equal to seven till he comes to be able to count to seven, and has got the name and *idea* of equality; and then upon explaining those words, he presently assents to, or rather perceives the truth of that proposition. But neither does he then readily assent, because it is an innate truth, nor was his assent wanting till then because he wanted the *use of reason*; but the truth of it appears to him as soon as he has settled in his mind the clear and distinct *ideas* that these names stand for. And then he knows the truth of that proposition upon the same grounds and by the same means that he knew before that a rod and cherry are not the same thing, and upon the same grounds also that he may come to know afterwards that *It is impossible for the same thing to be, and not to be*, as shall be more fully shown hereafter. So that the later it is before anyone comes to have those general *ideas* about which those maxims are, or to know the signification of those general terms that stand for them, or to put together in his mind the *ideas* they stand for, the later also will it be before he comes to assent to those maxims; whose terms, with the *ideas* they stand for, being no more innate than those of a cat or a weasel, he must stay till time and observation have acquainted him with them; and then he will be in a capacity to know the truth of these maxims, upon the first occasion that shall make him put together those *ideas* in his mind and observe whether they agree or disagree, according as is expressed in those propositions. And therefore it is that a man knows that eighteen and nineteen are equal to thirty-seven, by the same self-evidence that he knows one and two to be equal to three; yet a child knows this not so soon as the other, not for want of the use of reason, but because the *ideas* the words eighteen, nineteen, and thirty-seven stand for are not so soon got as those which are signified by one, two, and three.

17.   This evasion therefore of general assent when men come to the use of reason failing as it does, and leaving no difference between those sup-posed innate and other truths that are afterwards acquired and learnt, men have endeavoured to secure an universal assent to those they call maxims by saying they are generally *assented to, as soon as proposed*, and the terms they are proposed in understood; seeing all men, even children, as soon as they hear and understand the terms, assent to these propositions, they think it is sufficient to prove them innate. For since men never fail, after they have once understood the words, to acknowledge them for undoubted truths, they would infer that certainly these propositions were first lodged in the understanding which, without any teaching, the mind at very first proposal immediately closes with and assents to, and after that never doubts again.

18.   In answer to this, I demand whether ready *assent* given to a proposition, *upon first hearing* and understanding the terms, be a certain mark of an innate principle? If it be not, such a general assent is in vain urged as a proof of them; if it be said that it is a mark of innate, they must then allow all such propositions to be innate which are generally assented to as soon as heard, whereby they will find themselves plentifully stored with innate principles. For upon the same ground, viz. of assent at first hearing and understanding the terms, that men would have those maxims pass for innate, they must also admit several propositions about numbers to be innate; and thus, that *One and two are equal to three*, that *Two and two are equal to four*, and a multitude of other the like propositions in numbers that everybody assents to at first hearing and understanding the terms, must have a place amongst these innate axioms. Nor is this the prerogative of numbers alone, and propositions made about several of them; but even natural philosophy and all the other sciences afford propositions which are sure to meet with assent as soon as they are understood. That *Two bodies cannot be in the same place* is a truth that nobody any more sticks at than at these maxims that *It is impossible for the same thing to be and not to be*, that *White is not black*, that *A square is not a circle*, that *Yellowness is not sweetness*. These and a million of other such propositions, as many at least as we have distinct *ideas*, every man in his wits, at first hearing and knowing what the names stand for, must necessarily assent to. If these men will be true to their own rule and have *assent at first hearing and understanding the terms* to be a mark of

innate, they must allow not only as many innate propositions as men have distinct *ideas*, but as many as men can make propositions wherein different *ideas* are denied one of another. Since every proposition wherein one different *idea* is denied of another will as certainly find assent at first hearing and understanding the terms as this general one, *It is impossible for the same to be, and not to be*, or that which is the foundation of it and is the easier understood of the two, *The same is not different*: by which account they will have legions of innate propositions of this one sort, without mentioning any other. But since no proposition can be innate unless the *ideas* about which it is be innate, this will be to suppose all our *ideas* of colours, sounds, tastes, figure, etc., innate, than which there cannot be anything more opposite to reason and experience. Universal and ready assent upon hearing and understanding the terms is (I grant) a mark of self-evidence; but self-evidence, depending not on innate impressions but on something else (as we shall show hereafter), belongs to several propositions, which nobody was yet so extravagant as to pretend to be innate.

19.   Nor let it be said that those more particular self-evident propositions which are assented to at first hearing, as that *One and two are equal to three*, that *Green is not red*, etc., are received as the consequences of those more universal propositions which are looked on as innate principles, since anyone who will but take the pains to observe what passes in the understanding will certainly find that these and the like less general propositions are certainly known and firmly assented to by those who are utterly ignorant of those more general maxims, and so, being earlier in the mind than those (as they are called) first principles, cannot owe to them the assent wherewith they are received at first hearing.

20.   If it be said that these propositions, viz., *Two and two are equal to four, Red is not blue*, etc., are not general maxims nor of any great use, I answer that makes nothing to the argument of universal assent upon hearing and understanding. For, if that be the certain mark of innate, whatever proposition can be found that receives general assent as soon as heard and understood, that must be admitted for an innate proposition, as well as this maxim, that *It is impossible for the same thing to be, and not to be*, they being upon this ground equal. And as to the difference of being more general, that makes this maxim more remote from being innate, those general and abstract *ideas* being more strangers to our first apprehensions than those of more particular self-evident propositions, and therefore it is longer before they are admitted and assented to by the growing understanding. And as to the usefulness of these magnified maxims, that perhaps will not be found so great as is generally conceived when it comes to its due place to be more fully considered.

21.   But we have not yet done with *assenting to propositions at first hearing and understanding their terms*. It is fit we first take notice that this, instead of being a mark that they are innate, is a proof of the contrary, since it supposes that several, who understand and know other things, are ignorant of these principles till they are proposed to them, and that one may be unacquainted with these truths till he hears them from others. For if they were innate, what need they be proposed in order to gaining assent, when, by being in the understanding, by a natural and original impression (if there were any such) they could not but be known before? Or doth the proposing them print them clearer in the mind than nature did? If so, then the consequence will be that a man knows them better after he has been thus taught them than he did before. Whence it will follow that these principles may be made more evident to us by others' teaching than nature has made them by impression: which will ill agree with the opinion of innate principles, and give but little authority to them, but on the contrary makes them unfit to be the foundations of all our other knowledge, as they are pretended to be. This cannot be denied: that men grow first acquainted with many of these self-evident truths upon their being proposed; but it is clear that whosoever does so finds in himself that he then begins to know a proposition which he knew not before, and which from thenceforth he never questions, not because it was innate, but because the consideration of the nature of the things contained in those words would not suffer him to think otherwise, how or whensoever he is brought to reflect on them. And if whatever is assented to at first hearing and understanding the terms must pass for an innate principle, every well-grounded observation drawn from particulars into a general rule must be innate. When yet it is certain that not all but only

sagacious heads light at first on these observations and reduce them into general propositions, not innate but collected from a preceding acquaintance and reflection on particular instances. These, when observing men have made them, unobserving men, when they are proposed to them, cannot refuse their assent to.

22.   If it be said the understanding hath an *implicit knowledge* of these principles, but not an explicit, before this first hearing (as they must who will say that they are in the understanding before they are known), it will be hard to conceive what is meant by a principle imprinted on the understanding implicitly, unless it be this, that the mind is capable of understanding and assenting firmly to such propositions. And thus all mathematical demonstrations, as well as first principles, must be received as native impressions on the mind; which I fear they will scarce allow them to be, who find it harder to demonstrate a proposition than assent to it when demonstrated. And few mathematicians will be forward to believe that all the diagrams they have drawn were but copies of those innate characters which nature had engraven upon their minds.

23.   There is, I fear, this further weakness in the foregoing argument, which would persuade us that therefore those maxims are to be thought innate which men *admit at first hearing*, because they assent to propositions which they are not taught nor do receive from the force of any argument or demonstration, but a bare explication or understanding of the terms. Under which there seems to me to lie this fallacy, that men are supposed not to be *taught* nor to *learn* anything *de novo*, when, in truth, they are taught and do learn something they were ignorant of before. For, first, it is evident they have learned the terms and their signification, neither of which was born with them. But this is not all the acquired knowledge in the case: the *ideas* themselves, about which the proposition is, are not born with them, no more than their names, but got afterwards. So that in all propositions that are assented to at first hearing: the terms of all proposition, their standing for such *ideas*, and the *ideas* themselves that they stand for being neither of them innate, I would fain know what there is remaining in such propositions that is innate. For I would gladly have anyone name that proposition whose terms or *ideas* were either of them innate. We by degrees get *ideas* and names, and

learn their appropriated connection one with another; and then to propositions made in such terms, whose signification we have learnt, and wherein the agreement or disagreement we can perceive in our *ideas* when put together is expressed, we at first hearing assent; though to other propositions, in themselves as certain and evident, but which are concerning *ideas* not so soon or so easily got, we are at the same time no way capable of assenting. For though a child quickly assent to this proposition, that *An apple is not fire*, when by familiar acquaintance he has got the *ideas* of those two different things distinctly imprinted on his mind, and has learnt that the names *apple* and *fire* stand for them: yet it will be some years after, perhaps, before the same child will assent to this proposition, that *It is impossible for the same thing to be, and not to be.* Because, though perhaps the words are as easy to be learnt, yet the signification of them, being more large, comprehensive, and abstract than of the names annexed to those sensible things the child hath to do with, it is longer before he learns their precise meaning, and it requires more time plainly to form in his mind those general *ideas* they stand for. Till that be done, you will in vain endeavour to make any child assent to a proposition made up of such general terms; but as soon as ever he has got those *ideas* and learned their names, he forwardly closes with the one as well as the other of the forementioned propositions, and with both for the same reason, viz. because he finds the *ideas* he has in his mind to agree or disagree, according as the words standing for them are affirmed or denied one of another in the proposition. But if propositions be brought to him in words which stand for *ideas* he has not yet in his mind, to such propositions, however evidently true or false in themselves, he affords neither assent nor dissent but is ignorant. For words being but empty sounds, any further than they are signs of our *ideas* we cannot but assent to them as they correspond to those *ideas* we have, but no further than that. But the showing by what steps and ways knowledge comes into our minds, and the grounds of several degrees of assent, being the business of the following discourse, it may suffice to have only touched on it here, as one reason that made me doubt of those innate principles.

24.   To conclude this argument of *universal consent*, I agree with these defenders of innate

principles that if they are *innate* they must needs *have universal assent*. For that a truth should be innate and yet not assented to is to me as unintelligible as for a man to know a truth and be ignorant of it at the same time. But then, by these men's own confession, they cannot be innate, since they are not assented to by those who understand not the terms; nor by a great part of those who do understand them, but have yet never heard nor thought of those propositions; which I think, is at least one-half of mankind. But were the number far less, it would be enough to destroy *universal assent*, and thereby show these propositions not to be innate, if children alone were ignorant of them.

Leibniz, *New Essays on the Human Understanding*

Preface

[. . .] The question at issue is whether the soul itself is entirely void, like a tablet whereon nothing has yet been written (*tabula rasa*), as is the view of Aristotle and the author of the essay [i.e. Locke], and everything marked on it comes solely from the senses and from experience, or whether the soul contains originally the principles of various notions and doctrines, which external objects simply recall from time to time, as is my view and that of Plato, and even of the Schoolmen, and of all those who attribute this meaning to the passage from St. Paul (Rom. ii. 15), where he says that the law of God is writ in men's hearts. The Stoics call these principles *prolepses*, that is to say assumptions which are fundamental or taken as agreed in advance. The mathematicians call them *common notions* (κοιναὶ ἔννοιαι). Modern philosophers give them other fine names, and Julius Scaliger in particular called them *semina aeternitatis* ['seeds of eternity'] and again *zopyra*, meaning to say living fires, flashes of light, hidden within us, but caused to appear by the contact of the senses, like the sparks which the shock of the flint strikes from the steel. And it is not an unreasonable belief that these flashes are a sign of something divine and eternal, which makes its appearance above all in necessary truths. From this arises another question, whether all truths depend on experience, that is to say on induction

and on instances, or whether there are some which have another basis also. For if certain events can be foreseen before we have made any trial of them, it is clear that we contribute in those cases something of our own. The senses, although they are necessary for all our actual knowledge, are not sufficient to give us the whole of it, since the senses never give anything but instances, that is to say particular or individual truths. Now all the instances which confirm a general truth, however numerous they may be, are not sufficient to establish the universal necessity of this same truth, for it does not follow that what happened before will happen in the same way again. For example, the Greeks and the Romans, and all the other peoples of the earth known to the ancients, always observed that before the passage of twenty-four hours day changes to night and night to day. But they would have been wrong if they had believed that the same rule holds good everywhere, for since that time the contrary has been experienced during a visit to Nova Zembla. And any one who believed that in our zone at least this is a necessary and eternal truth which will last for ever, would likewise be wrong, since we must hold that the earth and even the sun do not exist of necessity, and that there may perhaps come a time when that beautiful star and its whole system will exist no longer, at least in its present form. From which it appears that necessary truths, such as we find in pure mathematics, and particularly in arithmetic and geometry, must have principles whose proof does not depend on instances, nor consequently on the testimony of the senses, although without the senses it would never have occurred to us to think of them. This is a distinction that should be carefully noted; and it is one which Euclid understood so well that he often proves by reason what is evident enough through experience and sensible images. Logic also, together with metaphysics and morals, the one of which forms natural theology and the other natural jurisprudence, are full of such truths; and consequently proof of them can only arise from inner principles, which are called innate. It is true that we must not imagine that we can read in the soul these eternal laws of reason as in an open book, as the edict of the praetor can be read in his *album* without trouble or deep scrutiny. But it is enough that we can find them in ourselves by dint of attention, opportunities for which are afforded by the senses. The success of experiments serves also as a confirmation of reason, more or less as verifications serve in arithmetic to help us to avoid erroneous calculation when the reasoning is long. It is in this also that the knowledge of men differs from that of the brutes: the latter are purely empirical, and guide themselves solely by particular instances; for, as far as we can judge, they never go so far as to form necessary propositions; whereas men are capable of the demonstrative sciences. This also is why the faculty the brutes have of making *sequences* of ideas is something inferior to the reason which is in man. The sequences of the brutes are just like those of the pure empiricists who claim that what has happened sometimes will happen again in a case where what strikes them is similar, without being capable of determining whether the same reasons hold good. It is because of this that it is so easy for men to catch animals, and so easy for pure empiricists to make mistakes. And people whom age and experience has rendered skilful are not exempt from this when they rely too much on their past experience, as some have done in civil and military affairs; they do not pay sufficient attention to the fact that the world changes, and that men become more skilful by discovering countless new contrivances, whereas the stags and hares of today are no more cunning than those of yesterday. The sequences of the brutes are but a shadow of reasoning, that is to say, they are but connexions of imagination, transitions from one image to another; for in a fresh experience, which appears like the preceding one, there is the expectation that what was hitherto joined thereto will occur again, as though the things were connected in fact, because their images are connected in the memory. It is true that reason also teaches us to expect in the ordinary course of events to see occur in the future what conforms to a long experience of the past, but it is not therefore a necessary and infallible truth, and we may cease to be successful when we least expect it, when the reasons which have maintained it change. This is why the wisest people do not rely on it to the extent of not trying to discover, if it is possible, something of the reason of what happens, so as to judge when exceptions must be made. For reason alone is capable of setting up rules which are certain, and of supplying what is lacking to those which are not certain, by inserting the exceptions, and in short

of finding connexions which are certain in the force of necessary consequences. This often provides the means of foreseeing the event, without its being necessary to experience the sensible connexions between images which is all that the brutes can do; so that to vindicate the existence within us of the principles of necessary truths is also to distinguish man from the brutes.

Perhaps our gifted author will not entirely dissociate himself from my opinion. For after having devoted the whole of his first book to the rejection of innate ideas, understood in a certain sense, he yet admits in the beginning of the second and in what follows that ideas whose origin is not in sensation arise from reflexion. Now reflexion is nothing but an attention to what is in us, and the senses do not give us what we already bring with us. This being so, can we deny that there is a great deal that is innate in our mind, since we are innate, so to speak, to ourselves, and since there is in ourselves being, unity, substance, duration, change, activity, perception, pleasure, and a thousand other objects of our intellectual ideas? And since these objects are immediate to our understanding and are always present (although they cannot always be apperceived on account of our distractions and our needs),[1] why be surprised that we say that these ideas, and everything which depends on them, are innate in us? This is why I have taken as an illustration a block of veined marble, rather than a wholly uniform block or blank tablets, that is to say what is called *tabula rasa* in the language of the philosophers. For if the soul were like these blank tablets, truths would be in us in the same way as the figure of Hercules is in a block of marble, when the marble is completely indifferent whether it receives this or some other figure. But if there were veins in the stone which marked out the figure of Hercules rather than other figures, this stone would be more determined thereto, and Hercules would be as it were in some manner innate in it, although labour would be needed to uncover those veins, and to clear them by polishing, and by cutting away what prevents them from appearing. It is in this way that ideas and truths are innate in us, like natural inclinations and dispositions, natural habits or potentialities, and not like activities, although these potentialities are always accompanied by some activities which correspond to them, though they are often imperceptible.

It seems that our gifted author claims that there is in us nothing *potential*, nor even anything which we do not always actually apperceive; but he cannot take this quite strictly, otherwise his opinion would be too paradoxical, since acquired habits also and the contents of our memory are not always apperceived, and do not even always come to our aid when needed, although we often easily recall them to mind on some trivial occasion which reminds us of them, in the same way as we only need the beginning of a song to make us remember the rest. Moreover he limits his doctrine in other places by saying that there is nothing in us which we have not at least previously apperceived. But besides the fact that nobody can guarantee by reason alone how far our past apperceptions which may have been forgotten may have gone, especially in view of the Platonic doctrine of reminiscence, which, mythical though it is, is not incompatible, in part at least, with bare reason: besides this, I say, why should it be necessary that everything should be acquired by us by apperceptions of external things, and nothing be able to be unearthed in ourselves? Is our soul of itself alone so empty that

apart from images borrowed from without it is nothing? This is not, I am convinced, an opinion that our judicious author could approve. And where are there to be found tablets which have not in themselves a certain amount of variety? We shall never see a perfectly level and uniform surface. Why, therefore, should we not also be able to provide some sort of thought from deep within ourselves, when we are willing to delve there? Thus I am led to believe that fundamentally his opinion on this point does not differ from mine, or rather from the common opinion, inasmuch as he recognises two sources of our knowledge, the senses and reflexion. . . .

Note

1   "Apperception" is Leibniz's term for conscious perception. It is an important part of his philosophy that there are "at all times an infinite number of *perceptions* in us, though without apperception and without reflexion" (*New Essays on the Human Understanding*, Preface, in *Philosophical Writings*, ed. Parkinson, p. 155).

10

(A) Giambattista Vico, *The New Science* (1744), "Poetic Wisdom"
(B) David Hume, *An Enquiry Concerning Human Understanding*, "Of the Idea of Necessary Connexion" and "Of the Academical or Sceptical Philosophy"

Introduction

The following selections present work by early modern philosophers who called into question the pretensions of reason, in the case of David Hume by deploying the philosophical tropes of skepticism, with the Neopolitan philosopher Giambattista Vico (1668–1744) by invoking those of Renaissance humanism, in particular rhetoric and philology. Well known for his cyclical and developmental theory of history, which appears to have influenced Karl Marx (V.19) among others, Vico argued that modern rationality exhibits a kind of "barbarism" for having forgotten its origins in mytho-poetic thought. According to Vico, truth is acquired neither by reason working through the relations and implications of ideas nor by reason stitching together synthetically the ideas found in experience.[1] Rather, according to Vico, arguments, reasoning, and hence knowledge originate in *topoi* or places of thinking generated by the inventive acts (*inventio* or *ingenium*) of "*fantasia*" (roughly translatable as "poetic imagination").[2] In fact, for Vico the "expressiveness" and "beauty"

(A) *From* Giambattista Vico, *The New Science of Giambattista Vico*, ed. T. G. Bergen and M. H. Fisch. New York: Anchor Books, 1961, pp. 69–87. (B) *From* David Hume, *Enquiries*, 2nd edition, ed. L. A. Selby-Bigge. Oxford: Oxford University Press, 1902, pp. 60–79 (Section 7), 148–65 (Section 12) (asterisked notes are Hume's own).

of language *is* its "truth" (§445). In that sense, poetic language not only fuses knowing and making; it fuses knowledge and the world. As God is the supreme maker, God is also the supreme knower.[3] For both the divine and the human, "*verum ipsum factum*" ("the true is the made") – not simply found, discovered, or given.

Within these originary *topoi* the universality of the reason and the particularity of sensation had been fused together in what Vico calls "imaginative universals." The modern "barbarism of reason," however, rends this primordial unity. Moderns forget how the various abstract concepts used by the intellect in modern science and philosophy originate in mytho-poetic thought, and as a result philosophy not only becomes alienated from the concrete world of humanity and history; it also claims for itself a false transcendence, a specious universality, and a baseless authority over the world. The nominalist break from the divinely-generated order of forms had, as in the case of Nicholas of Cusa (IV.11), deepened the radical transcendence of God from the world and freed the human mind to root intelligible orders in its own creativity. Vico understood that locating the possibility of knowing in human making was to attribute to human beings a capacity to know human things (e.g. history, society, politics, art) in a way that surpasses their capacity to know the natural world (which humans do not make). Hence for Vico, the human sciences and "poetic arts" offer a different and superior understanding than the natural and "philosophical" sciences.

Natural science, in fact, is not in Vico's terms truly a "science" (*scienza*) at all; it is, rather, merely a "consciousness" (*coscienza*) of things humanity has not made.

"The first thing anyone hears of Hume is that he was a sceptic."[4] Quite possibly – but in any case the position Scottish philosopher David Hume (1711–76) developed concerning skepticism is a complicated one. In *A Treatise of Human Nature* (1739–40) Hume veers from a sustained defense of what he calls "total" skepticism, judging it to be "cold and strain'd and ridiculous," something to set aside after a good dinner and game of backgammon (1.4.7); and yet in other sections of the same text he refers to himself as a "sceptic." In the final pages of the *Enquiry Concerning Human Understanding*,[5] which we have selected here, Hume describes his own thought as kind of a "mitigated" scepticism, a way of thinking that steers between the Scylla and Charybdis of "dogmatism" and the excesses of total skepticism (see II.4 above). Comparing Hume's thought to what in ancient times went by the names of "Pyrrhonian" and "Academic" skepticism, however, one finds a mixture of elements from both schools of thought.

Unlike Descartes, Hume accepts that skeptical arguments are largely successful. In Pyrrhonian fashion they undermine the criteria that were then the twin pillars of knowledge of reality beyond us: (1) "sensation"; and (2) "reason." Rejecting Berkeley's metaphysical speculations, Hume holds that reasoning at its best only tells us about ideas themselves; and experience tells us only about the way things appear to us – "experience is, and must be entirely silent" about external reality. As a consequence, Hume rejects the projects of traditional metaphysics (knowing ultimate reality) and theology (knowing the divine) altogether. In the (in)famous passage with which he closes the first *Enquiry*, he goes so far as to instruct his readers to burn as rubbish any text that purports to present knowledge about topics beyond the reach of the two prongs of what has come to be known as "Hume's fork" – (a) "relations of ideas" ("abstract reasoning concerning quantity or number") and (b) "matters of fact" ("experimental reasoning").

But while Hume's work subverts the projects of rationalistic science, metaphysics, and theology, his objective is not entirely destructive. Some commentators have discerned in Hume's appeals to "nature" and common life a genuine and interesting response to "excessive" skepticism.[6] In both the *Treatise* and the first *Enquiry*, Hume stresses that we are compelled, in accordance with our human nature, both to act and to think on the basis of "customary" and ineradicable convictions.[7] In the case, for example, of the necessary connexion between causes and effects (§7 below), Hume brackets the metaphysical question of the nature and even the very existence of that connection, explaining instead how that most basic element of scientific reasoning is not itself rationally justifiable but is grounded for us in nothing more than habit, custom, and what seems to be natural to us.

Clearly, however, as it does not prove skepticism to be false, Hume's tack is not a rebuttal of skepticism. But his analysis does indicate that human beings' way of being in the world is not most basically one of knowing. So far as science and philosophy go, it also shows that our theorizing ought to be built not, as Descartes argued, upon claims to absolute *truth* but instead according to the criteria characteristic of Academical skepticism – *durability*, *usefulness*, *ease*, an appropriate fit with human *custom* and *nature*, as well as the capacity to *satisfy* the demands of critical scrutiny.[8]

Notes

1 By contrast, Locke writes: "all the art of rhetoric, besides order; all the artificial and figurative application of words eloquence hath invented, are for nothing else but to insinuate wrong ideas, move the passions, and thereby mislead the judgment; and so indeed are perfect cheats." *An Essay Concerning Human Understanding*, ed. A. C. Fraser, Oxford: Clarendon Press, 1894, II.146.

2 G. Vico, *The New Science*, §§495–497; Vico also describes imagination as "compound or extended memory" (§211, §819). Aristotle writes: "Every systematic treatment of argumentation has two branches, one connected with invention of arguments and the other with judgments of their validity" (*Topics* II.6).

3 Cf. S. Rudnick Luft, *Vico's Uncanny Humanism*, Ithaca, NY: Cornell University Press, 2003; R. Manson, *The Theory of Knowledge of Giambattista Vico*, New York: Archon Books, 1969, p. 17.

4 E. Craig, *The Mind of God and the Works of Man*, Oxford: Clarendon Press, 1987, p. 81.

5 This "first" enquiry was originally published in 1748 as *An Essay on the Principles of Human Understanding*. Hume's "second" enquiry, *An Enquiry Concerning the Principles of Moral*, was published in 1750.

6 See R. H. Popkin, "David Hume: His Pyrrhonism and His Critique of Pyrrhonism,"

in *Hume*, ed. V. Chappell, Notre Dame, IN: University of Notre Dame Press, 1966; and P. F. Strawson, *Skepticism and Naturalism: Some Varieties*, London: Methuen, 1985.

7 Hume's deference to custom and tradition generally mark a point of similarity between his thought and that of Edmund Burke (V.15).

8 With these criteria Hume anticipates something of the pragmatists (II.18).

(A) Vico, *The New Science* (1744), "Poetic Wisdom"

[Prolegomena]

Introduction 361 We have said above in the Axioms that all the histories of the gentile nations have had fabulous beginnings, that among the Greeks (who have given us all we know of gentile antiquity) the first sages were the theological poets, and that the nature of everything born or made betrays the crudeness of its origin. It is thus and not otherwise that we must conceive the origins of poetic wisdom. And as for the great and sovereign esteem in which it has been handed down to us, this has its origin in the two conceits, that of nations and that of scholars, and it springs even more from the latter than from the former. For just as Manetho, the Egyptian high priest, translated all the fabulous history of Egypt into a sublime natural theology, so the Greek philosophers translated theirs into philosophy. And they did so not merely for the reason that the histories as they had come down to both alike were most unseemly, but for the following five reasons as well.

362 The first was reverence for religion, for the gentile nations were everywhere founded by fables on religion. The second was the grand effect thence derived, namely this civil world, so wisely ordered that it could only be the effect of a superhuman wisdom. The third was the occasions which, as we shall see, these fables, assisted by the veneration of religion and the credit of such great wisdom, gave the philosophers for instituting research and for meditating lofty things in philosophy. The fourth was the ease with which

they were thus enabled, as we shall also show farther on, to explain their sublime philosophical meditations by means of the expressions happily left them by the poets. The fifth and last, which is the sum of them all, is the confirmation of their own meditations which the philosophers derived from the authority of religion and the wisdom of the poets. Of these five reasons, the first two and the last contain the praises of the divine wisdom which ordained this world of nations, and the witness the philosophers bore to it even in their errors. The third and fourth are deceptions permitted by divine providence, that thence there might arise philosophers to understand and recognize it for what it truly is, an attribute of the true God.

363 Throughout this book it will be shown that as much as the poets had first sensed in the way of vulgar wisdom, the philosophers later understood in the way of esoteric wisdom; so that the former may be said to have been the sense and the latter the intellect of the human race. What Aristotle* said of the individual man is therefore true of the race in general: *Nihil est in intellectu quin prius fuerit in sensu*. That is, the human mind does not understand anything of which it has had no previous impression (which our modern metaphysicians call "occasion") from the senses. Now the mind uses the intellect when, from something it senses, it gathers something which does not fall under the senses; and this is the proper meaning of the Latin verb *intelligere*.

---

* *On the Soul* 432a 7–8. [*De anima*]

[Chapter I] Wisdom in General 364 Now, before discussing poetic wisdom, it is necessary for
us to see what wisdom in general is. Wisdom is
the faculty which commands all the disciplines by
which we acquire all the sciences and arts that
make up humanity. . . . Man, in his proper being
as man, consists of mind and spirit, or, if we
prefer, of intellect and will. It is the function
of wisdom to fulfill both these parts in man, the
second by way of the first, to the end that by a
mind illuminated by knowledge of the highest
institutions, the spirit may be led to choose the
best. The highest institutions in this universe
are those turned toward and conversant with
God; the best are those which look to the good
of all mankind. The former are called religious
institutions, the latter secular. True wisdom, then,
should teach the knowledge of religious institutions in order to conduct secular institutions
to the highest good. We believe that this was the
plan upon which Marcus Terentius Varro, who
earned the title "most learned of the Romans,"
erected his great work, [*The Antiquities*] *of Religious and Secular Institutions*, of which the injustice of time has unhappily bereft us, We shall treat
of these institutions in the present book so far as
the weakness of our education and the meager-
ness of our erudition permit.

365 Wisdom among the gentiles began with
the Muse, defined by Homer in a golden passage
of the *Odyssey* as "knowledge of good and evil,"
and later called divination. It was on the natural
prohibition of this practice, as something
naturally denied to man, that God founded the
true religion of the Hebrews, from which our
Christian religion arose. The Muse must thus
have been properly at first the science of divin-
ing by auspices, and this was the vulgar wisdom
of all nations, of which we shall have more to
say presently. It consisted in contemplating God
under the attribute of his providence, so that from
divinari his essence came to be called divinity. We
shall see presently that the theological poets,
who certainly founded the humanity of Greece,
were versed in this wisdom, and this explains
why the Latins called the judicial astrologers
"professors of wisdom." Wisdom was later
attributed to men renowned for useful counsels
given to mankind, as in the case of the Seven
Sages of Greece. The attribution was afterward
extended to men who for the good of peoples and
nations wisely ordered and governed common-

wealths. Still later the word "wisdom" came to
mean knowledge of natural divine things; that
is, metaphysics, called for that reason divine
science, which, seeking knowledge of man's
mind in God, and recognizing God as the source
of all truth, must recognize him as the regulator
of all good. So that metaphysics must essentially
work for the good of the human race, whose
preservation depends on the universal belief in
a provident divinity. [. . .] Finally among the
Hebrews, and thence among us Christians, wisdom was called the science of eternal things
revealed by God; a science which, among the
Tuscans, considered as knowledge of the true good
and true evil, perhaps owed to that fact the first
name they gave it, "science in divinity".

366 We must therefore distinguish three
kinds of theology. [. . .] First, poetic theology, that
of the theological poets, which was the civil
theology of all the gentile nations. Second, natural theology, that of the metaphysicians. [. . .]
Third, our Christian theology, a mixture of civil
and natural with the loftiest revealed theology;
all three united in the contemplation of divine
providence, which has so conducted human
institutions that, starting from the poetic theology which regulated them by certain sensible
signs believed to be divine counsels sent to man
by the gods, and by means of the natural theology which demonstrates providence by eternal
reasons which do not fall under the senses, the
nations were disposed to receive revealed theology in virtue of a supernatural faith, superior
not only to the senses but to human reason
itself.

*[Chapter II] Exposition and Division of Poetic
Wisdom* 367 But because metaphysics is the
sublime science which distributes their determinate subject matters to all the so-called subaltern
sciences; and because the wisdom of the ancients
was that of the theological poets, who without
doubt were the first sages of the gentile world; and
because the origins of all things must by nature
have been crude: for all these reasons we must trace
the beginnings of poetic wisdom to a crude metaphysics. From this, as from a trunk, there branch
out from one limb logic, morals, economics, and
politics, all poetic; and from another, physics,
the mother of cosmography and astronomy,
the latter of which gives their certainty to its
two daughters, chronology and geography – all

likewise poetic. We shall show clearly and distinctly how the founders of gentile humanity by means of their natural theology (or metaphysics) imagined the gods; how by means of their logic they invented languages; by morals, created heroes; by economics, founded families, and by politics, cities; by their physics, established the beginnings of things as all divine; by the particular physics of man, in a certain sense created themselves; by their cosmography, fashioned for themselves a universe entirely of gods; by astronomy, carried the planets and constellations from earth to heaven; by chronology, gave a beginning to [measured] times; and how by geography the Greeks, for example, described the [whole] world within their own Greece.

368   Thus our Science comes to be at once a history of the ideas, the customs, and the deeds of mankind. From these three we shall derive the principles of the history of human nature, which we shall show to be the principles of universal history, which principles it seems hitherto to have lacked.

[Chapter III] The Universal Flood and the Giants [369–373   The founders of gentile humanity, the giants, were men of the races of Ham, Japheth, and Shem who had renounced the true religion of Noah, their common ancestor. They owed their size to the wild and strenuous life of wanderers in the dense forest that covered the earth after the flood. (Of these giants there were two kinds: the first, autochthons, sons of Earth, or nobles, from whom, as being giants in the primary sense of the term, the age of giants took its name; the second, less properly so called, those other giants who were subjugated by the first.) Only the Hebrews retained the normal human stature, to which the descendants of the giants gradually returned.]

[Section I: Poetic Metaphysics]

[Chapter I] Poetic Metaphysics as the Origin of Poetry, Idolatry, Divination, and Sacrifices   374 From these first men, stupid, insensate, and horrible beasts, all the philosophers and philologians should have begun their investigations of the wisdom of the ancient gentiles; that is, from the giants in the proper sense in which we have just taken them. . . . And they should have begun

with metaphysics, which seeks its proofs not in the external world but within the modifications of the mind of him who meditates it. For since this world of nations has certainly been made by men, it is within these modifications that its principles should have been sought. And human nature, so far as it is like that of animals, carries with it this property, that the senses are its sole way of knowing things.

375   Hence poetic wisdom, the first wisdom of the gentile world, must have begun with a metaphysics not rational and abstract like that of learned men now, but felt and imagined as that of these first men must have been, who, without power of ratiocination, were all robust sense and vigorous imagination. This metaphysics was their poetry, a faculty born with them (for they were furnished by nature with these senses and imaginations); born of their ignorance of causes, for ignorance, the mother of wonder, made everything wonderful to men who were ignorant of everything. Their poetry was at first divine, because they imagined the causes of the things they felt and wondered at to be gods. (This is now confirmed by the American Indians, who call gods all the things that surpass their small understanding. We may add the ancient Germans dwelling about the Arctic Ocean, of whom Tacitus tells that they spoke of hearing the sun pass at night from west to east through the sea, and affirmed that they saw the gods. These very rude and simple nations help us to a much better understanding of the founders of the gentile world with whom we are now concerned.) At the same time they gave the things they wondered at substantial being after their own ideas, just as children do, whom we see take inanimate things in their hands and play with them and talk to them as though they were living persons.

376   In such fashion the first men of the gentile nations, children of nascent mankind, created things according to their own ideas. But this creation was infinitely different from that of God. For God, in his purest intelligence, knows things, and, by knowing them, creates them; but they, in their robust ignorance, did it by virtue of a wholly corporeal imagination. And because it was quite corporeal, they did it with marvelous sublimity; a sublimity such and so great that it excessively perturbed the very persons who by imagining did the creating, for which they were called "poets," which is Greek for "creators". Now

this is the threefold labor of great poetry: (1) to invent sublime fables suited to the popular understanding, (2) to perturb to excess, with a view to the end proposed: (3) to teach the vulgar to act virtuously, as the poets have taught themselves; as will presently be shown. Of this nature of human institutions it remained an eternal property, expressed in a noble phrase of Tacitus, that frightened men vainly "no sooner imagine than they believe" (*fingunt simul creduntque*).

377   Of such natures must have been the first founders of gentile humanity when [. . .] at last the sky fearfully rolled with thunder and flashed with lightning, as could not but follow from the bursting upon the air for the first time of an impression so violent. Thereupon a few giants, who must have been the most robust, and who were dispersed through the forests on the mountain heights where the strongest beasts have their dens, were frightened and astonished by the great effect whose cause they did not know, and raised their eyes and became aware of the sky. And because in such a case the nature of the human mind leads it to attribute its own nature to the effect, and because in that state their nature was that of men all robust bodily strength, who expressed their very violent passions by shouting and grumbling, they pictured the sky to themselves as a great animated body, which in that aspect they called Jove, the first god of the so-called greater gentes, who meant to tell them something by the hiss of his bolts and the clap of his thunder. And thus they began to exercise that natural curiosity which is the daughter of ignorance and the mother of knowledge, and which, opening the mind of man, gives birth to wonder. [. . .]

378   But the nature of our civilized minds is so detached from the senses, even in the vulgar, by abstractions corresponding to all the abstract terms our languages abound in, and so refined by the art of writing, and as it were spiritualized by the use of numbers, because even the vulgar know how to count and reckon, that it is naturally beyond our power to form the vast image of this mistress called "Sympathetic Nature." Men shape the phrase with their lips but have nothing in their minds; for what they have in mind is falsehood, which is nothing; and their imagination no longer avails to form a vast false image. It is equally beyond our power to enter into the vast imagination of those first men, whose minds

were not in the least abstract, refined, or spiritualized, because they were entirely immersed in the senses, buffeted by the passions, buried in the body. That is why we said above that we can scarcely understand, still less imagine, how those first men thought who founded gentile humanity.

379   In this fashion the first theological poets created the first divine fable, the greatest they ever created: that of Jove, king and father of men and gods, in the act of hurling the lightning bolt; an image so popular, disturbing, and instructive that its creators themselves believed in it, and feared, revered, and worshiped it in frightful religions. Whatever these men saw, imagined, or even made or did themselves they believed to be Jove; and to all of the universe that came within their scope, and to all its parts, they gave the being of animate substance. This is the civil history of the expression "All things are full of Jove" (*Iovis omnia plena*) . . . But for the theological poets Jove was no higher than the mountain peaks. The first men, who spoke by signs, naturally believed that lightning bolts and thunderclaps were signs made to them by Jove; whence from *nuo*, to make a sign, came *numen*, the divine will, by an idea more than sublime and worthy to express the divine majesty. They believed that Jove commanded by signs, that such signs were real words, and that nature was the language of Jove. The science of this language the gentiles universally believed to be divination, which by the Greeks was called theology, meaning the science of the language of the gods. Thus Jove acquired the fearful kingdom of the lightning and became the king of men and gods; and he acquired the two titles, that of best (*optimus*) in the sense of strongest (*fortissimus*) (as by a reverse process *fortis* meant in early Latin what *bonus* did in late), and that of greatest (*maximus*) from his vast body, the sky itself. From the first great benefit he conferred on mankind by not destroying it with his bolts, he received the title *Soter*, or savior. (This is the first of the three principles we have taken for our Science.) And for having put an end to the feral wandering of these few giants, so that they became the princes of the gentes, he received the epithet *Stator*, stayer or establisher. The Latin philologians explain this epithet too narrowly from Jove, invoked by Romulus, having stopped the Romans in their flight from the battle with the Sabines.

380 Every gentile nation had its Jove. [...] Thus the many Joves the philologians wonder at are so many physical histories preserved for us by the fables, which prove the universality of the flood.

381 Thus, in accordance with what has been said about the principles of the poetic characters, Jove was born naturally in poetry as a divine character or imaginative universal, to which everything having to do with the auspices was referred by all the ancient gentile nations, which must therefore all have been poetic by nature. Their poetic wisdom began with this poetic metaphysics, which contemplated God by the attribute of his providence; and they were called theological poets, or sages who understood the language of the gods expressed in the auspices of Jove; and were properly called divine in the sense of diviners, from *divinari*, to divine or predict. Their science was called Muse, defined by Homer as the knowledge of good and evil; that is, divination, on the prohibition of which God ordained his true religion for Adam. Because they were versed in this mystic theology, the Greek poets, who explained the divine mysteries of the auspices and oracles, were called *mystae*, which Horace learnedly renders "interpreters of the gods." Every gentile nation had its own sybil versed in this science, and we find mention of twelve of them. Sybils and oracles are the most ancient institutions of the gentile world.

382 All the things here discussed agree with that golden passage on the origins of idolatry: that the first people, simple and rough, invented the gods "from terror of present power". Thus it was fear which created gods in the world; not fear awakened in men by other men, but fear awakened in men by themselves. Along with this origin of idolatry is demonstrated likewise the origin of divination, which was brought into the world at the same birth. The origins of these two were followed by that of the sacrifices made to procure or rightly understand the auspices.

383 That such was the origin of poetry is finally confirmed by this eternal property of it: that its proper material is the credible impossibility. It is impossible that bodies should be minds, yet it was believed that the thundering sky was Jove. And nothing is dearer to poets than singing the marvels wrought by sorceresses by means of incantations. All this is to be explained by a hidden sense the nations have of the omnipotence of God. From this sense springs another by which all peoples are naturally led to do infinite honors to divinity. In this manner the poets founded religions among the gentiles.

384 All that has been so far said here upsets all the theories of the origin of poetry from Plato and Aristotle down to Patrizzi, Scaliger, and Castelvetro. For it has been shown that it was deficiency of human reasoning power that gave rise to poetry so sublime that the philosophies which came afterward, the arts of poetry and of criticism, have produced none equal or better, and have even prevented its production. Hence it is Homer's privilege to be, of all the sublime, that is, the heroic poets, the first in the order of merit as well as in that of age. This discovery of the origins of poetry does away with the opinion of the matchless wisdom of the ancients, so ardently sought after from Plato to Bacon's *De sapientia veterum*. For the wisdom of the ancients was the vulgar wisdom of the lawgivers who founded the human race, not the esoteric wisdom of great and rare philosophers. Whence it will be found, as it has been in the case of Jove, that all the mystic meanings of lofty philosophy attributed by the learned to the Greek fables and the Egyptian hieroglyphics are as impertinent as the historical meanings they both must have had are natural.

[Chapter II] Corollaries Concerning the Principal Aspects of this Science I 385 From what has been said up to this point it is concluded that divine providence, apprehended by such human sense as could have been possessed by rough, wild, and savage men who in despair of nature's succors desired something superior to nature to save them (which is the first principle on which we established the method of this Science), permitted them to be deceived into fearing the false divinity of Jove because he could strike them with lightning. Thus, through the thick clouds of those first tempests, intermittently lit by those flashes, they made out this great truth: that divine providence watches over the welfare of all mankind. So that this Science becomes in this principal aspect a rational civil theology of divine providence, which began in the vulgar wisdom of the lawgivers, who founded the nations by contemplating God under the attribute of providence, and which is completed

by the esoteric wisdom of the philosophers, who give a rational demonstration of it in their natural theology.

II 386 Here begins also a philosophy of authority, a second principal aspect of this Science, taking the word "authority" in its original meaning of property. The word is always used in this sense in the Law of the Twelve Tables, and the term *auctores* was accordingly applied to those from whom we derive title to property. *Auctor* certainly comes from *autos* (= *proprius* or *suus ipsius*); and many scholars write *autor* and *autoritas*, leaving out the aspirate.

387 Authority was at first divine; the authority by which divinity appropriated to itself the few giants we have spoken of, by properly casting them into the depths and recesses of the caves under the mountains. This is the iron ring by which the giants, dispersed upon the mountains, were kept chained to the earth by fear of the sky and of Jove, wherever they happened to be when the sky first thundered. Such were Tityus and Prometheus, chained to a high rock with their hearts being devoured by an eagle; that is, by the religion of Jove's auspices. Their being rendered immobile by fear was expressed by the Latins in the heroic phrase *terrore defixi*, and the artists depict them chained hand and foot with such links upon the mountains. Of these links was formed the great chain of which [. . .] Jove, to prove that he is king of men and gods, asserts that if all the gods and men were to take hold of one end, he alone at the other end would be able to drag them all. The Stoics would have the chain represent the eternal series of causes by which their Fate holds the world girdled and bound, but let them look out lest they be entangled in it themselves, because the dragging of men and gods by this chain depends on the will of Jove, yet they would have Jove subject to Fate.

388 Upon this divine authority followed human authority in the full philosophic sense of the term; that is, the property of human nature which not even God can take from man without destroying him. [. . .] This authority is the free use of the will, the intellect on the other hand being a passive power subject to truth. For from this first point of all human things, men began to exercise the freedom of the human will to hold in check the motions of the body, either to subdue them entirely or to give them better direction (this

being the impulse proper to free agents). Hence it was that the giants gave up the bestial custom of wandering through the great forest of the earth and habituated themselves to the quite contrary custom of remaining settled and hidden for a long period in their caves.

389 This authority of human nature was followed by the authority of natural law; for, having occupied and remained settled for a long time in the places where they chanced to find themselves at the time of the first thunderbolts, they became lords of them by occupation and long possession, the source of all dominion in the world. These are those "few whom just Jupiter loved" (*pauci quos aequus amavit/Iupiter*) whom the philosophers later metamorphosed into men favored by God with natural aptitudes for science and virtue. But the historical significance of this phrase is that in the recesses and depths [of the caves] they became the princes of the so-called greater gentes, who counted Jove the first god. These were the ancient noble houses, branching out into many families, of which the first kingdoms and the first cities were composed. Their memory was preserved in those fine heroic Latin phrases: *condere gentes, condere regna, condere urbes; fundare gentes, fundare regna, fundare urbes.*

390 This philosophy of authority follows the rational civil theology of providence because, by means of the former's theological proofs, the latter with its philosophical ones makes clear and distinct the philological ones; and with reference to the institutions of the most obscure antiquity of the nations it reduces to certitude the human will, which is by its nature most uncertain – which is as much as to say that it reduces philology to the form of a science.

III 391 The third principal aspect is a history of human ideas. These began with divine ideas by way of contemplation of the heavens with the bodily eyes. Thus in their science of augury the Romans used the verb *contemplari* for observing the parts of the sky whence the auguries came or the auspices were taken. These regions, marked out by the augurs with their wands, were called temples of the sky (*templa coeli*), whence must have come to the Greeks their first *theoremata* and *mathemata*, things divine or sublime to contemplate, which eventuated in metaphysical and mathematical abstractions. This is the civil history of the saying "From Jove the muse began" (*A*

Iove principium musae). For we have just seen that Jove's bolts produced the first muse, which Homer defines as "knowledge of good and evil". At this point it was all too easy for the philosophers later to intrude the dictum that the beginning of wisdom is piety. The first muse must have been Urania, who contemplated the heavens to take the auguries. Later she came to stand for astronomy, as will presently be shown. Just as poetic metaphysics was above divided into all its subordinate sciences, each sharing the poetic nature of their mother, so this history of ideas will present the rough origins both of the practical sciences in use among the nations and of the speculative sciences which are now cultivated by the learned.

IV 392   The fourth aspect is a philosophical criticism which grows out of the aforesaid history of ideas. Such a criticism will render true judgment upon the founders of the nations, which must have taken well over a thousand years to produce the writers who are the subjects of philological criticism. Beginning with Jove, our philosophical criticism will give us a natural theogony, or generation of the gods, as it took form naturally in the minds of the founders of the gentile world, who were by nature theological poets. The twelve gods of the so-called greater gentes, the ideas of whom were imagined by them from time to time on certain occasions of human necessity or utility, are assigned to twelve short epochs, into which we divide the period in which the fables were born. Thus this natural theogony will give us a rational chronology of poetic history for at least nine hundred years before vulgar history (which came after the heroic period) had its first beginnings.

V 393   The fifth aspect is an ideal eternal history traversed in time by the histories of all nations. Wherever, emerging from savage, fierce, and bestial times, men begin to domesticate themselves by religion, they begin, proceed, and end by those stages which are investigated here in Book Two, to be encountered again in Book Four, where we shall treat of the course the nations run, and in Book Five, where we shall treat of the recourse of human institutions.

VI 394   The sixth is a system of the natural law of the gentes. The three princes of this doctrine, Hugo Grotius, John Selden, and Samuel Pufendorf, should have taken their start from the beginnings of the gentes, where their subject matter begins. But all three of them err together in this respect, by beginning in the middle; that is, with the latest times of the civilized nations (and thus of men enlightened by fully developed natural reason), from which the philosophers emerged and rose to meditation of a perfect idea of justice.

398   For all these reasons, we begin our treatment of law – the Latin for which is *ius*, contraction of the ancient *Ious* (Jove) – at this most ancient point of all times, at the moment when the idea of Jove was born in the minds of the founders of the nations. [. . .] This then is our point of departure for the discussion of law, which was originally divine, in the proper sense expressed by divination, the science of Jove's auspices, which were the religious institutions by which the nations regulated all secular institutions. These two classes of institutions taken together make up the adequate subject matter of jurisprudence. Thus our treatment of natural law begins with the idea of divine providence, in the same birth with which was born the idea of law. For law began naturally to be observed, in the manner examined above, by the founders of the gentes properly so called, those of the most ancient order, which were called the greater gentes, whose first god was Jove.

VII 399   The seventh and last of the principal aspects of this Science is that of the principles of universal history. It begins with this first moment of all human institutions of the gentile world, with the first of the three ages of the world which the Egyptians said had elapsed before them; namely, the age of the gods, in which heaven began to reign on earth and to bestow great benefits on men. [. . .] This is the golden age of the Greeks, in which the gods consorted with men on earth, as we have seen Jove begin to do. Starting with this first age of the world, the Greek poets in their fables have faithfully narrated the universal flood and the existence of giants in nature, and thus have truly narrated the beginnings of profane universal history. Yet later men were unable to enter into the imaginations of the first men who founded the gentile world, which made them think they saw the gods. [. . .] For all these reasons profane universal history has hitherto lacked its beginning, and, for lack of the rational chronology of poetic history, it has lacked its continuity as well.

[Section II: Poetic Logic]

[*Chapter I*] *Poetic Logic* 400 That which is metaphysics insofar as it contemplates things in all the forms of their being, is logic insofar as it considers things in all the forms by which they may be signified. Accordingly, as poetry has been considered by us above as a poetic metaphysics in which the theological poets imagined bodies to be for the most part divine substances, so now that same poetry is considered as poetic logic, by which it signifies them.

401 "Logic" comes from *logos*, whose first and proper meaning was *fabula*, fable, carried over into Italian as *favella*, speech. In Greek the fable was also called *mythos*, myth, whence comes the Latin *mutus*, mute. For speech was born in mute times as mental [or sign] language, which Strabo in a golden passage says existed before vocal or articulate [language]; whence *logos* means both word and idea. It was fitting that the matter should be so ordered by divine providence in religious times, for it is an eternal property of religions that they attach more importance to meditation than to speech. Thus the first language in the first mute times of the nations must have begun with signs, whether gestures or physical objects, which had natural relations to the ideas [to be expressed]. For this reason *logos*, or word, meant also deed to the Hebrews and thing to the Greeks. [. . .] Similarly, *mythos* came to be defined for us as *vera narratio*, or true speech, the natural speech which first Plato and then Iamblichus said had been spoken in the world at one time. But this was mere conjecture on their part, and Plato's effort to recover this speech in the *Cratylus* was therefore vain, and he was criticized for it by Aristotle and Galen. For that first language, spoken by the theological poets, was not a language in accord with the nature of the things it dealt with (as must have been the sacred language invented by Adam, to whom God granted divine onomathesia, the giving of names to things according to the nature of each), but was a fantastic speech making use of physical substances endowed with life and most of them imagined to be divine.

402 This is the way in which the theological poets apprehended Jove, Cybele or Berecynthia, and Neptune, for example, and, at first mutely pointing, explained them as substances of the sky, the earth, and the sea, which they imagined to be animate divinities and were therefore true to their senses in believing them to be gods. By means of these three divinities, in accordance with what we have said above concerning poetic characters, they explained everything appertaining to the sky, the earth, and the sea. And similarly by means of the other divinities they signified the other kinds of things appertaining to each, denoting all flowers, for instance, by Flora, and all fruits by Pomona. We nowadays reverse this practice in respect of spiritual things, such as the faculties of the human mind, the passions, virtues, vices, sciences, and arts; for the most part the ideas we form of them are so many feminine personifications, to which we refer all the causes, properties, and effects that severally appertain to them. For when we wish to give utterance to our understanding of spiritual things, we must seek aid from our imagination to explain them and, like painters, form human images of them. But these theological poets, unable to make use of the understanding, did the opposite and more sublime thing: they attributed senses and passions, as we saw not long since, to bodies, and to bodies as vast as sky, sea, and earth. Later, as these vast imaginations shrank and the power of abstraction grew, the personifications were reduced to diminutive signs. Metonymy drew a cloak of learning over the prevailing ignorance of these origins of human institutions, which have remained buried until now. Jove becomes so small and light that he is flown about by an eagle. Neptune rides the waves in a fragile chariot. And Cybele rides seated on a lion.

403 Thus the mythologies, as their name indicates, must have been the proper languages of the fables; the fables being imaginative class concepts, as we have shown, the mythologies must have been the allegories corresponding to them. Allegory is defined as *diversiloquium* insofar as, by identity not of proportion but (to speak scholastically) of predicability, allegories signify the diverse species or the diverse individuals comprised under these genera. So that they must have a univocal signification connoting a quality common to all their species and individuals (as Achilles connotes an idea of valor common to all strong men, or Ulysses an idea of prudence common to all wise men); such that these allegories must be the etymologies of the poetic languages, which would make their origins

all univocal, whereas those of the vulgar languages are more often analogous. We also have the definition of the word "etymology" itself as meaning *veriloquium*, just as fable was defined as *vera narratio*.

(B) Hume, *An Enquiry Concerning Human Understanding*

Section VII: Of the Idea of Necessary Connexion

48 *Part I* THE great advantage of the mathematical sciences above the moral consists in this, that the ideas of the former, being sensible, are always clear and determinate, the smallest distinction between them is immediately perceptible, and the same terms are still expressive of the same ideas, without ambiguity or variation. An oval is never mistaken for a circle, nor an hyperbola for an ellipsis. The isosceles and scalenum are distinguished by boundaries more exact than vice and virtue, right and wrong. If any term be defined in geometry, the mind readily, of itself, substitutes, on all occasions, the definition for the term defined: Or even when no definition is employed, the object itself may be presented to the senses, and by that means be steadily and clearly apprehended. But the finer sentiments of the mind, the operations of the understanding, the various agitations of the passions, though really in themselves distinct, easily escape us, when surveyed by reflection; nor is it in our power to recall the original object, as often as we have occasion to contemplate it. Ambiguity, by this means, is gradually introduced into our reasonings: Similar objects are readily taken to be the same: And the conclusion becomes at last very wide of the premises.

One may safely, however, affirm, that, if we consider these sciences in a proper light, their advantages and disadvantages nearly compensate each other, and reduce both of them to a state of equality. If the mind, with greater facility, retains the ideas of geometry clear and determinate, it must carry on a much longer and more intricate chain of reasoning, and compare ideas much wider of each other, in order to reach the abstruser truths of that science. And if moral ideas are apt, without extreme care, to fall into obscurity and confusion, the inferences are always much shorter in these disquisitions, and the intermediate steps, which lead to the conclusion, much fewer than in the sciences which treat of quantity and number. In reality, there is scarcely a proposition in Euclid so simple, as not to consist of more parts, than are to be found in any moral reasoning which runs not into chimera and conceit. Where we trace the principles of the human mind through a few steps, we may be very well satisfied with our progress; considering how soon nature throws a bar to all our enquiries concerning causes, and reduces us to an acknowledgment of our ignorance. The chief obstacle, therefore, to our improvement in the moral or metaphysical sciences is the obscurity of the ideas, and ambiguity of the terms. The principal difficulty in the mathematics is the length of inferences and compass of thought, requisite to the forming of any conclusion. And, perhaps, our progress in natural philosophy is chiefly retarded by the want of proper experiments and phaenomena, which are often discovered by chance, and cannot always be found, when requisite, even by the most diligent and prudent enquiry. As moral philosophy seems hitherto to have received less improvement than either geometry or physics, we may conclude, that, if there be any difference in this respect among these sciences, the difficulties, which obstruct the progress of the former, require superior care and capacity to be surmounted.

There are no ideas, which occur in metaphysics, more obscure and uncertain, than those of *power, force, energy* or *necessary connexion*, of which it is every moment necessary for us to treat in all our disquisitions. We shall, therefore, endeavour, in this section, to fix, if possible, the precise meaning of these terms, and thereby remove some part of that obscurity, which is so much complained of in this species of philosophy.   49

It seems a proposition, which will not admit of much dispute, that all our ideas are nothing but copies of our impressions, or, in other words, that it is impossible for us to *think* of any thing, which we have not antecedently *felt*, either by our external or internal senses. I have endeavoured to explain and prove this proposition, and have expressed my hopes, that, by a proper application of it, men may reach a greater clearness and precision in philosophical reasonings, than what they have hitherto been able to attain. Complex ideas may, perhaps, be well known by definition, which is nothing but an enumeration of those parts or simple ideas, that compose them. But when we have pushed up definitions to the most simple ideas, and find still some ambiguity and obscurity; what resource are we then possessed of? By what invention can we throw light upon these ideas, and render them altogether precise and determinate to our intellectual view? Produce the impressions or original sentiments, from which the ideas are copied. These impressions are all strong and sensible. They admit not of ambiguity. They are not only placed in a full light themselves, but may throw light on their correspondent ideas, which lie in obscurity. And by this means, we may, perhaps, attain a new microscope or species of optics, by which, in the moral sciences, the most minute, and most simple ideas may be so enlarged as to fall readily under our apprehension, and be equally known with the grossest and most sensible ideas, that can be the object of our enquiry.

50   To be fully acquainted, therefore, with the idea of power or necessary connexion, let us examine its impression; and in order to find the impression with greater certainty, let us search for it in all the sources, from which it may possibly be derived.

When we look about us towards external objects, and consider the operation of causes, we are never able, in a single instance, to discover any power or necessary connexion; any quality, which binds the effect to the cause, and renders the one an infallible consequence of the other. We only find, that the one does actually, in fact, follow the other. The impulse of one billiard-ball is attended with motion in the second. This is the whole that appears to the *outward* senses. The mind feels no sentiment or *inward* impression from this succession of objects: Consequently, there is not, in any single, particular instance of cause and effect, any thing which can suggest the idea of power or necessary connexion.

From the first appearance of an object, we never can conjecture what effect will result from it. But were the power or energy of any cause discoverable by the mind, we could foresee the effect, even without experience; and might, at first, pronounce with certainty concerning it, by mere dint of thought and reasoning.

In reality, there is no part of matter, that does ever, by its sensible qualities, discover any power or energy, or give us ground to imagine, that it could produce any thing, or be followed by any other object, which we could denominate its effect. Solidity, extension, motion; these qualities are all complete in themselves, and never point out any other event which may result from them. The scenes of the universe are continually shifting, and one object follows another in an uninterrupted succession; but the power of force, which actuates the whole machine, is entirely concealed from us, and never discovers itself in any of the sensible qualities of body. We know, that, in fact, heat is a constant attendant of flame; but what is the connexion between them, we have no room so much as to conjecture or imagine. It is impossible, therefore, that the idea of power can be derived from the contemplation of bodies, in single instances of their operation; because no bodies ever discover any power, which can be the original of this idea.*

Since, therefore, external objects as they appear 51 to the senses, give us no idea of power or necessary connexion, by their operation in particular instances, let us see, whether this idea be derived from reflection on the operations of our own minds, and be copied from any internal impression. It may be said, that we are every moment conscious of internal power; while we feel, that, by the simple command of our will, we can move the organs of our body, or direct the faculties of our mind. An act of volition produces motion in our limbs, or raises a new idea in our imagination. This influence of the will we know by consciousness. Hence we acquire the idea of power or energy; and are certain, that we ourselves and all other intelligent beings are possessed of power. This idea, then, is an idea of reflection, since it arises from reflecting on the operations of our own mind, and on the command which is exercised by will, both over the organs of the body and faculties of the soul.

* Mr Locke, in his chapter of power, says that, finding from experience, that there are several new productions in nature, and concluding that there must somewhere be a power capable of producing them, we arrive at last by this reasoning at the idea of power. But no reasoning can ever give us a new, original, simple idea; as this philosopher himself confesses. This, therefore, can never be the origin of that idea.

52   We shall proceed to examine this pretension; and first with regard to the influence of volition over the organs of the body. This influence, we may observe, is a fact, which, like all other natural events, can be known only by experience, and can never be foreseen from any apparent energy or power in the cause, which connects it with the effect, and renders the one an infallible consequence of the other. The motion of our body follows upon the command of our will. Of this we are every moment conscious. But the means, by which this is effected; the energy, by which the will performs so extraordinary an operation; of this we are so far from being immediately conscious, that it must for ever escape our most diligent enquiry.

For *first*; is there any principle in all nature more mysterious than the union of soul with body; by which a supposed spiritual substance acquires such an influence over a material one, that the most refined thought is able to actuate the grossest matter? Were we empowered, by a secret wish, to remove mountains, or control the planets in their orbit; this extensive authority would not be more extraordinary, nor more beyond our comprehension. But if by consciousness we perceived any power or energy in the will, we must know this power; we must know its connexion with the effect; we must know the secret union of soul and body, and the nature of both these substances; by which the one is able to operate, in so many instances, upon the other.

Secondly, We are not able to move all the organs of the body with a like authority; though we cannot assign any reason besides experience, for so remarkable a difference between one and the other. Why has the will an influence over the tongue and fingers, not over the heart or liver? This question would never embarrass us, were we conscious of a power in the former case, not in the latter. We should then perceive, independent of experience, why the authority of will over the organs of the body is circumscribed within such particular limits. Being in that case fully acquainted with the power or force, by which it operates, we should also know, why its influence reaches precisely to such boundaries, and no farther.

A man, suddenly struck with palsy in the leg or arm, or who had newly lost those members, frequently endeavours, at first to move them, and employ them in their usual offices. Here he is as much conscious of power to command such limbs, as a man in perfect health is conscious of power to actuate any member which remains in its natural state and condition. But consciousness never deceives. Consequently, neither in the one case nor in the other, are we ever conscious of any power. We learn the influence of our will from experience alone. And experience only teaches us, how one event constantly follows another; without instructing us in the secret connexion, which binds them together, and renders them inseparable.

Thirdly, We learn from anatomy, that the immediate object of power in voluntary motion, is not the member itself which is moved, but certain muscles, and nerves, and animal spirits, and, perhaps, something still more minute and more unknown, through which the motion is successively propagated, ere it reach the member itself whose motion is the immediate object of volition. Can there be a more certain proof, that the power, by which this whole operation is performed, so far from being directly and fully known by an inward sentiment or consciousness, is, to the last degree, mysterious and unintelligible? Here the mind wills a certain event: Immediately another event, unknown to ourselves, and totally different from the one intended, is produced: This event produces another, equally unknown: Till at last, through a long succession, the desired event is produced. But if the original power were felt, it must be known: Were it known, its effect also must be known; since all power is relative to its effect. And *vice versa*, if the effect be not known, the power cannot be known nor felt. How indeed can we be conscious of a power to move our limbs, when we have no such power; but only that to move certain animal spirits, which, though they produce at last the motion of our limbs, yet operate in such a manner as is wholly beyond our comprehension?

We may, therefore, conclude from the whole, I hope, without any temerity, though with assurance; that our idea of power is not copied from any sentiment or consciousness of power within ourselves, when we give rise to animal motion, or apply our limbs to their proper use and office. That their motion follows the command of the will is a matter of common experience, like other natural events: But the power or energy by which this is effected, like that in other natural events, is unknown and inconceivable.*

53   Shall we then assert, that we are conscious of a power or energy in our own minds, when, by an act or command of our will, we raise up a new idea, fix the mind to the contemplation of it, turn it on all sides, and at last dismiss it for some other idea, when we think that we have surveyed it with sufficient accuracy? I believe the same arguments will prove, that even this command of the will gives us no real idea of force or energy.

First, It must be allowed, that, when we know a power, we know that very circumstance in the cause, by which it is enabled to produce the effect: For these are supposed to be synonimous. We must, therefore, know both the cause and effect, and the relation between them. But do we pretend to be acquainted with the nature of the human soul and the nature of an idea, or the aptitude of the one to produce the other? This is a real creation; a production of something out of nothing: Which implies a power so great, that it may seem, at first sight, beyond the reach of any being, less than infinite. At least it must be owned, that such a power is not felt, nor known, nor even conceivable by the mind. We only feel the event, namely, the existence of an idea, consequent to a command of the will: But the manner, in which this operation is performed, the power by which it is produced, is entirely beyond our comprehension.

---

* It may be pretended, that the resistance which we meet with in bodies, obliging us frequently to exert our force, and call up all our power, this gives us the idea of force and power. It is this *nisus*, or strong endeavour, of which we are conscious, that is the original impression from which this idea is copied. But, first, we attribute power to a vast number of objects, where we never can suppose this resistance or exertion of force to take place; to the Supreme Being, who never meets with any resistance; to the mind in its command over its ideas and limbs, in common thinking and motion, where the effect follows immediately upon the will, without any exertion or summoning up of force; to inanimate matter, which is not capable of this sentiment. *Secondly*, This sentiment of an endeavour to overcome resistance has no known connexion with any event: What follows it, we know by experience; but could not know it *a priori*. It must, however, be confessed, that the animal *nisus*, which we experience, though it can afford no accurate precise idea of power, enters very much into that vulgar, inaccurate idea, which is formed of it.

Secondly, The command of the mind over itself is limited, as well as its command over the body; and these limits are not known by reason, or any acquaintance with the nature of cause and effect, but only by experience and observation, as in all other natural events and in the operation of external objects. Our authority over our sentiments and passions is much weaker than that over our ideas; and even the latter authority is circumscribed within very narrow boundaries. Will any one pretend to assign the ultimate reason of these boundaries, or show why the power is deficient in one case, not in another.

Thirdly, This self-command is very different at different times. A man in health possesses more of it than one languishing with sickness. We are more master of our thoughts in the morning than in the evening: Fasting, than after a full meal. Can we give any reason for these variations, except experience? Where then is the power, of which we pretend to be conscious? Is there not here, either in a spiritual or material substance, or both, some secret mechanism or structure of parts, upon which the effect depends, and which, being entirely unknown to us, renders the power or energy of the will equally unknown and incomprehensible?

Volition is surely an act of the mind, with which we are sufficiently acquainted. Reflect upon it. Consider it on all sides. Do you find anything in it like this creative power, by which it raises from nothing a new idea, and with a kind of *Fiat*, imitates the omnipotence of its Maker, if I may be allowed so to speak, who called forth into existence all the various scenes of nature? So far from being conscious of this energy in the will, it requires as certain experience as that of which we are possessed, to convince us that such extraordinary effects do ever result from a simple act of volition.

The generality of mankind never find any 54 difficulty in accounting for the more common and familiar operations of nature – such as the descent of heavy bodies, the growth of plants, the generation of animals, or the nourishment of bodies by food: But suppose that, in all these cases, they perceive the very force or energy of the cause, by which it is connected with its effect, and is for ever infallible in its operation. They acquire, by long habit, such a turn of mind, that, upon the appearance of the cause, they immediately expect with assurance its usual attendant, and hardly conceive it possible that any other event could result from it. It is only on the discovery of extraordinary phaenomena, such as earthquakes, pestilence, and prodigies of any kind, that they find themselves at a loss to assign a proper cause, and to explain the manner in which the effect is produced by it. It is usual for men, in such difficulties, to have recourse to some invisible intelligent principle as the immediate cause of that event which surprises them, and which, they think, cannot be accounted for from the common powers of nature. But philosophers, who carry their scrutiny a little farther, immediately perceive that, even in the most familiar events, the energy of the cause is as unintelligible as in the most unusual, and that we only learn by experience the frequent *Conjunction* of objects, without being ever able to comprehend anything like

55 *Connexion* between them. Here, then, many philosophers think themselves obliged by reason to have recourse, on all occasions, to the same principle, which the vulgar never appeal to but in cases that appear miraculous and supernatural. They acknowledge mind and intelligence to be, not only the ultimate and original cause of all things, but the immediate and sole cause of every event which appears in nature. They pretend that those objects which are commonly denominated *causes*, are in reality nothing but *occasions*; and that the true and direct principle of every effect is not any power or force in nature, but a volition of the Supreme Being, who wills that such particular objects should for ever be conjoined with each other. Instead of saying that one billiard-ball moves another by a force which it has derived from the author of nature, it is the Deity himself, they say, who, by a particular volition, moves the second ball, being determined to this operation by the impulse of the first ball, in consequence of those general laws which he has laid down to himself in the government of the universe. But philosophers advancing still in their inquiries, discover that, as we are totally ignorant of the power on which depends the mutual operation of bodies, we are no less ignorant of that power on which depends the operation of mind on body, or of body on mind; nor are we able, either from our senses or consciousness, to assign the ultimate principle in one case more than in the other. The same ignorance, therefore, reduces them to the same conclusion. They assert that the Deity is the immediate cause of the union

between soul and body; and that they are not the organs of sense, which, being agitated by external objects, produce sensations in the mind; but that it is a particular volition of our omnipotent Maker, which excites such a sensation, in consequence of such a motion in the organ. In like manner, it is not any energy in the will that produces local motion in our members: It is God himself, who is pleased to second our will, in itself impotent, and to command that motion which we erroneously attribute to our own power and efficacy. Nor do philosophers stop at this conclusion. They sometimes extend the same inference to the mind itself, in its internal operations. Our mental vision or conception of ideas is nothing but a revelation made to us by our Maker. When we voluntarily turn our thoughts to any object, and raise up its image in the fancy, it is not the will which creates that idea: It is the universal Creator, who discovers it to the mind, and renders it present to us.

Thus, according to these philosophers, every 56 thing is full of God. Not content with the principle, that nothing exists but by his will, that nothing possesses any power but by his concession: They rob nature, and all created beings, of every power, in order to render their dependence on the Deity still more sensible and immediate. They consider not that, by this theory, they diminish, instead of magnifying, the grandeur of those attributes, which they affect so much to celebrate. It argues surely more power in the Deity to delegate a certain degree of power to inferior creatures than to produce every thing by his own immediate volition. It argues more wisdom to contrive at first the fabric of the world with such perfect foresight that, of itself, and by its proper operation, it may serve all the purposes of providence, than if the great Creator were obliged every moment to adjust its parts, and animate by his breath all the wheels of that stupendous machine.

But if we would have a more philosophical confutation of this theory, perhaps the two following reflections may suffice.

First, it seems to me that this theory of the 57 universal energy and operation of the Supreme Being is too bold ever to carry conviction with it to a man, sufficiently apprized of the weakness of human reason, and the narrow limits to which it is confined in all its operations. Though the chain of arguments which conduct to it were ever so logical, there must arise a strong suspicion, if not an absolute assurance, that it has carried us quite beyond the reach of our faculties, when it leads to conclusions so extraordinary, and so remote from common life and experience. We are got into fairy land, long ere we have reached the last steps of our theory; and *there* we have no reason to trust our common methods of argument, or to think that our usual analogies and probabilities have any authority. Our line is too short to fathom such immense abysses. And however we may flatter ourselves that we are guided, in every step which we take, by a kind of verisimilitude and experience, we may be assured that this fancied experience has no authority when we thus apply it to subjects that lie entirely out of the sphere of experience. But on this we shall have occasion to touch afterwards.

Secondly, I cannot perceive any force in the arguments on which this theory is founded. We are ignorant, it is true, of the manner in which bodies operate on each other: Their force or energy is entirely incomprehensible: But are we not equally ignorant of the manner or force by which a mind, even the supreme mind, operates either on itself or on body? Whence, I beseech you, do we acquire any idea of it? We have no sentiment or consciousness of this power in ourselves. We have no idea of the Supreme Being but what we learn from reflection on our own faculties. Were our ignorance, therefore, a good reason for rejecting any thing, we should be led into that principle of denying all energy in the Supreme Being as much as in the grossest matter. We surely comprehend as little the operations of one as of the other. Is it more difficult to conceive that motion may arise from impulse than that it may arise from volition? All we know is our profound ignorance in both cases.*

Part II   58   But to hasten to a conclusion of this argument, which is already drawn out to too great a length: We have sought in vain for an idea of power or necessary connexion in all the sources from which we could suppose it to be derived. It appears that, in single instances of the operation of bodies, we never can, by our utmost scrutiny, discover any thing but one event following another, without being able to comprehend any force or power by which the cause operates, or any connexion between it and its supposed effect. The same difficulty occurs in contemplating the operations of mind on body – where we observe the motion of the latter to follow upon the volition of the former, but are not able to observe or conceive the tie which binds together the motion and volition, or the energy by which the mind produces this effect. The authority of the will over its own faculties and ideas is not a whit more comprehensible: So that, upon the whole, there appears not, throughout all nature, any one instance of connexion which is conceivable by us. All events seem entirely loose and separate. One event follows another; but we never can observe any tie between them. They seem *conjoined*, but never *connected*. And as we can have no idea of any thing which never appeared to our outward sense or inward sentiment, the necessary conclusion *seems* to be that we have no idea of connexion or power at all, and that these words are absolutely without any meaning, when employed either in philosophical reasonings or common life.

---

* I need not examine at length the *vis inertiae* which is so much talked of in the new philosophy, and which is ascribed to matter. We find by experience, that a body at rest or in motion continues for ever in its present state, till put from it by some new cause; and that a body impelled takes as much motion from the impelling body as it acquires itself. These are facts. When we call this a *vis inertiae*, we only mark these facts, without pretending to have any idea of the inert power; in the same manner as, when we talk of gravity, we mean certain effects, without comprehending that active power. It was never the meaning of Sir Isaac Newton to rob second causes of all force or energy; though some of his followers have endeavoured to establish that theory upon his authority. On the contrary, that great philosopher had recourse to an etherial active fluid to explain his universal attraction; though he was so cautious and modest as to allow, that it was a mere hypothesis, not to be insisted on, without more experiments. I must confess, that there is something in the fate of opinions a little extraordinary. Descartes insinuated that doctrine of the universal and sole efficacy of the Deity, without insisting on it. Malebranche and other Cartesians made it the foundation of all their philosophy. It had, however, no authority in England. Locke, Clarke, and Cudworth, never so much as take notice of it, but suppose all along, that matter has a real, though subordinate and derived power. By what means has it become so prevalent among our modern metaphysicians?

59   But there still remains one method of avoiding this conclusion, and one source which we have not yet examined. When any natural object or event is presented, it is impossible for us, by any sagacity or penetration, to discover, or even conjecture, without experience, what event will result from it, or to carry our foresight beyond that object which is immediately present to the memory and senses. Even after one instance or experiment where we have observed a particular event to follow upon another, we are not entitled to form a general rule, or foretell what will happen in like cases; it being justly esteemed an unpardonable temerity to judge of the whole course of nature from one single experiment, however accurate or certain. But when one particular species of event has always, in all instances, been conjoined with another, we make no longer any scruple of foretelling one upon the appearance of the other, and of employing that reasoning, which can alone assure us of any matter of fact or existence. We then call the one object, *Cause*; the other, *Effect*. We suppose that there is some connexion between them; some power in the one, by which it infallibly produces the other, and operates with the greatest certainty and strongest necessity.

It appears, then, that this idea of a necessary connexion among events arises from a number of similar instances which occur of the constant conjunction of these events; nor can that idea ever be suggested by any one of these instances, surveyed in all possible lights and positions. But there is nothing in a number of instances, different from every single instance, which is supposed to be exactly similar; except only, that after a repetition of similar instances, the mind is carried by habit, upon the appearance of one event, to expect its usual attendant, and to believe that it will exist. This connexion, therefore, which we *feel* in the mind, this customary transition of the imagination from one object to its usual attendant, is the sentiment or impression from which we form the idea of power or necessary connexion. Nothing farther is in the case. Contemplate the subject on all sides; you will never find any other origin of that idea. This is the sole difference between one instance, from which we can never receive the idea of connexion, and a number of similar instances, by which it is suggested. The first time a man saw the communication of motion by impulse, as by the shock of two billiard balls, he could not pronounce that the one event was *connected*: but only that it was *conjoined* with the other. After he has observed several instances of this nature, he then pronounces them to be *connected*. What alteration has happened to give rise to this new idea of *connexion*? Nothing but that he now *feels* these events to be *connected* in his imagination, and can readily foretell the existence of one from the appearance of the other. When we say, therefore, that one object is connected with another, we mean only that they have acquired a connexion in our thought, and give rise to this inference, by which they become proofs of each other's existence: A conclusion which is somewhat extraordinary, but which seems founded on sufficient evidence. Nor will its evidence be weakened by any general diffidence of the understanding, or sceptical suspicion concerning every conclusion which is new and extraordinary. No conclusions can be more agreeable to scepticism than such as make discoveries concerning the weakness and narrow limits of human reason and capacity.

And what stronger instance can be produced 60 of the surprising ignorance and weakness of the understanding than the present? For surely, if there be any relation among objects which it imports to us to know perfectly, it is that of cause and effect. On this are founded all our reasonings concerning matter of fact or existence. By means of it alone we attain any assurance concerning objects which are removed from the present testimony of our memory and senses. The only immediate utility of all sciences, is to teach us, how to control and regulate future events by their causes. Our thoughts and enquiries are, therefore, every moment, employed about this relation: Yet so imperfect are the ideas which we form concerning it, that it is impossible to give any just definition of cause, except what is drawn from something extraneous and foreign to it. Similar objects are always conjoined with similar. Of this we have experience. Suitably to this experience, therefore, we may define a cause to be *an object, followed by another, and where all the objects similar to the first are followed by objects similar to the second*. Or in other words *where, if the first object had not been, the second never had existed*. The appearance of a cause always conveys the mind, by a customary transition, to the idea of the effect. Of this also we have experience. We may, therefore, suitably to this experience, form another definition of cause, and call it, *an object followed by another, and whose appearance always conveys the thought to that other.* But though both these definitions be drawn from circumstances foreign to the cause, we cannot remedy this inconvenience, or attain any more perfect definition, which may point out that circumstance in the cause, which gives it a connexion with its effect. We have no idea of this connexion, nor even any distinct notion what it is we desire to know, when we endeavour at a conception of it. We say, for instance, that the vibration of this string is the cause of this particular sound. But what do we mean by that affirmation? We either mean *that this vibration is followed by this sound, and that all similar vibrations have been followed by similar sounds:* Or, *that this vibration is followed by this sound, and that upon the appearance of one the mind anticipates the senses, and forms immediately an idea of the other.* We may consider the relation of cause and effect in either of these two lights; but beyond these, we have no idea of it.*

61   To recapitulate, therefore, the reasonings of this section: Every idea is copied from some preceding impression or sentiment; and where we cannot find any impression, we may be certain that there is no idea. In all single instances of the operation of bodies or minds, there is nothing that produces any impression, nor consequently can suggest any idea of power or necessary connexion. But when many uniform

instances appear, and the same object is always followed by the same event; we then begin to entertain the notion of cause and connexion. We then *feel* a new sentiment or impression, to wit, a customary connexion in the thought or imagination between one object and its usual attendant; and this sentiment is the original of that idea which we seek for. For as this idea arises from a number of similar instances, and not from any single instance, it must arise from that circumstance, in which the number of instances differ from every individual instance. But this customary connexion or transition of the imagination is the only circumstance in which they differ. In every other particular they are alike. The first instance which we saw of motion communicated by the shock of two billiard balls (to return to this obvious illustration) is exactly similar to any instance that may, at present, occur to us; except only, that we could not, at first, *infer* one event from the other; which we are enabled to do at present, after so long a course of uniform experience. I know not whether the reader will readily apprehend this reasoning. I am afraid that, should I multiply words about it, or throw it into a greater variety of lights, it would only become more obscure and intricate. In all abstract reasonings there is one point of view which, if we can happily hit, we shall go farther towards illustrating the subject than by all the eloquence and copious expression in the world. This point of view we should endeavour to

---

* According to these explications and definitions, the idea of *power* is relative as much as that of *cause*; and both have a reference to an effect, or some other event constantly conjoined with the former. When we consider the *unknown* circumstance of an object, by which the degree or quantity of its effect is fixed and determined, we call that its power: And accordingly, it is allowed by all philosophers, that the effect is the measure of the power. But if they had any idea of power, as it is in itself, why could not they Measure it in itself? The dispute whether the force of a body in motion be as its velocity, or the square of its velocity; this dispute, I say, need not be decided by comparing its effects in equal or unequal times; but by a direct mensuration and comparison.

As to the frequent use of the words, Force, Power, Energy, &c., which every where occur in common conversation, as well as in philosophy; that is no proof, that we are acquainted, in any instance, with the connecting principle between cause and effect, or can

account ultimately for the production of one thing to another. These words, as commonly used, have very loose meanings annexed to them; and their ideas are very uncertain and confused. No animal can put external bodies in motion without the sentiment of a *nisus* or endeavour; and every animal has a sentiment or feeling from the stroke or blow of an external object, that is in motion. These sensations, which are merely animal, and from which we can *à priori* draw no inference, we are apt to transfer to inanimate objects, and to suppose, that they have some such feelings, whenever they transfer or receive motion. With regard to energies, which are exerted, without our annexing to them any idea of communicated motion, we consider only the constant experienced conjunction of the events; and as we *feel* a customary connexion between the ideas, we transfer that feeling to the objects; as nothing is more usual than to apply to external bodies every internal sensation, which they occasion.

reach, and reserve the flowers of rhetoric for subjects which are more adapted to them.

Section XII: Of the Academical or Sceptical Philosophy

116 *Part I* There is not a greater number of philosophical reasonings, displayed upon any subject, than those, which prove the existence of a Deity, and refute the fallacies of *Atheists*; and yet the most religious philosophers still dispute whether any man can be so blinded as to be a speculative atheist. How shall we reconcile these contradictions? The knights errant, who wandered about to clear the world of dragons and giants, never entertained the least doubt with regard to the existence of these monsters.

The *Sceptic* is another enemy of religion, who naturally provokes the indignation of all divines and graver philosophers; though it is certain, that no man ever met with any such absurd creature, or conversed with a man, who had no opinion or principle concerning any subject, either of action or speculation. This begets a very natural question: What is meant by a sceptic? And how far it is possible to push these philosophical principles of doubt and uncertainty?

There is a species of scepticism, *antecedent* to all study and philosophy, which is much inculcated by Descartes and others, as a sovereign preservative against error and precipitate judgement. It recommends an universal doubt, not only of all our former opinions and principles, but also of our very faculties; of whose veracity, say they, we must assure ourselves, by a chain of reasoning, deduced from some original principle, which cannot possibly be fallacious or deceitful. But neither is there any such original principle, which has a prerogative above others, that are self-evident and convincing: or if there were, could we advance a step beyond it, but by the use of those very faculties, of which we are supposed to be already diffident. The Cartesian doubt, therefore, were it ever possible to be attained by any human creature (as it plainly is not) would be entirely incurable; and no reasoning could ever bring us to a state of assurance and conviction upon any subject.

117 It must, however, be confessed, that this species of scepticism, when more moderate, may be understood in a very reasonable sense, and is a necessary preparative to the study of philosophy, by preserving a proper impartiality in our judgements, and weaning our mind from all those prejudices, which we may have imbibed from education or rash opinion. To begin with clear and self-evident principles, to advance by timorous and sure steps, to review frequently our conclusions, and examine accurately all their consequences; though by these means we shall make both a slow and a short progress in our systems; are the only methods, by which we can ever hope to reach truth, and attain a proper stability and certainty in our determinations.

There is another species of scepticism, *consequent* to science and enquiry, when men are supposed to have discovered, either the absolute fallaciousness of their mental faculties, or their unfitness to reach any fixed determination in all those curious subjects of speculation, about which they are commonly employed. Even our very senses are brought into dispute, by a certain species of philosophers; and the maxims of common life are subjected to the same doubt as the most profound principles or conclusions of metaphysics and theology. As these paradoxical tenets (if they may be called tenets) are to be met with in some philosophers, and the refutation of them in several, they naturally excite our curiosity, and make us enquire into the arguments, on which they may be founded.

I need not insist upon the more trite topics, employed by the sceptics in all ages, against the evidence of *sense*; such as those which are derived from the imperfection and fallaciousness of our organs, on numberless occasions; the crooked appearance of an oar in water; the various aspects of objects, according to their different distances; the double images which arise from the pressing one eye; with many other appearances of a like nature. These sceptical topics, indeed, are only sufficient to prove, that the senses alone are not implicitly to be depended on; but that we must correct their evidence by reason, and by considerations, derived from the nature of the medium, the distance of the object, and the disposition of the organ, in order to render them, within their sphere, the proper *criteria* of truth and falsehood. There are other more profound arguments against the senses, which admit not of so easy a solution.

It seems evident, that men are carried, by a 118 natural instinct or prepossession, to repose faith in their senses; and that, without any reasoning, or even almost before the use of reason, we always suppose an external universe, which depends not on our perception, but would exist, though we and every sensible creature were absent or annihilated. Even the animal creation are governed by a like opinion, and preserve this belief of external objects, in all their thoughts, designs, and actions.

It seems also evident, that, when men follow this blind and powerful instinct of nature, they always suppose the very images, presented by the senses, to be the external objects, and never entertain any suspicion, that the one are nothing but representations of the other. This very table, which we see white, and which we feel hard, is believed to exist, independent of our perception, and to be something external to our mind, which perceives it. Our presence bestows not being on it: our absence does not annihilate it. It preserves its existence uniform and entire, independent of the situation of intelligent beings, who perceive or contemplate it.

But this universal and primary opinion of all men is soon destroyed by the slightest philosophy, which teaches us, that nothing can ever be present to the mind but an image or perception, and that the senses are only the inlets, through which these images are conveyed, without being able to produce any immediate intercourse between the mind and the object. The table, which we see, seems to diminish, as we remove farther from it: but the real table, which exists independent of us, suffers no alteration: it was, therefore, nothing but its image, which was present to the mind. These are the obvious dictates of reason; and no man, who reflects, ever doubted, that the existences, which we consider, when we say, *this house* and *that tree*, are nothing but perceptions in the mind, and fleeting copies or representations of other existences, which remain uniform and independent.

119   So far, then, are we necessitated by reasoning to contradict or depart from the primary instincts of nature, and to embrace a new system with regard to the evidence of our senses. But here philosophy finds herself extremely embarrassed, when she would justify this new system, and obviate the cavils and objections of the sceptics. She can no longer plead the infallible and irresistible instinct of nature: for that led us to a quite different system, which is acknowledged fallible and even erroneous. And to justify this pretended philosophical system, by a chain of clear and convincing argument, or even any appearance of argument, exceeds the power of all human capacity.

By what argument can it be proved, that the perceptions of the mind must be caused by external objects, entirely different from them, though resembling them (if that be possible) and could not arise either from the energy of the mind itself, or from the suggestion of some invisible and unknown spirit, or from some other cause still more unknown to us? It is acknowledged, that, in fact, many of these perceptions arise not from anything external, as in dreams, madness, and other diseases. And nothing can be more inexplicable than the manner, in which body should so operate upon mind as ever to convey an image of itself to a substance, supposed of so different, and even contrary a nature.

It is a question of fact, whether the perceptions of the senses be produced by external objects, resembling them: how shall this question be determined? By experience surely; as all other questions of a like nature. But here experience is, and must be entirely silent. The mind has never anything present to it but the perceptions, and cannot possibly reach any experience of their connexion with objects. The supposition of such a connexion is, therefore, without any foundation in reasoning.

To have recourse to the veracity of the su- 120 preme Being, in order to prove the veracity of our senses, is surely making a very unexpected circuit. If his veracity were at all concerned in this matter, our senses would be entirely infallible; because it is not possible that he can ever deceive. Not to mention, that, if the external world be once called in question, we shall be at a loss to find arguments, by which we may prove the existence of that Being or any of his attributes.

This is a topic, therefore, in which the pro- 121 founder and more philosophical sceptics will always triumph, when they endeavour to introduce an universal doubt into all subjects of human knowledge and enquiry. Do you follow the instincts and propensities of nature, may they say, in assenting to the veracity of sense? But these lead you to believe that the very perception or sensible image is the external object. Do you disclaim this principle, in order to embrace a more rational opinion, that the perceptions are only representations of something external? You here depart from your natural propensities and more obvious sentiments; and yet are not able to satisfy your reason, which can never find any convincing argument from experience to prove, that the perceptions are connected with any external objects.

122　　There is another sceptical topic of a like nature, derived from the most profound philosophy; which might merit our attention, were it requisite to dive so deep, in order to discover arguments and reasonings, which can so little serve to any serious purpose. It is universally allowed by modern enquirers, that all the sensible qualities of objects, such as hard, soft, hot, cold, white, black, &c. are merely secondary, and exist not in the objects themselves, but are perceptions of the mind, without any external archetype or model, which they represent. If this be allowed, with regard to secondary qualities, it must also follow, with regard to the supposed primary qualities of extension and solidity; nor can the latter be any more entitled to that denomination than the former. The idea of extension is entirely acquired from the senses of sight and feeling; and if all the qualities, perceived by the senses, be in the mind, not in the object, the same conclusion must reach the idea of extension, which is wholly dependent on the sensible ideas or the ideas of secondary qualities. Nothing can save us from this conclusion, but the asserting, that the ideas of those primary qualities are attained by *Abstraction*, an opinion, which, if we examine it accurately, we shall find to be unintelligible, and even absurd. An extension, that is neither tangible nor visible, cannot possibly be conceived: and a tangible or visible extension, which is neither hard nor soft, black nor white, is equally beyond the reach of human conception. Let any man try to conceive a triangle in general, which is neither *Isosceles* nor *Scalenum*, nor has any particular length or proportion of sides; and he will soon perceive the absurdity of all the scholastic notions with regard to abstraction and general ideas.*

* This argument is drawn from Dr Berkeley; and indeed most of the writings of that very ingenious author form the best lessons of scepticism, which are to be found either among the ancient or modern philosophers, Bayle not excepted. He professes, however, in his title-page (and undoubtedly with great truth) to have composed his book against the sceptics

Thus the first philosophical objection to 123 the evidence of sense or to the opinion of external existence consists in this, that such an opinion, if rested on natural instinct, is contrary to reason, and if referred to reason, is contrary to natural instinct, and at the same time carries no rational evidence with it, to convince an impartial enquirer. The second objection goes farther, and represents this opinion as contrary to reason: at least, if it be a principle of reason, that all sensible qualities are in the mind, not in the object. Bereave matter of all its intelligible qualities, both primary and secondary, you in a manner annihilate it, and leave only a certain unknown, inexplicable *something*, as the cause of our perceptions; a notion so imperfect, that no sceptic will think it worth while to contend against it.

Part II　It may seem a very extravagant attempt of the sceptics to destroy *reason* by argument and ratiocination; yet is this the grand scope of all their enquiries and disputes. They endeavour to find objections, both to our abstract reasonings, and to those which regard matter of fact and existence.

The chief objection against all *abstract* reasonings is derived from the ideas of space and time; ideas, which, in common life and to a careless view, are very clear and intelligible, but when they pass through the scrutiny of the profound sciences (and they are the chief object of these sciences) afford principles, which seem full of absurdity and contradiction. No priestly *dogmas*, invented on purpose to tame and subdue the rebellious reason of mankind, ever shocked commonsense more than the doctrine of the infinite divisibility of extension, with its consequences;[1] as they are pompously displayed by all geometricians and metaphysicians, with a kind of triumph and exultation. A real quantity, infinitely less than any finite quantity, containing quantities infinitely less than itself, and so on *in infinitum*; this is an edifice so bold and prodigious, that it is too

as well as against the atheists and free-thinkers. But that all his arguments, though otherwise intended, are, in reality, merely sceptical, appears from this, *that they admit of no answer and produce no conviction*. Their only effect is to cause that momentary amazement and irresolution and confusion, which is the result of scepticism.

weighty for any pretended demonstration to support, because it shocks the clearest and most natural principles of human reason.* But what renders the matter more extraordinary, is, that these seemingly absurd opinions are supported by a chain of reasoning, the clearest and most natural; nor is it possible for us to allow the premises without admitting the consequences. Nothing can be more convincing and satisfactory than all the conclusions concerning the properties of circles and triangles; and yet, when these are once received, how can we deny, that the angle of contact between a circle and its tangent is infinitely less than any rectilineal angle, that as you may increase the diameter of the circle *in infinitum*, this angle of contact becomes still less, even *in infinitum*, and that the angle of contact between other curves and their tangents may be infinitely less than those between any circle and its tangent, and so on, *in infinitum*? The demonstration of these principles seems as unexceptionable as that which proves the three angles of a triangle to be equal to two right ones, though the latter opinion be natural and easy, and the former big with contradiction and absurdity. Reason here seems to be thrown into a kind of amazement and suspence, which, without the suggestions of any sceptic, gives her a diffidence of herself, and of the ground on which she treads. She sees a full light, which illuminates certain places; but that light borders upon the most profound darkness. And between these she is so dazzled and confounded, that she scarcely can pronounce with certainty and assurance concerning any one object.

125   The absurdity of these bold determinations of the abstract sciences seems to become, if possible, still more palpable with regard to time than extension. An infinite number of real parts

of time, passing in succession, and exhausted one after another, appears so evident a contradiction, that no man, one should think, whose judgement is not corrupted, instead of being improved, by the sciences, would ever be able to admit of it.

Yet still reason must remain restless, and unquiet, even with regard to that scepticism, to which she is driven by these seeming absurdities and contradictions. How any clear, distinct idea can contain circumstances, contradictory to itself, or to any other clear, distinct idea, is absolutely incomprehensible; and is, perhaps, as absurd as any proposition, which can be formed. So that nothing can be more sceptical, or more full of doubt and hesitation, than this scepticism itself, which arises from some of the paradoxical conclusions of geometry or the science of quantity.†

The sceptical objections to *moral* evidence,   126 or to the reasonings concerning matter of fact, are either *popular* or *philosophical*. The popular objections are derived from the natural weakness of human understanding; the contradictory opinions, which have been entertained in different ages and nations; the variations of our judgement in sickness and health, youth and old age, prosperity and adversity; the perpetual contradiction of each particular man's opinions and

---

* Whatever disputes there may be about mathematical points, we must allow that there are physical points; that is, parts of extension, which cannot be divided or lessened, either by the eye or imagination. These images, then, which are present to the fancy or senses, are absolutely indivisible, and consequently must be allowed by mathematicians to be infinitely less than any real part of extension; and yet nothing appears more certain to reason, than that an infinite number of them composes an infinite extension. How much more an infinite number of those infinitely small parts of extension, which are still supposed infinitely divisible.

† It seems to me not impossible to avoid these absurdities and contradictions, if it be admitted, that there is no such thing as abstract or general ideas, properly speaking; but that all general ideas are, in reality, particular ones, attached to a general term, which recalls, upon occasion, other particular ones, that resemble, in certain circumstances, the idea, present to the mind.[2] Thus when the term Horse is pronounced, we immediately figure to ourselves the idea of a black or a white animal, of a particular size or figure: But as that term is also usually applied to animals of other colours, figures and sizes, these ideas, though not actually present to the imagination, are easily recalled; and our reasoning and conclusion proceed in the same way, as if they were actually present. If this be admitted (as seems reasonable) it follows that all the ideas of quantity, upon which mathematicians reason, are nothing but particular, and such as are suggested by the senses and imagination, and consequently, cannot be infinitely divisible. It is sufficient to have dropped this hint at present, without prosecuting it any farther. It certainly concerns all lovers of science not to expose themselves to the ridicule and contempt of the ignorant by their conclusions; and this seems the readiest solution of these difficulties.

sentiments; with many other topics of that kind. It is needless to insist farther on this head. These objections are but weak. For as, in common life, we reason every moment concerning fact and existence, and cannot possibly subsist, without continually employing this species of argument, any popular objections, derived from thence, must be insufficient to destroy that evidence. The great subverter of *Pyrrhonism* or the excessive principles of scepticism is action, and employment, and the occupations of common life. These principles may flourish and triumph in the schools; where it is, indeed, difficult, if not impossible, to refute them. But as soon as they leave the shade, and by the presence of the real objects, which actuate our passions and sentiments, are put in opposition to the more powerful principles of our nature, they vanish like smoke, and leave the most determined sceptic in the same condition as other mortals.

127   The sceptic, therefore, had better keep within his proper sphere, and display those *philosophical* objections, which arise from more profound researches. Here he seems to have ample matter of triumph; while he justly insists, that all our evidence for any matter of fact, which lies beyond the testimony of sense or memory, is derived entirely from the relation of cause and effect; that we have no other idea of this relation than that of two objects, which have been frequently *conjoined* together; that we have no argument to convince us, that objects, which have, in our experience, been frequently conjoined, will likewise, in other instances, be conjoined in the same manner; and that nothing leads us to this inference but custom or a certain instinct of our nature; which it is indeed difficult to resist, but which, like other instincts, may be fallacious and deceitful. While the sceptic insists upon these topics, he shows his force, or rather, indeed, his own and our weakness; and seems, for the time at least, to destroy all assurance and conviction. These arguments might be displayed at greater length, if any durable good or benefit to society could ever be expected to result from them.

128   For here is the chief and most confounding objection to *excessive* scepticism, that no durable good can ever result from it; while it remains in its full force and vigour. We need only ask such a sceptic, *What his meaning is? And what he proposes by all these curious researches?* He is immediately at a loss, and knows not what to answer. A Copernican or Ptolemaic, who supports each his different system of astronomy, may hope to produce a conviction, which will remain constant and durable, with his audience. A Stoic or Epicurean displays principles, which may not only be durable, but which have an effect on conduct and behaviour. But a Pyrrhonian cannot expect, that his philosophy will have any constant influence on the mind: or if it had, that its influence would be beneficial to society. On the contrary, he must acknowledge, if he will acknowledge anything, that all human life must perish, were his principles universally and steadily to prevail. All discourse, all action would immediately cease; and men remain in a total lethargy, till the necessities of nature, unsatisfied, put an end to their miserable existence. It is true; so fatal an event is very little to be dreaded. Nature is always too strong for principle. And though a Pyrrhonian may throw himself or others into a momentary amazement and confusion by his profound reasonings; the first and most trivial event in life will put to flight all his doubts and scruples, and leave him the same, in every point of action and speculation, with the philosophers of every other sect, or with those who never concerned themselves in any philosophical researches. When he awakes from his dream, he will be the first to join in the laugh against himself, and to confess, that all his objections are mere amusement, and can have no other tendency than to show the whimsical condition of mankind, who must act and reason and believe; though they are not able, by their most diligent enquiry, to satisfy themselves concerning the foundation of these operations, or to remove the objections, which may be raised against them.

Part III   There is, indeed, a more *mitigated* scep-   129 ticism or *academical* philosophy,[3] which may be both durable and useful, and which may, in part, be the result of this Pyrrhonism, or *excessive* scepticism, when its undistinguished doubts are, in some measure, corrected by commonsense and reflection. The greater part of mankind are naturally apt to be affirmative and dogmatical in their opinions; and while they see objects only on one side, and have no idea of any counterpoising argument, they throw themselves precipitately into the principles, to which they are inclined; nor have they any indulgence for those who entertain opposite sentiments. To hesitate or balance perplexes their understanding, checks their passion, and suspends their action. They are, therefore, impatient till they escape from a state, which to them is so uneasy: and they think, that they can never remove themselves far enough from it, by the violence of their affirmations and obstinacy of their belief. But could such dogmatical reasoners become sensible of the strange infirmities of human understanding, even in its most perfect state, and when most accurate and cautious in its determinations; such a reflection would naturally inspire them with more modesty and reserve, and diminish their fond opinion of themselves, and their prejudice against antagonists. The illiterate may reflect on the disposition of the learned, who, amidst all the advantages of study and reflection, are commonly still diffident in their determinations: and if any of the learned be inclined, from their natural temper, to haughtiness and obstinacy, a small tincture of Pyrrhonism might abate their pride, by showing them, that the few advantages, which they may have attained over their fellows, are but inconsiderable, if compared with the universal perplexity and confusion, which is inherent in human nature. In general, there is a degree of doubt, and caution, and modesty, which, in all kinds of scrutiny and decision, ought for ever to accompany a just reasoner.

130   Another species of *mitigated* scepticism which may be of advantage to mankind, and which may be the natural result of the Pyrrhonian doubts and scruples, is the limitation of our enquiries to such subjects as are best adapted to the narrow capacity of human understanding. The *imagination* of man is naturally sublime, delighted with whatever is remote and extraordinary, and running, without control, into the most distant parts of space and time in order to avoid the objects, which custom has rendered too familiar to it. A correct *Judgement* observes a contrary method, and avoiding all distant and high enquiries, confines itself to common life, and to such subjects as fall under daily practice and experience; leaving the more sublime topics to the embellishment of poets and orators, or to the arts of priests and politicians. To bring us to so salutary a determination, nothing can be more serviceable, than to be once thoroughly convinced of the force of the Pyrrhonian doubt, and of the impossibility, that anything, but the strong power of natural instinct, could free us from it. Those who have a propensity to philosophy, will still continue their researches; because they reflect, that, besides the immediate pleasure, attending such an occupation, philosophical decisions are nothing but the reflections of common life, methodized and corrected. But they will never be tempted to go beyond common life, so long as they consider the imperfection of those faculties which they employ, their narrow reach, and their inaccurate operations. While we cannot give a satisfactory reason, why we believe, after a thousand experiments, that a stone will fall, or fire burn; can we ever satisfy ourselves concerning any determination, which we may form, with regard to the origin of worlds, and the situation of nature, from, and to eternity?

This narrow limitation, indeed, of our enquiries, is, in every respect, so reasonable, that it suffices to make the slightest examination into the natural powers of the human mind and to compare them with their objects, in order to recommend it to us. We shall then find what are the proper subjects of science and enquiry.

It seems to me, that the only objects of the   131 abstract sciences or of demonstration are quantity and number, and that all attempts to extend this more perfect species of knowledge beyond these bounds are mere sophistry and illusion. As the component parts of quantity and number are entirely similar, their relations become intricate and involved; and nothing can be more curious, as well as useful, than to trace, by a variety of mediums, their equality or inequality, through their different appearances. But as all other ideas are clearly distinct and different from each other, we can never advance farther, by our utmost scrutiny, than to observe this diversity, and, by an obvious reflection, pronounce one thing not to be another. Or if there be any difficulty in these decisions, it proceeds entirely from the undeterminate meaning of words, which is corrected by juster definitions. That *the square of the hypothenuse is equal to the squares of the other two sides*, cannot be known, let the terms be ever so exactly defined, without a train of reasoning and enquiry. But to convince us of this proposition, *that where there is no property, there can be no injustice*, it is only necessary to define the terms, and explain injustice to be a violation of property. This proposition is, indeed, nothing but a more imperfect definition. It is the same case with all those pretended syllogistical reasonings, which may be found in every other branch of learning, except the sciences of quantity and number; and these may safely, I think, be pronounced the only proper objects of knowledge and demonstration.

132   All other enquiries of men regard only matter of fact and existence; and these are evidently incapable of demonstration. Whatever *is* may *not be*. No negation of a fact can involve a contradiction. The non-existence of any being, without exception, is as clear and distinct an idea as its existence. The proposition, which affirms it not to be, however false, is no less conceivable and intelligible, than that which affirms it to be. The case is different with the sciences, properly so called. Every proposition, which is not true, is there confused and unintelligible. That the cube root of 64 is equal to the half of 10, is a false proposition, and can never be distinctly conceived. But that Cæsar, or the angel Gabriel, or any being never existed, may be a false proposition, but still is perfectly conceivable, and implies no contradiction.

The existence, therefore, of any being can only be proved by arguments from its cause or its effect; and these arguments are founded entirely on experience. If we reason *a priori*, anything may appear able to produce anything. The falling of a pebble may, for aught we know, extinguish the sun; or the wish of a man control the planets in their orbits. It is only experience, which teaches us the nature and bounds of cause and effect, and enables us to infer the existence of one object from that of another.* Such is the foundation of moral reasoning, which forms the greater part of human knowledge, and is the source of all human action and behaviour.

---

* That impious maxim of the ancient philosophy, *Ex nihilo, nihil fit*, by which the creation of matter was excluded, ceases to be a maxim, according to this philosophy. Not only the will of the supreme Being may create matter; but, for aught we know *a priori*, the will of any other being might create it, or any other cause, that the most whimsical imagination can assign.

Moral reasonings are either concerning particular or general facts. All deliberations in life regard the former; as also all disquisitions in history, chronology, geography, and astronomy.

The sciences, which treat of general facts, are politics, natural philosophy, physic, chemistry, where the qualities, causes and effects of a whole species of objects are enquired into.

Divinity or Theology, as it proves the existence of a Deity, and the immortality of souls, is composed partly of reasonings concerning particular, partly concerning general facts. It has a foundation in *reason*, so far as it is supported by experience. But its best and most solid foundation is *faith* and divine revelation.

Morals and criticism are not so properly objects of the understanding as of taste and sentiment. Beauty, whether moral or natural, is felt, more properly than perceived. Or if we reason concerning it, and endeavour to fix its standard, we regard a new feet, to wit, the general taste of mankind, or some such fact, which may be the object of reasoning and enquiry.

When we run over libraries, persuaded of these principles, what havoc must we make? If we take in our hand any volume; of divinity or school metaphysics, for instance; let us ask, *Does it contain any abstract reasoning concerning quantity or number?* No. *Does it contain any experimental reasoning concerning matter of fact and existence?* No. Commit it then to the flames: for it can contain nothing but sophistry and illusion.

Notes

1   Consequences such as the paradoxical ones drawn by Zeno concerning motion.
2   Here Hume is siding with Berkeley, and against Locke, on the issue of whether we can form abstract general ideas.
3   "Academical philosophy" here refers to the brand of skepticism advanced by Carneades (second century BCE) and other teachers at the Academy in Athens founded by Plato.

11

Thomas Reid, *Essays on the Intellectual Powers Of Man,* Essay 6, Chapter 5

Introduction

Rightly or not, David Hume (II.10) was perceived by his contemporaries as a radical skeptic whose powerful case needed to be answered if the possibility of knowledge was to be restored. In the following text (II.12), we shall encounter the most famous of these responses, Immanuel Kant's. But important, too – and in the English-language tradition, arguably, of more enduring influence – was the response of Hume's fellow Scot, and Adam Smith's successor in the Chair of Moral Philosophy at Glasgow, Thomas Reid (1710–96). Indeed, it is not Hume's tomb that lords over Edinburgh from an eyrie near the faux-Parthenon on Calton Hill but the tomb of Dugald Stewart, a prominent member of the Scottish "Commonsense School" of philosophy of which Reid was a pre-eminent member.

Reid's refutation of skepticism was of an entirely different kind from that of Descartes and his rationalist followers, who are indeed as much a target of his criticisms as the skeptics are. Their arguments, for example, to "support the authority of our senses" – by, say, appealing to a non-deceiving God – are "very weak" and "easily refuted." But nor was Reid an empiricist of the seventeenth- or eighteenth-century ilk. For him, both

From Thomas Reid, *Essays on the Intellectual Powers of Man*, ed. A.D. Woozley. London: Macmillan, 1941, pp. 372–91 (notes and one passage omitted).

schools of thought share the mistaken assumption that our commonsense beliefs must either be suspended (rejected even) or justified by something more foundational – rational deduction either from a handful of self-evident axioms (like the *cogito*) or from "immediate" experience of our own "ideas" or "impressions."

In Reid's view, there are a large number of commonsense "first principles" – including the 12 "factual" or "contingent" ones discussed in the pages selected below – which are themselves certainly true and which allow people to arrive at countless other, more particular truths. Reid's list is not intended to be exhaustive, but it does contain most of the general claims argued about by epistemologists – for example, that people have knowledge of other minds and of the similarity of the future to the past.

By "commonsense," he means "that degree of judgement which is common to men with whom we can converse and transact business," and by "first principles" those "propositions which are no sooner understood than they are believed".[1] Since these principles, once understood, cannot but be believed true, they deserve to be called items of knowledge. Reid is therefore using the term "knowledge" rather more generously, and surely more in accordance with standard usage, than the philosophers he discusses. For even those, like Locke (II.9), who would not normally be regarded as skeptics, tend to confine the term to judgments about the relations among ideas, in effect restricting knowledge, "truly" or "strictly" so-called, to the necessary truths of mathematics and logic and to minimal statements about immediate sense-experience (about, say, differences in color between two "impressions").

Reid is not a "commonsense philosopher" simply because he defends the pronouncements of common sense, such as that there exists an external world or that we can know about the past. After all, Descartes eventually came to endorse many of the ordinary beliefs he originally determined to doubt. What invites that label is Reid's insistence, first, that common sense neither needs, nor can be given, the kind of rational foundation which Descartes tries to provide; and, second, that one is perfectly entitled to accept commonsense beliefs despite being unable to specify why or how they belong to common sense.[2]

Although we do not have to justify our commonsense principles in order to count as possessors of knowledge, Reid himself does offer some general reasons why they should not be called into question. For one thing, as his seventh principle (really a meta-principle) proclaims, "the natural faculties," such as memory and reason, "by which we distinguish truth from error, are not fallacious" – or, at least, cannot be regarded as fallacious since, providing us with "evidence," they "force" us to accept certain things as true.[3] For another thing, the first principles should be thought of less as "general propositions" to be mulled over by philosophers than as practical principles implicitly governing everyday discourse, belief, and behavior – those of would-be skeptics as much as everyone else. Hence, to question the reliability of our "natural faculties" would not only render us "absolute sceptics," but render unintelligible our capacity to "converse and transact business" with one another.

As earlier remarked, Reid has been an important influence on English-language, especially British, philosophy. Indeed, it is something of an injustice in the history of ideas that "a defense of commonsense" should be so closely associated with G. E. Moore's article of that name, given that, as Reid's editor puts it, "there is scarcely a thought" in that article "which we would be surprised to find in the *Intellectual Powers*."[4]

Notes

1 *Essays on the Intellectual Powers of Man*, ed. Woozley, pp. 331, 358.

2 See N. Lemos, "Commonsensism and Critical Cognitivism," in *A Companion to Epistemology*, ed. J. Dancy and E. Sosa, Oxford: Blackwell, 1992, p. 72.

3 On this meta-principle and Reid's philosophy as a whole, see Keith Lehrer, *Thomas Reid*, London: Routledge, 1989.

4 *Essays on the Intellectual Powers of Man*, ed. Woozley, p. xxxviii.

Reid, *Essays on the Intellectual Powers of Man*

Essay 6, Chapter 5: The First Principles of Contingent Truths

"Surely", says Bishop Berkeley, "it is a work well deserving our pains to make a strict inquiry concerning the first principles of knowledge; to sift and examine them on all sides" [*Principles*, Introd. 4]. [. . .]

But in order that such an Inquiry may be actually made, it is necessary that the first principles of knowledge be distinguished from other truths, and presented to view, that they may be sifted and examined on all sides. In order to this end I shall attempt a detail of those I take to be such, and of the reasons why I think them entitled to that character.

The truths that fell within the compass of human knowledge, whether they be self-evident or deduced from those that are self-evident, may be reduced to two classes. They are either necessary and immutable truths whose contrary is impossible, or they are contingent and mutable, depending upon some effect of will and power which had a beginning, and may have an end.

That a cone is the third part of a cylinder of the same base and the same altitude is a necessary truth. It depends not upon the will and power of any being. It is immutably true, and the contrary impossible. That the sun is the centre about which the earth and the other planets of our system perform their revolutions, is a truth;

but it is not a necessary truth. It depends upon the power and will of that Being who made the sun and all the planets, and who gave them those motions that seemed best to him.

If all truths were necessary truths there would be no occasion for different tenses in the verbs by which they are expressed. What is true in the present time would be true in the past and future, and there would be no change or variation of anything in nature.

We use the present tense in expressing necessary truths, but it is only because there is no flexion of the verb which includes all times. When I say that three is the half of six, I use the present tense only; but I mean to express not only what now is, but what always was, and always will be; and so every proposition is to be understood by which we mean to express a necessary truth. Contingent truths are of another nature. As they are mutable, they may be true at one time and not at another, and, therefore, the expression of them must include some point or period of time.

The distinction commonly made between abstract truths and those that express matters of fact, or real existences, coincides in a great measure, but not altogether, with that between necessary and contingent truths. The necessary truths that fall within our knowledge are for the most part abstract truths. We must except the existence and nature of the Supreme Being, which is necessary. Other existence are the effects of will and power. They had a beginning, and are mutable. Their nature is such as the Supreme Being was pleased to give them. Their attributes and relations must depend upon the nature God has given them, the powers with which he has endowed them, and the situation in which he hath placed them.

The conclusions deduced by reasoning from first principles will commonly be necessary or contingent, according as the principles are from which they are drawn. On the one hand, I take it to be certain that whatever can, by just reasoning, be inferred from a principle that is necessary must be a necessary truth, and that no contingent truth can be inferred from principles that are necessary.

Thus, as the axioms in mathematics are all necessary truths, so are all the conclusions drawn from them; that is, the whole body of that science. But from no mathematical truth can we deduce the existence of anything, not even of the objects of the science.

On the other hand, I apprehend there are very few cases in which we can, from principles that are contingent, deduce truths that are necessary. I can only recollect one instance of this kind – namely, that from the existence of things contingent and mutable we can infer the existence of an immutable and eternal cause of them.

As the minds of men are occupied much more about truths that are contingent than about those that are necessary, I shall first endeavour to point out the principles of the former kind.

1. *First*, then, I hold, as a first principle, the existence of everything of which I am conscious.

Consciousness is an operation of the understanding of its own kind and cannot be logically defined. The objects of it are our present pains, our pleasures, our hopes, our fears, our desires, our doubts, our thoughts of every kind; in a word, all the passions and all the actions and operations of our own minds while they are present. We may remember them when they are past, but we are conscious of them only while they are present.

When a man is conscious of pain he is certain of its existence; when he is conscious that he doubts or believes, he is certain of the existence of those operations.

But the irresistible conviction he has of the reality of those operations is not the effect of reasoning; it is immediate and intuitive. The existence therefore of those passions and operations of our minds of which we are conscious is a first principle which nature requires us to believe upon her authority.

If I am asked to prove that I cannot be deceived by consciousness – to prove that it is not a fallacious sense – I can find no proof. I cannot find any antecedent truth from which it is deduced or upon which its evidence depends. It seems to disdain any such derived authority and to claim my assent in its own right.

If any man could be found so frantic as to deny that he thinks, while he is conscious of it, I may wonder, I may laugh, or I may pity him, but I cannot reason the matter with him. We have no common principles from which we may reason, and therefore can never join issue in an argument.

I cannot reconcile this immediate knowledge of the operations of our own minds with Mr Locke's theory that all knowledge consists in perceiving the agreement and disagreement of ideas. What are the ideas from whose comparison the knowledge of our own thoughts results? Or what are the agreements or disagreements which convince a man that he is in pain when he feels it?

Neither can I reconcile it with Mr Hume's theory that to believe the existence of anything is nothing else than to have a strong and lively conception of it, or, at most, that belief is only some modification of the idea which is the object of belief. For, not to mention that propositions, not ideas, are the object of belief, in all that variety of thoughts and passions of which we are conscious we believe the existence of the weak as well as of the strong the faint as well as the lively. No modification of the operations of our minds disposes us to the least doubt of their real existence.

As, therefore, the real existence of our thoughts, and of all the operations and feelings of our own minds, is believed by all men – as we find ourselves incapable of doubting it, and as incapable of offering any proof of it – it may justly be considered as a first principle, or dictate of commonsense.

But although this principle rests upon no other, a very considerable and important branch of human knowledge rests upon it.

For from this source of consciousness is derived all that we know, and indeed all that we can know, of the structure and of the powers of our own minds; from which we may conclude that there is no branch of knowledge that stands upon a firmer foundation, for surely no kind of evidence can go beyond that of consciousness.

How does it come to pass, then, that in this branch of knowledge there are so many and so contrary systems? so many subtle controversies that are never brought to an issue? and so little fixed and determined? Is it possible that philosophers should differ most where they have the surest means of agreement – where everything is built upon a species of evidence which all men acquiesce in and hold to be the most certain?

This strange phenomenon may, I think, be accounted for if we distinguish between consciousness and reflection, which are often improperly confounded.

The first is common to all men at all times, but is insufficient of itself to give us clear and distinct notions of the operations of which we are conscious, and of their mutual relations and minute distinctions. The second – to wit, attentive reflection upon those operations, making them objects of thought, surveying them attentively, and examining them on all sides – is so far from being common to all men that it is the lot of very few. The greatest part of men, either through want of capacity or from other causes, never reflect attentively upon the operations of their own minds. The habit of this reflection, even in those whom nature has fitted for it, is not to be attained without much pains and practice.

2. Another first principle, I think, is, That the thoughts of which I am conscious are the thoughts of a being which I call *myself*, my *mind*, my *person*.

The thoughts and feelings of which we are conscious are continually changing, and the thought of this moment is not the thought of the last; but something which I call myself remains under this change of thought. This self has the same relation to all the successive thoughts I am conscious of – they are all my thoughts; and every thought which is not my thought must be the thought of some other person.

If any man asks a proof of this, I confess I can give none; there is an evidence in the proposition itself which I am unable to resist. Shall I think that thought can stand by itself without a thinking being? or that ideas can feel pleasure or pain? My nature dictates to me that it is impossible.

Here we must leave Mr Hume, who conceives it to be a vulgar error that, besides the thoughts we are conscious of, there is a mind which is the subject of those thoughts. If the mind be anything else than impressions and ideas, it must be a word without a meaning. The mind therefore, according to this philosopher, is a word which signifies a bundle of perceptions; or, when he defines it more accurately – "It is that succession of related ideas and impressions of which we have an intimate memory and consciousness" [*Treatise*, II.1.2].

I am therefore that succession of related ideas and impressions of which I have the intimate memory and consciousness.

But who is the *I* that has this memory and consciousness of a succession of ideas and impressions? Why, it is nothing but that succession itself.

Hence, I learn that this succession of ideas and impressions intimately remembers and is conscious of itself. I would wish to be further instructed whether the impressions remember and are conscious of the ideas, or the ideas remember and are conscious of the impressions, or if both remember and are conscious of both, and whether the ideas remember those that come after them as well as those that were before them. These are questions naturally arising from this system that have not yet been explained.

This, however, is clear, that this succession of ideas and impressions not only remembers and is conscious, but that it judges, reasons, affirms, denies – nay, that it eats and drinks and is sometimes merry and sometimes sad.

If these things can be ascribed to a succession of ideas and impressions, in a consistency with commonsense, I should be very glad to know what is nonsense.

3.   Another first principle I take to be – That those things did really happen which I distinctly remember.

This has one of the surest marks of a first principle, for no man ever pretended to prove it, and yet no man in his wits calls it in question: the testimony of memory, like that of consciousness, is immediate; it claims our assent upon its own authority.

Mr Hume has not, as far as I remember, directly called in question the testimony of memory, but he has laid down the premises by which its authority is overturned, leaving it to his reader to draw the conclusion.

Indeed the theory concerning ideas, so generally received by philosophers, destroys all the authority of memory as well as the authority of the senses. Descartes, Malebranche, and Locke were aware that this theory made it necessary for them to find out arguments to prove the existence of external objects which the vulgar believe upon the bare authority of their senses; but those philosophers were not aware that this theory made it equally necessary for them to find arguments to prove the existence of things past which we remember, and to support the authority of memory.

All the arguments they advanced to support the authority of our senses were easily refuted by Bishop Berkeley and Mr Hume, being indeed very weak and inconclusive. And it would have been as easy to answer every argument they could have brought, consistent with their theory, to support the authority of memory.

For according to that theory the immediate object of memory, as well as of every other operation of the understanding, is an idea present in the mind. And from the present existence of this idea of memory I am left to infer, by reasoning, that six months or six years ago there did exist an object similar to this idea.

But what is there in the idea that can lead me to this conclusion? What mark does it bear of the date of its archetype? Or what evidence have I that it had an archetype and that it is not the first of its kind?

Perhaps it will be said that this idea or image in the mind must have had a cause.

I admit that if there is such an image in the mind, it must have had a cause, and a cause able to produce the effect; but what can we infer from its having a cause? Does it follow that the effect is a type, an image, a copy of its cause? Then it will follow that a picture is an image of the painter, and a coach of the coachmaker.

A past event may be known by reasoning; but that is not remembering it. When I remember a thing distinctly, I disdain equally to hear reasons for it or against it. And so I think does every man in his senses.

4.   Another first principle is, Our own personal identity and continued existence, as far back as we remember anything distinctly.

This we know immediately, and not by reasoning. It seems, indeed, to be a part of the testimony of memory. Everything we remember has such a relation to ourselves as to imply necessarily our existence at the time remembered. And there cannot be a more palpable absurdity than that a man should remember what happened before he existed. He must therefore have existed as far back as he remembers anything distinctly, if his memory be not fallacious. This principle, therefore, is so connected with the last mentioned that it may be doubtful whether both ought not to be included in one. Let everyone judge of this as he sees reason. The proper notion of identity, and the sentiments of Mr Locke on this subject, have been considered before under the head of Memory [see *Essay* 3].

5.   Another first principle is, That those things do really exist which we distinctly perceive by our senses, and are what we perceive them to be.

It is too evident to need proof that all men are by nature led to give implicit faith to the distinct testimony of their senses, long before they are capable of any bias from prejudices of education or of philosophy.

How came we at first to know that there are certain beings about us whom we call father, and mother, and sisters, and brothers, and nurse? Was it not by the testimony of our senses? How did these persons convey to us any information or instruction? Was it not by means of our senses?

It is evident we can have no communication, no correspondence or society with any created being but by means of our senses. And until we rely upon their testimony, we must consider ourselves as being alone in the universe, without any fellow-creature, living or inanimate, and be left to converse with our own thoughts.

Bishop Berkeley surely, did not duly consider that it is by means of the material world that we have any correspondence with thinking beings, or any knowledge of their existence; and that, by depriving us of the material world, he deprived us at the same time of family, friends, country, and every human creature; of every object of affection, esteem, or concern, except ourselves.

When I consider myself as speaking to men who hear me, and can judge of what I say, I feel that respect which is due to such an audience. I feel an enjoyment in a reciprocal communication of sentiments with candid and ingenious friends, and my soul blesses the Author of my being, who has made me capable of this manly and rational entertainment.

But the Bishop shows me that this is all a dream; that I see not a human face; that all the objects I see, and hear, and handle, are only the ideas of my own mind; ideas are my only companions. Cold company indeed! Every social affection freezes at the thought!

This dismal system, which, if it could be believed, would deprive men of every social comfort, a very good Bishop, by strict and accurate reasoning, deduced from the principles commonly received by philosophers concerning ideas. The fault is not in the reasoning, but in the principles from which it is drawn.

All the arguments urged by Berkeley and Hume against the existence of a material world are grounded upon this principle – that we do not perceive external objects themselves, but certain images or ideas in our own minds. But this is no dictate of commonsense, but directly contrary to the sense of all who have not been taught it by philosophy.

We have before examined the reasons given by philosophers to prove that ideas, and not external objects, are the immediate objects of perception, and the instances given to prove the senses fallacious.[1] Without repeating what has before been said upon those points, we shall only here observe that, if external objects be perceived immediately, we have the same reason to believe their existence as philosophers have to believe the existence of ideas, while they hold them to be the immediate objects of perception.

6.   Another first principle, I think, is, That we have some degree of power over our actions, and the determinations of our will.

All power must be derived from the fountain of power and of every good gift. Upon his good pleasure its continuance depends, and it is always subject to his control.

Beings to whom God has given any degree of power and understanding to direct them to the proper use of it must be accountable to their Maker. But those who are entrusted with no power can have no account to make; for all good conduct consists in the right use of power, all bad conduct in the abuse of it.

It is not easy to say in what way we first get the notion or idea of *power*. It is neither an object of sense nor of consciousness. We see events, one succeeding another; but we see not the power by which they are produced. We are conscious of the operations of our minds; but power is not an operation of mind. If we had no notions but such as are furnished by the external senses and by consciousness, it seems to be impossible that we should ever have any conception of power. Accordingly Mr Hume, who has reasoned the most accurately upon this hypothesis, denies that we have any idea of power, and clearly refutes the account given by Mr Locke of the origin of this idea.

But it is in vain to reason from a hypothesis against a fact the truth of which every man may see by attending to his own thoughts. It is evident that all men, very early in life, not only have an idea of power, but a conviction that they have some degree of it in themselves; for this conviction is necessarily implied in many operations of mind which are familiar to every man, and without which no man can act the part of a reasonable being.

First, It is implied in every act of volition. "Volition, it is plain," says Mr Locke, "is an act of the mind, knowingly exerting that dominion which it takes itself to have over any part of the man, by employing it in, or withholding it from, any particular action" [*Essay Concerning Human Understanding*, II. 21.15]. Every volition, therefore, implies a conviction of power to do the action willed. A man may desire to make a visit to the moon, or to the planet Jupiter, but nothing but insanity could make him will to do so. And if even insanity produced this effect, it must be by making him think it to be in his power.

Secondly, This conviction is implied in all deliberation, for no man in his wits deliberates whether he shall do what he believes not to be in his power. *Thirdly*, The same conviction is implied in every resolution or purpose formed in consequence of deliberation. A man may as well form a resolution to pull the moon out of her sphere as to do the most insignificant action which he believes not to be in his power. The same thing may be said of every promise or contract wherein a man plights his faith, for he is not an honest man who promises what he does not believe he has power to perform.

As these operations imply a belief of some degree of power in ourselves, so there are others equally common and familiar which imply a like belief with regard to others.

When we impute to a man any action or omission as a ground of approbation or of blame, we must believe he had power to do otherwise. The same is implied in all advice, exhortation, command, and rebuke, and in every case in which we rely upon his fidelity in performing any engagement of executing any trust.

7.   Another first principle is, That the natural faculties, by which we distinguish truth from error, are not fallacious.[2] If any man should demand a proof of this, it is impossible to satisfy him. For suppose it should be mathematically demonstrated, this would signify nothing in this case, because, to judge of a demonstration, a man must trust his faculties, and take for granted the very thing in question.

If a man's honesty were called in question, it would be ridiculous to refer it to the man's own word whether he be honest or not. The same absurdity there is in attempting to prove by any kind of reasoning, probable or demonstrative, that our reason is not fallacious, since the very point in question is whether reasoning may be trusted.

How then come we to be assured of this fundamental truth on which all others rest? Perhaps evidence, as in many other respects it resembles light, so in this also – that, as light, which is the discoverer of all visible objects, discovers itself at the same time, so evidence, which is the voucher for all truth, vouches for itself at the same time.

This, however, is certain, that such is the constitution of the human mind that evidence discerned by us forces a corresponding degree of assent. And a man who perfectly understood a just syllogism, without believing that the conclusion follows from the premises, would be a greater monster than a man born without hands or feet.

We may here take notice of a property of the principle under consideration that seems to be common to it with many other first principles, and which can hardly be found in any principle that is built solely upon reasoning; and that is, that in most men it produces its effect without ever being attended to, or made an object of thought. No man ever thinks of this principle unless when he considers the grounds of scepticism; yet it invariably governs his opinions. When a man in the common course of life gives credit to the testimony of his senses, his memory, or his reason, he does not put the question to himself whether these faculties may deceive him, yet the trust he reposes in them supposes an inward conviction that, in that instance at least, they do not deceive him.

It is another property of this and of many first principles, that they force assent in particular instances more powerfully than when they are turned into a general proposition. Many sceptics have denied every general principle of science, excepting perhaps the existence of our present thoughts; yet these men reason, and refute, and prove, they assent and dissent in particular cases. They use reasoning to overturn all reasoning, and judge that they ought to have no judgment, and see clearly that they are blind. Many have in general maintained that the senses are fallacious, yet there never was found a man so sceptical as not to trust his senses in particular instances when his safety required it; and it may be observed of those who have professed scepticism that their scepticism lies in generals, while in particulars they are no less dogmatical than others.

8. Another first principle relating to existence is, That there is life and intelligence in our fellow-men with whom we converse.

As soon as children are capable of asking a question or of answering a question, as soon as they show the signs of love, of resentment, or of any other affection, they must be convinced that those with whom they have this intercourse are intelligent beings.

It is evident they are capable of such intercourse long before they can reason. Everyone knows that there is a social intercourse between the nurse and the child before it is a year old. It can at that age understand many things that are said to it.

It can by signs ask and refuse, threaten and supplicate. It clings to its nurse in danger, enters into her grief and joy, is happy in her soothing and caresses, and unhappy in her displeasure. That these things cannot be without a conviction in the child that the nurse is an intelligent being, I think must be granted.

Now I would ask how a child of a year old comes by this conviction? Not by reasoning surely, for children do not reason at that age. Nor is it by external senses, for life and intelligence are not objects of the external senses.

By what means, or upon what occasions, nature first gives this information to the infant mind is not easy to determine. We are not capable of reflecting upon our own thoughts at that period of life, and before we attain this capacity we have quite forgot how or on what occasion we first had this belief; we perceive it in those who are born blind and in others who are born deaf; and therefore nature has not connected it solely either with any object of sight or with any object of hearing. When we grow up to the years of reason and reflection, this belief remains. No man thinks of asking himself what reason he has to believe that his neighbour is a living creature. He would be not a little surprised if another person should ask him so absurd a question, and perhaps could not give any reason which would not equally prove a watch or a puppet to be a living creature.

But though you should satisfy him of the weakness of the reasons he gives for his belief, you cannot make him in the least doubtful. This belief stands upon another foundation than that of reasoning, and therefore, whether a man can give good reasons for it or not, it is not in his power to shake it off.

Setting aside this natural conviction, I believe the best reason we can give to prove that other men are living and intelligent is that their words and actions indicate like powers of understanding as we are conscious of in ourselves. The very same argument applied to the works of nature leads us to conclude that there is an intelligent Author of nature, and appears equally strong and obvious in the last case as in the first; so that it may be doubted whether men, by the mere exercise of reasoning, might not as soon discover the existence of a Deity as that other men have life and intelligence.

9. Another first principle I take to be, That certain features of the countenance, sounds of the voice, and gestures of the body, indicate certain thoughts and dispositions of mind.

That many operations of the mind have their natural signs in the countenance, voice, and gesture, I suppose every man will admit. The only question is whether we understand the signification of those signs by the constitution of our nature, by a kind of natural perception similar to the perceptions of sense; or whether we gradually learn the signification of such signs from experience, as we learn that smoke is a sign of fire or that freezing of water is a sign of cold. I take the first to be the truth.

It seems to me incredible that the notions men have of the expression of features, voice, and gesture are entirely the fruit of experience. Children, almost as soon as born, may be frighted and thrown into fits by a threatening or angry tone of voice.

The countenance and gesture have an expression no less strong and natural than the voice. The first time one sees a stern and fierce look, a contracted brow, and a menacing posture, he concludes that the person is inflamed with anger. Shall we say that, previous to experience, the most hostile countenance has as agreeable an appearance as the most gentle and benign? This surely would contradict all experience, for we know that an angry countenance will fright a child in the cradle. Who has not observed that children, very early, are able to distinguish what is said to them in jest from what is said in earnest, by the tone of the voice and the features of the face? They judge by these natural signs, even when they seem to contradict the artificial.

If it were by experience that we learn the meaning of features, and sound, and gesture, it might be expected that we should recollect the time when we first learned those lessons, or at least some of such a multitude.

Those who give attention to the operations of children can easily discover the time when they have their earliest notices from experience – such as that flame will burn or that knives will cut. But no man is able to recollect in himself, or to observe in others, the time when the expression of the face, voice, and gesture were learned.

Nay, I apprehend that it is impossible that this should be learned from experience.

When we see the sign, and see the thing signified always conjoined with it, experience may be the instructor and teach us how that sign is to be interpreted. But how shall experience instruct us when we see the sign only, when the thing signified is invisible? Now, this is the case here: the thoughts and passions of the mind, as well as the mind itself, are invisible, and therefore their connection with any sensible sign cannot be first discovered by experience; there must be some earlier source of this knowledge.

Nature seems to have given to men a faculty or sense by which this connection is perceived. And the operation of this sense is very analogous to that of the external senses.

When I grasp an ivory ball in my hand, I feel a certain sensation of touch. In the sensation there is nothing external, nothing corporeal. The sensation is neither round nor hard; it is an act of feeling of the mind from which I cannot, by reasoning, infer the existence of any body. But by the constitution of my nature, the sensation carries along with it the conception and belief of a round hard body really existing in my hand.

In like manner when I see the features of an expressive face, I see only figure and colour variously modified. But by the constitution of my nature the visible object brings along with it the conception and belief of a certain passion or sentiment in the mind of the person.

In the former case a sensation of touch is the sign, and the hardness and roundness of the body I grasp is signified by that sensation. In the latter case the features of the person is the sign, and the passion or sentiment is signified by it.

10.   Another first principle appears to me to be, That there is a certain regard due to human testimony in matters of fact, and even to human authority in matters of opinion.

11.   There are many events depending upon the will of man in which there is a self-evident probability, greater or less, according to circumstances.

There may be in some individuals such a degree of frenzy and madness that no man can say what they may or may not do. Such persons we find it necessary to put under restraint, that as far as possible they may be kept from doing harm to themselves or to others. They are not considered as reasonable creatures or members of society. But as to men who have a sound mind, we depend upon a certain degree of regularity in their conduct, and could put a thousand different cases wherein we could venture ten to one that they will act in such a way and not in the contrary.

If we had no confidence in our fellow-men that they will act such a part in such circumstances, it would be impossible to live in society with them. For that which makes men capable of living in society, and uniting in a political body under government, is that their actions will always be regulated, in a great measure, by the common principles of human nature.

It may always be expected that they will regard their own interest and reputation, and that of their families and friends; that they will repel injuries, and have some sense of good offices; and that they will have some regard to truth and justice, so far at least as not to swerve from them without temptation.

It is upon such principles as these that all political reasoning is grounded. Such reasoning is never demonstrative, but it may have a very great degree of probability, especially when applied to great bodies of men.

12.   The last principle of contingent truths I mention is, That, in the phenomena of nature, what is to be will probably be like to what has been in similar circumstances.

We must have this conviction as soon as we are capable of learning anything from experience, for all experience is grounded upon a belief that the future will be like the past. Take away this principle and the experience of a hundred years makes us no wiser with regard to what is to come.

This is one of those principles which, when we grow up and observe the course of nature, we can confirm by reasoning. We perceive that nature is governed by fixed laws, and that, if it were not so, there could be no such thing as prudence in human conduct; there would be no fitness in any means to promote an end, and what on one occasion promoted it might as probably on another occasion obstruct it.

But the principle is necessary for us before we are able to discover it by reasoning, and therefore is made a part of our constitution and produces its effects before the use of reason.

This principle remains in all its force when we come to the use of reason, but we learn to be more cautious in the application of it. We observe more carefully the circumstances on which the past event depended, and learn to distinguish them from those which were accidentally conjoined with it.

In order to this, a number of experiments, varied in their circumstances, is often necessary. Sometimes a single experiment is thought sufficient to establish a general conclusion. Thus, when it was once found that, in a certain degree of cold, quicksilver became a hard and malleable metal, there was good reason to think that the same degree of cold will always produce this effect to the end of the world.

I need hardly mention that the whole fabric of natural philosophy is built upon this principle, and if it be taken away, must tumble down to the foundation.

Therefore the great Newton lays it down as an axiom, or as one of his laws of philosophising, in these words, *Effectuum naturalium ejusdem generis easdem esse causas* [Similar effects have similar causes]. This is what every man assents to, as soon as he understands it, and no man asks a reason for it. It has, therefore, the most genuine marks of a first principle.

It is very remarkable that, although all our expectation of what is to happen in the course of nature is derived from the belief of this prin-ciple, yet no man thinks of asking what is the ground of this belief.

Mr Hume, I think, was the first who put this question; and he has shown clearly and invinc-ibly that it is neither grounded upon reasoning nor has that kind of intuitive evidence which mathematical axioms have. It is not a necessary truth [*Treatise*, I.3.6].

He has endeavoured to account for it upon his own principles. It is not my business, at present, to examine the account he has given of this uni-versal belief of mankind; because, whether his account of it be just or not (and I think it is not), yet as this belief is universal among mankind, and is not grounded upon any antecedent reasoning but upon the constitution of the mind itself, it must be acknowledged to be a first principle in the sense in which I use that word.

I do not at all affirm that those I have men-tioned are all the first principles from which we may reason concerning contingent truths. Such enumerations, even when made after much reflection, are seldom perfect.

Notes

1 See Essay 2, ch. 7. Reid was one of the first to argue against the *idée fixe* of seventeenth–eighteenth-century philosophers that what we immediately perceive can only be our own "ideas" or "impressions."

2 This principle might seem redundant, a mere summary of other principles which assert the reli-ability of such faculties as memory and perception. But, as Reid soon explains, this principle in fact sup-ports the others, the point being that any *natural* faculty must, for the reasons he gives, be deemed reliable. That memory, etc. are indeed *natural* fac-ulties therefore provides a consideration in favor of trusting their pronouncements.

Immanuel Kant, *Critique of Pure Reason*, Introduction (Second Edition), Sections I–VI (excerpt)

Introduction

Critique of Pure Reason, Immanuel Kant's (1724–1804) greatest work – the greatest, arguably, in modern philosophy – ranges over metaphysical, ethical, religious, and other issues, not just those of epistemology. Its fundamental concern, however, is with the possibility and nature of our knowledge of objective reality. Central to Kant's enterprise, a distinguished commentator writes, is the notion of the "epistemic condition(s) . . . necessary for the representation of . . . an objective state of affairs."[1] Kant's revolutionary thesis in the book, which he compares to Copernicus's revolution in astronomy, is that such representations and knowledge are possible, not through "conforming" our "intuitions" to mind-independent objects, but through the material of experience having been acted upon so that the objects of experience always already "conform" to our cognitive powers (Preface, B xvi–xviii).[2]

In the "Introduction" to the Second Edition (1787), Kant does not attempt to defend that thesis, but he prepares the ground for it and, in doing so, makes a number of distinctions which, ever since, have been staple topics of discussion

From Immanuel Kant, *Critique of Pure Reason*, trans. W. S. Pluhar. Indianapolis, IN: Hackett, 1996, pp. 43–63 (some notes omitted; asterisked notes are the translator's).

in epistemology. These distinctions are crucial to draw if, as he sees it, the sorry state of philosophy in his time is to be reformed. Both major trends of eighteenth-century philosophy – empiricism as represented, especially, by Hume (II.10), and the "dogmatic," rationalist metaphysics of Leibniz and others (III.15) – result in skepticism toward our capacity for objective knowledge, though for contrasting reasons.

Humean empiricism, by resting knowledge on immediate experience of "impressions" and "ideas," directly results in skepticism concerning the external world, the course of future experience, and so on. It was, however, Hume who, as Kant elsewhere wrote, "interrupted my dogmatic slumber,"[3] and did so by anticipating Kant's own appreciation that "dogmatic" metaphysical speculation, unhinged from ordinary experience, leads to irresolvable "stand-offs" or "antinomies" over such questions as whether the universe had a beginning and whether there exists a necessary being (God). That it does so only serves to discredit reason, and hence to foster a skeptical attitude toward philosophical claims to knowledge (B 23).

If progress is to be made, and the central question about knowledge properly posed, we need, first, clearly to distinguish between "intuitions" (including perceptions) and concepts, and also to distinguish among the respective faculties – "sensibility" and "understanding" – to which they belong. Empiricists are wrong to treat concepts as pale copies of perceptions, just as Leibniz et al. are wrong to regard the latter as confused forms of understanding. With that distinction firmly in place, we can ask about the respective contributions to knowledge of the two faculties. In particular, we will distinguish the correct claim that "all our cognition starts with experience" from the false (empiricist) one that it all arises from experience, for the latter ignores what our understanding actively "supplies from itself." Equally, by keeping the former, correct claim in mind, we shall not be seduced by a "dogmatic" rationalism, which ignores the requirement for metaphysical assertions to retain application to "possible objects of experience." Indeed, in this sense Kant transforms "metaphysics" from the "speculative" project of apprehending a "transcendent" reality, beyond experience, to the "transcendental" project of disclosing the conditions necessary for the very possibility of experience. Kant's transcendental philosophy, correlatively, embraces strict epistemological limits. "Knowledge" proper, according to Kant, is restricted to the world as it "appears" to us (as "phenomena"); because the phenomenal world of experience is mediated by sensation and shaped by our cognitive apparatus, we cannot "know" the world as it is "in itself" (as "noumena").

Once the grip of the idea that all knowledge arises from experience, in the sense of having to be legitimated by it, has been loosened, it should be obvious, Kant thinks – invoking another distinction – that we have "*a priori,*" as well as "*a posteriori,*" knowledge–knowledge whose "ground" is different from experience, as well as knowledge whose "ground" is experience. Indeed, all necessary and strictly universal truths, such as those of mathematics, will be *a priori,* for experience can only vindicate contingent and particular truths. One need not conduct experiments to confirm that all triangles have three sides, because that truth is prior to all possible experience (an *a priori* truth); but the particular experience of experiments is necessary to determine the boiling point of water (an *a posteriori* truth).

Previous philosophers have not, of course, denied the existence of *a priori* truths, but they have generally treated them all, in the terms of Kant's next distinction, as "analytic" ones, not as "synthetic." "Analytic" statements are said to be true or false on the basis of their concepts; more pre-

cisely, because in a true analytical statement the subject term contains the meaning of the predicate term, and the statement may be thought of as an analysis of the subject term – e.g. "All bachelors are unmarried." "Synthetic" statements, by contrast, synthesize or bind together a predicate to a subject that does not contain it. Determining the truth or falsehood of synthetic statements, therefore, requires comparing them to the world to see if their terms have been bound together accurately, rather than looking into the contents of the subject term – e.g. "The temperature at which ordinary book paper burns is 451 degrees Fahrenheit."

It is Kant's most important epistemological claim that while many *a priori* truths are analytic, some are not. "7 + 5 = 12;" "The quantity of matter in the universe is constant;" and "Every event has a cause" – to take examples, from mathematics, natural science, and metaphysics – are all, according to Kant, synthetic *a priori* truths. Hence the ground of their truth is a different and more puzzling thing than the relations between concepts or the meanings of words.

Kant, we know, will argue that this ground is our own cognitive powers which, so to speak, "give the orders" to how things must be if they are to be objects of our experience.[4] (This delineation of a transcendentally active ordering, perhaps even creative, mind was to exert a mighty influence on Romanticism and nineteenth-century idealist thought.) In the "Introduction," however, Kant contents himself with formulating, in the light of the above distinctions, the fundamental question that philosophy must address, "How are synthetic judgements possible *a priori*?" As later chapters in this Part of the present volume will show, this is indeed the question that most later philosophers have felt obliged either to answer or to reject.

Notes

1 H. E. Allison, *Kant's Transcendental Idealism: An Interpretation and Defense*, New Haven, CT: Yale University Press, 1983, p. 10.
2 Page numbers in the margins prefixed by B refer to material added or changed in the Second Edition; those prefixed by A to material in the First Edition, much of which is retained in the later edition.

3 I. Kant, *Prolegomena to Any Future Meta-physics*, trans. P. G. Lucas, Manchester: Manchester University Press, 1962, p. 9.

4 Gilles Deleuze, *Kant's Critical Philosophy: The Doctrine of the Faculties*, trans. H. Tomlinson and B. Habberjam, London: Athlone, 1984, p. 14.

Kant, *Critique of Pure Reason,* Introduction [Second Edition]

I*   On the Distinction between Pure and Empirical Cognition

There can be no doubt that all our cognition begins with experience. For what else might rouse our cognitive power to its operation if objects stirring our senses did not do so? In part these objects by themselves bring about presentations. In part they set in motion our understanding's activity, by which it compares these presentations, connects or separates them, and thus processes the raw material of sense impressions into a cognition of objects that is called experience. *In terms of time,* therefore, no cognition in us precedes experience, and all our cognition begins with experience.

But even though all our cognition starts **with** experience, that does not mean that all of it arises **from** experience. For it might well be that even our experiential cognition is composite, consisting of what we receive through impressions and what our own cognitive power supplies from itself (sense impressions merely prompting it to do so). If our cognitive power does make such an addition, we may not be able to distinguish it from that basic material until long practice has made us attentive to it and skilled in separating it from the basic material. B2

This question, then, whether there is such a cognition that is independent of experience and even of all impressions of the senses, is one that cannot be disposed of as soon as it comes to light, but that at least still needs closer investigation. Such cognitions are called *a priori cognitions*; they are distinguished from empirical cognitions, whose sources are a posteriori, namely, in experience.

But that expression, [viz., *a priori*,] is not yet determinate enough to indicate adequately the full meaning of the question just posed. For it is customary, I suppose, to say of much cognition derived from experiential sources that we can or do partake of it a priori. We say this because we

* Sections I and II in B replace the first two paragraphs (and section heading) from Section I in A. The Introduction in A starts as follows:

INTRODUCTION [FIRST EDITION]

A1 I. The Idea of Transcendental Philosophy

Experience is, without doubt, the first product to which our understanding gives rise, by working on the raw material of sense impressions. That is precisely why experience is our first instruction, and why, as it progresses, it is so inexhaustible in new information – so much so that if the lives of all future generations are strung together, they will never be lacking in new knowledge that can be gathered on that soil. Yet experience is far from being our understanding's only realm, and our understanding cannot be confined to it. Experience, does indeed tell us what is, but not that it must necessarily be so and not otherwise. And that is precisely why experience gives us no true universality; and reason, which is so eager for that [universal]

A2 kind of cognitions, is more stimulated by experience than satisfied. Now, such universal cognitions, which

are at the same time characterized by intrinsic necessity, must be independent of experience, clear and certain by themselves. Hence they are called a priori cognitions; by contrast, what is borrowed solely from experience is, as we put it, cognized only a posteriori, or empirically.

Now, it turns out – what is extremely remarkable – that even among our experiences there is an admixture of cognitions that must originate a priori, and that serve perhaps only to give coherence to our presentations of the senses. For even if we remove from our experiences everything belonging to the senses, there still remain certain original concepts, and judgments generated from these, that must have arisen entirely a priori, independently of experience. These concepts and judgments must have arisen in this way because through them we can – or at least we believe that we can – say more about the objects that appear to the senses than mere experience would teach us; and through them do assertions involve true universality and strict necessity, such as merely empirical cognition cannot supply.

derive the cognition not directly from experience but from a universal rule, even though that rule itself was indeed borrowed by us from experience. Thus if someone has undermined the foundation of his house, we say that he could have known a priori that the house would cave in, i.e., he did not have to wait for the experience of its actually caving in. And yet he could not have known this completely a priori. For he did first have to find out through experience that bodies have weight and hence fall when their support is withdrawn.

In what follows, therefore, we shall mean by a priori cognitions not those that occur independently of this or that experience, but those B3 that occur *absolutely* independently of all experience. They contrast with empirical cognitions, which are those that are possible only a posteriori, i.e., through experience. But we call a priori cognitions *pure* if nothing empirical whatsoever is mixed in with them. Thus, e.g., the proposition, Every change has its cause, is an a priori proposition; yet it is not pure, because change is a concept that can be obtained only from experience.

II We are in Possession of Certain A Priori Cognitions, and Even Common Understanding Is Never without Them

What matters here is that we find a characteristic by which we can safely distinguish a pure cognition from empirical ones. Now, experience does indeed teach us that something is thus or thus, but not that it cannot be otherwise. **First**, then, if we find a proposition such that in thinking it we think at the same time its *necessity*, then it is an a priori judgment; and if, in addition, it is not derived from any proposition except one that itself has the validity of a necessary proposition, then it is absolutely a priori. **Second**, experience never provides its judgments with true or strict *universality*, but only (through induction) with assumed and comparative universality; hence [there] we should, properly speaking, say [merely] B4 that as far as we have observed until now, no exception is to be found to this or that rule. If, therefore, a judgment is thought with strict universality, i.e., thought in such a way that no exception whatever is allowed as possible, then the judgment is not derived from experience, but is valid absolutely a priori. Hence empirical universality is only [the result of] our choosing to upgrade validity from one that holds in most cases to one that holds in all, as, e.g., in the proposition, All bodies have weight. But when universality is strict and belongs to a judgment essentially, then it points to a special cognitive source for the judgment, viz., a power of a priori cognition. Hence necessity and strict universality are safe indicators of a priori cognition, and they do moreover belong together inseparably. It is nevertheless advisable to make separate use of the two criteria, even though each is infallible by itself. For, in using them, there are times when showing the empirical limitedness of a cognition is easier than showing the contingency of the judgments based on it; and there are times when showing the unlimited universality that we attribute to a judgment is more convincing than is showing the judgment's necessity.

Now, it is easy to show that in human cognition there actually are such judgments [as we are looking for, viz.], judgments that are necessary and in the strictest sense universal, and hence are pure a priori judgments. If we want an example from the sciences, we need only look to all the propositions of mathematics; if we want one B5 from the most ordinary use of understanding, then we can use the proposition that all change must have a cause. Indeed, in this latter proposition the very concept of a cause so manifestly contains the concept of a necessity in [the cause's] connection with an effect, and of a strict universality of the rule [governing that connection], that the concept of a cause would get lost entirely if we derived it as *Hume* did: viz., from a repeated association of what happens with what precedes, and from our resulting habit* of connecting presentations (hence from a merely subjective necessity). But we do not need such examples in order to prove that pure a priori principles actual[ly exist] in our cognition. We could, alternatively, establish that these principles are indispensable for the possibility of experience as such, and hence establish [their existence] a priori. For where might even

---

* Or 'custom': *Enquiry Concerning Human Understanding*, V, Pt. I, and cf. VII, Pt. II. Cf. also below, B 19–20, 127.

experience get its certainty if all the rules by which it proceeds were always in turn empirical and hence contingent, so that they could hardly be considered first principles? But here we may settle for having established as a matter of fact [that there is a] pure use of our cognitive power, and to have established what its indicators, are. However, we can see such an a priori origin not merely in judgments, but even in some concepts. If from your experiential concept of a *body* you gradually omit everything that is empirical in a body – the color, the hardness or softness, the weight, even the impenetrability – there yet remains the *space* that was occupied by the body B6 (which has now entirely vanished), and this space you cannot omit [from the concept]. Similarly, if from your empirical concept of any object whatever, corporeal or incorporeal, you omit all properties that experience has taught you, you still cannot take away from the concept the property through which you think the object either as a *substance* or as *attaching* to a substance (even though this concept of substance is more determinate than that of an object as such). Hence you must, won over by the necessity with which this concept of substance forces itself upon you, admit that this concept resides a priori in your cognitive power.

III   Philosophy Needs a Science[1] That Will Determine the Possibility, the Principles, and the Range of All A Priori Cognitions*

Much more significant yet than all the preceding is the fact that there are certain cognitions that [not only extend to but] even leave the realm of all possible experiences. These cognitions, by A3 means of concepts to which no corresponding object can be given in experience at all, appear to expand the range of our judgments beyond all bounds of experience.

And precisely in these latter cognitions, which go beyond the world of sense, where experience

* The text of A continues, together with that of B, just below. The section number and heading were added in B.

cannot provide us with any guide or correction, reside our reason's inquiries. We regard these B7 inquiries as far superior in importance, and their final aim as much more sublime, than anything that our understanding can learn in the realm of appearances. Indeed, we would sooner dare anything, even at the risk of error, than give up such treasured inquiries [into the unavoidable problems of reason], whether on the ground that they are precarious somehow, or from disdain and indifference. These unavoidable problems of reason themselves are *God, freedom, and immortality*. But the science whose final aim, involving the science's entire apparatus, is in fact directed solely at solving these problems is called *metaphysics*. Initially, the procedure of metaphysics is *dogmatic*, i.e., [metaphysics], without first examining whether reason is capable or incapable of so great an enterprise, confidently undertakes to carry it out.[2]

Now, suppose that we had just left the terrain of experience. Would we immediately erect an edifice by means of what cognitions we have, though we do not know from where? Would we erect it on credit, i.e., on principles whose origin is unfamiliar to us? It does seem natural that we would not, but that we would first seek assurance through careful inquiries that the foundation had been laid. In other words, it does seem natural that we would, rather, long since have raised the question as to just how our understanding could arrive at all these a priori cognitions, and what might be their range, validity, and value. And A4 in fact nothing would be more natural, if by the term *natural* we mean what properly and reasonably ought to happen. If, on the other hand, we B8 mean by this term what usually happens, then nothing is more natural and comprehensible than the fact that for a long time this inquiry had to remain unperformed. For, one part of these [a priori] cognitions, viz., the mathematical ones, possess long-standing reliability, and thereby raise favorable expectations concerning other [a priori] cognitions as well, even though these may be of a quite different nature. Moreover, once we are beyond the sphere of experience, we are assured of not being refuted by experience. The appeal of expanding our cognitions is so great that nothing but hitting upon a clear contradiction can stop our progress. On the other hand, we can avoid such contradiction by merely being cautious in our inventions – even though they remain nonetheless inventions. Mathematics provides us with a splendid example of how much we can achieve, independently of experience, in a priori cognition. Now, it is true that mathematics deals with objects and cognitions only to the extent that they can be exhibited in intuition. But this detail is easily overlooked because that intuition can itself be given a priori and hence is rarely distinguished

A5 from a mere pure concept. Captivated by such a proof of reason's might, our urge to expand [our cognitions] sees no boundaries. When the light dove parts the air in free flight and feels the air's resistance, it might come to think that it would do much better still in space devoid of air. In the

B9 same way *Plato* left the world of sense because it sets such narrow limits to our understanding; on the wings of the ideas, he ventured beyond that world and into the empty space of pure understanding. He did not notice that with all his efforts he made no headway. He failed to make headway because he had no resting point against which – as a foothold, as it were – he might brace himself and apply his forces in order to set the understanding in motion. But [Plato is no exception]: it is human reason's usual fate, in speculation, to finish its edifice as soon as possible, and not to inquire until afterwards whether a good foundation has in fact been laid for it. Then all sorts of rationalizations are hunted up in order to reassure us that the edifice is sturdy, or, preferably, even to reject altogether so late and risky an examination of it. But what keeps us, while we are building, free from all anxiety and suspicion, and flatters us with a seeming thoroughness, is the following. A large part – perhaps the largest – of our reason's business consists in dissecting what concepts of objects we already have. This [procedure] supplies us with a multitude of cognitions. And although these cognitions are nothing more

A6 than clarifications or elucidations of what has already been thought in our concepts (although thought as yet in a confused way), they are yet rated equal to new insights at least in form, even though in matter or content they do not expand the concepts we have but only spell them out.

B10 Now since this procedure yields actual a priori cognitions that progresses in a safe and useful way, reason uses this pretense, though without itself noticing this, to lay claim surreptitiously to assertions of a quite different kind. In these assertions, reason adds to given concepts others quite foreign to them, doing so moreover a priori. Yet how reason arrived at these concepts is not known; indeed, such a question is not even thought of. Hence I shall deal at the very outset with the distinction between these two kinds of cognition.

IV   On the Distinction between Analytic and Synthetic Judgments

In all judgments in which we think the relation of a subject to the predicate (I here consider affirmative judgments only, because the application to negative judgments is easy afterwards), this relation is possible in two ways. Either the predicate B belongs to the subject A as something that is (covertly) contained in this concept A; or B, though connected with concept A, lies quite outside it. In the first case I call the judgment *analytic*; in the second, *synthetic*. Hence A7 (affirmative) analytic judgments are those in which the predicate's connection with the subject is thought by [thinking] identity, whereas those B11 judgments in which this connection is thought without [thinking] identity are to be called synthetic. Analytic judgments could also be called *elucidatory*. For they do not through the predicate add anything to the concept of the subject; rather, they only dissect the concept, breaking it up into its component concepts which had already been thought in it (although thought confusedly). Synthetic judgments, on the other hand, could also be called *expansive*. For they do add to the concept of the subject a predicate that had not been thought in that concept at all and could not have been extracted from it by any dissection. For example, if I say: All bodies are extended – then this is an analytic judgment. For I do not need to go beyond the concept that I link with the word body in order to find that extension is connected with it. All I need to do in order to find this predicate in the concept is to dissect the concept, i.e., become conscious of the manifold that I always think in it. Hence the judgment is analytic. By contrast, if I say: All bodies are heavy – then the predicate is something quite different from what I think in the mere concept of a body as such. Hence adding such a predicate yields a synthetic judgment.[3]

Experiential judgments, as such, are one and all synthetic. For to base an analytic judgment on experience would be absurd, because in its case I can formulate my judgment without going outside my concept, and hence do not need for it any testimony of experience. Thus the [analytic] proposition that bodies are extended is one that holds a priori and is not an experiential judgment. For before I turn to experience, I already have in the concept [of body] all the conditions required for my judgment. I have only to extract from it, in accordance with the principle of contradiction, the predicate [of extension]; in doing so, I can at the same time become conscious of the judgment's necessity, of which experience would not even inform me. On the other hand, though in the concept of a body as such I do not at all include the predicate of heaviness, yet the concept designates an object of experience by means of part of this experience; hence I can [synthetically] add to this part further parts, of the same experience, in addition to those that belonged to the concept of a body as such. I can begin by cognizing the concept of a body *analytically* through the char-

---

* This paragraph in B replaces the following two in A:

Now, this shows clearly: (1) that analytic judgments do not at all expand our cognition, but spell out and make understandable to myself the concept that I already have; (2) that in synthetic judgments, where the predicate does not lie within the concept of the subject, I must have besides this concept something else (X) on which the understanding relies in order to cognize nonetheless that the predicate belongs to that concept.

In empirical judgments, or in judgments of experience, it is not difficult at all to find this X. For here this X is the complete experience of the object that I think by means of a concept A, the concept amounting only to part of the experience. For although in the concept of a body as such I do not at all include the predicate of heaviness, yet the concept designates the complete experience [of a body] by means of part of it; hence I can add to this part, as belonging to it, further parts of the same experience. I can begin by cognizing the concept of a body analytically through the characteristics of extension, impenetrability, shape, etc., all of which are thought in this concept. But then I expand my cognition: by looking back to the experience from which I have abstracted this concept of body, I also find heaviness to be always connected with the above characteristics. Hence experience is the X that lies outside the concept A and makes possible the synthesis of the predicate B of heaviness with the concept A.

acteristics of extension, impenetrability, shape, etc., all of which are thought in this concept. But then I expand my cognition: by looking back to the experience from which I have abstracted this concept of body, I also find heaviness to be always connected with the above characteristics; and so I add it, as a predicate, to that concept *synthetically*. Hence experience is what makes possible the synthesis of the predicate of heaviness with the concept of body. For although neither of the two concepts is contained in the other, yet they belong to each other, though only contingently, as parts of a whole; that whole is experience, which is itself a synthetic combination of intuitions.

In synthetic judgments that are a priori, how- A9 ever, this remedy is entirely lacking. If I am to go beyond the concept A in order to cognize another B13 concept B as combined with it, I rely on something that makes the synthesis possible: what is that something, considering that here I do not have the advantage of looking around for it in the realm of experience? Take the proposition: Everything that happens has its cause. – In the concept of something that happens I do indeed think an existence preceded by a time, etc., and from this one can obtain analytic judgments. But the concept of a cause lies quite outside that earlier concept and indicates something different from what happens; hence it is not part of what is contained in this latter presentation. In speaking generally of what happens, how can I say about it something quite different from it, and cognize as belonging to it – indeed, belonging to it necessarily – the concept of cause, even though this concept is not contained in the concept of what happens? What is here the unknown = X on which the understanding relies when it believes that it discovers, outside the concept A, a predicate B that is foreign to concept A but that the understanding considers nonetheless to be connected with that concept? This unknown cannot be experience. For in adding the presentation of cause to the presentation of what happens, the above principle does so not only with greater universality than experience can provide, but also with the necessity's being expressed; hence it does so entirely a priori and on the basis of mere concepts. Now, on such synthetic, i.e., expansive, principles depends the whole final aim of our speculative a priori cognition. For, analytic principles A10 are indeed exceedingly important and needed, but only for attaining that distinctness in concepts B14

B12 (margin, left column)

which is required for a secure and extensive synthesis that, as such, will actually be a new acquisition [of cognition].

V All Theoretical Sciences of Reason Contain Synthetic A Priori Judgments as Principles

1. *Mathematical judgments are one and all synthetic.* Although this proposition is incontestably certain and has very important consequences, it seems thus far to have escaped the notice of those who have analyzed human reason; indeed, it seems to be directly opposed to all their conjectures. For they found that all the inferences made by mathematicians proceed (as the nature of all apodeictic certainty requires) according to the principle of contradiction; and thus they came to be persuaded that the principle of contradiction is also the basis on which we cognize the principles [of mathematics]. In this they were mistaken. For though we can indeed gain insight into a synthetic proposition according to the principle of contradiction, we can never do so [by considering] that proposition by itself, but can do so only by presupposing another synthetic proposition from which it can be deduced.

We must note, first of all, that mathematical propositions, properly so called, are always a priori judgments rather than empirical ones; for they carry with them necessity, which we B15 could never glean from experience. But if anyone refuses to grant that all such propositions are a priori – all right: then I restrict my assertion to *pure mathematics*, in the very concept of which is implied that it contains not empirical but only pure a priori cognition.

It is true that one might at first think that the proposition $7 + 5 = 12$ is a merely analytic one that follows, by the principle of contradiction, from the concept of a sum of seven and five. Yet if we look more closely, we find that the concept of the sum of 7 and 5 contains nothing more than the union of the two numbers into one; but in [thinking] that union we are not thinking in any way at all what that single number is that unites the two. In thinking merely that union of seven and five, I have by no means already thought the concept of twelve; and no matter how long I dissect my concept of such a possible sum, still I shall never find in it that twelve. We must go beyond

these concepts and avail ourselves of the intuition corresponding to one of the two: e.g., our five fingers, or (as *Segner* does in his *Arithmetic*) five dots. In this way we must gradually add, to the concept of seven, the units of the five given in intuition. For I start by taking the number 7. Then, for the concept of the 5, I avail myself of the fingers of my hand as intuition. Thus, in that image of mine, I gradually add to the number 7 the units that I previously gathered together in order to B16 make up the number 5. In this way I see the number 12 arise. That 5 *were to be added* to 7, this I had indeed already thought in the concept of a sum $= 7 + 5$, but not that this sum is equal to the number 12. Arithmetic propositions are therefore always synthetic. We become aware of this all the more distinctly if we take larger numbers. For then it is very evident that, no matter how much we twist and turn our concepts, we can never find the [number of the] sum by merely dissecting our concepts, i.e., without availing ourselves of intuition.

Just as little are any principles of pure geometry analytic. That the straight line between two points is the shortest is a synthetic proposition. For my concept of *straight* contains nothing about magnitude, but contains only a quality. Therefore the concept of shortest is entirely added to the concept of a straight line and cannot be extracted from it by any dissection. Hence we must here avail ourselves of intuition; only by means of it is the synthesis possible.

It is true that a few propositions presupposed by geometricians are actually analytic and based on the principle of contradiction. But, like identical propositions, they serve not as principles but only [as links in] the chain of method. B17 Examples are $a = a$; the whole is equal to itself; or $(a + b) > a$, i.e., the whole is greater than its part. And yet even these principles, although they hold according to mere concepts, are admitted in mathematics only because they can be exhibited in intuition. [As for mathematics generally,] what commonly leads us to believe that the predicate of its apodeictic judgments is contained in our very concept, and that the judgment is therefore analytic, is merely the ambiguity with which we express ourselves. For we say that we *are to* add in thought a certain predicate to a given concept, and this necessity adheres indeed to the very concepts. But here the question is not what we *are to* add in thought to the given concept, but what we *actually* think in the concept, even if only obscurely; and there we find that, although the predicate does indeed adhere necessarily to such concepts, yet it does so not as something thought in the concept itself, but by means of an intuition that must be added to the concept.

2.   *Natural science (physica) contains synthetic a priori judgments as principles.* Let me cite as examples just a few propositions: e.g., the proposition that in all changes in the corporeal world the quantity of matter remains unchanged; or the proposition that in all communication of motion, action and reaction must always be equal to each other. Both propositions are clearly not only necessary, and hence of a priori origin, but also synthetic. For in the concept of matter I do not think permanence, but think merely the matter's being present in space insofar as it occupies space. Hence I do actually go beyond the concept of matter, in order to add to it a priori in thought something that I have not thought *in it*. Hence the proposition is thought not analytically but synthetically and yet a priori, and the same occurs in the remaining propositions of the pure part of natural science.

B18

3.   *Metaphysics* is to *contain synthetic a priori cognitions.* This holds even if metaphysics is viewed as a science that thus far has merely been attempted, but that because of the nature of human reason is nonetheless indispensable. Metaphysics is not at all concerned merely to dissect concepts of things that we frame a priori, and thereby to elucidate them analytically. Rather, in metaphysics we want to expand our a priori cognition. In order to do this, we must use principles which go beyond the given concept and which add to it something that was not contained in it; and, by means of such synthetic a priori judgments, we must presumably go so far beyond such concepts that even experience can no longer follow us; as in the proposition: The world must have a first beginning – and others like that. And hence metaphysics consists, at least *in terms of its purpose*, of nothing but synthetic a priori propositions.

B19   VI   The General Problem of
               Pure Reason

Much is gained already when we can bring a multitude of inquiries under the formula of a single problem. For we thereby facilitate not only our own business by defining it precisely, but also – for anyone else who wants to examine it – the judgment as to whether or not we have carried out our project adequately. Now the proper problem of pure reason is contained in this question:

How are synthetic judgments possible a priori?

That metaphysics has thus far remained in such a shaky state of uncertainty and contradictions is attributable to a sole cause: the fact that this problem, and perhaps even the distinction between *analytic* and *synthetic* judgments, has not previously occurred to anyone. Whether metaphysics stands or falls depends on the solution of this problem, or on an adequate proof that the possibility which metaphysics demands to see explained does not exist at all. *David Hume* at least came closer to this problem than any other philosopher. Yet he did not think of it nearly determinately enough and in its universality, but merely remained with the synthetic proposition about the connection of an effect with its causes (*principium causalitatis*). He believed he had discovered that such a proposition is quite impossible a priori. Thus, according to his conclusions, everything that we call metaphysics would amount to no more than the delusion of a supposed rational insight into what in fact is merely borrowed from experience and has, through habit, acquired a seeming necessity. This assertion, which destroys all pure philosophy, would never have entered Hume's mind if he had envisaged our problem in its universality. For he would then have seen that by his argument there could be no pure mathematics either, since it certainly does contain synthetic a priori propositions; and from such an assertion his good sense would surely have saved him.

B20

In solving the above problem we solve at the same time another one, concerning the possibility of the pure use of reason in establishing and carrying out all sciences that contain theoretical a priori cognition of objects; i.e., we also answer these questions:

How is pure mathematics possible?
How is pure natural science possible?

Since these sciences are actually given [as existent], it is surely proper for us to ask **how** they are possible; for that they must be possible is proved by their being actual.* As regards *metaphysics*, however, there are grounds on which everyone must doubt its possibility: its progress thus far has been poor; and thus far not a single metaphysics has been put forth of which we can say, as far as the essential purpose of metaphysics is concerned, that it is actually at hand.

Yet in a certain sense this *kind of cognition* must likewise be regarded as given; and although metaphysics is not actual as a science, yet it is actual as a natural predisposition (i.e., as a *metaphysica naturalis*). For human reason, impelled by its own need rather than moved by the mere vanity of gaining a lot of knowledge, proceeds irresistibly to such questions as cannot be answered by any experiential use of reason and any principles taken from such use. And thus all human beings, once their reason has expanded to [the point where it can] speculate, actually have always had in them, and always will have in them, some metaphysics. Now concerning it, too, there is this question:

B22   **How is metaphysics as a natural predisposition possible?** i.e., how, from the nature of universal human reason, do the questions arise that pure reason poses to itself and is impelled, by its own need, to answer as best it can?

Thus far, however, all attempts to answer these natural questions – e.g., whether the world has a beginning or has been there from eternity, etc. – have met with unavoidable contradictions. Hence we cannot settle for our mere natural predisposition for metaphysics, i.e., our pure power of reason itself, even though some metaphysics or other (whichever it might be) always arises from it. Rather, it must be possible, by means of this predisposition, to attain certainty either concerning our knowledge or lack of knowledge of the objects [of metaphysics], i.e., either concerning a decision about the objects that its questions deal with, or certainty concerning the ability or inability of reason to make judgments about these objects. In other words, it must be possible to expand our pure reason in a reliable way, or to set for it limits that are determinate and safe. This last question, which flows from the general problem above, may rightly be stated thus:

How is metaphysics as science possible?

Ultimately, therefore, critique of pure reason leads necessarily to science; the dogmatic use of pure reason without critique, on the other hand, to baseless assertions that can always be opposed B23 by others that seem equally plausible, and hence to *skepticism*.

This science, moreover, cannot be overly, forbiddingly voluminous. For it deals not with objects of reason, which are infinitely diverse, but merely with [reason] itself. [Here reason] deals with problems that issue entirely from its own womb; they are posed to it not by the nature of things distinct from it, but by its own nature. And thus, once it has become completely acquainted with its own ability regarding the objects that it may encounter in experience, reason must find it easy to determine, completely and safely, the range and the bounds of its use [when] attempted beyond all bounds of experience.

Hence all attempts that have been made thus far to bring a metaphysics about *dogmatically* can and must be regarded as if they had never occurred. For whatever is analytic in one metaphysics or another, i.e., is mere dissection of the concepts residing a priori in our reason, is only a prearrangement for metaphysics proper, and is not yet its purpose at all. That purpose is to expand our a priori cognition synthetically, and for this purpose the dissection of reason's a priori concepts is useless. For it shows merely what is contained in these concepts; it does not show how we arrive at such concepts a priori, so that we could then also determine the valid use of such concepts in regard to the objects of all cognition generally. Nor do we need much self-denial to give B24 up all these claim; for every metaphysics put forth thus far has long since been deprived of its reputation by the fact that it gave rise to undeniable, and in the dogmatic procedure indeed unavoidable, contradictions of reason with itself. A different treatment, completely opposite to the one used thus far, must be given to metaphysics – a science, indispensable to human reason,

---

* This actuality may still be doubted by some in the case of pure natural science. Yet we need only examine the propositions that are to be found at the beginning of physics proper (empirical physics), such as those about the permanence of the quantity of matter, about inertia, about the equality of action and reaction, etc., in order to soon be convinced that these propositions themselves amount to a *physica pura* (or *physica rationalis*). Such a physics, as a science in its own right, surely deserves to be put forth separately and in its whole range, whether this range be narrow or broad.

whose every new shoot can indeed be lopped off but whose root cannot be eradicated. We shall need more perseverance in order to keep from being deterred – either from within by the difficulty of this science or from without by people's resistance to it – from thus finally bringing it to a prosperous and fruitful growth.

Notes

1 The German word *Wissenschaft* is wider in application than our word "science," and applies to philosophy and history as much as to physics. When he has science in the contemporary English sense in mind, Kant writes of "natural science."

2 Here we get a foretaste of Kant's discussion in Division II of the book, "Transcendental Dialectic," of such "ideas of reason" as God and freedom which, while beyond the reach of our understanding, have a "regulative" use and are essential to morality.

3 Most later philosophers, even those who accept an analytic/synthetic distinction, question Kant's ways of making that distinction. The tendency has been to express it in linguistic terms: for example, an analytic truth is one true in virtue, simply, of the meanings of the component terms – any other truth being a synthetic one.

13

G. W. F. Hegel, *Phenomenology of Spirit*, Sections 73–103

Introduction

In the Introduction to, and opening Section ("Sense-Certainty"), of his most famous work, *Phenomenology of Spirit* (1807), the German philosopher Georg Wilhelm Friedrich Hegel (1770–1831) does not mention Kant by name, but it is two central components of Kant's epistemology that he is attacking here, while at the same time indicating his own approach to the examination of cognition. As we saw in II.12 above, Kant insists that the scope and limits of knowledge must first be submitted to a "critique" before claims to knowledge can properly be made – a critique which shows, Kant argues, that knowledge is restricted to how the world appears to us, and cannot therefore extend to the nature of reality "in itself." This conclusion is partly based on Kant's sharp distinction between "sensible intuitions" (the immediate deliverances of sensory experience) and the "pure concepts of the understanding," which we then employ to organize such data. For if concepts simply organize sensory data, dependent as these are on our particular "forms of sensibility," there can be no reason to suppose that concepts correspond to how things are *in themselves*.

From G. W. F. Hegel, *Phenomenology of Spirit*, trans. A. V. Miller. Oxford: Oxford University Press, 1977, pp. 46–62 (note omitted).

Definitive of Hegel's "Absolute Idealism" (see the selection from Hegel in III.18) is his rejection of the Kantian "antithesis of being and knowing" (*Phenomenology of Spirit* §37), of an "impassable gulf" between "our" world and reality "in itself." We are, as Hegel sees it, already primed to accept such an antithesis if, like Kant, we speak of cognition as an "instrument" for discovering truth: for, since we cannot dispense with the instrument, there is no way of factoring out its contribution to the knowledge we take ourselves as having. As some modern writers express it, there is not, even in principle, the possibility of gaining a detached, "sideways on" view of the relationship between our conceptual schemes and reality.[1] Elsewhere, Hegel compares the critique of knowledge prior to making knowledge claims to learning how to swim before getting into the water (*Encyclopedia Logic* §41). Just as one only learns to swim through being in the water, so any appraisal of claims to knowledge must come from within ongoing epistemic practices, not from an "external" standpoint.

But how does the philosopher, immersed in these practices, evaluate claims to knowledge, or find a "criterion" for judging the adequacy of concepts to their alleged objects? Hegel's answer is by "looking on" at the history of consciousness itself – at centuries of experience during which, as he puts it, the work of testing the adequacy of concepts has already gone on. His point is that, at any given time, people not only make claims to knowledge, but operate with an implicit understanding of what knowledge consists in. These can and do come into conflict: for example, claims to knowledge of God might conflict with the prevailing empiricist or verificationist ethos of the period. When this happens, something has to give: either the knowledge claims must be abandoned, or the understanding of the nature of knowledge must be revised. Eventually the stage is reached where there is no such conflict: our epistemic practices are then "at peace," and a "true Science" has arrived. Epistemology, then, is not the doomed attempt to compare consciousness with reality, but the viable one of a "comparison of consciousness with itself."

Hegel's brief discussion of "sense-certainty" is important for two reasons. First, it paradigmatically illustrates Hegel's procedure of identifying contradictions between people's claims to knowledge and their implicit criterion of knowledge. Second, it is an attempt to dissolve the intuitions *versus* concepts dichotomy to which, as one commentator writes, "virtually all of Kant's dualisms could be traced back."[2] By "sense-certainty," Hegel means the idea that our primary and perhaps only kind of knowledge is that of immediate acquaintance with sensory particulars – that knowledge is of what is "here and now." He then argues that as soon as we look at the judgments taken to register such knowledge – "Now is night," "Here is a tree," and so on – it quickly emerges that much more than acquaintance with sensory data is involved, notably an understanding of con-

cepts, including temporal and spatial ones. As Charles Taylor writes, "sensible certainty turns out to be unrealizable . . . in its claim to immediate contact with sensible particulars, without the mediation of general terms."[3] In short, we never encounter pure, naked, uninterpreted sensations or sense-data (see Chapters II.20 and II.21 in this volume); and there is no (intuitive) perception distinct from (conceptual) understanding. Rather, there is, as he elsewhere puts it, "perceptive understanding" or "understanding perception."[4] In effect, Hegel is here exposing "the myth of the given" that a number of twentieth-century philosophers, such as Wilfrid Sellars, have identified as the central fault of empiricist epistemology.

Notes

1 See J. McDowell, *Mind and World*, Cambridge, MA: Harvard University Press, 1994.
2 P. Guyer, "Absolute Idealism and the Rejection of Kantian Dualism," in K. Ameriks, ed., *The Cambridge Companion to German Idealism*, Cambridge: Cambridge University Press, 2000, p. 54.
3 C. Taylor, *Hegel*, Cambridge: Cambridge University Press, 1975, p. 142.
4 From Hegel's *Lectures on the History of Philosophy*, quoted in F. Beiser, ed., *The Cambridge Companion to Hegel*, Cambridge: Cambridge University Press, p. 192.

Hegel Phenomenology of Spirit

Introduction

73. It is a natural assumption that in philosophy, before we start to deal with its proper subject-matter, viz. the actual cognition of what truly is, one must first of all come to an understanding about cognition, which is regarded either as the instrument to get hold of the Absolute, or as the medium through which one discovers it. A certain uneasiness seems justified, partly because there are different types of cognition, and one of them might be more appropriate than another for the attainment of this goal, so

that we could make a bad choice of means; and partly because cognition is a faculty of a definite kind and scope, and thus, without a more precise definition of its nature and limits, we might grasp clouds of error instead of the heaven of truth. This feeling of uneasiness is surely bound to be transformed into the conviction that the whole project of securing for consciousness through cognition what exists in itself is absurd, and that there is a boundary between cognition and the Absolute that completely separates them. For, if cognition is the instrument for getting hold of absolute being, it is obvious that the use of an instrument on a thing certainly does not let it be what it is for itself, but rather sets out to reshape and alter it. If, on the other hand, cognition is not an instrument of our activity but a more or less passive medium through which the light of truth reaches us, then again we do not receive the truth as it is in itself, but only as it exists through and in this medium. Either way we employ a means which immediately brings about the opposite of its own end; or rather, what is really absurd is that we should make use of a means at all.

It would seem, to be sure, that this evil could be remedied through an acquaintance with the way in which the *instrument* works; for this would enable us to eliminate from the representation of the Absolute which we have gained through it whatever is due to the instrument, and thus get the truth in its purity. But this 'improvement' would in fact only bring us back to where we were before. If we remove from a reshaped thing what the instrument has done to it, then the thing – here the Absolute – becomes for us exactly what it was before this [accordingly] superfluous effort. On the other hand, if the Absolute is supposed merely to be brought nearer to us through this instrument, without anything in it being altered, like a bird caught by a lime-twig, it would surely laugh our little ruse to scorn, if it were not with us, in and for itself, all along, and of its own volition. For a ruse is just what cognition would be in such a case, since it would, with its manifold exertions, be giving itself the air of doing something quite different from creating a merely immediate and therefore effortless relationship. Or, if by testing cognition, which we conceive of as a *medium*, we get to know the law of its refraction, it is again useless to subtract this from the end result. For it is not the refraction of the ray, but the ray itself whereby truth reaches us, that is cognition; and if this were removed, all that would be indicated would be a pure direction or a blank space.

74. Meanwhile, if the fear of falling into error sets up a mistrust of Science, which in the absence of such scruples gets on with the work itself, and actually cognizes something, it is hard to see why we should not turn round and mistrust this very mistrust. Should we not be concerned as to whether this fear of error is not just the error itself? Indeed, this fear takes something – a great deal in fact – for granted as truth, supporting its scruples and inferences on what is itself in need of prior scrutiny to see if it is true.

To be specific, it takes for granted certain ideas about cognition as an *instrument* and as a *medium*, and assumes that there is a *difference between ourselves and this cognition*. Above all, it presupposes that the Absolute stands on one side and cognition on the other, independent and separated from it, and yet is something real; or in other words, it presupposes that cognition which, since it is excluded from the Absolute, is surely outside of the truth as well, is nevertheless true, an assumption whereby what calls itself fear of error reveals itself rather as fear of the truth.

75. This conclusion stems from the fact that the Absolute alone is true, or the truth alone is absolute. One may set this aside on the grounds that there is a type of cognition which, though it does not cognize the Absolute as Science aims to, is still true, and that cognition in general, though it be incapable of grasping the Absolute, is still capable of grasping other kinds of truth. But we gradually come to see that this kind of talk which goes back and forth only leads to a hazy distinction between an absolute truth and some other kind of truth, and that words like 'absolute', 'cognition', etc. presuppose a meaning which has yet to be ascertained.

76. Instead of troubling ourselves with such useless ideas and locutions about cognition as 'an instrument for getting hold of the Absolute', or as 'a medium through which we view the truth' (relationships which surely, in the end, are what all these ideas of a cognition cut off from the Absolute, and an Absolute separated from cognition, amount to); instead of putting up with excuses which create the incapacity of Science by assuming relationships of this kind in order to be exempt from the hard work of Science, while at the same time giving the impression of working seriously and zealously; instead of bothering to refute all these ideas, we could reject them out of hand as adventitious and arbitrary, and the words associated with them like 'absolute', 'cognition', 'objective' and 'subjective', and countless others whose meaning is assumed to be generally familiar, could even be regarded as so much deception. For to give the impression that their meaning is generally well known, or that their Notion is comprehended, looks more like an attempt to avoid the main problem, which is precisely to provide this Notion. We could, with better justification, simply spare ourselves the trouble of paying any attention whatever to such

ideas and locutions; for they are intended to ward off Science itself, and constitute merely an empty appearance of knowing, which vanishes immediately as soon as Science comes on the scene. But Science, just because it comes on the scene, is itself an appearance: in coming on the scene it is not yet Science in its developed and unfolded truth. In this connection it makes no difference whether we think of Science as the appearance because it comes on the scene alongside another mode of knowledge, or whether we call that other untrue knowledge its manifestation. In any case Science must liberate itself from this semblance, and it can do so only by turning against it. For, when confronted with a knowledge that is without truth, Science can neither merely reject it as an ordinary way of looking at things, while assuring us that its Science is a quite different sort of cognition for which that ordinary knowledge is of no account whatever; nor can it appeal to the vulgar view for the intimations it gives us of something better to come. By the former *assurance*, Science would be declaring its power to lie simply in its *being*; but the untrue knowledge likewise appeals to the fact that *it is*, and *assures* us that for it Science is of no account. *One* bare assurance is worth just as much as another. Still less can Science appeal to whatever intimations of something better it may detect in the cognition that is without truth, to the signs which point in the direction of Science. For one thing, it would only be appealing again to what merely *is*; and for another, it would only be appealing to itself, and to itself in the mode in which it exists in the cognition that is without truth. In other words, it would be appealing to an inferior form of its being, to the way it appears, rather than to what it is in and for itself. It is for this reason that an exposition of how knowledge makes its appearance will here be undertaken.

77. Now, because it has only phenomenal knowledge for its object, this exposition seems not to be Science, free and self-moving in its own peculiar shape; yet from this standpoint it can be regarded as the path of the natural consciousness which presses forward to true knowledge; or as the way of the Soul which journeys through the series of its own configurations as though they were the stations appointed for it by its own nature, so that it may purify itself for the life of the Spirit, and achieve finally, through a completed experience of itself, the awareness of what it really is in itself.

78. Natural consciousness will show itself to be only the Notion of knowledge, or in other words, not to be real knowledge. But since it directly takes itself to be real knowledge, this path has a negative significance for it, and what is in fact the realization of the Notion, counts for it rather as the loss of its own self; for it does lose its truth on this path. The road can therefore be regarded as the pathway of *doubt*, or more precisely as the way of despair. For what happens on it is not what is ordinarily understood when the word 'doubt' is used: shilly-shallying about this or that presumed truth, followed by a return to that truth again, after the doubt has been appropriately dispelled – so that at the end of the process the matter is taken to be what it was in the first place. On the contrary, this path is the conscious insight into the untruth of phenomenal knowledge, for which the supreme reality is what is in truth only the unrealized Notion. Therefore this thoroughgoing scepticism is also not the scepticism with which an earnest zeal for truth and Science fancies it has prepared and equipped itself in their service: the *resolve*, in Science, not to give oneself over to the thoughts of others, upon mere authority, but to examine everything for oneself and follow only one's own conviction, or better still, to produce everything oneself, and accept only one's own deed as what is true.

The series of configurations which consciousness goes through along this road is, in reality, the detailed history of the *education* of consciousness itself to the standpoint of Science. That zealous resolve represents this education simplistically as something directly over and done with in the making of the resolution; but the way of the Soul is the actual fulfilment of the resolution, in contrast to the untruth of that view. Now, following one's own conviction is, of course, more than giving oneself over to authority; but changing an opinion accepted on authority into an opinion held out of personal conviction, does not necessarily alter the content of the opinion, or replace error with truth. The only difference between being caught up in a system of opinions and prejudices based on personal conviction, and being caught up in one based on the authority of others, lies in the added conceit that is innate in the former position. The scepticism that is directed against the whole range of phenomenal consciousness, on the other hand, renders the Spirit for the first time competent to examine what truth is. For it brings about a state of despair about all the so-called natural ideas, thoughts, and opinions, regardless of whether they are called one's own or someone else's, ideas with which the consciousness that sets about the examination [of truth] *straight away* is still filled and hampered, so that it is, in fact, incapable of carrying out what it wants to undertake.

79.   The necessary progression and interconnection of the forms of the unreal consciousness will by itself bring to pass the *completion* of the series. To make this more intelligible, it may be remarked, in a preliminary and general way, that the exposition of the untrue consciousness in its untruth is not a merely *negative* procedure. The natural consciousness itself normally takes this one-sided view of it; and a knowledge which makes this one-sidedness its very essence is itself one of the patterns of incomplete consciousness which occurs on the road itself, and will manifest itself in due course. This is just the scepticism which only ever sees pure nothingness in its result and abstracts from the fact that this nothingness is specifically the nothingness of that *from which it results*. For it is only when it is taken as the result of that from which it emerges, that it is, in fact, the true result; in that case it is itself a *determinate* nothingness, one which has a *content*. The scepticism that ends up with the bare abstraction of nothingness or emptiness cannot get any further from there, but must wait to see whether something new comes along and what it is, in order to throw it too into the same empty abyss. But when, on the other hand, the result is conceived as it is in truth, namely, as a *determinate* negation, a new form has thereby immediately arisen, and in the negation the transition is made through which the progress through the complete series of forms comes about of itself.

80.   But the *goal* is as necessarily fixed for knowledge as the serial progression; it is the point where knowledge no longer needs to go beyond itself, where knowledge finds itself, where Notion corresponds to object and object to Notion. Hence the progress towards this goal is also unhalting, and short of it no satisfaction is to be found at any of the stations on the way. Whatever is confined within the limits of a natural life cannot by its own efforts go beyond its immediate existence; but it is driven beyond it by something else, and this uprooting entails its

death. Consciousness, however, is explicitly the *Notion* of itself. Hence it is something that goes beyond limits, and since these limits are its own, it is something that goes beyond itself. With the positing of a single particular the beyond is also established for consciousness, even if it is only *alongside* the limited object as in the case of spatial intuition. Thus consciousness suffers this violence at its own hands: it spoils its own limited satisfaction. When consciousness feels this violence, its anxiety may well make it retreat from the truth, and strive to hold on to what it is in danger of losing. But it can find no peace. If it wishes to remain in a state of unthinking inertia, then thought troubles its thoughtlessness, and its own unrest disturbs its inertia. Or, if it entrenches itself in sentimentality, which assures us that it finds everything to be *good in its kind*, then this assurance likewise suffers violence at the hands of Reason, for, precisely in so far as something is merely a kind, Reason finds it *not* to be good. Or, again, its fear of the truth may lead consciousness to hide, from itself and others, behind the pretension that its burning zeal for truth makes it difficult or even impossible to find any other truth but the unique truth of vanity – that of being at any rate cleverer than any thoughts that one gets by oneself or from others. This conceit which understands how to belittle every truth, in order to turn back into itself and gloat over its own understanding, which knows how to dissolve every thought and always find the same barren Ego instead of any content – this is a satisfaction which we must leave to itself, for it flees from the universal, and seeks only to be for itself.

81.   In addition to these preliminary general remarks about the manner and the necessity of the progression, it may be useful to say something about the *method of carrying out the inquiry*. If this exposition is viewed as a way of *relating Science* to *phenomenal* knowledge, and as an investigation and *examination of the reality of cognition*, it would seem that it cannot take place without some presupposition which can serve as its underlying *criterion*. For an examination consists in applying an accepted standard, and in determining whether something is right or wrong on the basis of the resulting agreement or disagreement of the thing examined; thus the standard as such (and Science likewise if it were the criterion) is accepted as the *essence* or as the *in-itself*. But

here, where Science has just begun to come on the scene, neither Science nor anything else has yet justified itself as the essence or the in-itself; and without something of the sort it seems that no examination can take place.

82.   This contradiction and its removal will become more definite if we call to mind the abstract determinations of truth and knowledge as they occur in consciousness. Consciousness simultaneously *distinguishes* itself from something, and at the same time *relates* itself to it, or, as it is said, this something exists *for* consciousness; and the determinate aspect of this *relating*, or of the *being* of something for a consciousness, is *knowing*. But we distinguish this being-for-another from *being-in-itself*; whatever is related to knowledge or knowing is also distinguished from it, and posited as existing outside of this relationship; this *being-in-itself* is called *truth*. Just what might be involved in these determinations is of no further concern to us here. Since our object is phenomenal knowledge, its determinations too will at first be taken directly as they present themselves; and they do present themselves very much as we have already apprehended them.

83.   Now, if we inquire into the truth of knowledge, it seems that we are asking what knowledge is *in itself*. Yet in this inquiry knowledge is *our* object, something that exists *for us*; and the *in-itself* that would supposedly result from it would rather be the being of knowledge *for us*. What we asserted to be its essence would be not so much its truth but rather just our knowledge of it. The essence or criterion would lie within ourselves, and that which was to be compared with it and about which a decision would be reached through this comparison would not necessarily have to recognize the validity of such a standard.

84.   But the dissociation, or this semblance of dissociation and presupposition, is overcome by the nature of the object we are investigating. Consciousness provides its own criterion from within itself, so that the investigation becomes a comparison of consciousness with itself; for the distinction made above falls within it. In consciousness one thing exists *for* another, i.e. consciousness regularly contains the determinateness of the moment of knowledge; at the same time, this other is to consciousness not merely *for it*, but is also outside of this relationship, or exists *in itself*: the moment of truth. Thus in

what consciousness affirms from within itself as *being-in-itself* or the *True* we have the standard which consciousness itself sets up by which to measure what it knows. If we designate *knowledge* as the Notion, but the essence or the *True* as what exists, or the *object*, then the examination consists in seeing whether the Notion corresponds to the object. But if we call the *essence* or in-itself of the *object* the *Notion*, and on the other hand understand by the *object* the Notion itself as *object*, viz. as it exists *for an other*, then the examination consists in seeing whether the object corresponds to its Notion. It is evident, of course, that the two procedures are the same. But the essential point to bear in mind throughout the whole investigation is that these two moments, 'Notion' and 'object', 'being-for-another' and 'being-in-itself', both fall *within* that knowledge which we are investigating. Consequently, we do not need to import criteria, or to make use of our own bright ideas and thoughts during the course of the inquiry; it is precisely when we leave these aside that we succeed in contemplating the matter in hand as it is *in and for itself*.

85.   But not only is a contribution by us superfluous, since Notion and object, the criterion and what is to be tested, are present in consciousness itself, but we are also spared the trouble of comparing the two and really *testing* them, so that, since what consciousness examines is its own self, all that is left for us to do is simply to look on. For consciousness is, on the one hand, consciousness of the object, and on the other, consciousness of itself; consciousness of what for it is the True, and consciousness of its knowledge of the truth. Since both are *for* the same consciousness, this consciousness is itself their comparison; it is for this same consciousness to know whether its knowledge of the object corresponds to the object or not. The object, it is true, seems only to be for consciousness in the way that consciousness knows it; it seems that consciousness cannot, as it were, get behind the object as it exists for consciousness so as to examine what the object is *in itself*, and hence, too, cannot test its own knowledge by that standard. But the distinction between the in-itself and knowledge is already present in the very fact that consciousness knows an object at all. Something is *for it* the in-*itself*; and knowledge, or the being of the object for consciousness, is, *for it*, another moment. Upon this distinction, which is present as a fact,

the examination rests. If the comparison shows that these two moments do not correspond to one another, it would seem that consciousness must alter its knowledge to make it conform to the object. But, in fact, in the alteration of the knowledge, the object itself alters for it too, for the knowledge that was present was essentially a knowledge of the object: as the knowledge changes, so too does the object, for it essentially belonged to this knowledge. Hence it comes to pass for consciousness that what it previously took to be the *in-itself* is not an *in-itself*, or that it was only an in-itself *for consciousness*. Since consciousness thus finds that its knowledge does not correspond to its object, the object itself does not stand the test; in other words, the criterion for testing is altered when that for which it was to have been the criterion fails to pass the test; and the testing is not only a testing of what we know, but also a testing of the criterion of what knowing is.

86.   *Inasmuch as the new true object issues from it*, this *dialectical* movement which consciousness exercises on itself and which affects both its knowledge and its object, is precisely what is called *experience* [*Erfahrung*]. In this connection there is a moment in the process just mentioned which must be brought out more clearly, for through it a new light will be thrown on the exposition which follows. Consciousness knows *something*; this object is the essence or the *in-itself*; but it is also for consciousness the in-itself. This is where the ambiguity of this truth enters. We see that consciousness now has two objects: one is the first *in-itself*, the second is the *being-for-consciousness of this in-itself*. The latter appears at first sight to be merely the reflection of consciousness into itself, i.e. what consciousness has in mind is not an object, but only its knowledge of that first object. But, as was shown previously, the first object, in being known, is altered for consciousness; it ceases to be the in-itself, and becomes something that is the *in-itself* only *for consciousness*. And this then is the True: the being-for-consciousness of this in-itself. Or, in other words, this is the *essence*, or the *object* of consciousness. This new object contains the nothingness of the first, it is what experience has made of it.

87.   This exposition of the course of experience contains a moment in virtue of which it does not seem to agree with what is ordinarily understood by experience. This is the moment of transition from the first object and the knowledge of it, to the other object, which experience is said to be about. Our account implied that our knowledge of the first object, or the being-*for-consciousness* of the first in-itself, itself becomes the second object. It usually seems to be the case, on the contrary, that our experience of the untruth of our first notion comes by way of a second object which we come upon by chance and externally, so that our part in all this is simply the pure *apprehension* of what is in and for itself. From the present viewpoint, however, the new object shows itself to have come about through a *reversal of consciousness itself*. This way of looking at the matter is something contributed by *us*, by means of which the succession of experiences through which consciousness passes is raised into a scientific progression – but it is not known to the consciousness that we are observing. But, as a matter of fact, we have here the same situation as the one discussed in regard to the relation between our exposition and scepticism, viz. that in every case the result of an untrue mode of knowledge must not be allowed to run away into an empty nothing, but must necessarily be grasped as the nothing *of that from which it results* – a result which contains what was true in the preceding knowledge. It shows up here like this: since what first appeared as the object sinks for consciousness to the level of its way of knowing it, and since the in-itself becomes a *being-for-consciousness* of the in-itself, the latter is now the new object. Herewith a new pattern of consciousness comes on the scene as well, for which the essence is something different from what it was at the preceding stage. It is this fact that guides the entire series of the patterns of consciousness in their necessary sequence. But it is just this necessity itself, or the *origination* of the new object, that presents itself to consciousness without its understanding how this happens, which proceeds for us, as it were, behind the back of consciousness. Thus in the movement of consciousness there occurs a moment of *being-in-itself* or *being-for-us* which is not present to the consciousness comprehended in the experience itself. The *content*, however, of what presents itself to us does exist *for it*; we comprehend only the formal aspect of that content, or its pure origination. *For it*, what has thus arisen exists only as an object; *for us*, it appears at the same time as movement and a process of becoming.

88. Because of this necessity, the way to Science is itself already *Science*, and hence, in virtue of its content, is the Science of the *experience of consciousness*.

89. The experience of itself which consciousness goes through can, in accordance with its Notion, comprehend nothing less than the entire system of consciousness, or the entire realm of the truth of Spirit. For this reason, the moments of this truth are exhibited in their own proper determinateness, viz. as being not abstract moments, but as they are for consciousness, or as consciousness itself stands forth in its relation to them. Thus the moments of the whole are *patterns of consciousness*. In pressing forward to its true existence, consciousness will arrive at a point at which it gets rid of its semblance of being burdened with something alien, with what is only for it, and some sort of 'other', at a point where appearance becomes identical with essence, so that its exposition will coincide at just this point with the authentic Science of Spirit. And finally, when consciousness itself grasps this its own essence, it will signify the nature of absolute knowledge itself.

A. CONSCIOUSNESS

I Sense-certainty: or the 'This' and 'Meaning' [Meinen]

90. The knowledge or knowing which is at the start or is immediately our object cannot be anything else but immediate knowledge itself, a knowledge of the immediate or of what simply is. Our approach to the object must also be immediate or receptive; we must alter nothing in the object as it presents itself. In apprehending it, we must refrain from trying to comprehend it.

91. Because of its concrete content, sense-certainty immediately appears as the *richest* kind of knowledge, indeed a knowledge of infinite wealth for which no bounds can be found, either when we *reach out* into space and time in which it is dispersed, or when we take a bit of this wealth, and by division *enter into* it. Moreover, sense-certainty appears to be the *truest* knowledge; for it has not as yet omitted anything from the object, but has the object before it in its perfect entirety. But, in the event, this very *certainty* proves itself to be the most abstract and poorest *truth*. All that it says about what it knows is just

that it *is*; and its truth contains nothing but the sheer *being* of the thing [*Sache*]. Consciousness, for its part, is in this certainty only as a pure 'I'; or I am in it only as a pure 'This', and the object similarly only as a pure 'This'. I, *this* particular I, am certain of *this* particular thing, not because I, *qua* consciousness, in knowing it have developed myself or thought about it in various ways; and also not because *the thing* of which I am certain, in virtue of a host of distinct qualities, would be in its own self a rich complex of connections, or related in various ways to other things. Neither of these has anything to do with the truth of sense-certainty: here neither I nor the thing has the significance of a complex process of mediation; the 'I' does not have the significance of a manifold imagining or thinking; nor does the 'thing' signify something that has a host of qualities. On the contrary, the thing *is*, and it *is*, merely because it *is*. It *is*; this is the essential point for sense-knowledge, and this pure *being*, or this simple immediacy, constitutes its *truth*. Similarly, certainty as a *connection* is an *immediate* pure connection: consciousness is 'I', nothing more, a pure 'This'; the singular consciousness knows a pure 'This', or the single item.

92. But when we look carefully at this *pure being* which constitutes the essence of this certainty, and which this certainty pronounces to be its truth, we see that much more is involved. An actual sense-certainty is not merely this pure immediacy, but an *instance* of it. Among the countless differences cropping up here we find in every case that the crucial one is that, in sense-certainty, pure being at once splits up into what we have called the two 'Thises', one 'This' as 'I', and the other 'This' as object. When *we* reflect on this difference, we find that neither one nor the other is only *immediately* present in sense-certainty, but each is at the same time *mediated*: I have this certainty *through* something else, viz. the thing; and it, similarly, is in sense-certainty *through* something else, viz. through the 'I'.

93. It is not just we who make this distinction between essence and instance, between immediacy and mediation; on the contrary, we find it within sense-certainty itself, and it is to be taken up in the form in which it is present there, not as we have just defined it. One of the terms is posited in sense-certainty in the form of a simple, immediate being, or as the essence, the *object*; the other, however, is posited as what is

unessential and mediated, something which in sense-certainty is not *in itself* but through [the mediation of] an other, the 'I', a *knowing* which knows the object only because the *object* is, while the knowing may either be or not be. But the object *is*: it is what is true, or it is the essence. It is, regardless of whether it is known or not; and it remains, even it is not known, whereas there is no knowledge if the object is not there.

94. The question must therefore be considered whether in sense-certainty itself the object is in fact the kind of essence that sense-certainty proclaims it to be; whether this notion of it as the essence corresponds to the way it is present in sense-certainty. To this end, we have not to reflect on it and ponder what it might be in truth, but only to consider the way in which it is present in sense-certainty.

95. It is, then, sense-certainty itself that must be asked: 'What is the *This*?' If we take the 'This' in the twofold shape of its being, as 'Now' and as 'Here', the dialectic it has in it will receive a form as intelligible as the 'This' itself is. To the question: 'What is Now?', let us answer, e.g. 'Now is Night.' In order to test the truth of this sense-certainty a simple experiment will suffice. We write down this truth; a truth cannot lose anything by being written down, any more than it can lose anything through our preserving it. If *now*, *this noon*, we look again at the written truth we shall have to say that it has become stale.

96. The Now that is Night is *preserved*, i.e. it is treated as what it professes to be, as something that *is*; but it proves itself to be, on the contrary, something that is *not*. The Now does indeed preserve itself, but as something that is *not* Night; equally, it preserves itself in face of the Day that it now is, as something that also is not Day, in other words, as a *negative* in general. This self-preserving Now is, therefore, not immediate but mediated; for it is determined as a permanent and self-preserving Now *through* the fact that something else, viz. Day and Night, is *not*. As so determined, it is still just as simply Now as before, and in this simplicity is indifferent to what happens in it; just as little as Night and Day are its being, just as much also is it Day and Night; it is not in the least affected by this its other-being. A simple thing of this kind which *is* through negation, which is neither This nor That, a *not-This*, and is with equal indifference This as well as That – such a thing we call a *universal*. So it is

in fact the universal that is the true [content] of sense-certainty.

97. It is as a universal too that we *utter* what the sensuous [content] is. What we say is: 'This', i.e. the *universal* This; or, 'it is', i.e. *Being in general*. Of course, we do not *envisage* the universal This or Being in general, but we *utter* the universal; in other words, we do not strictly say what in this sense-certainty we *mean* to say. But language, as we see, is the more truthful; in it, we ourselves directly refute what we *mean* to say, and since the universal is the true [content] of sense-certainty and language expresses this true [content] alone, it is just not possible for us ever to say, or express in words, a sensuous being that we *mean*.

98. The same will be the case with the other form of the 'This', with 'Here'. 'Here' is, e.g., the tree. If I turn round, this truth has vanished and is converted into its opposite: 'No tree is here, but a house instead'. 'Here' itself does not vanish; on the contrary, it abides constant in the vanishing of the house, the tree, etc., and is indifferently house or tree. Again, therefore, the 'This' shows itself to be a *mediated simplicity*, or a *universality*.

99. *Pure being* remains, therefore, as the essence of this sense-certainty, since sense-certainty has demonstrated in its own self that the truth of its object is the universal. But this pure being is not an immediacy, but something to which negation and mediation are essential; consequently, it is not what we *mean* by 'being', but is 'being' defined as an abstraction, or as the pure universal; and our 'meaning', for which the true [content] of sense-certainty is *not* the universal, is all that is left over in face of this empty or indifferent Now and Here.

100. When we compare the relation in which knowing and the object first came on the scene, with the relation in which they now stand in this result, we find that it is reversed. The object, which was supposed to be the essential element in sense-certainty, is now the unessential element; for the universal which the object has come to be is no longer what the object was supposed essentially to be for sense-certainty. On the contrary, the certainty is now to be found in the opposite element, viz. in knowing, which previously was the unessential element. Its truth is in the object as *my* object, or in its being *mine* [*Meinen*]; it is, because *I* know it. Sense-certainty, then, though indeed expelled from the object, is not yet thereby overcome, but only driven back

into the 'I'. We have now to see what experience shows us about its reality in the 'I'.

101.   The force of its truth thus lies now in the 'I', in the immediacy of my *seeing, hearing,* and so on; the vanishing of the single Now and Here that we mean is prevented by the fact that *I* hold them fast. 'Now' is day because I see it; 'Here' is a tree for the same reason. But in this relationship sense-certainty experiences the same dialectic acting upon itself as in the previous one. I, *this* 'I', see the tree and assert that 'Here' is a tree; but another 'I' sees the house and maintains that 'Here' is not a tree but a house instead. Both truths have the same authentication, viz. the immediacy of seeing, and the certainty and assurance that both have about their knowing; but the one truth vanishes in the other.

102.   What does not disappear in all this is the 'I' as *universal,* whose seeing is neither a seeing of the tree nor of this house, but is a simple seeing which, though mediated by the negation of this house, etc., is all the same simple and indifferent to whatever happens in it, to the house, the tree, etc. The 'I' is merely universal like 'Now', 'Here', or 'This' in general; I do indeed *mean* a single 'I', but I can no more say what I *mean* in the case of 'I' than I can in the case of 'Now' and 'Here'. When I say 'this Here', 'this Now', or a 'single item', I am saying all Thises, Heres, Nows, all single items. Similarly, when I say 'I', this singular 'I', I say in general all 'Is'; everyone is what I say, everyone is 'I', this singular 'I'. When Science is faced with the demand – as if it were an acid test it could not pass – that it should deduce, construct, find *a priori,* or however it is put, something called 'this thing' or 'this one man', it is reasonable that the demand should *say* which 'this thing', or which 'this particular man' is *meant*; but it is impossible to say this.

103.   Sense-certainty thus comes to know by experience that its essence is neither in the object nor in the 'I', and that its immediacy is neither an immediacy of the one nor of the other; for in both, what I *mean* is rather something unessential, and the object and the 'I' are universals in which that 'Now' and 'Here' and 'I' which I *mean* do not have a continuing being, or *are* not. Thus we reach the stage where we have to posit the *whole* of sense-certainty itself as its *essence,* and no longer only one of its moments, as happened in the two cases where first the object confronting the 'I', and then the 'I', were supposed to be its reality. Thus it is only sense-certainty as a *whole* which stands firm within itself as *immediacy* and by so doing excludes from itself all the opposition which has hitherto obtained.

14

John Stuart Mill, *A System of Logic*, Book II, Chapters V–VII (selections)

Introduction

John Stuart Mill (1806–73), the most famous British philosopher of the nineteenth century, is primarily read today as a utilitarian moral philosopher and as a leading champion of political liberalism and the emancipation of women. (Extracts from his *Utilitarianism* and *On Liberty* are included as texts I.16 and V.18 in the present volume.) He was also the author, however, of two massive works – *A System of Logic* (1843) and *An Examination of Sir William Hamilton's Philosophy* (1865) – in which he elaborated and defended the radically empiricist position that informs all his thinking, including his moral and political philosophy.

All that is truly given to us, Mill holds, are the mind's "outward feelings or sensations, and its inward feelings" (*Logic* IV.I.2), so that any knowledge we possess must be built up, through inductive inference, from these sensations and feelings. One predictable objection to this claim is that our knowledge includes knowledge of necessary or *a priori* truths, ones of a kind that sensory experience is surely incapable of guaranteeing. In the selections from *A System of Logic* that follow, we see how Mill attempts to respond

From John Stuart Mill, *A System of Logic: Ratiocinative and Inductive*, London: Longmans, Green & Co., 1886, pp. 147–9, 151–3, 164–70, 183–4 (notes omitted).

to this objection by discussing the status of various propositions or principles – those of geometry, mathematics, and logic respectively – which have traditionally deemed to be necessarily and *a priori* true.

Mill's empiricist predecessors, such as David Hume (II.10), had conceded that not all truths are established by experience, but had treated these truths as merely "verbal" or "trivial." In the terminology of Kant (II.12), these necessary truths are "analytic," true in virtue of the meanings of the component terms. Mill does not deny that there are such "purely verbal" truths, like "All bachelors are unmarried," which "give no information" about reality at all (*Logic* I.VI.4). What he does deny, however, is that geometrical, mathematical and logical truths are of this "purely verbal" type. To this extent, he is agreeing with Kant – for whom 7 + 5 = 12, for example, is not an analytic truth. Where he disagrees with Kant, and indeed with nearly all other philosophers, is in his bold denial that such truths are necessary and *a priori* at all. The necessity normally assigned to these propositions is, he maintains, an "illusion." Granted, we might speak of the theorems of geometry as "necessary" in the sense that they follow from certain "hypotheses" or axioms; but since these latter are only "experimental truths," ones constantly confirmed by experience, the necessity attaching to theorems is not of a distinctive, *a priori* kind. If there is anything distinctive about them at all, this is simply the sheer scale of their daily confirmation.

The same applies to an arithmetical proposition like $3 = 2 + 1$. While this formulation could be treated as a definition or an analysis of "3," doing so is possible only because the equation itself registers the "physical fact" that whenever objects are experienced as a trio they can be separated so as to be experienced as a pair and a single object. The two principles of logic that Mill discusses – those of Contradiction and Excluded Middle – are also, in his view, empirical, but not through describing the world or our experience of it. Rather, the principles record the introspectively given relations between states of belief. Thus, following Herbert Spencer (1820–1903), Mill treats the second principle as recording the psychological "law" that "positive" and "negative" modes of entertaining a proposition exclude one another.

While Mill presents his account of the various kinds of so-called necessary or *a priori* truths as a requirement of an authentic empiricism, there occasionally shows through his discussion an attitude more often associated with pragmatism. For example, his point with respect to some theorems of geometry is less that these are evidentially guaranteed *descriptions* of experience than that we, abstracting from features of experience not relevant to certain enquiries, employ them as indispensable *tools* in conducting these enquiries. It is not that the propositions are, in themselves, immune to refutation by possible experience as that we, for our purposes, insulate them against refutation. It is along such lines, perhaps, that Mill might have revised and defended his approach in the face of the strident criticisms of his "psychologism" famously leveled by the logician Gottlob Frege (1848–1925).[1] If so, this approach might have come close to the one advanced by W. V. O. Quine (1908–2000) in his seminal 1951 paper, "Two Dogmas of Empiricism" (see II.25 below).

Note

1　Cf. G. Frege, *The Foundations of Arithmetic*, trans. J. L. Austin, Oxford: Blackwell, 1974.

Mill, *A System of Logic*

Book II

Chapter V: Of Demonstration and Necessary Truths § 1. If, as laid down in the two preceding chapters, the foundation of all sciences, even deductive or demonstrative sciences, is Induction; if every step in the ratiocinations even of geometry is an act of induction; and if a train of reasoning is but bringing many inductions to bear upon the same subject of inquiry, and drawing a case within one induction by means of another; wherein lies the peculiar certainty always ascribed to the sciences which are entirely, or almost entirely, deductive? Why are they called the Exact Sciences? Why are mathematical certainty, and the evidence of demonstration, common phrases to express the very highest degree of assurance attainable by reason? Why are mathematics by almost all philosophers, and (by some) even those branches of natural philosophy which, through the medium of mathematics, have been converted into deductive sciences, considered to be independent of the evidence of experience and observation, and characterised as systems of Necessary Truth?

The answer I conceive to be, that this character of necessity ascribed to the truths of mathematics, and even (with some reservations to be hereafter made) the peculiar certainty attributed to them, is an illusion; in order to sustain which, it is necessary to suppose that those truths relate to, and express the properties of purely imaginary objects. It is acknowledged that the conclusions of geometry are deduced, partly at least, from the so-called Definitions, and that those definitions are assumed to be correct representations, as far as they go, of the objects with which geometry is conversant. Now we have pointed out that, from a definition as such, no proposition, unless it be one concerning the meaning of a word, can ever follow; and that what apparently follows from a definition, follows in reality from an implied assumption that there exists a real thing conformable thereto. This assumption in the case of the definitions of geometry, is not strictly true: there exist no real things exactly conformable to the definitions. There exist no points without magnitude; no lines without breadth, nor perfectly straight; no circles with all their radii exactly equal, nor squares with all their angles perfectly right. It will perhaps be said that the assumption does not extend to the actual, but only to the possible existence of such things. I answer that, according to any test we have of possibility, they are not even possible. Their existence, so far as we can form any judgment, would seem to be inconsistent with the physical constitution of our planet at least, if not of the universe. To get rid of this difficulty, and at the same time to save the credit of the supposed system of necessary truth, it is customary to say that the points, lines, circles, and squares which are the subject of geometry, exist in our conceptions merely, and are part of our minds; which minds, by working on their own materials, construct an *à priori* science, the evidence of which is purely mental, and has nothing whatever to do with outward experience. By howsoever high authorities this doctrine may have been sanctioned, it appears to me psychologically incorrect. The points, lines, circles, and squares which any one has in his mind, are (I apprehend) simply copies of the points, lines, circles, and squares which he has known in his experience. Our idea of a point I apprehend to be simply our idea of the *minimum visibile*, the smallest portion of surface which we can see. A line as defined by geometers is wholly inconceivable. We can reason about a line as if it had no breadth; because we have a power, which is the foundation of all the control we can exercise over the operations of our minds; the power, when a perception is present to our senses or a conception to our intellects, of *attending* to a part only of that perception or conception, instead of the whole. But we cannot *conceive* a line without breadth; we can form no mental picture of such a line; all the lines which we have in our minds are lines possessing breadth. If any one doubts this, we may refer him to his own experience. I much question if any one who fancies that he can conceive what is called a mathematical line, thinks so from the evidence of his consciousness: I suspect it is rather because he supposes that unless such a conception were possible, mathematics could not exist as a science: a supposition which there will be no difficulty in showing to be entirely groundless.

Since, then, neither in nature, nor in the human mind, do there exist any objects exactly corresponding to the definitions of geometry, while yet that science cannot be supposed to be conversant about non-entities; nothing remains but to consider geometry as conversant with such lines, angles, and figures as really exist; and the definitions, as they are called, must be regarded as some of our first and most obvious generalisations concerning those natural objects. The correctness of those generalisations, *as* generalisations, is without a flaw: the equality of all the radii of a circle is true of all circles, so far as it is true of any one: but it is not exactly true of any circle; it is only nearly true; so nearly that no error of any importance in practice will be incurred by feigning it to be exactly true. When we have occasion to extend these inductions, or their consequences, to cases in which the error would be appreciable – to lines of perceptible breadth or thickness, parallels which deviate sensibly from equidistance, and the like – we correct our conclusions by combining with them a fresh set of propositions relating to the aberration; just as we also take in propositions relating to the physical or chemical properties of the material, if those properties happen to introduce any modification into the result; which they easily may, even with respect to figure and magnitude, as in the case, for instance, of expansion by heat. So long, however, as there exists no practical necessity for attending to any of the properties of the object except its geometrical properties, or to any of the natural irregularities in those, it is convenient to neglect the consideration of the other properties and of the irregularities, and to reason as if these did not exist: accordingly, we formally announce in the definitions, that we intend to proceed on this plan. But it is an error to suppose, because we resolve to confine our attention to a certain number of the properties of an object, that we therefore conceive, or have an idea of, the object denuded of its other properties. We are thinking, all the time, of precisely such objects as we have seen and touched, and with all the properties which naturally belong to them; but, for scientific convenience, we feign them to be divested of all properties, except those which are material to our purpose, and in regard to which we design to consider them.

The peculiar accuracy, supposed to be characteristic of the first principles of geometry thus appears to be fictitious. The assertions on which the reasonings of the science are founded do not, anymore than in other sciences, exactly correspond with the fact, but we suppose that they do so for the sake of tracing the consequences which follow from the supposition. The opinion of Dugald Steward respecting the foundations of geometry, is, I conceive, substantially correct;[1] that it is built on hypotheses; that it owes to this alone the peculiar certainty supposed to distinguish it; and that in any science whatever, by reasoning from a set of hypotheses, we may obtain a body of conclusions as certain as those of geometry, that is, as strictly in accordance with the hypotheses, and as irresistibly compelling assent, *on condition* that those hypotheses are true.

When, therefore, it is affirmed that the conclusions of geometry are necessary truths, the necessity consists in reality only in this, that they correctly follow from the suppositions from which they are deduced. Those suppositions are so far from being necessary, that they are not even true; they purposely depart, more or less widely, from the truth. The only sense in which necessity can be ascribed to the conclusions of any scientific investigation, is that of legitimately following from some assumption, which, by the conditions of the inquiry, is not to be questioned. In this relation, of course, the derivative truths of every deductive science must stand to the inductions, or assumptions, on which the science is founded, and which, whether true or untrue, certain or doubtful in themselves, are always supposed certain for the purposes of the particular science. And therefore the conclusions of all deductive sciences were said by the ancients to be necessary propositions. We have observed already that to be predicated necessarily was characteristic of the predicable Proprium, and that a proprium was any property of a thing which could be deduced from its essence, that is, from the properties included in its definition.

[...]

§ 4. It remains to inquire, what is the ground of our belief in axioms – what is the evidence on which they rest? I answer, they are experimental truths; generalisations from observation. The proposition, Two straight lines cannot enclose a space – or, in other words, two straight lines which have once met do not meet again, but continue to diverge – is an induction from the evidence of our senses.

This opinion runs counter to a scientific prejudice of long standing and great strength, and there is probably no proposition enunciated in this work for which a more unfavourable reception is to be expected. It is, however, no new opinion; and even if it were so, would be entitled to be judged, not by its novelty, but by the strength of the arguments by which it can be supported. I consider it very fortunate that so eminent a champion of the contrary opinion as Dr Whewell has found occasion for a most elaborate treatment of the whole theory of axioms, in attempting to construct the philosophy of the mathematical and physical sciences on the basis of the doctrine against which I now contend.[2] Whoever is anxious that a discussion should go to the bottom of the subject must rejoice to see the opposite side of the question worthily represented. If what is said by Dr Whewell, in support of an opinion which he has made the foundation of a systematic work, can be shown not to be conclusive, enough will have been done, without going elsewhere in quest of stronger arguments and a more powerful adversary.

It is not necessary to show that the truths which we call axioms are originally *suggested* by observation, and that we should never have known that two straight lines cannot enclose a space if we had never seen a straight line: thus much being admitted by Dr Whewell and by all, in recent times, who have taken his view of the subject. But they contend that it is not experience which *proves* the axiom; but that its truth is perceived *a priori*, by the constitution of the mind itself, from the first moment when the meaning of the proposition is apprehended, and without any necessity for verifying it by repeated trials, as is requisite in the case of truths really ascertained by observation.

They cannot, however, but allow that the truth of the axiom, Two straight lines cannot enclose a space, even if evident independently of experience, is also evident from experience. Whether the axiom needs confirmation or not, it receives confirmation in almost every instant of our lives, since we cannot look at any two straight lines which intersect one another without seeing that from that point they continue to diverge more and more. Experimental proof crowds in upon us in such endless profusion, and without one instance in which there can be even a suspicion of an exception to the rule, that we should soon have stronger ground for believing the axiom, even as an experimental truth, than we have for almost any of the general truths which we confessedly learn from the evidence of our senses. Independently of *a priori* evidence we should certainly believe it with an intensity of conviction far greater than we accord to any ordinary physical truth: and this too at a time of life much earlier than that from which we date almost any part of our acquired knowledge, and much too early to admit of our retaining any recollection of the history of our intellectual operations at that period. Where then is the necessity for assuming that our recognition of these truths has a different origin from the rest of our knowledge, when its existence is perfectly accounted for by supposing its origin to be the same? when the causes which produce belief in all other instances exist in this instance, and in a degree of strength as much superior to what exists in other cases as the intensity of the belief itself is superior? The burden of proof lies on the advocates of the contrary opinion: it is for them to point out some fact inconsistent with the supposition that this part of our knowledge of nature is derived from the same sources as every other part.

This, for instance, they would be able to do, if they could prove chronologically that we had the conviction (at least practically) so early in infancy as to be anterior to those impressions on the senses, upon which, on the other theory, the conviction is founded. This however, cannot be proved: the point being too far back to be within the reach of memory, and too obscure for external observation.

[. . .]

Chapter VI: The Same Subject Continued § 1. In the examination which formed the subject of the last chapter into the nature of the evidence of those deductive sciences which are commonly represented to be systems of necessary truth, we have been led to the following conclusions. The results of those sciences are indeed necessary, in the sense of necessarily following from certain first principles, commonly called axioms and definitions; that is, of being certainly true if those axioms and definitions are so; for the word necessity, even in this acceptation of it, means no more than certainty. But their claim to the character of necessity in any sense beyond this, as implying an evidence independent of and superior to observation and experience, must depend

on the previous establishment of such a claim in favour of the definitions and axioms themselves. With regard to axioms, we found that, considered as experimental truths, they rest on superabundant and obvious evidence. We inquired whether, since this is the case, it be imperative to suppose any other evidence of those truths than experimental evidence, any other origin for our belief of them than an experimental origin. We decided that the burden of proof lies with those who maintain the affirmative, and we examined, at considerable length, such arguments as they have produced. The examination having led to the rejection of those arguments, we have thought ourselves warranted in concluding that axioms are but a class, the most universal class, of inductions from experience; the simplest and easiest cases of generalisation from the facts furnished to us by our senses or by our internal consciousness.

While the axioms of demonstrative sciences thus appeared to be experimental truths, the definitions, as they are incorrectly called, in those sciences, were found by us to be generalisations from experience which are not even, accurately speaking, truths; being propositions in which, while we assert of some kind of object some property or properties which observation shows to belong to it, we at the same time deny that it possesses any other properties, though in truth other properties do in every individual instance accompany, and in almost all instances modify, the property thus exclusively predicated. The denial, therefore, is a mere fiction or supposition, made for the purpose of excluding the consideration of those modifying circumstances, when their influence is of too trifling amount to be worth considering, or adjourning it, when important, to a more convenient moment.

From these considerations it would appear that Deductive or Demonstrative Sciences are all, without exception, Inductive Sciences; that their evidence is that of experience; but that they are also, in virtue of the peculiar character of one indispensable portion of the general formulæ according to which their inductions are made, Hypothetical Sciences. Their conclusions are only true on certain suppositions, which are, or ought to be, approximations to the truth, but are seldom, if ever, exactly true; and to this hypothetical character is to be ascribed the peculiar certainty which is supposed to be inherent in demonstration.

What we have now asserted, however, cannot be received as universally true of Deductive or Demonstrative Sciences, until verified by being applied to the most remarkable of all those sciences, that of Numbers; the theory of the Calculus; Arithmetic and Algebra. It is harder to believe of the doctrines of this science than of any other, either that they are not truths *a priori*, but experimental truths, or that their peculiar certainty is owing to their being not absolute, but only conditional truths. This, therefore, is a case which merits examination apart; and the more so, because on this subject we have a double set of doctrines to contend with; that of the *a priori* philosophers on one side; and on the other, a theory the most opposite to theirs, which was at one time very generally received, and is still far from being altogether exploded among metaphysicians.

§ 2.   This theory attempts to solve the difficulty apparently inherent in the case, by representing the propositions of the science of numbers as merely verbal, and its processes as simple transformations of language, substitutions of one expression for another. The proposition, Two and one is equal to three, according to these writers, is not a truth, is not the assertion of a really existing fact, but a definition of the word three; a statement that mankind have agreed to use the name three as a sign exactly equivalent to two and one; to call by the former name whatever is called by the other more clumsy phrase. According to this doctrine the longest process in algebra is but a succession of changes in terminology, by which equivalent expressions are substituted one for another; a series of translations of the same fact, from one into another language; though how, after such a series of translations, the fact itself comes out changed, (as when we demonstrate a new geometrical theorem by algebra,) they have not explained; and it is a difficulty which is fatal to their theory.

It must be acknowledged that there are peculiarities in the processes of arithmetic and algebra which render the theory in question very plausible, and have not unnaturally made those sciences the stronghold of Nominalism. The doctrine that we can discover facts, detect the hidden processes of nature, by an artful manipulation of language, is so contrary to common sense, that a person must have made some advances in philosophy to believe it; men fly to so paradoxical a belief to avoid, as they think, some even greater difficulty, which the vulgar do not see. What has led many to believe that reasoning is a mere verbal process is, that no other theory seemed reconcilable with the nature of the Science of Numbers. For we do not carry any ideas along with us when we use the symbols of arithmetic or of algebra. In a geometrical demonstration we have a mental diagram, if not one on paper; AB, AC, are present to our imagination as lines, intersecting other lines, forming an angle with one another, and the like; but not so *a* and *b*. These may represent lines or any other magnitudes, but those magnitudes are never thought of; nothing is realised in our imagination but *a* and *b*. The ideas which, on the particular occasion, they happen to represent, are banished from the mind during every intermediate part of the process, between the beginning, when the premises are translated from things into signs, and the end, when the conclusion is translated back from signs into things. Nothing, then, being in the reasoner's mind but the symbols, what can seem more inadmissible than to contend that the reasoning process has to do with anything more? We seem to have come to one of Bacon's Prerogative Instances; an *experimentum crucis* on the nature of reasoning itself.

Nevertheless, it will appear on consideration, that this apparently so decisive instance is no instance at all; that there is in every step of an arithmetical or algebraical calculation a real induction, a real inference of facts from facts; and that what disguises the induction is simply its comprehensive nature and the consequent extreme generality of the language. All numbers must be numbers of something; there are no such things as numbers in the abstract. *Ten* must mean ten bodies, or ten sounds, or ten beatings of the pulse. But though numbers must be numbers of something, they may be numbers of anything. Propositions, therefore, concerning numbers have the remarkable peculiarity that they are propositions concerning all things whatever; all objects, all existences of every kind, known to our experience. All things possess quantity; consist of parts which can be numbered; and in that character possess all the properties which are called properties of numbers. That half of four is two, must be true whatever the word four represents, whether four hours, four miles, or four pounds weight. We need only conceive a thing divided into four equal parts (and all things may be conceived as so divided) to be able to predicate of it every property of the number four, that is, every arithmetical proposition in which the number four stands on one side of the equation. Algebra extends the generalisation still farther: every number represents that particular number of all things without distinction, but every algebraical symbol does more, it represents all numbers without distinction. As soon as we conceive a thing divided into equal parts, without knowing into what number of parts, we may call it *a* or *x*, and apply to it, without danger of error, every algebraical formula in the books. The proposition, $2(a + b) = 2a + 2b$, is a truth co-extensive with all nature. Since then algebraical truths are true of all things whatever, and not, like those of geometry, true of lines only or of angles only, it is no wonder that the symbols should not excite in our minds ideas of any things in particular. When we demonstrate the forty-seventh proposition of Euclid, it is not necessary that the words should raise in us an image of all right-angled triangles, but only of some one right-angled triangle; so in algebra we need not, under the symbol *a*, picture to ourselves all things whatever, but only some one thing; why not, then, the letter itself? The mere written characters, *a, b, x, y, z*, serve as well for representatives of Things in general, as any more complex and apparently more concrete conception. That we are conscious of them, however, in their character of things, and not of mere signs, is evident from the fact that our whole process of reasoning is carried on by predicating of them the properties of things. In resolving an algebraic equation, by what rules do we proceed? By applying at each step to *a, b*, and *x*, the proposition that equals added to equals make equals; that equals taken from equals leave equals; and other propositions founded on these two. These are not properties of language, or of signs as such, but of magnitudes, which is as much as to say, of all things. The inferences, therefore, which are successively drawn, are inferences concerning things, not symbols; though as any Things whatever will serve the turn, there is no necessity for keeping the idea of the Thing at all distinct, and consequently the process of thought may, in this case, be allowed without danger to do what all processes of thought, when they have been performed often, will do if permitted, namely, to become entirely

mechanical. Hence the general language of algebra comes to be used familiarly without exciting ideas, as all other general language is prone to do from mere habit, though in no other case than this can it be done with complete safety. But when we look back to see from whence the probative force of the process is derived, we find that at every single step, unless we suppose ourselves to be thinking and talking of the things, and not the mere symbols, the evidence fails.

There is another circumstance, which, still more than that which we have now mentioned, gives plausibility to the notion that the propositions of arithmetic and algebra are merely verbal. That is, that when considered as propositions respecting Things, they all have the appearance of being identical propositions. The assertion, Two and one is equal to three, considered as an assertion respecting objects, as for instance "Two pebbles and one pebble are equal to three pebbles," does not affirm equality between two collections of pebbles, but absolute identity. It affirms that if we put one pebble to two pebbles, those very pebbles are three. The objects, therefore, being the very same, and the mere assertion that "objects are themselves" being insignificant, it seems but natural to consider the proposition Two and one is equal to three, as asserting mere identity of signification between the two names.

This, however, though it looks so plausible, will not bear examination. The expression "two pebbles and one pebble," and the expression "three pebbles," stand indeed for the same aggregation of objects, but they by no means stand for the same physical fact. They are names of the same objects, but of those objects in two different states: though they *de*note the same things, their *con*notation is different. Three pebbles in two separate parcels, and three pebbles in one parcel, do not make the same impression on our senses; and the assertion that the very same pebbles may by an alteration of place and arrangement be made to produce either the one set of sensations or the other, though a very familiar proposition, is not an identical one. It is a truth known to us by early and constant experience – an inductive truth; and such truths are the foundation of the science of Numbers. The fundamental truths of that science all rest on the evidence of sense; they are proved by showing to our eyes and our fingers that any given number of objects, ten balls, for example, may by separation and rearrangement exhibit to our senses all the different sets of numbers the sum of which is equal to ten. All the improved methods of teaching arithmetic to children proceed on a knowledge of this fact. All who wish to carry the child's *mind* along with them in learning arithmetic; all who wish to teach numbers, and not mere ciphers – now teach it through the evidence of the senses, in the manner we have described.

We may, if we please, call the proposition, "Three is two and one," a definition of the number three, and assert that arithmetic, as it has been asserted that geometry, is a science founded on definitions. But they are definitions in the geometrical sense, not the logical; asserting not the meaning of a term only, but along with it an observed matter of fact. The proposition, "A circle is a figure bounded by a line which has all its points equally distant from a point within it," is called the definition of a circle; but the proposition from which so many consequences follow, and which is really a first principle in geometry, is, that figures answering to this description exist. And thus we may call "Three is two and one" a definition of three; but the calculations which depend on that proposition do not follow from the definition itself, but from an arithmetical theorem presupposed in it, namely, that collections of objects exist, which while they impress the senses thus, $^0 {}_0 {}^0$, may be separated into two parts, thus, ∘∘ ∘. This proposition being granted, we term all such parcels Threes, after which the enunciation of the above-mentioned physical fact will serve also for a definition of the word Three.

The Science of Numbers is thus no exception to the conclusion we previously arrived at, that the processes even of deductive sciences are altogether inductive, and that their first principles are generalisations from experience. It remains to be examined whether this science resembles geometry in the further circumstance that some of its inductions are not exactly true; and that the peculiar certainty ascribed to it, on account of which its propositions are called necessary truths, is fictitious and hypothetical, being true in no other sense than that those propositions legitimately follow from the hypothesis of the truth of premises which are avowedly mere approximations to truth.

§ 3.   The inductions of arithmetic are of two sorts: first, those which we have just expounded,

such as One and one are two, Two and one are three, &c., which may be called the definitions of the various numbers, in the improper or geometrical sense of the word Definition; and secondly, the two following axioms: The sums of equals are equal, The differences of equals are equal. These two are sufficient; for the corresponding propositions respecting unequals may be proved from these by a *reductio ad absurdum.*

These axioms, and likewise the so-called definitions, are, as has already been said, results of induction; true of all objects whatever, and, as it may seem, exactly true, without the hypothetical assumption of unqualified truth where an approximation to it is all that exists. The conclusions, therefore, it will naturally be inferred, are exactly true, and the science of numbers is an exception to other demonstrative sciences in this, that the categorical certainty which is predicable of its demonstrations is independent of all hypothesis.

On more accurate investigation, however, it will be found that, even in this case, there is one hypothetical element in the ratiocination. In all propositions concerning numbers, a condition is implied, without which none of them would be true; and that condition is an assumption which may be false. The condition is, that 1 = 1; that all the numbers are numbers of the same or of equal units. Let this be doubtful, and not one of the propositions of arithmetic will hold true. How can we know that one pound and one pound make two pounds, if one of the pounds may be troy, and the other avoirdupois? They may not make two pounds of either, or of any weight. How can we know that a forty-horse power is always equal to itself, unless we assume that all horses are of equal strength? It is certain that 1 is always equal in *number* to 1; and where the mere number of objects, or of the parts of an object, without supposing them to be equivalent in any other respect, is all that is material, the conclusions of arithmetic, so far as they go to that alone, are true without mixture of hypothesis. There are such cases in statistics; as, for instance, an inquiry into the amount of the population of any country. It is indifferent to that inquiry whether they are grown people or children, strong or weak, tall or short; the only thing we want to ascertain is their number. But whenever, from equality or inequality of number, equality or inequality in any other respect is to be inferred, arithmetic carried into such inquiries becomes as hypothetical a science as geometry. All units must be assumed to be equal in that other respect; and this is never accurately true, for one actual pound weight is not exactly equal to another, nor one measured mile's length to another; a nicer balance, or more accurate measuring instruments, would always detect some difference.

What is commonly called mathematical certainty, therefore, which comprises the twofold conception of unconditional truth and perfect accuracy, is not an attribute of all mathematical truths, but of those only which relate to pure Number, as distinguished from Quantity in the more enlarged sense; and only so long as we abstain from supposing that the numbers are a precise index to actual quantities. The certainty usually ascribed to the conclusions of geometry, and even to those of mechanics, is nothing whatever but certainty of inference. We can have full assurance of particular results under particular suppositions, but we cannot have the same assurance that these suppositions are accurately true, nor that they include all the data which may exercise an influence over the result in any given instance.

Chapter VII [. . .] As I have hitherto said nothing of the two axioms in question, those of Contradiction and of Excluded Middle, it is not unseasonable to consider them here. The former asserts that an affirmative proposition and the corresponding negative proposition cannot both be true; which has generally been held to be intuitively evident. Sir William Hamilton and the Germans consider it to be the statement in words of a form or law of our thinking faculty.[3] Other philosophers, not less deserving of consideration, deem it to be an identical proposition, an assertion involved in the meaning of the terms; a mode of defining Negation, and the word Not.

I am able to go one step with these last. An affirmative assertion and its negative are not two independent assertions, connected with each other only as mutually incompatible. That if the negative be true, the affirmative must be false, really is a mere identical proposition; for the negative proposition asserts nothing but the falsity of the affirmative, and has no other sense or meaning whatever. The Principium Contradictionis should therefore put off the ambitious phraseology which gives it the air of a fundamental

antithesis pervading nature, and should be enunciated in the simpler form, that the same proposition cannot at the same time be false and true. But I can go no farther with the Nominalists; for I cannot look upon this last as a merely verbal proposition. I consider it to be, like other axioms, one of our first and most familiar generalisations from experience. The original foundation of it I take to be, that Belief and Disbelief are two different mental states, excluding one another. This we know by the simplest observation of our own minds. And if we carry our observation outwards, we also find that light and darkness, sound and silence, motion and quiescence, equality and inequality, preceding and following, succession and simultaneousness, any positive phenomenon whatever and its negative, are distinct phenomena, pointedly contrasted, and the one always absent where the other is present. I consider the maxim in question to be a generalisation from all these facts.

In like manner as the Principle of Contradiction (that one of two contradictories must be false) means that an assertion cannot be *both* true and false, so the Principle of Excluded Middle, or that one of two contradictories must be true, means that an assertion must be *either* true or false: either the affirmative is true, or otherwise the negative is true, which means that the affirmative is false. I cannot help thinking this principle a surprising specimen of a so called necessity of Thought, since it is not even true, unless with a large qualification. A proposition must be either true or false, *provided* that the predicate be one which can in any intelligible sense be attributed to the subject (and as this is always assumed to be the case in treatises on logic, the axiom is always laid down there as of absolute truth). "Abracadabra is a second intention" is neither true nor false. Between the true and the false there is a third possibility, the Unmeaning; and this alternative is fatal to Sir William Hamilton's extension of the maxim to Noumena.[4] That Matter must either have a minimum of divisibility or be infinitely divisible, is more than we can ever know. For in the first place, Matter, in any other than the phenomenal sense of the term, may not exist; and it will scarcely be said that a non-entity must be either infinitely or finitely divisible. In the second place, though matter, considered as the occult cause of our sensations, do really exist, yet what we call divisibility may be an attribute only of our sensations of sight and touch, and not of their uncognisable cause. Divisibility may not be predicable at all, in any intelligible sense, of Things in Themselves, nor therefore of Matter in itself; and the assumed necessity of being either infinitely or finitely divisible may be an inapplicable alternative. On this question I am happy to have the full concurrence of Mr Herbert Spencer, from whose paper in the *Fortnightly Review* I extract the following passage.[5] The germ of an idea identical with that of Mr Spencer may be found in the present chapter, about a page back, but in Mr Spencer it is not an undeveloped thought, but a philosophical theory.

"When remembering a certain thing as in a certain place, the place and the thing are mentally represented together; while to think of the non-existence of the thing in that place implies a consciousness in which the place is represented, but not the thing. Similarly, if instead of thinking of an object as colourless, we think of its having colour, the change consists in the addition to the concept of an element that was before absent from it – the object cannot be thought of first as red and then as not red, without one component of the thought being totally expelled from the mind by another. The law of the Excluded Middle, then, is simply a generalisation of the universal experience that some mental states are directly destructive of other states. It formulates a certain absolutely constant law, that the appearance of any positive mode of con-sciousness cannot occur without excluding a correlative negative mode; and that the negative mode cannot occur without excluding the correlative positive mode, the antithesis of positive and negative being, indeed, merely an expression of this experience. Hence it follows that if consciousness is not in one of the two modes it must be in the other."

Notes

1 Dugald Stewart (1753–1828) was a leading representative of Scottish "Common Sense Philosophy."
2 William Whewell (1794–1866) was an important historian and philosopher of science. His account of induction, as well as his position on the nature of necessary truths, is a main critical target of Mill's in *A System of Logic*.
3 Sir William Hamilton (1788–1856) was a Scottish philosopher heavily influenced by Kant (one of "the Germans" referred to here), and the subject of a major critical study by Mill.
4 "Noumena" is Kant's term for things which, unlike "phenomena," cannot be known empirically. For Kant and Hamilton, noumena coincide with "things in themselves." Mill's point in this paragraph is that since noumena, if they exist at all, are unknowable, it is illegitimate of Hamilton to assert that they are subject to the Principle of the Excluded Middle with respect to a property like divisibility.
5 Herbert Spencer (1820–1903) – positivist philosopher, social reformer, and the main champion of "Social Darwinism" – was, after Mill, the most famous British philosopher of the nineteenth century.

Arthur Schopenhauer, "On the Possibility of Knowing the Thing-in-Itself"

Introduction

Arthur Schopenhauer's (1788–1860) eclectic mind drew upon natural science, Hinduism, Buddhism, the philosophical work of Plato (II.1), and Immanuel Kant (II.12), as well contemporary German idealists and Romantics like Johann Gottlieb Fichte (1762–1814), Friedrich D. E. Schleiermacher (1768–1834), and Goethe (1749–1832). His doctoral dissertation, *On the Fourfold Root of the Principle of Sufficient Reason* (1813), explored and challenged the idea that reality is fundamentally rational.[1]

After periods in Göttingen and Berlin, Schopenhauer settled in Dresden, where he immersed himself in writing his magnum opus, *The World as Will and Representation* (1818; second enlarged edition 1844). The text draws upon but also pushes past the limitations established by Kant's "critical philosophy" and grounds both the world and the self in a metaphysical "Will" (*Wille*) that lies in some sense beneath or behind phenomenal reality – reality as we experience it. Schopenhauer's idea would later inform the work of Friedrich Nietzsche (1844–1900), which also

From Arthur Schopenhauer, *The World as Will and Representation*, Vol. II, Chapter 18, trans. E. F. J. Payne, New York: Dover Publications, Inc., 1958, pp. 191–200.

at times adopts a metaphysic of Will, as well as Sigmund Freud's (1856–1939) theory of the unconscious.

Aristotelian and scholastic philosophy had defined "substance" as that which exists independently of other things (i.e., as that which can exist whether or not other things exist; III.4). While Big Ben exists independently of other substances (for example, Paris's, Eiffel Tower), predicates like Big Ben's color and shape cannot exist independently, separate from Big Ben itself. Colors and shapes cannot exist on their own; they can only exist "in" or inhere in some substance (on this topic see Aristotle's *Categories*).

Descartes had laid the groundwork for a fundamental reorientation in metaphysics by redefining substance as, in the first place, not what exists independently but instead as what is clearly and distinctly *conceived* as existing independently (III.12). Inverting the traditional understanding of Parmenides' remark that "it is the same for thinking as for being" (III.2), Descartes argued that whatever is clearly and distinctly conceived to be the case must really be the case. Kant's self-styled "Copernican Revolution" in philosophy follows Descartes's lead and renders "substance" not as the way things stand "in themselves" (*an sich*) but, rather, as one of rules by which conscious beings must organize sensations into objects of experience. "Substance" for Kant, in other words, is one of the 12 *a priori* "categories" (or "pure concepts of the understanding") through which any and every object must be conceived.

Conscious beings don't draw these *a priori* categories *from* things; rather they legislate *to* every possible thing its general categorical dimensions, including its being a substance in which predicates inhere.

But the Kantian revolution comes at a rather high cost to metaphysics. Because, according to Kant, we cannot experience things directly but only through the sensible intuitions of our sensory faculties, we can only know things as *representations* (*Vorstellungen*) or *phenomena*. While we can determine that the *a priori* conditions governing all possible experience require that reality *as we experience it* must be composed of substances, we cannot, according to Kant, know that things are substances *in themselves*. Reality, as it is in itself – as *noumena* – remains beyond our reach. Metaphysics, therefore, for Kantians cannot be a transcending science of ultimate reality but only a "transcendental" interrogation of the *a priori* conditions of any possible experience of the world and our selves (II.12).

Kant himself had explored ways of skirting the limits of metaphysical knowledge by arguing that there remains warrant for using metaphysical ideas to "regulate" our investigations into reality (*Critique of Pure Reason*, 1781) and for "postulating" the existence of God, freedom, and immortality (*Critique of Practical Reason*, 1788). In moral action, Kant maintained, we acquire a "consciousness" (if not "knowledge") of our freedom. More importantly, however – so far as concerns Schopenhauer – Kant points to aesthetic experience as a special way to "comprehend" (if not precisely "know") reality in itself. In experiences of sublimity – such as we find in contemplating the starry heavens or a raging storm – our freedom and immortality present themselves through what Kant calls a "negative exhibition." In the organic fit of the elements of nature, we discern the "purposiveness" (if not actually the purposes) of things. Through its beauty, nature appears to us "by analogy with art" rather than as "sheer purposeless mechanism." "Hence," Kant writes, "even though this beauty does not actually expand our cognition of natural objects, it does expand our concept of nature" (*Critique of Judgment*, 1790).

Schopenhauer develops Kant's claims about aesthetic comprehension, arguing that in aesthetic contemplation artistic "genius" penetrates beyond the merely phenomenal representations of ordinary experience (the representations to which science is confined) and achieves temporary freedom and release from the tumultuous strife of the Will. In music this release is most profound (a view that would influence Richard Wagner), as music has least to do with spatial reality, and as it calls upon the special qualities of inner experience that Kant, according to Schopenhauer, had misunderstood.[2]

Against Kant, for whom our inner, subjective life is as much an experience of phenomenal representations as that of the external, spatial-material world, Schopenhauer maintains that our inner life transcends the representational limitations of time and space (e.g. thoughts and feelings have no shape), giving us direct accesses to noumenal reality. That direct access exposes reality in itself as surging, driving, unfolding Will; and on the basis of this inward apprehension Schopenhauer extrapolates to a claim about the metaphysical basis of the world in its entirety. The play of forces that compose material objects; the persistent power of life, heartbeat, and breath; the drives, thought, and feelings that animate our minds; the wind, the up-surging mountain ranges, the tides and the seas; the movement of the planets and the galaxies – all are expressions of Will. Not only, however, the primordial basis of individual objects, Will also crystallizes itself in that series of unchanging patterns underwriting the possibility of knowledge of the world that Plato called the "Forms."

Schopenhauer's view is often thought of as pessimistic – not only because the Will resists our attempts to know it, but also because the Will's churning, irrational dynamics ultimately devour us. Romantics drank deeply from Schopenhauer's metaphysical well, maintaining that reality is fundamentally non-rational, more akin and more accessible to instinct, drive, and feeling than to ratiocination, logical order, and mechanism.

Notes

1   P. Gardiner, *Schopenhauer*, Harmondsworth: Penguin, 1963.
2   D. W. Hamlyn. *Schopenhauer*, London: Routledge & Kegan Paul, 1980.

Schopenhauer, On the Possibility of Knowing the Thing-in-Itself

In 1836, under the title *Ueber den Willen in der Natur* (second edition, 1854), I already published the really essential supplement to this book, which contains the most characteristic and important step of my philosophy, namely the transition from the phenomenon to the thing-in-itself, given up by Kant as impossible. We should make a great mistake if we tried to regard the statements of others, with which I have there associated my explanations, as the real and proper material and subject of that work, a work small in volume but important as regards its contents. On the contrary, those statements are merely the occasion from which I have started, and I have there discussed that fundamental truth of my teaching with greater distinctness than anywhere else, and brought it down to the empirical knowledge of nature. This has been done most exhaustively and stringently under the heading "Physical Astronomy"; so that I cannot hope ever to find a more correct and accurate expression of that core of my philosophy than what is there recorded. Whoever wishes to know my philosophy thoroughly and investigate it seriously must first take that chapter into consideration. Therefore all that is said in that small work would in general constitute the main subject-matter of the present supplements, if it had not to be excluded as having preceded them; whereas I here assume it to be known, since otherwise what is best would be missing.

First of all, I will make a few preliminary observations from a more general point of view as to the sense in which we can speak of a knowledge of the thing-in-itself, and of the necessary limitation of this sense.

What is *knowledge*? It is above all else and essentially *representation*. What is *representation*? A very complicated *physiological* occurrence in an animal's brain, whose result is the consciousness of a *picture or image* at that very spot. Obviously the relation of such a picture to something entirely different from the animal in whose brain it exists can only be a very indirect one. This is perhaps the simplest and most intelligible way of disclosing the *deep gulf between the ideal and the real*. This is one of the things of which, like the

earth's motion, we are not immediately aware; the ancients, therefore, did not notice it, just as they did not observe the earth's motion. On the other hand, once first demonstrated by Descartes, it has ever since given philosophers no rest. But after Kant had at last shown most thoroughly the complete diversity of the ideal and the real, it was an attempt as bold as it was absurd, yet quite correctly calculated with regard to the power of judgement of the philosophical public in Germany and thus crowned with brilliant success, to try to assert the *absolute identity* of the two by dogmatic utterances referring to a so-called intellectual intuition. On the contrary, a subjective and an objective existence, a being for self and a being for others, a consciousness of one's own self and a consciousness of other things, are in truth given to us immediately, and the two are given in such a fundamentally different way that no other difference compares with this. About *himself* everyone knows directly, about everything else only very indirectly. This is the fact and the problem.

On the other hand, it is no longer the essential point here, but one of secondary importance, whether, through further processes in the interior of the brain, universal concepts (*universalia*) are abstracted from the representations or pictures of perception that have arisen in the brain, for the purpose of further combinations, whereby knowledge becomes *rational*, and is then called *thinking*. For all such *concepts* borrow their contents only from the representation of perception, which is therefore *primary knowledge*, and thus is alone taken into consideration when we investigate the relation between the ideal and the real. Accordingly, it is evidence of a complete ignorance of the problem, or at any rate it is very inept, to want to describe this relation as that between *being* and *thinking*. In the first place, *thinking* has a relation only to *perceiving*, but *perceiving* has a relation to the *being-in-itself* of what is perceived, and this last is the great problem with which we are here concerned. On the other hand, empirical being, as it lies before us, is simply nothing but being-given in perception; but the relation of this to *thinking* is no riddle, for the concepts, and hence the immediate material of thinking, are obviously *abstracted* from perception, as no reasonable person can doubt. Incidentally, we can see how important the choice of expressions in philosophy is from the fact that the inept expression censured above, and the misunderstanding that has arisen from it, have become the foundation of the whole Hegelian pseudo-philosophy that has engrossed the attention of the German public for twenty-five years.

But if it should be said that "perception is already knowledge of the thing-in-itself, for it is the effect of that which exists outside us, and as this *acts*, so it *is*; its action is just its being"; then to this we reply: (1) that the law of causality, as has been sufficiently proved, is of subjective origin, as is also the sensation of the senses from which the perception comes; (2) that time and space, in which the object presents itself, are likewise of subjective origin; (3) that, if the being of the object consists merely in its acting, this means that it consists merely in the changes produced by it in others; consequently, itself and in itself it is nothing at all. Only of *matter* is it true, as I have said in the text and discussed in the essay *On the Principle of Sufficient Reason* at the end of § 21, that its being consists in its acting, that it is through and through only causality, and thus is causality itself objectively perceived, but that it is thus nothing in itself (ἡ ὕλη τὸ ἀληθινὸν ψεῦδος, *materia mendacium verax*);* on the contrary, as an ingredient of the perceived object it is a mere abstraction, which by itself alone cannot be given in any experience. It will be fully considered later on in a chapter to itself. Yet the perceived object must be something *in itself*, and not merely *something for others*; for otherwise it would be positively only representation, and we should have an absolute idealism that in the end would become theoretical egoism, in which all reality disappears, and the world becomes a mere subjective phantasm. However, if, without questioning further, we stop altogether at the *world as representation*, then of course it is immaterial whether I declare objects to be representations in my head or phenomena that exhibit themselves in time and space, since time and space themselves are only in my head. In this sense, then, an identity of the ideal and the real might still be affirmed; yet since Kant, this would be to say nothing new. Moreover, the inner nature of things and of the phenomenal world would

obviously not be exhausted in this way, but with it we should still always be only on the *ideal* side. The *real* side must be something *toto genere* different from the *world as representation*, namely that which things are *in themselves*; and it is this complete diversity between the ideal and the real that Kant has demonstrated most thoroughly.

Locke had denied knowledge of things as they are in themselves to the senses; but Kant denied it also to the perceiving *understanding*. Under this name I embrace here what he calls *pure* sensibility and the law of causality that brings about empirical perception, in so far as this law is given *a priori*. Not only are both right, but it can also be seen quite directly that there is a contradiction in the assertion that a thing is known according to what it is in and by itself, in other words, outside our knowledge. For, as I have said, all knowing is essentially a making of representations; but my making of representations, just because it is mine, can never be identical with the being-in-itself of the thing outside me. The being in and by itself of every thing must necessarily be *subjective*. But in the representation of another, it exists just as necessarily as something *objective*, a difference that can never be entirely reconciled. For through this the whole mode of its existence is fundamentally changed; as something objective, it presupposes a foreign subject, and exists as the representation of that subject; moreover, as Kant has shown, it has entered forms foreign to its own nature, just because they belong to that foreign subject whose knowledge becomes possible only through them. If, absorbed in this reflection, I perceive, let us say, lifeless bodies of easily observable size and regular comprehensible form, and then attempt to conceive this spatial existence in its three dimensions as their being-in-itself, and consequently as the existence that is subjective to the things, then I at once feel the impossibility of the thing, since I can never think of those objective forms as the being that is subjective to the things. On the contrary, I become directly conscious that what I represent there is a picture or image, brought about in my brain and existing only for me as the knowing subject, and that this picture cannot constitute the ultimate, and therefore subjective, being-in-and-by-itself of even these lifeless bodies. On the other hand, I cannot assume that even these lifeless bodies exist simply and solely in my representation, but as they

* Matter is a lie and yet true." [Tr.]

have unfathomable properties, and, by virtue of these, activity, I must concede them a *being-in-itself* of some kind. But this very inscrutability of the properties, pointing as it certainly does on the one hand to something existing independently of our knowledge, on the other hand gives the empirical proof that, because our knowledge consists only in the *framing of representations* by means of subjective forms, such knowledge always furnishes mere *phenomena*, not the being-in-itself of things. From this it can be explained that in all we know, a certain something remains hidden from us as being quite unfathomable, and we must confess that we are unable to understand even the commonest and simplest phenomena. For not merely do the highest productions of nature, namely living beings, or the *complicated* phenomena of the inorganic world remain inscrutable to us, but even every rock-crystal, even iron pyrites, are, by virtue of their crystallographical, optical, chemical, and electrical properties, an abyss of incomprehensibilities and mysteries for our searching consideration and investigation. This could not be so if we knew things as they are in themselves; for then at any rate the simpler phenomena, the path to whose properties was not barred to us by ignorance, would of necessity be thoroughly intelligible to us, and their whole being and inner nature could not fail to pass over into knowledge. Therefore it lies not in the defectiveness of our acquaintance with things, but in the very nature of knowledge itself. For if our perception, and thus the whole empirical apprehension of the things that present themselves to us, is already determined essentially and principally by our cognitive faculty and by its forms and functions, then it must be that things exhibit themselves in a manner quite different from their own inner nature, and that therefore they appear as through a mask. This mask enables us always merely to assume, never to know, what is hidden beneath it; and this something then gleams through as an inscrutable mystery. Never can the nature of anything pass over into knowledge wholly and without reserve; but still less can anything real be constructed *a priori*, like something mathematical. Therefore the empirical inscrutability of all the beings of nature is an *a posteriori* proof of the ideality, and merely phenomenal actuality, of their empirical existence.

In consequence of all this, on the path of *objective knowledge*, thus starting from the *representa-tion*, we shall never get beyond the representation, i.e., the phenomenon. We shall therefore remain at the outside of things; we shall never be able to penetrate into their inner nature, and investigate what they are in themselves, in other words, what they may be by themselves. So far I agree with Kant. But now, as the counterpoise to this truth, I have stressed that other truth that we are not merely the *knowing subject*, but that *we ourselves* are also among those realities or entities we require to know, that *we ourselves are the thing-in-itself*. Consequently, a way *from within* stands open to us to that real inner nature of things to which we cannot penetrate *from without*. It is, so to speak, a subterranean passage, a secret alliance, which, as if by treachery, places us all at once in the fortress that could not be taken by attack from without. Precisely as such, the *thing-in-itself* can come into consciousness only quite directly, namely by *it itself being conscious of itself*; to try to know it objectively is to desire something contradictory. Everything objective is representation, consequently appearance, in fact mere phenomenon of the brain.

Kant's principal result may be summarized in its essence as follows: "All concepts which do not have as their basis a perception in space and time (sensuous perception), or in other words, have not been drawn from such a perception, are absolutely empty, that is to say, they give us no knowledge. But as perception can furnish only *phenomena*, not things-in-themselves, we too have absolutely no knowledge of things-in-themselves." I admit this of everything, but not of the knowledge everyone has of his own *willing*. This is neither a perception (for all perception is spatial), nor is it empty; on the contrary, it is more real than any other knowledge. Further, it is not *a priori*, like merely formal knowledge, but entirely *a posteriori*; hence we are unable to anticipate it in the particular case, but in this are often guilty of error concerning ourselves. In fact, our *willing* is the only opportunity we have of understanding simultaneously from within any event that outwardly manifests itself; consequently, it is the one thing known to us *immediately*, and not given to us merely in the representation, as all else is. Here, therefore, lies the datum alone capable of becoming the key to everything else, or, as I have said, the only narrow gateway to truth. Accordingly, we must learn to understand nature from ourselves, not ourselves from nature. What is directly known to us must give us the explanation of what is only indirectly known, not conversely. Do we understand, let us say, the rolling away of a ball when it has received an impulse more thoroughly than we understand our own movement when we have perceived a motive? Many may think so, but I say that the reverse is the case. However, we shall arrive at the insight that in both the occurrences just mentioned what is essential is identical, although identical in the same way as the lowest audible note of harmony is identical with the note of the same name ten octaves higher.

Meanwhile it is to be carefully noted, and I have always kept it in mind, that even the inward observation we have of our own will still does not by any means furnish an exhaustive and adequate knowledge of the thing-in-itself. It would do so if it were a wholly immediate observation. But such observation is brought about by the will, with and by means of corporization, providing itself also with an intellect (for the purpose of its relations with the external world), and then through this intellect knowing itself in self-consciousness (the necessary reverse of the external world); but this knowledge of the thing-in-itself is not wholly adequate. In the first place, such knowledge is tied to the form of the representation; it is perception or observation, and as such falls apart into subject and object. For even in self-consciousness, the I is not absolutely simple, but consists of a knower (intellect) and a known (will); the former is not known and the latter is not knowing, although the two flow together into the consciousness of an I. But on this very account, this I is not *intimate* with itself through and through, does not shine through so to speak, but is opaque, and therefore remains a riddle to itself. Hence even in inner knowledge there still occurs a difference between the being-in-itself of its object and the observation or perception of this object in the knowing subject. But the inner knowledge is free from two forms belonging to outer knowledge, the form of *space* and the form of *causality* which brings about all sense-perception. On the other hand, there still remains the form of *time*, as well as that of being known and of knowing in general. Accordingly, in this inner knowledge the thing-in-itself has indeed to a great extent cast off its veils, but still does not appear quite naked. In consequence of the form of time which still adheres to it, everyone knows his *will* only in its successive individual *acts*, not as a whole, in and by itself. Hence no one knows his character a priori, but he becomes acquainted with it only by way of experience and always imperfectly. Yet the apprehension in which we know the stirrings and acts of our own will is far more immediate than is any other. It is the point where the thing-in-itself enters the phenomenon most immediately, and is most closely examined by the knowing subject; therefore the event thus intimately known is simply and solely calculated to become the interpreter of every other.

For in the case of every emergence of an act of will from the obscure depths of our inner being into the knowing consciousness, there occurs a direct transition into the phenomenon of the thing-in-itself that lies outside time. Accordingly, the act of will is indeed only the nearest and clearest *phenomenon* of the thing-in-itself; yet it follows from this that, if all the other phenomena could be known by us just as immediately and intimately, we should be obliged to regard them precisely as that which the will is in us. Therefore in this sense I teach that the inner nature of every thing is *will*, and I call the will the thing-in-itself. In this way, Kant's doctrine of the inability to know the thing-in-itself is modified to the extent that the thing-in-itself is merely not absolutely and completely knowable; that nevertheless by far the most immediate of its phenomena, distinguished *toto genere* from all the rest by this immediateness, is its representative for us. Accordingly we have to refer the whole world of phenomena to that one in which the thing-in-itself is manifested under the lightest of all veils, and still remains phenomenon only in so far as my intellect, the only thing capable of knowledge, still always remains distinguished from me as the one who wills, and does not cast off the knowledge-form of *time*, even with *inner* perception.

Accordingly, even after this last and extreme step, the question may still be raised what that will, which manifests itself in the world and as the world, is ultimately and absolutely in itself; in other words, what it is, quite apart from the fact that it manifests itself as *will*, or in general *appears*, that is to say, *is known* in general. This question can *never* be answered, because, as I have said, being-known of itself contradicts being-in-itself, and everything that is known is as such only phenomenon. But the possibility of this question shows that the thing-in-itself, which we know most immediately in the will, may have, entirely outside all possible phenomenon, determinations, qualities, and modes of existence which for us are absolutely unknowable and incomprehensible, and which then remain as the inner nature of the thing-in-itself, when this, as explained in the fourth book, has freely abolished itself as *will*, has thus stepped out of the phenomenon entirely, and as regards our knowledge, that is to say as regards the world of phenomena, has passed over into empty nothingness. If the will were positively and absolutely the thing-in-itself, then this nothing would be *absolute*, instead of which it expressly appears to us there only as a *relative* nothing.

I now proceed to supplement by a few relevant observations the establishment, given in our second book as well as in the work *On the Will in Nature*, of the doctrine that what makes itself known in the most immediate knowledge as will is precisely that which objectifies itself at different grades in all the phenomena of this world. I shall begin by producing a series of psychological facts proving first of all that in our own consciousness the *will* always appears as the primary and fundamental thing, and throughout asserts its preeminence over the intellect; that, on the other hand, the intellect generally turns out to be what is secondary, subordinate, and conditioned. This proof is the more necessary as all philosophers before me, from the first to the last, place the true and real inner nature or kernel of man in the *knowing* consciousness. Accordingly, they have conceived and explained the I, or in the case of many of them its transcendent hypostasis called soul, as primarily and essentially *knowing*, in fact *thinking*, and only in consequence of this, secondarily and derivatively, as *willing*. This extremely old, universal, and fundamental error, this colossal πρῶτον ψεῦδος and fundamental ὕστερον πρότερον,* must first of all be set aside, and instead of it the true state of the case must be brought to perfectly distinct consciousness. However, as this is done for the first time here after thousands of years of philosophizing, some detailed account will not be out of place. The remarkable phenomenon that in this fundamen-

tal and essential point all philosophers have erred, in fact have completely reversed the truth, might be partly explained, especially in the case of the philosophers of the Christian era, from the fact that all of them aimed at presenting man as differing as widely as possible from the animal. Yet they felt vaguely that the difference between the two was to be found in the intellect and not in the will. From this arose in them unconsciously the tendency to make the intellect the essential and principal thing, in fact to describe willing as a mere function of the intellect. Therefore the concept of a *soul*, as transcendent hypostasis, is not only inadmissible, as is established by the *Critique of Pure Reason*, but it becomes the source of irremediable errors by its establishing beforehand in its "simple substance" an indivisible unity of knowledge and of the will, the separation of which is precisely the path to truth. Therefore that concept can no longer occur in philosophy, but is to be left to German medical men and physiologists, who, laying aside scalpel and scoop, venture to philosophize with concepts they received when they were confirmed. They might perhaps try their luck with them in England. The French physiologists and zootomists have (till recently) kept themselves entirely free from this reproach.

The first consequence of their common fundamental error, which is very inconvenient to all these philosophers, is that, since in death the knowing consciousness obviously perishes, either they must admit death to be the annihilation of man, against which our inner nature revolts, or resort to the assumption of a continued existence of the knowing consciousness. For this a strong faith is required, since everyone's own experience has abundantly demonstrated to him the complete and general dependence of the knowing consciousness on the brain, and one can just as easily believe in a digestion without a stomach as in a knowing consciousness without a brain. My philosophy alone leads us out of this dilemma; in the first place it puts man's real inner nature not in consciousness, but in the will. This will is not essentially united with consciousness, but is related to consciousness, in other words to knowledge, as substance to accident, as something illuminated to light, as the string to the sounding-board; it comes into consciousness from within just as the corporeal world comes from without. Now we can grasp

* "The first false step." "Confusion of the earlier with the later, or of ground with consequent." [Tr.]

the indestructibility of this real kernel and true inner being that is ours, in spite of the obvious extinction of consciousness in death and its corresponding non-existence before birth. For the intellect is as fleeting and as perishable as is the brain, and is the brain's product, or rather its activity. But the brain, like the whole organism, is the product or phenomenon of, in short a secondary thing to, the will, and it is the will alone that is imperishable.

Søren Kierkegaard,
"Truth Is Subjectivity"

Introduction

There are a number of ways to think about
truth. Correspondence theories conceive of truth
as an alignment or conformity between thoughts
or words and things. Coherence theories portray
truth in terms of the fit of a statement in a system or web of other statements. Idealism conceives
of truth in terms of an identity between thought
and being, between the ideal and the real. One
may, in addition, speak of things being true in the
sense of being really or purely what they appear
to be, such as when one speaks of the true king,
rather than a pretender, a lover who is true, or a
true Highland malt. In this selection, however,
Danish philosopher Søren Kierkegaard (1813–
55) approaches the idea of "truth" in a still different way – by contrasting "subjective" against
"objective" senses of truth.

One may define "objective truth" as truth understood independently of any particular subject, any
particular individual. So, in terms of correspondence theories, a theory or statement might be true
objectively in the sense that its claims conform
to the way things are, even if no one is aware
of its being so. Objectively, for example, Einstein's

From Søren Kierkegaard, *Concluding Unscientific Postscript*, trans. D. Swenson and W. Lowrie, Princeton, NJ:
Princeton University Press, 1941, pp. 169–83 (some
notes omitted).

theory of general relativity was true before
Einstein was born. "What" is true was true in
ancient times as well as it is today, across cultures,
distances, and epochs. People's particular lives
and beliefs are, of course, irrelevant to this view
of truth.

G. W. F. Hegel (1770–1831), the principal
target of a great deal of Kierkegaard's critical
work, carried the notion of truth to the grandest
of scales – in Kierkegaard's view one in which the
place of individuals was even more profoundly
effaced. For Hegel, statements are true both to the
extent that the ideas they express are part of a
great system of true ideas of the universe and to
the extent that those ideas are self-conscious of
their identity with the things they seem to represent. Understanding how any particular idea fits in
with others and is part of the identity of thought
and being, however, ultimately depends upon a vast
dialectical process that yields the comprehension
of the whole of reality and *das absolute Wissen*
("absolute knowledge"). It is for this reason that
Hegel famously said, *Das Wahre ist das Ganze*
("the true is the whole").[1] No individual, however,
possesses or perhaps can possess this comprehensive knowledge. And so, Hegelian truth, perhaps
pre-eminently among variant theories of objective
truth, surpasses the individual.[2]

But for Kierkegaard (or at least the pseudonymous voice of the text, "Johannes Climacus," the
ladder), the individual and the particularities of
his or her existence must never be surpassed,
indeed *can* never be surpassed. Not only are, in

fact, statements and theories always understood only by individuals (whether objectively true or not); they *can* only be understood by individuals. Because of this, individual subjectivity simply cannot be ignored in considerations of what truth actually is for people. We existing individuals cannot acquire the independent, objective view of things that objective theories of truth pretend to have acquired – *sub specie aeternitatis*. We can only exist in relation to the truth as limited, subjective individuals. Kierkegaard is a philosopher of finitude. He writes: "Speculative philosophy is objective, and objectively there is no truth for existing individuals, but only approximations; for the existing individual is precluded from becoming altogether objective by the fact that he exists."[3]

Much of what Kierkegaard (or at least Climacus) determines to be crucial about individual subjects and their relationship to the truth is the necessity of utterly free choice. (In this he would be deeply influential to existentialist thought, for example that of Jean-Paul Sartre (see I.23) and Albert Camus.) Whether or not some particular scientific theory is objectively true or false (and it's important to note that Kierkegaard does not deny objective truth), it remains fully a matter of unconditioned individual choice to accept or reject it as true or false. Any criterion of truth can only be a criterion of truth if an individual accepts it as such. (Kierkegaard's writing under pseudonyms forces the reader to face his or her choice in deciding what the text means, and what to attribute or not attribute to Kierkegaard.)

What follows is the startling and radical idea that neither inference, nor intuition, nor evidence of any kind determines truth or falsehood for existing human beings. Finally, the epistemological standing of a statement or theory depends upon an individual choice. Continental epistemologists (both structuralist and post-structuralist), "standpoint" epistemologists, semioticists, and radical philosophers of science have been influenced by Kierkegaard on this score.[4]

Kierkegaard (Climacus) is interested, however, not only in establishing an understanding of *what* is true about the subjectivity of truth. He is concerned, in addition, with what it means to live in the truth, with *how* one lives in relation to truth, especially in relation to Christian truth. Too many in his own time, thought the Dane, had made "God" and "Christianity" into objects of objective, impersonal truth – advancing arguments, analyzing concepts, articulating logically coherent theories that have nothing to do with particular, existing individual life. Doing so had occluded their grasp of the way living in truth requires a deeply passionate, resolute existential choice to live accordingly – just as Socrates had made when he staked his life on the possibility of immortality. In light of this demand, Kierkegaard presents this "definition of truth: *An objective uncertainty, held fast through an appropriation-process of the most passionate inwardness, is the truth*, the highest truth there is for an *existing* individual." Re-achieving the subjectivity of truth in this sense is, if you'll pardon the pun, Kierkegaard's ultimate objective.

Notes

1 G. W. F. Hegel, *The Phenomenology of Spirit*, Preface, §22. (See II.13 and III.18 for selections from this work.)

2 A. Hannay and G. Marino, eds, *The Cambridge Companion to Kierkegaard*, Cambridge: Cambridge University Press, 1998.

3 L. Pojman, *The Logic of Subjectivity*, Tuscaloosa: University of Alabama Press, 1984.

4 M. Weston, *Kierkegaard and Modern Continental Philosophy*, London: Routledge, 1994.

Kierkegaard, "Truth Is Subjectivity"

Chapter II: The Subjective Truth, Inwardness; Truth Is Subjectivity

Whether truth is defined more empirically, as the conformity of thought and being, or more idealistically, as the conformity of being with thought, it is, in either case, important carefully to note what is meant by being. And in formulating the answer to this question it is likewise important to take heed lest the knowing spirit be tricked into losing itself in the indeterminate, so that it fantastically becomes a something that no existing human being ever was or can be, a sort of phantom with which the individual occupies himself upon occasion, but without making it clear to himself in terms of dialectical intermediaries how he happens to get into this fantastic realm, what significance being there has for him, and whether the entire activity that goes on out there does not resolve itself into a tautology within a recklessly fantastic venture of thought.

If being, in the two indicated definitions, is understood as empirical being, truth is at once transformed into a *desideratum*, and everything must be understood in terms of becoming; for the empirical object is unfinished and the existing cognitive spirit is itself in process of becoming. Thus the truth becomes an approximation whose beginning cannot be posited absolutely, precisely because the conclusion is lacking, the effect of which is retroactive. Whenever a beginning is *made*, on the other hand, unless through being unaware of this the procedure stamps itself as arbitrary, such a beginning is not the consequence of an immanent movement of thought, but is effected through a resolution of the will, essentially in the strength of faith. That the knowing spirit is an existing individual spirit, and that every human being is such an entity existing for himself, is a truth I cannot too often repeat; for the fantastic neglect of this is responsible for much confusion. Let no one misunderstand me. I happen to be a poor existing spirit like all other men; but if there is any lawful and honest manner in which I could be helped into becoming something extraordinary, like the pure I-am-I for example, I always stand ready gratefully to accept the gift and the benefaction. But if it can only be done in the manner indicated, by saying *ein zwei drei kokolorum*, or by tying a string around the little finger, and then when the moon is full, hiding it in some secret place – in that case I prefer to remain what I am, a poor existing human being.

The term "being," as used in the above definitions, must therefore be understood (from the systematic standpoint) much more abstractly, presumably as the abstract reflection of, or the abstract prototype for, what being is as concrete empirical being. When so understood there is nothing to prevent us from abstractly determining the truth as abstractly finished and complete; for the correspondence between thought and being is, from the abstract point of view, always

finished. Only with the concrete does becoming enter in, and it is from the concrete that abstract thought abstracts.

But if being is understood in this manner, the formula becomes a tautology. Thought and being mean one and the same thing, and the correspondence spoken of is merely an abstract self-identity. Neither formula says anything more than that the truth is, so understood as to accentuate the copula: the truth *is*, i.e. the truth is a reduplication. Truth is the subject of the assertion, but the assertion that it is, is the same as the subject; for this being that the truth is said to have is never its own abstract form. In this manner we give expression to the fact that truth is not something simple, but is in a wholly abstract sense a reduplication, a reduplication which is nevertheless instantly revoked.

Abstract thought may continue as long as it likes to rewrite this thought in varying phraseology, it will never get any farther. As soon as the being which corresponds to the truth comes to be empirically concrete, the truth is put in process of becoming, and is again by way of anticipation the conformity of thought with being. This conformity is actually realized for God, but it is not realized for any existing spirit, who is himself existentially in process of becoming.

For an existing spirit *qua* existing spirit, the question of the truth will again exist. The abstract answer has significance only for the abstraction into which an existing spirit is transformed when he abstracts from himself *qua* existing individual. This can be done only momentarily, and even in such moments of abstraction the abstract thinker pays his debt to existence by existing in spite of all abstraction. It is therefore an existing spirit who is now conceived as raising the question of truth, presumably in order that he may exist in it; but in any case the question is raised by someone who is conscious of being a particular existing human being. In this way I believe I can render myself intelligible to every Greek, as well as to every reasonable human being. If a German philosopher wishes to indulge a passion for making himself over, and, just as alchemists and necromancers were wont to garb themselves fantastically, first makes himself over into a superrational something for the purpose of answering this question of the truth in an extremely satisfactory manner, the affair is no concern of mine; nor is his extremely satisfactory answer, which is no doubt very satisfactory indeed – when you are fantastically transformed. On the other hand, whether it is or is not the case that a German professor behaves in this manner, can be readily determined by anyone who will concentrate enthusiastically upon seeking guidance at the hands of such a sage, without criticism but seeking merely to assimilate the wisdom in a docile spirit by proposing to shape his own life in accordance with it. Precisely when thus enthusiastically attempting to learn from such a German professor, one would realize the most apt of epigrams upon him. For such a speculative philosopher could hardly be more embarrassed than by the sincere and enthusiastic zeal of a learner who proposes to express and to realize his wisdom by appropriating it existentially. For this wisdom is something that the Herr Professor has merely imagined, and written books about, but never himself tried. Aye, it has never even occurred to him that this should be done. Like the custom clerk who writes what he could not himself read, satisfied that his responsibilities ended with the writing, so there are speculative philosophers who write what, when it is to be read in the light of action, shows itself to be nonsense, unless it is, perhaps, intended only for fantastic beings.

In that the question of truth is thus raised by an existing spirit *qua* existing, the above abstract reduplication that is involved in it again confronts him. But existence itself, namely, existence as it is in the individual who raises the question and himself exists, keeps the two moments of thought and being apart, so that reflection presents him with two alternatives. For an objective reflection the truth becomes an object, something objective, and thought must be pointed away from the subject. For a subjective reflection the truth becomes a matter of appropriation, of inwardness, of subjectivity, and thought must probe more and more deeply into the subject and his subjectivity.

But then what? Shall we be compelled to remain in this disjunction, or may we not here accept the offer of benevolent assistance from the principle of mediation, so that the truth becomes an identity of subject and object? Well, why not? But can the principle of mediation also help the existing individual while still remaining in existence himself to become the mediating principle, which is *sub specie aeterni*, whereas the poor existing individual is confined to the straitjacket of existence? Surely it cannot do any good to mock a man, luring him on by dangling before his eyes the identity of subject and object, when his situation prevents him from making use of this identity, since he is in process of becoming in consequence of being an existing individual. How can it help to explain to a man how the eternal truth is to be understood eternally, when the supposed user of the explanation is prevented from so understanding it through being an existing individual, and merely becomes fantastic when he imagines himself to be *sub specie aeterni*? What such a man needs instead is precisely an explanation of how the eternal truth is to be understood in determinations of time by one who as existing is himself in time, which even the worshipful Herr Professor concedes, if not always, at least once a quarter when he draws his salary.

The identity of subject and object posited through an application of the principle of mediation merely carries us back to where we were before, to the abstract definition of the truth as an identity of thought and being; for to determine the truth as an identity of thought and object is precisely the same thing as saying that the truth *is*, i.e. that the truth is a reduplication. The lofty wisdom has thus again merely been absentminded enough to forget that it was an existing spirit who asked about the truth. Or is the existing spirit himself the identity of subject and object, the subject-object? In that case I must press the question of where such an existing human being is, when he is thus at the same time also a subject-object? Or shall we perhaps here again first transform the existing spirit into something in general, and thereupon explain everything except the question asked, namely, how an existing subject is related to the truth *in concreto*; explain everything except the question that must in the next instance be asked, namely, how a particular existing spirit is related to this something in general, which seems to have not a little in common with a paper kite, or with the lump of sugar which the Dutch used to hang up under the loft for all to lick at.

So we return to the two ways of reflection; and we have not forgotten that it is an existing spirit who asks the question, a wholly individual human being. Nor can we forget that the fact that he exists is precisely what will make it impossible for him to proceed along both ways at once, while his earnest concern will prevent him from frivolously and fantastically becoming subject-object. Which of these two ways is now the way of truth for an existing spirit? For only the fantastic I-am-I is at once finished with both ways, or proceeds methodically along both ways simultaneously, a mode of ambulation which for an existing human is so inhuman that I dare not recommend it.

Since the inquirer stresses precisely the fact that he is an existing individual, then one of the above two ways which especially accentuates existence would seem to be especially worthy of commendation.

The way of objective reflection makes the subject accidental, and thereby transforms existence into something indifferent, something vanishing. Away from the subject the objective way of reflection leads to the objective truth, and while the subject and his subjectivity become indifferent, the truth also becomes indifferent, and this indifference is precisely its objective validity; for all interest, like all decisiveness, is rooted in subjectivity. The way of objective reflection leads to abstract thought, to mathematics, to historical knowledge of different kinds; and always it leads away from the subject, whose existence or non-existence, and from the objective point of view quite rightly, becomes infinitely indifferent. Quite rightly, since as Hamlet says, existence and non-existence have only subjective significance. At its maximum this way will arrive at a contradiction, and in so far as the subject does not become wholly indifferent to himself, this merely constitutes a sign that his objective striving is not objective enough. At its maximum this way will lead to the contradiction that only the objective has come into being, while the subjective has gone out; that is to say, the existing subjectivity has vanished, in that it has made an attempt to become what in the abstract sense is called subjectivity, the mere abstract form of an abstract objectivity. And yet, the objectivity which has thus come into being is, from the subjective point of view at the most, either an hypothesis or an approximation, because all eternal decisiveness is rooted in subjectivity.

However, the objective way deems itself to have a security which the subjective way does not have (and, of course, existence and existing cannot be thought in combination with objective security); it thinks to escape a danger which threatens the subjective way and this danger is at its maximum: madness. In a merely subjective determination of the truth, madness and truth become in the last analysis indistinguishable, since they may both have inwardness.* Nevertheless, perhaps I may here venture to offer a little remark, one which would seem to be not wholly superfluous in an objective age. The absence of inwardness is also madness. The objective truth as such, is by no means adequate to determine that whoever utters it is sane; on the contrary, it may even betray the fact that he is mad, although what he says may be entirely true, and especially objectively true. I shall here permit myself to tell a story, which without any sort of adaptation on my part comes direct from an asylum. A patient in such an institution seeks to escape, and actually succeeds in effecting his purpose by leaping out of a window, and prepares to start on the road to freedom, when the thought strikes him (shall I say sanely enough or madly enough?): "When you come to town you will be recognized, and you will at once be brought back here again; hence you need to prepare yourself fully to convince everyone by the objective truth of what you say, that all is in order as far as your sanity is concerned." As he walks along and thinks about this, he sees a ball lying on the ground, picks it up, and puts it into the tail pocket of his coat. Every step he takes the ball strikes him, politely speaking, on his hinder parts, and every time it thus strikes him he says: "Bang, the earth is round." He comes to the city, and at once calls on one of his friends; he wants to convince him that he is not crazy, and therefore walks back and forth, saying continually: "Bang, the earth is round!" But is not the earth round? Does the asylum still crave yet another sacrifice for this opinion, as in the time when all men believed it to be flat as a pancake? Or is

---

* Even this is not really true, however, for madness never has the specific inwardness of the infinite. Its fixed idea is precisely some sort of objectivity, and the contradiction of madness consists in embracing this with passion. The critical point in such madness is thus again not the subjective, but the little finitude which has become a fixed idea, which is something that can never happen to the infinite.

a man who hopes to prove that he is sane, by uttering a generally accepted and generally respected objective truth, insane? And yet it was clear to the physician that the patient was not yet cured; though it is not to be thought that the cure would consist in getting him to accept the opinion that the earth is flat. But all men are not physicians, and what the age demands seems to have a considerable influence upon the question of what madness is. Aye, one could almost be tempted sometimes to believe that the modern age, which has modernized Christianity, has also modernized the question of Pontius Pilate, and that its urge to find something in which it can rest proclaims itself in the question: What is madness? When a *Privatdocent*, every time his scholastic gown reminds him that he ought to say something, says *de omnibus dubitandum est*, and at the same time writes away at a system which offers abundant internal evidence in every other sentence that the man has never doubted anything at all: he is not regarded as mad.

Don Quixote is the prototype for a subjective madness, in which the passion of inwardness embraces a particular finite fixed idea. But the absence of inwardness gives us on the other hand the prating madness, which is quite as comical; and it might be a very desirable thing if an experimental psychologist would delineate it by taking a handful of such philosophers and bringing them together. In the type of madness which manifests itself as an aberrant inwardness, the tragic and the comic is that the something which is of such infinite concern to the unfortunate individual is a particular fixation which does not really concern anybody. In the type of madness which consists in the absence of inwardness, the comic is that though the something which the happy individual knows really is the truth, the truth which concerns all men, it does not in the slightest degree concern the much respected prater. This type of madness is more inhuman than the other. One shrinks from looking into the eyes of a madman of the former type lest one be compelled to plumb there the depths of his delirium; but one dares not look at a madman of the latter type at all, from fear of discovering that he has eyes of glass and hair made from carpet-rags; that he is, in short, an artificial product. If you meet someone who suffers from such a derangement of feeling, the derangement consisting in his not having any, you listen to what he says in a cold and awful dread, scarcely knowing whether it is a human being who speaks, or a cunningly contrived walking stick in which a talking machine has been concealed. It is always unpleasant for a proud man to find himself unwittingly drinking a toast of brotherhood with the public hangman; but to find oneself engaged in rational and philosophical conversation with a walking stick is almost enough to make a man lose his mind.

The subjective reflection turns its attention inwardly to the subject, and desires in this intensification of inwardness to realize the truth. And it proceeds in such fashion that, just as in the preceding objective reflection, when the objectivity had come into being, the subjectivity had vanished, so here the subjectivity of the subject becomes the final stage, and objectivity a vanishing factor. Not for a single moment is it forgotten that the subject is an existing individual, and that existence is a process of becoming, and that therefore the notion of the truth as identity of thought and being is a chimera of abstraction, in its truth only an expectation of the creature; not because the truth is not such an identity, but because the knower is an existing individual for whom the truth cannot be such an identity as long as he lives in time. Unless we hold fast to this, speculative philosophy will immediately transport us into the fantastic realism of the I-am-I, which modern speculative thought has not hesitated to use without explaining how a particular individual is related to it; and God knows, no human being is more than such a particular individual.

If an existing individual were really able to transcend himself, the truth would be for him something final and complete; but where is the point at which he is outside himself? The I-am-I is a mathematical point which does not exist, and in so far there is nothing to prevent everyone from occupying this standpoint; the one will not be in the way of the other. It is only momentarily that the particular individual is able to realize existentially a unity of the infinite and the finite which transcends existence. This unity is realized in the moment of passion. Modern philosophy has tried anything and everything in the effort to help the individual to transcend himself objectively, which is a wholly impossible feat; existence exercises its restraining influence, and if philosophers nowadays had not become mere scribblers in the service of a fantastic thinking and its preoccupation, they would long ago have perceived that suicide was the only tolerable practical interpretation of its striving. But the scribbling modern philosophy holds passion in contempt; and yet passion is the culmination of existence for an existing individual – and we are all of us existing individuals. In passion the existing subject is rendered infinite in the eternity of the imaginative representation, and yet he is at the same time most definitely himself. The fantastic I-am-I is not an identity of the infinite and the finite, since neither the one nor the other is real; it is a fantastic rendezvous in the clouds, an unfruitful embrace, and the relationship of the individual self to this mirage is never indicated.

All essential knowledge relates to existence, or only such knowledge as has an essential relationship to existence is essential knowledge. All knowledge which does not inwardly relate itself to existence, in the reflection of inwardness, is, essentially viewed, accidental knowledge; its degree and scope is essentially indifferent. That essential knowledge is essentially related to existence does not mean the above-mentioned identity which abstract thought postulates between thought and being; nor does it signify, objectively, that knowledge corresponds to something existent as its object. But it means that knowledge has a relationship to the knower, who is essentially an existing individual, and that for this reason all essential knowledge is essentially related to existence. Only ethical and ethico-religious knowledge has an essential relationship to the existence of the knower.

Mediation is a mirage, like the I-am-I. From the abstract point of view everything is and nothing comes into being. Mediation can therefore have no place in abstract thought, because it presupposes *movement*. Objective knowledge may indeed have the existent for its object; but since the knowing subject is an existing individual, and through the fact of his existence in process of becoming, philosophy must first explain how a particular existing subject is related to a knowledge of mediation. It must explain what he is in such a moment, if not pretty nearly *distrait*; where he is, if not in the moon? There is constant talk of mediation and mediation; is mediation then a man, as Peter Deacon believes that *Imprimatur* is a man? How does a human being manage to become something of this kind? Is this dignity, this great *philosophicum*, the fruit of study, or does the

magistrate give it away, like the office of deacon or grave-digger? Try merely to enter into these and other such plain questions of a plain man, who would gladly become mediation if it could be done in some lawful and honest manner, and not either by saying *ein zwei drei kokolorum*, or by forgetting that he is himself an existing human being, for whom existence is therefore something essential, and an ethico-religious existence a suitable *quantum satis*. A speculative philosopher may perhaps find it in bad taste to ask such questions. But it is important not to direct the polemic to the wrong point, and hence not to begin in a fantastic objective manner to discuss *pro* and *contra* whether there is a mediation or not, but to hold fast what it means to be a human being.

In an attempt to make clear the difference of way that exists between an objective and a subjective reflection, I shall now proceed to show how a subjective reflection makes its way inwardly in inwardness. Inwardness in an existing subject culminates in passion; corresponding to passion in the subject the truth becomes a paradox; and the fact that the truth becomes a paradox is rooted precisely in its having a relationship to an existing subject. Thus the one corresponds to the other. By forgetting that one is an existing subject, passion goes by the board and the truth is no longer a paradox; the knowing subject becomes a fantastic entity rather than a human being, and the truth becomes a fantastic object for the knowledge of this fantastic entity.

When the question of truth is raised in an objective manner, reflection is directed objectively to the truth, as an object to which the knower is related. Reflection is not focussed upon the relationship, however, but upon the question of whether it is the truth to which the knower is related. If only the object to which he is related is the truth, the subject is accounted to be in the truth. When the question of the truth is raised subjectively, reflection is directed subjectively to the nature of the individual's relationship; if only the mode of this relationship is in the truth, the individual is in the truth even if he should happen to be thus related to what is not true. *

---

* The reader will observe that the question here is about essential truth, or about the truth which is essentially related to existence, and that it is precisely for the sake of clarifying it as inwardness or as subjectivity that this contrast is drawn.

Let us take as an example the knowledge of God. Objectively, reflection is directed to the problem of whether this object is the true God; subjectively, reflection is directed to the question whether the individual is related to a something *in such a manner* that his relationship is in truth a God-relationship. On which side is the truth now to be found? Ah, may we not here resort to a mediation, and say: It is on neither side, but in the mediation of both? Excellently well said, provided we might have it explained how an existing individual manages to be in a state of mediation. For to be in a state of mediation is to be finished, while to exist is to become. Nor can an existing individual be in two places at the same time – he cannot be an identity of subject and object. When he is nearest to being in two places at the same time he is in passion; but passion is momentary, and passion is also the highest expression of subjectivity.

The existing individual who chooses to pursue the objective way enters upon the entire approximation-process by which it is proposed to bring God to light objectively. But this is in all eternity impossible, because God is a subject, and therefore exists only for subjectivity in inwardness. The existing individual who chooses the subjective way apprehends instantly the entire dialectical difficulty involved in having to use some time, perhaps a long time, in finding God objectively; and he feels this dialectical difficulty in all its painfulness, because every moment is wasted in which he does not have God.* That very instant he has God, not by virtue of any objective deliberation, but by virtue of the infinite passion of inwardness. The objective inquirer, on the other hand, is not embarrassed by such dialectical difficulties as are involved in devoting an entire period of investigation to finding God – since it is possible that the inquirer may die tomorrow; and if he lives he can scarcely regard

God as something to be taken along if convenient, since God is precisely that which one takes *a tout prix*, which in the understanding of passion constitutes the true inward relationship to God.

It is at this point, so difficult dialectically, that the way swings off for everyone who knows what it means to think, and to think existentially; which is something very different from sitting at a desk and writing about what one has never done, something very different from writing *de omnibus dubitandum* and at the same time being as credulous existentially as the most sensuous of men. Here is where the way swings off, and the change is marked by the fact that while objective knowledge rambles comfortably on by way of the long road of approximation without being impelled by the urge of passion, subjective knowledge counts every delay a deadly peril, and the decision so infinitely important and so instantly pressing that it is as if the opportunity had already passed.

Now when the problem is to reckon up on which side there is most truth, whether on the side of one who seeks the true God objectively, and pursues the approximate truth of the God-idea; or on the side of one who, driven by the infinite passion of his need of God, feels an infinite concern for his own relationship to God in truth (and to be at one and the same time on both sides equally, is as we have noted not possible for an existing individual, but is merely the happy delusion of an imaginary I-am-I): the answer cannot be in doubt for anyone who has not been demoralized with the aid of science. If one who lives in the midst of Christendom goes up to the house of God, the house of the true God, with the true conception of God in his knowledge, and prays, but prays in a false spirit; and one who lives in an idolatrous community prays with the entire passion of the infinite, although his eyes rest upon the image of an idol: where is there most truth? The one prays in truth to God though he worships an idol; the other prays falsely to the true God, and hence worships in fact an idol.

When one man investigates objectively the problem of immortality, and another embraces an uncertainty with the passion of the infinite: where is there most truth, and who has the greater certainty? The one has entered upon a never-ending approximation, for the certainty of immortality lies precisely in the subjectivity of the individual; the other is immortal, and fights

---

* In this manner God certainly becomes a postulate, but not in the otiose manner in which this word is commonly understood. It becomes clear rather that the only way in which an existing individual comes into relation with God, is when the dialectical contradiction brings his passion to the point of despair, and helps him to embrace God with the "category of despair" (faith). Then the postulate is so far from being arbitrary that it is precisely a life-necessity. It is then not so much that God is a postulate, as that the existing individual's postulation of God is a necessity.

for his immortality by struggling with the uncertainty. Let us consider Socrates. Nowadays everyone dabbles in a few proofs; some have several such proofs, others fewer. But Socrates! He puts the question objectively in a problematic manner: if there is an immortality. He must therefore be accounted a doubter in comparison with one of our modern thinkers with the three proofs? By no means. On this "if" he risks his entire life, he has the courage to meet death, and he has with the passion of the infinite so determined the pattern of his life that it must be found acceptable – if there is an immortality. Is any better proof capable of being given for the immortality of the soul? But those who have the three proofs do not at all determine their lives in conformity therewith; if there is an immortality it must feel disgust over their manner of life: can any better refutation be given of the three proofs? The bit of uncertainty that Socrates had, helped him because he himself contributed the passion of the infinite; the three proofs that the others have do not profit them at all, because they are dead to spirit and enthusiasm, and their three proofs, in lieu of proving anything else, prove just this. A young girl may enjoy all the sweetness of love on the basis of what is merely a weak hope that she is beloved, because she rests everything on this weak hope; but many a wedded matron more than once subjected to the strongest expressions of love, has in so far indeed had proofs, but strangely enough has not enjoyed *quod erat demonstrandum*. The Socratic ignorance, which Socrates held fast with the entire passion of his inwardness, was thus an expression for the principle that the eternal truth is related to an existing individual, and that this truth must therefore be a paradox for him as long as he exists; and yet it is possible that there was more truth in the Socratic ignorance as it was in him, than in the entire objective truth of the System, which flirts with what the times demand and accommodates itself to *Privatdocents*.

The objective accent falls on WHAT is said, the subjective accent on HOW it is said. This distinction holds even in the aesthetic realm, and receives definite expression in the principle that what is in itself true may in the mouth of such and such a person become untrue. In these times this distinction is particularly worthy of notice, for if we wish to express in a single sentence the difference between ancient times and our own, we should doubtless have to say: "In ancient times only an individual here and there knew the truth; now all know it, except that the inwardness of its appropriation stands in an inverse relationship to the extent of its dissemination.* Aesthetically the contradiction that truth becomes untruth in this or that person's mouth, is best construed comically: In the ethico-religious sphere, accent is again on the "how." But this is not to be understood as referring to demeanor, expression, or the like; rather it refers to the relationship sustained by the existing individual, in his own existence, to the content of his utterance. Objectively the interest is focussed merely on the thought-content, subjectively on the inwardness. At its maximum this inward "how" is the passion of the infinite, and the passion of the infinite is the truth. But the passion of the infinite is precisely subjectivity, and thus subjectivity becomes the truth. Objectively there is no infinite decisiveness, and hence it is objectively in order to annul the difference between good and evil, together with the principle of contradiction, and therewith also the infinite difference between the true and the false. Only in subjectivity is there decisiveness, to seek objectivity is to be in error. It is the passion of the infinite that is the decisive factor and not its content, for its content is precisely itself. In this manner subjectivity and the subjective "how" constitute the truth.

* *Stages on Life's Way*, Note on p. 426. Though ordinarily not wishing an expression of opinion on the part of reviewers, I might at this point almost desire it, provided such opinions, so far from flattering me, amounted to an assertion of the daring truth that what I say is something that everybody knows, even every child, and that the cultured know infinitely much better. If it only stands fast that everyone knows it, my standpoint is in order, and I shall doubtless make shift to manage with the unity of the comic and the tragic. If there were anyone who did not know it I might perhaps be in danger of being dislodged from my position of equilibrium by the thought that I might be in a position to communicate to someone the needful preliminary knowledge. It is just this which engages my interest so much, this that the cultured are accustomed to say: that everyone knows what the highest is. This was not the case in paganism, nor in Judaism, nor in the seventeen centuries of Christianity. Hail to the nineteenth century! Everyone knows it. What progress has been made since the time when only a few knew it. To make up for this, perhaps, we must assume that no one nowadays does it.

But the "how" which is thus subjectively accentuated precisely because the subject is an existing individual, is also subject to a dialectic with respect to time. In the passionate moment of decision, where the road swings away from objective knowledge, it seems as if the infinite decision were thereby realized. But in the same moment the existing individual finds himself in the temporal order, and the subjective "how" is transformed into a striving, a striving which receives indeed its impulse and a repeated renewal from the decisive passion of the infinite, but is nevertheless a striving.

When subjectivity is the truth, the conceptual determination of the truth must include an expression for the antithesis to objectivity, a memento of the fork in the road where the way swings off; this expression will at the same time serve as an indication of the tension of the subjective inwardness. Here is such a definition of truth: *An objective uncertainty held fast in an appropriation-process of the most passionate inwardness is the truth*, the highest truth attainable for an *existing* individual. At the point where the way swings off (and where this is cannot be specified objectively, since it is a matter of subjectivity), there objective knowledge is placed in abeyance. Thus the subject merely has, objectively, the uncertainty; but it is this which precisely increases the tension of that infinite passion which constitutes his inwardness. The truth is precisely the venture which chooses an objective uncertainty with the passion of the infinite. I contemplate the order of nature in the hope of finding God, and I see omnipotence and wisdom; but I also see much else that disturbs my mind and excites anxiety. The sum of all this is an objective uncertainty. But it is for this very reason that the inwardness becomes as intense as it is, for it embraces this objective uncertainty with the entire passion of the infinite. In the case of a mathematical proposition the objectivity is given, but for this reason the truth of such a proposition is also an indifferent truth.

But the above definition of truth is an equivalent expression for faith. Without risk there is no faith. Faith is precisely the contradiction between the infinite passion of the individual's inwardness and the objective uncertainty. If I am capable of grasping God objectively, I do not believe, but precisely because I cannot do this I must believe. If I wish to preserve myself in faith I must constantly be intent upon holding fast the objective uncertainty, so as to remain out upon the deep, over seventy thousand fathoms of water, still preserving my faith.

In the principle that subjectivity, inwardness, is the truth, there is comprehended the Socratic wisdom, whose everlasting merit it was to have become aware of the essential significance of existence, of the fact that the knower is an existing individual. For this reason Socrates was in the truth by virtue of his ignorance, in the highest sense in which this was possible within paganism. To attain to an understanding of this, to comprehend that the misfortune of speculative philosophy is again and again to have forgotten that the knower is an existing individual, is in our objective age difficult enough. "But to have made an advance upon Socrates without even having understood what he understood, is at any rate not "Socratic."

17

Friedrich Nietzsche, "On Truth and Lies in a Nonmoral Sense"

Introduction

Kant, we saw in II.12, regarded himself as securing the possibility of objective knowledge in arguing that certain things must be true of objects of experience in order for them to be experienced. Many of his contemporaries and successors, however, were more impressed – and sometimes depressed – by his admission that this knowledge only encompasses objects as experienced – "appearances" or "phenomena" – and not "things in themselves" or "noumena" (things considered apart from the epistemic conditions under which alone we can encounter them). This was the attitude, for example, of Arthur Schopenhauer (II.15) and of a young German Professor of Philology at Basel whom Schopenhauer had profoundly influenced, Friedrich Nietzsche (1844–1900).

In the remarkable essay of 1873 that follows – one whose insight has only been recently appreciated – Nietzsche subscribes to Kant's distinction between appearances and things in themselves and to his insistence on the unknowability of the latter. Nietzsche concludes, however, that there

From Friedrich Nietzsche, *Philosophy and Truth: Selections from Nietzsche's Notebooks of the Early 1870s*, ed. and trans. D. Breazeale. Atlantic Highlands, NJ: Humanities Press International, 1990, pp. 79–91, 93– 4, 97 (some notes and passages omitted; asterisked notes are the translator's).

can therefore be no truth or knowledge, as these are standardly understood – namely, in terms of agreement or correspondence with how things really are "apart from man." As he succinctly put it in an earlier note, "if Kant is right, then the sciences are wrong,"[1] since scientific claims purport to be true of an independent reality, not a merely "anthropomorphic" world. Since we are condemned to skepticism toward claims about that independent reality, there is no reason, Nietzsche holds, to regard these as anything but "lies" (in a "non-moral" sense). Where Kant, then, accentuates the positive (our knowledge of appearances), Nietzsche accentuates the negative (the gap between this and "real" knowledge).

There are two further, and perhaps more substantial, differences between the two philosophers. First, whereas for Kant the synthetic *a priori* principles presupposed by experience are fixed, universal principles of cognition, for Nietzsche the explanation of our compulsion to accept, say, the laws of logic or physics is a "naturalistic" one, in terms of our specifically human drives, interests and "welfare." Creatures with different drives, etc. would be under no similar compulsion to accept those laws.

Second and relatedly, Nietzsche emphasizes, in a manner Kant never did, the pivotal role of language in shaping our concepts and beliefs. "Logic," he writes, "is merely slavery within the fetters of language." Had we developed a very different language, we would have arrived at a correspondingly different logic. And we might

very well have developed a very different language, for there is arbitrariness and contingency
in our linguistic, and hence conceptual, categor-
izations. In the most famous part of the essay,
Nietzsche argues that language is essentially metaphorical – the result, in one case after another, of
applying a single word to things which may be quite
unalike. So-called truths, therefore, are themselves metaphors, but ones so well established
that we have forgotten this fact. (Quotation of the
description of truth as "a movable host of metaphors" is almost de rigueur for the postmodernists
Nietzsche has so decisively influenced.)[2]

Language plays a further important role in
Nietzsche's essay. Although, in a sense, all our
statements may be "lies," Nietzsche allows –
indeed, stresses – a workaday distinction between
truth and falsity, between knowledge and error. It
is crucial, if human beings are to "exist socially"
and so satisfy various needs, that they agree with
one another on many matters, including especially the "designations" they give to things for
purposes of communication and cooperation. In
the workaday sense, people speak truthfully when
they give to a thing its agreed, conventional designation. Here we find a very early version of that
understanding of truth and knowledge as products
of public agreement or consensus that was to
become familiar in the twentieth century.

Commentators differ as to how much of
Nietzsche's position in this early essay remains in
his later writings. Certainly he was to give up the
Kantian distinction between appearances and
things-in-themselves, and hence the kind of skep-

ticism which presupposes that distinction. But the
ideas seem to remain that workable notions of truth
and knowledge must be understood in terms of our
species-specific needs and drives (both biological
and social), that language decisively shapes our concepts and beliefs, and that allegedly *a priori* principles of judgment are simply ones "which must
be believed to be true, for the sake of the preservation of creatures like ourselves."[3]

(N.B. The passages following the essay proper are
from Nietzsche's sketch of proposed additions
to it.)

Notes

1 F. Nietzsche, "The Philosopher," in *Philosophy and Truth*, ed. and trans. D. Breazeale,
   p. 32.
2 See, e.g., P. de Man, *Allegories of Reading*,
   New Haven, CT: Yale University Press, 1979,
   pp. 103ff. For a contrasting interpretation, see
   M. Clark, *Nietzsche on Truth and Philosophy*,
   Cambridge: Cambridge University Press,
   1990, pp. 63ff.
3 F. Nietzsche, *Beyond Good and Evil*, §11, in
   Basic Writings of Nietzsche, trans. W.
   Kaufmann, New York: Modern Library, 1968,
   p. 209. For different accounts of the relation
   of "On Truth and Lies" to Nietzsche's later work,
   see: M. Clark, *Nietzsche on Truth and Philosophy*; and Peter Poellner, *Nietzsche and
   Metaphysics*, Oxford: Clarendon Press, 1995.

Nietzsche, "On Truth and Lies in a Nonmoral Sense"

1

Once upon a time, in some out of the way corner of that universe which is dispersed into
numberless twinkling solar systems, there was a
star upon which clever beasts invented knowing.
That was the most arrogant and mendacious
minute of "world history," but nevertheless, it
was only a minute. After nature had drawn a few
breaths, the star cooled and congealed, and the

clever beasts had to die. – One might invent such
a fable, and yet he still would not have adequately illustrated how miserable, how shadowy
and transient, how aimless and arbitrary the
human intellect looks within nature. There were
eternities during which it did not exist. And
when it is all over with the human intellect,
nothing will have happened. For this intellect
has no additional mission which would lead it
beyond human life. Rather, it is human, and
only its possessor and begetter takes it so
solemnly – as though the world's axis turned
within it. But if we could communicate with the

gnat, we would learn that he likewise flies through the air with the same solemnity, that he feels the flying center of the universe within himself. There is nothing so reprehensible and unimportant in nature that it would not immediately swell up like a balloon at the slightest puff of this power of knowing. And just as every porter wants to have an admirer, so even the proudest of men, the philosopher, supposes that he sees on all sides the eyes of the universe telescopically focused upon his action and thought.

It is remarkable that this was brought about by the intellect, which was certainly allotted to these most unfortunate, delicate, and ephemeral beings merely as a device for detaining them a minute within existence. For without this addition they would have every reason to flee this existence as quickly as Lessing's son [who died on the day of his birth]. The pride connected with knowing and sensing lies like a blinding fog over the eyes and senses of men, thus deceiving them concerning the value of existence. For this pride contains within itself the most flattering estimation of the value of knowing. Deception is the most general effect of such pride, but even its most particular effects contain within themselves something of the same deceitful character.

As a means for the preserving of the individual, the intellect unfolds its principal powers in dissimulation, which is the means by which weaker, less robust individuals preserve themselves – since they have been denied the chance to wage the battle for existence with horns or with the sharp teeth of beasts of prey. This art of dissimulation reaches its peak, in man. Deception, flattering, lying, deluding, talking behind the back, putting up a false front, living in borrowed splendor, wearing a mask, hiding behind convention, playing a role for others and for oneself – in short, a continuous fluttering around the *solitary* flame of vanity – is so much the rule and the law among men that there is almost nothing which is less comprehensible than how an honest and pure drive for truth could have arisen among them. They are deeply immersed in illusions and in dream images; their eyes merely glide over the surface of things and see "forms." Their senses nowhere lead to truth; on the contrary, they are content to receive stimuli and, as it were, to engage in a groping game on the backs of things. Moreover, man permits himself be deceived in his dreams every night of his life. His moral sentiment

does not even make an attempt to prevent this, whereas there are supposed to be men who have stopped snoring through sheer will power. What does man actually know about himself? Is he, indeed, ever able to perceive himself completely, as if laid out in a lighted display case? Does nature not conceal most things from him – even concerning his own body – in order to confine and lock him within a proud, deceptive consciousness, aloof from the coils of the bowels, the rapid flow of the blood stream, and the intricate quivering of the fibers! She threw away the key. And woe to that fatal curiosity which might one day have the power to peer out and down through a crack in the chamber of consciousness and then suspect that man is sustained in the indifference of his ignorance by that which is pitiless, greedy, insatiable, and murderous – as if hanging in dreams on the back of a tiger. Given this situation, where in the world could the drive for truth have come from?

Insofar as the individual wants to maintain himself against other individuals, he will under natural circumstances employ the intellect mainly for dissimulation. But at the same time, from boredom and necessity, man wishes to exist socially and with the herd; therefore, he needs to make peace and strives accordingly to banish from his world at least the most flagrant *bellum omni contra omnes*. This peace treaty brings in its wake something which appears to be the first step toward acquiring that puzzling truth drive: to wit, *that* which shall count as 'truth' from now on is established. That is to say, a uniformly valid and binding designation is invented for things, and this legislation of language likewise establishes the first laws of truth. For the contrast between truth and lie arises here for the first time. The liar is a person who uses the valid designations, the words, in order to make something which is unreal appear to be real. He says, for example, "I am rich," when the proper designation for his condition would be "poor." He misuses fixed conventions by means of arbitrary substitutions or even reversals of names. If he does this in a selfish and moreover harmful manner, society will cease to trust him and will thereby exclude him. What men avoid by excluding the liar is not so much being defrauded as it is being harmed by means of fraud. Thus, even at this stage, what they hate is basically not deception itself, but rather the unpleasant, hated consequences of certain sorts of deception. It is in a similarly restricted sense that man now wants nothing but truth: he desires the pleasant, life-preserving consequences of truth. He is indifferent toward pure knowledge which has no consequences; toward those truths which are possibly harmful and destructive he is even hostilely inclined. And besides, what about these linguistic conventions themselves? Are they perhaps products of knowledge, that is, of the sense of truth? Are designations congruent with things? Is language the adequate expression of all realities?

It is only by means of forgetfulness that man can ever reach the point of fancying himself to possess a "truth" of the grade just indicated. If he will not be satisfied with truth in the form of tautology, that is to say, if he will not be content with empty husks, then he will always exchange truths for illusions. What is a word? It is the copy in sound of a nerve stimulus. But the further inference from the nerve stimulus to a cause outside of us is already the result of a false and unjustifiable application of the principle of sufficient reason. If truth alone had been the deciding factor in the genesis of language, and if the standpoint of certainty had been decisive for designations, then how could we still dare to say "the stone is hard," as if "hard" were something otherwise familiar to us, and not merely a totally subjective stimulation! We separate things according to gender [in German], designating the tree as masculine and the plant as feminine. What arbitrary assignments! How far this oversteps the canons of certainty! We speak of a "snake": this designation touches only upon its ability to twist itself and could therefore also fit a worm. What arbitrary differentiations! What one-sided preferences, first for this, then for that property of a thing! The various languages placed side by side show that with words it is never a question of truth, never a question of adequate expression; otherwise, there would not be so many languages. The "thing in itself" (which is precisely what the pure truth, apart from any of its consequences, would be) is likewise something quite incomprehensible to the creator of language and something not in the least worth striving for. This creator only designates the relations of things to men, and for expressing these relations he lays hold of the boldest metaphors. To begin with, a nerve stimulus is transferred into an image:[1] first metaphor. The image, in turn, is

imitated in a sound: second metaphor. And each time there is a complete overleaping of one sphere, right into the middle of an entirely new and different one. One can imagine a man who is totally deaf and has never had a sensation of sound and music. Perhaps such a person will gaze with astonishment at Chladni's sound figures;[2] perhaps he will discover their causes in the vibrations of the string and will now swear that he must know what men mean by "sound." It is this way with all of us concerning language: we believe that we know something about the things themselves when we speak of trees, colors, snow, and flowers; and yet we possess nothing but metaphors for things – metaphors which correspond in no way to the original entities. In the same way that the sound appears as a sand figure, so the mysterious X of the thing in itself first appears as a nerve stimulus, then as an image, and finally as a sound. Thus the genesis of language does not proceed logically in any case, and all the material within and with which the man of truth, the scientist, and the philosopher later work and build, if not derived from never-never land, is at least not derived from the essence of things.

In particular, let us further consider the formation of concepts. Every word instantly becomes a concept precisely insofar as it is not supposed to serve as a reminder of the unique and entirely individual original experience to which it owes its origin; but rather, a word becomes a concept insofar as it simultaneously has to fit countless more or less similar cases – which means, purely and simply, cases which are never equal and thus altogether unequal. Every concept arises from the equation of unequal things. Just as it is certain that one leaf is never totally the same as another, so it is certain that the concept "leaf" is formed by arbitrarily discarding these individual differences and by forgetting the distinguishing aspects. This awakens the idea that, in addition to the leaves, there exists in nature the "leaf": the original model according to which all the leaves were perhaps woven, sketched, measured, colored, curled, and painted – but by incompetent hands, so that no specimen has turned out to be a correct, trustworthy, and faithful likeness of the original, model. We call a person "honest," and then we ask "why has he behaved so honestly today?" Our usual answer is, "on account of his honesty." Honesty! This in turn means that the leaf is the cause of the leaves. We know nothing whatsoever about an essential quality called "honesty"; but we do know of countless individualized and consequently unequal actions which we equate by omitting the aspects in which they are unequal and which we now designate as "honest" actions. Finally we formulate from them a *qualitas occulta* which has the name "honesty." We obtain the concept, as we do the form, by overlooking what is individual and actual; whereas nature is acquainted with no forms and no concepts, and likewise with no species, but only with an X which remains inaccessible and undefinable for us. For even our contrast between individual and species is something anthropomorphic and does not originate in the essence of things; although we should not presume to claim that this contrast does not correspond to the essence of things: that would of course be a dogmatic assertion and, as such, would be just as indemonstrable as its opposite.[3]

What then is truth? A movable host of metaphors, metonymies, and anthropomorphisms: in short, a sum of human relations which have been poetically and rhetorically intensified, transferred, and embellished, and which, after long usage, seem to a people to be fixed, canonical, and binding. Truths are illusions which we have forgotten are illusions; they are metaphors that have become worn out and have been drained of sensuous force, coins which have lost their embossing and are now considered as metal and no longer as coins.

We still do not yet know where the drive for truth comes from. For so far we have heard only of the duty which society imposes in order to exist: to be truthful means to employ the usual metaphors. Thus, to express it morally, this is the duty to lie according to a fixed convention, to lie with the herd and in a manner binding upon everyone. Now man of course forgets that this is the way things stand for him. Thus he lies in the manner indicated, unconsciously and in accordance with habits which are centuries old; and precisely *by means of this unconsciousness* and forgetfulness he arrives at his sense of truth. From the sense that one is obliged to designate one thing as "red," another as "cold," and a third as "mute," there arises a moral impulse in regard to truth. The venerability, reliability, and utility of truth is something which a person demonstrates for himself from the contrast with the liar, whom no one trusts and everyone excludes. As a "*rational*" being, he now places his behavior under the control of abstractions. He will no longer tolerate being carried away by sudden impressions, by intuitions. First he universalizes all these impressions into less colorful, cooler concepts, so that he can entrust the guidance of his life and conduct to them. Everything which distinguishes man from the animals depends upon this ability to volatilize perceptual metaphors in a schema, and thus to dissolve an image into a concept. For something is possible in the realm of these schemata which could never be achieved with the vivid first impressions: the construction of a pyramidal order according to castes and degrees, the creation of a new world of laws, privileges, subordinations, and clearly marked boundaries – a new world, one which now confronts that other vivid world of first impressions as more solid, more universal, better known, and more human than the immediately perceived world, and thus as the regulative and imperative world. Whereas each perceptual metaphor is individual and without equals and is therefore able to elude all classification, the great edifice of concepts displays the rigid regularity of a Roman columbarium* and exhales in logic that strength and coolness which is characteristic of mathematics. Anyone who has felt this cool breath [of logic] will hardly believe that even the concept – which is as bony, foursquare, and transposable as a die – is nevertheless merely the *residue of a metaphor*, and that the illusion which is involved in the artistic transference of a nerve stimulus into images is, if not the mother, then the grandmother of every single concept. But in this conceptual crap game "truth" means using every die in the designated manner, counting its spots accurately, fashioning the right categories, and never violating the order of caste and class rank. Just as the Romans and Etruscans cut up the heavens with rigid mathematical lines and confined a god within each of the spaces thereby delimited, as within a *templum*,† so every people has a similarly mathematically divided conceptual heaven above themselves and henceforth thinks

---

* A columbarium is a vault with niches for funeral urns containing the ashes of cremated bodies.
† A delimited space restricted to a particular purpose, especially a religiously sanctified area.

that truth demands that each conceptual god be sought only within *his own* sphere. Here one may certainly admire man as a mighty genius of construction, who succeeds in piling up an infinitely complicated dome of concepts upon an unstable foundation, and, as it were, on running water. Of course, in order to be supported by such a foundation, his construction must be like one constructed of spiders' webs: delicate enough to be carried along by the waves, strong enough not to be blown apart by every wind. As a genius of construction man raises himself far above the bee in the following way: whereas the bee builds with wax that he gathers from nature, man builds with the far more delicate conceptual material which he first has to manufacture from himself. In this he is greatly to be admired, but not on account of his drive for truth or for pure knowledge of things. When someone hides something behind a bush and looks for it again in the same place and finds it there as well, there is not much to praise in such seeking and finding. Yet this is how matters stand regarding seeking and finding "truth" within the realm of reason. If I make up the definition of a mammal, and then, after inspecting a camel, declare "look, a mammal," I have indeed brought a truth to light in this way, but it is a truth of limited value. That is to say, it is a thoroughly anthropomorphic truth which contains not a single point which would be "true in itself" or really and universally valid apart from man. At bottom, what the investigator of such truths is seeking is only the metamorphosis of the world into man. He strives to understand the world as something analogous to man, and at best he achieves by his struggles the feeling of assimilation. Similar to the way in which astrologers considered the stars to be in man's service and connected with his happiness and sorrow, such an investigator considers the entire universe in connection with man: the entire universe as the infinitely fractured echo of one original sound – man; the entire universe as the infinitely multiplied copy of one original picture – man. His method is to treat man as the measure of all things, but in doing so he again proceeds from the error of believing that he has these things [which he intends to measure] immediately before him as mere objects. He forgets that the original perceptual metaphors are metaphors and takes them to be the things themselves.

Only by forgetting this primitive world of metaphor can one live with any repose, security, and consistency: only by means of the petrification and coagulation of a mass of images which originally streamed from the primal faculty of human imagination like a fiery liquid, only in the invincible faith that *this* sun, *this* window, *this* table is a truth in itself, in short, only by forgetting that he himself is an *artistically creating* subject, does man live with any repose, security, and consistency. If but for an instant he could escape from the prison walls of this faith, his "self consciousness" would be immediately destroyed. It is even a difficult thing for him to admit to himself that the insect or the bird perceives an entirely different world from the one that man does, and that the question of which of these perceptions of the world is the more correct one is quite meaningless, for this would have to have been decided previously in accordance with the criterion of the *correct perception*, which means, in accordance with a criterion which is *not available*. But in any case it seems to me that "the correct perception" – which would mean "the adequate expression of an object in the subject" – is a contradictory impossibility. For between two absolutely different spheres, as between subject and object, there is no causality, no correctness, and no expression; there is, at most, an *aesthetic* relation: I mean, a suggestive transference, a stammering translation into a completely foreign tongue – for which there is required, in any case, a freely inventive intermediate sphere and mediating force. "Appearance" is a word that contains many temptations, which is why I avoid it as much as possible. For it is not true that the essence of things "appears" in the empirical world. A painter without hands who wished to express in song the picture before his mind would, by means of this substitution of spheres, still reveal more about the essence of things than does the empirical world. Even the relationship of a nerve stimulus to the generated image is not a necessary one. But when the same image has been generated millions of times and has been handed down for many generations and finally appears on the same occasion every time for all mankind, then it acquires at last the same meaning for men it would have if it were the sole necessary image and if the relationship of the original nerve stimulus to the generated image were a strictly causal one. In the same manner, an eternally repeated dream would certainly be felt and judged to be reality. But the hardening and congealing of a metaphor guarantees absolutely nothing concerning its necessity and exclusive justification.

Every person who is familiar with such considerations has no doubt felt a deep mistrust of all idealism of this sort: just as often as he has quite clearly convinced himself of the eternal consistency, omnipresence, and infallibility of the laws of nature. He has concluded that so far as we can penetrate here – from the telescopic heights to the microscopic depths – everything is secure, complete, infinite, regular, and without any gaps. Science will be able to dig successfully in this shaft forever, and all the things that are discovered will harmonize with and not contradict each other. How little does this resemble a product of the imagination, for if it were such, there should be some place where the illusion and unreality can be divined. Against this, the following must be said: if each of us had a different kind of sense perception – if we could only perceive things now as a bird, now as a worm, now as a plant, or if one of us saw a stimulus as red, another as blue, while a third even heard the same stimulus as a sound – then no one would speak of such a regularity of nature, rather, nature would be grasped only as a creation which is subjective in the highest degree. After all, what is a law of nature as such for us? We are not acquainted with it in itself, but only with its effects, which means in its relation to other laws of nature – which, in turn, are known to us only as sums of relations. Therefore all these relations always refer again to others and are thoroughly incomprehensible to us in their essence. All that we actually know about these laws of nature is what we ourselves bring to them – time and space, and therefore relationships of succession and number. But everything marvelous about the laws of nature, everything that quite astonishes us therein and seems to demand our explanation, everything that might lead us to distrust idealism: all this is completely and solely contained within the mathematical strictness and inviolability of our representations of time and space. But we produce these representations in and from ourselves with the same necessity with which the spider spins.[4] If we are forced to comprehend all things only under these forms, then it ceases to be amazing that in all things we actually comprehend nothing but these forms. For they must all bear within themselves the laws of number, and it is precisely number which is most astonishing in things. All that conformity to law, which impresses us so much in the movement of the stars and in chemical processes, coincides at bottom with those properties which we bring to things. Thus it is we who impress ourselves in this way. In conjunction with this, it of course follows that the artistic process of metaphor formation with which every sensation begins in us already presupposes these forms and thus occurs within them. The only way in which the possibility of subsequently constructing a new conceptual edifice from metaphors themselves can be explained is by the firm persistence of these original forms. That is to say, this conceptual edifice is an imitation of temporal, spatial, and numerical relationships in the domain of metaphor.

2

We have seen how it is originally *language* which works on the construction of concepts, a labor taken over in later ages by *science*. Just as the bee simultaneously constructs cells and fills them with honey, so science works unceasingly on this great columbarium of concepts, the graveyard of perceptions. It is always building new, higher stories and shoring up, cleaning, and renovating the old cells; above all, it takes pains to fill up this monstrously towering framework and to arrange therein the entire empirical world, which is to say, the anthropomorphic world. Whereas the man of action binds his life to reason and its concepts so that he will not be swept away and lost, the scientific investigator builds his hut right next to the tower of science so that he will be able to work on it and to find shelter for himself beneath those bulwarks which presently exist. And he requires shelter, for there are frightful powers which continuously break in upon him, powers which oppose scientific "truth" with completely different kinds of "truths" which bear on their shields the most varied sorts of emblems.

The drive toward the formation of metaphors is the fundamental human drive, which one cannot for a single instant dispense with in thought, for one would thereby dispense with man himself. This drive is not truly vanquished and scarcely subdued by the fact that a regular and rigid new world is constructed as its prison from its own ephemeral products, the concepts. It seeks a new realm and another channel for its activity, and it finds this in *myth* and in *art* generally. This drive continually confuses the conceptual categories and cells by bringing forward new transferences, metaphors, and metonymies. It continually manifests an ardent desire to refashion the world which presents itself to waking man, so that it will be as colorful, irregular, lacking in results and coherence, charming, and eternally new as the world of dreams. Indeed, it is only by means of the rigid and regular web of concepts that the waking man clearly sees that he is awake; and it is precisely because of this that he sometimes thinks that he must be dreaming when this web of concepts is torn by art. Pascal is right in maintaining that if the same dream came to us every night we would be just as occupied with it as we are with the things that we see every day. "If a workman were sure to dream for twelve straight hours every night that he was king," said Pascal, "I believe that he would be just as happy as a king who dreamt for twelve hours every night that he was a workman."* In fact, because of the way that myth takes it for granted that miracles are always happening, the waking life of a mythically inspired people – the Ancient Greeks, for instance – more closely resembles a dream than it does the waking world of a scientifically disenchanted thinker. When every tree can suddenly speak as a nymph, when a god in the shape of a bull can drag away maidens, when even the goddess Athena herself is suddenly seen in the company of Peisastratus driving through the market place of Athens with a beautiful team of horses – and this is what the honest Athenian believed – then, as in a dream, anything is possible at each moment, and all of nature swarms around man as if it were nothing but a masquerade of the gods, who were merely amusing themselves by deceiving men in all these shapes.

But man has an invincible inclination to allow himself to be deceived and is, as it were, enchanted with happiness when the rhapsodist tells him epic fables as if they were true, or when the actor in the theater acts more royally than any

* *Pensées*, number 386. Actually, Pascal says that the workman would be "almost as happy" as the king in this case!

real king. So long as it is able to deceive without *injuring*, that master of deception, the intellect, is free; it is released from its former slavery and celebrates its Saturnalia. It is never more luxuriant, richer, prouder, more clever and more daring. With creative pleasure it throws metaphors into confusion and displaces the boundary stones of abstractions, so that, for example, it designates the stream as "the moving path which carries man where he would otherwise walk." The intellect has now thrown the token of bondage from itself. At other times it endeavors, with gloomy officiousness, to show the way and to demonstrate the tools to a poor individual who covets existence; it is like a servant who goes in search of booty and prey for his master. But now it has become the master and it dares to wipe from its face the expression of indigence. In comparison with its previous conduct, everything that it now does bears the mark of dissimulation, just as that previous conduct did of distortion. The free intellect copies human life, but it considers this life to be something good and seems to be quite satisfied with it. That immense framework and planking of concepts to which the needy man clings his whole life long in order to preserve himself is nothing but a scaffolding and toy for the most audacious feats of the liberated intellect. And when it smashes this framework to pieces, throws it into confusion, and puts it back together in an ironic fashion, pairing the most alien things and separating the closest, it is demonstrating that it has no need of these makeshifts of indigence and that it will now be guided by intuitions rather than by concepts. There is no regular path which leads from these intuitions into the land of ghostly schemata, the land of abstractions. There exists no word for these intuitions; when man sees them he grows dumb, or else he speaks only in forbidden metaphors and in unheard-of combinations of concepts. He does this so that by shattering and mocking the old conceptual barriers he may at least correspond creatively to the impression of the powerful present intuition.

There are ages in which the rational man and the intuitive man stand side by side, the one in fear of intuition, the other with scorn for abstraction. The latter is just as irrational as the former is inartistic. They both desire to rule over life: the former, by knowing how to meet his principle needs by means of foresight, prudence, and regularity; the latter, by disregarding these needs and, as an "overjoyed hero," counting as real only that life which has been disguised as illusion and beauty. Whenever, as was perhaps the case in Ancient Greece, the intuitive man handles his weapons more authoritatively and victoriously than his opponent, then, under favorable circumstances, a culture can take shape and art's mastery over life can be established. All the manifestations of such a life will be accompanied by this dissimulation, this disavowal of indigence, this glitter of metaphorical intuitions, and, in general, this immediacy of deception: neither the house, nor the gait, nor the clothes, nor the clay jugs give evidence of having been invented because of a pressing need. It seems as if they were all intended to express an exalted happiness, an Olympian cloudlessness, and, as it were, a playing with seriousness. The man who is guided by concepts and abstractions only succeeds by such means in warding off misfortune, without ever gaining any happiness for himself from these abstractions. And while he aims for the greatest possible freedom from pain, the intuitive man, standing in the midst of a culture, already reaps from his intuition a harvest of continually inflowing illumination, cheer, and redemption – in addition to obtaining a defense against misfortune. To be sure, he suffers more intensely, *when* he suffers; he even suffers more frequently, since he does not understand how to learn from experience and keeps falling over and over again into the same ditch. He is then just as irrational in sorrow as he is in happiness: he cries aloud and will not be consoled. How differently the stoical man who learns from experience and governs himself by concepts is affected by the same misfortunes! This man, who at other times seeks nothing but sincerity, truth, freedom from deception, and protection against ensnaring surprise attacks, now executes a masterpiece of deception: he executes his masterpiece of deception in misfortune, as the other type of man executes his in times of happiness. He wears no quivering and changeable human face, but, as it were, a mask with dignified, symmetrical features. He does not cry; he does not even alter his voice. When a real storm cloud thunders above him, he wraps himself in his cloak, and with slow steps he walks from beneath it.

Drafts

177

[. . .] Truthfulness, considered as the foundation of all utterances and the presupposition for the maintenance of the human species, is a eudaemonic demand,* a demand which is opposed by the knowledge that the supreme welfare of men depends to a far greater extent upon *illusions*. Consequently, according to the eudaemonean principle, both truth *and lies* must be utilized – which is also the way it happens. [. . .]

[. . .] Analysis of the *belief in truth*: for all possession of truth is at bottom nothing but a belief that one possesses truth. The pathos, the feeling of duty, proceeds from *this belief*, not from the alleged truth. This belief in truth presupposes that the individual has an unconditional *power of knowledge*, as well as the conviction that no knowing being will ever have a greater power of knowledge; hence the belief in truth presupposes that the duty to speak the truth is binding upon all other knowing beings. The *relation* suspends the pathos of belief, that is to say, the human limitation, with the skeptical supposition that we are perhaps all in error.

But how is *skepticism* possible? It appears to be the truly *ascetic* standpoint of thought. For it does not believe in belief and thereby destroys everything that prospers by means of belief.

But even skepticism contains a belief: the belief in logic. Therefore what is most extreme is the surrender of logic, the *credo quia absurdum est*:† doubt concerning reason and thereby its negation. How this occurs as a consequence of asceticism. No one can *live* within such a denial of reason, no more than within pure asceticism. This demonstrates that belief in logic and belief as such is necessary for life, and consequently, that the realm of thinking is eudaemonic. But of course when life and eudaemonia are counted as arguments, then the demand for lies stands out in bold relief. Skepticism turns against the forbidden truth. There then remains no foundation

* I.e. a demand connected with the desire for human happiness.
† "I believe it because it is absurd"; a famous saying attributed to Tertullian (c. 160–220).

for pure truth in itself; the drive thereto is merely a disguised eudaemonistic drive.

Every natural process is fundamentally inexplicable to us. All we do in each case is to identify the setting in which the actual drama unfolds. Thus we speak of causality when we really see nothing but a succession of events. That this succession must always occur in a particular setting is a belief which is refuted with endless frequency.

Logic is merely slavery within the fetters of language. But language includes within itself an illogical element: metaphor, etc. The initial power produces an equation between things that are unequal, and is thus an operation of the imagination. The existence of concepts, forms, etc. is based upon this.

184

[...] Pure disinterested contemplation is possible only in regard to illusions which have been recognized as illusions, illusions which have no desire to entice us into belief and to this extent do not stimulate our wills at all.

Only a person who could contemplate the entire world *as an illusion* would be in a position to view it apart from desires and drives: the artist and the philosopher. Here instinctive drive comes to an end.

So long as one seeks the *truth* about the world he remains under the control of the drives. But he who desires *pleasure* rather than truth will desire the belief in truth, and consequently the pleasurable effects of this belief.

The world as an illusion: saint, artist, philosopher.

185

All eudaemonic drives awaken belief in the truth of things, in the truth of the world. Thus science in its entirety is directed toward becoming and not toward being.

187

I.   Truth as a cloak for quite different impulses and drives.
II. The pathos of truth is based upon belief.
III. The drive to lie is fundamental.
IV. Truth cannot be recognized. Everything which is knowable is illusion. The significance of art as truthful illusion.

Notes

1 Nietzsche's employment of the term "metaphor" takes seriously its original Greek sense of "transference." His general point is that, in the process which leads from things' impact upon our sensory organs to the formation of concepts, a number of "transfers" or transpositions – physiological, perceptual, linguistic – take place.

2 These are patterns in sand caused by sound vibrations.

3 Here Nietzsche is disagreeing with Kant, who *did* deny that our "anthropomorphic" conceptions can correspond to "the essence of things" in themselves.

4 Here Nietzsche follows Kant and Schopenhauer in holding that space and time are forms of perception, not features of reality in itself.

Charles S. Peirce, "Some Consequences of Four Incapacities" (excerpt) and "The Fixation of Belief"

Introduction

For much of the last century, the reputation and importance of the American philosopher Charles Sanders Peirce (1839–1914) were rather eclipsed by those of his younger pragmatist followers, William James (1842–1910) and John Dewey (1859–1952). More recently, however, and especially among epistemologists, Peirce is increasingly recognized as an original and radical critic of traditional approaches and a main inspiration for ideas, like that of "fallibilism," which loom large in contemporary discussion.[1]

Although he is generally referred to as "the founder of pragmatism," Peirce's position is far removed from the brand of humanistic anti-realism associated with that label by, for example, Richard Rorty.[2] Indeed, Peirce himself was so dismayed by James's deviation from the realist principle that the nature of things is "entirely independent of our opinions about them" that he disowned the "pragmatist" tag for fear of being associated with James. The issue of realism apart, however, it is clear even from the early piece on the "Four Incapacities" (1868) why Peirce is standardly classed as a pragmatist. For here, in the opening pages one finds, in brisk order,

From Charles S. Peirce, *Selected Writings*, ed. P. Wiener. New York: Dover, 1966, pp. 39–41, 92–112 (some notes and passages omitted; asterisked notes are the editor's).

some characteristically "practical" objections to Cartesian epistemology. The Cartesian merely pretends to cast doubt on all our beliefs; he or she ignores the social character of knowledge, within communities of enquirers; and fails to recognize that science's success depends, not on the certainty of its component claims and arguments, but on their holding together like the intertwined fibers in a strong cable.

In the later essay, "The Fixation of Belief" (1877), Peirce's pragmatism is on view in the attention which he, like Nietzsche during the same decade (see II.17 above), pays to the practical role which beliefs play in life. A belief is a guide to actions performed in order to "satisfy our desires," and something we are impelled to "fix" so as to escape from "irritating" and stultifying states of doubt. With belief understood in these terms, however, a serious question is raised (§V) which it is the main aim of the essay to address. Surely there are plenty of ways, other than rational scientific enquiry, whereby we can "fix" our beliefs – by letting political or divine authority decide for us, for example, or by indulging in metaphysical tastes. If these alternatives were equally effective in terms of enabling the satisfaction of desires, how could we prefer to engage in scientific enquiry?

Peirce cannot, without qualification, reply that only scientific method reliably leads to true beliefs, since he characterizes truth, as much as belief, in terms of "tend[ing] to satisfy desires." Perhaps the most interesting answers Peirce offers to his own question are the following. First, only by "fixing" beliefs according to scientific enquiry is justice done to the public character of belief. A person does not hold beliefs in isolation, but as a member of a community or, at any rate, of the human race. Each person will, therefore, be aware of conflicts between his or her own beliefs and those of other people: and, unless people are entirely ostrich-like, these conflicts will make them question their own beliefs and seek for consensus. It is Peirce's view that scientific enquiry has already proven itself by far the most effective procedure for approximating to relatively stable consensus. Second, Peirce contends, only scientific enquiry among the alternative ways of "fixing" beliefs is inspired by, and faithful to, a conviction that surely everyone at least implicitly feels. This is the realist conviction that there is a way "things really are," one which obtains quite independently of our opinions and to which we should seek to make our beliefs conform.

Both of these Peircean answers to his own question are contentious. Maybe scientific enquiry is not the most effective route toward stable consensus, and maybe it does not presuppose any realist commitment. But they are answers that no contemporary epistemologist could, or would want to, ignore.

Notes

1   For an excellent discussion of Peirce's general philosophy and his influence, see C. Hookway, *Peirce*, London: Routledge & Kegan Paul, 1985.
2   For a defense of Peircean pragmatism against such later interpretations of pragmatism, see S. Haack, *Evidence and Inquiry: Towards Reconstruction in Epistemology*, Oxford: Blackwell, 1993, Chapter 9.

Peirce, "Some Consequences of Four Incapacities"

Descartes is the father of modern philosophy, and the spirit of Cartesianism – that which principally distinguishes it from the scholasticism which it displaced – may be compendiously stated as follows:

1.   It teaches that philosophy must begin with universal doubt; whereas scholasticism had never questioned fundamentals.

2.   It teaches that the ultimate test of certainty is to be found in the individual consciousness; whereas scholasticism had rested on the testimony of sages and of the Catholic Church.

3.   The multiform argumentation of the Middle Ages is replaced by a single thread of inference depending often upon inconspicuous premises.

4.   Scholasticism had its mysteries of faith, but undertook to explain all created things. But there are many facts which Cartesianism not only does not explain but renders absolutely inexplicable, unless to say that "God makes them so" is to be regarded as an explanation.

In some, or all of these respects, most modern philosophers have been, in effect, Cartesians.

Now without wishing to return to scholasticism, it seems to me that modern science and modern logic require us to stand upon a very different platform from this.

1.   We cannot begin with complete doubt. We must begin with all the prejudices which we actually have when we enter upon the study of philosophy. These prejudices are not to be dispelled by a maxim, for they are things which it does not occur to us *can* be questioned. Hence this initial skepticism will be a mere self-deception, and not real doubt; and no one who follows the Cartesian method will ever be satisfied until he has formally recovered all those beliefs which in form he has given up. It is, therefore, as useless a preliminary as going to the North Pole would be in order to get to Constantinople by coming down regularly upon a meridian. A person may, it is true, in the course of his studies, find reason to doubt what he began by believing; but in that case he doubts because he has a positive reason for it, and not on account of the Cartesian maxim. Let us not pretend to doubt in philosophy what we do not doubt in our hearts.

2.   The same formalism appears in the Cartesian criterion, which amounts to this: "Whatever I am clearly convinced of, is true." If I were

really convinced, I should have done with reasoning and should require no test of certainty. But thus to make single individuals absolute judges of truth is most pernicious. The result is that metaphysicians will all agree that metaphysics has reached a pitch of certainty far beyond that of the physical sciences – only they can agree upon nothing else. In sciences in which men come to agreement, when a theory has been broached it is considered to be on probation until this agreement is reached. After it is reached, the question of certainty becomes an idle one, because there is no one left who doubts it. We individually cannot reasonably hope to attain the ultimate philosophy which we pursue; we can only seek it, therefore, for the *community* of philosophers. Hence, if disciplined and candid minds carefully examine a theory and refuse to accept it, this ought to create doubts in the mind of the author of the theory himself.

3.   Philosophy ought to imitate the successful sciences in its methods, so far as to proceed only from tangible premises which can be subjected to careful scrutiny, and to trust rather to the multitude and variety of its arguments than to the conclusiveness of any one. Its reasoning should not form a chain which is no stronger than its weakest link, but a cable whose fibers may be ever so slender, provided they are sufficiently numerous and intimately connected.

4.   Every unidealistic philosophy supposes some absolutely inexplicable, unanalyzable ultimate; in short, something resulting from mediation itself not susceptible of mediation. Now that anything *is* thus inexplicable can only be known by reasoning from, signs. But the only justification of an inference from signs is that the conclusion explains the fact. To suppose the fact absolutely inexplicable is not to explain it, and hence this supposition is never allowable. [. . .]

Peirce, "The Fixation of Belief"

I

Few persons care to study logic, because everybody conceives himself to be proficient enough in the art of reasoning already. But I observe that this satisfaction is limited to one's own ratiocination, and does not extend to that of other men.

We come to the full possession of our power of drawing inferences the last of all our faculties, for it is not so much a natural gift as a long and difficult art. The history of its practice would make a grand subject for a book. The mediæval schoolman, following the Romans, made logic the earliest of a boy's studies after grammar, as being very easy. So it was as they understood it. Its fundamental principle, according to them, was that all knowledge rests on either authority or reason; but that whatever is deduced by reason depends ultimately on a premise derived from authority. Accordingly, as soon as a boy was perfect in the syllogistic procedure, his intellectual kit of tools was held to be complete.

To Roger Bacon, that remarkable mind who in the middle of the thirteenth century was almost a scientific man, the schoolmen's conception of reasoning appeared only an obstacle to truth. He saw that experience alone teaches anything – a proposition which to us seems easy to understand, because a distinct conception of experience has been handed down to us from former generations; which to him also seemed perfectly clear, because its difficulties had not yet unfolded themselves. Of all kinds of experience, the best, he thought, was interior illumination, which teaches many things about nature which the external senses could never discover, such as the transubstantiation of bread.

Four centuries later, the more celebrated [Francis] Bacon, in the first book of his *Novum Organum*, gave his clear account of experience as something which must be opened to verification and re-examination. But, superior as Lord Bacon's conception is to earlier notions, a modern reader who is not in awe of his grandiloquence is chiefly struck by the inadequacy of his view of scientific procedure. That we have only to make some crude experiments, to draw up briefs of the results in certain blank forms, to go through these by rule, checking off everything disproved and setting down the alternatives, and that thus in a few years physical science would be finished up – what an idea! "He wrote on science like a Lord Chancellor,"* indeed, as Harvey, a genuine man of science, said.

The early scientists, Copernicus, Tycho Brahe, Kepler, Galileo, Harvey, and Gilbert, had

* Cf. J. Aubrey's *Brief Lives* (Oxford, ed. 1898), I, 299.

methods more like those of their modern brethren. Kepler undertook to draw a curve through the places of Mars; and his greatest service to science was in impressing on men's minds that this was the thing to be done if they wished to improve astronomy; that they were not to content themselves with inquiring whether one system of epicycles was better than another but that they were to sit down by the figures and find out what the curve, in truth, was. He accomplished this by his incomparable energy and courage, blundering along in the most inconceivable way (to us), from one irrational hypothesis to another, until, after trying twenty-two of these, he fell, by the mere exhaustion of his invention, upon the orbit which a mind well furnished with the weapons of modern logic would have tried almost at the outset.

In the same way, every work of science great enough to be remembered for a few generations affords some exemplification of the defective state of the art of reasoning of the time when it was written; and each chief step in science has been a lesson in logic. It was so when Lavoisier and his contemporaries took up the study of Chemistry. The old chemist's maxim had been *Lege, lege, lege, labora, ora, et relege.* Lavoisier's method was not to read and pray, not to dream that some long and complicated chemical process would have a certain effect, to put it into practice with dull patience, after its inevitable failure to dream that with some modification it would have another result, and to end by publishing the last dream as a fact: his way was to carry his mind into his laboratory, and to make of his alembics and cucurbits instruments of thought, giving a new conception of reasoning as something which was to be done with one's eyes open, by manipulating real things instead of words and fancies.

The Darwinian controversy is, in large part, a question of logic. Mr. Darwin proposed to apply the statistical method to biology. The same thing has been done in a widely different branch of science, the theory of gases. Though unable to say what the movement of any particular molecule of gas would be on a certain hypothesis regarding the constitution of this class of bodies, Clausius and Maxwell were yet able, by the application of the doctrine of probabilities, to predict that in the long run such and such a proportion of the molecules would, under given circumstances, acquire such and such velocities; that there would

take place, every second, such and such a number of collisions, etc.; and from these propositions they were able to deduce certain properties of gases, especially in regard to their heat-relations. In like manner, Darwin, while unable to say what the operation of variation and natural selection in every individual case will be, demonstrates that in the long run they will adapt animals to their circumstances. Whether or not existing animal forms are due to such action, or what position the theory ought to take, forms the subject of a discussion in which questions of fact and questions of logic are curiously interlaced.

II

The object of reasoning is to find out, from the consideration of what we already know, something else which we do not know. Consequently, reasoning is good if it be such as to give a true conclusion from true premises, and not otherwise. Thus, the question of validity is purely one of fact and not of thinking. A being the premises and B being the conclusion, the question is, whether these facts are really so related that if A is B is. If so, the inference is valid; if not, not. It is not in the least the question whether, when the premises are accepted by the mind, we feel an impulse to accept the conclusion also. It is true that we do generally reason correctly by nature. But that is an accident; the true conclusion would remain true if we had no impulse to accept it; and the false one would remain false, though we could not resist the tendency to believe in it.

We are, doubtless, in the main logical animals, but we are not perfectly so. Most of us, for example, are naturally more sanguine and hopeful than logic would justify. We seem to be so constituted that in the absence of any facts to go upon we are happy and self-satisfied; so that the effect of experience is continually to counteract our hopes and aspirations. Yet a lifetime of the application of this corrective does not usually eradicate our sanguine disposition. Where hope is unchecked by any experience, it is likely that our optimism is extravagant. Logicality in regard to practical matters is the most useful quality an animal can possess, and might, therefore, result from the action of natural selection; but outside of these it is probably of more advantage to the animal to have his mind filled with pleasing and encouraging visions, independently of their truth; and thus, upon unpractical subjects, natural selection might occasion a fallacious tendency of thought.

That which determines us, from given premises, to draw one inference rather than another is some habit of mind, whether it be constitutional or acquired. The habit is good or otherwise, according as it produces true conclusions from true premises or not; and an inference is regarded as valid or not, without reference to the truth or falsity of its conclusion specially, but according as the habit which determines it is such as to produce true conclusions in general or not. The particular habit of mind which governs this or that inference may be formulated in a proposition whose truth depends on the validity of the inferences which the habit determines; and such a formula is called a *guiding principle* of inference. Suppose, for example, that we observe that a rotating disk of copper quickly comes to rest when placed between the poles of a magnet, and we infer that this will happen with every disk of copper. The guiding principle is that what is true of one piece of copper is true of another. Such a guiding principle with regard to copper would be much safer than with regard to many other substances – brass, for example.

A book might be written to signalize all the most important of these guiding principles of reasoning. It would probably be, we must confess, of no service to a person whose thought is directed wholly to practical subjects, and whose activity moves along thoroughly beaten paths. The problems which present themselves to such a mind are matters of routine which he has learned once for all to handle in learning his business. But let a man venture into an unfamiliar field, or where his results are not continually checked by experience, and all history shows that the most masculine intellect will ofttimes lose his orientation and waste his efforts in directions which bring him no nearer to his goal, or even carry him entirely astray. He is like a ship on the open sea, with no one on board who understands the rules of navigation. And in such a case some general study of the guiding principles of reasoning would be sure to be found useful.

The subject could hardly be treated, however, without being first limited; since almost any fact may serve as a guiding principle. But it so happens that there exists a division among facts, such that in one class are all those which are absolutely essential as guiding principles, while in the other are all those which have any other interest as objects of research. This division is between those which are necessarily taken for granted in asking whether a certain conclusion follows from certain premises, and those which are not implied in that question. A moment's thought will show that a variety of facts are already assumed when the logical question is first asked. It is implied, for instance, that there are such states of mind as doubt and belief – that a passage from one to the other is possible, the object of thought remaining the same, and that this transition is subject to some rules which all minds are alike bound by. As these are facts which we must already know before we can have any clear conception of reasoning at all, it cannot be supposed to be any longer of much interest to inquire into their truth or falsity. On the other hand, it is easy to believe that those rules of reasoning which are deduced from the very idea of the process are the ones which are the most essential; and, indeed, that so long as it conforms to these it will, at least, not lead to false conclusions from true premises. In point of fact, the importance of what may be deduced from the assumptions involved in the logical question turns out to be greater than might be supposed, and this for reasons which it is difficult to exhibit at the outset. The only one which I shall here mention is that conceptions which are really products of logical reflections, without being readily seen to be so, mingle with our ordinary thoughts, and are frequently the causes of great confusion. This is the case, for example, with the conception of quality. A quality as such is never an object of observation. We can see that a thing is blue or green, but the quality of being blue and the quality of being green are not things which we see; they are products of logical reflections. The truth is that common sense, or thought as it first emerges above the level of the narrowly practical, is deeply imbued with that bad logical quality to which the epithet *metaphysical* is commonly applied; and nothing can clear it up but a severe course of logic.

III

We generally know when we wish to ask a question and when we wish to pronounce a judgment, for there is a dissimilarity between the sensation of doubting and that of believing.

But this is not all which distinguishes doubt from belief. There is a practical difference. Our beliefs guide our desires and shape our actions. The Assassins, or followers of the Old Man of the Mountain, used to rush into death at his least command, because they believed that obedience to him would insure everlasting felicity. Had they doubted this, they would not have acted as they did. So it is with every belief, according to its degree. The feeling of believing is a more or less sure indication of there being established in our nature some habit which will determine our actions. Doubt never has such an effect.

Nor must we overlook a third point of difference. Doubt is an uneasy and dissatisfied state from which we struggle to free ourselves and pass into the state of belief;[1] while the latter is a calm and satisfactory state which we do not wish to avoid, or to change to a belief in anything else. On the contrary, we cling tenaciously, not merely to believing, but to believing just what we do believe.

Thus, both doubt and belief have positive effects upon us, though very different ones. Belief does not make us act at once, but puts us into such a condition that we shall behave in a certain way, when the occasion arises. Doubt has not the least effect of this sort, but stimulates us to action until it is destroyed. This reminds us of the irritation of a nerve and the reflex action produced thereby; while for the analogue of belief, in the nervous system, we must look to what are called nervous associations – for example, to that habit of the nerves in consequence of which the smell of a peach will make the mouth water.

IV

The irritation of doubt causes a struggle to attain a state of belief. I shall term this struggle *inquiry*, though it must be admitted that this is sometimes not a very apt designation.

The irritation of doubt is the only immediate motive for the struggle to attain belief. It is certainly best for us that our beliefs should be such as may truly guide our actions so as to satisfy our desires; and this reflection will make us reject any belief which does not seem to have been so formed as to insure this result. But it will only do so by creating a doubt in the place of that belief.

With the doubt, therefore, the struggle begins, and with the cessation of doubt it ends. Hence, the sole object of inquiry is the settlement of opinion. We may fancy that this is not enough for us, and that we seek not merely an opinion, but a true opinion. But put this fancy to the test, and it proves groundless; for as soon as a firm belief is reached we are entirely satisfied, whether the belief be false or true. And it is clear that nothing out of the sphere of our knowledge can be our object, for nothing which does not affect the mind can be a motive for a mental effort. The most that can be maintained is that we seek for a belief that we shall *think* to be true. But we think each one of our beliefs to be true, and, indeed, it is mere tautology to say so.*

That the settlement of opinion is the sole end of inquiry is a very important proposition. It sweeps away, at once, various vague and erroneous conceptions of proof. A few of these may be noticed here.

1. Some philosophers have imagined that to start an inquiry it was only necessary to utter or question or set it down on paper, and have even recommended us to begin our studies with questioning everything! But the mere putting of a proposition into the interrogative form does not stimulate the mind to any struggle after belief. There must be a real and living doubt, and without all this, discussion is idle.

2. It is a very common idea that a demonstration must rest on some ultimate and absolutely indubitable propositions. These, according to one school, are first principles of a general nature; according to another, are first sensations. But, in point of fact, an inquiry, to have that completely satisfactory result called demonstration, has only to start with propositions perfectly free from all actual doubt. If the premises are not in fact doubted at all, they cannot be more satisfactory than they are.[2]

3. Some people seem to love to argue a point after all the world is fully convinced of it. But no further advance can be made. When doubt

* "For truth is neither more nor less than that character of a proposition which consists in this, that belief in the proposition would, with sufficient experience and reflection, lead us to such conduct as would tend to satisfy the desires we should then have. To say that truth means more than this is to say that it has no meaning at all." Peirce's note of 1903.

ceases, mental action on the subject comes to an end; and, if it did go on, it would be without a purpose, except that of self-criticism.

V

If the settlement of opinion is the sole object of inquiry, and if belief is of the nature of a habit, why should we not attain the desired end, by taking any answer to a question, which we may fancy, and constantly reiterating it to ourselves, dwelling on all which may conduce to that belief, and learning to turn with contempt and hatred from anything which might disturb it? This simple and direct method is really pursued by many men. I remember once being entreated not to read a certain newspaper lest it might change my opinion upon free-trade. "Lest I might be entrapped by its fallacies and misstatements" was the form of expression. "You are not," my friend said, "a special student of political economy. You might, therefore, easily be deceived by fallacious arguments upon the subject. You might, then, if you read this paper, be led to believe in protection. But you admit that free-trade is the true doctrine; and you do not wish to believe what is not true." I have often known this system to be deliberately adopted. Still oftener, the instinctive dislike of an undecided state of mind, exaggerated into a vague dread of doubt, makes men cling spasmodically to the views they already take. The man feels that if he only holds to his belief without wavering, it will be entirely satisfactory. Nor can it be denied that a steady and immovable faith yields great peace of mind. It may, indeed, give rise to inconveniences, as if a man should resolutely continue to believe that fire would not burn him, or that he would be eternally damned if he received his *ingesta* otherwise than through a stomach-pump. But then the man who adopts this method will not allow that its inconveniences are greater than its advantages. He will say, "I hold steadfastly to the truth and the truth is always wholesome." And in many cases it may very well be that the pleasure he derives from his calm faith overbalances any inconveniences resulting from its deceptive character. Thus, if it be true that death is annihilation, then the man who believes that he will certainly go straight to heaven when he dies, provided he have fulfilled certain simple observ-ances in this life, has a cheap pleasure which will not be followed by the least disappointment. A similar consideration seems to have weight with many persons in religious topics, for we frequently hear it said, "Oh, I could not believe so-and-so, because I should be wretched if I did." When an ostrich buries its head in the sand as danger approaches, it very likely takes the happiest course. It hides the danger, and then calmly says there is no danger; and, if it feels perfectly sure there is none, why should it raise its head to see? A man may go through life, systematically keeping out of view all that might cause a change in his opinions, and if he only succeeds – basing his method, as he does, on two fundamental psychological laws – I do not see what can be said against his doing so. It would be an egotistical impertinence to object that his procedure is irrational, for that only amounts to saying that his method of settling belief is not ours. He does not propose to himself to be rational, and indeed, will often talk with scorn of man's weak and illusive reason. So let him think as he pleases.

But this method of fixing belief, which may be called the method of tenacity, will be unable to hold its ground in practice. The social impulse is against it. The man who adopts it will find that other men think differently from him, and it will be apt to occur to him in some saner moment that their opinions are quite as good as his own, and this will shake his confidence in his belief. This conception, that another man's thought or sentiment may be equivalent to one's own, is a distinctly new step, and a highly important one. It arises from an impulse too strong in man to be suppressed, without danger of destroying the human species. Unless we make ourselves hermits, we shall necessarily influence each other's opinions; so that the problem becomes how to fix belief, not in the individual merely, but in the community.

Let the will of the state act, then, instead of that of the individual. Let an institution be created which shall have for its object to keep correct doctrines before the attention of the people, to reiterate them perpetually, and to teach them to the young; having at the same time power to prevent contrary doctrines from being taught, advocated, or expressed. Let all possible causes of a change of mind be removed from men's apprehensions. Let them be kept ignorant, lest they should learn of some reason to think otherwise than they do. Let their passions be enlisted, so that they may regard private and unusual opinions with hatred and horror. Then, let all men who reject the established belief be terrified into silence. Let the people turn out and tar-and-feather such men, or let inquisitions be made into the manner of thinking of suspected persons, and, when they are found guilty of forbidden beliefs, let them be subjected to some signal punishment. When complete agreement could not otherwise be reached, a general massacre of all who have not thought in a certain way has proved a very effective means of settling opinion in a country. If the power to do this be wanting, let a list of opinions be drawn up, to which no man of the least independence of thought can assent, and let the faithful be required to accept all these propositions, in order to segregate them as radically as possible from the influence of the rest of the world.

This method has, from the earliest times, been one of the chief means of upholding correct theological and political doctrines, and of preserving their universal or catholic character. In Rome, especially, it has been practiced from the days of Numa Pompilius to those of [Pope] Pius IX. This is the most perfect example in history; but wherever there is a priesthood – and no religion has been without one – this method has been more or less made use of. Wherever there is aristocracy, or a guild, or any association of a class of men whose interests depend or are supposed to depend on certain propositions, there will be inevitably found some traces of this natural product of social feeling. Cruelties always accompany this system; and when it is consistently carried out, they become atrocities of the most horrible kind in the eyes of any rational man. Nor should this occasion surprise, for the officer of a society does not feel justified in surrendering the interests of that society for the sake of mercy, as he might his own private interests. It is natural, therefore, that sympathy and fellowship should thus produce a most ruthless power.

In judging this method of fixing belief, which may be called the method of authority, we must, in the first place, allow its immeasurable mental and moral superiority to the method of tenacity. Its success is proportionally greater; and in fact it has over and over again worked the most majestic results. The mere structures of stone which it has caused to be put together – in Siam, for example, in Egypt, and in Europe – have many of them a sublimity hardly more than rivaled by the greatest works of nature. And, except the geological epochs, there are no periods of time so vast as those which are measured by some of these organized faiths. If we scrutinize the matter closely, we shall find that there has not been one of their creeds which has remained always the same; yet the change is so slow as to be imperceptible during one person's life, so that individual belief remains sensibly fixed. For the mass of mankind, then, there is perhaps no better method than this. If it is their highest impulse to be intellectual slaves, then slaves they ought to remain.

But no institution can undertake to regulate opinions upon every subject. Only the most important ones can be attended to, and on the rest men's minds must be left to the action of natural causes. This imperfection will be no source of weakness so long as men are in such a state of culture that one opinion does not influence another – that is, so long as they cannot put two and two together. But in the most priest-ridden states some individuals will be found who are raised above that condition. These men possess a wider sort of social feeling; they see that men in other countries and in other ages have held to very different doctrines from those which they themselves have been brought up to believe; and they cannot help seeing that it is the mere accident of their having been taught as they have, and of their having been surrounded with the manners and associations they have, that has caused them to believe as they do and not far differently. And their candor cannot resist the reflection that there is no reason to rate their own views at a higher value than those of other nations and other centuries; and this gives rise to doubts in their minds.

They will further perceive that such doubts as these must exist in their minds with reference to every belief which seems to be determined by the caprice either of themselves or of those who originated the popular opinions. The willful adherence to a belief, and the arbitrary forcing of it upon others, must, therefore, both be given up and a new method of settling opinions must be adopted, which shall not only produce an impulse to believe, but shall also decide what proposition it is which is to be believed. Let the action of natural preferences be unimpeded, then, and under their influence let men conversing together and regarding matters in different lights, gradually develop beliefs in harmony with natural causes. This method resembles that by which conceptions of art have been brought to maturity. The most perfect example of it is to be found in the history of metaphysical philosophy. Systems of this sort have not usually rested upon observed facts, at least not in any great degree. They have been chiefly adopted because their fundamental propositions seemed 'agreeable to reason.' This is an apt expression; it does not mean that which agrees with experience, but that which we find ourselves inclined to believe. Plato, for example, finds it agreeable to reason that the distances of the celestial spheres from one another should be proportional to the different lengths of strings which produce harmonious chords. Many philosophers have been led to their main conclusions by considerations like this; but this is the lowest and least developed form which the method takes, for it is clear that another man might find Kepler's [earlier] theory, that the celestial spheres are proportional to the inscribed and circumscribed spheres of the different regular solids, more agreeable to *his* reason. But the shock of opinions will soon lead men to rest on preferences of a far more universal nature. Take, for example, the doctrine that man only acts selfishly – that is, from the consideration that acting in one way will afford him more pleasure than acting in another. This rests on no fact in the world, but it has had a wide acceptance as being the only reasonable theory.

This method is far more intellectual and respectable from the point of view of reason than either of the others which we have noticed. But its failure has been the most manifest. It makes of inquiry something similar to the development of taste; but taste, unfortunately, is always more or less a matter of fashion, and accordingly, metaphysicians have never come to any fixed agreement, but the pendulum has swung backward and forward between a more material and a more spiritual philosophy, from the earliest times to the latest. And so from this, which has been called the *a priori* method, we are driven, in Lord Bacon's phrase, to a true induction. We have examined into this *a priori* method as something which promised to deliver our opinions from their accidental and capricious element. But development, while it is a

process which eliminates the effect of some casual circumstances, only magnifies that of others. This method, therefore, does not differ in a very essential way from that of authority. The government may not have lifted its finger to influence my convictions; I may have been left outwardly quite free to choose, we will say, between monogamy and polygamy, and appealing to my conscience only, I may have concluded that the latter practice is in itself licentious. But when I come to see that the chief obstacle to the spread of Christianity among a people of as high culture as the Hindoos has been a conviction of the immorality of our way of treating women, I cannot help seeing that, though governments do not interfere, sentiments in their development will be very greatly determined by accidental causes. Now, there are some people, among whom I must suppose that my reader is to be found, who, when they see that any belief of theirs is determined by any circumstance extraneous to the facts, will from that moment not merely admit in words that that belief is doubtful, but will experience a real doubt of it, so that it ceases in some degree at least to be a belief.

To satisfy our doubts, therefore, it is necessary that a method should be found by which our beliefs may be caused by nothing human, but by some external permanency – by something upon which our thinking has no effect. Some mystics imagine that they have such a method in a private inspiration from on high. But that is only a form of the method of tenacity, in which the conception of truth as something public is not yet developed. Our external permanency would not be external, in our sense, if it was restricted in its influence to one individual. It must be something which affects, or might affect, every man. And, though these affections are necessarily as various as are individual conditions, yet the method must be such that the ultimate conclusion of every man shall be the same, or would be the same if inquiry were sufficiently persisted in. Such is the method of science. Its fundamental hypothesis, restated in more familiar language, is this: There are real things, whose characters are entirely independent of our opinions about them; those realities affect our senses according to regular laws, and, though our sensations are as different as our relations to the objects, yet, by taking advantage of the laws of perception, we can ascertain by reasoning how things really are, and any man, if he have sufficient experience and reason enough about it, will be led to the one true conclusion. The new conception here involved is that of reality. It may be asked how I know that there are any realities. If this hypothesis is the sole support of my method of inquiry, my method of inquiry must not be used to support my hypothesis. The reply is this: (1) If investigation cannot be regarded as proving that there are real things, it at least does not lead to a contrary conclusion; but the method and the conception on which it is based remain ever in harmony. No doubts of the method, therefore, necessarily arise from its practice, as is the case with all the others. (2) The feeling which gives rise to any method of fixing belief is a dissatisfaction at two repugnant [i.e. conflicting] propositions. But here already is a vague concession that there is some *one* thing to which a proposition should conform. Nobody, therefore, can really doubt that there are realities, or, if he did, doubt would not be a source of dissatisfaction. The hypothesis, therefore, is one which every mind admits. So that the social impulse does not cause men to doubt it. (3) Everybody uses the scientific method about a great many things, and only ceases to use it when he does not know how to apply it. (4) Experience of the method has not led us to doubt it, but, on the contrary, scientific investigation has had the most wonderful triumphs in the way of settling opinion. These afford the explanation of my not doubting the method or the hypothesis which it supposes; and not having any doubt, nor believing that anybody else whom I could influence has, it would be the merest babble for me to say more about it. If there be anybody with a living doubt upon the subject, let him consider it.

To describe the method of scientific investigation is the object of this series of papers. At present I have only room to notice some points of contrast between it and other methods of fixing belief.

This is the only one of the four methods which presents any distinction of a right and a wrong way. If I adopt the method of tenacity and shut myself out from all influences, whatever I think necessary to doing this is necessary according to that method. So with the method of authority: the state may try to put down heresy by means which, from a scientific point of view, seems very ill-calculated to accomplish its purposes; but the only test *on that method* is what the state thinks, so that it cannot pursue the method wrongly. So with the *a priori* method. The very essence of it is to think as one is inclined to think. All metaphysicians will be sure to do that, however they may be inclined to judge each other to be perversely wrong. The Hegelian system recognizes every natural tendency of thought as logical, although it is certain to be abolished by counter-tendencies. Hegel thinks there is a regular system in the succession of these tendencies, in consequence of which, after drifting one way and the other for a long time, opinion will at last go right. And it is true that metaphysicians get the right ideas at last; Hegel's system of Nature represents tolerably the science of his day; and one may be sure that whatever scientific investigation has put out of doubt will presently receive *a priori* demonstration on the part of the metaphysicians. But with the scientific method the case is different. I may start with known and observed facts to proceed to the unknown; and yet the rules which I follow in doing so may not be such as investigation would approve. The test of whether I am truly following the method is not an immediate appeal to my feelings and purposes, but, on the contrary, itself involves the application of the method. Hence it is that bad reasoning as well as good reasoning is possible; and this fact is the foundation of the practical side of logic.

It is not to be supposed that the first three methods of settling opinion present no advantage whatever over the scientific method. On the contrary, each has some peculiar convenience of its own. The *a priori* method is distinguished for its comfortable conclusions. It is the nature of the process to adopt whatever belief we are inclined to, and there are certain flatteries to one's vanities which we all believe by nature, until we are awakened from our pleasing dream by rough facts. The method of authority will always govern the mass of mankind; and those who wield the various forms of organized force in the state will never be convinced that dangerous reasoning ought not to be suppressed in some way. If liberty of speech is to be untrammeled from the grosser forms of constraint, then uniformity of opinion will be secured by a moral terrorism to which the respectability of society will give its thorough approval. Following the method of authority is the path of peace. Certain nonconformities are permitted; certain others (considered unsafe) are forbidden. These are different in different countries and in different ages; but, wherever you are let it be known that you seriously hold a tabooed belief, and you may be perfectly sure of being treated with a cruelty no less brutal but more refined than hunting you like a wolf. Thus, the greatest intellectual benefactors of mankind have never dared, and dare not now, to utter the whole of their thought; and thus a shade of *prima facie* doubt is cast upon every proposition which is considered essential to the security of society. Singularly enough, the persecution does not all come from without; but a man torments himself and is oftentimes most distressed at finding himself believing propositions which he has been brought up to regard with aversion. The peaceful and sympathetic man will, therefore, find it hard to resist the temptation to submit his opinions to authority. But most of all I admire the method of tenacity for its strength, simplicity, and directness. Men who pursue it are distinguished for their decision of character, which becomes very easy with such a mental rule. They do not waste time in trying to make up their minds to what they want, but, fastening like lightning upon whatever alternative comes first, they hold to it to the end, whatever happens, without an instant's irresolution. This is one of the splendid qualities which generally accompany brilliant, unlasting success. It is impossible not to envy the man who can dismiss reason, although we know how it must turn out at last.

Such are the advantages which the other methods of settling opinions have over scientific investigation. A man should consider well of them; and then he should consider that, after all, he wishes his opinions to coincide with the fact, and that there is no reason why the results of those first three methods should do so. To bring about this effect is the prerogative of the method of science. Upon such considerations he has to make his choice – a choice which is far more than the adoption of any intellectual opinion, which is one of the ruling decisions of his life, to which when once made he is bound to adhere. The force of habit will sometimes cause a man to hold on to old beliefs after he is in a condition to see that they have no sound basis. But reflection upon the state of the case will overcome these habits, and he ought to allow reflection full weight. People sometimes shrink from doing this, having an idea that beliefs are wholesome which they cannot help feeling rest on nothing.

But let such persons suppose an analogous though different case from their own. Let them ask themselves what they would say to a reformed Mussulman who should hesitate to give up his old notions in regard to the relations of the sexes; or to a reformed Catholic who should still shrink from the Bible. Would they not say that these persons ought to consider the matter fully, and clearly understand the new doctrine, and then ought to embrace it in its entirety? But, above all, let it be considered that what is more wholesome than any particular belief is integrity of belief; and that to avoid looking into the support of any belief from a fear that it may turn out rotten is quite as immoral as it is disadvantageous. The person who confesses that there is such a thing as truth, which is distinguished from falsehood simply by this, that if acted on it should, on full consideration, carry us to the point we aim at and not astray, and then, though convinced of this, dares not know the truth and seeks to avoid it, is in a sorry state of mind, indeed.

Yes, the other methods do have their merits: a clear logical conscience does cost something – just as any virtue, just as all that we cherish, costs us dear. But, we should not desire it to be otherwise. The genius of a man's logical method should be loved and reverenced as his bride, whom he has chosen from all the world. He need not condemn the others; on the contrary, he may honor them deeply, and in doing so he only honors her the more. But she is the one that he has chosen, and he knows that he was right in making that choice. And having made it, he will work and fight for her, and will not complain that there are blows to take, hoping that there may be as many and as hard to give, and will strive to be the worthy knight and champion of her from the blaze of whose splendors he draws his inspiration and his courage.

Notes

1 In a note of 1903, Peirce attempts to rebut a predictable objection based on the existence of enquiring minds which seek out doubts. Admitting such exceptions, Peirce insists that "doubt essentially involves a struggle to escape it".

2 Here Peirce is expressing the position which he himself describes as "fallibilist." Any belief might conceivably be false, but that is no reason *per se* to doubt that it is actually true.

19

Edmund Husserl, *The Idea of Phenomenology*, Lectures I–II

Introduction

In several of the preceding texts, the authors represented all challenge the epistemological enterprise as conceived of and executed by Descartes. Reid, Kant, Kierkegaard, Nietzsche, and Peirce each, in his own way, rejects the idea that the endeavor should or could be one of establishing the domain of knowledge by reflecting on the immediate certainties of subjective experience which remain when everything else has been subjected to methodological doubt. The Cartesian approach, albeit modified, was to make a resounding return, however, in the philosophy of the Moravian-born philosopher, Edmund Husserl (1859–1938).

Husserl refers to his philosophical attitude and method as phenomenology. The aim of phenomenology is to provide "fundamental" descriptions, free from distortion by theoretical presuppositions and prejudices, of "things themselves," of "phenomena." In the 1907 lectures comprising *The Idea of Phenomenology*, Husserl has a more radical understanding of the execution of this aim than in his earlier *Logical Investigations* (1900–01) and

is, in effect, embarking on the course which was to end at the transcendental idealism of *Cartesian Meditations* over two decades later in 1929.[1] Phenomenology, he now urges, must begin with a thorough "critique of cognition," for our ordinary claims to knowledge, reflecting a "naive" and "natural attitude" toward the world, turn out to involve a host of prejudices and give rise to "abysmal difficulties." None of us really understands how, or even whether, our cognitions "grasp" or "reach out to" the transcendent realm of objects we naturally assume they do. Hence we are in no position to refute total skepticism, solipsism and the possibility that our thinking is incoherent (for, so far, the existence of laws of logic remains a mere assumption).

We require, then, a "new beginning," albeit one reminiscent of Descartes's approach. Husserl does not share Descartes's ambition to arrive, after a process of doubting, at the existence of an immaterial "thinking thing," the *cogito*, and still less the ambitions of proving the existence of a God and, via Him, of the material world. Descartes's achievement, for Husserl, was to have revealed a realm of objects immediately given to consciousness and hence indubitable – namely, cognitions or mental acts themselves, abstracted from their possible (and problematic) relation to objects in an actual world.

In his 1907 lectures, Husserl introduces the notion which henceforth plays a central role in his thinking, that of the "phenomenological reduction." The phenomenologist's first task, if he or she is

From Edmund Husserl, *The Idea of Phenomenology*, trans. W. P. Alston. The Hague: Martinus Nijhoff, 1964, pp. 13–32 (some notes omitted; asterisked note is the translator's).

to expose and describe what is indubitably given to consciousness, is not to doubt, but rather simply to "bracket" or "abstain from" our "natural" beliefs. For such purposes, actual objects (if such there be) are "reduced" to what is immediately given in perception, imagination or whatever. This "abstention" or *epochē* (the Greek word for "cessation") is radical (see II.4). The existence of the external world, and of ourselves as embodied, empirical egos within it, must be "bracketed."[2] So, for example, to understand the nature or "essence" or essential meaning (*Wesen*) of knowledge or cognition itself, we must ignore our assumed relationship to a material world so as to focus solely on the mental acts of cognition, thereby enabling us to "intuit" or "see" wherein their "essence" consists. Having done so, the phenomenologist is then in a position to purely describe that essence, laying it bare to others – the work of phenomenology.

At one point, importantly, Husserl is anxious to ward off a misinterpretation of his proposal. It might seem that he intends to confine knowledge to what is "immanent" in the sense of being "contained in" our minds, to "ideas" and "impressions," in the familiar seventeenth- and eighteenth-century manner. He argues, however, that something – an "essence," say – can be "immanent" in the sense of being directly given to consciousness without thereby being an ingredient in consciousness. It is a mistake, committed by Locke, Hume, and others to confuse the two senses of "immanence," and a mistake that precludes any possible knowledge of the transcendent or extra-mental.

Husserl's epistemology has been extremely influential although, it must be said, primarily by way of serving as a target for later philosophers, including many, like Martin Heidegger and Maurice Merleau-Ponty (see II.22 and II.24 below), who belong within a broadly phenomenological tradition. For these writers, we are too much "beings-in-the-world" and too much creatures of interpretation for us to "bracket" that world. So, what the attempt at phenomenological reduction ultimately shows is the impossibility of any complete reduction.[3] Certainly Husserl's approach is badly at odds with some currently favored ones in English-language philosophy. As a champion of "the given" which constitutes the foundation of all knowledge, Husserl is therefore, for many critics, defending a "myth" first exposed as such by Hegel (II.13). And his condemnation of the intrusion into the theory of knowledge of scientific, including biological, considerations as "extremely irrelevant" and "exceedingly dangerous" puts him at total odds with the program of "naturalizing epistemology" and, indeed, naturalism in general.

Notes

1 For a detailed account of the development of Husserl's thought, see H. Spiegelberg, *The Phenomenological Movement*, The Hague: Martinus Nijhoff, 1982.

2 For a clear account of the phenomenological reduction and other central notions in Husserl's thought, see M. Hammond, J. Howarth, and R. Keat, *Understanding Phenomenology*, Oxford: Blackwell, 1991, Chapters 1–2.

3 M. Merleau-Ponty, *Phenomenology of Perception*, London: Routledge & Kegan Paul, 1962, p. 85.

Husserl, *The Idea of Phenomenology*

Lecture I

[THE NATURAL ATTITUDE IN THINKING AND SCIENCE OF THE NATURAL SORT. THE PHILOSOPHIC (REFLECTIVE) ATTITUDE IN THINKING. THE CONTRADICTIONS OF REFLECTION ON COGNITION, WHEN ONE REFLECTS IN THE NATURAL ATTITUDE, THE DUAL TASK OF TRUE CRITICISM OF COGNITION. TRUE CRITICISM OF COGNITION AS PHENOMENOLOGY OF COGNITION. THE NEW DIMENSION BELONGING TO PHILOSOPHY; ITS PECULIAR METHOD IN CONTRAST TO SCIENCE.]

In earlier lectures I distinguished between *science of the natural sort* and *philosophic science*. The former originates from the natural, the latter from the philosophic attitude of mind.

The *natural attitude of mind* is as yet unconcerned with the critique of cognition. Whether in the act of intuiting or in the act of thinking, in the natural mode of reflection we are turned to *the objects* as they are given to us each time and as a matter of course, even though they are given in different ways and in different modes of being, according to the source and level of our cognition. In perception, for instance, a thing stands before our eyes as a matter of course. It is there, among other things, living or lifeless, animate or inanimate. It is, in short, within a world of which part is perceived, as are the individual things themselves, and of which part is contextually supplied by memory from whence it spreads out into the indeterminate and the unknown.

Our judgments relate to this world. We make (sometimes singular, sometimes universal) judgments about things, their relations, their changes, about the conditions which functionally determine their changes and about the laws of their variations. We find an expression for what immediate experience presents. In line with our experiential motives we draw inferences from the directly experienced (perceived and remembered) to what is not experienced. We generalize, and then apply again general knowledge to particular cases or deduce analytically new generalizations from general knowledge. Isolated cognitions do not simply follow each other in the manner of mere succession. They enter into logical relations with each other, they follow from one another, they "cohere" with one another, they support one another, thereby strengthening their logical power.

On the other hand, they also clash and contradict one another. They do not agree with one another, they are falsified by *assured* cognition, / and their claim to be cognition is discredited. Perhaps the contradictions arise in the sphere that belongs to laws governing the pure predicational form: we have equivocated, we have inferred fallaciously, we have miscounted or miscomputed. In these cases we restore formal consistency. We resolve the equivocation and the like.

Or the contradictions disturb our expectation of connections based on past experience: empirical evidence conflicts with empirical evidence. Where do we look for help? We now weigh the reasons for different possible ways of deciding or providing an explanation. The weaker must give way to the stronger, and the stronger, in turn, are of value as long as they will stand up, i.e., as long

as they in turn do not have to come into a similar logical conflict with new cognitional motives introduced by a broader sphere of cognition.

Thus, natural knowledge makes strides. It progressively takes possession of a reality at first existing for us as a matter of course and as something to be investigated further as regards its extent and content, its elements, its relations and laws. Thus the various sciences of the natural sort (*natürlichen Wissenschaften*) come into being and flourish, the natural sciences (*Naturwissenschaften*) as the sciences of physics and psychology, the sciences of culture (*Geisteswissenschaften*) and, on the other side, the mathematical sciences, the sciences of numbers, classes, relations, etc. The latter sciences deal not with actual but rather with ideal objects; they deal with what is valid *per se*, and for the rest with what are from the first unquestionable possibilities.

In every step of natural cognition pertaining to the sciences of the natural sort, difficulties arise and are resolved, either by *pure logic* or by appeal to *facts*, on the basis of motives or reasons which lie in the things themselves and which, as it were, come from things in the form of *requirements* that they themselves make on our thinking.

Now let, us contrast the natural *mode (or habit)* of *reflection* with the *philosophical*.

With the awakening of reflection about the relation of cognition to its object, abysmal difficulties arise. / Cognition, the thing most taken for <19> granted in natural thinking, suddenly emerges as a mystery. But I must be more exact. What is *taken for granted* in natural thinking is the possibility of cognition. Constantly busy producing results, advancing from discovery to discovery in newer and newer branches of science, natural thinking finds no occasion to raise the question of the possibility of cognition as such. To be sure, as with everything else in the world, *cognition*, too, will appear as a problem in a *certain manner*, becoming an object of natural investigation. Cognition is a fact in nature. It is the experience of a cognizing organic being. It is a psychological fact. As any psychological fact, it can be described according to its kinds and internal connections, and its genetic relations can be investigated. On the other hand cognition is essentially *cognition of what objectively is*; and it is cognition through the *meaning* which is intrinsic to it; by virtue of this meaning it is *related* to what objectively is. Natural thinking is also already active in this relating. It investigates in their *formal* generality the *a priori* connections of meanings and postulated meanings and the *a priori* principles which belong to objectivity *as such*; there comes into being a *pure grammar* and at higher stages a pure logic (a whole complex of disciplines owing to its different possible delimitations), and there arises once more a normative and practical logic in the form of an art of thinking, and, especially, of scientific thinking.

So far, we are still in the realm of *natural* thinking.

However, the correlation between cognition as mental process, its referent (*Bedeutung*) and what objectively is, which has just been touched upon in order to contrast the psychology of cognition with pure logic and ontology, is the source of the deepest and most difficult problems. Taken collectively, they are the problem of the possibility of cognition.

<20> Cognition in all of its manifestations is a psychic act; it is the cognition of a cognizing subject. The objects cognized stand over and against the cognition. But how can we be certain of the correspondence between cognition and the object cognized? How can knowledge transcend itself and reach its object reliably? The unproblematic manner in which the object of cognition is given to natural thought to be cognized now becomes an enigma. In perception the perceived thing is believed to be directly given. Before my perceiving eyes stands the thing. I see it, and I grasp it. Yet the perceiving is simply a mental act of mine, of the perceiving subject. Likewise, memory and expectation are subjective processes; and so are all thought processes built upon them and through which we come to posit that something really is the case and to determine any *truth* about what is. How do I, the cognizing subject, know if I can ever really know, that there exist not only my own mental processes, these acts of cognizing, but also that which they apprehend? How can I ever know that there is anything at all which could be set over against cognition as its object?

Shall I say: only phenomena are truly given to the cognizing subject, he never does and never can break out of the circle of his own mental processes, so that in truth he could only say: I exist, and all that is not-I is mere phenomenon dissolving into phenomenal connections? Am I then to become a solipsist? This is a hard requirement. Shall I,

with Hume, reduce all transcendent objectivity to fictions lending themselves to psychological explanation but to no rational justification? But this, too, is a hard requirement. Does not Hume's psychology, along with any psychology, transcend the sphere of immanence? By working with such concepts as habit, human nature, sense-organ, stimulus and the like, is it not working with transcendent existences (and transcendent by its own avowal), while its aim is to degrade to the status of fictions everything that transcends actual "impressions" and "ideas"?

But what is the use of invoking the specter of contradictions when / logic itself is in question <21> and becomes problematic. *Indeed, the real meaning of logical lawfulness* which natural thinking would not dream of questioning, now becomes *problematic* and *dubious*. Thoughts of a biological order intrude. We are reminded of the modern theory of evolution, according to which man has evolved in the struggle for existence and by natural selection, and with him his intellect too has evolved naturally and along with his intellect all of its characteristic forms, particularly the logical forms. Accordingly, is it not the case that the logical forms and laws express the accidental peculiarity of the human species, which could have been different and which will be different in the course of future evolution? Cognition is, after all, only *human cognition*, bound up with *human intellectual forms*, and unfit to reach the very nature of things, to reach the things in themselves.

But at once another piece of absurdity arises. Can the cognitions by which such a view operates and the possibilities which it ponders make any sense themselves if the laws of logic are given over to such relativism? Does not the truth that there is this and that possibility implicitly presuppose the absolute validity of the principle of non-contradiction, according to which any given truth excludes its contradictory?

These examples should suffice. The possibility of cognition has become enigmatic throughout. If we immerse ourselves in the sciences of the natural sort, we find everything clear and comprehensible, to the extent to which they have developed into exact sciences. We are certain that we are in possession of objective truth, based upon reliable methods of reaching (objective) reality. But whenever we reflect, we fall into errors and confusions. We become entangled in patent difficulties and even self-contradictions.

We are in constant danger of becoming sceptics, or still worse, we are in danger of falling into any one of a number of scepticisms all of which have, sad to say, one and the same characteristic: absurdity.

The playground of these unclear and inconsistent theories as well as the endless quarrels associated with them / is the *theory of knowledge*, and <22> *metaphysics* which is bound up with it historically and in subject matter. The task of the theory of knowledge or the critique of theoretical reason is, first of all, a critical one. It must brand the well-nigh inevitable mistakes which ordinary reflection makes about the relation of cognition, its meaning and its object, thereby refuting the concealed as well as the unconcealed sceptical theories concerning the essence of cognition by demonstrating their absurdity.

Furthermore, the positive task of the theory of knowledge is to solve the problems of the relations among cognition, its meaning and its object by inquiring into the essence of cognition. Among these, there is the problem of explicating the essential meaning of being a cognizable object or, what comes to the same thing, of being an object at all: of the meaning which is prescribed (for being an object at all) by the correlation *a priori* (or essential correlation) between cognition and being an object of cognition. And this naturally applies also to all basic forms of being an object which are predetermined by the nature of cognition. (To the ontological, the apophantic* as well as the metaphysical forms.)

Precisely by solving these problems the theory of knowledge qualifies as the critique of cognition, more exactly, as *the critique of natural cognition* in all the sciences of a natural sort. It puts us, in other words, in a position to interpret in an accurate and definitive way the teachings of these sciences about what exists. For the confusions of the theory of knowledge into which we are led by natural (pre-epistemological) reflection on the possibility of cognition (on the possibility of cognition's reaching its object) involve not just false views about the essence of cognition, but also self-contradictory, and, therefore, fundamentally misleading *interpretations* of the being that is cognized in the sciences of the

natural sort. So, one and the same science is interpreted in materialistic, spiritualistic, dualistic, psychomonistic, positivistic and many other ways, depending upon what interpretation is thought to be the necessary consequence of those pre-epistemological reflections. Only with epistemological reflection do we arrive at the distinction between / the sciences of a natural sort <23> and philosophy. Epistemological reflection first brings to light that the sciences of a natural sort are not yet the ultimate science of being. We need a science of being in the absolute sense. This science, which we call *metaphysics*, grows out of a "critique" of natural cognition in the individual sciences. It is based on what is learned in the general critique of cognition about the essence of cognition and what it is to be an object of cognition of one basic type or other, i.e., in accordance with the different fundamental correlations between cognizing and being an object of cognition.

If then we disregard any metaphysical purpose of the critique of cognition and confine ourselves purely to the task *of clarifying the essence of cognition and of being an object of cognition, then this will be phenomenology of cognition and of being an object of cognition* and will be the first and principal part of phenomenology as a whole.

Phenomenology: this denotes a science, a system of scientific disciplines. But it also and above all denotes a method and an attitude of mind, the specifically *philosophical attitude* of mind, the specifically *philosophical method*.

In contemporary philosophy, insofar as it claims to be a serious science, it has become almost a commonplace that there can be only one method for achieving cognition in all the sciences as well as in philosophy. This conviction accords wholly with the great philosophical traditions of the seventeenth century, which also thought that philosophy's salvation lay wholly in its taking as a model of method the exact sciences, and above all, mathematics and mathematical natural science. This putting philosophy methodologically on a par with the other sciences goes hand in hand with treating them alike with respect to subject matter. It is still the prevailing opinion that philosophy and, more specifically, ontology and the general theory of knowledge not only relate to all the other sciences, but also that they can be grounded upon the conclusions of those other sciences: / in the same way in which sciences are <24> built upon one another, and the conclusions of

---

* Tr. note: In Husserl the word "apophantic" refers to predicative judgements or to the theory of such judgements.

one of them can serve as premises for the others. I am reminded of the favorite ploy of basing the theory of knowledge on the psychology of cognition and biology. In our day, reactions against these fatal prejudices are multiplying. And prejudices they are.

In the sphere of ordinary inquiry one science can readily build upon another, and the one can serve the other as a model of method even though to a limited extent determined by the nature of the areas of inquiry in question. *But philosophy lies in a wholly new dimension.* It needs an *entirely new point of departure* and an entirely new method distinguishing it in principle from any "natural" science. This is why the logical procedures that give the sciences of a natural sort unity have a unitary character in principle in spite of the special methods which change from one science to another: while the methodological procedures of philosophy have by contrast and in principle a new unity. This is also why *pure* philosophy, within the whole of the critique of cognition and the "critical" disciplines generally, must disregard, and must refrain from using, the intellectual achievements of the sciences of a natural sort and of scientifically undisciplined natural wisdom and knowledge.

To anticipate, this doctrine, the grounds for which will be given in more detail in the sequel, is recommended by the following considerations.

In the sceptical mood which critical reflection about cognition necessarily begets (I mean the reflection that comes first, the one that comes before the scientific critique of cognition and which takes place on the natural level of thought) every science of the natural sort and every method characteristic of such a science ceases to count as something we properly possess. For cognition's reaching its object has become enigmatic and dubious as far as its meaning and possibility are concerned, and exact cognition becomes thereby no less enigmatic than inexact, <25> scientific knowledge no / less than the pre-scientific. The possibility of cognition becomes questionable, more precisely, how it can possibly reach an objectivity which, after all, is in itself whatever it is. Behind this lies the following: What is in question is what cognition can accomplish, the meaning of its claim to validity and correctness, the meaning of the distinction between valid real and merely apparent cognition; on the other hand, also the meaning of being an object which exists and exists as what it is whether

it is cognized or not and which as an object is an object of possible cognition, in principle cognizable, even if in fact it has never been and never will be cognized, but is in principle perceptible, imaginable, determinable by predicates in a possible judgment, etc.

However, it is impossible to see how working with presuppositions which are taken from natural cognition, no matter how "exactly founded" they are in it, can help us to resolve the misgivings which arise in the critique of cognition, to find the answers to its problems. If the meaning and value of natural cognition *as such* together with *all* of its methodological presuppositions and all of its exact foundations have become problematic, then this strikes at every proposition which natural cognition presupposes in its starting-point and at every allegedly exact method of giving a foundation. Neither the most exact mathematics nor mathematical natural science has here the slightest advantage over any actual or alleged cognition through ordinary experience. It is then clear that there can be no such talk as that philosophy (which begins in the critique of cognition and which, whatever else it is, is rooted in the critique of cognition) has to model itself after the exact sciences methodologically (or even as regards subject matter!), or that it has to adopt as a standard their methodology, or that it is philosophy's task to implement and to complete the work done in the exact sciences according to a single method, in principle the same for all the sciences. In contradistinction to all natural cognition, philosophy lies, I repeat, within a new dimension; and what corresponds to this new dimension, even if, as the phrase suggests, it is essentially connected with the old dimensions, is a *new* and *radically new method* which / is set over <26> against the "natural" method. He who denies this has failed to understand entirely the whole of the level at which the characteristic problem of the critique of cognition lies, and with this he has failed to understand what philosophy really wants to do and should do, and what gives it its own character and authority *vis-à-vis* the whole of natural cognition and science of the natural sort.

Lecture II

[THE BEGINNING OF THE CRITIQUE OF COGNITION; TREATING AS QUESTIONABLE EVERY (CLAIM TO) KNOWING. REACHING THE GROUND OF ABSOLUTE

CERTAINTY IN PURSUANCE OF DESCARTES'S METHOD OF DOUBT. THE SPHERE OF THE THINGS THAT ARE ABSOLUTELY GIVEN. REVIEW AND AMPLIFICATION: REFUTATION OF THE ARGUMENT AGAINST THE POSSIBILITY OF A CRITIQUE OF COGNITION. THE RIDDLE OF NATURAL COGNITION: TRANSCENDENCE. DISTINCTION BETWEEN THE TWO CONCEPTS OF IMMANENCE AND TRANSCENDENCE. THE INITIAL PROBLEM OF THE CRITIQUE OF COGNITION THE POSSIBILITY OF TRANSCENDENT COGNITION. THE PRINCIPLE OF EPISTEMOLOGICAL REDUCTION.]

<29> At the outset of the critique of cognition the entire world of nature, physical and psychological, as well as one's own human self together with all the sciences which have to do with these objective matters, are *put in question*. Their being, their validity are left up in the air.

Now the question is: How can *the critique of cognition get under way*? The critique of cognition is the attempt of cognition to find a scientific understanding of itself and to establish objectively what cognition is in its essence, what is the meaning of the relation to an object which is implicit in the claim to cognition and what its objective validity or the reaching of its object comes to if it is to be cognition in the true sense. Although the ἐποχή [epoche], which the critique of cognition must employ, begins with the doubt of all cognition, its own included, it cannot remain in such doubt nor can it refuse to take as valid everything given, including that which it brings to light itself. If it must presuppose nothing as *already given*, then it must begin with some cognition which it does not take unexamined from elsewhere but rather gives to itself, which it itself posits as primal.

This primal cognition must contain nothing of the unclarity and the doubt which otherwise give to cognition the character of the enigmatic and problematic so that we are finally in the embarrassing position of having to say that cognition as such is a problem, something incomprehensible, in need of elucidation and dubious in its claims. Or, to speak differently: If we are not allowed to take anything as already given because our lack of clarity about cognition implies that we cannot understand what it could mean for something *to be known in itself* yet *in the context of cognition*, then it must after all be possible to make evident something which

we have to acknowledge as absolutely given and indubitable; / insofar, that is, as it is given with <30> such complete clarity that every question about it will and must find an immediate answer.

And now we recall the Cartesian doubt. Reflecting on the multifarious possibilities of error and deception, I might reach such a degree of sceptical despair that I finally say: Nothing is certain, everything is doubtful. But it is at once evident that not everything is doubtful, for while I am judging that everything is doubtful, it is indubitable that I am so judging; and it would be absurd to want to persist in a universal doubt. And in every case of a definite doubt, it is indubitably certain that I have this doubt. And likewise with every *cogitatio*. Howsoever I perceive, imagine, judge, infer, howsoever these acts may be certain or uncertain, whether or not they have objects that exist as far as the perceiving itself is concerned, it is absolutely clear and certain that I am perceiving this or that, and as far as the judgment is concerned that I am judging of this or that, etc.

Descartes introduced these considerations for other purposes.[1] But with suitable modifications, we can use them here.

If we inquire into the essence of cognition, then whatever status it and our doubts about its reaching the object may have one thing is clear: that cognition itself is a name for a manifold sphere of being which can be given to us absolutely, and which can be given absolutely each time in the particular case. The thought processes which I really perform are given to me insofar as I *reflect* upon them, receive them and set them up in a pure "*seeing*." I can speak vaguely about cognition, perception, imagination, experience, judgment, inference, etc.; but then, when I reflect, all that is given, and absolutely given at that, is this phenomenon of vaguely "talking about and intending cognition, experience, judgment, etc." Even this phenomenon of vagueness is one of those that comes under the heading of cognition in the broadest sense. I can, however, have an actual perception and inspect it. I can, moreover, represent to myself in imagination or memory a perception and survey it as so given to imagination. In that case I am no longer / vacuously talking about <31> perception or having a vague intension or idea of it. Instead, perception itself stands open to my inspection as actually or imaginatively given to me. And the same is true of every intellectual process, of every form of thinking and cognizing.

I have here put on the same level the "seeing" [act of] reflective perception and [the "seeing" act of reflective] imagination. If one followed the Cartesian view, one would have to emphasize perception first; it would in some measure correspond to the so-called inner perception of traditional epistemology, though this is an ambivalent concept.

Every intellectual process and indeed every mental process whatever, while being enacted, *can be made the object of a pure "seeing" and understanding, and is something absolutely given in this "seeing."* It is given as something that is, that is here and now, and whose being cannot be sensibly *doubted.* To be sure, I can wonder what sort of being this is and how this mode of being is related to other modes. It is true I can wonder what givenness means *here,* and reflecting further I can "see" the "seeing" itself in which this givenness, or this mode of being, is constituted. But all the same I am now working on an absolute foundation: namely, this perception is, and remains as long as it lasts, something absolute, something here and now, something that in itself is what it is, something by which I can measure as by an ultimate standard what being and being given can mean and here must mean, at least, obviously, as far as the sort of being and being given is concerned which a "here and now" exemplifies. And that goes for all specific ways of thinking, whenever they are given. All of these, however, can also be data in imagination; they can "as it were" stand before our eyes and yet not stand before them as actualities, as actually accomplished perceptions, judgments, etc.; even then, they are, in a certain, sense, data. They are there *open to intuition.* We talk about them not in just vague hints and empty intention. We inspect them, and while inspecting them we can observe their essence, their constitution, their intrinsic character, and we can make our speech conform in a pure measure to what is "seen" in its full clarity. But this requires to be <32> supplemented / by a discussion of the concept and cognition of essences.

For the moment we keep it firmly in mind that a sphere of the absolutely given can be indicated at the outset; and this is just the sphere we need if it is to be possible to aim at a theory of knowledge. Indeed, lack of clarity with regard to the meaning or essence of cognition requires a science of cognition, a science whose sole end is to clarify the essential nature of cognition. It is not to explain cognition as a psychological fact; it is not to inquire into the natural causes and laws of the development and occurrence of cognitions. Such inquiry is the task of a science of the natural sort, of a psychology which deals with the mental processes of persons who are undergoing them. Rather, the task of the critique of cognition is to clarify, to cast light upon, the essence of cognition and the legitimacy of its claim to validity that belongs to its essence; and what else can this mean but to make the essence of cognition directly self-given.

Recapitulation and Amplification. In its constantly successful progress in the various sciences, cognition of the natural sort is altogether self-assured that it reaches the object and has no cause to worry about the possibility of cognition and about the meaning of cognized objectivity. But as soon as we begin to reflect on the correlation between cognition and reality (and eventually also on the ideal meanings on the one hand and, on the other, on the objects of cognition) there arise difficulties, absurdities, inconsistent yet seemingly well-founded theories which drive one to the admission that the possibility of cognition as far as its reaching the object is concerned is an enigma.

A new science, the critique of cognition, is called for. Its job is to resolve confusions and to clarify the essence of cognition. Upon the success of this science depends the possibility of a metaphysics, a science of being in the absolute and fundamental sense. But how / can such a science <33> of cognition in general get started? That which a science questions it cannot use as a presupposition. But what is in question is the possibility of all cognition in that the critique of cognition regards as problematic the possibility of cognition in general and its capacity to reach the object. Once it is launched, the critique of cognition cannot take any cognition for granted. Nor can it take over anything whatever from pre-scientific cognition. All cognition bears the mark of being questionable.

Without some cognition given at the outset, there is also no advancement of cognition. The critique of cognition cannot, therefore, begin. There can be no such science at all.

I already suggested that in all this there is an element of truth. In the beginning no cognition can be assumed *without examination.* However, even if the critique of cognition must not take over any antecedent cognition it still can begin by *giving* itself cognition, and naturally cognition which it does not base on, or logically derive from, anything else as this would presuppose some other immediate cognition already given. It must rather base itself on the cognition which is immediately evident and of such a kind that, as absolutely clear and indubitable, it excludes every doubt of its possibility and contains none of the puzzles which had led to all the sceptical confusions. I then pointed to the *Cartesian method of doubt* and to the domain of the absolutely given, viz., of absolute cognition which comes under the heading of evidence (*Evidenz*) of the *cogitatio*. It remained to be shown that the *immanence* of this cognition makes it an appropriate point of departure for the theory of cognition; that, furthermore, *because of this immanence*, it is free of the puzzlement which is the source of all sceptical embarrassment. Finally, it remained to be shown *that immanence is the generally necessary characteristic of all epistemological cognition*, and that it is nonsensical not only at the start but also in general to borrow from the sphere of transcendence, in other words, to try to found the theory of cognition on psychology or on any science whatever of the natural sort.

<34>   I may add the following: there is a plausible argument / to the effect that the theory of knowledge cannot get started because it questions cognition as such and hence regards as questionable every cognition with which we might begin. Moreover, it is alleged that if all cognition must be a riddle to the epistemologist, so must any initial cognition with which epistemology itself begins be a riddle. I repeat that this plausible argument is a deception. The deception is due to the vague generality of the wording. Cognition in general "is questioned." Surely, however, it is not denied that there is cognition in general (such denial would lead to contradiction); rather, cognition presents a certain problem, namely, of how it can accomplish a certain task attributed to it, namely, the task of reaching the object: I may even doubt whether this task can be accomplished at all. But doubt as I may, this doubt is a first step toward canceling itself out because some cognitions can be brought to light which render such doubt groundless. Moreover, if I begin by not understanding cognition at all, then this incomprehension with its inde-

terminate universality admittedly encompasses every cognition. But that is not to say that every cognition I might run up against in the future has to remain forever incomprehensible. It may be that there is a big puzzle to begin with connected with a particular class of cognitions, those that thrust themselves most immediately to the fore, and that I now reach a general embarrassment and say: cognition as such is a riddle, even though it soon appears that the riddle does not belong to certain other kinds of cognition. And, as we shall see presently, this is indeed the case.

I said that the cognitions with which the critique of cognition must begin must contain nothing doubtful or questionable. They must contain none of that which precipitates epistemological confusion and gives impetus to the critique of cognition. We have to show that this holds true of the sphere of the *cogitatio*. For this we need a more deeply probing reflection, one that will bring us substantial advantages.

If we look closer at what is so enigmatic and what, in the course of subsequent reflection on the possibility of cognition, causes embarrassment, we will find it to be the transcendence of cognition. All cognition of the natural sort, and especially the prescientific, is cognition which makes its object transcendent. / It posits objects <35> as existent, claims to reach matters of fact which are not "strictly given to it," are not "immanent" to it.

But on closer view, this *transcendence* is admittedly *ambiguous*. One thing one can mean by transcendence is that the object of cognition is not genuinely (*reell*) contained in the cognitive act so that one would be meaning by "being truly given" or "immanently given" that the object of the cognitive act is genuinely contained in the act: the cognitive act, the *cogitatio*, has genuine abstract parts genuinely constituting it: but the physical thing which it intends or supposedly perceives or remembers, etc., is not to be found in the *cogitatio* itself, as a mental process; the physical thing is not to be found as a genuine (*reell*) concrete part (*Stück*), not as something which really exists within the *cogitatio*. So the question is: how can the mental process so to speak transcend itself? *Immanent here means then genuinely (reell) immanent in the cognitive mental process.*

But there is still *another transcendence* whose opposite is an altogether different immanence, namely, *absolute* and *clear givenness, self-givenness in the absolute sense.* This givenness, which rules out any meaningful doubt, consists of a simply immediate "seeing" and apprehending of the intended object itself as it is, and it constitutes the precise concept of evidence (*Evidenz*) understood as immediate evidence. All cognition which is not evident, which though it intends or posits something objective yet *does not see it itself,* is transcendent in this second sense. In such cognition we go beyond what at any time *is truly given,* beyond what can be *directly "seen"* and *apprehended.* At this point we may ask: How can cognition posit something as existing that is not directly and truly given in it?

At first, before we come to a deeper level of critical epistemological reflection, these two kinds of immanence and transcendence run confusedly into each other. It is indeed clear that whoever raises the first question about the possibility of genuine (*reell*) transcendence is at the same time really also raising the second question: namely, how can there be transcendence beyond the realm of evident givenness? In this there is the unspoken supposition that the only actually understandable, unquestionable, absolutely evident givenness is the givenness of *the abstract part genuinely (reell)* <36> *contained* within the cognitive act, / and this is why anything in the way of a cognized objectivity that is not genuinely (*reell*) contained within that act is regarded as a puzzle and as problematic. We shall soon hear that this is a fatal mistake.

One may now construe transcendence in one sense or the other, or, at first even ambiguously, but transcendence is both the initial and the central problem of the critique of cognition. It is the riddle that stands in the path of cognition of the natural sort and is the incentive for new investigations. One could at the outset designate the solution to this problem as being the task of the critique of cognition. One would thereby delimit the new discipline in a preliminary fashion, instead of generally designating as its theme the problem of the essence of any cognition whatever.

If then the riddle connected with the initial establishment of the discipline lies *here,* it becomes more definitely clear what must not be claimed as presupposed. *Nothing transcendent must be used as a presupposition.* If I do not understand *how* it is possible that cognition reach something

transcendent, then I also do not know *whether* it is possible. The scientific warrant for believing in a transcendent existence is of no help. For every mediated warrant goes back to something immediate; and it is the unmediated which contains the riddle.

Still someone might say: "It is certain that mediated no less than immediate cognition contains the riddle. But it is only the *how* that is puzzling, whereas the *that* is absolutely certain. No sensible man will doubt the existence of the world, and the sceptic in action belies his own creed." Very well. Then let us answer him with a more powerful and far-reaching argument. For it proves that the theory of cognition has, *neither at the outset nor throughout its course,* any license to fall back upon the content of the sciences of a natural sort which treat their object as transcendent. What is proved is the fundamental thesis *that the theory of knowledge can never be based upon any science of the natural sort, no matter what the more specific nature of that science may be.* Hence we ask: What will our opponent do with his transcendent knowledge? We put freely at his disposal the entire stock of transcendent truths contained in the objective / sciences, and we take <37> it that those truths are not altered by the emergence of the puzzle of how a science of the transcendent is possible. What will he now do with his all-embracing knowledge? How does he think he can go from the "that" to the "how"? That he knows for a fact that cognition of the transcendent is actual guarantees as logically obvious that cognition of the transcendent is possible. But the riddle is, *how* is it possible? Can he solve it even if he presupposes all the sciences, all or any cognition of the transcendent? Consider: What more does he really need? That cognition of the transcendent is possible he takes for granted, even as analytically certain in saying to himself, there is in my case knowledge of the transcendent. What he lacks is obvious. He is unclear about the relation to transcendence. He is unclear about the "reaching the transcendent" which is ascribed to cognition, to knowledge. Where and how can he achieve clarity? He could do so if the essences of this relation were somehow *given* to him, so that he could "see" it and could directly inspect the unity of cognition and its object, a unity denoted by the locution "reaching the object." He would thereby not only know this unity to be possible, but he would have this possibility clearly before him. The possibility itself counts for him as something transcendent, as a possibility which is known but not of itself given, "seen." He obviously thinks: cognition is a thing apart from its object; cognition is given but the object of cognition is not given; and yet cognition is supposed to relate to the object, to cognize it. How can I understand this possibility? Naturally the reply is: I could understand it only if the relation itself were given as something to be "seen." As long as the object is, and remains, something transcendent, and cognition and its objects are actually separate, then indeed he can see nothing here, and his hopes for reaching a solution, perhaps even by way of falling back on transcendent presuppositions, are patent folly.

<38> However, if he is to be consistent with these views, he should give up his starting point: he should acknowledge that in this case cognition of the transcendent is impossible, and that his pretence to know is mere prejudice. Then the problem is no longer: How is cognition of the transcendent possible? But rather, How do we account for the prejudice which ascribes a transcendent feat to cognition? And this exactly was the path Hume took.

Let us emphatically reject that approach and let us go on to illustrate the basic idea that the problem of the "how" (how cognition of the transcendent is possible and even more generally, how cognition is possible at all) can never be answered on the basis of a prior knowledge of the transcendent, of prior judgments about it, no matter whence the knowledge or the judgments are borrowed, not even if they are taken from the exact sciences. Here is an illustration: A man born deaf knows that there are sounds, that sounds produce harmonies and that a splendid art depends upon them. But he cannot understand *how* sounds do this, how musical compositions are possible. Such things he cannot *imagine*, i.e., he cannot "see" and in "seeing" grasp the "how" of such things. His knowledge about what exists helps him in no way, and it would be absurd if he were to try to deduce the *how* of music from his knowledge, thinking that thereby he could achieve clarity about the possibility of music through conclusions drawn from things of which he is cognizant. It will not do to draw conclusions from existences of which one knows but which one cannot "see." "Seeing" does not lend itself to demonstration or deduction. It is patently absurd to try to explain possibilities (and unmediated possibilities at that) by drawing logical conclusions from non-intuitive knowledge. Even if I could be wholly certain that there are transcendent worlds, even if I accept the whole content of the sciences of a natural sort, even then I cannot borrow from them. I must never fancy that by relying on transcendent presuppositions and scientific inferences I can arrive where I want to go in the critique of cognition – namely, to assess the possibility of a transcendent objectivity of cognition. And that goes not just for the beginning but for the whole course of the critique of cognition, so long as there still remains the problem of *how cognition is possible.* / And, evidently, <39> that goes not just for the problem of transcendent objectivity but also for the elucidation of every possibility.

If we combine this with the extraordinarily strong inclination to make a transcendently oriented judgment and thus to fall into a μετάβασις εἰς ἄλλο γένος [a change into some other kind] in every case where a thought process involves transcendence and a judgment has to be based upon it, then we arrive at a sufficient and complete deduction of the *epistemological principle* that an epistemological *reduction* has to be accomplished in the case of every epistemological inquiry of whatever sort of cognition. That is to say, everything transcendent that is involved must be bracketed, or be assigned the index of indifference, of epistemological nullity, an index which indicates: the existence of all these transcendencies, whether I believe in them or not, is not here my concern; this is not the place to make judgments about them; they are entirely irrelevant.

All the basic errors of the theory of knowledge go hand in hand with the above mentioned μετάβασις, on the one hand the basic error of psychologism, on the other that of anthropologism and biologism. The μετάβασις is so exceedingly dangerous, partly because the proper sense of the problem is never made clear and remains totally lost in it, and partly because even those who have become clear about it find it hard to remain clear and slip easily, as their thinking proceeds, back into the temptations of the natural modes of thought and judgment as well as into the false and seductive conceptions of the problems which grow on their basis.

Note

1 Husserl's "purpose" differs from Descartes's in the following general way. He was not concerned initially to doubt nearly all our beliefs in order, later, to reinstate them on a firm basis. The purpose of the Husserlian *epochē* is to "purify" consciousness and its immediate objects by ignoring everything extraneous. This abstention is not something the phenomenologist can ever abandon, since it is the standing prerequisite of that focusing on "things themselves" or phenomena which is his job.

Bertrand Russell, "Knowledge by Acquaintance and Knowledge by Description"

Introduction

The English language is sometimes faulted for more than stinginess in employing the single word "know" where other languages enlist two – "*connaître*" and "*savoir*" in French, "*kennen*" and "*wissen*" in German, for example.[1] Whereas the English both know London and that London is foggy, Germans *kennen* Berlin but *wissen* that Berlin is damp. Failure to heed this distinction between knowing things (places, people, etc.) and knowing about them or that they are such-and-such has, at any rate, been held responsible for misguided assumptions in epistemology – for instance, for the view that all knowledge (*Wissenschaft*) is a matter of the presence to the mind of certain items, such as "ideas," which we know (*kennen*).[2]

The English logician and philosopher Bertrand Russell (1872–1970) was not the first to call attention to the importance of the distinction and to label the former kind of knowledge "knowledge by acquaintance."[3] But he was perhaps the first to attempt a precise account of it and a demonstration of its centrality for the theory of knowledge. The distinction's importance, for Russell, is due to his conviction that all other knowledge is "ultimately reducible to knowledge concerning what is known by acquaintance" – a principle which he

From Bertrand Russell, *The Problems of Philosophy*. Oxford: Oxford University Press, 1959, pp. 46–59.

takes to be equivalent to the truism that we cannot make judgments about things "without knowing what it is that we are judging about."

Two questions are raised by this conviction. First, what are the things we can know by acquaintance? Second, how is it that we may have knowledge about things when we are not acquainted with them? That second question may not seem a daunting one given our everyday, liberal understanding of acquaintance, on which someone may be acquainted with people, places, periods of history, philosophical movements and so on. So massive, on this understanding, is the domain of people's acquaintance that it hardly seems puzzling how, on such a basis, knowledge about things outside that domain could be built up.

Russell, however, writes in the tradition of British empiricism and takes a much narrower view of what, strictly, we can be acquainted with.[4] Somewhat in the manner of Husserl (see II.19 above), it is only "subjective things" – sense-data, concepts (or "universals") and possibly one's own self – which, for Russell, are objects of acquaintance. The second question therefore becomes urgent: for without an answer to it, we do not understand, says Russell, "what enables us to pass beyond the limits of our private experience" to knowledge of, say, tables and people.

Russell's answer is that "knowledge of," "knowledge about," or "knowledge that" is "knowledge by description." The answer is reached by reflecting on an apparent implication of his narrow construal of acquaintance. If we cannot be acquainted with the actual table, then the expression "this table" cannot, as we naively imagine, really "stand for" or "mean" the table. Now in earlier writings on logic, notably "On Denoting" (1905), Russell had developed his "theory of descriptions" to resolve paradoxes which arise when expressions that only apparently "stand for" objects are construed as really doing so. For example, if "The Golden Mountain does not exist" is construed as being about something referred to by the noun-phrase, it would, in effect, require the existence of the very thing whose existence it denies. Russell's proposal was that such expressions are not names or denoting terms but concealed descriptions, so that statements containing them are to the effect that something does (or does not) fit a certain description.

Russell exploits this proposal when explaining the nature of our knowledge of things with which we cannot be acquainted. To know, say, that the table is brown is to know that there is something of which a certain description is true, where all the terms in the description genuinely stand for items of acquaintance, notably sense-data and concepts. It is Russell's view, argued for in an earlier chapter of *The Problems of Philosophy*, that we have at least very strong reasons to believe that there exist actual tables causing our sense-data, and so that there are objects fitting such descriptions as "cause such-and-such sense-data."

It is not only Russell's empiricist restriction of items of acquaintance to "private experience" that has attracted later criticism. His distinction between knowledge by acquaintance and by description remains contentious even when a more generous list of items is allowed. By opposing the two kinds of knowledge, Russell is in effect holding that there can, indeed must, be direct knowledge that is non-propositional in form, unmediated by conceptual judgment. (For a contrasting view, Hegel's, see II.13). For many critics, the mere presence to perceptual awareness of a color or whatever cannot, in the absence of judgment, constitute a case of knowledge at all. If the critics are right, then perhaps there is only knowledge by description, important as acquaintance might be in the aetiology of knowledge-claims. Perhaps the English language, arguably, is not after all to be faulted for failing to mark two supposedly distinct kinds of knowledge.

Notes

1 Perhaps remnants in English and Scots-English of a second word for "know" or "knowing" include "cunning" or "canny," as in "a canny man."

2 See J. Bennett, *Locke, Berkeley and Hume: Central Themes*, Oxford: Clarendon Press, 1971.

3 See D. B. Martens, "Knowledge by Acquaintance/by Description," in *A Companion to Epistemology*, ed. J. Dancy and E. Sosa, Oxford: Blackwell, 1992. Russell's first discussion of the distinction was in a 1911 article bearing the same name as the somewhat amended and simplified Chapter V in *The Problems of Philosophy* of 1912.

4 For an excellent account of Russell's relation to the empiricist tradition, see D. Pears, *Bertrand Russell and the British Tradition in Philosophy*, London: Fontana, 1967.

Russell, "Knowledge by Acquaintance and Knowledge by Description"

In the preceding chapter we saw that there are two sorts of knowledge: knowledge of things, and knowledge of truths. In this chapter we shall be concerned exclusively with knowledge of things, of which in turn we shall have to distinguish two kinds. Knowledge of things, when it is of the kind we call knowledge by *acquaintance*, is essentially simpler than any knowledge of truths, and logically independent of knowledge of truths, though it would be rash to assume that human beings ever, in fact, have acquaintance with things without at the same time knowing some truth about them. Knowledge of things by *description*, on the contrary, always involves, as we shall find in the course of the present chapter, some knowledge of truths as its source and ground. But first of all we must make clear what we mean by 'acquaintance' and what we mean by 'description'.

We shall say that we have *acquaintance* with any-thing of which we are directly aware, without the intermediary of any process of inference or any knowledge of truths. Thus in the presence of my table I am acquainted with the sense-data that make up the appearance of my table – its colour, shape, hardness, smoothness, etc.; all these are things of which I am immediately conscious when I am seeing and touching my table. The par-ticular shade of colour that I am seeing may have many things said about it – I may say that it is brown, that it is rather dark, and so on. But such statements, though they make me know truths *about* the colour, do not make me know the colour itself any better than I did before: so far as concerns knowledge of the colour itself, as opposed to knowledge of truths about it, I know the colour perfectly and completely when I see it, and no further knowledge of it itself is even theoretically possible. Thus the sense-data which make up the appearance of my table are things with which I have acquaintance, things immedi-ately known to me just as they are.

My knowledge of the table as a physical object, on the contrary, is not direct knowledge. Such as it is, it is obtained through acquaintance with the sense-data that make up the appearance of the table. We have seen that it is possible, without absurdity, to doubt whether there is a table at all, whereas it is not possible to doubt the sense-data. My knowledge of the table is of the kind which we shall call 'knowledge by descrip-tion'. The table is 'the physical object which causes such-and-such sense-data'. This *describes* the table by means of the sense-data. In order to know anything at all about the table, we must know truths connecting it with things with which we have acquaintance: we must know that 'such-and-such sense-data are caused by a physical object'. There is no state of mind in which we are directly aware of the table; all our knowledge of the table is really knowledge of *truths*, and the actual thing which is the table is not, strictly speaking, known to us at all. We know a descrip-tion, and we know that there is just one object to which this description applies, though the object itself is not directly known to us. In such a case, we say that our knowledge of the object is knowledge by description.

All our knowledge, both knowledge of things and knowledge of truths, rests upon acquain-tance as its foundation. It is therefore important to consider what kinds of things there are with which we have acquaintance.

Sense-data, as we have already seen, are among the things with which we are acquainted; in fact, they supply the most obvious and striking ex-ample of knowledge by acquaintance. But if they were the sole example, our knowledge would be very much more restricted than it is. We should only know what is now present to our senses: we could not know anything about the past – not even that there was a past – nor could we know any truths about our sense-data, for all knowledge of truths, as we shall show, demands acquaintance with things which are of an essentially different character from sense-data, the things which are sometimes called 'abstract ideas', but which we shall call 'universals'. We have therefore to con-sider acquaintance with other things besides sense-data if we are to obtain any tolerably ade-quate analysis of our knowledge.

The first extension beyond sense-data to be con-sidered is acquaintance by *memory*. It is obvious that we often remember what we have seen or heard or had otherwise present to our senses, and that in such cases we are still immediately aware of what we remember, in spite of the fact that it appears as past and not as present. This imme-diate knowledge by memory is the source of all our knowledge concerning the past: without it, there could be no knowledge of the past by inference, since we should never know that there was anything past to be inferred.

The next extension to be considered is acquaintance by *introspection*. We are not only aware of things, but we are often aware of being aware of them. When I see the sun, I am often aware of my seeing the sun; thus 'my seeing the sun' is an object with which I have acquaintance. When I desire food, I may be aware of my desire for food; thus 'my desiring food' is an object with which I am acquainted. Similarly we may be aware of our feeling pleasure or pain, and gener-ally of the events which happen in our minds. This kind of acquaintance, which may be called self-consciousness, is the source of all our knowledge of mental things. It is obvious that it is only what goes on in our own minds that can be thus known immediately. What goes on in the minds of others is known to us through our perception of their bodies, that is, through the sense-data in us which are associated with their bodies. But for our acquaintance with the contents of our own minds, we should be unable to imagine the minds of others, and therefore we could never arrive at the knowledge that they have minds. It seems natural to suppose that self-consciousness is one of the things that distinguish men from animals; animals, we may suppose, though they have acquaintance with sense-data, never become aware of this acquaintance. I do not mean that they *doubt* whether they exist, but that they have never become conscious of the fact that they have sensations and feelings, nor therefore of the fact that they, the subjects of their sensations and feelings, exist.

We have spoken of acquaintance with the contents of our minds as *self*-consciousness, but it is not, of course, consciousness of our *self*: it is consciousness of particular thoughts and feelings. The question whether we are also acquainted with our bare selves, as opposed to particular thoughts and feelings, is a very difficult one, upon which it would be rash to speak positively. When we try to look into ourselves we always seem to come upon some particular thought or feeling, and not upon the 'I' which has the thought or feeling. Nevertheless there are some reasons for thinking that we are acquainted with the 'I', though the acquaintance is hard to disentangle from other things. To make clear what sort of reason there is, let us consider for a moment what our acquaintance with particular thoughts really involves.

When I am acquainted with 'my seeing the sun', it seems plain that I am acquainted with two different things in relation to each other. On the one hand there is the sense-datum which represents the sun to me, on the other hand there is that which sees this sense-datum. All acquaintance, such as my acquaintance with the sense-datum which represents the sun, seems obviously a relation between the person acquainted and the object with which the person is acquainted. When a case of acquaintance is one with which I can be acquainted (as I am acquainted with my acquaintance with the sense-datum representing the sun), it is plain that the person acquainted is myself. Thus, when I am acquainted with my seeing the sun, the whole fact with which I am acquainted is 'Self-acquainted-with-sense-datum'.

Further, we know the truth 'I am acquainted with this sense-datum'. It is hard to see how we could know this truth, or even understand what is meant by it, unless we were acquainted with

something which we call 'I'. It does not seem necessary to suppose that we are acquainted with a more or less permanent person, the same today as yesterday, but it does seem as though we must be acquainted with that thing, whatever its nature, which sees the sun and has acquaintance with sense-data. Thus, in some sense it would seem we must be acquainted with our Selves as opposed to our particular experiences. But the question is difficult, and complicated arguments can be adduced on either side. Hence, although acquaintance with ourselves seems *probably* to occur, it is not wise to assert that it undoubtedly does occur.

We may therefore sum up as follows what has been said concerning acquaintance with things that exist. We have acquaintance in sensation with the data of the outer senses, and in introspection with the data of what may be called the inner sense – thoughts, feelings, desires, etc.; we have acquaintance in memory with things which have been data either of the outer senses or of the inner sense. Further, it is probable, though not certain, that we have acquaintance with Self, as that which is aware of things or has desires towards things.

In addition to our acquaintance with particular existing things, we also have acquaintance with what we shall call *universals*, that is to say, general ideas, such as *whiteness, diversity, brotherhood*, and so on. Every complete sentence must contain at least one word which stands for a universal, since all verbs have a meaning which is universal. We shall return to universals later on, in Chapter IX; for the present, it is only necessary to guard against the supposition that whatever we can be acquainted with must be something particular and existent. Awareness of universals is called *conceiving*, and a universal of which we are aware is called a *concept*.

It will be seen that among the objects with which we are acquainted are not included physical objects (as opposed to sense-data), nor other people's minds. These things are known to us by what I call 'knowledge by description', which we must now consider.

By a 'description' I mean any phrase of the form 'a so-and-so' or 'the so-and-so'. A phrase of the form 'a so-and-so' I shall call an 'ambiguous' description; a phrase of the form 'the so-and-so' (in the singular) I shall call a 'definite' description. Thus 'a man' is an ambiguous description, and 'the man with the iron mask' is a definite description. There are various problems connected with ambiguous descriptions, but I pass them by, since they do not directly concern the matter we are discussing, which is the nature of our knowledge concerning objects in cases where we know that there is an object answering to a definite description, though we are not *acquainted* with any such object. This is a matter which is concerned exclusively with *definite* descriptions. I shall therefore, in the sequel, speak simply of 'descriptions' when I mean 'definite descriptions'. Thus a description will mean any phrase of the form 'the so-and-so' in the singular.

We shall say that an object is 'known by description' when we know that it is 'the so-and-so', i.e. when we know that there is one object, and no more, having a certain property; and it will generally be implied that we do not have knowledge of the same object by acquaintance. We know that the man with the iron mask existed, and many propositions are known about him; but we do not know who he was. We know that the candidate who gets the most votes will be elected, and in this case we are very likely also acquainted (in the only sense in which one can be acquainted with some one else) with the man who is, in fact, the candidate who will get most votes; but we do not know which of the candidates he is, i.e. we do not know any proposition of the form 'A is the candidate who will get most votes' where A is one of the candidates by name. We shall say that we have 'merely descriptive knowledge' of the so-and-so when, although we know that the so-and-so exists, and although we may possibly be acquainted with the object which is, in fact, the so-and-so, yet we do not know any proposition '*a* is the so-and-so', where *a* is something with which we are acquainted.

When we say 'the so-and-so exists', we mean that there is just one object which is the so-and-so. The proposition '*a* is the so-and-so' means that *a* has the property so-and-so, and nothing else has. 'Mr A. is the Unionist candidate for this constituency' means 'Mr A. is a Unionist candidate for this constituency, and no one else is'. 'The Unionist candidate for this constituency exists' means 'some one is a Unionist candidate for this constituency, and no one else is'. Thus, when we are acquainted with an object which is the so-and-so, we know that the so-and-so exists; but we may

know that the so-and-so exists when we are not acquainted with any object which we know to be the so-and-so, and even when we are not acquainted with any object which, in fact, is the so-and-so.

Common words, even proper names, are usually really descriptions. That is to say, the thought in the mind of a person using a proper name correctly can generally only be expressed explicitly if we replace the proper name by a description. Moreover, the description required to express the thought will vary for different people, or for the same person at different times. The only thing constant (so long as the name is rightly used) is the object to which the name applies. But so long as this remains constant, the particular description involved usually makes no difference to the truth or falsehood of the proposition in which the name appears.

Let us take some illustrations. Suppose some statement made about Bismarck. Assuming that there is such a thing as direct acquaintance with oneself, Bismarck himself might have used his name directly to designate the particular person with whom he was acquainted. In this case, if he made a judgement about himself, he himself might be a constituent of the judgement. Here the proper name has the direct use which it always wishes to have, as simply standing for a certain object, and not for a description of the object. But if a person who knew Bismarck made a judgement about him, the case is different. What this person was acquainted with were certain sense-data which he connected (rightly, we will suppose) with Bismarck's body. His body, as a physical object, and still more his mind, were only known as the body and the mind connected with these sense-data. That is, they were known by description. It is, of course, very much a matter of chance which characteristics of a man's appearance will come into a friend's mind when he thinks of him; thus the description actually in the friend's mind is accidental. The essential point is that he knows that the various descriptions all apply to the same entity, in spite of not being acquainted with the entity in question.

When we, who did not know Bismarck, make a judgement about him, the description in our minds will probably be some more or less vague mass of historical knowledge – far more, in most cases, than is required to identify him. But, for the sake of illustration, let us assume that we think of him as 'the first Chancellor of the German Empire'. Here all the words are abstract except 'German'. The word 'German' will, again, have different meanings for different people. To some it will recall travels in Germany, to some the look of Germany on the map, and so on. But if we are to obtain a description which we know to be applicable, we shall be compelled, at some point, to bring in a reference to a particular with which we are acquainted. Such reference is involved in any mention of past, present, and future (as opposed to definite dates), or of here and there, or of what others have told us. Thus it would seem that, in some way or other, a description known to be applicable to a particular must involve some reference to a particular with which we are acquainted, if our knowledge about the thing described is not to be merely what follows *logically* from the description. For example, 'the most long-lived of men' is a description involving only universals, which must apply to some man, but we can make no judgements concerning this man which involve knowledge about him beyond what the description gives. If, however, we say, 'The first Chancellor of the German Empire was an astute diplomatist', we can only be assured of the truth of our judgement in virtue of something with which we are acquainted – usually a testimony heard or read. Apart from the information we convey to others, apart from the fact about the actual Bismarck, which gives importance to our judgement, the thought we really have contains the one or more particulars involved, and otherwise consists wholly of concepts.

All names of places – London, England, Europe, the Earth, the Solar System – similarly involve, when used, descriptions which start from some one or more particulars with which we are acquainted. I suspect that even the Universe, as considered by metaphysics, involves such a connexion with particulars. In logic, on the contrary, where we are concerned not merely with what does exist, but with whatever might or could exist or be, no reference to actual particulars is involved.

It would seem that, when we make a statement about something only known by description, we often *intend* to make our statement, not in the form involving the description, but about the actual thing described. That is to say, when we say anything about Bismarck, we should like, if we could, to make the judgement which Bismarck alone can make, namely, the judgement of which he himself is a constituent. In this we are necessarily defeated, since the actual Bismarck is unknown to us. But we know that there is an object B, called Bismarck, and that B was an astute diplomatist. We can thus *describe* the proposition we should like to affirm, namely, 'B was an astute diplomatist', where B is the object which was Bismarck. If we are describing Bismarck as 'the first Chancellor of the German Empire', the proposition we should like to affirm may be described as 'the proposition asserting, concerning the actual object which was the first Chancellor of the German Empire, that this object was an astute diplomatist'. What enables us to communicate in spite of the varying descriptions we employ is that we know there is a true proposition concerning the actual Bismarck, and that however we may vary the description (so long as the description is correct) the proposition described is still the same. This proposition, which is described and is known to be true, is what interests us; but we are not acquainted with the proposition itself, and do not know *it*, though we know it is true.

It will be seen that there are various stages in the removal from acquaintance with particulars: there is Bismarck to people who knew him; Bismarck to those who only know of him through history; the man with the iron mask; the longest-lived of men. These are progressively further removed from acquaintance with particulars; the first comes as near to acquaintance as is possible in regard to another person; in the second, we shall still be said to know 'who Bismarck was'; in the third, we do not know who was the man with the iron mask, though we can know many propositions about him which are not logically deducible from the fact that he wore an iron mask; in the fourth, finally, we know nothing beyond what is logically deducible from the definition of the man. There is a similar hierarchy in the region of universals. Many universals, like many particulars, are only known to us by description. But here, as in the case of particulars, knowledge concerning what is known by description is ultimately reducible to knowledge concerning what is known by acquaintance.

The fundamental principle in the analysis of propositions containing descriptions is this: *Every proposition which we can understand must be composed wholly of constituents with which we are acquainted.*

We shall not at this stage attempt to answer all the objections which may be urged against this fundamental principle. For the present, we shall merely point out that, in some way or other, it must be possible to meet these objections, for it is scarcely conceivable that we can make a judgement or entertain a supposition without knowing what it is that we are judging or supposing about. We must attach *some* meaning to the words we use, if we are to speak significantly and not utter mere noise; and the meaning we attach to our words must be something with which we are acquainted. Thus when, for example, we make a statement about Julius Caesar, it is plain that Julius Caesar himself is not before our minds, since we are not acquainted with him. We have in mind some *description* of Julius Caesar: 'the man who was assassinated on the Ides of March', 'the founder of the Roman Empire', or, perhaps, merely 'the man whose name was *Julius Caesar*'. (In this last description, *Julius Caesar* is a noise or shape with which we are acquainted.) Thus our statement does not mean quite what it seems to mean, but means something involving, instead of Julius Caesar, some description of him which is composed wholly of particulars and universals with which we are acquainted.

The chief importance of knowledge by description is that it enables us to pass beyond the limits of our private experience. In spite of the fact that we can only know truths which are wholly composed of terms which we have experienced in acquaintance, we can yet have knowledge by description of things which we have never experienced. In view of the very narrow range of our immediate experience, this result is vital, and until it is understood, much of our knowledge must remain mysterious and therefore doubtful.

21

(A) Moritz Schlick, "On the Foundation of Knowledge"
(B) Karl Popper, *The Logic of Scientific Discovery*, Chapter 10 (abridged)

Introduction

Moritz Schlick (1882–1936) was the founder and main organizer of the famous Vienna Circle in the 1920–30s, a group of scientists and philosophers who formed the epicenter of the Logical Positivist movement. That movement is best known for the theory of meaning to which it subscribed, according to which propositions (other than "trivial," analytic ones) are meaningful only if, in some (disputed) sense, they are verifiable. On such a theory, meaning is understood in epistemic terms – in terms, that is, of conditions of knowledge, a topic that was bound to be of central concern to the Positivists given their shared ambition to establish the credentials of scientific enquiry at the same time as dismissing those of "metaphysics."

For at least two reasons, many in the Vienna Circle were dissatisfied with the foundationalist approach, still apparent in Russell (see II.20

(A) *From* Oswald Hanfling, ed., *Essential Readings in Logical Positivism.* Oxford: Blackwell, 1981, pp. 178–96 (notes omitted); originally in Schlick's *Philosophical Papers*, Vol. II (1925–36), ed. H. L. Mulder and B. van de Velde-Schlick (D. Reidel, 1979). (B) *From* Karl Popper, *The Logic of Scientific Discovery*, London: Routledge Classics, 2002, pp. 248–52, 264–70, 273–82 (some notes omitted).

above), of a more traditional empiricism. On that approach, typically, the "basic propositions" on which the edifice of knowledge rests are regarded as "subjective" ones corresponding to indubitable mental data or experiences. For many Positivists, this approach not only creates the dilemma of how so public and communicable an enterprise as science could rest upon purely "private" foundations, but it also falls foul of Ludwig Wittgenstein's strictures, in his *Tractatus Logico-Philosophicus*, against talking about the relation between language and reality. As they construed this work, which had strongly influenced them, it condemned any such talk as "metaphysical" and hence "nonsense."

Much of the interest of Schlick's 1933 paper "On the Foundation of Knowledge" resides in his critical exposure of some of the more radical attempts, by fellow members of the Circle, to identify and define a set of fundamental (or "protocol") propositions in a manner that avoided the alleged pitfalls of more traditional foundationalist approaches. For example, Schlick describes and rejects the proposals of Rudolf Carnap (1891–1970), Otto Neurath (1882–1945), and others to define these protocol propositions in terms of their *coherence* within a body of scientific statements, or of the *structural role* (as axioms, say) conferred on them by scientists.[1]

It is Schlick's view that all such proposals make it impossible properly to respond to skepticism and relativism. Any adequate response must, he insists, share the traditional insight that fundamental propositions are those that record personal experiences of pain, color, or whatever. In this respect, Schlick belonged to the more conservative wing of the Logical Positivist movement. Indeed, in a later article he wryly notes his reputation, within the Vienna Circle, as a "metaphysician and poet."[2] But in at least two other respects, Schlick's foundationalism differs from that of the older empiricist tradition.

First he rejects, or at any rate downplays, the genetic role traditionally attributed to basic observations, their role as building blocks on which we then erect a body of scientific knowledge. The real role of basic propositions ("affirmations," as Schlick calls them) is that of verifying or falsifying scientific hypotheses, whatever the source of these latter might be. Paradoxically, as it were, "affirmations" serve to "found" other propositions by "coming at the end," for they are the indubitable truths which scientific hypotheses must entail or at least lead us toward if these hypotheses are to be accepted.

Second, and rather puzzlingly, Schlick's "affirmations" turn out not really to be propositions at all, for a proposition, as something articulated and spoken or written down, is not something indubitable. And whereas propositions refer to or are about perceptions, the "affirmations" themselves mention no perceptions and so are not really about them. "Affirmations" are, rather, the "occasions" for the most basic propositions we can articulate, as if through a process of "combustion."

Schlick, it seems, is open to the kind of criticism that could also be leveled against Russell (see the introductory remarks to II.20). The allegedly foundational items in the edifice of knowledge do not, in Schlick's account, look like structured, cognitive claims at all, and this suggests that their role in supporting or verifying the claims of science is obscure. If, for example, Schlick's "affirmation" of pain amounts to no more than simply having the pain, then it is hard to see that such "affirmations" can be entailed by hypotheses and so serve to verify them.[3] Perhaps Schlick recognizes this, for at the end of the paper he switches to a rhetorical mode of indicating his view – talking, for example, of scientific knowledge not as entailing "affirmations," but as "flickering out" toward them.[4] It is not perhaps surprising, given the difficulties Schlick runs into, that some of the views he criticizes in the first half of his

paper currently enjoy rather more favor than his own.

Among the most significant difficulties the Positivists in general ran into, however, were those raised by Karl Popper (1902–94). Popper vigorously attacked Wittgenstein's contention (see II.23 in this volume) that there were no genuine philosophical problems, but only confusions resulting from the misuse of language. But Popper also rejected the emphasis on verification in positivist thought, in particular verification as an adequate description of the logic of scientific reasoning. Popper recognized that while it is difficult enough to explain how the meaningfulness of basic terms and propositions is tied to sensations, observations, or occasions for using them, it is logically impossible to verify the sort of sentences that typically compose scientific hypotheses and scientific laws. While experimental testing, for example, can verify that some objects in the universe exhibit attraction to one another according to Newton's inverse-square law, it is simply not possible to verify that all material objects in the universe conform to the law. Universal claims, except in restricted circumstances, simply cannot be verified. But they can be falsified. It is impossible to verify the universal claim "all swans are white," unless one can check every swan in the universe (perhaps even the past and future universes); but simply encountering a single black swan falsifies the claim. The progress of science, then, works like the process of natural selection in evolution. Contrary to the model advanced by Francis Bacon (II.7), scientists do not make observations and then inductively draw forth hypotheses from them that are then confirmed by experiment. Rather, scientific theorists speculatively propose hypotheses that then experimental scientists (sometimes the same individuals) try to disprove. Those hypotheses that survive the acid tests of falsification are admitted into the body of scientific "knowledge" – provisionally, that is, with the understanding that new evidence may at some time come to light that will falsify them.

Notes

1 Much of Schlick's criticism is directed against Carnap's paper "Über Protokollsätze", in *Erkenntnis 3,* 1932.

2 "Facts and Propositions", also in *Essential Readings in Logical Positivism*, ed. Oswald Hanfling, p. 196.

3 On this issue, see J. McDowell, *Mind and World*, Cambridge, MA: Harvard University Press, 1995.

4 For a useful discussion of Schlick's epistemology, see B. S. Gower, "Realism and Empiricism in Schlick's Philosophy", in *Science and Subjectivity*, ed. D. Bell and W. Vossenkuhl, Berlin: Akademie Verlag, 1993.

(A) Schlick, "On the Foundation of Knowledge"

I

All great attempts at establishing a theory of knowing arise from the problem of the reliability of human cognition, and this question again arises from the wish for absolute certainty of knowledge.

That the statements of everyday life and of science can ultimately lay claim only to probable status, and that even the most universal findings of inquiry, confirmed in all experience, can only have the character of hypotheses – this is an insight that has repeatedly spurred philosophers from the time of Descartes, and less clearly, indeed, from antiquity onwards, to seek for an unshakeable foundation, immune from all doubt and forming the firm basis on which the tottering edifice of our knowledge is reared. The unsafeness of the structure has mostly been put down to the fact that it was impossible – perhaps in principle – to build anything more solid by the power of human thought; but this did not prevent a search for the natural bedrock which is there *before* building commences, and does not itself sway.

This search is a praiseworthy honest endeavour, and also exerts an influence among 'relativists' and 'skeptics' who would dearly like to be ashamed of it. It makes its appearance in various forms and leads to strange differences of opinion. The question of 'protocol propositions', their function and structure, is the latest form in which philosophy, or rather the radical empiricism of our day, invests the problem of the ultimate ground of knowledge.

As the name implies, 'protocol propositions' originally meant those propositions which in absolute simplicity, without any forming, change or addition, set forth the *facts*, whose elaboration constitutes the substance of all science, and which are prior to all knowledge, to every claim about the world. It makes no sense to speak of uncertain facts – it is only statements, only our knowledge that can be uncertain; and if it is therefore possible to reproduce the raw facts quite purely in 'protocol propositions', the latter seem to be the absolute indubitable starting-points of all knowledge. They are indeed again left behind, the moment we go over to propositions which are really useable in life or science (such a transition appears to be that from 'singular' to 'general' statements), but they constitute, for all that, the firm basis to which all our knowledge owes the whole of whatever validity it may still possess.

It makes no difference here whether these so-called protocol propositions are ever indeed formulated, i.e., actually uttered, written or even merely explicitly 'thought'; it is important only to know what propositions the designations actually made are based on, and to be able at any time to reconstruct them. If a research worker, for example, records that 'under such and such circumstances the pointer stands at 10.5', he knows that this means 'two black lines coincide', and that the words 'under such and such circumstances' (which we here suppose to be enumerated), are likewise to be resolved into particular protocol propositions, which he could also state exactly in principle if he wanted to, though it might be a trouble to do so.

The fact is clear, and to my knowledge has not been contested by anyone, that knowledge in life and in the research situation *begins* in *some* sense with the establishing of facts, and that 'protocol propositions', in which this establishment takes place, stand in a like sense at the *beginning* of science. What is this sense? Is the 'beginning' to be understood in a temporal sense or a logical one?

Here already we find a great deal of wavering and unclarity. When I said above that it did not matter whether the crucial propositions were also uttered or enunciated as protocols, this obviously implies that they do not have to stand at the beginning *in time*, but can equally well be brought in afterwards, if this should be required. And required it will be, whenever we wish to make clear the real meaning of the sentence actually written down. So is the talk about protocol propositions to be understood in a *logical* sense? In that case they would be marked out by specific logical properties, by their structure, their position in the system of science, and the task would arise of actually specifying these properties. In fact, this is the form in which [Rudolf] Carnap, for example, expressly posed the problem of protocol propositions at an earlier stage, whereas later he declared it a question to be settled by arbitrary decision.

On the other side we find numerous arguments apparently presupposing that we are to count as 'protocol propositions' only such statements as also take precedence in time over the other assertions of science. And is this not correct? For we have to remember that we are dealing here with the ultimate foundation of our knowledge of *reality*, and that it cannot suffice for this purpose to treat the propositions merely as if they were 'ideal structures' (as in Platonizing fashion it was earlier the custom to say). On the contrary, we have to concern ourselves with real happenings, with the temporally occurring events in which the passing of judgement consists, and hence with mental acts of 'thinking' or physical acts of 'speaking' or 'writing'. Since the mental acts of judgement appear fitted to serve as a basis for intersubjectively valid knowledge only after having been translated into oral or written expression (i.e., into a physical sign-system), it was proposed to regard as 'protocol propositions' certain spoken, written or printed sentences, i.e., certain signcomplexes consisting of sounds, writing fluid or printer's ink, which if rendered out of the customary abbreviations into a fully articulate language would signify somewhat as follows: 'Mr So-and-so, at such-and-such a time and place, is observing this or that'. (This view was particularly upheld by Otto Neurath.) And in fact, if we retrace the road whereby we have actually arrived at all our knowledge, we undoubtedly always come upon these same sources: printed sentences in books, words from the mouth of the teacher, and our own observations (in the latter case we are ourselves Mr So-and-so).

According to this view, protocol propositions would be real occurrences in the world, and would have to be prior in time to the other real processes constituting the 'construction of science', or even the production of knowledge in an individual.

I don't know how far the distinction here drawn between the logical and temporal priority of protocol propositions may correspond to differences in the view actually taken by particular authors – but that is no part of our present concern. For our purpose is not to determine who has said the right thing, but what the right thing *is*. And in this our distinction of the two standpoints will serve us well.

De facto, both views might be compatible, for the propositions recording simple data of observation and standing at the beginning in time could at the same time be those which, in virtue of their structure, must constitute the logical starting-point of science.

II

The question which ought first to interest us is this: what progress is attained by formulating the problem of the ultimate foundation of knowledge with the aid of the concept of 'protocol proposition'? The answering of this question should prepare us for the solution of the problem itself.

It seems to me to signify a great improvement in method, to try to arrive at the foundation of knowledge by searching, not for the primary *facts*, but for the primary *propositions*. But it seems to me also that there has been no understanding of how to make proper use of this advantage, and this perhaps because there has been no real awareness that at bottom the issue was none other than this old problem of the foundation of knowledge. I believe, in fact, that the view arrived at by these considerations about protocol propositions is untenable. They lead towards a peculiar relativism, which seems to be a necessary consequence of the view that regards protocol propositions as empirical facts, on which, as time goes on, the edifice of knowledge is raised.

For as soon as one asks about the certainty with which one may maintain the truth of protocol propositions regarded in this fashion, one has to admit that it is exposed to all manner of doubt.

There is a sentence in a book which says, for example, that So-and-so made such-and-such an observation with such-and-such an instrument.

Although, given certain assumptions, one may have the utmost confidence in this statement, it, and hence the observation, can never be regarded as *absolutely* assured. For the possibilities of error are innumerable. So-and-so can inadvertently or deliberately have noted down something which fails to give a correct report of the fact observed; in writing or printing an error may have crept in – indeed the very assumption that the letters in a book preserve their shape even for a minute and do not rearrange themselves 'on their own' into new sentences, is an empirical hypothesis, which as such can never be strictly verified, since every verification would depend on similar assumptions, on the presupposition that our memory does not deceive us at least over short periods, and so forth.

This means of course – and some of our authors have been almost triumphant in pointing it out – that protocol propositions so conceived are in principle exactly the same in character as all other statements of science: they are hypotheses and nothing else. They are anything but irrefutable and can be employed in the construction of the knowledge-system only so long as they are supported, or at least not contradicted, by other hypotheses. We therefore reserve the right to make corrections at any time even to protocol propositions, and such corrections are often enough made, indeed, whenever we eliminate certain protocol data and maintain afterwards that they must have been due to some kind of error.

Even in propositions asserted by ourselves, we never in principle exclude the possibility of error. We admit that at the moment of passing judgement our mind was perhaps utterly confused, and that an experience we now claim to have had two seconds ago might be declared on subsequent examination to have been a hallucination, or even to have never happened at all.

It is clear, then, that for anyone in search of a firm foundation for knowledge the view outlined provides, in its 'protocol propositions', *nothing* of the kind. On the contrary, its only real outcome is that the distinction at first introduced between protocol and other propositions is subsequently done away with again as meaningless. We may therefore understand how the view was arrived at that any propositions we please may be picked out from science and designated as 'protocol propositions', and that it is merely a matter of

expediency which ones we care to choose for the purpose.

But can we agree to this? Are there really only grounds of expediency? Is it not rather a question of where the particular propositions come from, of what their origin and history may be? What meaning, in any case, does expediency have here? What is the purpose pursued in setting up and selecting the propositions?

The purpose can only be that of science itself, namely to provide a *true* account of the facts. We think it self-evident that the problem of the foundation of all knowledge is nothing else but the question of the criterion of truth. The term 'protocol propositions' was undoubtedly first introduced so that by means of it certain propositions might be singled out, by whose truth it should then be possible to measure, as if by a yardstick, the truth of all other statements. According to the view described, this yardstick has now turned out to be just as relative as, say, all the standards of measurement in physics. And that view with its consequences has been commended [by Carnap], also, as an eviction of the last remnant of 'absolutism' from philosophy.

But then what do we have left as a criterion of truth? Since we are not to have it that all statements of science are to accord with a specific set of protocol propositions, but rather that all propositions are to accord with all others, where each is regarded as in principle corrigible, truth can consist only in the *mutual agreement of the propositions with one another*.

III

This doctrine (expressly stated and defended in the above context by Otto Neurath, for example) is well known in the history of modern philosophy. In England it is commonly referred to as the 'coherence theory of truth' and contrasted with the older 'correspondence theory' (on which it should be noted that the term 'theory' is by no means appropriate here, since remarks about the nature of truth are quite different in character from scientific theories, which always consist of a system of hypotheses).

The two views are usually contrasted by saying that on the first or traditional theory the truth of a proposition consists in its agreement with the facts, whereas on the second or 'coherence' theory it consists in its agreement with the system of all other propositions.

I shall not here investigate in general whether the formulation of the latter doctrine cannot also be so interpreted as to draw attention to something perfectly correct (namely that there is a quite specific sense in which, as Wittgenstein puts it, we 'cannot get out of language'); my business here is to show, rather, that in the interpretation that must be given to it in our present context, the doctrine is wholly untenable.

If the truth of a proposition is to consist in its coherence or agreement with other propositions, we have to be clear about what is meant by 'agreement', and *which* propositions the 'others' are supposed to be.

The first point should be easy enough to dispose of. Since it cannot be intended that the statement under examination says the *same* as the others, the only alternative is that it merely has to be *consistent* with them, and hence that no contradiction shall obtain between them and it. Truth would thus consist simply in absence of contradiction. But now the question of whether truth can be straightforwardly identified with freedom from contradiction, ought no longer to be a matter of discussion. It should long since have been generally recognized that non-contradiction and truth (if one wishes to employ this word at all) can be equated only in propositions of a tautological character, e.g., in those of pure geometry. But in propositions of that kind all connection with reality is deliberately severed; they are merely formulae within an established calculus. Of the statements of *pure* geometry it makes no sense to ask whether they agree with the facts of the world or not; in order to be called true or correct, they merely have to be consistent with the axioms arbitrarily laid down at the outset (though it is customarily also required that they should *follow* from these). Here we are confronted with precisely what in earlier days was designated *formal* truth and distinguished from *material* truth.

The latter is the truth of synthetic propositions or factual statements, and if it is desired to describe them by means of the concept of non-contradiction or consistency with other propositions, this can be done only by saying that they may not stand in contradiction to certain *quite specific* statements, namely those very statements which record 'facts of immediate observation'. It

is not consistency with *any* sort of propositions you please that can serve as the criterion of truth; what is required, rather, is conformity with certain very particular statements which can by no means be chosen at will. In other words, the criterion of non-contradiction alone is utterly inadequate for material truth; it is wholly a matter, rather, of consistency with very special statements of a peculiar kind; and for *this* consistency there is nothing to prevent – indeed everything, in my view, to justify – our employment of the good old phrase 'agreement with reality'.

The astonishing error of the 'coherence theory' can only be explained by the fact that, in setting up and elaborating this theory, attention was invariably paid only to propositions actually occurring in science, and that these alone were employed as examples. The non-contradictory connection between them was then in fact sufficient, but only because these propositions are already of a quite definite kind. For in a certain sense (yet to be described) they have their 'origin' in observational propositions, and derive, as one may confidently say in the traditional terms, 'from experience'.

Anyone who takes coherence seriously as the sole criterion of truth must consider any fabricated tale to be no less true than a historical report or the pro-positions in a chemistry text-book, so long as the tale is well enough fashioned to harbour no contradictions anywhere. With the aid of fantasy I can portray a grotesque world of adventure; the coherence philosopher has to believe in the truth of my account, provided only that I have a care for the mutual consistency of my claims and discreetly avoid any collision with the customary description of the world, by laying the sense of my recital on a distant star, where observation is no longer possible. Indeed, strictly speaking, I have no need at all of such discretion; I can equally well insist that others have to adjust themselves to my story, and not the other way round. The others cannot even object, in that case, that this procedure conflicts with observation, for according to the coherence theory no 'observations' of any kind are involved here, but only the consistency of the statements in question.

Since it does not occur to anybody to suppose the propositions in a storybook true, and those in a physics book false, the coherence view is a total failure. Something else must be added to coherence, namely a principle whereby consistency is to be established, and this alone would then be the actual criterion.

If I am given a set of statements, some of which are also contradictory, I can indeed achieve consistency in various ways, in that on one occasion, for example, I pick out certain statements and abandon or correct them, while on another I do the same with those which contradict the first.

This brings out the logical impossibility of the coherence view; it provides absolutely no unambiguous criterion of truth, for by means of it I can arrive at as many internally non-contradictory proposition-systems as I like, although they are not consistent with each other.

The absurdity is avoided only by not permitting the abandonment or correction of any statements you please, but rather by specifying those which are to be upheld, and to which the remainder have to conform.

IV

The coherence theory is now disposed of, and we have long ago arrived in the meantime at the second point of our critical deliberations, namely the question whether *all* propositions are corrigible, or whether there are also some which cannot be shaken. The latter would in fact form the 'foundation' of all knowledge that we were in search of, and towards which we have so far advanced not a single step.

By what rule, then are we to seek out those propositions which themselves remain unaltered, and with which all others must be brought into agreement? In what follows we shall speak of them not as 'protocol propositions', but as 'fundamental propositions', since it is in fact doubtful whether they occur at all in the protocols of science.

The first thing, no doubt, would be to look for the desired rule in a sort of economy-principle, and to say, in other words, that those propositions are to be chosen as fundamental whose adoption requires a *minimum* of changes in the entire system of statements, in order to free it from all contradiction.

It deserves to be noted that such a rule of economy would not establish some particular set of statements once and for all as fundamental propositions; it might happen, rather, that with the progress of knowledge the fundamental pro-

positions that had hitherto served as such were again downgraded, since it had turned out more economical to drop them in favour of newly discovered propositions which from then on – until further notice – would play the part of a foundation. So while the standpoint would indeed be no longer that of pure coherence, but rather one of economy, it would be equally prone to 'relativism'.

It seems to me beyond question that the supporters of the view just criticized were in fact taking the economy principle as their true guideline, whether they stated this or left it unsaid; I have therefore already assumed above that in the relativistic theory it is grounds of expediency that determine the choice of 'protocol propositions', and I asked: 'Can we agree to this?'

To this question I now give the answer 'No!'. It is not in fact economic expediency, but properties of a wholly different kind, which mark out the truly fundamental propositions.

The process of choosing these propositions could be called economic if it consisted, say, in an accommodation to the opinions (or 'protocol propositions') of the majority of inquirers. Now it is indeed the case that we accept a fact, e.g., of geography or history, or even a natural law, as indubitably established, if we very often find its existence mentioned in the places appropriate to such reports. It then simply does not occur to us to want to check it again for ourselves. We therefore concur with what is universally acknowledged. But the reason for this is that we know precisely in what way such factual statements ordinarily come to be made, and this way inspires our confidence; it is not because it corresponds to the majority view.

On the contrary, it could only attain to universal acknowledgement because each individual feels the same confidence. Whether and to what extent we declare a statement to be corrigible or capable of annulment depends entirely *on its origin*, and (apart from quite special cases) in no way on whether its retention requires the correcting of very many other statements, and perhaps a rearrangement of the whole system of knowledge.

Before the economy-principle can be applied, we have to know: *which* propositions is it to apply to? And if the principle were to be the *only* decisive rule, the answer could only be: well, to *all* propositions that are advanced, or ever have been advanced, with the claim to validity. In point of fact, the clause 'with the claim to validity' should be left out, for how are we to distinguish such propositions from those advanced purely arbitrarily, having been thought up as a joke, or in order to mislead? This distinction simply cannot be formulated, without taking the *origin* of the statements into account. So we find ourselves repeatedly referred back to the question of their source. Without having classified the statements according to their origin, any application of the economic principle of compatibility would be utterly absurd. But once we have investigated the propositions in respect of their origin, we notice right away that in so doing we have already at the same time ranged them in an order of validity, that – apart from certain special cases in still uncompleted areas of science – there is simply no room for any application of the economy-principle, and that the order in question simultaneously points the way to the foundations we are seeking.

V

At this point, indeed, the most extreme caution is called for. For here we hit upon the very path which has been followed from time immemorial, by all who have embarked on the journey to the ultimate grounds of truth. And the goal has always failed of achievement. For in this ordering of propositions according to their origin, which I attempt in order to judge their certainty, an exceptional position is immediately taken by those which I advance *myself*. And of these, a secondary position is again occupied by those lying in the past, since we believe that their certainty can be impaired by 'deceptions of memory' – and the more so, in general, the further back in time they lie. At the forefront, however, as immune from all doubt, stand those propositions which give expression to a matter of personal 'perception' or 'experience' (or whatever the term may be) that lies *in the present*. And however clear and simple this may appear to be, the philosophers have fallen into a hopeless labyrinth as soon as they have actually tried to employ propositions of the last-mentioned kind as the foundation of all knowledge. Some puzzling alleys in this labyrinth include, for example, those formulae and arguments which, under such names as 'evidence of inner perception', 'solipsism', 'solipsism

of the moment', 'self-certainty of consciousness', and so on, have been at the heart of so many philosophical disputes. The most famous destination to which pursuit of this path has led is the Cartesian *cogito ergo sum*, already reached beforehand, as it happens, by St. Augustine. And as to the *cogito ergo sum*, our eyes have nowadays been sufficiently opened by logic: we know that it is simply a pseudo-proposition, which again does not become a genuine statement through being expressed in the form: *cogitatio est* – 'contents of consciousness exist'. Such a proposition, which itself says nothing, can in no sense serve as the foundation of anything; it is not itself a piece of knowledge, and none is based upon it; it can lend no assurance to anything we know.

There is therefore the utmost danger that in pursuing the path recommended we may arrive at nothing but empty word-patterns, instead of the foundation we seek. It was, indeed, from the wish to obviate this danger that the critical theory of protocol propositions arose. But its chosen way out was unable to satisfy us; its *essential* defect consists in failing to recognize the differing status of propositions, most clearly revealed in the fact that for the system of knowledge which anyone accepts as the 'correct' one, his *own* propositions still ultimately play the only decisive role.

It is theoretically conceivable that the statements made by everyone else about the world should be in no way confirmed by my own observations. It might be the case that all the books I read and all the pronouncements I hear are in perfect agreement among themselves and never contradict one another, but that they are utterly irreconcilable with a large part of my own observation propositions. (In this case, the problem of language-learning and its use for communication would create certain difficulties, but they are soluble by means of certain assumptions as to whereabouts alone the contradictions are to appear.) According to the theory under criticism, in such a case I would simply have to sacrifice my own 'protocol propositions', since they are certainly at odds with the overwhelming mass of the others, which do harmonize together, and which there can be no possible expectation of correcting by reference to my own limited and fragmentary experience.

But what would really happen in the case supposed? Well, I would not give up my own observation propositions under any circumstances, for I find, rather, that I can only adopt a system of knowledge which they fit into without mutilation. And such a system I should always be able to construct. I need only regard other people as dreaming fools, whose madness has uncommon method in it – or to put it more concretely – I would say that the others are actually living in a different world from mine, which has only just so much in common with the latter as to permit communication in the same language. In any event, and whatever the world-picture I construct, I would always test its truth only by my own experience; this support I would never allow to be taken from me, my own observation propositions would always be the final criterion. I would proclaim, as it were: 'What I see, I see!'.

VI

In the light of these critical preliminaries, it is clear in what direction we have to seek for the solution of the difficulties that bewilder us; we must utilize stretches of the Cartesian road, so far as they are sound and passable, but then must beware of losing ourselves in the *cogito ergo sum* and similar absurdities. This we may do by attaining clarity as to the meaning and role which are in fact possessed by propositions stating what is 'immediately observed'.

What actually lies behind the statement that they are 'absolutely certain'? And in what sense can they be designated as the ultimate ground of all knowledge?

Let us first consider the second question. If we suppose that I at once take note of every observation – it makes no difference in principle whether I do so on paper or in memory – and now start out from thence to construct science, I would have before me genuine 'protocol propositions', standing temporally at the outset of knowledge. From them the remaining propositions of science would gradually be evolved through the process which we call 'induction', and which consists simply in the fact that, stimulated or incited by the protocol propositions, I tentatively set up general propositions ('hypotheses'), from which these first propositions, along with innumerable others, logically follow. Now if these others say the *same* as later observation statements, obtained under quite specific cir-

cumstances that have to be exactly stated in advance, then the hypotheses continue to rank as confirmed so long as observation statements do not crop up which are in contradiction to the propositions derived from the hypotheses, and hence to the hypotheses themselves. So long as this does not happen, we believe ourselves to have guessed correctly at a law of nature. Induction is therefore nothing else but a methodically guided guessing, a psychological, biological process whose execution has certainly nothing to do with 'logic'.

Here we have a schematic description of the actual procedure of science. It is clear what role is played in it by assertions about the 'immediately perceived'. They are not identical with statements written or remembered, i.e., with what could properly be called 'protocol propositions', but are the *occasion* for framing them. As we have long since conceded, the protocol propositions preserved in a book or in memory are doubtless to be compared in their validity with *hypotheses*, for if we have such a proposition before us, it is a mere assumption that it is true, that it accords with the observation statement which gave rise to it. (Perhaps, indeed, it was not occasioned by any observation statement, but arose out of some game or other.) What I call an observation-statement cannot be identical with a real protocol proposition, if only because in a certain sense it cannot be noted down at all – a point to be dealt with shortly.

In the schema of knowledge-construction that I have described, therefore, the role of the observation statements is firstly that of standing in time at the outset of the whole process, occasioning it and setting it to work. How much of their content enters into knowledge, remains as first essentially undecided. With some justice the observation statements can therefore be regarded as the ultimate origin of all knowledge, but ought they to be designated as its foundation, its ultimate certain ground? This is scarcely advisable, for this 'origin' is still connected in too questionable a manner with the edifice of knowledge. Moreover, we have certainly conceived the true process in a schematically simplified fashion. In reality, what is actually stated in a protocol is less closely connected with the observed as such, and in general we should not even assume that pure observation statements are interpolated at all between the observation and the 'protocol'.

But now it seems that these propositions, the statements about the immediately perceived, or 'affirmations' [*Konstatierungen*], as we might also call them, have yet another function to perform, namely in confirming hypotheses, or in *verification*.

Science makes prophecies that are tested by 'experience'. It is in making predictions that its essential function lies. It says, for example: 'If, at such and such a time, you look through a telescope focussed in such and such a manner, you will see a speck of light (a star) coinciding with a black line (cross-wires).' Let us assume that on following these instructions the event prophesied actually occurs; this means, of course, that we make an affirmation for which we are prepared; we pass an observational judgement that we *expected*, and have in doing so a sense of *fulfilment*, a wholly characteristic satisfaction; we are *content*. It is quite proper to say that the affirmations or observation statements have fulfilled their true mission, as soon as this peculiar satisfaction is obtained.

And we obtain it at the very moment in which the affirmation occurs, the observation statement is made. This is of the utmost importance, for it means that the function of propositions about the *presently* experienced itself lies in the present. We saw, indeed, that they have, as it were, no duration, that as soon as they are over we have available in their stead only designations or memory traces, which can play only the role of hypotheses and are thereby lacking in ultimate certainty. Upon affirmations no logically tenable structure can be erected, for they are already gone at the moment building begins. If they stand in time at the outset of the process of knowledge, they are logically of no use. It is quite otherwise, however, when they come at the end; they complete the act of verification (or falsification), and at the moment of their appearance have already performed their duty. Nothing else is logically deduced from them, no conclusions are drawn from them, they are an absolute end.

Psychologically and biologically, of course, the satisfaction they produce is the beginning of a new process of knowledge: the hypotheses whose verification concludes in them are regarded as confirmed, the framing of more extensive hypotheses is attempted, and the seeking and guessing after universal laws resumes its progress. For these temporally subsequent processes the obser-

vation statements therefore form the origin and incentive, in the sense already described.

By means of these considerations it seems to me that a new and vivid light is thrown upon the question of the ultimate foundation of knowledge; we get a clear picture of how the system of our knowledge is built up, and of the role that 'affirmations' play in it.

Knowledge is originally a means in the service of life. In order to fit into his environment and to accommodate his actions to events, man must in some degree be able to foresee these events. For this he needs universal propositions, findings of knowledge, and these he can make use of only insofar as the prophecies really come to pass. Now in science this character of knowledge remains completely intact; the only difference is that it no longer serves the purposes of life, and is not pursued for the sake of utility. Once the prediction comes to pass, the aim of science is achieved: the joy in knowledge is joy in verification, the exaltation of having guessed correctly. And this it is that the observation statements convey to us; in them science, as it were, attains its goal, and for their sake it exists. The question concealed behind the problem of the absolutely certain foundation of knowledge is, so to speak, that of the legitimacy of the satisfaction which verification fills us with. Are our predictions actually realized? In every single case of verification or falsification an 'affirmation' answers unambiguously with yes or no, with joy of fulfilment or disillusion. The affirmations are final.

Finality is a very suitable word to describe the significance of observation statements. They are an absolute end, and in them the current task of knowledge is fulfilled. That the joy in which they culminate, and the hypotheses they leave behind, are then the beginning of a new task, is no longer their affair. Science does not rest on them, but leads to them, and they show that it has led aright. They are really the absolutely fixed points; we are glad to reach them, even if we cannot rest there.

VII

What does this fixity consist in? We come here to the question earlier postponed for the time being: In what sense can we speak of the 'absolute certainty' of observation statements?

I should like to elucidate this by first saying something about a quite different kind of proposition, namely *analytic propositions*, and then comparing these with 'affirmations'. In analytic judgements the question of their validity notoriously poses no problem. They are valid *a priori*, we must not and cannot be convinced of their correctness by experience, because they say nothing whatever about the objects of experience. Hence, too, they possess only 'formal truth' i.e., they are not 'true' because they correctly express any facts; their truth, rather, consists solely in the fact that they are framed with formal correctness, i.e., conform to our arbitrarily established definitions.

But now some philosophical authors have felt obliged to ask: 'Well, how do I know in the given case whether a proposition is really in accordance with the definitions, and so is really analytic and therefore indubitable? Must I not bear in mind the proposed definitions, the meaning of all the words employed, while I utter, hear or read the proposition? But can I be sure that my mental capacities are equal to this? Is it not possible, for example, that by the end of the proposition, were it to last only for a second, I might have forgotten the beginning or wrongly remembered it? Must I not therefore admit that for psychological reasons I am never sure of the validity even of an analytic judgement?'

To this it must be replied that the possibility of malfunction in the mental mechanism must naturally always be conceded, but that the consequences that follow from it are not correctly described in the skeptical questions just propounded.

It can happen that through weakness of memory, and a thousand other causes, we fail to understand a proposition, or understand it wrongly (i.e., otherwise than it was intended) – but what is the significance of that? Well, so long as I have not understood a proposition, it is for me no statement at all, but a mere string of words, sounds or characters. In this case there is no problem, for only of a proposition can one ask if it is analytic or synthetic, not of an uncomprehended string of words. If, however, I have interpreted a series of words wrongly, but at all events as some sort of proposition – then I know of *this* particular proposition whether it is analytic, and so valid *a priori*, or not. It should not be thought that I could have grasped a proposition as such and then still be in doubt about its analytic character, for if it is analytic, I have only

just then understood it, when I have understood it as analytic, For to understand means in fact nothing else but to be clear about the rules for employment of the words involved; but it is precisely such rules which make the proposition analytic.[1] If I do not know whether a word-complex constitutes an analytic proposition or not, this means simply that at this moment I am without rules for employment of the words, and thus have failed entirely to understand the proposition. The situation is, therefore, that either I have understood nothing whatever, and then there is no more to be said, or else I know whether the proposition that I *have* understood is analytic or synthetic (which is not to assume, of course, that in so doing these words hover before me, or are even known to me). In the case of an analytic proposition, I then know at the same time that it is valid and possesses formal truth.

The foregoing doubts about the validity of analytic propositions were thus misplaced. I can indeed doubt whether I have correctly grasped the meaning of some sign-complex, and even whether I shall ever understand the meaning of a given word-series at all; but I cannot ask whether I am also really able to discern the correctness of an analytic proposition. For in an analytic judgement, to understand its meaning and to discern its *a priori* validity, are *one and the same process*. A synthetic statement, by contrast, is characterized by the fact that if I have merely discerned its meaning, I have no notion whether it is true or false; its truth is established only by a comparison with experience. The process of discerning the meaning is here entirely different from that of verification.

There is only one exception to this. And here we return to our 'affirmations'. For these are always of the form 'Here now so-and-so', e.g., 'Here now two black spots coincide', or 'Here now blue is bounded by yellow', or even 'Here now pain . . .', etc. What is common to all these statements is that they contain *demonstrative* terms having the meaning of a present gesture, i.e., their rules of use stipulate that in making the statement in which they occur, an experience occurs, attention is directed to something observed. The meaning of the words 'here', 'now', 'this here', etc. cannot be stated by means of general definitions in words, but only through such words assisted by pointings and gesticulations. 'This here' makes sense only in combination with a gesture. In order, therefore, to understand the significance of such an observation statement, one must simultaneously make the gesture, one must in some way point to reality.

In other words, I can understand the meaning of an 'affirmation' only on and by way of a comparison with the facts, i.e., a carrying-out of the process required for the verification of all synthetic propositions. But whereas in all other synthetic statements, establishing the meaning and establishing the truth are separate, clearly distinguishable processes, in observation statements they coincide, just as they do in analytic judgements. However different the 'affirmations' may be from analytic propositions, they have this in common, that in both the process of understanding is at the same time the process of verification. Along with their meaning I simultaneously grasp their truth. To ask of an affirmation whether I might perhaps be mistaken about its truth, makes no more sense than with a tautology. Both have absolute validity. The analytical or tautological proposition, however, is at the same time devoid of content, whereas the observation statement gives us the satisfaction of a genuine acquaintance with reality.

It has now become clear, let us hope, that everything here turns upon the character of immediacy which is peculiar to observation statements, and to which they owe their value both positive and negative; the positive value of absolute validity, and the negative value of being useless as an enduring foundation.

The misunderstanding of this character is in large part responsible for the unfortunate issue concerning protocol propositions which formed the starting-point of our inquiry. When I make the affirmation 'Here now blue', that is *not* the same as the protocol proposition 'On such-and-such a date in April 1934, at such-and-such a time and place, Schlick perceived blue'. For the latter proposition is a hypothesis, and as such is always fraught with uncertainty. It is equivalent to the statement '(at the given time and place) . . . Schlick made the affirmation "Here now blue"'. And clearly this statement is not identical with the affirmation occurring in it. In protocol propositions the reference is *always* to perceptions (or they are to be supplied mentally; the personal identity of the perceiving observer is important for a scientific protocol), while in affirmations they are *never* mentioned. A genuine affirmation can-

not be written down, for as soon as I put down the demonstrative terms 'here' and 'now', they lose their meaning. Nor can they be replaced by an indication of time and place, for as soon as this is attempted, the observation statement is unavoidably replaced, as we have seen, by a protocol proposition, which as such has an altogether different nature.

VIII

The problem of the foundation of knowledge has now, I believe, been elucidated.

If we look on science as a system of propositions, whose logical interconnection is the only feature of interest to us as logicians, then the question of their foundation, which in that case would be a 'logical' one, can be answered as we please, for we are free to define the foundation at will. In an abstract proposition-system, after all, there is intrinsically no priority and no posteriority. The most general propositions of science, i.e., those which are most commonly selected as 'axioms', could be designated, for example, as its ultimate foundation; but the name could equally well be reserved for the most specific propositions of all, which would then in fact actually correspond to the protocols written down; or some other choice would be possible. But the propositions of science are one and all *hypotheses*, the moment they are seen from the standpoint of their truth-value, or validity.

If we turn our attention to the connection of science with reality, and see in the system of its propositions what it really is, namely a means of orienting oneself among the facts, of attaining to the joy of confirmation, the feeling of finality, then the problem of the 'foundation' will automatically transform itself into that of the unshakeable points of contact between knowledge and reality. These absolutely fixed points, the affirmations, we have come to know in their particularity; they are the only synthetic propositions *which are not hypotheses*. In no sense do they lie at the basis of science, but knowledge, as it were, flickers out to them, reaching each one for a moment only, and at once consuming it. And newly fed and strengthened, it then flares on toward the next.

These moments of fulfilment and combustion are of the essence. From them comes all the light of knowledge. And it is this light for whose source the philosopher is actually asking, when he seeks the foundation of all knowledge.

Note

1   The idea that *a priori* propositions are all analytic, and that analytic truths are determined simply by rules for the employment of their component terms, was popular among the Logical Positivists, and an important aspect of their overall epistemology.

(B)   Popper, *The Logic of Scientific Discovery*

Chapter 10: Corroboration or How a Theory Stands Up to Tests

Theories are not verifiable, but they can be 'corroborated'.

The attempt has often been made to describe theories as being neither *true* nor *false*, but instead more or less *probable*. Inductive logic, more especially, has been developed as a logic which may ascribe not only the two values 'true' and 'false' to statements, but also degrees of probability; a type of logic which will here be called '*probability logic*'. According to those who believe in probability logic, induction should determine the degree of probability of a statement. And a principle of induction should either *make it sure* that the induced statement is 'probably valid' or else it should *make it probable*, in its turn – for the principle of induction might itself be only 'probably valid'. Yet in my view, the whole problem of the probability of hypotheses is misconceived. Instead of discussing the 'probability' of a hypothesis we should try to assess what tests, what trials, it has withstood; that is, we should try to assess how far it has been able to prove its fitness to survive by standing up to tests. In brief, we should try to assess how far it has been 'corroborated'.*

79   Concerning the So-called Verification of Hypotheses

The fact that theories are not verifiable has often been overlooked. People often say of a theory that it is verified when some of the predictions derived from it have been verified. They may perhaps admit that the verification is not completely impeccable from a logical point of view, or that a statement can never be finally established by establishing some of its consequences. But they are apt to look upon such objections as due to somewhat unnecessary scruples. It is quite true, they say, and even trivial, that we cannot know for certain whether the sun will rise tomorrow; but this uncertainty may be neglected: the fact that theories may not only be improved but that they can also be *falsified by new experiments* presents to the scientist a serious possibility which may at any moment become actual; but never yet has a theory had to be regarded as falsified owing to the sudden breakdown of a well-confirmed law. It never happens that old experiments one day yield new results. What happens is only that new experiments decide against an old theory. The old theory, even when it is superseded, often retains its validity as a kind of limiting case of the new theory; it still applies, at least with a high degree of approximation, in those cases in which it was successful before. In short, regularities which are directly testable by experiment do not change. Admittedly it is conceivable, or logically possible, that they might change; but this possibility is disregarded by empirical science and does not affect its methods. On the contrary, scientific method presupposes *the immutability of natural processes*, or the 'principle of the uniformity of nature'.

There is something to be said for the above argument, but it does not affect my thesis. It expresses the metaphysical faith in the existence of regularities in our world (a faith which I share, and without which practical action is

---

* I introduced the terms '*corroboration*' ('*Bewährung*') and especially '*degree of corroboration*' ('*Grad der Bewährung*', '*Bewährungsgrad*') in my book because I wanted a *neutral* term to describe the degree to which a hypothesis has stood up to severe tests, and thus 'proved its mettle'. By 'neutral' I mean a term not pre-judging the issue whether, by standing up to tests, the

hypothesis becomes 'more probable', in the sense of the probability calculus. In other words, I introduced the term 'degree of corroboration' mainly in order to be able to discuss the problem whether or not 'degree of corroboration' could be identified with 'probability' (either in a frequency sense or in the sense of Keynes, for example).

hardly conceivable). Yet the question before us – the question which makes the non-verifiability of theories significant in the present context – is on an altogether different plane. Consistently with my attitude towards other metaphysical questions, I abstain from arguing for or against faith in the existence of regularities in our world. But I shall try to show that *the non-verifiability of theories is methodologically important*. It is on this plane that I oppose the argument just advanced.

I shall therefore take up as relevant only one of the points of this argument – the reference to the so-called 'principle of the uniformity of nature'. This principle, it seems to me, expresses in a very superficial way an important method-ological rule, and one which might be derived, with advantage, precisely from a consideration of the non-verifiability of theories.

Let us suppose that the sun will not rise tomorrow (and that we shall nevertheless continue to live, and also to pursue our scientific interests). Should such a thing occur, science would have to try to *explain it*, *i.e.* to derive it from laws. Existing theories would presumably require to be drastically revised. But the revised theories would not merely have to account for the new state of affairs: *our older experiences would also have to be derivable from them*. From the methodo-logical point of view one sees that the principle of the uniformity of nature is here replaced by the postulate of *the invariance of natural laws*, with respect to both space and time. I think, therefore, that it would be a mistake to assert that natural regularities do not change. (This would be a kind of statement that can neither be argued against nor argued for.) What we should say is, rather, that it is part of our *definition* of natural laws if we postulate that they are to be invariant with respect to space and time; and also if we pos-tulate that they are to have no exceptions. Thus from a methodological point of view, the pos-sibility of falsifying a corroborated law is by no means without significance. It helps us to find out what we demand and expect from natural laws. And the 'principle of the uniformity of nature' can again be regarded as a metaphysical interpreta-tion of a methodological rule – like its near relative, the 'law of causality'.

One attempt to replace metaphysical state-ments of this kind by principles of method leads to the 'principle of induction', supposed to gov-ern the method of induction, and hence that

of the verification of theories. But this attempt fails, for the principle of induction is itself meta-physical in character. As I have pointed out in section 1, the assumption that the principle of induction is empirical leads to an infinite regress. It could therefore only be introduced as a primi-tive proposition (or a postulate, or an axiom). This would perhaps not matter so much, were it not that the principle of induction would have in any case to be treated as a *non-falsifiable statement*. For if this principle – which is supposed to vali-date the inference of theories – were itself falsifiable, then it would be falsified with the first falsified theory, because this theory would then be a conclusion, derived with the help of the principle of induction; and this principle, as a premise, will of course be falsified by the *modus tollens* whenever a theory is falsified which was derived from it. But this means that a falsifiable principle of induction would be falsified anew with every advance made by science. It would be necessary, therefore, to introduce a principle of induction assumed not to be falsifiable. But this would amount to the misconceived notion of a synthetic statement which is *a priori* valid, *i.e.* an irrefutable statement about reality.

Thus if we try to turn our metaphysical faith in the uniformity of nature and in the verifi-ability of theories into a theory of knowledge based on inductive logic, we are left only with the choice between an infinite regress and *apriorism*.

[. . .]

82   The Positive Theory of Corroboration: How a Hypothesis May 'Prove its Mettle'

Cannot the objections I have just been advanc-ing [in § 80–1] against the probability theory of induction be turned, perhaps, against my own view? It might well seem that they can; for these objections are based on the idea of an *appraisal*. And clearly, I have to use this idea too. I speak of the '*corroboration*' of a theory; and corrobora-tion can only be expressed as an appraisal. (In this respect there is no difference between corrobor-ation and probability.) Moreover, I too hold that hypotheses cannot be asserted to be 'true' state-ments, but that they are 'provisional conjectures' (or something of the sort); and this view, too, can only be expressed by way of an appraisal of these hypotheses.

The second part of this objection can easily be answered. The appraisal of hypotheses which indeed I am compelled to make use of, and which describes them as 'provisional conjectures' (or something of the sort) has the status of a *tautology*. Thus it does not give rise to difficulties of the type to which inductive logic gives rise. For this description only paraphrases or interprets the assertion (to which it is equivalent by definition) that strictly universal statements, *i.e.* theories, cannot be derived from singular statements.

The position is similar as regards the first part of the objection which concerns appraisals stating that a theory is corroborated. The appraisal of the corroboration is not a hypothesis, but can be derived if we are given the theory as well as the accepted basic statements. It asserts the fact that these basic statements do not contradict the theory, and it does this with due regard to the degree of testability of the theory, and to the severity of the tests to which the theory has been subjected, up to a stated period of time.

We say that a theory is 'corroborated' so long as it stands up to these tests. The appraisal which asserts corroboration (the corroborative appraisal) establishes certain fundamental relations, viz. compatibility and incompatibility. We regard incompatibility as falsification of the theory. But compatibility alone must not make us attribute to the theory a positive degree of corroboration: the mere fact that a theory has not yet been falsified can obviously not be regarded as sufficient. For nothing is easier than to construct any number of theoretical systems which are compatible with any given system of accepted basic statements. (This remark applies also to all 'metaphysical' systems.)

It might perhaps be suggested that a theory should be accorded some positive degree of corroboration if it is compatible with the system of accepted basic statements, and if, in addition, part of this system can be derived from the theory. Or, considering that basic statements are not derivable from a purely theoretical system (though their negations may be so derivable), one might suggest that the following rule should be adopted: a theory is to be accorded a positive degree of corroboration if it is compatible with the accepted basic statements and if, in addition,

a non-empty sub-class of these basic statements is derivable from the theory in conjunction with the other accepted basic statements.

I have no serious objections to this last formulation, except that it seems to me insufficient for an adequate characterization of the positive degree of corroboration of a theory. For we wish to speak of theories as being better, or less well, corroborated. But the *degree of corroboration* of a theory can surely not be established simply by counting the number of the corroborating instances, *i.e.* the accepted basic statements which are derivable in the way indicated. For it may happen that one theory appears to be far less well corroborated than another one, even though we have derived very many basic statements with its help, and only a few with the help of the second. As an example we might compare the hypothesis 'All crows are black' with the hypothesis 'the electronic charge has the value determined by Millikan'. Although in the case of a hypothesis of the former kind, we have presumably encountered many more corroborative basic statements, we shall nevertheless judge Millikan's hypothesis to be the better corroborated of the two.

This shows that it is not so much the number of corroborating instances which determines the degree of corroboration as *the severity of the various tests* to which the hypothesis in question can be, and has been, subjected. But the severity of the tests, in its turn, depends upon the *degree of testability*, and thus upon the simplicity of the hypothesis: the hypothesis which is falsifiable in a higher degree, or the simpler hypothesis, is also the one which is corroborable in a higher degree. Of course, the degree of corroboration actually attained does not depend *only* on the degree of falsifiability: a statement may be falsifiable to a high degree yet it may be only slightly corroborated, or it may in fact be falsified. And it may perhaps, without being falsified, be superseded by a better testable theory from which it – or a sufficiently close approximation to it – can be deduced. (In this case too its degree of corroboration is lowered.)

The degree of corroboration of two statements may not be comparable in all cases, any more than the degree of falsifiability: we cannot define a numerically calculable degree of corroboration, but can speak only roughly in terms of positive degree of corroboration, negative degrees of corroboration, and so forth. Yet we can lay down various rules; for instance the rule that we shall not continue to accord a positive degree of corroboration to a theory which has been falsified by an inter-subjectively testable experiment based upon a falsifying hypothesis (cf. sections 8 and 22). (We may, however, under certain circumstances accord a positive degree of corroboration to another theory, even though it follows a kindred line of thought. An example is Einstein's photon theory, with its kinship to Newton's corpuscular theory of light.) In general we regard an inter-subjectively testable falsification as final (provided it is well tested): this is the way in which the asymmetry between verification and falsification of theories makes itself felt. Each of these methodological points contributes in its own peculiar way to the historical development of science as a process of step by step approximations. A corroborative appraisal made at a later date – that is, an appraisal made after new basic statements have been added to those already accepted – can replace a positive degree of corroboration by a negative one, but not *vice versa*. And although I believe that in the history of science it is always the theory and not the experiment, always the idea and not the observation, which opens up the way to new knowledge, I also believe that it is always the experiment which saves us from following a track that leads nowhere: which helps us out of the rut, and which challenges us to find a new way.

Thus the degree of falsifiability or of simplicity of a theory enters into the appraisal of its corroboration. And this appraisal may be regarded as one of the logical relations between the theory and the accepted basic statements: as an appraisal that takes into consideration the severity of the tests to which the theory has been subjected.

83   Corroborability, Testability, and Logical Probability*

In appraising the degree of corroboration of a theory we take into account its degree of falsifiability. A theory can be the better corroborated

* If the terminology is accepted which I first explained in my note in Mind, 1938, then the word 'absolute' should be inserted here throughout before 'logical probability' (in contradistinction to 'relative' or 'conditional' logical probability).

the better testable it is. Testability, however, is converse to the concept of *logical probability*, so that we can also say that an appraisal of corroboration takes into account the logical probability of the statement in question. And this, in turn, as was shown in section 72, is related to the concept of objective probability – the probability of events. Thus by taking logical probability into account the concept of corroboration is linked, even if perhaps only indirectly and loosely, with that of the probability of events. The idea may occur to us that there is perhaps a connection here with the doctrine of the probability of hypotheses criticized above.

When trying to appraise the degree of corroboration of a theory we may reason somewhat as follows. Its degree of corroboration will increase with the number of its corroborating instances. Here we usually accord to the first corroborating instances far greater importance than to later ones: once a theory is well corroborated, further instances raise its degree of corroboration only very little. This rule however does not hold good if these new instances are very different from the earlier ones, that is if they corroborate the theory in a *new field of application*. In this case, they may increase the degree of corroboration very considerably. The degree of corroboration of a theory which has a higher degree of universality can thus be greater than that of a theory which has a lower degree of universality (and therefore a lower degree of falsifiability). In a similar way, theories of a higher degree of precision can be better corroborated than less precise ones. One of the reasons why we do not accord a positive degree of corroboration to the typical prophecies of palmists and soothsayers is that their predictions are so cautious and imprecise that the logical probability of their being correct is extremely high. And if we are told that more precise and thus logically less probable predictions of this kind have been successful, then it is not, as a rule, their success that we are inclined to doubt so much as their alleged logical improbability: since we tend to believe that such prophecies are non-corroborable, we also tend to argue in such cases from their low degree of corroborability to their low degree of testability.

If we compare these views of mine with what is implicit in (inductive) probability logic, we get a truly remarkable result. According to my view, the corroborability of a theory – and also the degree of corroboration of a theory which has in fact passed severe tests, stand both, as it were, in inverse ratio to its logical probability; for they both increase with its degree of testability and simplicity. *But the view implied by probability logic is the precise opposite of this.* Its upholders let the probability of a hypothesis increase in *direct proportion* to its logical probability – although there is no doubt that they *intend* their 'probability of a hypothesis' to stand for much the same thing that I try to indicate by 'degree of corroboration'.*

84   Remarks Concerning the Use of the Concepts 'True' and 'Corroborated'

In the logic of science here outlined it is possible to avoid using the concepts 'true' and 'false'.† Their

---

* The last lines of this paragraph, especially from the italicized sentence on (it was not italicized in the original) contain the crucial point of my criticism of the probability theory of induction. The point may be summarized as follows.

We want *simple* hypotheses – hypotheses of a high *content*, a high degree of *testability*. These are also the highly *corroborable* hypotheses, for the degree of corroboration of a hypothesis depends mainly upon the severity of its test, and thus upon its testability. Now we know that testability is the same as high (absolute) logical *improbability*, or low (absolute) logical *probability*.

But if two hypotheses, h_1 and h_2, are comparable with respect to their content, and thus with respect to their (absolute) logical probability, then the following holds: let the (absolute) logical probability of h_1 be smaller than that of h_2. Then, whatever the evidence e, the (relative) logical probability of h_1 given e can never exceed that of h_2 given e. Thus the *better testable and better corroborable hypothesis can never obtain a higher probability, on the given evidence, than the less testable one.* But this entails that *degree of corroboration cannot be the same as probability.* This is the crucial result. My later remarks in the text merely draw the conclusion from it: if you value high probability, you must say very little – or better still, nothing at all: tautologies will always retain the highest probability.

† Not long after this was written, I had the good fortune to meet Alfred Tarski who explained to me the fundamental ideas of his theory of truth. It is a great pity that this theory – one of the two great discoveries in the field of logic made since *Principia Mathematica* – is still often misunderstood and misrepresented. It cannot be to strongly emphasized that Tarski's idea of truth (for whose definition with respect to formalized

---

place may be taken by logical considerations about derivability relations. Thus we need not say: 'The prediction *p* is true provided the theory *t* and the basic statement *b* are true.' We may say, instead, that the statement *p* follows from the (non-contradictory) conjunction of *t* and *b*. The falsification of a theory may be described in a similar way. We need not say that the theory is 'false', but we may say instead that it is contradicted by a certain set of accepted basic statements. Nor need we say of basic statements that they are 'true' or 'false', for we may interpret their acceptance as the result of a conventional decision, and the accepted statements as results of this decision.

This certainly does not mean that we are forbidden to use the concepts 'true' and 'false', or that their use creates any particular difficulty. The very fact that we can avoid them shows that they cannot give rise to any new fundamental problem. The use of the concepts 'true' and 'false' is quite analogous to the use of such concepts as '*tautology*', '*contradiction*', '*conjunction*', '*implication*' and others of the kind. These are non-empirical concepts, logical concepts. They describe or appraise a statement irrespective of any changes in the empirical world. Whilst we assume that the properties of physical objects (of 'genidentical' objects in Lewin's sense) change with the passage of time, we decide to use these logical predicates in such a way that the logical

languages Tarski gave a method) is the same idea which Aristotle had in mind and indeed most people (except pragmatists): the idea that truth is *correspondence with the facts* (or with reality). But what can we possibly mean if we say of a *statement* that it corresponds with the *facts* (or with reality)? Once we realize that this correspondence cannot be one of structural similarity, the task of elucidating this correspondence seems hopeless; and as a consequence, we may become suspicious of the concept of truth, and prefer not to use it. Tarski solved (with respect to formalized languages) this apparently hopeless problem by making use of a semantic metalanguage, reducing the idea of correspondence to that of 'satisfaction' or 'fulfilment'.

As a result of Tarski's teaching, I no longer hesitate to speak of 'truth' and 'falsity'. And like everybody else's views (unless he is a pragmatist), my views turned out, as a matter of course, to be consistent with 'Tarski's theory of absolute truth. Thus although my views on formal logic and its philosophy were revolutionized by Tarski's theory, my views on science and its philosophy were fundamentally unaffected, although clarified.

properties of statements become timeless: if a statement is a tautology, then it is a tautology once and for all. This same timelessness we also attach to the concepts 'true' and 'false', in agreement with common usage. It is not common usage to say of a statement that it was perfectly true yesterday but has become false today. If yesterday we appraised a statement as true which today we appraise as false, then we implicitly assert today that *we were mistaken yesterday*; that the statement was false even yesterday – timelessly false – but that we erroneously 'took it for true'.

Here one can see very clearly the difference between truth and corroboration. The appraisal of a statement as corroborated or as not corroborated is also a logical appraisal and therefore also timeless; for it asserts that a certain logical relation holds between a theoretical system and some system of accepted basic statements. But we can never simply say of a statement that it is as such, or in itself, 'corroborated' (in the way in which we may say that it is 'true'). We can only say that it is *corroborated with respect to some system of basic statements* – a system accepted up to a particular point in time. 'The corroboration which a theory has received up to yesterday' is *logically not identical* with 'the corroboration which a theory has received up to today'. Thus we must attach a subscript, as it were, to every appraisal of corroboration – a subscript characterizing the system of basic statements to which the corroboration relates (for example, by the date of its acceptance).

Corroboration is therefore not a 'truth value'; that is, it cannot be placed on a par with the concepts 'true' and 'false' (which are free from temporal subscripts); for to one and the same statement there may be any number of different corroboration values, of which indeed all can be 'correct' or 'true' at the same time. For they are values which are logically derivable from the theory and the various sets of basic statements accepted at various times.

The above remarks may also help to elucidate the contrast between my views and those of the pragmatists who propose to *define* 'truth' in *terms of the success of a theory – and thus of its usefulness, or of its confirmation or of its corroboration.* If their intention is merely to assert that a logical appraisal of the success of a theory can be no more than an appraisal of its corroboration, I can agree. But I think that it would be far from

'*useful*' to identify the concept of corroboration with that of truth.* This is also avoided in ordinary usage. For one might well say of a theory that it has hardly been corroborated at all so far, or that it is still uncorroborated. But we should not normally say of a theory that it is hardly true at all so far, or that it is still false.

85   The Path of Science

One may discern something like a general direction in the evolution of physics – a direction from theories of a lower level of universality to theories of a higher level. This is usually called the 'inductive' direction; and it might be thought that the fact that physics advances in this 'inductive' direction could be used as an argument in favour of the inductive method.

Yet an advance in the inductive direction does not necessarily consist of a sequence of inductive inferences. Indeed we have shown that it may be explained in quite different terms – in terms of degree of testability and corroborability. For a theory which has been well corroborated can only be superseded by one of a higher level of universality; that is, by a theory which is better testable and which, in addition, *contains* the old, well corroborated theory – or at least a good approximation to it. It may be better, therefore, to describe that trend – the advance towards theories of an ever higher level of universality – as 'quasi-inductive'.

The quasi-inductive process should be envisaged as follows. Theories of some level of universality are proposed, and deductively tested; after that, theories of a higher level of universality are proposed, and in their turn tested with the help of those of the previous levels of universality, and so on. The methods of testing are invariably based on deductive inferences from the higher to the lower level; on the other hand, the levels of universality are reached, in the order of time, by proceeding from lower to higher levels.

The question may be raised: 'Why not invent theories of the highest level of universality

---

* Thus if we were to define 'true' as 'useful' (as suggested by some pragmatists), or else as 'successful' or 'confirmed' or 'corroborated', we should only have to introduce a new 'absolute' and 'timeless' concept to play the role of 'truth'.

straight away? Why wait for this quasi-inductive evolution? Is it not perhaps because there is after all an inductive element contained in it?' I do not think so. Again and again suggestions are put forward – conjectures, or theories – of all possible levels of universality. Those theories which are on too high a level of universality, as it were (that is, too far removed from the level reached by the testable science of the day) give rise, perhaps, to a 'metaphysical system'. In this case, even if from this system statements should be deducible (or only semi-deducible, as for example in the case of Spinoza's system), which belong to the prevailing scientific system, there will be no *new* testable statement among them; which means that no crucial experiment can be designed to test the system in question.* If, on the other hand, a crucial experiment can be designed for it, then the system will contain, as a first approximation, some well corroborated theory, and at the same time also something new – and something that can be tested. Thus the system will not, of course, be 'metaphysical'. In this case, the system in question may be looked upon as a new advance in the quasi-inductive evolution of science. This explains why a link with the science of the day is as a rule established only by those theories which are proposed in an attempt to meet the current problem situation; that is, the current difficulties, contradictions, and falsifications. In proposing a solution to these difficulties, these theories may point the way to a crucial experiment.

To obtain a picture or model of this quasi-inductive evolution of science, the various ideas and hypotheses might be visualized as particles suspended in a fluid. Testable science is the precipitation of these particles at the bottom of the vessel: they settle down in layers (of universality). The thickness of the deposit grows with the number of these layers, every new layer corresponding to a theory more universal than those beneath it. As the result of this process ideas previously floating in higher metaphysical regions may sometimes be reached by the growth of science, and thus make contact with it, and settle.

Examples of such ideas are atomism; the idea of a single physical 'principle' or ultimate element (from which the others derive); the theory of terrestrial motion (opposed by Bacon as fictitious); the age-old corpuscular theory of light; the fluid-theory of electricity (revived as the electron-gas hypothesis of metallic conduction). All these metaphysical concepts and ideas may have helped, even in their early forms, to bring order into man's picture of the world, and in some cases they may even have led to successful predictions. Yet an idea of this kind acquires scientific status only when it is presented in falsifiable form; that is to say, only when it has become possible to decide empirically between it and some rival theory.

My investigation has traced the various consequences of the decisions and conventions – in particular of the criterion of demarcation – adopted at the beginning of this book. Looking back, we may now try to get a last comprehensive glimpse of the picture of science and of scientific discovery which has emerged. (What I have here in mind is not a picture of science as a biological phenomenon, as an instrument of adaptation, or as a roundabout method of production: I have in mind its epistemological aspects.)

Science is not a system of certain, or well-established, statements; nor is it a system which steadily advances towards a state of finality. Our science is not knowledge (*epistēmē*): it can never claim to have attained truth, or even a substitute for it, such as probability.

Yet science has more than mere biological survival value. It is not only a useful instrument. Although it can attain neither truth nor probability, the striving for knowledge and the search for truth are still the strongest motives of scientific discovery.

We do not know: we can only guess. And our guesses are guided by the unscientific, the metaphysical (though biologically explicable) faith in laws, in regularities which we can uncover – discover. Like Bacon, we might describe our own contemporary science – 'the method of reasoning which men now ordinarily apply to nature' – as consisting of 'anticipations, rash and premature' and as 'prejudices'†

---

* It should be noted that I mean by a crucial experiment one that is designed to refute a theory (if possible) and more especially one which is designed to bring about a decision between two competing theories by refuting (at least) one of them – without, of course, proving the other.

† Bacon, *Novum Organum* I, 26. (See II. 7 of this volume.]

But these marvellously imaginative and bold conjectures or 'anticipations' of ours are carefully and soberly controlled by systematic tests. Once put forward, none of our 'anticipations' are dogmatically upheld. Our method of research is not to defend them, in order to prove how right we were. On the contrary, we try to overthrow them. Using all the weapons of our logical, mathematical, and technical armoury, we try to prove that our anticipations were false – in order to put forward, in their stead, new unjustified and unjustifiable anticipations, new 'rash and premature prejudices', as Bacon derisively called them.*

It is possible to interpret the ways of science more prosaically. One might say that progress can '. . . come about only in two ways: by gathering new perceptual experiences, and by better organizing those which are available already'.† But this description of scientific progress, although not actually wrong, seems to miss the point. It is too reminiscent of Bacon's induction: too suggestive of his industrious gathering of the 'countless grapes, ripe and in season',‡ from which he expected the wine of science to flow: of his myth of a scientific method that starts from observa-

tion and experiment and then proceeds to theories. (This legendary method, by the way, still inspires some of the newer sciences which try to practice it because of the prevalent belief that it is the method of experimental physics.)

The advance of science is not due to the fact that more and more perceptual experiences accumulate in the course of time. Nor is it due to the fact that we are making ever better use of our senses. Out of uninterpreted sense-experiences science cannot be distilled, no matter how industriously we gather and sort them. Bold ideas, unjustified anticipations, and speculative thought, are our only means for interpreting nature: our only organon, our only instrument, for grasping her. And we must hazard them to win our prize. Those among us who are unwilling to expose their ideas to the hazard of refutation do not take part in the scientific game.

Even the careful and sober testing of our ideas by experience is in its turn inspired by ideas: experiment is planned action in which every step is guided by theory. We do not stumble upon our experiences, nor do we let them flow over us like a stream. Rather, we have to be active: we have to '*make*' our experiences. It is we who always formulate the questions to be put to nature; it is we who try again and again to put these question so as to elicit a clear-cut 'yes' or 'no' (for nature does not give an answer unless pressed for it). And in the end, it is again we who give the answer; it is we ourselves who, after severe scrutiny, decide upon the answer to the question which we put to nature – after protracted and earnest attempts to elicit from her an unequivocal 'no'. 'Once and for all', says Weyl,§ with whom I fully agree, 'I wish to record my unbounded admiration for the work of the experimenter in his struggle to wrest *interpretable facts* from an unyielding Nature who knows so well how to meet our theories with a decisive *No* – or with an inaudible *Yes*.'

The old scientific ideal of *epistēmē* – of absolutely certain, demonstrable knowledge – has proved to be an idol. The demand for scientific objectivity makes it inevitable that every scientific statement must remain *tentative for ever*. It may

---

* Bacon's 'anticipation' ('*anticipatio*'; *Novum Organum* I, 26) *means almost the same as* '*hypothesis*' (*in my usage*). *Bacon held that, to prepare the mind for the intuition of the true essence or nature of a thing, it has to be meticulously cleansed of all anticipations, prejudices, and idols. For the source of all error is the impurity of our own minds: Nature itself does not lie. The main function of eliminative induction is (as with Aristotle) to assist the purification of the mind.*

† P. Frank, *Das Kausalgesetz und seine Grenzen*, 1932. The view that the progress of science is due to the accumulation of perceptual experiences is still widely held (cf. my second Preface, 1958). My denial of this view is closely connected with the rejection of the doctrine that science or knowledge is bound to advance since our experiences are bound to accumulate. As against this, I believe that the advance of science depends upon the free competition of thought, and thus upon freedom, and that it must come to an end if freedom is destroyed (though it may well continue for some time in some fields, especially in technology). This view is more fully expounded in my *Poverty of Historicism* (section 32). I also argue there (in the Preface) that the growth of our knowledge is unpredictable by scientific means, and that, as a consequence, the future course of our history is also unpredictable.

‡ Bacon, *Novum Organum* I, 123.

§ H. Weyl, *Gruppentheorie und Quantenmechanik*, Leipzig: Hirzel, 1931, p. 2. English translation by H. P. Robertson: *The Theory of Groups and Quantum Mechanics* (1931), p. xx.

indeed be corroborated, but every corroboration is relative to other statements which, again, are tentative. Only in our subjective experiences of conviction, in our subjective faith, can we be 'absolutely certain'.

With the idol of certainty (including that of degrees of imperfect certainty or probability) there falls one of the defences of obscurantism which bar the way of scientific advance. For the worship of this idol hampers not only the boldness of our questions, but also the rigour and the integrity of our tests. The wrong view of science betrays itself in the craving to be right; for it is not his *possession* of knowledge, of irrefutable truth, that makes the man of science, but his persistent and recklessly critical *quest* for truth.

Has our attitude, then, to be one of resignation? Have we to say that science can fulfil only its biological task; that it can, at best, merely prove its mettle in practical applications which may corroborate it? Are its intellectual problems insoluble? I do not think so. Science never pursues the illusory aim of making its answers final, or even probable. Its advance is, rather, towards an infinite yet attainable aim: that of ever discovering new, deeper, and more general problems, and of subjecting our ever tentative answers to ever renewed and ever more rigorous tests.

Addendum, 1972
In the preceding chapter of my book (which was the final chapter) I tried to make clear that by the *degree of corroboration* of a theory I mean a brief report that summarizes the way in which the theory has stood up to tests, and how severe these tests were.

I have never deviated from this view; see for example the beginnings of the new Appendices [. . .]. Here I wish to add the following points:

(1) The logical and methodological problem of induction is not insoluble, but my book offered a negative solution: (a) *We can never rationally justify a theory*, that is to say, our belief in the truth of a theory, or in its being probably true. This negative solution is compatible with the following positive solution, contained in the *rule of preferring* theories which are better corroborated than others: (b) *We can sometimes rationally justify the preference* for a theory in the light of its corroboration, that is, of the present state of the critical discussion of the competing theories, which are critically discussed and compared from the point of view of assessing their nearness to the truth (verisimilitude). The current state of this discussion may, in principle, be reported in the form of their degrees of corroboration. The degree of corroboration is not, however, a measure of verisimilitude (such a measure would have to be timeless) but only a report of what we have been able to ascertain up to a certain moment of time, about the comparative claims of the competing theories by judging the available reasons which have been proposed for and against their verisimilitude.

(2) A metaphysical problem raised by the idea of verisimilitude is: are there genuine regularities in nature? My reply is 'yes'. One of the arguments (non-scientific but perhaps 'transcendental') in favour of this reply is: if no regularities were apparent in nature then neither observations nor language could exist: neither a descriptive nor an argumentative language.

(3) The force of this reply depends on some kind of commonsense realism.

(4) The pragmatic problem of induction solves itself: the practical preference for the theory which in the light of the rational discussion appears to be nearer to the truth is risky but rational.

(5) The psychological problem (why do we *believe* that the theory so chosen will continue to be worthy of our trust?) is, I suggest, trivial: a belief or trust is always irrational, but it may be important for action.

(6) Not all possible 'problems of induction' are solved in this way.

22

Martin Heidegger, "*Dasein*, Disclosedness, and Truth"

Introduction

Perhaps the most common theory of knowledge in the history of philosophy conceives of truth as a "correspondence" or conformity between the intellect (thoughts or statements) and things – the *adaequatio intellectus et rei*. We've seen Aquinas, following Ibn Sina (Avicenna), appeal to this conception (II.6 in this volume); and the view has been attributed to thinkers as far back as Aristotle (*De interpretatione* I.16a6). German phenomenologist Martin Heidegger (1889–1976) argues that the correspondence theory – and indeed all other theories that conceive truth as a property of language, thought, or judgment – is derivative and contributes to a widespread forgetting of a deeper sense of truth, the "primordial" truth that makes any theory of truth meaningful.

Correspondence accounts of truth fail, according to Heidegger, for a number of reasons. In the first place, it's not at all clear that the idea of correspondence adequately explains what precisely it means for words or thoughts to agree with things. Taken by itself, as Heidegger explains in *Vom Wesen der Wahrheit* (*On the Essence of Truth*, 1931–2), that a proposition corresponds

to a thought that corresponds to a thing just isn't sufficient: "The proposition corresponds with what is known in knowledge; thus with what is true. The true? So, does the correspondence of the proposition amount to correspondence with something corresponding? A fine definition! Truth is correspondence with a correspondence, the latter itself corresponds with a correspondence, and so forth. . . . What presents itself as self-evident is utterly obscure."[1]

Moreover, as Heidegger explains in this selection from *Sein und Zeit* (*Being and Time*, 1927), correspondence theories, like scientific theories, like any theory, presupposes that truth is a general feature of human existence – of the kind of world human beings inhabit. Truth is, in short, what Heidegger calls an "*existentiale*" of "*Dasein*." (*Dasein* was translated by Jean-Paul Sartre as "human reality," but perhaps is better and certainly more literally understood as the "there-being" humans inhabit).[2] What any truth-claim presupposes is that humans inhabit a reality in which entities can be disclosed, in which things can appear and be apprehended as what they are. Without the prior condition that truth can be disclosed, claiming that a statement is true (or false, or even dubious) would be incoherent. Procedures for establishing, expressing, or certifying truth would be worse than pointless; they would be senseless.

Dasein in its very essence is a "truing" – in Heidegger's terminology, alternatively, a disclosing, a lighting, a clearing, an uncovering, or

From Martin Heidegger, *Being and Time*, J. Macquarrie and E. Robinson, San Francisco: Harper & Row, 1962, pp. 256–69.

un-concealing of things. As such, "truth" most basically isn't a property of sentences or theories, or even of the relationship of sentences-theories to things. It is that basic disclosedness of reality on the basis of which "truth" as a term attributed to sentences-thoughts-theories is secondarily possible. According to Heidegger, this primordial kind of truth has been forgotten or hidden by the history of western philosophy – although the ancient Greeks, who understood truth as *aletheia* ("un-forgetfulness" or "unveiledness") had a clearer understanding of it. Why?

In a way that echoes Bacon's scrutiny of various "idols" of the mind, Heidegger develops an error theory that explains the forgetfulness of the basic truing of being to which philosophy has been subject for so long. As it turns out, *Dasein* characteristically finds itself "thrown" into a world of entities or things and into a world of projects and concerns he calls "care." *Dasein* is also characteristically linguistic. That is, it is through language that the disclosure of entities is given expression. Both as linguistic and social beings, however, humans are also susceptible to a kind of "fallenness." People are subject to apprehending their existence as it is publicly understood by an everyday, impersonal "one" (*das man*), by the "they," and by "idle-talk" rather than as it actually is. (In this Heidegger also echoes

Kierkegaard's critique of impersonal objective theories of truth.) Because of *Dasein*'s thrownness and fallenness, people are inclined to interpret being itself as if it were a specific being, entity, or thing. (My calling being "it" in the preceding sentence is a case in point.) But *Dasein* and being itself are not themselves things. Being is the "there" of temporality where individual beings appear. *Dasein*, therefore, serves not only to disclose entities as what they are; *Dasein* also, sometimes simultaneously, hides them.

Like someone pointing out that we've been holding in our hand the very thing we've been looking for everywhere else, Heidegger aims to help us re-apprehend the primordial truth that is "there" in every one of our inquiries, that makes scientific truth and other forms of theoretical truth possible, but that we have covered over with centuries of looking elsewhere.

Notes

1 Martin Heidegger, *The Essence of Truth*, trans. T. Sandler, New York: Continuum, 2002, pp. 2–3.
2 J. P. Fell, *Heidegger and Sartre: An Essay on Being and Place*, New York: Columbia University Press, 1983.

Heidegger, *Dasein, Disclosedness, and Truth*

From time immemorial, philosophy has associated truth and Being. Parmenides was the first to discover the Being of entities, and he 'identified' Being with the perceptive understanding of Being: τὸ γὰρ αὐτὸ νοεῖν ἐστίν τε καὶ εἶναι.* Aristotle, in outlining the history of how the
213 ἀρχαί [archai] have been uncovered,† emphasizes that the philosophers before him, under the guidance of 'the things themselves' have been compelled to inquire further: αὐτὸ τὸ πρᾶγμα

---

* Diels, Fragment 5. [This fragment may be translated in more than one way: e.g., 'for thought and being are the same thing' (Fairbanks); 'it is the same thing that can be thought and can be' (Burnet). –Tr.]
† Aristotle, *Metaphysics A*.

ὡδοποίησεν αὐτοῖς καὶ συνηνάγκασε ζητεῖν.‡ He is describing the same fact when he says that ἀναγκαζόμενος δ᾽ἀκολουθεῖν τοῖς φαινομένοις§ – that he (Parmenides) was compelled to follow that which showed itself in itself. In another passage he remarks that these thinkers carried on their researches ὑπ᾽ αὐτῆς τῆς ἀληθείας ἀναγκαζόμενοι** – 'compelled by the "truth" itself'. Aristotle describes these researches as φιλοσοφεῖν περὶ τῆς ἀληθείας†† – '"philosophizing" about the "truth"' – or even as ἀποφαίνεσθαι περὶ τῆς ἀληθείας§§ – as exhibiting something and letting it be seen with

---

‡ Aristotle, *Metaphysics A*, 984a18 ff. ['. . . the very fact showed them the way and joined in forcing them to investigate the subject'. (Ross) –Tr.]
§ Aristotle, *Metaphysics A*, 986b31.
** Aristotle, *Metaphysics A*, 984b10.
†† Aristotle, *Metaphysics A*, 983b2.
§§ Aristotle, *Metaphysics aI*, 993b17.

regard to the 'truth' and within the range of the 'truth'. Philosophy itself is defined as ἐπιστήμη τῆς ἀληθείας* – 'the science of the "truth"'. But it is also characterized as ἐπιστήμη, ἣ θεωρεῖ τὸ ὄν ᾗ ὄν† –a 'science which contemplates entities as entities' that is, with regard to their Being.

What is signified here by 'carrying on researches into the "truth"' by "science of the 'truth'"? In such researches is 'truth' made a theme as it would be in a theory of knowledge or of judgment? Manifestly not, for 'truth' signifies the same as 'thing' ['Sache'], 'something that shows itself. But what then does the expression 'truth' signify if it can be used as a term for 'entity' and 'Being'?

If, however, *truth* rightfully has a primordial connection with *Being*, then the phenomenon of truth comes within the range of the problematic of fundamental ontology. In that case, must not this phenomenon have been encountered already within our preparatory fundamental analysis, the analytic of Dasein? What ontico-ontological connection does 'truth' have with Dasein and with that ontical characteristic of Dasein which we call the 'understanding of Being'? Can the reason why Being necessarily goes together with truth and *vice versa* be pointed out in terms of such understanding?

These questions are not to be evaded. Because Being does indeed 'go together' with truth, the phenomenon of truth has already been one of the themes of our earlier analyses, though not explicitly under this title. In giving precision to the problem of Being, it is now time to delimit the phenomenon of truth explicitly and to fix the problems which it comprises. In doing, this, we should not just take together what we have previously taken apart. Our investigation requires a new approach.

Our analysis takes its departure from the *traditional conception of truth*, and attempts to lay bare the ontological foundations of that conception *(a)*. In terms of these foundations the *primordial* phenomenon of truth becomes visible. We can then exhibit the way in which the traditional conception of truth has been *derived* from this phenomenon *(b)*. Our investigation will make it plain that to the question of the 'essence' of truth,

there belongs necessarily the question of the *kind of Being* which truth possesses. Together with this we must clarify the ontological meaning of the kind of talk in which we say that 'there is truth', and we must also clarify the kind of necessity with which 'we must presuppose' that 'there is' truth *(c)*.

(a)   The Traditional Conception of Truth, and its Ontological Foundations

There are three theses which characterize the way in which the essence of truth has been traditionally taken and the way it is supposed to have been first defined: (1) that the 'locus' of truth is assertion (judgment); (2) that the essence of truth lies in the 'agreement' of the judgment with its object; (3) that Aristotle, the father of logic, not only has assigned truth to the judgment as its primordial locus but has set going the definition of "truth" as 'agreement'.

Here it is not our aim to provide a history of the concept of truth, which would be presented only on the basis of a history of ontology. We shall produce our analytical discussions by alluding to some familiar matters.

Aristotle says that the παδήματα τῆς ψυχῆς are τῶν πραγμάτων ὁμοιώματα‡ – that the soul's 'Experiences', its νοήματα ('representations'), are likenings of Things. This assertion, which is by no means proposed as an explicit definition of the essence of truth, has also given occasion for developing the later formulation of the essence of truth as *adaequatio intellectus et rei*. Thomas Aquinas, who refers this definition to Avicenna (who has taken it over from Isaac Israeli's tenth-century '*Book of Definitions*') also uses for "*adaequatio*" (likening) the terms "*correspondentia*" ("correspondence") and "*convenientia*" ("coming together").§

The neo-Kantian epistemology of the nineteenth century often characterized this definition of "truth" as an expression of a methodologically retarded naive realism, and declared it to be irreconcilable with formulation of this question which has undergone Kant's 'Copernican revolution'. But Kant too adhered to this conception

215

---

* Aristotle, *Metaphysics* aI, 993b20.
† Aristotle, *Metaphysics* Γ, 1003a21.

‡ Aristotle, *De interpretatione*, I, 16a6.
§ Thomas Aquinas, from *De veritate*, [Part II.6].

of truth, so much so that he did not even bring it up for discussion; this has been overlooked though Brentano has already called our attention to it. 'The old and celebrated question with which it was supposed that one might drive the logicians into a corner is this: *"what is truth?"* The explanation of the name of truth – namely, that it is the agreement of knowledge with its object – will here be granted and presupposed. . . .

'If truth consists in the agreement of knowledge with its object, then this object must thus be distinguished from others; for knowledge is false if it does not agree with the object to which it is related, even if it should contain something which might well be valid for other objects.' And in the introduction to the "Transcendental Dialectic" Kant states: 'Truth and illusion are not in the object so far as it is intuited, but in the judgment about it so far as it is thought'.*

Of course this characterization of truth as 'agreement', *adaequatio*, ὁμοίωσις, is very general and empty. Yet it will still have some justification if it can hold its own without prejudice to any of the most various Interpretations which that distinctive predicate "knowledge" will support. We are now inquiring into the foundations of this 'relation'. *What else is tacitly posited in this relational totality of the adaequatio intellectus et rei? And what ontological character does that which is thus posited have itself?*

What in general does one have in view when one uses the term 'agreement'? The agreement of something with something has the formal character of a relation of something to something. Every agreement, and therefore 'truth' as well, is a relation. But not every relation is an agreement. A sign points *at* what is indicated. Such indicating is a relation, but not an agreement of the sign with what is indicated. Yet manifestly not every agreement is a *convenientia* of the kind that is fixed upon in the definition of 'truth'. The number '6' agrees with '16 minus 10'. These 216 numbers agree; they are equal with regard to the question of 'how much?' Equality is *one* way of agreeing. Its structure is such that something like a 'with-regard-to' belongs to it. In the *adaequatio* something gets related; what is that with regard to which it agrees? In clarifying the 'truth-

relation' we must notice also what is peculiar to the terms of this relation. With regard to what do *intellectus* and *res* agree? In their kind of Being and their essential content do they give us anything at all with regard to which they can agree? If it is impossible for *intellectus* and *res* to be equal because they are not of the same species, are they then perhaps similar? But knowledge is still supposed to 'give' the thing *just as* it is. This 'agreement' has the Relational character of the 'just as' ['*So – Wie*']. In what way is this relation possible as a relation between *intellectus* and *res*? From these questions it becomes plain that to clarify the structure of truth it is not enough simply to presuppose this relational totality, but we must go back and inquire into the context of Being which provides the support for this totality as such.

Must we, however, bring up here the 'epistemological' problematic as regards the subject–Object relation, or can our analysis restrict itself to Interpreting the 'immanent consciousness of truth', and thus remain 'within the sphere' of the subject? According to the general opinion, what is true is knowledge. But knowledge is judging. In judgment one must distinguish between the judging as a *Real* psychical process, and that which is judged, as an *ideal* content. It will be said of the latter that it is 'true'. The Real psychical process, however, is either present-at-hand or not. According to this opinion, the ideal content of judgment stands in a relationship of agreement. This relationship thus pertains to a connection between an ideal content of judgment and the Real Thing as that which is judged *about*. Is this agreement Real or ideal in its kind of Being, or neither of these? How *are we to take ontologically the relation between an ideal entity and something that is Real and present-at-hand?* Such a relation indeed subsists [*besteht*]; and in factical judgments it subsists not only as a relation between the content of judgment and the Real Object, but likewise as a relation between the ideal content and the Real act of judgment. And does it manifestly subsist 'more inwardly' in this latter case?

Or is the ontological meaning of the relation between Real and ideal (μέθεξις) something about which we must not inquire? Yet the relation is to be one which *subsists*. What does such 'subsisting' [*Bestand*] mean ontologically?

Why should this not be a legitimate question? Is it accidental that no headway has been made with this problem in over two thousand years? Has 217

---

* Immanuel Kant, *Critique of Pure Reason.* [See II.12 of the current volume.]

the question already been perverted in the very way it has been approached – in the ontologically unclarified separation of the Real and the ideal?

And with regard to the 'actual' judging of what is judged, is the separation of the Real act of judgment from the ideal content altogether unjustified? Does not the actuality of knowing and judging get broken asunder into two ways of Being – two 'levels' which can never be pieced together in such a manner as to reach the kind of Being that belongs to knowing? Is not psychologism correct in holding out against this separation, even if it neither clarifies ontologically the kind of Being which belongs to the thinking of that which is thought, nor is even so much as acquainted with it as a problem?

If we go back to the distinction between the act of judgment and its content, we shall not advance our discussion of the question of the kind of Being which belongs to the *adaequatio*; we shall only make plain the indispensability of clarifying the kind of Being which belongs to knowledge itself. In the analysis which this necessitates we must at the same time try to bring into view a phenomenon which is characteristic of knowledge – the phenomenon of truth. When does truth become phenomenally explicit in knowledge itself? It does so when such knowing demonstrates itself as *true*. By demonstrating itself it is assured of its truth. Thus in the phenomenal context of demonstration, the relationship of agreement must become visible.

Let us suppose that someone with his back turned to the wall makes the true assertion that 'the picture on the wall is hanging askew.' This assertion demonstrates itself when the man who makes it, turns round and perceives the picture hanging askew on the wall. What gets demonstrated in this demonstration? What is the meaning of 'confirming' [*Bewährung*] such an assertion? Do we, let us say, ascertain some agreement between our 'knowledge' or 'what is known' and the Thing on the wall? Yes and no, depending upon whether our Interpretation of the expression 'what is known' is phenomenally appropriate. If he who makes the assertion judges without perceiving the picture, but 'merely represents' it to himself, to what is he related"? To 'representations', shall we say? Certainly not, if 'representation' is here supposed to signify representing, as a psychical process. Nor is he related to 'representations' in the sense of what

is thus 'represented', if what we have in mind here is a 'picture' of that Real Thing which is on the wall.* The asserting which 'merely represents' is related rather, in that sense which is most its own to the Real picture on the wall. What one has in mind is the Real picture, and nothing else. Any Interpretation in which something else is here slipped in as what one supposedly has in mind in an assertion that merely represents, belies the phenomenal facts of the case as to that about 218 which the assertion gets made. Asserting is a way of Being towards the Thing itself that is. And what does one's perceiving of it demonstrate? Nothing else than *that* this Thing *is* the very entity which one has in mind in one's assertion. What comes up for confirmation is that this entity is pointed out by the Being in which the assertion is made – which is Being towards what is put forward in the assertion; thus what is to be confirmed is *that* such Being *uncovers* the entity towards which it is. What gets demonstrated is the Being-uncovering of the assertion. In carrying out such a demonstration, the knowing remains related solely to the entity itself. In this entity the confirmation, as it were, gets enacted. The entity itself which one has in mind shows itself *just as* it is in itself; that is to say, it shows that it, in its selfsameness, is just as *it* gets pointed out in the assertion as being – just as *it* gets uncovered as being. Representations do not get compared, either among themselves or in *relation to* the Real Thing. What is to be demonstrated is not an agreement of knowing with its object, still less of the psychical with the physical; but neither is it an agreement between 'contents of consciousness' among themselves. What is to be demonstrated

---

* 'Er is auch nicht auf Vorstellungen bezogen im Sinne des Vorgestellten, sofern damit gemeint wird ein "Bild" von dem realen Ding an der Wand'. While we follow tradition in translating 'Vorstellung' as 'representation', the literal meaning is somewhat closer to 'putting before us'. In this sense our 'picture' or 'image' ('Bild') of the actual picture ('Bild') on the wall, is itself something which we have 'put before us' and which is thus 'vorgestellt', though in English we would hardly call it 'that which we represent'. [Heidegger later came to criticize the modern era and its technological humanism as *Gestell*, as falsely believing that the meaning of beings is placed or put there solely by human agency. See, for example, 'The Question concerning Technology' (1954).]

is solely the Being-uncovered [*Entdeckt-sein*] of the entity itself – that *entity in* the 'how' of its uncoveredness. This uncoveredness is confirmed when that which is put forward in the assertion (namely the entity itself) shows itself *as that very same thing*. '*Confirmation*' signifies *the entity's showing itself in its selfsameness*.* The confirmation is accomplished on the basis of the entity's showing itself. This is possible only in such a way that the knowing which asserts and which gets confirmed is, in its ontological meaning, itself a *Being towards* Real entities, and a Being that *uncovers*.

To say that an assertion "is *true*" signifies that it uncovers the entity as it is in itself. Such an assertion asserts, points out, 'lets' the entity 'be seen' (ἀπόφανσις) in its uncoveredness. The *Being-true (truth)* of the assertion must be understood as *Being-uncovering*. Thus, truth has by no means the

219 structure of an agreement between knowing and the object in the sense (*if* a likening of one entity (the subject) to another (the Object).

Being-true as Being-uncovering, is in turn ontologically possible only on the basis of Being-in-the-world. This latter phenomenon, which we have known as a basic state of Dasein, is the *foundation* for the primordial phenomenon of truth. We shall now follow this up more penetratingly.

(b) The Primordial Phenomenon of Truth and the Derivative Character of the Traditional Conception of Truth

'Being-true' ('truth') means Being-uncovering. But is not this a highly arbitrary way to define 'truth'? By such drastic ways of defining this concept we may succeed in eliminating the idea of agreement from the conception of truth. Must we not pay for this dubious gain by plunging the 'good' old tradition into nullity? But while our definition is seemingly *arbitrary*, it contains only the *necessary* Interpretation of what was primordially surmised in the *oldest* tradition of ancient philosophy and even understood in

a pre-phenomenological manner. If a λόγος as ἀπόφανσις is to be true, its Being-true is ἀληθεύειν in the manner of ἀποφαίνεσθαι – of taking entities out of their hiddenness and letting them be seen in their unhiddenness (their uncoveredness). The ἀλήθεια which Aristotle equates with πρᾶγμα and φαινόμενα in the passages cited above, signifies, the 'things themselves'; it signifies what shows itself – *entities in the 'how' of their uncoveredness*. And is it accidental that in one of the fragments of Heraclitus – the oldest fragments of philosophical doctrine in which the λόγος is *explicitly* handled – the phenomenon of truth in the sense of uncoveredness (unhiddenness), as we have set it forth, shows through?† Those who are lacking in understanding are contrasted with the λόγος, and also with him who speaks that λόγος, and understands it. The λόγος is φράζων ὅπως ἔχει: it tells how entities comport themselves. But to those who are lacking in understanding, what they do remains hidden – λανθάνει. They forget it (ἐπιλανθάνονται); that is, for them it sinks back into hiddenness. Thus to the λόγος belongs unhiddenness – ἀ-λήθεια. To translate this word as 'truth', and, above all, to define this expression conceptually in theoretical ways, is to cover up the meaning of what the Greeks made 'self-evidently' basic for the terminological use of ἀλήθεια as a pre-philosophical way of understanding it.

In citing such evidence we must avoid unin- 220 hibited word mysticism. Nevertheless, the ultimate business of philosophy is to preserve the *force of the most elemental words* in which Dasein expresses itself, and to keep the common understanding from leveling them off to that unintelligibility which functions in turn as a source of pseudo-problems.

We have now given a phenomenal demonstration of what we set forth earlier as to λόγος and ἀλήθεια in, so to speak, a dogmatic Interpretation. In proposing our 'definition' of 'truth' we have not *shaken off* the tradition, but we have *appropriated* it primordially; and we shall have done so all the more if we succeed in demonstrating that the idea of agreement is one to which theory had to come on the basis of the

---

* On the idea of demonstration as 'identification' cf. Husserl, *Logische Untersuchungen*, vol. II, part 2, *Untersuchungen* VI. On 'evidence and truth' see *ibid.*, Sections 36–39.

† Cf. Diels, *Die Fragmente der Vorsokratiker*, Heracleitus fragment B1.

primordial phenomenon of truth, and if we can show how this came about.

Moreover, the 'definition' of 'truth' as 'uncoveredness' and as 'Being-uncovering', is not a mere explanation of a word. Among those ways in which Dasein comports itself there are some which we are accustomed in the first instance to call 'true'; from the analysis of these our definition emerges. Being-true as Being-uncovering, is a way of Being for Dasein. What makes this very uncovering possible must necessarily be called 'true' in a still more primordial sense. *The most primordial phenomenon of truth is first shown by* the *existential-ontological foundations of uncovering.*

Uncovering is a way of Being for Being-in-the-world. Circumspective concern, or even that concern in which we tarry and look at something, uncovers entities within-the-world. These entities become that which has been uncovered. They are 'true' in a second sense. What is primarily 'true' – that is, uncovering – is Dasein. 'Truth' in the second sense does not mean Being-uncovering (uncovering), but Being-uncovered (uncoveredness).

Our earlier analysis of the worldhood of the world and of entities within-the-world has shown, however, that the uncoveredness of entities within-the-world is *grounded* in the world's disclosedness. But disclosedness is that basic character of Dasein according to which it *is* its 'there'. Disclosedness is constituted by state-of-mind, understanding, and discourse, and pertains equiprimordially to the world, to Being-in, and to the Self. In its very structure, care is *ahead of itself* – Being already in a world – as Being alongside entities within-the-world; and in this structure the disclosedness of Dasein lies hidden. *With* and *through* it is uncoveredness; hence only 221 with Dasein's *disclosedness* is the *most primordial* phenomenon of truth attained. What we have pointed out earlier with regard to the existential Constitution of the 'there', and in relation to the everyday Being of the 'there' pertains to the most primordial phenomenon of truth, nothing less. In so far as Dasein *is* its disclosedness essentially, and discloses and uncovers as something disclosed to this extent it is essentially 'true'. *Dasein is 'in the truth'.* This assertion has meaning ontologically. It does not purport to say that ontically Dasein is introduced 'to all the truth' either always or just in every case, but rather that the disclosedness of

its ownmost Being belongs to its existential constitution.

If we accept the results we have obtained earlier, the full existential meaning of the principle that 'Dasein is in the truth' can be restored by considerations:

(1) To Dasein's state of Being, *disclosedness in general* essentially belongs. It embraces the whole of that structure-of-Being which has become explicit through the phenomenon of care. To care belongs not only Being-in-the-world but also Being alongside entities within-the-world. The uncoveredness of such entities is equiprimordial with the Being of Dasein and its disclosedness.

(2) To Dasein's state of Being belongs *thrownness*; indeed it is constitutive for Dasein's disclosedness. In thrownness is revealed that in each case Dasein, as my Dasein and this Dasein, is already in a definite world and alongside a definite range of definite entities within-the-world. Disclosedness is essentially factical.

(3) To Dasein's state of Being belongs *projection* – disclosive Being towards its potentiality-for-Being. As something that understands, Dasein *can* understand *itself* in terms of the 'world' and Others or in terms of its ownmost potentiality-for-Being. The possibility just mentioned means that Dasein discloses itself to itself in and as its ownmost potentiality-for-Being. This *authentic* disclosedness shows the phenomenon of the most primordial truth in the mode of authenticity. The most primordial, and indeed the most authentic, disclosedness in which Dasein, as a potentiality-for-Being, can be, is the *truth of existence*. This becomes existentially and ontologically definite only in connection with the analysis of Dasein's authenticity.

(4) To Dasein's state of Being belongs falling. Proximally and for the most part Dasein is lost 222 in its 'world'. Its understanding, as a projection upon possibilities of Being, has diverted itself thither. Its absorption in the 'they' signifies that it is dominated by the way things are publicly interpreted. That which has been uncovered and disclosed stands in a mode in which it has been disguised and closed off by idle talk, curiosity, and ambiguity. Being towards entities has not been extinguished, but it has been uprooted. Entities have not been completely hidden; they are precisely the sort of thing that has been uncovered, but at the same time they have been disguised.

They show themselves, but in the mode of semblance. Likewise what has formerly been uncovered sinks back again, hidden and disguised. *Because Dasein is essentially falling, its state of Being is such that it is in 'untruth'. This* term, like the expression 'falling', is here used ontologically. If we are to use it in existential analysis, we must avoid giving it any ontically negative 'evaluation'. To be closed off and covered up belongs to Dasein's *facticity.* In its full existential-ontological meaning, the proposition that 'Dasein is in the truth' states equiprimordially that 'Dasein is in untruth'. But only in so far as Dasein has been disclosed has it also been closed off; and only in so far as entities within-the-world have been uncovered along with Dasein, have such entities, as possibly encounterable within-the-world, been covered up (hidden) or disguised.

It is therefore essential that Dasein should explicitly appropriate what has already been uncovered, defend it *against* semblance and disguise, and assure itself of its uncoveredness again and again. The uncovering of anything new is never done on the basis of having something completely hidden, but takes its departure rather from uncoveredness in the mode of semblance. Entities look as if... That is, they have, in a certain way, been uncovered already, and yet they are still disguised.

Truth (uncoveredness) is something that must always first be wrested from entities. Entities get snatched out of their hiddenness. The factical uncoveredness of anything is always, as it were, a kind of *robbery.* Is it accidental that when the Greeks express themselves as to the essence of truth, they use a *privative* expression – ἀ-λήθεια? When Dasein so expresses itself, does not a primordial understanding of its own Being thus make itself known – the understanding (even if it is only pre-ontological) that Being-in-untruth makes up an essential characteristic of Being-in-the world?

The goddess of Truth who guides Parmenides, puts two pathways before him, one of uncovering, one of hiding; but this signifies nothing else than that Dasein is already both in the truth and in untruth. The way of uncovering is achieved only in κρίνειν λόγῳ – distinguishing between these understandingly, and making one's decision for the one rather than the other.

The existential-ontological condition for the fact that Being-in-the-world is characterized by 'truth' and 'untruth', lies in that state of Dasein's Being which we have designated as *thrown projection.* This is something that is constitutive for the structure of care.

The upshot of our existential-ontological Interpretation of the phenomenon of truth is (1) that truth, in the most primordial sense, is Dasein's disclosedness, to which the uncoveredness of entities within-the-world belongs; and (2) that Dasein is equiprimordially both in the truth and in untruth.

Within the horizon of the traditional Interpretation of the phenomenon of truth, our insight into these principles will not be complete until it can be shown: (1) that truth, understood as agreement, originates from disclosedness by way of definite modification; (2) that the kind of being which belongs to disclosedness itself is such that its derivative modification first comes into view and leads the way for the theoretical explication of the structure of truth.

Assertion and its structure (namely, the apophantical 'as') are founded upon interpretation and its structure (viz, the hermeneutical 'as') and also upon understanding – upon Dasein's disclosedness. Truth, however, is regarded as a distinctive character of assertion as so derived. Thus the roots of the truth of assertion reach back to the disclosedness of the understanding. But over and above these indications of how the truth of assertion has originated, the phenomenon of *agreement* must now be exhibited *explicitly* in its derivative character.

Our Being alongside entities within-the-world is concern, and this is Being which uncovers. To Dasein's disclosedness, however, discourse belongs essentially. Dasein expresses itself [*spricht sich aus*]: it expresses *itself* as a Being-towards entities – a Being-towards which uncovers. And in assertion it expresses itself as such about entities which have been uncovered. Assertion communicates entities in the 'how' of their uncoveredness. When Dasein is aware of the communication, it brings itself in its awareness into an uncovering Being-towards the entities discussed. The assertion which is expressed is about something, and in what it is about [*in ihrem Worüber*] it contains the uncoveredness of these entities. This uncoveredness is preserved in what is expressed. What is expressed becomes, as it were, something ready-to-hand within-the-world which can be taken up and spoken again.* Because the uncoveredness has been preserved, that which is expressed (which thus is ready-to-hand) has in itself a relation to any entities about which it is an assertion. Any uncoveredness is an uncoveredness of something. Even when Dasein speaks over again what someone else has said, it comes into a Being-towards the very entities which have been discussed. But it has been exempted from having to uncover them again, primordially, and it holds that it has been thus exempted.

Dasein need not bring itself face to face with entities themselves in an 'original' experience; but it nevertheless remains in a Being-towards these entities. In a large measure uncoveredness gets appropriated not by one's own uncovering, but rather by hearsay of something that has been said.

Absorption in something that has been said belongs to the kind of Being which the 'they' possesses. That which has been expressed as such takes over Being-towards those entities which have been uncovered in the assertion. If, however, these entities are to be appropriated explicitly with regard to their uncoveredness, this amounts to saying that the assertion is to be demonstrated as one that uncovers. But the assertion expressed is something ready-to-hand, and indeed in such a way that, as something by which uncoveredness is preserved, it has in itself a relation to the entities uncovered. Now to demonstrate that it is something which uncovers [*ihres Entdeckend-seins*] means to demonstrate how the assertion by which the uncoveredness is preserved is related *to* these entities. The assertion is something ready-to-hand. The entities to which it is related as something that uncovers, are either ready-to-hand or present-at-hand within-the-world. The relation itself presents itself thus, as one that is present-at-hand. But this relation lies in the fact that the uncoveredness preserved in the assertion is in each case an uncoveredness of something.

The judgment 'contains something which holds for the objects' (Kant). But the relation itself now acquires the character of presence-at-hand by getting switched over to a relationship between things which are present-at-hand. The uncoveredness of something becomes the present-at-hand conformity of one thing which is present-at-hand – the assertion expressed – *to* something else which is present-at-hand – the entity under discussion. And if this conformity is seen only as a relationship between things which are present-at-hand – that is, if the kind of Being which belongs to the terms of this relationship has not been discriminated and is understood as something merely present-at-hand – then the relation shows itself as an agreement of two things which are present-at-hand, an agreement which is present-at-hand itself.

When the assertion has been expressed, the un- 225 *coveredness of the entity moves into the kind of Being of that which is ready-to-hand within-the-world. But now to the extent that in this uncoveredness,* as an uncoveredness of something, *a relationship to something present-at-hand persists, the uncoveredness (truth) becomes, for its part, a relationship between things which are present-at-hand (intellectus and res) a relationship that is present-at-hand itself.*

Though it is founded upon Dasein's disclosedness, the existential phenomenon of uncoveredness becomes a property which is present-at-hand but in which there still lurks a relational character; and as such a property, it gets broken asunder into a relationship which is present-at-hand. Truth as disclosedness and as a Being towards uncovered entities – a Being which itself uncovers – has become truth as agreement between things which are present-at-hand within-the-world. And thus we pointed out the ontologically derivative character of the traditional conception of truth.

Yet that which is last in the order of the way things are connected in their foundations existentially and ontologically, is regarded ontically and factically as that which is first and closest to us. The necessity of this Fact, however, is based in turn upon the kind of Being which Dasein itself possesses. Dasein, in its concernful absorption, understands itself in terms of what it encounters within-the-world. The uncoveredness which belongs to uncovering, is something that we come across proximally within-the-world in that which has been expressed [im *Aus*gesprochenen]. Not only truth, however, is encountered as present-at-hand: in general our understanding of Being

---

* [Beings that exist as "ready-to-hand" (*zuhanden*) are beings disclosed through our concerns and our projects, as well as through the way we use them. This for Heidegger is the primary mode of beings. A derivative mode of being, which has misleadingly been posited by the metaphysical and scientific traditions as primary, is what Heidegger calls being "present-at-hand" (*vorhanden*) – existing independently of human beings and their engagement with the world. Heidegger's *destruktion* of this inverted "metaphysics of presence" is central to his phenomenological labor. – Eds]

is such that every entity is understood in the first instance as present-at-hand. If the 'truth' which we encounter proximally in an ontical manner is considered ontologically in the way that is closest to us, then the λόγος (the assertion) gets understood as λόγος τινός – as an assertion about something, an uncoveredness of something; but the phenomenon gets Interpreted as something present-at-hand with regard to its possible presence-at-hand. Yet because presence-at-hand has been equated with the meaning of Being in general, the question of whether this kind of Being of truth is a primordial one, and whether there is anything primordial in that structure of it which we encounter as closest to us, *can* not come alive at all. *The primordial phenomenon of truth has been covered up by Dasein's very understanding of Being – that understanding which is proximally the one that prevails, and which even today has not been surmounted* explicitly *and in principle.*

At the same time, however, we must not overlook the fact that while this way of understanding Being (the way which is closest to us) is one which the Greeks were the first to develop as a branch of knowledge and to master, the primordial understanding of truth was simultaneously alive among them, even if pre-ontologically – at least in Aristotle.*

226   Aristotle never defends the thesis that the primordial 'locus' of truth is in the judgment. He says

* Cf. Aristotle, *Ethica Nicomachea* Z and *Metaphysica* Θ 10.

rather that the λόγος is that way of Being in which Dasein can *either* uncover *or* cover up. This *double possibilly* is what is distinctive in the Being-true of the λόγος: the λόγος is that way of comporting oneself which can *also cover things* up. And because Aristotle never upheld the thesis we have mentioned, he was also never in a situation to 'broaden' the conception of truth in the λόγος to include pure νοεῖν. The truth of αἴσθησις and of the seeing of 'ideas' is the primordial kind of uncovering. And only because νόησις primarily uncovers, can, the λόγος as διανοεῖν also have uncovering as its function.

Not only is it wrong to invoke Aristotle for the thesis that the genuine "locus" of truth lies in the judgment; even in its content this thesis fails to recognize the structure of truth. Assertion is not the primary 'locus' of truth. *On the contrary,* whether as a mode in which uncoveredness is appropriated or as a way of Being-in-the-world, assertion is grounded in Dasein's uncovering, or rather in its *disclosedness.* The most primordial 'truth' is the 'locus' of assertion; it is the ontological condition for the possibility that assertions can be either true or false – that they may uncover or cover things up.

Truth, understood in the most primordial sense, belongs to the basic constitution of Dasein. The term signifies an *existentiale.* But herewith we have already sketched out our answers to the question of what kind of Being truth possesses, and to the question of in what sense it is necessary to presuppose that 'there is truth'.

23

Ludwig Wittgenstein, *Philosophical Investigations* (§§60–81, 112–16, 269–75)

Introduction

Arguably one of the most important philosophers of the twentieth century, Ludwig Wittgenstein (1889–1951) was born in Vienna, the youngest of eight children. The Wittgenstein family was one of the wealthiest in Europe and was also deeply involved in the dynamic arts scene in Vienna. Composers and artists such as Brahms and Mahler were frequent guests in the family home, and the Wittgenstein children all received a musical education. The family patronized the Secession movement. Ludwig, however, was drawn to technical subjects. He attended the *Realschule* in Linz, at the same time Adolf Hitler was enrolled there, and then went on to study engineering in Berlin and in Manchester, where he conducted research toward a doctorate in aeronautics.

Reading the work of Bertrand Russell (II.20 in this volume) and Gottlob Frege (1848–1925) led Wittgenstein into the study of philosophy, and in 1911 he joined Russell at Trinity College of Cambridge University in pursuing ideas in the philosophy of logic. With the outbreak of World War I, Wittgenstein volunteered for the Austrian army and after engaging in a number of battles

From Ludwig Wittgenstein, *Philosophical Investigations*, trans. G. E. M. Anscombe, 3rd edition, New York: Macmillan Publishing Co., 1958, pp. 29–38, 47–8, 94–6.

on the Russian front was awarded several medals for bravery. He was captured and interred in a camp near the monastery of Monte Casino in Italy, where Thomas Aquinas had lived. While serving in the military and during his internment, Wittgenstein completed his first major work, the *Tractatus Logico-Philosophicus* (1922).

Epistemologically, the *Tractatus* relies on a "picture theory" of language. Influenced by the work of theorists in science and engineering, Wittgenstein came to think that the fundamental elements in language somehow picture or correspond to fundamental facts in the world. Both the elements of sentences and the elements of the world occupy, according to this view, "logical space" that sets out the possibilities of their combination. "Atomic sentences" of this sort, then, either singly or in molecular combination, "say" meaningful things about the world. Not all language, however, is meaningful in this sense or, anyway, says things clearly. Knowledge, accordingly, is achieved by logically analyzing and purifying language, eliminating or partitioning those portions of language that are "nonsense" or "nonsensical," and saying clearly what it is possible to say. Matters of ethics, aesthetics, and religious expression, however, cannot be said clearly, and trying to say them produces nonsensical philosophy. Such matters can only be "shown," and so about them the best people can do is remain silent. Wittgenstein's views were extremely influential with the Vienna Circle and logical positivists elsewhere.

Returning after the war to Cambridge, where he would spend much of the rest of his life, Wittgenstein came to think, however, of some of these ideas as mistaken. He concluded that language acquires meaning not through correspondence or picturing the world but instead through the role words play in various "language-games" (*Sprachspiele*) and "forms of life" (*Lebensformen*). It is from these phases of Wittenstein's thought that the following selections from his posthumous *Philosophical Investigations* (1953) have been taken.

Contrary to his views in the *Tractatus*, in his later work Wittgenstein maintained that it is mistaken to think that logically analyzing language somehow lays bare its inner, hidden core – its essential meaning. There is, rather, no essential logical structure the discovery of which will produce a better, more ideal language: "To say, however, that a sentence in (b) is an 'analysed' form of one in (a) readily seduces us into thinking that the former is the more fundamental form; that it alone shews what is meant by the other, and so on."

His work on this topic has had a powerful subversive effect not only upon the idea that words have essential meanings but also upon the aspiration to achieve knowledge by apprehending the "essential" natures of things. Terms like "human" or "game" do not, according to Wittgenstein, refer to some common essential feature that each thing they describe possesses. Instead, such terms point to things linked together for different purposes in different contexts by "family resemblances," each member of the linked group resembling some others in context-relevant ways, but perhaps not in a universally common way – "we see a complicated network of similarities overlapping and crisscrossing: sometimes overall similarities, sometimes similarities of detail." What is regarded as "essential" or "inessential" about whatever one is investigating, depends upon the language-game one is playing, and playing with others: "One thinks that one is tracing the outline of the thing's nature over and over again, and one is merely tracing round the frame through which we look at it."

To understand what it is to know something, then, means coming to understand the "grammar" of the word "know" – the way the word "know" is used in various language-games. Commonly, to "know" something (unlike to "believe" something) means to be able to do something that provides convincing grounds or support for the claim – where what is to count as proper grounds is internal to that game. In this context, the very possibility of doubt implies the possibility of knowledge. So, according to Wittgenstein, it can only be possible to doubt if it is also possible to know. One can in addition, however, in a different way "know" something but not be able to "say" that knowledge in a formula, as for example when one knows what a clarinet sounds like. In other instances, it simply makes no sense to speak of knowledge – for example to say, except in some strange context, "I know I am in pain."

In these ways, Wittgenstein's work bears import for the epistemological issue of skepticism. Notably, Wittgenstein argues that a "private language" (and therefore solipsism) is impossible because the very possibility of meaningful language requires a public world, populated by other people with whom one is engaged, who can correct and respond to one's usage. Furthermore, Wittgenstein's investigations into the meaningful uses of words reveals that specific statements about the world are simply certain and cannot be meaningfully doubted. They are indubitable, however, not because they are grounded in some sort of cognitive bedrock such as immediate observation, sense-data, or intuition. Rather, they are grounded in what we do – the forms of life according to which we actually act in the world. Indubitable statements of this sort, as they were discussed in *On Certainty* (the text on which Wittgenstein was working when he died), have come to be called "hinge propositions," propositions upon which the very forms of life in which we are engaged turn. Forms of life, then, not perceptions or self-evident truths serve for Wittgenstein as epistemological foundations, and our lives "show" us their truth (*On Certainty*, §7).

Wittgenstein, Philosophical Investigations

60.   When I say: "My broom is in the corner", – is this really a statement about the broomstick and the brush? Well, it could at any rate be replaced by a statement giving the position of the stick and the position of the brush. And this statement is surely a further analysed form of the first one. – But why do I call it "further analysed"? – Well, if the broom is there, that surely means that the stick and brush must be there, and in a particular relation to one another; and this was as it were hidden in the sense of the first sentence, and is *expressed* in the analysed sentence. Then does someone who says that the broom is in the corner really mean: the broomstick is there, and so is the brush, and the broomstick is fixed in the brush? – If we were to ask anyone if he meant this he would probably say that he had not thought specially of the broomstick or specially of the brush at all. And that would be the *right* answer, for he meant to speak neither of the stick nor of the brush in particular. Suppose that, instead of saying "Bring me the broom", you said "Bring me the broomstick and the brush which is fitted on to it."! – Isn't the answer: "Do you want the broom? Why do you put it so oddly?" – Is he going to understand the further analysed sentence better? – This sentence, one might say, achieves the same as the ordinary one, but in a more round-about way. – Imagine a language-game in which someone is ordered to bring certain objects which are composed of several parts, to move them about, or something else of the kind. And two ways of playing it: in one (a) the composite objects (brooms, chairs, tables, etc.) have names, as in (§15); in the other (b) only the parts are given names and the wholes are described by means of them. – In what sense is an order in the second game an analysed form of an order in the first? Does the former lie concealed in the latter, and is it now brought out by analysis? – True, the broom is taken to pieces when one separates broomstick and brush; but does it follow that the order to bring the broom also consists of corresponding parts?

61.   "But all the same you will not deny that a particular order in (a) means the same as one in (b); and what would you call the second one, if not an analysed form of the first?" – Certainly I too should say that an order in (a) had the same meaning as one in (b); or, as I expressed it earlier: they achieve the same. And this means that if I were shewn an order in (a) and asked: "Which order in (b) means the same as this?" or again "Which order in (b) does this contradict?" I should give such-and-such an answer. But that is not to say that we have come to a *general* agreement about the use of the expression "to have the same meaning" or "to achieve the same". For it may be asked in what cases we say: "These are merely two forms of the same game."

62.   Suppose for instance that the person who is given the orders in (a) and (b) has to look up a table co-ordinating names and pictures before bringing what is required. Does he do *the same* when he carries out an order in (a) and the corresponding one in (b)? – Yes and no. You may say: "The *point* of the two orders is the same". I should say so too. – But it is not clear everywhere what should be called the 'point' of an order. (Similarly one may say of certain objects that they have this or that purpose. The essential thing is that this is a *lamp*, that it serves to give light; – that it is an ornament to the room, fills an empty space, etc., is not essential. But there is not always a sharp distinction between essential and inessential.)

63.   To say, however, that a sentence in (b) is an 'analysed' form of one in (a) readily seduces us into thinking that the former is the more fundamental form; that it alone shews what is meant by the other, and so on. For example, we think: If you have only the unanalysed form you miss the analysis; but if you know the analysed form that gives you everything. – But may I not say that an aspect of the matter is lost on you in the *latter* case as well as the former?

64.   Let us imagine language-game (§48) altered so that names signify not monochrome squares but rectangles each consisting of two such squares. Let such a rectangle, which is half red half green, be called "U"; a half green half white one, "V"; and so on. Could we not imagine people who had names for such combinations of colour, but not for the individual colours? Think of the cases where we say: "This arrangement of colours (say the French tricolor) has a quite special character."

In what sense do the symbols of this language-game stand in need of analysis? How far is it even *possible* to replace this language-game by (§48)? – It is just *another* language-game; even though it is related to (§48).

65.   Here we come up against the great question that lies behind all these considerations. – For someone might object against me: "You take the easy way out! You talk about all sorts of language-games, but have nowhere said what the essence of a language-game, and hence of language, is: what is common to all these activities, and what makes them into language or parts of language. So you let yourself off the very part of the investigation that once gave you yourself most headache, the part about the *general form of propositions* and of language."

And this is true. – Instead of producing something common to all that we call language, I am saying that these phenomena have no one thing in common which makes us use the same word for all, – but that they are *related* to one another in many different ways. And it is because of this relationship, or these relationships, that we call them all "language". I will try to explain this.

66.   Consider for example the proceedings that we call "games". I mean board-games, card-games, ball-games, Olympic games, and so on. What is common to them all? – Don't say: "There *must* be something common, or they would not be called 'games'" – but *look and see* whether there is anything common to all. – For if you look at them you will not see something that is common to *all*, but similarities, relationships, and a whole series of them at that. To repeat: don't think, but look! – Look for example at board-games, with their multifarious relationships. Now pass to card-games; here you find many correspondences with the first group, but many common features drop out, and others appear. When we pass next to ball-games, much that is common is retained, but much is lost. – Are they all 'amusing'? Compare chess with noughts and crosses. Or is there always winning and losing, or competition between players? Think of patience. In ball-games there is winning and losing; but when a child throws his ball at the wall and catches it again, this feature has disappeared. Look at the parts played by skill and luck; and at the difference between skill in

chess and skill in tennis. Think now of games like ring-a-ring-a-roses; here is the element of amusement, but how many other characteristic features have disappeared! And we can go through the many, many other groups of games in the same way; can see how similarities crop up and disappear.

And the result of this examination is: we see a complicated network of similarities overlapping and criss-crossing: sometimes overall similarities, sometimes similarities of detail.

67.   I can think of no better expression to characterize these similarities than "family resemblances"; for the various resemblances between members of a family: build, features, colour of eyes, gait, temperament, etc., etc. overlap and criss-cross in the same way. – And I shall say: 'games' form a family.

And for instance the kinds of number form a family in the same way. Why do we call something a "number"? Well, perhaps because it has a – direct – relationship with several things that have hitherto been called number; and this may be said to give it an indirect relationship to other things that we call the same name. And we extend our concept of number as in spinning a thread we twist fibre on fibre. And the strength of the thread does not reside in the fact that some one fibre runs through its whole length, but in the overlapping of many fibres.

But if someone wished to say: "There is something common to all these constructions – namely the disjunction of all their common properties" – I should reply: Now you are only playing with words. One might as well say: "Something runs through the whole thread – namely the continuous overlapping of these fibres".

68.   "All right: the concept of number is defined for you as the logical sum of these individual interrelated concepts: cardinal numbers, rational numbers, real numbers, etc.; and in the same way the concept of a game as the logical sum of a corresponding set of sub-concepts." – It need not be so. For I may give the concept 'number' rigid limits in this way, that is, use the word "number" for a rigidly limited concept, but I may also use it so that the extension of the concept is *not* closed by a frontier. And this is how we do use the word "game". For how is the concept of a game bounded? What still counts as a

game and what no longer does? Can you give the boundary? No. You can *draw* one; for none has so far been drawn. (But that never troubled you before when you used the word "game".)

"But then the use of the word is unregulated, the 'game' we play with it is unregulated." – It is not everywhere circumscribed by rules; but no more are there any rules for how high one throws the ball in tennis, or how hard; yet tennis is a game for all that and has rules too.

69. How should we explain to someone what a game is? I imagine that we should describe *games* to him, and we might add: "This *and similar things* are called 'games'". And do we know any more about it ourselves? Is it only other people whom we cannot tell exactly what a game is? – But this is not ignorance. We do not know the boundaries because none have been drawn. To repeat, we can draw a boundary – for a special purpose. Does it take that to make the concept usable? Not at all! (Except for that special purpose.) No more than it took the definition: 1 pace = 75 cm. to make the measure of length 'one pace' usable. And if you want to say "But still, before that it wasn't an exact measure", then I reply: very well, it was an inexact one. – Though you still owe me a definition of exactness.

70. "But if the concept 'game' is uncircumscribed like that, you don't really know what you mean by a 'game'." – When I give the description: "The ground was quite covered with plants" – do you want to say I don't know what I am talking about until I can give a definition of a plant?

My meaning would be explained by, say, a drawing and the words "The ground looked roughly like this". Perhaps I even say "it looked *exactly* like this." – Then were just *this* grass and *these* leaves there, arranged just like this? No, that is not what it means. And I should not accept any picture as exact in *this* sense.

71. One might say that the concept 'game' is a concept with blurred edges. – "But is a blurred concept a concept at all?" – Is an indistinct photograph a picture of a person at all? Is it even always an advantage to replace an indistinct picture by a sharp one? Isn't the indistinct one often exactly what we need?

Frege compares a concept to an area and says that an area with vague boundaries cannot be

called an area at all. This presumably means that we cannot do anything with it. – But is it senseless to say: "Stand roughly there"? Suppose that I were standing with someone in a city square and said that. As I say it I do not draw any kind of boundary, but perhaps point with my hand – as if I were indicating a particular *spot*. And this is just how one might explain to someone what a game is. One gives examples and intends them to be taken in a particular way. – I do not, however, mean by this that he is supposed to see in those examples that common thing which I – for some reason – was unable to express; but that he is now to *employ* those examples in a particular way. Here giving examples is not an *indirect* means of explaining – in default of a better. For any general definition may be misunderstood too. The point is that *this* is how we play the game. (I mean the language-game with the word "game".)

72. *Seeing what is common.* Suppose I shew someone various multicoloured pictures, and say: "The colour you see in all these is called 'yellow ochre'". – This is a definition, and the other will get to understand it by looking for and seeing what is common to the pictures. Then he can look *at*, can point *to*, the common thing.

Compare with this a case in which I shew him figures of different shapes all painted the same colour, and say: "What these have in common is called 'yellow ochre'".

And compare this case: I shew him samples of different shades of blue and say: "The colour that is common to all these is what I call 'blue'".

73. When someone defines the names of colours for me by pointing to samples and saying "This colour is called 'blue', this 'green' . . . . ." this case may be compared in many respects to putting a table in my hands, with the words written under the colour-samples. – Though this comparison may mislead in many ways. – One is now inclined to extend the comparison: to have understood the definition means to have in one's mind an idea of the thing defined, and that is a sample or picture. So if I am shewn various different leaves and told "This is called a 'leaf'", I get an idea of the shape of a leaf, a picture of it in my mind. – But what does the picture of a leaf look like when it does not shew us any particular shape, but 'what is common to all shapes of leaf'? Which shade is the 'sample in my mind' of

the colour green – the sample of what is common to all shades of green?

"But might there not be such 'general' samples? Say a schematic leaf, or a sample of *pure* green?" – Certainly there might. But for such a schema to be understood as a *schema*, and not as the shape of a particular leaf, and for a slip of pure green to be understood as a sample of all that is greenish and not as a sample of pure green – this in turn resides in the way the samples are used.

Ask yourself: what *shape* must the sample of the colour green be? Should it be rectangular? Or would it then be the sample of a green rectangle? – So should it be 'irregular' in shape? And what is to prevent us then from regarding it – that is, from using it – only as a sample of irregularity of shape?

74.   Here also belongs the idea that if you see this leaf as a sample of 'leaf shape in general' you *see* it differently from someone who regards it as, say, a sample of this particular shape. Now this might well be so – though it is not so – for it would only be to say that, as a matter of experience, if you *see* the leaf in a particular way, you use it in such-and-such a way or according to such-and-such rules. Of course, there is such a thing as seeing in *this* way or *that*; and there are also cases where whoever sees a sample like *this* will in general use it in *this* way, and whoever sees it otherwise in another way. For example, if you see the schematic drawing of a cube as a plane figure consisting of a square and two rhombi you will, perhaps, carry out the order "Bring me something like this" differently from someone who sees the picture three-dimensionally.

75.   What does it mean to know what a game is? What does it mean, to know it and not be able to say it? Is this knowledge somehow equivalent to an unformulated definition? So that if it were formulated I should be able to recognize it as the expression of my knowledge? Isn't my knowledge, my concept of a game, completely expressed in the explanations that I could give? That is, in my describing examples of various kinds of game; shewing how all sorts of other games can be constructed on the analogy of these; saying that I should scarcely include this or this among games; and so on.

76.   If someone were to draw a sharp boundary I could not acknowledge it as the one that I

too always wanted to draw, or had drawn in my mind. For I did not want to draw one at all. His concept may then be said to be not the same as mine, but akin to it. The kinship is that of two pictures, one of which consists of colour patches with vague contours, and the other of patches similarly shaped and distributed, but with clear contours. The kinship is just as undeniable as the difference.

77.   And if we carry this comparison still further it is clear that the degree to which the sharp picture *can* resemble the blurred one depends on the latter's degree of vagueness. For imagine having to sketch a sharply defined picture 'corresponding' to a blurred one. In the latter there is a blurred red rectangle: for it you put down a sharply defined one. Of course – several such sharply defined rectangles can be drawn to correspond to the indefinite one. – But if the colours in the original merge without a hint of any outline won't it become a hopeless task to draw a sharp picture corresponding to the blurred one? Won't you then have to say: "Here I might just as well draw a circle or heart as a rectangle, for all the colours merge. Anything – and nothing – is right." – And this is the position you are in if you look for definitions corresponding to our concepts in aesthetics or ethics.

In such a difficulty always ask yourself: How did we *learn* the meaning of this word ("good" for instance)? From what sort of examples? in what language-games? Then it will be easier for you to see that the word must have a family of meanings.

78.   Compare *knowing* and *saying*:
> how many feet high Mont Blanc is –
> how the word "game" is used –
> how a clarinet sounds.

If you are surprised that one can know something and not be able to say it, you are perhaps thinking of a case like the first. Certainly not of one like the third.

79.   Consider this example. If one says "Moses did not exist", this may mean various things. It may mean: the Israelites did not have a *single* leader when they withdrew from Egypt – or: their leader was not called Moses – or: there cannot have been anyone who accomplished all that the Bible relates of Moses – or: etc. etc. – We

may say, following Russell: the name "Moses" may be defined by means of various descriptions. For example, as "the man who led the Israelites through the wilderness", "the man who lived at that time and place and was then called 'Moses'", "the man who as a child was taken out of the Nile by Pharaoh's daughter" and so on. And according as we assume one definition or another the proposition "Moses did exist" acquires a different sense, and so does every other proposition about Moses. – And if we are told "N did not exist", we do ask: "What do you mean? Do you want to say ...... or ...... etc.?"

But when I make a statement about Moses, – am I always ready to substitute some *one* of these descriptions for "Moses"? I shall perhaps say: By "Moses" I understand the man who did what the Bible relates of Moses, or at any rate a good deal of it. But how much? Have I decided how much must be proved false for me to give up my proposition as false? Has the name "Moses" got a fixed and unequivocal use for me in all possible cases? – Is it not the case that I have, so to speak, a whole series of props in readiness, and am ready to lean on one if another should be taken from under me, and vice versa? – Consider another case. When I say "N is dead", then something like the following may hold for the meaning of the name "N": I believe that a human being has lived, whom I (1) have seen in such-and-such places, who (2) looked like this (pictures), (3) has done such-and-such things, and (4) bore the name "N" in social life. – Asked what I understand by "N", I should enumerate all or some of these points, and different ones on different occasions. So my definition of "N" would perhaps be "the man of whom all this is true". – But if some point now proves false? – Shall I be prepared to declare the proposition "N is dead" false – even if it is only something which strikes me as incidental that has turned out false? But where are the bounds of the incidental? – If I had given a definition of the name in such a case, I should now be ready to alter it.

And this may be expressed like this: I use the name "N" without a *fixed* meaning. (But that detracts as little from its usefulness, as it detracts from that of a table that it stands on four legs instead of three and so sometimes wobbles.)

Should it be said that I am using a word whose meaning I don't know, and so am talking nonsense? – Say what you choose, so long as it does not prevent you from seeing the facts. (And when you see them there is a good deal that you will not say.)

(The fluctuation of scientific definitions: what to-day counts as an observed concomitant of a phenomenon will to-morrow be used to define it.)

80. I say "There is a chair". What if I go up to it, meaning to fetch it, and it suddenly disappears from sight? – "So it wasn't a chair, but some kind of illusion". – But in a few moments we see it again and are able to touch it and so on. – "So the chair was there after all and its disappearance was some kind of illusion". – But suppose that after a time it disappears again – or seems to disappear. What are we to say now? Have you rules ready for such cases – rules saying whether one may use the word "chair" to include this kind of thing? But do we miss them when we use the word "chair"; and are we to say that we do not really attach any meaning to this word, because we are not equipped with rules for every possible application of it?

81. F. P. Ramsey once emphasized in conversation with me that logic was a 'normative science'. I do not know exactly what he had in mind, but it was doubtless closely related to what only dawned on me later: namely, that in philosophy we often *compare* the use of words with games and calculi which have fixed rules, but cannot say that someone who is using language *must* be playing such a game. – But if you say that our languages only *approximate* to such calculi you are standing on the very brink of a misunderstanding. For then it may look as if what we were talking about were an *ideal* language. As if our logic were, so to speak, a logic for a vacuum. – Whereas logic does not treat of language – or of thought – in the sense in which a natural science treats of a natural phenomenon, and the most that can be said is that we *construct* ideal languages. But here the word "ideal" is liable to mislead, for it sounds as if these languages were better, more perfect, than our everyday language; and as if it took the logician to shew people at last what a proper sentence looked like.

All this, however, can only appear in the right light when one has attained greater clarity about the concepts of understanding, meaning, and thinking. For it will then also become clear what may lead us (and did lead me) to think that if anyone utters a sentence and *means* or *understands* it he is operating a calculus according to definite rules.

[. . .]

112. A simile that has been absorbed into the forms of our language produces a false appearance, and this disquiets us. "But *this* isn't how it is!" – we say. "Yet *this* is how it has to *be*!"

113. "But *this* is how it is –" I say to myself over and over again. I feel as though, if only I could fix my gaze absolutely sharply on this fact, get it in focus, I must grasp the essence of the matter.

114. (*Tractatus Logico-Philosophicus*, 4.5): "The general form of propositions is: This is how things are." – That is the kind of proposition that one repeats to oneself countless times. One thinks that one is tracing the outline of the thing's nature over and over again, and one is merely tracing round the frame through which we look at it.

115. A *picture* held us captive. And we could not get outside it, for it lay in our language and language seemed to repeat it to us inexorably.

116. When philosophers use a word – "knowledge", "being", "object", "I", "proposition", "name" – and try to grasp the *essence* of the thing, one must always ask oneself: is the word ever actually used in this way in the language which is its original home? –

What *we* do is to bring words back from their metaphysical to their everyday use.

[. . .]

269. Let us remember that there are certain criteria in a man's behaviour for the fact that he does not understand a word: that it means nothing to him, that he can do nothing with it. And criteria for his 'thinking he understands', attaching some meaning to the word, but not the right one. And, lastly, criteria for his understanding the word right. In the second case one might speak of a subjective understanding. And sounds which no one else understands but which I '*appear to understand*' might be called a "private language".

270. Let us now imagine a use for the entry of the sign "S" in my diary. I discover that whenever I have a particular sensation a manometer shews that my blood-pressure rises. So I shall be able to say that my blood-pressure is rising without using any apparatus. This is a useful result. And now it seems quite indifferent whether I have recognized the sensation *right* or not. Let us suppose I regularly identify it wrong, it does not matter in the least. And that alone shews that the hypothesis that I make a mistake is mere show. (We as it were turned a knob which looked as if it could be used to turn on some part of the machine; but it was a mere ornament, not connected with the mechanism at all.)

And what is our reason for calling "S" the name of a sensation here? Perhaps the kind of way this sign is employed in this language-game. – And why a "particular sensation," that is, the same one every time? Well, aren't we supposing that we write "S" every time?

271. "Imagine a person whose memory could not retain *what* the word 'pain' meant – so that he constantly called different things by that name – but nevertheless used the word in a way fitting in with the usual symptoms and presuppositions of pain" – in short he uses it as we all do. Here I should like to say: a wheel that can be turned though nothing else moves with it, is not part of the mechanism.

272. The essential thing about private experience is really not that each person possesses his own exemplar, but that nobody knows whether other people also have *this* or something else. The assumption would thus be possible – though unverifiable – that one section of mankind had one sensation of red and another section another.

273. What am I to say about the word "red"? – that it means something 'confronting us all' and that everyone should really have another word, besides this one, to mean his *own* sensation of red? Or is it like this: the word "red" means something known to everyone; and in addition, for each person, it means something known only to him? (Or perhaps rather: it *refers* to something known only to him.)

274. Of course, saying that the word "red" "refers to" instead of "means" something private

does not help us in the least to grasp its function; but it is the more psychologically apt expression for a particular experience in doing philosophy. It is as if when I uttered the word I cast a sidelong glance at the private sensation, as it were in order to say to myself: I know all right what I mean by it.

275.　Look at the blue of the sky and say to yourself "How blue the sky is!" – When you do it spontaneously – without philosophical intentions – the idea never crosses your mind that this impression of colour belongs only to *you*. And you have no hesitation in exclaiming that to someone else. And if you point at anything as you say the words you point at the sky. I am saying: you have not the feeling of pointing-into-yourself, which often accompanies 'naming the sensation' when one is thinking about 'private language'. Nor do you think that really you ought not to point to the colour with your hand, but with your attention. (Consider what it means "to point to something with the attention".)

24

Maurice Merleau-Ponty, *Phenomenology of Perception*, "Preface"

Introduction

French philosopher Maurice Merleau-Ponty (1908–61), in this selection from his 1945 work, *Phénoménologie de la perception*,[1] presents one of the most succinct statements of the phenomenological project and its relationship to scientific and philosophical theories aimed at explaining the world, determining knowledge, and apprehending truth.

Merleau-Ponty argues that preceding philosophy has largely been hobbled by its theoretical starting points. Beginning with a world of objects, realisms and naturalisms of various sorts have struggled in vain to account properly for subjectivity and the central, irreducible role thinkers like Descartes, Kant, and Kierkegaard have shown us subjectivity must play in any proper account of the world. Object-centered theories inevitably mask the import of subjectivity and attempt to reduce the subject to some kind of natural object. On the other hand, those philosophers who have begun with subjectivity have found themselves unable to construct an adequate bridge to the world and account for its objective features, features that somehow surpass the subject and exist beyond it. Subject-centered philosophies deny that objects transcend us and are in important ways simply

From Maurice Merleau-Ponty, *Phenomenology of Perception*, trans. C. Smith, New York: The Humanities Press, 1962, pp. vii–xxi.

given. They transmute objects into mental perceptions in the theater of the mind (Berkeley, III.16), or else pretend that they are products of synthetic mental activity (Kant, III.17), or else define them as manifestations of an absolute idea, mind, or spirit (Hegel, III.18).[2]

For Edmund Husserl (1859–1938) (see II.19 above), who founded the phenomenological movement, and for Merleau-Ponty, subjects and objects are given at one blow, together with the world that subsumes them. The world cannot be reduced either to simple subjective or objective things; and neither subjects nor objects can be reduced to one another. Rather, both subjects and objects appear interdependently within a world. It is the task of phenomenology to bring us back to an awareness of that world, its basic or primordial meaningfulness, and the prior unity of subjects and objects within it.[3]

One reason subjects do not exist separately from objects is because of a radical re-conceptualization of consciousness developed by Husserl according to which consciousness is essentially "intentional."[4] For Husserl, as for Merleau-Ponty, all consciousness is consciousness *of* something beyond itself; and, correlatively, all objects are objects *of* a consciousness that as a matter of intentionality apprehends them as objects. Merleau-Ponty follows Heidegger in pointing to a primordial "truing" (II.22) and deepens Husserl's insight by arguing that acts of consciousness (*noesis*) together with objects of consciousness (*noema*) are themselves grounded in a primordial openness he calls "perception."

By its very nature, therefore, consciousness is grounded in perception and cannot be cut off from the world in a sealed realm of subjectivity or interiority. The *solus ipse* (a self-alone) is simply impossible; and no object can appear as an object unless it is apprehended by a consciousness that transcends itself by intentionally apprehending it. Indeed, neither subjects nor objects exist separated from other subjects and objects. Objects and subjects exist essentially in "situations," in a world of meanings and relationships, where those relationships are not superficial or external but are actually constitutive of what the subjects and objects are. Our world is a world of subjects and objects meaningfully related to other subjects and objects in situations. Phenomenology, then, self-consciously attempts to overcome the misleading alternatives of realism and idealism. "Probably the chief gain from phenomenology," writes Merleau-Ponty, "is to have united extreme subjectivism and extreme objectivism in its notion of the world or of rationality."

The phenomenological method that Merleau-Ponty, following Husserl, enlists in order to accomplish the task of disclosing the essential features of the primordial, pre-theoretic world we all share he calls "reduction." Phenomenological reduction may be thought of as an attempt to strip away the accretions of centuries of philosophical and scientific theory that have occluded our consciousness of the basic world in which we exist. Phenomenological reduction attempts to achieve a special kind of "description," that tries to disclose "the things themselves" – that is, things as they compose a primordial, pre-theoretic existence that is the *explandum* of all possible explanations. Merleau-Ponty, however, criticizes Husserl for supposing that "reduction" can be taken to the extreme of "bracketing," of suspending belief in, the external world.

In addition, phenomenological reduction as an "eidetic" project attempts to lay bare the essential and general features of that world as a set of essential meanings (*Wesen*): "The whole universe of science," says Merleau-Ponty, "is built upon the world as directly experienced, and if we want to subject science itself to rigorous scrutiny and arrive at a precise assessment of its meaning and scope, we must begin by reawakening the basic experience of the world of which science is the second-order expression. Science has not and never will have, by its nature, the same significance *qua*

form of being as the world which we perceive, for the simple reason that it is a rationale or explanation of that world."

Merleau-Ponty's phenomenological method is intrinsically pluralistic and argues for a kind of interdisciplinary cognition, when it comes to the epistemological projects of theory. What's crucial is to interpret the meaning of any theoretical enterprise properly – that is, in light of a phenomenological interrogation, to lay bare the "essence" of the kind of being the inquiry addresses and the kind of meaning each different kind of science and literature conveys: "We must seek an understanding from all these angles simultaneously. . . . All these views are true provided that they are not isolated, that we delve deeply into history and reach the unique core of existential meaning which emerges in each perspective."

That there is a "unique core" or a basic, pre-theoretical, life-world (*Lebenswelt*) that's shared across different cultures, different conceptual schemes, and different histories, is a deeply controversial idea. Through phenomenological reduction and reflection, Merleau-Ponty would apprehend a basic world that exists prior to the meaning of language and, in fact, underwrites the possibility that language has meaning. Phenomenological reflection would also claim to disclose the essential meanings of the social and natural worlds we inhabit. Philosophers of language from both the analytic and continental traditions, however, have questioned whether doing so is at all possible. On the other hand, while it makes perfect sense to say that medieval Europeans and the ancient Chinese produced different theoretical explanations of world, does it really make sense to say they lived in different worlds?

Notes

1   Maurice Merleau-Ponty, *Phénoménologie de la perception*, Paris: Gallimard, 1945.

2   See R. D. Cumming, *Starting Point: An Introduction to the Dialectic of Existence*, Chicago: University of Chicago Press, 1979.

3   See J. Sallis, *Phenomenology and the Return to Beginnings*, Pittsburgh, PA: Duquesne University Press, 1973.

4   Jean-Paul Sartre, "Intentionality: A Fundamental Idea of Husserl's Phenomenology," trans. J. P. Fell, *British Journal for Phenomenology* 1.2 (1970): 4–5.

Merleau-Ponty,
Phenomenology of Perception

Preface

What is phenomenology? It may seem strange that this question has still to be asked half a century after the first works of Husserl. The fact remains that it has by no means been answered. Phenomenology is the study of essences; and according to it, all problems amount to finding definitions of essences: the essence of perception, or the essence of consciousness, for example. But phenomenology is also a philosophy which puts essences back into existence, and does not expect to arrive at an understanding of man and the world from any starting point other than that of their 'facticity'. It is a transcendental philosophy which places in abeyance the assertions arising out of the natural attitude, the better to understand them; but it is also a philosophy for which the world is always 'already there' before reflection begins – as an inalienable presence; and all its efforts are concentrated upon re-achieving a direct and primitive contact with the world, and endowing that contact with a philosophical status. It is the search for a philosophy which shall be a 'rigorous science', but it also offers an account of space, time and the world as we 'live' them. It tries to give a direct description of our experience as it is, without taking account of its psychological origin and the causal explanations which the scientist, the historian or the sociologist may be able to provide. Yet Husserl in his last works mentions a 'genetic phenomenology',* and even a 'constructive phenomenology'.† One may try to do away with these contradictions by making a distinction between Husserl's and Heidegger's phenomenologies; yet the whole of *Sein und Zeit* springs from an indication given by Husserl and amounts to no more than an explicit account of the '*naturlicher Weltbegriff*'or the '*Lebenswelt*' which Husserl, towards the end of his life, identified as the central theme of phenomenology, with the result that the contradiction reappears in

Husserl's own philosophy. The reader pressed for time will be inclined to give up the idea of covering a doctrine which says everything, and will wonder whether a philosophy which cannot define its scope deserves all the discussion which has gone on around it, and whether he is not faced rather by a myth or a fashion.

Even if this were the case, there would still be a need to understand the prestige of the myth and the origin of the fashion, and the opinion of the responsible philosopher must be that *phenomenology can be practised and identified as a manner or style of thinking, that it existed as a movement before arriving at complete awareness of itself as a philosophy*. It has been long on the way, and its adherents have discovered it in every quarter, certainly in Hegel and Kierkegaard, but equally in Marx, Nietzsche and Freud. A purely linguistic examination of the texts in question would yield no proof; we find in texts only what we put into them, and if ever any kind of history has suggested the interpretations which should be put on it, it is the history of philosophy. We shall find in ourselves, and nowhere else, the unity and true meaning of phenomenology. It is less a question of counting up quotations than of determining and expressing in concrete form this *phenomenology for ourselves* which has given a number of present-day readers the impression, on reading Husserl or Heidegger, not so much of encountering a new philosophy as of recognizing what they had been waiting for. Phenomenology is accessible only through a phenomenological method. Let us, therefore, try systematically to bring together the celebrated phenomenological themes as they have grown spontaneously together in life. Perhaps we shall then understand why phenomenology has for so long remained at an initial stage, as a problem to be solved and a hope to be realized.

It is a matter of describing, not of explaining or analyzing. Husserl's first directive to phenomenology, in its early stages, to be a 'descriptive psychology', or to return to the 'things themselves', is from the start a rejection of science. I am not the outcome or the meeting-point of numerous causal agencies which determine my bodily or psychological make-up. I cannot conceive myself as nothing but a bit of the world, a mere object of biological, psychological or sociological investigation. I cannot shut my self up within the realm of science. All my knowledge of the world, even my scientific knowledge, is gained from my own

---

* [Edmund Husserl,] *Méditations cartésiennes*, [Paris: Colin, 1931], pp. 120 ff.

† [Edmund Husserl,] *6th Méditations cartésiennes*. [*Sixth Cartesian Meditation*, ed. E. Fink, trans. R. Bruzina, Bloomington: Indiana University Press, 1995.]

particular point of view, or from some experience of the world without which the symbols of science would be meaningless. The whole universe of science is built upon the world as directly experienced, and if we want to subject science itself to rigorous scrutiny and arrive at a precise assessment of its meaning and scope, we must begin by reawakening the basic experience of the world of which science is the second-order expression. Science has not and never will have, by its nature, the same significance *qua* form of being as the world which we perceive, for the simple reason that it is a rationale or explanation of that world. I am, not a 'living creature' nor even a 'man', nor again even 'a consciousness' endowed with all the characteristics which zoology, social anatomy or inductive psychology recognize in these various products of the natural or historical process – I am the absolute source, my existence does not stem from my antecedents, from my physical and social environment; instead it moves out towards them and sustains them, for I alone bring into being for myself (and therefore into being in the only sense that the word can have for me) the tradition which I elect to carry on, or the horizon whose distance from me would be abolished – since that distance is not one of its properties – if I were not there to scan it with my gaze. Scientific points of view, according to which my existence is a moment of the world's, are always both naïve and at the same time dishonest, because they take for granted, without explicitly mentioning it, the other point of view, namely that of consciousness, through which from the outset a world forms itself round me and begins to exist for me. To return to things themselves is to return to that world which precedes knowledge, of which knowledge always *speaks*, and in relation to which every scientific schematization is an abstract and derivative sign-language, as is geography in relation to the countryside in which we have learnt beforehand what a forest, a prairie or a river is.

This move is absolutely distinct from the idealist return to consciousness, and the demand for a pure description excludes equally the procedure of analytical reflection on the one hand, and that of scientific explanation on the other. Descartes and particularly Kant *detached* the subject, or consciousness, by showing that I could not possibly apprehend anything as existing unless I first

of all experienced myself as existing in the act of apprehending it. They presented consciousness, the absolute certainty of my existence for myself, as the condition of there being anything at all; and the act of relating as the basis of relatedness. It is true that the act of relating is nothing if divorced from the spectacle of the world in which relations are found; the unity of consciousness in Kant is achieved simultaneously with that of the world. And in Descartes methodical doubt does not deprive us of anything, since the whole world, at least in so far as we experience it, is reinstated in the *Cogito*, enjoying equal certainty, and simply labeled 'thought about . . .'. But the relations between subject and world are not strictly bilateral: if they were, the certainty of the world would, in Descartes, be immediately given with that of the *Cogito*, and Kant would not have talked about his 'Copernican revolution'. Analytical reflection starts from our experience of the world and goes back to the subject as to a condition of possibility distinct from that experience, revealing the all-embracing synthesis as that without which there would be no world. To this extent it ceases to remain part of our experience and offers, in place of an account, a reconstruction. It is understandable, in view of this, that Husserl, having accused Kant of adopting a 'faculty psychologism',* should have urged, in place of a noetic analysis which bases the world on the synthesizing activity of the subject, his own *'noematic reflection' which remains within the object and, instead of begetting it, brings to light its fundamental unity.*

The world is there before any possible analysis of mine, and it would be artificial to make it the outcome of a series of syntheses which link, in the first place sensations, then aspects of the object corresponding to different perspectives, when both are nothing but products of analysis, with no sort of prior reality. Analytical reflection believes that it can trace back the course followed by a prior constituting act and arrive, in the 'inner man' – to use Saint Augustine's expression – at a constituting power which has always been identical with that inner self. Thus reflection itself is carried away and transplanted in an impregnable subjectivity, as yet untouched

---

* [Edmund Husserl,] *Logische Untersuchungen, Prolegomena zur reinen Logik,* [Halle: Niemeyer, 1928], p. 93.

by being and time. But this is very ingenuous, or at least it is an incomplete form of reflection which loses sight of its own beginning. When I begin to reflect my reflection bears upon an unreflective experience; moreover my reflection cannot be unaware of itself as an event, and so it appears to itself in the light of a truly creative act, of a changed structure of consciousness, and yet it has to recognize, as having priority over its own operations, the world which is given to the subject, because the subject is given to himself. The real has to be described, not constructed or formed. Which means that I cannot put perception into the same category as the syntheses represented by judgements, acts or predications. My field of perception is constantly filled with a play of colours, noises and fleeting tactile sensations which I cannot relate precisely to the context of my clearly perceived world, yet which I nevertheless immediately 'place' in the world, without ever confusing them with my daydreams. Equally constantly I weave dreams round things. I imagine people and things whose presence is not incompatible with the context, yet who are not in fact involved in it: they are ahead of reality, in the realm of the imaginary. If the reality of my perception were based solely on the intrinsic coherence of 'representations', it ought to be forever hesitant and, being wrapped up in my conjectures on probabilities, I ought to be ceaselessly taking apart misleading syntheses, and reinstating in reality stray phenomena which I had excluded in the first place. But this does not happen. The real is a closely woven fabric. It does not await our judgement before incorporating the most surprising phenomena, or before rejecting the most plausible figments of our imagination. Perception is not a science of the world, it is not even an act, a deliberate taking up of a position; it is the background from which all acts stand out, and is presupposed by them. The world is not an object such that I have in my possession the law of its making; it is the natural setting of, and field for, all my thoughts and all my explicit perceptions. Truth does not 'inhabit' only 'the inner man',* or more accurately, there is no inner man, man is in the world, and only in the world does he know himself. When I return to myself

from an excursion into the realm of dogmatic common sense or of science, I find, not a source of intrinsic truth, but a subject destined to be in the world.

All of which reveals the true meaning of the famous phenomenological reduction. There is probably no question over which Husserl has spent more time – or to which he has more often returned, since the 'problematic of reduction' occupies an important place in his unpublished work. For a long time, and even in recent texts, the reduction is presented as the return to a transcendental consciousness before which the world is spread out and completely transparent, quickened through and through by a series of apperceptions which it is the philosopher's task to reconstitute on the basis of their outcome. Thus my sensation of redness *is perceived as* the manifestation of a certain redness experienced, this in turn as the manifestation of a red surface, which is the manifestation of a piece of red cardboard, and this finally is the manifestation or outline of a red thing, namely this book. We are to understand, then, that it is the apprehension of a certain *hylè*, as indicating a phenomenon of a higher degree, the *Sinngebung*, or active meaning-giving operation which may be said to define consciousness, so that the world is nothing but 'world-as-meaning', and the phenomenological reduction is idealistic, in the sense that there is here a transcendental idealism which treats the world as an indivisible unity of value shared by Peter and Paul, in which their perspectives blend. 'Peter's consciousness' and 'Paul's consciousness' are in communication, the perception of the world 'by Peter' is not Peter's doing any more than its perception 'by Paul' is Paul's doing; in each case it is the doing of pre-personal forms of consciousness, whose communication raises no problem, since it is demanded by the very definition of consciousness, meaning or truth. In so far as I am a consciousness, that is, in so far as something has meaning for me, I am neither here nor there, neither Peter nor Paul; I am in no way distinguishable from an 'other' consciousness, since we are immediately in touch with the world and since the world is, by definition, unique, being the system in which all truths cohere. A logically consistent transcendental idealism rids the world of its opacity and its transcendence. The world is precisely that thing of which we form a representation, not as men

---

* *In te redi; in interiore homine habitat veritas* (Saint Augustine).

or as empirical subjects, but in so far as we are all one light and participate in the One without destroying its unity. Analytical reflection knows nothing of the problem of other minds, or of that of the world, because it insists that with the first glimmer of consciousness there appears in me theoretically the power of reaching some universal truth, and that the other person, being equally without thisness, location or body, the Alter and the Ego are one and the same in the true world which is the unifier of minds. There is no difficulty in understanding how I can conceive the Other, because the I and consequently the Other are not conceived as part of the woven stuff of phenomena; they have validity rather than existence. There is nothing hidden behind these faces and gestures, no domain to which I have no access, merely a little shadow which owes its very existence to the light. For Husserl, on the contrary, it is well known that there is a problem of other people, and the *alter ego* is a paradox. If the other is truly for himself alone, beyond his being for me, and if we are for each other and not both for God, we must necessarily have some appearance for each other. He must and I must have an outer appearance, and there must be, besides the perspective of the For Oneself – my view of myself and the other's of himself – a perspective of For Others – my view of others and theirs of me. Of course, these two perspectives, in each one of us, cannot be simply juxtaposed, for in that case it is not I that *the other would see*, nor *he* that I *should see*. I must be the exterior that I present to others, and the body of the other must be the other himself. This paradox and the dialectic of the Ego and the Alter are possible only provided that the Ego and the Alter Ego are defined by their situation and are not freed from all inherence; that is, provided that philosophy does not culminate in a return to the self, and that I discover by reflection not only my presence to myself, but also the possibility of an 'outside spectator'; that is, again, provided that at the very moment when I experience my existence – at the ultimate extremity of reflection – I fall short of the ultimate density which would place me outside time, and that I discover within myself a kind of internal weakness standing in the way of my being totally individualized: a weakness which exposes me to the gaze of others as a man among men or at least as a consciousness among consciousnesses. Hitherto the Cogito depreciated the per-

ception of others, teaching me as it did that the I is accessible only to itself, since it defined *me* as the thought which I have of myself, and which clearly I am alone in having, at least in this ultimate sense. For the 'other' to be more than an empty word, it is necessary that my existence should never be reduced to my bare awareness of existing, but that it should take in also the awareness that *one* may have of it, and thus include my incarnation in some nature and the possibility, at least, of a historical situation. The Cogito must reveal me in a situation, and it is on this condition alone that transcendental subjectivity can, as Husserl puts it,* *be* an intersubjectivity. As a meditating Ego, I can clearly distinguish from myself the world and things, since I certainly do not exist in the way in which things exist. I must even set aside from myself my body understood as a thing among things, as a collection of physico-chemical processes. But even if the *cogitatio*, which I thus discover, is without location in objective time and space, it is not without place in the phenomenological world, The world, which I distinguished from myself as the totality of things or of processes linked by causal relationships, I rediscover 'in me' as the permanent horizon of all my *cogitationes* and as a dimension in relation to which I am constantly situating myself. The true *Cogito* does not define the subject's existence in terms of the thought he has of existing, and furthermore does not convert the indubitability of the world into the indubitability of thought about the world, nor finally does it replace the world itself by the world as meaning. On the contrary it recognizes my thought itself as an inalienable fact, and does away with any kind of idealism in revealing me as 'being-in-the-world'.

It is because we are through and through compounded of relationships with the world that for us the only way to become aware of the fact is to suspend the resultant activity, to refuse it our complicity (to look at it *ohne mitzumachen,* as Husserl often says), or yet again, to put it 'out of play'. Not because we reject the

---

* [Edmund Husserl,] *Die Krisis der europäishen Wissenshaften und die tranzendentale Phänomenologie,* III. [See Edmund Husserl, *Crisis of European Science and Transcendental Phenomenology,* trans. D. Carr, ed. W. Biemel, Evanston: Northwestern University Press, 1970.]

certainties of common sense and a natural attitude to things – they are, on the contrary, the constant theme of philosophy – but because, being the presupposed basis of any thought, they are taken for granted, and go unnoticed, and because in order to arouse them and bring them to view, we have to suspend for a moment our recognition of them. The best formulation of the reduction is probably that given by Eugen Fink, Husserl's assistant, when he spoke of 'wonder' in the face of the world.* Reflection does not withdraw from the world towards the unity of consciousness as the world's basis; it steps back to watch the forms of transcendence fly up like sparks from a fire; it slackens the intentional threads which attach us to the world and thus brings them to our notice; it alone is consciousness of the world because it reveals that world as strange and paradoxical. Husserl's transcendental is not Kant's and Husserl accuses Kant's philosophy of being 'worldly', because it *makes use* of our relation to the world, which is the motive force of the transcendental deduction, and makes the world immanent in the subject, instead of *being filled with wonder* at it and conceiving the subject as a process of transcendence towards the world. All the misunderstandings with his interpreters, with the existentialist 'dissidents' and finally with himself, have arisen from the fact that in order to see the world and grasp it as paradoxical, we must break with our familiar acceptance of it and, also, from the fact that from this break we can learn nothing but the unmotivated upsurge of the world. The most important lesson which the reduction teaches us is the impossibility of a complete reduction. This is why Husserl is constantly re-examining the possibility of the reduction. If we were absolute mind, the reduction would present no problem. But since, on the contrary, we are in the world, since indeed our reflections are carried out in the temporal flux on to which we are trying to seize (since they *sich einströmen*, as Husserl says), there is no thought which embraces all our thought. The philosopher, as the unpublished works declare, is a perpetual beginner, which means that he takes for granted

nothing that men, learned or otherwise, believe they know. It means also that philosophy itself must not take itself for granted, in so far as it may have managed to say something true; that it is an ever-renewed experiment in making its own beginning; that it consists wholly in the description of this beginning, and finally, that radical reflection amounts to a consciousness of its own dependence on an unreflective life which is its initial situation, unchanging, given once and for all. Far from being, as has been thought, a procedure of idealistic philosophy, phenomenological reduction belongs to existential philosophy: Heidegger's 'being-in-the-world' appears only against the background of the phenomenological reduction.

A misunderstanding of a similar kind confuses the notion of the essences in Husserl. Every reduction, says Husserl, as well as being transcendental is necessarily eidetic. That means that we cannot subject our perception of the world to philosophical scrutiny without ceasing to be identified with that act of positing the world, with that interest in it which delimits us, without drawing back from our commitment which is itself thus made to appear as a spectacle, without passing from the *fact* of our existence to its *nature*, from the Dasein to the Wesen. But it is clear that the essence is here not the end, but a means, that our effective involvement in the world is precisely what has to be understood and made amenable to conceptualization, for it is what polarizes all our conceptual particularizations. The need to proceed by way of essences does not mean that philosophy takes them as its object, but, on the contrary, that our existence is too tightly held in the world to be able to know itself as such at the moment of its involvement, and that it requires the field of ideality in order to become acquainted with and to prevail over its facticity. The Vienna Circle, as is well known, lays it down categorically that we can enter into relations only with meanings. For example, 'consciousness' is not for the Vienna Circle identifiable with what we are. It is a complex meaning which has developed late in time, which should be handled with care, and only after the many meanings which have contributed, throughout the word's semantic development, to the formation of its present one have been made explicit. Logical positivism of this kind is the antithesis of Husserl's thought. Whatever the subtle changes of meaning which

---

* *Die phänomenologische Philosophie Edmund Husserls in der gegenwärtigen Kritik*, pp. 331 and ff. [See Ronald Bruzina, *Edmund Husserl and Eugen Fink: Beginnings and Ends in Phenomenology, 1928–1938*, New Haven: Yale University Press, 2004.]

have ultimately brought us, as a linguistic acqui-sition, the word and concept of consciousness, we enjoy direct access to what it designates. For we have the experience of ourselves, of that con-sciousness which we are, and it is on the basis of this experience that all linguistic connotations are assessed, and precisely through it that language comes to have any meaning at all for us. 'It is that as yet dumb experience . . . which we are concerned to lead to the pure expression of its own mean-ing.'* Husserl's essences are destined to bring back all the living relationships of experience, as the fisherman's net draws up from the depths of the ocean quivering fish and seaweed. Jean Wahl is therefore wrong in saying that 'Husserl separ-ates essences from existence'.† The separated essences are those of language. It is the office of language to cause essences to exist in a state of separation which is in fact merely apparent, since through language they still rest upon the ante-predicative life of consciousness. In the silence of primary consciousness can be seen appearing not only what words mean, but also what things mean: the core of primary meaning round which the acts of naming and expression take shape.

Seeking the essence of consciousness will there-fore not consist in developing the *Wortbedeutung* of consciousness and escaping from existence into the universe of things said; it will consist in rediscovering my actual presence to myself, the fact of my consciousness which is in the last resort what the word and the concept of con-sciousness mean. Looking for the world's essence is not looking for what it is as an idea once it has been reduced to a theme of discourse; it is looking for what it is as a fact for us, before any thematization. Sensationalism 'reduces' the world by noticing that after all we never experience anything but states of ourselves. Transcendental idealism too 'reduces' the world since, in so far as it guarantees the world, it does so by regard-ing it as thought or consciousness of the world, and as the mere correlative of our knowledge, with the result that it becomes immanent in consciousness and the aseity of things is thereby done away with. The eidetic reduction is, on the other hand, the determination to bring the world to light as it is before any falling back on ourselves has occurred, it is the ambition to make reflection emulate the unreflective life of consciousness. I aim at and perceive a world. If I said, as do the sensationalists, that we have here only 'states of consciousness', and if I tried to distinguish my perceptions from my dreams with the aid of 'criteria', I should overlook the phenomenon of the world. For if I am able to talk about 'dreams' and 'reality', to bother my head about the distinction between imaginary and real, and cast doubt upon the 'real', it is because this distinction is already made by me before any analysis; it is because I have an experience of the real as of the imaginary, and the problem then becomes one not of asking how critical thought can provide for itself secondary equivalents of this distinction, but of making explicit our primordial knowledge of the 'real', of describing our per-ception of the world as that upon which our idea of truth is for ever based. We must not, therefore, wonder whether we really perceive a world, we must instead say: the world is what we perceive. In more general terms we must not wonder whether our self-evident truths are real truths, or whether, through some perversity inherent in our minds, that which is self-evident for us might not be illusory in relation to some truth in itself. For in so far as we talk about illusion, it is because we have identified illusions, and done so solely in the light of some perception which at the same time gave assurance of its own truth. It follows that doubt, or the fear of being mistaken, testifies as soon as it arises to our power of unmasking error, and that it could never finally tear us away from truth. We are in the realm of truth and it is 'the experience of truth' which is self-evident.‡ To seek the essence of perception is to declare that perception is, not presumed true, but defined as access to truth. So, if I now wanted, according to idealistic principles, to base this *de facto* self-evident truth, this irresistible belief, on some absolute self-evident truth, that

* [Edmund Husserl,] *Méditations cartésiennes*, [Paris: Colin, 1931], p. 33.
† *Reaslisme, dialectique et mystère*, l'Arbalète, Autumn, 1942, unpaginated.

‡ [Edmund Husserl,] *Das Erlebnis der Wahrheit* (*Logische Untersuchungen, Prolegomena zur reinen Logik*) p. 190. [See Edmund Husserl, *Logical Invest-igations*, trans. N. Findlay, ed. D. Moran, London: Routledge, 2001, Vol. II, Part 2, Section One, Chapter 5, 'The Ideal Adequation: Self-Evidence and Truth'.]

is, on the absolute clarity which my thoughts have for me; if I tried to find in myself a creative thought which bodied forth the framework of the world or illumined it through and through, I should once more prove unfaithful to my experience of the world, and should be looking for what makes that experience possible instead of looking for what it is. The self-evidence of perception is not adequate thought or apodeictic self-evidence. 'The world is not what I think' but what I live through. I am open to the world, I have no doubt that I am in communication with it, but I do not possess it; it is inexhaustible. 'There is a world', or rather: 'There is the world'; I can never completely account for this ever-reiterated assertion in my life. This facticity of the world is what constitutes the *Weltlichkeit der Welt*, what causes the world to be the world; just as the facticity of the *cogito is* not an imperfection in itself, but rather what assures me of my existence. The eidetic method is the method of a phenomenological positivism which bases the possible on the real.

We can now consider the notion of intentionality, too often cited as the main discovery of phenomenology, whereas it is understandable only through the reduction. 'All consciousness is consciousness of something'; there is nothing new in that. Kant showed, in the *Refutation of Idealism*, that inner perception is impossible without outer perception, that the world, as a collection of connected phenomena, is anticipated in the consciousness of my unity, and is the means whereby I come into being as a consciousness. What distinguishes intentionality from the Kantian relation to a possible object is that the unity of the world, before being posited by knowledge in a specific act of identification, is 'lived' as ready-made or already there. Kant himself shows in the *Critique of Judgement* that there exists a unity of the imagination and the understanding and a unity of subjects *before the object*, and that, in experiencing the beautiful, for example, I am aware of a harmony between sensation and concept, between myself and others, which is itself without any concept. Here the subject is no longer the universal thinker of a system of objects rigorously interrelated, the positing power who subjects the manifold to the law of the understanding, in so far as he is to be able to put together a world – he discovers and enjoys his own nature as spontaneously in harmony with the law of the understanding. But if

the subject has a nature, then the hidden art of the imagination must condition the categorial activity. It is no longer merely the aesthetic judgement, but knowledge too which rests upon this art, an art which forms the basis of the unity of consciousness and of consciousnesses.

Husserl takes up again the *Critique of Judgement* when he talks about a teleology of consciousness. It is not a matter of duplicating human consciousness with some absolute thought which, from outside, is imagined as assigning to it its aims. It is a question of recognizing consciousness itself as a project of the world, meant for a world which it neither embraces nor possesses, but towards which it is perpetually directed – and the world as this pre-objective individual whose imperious unity decrees what knowledge shall take as its goal. This is why Husserl distinguishes between intentionality of act, which is that of our judgements and of those occasions when we voluntarily take up a position – the only intentionality discussed in the *Critique of Pure Reason* – and operative intentionality (*fungierende Intentionalität*), or that which produces the natural and ante-predicative unity of the world and of our life, being apparent in our desires, our evaluations and in the landscape we see, more clearly than in objective knowledge, and furnishing the text which our knowledge tries to translate into precise language. Our relationship to the world, as it is untiringly enunciated within us, is not a thing which can be any further clarified by analysis; philosophy can only place it once more before our eyes and present it for our ratification.

Through this broadened notion of intentionality, phenomenological 'comprehension' is distinguished from traditional 'intellection', which is confined to 'true and immutable natures', and so phenomenology can become a phenomenology of origins. Whether we are concerned with a thing perceived, a historical event or a doctrine, to 'understand' is to take in the total intention not only what these things are for representation (the 'properties' of the thing perceived, the mass of 'historical facts', the 'ideas' introduced by the doctrine) – but the unique mode of existing expressed in the properties of the pebble, the glass or the piece of wax, in all the events of a revolution, in all the thoughts of a philosopher. It is a matter, in the case of each civilization, of finding the Idea in the Hegelian sense, that is, not a law of the physico-mathematical type, discoverable by objective thought, but that formula which sums up some unique manner of behaviour towards others, towards Nature, time and death: a certain way of patterning the world which the historian should be capable of seizing upon and making his own. These are the *dimensions* of history. In this context there is not a human word, not a gesture, even one which is the outcome of habit or absentmindedness, which has not some meaning. For example, I may have been under the impression that I lapsed into silence through weariness, or some minister may have thought he had uttered merely an appropriate platitude, yet my silence or his words immediately take on a significance, because my fatigue or his falling back upon a ready-made formula are not accidental, for they express a certain lack of interest, and hence some degree of adoption of a definite position in relation to the situation.

When an event is considered at close quarters, at the moment when it is lived through, everything seems subject to chance: one man's ambition, some lucky encounter, some local circumstance or other appears to have been decisive. But chance happenings offset each other, and facts in their multiplicity coalesce and show up a certain way of taking a stand in relation to the human situation, reveal in fact an *event* which has its definite outline and about which we can talk. Should the starting-point for the understanding of history be ideology, or politics, or religion, or economics? Should we try to understand a doctrine from its overt content, or from the psychological makeup and the biography of its author? We must seek an understanding from all these angles simultaneously, everything has meaning, and we shall find this same structure of being underlying all relationships, All these views are true provided that they are not isolated, that we delve deeply into history and reach the unique core of existential meaning which emerges in each perspective. It is true, as Marx says, that history does not walk on its head, but it is also true that it does not think with its feet. Or one should say rather that it is neither its 'head' not its 'feet' that we have to worry about, but its body. All economic and psychological explanations of a doctrine are true, since the thinker never thinks from any starting-point but the one constituted by what he is. Reflection even on a doctrine will be complete only if it succeeds in linking up with the doctrine's history and the extraneous explanations of it, and in putting back the causes and meaning of the doctrine in an existential structure. There is, as Husserl says, a 'genesis of meaning' *(Sinngenesis)*,* which alone, in the last resort, teaches us what the doctrine 'means.' Like understanding, criticism must be pursued at all levels, and naturally, it will be insufficient, for the refutation of a doctrine, to relate it to some accidental event in the author's life: its significance goes beyond, and there is no pure accident in existence or in coexistence, since both absorb random events and transmute them into the rational.

Finally, as it is indivisible in the present, history is equally so in its sequences. Considered in the light of its fundamental dimensions, all periods of history appear as manifestations of a single existence, or as episodes in a single drama – without our knowing whether it has an ending. Because we are in the world, we are *condemned to meaning*, and we cannot do or say anything without its acquiring a name in history.

Probably the chief gain from phenomenology is to have united extreme subjectivism and extreme objectivism in its notion of the world or of rationality. Rationality is precisely measured by the experiences in which it is disclosed. To say that there exists rationality is to say that perspectives blend, perceptions confirm each other, a meaning emerges. But it should not be set in a realm apart, transposed into absolute Spirit, or into a world in the realist sense. The phenomenological world is not pure being, but the sense which is revealed where the paths of my various experiences intersect, and also where my own and other people's intersect and engage each other like gears. It is thus inseparable from subjectivity and intersubjectivity, which find their unity when I either take up my past experiences in those of the present, or other people's in my own. For the first time the philosopher's thinking is sufficiently conscious not to anticipate itself and endow its own results with reified form in the world. The philosopher tries to conceive

* The usual term in the unpublished writings. The idea is already to be found in the *Formale und transzendentale Logik*, pp. 184 and ff. [See Edmund Husserl, *Formal and Transcendental Logic*, trans. D. Cairns, The Hague: Martinus Nijhoff, 2002; and see Suzanne Bachelard, *A Study of Husserl's Formal and Transcendental Logic*, Evanston: Northwestern University Press, 1990.]

the world, others and himself and their inter-relations. But the meditating Ego, the 'impartial spectator' *(uninteressierter Zuschauer)** do not rediscover an already given rationality, they 'establish themselves',† and establish it, by an act of initiative which has no guarantee in being, its justification resting entirely on the effective power which it confers on us of taking our own history upon ourselves.

The phenomenological world is not the bring-ing to explicit expression of a pre-existing being, but the laying down of being. Philosophy is not the reflection of a pre-existing truth, but, like art, the act of bringing truth into being. One may well ask how this creation is *possible*, and if it does not recapture in things a preexisting Reason. The answer is that the only preexistent Logos is the world itself, and that the philosophy which brings it into visible existence does not begin by being *possible*; it is actual or real like the world of which it is a part, and no explanatory hypo-thesis is clearer than the act whereby we take up this unfinished world in an effort to complete and conceive it. Rationality is not a *problem*. There is behind it no unknown quantity which has to be determined by deduction, or, beginning with it, demonstrated inductively. We witness every minute the miracle of related experiences, and yet nobody knows better than we do how this mir-acle is worked, for we are ourselves this network of relationships. The world and reason are not problematical. We may say, if we wish, that they are mysterious, but their mystery defines them: there can be no question of dispelling it by some 'solution', it is on the hither side of all solutions.

True philosophy consists in relearning to look at the world, and in this sense a historical account can give meaning to the world quite as 'deeply' as a philosophical treatise. We take our fate in our hands, we become responsible for our history through reflection, but equally by a decision on which we stake our life, and in both cases what is involved is a violent act which is validated by being performed.

Phenomenology, as a disclosure of the world, rests on itself, or rather provides its own founda-tion. All knowledge is sustained by a 'ground' of postulates and finality by our communication with the world as primary embodiment of rationality. Philosophy, as radical reflection, dis-penses in principle with this resource. As, how-ever, it too is in history, it too exploits the world and constituted reason. It must therefore put to itself the question which it puts to all branches of knowledge, and so duplicate itself infinitely, being, as Husserl says, a dialogue or infinite meditation, and, in so far as it remains faithful to its intention, never knowing where it is going. The unfinished nature of phenomenology and the inchoative atmosphere which has surrounded it are not to be taken as a sign of failure, they were inevitable because phenomenology's task was to reveal the mystery of the world and of reason.‡ If phenomenology was a movement before becoming a doctrine or a philosophical system, this was attributable neither to accident, nor to fraudulent intent. It is as painstaking as the works of Balzac, Proust, Valéry or Cézanne – by reason of the same kind of attentiveness and wonder, the same demand for awareness, the same will to seize the meaning of the world or of history as that meaning comes into being. In this way it merges into the general effort of modern thought.

* [Edmund Husserl,] *6th Méditations cartésiennes.* [*Sixth Cartesian Meditation*, ed. E. Fink, trans. R. Bruzina, Bloomington: Indiana University Press, 1995.]
† Ibid.

‡ We are indebted for this last expression to G. Gusdorf, who may well have used it in another sense.

W. V. O. Quine, "Two Dogmas of Empiricism"

Introduction

One of the leading figures of the analytic tradition in philosophy, W. V. O. Quine (1908–2000) was born in Akron, Ohio, and educated at Oberlin College and Harvard University, writing his PhD under the direction of Bertrand Russell's collaborator, Alfred North Whitehead. While traveling in Europe in 1932–3, he became acquainted with the logician Alfred Tarski as well as Rudolf Carnap and various other members of the Vienna Circle of logical positivists, whose work he would come to criticize in this 1951 essay and elsewhere.

"Two Dogmas" works to subvert two central pillars of empiricist theory – the "analytic-synthetic" distinction and semantic "reductionism." Quine's aim is to re-conceptualize truth; and indeed if he is right, then a number of dramatic conclusions follow. In the first place, it would follow that truths cannot be divided neatly, as philosophers have long maintained – into two classes, "analytic" and "synthetic."

David Hume (1711–76), in his *Enquiry Concerning Human Understanding* (1748), had distinguished between truths dependent upon 'relations of ideas' (the negation of which imply a contradiction) and truths dependent on observed

'matters of fact' (II.10).[1] As we saw in II.12, Immanuel Kant (1724–1804) in his *Critique of Pure Reason* (1780) articulated a similar, though not identical, distinction between 'analytic' and 'synthetic' judgments. In synthetic judgments, the meaning of the predicate term is independent of the subject term in the sense that one can't tell by the meanings of the terms alone whether sentences using those terms are true or false – for example, "All apartments in that building are leased by bachelors." In analytic judgments, by contrast, one simply analyses or unpacks the meaning of a given subject term to determine the truth of the sentence. That is to say, the meaning of the subject term in a true analytic statement somehow already 'contains' the meaning of the predicate – "All bachelors are unmarried men."

One needn't consult observation and experience to determine the truth or falsehood of this last sentence by, for instance, conducting a survey of bachelors to discover what fraction is unmarried. Indeed, should any bachelor queried in such a pointless affair answer that he is married, his answer could not be taken seriously. It must be false. In such cases, the concepts dictate what the facts can possibly be; the facts don't determine the answer to the question.

In "Two Dogmas of Empiricism," Quine challenges the analytic/synthetic distinction by interrogating the concept of analyticity and concluding that in significant ways it's incoherent. While sentences like "No unmarried man is married" preserve a kind of simple "logical" sense of ana-

From Willard Van Orman Quine, *From a Logical Point of View: Logico-Philosophical Essays*, 2nd edn, New York: Harper & Row, 1961. pp. 20–46.

lyticity (because the subject and predicate terms are the same or at least class complements), other purportedly analytic statements, where the predicate is said to be "synonymous" or contained by the subject, cannot be adequately explained.

If the first four sections of Quine's article militate against determining truth by an analysis of ideas or meanings, the last two sections militate against determining truth through observation, experiment, and experience. Positivist Rudolf Carnap (1891–1970), like many empiricists before him, maintained that statements about matters of fact face empirical testing independently of other statements. Quine opposes this reductionist view with a position that's come to be known as semantic "holism." Quine argues that statements whose truth and falsehood is determined by checking them against experience face testing as part of a larger whole or "web"[2] – that indeed, in a sense, when a single sentence (e.g. a scientific hypothesis) is tested, the entire language, or at least large sectors of it, are tested as well.

Part of the reason for this is that sentences are connected through logical relations. So, establishing that one sentence is true or false may entail establishing that many other sentences are true or false. There is another reason, however, for semantic holism. Quine argues that, through careful revisions elsewhere, the web can resist changes to *any* given statement in the face of apparently contrary experience or experimentation.[3] As a result, empirical evidence can never fully determine the truth or falsehood of statements. (Because of this Quine holds that all scientific theories are "underdetermined" by the evidence.) Conversely, any statement – even of mathematics or the analytic statements of logic – can be abandoned as false, so long as the proper revisions are

made elsewhere. Quine's conclusion, then, undermines both the claim that scientific reasoning progresses through procedures of verification (Carnap) and the claim that is does so through falsification (Popper, II.21).

Moreover, since statements don't confront experience in isolation and any statement can either be revised or resist revision, there is no difference in kind between the knowledge claims of ancient and modern science, or indeed between the claims of science and those of mythology. If we are to decide among explanations and theories, we cannot turn in a "crucial" or definitive way to experimentation. We must consider other criteria – perhaps culturally specific criteria – as well. For Quine, pragmatic issues of usefulness, efficiency, and simplicity are decisive.

Notes

1 David Hume, *Enquiry Concerning Human Understanding*, ed. P. H. Nidditch and L. A. Selby-Bigge, Oxford: Clarendon Press, 1975, p. 25. Similarly, French natural philosopher, Comte de Buffon, (1707–88) had, in the "Premier discours: De la manière d'étudier et de traiter l'histoire naturelle," of his *Histoire naturelle* (1749), argued that truths can be divided between those that are "abstract" or "mathematical" and depend only upon the definitions of terms and those that are "physical" and depend upon the facts of the world.

2 W. V. O. Quine and J. S. Ullian, *The Web of Belief*, New York: Random House, 1970.

3 In this Quine follows Pierre Duhem (1861–1916), *La théorie physique: son objet et sa structure* (1906).

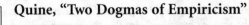

Quine, "Two Dogmas of Empiricism"

Modern empiricism has been conditioned in large part by two dogmas. One is a belief in some fundamental cleavage between truths which are *analytic*, or grounded in meanings independently of matters of fact, and truths which are *synthetic*, or grounded in fact. The other dogma is *reductionism*: the belief that each meaningful statement is equivalent to some logical construct upon terms which refer to immediate experience. Both dogmas, I shall argue, are ill-founded. One effect of abandoning them is, as we shall see, a blurring of the supposed boundary between speculative metaphysics and natural science. Another effect is a shift toward pragmatism.

1   Background for Analyticity

Kant's cleavage between analytic and synthetic truths was foreshadowed in Hume's distinction between relations of ideas and matters of fact, and in Leibniz's distinction between truths of reason and truths of fact. Leibniz spoke of the truths of reason as true in all possible worlds. Picturesqueness aside, this is to say that the truths of reason are those which could not possibly be false. In the same vein we hear analytic statements defined as statements whose denials are self-contradictory. But this definition has small explanatory value; for the notion of self-contradictoriness, in the quite broad sense needed for this definition of analyticity, stands in exactly the same need of clarification as does the notion of analyticity itself. The two notions are the two sides of a single dubious coin.

Kant conceived of an analytic statement as one that attributes to its subject no more than is already conceptually contained in the subject. This formulation has two shortcomings: it limits itself to statements of subject–predicate form, and it appeals to a notion of containment which is left at a metaphorical level. But Kant's intent, evident more from the use he makes of the notion of analyticity than from his definition of it, can be restated thus: a statement is analytic when it is true by virtue of meanings and independently of fact. Pursuing this line, let us examine the concept of *meaning* which is presupposed.

Meaning, let us remember, is not to be identified with naming. Frege's example of 'Evening Star' and 'Morning Star', and Russell's of 'Scott' and 'the author of *Waverley*', illustrate that terms can name the same thing but differ in meaning. The distinction between meaning and naming is no less important at the level of abstract terms. The terms '9' and 'the number of the planets' name one and the same abstract entity but presumably must be regarded as unlike in meaning; for astronomical observation was needed, and not mere reflection on meanings, to determine the sameness of the entity in question.

The above examples consist of singular terms, concrete and abstract. With general terms, or predicates, the situation is somewhat different but parallel. Whereas a singular term purports to name an entity, abstract or concrete, a general term does not; but a general term is *true of* an entity, or of each of many, or of none. The class of all entities of which a general term is true is called the *extension* of the term. Now paralleling the contrast between the meaning of a singular term and the entity named, we must distinguish equally between the meaning of a general term and its extension. The general terms 'creature with a heart' and 'creature with kidneys', for example, are perhaps alike in extension but unlike in meaning.

Confusion of meaning with extension, in the case of general terms, is less common than confusion of meaning with naming in the case of singular terms. It is indeed a commonplace in philosophy to oppose intension (or meaning) to extension, or, in a variant vocabulary, connotation to denotation.

The Aristotelian notion of essence was the forerunner, no doubt, of the modern notion of intension or meaning. For Aristotle it was essential in men to be rational, accidental to be two-legged. But there is an important difference between this attitude and the doctrine of meaning. From the latter point of view it may indeed be conceded (if only for the sake of argument) that rationality is involved in the meaning of the word 'man' while two-leggedness is not; but two-leggedness may at the same time be viewed as involved in the meaning of 'biped' while rationality is not. Thus from the point of view of the doctrine of meaning it makes no sense to say of the actual individual, who is at once a man and a biped, that his rationality is essential and his two-leggedness accidental or vice versa. Things had essences, for Aristotle, but only linguistic forms have meanings. Meaning is what essence becomes when it is divorced from the object of reference and wedded to the word.

For the theory of meaning a conspicuous question is the nature of its objects: what sort of things are meanings? A felt need for meant entities may derive from an earlier failure to appreciate that meaning and reference are distinct. Once the theory of meaning is sharply separated from the theory of reference, it is a short step to recognizing as the primary business of the theory of meaning simply the synonymy of linguistic forms and the analyticity of statements; meanings themselves, as obscure intermediary entities, may well be abandoned.

The problem of analyticity then confronts us anew. Statements which are analytic by general philosophical acclaim are not, indeed, far to seek.

They fall into two classes. Those of the first class, which may be called *logically true*, are typified by:

(1) No unmarried man is married.

The relevant feature of this example is that it not merely is true as it stands, but remains true under any and all reinterpretations of 'man' and 'married'. If we suppose a prior inventory of *logical* particles, comprising 'no', 'un-', 'not', 'if', 'then', 'and', etc., then in general a logical truth is a statement which is true and remains true under all reinterpretations of its components other than the logical particles.

But there is also a second class of analytic statements, typified by:

(2) No bachelor is married.

The characteristic of such a statement is that it can be turned into a logical truth by putting synonyms for synonyms; thus (2) can be turned into (1) by putting 'unmarried man' for its synonym 'bachelor'. We still lack a proper characterization of this second class of analytic statements, and therewith of analyticity generally, inasmuch as we have had in the above description to lean on a notion of "synonymy" which is no less in need of clarification than analyticity itself.

In recent years Carnap has tended to explain analyticity by appeal to what he calls state-descriptions.* A state-description is any exhaustive assignment of truth values to the atomic, or noncompound, statements of the language. All other statements of the language are, Carnap assumes, built up of their component clauses by means of the familiar logical devices, in such a way that the truth value of any complex statement is fixed for each state-description by specifiable logical laws. A statement is then explained as analytic when it comes out true under every state description. This account is an adaptation of Leibniz's "true in all possible worlds." But note that this version of analyticity serves its purpose only if the atomic statements of the language are,

unlike 'John is a bachelor' and 'John is married', mutually independent. Otherwise there would be a state-description which assigned truth to 'John is a bachelor' and to 'John is married', and consequently 'No bachelors are married' would turn out synthetic rather than analytic under the proposed criterion. Thus the criterion of analyticity in terms of state-descriptions serves only for languages devoid of extralogical synonym-pairs, such as 'bachelor' and 'unmarried man' – synonym-pairs of the type which give rise to the "second class" of analytic statements. The criterion in terms of state-descriptions is a reconstruction at best of logical truth, not of analyticity.

I do not mean to suggest that Carnap is under any illusions on this point. His simplified model language with its state-descriptions is aimed primarily not at the general problem of analyticity but at another purpose, the clarification of probability and induction. Our problem, however, is analyticity; and here the major difficulty lies not in the first class of analytic statements, the logical truths, but rather in the second class, which depends on the notion of synonymy.

2 Definition

There are those who find it soothing to say that the analytic statements of the second class reduce to those of the first class, the logical truths, by *definition*; 'bachelor', for example, is *defined* as 'unmarried man'. But how do we find that 'bachelor' is defined as 'unmarried man'? Who defined it thus, and when? Are we to appeal to the nearest dictionary, and accept the lexicographer's formulation as law? Clearly this would be to put the cart before the horse. The lexicographer is an empirical scientist, whose business is the recording of antecedent facts; and if he glosses 'bachelor' as 'unmarried man' it is because of his belief that there is a relation of synonymy between those forms, implicit in general or preferred usage prior to his own work. The notion of synonymy presupposed here has still to be clarified, presumably in terms relating to linguistic behavior. Certainly the "definition" which is the lexicographer's report of an observed synonymy cannot be taken as the ground of the synonymy.

Definition is not, indeed, an activity exclusively of philologists. Philosophers and scientists

---

* [Rudolf] Carnap [*Meaning and Necessity*, Chicago: University of Chicago Press, 1947], pp. 9ff; [*Logical Foundations of Possibility*, Chicago: University of Chicago Press, 1950], pp. 70ff.

frequently have occasion to "define" a recondite term by paraphrasing it into terms of a more familiar vocabulary. But ordinarily such a definition, like the philologist's, is pure lexicography, affirming a relation of synonymy antecedent to the exposition in hand.

Just what it means to affirm synonymy, just what the interconnections may be which are necessary and sufficient in order that two linguistic forms be properly describable as synonymous, is far from clear; but, whatever these interconnections may be, ordinarily they are grounded in usage. Definitions reporting selected instances of synonymy come then as reports upon usage.

There is also, however, a variant type of definitional activity which does not limit itself to the reporting of pre-existing synonymies. I have in mind what Carnap calls *explication* – an activity to which philosophers are given, and scientists also in their more philosophical moments. In explication the purpose is not merely to paraphrase the definiendum into an outright synonym, but actually to improve upon the definiendum by refining or supplementing its meaning. But even explication, though not merely reporting a preexisting synonymy between definiendum and definiens, does rest nevertheless on *other* preexisting synonymies. The matter may be viewed as follows. Any word worth explicating has some contexts which, as wholes, are clear and precise enough to be useful; and the purpose of explication is to preserve the usage of these favored contexts while sharpening the usage of other contexts. In order that a given definition be suitable for purposes of explication, therefore, what is required is not that the definiendum in its antecedent usage be synonymous with the definiens, but just that each of these favored contexts of the definiendum, taken as a whole in its antecedent usage, be synonymous with the corresponding context of the definiens.

Two alternative definientia may be equally appropriate for the purposes of a given task of explication and yet not be synonymous with each other; for they may serve interchangeably within the favored contexts but diverge elsewhere. By cleaving to one of these definientia rather than the other, a definition of explicative kind generates, by fiat, a relation of synonymy between definiendum and definiens which did not hold before. But such a definition still owes its explicative function, as seen, to pre-existing synonymies.

There does, however, remain still an extreme sort of definition which does not hark back to prior synonymies at all: namely, the explicitly conventional introduction of novel notations for purposes of sheer abbreviation. Here the definiendum becomes synonymous with the definiens simply because it has been created expressly for the purpose of being synonymous with the definiens. Here we have a really transparent case of synonymy created by definition; would that all species of synonymy were as intelligible. For the rest, definition rests on synonymy rather than explaining it.

The word 'definition' has come to have a dangerously reassuring sound, owing no doubt to its frequent occurrence in logical and mathematical writings. We shall do well to digress now into a brief appraisal of the role of definition in formal work.

In logical and mathematical systems either of two mutually antagonistic types of economy may be striven for, and each has its peculiar practical utility. On the one hand we may seek economy of practical expression – ease and brevity in the statement of multifarious relations. This sort of economy calls usually for distinctive concise notations for a wealth of concepts. Second, however, and oppositely, we may seek economy in grammar and vocabulary; we may try to find a minimum of basic concepts such that, once a distinctive notation has been appropriated to each of them, it becomes possible to express any desired further concept by mere combination and iteration of our basic notations. This second sort of economy is impractical in one way, since a poverty in basic idioms tends to a necessary lengthening of discourse. But it is practical in another way: it greatly simplifies theoretical discourse *about* the language, through minimizing the terms and the forms of construction wherein the language consists.

Both sorts of economy, though prima facie incompatible, are valuable in their separate ways. The custom has consequently arisen of combining both sorts of economy by forging in effect two languages, the one a part of the other. The inclusive language, though redundant in grammar and vocabulary, is economical in message lengths, while the part, called primitive notation, is economical in grammar and vocabulary. Whole and part are correlated by rules of translation whereby each idiom not in primitive notation is equated to some complex built up of primitive notation. These rules of translation are the so-called *definitions* which appear in formalized systems. They are best viewed not as adjuncts to one language but as correlations between two languages, the one a part of the other.

But these correlations are not arbitrary. They are supposed to show how the primitive notations can accomplish all purposes, save brevity and convenience, of the redundant language. Hence the definiendum and its definiens may be expected, in each case, to be related in one or another of the three ways lately noted. The definiens may be a faithful paraphrase of the definiendum into the narrower notation, preserving a direct synonymy* as of antecedent usage; or the definiens may, in the spirit of explication, improve upon the antecedent usage of the definiendum; or finally, the definiendum may be a newly created notation, newly endowed with meaning here and now.

In formal and informal work alike, thus, we find that definition – except in the extreme case of the explicitly conventional introduction of new notations – hinges on prior relations of synonymy. Recognizing then that the notion of definition does not hold the key to synonymy and analyticity, let us look further into synonymy and say no more of definition.

3 Interchangeability

A natural suggestion, deserving close examination, is that the synonymy of two linguistic forms consists simply in their interchangeability in all contexts without change of truth value – interchangeability, in Leibniz's phrase, *salva veritate*.† Note that synonyms so conceived need not even

* According to an important variant sense of 'definition', the relation preserved may be the weaker relation of mere agreement in reference [. . .]. But definition in this sense is better ignored in the present connection, being irrelevant to the question of synonymy.
† Cf. Lewis [*A Survey of Symbolic Logic*, Berkeley: University of California Press, 1918], p. 373. [Leibniz's phrase appears in "General Science" (1677) and means, literally, "saving the truth"; it is used to characterize substituting difference expressions in a sentence "without altering the truth value" of the sentence.]

be free from vagueness, as long as the vaguenesses match.

But it is not quite true that the synonyms 'bachelor' and 'unmarried man' are everywhere interchangeable *salva veritate*. Truths which become false under substitution of 'unmarried man' for 'bachelor' are easily constructed with the help of 'bachelor of arts' or 'bachelor's buttons'; also with the help of quotation, thus:

'Bachelor' has less than ten letters.

Such counterinstances can, however, perhaps be set aside by treating the phrases 'bachelor of arts' and 'bachelor's buttons' and the quotation 'bachelor' each as a single indivisible word and then stipulating that the interchangeability *salva veritate* which is to be the touchstone of synonymy is not supposed to apply to fragmentary occurrences inside of a word. This account of synonymy, supposing it acceptable on other counts, has indeed the drawback of appealing to a prior conception of "word" which can be counted on to present difficulties of formulation in its turn. Nevertheless some progress might be claimed in having reduced the problem of synonymy to a problem of word-hood. Let us pursue this line a bit, taking "word" for granted.

The question remains whether interchangeability *salva veritate* (apart from occurrences within words) is a strong enough condition for synonymy, or whether, on the contrary, some heteronymous expressions might be thus interchangeable. Now let us be clear that we are not concerned here with synonymy in the sense of complete identity in psychological associations or poetic quality; indeed no two expressions are synonymous in such a sense. We are concerned only with what may be called *cognitive* synonymy. Just what this is cannot be said without successfully finishing the present study; but we know something about it from the need which arose for it in connection with analyticity in §1. The sort of synonymy needed there was merely such that any analytic statement could be turned into a logical truth by putting synonyms for synonyms. Turning the tables and assuming analyticity, indeed, we could explain cognitive synonymy of terms as follows (keeping to the familiar example): to say that 'bachelor' and 'unmarried man' are cognitively synonymous is to say no more nor less than that the statement:

(3) All and only bachelors are unmarried men is analytic.*

What we need is an account of cognitive synonymy not presupposing analyticity – if we are to explain analyticity conversely with help of cognitive synonymy as undertaken in §1. And indeed such an independent account of cognitive synonymy is at present up for consideration, namely, interchangeability *salva veritate* everywhere except within words. The question before us, to resume the thread at last, is whether such interchangeability is a sufficient condition for cognitive synonymy. We can quickly assure ourselves that it is, by examples of the following sort. The statement:

(4) Necessarily all and only bachelors are bachelors

is evidently true, even supposing 'necessarily' so narrowly construed as to be truly applicable only to analytic statements. Then, if 'bachelor' and 'unmarried man' are interchangeable *salva veritate*, the result:

(5) Necessarily all and only bachelors are unmarried men

of putting 'unmarried man' for an occurrence of 'bachelor' in (4) must, like (4), be true. But to say that (5) is true is to say that (3) is analytic, and hence that 'bachelor' and 'unmarried man' are cognitively synonymous.

Let us see what there is about the above argument that gives it its air of hocus-pocus. The condition of interchangeability *salva veritate* varies in its force with variations in the richness of the language at hand. The above argument supposes we are working with a language rich enough to contain the adverb 'necessarily', this

adverb being so construed as to yield truth when and only when applied to an analytic statement. But can we condone a language which contains such an adverb? Does the adverb really make sense? To suppose that it does is to suppose that we have already made satisfactory sense of 'analytic'. Then what are we so hard at work on right now?

Our argument is not flatly circular, but something like it. It has the form, figuratively speaking, of a closed curve in space.

Interchangeability *salva veritate* is meaningless until relativized to a language whose extent is specified in relevant respects. Suppose now we consider a language containing just the following materials. There is an indefinitely large stock of one-place predicates (for example, 'F' where 'Fx' means that x is a man) and many-place predicates (for example, 'G' where 'Gxy' means that x loves y), mostly having to do with extralogical subject matter. The rest of the language is logical. The atomic sentences consist each of a predicate followed by one or more variables 'x', 'y', etc.; and the complex sentences are built up of the atomic ones by truth functions ('not', 'and', 'or', etc.) and quantification. In effect such a language enjoys the benefits also of descriptions and indeed singular terms generally, these being contextually definable in known ways. Even abstract singular terms naming classes, classes of classes, etc., are contextually definable in case the assumed stock of predicates includes the two-place predicate of class membership. Such a language can be adequate to classical mathematics and indeed to scientific discourse generally, except in so far as the latter involves debatable devices such as contrary-to-fact conditionals or modal adverbs like 'necessarily'. Now a language of this type is extensional, in this sense: any two predicates which agree extensionally (that is, are true of the same objects) are interchangeable *salva veritate*.†

In an extensional language, therefore, interchangeability *salva veritate* is no assurance of cognitive synonymy of the desired type. That 'bachelor' and 'unmarried man' are interchangeable *salva veritate* in an extensional language assures us of no more than that (3) is true. There is no assurance here that the extensional agree-

* This is cognitive synonymy in a primary, broad sense. Carnap ([*Meaning and Necessity*, Chicago: University of Chicago Press, 1947], pp. 56ff) and Lewis ([*An Analysis of Knowledge and Valuation*, La Salle, IL: Open Court, 1946], pp. 83ff) have suggested how, once this notion is at hand, a narrower sense of cognitive synonymy which is preferable for some purposes can in turn be derived. But this special ramification of concept-building lies aside from the present purposes and must not be confused with the broad sort of cognitive synonymy here concerned.

† This is the substance of Quine [*Mathematical Logic*, New York: Norton, 1940; Cambridge, MA: Harvard University Press, 1951], *121.

ment of 'bachelor' and 'unmarried man' rests on meaning rather than merely on accidental matters of fact, as does the extensional agreement of 'creature with a heart' and 'creature with kidneys'.

For most purposes extensional agreement is the nearest approximation to synonymy we need care about. But the fact remains that extensional agreement falls far short of cognitive synonymy of the type required for explaining analyticity in the manner of §1. The type of cognitive synonymy required there is such as to equate the synonymy of 'bachelor' and 'unmarried man' with the analyticity of (3), not merely with the truth of (3).

So we must recognize that interchangeability *salva veritate*, if construed in relation to an extensional language, is not a sufficient condition of cognitive synonymy in the sense needed for deriving analyticity in the manner of §1. If a language contains an intensional adverb 'necessarily' in the sense lately noted, or other particles to the same effect, then interchangeability *salva veritate* in such a language does afford a sufficient condition of cognitive synonymy; but such a language is intelligible only in so far as the notion of analyticity is already understood in advance.

The effort to explain cognitive synonymy first, for the sake of deriving analyticity from it afterward as in §1, is perhaps the wrong approach. Instead we might try explaining analyticity somehow without appeal to cognitive synonymy. Afterward we could doubtless derive cognitive synonymy from analyticity satisfactorily enough if desired. We have seen that cognitive synonymy of 'bachelor' and 'unmarried man' can be explained as analyticity of (3). The same explanation works for any pair of one-place predicates, of course, and it can be extended in obvious fashion to many-place predicates. Other syntactical categories can also be accommodated in fairly parallel fashion. Singular terms may be said to be cognitively synonymous when the statement of identity formed by putting '=' between them is analytic. Statements may be said simply to be cognitively synonymous when their biconditional (the result of joining them by 'if and only if') is analytic.* If we care to lump

all categories into a single formulation, at the expense of assuming again the notion of "word" which was appealed to early in this section, we can describe any two linguistic forms as cognitively synonymous when the two forms are interchangeable (apart from occurrences within "words") *salva* (no longer *veritate* but) *analyticitate*. Certain technical questions arise, indeed, over cases of ambiguity or homonymy; let us not pause for them, however, for we are already digressing. Let us rather turn our backs on the problem of synonymy and address ourselves anew to that of analyticity.

4   Semantical Rules

Analyticity at first seemed most naturally definable by appeal to a realm of meanings. On refinement, the appeal to meanings gave way to an appeal to synonymy or definition. But definition turned out to be a will-o'-the-wisp, and synonymy turned out to be best understood only by dint of a prior appeal to analyticity itself. So we are back at the problem of analyticity.

I do not know whether the statement 'Everything green is extended' is analytic. Now does my indecision over this example really betray an incomplete understanding, an incomplete grasp of the "meanings", of 'green' and 'extended'? I think not. The trouble is not with 'green' or 'extended', but with 'analytic'.

It is often hinted that the difficulty in separating analytic statements from synthetic ones in ordinary language is due to the vagueness of ordinary language and that the distinction is clear when we have a precise artificial language with explicit "semantical rules." This, however, as I shall now attempt to show, is a confusion.

The notion of analyticity about which we are worrying is a purported relation between statements and languages: a statement S is said to be *analytic for* a language L, and the problem is to make sense of this relation generally, that is, for variable 'S' and 'L'. The gravity of this problem is not perceptibly less for artificial languages than for natural ones. The problem of making sense of the idiom 'S is analytic for L', with variable 'S' and 'L', retains its stubbornness even if we limit the range of the variable 'L' to artificial languages. Let me now try to make this point evident.

---

* The 'if and only if' itself is intended in the truth functional sense. See Carnap [*Meaning and Necessity*, Chicago: University of Chicago Press, 1947], p. 14.

For artificial languages and semantical rules we look naturally to the writings of Carnap. His semantical rules take various forms, and to make my point I shall have to distinguish certain of the forms. Let us suppose, to begin with, an artificial language L_0 whose semantical rules have the form explicitly of a specification, by recursion or otherwise, of all the analytic statements of L_0. The rules tell us that such and such statements, and only those, are the analytic statements of L_0. Now here the difficulty is simply that the rules contain the word 'analytic', which we do not understand! We understand what expressions the rules attribute analyticity to, but we do not understand what the rules attribute to those expressions. In short, before we can understand a rule which begins 'A statement S is analytic for language L_0 if and only if...', we must understand the general relative term 'analytic for'; we must understand 'S is analytic for L' where 'S' and 'L' are variables.

Alternatively we may, indeed, view the so-called rule as a conventional definition of a new simple symbol 'analytic-for-L_0', which might better be written untendentiously as 'K' so as not to seem to throw light on the interesting word 'analytic'. Obviously any number of classes K, M, N, etc. of statements of L_0 can be specified for various purposes or for no purpose; what does it mean to say that K, as against M, N, etc., is the class of the "analytic" statements of L_0?

By saying what statements are analytic for L_0 we explain 'analytic-for-L_0' but not 'analytic', not 'analytic for'. We do not begin to explain the idiom 'S is analytic for L' with variable 'S' and 'L', even if we are content to limit the range of 'L' to the realm of artificial languages.

Actually we do know enough about the intended significance of 'analytic' to know that analytic statements are supposed to be true. Let us then turn to a second form of semantical rule, which says not that such and such statements are analytic but simply that such and such statements are included among the truths. Such a rule is not subject to the criticism of containing the un-understood word 'analytic'; and we may grant for the sake of argument that there is no difficulty over the broader term 'true'. A semantical rule of this second type, a rule of truth, is not supposed to specify all the truths of the language; it merely stipulates, recursively or otherwise, a certain multitude of statements

which, along with others unspecified, are to count as true. Such a rule may be conceded to be quite clear. Derivatively, afterward, analyticity can be demarcated thus: a statement is analytic if it is (not merely true but) true according to the semantical rule.

Still there is really no progress. Instead of appealing to an unexplained word 'analytic', we are now appealing to an unexplained phrase 'semantical rule'. Not every true statement which says that the statements of some class are true can count as a semantical rule – otherwise all truths would be "analytic" in the sense of being true according to semantical rules. Semantical rules are distinguishable, apparently, only by the fact of appearing on a page under the heading 'Semantical Rules'; and this heading is itself then meaningless.

We can say indeed that a statement is *analytic-for-L_0* if and only if it is true according to such and such specifically appended "semantical rules," but then we find ourselves back at essentially the same case which was originally discussed: 'S is analytic-for-L_0 if and only if....' Once we seek to explain 'S is analytic for L' generally for variable 'L' (even allowing limitation of 'L' to artificial languages), the explanation 'true according to the semantical rules of L' is unavailing; for the relative term 'semantical rule of' is as much in need of clarification, at least, as 'analytic for'.

It may be instructive to compare the notion of semantical rule with that of postulate. Relative to a given set of postulates, it is easy to say what a postulate is: it is a member of the set. Relative to a given set of semantical rules, it is equally easy to say what a semantical rule is. But given simply a notation, mathematical or otherwise, and indeed as thoroughly understood a notation as you please in point of the translations or truth conditions of its statements, who can say which of its true statements rank as postulates? Obviously the question is meaningless – as meaningless as asking which points in Ohio are starting points. Any finite (or effectively specifiable infinite) selection of statements (preferably true ones, perhaps) is as much a set of postulates as any other. The word 'postulate' is significant only relative to an act of inquiry; we apply the word to a set of statements just in so far as we happen, for the year or the moment, to be thinking of those statements in relation to the statements which can be reached from them by some set of transformations to which we have seen fit to direct our attention. Now the notion of semantical rule is as sensible and meaningful as that of postulate, if conceived in a similarly relative spirit – relative, this time, to one or another particular enterprise of schooling unconversant persons in sufficient conditions for truth of statements of some natural or artificial language L. But from this point of view no one signalization of a subclass of the truths of L is intrinsically more a semantical rule than another; and, if 'analytic' means 'true by semantical rules', no one truth of L is analytic to the exclusion of another.*

It might conceivably be protested that an artificial language L (unlike a natural one) is a language in the ordinary sense *plus* a set of explicit semantical rules – the whole constituting, let us say, an ordered pair; and that the semantical rules of L then are specifiable simply as the second component of the pair L. But, by the same token and more simply, we might construe an artificial language L outright as an ordered pair whose second component is the class of its analytic statements; and then the analytic statements of L become specifiable simply as the statements in the second component of L. Or better still, we might just stop tugging at our bootstraps altogether.

Not all the explanations of analyticity known to Carnap and his readers have been covered explicitly in the above considerations, but the extension to other forms is not hard to see. Just one additional factor should be mentioned which sometimes enters: sometimes the semantical rules are in effect rules of translation into ordinary language, in which case the analytic statements of the artificial language are in effect recognized as such from the analyticity of their specified translations in ordinary language. Here certainly there can be no thought of an illumination of the problem of analyticity from the side of the artificial language.

From the point of view of the problem of analyticity the notion of an artificial language with semantical rules is a *feu follet par excellence*. Semantical rules determining the analytic state-

---

* The foregoing paragraph was not part of the present essay as originally published. It was prompted by Martin [R. M. Martin, "On 'Analytic'," *Philosophical Studies* 3 (1952), 42–7], as was the end of Essay VII.

ments of an artificial language are of interest only in so far as we already understand the notion of analyticity; they are of no help in gaining this understanding.

Appeal to hypothetical languages of an artificially simple kind could conceivably be useful in clarifying analyticity, if the mental or behavioral or cultural factors relevant to analyticity – whatever they may be – were somehow sketched into the simplified model. But a model which takes analyticity merely as an irreducible character is unlikely to throw light on the problem of explicating analyticity.

It is obvious that truth in general depends on both language and extralinguistic fact. The statement 'Brutus killed Caesar' would be false if the world had been different in certain ways, but it would also be false if the word 'killed' happened rather to have the sense of 'begat'. Thus one is tempted to suppose in general that the truth of a statement is somehow analyzable into a linguistic component and a factual component. Given this supposition, it next seems reasonable that in some statements the factual component should be null; and these are the analytic statements. But, for all its a priori reasonableness, a boundary between analytic and synthetic statements simply has not been drawn. That there is such a distinction to be drawn at all is an unempirical dogma of empiricists, a metaphysical article of faith.

5   The Verification Theory and Reductionism

In the course of these somber reflections we have taken a dim view first of the notion of meaning, then of the notion of cognitive synonymy, and finally of the notion of analyticity. But what, it may be asked, of the verification theory of meaning? This phrase has established itself so firmly as a catchword of empiricism that we should be very unscientific indeed not to look beneath it for a possible key to the problem of meaning and the associated problems.

The verification theory of meaning, which has been conspicuous in the literature from Peirce onward, is that the meaning of a statement is the method of empirically confirming or infirming it. An analytic statement is that limiting case which is confirmed no matter what.

As urged in §1, we can as well pass over the question of meanings as entities and move straight to sameness of meaning, or synonymy. Then what the verification theory says is that statements are synonymous if and only if they are alike in point of method of empirical confirmation or infirmation.

This is an account of cognitive synonymy not of linguistic forms generally, but of statements.* However, from the concept of synonymy of statements we could derive the concept of synonymy for other linguistic forms, by considerations somewhat similar to those at the end of §3. Assuming the notion of "word," indeed, we could explain any two forms as synonymous when the putting of the one form for an occurrence of the other in any statement (apart from occurrences within "words") yields a synonymous statement. Finally, given the concept of synonymy thus for linguistic forms generally, we could define analyticity in terms of synonymy and logical truth as in §1. For that matter, we could define analyticity more simply in terms of just synonymy of statements together with logical truth; it is not necessary to appeal to synonymy of linguistic forms other than statements. For a statement may be described as analytic simply when it is synonymous with a logically true statement.

So, if the verification theory can be accepted as an adequate account of statement synonymy, the notion of analyticity is saved after all. However, let us reflect. Statement synonymy is said to be likeness of method of empirical confirmation or infirmation. Just what are these methods which are to be compared for likeness? What, in other words, is the nature of the relation between a statement and the experiences which contribute to or detract from its confirmation?

---

* The doctrine can indeed be formulated with terms rather than statements as the units. Thus [C. I.] Lewis describes the meaning of a term as "*a criterion in mind*, by reference to which one is able to apply or refuse to apply the expression in question in the case of presented, or imagined, things or situations" ([*An Analysis of Knowledge and Valuation*, La Salle, IL: Open Court, 1946], p. 133). – For an instructive account of the vicissitudes of the verification theory of meaning, centered however on the question of mean-ing*fulness* rather than synonymy and analyticity, see Hempel.

The most naïve view of the relation is that it is one of direct report. This is *radical reductionism*. Every meaningful statement is held to be translatable into a statement (true or false) about immediate experience. Radical reductionism, in one form or another, well antedates the verification theory of meaning explicitly so called. Thus Locke and Hume held that every idea must either originate directly in sense experience or else be compounded of ideas thus originating; and taking a hint from Tooke we might rephrase this doctrine in semantical jargon by saying that a term, to be significant at all, must be either a name of a sense datum or a compound of such names or an abbreviation of such a compound. So stated, the doctrine remains ambiguous as between sense data as sensory events and sense data as sensory qualities; and it remains vague as to the admissible ways of compounding. Moreover, the doctrine is unnecessarily and intolerably restrictive in the term-by-term critique which it imposes. More reasonably, and without yet exceeding the limits of what I have called radical reductionism, we may take full statements as our significant units – thus demanding that our statements as wholes be translatable into sense-datum language, but not that they be translatable term by term.

This emendation would unquestionably have been welcome to Locke and Hume and Tooke, but historically it had to await an important reorientation in semantics – the reorientation whereby the primary vehicle of meaning came to be seen no longer in the term but in the statement. This reorientation, seen in Bentham and Frege, underlies Russell's concept of incomplete symbols defined in use; also it is implicit in the verification theory of meaning, since the objects of verification are statements.

Radical reductionism, conceived now with statements as units, set itself the task of specifying a sense-datum language and showing how to translate the rest of significant discourse, statement by statement, into it. Carnap embarked on this project in the *Aufbau*.†

The language which Carnap adopted as his starting point was not a sense-datum language in the narrowest conceivable sense, for it included also the notations of logic, up through higher set

---

† [*Der logische Aufbau der Welt*, 1928.]

theory. In effect it included the whole language of pure mathematics. The ontology implicit in it (that is, the range of values of its variables) embraced not only sensory events but classes, classes of classes, and so on. Empiricists there are who would boggle at such prodigality. Carnap's starting point is very parsimonious, however, in its extralogical or sensory part. In a series of constructions in which he exploits the resources of modern logic with much ingenuity, Carnap succeeds in defining a wide array of important additional sensory concepts which, but for his constructions, one would not have dreamed were definable on so slender a basis. He was the first empiricist who, not content with asserting the reducibility of science to terms of immediate experience, took serious steps toward carrying out the reduction.

If Carnap's starting point is satisfactory, still his constructions were, as he himself stressed, only a fragment of the full program. The construction of even the simplest statements about the physical world was left in a sketchy state. Carnap's suggestions on this subject were, despite their sketchiness, very suggestive. He explained spatio-temporal point-instants as quadruples of real numbers and envisaged assignment of sense qualities to point-instants according to certain canons. Roughly summarized, the plan was that qualities should be assigned to point-instants in such a way as to achieve the laziest world compatible with our experience. The principle of least action was to be our guide in constructing a world from experience.

Carnap did not seem to recognize, however, that his treatment of physical objects fell short of reduction not merely through sketchiness, but in principle. Statements of the form 'Quality q is at point-instant $x;y;z;t$' were, according to his canons, to be apportioned truth values in such a way as to maximize and minimize certain overall features, and with growth of experience the truth values were to be progressively revised in the same spirit. I think this is a good schematization (deliberately oversimplified, to be sure) of what science really does; but it provides no indication, not even the sketchiest, of how a statement of the form 'Quality q is at $x;y;z;t$' could ever be translated into Carnap's initial language of sense data and logic. The connective 'is at' remains an added undefined connective; the canons counsel us in its use but not in its elimination.

Carnap seems to have appreciated this point afterward; for in his later writings he abandoned all notion of the translatability of statements about the physical world into statements about immediate experience. Reductionism in its radical form has long since ceased to figure in Carnap's philosophy.

But the dogma of reductionism has, in a subtler and more tenuous form, continued to influence the thought of empiricists. The notion lingers that to each statement, or each synthetic statement, there is associated a unique range of possible sensory events such that the occurrence of any of them would add to the likelihood of truth of the statement, and that there is associated also another unique range of possible sensory events whose occurrence would detract from that likelihood. This notion is of course implicit in the verification theory of meaning.

The dogma of reductionism survives in the supposition that each statement, taken in isolation from its fellows, can admit of confirmation or infirmation at all. My countersuggestion, issuing essentially from Carnap's doctrine of the physical world in the *Aufbau*, is that our statements about the external world face the tribunal of sense experience not individually but only as a corporate body.*

The dogma of reductionism, even in its attenuated form, is intimately connected with the other dogma – that there is a cleavage between the analytic and the synthetic. We have found ourselves led, indeed, from the latter problem to the former through the verification theory of meaning. More directly, the one dogma clearly supports the other in this way: as long as it is taken to be significant in general to speak of the confirmation and infirmation of a statement, it seems significant to speak also of a limiting kind of statement which is vacuously confirmed, *ipso facto*, come what may; and such a statement is analytic.

The two dogmas are, indeed, at root identical. We lately reflected that in general the truth of statements does obviously depend both upon language and upon extralinguistic fact; and we noted that this obvious circumstance carries in its

* This doctrine was well argued by Pierre Duhem [*La théorie physique: son objet et sa structure*, Paris, 1906], pp. 303–328. Or see Armand Lowinger [*The Methodology of Pierre Duhem*, New York: Columbia University Press, 1941], pp. 132–140.

train, not logically but all too naturally, a feeling that the truth of a statement is somehow analyzable into a linguistic component and a factual component. The factual component must, if we are empiricists, boil down to a range of confirmatory experiences. In the extreme case where the linguistic component is all that matters, a true statement is analytic. But I hope we are now impressed with how stubbornly the distinction between analytic and synthetic has resisted any straightforward drawing. I am impressed also, apart from prefabricated examples of black and white balls in an urn, with how baffling the problem has always been of arriving at any explicit theory of the empirical confirmation of a synthetic statement. My present suggestion is that it is nonsense, and the root of much nonsense, to speak of a linguistic component and a factual component in the truth of any individual statement. Taken collectively, science has its double dependence upon language and experience; but this duality is not significantly traceable into the statements of science taken one by one.

The idea of defining a symbol in use was, as remarked, an advance over the impossible term-by-term empiricism of Locke and Hume. The statement, rather than the term, came with Bentham to be recognized as the unit accountable to an empiricist critique. But what I am now urging is that even in taking the statement as unit we have drawn our grid too finely. The unit of empirical significance is the whole of science.

6   Empiricism without the Dogmas

The totality of our so-called knowledge or beliefs, from the most casual matters of geography and history to the profoundest laws of atomic physics or even of pure mathematics and logic, is a man-made fabric which impinges on experience only along the edges. Or, to change the figure, total science is like a field of force whose boundary conditions are experience. A conflict with experience at the periphery occasions readjustments in the interior of the field. Truth values have to be redistributed over some of our statements. Re-evaluation of some statements entails re-evaluation of others, because of their logical interconnections – the logical laws being in turn simply certain further statements of the system, certain further elements of the field.

Having re-evaluated one statement we must re-evaluate some others, which may be statements logically connected with the first or may be the statements of logical connections themselves. But the total field is so underdetermined by its boundary conditions, experience, that there is much latitude of choice as to what statements to re-evaluate in the light of any single contrary experience. No particular experiences are linked with any particular statements in the interior of the field, except indirectly through considerations of equilibrium affecting the field as a whole.

If this view is right, it is misleading to speak of the empirical content of an individual statement – especially if it is a statement at all remote from the experiential periphery of the field. Furthermore it becomes folly to seek a boundary between synthetic statements, which hold contingently on experience, and analytic statements, which hold come what may. Any statement can be held true come what may, if we make drastic enough adjustments elsewhere in the system. Even a statement very close to the periphery can be held true in the face of recalcitrant experience by pleading hallucination or by amending certain statements of the kind called logical laws. Conversely, by the same token, no statement is immune to revision. Revision even of the logical law of the excluded middle has been proposed as a means of simplifying quantum mechanics; and what difference is there in principle between such a shift and the shift whereby Kepler superseded Ptolemy, or Einstein Newton, or Darwin Aristotle?

For vividness I have been speaking in terms of varying distances from a sensory periphery. Let me try now to clarify this notion without metaphor. Certain statements, though *about* physical objects and not sense experience, seem peculiarly germane to sense experience – and in a selective way: some statements to some experiences, others to others. Such statements, especially germane to particular experiences, I picture as near the periphery. But in this relation of "germaneness" I envisage nothing more than a loose association reflecting the relative likelihood, in practice, of our choosing one statement rather than another for revision in the event of recalcitrant experience. For example, we can imagine recalcitrant experiences to which we would surely be inclined to accommodate our system by re-evaluating just the statement that there are brick houses on Elm Street, together with related statements on the same topic. We can imagine other recalcitrant experiences to which we would be inclined to accommodate our system by re-evaluating just the statement that there are no centaurs, along with kindred statements. A recalcitrant experience can, I have urged, be accommodated by any of various alternative re-evaluations in various alternative quarters of the total system; but, in the cases which we are now imagining, our natural tendency to disturb the total system as little as possible would lead us to focus our revisions upon these specific statements concerning brick houses or centaurs. These statements are felt, therefore, to have a sharper empirical reference than highly theoretical statements of physics or logic or ontology. The latter statements may be thought of as relatively centrally located within the total network, meaning merely that little preferential connection with any particular sense data obtrudes itself.

As an empiricist I continue to think of the conceptual scheme of science as a tool, ultimately, for predicting future experience in the light of past experience. Physical objects are conceptually imported into the situation as convenient intermediaries – not by definition in terms of experience, but simply as irreducible posits comparable, epistemologically, to the gods of Homer. For my part I do, qua lay physicist, believe in physical objects and not in Homer's gods; and I consider it a scientific error to believe otherwise. But in point of epistemological footing the physical objects and the gods differ only in degree and not in kind. Both sorts of entities enter our conception only as cultural posits. The myth of physical objects is epistemologically superior to most in that it has proved more efficacious than other myths as a device for working a manageable structure into the flux of experience.

Positing does not stop with macroscopic physical objects. Objects at the atomic level are posited to make the laws of macroscopic objects, and ultimately the laws of experience, simpler and more manageable; and we need not expect or demand full definition of atomic and subatomic entities in terms of macroscopic ones, any more than definition of macroscopic things in terms of sense data. Science is a continuation of common sense, and it continues the common-sense expedient of swelling ontology to simplify theory.

Physical objects, small and large, are not the only posits. Forces are another example; and indeed we are told nowadays that the boundary between energy and matter is obsolete. Moreover, the abstract entities which are the substance of mathematics – ultimately classes and classes of classes and so on up – are another posit in the same spirit. Epistemologically these are myths on the same footing with physical objects and gods, neither better nor worse except for differences in the degree to which they expedite our dealings with sense experiences.

The over-all algebra of rational and irrational numbers is underdetermined by the algebra of rational numbers, but is smoother and more convenient; and it includes the algebra of rational numbers as a jagged or gerrymandered part. Total science, mathematical and natural and human, is similarly but more extremely underdetermined by experience. The edge of the system must be kept squared with experience; the rest, with all its elaborate myths or fictions, has as its objective the simplicity of laws.

Ontological questions, under this view, are on a par with questions of natural science.* Consider the question whether to countenance classes as entities. This, as I have argued elsewhere, is the question whether to quantify with respect to variables which take classes as values. Now Carnap [6] has maintained that this is a question not of matters of fact but of choosing a convenient language form, a convenient conceptual scheme or framework for science.† With this I agree, but only on the proviso that the same be conceded regarding scientific hypotheses generally. Carnap ([6], p. 32n) has recognized that he is able to preserve a double standard for ontological questions and scientific hypotheses only by assuming an absolute distinction between the analytic and the synthetic; and I need not say again that this is a distinction which I reject.

The issue over there being classes seems more a question of convenient conceptual scheme; the issue over there being centaurs, or brick houses

---

* "L'ontologie fait corps avec la science elle-même et ne peut en être separée." [Emile] Meyerson [*Identité et realité*, Paris, 1908, 4th edn, 1932], p. 439.
† [Rudolf Carnap, "Empiricism, Semantics, 2nd Ontology." *Revue internationale de philosophie* 4 (1950); 20–40.]

on Elm Street, seems more a question of fact. But I have been urging that this difference is only one of degree, and that it turns upon our vaguely pragmatic inclination to adjust one strand of the fabric of science rather than another in accommodating some particular recalcitrant experience. Conservatism figures in such choices, and so does the quest for simplicity.

Carnap, Lewis, and others take a pragmatic stand on the question of choosing between language forms, scientific frameworks; but their pragmatism leaves off at the imagined boundary between the analytic and the synthetic. In repudiating such a boundary I espouse a more thorough pragmatism. Each man is given a scientific heritage plus a continuing barrage of sensory stimulation; and the considerations which guide him in warping his scientific heritage to fit his continuing sensory promptings are, where rational, pragmatic.

III

Metaphysics

1

Tao Te Ching (selections)

Introduction

Hardly any books in world literature have inspired more translations and commentaries than the short work (only 5,000 Chinese characters) known as the *Tao Te Ching* (*Dao De Jing*, in Pinyin transliteration). The usual English rendition of the title is "The Book of the Way (*tao*) and Its Virtue (*te*)," though some translators prefer "power" to "virtue" – for the virtue of which the book speaks is, for the most part, not moral excellence, but something more akin to the "efficacy" of a plant or mineral to which scientists once referred as its virtue. Opinions on the book's date and authorship vary wildly: some commentators cling to the traditional view that it was written by Lao Tzu (Laozi, or "Old Master"), a contemporary of Confucius in the sixth century BCE, while others hold that Lao Tzu was a mythical figure and the book a fourth- or third-century compilation. A compromise opinion is that Lao Tzu may have been real enough, but that most of the chapters are later accretions.[1]

What is not similarly in dispute is the massive influence of the book – immediately on Taoist thinkers such as Chuang Tzu (see I.5 and II.3 of

From A Source Book in Chinese Philosophy, trans. and compiled by Wing-Tsit Chan. Princeton, NJ: Princeton University Press, 1969, pp. 139–50, 152–4, 156–64, 166, 172 (some notes and passages omitted; asterisked notes are the translator's).

this volume) and later on almost every development in Chinese philosophy, including Chan or Zen Buddhism. Its influence has not been confined, moreover, to the East. In our own century, that influence is palpable in the later writings of Martin Heidegger (III.24), who even embarked on an abortive project to translate the work.[2]

Like other famous works from the "classic age" of Chinese philosophy, such as Confucius's *Analects* (V.3), the *Tao Te Ching* has a primarily practical purpose: to advise the author's contemporaries in those troubled and bellicose times, especially the rulers of states, on how to live – and enable others to live – prudently, safely, and contentedly. (On the political aspects of the work, see V.1 of this volume.) The advice given by Lao Tzu (assuming he was the author) is, on the surface, no different from that offered by other authors of the time. The wise person or ruler must live "in accord with" the Tao, the Way, for "whatever is contrary to Tao will soon perish" (Ch. 55). Lao Tzu, however, invested the notion of Tao with much greater metaphysical significance than had other writers, for whom the Way was often no more than the natural order of the world. As the resounding opening lines of the *Tao Te Ching* tell us, the Tao is the eternal, nameless, and ultimate origin of everything. (In the original text, whose chapters were later reordered, such metaphysical passages came after the advisory ones, which indicates that the book's purpose was primarily practical, but hardly, as some have held, that the metaphysics was only an "afterthought.")[3]

The *Tao Te Ching* makes at least four claims of metaphysical interest – claims of a general kind, moreover, which has had recurrent appeal to thinkers during the whole history of philosophy. First and foremost there is the idea that, in order for any thing, any being, to exist, there must be a "profound" origin or source that cannot itself be conceived as a thing or a being. This is the point of the references to the Tao as "non-being" or "nothing." The Tao is not some remarkable entity or person, a God, who created the universe *ex nihilo*. While it is the source of all things, their precondition, it is nothing over and above or outside them – no more than the melody, which, so to speak, holds the notes together, is something *in addition* to those notes.[4] Second, there is the insistence that the "eternal Tao" is ineffable, "nameless" in the sense of resisting informative description. It was to be left to Chuang Tzu, with his reflections on the limits of language, to clarify why the Tao must be ineffable, but hints are afforded in the *Tao Te Ching* – in Chapters 14 and 25, for example, where it is implied that the Tao is too "undifferentiated" and "vague" for informative descriptions to be given of it.

Third, there is the claim that, while the "eternal Tao" is unknowable and ineffable, it nevertheless presents aspects to us – the "named Tao" – which can be discerned in the operations of the natural world. We can discern, for instance, that the Tao operates according to a principle of "reversal," an oscillation back and forth between "opposites," like heat and cold, which prevents things going beyond limits in a way fatal for the stability of the natural order. We can discern, too,

that the Tao's "actions," like that of water (Ch. 8), display that spontaneity and effortlessness which Taoists call *wu wei* ("actionless action"). Finally, there is the claim, required if the metaphysical claims are to be of practical import, that insight into the Way enables a proper human life. The good person or sage is one who, in certain respects, emulates the Way, above all by renouncing those conventions or artifices (so admired by Confucians) as well as that febrile striving antithetical to *wu wei*, which indicate that the Tao has been "lost."

The *Tao Te Ching*, then, is one of philosophy's earliest invitations to share a metaphysical vision of a source of all things which, while ineffable, affords us intimations of its nature – a nature which to ignore or oppose is to "perish."

Notes

1   The three opinions mentioned are those of, respectively: Wing-Tsit Chin in his preamble to the translation we have selected; Arthur Waley, *The Way and Its Power*, London: Unwin, 1977; and Fung Yu-Lan, *A Short History of Chinese Philosophy*, New York: Free Press, 1966.

2   See R. May, *Heidegger's Hidden Sources: East Asian Influences on His Work*, London: Routledge, 1996.

3   See C. Wei-hsun Fu, "Daoism in Chinese Philosophy," in B. Carr and I. Mahalingam, eds, *Companion Encyclopedia of Asian Philosophy*, London: Routledge, 1997, p. 554.

4   The analogy is Raymond M. Smullyan's, *The Tao is Silent*, San Francisco: Harper, 1977.

Tao-Te Ching

1.   The Tao (way) that can be told of is not the eternal Tao;
    The name that can be named is not the eternal name.
    The Nameless is the origin of Heaven and Earth;
    The Named is the mother of all things.
    Therefore let there always be non-being so we may see their subtlety [or mystery].
    And let there always be being so we may see their outcome.

The two are the same,
    But after they are produced, they have different names.
    They both may be called deep and profound (*hsüan*).
    Deeper and more profound,
    The door of all subtleties!

2.   When the people of the world all know beauty as beauty,
    There arises the recognition of ugliness.
    When they all know the good as good,
    There arises the recognition of evil.

Therefore:
  Being and non-being produce each other;
  Difficult and easy complete each other;
  Long and short contrast each other;
  High and low distinguish each other;
  Sound and voice harmonize with each other;
  Front and back follow each other.
  Therefore the sage manages affairs without action (*wu-wei*)
  And spreads doctrines without words.
  All things arise, and he does not turn away from them.
  He produces them, but does not take possession of them.
  He acts, but does not rely on his own ability.
  He accomplishes his task, but does not claim credit for it.
  It is precisely because he does not claim credit that his accomplishment remains with him.

[. . .]

4. Tao is empty (like a bowl),
  It may be used but its capacity is never exhausted.
  It is bottomless, perhaps the ancestor of all things.
  It blunts its sharpness,
  It unties its tangles.
  It softens its light.
  It becomes one with the dusty world.
  Deep and still, it appears to exist forever.
  I do not know whose son it is.
  It seems to have existed before the Lord.

[. . .]

6. The spirit of the valley never dies.
    It is called the subtle and profound female.
  The gate of the subtle and profound female
    Is the root of Heaven and Earth.
  It is continuous, and seems to be always existing.
  Use it and you will never wear it out.

[. . .]

8. The best (man) is like water.
  Water is good; it benefits all things and does not compete with them.

It dwells in (lowly) places that all disdain.
This is why it is so near to Tao.
[The best man] in his dwelling loves the earth.
In his heart, he loves what is profound.
In his associations, he loves humanity.
In his words, he loves faithfulness.
In government, he loves order.
In handling affairs, he loves competence.
In his activities, he loves timeliness.
It is because he does not compete that he is without reproach.

[. . .]

10. Can you keep the spirit and embrace the One without departing from them?
  Can you concentrate your vital force (*ch'i*) and achieve the highest degree of weakness like an infant?
  Can you clean and purify your profound insight so it will be spotless?
  Can you love the people and govern the state without knowledge (cunning)?
  Can you play the role of the female in the opening and closing of the gates of Heaven?
  Can you understand all and penetrate all without taking any action?
    To produce things and to rear them,
      To produce, but not to take possession of them,
      To act, but not to rely on one's own ability,
      To lead them, but not to master them –
    This is called profound and secret virtue (*hsüan-te*).

11. Thirty spokes are united around the hub to make a wheel,
    But it is on its non-being that the utility of the carriage depends.
  Clay is molded to form a utensil,
    But it is on its non-being that the utility of the utensil depends.
  Doors and windows are cut out to make a room,
    But it is on its non-being that the utility of the room depends.
  Therefore turn being into advantage, and turn non-being into utility.

[. . .]

14. We look at it and do not see it;
      Its name is The Invisible.
    We listen to it and do not hear it;
      Its name is The Inaudible.
    We touch it and do not find it;
      Its name is The Subtle (formless).
    These three cannot be further inquired into,
    And hence merge into one.
    Going up high, it is not bright, and coming
      down low, it is not dark.
    Infinite and boundless, it cannot be given any
      name;
    It reverts to nothingness.
    This is called shape without shape,
    Form (*hsiang*) without object.
    It is The Vague and Elusive.
    Meet it and you will not see its head.
    Follow it and you will not see its back.
    Hold on to the Tao of old in order to mas-
      ter the things of the present.
    From this one may know the primeval
      beginning [of the universe].[1]
    This is called the bond [*chi*] of Tao.*

15. Of old those who were the best rulers
      were subtly mysterious and profoundly
      penetrating;
    Too deep to comprehend.
    And because they cannot be comprehended,
    I can only describe them arbitrarily:
    Cautious, like crossing a frozen stream in
      the winter,
    Being at a loss, like one fearing danger on
      all sides,
    Reserved, like one visiting,
    Supple and pliant, like ice about to melt,
    Genuine, like a piece of uncarved wood,†
    Open and broad, like a valley,
    Merged and undifferentiated, like muddy
      water.

    Who can make muddy water gradually
      clear through tranquillity?
    Who can make the still gradually come to
      life through activity?

He who embraces this Tao does not want
  to fill himself to overflowing.
It is precisely because there is no
  overflowing that he is beyond wearing
  out and renewal.

16. Attain complete vacuity,
    Maintain steadfast quietude.
    All things come into being,
    And I see thereby their return.
    All things flourish,
    But each one returns to its root.
    This return to its root means tranquillity.
    It is called returning to its destiny.
    To return to destiny is called the eternal
      (Tao).
    To know the eternal is called enlighten-
      ment.
    Not to know the eternal is to act blindly to
      result in disaster.
    He who knows the eternal is all-embracing.
    Being all-embracing, he is impartial.
    Being impartial, he is kingly (universal).
    Being kingly, he is one with Nature.
    Being one with Nature, he is in accord with
      Tao.
    Being in accord with Tao, he is everlasting,
    And is free from danger throughout his life-
      time.

[. . .]

18. When the great Tao declined,
    The doctrines of humanity (*jen*) and right-
      eousness (*i*) arose.
    When knowledge and wisdom appeared,
    There emerged great hypocrisy.
    When the six family relationships‡ are not
      in harmony,
    There will be the advocacy of filial piety and
      deep love to children.
    When a country is in disorder,
    There will be praise of loyal ministers.[2]

[. . .]

20. Abandon learning and there will be no sorrow.
    How much difference is there between
      "Yes, sir," and "Of course not"?

---

* *Chi*, literally a thread, denotes tradition, discipline,
principle, order, essence, etc. Generally it means the
system, principle, or continuity that binds things
together.
† *P'u*, literally an uncarved wood, has come to mean
in Taoism simplicity, plainness, genuineness, etc.

‡ Father, son, elder brother, younger brother, husband, and wife.

How much difference is there between "good" and "evil"?

What people dread, do not fail to dread.

But, alas, how confused, and the end is not yet.

The multitude are merry, as though feasting on a day of sacrifice,

Or like ascending a tower at springtime.

I alone am inert, showing no sign (of desires),

Like an infant that has not yet smiled.

Wearied, indeed, I seem to be without a home.

The multitude all possess more than enough,

I alone seem to have lost all.

Mine is indeed the mind of an ignorant man,

Indiscriminate and dull!

Common folks are indeed brilliant;

I alone seem to be in the dark.

Common folks see differences and are clear-cut;

I alone make no distinctions.

I seem drifting as the sea;

Like the wind blowing about, seemingly without destination.

The multitude all have a purpose;

I alone seem to be stubborn and rustic.

I alone differ from others,

And value drawing sustenance from Mother (Tao).

21. The all-embracing quality of the great virtue (*te*) follows alone from the Tao.

The thing that is called Tao is eluding and vague.

Vague and eluding, there is in it the form.

Eluding and vague, in it are things.

Deep and obscure, in it is the essence.*

The essence is very real; in it are evidences.

From the time of old until now, its name (manifestations) ever remains,

By which we may see the beginning of all things.

How do I know that the beginnings of all things are so?

Through this (Tao).

* The word *ching* (essence) also means intelligence, spirit, life-force.

[...]

25. There was something undifferentiated and yet complete,

Which existed before heaven and earth.

Soundless and formless, it depends on nothing and does not change.

It operates everywhere and is free from danger.

It may be considered the mother of the universe.

I do not know its name; I call it Tao.

If forced to give it a name, I shall call it Great.

Now being great means functioning everywhere.

Functioning everywhere means far-reaching.

Being far-reaching means returning to the original point.

Therefore Tao is great.

Heaven is great.

Earth is great.

And the king is also great.

There are four great things in the universe, and the king is one of them.

Man models himself after Earth.

Earth models itself after Heaven.

Heaven models itself after Tao.

And Tao models itself after Nature.

[...]

28. He who knows the male (active force) and keeps to the female (the passive force or receptive element)

Becomes the ravine of the world.

Being the ravine of the world,

He will never depart from eternal virtue,

But returns to the state of infancy.

He who knows the white (glory) and yet keeps to the black (humility),

Becomes the model for the world.

Being the model for the world,

He will never deviate from eternal virtue,

But returns to the state of the Ultimate of Non-being.

He who knows glory but keeps to humility,

Becomes the valley of the world.

Being the valley of the world,

He will be proficient in eternal virtue,

And returns to the state of simplicity (uncarved wood).

When the uncarved wood is broken up, it is turned into concrete things (as Tao is transformed into the myriad things).

But when the sage uses it, he becomes the leading official.

Therefore the great ruler does not cut up.

[...]

32. Tao is eternal and has no name.

Though its simplicity seems insignificant, none in the world can master it.

If kings and barons would hold on to it, all things would submit to them spontaneously.

Heaven and earth unite to drip sweet dew.

Without the command of men, it drips evenly over all.

As soon as there were regulations and institutions, there were names (differentiation of things).

As soon as there are names, know that it is time to stop.

It is by knowing when to stop that one can be free from danger.

Analogically, Tao in the world (where everything is embraced by it), may be compared to rivers and streams running into the sea.

[...]

34. The Great Tao flows everywhere.

It may go left or right.

All things depend on it for life, and it does not turn away from them.

It accomplishes its task, but does not claim credit for it.

It clothes and feeds all things but does not claim to be master over them.

Always without desires, it may be called The Small.

All things come to it and it does not master them; it may be called The Great.

Therefore (the sage) never strives himself for the great, and thereby the great is achieved.

35. Hold fast to the great form (Tao),

And all the world will come.

They come and will encounter no harm;

But enjoy comfort, peace, and health.

When there are music and dainties,

Passing strangers will stay.

But the words uttered by Tao,

How insipid and tasteless!

We look at Tao; it is imperceptible.

We listen to it; it is inaudible.

We use it; it is inexhaustible.

[...]

38. [...], only when Tao is lost does the doctrine of virtue arise.

When virtue is lost, only then does the doctrine of humanity arise.

When humanity is lost, only then does the doctrine of righteousness arise.

When righteousness is lost, only then does the doctrine of propriety [li]* arise.

Now, propriety is a superficial expression of loyalty and faithfulness, and the beginning of disorder.

Those who are the first to know have the flowers (appearance) of Tao but are the beginning of ignorance.

For this reason the great man dwells in the thick (substantial), and does not rest with the thin (superficial).

He dwells in the fruit (reality), and does not rest with the flower (appearance).

Therefore he rejects the one, and accepts the other.

39. Of old those that obtained the One:

Heaven obtained the One and became clear.

Earth obtained the One and became tranquil.

The spiritual beings obtained the One and became divine.

The valley obtained the One and became full.

The myriad things obtained the One and lived and grew.

Kings and barons obtained the One and became rulers of the empire.

What made them so is the One.

If heaven had not thus become clear,

It would soon crack.

If the earth had not thus become tranquil,

It would soon be shaken.

---

* In a narrow sense, li means rites, ritual, ceremonies, etc., but in a broad sense it means rules of behavior or principles of conduct.

If the spiritual beings had not thus become
   divine,
They would soon wither away.
If the valley had not thus become full,
It would soon become exhausted.
If the myriad things had not thus lived and
   grown,
They would soon become extinct.
If kings and barons had not thus become
   honorable and high in position,
They would soon fall.
Therefore humble station is the basis of
   honor.
The low is the foundation of the high.
For this reason kings and barons call them-
   selves the orphaned, the lonely ones, the
   unworthy.
Is this not regarding humble station as the
   basis of honor?
Is it not?
Therefore enumerate all the parts of a char-
   iot as you may, and you still have no
   chariot.
Rather than jingle like the jade,
Rumble like the rocks.

40. Reversion is the action of Tao.
   Weakness is the function of Tao.
   All things in the world come from being.
   And being comes from non-being.

41. [. . .] Tao is hidden and nameless.
   Yet it is Tao alone that skillfully provides for
      all and brings them to perfection.

42. Tao produced the One.
   The One produced the two.
   The two produced the three.
   And the three produced the ten thousand
      things.[3]
   The ten thousand things carry the yin and
      embrace the yang,* and through the
      blending of the material force (*ch'i*)† they
      achieve harmony. [. . .]

43. The softest things in the world overcome the
   hardest things in the world.

---

* Yin is the passive, female cosmic principle or force
while yang is the active or male principle.
† Variously translated as matter, matter-energy, vital
force, breath, etc.

Non-being penetrates that in which there is
   no space.
Through this I know the advantage of taking no action.
Few in the world can understand teaching
   without words and the advantage of taking no action.

[. . .]

47. One may know the world without going out
   of doors.
   One may see the Way of Heaven without
      looking through the windows,
   The further one goes, the less one knows.
   Therefore the sage knows without going
      about,
   Understands without seeing,
   And accomplishes without any action.

[. . .]

51. Tao produces them (the ten thousand things).
   Virtue fosters them.
   Matter gives them physical form.[4]
   The circumstances and tendencies complete
      them.
   Therefore the ten thousand things esteem Tao
      and honor virtue.
   Tao is esteemed and virtue is honored
      without anyone's order.
   They always come spontaneously.
   Therefore Tao produces them and virtue
      fosters them.
   They rear them and develop them.
   They give them security and give them peace.
   They nurture them and protect them.
   (Tao) produces them but does not take
      possession of them.
   It acts, but does not rely on its own ability.
   It leads them but does not master them.
   This is called profound and secret virtue.

52. There was a beginning of the universe
   Which may be called the Mother of the
      Universe.
   He who has found the mother (Tao)
   And thereby understands her sons (things)
   And having understood the sons,
   Still keeps to its mother,
   Will be free from danger throughout his
      lifetime.

[...]

55. [...] To know harmony means to be in
    accord with the eternal.
    To be in accord with the eternal means to
    be enlightened.
    To force the growth of life means ill omen.
    For the mind to employ the vital force with-
    out restraint means violence.
    After things reach their prime, they begin to
    grow old,
    Which means being contrary to Tao.
    Whatever is contrary to Tao will soon perish.

56. He who knows does not speak.
    He who speaks does not know.
    Close the mouth.
    Shut the doors (of cunning and desires).
    Blunt the sharpness.
    Untie the tangles.
    Soften the light.
    Become one with the dusty world.
    This is called profound identification.

[...]

70. My doctrines are very easy to understand and
    very easy to practice,
    But none in the world can understand or
    practice them.
    My doctrines have a source (Nature); my
    deeds have a master (Tao).
    It is because people do not understand this
    that they do not understand me.
    Few people know me, and therefore I am
    highly valued.

Therefore the sage wears a coarse cloth on
top and carries jade within his bosom.

71. To know that you do not know is the best.
    To pretend to know when you do not know
    is a disease.
    Only when one recognizes this disease as a
    disease can one be free from the disease.
    The sage is free from the disease.
    Because he recognizes this disease to be dis-
    ease, he is free from it. [...]

Notes

1   References to Tao as the "beginning" or "origin" of
    the universe should not be taken in a temporal sense,
    but an ontological one. Tao is the precondition of
    "the dusty world," but does not pre-exist it.
2   The target in this chapter, and several others (e.g.
    ch. 38), is Confucian ethics, in which "righteous-
    ness," "propriety," and "filial piety" figure promin-
    ently. The point made is that such conventional
    and "artificial" virtues would not be required had
    people not forgotten or departed from the Way.
3   The intended referents of "one," "two," and
    "three" have been much disputed. But perhaps,
    like Chuang Tzu, we should be impatient with
    attempts to determine an exact literal meaning and
    instead treat the passage as simply indicating the
    development of the Tao from simplicity to com-
    plexity and differentiation. "The ten thousand
    things," incidentally, is a conventional Chinese
    expression for the totality of things.
4   This makes clear that "virtue" is not necessarily a
    human and moral feature. Here it seems to refer to
    a thing's essential form as distinct from the matter
    of which it is composed.

2

(A) Heraclitus of Ephesus, selected fragments
(B) Parmenides of Elea, from "The Way of Truth" (fr. 344–55)

Introduction

Heraclitus (Ηράκλειτος ὸ Εφέσιος, c. 535–475 BCE) lived in the wealthy, bustling, multicultural port city of Ephesus in Ionia – today Efes on the west coast of Turkey. His life spanned the period when Greece succeeded in acquiring a sense of collective identity and power as it freed itself from Persian rule.

As with so many thinkers of his age, we know Heraclitus's thought only through fragments relayed to us at second hand. Although he is credited with a book entitled, *On Nature*, these fragments seem to indicate that Heraclitus presented his thought in the form of short remarks or aphorisms. Other philosophers have chosen this difficult technique – Nietzsche and Wittgenstein (II.23), for example. It is, however, a method that yields particularly arduous (perhaps intentional) interpretative difficulties, and perhaps largely for this reason Heraclitus has earned the label, "the Obscure."

Metaphysically, nevertheless, Heraclitus's thought has been of towering significance. Through Plato and Aristotle, Heraclitus has been associated

(A) *From* G. S. Kirk, ed., *Heraclitus: The Cosmic Fragments*, Cambridge: Cambridge University Press, 1970, pp. 48, 57, 65, 97, 105, 113, 116, 135, 155, 168, 180, 184, 203, 238, 245, 250, 258, 284, 307, 325, 339, 345, 349, 362, 367, 381, 386, 392. (B) *From* G. S. Kirk and J. E. Raven, *The Presocratic Philosophers*, Cambridge: Cambridge University Press, 1957, pp. 269–81.

with the doctrine that everything changes or is in a process of changing. The idea is famously summed up in the phrase, *panta rhei* (everything moves),[1] as well as in Heraclitus's Fragment 91: "Upon those who step into the same rivers, different and again different waters flow." But reducing Heraclitus's thought to the doctrine of universal flux would be a simplification to the point of distortion. While indeed Heraclitus does seem to understand that the various things of the world come to be and pass away (i.e., they "become"), he recognizes that they do not do so in a haphazard or chaotic fashion. Change for Heraclitus takes place according to an independent, largely hidden natural law or *logos*. And the components of change seem to be not just anything at all but a set of connected opposites (wet-dry, hot-cold, etc.), two sides of the same metaphysical coin existing in a kind of dynamic, creative tension – like the tension of a bow or a stringed instrument.[2] These dynamic opposites may themselves, it seems, be the manifestation of an even more basic or elemental substance, a cosmic fire that periodically (or perhaps at each moment) consumes the world and then gives it birth again in an endless cycle.

Many of the early Greek philosophers seemed to have been interested in exploring the idea that all of the multifarious phenomena of the world are grounded in a small, comprehensible set of basic elements or principles, much as modern physics has tried to explain the natural world by a finite set of elements, a comprehensible set of natural laws, and the various knottings and unknottings of energy fields. Philosophers have called these basic elements and principles *archai* (*archē* singular) – a word from which the modern words "mon-archy" and "arche-ology" originate. One might even say that metaphysics is the attempt to discern the *archai* of reality. If so, we might tersely describe Heraclitus's view of reality's *archai* as a set of internally connected and contesting opposites that compose an orderly process governed by the *logos* and manifesting the elemental cosmic fire.

Parmenides (Παρμενίδης ὁ Ελεάτης, b. early fifth century BCE), with whom Heraclitus is often paired, hailed from the other end of ancient Hellas – the city-state of Elea (now Velia) in the south of the Italian peninsula. The vision of reality he presents in his poem, conventionally entitled "On Nature," precipitates what philosophers have called the "appearance-reality" distinction. What humans experience cannot be reality because only "what-is" (*ti esti*) can be real, and what-appears to us in experience seems full of "what-is-not" (*ouk esti*). The present "is," so the present is real; but the past and the future "are not," so reality cannot be past or future. What exists in an unchanging state "is," but what-changes or "becomes" moves from what-it-is to what-it-is-not; so, reality cannot change. By the end of his investigation, Parmenides has determined that reality is only what is present, singular, indivisible, unchanging, spherical, unmoving, and without origin or end – that is to say, reality is pure "being" and in no way "becoming."

The shadow of Parmenides's view falls heavily across the history of philosophy. It crystallized ideas about being as singular, eternal, unchanging, and apprehensible principally by reason, even against the apparent evidence of the senses.

Indeed, a great deal of subsequent metaphysics may be understood as the attempt to reconcile the demands of Parmenides with those of Heraclitus, to offer an explanation of the world that accounts both for being and becoming, unity and plurality, change and stability, difference and sameness, truth and appearance, the claims of reason and the evidence of observation. Plato's postulation of a world of changing phenomenal appearances (the Heraclitean dimensions of existence) rooted in a world of unchanging forms (the Parmenidean) like Democritus's postulation of changing sensible objects (the Heraclitean) composed of intellectually apprehensible atoms (the Parmenidean) represent just two such attempts to reconcile Heraclitean and Parmenidean demands.[3]

Notes

1 Plato, *Theaetetus* 152e–160d, *Cratylus* 401d–402a. Aristotle, *De anima* 405a28, *Topics* 104b21, *Metaphysics* 987a32. For a critique of Plato's interpretation, see G. S. Kirk, "The Problem of Cratylus," *Australian Journal of Philosophy* 72 (1951): 243ff.

2 Charles H. Kahn, *The Art and Thought of Heraclitus*, new edition, Cambridge: Cambridge University Press, 2003.

3 W. K. C. Guthrie, *A History of Greek Philosophy: The Presocratic Tradition from Parmenides to Democritus*, Cambridge: Cambridge University Press, 2003, pp. xiiiff.

Heraclitus of Ephesus, Selected Fragments

[frr. 108–13] Those who speak with sense must rely on what is common to all, as a city must rely on its law, and with much greater reliance: for all the laws of men are nourished by one law, the divine law; for it has as much power as it wishes and is sufficient for all and is still left over. [Stobaeus, *Florilegium* I, 179]

[After fr. I] Therefore it is necessary to follow the common: but although the Logos is common the many live as though they had a private understanding. [Sextus Empiricus, *Aversus mathematicos* VII, 133]

Listening not to me but to the Logos, it is wise to agree that all things are one. [fr. 51 follows; Hippolytus, *Refutatio*, IX, 9.1]

[After fr. 58] Of letters, the way is straight and crooked: it is one, and the same [fr. 60; Hippolytus, *Refutatio* IX, 10.4]

[After fr. 59] The way up and down is one and the same. [fr. 61 follows; Hippolytus, *Refutatio* IX, 10.4]

Beginning and end in a circle are common. [Porphyrius, *Pu. Hom.* Ad *Il.* XIV, 200]

For the bow the name is life, but the work is death. [*Etymologicum magnum*, s.v.]

And as the same thing there exists in us living and dead and the waking and the sleeping and young and old: for these things having changed round are those, and those things having changed round [again] are these ones. [Plutarch, *Consolatio ad Apollonium*, 10.106E]

Teacher of most men is Hesiod: they are sure that he knows very many things, who continually failed to recognize day and night: for they are one. [fr. 58 follows]

Things taken together are whole and not *whole*, something which is being, brought together and brought apart, which is in tune and out of tune: out of all things can be made a unity; and out of a unity, all things. [pseudo-Aristotle, *De mundo* 5, 396b7]

To god all things are beautiful and good and just, but men have supposed some things to be unjust, others just. [Porphyrius, *Qu. Hom.* ad *Il.* IV, 4]

God is day night, winter summer, war peace, satiety hunger, and undergoes alteration in the way that fire, when it is mixed with species, is named according to the scent of each of them. [Hippolytus, *Refutatio* IX, 10.8]

They do not apprehend how being at variance it agrees with itself: there is a connexion working in both directions, as in the bow and the lyre. [Hippolytus, *Refutatio* IX, 9.1]

One must know that war is common and right is strife and that all things are happening by strife and necessity. [Origen, *Contra Celsum* VI, 42]

War is the father of all and king of all, and some he shows as gods, others as men; some he makes slaves and others free. [fr. 54 follows]

Changing it rests. . . . It is weariness to toil for and be ruled by the same. [Plotinus, *Enneads* IV, 8, I]

Every animal is driven to pasture with a blow. [pseudo-Aristotle, *De mundo* 6, 401a8]

Sun will not overstep his measures; if he does, the Erinyes, the minions of Justice, will find him out. [Plutarch, *De exil.*, 11, 604A]

This (world-)order did none of gods or men make, but it always was and is and shall be: an everliving fire, kindling in measures and going out in measures. [fr. 31 follows; Clement, *Stromateis* V, 104, I]

Fire's changes: first sea, and of sea the half is earth, the half lightning-flash. . . . [Earth] is dispersed as sea and is measured so as to form the same proportion as existed before it became earth. [Clement *Stromateis* V, 104.3]

For souls it is death to become water, for water it is death to become earth; out of earth water comes-to-be, and out of water, soul. [Clement, *Stromateis* VI, 17.1]

All things are an equal exchange for fire and fire for all things, as goods are for gold and gold for goods. [Plutarch *de E* 8, 388d-e]

Thunderbolt steers all things. [fr. 64; Hippolytus, *Refutatio* IX, 10.6]

How could anyone escape the notice of that which never sets? [Clement, *Paedagogus* II, 99.5]

Upon those who step into the same rivers different and again different waters flow. [Arius Didymus *ap.* Eusebium *P.E.* XV, 20]

It scatters and [again] gathers . . . it comes together and flows away, [and] approaches and departs. [Plutarch *de E* 18, 392b]

Wisdom is one thing: to be skilled in true judgement, how all things are steered through all. [fr. 42 follows; Diogenes Laertius IX.1]

One thing, the only truly wise, does not and does consent to be called by the name of Zeus. [fr. 33 follows; Clement Stromateis V.115.1]

Parmenides of Elea, from "The Way of Truth"

344 Come now, and I will tell thee – and do thou hearken and carry my word away – the only ways of enquiry that can be thought of [literally, 'that exist for thinking', the old dative sense of the infinitive]: the one way, that it is and cannot not-be, is the path of Persuasion, for it attends upon Truth; the other, that it is-not and needs must not-be, that I tell thee is a path altogether unthinkable. For thou couldst not know that which is-not (that is impossible) nor utter it; for the same thing can be thought as can be

[construction as above, literally 'the same thing exists for thinking and for being'].

345   That which can be spoken and thought needs must be [construction as in 344]; for it is possible for it, but not for nothing, to be; that is what I bid thee ponder. This is the first way of enquiry from which I hold thee back, and then from that way also on which mortals wander knowing nothing, two-headed; for helplessness guides the wandering thought in their breasts; they are carried along, deaf and blind at once, altogether dazed – hordes devoid of judgement, who are persuaded that to be and to be-not are the same, yet not the same, and that of all things the path is backward-turning.

346   For never shall this be proved, that things that are not are, but do thou hold back thy thought from this way of enquiry, nor let custom, born of much experience, force thee to let wander along this road thy aimless eye, thy echoing ear or thy tongue; but do thou judge by reason the strife-encompassed proof that I have spoken.

347   One way only is left to be spoken of, that it is; and on this way are full many signs that what is is uncreated and imperishable, for it is entire, immovable and without end. It was not in the past, nor shall it be, since it is now, all at once, one, continuous; for what creation wilt thou seek for it? how and whence did it grow? Nor shall I allow thee to say or to think, 'from that which is not'; for it is not to be said or thought that it is not. And what need would have driven it on to grow, starting from nothing, at a later time rather than an earlier? Thus it must either completely be or be not. Nor will the force of true belief allow that, beside what is, there could also arise anything from what is not; therefore justice looseth not her fetters to allow it to come into being or perish, but holdeth it fast; and the decision on these matters rests here: it is or it is not. But it has surely been decided, as it must be, to leave alone the one way as unthinkable and nameless (for it is no true way), and that the other is real and true. How could what is thereafter Perish? and how could it come into being? For if it came into being, it is not, nor if it is going to be in the future. So coming into being is extinguished and perishing unimaginable.

348   Nor is it divisible, since it is all alike; nor is there more here and less there, which would prevent it from cleaving together, but it is all full

of what is. So it is all continuous; for what is clings close to what is.

349   Look steadfastly at things which, though far off, are yet present to thy mind; for thou shalt not cut off what is from clinging to what is, neither scattering itself everywhere in order nor crowding together.

350   But, motionless within the limits of mighty bonds, it is without beginning or end, since coming into being and perishing have been driven far away, cast out by true belief. Abiding the same in the same place it rests by itself, and so abides firm where it is; for strong Necessity holds it firm within the bonds of the limit that keeps it back on every side, because it is not lawful that what is should be unlimited; for it is not in need – if it were, it would need all.

351   But since there is a furthest limit, it is bounded on every side, like the bulk of a well-rounded sphere, from the centre equally balanced in every direction; for it needs must not be somewhat more here or somewhat less there. For neither is there that which is not, which might stop it from meeting its like, nor can what is be more here and less there than what is, since it is all inviolate; for being equal to itself on every side, it rests uniformly within its limits.

352   What can be thought is only the thought that it is. [The infinitive by itself seldom bears the sense of the infinitive with article – i.e. 'thinking'; the construction must be the same as in 344 and 345 – that is: the only thing that exists for thinking is the thought that it is.] For you will not find thought without what is, in relation to which it is uttered; for there is not, nor shall be, anything else besides that is since Fate fettered it to be entire and immovable. Wherefore all these are mere names which mortals laid down believing them to be true – coming into being and perishing, being and not being, change of place and variation of bright colour.

353   [Parmenides effects the transition from the objects of reason to the objects of sense, or, as he himself puts it, from truth to seeming, when he writes]: 'Here I end my trustworthy discourse and thought concerning truth; henceforth learn the beliefs of mortal men, listening to the deceitful ordering of my words'; and he then himself makes the elemental principles of created things the primary opposition of light and darkness, as he calls them, or fire and earth, or dense and rare, or sameness and difference; for he says

immediately after the lines quoted above: 'For they made up their minds to name two forms, of which they must not name one only – that is where they have gone astray – and distinguished them as opposite in appearance and assigned to them manifestations different one from the other – to one the aitherial flame of fire, gentle and very light, in every direction identical with itself, but not with the other; and that other too is in itself just the opposite, dark night, dense in appearance and heavy.

The whole ordering of these I tell thee as it seems likely, that so no thought of mortal men shall ever outstrip thee.'

354   [. . .] to give an account, in accordance with Popular opinion, of the coming into being of sensible things, he makes the first principles two [. . .]

355   [. . .] but being forced to comply with sensible things, and supposing the existence of that which is one in formula but more than one according to our sensations, he now posits two causes and two first principles. [. . .]

Plato, *Phaedrus* 245–50

Introduction

Although the Way indicated in the *Tao Te Ching* (see III.1 above) is intangible and invisible, it is not dualistically opposed, as an "other world," to the everyday "dusty world." In the *Phaedrus* dialogue of the great Athenian philosopher, Plato (c. 427–347 BCE), however, we are introduced to just such an opposition – between a realm of "existence absolute" and the ordinary empirical world whose contents are but "copies" of the "universals" or "essences" comprised in the former (247). Only if the soul were not "enshrined in that living tomb," the body, could it attain knowledge of the absolute realm – or, rather, fully recapture the knowledge it enjoyed prior to that enshrinement. As it is, nearly all of us are condemned to mere "opinion" about the world of "copies." The Plato of *Phaedrus*, then, is perhaps the earliest and certainly the greatest western thinker to have promulgated the triple dualisms of "the two worlds," soul *versus* body, and transcendent knowledge *versus* mere "opinion."

In *Phaedrus*, as in related writings – notably, Diotima's speech in the *Symposium* (see IV.1) and the central Books of *Republic* (see II.1) – Plato represents his metaphysical vision in the form of allegory or "figure." Only someone who experiences

From *The Dialogues of Plato*, Vol. I, trans. B. Jowett. New York: Macmillan & Co., 1892. pp. 451–57 (one note omitted; asterisked note is the translator's).

"existence absolute" could, if language allowed, provide a literal account of it; and Plato makes no personal claim to any such experience. Plato's figurative presentation creates a problem, of course, for as one commentator puts it, it is not "permissible to extract metaphysics from mythical details . . . [included] for the coherency of the pictorial representation."[1] The charioteer allegory of *Phaedrus* is "one of the highest points in Plato's achievement as artist and poet,"[2] and presumably we are to take as merely poetic references such as those to a supra-heavenly vault and the 10 millennia it takes a soul to grow wings. On the other hand, there is no reason to doubt Plato's commitment to the literal, or near-literal, truth of those doctrines, briefly indicated in the dialogue, which are elaborated and defended elsewhere, notably in *Republic* (see II.1).

These doctrines include: (a) the distinction between the realm of "universals," or as Plato elsewhere calls them, "Forms," "Types," or "Ideas" (*ēide*), and the world of ordinary things which are their "copies;" (b) the doctrine of *anamnesis*, according to which our present understanding is due to dim recollection of the Forms experienced by the soul prior to its embodiment; (c) the idea that while reason may lead us towards an understanding of "existence absolute," this is finally a matter of enjoying a "beatific" or "mystic" vision; (d) the immortality of the soul; (e) the distinctness of soul from body, in which it unfortunately gets stuck "like an oyster in its shell" (250); (f) the "transmigration" of souls from body to body;

and (g) the "tripartite" nature of the soul – rational, "spirited" and "appetitive."

The bulk of *Phaedrus* is concerned not with metaphysics, but with the nature of sexual love and the status of rhetoric. We join the dialogue at the point where Plato's mouthpiece, Socrates,[3] is challenging the view that the "temperate" person is superior to the lover since the latter is "mad," "possessed," or "beside himself." He intends to show that there is a divine madness, manifested in sexual desires, the real significance of which the lover is typically unaware, but which is properly understood as a displaced yearning for absolute beauty. Since the object of this absolute *eros* is the Form of beauty, Socrates needs, therefore, first to give an account of how the soul, which must be immaterial and immortal, originally encountered it. The charioteer allegory provides that account.

It would be a mistake to think that Plato's admiration for the person of divine madness or passion entails any rejection of reason. "What emerges with particular clarity from the *Phaedrus* is that it is reason itself which longs for Beauty" and the other Forms.[4] It is a prior knowledge of Beauty, not the esthetic thrills it may have afforded, which the lover unconsciously seeks to recollect. And the "madness" or passion of the philosopher – the lover (from Gk *philia*) of wisdom (from Gk *sophia*) – is a rational passion to know and understand "existence absolute."[5]

Notes

1   A. E. Taylor, *Plato: The Man and His Work*, London: Methuen, 1937, p. 307.
2   W. Hamilton, Introduction to Plato's *Phaedrus and Letters VII and VIII*, Harmondsworth: Penguin, 1973, p. 10.
3   *Phaedrus* belongs to Plato's so-called "middle period" when, it is generally agreed, many of the views expressed by the character Socrates, especially those of a metaphysically momentous nature, are probably not those of the historical Socrates.
4   C. Rowe, "Plato: Aesthetics and Psychology," in C. C. W. Taylor, ed., *From the Beginning to Plato*, London: Routledge, 1997, p. 435.
5   Compare this gesture with the philosophical aspirations of Plotinus (I.10, III.6), Augustine (IV.3) and Boethius (IV.4).

Plato, *Phaedrus*

245   [. . .] I might tell of many other noble deeds which have sprung from inspired madness. And therefore, let no one frighten or flutter us by saying that the temperate friend is to be chosen rather than the inspired, but let him further show that love is not sent by the gods for any good to lover or beloved; if he can do so we will allow him to carry off the palm. And we, on our part, will prove in answer to him that the madness of love is the greatest of heaven's blessings, and the proof shall be one which the wise will receive, and the witling disbelieve. But first of all, let us view the affections and actions of the soul divine and human, and try to ascertain the truth about them. The beginning of our proof is as follows: –

The soul through all her being is immortal, for that which is ever in motion is immortal; but that which moves another and is moved by another, in ceasing to move ceases also to live. Only the self-moving, never leaving itself, never ceases to move, and is the fountain and beginning of motion to all that moves besides. Now, the beginning is unbegotten, for that which is begotten has a beginning; but the beginning is begotten of nothing, for if it were begotten of something, then the begotten would not come from a beginning. But if unbegotten, it must also be indestructible; for if beginning were destroyed, there could be no beginning out of anything, nor anything out of a beginning; and all things must have a beginning. And therefore the self-moving is the beginning of motion; and this can neither be destroyed nor begotten, else the whole heavens and all creation would collapse and stand still, and never again have motion or birth. But if the self-moving is proved to be immortal, he who affirms that self-motion is the very idea and essence of the soul will not be put to confusion. For the body which is moved from without is soulless; but that which is moved from within has a soul, such motion being inherent in the soul. But if this is true, must not the soul be the

246 self-moving, and therefore of necessity unbegotten and immortal? Enough of the soul's immortality.

Of the nature of the soul, though her true form be ever a theme of large and more than mortal discourse, let me speak briefly, and in a figure. And let the figure be composite – a pair of winged horses and a charioteer.[1] Now the winged horses and the charioteers of the gods are all of them noble and of noble descent, but those of other races are mixed; the human charioteer drives his in a pair; and one of them is noble and of noble breed, and the other is ignoble and of ignoble breed; and the driving of them of necessity gives a great deal of trouble to him. I will endeavour to explain to you in what way the mortal differs from the immortal creature. The soul in her totality has the care of inanimate being everywhere, and traverses the whole heaven in divers forms appearing; – when perfect and fully winged she soars upward, and orders the whole world; whereas the imperfect soul, losing her wings and drooping in her flight at last settles on the solid ground – there, finding a home, she receives an earthly frame which appears to be self-moved, but is really moved by her power; and this composition of soul and body is called a living and mortal creature. For immortal no such union can be reasonably believed to be; although fancy, not having seen nor surely known the nature of God, may imagine an immortal creature having both a body and also a soul which are united throughout all time. Let that, however, be as God wills, and be spoken of acceptably to him. And now let us ask the reason why the soul loses her wings!

The wing is the corporeal element which is most akin to the divine, and which by nature tends to soar aloft and carry that which gravitates downwards into the upper region, which is the habitation of the gods. The divine is beauty, wisdom, goodness, and the like; and by these the wing of the soul is nourished, and grows apace; but when fed upon evil and foulness and the opposite of good, wastes and falls away. Zeus, the mighty lord, holding the reins of a winged chariot, leads the way in heaven, ordering all and taking care of all; and there follows him the

247 array of gods and demi-gods, marshalled in eleven bands; Hestia alone abides at home in the house of heaven;[2] of the rest they who are reckoned among the princely twelve march in their appointed order. They see many blessed sights in the inner heaven, and there are many ways to and fro, along which the blessed gods are passing, every one doing his own work; he may follow who will and can, for jealousy has no place in the celestial choir. But when they go to banquet and festival, then they move up the steep to the top of the vault of heaven. The chariots of the gods in even poise, obeying the rein, glide rapidly; but the others labour, for the vicious steed goes heavily, weighing down the charioteer to the earth when his steed has not been thoroughly trained: – and this is the hour of agony and extremest conflict for the soul. For the immortals, when they are at the end of their course, go forth and stand upon the outside of heaven, and the revolution of the spheres carries them round, and they behold the things beyond. But of the heaven which is above the heavens, what earthly poet ever did or ever will sing worthily? It is such as I will describe; for I must dare to speak the truth, when truth is my theme. There abides the very being with which true knowledge is concerned; the colourless, formless, intangible essence, visible only to mind, who is the pilot of the soul. The divine intelligence, being nurtured upon mind and pure knowledge, and the intelligence of every soul which is capable of receiving the food proper to it, rejoices at beholding reality, and once more gazing upon truth, is replenished and made glad, until the revolution of the worlds brings her round again to the same place. In the revolution she beholds justice, and temperance, and knowledge absolute, not in the form of generation or of relation, which men call existence, but knowledge absolute in existence absolute; and beholding the other true existences in like manner, and feasting upon them, she passes down into the interior of the heavens and returns home; and there the charioteer putting up his horses at the stall, gives them ambrosia to eat and nectar to drink.

Such is the life of the gods; but of other souls, 248 that which follows God best and is likest to him lifts the head of the charioteer into the outer world, and is carried round in the revolution, troubled indeed by the steeds, and with difficulty beholding true being; while another only rises and falls, and sees, and again fails to see by reason of the unruliness of the steeds. The rest of the souls are also longing after the upper world and they all follow, but not being strong enough they are carried round below the surface, plunging, treading on one another, each striving to be first;

and there is confusion and perspiration and the extremity of effort; and many of them are lamed or have their wings broken through the ill-driving of the charioteers; and all of them after a fruitless toil, not having attained to the mysteries of true being, go away, and feed upon opinion. The reason why the souls exhibit this exceeding eagerness to behold the plain of truth is that pasturage is found there, which is suited to the highest part of the soul; and the wing on which the soul soars is nourished with this. And there is a law of Destiny, that the soul which attains any vision of truth in company with a god is preserved from harm until the next period, and if attaining always is always unharmed. But when she is unable to follow, and fails to behold the truth, and through some ill-hap sinks beneath the double load of forgetfulness and vice, and her wings fall from her and she drops to the ground, then the law ordains that this soul shall at her first birth pass, not into any other animal, but only into man; and the soul which has seen most of truth shall come to the birth as a philosopher, or artist, or some musical and loving nature; that which has seen truth in the second degree shall be some righteous king or warrior chief; the soul which is of the third class shall be a politician, or economist, or trader; the fourth shall be a lover of gymnastic toils, or a physician; the fifth shall lead the life of a prophet or hierophant; to the sixth the character of a poet or some other imitative artist will be assigned; to the seventh the life of an artisan or husbandman; to the eighth that of a sophist or demagogue; to the ninth that of a tyrant; – all these are states of probation, in which he who does righteously improves, and he who does unrighteously, deteriorates his lot.

Ten thousand years must elapse before the soul of each one can return to the place whence she came, for she cannot grow her wings in less; only the soul of a philosopher, guileless and true, or the soul of a lover, who is not devoid of philosophy, may acquire wings in the third of the recurring periods of a thousand years; – these, if they choose this higher life three times in succession, have wings given them, and go away at 249 the end of three thousand years. But the other souls* receive judgment when they have completed their first life, and after the judgment they

* The philosopher alone is not subject to judgment, for he has never lost the vision of truth.

go, some of them to the houses of correction which are under the earth, and are punished; others to some place in heaven whither they are lightly borne by justice, and there they live in a manner worthy of the life which they led here when in the form of men. And at the end of the first thousand years the good souls and also the evil souls both come to draw lots and choose their second life, and they may take any which they please. The soul of a man may pass into the life of a beast, or from the beast return again into the man. But the soul which has never seen the truth will not pass into the human form. For a man must have intelligence of universals, and be able to proceed from the many particulars of sense to one conception of reason; – this is the recollection of those things which our soul once saw while following God, when, regardless of that which we now call being, she raised her head up towards the true being.[3] And therefore the mind of the philosopher alone has wings; and this is just, for he is always, according to the measure of his abilities, clinging in recollection to those things in which God abides, and in which abiding He is Divine. And he who employs aright these memories is ever being initiated into perfect mysteries and alone becomes truly perfect. But, as he forgets earthly interests and is rapt in the divine, the vulgar deem him mad, and rebuke him; they do not see that he is inspired.

Thus far I have been speaking of the fourth and last kind of madness, which is imputed to him who, when he sees the beauty of earth, is transported with the recollection of the true beauty; he would like to fly away, but he cannot; he is like a bird fluttering and looking upward and careless of the world below; and he is therefore thought to be mad. And I have shown this of all inspirations to be the noblest and highest and the offspring of the highest to him who has or shares in it, and that he who loves the beautiful is called a lover because he partakes of it. For, as has been already said, every soul of man has in the way of nature beheld true being; this was the condition of her passing into the form of man. But all 250 souls do not easily recall the things of the other world; they may have seen them for a short time only, or they may have been unfortunate in their earthly lot, and, having had their hearts turned to unrighteousness through some corrupting influence, they may have lost the memory of the holy things which once they saw. Few only retain an adequate remembrance of them; and they, when they behold here any image of that other world, are rapt in amazement; but they are ignorant of what this rapture means, because they do not clearly perceive. For there is no light of justice or temperance or any of the higher ideas which are precious to souls in the earthly copies of them: they are seen through a glass dimly; and there are few who, going to the images, behold in them the realities, and these only with difficulty. There was a time when with the rest of the happy band they saw beauty shining in brightness, – we philosophers following in the train of Zeus, others in company with other gods; and then we beheld the beatific vision and were initiated into a mystery which may be truly called most blessed, celebrated by us in our state of innocence, before we had any experience of evils to come, when we were admitted to the sight of apparitions innocent and simple and calm and happy, which we beheld shining in pure light, pure ourselves and not yet enshrined in that living tomb which we carry about, now that we are imprisoned in the body, like an oyster in his shell.

Notes

1 Jowett's translation ignores the word *sumphutos* in the Greek text, which signifies that the two horses and the charioteer are "grown together" into an uneasy unity. Plato's figure is to be compared with the tripartite account of the soul in Book IV of the *Republic*. Sections 253–5 of *Phaedrus* make it clearer that the charioteer corresponds to the rational part, while the two horses correspond to "spiritedness" (or "mettle," *thumos*) and "appetite" respectively.

2 Hestia was the goddess of the hearth and a symbol of the earth. Presumably the point of her remaining at home is to emphasize the divide between earth and the realm of the Forms.

3 Plato's most detailed account of "recollection" is in his *Meno*.

4

Aristotle, *Metaphysics,*
Books I.1–3 (abridged),
VII, VIII, and XII

Introduction

Plato's theory of "Forms" (or Ideas, or Types, *ēide*) was soon to come under attack from his most famous pupil, Aristotle (384–22 BCE), above all in those writings of Aristotle, which, in a collected edition, came after (*meta*) his writings on nature (*ta phusika*). *Metaphysics* is a wide-ranging work, but its main concerns are interconnected and each of them comes to center on the notion of substance (*ousia*), the subject of the work's most famous (and, unfortunately, very difficult) section, Book VII (or *Z*).

Three main themes are the nature of being or the meaning of "is," change and the explanation of coming-to-be and ceasing-to-be, and the criteria for identity. Just about anything we speak of can be said to be, including health, smiles, and colors: but, for Aristotle, being must belong "primarily" to what "underlies," stands-under (*hypokeimenon*), or supports such states, occurrences or properties, for – *pace* the Cheshire Cat's smile – they are incapable of independent existence. "Substance" is first introduced (Ch. 1)

From The Basic Works of Aristotle, ed. R. McKeon, New York: Random House, 1941, pp. 689–93, 872–88 (some notes omitted). *From A New Aristotle Reader*, ed. J. L. Ackrill, trans. W. D. Ross (revised by J. Barnes). Oxford: Clarendon Press, 1987, pp. 284–9, 291–6, 306–14 [some passages omitted].

as the name for the *underlying* factor. It is the name, too, for the relatively *stable* and *persistent* things we must assume in order to make sense of the idea of change. For change to occur, there must be something that persists in order to undergo the change. Finally, it is a substance we are trying to specify when answering questions about anything's *identity*, such as "What is it?" or "What makes it the same thing over time and distinguishes it from anything else?"

Whether or not a single concept of substance can apply to "underlying," independently existing entities, to what remains the same as a thing changes, and that to which anything owes its essential identity, is a moot question.[1] But it is Aristotle's view that it can, and in Book VII, especially, he explores this concept with the aim of showing what substance is. With two views of substance – of what, fundamentally, there is – he takes issue. First, substance is not, as the "naturalists" like Democritus (c. 460–c. 370 BCE) had held, matter. When we ask what something is, we are asking about something "separable and individual," not about some general stuff of which it may be composed. (Elsewhere Aristotle had argued that ultimate or "prime" matter was anyway unknowable, and hence could not be used to determine a thing's nature. *Physics* 193ff.) Second, and at the other extreme, substance cannot be identified with abstract Platonic Forms or Ideas, held to exist independently of or "apart from" the particular things that "participate" in them. For one thing, such Forms would be useless for explaining how things come into being (Ch. 8). For another, insuperable logical problems arise once we press such questions as whether the Form of, say, animals is the same or a different one in the case of each different species, or how particular humans relate to the "human-in-itself" which is alleged to be their Form (Ch. 13ff). Other arguments against Platonic Forms are marshaled in Book XIII.

In *Metaphysics*, moreover, Aristotle is no longer content, it seems, with the "robustly common-sensical"[2] answer to the question, "What are substances?," offered in his *Categories*, where by "primary substances" he meant individual concrete things, animals, plants or whatever. (Though see the beginning of Ch. 15.) His considered answer now is that a substance is a "form" of something (not to be confused with a Platonic "Form"). By a "form" (*ēidos, morphos*), Aristotle means the "essence" (the "what-it-is," *ti esti*) of something – that which makes it what it is – rather than the object itself considered as a spatio-temporal particular.[3] It may sound odd to equate substances with essences, but in the first place we should set aside the "stuff-like" connotations that the word "substance" acquired in later philosophical and vernacular parlance (the Greek *ousia*, an Aristotelian term of art, was coined from the participle of the verb "to be"). And, second, we need to recall a main role Aristotle intended the term to play – namely, to refer to what can exist independently (unlike a smile or a color, which must be of somebody or something). His thought seems to be that the concrete individual Socrates is not, in the relevant sense, suitably independent, since his existence depends on his essence. A certain snub-nosed Greek philosopher was Socrates, or at least human, only because of a unique essence he embodied.[4] It is hard to exaggerate the import-ance of Aristotle's "independence" criterion for substance. Crucially, it helps explain the "theological" turn in Book XII of *Metaphysics* (comparable, in some respects, to a similar turn at the end of the *Nicomachean* Ethics (see I.2), where Aristotle intimates that, strictly speaking, only God may be a substance (compare Spinoza, III.13). This is presumably because God, being immaterial, is not dependent, like Socrates, on matter.

Despite, or perhaps because of, the difficulties and ambiguities in Aristotle's discussion of substance, it is one that – alongside such related discussions of form/matter, actuality/potentiality, essence/accident – has continued to influence, indeed to shape, all subsequent metaphysical debate in the West.

Notes

1   See M. C. Nussbaum, "Aristotle," in J. Kim and E. Sosa, eds, *A Companion to Metaphysics*, Oxford: Blackwell, 1995, pp. 24–31, for a succinct discussion of possible tensions in Aristotle's notion of "substance."

2   J. Barnes, *Aristotle*, Oxford: Oxford University Press, 1985, p. 46.

3   For a clear discussion of Aristotle on substance as form, see J. Lear, *Aristotle: The Desire to Understand*, Cambridge: Cambridge University Press, 1988.

4   Determining what makes individuals – the principle of individuation – so that we have a world where each is both an individual and a member of a general group (a "this-such"), will become an important topic of metaphysics (see III.11).

Aristotle, *Metaphysics*

Book A (I)

980ª   **1**   All men by nature desire to know. An indication of this is the delight we take in our senses; for even apart from their usefulness they are loved for themselves; and above all others the sense of sight. For not only with a view to action, but even when we are not going to do anything, we prefer seeing (one might say) to everything else. The reason is that this, most of all the senses, makes us know and brings to light many differences between things.

By nature animals are born with the faculty of sensation, and from sensation memory is produced in some of them, though not in others. And therefore the former are more intelligent and apt   980ᵇ at learning than those which cannot remember; those which are incapable of hearing sounds are intelligent though they cannot be taught, e. g. the bee, and any other race of animals that may be like it; and those which besides memory have this sense of hearing can be taught.

The animals other than man live by appearances and memories, and have but little of connected experience; but the human race lives also by art and reasonings. Now from memory experience is produced in men; for the several memories of the same thing produce finally the capacity for a single experience. And experience seems pretty much like science and art, but really science and art come to men *through* experience; for 'experience made art', as Polus says,* 'but inexperience luck'. Now art arises when from many notions gained by experience one universal judgement about a class of objects is produced. For to have a judgement that when Callias was ill of this disease this did him good, and similarly in the case of Socrates and in many individual cases, is a matter of experience; but to judge that it has done good to all persons of a certain constitution, marked off in one class, when they were ill of this disease, e. g. to phlegmatic or bilious people when burning with fever – this is a matter of art.

With a view to action experience seems in no respect inferior to art, and men of experience succeed even better than those who have theory without experience. (The reason is that experience is knowledge of individuals, art of universals, and actions and productions are all concerned with the individual; for the physician does not cure *man*, except in an incidental way, but Callias or Socrates or some other called by some such individual name, who happens to be a man. If, then, a man has the theory without the experience, and recognizes the universal but does not know the individual included in this, he will often fail to cure; for it is the individual that is to be cured.) But yet we think that *knowledge* and *understanding* belong to art rather than to experience, and we suppose artists to be wiser than men of experience (which implies that Wisdom depends in all cases rather on knowledge); and this because the former know the cause, but the latter do not. For men of experience know that

the thing is so, but do not know why, while the others know the 'why' and the cause. Hence we think also that the master-workers in each craft are more honourable and know in a truer sense and are wiser than the manual workers, because they know the causes of the things that are done (we think the manual workers are like certain lifeless things which act indeed, but act without knowing what they do, as fire burns – but while the lifeless things perform each of their functions by a natural tendency, the labourers perform them through habit); thus we view them as being wiser not in virtue of being able to act, but of having the theory for themselves and knowing the causes. And in general it is a sign of the man who knows and of the man who does not know, that the former can teach, and therefore we think art more truly knowledge than experience is; for artists can teach, and men of mere experience cannot.

Again, we do not regard any of the senses as Wisdom; yet surely these give the most authoritative knowledge of particulars. But they do not tell us the 'why' of anything – e. g. why fire is hot; they only say *that* it is hot.

At first he who invented any art whatever that went beyond the common perceptions of man was naturally admired by men, not only because there was something useful in the inventions, but because he was thought wise and superior to the rest. But as more arts were invented, and some were directed to the necessities of life, others to recreation, the inventors of the latter were naturally always regarded as wiser than the inventors of the former, because their branches of knowledge did not aim at utility. Hence when all such inventions were already established, the sciences which do not aim at giving pleasure or at the necessities of life were discovered, and first in the places where men first began to have leisure. This is why the mathematical arts were founded in Egypt; for there the priestly caste was allowed to be at leisure.

We have said in the *Ethics*† what the difference is between art and science and the other kindred faculties; but the point of our present discussion is this, that all men suppose what is called Wisdom to deal with the first causes and the

981ᵃ (margin, left column)

981ᵇ (margin, right column)

---

* Cf. Plato, *Gorgias* 448 c, 462 bc. [Cf. *Nicomachean Ethics* 1176a1 – Eds]

† 1139ᵇ 14–1141ᵇ 8.

principles of things; so that, as has been said before, the man of experience is thought to be wiser than the possessors of any sense-perception whatever, the artist wiser than the men of experience, the master-worker than the mechanic, and the theoretical kinds of knowledge to be more of the nature of Wisdom than the productive. 982ª Clearly then Wisdom is knowledge about certain principles and causes.

2 Since we are seeking this knowledge, we must inquire of what kind are the causes and the principles, the knowledge of which is Wisdom. If one were to take the notions we have about the wise man, this might perhaps make the answer more evident. We suppose first, then, that the wise man knows all things, as far as possible, although he has not knowledge of each of them in detail; secondly, that he who can learn things that are difficult, and not easy for man to know, is wise (sense-perception is common to all, and therefore easy and no mark of Wisdom); again, that he who is more exact and more capable of teaching the causes is wiser, in every branch of knowledge; and that of the sciences, also, that which is desirable on its own account and for the sake of knowing it is more of the nature of Wisdom than that which is desirable on account of its results, and the superior science is more of the nature of Wisdom than the ancillary; for the wise man must not be ordered but must order, and he must not obey another, but the less wise must obey *him*.

Such and so many are the notions, then, which we have about Wisdom and the wise. Now of these characteristics that of knowing all things must belong to him who has in the highest degree universal knowledge; for he knows in a sense all the instances that fall under the universal. And these things, the most universal, are on the whole the hardest for men to know; for they are farthest from the senses. And the most exact of the sciences are those which deal most with first principles; for those which involve fewer principles are more exact than those which involve additional principles, e. g. arithmetic than geometry. But the science which investigates causes is also *instructive*, in a higher degree, for the people who instruct us are those who tell the causes of each thing. And understanding and knowledge pursued for their own sake are found most in the knowledge of that which is most knowable (for he who chooses to know for the sake of knowing will choose most readily that which is most truly knowledge, and such is the knowledge of that which is most 982ᵇ knowable); and the first principles and the causes are most knowable; for by reason of these, and from these, all other things come to be known, and not these by means of the things subordinate to them. And the science which knows to what end each thing must be done is the most authoritative of the sciences, and more authoritative than any ancillary science; and this end is the good of that thing, and in general the supreme good in the whole of nature. Judged by all the tests we have mentioned, then, the name in question falls to the same science; this must be a science that investigates the first principles and causes; for the good, i.e. the end, is one of the causes.

That it is not a science of production is clear even from the history of the earliest philosophers. For it is owing to their wonder that men both now begin and at first began to philosophize; they wondered originally at the obvious difficulties, then advanced little by little and stated difficulties about the greater matters, e. g. about the phenomena of the moon and those of the sun and of the stars, and about the genesis of the universe. And a man who is puzzled and wonders thinks himself ignorant (whence even the lover of myth is in a sense a lover of Wisdom, for the myth is composed of wonders); therefore since they philosophized in order to escape from ignorance, evidently they were pursuing science in order to know, and not for any utilitarian end. And this is confirmed by the facts; for it was when almost all the necessities of life and the things that make for comfort and recreation had been secured, that such knowledge began to be sought. Evidently then we do not seek it for the sake of any other advantage; but as the man is free, we say, who exists for his own sake and not for another's, so we pursue this as the only free science, for it alone exists for its own sake.

Hence also the possession of it might be justly regarded as beyond human power; for in many ways human nature is in bondage, so that according to Simonides 'God alone can have this privilege', and it is unfitting that man should not be content to seek the knowledge that is suited to him. If, then, there is something in what the poets say, and jealousy is natural to the 983ª divine power, it would probably occur in this case above all, and all who excelled in this knowledge would be unfortunate. But the divine power cannot be jealous (nay, according to the proverb, 'bards tell many a lie'), nor should any other science be thought more honourable than one of this sort. For the most divine science is also most honourable; and this science alone must be, in two ways, most divine. For the science which it would be most meet for God to have is a divine science, and so is any science that deals with divine objects; and this science alone has both these qualities; for (1) God is thought to be among the causes of all things and to be a first principle, and (2) such a science either God alone can have, or God above all others. All the sciences, indeed, are more necessary than this, but none is better.

Yet the acquisition of it must in a sense end in something which is the opposite of our original inquiries. For all men begin, as we said, by wondering that things are as they are, as they do about self-moving marionettes, or about the solstices or the incommensurability of the diagonal of a square with the side; for it seems wonderful to all who have not yet seen the reason, that there is a thing which cannot be measured even by the smallest unit. But we must end in the contrary and, according to the proverb, the better state, as is the case in these instances too when men learn the cause; for there is nothing which would surprise a geometer so much as if the diagonal turned out to be commensurable.

We have stated, then, what is the nature of the science we are searching for, and what is the mark which our search and our whole investigation must reach.

3 Evidently we have to acquire knowledge of the original causes (for we say we know each thing only when we think we recognize its first cause), and causes are spoken of in four senses. In one of these we mean the substance, i.e. the essence (for the 'why' is reducible finally to the definition, and the ultimate 'why' is a cause and principle); in another the matter or substratum, in a third the source of the change, and in a fourth the cause opposed to this, the purpose and the good 983ᵇ (for this is the end of all generation and change). We have studied these causes sufficiently in our work on nature,* but yet let us call to our aid those

who have attacked the investigation of being and philosophized about reality before us. For obviously they too speak of certain principles and causes; to go over their views, then, will be of profit to the present inquiry, for we shall either find another kind of cause, or be more convinced of the correctness of those which we now maintain.

Of the first philosophers, then, most thought the principles which were of the nature of matter were the only principles of all things.

Book VII (Z)

1 There are several senses in which a thing may 1028ᵃ be said to be, as we pointed out previously in our book on the various senses of the words; for in one sense it means what a thing is or a 'this', and in another sense it means that a thing is of a certain quality or quantity or has some such predicate asserted of it. While 'being' has all these senses, obviously that which is primarily is the 'what', which indicates the substance of the thing. For when we say of what quality a thing is, we say that it is good or beautiful, but not that it is three cubits long or that it is a man; but when we say *what* it is, we do not say 'white' or 'hot' or 'three cubits long', but 'man' or 'God'. And all other things are said to be because they are, some of them, quantities of that which *is* in this primary sense, others qualities of it, other affections of it, and others some other determination of it. And so one might raise the question whether 'to walk' and 'to be healthy' and 'to sit' signify in each case something that is, and similarly in any other case of this sort; for none of them is either self-subsistent or capable of being separated from substance, but rather, if anything, it is that which walks or is seated or is healthy that is an existent thing. Now these are seen to be more real because there is something definite which underlies them; and this is the substance or individual, which is implied in such a predicate; for 'good' or 'sitting' are not used without this. Clearly then it is in virtue of this category that each of the others *is*. Therefore that which is primarily and *is* simply (not is something) must be substance.

Now there are several senses in which a thing is said to be primary; but substance is primary in every sense – in formula, in order of knowledge,

* *Physics.* ii. 3, 7.

in time. For of the other categories none can exist independently, but only substance. And in formula also this is primary; for in the formula of each term the formula of its substance must be present. And we think we know each thing most fully, when we know what it is, e.g. what man is or what fire is, rather than when we know its quality, its quantity, or where it is; since we know each of these things also, only when we know *what* the quantity or the quality *is*.

And indeed the question which, both now and of old, has always been raised, and always been the subject of doubt, viz. what being is, is just the question, what is substance? For it is this that some assert to be one, others more than one, and that some assert to be limited in number, other unlimited. And so we also must consider chiefly and primarily and almost exclusively what that is which *is* in this sense.

2 Substance is thought to belong most obviously to bodies; and so we say that both animals and plants and their parts are substances, and so are natural bodies such as fire and water and earth and everything of the sort, and all things that are parts of these or composed of these (either of parts or of the whole bodies), e.g. the heaven and its parts, stars and moon and sun. But whether these alone are substances, or there are also others, or only some of these, or some of these and some other things are substances, or none of these but only some other things, must be considered. Some think the limits of body, i.e. surface, line, point, and unit, are substances, and more so than body or the solid. Further, some do not think there is anything substantial besides sensible things, but others think there are eternal substances which are more in number and more real, e.g. Plato posited two kinds of substance – the Forms and the objects of mathematics – as well as a third kind, viz. the substance of sensible bodies. And Speusippus made still more kinds of substance, beginning with the One, and making principles for each kind of substance, one for numbers, another for spatial magnitudes, and then another for the soul; and in this way he multiplies the kinds of substance. And some say Forms and numbers have the same nature, and other things come after them, e.g. lines and planes, until we come to the substance of the heavens and to sensible bodies.

Regarding these matters, then, we must inquire which of the common statements are right and which are not right, and what things are substances, and whether there are or are not any besides sensible substances, and how sensible substances exist, and whether there is a separable substance (and if so why and how) or there is no substance separable from sensible substances; and we must first sketch the nature of substance.

3 The word 'substance' is applied, if not in more senses, still at least to four main objects: for both the essence and the universal and the genus are thought to be the substance of each thing, and fourthly the substratum. Now the substratum is that of which other things are predicated, while it is itself not predicated of anything else. And so we must first determine the nature of this; for that which underlies a thing primarily is thought to be in the truest sense its substance. And in one sense matter is said to be of the nature of substratum, in another shape, and in a third sense, the compound of these. By the matter I mean, for instance, the bronze, by the shape the plan of its form, and by the compound of these (the concrete thing) the statue. Therefore if the form is prior to the matter and more real, it will be prior to the compound also for the same reason.

We have now outlined the nature of substance, showing that it is that which is not predicated of a subject, but of which all else is predicated. But we must not merely state the matter thus; for this is not enough. The statement itself is obscure, and further, on this view, *matter* becomes substance. For if this is not substance, it is beyond us to say what else is. When all else is taken away evidently nothing but matter remains. For of the other elements some are affections, products, and capacities of bodies, while length, breadth, and depth are quantities and not substances. For a quantity is not a substance; but the substance is rather that to which these belong primarily. But when length and breadth and depth are taken away we see nothing left except that which is bounded by these, whatever it be; so that to those who consider the question thus matter alone must seem to be substance. By matter I mean that which in itself is neither a particular thing nor of a certain quantity nor assigned to any other of the categories

1028^b

1029

by which being is determined. For there is something of which each of these is predicated, so that its being is different from that of each of the predicates; for the predicates other than substance are predicated of substance, while substance is predicated of matter. Therefore the ultimate substratum is of itself neither a particular thing nor of a particular quantity nor otherwise positively characterized; nor yet negatively, for negations also will belong to it only by accident.

For those who adopt this point of view, then, it follows that matter is substance. But this is impossible; for both separability and individuality are thought to belong chiefly to substance. And so form and the compound of form and matter would be thought to be substance, rather than matter. The substance compounded of both, i.e. of matter and shape, may be dismissed; for it is posterior and its nature is obvious. And matter also is in a sense manifest. But we must inquire into the third kind of substance; for this is the most difficult.

1029^b It is agreed that there are some substances among sensible things, so that we must look first among these. For it is an advantage to advance to that which is more intelligible. For learning proceeds for all in this way – through that which is less intelligible by nature to that which is more intelligible . . .

4 Since at the start we distinguished the various marks by which we determine substance, and one of these was thought to be the essence, we must investigate this. And first let us say something about it in the abstract. The essence of each thing is what it is said to be in virtue of itself. For being you is not being musical; for you are not musical in virtue of yourself. What, then, you are in virtue of yourself is your essence.

But not the whole of this is the essence of a thing; not that which something is in virtue of itself in the way in which a surface is white, because being a surface is not being white. But again the combination of both – being a white surface – is not the essence of surface. Why? Because 'surface' itself is repeated. The formula, therefore, in which the term itself is not present but its meaning is expressed, this is the formula of the essence of each thing. Therefore if to be a white surface is to be a smooth surface, to be white and to be smooth are one and the same. . . .

. . . the essence is what something is; but when one thing is said of another, that is not what a 'this' is, e.g. white man is not what a 'this' is since being a 'this' belongs only to substances. Therefore there is an essence only of those things whose formula is a definition. But we have a definition not where we have a word and a formula identical in meaning (for in that case all formulae would be definitions; for there will be some name for any formula whatever, so that even the *Iliad* would be a definition), but where there is a formula of something primary; and primary things are those which do not involve one thing's being said of another. Nothing, then, which is not a species of a genus will have an *essence* – only species will have it, for in these the subject is not thought to participate in the attribute and to have it as an affection, nor to have it by accident; but for everything else as well, if it has a name, there will be a formula of its meaning – viz. that this attribute belongs to this subject; or instead of a simple formula we shall be able to give a more accurate one; but there will be no definition nor essence. . . .

. . . essence will belong, just as the 'what' does, primarily and in the simple sense to substance, and in a secondary way to the other categories also, – not essence simply, but the essence of a quality or of a quantity. For it must be either homonymously that we say these *are*, or by making qualifications and abstractions (in the way in which that which is not known may be said to be known), – the truth being that we use the word neither homonymously nor in the same sense, but just as we apply the word 'medical' when there is a *reference* to one and the same thing, not *mean-* 1030^b *ing* one and the same thing, nor yet speaking homonymously; for a patient and an operation and an instrument are called medical neither homonymously nor in virtue of one thing, but with reference to one thing. But it does not matter in which of the two ways one likes to describe the facts; this is evident, that definition and essence in the primary and simple sense belong to substances. Still they belong to other things as well in a similar way, but not primarily. For if we suppose this it does not follow that there is a definition of every word which means the same as any formula; it must mean the same as a particular kind of formula; and this condition is satisfied if it is a formula of something which is one, not by continuity like the *Iliad* or the things that are one by being bound together, but in one of the main senses of 'one' which answer to the senses of 'is'; now 'that which is' in one sense denotes an individual, in another a quantity, in another a quality. And so there can be a formula or definition of white man, but not in the sense in which there is a definition either of white or of a substance. . . .

6   We must inquire whether each thing and its essence are the same or different. This is of some use for the inquiry concerning substance; for each thing is thought to be not different from its substance, and the essence is said to be the substance of each thing.

Now in the case of things with accidental attributes the two would be generally thought to be different, e.g. white man would be thought to be different from the essence of white man. For if they are the same, the essence of man and that of white man are also the same; for a man and a white man are the same, as people say, so that the essence of white man and that of man would be also the same. But probably it is not necessary that things with accidental attributes should be the same. For the extreme terms are not in the same way the same. – Perhaps *this* might be thought to follow, that the extreme terms, the accidents, should turn out to be the same, e.g. the essence of white and that of musical; but this is not actually thought to be the case.

But in the case of so-called self-subsistent things, is a thing necessarily the same as its essence? E.g. if there are some substances which have no other substances nor entities prior to them – substances such as some assert the Ideas to be? If the essence of good is to be different from the Idea of good, and the essence of animal from the Idea of animal, and the essence of being from 1031^b the Idea of being, there will, firstly, be other substances and entities and Ideas besides those which are asserted, and, secondly, these others will be prior substances if the essence is substance. And if the posterior substances are severed from one another, there will be no knowledge of the ones and the others will have no being. (By 'severed' I mean, if the Idea of good has not the essence of good, and the latter has not the property of being good.) For there is knowledge of each thing only when we know its essence. And the case

is the same for other things as for the good; so that if the essence of good is not good, neither will the essence of being be, nor the essence of unity be one. And all essences alike exist or none of them does; so that if the essence of being is not, neither will any of the others be. Again, that which has not the property of being good is not good. The good, then, must be one with the essence of good, and the beautiful with the essence of beauty, and so with all things which do not depend on something else but are self-subsistent and primary. For it is enough if they are this, even if there are no Forms; and perhaps all the more if there are Forms. – At the same time it is clear that if there are Ideas such as some people say there are, the substratum of them will not be substance; for these must be substances, and not predicable of a substratum; for if they were they would exist only by being participated in. – Each thing then and its essence are one and the same in no merely accidental way, as is evident both from the preceding arguments and because to *know* each thing, at least, is to know its essence, so that even by the exhibition of instances it becomes clear that both must be one.

(But of an accidental term, e.g. 'the musical' or 'the white', since it has two meanings, it is not true to say that it itself is identical with its essence; for both that to which the accidental quality belongs, and the accidental quality, are white, so that in a sense the accident and its essence are the same, and in a sense they are not; for the essence of white is not the same as the man or the white man, but it is the same as the attribute white.)

The absurdity of the separation would appear also if one were to assign a name to each of the essences; for there would be another essence besides the original one; e.g. to the essence of horse there will belong a second essence. Yet why should not some things be their essences from the start, since essence is substance? But not only are 1032 a thing and its essence one, but the formula of them is also the same, as is clear even from what has been said; for it is not by accident that the essence of one, and the one, are one. Further, if they were different, the process would go on to infinity; for we should have the essence of one, and the one, so that in their case also the same infinite regress would be found. Clearly, then, each primary and self-subsistent thing is one and the same as its essence.

Now the sophistical objections to this position, and the question whether Socrates and to be Socrates are the same thing, are obviously answered in the same way; for there is no difference either in the standpoint from which the question would be asked, or in that from which one could answer it successfully. We have explained, then, in what sense each thing is the same as its essence and in what sense it is not.

7 Of things that come to be some come to be by nature, some by art, some spontaneously. Now everything that comes to be comes to be by the agency of something and from something and comes be something. And the something which I say it comes to be may be found in any category; it may come to be either a 'this' or of some quantity or of some quality or somewhere.

Now natural comings to be are the comings to be of those things which come to be by nature; and that out of which they come to be is what we call matter; and that by which they come to be is something which exists naturally; and the something which they come to be is a man or a plant or one of the things of this kind, which we say are substances if anything is. All things that come to be either by nature or by art have matter, for each of them is capable both of being and of not being, and this capacity is the matter in each. And, in general, both that from which they are produced is nature, and the type according to which they are produced is nature (for that which is produced, e.g. a plant or an animal, has a nature), and so is that by which they are produced – the so-called 'formal' nature, which is specifically the same as the nature of the thing produced (though it is in another individual); for man begets man.

Thus, then, are natural products produced; all other productions are called 'makings'. And all makings proceed either from art or from a capacity or from thought. Some of them happen also spontaneously or by chance just as natural products sometimes do; for there also the same things sometimes are produced without seed as well as from seed. Concerning these cases, then, we must inquire later, but from art proceed the things of which the form is in the soul. (By form I mean the essence of each thing and its primary substance.) For even contraries have in a sense the same form; for the substance of a privation is the opposite substance, e.g. health is the substance of disease; for it is by its absence that disease exists; and health is the formula and the knowledge in the soul.

... Therefore, as we say, it is impossible that anything should be produced if there were nothing before. Obviously then some part of the result will pre-exist of necessity; for the matter is a part; for this is present in the process and it is this that becomes something. But do some also of the elements in the *formula* pre-exist? Well, we describe in both ways what bronze circles are; we describe both the matter by saying it is bronze, and the form by saying that it is such and such a figure; and figure is the proximate genus in which it is placed. The bronze circle, then, has its matter *in its formula*.

And as for that out of which as matter they are produced, some things are said, when they have been produced, to be not it but of it, e.g. the statue is not stone but of stone. But though what becomes healthy is a man, a man is not what the healthy product is said to come from. The reason is that though a thing comes both from its privation and from its substratum, which we call its matter (e.g. what becomes healthy is both a man and an invalid), it is said to come rather from its privation (e.g. it is from an invalid rather than from a man that a healthy subject is produced). And so the healthy subject is not said to *be* an invalid, but to be a man, and a healthy man. But as for the things whose privation is obscure and nameless, e.g. in bronze the privation of a particular shape or in bricks and timber the privation of arrangement as a house, the thing is thought to be produced *from* these materials, as in the former case the healthy man is produced *from* an invalid. And so, as there also a thing is not said to be that from which it comes, here the statue is not said to be wood but is said by a verbal change to be not wood but wooden, not bronze but of bronze, not stone but of stone, and the house is said to be not bricks but of bricks (since we should not say without qualification, if we looked at things carefully, even that a statue is produced from wood or a house from bricks, because its coming to be implies change in that from which it comes, and not permanence). For this reason, then, we use this way of speaking.

1033ᵃ marginal — 1033ᵃ

032ᵇ marginal — 032ᵇ

8 Since anything which is produced is produced by something (and this I call the starting-point of the production), and from something (and let this be taken to be not the privation but the matter; for the meanings we attach to these have already been distinguished), and since something is produced (and this is either a sphere or a circle or whatever else it may chance to be), just as we do not make the substratum – the bronze – so we do not make the sphere, except incidentally, because the bronze sphere is a sphere and we make the former. For to make a 'this' is to make a 'this' out of the general substratum. I mean that to make the bronze round is not to make the round or the sphere, but something else, i.e. to produce this form in something else. For if we make the form, we must make it out of something else; for this was assumed. E.g. we make a bronze sphere; and that in the sense that out of this, which is bronze, we make this other, which is a sphere. If, then, we make the sphere itself, clearly we must make it in the same way, and the processes of making will regress to infinity. Obviously then the form also, or whatever we ought to call the shape of the sensible thing, is not produced, nor does production relate to it, – i.e. the essence is not produced; for this is that which is made to be in something else by art or by nature or by some capacity. But that there is a *bronze sphere*, this we make. For we make it out of bronze and the sphere; we bring the form into this particular matter, and the result is a bronze sphere. But if the essence of sphere in general is produced, something must be produced out of something. For the product will always have to be divisible, and one part must be this and another that, I mean the one must be matter and the other form. If then a sphere is the figure whose circumference is at all points equidistant from the centre, part of this will be the medium in which the thing made will be, and part will be in that medium, and the whole will be the thing produced, which corresponds to the bronze sphere. It is obvious then from what has been said that the thing, in the sense of form or substance, is not produced, but the concrete thing which gets its name from this is produced, and that in everything which comes to be matter is present, and one part of the thing is matter and the other form.

Is there then a sphere apart from the individual spheres or a house apart from the bricks?

Rather we may say that no 'this' would ever have been coming to be, if this had been so. The 'form' however means the 'such', and is not a 'this' – a definite thing; but the artist makes, or the father generates, a 'such' out of a 'this'; and when it has been generated, it is a 'this such'. And the whole 'this', Callias or Socrates, is analogous to this bronze sphere, but man and animal to bronze sphere in general. Obviously then the cause which consists of the Forms (taken in the sense in which some maintain the existence of the Forms, i.e. if they are something apart from the individuals) is useless with regard both to comings-to-be and to substances; and the Forms need not, for this reason at least, be self-subsistent substances. In some cases it is even obvious that the producer is of the same kind as the produced (not, however, the same nor one in number, but in form), e.g. in the case of natural products (for man produces man), unless something happens contrary to nature, e.g. the production of a mule by a horse. And even these cases are similar; for that which would be found to be common to horse and ass, the genus next above them, has not received a name, but it would doubtless be both, as the mule is both. Obviously, therefore, it is quite unnecessary to set up a Form as a pattern (for we should have looked for Forms in these cases if any; for these are substances if anything is so); the begetter is adequate to the making of the product and to the causing of the form in the matter. And when we have the whole, such and such a form in this flesh and in these bones, this is Callias or Socrates; and they are different in virtue of their matter (for that is different), but the same in form; for their form is indivisible. . . .

13 Let us again return to the subject of our inquiry, which is substance. As the substrate and the essence and the compound of these are called substance, so also is the universal. About two of these we have spoken; about the essence and about the substrate, of which we have said that it underlies in two senses, either being a 'this' – which is the way in which an animal underlies its attributes –, or as the matter underlies the complete reality. The universal also is thought by some to be in the fullest sense a cause, and a principle; therefore let us attack the discussion of this point also. For it seems impossible that any universal term should be the name of a substance. For primary substance is that kind of substance which is peculiar to an individual, which does not belong to anything else; but the universal is common, since that is called universal which naturally belongs to more than one thing. Of which individual then will this be the substance? Either of all or of none. But it cannot be the substance of all; and if it is to be the substance of one, this one will be the others also; for things whose substance is one and whose essence is one are themselves also one.

Further, substance means that which is not predicable of a subject, but the universal is predicable of some subjects always.

But perhaps the universal, while it cannot be substance in the way in which the essence is so, can be present in this, e.g. animal can be present in man and horse. Then clearly there is a formula of the universal. And it makes no difference even if there is not a formula of everything that is in the substance; for none the less the universal will be the substance of something. Man is the substance of the individual man in whom it is present; therefore the same will happen again, for a substance, e.g. animal, must be the substance of that in which it is present as something peculiar to it. And further it is impossible and absurd that the 'this', i.e. the substance, if it consists of parts, should not consist of substances nor of what is a 'this', but of quality; for that which is not substance, i.e. the quality, will then be prior to substance and to the 'this'. Which is impossible; for neither in formula nor in time nor in coming to be can the affections be prior to the substance; for then they would be separable from it. Further, in Socrates there will be a substance in a substance, so that he will be the substance of two things. And in general it follows, if man and such things are substances, that none of the elements in their formulae is the substance of anything, nor does it exist apart from the species or in anything else; I mean, for instance, that no animal exists apart from the particular animals, nor does any other of the elements present in formulae exist apart.

039ᵃ If, then, we view the matter from these standpoints, it is plain that no universal attribute is a substance, and this is plain also from the fact that no common predicate indicates a 'this', but rather a 'such'. If not, many difficulties follow and especially the 'third man'.

The conclusion is evident also from the following consideration – that a substance cannot consist of substances present in it actually (for things that are thus actually two are never actually one, though if they are *potentially* two, they can be one, e.g. the double line consists of two halves – potentially; for the *actualization* of the halves divides them from one another; therefore if the substance is one, it will not consist of substances present in it); and according to the argument which Democritus states rightly; he says one thing cannot come from two nor two from one; for he identifies his indivisible magnitudes with substances. It is clear therefore that the same will hold good of number, if number is a synthesis of units, as is said by some; for two is either not one, or there is no unit present in it actually.

The consequence of this view involves a difficulty. If no substance can consist of universals because a universal indicates a 'such', not a 'this', and if no composite substance can be composed of actual substances, every substance would be incomposite, so that there would not even be a formula of any substance. But it is thought by all and has been previously stated that it is either only, or primarily, substance that can be defined; yet now it seems that not even substance can. There cannot, then, be a definition of anything; or rather in a sense there can be, and in a sense there cannot. And what we say will be plainer from what follows.

14 It is clear also from these very facts what consequences confront those who say the Ideas are substances and can exist apart, and at the same time make the Form consist of the genus and the differentiae. For if the Forms exist and animal is present in man and horse, it is either one and the same in number, or different. (In formula it is clearly one; for he who states the formula unfolds the same formula in either case.) If there is a man-in-himself who is a 'this' and exists apart, the parts of which he consists, e.g. animal and two-footed, must indicate a 'this' and be things existing apart and substances; therefore animal too must be of this sort.

Now if animal, which is in the horse and in man, 1039ᵇ is one and the same, as you are one and the same with yourself, how will the one in things that exist apart be one, and how will this animal escape being divided even from itself?

Further, if it is to share in two-footed and many-footed, an impossible conclusion follows; for contrary attributes will belong at the same time to it although it is one and a this. If it does not, what is the relation implied when one says the animal is two-footed or has feet? But perhaps these are put together and are in contact, or are mixed. Yet all these are absurd.

But suppose the Form to be different in each species. Then there will be practically an infinite number of things whose *substance* is animal; for it is not by accident that man has animal for one of its elements. Further, animal-in-itself will be many. For the animal in each species will be the substance of the species; for it is not dependent on anything else; if it were, that other would be an element in man, i.e. would be the genus of man. And further all the elements of which man is composed will be Ideas. Now nothing can be the Idea of one thing and the substance of another; this is impossible. Each, then, of the Ideas present in the species of animals will be the ideal animal. Further, from what will these Ideas be derived; how will they be derived from the ideal animal? Or how can an Idea of animal whose essence is simply animal exist apart from the ideal animal? Further, in the case of sensible things both these consequences and others still more absurd follow. If, then, these consequences are impossible, clearly there are not Forms of sensible things in the sense in which some maintain their existence.

15 Since substance is of two kinds, the concrete thing and the formula (I mean that one kind of substance is the formula taken with the matter, while another kind is the formula in its generality), substances in the former sense are capable of destruction (for they are capable also of generation), but there is no destruction of the formula in the sense that it is ever in course of being destroyed; for there is no generation of it (the being of house is not generated, but only the being of *this* house), but without generation and destruction formulae are and are not; for it has been shown that no one produces nor makes these. For this reason, also, there is neither definition nor demonstration of sensible individual substances, because they have matter whose nature is such that they are capable both of being and of not being; for which reason all the individual instances of them are destructible.

If then demonstration is of necessary truths and definition involves knowledge, and if, just as knowledge cannot be sometimes knowledge and sometimes ignorance, but the state which varies thus is opinion, so too demonstration and definition cannot vary thus, but it is opinion that deals with that which can be otherwise than as it is, clearly there can neither be definition nor demonstration of sensible individuals. For perishing things are obscure to those who have knowledge of them, when they have passed from our perception; and though the formulae remain in the soul unchanged, there will no longer be either definition or demonstration. Therefore when one of those who aim at definition defines any individual, he must recognize that his definition may always be overthrown; for it is not possible to define such things.

Nor is it possible to define any Idea. For the Idea is, as its supporters say, an individual, and can exist apart; and the formula must consist of words; and he who defines must not invent a word (for it would be unknown), but the established words are common to each of a number of things; these then must apply to something besides the thing defined; e.g. if one were defining you, he would say 'an animal which is lean' or 'white', or something else which will apply also to some one other than you. If anyone were to say that perhaps all the attributes taken apart may belong to many subjects, but together they belong only to this one, we must reply firstly that they belong also to both the elements, e.g. two-footed animal belongs to animal and to the two-footed. And where the elements are eternal this is even necessary, since the elements are prior to and parts of the compound; what is more, they can also exist apart, if 'man' can exist apart. For either neither or both can. If, then, neither can, the genus will not exist apart from the species; but if it does, the differentia will also. Secondly, we must reply that they are prior in being; and things which are prior to others are not destroyed when the others are.

Again, if the Ideas consist of Ideas (as they must, since elements are simpler than the compound), it will be further necessary that the elements of which the Idea consists, e.g. animal and two-footed, should be predicated of many subjects. If not, how will they be known? For there will then be an Idea which cannot be predicated of more subjects than one. But this is not thought

1040

possible – every Idea is thought to be capable of being shared.

As has been said, then, people do not realize that it is impossible to define in the case of eternal things, especially those which are unique, like the sun or the moon. For they err not only by adding attributes after whose removal the sun would still exist, e.g. 'going round the earth' or 'night-hidden' (for from their view it follows that if it stands still or is visible, it will no longer be the sun; but it is strange if this is so; for the 'sun' means a certain *substance*); but also by the mention of attributes which can belong to another subject; e.g. if another thing with the stated attributes comes into existence, clearly it will be a sun; the formula therefore is general. But the sun was supposed to be an individual, like Cleon or Socrates. Why does not one of the supporters of the Ideas produce a definition of an Idea? It would become clear, if they tried, that what has now been said is true.

16 Evidently even of the things that are thought to be substances, most are only potentialities, – e.g. the parts of animals (for none of them exists separately; and when they *are* separated, then they too exist, all of them, merely as matter) and earth and fire and air; for none of them is one, but they are like a heap before it is fused by heat and some one thing is made out of the bits. One might suppose especially that the parts of living things and the corresponding parts of the soul are both, i.e. exist both actually and potentially, because they have sources of movement in something in their joints; for which reason some animals live when divided. Yet all the parts must exist only potentially, when they are one and continuous by nature, – not by force or even by growing together, for such a phenomenon is an abnormality.

Since the term 'unity' is used like the term 'being', and the substance of that which is one is one, and things whose substance is numerically one are numerically one, evidently neither unity nor being can be the substance of things, just as being an element or a principle cannot be the substance, but we seek *what* the principle is, that we may refer the thing to something more intelligible. Now of these things being and unity are more substantial than principle or element or cause, but not even the former are substance, since

in general nothing that is common is substance; for substance does not belong to anything but to itself and to that which has it, of which it is the substance. Further, that which is one cannot be in many things at the same time, but that which is common is present in many things at the same time; so that clearly no universal exists apart from the individuals.

But those who say the Forms exist, in one respect are right, in saying the Forms exist apart, if they are substances; but in another respect they are not right, because they say the one *in* many is a Form. The reason for their doing this is that they cannot say what are the substances of this sort, the imperishable substances which exist apart from the individual and sensible substances. They make them, then, the same in kind as the perishable things (for this kind of substance we know) – man himself and the horse itself, adding to the sensible things the word 'itself'. Yet even if we had not seen the stars, none the less, I suppose, would there be eternal substances besides those which we knew; so that now also if we do not know what eternal substances there are, yet it is doubtless necessary that some should exist. Clearly, then, no universal term is the name of a substance, and no substance is composed of substances.

17 We should say what, and what sort of thing, substance is, taking another starting-point; for perhaps from this we shall get a clear view also of that substance which exists apart from sensible substances. Since, then, substance is a principle and a cause, let us attack it from this standpoint. The 'why' is always sought in this form – 'why does one thing attach to another?' For to inquire why the musical man is a musical man, is either to inquire – as we have said – why the man is musical, or it is something else. Now 'why a thing is itself' is doubtless a meaningless inquiry; for the fact or the existence of the thing must already be evident (e.g. that the moon is eclipsed), but the fact that a thing is itself is the single formula and the single cause to all such questions as why the man is man, or the musical musical, unless one were to say that each thing is inseparable from itself; and its being one just meant this. This, however, is common to all things and is a short and easy way with the question. But we *can* inquire why man is an animal of such and such a nature. Here, then, we are evidently not inquiring why he who is a man is a man. We are inquiring, then, why something is predicable of something; that it is predicable must be clear; for if not, the inquiry is an inquiry into nothing. E.g. why does it thunder? – why is sound produced in the clouds? Thus the inquiry is about the predication of one thing of another. And why are certain things, i.e. stones and bricks, a house? Plainly we are seeking the cause. And this is the essence (to speak abstractly), which in some cases is that for the sake of which, e.g. perhaps in the case of a house or a bed, and in some cases is the first mover; for this also is a cause. But while the efficient cause is sought in the case of genesis and destruction, the final cause is sought in the case of being also.

The object of the inquiry is most overlooked where one term is not expressly predicated of 1041ᵇ another (e.g. when we inquire why man is), because we do not distinguish and do not say definitely 'why do these parts form this whole?' But we must distinguish the elements before we begin to inquire; if not, it is not clear whether the inquiry is significant or unmeaning. Since we must know the existence of the thing and it must be given, clearly the question is *why* the matter is some individual thing, e.g. why are these materials a house? Because that which was the essence of a house is present. And why is this individual thing, or this body in this state, a man? Therefore what we seek is the cause, i.e. the form, by reason of which the matter is some definite thing; and this is the substance of the thing. Evidently, then, in the case of simple things no inquiry nor teaching is possible; but we must inquire into them in a different way.

As regards that which is compounded out of something so that the whole is one – not like a heap, however, but like a syllable, – the syllable is not its elements, *ba* is not the same as *b* and *a*, nor is flesh fire and earth; for when they are dissolved the wholes, i.e. the flesh and the syllable, no longer exist, but the elements of the syllable exist, and so do fire and earth. The syllable, then, is something – not only its elements (the vowel and the consonant) but also something else; and the flesh is not only fire and earth or the hot and the cold, but also something else. Since, then, that something must be either an element or composed of elements, if it is an element the same argument will again apply; for flesh will consist of this and fire and earth and something still

further, so that the process will go on to infinity; while if it is a compound, clearly it will be a compound not of one but of many (or else it will itself be that one), so that again in this case we can use the same argument as in the case of flesh or of the syllable. But it would seem that this is something, and not an element, and that it is the cause which makes *this* thing flesh and *that* a syllable. And similarly in all other cases. And this is the substance of each thing; for this is the primary cause of its being; and since, while some things are not substances, as many as are substances are formed naturally and by nature, their substance would seem to be this nature, which is not an element but a principle. An *element* is that into which a thing is divided and which is present in it as matter, e.g. *a* and *b* are the elements of the syllable.

Book VIII (H)

1 We must draw our conclusions from what has 1042 been said, and sum up our results, and put the finishing touch to our inquiry. We have said that the causes, principles, and elements of substances are the object of our search. And some substances are recognized by all thinkers, but some have been advocated by particular schools. Those generally recognized are the natural substances, i.e. fire, earth, water, air, etc., the simple bodies; secondly, plants and their parts, and animals and the parts of animals; and finally the heavens and the parts of the heavens. Some particular schools say that Forms and the objects of mathematics are substances. And it follows from our arguments that there are other substances, the essence and the substratum. Again, in another way the genus seems more substantial than the species, and the universal than the particulars. And with the universal and the genus the Ideas are connected; it is in virtue of the same argument that they are thought to be substances. And since the essence is substance, and the definition is formula of the essence, for this reason we have discussed definition and essential predication. Since the definition is a formula, and a formula has parts, we had to consider with respect to the notion of part, what are parts of the substance and what are not, and whether the same things are also parts of the definition. Further, then, neither the universal nor the genus is a substance; we must inquire later into the Ideas and the objects of mathematics; for some say these exist apart from sensible substances.

But now let us resume the discussion of the generally recognized substances. These are the sensible substances, and sensible substances all have matter. The substratum is substance, and this is in one sense the matter (and by matter I mean that which, not being a 'this' actually, is potentially a 'this'), and in another sense the formula or form (which being a 'this' can be separately formulated), and thirdly the complex of matter and form, which alone is generated and destroyed, and is, without qualification, capable of separate existence; for of substances in the sense of formulae some are separable and some are not.

But clearly matter also is substance;[1] for in all the opposite changes that occur there is something which underlies the changes, e.g. in respect of place that which is now here and again elsewhere, and in respect of increase that which is now of one 042^b size and again less or greater, and in respect of alteration that which is now healthy and again diseased; and similarly in respect of substance there is something that is now being generated and again being destroyed, and now underlies the process as a 'this' and again underlies it as the privation of positive character. In this last change the others are involved. But in either one or two of the others this is not involved; for it is not necessary if a thing has matter for change of place that it should also have matter for generation and destruction.

Book Λ (XII)

1 The subject of our inquiry is substance; for the principles and the causes we are seeking are those of substances. For if the universe is of the nature of a whole, substance is its first part; and if it coheres merely by virtue of serial succession, on this view also substance is first, and is succeeded by quality, and then by quantity. At the same time these latter are not even being in the full sense, but are qualities and movements of it – or else even the not-white and the not-straight would be being; at least we say even these *are*, e. g. 'there is a not-white'. Further, none of the categories other than substance can exist apart. And the early philosophers also in practice testify to the primacy

of substance; for it was of substance that they sought the principles and elements and causes. The thinkers of the present day tend to rank universals as substances (for genera are universals, and these they tend to describe as principles and substances, owing to the abstract nature of their inquiry); but the thinkers of old ranked particular things as substances, e. g. fire and earth, not what is common to both, body.

There are three kinds of substance – one that is sensible (of which one subdivision is eternal and another is perishable; the latter is recognized by all men, and includes e. g. plants and animals), of which we must grasp the elements, whether one or many; and another that is immovable, and this certain thinkers assert to be capable of existing apart, some dividing it into two, others identifying the Forms and the objects of mathematics, and others positing, of these two, only the objects of mathematics. The former two kinds of substance are the subject of physics (for they imply move- 1069^b ment); but the third kind belongs to another science, if there is no principle common to it and to the other kinds.

2 Sensible substance is changeable. Now if change proceeds from opposites or from intermediates, and not from all opposites (for the voice is not-white [but it does not therefore change to white]), but from the contrary, there must be something underlying which changes into the contrary state; for the *contraries* do not change. Further, something persists, but the contrary does not persist; there is, then, some third thing besides the contraries, viz. the matter. Now since changes are of four kinds – either in respect of the 'what' or of the quality or of the quantity or of the place, and change in respect of 'thisness' is simple generation and destruction, and change in quantity is increase and diminution, and change in respect of an affection is alteration, and change of place is motion, changes will be from given states into those contrary to them in these several respects. The matter, then, which changes must be capable of both states. And since that which 'is' has two senses, we must say that everything changes from that which is potentially to that which is actually, e. g. from potentially white to actually white, and similarly in the case of increase and diminution. Therefore not only can a thing come to be, incidentally, out of that which is not, but also all things come to be out of that which is, but is potentially, and is not actually. And this is the 'One' of Anaxagoras; for instead of 'all things were together' – and the 'Mixture' of Empedocles and Anaximander and the account given by Democritus – it is better to say 'all things were together potentially but not actually'. Therefore these thinkers seem to have had some notion of matter. Now all things that change have matter, but different matter; and of eternal things those which are not generable but are movable in space have matter – not matter for generation, however, but for motion from one place to another.

One might raise the question from what sort of non-being generation proceeds; for 'non-being' has three senses. If, then, one form of non-being exists potentially, still it is not by virtue of a potentiality for any and every thing, but different things come from different things; nor is it satisfactory to say that 'all things were together'; for they differ in their matter, since otherwise why did an infinity of things come to be, and not one thing? For 'reason' is one, so that if matter also were one, that must have come to be in actuality which the matter was in potency. The causes and the principles, then, are three, two being the pair of contraries of which one is definition and form and the other is privation, and the third being the matter.

3 Note, next, that neither the matter nor the form comes to be – and I mean the last matter and form. For everything that changes is something and is changed by something and into something. 1070ᵃ That by which it is changed is the immediate mover; that which is changed, the matter; that into which it is changed, the form. The process, then, will go on to infinity, if not only the bronze comes to be round but also the round or the bronze comes to be; therefore there must be a stop.

Note, next, that each substance comes into being out of something that shares its name. (Natural objects and other things both rank as substances.) For things come into being either by art or by nature or by luck or by spontaneity. Now art is a principle of movement in something other than the thing moved, nature is a principle in the thing itself (for man begets man), and the other causes are privations of these two.

There are three kinds of substance – the matter, which is a 'this' in appearance (for all things that are characterized by contact and not by organic unity are matter and substratum, e. g. fire, flesh, head; for these are all matter, and the last matter is the matter of that which is in the full sense substance); the nature, which is a 'this' or positive state towards which movement takes place; and again, thirdly, the particular substance which is composed of these two, e. g. Socrates or Callias. Now in some cases the 'this' does not exist apart from the composite substance, e. g. the form of house does not so exist, unless the art of building exists apart (nor is there generation and destruction of these forms, but it is in another way that the house apart from its matter, and health, and all ideals of art, exist and do not exist); but if the 'this' exists apart from the concrete thing, it is only in the case of natural objects. And so Plato was not far wrong when he said that there are as many Forms as there are kinds of natural object (if there *are* Forms distinct from the things of this earth). The moving causes exist as things preceding the effects, but causes in the sense of definitions are simultaneous with their effects. For when a man is healthy, then health also exists; and the shape of a bronze sphere exists at the same time as the bronze sphere. (But we must examine whether any form also survives afterwards. For in some cases there is nothing to prevent this; e.g. the soul may be of this sort – not all soul but the reason; for presumably it is impossible that *all* soul should survive.) Evidently then there is no necessity, on this ground at least, for the existence of the Ideas. For man is begotten by man, a given man by an individual father; and similarly in the arts; for the medical art is the formal cause of health.

4 The causes and the principles of different things are in a sense different, but in a sense, if one speaks universally and analogically, they are the same for all. For one might raise the question whether the principles and elements are different or the same for substances and for relative terms, and similarly in the case of each of the categories. But it would be paradoxical if they were the same for all. For then from the same elements will proceed relative terms and substances. What then will this common element be? For (1) 1070ᵇ (a) there is nothing common to and distinct from substance and the other categories, viz. those which are predicated; but an element is prior to the things of which it is an element. But again (*b*) substance is not an element in relative terms, nor is any of these an element in substance. Further, (2) how can all things have the same elements? For none of the elements can be the same as that which is composed of elements, e. g. *b* or *a* cannot be the same as *ba*. (None, therefore, of the intelligibles, e. g. being or unity, is an element; for these are predicable of each of the compounds as well.) None of the elements, then, will be either a substance or a relative term; but it must be one or other. All things, then, have not the same elements.

Or, as we are wont to put it, in a sense they have and in a sense they have not; e. g. perhaps the elements of perceptible bodies are, as *form*, the hot, and in another sense the cold, which is the *privation*; and, as *matter*, that which directly and of itself potentially has these attributes; and substances comprise both these and the things composed of these, of which these are the principles, or any unity which is produced out of the hot and the cold, e.g. flesh or bone; for the product must be different from the elements. These things then have the same elements and principles (though specifically different things have specifically different elements); but *all* things have not the same elements in this sense, but only analogically; i. e. one might say that there are three principles – the form, the privation, and the matter. But each of these is different for each class; e.g. in colour they are white, black, and surface, and in day and night they are light, darkness, and air.

Since not only the elements present in a thing are causes, but also something external, i. e. the moving cause, clearly while 'principle' and 'element' are different both are causes, and 'principle' is divided into these two kinds and that which acts as producing movement or rest is a principle and a substance. Therefore analogically there are three elements, and four causes and principles; but the elements are different in different things, and the proximate moving cause is different for different things. Health, disease, body; the moving cause is the medical art. Form, disorder of a particular kind, bricks; the moving cause is the building art. And since the moving cause in the case of natural things is – for man, for instance, man, and in the products of thought the form or its contrary, there will be in a sense three causes, while in a sense there are four. For the medical art is in some sense health, and the building art is the form of the house, and man begets man;

further, besides these there is that which as first of all things moves all things.

5 Some things can exist apart and some cannot, and it is the former that are substances. And therefore all things have the same causes, because, 1071ᵃ without substances, modifications and movements do not exist. Further, these causes will probably be soul and body, or reason and desire and body.

And in yet another way, analogically identical things are principles, i. e. actuality and potency; but these also are not only different for different things but also apply in different ways to them. For in some cases the same thing exists at one time actually and at another potentially, e. g. wine or flesh or man does so. (And these two fall under the above-named causes. For the form exists actually, if it can exist apart, and so does the complex of form and matter, and the privation, e. g. darkness or disease; but the matter exists potentially; for this is that which can become qualified either by the form or by the privation.) But the distinction of actuality and potentiality applies in another way to cases where the matter of cause and of effect is not the same, in some of which cases the form is not the same but different; e.g. the cause of man is (1) the elements in man (viz. fire and earth as matter, and the peculiar form), and further (2) something else outside, i.e. the father, and (3) besides these the sun and its oblique course, which are neither matter nor form nor privation of man nor of the same species with him, but moving causes.

Further, one must observe that some causes can be expressed in universal terms, and some cannot. The proximate principles of all things are the 'this' which is proximate in actuality, and another which is proximate in potentiality. The universal causes, then, of which we spoke do not *exist*. For it is the individual that is the originative principle of the individuals. For while man is the originative principle of man universally, there *is* no universal man, but Peleus is the originative principle of Achilles, and your father of you, and this particular *b* of this particular *ba*, though *b* in general is the originative principle of *ba* taken without qualification.

Further, if the causes of substances are the causes of all things, yet different things have different causes and elements, as was said; the causes of things that are not in the same class,

e. g. of colours and sounds, of substances and quantities, are different except in an analogical sense; and those of things in the same species are different, not in species, but in the sense that the causes of different individuals are different, your matter and form and moving cause being different from mine, while in their universal definition they are the same. And if we inquire what are the principles or elements of substances and relations and qualities – whether they are the same or different – clearly when the names of the causes are used in several senses the causes of each are the same, but when the senses are distinguished the causes are not the same but different, except that in the following senses the causes of all are the same. They are (1) the same or analogous in this sense, that matter, form, privation, and the moving cause are common to all things; and (2) the causes of substances may be treated as causes of all things in this sense, that when substances are removed all things are removed; further, (3) that which is first in respect of complete reality is the cause of all things. But in another sense there are different first causes, viz. all the contraries which are neither generic nor ambiguous terms; and, further, the matters of different things are different. We have stated, then, what are the principles of sensible things and how many they are, and in what sense they are the same and in what sense different.

1071ᵇ

6 Since there were* three kinds of substance, two of them physical and one unmovable, regarding the latter we must assert that it is necessary that there should be an eternal unmovable substance. For substances are the first of existing things, and if they are all destructible, all things are destructible. But it is impossible that movement should either have come into being or cease to be (for it must always have existed), or that time should. For there could not be a before and an after if time did not exist. Movement also is continuous, then, in the sense in which time is; for time is either the same thing as movement or an attribute of movement. And there is no continuous movement except movement in place, and of this only that which is circular is continuous.

But if there is something which is capable of moving things or acting on them, but is not actually doing so, there will not necessarily be movement; for that which has a potency need not exercise it. Nothing, then, is gained even if we suppose eternal substances, as the believers in the Forms do, unless there is to be in them some principle which can cause change; nay, even this is not enough, nor is another substance besides the Forms enough; for if it is not to *act*, there will be no movement. Further, even if it acts, this will not be enough, if its essence is potency; for there will not be *eternal* movement, since that which is potentially may possibly not be. There must, then, be such a principle, whose very essence is actuality. Further, then, these substances must be without matter; for they must be eternal, if *anything* is eternal. Therefore they must be actuality.

Yet there is a difficulty; for it is thought that everything that acts is able to act, but that not everything that is able to act acts, so that the potency is prior. But if this is so, nothing that is need be; for it is possible for all things to be capable of existing but not yet to exist.

Yet if we follow the theologians who generate the world from night, or the natural philosophers who say that 'all things were together', the same impossible result ensues. For how will there be movement, if there is no actually existing cause? Wood will surely not move itself – the carpenter's art must act on it; nor will the menstrual blood nor the earth set themselves in motion, but the seeds must act on the earth and the *semen* on the menstrual blood.

This is why some suppose eternal actuality – e. g. Leucippus and Plato;† for they say there is always movement. But why and what this movement is they do not say, nor, if the world moves in this way or that, do they tell us the cause of its doing so. Now nothing is moved at random, but there must always be something present to move it; e. g. as a matter of fact a thing moves in one way by nature, and in another by force or through the influence of reason or something else. (Further, what sort of movement is primary? This makes a vast difference.) But again for Plato, at least, it is not permissible to name here that which he sometimes supposes to be the 1072 source of movement – that which moves itself;‡

* Cf. 1069ᵃ 30.

† Cf. *Timaeus*, 30 A.
‡ Cf. *Timaeus*, 34 B.

for the soul is later, and coeval with the heavens, according to his account.* To suppose potency prior to actuality, then, is in a sense right, and in a sense not; and we have specified these senses.† That actuality is prior is testified by Anaxagoras (for his 'reason' is actuality) and by Empedocles in his doctrine of love and strife, and by those who say that there is always movement, e. g. Leucippus. Therefore chaos or night did not exist for an infinite time, but the same things have always existed (either passing through a cycle of changes or obeying some other law), since actuality is prior to potency. If, then, there is a constant cycle, something must always remain, acting in the same way. And if there is to be generation and destruction, there must be something else which is always acting in different ways. This must, then, act in one way in virtue of itself, and in another in virtue of something else – either of a third agent, therefore, or of the first. Now it must be in virtue of the first. For otherwise this again causes the motion both of the second agent and of the third. Therefore it is better to say 'the first'. For it was the cause of eternal uniformity; and something else is the cause of variety, and evidently both together are the cause of eternal variety. This, accordingly, is the character which the motions actually exhibit. What need then is there to seek for other principles?

7 Since (1) this is a possible account of the matter, and (2) if it were not true, the world would have proceeded out of night and 'all things together' and out of non-being, these difficulties may be taken as solved. There is, then, something which is always moved with an unceasing motion, which is motion in a circle; and this is plain not in theory only but in fact. Therefore the first heaven must be eternal. There is therefore also something which moves it. And since that which is moved and moves is intermediate, there is something which moves without being moved, being eternal, substance, and actuality. And the object of desire and the object of thought move in this way; they move without being moved. The primary objects of desire and of thought are the same. For the apparent good is the object of appetite, and the real good is the primary object

of rational wish. But desire is consequent on opinion rather than opinion on desire; for the thinking is the starting-point. And thought is moved by the object of thought, and one of the two columns of opposites is in itself the object of thought; and in this, substance is first, and in substance, that which is simple and exists actually. (The one and the simple are not the same; for 'one' means a measure, but 'simple' means that the thing itself has a certain nature.) But the beautiful, also, and that which is in itself desirable are in the same column; and the first in any class is always best, or analogous to the best.

That a final cause may exist among unchangeable entities is shown by the distinction of its meanings. For the final cause is (*a*) some being for whose good an action is done, and (*b*) something at which the action aims; and of these the latter exists among unchangeable entities though the former does not. The final cause, then, produces motion as being loved, but all other things move by being moved. 1072^b

Now if something is moved it is capable of being otherwise than as it is. Therefore if its actuality is the primary form of spatial motion, then in so far as it is subject to change, in *this* respect it is capable of being otherwise – in place, even if not in substance. But since there is something which moves while itself unmoved, existing actually, this can in no way be otherwise than as it is. For motion in space is the first of the kinds of change, and motion in a circle the first kind of spatial motion; and this the first mover *produces*. The first mover, then, exists of necessity; and in so far as it exists by necessity, its mode of being is good, and it is in this sense a first principle. For the necessary has all these senses – that which is necessary perforce because it is contrary to the natural impulse, that without which the good is impossible, and that which cannot be otherwise but can exist only in a single way.

On such a principle, then, depend the heavens and the world of nature. And it is a life such as the best which we enjoy, and enjoy for but a short time (for it is ever in this state, which we cannot be), since its actuality is also pleasure. (And for this reason are waking, perception, and thinking most pleasant, and hopes and memories are so on account of these.) And thinking in itself deals with that which is best in itself, and that which is thinking in the fullest sense with that which is best in the fullest sense. And thought thinks on itself

---

* Cf. *Phaedrus*, 245 c; *Laws*, 894 E.
† Cf. 1071^b 22–26.

because it shares the nature of the object of thought; for it becomes an object of thought in coming into contact with and thinking its objects, so that thought and object of thought are the same. For that which is *capable* of receiving the object of thought, i. e. the essence, is thought. But it is *active* when it *possesses* this object. Therefore the possession rather than the receptivity is the divine element which thought seems to contain, and the act of contemplation is what is most pleasant and best. If, then, God is always in that good state in which we sometimes are, this compels our wonder; and if in a better this compels it yet more. And God *is* in a better state. And life also belongs to God; for the actuality of thought is life, and God is that actuality; and God's self-dependent actuality is life most good and eternal. We say therefore that God is a living being, eternal, most good, so that life and duration continuous and eternal belong to God; for this *is* God.

Those who suppose, as the Pythagoreans and Speusippus do, that supreme beauty and goodness are not present in the beginning, because the beginnings both of plants and of animals are *causes*, but beauty and completeness are in the *effects* of these, are wrong in their opinion. For the seed comes from other individuals which are prior and complete, and the first thing is not seed but the complete being; e. g. we must say that 1073ª before the seed there is a man – not the man produced from the seed, but another from whom the seed comes.

It is clear then from what has been said that there is a substance which is eternal and unmovable and separate from sensible things. It has been shown also that this substance cannot have any magnitude but is without parts and indivisible (for it produces movement through infinite time, but nothing finite has infinite power; and, while every magnitude is either infinite or finite, it cannot, for the above reason, have finite magnitude, and it cannot have infinite magnitude because there is no infinite magnitude at all). But it has also been shown that it is impassive and unalterable; for all the other changes are posterior to change of place.

8 It is clear, then, why these things are as they are. But we must not ignore the question whether we have to suppose one such substance or more than one, and if the latter, how many; we must

also mention, regarding the opinions expressed by others, that they have said nothing about the number of the substances that can even be clearly stated. For the theory of Ideas has no special discussion of the subject; for those who speak of Ideas say the Ideas are numbers, and they speak of numbers now as unlimited, now as limited by the number 10; but as for the reason why there should be just so many numbers, nothing is said with any demonstrative exactness. We however must discuss the subject, starting from the presuppositions and distinctions we have mentioned. The first principle or primary being is not movable either in itself or accidentally, but produces the primary eternal and single movement. But since that which is moved must be moved by something, and the first mover must be in itself unmovable, and eternal movement must be produced by something eternal and a single movement by a single thing, and since we see that besides the simple spatial movement of the universe, which we say the first and unmovable substance produces, there are other spatial movements – those of the planets – which are eternal (for a body which moves in a circle is eternal and unresting; we have proved these points in the physical treatises), each of *these* movements also must be caused by a substance both unmovable in itself and eternal. For the nature of the stars is eternal just because it is a certain kind of substance, and the mover is eternal and prior to the moved, and that which is prior to a substance must be a substance. Evidently, then, there must be substances which are of the same number as the movements of the stars, and in their nature eternal, and in themselves unmovable, and without magnitude, for the reason before mentioned.

That the movers are substances, then, and 1073 that one of these is first and another second according to the same order as the movements of the stars, is evident. But in the number of the movements we reach a problem which must be treated from the standpoint of that one of the mathematical sciences which is most akin to philosophy – viz. of astronomy; for this science speculates about substance which is perceptible but eternal, but the other mathematical sciences, i. e. arithmetic and geometry, treat of no substance. That the movements are more numerous than the bodies that are moved is evident to those who have given even moderate attention to the matter; for each of the planets has more than one movement.

But as to the actual number of these movements, we now – to give some notion of the subject – quote what some of the mathematicians say, that our thought may have some definite number to grasp; but, for the rest, we must partly investigate for ourselves, partly learn from other investigators, and if those who study this subject form an opinion contrary to what we have now stated, we must esteem both parties indeed, but follow the more accurate.

Eudoxus supposed that the motion of the sun or of the moon involves, in either case, three spheres, of which the first is the sphere of the fixed stars, and the second moves in the circle which runs along the middle of the zodiac, and the third in the circle which is inclined across the breadth of the zodiac; but the circle in which the moon moves is inclined at a greater angle than that in which the sun moves. And the motion of the planets involves, in each case, four spheres, and of these also the first and second are the same as the first two mentioned above (for the sphere of the fixed stars is that which moves all the other spheres, and that which is placed beneath this and has its movement in the circle which bisects the zodiac is common to all), but the *poles* of the third sphere of each planet are in the circle which bisects the zodiac, and the motion of the fourth sphere is in the circle which is inclined at an angle to the equator of the third sphere; and the poles of the third sphere are different for each of the other planets, but those of Venus and Mercury are the same.

Callippus made the position of the spheres the same as Eudoxus did, but while he assigned the same number as Eudoxus did to Jupiter and to Saturn, he thought two more spheres should be added to the sun and two to the moon, if one is to explain the observed facts; and one more to each of the other planets.

But it is necessary, if all the spheres combined are to explain the observed facts, that for each of the planets there should be other spheres (one fewer than those hitherto assigned) which counteract those already mentioned and bring back to the same position the outermost sphere of the star which in each case is situated below the star in question; for only thus can all the forces at work produce the observed motion of the planets. Since, then, the spheres involved in the movement of the planets themselves are – eight for Saturn and Jupiter and twenty-five for the others, and of

1074ª

these only those involved in the movement of the lowest-situated planet need not be counteracted, the spheres which counteract those of the outermost two planets will be six in number, and the spheres which counteract those of the next four planets will be sixteen; therefore the number of all the spheres – both those which move the planets and those which counteract these – will be fifty-five. And if one were not to add to the moon and to the sun the movements we mentioned, the whole set of spheres will be forty-seven in number.

Let this, then, be taken as the number of the spheres, so that the unmovable substances and principles also may probably be taken as just so many; the assertion of *necessity* must be left to more powerful thinkers. But if there can be no spatial movement which does not conduce to the moving of a star, and if further every being and every substance which is immune from change and in virtue of itself has attained to the best must be considered an end, there can be no other being apart from these we have named, but this must be the number of the substances. For if there are others, they will cause change as being a final cause of movement; but there cannot *be* other movements besides those mentioned. And it is reasonable to infer this from a consideration of the bodies that are moved; for if everything that moves is for the sake of that which is moved, and every movement belongs to something that is moved, no movement can be for the sake of itself or of another movement, but all the movements must be for the sake of the stars. For if there is to be a movement for the sake of a movement, this latter also will have to be for the sake of something else; so that since there cannot be an infinite regress, the end of every movement will be one of the divine bodies which move through the heaven.

(Evidently there is but one heaven. For if there are many heavens as there are many men, the moving principles, of which each heaven will have one, will be one in form but in *number* many. But all things that are many in number have matter; for one and the same definition, e. g. that of man, applies to many things, while Socrates is one. But the primary essence has not matter; for it is complete reality. So the unmovable first mover is one both in definition and in number; so too, therefore, is that which is moved always and continuously; therefore there is one heaven alone.)

1074^b   Our forefathers in the most remote ages have handed down to their posterity a tradition, in the form of a myth, that these bodies are gods and that the divine encloses the whole of nature. The rest of the tradition has been added later in mythical form with a view to the persuasion of the multitude and to its legal and utilitarian expediency; they say these gods are in the form of men or like some of the other animals, and they say other things consequent on and similar to these which we have mentioned. But if one were to separate the first point from these additions and take it alone – that they thought the first substances to be gods, one must regard this as an inspired utterance, and reflect that, while probably each art and each science has often been developed as far as possible and has again perished, these opinions, with others, have been preserved until the present like relics of the ancient treasure. Only thus far, then, is the opinion of our ancestors and of our earliest predecessors clear to us.

9 The nature of the divine thought involves certain problems; for while thought is held to be the most divine of things observed by us, the question how it must be situated in order to have that character involves difficulties. For if it thinks of nothing, what is there here of dignity? It is just like one who sleeps. And if it thinks, but this depends on something else, then (since that which is its substance is not the act of thinking, but a potency) it cannot be the best substance; for it is through thinking that its value belongs to it. Further, whether its substance is the faculty of thought or the act of thinking, what does it think of? Either of itself or of something else; and if of something else, either of the same thing always or of something different. Does it matter, then, or not, whether it thinks of the good or of any chance thing? Are there not some things about which it is incredible that it should think? Evidently, then, it thinks of that which is most divine and precious, and it does not change; for change would be change for the worse, and this would be already a movement. First, then, if 'thought' is not the act of thinking but a potency, it would be reasonable to suppose that the continuity of its thinking is wearisome to it. Secondly, there would evidently be something else more precious than thought, viz. that which is thought of. For both thinking and the act of thought will belong even to one who thinks of the worst thing in the world, so that if this ought to be avoided (and it ought, for there are even some things which it is better not to see than to see), the act of thinking cannot be the best of things. Therefore it must be of itself that the divine thought thinks (since it is the most excellent of things), and its thinking is a thinking on thinking.

But evidently knowledge and perception and opinion and understanding have always something else as their object, and themselves only by the way. Further, if thinking and being thought of are different, in respect of which does goodness belong to thought? For to *be* an act of thinking and to *be* an object of thought are not the same thing. We answer that in some cases the knowledge is the object. In the productive sciences it 1075 is the substance or essence of the object, matter omitted, and in the theoretical sciences the definition or the act of thinking is the object. Since, then, thought and the object of thought are not different in the case of things that have not matter, the divine thought and its object will be the same, i. e. the thinking will be one with the object of its thought.

A further question is left – whether the object of the divine thought is composite; for if it were, thought would change in passing from part to part of the whole. We answer that everything which has not matter is indivisible – as human thought, or rather the thought of composite beings, is in a certain period of time (for it does not possess the good at this moment or at that, but its best, being something *different* from it, is attained only in a whole period of time), so throughout eternity is the thought which has *itself* for its object.

10 We must consider also in which of two ways the nature of the universe contains the good and the highest good, whether as something separate and by itself, or as the order of the parts. Probably in both ways, as an army does; for its good is found both in its order and in its leader, and more in the latter; for he does not depend on the order but it depends on him. And all things are ordered together somehow, but not all alike – both fishes and fowls and plants; and the world is not such that one thing has nothing to do with another, but they are connected. For all are ordered together to one end, but it is as in a house, where the freemen are least at liberty to act at random, but all things or most things are already ordained for them, while the slaves and the animals do little for the common good, and for the most part live at random; for this is the sort of principle that constitutes the nature of each. I mean, for instance, that all must at least come to be dissolved into their elements, and there are other functions similarly in which all share for the good of the whole.

We must not fail to observe how many impossible or paradoxical results confront those who hold different views from our own, and what are the views of the subtler thinkers, and which views are attended by fewest difficulties. All make all things out of contraries. But neither 'all things' nor 'out of contraries' is right; nor do these thinkers tell us how all the things in which the contraries are present can be made out of the contraries; for contraries are not affected by one another. Now for us this difficulty is solved naturally by the fact that there is a third element. These thinkers however make one of the two contraries matter; this is done for instance by those who make the unequal matter for the equal, or the many matter for the one. But this also is refuted in the same way; for the one matter which underlies any pair of contraries is contrary to nothing. Further, all things, except the one, will, on the view we are criticizing, partake of evil; for the bad itself is one of the two elements. But the other school does not treat the good and the bad even as principles; yet in all things the good is in the highest degree a principle. The school we first mentioned is right in saying that it is a principle, but *how* the good is a principle they do not say – whether as end or as mover or as form.

1075ᵇ Empedocles also has a paradoxical view; for he identifies the good with love, but this is a principle both as mover (for it brings things together) and as matter (for it is part of the mixture). Now even if it happens that the same thing is a principle both as matter and as mover, still the being, at least, of the two is not the same. In which respect then is love a principle? It is paradoxical also that strife should be imperishable; the nature of his 'evil' is just strife.

Anaxagoras makes the good a motive principle; for his 'reason' moves things. But it moves them for an end, which must be something other than it, except according to *our* way of stating the case; for, on our view, the medical art is in a sense health. It is paradoxical also not to suppose a contrary to the good, i. e. to reason. But all who speak of the contraries make no use of the contraries, unless we bring their views into shape. And why some things are perishable and others imperishable, no one tells us; for they make all existing things out of the same principles. Further, some make existing things out of the non-existent; and others to avoid the necessity of this make all things one.

Further, why should there always be becoming, and what is the cause of becoming? – this no one tells us. And those who suppose two principles must suppose another, a superior principle, and so must those who believe in the Forms; for why did things come to participate, or why do they participate, in the Forms? And all other thinkers are confronted by the necessary consequence that there is something contrary to Wisdom, i.e. to the highest knowledge; but *we* are not. For there is nothing contrary to that which is primary; for all contraries have matter, and things that have matter exist only potentially; and the ignorance which is contrary to any knowledge leads to an object contrary to the object of the knowledge; but what is primary has no contrary.

Again, if besides sensible things no others exist, there will be no first principle, no order, no becoming, no heavenly bodies, but each principle will have a principle before it, as in the accounts of the theologians and all the natural philosophers. But if the Forms or the numbers are to exist, they will be causes of nothing; or if not that, at least not of movement. Further, how is extension, i. e. a *continuum*, to be produced out of unextended parts? For number will not, either as mover or as form, produce a *continuum*. But again there cannot be any *contrary* that is also essentially a productive or moving principle; or it would be possible not to be. Or at least its action would be posterior to its potency. The world, then, would not be eternal. But it is; one of these premisses, then, must be denied. And we have said how this must be done. Further, in virtue of what the numbers, or the soul and the body, or in general the form and the thing, are one – of this no one tells us anything; nor can any one tell, unless he says, as we do, that the mover makes them one. And those who say mathematical number is first and go on to generate one kind of substance after another and give different principles for each, make the substance of the universe a mere 1076ᵃ series of episodes (for one substance has no influence on another by its existence or non-existence), and they give us many governing principles; but the world refuses to be governed badly.

'The rule of many is not good; one ruler let there be.'

Note

1   This is hard to square with the earlier denial that matter is substance, e.g. in Book VII, Ch. 3. Critics will see, in this apparent inconsistency, an indication that no one concept of substance can do all the work to which Aristotle would like to put it.

5

(A)   Gotama (the Buddha), Sayings on "Conditioned Genesis"
(B)   *Lalitavistara*, XIII, 95–117
(C)   Nāgārjuna, *Madhyamaka-Kārikā*, Dedication and Chapter XXV

Introduction

In III.4, we saw the important place occupied in Aristotle's *Metaphysics* by causality, broadly construed. A similarly broad notion played an even more central part in a remarkably rich eastern metaphysical tradition, Buddhism – from the Buddha himself (Siddhatha Gotama, c. 563–c. 483 BCE) to the greatest of Buddhist philosophers, the south Indian monk Nāgārjuna (c. second to third century CE), and beyond.

Among the wider public, the best-known doctrines of the Buddha are those of the "Four Noble Truths," concerning the origin and elimination of "suffering," and the "Eightfold Path" ("right action," "right mindfulness," and so on), which details the means to the ending of "suffering."[1] But neither doctrine, widespread in Indian religion at large, was distinctive of the Buddha's thought in the way that two underlying doctrines of a more metaphysical character were. These were the theses of "conditioned genesis" (*paṭiccasamuppāda* in Pali; alternatively translated, *inter alia*, as "dependent arising" and "relative conditioning") and of "not-self" (*anatta*). What distinguishes Buddhism from other Indian schools is the insist-

(A) and (B) *From Buddhist Texts Through the Ages*, trans. and ed. E. Conze, Boston, MA: Shambhala, 1990, pp. 65–70, 91–4, 158–61 (some notes omitted). (C) *From* T. Stcherbatsky, *The Conception of Buddhist Nirvāṇa*, Delhi: Motilal Banarsidass, 1977, pp. 77, 81–4.

ence that it is through grasping these two theses that "suffering" may be ended and "liberation" from the everyday world (*saṃsāra*) achieved. "Who sees Conditioned Genesis," spoke the Buddha, "sees Dhamma [true doctrine]."

The two theses are closely related: it is because people and things are not self-subsistent, because everything is reciprocally conditioned in a circular chain,[2] that there are no "selves," in the sense of enduring, unchanging substances (mental or physical) underlying the changing phenomena we observe. (Compare the positions of Spinoza and Leibniz in III.13 and 15 below.) Hence, for example, we must reject the Vedantin view (see III.7 below) that people have "true selves" that are identical with absolute reality, Brahman.

The two theses are also intimately connected with other famous Buddhist concepts, notably those of "Nirvāṇa" and "emptiness" (*śūnyatā*). Nirvāṇa, the goal of the Eightfold Path, is "the stopping of [conditioned] becoming," of the cycle of birth-and-death, and the world is "empty" because everything is "empty of self," a "no-thing" if "thing" is understood as "substance."

The Buddha regarded abstract metaphysical speculation about reality as "unprofitable," so that it was left to later thinkers to develop the implications of his remarks on "conditioned genesis" and related notions into a systematic position. Early Theravada Buddhists, for example, tended towards a "realist" interpretation of things, but with an insistence that these are analyzable into the constituents or "atoms" on which they depend.

By contrast, later Buddhists of the "mind only" school understood the Buddha's account of the chain of dependence to imply that reality is an interconnected process of mental events. In one text we have selected, the *Lalitavistara*, one discerns the "atomist" approach, but with a pronounced tendency as well to regard a world of merely conditioned things as a "mock show."[3]

Perhaps the most interesting and radical interpretation of the Buddha's sayings was that of Nāgārjuna, the main representative of the Mahayana school known as Madhyamaka ("middle way").[4] (Nāgārjuna's equally radical views on knowledge may be found in II.5(B) of this volume.) He is often described as a "nihilist" – unsurprisingly, perhaps, when one reads the "Dedication" below, which seems to deny the existence of anything whatever. But his position is a good deal more subtle. Nāgārjuna's insight was that, with "selves" or substances rejected, it is hard to see what sense to make of causality and conditioning, in which case we cannot rest content with a view of reality as a causally conditioned whole.

This does not mean, however, that we can regard the familiar world as an illusion, as nonexistent. For one thing, that would imply a contrast with some true world, of Nirvāṇa perhaps: but postulating such an "other world" is to remain in the grip of the substantialist idea of self. Nirvāṇa is not any kind of entity, but rather the familiar world considered in abstraction from all causal concepts (Ch. 25, Verse IX). As such, it is a "limit" to thought, about which nothing informative can be said. For another thing, dismissing the world as illusory or non-existent would wrongly assume that words like "illusion" and "exist," which have a use within the everyday world, can be used to talk about that world as a whole. For Nāgārjuna, as for Wittgenstein in his *Tractatus Logico-Philosophicus* (1922), the world as a whole is not a mere nothing, but we must greet it

with silence, with "the cessation of all thought." Therein, for the Buddhist, lies "bliss."

Notes

1 Useful introductory accounts of the Buddha's thought are W. Rahula, *What the Buddha Taught*, New York: Grove, 1962; and P. Harvey, *An Introduction to Buddhism*, Cambridge: Cambridge University Press, 1990.

2 As in the extract from the *Vinaya-piṭaka* below, "conditioned genesis" is often explained in terms of a 12-link chain of mutually dependent factors (consciousness, mind-and-body, craving, etc.). The general point, though, is the one stated in the previous extract: "If this is that comes to be; from the arising of this that arises."

3 This work, of uncertain date, is, in the main, an account of the Buddha's life and the primary inspiration, incidentally, for Sir Edwin Arnold's long poem, *The Light of Asia*. Commentators vary on where to "place" it philosophically, marking as it does a relatively early work with anticipations of later Mahayana themes.

4 It is the "middle school" since it attempts to steer between robust assertion of the world's reality and nihilistic denial of this. Inspiration was sought from such remarks of the Buddha as: "'Everything exists,' this is one extreme; 'Nothing exists,' this is the other extreme. Avoiding both extremes the [Buddha] teaches a doctrine of the middle" (*Samyutta Nikāya*, 2.12.15). On Nāgārjuna, see P. Williams, *Mahāyāna Buddhism*, 2nd edition, London: Routledge, 2008, and K. K. Inada, *Nāgārjuna*, Tokyo: Hokuseido, 1970, which offers a more scholarly, but less accessible, translation of the *Madhyamaka-Kārikā* than the one from which we have selected.

(A)   Gotama, Sayings on "Conditioned Genesis"

Who sees Conditioned Genesis sees Dhamma [true doctrine]; who sees Dhamma sees Conditioned Genesis.

Majjhima-nikāya I, 190–91

This body, monks, is not yours, nor does it belong to others. It should be regarded (as the product of) former karma,[1] effected through what has been willed and felt. In regard to it, the instructed disciple of the Ariyans well and wisely reflects on Conditioned Genesis itself:[2] If this is that comes to be; from the arising of this that arises; if this is not that does not come to be; from the stopping of this that is stopped. That is to say: [. . .]

Samyutta-nikāya II, 64–65

Conditioned by ignorance are the karma-formations;* conditioned by the karma-formations is consciousness; conditioned by consciousness is mind-and-body; conditioned by mind-and-body are the six sense-fields; conditioned by the six sense-fields is impression; conditioned by impression is feeling; conditioned by feeling is craving; conditioned by craving is grasping; conditioned by grasping is becoming; conditioned by becoming is birth; conditioned by birth there come into being ageing and dying, grief, sorrow, suffering, lamentation and despair. Thus is the origin of this whole mass of suffering.

But from the stopping of ignorance is the stopping of the karma-formations; from the stopping of the karma-formations is the stopping of consciousness; from the stopping of consciousness is the stopping of mind-and-body; from the stopping of mind-and-body is the stopping of the six sense-fields; from the stopping of the six sense-fields is the stopping of impression; from the stopping of impression is the stopping of feeling; from the stopping of feeling is the stopping of craving; from the stopping of craving is the stopping of grasping; from the stopping of grasping is the stopping of becoming; from the stopping of becoming is the stopping of birth; from the stopping of birth, ageing and dying, grief, sorrow, suffering, lamentation and despair are stopped. Thus is the stopping of this whole mass of suffering.

Vinaya-piṭaka I, 1

From the arising of ignorance is the arising of the karma-formations; from the stopping of ignorance is the stopping of the karma-formations. This ariyan[2] eightfold Way is itself the course leading to the stopping of the karma-formations, that is to say: right view, right thought, right speech, right action, right mode of livelihood, right endeavour, right mindfulness, right concentration.

When an ariyan disciple comprehends 'condition' thus, its arising, its stopping and the course leading to its stopping thus, he is called an ariyan disciple who is possessed of right view, of vision, one who has come into this true Dhamma, who sees this true Dhamma, who is endowed with the knowledge and lore of a learner, who has attained the stream of Dhamma, who is an Ariyan of penetrating wisdom, and who stands knocking at the door of the Deathless.

Samyutta-nikāya II, 43

And what is ageing and dying? Whatever for this or that class of beings is ageing, decrepitude, breaking up, hoariness, wrinkling of the skin, dwindling of the life-span, overripeness of the sense-faculties: this is called ageing. Whatever for this or that being in this or that class of beings is the falling and deceasing, the breaking, the disappearance, the mortality and dying,[3] the passing away, the breaking of the khandhas,[3] the laying down of the body: this is called dying. This is called ageing and dying.

And what is birth? Whatever for this or that being in this or that class of beings is the conception, the birth, the descent, the production, the appearance of the khandhas, the acquiring of the sensory fields: this is called birth.

And what is becoming? There are these three becomings: sensuous becoming, fine-material becoming, immaterial becoming.

And what is grasping? There are four graspings: after sense-pleasures, after speculative view, after rite and custom, after the theory of self.

And what is craving? There are six classes of craving: for material shapes, sounds, smells, tastes, touches and mental objects.

And what is feeling? There are six classes of feeling: feeling due to visual, auditory, olfactory, gustatory, physical and mental impact.

And what is impression? There are six classes of impression: visual, auditory, olfactory, gustatory, physical and mental.

And what are the six sensory fields? The field of the eye, ear, nose, tongue, body, mind.

And what is mind-and-body? Feeling, perception, volition, impression, wise attention: this is called mind. The four great elements† and the material shape derived from them: this is called

---

* The Saṁkhāra are karma-formations or karmical formations, in the sense of 'forming', as opposed to 'formed'. As such they may be said to represent the volitional activity (cetanā) of body (kāya), speech (vacì) and mind (mano).

† Earth, water, fire and air.

body. Such is mind and such is body. This is called mind-and-body.

And what is consciousness? There are six classes of consciousness: visual, auditory, olfactory, gustatory, physical and mental consciousness.

And what are the karma-formations? There are three: karma formations of body, of speech, of thought.

And what is ignorance? Whatever is the unknowing in regard to suffering, its arising, its stopping and the course leading to its stopping – this is called ignorance.

Majjhima-nikāya I, 49–54

"Is suffering wrought by oneself, good Gotama?"

"No, Kassapa."

"Then by another?"

"No."

"Then by both oneself and another?"

"No, Kassapa."

"Well then, has the suffering that has been wrought neither by myself nor by another come to me by chance?"

"No, Kassapa."

"Then, is there not suffering?"

"No, Kassapa, it is not that there is not suffering. For there *is* suffering."

"Well then, the good Gotama neither knows nor sees suffering."

"It is not that I do not know suffering, do not see it. I know it, I see it."

"To all my questions, good Gotama, you have answered 'No', and you have said that you know suffering and see it. Lord, let the Lord explain suffering to me, let him teach me suffering."

"Whoso says, 'He who does (a deed) is he who experiences (its result)', is thereby saying that from the being's beginning suffering was wrought by (the being) himself – this amounts to the Eternity-view. Whoso says, 'One does (a deed), another experiences (the result)', is thereby saying that when a being is smitten by feeling the suffering was wrought by another – this amounts to the Annihilation-view."

"Avoiding both these dead-ends, Kassapa, the Tathagata[4] teaches Dhamma by the man: conditioned by ignorance are the karma-formations [. . .]. Thus is the origin of this whole mass of suffering. By the utter stopping of that very ignorance is the stopping of the karma-formations [. . .]. Thus is the stopping of this whole mass of suffering."

Samyutta-nikāya II, 19–21

Once when the Lord was staying among the Kurus, the venerable Ananda approached him and said: "It is wonderful, Lord, that while Conditioned Genesis is so deep and looks so deep, to me it seems perfectly clear."

"Do not speak like that, Ananda. For this Conditioned Genesis is deep and looks deep too. It is from not awakening to this Dhamma, Ananda, from not penetrating it, that this generation, become tangled like a ball of thread, covered as with blight, twisted up like a grass-rope, cannot overpass the sorrowful state, the bad bourn, the abyss, the circling on (saṃsāra)."

Dīgha-nikāya II, 55

"To what extent is the world called 'empty', Lord?"

"Because it is empty of self or of what belongs to self, it is therefore said: 'The world is empty.' And what is empty of self and what belongs to self? The eye, material shapes, visual consciousness, impression on the eye – all these are empty of self and of what belongs to self. So too are ear, nose, tongue, body and mind (and their appropriate sense-data, appropriate consciousness and the impression on them of their appropriate sense-data – *as above*): they are all empty of self and of what belongs to self. Also that feeling which arises, conditioned by impression on the eye, ear, nose, tongue, body, mind, whether it be pleasant or painful or neither painful nor pleasant – that too is empty of self and of what belongs to self. Wherefore is the world called empty because it is empty of self and of what belongs to self."

Samyutta-nikāya IV, 54

And what is the freedom of mind that is empty? As to this, a monk forest-gone or gone to the root of a tree or to an empty place reflects thus: This is empty of self or of what belongs to self. This is called the freedom of mind that is empty. . . . To the extent that the freedoms of mind are immeasurable, are of no-thing, are signless, of them all unshakable freedom of mind is pointed to as chief, for it is empty of passion, empty of aversion, empty of confusion.

Majjhima-nikāya I, 297–98

The stopping of becoming is Nirvāna.

Samyutta-nikāya II, 117

It is called Nirvāṇa because of the getting rid of craving.

Samyutta-nikāya I, 39

That monk of wisdom here, devoid of desire and passion, attains to deathlessness, peace, the unchanging state of Nirvāṇa.

Suttanipāta, 204

For those who in mid-stream stay, in great peril in the flood – for those adventuring on ageing and dying – do I proclaim the Isle:
Where is no-thing, where naught is grasped, this is the Isle of No-beyond. Nirvāṇa do I call it – the utter extinction of ageing and dying.

Suttanipāta, 1093–94

"To what extent, Lord, is one a speaker of Dhamma?"
"Monk, if one teaches Dhamma for the turning away from material shape, from feeling, perception, the impulses, consciousness, for dispassion in regard to them, for their cessation, it is fitting to call him a monk who is a speaker of Dhamma. If he is himself faring along for the turning away from material shape and so on, for dispassion in regard to them, for their cessation, it is fitting to call him a monk who is faring along in accordance with Dhamma. Monk, if he is freed by this turning away, by dispassion in regard to these things, by their cessation, it is fitting to call him a monk who has attained Nirvāṇa here and now."

Samyutta-nikāya III, 163–64

A wanderer who ate rose-apples spoke thus to the venerable Sariputta:
"Reverend Sariputta, it is said: 'Nirvāṇa, Nirvāṇa.' Now, what, your reverence, is Nirvāṇa?"
"Whatever, your reverence, is the extinction of passion, of aversion, of confusion, this is called Nirvāṇa."
"Is there a way, your reverence, is there a course for the realization of this Nirvāṇa?"
"There is, your reverence."
"What is it, your reverence?"
"This ariyan eightfold Way itself is for the realization of Nirvāṇa, that is to say right view, right thought, right speech, right action, right mode of livelihood, right endeavour, right mindfulness, right concentration."

"Goodly, your reverence, is the Way, goodly the course for the realization of this Nirvāṇa. But for certain it needs diligence."

Samyutta-nikāya IV, 251–52

As this, Ananda, he perceives thus: This is the real, this the excellent, namely the calm of all the impulses, the casting out of all 'basis', the extinction of craving, dispassion, stopping, Nirvāṇa.

Anguttara-nikāya V, 322

There is, monks, that plane where there is neither extension nor ... motion nor the plane of infinite ether ... nor that of neither-perception-nor-non-perception, neither this world nor another, neither the moon nor the sun. Here, monks, I say that there is no coming or going or remaining or deceasing or uprising, for this is itself without support, without continuance, without mental object – this is itself the end of suffering.
There is, monks, an unborn, not become, not made, uncompounded, and were it not, monks, for this unborn, not become, not made, uncompounded, no escape could be shown here for what is born, has become, is made, is compounded. But because there is, monks, an unborn, not become, not made, uncompounded, therefore an escape can be shown for what is born, has become, is made, is compounded.[5]

Udāna, 80–81

(B)   *Lalitavistara*, XIII, 95–117

The following stanzas were spoken by the Gods to remind the Buddha that the time had come to leave his home:

95. Impermanent and unstable are all conditioned things,
Essentially brittle, like an unbaked pot.
Like some borrowed article, like a town built on sand,
They last for a short while only.

96. These complexes are doomed to destruction,
Like plaster washed away by the rainy season,
Like sand on a river's bank.
They are subject to conditions, and their own-being is hard to get at.

97. Like the flame of a lamp are the complexes.
     Suddenly it arises, soon it is doomed to
        stop.
     Without any staying power they are, like air,
        or a mass of foam,
     Unsubstantial and weak in themselves.

98. Complexes have no inner might, are void
        in themselves;
     Rather like the stem of the plantain tree,
        when reflects on them,
     Like a mock show which deludes the
        mind,
     Like an empty fist with which a child is
        teased.

99. Everything that is a complex event
     Proceeds by way of causes and conditions,
     And the events mutually cause and condi-
        tion each other.
     This fact is not understood by foolish
        people.

100. Out of pieces of Munja-grass a rope is
        twisted
     By the force of effort;
     Well-buckets are raised by several revolu-
        tions of the wheel;
     Yet each revolution, by itself, can do
        nothing.

101. Just so, the turning of all the components
        of becoming
     Results from their mutual interaction;
     In each of them singly it cannot be
        apprehended,
     Either at the beginning or at the end.

102. Where there is a seed, there is the sprout;
     But the seed is by its nature not the sprout,
     Nor is it other than that, nor just that.
     Just so the true nature of Dharma is
        neither annihilated nor eternal.[6]

103. Ignorance is the condition of all condi-
        tioned things;
     But in real truth these conditioned things
        are not.
     For conditioned things and ignorance are
        just empty,
     By their own inner nature without any
        ability to act.

104. One can see the impression made by a seal,
     But the transmission of the seal one can-
        not apprehend.
     It is not therein, nor anywhere else.
     Just so are conditioned things not annihi-
        lated or eternal.

105. Dependent on eye and sight-object
     An act of eye-consciousness springs up
        here.
     But the sight-object is not based on the eye,
     Nor has any sight-object been transferred
        to the eye.

106. Without self and impure are these dharmas;
     Yet one imagines that they are with self and
        pure.
     The act of eye-consciousness springs up
        from that
     Which is pervertedly seen, which is dis-
        criminated although it does not exist.

107. The wise discern of an act of consciousness
     The origin and the stopping, the produc-
        tion and the passing away.
     The Yogin sees that it has come from
        nowhere, gone to nowhere,
     That it is empty, and like unto a mock
        show.

108. Conditioned by the concourse of three
        factors, –
     The tinderstick, the fuel, the exertion of the
        hand, –
     Does fire arise; it does its work,
     And then it quickly stops again.

109. Then a wise man searches all around
     Whence it has come and whither it goes.
     Through every region, in every direction he
        searches.
     He cannot find it as it was before it came
        or went.

110. Skandhas, sense-fields, elements, craving
        and ignorance,
     These are the conditions which bring
        about our deeds.
     Where they are complete one thinks of a
        being.
     In ultimate truth such a being can never be
        found.

111. When words are uttered the conditions are
     The throat, the lips, the palate and the
        rolling of the tongue.
     But the words have not come from the
        throat or the palate,
     And in each single of these conditions they
        cannot be found.

112. Speech comes about when all these condi-
        tions are complete,
     With mind and intellect as the driving
        force.
     Invisible and immaterial are mind and
        speech;
     Without or within they cannot be found.

113. The wise man discerns the rise and fall,
     Of speech, or song, or noise, or any sound.
     They are but momentary and empty,
     All speech is similar to an echo.

114. From a lute, or other stringed musical
        instruments,
     Sound comes forth when three conditions
        are present –
     The strings, the wooden body, and the
        hand's exertion.
     It is their concourse which brings forth the
        sound.

115. Then the wise man searches all around
     Whence it has come and whither it goes.
     Through every region, in every direction he
        searches,
     He cannot find the sound as it was before
        it came.

116. Thus immersed in causes and conditions
     Proceeds all that belongs to this condi-
        tioned world.
     The Yogin again with his vision of the
        truly real
     Sees the complexes as empty and without
        inner might.

117. The skandhas, the sense-fields, the elements
     They are empty inward, empty outward.
     The beings are separated from their self
        and homeless,
     The dharmas marked with the own-being
        of space.

                              Lalitavistara XIII, 95–117

(C) Nāgārjuna,
Madhyamaka-Kārikā

Dedication

The Perfect Buddha,
The foremost of all Teachers I salute.
He has proclaimed
The principle of Universal Relativity [condi-
   tioned genesis],
'Tis like blissful (Nirvāna),
Quiescence of Plurality.
There is nothing disappears,
Nor anything appears,
Nothing has an end.
Nor is there anything eternal,
Nothing is identical with itself,
Nor is there anything differentiated,
Nothing moves,
Neither hither nor thither.

Chapter XXV

Examination of Nirvāna

I[7]

If everything is relative,
No (real) origination, no (real) annihilation,
How is Nirvāna, then conceived?
Through what deliverance, through what
   annihilation?

II

Should every thing be real in substance,
No (new) creation, no (new) destruction,
How should Nirvāna then be reached?
Through what deliverance, through what
   annihilation?

III

What neither is released, nor is it ever reached,
What neither is annihilation, nor is it eternality,
What never disappears, nor has it been created,
This is Nirvāna. It escapes precision.

IV

Nirvāna, first of all, is not a kind of Ens [entity,
   substance].
It would then have decay and death.
There altogether is no Ens.
Which is not subject to decay and death.

V

If Nirvāṇa is Ens,
It is produced by causes,
Nowhere and none the entity exists
Which would not be produced by causes.

VI

If Nirvāṇa is Ens,
How can it lack substratum,
There whatsoever is no Ens
Without any substratum.

VII

If Nirvāṇa is not an Ens,
Will it be then a non-Ens?
Wherever there is found no Ens,
There is neither a (corresponding) non-Ens.[8]

VIII

Now, if Nirvāṇa is a non-Ens,
How can it then be independent?
For sure, an independent non-Ens
Is nowhere to be found.

IX

Coordinated here or caused are (separate) things,
We call this world Phenomenal;
But just the same is called Nirvāṇa,
When from causality abstracted.

X

The Buddha has declared
That Ens and non-Ens should both be rejected.
Neither as Ens nor as a non-Ens
Nirvāṇa therefore is conceived.

XI

If Nirvāṇa were both Ens and non-Ens,
Final Deliverance would be also both,
Reality and unreality together,
This never could be possible.

XII

If Nirvāṇa were both Ens and non-Ens,
Nirvāṇa could not be uncaused.
Indeed the Ens and the non-Ens
Are both dependent on causation.

XIII

How can Nirvāṇa represent
An Ens and a non-Ens together?
Nirvāṇa is indeed uncaused,
Both Ens and non-Ens are productions.

XIV

How can Nirvāṇa represent
(The place of Ens and non-Ens together –
    As light and darkness in one spot)
They cannot be simultaneously present.

XV

If it were clear, indeed,
What an Ens means, and what a non-Ens,
We could then understand the doctrine.
About Nirvāṇa being neither Ens nor non-Ens.

XVI

If Nirvāṇa is neither Ens nor non-Ens,
No one can really understand
This doctrine which proclaims at once
Negation of them both together.

XVII

What is the Buddha after Nirvāṇa?
Does he exist or does he not exist,
Or both, or neither?
We never will conceive it.

XVIII

What is the Buddha then at life time?
Does he exist, or does he not exist,
Or both, or neither?
We never will conceive it.

XIX

There is no difference at all
Between Nirvāṇa and Saṁsāra,
There is no difference at all
Between Saṁsāra and Nirvāṇa.

XX

What makes the limit of Nirvāṇa
Is also then the limit of Saṁsāra.
Between the two we cannot find
The slightest shade of difference.

XXI

(Insoluble are antinomic) views
Regarding what exists beyond Nirvāṇa,
Regarding what the end of this world is,
Regarding its beginning.

XXII

Since everything is relative (we do not know),
What is finite and what is infinite,
What means finite and infinite at once,
What means negation of both issues?

XXIII

What is identity, and what is difference?
What is eternity what non-eternity,
What means eternity and non-eternity together,
What means negation of both issues?

XXIV

The bliss consists in the cessation of all thought,
In the quiescence of Plurality.
No (separate) Reality was preached at all,
Nowhere and none by Buddha.

Notes

1　*Karma* means intentional action. Buddhism shares the standard Indian view that such action must "bear fruit," good or bad, in the present or a future lifetime of the agent, according to its moral quality.

2　"Ariyan (or Aryan)" was the name of the central asian invaders of India in the second millennium BCE (and of their language). It came to mean, as here, "noble" or "holy."

3　The *khandhas* (*skhandhas* in Sanskrit) are the "five aggregates" which comprise a person: matter, sensation, perception, mental formations, and consciousness.

4　*Tathagata*, literally "the thus-gone," is a familiar epithet for a Buddha or "enlightened one."

5　This passage reflects a more metaphysically adventurous view of Nirvāṇa than do the Buddha's usual remarks, and for that reason its authenticity has been questioned. The suggestion that Nirvāṇa is some uncompounded plane of existence underlying or transcending the world is one that some Buddhists took up and elaborated, but which others, such as Nāgārjuna, clearly reject.

6　The unpluralizable word *Dharma* (*Dhamma* in Pali), here, does not mean "true (Buddhist) doctrine," as on p. 614, but "reality" or "the world," which is comprised of *dharmas*, in the plural – the constituents of the world (see Verse 106). These three senses of "*dharma*" do not exhaust this versatile word: it can also mean "law" and "duty."

7　Verse I expresses an imagined critic's objection to regarding everything as relative or conditioned. Verse II is in Nāgārjuna's own voice and argues that the critic's worry, concerning the status of Nirvāṇa, remains when things are considered as absolute or unconditioned. If things are unconditioned, how can they be annihilated or extinguished so that Nirvāṇa (literally, "extinction") is reached?

8　Nāgārjuna is making two points here. (a) Although Nirvāṇa is not an entity or substance, for it is "empty," one cannot just bluntly deny its existence. At the same time, (b) it would be an error to reify "emptiness," to treat what is a "no-thing," Nirvāṇa, as a special kind of thing.

6

Plotinus, *The Enneads* V.1

Introduction

Prior to the twentieth century, the Egyptian-born
Neo-Platonist, Plotinus (205–270), was commonly known as an interesting, if eccentric, coda
to Greek philosophy and as a powerful influence on Augustine and, through him, on medieval
Christian philosophy at large. In recent years,
however, Plotinus's metaphysics – which rivals
Hegel's in its systematic ambitions – has become
an object of critical attention in its own right, with
one author even declaring him to have been the
"greatest of the Greek philosophers."[1]

Plotinus was a late starter, only beginning to
write 10 years after arriving in Rome as a teacher
at the age of 40. Although scornful of civic and
other mundane activities, Plotinus – who, according to his disciple and biographer, Porphyry, was
"ashamed of being in the body"[2] – attempted,
unsuccessfully, to set up an ideal city, ruled by
philosopher-kings, to be called "Platonopolis."
Largely thanks to Porphyry, who organized them
into Books of nine sections or "tractates" each
(hence the name "Enneads"), his writings had more
success.

Plotinus's main philosophical inspiration was
Plato's accounts, in the *Symposium* and the
Phaedrus (see III.3 above), of the soul's ascent

From Plotinus, *The Enneads*, trans. S. McKenna,
London: Penguin, 1991, pp. 347–56, 358–60 (Sections
8–9 and notes omitted).

from a base, worldly existence to union with
The Good. Despite some important differences,
Plotinus's system corresponds to the Platonic
triad of the Good, the Forms, and the Soul. (In
the two sections omitted from our selection,
Plotinus spells out what he takes to be his philosophical debts, not only to Plato, but to various
Pre-Socratic thinkers such as Parmenides.) In
the First Tractate of the Fifth Ennead, Plotinus
provides a compact sketch of his overall metaphysical position. There are, he argues, three
fundamental layers of existence, which he calls
"hypostases," after a Greek word that literally
means "what stands under." These three are the
"One," "*noûs*" or the "Intellectual-Principle"
(as his translator renders it), and "Soul."

The three hypostases are hierarchically – or, as
Plotinus prefers, concentrically – ordered in relation to one another. Soul "emanates" or "radiates" from the Intellectual-Principle, which, in
its turn, emanates or radiates from the One. The
picture seems to be something like the following.
All beings and creatures in the world require the
activity of Soul operating on shapeless, formless
"matter" in order to give them an identity. Soul
is able to do this only through its acquaintance
with the Forms that constitute one aspect of the
Intellectual-Principle. This Principle cannot, however, be the "primal" reality, since it emanates from
an indivisible and ineffable One.

Plotinus's arguments in support of this picture
are not easy to articulate, partly because he
expresses them in highly figurative language. But

there seem to be two types of argument, which one might dub "centrifugal" and "centripetal" respectively. The former, beginning with the assumption of an indivisible One, is to the effect that the One – like anything which is known to us, such as fire – is bound to impart aspects of itself beyond itself. Somewhat like God, as conceived by some theologians, the One must, by its very nature, express and externalize itself. It does so, initially, in the Intellectual-Principle, which, in its turn, must impart itself to the activities of Soul, the "life-principle" responsible for the beings and creatures of familiar experience.

The "centripetal" argument attempts to derive the Intellectual-Principle, and then the One, from the activities of Soul. Here the crucial role is played by the idea of unity. Something – a table, say – only exists in virtue of a Soul-imparted unity among its diverse features. But Soul itself is complex and hence must owe its unity and existence to something more unitary than itself – the Intellectual-Principle. But this Principle is not itself a perfect unity, since it is composed of

Forms and the "intellection" of those Forms. Hence, the Principle must depend upon, "emanate" from, a more perfect unity – the One itself.

Despite the somewhat baroque structure of Plotinus's thought, his vision is an essentially simple one that bears comparison with, for example, that of Taoism (see III.1 above). Our complex world of experience is ultimately explicable only as deriving from something utterly simple and indivisible, and the path of the wise person is an ascent from this complex, and superficial, world towards an intimacy or union with the ineffable "Way" that holds sway over everything and from which everything emanates.

Notes

1 S.R.L. Clark, *God's World and the Great Awakening*, Oxford: Clarendon Press, 1991, p. 205.
2 "On the Life of Plotinus," in *The Enneads*, trans. S. McKenna, p. cii.

Plotinus, *The Enneads* V

First Tractate

The three initial hypostases 1. What can it be that has brought the souls to forget the father, God, and, though members of the Divine and entirely of that world, to ignore at once themselves and It?

The evil that has overtaken them has its source in self-will, in the entry into the sphere of process, and in the primal differentiation with the desire for self-ownership. They conceived a pleasure in this freedom and largely indulged their own motion; thus they were hurried down the wrong path, and in the end, drifting further and further, they came to lose even the thought of their origin in the Divine. A child wrenched young from home and brought up during many years at a distance will fail in knowledge of its father and of itself: the souls, in the same way, no longer discern either the divinity or their own nature; ignorance of their rank brings self-depreciation; they misplace their respect, honouring everything more than themselves; all their awe and

admiration is for the alien, and, clinging to this, they have broken apart, as far as a soul may, and they make light of what they have deserted; their regard for the mundane and their disregard of themselves bring about their utter ignoring of the Divine.

Admiring pursuit of the external is a confession of inferiority; and nothing thus holding itself inferior to things that rise and perish, nothing counting itself less honourable and less enduring than all else it admires could ever form any notion of either the nature or the power of God.

A double discipline must be applied if human beings in this pass are to be reclaimed, and brought back to their origins, lifted once more towards the Supreme and One and First.

There is the method, which we amply exhibit elsewhere, declaring the dishonour of the objects which the Soul holds here in honour; the second teaches or recalls to the Soul its race and worth; this latter is the leading truth, and, clearly brought out, is the evidence of the other.

It must occupy us now, for it bears closely upon our inquiry (as to the Divine Hypostases) to which it is the natural preliminary: the seeker is soul and it must start from a true notion of the nature and quality by which soul may undertake the search; it must study itself in order to learn whether it has the faculty for the inquiry, the eye for the object proposed, whether in fact we ought to seek; for if the object is alien the search must be futile, while if there is relationship the solution of our problems is at once desirable and possible.

2.　Let every soul recall, then, at the outset the truth that soul is the author of all living things, that it has breathed the life into them all, whatever is nourished by earth and sea, all the creatures of the air, the divine stars in the sky; it is the maker of the sun; itself formed and ordered this vast heaven and conducts all that rhythmic motion: and it is a principle distinct from all these to which it gives law and movement and life, and it must of necessity be more honourable than they, for they gather or dissolve as soul brings them life or abandons them, but soul, since it never can abandon itself, is of eternal being.

How life was purveyed to the universe of things and to the separate beings in it may be thus conceived:

That great soul must stand pictured before another soul, one not mean, a soul that has become worthy to look, emancipate from the lure, from all that binds its fellows in bewitchment, holding itself in quietude. Let not merely the enveloping body be at peace, body's turmoil stilled, but all that lies around, earth at peace, and sea at peace, and air and the very heavens. Into that heaven, all at rest, let the great soul be conceived to roll inward at every point, penetrating, permeating, from all sides pouring in its light. As the rays of the sun throwing their brilliance upon a louring cloud make it gleam all gold, so the soul entering the material expanse of the heavens has given life, has given immortality: what was abject it has lifted up; and the heavenly system, moved now in endless motion by the soul that leads it in wisdom, has become a living and a blessed thing; the soul domiciled within, it takes worth where, before the soul, it was stark body – clay and water – or, rather, the blankness of Matter, the absence of Being, and, as an author [Homer] says, 'the execration of the Gods'.

The Soul's nature and power will be brought out more clearly, more brilliantly, if we consider next how it envelops the heavenly system and guides all to its purposes: for it has bestowed itself upon all that huge expanse so that every interval, small and great alike, all has been ensouled.

The material body is made up of parts, each holding its own place, some in mutual opposition and others variously separated; the Soul is in no such condition; it is not whittled down so that life tells of a part of the Soul and springs where some such separate portion impinges; each separate life lives by the Soul entire, omnipresent in the likeness of the engendering father, entire in unity and entire in diffused variety. By the power of the Soul the manifold and diverse heavenly system is a unit: through soul this universe is a God: and the sun is a God because it is ensouled; so too the stars: and whatsoever we ourselves may be, it is all in virtue of soul; for 'dead is viler than dung'.

This, by which the gods are divine, must be the oldest God of them all: and our own soul is of that same Ideal nature, so that to consider it, purified, freed from all accruement, is to recognize in ourselves that same value which we have found soul to be, honourable above all that is bodily. For what is body but earth, and even if it be fire (as Stoics think), what (but soul) is its burning power? So it is with all the compounds of earth and fire, even with water and air added to them.

If, then, it is the presence of soul that brings worth, how can a man slight himself and run after other things? You honour the Soul elsewhere; honour then yourself.

3.　The Soul once seen to be thus precious, thus divine, you may hold the faith that by its possession you are already nearing God: in the strength of this power make upwards towards Him: at no great distance you must attain: there is not much between.

But over this divine, there is a still diviner: grasp the upward neighbour of the Soul, its prior and source.

Soul, for all the worth we have shown to belong to it, is yet a secondary, an image of the Intellectual-Principle: reason uttered is an image of the reason stored within the Soul, and in the same way soul is an utterance of the Intellectual-Principle: it is even the total of its activity, the entire stream of life sent forth by that Principle to the production of further being: it is the forthgoing heat of a fire which has also heat essentially inherent. But within the Supreme we must see energy not as an overflow but in the double aspect of integral inherence with the establishment of a new being. Sprung, in other words, from the Intellectual-Principle, soul is intellective, but with an intellection operating by the method of reasonings: for its perfecting it must look to that Divine Mind, which may be thought of as a father watching over the development of his child born imperfect in comparison with himself.

Thus its substantial existence comes from the Intellectual-Principle; and the Reason within it becomes Act in virtue of its contemplation of that prior; for its thought and act are its own intimate possession when it looks to the Supreme Intelligence; those only are soul-acts which are of this intellective nature and are determined by its own character; all that is less noble is foreign (traceable to Matter) and is accidental to the Soul in the course of its peculiar task.

In two ways, then, the Intellectual-Principle enhances the divine quality of the Soul, as father and as immanent presence; nothing separates them but the fact that they are not one and the same, that there is succession, that over against a recipient there stands the Ideal-Form received; but this recipient, Matter to the Supreme Intelligence, is also noble as being at once informed by divine intellect and uncompounded.

What the Intellectual-Principle must be is carried in the single word that Soul, itself so great, is still inferior.

4. But there is yet another way to this knowledge:

Admiring the world of sense as we look out upon its vastness and beauty and the order of its eternal march, thinking of the gods within it, seen and hidden, and the celestial spirits and all the life of animal and plant, let us mount to its archetype, to the yet more authentic sphere: there we are to contemplate all things as members of the Intellectual – eternal in their own right, vested with a self-springing consciousness and life – and, presiding over all these, the unsoiled Intelligence and the unapproachable wisdom.

That archetypal world is the true Golden Age, age of Kronos, whose very name suggests (in Greek) Abundance (κόρος) and Intellect (νοῦς). For here is contained all that is immortal: nothing here but is Divine Mind; all is God; this is the place of every soul. Here is rest unbroken: for how can that seek change, in which all is well; what

need that reach to, which holds all within itself; what increase can that desire, which stands utterly achieved? All its content, thus, is perfect, that itself may be perfect throughout, as holding nothing that is less than the divine, nothing that is less than intellective. Its knowing is not by search but by possession, its blessedness inherent, not acquired; for all belongs to it eternally and it holds the authentic Eternity imitated by Time which, circling round the Soul, makes towards the new thing and passes by the old. Soul deals with thing after thing – now Socrates; now a horse: always some one entity from among beings – but the Intellectual-Principle is all and therefore its entire content is simultaneously present in that identity: this is pure being in eternal actuality; nowhere is there any future, for every then is a now; nor is there any past, for nothing there has ever ceased to be; everything has taken its stand for ever, an identity well pleased, we might say, to be as it is; and everything, in that entire content, is Intellectual-Principle and Authentic-Existence; and the total of all is Intellectual-Principle entire and Being entire. Intellectual-Principle by its intellective act establishes Being, which in turn, as the object of intellection, becomes the cause of intellection and of existence to the Intellectual-Principle – though, of course, there is another cause of intellection which is also a cause to Being, both rising in a source distinct from either.

Now while these two are coalescents, having their existence in common, and are never apart, still the unity they form is two-sided; there is Intellectual-Principle as against Being, the intellectual agent as against the object of intellection; we consider the intellective act and we have the Intellectual-Principle; we think of the object of that act and we have Being.

Such difference there must be if there is to be any intellection; but similarly there must also be identity (since, in perfect knowing, subject and object are identical).

Thus the Primals (the first 'Categories') are seen to be: Intellectual-Principle; Existence; Difference; Identity: we must include also Motion and Rest: Motion provides for the intellectual act, Rest preserves identity as Difference gives at once a Knower and a Known, for, failing this, all is one, and silent.

So too the objects of intellection (the ideal content of the Divine Mind) – identical in virtue of the self-concentration of the principle which is their common ground – must still be distinct each from another; this distinction constitutes Difference.

The Intellectual Cosmos thus a manifold, Number and Quantity arise: Quality is the specific character of each of these Ideas which stand as the principles from which all else derives.

5.   As a manifold, then, this God, the Intellectual-Principle, exists above the Soul here, the Soul which once for all stands linked a member of the divine, unless by a deliberate apostasy.

Bringing itself close to the divine Intellect, becoming, as it were, one with this, it seeks still further: what Being, now, has engendered this God, what is the Simplex preceding this multiple; what the cause at once of its existence and of its existing as a manifold; what the source of this Number, this Quantity?

Number, Quantity, is not primal: obviously before even duality, there must stand the unity.

The Dyad is a secondary; deriving from unity, it finds in unity the determinant needed by its native indetermination: once there is any determination, there is Number, in the sense, of course, of the real (the archetypal) Number. And the Soul is such a number or quantity. For the Primals are not masses or magnitudes; all of that gross order is later real only to the sense-thought; even in seed the effective reality is not the moist substance but the unseen – that is to say Number (as the determinant of individual being) and the Reason-Principle (of the product to be).

Thus by what we call the Number and the Dyad of that higher realm, we mean Reason Principles and the Intellectual-Principle: but while the Dyad is undetermined – representing, as it were, the underlie (or Matter) of the Intellectual World – the number which rises from the Dyad and The One is always a Form-Idea: thus the Intellectual-Principle is, so to speak, shaped by the Ideas rising within it – or rather, it is shaped in a certain sense by The One and in another sense by itself, since its potential vision becomes actual and intellection is, precisely, an act of vision in which subject and object are identical.

6.   But how and what does the Intellectual-Principle see and, especially, how has it sprung from that which is to become the object of its vision?

The mind demands the existence of these Beings, but it is still in trouble over the problem endlessly debated by the most ancient philosophers: from such a unity as we have declared The One to be, how does anything at all come into substantial existence, any multiplicity, dyad, or number? Why has the Primal not remained self-gathered so that there be none of this profusion of the manifold which we observe in existence and yet are compelled to trace to that absolute unity?

In venturing an answer, we first invoke God Himself, not in loud word but in that way of prayer which is always within our power, leaning in soul towards Him by aspiration, alone towards the alone. But if we seek the vision of that great Being within the Inner Sanctuary – self-gathered, tranquilly remote above all else – we begin by considering the images stationed at the outer precincts, or, more exactly to the moment, the first image that appears. How the Divine Mind comes into being must be explained:

Everything moving has necessarily an object towards which it advances; but since the Supreme can have no such object, we may not ascribe motion to it: anything that comes into being after it can be produced only as a consequence of its unfailing self-intention; and, of course, we dare not talk of generation in time, dealing as we are with eternal Beings: where we speak of origin in such reference, it is in the sense, merely, of cause and subordination: origin from the Supreme must not be taken to imply any movement in it: that would make the Being resulting from the movement not a second principle but a third: the Movement would be the second hypostasis.

Given this immobility in the Supreme, it can neither have yielded assent nor uttered decree nor stirred in any way towards the existence of a secondary.

What happened, then? What are we to conceive as rising in the neighbourhood of that immobility?

It must be a circumradiation – produced from the Supreme but from the Supreme unaltering – and may be compared to the brilliant light encircling the sun and ceaselessly generated from that unchanging substance.

All existences, as long as they retain their character, produce – about themselves, from their essence, in virtue of the power which must be in them – some necessary, outward-facing hypostasis continuously attached to them and

representing in image the engendering archetypes: thus fire gives out its heat; snow is cold not
merely to itself; fragrant substances are a notable
instance; for, as long as they last, something is
diffused from them and perceived wherever they
are present.

Again, all that is fully achieved engenders:
therefore the eternally achieved engenders eternally an eternal being. At the same time, the offspring is always minor: what then are we to
think of the All-Perfect but that it can produce
nothing less than the very greatest that is later than
itself? This greatest, later than the divine unity,
must be the Divine Mind, and it must be the
second of all existence, for it is that which sees
The One on which alone it leans while the First
has no need whatever of it. The offspring of the
prior to Divine Mind can be no other than that
Mind itself and thus is the loftiest being in the
universe, all else following upon it – the Soul,
for example, being an utterance and act of the
Intellectual-Principle as that is an utterance and
act of The One. But in soul the utterance is
obscured, for soul is an image and must look to
its own original: that Principle, on the contrary,
looks to the First without mediation – thus
becoming what it is – and has that vision not as
from a distance but as the immediate next with
nothing intervening, close to the One as Soul
to it.

The offspring must seek and love the begetter;
and especially so when begetter and begotten
are alone in their sphere; when, in addition, the
begetter is the highest Good, the offspring (inevitably seeking its good) is attached by a bond of
sheer necessity, separated only in being distinct.

7. We must be more explicit:

The Intellectual-Principle stands as the image
of The One, firstly because there is a certain
necessity that the first should have its offspring,
carrying onward much of its quality, in other
words that there be something in its likeness as
the sun's rays tell of the sun. Yet The One is not
an Intellectual-Principle; how then does it
engender an Intellectual-Principle?

Simply by the fact that in its self-quest it
has vision: this very seeing is the Intellectual-
Principle. Any perception of the external indicates
either sensation or intellection, sensation symbolized by line, intellection by a circle . . . [corrupt
passage].

Of course the divisibility belonging to the circle does not apply to The One; here, to be sure,
is a unity, but there the Unity which is the
potentiality of all existence.

The items of this potentiality the divine intellection brings out, so to speak, from the unity
and knows them in detail, as it must if it is to be
an intellectual principle.

It has besides a consciousness, as it were,
within itself of this same potentiality; it knows that
it can of itself beget an hypostasis and can determine its own Being by the virtue emanating
from its prior; it knows that its nature is in some
sense a definite part of the content of that First;
that it thence derives its essence, that its strength
lies there, and that its Being takes perfection as a
derivative and a recipient from the First. It sees
that, as a member in some sense of the realm of
division and part, it receives life and intellection
and all else it has and is, from the undivided and
partless, since that First is no member of existence,
but can be the source of all on condition only of
being held down by no one distinctive shape but
remaining the undeflected unity.

To be all in itself would place it in the realm
of Being. And so the First is not a thing among
the things contained by the Intellectual-Principle
though the source of all. In virtue of this source
things of the later order are essential beings; for
from that fact there is determination; each has
its form: what has being cannot be envisaged as
outside of limit; the nature must be held fast by
boundary and fixity; though to the Intellectual
Beings this fixity is no more than determination
and form, the foundations of their substantial
existence.

A being of this quality, like the Intellectual-
Principle, must be felt to be worthy of the all-pure:
it could not derive from any other than from the
first principle of all; as it comes into existence, all
other beings must be simultaneously engendered
– all the beauty of the Ideas, all the Gods of the
Intellectual realm. And it still remains pregnant
with this offspring; for it has, so to speak, drawn
all within itself again, holding them lest they
fall away towards Matter to be brought up in
the House of Rhea (in the realm of flux). This is
the meaning hidden in the Mysteries, and in the
Myths of the gods: Kronos, as the wisest, exists
before Zeus; he must absorb his offspring that,
full within himself, he may be also an Intellectual-
Principle manifest in some product of his plenty;

afterwards, the myth proceeds, Kronos engenders Zeus, who already exists as the (necessary and eternal) outcome of the plenty there; in other words the offspring of the Divine Intellect, perfect within itself, is Soul (the life-principle carrying forward the Ideas in the Divine Mind). The perfection entails the offspring; a power so vast could not remain unfruitful.

Now, even in the Divine the engendered could not be the very highest; it must be a lesser, an image; it will be undetermined, as its progenitor was, but will receive determination, and, so to speak, its shaping idea, from the progenitor.

Yet the offspring of the Intellectual-Principle must be a Reason-Principle, that is to say, a substantial existence (hypostasis) identified with the principle of deliberative thought (in the Timaeus); such then is that (higher Soul) which circles about the Divine Mind, its light, its image inseparably attached to it: on the upper level united with it, filled from it, enjoying it, participant in its nature, intellective with it, but on the lower level in contact with the realm beneath itself, or, rather, generating in turn an offspring which must lie beneath; of this lower we will treat later; so far we deal still with the Divine.

[. . .]

10.   We have shown the inevitability of certain convictions as to the scheme of things:

There exists a Principle which transcends Being; this is The One, whose nature we have sought to establish in so far as such matters lend themselves to proof. Upon The One follows immediately the Principle which is at once Being and the Intellectual-Principle. Third comes the Principle, Soul.

Now just as these three exist for the system of Nature, so, we must hold, they exist for ourselves. I am not speaking of the material order – all that is separable – but of what lies beyond the sense realm in the same way as the Primals are beyond all the heavens; I mean the corresponding aspect of man, what Plato calls the Interior Man.

Thus our soul, too, is a divine thing, belonging to another order than sense; such is all that holds the rank of soul, but (above the life-principle) there is the Soul perfected as containing Intellectual-Principle with its double phase, reasoning and giving the power to reason. The

reasoning phase of the soul, needing no bodily organ for its thinking but maintaining, in purity, its distinctive Act that its thought may be uncontaminated – this we cannot err in placing, separate and not mingled into body, within the first Intellectual. We may not seek any point of space in which to seat it; it must be set outside of all space: its distinct quality, its separateness, its immateriality, demand that it be a thing alone, untouched by all of the bodily order. That is why we read of the universe, that the Demiurge cast the Soul around it from without – understand that phase of soul which is permanently seated in the Intellectual – and of ourselves that the charioteer's head reaches upwards towards the heights.

The admonition to sever soul from body is not, of course, to be understood spatially – that separation stands made in Nature – the reference is to holding our rank, to use of our thinking, to an attitude of alienation from the body in the effort to lead up and attach to the over-world, equally with the other, that phase of soul seated here and, alone, having to do with body, creating, moulding, spending its care upon it.[1]

11.   Since there is a Soul which reasons upon the right and good – for reasoning is an inquiry into the rightness and goodness of this rather than that – there must exist some permanent Right, the source and foundation of this reasoning in our soul; how, else, could any such discussion be held? Further, since the Soul's attention to these matters is intermittent, there must be within us an Intellectual-Principle acquainted with that Right not by momentary act but in permanent possession. Similarly there must be also the principle of this principle, its cause, God. This Highest cannot be divided and allotted, must remain intangible but not bound to space, it may be present at many points, wheresoever there is anything capable of accepting one of its manifestations: thus a centre is an independent unity; everything within the circle has its term at the centre; and to the centre the radii bring each their own. Within our nature is such a centre by which we grasp and are linked and held; and those of us are firmly in the Supreme whose being is concentrated There.

12.   Possessed of such powers, how does it happen that we do not lay hold of them, but for the most part, let these high activities go idle – some,

even, of us never bringing them in any degree to effect?

The answer is that all the Divine Beings are unceasingly about their own act, the Intellectual-Principle and its Prior always self-intent; and so, too, the Soul maintains its unfailing movement; for not all that passes in the soul is, by that fact, perceptible; we know just as much as impinges upon the faculty of sense. Any activity not transmitted to the sensitive faculty has not traversed the entire Soul: we remain unaware because the human being includes sense-perception; man is not merely a part (the higher part) of the Soul but the total.

None the less every being of the order of soul is in continuous activity as long as life holds, continuously executing to itself its characteristic act: knowledge of the act depends upon transmission and perception. If there is to be perception of what is thus present, we must turn the perceptive faculty inward and hold it to attention there. Hoping to hear a desired voice we let all others pass and are alert for the coming at last of that most welcome of sounds: so here, we must let the hearings of sense go by, save for sheer necessity, and keep the Soul's perception bright and quick to the sounds from above.

Note

1 There are several references to Plato's dialogues in the last three paragraphs of Section 10. On "the interior man," see *Republic*, Book IX 589a; on "the Demiurge," see *Timaeus* 36e; on the "severing of soul from body," see *Phaedo* 67-c-d.

7

Śaṃkara, *Brahmasūtrabhāṣya*
(selections)

Introduction

Criticism of what he saw as the "nihilistic" position of Buddhist thinkers such as Nāgārjuna occurs in several writings of the eighth to ninth century CE Indian philosopher Śaṃkara (or Śaṅkara) – the author, despite his short life, of a large corpus of works and perhaps the most revered figure of philosophical Hinduism. But it is his own position that is articulated in the following selections from his greatest work, "the single most influential text in India today,"[1] a massive Commentary (*bhāṣya*) on the *Brahmasūtras* (or *Vedāntasūtras*). These were a collection of short verses, attributed to one Bādarāyaṇa, and of uncertain date, which interpreted the doctrines found in the *Upaniṣads*, themselves philosophical reflections on the Vedic scriptures.

Śaṃkara was the leading exponent of the philosophy of Advaita Vedanta (non-dualist Vedanta, with "Vedanta" – literally, "end of the Veda" – here referring to the systematic interpretation of such texts as the *Upaniṣads* and the *Bhagavadgītā*). As its name implies, Śaṃkara's position was a monistic one, and very radically so. The nearest parallel in the western tradition,

perhaps, is the "absolute idealism" of F. H. Bradley (see III.20 below) or the radical monism of Parmenides (III.2). For Śaṃkara, there is not simply just one kind of being, but only one being or entity – Brahman (the favored term for "absolute reality," and not to be confused with the Hindu god, Brahmā). Śaṃkara's main metaphysical tenets can be summarized as follows:

(a) Nothing is real other than a unitary, ineffable being, Brahman.
(b) Everything taken to exist by ordinary people or philosophers is either illusion or it is identical with Brahman.
(c) Individual selves are only "appearances" of a single Self or "pure consciousness," Ātman, which is itself identical with Brahman.

To these metaphysical claims, Śaṃkara adds an epistemological one to the effect that:

(d) Failure to recognize the truth of (a)–(c) is due to our mistakenly "superimposing" upon Brahman/Ātman features which do not belong to it;

in addition, he enters a soteriological claim holding that:

(e) Full appreciation of these metaphysical truths will lead to happiness and "liberation" (*mokṣa*) from the cycle of rebirth in the "apparent" world.

From E. Deutsch and J. A. B. van Buitenen, eds, *A Source Book of Advaita Vedanta*, trans. G. Thibaut. Honolulu: University Press of Hawaii, 1971, pp. 151–6, 58–60, 162–5, 173–85, 189–90, 196–8.

Śaṁkara's argument for the above metaphysical claims is almost entirely an argument from testimony. Properly understood, he insists, such famous and authoritative Upaniṣadic utterances as "That thou art" assert the identity of Self, and everything that truly exists, with Brahman. Not even the scriptures, however, can provide informative descriptions of Brahman: for, although it may be grasped through "direct intuition" and a "self-luminous flash," it lacks all those features of the "apparent" world that language is capable of articulating. Thus, although Brahman might be called "conscious" and "blissful," the senses of these terms are at best analogous to the ones they bear when applied to minds and their states. Indeed, for Śaṁkara the very existence, albeit only "apparent," of the pluralistic world of things, properties, and persons is the product, in some sense, of the imposition of linguistic classifications on what is, in itself, seamless (11.1.27).

Such religious mysticism might seem to leave little scope for philosophical elaboration. But Śaṁkara displays his philosophical acumen in at least three ways in the passages selected. First, in his Introduction, he analyzes the notion of "superimposition," which he will later deploy in order to explain how our ignorance of Brahman, our confusion of reality with the world of illusion or *maya*, arises. Second, especially in Part I, he offers us various analogies – for example, that of Space and the spaces inside jugs and the like – to help give us a handle on his claim that what is really One (Brahman/Ātman) can appear as many (things/selves). Finally, and at most length, he considers and attempts to refute a battery of objections, whether common-sense ones or those leveled by rival schools, to his position.

The set of objections he takes most seriously concern causality, above all the following one. If, as scripture tells us, Brahman is the cause and origin of the world, how can we deny the real existence of a world distinct from Brahman?

Here, in Part II, Śaṁkara defends the view that effects are really identical with causes against both the more moderate Sāmkhyan view that effects are "implicit" in their causes and the radically opposed view, associated with David Hume (1711–76), that causes and effects are entirely distinct (see II.10).[2]

Our selection ends with an important discussion of dreams and sleep. Śaṁkara is keen to insist that his position does not entail that the "apparent" world is no different in status from that of "the world of dreams." Dreams, however, also provide him with a useful analogy. Just as the world of dreams is "daily sublated" or contradicted by waking experience, so the illusory character of the latter is revealed in direct intuitive experience of Brahman. Ultimately, indeed, it is the testimony of those who have enjoyed such direct experience, as recorded in scripture, which convinces Śaṁkara of the truth of his doctrine of the "absolute unity" of reality.

The works referred to by Śaṁkara in abbreviated form in the following selections are: the Taittirīya, Chāndogya, Bṛhadāraṇyaka, Muṇḍaka, and Kaṭha *Upaniṣads*; the *Aiterya Āraṇyaka*; and Gauḍapāda's *Kārikās* on the *Māṇḍukya Upaniṣad*.

Notes

1 Karl H. Potter, ed., *Encyclopedia of Indian Philosophies: Advaita Vedanta Up to Śaṁkara and His Pupils*, Delhi: Motilal Banarsidass, 1981, p. 119. This book contains a useful reduction of the *Brahmasūtrabhāṣya*.

2 For an especially useful discussion of Śaṁkara's views on causality, see B. Carr, "Śaṅkarācāya," in B. Carr and I. Mahalingam, eds, *Companion Encyclopedia of Asian Philosophy*, London: Routledge, 1997.

Śaṁkara, *Brahmasūtrabhāṣya*

Introduction

It is a matter not requiring any proof that the object and the subject whose respective spheres are the notion of the 'Thou' (the Non-Ego) and

the 'Ego,' and which are opposed to each other as much as darkness and light are, cannot be identified. All the less can their respective attributes be identified. Hence it follows that it is wrong to superimpose upon the subject – whose Self is intelligence, and which has for its sphere the notion of the Ego – the object whose sphere is the notion of the Non-Ego, and the attributes of the object, and vice versa to superimpose the subject and the attributes of the subject on the object. In spite of this it is on the part of man a natural procedure – which has its cause in wrong knowledge – not to distinguish the two entities (object and subject) and their respective attributes, although they are absolutely distinct, but to superimpose upon each the characteristic nature and the attributes of the other, and thus, coupling the Real and Unreal, to make use of expressions such as 'That am I' 'That is mine.' – But what have we to understand by the term 'superimposition?' – The apparent presentation, in the form of remembrance, to consciousness of something previously observed, in some other thing.

Some indeed define the term 'superimposition' as the superimposition of the attributes of one thing on another thing. Others, again, define superimposition as the error founded on the non-apprehension of the difference of that which is superimposed from that on which it is superimposed. Others, again, define it as the fictitious assumption of attributes contrary to the nature of that thing on which something else is superimposed. But all these definitions agree in so far as they represent superimposition as the apparent presentation of the attributes of one thing in another thing. And therewith agrees also the popular view which is exemplified by expressions such as the following: 'Mother-of-pearl appears like silver,' 'The moon although one only appears as if she were double.' But how is it possible that on the interior Self which itself is not an object there should be superimposed objects and their attributes? For every one superimposes an object only on such other objects as are placed before him (i.e. in contact with his sense-organs), and you have said before that the interior Self which is entirely disconnected from the idea of the Thou (the Non-Ego) is never an object. It is not, we reply, non-object in the absolute sense. For it is the object of the notion of the Ego, and the interior Self is well known to exist on account of its immediate (intuitive) presentation. Nor is it an exceptionless rule that objects can be superimposed only on such other objects as are before us, i.e. in contact with our sense-organs; for non-discerning men superimpose on the ether, which is not the object of sensuous perception, dark-blue colour.

Hence it follows that the assumption of the Non-Self being superimposed on the interior Self is not unreasonable.

This superimposition thus defined, learned men consider to be Nescience (*avidyā*), and the ascertainment of the true nature of that which is (the Self) by means of the discrimination of that (which is superimposed on the Self), they call knowledge (*vidyā*). There being such knowledge (neither the Self nor the Non-Self) are affected in the least by any blemish or (good) quality produced by their mutual superimposition. The mutual superimposition of the Self and the Non-Self, which is termed Nescience, is the presupposition on which there base all the practical distinctions – those made in ordinary life as well as those laid down by the Veda – between means of knowledge, objects of knowledge (and knowing persons), and all scriptural texts, whether they are concerned with injunctions and prohibitions (of meritorious and non-meritorius actions), or with final release. – But how can the means of right knowledge such as perception, inference, &c., and scriptural texts have for their object that which is dependent on Nescience? – Because we reply, the means of right knowledge cannot operate unless there be a knowing personality, and because the existence of the latter depends on the erroneous notion that the body, the sense, and so on, are identical with, or belong to, the Self of the knowing person. For without the employment of the senses, perception and the other means of right knowledge cannot operate. And without a basis (i.e. the body) the senses cannot act. Nor does anybody act by means of a body on which the nature of the Self is not superimposed. Nor can, in the absence of all that, the Self which, in its own nature is free from all contact, become a knowing agent. And if there is no knowing agent, the means of right knowledge cannot operate (as said above). Hence perception and the other means of right knowledge, and the Vedic texts have for their object that which is dependent on Nescience. [. . .]

[. . .] That by superimposition we have to understand the notion of something in some other thing we have already explained. (The superimposition of the Non-Self will be understood more definitely from the following examples.) Extra-personal attributes are superimposed on the Self, if a man considers himself sound and entire, or the contrary, as long as his wife, children, and so on are sound and entire or not. Attributes of the body are superimposed on the Self, if a man thinks of himself (his Self) as stout, lean, fair, as standing, walking, or jumping. Attributes of the sense-organs, if he thinks 'I am mute, or deaf, or one-eyed, or blind.' Attributes of the internal organ when he considers himself subject to desire, intention, doubt, determination, and so on. Thus the producer of the notion of the Ego (i.e. the internal organ) is superimposed on the interior Self, which, in reality, is the witness of all the modifications of the internal organ, and vice versa the interior Self, which is the witness of everything, is superimposed on the internal organ, the senses, and so on. In this way there goes on this natural beginning – and endless super-imposition, which appears in the form of wrong conception, is the cause of individual souls appearing as agents and enjoyers (of the results of their actions), and is observed by every one.

(Sūtra. Then therefore the enquiry into Brahman.)

The word 'then' is here to be taken as denoting immediate consecution; not as indicating the introduction of a new subject to be entered upon; for the enquiry into Brahman (more literally, the desire of knowing Brahman) is not of that nature. [. . .]

If, then, the word 'then' intimates immediate consecution it must be explained on what antecedent the enquiry into Brahman specially depends; just as the enquiry into active religious duty . . . specially depends on the antecedent reading of the Veda.

[. . .] Well, then, we maintain that the antecedent conditions are the discrimination of what is eternal and what is non-eternal; the renunciation of all desire to enjoy the fruit (of one's actions) both here and hereafter; the acquirement of tranquillity, self-restraint, and the other means, and the desire of final release. If these conditions exist, a man may, either before entering on an enquiry into active religious duty or after that, engage in the enquiry into Brahman and come to know it; but not otherwise. The word 'then' therefore intimates that the enquiry into Brahman is subsequent to the acquisition of the above-mentioned (spiritual) means. [. . .]

But, it may be asked, is Brahman known or not known (previously to the enquiry into its nature)? If it is known we need not enter on an enquiry concerning it; if it is not known we can not enter on such an enquiry.[1]

We reply that Brahman is known. Brahman, which is all-knowing and endowed with all powers, whose essential nature is eternal purity, intelligence, and freedom, exists. For if we consider the derivation of the word 'Brahman,' from the root *brh*, 'to be great,' we at once understand that eternal purity, and so on, belong to Brahman. Moreover the existence of Brahman is known on the ground of its being the Self of every one. For every one is conscious of the existence of (his) Self, and never thinks 'I am not.' If the existence of the Self were not known, every one would think 'I am not.' And this Self (of whose existence all are conscious) is Brahman. But if Brahman is generally known as the Self, there is no room for an enquiry into it! Not so, we reply; for there is a conflict of opinions as to its special nature. Unlearned people and the Lokāyatikas [materialists] are of opinion that the mere body endowed with the quality of intelligence is the Self; others that the organs endowed with intelligence are the Self; others maintain that the internal organ is the Self; others, again, that the Self is a mere momentary idea; others, again, that it is the Void. Others, again (to proceed to the opinion of such as acknowledge the authority of the Veda), maintain that there is a transmigrating being different from the body, and so on, which is both agent and enjoyer (of the fruits of action); others teach that that being is enjoying only, not acting; others believe that in addition to the individual souls, there is an all-knowing, all-powerful Lord. Others, finally, (i.e. the Vedāntins) maintain that the Lord is the Self of the enjoyer (i.e. of the individual soul whose individual existence is apparent only, the product of Nescience).

Thus there are many various opinions, basing part of them on sound arguments and scriptural texts, part of them on fallacious arguments and scriptural texts misunderstood. If therefore a man would embrace some one of these opinions without previous consideration, he would bar himself from the highest beatitude and incur grievous loss. [. . .] (I, 1, 1)

[. . .] The full sense of the [next] Sūtra [. . .] is: That omniscient omnipotent cause from which proceed the origin, subsistence, and dissolution of this world – which world is differentiated by names and forms, contains many agents and enjoyers, is the abode of the fruits of actions, these fruits having their definite places, time, and causes, and the nature of whose arrangement cannot even be conceived by the mind – that cause, we say, is Brahman. [. . .]

[. . .] [T]he knowledge of the real nature of a thing does not depend on the notions of man, but only on the thing itself. For to think with regard to a post, 'this is a post or a man, or something else,' is not knowledge of truth; the two ideas, 'it is a man or something else,' being false, and only the third idea, 'it is a post,' which depends on the thing itself, falling under the head of true knowledge. Thus true knowledge of all existing things depends on the things themselves, and hence the knowledge of Brahman all depends altogether on the thing, i.e. Brahman itself. – But, it might be said, as Brahman is an existing substance, it will be the object of the other means of right knowledge also, and from this it follows that a discussion of the Vedānta-texts is purposeless. – This we deny; for as Brahman is not an object of the senses, it has no connection with those other means of knowledge. For the senses have, according to their nature, only external things for their objects, not Brahman. If Brahman were an object of the senses, we might perceive that the world is connected with Brahman as its effect; but as the effect only (i.e. the world) is perceived, it is impossible to decide (through perception) whether it is connected with Brahman or something else. Therefore the Sūtra under discussion is not meant to propound inference (as the means of knowing Brahman), but rather to set forth a Vedānta-text. – Which, then, is the Vedānta-text which the Sūtra points at as having to be considered with reference to the characteristics of Brahman? – It is the passage Taitt. Up. III, 1, 'Bhṛigu Vāruṇi went to his father Varuṇa, saying, Sir, teach me Brahman,' &c., up to 'That from whence these beings are born, that by which, when born, they live, that into which they enter at their death, try to know that. That is Brahman.' The sentence finally determining the sense of this passage is found III, 6: 'From bliss these beings are born; by bliss, when born, they live; into bliss they enter at their death.' Other passages also are to be adduced which declare the cause to be the almighty Being, whose essential nature is eternal purity, intelligence, and freedom. (I, 1, 2)

[. . .] But how about the objection raised [. . .] that the information about Brahman cannot be held to have a purpose in the same way as the statement about a rope has one, because a man even after having heard about Brahman continues to belong to this transmigratory world? – We reply as follows: It is impossible to show that a man who has once understood Brahman to be the Self, belongs to the transmigratory world in the same sense as he did before, because that would be contrary to the fact of his being Brahman. For we indeed observe that a person who imagines the body, and so on, to constitute the Self, is subject to fear and pain, but we have no right to assume that the same person after having, by means of the Veda, comprehended Brahman to be the Self, and thus having got over his former imaginings, will still in the same manner be subject to pain and fear whose cause is wrong knowledge. [. . .] Thus *śruti* [reliable testimony] also declares, 'When he is free from the body, then neither pleasure nor pain touches him' (Ch. Up. VIII, 12, 1). If it should be objected that the condition of being free from the body follows on death only, we demur, since the cause of man being joined to the body is wrong knowledge. For it is not possible to establish the state of embodiedness upon anything else but wrong knowledge. And that the state of disembodiedness is eternal on account of its not having actions for its cause, we have already explained. The objection again, that embodiedness is caused by the merit and demerit effected by the Self (and therefore real), we refute by remarking that as the (reality of the) conjunction of the Self with the body is itself not established, the circumstance of merit and demerit being due to the action of the Self is likewise not established; for (if we should try to get over this difficulty by representing the Self's embodiedness as caused by merit and demerit) we should commit the logical fault of making embodiedness dependent on merit and demerit, and again merit and demerit on embodiedness. And the assumption of an endless retrogressive chain (of embodied states and merit and demerit) would be no better than a chain of blind men (who are unable to lead one another). [. . .]

[. . .] As long as the knowledge of the Self, which Scripture tells us to search after, has not arisen, so long the Self is knowing subject; but that same subject is that which is searched after, viz. (the highest Self) free from all evil and blemish.

Just as the idea of the Self being the body is assumed as valid (in ordinary life), so all the ordinary sources of knowledge (perception and the like) are valid only until the one Self is ascertained.' (I, 1, 4)

But to raise a new objection, there exists no transmigrating soul different from the Lord and obstructed by impediments of knowledge; for *śruti* expressly declares that 'there is no other seer but he; there is no other knower but he' (Bṛh. Up. III, 7, 23). How then can it be said that the origination of knowledge in the transmigrating soul depends on a body, while it does not do so in the case of the Lord? – True, we reply. There is in reality no transmigrating soul different from the Lord. Still the connexion (of the Lord) with limiting adjuncts, consisting of bodies and so on, is assumed, just as we assume the ether to enter into connexion with divers limiting adjuncts such as jars, pots, caves, and the like. And just as in consequence of connexion of the latter kind such conceptions and terms as 'the hollow (space) of a jar,' &c. are generally current, although the space inside a jar is not really different from universal space, and just as in consequence thereof there generally prevails the false notion that there are different spaces such as the space of a jar and so on; so there prevails likewise the false notion that the Lord and the transmigrating soul are different; a notion due to the non-discrimination of the (unreal) connexion of the soul with the limiting conditions, consisting of the body and so on. That the Self, although in reality the only existence, imparts the quality of Selfhood to bodies and the like which are Not-Self is a matter of observation, and is due to mere wrong conception, which depends in its turn on antecedent wrong conception. And the consequence of the soul thus involving itself in the transmigratory state is that its thought depends on a body and the like. (I, 1, 5)

[. . .] The individual soul (*jīva*) is called awake as long as being connected with the various external objects by mean of the modifications of the mind – which thus constitute limiting adjuncts of the soul – it apprehends those external objects, and identifies itself with the gross body, which is one of those external objects. When, modified by the impressions which the external objects have left, it sees dreams, it is denoted

by the term 'mind.' When, on the cessation of the two limiting adjuncts (i.e. the subtle and the gross bodies), and the consequent absence of the modifications due to the adjuncts, it is, in the state of deep sleep, merged in the Self as it were, then it is said to be asleep (resolved into the Self). [. . .] (I, 1, 9)

In what precedes we have shown, availing ourselves of appropriate arguments, that the Vedānta-texts exhibited under Sūtras I, 1-11, are capable of proving that the all-knowing, all-powerful Lord is the cause of the origin, subsistence, and dissolution of the world. And we have explained, by pointing to the prevailing uniformity of view (I, 10), that all Vedānta-texts whatever maintain an intelligent cause. The question might therefore be asked, 'What reason is there for the subsequent part of the *Vedāntasūtras?*' (as the chief point is settled already.)

To this question we reply as follows: Brahman is apprehended under two forms; in the first place as qualified by limiting conditions owing to the multiformity of the evolutions of name and form (i.e. the multiformity of the created world[)]; in the second place as being the opposite of this, i.e. free from all limiting conditions whatever. [. . .][2]

Although one and the same Self is hidden in all beings movable as well as immovable, yet owing to the gradual rise of excellence of the minds which form the limiting conditions (of the Self), Scripture declares that the Self, although eternally unchanging and uniform, reveals itself in a graduated series of beings, and so appears in forms of various dignity and power; compare, for instance (Ait. Ār. II, 3, 2, 1), 'He who knows the higher manifestation of the Self in him,' &c. [. . .] (I, 1, 11)

[. . .] [W]e see that in ordinary life, the Self, which in reality is never anything but the Self, is, owing to non-comprehension of the truth, identified with the Non-Self, i.e. the body and so on; whereby it becomes possible to speak of the Self in so far as it is identified with the body, and so on, as something not searched for but to be searched for, not heard but to be heard, not seized but to be seized, not perceived but to be perceived, not known but to be known, and the like. Scripture, on the other hand, denies, in such passages as 'there is no other seer but he' (Bṛh. Up. III, 7, 23), that there is in reality any seer or hearer different from the all-knowing highest Lord. (Nor can it be said that the Lord is unreal because he is identical with the unreal individual soul; for) the Lord differs from the soul (*vijñānātman*) which is embodied, acts and enjoys, and is the product of Nescience, in the same way as the real juggler who stands on the ground differs from the illusive juggler, who, holding in his hand a shield and a sword, climbs up to the sky by means of a rope; or as the free unlimited ether differs from the ether of a jar, which is determined by its limiting adjunct, (viz. the jar.) [. . .] (I, 1, 17)

[. . .] [A]s the passages, 'I am Brahman,' 'That art thou,' and others, prove, there is in reality no such thing as an individual soul absolutely different from Brahman, but Brahman, in so far as it differentiates itself through the mind (*buddhi*) and other limiting conditions, is called individual soul, agent, enjoyer.

[. . .] If there were no objects there would be no subjects; and if there were no subjects there would be no objects. For on either side alone nothing could be achieved. [. . .] (I, 1, 31)

True, we reply, (there is in reality one universal Self only.) But the highest Self in so far as it is limited by its adjuncts, viz. the body, the senses, and the mind (*mano-buddhi*), is, by the ignorant, spoken of as if it were embodied. Similarly the ether, although in reality unlimited, appears limited owing to certain adjuncts, such as jars and other vessels. With regard to this (unreal limitation of the one Self) the distinction of objects of activity and of agents may be practically assumed, as long as we have not learned – from the passage, 'That art thou' – that the Self is one only. As soon, however, as we grasp the truth that there is only one universal Self, there is an end to the whole practical view of the world with its distinction of bondage, final release, and the like. (I, 2, 6)

[. . .] The declaration of the difference of the embodied Self and the internal ruler has its reason in the limiting adjunct, consisting of the organs of action, presented by Nescience, and is not absolutely true. For the Self within is one only; two internal Selfs are not possible. But owing to its limiting adjunct the one Self is practically treated as if it were two; just as we make a distinction between the ether of the jar and the universal ether. Hence there is room for those scriptural passages which set forth the distinction of knower and object of knowledge, for perception and the other means of proof, for the intuitive knowledge of the apparent world, and for that part of Scripture which contains injunctions and prohibitions. In accordance with this, the scriptural passage, 'Where there is duality, as it were, there one sees another,' declares that the whole practical world exists only in the sphere of Nescience; while the subsequent passage, 'But when the Self only is all this, how should he see another?' declares that the practical world vanishes in the sphere of true knowledge. (I, 2, 20)

[. . .] That same highest Brahman constitutes – as we know from passages such as 'that art thou' – the real nature of the individual soul, while its second nature, i.e. that aspect of it which depends on fictitious limiting conditions, is not its real nature. For as long as the individual soul does not free itself from Nescience in the form of duality – which Nescience may be compared to the mistake of him who in the twilight mistakes a post for a man – and does not rise to the knowledge of the Self, whose nature is unchangeable, eternal Cognition – which expresses itself in the form 'I am Brahman' – so long it remains the individual soul. But when, discarding the aggregate of body, sense-organs and mind, it arrives, by means of Scripture, at the knowledge that it is not itself that aggregate, that it does not form part of transmigratory existence, but is the True, the Real, the Self, whose nature is pure intelligence; then knowing itself to be of the nature of unchangeable, eternal Cognition, it lifts itself above the vain conceit of being one with this body, and itself becomes the Self, whose nature is unchanging, eternal Cognition. As is declared in such scriptural passages as 'He who knows the highest Brahman becomes even Brahman' (Mu. Up. III, 2, 9). And this is the real nature of the individual soul by means of which it arises from the body and appears in its own form.

[. . .] Before the rise of discriminative knowledge the nature of the individual soul, which is (in reality) pure light, is non-discriminated as it were from its limiting adjuncts consisting of body, senses, mind, sense-objects and feelings, and appears as consisting of the energies of seeing and so on. Similarly – to quote an analogous case from ordinary experience – the true nature of a pure crystal, i.e. its transparency and whiteness, is, before the rise of discriminative knowledge (on the part of the observer,) nondiscriminated as it were from any limiting adjuncts of red or blue colour; while, as soon as through some means of true cognition discriminative knowledge has arisen, it is said to have now accomplished its true nature, i.e. transparency and whiteness, although in reality it had already done so before. (I, 3, 19)

[...] Brahman has been defined as that from which there proceed the origination, sustentation, and retractation of this world. Now as this definition comprises alike the relation of substantial causality in which clay and gold, for instance, stand to golden ornaments and earthen pots, and the relation of operative causality in which the potter and the goldsmith stand to the things mentioned; a doubt arises to which of these two kinds the causality of Brahman belongs. [...]

[...] Now the knowledge of everything is possible through the cognition of the material cause, since the effect is non-different from the material cause. On the other hand, effects are not non-different from their operative cause; for we know from ordinary experience that the carpenter, for instance, is different from the house he has built. – The illustrative example referred to is the one mentioned (Ch. Up. VI, 1, 4), 'My dear, as by one clod of clay all that is made of clay is known, the modification (i.e. the effect) being a name merely which has its origin in speech, while the truth is that it is clay merely;' which passage again has reference to the material cause. [...] The Self is thus the operative cause, because there is no other ruling principle, and the material cause because there is no other substance from which the world could originate. (I, 4, 23)

There is nothing objectionable in our system. – The objection that the effect when being reabsorbed into its cause would inquinate [pollute] the latter with its qualities does not damage our position 'because there are parallel instances' [...] of effects not inquinating with their qualities the causes into which they are reabsorbed. Things, for instance, made of clay, such as pots, &c., which in their state of separate existence are of various

descriptions, do not, when they are reabsorbed into their original matter (i.e. clay), impart to the latter their individual qualities; nor do golden ornaments impart their individual qualities to their elementary material, i.e. gold, into which they may finally be reabsorbed. Nor does the fourfold complex of organic beings which springs from earth impart its qualities to the latter at the time of reabsorption. You [the objector], on the other hand, have not any instances to quote in your favour. For reabsorption could not take place at all if the effect when passing back into its causal substance continued to subsist there with all its individual properties. And that in spite of the non-difference of cause and effect the effect has its Self in the cause, but not the cause in the effect, is a point which we shall render clear later on, under II, 1, 14.

[...] We can quote other examples in favour of our doctrine. As the magician is not at any time affected by the magical illusion produced by himself, because it is unreal, so the highest Self is not affected by the world-illusion. And as one dreaming person is not affected by the illusory visions of his dream because they do not accompany the waking state and the state of dreamless sleep; so the one permanent witness of the three states (viz. the highest Self which is the one unchanging witness of the creation, subsistence, and reabsorption of the world) is not touched by the mutually exclusive three states. For that the highest Self appears in those three states, is a mere illusion, not more substantial than the snake for which the rope is mistaken in the twilight. With reference to this point teachers knowing the true tradition of the Vedanta have made the following declaration, 'When the individual soul which is held in the bonds of slumber by the beginningless *māyā* awakes, then it knows the eternal, sleepless, dreamless non-duality' (Gauḍap. Kār. I, 16). (II, 1, 11)

[...] Another objection, based on reasoning, is raised against the doctrine of Brahman being the cause of the world. [...]

[...] The distinction of enjoyers and objects of enjoyment is well known from ordinary experience, the enjoyers being intelligent, embodied souls, while sound and the like are the objects of enjoyment. Devadatta, for instance, is an enjoyer, the dish (which he eats) an object of enjoyment. The distinction of the two would be reduced to non-existence if the enjoyer passed over into the object of enjoyment, and vice versa. Now this passing over of one thing into another would actually result from the doctrine of the world being non-different from Brahman. But the sublation of a well-established distinction is objectionable, not only with regard to the present time when that distinction is observed to exist, but also with regard to the past and the future, for which it is inferred. The doctrine of Brahman's causality must therefore be abandoned, as it would lead to the sublation of the well-established distinction of enjoyers and objects of enjoyment.

To the preceding objection we reply, 'It may exist as in ordinary experience.' Even on our philosophic view the distinction may exist, as ordinary experience furnishes us with analogous instances. We see, for instance, that waves, foam, bubbles, and other modifications of the sea, although they really are not different from the seawater, exist, sometimes in the state of mutual separation, sometimes in the state of conjunction, &c. From the fact of their being non-different from the seawater, it does not follow that they pass over into each other; and, again, although they do not pass over into each other, still they are not different from the sea. So it is in the case under discussion also. The enjoyers and the objects of enjoyment do not pass over into each other, and yet they are not different from the highest Brahman. And although the enjoyer is not really an effect of Brahman, since the unmodified creator himself, in so far as he enters into the effect, is called the enjoyer (according to the passage, 'Having created he entered into it,' Taitt. Up. II, 6), still after Brahman has entered into its effects it passes into a state of distinction, in consequence of the effect acting as a limiting adjunct; just as the universal ether is divided by its contact with jars and other limiting adjuncts. The conclusion is, that the distinction of enjoyers and objects of enjoyment is possible, although both are non-different from Brahman, their highest cause, as the analogous instance of the sea and its waves demonstrates. (II, 1, 13)

The refutation contained in the preceding Sutra was set forth on the condition of the practical distinction of enjoyers and objects of enjoyment being acknowledged. In reality, however, that distinction does not exist because there is understood to be non-difference (identity) of

cause and effect. The effect is this manifold world consisting of ether and so on; the cause is the highest Brahman. Of the effect it is understood that in reality it is non-different from the cause, i.e. has no existence apart from the cause. – How so? – 'On account of the scriptural word "origin" and others.' The word 'origin' is used in connexion with a simile, in a passage undertaking to show how through the knowledge of one thing everything is known; viz. Ch. Up. VI, 1, 4, 'As, my dear, by one clod of clay all that is made of clay is known, the modification (i.e. the effect; the thing made of clay) being a name merely which has its origin in speech, while the truth is that it is clay merely; thus,' &c. – The meaning of this passage is that, if there is known a lump of clay which really and truly is nothing but clay, there are known thereby likewise all things made of clay, such as jars, dishes, pails, and so on, all of which agree in having clay for their true nature. For these modifications or effects are names only, exist through or originate from speech only, while in reality there exists no such thing as a modification. In so far as they are names (individual effects distinguished by names) they are untrue; in so far as they are clay they are true. – This parallel instance is given with reference to Brahman; applying the phrase 'having its origin in speech' to the case illustrated by the instance quoted we understand that the entire body of effects has no existence apart from Brahman. [. . .] We therefore must adopt the following view. In the same way as those parts of ethereal space which are limited by jars and waterpots are not really different from the universal ethereal space, and as the water of a mirage is not really different from the surface of the salty steppe – for the nature of that water is that it is seen in one moment and has vanished in the next, and moreover, it is not to be perceived by its own nature (i.e. apart from the surface of the desert –; so this manifold world with its objects of enjoyment, enjoyers and so on has no existence apart from Brahman. – But – it might be objected – Brahman has in itself elements of manifoldness. As the tree has many branches, so Brahman possesses many powers and energies dependent on those powers. Unity and manifoldness are therefore both true. Thus, a tree considered in itself is one, but it is manifold if viewed as having branches; so the sea in itself is one, but manifold as having waves and foam; so the clay in itself is one, but manifold if viewed with regard to the jars and dishes made of it. On this assumption the process of final release resulting from right knowledge may be established in connexion with the element of unity (in Brahman), while the two processes of common worldly activity and of activity according to the Veda – which depend on the *karmakāṇḍa* [ritual activity] – may be established in connexion with the element of manifoldness. And with this view the parallel instances of clay &c. agree very well.

This theory, we reply, is untenable because in the instance (quoted in the Upaniṣad) the phrase 'as clay they are true' asserts the cause only to be true while the phrase 'having its origin in speech' declares the unreality of all effects. And with reference to the matter illustrated by the instance given (viz. the highest cause, Brahman) we read, 'In that all this has its Self;' and, again, 'That is true,' whereby it is asserted that only the one highest cause is true. The following passage again, 'That is the Self; thou art that, O Śvetaketu!' teaches that the embodied soul (the individual soul) also is Brahman. (And we must note that) the passage distinctly teaches that the fact of the embodied soul having its Self in Brahman is self-established, not be accomplished by endeavour. This doctrine of the individual soul having its Self in Brahman, if once accepted as the doctrine of the Veda, does away with the independent existence of the individual soul, just as the idea of the rope does away with the idea of the snake (for which the rope had been mistaken). And if the doctrine of the independent existence of the individual soul has to be set aside, then the opinion of the entire phenomenal world – which is based on the individual soul – having an independent existence is likewise to be set aside. But only for the establishment of the latter an element of manifoldness would have to be assumed in Brahman, in addition to the element of unity. – Scriptural passages also (such as 'When the Self only is all this, how should he see another?' Bṛh. Up. II, 4, 13) declare that for him who sees that everything has its Self in Brahman the whole phenomenal world with its actions, agents, and results of actions is non-existent. Nor can it be said that this non-existence of the phenomenal world is declared (by Scripture) to be limited to certain states; for the passage 'Thou art that' shows that the general fact of Brahman being the Self of all is not limited by any particular state.

Other objections are started. – If we acquiesce in the doctrine of absolute unity, the ordinary means of right knowledge, perception, &c., become invalid because the absence of manifoldness deprives them of their objects; just as the idea of a man becomes invalid after the right idea of the post (which at first had been mistaken for a man) has presented itself. Moreover, all the texts embodying injunctions and prohibitions will lose their purport if the distinction on which their validity depends does not really exist. And further, the entire body of doctrine which refers to final release will collapse, if the distinction of teacher and pupil on which it depends is not real. And if the doctrine of release is untrue, how can we maintain the truth of the absolute unity of the Self, which forms an item of that doctrine?

These objections, we reply, do not damage our position because the entire complex of phenomenal existence is considered as true as long as the knowledge of Brahman being the Self of all has not arisen; just as the phantoms of a dream are considered to be true until the sleeper wakes. For as long as a person has not reached the true knowledge of the unity of the Self, so long it does not enter his mind that the world of effects with its means and objects of right knowledge and its results of actions is untrue; he rather, in consequence of his ignorance, looks on mere effects (such as body, offspring, wealth, &c.) as forming part of and belonging to his Self, forgetful of Brahman being in reality the Self of all. Hence, as long as true knowledge does not present itself, there is no reason why the ordinary course of secular and religious activity should not hold on undisturbed. The case is analogous to that of a dreaming man who in his dream sees manifold things, and, up to the moment of waking, is convinced that his ideas are produced by real perception without suspecting the perception to be a merely apparent one. – But how (to restate an objection raised above) can the Vedanta-texts if untrue convey information about the true being of Brahman? We certainly do not observe that a man bitten by a rope-snake (i.e. a snake falsely imagined in a rope) dies, nor is the water appearing in a mirage used for drinking or bathing. – This objection, we reply, is without force (because as a matter of fact we do see real effects to result from unreal causes), for we observe that death sometimes takes place from imaginary venom, (when a man imagines himself to have been bitten by a venomous snake,) and effects (of what is perceived in a dream) such as the bite of a snake or bathing in a river take place with regard to a dreaming person. – But, it will be said, these effects themselves are unreal! – These effects themselves, we reply, are unreal indeed; but not so the consciousness which the dreaming person has of them. This consciousness is a real result; for it is not sublated by the waking consciousness. The man who has risen from sleep does indeed consider the effects perceived by him in his dream such as being bitten by a snake, bathing in a river, &c. to be unreal, but he does not on that account consider the consciousness he had of them to be unreal likewise.

[...] Thus the Lord depends (as Lord) upon the limiting adjuncts of name and form, the products of Nescience; just as the universal ether depends (as limited ether, such as the ether of a jar, &c.) upon the limiting adjuncts in the shape of jars, pots, &c. He (the Lord) stands in the realm of the phenomenal in the relation of a ruler to the so-called jīvas (individual souls) or cognitional Selfs (*vijñānātman*), which indeed are one with his own Self – just as the portions of ether enclosed in jars and the like are one with the universal ether – but are limited by aggregates of instruments of action (i.e. bodies) produced from name and form, the presentations of Nescience. Hence the Lord's being a Lord, his omniscience, his omnipotence, &c. all depend on the limitation due to the adjuncts whose Self is Nescience; while in reality none of these qualities belong to the Self whose true nature is cleared, by right knowledge, from all adjuncts whatever. [...] (II, 1, 14)

That the effect exists before its origination and is non-different from the cause, follows from reasoning as well as from a further scriptural passage.

We at first set forth the argumentation. – Ordinary experience teaches us that those who wish to produce certain effects, such as curds, or earthen jars, or golden ornaments, employ for their purpose certain determined causal substances such as milk, clay, and gold; those who wish to produce sour milk do not employ clay, nor do those who intend to make jars employ milk and so on. But, according to that doctrine which teaches that the effect is non-existent (before its actual production), all this should be possible. For if before their actual origination all effects are equally non-existent in any causal substance, why then should curds be produced from milk only and not from clay also, and jars from clay only and not from milk as well? – Let us then maintain, the *asatkāryavādin* rejoins,[3] that there is indeed an equal non-existence of any effect in any cause, but that at the same time each causal substance has a certain capacity reaching beyond itself (*atiśaya*) for some particular effect only and not for other effects; that, for instance, milk only, and not clay, has a certain capacity for curds; and clay only, and not milk, an analogous capacity for jars. – What, we ask in return, do you understand by that '*atiśaya*'? If you understand by it the antecedent condition of the effect (before its actual origination), you abandon your doctrine that the effect does not exist in the cause, and prove our doctrine according to which it does so exist. If, on the other hand, you understand by the *atiśaya* a certain power of the cause assumed to the end of accounting for the fact that only one determined effect springs from the cause, you must admit that the power can determine the particular effect only if it neither is other (than cause and effect) nor non-existent; for if it were either, it would not be different from anything else which is either non-existent or other than cause and effect, (and how then should it alone be able to produce the particular effect?). Hence it follows that that power is identical with the Self of the cause, and that the effect is identical with the Self of that power. – Moreover, as the ideas of cause and effect on the one hand and of substance and qualities on the other hand are not separate ones, as, for instance, the ideas of a horse and a buffalo, it follows that the identity of the cause and the effect as well as of the substance and its qualities has to be admitted. (Let it then be assumed, the opponent rejoins, that the cause and the effect, although really different, are not apprehended as such, because they are connected by the so-called *samavāya* connexion.) – If, we reply, you assume the *samavāya* connexion between cause and effect,[4] you have either to admit that the *samavāya* itself is joined by a certain connexion to the two terms which are connected by *samavāya*, and then that connexion will again require a new connexion (joining it to the two terms which it binds together), and you will thus be compelled to postulate an infinite series of connexions; or else you will have to maintain that the *samavāya* is not joined by any connexion to the terms which it binds together, and from that will result the dissolution of the bond which connects the two terms of the *samavāya* relation. – Well then, the opponent rejoins, let us assume that the *samavāya* connexion as itself being a connexion may be connected with the terms which it joins without the help of any further connexion. – Then, we reply, conjunction (*samyoga*) also must be connected with the two terms which it joins without the help of the *samavāya* connexion; for conjunction also is a kind of connexion. – Moreover, as substances, qualities, and so on are apprehended as standing in the relation of identity, the assumption of the *samavāya* relation has really no purport.

In what manner again do you – who maintain that the cause and the effect are joined by the *samavāya* relation – assume a substance consisting of parts which is an effect to abide in its causes, i.e. in the material parts of which it consists? Does it abide in all the parts taken together or in each particular part? – If you say that it abides in all parts together, it follows that the whole as such cannot be perceived, as it is impossible that all the parts should be in contact with the organs of perception. (And let it not be objected that the whole may be apprehended through some of the parts only), for manyness which abides in all its substrates together (i.e. in all the many things), is not apprehended so long as only some of those substrates are apprehended. – Let it then be assumed that the whole abides in all the parts by the mediation of intervening aggregates of parts. – In that case, we reply, we should have to assume other parts in addition to the primary originative parts of the whole, in order that by means of those other parts the whole could abide in the primary parts in the manner indicated by you. For we see (that one thing which abides in another abides there by means of parts different from those of that other thing), that the sword, for instance, pervades the sheath by means of parts different from the parts of the sheath. But an assumption of that kind would lead us into a regressus in infinitum, because in order to explain how the whole abides in certain given parts we should always have to assume further parts. – Well, then, let us maintain the second alternative, viz. that the whole abides in each particular part. – That also cannot be admitted; for if the whole is present in one part it cannot be present in other parts also; not any more than Devadatta can be present in Śrughna and in Pāṭaliputra on one and the same day. If the whole were present in more than one part, several wholes would result, comparable to Devadatta and Yajñadatta, who, as being two different persons, may live one of them at Śrughna and the other at Pāṭaliputra. – If the opponent should rejoin that the whole may be fully present in each part, just as the generic character of the cow is fully present in each individual cow; we point out that the generic attributes of the cow are visibly perceived in each individual cow, but that the whole is not thus perceived in each particular part. If the whole were fully present in each part, the consequence would be that the whole would produce its effects indifferently with any of its parts; a cow, for instance, would give milk from her horns or her tail. But such things are not seen to take place. [. . .] (II, 1, 18)

Your assertion that the intelligent Brahman alone, without a second, is the cause of the world cannot be maintained, on account of the observation of employment (of instruments). For in ordinary life we see that potters, weavers, and other handicraftsmen produce jars, cloth, and the like, after having put themselves in possession of the means thereto by providing themselves with various implements, such as clay, staffs, wheels, string, &c.; Brahman, on the other hand, you conceive to be without any help; how then can it act as a creator without providing itself with instruments to work with? – We therefore maintain that Brahman is not the cause of the world.

This objection is not valid, because causation is possible in consequence of a peculiar constitution of the causal substance, as in the case of milk. Just as milk and water turn into curds and ice respectively, without any extraneous means, so it is in the case of Brahman also. And if you object to this analogy for the reason that milk, in order to turn into curds, does require an extraneous agent, viz. heat, we reply that milk by itself also undergoes a certain amount of definite change, and that its turning is merely accelerated by heat. If milk did not possess that capability of itself, heat could not compel it to turn; for we see that air or ether, for instance, is not compelled by the action of heat to turn into sour milk. By the co-operation of auxiliary means the milk's capability of turning into sour milk is merely completed. The absolutely complete power of Brahman, on the other hand, does not require to be supplemented by any extraneous help. [. . .] (II, 1, 24)

[. . .] [W]e maintain that the (alleged) break in Brahman's nature is a mere figment of Nescience. By a break of that nature a thing is not really broken up into parts, not any more than the moon is really multiplied by appearing double to a person of defective vision. By that element of plurality which is the fiction of Nescience, which is characterised by name and form, which is evolved as well as non-evolved, which is not to be defined either as the Existing or the Non-existing, Brahman becomes the basis of this entire apparent world with its changes, and so on, while in its true and real nature it at the same time remains unchanged, lifted above the phenomenal universe. And as the distinction of names and forms, the fiction of Nescience, originates entirely from speech only, it does not militate against the fact of Brahman being without parts. – Nor have the scriptural passages which speak of Brahman as undergoing change the purpose of teaching the fact of change; for such instruction would have no fruit. They rather aim at imparting instruction about Brahman's Self as raised above this apparent world; that being an instruction which we know to have a result of its own. [. . .] (II, 1, 27)

[. . .] It is not true that the world of dreams is real; it is mere illusion and there is not a particle of reality in it. – Why? – 'On account of its nature not manifesting itself with the totality,' i.e. because the nature of the dream world does not manifest itself with the totality of the attributes of real things. – What then do you mean by the 'totality'? – The fulfilment of the conditions of place, time, and cause, and the circumstance of non-refutation. All these have their sphere in real things, but cannot be applied to dreams. In the first place there is, in a dream, no space for chariots and the like; for those cannot possibly find room in the limited confines of the body. [. . .] In the second place we see that dreams are in conflict with the conditions of time. One person lying asleep at night dreams that it is day in the Bhārata Varṣa; another lives, during a dream which lasts one [brief period] only, through many crowds of years. – In the third place there do not exist in the state of dreaming the requisite efficient causes for either thought or action;

for as, in sleep, the organs are drawn inward, the dreaming person has no eyes, &c. for perceiving chariots and other things; and whence should he, in the space of the twinkling of an eye, have the power of – or procure the material for – making chariots and the like? – In the fourth place the chariots, horses, &c., which the dream creates, are refuted, i.e. shown not to exist by the waking state. And apart from this, the dream itself refutes what it creates, as its end often contradicts its beginning; what at first was considered to be a chariot turns, in a moment, into a man, and what was conceived to be a man has all at once become a tree. [. . .] (III, 2, 3)

[. . .] We only maintain that the world connected with the intermediate state (i.e. the world of dreams) is not real in the same sense as the world consisting of ether and so on is real. On the other hand we must remember that also the so-called real creation with its ether, air, &c., is not absolutely real; for as we have proved before (II, 1, 14) the entire expanse of things is mere illusion. The world consisting of ether, &c. remains fixed and distinct up to the moment when the soul cognizes that Brahman is the Self of all; the world of dreams on the other hand is daily sublated by the waking state. That the latter is mere illusion has, therefore, to be understood with a distinction. (III, 2, 4)

We now attempt to ascertain, on the ground *śruti*, the nature of that Brahman with which the individual soul becomes united in the state of deep sleep and so on, in consequence of the cessation of the limiting adjuncts. – The scriptural passages which refer to Brahman are of a double character; some indicate that Brahman is affected by difference, so, e.g. 'He to whom belong all works, all desires, all sweet odours and tastes' (Ch. Up. III, 14, 2); others, that it is without difference, so, e.g. 'It is neither coarse nor fine, neither short nor long,' &c. (Bṛh. Up. III, 8, 8). Have we, on the ground of these passages, to assume that Brahman has a double nature, or either nature, and, if either, that it is affected with difference, or without difference? This is the point to be discussed.

The [objector] maintains that, in conformity with the scriptural passages which indicate a double nature, a double nature is to be ascribed to Brahman.

To this we reply as follows. – At any rate the highest Brahman cannot, by itself, possess double characteristics; for on account of the contradiction implied therein, it is impossible to admit that one and the same thing should by itself possess certain qualities, such as colour, &c., and should not possess them. – Nor is it possible that Brahman should possess double characteristics 'on account of place,' i.e. on account of its conjunction with its limiting adjuncts, such as earth, &c. For the connexion with limiting adjuncts is unavailing to impart to a thing of a certain nature an altogether different nature. The crystal, e.g. which is in itself clear, does not become dim through its conjunction with a limiting adjunct in the form of red colour; for that it is pervaded by the quality of dimness is an altogether erroneous notion. In the case of Brahman the limiting adjuncts are, moreover, presented by Nescience merely. Hence (as the *upadhis* [limitations] are the product of Nescience) if we embrace either of the two alternatives, we must decide in favour of that according to which Brahma is absolutely devoid of all difference, not in favour of the opposite one. For all passages whose aim it is to represent the nature of Brahman (such as, 'It is without sound, without touch, without form, without decay,' Ka. Up. I, 3, 15) teach that it is free from all difference. (III, 2, 11)

Just as the light of the sun or the moon after having passed through space enters into contact with a finger or some other limiting adjunct, and, according as the latter is straight or bent, itself becomes straight or bent as it were; so Brahman also assumes, as it were, the form of the earth and the other limiting adjuncts with which it enters into connexion. Hence there is no reason why certain texts should not teach, with a view to meditative worship, that Brahman has that and that form. [. . .] (III, 2, 15)

Notes

1   Readers will be reminded here of Plato's puzzle, in the *Meno*, as to how one can seek knowledge without already knowing what one is seeking. Śaṃkara's solution is that while we know Brahman in the sense of being acquainted with it in the form of our true Self, most of us do not know what it is and indeed entertain mistaken theories about it.

2   This is the famous distinction between *saguṇa* (qualified/conditioned) and *nirguṇa* (unqualified/unconditioned) Brahman or reality. The former is Brahman as manifested in the apparent world; the latter, Brahman as it truly is in itself.

3   *Asatkāryavāda* is the doctrine that the effect does *not* already exist in the cause.

4   *Samavāya* is usually translated as "inherence." The argument that follows is strikingly similar to F. H. Bradley's "infinite regress" argument against the possibility of "external," including causal, relations between different things. See his *Appearance and Reality*, Oxford: Oxford University Press, 1969, ch. 3.

8

Ibn Sina (Avicenna), *Kitab al-Shifa*, Book I, Chapters Six and Seven, Book II, Chapters Two and Three

Introduction

In 1952 the Iranian government erected in the center of the town of Hamadan a towering conical mausoleum in memory of a thinker whom Thomas Aquinas called simply "the Commentator" and who has been described variously as the most important philosopher of the Islamic tradition and the most influential philosopher of the pre-modern world. Indeed, the man memorialized by the 12-pillared colossus of Hamadan is the only medieval philosopher to have made a significant impact upon all three medieval Abrahamic philosophical traditions – Jewish, Christian, and Muslim. Curiously, however, even today few people in the West know this thinker by name. He was called "Abu Ali al-Husayn Ibn Abd Allah Ibn Sina," or just "Ibn Sina" for short. In the west his name has been Latinized through the Hebrew to simply "Avicenna."

Avicenna was born in 980 in the ancient city of Balkh (or Bactra) in present-day Afghanistan, near today's border with Uzbekistan. He died in 1037 in Hamadan en route to Istfahan. At the time of Avicenna's birth, Balkh was an important city in the eastern Persian province of Khorasan,

and his father was a governor in the Samanid government there. His father's position gave Avicenna access to a first rate education, and he was quickly recognized as an intellectual prodigy. Avicenna's adulthood led him into the leading halls of power of his place and time, but his life was nevertheless unsettled and itinerant. He gained renown, like many other Muslim philosophers, as a physician as well as a mathematician and general polymath. Perhaps unlike many others, however, he was also well known for his carnal exploits.

The author of hundreds of volumes, Avicenna is principally remembered today for two works: first the *al-Qanun fi Tibb* (*The Canon of Medicine*), which became an indispensable medical text in European as well as near Eastern universities even into the nineteenth century; and second his highly influential philosophical treatise, the *Kitab al-Shifa*, whose title (*The Book of Healing* or *The Cure for Ignorance*) indicates the continuity in Avicenna's own mind between medicine and philosophy.

Avicenna's philosophical accomplishment must be understood in the context of the intellectual tradition known as *falsafa* (from the Greek, *philosophia*).[1] *Falsafa* may be understood as the stream of thought rooted in the translation into Arabic of Greek philosophical works by the "House of Wisdom" in Baghdad from the eighth through early tenth centuries. It was, indeed, because of this massive translation project that many ancient works were able to survive into the

From Avicenna, *The Metaphysics of* The Healing, ed. and trans. M. E. Marmura, Provo, UT: Brigham Young University Press, 2005, pp. 29–38, 48–63 (notes omitted).

modern world. Those employed with philosophical texts at the House of Wisdom included non-Muslims as well as Muslims and were known collectively as *falâsifa*. Although *falsafa* focused largely on the works of Aristotle, it also exhibited a decidedly neo-Platonic cast, especially since through a series of accidents one of its most influential texts, the *Theology* attributed Aristotle, was actually a compendium of work drawn from the *Enneads* written by the neo-Platonic philosopher, Plotinus (205–270; I.10; III.6 above).

Systematic structure was brought to *falsafa* by first the Arab thinker al-Kindi (aka Alkindus; 805–873) and then by the Persian or Turkic al-Farabi (aka Abunaser; c. 872–c. 950). Two questions dominated their thought, questions which in various ways would wind through much of Islamic philosophy and indeed medieval philosophy generally. One of these questions was fundamentally epistemological, namely the extent to which revelation, especially Holy Scripture, and Greek philosophical science are consistent with one another in their knowledge claims, and even whether they are about the same subject matter. The other question was metaphysical and aimed to determine the ultimate nature of reality.

Avicenna's metaphysical thought is distinctive in a number of ways. In the following selection we have focused on his ideas about necessary and contingent being. More than any philosopher preceding him, and perhaps more than any of his successors, Avicenna was concerned to identify God with necessary being, or the being that exists by virtue of its own necessity (the "Necessary Existent"). Contingent being, by contrast, is the sort of being that might exist or might not exist. What set Avicenna apart was his wholesale attempt to derive the divine attributes from that necessity. He argued, for example, that God's omniscience followed from God's necessity because if there were something that God did not know, God would be merely a potential being with respect to acquiring that knowledge; thence God would not be a necessary being. Accordingly, Avicenna writes: "Whatever is a necessary existent in itself is a necessary existent in all its aspects". . . . So, "the Necessary Existent is not [dependent on] relation, is neither changing nor multiple, and has nothing associated with His existence that is proper to Himself." While the influence of Parmenides' demanding requirements for "what is" (*ti est*) remain evident here (see III.2 above), Avicenna's

radical incorporation of the logical ideas of "necessity" and "contingency" into philosophical speculation about the ultimate nature of reality were crucial for the course of metaphysics.[2]

Avicenna's metaphysics of terrestrial being argue that corporeal being is always composed of both matter and form, and accordingly the quasi-Aristotelian idea of "prime matter (*hylē*)" as matter that exists without form is incoherent. Using an example that seems to anticipate Descartes's famous "ball of wax experiment" in Meditation II of his *Meditations on First Philosophy* (II.8, III.12), Avicenna argues for a conception of corporeal being very much like Descartes's modern concept of "extension" (*res extensa*). Avicenna argues that while there may be atoms that are, as things happen to stand, not divided, corporeal substance cannot be in principle impossible to divide. Corporeality must have surfaces that are always subject to division, at least conceptually.

What has come to be known as Avicenna's "flying man" argument argues that the self or mind is metaphysically distinct from the body.[3] By imagining a newly created and fully functional adult human being suspended in a space devoid of all sensory input and without any memories, Avicenna invites his readers to conclude that such a being would still be able to affirm the "existence of its self." Since the being has no awareness of its body but still possesses an awareness of its self, the two must be different metaphysically: "it is not possible," Avicenna writes, "for the thing of which one is aware and not aware to be one in any respect." Avicenna advanced this line of reasoning 600 years before Descartes.

Notes

1   R. Wisnovsky, *Avicenna's Metaphysics in Context*, Ithaca, NY: Cornell University Press, 2003.

2   D. Gutas, *Avicenna and the Aristotelian Tradition: Introduction to Reading Avicenna's Philosophical Works*, Leiden: Brill, 1988.

3   E. Gilson, "Les sources gréco-arabe de l'augustinisme avicennisant," *Archives d'histoire doctrinale et littéraire du moyen âge* 4 (1929–30): 41n1. At *De anima* 2.1, 412a27–29 and 412b5–6 Aristotle calls the soul-mind (*psychē*) the "the first actuality [or perfection,

'entelecheia') of the body." Whether according to Aristotle the soul and body were separable became in the middle ages a subject of great dispute. Compare *De anima* 403a10 and 408b17ff., as well as the general issue of whether the "active intellect" (*nôus poietikos*) is capable of existence independent of the body.

Ibn Sina (Avicenna), *Kitab al-Shifa*

Book I, Chapter [Six]

On commencing a discourse on the Necessary Existent and the possible existent; that the Necessary Existent has no cause; that the possible existent is caused; that the Necessary Existent has no equivalent in existence and is not dependent [in existence] on another (1) We will now return to what we were [discussing] and say: There are specific properties that belong individually each to the Necessary Existent and the possible existent. We thus say: The things that enter existence bear a [possible] twofold division in the mind. Among them there will be that which, when considered in itself, its existence would be not necessary. It is [moreover] clear that its existence would also not be impossible, since otherwise it would not enter existence. This thing is within the bound of possibility. There will also be among them that which, when considered in itself, its existence would be necessary.

(2) We thus say: That which in itself is a necessary existent has no cause, while that which in itself is a possible existent has a cause. Whatever is a necessary existent in itself is a necessary existent in all its aspects. The existence of the Necessary Existent cannot be equivalent to the existence of another where each would equal the other as regards necessary existence, becoming [thereby] necessary concomitants. The existence of the Necessary Existent cannot at all be a composite, [deriving] from multiplicity. The true nature of the Necessary Existent can in no manner be shared by another. From our verifying [all] this, it follows necessarily that the Necessary Existent is not [dependent on] relation, is neither changing nor multiple, and has nothing associated with His existence that is proper to Himself.

(3) That the Necessary Existent has no cause is obvious. For if in His existence the Necessary Existent were to have a cause, His existence would be by [that cause]. But whatever exists by something [else], if considered in itself, apart from another, existence for it would not be necessary. And every [thing] for which existence is not [found to be] necessary – if [the thing is] considered in itself, apart from another – is not a necessary existent in itself. It is thus evident that if what is in itself a necessary existent were to have a cause, it would not be in itself a necessary existent. Thus, it becomes clear that the Necessary Existent has no cause. From this it is [also] clear that it is impossible for a thing to be [both] a necessary existent in itself and a necessary existent though another. [This is] because, if its existence is rendered necessary through another, it cannot exist without the other. But [if anything] whatsoever cannot exist without another, its existence [as] necessary in itself is impossible. For if it were necessary in itself, then it would have to come into existence, there being no influence on its existence by way of necessity from that which is other and which affects the existence of something else. [But since such an influence has been supposed,] its existence would not be necessary in itself.

(4) Moreover, whatever is possible in existence when considered in itself, its existence and nonexistence are both due to a cause. [This is] because, if it comes into existence, then existence, as distinct from nonexistence, would have occurred to it. [Similarly,] if it ceases to exist, then nonexistence, as distinct from existence, would have occurred to it. Hence, in each of the two cases, what occurs to the thing must either occur through another or not. If [it occurs] through another, then [this] other is the cause. And if it did not exist through another, [then the nonexistence of the other is the cause of its nonexistence].

(5) Hence, it is clear that whatever exists after nonexistence has been specified with something possible other than itself. The case is the same with nonexistence. This is because the thing's quiddity is either sufficient for this specification or not. If its quiddity is sufficient for either of the two states of affairs [existence or nonexistence]

to obtain, then that thing would be in itself of a necessary quiddity, when [the thing] has been supposed not to be necessary [in itself]. And this is contradictory. If [on the other hand] the existence of its quiddity is not sufficient [for specifying the possible with existence] – [the latter] being, rather, something whose existence is added to it – then its existence would be necessarily due to some other thing. [This,] then, would be its cause. Hence, it has a cause. In sum, then, either of the two things [existence or nonexistence] would obtain necessarily for [the possible that was] due, not to itself, but to a cause. The existential idea would be realized through a cause (namely, an existential cause); and the nonexistential idea [would be realized] through a cause (namely, the absence of the [former] existential idea, as you have known).

(6) We thus say: [The possible in itself] must become necessary through a cause and with respect to it. For, if it were not necessary, then with the existence of the cause and with respect to it, it would [still] be possible. It would then be possible for it to exist or not to exist, being specified with neither of the two states. [Once again,] from the beginning this would be in need of the existence of a third thing through which either existence (as distinct from nonexistence) or nonexistence (as distinct from existence) would be assigned for [the possible] when the cause of its existence with [this state of affairs] would not have been specified. This would be another cause, and the discussion would extend to an infinite regress. And, if it regresses infinitely, the existence of the possible, with all this, would not have been specified by it. As such, its existence would not have been realized. This is impossible, not only because this leads to an infinity of causes – for this is a dimension, the impossibility of which is still open to doubt in this place – but because no dimension has been arrived at through which its existence is specified, when it has been supposed to be existing. Hence, it has been shown to be true that whatever is possible in its existence does not exist unless rendered necessary with respect to its cause.

(7) We [further] say: It is impossible for the Necessary Existent to be equivalent to another necessary existent so that this would exist with that and that would exist with this, neither being the cause of the other [but] both, rather, being equal with respect to the matter of the necessity of existence. [This is] because, if the essence of the one is considered in itself, apart from the other, then it would have to be either [(a)] necessary in itself or [(b)] not necessary in itself.

(8) If [(a)] necessary in itself, then either it would have also a necessity with respect to the other, whereby a thing would be both a necessary existent in itself and a necessary existent through another (which, as we have seen, is impossible); or it would have no necessity by reason of another and, hence, it would not be necessary for its existence to be consequent on the existence of the other, and it follows necessarily that its existence would have no relation with the other such that it exists only when this other exists.

(9) But, if [(b)] it is not necessary in itself, then, considered in itself, it must be possible in existence and considered, with respect to the other, necessary in existence. From this it follows that either the other is of the same [state] or [it is] not. [If not, then it would not be equivalent in existence.] If the other is of the same [state], then it follows that the necessity of existence of this [one] derives from that [other] when that [other] is either [(i)] within the bounds of possible existence or [(ii)] within the bounds of necessary existence.

(10) If the necessary existence of this [one] derives from that [other] – that [other] being within the bounds of necessary existence – and does not derive from itself or some prior third thing, as we have stated in a previous context, but [derives] from that from which it comes to be, then a condition of the necessary existence of this [one] becomes the necessary existence of what occurs thereafter [as a consequence of] its necessary existence, the posteriority [here] being in essence. As such, no necessary existence is realized at all for it. If [on the other hand] the necessary existence of this [one] derives from that [other] – [that other] being within the bounds of possibility – then the necessary existence of this [one] derives from the essence of that [other] when [that other] is within the bounds of possibility. The essence of that [other] which is within the bounds of possibility would bestow necessary existence on this [one], having derived not possibility but necessity from this [one]. Thus, the cause of [that one] is the possible existence of this [one], whereas the possible existence of this [one] is not caused by that [other]. As such, the two cannot be equivalent – I mean, that whose

causality is essential and that which is essentially caused.

(11) Another [circumstance] occurs [relating to the above argument]: namely, that, if the possible existence of that [one] is the cause of the necessary existence of this [one], then the existence of [the latter] is not connected with the necessary existence of [the former], but only with its possibility. It follows, then, that the existence of [the latter] is possible with the non-existence of [the former], when both have been supposed to be equivalent – and this is contradictory. Hence, it is impossible for the two to be existentially equivalent in the circumstance of not being attached to an external cause. Rather, one must be the one that is essentially prior, or else there must be some other external cause that either necessitates both by necessitating the relation between them or necessitates the relation between them by necessitating them.

(12) The two related things [are such that] one is not necessitated *by* the other but is [necessary] *with* the other, that which necessitates them being the cause that brought them together (and also the two substances or two subjects described by the two [relatives]). The existence of the two subjects or substances alone is not sufficient to [make] the two [related], a third thing that combines the two [being required]. This is because the existence of each of the two and its true nature would either consist in their being with the other [or not]. [If they consist in being with the other,] then the existence of [each] in itself would not be necessary. It thus becomes possible and, hence, becomes caused. Its cause, as we have stated, would not be equivalent [to it] in existence. As such, its cause would therefore be something else, and hence [the existent] and its cause would not be the cause of the relation between the two, but [the cause would be] that other.

(13) [If, on the other hand, the existence and true nature of each] does not consist in [being with the other], then the conjunction of the two would be an occurrence pertaining to the proper existence of each and consequent to it. Also, the existence proper to the one would not be due to its equivalence inasmuch as it is equivalent, but due to a prior cause, if it is caused. Then its existence would be due either [(a)] to its companion, not inasmuch as the latter is its equivalent, but due to the existence that is proper to its companion (and, as such, they would not be

equivalent, but, rather, [an instance of] cause and effect, its companion being also a cause of the imagined relation between them, as in the case of father and son); or [(b)] they would be equivalent, belonging to the class of equivalents where one is not the cause of the other, the relation [of concomitance] being necessary for their existence. As such, the primary cause of the relation would be something external that brings about the existence of both, as you have known, the relation being accidental. Hence, there would be no equivalence there, except in terms of a differing or a necessary concomitant accident. But this is something other than that with which we are concerned. There would necessarily be a cause for that which is accidental; and the two things, as far as equivalence is concerned, would both be caused.

Book I, Chapter [Seven]

That the Necessary Existent is one (1) We further say: The Necessary Existent must be one entity. Otherwise, let [us suppose the Necessary Existent were] a multiplicity in which each [member] is a necessary existent. It would then follow that each, with respect to the meaning which is its true nature, either would not differ at all from [any] other [member] or would differ from it. If it does not differ from the other in the meaning that belongs to [itself] essentially, differing from [the other] only in not being it – and this is inescapably a difference – then it differs from it in [something] other than the meaning. This is because the meaning in both does not differ; [but] something has conjoined [with] it, in terms of which it becomes "this" or in "this" (or it was conjoined by the very fact of being "this" or in "this"), while this [thing] that conjoins [with] it did not conjoin [with] the other. Rather, it is through [what the former has] that [the other] becomes "that," or [through] the very fact that "that" is "that." This is some [kind] of specification that has attached to that meaning through which there is a difference between the two [necessary existents]. Hence, each of the two differs from the other through [this thing that conjoined the one, but not the other,] but would not differ from it in [that it has] the same meaning. It would thus differ from it in [something] other than this meaning.

(2) [Now,] the things that are other than the meaning but which attach to the meaning are the accidents and unessential sequels. These sequels either occur to the thing's existence inasmuch as it is that existence ([in which case] it is necessary that everything in this existence [must] agree, when [in fact] these were supposed to be different – and this is contradictory), or [these sequels] occur to [the thing's existence] from external causes, not from [the thing's] quiddity itself. [As such,] it would then follow that, if it were not for that cause, [the sequels] would not have occurred; and, if it were not for that cause, [the existent] would not be different [from another]; and, if it were not for that cause, the essences either would or would not be one; and if it were not for that cause, "this" by itself would not be a necessary existent, [nor] "that" by itself a necessary existent – [that is,] not with respect to existence, but with respect to the accidents.

(3) Thus, the necessity of existence of each, particular to each and singled out [for each], would be derived from another. But it has been stated that whatever is a necessary existent through another is not a necessary existent in itself; rather, within its own domain it is a possible existent. It would then [follow] that, although each one of this [supposed multiplicity] is in itself a necessary existent, it is [also], within its own domain, a possible existent – and this is impossible.

(4) Let us now suppose that [each member of the supposed multiplicity] differs from the [other] in some basic meaning, after agreeing with it in the meaning [of being a necessary existent]. It follows, then, that either that [basic] meaning would be a condition for the necessity of existence, or it would not. If it is a condition for the necessity of existence, it is obvious that everything that is a necessary existent must agree with respect to it. If it is not a condition for the necessity of existence, then the necessity of existence would have been established [as] a necessity of existence without it, [the latter] intruding on it, occurring accidentally to it, and [being] related to it after that [existence] has been completed as a necessary existence. But we have denied this as impossible, showing its falsity. Hence, [each member of the supposed multiplicity] cannot differ from [the other] in [the supposed basic] meaning.

(5) Indeed, we must add further clarification of this, [taking it] from another aspect –

namely, that division of the meaning of necessary existence in [the supposed] multiplicity must conform to [only] one of two alternatives. It would have to be either by way of its division in terms of differentiae or by way of its division in terms of accidents. [Now,] it is known that differentiae are not included in the definition of that which stands as genus, for they do not confer on the genus its true nature, conferring on it only actual subsistence. This is exemplified by "the rational," for "the rational" does not confer on animal the meaning of "animality" but confers on it subsistence in actuality, as a specific existing entity. It must also be the case that the differentiae of necessary existence, if [such attribution] is correct, would have to be such that they do not confer on necessary existence its true nature but would confer on it actual existence. But this is impossible in two respects.

(6) One of the two is that the true nature of necessary existence is nothing but the very assuredness of existence, unlike the true nature of animality, which is something other than the assuredness of existence (existence being either a necessary concomitant of it or an intruder on it, as you have known). Hence, the conferring of existence upon unnecessary existence would necessarily be the conferring of a condition [constituent] of its true nature. But the permissibility of this [to obtain] between differentiae and genus has been denied as impossible.

(7) The second respect is that it would follow that the reality of necessary existence is dependent on its being realized in actuality through that which necessitates it, [in which case] the sense in which a thing is a necessary existent would be that it is a necessary existent though another. But what we are discussing [here] is necessary existence in itself. Thus, the thing which is a necessary existent in itself would be a necessary existent through another; and we have refuted this.

(8) It has thus become clear that the division of necessary existence into these matters would not be the division of the generic meaning into differentiae. Hence, it has become evident that the meaning that entails necessary existence cannot be a generic meaning, divisible by differentiae and accidents. It thus remains that it would be a meaning [in terms of] species. We thus say: It would not be possible for its kind of species to be predicated of many, because, if the individuals of the one species, as we have shown, do not

differ in the essential meaning, they must then differ only in terms of accidents. But we have prohibited the possibility of this in necessary existence. It may be possible to show this by a kind of summary, where the purpose would turn out [to be] what we mean. We thus say:

(9) If necessary existence is an attribute of the thing, existing for it, then [there are two alternatives. The first is that] it would be necessary, as regards this attribute – that is, necessary existence – that that very attribute should exist for this [thing] to which it is attributed. As such, any other [hypothetical attribute] of [the kind] cannot exist except as an attribute of that [one] thing. Hence, it would be impossible for [such an attribute] to exist for another and it must, hence, exist for [that thing] alone. [The second alternative is that] the existence [of the attribute] is possible but not necessary for it. As such, it would be possible for that thing not to be a necessary existent in itself when it is a necessary existent in itself – and this is a contradiction. Hence, necessary existence [belongs] to only one [existent].

(10) If [to this] someone were to say, "Its existence for this [thing] does not prevent its existence as an attribute for the other, and its being an attribute of the other does not falsify its being an attribute of [the former]," we say:

(11) We are speaking of the assigning of necessary existence as an attribute [to the thing] inasmuch as it belongs to it and inasmuch as no attention is paid to the other. For this [necessary existence] is not an identical attribute of the other but is similar to it, [where] what is necessary in it is the very same thing which would be necessary in the other. To put it in another way, we say:

(12) [In order for] each one of [the hypothesized necessary existents] to be a necessary existent and to be the specific thing that it is, it [must be] either one [and the same – in which case] whatever is a necessary existent is itself [that] thing and no other [– or not one and the same]. If its being a necessary existent is other than its being the very same thing [that] it is, then the conjunction of the Necessary Existent with [the fact] that it is the very thing that it is would have to be due either to itself, or to a necessitating ground, or to a cause other than itself. If due to itself and to the fact that it is a necessary existent, then whatever is a necessary existent would have to be this very thing. If due to a necessitating

ground and cause other than it, then it would have a cause for being this very thing. Hence, there would be a cause for the specific property of its singular existence. It is, then, caused.

(13) The Necessary Existent is therefore one in [its] entirety (not as species are [subsumed] under genus) and one in number (not as individuals [subsumed] under species). Rather, it is a meaning, the explication of whose term belongs only to it; and its existence is not shared by any other. We will clarify this further in another place. These are the specific properties with which the Necessary Existent is exclusively endowed.

(14) As regards the possible existent, from this its specific property has become evident – namely, that it necessarily needs some other thing to render it existing in actuality. Whatever is a possible existent is always, considered in itself, a possible existent; but it may happen that its existence becomes necessary through another. This may either occur to it always, or else its necessary existence through another may not be permanent – occurring, rather, at one time and not another. This [latter] must have matter that precedes its existence in time, as we will clarify. That whose existence is always necessitated by another is also not simple in its true nature. [This is] because what belongs to it [when] considered in itself is other than what belongs to it from another. It attains its haecceity in existence from both together. For this reason, nothing other than the Necessary Existent, considered in Himself, is stripped of associating with what is in potentiality and [what is within the realm of] possibility. He is the single existent, [every] other [being] a composite [dual].

Book II, Chapter [Two]

On ascertaining corporeal substance and what is composed from it (1) The first thing [this involves] is knowledge of body and ascertaining its nature.

(2) As for showing that body is a single continuous substance not composed of indivisible parts, [this is something that] we have completed [discussing]. As regards ascertaining and defining it, it is customarily said that body is a long, wide, and deep substance; hence, one must look into the manner of this. But, by each of the

expressions "length," "width," and "depth," one understands a variety of things. Thus, sometimes "length" is said of a line in whatever manner it happens to be; sometimes "length" is said of the greater in magnitude of the two lines that encompass a surface; sometimes "length" is said of the greatest of various extended, intersecting dimensions in whatever manner they happen to be, regardless of whether they are lines or not; sometimes "length" is said of the supposed distance between the head and its opposite – whether foot or tail – in animals. As regards "width," this is said of the surface itself, and of the lesser in magnitude of two distances, and of the dimension connecting right and left. "Depth" is [also] said of a thing such as the dimension connecting two surfaces, being so termed when one takes it starting from the top, [whereas] if one starts from the bottom it is termed "height." These, then, are the popular perspectives in this.

(3) It is not necessary that in every body there should be an actual line. For, as long as a sphere is not moving, it does not have a line at all in actuality, nor is an axis assigned to it. It is not a condition that, for the sphere to be a body, it should be moving, whereby an axis or some other line would appear in it. For it is realized as a body through that which realizes corporeality, motion occurring to it thereafter either accidentally or as a necessary concomitant. Moreover, body inasmuch as it is body does not necessarily need to have a surface. This is only required in it inasmuch as [body] is finite. But to be realized as a body, and for us to know it as a body, it is not required that it should be finite. Rather, finitude is an accidental occurrence that is a necessary concomitant of it. For this reason, when conceptualizing body, the conception [of finitude] as belonging to body is not required. Whoever conceives an infinite body does not conceive a body which is "not body"; and [moreover] absence of finitude is only conceived for that which is conceived as body. But [an individual] would have erred [in this] in the way someone [errs] who says that "body is an organ." For in this he would have erred [in the realm] of assent [to the truth or falsehood of a proposition] but not in the conception of [each of] its two simple constituents – namely, the subject and the predicate.

(4) [To continue,] then, if body, in its realization as body, must have surfaces, it may be a body that is enclosed by [only] one surface – [this body] being the sphere. Moreover, it is not a condition for the body to be a body that it should have unequal dimensions. For the cube is also a body, and although it is enclosed by six edges, yet it does not [require] unequal dimensions in order to have "length," "width," and "depth" in one of the meanings [of this term]. Nor, moreover, is its being body dependent on its being placed under the heaven so that the different directions would obtain for it in accordance with the direction of the world or [so that], in another sense, it would have length, width, and depth ([this] even though [body] must be either a heaven or within a heaven). From this it is clear that, for a body to be body in actuality, it is not necessary that there should in actuality be three dimensions in body in the manner [normally] understood by these three dimensions.

(5) If this, then, is the state of affairs, how can we compel ourselves to suppose three dimensions existing in actuality in the body [in order] for [the latter] to be a body? Rather, the meaning of the description of a body is that the body is the substance for which it is possible for you to begin by postulating in it a dimension in whatever manner you desire. The thing you begin with would be the length. Then you could also postulate another dimension intersecting the other perpendicularly at bases. This second dimension would be the width. You could then postulate a third dimension intersecting the other two at bases where the three meet at one place. You are not able, however, to postulate a perpendicular dimension other than these three.

(6) It is due to the body's having this description that one refers to body as being long, wide, and deep, just as it is said that body is that which is divisible in [terms] of all dimensions. It is not meant by this that it is divided in actuality, as something completed; rather, [it is understood] as being of a nature that this division is postulated of it.

(7) This, then, is how body should be defined – namely, that it is the substance that has this form by virtue of which it is what it is and that the rest of the dimensions postulated between its limits, and also its limits, its shapes, and its position, are not matters that render it subsistent but are, rather, sequels to its substance. It may be the case that some bodies would have some or all of these [things] as necessary concomitants;

or it may be that all of these [things], or only some of them, would not become necessary concomitants of some bodies.

(8) If you were to take a piece of wax and give it a shape that imposes on it actual dimensions between these limits that are numbered, measured, and limited, and if you were then to change that shape, none of those [former dimensions] would remain in actuality [as] individually one [and the same], having that [previous] limit and measure. Rather, new dimensions, numerically different from those [previous ones], would have taken [their] place. These are the dimensions that belong to the category of quantity.

(9) If it happens that a body – like the celestial sphere, for example – has one [set] of dimensions as a necessary concomitant, this does not belong to it inasmuch as it is body, but by virtue of another nature that preserves its secondary perfections. For corporeality, in reality, is the form of a continuum that is receptive of the hypothesized three dimensions of which we spoke. This meaning is other than measure and other than mathematical corporeality. For this body, inasmuch as it has this form, does not differ from another body in being larger or smaller and does not relate to it by being equal [to it], [or by being] measured by it, [or by] measuring it, [or by] sharing [something with it], or [by] being different [from it]. This [relation] would belong to it only inasmuch as it is something measured and inasmuch as part of it [is used to] measure it numerically. This consideration is other than the consideration of corporeality, which we have mentioned. These are matters that we have explained to you in a simpler way in another place, which you [may] need for help.

(10) It is for this reason that the one body is rarefied and condensed through heating and cooling so that, while its corporeality (which we have mentioned) does not vary and change, the measure of its corporeality becomes different. Hence, natural body is a substance having [such a] description.

(11) As for our saying "mathematical body," either one intends by it the form of [the above] (inasmuch as it is limited and quantified [when] taken in the soul, not in [external] existence), or one intends by it some measure that has continuity [that is] also of this description (inasmuch as it has a continuum that is limited and measured, whether in a soul or in matter). It is as though

mathematical body is [something] that in itself occurs to this body we have explained, the surface [of mathematical body] being its limit, and the line being the limit of its limit. We will be clarifying the discussion of [this mathematical body] hereafter and examining the manner in which continuity belongs to it, and [also] the manner in which it belongs to natural body.

(12) We first say: It is of the nature of bodies to be divided, but observations are not sufficient for establishing this. For someone may say: "Nothing among observed bodies is a body that is purely one. Rather, [observed bodies] are composed of bodies. Unitary bodies are not perceived by the senses and cannot be divided in any manner whatsoever."

(13) [Now,] we have said [something] in refutation of this [view] through demonstrations pertaining to [natural science], particularly against the doctrine that is easiest to refute – namely, the doctrine of those who differentiate between [the indivisible bodies] in terms of shape. However, should someone say, "Their natures and their shapes are similar," then his doctrine and his theoretical view must be refuted by what I say.

(14) We thus say: If he makes the smallest of bodies indivisible both potentially and actually, so that it becomes altogether like a point, then that [indivisible] body becomes necessarily governed by the [same] rule that governs a point with respect to the impossibility of a sensible body's being composed from it. If [however] this is not the case, but, rather, that in itself it is such that one part of it can be set apart from another part, and yet it does not submit to [any actual] division separating [those] two parts (whose supposition [as separated parts] in [such a division] is possible [only] as [an act] of the estimative faculty), then we would say:

(15) It is either the case that the state [obtaining] between the one part [of the atom] and the other [part] – [this state] differing from the state obtaining between one [atom] and another in that [the atoms] do not coagulate and the parts do not separate – is [either] due to the nature of the thing and its substance or [due] to a cause extraneous to nature and substance. If it is [due to] a cause extraneous to nature and substance, then it would either have to be a cause in terms of which nature and substance are in actuality rendered subsistent (as with [the relation] of form to substance and of receptacle to accident)

or a cause through which [such] rendering of subsistence does not take place.

(16) If it is a cause in which [such] substantiation does not take place, then it becomes possible, in terms of nature and substance, that [among the atoms] there would be coagulation after separation and separation after coagulation, in which case this corporeal nature, considered in itself, would be receptive of division but would not divide due to an external cause. And this much is sufficient for our purpose.

(17) If this cause is one through which each of the [indivisible] parts [or atoms] is rendered subsistent either in a manner pertaining to its nature and quiddity or in a manner pertaining to its actual existence [and] not to its quiddity (in which case there would be variance [between one atom and another]), then it would happen as a first [consequence] that these [atomic] bodies would differ in [their] substances. But those [whom we are refuting] do not uphold [this view]. Secondly, [it follows] that it is not the corporeal nature these [atoms] possess which [renders their divisibility] impossible; rather, this [divisibility] is impossible for them in terms of the form of [what differentiates them as a] species. This we do not disallow. For it is possible that something should attach to corporeality, rendering that body subsisting as a species receptive neither of division nor of contact with another [body]. And this is what we maintain about the [celestial] sphere. What is needed here is [to establish] that the nature of corporeality insofar as it is the nature of corporeality does not prevent [the divisibility of bodies].

(18) We first say: We have verified for ourselves that corporeality inasmuch as it is corporeality is not unreceptive of division, for it lies in all the natures of corporeality to receive division. From this it becomes clear that the dimensions and form of the body subsist in something. [This is] because these dimensions are [either] the connections themselves or something that occurs to the connections (as we shall verify), and [because they] are not things to which connection occurs. For the expression "dimensions" is a name for the contiguous magnitudes themselves, not for the things to which connection occurs. The thing which is the connection itself or which is connected in itself cannot remain its identical self [once] the connection ceases to be. For, if the connection of every dimension is

separated, that dimension ceases and two other dimensions come to be. The case is similar when connection takes place – I mean, connection in the sense that it is a differentia, not an accident. This we have explained in another place. For then another dimension would have occurred and each one that had been with its special characteristic would have ceased to be. Hence, in bodies there is something that is the subject for connection and separation and for what occurs to connection by way of limited measures.

(19) Also, body inasmuch as it is body that has the form of corporeality is something in actuality; and inasmuch as it is disposed [for reception], then in whatever disposition you wish for it, it is in potentiality. [Now,] the thing inasmuch as it is a thing potentially is not some other thing inasmuch as it is in actuality. Potentiality [however] would not belong to the body inasmuch as it has actuality. Hence, the form of the body conjoins something belonging to it which is other than its being a form. Body, then, would be a substance composed of something from which it has potentiality and something from which it has actuality. That through which it has actuality is its form, and that from which it is potential is its matter – namely, hyle.

(20) A questioner, however, may ask and say, "Hyle is also composite. This is because it is in itself hyle, and a substance in actuality, and [yet] is also disposed [to receive form]."

(21) We say, "The substance of hyle and its being in actuality hyle is not some other thing, except that it is a substance disposed for [the reception] of [such and such] a thing. The substantiality it has does not render it anything in actuality but merely prepares it to become something actual through form. The meaning of its substantiality is nothing but that it is "a something" that is not in a subject. The affirmation here is that it is "a something." As regards its not being in a subject, [this] is a negation. [The fact] that it is "a something" does not necessitate that it be a specific thing in actuality, because this is general, and a thing does not become a thing in actuality through a general state of affairs as long as it does not possess a differentia proper to it. Its differentia is that it is prepared [for the reception] of all things. Its form (which is thought of as belonging to it) consists in its being prepared, receptive.

(22) Therefore, here there is no [first] true nature belonging to hyle through which it is

rendered [something] in actuality, and [then] another true nature [that renders it something] in potentiality – unless a true nature comes to it from the outside through which it becomes [something] in actuality, remaining [something] in potentiality in itself and when considered in terms of [its] existence [as an] entity. This true nature would be the form. [But] the relation of hyle to these two meanings is more akin to the relation of the simple to what is a genus and a differentia than it is to that which is a composite of what is matter and form.

(23)　From this it has become evident that the form of corporeality inasmuch as it is the form of corporeality is in need of matter. And, because the nature of the form of corporeality inasmuch as it is the form of corporeality does not vary in itself – for it is one simple nature – it cannot become varied in species through differentiae that enter into it inasmuch as it is [the form of] corporeality. Should differentiae enter into it, these would be things added to it from the outside and would also consist of one of the forms that attach to matter. The [rule] governing [these forms in relation to hyle] would not be the [rule] governing real differentiae.

(24)　The demonstration of this is that, if corporeality differs from another corporeality, this would be either because this [one] is hot, that one cold, or [because] this has a celestial nature, that a terrestrial nature. This is unlike measure, which is not a realized thing in itself so long as it has not become varied in species by being a line, a surface, or a body. And [this is] like number, which is not a realized thing so long as it has not become varied in species [such] as [being] two, three, or four. Moreover, if [measure] becomes realized, its realization does not come about through the addition to it of some external thing where there would be, besides the generic nature – such as "measureness" and "being numeral" – a subsisting indicated nature to which another nature is added and through which [the generic nature] becomes varied in species. Rather, the nature of "twoness" itself is the [characteristic of] "being numeral" that is predicated of "twoness" and is proper to it; and longitude itself is the "measureness" that is predicated of it and is proper to it.

(25)　However, this is not the case here. But, if another form is added to corporeality, then that form, which is thought to be a differentia, and cor-

poreality would not, through their combination, be corporeality. Rather, corporeality would be one of the two that is in itself achieved, realized. For, here, we mean by corporeality that which is akin to form, not akin to genus. You have known the difference between the two in the *Book of Demonstration*. Here you will have [further] clarification and explanation of this.

(26)　You have, however, ascertained through what has been made clear to you the difference between the two. In the case of what is akin to measure, it is possible for its species to differ through things that belong to them in themselves, whereas absolute measure does not have any of these things in itself. This is because no stable essence is realized for the absolute measure unless it is a line or a surface. Once it is realized as either line or surface, then it is possible for the line in itself to have a difference from the surface through a differentia that renders the nature of "measureness" realized as either line or surface.

(27)　As for the corporeality which we are discussing [however] it is in itself a realized nature whose specific kind is not realized through something that joins it, so that, if we imagine that no [added] meaning joins corporeality but that it is [only] corporeality, [then it is not the case that] it would be impossible to have attained for ourselves [as objects of knowledge] anything but matter and connection alone. Likewise, if we affirm some other thing with the connection, this is not because the connection in itself is not realized for us except by adding and conjoining [this thing] to it. Rather, it is shown through other arguments that connection does not exist in act by itself. For a thing not to exist in act, however, does not [mean] that its nature is not realized. For whiteness and blackness [are such that] each of them is of a realized nature as a specific idea in its most complete manner – which is [realization] in itself. [Yet,] it is impossible for [such a thing as whiteness or blackness] to exist in act except in matter.

(28)　Absolute measure, on the other hand, cannot be realized as a nature to which one points unless it is necessarily made a line or a surface in order that it would be possible for it to exist. [This is] not [to say] that measure can exist as measure and that as a consequence thereafter there would exist a line or a surface that constitutes a state of affairs that [could not] exist in actuality without [measure]. And even though [measure] realizes its essence, this is not similar to [corporeality]. Rather, corporeality is conceived to exist through the causes belonging to it ([causes] through which and by which it exists, being only corporeality, without [anything] additional), whereas measure is not conceived to exist through the causes belonging to it ([causes] through which and by which it exists, being only measure, without [anything] additional). For, this measure in itself requires differentiae so as to exist as a realized thing. These differentiae are essential to it [so] that, when realized, they do not require it to be [something] other than [that] measure. It is thus possible for one measure to differ from another measure in terms of something which it possesses essentially.

(29) As regards the form of corporeality inasmuch as it is corporeality, it is one nature – simple, realized, with no variance in it. The pure form of corporeality does not differ from [another] pure form of corporeality through a differentia included in [the definition of] corporeality. What adheres to it consequentially is something extraneous to its nature. Hence, it is not possible that one corporeality should need matter and [another] corporeality should not need matter. The external things that attach to it consequentially do not in any way render it not in need of matter. [This is] because the need for matter belongs essentially to corporeality and to whatever possesses matter – and it belongs to corporeality inasmuch as it is corporeality, not inasmuch as it is corporeality with a consequential [attachment].

(30) It thus has become clear that bodies are composed of matter and form.

Book II, Chapter [Three]

That corporeal matter is not devoid of form (1) We now say: This corporeal matter cannot exist devoid of form in actuality. One of the things that quickly clarifies this is [what] we have shown: namely, that every existence that has something in actuality existing in it [that is] realized and subsistent and in which there is also a disposition to receive another thing – [every] such existence is composed of matter and form, the last matter not being composed of matter and form.

(2) Also, if [corporeal matter] were to separate from corporeal form, then either it would have a position and a bound within the existence that it then would have, or it would not. If it were to have a position and a space and [hence] could be divided, then it would necessarily have measure, whereas it was postulated to have no measure. And if it were not possible for it to be divided, but it had a position, then it would necessarily be a point with which a line could terminate. [But,] as you have learned from several places, [the point] cannot exist [independently] as a single entity, separated spatially [in a confine all its own].

(3) If [on the other hand] this substance has neither position nor [spatial] reference – being, rather, akin to substances in intellectual apprehension – then it would follow either [(a)] that the realized dimension in its entirety would indwell in it all at once, or [(b)] that [this substance] would itself move continuously toward the perfection of its measure. [But] if measure indwells in it all at once and [this] necessarily comes about with the [substance's] acquiring of measure in a specific spatial confine, then measure would have encountered it as [something] having a specific confine – otherwise, no one confine would have been more appropriate for it than [any] other. [Measure] would have then encountered it where [the specific confine] became related to it. Hence, [measure] would have necessarily encountered it while being in the confine it is in. That substance, then, would have been in a confine (although, perhaps, a confine not experienced by the senses) when it was supposed to have had no confine at all – and this is a contradiction. Nor is it possible that its occupying a confine should have occurred to it all at once as a result of the reception of measure. [This is] because, if measure were to come to it when it was not within a confine, then that measure would have connected with it in no confine. It would, then, not come to it in one specific confine from among the various possible confines to which it may belong. [Measure] would, then, have no confine – and this is impossible. Or, alternatively, [measure] would exist in every confine that can possibly belong to it [and would] not [be] confined to some specific one – and this is also impossible.

(4) This is seen more clearly [when, through exercising] our estimative faculty, we think of the matter of some clod of clay that is separated

[from its form], the form of that clod occurring in it thereafter. [The form] cannot occur in it when [the clod] is not in a consigned place, nor is it possible for that clod to exist in every confine that is potentially a natural confine to that clay clod. For, being a clod does not render it an occupant of every confine of its species, nor does it render it more fit to be in one direction of its confine than another. It can exist only in one specific direction within the general totality of the confine. Nor can it come to be in a specific direction when there is no circumstance specifying [such a direction], for [here] there is nothing except the connection of a form with matter, and this has the common possibility [of occurring] in any of the natural directions of the parts of the earth. [Now,] you have known that such an occurrence in a direction of the confine takes place in the way it does only either [(1)] by dint of its occurring close to it through the compulsion of a compelling [agent] that specifies that proximity, directing it through uniform motion to that very confine, or [(2)] by its coming to be there initially. With [its initial existence] in this proximity, or with its occurrence, [then] through being transported by a transporter, there is specification. But we have spoken fully about this. Hence, after abstraction [from form], the matter that belongs to the clod does not become specified [with a consigned place]. Moreover, the form of being a clod is not in any [specific] direction unless it has an appropriate relation to that direction. It is due to this relation – not, first of all, to its actually being matter, nor, secondly, to its actually acquiring form – that it became specified with [the direction]. And that relation is a position [of a kind].

(5)   The case is similar if the reception of measure in its entirety [by the hypothesized formless matter] occurs not all at once but in a spread-out fashion – where whatever is such that it spreads out has directions, and where whatever has directions [also] has position. That substance would then have a position and a confine, whereas it was stated that it had neither position nor confine – and this is contradictory.

(6)   What has necessitated all [these absurd consequences] is our supposition that [matter] separates from corporeal form. It is thus impossible that [matter] should exist in actuality unless it is rendered subsistent by corporeal form. For how can an entity that possesses a confine neither in potentiality nor in actuality [be such as to] receive

measure? It has become evident, then, that matter never remains separated [from form].

(7)   Again, either [matter's] existence would have to be the existence of a recipient (in which case it would always be receptive of some thing [or another] that it is never deprived of receiving), or it would have a special existence that is subsistent [to begin with], which it then follows that it receives. [In this latter case] it would, in its special subsisting existence, possess neither quantity nor a confine. Corporeal measure would then be [the thing] that occurred to it, rendering itself such that it potentially possessed parts – [this] after it became due for [corporeal measure] to render subsistent a substance that in itself is without a confine, quantity, or receptivity of division.

(8)   If its special existence through which it subsists would basically not endure when [it became] multiple, then to that which subsists in being without a confine and which is divisible neither in estimation nor in supposition, it would happen that that through which it is rendered subsistent ceases to be due to the occurrence to it of an accident, even though that unity [hypothesized for its special existence] is not due to that which rendered prime matter subsistent, but to something else. Then that which we have supposed as a special existence for it would not be a special existence through which it is rendered subsistent. Matter, then, would have a form that comes to it through which it becomes one in potency and act and another form coming to it through which it does not become one in potency and act. There would then be something in common between the two things – namely, the one recipient of the two states of affairs, [a recipient] of a nature [such] that at one time it would not have the potentiality to be divided and at another time [it would have] the potentiality to be divided. [By potentiality] I mean proximate potentiality that has no intermediary.

(9)   Let us now suppose [such] a substance and [suppose further] that it has become two in actuality, each numerically different from the other and each governed by the rule that it [can] separate from corporeal form. Then let each of the two separate from corporeal form so that each of the two would remain one substance potentially and actually. Let us [now] suppose [one of the two] in itself not to have been divided, except that corporeal form has been removed from it, so that it remains one substance potentially and

actually. It would then follow that that which has remained a substance ([although] not a body) would in itself either be similar to that which is akin to being part of it and which likewise has remained separate [from corporeal] form or [would be] different from it. If [it is] different, then this would be due either to [the fact] that this [one] has continued to exist while the other ceased (or [to] the converse of this); or else [to the fact] that both have continued to exist but that one has been specified with a quality or form that exists only for it; or [else to the fact] that, after their agreement, the two differ in surpassing [each other] in terms of measure, quality, or some other thing.

(10) If one of the two remains [in existence] and the other ceases to exist, the nature [of both] being one [and the same] and similar (where only the removal of corporeal form has rendered the one nonexistent), then [this removal of form] must [also] render that very other as nonexistent. And if one is particularized by some quality – the nature [of the two] being one [and the same, with] no other occurrence taking place except the separation of the corporeal form and no new occurrence taking place with this state other than that which is a necessary concomitant of this state – then it follows necessarily that the state of the other must be similar.

(11) If [to this] it is [then] said, "The first two, while two, are united and, hence, become one," we say: It is impossible for two substances to unite. For, if they were to unite, each of the two [still] existing, then they would be two, not one. And if they were to unite, one being nonexistent and the other existent, then how would the nonexistent unite with the existent? If both, by their union, were to become nonexistent and a third thing should come into existence from the two, then they would not be united but would be two corruptible things, and between them and the third [thing] there would be common matter. But we are speaking about matter itself, not about something having matter. [On the other hand,] if they differ in that [the one] surpasses [the other] in measure or some other thing, then they would necessarily have to exist devoid of corporeal form while yet possessing the form of being a measure. But this is contradictory. As for the two not differing in any respect [if this were so] then the rule governing [the one] thing (if that which is other [than it] were not separated from

it) would be the very same governing rule when it has dissociated from [the] other – [this] when its rule governing another and the rule that governs it alone are one and the same in all respects – and this is contradictory. [By this I mean] that it is [contradictory] for a rule governing part of the subject and for the rule governing all of it to be one and the same in all respects. I mean that a thing would not decrease when something was not taken away from it as it would if something was taken away; and the self-same rule would govern it, both when something was not added to it and when something was added to it.

(12) In brief, there is in the very nature of everything that at one time or another can become two a disposition toward divisibility which cannot separate from it. It may happen that it is prevented from [dividing] by an accidental occurrence other than the disposition of its essence. And this disposition is impossible except through the conjoining of measure to the essence.

(13) It thus remains that matter is never stripped of corporeal form. And, because this substance has become a measure through some quantity that indwelled in it, it is not in itself measure. Hence, it is not necessary for its essence to be specified with the reception of one particular dimension rather than another and with one magnitude rather than another, even though the corporeal form is one. The relation of any quantity whose existence is possible to that which in itself is neither divisible nor quantified and which becomes divided and quantified only through another is one [and the same]. Otherwise, it would have a quantity in itself corresponding to that which equals [such hypothesized substance], not to that which exceeds it.

(14) From this it becomes evident that matter can contract through condensation and expand through rarefaction. This is something observed by the senses. Indeed, its specification with quantity must be necessarily due to a cause that decrees that quantity to be in existence. Either that cause must be one of the forms and accidents that exist in matter, or [it must be] an external cause. If it is an external cause, then either [(a)] it must bestow that measured amount through the mediation of some other thing, or by reason of a special disposition (in which case the rule governing this and the first alternative [above] becomes one and the same,

reducing [to the fact] that bodies have different measures due to their different circumstances); or [(b)] the bestowal is not due to this [external cause] and its mediation (in which case bodies would be equally deserving of quantity and are [all] equal in size, which is false).

(15) Also, in addition to this, it is not necessary that from that cause there should proceed one specific size rather than another size, except by reason of something. By this "something" I mean a condition that is added to matter, rendering it deserving of that specific quantity [that it has] – not by its actually being matter, neither by its being matter that has [a giver of forms] that informs it with quantity, but in that [the] matter will have something because of which it deserves to be informed by the [giver] of the form with that size and quantity. It is possible for [matter] to differ absolutely in species, and it is possible for it to differ in being stronger and weaker ([while] not [differing] absolutely in species), even though the difference in being the stronger or the weaker may be close to the difference in species. But in the difference between [one matter and another] in terms of absolute species, and in the difference between [one

matter and another in terms of which is] the stronger [or] the weaker, there is a contrariety known to the perceptive examiners. For it is known that hyle in itself may be disposed [to receive] different measures. This is also a principle of natural philosophy.

(16) Also, every body is necessarily specified with one spatial confine. It does not have this confine proper to it inasmuch as it is body; otherwise, each body would be thus [specified with the same spatial confine]. Hence, it is necessarily specified with a confine by reason of some form it has in itself. This is evident. For, either it is not receptive to varieties [of shapes] and to differences in detail so that it thus becomes [receptive of these] due to some form – not in that it is receptive of [them] inasmuch as it is body – or else it is [in itself] receptive of them, either easily or with difficulty. Whatever the case, [body] would possess one of the forms mentioned in the natural sciences. Hence, corporeal matter does not exist separate from form. Matter, hence, is rendered subsistent in act through form. Thus, when matter is abstracted [from form] in the estimative faculty, then what was done to it is [something] that does not hold in [external] existence.

Chu Hsi, *Recorded Sayings* (selections)

Introduction

In 1313, the Mongol emperor of China ordered that all civil servants and officials should be examined in the "Four Books" – the Confucian classics, including Confucius's *Analects* (see V.3 of this volume) – as interpreted in the twelfth century commentaries of Chu Hsi (or Zhuxi). This order was followed until 1905. This is one reason why the "School of *Li* ('principle')," or "Ch'eng-Chu School" – named after Ch'eng Yi (1033–1108) and Chu Hsi (1130–1200) – "remained the most influential single system of philosophy until the introduction of Western philosophy in China" in the twentieth century.[1] Another reason is that the Neo-Confucian position brought to completion by Chu was the most systematic and speculatively ambitious product of a philosophical tradition more noted for its emphasis on "practical" concerns and human affairs than on metaphysical issues.

This last point should not be taken to mean that Chu lacked any interest in "practical" and public life. On the contrary, much of his career was spent as a public servant, involved in the reform of education, agriculture and the army – often, it seems, to the detriment of this career, since his

From Wing-Tsit Chan, *A Source Book in Chinese Philosophy*, Princeton, NJ: Princeton University Press, 1963, pp. 623–43 (translator's comments and notes omitted).

uncompromising insistence on integrity and dedication in public life appears to have offended many imperial officials. He was frequently dismissed from office and, on one occasion, narrowly escaped execution. More importantly, it was necessary, in his view, to address metaphysical issues if one is properly to understand human nature and the bases for both morality and political action. Without "the investigation of things" and "the extension of knowledge," there can be no rational ground for moral reform and social policy.

Thus his remarks on "physical nature" (§§62–70 below) are made in the context of the question that had preoccupied Confucian thinkers of the classical period, such as Mencius and Hsun Tzu (see I.4). This was the question of whether human beings are by nature good, and if they are, why it is that so many of them behave in an evil manner. Chu's solution requires an appeal to a distinction between man's "original nature," which is constituted by "principle" (*Li*) and his "physical nature," which is the joint product of *Li* and "material force" (*Ch'i*). Although all human beings are good according to their essential or "original nature," they are differently "endowed" with *Ch'i* so that, in the case of some people, their essential nature is, as it were, occluded by "turbid" matter.

The distinction between *Li* and *Ch'i* is central to Chu's more general picture of reality, for everything – not just people – is to be viewed as a combination of the two. Hence in §§100–113, Chu turns to clarification of the distinction and to raising questions concerning the "priority" or otherwise of one over the other. Readers are bound to be reminded here of Plato's and Aristotle's discussions of the relationship between the Forms and material objects – of, for example, the issue of whether Forms can have any existence independently of the particulars which instantiate them (see III.3 and III.4). Echoes of Plato and Aristotle appear to be even louder when, in §§114–122, Chu introduces the idea of "the Great Ultimate" (*T'ai Chi*). For some of his remarks make this sound akin to Plato's Form of the Good, since *T'ai Chi* not only "contains" all "principles" but is also "the highest good." Other remarks, however, indicate a kinship with Aristotle's "prime mover," as when *T'ai Chi* is said to "make possible" the "cycle" of *yin* and *yang*, those opposing but collaborating tendencies to "action" and "tranquillity" whose "circulations" produce the earth and material things as some kind of "sediment."

Perhaps, however, it is a mistake to assimilate Chu Hsi's concerns too closely to those of the Greeks. As the great scholar of Chinese science, Joseph Needham, argues, "*Li* was not in any strict sense metaphysical . . . but rather the invisible organizing fields or forces . . . within the natural world."[2] If so, "the Great Ultimate" might be better construed, not as a metaphysical Form of Forms, or "prime mover," but as the most general pattern and structure of physical processes. Chu Hsi, on this view, is less the inheritor of hoary metaphysical disputes, than the precursor of later developments in the natural sciences. How this would leave his attempt to solve the Confucian version of "the problem of evil" – a solution that seemed to require a distinction between a person's physical and non-physical nature – is unclear.

Notes

1 Fung Yu-Lan, *A Short History of Chinese Philosophy*, trans. D. Bodde, New York: Free Press, 1966, p. 294.
2 J. Needham, *Science and Civilization in China*, Vol. 2, Cambridge: Cambridge University Press, 1956, p. 475.

Chu Hsi, *Recorded Sayings*

5. Physical Nature

62. Nature is principle only. However, without the material force and concrete stuff of the universe, principle would have nothing in which to inhere. When material force is received in its state of clearness, there will be no obscurity or obstruction and principle will express itself freely. If there is obscurity or obstruction, then in its operation of principle, the Principle of Heaven will dominate if the obstruction is small and human selfish desire will dominate if the obstruction is great. From this we know that original nature is perfectly good. This is the nature described by Mencius as "good," by Master Chou Tun-i as "pure and perfectly good," and by Master Ch'eng I as "the fundamental character of our nature" and "the nature traced to the source of our being." However, it will be obstructed if physical nature contains impurity. Hence, [as Chang Tsai said] "In physical nature there is that which the superior man denies to be his original nature," and "If one learns to return to the original nature endowed by Heaven and Earth, then it will be preserved." In our discussion of nature, we must include physical nature before the discussion can be complete. (43:2b–3a)

63. When we speak of the nature of Heaven and Earth, we refer to principle alone. When we speak of the physical nature, we refer to principle and material force combined. Before material force existed, basic nature was already in existence. Material force does not always exist, but nature is eternal. Although nature is implanted in material force, yet material force is still material force and nature is still nature, without being confused or mixed up. As to its immanence in things and universal existence, regardless of whether material force is refined or coarse, there is nothing without its principle. (43:3a–b)

64. The physical nature is no different from the nature of Heaven and Earth. The point is that the nature of Heaven and Earth runs through the physical nature. For example, the good nature is like water. The physical nature is as though you sprinkled some sauce and salt in it and it then acquired a peculiar flavor. (43:4a)

65. The nature of all men is good, and yet there are those who are good from their birth and those who are evil from their birth. This is because of the difference in material force with which they are endowed. The revolutions of the universe consist of countless variety and are endless. But these may be seen: If the sun and moon are clear and bright, and the climate temperate and reasonable, the man born at such a time and endowed with such material force, which is clear, bright, well-blended, and strong, should be a good man. But if the sun and moon are darkened and gloomy, and the temperature abnormal, all this is evidence of violent material force. There is no doubt that if a man is endowed with such material force, he will be a bad man. The objective of learning is to transform this material endowment. (43:4b)

66. Nature is like water. If it flows in a clean channel, it is clear, if it flows in a dirty channel, it becomes turbid. When physical nature that is clear and balanced is received, it will be preserved in its completeness. This is true of man. When physical nature that is turbid and unbalanced is received, it will be obscured. This is true of animals. Material force may be clear or turbid. That received by men is clear and that received by animals is turbid. Men mostly have clear material force; hence the difference between them and animals. However, there are some whose material force is turbid, and they are not far removed from animals. (43:7a–b)

67. Someone asked about the inequality in the clearness of the material endowment. The Teacher said: The differences in the material endowment are not limited to one kind and are not described only in terms of clearness and turbidity. There are men who are so bright that they know everything. Their material force is clear, but what they do may not all be in accord with principle. The reason is that their material force is not pure. There are others who are respectful, generous, loyal, and faithful. Their material force is pure, but in their knowledge they do not always penetrate principle. The reason is that their material force is not clear. From this you can deduce the rest. (42:8a)

68. Although nature is the same in all men, it is inevitable that [in most cases] the various elements in their material endowment are unbalanced. In some men the material force of Wood predominates. In such cases, the feeling of commiseration is generally uppermost, but the feeling of shame, of deference and compliance, and of right and wrong are impeded by the predominating force and do not emanate into action. In others, the material force of Metal predominates. In such cases, the feeling of shame is generally uppermost, but the other feelings are impeded and do not emanate into action. So with the material forces of Water and Fire. It is only when yin and yang are harmonized and the five moral natures (of humanity, righteousness, propriety, wisdom, and good faith) are all complete that a man has the qualities of the Mean and correctness and becomes a sage. (43:8a–b)

69. *Question*: Men often differ in the degree of clearness and purity. These are of course due to material endowment. By necessity their minds differ depending on their material endowment. Now, the mouth, the ear, and the eye, as well as the mind are all organs. Why is it that Heaven, in imparting the physical nature, invests the qualities of clearness and turbidity and purity and impurity only in the mind but not in the mouth, ear, or eye?.... *Answer*: The mouth, ear, and eye also differ in clearness and turbidity and in purity and impurity. For example, people like I-ya (famous cook of the seventh century B.C.), the musicmaster Kuang (music-master shortly before Confucius), and Li-lou (legendary figure famous for power of vision) preserved clearness in the highest degree. It is the same with the mind. (43:17a–b)

70. Question about man's nature and destiny. *Answer*: If those born wise are completely and perfectly good, material force is there as material force and principle is there as principle, without any connection between each other. In such cases, there is no need to speak of the physical nature. But in the cases of men inferior to those born wise, [those who learn through study to be wise, those who learn through hard work, and those who work hard but still do not learn], even the Principle of Nature is not deficient. Nevertheless it is tied up with material force. When material force is clear, principle will be obvious. When material force is turbid, principle will be obscured. The two – material force and principle – always go together, and therefore we designate this state as physical nature. It means that principle advances or retards depending on material force, and not to consider physical nature as the nature and destiny.

Answer: In the cases of those who are born wise, material force is extremely clear and principle is not obstructed. In the cases of those who learn to be wise and those below them, the clearness or turbidity of material force varies in degree. Whether principle is complete or incomplete depends on this. (43:18a)

[. . .]

8. The Mind, the Nature, and the Feelings

85. The nature is comparable to the Great Ultimate, and the mind to yin and yang. The Great Ultimate exists only in the yin and yang, and cannot be separated from them. In the final analysis, however, the Great Ultimate is the Great Ultimate and yin and yang are yin and yang. So it is with nature and mind. They are one and yet two, two and yet one, so to speak. Philosopher Han Yü (768–824) described nature as humanity, righteousness, propriety, wisdom, and faithfulness and the feelings as pleasure, anger, sorrow, and joy. This is an advance over other philosophers on the problem of human nature. As to his division of human nature into three grades (superior, medium, and inferior), he has only explained material force but not nature. (45:1a)

86. Although nature is a vacuity, it consists of concrete principles. Although the mind is a distinct entity, it is vacuous, and therefore embraces all principles. This truth will be apprehended only when people examine it for themselves. (45:2a)

87. Nature consists of principles embraced in the mind, and the mind is where these principles are united. (45:2a)

88. Nature is principle. The mind is its embracement and reservoir, and issues it forth into operation. (45:2a)

89. Some time ago I read statements by Wu-feng (Hu Hung, 1100-1155) in which he spoke of the mind only in contrast to nature, leaving the feelings unaccounted for. Later when I read Heng-ch'ü's (Changtsai's) doctrine that "the mind commands man's nature and feelings," I realized that it was a great contribution. Only then did I find a satisfactory account of the feelings. His doctrine agrees with that of Mencius. In the words of Mencius, "the feeling of commiseration is the beginning of humanity." Now humanity is nature, and commiseration is feeling. In this, the mind can be seen through the feelings. He further said, "Humanity, righteousness, propriety, and wisdom are rooted in the mind." In this, the mind is seen through nature. For the mind embraces both nature and the feelings. Nature is substance and feelings are function. (45:3a–b)

90. Nature is the state before activity begins, the feelings are the state when activity has started, and the mind includes both of these states. For nature is the mind before it is aroused, while feelings are the mind after it is aroused, as is expressed in [Chang Tsai's] saying, "The mind commands man's nature and feelings." Desire emanates from feelings. The mind is comparable to water, nature is comparable to the tranquillity of still water, feeling is comparable to the flow of water, and desire is comparable to its waves. Just as there are good and bad waves, so there are good desires, such as when "I want humanity," and bad desires which rush out like wild and violent waves. When bad desires are substantial, they will destroy the Principle of Heaven, as water bursts a dam and damages everything. When Mencius said that "feelings enable people to do good," he meant that the correct feelings flowing from our nature are originally all good. (45:4a)

91. The mind means master. It is master whether in the state of activity or in the state of tranquillity. It is not true that in the state of tranquillity there is no need of a master and there is a master only when the state becomes one of activity. By master is meant an all-pervading control and command existing in the mind by itself. The mind unites and apprehends nature and the feelings, but it is not united with them as a vague entity without any distinction. (45:4a–b)

92. In his reply to Heng-ch'ü's dictum that "nature in the state of calmness cannot be without activity," Ming-tao's (Ch'eng Hao's) idea is that we should not hate things and events nor chase after them. Nowadays people who hate things avoid them completely, and who chase after them are continuously lured away by them. The best thing is neither to shun away from things nor to drift with them, but to face and respond to them in various ways. For Heng-ch'ü's idea was to cut ourselves from the external world and achieve calmness internally, whereas Ming-tao's idea was that the internal and the external must

be harmonized and unified. If (as Ming-tao said) that nature is calm "whether it is in a state of activity or in a state of tranquillity," then in our response to things we will naturally not be bound by them. If nature can be calmed only in a state of tranquillity, I am afraid that in time of activity it will be tempted and carried away by external things. (45:11b–12a)

93. *Question*: Is it correct to suppose that sages never show any anger?

Answer: How can they never show anger? When they ought to be angry, they will show it in their countenances. But if one has to punish someone for his crime and purposely smiles, that would be wrong.

Question: In that case, does it not show some feeling of wrath?

Answer: When Heaven is angry, thunder is also aroused. When sage-emperor Shun executed the four cruel criminals, he must have been angry at that time. When one becomes angry at the right time, he will be acting in the proper degree. When the matter is over, anger disappears, and none of it will be retained. (45:14b–15a)

94. *Question*: "How can desires be checked? Simply by thought. In learning there is nothing more important than thought. Only thought can check desires." Someone said that if thought is not correct, it will not be adequate to check desires. Instead, it will create trouble. How about "having no depraved thoughts"?

Answer: Thoughts that are not correct are merely desires. If we think through the right and wrong, and the ought and ought-not of a thing, in accordance with its principle, then our thought will surely be correct. (45:19b)

[. . .]

10. Principle (Li) and Material Force (Ch'i)

100. In the universe there has never been any material force without principle or principle without material force. (49:1a)

101. *Question*: Which exists first, principle or material force?

Answer: Principle has never been separated from material force. However, principle "exists before physical form [and is therefore without it]"

whereas material force "exists after physical form [and is therefore with it]." Hence when spoken of as being before or after physical form, is there not the difference of priority and posteriority? Principle has no physical form, but material force is coarse and contains impurities. (49:1a–b)

102. Fundamentally principle and material force cannot be spoken of as prior or posterior. But if we must trace their origin, we are obliged to say that principle is prior. However, principle is not a separate entity. It exists right in material force. Without material force, principle would have nothing to adhere to. As material force, there are the Agents (or Elements) of Metal, Wood, Water, and Fire. As principle, there are humanity, righteousness, propriety, and wisdom. (49:1b)

103. Question about the relation between principle and material force.

Answer: I-ch'uan (Ch'eng I) expressed it very well when he said that principle is one but its manifestations are many. When heaven, earth, and the myriad things are spoken of together, there is only one principle. As applied to man, however, there is in each individual a particular principle. (49:1b)

104. *Question*: What are the evidences that principle is in material force?

Answer: For example, there is order in the complicated interfusion of the yin and the yang and of the Five Agents. Principle is there. If material force does not consolidate and integrate, principle would have nothing to attach itself to. (49:2b)

105. *Question*: May we say that before heaven and earth existed there was first of all principle?

Answer: Before heaven and earth existed, there was after all only principle. As there is this principle, therefore there are heaven and earth. If there were no principle, there would also be no heaven and earth, no man, no things, and in fact, no containing or sustaining (of things by heaven and earth) to speak of. As there is principle, there is therefore material force to operate everywhere and nourish and develop all things.

Question: Is it principle that nourishes and develops all things?

Answer: As there is this principle, therefore there is this material force operating, nourishing, and developing. Principle itself has neither physical form nor body. (49:3a–b)

106. K'o-chi asked: When the creative process disposes of things, is it the end once a thing is gone,

or is there a principle by which a thing that is gone may return?

Answer: It is the end once a thing is gone. How can there be material force that has disintegrated and yet integrates once more? (49:3b–4a)

107.   *Question*: "The Lord on High has conferred even on the inferior people a moral sense." "When Heaven is about to confer a great responsibility on any man . . ." "Heaven, to protect the common people, made for them rulers." "Heaven, in the production of things, is sure to be bountiful to them, according to their natural capacity." "On the good-doer, the Lord on High sends down all blessings, and on the evil-doer, He sends down all miseries." "When Heaven is about to send calamities to the world, it will always first produce abnormal people as a measure of their magnitude." In passages like these, does it mean that Heaven has no personal consciousness and the passages are merely deductions from principle?

Answer: These passages have the same meaning. It is simply that principle operates this way. (49:4a)

108.   Principle attaches to material force and thus operates. (49:4b)

109.   Throughout the universe there are both principle and material force. Principle refers to the Way, which exists before physical form [and is without it] and is the root from which all things are produced. Material force refers to material objects, which exists after physical form [and is with it]; it is the instrument by which things are produced. Therefore in the production of man and things, they must be endowed with principle before they have their nature, and they must be endowed with material force before they have physical form. (49:5b)

110.   What are called principle and material force are certainly two different entities. But considered from the standpoint of things, the two entities are merged one with the other and cannot be separated with each in a different place. However, this does not destroy the fact that the two entities are each an entity in itself. When considered from the standpoint of principle, before things existed, their principles of being had already existed. Only their principles existed, however, but not yet the things themselves. Whenever one studies these aspects, one should clearly recognize and distinguish them, and consider both principle and material force from the

beginning to the end, and then one will be free from error. (49:5b–6a)

111.   There is principle before there can be material force. But it is only when there is material force that principle finds a place to settle. This is the process by which all things are produced, whether large as heaven and earth or small as ants. Why should we worry that in the creative process of Heaven and Earth, endowment may be wanting? Fundamentally, principle cannot be interpreted in the senses of existence or nonexistence. Before Heaven and Earth came into being, it already was as it is. (49:6a)

112.   Considering the fact that all things come from one source, we see that their principle is the same but their material force different. Looking at their various substances, we see that their material force is similar but their principle utterly different. The difference in material force is due to the inequality of its purity or impurity, whereas the difference in principle is due to its completeness or partiality. If you will please examine thoroughly, there should be no further doubt. (49:7a)

113.   The nature of man and things is nothing but principle and cannot be spoken of in terms of integration and disintegration. That which integrates to produce life and disintegrates to produce death is only material force. What we called the spirit, the heavenly and earthly aspects of the soul (*hun-p'o*), and consciousness are all effects of material force. Therefore when material force is integrated, there are these effects. When it is disintegrated, there are no more. As to principle, fundamentally it does not exist or cease to exist because of such integration or disintegration. As there is a certain principle, there is the material force corresponding to it, and as this material force integrates in a particular instance, its principle is also endowed in that instance. (49:8a)

11.   The Great Ultimate

114.   The Great Ultimate is nothing other than principle. (49:8b)

115.   *Question*: The Great Ultimate is not a thing existing in a chaotic state before the formation of heaven and earth, but a general name for the principles of heaven and earth and the myriad things. Is that correct?

Answer: The Great Ultimate is merely the principle of heaven and earth and the myriad things. With respect to heaven and earth, there is the Great Ultimate in them. With respect to the myriad things, there is the Great Ultimate in each and every one of them. Before heaven and earth existed, there was assuredly this principle. It is the principle that "through movement generates the yang." It is also this principle that "through tranquillity generates the yin." (49:8b–9a)

116.   *Question:* [You said,] "Principle is a single, concrete entity, and the myriad things partake it as their substance. Hence each of the myriad things possesses in it a Great Ultimate." According to this theory, does the Great Ultimate not split up into parts?

Answer: Fundamentally there is only one Great Ultimate, yet each of the myriad things has been endowed with it and each in itself possesses the Great Ultimate in its entirety. This is similar to the fact that there is only one moon in the sky but when its light is scattered upon rivers and lakes, it can be seen everywhere. It cannot be said that the moon has been split. (49:10b–IIa)

117.   The Great Ultimate has neither spatial restriction nor physical form or body. There is no spot where it may be placed. When it is considered in the state before activity begins, this state is nothing but tranquillity. Now activity, tranquillity, yin, and yang all exist only after physical form [and are with it]. However, activity is after all the activity of the Great Ultimate and tranquillity is also its tranquillity, although activity and tranquillity themselves are not the Great Ultimate. This is why Master Chou Tun-i only spoke of that state as Non-ultimate. While the state before activity begins cannot be spoken of as the Great Ultimate, nevertheless the principles of pleasure, anger, sorrow, and joy are already inherent in it. Pleasure and joy belong to yang and anger and sorrow belong to yin. In the initial stage the four are not manifested, but their principles are already there. As contrasted with the state after activity begins, it may be called the Great Ultimate. But still it is difficult to say. All this is but a vague description. The truth must be personally realized by each individual himself. (49:11a–b)

118.   Someone asked about the Great Ultimate. *Reply:* The Great Ultimate is simply the principle of the highest good. Each and every person has in him the Great Ultimate and each and every thing has in it the Great Ultimate. What Master Chou calls the Great Ultimate is a name to express all the virtues and the highest good in Heaven and Earth, man, and things. (49:11b)

119.   The Great Ultimate is similar to the top of a house or the zenith of the sky, beyond which point there is no more. It is the ultimate of principle. Yang is active and yin is tranquil. In these it is not the Great Ultimate that acts or remains tranquil. It is simply that there are the principles of activity and tranquillity. Principle is not visible; it becomes visible through yin and yang. Principle attaches itself to yin and yang as a man sits astride a horse. As soon as yin and yang produce the Five Agents, they are confined and fixed by physical nature and are thus differentiated into individual things each with its nature. But the Great Ultimate is in all of them. (49:14a)

120.   The Great Ultimate contains all principles of the Five Agents and yin and yang. It is not an empty thing. If it were a void, it would approach the Buddhist theory of dharma-nature (which maintains that the nature of dharmas, that is, elements of existence, are void). (49:14a)

121.   *Question:* Is the Great Ultimate the highest principle of the human mind?

Answer: There is an ultimate in every thing or event. That is the ultimate of principle.

Someone asked: Like humanity on the part of the ruler and respect on the part of ministers. These are ultimates.

Answer: These are ultimates of a particular thing or event. When all principles of heaven and earth and the myriad things are put together, that is the Great Ultimate. The Great Ultimate originally has no such name. It is merely a name to express its character. (49:14b–15a)

122.   There is no other event in the universe except yin and yang succeeding each other in an unceasing cycle. This is called Change. However, for these activity and tranquillity, there must be the principles which make them possible. This is the Great Ultimate. (49:16a)

12.   Heaven and Earth

123.   In the beginning of the universe there was only material force consisting of yin and yang. This force moved and circulated, turning this way and that. As this movement gained speed, a mass

of sediment was compressed (pushed together), and since there is no outlet for this, it consolidated to form the earth in the center of the universe. The clear part of material force formed the sky, the sun, and moon, and the stars and zodiacal spaces. It is only on the outside that the encircling movement perpetually goes on. The earth exists motionless in the center of the system, not at the bottom. (49:19a)

124. In the beginning of the universe, when it was still in a state of undifferentiated chaos, I imagine there were only water and fire. The sediment from water formed the earth. If today we climb the high mountains and look around, we will see ranges of mountains in the shape of waves. This is because the water formed them like this, though we do not know in what period they solidified. The solidification was at first very soft, but in time it became hard.

Question: I imagine it is like the tide rushing upon and making waves in the sand.

Answer: Yes. The most turbid water formed the earth and the purest fire became wind, thunder, lightning, the stars, and the like. (49:19b–20a)

125. *Question*: From the beginning of the universe to this day, it has not yet been ten thousand years. I do not know how things looked before then.

Answer: The past is to be understood in the same way.

Further question: Can the universe be destroyed?

Answer: It is indestructible. But in time man will lose all moral principles and everything will be thrown together in a chaos. Man and things will all die out, and then there will be a new beginning.

Further question: How was the first man created?

Answer: Through the transformation of material force. When the essence of yin and yang and the Five Agents are united, man's physical form is established. This is what the Buddhists call production by transformation. There are many such productions today, such as lice. (49:20a)

126. *Question*: With reference to the mind of Heaven and Earth and the Principle of Heaven and Earth. Principle is moral principle. Is mind the will of a master?

Answer: The mind is the will of a master, it is true, but what is called master is precisely

principle itself. It is not true that outside of the mind there is principle, or that outside of principle there is a mind. (49:23a)

127. Heaven and Earth have no other business except to have the mind to produce things. The material force of one origin (the Great Ultimate including principle and material force) revolves and circulates without a moment of rest, doing nothing except creating the myriad things.

Question: Master Ch'eng I said, "Heaven and Earth create and transform without having any mind of their own. The sage has a mind of his own but does not take any [unnatural] action."

Answer: That shows where Heaven and Earth have no mind of their own. It is like this: The four seasons run their course and the various things flourish. When do Heaven and Earth entertain any mind of their own? As to the sage, he only follows principle. What action does he need to take? This is the reason why Ming-tao (Ch'eng Hao) said, "The constant principle of Heaven and Earth is that their mind is in all things and yet they have no mind of their own. The constant principle of the sage is that his feelings are in accord with all creation, and yet he has no feelings of his own." This is extremely well said.

Question: Does having their mind in all things not mean to pervade all things with their mind without any selfishness?

Answer: Heaven and Earth reach all things with this mind. When man receives it, it then becomes the human mind. When things receive it, it becomes the mind of things (in general). And when grass, trees, birds, animals receive it, it becomes the mind of grass, trees, birds, and animals (in particular). All of these are simply the one mind of Heaven and Earth. Thus we must understand in what sense Heaven and Earth have mind and in what sense they have no mind. We cannot be inflexible. (49:23b–24a)

128. When the myriad things are born and grow, that is the time when Heaven and Earth have no mind. When dried and withered things desire life, that is the time when Heaven and Earth have mind. (49:24a)

129. The Lord (*Ti*) is principle acting as master. (49:25a)

[. . .]

Thomas Aquinas, *De ente et essentia*, Introduction and Chapters I–II, IV–V

Introduction

Born to an aristocratic family in the Kingdom of Naples in the south of Italy, Thomas Aquinas (1225–74) would become one of the leading intellectuals of the thirteenth century and perhaps still today the dominant intellectual force of the Roman Catholic Church. After joining the Dominican order, Aquinas studied and lectured at the universities of Paris and Cologne, and in Rome during the heady years when the value and place of Aristotle was under intense debate among Christian scholars. Aquinas's comprehensive grasp of a vast range of philosophical and theological writing made it possible for him to synthesize the work of neo-Platonists, Aristotelians, Christian and Islamic scholars and religious thinkers into a massive and complex philosophical vision.

The first four chapters of *De ente et essentia* ("On Being and Essence") articulate and modify a number of metaphysical claims culled from Aristotelian metaphysics (see III.4 in this volume). The result Aquinas gathers in Chapter V into a threefold schema of modes or ways of "possessing an essence" – in short, a threefold schema of beings. Those three are as follows: (1) God; (2) created intellectual substances; and (3) sub-

From Thomas Aquinas, *On Being and Essence*, trans. A. Maurer. Toronto: The Pontifical Institute of Medieval Studies, 1949, pp. 25–59 (some notes omitted).

stances composed of matter and form (i.e. perceptible sublunar and celestial things). What's most important to see is that Aquinas advances his conception of "the way of possessing an essence" as the blade by which he attempts to cut his distinctions among beings.

First, Thomas cleaves God from everything else, characterizing Him as an utterly unique being, the single being whose "essence is its very act of existence." That is to say, God is the only being whose very nature is to exist. A number of consequences follow: God is a member of no genus or species. God, in other words, is not an instance of a certain "type" or "kind" of being. Apples are apples because they possess the form or essence of apples. But God is not God because God has the form or essence of a god. "God," says Aquinas, "is only an act of existing" – pure *esse*. As a pure act of existing (pure *esse*), God is in some sense non-composite and, following Augustine, absolutely simple. In this Aquinas develops through metaphysical philosophy the way God describes himself to Moses through the burning bush: "I Am Who Am" (*Exodus* 3:13–15). Since "a thing is intelligible only through its definition and essence," there's clearly a sense in which God is, for Thomas, fundamentally unknowable to the human mind (see II.6 in this volume).

Moreover, for all beings other than God, essence and being (or what he calls the "act of existing") remain distinct. In Chapter IV Thomas maintains that "every essence or quiddity can be understood without its act of existing being understood." For everything besides God, existence must be "added" to a thing – in short, except for God existence is inessential. Since "that thing which has the nature cause can have the act of existing without the other thing" and God is the first cause, for Thomas the existence of God does not logically entail the existence of anything else.

This is an important move for Thomas. Cleaving being from essence with the concept of "act of existence," Thomas renders the existence of entities other than God contingent, even gratuitous. With this gesture, Thomas makes room for the Creation, and in doing so he undertakes a fundamental revision of Aristotle, for whom being and essence are synonymous or at least coextensive in their both being grounded in "form" (*ēidos, morphos*).

This move also marks a revision of Aristotle's notions of "potency" and "actuality." Aristotle had drawn a fairly tight (though certainly not perfect) correspondence between the notions of form/matter and act/potency, respectively. Thomas tears this correspondence apart.

In his account, the essence (the *ti esti* or "what-it-is") of immaterial substances remains nothing besides their form; they are, after all, purely formal entities. But since Thomas renders existence distinct from essence, forms may not be actual existents. Since they must receive existence, some degree of potentiality is, if you will, built into the essences or forms of immaterial substances: "that quiddity or form which an intelligence is must be in potency with respect to the act of existence

which it receives from God." Matter is no longer the locus of potency. By this strategy Thomas clears a space between God and humanity for created intelligences (angels), which though purely formal are not necessarily actual. Aristotle's the prime movers were, by contrast, both purely formal and, necessarily, purely actual.

Humans, for Aquinas, simultaneously maintain an affinity with angels (by virtue of their souls being intellectual, immaterial substances) and with lower animals. The human form is lowest among intelligences in grade of perfection and hence "is so near to material things that the material thing is drawn to participate in its act of existing." Yet, "human" simultaneously stands above the soul-mind-forms of other animals since it partakes so much in intelligence. But can the "propinquity" Aquinas posits of the human soul to the forms of strictly material things satisfactorily bridge the Aristotelian border between sensible-composite and purely formal substances?

The Aristotelian framework Thomas adopts also confronts him with the difficult challenge of accounting for the individuality of immaterial souls. Like Aristotle, Thomas construes body and soul as "one" composite with one act of existing. Matter individuates form, yielding individual men and women who nevertheless possess universal human forms. But is the mind individual only through the soul's relation to a particular body? Thomas's section of Chapter V devoted to immaterial substances is the longest section of that chapter because of his struggle to deal with this problem.

Aquinas, *De ente et essentia*

Introduction

A small mistake in the beginning is a great one in the end, according to the Philosopher* in the first book of the *De Caelo et Mundo*.† Moreover, as Avicenna declares early in his *Metaphysics*, what the intellect first conceives is being and essence. Consequently, lest we fall into error through ignorance of them, we ought to state, with

a view to disclosing the difficulty they involve: [1] what is meant by the terms *being* and *essence*; [2] how they are found in diverse things; and [3] how they are related to the intentions of logic, namely, genus, species and difference.

Chapter I: The General Meaning of the Terms Being and Essence

Now, we ought to acquire knowledge of the simple from the composite and arrive at what is prior from what is posterior, so that, beginning with easier matters, we may advance more suitably in knowledge. For this reason we ought to

---

* I, 5, 271b–13. [The "Philosopher" is Aristotle; the "Commentator" is Averroës, also known as Ibn Rushd.]
† I, 6, fol. 72rb.

go from the meaning of being to the meaning of essence.*

It should be known that being of itself is spoken of in two ways, as the Philosopher says in the fifth book of the *Metaphysics.*† In the first way it is divided into the ten categories; in the second way it signifies the truth of propositions. The difference between the two is that in the second sense we can call everything being about which we can form an affirmative proposition, even though it may posit nothing in reality. Thus, we call even privations and negations beings, for we say that affirmation *is* opposed to negation, and that blindness *is* in the eye. But, in the first sense, only that can be called being which posits something in reality. In this sense of the word, then, blindness and the like are not beings.

So, the term *essence* is not taken from being in the second sense of the word. For, as is clear in the case of privations, in that sense we call some things beings which do not have an essence. Essence is rather taken from being in the first sense. That is the reason why the Commentator declares in the same place‡ that being in the first sense of the word is that which signifies the essence of a thing.

And because, as we have said, being in this sense is divided into the ten categories, essence must signify something common to all natures, through which natures different beings are placed in different genera and species. For example, humanity is the essence of man, and so with other things.

Moreover, since that by which a thing is constituted in its proper genus or species is what is signified by the definition expressing what the thing is, philosophers have taken to using the word *quiddity* for the word essence. The Philosopher frequently calls this the *what a thing was to be,*§ in other words, that by which a thing is a *what.* It is also called form, inasmuch as form signifies the determination of each thing, as Avicenna says in the second book of his *Metaphysics.* Furthermore, it is called by another name, namely, *nature,* using nature in the first of the four senses given by Boethius in the treatise *De Duabus Naturis.* In this sense every being which the intellect can in any way grasp is called a nature; for a thing is intelligible only by its definition and essence. Thus the Philosopher, too, declares in the fifth book of the *Metaphysics*** that every substance is a nature. In this sense of the word, however, nature seems to mean the thing's essence as ordered to its proper activity, for nothing is without its proper activity. The term *quiddity,* on the other hand, is derived from what the definition signifies, while essence means that through which and in which a being has its act of existing [*esse*].

Now, being is predicated absolutely and primarily of substances; it is predicated secondarily and as in a qualified sense of accidents. For this reason essence is truly and properly in substances, but in accidents it is present in a certain manner and in a qualified sense.

Some substances, furthermore, are simple and some composite, and essence is in both. But, in simple substances it is present more truly and excellently, inasmuch as they also have the act of existing [*esse*] in a more excellent way; for they are the cause of composite substances – at least this is true of God, the first of the simple substances. But, because the essences of the simple substances are more hidden from us, we ought to begin with the essences of composite substances, so that, beginning with easier matters, we may advance more suitably in knowledge.

Chapter II: Essence as Found in Composite Substances

Form and matter are found in composite substances, for example, soul and body in man. It cannot be said, however, that either one of these alone is called the essence. That matter alone is not the essence of a thing is evident, for through its essence a thing is knowable and fixed in its species and genus. But, matter is not a principle

---

* Being (*ens*) is the existing thing (*id quod habet esse*), including both essence and the act of existing. It is thus complex or composite. Essence is one of its components, and its notion is disengaged only after we know being. Being is also posterior to essence, not in time, but in nature, since what is composite is naturally posterior to its constitutive principles.

† V, 7, 1017a22–35.

‡ Averroes, *In V Meta.*, 7, t. c. 14, fol. 55 a56.

§ *Quod quid erat esse.* A literal translation of Aristotle's: *TO TI HN EINAI.* See Aristotle, *Post. Anal.* I, 22, 82b38; *De Anima.* III. 6, 430b28; *Meta.*, VII, 3, 1028b34.

** V, 4, 1014b35.

of knowledge, nor does it determine anything in a genus or species. Only that which is actually something does this. Neither can the form alone of a composite substance be called its essence, although some would endeavor to assert it. For it is evident from what has been said that essence is what the definition of a thing signifies. Now, the definition of physical substances includes not only form but matter; otherwise there would be no difference between physical and mathematical definitions. Neither can it be said that the definition of a physical substance includes matter as something added to its essence, or as a being outside of its essence, because this manner of definition is proper to accidents, which do not have a perfect essence. That is the reason why the definition of accidents must include their subject which is outside their genus.

Evidently, then, essence embraces matter and form. We cannot say, however, that essence signifies the relation existing between matter and form, or something added to them. This would of necessity be accidental or extraneous to the thing, and it would not enable us to know the thing: none of which characteristics befits essence. For, through form, which is the actuality of matter, matter is rendered being in act and a substance [*hoc aliquid*]. What is added to it later, then, does not make matter to be actual without any qualification, but to be actually *such*, as accidents likewise do. Whiteness, for instance, makes a being actually white. Accordingly, when such a form is acquired, we do not say something comes into being purely and simply, but in a certain respect.

It remains, then, that the word *essence* in composite substances signifies the composite of matter and from. In agreement with this is Boethius' statement in his commentary on the *Categories*, where he says that *usia* signifies the composite. *Usia* in Greek is the same as essence in our language, as Boethius himself says in *De Duabus Naturis*. Avicenna, too, declares that the quiddity of composite substances is the composition itself of form and matter. The Commentator also asserts in his exposition on the seventh book of the *Metaphysics*: "The nature which species have in things subject to generation is a mean, that is, a composite of matter and form." Reason likewise is in agreement with this, because the act of existing of a composite substance belongs neither to the form alone nor to the matter alone, but

to the composite itself. Now, essence is that according to which a thing is said to be. On this account, the essence, by reason of which a thing is called a being, cannot be either form alone or matter alone, but is the two together, even though the form alone in its own way is the cause of such an act of existing. We see in the case of other things composed of several principles that they do not take their name from one of these principles alone, but from that which includes both. This is evident in the case of savors. Sweetness is caused by the action of the hot dissolving the moist. Although in this way heat is the cause of sweetness, a body is not called sweet from its heat, but from the savor which includes the hot and the moist.

However, since matter is the principle of individuation, it might perhaps seem to follow that the essence which includes within itself both matter and form is only particular and not universal. If this were so, it would follow that, the essence being what the definition signifies, universals would have no definition. Hence, we must realize that the matter which is the principle of individuation is not any matter whatsoever, but only designated matter [*materia signata*]. By designated matter I mean matter considered under determined dimensions. Now, we do not include matter of this sort in the definition of man as man, but we would include it in Socrates' definition if Socrates had a definition. The definition of man, however, does include undesignated matter. For we do not include in the definition of man this particular bone and this particular flesh, but simply bone and flesh, which are the undesignated matter of man.

It is clear, then, that the difference between the essence of Socrates and the essence of man is simply between what is designated and what is not. This is why the Commentator declares in his exposition on the seventh book of the *Metaphysics*: "Socrates is nothing else than animality and rationality, which are his quiddity."

The generic and specific essence also differ as designated and undesignated. In this case, however, there is a different mode of designation from the preceding. The designation of the individual with respect to the species is through matter determined by dimensions, while the designation of the species with respect to the genus is through the constitutive difference taken from the thing's form. The designation in the species with respect to the genus is not, however, through anything in the specific essence which is in no way in the generic essence; rather, whatever is in the species is also in the genus as undetermined. For, if *animal* were not the whole that man is, but a part of it, it would not be predicated of it, since no integral part may be predicated of its whole.

We can see how this is so if we observe the difference between *body* as part of animal and *body* as genus. For body cannot be a genus in the same way as it is an integral part. Thus, the word *body* has several meanings. Body in the genus substance means that which has such a nature that three dimensions can be designated in it. But the three designated dimensions themselves are a body according as body is in the genus quantity.

Now, it is possible that a being having one perfection may also possess further perfection. This is evident in the case of man, who has a sensitive nature and, besides this, an intellectual nature. Similarly, over and above the perfection of having such a form that three dimensions can be designated in it, another perfection can be added, such as life, or something of the kind. The word *body*, therefore, can signify something having a form such that it admits the possibility of designating in it three dimensions, to the exclusion of any further perfection following upon that form. If anything else is added, it is outside the meaning of *body* in this sense of the word. In this sense body will be an integral and material part of animal, because soul then will not be included in the meaning of the word *body*, and it will be additional to body itself; so that, as parts, these two – soul and body – constitute the animal.

We also can understand by the word *body* a thing having a form such that three dimensions can be designated in it, no matter what that form may be, whether some further perfection can come from it or not. In this sense body will be the genus of animal, because there is nothing to be found in animal which is not implicitly contained in body. Soul is not another form than that through which three dimensions could be designated in that thing. Consequently, when we said that a body is that which has a form such that in virtue of it three dimensions can be designated in the body, it was understood of whatever the form might be, whether animality, or stoneness, or any other form. Thus, the form of animal is implicitly contained in the form of body, inasmuch as body is its genus. Animal likewise bears the same

relation to man. For, if *animal* were the name simply of a thing having a perfection such that it is capable of sensation and movement through an intrinsic principle, to the exclusion of another perfection, then any other additional perfection would be related to animal as a part, and not as implicitly contained in the notion of animal; so, animal would not be a genus. But it is a genus inasmuch as it signifies a thing from whose form sensation and movement can issue, no matter what that form may be, whether it be simply a sensitive soul or a soul that is both sensitive and rational.

The genus, then, signifies indeterminately everything in the species. It does not indicate the matter alone. Similarly, the difference also signifies the whole and does not indicate merely the form. The definition, too, signifies the whole, and so also does the species, although they do so in different ways. The genus signifies the whole as a name expressing what is material in the thing without the proper form's determination. The genus, then, is taken from matter, even though it is not matter; as it is evident that body means that which has a perfection such that three dimensions can be indicated in it, and this perfection is related as matter with respect to further perfection. Difference, however, signifies the whole as a name drawn from the form, taken in a determinate way, without determinate matter being included in its primary notion. This is evident when we say *animated*, in other words, *that which has a soul*. For we do not determine what that thing is, whether it is a body or something else. Thus, Avicenna declares that the genus is not understood in the difference as a part of its essence, but only as a being outside of its essence, in the same way that the subject is contained in the notion of its attributes. For this reason, too, as the Philosopher says in the third book of the *Metaphysics** and in the fourth book of the *Topics*,† we do not, properly speaking, predicate the genus of the difference, except perhaps as a subject is predicated of its attribute. But the definition or species embraces both, namely, the determinate matter expressed by the word *genus*, and the determinate form expressed by the word *difference*.

---

* III, 3, 998b24.
† IV, 2, 122b20.

From this it is evident why genus, species and difference are related proportionately to matter, form and composite in the world of things, although they are not identical with them. Genus is not matter, but is taken from matter as signifying the whole; and difference is not form, but is taken from form as signifying the whole. Thus we say that man is a rational animal, not that he is composed of animal and rational as we say that he is composed of soul and body. We say that man is made up of soul and body as two things constitute a third thing which is neither one of them, for man is neither soul nor body. But if, in a sense, we may say that man is made up of animal and rational, it will not be as a third thing is made up of two things but as a third concept of two concepts. The concept *animal* expresses the nature of a thing without the determination of a special form, on the basis of that which is material with respect to the ultimate perfection. But the concept of the difference *rational* consists in the determination of the special form. And from these two concepts there is formed the concept of the species or definition. Accordingly, just as we do not predicate of a composite thing the several things which compose it, in the same way neither do we predicate of a concept those concepts from which it is formed. We do not say that definition is genus or difference.

Now, although genus signifies the whole essence of the species, it is not required that different species in the same genus have one essence. For the unity of the genus comes from its very indetermination or indifference; not in such a way, it is true, that the genus expresses a nature numerically identical in different species, to which might be joined another thing – the difference – determining it as form determines matter which is numerically one. On the contrary, the genus expresses some form – although not in a determinate way this one or that one – which the difference signifies determinately, and which is not other than that which the genus signified indeterminately. That is why the Commentator declares in the eleventh book of the *Metaphysics* that prime matter is said to be one because of the removal of all forms, whereas genus is called one because of the commonness of the designated form. It is thus clear that, by adding the difference and removing the indetermination which was the cause of the unity of the genus, essentially diverse species remain.

As we have said, the nature of the species is indeterminate with respect to the individual, as the nature of the genus is with respect to the species. As a consequence, just as the genus, predicated of the species, implies indistinctly in its signification everything which is determinately in the species, so too the species, predicated of the individual, must signify, although indistinctly, everything essentially in the individual. In this way the word *man* expresses the essence of the species, and so man is predicated of Socrates. But if the nature of the species is signified in precision from designated matter, which is the principle of individuation, then it will have the role of a part. This is the way it is signified by the word *humanity*, for humanity expresses that by reason of which man is man. Now, it is not designated matter by which man is man; so it is not in any way included among the things by which man is man. Since the concept of humanity, then, includes only those things by which man is man, it manifestly excludes or omits from its signification designated matter. And because the part is not predicated of the whole, humanity is predicated neither of man nor of Socrates. Hence, Avicenna declares that the quiddity of a composite is not the composite itself whose quiddity it is, although the quiddity itself be composite. Although humanity, for instance, is composite, it is not man; it must be received in something which is designated matter.

As we have already said, relative to the genus the species is designated by forms, while relative to the species the individual is designated by matter. In consequence, the word expressing that from which the generic nature is taken in precision from the determinate form completing the species must signify the material part of the whole, as body is the material part of man. But the word expressing that from which the specific nature is taken in precision from designated matter signifies the formal part.

By humanity, therefore, we mean a certain form, called the form of the whole. It is not as something added to the essential parts, namely, form and matter, as the form of a house is added to its integral parts; rather, it is the form which is the whole, embracing both form and matter, excluding, however, those things which enable matter to be designated.

The word *man* and the word *humanity*, then, clearly signify man's essence, but, as we have said, they do so in different ways. The word *man* expresses it as a whole, inasmuch as it does not exclude the designation of matter; but it contains it implicitly and indistinctly, as we said previously the genus contains the difference. For this reason the word *man* is predicated of individuals. The word *humanity*, on the other hand, signifies man's essence as a part, because it signifies only what belongs to man as man, excluding all designation of matter. Therefore it is not predicated of individual men. And this is why we sometimes find the word *essence* predicated of a thing (for we say that Socrates is a certain essence), and sometimes denied (as when we say that Socrates' essence is not Socrates).

Chapter IV: Essence as Found in Separate Substances

It remains for us to see in what way essence is in separated substances, namely, in the soul, in the intelligences and in the First Cause.

Although everyone admits the simplicity of the First Cause some try to introduce the composition of matter and form in the intelligences and in souls. The originator of this doctrine seems to have been Avicebron, the author of the *Fons Vitae*. But it is not in accord with what philosophers generally say, since they call these substances separated from matter, and they prove that they are entirely immaterial. The strongest demonstration of this is from their power of understanding. We see that forms are not actually intelligible unless they are separated from matter and material conditions; nor are they rendered actually intelligible except through the power of an intelligent substance which receives them within itself and produces them. Every intelligent substance, then, must be in every way free from matter, neither having matter as a part of itself, nor being, like material forms, a form impressed on matter. Nor can it be asserted that not any matter whatsoever, but only corporeal matter, stands in the way of intelligibility. If corporeal matter alone stood in the way of intelligibility, then matter must impede intelligibility because of its corporeal form, since matter is called corporeal only when it exists under a corporeal form. But this is impossible, because a corporeal form itself, like other forms, is actually intelligible when abstracted from matter.

Hence there is in no way a composition of matter and form in a soul or an intelligence so that matter may be thought to exist in them as it does in corporeal substances. There is in them, however, a composition of form and act of existing [*esse*]. Thus, in the commentary on the ninth proposition of the *Liber de Causis*,* it is said that an intelligence is a being having form and act of existing; and form is understood here as the essence itself or the simple nature.

It is easy to see how this is so. Whatever things are so related to each other that one is the cause of the other's existing, the one which is the cause can exist without the other, but not conversely. Now, we find the relation of matter and form such that form makes matter exist. It is thus impossible that matter exist without some form. On the other hand, it is not impossible that some form exist without matter, for form as such does not depend on matter. If we find some forms which can exist only in matter, this happens to them because they are far removed from the First Principle, which is primary and pure act. So, those forms closest to the First Principle subsist in virtue of themselves without matter. For, as we have said, not every kind of form requires matter, and the intelligences are forms of this sort. It is not necessary, then, that the essences or quiddities of these substances be other than form itself.

Accordingly, the essence of a composite substance differs from that of a simple substance in that the essence of the composite substance is not from alone, but includes form and matter. The essence of a simple substance, on the contrary, is form alone. Two other differences follow upon this. The first is that we can signify the essence of a composite substance as a whole or as part. This happens, as we have said, because of the designation of matter. We may not predicate, then, in just any way the essence of a composite thing of the composite thing itself. We cannot say, for instance, that man is his quiddity. But the essence of a simple being, which is its form, cannot be signified except as a whole, since nothing is there besides the form as receiving the form.

* O. Bardenhewer, *Die pseudo-aristotelische Schrift "Ueber das reine Gute" bekannt unter dem Namen "Liber de Causis"*, 8, p. 173. The *Liber de Causis* is a Latin translation of a neoplatonic work whose contents are taken from Proclus' *Elements of Theology*.

Thus, no matter in what way the essence of a simple substance is considered, it may be predicated of the substance. That is why Avicenna says: "The quiddity of a simple thing is the simple thing itself because there is nothing else receiving it."

The second difference is that the essences of composite beings are multiplied according to the division of designated matter, because they are received in it. That is why it happens that some beings are specifically the same and numerically diverse. But, since the essence of a simple substance is not received in matter, it cannot be multiplied in this way. Of necessity, therefore, we do not find among those substances many individuals of the same species; but, as Avicenna clearly states, there are as many species among them as there are individuals.

Although substances of this kind are forms alone and immaterial, they are not in every way simple so as to be pure act. They do have an admixture of potency, which is evident from the following consideration. Whatever does not belong to the notion of an essence or quiddity comes from without and enters into composition with the essence, for no essence is intelligible without its parts. Now, every essence or quiddity can be understood without anything being known of its existing. I can know what a man or a phoenix is and still be ignorant whether it exists in reality. From this it is clear that the act of existing is other than essence or quiddity unless, perhaps, there is a being whose quiddity is its very act of existing. And there can be only one such being, the First Being. For nothing can be multiplied except: [1] through the addition of some difference, as the generic nature is multiplied into species; or [2] by the form being received in different parts of matter, as the specific nature is multiplied in different individuals; or [3] by one thing being separate and another thing being received in something – for instance, if there were a separated heat, by reason of its very separation it would be different from heat which is not separated. But, should there exist some being which is simply the act of existing, so that the act of existing be itself subsistent, a difference cannot be added to this act of existing. Otherwise, it would not be purely and simply the act of existing, but the act of existing plus a certain form. Much less can matter be added to it, because then it would not be a subsistent, but a material, act of existing. So we conclude that there can only

be one such being which is its very act of existing. With this exception, in every other thing its act of existing is other than its quiddity, nature or form. The intelligences' act of existing must therefore be over and above their form, and for that reason it has been said that an intelligence is form and act of existing.

Now, whatever belongs to a being is either caused by the principles of its nature, as the capability of laughter in man, or it comes to it from some extrinsic principle, as light in the air from the sun's influence. But it is impossible that the act of existing be caused by a thing's form or its quiddity, (I say *caused* as by an efficient cause); for then something would be the cause of itself and would bring itself into existence – which is impossible. Everything, then, which is such that its act of existing is other than its nature must needs have its act of existing from something else. And since every being which exists through another is reduced, as to its first cause, to one existing in virtue of itself, there must be some being which is the cause of the existing of all things because it itself is the act of existing alone. If that were not so, we would proceed to infinity among causes, since, as we have said, every being which is not the act of existing alone has a cause of its existence. Evidently, then, an intelligence is form and act of existing, and it has its act of existing from the First Being which is simply the act of existing. This is the First Cause, God.

Now, every being receiving something from another is potential with respect to what it receives, and what is received in it is its act. The quiddity itself, then, or the form which is the intelligence must be potential with respect to the existence which it receives from God, and that existence [*esse*] is received as an act. Potency and act are thus found in the intelligences, but not form and matter except in an equivocal sense. So, too, as the Commentator says in his exposition on the third book of the *De Anima, to suffer, to receive, to be a subject of,* and all characteristics of this sort which seem to belong to things by reason of matter, belong equivocally to intellectual and corporeal substances.

Furthermore, since the quiddity of an intelligence is, as we have said, the intelligence itself, its quiddity or essence is identical with itself, and the act of existing it receives from God is that whereby it subsists in the world of things. For that reason some assert that a substance of this kind is composed of *that by which it is* [*quo est*] and *that which it is* [*quod est*], or, as Boethius says, of *that which it is* [*quod est*] and its *act of existing* [*esse*]. Since, then, both potency and act are in the intelligences, finding a multitude among them will not be difficult, whereas it would be impossible if there were no potency in them. Thus, the Commentator declares in his exposition on the third book of the *De Anima* that, if we did not know the nature of the possible intellect, we could not find multitude among separated substances.

These substances are accordingly distinct from one another by reason of their degree of potency and act. A superior intelligence, closer to the First Being, has more act and less potency, and so on with the others. This gradation terminates in the human soul which holds the lowest degree among intellectual substances. As the Commentator states in his exposition on the third book of the *De Anima*, the possible intellect of the human soul bears the same relation to intelligible forms that prime matter, holding the lowest position in sensible existence, bears to sensible forms. That is why the Philosopher compares it to a blank tablet on which nothing is written.* Having more potency than the other intellectual substances, the human soul is so close to matter that a material thing is drawn to share in its own act of existing, so that from soul and body there results in the one composite one act of existing, although in so far as it is the soul's act of existing it is not dependent on the body. Posterior to that form which is the soul, other forms are found still more potential and close to matter, to such a point that they do not exist without matter. Among these forms, too, we find an order and hierarchy, until we reach the primary forms of the elements, which are closest to matter. Being so close to matter, they operate only according to the exigencies of active and passive qualities and other dispositions which prepare matter to receive form.

Chapter V: Essence as Found in Different Beings

It is evident from the foregoing how essence is found in different beings. Indeed, we find in substances a threefold manner of having essence. There is a being, God, whose essence is His very act of existing. That explains why we find some philosophers asserting that God does not have a quiddity or essence, because His essence is not other than His act of existing. From this it follows that He is not in a genus, for the quiddity of anything in a genus must be other than its act of existing, since the different beings within a genus or species have the same generic or specific quiddity or nature, whereas their act of existing is diverse.

If we say, moreover, that God is purely and simply the act of existing, we need not fall into the mistake of those who assert that God is that universal existence whereby each thing formally exists. The act of existing which is God is such that no addition can be made to it. Consequently, in virtue of its very purity it is the act of existing distinct from every act of existing. That is why, in the commentary on the ninth proposition of the *Liber de Causis*, it is said that the First Cause, being purely and simply the act of existing, is individualized by its unalloyed perfection. But just as existing-in-general [*esse commune*] does not include in its notion any addition, so neither does it imply any exclusion of addition; otherwise, nothing could be understood to exist in which something would be added over and above the act of existing.

Similarly, although God is simply the act of existing, it is not necessary that He lack the other perfections or excellences. On the contrary, He possesses all perfections of all genera of beings; so He is said to be unqualifiedly perfect, as the Philosopher and Commentator assert in the fifth book of the *Metaphysics*.† But He possesses these perfections in a more excellent way than all things, for in Him they are one, while in other things they are diversified. The reason for this is that all these perfections are His according to His simple act of existing. So, too, if someone through one quality could perform the operations of all the qualities, he would in that one quality possess all the qualities. In the same way, God possesses all perfections in His very act of existing.

In a second way, we find essence in created intellectual substances. Their act of existing is other than their essence, although their essence is immaterial. Their act of existing is thus not a

---

* Aristotle, *De Anima*, III, 4, 430al.

† Aristotle, *Meta.*, V, 16, 1021b30.

separated, but a received, one; and it is therefore limited and restricted to the capacity of the receiving nature. Their nature or quiddity, however, is separated and unreceived in any matter. Thus the *Liber de Causis* states that the intelligences are unlimited from below and limited from above. They are limited as to their act of existing which they receive from above, but they are unlimited from below because their forms are not limited to the capacity of some matter receiving them.

Consequently, in these substances, as we have said, we do not find many individuals in one species, except in the case of the human soul because of the body to which it is united. Although the soul's individuation depends on the body for the occasion of its beginning, since it comes into possession of its individuated act of existing only in the body of which it is the act, it is not necessary that the individuation come to an end when the body is removed. Since its act of existing is independent, once it has acquired an individuated act of existing from its being made the form of this particular body, that act of existing always remains individuated. Hence, Avicenna states that the individuation, and multiplication of souls depend on the body for their beginning but not for their end.

What is more, because the quiddity in these substances is not identical with their act of existing, they are able to be placed in a category. So, we find in them genus, species and difference, although their proper differences are hidden from us. But even in the case of sensible things the essential differences themselves are unknown to us; hence, we have to signify them by the accidental differences which arise from the essential, as we designate a cause by its effect. *Biped*, for instance, is given as the difference of man. With regard to immaterial substances, we do not know their proper accidents; hence, we cannot designate their differences either through themselves or through their accidental differences.

We should observe, however, that genus and difference are not taken in the same way in these substances, and in sensible substances. In sensible substances the genus is taken from what is material in a thing, while the difference is taken from what is formal in it. And so, Avicenna says, in the beginning of his *De Anima*, that in things composed of matter and form the form is the simple difference of what is constituted by it; not that

the form itself is the difference, but that it is the principle of the difference, as the same author declares in his *Metaphysics*. A difference of this sort is called a *simple difference*, because it is drawn from a part of the thing's quiddity, namely, the form. But, since immaterial substances are simple quiddities, their difference cannot be taken from a part of the quiddity, but from the whole quiddity. So, Avicenna says in the beginning of the *De Anima* that only those species whose essences are composed of matter and form have a simple difference.

In immaterial substances the genus is likewise taken from the whole essence, although in a different way. One separated substance agrees with another in being immaterial, and they are different from each other in their degree of perfection in proportion as they withdraw from potentiality and approach pure act. We take their genus, then, from what follows upon their being immaterial, for example, intellectuality and the like. Their difference, which in fact is unknown to us, is taken from what follows upon their degree of perfection.

These differences, moreover, need not be accidental because they correspond to greater and less degrees of perfection, which do not vary the species. True, the degrees of perfection in receiving the same form do not vary the species, for instance, the more white and less white in participating in the same nature of whiteness. But a diverse grade of perfection in the forms themselves or the participated natures does vary the species. Thus, according to the Philosopher in the seventh book of the *De Animalibus*,* nature advances by grades from plants to animals by way of certain beings which are intermediate between animals and plants. Nor is it necessary that intellectual substances be always separated by two real differences, because, as the Philosopher states in the eleventh book of the *De Animalibus*,† this cannot happen in all things.

We find essence in a third way in substances composed of matter and form. Their act of

---

* *Historia Animalium*, VIII, 1, 588b4–14. Michael Scot translated Aristotle's three works on animals from the Arabian under the title of *De Animalibus*. Books 1–10 correspond to *Historia Animalium*; 11–14 to *De Partibus Animalium*.
† *De Partibus Animalium*, 1, 2, 642b5.

existing is received and limited because they have it from another; what is more, their nature or quiddity is received in designated matter. So, they are limited both from above and from below. Moreover, because of the division of designated matter, individuals can now be multiplied in one species. As for the manner in which the essence of these substances is related to logical intentions, we have explained that in a previous chapter.

11

Duns Scotus, *Ordinatio* I (abridged)[1]

Introduction

John Duns Scotus (1266–1308) seems to have been born in Scotland, in the town of Duns, just west of Berwick-upon-Tweed. Receiving an early education on perhaps the Hebridean island of North Uist or in Dumfries, Scotus joined the Franciscans and was ordained in Northampton in 1291. Studying at both Oxford and Paris, Scotus rose first to become a master and then regent. Transferred to Cologne, Scotus met there an untimely death. Arguably the most important scholastic metaphysician after Thomas Aquinas (III.10), Scotus in many ways defined the terms with which institutional European philosophy would be engaged during the fourteenth century, and he anticipated modern naturalism. Later, Renaissance thinkers' mockery of those who followed Scotus – and indeed all those caught up in the recondite thought of scholastic philosophy – as "dunces" gave rise to the abusive term still in use today.[2]

Perhaps Scotus's most important metaphysical achievement was his doctrine of "transcendentals." The term "transcendental" as Scotus deployed it includes both the sense of (a) rising above or beyond ordinary experience to reach something divine and (b) Immanuel Kant's usage in describing investigations into the necessary conditions of the

From Duns Scotus, *Duns Scotus: Philosophical Writings*, ed. A. Wolter, Edinburgh: Thomas Nelson and Sons, Ltd., 1962, pp. 2–12.

possibility of knowledge and experience generally. Epistemologically, Scotus maintains that the natural powers of the human intellect are sufficient to know God in important ways without revelation. What makes this possible is something metaphysical with regard to the nature of reality – namely, the "transcendentals." Tersely put, transcendentals are features of reality that all beings share – e.g. being, unity, goodness. Comprising the absolutely most general common ground of things, supernatural as well as natural, transcendentals serve as epistemological and metaphysical bridges between the human and the divine. Among the important conclusions one can draw from Scotus's doctrine is that God and the divine are not utterly distinct from natural creatures.[3]

Revealed theologians and illuminationists – such as Augustine, al-Farabi and Henry of Ghent – held that human knowledge requires revelation or illumination of the natural faculties of mind by something supernatural, namely God. Natural theologians, by contrast, while not excluding revelation, maintained that natural, unaided human faculties can themselves acquire knowledge, including knowledge of the divine. People can naturally achieve knowledge, the natural theologians say, either negatively by considering what God is not (e.g. Maimonides) or more positively by understanding what God is (Aquinas).

According to Scotus, however, Aquinas's positive theology threatened to undermine the very possibility of natural theology because Thomas limits the human intellect's apprehension of God to the equivocal language of analogy.[4] It is only if, Scotus argued, we can think and speak "univocally," that is, in precisely the same way, about God and creatures, that we are justified in claiming to know the divine. Scotus's arguments about the univocity of the transcendentals were devastating to illuminationism. They also foreshadowed the wider, modern naturalistic shift in focus from divine intercession to the natural powers of mind as a source of knowledge and understanding.[5]

Scotus, however, not only departed from the scholastic tradition through his doctrine of the univocity of the transcendentals; he also broke with it on the relation of universal "forms" (such as "dog") to individuals (such as any particular dog). His strategy was to close the gap between universals and particulars by claiming that forms carry within them a principle of individuation or "thisness," which he called "*haecceitas.*" It is by virtue of haecceity, according to Scotus, that universal forms are able to contract into particulars.

According, however, to another Franciscan, William of Ockham (1288–1348), Scotus's account of the relationship between universals and particulars is incoherent – as is, in fact, every doctrine of universals that maintains that they exist outside the mind. Born in Surrey, Ockham (or Occam) is best known, perhaps, for the principle of ontological "parsimony" or "simplicity" attributed to him: *entia non sunt multiplicanda sine necessitate* ("entities should not be multiplied without necessity"). While Ockham never actually articulated this principle, he does hold to a variant of the Principle of Sufficient Reason, maintaining that nothing exists without a reason for its existence; hence, in his own words: "For nothing ought to be posited without a reason given, unless it is self-evident or known by experience or proved by the authority of Sacred Scripture."[6] While Scotus's idea of transcendentals would influence scores of ontologists and metaphysicians, including twentieth-century philosophers like Martin Heidegger (III.24), Ockham's rejection of realistic conceptions of universal forms, the principle of parsimony, and the principle of sufficient reason would become central features of modern philosophy and science.

Notes

1 Part of the 1300–02 Oxford edition of Scotus's *Commentary on the Sentences of Peter Lombard*.
2 R. Cross, *Duns Scotus*. New York: Oxford University Press, 1999.
3 John Duns Scotus, "Man's Natural Knowledge of God," in *Philosophical Writings: A Selection*, trans. A. Wolter, Indianapolis, IN: Hackett Publishing Co., 1987. A. Wolter, *The Transcendentals and their Function in the Metaphysics of Duns Scotus*, St Bonaventure, NY: The Fransciscan Institute, 1946. In a not terribly distant way, Newton had showed that the celestial and terrestrial objects are governed by the same laws.
4 T. Aquinas, *Summa Theologica*. I, Q13, a.10, ad 4. See also II.6 in this volume.
5 T. Williams, ed., *The Cambridge Companion to Duns Scotus*, Cambridge: Cambridge University Press, 2000.
6 William of Ockham, *Ordinatio I* (from Ockham's *Commentary on the Sentences of Peter Lombard*), D. 30, Q. 1.

Duns Scotus, *Ordinatio*

[I. Concerning Metaphysics]

[1. Metaphysics, the science of the Transcendentals] There must necessarily exist some universal science which considers the transcendentals as such. This science we call "metaphysics", from "meta", which means "beyond", and "the science of nature". It is, as it were, the transcending science, because it is concerned with the transcendentals.

[2. Concept and Articulation of the Transcendental] Now a doubt arises as to what kind of predicates are those which are predicated formally of God, for instance, "wise", "good", and the like. I answer that before "being" is divided into the ten categories, it is divided into infinite and finite. For the latter, namely finite being, is common to the ten genera. Whatever pertains to "being", then, in so far as it remains indifferent to finite and infinite, or as proper to the Infinite Being, does not belong to it as determined to a genus, but prior to any such determination,

and therefore as transcendental and outside any genus. Whatever [predicates] are common to God and creatures are of such kind, pertaining as they do to being in its indifference to what is infinite and finite. For in so far as they pertain to God they are infinite, whereas in so far as they belong to creatures they are finite. They belong to "being", then, prior to the division into the ten genera. Anything of this kind, consequently, is transcendental.

But then another doubt arises. How can wisdom be considered a transcendental if it is not common to all beings, for transcendentals seem to be common to all? I answer that just as it is not of the nature of a supreme genus to have many species contained under it, but it is of its nature not to have any genus over and above it (the category of "when", for instance, is a supreme genus since it has no genus over and above it, although it has few, if any, species contained under it), so also whatever is not contained under any genus is transcendental. Hence, not to have any predicate above it except "being" pertains to the very notion of a transcendental. That it be common to many inferior notions, however, is purely incidental. This is evident too from the fact that "being" possesses not only attributes which are coextensive with it, such as "one", "true" and "good", but also attributes which are opposed to one another such as "possible-or-necessary", "act-or-potency", and suchlike.

But if the coextensive attributes are transcendental because they pertain to "being" as not determined to a definite genus, then the disjunctive attributes are transcendental too. And both members of the disjunction are transcendental since neither determines its determinable element to a definite genus. Nevertheless, one member of the disjunction is proper and pertains formally to one being alone, for instance, "necessary" in the disjunction "necessary-or-possible", or "infinite" in the disjunction "finite-or-infinite", and so also with the others.

And so "wisdom", or anything else, for that matter, which is common to God and creatures, can be transcendental. A transcendental, however, may also be predicated of God alone, or again it may be predicated about God and some creature. It is not necessary, then, that a transcendental as transcendental be predicated of every being, unless it be coextensive with the first of the transcendentals, namely "being".

[3. Primacy of "Being" among the other Transcendentals] And I say that ... since nothing can be more common than "being", and that "being" cannot be predicated univocally and *in quid* of all that is of itself intelligible (because it cannot be predicated in this way of the ultimate differences or of its attributes), it follows that we have no object of the intellect that is primary by reason of a commonness *in quid* in regard to all that is of itself intelligible.

And yet, notwithstanding, I say that "being" is the first object of the intellect, because in it a twofold primacy concurs, namely, a primacy of commonness and of virtuality. For whatever is of itself intelligible either includes essentially the notion of "being" or is contained virtually or essentially in something else which does include "being" essentially. For all genera, species, individuals, and the essential parts of genera, and the Uncreated Being all include "being" quidditatively. All the ultimate differences are included essentially in some of these. All the attributes of "being" are virtually included in "being" and in those things which come under "being".

Hence, all to which "being" is not univocal *in quid* are included in those to which "being" is univocal in this way. And so it is clear that "being" has a primacy of commonness in regard to the primary intelligibles, that is, to the quidditative concepts of the genera, species, individuals, and all their essential parts, and to the Uncreated Being. It has a virtual primacy in regard to the intelligible elements included in the first intelligibles, that is, in regard to the qualifying concepts of the ultimate differences and proper attributes.

My supposition that "being" is predicated commonly *in quid* of all the aforementioned quidditative concepts is established by the two arguments used in the initial question to prove that being is predicated commonly of created and uncreated being. That what I have supposed may be evident, I now explain these reasons a little.

I explain the first reason thus. Of each of the aforementioned concepts, the intellect can be certain that it is a being and still be in doubt about the differences which delimit "being" to the concept in question. And so the concept of being, in so far as it agrees with the concept in question, is other than the dubious concepts which come under it. But it is other in such a way that it is included in both of the concepts which come under it, for these limiting differences presuppose the same concept of being which they limit.

The second reason I explain as follows: We argued that God cannot be known naturally unless being is univocal to the created and uncreated. We can argue in the same way of substance and accident, for substance does not immediately move our intellect to know the substance itself, but only the sensible accident does so. From this it follows that we can have no quidditative concept of substance except such as could be abstracted from the concept of an accident. But the only quidditative concept of this kind that can be abstracted from that of an accident is the concept of being.

Our assumption that substance does not immediately move our intellect to know the substance itself, we prove thus: If something moves the intellect when it is present, then whenever the intellect is not so moved, it will be able to know naturally that this object is absent. This is clear from the *De anima*, BK. II, according to which the sense of sight can perceive darkness when, presumably, light is not present, and the sense, in consequence, is not moved. Therefore, if substance immediately moved the intellect naturally to know the substance itself, it would follow that when a substance was absent, the intellect could know that it was not present. Hence, it could know naturally that the substance of bread does not exist in the Consecrated Victim of the Altar, which is clearly false. Naturally, then, we have no quidditative concept of substance caused immediately by substance itself. Our only quidditative concept thereof is that caused by, or first abstracted from, an accident, and this is none other than the concept of being.

By the same token, our conclusion holds for the essential parts of substance. For if neither matter nor form move the intellect to an act of knowledge about themselves, I ask "What simple concept shall we have of matter or form?" If you say that it is some relative concept, for instance, of some part, or that it is an incidental concept, for instance, of some property of matter or form, then I ask "What is the quidditative concept to which this incidental or relative concept is attributed?" And if there is no quidditative concept, there will be nothing to which this incidental concept may be attributed. But the only quidditative concept possible is caused by, or abstracted from, that which does move the intellect, viz. an accident. And this will be the concept

of being. Consequently, nothing is known of the essential parts of substance unless "being" is univocal, common to them and to the accidents.

These reasons do not imply that "being" is predicated *in quid* of the ultimate differences and attributes.

The first does not, for the intellect [according to the argument] is certain that some such thing is a being while it doubts whether it is this being or that. The intellect, however, is certain that it [viz. an ultimate difference or attribute] is not being quidditatively, but it is as it were "being" by way of accidental predication.

Or another and better way. Every such concept is irreducibly simple and therefore one part of it cannot be conceived while another part remains unknown, as is evident from the statement of the Philosopher (in *Metaphysics*, BK. IX, near the end) that there is no deception regarding irreducibly simple concepts as there is regarding the quiddity of what is complex. This is not to be understood as though the simple intellect is formally deceived regarding the knowledge of quiddities, for in simple intellection there is neither truth nor falsity. In regard to a quiddity that is composed, however, the simple intellect can be virtually deceived. For if such a notion is false in itself, then it includes virtually a false proposition. But what is irreducibly simple includes a false proposition neither virtually nor formally, and therefore there is no deception in its regard. Either it is grasped totally or not at all, in which case it remains completely unknown. Of no irreducibly simple concept, therefore, can we be certain of one part and doubtful about another.

From this, it is clear also as far as the second reason stated above is concerned, that what is so irreducibly simple remains completely unknown unless it is grasped fully as it is in itself.

A third reply is possible regarding the first reason. This concept of which we are certain is other than those of which we are in doubt. Now if this same element of which we are certain is preserved with both of the doubtful concepts, it is truly univocal in the sense that it is grasped with both of them. It is not necessary, however, that it be contained in both of them *in quid*, but it may either be contained *in quid* or be univocal to them as determinable is univocal to determinant, or as what can be denominated to what denominates. To put it briefly, then, "being" is univocal for all. But for concepts that are not irreducibly simple, it is predicated of them univocally *in quid*; for concepts irreducibly simple, it is univocal as something determinable or denominable, but it is not univocal in the sense that it is predicated of them *in quid*, for that would be a contradiction.

And so it is clear how in "being" there concurs a twofold primacy, namely, a primacy of commonness *in quid* in regard to all concepts that are not irreducibly simple and a primacy of virtuality in itself or in its inferiors regarding all concepts which are irreducibly simple.

[4. On the Deduction of the Attributes of "Being"] I say that this disjunction "necessary-or-possible", like the countless other such found among beings, is an attribute of "being" that is equivalent to a coextensive attribute. But the coextensive attributes, as something more common, are affirmed immediately of "being", because "being" is an irreducibly simple concept and consequently no middle term can exist between "being" and its attribute, for neither has a definition that might serve as a middle term. Also, if there is some attribute of "being" that is not immediate, it is difficult to see what prior attribute could be used as a middle term to link it with "being", for it is not easy to discern any order among the attributes of "being". And even if we knew of such an order among them, any propositions about them we might use as premises seem scarcely more evident than the conclusions. In the disjunctive attributes, however, while the entire disjunction cannot be demonstrated from "being", nevertheless as a universal rule by positing the less perfect extreme of some being we can conclude that the more perfect extreme is realised in some other being. Thus it follows that if some being is finite, then some being is infinite. And if some being is contingent, then some being is necessary. For in such cases it is not possible for the more imperfect extreme of the disjunction to be existentially predicated of "being", particularly taken, unless the more perfect extreme be existentially verified of some other being upon which it depends.

But we see that the less perfect member of such a disjunction cannot be established in this fashion, for if the more perfect exists in some being, there is no necessity on this score that the less perfect should exist in some other being, unless, of course, the two extremes of the disjunction should happen to be correlatives, such as "cause" and "caused". Consequently, this disjunction "necessary-or-contingent", cannot be established of "being" through some prior medium. Neither could the contingent part of the disjunction be established of anything on the supposition that something necessary exists. The proposition: "Some being is contingent", therefore, seems to be a primary truth and is not demonstrable by an *a priori* demonstration, which gives the reason for the fact. That is why the Philosopher, in arguing against the theory that future events are necessary, makes no attempt to deduce from it something even more impossible than the hypothesis, but he deduces from it an impossibility that is more apparent to us, namely, that there would be no need to deliberate [about the future]. And therefore, those who deny such manifest things need punishment or knowledge or sense, for as Avicenna puts it (*Metaphysics* i): "Those who deny a first principle should be beaten or exposed to fire until they concede that to burn and not to burn, or to be beaten and not to be beaten, are not identical". And so too, those who deny that some being is contingent should be exposed to torments until they concede that it is possible for them not to be tormented.

[5. Being as the Subject and God as the Goal of Metaphysics] We must first see whether metaphysics, the first and highest of the naturally acquired habits perfecting man's intellect in the present life, has God as its first object.

On this point there is a controversy between Avicenna and Averroes. Avicenna claims that God is not the subject of metaphysics, because no science proves [the existence of] its own subject. The metaphysician, however, proves that God exists. Averroes reproves Avicenna in his final comment on the *Physics*, BK. I, because he wishes, by using the same major premise against Avicenna, to prove that God and the pure spirits are the subject of metaphysics, and that God's existence is not proved in metaphysics, since it is only by means of motion, which pertains to the science of natural philosophy, that any kind of pure spirit can be proved to exist.

It seems to me, however, that of the two, Avicenna has spoken better. Wherefore I argue against Averroes as follows. The proposition they both hold, viz. "No science proves the existence of its subject" is true, because of the priority the subject holds in regard to the science. For if the subject were posterior to the science, then its existence would have to be established in some lower science, where it would be conceived under some inferior aspect which is inadequate for its role as the object [of the higher science]. Now a subject enjoys a greater priority over the lower than over the higher science. If the highest science, therefore, cannot prove that its subject exists, it is even less possible for a lower science to do so.

Or to put the argument in another way, if the philosopher of nature can prove that God exists, then God's existence is a conclusion of natural philosophy. Now if metaphysics cannot prove the existence of God in this way, then God's existence is presupposed as a principle in metaphysics. Consequently, a conclusion of natural philosophy is a principle of metaphysics, and therefore the philosophy of nature is prior to metaphysics.

Again, if a certain property can exist only in virtue of such and such a cause, from every such property that appears in the effect, we can infer the existence of the cause. Now it is not just such properties of the effect as are treated in the philosophy of nature that are possible only on condition that God exists, for the same is true of the properties treated of in metaphysics. Not only does motion presuppose a mover, but a being that is posterior presupposes one that is prior. Consequently, from the priority that exists among beings the existence of the First Being can be inferred, and this can be done in a more perfect way than the existence of a Prime Mover can be established in natural philosophy. We can infer, then, in metaphysics from act and potency, finiteness and infinity, multitude and unity, and many other such metaphysical properties, that God or the First Being exists.

So far as this article is concerned, then, I say that God is not the subject of metaphysics,

because, as has been proved above in the first question, there is but one science that has God as its first subject, and this is not metaphysics. And this is proved in the following manner. Of every subject, also of a subordinate science, it is known through the senses that it is of such a nature that to exist is not repugnant to it, as is evident of the subject of optics, for the existence of a visible line is grasped immediately from the senses. Just as principles are grasped immediately once the terms are apprehended through the medium of the senses, so likewise if a subject, is not to be posterior to, or less known than, its principle, it must needs be grasped through the senses. But no proper notion that we can form of God is apprehended immediately by man's intellect in this life. Therefore, we can have no naturally acquired science about God under some notion proper to Himself. Proof of the minor: The first [proper] concept we have of God is that He is the First Being. But this notion is not grasped through the senses, but we must first ascertain that the union of these two terms is compatible. Before we can know this compatibility, however, it is necessary that we demonstrate that some being is first. Therefore, etc.

Hence, I concede with Avicenna that God is not the subject of metaphysics. The Philosopher's statement (*Metaphysics*, BK. I) that metaphysics is concerned with the highest causes, presents no difficulty. For he speaks here as he did in the *Prior Analytics*, BK. I, where he says: "First it is necessary to determine with what [Prior Analytics] is concerned and what it has to do. It is concerned with demonstration and has to do with the demonstrative branch of learning, that is with the general science of demonstrating or syllogising". Hence, "concerned with" denotes properly the circumstance of the final cause just as much as it does that of the material cause. Wherefore, metaphysics is concerned with the highest causes as its end. In knowing them, metaphysical science attains its goal.

12

René Descartes, *Principles of Philosophy*, Part One, and selected correspondence with Princess Elisabeth of Bohemia

Introduction

The line between epistemology and metaphysics, hardly a sharp or undisputed one, was something that earlier thinkers were less prone to harp upon than contemporary philosophers. Descartes (1596–1650), generally regarded as the initiator of "modern philosophy," is often congratulated – or condemned – for putting epistemological concerns at the forefront of philosophy, above all by his systematic subjection of our usual beliefs to "methodological doubt." But, for Descartes, investigation of human knowledge and its limits quickly generates metaphysical results. The most prominent example in his writings is his "dualism" – the conclusion that mind and body are different substances, drawn from the premise that what can be clearly and distinctly conceived as existing separately can in reality exist separately. To take another example, Descartes thinks that the exist-

From Descartes: Selected Philosophical Writings, trans. J. Cottingham, R. Stoothoff, and D. Murdoch. Cambridge: Cambridge University Press, 1988, pp. 160–6, 169–70, 172–85, 188 (some passages and notes omitted; asterisked notes are the translators'). *Also from* Princess Elisabeth, "Selections from Her Correspondence with Descartes," in M. Atherton, ed., *Women Philosophers of the Early Modern Period*, Indianapolis, IN: Hackett Publishing Co., 1994, pp. 11–21.

ence of God can be inferred from the fact that we possess a certain concept, the concept of a perfect being. In *Principles of Philosophy* (1644), a late and synoptic work, as in other writings, we find, therefore, a shuttling back and forth between what today's philosophers would think of as epistemological and metaphysical concerns.

Part One of the *Principia philosophiae* provides a virtual overview of most of Descartes's distinctive and influential claims. Our selection retains the somewhat *al presto* rehearsal (Articles 1–7) of his methodological doubt and the famous claim that doubt cannot extend to the existence of the "thinking thing" which is doing the doubting: "I think, therefore I am" or "I am thinking, therefore I exist." Those Articles are followed by ones in which Descartes not only tries to establish God's existence, but where he also tries to show that if and only if God exists can we legitimately regain confidence in what was earlier subjected to doubt – at any rate, in those matters that are open to "clear and distinct perception."

It is important to note that while Descartes thinks we can know that God exists, he insists that our knowledge of God is very limited. This insistence has two significant implications for Descartes's overall metaphysics. First, it enables him to sidestep a problem about free will.[1] We may not understand how our free will is compatible with divine preordination, but given the opacity of God's powers, it would be "absurd" to let that puzzle weaken our confidence in our freedom (Art. 41). Second, "we shall entirely banish . . . the search for final causes" (Art. 28) – the attempt, that is, to explain events in terms of teleological ends or purposes. Instead inquirers should focus solely on the antecedent, "efficient" causes of things. (This eschewal of final causes by Descartes, Bacon, and other figures of the time is usually regarded as integral to "modern" thinking.)

The latter half of Part One of the *Principles* consists, primarily, in Descartes's attempts to specify what is "clearly and distinctly" given to perception or thought, and in effect to delineate the broad structure of reality. As for Aristotle (III.4), pride of place in that structure is given to substance. Substance is what "depend[s] on no other thing for its existence" (Art. 51) – which means that, as Aristotle again hinted, the only substance strictly speaking is God.[2] Speaking slightly more loosely, however, one can postulate that there are just two further substances – mind (*res cogitans*) and matter (*res extensa*), whose "essences" or "natures" are "thought" and "extension," respectively. Speaking still more loosely, one may talk of the many substances – the individual minds and physical objects – which "pertain to" mind or matter. Since Descartes establishes what is and is not to count as substance solely on the basis of concepts of them, one might say that Descartes transmutes Aristotle's definition of a "primary substance" as something that *exists independently* into something that can be *conceived to exist independently*.

Many have bridled at Cartesian dualism, and even today philosophers working in the philosophy of mind continue to struggle with its legacy, perhaps most notably in what has recently been referred to as "the hard problem" of consciousness.[3] Among Descartes's earliest critics was his correspondent, Princess Elisabeth of Bohemia (1618–80). Female philosophers of the early modern period rarely published treatises, and so their philosophical achievements must be found elsewhere, often in epistolary texts. Elisabeth, for example, corresponded with Descartes and with Leibniz; some of the work from Elisabeth's 1645 letters to Descartes even found its way into his *Passions of the Soul* (1649). Elisabeth is among the first to point out, in a set of letters we present here, what has become recognized as perhaps the most devastating shortcoming of Cartesian dualism, the "interaction problem" – the problem of how mind and body, if two different substances with different essential properties, can possibly

cause effects to occur in one another. Descartes's letter of June 28, 1643, to Elisabeth suggests that the "union" or connection between the two is somehow "primitive" or basic, that it can be directly apprehended but not explained by anything more fundamental. While Spinoza addresses this problem by denying that mind and body are separate substances (III.13), Leibniz maintains that God has created mind and body with a "preestablished harmony" between the independent acts of one another (III.15). Within the Cartesian tradition, "occasionalists" like Nicolas Malebranche (1638–1715) argue that while mind and body do not themselves interact, God intercedes to cause the proper effects in each of them, creating the appearance of interaction.

On the question of "Forms" or "universals" (properties, roughly), which so vexed the ancients and the medievals, Descartes rejects the "realist" view that these exist independently of thought and the particular things that have properties. They arise, he says, solely from the "use" toward which thinking things put their "ideas" (Art. 59).

In Articles 69–70 one may note a brief, but seminal, articulation of a view that not only indicates Descartes's debt to the emerging, Galilean science of his day, but was also to influence John Locke (III.14) and later advocates of science as the provider of an "absolute" account of the world.[4] In effect, Descartes is making the distinction between "primary" and "secondary" qualities, though he does not use those expressions, and insisting that only the former – shape, motion, and the like – belong genuinely "in the objects" themselves. In the case of color, smell, and so on, there is nothing in the objects resembling that "of which we have sensory awareness."

In Part One of the Principles, then, one encounters, in staccato form, not only an account of the powers and limits of human knowledge, and of the reasons people tend to overstep those limits, but also a delineation of Descartes's world: a world created and governed by a perfect God who has laid down causal laws for its operation, and a world consisting of two interacting substances – mind, whose nature is to be explored by rational introspection, and body, whose nature is to be revealed by geometry and the sciences. One is offered, in effect, the epistemology and metaphysics that have set the agenda for modern philosophy and with which in the rest of this volume most of the authors represented are visibly grappling.

Notes

1 It is hard to exaggerate the importance Descartes attaches to our free will, especially to our freedom to withhold belief. It is here, as much as anywhere perhaps, that his "modernity" resides. See Hans Blumenberg, *The Legitimacy of the Modern Age*, Boston, MA: MIT Press, 1985, Part 2.

2 Not making this clear serves, among other things, Benedict de Spinoza's (III.13) criticism of Descartes in his *Principles of Descartes's Philosophy* (1663).

3 D. J. Chalmers, *The Conscious Mind*, Oxford: Oxford University Press, 1997.

4 On Descartes and the "absolute," scientific picture of the world, see B. Williams, *Descartes*, Harmondsworth: Penguin, 1978.

Descartes, *Principles of Philosophy*

Part One

The principles of human knowledge

1. *The seeker after truth must, once in the course of his life, doubt everything, as far as is possible.*

Since we began life as infants, and made various judgements concerning the things that can be perceived by the senses before we had the full use of our reason, there are many preconceived opinions that keep us from knowledge of the truth. It seems that the only way of freeing ourselves from these opinions is to make the effort, once in the course of our life, to doubt everything which we find to contain even the smallest suspicion of uncertainty.

2. *What is doubtful should even be considered as false.*

Indeed, it will even prove useful, once we have doubted these things, to consider them as false, so that our discovery of what is most certain and easy to know may be all the clearer.

3. *This doubt should not meanwhile be applied to ordinary life.*

This doubt, while it continues, should be kept in check and employed solely in connection with the contemplation of the truth. As far as ordinary life is concerned, the chance for action would frequently pass us by if we waited until we could free ourselves from our doubts, and so we are often compelled to accept what is merely probable. From time to time we may even have to make a choice between two alternatives, even though it is not apparent that one of the two is more probable than the other.

4. *The reasons for doubt concerning the things that can be perceived by the senses.*

Given, then, that our efforts are directed solely to the search for truth, our initial doubts will be about the existence of the objects of sense-perception and imagination. The first reason for such doubts is that from time to time we have caught out the senses when they were in error, and it is prudent never to place too much trust in those who have deceived us even once. The second reason is that in our sleep we regularly seem to have sensory perception of, or to imagine, countless things which do not exist anywhere; and if our doubts are on the scale just outlined, there seem to be no marks by means of which we can with certainty distinguish being asleep from being awake.

5. *The reasons for doubting even mathematical demonstrations.*

Our doubt will also apply to other matters which we previously regarded as most certain – even the demonstrations of mathematics and even the principles which we hitherto considered to be self-evident. One reason for this is that we have sometimes seen people make mistakes in such matters and accept as most certain and self-evident things which seemed false to us. Secondly, and most importantly, we have been told that there is an omnipotent God who created us. Now we do not know whether he may have wished to make us beings of the sort who are always deceived even in those matters which seem to us supremely evident; for such constant deception seems no less a possibility than the occasional deception which, as we have noticed on previous occasions, does occur. We may of course suppose that our existence derives not from a supremely powerful God but either from ourselves or from some other source; but in that case, the less powerful we make the author of our coming into being, the

6

more likely it will be that we are so imperfect as to be deceived all the time.

6. *We have free will, enabling us to withhold our assent in doubtful matters and hence avoid error.*
But whoever turns out to have created us, and however powerful and however deceitful he may be, in the meantime we nonetheless experience within us the kind of freedom which enables us always to refrain from believing things which are not completely certain and thoroughly examined. Hence we are able to take precautions against going wrong on any occasion.

7. *It is not possible for us to doubt that we exist while we are doubting; and this is the first thing we come to know when we philosophize in an orderly way.*

7 In rejecting – and even imagining to be false – everything which we can in any way doubt, it is easy for us to suppose that there is no God and no heaven, and that there are no bodies, and even that we ourselves have no hands or feet, or indeed any body at all. But we cannot for all that suppose that we, who are having such thoughts, are nothing. For it is a contradiction to suppose that what thinks does not, at the very time when it is thinking, exist. Accordingly, this piece of knowledge – *I am thinking, therefore I exist* – is the first and most certain of all to occur to anyone who philosophizes in an orderly way.

8. *In this way we discover the distinction between soul and body, or between a thinking thing and a corporeal thing.*
This is the best way to discover the nature of the mind and the distinction between the mind and the body. For if we, who are supposing that everything which is distinct from us is false, examine what we are, we see very clearly that neither extension nor shape nor local motion, nor anything of this kind which is attributable to a body, belongs to our nature, but that thought alone belongs to it. So our knowledge of our thought is prior to, and more certain than, our knowledge of any corporeal thing; for we have already perceived it, although we are still in doubt about other things.

9. *What is meant by 'thought'.*
By the term 'thought', I understand everything which we are aware of as happening within us,

in so far as we have awareness of it. Hence, *thinking* is to be identified here not merely with understanding, willing and imagining, but also with sensory awareness. For if I say 'I am seeing, or I am walking, therefore I exist', and take this as applying to vision or walking as bodily activities, then the conclusion is not absolutely certain. This is because, as often happens during sleep, it is possible for me to think I am seeing or walking, though my eyes are closed and I am not moving about; such thoughts might even be possible if I had no body at all. But if I take 'seeing' or 'walking' to apply to the actual sense or awareness of seeing or walking, then the conclusion is quite certain, since it relates to the mind, which 8 alone has the sensation or thought that it is seeing or walking.

10. *Matters which are very simple and self-evident are only rendered more obscure by logical definitions, and should not be counted as items of knowledge which it takes effort to acquire.*
I shall not here explain many of the other terms which I have already used or will use in what follows, because they seem to me to be sufficiently self-evident. I have often noticed that philosophers make the mistake of employing logical definitions in an attempt to explain what was already very simple and self-evident; the result is that they only make matters more obscure. And when I said that the proposition *I am thinking, therefore I exist* is the first and most certain of all to occur to anyone who philosophizes in an orderly way, I did not in saying that deny that one must first know what thought, existence and certainty are, and that it is impossible that that which thinks should not exist, and so forth. But because these are very simple notions, and ones which on their own provide us with no knowledge of anything that exists, I did not think they needed to be listed.

11. *How our mind is better known than our body.*
In order to realize that the knowledge of our mind is not simply prior to and more certain than the knowledge of our body, but also more evident, we should notice something very well known by the natural light: nothingness possesses no attributes or qualities. It follows that, wherever we find some attributes or qualities, there is necessarily some thing or substance to be found for them to belong to; and the more

attributes we discover in the same thing or substance, the clearer is our knowledge of that substance. Now we find more attributes in our mind than in anything else, as is manifest from the fact that whatever enables us to know anything else cannot but lead us to a much surer knowledge of our own mind. For example, if I judge that the earth exists from the fact that I touch it or see it, 9 this very fact undoubtedly gives even greater support for the judgement that my mind exists. For it may perhaps be the case that I judge that I am touching the earth even though the earth does not exist at all; but it cannot be that, when I make this judgement, my mind which is making the judgement does not exist. And the same applies in other cases <regarding all the things that come into our mind, namely that we who think of them exist, even if they are false or have no existence>.

12. *Why this fact does not come to be known to all alike.*
Disagreement on this point has come from those who have not done their philosophizing in an orderly way; and the reason for it is simply that they have never taken sufficient care to distinguish the mind from the body. Although they may have put the certainty of their own existence before that of anything else, they failed to realize that they should have taken 'themselves' in this context to mean their minds alone. They were inclined instead to take 'themselves' to mean only their bodies – the bodies which they saw with their eyes and touched with their hands, and to which they incorrectly attributed the power of sense-perception; and this is what prevented them from perceiving the nature of the mind.

13. *The sense in which knowledge of all other things depends on the knowledge of God.*
The mind, then, knowing itself, but still in doubt about all other things, looks around in all directions in order to extend its knowledge further. First of all, it finds within itself ideas of many things; and so long as it merely contemplates these ideas and does not affirm or deny the existence outside itself of anything resembling them, it cannot be mistaken. Next, it finds certain common notions from which it constructs various proofs; and, for as long as it attends to them, it is completely convinced of their truth. For example, the mind has within itself ideas of numbers and shapes, and

it also has such common notions as: *If you add equals to equals the results will be equal;* from these it is easy to demonstrate that the three angles of a triangle equal two right angles, and so on. And so the mind will be convinced of the truth of this and similar conclusions, so long as it attends to the premises from which it deduced them. But it cannot attend to them all the time; and subsequently,* recalling that it is still ignorant as to whether it may have been created with the kind of nature that makes it go wrong even in matters which appear most evident, the mind 10 sees that it has just cause to doubt such conclusions, and that the possession of certain knowledge will not be possible until it has come to know the author of its being.

14. *The existence of God is validly inferred from the fact that necessary existence is included in our concept of God.*
The mind next considers the various ideas which it has within itself, and finds that there is one idea – the idea of a supremely intelligent, supremely powerful and supremely perfect being – which stands out from all the others. <And it readily judges from what it perceives in this idea, that God, who is the supremely perfect being, is, or exists. For although it has distinct ideas of many other things it does not observe anything in them to guarantee the existence of their object.> In this one idea the mind recognizes existence – not merely the possible and contingent existence which belongs to the ideas of all the other things which it distinctly perceives, but utterly necessary and eternal existence. Now on the basis of its perception that, for example, it is necessarily contained in the idea of a triangle that its three angles should equal two right angles, the mind is quite convinced that a triangle does have three angles equalling two right angles. In the same way, simply on the basis of its perception that necessary and eternal existence is contained in the idea of a supremely perfect being, the mind must clearly conclude that the supreme being does exist.[1]

15. *Our concepts of other things do not similarly contain necessary existence, but merely contingent existence.*

* '. . . when it happens that it remembers a conclusion without attending to the sequence which enables it to be demonstrated' (added in French version).

The mind will be even more inclined to accept this if it considers that it cannot find within itself an idea of any other thing such that necessary existence is seen to be contained in the idea in this way. And from this it understands that the idea of a supremely perfect being is not an idea which was invented by the mind, or which represents some chimera, but that it represents a true and immutable nature which cannot but exist, since necessary existence is contained within it.

16. *Preconceived opinions prevent the necessity of the existence of God from being clearly recognized by everyone.*

Our mind will, as I say, easily accept this, provided that it has first of all completely freed itself from preconceived opinions. But we have got into the habit of distinguishing essence from existence in the case of all other things; and we are also in the habit of making up at will various 11 ideas of things which do not exist anywhere and have never done so. Hence, at times when we are not intent on the contemplation of the supremely perfect being, a doubt may easily arise as to whether the idea of God is not one of those which we made up at will, or at least one of those which do not include existence in their essence.

17. *The greater the objective perfection in any of our ideas, the greater its cause must be.*

When we reflect further on the ideas that we have within us, we see that some of them, in so far as they are merely modes of thinking, do not differ much one from another; but in so far as one idea represents one thing and another represents another, they differ widely; and the greater the amount of objective* perfection they contain within themselves, the more perfect their cause must be. For example, if someone has within himself the idea of a highly intricate machine, it would be fair to ask what was the cause of his possession of the idea: did he somewhere see such a machine made by someone else; or did he make such a close study of mechanics, or is his own ingenuity so great, that he was able to think it up on his own, although he never saw it anywhere? All the intricacy which is contained in the idea merely objectively – as in a picture – must be contained in its cause, whatever kind of cause it turns out to be; and it must be contained not merely objectively or representatively, but in actual reality, either formally or eminently,† at least in the case of the first and principal cause.

18. *This gives us a second reason for concluding that God exists.*

Since, then, we have within us the idea of God, or a supreme being, we may rightly inquire into the cause of our possession of this idea. Now we find in the idea such immeasurable greatness that we are quite certain that it could have been placed in us only by something which truly possesses the sum of all perfections, that, by a God who really exists. For it is very evident by the natural light not only that nothing comes from nothing but also that what is more perfect cannot be produced by – that is, cannot have as its 12 efficient and total cause – what is less perfect. Furthermore, we cannot have within us the idea or image of anything without there being somewhere, either within us or outside us, an original which contains in reality all the perfections belonging to the idea. And since the supreme perfections of which we have an idea are in no way to be found in us, we rightly conclude that they reside in something distinct from ourselves, namely God – or certainly that they once did so, from which it most evidently follows that they are still there.

[. . .]

28. *It is not the final but the efficient causes of created things that we must inquire into.*

When dealing with natural things we will, then, never derive any explanations from the purposes which God or nature may have had in view when creating them <and we shall entirely banish from our philosophy the search for final causes>. For we should not be so arrogant as to suppose that we can share in God's plans. We 16 should, instead, consider him as the efficient cause of all things; and starting from the divine attributes which by God's will we have some knowledge of, we shall see, with the aid of our

---

* If an idea represents some object which is F, the idea is said to possess 'objective' F-ness, or to contain F-ness 'objectively'.

† To possess a property *formally* is to possess it strictly as defined; to possess it *eminently* is to possess it in some higher or more perfect form.

God-given natural light, what conclusions should be drawn concerning those effects which are apparent to our senses.* At the same time we should remember, as noted earlier, that the natural light is to be trusted only to the extent that it is compatible with divine revelation.

29. *God is not the cause of our errors.*

The first attribute of God that comes under consideration here is that he is supremely truthful and the giver of all light. So it is a complete contradiction to suppose that he might deceive us or be, in the strict and positive sense, the cause of the errors to which we know by experience that we are prone. For although the ability to deceive may perhaps be regarded among us men as a sign of intelligence, the will to deceive must undoubtedly always come from malice, or from fear and weakness, and so cannot belong to God.

30. *It follows that everything that we clearly perceive is true; and this removes the doubts mentioned earlier.*

It follows from this that the light of nature or faculty of knowledge which God gave us can never encompass any object which is not true in so far as it is indeed encompassed by this faculty, that is, in so far as it is clearly and distinctly perceived. For God would deserve to be called a deceiver if the faculty which he gave us was so distorted that it mistook the false for the true <even when we were using it properly>. This disposes of the most serious doubt, which arose from our ignorance about whether our nature might not be such as to make us go wrong even in matters which seemed to us utterly evident. Indeed, this argument easily demolishes all the other reasons for doubt which were mentioned earlier. Mathematical truths should no longer be suspect, since they are utterly clear to us. And as for our senses, if we notice anything here that is clear and distinct, no matter whether we are awake or asleep, then provided we separate it from what is confused and obscure we will easily recognize – whatever the thing in question – which are the aspects that may be regarded as true.

17

* '... and we shall be assured that what we have once clearly and distinctly perceived to belong to the nature of these things has the perfection of being true' (added in French version, which also omits the last sentence of this article).

[...]

39. *The freedom of the will is self-evident.*

That there is freedom in our will, and that we have power in many cases to give or withhold our assent at will, is so evident that it must be counted among the first and most common notions that are innate in us. This was obvious earlier on when, in our attempt to doubt everything, we went so far as to make the supposition of some supremely powerful author of our being who was attempting to deceive us in every possible way. For in spite of that supposition, the freedom which we experienced within us was nonetheless so great as to enable us to abstain from believing whatever was not quite certain or fully examined. And what we saw to be beyond doubt even during the period of that supposition is as self-evident and as transparently clear as anything can be.

20

40. *It is also certain that everything was preordained by God.*

But now that we have come to know God, we perceive in him a power so immeasurable that we regard it as impious to suppose that we could ever do anything which was not already preordained by him. And we can easily get ourselves into great difficulties if we attempt to reconcile this divine preordination with the freedom of our will, or attempt to grasp both these things at once.

41. *How to reconcile the freedom of our will with divine preordination.*

But we shall get out of these difficulties if we remember that our mind is finite, while the power of God is infinite – the power by which he not only knew from eternity whatever is or can be, but also willed it and preordained it. We may attain sufficient knowledge of this power to perceive clearly and distinctly that God possesses it; but we cannot get a sufficient grasp of it to see how it leaves the free actions of men undetermined. Nonetheless, we have such close awareness of the freedom and indifference which is in us, that there is nothing we can grasp more evidently or more perfectly. And it would be absurd, simply because we do not grasp one thing, which we know must by its very nature be beyond our comprehension, to doubt something else of which we have an intimate grasp and which we experience within ourselves.

42. *Although we do not want to go wrong, nevertheless we go wrong by our own will.*

Now that we know that all our errors depend on the will, it may seem surprising that we should ever go wrong, since there is no one who wants to go wrong. But there is a great difference between choosing to go wrong and choosing to give one's assent in matters where, as it happens, error is to be found. And although there is in fact no one who expressly wishes to go wrong, there is scarcely anyone who does not often wish to give his assent to something which, though he does not know it, contains some error. Indeed, precisely because of their eagerness to find the truth, people who do not know the right method of finding it often pass judgement on things of which they lack perception, and this is why they fall into error.

43. *We never go wrong when we assent only to what we clearly and distinctly perceive.*

It is certain, however, that we will never mistake the false for the true provided we give our assent only to what we clearly and distinctly perceive. I say that this is certain, because God is not a deceiver, and so the faculty of perception which he has given us cannot incline to falsehood; and the same goes for the faculty of assent, provided its scope is limited to what is clearly perceived. And even if there were no way of proving this, the minds of all of us have been so moulded by nature that whenever we perceive something clearly, we spontaneously give our assent to it and are quite unable to doubt its truth.

[...]

45. *What is meant by a clear perception, and by a distinct perception.*

Indeed there are very many people who in their entire lives never perceive anything with sufficient accuracy to enable them to make a judgement about it with certainty. A perception which can serve as the basis for a certain and indubitable judgement needs to be not merely clear but also distinct. I call a perception 'clear' when it is present and accessible to the attentive mind – just as we say that we see something clearly when it is present to the eye's gaze and stimulates it with a sufficient degree of strength and accessibility. I call a perception 'distinct' if, as well as being clear, it is so sharply separated from all other

perceptions that it contains within itself only what is clear.

46. *The example of pain shows that a perception can be clear without being distinct, but cannot be distinct without being clear.*

For example, when someone feels an intense pain, the perception he has of it is indeed very clear, but is not always distinct. For people commonly confuse this perception with an obscure judgement they make concerning the nature of something which they think exists in the painful spot and which they suppose to resemble the sensation of pain; but in fact it is the sensation alone which they perceive clearly. Hence a perception can be clear without being distinct, but not distinct without being clear.

47. *In order to correct the preconceived opinions of our early childhood we must consider the simple notions and what elements in each of them are clear.*

In our childhood the mind was so immersed in the body that although there was much that it perceived clearly, it never perceived anything distinctly. But in spite of this the mind made judgements about many things, and this is the origin of the many preconceived opinions which most of us never subsequently abandon. To enable us to get rid of these preconceived opinions, I shall here briefly list all the simple notions which are the basic components of our thoughts; and in each case I shall distinguish the clear elements from those which are obscure or liable to lead us into error.

48. *All the objects of our perception may be regarded either as things or affections of things, or as eternal truths. The former are listed here.*

All the objects of our perception we regard either as things, or affections of things, or else as eternal truths which have no existence outside our thought. The most general items which we regard as things are *substance, duration, order, number* and any other items of this kind which extend to all classes of things. But I recognize only two ultimate classes of things: first, intellectual or thinking things, i.e. those which pertain to mind or thinking substance; and secondly, material things, i.e. those which pertain to extended substance or body. Perception, volition and all the modes both of perceiving and of willing are referred to thinking substance; while to extended substance belong size (that is, extension in length, breadth and depth), shape, motion, position, divisibility of component parts and the like. But we also experience within ourselves certain other things which must not be referred either to the mind alone or to the body alone. These arise . . . from the close and intimate union of our mind with the body. This list includes, first, appetites like hunger and thirst; secondly, the emotions or passions of the mind which do not consist of thought alone, such as the emotions of anger, joy, sadness and love; and finally, all the sensations, such as those of pain, pleasure, light, colours, sounds, smells, tastes, heat, hardness and the other tactile qualities.

49.   *It is not possible – or indeed necessary – to give a similar list of eternal truths.*

Everything in the preceding list we regard either as a thing or as a quality or mode of a thing. But when we recognize that it is impossible for anything to come from nothing, the proposition *Nothing comes from nothing* is regarded not as a really existing thing, or even as a mode of a thing, but as an eternal truth which resides within our mind. Such truths are termed common notions 24 or axioms. The following are examples of this class: *It is impossible for the same thing to be and not to be at the same time; What is done cannot be undone; He who thinks cannot but exist while he thinks*; and countless others. It would not be easy to draw up a list of all of them; but nonetheless we cannot fail to know them when the occasion for thinking about them arises, provided that we are not blinded by preconceived opinions.

[. . .]

51.   *What is meant by 'substance' – a term which does not apply univocally to God and his creatures.*

In the case of those items which we regard as things or modes of things, it is worthwhile examining each of them separately. By *substance* we can understand nothing other than a thing which exists in such a way as to depend on no other thing for its existence. And there is only one substance which can be understood to depend on no other thing whatsoever, namely God. In the case of all other substances, we perceive that they can exist

only with the help of God's concurrence. Hence the term 'substance' does not apply *univocally*, as they say in the Schools, to God and to other things; that is, there is no distinctly intelligible meaning of the term which is common to God and his creatures. <In the case of created things, some are of such a nature that they cannot exist without other things, while some need only the ordinary concurrence of God in order to exist. We make this distinction by calling the latter 'substances' and the former 'qualities' or 'attributes' of those substances.>

52.   *The term 'substance' applies univocally to mind and to body. How a substance itself is known.*

But as for corporeal substance and mind (or 25 created thinking substance), these can be understood to fall under this common concept: things that need only the concurrence of God in order to exist. However, we cannot initially become aware of a substance merely through its being an existing thing, since this alone does not of itself have any effect on us. We can, however, easily come to know a substance by one of its attributes, in virtue of the common notion that nothingness possesses no attributes, that is to say, no properties or qualities. Thus, if we perceive the presence of some attribute, we can infer that there must also be present an existing thing or substance to which it may be attributed.

53.   *To each substance there belongs one principal attribute; in the case of mind, this is thought, and in the case of body it is extension.*

A substance may indeed be known through any attribute at all; but each substance has one principal property which constitutes its nature and essence, and to which all its other properties are referred. Thus extension in length, breadth and depth constitutes the nature of corporeal substance; and thought constitutes the nature of thinking substance. Everything else which can be attributed to body presupposes extension, and is merely a mode of an extended thing; and similarly, whatever we find in the mind is simply one of the various modes of thinking. For example, shape is unintelligible except in an extended thing; and motion is unintelligible except as motion in an extended space; while imagination, sensation and will are intelligible only in a thinking thing. By contrast, it is possible to understand extension without shape or movement, and thought without imagination or sensation, and so on; and this is quite clear to anyone who gives the matter his attention.

54. *How we can have clear and distinct notions of thinking substance and of corporeal substance, and also of God.*

Thus we can easily have two clear and distinct notions or ideas, one of created thinking substance, and the other of corporeal substance, provided we are careful to distinguish all the attributes of thought from the attributes of extension. We can also have a clear and distinct idea of uncreated and independent thinking substance, that is of God. Here we must simply avoid supposing that the idea adequately represents everything which is to be found in God; and we must not invent any additional features, but concentrate only on what is really contained in the idea and on what we clearly perceive to belong to the nature of a supremely perfect being. And certainly no one can deny that we possess such an idea of God, unless he reckons that there is absolutely no knowledge of God to be found in the minds of men.

55. *How we can also have a distinct understanding of duration, order and number.*

We shall also have a very distinct understanding of *duration, order* and *number*, provided we do not mistakenly tack on to them any concept of substance. Instead, we should regard the duration of a thing simply as a mode under which we conceive the thing in so far as it continues to exist. And similarly we should not regard order or number as anything separate from the things which are ordered and numbered, but should think of them simply as modes under which we consider the things in question.

56. *What modes, qualities and attributes are.*

By *mode*, as used above, we understand exactly the same as what is elsewhere meant by an *attribute* or *quality*. But we employ the term *mode* when we are thinking of a substance as being affected or modified; when the modification enables the substance to be designated as a substance of such and such a kind, we use the term *quality*; and finally, when we are simply thinking in a more general way of what is in a substance, we use the term *attribute*. Hence we do not, strictly speaking, say that there are modes or

qualities in God, but simply attributes, since in the case of God, any variation is unintelligible. And even in the case of created things, that which always remains unmodified – for example existence or duration in a thing which exists and endures – should be called not a quality or a mode but an attribute.

57. *Some attributes are in things and others in thought. What duration and time are.*

Now some attributes or modes are in the very things of which they are said to be attributes or modes, while others are only in our thought. For example, when time is distinguished from duration taken in the general sense and called the measure of movement, it is simply a mode of thought. For the duration which we understand to be involved in movement is certainly no different from the duration involved in things which do not move. This is clear from the fact that if there are two bodies moving for an hour, one slowly and the other quickly, we do not reckon the amount of time to be greater in the latter case than the former, even though the amount of movement may be much greater. But in order to measure the duration of all things, we compare their duration with the duration of the greatest and most regular motions which give rise to years and days, and we call this duration 'time'. Yet nothing is thereby added to duration, taken in its general sense, except for a mode of thought.

58. *Number and all universals are simply modes of thinking.*

In the same way, number, when it is considered simply in the abstract or in general, and not in any created things, is merely a mode of thinking; and the same apples to all the other *universals*, as we call them.

59. *How universals arise. The five common universals: genus, species, differentia, property, accident.*

These universals arise solely from the fact that we make use of one and the same idea for thinking of all individual items which resemble each other: we apply one and the same term to all the things which are represented by the idea in question, and this is the universal term. When we see two stones, for example, and direct our attention not to their nature but merely to the fact that there are two of them, we form the idea of the number which we call 'two'; and when we later see two birds or two trees, and consider not their nature but merely the fact that there are two of them, we go back to the same idea as before. This, then, is the universal idea; and we always

28 designate the number in question by the same universal term 'two'. In the same way, when we see a figure made up of three lines, we form an idea of it which we call the idea of a triangle; and we later make use of it as a universal idea, so as to represent to our mind all the other figures made up of three lines. Moreover, when we notice that some triangles have one right angle, and others do not, we form the universal idea of a right-angled triangle; since this idea is related to the preceding idea as a special case, it is termed a *species*. And the rectangularity is the universal *differentia* which distinguishes all right-angled triangles from other triangles. And the fact that the square on the hypotenuse is equal to the sum of the squares on the other two sides is a *property* belonging to all and only right-angled triangles. Finally, if we suppose that some right-angled triangles are in motion while others are not, this will be a universal *accident* of such triangles. Hence five universals are commonly listed: *genus, species, differentia, property* and *accident*.

60. *Three sorts of distinction: firstly, what is meant by a 'real distinction'.*

Now number, in things themselves, arises from the distinction between them. But *distinction* can be taken in three ways: as a *real* distinction, a *modal* distinction, or a *conceptual* distinction. Strictly speaking, a *real* distinction exists only between two or more substances; and we can perceive that two substances are really distinct simply from the fact that we can clearly and distinctly understand one apart from the other. For when we come to know God, we are certain that he can bring about anything of which we have a distinct understanding. For example, even though we may not yet know for certain that any extended or corporeal substance exists in reality, the mere fact that we have an idea of such a substance enables us to be certain that it is capable of existing. And we can also be certain that, if it exists,

29 each and every part of it, as delimited by us in our thought, is really distinct from the other parts of the same substance. Similarly, from the mere fact that each of us understands himself to

be a thinking thing and is capable, in thought, of excluding from himself every other substance, whether thinking or extended, it is certain that each of us, regarded in this way, is really distinct from every other thinking substance and from every corporeal substance. And even if we suppose that God has joined some corporeal substance to such a thinking substance so closely that they cannot be more closely conjoined, thus compounding them into a unity, they nonetheless remain really distinct. For no matter how closely God may have united them, the power which he previously had of separating them, or keeping one in being without the other, is something he could not lay aside; and things which God has the power to separate, or to keep in being separately, are really distinct.

61. *What is meant by a 'modal distinction'.*

A *modal distinction* can be taken in two ways: firstly, as a distinction between a mode, properly so called, and the substance of which it is a mode; and secondly, as a distinction between two modes of the same substance. The first kind of modal distinction can be recognized from the fact that we can clearly perceive a substance apart from the mode which we say differs from it, whereas we cannot, conversely, understand the mode apart from the substance. Thus there is a modal distinction between shape or motion and the corporeal substance in which they inhere; and similarly, there is a modal distinction between affirmation or recollection and the mind. The second kind of modal distinction is recognized from the fact that we are able to arrive at knowledge of one mode apart from another, and *vice versa*, whereas we cannot know either mode apart from the substance in which they both inhere. For example, if a stone is in motion and is square-shaped, I can understand the square shape without the motion and, conversely, the motion without the square shape; but I can understand neither the motion nor the shape 30 apart from the substance of the stone. A different case, however, is the distinction by which the mode of one substance is distinct from another substance or from the mode of another substance. An example of this is the way in which the motion of one body is distinct from another body, or from the mind; or the way in which motion differs from doubt. It seems more appropriate to call this kind of distinction a real distinction, rather than a modal distinction, since the modes in question cannot be clearly understood apart from the really distinct substances of which they are modes.

62. *What is meant by a 'conceptual distinction'.*
Finally, a *conceptual distinction* is a distinction between a substance and some attribute of that substance without which the substance is unintelligible; alternatively, it is a distinction between two such attributes of a single substance. Such a distinction is recognized by our inability to form a clear and distinct idea of the substance if we exclude from it the attribute in question, or, alternatively, by our inability to perceive clearly the idea of one of the two attributes if we separate it from the other. For example, since a substance cannot cease to endure without also ceasing to be, the distinction between the substance and its duration is merely a conceptual one. And in the case of all the modes of thought which we consider as being in objects, there is merely a conceptual distinction between the modes and the object which they are thought of as applying to; and the same is true of the distinction between the modes themselves when these are in one and the same object. I am aware that elsewhere I did lump this type of distinction with the modal distinction, namely at the end of my Replies to the First Set of Objections to the *Meditations on First Philosophy*; but that was not a suitable place for making a careful distinction between the two types; it was enough for my purposes to distinguish both from the real distinction.

63. *How thought and extension may be distinctly recognized as constituting the nature of mind and of body.*
Thought and extension can be regarded as constituting the natures of intelligent substance and corporeal substance; they must then be considered as nothing else but thinking substance itself and extended substance itself – that is, as mind and body. In this way we will have a very clear and distinct understanding of them. Indeed, it is much easier for us to have an understanding of extended substance or thinking substance than it is for us to understand substance on its own, leaving out the fact that it thinks or is extended. For we have some difficulty in abstracting the notion of substance from the notions of thought and extension, since the distinction between

these notions and the notion of substance itself is merely a conceptual distinction. A concept is not any more distinct because we include less in it; its distinctness simply depends on our carefully distinguishing what we do include in it from everything else.

64. *How thought and extension may also be distinctly recognized as modes of a substance.*
Thought and extension may also be taken as modes of a substance, in so far as one and the same mind is capable of having many different thoughts; and one and the same body, with its quantity unchanged, may be extended in many different ways (for example, at one moment it may be greater in length and smaller in breadth or depth, and a little later, by contrast, it may be greater in breadth and smaller in length). The distinction between thought or extension and the substance will then be a modal one; and our understanding of them will be capable of being just as clear and distinct as our understanding of the substance itself, provided they are regarded not as substances (that is, things which are separate from other things) but simply as modes of things. By regarding them as being in the substances of which they are modes, we distinguish them from the substances in question and see them for what they really are. If, on the other hand, we attempted to consider them apart from the substances in which they inhere, we would be regarding them as things which subsisted in their own right, and would thus be confusing the ideas of a mode and a substance.

65. *How the modes of thought and extension are to be known.*
There are various modes of thought such as understanding, imagination, memory, volition, and so on; and there are various modes of extension, or modes which belong to extension, such as all shapes, the positions of parts and the motions of the parts. And, just as before, we shall arrive at the best perception of all these items if we regard them simply as modes of the things in which they are located. As far as motion is concerned, it will be best if we think simply of local motion, without inquiring into the force which produces it. . . .

66. *How sensations, emotions and appetites may be clearly known, despite the fact that we are*

frequently wrong in our judgements concerning them.

There remains sensations, emotions and appetites [see art. 48]. These may be clearly perceived provided we take great care in our judgements concerning them to include no more than what is strictly contained in our perception – no more than that of which we have inner awareness. But this is a very difficult rule to observe, at least with regard to sensations. For all of us have, from our early childhood, judged that all the objects of our sense-perception are things existing outside our minds and closely resembling our sensations, i.e. the perceptions that we had of them. Thus, on seeing a colour, for example, we supposed we were seeing a thing located outside us which closely resembled the idea of colour that we experienced within us at the time. And this was something that, because of our habit of making such judgements, we thought we saw clearly and distinctly – so much so that we took it for something certain and indubitable.

67. *We frequently make mistakes, even in our judgements concerning pain.*

The same thing happens with regard to everything else of which we have sensory awareness, even to pleasure and pain. For, although we do not suppose that these exist outside us, we generally regard them not as being in the mind alone, or in our perception, but as being in the hand or foot or in some other part of our body. But the fact that we feel a pain as it were in our foot does not make it certain that the pain exists outside our mind, in the foot, any more than the fact that we see light as it were in the sun, makes it certain the light exists outside us, in the sun. Both these beliefs are preconceived opinions of our early childhood, as will become clear below.

68. *How to distinguish what we clearly know in such matters from what can lead us astray.*

In order to distinguish what is clear in this connection from what is obscure, we must be very careful to note that pain and colour and so on are clearly and distinctly perceived when they are regarded merely as sensations or thoughts. But when they are judged to be real things existing outside our mind, there is no way of understanding what sort of things they are. If someone says he sees colour in a body or feels pain in a limb, this amounts to saying that he sees or feels something

there of which he is wholly ignorant, or, in other words, that he does not know what he is seeing or feeling. Admittedly, if he fails to pay sufficient attention, he may easily convince himself that he has some knowledge of what he sees or feels, because he may suppose that it is something similar to the sensation of colour or pain which he experiences within himself. But if he examines the nature of what is represented by the sensation of colour or pain – what is represented as existing in the coloured body or the painful part – he will realize that he is wholly ignorant of it.

69. *We know size, shape and so forth in quite a different way from the way in which we know colours, pains and the like.*

This will be especially clear if we consider the wide gap between our knowledge of those features of bodies which we clearly perceive, as stated earlier [in art. 48], and our knowledge of those features which must be referred to the senses, as I have just pointed out. To the former class belong the size of the bodies we see, their shape, motion, position, duration, number and so on (by 'motion' I mean local motion: philosophers have imagined that there are other kinds of motion distinct from local motion, thereby only making the nature of motion less intelligible to themselves).* To the latter class belong the colour in a body, as well as pain, smell, taste and so on. It is true that when we see a body we are just as certain of its existence in virtue of its having a visible colour as we are in virtue of its having a visible shape; but our knowledge of what it is for the body to have a shape is much clearer than our knowledge of what it is for it to be coloured.

70. *There are two ways of making judgements concerning the things that can be perceived by the senses: the first enables us to avoid error, while the second allows us to fall into error.*

It is clear, then, that when we say that we perceive colours in objects, this is really just the same as saying that we perceive something in the objects whose nature we do not know, but which

33

34

---

* By 'local motion' is meant, roughly, movement from place to place. Scholastic philosophers, following Aristotle, sometimes classifed any alteration (e.g. a quantitative or a qualitative change) as a type of motion; various other distinctions, e.g. that between 'natural' and 'violent' motion, were also commonplace.

produces in us a certain very clear and vivid sensation which we call the sensation of colour. But the way in which we make our judgement can vary very widely. As long as we merely judge that there is in the objects (that is, in the things, whatever they may turn out to be, which are the source of our sensations) something whose nature we do not know, then we avoid error; indeed, we are actually guarding against error, since the recognition that we are ignorant of something makes us less liable to make any rash judgement about it. But it is quite different when we suppose that we perceive colours in objects. Of course, we do not really know what it is that we are calling a colour; and we cannot find any intelligible resemblance between the colour which we suppose to be in objects and that which we experience in our sensation. But this is something we do not take account of; and, what is more, there are many other features, such as size, shape and number which we clearly perceive to be actually or at least possibly present in objects in a way exactly corresponding to our sensory perception or understanding. And so we easily fall into the

35 error of judging that what is called colour in objects is something exactly like the colour of which we have sensory awareness; and we make the mistake of thinking that we clearly perceive what we do not perceive at all.

[. . .]

75. *Summary of the rules to be observed in order to philosophize correctly.*

In order to philosophize seriously and search out the truth about all the things that are capable of being known, we must first of all lay aside all our preconceived opinions, or at least we must take the greatest care not to put our trust in any of the opinions accepted by us in the past until we have first scrutinized them afresh and confirmed their truth. Next, we must give our attention in an orderly way to the notions that we have within us, and we must judge to be true all and only those whose truth we clearly and distinctly recognize when we attend to them in this way. When we do this we shall realize, first of all, that we exist in so far as our nature consists in thinking; and we shall simultaneously realize both that there is a God, and that we depend on him, and also that a consideration of his attributes enables us to investigate the truth of other

things, since he is their cause. Finally, we will see that besides the notions of God and of our mind, we have within us knowledge of many propositions which are eternally true, such as 'Nothing comes from nothing'. We shall also find that we have knowledge both of a corporeal or extended nature which is divisible, moveable, and so on, and also of certain sensations which affect us, such as the sensations of pain, colours, tastes and so on (though we do not yet know the cause of our being affected in this way). When we contrast all this knowledge with the confused thoughts we had before, we will acquire the habit of forming clear and distinct concepts of all the things that can be known. These few instructions seem to me to contain the most important principles of human 39 knowledge.

[. . .]

Note

1   This "ontological argument" for God's existence reminds one, of course, of St Anselm's reasoning IV.5. According to him, God's "essence" – that of a supremely great being – requires that God actually exist, since an imaginary or fictional God would not be as great as an existing one.

Descartes, Selected Correspondence with Princess Elisabeth of Bohemia

Elisabeth to Descartes*

The Hague, 6/16 May 1643

Monsieur,

I have learned, with very great joy and regret, the intention you had to see me a few days ago, and I have been equally moved, both by your charity in consenting to communicate with an ignorant and indocile person, and by the misfortune that stole me away from so profitable a conversation. M. Pollot greatly augmented this latter passion by repeating to me the solution you gave him of the obscurities in the physics of M. Regius, concerning which I would have been

* Selections from J. Blom, trans., *Descartes: His Moral Philosophy and Psychology* (New York: New York University, 1978), 105–116.

better instructed from your own mouth, as also about a question I proposed to the said professor when he was in this city, and in regard to which he directed me back to you to receive the required satisfaction. The shame of showing you so unruly a style has prevented me to date from asking this favor of you by letter.

But today M. Pollot gave me such assurance of your good will toward everyone, and especially toward me, that, banishing every other consideration from mind, save that of availing myself of it, I beseech you tell me how the soul of man (since it is but a thinking substance) can determine the spirits of the body to produce voluntary actions. For it seems every determination of movement happens from an impulsion of the thing moved, according to the manner in which it is pushed by that which moves it, or else, depends on the qualification and figure of the superficies of this latter. Contact is required for the first two conditions, and extension for the third. You entirely exclude extension from your notion of the soul, and contact seems to me incompatible with an immaterial thing. That is why I ask of you a definition of the soul more particular than in your metaphysic – that is to say, for a definition of the substance separate from its action, thought. For although we suppose them inseparable (which nonetheless is difficult to prove regarding infants in their mother's womb and deep faints), still, like the attributes of God, we can, by considering them separately, acquire a more perfect idea of them.

Knowing you to be the best doctor for my soul, I therefore freely reveal to you the weaknesses of its speculations, and I trust that in observing the oath of Hippocrates you will furnish it remedies without publicizing them; that I ask of you, as likewise, that you bear these importunities of . . . etc.

Descartes to Elisabeth

Egmond du Hoef, 21 May 1643

Madame,

The favor with which Your Highness has honored me, in granting me receive her commands in writing, surpasses anything I had ever dared hope for; and it compensates for my flaws better than would that which I passionately desired – to receive those commands from your lips had I been

able to be admitted to the honor of paying you reverence, and of offering you my very-humble services, when I was last at the Hague. For I would have had too many marvels to admire at the same time; and seeing a discourse more than human flow from a frame so similar to those painters bestow upon angels, I would have been ravished, just as, it seems to me, are bound to be they who, in coming from earth, enter for the first time upon heaven. In such wise was I rendered less capable of responding to Your Highness – who undoubtedly already noticed this flaw in me – when I previously had the honor of speaking to her; and it is your clemency that has wished to compensate for that flaw by placing the traces of your thoughts upon paper, where, rereading them several times, and accustoming myself to consider them, I am indeed less dazzled, yet have only so much the more admiration for them, recognizing that they do not seem ingenious merely at first sight, but proportionately more judicious and solid the further one examines them.

And I can in all honesty say that the question Your Highness proposes seems to me that which can be asked with the greatest justification in sequel to the writings I have published. For, there being two things in the human soul on which depends all the knowledge we can have of its nature – the first, that it thinks, and the second, that being united to the body, it can act and suffer with it – I have said nearly nothing of this latter, and have studied only to understand well the first, since my principal design was to prove the distinction that exists between the soul and the body, for which the first alone could suffice, while the other would have been an impediment. But since Your Highness is so discerning that one cannot hide anything from her, I shall try here to explain the manner in which I conceive the union of the soul with the body, and how it has the force to move the body.

Firstly, I consider that in us are certain primitive notions that are like originals on whose model we form all our other knowledge. And there are but very few such notions; for, after the most general ones – of being, number, duration, etc. – which refer to everything we can conceive, we have, as regards body in particular, only the notion of extension, from which follow those of figure and movement; and, as regards the soul alone, we have only that of thought, in which are comprised the perceptions of the understanding and the inclinations of the will; finally, for the soul and the body together, we have only that of their union, on which depends that of the force of the soul for moving the body, and of the body for acting upon the soul by causing its feelings and passions.

I consider also that all human knowledge consists only in carefully distinguishing these notions, and in attributing each of them only to the things to which they pertain. For when we wish to explain some difficulty by means of a notion that does not pertain to it, we cannot fail to make a mistake. And that occurs whenever we wish to explain one of these notions by another – for since they are primitive, each of them cannot be understood except through itself. And inasmuch as the use of the senses has rendered the notions of extension, figures, and movements very much more familiar to us than the others, the principal cause of our errors consists in that we ordinarily wish to employ them to explain things to which they do not pertain, as when one wishes to employ the imagination to conceive the nature of the soul, or else, when one wishes to conceive the manner in which the soul moves the body after the fashion in which a body is moved by another body.

That is why, having tried to clarify in the *Meditations* Your Highness has deigned to read, the notions that pertain to the soul alone and distinguish them from those that pertain to the body alone, the first thing I should in sequel explain is the manner of conceiving whatever pertains to the union of the soul with the body, leaving aside things that pertain to the body alone or to the soul alone. In this regard it seems to me that what I wrote at the end of my Response to the sixth objections can be of use; for we cannot seek these simple notions other than in our soul – in our soul which, although it has all of them in it by its nature, does not always sufficiently distinguish them one from another, or else fails to attribute them to the objects to which they should be attributed.

Thus I believe that we hitherto confused the notion of the force by which the soul acts on the body with that by which one body acts upon another; and that we have attributed both, not to the soul, for as yet we did not recognize it, but to different qualities of bodies, such as weight, heat, and so forth which we imagined as being real – or, as having an existence distinct from that of body, and consequently as being substances, although we called them qualities. And in order

to conceive them, we have sometimes used the notions that are in us for knowing body, and sometimes those that are for knowing the soul, according as what we attributed to them has been material or immaterial. For example, in supposing weight a real quality, of which we possess no other knowledge save that it has the force of moving the body in which it exists toward the center of the earth, we have no difficulty conceiving how it moves this body, nor how it is joined to it; and we do not think that happens by means of an actual touching of one surface against another, for we experience in our own selves that we have a particular notion for conceiving it; yet I believe that in applying this notion to weight – which, as I hope to show in physics, is nothing really distinct from body – we are abusing what has been given us for conceiving the manner in which the soul moves the body.

I would show myself insufficiently aware of the incomparable wit of Your Highness if I employed more words in explaining myself, and I would be too presumptuous if I dared think my response ought satisfy her entirely; but I shall try to avoid both by adding nothing further here save that, if I am capable of writing or saying anything that can be agreeable to her, I will always consider it a very great favor to take up my pen or to go to the Hague on such account; and that there is nothing in the world so dear to me as to obey her commands. But I can find no room here for observing the oath of Hippocrates as she enjoins me; for she has communicated nothing to me that does not merit being seen and admired by all. I can only say, regarding this matter, that infinitely esteeming your letter, I shall treat it as misers do their treasures – which they stash away all the more they esteem them, and, by begrudging everyone else the sight of them, take their sovereign contentment in looking upon them. And thus I shall be very willing to enjoy all to myself the good of looking upon it; and my greatest ambition is to be able to say, and truly to be, . . . etc.

Elisabeth to Descartes

The Hague, 10/20 June 1643

Monsieur Descartes,
Your good will not only shows forth, as I had been given to understand it would, in pointing

out and correcting the flaws in my reasoning, but also in that, to render my recognizing them less annoying, you try – to the prejudice of your judgment – to console me by means of false praises that would have been necessary to encourage me to take the remedy had not my nourishment, in a place where the ordinary fashion of conversation has accustomed me to hear praises from persons incapable of speaking the truth, led me to suppose I could never err in believing the opposite of their discourse, and thereby to render reflection upon my imperfections so familiar as to cause me no more emotion than I require in connection with the desire to rid myself of them.

That makes me confess, without shame, that I have discovered in myself all the causes of error you note in your letter, and that I have been as yet unable to banish them entirely, since the life I am constrained to lead does not allow me enough free time to acquire a habit of meditation in accordance with your rules. Sometimes the interests of my household, which I must not neglect, sometimes conversations and civilities I cannot eschew, so thoroughly deject this weak mind with annoyances or boredom that it remains, for a long time afterward, useless for anything else: which will serve, I hope, to excuse my stupidity in being unable to comprehend, from what you had previously said concerning weight, the idea by which we should judge how the soul (nonextended and immaterial) can move the body; nor why this power, that you have then under the name of quality falsely attributed to it as carrying the body toward the center of the earth, ought persuade us that body can be pushed by something immaterial any more than the demonstration of a contrary truth (as you promise in your physics) confirms us in the opinion of its impossibility; principally, because this idea (not being able to claim to the same perfection and objective reality as that of God) can be feigned out of ignorance of what truly moves these bodies toward the center; and then, since no material cause presents itself to the senses, one would have attributed it – which I have only been able to conceive as a negation of matter – to its contrary, the immaterial, which cannot have any communication with it.

And I admit it would be easier for me to concede matter and extension to the soul, than the capacity of moving a body and of being moved, to an immaterial being. For, if the first occurred through 'information', the spirits that perform the movement would have to be intelligent, which you accord to nothing corporeal. And although in your metaphysical meditations you show the possibility of the second, it is, however, very difficult to comprehend that a soul, as you have described it, after having had the faculty and habit of reasoning well, can lose all of it on account of some vapors, and that, although it can subsist without the body and has nothing in common with it, is yet so ruled by it.

But, since you have undertaken to instruct me, I entertain these opinions only as friends that I do not intend to keep, assuring myself you will explain the nature of an immaterial substance and the manner of its actions and passions in the body just as well as all the other things you have wished to teach. I ask you also to believe there is no one upon whom you can bestow this charity more aware of the obligation she owes you for it than . . . etc.

Descartes to Elisabeth

Egmond du Hoef, 28 June 1643

Madame,

I am very greatly obliged to Your Highness in that, having experienced from my preceding remarks that I badly explain myself concerning the question it has pleased her to propose to me, she again deigns to have the patience to listen to me regarding the same subject, and to give me an opportunity to note the things I had omitted. The principal omissions seem to be that, having distinguished three kinds of ideas or primitive notions, each of which are recognized in a particular manner and not by the comparison of one with another, namely, the notion we have of the soul, of the body, and of the union existing between the soul and the body, I should have explained the difference that exists among these three sorts of notions, and among the operations of the soul by which we have them, and should have stated the means of rendering each of them familiar and easy for ourselves; then, in sequel, having said why I used the comparison to weight, I should have made it plain that, although one wishes to conceive the soul as material (which is properly to conceive its union with the body), one cannot fail to recognize afterward that it is separable from it. That, I believe, is everything Your Highness has enjoined me discuss here.

First, then, I note a great difference among these three kinds of notions, in that the soul conceives itself only by the pure understanding; body – that is to say, extension, figures, and movements – can likewise be recognized by the understanding alone, but very much better by the understanding aided by the imagination; and finally, the things that pertain to the union of the soul and the body are recognized only obscurely by the understanding alone or even by the understanding as aided by the imagination; yet they are known very clearly by the senses. From that it comes about that those who never philosophize, and who make use only of their senses, do not doubt that the soul moves the body and the body acts upon the soul; but they consider the one and the other as a single thing, that is to say, they conceive their union; for to conceive the union existing between two things is to conceive them as one thing alone. The metaphysical thoughts that exercise the pure understanding serve to render the notion of the soul more familiar to us; and the study of mathematics, which principally exercises the imagination in considering figures and movements, accustoms us to form very distinct notions of body; and finally, it is by availing oneself only of life and ordinary conversations, and by abstaining from meditating and studying things that exercise the imagination, that one learns to conceive the union of the soul and the body.

I almost fear that Your Highness may think I am not speaking seriously here; but that would be contrary to the respect I owe her and shall never fail to render her. And I can truly say that the principal rule I have always observed in my studies, and of which I believe I have made very good use in acquiring some knowledge, has been that I have never employed save very few hours each day at thoughts that occupy the imagination, and very few hours per year at those that occupy the understanding alone, and that I have devoted all the rest of my time to the respite of my senses and the repose of my mind; I even reckon among the exercises of the imagination all serious conversations, and everything that requires attention. That is what made me retire to the country. For although, were I in the most densely occupied city in the world, I could have as many more hours to myself as I now employ at studying, nevertheless I could not so usefully employ them, since my soul would be wearied by the attention required by the bustle of life. And I here take liberty of writing to Your Highness to testify to her how truly I admire that, among the affairs and cares never relenting for persons who are at once of great mind and great birth, she has yet been able to devote herself to the meditations required to recognize well the distinction that exists between the soul and the body.

But I have judged that it was those meditations, rather than thoughts that require less attention, that have made her find obscurity in the notion we have of their union; for it does not seem to me that the human mind is capable of conceiving very distinctly, and at the same time, both the distinction between the soul and the body, and also their union; because to do so it is necessary to conceive them as one thing alone, and at the same time to conceive them as two, which is the contrary. And for this reason (supposing Your Highness still had the reasons that prove the distinction of the soul and the body very present to her mind, and not wishing to ask her to rid herself of them in order to represent the notion that everyone always experiences in himself without philosophizing – namely, that it is one person alone who, at the same time, has a body and thought of such nature that this thought can move the body and feel the accidents that happen to it), I previously made use of the comparison with weight and other qualities we commonly imagine united to some body, just as thought is united to ours; and I am not concerned that this comparison limped in that such qualities are not real, as one is wont to image them, because I believed Your Highness was already entirely persuaded that the soul is a substance distinct from the body

But, since Your Highness notes it is easier to attribute matter and extension to the soul than to attribute to it, when it has no matter, a capacity to move a body and be moved by one, I ask her to please freely attribute this matter and this extension to the soul; for that is nothing but to conceive it united to the body. And having conceived that well, and having experienced it in herself, it will be easy for her to appreciate that the matter she shall have attributed to this thought is not thought itself, but rather that the extension of this matter is of another nature than the extension of this thought, in that the first is determined to a certain place, from which it excludes every other extension of body, which the second does not. And thus Your Highness will not fail to return easily to the knowledge of the distinction of the soul and the body, notwithstanding that she has conceived their union.

Finally, just as I believe it very necessary, once in one's life, to have well understood the principles of metaphysics, since it is they that provide us with knowledge of God and our soul, I also believe it would be very harmful to occupy one's understanding in frequently meditating upon them because it could not be so healthy to abandon the functions of the imagination and senses; but the best procedure is to content oneself with retaining in one's memory and belief those conclusions one has once extracted from them, and then to devote the rest of the time remaining for studying to thoughts wherein the understanding acts along with the imagination and the senses.

My extreme devotion to the service of Your Highness makes me hope my frankness will not be disagreeable to her, and it would have led me to engage here in a longer discourse, wherein I would have tried to clarify on this occasion all the difficulties attaching to the question proposed; but troublesome news from Utrecht, where the magistrate summons me to verify what I have written about one of their ministers – that he is indeed a man who has most scandalously calumniated me, and that what I have written about him in my just defense is only too well known to everyone – compels me to finish here, in order to go consult about the means of extricating myself, as soon as possible, from these chicaneries.* I am, . . . etc.

Elisabeth to Descartes

The Hague, 1 July 1643
Monsieur Descartes,

I see that my regard for your instructions, and the desire to avail myself of them, does not

* Descartes was summoned to defend what he had written in his *Epistle to Voetius.*

inconvenience you as much as does the ingratitude of they who deprive themselves, and would wish deprive all mankind, of them; nor would I have dispatched this new effect of my ignorance before knowing you acquitted of that of their bigotedness, except that M. Van Bergen obliged me write sooner by his civility in resolving to remain in this city until I should give him a response to your letter of 28 June in which you clearly point out the three sorts of notions we possess, their objects, and the manner of using them properly.

I too find that the senses show me that the soul moves the body; but they fail to teach me (any more than the understanding and the imagination) the manner in which she does it. And, in regard to that, I think there are unknown properties in the soul that might suffice to reverse what your metaphysical meditations, with such good reasons, persuaded me concerning her inextension. And this doubt seems founded upon the rule you lay down there in speaking of the true and the false – namely, that all our errors occur from forming judgments about what we do not sufficiently perceive. Although extension is not necessary to thought, yet not being contradictory to it, it will be able to belong to some other function of the soul less essential to her. At least that avoids the contradiction of the scholastics – namely, that the entire soul is in the entire body and entirely in each of its parts. I do not excuse myself for confusing the notion of the soul with that of the body for the same reason as do ordinary people; but that does not dispel for me the first doubt, and I will despair of finding certitude in any matter unless you provide me with it – you who alone have prevented me from being the skeptic I was inclined to be by my first reasoning.

Although I owe you this admission, by way of rendering you thanks, I should nevertheless think it very imprudent, except that I know, as much from the experience I have already had of them as by reputation, that your good will and generosity equal the rest of your merits. You cannot give witness of them in any more obliging manner than by the elucidations and advice you share with me, and which I prize above the greatest treasures that could be possessed by . . . etc.

13

Benedict Spinoza, *Ethics*,
Part I (selections)

Introduction

In the Preface to Part V of his *Ethics*, the Dutch philosopher of Jewish-Spanish descent, Benedict Spinoza (1632–77; see I.13 of this volume for details of Spinoza's life), accuses Descartes's "interactionist" account of mental and material substances (III.12) of being an "occult" doctrine unworthy of "so great a man." Like other critical admirers of Descartes, such as Thomas Hobbes (V.10), Spinoza's metaphysics was largely inspired by an ambition to articulate a system that would be free from the implausibility, as they saw it, of the Frenchman's mind-body dualism. It is in Part II of his posthumously published *Ethics* (1677) that Spinoza develops his own, extremely difficult view of mind and body – or "thought" and "extension" – as two "attributes" or "aspects" (*attributa*) of a single substance (*substantium*), as two incommensurable ways in which we humans are compelled to view and describe the same reality. In the first part, entitled "Of God," Spinoza undertakes the prior tasks of establishing that there is just one substance and of drawing out crucial implications of that claim.

"Of God" has a somewhat musical structure, with the first section constituting a crescendo that climaxes in the Propositions (P14 and P15)

From Benedict de Spinoza, *Ethics*, ed. and trans. E. Curley. Harmondsworth: Penguin, 1996, pp. 1–10, 13–23, 25 (some passages omitted).

maintaining that there is a single substance, God, and that "whatever is, is in God," while the remaining sections explore those themes and their modulations (the eternal nature of substance, for example). Spinoza, then, was a "monist," but of a different type from Śaṁkara (III.7 above). For one thing, he has no tendency to relegate physical objects and people – which are "modes" (*modi* or *modificationes*) that are "of" or "in," the one substance – to the realm of illusion. Nor does he appeal, by way of argument, to any special "mystical experience" of oneness or unity. Indeed, he eschews appeal to experience of any sort. Spinoza was an arch-rationalist, as the Euclidean layout of *Ethics*, with its apparatus of axioms, corollaries, lemmas, scholia, etc., might indicate. It was not simply that Spinoza thought that pure reason, unaided by empirical evidence, was the proper tool for arriving at metaphysical truth. He was also a "causal rationalist,"[1] holding it to be clearer than "the noon light that there is absolutely nothing . . . contingent" (P33), so that to the fully rational mind everything which is or happens will be recognizable as strictly necessary.

The ascent to the central Propositions 14–15 is achieved, above all, by reflection on the notion of substance, specifically by taking to its logical conclusion, in Spinoza's view, the traditional idea, stemming from Aristotle (III.4 above), that substance is "independent" – or, as he himself puts it, what is "in itself" and "whose concept does not require the concept of another thing" (Definition 3). Descartes himself had said that, on such a characterization, there is, strictly speaking, only one substance, God. For Spinoza, we should never speak less than strictly. Hence, if we stick to the "independence" criterion, we are forced to concede that there must be exactly one substance. There must be at least one, since it belongs to the notion of substance that it is a cause of itself, and so must exist. There cannot be more than one since, *inter alia*, a second would "limit," and hence be incompatible with, the complete "independence," as well as the "infinite" nature, of the first.

It is less easy to understand why Spinoza calls this one substance "God," a difficulty compounded for some readers by his later remark that this "eternal and infinite being" may be called "God or Nature" (*deus sive natura*; IV Preface). In some commentators' views, Spinoza was in effect a closet atheist who, for reasons of prudence in an intolerant age, needed to retain the rhetorical trappings of religion. But it is more plausible to hold that Spinoza, if not the "God-intoxicated" figure described by Novalis (1772–1801), regarded his one substance as enjoying sufficiently many of the essential features traditionally associated with God – necessity, eternity, self-causation, freedom (in the sense of being unlimited by anything else), and so on. It is true that Spinoza's God is, under one aspect, extended matter, but as one commentator points out, the effect of his "conception rather raises our conception of matter than lowers our conception of God," in somewhat the same manner as does William Wordsworth's (1770–1850) pantheistic picture of the world as "rolled through" by "something far more deeply interfused."[2] In this connection, one should remark that the "Nature" which seems, for Spinoza, to be synonymous with "God," is *natura naturans*, the dynamic "expression" of a "free" causal process, not *natura naturata*, the finished products, as it were – trees, stones, people – of that process (P. 29). (We have had to omit some of the more obviously "theological" passages where Spinoza compares and contrasts his view with traditional ones).

Spinoza's *Ethics* is rationalist metaphysics on the grand and ambitious scale. It will be intriguing to compare his position to the very different one reached by an equally ambitious rationalist, Leibniz (III.15 below), on the basis, ironically, of strikingly similar premisses.[3]

Notes

1 See J. Bennett, *A Study in Spinoza's Ethics*, Cambridge: Cambridge University Press, 1984.

2 T. L. S. Sprigge, *Theories of Existence: A Sequence of Essays on the Fundamental Questions of Philosophy*, Harmondsworth: Penguin, 1984, p. 157.

3 In the following text, the following abbreviations used are: D = definition, A = axiom, P = Proposition, Dem. = Demonstration, Exp. = explanation, Cor. = corollary, Schol. = Scholium, NS = *Nagelate Schriften* (i.e. material from a Dutch translation of original Latin).

Spinoza, *Ethics*

First Part of the Ethics: Of God

Definitions D1: By cause of itself I understand that whose essence involves existence, *or* that whose nature cannot be conceived except as existing.

D2: That thing is said to be finite in its own kind that can be limited by another of the same nature.

For example, a body is called finite because we always conceive another that is greater. Thus a thought is limited by another thought. But a body is not limited by a thought nor a thought by a body.

D3: By substance I understand what is in itself and is conceived through itself, that is, that whose concept does not require the concept of another thing, from which it must be formed.

D4: By attribute I understand what the intellect perceives of a substance, as constituting its essence.

D5: By mode I understand the affections of a substance, *or* that which is in another through which it is also conceived.

D6: By God I understand a being absolutely infinite, that is, a substance consisting of an infinity of attributes, of which each one expresses an eternal and infinite essence.

Exp.: I say absolute infinite, not infinite in its own kind; for if something is only infinite in its own kind, we can deny infinite attributes of it [NS: (i.e., we can conceive infinite attributes which do not pertain to its nature)]; but if something is absolutely infinite, whatever expresses essence and involves no negation pertains to its essence.

D7: That thing is called free which exists from the necessity of its nature alone, and is determined to act by itself alone. But a thing is called necessary, or rather compelled, which is determined by another to exist and to produce an effect in a certain and determinate manner.

D8: By eternity I understand existence itself, insofar as it is conceived to follow necessarily from the definition alone of the eternal thing.

Exp.: For such existence, like the essence of a thing, is conceived as an eternal truth, and on that account cannot be explained by duration or time, even if the duration is conceived to be without beginning or end.

Axioms   A1: Whatever is, is either in itself or in another.

A2: What cannot be conceived through another, must be conceived through itself.

A3: From a given determinate cause the effect follows necessarily; and conversely, if there is no determinate cause, it is impossible for an effect to follow.

A4: The knowledge of an effect depends on, and involves, the knowledge of its cause.

A5: Things that have nothing in common with one another also cannot be understood through one another, *or* the concept of the one does not involve the concept of the other.

I/47   A6: A true idea must agree with its object.

A7: If a thing can be conceived as not existing, its essence does not involve existence.

Propositions   P1: *A substance is prior in nature to its affections.*

Dem.: This is evident from D3 and D5.

P2: *Two substances having different attributes have nothing in common with one another.*

Dem.: This is also evident from D3. For each must be in itself and be conceived through itself, *or* the concept of the one does not involve the concept of the other.

P3: *If things have nothing in common with one another, one of them cannot be the cause of the other.*

Dem.: If they have nothing in common with one another, then (by A5) they cannot be understood through one another, and so (by A4) one cannot be the cause of the other, q.e.d.

P4: *Two or more distinct things are distinguished from one another, either by a difference in the attributes of the substances or by a difference in their affections.*

Dem.: Whatever is, is either in itself or in another (by A1), that is (by D3 and D5), outside the intellect there is nothing except substances and their affections. Therefore, there is nothing outside the intellect through which a number of things can be distinguished from one another   II/48 except substances, *or* what is the same (by D4), their attributes and their affections, q.e.d.

P5: *In Nature there cannot be two or more substances of the same nature or attribute.*

Dem.: If there were two or more distinct substances, they would have to be distinguished from one another either by a difference in their attributes, or by a difference in their affections (by P4). If only by a difference in their attributes, then it will be conceded that there is only one of the same attribute. But if by a difference in their affections, then since a substance is prior in nature to its affections (by P1), if the affections are put to one side and [the substance] is considered in itself, that is (by D3 and A6), considered truly, one cannot be conceived to be distinguished from another, that is (by P4), there cannot be many, but only one [of the same nature *or* attribute], q.e.d.

P6: *One substance cannot be produced by another substance.*

Dem.: In Nature there cannot be two substances of the same attribute (by P5), that is (by

P2), which have something in common with each other. Therefore (by P3) one cannot be the cause of the other, *or* cannot be produced by the other, q.e.d.

Cor.: From this it follows that a substance cannot be produced by anything else. For in Nature there is nothing except substances and their affections, as is evident from A1, D3, and D5. But it cannot be produced by a substance (by P6). Therefore, substance absolutely cannot be produced by anything else, q.e.d.

Alternatively: This is demonstrated even more easily from the absurdity of its contradictory. For if a substance could be produced by something else, the knowledge of it would have to depend on the knowledge of its cause (by A4). And so (by D3) it would not be a substance.

II/49 P7: *It pertains to the nature of a substance to exist.*

Dem.: A substance cannot be produced by anything else (by P6C); therefore it will be the cause of itself, that is (by D1), its essence necessarily involves existence, *or* it pertains to its nature to exist, q.e.d.

P8: *Every substance is necessarily infinite.*

Dem.: A substance of one attribute does not exist unless it is unique (P5), and it pertains to its nature to exist (P7). Of its nature, therefore, it will exist either as finite or as infinite. But not as finite. For then (by D2) it would have to be limited by something else of the same nature, which would also have to exist necessarily (by P7), and so there would be two substances of the same attribute, which is absurd (by P5). Therefore, it exists as infinite, q.e.d.

Schol. 1: Since being finite is really, in part, a negation, and being infinite is an absolute affirmation of the existence of some nature, it follows from P7 alone that every substance must be infinite. [NS: For if we assumed a finite substance, we would, in part, deny existence to its nature, which (by P7) is absurd.]

Schol. 2: I do not doubt that the demonstration of P7 will be difficult to conceive for all who judge things confusedly, and have not been accustomed to know things through their first causes – because they do not distinguish between the modifications of substances and the substances themselves, nor do they know how things are produced. So it happens that they fictitiously ascribe to substances the beginning

which they see that natural things have; for those who do not know the true causes of things confuse everything and without any conflict of mind feign that both trees and men speak, imagine that men are formed both from stones and from seed, and that any form whatever is changed into any other. So also, those who confuse the divine nature with the human easily ascribe human affects to God, particularly so long as they are also ignorant of how those affects are produced in the mind.

But if men would attend to the nature of II/5 substance, they would have no doubt at all of the truth of P7. Indeed, this proposition would be an axiom for everyone, and would be numbered among the common notions. For by substance they would understand what is in itself and is conceived through itself, that is, that the knowledge of which does not require the knowledge of any other thing. But by modifications they would understand what is in another, those things whose concept is formed from the concept of the thing in which they are.

This is how we can have true ideas of modifications which do not exist; for though they do not actually exist outside the intellect, nevertheless their essences are comprehended in another in such a way that they can be conceived through it. But the truth of substances is not outside the intellect unless it is in them themselves, because they are conceived through themselves.

Hence, if someone were to say that he had a clear and distinct, that is true, idea of a substance, and nevertheless doubted whether such a substance existed, that would indeed be the same as if he were to say that he had a true idea, and nevertheless doubted whether it was false (as is evident to anyone who is sufficiently attentive). Or if someone maintains that a substance is created, he maintains at the same time that a false idea has become true. Of course nothing more absurd can be conceived. So it must be confessed that the existence of a substance, like its essence, is an eternal truth.

And from this we can infer in another way that there is only one [substance] of the same nature, which I have considered it worth the trouble of showing here. But to do this in order, it must be noted,

I. that the true definition of each thing neither involves nor expresses anything except the nature of the thing defined.

From which it follows,

II.   that no definition involves or expresses any certain number of individuals,

since it expresses nothing other than the nature of the thing defined. For example, the definition of the triangle expresses nothing but the simple nature of the triangle, but not any certain number of triangles. It is to be noted,

III.   that there must be, for each existing thing, a certain cause on account of which it exists.

Finally, it is to be noted,

IV.   that this cause, on account of which a thing exists, either must be contained in the very nature and definition of the existing thing (*viz. that it pertains to its nature to exist*) or must be outside it.

From these propositions it follows that if, in Nature, a certain number of individuals exists, there must be a cause why those individuals, and why neither more nor fewer, exist.

I/51   For example, if twenty men exist in Nature (*to make the matter clearer, I assume that they exist at the same time, and that no others previously existed in Nature*), it will not be enough (i.e., *to give a reason why twenty men exist*) to show the cause of human nature in general; but it will be necessary in addition to show the cause why not more and not fewer than twenty exist. For (by III) there must necessarily be a cause why each [NS: particular man] exists. But this cause (by II and III) cannot be contained in human nature itself, since the true definition of man does not involve the number 20. So (by IV) the cause why these twenty men exist, and consequently, why each of them exists, must necessarily be outside each of them.

For that reason it is to be inferred absolutely that whatever is of such a nature that there can be many individuals [of that nature] must, to exist, have an external cause to exist. Now since it pertains to the nature of a substance to exist (by what we have already shown in this scholium), its definition must involve necessary existence, and consequently its existence must be inferred from its definition alone. But from its definition (as we have shown from II and III) the existence of a number of substances cannot follow. Therefore it follows necessarily from this, that there exists only one of the same nature, as was proposed.

P9: *The more reality or being each thing has, the more attributes belong to it.*

Dem.: This is evident from D4.

P10: *Each attribute of a substance must be conceived through itself.*

Dem.: For an attribute is what the intellect perceives concerning a substance, as constituting its essence (by D4); so (by D3) it must be conceived through itself, q.e.d.

Schol.: From these propositions it is evident that II/52 although two attributes may be conceived to be really distinct (i.e., one may be conceived without the aid of the other), we still cannot infer from that that they constitute two beings, *or* two different substances. For it is of the nature of a substance that each of its attributes is conceived through itself, since all the attributes it has have always been in it together, and one could not be produced by another, but each expresses the reality, *or* being of substance.

So it is far from absurd to attribute many attributes to one substance. Indeed, nothing in Nature is clearer than that each being must be conceived under some attribute, and the more reality, or being it has, the more it has attributes which express necessity, *or* eternity, and infinity. And consequently there is also nothing clearer than that a being absolutely infinite must be defined (as we taught in D6) as a being that consists of infinite attributes, each of which expresses a certain eternal and infinite essence.

But if someone now asks by what sign we shall be able to distinguish the diversity of substances, let him read the following propositions, which show that in Nature there exists only one substance, and that it is absolutely infinite. So that sign would be sought in vain.

P11: *God, or a substance consisting of infinite attributes, each of which expresses eternal and infinite essence, necessarily exists.*

Dem.: If you deny this, conceive, if you can, that God does not exist. Therefore (by A7) his essence does not involve existence. But this (by P7) is absurd. Therefore God necessarily exists, q.e.d.

Alternatively: For each thing there must be assigned a cause, *or* reason, both for its existence

and for its nonexistence. For example, if a triangle exists, there must be a reason *or* cause
why it exists; but if it does not exist, there must
also be a reason *or* cause which prevents it from
existing, *or* which takes its existence away.

But this reason, *or* cause, must either be contained in the nature of the thing, or be outside
it. For example, the very nature of a square circle indicates the reason why it does not exist,
namely, because it involves a contradiction. On
the other hand, the reason why a substance
exists also follows from its nature alone, because
it involves existence (see P7). But the reason why
a circle or triangle exists, or why it does not
exist, does not follow from the nature of these
things, but from the order of the whole of corporeal Nature. For from this [order] it must
follow either that the triangle necessarily exists now
or that it is impossible for it to exist now. These
things are evident through themselves; from
them it follows that a thing necessarily exists if
there is no reason or cause which prevents it from
existing. Therefore, if there can be no reason or
cause which prevents God from existing, or
which takes his existence away, it must certainly
be inferred that he necessarily exists.

But if there were such a reason, *or* cause, it
would have to be either in God's very nature or
outside it, that is, in another substance of another
nature. For if it were of the same nature, that very
supposition would concede that God exists. But
a substance which was of another nature [NS: than
the divine] would have nothing in common with
God (by P2), and therefore could neither give
him existence nor take it away. Since, then, there
can be, outside the divine nature, no reason, *or*
cause, which takes away the divine existence, the
reason will necessarily have to be in his nature
itself, if indeed he does not exist. That is, his nature
would involve a contradiction [NS: as in our second example]. But it is absurd to affirm this of a
Being absolutely infinite and supremely perfect.
Therefore, there is no cause, *or* reason, either in
God or outside God, which takes his existence
away. And therefore, God necessarily exists,
q.e.d.

Alternatively: To be able not to exist is to lack
power, and conversely, to be able to exist is to have
power (as is known through itself). So, if what now
necessarily exists are only finite beings, then
finite beings are more powerful than an absolutely
infinite Being. But this, as is known through

itself, is absurd. So, either nothing exists or an
absolutely infinite Being also exists. But we exist,
either in ourselves, or in something else, which
necessarily exists (see A1 and P7). Therefore an
absolutely infinite Being – that is (by D6), God
– necessarily exists, q.e.d.

Schol.: In this last demonstration I wanted to
show God's existence a posteriori, so that the
demonstration would be perceived more easily –
but not because God's existence does not follow
a priori from the same foundation. For since
being able to exist is power, it follows that the more
reality belongs to the nature of a thing, the more
powers it has, of itself, to exist. Therefore, an absolutely infinite Being, *or* God, has, of himself, an
absolutely infinite power of existing. For that
reason, he exists absolutely.

Still, there may be many who will not easily be
able to see how evident this demonstration is,
because they have been accustomed to contemplate only those things that flow from external
causes. And of these, they see that those which
quickly come to be, that is, which easily exist, also
easily perish. And conversely, they judge that
those things to which they conceive more things
to pertain are more difficult to do, that is, that
they do not exist so easily. But to free them from
these prejudices, I have no need to show here in
what manner this proposition – *what quickly
comes to be, quickly perishes* – is true, nor
whether or not all things are equally easy in
respect to the whole of Nature. It is sufficient to
note only this, that I am not here speaking of things
that come to be from external causes, but only of
substances that (by P6) can be produced by no
external cause.

For things that come to be from external
causes – whether they consist of many parts or
of few – owe all the perfection or reality they have
to the power of the external cause; and therefore
their existence arises only from the perfection
of their external cause, and not from their own
perfection. On the other hand, whatever perfection substance has is not owed to any external
cause. So its existence must follow from its
nature alone; hence its existence is nothing but
its essence.

Perfection, therefore, does not take away the
existence of a thing, but on the contrary asserts
it. But imperfection takes it away. So there is nothing of whose existence we can be more certain
than we are of the existence of an absolutely

infinite, *or* perfect, Being – that, God. For since his essence excludes all imperfection, and involves absolute perfection, by that very fact it takes away every cause of doubting his existence, and gives the greatest certainty concerning it. I believe this will be clear even to those who are only moderately attentive.

I/55 P12: *No attribute of a substance can be truly conceived from which it follows that the substance can be divided.*

Dem.: For the parts into which a substance so conceived would be divided either will retain the nature of the substance or will not. If the first [NS: viz. they retain the nature of the substance], then (by P8) each part will have to be infinite, and (by P7) its own cause, and (by P5) each part will have to consist of a different attribute. And so many substances will be able to be formed from one, which is absurd (by P6). Furthermore, the parts (by P2) would have nothing in common with their whole, and the whole (by D4 and P10) could both be and be conceived without its parts, which is absurd, as no one will be able to doubt.

But if the second is asserted, namely, that the parts will not retain the nature of substance, then since the whole substance would be divided into equal parts, it would lose the nature of substance, and would cease to be, which (by P7) is absurd.

P13: *A substance which is absolutely infinite is indivisible.*

Dem.: For if it were divisible, the parts into which it would be divided will either retain the nature of an absolutely infinite substance or they will not. If the first, then there will be a number of substances of the same nature, which (by P5) is absurd. But if the second is asserted, then (as above [NS: P12]), an absolutely infinite substance will be able to cease to be, which (by P11) is also absurd.

Cor.: From these [propositions] it follows that no substance, and consequently no corporeal substance, insofar as it is a substance, is divisible.

Schol.: That substance is indivisible, is understood more simply merely from this, that the nature of substance cannot be conceived unless as infinite, and that by a part of substance nothing can be understood except a finite substance, II/56 which (by P8) implies a plain contradiction.

P14: *Except God, no substance can be or be conceived.*

Dem.: Since God is an absolutely infinite being, of whom no attribute which expresses an essence of substance can be denied (by D6), and he necessarily exists (by P11), if there were any substance except God, it would have to be explained through some attribute of God, and so two substances of the same attribute would exist, which (by P5) is absurd. And so except God, no substance can be or, consequently, be conceived. For if it could be conceived, it would have to be conceived as existing. But this (by the first part of this demonstration) is absurd. Therefore, except for God no substance can be or be conceived, q.e.d.

Cor. 1: From this it follows most clearly, first, that God is unique, that is (by D6), that in Nature there is only one substance, and that it is absolutely infinite (as we indicated in P10S).

Cor. 2: It follows, second, that an extended thing and a thinking thing are either attributes of God, or (by A1) affections of God's attributes.

P15: *Whatever is, is in God, and nothing can be or be conceived without God.*

Dem.: Except for God, there neither is, nor can be conceived, any substance (by P14), that is (by D3), thing that is in itself and is conceived through itself. But modes (by D5) can neither be nor be conceived without substance. So they can be in the divine nature alone, and can be conceived through it alone. But except for substances and II/57 modes there is nothing (by A1). Therefore, [NS: everything is in God and] nothing can be or be conceived without God, q.e.d.

Schol.: [I] There are those who feign a God, like man, consisting of a body and a mind, and subject to passions. But how far they wander from the true knowledge of God, is sufficiently established by what has already been demonstrated. Them I dismiss. For everyone who has to any extent contemplated the divine nature denies that God is corporeal. They prove this best from the fact that by body we understand any quantity, with length, breadth, and depth, limited by some certain figure. Nothing more absurd than this can be said of God, namely, of a being absolutely infinite. But meanwhile, by the other arguments by which they strive to demonstrate this same conclusion they clearly show that they entirely remove corporeal, *or* extended, substance itself from the divine nature. And they maintain that it has been created by God. But by what divine power could it be created? They are completely ignorant of that. And this shows clearly that they do not understand what they themselves say. At any rate, I have demonstrated clearly enough – in my judgment, at least – that no substance can be produced or created by another thing (see P6C and P8S2). Next, we have shown (P14) that except for God, no substance can either be or be conceived, and hence [in P14C2] we have concluded that extended substance is one of God's infinite attributes. [. . .]

[. . .]

II/60   All things, I say, are in God, and all things that happen, happen only through the laws of God's infinite nature and follow (as I shall show) from the necessity of his essence. So it cannot be said in any way that God is acted on by another, or that extended substance is unworthy of the divine nature, even if it is supposed to be divisible, so long as it is granted to be eternal and infinite. But enough of this for the present.

P16: *From the necessity of the divine nature there must follow infinitely many things in infinitely many modes, (i.e., everything which can fall under an infinite intellect).*

Dem.: This proposition must be plain to anyone, provided he attends to the fact that the intellect infers from the given definition of any thing a number of properties that really do follow necessarily from it (that is, from the very essence of the thing); and that it infers more properties the more the definition of the thing expresses reality, that is, the more reality the essence of the defined thing involves. But since the divine nature has absolutely infinite attributes (by D6), each of which also expresses an essence infinite in its own kind, from its necessity there must follow infinitely many things in infinite modes (i.e., everything which can fall under an infinite intellect), q.e.d.

Cor. 1: From this it follows that God is the efficient cause of all things which can fall under an infinite intellect.

II/61   Cor. 2: It follows, second, that God is a cause through himself and not an accidental cause.

Cor. 3: It follows, third, that God is absolutely the first cause.

P17: *God acts from the laws of his nature alone, and is compelled by no one.*

Dem.: We have just shown (P16) that from the necessity of the divine nature alone, or (what is the same thing) from the laws of his nature alone, absolutely infinite things follow, and in P15 we have demonstrated that nothing can be or be conceived without God, but that all things are in God. So there can be nothing outside him by which he is determined or compelled to act. Therefore, God acts from the laws of his nature alone, and is compelled by no one, q.e.d.

Cor. 1: From this it follows, first, that there is no cause, either extrinsically or intrinsically, which prompts God to action, except the perfection of his nature.

Cor. 2: It follows, second, that God alone is a free cause. For God alone exists only from the necessity of his nature (by P11 and P14C1), and acts from the necessity of his nature (by P17). Therefore (by D7) God alone is a free cause, q.e.d.

Schol.: [I.] Others think that God is a free cause because he can (so they think) bring it about that the things which we have said follow from his nature (i.e., which are in his power) do not happen or are not produced by him. But this is the same as if they were to say that God can bring it about that it would not follow from the nature of a triangle that its three angles are equal to two right angles; *or* that from a given cause the effect would not follow – which is absurd.   II/62

Further, I shall show later, without the aid of this proposition, that neither intellect nor will pertain to God's nature. Of course I know there are many who think they can demonstrate that a supreme intellect and a free will pertain to God's nature. For they say they know nothing they can ascribe to God more perfect than what is the highest perfection in us.

Moreover, though they conceive God to actually understand in the highest degree, they still do not believe that he can bring it about that all the things he actually understands exist. For they think that in that way they would destroy God's power. If he had created all the things in his intellect (they say), then he would have been able to create nothing more, which they believe to be incompatible with God's omnipotence. So they prefer to maintain that God is indifferent to all things, not creating anything except what he has decreed to create by some absolute will.

But I think I have shown clearly enough (see P16) that from God's supreme power, *or* infinite nature, infinitely many things in infinitely many modes, that is, all things, have necessarily flowed, or always follow, by the same necessity and in the same way as from the nature of a triangle it follows, from eternity and to eternity, that its three angles are equal to two right angles. So God's omnipotence has been actual from eternity and will remain in the same actuality to eternity. And in this way, at least in my opinion, God's omnipotence is maintained far more perfectly.

Indeed – to speak openly – my opponents seem to deny God's omnipotence. For they are forced to confess that God understands infinitely many creatable things, which nevertheless he will never be able to create. For otherwise, if he created everything he understood [NS: to be creatable] he would (according to them) exhaust his omnipotence and render himself imperfect. Therefore to maintain that God is perfect, they are driven to maintain at the same time that he cannot bring about everything to which his power extends. I do not see what could be feigned which would be more absurd than this or more contrary to God's omnipotence....

P18: *God is the immanent, not the transitive, cause of all things.*

I/64   Dem.: Everything that is, is in God, and must be conceived through God (by P15), and so (by P16C1) God is the cause of [NS: all] things, which are in him. That is the first [thing to be proven]. And then outside God there can be no substance (by P14), that is (by D3), thing which is in itself outside God. That was the second. God, therefore, is the immanent, not the transitive cause of all things, q.e.d.

P19: *God is eternal, or all God's attributes are eternal.*

Dem.: For God (by D6) is substance, which (by P11) necessarily exists, that is (by P7), to whose nature it pertains to exist, or (what is the same) from whose definition it follows that he exists; and therefore (by D8), he is eternal.

Next, by God's attributes are be understood what (by D4) expresses an essence of the divine substance, that is, what pertains to substance. The attributes themselves, I say, must involve it itself. But eternity pertains to the nature of substance (as I have already demonstrated from P7).

Therefore each of the attributes must involve eternity, and so, they are all eternal, q.e.d.

Schol.: This proposition is also as clear as possible from the way I have demonstrated God's existence (P11). For from that demonstration, I say, it is established that God's existence, like his essence, is an eternal truth. And then I have also demonstrated God's eternity in another way (*Descartes' Principles* IP19), and there is no need to repeat it here.

P20: *God's existence and his essence are one and the same.*

Dem.: God (by P19) and all of his attributes are eternal, that is (by D8), each of his attributes expresses existence. Therefore, the same attributes of God which (by D4) explain God's eternal essence at the same time explain his eternal existence, that is, that itself which constitutes God's   II/65 essence at the same time constitutes his existence. So his existence and his essence are one and the same, q.e.d.

Cor. 1: From this it follows, first, that God's existence, like his essence, is an eternal truth.

Cor. 2: It follows, second, that God, *or* all of God's attributes, are immutable. For if they changed as to their existence, they would also (by P20) change as to their essence, that is (as is known through itself), from being true become false, which is absurd.

P21: *All the things which follow from the absolute nature of any of God's attributes have always had to exist and be infinite, or are, through the same attribute, eternal and infinite.*

Dem.: If you deny this, then conceive (if you can) that in some attribute of God there follows from its absolute nature something that is finite and has a determinate existence, *or* duration, for example, God's idea in thought. Now since thought is supposed to be an attribute of God, it is necessarily (by P11) infinite by its nature. But insofar as it has God's idea, [thought] is supposed to be finite. But (by D2) [thought] cannot be conceived to be finite unless it is determined through thought itself. But [thought can] not [be determined] through thought itself, insofar as it constitutes God's idea, for to that extent [thought] is supposed to be finite. Therefore, [thought must be determined] through thought insofar as it does not constitute God's idea, which [thought] nevertheless (by P11) must necessarily exist. Therefore, there is thought which does not constitute God's idea, and on that account God's idea does not follow necessarily from the nature [of this thought] insofar as it is absolute thought (for [thought] is conceived both as constituting God's idea and as not constituting it). [That God's idea does not follow from thought, insofar as it is absolute thought] is contrary to the hypothesis. So if God's idea in thought, or anything else in any attribute of God (for it does not matter what example is taken, since the demonstration is universal), follows from the necessity of the absolute nature of the attribute itself, it must necessarily be infinite. This was the first thing to be proven.

II/66 Next, what follows in this way from the necessity of the nature of any attribute cannot have a determinate [NS: existence, or] duration. For if you deny this, then suppose there is, in some attribute of God, a thing which follows from the necessity of the nature of that attribute – for example, God's idea in thought – and suppose that at some time [this idea] did not exist or will not exist. But since thought is supposed to be an attribute of God, it must exist necessarily and be immutable (by P11 and P20C2). So beyond the limits of the duration of God's idea (for it is supposed that at some time [this idea] did not exist or will not exist) thought will have to exist without God's idea. But this is contrary to the hypothesis, for it is supposed that God's idea follows necessarily from the given thought. Therefore, God's idea in thought, or anything else which follows necessarily from the absolute nature of some attribute of God, cannot have a determinate duration, but through the same attribute is eternal. This was the second thing [NS: to be proven]. Note that the same is to be affirmed of any thing which, in some attribute of God, follows necessarily from God's absolute nature.

P22: *Whatever follows from some attribute of God insofar as it is modified by a modification which, through the same attribute, exists necessarily and is infinite, must also exist necessarily and be infinite.*

Dem.: The demonstration of this proposition proceeds in the same way as the demonstration of the preceding one.

P23: *Every mode which exists necessarily and is infinite has necessarily had to follow either from the absolute nature of some attribute of God, or from some attribute, modified by a modification which exists necessarily and is infinite.*

Dem.: For a mode is in another, though which it must be conceived (by D5), that is (by P15), II/67 is in God alone, and can be conceived through God alone. So if a mode is conceived to exist necessarily and be infinite, [its necessary existence and infinity] must necessarily be inferred, *or* perceived through some attribute of God, insofar as that attribute is conceived to express infinity and necessity of existence, *or* (what is the same, by D8) eternity, that is (by D6 and P19), insofar as it is considered absolutely. Therefore, the mode, which exists necessarily and is infinite, has had to follow from the absolute nature of some attribute of God – either immediately (see P21) or by some mediating modification, which follows from its absolute nature, that is (by P22), which exists necessarily and is infinite, q.e.d.

P24: *The essence of things produced by God does not involve existence.*

Dem.: This is evident from D1. For that whose nature involves existence (considered in itself), is its own cause, and exists only from the necessity of its nature.

Cor.: From this it follows that God is not only the cause of things' beginning to exist, but also of their persevering in existing, *or* (to use a Scholastic term) God is the cause of the being of things. For – whether the things [NS: produced] exist or not – so long as we attend to their essence, we shall find that it involves neither existence nor duration. So their essence can be the cause neither of their existence nor of their duration, but only God, to whose nature alone it pertains to exist [, can be the cause] (by P14C1).

P25: *God is the efficient cause, not only of the existence of things, but also of their essence.*

Dem.: If you deny this, then God is not the cause of the essence of things; and so (by A4) the essence of things can be conceived without God. But (by P15) this is absurd. Therefore II/68 God is also the cause of the essence of things, q.e.d.

Schol.: This proposition follows more clearly from P16. For from that it follows that from the given divine nature both the essence of things and their existence must necessarily be inferred; and in a word, God must be called the cause of all things in the same sense in which he is called the cause of himself. This will be established still more clearly from the following corollary.

Cor.: Particular things are nothing but affections of God's attributes, *or* modes by which God's attributes are expressed in a certain and determinate way. The demonstration is evident from P15 and D5.

P26: *A thing which has been determined to produce an effect has necessarily been determined in this way by God; and one which has not been determined by God cannot determine itself to produce an effect.*

Dem.: That through which things are said to be determined to produce an effect must be something positive (as is known through itself). And so, God, from the necessity of his nature, is the efficient cause both of its essence and of its existence (by P25 and 16); this was the first thing. And from it the second thing asserted also follows very clearly. For if a thing which has not been determined by God could determine itself, the first part of this [NS: proposition] would be false, which is absurd, as we have shown.

P27: *A thing which has been determined by God to produce an effect, cannot render itself undetermined.*

Dem.: This proposition is evident from A3.

I/69 P28: *Every singular thing, or any thing which is finite and has a determinate existence, can neither exist nor be determined to produce an effect unless it is determined to exist and produce an effect by another cause, which is also finite and has a determinate existence; and again, this cause also can neither exist nor be determined to produce an effect unless it is determined to exist and produce an effect by another, which is also finite and has a determinate existence, and so on, to infinity.*

Dem.: Whatever has been determined to exist and produce an effect has been so determined by God (by P26 and P24C). But what is finite and has a determinate existence could not have been produced by the absolute nature of an attribute of God; for whatever follows from the absolute nature of an attribute of God is eternal and infinite (by P21). It had, therefore, to follow either from God or from an attribute of God insofar as it is considered to be affected by some mode. For there is nothing except substance and its modes (by A1, D3, and D5) and modes (by P25C) are nothing but affections of God's

attributes. But it also could not follow from God, or from an attribute of God, insofar as it is affected by a modification which is eternal and infinite (by P22). It had, therefore, to follow from, or be determined to exist and produce an effect by God or an attribute of God insofar as it is modified by a modification which is finite and has a determinate existence. This was the first thing to be proven.

And in turn, this cause, *or* this mode (by the same reasoning by which we have already demonstrated the first part of this proposition) had also to be determined by another, which is also finite and has a determinate existence; and again, this last (by the same reasoning) by another, and so always (by the same reasoning) to infinity, q.e.d.

Schol.: Since certain things had to be produced by God immediately, namely, those which follow necessarily from his absolute nature, and others (which nevertheless can neither be nor be conceived without God) had to be produced by the mediation of these first things, it follows: II/70

I. That God is absolutely the proximate cause of the things produced immediately by him, and not [a proximate cause] in his own kind, as they say. For God's effects can neither be nor be conceived without their cause (by P15 and P24C).

II. That God cannot properly be called the remote cause of singular things, except perhaps so that we may distinguish them from those things that he has produced immediately, or rather, that follow from his absolute nature. For by a remote cause we understand one which is not conjoined in any way with its effect. But all things that are, are in God, and so depend on God that they can neither be nor be conceived without him.

P29: *In nature there is nothing contingent, but all things have been determined from the necessity of the divine nature to exist and produce an effect in a certain way.*

Dem.: Whatever is, is in God (by P15); but God cannot be called a contingent thing. For (by P11) he exists necessarily, not contingently. Next, the modes of the divine nature have also followed from it necessarily and not contingently (by P16) – either insofar as the divine nature is considered absolutely (by P21) or insofar as it is considered to be determined to act in a certain way (by P28). Further, God is the cause of these modes not only insofar as they simply exist (by P24C), but also (by P26) insofar as they are considered to be determined to produce an effect. For if they have not been determined by God, then (by P26) it is impossible, not contingent, that they II/71 should determine themselves. Conversely (by P27) if they have been determined by God, it is not contingent, but impossible, that they should render themselves undetermined. So all things have been determined from the necessity of the divine nature, not only to exist, but to exist in a certain way, and to produce effects in a certain way. There is nothing contingent, q.e.d.

Schol.: Before I proceed further, I wish to explain here – or rather to advise [the reader] – what we must understand by *Natura naturans* and *Natura naturata*. For from the preceding I think it is already established that by *Natura naturans* we must understand what is in itself and is conceived through itself, *or* such attributes of substance as express an eternal and infinite essence, that is (by P14C1 and P17C2), God, insofar as he is considered as a free cause.

But by *Natura naturata* I understand whatever follows from the necessity of God's nature, *or* from any of God's attributes, that is, all the modes of God's attributes insofar as they are considered as things which are in God, and can neither be nor be conceived without God.

P30: *An actual intellect, whether finite or infinite, must comprehend God's attributes and God's affections, and nothing else.*

Dem.: A true idea must agree with its object (by A6), that is (as is known through itself), what is contained objectively in the intellect must necessarily be in Nature. But in Nature (by P14C1) there is only one substance, namely, God, and there are no affections other than those which are in God (by P15) and which can neither be nor be conceived without God (by P15). Therefore, an actual intellect, whether finite or infinite, must comprehend God's attributes and God's affections, and nothing else, q.e.d.

P31: *The actual intellect, whether finite or infinite, like will, desire, love, and the like, must be referred to* Natura Naturata, *not to* Natura naturans.

II/72   Dem.: By intellect (as is known through itself) we understand not absolute thought, but only a certain mode of thinking, which mode differs from the others, such as desire, love, and the like, and so (by D5) must be conceived through

absolute thought, that is (by P15 and D6), it must be so conceived through an attribute of God, which expresses the eternal and infinite essence of thought, that it can neither be nor be conceived without [that attribute]; and so (by P29S), like the other modes of thinking, it must be referred to *Natura naturata*, not to *Natura naturans*, q.e.d.

Schol.: The reason why I speak here of actual intellect is not because I concede that there is any potential intellect, but because, wishing to avoid all confusion, I wanted to speak only of what we perceive as clearly as possible, that is, of the intellection itself. We perceive nothing more clearly than that. For we can understand nothing that does not lead to more perfect knowledge of the intellection.

P32: *The will cannot be called a free cause, but only a necessary one.*

Dem.: The will, like the intellect, is only a certain mode of thinking. And so (by P28) each volition can neither exist nor be determined to produce an effect unless it is determined by another cause, and this cause again by another, and so on, to infinity. Even if the will be supposed to be infinite, it must be determined to exist and produce an effect by God, not insofar as he is an absolutely infinite substance, but insofar as he has an attribute that expresses the infinite and eternal essence of thought (by P23). So in whatever way it is conceived, whether as finite or as infinite, it requires a cause by which it is determined to exist and produce an effect. And so (by D7) it cannot be called a free cause, but only a necessary or compelled one, q.e.d.

Cor. 1: From this it follows, first, that God does II/73 not produce any effect by freedom of the will.

Cor. 2: It follows, second, that will and intellect are related to God's nature as motion and rest are, and as are absolutely all natural things, which (by P29) must be determined by God to exist and produce an effect in a certain way. For the will, like all other things, requires a cause by which it is determined to exist and produce an effect in a certain way. And although from a given will, *or* intellect infinitely many things may follow, God still cannot be said, on that account, to act from freedom of the will, any more than he can be said to act from freedom of motion and rest on account of those things that follow from motion and rest (for infinitely many things also follow from motion and rest). So will does not pertain to God's nature any more than do the other natural things, but is related to him in the same way as motion and rest, and all the other things which, as we have shown, follow from the necessity of the divine nature and are determined by it to exist and produce an effect in a certain way.

P33: *Things could have been produced by God in no other way, and in no other order than they have been produced.*

Dem.: For all things have necessarily followed from God's given nature (by P16), and have been determined from the necessity of God's nature to exist and produce an effect in a certain way (by P29). Therefore, if things could have been of another nature, or could have been determined to produce an effect in another way, so that the order of Nature was different, then God's nature could also have been other than it is now, and therefore (by P11) that [other nature] would also have had to exist, and consequently, there could have been two or more Gods, which is absurd (by P14C1). So things could have been produced in no other way and no other order, and so on, q.e.d.

Schol. 1: Since by these propositions I have shown more clearly than the noon light that there is absolutely nothing in things on account of which they can be called contingent, I wish now to explain briefly what we must understand by contingent – but first, what [we must understand] by necessary and impossible.

A thing is called necessary either by reason of its essence or by reason of its cause. For a thing's existence follows necessarily either from its essence and definition or from a given efficient cause. And a thing is also called impossible from these same causes – namely, either because its essence, *or* definition, involves a contradiction, or because there is no external cause which has been determined to produce such a thing.

But a thing is called contingent only because of a defect of our knowledge. For if we do not know that the thing's essence involves a con-

tradiction, or if we do know very well that its essence does not involve a contradiction, and nevertheless can affirm nothing certainly about its existence, because the order of causes is hidden from us, it can never seem to us either necessary or impossible. So we call it contingent or possible.

Schol. 2: From the preceding it clearly follows that things have been produced by God with the highest perfection, since they have followed necessarily from a given most perfect nature. Nor does this convict God of any imperfection, for his perfection compels us to affirm this. Indeed, from the opposite, it would clearly follow (as I have just shown), that God is not supremely perfect; because if things had been produced by God in another way, we would have to attribute to God another nature, different from that which we have been compelled to attribute to him from the consideration of the most perfect being. . . .

P34: *God's power is his essence itself.* II/77

Dem.: For from the necessity alone of God's essence it follows that God is the cause of himself (by P11) and (by P16 and P16C) of all things. Therefore, God's power, by which he and all things are and act, is his essence itself, q.e.d.

P35: *Whatever we conceive to be in God's power, necessarily exists.*

Dem.: For whatever is in God's power must (by P34) be so comprehended by his essence that it necessarily follows from it, and therefore necessarily exists, q.e.d.

P36: *Nothing exists from whose nature some effect does not follow.*

Dem.: Whatever exists expresses the nature, *or* essence of God in a certain and determinate way (by P25C), that is (by P34), whatever exists expresses in a certain and determinate way the power of God, which is the cause of all things. So (by P16), from [NS: everything which exists] some effect must follow, q.e.d.

14

John Locke, *An Essay Concerning Human Understanding*, Book II, Chapters VIII and XXIII

Introduction

A seventeenth-century philosopher more congenial than Descartes and Spinoza to the predominant empiricist temper of our times is John Locke (1632–1704). Both as the "father" of British Empiricism and as one of the first to appreciate the philosophical significance of modern science, Locke's *Essay* (1690) has great appeal in an age whose received wisdom is that of an empirically and scientifically minded intelligentsia. Indeed, Locke is frequently hailed as the prime inspiration for a metaphysics of "scientific realism" whose central tenet is that objective, independent reality is what is articulated by the natural sciences, at any rate by an "ideal physics."[1] Scientific realists sometimes need reminding that their position is a metaphysical one. It is, after all, one thing to subscribe to various propositions of physics, quite another to hold that those propositions uniquely describe how the world objectively and independently is.

There are two discussions of Locke's in particular that have been inspirational for scientific realists. The first of these, found in Book II, Chapter VIII, argues for a radical distinction

From John Locke, *An Essay Concerning Human Understanding*, Vol. I, ed. J. W. Yolton. London: J. M. Dent & Sons, 1961, pp. 103–11, 244–50 (opening paragraphs of Chapter VIII omitted).

between "primary" qualities, such as shape and motion, and "secondary" ones, such as color and smell. We briefly encountered this distinction, though not drawn in those terms, in Descartes's *Principles of Philosophy* (III.12 above), but Locke's discussion owes more to the scientist Robert Boyle (1627–91), who had made the distinction on the basis of his "corpuscular theory" of the material world. For many years, the tendency was to interpret Locke as holding that only primary qualities belong to external objects, with secondary ones belonging only "in the mind," to our perceptual "ideas" or sensations. Certainly some of Locke's remarks suggest that interpretation, as when he asserts that yellowness, unlike solidity, is "not actually in gold." But his more considered view seems to be that color does belong to objects, but only as a "power" which they have, due to their primary features, to produce certain sensations in the mind. The crucial difference between primary and secondary qualities is, therefore, that only the former *represent* or have any "resemblance" to our "ideas" or experiences of them – a claim sharply criticized, as we will see in III.16 by George Berkeley. From the scientific realist's point of view, it perhaps matters little in which of these ways the distinction is drawn. Either way – whether color is "in the mind" alone or reduced to primary qualities and their powers – we are not required to include, in our basic account of material reality, any concepts which do not figure in the physicist's mathematicized depiction of the universe.[2]

Locke's second discussion, scattered at various places in the *Essay*, but beginning with Book II, Ch. XXIII, is not unrelated to the first: it concerns substances and our concepts of them. Unlike Descartes and Spinoza (see III.12 and 13 above), Locke's main emphasis is not upon substances as entities capable of existing, or conceived as existing, "independently," but as what "stand under," "support," or "hold together" the various properties attributed to, say, gold or some animal. Locke complains that Aristotelian and medieval (III.4, 10 and 11) views of "substantial forms" fail to honor a crucial distinction between our *idea* of a substance like gold and the *intrinsic nature* of that substance. They have wrongly conflated what, in Book III, he calls "nominal" and "real" essence, for they have failed to distinguish between the question of our usual criteria for judging that something is gold and that of gold's underlying nature. A person's concept of a substance is a combination of an idea of its properties and "a supposition of he knows not what support" these properties have. The substance itself, Locke seems to suggest, might be identified with that "real constitution," inaccessible to ordinary perception but available in principle to scientific investigation, which serves as that "support."

The appeal of this position to the scientific realist is not hard to discern. If the above interpretation of Locke is right, then in order to know what a thing or a creature really and basically is, it is not our everyday understanding of its "manifest" features which should be consulted, but scientific understanding of a physical constitution underlying such features. Indeed, the possibility is always there that everyday allocation of objects or creatures to species and kinds may be overturned by scientific discoveries concerning the inner physical constitutions. "Natural kinds," defined in terms of such constitutions, may have no close fit with the pre-scientific categories employed for dividing up the world's furniture.[3]

For Locke himself, his claim about the (presently) unknown natures of substances had further and welcome implications for the philosophy of mind. First, we should not deny that there exists mental substance simply because its nature is unknown, for the position is no different in the case of material substance. Second, it was premature of Descartes to insist that mind and body were substances of radically different kinds. Granted, mental properties and spatial ones are strikingly different, but for Locke there can be no *a priori* reason to insist that the substances that "hold together" or "stand under" both sets of properties are themselves of different natures.

Notes

1 See, for example, M. Devitt, *Realism and Truth*, Oxford: Blackwell, 1991, for an expression of one scientific realist's debt to Locke.

2 For a clear discussion of Locke's distinction and its relation to science, see J. Mackie, *Problems from Locke*, Oxford: Clarendon Press, 1976 and E. J. Lowe, *Locke on Human Understanding*, London: Routledge, 1995.

3 See Saul A. Kripke, *Naming and Necessity*, Cambridge, MA: Harvard University Press, 1980, for the best-known contemporary development of this line of thought.

Locke, *An Essay Concerning Human Understanding*

Book II

Chapter VIII
SOME FURTHER CONSIDERATIONS CONCERNING OUR SIMPLE IDEAS

[...]

7. To discover the nature of our *ideas* the better, and to discourse of them intelligibly, it will be convenient to distinguish them as they are *ideas* or perceptions in our minds, and as they are modifications of matter in the bodies that cause such perceptions in us: that so we *may not* think (as perhaps usually is done) that they are exactly the images and *resemblances* of something inherent in the subject: most of those of sensation being in the mind no more the likeness of something existing without us, than the names that stand for them are the likeness of our *ideas*, which yet upon hearing they are apt to excite in us.

8. Whatsoever the mind perceives in itself, or is the immediate object of perception, thought,

or understanding, that I call *idea*; and the power to produce any *idea* in our mind, I call *quality* of the subject wherein that power is. Thus a snowball having the power to produce in us the *ideas* of *white*, *cold*, and *round*, the power to produce those *ideas* in us as they are in the snowball I call *qualities*; and as they are sensations or perceptions in our understandings, I call them *ideas*; which *ideas*, if I speak of sometimes as in the things themselves, I would be understood to mean those qualities in the objects which produce them in us.

9. Qualities thus considered in bodies are:

First, such as are utterly inseparable from the body, in what state soever it be; such as in all the alterations and changes it suffers, all the force can be used upon it, it constantly keeps; and such as sense constantly finds in every particle of matter which has bulk enough to be perceived; and the mind finds inseparable from every particle of matter, though less than to make itself singly be perceived by our senses. V.g., take a grain of wheat, divide it into two parts, each part has still *solidarity, extension, figure*, and *mobility*; divide it again, and it retains still the same qualities; and so divide it on, till the parts become insensible: they must retain still each of them all those qualities. For division (which is all that a mill or pestle or any other body does upon another in reducing it to insensible parts) can never take away either solidity, extension, figure, or mobility from any body, but only makes two or more distinct separate masses of matter, of that which was but one before; all which distinct masses, reckoned as so many distinct bodies, after division make a certain number. These I call *original* or *primary qualities* of body; which I think we may observe to produce simple *ideas* in us, viz. solidity, extension, figure, motion or rest, and number.

10. Secondly, such *qualities* which in truth are nothing in the objects themselves but powers to produce various sensations in us by their *primary qualities*, i.e. by the bulk, figure, texture, and motion of their insensible parts, as colours, sounds, tastes, etc. These I call *secondary qualities*. To these might be added a third sort, which are allowed to be barely powers, though they are as much real qualities in the subject as those which I, to comply with the common way of speaking, call *qualities*, but for distinction, *secondary qualities*. For the power in fire to produce a new colour, or consistency in wax or clay, by its primary qualities, is as much a quality in fire as

the power it has to produce in me a new *idea or* sensation of warmth or burning, which I felt not before, by the same primary qualities, viz. the bulk, texture, and motion of its insensible parts.

11. The next thing to be considered is how *bodies* produce *ideas* in us; and that is manifestly *by impulse*, the only way which we can conceive bodies operate in.

12. If then external objects be not united to our minds when they produce *ideas* in it and yet we perceive *these original qualities* in such of them as singly fall under our senses, it is evident that some motion must be thence continued by our nerves or animal spirits, by some parts of our bodies, to the brains or the seat of sensation, there to *produce in our minds the particular ideas we have of them*. And since the extension, figure, number, and motion of bodies of an observable bigness may be perceived at a distance *by* the sight, it is evident some singly imperceptible bodies must come from them to the eyes, and thereby convey to the brain some *motion*, which produces these *ideas* which we have of them in us.

13. After the same manner that the *ideas* of these original qualities are produced in us, we may conceive that the *ideas of secondary qualities* are also *produced*, viz. *by the operation of insensible particles on our senses*. For it being manifest that there are bodies and good store of bodies, each whereof are so small that we cannot by any of our senses discover either their bulk, figure, or motion, as is evident in the particles of the air and water and others extremely smaller than those, perhaps as much smaller than the particles of air or water as the particles of air or water are smaller than peas or hail-stones: let us suppose at present that the different motions and figures, bulk and number, of such particles, affecting the several organs of our senses, produce in us those different sensations which we have from the colours and smells of bodies: v.g. that a violet, by the impulse of such insensible particles of matter, of peculiar figures and bulks, and in different degrees and modifications of their motions, causes the *ideas* of the blue colour and sweet scent of that flower to be produced in our minds. It being no more impossible to conceive that God should annex such *ideas* to such motions, with which they have no similitude, than that he should annex the *idea* of pain to the motion of a piece of steel dividing our flesh, with which that *idea* hath no resemblance.

14. What I have said concerning *colours* and *smells* may be understood also of *tastes* and *sounds, and other the like sensible qualities*; which, whatever reality we by mistake attribute to them, are in truth nothing in the objects themselves but powers to produce various sensations in us, and depend *on those primary qualities*, viz. bulk, figure, texture, and motion of parts, as I have said.

15. From whence I think it easy to draw this observation: that the *ideas of primary qualities* of bodies *are resemblances* of them, and their patterns do really exist in the bodies themselves; but the *ideas produced* in us *by* these *secondary qualities have no resemblance* of them at all. There is nothing like our *ideas* existing in the bodies themselves. They are, in the bodies we denominate from them, only a power to produce those sensations in us; and what is sweet, blue, or warm in *idea* is but the certain bulk, figure, and motion of the insensible parts in the bodies themselves, which we call so.

16. *Flame* is denominated *hot* and *light*; snow, *white* and *cold*; and *manna, white* and *sweet*, from the *ideas* they produce in us. Which qualities are commonly thought to be the same in those bodies that those *ideas* are in us, the one the perfect resemblance of the other, as they are in a mirror, and it would by most men be judged very extravagant if one should say otherwise. And yet he that will consider that *the same fire* that at one distance *produces* in us the sensation of *warmth* does, at a nearer approach, produce in us the far different sensation of *pain*, ought to bethink himself what reason he has to say that his *idea* of *warmth*, which was produced in him by the fire, is actually *in the fire*; and his *idea* of *pain*, which the same fire produced in him the same way, is *not* in the *fire*. Why are whiteness and coldness in snow, and pain not, when it produces the one and the other *idea* in us; and can do neither, but by the bulk, figure, number, and motion of its solid parts?

17. The particular *bulk, number, figure, and motion of the parts of fire or snow are really in them*, whether anyone's senses perceive them or no; and therefore they may be called *real qualities*, because they really exist in those bodies. But *light, heat, whiteness*, or *coldness are no more really in them than sickness or pain is in* manna. Take away the sensation of them; let not the eyes see light or colours, nor the ears hear sounds; let the palate not taste, nor the nose smell; and all colours, tastes,

odours, and sounds, as they are such particular *ideas*, vanish and cease, and are reduced to their causes, i.e. bulk, figure, and motion of parts.[1]

18. A piece of *manna* of a sensible bulk is able to produce in us the *idea* of a round or square figure; and by being removed from one place to another, the *idea* of motion. This *idea* of motion represents it as it really is in the *manna* moving; a circle or square are the same, whether in *idea* or existence, in the mind or in the *manna*; and this, both *motion and figure, are really in the manna*, whether we take notice of them or no: this everybody is ready to agree to. Besides, *manna*, by the bulk, figure, texture, and motion of its parts, has a power to produce the sensations of sickness, and sometimes of acute pains or gripings in us. That these *ideas of sickness and pain are not in the* manna, but effects of its operations on us, and are nowhere when we feel them not: this also everyone readily agrees to. And yet men are hardly to be brought to think that *sweetness and whiteness are not really in* manna, which are but the effects of the operations of *manna*, by the motion, size, and figure of its particles, on the eyes and palate, as the pain and sickness caused by *manna* are confessedly nothing but the effects of its operations on the stomach and guts, by the size, motion, and figure of its insensible parts (for by nothing else can a body operate, as has been proved): as if it could not operate on the eyes and palate and thereby produce in the mind particular distinct *ideas* which in itself it has not, as well as we allow it can operate on the guts and stomach and thereby produce distinct *ideas* which in itself it has not. These *ideas* being all effects of the operations of *manna* on several parts of our bodies by the size, figure, number, and motion of its parts, why those produced by the eyes and palate should rather be thought to be really in the *manna* than those produced by the stomach and guts; or why the pain and sickness, *ideas* that are the effects of *manna*, should be thought to be nowhere, when they are not felt: and yet the sweetness and whiteness, effects of the same *manna* on other parts of the body by ways equally as unknown, should be thought to exist in the *manna*, when they are not seen nor tasted, would need some reason to explain.

19. Let us consider the red and white colours in *porphyry*. Hinder light but from striking on it, and its colours vanish: it no longer produces any such *ideas* in us; upon the return of light it

produces these appearances on us again. Can anyone think any real alterations are made in the *porphyry* by the presence or absence of light; and that those *ideas* of whiteness and redness are really in *porphyry* in the light, when it is plain *it has no colour in the dark*? It has, indeed, such a configuration of particles, both night and day, as are apt, by the rays of light rebounding from some parts of that hard stone, to produce in us the *idea* of redness, and from others the *idea* of whiteness; but whiteness or redness are not in it at any time, but such a texture that hath the power to produce such a sensation in us.

20.   Pound an almond, and the clear white *colour* will be altered into a dirty one, and the sweet *taste* into an oily one. What real alteration can the beating of the pestle make in any body, but an alteration of the *texture* of it?

21.   *Ideas* being thus distinguished and understood, we may be able to give an account how the same water, at the same time, may produce the *idea* of cold by one hand and of heat by the other, whereas it is impossible that the same water, if those *ideas* were really in it, should at the same time be both hot and cold. For if we imagine *warmth* as it is *in our hands* to be *nothing but a certain sort and degree of motion in the minute particles of our nerves, or animal spirits,* we may understand how it is possible that the same water may at the same time produce the sensation of heat in one hand and cold in the other; which yet figure never does, that never producing the *idea* of a square by one hand which has produced the *idea* of a globe by another. But if the sensation of heat and cold be nothing but the increase or diminution of the motion of the minute parts of our bodies, caused by the corpuscles of any other body, it is easy to be understood that, if that motion be greater in one hand than in the other, if a body be applied to the two hands, which has in its minute particles a greater motion than in those of one of the hands, and a less than in those of the other, it will increase the motion of the one hand and lessen it in the other, and so cause the different sensations of heat and cold that depend thereon.

22.   I have in what just goes before been engaged in physical inquiries a little further than perhaps I intended. But, it being necessary to make the nature of sensation a little understood; and to make the *difference between the qualities in bodies, and the* ideas *produced by them in the*

mind, to be distinctly conceived, without which it were impossible to discourse intelligibly of them: I hope I shall be pardoned this little excursion into natural philosophy, it being necessary in our present inquiry to distinguish the *primary* and *real qualities* of bodies, which are always in them (viz. solidity, extension, figure, number, and motion or rest; and are sometimes perceived by us, viz. when the bodies they are in are big enough singly to be discerned), from those *secondary* and *imputed qualities*, which are but the powers of several combinations of those primary ones, when they operate without being distinctly discerned; whereby we also may come to know what *ideas* are, and what are not, resemblances of something really existing in the bodies we denominate from them.

23.   The *qualities*, then, that are in *bodies*, rightly considered, are of *three sorts*:

First, The *bulk, figure, number, situation,* and *motion or rest* of their solid parts. Those are in them, whether we perceive them or no; and when they are of that size that we can discover them, we have by these an *idea* of the thing as it is in itself, as is plain in artificial things. These I call *primary qualities.*

Secondly, The *power* that is in any body, by reason of *its* insensible *primary qualities*, to operate after a peculiar manner on any of our senses, and thereby *produce in us* the *different ideas* of several colours, sounds, smells, tastes, etc. These are usually called sensible qualities.

Thirdly, The *power* that is in any body, *by* reason of the particular constitution of *its primary qualities, to* make such a *change in the bulk, figure, texture, and motion of another body,* as to make it operate on our senses differently from what it did before. Thus the sun has a power to make wax white, and fire to make lead fluid. These *are* usually called powers.

The first of these, as has been said, I think may be properly called *real, original,* or *primary qualities,* because they are in the things themselves, whether they are perceived or no; and upon their different modifications it is that the secondary qualities depend.

The other two are only powers to act differently upon other things, which powers result from the different modifications of those primary qualities.

24.   But though *these two latter sorts of qualities are powers barely,* and nothing but powers relating to several other bodies and resulting

from the different modifications of the original qualities, yet they are generally otherwise thought of. For *the second sort*, viz. the powers to produce several *ideas* in us by our senses, *are looked upon as real qualities in the things* thus affecting us; but *the third sort are called and esteemed barely powers*, v.g. the *idea* of heat or light which we receive by our eyes or touch from the sun are commonly thought *real qualities* existing in the sun and something more than mere powers in it. But when we consider the sun in reference to wax, which it melts or blanches, we look upon the whiteness and softness produced in the wax not as qualities in the sun but effects produced by *powers* in it: whereas, if rightly considered, these qualities of light and warmth, which are perceptions in me when I am warmed or enlightened by the sun, are no otherwise in the sun than the changes, made in the wax when it is blanched or melted, are in the sun. They are all of them equally powers in the sun, depending on its primary qualities; whereby it is able in the one case so to alter the bulk, figure, texture, or motion of some of the insensible parts of my eyes or hands as thereby to produce in me the *idea* of light or heat; and in the other, it is able so to alter the bulk, figure, texture, or motion of the insensible parts of the wax, as to make them fit to produce in me the distinct *ideas* of white and fluid.

25. The reason *why the one are ordinarily taken for real qualities and the other only for bare powers seems* to be because the *ideas* we have of distinct colours, sounds, etc., containing nothing at all in them of bulk, figure, or motion, we are apt to think them the effects of these primary qualities which appear not to our senses to operate in their production, and with which they have not any apparent congruity or conceivable connexion. Hence it is that we are so forward to imagine that those *ideas* are the resemblances of something really existing in the objects themselves, since sensation discovers nothing of bulk, figure, or motion of parts in their production, nor can reason show how bodies by their bulk, figure, and motion should produce in the mind the *ideas* of blue or yellow, etc. But in the other case, in the operations of bodies changing the qualities one of another, we plainly discover that the quality produced hath commonly no resemblance with anything in the thing producing it; wherefore we look on it as a bare effect of power. For, though receiving the *idea* of heat or light from the sun,

we are apt to think it is a perception and resemblance of such a quality in the sun: yet when we see wax or a fair face receive change of colour from the sun, we cannot imagine that to be the reception or resemblance of anything in the sun, because we find not those different colours in the sun itself. For, our senses being able to observe a likeness or unlikeness of sensible qualities in two different external objects, we forwardly enough conclude the production of any sensible quality in any subject to be an effect of bare power, and not the communication of any quality which was really in the efficient, when we find no such sensible quality in the thing that produced it. But our senses not being able to discover any unlikeness between the *idea* produced in us and the quality of the object producing it, we are apt to imagine that our *ideas* are resemblances of something in the objects, and not the effects of certain powers placed in the modification of their primary qualities, with which primary qualities the *ideas* produced in us have no resemblance.

26. To conclude, beside those beforementioned *primary qualities* in bodies, viz. bulk, figure, extension, number, and motion of their solid parts: all the rest, whereby we take notice of bodies and distinguish them one from another, are nothing else but several powers in them, depending on those primary qualities; whereby they are fitted, either by immediately operating on our bodies to produce several different *ideas* in us, or else, by operating on other bodies, so to change their primary qualities as to render them capable of producing *ideas* in us different from what before they did. The former of these, I think, may be called *secondary qualities immediately perceivable*, the latter *secondary qualities, mediately perceivable*.

Chapter XXIII
OF OUR COMPLEX IDEAS OF SUBSTANCES
1. The mind being, as I have declared, furnished with a great number of the simple *ideas* conveyed in by the *senses*, as they are found in exterior things, or by *reflection* on its own operations, takes notice also that a certain number of these simple *ideas* go constantly together; which, being presumed to belong to one thing, and words being suited to common apprehensions and made use of for quick dispatch, are called, so united in one subject, by one name; which, by inadvertency, we are apt afterward to talk of and

consider as one simple *idea*, which indeed is a complication of many *ideas* together: because, as I have said, not imagining how these simple *ideas* can subsist by themselves, we accustom ourselves to suppose some *substratum* wherein they do subsist, and from which they do result; which therefore we call *substance*.

2. So that if anyone will examine himself concerning his *notion of pure substance in general*, he will find he has no other *idea* of it at all, but only a supposition of he knows not what support of such qualities which are capable of producing simple *ideas* in us; which qualities are commonly called accidents. If anyone should be asked what is the subject wherein colour or weight inheres, he would have nothing to say but, the solid extended parts; and if he were demanded what is it that that solidity and extension adhere in, he would not be in a much better case than the *Indian* before-mentioned who, saying that the world was supported by a great elephant, was asked what the elephant rested on, to which his answer was, a great tortoise; but being again pressed to know what gave support to the broad-backed tortoise, replied, something, he knew not what. And thus here, as in all other cases where we use words without having clear and distinct *ideas*, we talk like children who, being questioned what such a thing is which they know not, readily give this satisfactory answer, that it is *something*; which in truth signifies no more, when so used, either by children or men, but that they know not what, and that the thing they pretend to know and talk of is what they have no distinct *idea* of at all, and so are perfectly ignorant of it and in the dark. The *idea* then we have, to which we give the general name substance, being nothing but the supposed, but unknown, support of those qualities we find existing, which we imagine cannot subsist *sine re substante*, without something to support them, we call that support *substantia*; which, according to the true import of the word, is, in plain *English*, *standing under* or *upholding*.

3. An obscure and relative *idea* of substance in general being thus made, we come to have the *ideas of particular sorts of substances* by collecting such combinations of simple *ideas* as are, by experience and observation of men's senses, taken notice of to exist together, and are therefore supposed to flow from the particular internal constitution or unknown essence of that substance. Thus we come to have the *ideas* of a man, horse,

gold, water, etc.; of which substances, whether anyone has any other clear *idea*, further than of certain simple *ideas* co-existent together, I appeal to everyone's own experience. It is the ordinary qualities observable in iron, or a diamond, put together that make the true complex *idea* of those substances, which a smith or a jeweller commonly knows better than a philosopher; who, whatever substantial forms he may talk of, has no other *idea* of those substances than what is framed by a collection of those simple *ideas* which are to be found in them: only we must take notice that our complex *ideas* of substances, besides all these simple *ideas* they are made up of, have always the confused *idea* of *something* to which they belong, and in which they subsist; and therefore when we speak of any sort of substance, we say it is a *thing* having such or such qualities: as body is a *thing* that is extended, figured, and capable of motion; a spirit, a *thing* capable of thinking; and so hardness, friability, and power to draw iron, we say, are qualities to be found in a loadstone. These and the like fashions of speaking intimate that the substance is supposed always *something* besides the extension, figure, solidity, motion, thinking or other observable *ideas*, though we know not what it is.

4. Hence, when we talk or think of any particular sort of corporeal substances, as *horse*, *stone*, etc., though the *idea* we have of either of them be but the complication or collection of those several simple *ideas* of sensible qualities, which we use to find united in the thing called *horse* or *stone*: yet, because we cannot conceive how they should subsist alone, nor one in another, we suppose them existing in and supported by some common subject; *which support we denote by the name substance*, though it be certain we have no clear or distinct *idea* of that *thing* we suppose a support.

5. The same thing happens concerning the operations of the mind, viz. thinking, reasoning, fearing, etc., which we concluding not to subsist of themselves, nor apprehending how they can belong to body or be produced by it, we are apt to think these the actions of some other *substance*, which we call *spirit*; whereby yet it is evident that, having no other *idea* or notion of matter but *something* wherein those many sensible qualities which affect our senses do subsist, by supposing a substance wherein *thinking, knowing, doubting*, and a power of moving, etc., do

subsist, *we have as clear a notion of the substance of spirit as we have of body*: the one being supposed to be (without knowing what it is) the *substratum* to those simple *ideas* we have from without; and the other supposed (with a like ignorance of what it is) to be the *substratum* to those operations which we experiment in ourselves within. It is plain then that the *idea* of corporeal *substance* in matter is as remote from our conceptions and apprehensions as that of spiritual *substance*, or *spirit*; and therefore, from our not having any notion of the *substance* of spirit, we can no more conclude its non-existence than we can, for the same reason, deny the existence of body: it being as rational to affirm there is no body, because we have no clear and distinct *idea* of the *substance* of matter, as to say there is no spirit, because we have no clear and distinct *idea* of the *substance* of a spirit.

6. Whatever therefore be the secret and abstract nature of *substance* in general, all *the* ideas *we have of particular distinct sorts of substances* are nothing but several combinations of simple *ideas*, co-existing in such, though unknown, cause of their union as makes the whole subsist of itself. It is by such combinations of simple *ideas* and nothing else that we represent particular sorts of *substances* to ourselves; such are the *ideas* we have of their several species in our minds; and such only do we, by their specific names, signify to others, v.g. *man, horse, sun, water, iron*; upon hearing which words, everyone who understands the language frames in his mind a combination of those several simple *ideas* which he has usually observed or fancied to exist together under that denomination, all which he supposes to rest in and be, as it were, adherent to that unknown common subject which inheres not in anything else. Though in the meantime it be manifest, and everyone upon inquiry into his own thoughts will find, that he has no other *idea* of any *substance*, v.g., let it be *gold, horse, iron, man, vitriol, bread*, but what he has barely of those sensible qualities which he supposes to inhere, with a supposition of such a *substratum* as gives, as it were, a support to those qualities or simple *ideas* which he has observed to exist united together. Thus, the *idea* of the *sun*, what is it but an aggregate of those several simple *ideas*, bright, hot, roundish, having a constant regular motion, at a certain distance from us, and perhaps some other: as he who thinks and discourses of the *sun* has been more or less accurate in observing those sensible qualities, *ideas*, or properties, which are in that thing which he calls the *sun*.

7. For he has the perfectest *idea* of any of the particular sorts of *substances*, who has gathered and put together most of those simple *ideas* which do exist in it; among which are to be reckoned its active powers and passive capacities, which, though not simple *ideas*, yet in this respect, for brevity's sake, may conveniently enough be reckoned amongst them. Thus, the power of drawing iron is one of the *ideas* of the complex one of that substance we call a *loadstone*; and a power to be so drawn is a part of the complex one we call *iron*: which powers pass for inherent qualities in those subjects. Because every *substance*, being as apt, by the powers we observe in it, to change some sensible qualities in other subjects as it is to produce in us those simple *ideas* which we receive immediately from it, does, by those new sensible qualities introduced into other subjects, discover to us those powers which do thereby mediately affect our senses, as regularly as its sensible qualities do it immediately: v.g. we immediately by our senses perceive in *fire* its heat and colour, which are, if rightly considered, nothing but powers in it to produce those *ideas* in us; we also by our senses perceive the colour and brittleness of *charcoal*, whereby we come by the knowledge of another power in fire, which it has to change the colour and consistency of wood. By the former, fire immediately, by the latter, it mediately discovers to us these several powers; which therefore we look upon to be a part of the qualities of fire, and so make them a part of the complex *idea* of it. For all those powers that we take cognizance of terminating only in the alteration of some sensible qualities in those subjects on which they operate, and so making them exhibit to us new sensible *ideas*, therefore it is that I have reckoned these powers amongst the simple *ideas* which make the complex ones of the sorts of *substances*, though these powers considered in themselves are truly complex *ideas*. And in this looser sense, I crave leave to be understood when I name any of these *potentialities amongst the simple ideas*, which we recollect in our minds when we think *of particular substances*. For the powers that are severally in them are necessary to be considered, if we will have true distinct notions of the several sorts of substances.

8. Nor are we to wonder that *powers make a great part of our complex* ideas *of substances*, since

their secondary qualities are those which in most of them serve principally to distinguish substances one from another, and commonly make a considerable part of the complex *idea* of the several sorts of them. For, our senses failing us in the discovery of the bulk, texture, and figure of the minute parts of bodies, on which their real constitutions and differences depend, we are fain to make use of their secondary qualities as the characteristical notes and marks whereby to frame *ideas* of them in our minds and distinguish them one from another: all which secondary qualities, as has been shown, are nothing but bare powers. For the colour and taste of *opium* are, as well as its soporific or anodyne virtues, mere powers, depending on its primary qualities, whereby it is fitted to produce different operations on different parts of our bodies.

9.   The ideas *that make our complex ones of corporeal substances* are of these three sorts. *First*, the *ideas* of the primary qualities of things, which are discovered by our senses, and are in them even when we perceive them not; such are the bulk, figure, number, situation, and motion of the parts of bodies, which are really in them, whether we take notice of them or no. *Secondly*, the sensible secondary qualities, which, depending on these, are nothing but the powers those substances have to produce several *ideas* in us by our senses; which *ideas* are not in the things themselves otherwise than as anything is in its cause. *Thirdly*, the aptness we consider in any substance to give or receive such alterations of primary qualities, as that the substance so altered should produce in us different *ideas* from what it did before: these are called active and passive powers; all which powers, as far as we have any notice or notion of them, terminate only in sensible simple *ideas*. For whatever alteration a *loadstone* has the power to make in the minute particles of iron, we should have no notion of any power it had at all to operate on iron, did not its sensible motion discover it; and I doubt not but there are a thousand changes that bodies we daily handle have a power to cause in one another, which we never suspect, because they never appear in sensible effects.

10.   *Powers* therefore justly make a great part *of our complex* ideas *of substances*. He that will examine his complex *idea* of gold will find several of its *ideas* that make it up to be only powers, as the power of being melted, but of not

spending itself in the fire, of being dissolved in *aqua regia*, are *ideas* as necessary to make up our complex *idea* of gold as its colour and weight; which, if duly considered, are also nothing but different powers. For, to speak truly, yellowness is not actually in gold, but is a power in gold to produce that *idea* in us by our eyes, when placed in a due light; and the heat, which we cannot leave out of our *idea* of the sun, is no more really in the sun, than the white colour it introduces into wax. These are both equally powers in the sun, operating, by the motion and figure of its insensible parts, so on a man as to make him have the *idea* of heat; and so on wax, as to make it capable to produce in a man the *idea* of white.

11.   Had we senses acute enough to discern the minute particles of bodies and the real constitution on which their sensible qualities depend, I doubt not but they would produce quite different *ideas* in us; and that which is now the yellow colour of gold would then disappear, and instead of it we should see an admirable texture of parts, of a certain size and figure. This microscopes plainly discover to us; for what to our naked eyes produces a certain colour is, by thus augmenting the acuteness of our senses, discovered to be quite a different thing; and the thus altering, as it were, the proportion of the bulk of the minute parts of a coloured object to our usual sight produces different *ideas* from what it did before. Thus sand, or pounded glass, which is opaque and white to the naked eye, is pellucid in a microscope; and a hair seen this way loses its former colour and is in a great measure pellucid, with a mixture of some bright sparkling colours, such as appear from the refraction of diamonds and other pellucid bodies. Blood to the naked eye appears all red, but by a good microscope, wherein its lesser parts appear, shows only some few globules of red, swimming in a pellucid liquor; and how these red globules would appear, if glasses could be found that yet could magnify them a thousand or ten thousand times more, is uncertain. [. . .]

Note

1   In this paragraph there is clearly oscillation between denying that secondary qualities belong to objects and identifying them with the causal powers of the objects' primary qualities.

15

Gottfried Wilhelm von Leibniz, *Monadology*

Introduction

In Bertrand Russell's opinion, it was the "lamentable waste of time in the endeavour to please" his princely patrons that prevented the German polymath, Gottfried Wilhelm von Leibniz (1646–1716), from writing an extensive exposition of his metaphysical system.[1] On a more generous view, the reason was Leibniz's "unachievable ambition to excel in every sphere of intellectual and political activity."[2] But while Leibniz left no comprehensive, systematic account of his thought, he did, in his *Monadologie* of 1714, provide a relatively complete statement of his views. The work defies useful summary, since it is itself a useful summary, bold and clear, of one of the most complex and ambitious of metaphysical systems. Most of Leibniz's distinctive theses – the Principles of Sufficient Reason and of the Identity of Indiscernibles, for example – are all there. More valuable then, by way of a preamble, than an attempt at summary is to place Leibniz's position in relation to those of his predecessors, above all Spinoza (see III.13 above).

Leibniz was a critical admirer of the three seventeenth-century philosophers represented in the preceding three chapters. An aim that Leibniz

From Gottfried Wilhelm Leibniz, *Philosophical Writings*, ed. G. H. R. Parkinson, trans. M. Morris and G. H. R. Parkinson. London: J. M. Dent & Sons, 1973, pp. 179–94 (asterisked note is the translators').

shared with Spinoza and Locke was to develop a philosophy that would not entail Descartes's dualistic dichotomy between mind and body. Against Locke, however, Leibniz sided with the two rationalists in holding up the self-evident truths of reason and their logical implications as the only proper objects of knowledge. (For Leibniz's defense of innate ideas against Locke's insistence that all knowledge derives from experience, see II.9.) Leibniz regarded the work of Spinoza, whom he journeyed to the Hague in November 1676 to visit, through the lens of the widespread and certainly mistaken view that it was a "brutal" materialism whose references to God were little more than decorative.[3]

In fact, there are deep similarities between Spinoza's and Leibniz's metaphysics: and this is so despite some apparently radical differences. Whereas for the Dutchman there is just one substance ("God or Nature"), for the German reality is composed of countless simple substances ("monads"). For Spinoza, the idea of God as a creator of independent substances is absurd, while for Leibniz that is precisely what God is. Whereas, for Spinoza, there are no contingencies, Leibniz distinguishes between the necessary truths of reason and contingent truths. And while Spinoza advocated a liberal, secular, democratic society, Leibniz remained a stalwart defender of theocracy.

Reflection on what Leibniz intends by the distinction between necessary and contingent truths, however, soon begins to soften the contrast between the two thinkers. For Leibniz, the truth "that, say, Adam ate the apple is, as it were, only contingent for us, with our limited understanding." Had we a "complete concept" of Adam, in the way God does, we would recognize that eating the apple belonged to that concept, so that someone who refused Eve's offer, however like Adam in other respects, could not have been Adam. Moreover, though lacking "complete concepts," we can reflect that everything that happens does so in accordance with a necessity to which God, by his nature, is subject – namely to determine everything "for the best." This view, one almost identical to Spinoza's, also underwrites his theodicy, his explanation for the existence of evil (see IV.13).

Furthermore, while Spinoza and Leibniz disagree about the number of substances, their concepts of substance are nevertheless similar. A substance is "independent," so that it cannot be causally affected by anything outside it. In Leibniz's famous remark, "monads have no windows, by which anything could come in or go out" (§7 below). As such, the development of any monadic substance must be due to something internal to it, which Leibniz calls "appetition." "In a manner of speaking," remarks one commentator, "monads were gonads."[4]

Spinoza and Leibniz's disagreement over the number of substances – one *versus* an infinity – is due to the following difference. Spinozan substance is independent *tout court*, while for Leibniz – here following Descartes – a (simple) substance is something that "does not depend on anything except . . . God."[5] Nor is this a disagreement that prevents Leibniz's conception of reality being almost as holistic as Spinoza's. While there really are distinct monads, not just "modes" of a single substance, each of these "mirrors" or "expresses" all other monads in a grand system of "pre-established harmony." Were we to possess divine knowledge, we could "read off" from our knowledge of each monad how everything else in the universe must be.

Leibniz cannot subscribe, in so many words, to Spinoza's alternative to Cartesian dualism, for this requires treating mind and body as merely different "attributes" of God/Nature. Instead, Leibniz argues that matter does not exist at the level of ultimate reality, being merely a "chimera" constructed out of distinct "incorporeal" monads. At a less deep level, however, one may still speak of bodies in the same unobjectionable way one speaks of flocks or armies, even though these have no existence beyond their individual members. But it would remain a mistake to suppose, with Descartes, that souls and bodies "interact." Rather, there is "pre-established harmony" between mental and bodily events: in particular between events in a given mind and events in a given body where the harmony is sufficiently obvious to permit speaking – at the conventional level – of the body in question as that mind's, or person's, body. *My* body, that is, is an aggregate of events that are "mirrored" with special vivacity and clarity in the mental events that take place in the monad which *I* am.

Leibniz's philosophy, like Spinoza's, is metaphysics on the grand scale; and it became a major influence on eighteenth-century philosophy. It is unsurprising, therefore, that Leibniz was also to become (as we shall see in III.17 below) one of the main targets of Immanuel Kant's attack on "dogmatic" and "speculative" metaphysics.

Notes

1   Quoted in J. Cottingham, *The Rationalists*, Oxford: Oxford University Press, 1990, p. 26.
2   G. MacDonald Ross, *Leibniz*, Oxford: Oxford University Press, 1984, p. 26.
3   See M. Stewart, *The Courtier and the Heretic: Leibniz, Spinoza, and the Fate of the Modern World*, New York: W. W. Norton, 2006.
4   Ross, *Leibniz*, p. 107.
5   See *Metaphysical Consequences of the Principle of Reason*, also in *Leibniz's Philosophical Writings*, p. 175.

Leibniz, *Monadology*

1.   The *monad*, of which we shall speak here, is nothing but a simple substance which enters into compounds; *simple*, that is to say, without parts.

2.   And there must be simple substances, because there are compounds; for the compound is nothing but a collection or *aggregatum* of simples.

3.   Now where there are no parts, there neither extension, nor shape, nor divisibility is possible.

And these monads are the true atoms of nature and, in a word, the elements of things.

4. Moreover, there is no fear of dissolution, and there is no conceivable way in which a simple substance could perish in the course of nature.

5. For the same reason there is no way in which a simple substance could begin in the course of nature, since it cannot be formed by means of compounding.

6. Thus it may be said that monads can only begin and end all at once, that is to say they can only begin by creation and end by annihilation, whereas what is compound begins or ends by parts.

7. There is also no means of explaining how a monad can be altered or changed within itself by any other created thing, since it is impossible to displace anything in it or to conceive of the possibility of any internal motion being started, directed, increased, or diminished within it, as can occur in compounds, where change among the parts takes place. Monads have no windows, by which anything could come in or go out. Accidents cannot become detached, or wander about outside substances, as the 'sensible species' of the Scholastics used to do.[1] Thus neither substance nor accident can enter a monad from without.

8. Monads, however, must have some qualities, otherwise they would not be beings at all. And if simple substances did not differ by their qualities, there would be no way of perceiving any change in things, since what is in the compound can only come from its simple ingredients; and if monads were without qualities, they would be indistinguishable from one another, since they do not differ in quantity either. And consequently, supposing space to be a plenum, each place would always only receive, when motion occurred, the equivalent of what it had before; and one state of things would be indistinguishable from another.

9. Indeed, every monad must be different from every other. For there are never in nature two beings which are precisely alike, and in which it is not possible to find some difference which is internal, or based on some intrinsic denomination.[2]

10. I also take it as granted that every created thing, and consequently the created monad also, is subject to change, and indeed that this change is continual in each one.

11. It follows from what we have just said, that the natural changes of monads come from an *internal principle*, since an external cause would be unable to influence their inner being.

12. But besides the principle of change, there must be *differentiation within that which changes*, to constitute as it were the specification and variety of simple substances.

13. This differentiation must involve a plurality within the unity or the simple. For since very natural change takes place by degrees, something changes, and something remains; and consequently the simple must contain a large number of affections and relations, although it has no parts.

14. The passing state, which involves and represents a plurality within the unity or simple substance, is nothing other than what is called *perception*, which must be carefully distinguished from apperception or consciousness, as will appear presently. And herein lies the great mistake of the Cartesians, that they took no account of perceptions which are not apperceived. It is this also which made them believe that minds alone are monads, and that neither brutes nor other entelechies [see §18] have souls. For the same reason also they fell into the common error of confusing death, properly so called, with a prolonged unconsciousness; and this made them favour the Scholastic conviction that souls are entirely separate from bodies, and even confirmed some ill-balanced minds in the opinion that souls are mortal.

15. The action of the internal principle which produces the change or passage from one perception to another may be called *appetition*; it is true that the appetite cannot always attain completely the whole of the perception towards which it tends, but it always attains something of it, and arrives at new perceptions.

16. We ourselves experience plurality within a simple substance, when we find that the least thought which we apperceive involves a variety in its object. So everyone who acknowledges that the soul is a simple substance must acknowledge this plurality within the monad; and M. [Pierre] Bayle should not have found any difficulty in this, as he does in his *Dictionary*, in the article 'Rorarius'.

17. We are moreover obliged to confess that *perception* and that which depends on it *cannot be explained mechanically*, that is to say by figures and motions. Suppose that there were a machine

so constructed as to produce thought, feeling, and perception, we could imagine it increased in size while retaining the same proportions, so that one could enter as one might a mill. On going inside we should only see the parts impinging upon one another; we should not see anything which would explain a perception. The explanation of perception must therefore be sought in a simple substance, and not in a compound or in a machine. Moreover, there is nothing else whatever to be found in the simple substance except just this, viz. perceptions and their changes. It is in this alone that all the *internal actions* of simple substances must consist.

18. We may give the name *entelechies* to all created simple substances or monads. For they have in themselves a certain perfection (ἔχουσι τὸ ἐντελές), there is a self-sufficiency (αὐτάρκεια) in them which makes the sources of their internal actions – incorporeal automata, if I may so put it.

19. If we wish to give the name 'soul' to everything which has *perceptions* and *appetites* in the general sense I have just explained, all created simple substances or monads might be called souls; but as feeling is something more than a simple perception, I agree that the general name – monad or entelechy – should be enough for simple substances which have no more than that, and that those only should be called souls, whose perception is more distinct and is accompanied by memory.

20. For we experience within ourselves a state, in which we remember nothing and have no distinguishable perception; as when we fall into a swoon, or when we are overcome by a deep dreamless sleep. In this state the soul does not sensibly differ from a simple monad; but as this state is not permanent, and as the soul emerges from it, the soul is something more.

21. And it does not follow that when in that state the simple substance has no perception at all. Indeed, that is not possible for the above reasons; for it cannot perish, nor can it subsist without some affection in some way, and this affection is nothing but its perception. But when there are a very great number of small perceptions with nothing to distinguish them, we are stupefied, just as it happens that if we go on turning round in the same direction several times running, we become giddy and go into a swoon, so that we can no longer distinguish anything at

all. And death can throw animals* into this state for a time.

22. And as every state of a simple substance is a natural consequence of its preceding state, so that the present state of it is big with the future,

23. and since, on awakening from our stupor, we apperceive our perceptions, it must be the case that we received the perceptions the moment before, though we did not apperceive them; for a perception cannot arise in the course of nature except from another perception, as one motion can only arise in the course of nature from another motion.

24. From this we see that if we had nothing in our perceptions to distinguish them, nothing so to speak heightened and of a keener savour, we should always be in this stupor. And this is the state of bare monads.

25. We see also that Nature has given heightened perceptions to animals from the care she has taken to provide them with organs which collect several rays of light, or several undulations of the air, so as to make these more effective by being united. There is something of the kind in smell, taste, and touch, and perhaps in many other senses which are unknown to us. I will explain later how what occurs in the soul represents what takes place in the organs.

26. Memory provides souls with a kind of *consecutiveness*, which copies reason but must be distinguished from it. What I mean is this: we often see that animals, when they have a perception of something which strikes them, and of which they had a similar perception previously, are led, by the representation of their memory, to expect what was united with his perception before, and are moved to feelings similar to those they had before. For example, when dogs are shown a stick, they remember the pain which it has caused them in the past, and howl or run away.

27. The powerful imagination, which strikes and moves them, arises either from the magnitude or from the number of the preceding perceptions. For often a vivid impression has in a moment the effect of long *habit*, or of many moderate perceptions oft repeated.

---

* By 'animals' Leibniz means all living creatures up to and including man. The lower animals as distinguished from man, he refers to as 'brutes'.

28. Men act like brutes in so far as the sequences of their perceptions arise through the principle of memory only, like those empirical physicians who have mere practice without theory. We are all merely empiricists as regards three-fourths of our actions. For example, when we expect it to be day tomorrow, we are behaving as empiricists, because until now it has always happened thus. The astronomer alone knows this by reason.

29. But it is the knowledge of necessary and eternal truths which distinguishes us from mere animals, and gives us *reason* and the sciences, raising us to knowledge of ourselves and God. It is this in us which we call the rational soul or *mind*.

30. Further it is by the knowledge of necessary truths and by their abstractions that we are raised to *acts of reflection*, which make us think of what is called the *self*, and consider that this or that is within *us*. And it is thus that in thinking of ourselves, we think of being, of substance, of the simple and the compound, of the immaterial and of God himself, conceiving that what is limited in us, in him is limitless. And these acts of reflection provide the chief objects of our reasonings.

31. Our reasonings are based on two great principles: the *principle of contradiction*, by virtue of which we judge to be false that which involves a contradiction, and true that which is opposed or contradictory to the false;

32. and the *principle of sufficient reason*, by virtue of which we consider that no fact can be real or existing and no proposition can be true unless there is a sufficient reason, why it should be thus and not otherwise, even though in most cases these reasons cannot be known to us.

33. There are also two kinds of *truths*: truths of *reasoning* and truths of *fact*. Truths of reasoning are necessary and their opposite is impossible; those of fact are contingent and their opposite is possible. When a truth is necessary, the reason for it can be found by analysis, that is, by resolving it into simpler ideas and truths until the primary ones are reached.

34. It is in this way that in mathematics speculative *theorems* and practical *canons* are reduced by analysis to *definitions*, *axioms*, and *postulates*.

35. Finally there are simple ideas of which no definition can be given; there are also axioms and postulates, or in a word *primary principles*, which cannot be proved and have no need of proof. These are *identical propositions*, whose opposite contains an express contradiction.[3]

36. But a *sufficient reason* also must be found in the case of *contingent truths* or *truths of fact*; that is to say, in the case of the series of things spread over the universe of created things; here resolution into particular reasons might go on into endless detail on account of the immense variety of things in nature and the division of bodies *ad infinitum*. There are an infinite number of shapes and motions, both present and past, which enter into the efficient cause of my present writing; and there are an infinite number of minute inclinations and dispositions of my soul, both present and past, which enter into its final cause.

37. And as all this differentiation involves only other prior or more differentiated contingent things, all of which need a similar analysis to explain them, we are no further advanced: and the sufficient or ultimate reason must be outside the succession or *series* of this differentiation of contingent things, however infinite it may be.

38. This is why the ultimate reason of things must lie in a necessary substance, in which the differentiation of the changes only exists eminently as in their source; and this is what we call *God*.

39. Now since this substance is a sufficient reason of all this differentiation, which it itself likewise all connected, *there is only one God, and this God is enough*.

40. We may also judge that since this Supreme Substance, who is unique, universal, and necessary, has nothing outside himself independent of himself, and is a simple consequence of possible being, he must be incapable of being limited, and must contain just as much reality as is possible.

41. Whence it follows that God is absolutely perfect, since *perfection* is nothing but magnitude of positive reality, in the strict sense, setting aside the limits or bounds in things which are limited. And there, where there are no bounds, that is to say in God, perfection is absolutely infinite.

42. It follows also that created things owe their perfections to the influence of God, but that they owe their imperfections to their own nature, which is incapable of being without limits. For it is in this that they are distinguished from God.

43. It is true likewise, that in God is the source not only of existences but also of essences,

in so far as they are real, that is of all the reality there is in possibility. This is because the Understanding of God is the region of eternal truths or of the ideas on which they depend, and because without him there would be nothing real in the possibilities – not only nothing existent, but also nothing possible.

44.   For if there is a reality in essences or possibilities, or indeed in eternal truths, this reality must be founded on something existent and actual; and consequently on the existence of the Necessary Being in whom essence involves existence, or in whom it is enough to be possible in order to be actual.

45.   Thus God alone (or the Necessary Being) has the privilege that he must exist if he is possible. And as nothing can prevent the possibility of that which has no limits, no negation, and consequently no contradiction, this alone is sufficient for us to know the existence of God *a priori*. We have proved it also by the reality of eternal truths. And we have now just proved it *a posteriori* also, since there exist contingent beings, which can only have their ultimate or sufficient reason the Necessary Being, who has the reason for his existence in himself.

46.   We must not, however, imagine, as some do, that because the eternal truths are dependent on God, they are therefore arbitrary and depend on his will, as Descartes, and after him M. [Pierre] Poiret, seem to have thought. This is true only of contingent truths, whose principle is *fitness* or the choice of *the best*; whereas necessary truths depend solely on his understanding, of which they are the internal object.

47.   Thus God alone is the primary Unity, or original simple substance, from which all monads, created and derived, are produced, and are born, so to speak, by continual fulgurations of the Divinity from moment to moment, limited by the receptivity of the created being, which is of its essence limited.

48.   There is in God *power*, which is the source of everything, *knowledge*, which contains the differentiation of the ideas, and finally *will*, which causes changes and productions according to the principle of what is best. And these correspond to what provides the ground or basis in created monads, the perceptive faculty and the appetitive faculty. But in God these attributes are absolutely infinite or perfect, while in created monads or in *entelechies* (or *perfectihabiae*, as

Hermolaus Barbarus translated this word) there are only limitations of them, in proportion to the perfection there is in the monad.

49.   The created thing is said to *act* outwardly in so far as it has perfection, and to be *passively affected* by another in so far as it is imperfect. Thus *activity* is attributed to the monad in so far as it has distinct perceptions, and *passivity* in so far as it has confused perceptions.

50.   And one created thing is more perfect than another when there is found in it that which explains *a priori* what happens in the other; and it is because of this that we say that it acts upon the other.

51.   But in simple substances the influence of one monad over another is *ideal* only; it can have its effect only through the intervention of God, inasmuch as in the ideas of God a monad rightly demands that God, in regulating the rest from the beginning of things, should have regard to itself. For since it is impossible for a created monad to have a physical influence on the inner nature of another, this is the only way in which one can be dependent on another.

52.   And this is why actions and passions are mutual between created things. For when God compares two simple substances he finds in each reasons which oblige him to adapt the other to it, and consequently what is active in certain aspects is passive from another point of view: *active* in so far as what is distinctly known in it explains what occurs in another, and *passive* in so far as the reason for what occurs in it is found in what is distinctly known in another.

53.   Now as there is an infinite number of possible universes in the ideas of God, and as only one can exist, there must be a sufficient reason for God's choice, determining him to one rather than to another.

54.   And this reason can only be found in the *fitness*, or in the degrees of perfection, which these worlds contain, each possible world having the right to claim existence in proportion to the perfection which it involves.

55.   And it is this which causes the existence of the best, which God knows through his wisdom, chooses through his goodness, and produces through his power.

56.   Now this *connexion* or adaptation of all created things with each, and of each with all the rest, means that each simple substance has relations which express all the others, and that

consequently it is a perpetual living mirror of the universe.

57.   And just as the same town, when looked at from different sides, appears quite different and is, as it were, multiplied *in perspective*, so also it happens that because of the infinite number of simple substances, it is as if there were as many different universes, which are however but different perspectives of a single universe in accordance with the different point of view of each monad.

58.   And this is the means of obtaining as much variety as possible, but with the greatest order possible; that is to say, it is the means of obtaining as much perfection as possible.

59.   Further it is this hypothesis alone (which I venture to regard as proved) which properly exalts the greatness of God. This M. Bayle recognised, when in his *Dictionary* (in the article 'Rorarius') he made objections, in which he was even inclined to believe that I attributed too much to God, and more than is possible. But he could not advance any reason why this universal harmony, which causes each substance exactly to express all the others through the relations which it has with them, should be impossible.

60.   Moreover, there are evident from what I have just said the *a priori* reasons why things could not be otherwise than they are: namely, because God in regulating the whole had regard to each part, and particularly to each monad. The nature of the monad is representative, and consequently nothing can limit it to representing a part of things only, although it is true that its representation is confused as regards the detail of the whole universe and can only be distinct as regards a small part of things; that is to say as regards those which are either the nearest or the largest in relation to each of the monads; otherwise each monad would be a divinity. It is not in the object, but in the modification of the knowledge of the object, that monads are limited. In a confused way they all go towards the infinite, towards the whole; but they are limited and distinguished from one another by the degrees of their distinct perceptions.

61.   And in this the compounds agree with the simples. For as the whole is a plenum, which means that the whole of matter is connected, and as in a plenum every movement has some effect on distant bodies in proportion to their distance, so that each body not only is affected by those which touch it, and is in some way sensitive to whatever happens to them, but also by means of them is sensitive to those which touch the first bodies by which it is itself directly touched; it follows that this communication stretches out indefinitely. Consequently every body is sensitive to everything which is happening in the universe, so much so that one who saw everything could read in each body what is happening everywhere, and even what has happened or what will happen, by observing in the present the things that are distant in time as well as in space; σύμπνοια πάντα ['Everything is in League'], as Hippocrates said. But a soul can read in itself only what is distinctly represented there; it is unable to develop all at once all the things that are folded within it, for they stretch to infinity.

62.   Thus although each created monad represents the whole universe, it represents more distinctly the body which is particularly affected by it, and whose entelechy it is: and as this body expresses the whole universe by the connexion of all matter in the plenum, the soul represents the whole universe also in representing the body which belongs to it in a particular way.

63.   The body belonging to a monad, which is that body's entelechy or soul, constitutes together with the entelechy what may be called a *living thing*, and with the soul what is called an *animal*. Now this body of a living thing or animal is always organic; for since every monad is in its way a mirror of the universe, and since the universe is regulated in a perfect order, there must also be an order in that which represents it, that is to say in the perceptions of the soul, and consequently in the body, according to which order the universe is represented therein.

64.   Thus each organic body of a living thing is a kind of divine machine, or natural automaton, which infinitely surpasses all artificial automata. Because a machine which is made by the art of man is not a machine in each of its parts; for example, the tooth of a metal wheel has parts or fragments which as far as we are concerned are not artificial and which have about them nothing of the character of a machine, in relation to the use for which the wheel was intended. But the machines of nature, that is to say living bodies, are still machines in the least of their parts *ad infinitum*. This it is which makes the difference between nature and art, that is to say between Divine art and ours.

65.   And the Author of nature was enabled to practise this divine and infinitely marvellous artifice, because each portion of matter is not only infinitely divisible, as the ancients recognised, but is also actually subdivided without limit, each part into further parts, of which each one has some motion of its own: otherwise it would be impossible for each portion of matter to express the whole universe.

66.   Whence it is evident that there is a world of created beings – living things, animals, entelechies, and souls – in the least part of matter.

67.   Each portion of matter may be conceived as a garden full of plants, and as a pond full of fish. But every branch of each plant, every member of each animal, and every drop of their liquid parts is itself likewise a similar garden or pond.

68.   And although the earth and the air interspersed between the plants in the garden, or water interspersed between the fish in the pond, are neither plant nor fish, yet they still contain them, though most usually of a subtlety which renders them imperceptible to us.

69.   Thus there is nothing waste, nothing sterile, nothing dead in the universe; no chaos, no confusions, save in appearance. We might compare this to the appearance of a pond in the distance, where we can see the confused movement and swarming of the fish, without distinguishing the fish themselves.

70.   Thus we see that each living body has a dominant entelechy, which in the case of an animal is the soul, but the members of this living body are full of other living things, plants and animals, of which each has in turn its dominant entelechy or soul.

71.   But we must not imagine, as some have done who have misunderstood my view, that each soul has a mass or portion of matter appropriate or attached to itself for ever, and that it consequently possesses other inferior living things, for ever destined to its service. For all bodies are in a perpetual flux like rivers, and parts are passing in and out of them continually.

72.   Thus the soul only changes its body bit by bit and by degrees, so that it is never despoiled of all its organs all together; in animals there is often metamorphosis, but never metempsychosis, nor transmigration of souls: neither are there any entirely *separate souls*, nor *superhuman spirits* without bodies. God alone is entirely detached from body.

73.   It is because of this also that there is never, strictly speaking, absolute generation nor perfect death, consisting in the separation of the soul. And what we call *generation* is a development and a growth, while what we call *death* is an envelopment and a diminution.

74.   Philosophers have been much embarrassed over the origin of forms, entelechies or souls. But today when exact researches on plants, insects, and animals have revealed the fact that the organic bodies of nature are never produced from a chaos or from putrefaction, but always from seeds, wherein there was certainly some *preformation*, we conclude not only that the organic body was already present before conception, but also that there was a soul in this body; that, in a word, the animal itself was present, and that by means of conception it was merely prepared for a great transformation, so as to become an animal of another kind. We even see something of this kind apart from birth, as when worms become flies, and caterpillars become butterflies.

75.   The *animals*, of which some are raised by means of conception to the rank of the larger animals, may be called *spermatic*; but those among them which remain in their own kind (and they are the greater number) are born, multiply, and are destroyed like the large animals; and there is only a small number of elect ones who pass into a greater theatre.

76.   But this is only half the truth. And so I have judged that if the animal never begins naturally, neither does it end naturally; and that not only will there be no birth, but also no complete destruction, no death, strictly speaking. And these reasonings, which are *a posteriori* and derived from experience, agree perfectly with the principles which I have deduced *a priori* above.

77.   Thus one may say that not only is the soul (the mirror of an indestructible universe) itself indestructible, but so also is the animal itself, although its machine may often perish in part, and cast off or put on particular organic integuments.

78.   These principles provide me with a way of explaining naturally the union, or rather the conformity, of the soul and the organic body. The soul follows its own laws, and the body its own likewise, and they accord by virtue of the *harmony pre-established* among all substances, since they are all representations of one and the same universe.

79.   Souls act according to the laws of final causes by appetitions, ends, and means. Bodies

act according to the laws of efficient causes by motions. And the two kingdoms, of efficient and of final causes, are in harmony with one another.

80. Descartes recognised that souls cannot give force to bodies because there is always the same quantity of force in matter. He believed, however, that the soul could change the direction of bodies. But this is because in his day the law of nature was not known which affirms the conservation of the same total direction in matter.[4] Had he noticed this, he would have stumbled upon my system of Pre-established Harmony.

81. Under this system, bodies act as though, *per impossibile*, there were no souls: and souls act as if there were no bodies, and both act as if each influenced the other.

82. As for minds or rational souls, although I find that what I have just been saying is at bottom true of all living beings and animals (that is to say that the animal and the soul only begin with the world and do not come to an end any more than the world comes to an end), yet rational animals are peculiar in this, that their little spermatic animals, so long as they are that merely, have only ordinary or sensitive souls; but as soon as those which are, so to speak, elect arrive by an actual conception at human nature, then their sensitive souls are raised to the rank of reason and to the prerogative of minds.

83. Among other differences which exist between ordinary souls and minds, some of which I have already pointed out, there is also this, that souls in general are the living mirrors or images of the universe of created things, whereas minds are also images of the Divinity himself, or the Author of nature, capable of knowing the system of the universe, and of imitating something of it by architectonic patterns, each mind being as it were a little divinity in its own department.

84. This it is which renders minds capable of entering into a kind of society with God, and makes his relation to them not only that of an inventor to his machine (which is God's relation to the rest of created things) but also that of a prince to his subjects, and even of a father to his children.

85. From this it is easy to conclude that the assemblage of all minds must make up the City of God, that is to say the most perfect possible state under the most perfect of monarchs.

86. This City of God, this truly universal monarchy, is a moral world in the natural world,

and is the most exalted and the most divine of God's works, and in it truly consists his glory, since he could not be glorified if his greatness and goodness were not known and wondered at by minds: it is also in relation to this divine City that he may properly be said to have goodness, whereas his wisdom and power are manifested everywhere.

87. As we have established above a perfect harmony between two natural kingdoms, the one of efficient and the other of final causes, we ought here also to point out another harmony between the physical kingdom of nature and the moral kingdom of grace; that is to say between God as Architect of the machine of the universe, and God as Monarch of the divine City of Minds.

88. This harmony means that things conduce to grace by the very ways of nature, and that this globe, for example, must be destroyed and repaired by natural ways at the times demanded by the government of minds for the chastisement of some and the reward of others.

89. It can further be said that God as Architect satisfies God as Lawgiver in everything, and that thus sins carry their punishment with them by the order of nature, and by virtue of the mechanical structure of things itself; and that in the same way noble actions will attract their rewards by ways which are mechanical as far as bodies are concerned, although this cannot and should not always happen immediately.

90. Finally, under this perfect government there will be no good action without reward, no evil action without punishment, and everything must turn out for the good of the righteous, of those, that is, who are not dissatisfied in this great State, who trust in Providence when they have done their duty, and who love and imitate fittingly the Author of all good, delighting in the consideration of his perfections after the manner of true *pure love*, which makes us take pleasure in the happiness of the beloved. This it is which makes the wise and virtuous work for whatever seems to conform with the presumptive or antecedent will of God, and yet leaves them satisfied with what God in fact causes to happen by his secret will, which is consequent and decisive,[5] recognising as they do that if we could sufficiently understand the order of the universe, we should find that it surpasses all the desires of the most wise, and that it is impossible to make it better than it is, not only for the whole in

general, but also for ourselves in particular, if we are attached as we should be to the Author of the whole, not merely as to the Architect and efficient Cause of our being, but also as to our Master and the final Cause which must constitute the whole end of our will, and which alone can constitute our happiness.

Notes

1 The reference here is probably to the properties which, according to some medieval philosophers, transferred themselves from objects on to the mind.
2 This is one of Leibniz's many statements of his principle of "the identity of indiscernibles." If x and y are different objects, x must possess at least one property which y lacks.
3 The point in these sections is that a "truth of reasoning" is such that, on analysis of its terms, denial of it would be an explicit contradiction. For example, "All vixens are foxes" can be analyzed as "All female foxes are foxes," a statement whose denial is plainly a contradiction. Leibniz's view, in later philosophical parlance, is that all necessary truths are "analytic."
4 This somewhat obscure point is explained at greater length in "Explanation of the New System," §20, also in Leibniz's *Philosophical Writings*.
5 The translator explains that "'Consequent will'" refers to God's decisions (hence it is called 'decisive' in the *Monadology*), whereas the antecedent will only inclines."

16

George Berkeley, *Of the Principles of Human Knowledge*, Part I (Sections 1–37)

Introduction

Idealism – the broad view that reality is "ideal" or somehow "mental" – can come in many shapes and sizes. We have encountered idealist systems in earlier chapters: in Plato's "Ideas" or "Forms" (see III.3), in Śaṃkara's view that Brahman or the Absolute is consciousness and the familiar physical world some kind of "illusion" (III.7), and in Leibniz's claim that everything ultimately consists in monads, all of which are, if not minds, then certainly "incorporeal" and mind-*like* (III.15). Neither Śaṃkara nor Leibniz was concerned to deny the offence to commonsense caused by their theories. The Irish-born Anglican Bishop, George Berkeley (1685–1752), on the other hand, despite attracting charges of insanity and being a butt of Dr Johnson's jokes, argued that one of the main merits of his empiricist idealism was its consonance with commonsense. While noting the "opinion strangely prevailing" that houses and mountains exist independently of being perceived (§4), he insists that this conflicts with the far more deeply and generally rooted convictions that we really do perceive such objects and do know for certain that they exist – convictions, he argues, which his own immaterialism alone can secure. For

From George Berkeley, *Philosophical Works*, ed. M. R. Ayers, London: J. M. Dent & Sons, 1995, pp. 77–87 (notes omitted).

him, it is "obvious," on just a little reflection, that all the things that compose the world have no existence "without a mind, that their being is to be perceived" (§6).

Berkeley's claim, spelt out at the beginning of Part I of his *Treatise Concerning the Principles of Human Knowledge* (1710), is that we never perceive anything but our own perceptions or "ideas," and that objects such as houses are nothing but "collections of ideas" which minds do or might experience. He goes on to argue that belief in a material world independent of perception is at best unsupported and superfluous, at worst incoherent. Our ideas do have an outside cause, but this is God, not matter. Our selection ends with the early stages of Berkeley's attempt to show that his position is perfectly consonant with commonsense assumptions which it might seem to threaten, such as that there is a genuine difference between veridical and illusory experiences.

One main target is the work of John Locke (III.14 above). Already in his Introduction, Berkeley has rejected Locke's doctrine of "abstract general ideas." In Part I, in addition, Locke's distinction between primary and secondary qualities and his notion of material substances that "support" qualities are both dismissed. Features that Locke takes to distinguish secondary qualities, such as their relativity to perceivers, are, Berkeley argues, equally true of size, solidity and other allegedly primary qualities. More crucially, Locke's claim that, in the case of primary qualities, our ideas of them "resemble" qualities possessed by mind-independent objects, is declared to be absurd, for "an idea can be like nothing but an idea" (§8). As for the notion of substances or substrata, this is declared not to be false but, instead, in what would become one of the central critical gestures of modern philosophy, unintelligible.

Although Berkeley spends significant time attacking Locke's views, though not as much as in his *Three Dialogues between Hylas and Philonous* (1713), he states (§22) that he has been "needlessly prolix" and that, "in a line or two," the immaterialist thesis can be secured by another argument. This so-called "master argument" is to the effect that the attempt even to conceive of unperceived or unthought things is self-defeating, for in imagining them one in effect perceives or thinks them, so that in every case they turn out simply to be ideas after all. As it stands, this argument has unwelcome implications for Berkeley's own philosophy. It would seem to show, for example, that in trying to conceive of God one turns God into an idea in one's mind. On a charitable interpretation, however, the argument is driving at an important thought: the impossibility of conceiving of anything except from perspectives that cannot be transcended in order to arrive at a conception of how anything in itself is.[1]

In the pages we have selected, one finds Berkeley apparently proposing two very different accounts of what it is for a tree or a house to exist when no one perceives it. (Clearly, if Berkeley is to succeed in reconciling his idealism with commonsense, some account of this is imperative.) In §3, the suggestion seems to be the "phenomenalist" one – elaborated by J. S. Mill (III.19) – that something can exist, though unperceived, only in the sense that someone *would* perceive it if suitably placed to do so.[2] But Berkeley's more considered and constant view is the one indicated in Ronald Knox's famous limerick about the unperceived tree in the Quad:

I am always about in the Quad.
And that's why the tree
Will continue to be,
Since observed by *Yours Faithfully*, GOD.

More prosaically, an actual object unperceived by any human or animal observer is nevertheless always being perceived, as ideas in the mind of God.

For Berkeley, God's existence is not a matter of mere faith. As he argues in Part 1 (§§29ff.), there must be some extremely powerful cause of the ideas people perceive, since we are aware of ourselves as the passive recipient of most of these. Since that cause cannot be matter, it must be an immaterial mind – a cause that has the further advantage of being intelligible, unlike matter, by way of analogy with one's own self. Berkeley, arguably, is at his philosophically and theologically most acute, when showing the sheer redundancy of materialist hypotheses in accounting for our experiences once the existence of God is admitted. And the vision he offers is surely one that, for religious persons, might be a deeply satisfying one: the vision of human beings, whenever they see, smell, touch, taste, or think being in direct receipt of ideas granted to them by God.

Notes

1   See H. Robinson, "Berkeley," in N. Bunnin and E. P. Tsui-James, eds, *The Blackwell Companion to Philosophy*, Oxford: Blackwell, 1996, pp. 564ff. See also, the same author's *Objections to Physicalism*, Oxford: Oxford University Press, 1995, and J. Foster, *The Case for Idealism*, London: Routledge, 1982, for modern-day defences of Berkeleyan idealism.

2   See G. J. Warnock, *Berkeley*, Harmondsworth: Penguin, 1953, for a phenomenalist reading of Berkeley.

Berkeley, *Principles of Human Knowledge*

Part I

1.   It is evident to anyone who takes a survey of the objects of human knowledge, that they are either ideas actually imprinted on the senses, or else such as are perceived by attending to the passions and operations of the mind, or lastly ideas formed by help of memory and imagination, either compounding, dividing, or barely representing those originally perceived in the aforesaid ways. By sight I have the ideas of light and colours with their several degrees and variations. By touch I perceive, for example, hard and soft, heat and cold,

motion and resistance, and of all these more and less either as to quantity or degree. Smelling furnishes me with odours; the palate with tastes, and hearing conveys sounds to the mind in all their variety of tone and composition. And as several of these are observed to accompany each other, they come to be marked by one name, and so to be reputed as one thing. Thus, for example, a certain colour, taste, smell, figure and consistence having been observed to go together, are accounted one distinct thing, signified by the name *apple*. Other collections of ideas constitute a stone, a tree, a book, and the like sensible things; which, as they are pleasing or disagreeable, excite the passions of love, hatred, joy, grief, and so forth.

2. But besides all that endless variety of ideas or objects of knowledge, there is likewise something which knows or perceives them, and exercises divers operations, as willing, imagining, remembering about them. This perceiving, active being is what I call *mind, spirit, soul* or *myself*. By which words I do not denote any one of my ideas, but a thing entirely distinct from them, wherein they exist, or, which is the same thing, whereby they are perceived; for the existence of an idea consists in being perceived.

3. That neither our thoughts, nor passions, nor ideas formed by the imagination, exist without the mind, is what everybody will allow. And it seems no less evident that the various sensations or ideas imprinted on the sense, however blended or combined together (that is, whatever objects they compose) cannot exist otherwise than in a mind perceiving them. I think an intuitive knowledge may be obtained of this, by anyone that shall attend to what is meant by the term *exist* when applied to sensible things. The table I write on, I say, exists, that is, I see and feel it; and if I were out of my study I should say it existed, meaning thereby that if I was in my study I might perceive it, or that some other spirit actually does perceive it. There was an odour, that is, it was smelled; there was a sound, that is to say, it was heard; a colour or figure, and it was perceived by sight or touch. This is all that I can understand by these and the like expressions. For as to what is said of the absolute existence of unthinking things without any relation to their being perceived, that seems perfectly unintelligible. Their *esse* is *percipi*, nor is it possible they should have any existence, out of the minds or thinking things which perceive them.

4. It is indeed an opinion strangely prevailing amongst men, that houses, mountains, rivers, and in a word all sensible objects have an existence natural or real, distinct from their being perceived by the understanding. But with how great an assurance and acquiescence soever this principle may be entertained in the world; yet whoever shall find in his heart to call it in question, may, if I mistake not, perceive it to involve a manifest contradiction. For what are the forementioned objects but the things we perceive by sense, and what do we perceive besides our own ideas or sensations; and is it not plainly repugnant that any one of these or any combination of them should exist unperceived?

5. If we thoroughly examine this tenet, it will, perhaps, be found at bottom to depend on the doctrine of *abstract ideas*.[1] For can there be a nicer strain of abstraction than to distinguish the existence of sensible objects from their being perceived, so as to conceive them existing unperceived? Light and colours, heat and cold, extension and figures, in a word the things we see and feel, what are they but so many sensations, notions, ideas or impressions on the sense; and is it possible to separate, even in thought, any of these from perception? For my part I might as easily divide a thing from itself. I may indeed divide in my thoughts or conceive apart from each other those things which, perhaps, I never perceived by sense so divided. Thus I imagine the trunk of a human body without the limbs, or conceive the smell of a rose without thinking on the rose itself. So far I will not deny I can abstract, if that may properly be called *abstraction*, which extends only to the conceiving separately such objects, as it is possible may really exist or be actually perceived asunder. But by conceiving or imagining power does not extend beyond the possibility of real existence or perception. Hence as it is impossible for me to see or feel anything without an actual sensation of that thing, so is it impossible for me to conceive in my thoughts any sensible thing or object distinct from the sensation or perception of it.

6. Some truths there are so near and obvious to the mind, that a man need only open his eyes to see them. Such I take this important one to be, to wit, that all the choir of heaven and furniture of the earth, in a word all those bodies which compose the mighty frame of the world, have not any subsistence without a mind, that their being is to

be perceived or known; that consequently so long as they are not actually perceived by me, or do not exist in my mind or that of any other created spirit, they must either have no existence at all, or else subsist in the mind of some eternal spirit: it being perfectly unintelligible and involving all the absurdity of abstraction, to attribute to any single part of them an existence independent of a spirit. To be convinced of which, the reader need only reflect and try to separate in his own thoughts the being of a sensible thing from its being perceived.

7. From what has been said, it follows, there is not any other substance than *spirit*, or that which perceives. But for the fuller proof of this point, let it be considered, the sensible qualities are colour, figure, motion, smell, taste, and such like, that is, the ideas perceived by sense. Now for an idea to exist in an unperceiving thing, is a manifest contradiction; for to have an idea is all one as to perceive: that therefore wherein colour, figure, and the like qualities exist, must perceive them; hence it is clear there can be no unthinking substance or *substratum* of those ideas.

8. But say you, though the ideas themselves do not exist without the mind, yet there may be things like them whereof they are copies or resemblances, which things exist without the mind, in an unthinking substance. I answer, an idea can be like nothing but an idea; a colour or figure can be like nothing but another colour or figure. If we look but ever so little into our thoughts, we shall find it impossible for us to conceive a likeness except only between our ideas. Again, I ask whether those supposed originals or external things, of which our ideas are the pictures or representations, be themselves perceivable or no? If they are, then they are ideas, and we have gained our point; but if you say they are not, I appeal to anyone whether it be sense, to assert a colour is like something which is invisible; hard or soft, like something which is intangible; and so of the rest.

9. Some there are who make a distinction betwixt *primary* and *secondary* qualities: by the former, they mean extension, figure, motion, rest, solidity or impenetrability and number: by the latter they denote all other sensible qualities, as colours, sounds, tastes, and so forth. The ideas we have of these they acknowledge not to be the resemblances of anything existing without the

mind or unperceived; but they will have our ideas of the primary qualities to be patterns or images of things which exist without the mind, in an unthinking substance which they call *matter*. By matter therefore we are to understand an inert, senseless substance, in which extension, figure, and motion, do actually subsist. But it is evident from what we have already shewn, that extension, figure and motion are only ideas existing in the mind, and that an idea can be like nothing but another idea, and that consequently neither they nor their archetypes can exist in an unperceiving substance. Hence it is plain, that the very notion of what is called *matter* or *corporeal substance*, involves a contradiction in it.

10. They who assert that figure, motion, and the rest of the primary or original qualities do exist without the mind, in unthinking substances, do at the same time acknowledge that colours, sounds, heat, cold, and such like secondary qualities, do not, which they tell us are sensations existing in the mind alone, that depend on and are occasioned by the different size, texture and motion of the minute particles of matter. This they take for an undoubted truth, which they can demonstrate beyond all exception. Now if it be certain, that those original qualities are inseparably united with the other sensible qualities, and not, even in thought, capable of being abstracted from them, it plainly follows that they exist only in the mind. But I desire anyone to reflect and try, whether he can by any abstraction of thought, conceive the extension and motion of a body, without all other sensible qualities. For my own part, I see evidently that it is not in my power to frame an idea of a body extended and moved, but I must withal give it some colour or other sensible quality which is acknowledged to exist only in the mind. In short, extension, figure and motion, abstracted from all other qualities, are inconceivable. Where therefore the other sensible qualities are, there must these be also, to wit, in the mind and nowhere else.

11. Again, *great* and *small*, *swift* and *slow*, are allowed to exist nowhere without the mind, being entirely relative, and changing as the frame or position of the organs of sense varies. The extension therefore which exists without the mind, is neither great nor small, the motion neither swift nor slow, that is, they are nothing at all. But say you, they are extension in general, and motion in general: thus we see how much the tenet of

extended, moveable substances existing without the mind, depends on that strange doctrine of *abstract ideas*. And here I cannot but remark, how nearly the vague and indeterminate description of matter or corporeal substance, which the modern philosophers are run into by their own principles, resembles that antiquated and so much ridiculed notion of *materia prima* ['prime matter'], to be met with in Aristotle and his followers. Without extension solidity cannot be conceived; since therefore it has been shewn that extension exists not in an unthinking substance, the same must also be true of solidity.

12. That number is entirely the creature of the mind, even though the other qualities be allowed to exist without, will be evident to whoever considers, that the same thing bears a different denomination of number, as the mind views it with different respects. Thus, the same extension is one or three or thirty-six, according as the mind considers it with reference to a yard, a foot, or an inch. Number is so visibly relative, and dependent on men's understanding, that it is strange to think how anyone should give it an absolute existence without the mind. We say one book, one page, one line; all these are equally units, though some contain several of the others. And in each instance it is plain, the unit relates to some particular combination of ideas arbitrarily put together by the mind.

13. Unity I know some will have to a simple or uncompounded idea, accompanying all other ideas into the mind. That I have any such idea answering the word *unity*, I do not find; and if I had, methinks I could not miss finding it; on the contrary it should be the most familiar to my understanding, since it is said to accompany all other ideas, and to be perceived by all the ways of sensation and reflexion. To say no more, it is an *abstract idea*.

14. I shall farther add, that after the same manner, as modern philosophers prove certain sensible qualities to have no existence in matter, or without the mind, the same thing may be likewise proved of all other sensible qualities whatsoever. Thus, for instance, it is said that heat and cold are affections only of the mind, and not at all patterns of real beings, existing in the corporeal substances which excite them, for that the same body which appears cold to one hand, seems warm to another. Now why may we not as well argue that figure and extension are not patterns or resemblances of qualities existing in matter, because to the same eye at different stations, or eyes of a different texture at the same station, they appear various, and cannot therefore be the images of anything settled and determinate without the mind? Again, it is proved that sweetness is not really in the sapid thing, because the thing remaining unaltered the sweetness is changed into bitter, as in case of a fever or otherwise vitiated palate. Is it not as reasonable to say, that motion is not without the mind, since if the succession of ideas in the mind become swifter, the motion, it is acknowledged, shall appear slower without any alteration in any external object.

15. In short, let anyone consider those arguments, which are thought manifestly to prove that colours and tastes exist only in the mind, and he shall find they may with equal force, be brought to prove the same thing of extension, figure, and motion. Though it must be confessed this method of arguing doth not much prove that there is no extension or colour in an outward object, as that we do not know by sense which is the true extension or colour of the object. But the arguments foregoing plainly shew it to be impossible that any colour or extension at all, or other sensible quality whatsoever, should exist in an unthinking subject without the mind, or in truth, that there should be any such thing as an outward object.

16. But let us examine a little the received opinion. It is said extension is a mode or accident of matter, and that matter is the *substratum* that supports it. Now I desire that you would explain what is meant by matter's *supporting* extension: say you, I have no idea of matter, and therefore cannot explain it. I answer, though you have no positive, yet if you have any meaning at all, you must at least have a relative idea of matter; though you know not what it is, yet you must be supposed to know what relation it bears to accidents, and what is meant by its supporting them. It is evident *support* cannot here be taken in its usual or literal sense, as when we say that pillars support a building: in what sense therefore must it be taken?

17. If we inquire into what the most accurate philosophers declare themselves to mean by *material substance*; we shall find them acknowledge, they have no other meaning annexed to those sounds, but the idea of being in general, together

with the relative notion of its supporting accidents. The general idea of being appeareth to me the most abstract and incomprehensible of all other; and as for its supporting accidents, this, as we have just now observed, cannot be understood in the common sense of those words; it must therefore be taken in some other sense, but what that is they do not explain. So that when I consider the two parts or branches which make the signification of the words *material substance*, I am convinced there is no distinct meaning annexed to them. But why should we trouble ourselves any farther, in discussing this material *substratum* or support of figure and motion, and other sensible qualities? Does it not suppose they have an existence without the mind? And is not this a direct repugnancy, and altogether inconceivable?

18.   But though it were possible that solid, figured, moveable substances may exist without the mind, corresponding to the ideas we have of bodies, yet how is it possible for us to know this? Either we must know it by sense, or by reason. As for our senses, by them we have the knowledge only of our sensations, ideas, or those things that are immediately perceived by sense, call them what you will: but they do not inform us that things exist without the mind, or unperceived, like to those which are perceived. This the materialists themselves acknowledge. It remains therefore that if we have any knowledge at all of external things, it must be by reason, inferring their existence from what is immediately perceived by sense. But what reason can induce us to believe the existence of bodies without the mind, from what we perceive, since the very patrons of matter themselves do not pretend, there is any necessary connexion betwixt them and our ideas? I say it is granted on all hands (and what happens in dreams, phrensies, and the like, puts it beyond dispute) that it is possible we might be affected with all the ideas we have now, though no bodies existed without, resembling them. Hence it is evident the supposition of external bodies is not necessary for the producing our ideas: since it is granted they are produced sometimes, and might possibly be produced always in the same order we see them in at present, without their concurrence.

19.   But though we might possibly have all our sensations without them, yet perhaps it may be thought easier to conceive and explain the manner of their production, by supposing external bodies in their likeness rather than otherwise; and so it might be at least probable there are such things as bodies that excite their ideas in our minds. But neither can this be said; for though we give the materialists their external bodies, they by their own confession are never the nearer knowing how our ideas are produced: since they own themselves unable to comprehend in what manner body can act upon spirit, or how it is possible it should imprint any idea in the mind. Hence it is evident the production of ideas or sensations in our minds, can be no reason why we should suppose matter or corporeal substances, since that is acknowledged to remain equally inexplicable with, or without this supposition. If therefore it were possible for bodies to exist without the mind, yet to hold they do so, must needs be a very precarious opinion; since it is to suppose, without any reason at all, that God has created innumerable beings that are entirely useless, and serve to no manner of purpose.

20.   In short, if there were external bodies, it is impossible we should ever come to know it; and if there were not, we might have the very same reasons to think there were that we have now. Suppose, what no one can deny possible, an intelligence, without the help of external bodies, to be affected with the same train of sensations or ideas that you are, imprinted in the same order and with like vividness in his mind. I ask whether that intelligence hath not all the reason to believe the existence of corporeal substances, represented by his ideas, and exciting them in his mind, that you can possibly have for believing the same thing? Of this there can be no question; which one consideration is enough to make any reasonable person suspect the strength of whatever arguments he may think himself to have, for the existence of bodies without the mind.

21.   Were it necessary to add any farther proof against the existence of matter, after what has been said, I could instance several of those errors and difficulties (not to mention impieties) which have sprung from that tenet. It has occasioned numberless controversies and disputes in philosophy, and not a few of far greater moment in religion. But I shall not enter into the detail of them in this place, as well because I think, arguments *a posteriori* are unnecessary for confirming what has been, if I mistake not, sufficiently demonstrated *a priori*, as because I shall hereafter find occasion to say somewhat of them.

22. I am afraid I have given cause to think me needlessly prolix in handling this subject. For to what purpose is it to dilate on that which may be demonstrated with the utmost evidence in a line or two, to anyone that is capable of the least reflexion? It is but looking into your own thoughts, and so trying whether you can conceive it possible for a sound, or figure, or motion, or colour, to exist without the mind, or unperceived. This easy trial may make you see, that what you contend for, is a downright contradiction. Insomuch that I am content to put the whole upon this issue; if you can but conceive it possible for one extended moveable substance, or in general, for any one idea or anything like an idea, to exist otherwise than in a mind perceiving it, I shall readily give up the cause: and as for all that *compages* of external bodies which you contend for, I shall grant you its existence, though you cannot either give me any reason why you believe it exists, or assign any use to it when it is supposed to exist. I say, the bare possibility of your opinion's being true, shall pass for an argument that it is so.

23. But say you, surely there is nothing easier than to imagine trees, for instance, in a park, or books existing in a closet, and nobody by to perceive them. I answer, you may so, there is no difficulty in it: but what is all this, I beseech you, more than framing in your mind certain ideas which you call *books* and *trees*, and at the same time omitting to frame the idea of anyone that may perceive them? But do not you yourself perceive or think of them all the while? This therefore is nothing to the purpose: it only shows you have the power of imagining or forming ideas in your mind; but it doth not shew that you can conceive it possible, the objects of your thought may exist without the mind: to make out this, it is necessary that you conceive them existing unconceived or unthought of, which is a manifest repugnancy. When we do our utmost to conceive the existence of external bodies, we are all the while only contemplating our own ideas. But the mind taking no notice of itself, is deluded to think it can and doth conceive bodies existing unthought of or without the mind; though at the same time they are apprehended by or exist in itself. A little attention will discover to anyone the truth and evidence of what is here said, and make it unnecessary to insist on any other proofs against the existence of material substance.

24. It is very obvious, upon the least inquiry into our own thoughts, to know whether it be possible for us to understand what is meant, by the *absolute existence of sensible objects in themselves, or without the mind.* To me it is evident those words mark out either a direct contradiction, or else nothing at all. And to convince others of this, I know no readier or fairer way, than to entreat they would calmly attend to their own thoughts: and if by this attention, the emptiness or repugnancy of those expressions does appear, surely nothing more is requisite for their conviction. It is on this therefore that I insist, to wit, that the absolute existence of unthinking things are words without a meaning, or which include a contradiction. This is what I repeat and inculcate, and earnestly recommend to the attentive thoughts of the reader.

25. All our ideas, sensations, or the things which we perceive, by whatsoever names they may be distinguished, are visibly inactive, there is nothing of power or agency included in them. So that one idea or object of thought cannot produce, or make any alternation in another. To be satisfied of the truth of this, there is nothing else requisite but a bare observation of our ideas. For since they and every part of them exist only in the mind, it follows that there is nothing in them but what is perceived. But whoever shall attend to his ideas, whether of sense or reflexion, will not perceive in them any power or activity; there is therefore no such thing contained in them. A little attention will discover to us that the very being of an idea implies passiveness and inertness in it, insomuch that it is impossible for an idea to do anything, or, strictly speaking, to be the cause of anything: neither can it be the resemblance or pattern of any active being, as is evident from *Sect.* 8. Whence it plainly follows that extension, figure and motion, cannot be the cause of our sensations. To say therefore, that these are the effects of powers resulting from the configuration, number, motion, and size of corpuscles, must certainly be false.

26. We perceive a continual succession of ideas, some are anew excited, others are changed or totally disappear. There is therefore some cause of these ideas whereon they depend, and which produces and changes them. That this cause cannot be any quality or idea or combination of ideas, is clear from the preceding section. It must therefore be a substance; but it has been

shewn that there is no corporeal or material substance: it remains therefore that the cause of ideas is an incorporeal active substance or spirit.

27.   A spirit is one simple, undivided, active being: as it perceives ideas, it is called the *understanding*, and as it produces or otherwise operates about them, it is called the *will*. Hence there can be no idea formed of a soul or spirit: for all ideas whatever, being passive and inert, *vide Sect.* 25, they cannot represent unto us, by way of image or likeness, that which acts. A little attention will make it plain to anyone, that to have an idea which shall be like that active principle of motion and change of ideas, is absolutely impossible. Such is the nature of *spirit* or that which acts, that it cannot be of itself perceived, but only by the effects which it produceth. If any man shall doubt of the truth of what is here delivered, let him but reflect and try if he can frame the idea of any power or active being; and whether he hath ideas of two principal powers, marked by the names *will* and *understanding*, distinct from each other as well as from a third idea of substance or being in general, with a relative notion of its supporting or being the subject of the aforesaid powers, which is signified by the name *soul or spirit*. This is what some hold; but so far as I can see, the words *will, soul, spirit*, do not stand for different ideas, or in truth, for any idea at all, but for something which is very different from ideas, and which being an agent cannot be like unto, or represented by, any idea whatsoever. Though it must be owned at the same time, that we have some notion of soul, spirit, and the operations of the mind, such as willing, loving, hating, in as much as we know or understand the meaning of those words.

28.   I find I can excite ideas in my mind at pleasure, and vary and shift the scene as oft as I think fit. It is no more than willing, and straightway this or that idea arises in my fancy: and by the same power it is obliterated, and makes way for another. This making and unmaking of ideas doth very properly denominate the mind active. Thus much is certain, and grounded on experience: but when we talk of unthinking agents, or of exciting ideas exclusive of volition, we only amuse ourselves with words.

29.   But whatever power I may have over my own thoughts, I find the ideas actually perceived by sense have not a like dependence on my will. When in broad day-light I open my eyes, it is not in my power to choose whether I shall see or no, or to determine what particular objects shall present themselves to my view; and so likewise as to the hearing and other senses, the ideas imprinted on them are not creatures of my will. There is therefore some other will or spirit that produces them.

30.   The ideas of sense are more strong, lively, and distinct than those of the imagination; they have likewise a steadiness, order, and coherence, and are not excited at random, as those which are the effects of human wills often are, but in a regular train or series, the admirable connexion whereof sufficiently testifies the wisdom and benevolence of its Author. Now the set rules or established methods, wherein the mind we depend on excites in us the ideas of sense, are called the *Laws of Nature*: and these we learn by experience, which teaches us that such and such ideas are attended with such and such other ideas, in the ordinary course of things.

31.   This gives us a sort of foresight, which enables us to regulate our actions for the benefit of life. And without this we should be eternally at a loss: we could not know how to act anything that might procure us the least pleasure, or remove the least pain of sense. That food nourishes, sleep refreshes, and fire warms us; that to sow in the seed-time is the way to reap in the harvest, and, in general, that to obtain such or such ends, such or such means are conducive, all this we know, not by discovering any necessary connexion between our ideas, but only by the observation of the settled laws of Nature, without which we should be all in uncertainty and confusion, and a grown man no more know how to manage himself in the affairs of life, than an infant just born.

32.   And yet this consistent uniform working, which so evidently displays the goodness and wisdom of that governing spirit whose will constitutes the Laws of Nature, is so far from leading our thoughts to him, that it rather sends them a wandering after second causes. For when we perceive certain ideas of sense constantly followed by other ideas, and we know this is not of our doing, we forthwith attribute power and agency to the ideas themselves, and make one the cause of another, than which nothing can be more absurd and unintelligible. Thus, for example, having observed that when we perceive by sight a certain round luminous figure, we at the same

time perceive by touch the idea or sensation called *heat*, we do from thence conclude the sun to be the cause of heat. And in like manner perceiving the motion and collision of bodies to be attended with sound, we are inclined to think the latter an effect of the former.

33. The ideas imprinted on the senses by the Author of Nature are called *real things*: and those excited in the imagination being less regular, vivid and constant, are more properly termed *ideas*, or *images of things*, which they copy and represent. But then our sensations, be they never so vivid and distinct, are nevertheless *ideas*, that is, they exist in the mind, or are perceived by it, as truly as the ideas of its own framing. The ideas of sense are allowed to have more reality in them, that is, to be more strong, orderly, and coherent than the creatures of the mind; but this is no argument that they exist without the mind. They are also less dependent on the spirit, or thinking substance which perceives them, in that they are excited by the will of another and more powerful spirit: yet still they are *ideas*, and certainly no *idea*, whether faint or strong, can exist otherwise than in a mind perceiving it.

34. Before we proceed any farther, it is necessary to spend some time in answering objections which may probably be made against the principles hitherto laid down. In doing of which, if I seem too prolix to those of quick apprehensions, I hope it may be pardoned, since all men do not equally apprehend things of this nature; and I am willing to be understood by everyone. First then, it will be objected that by the foregoing principles, all that is real and substantial in Nature is banished out of the world: and instead thereof a chimerical scheme of ideas takes place. All things that exist, exist only in the mind, that is, they are purely notional. What therefore becomes of the sun, moon, and stars? What must we think of houses, rivers, mountains, trees, stones; nay, even of our own bodies? Are all these but so many chimeras and illusions on the fancy? To all which, and whatever else of the same sort may be objected, I answer, that by the principles premised, we are not deprived of any one thing in Nature. Whatever we see, feel, hear, or any wise conceive or understand, remains as secure as ever, and is as real as ever. There is a *rerum natura*, and the distinction between realities and chimeras retains its full force. This is evident from *Sect.* 29, 30, and 33, where we have shewn

what is meant by *real things* in opposition to *chimeras*, or ideas of our own framing; but then they both equally exist in the mind, and in that sense are alike *ideas*.

35. I do not argue against the existence of any one thing that we can apprehend, either by sense or reflexion. That the things I see with mine eyes and touch with my hands do exist, really exist, I make not the least question. The only thing whose existence we deny, is that which philosophers call matter or corporeal substance. And in doing of this, there is no damage done to the rest of mankind, who, I dare say, will never miss it. The atheist indeed will want the colour of an empty name to support his impiety; and the philosophers may possibly find, they have lost a great handle for trifling and disputation.

36. If any man thinks this detracts from the existence or reality of things, he is very far from understanding what hath been premised in the plainest terms I could think of. Take here an abstract of what has been said. There are spiritual substances, minds, or human souls, which will or excite ideas in themselves at pleasure: but these are faint, weak, and unsteady in respect of others they perceive by sense, which being impressed upon them according to certain rules or laws of Nature, speak themselves the effects of a mind more powerful and wise than human spirits. These latter are said to have more *reality* in them than the former: by which is meant that they are more affecting, orderly, and distinct, and that they are not fictions of the mind perceiving them. And in this sense, the sun that I see by day is the real sun, and that which I imagine by night is the idea of the former. In the sense here given of *reality*, it is evident that every vegetable, star, mineral, and in general each part of the mundane system, is as much a *real being* by our principles as by any other. Whether others mean anything by the term *reality* different from what I do, I entreat them to look into their own thoughts and see.[2]

37. It will be urged that thus much at least is true, to wit, that we take away all corporeal substances. To this my answer is, that if the word *substance* be taken in the vulgar sense, for a combination of sensible qualities, such as extension, solidity, weight, and the like; this we cannot be accused of taking away. But if it be taken in a philosophic sense, for the support of accidents or qualities without the mind: then indeed I

acknowledge that we take it away, if one may be said to take away that which never had any existence, not even in the imagination. [. . .]

Notes

1   As Berkeley understands it, this is Locke's doctrine to the effect that a general concept, like *triangle*, is an indefinite image formed by abstraction from particular ideas, such as perceptions of particular triangles. Berkeley insists, in the Introduction to the *Principles*, that all ideas are particular, though they may be put to general use by being made to "stand for" other ideas. For example, I may use an idea of a particular triangle to represent triangles at large. Berkeley does not explain how the doctrine of materialism depends on that of abstract ideas. Presumably, though, the thought is this. If we do have an idea of matter or materiality at all, it must be an abstract one: since there are no abstract ideas, then we do not have such an idea.

2   This section records as robustly as any Berkeley's conviction that his idealism disposes of skepticism about the reality of physical objects. Many commentators, including Hume, think that Berkeley's denial of matter gives to the skeptic everything the latter could want. Berkeley's view, however, is that if a house simply is a collection of ideas perceived by us or by God, then its existence is as certain as that of ideas. There is, so to speak, no gap between ideas and objects of the kind the skeptic exploits in trying to cast doubt on a correspondence between the order of ideas and the order of things.

Immanuel Kant, *Critique of Pure Reason* I.1 (2nd edition), "Transcendental Aesthetic," Sections 1–3, 8

Introduction

Immanuel Kant (1724–1804) perceived metaphysics in his day as a "combat ground" on which rival thinkers were "groping about" with no clear criteria for adjudicating among their competing systems. If what should be the greatest of the sciences is to overcome this "shaky state of uncertainty and contradictions," its protagonists must first attend to what he would call a "transcendental" question, "How is metaphysics possible?" In the Introduction to his greatest work, *Critique of Pure Reason* (1781 and 1787), Kant converted this question into "How are synthetic *a priori* judgements possible?" These are judgments that, while necessarily true and so immune to refutation by experience, are not merely "trivial" analytic judgments guaranteed by the meanings of the concepts they contain. They include, for example, the principle that everything takes place according to the law of causality, as well as the truths of mathematics. (For Kant's account of *a priori* and analytic truths, see II.12 of this volume.) Kant's revolutionary answer to the question of how such judgments are possible not only indicates the proper method for metaphysics; it is

also the key to the development of his own metaphysical system of Transcendental Idealism.

Much of Kant's enquiry concerns the *a priori* conditions for the possibility of *understanding* anything: but he sharply distinguishes these from the conditions of our *sensibility* or "sensory intuitions." Along these lines, the "Transcendental Aesthetic" – which has nothing to do with "aesthetics" in the modern sense of enquiry into art and properties like beauty – attempts to establish the "principles of *a priori* sensibility." Kant's first central claim, here, is that the formal *a priori* conditions of the mind's intuitions of "outer" objects and its own "inner" states are space and time, respectively. Our selection focuses on the former (most of Kant's claims about time are closely analogous to those he makes about space, as §8 makes clear). The insistence that our experience of what is "outer" must be spatial is not the dull point that what is spatially outside us gets experienced as such, but the contentious claim that it's possible for objects to be "outer," in the sense of being objective – distinct, that is, from our own "inner" states – only because they can be spatially locatable.[1]

Space, like time, has always been a topic of metaphysical interest, not least because of the puzzles about infinity it seems to generate. Kant himself addresses such issues later in the *Critique*; but in the Transcendental Aesthetic several of the points he makes about space are of interest in their own right – for example, his rejection of Leibniz's view that space is simply a relation between objects or their parts. But in the context of the present

From Immanuel Kant, *Critique of Pure Reason*, trans. W. S. Pluhar, Indianapolis, IN: Hackett Publishing Co., Inc., 1996, pp. 71–84, 94–104 (most notes omitted; asterisked note is Kant's).

volume, it is the strategic place of Kant's discussion in his overall metaphysics that is crucial.

The startling conclusion Kant draws from his enquiries concerning space is that space is not a property or the field of things as they are in themselves (*an sich*) – the mistake of realist metaphysics. Instead, space is only "the subjective condition of sensibility" under which objects are experienced by us. Hence it is "only from the human standpoint" that we may speak of space, of extended things, and so on (B 42). Given how central a feature of the empirical world its spatial order surely is, then, if Kant's conclusion is correct, he is well on the way to establishing his general thesis that how this world must be is due to our "imposition" of form, structure, and intelligibility on it. The world of experience, then, is partly *given* to us and partly *structured* by us. Kant's conclusion may seem to put him on the side of Berkeley (III.16), and against Locke (III.14), by denying that space is a feature of the external world. But Kant insists that he is an "empirical realist" about space. That's because although for Kant the world as we experience it (empirical reality) is spatially and temporally ordered by the subjective "pure forms of sensibility," that ordering is *a priori* universal, always-already holding for all possible experience among any beings capable of experiencing the world as we inhabit it. From the transcendental viewpoint, of course, even "outer" objects are merely "phenomena," "appearances" (*Erscheinungen*) of things-in-themselves (*Dinge an sich*), the nature of these latter being completely unknowable. The devastating implications of Kant's critical transcendental philosophy for dogmatic speculative metaphysics are clear and led the poet Heinrich Heine to call him "the great destroyer in the realm of thought," who "exceeded Maximillian Robespierre in terrorism."[2]

Kant deploys a number of arguments to establish the "ideality" of space, and commentators differ as to which of these is the weightiest.[3] One is "the argument from geometry" (B 41, 47ff.), according to which Euclid's propositions are synthetic *a priori* truths – something they could not be if they were, *per impossibile*, descriptions of how things-in-themselves are. Another rests on the claim that "through outer sense we are given nothing but mere relational presentations," and hence we cannot penetrate "the intrinsic character belonging to the object in itself" (B 67).[4] But

perhaps Kant's most powerful argument is what has been called "the argument from elimination."[5] There are only so many ways in which one could try to account for our *a priori* knowledge that objects are spatial – Leibniz's relational theory, for example. If, as Kant tries to show, all but his own account definitely fail, then, like it or not, his must win the day.

Needless to say, Kant's arguments and conclusion have often been challenged. Certainly "the argument from geometry" is open to the charge that Kant fails to distinguish between treating Euclid's theorems as uninterpreted, "formal" consequences of definitions and regarding them as interpreted accounts of physically reality. Treated one way, they are necessarily true, but only "analytic." Treated the other way, they are "synthetic," but may not be true at all, let alone necessarily or *a priori* true. Other critics, while conceding that space and time may be *a priori* forms of our sensibility, are puzzled as to why this should rule out the possibility that they are also features of things-in-themselves.[6] Nevertheless, Kant's philosophy of space and time, like his wider metaphysics to which it is integral, continues to have its champions. Metaphysics, despite Kant's efforts, remains the "combat ground" it was in his own day.

Notes

1   P. F. Strawson, *The Bounds of Sense: An Essay on Kant's Critique of Pure Reason*, London: Methuen, 1966, skillfully explains this and many other points.

2   H. Heine (1797–1856), *Concerning the History of Religion and Philosophy in Germany* (1834).

3   See the dispute between P. F. Strawson (*The Bounds of Sense*), and H. E. Allison, *Kant's Transcendental Idealism*, New Haven, CT: Yale University Press, 1983, over the weight to be attached to "the argument from geometry," discussed in what follows.

4   R. Langton, *Kantian Humility: Our Ignorance of Things in Themselves*, Oxford: Clarendon Press, 1998, puts this argument of Kant's to interesting use.

5   See H. E. Allison, *Kant's Transcendental Idealism*.

6   See, for example, S. Körner, *Kant*, Harmondsworth: Penguin, 1955.

Kant, *Critique of Pure Reason*

Transcendental Aesthetic

§1 In whatever way and by whatever means a cognition may refer to objects, still *intuition* is that by which a cognition refers to objects directly, and at which all thought aims as a means. Intuition, however, takes place only insofar as the object is given to us; but that, in turn, is possible only – for us human beings, at any rate[1] – by the mind's being affected in a certain manner. The capacity (a receptivity) to acquire presentations as a result of the way in which we are affected by objects is called **sensibility**. Hence by means of sensibility objects are *given* to us, and it alone supplies us with *intuitions*. Through understanding, on the other hand, objects are *thought*, and from it arise *concepts*. But all thought must, by means of certain characteristics, refer ultimately to intuitions, whether it does so straightforwardly (*directe*) or circuitously (*indirecte*); and hence it must, in us [human beings], refer ultimately to sensibility, because no object can be given to us in any other manner than through sensibility.

34
20   The effect of an object on our capacity for presentation, insofar as we are affected by the object, is *sensation*. Intuition that refers to the object through sensation is called *empirical* intuition. The undetermined object of an empirical intuition is called *appearance*.

Whatever in an appearance corresponds to sensation I call its *matter*; but whatever in an appearance brings about the fact that the manifold of the appearance can be ordered in certain relations I call the *form* of appearance. Now, that in which alone sensations can be ordered and put into a certain form cannot itself be sensation again. Therefore, although the matter of all appearance is given to us only a posteriori, the form of all appearance must altogether lie ready for the sensations a priori in the mind; and hence that form must be capable of being examined apart from all sensation.

All presentations in which nothing is found that belongs to sensation I call *pure* (in the transcendental sense of the term). Accordingly, the pure form of sensible intuitions generally, in which everything manifold in experience is intuited in certain relations, will be found in the mind a priori. This pure form of sensibility will also

35 itself be called *pure intuition*. Thus, if from the

presentation of a body I separate what the understanding thinks in it, such as substance, force, divisibility, etc., and if I similarly separate from it what belongs to sensation in it, such as impenetrability, hardness, color, etc., I am still left with something from this empirical intuition,   A 21 namely, extension and shape. These belong to pure intuition, which, even if there is no actual object of the senses or of sensation, has its place in the mind a priori, as a mere form of sensibility.

There must, therefore, be a science of all principles of a priori sensibility; I call such a science *transcendental aesthetic*. It constitutes the first   B 36 part of the transcendental doctrine of elements, and stands in contrast to that [part of the] transcendental doctrine of elements which contains the principles of pure thought and is called transcendental logic.

Hence in the transcendental aesthetic we   A 22 shall, first of all, *isolate* sensibility, by separating from it everything that the understanding through its concepts thinks [in connection] with it, so that nothing other than empirical intuition will remain. Second, we shall also segregate from sensibility everything that belongs to sensation, so that nothing will remain but pure intuition and the mere form of appearances, which is all that sensibility can supply a priori. In the course of that inquiry it will be found that there are two pure forms of sensible intuition, which are principles for a priori cognition: viz., space and time. We now proceed to the task of examining these.

Section I   Space

§2 Metaphysical Exposition of this Concept   By means of outer sense (a property of our mind) we present objects as outside us, and present them one and all in space. In space their shape, magnitude, and relation to one another are determined or determinable. By means of inner sense the mind intuits itself, or its inner state. Although inner sense provides no intuition of the soul itself as an object, yet there is a determinate form under which alone [as condition] we can   A 23 intuit the soul's inner state. [That form is time.] Thus everything belonging to our inner determinations is presented in relations of time. Time cannot be intuited outwardly, any more than space can be intuited as something within us. What, then, are space and time? Are they actual

beings? Are they only determinations of things, or, for that matter, relations among them? If so, are they at least determinations or relations that would belong to things intrinsically also, i.e., even if these things were not intuited? Or are they determinations and relations that adhere only to the form of intuition and hence to the subjective character of our mind, so that apart from that character these predicates cannot be ascribed to any thing at all? In order to inform ourselves on these points, let us first of all give an exposition of the concept of space. Now, by *exposition* (*expositio*) I mean clear (even if not comprehensive) presentation of what belongs to a concept; and such exposition is *metaphysical* if it contains what exhibits the concept as *given a priori*.

1. Space is not an empirical concept that has been abstracted from outer experiences. For the presentation of space must already lie at the basis in order for certain sensations to be referred to something outside me (i.e., referred to something in a location of space other than the location in which I am). And it must similarly already lie at the basis in order for me to be able to present [the objects of] these sensations as outside and *alongside* one another, and hence to present them not only as different but as being in different locations. Accordingly, the presentation of space cannot be one that we take from the relations of outer appearance by means of experience; rather, only through the presentation of space is that outer experience possible in the first place.

2. Space is a necessary a priori presentation that underlies all outer intuitions. We can never have a presentation of there being no space, even though we are quite able to think of there being no objects encountered in it. Hence space must be regarded as the condition for the possibility of appearances, and not as a determination dependent on them. Space is an a priori presentation that necessarily underlies outer appearances.

3. Space is not a discursive or, as we say, universal concept of things as such; rather, it is a pure intuition. For, first, we can present only one space; and when we speak of many spaces, we mean by that only parts of one and the same unique space. Nor, second, can these parts precede the one all-encompassing space, as its constituents, as it were (from which it can be assembled); rather, they can be thought only as *in it*. Space is essentially one; the manifold in it,

and hence also the universal concept of spaces as such, rests solely on [our bringing in] limitations. It follows from this that, as far as space is concerned, an a priori intuition of it (i.e., one that is not empirical) underlies all concepts of space. By the same token, no geometric principles – e.g., the principle that in a triangle two sides together are greater than the third – are ever derived from universal concepts of *line* and *triangle*; rather, they are all derived from intuition, and are derived from it moreover a priori, with apodeictic certainty.

4. We present space as an infinite *given* magnitude. Now it is true that every concept must be thought as a presentation that is contained in an infinite multitude of different possible presentations (as their common characteristic) and hence the concept contains these presentations *under itself*. But no concept, as such, can be thought as containing an infinite multitude of presentations *within itself*. Yet that is how we think space (for all parts of space, *ad infinitum*, are simultaneous). Therefore the original presentation of space is an a priori *intuition*, not a *concept*.

§3 Transcendental Exposition of the Concept of Space By a *transcendental exposition* I mean the explication of a concept as a principle that permits insight into the possibility of other synthetic a priori cognitions. Such explication requires (1) that cognitions of that sort do actually flow from the given concept, and (2) that these cognitions are possible only on the presupposition of a given way of explicating that concept.

Geometry is a science that determines the properties of space synthetically and yet a priori. What, then, must the presentation of space be in order for such cognition of space to be possible? Space must originally be intuition. For from a mere concept one cannot obtain propositions that go beyond the concept; but we do obtain such propositions in geometry (Introduction, V). This intuition must, however, be encountered in us a priori, i.e., prior to any perception of an object; hence this intuition must be pure rather than empirical. For geometric propositions are one and all apodeictic, i.e. linked with the consciousness of their necessity – e.g., the proposition that space has only three dimensions. But propositions of that sort cannot be empirical judgments or judgments of experience; nor can they be inferred from such judgments (Introduction, II).

B 38

A 24

B 39

A 25

B 4

B 4

How, then, can the mind have an outer intuition which precedes the objects themselves, and in which the concept of these objects can be determined a priori? Obviously, this can be so only insofar as this intuition resides merely in the subject, as the subject's formal character of being affected by objects and of thereby acquiring from them *direct presentation*, i.e., *intuition*, and hence only as form of outer *sense* in general.

Our explication of the concept of space is, therefore, the only one that makes comprehensible the *possibility of geometry* as a [kind of] synthetic a priori cognition. Any way of explicating the concept that fails to make this possibility comprehensible, even if it should otherwise seem to have some similarity to ours, can be distinguished from it most safely by these criteria.

26

42 *Conclusions from the Above Concepts* (a) Space represents no property whatever of any things in themselves, nor does it represent things in themselves in their relation to one another. That is, space represents no determination of such things, no determination that adheres to objects themselves and that would remain even if we abstracted from all subjective conditions of intuition. For determinations, whether absolute or relative, cannot be intuited prior to the existence of the things to which they belong, and hence cannot be intuited a priori.

(b) Space is nothing but the mere form of all appearances of outer senses; i.e., it is the subjective condition of sensibility under which alone outer intuition is possible for us. Now, the subject's receptivity for being affected by objects precedes necessarily all intuitions of these objects. Thus we can understand how the form of all appearances can be given in the mind prior to all actual perceptions, and hence given a priori; and we can understand how this form, as a pure intuition in which all objects must be determined, can contain, prior to all experience, principles for the relations among these objects.

Only from the human standpoint, therefore, can we speak of space, of extended beings, etc. If we depart from the subjective condition under which alone we can – viz, as far as we may be affected by objects – acquire outer intuition, then the presentation of space means nothing whatsoever. This predicate is ascribed to things only insofar as they appear to us, i.e., only insofar as they are objects of sensibility. The constant

43

27

form of this receptivity which we call sensibility is a necessary condition of all relations in which objects are intuited as outside us; and if we abstract from these objects, then the form of that receptivity is a pure intuition that bears the name of space. We cannot make the special conditions of sensibility to be conditions of the possibility of things, but only of the possibility of their appearances. Hence we can indeed say that space encompasses all things that appear to us externally, but not that it encompasses all things in themselves, intuited or not, or intuited by whatever subject. For we can make no judgment at all about the intuitions of other thinking beings, as to whether they are tied to the same conditions that limit our intuition and that are valid for us universally. If the limitation on a judgment is added to the concept of the subject [term], then the judgment holds unconditionally. The proposition, All things are side by side in space, holds under the limitation: if these things are taken as objects of our sensible intuition. If I here add the condition to the concept and say, All things considered as outer appearances are side by side in space, then this rule holds universally and without limitation. Accordingly, our exposition teaches that space is *real* (i.e., objectively valid) in regard to everything that we can encounter externally as object, but teaches at the same time that space is *ideal* in regard to things when reason considers them in themselves, i.e., without taking into account the character of our sensibility. Hence we assert that space is *empirically real* (as regards all possible outer experience), despite asserting that space is *transcendentally ideal*, i.e., that it is nothing as soon as we omit [that space is] the condition of the possibility of all experience and suppose space to be something underlying things in themselves.

B 44

A 28

Besides space, on the other hand, no other subjective presentation that is referred to something external could be called an a priori objective presentation. For from none of them can we derive synthetic a priori propositions, as we can from intuition in space (§3). Hence, strictly speaking, ideality does not apply to them, even though they agree with the presentation of space inasmuch as they belong merely to the subjective character of the kind of sense involved. They may belong, e.g., to the sense of sight, of hearing, or of touch, by [being] sensations of colors, sounds, or heat. Yet because they are mere sensations rather than intuitions, they do not allow us to cognize any object at all, let alone a priori.

B 45 The only aim of this comment is to forestall an error: it might occur to someone to illustrate the ideality of space asserted above by means of examples such as colors or taste, etc. These are thoroughly insufficient for this, because they are rightly regarded not as properties of things, but merely as changes in ourselves as subjects, changes that may even be different in different people. For in this case, something that originally is itself only appearance – e.g., a rose – counts as a thing in itself in the empirical meaning of this

A 30 expression, a thing in itself that in regard to color can nonetheless appear differently to every eye. The transcendental concept of appearances in space, on the other hand, is a critical reminder. It reminds us that nothing whatever that is intuited in space is a thing in itself, and that space is not a form of things, one that might belong to them as they are in themselves. Rather, what we call external objects are nothing but mere presentations of our sensibility. The form of this sensibility is space; but its true correlate, i.e., the thing in itself, is not cognized at all through these presentations, and cannot be. Nor, on the other hand, is the thing in itself ever at issue in experience. [. . .]

B 59 *§8 General Comments on Transcendental Aesthetic*
I. In order to forestall any misinterpretation of our opinion regarding the basic character of

A 42 sensible cognition as such, we must first explain as distinctly as possible what that opinion is.

What we have tried to say, then, is the following. All our intuition is nothing but the presentation of appearance. The things that we intuit are not in themselves what we intuit them as being. Nor do their relations in themselves have the character that they appear to us as having. And if we annul ourselves as subject, or even annul only the subjective character of the senses generally, then this entire character of objects and all their relations in space and time – indeed, even space and time themselves – would vanish; being appearances, they cannot exist in themselves, but can exist only in us. What may be the case regarding objects in themselves and apart from all this receptivity of our sensibility remains to us entirely unknown. All we know is the way in which we perceive them. That way is peculiar to us and does not necessarily have to apply to all

beings, even though it applies necessarily to all human beings. Solely with that way of perceiving B 6 are we dealing here. Space and time are its pure forms; sensation as such as its matter. Only that way of perceiving can we cognize a priori, i.e., prior to all actual perception, and that is why it is called pure intuition. Sensation, on the other hand, is that component in our cognition on whose account it is called a posteriori cognition, i.e., empirical intuition. The forms [of intuition] attach to our sensibility with absolute necessity, no matter of what kind our sensations may be; A 4 the sensations can differ very much. Even if we could bring this institution of ours to the highest degree of distinctiveness, that would still not get us closer to the character of objects in themselves. For what we would cognize, and cognize completely, would still be only our way of intuiting, i.e., our sensibility; and we would always cognize it only under the conditions attaching to the subject originally: space and time. What objects may be in themselves would still never become known to us, not even through the most enlightened cognition of what alone is given to us, viz., their appearance.

Hence we must reject the view that our entire sensibility is nothing but our confused presentation of things, a presentation that contains solely what belongs to them in themselves, but contains it only by way of an accumulation of characteristics and partial presentations that we do not consciously discriminate. For this view falsifies the concept of sensibility and of appearance, thus rendering the entire doctrine of sensibility useless and empty. The distinction between an indistinct and a distinct presentation is merely logical B 6 and does not concern the content. No doubt the concept of *rightness* as employed by common sense contains just the same as can be extricated from it by the most subtle speculation, except that in its common and practical use one is not conscious of the diverse presentations contained in that thought. But that does not entitle us to say that the common concept is sensible and contains a mere appearance. For rightness cannot be an A 4 appearance at all; rather, its concept lies in the understanding, and we present by it a character of acts (their moral character) which belongs to them in themselves. On the other hand, when a *body* is presented in intuition, this presentation contains nothing whatever that could belong to an object in itself. It contains, rather, merely the appearance of something, and the way we are affected by that something. This receptivity of our cognitive capacity is called sensibility; and even if we were to see through that appearance and to its very bottom, yet this receptivity remains as different as day and night from cognition of the object in itself.

Hence the philosophy of Leibniz and [Christian] Wolff, by considering the distinction between what is sensible and what is intellectual as a merely logical one, has imposed an entirely wrong point of view on all investigations about the nature and origin of our cognitions. For plainly the distinction is transcendental, and does not concern merely the form of these cognitions, i.e., their distinctness or indistinctness, 62 but concerns their origin and content. Hence sensibility does not merely fail to provide us with a distinct cognition of the character of things in themselves; it provides us with none whatsoever. And once we remove our subjective character, then the presented object, along with the properties contributed to it by sensible intuition, is not to be found anywhere at all; nor can it possibly be found, because this subjective character is precisely what determines the form of that object as appearance.

45　It is true that we commonly make this distinction about appearances: we distinguish what attaches to their intuition essentially and holds for the sense of every human being in general, from what belongs to that intuition only contingently by being valid only for a special position of this or that sense, or for the special organization of that sense, but not valid for the relation of [the intuition to] sensibility in general. We then speak of the first kind of cognition as presenting the object in itself, and of the second as presenting only its appearance. This distinction, however, is only empirical. If (as is commonly done) we fail to go beyond it and do not (as we ought to do) regard that empirical intuition in turn as mere appearance, in which nothing whatever belonging to some thing in itself is to be found, then our transcendental distinction is lost. We then 63 believe after all that we cognize things in themselves, even though in the world of sense, however deeply we explore its objects, we deal with nothing whatever but appearances. Thus it is true, e.g., that when during a rain accompanied by sunshine we see a rainbow, we will call it a mere appearance, while calling the rain the thing in itself.

And this is indeed correct, provided that we here take the concept of a thing in itself as meaning only something physical. We then mean by it something that in general experience, and in all its different positions in relation to the senses, is yet determined thus, and not otherwise, in intuition. But suppose that we take this empirical something as such, and that – without being A 46 concerned about its being the same for the sense of every human being – we ask whether it presents also an object in itself (not whether it presents the rain drops, for these, as appearances, will already be empirical objects). In that case our question about the presentation's relation to the object is transcendental, and the answer is: Not only are these drops mere appearances; rather, even their round shape, and indeed even the space in which they fall, are nothing in themselves. They are, rather, mere modifications, or foundations, of our sensible intuition. The transcendental object, however, remains unknown to us.

Our second important concern in this transcendental aesthetic is that it should not merely gain some favor as a plausible hypothesis, but should be as certain and indubitable as can possibly be demanded of a theory that is to serve as an organon. In order to make this certainty fully evident, let us select some case that can render the B 64 validity of this organon obvious and can serve to clarify further what has been set forth in §3.

Suppose, then, that space and time are in themselves objective, and are conditions of the possibility of things in themselves. We then find, in the first place, that we encounter a large number of synthetic a priori propositions about both space and time – above all about space, which we shall therefore investigate here as our prime example. The propositions of geometry are cognized synthetically a priori and with apodeictic A 47 certainty. And so I ask: From where do you obtain such propositions, and on what does the understanding rely in order to arrive at such absolutely necessary and universally valid truths? There is no other way [to arrive at truths] than through concepts or through intuition. But these concepts and intuitions are both given either a priori or a posteriori. The a posteriori ones, i.e., empirical concepts as well as the empirical intuition on which they are based, can yield only such synthetic propositions as are likewise merely empirical, i.e., propositions of experience. As such, these propositions can never contain necessity and

absolute universality; yet these are what characterize all geometric propositions.[2] The first and sole
means of arriving at such cognitions is a priori,
through mere concepts or through intuitions.
From mere concepts, however, we clearly can
obtain no synthetic cognition at all, but only
B 65 analytic cognition. Just take the proposition that
two straight lines cannot enclose any space and
hence do not permit [construction of], any
figure, and try to derive it from the concept of
straight lines and of the number two. Or take the
proposition that three straight lines permit [con-
struction of] a figure, and try similarly to derive
it from these mere concepts. All your endeavor
is futile, and you find yourselves compelled to have
recourse to intuition, as indeed geometry always
A 48 does. Hence you give yourselves an object in
intuition. But of which kind is this intuition?
Is it a pure a priori intuition or an empirical one?
If it were an empirical intuition, then it could
never turn into a universally valid proposition,
let alone an apodeictic one; for experience can
never supply anything like that. Hence you must
give your object to yourselves a priori in intuition,
and base your synthetic proposition on this
object. Now suppose that there did not lie within
you a power to intuit a priori; that this subjective condition were not, as regards its form, at the
same time the universal a priori condition under
which alone the object of this (outer) intuition is
itself possible; and that the object (the triangle)
were something in itself, even apart from any relation to yourselves as subject. If that were so, how
could you say that what necessarily lies in [or
belongs to] your subjective conditions for constructing a triangle must also belong necessarily
to the triangle itself? For, after all, you could not
add to your concepts (of three lines) anything new
B 66 (the figure) that would therefore have to be met
with necessarily in the object, since this object
would be given prior to your cognition rather than
through it. Hence you could not synthetically
a priori establish anything whatsoever about
external objects if space (and similarly time) were
not a mere form of your intuition, an intuition
that a priori contains conditions under which
alone things can be external objects for you – these
objects being nothing in themselves, apart from
these subjective conditions. Therefore the following is not merely possible – or probable, for
A 49 that matter – but indubitably certain: Space and
time, as the necessary conditions of all (outer and

inner) experience, are merely subjective conditions
of all our intuition. Hence in relation to these conditions all objects are mere appearances, and are
not given to us in this way on their own. And that
is why much can be said a priori about these
objects as regards their form, but not the least can
ever be said about the thing in itself that may
underlie these appearances.

II. This theory, according to which both
outer and inner sense are ideal and hence all
objects of the senses are mere appearances, can
be confirmed superbly by the following observation. Whatever in our cognition belongs to
intuition (excluding, therefore, what are not
cognitions at all, i.e., both the feeling of pleasure
and displeasure and the will) contains nothing but
mere relations: of places in an intuition (exten- B 67
sion), of change of places (motion), and of laws
according to which this change is determined
(motive forces). But what is present in that
place, or what effect – besides the change of
place – it produces in the things themselves, is not
given to us by [what belongs to intuition]. Now
through mere relations we do not, of course,
cognize a thing in itself. Hence our judgment must
surely be this: since through outer sense we are
given nothing but mere relational presentations,
outer sense can, by the same token, contain in its
presentation only the relation of an object to the
subject, but not the intrinsic character belonging
to the object in itself. The same applies to inner
intuition. For not only does the proper material
in it, with which we occupy our mind, consist in
presentations of *outer senses*; but the time in
which we place these presentations, and which itself
precedes the consciousness of them in experience
and underlies, as formal condition, the way in
which we place them within the mind, already contains relations: of succession, of simultaneity,
and of what is simultaneous with succession (the
permanent). Now, presentation that can precede
all acts of thinking anything is intuition; and if
this intuition contains nothing but relations
then it is the form of intuition. But this form does
not present anything except insofar as something is being placed within the mind. Therefore B 68
this form can be nothing but the way in which
the mind is affected by its own activity – viz., this
placing of its presentation – and hence affected
by itself; i.e., it is an inner sense insofar as that
sense's form is concerned. Whatever is presented
through a sense is, to that extent, always appear-

ance. Hence either we must not grant that there is an inner sense at all; or we must grant that the subject who is the object of this sense can be presented through it only as appearance, and not as he would judge himself if his intuition were self-activity only, i.e., if it were intellectual intuition. What underlies this whole difficulty is this: how can a subject inwardly intuit himself? But this difficulty is shared by every theory. The consciousness of oneself (apperception) is the simple presentation of the *I*; and if through this consciousness by itself all the manifold in the subject were given *self-actively*, then the inner intuition would be intellectual. But in man this consciousness requires also inner perception of the manifold given in the subject beforehand; and the way in which this manifold is given in the mind – viz., without spontaneity – must, for the sake of marking this distinction, be called sensibility. If the power to become conscious of oneself is to locate (apprehend) what lies in the mind, then it must affect the mind; and only in that way can it produce an intuition of itself. But the form of this intuition lies at the basis beforehand in the mind; and this form determines, in the presentation of time, the way in which the manifold is [placed] together in the mind. And thus this power does not intuit itself as it would if it presented itself directly and self-actively; rather, it intuits itself according to the way in which it is affected from within, and hence intuits itself as it appears to itself, not as it is.

III. I am saying, then, that the intuition of external objects and the self-intuition of the mind both present these objects and the mind, in space and in time, as they affect our senses, i.e., as they appear. But I do not mean by this that these objects are a mere *illusion*. For when we deal with appearance, the objects, and indeed even the properties that we ascribe to them, are always regarded a something actually given – except that insofar as the object's character depends only on the subject's way of intuiting this given object in its relation to him, we do also distinguish this object as *appearance* from the same object as object *in itself*. Thus when I posit both bodies and my soul as being in accordance with the quality of space and time, as condition of their existence, I do indeed assert that this quality lies in my way of intuiting and not in those objects in themselves. But in asserting this I am not saying that the bodies merely *seem* to be outside me,

or that my soul only *seems* to be given in my self-consciousness. It would be my own fault if I turned into mere illusion what I ought to class with appearance.* This is not, however, what happens if we follow our principle that all our sensible intuitions are ideal. On the contrary: it is when we attribute *objective reality* to those forms of presentation that we cannot prevent everything from being thereby transformed into mere *illusion*. For suppose that we regard space and time as properties that, as far as their very possibility is concerned, must be found in things in themselves. And now reflect on the absurdities in which we then become entangled, inasmuch as [we then have] two infinite things that must not be substances nor anything actually inhering in substances, but that yet must be something existent – indeed, must be the necessary condition for the existence of all things – and must moreover remain even if all existing things are annulled. If we thus reflect on this supposition, then we can hardly blame the good *Berkeley* for downgrading bodies to mere illusion.[3] Indeed, even our own existence, which would in this way be made dependent on the self-subsistent reality of a nonentity such as time would be, would be transformed along with this time into nothing but illusion – an absurdity of which no one thus far has made himself guilty.

IV. In natural theology we think an object [viz. God] that not only cannot possibly be an object of intuition for us, but that cannot in any way be

* The predicates of the appearance can be ascribed to the object itself in relation to our sense: e.g., to the rose, the red color or the scent. But what is mere illusion can never be ascribed as predicate to an object, precisely because illusion ascribes to the object taken *by itself* what belongs to it only in relation to the senses or in general to the subject – an example being the two handles intially ascribed to Saturn. If something is not to be met with at all in the object in itself, but is always to be met with in the object's relation to the subject and is inseparable from the presentation of the object, then it is appearance. And thus the predicates of space and time are rightly ascribed to objects of the senses, as such; and in this there is no illusion. Illusion first arises if, by contrast, I ascribe the redness to the rose *in itself*, or the handles to Saturn, or extension to all external objects *in themselves*, without taking account of – and limiting my judgment to – a determinate relation of these objects to the subject.

B 69

B 70

B 71

an object of sensible intuition even to itself. [When we think of God in this way,] we take great care to remove the conditions of time and space from all his intuition. (All his cognition must be intuition rather than *thought*, which always manifests limits.) But what right do we have to do this if we have beforehand turned space and time into forms of things in themselves – such forms, moreover, as are a priori conditions of the existence of things and hence would remain even if we had annulled the things themselves? For as conditions of all existence in general, they would B 72 have to be conditions also of the existence of God. If we are not to make space and time objective forms of all things, then we are left with only one alternative: we must make them subjective forms of our kind of intuition, inner and outer. Our kind of intuition is called sensible because it is *not original*. I.e., it is not such that through this intuition itself the existence of its object is given (the latter being a kind of intuition that, as far as we can see, can belong only to the original being). Rather, our kind of intuition is dependent on the existence of the object, and hence is possible only by the object's affecting the subject's capacity to present.

There is, moreover, no need for us to limit this kind of intuition – intuition in space and time – to the sensibility of man. It may be (though we cannot decide this) that any finite thinking being must necessarily agree with man in this regard. Yet even if this kind of intuition were thus universally valid, it would not therefore cease to be sensibility. It would remain sensibility precisely because it is derivative (*intuitus derivativus*) rather than original (*intuitus originarius*), and hence is not intellectual intuition. For the reason just set forth, intellectual intuition seems to belong solely to the original being, and never to a being that is dependent as regards both its

existence and its intuition (an intuition that determines that being's existence by reference to given objects). This last remark, however, must be considered as included in our aesthetic theory only as an illustration, not as a basis of proof.

Concluding the Transcendental Aesthetic Thus B 73 in our pure a priori intuitions, space and time, we now have one of the components required for solving the general problem of transcendental philosophy: *How are synthetic propositions possible a priori?* When in an a priori judgment about space and time we want to go beyond the given concept, we encounter what cannot be discovered a priori in the given concept, but can indeed be so discovered in the intuition corresponding to that concept and can be combined with it synthetically. Because of this, however, such judgments can never reach beyond objects of the senses, and can hold only for objects of possible experience.

Notes

1 Here and elsewhere Kant's wording suggests that his thesis is limited to specifically *human* capacities and limitations. But in other places, it looks as if his claims are meant to apply to all rational creatures whose knowledge, unlike that of God's, requires experience.

2 This "argument from geometry" is more fully expounded by Kant in his *Prolegomena to Any Future Metaphysics*, Manchester: Manchester University Press, 1953, pp. 36–51.

3 Berkeley, as we may see from III. 16 above, would certainly reject the charge of "downgrading bodies to mere illusion." But whatever the propriety of Kant's use of the term "illusion," his claim that Berkeley treats spatial properties as no different in status from, say, colors and smells, is accurate.

18

G. W. F. Hegel, *Phenomenology of Spirit*, Preface

Introduction

In the Preface to his book *Phenomenology of Spirit* (1807) – an introduction, in effect, to his entire mature philosophy – the German philosopher, Georg Wilhelm Friedrich Hegel (1770–1831), sketches one of the most startling and ambitious metaphysical visions in the history of philosophy. Startling, since it maintains that reality as such, or "the Absolute," is "Subject" or "Spirit" (*Geist*); ambitious, since it proclaims that not only can this Absolute be rationally articulated by philosophical "Science" (*Wissenschaft*), but that in terms of this articulation the necessity of all significant developments both in the natural world and in human history can be demonstrated. As Hegel elsewhere put it, "history is the development of Spirit in time, as nature is . . . of the Idea in space" (*Introduction to the Lectures on the Philosophy of History*).

Hegel refers to his metaphysics as "Absolute Idealism," which he contrasts with Kant's "Transcendental Idealism" (III.17). For Kant, what is "ideal" (i.e. mind-dependent) is only the empirical or "phenomenal" world (not things in themselves), and the mind on which it is dependent is the individual human mind. For Hegel, by contrast,

From G. W. F. Hegel, *Phenomenology of Spirit*, trans. A. V. Miller, Oxford: Oxford University Press, 1977, pp. 3–22 (some sections omitted).

who rejects the distinction between "appearances" and things in themselves, everything is "ideal" in the sense of having its "ground" in what he calls "the universal divine idea" (*Encyclopedia Logic* §45). This includes individual human minds, which – though they are the pre-eminent "vehicles" of *Geist* – have their "Substance" or "ground" in "the world-spirit."

Precisely because human beings are "vehicles" of Spirit, the story of Spirit's development is, in effect, the history of human experience, practices and institutions – scientific, political, artistic and so on. And it is the telling of this history that Hegel has in mind by "the phenomenology of Spirit." That, in this way, we can tell the story of Spirit, means that it is something rationally articulatable, and therefore is what Hegel calls a "Concept" or "Notion" (*Begriff*), or rather *the* Concept. Hence we find Hegel, in the early sections of the Preface, strenuously rejecting the view – of Novalis and F. W. Schelling among several other contemporaries[1] – that Absolute Spirit is essentially mysterious, the object not of conceptual articulation but at best of a special and ineffable "intuition." We also find him, despite his own occasional invocation of religious language, rejecting any equation of Spirit with God, at any rate with the personal creator-God of monotheism. (As Hegel will explain toward the end of his book, religion gives figurative expression to the literal truth of his own metaphysics.)

That there is a (hi)story of Spirit to tell also indicates that, for Hegel, Spirit is *essentially* developmental or progressive. This, in turn, entails that there is a "goal" or end-state to which Spirit moves. This goal is Spirit's coming to self-conscious recognition – in and through the understanding achieved by its primary "vehicles," human thought and practices – of what it truly is, namely the "whole" of which everything that has hitherto seemed alien to Spirit is only an aspect. In Hegel-speak, when this goal is reached, Spirit is now "actual," not merely "potential," and "The Concept" becomes what he calls "The Idea."

While, in other works, Hegel does offer arguments in favor of his Absolute Idealism – to the effect that any rival conception of reality contains contradictions – in the case of *Phenomenology of Spirit* it is the book as a whole that is the argument. For the book is one long invitation, in effect, to appreciate that there can be no final distinction between how the world really is and Spirit's (and our own) conceptions of the world, between "Being and Thought," as Hegel puts it. Correlatively, the *Phenomenology* invites readers to appreciate how, as Hegel argues in the Introduction to the book, as our forms of knowledge change, so do the "objects" that are known (see II.13 of this volume). The *Phenomenology*'s invitation is one that many later philosophers, such as Michel Foucault (1926–1984) and Richard

Rorty (1931–2007) have accepted, even when they at the same time reject, or deem unintelligible, Hegel's notion of Spirit as a "divine idea" of which the world is but "the superficial outer rind." Other recent philosophers, it is worth noting, have preferred to treat such descriptions of Spirit as mere rhetoric on Hegel's part. Plausibly or otherwise, they hold that Hegel's idealism is not "a thorough-going spiritualist doctrine," but a "relatively modest doctrine concerning the conceptual structure of the world and humanity's historical development."[2]

Notes

1 See, especially, F. W. Schelling (1775–1854), *Ideas for a Philosophy of Nature*, trans. E. Harris and P. Heath, Cambridge: Cambridge University Press, 1988. Novalis (Friedrich Leopold, Freiherr von Hardenberg) (1772–1801).

2 See M. Inwood, *A Hegel Dictionary*, Oxford: Blackwell, 1992, p. 130. Inwood may have in mind such commentators as Robert B. Pippin, *Hegel's Idealism: The Satisfactions of Self-Consciousness*, Cambridge: Cambridge University Press, 1989.

Hegel, *Phenomenology of Spirit*

Preface

[. . .]

5. The true shape in which truth exists can only be the scientific system of such truth. To help bring philosophy closer to the form of Science, to the goal where it can lay aside the title '*love of knowing*' and be *actual* knowing – that is what I have set myself to do. The inner necessity that knowing should be Science lies in its nature, and only the systematic exposition of philosophy itself provides it. But the *external* necessity, so far as it is grasped in a general way, setting aside accidental matters of person and motivation, is the same as the inner, or in other words it lies in the shape in which time sets forth the sequential existence of its moments. To show that now is

the time for philosophy to be raised to the status of a Science would therefore be the only true justification of any effort that has this aim, for to do so would demonstrate the necessity of the aim, would indeed at the same time be the accomplishing of it.

6. To lay down that the true shape of truth is scientific – or, what is the same thing, to maintain that truth has only the Notion as the element of its existence – seems, I know, to contradict a view which is in our time as prevalent as it is pretentious, and to go against what that view implies. Some explanation therefore seems called for, even though it must for the present be no more than a bare assertion, like the view that it contradicts. If, namely, the True exists only in what, or better *as* what, is sometimes called intuition, sometimes immediate knowledge of the Absolute, religion or being – not at the centre of divine love but the being of the divine love itself – then

what is required in the exposition of philosophy is, from this viewpoint, rather the opposite of the form of the Notion. For the Absolute is not supposed to be comprehended, it is to be felt and intuited; not the Notion of the Absolute, but the feeling and intuition of it, must govern what is said, and must be expressed by it.

7.   If we apprehend a demand of this kind in its broader context, and view it as it appears at the stage which self-conscious Spirit has presently reached, it is clear that Spirit has now got beyond the substantial life it formerly led in the element of thought, that it is beyond the immediacy of faith, beyond the satisfaction and security of the certainty that consciousness then had, of its reconciliation with the essential being, and of that being's universal presence both within and without. It has not only gone beyond all this into the other extreme of an insubstantial reflection of itself into itself, but beyond that too. Spirit has not only lost its essential life; it is also conscious of this loss, and of the finitude that is its own content. Turning away from the empty husks, and confessing that it lies in wickedness, it reviles itself for so doing, and now demands from philosophy, not so much *knowledge* of what it *is*, as the recovery through its agency of that lost sense of solid and substantial being. Philosophy is to meet this need, not by opening up the fast-locked nature of substance, and raising this to self-consciousness, not by bringing consciousness out of its chaos back to an order based on thought, nor to the simplicity of the Notion, but rather by running together what thought has put asunder, by suppressing the differentiations of the Notion and restoring the *feeling* of essential being: in short, by providing edification rather than insight. The 'beautiful', the 'holy', the 'eternal', 'religion', and 'love' are the bait required to arouse the desire to bite; not the Notion, but ecstasy, not the cold march of necessity in the thing itself, but the ferment of enthusiasm, these are supposed to be what sustains and continually extends the wealth of substance.

8.   In keeping with this demand is the strenuous, almost over-zealous and frenzied effort to tear men away from their preoccupation with the sensuous, from their ordinary, private [*einzelne*] affairs, and to direct their gaze to the stars; as if they had forgotten all about the divine, and were ready like worms to content themselves with dirt and water. Formerly they had a heaven adorned with a vast wealth of thoughts and imagery. The meaning of all that is, hung on the thread of light by which it was linked to that heaven. Instead of dwelling in this world's presence, men looked beyond it, following this thread to an other-worldly presence, so to speak. The eye of the Spirit had to be forcibly turned and held fast to the things of this world; and it has taken a long time before the lucidity which only heavenly things used to have could penetrate the dullness and confusion in which the sense of worldly things was enveloped, and so make attention to the here and now as such, attention, to what has been called 'experience', an interesting and valid enterprise. Now we seem to need just the opposite: sense is so fast rooted in earthly things that it requires just as much force to raise it. The Spirit shows itself as so impoverished that, like a wanderer in the desert craving for a mere mouthful of water, it seems to crave for its refreshment only the bare feeling of the divine in general. By the little which now satisfies Spirit, we can measure the extent of its loss.

9.   This modest complacency in receiving, or this sparingness in giving, does not, however, befit Science. Whoever seeks mere edification, and whoever wants to shroud in a mist the manifold variety of his earthly existence and of thought, in order to pursue the indeterminate enjoyment of this indeterminate divinity, may look where he likes to find all this. He will find ample opportunity to dream up something for himself. But philosophy must beware of the wish to be edifying.

10.   Still less must this complacency which abjures Science claim that such rapturous haziness is superior to Science. This prophetic talk supposes that it is staying right in the centre and in the depths, looks disdainfully at determinateness (*Horos*), and deliberately holds aloof from Notion and Necessity as products of that reflection which is at home only in the finite. But just as there is an empty breadth, so too there is an empty depth; and just as there is an extension of substance that pours forth as a finite multiplicity without the force to hold the multiplicity together, so there is an intensity without content, one that holds itself in as a sheer force without spread, and this is in no way distinguishable from superficiality. The power of Spirit is only as great as its expression, its depth only as deep as it dares to spread out and lose itself in its

exposition. Moreover, when this non-conceptual, substantial knowledge professes to have sunk the idiosyncrasy of the self in essential being, and to philosophize in a true and holy manner, it hides the truth from itself: by spurning measure and definition, instead of being devoted to God, it merely gives free rein both to the contingency of the content within it, and to its own caprice. Such minds, when they give themselves up to the uncontrolled ferment of [the divine] substance, imagine that, by drawing a veil over self-consciousness and surrendering understanding they become the beloved of God to whom He gives wisdom in sleep; and hence what they in fact receive, and bring to birth in their sleep, is nothing but dreams.

11.   Besides, it is not difficult to see that ours is a birth-time and a period of transition to a new era. Spirit has broken with the world it has hitherto inhabited and imagined, and is of a mind to submerge it in the past, and in the labour of its own transformation [. . .]

[. . .]

13.   While the initial appearance of the new world is, to begin with, only the whole veiled in its *simplicity,* or the general foundation of the whole, the wealth of previous existence is still present to consciousness in memory. Consciousness misses in the newly emerging shape its former range and specificity of content, and even more the articulation of form whereby distinctions are securely defined, and stand arrayed in their fixed relations. Without such articulation, Science lacks universal intelligibility, and gives the appearance of being the esoteric possession of a few individuals: an esoteric possession, since it is as yet present only in its Notion or in its inwardness; of a few individuals, since its un-diffused manifestation makes its existence something singular. Only what is completely determined is at once exoteric, comprehensible, and capable of being learned and appropriated by all. The intelligible form of Science is the way open and equally accessible to everyone, and consciousness as it approaches Science justly demand that it be able to attain to rational knowledge by way of the ordinary understanding; for the understanding is thought, the pure 'I' as such; and what is intelligible is what is already familiar and common to Science and the unscientific consciousness alike, the latter through its having afforded direct access to the former.

14.   Science in its early stages, when it has attained neither to completeness of detail nor perfection of form, is vulnerable to criticism. But it would be as unjust for such criticism to strike at the very heart of Science, as it is untenable to refuse to honour the demand for its further development. This polarization seems to be the Gordian knot with which scientific culture is at present struggling, and which it still does not properly understand. One side boasts of its wealth of material and intelligibility, the other side at least scorns this intelligibility, and flaunts its immediate rationality and divinity. Even if the former side is reduced to silence, whether by the force of truth alone or by the blustering of the other, and even if, in respect of fundamentals, it feels itself outmatched, it is by no means satisfied regarding the said demands; for they are justified, but not fulfilled. Its silence stems only half from the triumph of its opponent, and half from the boredom and indifference which tend to result from the continual awakening of expectations through unfulfilled promises.

15.   As for content, the other side make it easy enough for themselves at times to display a great expanse of it. They appropriate a lot of already familiar and well-ordered material; by focusing on rare and exotic instances they give the impression that they have hold of everything else which scientific knowledge had already embraced in its scope, and that they are also in command of such material as is as yet unordered. It thus appears that everything has been subjected to the absolute Idea, which therefore seems to be cognized in everything and to have matured into an expanded science. But a closer inspection shows that this expansion has not come about through one and the same principle having spontaneously assumed different shapes, but rather through the shapeless repetition of one and the same formula, only externally applied to diverse materials, thereby obtaining merely a boring show of diversity. The Idea, which is of course true enough on its own account, remains in effect always in its primitive condition, if its development involves nothing more than this sort of repetition of the same formula. When the knowing subject goes around applying this single inert form to whatever it encounters, and dipping the material into this placid element from outside, this

is no more the fulfilment of what is needed, i.e. a self-originating, self-differentiating wealth of shapes, than any arbitrary insights into the content. Rather it is a monochromatic formalism which only arrives at the differentiation of its material since this has been already provided and is by now familiar.

16. Yet this formalism maintains that such monotony and abstract universality are the Absolute, and we are assured that dissatisfaction with it indicates the inability to master the absolute standpoint and to keep hold of it. Time was when the bare possibility of imagining something differently was sufficient to refute an idea, and this bare possibility, this general thought, also had the entire positive value of an actual cognition. Nowadays we see all value ascribed to the universal Idea in this nonactual form, and the undoing of all distinct, determinate entities (or rather the hurling of them all into the abyss of vacuity without further development or any justification) is allowed to pass muster as the speculative mode of treatment. Dealing with something from the perspective of the Absolute consists merely in declaring that, although one has been speaking of it just now as something definite, yet in the Absolute, the A=A, there is nothing of the kind, for there all is one. To pit this single insight, that in the Absolute everything is the same, against the full body of articulated cognition, which at least seeks and demands such fulfilment, to palm off its Absolute as the night in which, as the saying goes, all cows are black – this is cognition naïvely reduced to vacuity. The formalism which recent philosophy denounces and despises, only to see it reappear in its midst, will not vanish from Science, however much its inadequacy may be recognized and felt, till the cognizing of absolute actuality has become entirely clear as to its own nature. Since the presentation of a general idea in outline, before any attempt to follow it out in detail, makes the latter attempt easier to grasp, it may be useful at this point to give a rough idea of it, at the same time taking the opportunity to get rid of certain habits of thought which impede philosophical cognition.

17. In my view, which can be justified only by the exposition of the system itself, everything turns on grasping and expressing the True, not only as *Substance*, but equally as *Subject*. At the same time, it is to be observed that substantiality embraces the universal, or the *immediacy of knowledge* itself, as well as that which is *being* or immediacy *for* knowledge. If the conception of God as the one Substance shocked the age in which it was proclaimed, the reason for this was on the one hand an instinctive awareness that, in this definition, self-consciousness was only submerged and not preserved. On the other hand, the opposite view, which clings to thought as thought, to *universality* as such, is the very same simplicity, is undifferentiated, unmoved substantiality. And if, thirdly, thought does unite itself with the being of Substance, and apprehends immediacy or intuition as thinking, the question is still whether this intellectual intuition does not again fall back into inert simplicity, and does not depict actuality itself in a non-actual manner.

18. Further, the living Substance is being which is in truth *Subject*, or, what is the same, is in truth actual only in so far as it is the movement of positing itself, or is the mediation of its self-othering with itself. This Substance is, as Subject, pure, *simple negativity*, and is for this very reason the bifurcation of the simple; it is the doubling which sets up opposition, and then again the negation of this indifferent diversity and of its antithesis [the immediate simplicity]. Only this self-*restoring* sameness, or this reflection in otherness within itself – not an *original* or *immediate* unity as such – is the True. It is the process of its own becoming, the circle that presupposes its end as its goal, having its end also as its beginning; and only by being worked out to its end, is it actual.

19. Thus the life of God and divine cognition may well be spoken of as a disporting of Love with itself; but this idea sinks into mere edification, and even insipidity, if it lacks the seriousness, the suffering, the patience, and the labour of the negative. *In itself*, that life is indeed one of untroubled equality and unity with itself, for which otherness and alienation, and the overcoming of alienation, are not serious matters. But this *in-itself* is abstract universality, in which the nature of the divine life *to be for itself*, and so too the self-movement of the form, are together left out of account. If the form is declared to be the same as the essence, then it is *ipso facto* a mistake to suppose that cognition can be satisfied with the in-itself or the essence, but can get along without the form – that the absolute principle or absolute intuition makes the working-out of the

former, or the development of the latter, super-fluous. Just because the form is as essential to the essence as the essence is to itself, the divine essence is not to be conceived and expressed merely as essence, i.e. as immediate substance or pure self-contemplation of the divine, but likewise as *form*, and in the whole wealth of the developed form. Only then is it conceived and expressed as an actuality.

20.   The True is the whole. But the whole is nothing other than the essence consummating itself through its development. Of the Absolute it must be said that it is essentially a *result*, that only in the *end* is it what it truly is; and that precisely in this consists its nature, viz. to be actual, sub-ject, the spontaneous becoming of itself. Though it may seem contradictory that the Absolute should be conceived essentially as a result, it needs little pondering to set this show of contradic-tion in its true light. The beginning, the prin-ciple, or the Absolute, as at first immediately enunciated, is only the universal. Just as when I say '*all* animals', this expression cannot pass for a zoology, so it is equally plain that the words, 'the Divine', 'the Absolute', 'the Eternal', etc., do not express what is contained in them; and only such words, in fact, do express the intuition as something immediate. Whatever is more than such a word, even the transition to a mere proposition, contains a *becoming-other* that has to be taken back, or is a mediation. But it is just this that is rejected with horror, as if absolute cogni-tion were being surrendered when more is made of mediation than in simply saying that it is nothing absolute, and is completely absent in the Absolute.

21.   But this abhorrence in fact stems from ignorance of the nature of mediation, and of absolute cognition itself. For mediation is nothing beyond self-moving selfsameness, or is reflection into self, the moment of the 'I' which is for itself pure negativity or, when reduced to its pure abstraction, *simple becoming*. The 'I', or becoming in general, this mediation, on account of its simple nature, is just immediacy in the process of becoming, and is the immediate itself. Reason is, therefore, misunderstood when reflection is excluded from the True, and is not grasped as a positive moment of the Absolute. It is reflection that makes the True a result, but it is equally reflection that overcomes the anti-thesis between the process of its becoming and the

result, for this becoming is also simple, and therefore not different from the form of the True which shows itself as *simple* in its result; the pro-cess of becoming is rather just this return into simplicity. Though the embryo is indeed *in itself* a human being, it is not so *for itself*; this it only is as cultivated Reason, which has *made* itself into what it is *in itself*. And that is when it for the first time is actual. But this result is itself a sim-ple immediacy, for it is self-conscious freedom at peace with itself, which has not set the antithesis on one side and left it lying there, but has been reconciled with it.

22.   What has just been said can also be ex-pressed by saying that Reason is *purposive activity*. The exaltation of a supposed Nature over a mis-conceived thinking, and especially the rejection of external teleology, has brought the form of purpose in general into discredit. Still, in the sense in which Aristotle, too, defines Nature as purposive activity, purpose is what is immediate and *at rest*, the unmoved which is also *self-moving*, and as such is Subject. Its power to move, taken abstractly, is *being-for-self* or pure negativity. The result is the same as the beginning, only because the *beginning* is the *purpose*; in other words, the actual is the same as its Notion only because the immediate, as purpose, contains the self or pure actuality within itself. The realized purpose, or the existent actuality, is movement and unfolded becoming; but it is just this unrest that is the self; and the self is like that immediacy and simplicity of the beginning because it is the result, that which has returned into itself, the latter being similarly just the self. And the self is the sameness and simplicity that relates itself to itself.

23.   The need to represent the Absolute as *Subject* has found expression in the propositions: *God is the eternal, the moral world-order, love*, and so on. In such propositions the True is only posited *immediately* as Subject, but is not presented as the movement of reflecting itself into itself. In a proposition of this kind one begins with the word 'God'. This by itself is a meaningless sound, a mere name; it is only the predicate that says *what God is*, gives Him content and meaning. Only in the end of the proposition does the empty beginning become actual knowledge. This being so, it is not clear why one does not speak merely of the eternal, of the moral world-order, and so on, or, as the ancients did, of pure notions like 'being',

'the One', and so on, in short, of that which gives the meaning without adding the *meaningless* sound as well. But it is just this word that indicates that what is posited is not a being [i.e. something that merely *is*], or essence, or a universal in general, but rather something that is reflected into itself, a Subject. But at the same time this is only anticipated. The Subject is assumed as a fixed point to which, as their support, the predicates are affixed by a movement belonging to the knower of this Subject, and which is not regarded as belonging to the fixed point itself; yet it is only through this movement that the content could be represented as Subject. The way in which this movement has been brought about is such that it cannot belong to the fixed point; yet, after this point has been presupposed, the nature of the movement cannot really be other than what it is, it can only be external. Hence, the mere anticipation that the Absolute is Subject is not only *not* the actuality of this Notion, but it even makes the actuality impossible; for the anticipation posits the subject as an inert point, whereas the actuality is self-movement.

[. . .]

25. That the True is actual only as system, or that Substance is essentially Subject, is expressed in the representation of the Absolute as *Spirit* – the most sublime Notion and the one which belongs to the modern age and its religion. The spiritual alone is the *actual*; it is essence, or that which has *being in itself*; it is that which *relates itself to itself and* is *determinate*, it is *other-being* and *being-for-self*, and in this determinateness, or in its self-externality, abides within itself; in other words, it is *in and for itself*. – But this being-in-and-for-itself is at first only for us, or *in itself*, it is spiritual *Substance*. It must also be this *for itself*, it must be the knowledge of the spiritual, and the knowledge of itself as Spirit, i.e. it must be an *object* to itself, but just as immediately a sublated object, reflected into itself. It is *for itself* only for *us*, in so far as its spiritual content is generated by itself. But in so far as it is also for itself for its own self, this self-generation, the pure Notion, is for it the objective element in which it has its existence, and it is in this way, in its existence for itself, an object reflected into itself. The Spirit that, so developed, knows itself as Spirit, is *Science*; Science is its actuality and

the realm which it builds for itself in its own element.

26. *Pure* self-recognition in absolute otherness, this Aether *as such*, is the ground and soil of Science or *knowledge in general*. The beginning of philosophy presupposes or requires that consciousness should dwell in this *element*. But this element itself achieves its own perfection and transparency only through the movement of its becoming [. . .].

27. It is this coming-to-be of *Science as such* or of *knowledge*, that is described in this *Phenomenology* of Spirit. Knowledge in its first phase, or *immediate Spirit*, is the non-spiritual, i.e. *sense-consciousness*. In order to become genuine knowledge, to beget the element of Science which is the pure Notion of Science itself, it must travel a long way and work its passage. This process of coming-to-be (considering the content and patterns it will display therein) will not be what is commonly understood by an initiation of the unscientific consciousness into Science; it will also be quite different from the 'foundation' of Science; least of all will it be like the rapturous enthusiasm which, like a shot from a pistol, begins straight away with absolute knowledge, and makes short work of other standpoints by declaring that it takes no notice of them.

28. The task of leading the individual from his uneducated standpoint to knowledge had to be seen in its universal sense, just as it was the universal individual, self-conscious Spirit, whose formative education had to be studied. As regards the relation between them, every moment, as it gains concrete form and a shape of its own, displays itself in the universal individual. The single individual is incomplete Spirit, a concrete shape in whose whole existence *one* determinateness predominates, the others being present only in blurred outline. In a Spirit that is more advanced than another, the lower concrete existence has been reduced to an inconspicuous moment; what used to be the important thing is now but a trace; its pattern is shrouded to become a mere shadowy outline. The individual whose substance is the more advanced Spirit runs through this past just as one who takes up a higher science goes through the preparatory studies he has long since absorbed, in order to bring their content to mind: he recalls them to the inward eye, but has no lasting interest in them. The single individual must also pass through the formative

stages of universal Spirit so far as their content is concerned, but as shapes which Spirit has already left behind, as stages on a way that has been made level with toil. Thus, as far as factual information is concerned, we find that what in former ages engaged the attention of men of mature mind, has been reduced to the level of facts, exercises, and even games for children; and, in the child's progress through school, we shall recognize the history of the cultural development of the world traced, as it were, in a silhouette. This past existence is the already acquired property of universal Spirit which constitutes the Substance of the individual, and hence appears externally to him as his inorganic nature. In this respect formative education, regarded from the side of the individual, consists in his acquiring what thus lies at hand, devouring his inorganic nature, and taking possession of it for himself. But, regarded from the side of universal Spirit as substance, this is nothing but its own acquisition of self-consciousness, the bringing-about of its own becoming and reflection into itself.

29. Science sets forth this formative process in all its detail and necessity, exposing the mature configuration of everything which has already been reduced to a moment and property of Spirit. The goal is Spirit's insight into what knowing is. Impatience demands the impossible, to wit, the attainment of the end without the means. But the *length* of this path has to be endured, because, for one thing, each moment is necessary; and further, each moment has to be *lingered* over, because each is itself a complete individual shape, and one is only viewed in absolute perspective when its determinateness is regarded as a concrete whole, or the whole is regarded as uniquely qualified by that determination. Since the Substance of the individual, the World-Spirit itself, has had the patience to pass through these shapes over the long passage of time, and to take upon itself the enormous labour of world-history, in which it embodied in each shape as much of its entire content as that shape was capable of holding, and since it could not have attained consciousness of itself by any lesser effort, the individual certainly cannot by the nature of the case comprehend his own substance more easily. Yet, at the same time, he does have less trouble, since all this has already been *implicitly* accomplished; the content is already the actuality reduced to a possibility, its immediacy overcome, and the

embodied shape reduced to abbreviated, simple determinations of thought. It is no longer existence in the form of *being-in-itself* – neither still in the original form [of an abstract concept], nor submerged in existence – but is now the *recollected in-itself*, ready for conversion into the form of *being-for-self*. How this is done must now be described more precisely.

[. . .]

31. Quite generally, the familiar, just because it is familiar, is not cognitively understood. The commonest way in which we deceive either ourselves or others about understanding is by assuming something as familiar, and accepting it on that account; with all its pros and cons, such knowing never gets anywhere, and it knows not why. Subject and object, God, Nature, Understanding, sensibility, and so on, are uncritically taken for granted as familiar, established as valid, and made into fixed points for starting and stopping. While these remain unmoved, the knowing activity goes back and forth between them, thus moving only on their surface. Apprehending and testing likewise consist in seeing whether everybody's impression of the matter coincides with what is asserted about these fixed points, whether it seems that way to him or not.

32. The *analysis* of an idea, as it used to be carried out, was, in fact, nothing else than ridding it of the form in which it had become familiar. To break an idea up into its original elements is to return to its moments, which at least do not have the form of the given idea, but rather constitute the immediate property of the self. This analysis, to be sure, only arrives at *thoughts* which are themselves familiar, fixed, and inert determinations. But what is thus *separated* and non-actual is an essential moment; for it is only because the concrete does divide itself, and make itself into something non-actual, that it is self-moving. The activity of dissolution is the power and work of the *Understanding*, the most astonishing and mightiest of powers, or rather the absolute power. The circle that remains self-enclosed and, like substance, holds its moments together, is an immediate relationship, one therefore which has nothing astonishing about it. But that an accident as such, detached from what circumscribes it, what is bound and is actual only in its context with others, should attain an existence

of its own and a separate freedom – this is the tremendous power of the negative; it is the energy of thought, of the pure 'I'. Death, if that is what we want to call this non-actuality, is of all things the most dreadful, and to hold fast what is dead requires the greatest strength. Lacking strength, Beauty hates the Understanding for asking of her what it cannot do. But the life of Spirit is not the life that shrinks from death and keeps itself untouched by devastation, but rather the life that endures it and maintains itself in it. It wins its truth only when, in utter dismemberment, it finds itself. It is this power, not as something positive, which closes its eyes to the negative, as when we say of something that it is nothing or is false, and then, having done with it, turn away and pass on to something else; on the contrary, Spirit is this power only by looking the negative in the face, and tarrying with it. This tarrying with the negative is the magical power that converts it into being. This power is identical with what we earlier called the Subject, which by giving determinateness an existence in its own element supersedes abstract immediacy, i.e. the immediacy which barely is, and thus is authentic substance: that being or immediacy whose mediation is not outside of it but which is this mediation itself.

33. The fact that the object represented becomes the property of pure self-consciousness, its elevation to universality in general, is only one aspect of formative education, not its fulfilment – The manner of study in ancient times differed from that of the modern age in that the former was the proper and complete formation of the natural consciousness. Putting itself to the test at every point of its existence, and philosophizing about everything it came across, it made itself into a universality that was active through and through. In modern times, however, the individual finds the abstract form ready-made; the effort to grasp and appropriate it is more the direct driving-forth of what is within and the truncated generation of the universal than it is the emergence of the latter from the concrete variety of existence. Hence the task nowadays consists not so much in purging the individual of an immediate, sensuous mode of apprehension, and making him into a substance that is an object of thought and that thinks, but rather in just the opposite, in freeing determinate thoughts from their fixity so as to give actuality to the universal, and

impart to it spiritual life. But it is far harder to bring fixed thoughts into a fluid state than to do so with sensuous existence. The reason for this was given above: fixed thoughts have the 'I', the power of the negative, or pure actuality, for the substance and element of their existence, whereas sensuous determinations have only powerless, abstract immediacy, or being as such. Thoughts become fluid when pure thinking, this inner *immediacy*, recognizes itself as a moment, or when the pure certainty of self abstracts from itself – not by leaving itself out, or setting itself aside, but by giving up the *fixity* of its self-positing, by giving up not only the fixity of the pure concrete, which the 'I' itself is, in contrast with its differentiated content, but also the fixity of the differentiated moments which, posited in the element of pure thinking, share the unconditioned nature of the 'I'. Through this movement the pure thoughts become *Notions*, and are only now what they are in truth, self-movements, circles, spiritual essences, which is what their substance is.

34. This movement of pure essences constitutes the nature of scientific method in general. Regarded as the connectedness of their content it is the necessary expansion of that content into an organic whole. Through this movement the path by which the Notion of knowledge is reached becomes likewise a necessary and complete process of becoming; so that this preparatory path ceases to be a casual philosophizing that fastens on to this or that object, relationship, or thought that happens to pop up in the imperfect consciousness, or tries to base the truth on the pros and cons, the inferences and consequences, of rigidly defined thoughts. Instead, this pathway, through the movement of the Notion, will encompass the entire sphere of secular consciousness in its necessary development.

35. Further, an exposition of this kind constitutes the *first* part of Science, because the existence of Spirit *qua* primary is nothing but the immediate or the beginning – but not yet its return into itself. The *element of immediate existence* is therefore what distinguishes this part of Science from the others. The statement of this distinction leads us into a discussion of some fixed ideas which usually crop up in this connection.

36. The immediate existence of Spirit, *consciousness*, contains the two moments of knowing and the objectivity negative to knowing. Since it is in this element [of consciousness] that Spirit

develops itself and explicates its moments, these moments contain that antithesis, and they all appear as shapes of consciousness. The Science of this pathway is the Science of the *experience* which consciousness goes through; the substance and its movement are viewed as the object of consciousness. Consciousness knows and comprehends only what falls within its experience; for what is contained in this is nothing but spiritual substance, and this, too, as *object* of the self. But Spirit becomes object because it is just this movement of becoming an *other to itself*, i.e. becoming an *object to itself*, and of suspending this otherness. And experience is the name we give to just this movement, in which the immediate, the unexperienced, i.e. the abstract, whether it be of sensuous [but still unsensed] being, or only thought of as simple, becomes alienated from itself and then returns to itself from this alienation, and is only then revealed for the first time in its actuality and truth, just as it then has become a property of consciousness also.

37.   The disparity which exists in consciousness between the 'I' and the substance which is its object is the distinction between them, the *negative* in general. This can be regarded as the *defect* of both, though it is their soul, or that which moves them. That is why some of the ancients conceived the *void* as the principle of motion, for they rightly saw the moving principle as the *negative*,

though they did not as yet grasp that the negative is the self. Now, although this negative appears at first as a disparity between the 'I' and its object, it is just as much the disparity of the substance with itself. Thus what seems to happen outside of it, to be an activity directed against it, is really its own doing, and Substance shows itself to be essentially Subject. When it has shown this completely, Spirit has made its existence identical with its essence; it has itself for its object just as it is, and the abstract element of immediacy, and of the separation of knowing and truth, is overcome. Being is then absolutely mediated; it is a substantial content which is just as immediately the property of the 'I', it is self-like or the Notion.

With this, the Phenomenology of Spirit is concluded. What Spirit prepares for itself in it, is the element of [true] knowing. In this element the moments of Spirit now spread themselves out in that *form of simplicity* which knows its object as its own self. They no longer fall apart into the antithesis of being and knowing, but remain in the simple oneness of knowing; they are the True in the form of the True, and their difference is only the difference of content. Their movement, which organizes itself in this element into a whole, is *Logic* or *speculative philosophy*.

[. . .]

19

John Stuart Mill, *An Examination of Sir William Hamilton's Philosophy*, Chapter XI

Introduction

In nineteenth-century Britain, hardly less than in Germany, metaphysical effort was devoted to dissolving or mitigating Kant's dichotomy between phenomena and unknowable things-in-themselves. Schopenhauer's identification (II.15) of the thing-in-itself with a cosmic will (*Wille*), partially apprehensible through esthetic and internal experience, had little appeal for the leading British empiricist of the century, J. S. Mill (1806–73). Not only did Schopenhauer's solution, like that of many German idealists, retain the idea of something beyond all possible perceptual experience, but the cosmic will was far too speculative a notion to be accepted by a philosopher for whom inductive generalization from observed data was the only legitimate form of inference.[1]

The chapter we have selected from Mill's massive book on the philosophy of Sir William Hamilton (1791–1856) begins with a related issue that may seem to belong more to psychology than metaphysics: why do we believe in an external, material reality at all? Mill's target is those philosophers – mainly members of the Scottish

From John Stuart Mill, *An Examination of Sir William Hamilton's Philosophy and of the Principal Philosophical Questions Discussed in his Writings*, ed. J. M. Robson. Toronto: University of Toronto Press, 1979, pp. 177–87 (most notes omitted; asterisked note is Mill's).

"commonsense school," and in particular Hamilton himself – who held that this belief is an intuitive, non-inferential one (see II.11).[2] Against them, Mill argues that belief in the external world is an "acquired product," at which we inevitably arrive on the basis of our experiences or "sensations" as governed by the laws of "associationist" psychology – such as that a given sensation causes us to think of other sensations with which it has been regularly associated.

Without quite appreciating the change, Mill shifts to metaphysics once he explains *what* precisely it is in which we come to believe as a result of our experiences and psychology. "Matter," he famously writes, "may be defined [as] a Permanent Possibility of Sensation." To believe there are external physical objects is to believe that, besides our actual sensations of color, shape, and so on, there are clusters of sensations we *would* experience under appropriate conditions. To such clusters we give names like "table" and "city." So, for example, to hold that Calcutta exists, even though no one is currently experiencing the place, means that under certain possible conditions, "I should still have the sensations which, if now present, would lead me to affirm that Calcutta exists here and now."

Mill, then, is what we would now call a "phenomenalist," a philosopher for whom belief in an external world is *reducible* to beliefs concerning future and possible perceptual phenomena (see II.19–21 of this volume). In effect, he is picking up on and elaborating a view briefly hinted at by

Bishop Berkeley (III.16) – a view which, in Berkeley's case but not, of course, in Mill's, was superseded by an account of external reality in terms of the experiences God is having.

Mill is satisfied that a permanent possibility of sensation "constitutes altogether our idea of external substance." For example, it answers to our conviction that such substances are "perdurable" – that they do not change in the way our actual sensations do. One might then expect Mill, like many later phenomenalists, to dismiss as entirely unmotivated and indeed as unintelligible the claim that external objects are unperceivable things-in-themselves. Consistently or otherwise, this is not, however, what he does; rather, he sees such a claim as one that ordinary people – and not just wayward metaphysicians – unsurprisingly, though illegitimately, tend to embrace. A main reason for this tendency is the natural, if unfortunate, psychological urge to move from the proper distinction between individual experiences and their causes to one between experience *as a whole* and its supposed cause. In Chapter XI, Mill does not make clear why this move is illegitimate, but his objection is grounded in his theory of inference according to which, as mentioned earlier, only inductive inference from observed cases to further, in principle, observable cases is permissible.[3] There is, within that theory, no room for a principle like that of "inference to the best explanation" which some philosophers have invoked by way of support for postulating unobservable entities as the cause of our experience as a whole.

Mill's ontology of actual and possible sensations is a parsimonious one, but not as parsimonious as that of some later phenomenalists. For in the Appendix to Chapters XI and XII, Mill baulks, with some evident disappointment, at attempting to reduce *minds* or *selves* to collections of sensations in the same manner that physical objects have been reduced to these. My mind, he argues, cannot be reduced to a cluster or, in Hume's phrase, "bundle" of sensations, since any sensation properly allocated to that cluster must already be recognizable as *mine*. Hence, we are forced to "ascribe a reality to the Ego – to my own Mind – different from that real existence as a Permanent Possibility, which is the only reality I acknowledge in Matter". There will, of course, be philosophers who feel that, despite Mill's own lively arguments, a robust sense of the reality of physical objects, as much as that of minds, resists any dissolution of them into mere possibilities of experience.

Notes

1   Mill's accounts of inference and induction are expounded in his *A System of Logic*, London: Longman & Green, 1886. See II.14 of this volume.

2   Besides Hamilton, principal members of the Scottish Common Sense School included Thomas Reid (1710–96), Dugald Stewart (1753–1828), and James McCosh (1811–94).

3   A clear exposition of this point, and of Mill's views at large, is J. Skorupski's in his *English-Language Philosophy 1750 to 1945*, Oxford: Oxford University Press, 1993, pp. 54ff.

Mill, *An Examination of Sir William Hamilton's Philosophy*

Chapter XI

We have seen Sir W. Hamilton at work on the question of the reality of Matter, by the introspective method, and, as it seems, with little result. Let us now approach the same subject by the psychological. I proceed, therefore, to state the case of those who hold that the belief in an external world is not intuitive, but an acquired product.

This theory postulates the following psychological truths, all of which are proved by experience, and are not contested, though their force is seldom adequately felt, by Sir W. Hamilton and the other thinkers of the introspective school.

It postulates, first, that the human mind is capable of Expectation. In other words, that after having had actual sensations, we are capable of forming the conception of Possible sensations; sensations which we are not feeling at the present moment, but which we might feel, and should feel if certain conditions were present, the nature of which conditions we have, in many cases, learnt by experience.

It postulates, secondly, the laws of the Association of Ideas. So far as we are here concerned, these laws are the following: 1st. Similar phænomena tend to be thought of together. 2nd. Phænomena which have either been experienced or conceived in close contiguity to one another, tend to be thought of together. The contiguity is of two kinds; simultaneity, and immediate succession. Facts which have been experienced or thought of simultaneously, recall the thought of one another. Of facts which have been experienced or thought of in immediate succession, the antecedent, or the thought of it, recalls the thought of the consequent, but not conversely. 3rd. Associations produced by contiguity become more certain and rapid by repetition. When two phænomena have been very often experienced in conjunction, and have not, in any single instance, occurred separately either in experience or in thought, there is produced between them what has been called Inseparable, or less correctly, Indissoluble Association: by which is not meant that the association must inevitably last to the end of life – that no subsequent experience or process of thought can possibly avail to dissolve it; but only that as long as no such experience or process of thought has taken place, the association is irresistible; it is impossible for us to think the one thing disjoined from the other. 4th. When an association has acquired this character of inseparability – when the bond between the two ideas had been thus firmly riveted, not only does the idea called up by association become, in our consciousness, inseparable from the idea which suggested it, but the facts or phænomena answering to those ideas come at last to seem inseparable in existence: things which we are unable to conceive apart, appear incapable of existing apart; and the belief we have in their coexistence, though really a product of experience, seems intuitive. Innumerable examples might be given of this law. One of the most familiar, as well as the most striking, is that of our acquired perceptions of sight. Even those who, with Mr [Samuel] Bailey, consider the perception of distance by the eye as not acquired, but intuitive, admit that there are many perceptions of sight which, though instantaneous and unhesitating, are not intuitive. What we see is a very minute fragment of what we think we see. We see artificially

that one thing is hard, another soft. We see artificially that one thing is hot, another cold. We see artificially that what we see is a book, or a stone, each of these being not merely an inference, but a heap of inferences, from the signs which we see, to things not visible. We see, and cannot help seeing, what we have learnt to infer, even when we know that the inference is erroneous, and that the apparent perception is deceptive. We cannot help seeing the moon larger when near the horizon, though we know that she is of precisely her usual size. We cannot help seeing a mountain as nearer to us and of less height, when we see it through a more than ordinarily transparent atmosphere.

Setting out from these premises, the Psychological Theory maintains, that there are associations naturally and even necessarily generated by the order of our sensations and of our reminiscences of sensation, which, supposing no intuition of an external world to have existed in consciousness, would inevitably generate the belief, and would cause it to be regarded as an intuition.

What is it we mean, or what is it which leads us to say, that the objects we perceive are external to us, and not a part of our own thoughts? We mean, that there is concerned in our perceptions something which exists when we are not thinking of it; which existed before we had ever thought of it, and would exist if we were annihilated; and further, that there exist things which we never saw, touched, or otherwise perceived, and things which never have been perceived by man. This idea of something which is distinguished from our fleeting impressions by what, in Kantian language, is called Perdurability; something which is fixed and the same, while our impressions vary; something which exists whether we are aware of it or not, and which is always square (or of some other given figure) whether it appears to us square or round – constitutes altogether our idea of external substance. Whoever can assign an origin to this complex conception, has accounted for what we mean by the belief in matter. Now all this, according to the Psychological Theory, is but the form impressed by the known laws of association, upon the conception or notion, obtained by experience, of Contingent Sensations; by which are meant, sensations that are not in our present consciousness, and individually never were in our consciousness at all, but which in virtue of the laws to which we have learnt by experience that our sensations are subject, we know that we should have felt under given supposable circumstances, and under these same circumstances, might still feel.

I see a piece of white paper on a table. I go into another room. If the phænomenon always followed me, or if, when it did not follow me, I believed it to disappear *è rerum naturâ* [from the natural order], I should not believe it to be an external object. I should consider it as a phantom – a mere affection of my senses: I should not believe that there had been any Body there. But, though I have ceased to see it, I am persuaded that the paper is still there. I no longer have the sensations which it gave me; but I believe that when I again place myself in the circumstances in which I had those sensations, that, when I go again into the room, I shall again have them; and further, that there has been no intervening moment at which this would not have been the case. Owing to this property of my mind, my conception of the world at any given instant consists, in only a small proportion, of present sensations. Of these I may at the time have none at all, and they are in any case a most insignificant portion of the whole which I apprehend. The conception I form of the world existing at any moment, comprises, along with the sensations I am feeling, a countless variety of possibilities of sensation: namely, the whole of those which past observation tells me that I could, under any supposable circumstances, experience at this moment, together with an indefinite and illimitable multitude of others which though I do not know that I could, yet it is possible that I might, experience in circumstances not known to me. These various possibilities are the important thing to me in the world. My present sensations are generally of little importance, and are moreover fugitive: the possibilities, on the contrary, are permanent, which is the character that mainly distinguishes our idea of Substance or Matter from our notion of sensation. These possibilities, which are conditional certainties, need a special name to distinguish them from mere vague possibilities, which experience gives no warrant for reckoning upon. Now, as soon as a distinguishing name is given, though it be only to the same thing regarded in a different aspect, one of the most familiar experiences of our mental nature teaches us, that the different name comes to be considered as the name of a different thing.

There is another important peculiarity of these certified or guaranteed possibilities of sensation; namely, that they have reference, not to single sensations, but to sensations joined together in groups. When we think of anything as a material substance, or body, we either have had, or we think that on some given supposition we should have, not some *one* sensation, but a great and even an indefinite number and variety of sensations, generally belonging to different senses, but so linked together, that the presence of one announces the possible presence at the very same instant of any or all of the rest. In our mind, therefore, not only is this particular Possibility of sensation invested with the quality of permanence when we are not actually feeling any of the sensations at all; but when we are feeling some of them, the remaining sensations of the group are conceived by us in the form of Present Possibilities, which might be realized at the very moment. And as this happens in turn to all of them, the group as a whole presents itself to the mind as permanent, in contrast not solely with the temporariness of my bodily presence, but also with the temporary character of each of the sensations composing the group; in other words, as a kind of permanent substratum, under a set of passing experiences or manifestations: which is another leading character of our idea of substance or matter, as distinguished from sensation.

Let us now take into consideration another of the general characters of our experience, namely, that in addition to fixed groups, we also recognise a fixed Order in our sensations; an Order of succession, which, when ascertained by observation, gives rise to the ideas of Cause and Effect, according to what I hold to be the true theory of that relation, and is on any theory the source of all our knowledge what causes produce what effects. Now, of what nature is this fixed order among our sensations? It is a constancy of antecedence and sequence. But the constant antecedence and sequence do not generally exist between one actual sensation and another. Very few such sequences are presented to us by experience. In almost all the constant sequences which occur in Nature, the antecedence and consequence do not obtain between sensations, but between the groups we have been speaking about, of which a very small portion is actual sensation, the greater part being permanent possibilities of sensation, evidenced to us by a small and variable number of sensations actually present. Hence, our ideas of causation, power, activity, do not become connected in thought with our sensations as *actual* at all, save in the few physiological cases where these figure by themselves as the antecedents in some uniform sequence. Those ideas become connected, not with sensations, but with groups of possibilities of sensation. The sensations conceived do not, to our habitual thoughts, present themselves as sensations actually experienced, inasmuch as not only any one or any number of them may be supposed absent, but none of them need be present. We find that the modifications which are taking place more or less regularly in our possibilities of sensation, are mostly quite independent of our consciousness, and of our presence or absence. Whether we are asleep or awake the fire goes out, and puts an end to one particular possibility of warmth and light. Whether we are present or absent the corn ripens, and brings a new possibility of food. Hence we speedily learn to think of Nature as made up solely of these groups of possibilities, and the active force in Nature as manifested in the modification of some of these by others. The sensations, though the original foundation of the whole, come to be looked upon as a sort of accident depending on us, and the possibilities as much more real than the actual sensations, nay, as the very realities of which these are only the representations, appearances, or effects. When this state of mind has been arrived at, then, and from that time forward, we are never conscious of a present sensation without instantaneously referring it to some one of the groups of possibilities into which a sensation of that particular description enters; and if we do not yet know to what group to refer it, we at least feel an irresistible conviction that it must belong to some group or other; *i.e.* that its presence proves the existence, here and now, of a great number and variety of possibilities of sensation, without which it would not have been. The whole set of sensations as possible, form a permanent background to any one or more of them that are, at a given moment, actual; and the possibilities are conceived as standing to the actual sensations in the relation of a cause to its effects, or of canvas to the figures painted on it, or of a root to the trunk, leaves, and flowers, or of a substratum to that which is spread over it, or, in transcendental language, of Matter to Form.

When this point has been reached, the Permanent Possibilities in question have assumed such unlikeness of aspect, and such difference of apparent relation to us, from any sensations, that it would be contrary to all we know of the constitution of human nature that they should not be conceived as, and believed to be, at least as different from sensations as sensations are from one another. Their groundwork in sensation is forgotten, and they are supposed to be something intrinsically distinct from it. We can withdraw ourselves from any of our (external) sensations, or we can be withdrawn from them by some other agency. But though the sensations cease, the possibilities remain in existence; they are independent of our will, our presence, and everything which belongs to us. We find, too, that they belong as much to other human or sentient beings as to ourselves. We find other people grounding their expectations and conduct upon the same permanent possibilities on which we ground ours. But we do not find them experiencing the same actual sensations. Other people do not have our sensations exactly when and as we have them: but they have our possibilities of sensation; whatever indicates a present possibility of sensations to ourselves, indicates a present possibility of similar sensations to them, except so far as their organs of sensation may vary from the type of ours. This puts the final seal to our conception of the groups of possibilities as the fundamental reality in Nature. The permanent possibilities are common to us and to our fellow-creatures; the actual sensations are not. That which other people become aware of when, and on the same grounds, as I do, seems more real to me than that which they do not know of unless I tell them. The world of Possible Sensations succeeding one another according to laws, is as much in other beings as it is in me; it has therefore an existence outside me; it is an External World.

If this explanation of the origin and growth of the idea of Matter, or External Nature, contains nothing at variance with natural laws, it is at least an admissible supposition, that the element of Non-ego which Sir W. Hamilton regards as an original datum of consciousness, and which we certainly do find in what we now call our consciousness, may not be one of its primitive elements – may not have existed at all in its first manifestations. But if this supposition be admissible, it ought, on Sir W. Hamilton's principles, to be received as true. The first of the laws laid down by him for the interpretation of Consciousness, the law (as he terms it) of Parsimony, forbids to suppose an original principle of our nature in order to account for phænomena which admit of possible explanation from known causes. If the supposed ingredient of consciousness be one which might grow up (though we cannot prove that it did grow up) through later experience; and if, when it had so grown up, it would, by known laws of our nature, appear as completely intuitive as our sensations themselves; we are bound, according to Sir W. Hamilton's and all sound philosophy, to assign to it that origin. Where there is a known cause adequate to account for a phænomenon, there is no justification for ascribing it to an unknown one. And what evidence does Consciousness furnish of the intuitiveness of an impression, except instantaneousness, apparent simplicity, and unconsciousness on our part of how the impression came into our minds? These features can only prove the impression to be intuitive, on the hypothesis that there are no means of accounting for them otherwise. If they not only might, but naturally would, exist, even on the supposition that it is not intuitive, we must accept the conclusion to which we are led by the Psychological Method, and which the Introspective Method furnishes absolutely nothing to contradict.

Matter, then, may be defined, a Permanent Possibility of Sensation. If I am asked, whether I believe in matter, I ask whether the questioner accepts this definition of it. If he does, I believe in matter: and so do all Berkeleians. In any other sense than this, I do not. But I affirm with confidence, that this conception of Matter includes the whole meaning attached to it by the common world, apart from philosophical, and sometimes from theological, theories. The reliance of mankind on the real existence of visible and tangible objects, means reliance on the reality and permanence of Possibilities of visual and tactual sensations, when no such sensations are actually experienced. We are warranted in believing that this is the meaning of Matter in the minds of many of its most esteemed metaphysical champions, though they themselves would not admit as much: for example, of Reid, Stewart, and Brown.[1] For these three philosophers alleged that all mankind, including Berkeley and Hume, really believed in Matter, inasmuch as unless

they did, they would not have turned aside to save themselves from running against a post. Now all which this manœuvre really proved is, that they believed in Permanent Possibilities of Sensation. We have therefore the unintentional sanction of these three eminent defenders of the existence of matter, for affirming, that to believe in Permanent Possibilities of Sensation is believing in Matter. It is hardly necessary, after such authorities, to mention Dr Johnson, or any one else who resorts to the *argumentatum baculinum* of knocking a stick against the ground.[2] Sir W. Hamilton, a far subtler thinker than any of these, never reasons in this manner. He never supposes that a disbeliever in what he means by Matter, ought in consistency to act in any different mode from those who believe in it. He knew that the belief on which all the practical consequences depend, is the belief in Permanent Possibilities of Sensation, and that if nobody believed in a material universe in any other sense, life would go on exactly as it now does. He, however, did believe in more than this, but, I think, only because it had never occurred to him that mere Possibilities of Sensation could, to our artificialized consciousness, present the character of objectivity which, as we have now shown, they not only can, but unless the known laws of the human mind were suspended, must necessarily, present.

Perhaps it may be objected, that the very possibility of framing such a notion of Matter as Sir W. Hamilton's – the capacity in the human mind of imagining an external world which is anything more than what the Psychological Theory makes it – amounts to a disproof of the theory. If (it may be said) we had no revelation in consciousness, of a world which is not in some way or other identified with sensation, we should be unable to have the notion of such a world. If the only ideas we had of external objects were ideas of our sensations, supplemented by an acquired notion of permanent possibilities of sensation, we must (it is thought) be incapable of conceiving, and therefore still more incapable of fancying that we perceive, things which are not sensations at all. It being evident however that some philosophers believe this, and it being maintainable that the mass of mankind do so, the existence of a perdurable basis of sensations, distinct from sensations themselves, is proved, it might be said, by the possibility of believing it.

Let me first restate what I apprehend the belief to be. We believe that we perceive a something closely related to all our sensations, but different from those which we are feeling at any particular minute; and distinguished from sensations altogether, by being permanent and always the same, while these are fugitive, variable, and alternately displace one another. But these attributes of the object of perception are properties belonging to all the possibilities of sensation which experience guarantees. The belief in such permanent possibilities seems to me to include all that is essential or characteristic in the belief in substance. I believe that Calcutta exists, though I do not perceive it, and that it would still exist if every percipient inhabitant were suddenly to leave the place, or be struck dead. But when I analyse the belief, all I find in it is, that were these events to take place, the Permanent Possibility of Sensation which I call Calcutta would still remain; that if I were suddenly transported to the banks of the Hoogly, I should still have the sensations which, if now present, would lead me to affirm that Calcutta exists here and now. We may infer, therefore, that both philosophers and the world at large, when they think of matter, conceive it really as a Permanent Possibility of Sensation. But the majority of philosophers fancy that it is something more; and the world at large, though they have really, as I conceive, nothing in their minds but a Permanent Possibility of Sensation, would, if asked the question, undoubtedly agree with the philosophers: and though this is sufficiently explained by the tendency of the human mind to infer difference of things from difference of names, I acknowledge the obligation of showing how it can be possible to believe in an existence transcending all possibilities of sensation, unless on the hypothesis that such an existence actually is, and that we actually perceive it.

The explanation, however, is not difficult. It is an admitted fact, that we are capable of all conceptions which can be formed by generalizing from the observed laws of our sensations. Whatever relation we find to exist between any one of our sensations and something different from *it*, that same relation we have no difficulty in conceiving to exist between the sum of all our sensations and something different from *them*. The differences which our consciousness recognises between one sensation and another, give us the general

notion of difference, and inseparably associate with every sensation we have, the feeling of its being different from other things: and when once this association has been formed, we can no longer conceive anything, without being able, and even being compelled, to form also the conception of something different from it. This familiarity with the idea of something different from *each* thing we know, makes it natural and easy to form the notion of something different from *all* things that we know, collectively as well as individually. It is true we can form no conception of what such a thing can be; our notion of it is merely negative; but the idea of a substance, apart from its relation to the impressions which we conceive it as making on our senses *is* a merely negative one. There is thus no psychological obstacle to our forming the notion of a something which is neither a sensation nor a possibility of sensation, even if our consciousness does not testify to it; and nothing is more likely than that the Permanent Possibilities of sensation, to which our consciousness does testify, should be confounded in our minds with this imaginary conception. All experience attests the strength of the tendency to mistake mental abstractions, even negative ones, for substantive realities; and the Permanent Possibilities of sensation which experience guarantees, are so extremely unlike in many of their properties to actual sensations, that since we are capable of imagining something which transcends sensation, there is a great natural probability that we should suppose these to be it.

But this natural probability is converted into certainty, when we take into consideration that universal law of our experience which is termed the law of Causation, and which makes us mentally connect with the beginning of everything, some antecedent condition, or Cause. The case of Causation is one of the most marked of all the cases in which we extend to the sum total of our consciousness, a notion derived from its parts. It is a striking example of our power to conceive, and our tendency to believe, that a relation which subsists between every individual item of our experience and some other item, subsists also between our experience as a whole, and something not within the sphere of experience. By this extension to the sum of all our experiences, of the internal relations obtaining between its several parts, we are led to consider sensation itself – the aggregate whole of our sensations – as deriving its origin from antecedent existences transcending sensation. That we should do this, is a consequence of the particular character of the uniform sequences, which experience discloses to us among our sensations. As already remarked, the constant antecedent of a sensation is seldom another sensation, or set of sensations, actually felt. It is much oftener the existence of a group of possibilities, not necessarily including any actual sensations, except such as are required to show that the possibilities are really present. Nor are actual sensations indispensable even for this purpose; for the presence of the object (which is nothing more than the immediate presence of the possibilities) may be made known to us by the very sensation which we refer to it as its effect. Thus, the real antecedent of an effect – the only antecedent which, being invariable and unconditional, we consider to be the cause – may be, not any sensation really felt, but solely the presence, at that or the immediately preceding moment, of a group of possibilities of sensation. Hence it is not with sensations as actually experienced, but with their Permanent Possibilities, that the idea of Cause comes to be identified: and we, by one and the same process, acquire the habit of regarding Sensation in general, like all our individual sensations, as an Effect, and also that of conceiving as the causes of most of our individual sensations, not other sensations, but general possibilities of sensation. If all these considerations put together do not completely explain and account for our conceiving these Possibilities as a class of independent and substantive entities, I know not what psychological analysis can be conclusive.

It may perhaps be said, that the preceding theory gives, indeed, some account of the idea of Permanent Existence which forms part of our conception of matter, but gives no explanation of our believing these permanent objects to be external, or out of ourselves. I apprehend, on the contrary, that the very idea of anything out of ourselves is derived solely from the knowledge experience give us of the Permanent Possibilities. Our sensations we carry with us wherever we go, and they never exist where we are not; but when we change our place we do not carry away with us the Permanent Possibilities of Sensation: they remain until we return, or arise and cease under conditions with which our presence has in general nothing to do. And more than all – they are, and will be after we have ceased to feel, Permanent Possibilities of Sensation to other beings than ourselves. Thus our actual sensations and the permanent possibilities of sensation, stand out in obtrusive contrast to one another: and when the idea of Cause has been acquired, and extended by generalization from the parts of our experience to its aggregate whole, nothing can be more natural than that the Permanent Possibilities should be classed by us as existences generically distinct from our sensations, but of which our sensations are the effect.*

The same theory which accounts for our ascribing to an aggregate of possibilities of sensation, a permanent existence which our sensations themselves do not possess, and consequently a greater reality than belongs to our sensations,

---

* My able American critic, Dr H. B. Smith, contends ... that these facts afford no proofs that objects *are* external to us. I never pretended that they do. I am accounting for our conceiving, or representing to ourselves, the Permanent Possibilities as real objects external to us. I do not believe that the real externality to us of anything, except other minds, is capable of proof. But the Permanent Possibilities are external to us in the only sense we need care about; they are not constructed by the mind itself, but merely recognised by it; in Kantian language, they are *given* to us, and to other beings in common with us. "Men cannot act, cannot live," says Professor [Alexander] Fraser, "without assuming an external world, in some conception of the term external. It is the business of the philosopher to explain what that conception ought to be. For ourselves we can conceive only – (1) An externality to our present and transient experience in *our own* possible experience past and future, and (2) An externality to our own conscious experience, in the contemporaneous, as well as in the past or future experience of *other minds*." The view I take of externality, in the sense in which I acknowledge it as real, could not be more accurately expressed than in Professor Fraser's words. Dr Smith's criticisms continually go wide of the mark because he has somehow imagined that I am defending, instead of attacking, the belief in Matter as an entity *per se*. As when he says that my reasoning assumes, contrary to my own opinion, "an *à priori* necessity and validity of the law of cause and effect, or invariable antecedence and consequence." This might fairly have been said if I were defending the belief in the supposed hidden cause of our sensations: but I am only accounting for it; and to do so I assume only the tendency, but not the legitimacy of the tendency, to extend all the laws of our own experience to a sphere beyond our experience.

also explains our attributing greater objectivity to the Primary Qualities of bodies than to the Secondary. For the sensations which correspond to what are called the Primary Qualities (as soon at least as we come to apprehend them by two senses, the eye as well as the touch) are always present when any part of the group is so. But colours, tastes, smells, and the like, being, in comparison, fugacious, are not, in the same degree, conceived as being always there, even when nobody is present to perceive them. The sensations answering to the Secondary Qualities are only occasional, those to the Primary, constant. The Secondary, moreover, vary with different persons, and with the temporary sensibility of our organs; the Primary, when perceived at all, are, as far as we know, the same to all persons and at all times.[3]

Notes

1 Thomas Reid (1710–96) was the leading representative of Scottish "commonsense philosophy," and Dugald Stewart (1735–1828) and Thomas Brown (1778–1820) were two of his main, if critical, followers.

2 An *argumentum baculinam* is literally an argument with a stick, hence an argument taking the form of a threat. The phrase hardly fits Dr Johnson's famous "argument" against Berkeley's immaterialism, which consisted in kicking a stone.

3 Although this paragraph argues for a significant distinction between shape etc. on the other hand and colors, tastes, etc. on the other, it is not, of course, a defense of Locke's distinction between primary and secondary qualities, which was between those qualities in mind-independent objects which do and those which do not resemble our experiences of them (see II. 9 in this volume).

F. H. Bradley, *Appearance and Reality*, Chapters XIII and XIV

Introduction

There "is no being . . . outside of . . . psychical existence." This stark statement by the leading "Oxford Idealist," F. H. Bradley (1846–1924), in his magnum opus *Appearance and Reality* (1893), might sound to put him in the same camp as George Berkeley (III.16) and J. S. Mill (III.19). Bradley's idealism, however, is of an entirely different stamp from Berkeley's and from Mill's atomistic phenomenalism, which Bradley saw as a pernicious doctrine intimately linked to an individualistic utilitarian ethics that he detested. (We omit the sections in Chapter XIV where he argues that his own metaphysics satisfies our moral aspirations.) Bradley's position has some affinity with that of the German Absolute Idealists, but still more with that of Śaṁkara (see III.7 above), as T. S. Eliot, who wrote a dissertation on Bradley, and several modern Indian philosophers have noted.

Chapters XIII and XIV, which succinctly state the kernel of Bradley's metaphysics, presuppose a number of earlier conclusions. The first is that a belief is true in virtue of its coherence with a total body of beliefs, and that its "degree of truth"

From F. H. Bradley, *Appearance and Reality: A Metaphysical Essay*, Oxford: Clarendon Press, 1930 (9th impression), pp. 119–30, 140–2 (middle sections of Ch. XIV and some notes omitted; asterisked note is Bradley's).

depends on how adequately it expresses this totality. Our everyday beliefs enjoy only a very limited degree of truth, since in affirming, say, that "the cat is on the mat," I severely abstract elements from the whole of reality, thereby giving little indication of what that whole is.[1] The second is that it is perverse to regard the world as a collection of elements that are somehow related to one another. "A relational way of thought . . . must give appearance, and not truth" (*Appearance and Reality*, p. 28). The notion of relations between a plurality of independent objects is, Bradley argues, incoherent. The argument, reminiscent of Śaṁkara, is that the notion involves a regress. For the cat and the mat to be spatially related, there must be a further relation between the cat, the mat, and that spatial relation – and so on.[2]

Combining these points, Bradley elaborates, in Chapter XIII, his claim that plurality is only "appearance," that reality as such, or the Absolute, is a single harmonious and systematic whole, within which each artificially abstracted element owes its identity to its place in that whole. Nothing, except that whole, enjoys the independence required to count as fully real. Echoes of Śaṁkara and, indeed, Spinoza (see III.13 above) are easy to hear.

This monistic claim, explains Bradley, only tells us of the "form" of absolute reality. There remains the question, what is its "matter" or nature? The unequivocal answer is that "this matter is experience. . . . [To] be real . . . must be to fall within sentience." The argument here is, perhaps, disappointingly curt, little more than a repetition of Berkeley's "master argument" (see III. 16 above) to the effect that we can never succeed in thinking or imagining something unthought or unimagined: "I can myself conceive of nothing else than the experienced." Be that as it may, Bradley's own idealism is far removed from Berkeley's and Mill's. For him, experience is not the sum of atomic sense-data, perceptions and so on taking place in individual minds or subjects. Individual minds, no less than particular sense-data, are artificial abstractions from the essentially seamless unity of experience as a whole. The subject–object distinction, like that between different subjects, belongs to the realm of appearance.

What can be said about experience as a whole, the "matter" of absolute reality? Very little, according to Bradley, since as soon as we try to think or speak about it we are bound to employ concepts and distinctions that distort its seamless character. Bradley does, however, think that, in certain kinds of familiar experiences, we get a glimmer or intimation of this whole. Thus, in "mere feeling," where our experience is as yet unarticulated into subject and object, thought and will, and so on, there is a sense, however dark, of a "unity which transcends and yet contains every manifold appearance." Bradley, here, is reversing a whole

tradition of western rationalism, according to which it is thought, not "mere feeling," which provides access to the nature of reality. Indeed, one suspects that Bradley is a mystic *manqué*, hinting at – without (like Śaṁkara) endorsing – the possibility of a special experience of the oneness of reality.

Bradley was an immensely influential philosopher at the turn of the century, one whom philosophers rather more in fashion today, such as William James and Bertrand Russell, saw that they needed to take on and refute if their own positions were to pass muster. It is to these positions that we turn in later chapters of Part III.

Notes

1 On degrees of truth, see Bradley's *Principles of Logic*, Oxford: Oxford University Press, 1883, and R. Wollheim's discussion in his *F. H. Bradley*, Baltimore, MD: Penguin, 1969, Ch. 4.

2 For an excellent discussion of Bradley's account of relations, see P. Hylton, *Russell, Idealism and the Emergence of Analytic Philosophy*, Oxford: Clarendon Press, 1990, pp. 48ff.

Bradley, *Appearance and Reality*

Chapter XIII

The result of our First Book has been mainly negative. We have taken up a number of ways of regarding reality, and we have found that they all are vitiated by self-discrepancy. The reality can accept not one of these predicates, at least in the character in which so far they have come. We certainly ended with a reflection which promised something positive. Whatever is rejected as appearance is, for that very reason, no mere nonentity. It cannot bodily be shelved and merely got rid of, and, therefore, since it must fall somewhere, it must belong to reality. To take it as existing somehow and somewhere in the unreal, would surely be quite meaningless. For reality must own and cannot be less than appearance, and that is the one positive result which, so far, we have reached.[1] But as to the character

which, otherwise, the real possesses, we at present know nothing; and a further knowledge is what we must aim at through the remainder of our search. The present Book, to some extent, falls into two divisions. The first of these deals mainly with the general character of reality, and with the defence of this against a number of objections. Then from this basis, in the second place, I shall go on to consider mainly some special features. But I must admit that I have kept to no strict principle of division. I have really observed no rule of progress, except to get forward in the best way that I can.

At the beginning of our inquiry into the nature of the real we encounter, of course, a general doubt or denial. To know the truth, we shall be told, is impossible, or is, at all events, wholly impracticable. We cannot have positive knowledge about first principles; and, if we could possess it, we should not know when actually we had got it. What is denied is, in short, the existence of a criterion. I shall, later on, in Chapter xxvii, have to deal more fully with the objections of a thorough-going scepticism, and I will here confine myself to what seems requisite for the present.

Is there an absolute criterion? This question, to my mind, is answered by a second question: How otherwise should we be able to say anything at all about appearance? For through the last Book, the reader will remember, we were for the most part criticizing. We were judging phenomena and were condemning them, and throughout we proceeded as if the self-contradictory could not be real. But this was surely to have and to apply an absolute criterion. For consider: you can scarcely propose to be quite passive when presented with statements about reality. You can hardly take the position of admitting any and every nonsense to be truth, truth absolute and entire, at least so far as you know. For, if you think at all so as to discriminate between truth and false-hood, you will find that you cannot accept open self-contradiction. Hence to think is to judge, and to judge is to criticize, and to criticize is to use a criterion of reality. And surely to doubt this would be mere blindness or confused self-deception. But if so, it is clear that, in rejecting the inconsistent as appearance, we are applying a positive knowledge of the ultimate nature of things. Ultimate reality is such that it does not contradict itself; here is an absolute criterion. And it is proved absolute by the fact that, either in endeavouring to deny it, or even in attempting to doubt it, we tacitly assume its validity.

One of these essays in delusion may be noticed briefly in passing. We may be told that our criterion has been developed by experience, and that therefore at least it may not be absolute. But why anything should be weaker for having been developed is, in the first place, not obvious. And, in the second place, the whole doubt, when understood, destroys itself. For the alleged origin of our criterion is delivered to us by knowledge which rests throughout on its application as an absolute test. And what can be more irrational than to try to prove that a principle is doubtful, when the proof through every step rests on its unconditional truth? It would, of course, not be irrational to take one's stand on this criterion, to use it to produce a conclusion hostile to itself, and to urge that therefore our whole knowledge is self-destructive, since it essentially drives us to what we cannot accept. But this is not the result which

our supposed objector has in view, or would welcome. He makes no attempt to show in general that a psychological growth is in any way hostile to metaphysical validity. And he is not pre-pared to give up his own psychological knowledge, which knowledge plainly is ruined if the criterion is *not* absolute. The doubt is seen, when we reflect, to be founded on that which it endeav-ours to question. And it has but blindly borne wit-ness to the absolute certainty of our knowledge about reality.

Thus we possess a criterion, and our criterion is supreme. I do not mean to deny that we might have several standards, giving us sundry pieces of information about the nature of things. But, be that as it may, we still have an over-ruling test of truth, and the various standards (if they exist) are certainly subordinate. This at once becomes evi-dent, for we cannot refuse to bring such standards together, and to ask if they agree. Or, at least, if a doubt is suggested as to their consistency, each with itself and with the rest, we are compelled, so to speak, to assume jurisdiction. And if they were guilty of self-contradiction, when examined or compared, we should condemn them as appearance. But we could not do that if they were not subject all to one tribunal. And hence, as we find nothing not subordinate to the test of self-consistency, we are forced to set that down as supreme and absolute.

But it may be said that this supplies us with no real information. If we think, then certainly we are not allowed to be inconsistent, and it is admitted that this test is unconditional and absolute. But it will be urged that, for knowledge about any matter, we require something more than a bare negation. The ultimate reality (we are agreed) does not permit self-contradiction, but a prohibition or an absence (we shall be told) by itself does not amount to positive knowledge. The denial of inconsistency, therefore, does not predicate any positive quality. But such an objection is untenable. It may go so far as to assert that a bare denial is possible, that we may reject a predicate though we stand on no positive basis, and though there is nothing special which serves to reject. This error has been refuted in my *Principles of Logic* (Book I, Chapter iii), and I do not propose to discuss it here. I will pass to another sense in which the objection may seem more plausible. The criterion, it may be urged, in itself is doubtless positive; but, for our knowledge and in effect, is merely negative. And it gives us therefore no information at all about reality, for, although knowledge is there, it cannot be brought out. The criterion is a basis, which serves as the foundation of denial; but, since this basis cannot be exposed, we are but able to stand on it and unable to see it. And it hence, in effect, tells us nothing, though there are assertions which it does not allow us to venture on. This objection, when stated in such a form, may seem plausible, and there is a sense in which I am prepared to admit that it is valid. If by the nature of reality we understand its full nature, I am not contending that this in a complete form is knowable. But that is very far from being the point here at issue. For the objection denies that we have a standard which gives *any* positive knowledge, *any* information, complete or incomplete, about the genuine reality. And this denial assuredly is mistaken.

The objection admits that we know what reality *does*, but it refuses to allow us any understanding of what reality *is*. The standard (it is agreed) both exists and possesses a positive character, and it is agreed that this character rejects inconsistency. It is admitted that we know this, and the point at issue is whether such knowledge supplies any positive information. And to my mind this question seems not hard to answer. For I cannot see how, when I observe a thing at work, I am to stand there and to insist that I know nothing of its nature. I fail to perceive how a function is nothing at all, or how it does not positively qualify that to which I attribute it. To know only so much, I admit, may very possibly be useless; it may leave us without the information which we desire most to obtain; but, for all that, it is not total ignorance.

Our standard denies inconsistency, and therefore asserts consistency. If we can be sure that the inconsistent is unreal, we must, logically, be just as sure that the reality is consistent. The question is solely as to the meaning to be given to consistency. We have now seen that it is not the bare exclusion of discord, for that is merely our abstraction, and is otherwise nothing. And our result, so far, is this. Reality is known to possess a positive character, but this character is at present determined only as that which excludes contradiction.

But we may make a further advance. We saw (in the preceding chapter) that all appearance must belong to reality. For what appears is, and whatever is cannot fall outside the real. And we may now combine this result with the conclusion just reached. We may say that everything, which appears, is somehow real in such a way as to be self-consistent. The character of the real is to possess everything phenomenal in a harmonious form.

I will repeat the same truth in other words. Reality is one in this sense that it has a positive nature exclusive of discord, a nature which must hold throughout everything that is to be real. Its diversity can be diverse only so far as not to clash, and what seems otherwise anywhere cannot be real. And, from the other side, everything which appears must be real. Appearance must belong to reality, and it must therefore be concordant and other than it seems. The bewildering mass of phenomenal diversity must hence somehow be at unity and self-consistent; for it cannot be elsewhere than in reality, and reality excludes discord. Or again we may put it so: the real is individual. It is one in the sense that its positive character embraces all differences in an inclusive harmony. And this knowledge, poor as it may be, is certainly more than bare negation or simple ignorance. So far as it goes, it gives us positive news about absolute reality.

Let us try to carry this conclusion a step further on. We know that the real is one; but its oneness so far, is ambiguous. Is it one system, possessing diversity as an adjective; or is its consistency, on the other hand, an attribute of independent realities? We have to ask, in short, if a plurality of reals is possible, and if these can merely coexist so as not to be discrepant? Such a plurality would mean a number of beings not dependent on each other. On the one hand they would possess somehow the phenomenal diversity, for that possession, we have seen, is essential. And, on the other hand, they would be free from external disturbance and from inner discrepancy. After the inquiries of our First Book the possibility of such reals hardly calls for discussion. For the internal states of each give rise to hopeless difficulties. And, in the second place, the plurality of the reals cannot be reconciled with their independence. I will briefly resume the arguments which force us to this latter result.

If the Many are supposed to be without internal quality, each would forthwith become nothing, and we must therefore take each as being internally somewhat. And, if they are to be plural, they must be a diversity somehow coexisting together. Any attempt again to take their togetherness as unessential seems to end in the unmeaning. We have no knowledge of a plural diversity, nor can we attach any sense to it, if we do not have it somehow as one. And, if we abstract from this unity, we have also therewith abstracted from the plurality, and are left with mere being.

Can we then have a plurality of independent reals which merely coexist? No, for absolute independence and coexistence are incompatible. Absolute independence is an idea which consists merely in one-sided abstraction. It is made by an attempted division of the aspect of several existence from the aspect of relatedness; and these aspects, whether in fact or thought, are really indivisible.

If we take the diversity of our reals to be such as we discover in feeling and at a stage where relations do not exist, that diversity is never found except as one integral character of an undivided whole. And if we forcibly abstract from that unity, then together with feeling we have destroyed the diversity of feeling. We are left not with plurality, but with mere being, or, if you prefer it, with nothing. Coexistence in feeling is hence an instance and a proof not of self-sufficiency, but of dependence, and beside this it would add a further difficulty. If the nature of our reals is the diversity found at a stage below relations, how are we to dispose of the mass of relational appearance? For that exists, and existing it must somehow qualify the world, a world the reality of which is discovered only at a level other than its own. Such a position would seem not easy to justify.

Thus a mode of togetherness such as we can verify in feeling destroys the independence of our reals. And they will fare no better if we seek to find their coexistence elsewhere. For any other verifiable way of togetherness must involve relations, and they are fatal to self-sufficiency. Relations, we saw, are a development of and from the felt totality. They inadequately express, and they still imply in the background that unity apart from which the diversity is nothing. Relations are unmeaning except within and on the basis of a substantial whole, and related terms, if made absolute, are forthwith destroyed. Plurality and relatedness are but features and aspects of a unity.

If the relations in which the reals somehow stand are viewed as essential, that, as soon as we understand it, involves at once the internal relativity of the reals. And any attempt to maintain the relations as merely external must fail.[2] For if, wrongly and for argument's sake, we admit processes and arrangements which do not qualify their terms, yet such arrangements, if admitted, are at any rate not ultimate. The terms would be prior and independent only with regard to *these* arrangements, and they would remain relative otherwise, and vitally dependent on some whole. And severed from this unity, the terms perish by the very stroke which aims to set them up as absolute.

The reals therefore cannot be self-existent, and, if self-existent, yet taken as the world they would end in inconsistency. For the relations, because they exist, must somehow qualify the world. The relations then must externally qualify the sole and self-contained reality, and that seems self-contradictory or meaningless.* And if it is urged that a plurality of independent beings may be unintelligible, but that after all some unintelligible facts must be affirmed – the answer is obvious. An unintelligible fact may be admitted so far as, first, it is a fact, and so far as, secondly, it has a meaning which does not contradict itself internally or make self-discrepant our view of the world. But the alleged independence of the reals is no fact, but a theoretical construction; and, so far as it has a meaning, that meaning contradicts itself, and issues in chaos. A reality of this kind may safely be taken as unreal.

We cannot therefore maintain a plurality save as dependent on the relations in which it stands. Or if desiring to avoid relations we fall back on

---

* To this brief statement we might add other fatal objections. There is the question of the reals' interaction and of the general order of the world. Here, whether we affirm or deny, we turn in a maze. The fact of knowledge plunges us again in a dilemma. If we do not know that the Many are, we cannot affirm them. But the knowledge of the Many seems compatible with the self-existence neither of what knows nor of what is known. Finally, if the relations are admitted to an existence somehow alongside of the reals, the sole reality of the reals is given up. The relations themselves have now become a second kind of real thing. But the connexion between these new reals and the old ones, whether we deny or affirm it, leads to insoluble problems.

the diversity given in feeling, the result is the same. The plurality then sinks to become merely an integral aspect in a single substantial unity, and the reals have vanished.

Chapter XIV

Our result so far is this. Everything phenomenal is somehow real; and the absolute must at least be as rich as the relative. And, further, the Absolute is not many; there are no independent reals. The universe is one in this sense that its differences exist harmoniously within one whole, beyond which there is nothing. Hence the Absolute is, so far, an individual and a system, but, if we stop here, it remains but formal and abstract. Can we then, the question is, say anything about the concrete nature of the system?

Certainly, I think this is possible. When we ask as to the matter which fills up the empty outline, we can reply in one word, that this matter is experience. And experience means something much the same as given and present fact. We perceive, on reflection, that to be real, or even barely to exist, must be to fall within sentience. Sentient experience, in short, is reality, and what is not this is not real. We may say, in other words, that there is no being or fact outside of that which is commonly called psychical existence. Feeling, thought, and volition (any groups under which we class psychical phenomena) are all the material of existence, and there is no other material, actual or even possible. This result in its general form seems evident at once; and, however serious a step we now seem to have taken, there would be no advantage at this point in discussing it at length. For the test in the main lies ready to our hand, and the decision rests on the manner in which it is applied. I will state the case briefly thus. Find any piece of existence, take up anything that any one could possibly call a fact, or could in any sense assert to have being, and then judge if it does not consist in sentient experience. Try to discover any sense in which you can still continue to speak of it, when all perception and feeling have been removed; or point out any fragment of its matter, any aspect of its being, which is not derived from and is not still relative to this source. When the experiment is made strictly, I can myself conceive of nothing else than the experienced. Anything, in no sense felt or perceived, becomes

to me quite unmeaning. And as I cannot try to think of it without realizing either that I am not thinking at all, or that I am thinking of it against my will as being experienced, I am driven to the conclusion that for me experience is the same as reality. The fact that falls elsewhere seems, in my mind, to be a mere word and a failure, or else an attempt at self-contradiction. It is a vicious abstraction whose existence is meaningless nonsense, and is therefore not possible.

This conclusion is open, of course, to grave objection, and must in its consequences give rise to serious difficulties. I will not attempt to anticipate the discussion of these, but before passing on, will try to obviate a dangerous mistake. For, in asserting that the real is nothing but experience, I may be understood to endorse a common error. I may be taken first to divide the percipient subject from the universe; and then, resting on that subject, as on a thing actual by itself, I may be supposed to urge that it cannot transcend its own states. Such an argument would lead to impossible results, and would stand on a foundation of faulty abstraction. To set up the subject as real independently of the whole, and to make the whole into experience in the sense of an adjective of that subject, seems to me indefensible. And when I contend that reality must be sentient, my conclusion almost consists in the denial of this fundamental error. For if, seeking for reality, we go to experience, what we certainly do *not* find is a subject or an object, or indeed any other thing whatever, standing separate and on its own bottom. What we discover rather is a whole in which distinctions can be made, but in which divisions do not exist. And this is the point on which I insist, and it is the very ground on which I stand, when I urge that reality is sentient experience. I mean that to be real is to be indissolubly one thing with sentience. It is to be something which comes as a feature and aspect within one whole of feeling, something which, except as an integral element of such sentience, has no meaning at all. And what I repudiate is the separation of feeling from the felt, or of the desired from desire, or of what is thought from thinking, or the division – I might add – of anything from anything else. Nothing is ever so presented as real by itself, or can be argued so to exist without demonstrable fallacy. And in asserting that the reality is experience, I rest throughout on this foundation. You cannot find fact unless in unity with sentience, and one cannot in the end be divided from the other, either actually or in idea. But to be utterly indivisible from feeling or perception, to be an integral element in a whole which is experienced, this surely is itself to *be* experience. Being and reality are, in brief, one thing with sentience; they can neither be opposed to, nor even in the end distinguished from it.

I am well aware that this statement stands in need of explanation and defence. This will, I hope, be supplied by succeeding chapters, and I think it better for the present to attempt to go forward. Our conclusion, so far, will be this, that the Absolute is one system, and that its contents are nothing but sentient experience. It will hence be a single and all-inclusive experience, which embraces every partial diversity in concord. For it cannot be less than appearance, and hence no feeling or thought, of any kind, can fall outside its limits. And if it is more than any feeling or thought which we know, it must still remain more of the same nature. It cannot pass into another region beyond what falls under the general head of sentience. For to assert that possibility would be in the end to use words without a meaning. We can entertain no such suggestion except as self-contradictory, and as therefore impossible.

This conclusion will, I trust, at the end of my work bring more conviction to the reader; for we shall find that it is the one view which will harmonize all facts. And the objections brought against it, when it and they are once properly defined, will prove untenable. But our general result is at present seriously defective; and we must now attempt to indicate and remedy its failure in principle. [. . .]

[. . .] And hence, for the present at least, we must believe that reality satisfies our whole being. Our main wants – for truth and life, and for beauty and goodness – must all find satisfaction. And we have seen that this consummation must somehow be experience, and be individual. Every element of the universe, sensation, feeling, thought and will, must be included within one comprehensive sentience. And the question which now occurs is whether really we have a positive idea of such sentience. Do we at all know what we mean when we say that it is actual?

Fully to realize the existence of the Absolute is for finite beings impossible. In order thus to know we should have to be [it], and then *we* should not exist. This result is certain, and all attempts to avoid it are illusory. But then the whole question turns on the sense in which we are to understand 'knowing'. What is impossible is to construct absolute life in its detail, to have the specific experience in which it consists. But to gain an idea of its main features – an idea true so far as it goes, though abstract and incomplete – is a different endeavour. And it is a task, so far as I see, in which we may succeed. For these main features, to some extent, are within our own experience; and again the idea of their combination is, in the abstract, quite intelligible. And surely no more than this is wanted for a knowledge of the Absolute. It is a knowledge which of course differs enormously from the fact. But it is true, for all that, while it respects its own limits; and it seems fully attainable by the finite intellect.

I will end this chapter by briefly mentioning the sources of such knowledge. First, in mere feeling, or immediate presentation, we have the experience of a whole (Chapters ix, xix, xxvi, xxvii). This whole contains diversity, and, on the other hand, is not parted by relations. Such an experience, we must admit, is most imperfect and unstable, and its inconsistencies lead us at once to transcend it. Indeed, we hardly possess it as more than that which we are in the act of losing. But it serves to suggest to us the general idea of a total experience, where will and thought and feeling may all once more be one. Further, this same unity, felt below distinctions, shows itself later in a kind of hostility against them. We find it in the efforts made both by theory and practice, each to complete itself and so to pass into the other. And, again, the relational form, as we saw, pointed everywhere to a unity. It implies a substantial totality beyond relations and above them, a whole endeavouring without success to realize itself in their detail. Further, the ideas of goodness, and of the beautiful, suggest in different ways the same result. They more or less involve the experience of a whole beyond relations though full of diversity. Now, if we gather (as we can) such considerations into one, they will assuredly supply us with a positive idea. We gain from them the knowledge of a unity which transcends and yet contains every manifold appearance. They supply not an experience but an abstract idea, and idea which we make by uniting given elements. And the mode of union, once more in the abstract, is actually given. Thus we know what is meant by an experience, which embraces all divisions, and yet somehow possesses the direct nature of feeling. We can form the general idea of an absolute experience in which phenomenal distinctions are merged, a whole become immediate at a higher stage without losing any richness. Our complete inability to understand this concrete unity in detail is no good ground for our declining to entertain it. Such a ground would be irrational, and its principle could hardly everywhere be adhered to. But if we can realize at all the general features of the Absolute, if we can see that somehow they come together in a way known vaguely and in the abstract, our result is certain. Our conclusion, so far as it goes, is real knowledge of the Absolute, positive knowledge built on experience, and inevitable when we try to think consistently. We shall realize its nature more clearly when we have confronted it with a series of objections and difficulties. If our result will hold against them all,

we shall be able to urge that in reason we are bound to think it true.

Notes

1 I take Bradley to mean two things in these rather confusing remarks. First, that while a merely apparent X is not a real X, its appearing as X is real enough. Second, given Bradley's doctrine of degrees of truth, experiencing an apparent aspect of the world is not necessarily, therefore, to be experiencing it in a totally unveridical way.

2 In Bradley's vocabulary, external relations – if there were any – would hold between independently existing and identifiable objects. According to him, there are no such external relations. An internal relation between X and Y, on the other hand, is one that must obtain between them in order for them to *be* X and Y. Since everything is internally related to everything else, it follows that the identity of any one thing logically depends on its place within a "harmonious" whole of things.

William James,
"The One and the Many"

Introduction

An important bone of metaphysical contention in several earlier chapters of this anthology has been that of the unity *versus* the plurality of the world. Is the world a single Spinozan substance (see III.13 in this volume) or an infinite number of Leibnizian monads (III.15)? An indivisible Bradleian Absolute (III.20) or a collection of atomic Millian sensations (III.19)? For the American psychologist and pragmatist philosopher, William James (1842–1910), the issue is not simply important but "the most central of all philosophic problems," the "most pregnant" one whose resolution has more implications for the rest of a philosopher's opinions than that of any other question.[1]

Although James notes, and without any animosity, a purely "mystical," primarily "eastern," version of monism, his focus is upon the more "talkative and explicit" versions of monism to be found in western philosophical literature. (Somewhat questionably, he associates monism and pluralism with rationalism and empiricism respectively.) The burden of argument, James holds, falls upon the monist – be he Parmenides (III.2), Spinoza, Bradley, or James's American contemporary, Josiah Royce (1855–1916). Not only

From J. J. McDermott, ed., *The Writings of William James*, Chicago: University of Chicago Press, 1977, pp. 258–70 (some notes omitted; asterisked notes are James's).

does science treat the world as composed of many, separable elements, but also our commonsense experience is evidently that of a plural world. To show that such treatment or experience is deluded would be a difficult task.

In James's view, the usual monistic arguments quite fail to discharge this task. Both Spinoza's appeal to the nature of underlying substance and more recent idealist appeals to an indivisible experience present to a single "noetic subject" verge on the meaningless, since these are hypotheses without testable, pragmatic consequences. He agrees, for example, with David Hume's criticism of the notion of material substance as an idle one that adds nothing of empirical significance to that of sensory data "united by the imagination" (II.10).

This is not to say that no sense can ever be attributed to remarks like: "The world is one" or "Reality is a unity." They may, for example, be drawing attention to the systematic causal connections we find, or expect to find, among things. Or they may remind us that we are able to take the world as a whole as an object of thought and speculation. The problem is that, if this is what monism amounts to, it is in no way incompatible with pluralism. Things need to be genuinely different from one another in order to be causally related, and the fact that we can think about the world as a whole does not mean that this whole is without genuinely distinguishable and separate items, intelligible independently of one another.

One might expect James to end here, content to conclude, as he almost does, that, in so far as sense can be made of monistic claims, the debate between monists and pluralists is over something of a non-issue. The "world is 'one' in some respects, and 'many' in others."[2] In contrast with some of his fellow pragmatists, however, James was, one might say, a highly "generous" pragmatist, putting few restrictions on the kinds of pragmatic pay-off or advantages that might speak in support of a belief. It is not, therefore, irrelevant to James that the monistic thesis may bring with it a sense of "stability and peace" and confer value and "dignity" on the world.[3] (This is an attitude that also informs James's discussion of mysticism: see IV.19 of this volume.)

When considerations like these are introduced, James seems to suggest, there is no universally compelling rational resolution of the issue: for the competing positions are attractive to human beings of different stamps. Monism, with its portrait of a stable, integrated world will appeal to the "more religious" person; pluralism, which emphasizes change and unpredictability, to the "more moral" one, since it allows for "melioristic" intervention by human beings in the course of events. Indeed, the crux of the debate, for James, comes to turn on the possibility of genuine "novelty" in the world, something that is required for belief in a freedom of the will, which is in turn necessary for adoption of an authentically moral point of view.[4] James leaves us in no doubt about his own "melioristic" and pluralistic sympathies, but it is a mark of his "generous" pragmatism that he is appreciatively aware of opposed sympathies.

Like Spinoza, Fichte, and Bradley before him, and in marked contrast with most later metaphysicians, James is a thinker for whom metaphysical issues are not to be finally divorced from the value that philosophical beliefs may have for the conduct of life.[5]

Notes

1　*Pragmatism* (1907), also in *The Writings of William James*, pp. 405–6. Besides James, other important pragmatists include C. S. Peirce (see II.18), John Dewey (1859–1952), and Richard Rorty (1931–2007).

2　Compare John William Miller (1895–1978), who worked to reconcile James and Royce; *The Midworld of Symbols and Functioning Objects*, New York: W. W. Norton, 1982.

3　See James's *The Varieties of Religious Experience: A Study in Human Nature*, New York: Longman, Green & Co., 1923, which copiously illustrates his "generosity" in refusing to confine the "experiences" that may support a belief to everyday sensory ones.

4　James was helped out of a severe depression in 1870 by his newly won conviction that freedom of the will genuinely exists. See his Diary entry for April 30, 1870, in *The Writings of William James*, pp. 7–8.

5　See Hilary Putnam, *Pragmatism: An Open Question*, Oxford: Blackwell, 1995, for a defense of this aspect of James's thought. See also R. Rorty, "Pragmatism as Romantic Polytheism," in *The Revival of Pragmatism*, ed. Morris Dickstein, Durham, NC: Duke University Press, 1998, pp. 21–36.

James, "The One and the Many"

The full nature, as distinguished from the full amount, of reality, we now believe to be given only in the perceptual flux. But, though the flux is continuous from next to next, nonadjacent portions of it are separated by parts that intervene, and such separation seems in a variety of cases to work a positive disconnection. The latter part, may contain no element surviving from the earlier part, may be unlike it, may forget it, may be shut off from it by physical barriers, or whatnot. Thus when we use our intellect for cutting up the flux and individualizing its members, we have (provisionally and practically at any rate) to treat an enormous number of these as if they were unrelated or related only remotely, to one another. We handle them piecemeal or distributively, and look at the entire flux as if it were their sum or collection. This encourages the empiricist notion, that the parts are distinct and that the whole is a resultant.

This doctrine rationalism opposes, contending that the whole is fundamental, that the parts derive from it and all belong with one-another, that the separations we uncritically accept are illusory, and that the entire universe, instead of being a sum, is the only genuine unit in existence, constituting (in the words often quoted from d'Alembert) '*un seul fait et une grande vérité*' ['one single fact and one great truth'].

The alternative here is known as that between pluralism and monism. It is the most pregnant of all the dilemmas of philosophy, although it is only in our time that it has been articulated distinctly. Does reality exist distributively? or collectively? – in the shape of *eaches, everys, anys, eithers*? or only in the shape of an *all* or *whole*! An identical content is compatible with either form obtaining, the Latin *omnes*, or *cuncti*, or the German *alle* or *sämmtliche* expressing the alternatives familiarly. Pluralism stands for the distributive, monism for the collective form of being.

Please note that pluralism need not be supposed at the outset to stand for any particular kind or amount of disconnection between the many things which it assumes. It only has the negative significance of contradicting monism's thesis that there is absolutely *no* disconnection. The irreducible outness of *any*thing, however infinitesimal, from *any*thing else, in *any* respect, would be enough, if it were solidly established, to ruin the monistic doctrine.

I hope that the reader begins to be pained here by the extreme vagueness of the terms I am using. To say that there is 'no disconnection', is on the face of it simply silly, for we find practical disconnections without number. My pocket is disconnected with Mr Morgan's bank-account, and King Edward VII's mind is disconnected with this book. Monism must mean that all such apparent disconnections are bridged over by some deeper absolute union in which it believes, and this union must in some way be more real than the practical separations that appear upon the surface.

In point of historical fact monism has generally kept itself vague and mystical as regards the ultimate principle of unity. To be One is more wonderful than to be many, so the principle of things must be One, but of that One no exact account is given. Plotinus simply calls it the One. 'The One is all things and yet no one of them. . . . For the very reason that none of them was in the One, are all derived from it. Furthermore, in order that they may be real existences, the One is not an existence, but the father of existences. And the generation of existence is as it were the first act of generation. Being perfect by reason of neither seeking nor possessing nor needing anything, the One overflows, as it were, and what overflows forms another hypostasis. . . . How should the most perfect and primal good stay shut up in itself as if it were envious or impotent? . . . Necessarily then something comes from it' [*Enneads*, Book V].

This is like the Hindoo doctrine of the Brahman, or of the Âtman. In the Bhagavat-gita the holy Krishna speaking for the One, says: "I am the immolation. I am the sacrificial rite. I am the libation offered to ancestors. I am the drug. I am the incantation. I am the sacrificial butter also. I am the fire. I am the incense. I am the father, the mother, the sustainer, the grandfather of the universe – the mystic doctrine, the purification, the syllable "Om" . . . the path, the supporter, the master, the witness, the habitation, the refuge, the friend, the origin, the dissolution, the place, the receptacle, the inexhaustible seed. I heat (the world) I withhold and pour out the rain. I am ambrosia and death, the existing and the non-existing. . . . I am the same to all beings. I have neither foe nor friend. . . . Place thy heart on me, worshipping me, sacrificing to me, saluting me' [*Bhagavadgita*, ch. iv].

I call this sort of monism mystical, for it not only revels in formulas that defy understanding,* but it accredits itself by appealing to states of illumination not vouchsafed to common men. Thus Porphyry, in his life of Plotinus, after saying that he himself once had such an insight, when 68 years old, adds that whilst he lived with Plotinus, the latter four times had the happiness

---

* Al-Ghazzali, the Mohammedan philosopher and mystic, gives a more theistic version of essentially the same idea: 'Allah is the guider aright and the leader astray; he does what he wills and decides what he wishes; there is no opposer of his decision and no repeller of his decree. He created the Garden, and created for it a people, then used them in obedience. And he created the Fire, and created for it a people, then used them in rebellion. . . . Then he said, as has been handed down from the Prophet: "These are in the Garden, and I care not; and these are in the Fire, and I care not." So he is Allah, the Most High, the King, the Reality. He is not asked concerning what he does; but they are asked.' (D. B. MacDonald's translation, in *Hartford Seminary Record*, January, 1910.) Compare for other quotations, W. James: *The Varieties of Religious Experience*, pp. 415–22.

of approaching the supreme God and consciously uniting with him in a real and ineffable act.

The regular mystical way of attaining the vision of the One is by ascetic training, fundamentally the same in all religious systems. But this ineffable kind of Oneness is not strictly philosophical, for philosophy is essentially talkative and explicit, so I must pass it by.

The usual philosophic way of reaching deeper oneness has been by the conception of substance. First used by the Greeks, this notion was elaborated with great care during the Middle Ages. Defined as any being that exists *per se*, so that it needs no further subject in which to inhere (*Ens ita per se existens, ut non indigent alio tamquam subjecto, cui inhaereat, ad existendum*) a 'substance' was first distinguished from all 'accidents' (which do require such a subject of inhesion – *cujus esse est inesse*). It was then identified with the 'principle of individuality' in things, and with their 'essence,' and divided into various types, for example into first and second, simple and compound, complete and incomplete, specific and individual, material and spiritual substances. God, on this view, is a substance, for he exists *per se*, as well as *a se*; but of secondary beings, he is the creator, not the substance, for once created, they also exist *per se* though not *a se*. Thus, for scholasticism, the notion of substance is only a partial unifier, and in its totality, the universe forms a pluralism from the substance-point-of-view.

Spinoza broke away from the scholastic doctrine. He began his 'Ethics' by demonstrating that only one substance is possible, and that that substance can only be the infinite and necessary God. This heresy brought reprobation on Spinoza, but it has been favored by philosophers and poets ever since. The pantheistic spinozistic unity was too sublime a prospect not to captivate the mind. It was not till Locke, Berkeley, and Hume began to put in their 'critical' work that the suspicion began to gain currency that the notion of substance might be only a word masquerading in the shape of an idea.*

Locke believed in substances, yet confessed that 'we have no such clear idea at all, but only an uncertain supposition of we know not what, which we take to be the substratum, or support of those ideas we do not know' [see III. 14 above]. He criticized the notion of personal substance as the principles of self-sameness in our different minds. *Experientially* our personal identity consists, he said, in nothing more than the functional and perceptible fact that our later states of mind continue and remember our earlier ones.

Berkeley applied the same sort of criticism to the notion of bodily substance. 'When I consider,' he says, 'the two parts ("being" in general, and "supporting accidents") which make the signification of the words "material substance," I am convinced there is no distinct meaning annexed to them. ... Suppose an intelligence without the help of external bodies to be affected with the same train of sensations that you are, imprinted in the same order, and with like vividness in his mind. I ask whether that intelligence hath not all the reason to believe the existence of corporeal substances, represented by his ideas, and exciting them in his mind, that you can possibly have for believing the same thing' [see III. 16 above]. Certain *grouped sensations*, in short, are all that corporeal substances are *known-as*, therefore the only meaning which the word 'matter' can claim is that it denotes such sensations and their groupings. They are the only verifiable aspect of the word.

The reader will recognize that in these criticisms our own pragmatic rule is used. What difference in practical experience is it supposed to make that we have each a personal substantial principle? This difference, that we can remember and appropriate our past, calling it 'mine.' What difference that in this book there is a substantial principle? This, that certain optical and tactile sensations cling permanently together in a cluster. The fact that

---

* No one believes that such words as 'winter,' 'army,' 'house,' denote substances. They designate collective facts, of which the parts are held together by means that can be experimentally traced. Even when we can't define what groups the effects together, as in 'poison,' 'sickness,' 'strength,' we don't assume a substance, but are willing that the word should designate some phenomenal agency yet to be found out. Nominalists treat all substances after this analogy, and consider 'matter,' 'gold,' 'soul,' as but the names of so many grouped properties, of which the bond of union must be, not some unknowable substance corresponding to the name, but rather some hidden portion of the whole phenomenal fact.

certain perceptual experiences do seem to *belong together* is thus all that the word substance means. Hume carries the criticism to the last degree of clearness. 'We have no idea of substance,' he says, 'distinct from that of a collection of particular qualities, nor have we any other meaning when we either talk or reason concerning it. The idea of a substance . . . is nothing but a collection of simple ideas that are united by the imagination and have a particular name assigned them by which we are able to recall that collection' [*Treatise on Human Nature*, I §6]. Kant's treatment of substance agrees with Hume's in denying all positive content to the notion. It differs in insisting that, by attaching shifting percepts to the permanent name, the category of substance unites them *necessarily* together, and thus makes nature intelligible. It is impossible to assent to this. The grouping of qualities becomes no more intelligible when you call substance a 'category' than when you call it a bare word.

Let us now turn our backs upon ineffable or unintelligible ways of accounting for the world's oneness, and inquire whether, instead of being a principle, the 'oneness' affirmed may not merely be a name like 'substance,' descriptive of the fact that certain *specific and verifiable connections* are found among the parts of the experiential flux. This brings us back to our pragmatic rule: Suppose there is a oneness in things, what may it be known-as? What differences to you and me will it make?

Our question thus turns upside down, and sets us on a much more promising inquiry. We can easily conceive of things that shall have no connection whatever with each other. We may assume them to inhabit different times and spaces, as the dreams of different persons do even now. They may be so unlike and incommensurable, and so inert towards one another, as never to jostle or interfere. Even now there may actually be whole universes so disparate from ours that we who know ours have no means of perceiving that they exist. We conceive their diversity, however; and by that fact the whole lot of them form what is known in logic as one 'universe of discourse.' To form a universe of discourse argues, as this example shows, no further kind of connection. The importance attached by certain monistic writers to the fact that any chaos may become a universe by being merely named, is to me incomprehensible. We must seek something

better in the way of oneness than this susceptibility of being mentally considered together, and named by a collective noun.

What connections may be perceived concretely or in point of fact, among the parts of the collection abstractly designated as our 'world'?

There are innumerable modes of union among its parts, some obtaining on a larger, some on a smaller scale. Not all the parts of our world are united *mechanically*, for some can move without the others moving. They all seem united by *gravitation*, however, so far as they are material things. Some again of these are united *chemically*, while others are not; and the like is true of thermic, optical, electrical, and other *physical* connections. These connections are specifications of what we mean by the word oneness when we apply it to our world. We should not call it one unless its parts were connected in these and other ways. But then it is clear that by the same logic we ought to call it 'many' so far as its parts are disconnected in these same ways, chemically inert towards one another or non-conductors to electricity, light and heat. In all these modes of union, some parts of the world prove to be conjoined with other parts, so that if you choose your line of influence and your items rightly, you may travel from pole to pole without an interruption. If, however, you choose them wrongly, you meet with obstacles and non-conductors from the outset, and cannot travel at all. There is thus neither absolute oneness nor absolute manyness from the physical point of view, but a mixture of well-definable modes of both. Moreover, neither the oneness nor the manyness seems the more essential attribute, they are co-ordinate features of the natural world.

There are plenty of other practical differences meant by calling a thing One. Our world, being strung along in time and space, has *temporal and spatial unity*. But time and space relate things by determinately sundering them, so it is hard to say whether the world ought more to be called 'one' or 'many' in this spatial or temporal regard.

The like is true of the *generic oneness* which comes from so many of the world's parts being similar. When two things are similar you can make inferences from the one which will hold good of the other, so that this kind of union among things, so far as it obtains, is inexpressibly precious from the logical point of view. But an infinite heterogeneity among things exists alongside of whatever likeness of kind we discover; and our world appears no more distinctly or essentially as a One than as a Many, from this generic point of view.

We have touched on the noetic[1] unity predicable of the world in consequence of our being able to mean the whole of it at once. Widely different from unification by an abstract designation, would be the concrete noetic union wrought by an all-knower of perceptual type who should be acquainted at one stroke with every part of what exists. In such an absolute all-knower idealists believe. Kant, they say, virtually replaced the notion of Substance, by the more intelligible notion of Subject. The 'I am conscious of it,' which on some witness's part must accompany every possible experience, means in the last resort, we are told, one individual witness of the total frame of things, world without end, amen. You may call his undivided act of omniscience instantaneous or eternal, whichever you like, for time is its object just as everything else is, and itself is not in time.

We shall find reasons later for treating noetic monism as an unverified hypothesis. Over against it there stands the noetic pluralism which we verify every moment when we seek information from our friends. According to this, everything in the world might be known by somebody, yet not everything by the same knower, or in one single cognitive act – much as all mankind is knit in one network of acquaintance, A knowing B, B knowing C, – Y knowing Z, and Z possibly knowing A again, without the possibility of anyone knowing everybody at once. This 'concatenated' knowing, going from next to next, is altogether different from the 'consolidated' knowing supposed to be exercised by the absolute mind. It makes a coherent type of universe in which the widest knower that exists may yet remain ignorant of much that is known to others.

There are other systems of concatenation besides the noetic concatenation. We ourselves are constantly adding to the connections of things, organizing labor-unions, establishing postal, consular, mercantile, railroad, telegraph, colonial, and other systems that bind us and things together in ever wider reticulations. Some of these systems involve others, some do not. You cannot have a telephone system without air and copper connections, but you can have air and copper connections without telephones. You cannot have love without acquaintance, but you can have acquaintance without love, etc. The same thing, moreover, can belong to many systems, as when a man is connected with other objects by heat, by gravitation, by love, and by knowledge.

From the point of view of these partial systems, the world hangs together from next to next in a variety of ways, so that when you are off of one thing you can always be on to something else, without ever dropping out of your world. Gravitation is the only positively known sort of connection among things that reminds us of the consolidated or monistic form of union. If a 'mass' should change anywhere, the mutual gravitation of all things would instantaneously alter.

Teleological and aesthetic unions are other forms of systematic union. The world is full of partial purposes, of partial stories. That they all form chapters of one supreme purpose and inclusive story is the monistic conjecture. They *seem*, meanwhile, simply to run alongside of each other – either irrelevantly, or, where they interfere, leading to mutual frustrations, – so the appearance of things is invincibly pluralistic from this purposive point of view.

It is a common belief that all particular beings have one origin and source, either in God, or in atoms all equally old. There is no real novelty, it is believed, in the universe, the new things that appear having either been eternally prefigured in the absolute, or being results of the same *primordia rerum*, atoms, or monads, getting into new mixtures. But the question of being is so obscure anyhow, that whether realities have burst into existence all at once, by a single 'bang,' as it were; or whether they came piecemeal, and have different ages (so that real novelties may be leaking into our universe all the time), may here be left an open question, though it is undoubtedly intellectually economical to suppose that all things are equally old, and that no novelties leak in.

These results are what the Oneness of the Universe is *known-as*. They *are* the oneness, pragmatically considered. A world coherent in any of these ways would be no chaos, but a universe of such or such a grade. (The grades might differ, however. The parts, e.g., might have space-relations, but nothing more; or they might also gravitate; or exchange heat; or know, or love one another, etc.)

Such is the cash-value of the world's unity, empirically realized. Its total unity is the sum of all the partial unities. It consists of them and follows upon them. Such an idea, however, outrages rationalistic minds, which habitually despise all this practical small-change. Such minds insist on a deeper, more through-and-through union of all things in the absolute, 'each in all and all in each,' as the prior condition of these empirically ascertained connections. But this may be only a case of the usual worship of abstractions, like calling 'bad weather' the cause of to-day's rain, etc., or accounting for a man's features by his 'face,' when really the rain *is* the bad weather, is what you *mean* by 'bad weather,' just as the features are what you mean by the face.

To sum up, the world is 'one' in some respects, and 'many' in others. But the respects must be distinctly specified, if either statement is to be more than the emptiest abstraction. Once we are committed to this soberer view, the question of the One or the Many may well cease to appear important. The amount either of unity or of plurality is in short only a matter for observation to ascertain and write down, in statements which will have to be complicated, in spite of every effort to be concise.

Values and Defects

We might dismiss the subject with the preceding chapter were it not for the fact that further consequences follow from the rival hypotheses, and make of the alternative of monism or pluralism what I called it on page [238], the most 'pregnant' of all the dilemmas of metaphysics.

To begin with, the attribute 'one' seems for many persons to confer a value, an ineffable illustriousness and dignity upon the world, with which the conception of it as an irreducible 'many' is believed to clash.

Secondly, a through-and-through noetic connection of everything with absolutely everything else is in some quarters held to be indispensable to the world's rationality. Only then might we believe that all things really do *belong* together, instead of being connected by the bare conjunctions 'with' or 'and.' The notion that this latter pluralistic arrangement may obtain is deemed 'irrational'; and of course it does make the world partly alogical or non-rational from a purely intellectual point of view.

Monism thus holds the oneness to be the more vital and essential element. The entire cosmos must be a consolidated unit, within which each member is determined by the whole to be just that, and from which the slightest incipiency of independence anywhere is ruled out. With Spinoza, monism likes to believe that all things follow from the essence of God as necessarily as from the nature of a triangle it follows that the angles are equal to two right angles. The whole is what yields the parts, not the parts the whole. The universe is *tight*, monism claims, not loose; and you must take the irreducible whole of it just as it is offered, or have no part or lot in it at all. The only alternative allowed by monistic writers is to confess the world's non-rationality – and no philosopher can permit himself to do that. The form of monism regnant at the present day in philosophic circles is *absolute idealism*. For this way of thinking, the world exists no otherwise than as the object of one infinitely knowing mind. The analogy that suggests the hypothesis here is that of our own finite fields of consciousness, which at every moment envisage a much-at-once composed of parts related variously, and in which both the conjunctions and the disjunctions that appear are there only in so far as we are there as their witnesses, so that they are both 'noetically' and monistically based.

We may well admit the sublimity of this noetic monism and of its vague vision of an underlying connection among all phenomena without exception.* It shows itself also able to confer religious stability and peace, and it invokes the authority of mysticism in its favor. Yet, on the other hand, like many another concept unconditionally carried out, it introduces into philosophy puzzles peculiar to itself, as follows:–

1.   It does not account for our finite consciousness. If nothing exists but as the Absolute Mind knows it, how can anything exist otherwise than as that Mind knows it? That Mind knows each thing in one act of knowledge, along with every other thing. Finite minds know things without other things, and this ignorance is the source of most of their woes. We are thus not simply objects to an all-knowing subject: we are

---

* In its essential features, Spinoza was its first prophet, Fichte and Hegel were its middle exponents, and Josiah Royce is its best contemporary representative.

subjects on our own account and know differently from its knowing.

2. It creates a problem of evil. Evil, for pluralism, presents only the practical problem of how to get rid of it. For monism the puzzle is theoretical: How – if Perfection be the source, should there be Imperfection? If the world as known to the Absolute be perfect, why should it be known otherwise, in myriads of inferior finite editions also? The perfect edition surely was enough. How do the breakage and dispersion and ignorance get in?

3. It contradicts the character of reality as perceptually experienced. Of our world, change seems an essential ingredient. There is history. There are novelties, struggles, losses, gains. But the world of the Absolute is represented as unchanging, eternal, or 'out of time,' and is foreign to our powers either of apprehension or of appreciation. Monism usually treats the sense-world as a mirage or illusion.

4. It is fatalistic. Possibility, as distinguished from necessity on the one hand and from impossibility on the other, is an essential category of human thinking. For monism, it is a pure illusion; for whatever is is necessary, and aught else is impossible, if the world be such a unit of fact as monists pretend.

Our sense of 'freedom' supposes that some things at least are decided here and now, that the passing moment may contain some novelty, be an original starting-point of events, and not merely transmit a push from elsewhere. We imagine that in some respects at least the future may not be co-implicated with the past, but may be really addable to it, and indeed addable in one shape or another, so that the next turn in events can at any given moment genuinely be ambiguous, i.e., possibly this, but also possibly that.

Monism rules out this whole conception of possibles, so native to our common-sense. The future and the past are linked, she is obliged to say; there can be no genuine novelty anywhere, for to suppose that the universe has a constitution simply additive, with nothing to link things together save what the words 'plus,' 'with,' or 'and' stand for, is repugnant to our reason.

Pluralism, on the other hand, taking perceptual experience at its face-value, is free from all these difficulties. It protests against working our ideas in a vacuum made of conceptual abstractions. Some parts of our world, it admits, cannot exist out of their wholes; but other, it says, can. To some extent the world *seems* genuinely additive: it may really be so. We cannot explain conceptually *how* genuine novelties can come; but if one did come we could experience *that* it came. We do, in fact, experience perceptual novelties all the while. Our perceptual experience overlaps our conceptual reason: the *that* transcends the *why*. So the common-sense view of life, as something really dramatic, with work done, and things decided here and now, is acceptable to pluralism. 'Free will' means nothing but real novelty; so pluralism accepts the notion of free will.

But pluralism, accepting a universe unfinished, with doors and windows open to possibilities uncontrollable in advance, gives us less religious certainty than monism, with its absolutely closed-in world. It is true that monism's religious certainty is not rationally based, but is only a faith that 'sees the All-Good in the All-Real.' In point of fact, however, monism is usually willing to exert this optimistic faith: its world is certain to be saved, yes, is saved already, unconditionally and from eternity, in spite of all the phenomenal appearances of risk.*

A world working out an uncertain destiny, as the phenomenal world appears to be doing, is an intolerable idea to the rationalistic mind.

Pluralism, on the other hand, is neither optimistic nor pessimistic, but melioristic, rather. The world, it thinks, may be saved, on condition that its parts shall do their best. But shipwreck in detail, or even on the whole, is among the open possibilities.

There is thus a practical lack of balance about pluralism, which contrasts with monism's peace of mind. The one is a more moral, the other a more religious view; and different men usually let this sort of consideration determine their belief.

So far I have sought only to show the respective implications of the rival doctrines without dogmatically deciding which is the more true. It is obvious that pluralism has three great advantages:–

1. It is more 'scientific,' in that it insists that when oneness is predicated, it shall mean definitely ascertainable conjunctive forms. With

---

* For an eloquent expression of the monistic position, from the religious point of view, read J. Royce: *The World and the Individual,* vol. ii, lectures 8, 9, 10.

these the disjunctions ascertainable among things are exactly on a par. The two are co-ordinate aspects of reality. To make the conjunctions more vital and primordial than the separations, monism has to abandon verifiable experience and proclaim a unity that is indescribable.

2. It agrees more with the moral and dramatic expressiveness of life.

3. It is not obliged to stand for any particular amount of plurality, for it triumphs over monism if the smallest morsel of disconnectedness is once found undeniably to exist. 'Ever not quite' is all it says to monism; while monism is obliged to prove that what pluralism asserts can in no amount whatever possibly be true – an infinitely harder task.

The advantages of monism, in turn, are its natural affinity with a certain kind of religious faith, and the peculiar emotional value of the conception that the world is a unitary fact.

So far has our use of the pragmatic rule brought us towards understanding this dilemma. The reader will by this time feel for himself the essential practical difference which it involves. The word 'absence' seems to indicate it. The monistic principle implies that nothing that is can in any way whatever be absent from anything else that is. The pluralistic principle, on the other hand, is quite compatible with some things being absent from operations in which other things find themselves singly or collectively engaged. *Which* things are absent from which other things, and *when*, – these of course are questions which a pluralistic philosophy can settle only by an exact study of details. The past, the present, and the future in perception, for example, are absent from one another, while in imagination they are present or absent as the case may be. If the time-content of the world be not one monistic block of being, if some part, at least, of the future, is added to the past without being virtually one therewith, or implicitly contained therein, then it is absent really as well as phenomenally and may be called an absolute novelty in the world's history in so far forth.

Towards this issue, of the reality or unreality of the novelty that appears, the pragmatic difference between monism and pluralism seems to converge. That we ourselves may be authors of genuine novelty is the thesis of the doctrine of free-will. That genuine novelties can occur means that from the point of view of what is already given, what comes may have to be treated as a matter of *chance*. We are led thus to ask the question: In what manner does new being come? Is it through and through the consequence of older being or is matter of chance so far as older being goes? – which is the same thing as asking: Is it original, in the strict sense of the word?

We connect again here with what was said [earlier]. We there agreed that being is a datum or gift and has to be begged by the philosopher; but we left the question open as to whether he must beg it all at once or beg it bit by bit or in instalments. The latter is the more consistently empiricist view.

Note

1 "Noetic" (from the Greek *noētos*) tends to mean, in modern philosophical parlance, that which is apprehended by the intellect rather than the senses. James is referring to that minimal unity the world possesses in virtue of our being able to regard it as a single object of thought.

Henri Bergson, *An Introduction to Metaphysics*, Second Part

Introduction

The French writer, Henri Bergson (1859–1941), was the most acclaimed and popular European philosopher of the years preceding World War I. This was due, in part, to the brilliance of his literary style – something recognized with the award of the Nobel Prize for Literature in 1927 – but also to Bergson's exciting, "vitalistic" metaphysical vision, one which chimed with early twentieth-century tendencies in the arts and, indeed, with the mood of the times. His influence on other philosophers of the period – notably William James (III.21) and A. N. Whitehead (III.25) – was immense. Bergson wrote relatively little after the war and, as a Jew, fell victim to Nazi persecution during the last year of his long life. By that time, his intellectual star had waned, having become a target of especially vigorous criticism by Bertrand Russell, not least for what many came to regard as his amateur forays into the natural sciences. In recent years, however, Bergson has received renewed attention, particularly from those philosophers, including many postmodernists, who share his reservations about the capacity of intellect and analysis to reveal the nature of reality.[1]

From Henri Bergson, *An Introduction to Metaphysics*, trans. T. E. Hulme, New York: Liberal Arts Press, 1949, pp. 48–61 (author's notes omitted).

Bergson's long article, *An Introduction to Metaphysics*, first published in 1903, is an admirably succinct summary of many of his central ideas, and forms a bridge between his earlier major works, such as *Matter and Memory* (1896), and his most famous book, *Creative Evolution* (1907). The article draws on the earlier works' main contention, that our mental life is a temporal process (*durée*) that we misleadingly construe as a sequence of discrete events. Such "events," as he puts it, are only "artificially taken snapshots," abstractions from a seamless, ongoing process. And the essay anticipates the cosmological vision expressed in the later work of a world that, as a whole, should be thought of by way of analogy with our mental life. Rather, as for Schopenhauer (II.15), knowledge of ourselves provides the key to an understanding of reality at large. For once we appreciate ourselves as personalities flowing through time, we should regard reality "as if a broad current of consciousness had penetrated" it.[2] Both we ourselves and the world as a whole must be understood as a "force" – in Bergson's famous phrase, an *élan vital* – that directs and forms their "superficial" manifestations.

Central to Bergson's discussion in his article is a contrast between science (or, more generally, intellectual, analytical enquiry) and "intuition." The former is indispensable for pragmatic reasons. If we are to act efficiently, we need artificially to break down the seamless flow of reality into discrete objects, events and states that we can then "act upon." But this is indeed artificial, for there is no reason to think, as we inveterately tend to do, that the world is itself structured in the way that our conceptual and linguistic schemes articulate it. For Bergson, as Russell nicely puts it, we are like the carvers of a chicken who are under the illusion that the chicken always was the separate portions into which we have cut it.[3] Intuition, by contrast – which "inverts" our usual analytical habits of thought – is a direct, non-conceptual and non-linguistic experience of the "movement," the "life," of both mind and the world. There is, Bergson insists, "nothing mysterious" in intuitive experience. On the contrary, it is at work when, for example, an author attends – but without as yet subjecting the process to analytical inspection – to the "impulse" to which he or she surrenders when composing a novel. "Metaphysical intuition," he writes, is of "the same kind": a direct, concept-free experience of reality available to a person who enters into the movement of reality, suspending intellectual presuppositions.

Bergson's distinction between a scientifically articulated world that is relative to ourselves and an ineffable reality in itself might seem similar to Kant's distinction between the phenomenal and noumenal realms (see III.17 above). But he is at some pains in *An Introduction to Metaphysics* to distinguish his position from Kant's. For one thing, Kant has an over-rigid conception of how the phenomenal world must be if it is to become an object of experience and scientific (Newtonian) articulation. More importantly, Bergson reiterates Schopenhauer's complaint that Kant ignores the possibility of a form of knowledge – most obviously in operation when we attend to our own mental life – which, while non-conceptual, provides access to the "inner reality" of the world. We are not therefore doomed, as Kant supposed, to remain in ignorance of, and plagued by irresolvable "antinomies" (see IV.17) with respect to, reality in itself.

Notes

1 See the editors' Introduction to the useful volume (itself a sign of Bergson's renaissance), *Henri Bergson: Key Writings*, ed. K. Ansell Pearson and J. Mullarkey, London: Continuum, 2002.
2 H. Bergson, *Creative Evolution*, trans. A. Mitchell, London: Macmillan, 1911, p. 191.
3 Bertrand Russell, *History of Western Philosophy*, London: Routledge, 1993, p. 759.

Bergson, *An Introduction to Metaphysics*

Second Part

[...]

[H]aving presented a general view of the method and made a first application of it, it may not be amiss to formulate, as precisely as we can, the principles on which it rests. Most of the following propositions have already received in this essay some degree of proof. We hope to demonstrate them more completely when we come to deal with other problems.

I.   *There is a reality that is external and yet given immediately to the mind.* Common-sense is right on this point, as against the idealism and realism of the philosophers.

II.   This reality is mobility. Not *things* made, but things in the making, not self-maintaining states, but only changing states, exist. Rest is never more than apparent, or, rather, relative. The consciousness we have of our own self in its continual flux introduces us to the interior of a reality, on the model of which we must represent other realities. *All reality, therefore, is tendency, if we agree to mean by tendency an incipient change of direction.*

III.   Our mind, which seeks for solid points of support, has for its main function in the ordinary course of life that of representing *states* and *things*. It takes, at long intervals, almost instantaneous views of the undivided mobility of the real. It thus obtains *sensations* and *ideas*. In this way it substitutes for the continuous the discontinuous, for motion stability, for tendency in process of change, fixed points marking a direction of change and tendency. This substitution is necessary to common-sense, to language, to practical life, and even, in a certain degree, which we shall endeavor to determine, to positive science. *Our intellect, when it follows its natural bent, pro-ceeds on the one hand by solid perceptions, and on the other by stable conceptions.* It starts from the immobile, and only conceives and expresses movement as a function of immobility. It takes up its position in ready-made concepts, and endeavors to catch in them, as in a net, something of the reality which passes. This is certainly not done in order to obtain an internal and meta-physical knowledge of the real, but simply in order to utilize the real, each concept (as also each sensation) being a *practical question* which our activity puts to reality and to which reality replies, as must be done in business, by a Yes or a No. But, in doing that, it lets that which is its very essence escape from the real.

IV. The inherent difficulties of metaphysic, the antinomies which it gives rise to, and the con-tradictions into which it falls, the division into antagonistic schools, and the irreducible opposi-tion between systems are largely the result of our applying, to the disinterested knowledge of the real, processes which we generally employ for practical ends. They arise from the fact that we place ourselves in the immobile in order to lie in wait for the moving thing as it passes, instead of replacing ourselves in the moving thing itself, in order to traverse with it the immobile positions. They arise from our professing to reconstruct reality – which is tendency and consequently mobility – with percepts and concepts whose function it is to make it stationary. With stoppages, however numerous they may be, we shall never make mobility; whereas, if mobility is given, we can, by means of diminution, obtain from it by thought as many stoppages as we desire. In other words, *it is clear that fixed concepts may be extracted by our thought from mobile reality; but there are no means of reconstructing the mobility of the real with fixed concepts.* Dogmatism, how-ever, in so far as it has been a builder of systems, has always attempted this reconstruction.

V. In this it was bound to fail. It is on this impotence and on this impotence only that the sceptical, idealist, critical doctrines really dwell: in fact, all doctrines that deny to our intelligence the power of attaining the absolute. But because we fail to reconstruct the living reality with stiff and ready-made concepts, it does not follow that we cannot grasp it in some other way. *The demon-strations which have been given of the relativity of our knowledge are therefore tainted with an*

original vice; they imply, like the dogmatism they attack, that all knowledge must necessarily start from concepts with fixed outlines, in order to clasp with them the reality which flows.

VI. But the truth is that our intelligence can follow the opposite method. It can place itself within the mobile reality, and adopt its ceaselessly changing direction; in short, can grasp it by means of that *intellectual sympathy* which we call intuition. This is extremely difficult. The mind has to do violence to itself, has to reverse the direction of the operation by which it habitually thinks, has perpetually to revise, or rather to recast, all its categories. But in this way it will attain to fluid concepts, capable of following reality in all its sinuosities and of adopting the very move-ment of the inward life of things. Only thus will a progressive philosophy be built up, freed from the disputes which arise between the various schools, and able to solve its problems naturally, because it will be released from the artificial expression in terms of which such problems are posited. *To philosophize, therefore, is to invert the habitual direction of the work of thought.*

VII. This inversion has never been practised in a methodical manner; but a profoundly con-sidered history of human thought would show that we owe to it all that is greatest in the sciences, as well as all that is permanent in metaphysics. The most powerful of the methods of investigation at the disposal of the human mind, the infinites-imal calculus, originated from this very inversion. Modern mathematics is precisely an effort to substitute the *being made* for the *ready made*, to follow the generation of magnitudes, to grasp motion no longer from without and in its displayed result, but from within and in its tendency to change; in short, to adopt the mobile continuity of the outlines of things. It is true that it is confined to the outline, being only the science of magnitudes. It is true also that it has only been able to achieve its marvelous applications by the invention of certain symbols, and that if the intuition of which we have just spoken lies at the origin of invention, it is the symbol alone which is concerned in the application. But metaphysics, which aims at no application, can and usually must abstain from converting intuition into symbols. Liberated from the obligation of working for practically useful results, it will indefinitely enlarge the domain of its investigations. What it may lose in comparison with science in utility and

exactitude, it will regain in range and extension. Though mathematics is only the science of
magnitudes, though mathematical processes
are applicable only to quantities, it must not be
forgotten that quantity is always quality in a
nascent state; it is, we might say, the limiting case
of equality. It is natural, then, that metaphysics
should adopt the generative idea of our mathematics in order to extend it to all qualities; that
is, to reality in general. It will not, by doing
this, in any way be moving towards universal
mathematics, that chimera of modern philosophy.
On the contrary, the farther it goes, the more
untranslatable into symbols will be the objects
it encounters. But it will at least have begun by
getting into contact with the continuity and
mobility of the real, just where this contact can
be most marvelously utilized. It will have contemplated itself in a mirror which reflects an
image of itself, much shrunken, no doubt, but for
that reason very luminous. It will have seen with
greater clearness what the mathematical processes borrow from concrete reality, and it will continue in the direction of concrete reality, and not
in that of mathematical processes. Having then
discounted beforehand what is too modest, and
at the same time too ambitious, in the following
formula, we may say that *the object of metaphysics is to perform* qualitative *differentiations
and integrations.*

VIII.   The reason why this object has been lost
sight of, and why science itself has been mistaken
in the origin of the processes it employs, is that
intuition, once attained, must find a mode of
expression and of application which conforms to
the habits of our thought, and one which furnishes
us, in the shape of well-defined concepts, with the
solid points of support which we so greatly need.
In that lies the condition of what we call exactitude and precision, and also the condition of the
unlimited extension of a general method to particular cases. Now this extension and this work
of logical improvement can be continued for
centuries, whilst the act which creates the method
lasts but for a moment. That is why we so often
take the logical equipment of science for science
itself, forgetting the metaphysical intuition from
which all the rest has sprung.

From the overlooking of this intuition proceeds
all that has been said by philosophers and by
men of science themselves about the "relativity"
of scientific knowledge. *What is relative is the
symbolic knowledge by pre-existing concepts, which
proceeds from the fixed to the moving, and not the
intuitive knowledge which installs itself in that
which is moving and adopts the very life of things.*
This intuition attains the absolute.

Science and metaphysics therefore come
together in intuition. A truly intuitive philosophy
would realize the much-desired union of science
and metaphysics. While it would make of metaphysics a positive science – that is, a progressive
and indefinitely perfectible one – it would at the
same time lead the positive sciences, properly so-
called, to become conscious of their true scope,
often far greater than they imagine. It would put
more science into metaphysics, and more metaphysics into science. It would result in restoring
the continuity between the intuitions which the
various sciences have obtained here and there in
the course of their history, and which they have
obtained only by strokes of genius.

IX.   That there are not two different ways of
knowing things fundamentally, that the various
sciences have their root in metaphysics, is what
the ancient philosophers generally thought.
Their error did not lie there. It consisted in their
being always dominated by the belief, so natural
to the human mind, that a variation can only
be the expression and development of what is
invariable. Whence it followed that action was
an enfeebled contemplation, duration a deceptive
and shifting image of immobile eternity, the
Soul a fall from the Idea. The whole of the philosophy which begins with Plato and culminates
in Plotinus is the development of a principle
which may be formulated thus: "There is more
in the immutable than in the moving, and we
pass from the stable to the unstable by a mere
diminution." Now it is the contrary which is
true.

Modern science dates from the day when
mobility was set up as an independent reality. It
dates from the day when Galileo, setting a ball
rolling down an inclined plane, firmly resolved
to study this movement from top to bottom for
itself, in itself, instead of seeking its principle in
the concepts of *high* and *low,* two immobilities
by which Aristotle believed he could adequately
explain the mobility. And this is not an isolated
fact in the history of science. Several of the great
discoveries, of those at least which have transformed the positive sciences or which have created new ones, have been so many soundings in

the depths of pure duration. The more living the reality touched, the deeper was the sounding.

But the lead-line sunk to the sea bottom brings up a fluid mass which the sun's heat quickly dries into solid and discontinuous grains of sand. And the intuition of duration, when it is exposed to the rays of the understanding, in like manner quickly turns into fixed, distinct, and immobile concepts. In the living mobility of things the understanding is bent on marking real or virtual stations, it notes departures and arrivals; for this is all that concerns the thought of man in so far as it is simply human. It is more than human to grasp what is happening in the interval. But philosophy can only be an effort to transcend the human condition.

Men of science have fixed their attention mainly on the concepts with which they have marked out the pathway of intuition. The more they laid stress on these residual products, which have turned into symbols, the more they attributed a symbolic character to every kind of science. And the more they believed in the symbolic character of science, the more did they indeed make science symbolical. Gradually they have blotted out all difference, in positive science, between the natural and the artificial, between the data of immediate intuition, and the enormous work of analysis which the understanding pursues round intuition. Thus they have prepared the way for a doctrine which affirms the relativity of all our knowledge.

But metaphysics has also labored to the same end.

How could the masters of modern philosophy, who have been renovators of science as well as of metaphysics, have had no sense of the moving continuity of reality? How could they have abstained from placing themselves in what we call concrete duration? They have done so to a greater extent than they were aware; above all, much more than they said. If we endeavor to link together, by a continuous connection, the intuitions about which systems have become organized, we find, together with other convergent and divergent lines, one very determinate direction of thought and of feeling. What is this latent thought? How shall we express the feeling? To borrow once more the language of the Platonists, we will say – depriving the words of their psychological sense, and giving the name of Idea to a certain settling down into easy intelligibility, and that of

Soul to a certain longing after the restlessness of life – that an invisible current causes modern philosophy to place the Soul above the Idea. It thus tends, like modern science, and even more so than modern science, to advance in an opposite direction to ancient thought.

But this metaphysics, like this science, has enfolded its deeper life in a rich tissue of symbols, forgetting something that, while science needs symbols for its analytical development, the main object of metaphysics is to do away with symbols. Here, again, the understanding has pursued its work of fixing, dividing, and reconstructing. It has pursued this, it is true, under a rather different form. Without insisting on a point which we propose to develop elsewhere, it is enough here to say that the understanding, whose function it is to operate on stable elements, may look for stability either in *relations* or in *things*. In so far as it works on concepts of relations, it culminates in *scientific* symbolism. In so far as it works on concepts of things, it culminates in *metaphysical* symbolism. But in both cases the arrangement comes from the understanding. Hence, it would fain believe itself independent. Rather than recognize at once what it owes to an intuition of the depths of reality, it prefers exposing itself to the danger that its whole work may be looked upon as nothing but an artificial arrangement of symbols. So that if we were to hold on to the letter of what metaphysicians and scientists say, and also to the material aspect of what they do, we might believe that the metaphysicians have dug a deep tunnel beneath reality, that the scientists have thrown an elegant bridge over it, but that the moving stream of things passes between these two artificial constructions without touching them.

One of the principal artifices of the Kantian criticism consisted in taking the metaphysician and the scientist literally, forcing both metaphysics and science to the extreme limit of symbolism to which they could go, and to which, moreover, they make their way of their own accord as soon as the understanding claims an independence full of perils. Having once overlooked the ties that bind science and metaphysics to intellectual intuition, Kant has no difficulty in showing that our science is wholly relative, and our metaphysics entirely artificial. Since he has exaggerated the independence of the understanding in both cases, since he has relieved both metaphysics and science of the intellectual intuition which served them as inward ballast, science with its relations presents to him no more than a film of form, and metaphysics, with its things, no more than a film of matter. Is it surprising that the first, then, reveals to him only frames packed within frames, and the second only phantoms chasing phantoms?

He has struck such telling blows at our science and our metaphysic that they have not even yet quite recovered from their bewilderment. Our mind would readily resign itself to seeing in science a knowledge that is wholly relative, and in metaphysics a speculation that is entirely empty. It seems to us, even at this present date, that the Kantian criticism applies to all metaphysics and to all science. In reality, it applies more especially to the philosophy of the ancients, as also to the form – itself borrowed from the ancients – in which the moderns have most often left their thought. It is valid against a metaphysic which claims to give us a *single* and completed system of things, against a science professing to be a *single* system of relations; in short, against a science and a metaphysic presenting themselves with the architectural simplicity of the Platonic theory of ideas or of a Greek temple. If metaphysics claims to be made up of concepts which were ours before its advent, if it consists in an ingenious arrangement of pre-existing ideas which we utilize as building material for an edifice, if, in short, it is anything else but the constant expansion of our mind, the ever-renewed effort to transcend our actual ideas and perhaps also our elementary logic, it is but too evident that, like all the works of pure understanding, it becomes artificial. And if science is wholly and entirely a work of analysis or of conceptual representation, if experience is only to serve therein as a verification for "clear ideas," if, instead of starting from multiple and diverse intuition – which insert themselves in the particular movement of each reality, but do not always dovetail into each other – it professes to be a vast mathematic, a single and closed-in system of relations, imprisoning the whole of reality in a network prepared in advance – it becomes a knowledge purely relative to human understanding. If we look carefully into the *Critique of Pure Reason*, we see that science for Kant did indeed mean this kind of *universal mathematic*, and metaphysics this practically unaltered *Platonism*. In truth, the dream of a universal mathematic is itself but a sur-

vival of Platonism. Universal mathematic is what the world of ideas becomes when we suppose that the Idea consists in a relation or in a law, and no longer in a thing. Kant took this dream of a few modern philosophers for a reality; more than this, he believed that all scientific knowledge was only a detached fragment of, or rather a stepping-stone to, universal mathematics. Hence the main task of the *Critique* was to lay the foundation of this mathematic – that is, to determine what the intellect must be, and what the object, in order that an uninterrupted mathematic may bind them together. And of necessity, if all possible experience can be made to enter thus into the rigid and already formed framework of our understanding, it is (unless we assume a pre-established harmony) because our understanding itself organizes nature, and finds itself again therein as in a mirror. Hence the possibility of science, which owes all its efficacy to its relativity, and the impossibility of metaphysics, since the latter finds nothing more to do than to parody with phantoms of things the work of conceptual arrangement which science practises seriously on relations. Briefly, *the whole* Critique of Pure Reason *ends in establishing that Platonism, illegitimate if Ideas are things, becomes legitimate if Ideas are relations, and that the ready-made idea, once brought down in this way from heaven to earth, is in fact, as Plato held, the common basis alike of thought and of nature. But the whole of the* Critique of Pure Reason *also rests on this postulate, that our intellect is incapable of anything but Platonizing* – that is, of pouring all possible experience into pre-existing moulds.

On this the whole question depends. If scientific knowledge is indeed what Kant supposed, then there is one simple science, preformed and even preformulated in nature, as Aristotle believed; great discoveries, then, serve only to illuminate, point by point, the already drawn line of this logic, immanent in things, just as on the night of a fête we light up one by one the rows of gas-jets which already outline the shape of some building. And if metaphysical knowledge is really what Kant supposed, it is reduced to a *choice* between two attitudes of the mind before all the great problems, both equally possible; its manifestations are so many arbitrary and always ephemeral choices between two solutions, virtually formulated from all eternity: it lives and dies by antinomies. But the truth is that modern science does not present this unilinear simplicity, nor does modern metaphysics these irreducible oppositions.

Modern science is neither one present nor simple. It rests, I freely admit, on ideas which in the end we find clear; but these ideas have gradually become clear through the use made of them; they owe most of their clearness to the light which the facts, and the applications to which they led, have by reflection shed on them – the clearness of a concept being scarcely anything more at bottom than the certainty, at last obtained, of manipulating the concept profitably. At its origin, more than one of these concepts must have appeared obscure, not easily reconcilable with the concepts already admitted into science, and indeed very near the border-line of absurdity. This means that science does not proceed by an orderly dovetailing together of concepts predestined to fit each other exactly. True and fruitful ideas are so many close contacts with currents of reality, which do not necessarily converge on the same point. However, the concepts in which they lodge themselves manage somehow, by rubbing off each other's corners, to settle down well enough together.

On the other hand, modern metaphysics is not made up of solutions so radical that they can culminate in irreducible oppositions. It would be so, no doubt, if there were no means of accepting at the same time and on the same level the thesis and the antithesis of the antinomies. But philosophy consists precisely in this, that by an effort of intuition one places oneself within that concrete reality, of which the *Critique* takes from without the two opposed views, thesis and antithesis. I could never imagine how black and white interpenetrate if I had never seen gray; but once I have seen gray I easily understand how it can be considered from two points of view, that of white and that of black. Doctrines which have a certain basis of intuition escape the Kantian criticism exactly in so far as they are intuitive; and these doctrines are the whole of metaphysics, provided we ignore the metaphysics which is fixed and dead in *theses*, and consider only that which is living in *philosophers*. The divergencies between the schools – that is, broadly speaking, between the groups of disciples formed round a few great masters – are certainly striking. But would we find them as marked between the masters themselves? Something here dominates the diversity of systems, something, we repeat,

which is simple and definite like a sounding, about which one feels that it has touched at greater or less depth the bottom of the same ocean, though each time it brings up to the surface very different materials. It is on these materials that the disciples usually work; in this lies the function of analysis. And the master, in so far as he formulates, develops, and translates into abstract ideas what he brings, is already in a way his own disciple. But the simple act which started the analysis, and which conceals itself behind the analysis, proceeds from a faculty quite different from the analytical. This is, by its very definition, intuition.

In conclusion, we may remark that there is nothing mysterious in this faculty. Every one of us has had occasion to exercise it to a certain extent. Any one of us, for instance, who has attempted literary composition, knows that when the subject has been studied at length, the materials all collected, and the notes all made, something more is needed in order to set about the work of composition itself, and that is an often very painful effort to place ourselves directly at the heart of the subject, and to seek as deeply as possible an impulse, after which we need only let ourselves go. This impulse, once received, starts the mind on a path where it rediscovers all the information it had collected, and a thousand other details besides; it develops and analyzes itself into terms which could be enumerated indefinitely. The farther we go, the more terms we discover; we shall never say all that could be said, and yet, if we turn back suddenly upon the impulse that we feel behind us, and try to seize it, it is gone; for it was not a thing, but the direction of a movement, and though indefinitely extensible, it is infinitely simple. Metaphysical intuition seems to be something of the same kind. What corresponds here to the documents and notes of literary composition is the sum of observations and experience gathered together by positive science. For we do not obtain an intuition from reality – that is, an intellectual sympathy with the most intimate part of it – unless we have won its confidence by a long fellowship with its superficial manifestations. And it is not merely a question of assimilating the most conspicuous facts; so immense a mass of facts must be accumulated and fused together, that in this fusion all the preconceived and premature ideas which observers may unwittingly have put into their observations will be certain to neutralize each other. In this way only can the bare materiality of the known facts be exposed to view. Even in the simple and privileged case which we have used as an example, even for the direct contact of the self with the self, the final effort of distinct intuition would be impossible to any one who had not combined and compared with each other a very large number of psychological analyses. The masters of modern philosophy were men who had assimilated all the scientific knowledge of their time, and the partial eclipse of metaphysics for the last half-century has evidently no other cause than the extraordinary difficulty which the philosopher finds to-day in getting into touch with positive science, which has become far too specialized. But metaphysical intuition, although it can be obtained only through material knowledge, is quite other than the mere summary or synthesis of that knowledge. It is distinct from these, we repeat, as the motor impulse is distinct from the path traversed by the moving body, as the tension of the spring is distinct from the visible movements of the pendulum. In this sense metaphysics has nothing in common with a generalization of facts, and nevertheless it might be defined as *integral experience*.

23

Bertrand Russell, *The Philosophy of Logical Atomism*, Lecture VIII

Introduction

Lecture VIII – the last of a series that Bertrand Russell (1872–1970) gave in London in 1918 – "point[s] to a few of the morals" of the earlier lectures for "various problems of metaphysics." In fact, it provides a succinct presentation of the metaphysical aspects of the logical atomism that he and his former student, Ludwig Wittgenstein (II.23), had been developing during the preceding years. (Despite Russell's claim in the Preface to be "explaining certain ideas . . . learnt from . . . Wittgenstein", it became clear, after the publication of the latter's *Tractatus Logico-Philosophicus* (1922), that there were important differences between the views of the two men.)

As the name "logical atomism" suggests, Russell's philosophy is a thoroughly pluralistic one, honoring "the common-sense belief that there are many separate things".[1] Lecture VIII, however, is concerned to articulate a metaphysics that does not at all belong to plain common-sense. The central claim is that nothing fundamentally exists except "ultimate simples," which turn out to be sense-data (the immediate, fleeting data of perception) and their simple properties

From Bertrand Russell, *Logic and Knowledge: Essays 1901–1950*, ed. R. C. Marsh, London: George Allen & Unwin, 1956, pp. 269–81.

(including relational properties). All "the familiar objects of daily life: tables, chairs, Piccadilly, Socrates, and so on" are at best "logical fictions". While it would be too crude bluntly to deny the existence of the table I take myself to have been working at over the months, the table must be treated simply as a "series" of related sense-data, not an "ultimate" constituent of reality. What can, however, be bluntly denied is that there is any empirical reason to postulate the existence, in any sense, of "metaphysical entities" which, by their very nature, are never "empirically given."

Russell's conclusions, then, are in the tradition of British empiricism.[2] He is, nevertheless, more ontologically generous than some of his predecessors in including qualities or properties, as well as sensory particulars, among the genuine constituents of reality. Russell's argument, which doesn't surface in Lecture VIII, is that any attempt to do away with universals, such as properties, requires the notion of "similarity" among particulars. But the notion of similarity itself is that of a relational property, and hence of a universal. In another respect, though, Russell is more parsimonious than, for example, John Stuart Mill (see III.19). For Russell, unlike Mill, shares the Humean view that the self is "fiction," reducible to a series of experiences related to one another over time.

Given the debt of his conclusions to the empiricist tradition, Russell's originality resides less in these conclusions than in his arguments for them.

Unlike earlier empiricists, he appeals, primarily, to the notion of *meaning* and other concepts of "philosophical grammar." In particular, Russell has argued in previous lectures that many, indeed nearly all, expressions that look like names – referring to genuine constituents of reality – are nothing of the sort. Rather, they are "incomplete symbols," ultimately analyzable into "logically proper names," which do so refer. Provision of the form of such analyses, an important feature of "analytic" philosophy, is the purpose of Russell's famous "theory of descriptions."

This theory, as it stands, does not tell us what the constituents of reality referred to by genuine names are. But we can, Russell thinks, say this much: they are entities that the names mean, so that they must exist if the names are to be meaningful at all. From this it follows, he has argued, that the entities must be "ultimate simples." If they were not, the words standing for them could be analyzed into simpler terms and so would not depend for their meaning on the actual existence of the entities. This still leaves the nature of the simples undetermined; and it is here that Russell's empiricist legacy comes into play. (It is here, too, where he parts company with Wittgenstein, who refuses to specify what entities count as ultimate simples.) Russell's reasoning is that – among particulars, at least – only sense-data fill the bill, for they alone are items whose existence one cannot be in error about and whose existence is therefore guaranteed in the very act of naming them – albeit with such descriptively uninformative names as "this" and "that." For Russell, then, only the parsimonious, seemingly "dry and dull,"

world of empiricism has the structure which corresponds to the structure of our language.

As an extra bonus, Russell briefly discusses William James's theory of "neutral monism." This is not monism in a sense that contradicts the pluralism that James elsewhere defends. It is not the doctrine that reality is a single indivisible unity, but the denial that mind and matter are two different kinds of entity, and hence a denial of Cartesian dualism. For the "neutral monist," as Russell clearly explains, the difference between mental and physical phenomena is a function of their "arrangement." Grouped in one way they count as mental; grouped in another way, they count as physical. Russell is sympathetic to this theory, though he raises a couple of difficulties it faces. Three years later, he was to endorse it more emphatically, writing that "the stuff of which the world of our experience is composed is . . . neither mind nor matter, but something more primitive."[3]

Notes

1   See P. Hylton, *Russell, Idealism and the Emergence of Analytic Philosophy*, Oxford: Clarendon Press, 1990, for a good account of Russell's overcoming of his early flirtation with Bradley's idealist monism.
2   See D. F. Pears, *Russell and the British Tradition in Philosophy*, London: Fontana, 1967, for a good account of Russell's relation to that tradition.
3   B. Russell, *The Analysis of Mind*, London: Allen & Unwin, 1921, p. 10.

Russell, *The Philosophy of Logical Atomism*

Lecture VIII "Excursus into Metaphysics: What There Is"

I come now to the last lecture of this course, and I propose briefly to point to a few of the morals that are to be gathered from what has gone before, in the way of suggesting the bearing of the doctrines that I have been advocating upon various problems of metaphysics. I have dealt hitherto upon what one may call philosophical

grammar, and I am afraid I have had to take you through a good many very dry and dusty regions in the course of that investigation, but I think the importance of philosophical grammar is very much greater than it is generally thought to be. I think that practically all traditional metaphysics is filled with mistakes due to bad grammar, and that almost all the traditional problems of metaphysics and traditional results – supposed results – of metaphysics are due to a failure to make the kind of distinctions in what we may call philosophical grammar with which we have been concerned in these previous lectures.

Take as a very simple example, the philosophy of arithmetic. If you think that 1, 2, 3, and 4, and the rest of the numbers, are in any sense entities, if you think that there are objects, having those names, in the realm of being, you have at once a very considerable apparatus for your metaphysics to deal with, and you have offered to you a certain kind of analysis of arithmetical propositions. When you say, e.g., that 2 and 2 are 4, you suppose in that case that you are making a proposition of which the number 2 and the number 4 are constituents, and that has all sorts of consequences, all sorts of bearings upon your general metaphysical outlook. If there has been any truth in the doctrines that we have been considering, all numbers are what I call logical fictions. Numbers are classes of classes, and classes are logical fictions, so that numbers are, as it were, fictions at two removes, fictions of fictions. Therefore you do not have, as part of the ultimate constituents of your world, these queer entities that you are inclined to call numbers. The same applies in many other directions.

One purpose that has run through all that I have said, has been the justification of analysis, i.e., the justification of logical atomism, of the view that you can get down in theory, if not in practice, to ultimate simples, out of which the world is built, and that those simples have a kind of reality not belonging to anything else. Simples, as I tried to explain, are of an infinite number of sorts. There are particulars and qualities and relations of various orders, a whole hierarchy of different sorts of simples, but all of them, if we were right, have in their various ways some kind of reality that does not belong to anything else. The only other sort of object you come across in the world is what we call *facts*, and facts are the sort of things that are asserted or denied by propositions, and are not properly entities at all in the same sense in which their constituents are. That is shown in the fact that you cannot name them. You can only deny, or assert, or consider them, but you cannot name them because they are not there to be named, although in another sense it is true that you cannot know the world unless you know the facts that make up the truths of the world; but the knowing of facts is a different sort of thing from the knowing of simples.

Another purpose which runs through all that I have been saying is the purpose embodied in the maxim called Occam's Razor. That maxim

comes in, in practice, in this way: take some science, say physics. You have there a given body of doctrine, a set of propositions expressed in symbols – I am including words among symbols – and you think that you have reason to believe that on the whole those propositions, rightly interpreted, are fairly true, but you do not know what is the actual meaning of the symbols that you are using. The meaning they have *in use* would have to be explained in some pragmatic way: they have a certain kind of practical or emotional significance to you which is a datum, but the logical significance is not a datum, but a thing to be sought, and you go through, if you are analysing a science like physics, these propositions with a view to finding out what is the smallest empirical apparatus – or the smallest apparatus, not necessarily wholly empirical – out of which you can build up these propositions. What is the smallest number of simple undefined things at the start, and the smallest number of undemonstrated premises, out of which you can define the things that need to be defined and prove the things that need to be proved? That problem, in any case that you like to take, is by no means a simple one, but on the contrary an extremely difficult one. It is one which requires a very great amount of logical technique; and the sort of thing that I have been talking about in these lectures is the preliminaries and first steps in that logical technique. You cannot possibly get at the solution of such a problem as I am talking about if you go at it in a straightforward fashion with just the ordinary acumen that one accumulates in the course of reading or in the study of traditional philosophy. You do need this apparatus of symbolical logic that I have been talking about. (The description of the subject as symbolical logic is an inadequate one. I should like to describe it simply as logic, on the ground that nothing else really is logic, but that would sound so arrogant that I hesitate to do so.)

Let us consider further the example of physics for a moment. You find, if you read the works of physicists, that they reduce matter down to certain elements – atoms, ions, corpuscles, or what not. But in any case the sort of thing that you are aiming at in the physical analysis of matter is to get down to very little bits of matter that still are just like matter in the fact that they persist through time, and that they travel about in space. They have in fact all the ordinary everyday properties of physical matter, not the matter that one has in ordinary life – they do not taste or smell or appear to the naked eye – but they have the properties that you very soon get to when you travel toward physics from ordinary life. Things of that sort, I say, are not the ultimate constituents of matter in any metaphysical sense. Those things are all of them, as I think a very little reflection shows, logical fictions in the sense that I was speaking of. At least, when I say they are, I speak somewhat too dogmatically. It is possible that there may be all these things that the physicist talks about in actual reality, but it is impossible that we should ever have any reason whatsoever for supposing that there are. That is the situation that you arrive at generally in such analyses. You find that a certain thing which has been set up as a metaphysical entity can either be assumed dogmatically to be real, and then you will have no possible argument either for its reality or against its reality; or, instead of doing that, you can construct a logical fiction having the same formal properties, or rather having formally analogous formal properties to those of the supposed metaphysical entity and itself composed of empirically given things, and that logical fiction can be substituted for your supposed metaphysical entity and will fulfil all the scientific purposes that anybody can desire. With atoms and the rest it is so, with all the metaphysical entities whether of science or of metaphysics. By metaphysical entities I mean those things which are supposed to be part of the ultimate constituents of the world, but not to be the kind of thing that is ever empirically given – I do not say merely not being itself empirically given, but not being the *kind* of thing that is empirically given. In the case of matter, you can start from what is empirically given, what one sees and hears and smells and so forth, all the ordinary data of sense, or you can start with some definite ordinary object, say this desk, and you can ask yourselves, 'What do I mean by saying that this desk that I am looking at now is the same as the one I was looking at a week ago?' The first simple ordinary answer would be that it *is* the same desk, it is actually identical, there is a perfect identity of substance, or whatever you like to call it. But when that apparently simple answer is suggested, it is important to observe that you cannot have an empirical reason for such a view as that, and if you hold it, you hold it simply because you like it and for no

other reason whatever. All that you really know is such facts as that what you see now, when you look at the desk, bears a very close similarity to what you saw a week ago when you looked at it. Rather more than that one fact of similarity I admit you know, or you may know. You might have paid some one to watch the desk continuously throughout the week, and might then have discovered that it was presenting appearances of the same sort all through that period, assuming that the light was kept on all through the night. In that way you could have established continuity. You have not in fact done so. You do not in fact know that that desk has gone on looking the same all the time, but we will assume that. Now the essential point is this: What is the empirical reason that makes you call a number of appearances, appearances of the same desk? What makes you say on successive occasions, I am seeing the same desk? The first thing to notice is this, that it does not matter what is the answer, so long as you have realized that the answer consists in something empirical and not in a recognized metaphysical identity of substance. There is something given in experience which makes you call it the same desk, and having once grasped that fact, you can go on and say, it is that something (whatever it is) that makes you call it the same desk which shall be *defined* as *constituting* it the same desk, and there shall be no assumption of a metaphysical substance which is identical throughout. It is a little easier to the untrained mind to conceive of an identity than it is to conceive of a system of correlated particulars, hung one to another by relations of similarity and continuous change and so on. That idea is apparently more complicated, but that is what is empirically given in the real world, and substance, in the sense of something which is continuously identical in the same desk, is not given to you. Therefore in all cases where you seem to have a continuous entity persisting through changes, what you have to do is to ask yourself what makes you consider the successive appearances as belonging to one thing. When you have found out what makes you take the view that they belong to the same thing, you will then see that that which has made you say so, is all that is *certainly* there in the way of unity. Anything that there may be over and above that, I shall recognize as something I cannot know. What I can know is that there are a certain series of appearances linked together, and the series of those appearances I shall define as being a desk. In that way the desk is reduced to being a logical fiction, because a series is a logical fiction. In that way all the ordinary objects of daily life are extruded from the world of what there is, and in their place as what there is you find a number of passing particulars of the kind that one is immediately conscious of in sense. I want to make clear that I am not *denying* the existence of anything; I am only refusing to affirm it. I refuse to affirm the existence of anything for which there is no evidence, but I equally refuse to deny the existence of anything against which there is no evidence. Therefore I neither affirm nor deny it, but merely say, that is not in the realm of the knowable and is certainly not a part of physics; and physics, if it is to be interpreted, must be interpreted in terms of the sort of thing that can be empirical. If your atom is going to serve purposes in physics, as it undoubtedly does, your atom has got to turn out to be a series of classes of particulars. The same process which one applies to physics, one will also apply elsewhere. The application to physics I explained briefly in my book on the *External World*, Chapters III and IV.[1]

I have talked so far about the unreality of the things we think real. I want to speak with equal emphasis about the reality of things we think unreal, such as phantoms and hallucinations. Phantoms and hallucinations, considered in themselves, are, as I explained in the preceding lectures, on exactly the same level as ordinary sense-data. They differ from ordinary sense-data only in the fact that they do not have the usual correlations with other things. In themselves they have the same reality as ordinary sense-data. They have the most complete and absolute and perfect reality that anything can have. They are part of the ultimate constituents of the world, just as the fleeting sense-data are. Speaking of the fleeting sense-data, I think it is very important to remove out of one's instincts any disposition to believe that the real is the permanent. There has been a metaphysical prejudice always that if a thing is really real, it has to last either forever or for a fairly decent length of time. That is to my mind an entire mistake. The things that are really real last a very short time. Again I am not denying that there *may* be things that last forever, or for thousands of years; I only say that those are not within our experience, and that the

real things that we know by experience last for a very short time, one tenth or half a second, or whatever it may be. Phantoms and hallucinations are among those, among the ultimate constituents of the world. The things that we call real, like tables and chairs, are systems, series of classes of particulars, and the particulars are the real things, the particulars being sense-data when they happen to be given to you. A table or chair will be a series of classes of particulars, and therefore a logical fiction. Those particulars will be on the same level of reality as a hallucination or a phantom. I ought to explain in what sense a chair is a series of classes. A chair presents at each moment a number of different appearances. All the appearances that it is presenting at a given moment make up a certain class. All those sets of appearances vary from time to time. If I take a chair and smash it, it will present a whole set of different appearances from what it did before, and without going as far as that, it will always be changing as the light changes, and so on. So you get a series in time of different sets of appearances, and that is what I mean by saying that a chair is a series of classes. That explanation is too crude, but I leave out the niceties, as that is not the actual topic I am dealing with. Now each single particular which is part of this whole system is linked up with the others in the system. Supposing, e.g. I take as my particular the appearance which that chair is presenting to me at this moment. That is linked up first of all with the appearance which the same chair is presenting to any one of you at the same moment, and with the appearance which it is going to present to me at later moments. There you get at once two journeys that you can take away from that particular, and that particular will be correlated in certain definite ways with the other particulars which also belong to that chair. That is what you mean by saying – or what you ought to mean by saying – that what I see before me is a real thing as opposed to a phantom. It means that it has a whole set of correlations of different kinds. It means that that particular, which is the appearance of the chair to me at this moment, is not isolated but is connected in a certain well-known familiar fashion with others, in the sort of way that makes it answer one's expectations. And so, when you go and buy a chair, you buy not only the appearance which it presents to you at that moment, but also those other appearances that it is going to present when it gets home. If it were a phantom chair, it would not present any appearances when it got home and would not be the sort of thing you would want to buy. The sort one calls real is one of a whole correlated system, whereas the sort you call hallucinations are not. The respectable particulars in the world are all of them linked up with other particulars in respectable, conventional ways. Then sometimes you get a wild particular, like a merely visual chair that you cannot sit on, and say it is a phantom, a hallucination, you exhaust all the vocabulary of abuse upon it. That is what one means by calling it unreal, because 'unreal' applied in that way is a term of abuse and never would be applied to a thing that *was* unreal because you would not be so angry with it.

I will pass on to some other illustrations. Take a person. What is it that makes you say, when you meet your friend Jones, 'Why, this is Jones'? It is clearly not the persistence of a metaphysical entity inside Jones somewhere, because even if there be such an entity, it certainly is not what you see when you see Jones coming along the street; it certainly is something that you are not acquainted with, not an empirical datum. Therefore plainly there is something in the empirical appearances which he presents to you, something in their relations one to another, which enables you to collect all these together and say, 'These are what I call the appearances of one person', and that something that makes you collect them together is not the persistence of a metaphysical subject, because that, whether there be such a persistent subject or not, is certainly not a datum, and that which makes you say 'Why, it is Jones' is a datum. Therefore Jones is not constituted as he is known by a sort of pin-point ego that is underlying his appearances, and you have got to find some correlations among the appearances which are of the sort that make you put all those appearances together and say, they are the appearances of one person. Those are different when it is other people and when it is yourself. When it is yourself, you have more to go by. You have not only what you look like, you have also your thoughts and memories and all your organic sensations, so that you have a much richer material and are therefore much less likely to be mistaken as to your own identity than as to someone else's. It happens, of course, that there are mistakes even as to one's own identity, in cases of multiple personality and so forth, but as a rule you will know that it is you because you have more to go by than other people have, and you would know it is you, not by a consciousness of the ego at all but by all sorts of things, by memory, by the way you feel and the way you look and a host of things. But all those are empirical data, and those enable you to say that the person to whom something happened yesterday was yourself. So if you can collect a whole set of experiences into one string as all belonging to you, and similarly other people's experiences can be collected together as all belonging to them by relations that actually are observable and without assuming the existence of the persistent ego. It does not matter in the least to what we are concerned with, what exactly is the given empirical relation between two experiences that makes us say, 'These are two experiences of the same person'. It does not matter precisely what that relation is, because the logical formula for the construction of the person is the same whatever that relation may be, and because the mere fact that you can know that two experiences belong to the same person proves that there is such an empirical relation to be ascertained by analysis. Let us call the relation R. We shall say that when two experiences have to each other the relation R, then they are said to be experiences of the same person. That is a definition of what I mean by 'experiences of the same person'. We proceed here just in the same way as when we are defining numbers. We first define what is meant by saying that two classes 'have the same number', and then define what a number is. The person who has a given experience x will be the class of all those experiences which are 'experiences of the same person' as the one who experiences x. You can say that two events are co-personal when there is between them a certain relation R, namely that relation which makes us say that they are experiences of the same person. You can define the person who has a certain experience as being those experiences that are co-personal with that experience, and it will be better perhaps to take them as a series than as a class, because you want to know which is the beginning of a man's life and which is the end. Therefore we shall say that a person is a certain series of experiences. We shall not deny that there may be a metaphysical ego. We shall merely say that it is a question that does not concern us in any way, because it is a matter about which we know nothing and can know nothing, and therefore it obviously cannot be a thing that comes into science in any way. What we know is this string of experiences that makes up a person, and that is put together by means of certain empirically given relations, such, e.g., as memory.

I will take another illustration, a kind of problem that our method is useful in helping to deal with. You all know the American theory of neutral monism, which derives really from William James and is also suggested in the work of Mach, but in a rather less developed form. The theory of neutral monism maintains that the distinction between the mental and the physical is entirely an affair of arrangement, that the actual material arranged is exactly the same in the case of the mental as it is in the case of the physical, but they differ merely in the fact that when you take a thing as belonging in the same context with certain other things, it will belong to psychology, while when you take it in a certain other context with other things, it will belong to physics, and the difference is as to what you consider to be its context, just the same sort of difference as there is between arranging the people in London alphabetically or geographically. So, according to William James, the actual material of the world can be arranged in two different ways, one of which gives you physics and the other psychology. It is just like rows or columns: in an arrangement of rows and columns, you can take an item as either a member of a certain row or a member of a certain column; the item is the same in the two cases, but its context is different.

If you will allow me a little undue simplicity I can go on to say rather more about neutral monism, but you must understand that I am talking more simply than I ought to do because there is not time to put in all the shadings and qualifications. I was talking a moment ago about the appearances that a chair presents. If we take any one of these chairs, we can all look at it, and it presents a different appearance to each of us. Taken all together, taking all the different appearances that that chair is presenting to all of us at this moment, you get something that belongs to physics. So that, if one takes sense-data and arranges together all those sense-data that appear to different people at a given moment

and are such as we should ordinarily say are appearances of the same physical object, then that class of sense-data will give you something that belongs to physics, namely, the chair at this moment. On the other hand, if instead of taking all the appearances that that chair presents to all of us at this moment, I take all the appearances that the different chairs in this room present to me at this moment, I get quite another group of particulars. All the different appearances that different chairs present to me now will give you something belonging to psychology, because that will give you my experiences at the present moment. Broadly speaking, according to what one may take as an expansion of William James, that should be the definition of the difference between physics and psychology.

We commonly assume that there is a phenomenon which we call seeing the chair, but what I call my seeing the chair according to neutral monism is merely the existence of a certain particular, namely the particular which is the sense-datum of that chair at that moment. And I and the chair are both logical fictions, both being in fact a series of classes of particulars, of which one will be that particular which we call my seeing the chair. That actual appearance that the chair is presenting to me now is a member of me and a member of the chair, I and the chair being logical fictions. That will be at any rate a view that you can consider if you are engaged in vindicating neutral monism. There is no simple entity that you can point to and say: this entity is physical and not mental. According to William James and neutral monists that will not be the case with any simple entity that you may take. Any such entity will be a member of physical series and a member of mental series. Now I want to say that if you wish to test such a theory as that of neutral monism, if you wish to discover whether it is true or false, you cannot hope to get any distance with your problem unless you have at your fingers' ends the theory of logic that I have been talking of. You never can tell otherwise what can be done with a given material, whether you can concoct out of a given material the sort of logical fictions that will have the properties you want in psychology and in physics. That sort of thing is by no means easy to decide. You can only decide it if you really have a very considerable technical facility in these matters. Having said that,

I ought to proceed to tell you that I have discovered whether neutral monism is true or not, because otherwise you may not believe that logic is any use in the matter. But I do not profess to know whether it is true or not. I feel more and more inclined to think that it may be true. I feel more and more that the difficulties that occur in regard to it are all of the sort that may be solved by ingenuity. But nevertheless there *are* a number of difficulties; there are a number of problems, some of which I have spoken about in the course of these lectures.[2] One is the question of belief and the other sorts of facts involving two verbs. If there are such facts as this, that, I think, may make neutral monism rather difficult, but as I was pointing out, there is the theory that one calls behaviourism, which belongs logically with neutral monism, and that theory would altogether dispense with those facts containing two verbs, and would therefore dispose of that argument against neutral monism. There is, on the other hand, the argument from emphatic particulars, such as 'this' and 'now' and 'here' and such words as that, which are not very easy to reconcile, to my mind, with the view which does not distinguish between a particular and experiencing that particular. But the argument about emphatic particulars is so delicate and so subtle that I cannot feel quite sure whether it is a valid one or not, and I think the longer one pursues philosophy, the more conscious one becomes how extremely often one has been taken in by fallacies, and the less willing one is to be quite sure that an argument is valid if there is anything about it that is at all subtle or elusive, at all difficult to grasp. That makes me a little cautious, and doubtful about all these arguments, and therefore although I am quite sure that the question of the truth or falsehood of neutral monism is not be solved except by these means, yet I do not profess to know whether neutral monism is true or is not. I am not without hopes of finding out in the course of time, but I do not profess to know yet.

As I said earlier in this lecture, one thing that our technique does, is to give us a means of constructing a given body of symbolic propositions with the minimum of apparatus, and every diminution in apparatus diminishes the risk of error. Suppose, e.g., that you have constructed your physics with a certain number of entities and a certain number of premises; suppose you discover that by a little ingenuity you can dispense with half of those entities and half of those premises, you clearly have diminished the risk of error, because if you had before 10 entities and 10 premises, then the 5 you have now would be all right, but it is not true conversely that if the 5 you have now are all right, the 10 must have been. Therefore you diminish the risk of error with every diminution of entities and premises. When I spoke about the desk and said I was not going to assume the existence of a persistent substance underlying its appearances, it is an example of the case in point. You have anyhow the successive appearances, and if you can get on without assuming the metaphysical and constant desk, you have a smaller risk of error than you had before. You would not necessarily have a smaller risk of error if you were tied down to *denying* the metaphysical desk. That is the advantage of Occam's Razor, that it diminishes your risk of error. Considered in that way you may say that the whole of our problem belongs rather to science than to philosophy. I think perhaps that is true, but I believe the only difference between science and philosophy is, that science is what you more or less know and philosophy is what you do not know. Philosophy is that part of science which at present people choose to have opinions about, but which they have no knowledge about. Therefore every advance in knowledge robs philosophy of some problems which formerly it had, and if there is any truth, if there is any value in the kind of procedure of mathematical logic, it will follow that a number of problems which had belonged to philosophy will have ceased to belong to philosophy and will belong to science. And of course the moment they become soluble, they become to a large class of philosophical minds uninteresting, because to many of the people who like philosophy, the charm of it consists in the speculative freedom, in the fact that you can play with hypotheses. You can think out this or that which *may* be true, which is a very valuable exercise until you discover what *is* true; but when you discover what is true the whole fruitful play of fancy in that region is curtailed, and you will abandon that region and pass on. Just as there are families in America who from the time of the Pilgrim Fathers onward had always migrated westward, toward the backwoods, because they did not like civilized life, so the philosopher has an adventurous disposition and likes to dwell in the region where there are still uncertainties. It is true that the transferring of a region from philosophy into science will make it distasteful to a very important and useful type of mind. I think that is true of a good deal of the applications of mathematical logic in the directions that I have been indicating. It makes it dry, precise, methodical, and in that way robs it of a certain quality that it had when you could play with it more freely. I do not feel that it is my place to apologize for that, because if it is true, it is true. If it is not true, of course, I do owe you an apology; but if it is, it is not my fault, and therefore I do not feel I owe any apology for any sort of dryness or dulness in the world. I would say this too, that for those who have any taste for mathematics, for those who like symbolic constructions, that sort of world is a very delightful one, and if you do not find it otherwise attractive, all that is necessary to do is to acquire a taste for mathematics, and then you will have a very agreeable world, and with that conclusion I will bring this course of lectures to an end.

Notes

1 *Our Knowledge of the External World*, Allen & Unwin, 1914.

2 The two rather technical problems that Russell mentions emerge from earlier lectures. (a) In Lecture IV, he has discussed "propositions involving two verbs," such as "I believe that Socrates is wise." The problem is whether such propositions record irreducible, *sui generis* mental facts. If they do, then these facts cannot also, in a different "arrangement," be physical facts. Russell, however, allows the possibility of a "behaviourist" analysis of such propositions which would remove the difficulty. (b) In Lecture II, Russell has argued that the only genuine logically proper names are terms like "this" and "that" when these are used, not to refer to a physical object, but "to stand for an actual object of sense," a sense-datum. The difficulty, I take it, is that with "This is red" so construed, it contrasts with the same words when used to state a fact about a physical object. The contrast seems to imply that there are two kinds of fact, sensory and physical, not one "neutral" fact which, according to the arrangement it is placed in, could count as either mental or physical.

24

Martin Heidegger, *Being and Time*, Sections 14, 15, 19, and 21

Introduction

The texts usually chosen from the writings of the German philosopher Martin Heidegger (1889–1976) to illustrate his metaphysical views – the "Introduction" to *Being and Time* (1927), for example, or the lecture "What is Metaphysics?" – are ones in which he talks about the task of metaphysics or ontology. (In his later work, Heidegger, like the logical positivists but for different reasons, uses the term "metaphysics" pejoratively.)[1] We have preferred, however, to choose some sections from *Being and Time* (*Sein und Zeit*) where Heidegger is engaged in ontology – in presenting part of his own account of the world and reality, and in contrasting that account with a more traditional one exemplified by, above all, Descartes.

That traditional ontology, Heidegger reasonably claims, is centered on the notion of substance. The world is a collection of logically independent substances, with objective properties that we can observe or cognize: a world of things "present-at-hand" (*vorhanden*), in his terminology. That conception, of course, had been criticized by earlier writers including, as one can see in other entries in this volume, Bradley and Whitehead (III.20 and

From Martin Heidegger, *Being and Time*, trans. J. Macquarrie and E. Robinson. Oxford: Blackwell, 1962, pp. 91–102, 122–3, 128–34 (some passages and most notes omitted; asterisked note is the translators').

III.25). Heidegger's rejection of it is, however, a distinctly original one. To understand Heidegger's critique, we need to be acquainted with what has preceded the chapter of *Being and Time*, "The Worldhood of the World," from which the following selections are taken.

The purpose of the book is to address "the question of Being," one which, Heidegger believes, philosophers have generally failed to do. They have focused on beings or entities, and not on the Being of these. In doing so, they have mistakenly come to understand Being as if it were itself an entity. (In Heidegger's jargon, they have focused on "ontical" questions about the properties of beings, not the "ontological" issue of their Being.) By "Being" (*Sein*) Heidegger means "that which determines entities as entities, that on the basis of which entities are already understood" (*Being and Time*, pp. 25–6). If we are to uncover these very general conditions for anything to be encountered or understood as the thing it is, enquiry should begin with that special being which has some grasp (however implicit and inchoate) of those conditions, that being for which Being is a question, the being that human beings endure – namely, what Heidegger calls, "*Dasein*" or literally "there-being."[2]

Reflection on *Dasein* soon reveals that its fundamental aspect is not knowledge or theoretical reason, but its "Being-in-the-world" as an engaged, purposeful agent. Being in the world, Heidegger emphasizes, is no mere matter of being spatially located in a universe. The notion of the "world" that *Dasein* is "in" must, therefore, be clarified if we are to progress towards uncovering the nature of Being, that "basis" on which entities are encountered and understood. The world, as he puts it, is an *"existentiale"* of *Dasein*, one of the necessary structural components in its analysis.

That world, Heidegger insists, is not all a collection of substances or things "present-at-hand." Rather it is a world of "equipment" or "gear" (*Zeug*), of things "ready-to-hand" (*zuhanden*), variously involved in our purposeful projects. We experience the world about us, in the first instance, as containing hammers, signposts, workshops, and the like, and not as mere lumps of spatially extended stuff. The world that *Dasein* is "in" is a vast "relational totality" of "significance," in which things are what they are in virtue of their meaningful relations to our "concerns," or generally what Heidegger calls "Care" (*Sorge*). That we "primordially" encounter the world in this way is not, moreover, a contingent matter: unless we did so, nothing would "light up" for us, "stand out" and hence be an object for attention and exploration. The merely "present-at-hand" world of traditional ontology is, therefore, an abstraction, parasitic on the "ready-to-hand" world of everyday engagement.

The defects of that traditional ontology are exposed in §21, where Heidegger argues that, on Descartes's account, it would be impossible to explain how we acquire any "access" to the world, how things could "show up" for us. It is hopeless, moreover, to construe "ready-to-hand" things, like hammers, as "really" being mere material lumps to which we subsequently and "subjectively" attach some value or purpose. The bifurcation of our experience of, say, a hammer into an "objective" perception of it as something with its cultural "skin off" and an evaluation of that thing's purpose is entirely untrue to the phenomenology of our encounter with "equipment" and with the world.

Heidegger's discussion raises many questions. One concerns how, given our "primordial" experience of the world as "equipment," we ever manage to attain the "objective" standpoint – that of the scientist, say – from which we look at and examine things in isolation from their involvement with our projects and concerns. Heidegger addresses this question in §16, where he argues that regarding things as merely "present-at-hand" emerges as a result of various "breakdowns" in our usual, engaged dealings with things.[3] Without denying that an "objective" standpoint is possible, Heidegger insists, however, that this standpoint is a derivative one and has no claim to be that from which things are experienced as they are in themselves. Another critical question is whether Heidegger, despite his protests, is not, after all, confusing "genetic," "anthropological" issues concerning how we come to experience and describe things with ontological ones concerning what fundamentally it is that we encounter.[4] This is a question that continues to divide his admirers and detractors.

Notes

1 See, e.g., Heidegger's "Letter on Humanism," in *Martin Heidegger: Basic Writings*, ed. D. F. Krell, London: Routledge & Kegan Paul, 1978.
2 Jean-Paul Sartre (I.23), taking a more human-centered approach, translated *Dasein* as "human reality."
3 For a good account of this and many other points, see H. L. Dreyfus, *Being-in-the-World: A Commentary on Heidegger's* Being and Time, *Division I*, Cambridge, MA: MIT Press, 1991.
4 The charge of only "doing anthropology" was made, early on, by Heidegger's teacher Edmund Husserl (1859–1938). See David E. Cooper, *Existentialism: A Reconstruction*, Oxford: Blackwell, 1999 (revised edition), Ch. 4, p. 64.

Heidegger, *Being and Time*

III

¶ 14. *The Idea of the Worldhood of the World in General* Being-in-the-world shall first be made visible with regard to that item of its structure which is the 'world' itself. To accomplish this task seems easy and so trivial as to make one keep taking for granted that it may be dispensed with. What can be meant by describing 'the world' as a phenomenon? It means to let us see what shows itself in 'entities' within the world. Here the first step is to enumerate the things that are 'in' the world: houses, trees, people, mountains, stars. We can *depict* the way such entities 'look', and we can give an *account* of occurrences in them and with them. This, however, is obviously a pre-phenomenological 'business' which cannot be at all relevant phenomenologically. Such a description is always confined to entities. It is ontical. But what we are seeking is Being. And we have formally defined 'phenomenon' in the phenomenological sense as that which shows itself as Being and as a structure of Being.

Thus, to give a phenomenological description of the 'world' will mean to exhibit the Being of those entities which are present-at-hand within the world, and to fix it in concepts which are categorial.[1] Now the entities within the world are Things – Things of Nature, and Things 'invested with value'. Their Thinghood becomes a problem; and to the extent that the Thinghood of Things 'invested with value' is based upon the Thinghood of Nature, our primary theme is the Being of Things of Nature – Nature as such. That characteristic of Being which belongs to Things of Nature (substances), and upon which everything is founded, is substantiality. What is its ontological meaning? By asking this, we have given an unequivocal direction to our inquiry.

But is this a way of asking ontologically about the 'world'? The problematic which we have thus marked out is one which is undoubtedly ontological. But even if this ontology should itself succeed in explicating the Being of Nature in the very purest manner, in conformity with the basic assertions about this entity, which the mathematical natural sciences provide, it will never reach the phenomenon that is the 'world'. Nature is itself an entity which is encountered within the world and which can be discovered in various way and at various stages.

Should we then first attach ourselves to those entities with which Dasein proximally and for the most part dwells – Things 'invested with value'? Do not these 'really' show us the world in which we live? Perhaps, in fact, they show us something like the 'world' more penetratingly. But these Things too are entities 'within' the world.

Neither the ontical depiction of entities within-the-world nor the ontological Interpretation of their Being is such as to reach the phenomenon of the 'world.' In both of these ways of access to 'Objective Being', the 'world' has already been 'presupposed', and indeed in various ways.

Is it possible that ultimately we cannot address ourselves to 'the world' as determining the nature of the entity we have mentioned? Yet we call this entity one which is "within-the-world". Is 'world' perhaps a characteristic of Dasein's Being? And in that case, does every Dasein 'proximally' have its world? Does not 'world' thus become something 'subjective'? How, then, can there be a 'common' world 'in' which, nevertheless, we *are*? And if we raise the question of the 'world', *what* world do we have in view? Neither the common world nor the subjective world, but *the worldhood of the world as such*. By what avenue do we meet this phenomenon?

'Worldhood' is an ontological concept, and stands for the structure of one of the constitutive items of Being-in-the-world. But we know Being-in-the-world as a way in which Dasein's character is defined existentially. Thus worldhood itself is an *existentiale*. If we inquire ontologically about the 'world', we by no means abandon the analytic of Dasein as a field for thematic study. Ontologically, 'world' is not a way of characterizing those entities which Dasein essentially is *not*; it is rather a characteristic of Dasein itself. This does not rule out the possibility that when we investigate the phenomenon of the 'world' we must do so by the avenue of entities within-the-world and the Being which they possess. The task of 'describing' the world phenomenologically is so far from obvious that even if we do no more than determine adequately what form it shall take, essential ontological clarifications will be needed.

This discussion of the word 'world', and our frequent use of it have made it apparent that it is used in several ways. By unravelling these we can get an indication of the different kinds of phenomena that are signified, and of the way in which they are interconnected.

1. "World" is used as an ontical concept, and signifies the totality of those entities which can be present-at-hand within the world.

2. "World" functions as an ontological term, and signifies the Being of those entities which we have just mentioned. And indeed 'world' can become a term for any realm which encompasses a multiplicity of entities: for instance, when one talks of the 'world' of a mathematician, 'world' signifies the realm of possible objects of mathematics.

3. "World" can be understood in another ontical sense – not, however, as those entities which Dasein essentially is not and which can be encountered within-the-world, but rather as that '*wherein*' a factical Dasein as such can be said to 'live'. "World" has here a pre-ontological existentiell signification.[2] Here again there are different possibilities: "world" may stand for the 'public' we-world, or one's 'own' closest (domestic) environment.

4. Finally, "world" designates the ontologico-existential concept of *worldhood*. Worldhood itself may have as its modes whatever structural wholes any special 'worlds' may have at the time; but it embraces in itself the *a priori* character of worldhood in general. We shall reserve the expression "world" as a term for our third signification. If we should sometimes use it in the first of these senses, we shall mark this with single quotation marks.

The derivative form 'worldly' will then apply terminologically to a kind of Being which belongs to Dasein, never to a kind which belongs to entities present-at-hand 'in' the world. We shall designate these latter entities as "belonging to the world" or "within-the-world".

A glance at previous ontology shows that if one fails to see Being-in-the-world as a state of Dasein, the phenomenon of worldhood likewise gets *passed over*. One tries instead to Interpret the world in terms of the Being of those entities which are present-at-hand within-the-world but which are by no means proximally discovered – namely, in terms of Nature. If one understands Nature ontologico-categorially, one finds that Nature is a limiting case of the Being of possible entities within-the-world. Only in some definite mode of its own Being-in-the-world can Dasein discover entities as Nature. This manner of knowing them has the character of depriving the world of its worldhood in a definite way. 'Nature', as the categorial aggregate of those structures of Being which a definite entity encountered within-the-world may possess, can never make *worldhood* intelligible. But even the phenomenon of 'Nature', as it is conceived, for instance, in romanticism, can be grasped ontologically only in terms of the concept of the world – that to say, in terms of the analytic of Dasein.

When it comes to the problem of analysing the world's worldhood ontologically, traditional ontology operates in a blind alley, if, indeed, it sees this problem at all. On the other hand, if we are to Interpret the worldhood of Dasein and the possible ways in which Dasein is made worldly, we must show *why* the kind of Being with which Dasein knows the world is such that it passes over 66 the phenomenon of worldhood both ontically and ontologically. But at the same time the very Fact of this passing-over suggests that we must take special precautions to get the right phenomenal point of departure for access to the phenomenon of worldhood, so that it will not get passed over.

Our method has already been assigned. The theme of our analytic is to be Being-in-the-world, and accordingly the very world itself; and these are to be considered within the horizon of average everydayness – the kind of Being which is *closest* to Dasein. We must make a study of everyday Being-in-the-world; with the phenomenal support which this gives us, something like the world must come into view.

That world of everyday Dasein which is closest to it, is the *environment*. From this existential character of average Being-in-the-world, our investigation will take its course towards the idea of worldhood in general. We shall seek the worldhood of the environment (environmentality) by going through an ontological Interpretation of those entities within-the-*environment* which we encounter as closest to us. The expression "environment" [Umwelt] contains in the 'environ' ["um"] a suggestion of spatiality. Yet the 'around' ["Umherum"] which is constitutive for the environment does not have a primarily 'spatial' meaning. Instead, the spatial character which incontestably belongs to any environment, can be clarified only in terms of the structure of worldhood. From this point of view, Dasein's spatiality, of which we have given an indication in Section 12, becomes phenomenally visible.[3] In ontology, however, an attempt has been made to start with spatiality and then to Interpret the Being of the 'world' as *res extensa*. In Descartes we find the most extreme tendency towards such an ontology of the 'world', with, indeed, a counter-orientation towards the *res cogitans* – which does not coincide with Dasein either ontically or ontologically. The analysis of worldhood which we are here attempting can be made clearer if we show how it differs from such an ontological tendency. Our analysis will be completed in three stages: (*A*) the analysis of environmentality and worldhood in general; (B) an illustrative contrast between our analysis of worldhood and Descartes' ontology of the 'world'; (C) the aroundness of the environment, and the 'spatiality' of Dasein.*

A. Analysis of Environmentality and Worldhood in General

¶ 15. *The Being of the Entities Encountered in the Environment* The Being of those entities which we encounter as closest to us can be exhibited phenomenologically if we take as our clue our 67 everyday Being-in-the-world, which we also call our *"dealings"* in the world and *with* entities within-the-world. Such dealings have already dispersed themselves into manifold ways of concern. The kind of dealing which is closest to us is as we have shown, not a bare perceptual cognition, but rather that kind of concern which manipulates things and puts them to use; and this has its own kind of 'knowledge'. The phenomenological question applies in the first instance to the Being of those entities which we encounter in such concern. To assure the kind of seeing which is here required, we must first make a remark about method.

In the disclosure and explication of Being, entities are in every case our preliminary and our accompanying theme; but our real theme is Being. In the domain of the present analysis, the entities we shall take as our preliminary theme are those which show themselves in our concern with the environment. Such entities are not thereby objects for knowing the 'world' theoretically; they are simply what gets used, what gets produced, and so forth. As entities so encountered, they become the preliminary theme for the purview of a 'knowing' which, as phenomenological, looks primarily towards Being, and which, in thus taking Being as its theme, takes these entities as its accompanying theme. This phenomenological interpretation is accordingly not a way of knowing those characteristics of entities which themselves are; it is rather a determination of the structure of the Being which entities possess. But as an investigation of Being, it brings to

completion, autonomously and explicitly, that understanding of Being which belongs already to Dasein and which 'comes alive' in any of its dealings with entities. Those entities which serve phenomenologically as our preliminary theme – in this case, those which are used or which are to be found in the course of production – become accessible when we put ourselves into the position of concerning ourselves with them in some such way. Taken strictly, this talk about "putting ourselves into such a position" is misleading; for the kind of Being which belongs to such concernful dealings is not one into which we need to put ourselves first. This is the way in which everyday Dasein always *is*: when I open the door, for instance, I use the latch. The achieving of phenomenological access to the entities which we encounter, consists rather in thrusting aside our interpretative tendencies, which keep thrusting themselves upon us and running along with us, and which conceal not only the phenomenon of such 'concern', but even more those entities themselves *as* encountered of their own accord *in* our concern with them. These entangling errors become plain if in the course of our investigation we now ask which entities shall be taken as our preliminary theme and established as the pre-phenomenal basis for our study.

One may answer: "Things." But with this obvious answer we have perhaps already missed 68 the pre-phenomenal basis we are seeking. For in addressing these entities as 'Things' (*res*), we have tacitly anticipated their ontological character. When analysis starts with such entities and goes on to inquire about Being, what it meets is Thinghood and Reality. Ontological explication discovers, as it proceeds, such characteristics of Being as substantiality, materiality, extendedness, side-by-side-ness, and so forth. But even pre-ontologically, in such Being as this, the entities which we encounter in concern are proximally hidden. When one designates Things as the entities that are 'proximally given', one goes ontologically astray, even though ontically one has something else in mind. What one really has in mind remains undetermined. But suppose one characterizes these 'Things' as Things 'invested with value'? What does "value" mean ontologically? How are we to categorize this 'investing' and Being-invested? Disregarding the obscurity of this structure of investiture with value, have we thus met that phenomenal characteristic of

* *A* is considered in Sections 15–18; *B* in Sections 19–21; *C* in Sections 22–24.

Being which belongs to what we encounter in our concernful dealings?

The Greeks had an appropriate term for 'Things': πράγματα [pragmata] – that is to say, that which one has to do with in one's concernful dealings (πρᾶξις) [praxis]. But ontologically, the specifically 'pragmatic' character of the πράγματα is just what the Greeks left in obscurity; they thought of these 'proximally' as 'mere Things'. We shall call those entities which we encounter in concern "*equipment*".[4] In our dealings we come across equipment for writing, sewing, working, transportation, measurement. The kind of Being which equipment possesses must be exhibited. The clue for doing this lies in our first defining what makes an item of equipment – namely, its equipmentality.

Taken strictly, there 'is' no such thing as *an* equipment. To the Being of any equipment there always belongs a totality of equipment, in which it can be this equipment that it is. Equipment is essentially 'something in-order-to'. . . . A totality of equipment is constituted by various ways of the 'in-order-to', such as serviceability, conduciveness, usability, manipulability.

In the 'in-order-to' as a structure there lies an *assignment* or *reference* of something to something. Only in the analyses which are to follow can the phenomenon which this term 'assignment' indicates be made visible in its ontological genesis. Provisionally, it is enough to take a look phenomenally at a manifold of such assignments. Equipment – in accordance with its equipmentality – always is *in terms of* its belonging to other equipment: ink-stand, pen, ink, paper, blotting pad, table, lamp, furniture, windows, doors, room. These 'Things' never show themselves proximally as they are for themselves, so as to add up to a sum of *realia* and fill up a room. What we encounter as closest to us (though not as something taken as a theme) is the room; and we encounter it not as something 'between four walls' in a geometrical spatial sense, but as equipment for residing. Out of this the 'arrange-69 ment' emerges, and it is in this that any 'individual' item of equipment shows itself. *Before* it does so, a totality of equipment has already been discovered.

Equipment can genuinely show itself only in dealings cut to its own measure (hammering with a hammer, for example); but in such dealings an entity of this kind is not *grasped* thematically as an occurring Thing, nor is the equipment-structure known as such even in the using. The hammering does not simply have knowledge about the hammer's character as equipment, but it has appropriated this equipment in a way which could not possibly be more suitable. In dealings such as this, where something is put to use, our concern subordinates itself to the "in-order-to" which is constitutive for the equipment we are employing at the time; the less we just stare at the hammer-Thing, and the more we seize hold of it and use it, the more primordial does our relationship to it become, and the more unveiledly is it encountered as that which it is – as equipment. The hammering itself uncovers the specific 'manipulability' of the hammer. The kind of Being which equipment possesses – in which it manifests itself in its own right – we call "*readiness-to-hand*". Only because equipment has *this* 'Being-in-itself' and does not merely occur, is it manipulable in the broadest sense and at our disposal. No matter how sharply we just *look* at the 'outward appearance' of Things in whatever form this takes, we cannot discover anything ready-to-hand. If we look at Things just 'theoretically', we can get along without understanding readiness-to-hand. But when we deal with them by using them and manipulating them, this activity is not a blind one; it has its own kind of sight, by which our manipulation is guided and from which it acquires its specific Thingly character. Dealings with equipment subordinate themselves to the manifold assignments of the 'in-order-to'. And the sight with which they thus accommodate themselves is *circumspection*.

'Practical' behaviour is not 'atheoretical' in the sense of "sightlessness". The way it differs from theoretical behaviour does not lie simply in the fact that in theoretical behaviour one observes, while in practical behaviour one *acts*, and that action must employ theoretical cognition if it is not to remain blind; for the fact that observation is a kind of concern is just as primordial as the fact that action has *its own* kind of sight. Theoretical behaviour is just looking, without circumspection. But the fact that this looking is non-circumspective does not mean that it follows no rules: it constructs a canon for itself in the form of *method*.

The ready-to-hand is not grasped theoretically at all, nor is it itself the sort of thing that circumspection takes proximally as a circum-spective theme. The peculiarity of what is proximally ready-to-hand is that, in its readiness-to-hand, it must, as it were, withdraw in order to be ready-to-hand quite authentically. That with which our everyday dealings proxim-ally dwell is not the tools themselves. On the contrary, that with which we concern ourselves primarily is the work – that which is to be pro-duced at the time; and this is accordingly ready-to-hand too. The work bears with it that referential totality within which the equipment is encountered.

70

The work to be produced, as the "*towards-which*" of such things as the hammer, the plane, and the needle, likewise has the kind of Being that belongs to equipment. The shoe which is to be produced is for wearing (footgear); the clock is manufactured for telling the time. The work which we chiefly encounter in our concernful dealings – the work that is to be found when one is "at work" on something – has a usability which belongs to it essentially; in this usability it lets us encounter already the "towards-which" for which *it* is usable. A work that someone has ordered *is* only by reason of its use and the assignment-context of entities which is discovered in using it.

But the work to be produced is not merely usable for something. The production itself is a using *of* something for something. In the work there is also a reference or assignment to 'mater-ials': the work is dependent on leather, thread, needles, and the like. Leather, moreover is pro-duced from hides. These are taken from animals, which someone else has raised. Animals also occur within the world without having been raised at all; and, in a way, these entities still produce themselves even when they have been raised. So in the environment certain entities become accessible which are always ready-to-hand, but which, in themselves, do not need to be produced. Hammer, tongs, and needle, refer in themselves to steel, iron, metal, mineral, wood, in that they consist of these. In equipment that is used, 'Nature' is discovered along with it by that use – the 'Nature' we find in natural products.

Here however, "Nature" is not to be understood as that which is just present-at-hand, nor as the *power of Nature*. The wood is a forest of timber,

the mountain a quarry of rock; the river is water-power, the wind is wind 'in the sails'. As the 'environment' is discovered, the 'Nature' thus discovered is encountered too. If its kind of Being as ready-to-hand is disregarded, this 'Nature' itself can be discovered and defined simply in its pure presence-at-hand. But when this happens, the Nature which 'stirs and strives', which assails us and enthralls us as landscape, remains hidden. The botanist's plants are not the flowers of the hedgerow; the 'source' which the geographer establishes for a river is not the 'springhead in the dale'.

The work produced refers not only to the "towards-which" of its usability and the "where-of" of which it consists: under simple craft conditions it also has an assignment to the per-son who is to use it or wear it. The work is cut to his figure; he 'is' there along with it as the work emerges. Even when goods are produced by the dozen, this constitutive assignment is by no means lacking; it is merely indefinite, and points to the random, the average. Thus along with the work, we encounter not only entities ready-to-hand but also entities with Dasein's kind of Being – entities for which, in their concern, the product becomes ready-to-hand; and together with these we encounter the world in which wearers and users live, which is at the same time ours. Any work with which one concerns oneself is ready-to-hand not only in the domestic world of the workshop but also in the *public world*. Along with the public world, the *environing Nature* is discovered and is accessible to everyone. In roads, streets, bridges, buildings, our concern discovers Nature as having some definite direc-tion. A covered railway platform takes account of bad weather; an installation for public light-ing takes account of the darkness, or rather of specific changes in the presence or absence of daylight – the 'position of the sun'. In a clock, account is taken of some definite constellation in the world-system. When we look at the clock, we tacitly make use of the 'sun's position', in accord-ance with which the measurement of time gets regulated in the official astronomical manner. When we make use of the clock-equipment, which is proximally and inconspicuously ready-to-hand, the environing Nature is ready-to-hand along with it. Our concernful absorption in whatever work-world lies closest to us, has a

71

function of discovering; and it is essential to this function that, depending upon the way in which we are absorbed, those entities within-the-world which are brought along in the work and with it (that is to say, in the assignments or references which are constitutive for it) remain discoverable in varying degrees of explicitness and with a varying circumspective penetration.

The kind of Being which belongs to these entities is readiness-to-hand. But this characteristic is not to be understood as merely a way of taking them, as if we were talking such 'aspects' into the 'entities' which we proximally encounter, or as if some world-stuff which is proximally present-at-hand in itself were 'given subjective colouring' in this way. Such an Interpretation would overlook the fact that in this case these entities would have to be understood and discovered beforehand as something purely present-at-hand, and must have priority and take the lead in the sequence of those dealings with the 'world' in which something is discovered and made one's own. But this already runs counter to the ontological meaning of cognition, which we have exhibited as a *founded* mode of Being-in-the-world. To lay bare what is just present-at-hand and no more, cognition must first penetrate *beyond* what is ready-to-hand in our concern. *Readiness-to-hand is the way in which entities as they are 'in themselves' are defined ontologico-categorially.* Yet only by reason of something present-at-hand, 'is there' anything ready-to-hand. Does it follow, however, granting this thesis for the nonce, that readiness-to-hand is ontologically founded upon presence-at-hand?

72 But even if, as our ontological Interpretation proceeds further, readiness-to-hand should prove itself to be the kind of Being characteristic of those entities which are proximally discovered within-the-world, and even if its primordiality as compared with pure presence-at-hand can be demonstrated, have all these explications been of the slightest help towards understanding the phenomenon of the world ontologically? In interpreting these entities within-the-world, however, we have always 'presupposed' the world. Even if we join them together, we still do not get anything like the 'world' as their sum. If, then, we start with the Being of these entities, is there any avenue that will lead us to exhibiting the phenomenon of the world? [. . .]

B. A Contrast between Our Analysis of Worldhood and Descartes' Interpretation of the World

89

Only step by step can the concept of worldhood and the structures which this phenomenon embraces be firmly secured in the course of our investigation. The Interpretation of the world begins, in the first instance, with some entity within-the-world, so that the phenomenon of the world in general no longer comes into view; we shall accordingly try to clarify this approach ontologically by considering what is perhaps the most extreme form in which it has been carried out. We not only shall present briefly the basic features of Descartes' ontology of the 'world', but shall inquire into its presuppositions and try to characterize these in the light of what we have hitherto achieved. The account we shall give of these matters will enable us to know upon what basically undiscussed ontological 'foundations' those Interpretations of the world which have come after Descartes – and still more those which preceded him – have operated.

Descartes sees the *extensio* as basically definitive ontologically for the world. In so far as extension is one of the constituents of spatiality (according to Descartes it is even identical with it), while in some sense spatiality remains constitutive for the world, a discussion of the Cartesian ontology of the 'world' will provide us likewise with a negative support for a positive explication of the spatiality of the environment and of Dasein itself. With regard to Descartes' ontology there are three topics which we shall treat: 1. the definition of the 'world' as *res extensa* (Section 19); 2. the foundations of this ontological definition (Section 20); 3. a hermeneutical discussion of the Cartesian ontology of the 'world' (Section 21). The considerations which follow will not have been grounded in full detail until the 'cogito sum' has been phenomenologically destroyed.

¶ 19. The Definition of the 'World' as res extensa
Descartes distinguishes the '*ego cogito*' from the '*res corporea*'. This distinction will thereafter be determinative ontologically for the distinction between 'Nature' and 'spirit'. No matter with how many variations of content the opposition between 'Nature' and 'spirit' may get set up ontically, its ontological foundations, and indeed

the very poles of this opposition, remain unclarified; this unclarity has its proximate roots in Descartes' distinction. What kind of understanding of Being does he have when he defines the Being of these entities? The term for the Being of an entity that is in itself, is "*substantia*".

90 Sometimes this expression means the *Being* of an entity as substance, *substantiality*; at other times it means the entity itself, *a substance*. That "*substantia*" is used in these two ways is not accidental; this already holds for the ancient conception of οὐσία [ousia]. [. . .]

[. . .]

§ 21. *Hermeneutical Discussion of the Cartesian Ontology of the "World"* The critical question now arises: does this ontology of the 'world' seek the phenomenon of the world at all, and if not, does it at least define some entity within-the-world fully enough so that the worldly character of this entity can be made visible in it? *To both questions we must answer "No"*. The entity which Descartes is trying to grasp ontologically and in principle with his "*extensio*", is rather such as to become discoverable first of all by going through an entity within-the-world which is proximally ready-to-hand – Nature. Though this is the case, and though any ontological characterization of this *latter* entity within-the-world may lead us into obscurity, even if we consider both the idea of substantiality and the meaning of the "*existit*" and "*ad existendum*" which have been brought into the definition of that idea, it still remains possible that through an ontology based upon a radical separation of God, the "I", and the 'world', the ontological problem of the world will in some sense get formulated and further advanced. If, however, this is not possible, we must then demonstrate explicitly not only that Descartes' conception of the world is ontologically defective, but that his Interpretation and the foundations on which it is based have led him to *pass over* both the phenomenon of the world and the Being of those entities within-the-world which are proximally ready-to-hand.

In our exposition of the problem of worldhood (Section 14), we suggested the importance of obtaining proper access to this phenomenon. So in criticizing the Cartesian point of departure, we must ask which kind of Being that belongs to Dasein we should fix upon as giving us an

appropriate way of access to those entities with whose Being as *extensio* Descartes equates the Being of the 'world'. The only genuine access to them lies in knowing [Erkennen], *intellectio*, in the sense of the kind of knowledge [Erkenntnis] we get in mathematics and physics. Mathematical knowledge is regarded by Descartes as the one manner of apprehending entities which can always give assurance that their Being has been securely grasped. If anything measures up in its own kind of Being to the Being that is accessible in mathematical knowledge, then it *is* in the authentic sense. Such entities are those *which always are what they are*. Accordingly, that which 96 can be shown to have the character of something that *constantly remains*, makes up the real Being of those entities of the world which get experienced. That which enduringly remains, really *is*. This is the sort of thing which mathematics knows. That which is accessible in an entity *through mathematics*, makes up its Being. Thus the Being of the 'world' is, as it were, dictated to it in terms of a definite idea of Being which lies veiled in the concept of substantiality, and in terms of the idea of a knowledge by which *such* entities are cognized. The kind of Being which belongs to entities within-the-world is something which they themselves might have been permitted to present; but Descartes does not let them do so. Instead he prescribes for the world its 'real' Being, as it were, on the basis of an idea of Being whose source has not been unveiled and which has not been demonstrated in its own right – an idea in which Being is equated with constant presence-at-hand. Thus his ontology of the world is not primarily determined by his leaning towards mathematics, a science which he chances to esteem very highly, but rather by his ontological orientation in principle towards Being as constant presence-at-hand, which mathematical knowledge is exceptionally well suited to grasp. In this way Descartes explicitly switches over philosophically from the development of traditional ontology to modern mathematical physics and its transcendental foundations.

The problem of how to get appropriate access to entities within-the-world is one which Descartes feels no need to raise. Under the unbroken ascendance of the traditional ontology, the way to get a genuine grasp of what really is has been decided in advance: it lies in νοεῖν [noeen] – 'beholding' in the widest sense;

διανοεῖν [dianoeen] or 'thinking' is just a more fully achieved form of νοεῖν and is founded upon it. *Sensatio* (αἴσθησις) [aesthesis], as opposed to *intellectio*, still remains possible as a way of access to entities by a beholding which is perceptual in character; but Descartes presents his 'critique' of it because he is oriented ontologically by these principles.

Descartes knows very well that entities do not proximally show themselves in their real Being. What is 'proximally' given is this waxen Thing which is coloured, flavoured, hard, and cold in definite ways, and which gives off its own special sound when struck. But this is not of any importance ontologically, nor, in general, is anything which is given through the senses. [. . .] The senses do not enable us to cognize any entity in its Being; they merely serve to announce the ways in which 'external' Things within-the-world are useful or harmful for human creatures encumbered with bodies. [. . .] they tell us nothing about entities in their Being. [. . .]

If we subject Descartes' Interpretation of the experience of hardness and resistance to a critical analysis, it will be plain how unable he is to let what shows itself in sensation present itself in its own kind of Being, or even to determine its character (Cf. Section 19).

Hardness gets taken as resistance. But neither hardness nor resistance is understood in a phenomenal sense, as something experienced in itself whose nature can be determined in such an experience. For Descartes, resistance amounts to no more than not yielding place – that is, not undergoing any change of location. So if a Thing resists, this means that it stays in a definite location relatively to some other Thing which is changing its location, or that it is changing its own location with a velocity which permits the other Thing to 'catch up' with it. But when the experience of hardness is Interpreted this way, the kind of Being which belongs to sensory perception is obliterated, and so is any possibility that the entities encountered in such perception should be grasped in their Being. Descartes takes the kind of Being which belongs to the perception of something, and translates it into the only kind he knows: the perception of something becomes a definite way of Being-present-at-hand-side-by-side of two *res extensae* which are present-at-hand; the way in which their movements are related is itself a mode of that *extensio* by which

the presence-at-hand of the corporeal Thing is primarily characterized. Of course no behaviour in which one feels one's way by touch can be 'completed' unless what can thus be felt has 'closeness' of a very special kind. But this does not mean that touching and the hardness which makes itself known in touching consist ontologically in different velocities of two corporeal Things. Hardness and resistance do not show themselves at all unless an entity has the kind of Being which Dasein – or at least something living – possesses.

Thus Descartes' discussion of possible kinds of *access* to entities within-the-world is dominated by an idea of Being which has been gathered from a definite realm of these entities themselves.

The idea of Being as permanent presence-at-hand not only gives Descartes a motive for identifying entities within-the-world with the world in general, and for providing so extreme a definition of their Being; it also keeps him from bringing Dasein's ways of behaving into view in a manner which is ontologically appropriate. But thus the road is completely blocked to seeing the founded character of all sensory and intellective awareness, and to understanding these as possibilities of Being-in-the-world. On the contrary, he takes the Being of 'Dasein' (to whose basic constitution Being-in-the-world belongs) in the very same way as he takes the Being of the *res extensa* – namely, as substance.

But with these criticisms, have we not fobbed off on Descartes a task altogether beyond his horizon, and then gone on to 'demonstrate' that he has failed to solve it? If Descartes does not know the phenomenon of the world, and thus knows no such thing as within-the-world-ness, how can he identify the world itself with certain entities within-the-world and the Being which they possess?

In controversy over principles, one must not only attach oneself to theses which can be grasped doxographically; one must also derive one's orientation from the objective tendency of the problematic, even if it does not go beyond a rather ordinary way of taking things. In his doctrine of the *res cogitans* and the *res extensa*, Descartes not only *wants to formulate* the problem of 'the "I" and the world'; he claims to have solved it in a radical manner. His *Meditations* make this plain. (See especially Meditations I and VI.) By taking his basic ontological orientation from

traditional sources and not subjecting it to positive criticism, he has made it impossible to lay
bare any primordial ontological problematic of
Dasein; this has inevitably obstructed his view of
the phenomenon of the world, and has made it
possible for the ontology of the 'world' to be
compressed into that of certain entities within-
the-world. The foregoing discussion should have
proved this.

One might retort, however, that even if in
point of fact both the problem of the world and
the Being of the entities encountered environ-
mentally as closest to us remain concealed,
Descartes has still laid the basis for characterizing ontologically that entity within-the-world
upon which, in its very Being, every other entity
is founded – material Nature. This would be the
fundamental stratum upon which all the other
strata of actuality within-the-world are built
up. The extended Thing as such would serve, in
the first instance, as the ground for those definite
99 characters which show themselves, to be sure, as
qualities, but which 'at bottom' are quantitative
modifications of the modes of the *extensio* itself.
These qualities, which are themselves reducible,
would provide the footing for such specific qualities as "beautiful", "ugly", "in keeping", "not in
keeping", "useful", "useless". If one is oriented
primarily by Thinghood, these latter qualities
must be taken as non-quantifiable value-predicates
by which what is in the first instance just a material Thing, gets stamped as something good. But
with this stratification, we come to those entities
which we have characterized ontologically as
equipment ready-to-hand. The Cartesian analysis of the 'world' would thus enable us for the first
time to build up securely the structure of what is
proximally ready-to-hand; all it takes is to round
out the Thing of Nature until it becomes a full-
fledged Thing of use, and this is easily done.

But quite apart from the specific problem
of the world itself, can the Being of what
we encounter proximally within-the-world be
reached ontologically by this procedure? When we
speak of material Thinghood, have we not tacitly
posited a kind of Being – the constant presence-
at-hand of Things – which is so far from having
been rounded out ontologically by subsequently
endowing entities with value-predicates, that
these value-characters themselves are rather just
ontical characteristics of those entities which
have the kind of Being possessed by Things?

Adding on value-predicates cannot tell us anything
at all new about the Being of goods, *but would
merely presuppose again that goods have pure
presence-at-hand as their kind of Being*. Values
would then be determinate characteristics which
a Thing possesses, and they would be *present-at-
hand*. They would have their sole ultimate ontological source in our previously laying down the
actuality of Things as the fundamental stratum.
But even pre-phenomenological experience
shows that in an entity which is supposedly a
Thing, there is something that will not become
fully intelligible through Thinghood alone. Thus
the Being of Things has to be rounded out.
What, then does the Being of values or their
'validity' [. . .] really amount to ontologically?
And what does it signify ontologically for Things
to be 'invested' with values in this way? As long
as these matters remain obscure, to reconstruct
the Thing of use in terms of the Thing of Nature
is an ontologically questionable undertaking,
even if one disregards the way in which the
problematic has been perverted in principle.
And if we are to reconstruct this Thing of use,
which supposedly comes to us in the first
instance 'with its skin off', does not this always
require *that we previously take a positive look at
the phenomenon whose totality such a reconstruction is to restore*? But if we have not given a
proper explanation beforehand of its ownmost
state of Being, are we not building our reconstruction without a plan? Inasmuch as this
reconstruction and 'rounding-out' of the tradi-   100
tional ontology of the 'world' results in our
reaching the same *entities* with which we started
when we analysed the readiness-to-hand of
equipment and the totality of involvements, it
seems as if the *Being* of these entities has in fact
been clarified or has at least become a *problem*.
But by taking *extensio* as a *proprietas*, Descartes
can hardly reach the Being of substance; and by
taking refuge in 'value'-characteristics we are
just as far from even catching a glimpse of Being
as readiness-to-hand, let alone permitting it to
become an ontological theme.

Descartes has narrowed down the question
of the world to that of Things of Nature as those
entities within-the-world which are proximally
accessible. He has confirmed the opinion that
to *know* an entity in what is supposedly the most
rigorous ontical manner is our only possible
access to the primary Being of the entity which

such knowledge reveals. But at the same time we must have the insight to see that in principle the 'roundings-out' of the Thing-ontology also operate on the same dogmatic basis as that which Descartes has adopted.

We have already intimated in Section 14 that passing over the world and those entities which we proximally encounter is not accidental, not an oversight which it would be simple to correct, but that it is grounded in a kind of Being which belongs essentially to Dasein itself. When our analytic of Dasein has given some transparency to those main structures of Dasein which are of the most importance in the framework of this problematic, and when we have assigned to the concept of Being in general the horizon within which its intelligibility becomes possible, so that readiness-to-hand and presence-at-hand also become primordially intelligible ontologically for the first time, only then can our critique of the Cartesian ontology of the world (an ontology which, in principle, is still the usual one today) come philosophically into its own.

To do this, we must show several things. [. . .]

1. Why was the phenomenon of the world passed over at the beginning of the onto-logical tradition which has been decisive for us (explicitly in the case of Parmenides), and why has this passing-over kept constantly recurring?
2. Why is it that, instead of the phenomenon thus passed over, entities within-the-world have intervened as an ontological theme?
3. Why are these entities found in the first instance in 'Nature'?
4. Why has recourse been taken to the phenom-enon of value when it has seemed necessary to round out such an ontology of the world?[5]

In the answers to these questions a positive understanding of the *problematic* of the world will be reached for the first time, the sources of our failure to recognize it will be exhibited, and the ground for rejecting the traditional ontology of the world will have been demonstrated. [101]

The world and Dasein and entities within-the-world are the ontologically constitutive states which are closest to us; but we have no guaran-tee that we can achieve the basis for meeting up with these as phenomena by the seemingly obvious procedure of starting with the Things of the world, still less by taking our orientation from what is supposedly the most rigorous knowledge of entities. Our observations on Descartes should have brought us this insight. [. . .]

Notes

1 Heidegger does not make it clear until a bit later that the view expressed in this paragraph is not his own, but the one he will be criticizing.
2 "Existential" and "existentiell" are Heideggerian terms of art. Dreyfus, *Being-in-the-World, op. cit.*, p. 20, explains them as follows: "*Existential* under-standing is a worked-out understanding of the ontological structures of existence, that is, of what it is to be Dasein. *Existentiell* understanding is an individual's understanding of his or her own way to be, that is, of what he or she is."
3 In that section, and also in Sections 23–4, Heidegger explains how different *Dasein*'s "spatial-ity" is from that of "present-at-hand" objects. For example, someone's being in his office is not a matter, merely, of a geometrical relationship to walls etc. Often, the relevant sense of "in" is like the one intended when we speak of someone being in the world of fashion or showbusiness.
4 The German word is "*Zeug*," which can mean tool, instrument *etc.* Heidegger, though, uses it in a col-lective sense. It should be stressed that, for him, even "things in Nature" are originally encountered as significant "equipment," e.g., the wood as "a forest of timber."
5 *Being and Time*, which remained uncompleted, does not address all these questions. They were, how-ever, to become the focus of many of Heidegger's later writings.

25

A. N. Whitehead, *Process and Reality*, Part I, Chapters I and II (selected sections)

Introduction

Process and Reality: An Essay in Cosmology (1929), the major work of the British emigré to Harvard, Alfred North Whitehead (1861–1947), emerged from the Gifford Lectures which he delivered in Edinburgh in 1927–8. Although Whitehead had been Bertrand Russell's collaborator on *Principia Mathematica* (1910–13), these Lectures display not so much the influence of his earlier work on logic as that of the "life philosophy" of Henri Bergson (III.22) and of recent currents in physics, notably Einsteinian relativity theory and quantum mechanics. Like Bergson and contemporary physicists, Whitehead aimed to develop a theory of the universe that would dispense with the "static," mechanical model of the world that still exerted an unfortunate grip, he believed, on most philosophers. The resulting metaphysics, highly influential in the United States, is known as "Process philosophy" or, as Whitehead calls it in the following pages, "the philosophy of organism."

The sections we have selected from *Process and Reality* give a fair idea of the shape of Whitehead's theory, but they also record his conception of "speculative philosophy" or meta-

From F. S. C. Northrop and M. W. Gross, eds, *Alfred North Whitehead: An Anthology*, Cambridge: Cambridge University Press, 1953, pp. 567–72, 576–87 (some notes omitted; asterisked notes are Whitehead's).

physics. Despite the attacks being launched on the metaphysical enterprise by the logical positivists during the 1920s (II.21), Whitehead's view of the enterprise is unapologetically in the tradition of Hegel (III.18). Speculative philosophy provides a "synoptic vision" of reality "in terms of which every element of our experience can be interpreted." While the sciences must be incorporated in this vision, it is the "self-denial of thought" to suppose that they alone can provide it.

Like the positivists, however, Whitehead focuses attention on issues of meaning and language, and he outbids Russell in regarding everyday language – its subject/predicate structure, for example – as a poor guide to the nature of reality: "no verbal statement is the adequate expression of a proposition." A main reason for this is that every statement is "elliptical," indicating far more by way of its relation to experience than it can actually state. This, in turn, is because experience and reality themselves are systematic wholes from which particular things and facts may only be artificially abstracted. To regard any such thing or fact as self-contained and independent is to commit "the fallacy of misplaced concreteness." This emphasis on the universe as being, not a collection of substances, but a totality of processes, within which everything is intimately interrelated, is the central thrust of "Process philosophy."[1]

Given this, it is unsurprising to find Whitehead criticizing Descartes's dualism, and even Spinoza's monism because of its sharp distinction between the two "modes" of thought and extension (see

III.12 and III.13). Later in *Process and Reality*, and still more in Lecture 8 of *Modes of Thought* (1938), Whitehead insists on the continuity between human mental processes and those going on at the "merely" material level, and hence on the artificiality of any dualistic division.

The opening section of Chapter II introduces some of Whitehead's main terms of art: "actual entity," "nexus," and "prehension." Unlike some monists, Whitehead does not treat reality as a single indivisible whole. It contains "actual entities," but these processes are "drops of experience, complex and interdependent," related to one another in a "nexus" or "togetherness." Instead of calling this relation "causality," which might connote an excessive degree of separation among the related items, Whitehead speaks of "prehension." This, he explains, should be thought of on the model of psychological phenomena, like desire and appetite. There are echoes here, as Whitehead notes, of Leibniz's monadology, not least in the suggestion that primitive, unconscious "mindlikeness" permeates the material universe (see III.15 above). In the words of one commentator, however, whereas Leibniz's monads are "windowless," in having no contact with other monads, a Whiteheadian "actual entity" is all window, for "in an important sense [it] *is* its relations to other beings."[2]

An area where Whitehead's thinking has had particular influence is the philosophy of religion: hence the emergence of the "Process theology" associated with such figures as Charles Hartshorne.[3] The inspiration, here, is Whitehead's reference to the "ultimate" and "creative" character of reality as "God": a reference he elsewhere justifies by attributing responsibility for "importance, value, and ideal" to the "creative" process. God, he makes clear, should not be thought of, in the manner of some monists, as an "Absolute" enjoying a more "eminent" reality than its "accidents." God, for Whitehead, is no way apart from reality or process itself.

Notes

1 See N. Rescher, 'The Promise of Process Philosophy', in his *Baffling Phenomena*, Savage, MD: Rowman & Littlefield, 1991.
2 D. W. Sherburne, 'Whitehead, Alfred North', in *A Companion to Metaphysics*, ed. J. Kim and E. Sosa, Oxford: Blackwell, 1995, p. 511.
3 See E. H. Cousins, ed., *Process Theology*, New York: Newman, 1971.

Whitehead, *Process and Reality*

Part I – The Speculative Scheme

Chapter I – Speculative Philosophy

SECTION I
This course of lectures is designed as an essay in Speculative Philosophy. Its first task must be to define 'speculative philosophy,' and to defend it as a method productive of important knowledge.

Speculative Philosophy is the endeavor to frame a coherent, logical, necessary system of general ideas in terms of which every element of our experience can be interpreted. By this notion of 'interpretation' I mean that everything of which we are conscious, as enjoyed, perceived, willed, or thought, shall have the character of a particular instance of the general scheme. Thus the philosophical scheme should be coherent, logical, and, in respect to its interpretation, applicable and adequate. Here 'applicable' means that some items of experience are thus interpretable, and 'adequate' means that there are no items incapable of such interpretation.

'Coherence,' as here employed, means that the fundamental ideas, in terms of which the scheme is developed, presuppose each other so that in isolation they are meaningless. This requirement does not mean that they are definable in terms of each other; it means that what is indefinable in one such notion cannot be abstracted from its relevance to the other notions. It is the ideal of speculative philosophy that its fundamental notions shall not seem capable of abstraction from each other. In other words, it is presupposed that no entity can be conceived in complete abstraction from the system of the universe, and that it is the business of speculative philosophy to exhibit this truth. This character is its coherence.

The term 'logical' has its ordinary meaning, including 'logical' consistency, or lack of contradiction, the definition of constructs in logical terms, the exemplification of general logical notions in specific instances, and the principles of inference. It will be observed that logical notions must themselves find their places in the scheme of philosophic notions.

It will also be noticed that this ideal of speculative philosophy has its rational side and its empirical side. The rational side is expressed by the terms 'coherent' and 'logical.' The empirical side is expressed by the terms 'applicable' and 'adequate.' But the two sides are bound together by clearing away an ambiguity which remains in the previous explanation of the term 'adequate.' The adequacy of the scheme over every item does not mean adequacy over such items as happen to have been considered. It means that the texture of observed experience, as illustrating the philosophic scheme, is such that all related experience must exhibit the same texture. Thus the philosophic scheme should be 'necessary', in the sense of bearing in itself its own warrant of universality throughout all experience, provided that we confine ourselves to that which communicates with immediate matter of fact. But what does not so communicate is unknowable, and the unknowable is unknown;* and so this universality defined by 'communication' can suffice.

This doctrine of necessity in universality means that there is an essence to the universe which forbids relationships beyond itself, as a violation of its rationality. Speculative philosophy seeks that essence.

SECTION II

Philosophers can never hope finally to formulate these metaphysical first principles. Weakness of insight and deficiencies of language stand in the way inexorably. Words and phrases must be stretched towards a generality foreign to their ordinary usage; and however such elements of language be stabilized as technicalities, they remain metaphors mutely appealing for an imaginative leap.

There is no first principle which is in itself unknowable, not to be captured by a flash of insight. But, putting aside the difficulties of language, deficiency in imaginative penetration forbids progress in any form other than that of

an asymptotic approach to a scheme of principles, only definable in terms of the ideal which they should satisfy.

The difficulty has its seat in the empirical side of philosophy. Our datum is the actual world, including ourselves; and this actual world spreads itself for observation in the guise of the topic of our immediate experience. The elucidation of immediate experience is the sole justification for any thought; and the starting point for thought is the analytic observation of components of this experience. But we are not conscious of any clear-cut complete analysis of immediate experience, in terms of the various details which comprise its definiteness. We habitually observe by the method of difference. Sometimes we see an elephant, and sometimes we do not. The result is that an elephant, when present, is noticed. Facility of observation depends on the fact that the object observed is important when present, and sometimes is absent.

The metaphysical first principles can never fail of exemplification. We can never catch the actual world taking a holiday from their sway. Thus, for the discovery of metaphysics, the method of pinning down thought to the strict systematization of detailed discrimination, already effected by antecedent observation, breaks down. This collapse of the method of rigid empiricism is not confined to metaphysics. It occurs whenever we seek the larger generalities. In natural science this rigid method is the Baconian method of induction, a method which, if consistently pursued, would have left science where it found it. What Bacon omitted was the play of a free imagination, controlled by the requirements of coherence and logic. The true method of discovery is like the flight of an aeroplane. It starts from the ground of particular observation; it makes a flight in the thin air of imaginative generalization; and it again lands for renewed observation rendered acute by rational interpretation. The reason for the success of this method of imaginative rationalization is that, when the method of difference fails, factors which are constantly present may yet be observed under the influence of imaginative thought. Such thought supplies the differences which the direct observation lacks. It can even play with inconsistency; and can thus throw light on the consistent, and persistent, elements in experience by comparison with what in imagination

---

* This doctrine is a paradox. Indulging in a species of false modesty, 'cautious' philosophers undertake its definition.

is inconsistent with them. The negative judgment is the peak of mentality. But the conditions for the success of imaginative construction must be rigidly adhered to. In the first place, this construction must have its origin in the generalization of particular factors discerned in particular topics of human interest; for example, in physics, or in physiology, or in psychology, or in aesthetics, or in ethical beliefs, or in sociology, or in languages conceived as storehouses of human experience. In this way the prime requisite, that anyhow there shall be some important application, is secured. The success of the imaginative experiment is always to be tested by the applicability of its results beyond the restricted locus from which it originated. In default of such extended application, a generalization started from physics, for example, remains merely an alternative expression of notions applicable to physics. The partially successful philosophic generalization will, if derived from physics, find applications in fields of experience beyond physics. It will enlighten observation in those remote fields, so that general principles can be discerned as in process of illustration, which in the absence of the imaginative generalization are obscured by their persistent exemplification.

Thus the first requisite is to proceed by the method of generalization so that certainly there is some application; and the test of some success is application beyond the immediate origin. In other words, some synoptic vision has been gained.

In this description of philosophic method, the term 'philosophic generalization' has meant 'the utilization of specific notions, applying to a restricted group of facts, for the divination of the generic notions which apply to all facts.'

In its use of this method natural science has shown a curious mixture of rationalism and irrationalism. Its prevalent tone of thought has been ardently rationalistic within its own borders, and dogmatically irrational beyond those borders. In practice such an attitude tends to become a dogmatic denial that there are any factors in the world not fully expressible in terms of its own primary notions devoid of further generalization. Such a denial is the self-denial of thought.

The second condition for the success of imaginative construction is unflinching pursuit of the two rationalistic ideals, coherence and logical perfection.

Logical perfection does not here require any detailed explanation. An example of its importance is afforded by the role of mathematics in the restricted field of natural science. The history of mathematics exhibits the generalization of special notions observed in particular instances. In any branches of mathematics, the notions presuppose each other. It is a remarkable characteristic of the history of thought that branches of mathematics developed under the pure imaginative impulse, thus controlled, finally receive their important application. Time may be wanted. Conic sections had to wait for eighteen hundred years. In more recent years, the theory of probability, the theory of tensors, the theory of matrices are cases in point.

The requirement of coherence is the great preservative of rationalistic sanity. But the validity of its criticism is not always admitted. If we consider philosophical controversies, we shall find that disputants tend to require coherence from their adversaries, and to grant dispensations to themselves. It has been remarked that a system of philosophy is never refuted; it is only abandoned. The reason is that logical contradictions, except as temporary slips of the mind – plentiful, though temporary – are the most gratuitous of errors; and usually they are trivial. Thus, after criticism, systems do not exhibit mere illogicalities. They suffer from inadequacy and incoherence. Failure to include some obvious elements of experience in the scope of the system is met by boldly denying the facts. Also while a philosophical system retains any charm of novelty, it enjoys a plenary indulgence for its failures in coherence. But after a system has acquired orthodoxy, and is taught with authority, it receives a sharper criticism. Its denials and its incoherences are found intolerable, and a reaction sets in.

Incoherence is the arbitrary disconnection of first principles. In modern philosophy Descartes' two kinds of substance, corporeal and mental, illustrate incoherence. There is, in Descartes' philosophy, no reason why there should not be a one-substance world, only corporeal, or a one-substance world, only mental. According to Descartes, a substantial individual 'requires nothing but itself in order to exist.' Thus this system makes a virtue of its incoherence. But on the other hand, the facts seem connected, while Descartes' system does not; for example, in the treatment of the body-mind problem. The

Cartesian system obviously says something that is true. But its notions are too abstract to penetrate into the nature of things.

The attraction of Spinoza's philosophy lies in its modification of Descartes' position into greater coherence. He starts with one substance, *causa sui*, and considers its essential attributes and its individualized modes, i.e. the '*affectiones substantiae.*' The gap in the system is the arbitrary introduction of the 'modes.' And yet, a multiplicity of modes is a fixed requisite, if the scheme is to retain any direct relevance to the many occasions in the experienced world.

The philosophy of organism is closely allied to Spinoza's scheme of thought. But it differs by the abandonment of the subject-predicate forms of thought, so far as concerns the presupposition that this form is a direct embodiment of the most ultimate characterization of fact. The result is that the 'substance-quality' concept is avoided; and that morphological description is replaced by description of dynamic process. Also Spinoza's 'modes' now become the sheer actualities; so that, though analysis of them increases our understanding, it does not lead us to the discovery of any higher grade of reality. The coherence, which the system seeks to preserve, is the discovery that the process, or concrescence, of any one actual entity involves the other actual entities among its components. In this way the obvious solidarity of the world receives its explanation.

In all philosophic theory there is an ultimate which is actual in virtue of its accidents. It is only then capable of characterization through its accidental embodiments, and apart from these accidents is devoid of actuality. In the philosophy of organism this ultimate is termed 'creativity'; and God is its primordial, non-temporal accident. In monistic philosophies, Spinoza's or absolute idealism, this ultimate is God, who is also equivalently termed 'The Absolute.' In such monistic schemes, the ultimate is illegitimately allowed a final, 'eminent' reality, beyond that ascribed to any of its accidents. In this general position the philosophy of organism seems to approximate more to some strains of Indian, or Chinese, thought, than to western Asiatic, or European, thought. One side makes process ultimate; the other side makes fact ultimate.

[...]

SECTION V

Every science must devise its own instruments. The tool required for philosophy is language. Thus philosophy redesigns language in the same way that, in a physical science, pre-existing appliances are redesigned. It is exactly at this point that the appeal to facts is a difficult operation. This appeal is not solely to the expression of the facts in current verbal statements. The adequacy of such sentences is the main question at issue. It is true that the general agreement of mankind as to experienced facts is best expressed in language. But the language of literature breaks down precisely at the task of expressing in explicit form the large generalities – the very generalities which metaphysics seeks to express.

The point is that every proposition refers to a universe exhibiting some general systematic metaphysical character. Apart from this background, the separate entities which go to form the proposition, and the proposition as a whole, are without determinate character. Nothing has been defined, because every definite entity requires a systematic universe to supply its requisite status. Thus every proposition proposing a fact must, in its complete analysis, propose the general character of the universe required for that fact. There are no selfsustained facts, floating in nonentity. This doctrine, of the impossibility of tearing a proposition from its systematic context in the actual world, is a direct consequence of the fourth and the twentieth of the fundamental categoreal explanations which we shall be engaged in expanding and illustrating.[1] A proposition can embody partial truth because it only demands a certain type of systematic environment, which is presupposed in its meaning. It does not refer to the universe in all its detail.

One practical aim of metaphysics is the accurate analysis of propositions; not merely of metaphysical propositions, but of quite ordinary propositions such as 'There is beef for dinner today,' and 'Socrates is mortal.' The one genus of facts which constitutes the field of some special science requires some common metaphysical presupposition respecting the universe. It is merely credulous to accept verbal phrases as adequate statements of propositions. The distinction between verbal phrases and complete propositions is one of the reasons why the logicians' rigid alternative, 'true or false,' is so largely irrelevant for the pursuit of knowledge.

The excessive trust in linguistic phrases has been the well-known reason vitiating so much of the philosophy and physics among the Greeks and among the medieval thinkers who continued the Greek traditions. For example John Stuart Mill writes: 'They (the Greeks) had great difficulty in distinguishing between things which their language confounded, or in putting mentally together things which it distinguished; and could hardly combine the objects in nature, into any classes but those which were made for them by the popular phrases of their own country; or at least could not help fancying those classes to be natural, and all others arbitrary and artificial. Accordingly, scientific investigation among the Greek schools of speculation and their followers in the Middle Ages, was little more than a mere sifting and analysing of the notions attached to common language. They thought that by determining the meaning of words they could become acquainted with facts.'* Mill then proceeds to quote from Whewell a paragraph illustrating the same weakness of Greek thought.†

But neither Mill, nor Whewell, tracks this difficulty about language down to its sources. They both presuppose that language does enunciate well-defined propositions. This is quite untrue. Language is thoroughly indeterminate, by reason of the fact that every occurrence presupposes some systematic type of environment.

For example, the word 'Socrates,' referring to the philosopher, in one sentence may stand for an entity presupposing a more closely defined background than the word 'Socrates,' with the same reference, in another sentence. The word 'mortal' affords an analogous possibility. A precise language must await a completed metaphysical knowledge.

The technical language of philosophy represents attempts of various schools of thought to obtain explicit expression of general ideas presupposed by the facts of experience. It follows that any novelty in metaphysical doctrines exhibits some measure of disagreement with statements of the facts to be found in current philosophical literature. The extent of disagreement measures the extent of metaphysical divergence. It is, therefore,

no valid criticism of one metaphysical school to point out that its doctrines do not follow from the verbal expression of the facts accepted by another school. The whole contention is that the doctrines in question supply a closer approach to fully expressed propositions.

The truth itself is nothing else than how the composite natures of the organic actualities of the world obtain adequate representation in the divine nature. Such representations compose the 'consequent nature' of God, which evolves in its relationship to the evolving world without derogation to the eternal completion of its primordial conceptual nature. In this way the 'ontological principle' is maintained [see Ch. 11, Sect. 1 following] – since there can be no determinate truth, correlating impartially the partial experiences of many actual entities, apart from one actual entity to which it can be referred. The reaction of the temporal world on the nature of God is considered subsequently in Part V: it is there termed 'the consequent nature of God.'

Whatever is found in 'practice' must lie within the scope of the metaphysical description. When the description fails to include the 'practice,' the metaphysics is inadequate and requires revision. There can be no appeal to practice to supplement metaphysics, so long as we remain contented with our metaphysical doctrines. Metaphysics is nothing but the description of the generalities which apply to all the details of practice.

No metaphysical system can hope entirely to satisfy these pragmatic tests. At the best such a system will remain only an approximation to the general truths which are sought. In particular, there are no precisely stated axiomatic certainties from which to start. There is not even the language in which to frame them. The only possible procedure is to start from verbal expressions which, when taken by themselves with the current meaning of their words, are ill-defined and ambiguous. These are not premises to be immediately reasoned from apart from elucidation by further discussion; they are endeavours to state general principles which will be exemplified in the subsequent description of the facts of experience. This subsequent elaboration should elucidate the meanings to be assigned to the words and phrases employed. Such meaning are incapable of accurate apprehension apart from a correspondingly accurate apprehension of the metaphysical background which the universe provides for

* Cf. *Logic*, Book V, Ch. III.
† Cf. Whewell's *History of the Inductive Sciences*.

them. But no language can be anything but elliptical, requiring a leap of the imagination to understand its meaning in its relevance to immediate experience. The position of metaphysics in the development of culture cannot be understood without remembering that no verbal statement is the adequate expression of a proposition.

An old established metaphysical system gains a false air of adequate precision from the fact that its words and phrases have passed into current literature. Thus propositions expressed in its language are more easily correlated to our flitting intuitions into metaphysical truth. When we trust these verbal statements and argue as though they adequately analysed meaning, we are led into difficulties which take the shape of negations of what in practice is presupposed. But when they are proposed as first principles they assume an unmerited air of sober obviousness. Their defect is that the true propositions which they do express lose their fundamental character when subjected to adequate expression. For example consider the type of propositions such as 'The grass is green,' and 'The whale is big.' This subject-predicate form of statement seems so simple, leading straight to a metaphysical first principle; and yet in these examples it conceals such complex, diverse meanings.

SECTION VI
It has been an objection to speculative philosophy that it is over-ambitious. Rationalism, it is admitted, is the method by which advance is made within the limits of particular sciences. It is, however, held that this limited success must not encourage attempts to frame ambitious schemes expressive of the general nature of things.

One alleged justification of this criticism is ill-success: European thought is represented as littered with metaphysical systems, abandoned and unreconciled.

Such an assertion tacitly fastens upon philosophy the old dogmatic test. The same criterion would fasten ill-success upon science. We no more retain the physics of the seventeenth century than we do the Cartesian philosophy of that century. Yet within limits, both systems express important truths. Also we are beginning to understand the wider categories which define their limits of correct application. Of course, in

that century, dogmatic views held sway; so that the validity both of the physical notions, and of the Cartesian notions, was misconceived. Mankind never quite knows what it is after. When we survey the history of thought, and likewise the history of practice, we find that one idea after another is tried out, its limitations defined, and its core of truth elicited. In application to the instinct for the intellectual adventures demanded by particular epochs, there is much truth in Augustine's rhetorical phrase, *Securus judicat orbis terrarum.*[2] At the very least, men do what they can in the way of systematization, and in the event achieve something. The proper test is not that of finality, but of progress.

But the main objection, dating from the sixteenth century and receiving final expression from Francis Bacon, is the uselessness of philosophic speculation. The position taken by this objection is that we ought to describe detailed matter of fact, and elicit the laws with a generality strictly limited to the systematization of these described details. General interpretation, it is held, has no bearing upon this procedure; and thus any system of general interpretation, be it true or false, remains intrinsically barren. Unfortunately for this objection, there are no brute, self-contained matters of fact, capable of being understood apart from interpretation as an element in a system. Whenever we attempt to express the matter of immediate experience, we find that its understanding leads us beyond itself, to its contemporaries, to its past, to its future, and to the universals in terms of which its definiteness is exhibited. But such universals, by their very character of universality, embody the potentiality of other fact with variant types of definiteness. Thus the understanding of the immediate brute fact requires its metaphysical interpretation as an item in a world with some systematic relation to it. When thought comes upon the scene, it finds the interpretations as matters of practice. Philosophy does not initiate interpretations. Its search for a rationalistic scheme is the search for more adequate criticism, and for more adequate justification, of the interpretations which we perforce employ. Our habitual experience is a complex of failure and success in the enterprise of interpretation. If we desire a record of uninterrupted experience, we must ask a stone to record its autobiography. Every scientific memoir in its record of the 'facts' is shot through and through with interpretation. The methodology of rational interpretation is the product of the fitful vagueness of consciousness. Elements which shine with immediate distinctness, in some circumstances, retire into penumbral shadow in other circumstances, and into black darkness on other occasions. And yet all occasions proclaim themselves as actualities within the flux of a solid world, demanding a unity of interpretation.

Philosophy is the self-correction by consciousness of its own initial excess of subjectivity. Each actual occasion contributes to the circumstances of its origin additional formative elements deepening its own peculiar individuality. Consciousness is only the last and greatest of such elements by which the selective character of the individual obscures the external totality from which it originates and which it embodies. An actual individual, of such higher grade, has truck with the totality of things by reason of its sheer actuality; but it has attained its individual depth of being by a selective emphasis limited to its own purposes. The task of philosophy is to recover the totality obscured by the selection. It replaces in rational experience what has been submerged in the higher sensitive experience and has been sunk yet deeper by the initial operations of consciousness itself. The selectiveness of individual experience is moral so far as it conforms to the balance of importance disclosed in the rational vision; and conversely the conversion of the intellectual insight into an emotional force corrects the sensitive experience in the direction of morality. The correction is in proportion to the rationality of the insight.

Morality of outlook is inseparably conjoined with generality of outlook. The antithesis between the general good and the individual interest can be abolished only when the individual is such that its interest is the general good, thus exemplifying the loss of the minor intensities in order to find them again with finer composition in a wider sweep of interest.

Philosophy frees itself from the taint of ineffectiveness by its close relations with religion and with science, natural and sociological. It attains its chief importance by fusing the two, namely, religion and science, into one rational scheme of thought. Religion should connect the rational generality of philosophy with the emotions and purposes springing out of existence in a particular society, in a particular epoch, and conditioned by particular antecedents. Religion is the translation of general ideas into particular thoughts, particular emotions, and particular purposes; it is directed to the end of stretching individual interest beyond its self-defeating particularity. Philosophy finds religion, and modifies it; and conversely religion is among the data of experience which philosophy must weave into its own scheme. Religion is an ultimate craving to infuse into the insistent particularity of emotion that non-temporal generality which primarily belongs to conceptual thought alone. In the higher organisms the differences of tempo between the mere emotions and the conceptual experiences produce a life-tedium, unless this supreme fusion has been effected. The two sides of the organism require a reconciliation in which emotional experiences illustrate a conceptual justification, and conceptual experiences find an emotional illustration.

This demand for an intellectual justification of brute experience has also been the motive power in the advance of European science. In this sense scientific interest is only a variant form of religious interest. Any survey of the scientific devotion to 'truth,' as an ideal, will confirm this statement. There is, however, a grave divergence between science and religion in respect to the phases of individual experience with which they are concerned. Religion is centred upon the harmony of rational thought with the sensitive reaction to the percepta from which experience originates. Science is concerned with the harmony of rational thought with the percepta themselves. When science deals with emotions, the emotions in question are percepta and not immediate passions – other people's emotion and not our own; at least our own in recollection, and not in immediacy. Religion deals with the formation of the experiencing subject; whereas science deals with the objects, which are the data forming the primary phase in this experience. The subject originates from, and amid, given conditions; science conciliates thought with this primary matter of fact; and religion conciliates the thought involved in the process with the sensitive reaction involved in that same process. The process is nothing else than the experiencing subject itself. In this explanation it is presumed that an experiencing subject is one occasion of sensitive reaction to an actual world. Science finds religious experiences among its percepta;

and religion finds scientific concepts among the conceptual experiences to be fused with particular sensitive reactions.

The conclusion of this discussion is, first, the assertion of the old doctrine that breadth of thought reacting with intensity of sensitive experience stands out as an ultimate claim of existence; secondly, the assertion that empirically the development of self-justifying thoughts has been achieved by the complex process of generalizing from particular topics, of imaginatively schematizing the generalizations, and finally by renewed comparison of the imagined scheme with the direct experience to which it should apply.

There is no justification for checking generalization at any particular stage. Each phase of generalization exhibits its own peculiar simplicities which stand out just at that stage, and at no other stage. There are simplicities connected with the motion of a bar of steel which are obscured if we refuse to abstract from the individual molecules; and there are certain simplicities concerning the behaviour of men which are obscured if we refuse to abstract from the individual peculiarities of particular specimens. In the same way, there are certain general truths, about the actual things in the common world of activity, which will be obscured when attention is confined to some particular detailed mode of considering them. These general truths, involved in the meaning of every particular notion respecting the actions of things, are the subject matter for speculative philosophy.

Philosophy destroys its usefulness when it indulges in brilliant feats of explaining away. It is then trespassing with the wrong equipment upon the field of particular sciences. Its ultimate appeal is to the general consciousness of what in practice we experience. Whatever thread of presupposition characterizes social expression throughout the various epochs of rational society, must find its place in philosophic theory. Speculative boldness must be balanced by complete humility before logic, and before fact. It is a disease of philosophy when it is neither bold nor humble, but merely a reflection of the temperamental presuppositions of exceptional personalities.

Analogously, we do not trust any recasting of scientific theory depending upon a single performance of an aberrant experiment, unrepeated. The ultimate test is always widespread, recurrent experience; and the more general the rationalistic scheme, the more important is this final appeal.

The useful function of philosophy is to promote the most general systematization of civilized thought. There is a constant reaction between specialism and common sense. It is the part of the special sciences to modify common sense. Philosophy is the welding of imagination and common sense into a restraint upon specialists, and also into an enlargement of their imaginations. By providing the generic notions philosophy should make it easier to conceive the infinite variety of specific instances which rest unrealized in the womb of nature.

Chapter II The Categoreal Scheme

SECTION I

This chapter contains an anticipatory sketch of the primary notions which constitute the philosophy of organism. The whole of the subsequent discussion in these lectures has the purpose of rendering this summary intelligible, and of showing that it embodies generic notions inevitably presupposed in our reflective experience – presupposed, but rarely expressed in explicit distinction. Four notions may be singled out from this summary, by reason of the fact that they involve some divergence from antecedent philosophical thought. These notions are, that of an 'actual entity,' that of a 'prehension,' that of a 'nexus,' and that of the 'ontological principle.' Philosophical thought has made for itself difficulties by dealing exclusively in very abstract notions, such as those of mere awareness, mere private sensation, mere emotion, mere purpose, mere appearance, mere causation. These are the ghosts of the old 'faculties,' banished from psychology, but still haunting metaphysics. There can be no 'mere' togetherness of such abstractions. The result is that philosophical discussion is enmeshed in the fallacy of 'misplaced concreteness.'* In the three notions – actual entity, prehension, nexus – an endeavour has been made to base philosophical thought upon the most concrete elements in our experience.

---

* Cf. my *Science and the Modern World*, Ch. III [also in the Whitehead *Anthology*].

'Actual entities' – also termed 'actual occasions' – are the final real things of which the world is made up. There is no going behind actual entities to find anything more real. They differ among themselves: God is an actual entity, and so is the most trivial puff of existence in far-off empty space. But, though there are gradations of importance, and diversities of function, yet in the principles which actuality exemplifies all are on the same level. The final facts are, all alike, actual entities; and these actual entities are drops of experience, complex and interdependent.

In its recurrence to the notion of a plurality of actual entities the philosophy of organism is through and through cartesian. The 'ontological principle' broadens and extends a general principle laid down by John Locke in his *Essay* (Bk II, Ch. XXIII, Sec. 7), when he asserts that 'power' is 'a great part of our complex ideas of substances.' The notion of 'substance' is transformed into that of 'actual entity'; and the notion of 'power' is transformed into the principle that the reasons for things are always to be found in the composite nature of definite actual entities – in the nature of God for reasons of the highest absoluteness, and in the nature of definite temporal actual entities for reasons which refer to a particular environment. The ontological principle can be summarized as: no actual entity, then no reason.

Each actual entity is analysable in an indefinite number of ways. In some modes of analysis the component elements are more abstract than in other modes of analysis. The analysis of an actual entity into 'prehensions' is that mode of analysis which exhibits the most concrete elements in the nature of actual entities. This mode of analysis will be termed the 'division' of the actual entity in question. Each actual entity is 'divisible' in an indefinite number of ways, and each way of 'division' yields its definite quota of prehensions. A prehension reproduces in itself the general characteristics of an actual entity: it is referent to an external world, and in this sense will be said to have a 'vector character'; it involves emotion, and purpose, and valuation, and causation. In fact, any characteristic of an actual entity is reproduced in a prehension. It might have been a complete actuality; but, by reason of a certain incomplete partiality, a prehension is only a subordinate element in an actual entity. A reference to the complete actuality is required to give the reason why such a prehension is what it is in respect to its subjective form. This subjective form is determined by the subjective aim at further integration, so as to obtain the 'satisfaction' of the completed subject. In other words, final causation and atomism are interconnected philosophical principles.

With the purpose of obtaining a one-substance cosmology, 'prehensions' are a generalization from Descartes' mental 'cogitations,' and from Locke's 'ideas,' to express the most concrete mode of analysis applicable to every grade of individual actuality. Descartes and Locke maintained a two-substance ontology – Descartes explicitly, Locke by implication. Descartes, the mathematical physicist, emphasized his account of corporeal substance; and Locke, the physician and the sociologist, confined himself to an account of mental substance. The philosophy of organism, in its scheme for one type of actual entities, adopts the view that Locke's account of mental substance embodies, in a very special form, a more penetrating philosophic description than does Descartes' account of corporeal substance. Nevertheless, Descartes' account must find its place in the philosophic scheme. On the whole, this is the moral to be drawn from the *Monadology* of Leibniz. His monads are best conceived as generalizations of contemporary notions of mentality. The contemporary notions of physical bodies only enter into his philosophy subordinately and derivatively. The philosophy of organism endeavours to hold the balance more evenly. But it does start with a generalization of Locke's account of mental operations.

Actual entities involve each other by reason of their prehensions of each other. There are thus real individual facts of the togetherness of actual entities, which are real, individual, and particular, in the same sense in which actual entities and the prehensions are real, individual, and particular. Any such particular fact of togetherness among actual entities is called a 'nexus' (plural form is written 'nexūs'). The ultimate facts of immediate actual experience are actual entities, prehensions, and nexūs. All else is, for our experience, derivative abstraction.

The explanatory purpose of philosophy is often misunderstood. Its business is to explain the emergence of the more abstract things from the more concrete things. It is a complete mistake to ask how concrete particular fact can be built up out of universals. The answer is, 'In no way.' The true philosophic question* is, How can concrete fact exhibit entities abstract from itself and yet participated in by its own nature?

In other words, philosophy is explanatory of abstraction, and not of concreteness. It is by reason of their instinctive grasp of this ultimate truth that, in spite of much association with arbitrary fancifulness and atavistic mysticism, types of Platonic philosophy retain their abiding appeal; they seek the forms in the facts. Each fact is more than its forms, and each form 'participates' throughout the world of facts. The definiteness of

* In this connection I may refer to the second chapter of my book *The Principle of Relativity* (Cambridge University, 1922) [also in the Whitehead *Anthology*].

fact is due to its forms; but the individual fact is a creature, and creativity is the ultimate behind all forms, inexplicable by forms, and conditioned by its creatures.

Notes

1   The "categoreal explanations" referred to are:
(iv) ". . . it belongs to the nature of a 'being' that it is a potential for every 'becoming'" (p. 590), and
(xx) "to 'function' means to contribute determination to the actual entities in the nexus of some actual world" (p. 593).
2   The sense of Augustine's remark is that a judgment which has the general consensus of mankind can be trusted.

26

Willard Van Orman Quine, "Ontological Relativity"

Introduction

With the "linguistic turn" of the early twentieth century, many philosophers in both the Anglo-American and in the continental traditions shifted the focus of metaphysical questions from "What is?" to "What is said to be?" In a way, this shift was presaged by Immanuel Kant, who in his *Critique of Pure Reason* (1780) rejected the scientific status of what he called "speculative metaphysics," the project of knowing reality as it is "in itself" (*an sich*). In its place, Kant advanced a "transcendental" metaphysics, which rather than attempting to apprehend reality itself delineates the conditions that make it possible to know the world as it appears (II.12 and III.17). Kant's rejection of traditional metaphysics precipitated out from centuries of struggle with skepticism, which undermined the ancient idea that what thinking determines to be true about reality must actually be true about reality – or as Parmenides remarked: "it is the same for thinking as for being" (Bk II, Ch.15; cf. frag. 344). Kant, one might say, turns Parmenides' idea on its head.

Aristotle (III.4) had demarcated 10 different categories of being that seem to take their clue from the way people speak of things in terms of

From W. V. O. Quine, *Ontological Relativity and Other Essays*, New York: Columbia University Press, 1969, pp. 26–68 (some notes amended).

substantives and predicates – as if the way we speak is somehow determined by the way reality is structured. But what if things work the other way around? What if it's not that reality determines thought and language but instead that thought and language determine the possibilities of what reality can be for us? Perhaps, as Ludwig Wittgenstein later maintained, "One thinks that one is tracing the outline of the thing's nature over and over again, and one is merely tracing round the frame through which we look at it."[1] Or, in the dictum attributed to Quine: "to be is to be the value of a bound variable."[2]

Accordingly, Kant supplanted Aristotle's 10 categories of being with 12 *a priori* categories of the understanding. Later, Wilhelm Dilthey (1833–1911) argued that the categories of the understanding are better thought of as historically conditioned expressions of culture, rather than as fixed and universal across time and space.[3] Language-centered philosophers of the twentieth century have reached a similar conclusion by arguing that language structures thought and, indeed, is perhaps in many ways coextensive with thought.

In the following essay, Quine explores the implications of just that idea, arguing against what he calls the "museum theory" of meaning. According to the museum theory, the meaning of words somehow exists independently of them such that people who speak different words in different languages (e.g. "rabbit" and "*lapin*") are saying the same thing when the meanings that underwrite those words are the same. But suppose words don't derive their meaning from being tied to mental ideas or to other independent realities, such as Plato's "forms." Suppose instead, as Quine argues, that the meaning of words derives from how we use them in various contexts, in relation to other words, on the basis of observation and imitation.

Part I of "Ontological Relativity" invites us to consider an anthropologist who discovers a society of people with whom no one has had contact before. The anthropologist notices her subjects seem to use the word "*gavagai*" where she would use "rabbit." But do the two words actually *mean* the same thing in the absence of independent "meanings" with which to compare them? In particular, for our purposes here, does the word "*gavagai*" carry the same metaphysical freight as "rabbit"? Consider all the many different metaphysical views that are consistent with the way "*gavagai*" is used but inconsistent with the common metaphysical view of rabbits. By "*gavagai*" the others may mean alternatively, "it rabbits" (in the way we say "it rains"), or "manifestation of rabbit-hood," or "group of undetached rabbit parts" – *ad infinitum*.

But how different is the situation each of us faces in relation to anyone else, including everyone else who speaks our own language, from that of the anthropologist? Of course, we can ask each other which among alternative metaphysical views is in play; and presumably, as the anthropologist

comes to master the language of *gavagai*, she can ask similar questions. In trying to discover what "*gavagai*" means to her subjects (or what "rabbit" means to her colleagues) she can appeal to what Quine calls a "background theory" – another sector of the relevant language that will clarify things, much in the same way that a given point in space acquires meaningful location by relating it to other points.

But in Part II of "Ontological Relativity" Quine argues that this solution only results in an infinite regress. If the metaphysic of "*gavagai*" (or "rabbit") is clarified through background theory X, what clarifies the terms of background theory X? Another background theory? It would seem then not only that ontology is relative to the language that binds the various variables of that language but also that the way those variables are bound is ultimately indefinite and without foundation – as it is, therefore, for any possible metaphysics.

Notes

1 L. Wittgenstein, *Philosophical Investigations*, trans. G. E. M. Anscombe, 3rd edn, New York: Macmillan Publishing Co., 1958, §114.
2 W. V. O. Quine, "On What There Is," *Review of Metaphysics* 2.5 (1948): 21–38.
3 R. A. Makkreel, *Dilthey: Philosopher of the Human Sciences*, Princeton, NJ: Princeton University Press, 1992.

Quine, "Ontological Relativity"

I

I listened to Dewey on Art as Experience when I was a graduate student in the spring of 1931. Dewey was then at Harvard as the first William James Lecturer. I am proud now to be at Columbia as the first John Dewey Lecturer.

Philosophically I am bound to Dewey by the naturalism that dominated his last three decades. With Dewey I hold that knowledge, mind, and meaning are part of the same world that they have to do with, and that they are to be studied in the same empirical spirit that animates natural science. There is no place for a prior philosophy.

When a naturalistic philosopher addresses himself to the philosophy of mind, he is apt to talk of language. Meanings are, first and foremost, meanings of language. Language is a social art which we all acquire on the evidence solely of other people's overt behavior under publicly recognizable circumstances. Meanings, therefore, those very models of mental entities, end up as grist for the behaviorist's mill. Dewey was explicit on the point: "Meaning . . . is not a psychic existence; it is primarily a property of behavior."*

Once we appreciate the institution of language in these terms, we see that there cannot be, in any

* J. Dewey, *Experience and Nature* (La Salle, Ill.: Open Court, 1925, 1958), p. 179.

useful sense, a private language. This point was stressed by Dewey in the twenties. "Soliloquy," he wrote, "is the product and reflex of converse with others" (170). Further along he expanded the point thus: "Language is specifically a mode of interaction of at least two beings, a speaker and a hearer; it presupposes an organized group to which these creatures belong, and from whom they have acquired their habits of speech. It is therefore a relationship" (185). Years later, Wittgenstein likewise rejected private language. When Dewey was writing in this naturalistic vein, Wittgenstein still held his copy theory of language.

The copy theory in its various forms stands closer to the main philosophical tradition, and to the attitude of common sense today. Uncritical semantics is the myth of a museum in which the exhibits are meanings and the words are labels. To switch languages is to change the labels. Now the naturalist's primary objection to this view is not an objection to meanings on account of their being mental entities, though that could be objection enough. The primary objection persists even if we take the labeled exhibits not as mental ideas but as Platonic ideas or even as the denoted concrete objects. Semantics is vitiated by a pernicious mentalism as long as we regard a man's semantics as somehow determinate in his mind beyond what might be implicit in his dispositions to overt behavior. It is the very facts about meaning, not the entities meant, that must be construed in terms of behavior.

There are two parts to knowing a word. One part is being familiar with the sound of it and being able to reproduce it. This part, the phonetic part, is achieved by observing and imitating other people's behavior, and there are no important illusions about the process. The other part, the semantic part, is knowing how to use the word. This part, even in the paradigm case, is more complex than the phonetic part. The word refers, in the paradigm case, to some visible object. The learner has now not only to learn the word phonetically, by hearing it from another speaker; he also has to see the object; and in addition to this, in order to capture the relevance of the object to the word, he has to see that the speaker also sees the object. Dewey summed up the point thus: "The characteristic theory about B's understanding of A's sounds is that he responds to the thing from the standpoint of A" (178). Each of us, as he learns his language, is a student of his neighbor's

behavior; and conversely, insofar as his tries are approved or corrected, he is a subject of his neighbor's behavioral study.

The semantic part of learning a word is more complex than the phonetic part, therefore, even in simple cases: we have to see what is stimulating the other speaker. In the case of words not directly ascribing observable traits to things, the learning process is increasingly complex and obscure; and obscurity is the breeding place of mentalistic semantics. What the naturalist insists on is that, even in the complex and obscure parts of language learning, the learner has no data to work with but the overt behavior of other speakers.

When with Dewey we turn thus toward a naturalistic view of language and a behavioral view of meaning, what we give up is not just the museum figure of speech. We give up an assurance of determinacy. Seen according to the museum myth, the words and sentences of a language have their determinate meanings. To discover the meanings of the native's words we may have to observe his behavior, but still the meanings of the words are supposed to be determinate in the native's *mind*, his mental museum, even in cases where behavioral criteria are powerless to discover them for us. When on the other hand we recognize with Dewey that "meaning . . . is primarily a property of behavior," we recognize that there are no meanings, nor likenesses nor distinctions of meaning, beyond what are implicit in people's dispositions to overt behavior. For naturalism the question whether two expressions are alike or unlike in meaning has no determinate answer, known or unknown, except insofar as the answer is settled in principle by people's speech dispositions, known or unknown. If by these standards there are indeterminate cases, so much the worse for the terminology of meaning and likeness of meaning.

To see what such indeterminacy would be like, suppose there were an expression in a remote language that could be translated into English equally defensibly in either of two ways, unlike in meaning in English. I am not speaking of ambiguity within the native language. I am supposing that one and the same native use of the expression can be given either of the English translations, each being accommodated by compensating adjustments in the translation of other words. Suppose both translations, along with these accommodations in each case, accord equally well with all observable behavior on the part of speakers of the remote language and speakers of English. Suppose they accord perfectly not only with behavior actually observed, but with all dispositions to behavior on the part of all the speakers concerned. On these assumptions it would be forever impossible to know of one of these translations that it was the right one, and the other wrong. Still, if the museum myth were true, there would be a right and wrong of the matter; it is just that we would never know, not having access to the museum. See language naturalistically, on the other hand, and you have to see the notion of likeness of meaning in such a case simply as nonsense.

I have been keeping to the hypothetical. Turning now to examples, let me begin with a disappointing one and work up. In the French construction "ne . . . rien" you can translate "rien" into English as "anything" or as "nothing" at will, and then accommodate your choice by translating "ne" as "not" or by construing it as pleonastic. This example is disappointing because you can object that I have merely cut the French units too small. You can believe the mentalistic myth of the meaning museum and still grant that "rien" of itself has no meaning, being no whole label; it is part of "ne . . . rien," which has its meaning as a whole.

I began with this disappointing example because I think its conspicuous trait – its dependence on cutting language into segments too short to carry meanings – is the secret of the more serious cases as well. What makes other cases more serious is that the segments they involve are seriously long: long enough to be predicates and to be true of things and hence, you would think, to carry meanings.

An artificial example which I have used elsewhere* depends on the fact that a whole rabbit is present when and only when an undetached part of a rabbit is present; also when and only when a temporal stage of a rabbit is present. If we are wondering whether to translate a native expression "gavagai" as "rabbit" or as "undetached rabbit part" or as "rabbit stage," we can never settle the matter simply by ostension – that is,

simply by repeatedly querying the expression "gavagai" for the native's assent or dissent in the presence of assorted stimulations.

Before going on to urge that we cannot settle the matter by non-ostensive means either, let me belabor this ostensive predicament a bit. I am not worrying, as Wittgenstein did, about simple cases of ostension. The color word "sepia," to take one of his examples,† can certainly be learned by an ordinary process of conditioning, or induction. One need not even be told that sepia is a color and not a shape or a material or an article. True, barring such hints, many lessons may be needed, so as to eliminate wrong generalizations based on shape, material, etc., rather than color, and so as to eliminate wrong notions as to the intended boundary of an indicated example, and so as to delimit the admissible variations of color itself. Like all conditioning, or induction, the process will depend ultimately also on one's own inborn propensity to find one stimulation qualitatively more akin to a second stimulation than to a third; otherwise there can never be any selective reinforcement and extinction of responses.‡ Still, in principle nothing more is needed in learning "sepia" than in any conditioning or induction.

But the big difference between "rabbit" and "sepia" is that whereas "sepia" is a mass term like "water," "rabbit" is a term of divided reference. As such it cannot be mastered without mastering its principle of individuation: where one rabbit leaves off and another begins. And this cannot be mastered by pure ostension, however persistent.

Such is the quandary over "gavagai": where one gavagai leaves off and another begins. The only difference between rabbits, undetached rabbit parts, and rabbit stages is in their individuation. If you take the total scattered portion of the spatiotemporal world that is made up of rabbits, and that which is made up of undetached rabbit parts, and that which is made up of rabbit stages, you come out with the same scattered portion of the world each of the three times. The only difference is in how you slice it. And how to slice it is what ostension or simple conditioning, however persistently repeated, cannot teach.

Thus consider specifically the problem of deciding between "rabbit" and "undetached

* Quine, *Word and Object* (Cambridge, Mass.: MIT Press, 1960), §12.

† L. Wittgenstein, *Philosophical Investigations* (New York: Macmillan, 1953), p. 14.

‡ Cf. *Word and Object*, §17.

rabbit part" as translation of "gavagai." No word of the native language is known, except that we have settled on some working hypothesis as to what native words or gestures to construe as assent and dissent in response to our pointings and queryings. Now the trouble is that whenever we point to different parts of the rabbit, even sometimes screening the rest of the rabbit, we are pointing also each time to the rabbit. When, conversely, we indicate the whole rabbit with a sweeping gesture, we are still pointing to a multitude of rabbit parts. And note that we do not have even a native analogue of our plural ending to exploit, in asking "gavagai?" It seems clear that no even tentative decision between "rabbit" and "undetached rabbit part" is to be sought at this level.

How would we finally decide? My passing mention of plural endings is part of the answer. Our individuating of terms of divided reference, in English, is bound up with a cluster of interrelated grammatical particles and constructions: plural endings, pronouns, numerals, the "is" of identity, and its adaptations "same" and "other." It is the cluster of interrelated devices in which quantification becomes central when the regimentation of symbolic logic is imposed. If in his language we could ask the native "Is this *gavagai* the same as that one?" while making appropriate multiple ostensions, then indeed we would be well on our way to deciding between "rabbit," "undetached rabbit part," and "rabbit stage." And of course the linguist does at length reach the point where he can ask what purports to be that question. He develops a system for translating our pluralizations, pronouns, numerals, identity, and related devices contextually into the native idiom. He develops such a system by abstraction and hypothesis. He abstracts native particles and constructions from observed native sentences and tries associating these variously with English particles and constructions. Insofar as the native sentences and the thus associated English ones seem to match up in respect of appropriate occasions of use, the linguist feels confirmed in these hypotheses of translation – what I call *analytical hypotheses.**

---

* *Word and Object*, §15. For a summary of the general point of view see also §I of "Speaking of Objects," Chapter 1 in this volume.

But it seems that this method, though laudable in practice and the best we can hope for, does not in principle settle the indeterminacy between "rabbit," "undetached rabbit part," and "rabbit stage." For if one workable overall system of analytical hypotheses provides for translating a given native expression into "is the same as," perhaps another equally workable but systematically different system would translate that native expression rather into something like "belongs with." Then when in the native language we try to ask "Is this *gavagai* the same as that?" we could as well be asking "Does this *gavagai* belong with that?" Insofar, the native's assent is no objective evidence for translating "gavagai" as "rabbit" rather than "undetached rabbit part" or "rabbit stage."

This artificial example shares the structure of the trivial earlier example "ne . . . rien." We were able to translate "rien" as "anything" or as "nothing," thanks to a compensatory adjustment in the handling of "ne." And I suggest that we can translate "gavagai" as "rabbit" or "undetached rabbit part" or "rabbit stage," thanks to compensatory adjustments in the translation of accompanying native locutions. Other adjustments still might accommodate translation of "gavagai" as "rabbithood," or in further ways. I find this plausible because of the broadly structural and contextual character of any considerations that could guide us to native translations of the English cluster of interrelated devices of individuation. There seem bound to be systematically very different choices, all of which do justice to all dispositions to verbal behavior on the part of all concerned.

An actual field linguist would of course be sensible enough to equate "gavagai" with "rabbit," dismissing such perverse alternatives as "undetached rabbit part" and "rabbit stage" out of hand. This sensible choice and others like it would help in turn to determine his subsequent hypotheses as to what native locutions should answer to the English apparatus of individuation, and thus everything would come out all right. The implicit maxim guiding his choice of "rabbit," and similar choices for other native words, is that an enduring and relatively homogeneous object, moving as a whole against a contrasting background, is a likely reference for a short expression. If he were to become conscious of this maxim, he might celebrate it as one of the linguistic universals, or traits of all languages, and he would have no trouble pointing out its psychological plausibility. But he would be wrong; the maxim is his own imposition, toward settling what is objectively indeterminate. It is a very sensible imposition, and I would recommend no other. But I am making a philosophical point.

It is philosophically interesting, moreover, that what is indeterminate in this artificial example is not just meaning, but extension; reference. My remarks on indeterminacy began as a challenge to likeness of meaning. I had us imagining "an expression that could be translated into English equally defensibly in either of two ways, unlike in meaning in English." Certainly likeness of meaning is a dim notion, repeatedly challenged. Of two predicates which are alike in extension, it has never been clear when to say that they are alike in meaning and when not; it is the old matter of featherless bipeds and rational animals, or of equiangular and equilateral triangles. Reference, extension, has been the firm thing; meaning, intension, the infirm. The indeterminacy of translation now confronting us, however, cuts across extension and intension alike. The terms "rabbit," "undetached rabbit part," and "rabbit stage" differ not only in meaning; they are true of different things. Reference itself proves behaviorally inscrutable.

Within the parochial limits of our own language, we can continue as always to find extensional talk clearer than intensional. For the indeterminacy between "rabbit," "rabbit stage," and the rest depended only on a correlative indeterminacy of translation of the English apparatus of individuation – the apparatus of pronouns, pluralization, identity, numerals, and so on. No such indeterminacy obtrudes so long as we think of this apparatus as given and fixed. Given this apparatus, there is no mystery about extension; terms have the same extension when true of the same things. At the level of radical translation, on the other hand, extension itself goes inscrutable.

My example of rabbits and their parts and stages is a contrived example and a perverse one, with which, as I said, the practicing linguist would have no patience. But there are also cases, less bizarre ones, that obtrude in practice. In Japanese there are certain particles, called "classifiers," which may be explained in either of two ways. Commonly they are explained as attaching to numerals, to form compound numerals of distinctive styles. Thus take the numeral for 5. If

you attach one classifier to it you get a style of "5" suitable for counting animals; if you attach a different classifier, you get a style of "5" suitable for counting slim things like pencils and chopsticks; and so on. But another way of viewing classifiers is to view them not as constituting part of the numeral, but as constituting part of the term – the term for "chopsticks" or "oxen" or whatever. On this view the classifier does the individuative job that is done in English by "sticks of" as applied to the mass term "wood," or "head of" as applied to the mass term "cattle."

What we have on either view is a Japanese phrase tantamount say to "five oxen," but consisting of three words;* the first is in effect the neutral numeral "5," the second is a classifier of the animal kind, and the last corresponds in some fashion to "ox." On one view the neutral numeral and the classifier go together to constitute a declined numeral in the "animal gender," which then modifies "ox" to give, in effect, "five oxen." On the other view the third Japanese word answers not to the individuative term "ox" but to the mass term "cattle"; the classifier applies to this mass term to produce a composite individuative term, in effect "head of cattle"; and the neutral numeral applies directly to all this without benefit of gender, giving "five head of cattle," hence again in effect "five oxen."

If so simple an example is to serve its expository purpose, it needs your connivance. You have to understand "cattle" as a mass term covering only bovines, and "ox" as applying to all bovines. That these usages are not the invariable usages is beside the point. The point is that the Japanese phrase comes out as "five bovines," as desired, when parsed in either of two ways. The one way treats the third Japanese word as an individuative term true of each bovine, and the other way treats that word rather as a mass term covering the unindividuated totality of beef on the hoof. These are two very different ways of treating the third Japanese word; and the three-word phrase as a whole turns out all right in both cases only because of compensatory differences in our account of the second word, the classifier.

This example is reminiscent in a way of our trivial initial example, "ne . . . rien." We were able to represent "rien" as "anything" or as

---

* To keep my account graphic I am counting a certain postpositive particle as a suffix rather than a word.

"nothing," by compensatorily taking "ne" as negative or as vacuous. We are able now to represent a Japanese word either as an individuative term for bovines or as a mass term for live beef, by compensatorily taking the classifier as declining the numeral or as individuating the mass term. However, the triviality of the one example does not quite carry over to the other. The early example was dismissed on the ground that we had cut too small; "rien" was too short for significant translation on its own, and "ne . . . rien" was the significant unit. But you cannot dismiss the Japanese example by saying that the third word was too short for significant translation on its own and that only the whole three-word phrase, tantamount to "five oxen," was the significant unit. You cannot take this line unless you are prepared to call a word too short for significant translation even when it is long enough to be a term and carry denotation. For the third Japanese word is, on either approach, a term: on one approach a term of divided reference, and on the other a mass term. If you are indeed prepared thus to call a word too short for significant translation even when it is a denoting term, then in a backhanded way you are granting what I wanted to prove: the inscrutability of reference.

Between the two accounts of Japanese classifiers there is no question of right and wrong. The one account makes for more efficient translation into idiomatic English; the other makes for more of a feeling for the Japanese idiom. Both fit all verbal behavior equally well. All whole sentences, and even component phrases like "five oxen," admit of the same net overall English translations on either account. This much is invariant. But what is philosophically interesting is that the reference or extension of shorter terms can fail to be invariant. Whether that third Japanese word is itself true of each ox, or whether on the other hand it is a mass term which needs to be adjoined to the classifier to make a term which is true of each ox – here is a question that remains undecided by the totality of human dispositions to verbal behavior. It is indeterminate in principle; there is no fact of the matter. Either answer can be accommodated by an account of the classifier. Here again, then, is the inscrutability of reference – illustrated this time by a humdrum point of practical translation.

The inscrutability of reference can be brought closer to home by considering the word "alpha," or again the word "green." In our use of these words and others like them there is a systematic ambiguity. Sometimes we use such words as concrete general terms, as when we say the grass is green, or that some inscription begins with an alpha. Sometimes on the other hand we use them as abstract singular terms, as when we say that green is a color and alpha is a letter. Such ambiguity is encouraged by the fact that there is nothing in ostension to distinguish the two uses. The pointing that would be done in teaching the concrete general term "green," or "alpha," differs none from the pointing that would be done in teaching the abstract singular term "green" or "alpha." Yet the objects referred to by the word are very different under the two uses; under the one use the word is true of many concrete objects, and under the other use it names a single abstract object.

We can of course tell the two uses apart by seeing how the word turns up in sentences: whether it takes an indefinite article, whether it takes a plural ending, whether it stands as singular subject, whether it stands as modifier, as predicate complement, and so on. But these criteria appeal to our special English grammatical constructions and particles, our special English apparatus of individuation, which, I already urged, is itself subject to indeterminacy of translation. So, from the point of view of translation into a remote language, the distinction between a concrete general and an abstract singular term is in the same predicament as the distinction between "rabbit," "rabbit part," and "rabbit stage." Here then is another example of the inscrutability of reference, since the difference between the concrete general and the abstract singular is a difference in the objects referred to.

Incidentally we can concede this much indeterminacy also to the "sepia" example, after all. But this move is not evidently what was worrying Wittgenstein.

The ostensive indistinguishability of the abstract singular from the concrete general turns upon what may be called "deferred ostension," as opposed to direct ostension. First let me define direct ostension. The *ostended point*, as I shall call it, is the point where the line of the pointing finger first meets an opaque surface. What characterizes *direct ostension*, then, is that the term which is being ostensively explained is true of something that contains the ostended point. Even such direct ostension has its uncertainties, of course, and these are familiar. There is the question how wide an environment of the ostended point is meant to be covered by the term that is being ostensively explained. There is the question how considerably an absent thing or substance might be allowed to differ from what is now ostended, and still be covered by the term that is now being ostensively explained. Both of these questions can in principle be settled as well as need be by induction from multiple ostensions. Also, if the term is a term of divided reference like "apple," there is the question of individuation: the question where one of its objects leaves off and another begins. This can be settled by induction from multiple ostensions of a more elaborate kind, accompanied by expressions like "same apple" and "another," if an equivalent of this English apparatus of individuation has been settled on; otherwise the indeterminacy persists that was illustrated by "rabbit," "undetached rabbit part," and "rabbit stage."

Such, then, is the way of direct ostension. Other ostension I call *deferred*. It occurs when we point at the gauge, and not the gasoline, to show that there is gasoline. Also it occurs when we explain the abstract singular term "green" or "alpha" by pointing at grass or a Greek inscription. Such pointing is direct ostension when used to explain the concrete general term "green" or "alpha," but it is deferred ostension when used to explain the abstract singular terms; for the abstract object which is the color green or the letter alpha does not contain the ostended point, nor any point.

Deferred ostension occurs very naturally when, as in the case of the gasoline gauge, we have a correspondence in mind. Another such example is afforded by the Gödel numbering of expressions. Thus if 7 has been assigned as Gödel number of the letter alpha, a man conscious of the Gödel numbering would not hesitate to say "Seven" on pointing to an inscription of the Greek letter in question. This is, on the face of it, a doubly deferred ostension: one step of deferment carries us from the inscription to the letter as abstract object, and a second step carries us thence to the number.

By appeal to our apparatus of individuation, if it is available, we can distinguish between the concrete general and the abstract singular use of the word "alpha"; this we saw. By appeal again to that apparatus, and in particular to identity, we can evidently settle also whether the word "alpha" in its abstract singular use is being used really to name the letter or whether, perversely, it is being used to name the Gödel number of the letter. At any rate we can distinguish these alternatives if also we have located the speaker's equivalent of the numeral "7" to our satisfaction; for we can ask him whether alpha *is* 7.

These considerations suggest that deferred ostension adds no essential problem to those presented by direct ostension. Once we have settled upon analytical hypotheses of translation covering identity and the other English particles relating to individuation, we can resolve not only the indecision between "rabbit" and "rabbit stage" and the rest, which came of direct ostension, but also any indecision between concrete general and abstract singular, and any indecision between expression and Gödel number, which come of deferred ostension. However, this conclusion is too sanguine. The inscrutability of reference runs deep, and it persists in a subtle form even if we accept identity and the rest of the apparatus of individuation as fixed and settled; even, indeed, if we forsake radical translation and think only of English.

Consider the case of a thoughtful protosyntactician. He has a formalized system of first-order proof theory, or protosyntax, whose universe comprises just expressions, that is, strings of signs of a specified alphabet. Now just what sorts of things, more specifically, are these expressions? They are types, not tokens. So, one might suppose, each of them is the set of all its tokens. That is, each expression is a set of inscriptions which are variously situated in space–time but are classed together by virtue of a certain similarity in shape. The concatenate $x \frown y$ of two expressions x and y, in a given order, will be the set of all inscriptions each of which has two parts which are tokens respectively of x and y and follow one upon the other in that order. But $x \frown y$ may then be the null set, though x and y are not null; for it may be that inscriptions belonging to x and y happen to turn up head to tail nowhere, in the past, present, or future. This danger increases with the lengths of x and y. But it is easily seen to violate a law of protosyntax which says that $x = z$ whenever $x \frown y = z \frown y$.

Thus it is that our thoughtful protosyntactician will not construe the things in his universe as sets of inscriptions. He can still take his atoms, the single signs, as sets of inscriptions, for there is no risk of nullity in these cases. And then, instead of taking his strings of signs as sets of inscriptions, he can invoke the mathematical notion of sequence and take them as sequences of signs. A familiar way of taking sequences, in turn, is as a mapping of things on numbers. On this approach an expression or string of signs becomes a finite set of pairs each of which is the pair of a sign and a number.

This account of expressions is more artificial and more complex than one is apt to expect who simply says he is letting his variables range over the strings of such and such signs. Moreover, it is not the inevitable choice; the considerations that motivated it can be met also by alternative constructions. One of these constructions is Gödel numbering itself, and it is temptingly simple. It uses just natural numbers, whereas the foregoing construction used sets of one-letter inscriptions and also natural numbers and sets of pairs of these. How clear is it that at just *this* point we have dropped expressions in favor of numbers? What is clearer is merely that in both constructions we were artificially devising models to satisfy laws that expressions in an unexplicated sense had been meant to satisfy.

So much for expressions. Consider now the arithmetician himself, with his elementary number theory. His universe comprises the natural numbers outright. Is it clearer than the protosyntactician's? What, after all, is a natural number? There are Frege's version, Zermelo's, and von Neumann's, and countless further alternatives, all mutually incompatible and equally correct. What we are doing in any one of these explications of natural number is to devise set-theoretic models to satisfy laws which the natural numbers in an unexplicated sense had been meant to satisfy. The case is quite like that of protosyntax.

It will perhaps be felt that any set-theoretic explication of natural number is at best a case of *obscurum per obscurius*; that all explications must assume something, and the natural numbers themselves are an admirable assumption to start with. I must agree that a construction of sets and set theory from natural numbers and arithmetic would be far more desirable than the familiar opposite. On the other hand our impression of

the clarity even of the notion of natural number itself has suffered somewhat from Gödel's proof of the impossibility of a complete proof procedure for elementary number theory, or, for that matter, from Skolem's and Henkin's observations that all laws of natural numbers admit nonstandard models.*

We are finding no clear difference between *specifying* a universe of discourse – the range of the variables of quantification – and *reducing* that universe to some other. We saw no significant difference between clarifying the notion of expression and supplanting it by that of number. And now to say more particularly what numbers themselves are is in no evident way different from just dropping numbers and assigning to arithmetic one or another new model, say in set theory.

Expressions are known only by their laws, the laws of concatenation theory, so that any constructs obeying those laws – Gödel numbers, for instance – are *ipso facto* eligible as explications of expression. Numbers in turn are known only by their laws, the laws of arithmetic, so that any constructs obeying those laws – certain sets, for instance – are eligible in turn as explications of number. Sets in turn are known only by their laws, the laws of set theory.

Russell pressed a contrary thesis, long ago. Writing of numbers, he argued that for an understanding of number the laws of arithmetic are not enough; we must know the applications, we must understand numerical discourse embedded in discourse of other matters. In applying number, the key notion, he urged, is *Anzahl*: there are *n* so-and-sos. However, Russell can be answered. First take, specifically, *Anzahl*. We can define "there are *n* so-and-sos" without ever deciding what numbers are, apart from their fulfillment of arithmetic. That there are *n* so-and-sos can be explained simply as meaning that the so-and-sos are in one-to-one correspondence with the numbers up to *n*.†

Russell's more general point about application can be answered too. Always, if the structure is there, the applications will fall into place. As

* See Leon Henkin, "Completeness in the theory of types," *Journal of Symbolic Logic* 15 (1950), 81–91, and references therein.
† For more on this theme see my *Set Theory and Its Logic* (Cambridge, Mass.; Harvard, 1963, 1969), §11.

paradigm it is perhaps sufficient to recall again this reflection on expressions and Gödel numbers: that even the pointing out of an inscription is no final evidence that our talk is of expressions and not of Gödel numbers. We can always plead deferred ostension.

It is in this sense true to say, as mathematicians often do, that arithmetic is all there is to number. But it would be a confusion to express this point by saying, as is sometimes said, that numbers are any things fulfilling arithmetic. This formulation is wrong because distinct domains of objects yield distinct models of arithmetic. Any progression can be made to serve; and to identify all progressions with one another, e.g., to identify the progression of odd numbers with the progression of evens, would contradict arithmetic after all.

So, though Russell was wrong in suggesting that numbers need more than their arithmetical properties, he was right in objecting to the definition of numbers as any things fulfilling arithmetic. The subtle point is that any progression will serve as a version of number so long and only so long as we stick to one and the same progression. Arithmetic is, in this sense, all there is to number: there is no saying absolutely what the numbers are; there is only arithmetic.*

II

I first urged the inscrutability of reference with the help of examples like the one about rabbits and rabbit parts. These used direct ostension, and the inscrutability of reference hinged on the indeterminacy of translation of identity and other individuative apparatus. The setting of these examples, accordingly, was radical translation: translation from a remote language on behavioral evidence, unaided by prior dictionaries. Moving then to deferred ostension and abstract objects, we found a certain dimness of reference pervading the home language itself.

Now it should be noted that even for the earlier examples the resort to a remote language was not really essential. On deeper reflection, radical

translation begins at home. Must we equate our neighbor's English words with the same strings of phonemes in our own mouths? Certainly not; for sometimes we do not thus equate them. Sometimes we find it to be in the interests of communication to recognize that our neighbor's use of some word, such as "cool" or "square" or "hopefully," differs from ours, and so we translate that word of his into a different string of phonemes in our idiolect. Our usual domestic rule of translation is indeed the homophonic one, which simply carries each string of phonemes into itself; but still we are always prepared to temper homophony with what Neil Wilson has called the "principle of charity."† We will construe a neighbor's word heterophonically now and again if thereby we see our way to making his message less absurd.

The homophonic rule is a handy one on the whole. That it works so well is no accident, since imitation and feedback are what propagate a language. We acquired a great fund of basic words and phrases in this way, imitating our elders and encouraged by our elders amid external circumstances to which the phrases suitably apply. Homophonic translation is implicit in this social method of learning. Departure from homophonic translation in this quarter would only hinder communication. Then there are the relatively rare instances of opposite kind, due to divergence in dialect or confusion in an individual, where homophonic translation incurs negative feedback. But what tends to escape notice is that there is also a vast mid-region where the homophonic method is indifferent. Here, gratuitously, we can systematically reconstrue our neighbor's apparent references to rabbits as really references to rabbit stages, and his apparent references to formulas as really references to Gödel numbers and vice versa. We can reconcile all this with our neighbor's verbal behavior, by cunningly readjusting our translations of his various connecting predicates so as to compensate for the switch of ontology. In short, we can reproduce the inscrutability of reference at home. It is of no avail to check on this fanciful version of our neighbor's meanings by asking him, say, whether he really means at a certain point

---

* Paul Benacerraf, "What numbers cannot be," *Philosophical Review* 74 (1965), 47–73, develops this point. His conclusions differ in some ways from those I shall come to.

† N. L. Wilson, "Substances without substrata," *Review of Metaphysics* 12 (1959), 521–539, p. 532.

to refer to formulas or to their Gödel numbers; for our question and his answer – "By all means, the numbers" – have lost their title to homophonic translation. The problem at home differs none from radical translation ordinarily so called except in the willfulness of this suspension of homophonic translation.

I have urged in defense of the behavioral philosophy of language, Dewey's, that the inscrutability of reference is not the inscrutability of a fact; there is no fact of the matter. But if there is really no fact of the matter, then the inscrutability of reference can be brought even closer to home than the neighbor's case; we can apply it to ourselves. If it is to make sense to say even of oneself that one is referring to rabbits and formulas and not to rabbit stages and Gödel numbers, then it should make sense equally to say it of someone else. After all, as Dewey stressed, there is no private language.

We seem to be maneuvering ourselves into the absurd position that there is no difference on any terms, interlinguistic or intralinguistic, objective or subjective, between referring to rabbits and referring to rabbit parts or stages; or between referring to formulas and referring to their Gödel numbers. Surely this is absurd, for it would imply that there is no difference between the rabbit and each of its parts or stages, and no difference between a formula and its Gödel number. Reference would seem now to become nonsense not just in radical translation but at home.

Toward resolving this quandary, begin by picturing us at home in our language, with all its predicates and auxiliary devices. This vocabulary includes "rabbit," "rabbit part," "rabbit stage," "formula," "number," "ox," "cattle"; also the two-place predicates of identity and difference, and other logical particles. In these terms we can say in so many words that this is a formula and that a number, this a rabbit and that a rabbit part, this and that the same rabbit, and this and that different parts. *In just those words.* This network of terms and predicates and auxiliary devices is, in relativity jargon, our frame of reference, or coordinate system. Relative to *it* we can and do talk meaningfully and distinctively of rabbits and parts, numbers and formulas. Next, as in recent paragraphs, we contemplate alternative denotations for our familiar terms. We begin to appreciate that a grand and ingenious permutation of these denotations, along with compensatory adjust-

ments in the interpretations of the auxiliary particles, might still accommodate all existing speech dispositions. This was the inscrutability of reference, applied to ourselves; and it made nonsense of reference. Fair enough; reference *is* nonsense except relative to a coordinate system. In this principle of relativity lies the resolution of our quandary.

It is meaningless to ask whether, in general, our terms "rabbit," "rabbit part," "number," etc., really refer respectively to rabbits, rabbit parts, numbers, etc., rather than to some ingeniously permuted denotations. It is meaningless to ask this absolutely; we can meaningfully ask it only relative to some background language. When we ask, "Does 'rabbit' really refer to rabbits?" someone can counter with the question: "Refer to rabbits in what sense of 'rabbits'?" thus launching a regress; and we need the background language to regress into. The background language gives the query sense, if only relative sense; sense relative in turn to it, this background language. Querying reference in any more absolute way would be like asking absolute position, or absolute velocity, rather than position or velocity relative to a given frame of reference. Also it is very much like asking whether our neighbor may not systematically see everything upside down, or in complementary color, forever undetectably.

We need a background language, I said, to regress into. Are we involved now in an infinite regress? If questions of reference of the sort we are considering make sense only relative to a background language, then evidently questions of reference for the background language make sense in turn only relative to a further background language. In these terms the situation sounds desperate, but in fact it is little different from questions of position and velocity. When we are given position and velocity relative to a given coordinate system, we can always ask in turn about the placing of origin and orientation of axes of that system of coordinates; and there is no end to the succession of further coordinate systems that could be adduced in answering the successive questions thus generated.

In practice of course we end the regress of coordinate systems by something like pointing. And in practice we end the regress of background languages, in discussions of reference, by acquiescing in our mother tongue and taking its words at face value.

Very well; in the case of position and velocity, in practice, pointing breaks the regress. But what of position and velocity apart from practice? what of the regress then? The answer, of course, is the relational doctrine of space; there is no absolute position or velocity; there are just the relations of coordinate systems to one another, and ultimately of things to one another. And I think that the parallel question regarding denotation calls for a parallel answer, a relational theory of what the objects of theories are. What makes sense is to say not what the objects of a theory are, absolutely speaking, but how one theory of objects is interpretable or reinterpretable in another.

The point is not that bare matter is inscrutable: that things are indistinguishable except by their properties. That point does not need making. The present point is reflected better in the riddle about seeing things upside down, or in complementary colors; for it is that things can be inscrutably switched even while carrying their properties with them. Rabbits differ from rabbit parts and rabbit stages not just as bare matter, after all, but in respect of properties; and formulas differ from numbers in respect of properties. What our present reflections are leading us to appreciate is that the riddle about seeing things upside down, or in complementary colors, should be taken seriously and its moral applied widely. The relativistic thesis to which we have come is this, to repeat: it makes no sense to say what the objects of a theory are, beyond saying how to interpret or reinterpret that theory in another. Suppose we are working within a theory and thus treating of its objects. We do so by using the variables of the theory, whose values those objects are, though there be no ultimate sense in which that universe can have been specified. In the language of the theory there are predicates by which to distinguish portions of this universe from other portions, and these predicates differ from one another purely in the roles they play in the laws of the theory. Within this background theory we can show how some subordinate theory, whose universe is some portion of the background universe, can by a reinterpretation be reduced to another subordinate theory whose universe is some lesser portion. Such talk of subordinate theories and their ontologies *is* meaningful, but only relative to the background theory with its own primitively adopted and ultimately inscrutable ontology.

To talk thus of theories raises a problem of formulation. A theory, it will be said, is a set of fully interpreted sentences. (More particularly, it is a deductively closed set: it includes all its own logical consequences, insofar as they are couched in the same notation.) But if the sentences of a theory are fully interpreted, then in particular the range of values of their variables is settled. How then can there be no sense in saying what the objects of a theory are?

My answer is simply that we cannot require theories to be fully interpreted, except in a relative sense, if anything is to count as a theory. In specifying a theory we must indeed fully specify, in our own words, what sentences are to comprise the theory, and what things are to be taken as values of the variables, and what things are to be taken as satisfying the predicate letters; insofar we do fully interpret the theory, *relative* to our own words and relative to our overall home theory which lies behind them. But this fixes the objects of the described theory only relative to those of the home theory; and these can, at will, be questioned in turn.

One is tempted to conclude simply that meaninglessness sets in when we try to pronounce on everything in our universe; that universal predication takes on sense only when furnished with the background of a wider universe, where the predication is no longer universal. And this is even a familiar doctrine, the doctrine that no proper predicate is true of everything. We have all heard it claimed that a predicate is meaningful only by contrast with what it excludes, and hence that being true of everything would make a predicate meaningless. But surely this doctrine is wrong. Surely self-identity, for instance, is not to be rejected as meaningless. For that matter, any statement of fact at all, however brutally meaningful, can be put artificially into a form in which it pronounces on everything. To say merely of Jones that he sings, for instance, is to say of everything that it is other than Jones or sings. We had better beware of repudiating universal predication, lest we be tricked into repudiating everything there is to say.

Carnap took an intermediate line in his doctrine of universal words, or *Allwörter*, in *The Logical Syntax of Language*. He did treat the predicating of universal words as "quasi-syntactical" – as a predication only by courtesy, and without empirical content. But universal words were for him not just any universally true predicates, like "is other than Jones or sings." They were a special breed of universally true predicates, ones that are universally true by the sheer meanings of their words and no thanks to nature. In his later writing this doctrine of universal words takes the form of a distinction between "internal" questions, in which a theory comes to grips with facts about the world, and "external" questions, in which people come to grips with the relative merits of theories.

Should we look to these distinctions of Carnap's for light on ontological relativity? When we found there was no absolute sense in saying what a theory is about, were we sensing the infactuality of what Carnap calls "external questions"? When we found that saying what a theory is about did make sense against a background theory, were we sensing the factuality of internal questions of the background theory? I see no hope of illumination in this quarter. Carnap's universal words were not just any universally true predicates, but, as I said, a special breed; and what distinguishes this breed is not clear. What I said distinguished them was that they were universally true by sheer meanings and not by nature; but this is a very questionable distinction. Talking of "internal" and "external" is no better.

Ontological relativity is not to be clarified by any distinction between kinds of universal predication – unfactual and factual, external and internal. It is not a question of universal predication. When questions regarding the ontology of a theory are meaningless absolutely, and become meaningful relative to a background theory, this is not in general because the background theory has a wider universe. One is tempted, as I said a little while back, to suppose that it is; but one is then wrong.

What makes ontological questions meaningless when taken absolutely is not universality but circularity. A question of the form "What is an F?" can be answered only by recourse to a further term: "An F is a G." The answer makes only relative sense: sense relative to the uncritical acceptance of "G."

We may picture the vocabulary of a theory as comprising logical signs such as quantifiers and the signs for the truth functions and identity, and in addition descriptive or nonlogical signs, which, typically, are singular terms, or names, and general terms, or predicates. Suppose next that in the statements which comprise the theory, that is, are true according to the theory, we abstract from the meanings of the nonlogical vocabulary and from the range of the variables. We are left with the logical form of the theory, or, as I shall say, the *theory form*. Now we may interpret this theory form anew by picking a new universe for its variables of quantification to range over, and assigning objects from this universe to the names, and choosing subsets of this universe as extensions of the one-place predicates, and so on. Each such interpretation of the theory form is called a model of it, if it makes it come out true. Which of these models is meant in a given actual theory cannot, of course, be guessed from the theory form. The intended references of the names and predicates have to be learned rather by ostension, or else by paraphrase in some antecedently familiar vocabulary. But the first of these two ways has proved inconclusive, since, even apart from indeterminacies of translation affecting identity and other logical vocabulary, there is the problem of deferred ostension. Paraphrase in some antecedently familiar vocabulary, then, is our only recourse; and such is ontological relativity. To question the reference of all the terms of our all-inclusive theory becomes meaningless, simply for want of further terms relative to which to ask or answer the question.

It is thus meaningless within the theory to say which of the various possible models of our theory form is our real or intended model. Yet even here we can make sense still of there being many models. For we might be able to show that for each of the models, however unspecifiable, there is bound to be another which is a permutation or perhaps a diminution of the first.

Suppose for example that our theory is purely numerical. Its objects are just the natural numbers. There is no sense in saying, from within that theory, just which of the various models of number theory is in force. But we can observe even from within the theory that, whatever 0, 1, 2, 3, etc. may be, the theory would still hold true if the 17 of this series were moved into the role of 0, and the 18 moved into the role of 1, and so on.

Ontology is indeed doubly relative. Specifying the universe of a theory makes sense only relative to some background theory, and only relative to some choice of a manual of translation of the one theory into the other. Commonly of course the background theory will simply be a containing theory, and in this case no question of a manual of translation arises. But this is after all just a degenerate case of translation still – the case where the rule of translation is the homophonic one.

We cannot know what something is without knowing how it is marked off from other things. Identity is thus of a piece with ontology. Accordingly it is involved in the same relativity, as may be readily illustrated. Imagine a fragment of economic theory. Suppose its universe comprises persons, but its predicates are incapable of distinguishing between persons whose incomes are equal. The interpersonal relation of equality of income enjoys, within the theory, the substitutivity property of the identity relation itself; the two relations are indistinguishable. It is only relative to a background theory, in which more can be said of personal identity than equality of income, that we are able even to appreciate the above account of the fragment of economic theory, hinging as the account does on a contrast between persons and incomes.

A usual occasion for ontological talk is reduction, where it is shown how the universe of some theory can by a reinterpretation be dispensed with in favor of some other universe, perhaps a proper part of the first. I have treated elsewhere* of the reduction of one ontology to another with help of a *proxy function*: a function mapping the one universe into part or all of the other. For instance, the function "Gödel number of" is a proxy function. The universe of elementary proof theory or protosyntax, which consists of expressions or strings of signs, is mapped by this function into the universe of elementary number theory, which consists of numbers.

The proxy function used in reducing one ontology to another need not, like Gödel numbering, be one-to-one. We might, for instance, be confronted with a theory treating of both expressions and ratios. We would cheerfully reduce all this to the universe of natural numbers, by invoking a proxy function which enumerates the expressions in the Gödel way, and enumerates the ratios by the classical method of short diagonals. This proxy function is not one-to-one, since

it assigns the same natural number both to an expression and to a ratio. We would tolerate the resulting artificial convergence between expressions and ratios, simply because the original theory made no capital of the distinction between them; they were so invariably and extravagantly unlike that the identity question did not arise. Formally speaking, the original theory used a two-sorted logic.

For another kind of case where we would not require the proxy function to be one-to-one, consider again the fragment of economic theory lately noted. We would happily reduce its ontology of persons to a less numerous one of incomes. The proxy function would assign to each person his income. It is not one-to-one; distinct persons give way to identical incomes. The reason such a reduction is acceptable is that it merges the images of only such individuals as never had been distinguishable by the predicates of the original theory. Nothing in the old theory is contravened by the new identities.

If on the other hand the theory that we are concerned to reduce or reinterpret is straight protosyntax, or a straight arithmetic of ratios or of real numbers, then a one-to-one proxy function is mandatory. This is because any two elements of such a theory are distinguishable in terms of the theory. This is true even for the real numbers, even though not every real number is uniquely specifiable; any two real numbers x and y are still distinguishable, in that $x < y$ or $y < x$ and never $x < x$. A proxy function that did not preserve the distinctness of the elements of such a theory would fail of its purpose of reinterpretation.

One ontology is *always* reducible to another when we are given a proxy function f that is one-to-one. The essential reasoning is as follows. Where P is any predicate of the old system, its work can be done in the new system by a new predicate which we interpret as true of just the correlates fx of the old objects x that P was true of. Thus suppose we take fx as the Gödel number of x, and as our old system we take a syntactical system in which one of the predicates is "is a segment of." The corresponding predicate of the new or numerical system, then, would be one which amounts, so far as its extension is concerned, to the words "is the Gödel number of a segment of that whose Gödel number is." The numerical predicate would not be given this devious form,

* Quine, *The Ways of Paradox* (New York: Random House, 1966), pp. 204ff.; or see *Journal of Philosophy*, 1964, pp. 214ff.

of course, but would be rendered as an appropriate purely arithmetical condition.

Our dependence upon a background theory becomes especially evident when we reduce our universe U to another V by appeal to a proxy function. For it is only in a theory with an inclusive universe, embracing U and V, that we can make sense of the proxy function. The function maps U into V and hence needs all the old objects of U as well as their new proxies in V.

The proxy function need not exist as an object in the universe even of the background theory. It may do its work merely as what I have called a "virtual class,"* and Gödel has called a "notion."† That is to say, all that is required toward a function is an open sentence with two free variables, provided that it is fulfilled by exactly one value of the first variable for each object of the old universe as value of the second variable. But the point is that it is only in the background theory, with its inclusive universe, that we can hope to write such a sentence and have the right values at our disposal for its variables.

If the new objects happen to be among the old, so that V is a subclass of U, then the old theory with universe U can itself sometimes qualify as the background theory in which to describe its own ontological reduction. But we cannot do better than that; we cannot declare our new ontological economies without having recourse to the uneconomical old ontology.

This sounds, perhaps, like a predicament: as if no ontological economy is justifiable unless it is a false economy and the repudiated objects really exist after all. But actually this is wrong; there is no more cause for worry here than there is in *reductio ad absurdum*, where we assume a falsehood that we are out to disprove. If what we want to show is that the universe U is excessive and that only a part exists, or need exist, then we are quite within our rights to assume all of U for the space of the argument. We show thereby that if all of U were needed then not all of U would be needed; and so our ontological reduction is sealed by *reductio ad absurdum*.

Toward further appreciating the bearing of ontological relativity on programs of ontological reduction, it is worth while to reexamine the philosophical bearing of the Löwenheim-Skolem theorem. I shall use the strong early form of the theorem,‡ which depends on the axiom of choice. It says that if a theory is true and has an indenumerable universe, then all but a denumerable part of that universe is dead wood, in the sense that it can be dropped from the range of the variables without falsifying any sentences.

On the face of it, this theorem declares a reduction of all acceptable theories to denumerable ontologies. Moreover, a denumerable ontology is reducible in turn to an ontology specifically of natural numbers, simply by taking the enumeration as the proxy function, if the enumeration is explicitly at hand. And even if it is not at hand, it exists; thus we can still think of all our objects as natural numbers, and merely reconcile ourselves to not always knowing, numerically, which number an otherwise given object is. May we not thus settle for an all-purpose Pythagorean ontology outright?

Suppose, afterward, someone were to offer us what would formerly have qualified as an ontological reduction – a way of dispensing in future theory with all things of a certain sort S, but still leaving an infinite universe. Now in the new Pythagorean setting his discovery would still retain its essential content, though relinquishing the form of an ontological reduction; it would take the form merely of a move whereby some numerically unspecified numbers were divested of some property of numbers that corresponded to S.

Blanket Pythagoreanism on these terms is unattractive, for it merely offers new and obscurer accounts of old moves and old problems. On this score again, then, the relativistic proposition seems reasonable: that there is no absolute sense in speaking of the ontology of a theory. It very creditably brands this Pythagoreanism itself as

---

* Quine, *Set Theory and Its Logic*, §§2f.
† Kurt Gödel, *The Consistency of the Continuum Hypothesis* (Princeton, N.J.: The University Press, 1940), p. 11.

‡ Thoralf Skolem, "Logisch-kombinatorische Untersuchungen über die Erfüllbarkeit oder Beweisbarkeit mathematischer Sätze nebst einem Theorem über dichte Mengen," *Skrifter utgit av Videnskapsselskapet i Kristiania*, 1919. 37 pp. Translation in Jean van Heijenoort, ed., *From Frege to Gödel: Source Book in the History of Mathematical Logic* (Cambridge, Mass.: Harvard, 1967), pp. 252–263.

meaningless. For there is no absolute sense in saying that all the objects of a theory are numbers, or that they are sets, or bodies, or something else; this makes no sense unless relative to some background theory. The relevant predicates – "number," "set," "body," or whatever – would be distinguished from *one another* in the background theory by the roles they play in the laws of that theory.

Elsewhere* I urged in answer to such Pythagoreanism that we have no ontological reduction in an interesting sense unless we can specify a proxy function. Now where does the strong Löwenheim–Skolem theorem leave us in this regard? If the background theory assumes the axiom of choice and even provides a notation for a general selector operator, can we in these terms perhaps specify an actual proxy function embodying the Löwenheim–Skolem argument?

The theorem is that all but a denumerable part of an ontology can be dropped and not be missed. One could imagine that the proof proceeds by partitioning the universe into denumerably many equivalence classes of indiscriminable objects, such that all but one member of each equivalence class can be dropped as superfluous; and one would then guess that where the axiom of choice enters the proof is in picking a survivor from each equivalence class. If this were so, then with help of Hilbert's selector notation we could indeed express a proxy function. But in fact the Löwenheim–Skolem proof has another structure. I see in the proof even of the strong Löwenheim–Skolem theorem no reason to suppose that a proxy function can be formulated anywhere that will map an indenumerable ontology, say the real numbers, into a denumerable one.

On the face of it, of course, such a proxy function is out of the question. It would have to be one-to-one, as we saw, to provide distinct images of distinct real numbers; and a one-to-one mapping of an indenumerable domain into a denumerable one is a contradiction. In particular it is easy to show in the Zermelo–Fraenkel system of set theory that such a function would neither exist nor admit even of formulation as a virtual class in the notation of the system.

The discussion of the ontology of a theory can make variously stringent demands upon the

background theory in which the discussion is couched. The stringency of these demands varies with what is being said about the ontology of the object theory. We are now in a position to distinguish three such grades of stringency.

The least stringent demand is made when, with no view to reduction, we merely explain what things a theory is about, or what things its terms denote. This amounts to showing how to translate part or all of the object theory into the background theory. It is a matter really of showing how we *propose*, with some arbitrariness, to relate terms of the object theory to terms of the background theory; for we have the inscrutability of reference to allow for. But there is here no requirement that the background theory have a wider universe or a stronger vocabulary than the object theory. The theories could even be identical; this is the case when some terms are clarified by definition on the basis of other terms of the same language.

A more stringent demand was observed in the case where a proxy function is used to reduce an ontology. In this case the background theory needed the unreduced universe. But we saw, by considerations akin to *reductio ad absurdum*, that there was little here to regret.

The third grade of stringency has emerged now in the kind of ontological reduction hinted at by the Löwenheim–Skolem theorem. If a theory has by its own account an indenumerable universe, then even by taking that whole unreduced theory as background theory we cannot hope to produce a proxy function that would be adequate to reducing the ontology to a denumerable one. To find such a proxy function, even just a virtual one, we would need a background theory essentially stronger than the theory we were trying to reduce. This demand cannot, like the second grade of stringency above, be accepted in the spirit of *reductio ad absurdum*. It is a demand that simply discourages any general argument for Pythagoreanism from the Löwenheim–Skolem theorem.

A place where we see a more trivial side of ontological relativity is in the case of a finite universe of named objects. Here there is no occasion for quantification, except as an inessential abbreviation; for we can expand quantifications into finite conjunctions and alternations. Variables thus disappear, and with them the question of a universe of values of variables. And the very

* *The Ways of Paradox*, pp. 204ff.

distinction between names and other signs lapses in turn, since the mark of a name is its admissibility in positions of variables. Ontology thus is emphatically meaningless for a finite theory of named objects, considered in and of itself. Yet we are now talking meaningfully of such finite ontologies. We are able to do so precisely because we are talking, however vaguely and implicitly, within a broader containing theory. What the objects of the finite theory are, makes sense only as a statement of the background theory in its own referential idiom. The answer to the question depends on the background theory, the finite foreground theory, and, of course, the particular manner in which we choose to translate or embed the one in the other.

Ontology is internally indifferent also, I think, to any theory that is complete and decidable. Where we can always settle truth values mechanically, there is no evident internal reason for interest in the theory of quantifiers nor, therefore, in values of variables. These matters take on significance only as we think of the decidable theory as embedded in a richer background theory in which the variables and their values are serious business.

Ontology may also be said to be internally indifferent even to a theory that is not decidable and does not have a finite universe, if it happens still that each of the infinitely numerous objects of the theory has a name. We can no longer expand quantifications into conjunctions and alternations, barring infinitely long expressions. We can, however, revise our semantical account of the truth conditions of quantification, in such a way as to turn our backs on questions of reference. We can explain universal quantifications as true when true under all substitutions; and correspondingly for existential. Such is the course that has been favored by Leśniewski and by Ruth Marcus.* Its nonreferential orientation is seen in the fact that it makes no essential use of name-

hood. That is, additional quantifications could be explained whose variables are place-holders for words of any syntactical category. *Substitutional* quantification, as I call it, thus brings no way of distinguishing names from other vocabulary, nor any way of distinguishing between genuinely referential or value-taking variables and other place-holders. Ontology is thus meaningless for a theory whose only quantification is substitutionally construed; meaningless, that is, insofar as the theory is considered in and of itself. The question of its ontology makes sense only relative to some translation of the theory into a background theory in which we use referential quantification. The answer depends on both theories and, again, on the chosen way of translating the one into the other.

A final touch of relativity can in some cases cap this, when we try to distinguish between substitutional and referential quantification. Suppose again a theory with an infinite lot of names, and suppose that, by Gödel numbering or otherwise, we are treating of the theory's notations and proofs within the terms of the theory. If we succeed in showing that every result of substituting a name for the variable in a certain open sentence is true in the theory, but at the same time we disprove the universal quantification of the sentence,† then certainly we have shown that the universe of the theory contained some nameless objects. This is a case where an absolute decision can be reached in favor of referential quantification and against substitutional quantification, without ever retreating to a background theory.

But consider now the opposite situation, where there is no such open sentence. Imagine on the contrary that, whenever an open sentence is such that each result of substituting a name in it can be proved, its universal quantification can be proved in the theory too. Under these circumstances we can construe the universe as devoid of nameless objects and hence reconstrue the quantifications as substitutional, but we need not. We could still construe the universe as containing nameless objects. It could just happen that the nameless ones are *inseparable* from the

---

* Ruth B. Marcus, "Modalities and intensional languages," *Synthese* 13 (1961), 303–322. I cannot locate an adequate statement of Stanislaw Leśniewski's philosophy of quantification in his writings; I have it from his conversations. E. C. Luschei, in *The Logical Systems of Leśniewski* (Amsterdam: North-Holland, 1962), pp. 108ff., confirms my attribution but still cites no passage. On this version of quantification see further "Existence and Quantification," in this volume.

† Such is the typical way of a numerically insegregative system, misleadingly called "ω-inconsistent." See my *Selected Logic Papers* (New York: Random House, 1966), pp. 118ff., or *Journal of Symbolic Logic*, 1953, pp. 122ff.

named ones, in this sense: it could happen that all properties of nameless objects that we can express in the notation of the theory are shared by named objects.

We could construe the universe of the theory as containing, e.g., all real numbers. Some of them are nameless, since the real numbers are indenumerable while the names are denumerable. But it could still happen that the nameless reals are inseparable from the named reals. This would leave us unable within the theory to prove a distinction between referential and substitutional quantification.* Every expressible quantification that is true when referentially construed remains true when substitutionally construed, and vice versa.

We might still make the distinction from the vantage point of a background theory. In it we might specify some real number that was nameless in the object theory; for there are always ways of strengthening a theory so as to name more real numbers, though never all. Further, in the background theory, we might construe the universe of the object theory as exhausting the real numbers. In the background theory we could, in this way, clinch the quantifications in the object theory as referential. But this clinching is doubly relative: it is relative to the background theory and to the interpretation or translation imposed on the object theory from within the background theory.

One might hope that this recourse to a background theory could often be avoided, even when the nameless reals are inseparable from the named reals in the object theory. One might hope by indirect means to show within the object theory that there are nameless reals. For we might prove within the object theory that the reals are indenumerable and that the names are denumerable and hence that there is no function whose arguments are names and whose values exhaust the real numbers. Since the relation of real numbers to their names would be such a function if each real number had a name, we would seem to have proved within the object theory itself that there are nameless reals and hence that quantification must be taken referentially.

However, this is wrong; there is a loophole. This reasoning would prove only that a relation of all

real numbers to their names cannot exist as an entity in the universe of the theory. This reasoning denies no number a name in the notation of the theory, as long as the name relation does not belong to the universe of the theory. And anyway we should know better than to expect such a relation, for it is what causes Berry's and Richard's and related paradoxes.

Some theories can attest to their own nameless objects and so claim referential quantification on their own; other theories have to look to background theories for this service. We saw how a theory might attest to its own nameless objects, namely, by showing that some open sentence became true under all constant substitutions but false under universal quantification. Perhaps this is the only way a theory can claim referential import for its own quantifications. Perhaps, when the nameless objects happen to be inseparable from the named, the quantification used in a theory cannot meaningfully be declared referential except through the medium of a background theory. Yet referential quantification is the key idiom of ontology.

Thus ontology can be multiply relative, multiply meaningless apart from a background theory. Besides being unable to say in absolute terms just what the objects are, we are sometimes unable even to distinguish objectively between referential quantification and a substitutional counterfeit. When we do relativize these matters to a background theory, moreover, the relativization itself has two components: relativity to the choice of background theory and relativity to the choice of how to translate the object theory into the background theory. As for the ontology in turn of the background theory, and even the referentiality of its quantification – these matters can call for a background theory in turn.

There is not always a genuine regress. We saw that, if we are merely clarifying the range of the variables of a theory or the denotations of its terms, and are taking the referentiality of quantification itself for granted, we can commonly use the object theory itself as background theory. We found that when we undertake an ontological reduction, we must accept at least the unreduced theory in order to cite the proxy function; but this we were able cheerfully to accept in the spirit of *reductio ad absurdum* arguments. And now in the end we have found further that if we care to question quantification itself, and settle whether

---

* This possibility was suggested by Saul Kripke.

it imports a universe of discourse or turns merely on substitution at the linguistic level, we in some cases have genuinely to regress to a background language endowed with additional resources. We seem to have to do this unless the nameless objects are separable from the named in the object theory.

Regress in ontology is reminiscent of the now familiar regress in the semantics of truth and kindred notions – satisfaction, naming. We know from Tarski's work how the semantics, in this sense, of a theory regularly demands an in some way more inclusive theory. This similarity should perhaps not surprise us, since both ontology and satisfaction are matters of reference. In their elusiveness, at any rate – in their emptiness now and again except relative to a broader background – both truth and ontology may in a suddenly rather clear and even tolerant sense be said to belong to transcendental metaphysics.*

* In developing these thoughts I have been helped by discussions with Saul Kripke, Thomas Nagel, and especially Burton Dreben.

IV
Philosophy of Religion

1

Plato, *Euthyphro* and the "Ladder of Loves" from *Symposium* (201c–212c)

Introduction

Thales of Miletus (fl. c. 585 BCE) has been called the first philosopher for holding that "all is water," but Thales is also supposed to have maintained that all is "full of gods" and that "soul is intermingled in the universe." Early Greek philosophers, despite their turn away from traditional religion, in fact remained deeply involved with topics related to the divine. Thales' successor Anaximander (c. 610–c. 546 BCE) was intrigued with a sort of supernatural infinitude, the "limitless" (ἄπειρον), as well as with how all things originate from it and return to it. Pythagoreans elaborated the manifestation of two related and quasi-divine principles, the "limited" and the "unlimited." Empedocles (c. 484–424 BCE) found in the universe twinned godlike principles, "love" (φιλία) and "strife" (νεῖκος). Anaxagoras (c. 500–c. 428 BCE), by contrast, discerned a great cosmic intelligence (*nôus*) guiding the separation and combining of all things.

While these early philosophers of the divine might be thought of as pursuing investigations aimed principally at metaphysical explanation

and moral instruction, another stream of early philosophical thought about the divine was more decidedly critical. Xenophanes (570–478 BCE) criticized the pantheon of Homer and Hesiod for its anthropomorphism, its polytheism, and for the moral failings of its deities: "if oxen, horses, and lions had hands or could paint . . . horses would paint horse-like images of gods and oxen oxen-like ones, and each would fashion bodies like their own." Plato (c. 424–c. 348 BCE), whose thought would become deeply influential to Christian and Islamic theology, combined all these preceding streams, developing critical as well as explanatory and instructive lines of thought in what might today be discerned as his philosophy of religion. There is perhaps no better place to see this than his dialogue, *Euthyphro*.

Plato's dialogues depicting the trial and death of Socrates (469–399 BCE) portray his teacher confronting the social and political authorities that had prosecuted him. In the *Apology*, which recounts the trial proper, Socrates cross-examines representatives of the political orators (Lycon), the craftsmen (Anytus), and the poets (Meletus) who had charged him with corrupting Athens' youth (23e). But the most important elements of these allegations of corruption also included the charge that Socrates somehow threatened Athens' official religious order.[1] To understand Plato's understanding of Socrates' response to that charge (and perhaps by extension something of Plato's philosophy of religion), one must turn to the *Euthyphro*. The *Euthyphro* is set in the law courts of the

From Plato, *The Trial and Death of Socrates*, trans. G. M. A. Grube, Indianapolis, IN: Hackett Publishing Co., Inc. 1975, pp. 3–20; and from Plato, *Symposium*, trans. B. Jowett, New York: Dover Publications, Inc., 1993, pp. 23–34.

Athenian *agora* where Socrates has come to answer the indictment brought against him. More pointedly, however, it's in this dialogue where Socrates directly confronts religious authorities, or at least those who make claim to religious authority.

The action of the dialogue turns upon Socrates exposing the confusion afflicting a young man he happens upon at the courts – Euthyphro – whose dogmatic misunderstanding of religious truth has led him to prosecute his own father (much as others are prosecuting Socrates). Through the dynamics of this drama, Plato legitimates what would become later traditions in western philosophy of subjecting claims to religious authority to relentless rational, analytic critique. The particular line of questioning Plato's Socrates undertakes with Euthyphro itself becomes a powerful and controversial critical device, one that many believe shows that appeals to the divine cannot by themselves, without rational justification, underwrite moral authority.

The crux of this vexing topic surfaces when Socrates presents Euthyphro with a simple but devastating question (10a–11c): "Is the pious [*to hosios*][2] loved by the gods because it is pious, or is it pious because it is loved by the gods?" More broadly, one might ask whether the deity commands what is morally good because it is in itself good; or is it good simply because the deity commands it? In part, Plato's pursuit of this issue exhibits his concern to establish a rational, objective foundation for moral truth, rather than make morality the arbitrary result of choice or will – even God's will (a theological position that has come to be known as moral "voluntarism"; see IV.10). Many, like Plato, have found voluntarism unappealing because it seems to imply that God could by an arbitrary act of will substitute what is now commanded to be good and obligatory with what is now commanded to be evil and prohibited. If God commanded rape and murder, it would then become the duty of every moral agent to rape and murder.[3]

If, on the other hand, what is pious and good are not so simply because a deity designates them to be, then it seems something very important follows regarding the divine nature: whatever else it is, the divine is not itself the ground of moral goodness or piety. An independent standard must exist, perhaps a rational standard that can be apprehended by the human intellect, perhaps a standard that constrains even the divine.

Plato's regard for the importance of reason in understanding the divine is also manifest in his dialogue, *Symposium*, whose *mise-en-scène* is a drinking party and oratory contest on the topic of love pitting Socrates against playwrights as well as legal and medical authorities. Socrates' speech in the *Symposium* relates his having been instructed by the priestess or seer, Diotima, about the way both "reason" (λόγος) and "desire" (ἔρως) are together necessary to acquire an apprehension of divine reality. In a way that would influence neo-Platonists like Plotinus (III.6), Proclus, and Augustine (IV.3; in particular, *Confessions* IX.10), as well as countless religious thinkers, Plato describes a process of transcendence where the love and apprehension of material objects through the senses gives way to the more abstract love and apprehension of persons, institutions, theories, and ideas through the intellect. Driven by the engine of desire towards the object of its most profound satisfaction and guided towards this final destination by the rational power of reason, the soul transcends the body, materiality, and other shadows of divinity, moving upwards until, in a flash, the beautiful itself, the unifying ground of all reality bursts forth. It may be important to keep in mind, however, that in his *Seventh Letter*, Plato denies ever having written anything directly about ultimate truth (341c–d), and in *Phaedrus* he calls into question the capacity of written works to convey philosophical thought at all (274bff.). Both gestures may indicate Plato's keen awareness of the limitations of human language or conceptualization concerning matters divine.

Notes

1   In the *Apology*, Plato recounts variously that Socrates was charged with "something like": (1) "studying things in the sky and below the earth" (19b, 23d), which might be naturalistic pre-Socratic philosophy like that of Anaxagoras et al., to whom Plato refers in the *Phaedo* (95a–100a), his dialogue about Socrates' execution; (2) making "the worse into the stronger argument" (*Apology*, 19b, 23d); (3) "teaching the same" (19b); and (4) "corrupting the young" (24b).

2   The term, *hosios*, means something like the state of mind or condition of one whose conduct accords with divine law; in this it is

related to the idea of the "holy" distinct, as the divine itself may be considered holy.

3 Duns Scotus (1266–1308) and William of Ockham (1287–1347) are often associated with

voluntarist positions (see IV.10 in this volume). From the implications of God being both free and omnipotent, Ockham argued that God can invert the moral universe at any time.

Plato, *Euthyphro*

2 EUTHYPHRO:* What's new, Socrates, to make you leave your usual haunts in the Lyceum and spend your time here by the king-archon's court? Surely you are not prosecuting anyone before the king-archon as I am?

SOCRATES: The Athenians do not call this a prosecution but an indictment, Euthyphro.

E: What is this you say? Someone must have indicted you, for you are not going to tell me that you have indicted someone else.

S: No indeed.

E: But someone else has indicted you?

S: Quite so.

E: Who is he?

S: I do not really know him myself, Euthyphro. He is apparently young and unknown. They call him Meletus, I believe. He belongs to the Pitthean deme, if you know anyone from that deme called Meletus, with long hair, not much of a beard, and a rather aquiline nose.

E: I don't know him, Socrates. What charge does he bring against you?

S: What charge? A not ignoble one I think, for it is no small thing for a young man to have knowledge of such an important subject. He says he knows how our young men are corrupted and who corrupts them. He is likely to be wise, and when he sees my ignorance corrupting his contemporaries, he proceeds to accuse me to the city as to their mother. I think he is the only one of our public men to start out the right way, for it is right to care first that the young should be as good as possible, just as a good farmer is likely to take care of the young plants first, and of the

others later. So, too, Meletus first gets rid of us who corrupt the young shoots, as he says, and then afterwards he will obviously take care of the older ones and become a source of great blessings for the city, as seems likely to happen to one who started out this way.

E: I could wish this were true, Socrates, but I fear the opposite may happen. He seems to me to start out by harming the very heart of the city by attempting to wrong you. Tell me, what does he say you do to corrupt the young?

S: Strange things, to hear him tell it, for he says that I am a maker of gods, and on the ground that I create new gods while not believing in the old gods, he has indicted me for their sake, as he puts it.

E: I understand, Socrates. This is because you say that the divine sign keeps coming to you.† So he has written this indictment against you as one who makes innovations in religious matters, and he comes to court to slander you, knowing that such things are easily misrepresented to the crowd. The same is true in my case. Whenever I speak of divine matters in the assembly and foretell the future, they laugh me down as if I were crazy; and yet I have foretold nothing that did not happen. Nevertheless, they envy all of us who do this. One need not worry about them, but meet them head-on.

S: My dear Euthyphro, to be laughed at does not matter perhaps, for the Athenians do not mind anyone they think clever, as long as he does not teach his own wisdom, but if they think that he makes others to be like himself they get angry, whether through envy, as you say, or for some other reason.

3

---

* We know nothing about Euthyphro except what we can gather from this dialogue. He is obviously a professional priest who considers himself an expert on ritual and on piety generally, and, it seems, is generally so considered. One Euthyphro is mentioned in Plato's *Cratylus* (396d) who is given to *enthousiasmos*, inspiration or possession, but we cannot be sure that it is the same person.

† In Plato, Socrates always speaks of his divine sign or voice as intervening to prevent him from doing or saying something (e.g., *Apology* 31d), but never positively. The popular view was that it enabled him to foretell the future, and Euthyphro here represents that view. Note, however, that Socrates dissociates himself from "you prophets" (3e).

E: I have certainly no desire to test their feelings towards me in this matter.

S: Perhaps you seem to make yourself but rarely available, and not to be willing to teach your own wisdom, but I'm afraid that my liking for people makes them think that I pour out to anybody anything I have to say, not only without charging a fee but even glad to reward anyone who is willing to listen. If then they were intending to laugh at me, as you say they laugh at you, there would be nothing unpleasant in their spending their time in court laughing and jesting, but if they are going to be serious, the outcome is not clear except to you prophets.

E: Perhaps it will come to nothing, Socrates, and you will fight your case as you think best, as I think I will mine.

S: What is your case, Euthyphro? Are you the defendant or the prosecutor?

E: The prosecutor.

S: Whom do you prosecute?

4 E: One whom I am thought crazy to prosecute.

S: Are you pursuing someone who will easily escape you?

E: Far from it, for he is quite old.

S: Who is it?

E: My father.

S: My dear sir! Your own father?

E: Certainly.

S: What is the charge? What is the case about?

E: Murder, Socrates.

S: Good heavens! Certainly, Euthyphro, most men would not know how they could do this and be right. It is not the part of anyone to do this, but of one who is far advanced in wisdom.

E: Yes, by Zeus, Socrates, that is so.

S: Is then the man your father killed one of your relatives? Or is that obvious, for you would not prosecute your father for the murder of a stranger.

E: It is ridiculous, Socrates, for you to think that it makes any difference whether the victim is a stranger or a relative. One should only watch whether the killer acted justly or not; if he acted justly, let him go, but if not, one should prosecute, even if the killer shares your hearth and table. The pollution is the same if you knowingly keep company with such a man and do not cleanse yourself and him by bringing him to justice. The victim was a dependent of mine, and when we were farming in Naxos he was a servant of ours.

He killed one of our household slaves in drunken anger, so my father bound him hand and foot and threw him in a ditch, then sent a man here to enquire from the priest what should be done. During that time he gave no thought or care to the bound man, as being a killer, and it was no matter if he died, which he did. Hunger and cold and his bonds caused his death before the messenger came back from the seer. Both my father and my other relatives are angry that I am prosecuting my father for murder on behalf of a murderer when he hadn't even killed him, they say, and even if he had, the dead man does not deserve a thought, since he was a killer. For, they say, it is impious for a son to prosecute his father for murder. But their ideas of the divine attitude to piety and impiety are wrong, Socrates.

S: Whereas, by Zeus, Euthyphro, you think that your knowledge of the divine, and of piety and impiety, is so accurate that, when those things happened as you say, you have no fear of having acted impiously in bringing your father to trial?

E: I should be of no use, Socrates, and Euthyphro would not be superior to the majority of men, if I did not have accurate knowledge of all 5 such things.

S: It is indeed most important, my admirable Euthyphro, that I should become your pupil, and as regards this indictment challenge Meletus about these very things and say to him: that in the past too I considered knowledge about the divine to be most important, and that now that he says that I am guilty of improvising and innovating about the gods I have become your pupil. I would say to him: "If, Meletus, you agree that Euthyphro is wise in these matters, consider me, too, to have the right beliefs and do not bring me to trial. If you do not think so, then prosecute that teacher of mine, not me, for corrupting the older men, me and his own father, by teaching me and by exhorting and punishing him." If he is not convinced, and does not discharge me or indict you instead of me, I shall repeat the same challenge in court.

E: Yes, by Zeus, Socrates, and, if he should try to indict me, I think I would find his weak spots and the talk in court would be about him rather than about me.

S: It is because I realize this that I am eager to become your pupil, my dear friend. I know that other people as well as this Meletus do not even seem to notice you, whereas he sees me so sharply and clearly that he indicts me for ungodliness. So tell me now, by Zeus, what you just now maintained you clearly knew: what kind of thing do you say that godliness and ungodliness are, both as regards murder and other things; or is the pious not the same and alike in every action, and the impious the opposite of all that is pious and like itself, and everything that is to be impious presents us with one form* or appearance in so far as it is impious?

E: Most certainly, Socrates.

S: Tell me then, what is the pious, and what the impious, do you say?

E: I say that the pious is to do what I am doing now, to prosecute the wrongdoer, be it about murder or temple robbery or anything else, whether the wrongdoer is your father or your mother or anyone else; not to prosecute is impious. And observe, Socrates, that I can quote the law as a great proof that this is so. I have already said to others that such actions are right, not to favour the ungodly, whoever they are. These people themselves believe that Zeus is the best and most 6 just of the gods, yet they agree that he bound his father because he unjustly swallowed his sons, and that he in turn castrated his father for similar reasons. But they are angry with me because I am prosecuting my father for his wrongdoing. They contradict themselves in what they say about the gods and about me.

S: Indeed, Euthyphro, this is the reason why I am a defendant in the case, because I find it hard to accept things like that being said about the gods, and it is likely to be the reason why I shall be told I do wrong. Now, however, if you, who have full knowledge of such things, share their opinions, then we must agree with them too, it would seem. For what are we to say, we who agree that we our-

selves have no knowledge of them? Tell me, by the god of friendship, do you really believe these things are true?

E: Yes, Socrates, and so are even more surprising things, of which the majority has no knowledge.

S: And do you believe that there really is war among the gods, and terrible enmities and battles, and other such things as are told by the poets, and other sacred stories such as are embroidered by good writers and by representations of which the robe of the goddess is adorned when it is carried up to the Acropolis? Are we to say these things are true, Euthyphro?

E: Not only these, Socrates, but, as I was saying just now, I will, if you wish, relate many other things about the gods which I know will amaze you.

S: I should not be surprised, but you will tell me these at leisure some other time. For now, try to tell me more clearly what I was asking just now, for, my friend, you did not teach me adequately when I asked you what the pious was, but you told me that what you are doing now, prosecuting your father for murder, is pious.

E: And I told the truth, Socrates.

S: Perhaps. You agree, however, that there are many other pious actions.

E: There are.

S: Bear in mind then that I did not bid you tell me one or two of the many pious actions but that form itself that makes all pious actions pious, for you agreed that all impious actions are impious and all pious actions pious through one form, or don't you remember?

E: I do.

S: Tell me then what this form itself is, so that I may look upon it, and using it as a model, say that any action of yours or another's that is of that kind is pious, and if it is not that it is not.

E: If that is how you want it, Socrates, that is how I will tell you.

S: That is what I want.

E: Well then, what is dear to the gods is 7 pious, what is not is impious.

S: Splendid, Euthyphro! You have now answered in the way I wanted. Whether your answer is true I do not know yet, but you will obviously show me that what you say is true.

E: Certainly.

S: Come then, let us examine what we mean. An action or a man dear to the gods is pious, but

---

* This is the kind of passage that makes it easier for us to follow the transition from Socrates' universal definitions to the Platonic theory of separately existent eternal universal Forms. The words *eidos* and *idea*, the technical terms for the Platonic Forms, commonly mean physical stature or bodily appearance. As we apply a common epithet, in this case pious, to different actions or things, these must have a common characteristic, present a common appearance or form, to justify the use of the same term, but in the early dialogues, as here, it seems to be thought of as immanent in the particulars and without separate existence. The same is true of 6d where the word "Form" is also used.

an action or a man hated by the gods is impious. They are not the same, but quite opposite, the pious and the impious. Is that not so?

E: It is indeed.

S: And that seems to be a good statement?

E: I think so, Socrates.

S: We have also stated that the gods are in a state of discord, that they are at odds with each other, Euthyphro, and that they are at enmity with each other. Has that, too, been said?

E: It has.

S: What are the subjects of difference that cause hatred and anger? Let us look at it this way. If you and I were to differ about numbers as to which is the greater, would this difference make us enemies and angry with each other, or would we proceed to count and soon resolve our difference about this?

E: We would certainly do so.

S: Again, if we differed about the larger and the smaller, we would turn to measurement and soon cease to differ.

E: That is so.

S: And about the heavier and the lighter, we would resort to weighing and be reconciled.

E: Of course.

S: What subject of difference would make us angry and hostile to each other if we were unable to come to a decision? Perhaps you do not have an answer ready, but examine as I tell you whether these subjects are the just and the unjust, the beautiful and the ugly, the good and the bad. Are these not the subjects of difference about which, when we are unable to come to a satisfactory decision, you and I and other men become hostile to each other whenever we do?

E: That is the difference, Socrates, about those subjects.

S: What about the gods, Euthyphro? If indeed they have differences, will it not be about these same subjects?

E: It certainly must be so.

S: Then according to your argument, my good Euthyphro, different gods consider different things to be just, beautiful, ugly, good, and bad, for they would not be at odds with one another unless they differed about these subjects, would they?

E: You are right.

S: And they like what each of them considers beautiful, good, and just, and hate the opposites of these?

E: Certainly.

S: But you say that the same things are considered just by some gods and unjust by others, and as they dispute about these things they are at odds and at war with each other. Is that not so?

E: It is.

S: The same things then are loved by the gods and hated by the gods, and would be both god-loved and god-hated.

E: It seems likely.

S: And the same things would be both pious and impious, according to this argument?

E: I'm afraid so.

S: So you did not answer my question, you surprising man. I did not ask you what same thing is both pious and impious, and it appears that what is loved by the gods is also hated by them. So it is in no way surprising if your present action, namely punishing your father, may be pleasing to Zeus but displeasing to Kronos and Ouranos, pleasing to Hephaestus but displeasing to Hera, and so with any other gods who differ from each other on this subject.

E: I think, Socrates, that on this subject no gods would differ from one another, that whoever has killed anyone unjustly should pay the penalty.

S: Well now, Euthyphro, have you ever heard any man maintaining that one who has killed or done anything else unjustly should not pay the penalty?

E: They never cease to dispute on this subject, both elsewhere and in the courts, for when they have committed many wrongs they do and say anything to avoid the penalty.

S: Do they agree they have done wrong, Euthyphro, and in spite of so agreeing do they nevertheless say they should not be punished?

E: No, they do not agree on that point.

S: So they do not say or do anything. For they do not venture to say this, or dispute that they must not pay the penalty if they have done wrong, but I think they deny doing wrong. Is that not so?

E: That is true.

S: Then they do not dispute that the wrongdoer must be punished, but they may disagree as to who the wrongdoer is, what he did and when.

E: You are right.

S: Do not the gods have the same experience, if indeed they are at odds with each other about the just and the unjust, as your argument maintains? Some assert that they wrong one another, while others deny it, but no one among gods or men ventures to say that the wrongdoer must not be punished.

E: Yes, that is true, Socrates, as to the main point.

S: And those who disagree, whether men or gods, dispute about each action, if indeed the gods disagree. Some say it is done justly, others unjustly. Is that not so?

E: Yes, indeed.

9   S: Come now, my dear Euthyphro, tell me, too, that I may become wiser, what proof you have that all the gods consider that man to have been killed unjustly who became a murderer while in your service, was bound by the master of his victim, and died in his bonds before the one who bound him found out from the seers what was to be done with him, and that it is right for a son to denounce and to prosecute his father on behalf of such a man. Come, try to show me a clear sign that all the gods definitely believe this action to be right. If you can give me adequate proof of this, I shall never cease to extol your wisdom.

E: This is perhaps no light task, Socrates, though I could show you very clearly.

S: I understand that you think me more dull-witted than the jury, as you will obviously show them that these actions were unjust and that all the gods hate such actions.

E: I will show it to them clearly, Socrates, if only they will listen to me.

S: They will listen if they think you show them well. But this thought came to me as you were speaking, and I am examining it, saying to myself: "If Euthyphro shows me conclusively that all the gods consider such a death unjust, to what greater extent have I learned from him the nature of piety and impiety? This action would then, it seems, be hated by the gods, but the pious and the impious were not thereby now defined, for what is hated by the gods has also been shown to be loved by them." So I will not insist on this point; let us assume, if you wish, that all the gods consider this unjust and that they all hate it. However, is this the correction we are making in our discussion, that what all the gods hate is impious, and what they all love is pious, and that what some gods love and others hate is neither or both? Is that how you now wish us to define piety and impiety?

E: What prevents us from doing so, Socrates?

S: For my part nothing, Euthyphro, but you look whether on your part this proposal will enable you to teach me most easily what you promised.

E: I would certainly say that the pious is what all the gods love, and the opposite, what all the gods hate, is the impious.

S: Then let us again examine whether that is a sound statement, or do we let it pass, and if one of us, or someone else, merely says that something is so, do we accept that it is so? Or should we examine what the speaker means?

E: We must examine it, but I certainly think that this is now a fine statement.

S: We shall soon know better whether it 10 is. Consider this: Is the pious loved by the gods because it is pious, or is it pious because it is loved by the gods?

E: I don't know what you mean, Socrates.

S: I shall try to explain more clearly: we speak of something being carried* and something carrying, of something being led and something leading, of something being seen and something seeing, and you understand that these things are all different from one another and how they differ?

E: I think I do.

S: So there is something being loved and something loving, and the loving is a different thing.

E: Of course.

S: Tell me then whether that which is being carried is being carried because someone carries it or for some other reason.

E: No, that is the reason.

---

* This is the present participle form of the verb *pheromenon*, literally *being-carried*. The following passage is somewhat obscure, especially in translation, but the general meaning is clear. Plato points out that this participle simply indicates the object of an action of carrying, seeing, loving, etc. It follows from the action and adds nothing new, the action being prior to it, not following from it, and a thing is said to be loved because someone loves it, not vice versa. To say therefore that the pious is being loved by the gods says no more than that the gods love it. Euthyphro, however, also agrees that the pious is loved by the gods because of its nature (because it is pious), but the fact of its being loved by the gods does not define that nature, and as a definition is therefore unsatisfactory. It only indicates a quality or affect of the pious, and the pious is therefore still to be defined (11a7).

S: And that which is being led is so because someone leads it, and that which is being seen because someone sees it?

E: Certainly.

S: It is not seen by someone because it is being seen but on the contrary it is being seen because someone sees it, nor is it because it is being led that someone leads it but because someone leads it that it is being led; nor does someone carry an object because it is being carried, but it is being carried because someone carries it. Is what I want to say clear, Euthyphro? I want to say this, namely, that if anything comes to be, or is affected, it does not come to be because it is coming to be, but it is coming to be because it comes to be; nor is it affected because it is being affected but because something affects it. Or do you not agree?

E: I do.

S: What is being loved is either something that comes to be or something that is affected by something?

E: Certainly.

S: So it is in the same case as the things just mentioned; it is not loved by those who love it because it is being loved, but it is being loved because they love it?

E: Necessarily.

S: What then do we say about the pious, Euthyphro? Surely that it is loved by all the gods, according to what you say?

E: Yes.

S: Is it loved because it is pious, or for some other reason?

E: For no other reason.

S: It is loved then because it is pious, but it is not pious because it is loved?*

E: Apparently.

* I quote an earlier comment of mine on this passage: "... it gives in a nutshell a point of view from which Plato never departed. Whatever the gods may be, they must by their very nature love the right because it is right." They have no choice in the matter. "This separation of the dynamic power of the gods from the ultimate reality, this setting up of absolute values above the gods themselves was not as unnatural to a Greek as it would be to us. ... The gods who ruled on Olympus ... were not creators but created beings. As in Homer, Zeus must obey the balance of Necessity, so the Platonic gods must conform to an eternal scale of values. They did not create them, cannot alter them, cannot indeed wish to do so." (*Plato's Thought*, Indianapolis: Hackett Publishing Co., 1980, pp. 152–3.)

S: And because it is loved by the gods it is being loved and is dear to the gods?

E: Of course.

S: The god-beloved is then not the same as the pious, Euthyphro, nor the pious the same as the god-beloved, as you say it is, but one differs from the other.

E: How so, Socrates?

S: Because we agree that the pious is beloved for the reason that it is pious, but it is not pious because it is loved. Is that not so?

E: Yes.

S: And that the god-beloved, on the other hand, is so because it is loved by the gods, by the very fact of being loved, but it is not loved because it is god-beloved.

E: True.

S: But if the god-beloved and the pious were the same, my dear Euthyphro, and the pious were loved because it was pious, then the god-beloved would be loved because it was god-beloved, and if the god-beloved was god-beloved because it was loved by the gods, then the pious would also be pious because it was loved by the gods; but now you see that they are in opposite cases as being altogether different from each other: the one is of a nature to be loved because it is loved, the other is loved because it is of a nature to be loved. I'm afraid, Euthyphro, that when you were asked what piety is, you did not wish to make its nature clear to me, but you told me an affect or quality of it, that the pious has the quality of being loved by all the gods, but you have not yet told me what the pious is. Now, if you will, do not hide things from me but tell me again from the beginning what piety is, whether loved by the gods or having some other quality – we shall not quarrel about that – but be keen to tell me what the pious and the impious are.

E: But Socrates, I have no way of telling you what I have in mind, for whatever proposition we put forward goes around and refuses to stay put where we establish it.

S: Your statements, Euthyphro, seem to belong to my ancestor, Daedalus. If I were stating them and putting them forward, you would perhaps be making fun of me and say that because of my kinship with him my conclusions in discussion run away and will not stay where one puts them. As these propositions are yours, however, we need some other jest, for they will not stay put for you, as you say yourself.

11

E: I think the same jest will do for our discussion, Socrates, for I am not the one who makes them go round and not remain in the same place; it is you who are the Daedalus; for as far as I am concerned they would remain as they were.

S: It looks as if I was cleverer than Daedalus in using my skill, my friend, in so far as he could only cause to move the things he made himself, but I can make other people's move as well as my own. And the smartest part of my skill is that I am clever without wanting to be, for I would rather have your statements to me remain unmoved than possess the wealth of Tantalus as well as the cleverness of Daedalus. But enough of this. Since I think you are making unnecessary difficulties, I am as eager as you are to find a way to teach me about piety, and do not give up before you do. See whether you think all that is pious is of necessity just.

E: I think so.

S: And is then all that is just pious? Or is all that is pious just, but not all that is just pious, but some of it is and some is not?

E: I do not follow what you are saying, Socrates.

S: Yet you are younger than I by as much as you are wiser. As I say, you are making difficulties because of your wealth of wisdom. Pull yourself together, my dear sir, what I am saying is not difficult to grasp. I am saying the opposite of what the poet said who wrote:

You do not wish to name Zeus, who had done it, and who made all things grow, for where there is fear there is also shame.

I disagree with the poet. Shall I tell you why?

E: Please do.

S: I do not think that "where there is fear there is also shame," for I think that many people who fear disease and poverty and many other such things feel fear, but are not ashamed of the things they fear. Do you not think so?

E: I do indeed.

S: But where there is shame there is also fear. For is there anyone who, in feeling shame and embarrassment at anything, does not also at the same time fear and dread a reputation for wickedness?

E: He is certainly afraid.

S: It is then not right to say "where there is fear there is also shame," but that where there is shame there is also fear, for fear covers a larger area than shame. Shame is a part of fear just as

odd is a part of number, with the result that it is not true that where there is number there is also oddness, but that where there is oddness there is also number. Do you follow me now?

E: Surely.

S: This is the kind of thing I was asking before, whether where there is piety there is also justice, but where there is justice there is not always piety, for the pious is a part of justice. Shall we say that, or do you think otherwise?

E: No, but like that, for what you say appears to be right.

S: See what comes next: if the pious is a part of the just, we must, it seems, find out what part of the just it is. Now if you asked me something of what we mentioned just now, such as what part of number is the even, and what number that is, I would say it is the number that is divisible into two equal, not unequal, parts. Or do you not think so?

E: I do.

S: Try in this way to tell me what part of the just the pious is, in order to tell Meletus not to wrong us any more and not to indict me for ungodliness, since I have learned from you sufficiently what is godly and pious and what is not.

E: I think, Socrates, that the godly and pious is the part of the just that is concerned with the care of the gods, while that concerned with the care of men is the remaining part of justice.

S: You seem to me to put that very well, but I still need a bit of information. I do not know yet what you mean by care, for you do not mean the care of the gods in the same sense as the care of other things, as, for example, we say, don't we, that not everyone knows how to care for horses, but the horse breeder does.

E: Yes, I do mean it that way.

S: So horse breeding is the care of horses.

E: Yes.

S: Nor does everyone know how to care for dogs, but the hunter does.

E: That is so.

S: So hunting is the care of dogs.

E: Yes.

S: And cattle raising is the care of cattle.

E: Quite so.

S: While piety and godliness is the care of the gods, Euthyphro. Is that what you mean?

E: It is.

S: Now care in each case has the same effect; it aims at the good and the benefit of the object cared for, as you can see that horses cared for by horse breeders are benefited and become better. Or do you not think so?

E: I do.

S: So dogs are benefited by dog breeding, cattle by cattle raising, and so with all the others. Or do you think that care aims to harm the object of its care?

E: By Zeus, no.

S: It aims to benefit the object of its care?

E: Of course.

S: Is piety then, which is the care of the gods, also to benefit the gods and make them better? Would you agree that when you do something pious you make some one of the gods better?

E: By Zeus, no.

S: Nor do I think that this is what you mean – far from it – but that is why I asked you what you meant by the care of gods, because I did not believe you meant this kind of care.

E: Quite right, Socrates, that is not the kind of care I mean.

S: Very well, but what kind of care of the gods would piety be?

E: The kind of care, Socrates, that slaves take of their masters.

S: I understand. It is likely to be a kind of service of the gods.

E: Quite so.

S: Could you tell me to the achievement of what goal service to doctors tends? Is it not, do you think, to achieving health?

E: I think so.

S: What about service to shipbuilders? To what achievement is it directed?

E: Clearly, Socrates, to the building of a ship.

S: And service to housebuilders to the building of a house?

E: Yes.

S: Tell me then, my good sir, to the achievement of what aim does service to the gods tend? You obviously know since you say that you, of all men, have the best knowledge of the divine.

E: And I am telling the truth, Socrates.

S: Tell me then, by Zeus, what is that excellent aim that the gods achieve, using us as their servants?

E: Many fine things, Socrates.

14   S: So do generals, my friend. Nevertheless you could easily tell me their main concern, which is to achieve victory in war, is it not?

E: Of course.

S: The farmers too, I think, achieve many fine things, but the main point of their efforts is to produce food from the earth.

E: Quite so.

S: Well then, how would you sum up the many fine things that the gods achieve?

E: I told you a short while ago, Socrates, that it is a considerable task to acquire any precise knowledge of these things, but, to put it simply, I say that if a man knows how to say and do what is pleasing to the gods at prayer and sacrifice, those are pious actions such as preserve both private houses and public affairs of state. The opposite of these pleasing actions are impious and overturn and destroy everything.

S: You could tell me in far fewer words, if you were willing, the sum of what I asked, Euthyphro, but you are not keen to teach me, that is clear. You were on the point of doing so, but you turned away. If you had given that answer, I should now have acquired from you sufficient knowledge of the nature of piety. As it is, the lover of inquiry must follow his beloved wherever it may lead him. Once more then, what do you say that piety and the pious are? Are they a knowledge of how to sacrifice and pray?

E: They are.

S: To sacrifice is to make a gift to the gods, whereas to pray is to beg from the gods?

E: Definitely, Socrates.

S: It would follow from this statement that piety would be a knowledge of how to give to, and beg from, the gods.

E: You understood what I said very well, Socrates.

S: That is because I am so desirous of your wisdom, and I concentrate my mind on it, so that no word of yours may fall to the ground. But tell me, what is this service to the gods? You say it is to beg from them and to give to them?

E: I do.

S: And to beg correctly would be to ask from them things that we need?

E: What else?

S: And to give correctly is to give them what they need from us, for it would not be skillful to bring gifts to anyone that are in no way needed.

E: True, Socrates.

S: Piety would then be a sort of trading skill between gods and men?

E: Trading yes, if you prefer to call it that.

S: I prefer nothing, unless it is true. But tell me, what benefit do the gods derive from the gifts they receive from us? What they give us is obvi-
15 ous to all. There is for us no good that we do not receive from them, but how are they benefited by what they receive from us? Or do we have such an advantage over them in the trade that we receive all our blessings from them and they receive nothing from us?

E: Do you suppose, Socrates, that the gods are benefited by what they receive from us?

S: What could those gifts from us to the gods be, Euthyphro?

E: What else, do you think, than honour, reverence, and what I mentioned just now, gratitude?

S: The pious is then, Euthyphro, pleasing to the gods, but not beneficial or dear to them?

E: I think it is of all things most dear to them.

S: So the pious is once again what is dear to the gods.

E: Most certainly.

S: When you say this, will you be surprised if your arguments seem to move about instead of staying put? And will you accuse me of being Daedalus who makes them move, though you are yourself much more skillful than Daedalus and make them go round in a circle? Or do you not realize that our argument has moved around and come again to the same place? You surely remember that earlier the pious and the god-beloved were shown not to be the same but different from each other. Or do you not remember?

E: I do.

S: Do you then not realize now that you are saying that what is dear to the gods is the pious? Is this not the same as the god-beloved? Or is it not?

E: It certainly is.

S: Either we were wrong when we agreed before, or, if we were right then, we are wrong now.

E: That seems to be so.

S: So we must investigate again from the beginning what piety is, as I shall not willingly give up before I learn this. Do not think me un-worthy, but concentrate your attention and tell the truth. For you know it, if any man does, and I must not let you go, like Proteus, before you tell me. If you had no clear knowledge of piety and impiety you would never have ventured to pros-ecute your old father for murder on behalf of a servant. For fear of the gods you would have been afraid to take the risk lest you should not be acting rightly, and would have been ashamed before men, but now I know well that you believe you have clear knowledge of piety and impiety. So tell me, my good Euthyphro, and do not hide what you think it is.

E: Some other time, Socrates, for I am in a hurry now, and it is time for me to go.

S: What a thing to do, my friend! By going you have cast me down from a great hope I had, that I would learn from you the nature of the pious and the impious and so escape Meletus' indict-
16 ment by showing him that I had acquired wisdom in divine matters from Euthyphro, and my ignor-ance would no longer cause me to be careless and inventive about such things, and that I would be better for the rest of my life.

Plato, "Ladder of Loves"

I grant the permission, said Phaedrus: put your questions. Socrates then proceeded as follows: –

In the magnificent discourse which you have uttered, I think that you were right, my dear Agathon, in saying that you would begin with the nature of love and then afterwards speak of his works – that is a way of beginning which I very much approve. And as you have spoken thus eloquently of the nature of love, will you answer me a further question? – Is love the love of some-thing or of nothing? And here I must explain myself: I do not want you to say that love is the love of a father or the love of a mother – that would be ridiculous; but to answer as you would, if I asked is a father a father of something? to which you would find no difficulty in replying, of a son or daughter: and that would be right.

Very true, said Agathon.

And you would say the same of a mother?

He assented.

Yet let me ask you one more question in order further to illustrate my meaning. Is not a bro-ther to be regarded essentially as a brother of something?

Certainly, he replied.

That is, of a brother or sister?

Yes, he said.

And now, said Socrates, I will ask about love:
– Is love of something or of nothing?

Of something, surely, he replied.

Keep in mind what this is, and tell me what
I want to know – whether love desires that of
which love is.

Yes, surely.

And does he possess, or does he not possess,
that which he loves and desires?

Probably not, I should say.

Nay, replied Socrates, I would have you consider whether necessarily is not rather the word.
The inference that he who desires something is
in want of something, and that he who desires
nothing is in want of nothing, is in my judgment,
Agathon, absolutely and necessarily true. What do
you think?

I think with you, said Agathon, in that.

Very good. And would he who is great desire to
be great, or he who is strong desire to be strong?

That would be inconsistent with our previous
admissions.

True. For he who is anything can not want to
be that which he is?

Very true.

But if, added Socrates, a man being strong
desired to be strong, or being swift desired to be
swift, or being healthy desired to be healthy (for
any one may be imagined to desire any quality
which he already has), in these cases there might
be an objection raised – they might be said to
desire that which they have already. I give the
example in order that we may avoid misconception. For as you may see, Agathon, these persons
must be supposed to have their respective
advantages at the time, whether they choose or
not; and surely no man can desire that which he
has. And therefore, when a person says, I am well
and wish to be well, or I am rich and wish to be
rich, and I desire simply what I have; we shall reply
to him: "You, my friend, having wealth and
health and strength, want to have the continuance
of them; for at this moment, whether you choose
or no, you have them. And when you say, I
desire that which I have and nothing else, is not
your meaning that you want to have what you now
have in the future?" He must allow this?

He must, said Agathon.

Then, said Socrates, this is equivalent to desiring not what he has or possesses already, but that
what he has may be preserved to him in the
future?

Very true, he said.

Then he and every one who desires, desires that
which he has not already, and which is future and
not present, and which he has not, and is not, and
of which he is in want; – these are the sort of things
which love and desire seek?

Very true, he said.

Then now, said Socrates, let us recapitulate
the argument. First, is not love of something, and
of something too which is wanting to a man?

Yes, he replied.

Remember further what you said in your
speech, or if you do not remember I will remind
you: you said that the love of the beautiful disposes
the empire of the gods, for that of deformed
things there is no love – did you not say something like that?

Yes, said Agathon.

Yes, my friend, and the remark is a just one.
And if this is true, love is the love of beauty and
not of deformity?

He assented.

And the admission has been already made
that love is of that which a man wants and has
not?

True, he said.

Then love wants and has not beauty?

Certainly, he replied.

And would you call that beautiful which
wants and does not possess beauty?

Certainly not.

Then would you still say that love is beautiful?

Agathon replied: I fear that I did not understand what I was saying.

Nay, Agathon, replied Socrates; but I should like
to ask you one more question: – Is not the good
also the beautiful?

Yes.

Then in wanting the beautiful, love wants also
the good?

I can not refute you, Socrates, said Agathon. And
let us suppose that what you say is true.

Say rather, dear Agathon, that you can not
refute the truth; for Socrates is easily refuted.

And now I will take my leave of you, and
rehearse the tale of love which I heard once
upon a time from Diotima of Mantineia, who was
a wise woman in this and many other branches
of knowledge. She was the same who deferred
the plague of Athens ten years by a sacrifice, and
was my instructress in the art of love. In the attempt which I am about to make I shall pursue

Agathon's method, and begin with his admissions, which are nearly if not quite the same which I made to the wise woman when she questioned me: this will be the easiest way, and I shall take both parts myself as well as I can. For, like Agathon, she spoke first of the being and nature of love, and then of his works. And I said to her in nearly the same words which he used to me, that love was a mighty god, and likewise fair; and she proved to me as I proved to him that, in my way of speaking about him, love was neither fair nor good. "What do you mean, Diotima," I said, "is love then evil and foul?" "Hush," she cried; "is that to be deemed foul which is not fair?" "Certainly," I said. "And is that which is not wise, ignorant? do you not see that there is a mean between wisdom and ignorance?" "And what is this?" I said. "Right opinion," she replied; "which, as you know, being incapable of giving a reason, is not knowledge (for how could knowledge be devoid of reason? nor again, ignorance, for neither can ignorance attain the truth), but is clearly something which is a mean between ignorance and wisdom." "Quite true," I replied. "Do not then insist," she said, "that what is not fair is of necessity foul, or what is not good evil; or infer that because love is not fair and good he is therefore foul and evil; for he is in a mean between them." "Well," I said, "love is surely admitted by all to be a great god." "By those who know or by those who don't know?" "By all." "And how, Socrates," she said with a smile, "can love be acknowledged to be a great god by those who say that he is not a god at all?" "And who are they?" I said. "You and I are two of them," she replied. "How can that be?" I said. "That is very intelligible," she replied; "as you yourself would acknowledge that the gods are happy and fair – of course you would – would you dare to say that any god was not?" "Certainly not," I replied. "And you mean by the happy, those who are the possessors of things good or fair?" "Yes." "And you admitted that love, because he was in want, desires those good and fair things of which he is in want?" "Yes, I admitted that." "But how can he be a god who has no share in the good or the fair?" "That is not to be supposed." "Then you see that you also deny the deity of love."

"What then is love?" I asked; "Is he mortal?" "No." "What then?" "As in the former instance, he is neither mortal nor immortal, but in a mean between them." "What is he then, Diotima?"

"He is a great spirit (δαίμων), and like all that is spiritual he is intermediate between the divine and the mortal." "And what is the nature of this spiritual power?" I said. "This is the power," she said, "which interprets and conveys to the gods the prayers and sacrifices of men, and to men the commands and rewards of the gods; and this power spans the chasm which divides them, and in this all is bound together, and through this the arts of the prophet and the priest, their sacrifices and mysteries and charms, and all prophecy and incantation, find their way. For God mingles not with man; and through this power all the intercourse and speech of God with man, whether awake or asleep, is carried on. The wisdom which understands this is spiritual; all other wisdom, such as that of arts or handicrafts, is mean and vulgar. Now these spirits or intermediate powers are many and divine, and one of them is love." "And who," I said, "was his father, and who his mother?" "The tale," she said, "will take time; nevertheless I will tell you. On the birthday of Aphrodite there was a feast of the gods, at which the god Poros or Plenty, who is the son of Metis or Discretion, was one of the guests. When the feast was over, Penia or Poverty, as the manner was, came about the doors to beg. Now Plenty, who was the worse for nectar (there was no wine in those days), came into the garden of Zeus and fell into a heavy sleep; and Poverty considering her own straitened circumstances, plotted to have him for a husband, and accordingly she lay down at his side and conceived Love, who partly because he is naturally a lover of the beautiful, and because Aphrodite is herself beautiful, and also because he was born on Aphrodite's birthday is her follower and attendant. And as his parentage is, so also are his fortunes. In the first place he is always poor, and anything but tender and fair, as the many imagine him; and he is hard-featured and squalid, and has no shoes, nor a house to dwell in; on the bare earth exposed he lies under the open heaven, in the streets, or at the doors of houses, taking his rest; and like his mother he is always in distress. Like his father too, whom he also partly resembles, he is always plotting against the fair and good; he is bold, enterprising, strong, a hunter of men, always at some intrigue or other, keen in the pursuit of wisdom, and never wanting resources; a philosopher at all times, terrible as an enchanter, sorcerer, sophist; for as he is neither mortal nor immortal, he is alive and flourishing at one moment when he is in plenty, and dead at another moment, and again alive by reason of his father's nature. But that which is always flowing in is always flowing out, and so he is never in want and never in wealth, and he is also in a mean between ignorance and knowledge. The truth of the matter is just this: No god is a philosopher or seeker after wisdom, for he is wise already; nor does any one else who is wise seek after wisdom. Neither do the ignorant seek after wisdom. For herein is the evil of ignorance, that he who is neither good nor wise is nevertheless satisfied: he feels no want, and has therefore no desire." "But who then, Diotima," I said, "are the lovers of wisdom, if they are neither the wise nor the foolish?" "A child may answer that question," she replied; "they are those who, like love, are in a mean between the two. For wisdom is a most beautiful thing, and love is of the beautiful; and therefore love is also a philosopher or lover of wisdom, and being a lover of wisdom is in a mean between the wise and the ignorant. And this again is a quality which Love inherits from his parents; for his father is wealthy and wise, and his mother poor and foolish. Such, my dear Socrates, is the nature of the spirit Love. The error in your conception of him was very natural, and as I imagine from what you say, has arisen out of a confusion of love and the beloved – this made you think that love was all beautiful. For the beloved is the truly beautiful, delicate, and perfect and blessed; but the principle of love is of another nature, and is such as I have described."

I said: "O thou stranger woman, thou sayest well, and now, assuming love to be such as you say, what is the use of him?" "That, Socrates," she replied, "I will proceed to unfold: of his nature and birth I have already spoken; and you acknowledge that love is of the beautiful. But some one will say: Of the beautiful in what, Socrates and Diotima – or rather let me put the question more clearly, and ask: When a man loves the beautiful, what does he love?" I answered her, "That the beautiful may be his." "Still," she said, "the answer suggests a further question, which is this: What is given by the possession of beauty?" "That," I replied, "is a question to which I have no answer ready." "Then," she said, "let me put the word 'good' in the place of the beautiful, and repeat the question: What does he who loves the good desire?"

"The possession of the good," I said. "And what does he gain who possesses the good?" "Happiness," I replied; "there is no difficulty in answering that." "Yes," she said, "the happy are made happy by the acquisition of good things. Nor is there any need to ask why a man desires happiness; the answer is already final." "That is true," I said. "And is this wish and this desire common to all? and do all men always desire their own good, or only some men? – what think you?" "All men," I replied; "the desire is common to all." "But all men, Socrates," she rejoined, "are not said to love, but only some of them; and you say that all men are always loving the same things." "I myself wonder," I said, "why that is." "There is nothing to wonder at," she replied; "the reason is that one part of love is separated off and receives the name of the whole, but the other parts have other names." "Give an example," I said. She answered me as follows: "There is poetry, which, as you know, is complex and manifold. And all creation or passage of non-being into being is poetry or making, and the processes of all art are creative; and the masters of arts are all poets." "Very true." "Still," she said, "you know that they are not called poets, but have other names; the generic term 'poetry' is confined to that specific art which is separated off from the rest of poetry, and is concerned with music and metre; and this is what is called poetry, and they who possess this kind of poetry are called poets." "Very true," I said. "And the same holds of love. For you may say generally that all desire of good and happiness is due to the great and subtle power of love; but those who, having their affections set upon him, are yet diverted into the paths of money-making or gymnastic philosophy, are not called lovers – the name of the genus is reserved for those whose devotion takes one form only – they alone are said to love, or to be lovers." "In that," I said, "I am of opinion that you are right." "Yes," she said, "and you hear people say that lovers are seeking for the half of themselves; but I say that they are seeking neither for the half, nor for the whole, unless the half or the whole be also a good. And they will cut off their own hands and feet and cast them away, if they are evil; for they love them not because they are their own, but because they are good, and dislike them not because they are another's, but because they are evil. There is nothing which men love but the good. Do you think that there is?" "Indeed," I answered, "I should say not." "Then," she said, "the conclusion of the whole matter is, that men love the good." "Yes," I said. "To which may be added that they love the possession of the good?" "Yes, that may be added." "And not only the possession, but the everlasting possession of the good?" "That may be added too." "Then, love," she said, "may be described generally as the love of the everlasting possession of the good?" "That is most true," I said.

"Then if this be the nature of love, can you tell me further," she said, "what is the manner of the pursuit? what are they doing who show all this eagerness and heat which is called love? Answer me that." "Nay, Diotima," I said, "if I had known I should not have wondered at your wisdom, or have come to you to learn." "Well," she said, "I will teach you; – love is only birth in beauty, whether of body or soul." "The oracle requires an explanation," I said; "I don't understand you." "I will make my meaning clearer," she replied. "I mean to say, that all men are bringing to the birth in their bodies and in their souls. There is a certain age at which human nature is desirous of procreation; and this procreation must be in beauty and not in deformity: and this is the mystery of man and woman, which is a divine thing, for conception and generation are a principle of immortality in the mortal creature. And in the inharmonical they can never be. But the deformed is always inharmonical with the divine, and the beautiful harmonious. Beauty, then, is the destiny or goddess of parturition who presides at birth, and therefore when approaching beauty the conceiving power is propitious, and diffuse, and benign, and begets and bears fruit: on the appearance of foulness she frowns and contracts in pain, and is averted and morose, and shrinks up, and not without a pang refrains from conception. And this is the reason why, when the hour of conception arrives, and the teeming nature is full, there is such a flutter and ecstasy about beauty whose approach is the alleviation of pain. For love, Socrates, is not, as you imagine, the love of the beautiful only." "What then?" "The love of generation and birth in beauty." "Yes," I said. "Yes, indeed," she replied. "But why of birth?" I said. "Because to the mortal, birth is a sort of eternity and immortality," she replied; "and as has been already admitted, all men will necessarily desire immortality together with good, if love is of the everlasting possession of the good."

And this she taught me at various times when she spoke of love. And on another occasion she said to me, "What is the reason, Socrates, of this love, and the attendant desire? See you not how all animals, birds as well as beasts, in their desire of procreation, are in agony when they take the infection of love; – this begins with the desire of union, to which is added the care of offspring, on behalf of whom the weakest are ready to battle against the strongest even to the uttermost, and to die for them, and will let themselves be tormented with hunger or suffer anything in order to maintain their offspring. Man may be supposed to do this from reason; but why should animals have these passionate feelings? Can you tell me why?" Again I replied, that I did not know. She said to me: "And do you expect ever to become a master in the art of love, if you do not know this?" "But that," I said, "Diotima, is the reason why I come to you, because, as I have told you already, I am aware that I want a teacher; and I wish that you would explain to me this and the other mysteries of love." "Marvel not at this," she said, "if you believe that love is of the immortal, as we have already admitted; for here again, and on the same principle too, the mortal nature is seeking as far as is possible to be everlasting and immortal: and this is only to be attained by generation, because the new is always left in the place of the old. For even in the same individual there is succession and not absolute unity: a man is called the same; but yet in the short interval which elapses between youth and age, and in which every animal is said to have life and identity, he is undergoing a perpetual process of loss and reparation – hair, flesh, bones, blood, and the whole body are always changing. And this is true not only of the body, but also of the soul, whose habits, tempers, opinions, desires, pleasures, pains, fears, never remain the same in any one of us, but are always coming and going. And what is yet more surprising is, that this is also true of knowledge; and not only does knowledge in general come and go, so that in this respect we are never the same; but particular knowledge also experiences a like change. For what is implied in the word 'recollection,' but the departure of knowledge, which is ever being forgotten and is renewed and preserved by recollection, appearing to be the same although in reality new, according to that law of succession by which all mortal things are preserved, not by absolute sameness of existence, but by substitution, the old worn-out mortality leaving another new and similar one behind – unlike the immortal in this, which is always the same and not another? And in this way, Socrates, the mortal body, or mortal anything, partakes of immortality; but the immortal in another way. Marvel not then at the love which all men have of their offspring; for that universal love and interest is for the sake of immortality."

When I heard this, I was astonished, and said: "Is this really true, O thou wise Diotima?" And she answered with all the authority of a sophist: "Of that, Socrates, you may be assured; – think only of the ambition of men, and you will marvel at their senselessness, unless you consider how they are stirred by the love of an immortality of fame. They are ready to run risks greater far than they would have run for their children, and to spend money and undergo any amount of toil, and even to die for the sake of leaving behind them a name which shall be eternal. Do you imagine that Alcestis would have died on behalf of Admetus, or Achilles after Patroclus, or your own Codrus in order to preserve the kingdom for his sons, if they had not imagined that the memory of their virtues, which is still retained among us, would be immortal? Nay," she said, "for I am persuaded that all men do all things for the sake of the glorious fame of immortal virtue, and the better they are the more they desire this; for they are ravished with the desire of the immortal.

"Men whose bodies only are creative, betake themselves to women and beget children – this is the character of their love; their offspring, as they hope, will preserve their memory and give them the blessedness and immortality which they desire in the future. But creative souls – for there are men who are more creative in their souls than in their bodies – conceive that which is proper for the soul to conceive or retain. And what are these conceptions? – wisdom and virtue in general. And such creators are all poets and other artists who may be said to have invention. But the greatest and fairest sort of wisdom by far is that which is concerned with the ordering of states and families, and which is called temperance and justice. And he who in youth has the seed of these implanted in him and is himself inspired, when he comes to maturity desires to beget and generate. And he wanders about seeking beauty that he may beget offspring – for in deformity he will beget

nothing – and embraces the beautiful rather than the deformed; and when he finds a fair and noble and well-nurtured soul, and there is union of the two in one person, he gladly embraces him, and to such an one he is full of fair speech about virtue and the nature and pursuits of a good man; and he tries to educate him; and at the touch and presence of the beautiful he brings forth the beautiful which he conceived long before, and the beautiful is ever present with him and in his memory even when absent, and in company they tend that which he brings forth, and they are bound together by a far nearer tie and have a closer friendship than those who beget mortal children, for the children who are their common offspring are fairer and more immortal. Who, when he thinks of Homer and Hesiod and other great poets, would not rather have their children than any ordinary human ones? Who would not emulate them in the creation of children such as theirs, which have preserved their memory and given them everlasting glory? Or who would not have such children as Lycurgus left behind to be the saviors, not only of Lacedaemon, but of Hellas, as one may say? There is Solon, too, who is the revered father of Athenian laws; and many others there are in many other places, both among Hellenes and barbarians. All of them have done many noble works, and have been the parents of virtue of every kind, and many temples have been raised in honor of their children, which were never raised in honor of the mortal children of any one.

"These are the lesser mysteries of love, into which even you, Socrates, may enter; to the greater and more hidden ones which are the crown of these, and to which, if you pursue them in a right spirit, they will lead, I know not whether you will be able to attain. But I will do my utmost to inform you, and do you follow if you can. For he who would proceed rightly in this matter should begin in youth to turn to beautiful forms; and first, if his instructor guide him rightly, he should learn to love one such form only – out of that he should create fair thoughts; and soon he would himself perceive that the beauty of one form is truly related to the beauty of another; and then if beauty in general is his pursuit, how foolish would he be not to recognize that the beauty in every form is one and the same! And when he perceives this he will abate his violent love of the one, which he will despise and deem a small thing, and will become a lover of all beautiful forms; this will lead him on to consider that the beauty of the mind is more honorable than the beauty of the outward form. So that if a virtuous soul have but a little comeliness, he will be content to love and tend him, and will search out and bring to the birth thoughts which may improve the young, until his beloved is compelled to contemplate and see the beauty of institutions and laws, and understand that all is of one kindred, and that personal beauty is only a trifle; and after laws and institutions he will lead him on to the sciences, that he may see their beauty, being not like a servant in love with the beauty of one youth or man or institution, himself a slave mean and calculating, but looking at the abundance of beauty and drawing towards the sea of beauty, and creating and beholding many fair and noble thoughts and notions in boundless love of wisdom; until at length he grows and waxes strong, and at last the vision is revealed to him of a single science, which is the science of beauty everywhere. To this I will proceed; please to give me your very best attention.

"For he who has been instructed thus far in the things of love, and who has learned to see the beautiful in due order and succession, when he comes towards the end will suddenly perceive a nature of wondrous beauty – and this, Socrates, is that final cause of all our former toils, which in the first place is everlasting – not growing and decaying, or waxing and waning; in the next place not fair in one point of view and foul in another, or at one time or in one relation or at one place fair, at another time or in another relation or at another place foul, as if fair to some and foul to others, or in the likeness of a face or hands or any other part of the bodily frame, or in any form of speech or knowledge, nor existing in any other being; as for example, an animal, whether in earth or heaven, but beauty only, absolute, separate, simple, and everlasting, which without diminution and without increase, or any change, is imparted to the ever-growing and perishing beauties of all other things. He who under the influence of true love rising upward from these begins to see that beauty, is not far from the end. And the true order of going or being

led by another to the things of love, is to use the beauties of earth as steps along which he mounts upwards for the sake of that other beauty, going from one to two, and from two to all fair forms, and from fair forms to fair actions, and from fair actions to fair notions, until from fair notions he arrives at the notion of absolute beauty, and at last knows what the essence of beauty is. This, my dear Socrates," said the stranger of Mantineia, "is that life above all others which man should live, in the contemplation of beauty absolute; a beauty which if you once beheld, you would see not to be after the measure of gold, and garments, and fair boys and youths, which when you now behold you are in fond amazement, and you and many a one are content to live seeing only and conversing with them without meat or drink, if that were possible – you only want to be with them and to look at them. But what if man had eyes to see the true beauty – the divine beauty, I mean, pure and clear and unalloyed, not clogged with the pollutions of mortality, and all the colors and vanities of human life – thither looking, and holding converse with the true beauty divine and simple, and bringing into being and educating true creations of virtue and not idols only? Do you not see that in that communion only, beholding beauty with the eye of the mind, he will be enabled to bring forth, not images of beauty, but realities; for he has hold not of an image but of a reality, and bringing forth and educating true virtue to become the friend of God and be immortal, if mortal man may. Would that be an ignoble life?"

Such, Phaedrus – and I speak not only to you, but to all men – were the words of Diotima; and I am persuaded of their truth. And being persuaded of them, I try to persuade others, that in the attainment of this end human nature will not easily find a better helper than love. And therefore, also, I say that every man ought to honor him as I myself honor him, and walk in his ways, and exhort others to do the same, even as I praise the power and spirit of love according to the measure of my ability now and ever.

The words which I have spoken, you, Phaedrus, may call an encomium of love, or anything else which you please.

2

Mānavadharmaśāstra, Chapters 1, 6 (abridged), and 12

Introduction

One of the most fundamental texts of Hindu thought, the *Mānavadharmaśāstra* or *Manusmṛti*, as it is also known, presents an indispensable vantage point for understanding Hindu philosophy. Composed by a collection of authors sometime around the beginning of the Common Era, the *Mānavadharmaśāstra* would become a crucial text in the more secular of the two main streams of Hindu thought.

While commonly referred to as "*Manusmṛti*," naming it as a "*smṛti*" or "traditional" text, the collected verses attributed to Manu are also named using the designator "*śāstra*," which indicates the text's standing as a treatise, a set of teachings, or a compendium of laws.[1] As such, it is one of the 19 *dharmaśāstra* of the *smṛti* literature. The voice of Adam-like "Manu," the mythological first man in Hindu cosmogony, delivers the 2,684 verses composing this text to a group of saints (*rishi*) eager for instruction about *dharma*, the central concept around which the following selection is drawn. Calling the text "*Mānava-dharmaśāstra*" also, however, contains a telling pun, because "*mānava*" is a common word for "human" as well as a genitive for Manu. Hence

From The Laws of Manu, trans. W. Doniger and B. K. Smith, London: Penguin Books, 1991, pp. 3–16, 124–7, 278–90 (some notes omitted).

Mānavadharmaśāstra carries at least two intertwined meanings: (1) "Manu's treatise on *dharma*"; and (2) the more expansive and universal, "the treatise on human *dharma*."

In any case, the early chapters of the *Mānavadharmaśāstra* retell Manu's story of the origin of the universe and human society within it. Although according to the narrative humans share a common nature and a common ancestor in Manu, they have been separated into a natural hierarchy of four orders or classes (*varṇa*), each comprising many castes (*jāti*), and each with its own duties, rights, and privileges.[2] The *Mānava-dharmaśāstra*'s account has been controversial because of at least apparent inconsistencies with the *Bhagavad-Gītā* and because of the especially privileged position the *Mānavadharmaśāstra* describes for Brahmins, a class whose status at the time of the text's authorship was under assault.[3]

The idea of *dharma* is complex and, indeed, equivocal. Like many highly nuanced philosophical terms, "*dharma*" is difficult, perhaps impossible, to translate. It carries meanings that include something like social-religious "duty," "right," "justice," "basic principle," "goodness," "merit," and "natural law." By means of this last inflection the idea of "*dharma*" suggests a philosophical resemblance to the family of natural law philosophies criss-crossing Western philosophy. John Stuart Mill (I.16) had argued in his 1874 essay, "On Nature," that "Conformity to nature has no connection whatever with right and wrong."[4] Nature, in fact, argues Mill, exhibits in its activities not only reckless, amoral indifference, it also commonly produces the sort of effects that would be considered grotesquely immoral if performed by human agents. Nevertheless, across cultures and across philosophical history, thinkers have commonly looked to the ways of nature for moral guidance and sustenance. Having somehow apprehended the terms of natural law (*lex naturalis*), moralists have called upon others to conform their lives to it, to follow and obey nature (*naturam sequi*) in order to achieve "natural goodness" and "natural justice" (*ius naturale*).

Asian thinkers looked to the *Tao*, a primordial force manifest in the natural world (V.1). Aristotle (V.5) had maintained that "Of political justice part is natural, part legal – natural, that which everywhere has the same force and does not exist by people's thinking this or that; legal, that which is originally indifferent, but when it is laid down is not indifferent."[5] Stoics (I.7 and I.8) like Zeno of Citium had posited a ruling rational order – other Stoics even a *pneuma* or breath-like spirit – providentially guiding the world, and underwriting the natural order both in terms of its operations and its moral purposes. Paul of Tarsus's "Letter to the Romans" (2:11–16) indicates still another sense of natural law, namely the idea that moral directives are naturally implanted into the internal constitution of human beings, perhaps into the structures of conscience, by God: "For when Gentiles, who do not have the law, by nature do what the law requires, they are a law to themselves, even though they do not have the law. They show that the work of the law is written on their hearts, while their conscience also bears witness." Evolutionary theorists like E. O. Wilson (b. 1929) have pursued a strangely similar gesture, suggesting that moral feelings and conduct have been engendered not by social arrangements but through natural selection.[6] Even modern ideas of universal human rights that transcend the particular positive rights stipulated by the world's governments are rooted in this rich tradition (see V.11–13 and V.16).

Manu describes, however, an apprehension or achievement of *dharma* not through the deliberation and contemplation of reason, not by attending to the voice of conscience, or by refining one's natural moral sentiments. One achieves a life conforming to *dharma* through the instruction of custom and Hinduism's sacred texts. Achieving a life of *dharma* results in a heightened engagement

with the world and ultimately to detachment from desire and corporeality, in "seeing the self in all living beings and all living beings in the self," and in finally escaping the cycle of reincarnation. The "supreme good" for human beings, or at least for men, is a kind of "self-knowledge," but subordinate goods like wealth and health flow, across all four periods of life's course (the *āshrama* or stages), to those whose lives are ordered through *dharma*, as well.[7] The Stoics and Pythagoreans had prescribed rationally grasping the natural order of the cosmos and incorporating it into one's own individual life. Manu, on the other hand, describes a process by which one realizes in conduct, perhaps more than conceptually, one's proper relationship with the world and the divinity that both transcends us and of which we are all manifestations.

Notes

1 Thence the collection's name is often translated as "The Laws of Manu." The tem, "*smṛti*," designates a sacred text of human composition, as opposed to Vedic texts, which are thought to have been produced through revelation (*śruti*).

2 The four *varṇa* comprise: Brahmins (scholars and priests), the Kshatriyas (kings and warriors), the Vaishyas (traders), and Shudras (servants).

3 The *Bhagavad-Gītā* is a Sanskrit text drawn from the longer of the two great Hindu epics, the *Mahābhārata*. Describing a conversation between the deity Krishna and the *Pāṇḍava* warrior Arjuna just before the start of the Mahābhārata war, the text delineates, among other things, crucial differences between Vedantic and Yogic philosophy. The *Gītā*, attributed in authorship to Vyāsa and dating from between 300 BCE and 300 CE, is commonly regarded as a traditional sacred text, or *smṛti*.

4 J. S. Mill, *The Utility of Religion and Theism* (1874).

5 Aristotle, *Nicomachean Ethics* VII.7 (1134b18ff.).

6 See E. O. Wilson, *Consilience* (1999); M. Ridley, *The Origins of Virtue* (1996); F. Hutcheson, *Essay on the Nature and Conduct of the Passions and Affections and Illustrations upon the Moral Sense* (1728); D. Hume,

Enquiry Concerning the Principles of Morals
(1751); and A. Smith, *The Theory of the
Moral Sentiments* (1759).
7 Under Hinduism's *āshrama* system, human
life is divided into four stages, each of roughly

25 years, and each with its own proper
dharma: the child, the developing householder, the mature householder, and the
elderly person withdrawing from the world
into spiritual freedom.

Mānavadharmaśāstra

Chapter 1

[*1*] The great sages approached Manu when he was seated in single-minded concentration; they exchanged mutual salutations in the proper manner and then they said this to him: [*2*] 'Sir, please tell us, properly and in order, the duties of all (four) classes and also of the people who are born between (two classes). [*3*] For you, lord, are the only one who knows the true meaning of what is to be done in this whole system made by the Self-existent one, that cannot be imagined and cannot be measured.'

[*4*] When the great and great-souled sages had properly asked him this, Manu, whose energy was boundless, honoured them and replied,

Listen! [*5*] Once upon a time this (universe) was made of darkness, without anything that could be discerned, without any distinguishing marks, impossible to know through reasoning or under-standing; it seemed to be entirely asleep. [*6*] Then the Lord who is Self-existent, himself unmanifest, caused this (universe) to become manifest; putting his energy into the great elements and every-thing else, he became visible and dispelled the darkness. [*7*] The one who can be grasped only by what is beyond the sensory powers, who is subtle, unmanifest, eternal, unimaginable, he of whom all creatures are made – he is the one who actually appeared.

[*8*] He thought deeply, for he wished to emit various sorts of creatures from his own body; first he emitted the waters, and then he emitted his semen in them. [*9*] That (semen) became a golden egg, as bright as the sun with his thousand rays; Brahmā himself, the grandfather of all people, was born in that (egg). [*10*] 'The waters

are born of man,' so it is said; indeed, the waters are the children of the (primordial) man. And since they were his resting place in ancient time, therefore he is traditionally known as Nārāyaṇa ('Resting on those born of man'), [*11*] The one who is the first cause, unmanifest, eternal, the essence of what is real and unreal, emitted the Man, who is known in the world as Brahmā.

[*12*] The Lord dwelt in that egg for a whole year, and then just by thinking he himself divided the egg into two. [*13*] Out of the two frag-ments he made the sky and the earth, and the atmosphere in the middle, and the eight cardinal directions, and the eternal place of the waters. [*14*] And out of himself he grew the mind-and-heart, the essence of what is real and unreal, and from mind-and-heart came the sense of 'I', the con-trolling consciousness of self, [*15*] and the great one which is the self, and all (material things that have) the three qualities, and, one by one, the five sensory powers that grasp the sensory objects.

[*16*] But by mingling the subtle parts of the six that have boundless energy with the minute particles of his own self, he made all living beings. [*17*] Since the six subtle parts of his physical form 'embody' these, therefore wise men call his physical form 'the body'. [*18*] The gross ele-ments enter into that with their innate activities, and the imperishable mind-and-heart that makes all living beings (enters) with its subtle parts. [*19*] But this (universe) arises from the subtle minute particles of the physical form of those seven Men of great energy, the perishable from the imperishable. [*20*] Each of these (elements) takes

[2] Here and throughout this translation, 'duty' will always be a translation of *dharma*, though other English renderings for *dharma* (such as 'religion', 'justice', 'law', and 'right') will also be used.

[11] The Man is *Puruṣa*, the primeval spirit.
[15] The great one is often identified with the supreme soul or *paramātman*. The qualities or charac-teristics (Sanskrit: *guṇas*) are the three constituent 'strands' of matter, entwined together like a braid: darkness or torpor (*tamas*), energy or passion (*rajas*), and lucidity or goodness (*sattva*).
[16] The six are the five sense organs and the mind, or the six elements.

on the quality of the one that precedes it, so that each is traditionally regarded as having as many qualities as the number of its position in the series.

[21] But in the beginning he made the individual names and individual innate activities and individual conditions of all things precisely in accordance with the words of the Veda. [22] And the Lord emitted the host of gods who have the breath of life and whose essence is the ritual, and the subtle host of the Amenables, and the everlasting sacrifice. [23] From fire, wind, and the sun he milked out the triple eternal Veda, consisting of the *Ṛg, Yajur,* and *Sāman,* so that the sacrifice could be accomplished. [24] He emitted time and the divisions of time, the constellations and planets, rivers, oceans, mountains, rough ground and smooth ground; [23] inner heat, speech, and sexual pleasure; desire and anger. Indeed, he emitted precisely this created universe because he wanted to emit these creatures.

[26] And in order to distinguish innate activities, he distinguished right from wrong, and he yoked these creatures with the pairs, happiness and unhappiness and so forth. [27] For, with the impermanent atomic particles of what are traditionally known as the five (elements), in their order this whole (universe) comes into being. [28] And whatever innate activity the Lord yoked each (creature) to at first, that (creature) by himself engaged in that very activity as he was created again and again. [29] Harmful or harmless, gentle or cruel, right or wrong, truthful or lying – the (activity) he gave to each (creature) in creation kept entering it by itself. [30] Just as the seasons by themselves take on the distinctive signs of the seasons as they change, so embodied beings by themselves take on their innate activities, each his own.

[31] Then, so that the worlds and people would prosper and increase, from his mouth he created the priest, from his arms the ruler, from his thighs the commoner, and from his feet the

servant. [32] He divided his own body into two and became a man with one half, a woman with the other half. In her the Lord emitted Virāj, [33] and that man, Virāj, generated ascetic heat and by himself emitted someone – you, who are the best of the twice-born, should know that the one whom he emitted was me, the creator of this whole (universe). [34] Because I wanted to emit creatures, I generated inner heat that is very hard to produce, and then at the start I emitted the ten great sages, lords of creatures: [35] Marīci, Atri and Angiras, Pulastya, Pulaha, Kratu, Pracetas, Vasiṣṭha, Bhṛgu, and Nārada.

[36] These emitted seven other Manus who had immeasurable brilliant energy, and the gods and the troops of the gods, and the great sages who had boundless energy; [37] and genies and ogres and ghouls, and centaurs and nymphs and demons, and dragons and snakes and supernatural birds, and the several classes of the ancestors; [38] and lightning, thunderbolts, and clouds, straight rainbows and curved rainbows, comets, whirlwinds, and meteors, and the higher and lower celestial lights; [39] quasi-men, monkeys, fish, and various kinds of birds, livestock, wild animals and humans, beasts of prey, (and) animals with two rows of teeth; [40] worms, bugs, and moths, lice, flies, and maggots, mosquitoes and gnats, and various stationary things.

[41] Thus this whole (universe), stationary and moving, was created by those great-souled ones at my command through the use of inner heat – each according to its own innate activity. [42] I will tell you now what sort of innate activity each sort of living being here is said to have, and also their order according to their birth.

[43] Livestock and wild animals, beasts of prey and animals with two rows of teeth, ogres, ghouls, and humans, are born from an embryonic sac. [44] Birds, snakes, crocodiles, fish, turtles, and various other species of this sort born on land or in water are born from eggs. [45] Mosquitoes and gnats, lice, flies, and maggots, and other species of this sort which originate from heat are born of sweat. [46] All the stationary (plants) that grow from the seed or node are born from shoots; herbs are those that bear many flowers and fruits and then die with the ripening of the fruit. [47]

---

[21] Innate activities (*karmans*) here designate different courses of action ('those that should be done and those that should not be done', or 'the proper activity of a priest versus the proper activity of a ruler'), or different sorts of rituals, or good and evil action ('performing a horse sacrifice versus killing a priest', as one commentary puts it), or *karmans* in the more technical sense of the accumulated consequences of past actions.

[26] 'Right' and 'wrong' render *dharma* and *adharma.*

[36] The Manus are the creators, each of whom presides over an Epoch of a Manu (*manvantara*).

(Trees) that have fruit but no flowers are traditionally known as Lords of the Forest; those that bear both flowers and fruit are called trees. [48] The various sorts of (plants that have) one root and those with many roots, the different species of grasses, and climbing vines and creepers all grow from a seed or a shoot. [49] Enveloped by a darkness that has many forms and is the result of their own innate activities, they have an internal consciousness and experience happiness and unhappiness. [50] In this terrible cycle of transmigration of living beings, which moves relentlessly on and on, the levels of existence are said to begin with Brahmā and to end with them.

[51] When the one whose prowess cannot be imagined had thus emitted this whole (universe), and me, he vanished once again into himself, pressing time against time. [52] For when the god awakens, this universe moves; and when he sleeps, and his soul is at rest, then everything closes its eyes. [53] And when he is fast asleep, embodied beings, whose souls are conditioned by their innate activities, cease from their own innate activities, and the mind-and-heart becomes faint. [54] And when, all at the same time, they are dissolved into that great soul, then the one who is the soul of all living beings turns back and sleeps happily. [55] Lodging in darkness, he remains there with the sensory powers for a long time and does not engage in his own innate activity; and then he moves out from that physical form. [56] He becomes the size of an atomic particle and enters into the seed of what moves and of what is still; and when he has united (with that) he leaves his (former) physical form. [57] Thus by means of waking and sleeping the imperishable one brings to life this whole (universe), moving and unmoving, and tirelessly destroys it.

[58] When he had made this teaching, he himself first made me grasp it according to the rules, and I taught it to Marīci and the other hermits. [59] Bhṛgu, here, will let you hear this teaching and leave nothing out; for that hermit came to understand it all, in its entirety, from me.

[60] When Manu had spoken to the great sage Bhṛgu in this way, Bhṛgu's soul rejoiced and he said to all the sages,

Listen! [61] There are six other Manus in the dynasty of that Manu who was born of the Self-existent (Brahmā); they have great souls and great energy and each emitted his own progeny. [62] They are the sons of 'Self-luminous', 'Uppermost', 'Dark', 'Wealthy', 'Gazing', and the radiant son of 'the Shining Sun'. [63] These seven Manus, beginning with the one born of the Self-existent (Brahmā), abound in brilliant energy; each one, in his own Epoch, created and pervaded this whole (universe), moving and unmoving.

[64] Eighteen blinks of an eye make up a period called a 'race-course', and thirty 'race-courses' make up one 'fraction'; thirty 'fractions' constitute a 'moment', and the same number (of 'moments') make up a day and a night. [65] The sun separates day and night, both for human beings and for gods; the night is for living beings to sleep, and the day is for them to move about in their activity. [66] A (human) month is a day and night for the ancestors, and it is divided into two lunar fortnights: the dark (fortnight) is the day for them to move about in their activity and the bright (fortnight) is the night for their sleep. [67] A (human) year is a day and night for the gods, and it too is divided into two parts: when the sun goes north it is their day, and when it goes south it is their night.

[68] Now learn, in summary, the measure of the night and day of Brahmā, and of the Ages, one by one, in order. [69] It is said that the Winning Age lasts for four thousand years; the twilight (preceding it) lasts for the same number of hundreds (of years), and the partial twilight (following it) is the same size. [70] In the three other (Ages) with their twilights and their partial twilights, the thousands and hundreds (of years) are calculated by subtracting one (from each progressive Age). [71] This period of four Ages, lasting for twelve thousand years, that has been enumerated first, is said to be an Age of the gods. [72] But the sum of a thousand Ages of the gods is known as a single day of Brahmā, and a night (of Brahmā) is exactly as long. [73] Those who know about days and nights know that an excellent day of Brahmā ends after a thousand Ages, and a night is exactly as long. [74] At the end of his day and night, the sleeper awakens, and when he is awake he emits mind-and-heart, the essence of what is real and unreal.

[75] Driven by the desire to create, mind-and-heart transforms creation; the ether is produced from that, and sound is known as the quality of the ether. [76] From the ether as it transforms itself comes the unpolluted and powerful wind, the vehicle of all odours, which is regarded as

having the quality of touch. [77] From wind, as it also transforms itself, comes light, shining and brilliant and dispelling darkness, and said to have the quality of form. [78] And from light as it transforms itself come the waters, which are traditionally known to have the quality of taste; and from the waters comes earth, with the quality of smell. This is the creation in the beginning.

[79] The Age of the gods, which was mentioned before, lasts for twelve thousand (years); when it is multiplied by seventy-one it is called an Epoch of a Manu. [80] The Epochs of a Manu are countless, and so are the emissions and reabsorptions (of the universe); as if he were playing, the Supreme Lord does this again and again. [81] In the Winning Age, religion [dharma] is entire, standing on all four feet, and so is truth; and men do not acquire any gain through irreligion. [82] But in the other (Ages), through (such wrong) gains, religion is brought down foot by foot; and because of theft, lying, and deceit, religion goes away foot by foot. [83] In the Winning Age, (people) are free from sickness, achieve all their goals, and (have) a lifespan of four hundred years; but in the Ages that begin with the Age of the Trey, their lifespan grows smaller foot by foot.

[84] The lifespan of mortals, which is mentioned in the Veda, the realized hopes of innate activities, and the special power of embodied beings bear fruit in the world according to the Age. [85] The religious duties of men are different in the Winning Age and in the Age of the Trey and the Age of the Deuce; they are different in the Losing Age, in proportion with the decrease of each Age. [86] Inner heat is said to be paramount in the Winning Age, and knowledge in the Age of the Trey; they say that sacrifice (is paramount) in the Age of the Deuce, and the one thing in the Losing Age is giving.

[87] But to protect this whole creation, the lustrous one made separate innate activities for those born of his mouth, arms, thighs, and feet. [88] For priests, he ordained teaching and learning, sacrificing for themselves and sacrificing for others, giving and receiving. [89] Protecting his subjects, giving, having sacrifices performed, studying, and remaining unaddicted to the sensory objects are, in summary, for a ruler. [90] Protecting his livestock, giving, having sacrifices performed, studying, trading, lending money, and farming the land are for a commoner. [91]

The Lord assigned only one activity to a servant: serving these (other) classes without resentment.

[92] A man is said to be purer above the navel; therefore the Self-existent one said that his mouth was the purest part of him. [93] The priest is the Lord of this whole creation, according to the law, because he was born of the highest part of the body, because he is the eldest, and because he maintains the Veda. [94] The Self-existent one emitted him from his own mouth, first, when he had generated inner heat, to convey the offerings to the gods and the ancestors, and to guard this whole (creation). [95] What living being is greater than him? For it is through his mouth that those (gods) who live in the triple heaven always eat their offerings, and the ancestors (eat) their offerings. [96] The best of living beings are those that have the breath of life; and (the best) of those that have the breath of life are those that live by their intelligence; the best of those that have intelligence are men; and priests are traditionally regarded as (the best) of men. [97] Among priests, learned men (are the best); among learned men, those who understand their obligations; among those who understand their obligations, those who fulfil them; and among those who fulfil them, those who know the Veda.

[98] The very birth of a priest is the eternal physical form of religion; for he is born for the sake of religion and is fit to become one with ultimate reality. [99] For when a priest is born he is born at the top of the earth, as the lord of all living beings, to guard the treasure of religion. [100] All of this belongs to the priest, whatever there is in the universe; the priest deserves all of this because of his excellence and his high birth. [101] The priest eats only what is his own, he wears what is his own, and he gives what is his own; other people eat through the priest's mercy.

[102] To distinguish the (priest's) innate activity and those of the rest (of the classes) in their order, the wise Manu, son of the Self-existent, made this teaching. [103] A learned priest – but no one else – should study it carefully and explain it to his pupils properly. [104] A priest who studies this teaching and has fulfilled his vow is not constantly smeared with the faults of the effects of past actions born of mind-and-heart, speech, and body. [105] He purifies the rows for

[97] *Brahman* may designate the Veda or ultimate reality.

seven generations in the past and seven in the future; and he alone deserves this entire earth. [106] This (teaching) is the best support for well-being; it increases intelligence; it is conducive to fame, long life, and the supreme good.

[107] This (teaching) describes religion in its entirety, as well as the virtues and vices of the effects of past actions and the eternal rule of conduct for the four classes. [108] The rule of conduct, the highest law, is described both in the revealed canon and in tradition; therefore a twice-born person who is self-possessed should always engage in it. [109] A priest who has slipped from (proper) conduct does not reap the fruit of the Veda; but one who is engaged in (proper) conduct is traditionally said to enjoy the full fruit. [110] When the hermits saw that the course of religion thus comes from (proper) conduct, they understood that (proper) conduct was the ultimate root of all inner heat.

[111] In this teaching, Manu has declared the origin of the universe and the rules for the transformative rituals, the carrying out of vows and attendance upon (a teacher) and the ultimate rule for the graduation bath; [112] the taking of a wife and the mark of (different kinds of) marriages, the regulations for the great sacrifices and the obligatory rule of the ceremonies for the dead; [113] the mark of the (various) means of livelihood, the vows of a Vedic graduate, what is to be eaten and not to be eaten, purification and the cleansing of things; [114] the application of the duties of women, the rules for the generation of inner heat, Freedom, and renunciation, all the duties of a king, and decision-making in lawsuits; [115] the regulations for questioning witnesses; the duties of husband and wife; the law for the division (of inheritances), gambling, and 'cleaning out thorns'; [116] attendance by commoners and servants, and the origin of confused classes; the religious duties of (all) classes in extremity, and the rules for restorations; [117] the threefold course of transmigration that arises from the effects of past actions; the supreme good, and the examination of the virtues and vices of the effects of past actions; [118] the obligatory duties of (particular) countries, castes, and families; and the duties of sects of heretics.

[106] The supreme good (niḥśreyasam param) is, literally, that which has no better, a term that generally refers to the knowledge that leads to Freedom.

[119] Learn this teaching, all of you, from me today, just as Manu told it to me long ago when I asked him.

Chapter 6 [abridged]

[. . .]

[73] Through the practice of meditation he [the ascetic] should realize the destination of the individual soul through higher and lower living beings, which is hard for people with imperfect souls to understand. [74] The man who has the ability to see correctly is not bound by the effects of his past actions, but the man who lacks this vision is caught up in the cycle of transmigration. [75] Through non-violence, lack of attachment of the sensory powers, Vedic rituals, and intense inner heat people achieve that place here on earth.

[76–7] He should abandon this foul-smelling, tormented, impermanent dwelling-place of living beings, filled with urine and excrement, pervaded by old age and sorrow, infested by illness, and polluted by passion, with bones for beams, sinews for cords, flesh and blood for plaster, and skin for the roof. [78] When he abandons this body, as a tree abandons the bank of a river or a bird abandons a tree, he is freed from a painful shark. [79] Casting the credit for his good deeds on to the people he likes and the discredit for his bad deeds on to those he dislikes, he reaches the eternal ultimate reality through the practice of meditation. [80] When through his natural emotion he becomes impervious to all natural emotions, then he wins lasting happiness here on earth and after death. [81] When he has gradually abandoned all attachments in this way and is freed from all the pairs, he is absorbed right into the ultimate reality.

[82] The entire subject of this discussion involves meditation, for no one who does not know about the soul enjoys the fruits of his rituals. [83] He should constantly chant the Veda about the sacrifice, the one about the gods, and the one about the soul, which is set down at

[75] 'That place' is the world of ultimate reality, or the condition of union with ultimate reality.

[81] The pairs are the dualisms of sensory perceptions, such as pain and pleasure, heat and cold, hunger and satiety, honour and dishonour.

the end of the Veda. [*84*] That is the refuge of those who do not know and of those who do know, of those who want to get to heaven and of those who long for the infinite. [*85*] A twice-born man who wanders as an ascetic after engaging in this sequence shakes off evil here on earth and reaches the highest ultimate reality.

[*86*] The duty of self-controlled ascetics has thus been taught to you; now learn about the activities that renouncers of the Veda should engage in.

[*87*] The chaste student of the Veda, the householder, the forest-dweller, and the ascetic – these four separate stages of life originate in the householder. [*88*] Any or all of these (stages of life), adopted in succession by a priest who does what has just been explained in accordance with the teaching, lead him to the highest level of existence. [*89*] But the householder is said to be the best of all of them, according to the rule of the revealed canon of the Veda, for he supports the other three. [*90*] Just as all rivers and streams culminate in the ocean, even so people in all stages of life culminate in the householder.

[*91*] Twice-born men in all four stages of life must constantly and carefully fulfil their ten-point duty. [*92*] The ten points of duty are patience, forgiveness, self-control, not stealing, purification, mastery of the sensory powers, wisdom, learning, truth, and lack of anger. [*93*] Those priests who study the ten points of duty carefully and, after they have learnt it, follow it, progress to the highest level of existence. [*94*] When a twice-born man has fulfilled his ten-point duty with concentration, learned the Vedānta according to the rules, and paid his (three) debts, he may become a renouncer.

[*95*] When he has renounced all innate activities and dispelled the faults of the effects of his past actions, when he has restrained himself and studied the Veda, he may live happily under the control of his sons. [*96*] When he has renounced actions in this way and regards as paramount what he himself should do, when he is without longing and has struck down his guilt by means of his renunciation, he attains the highest level of existence.

[*97*] The meritorious four-fold duty of the priest, which yields incorruptible fruits after

[*97*] Duty (*dharma*) is four-fold here in that it deals with the four stages of life (or *āśramas*). (It is also four-fold in dealing with the four classes, or *varṇas*.)

death, has thus been explained to you; now learn the duties of kings.

Chapter 12

[*1*] 'Unerring one, you have described the whole law of the four class (system); now teach us, accurately, the ultimate culmination of the fruits of actions.' [*2*] Bhṛgu the descendant of Manu, the soul of religion, said this in reply to the great sages:

Listen to the final conclusion about the whole performance of actions.

[*3*] The action that arises in the mind-and-heart, speech, and the body bears good and bad fruits; the highest, lowest, and middle levels of men's existences come from their actions. [*4*] Know that the mind-and-heart sets in motion the body's (action) here on earth, which is of three kinds and has three bases and ten distinctive marks. [*5*] The three kinds of mental action are thinking too much about things that belong to others, meditating in one's mind-and-heart about what is undesirable, and adhering to falsehoods. [*6*] The four kinds of speech (acts) are verbal abuse, lies, slander of all sorts, and unbridled chatter. [*7*] The three kinds of bodily (action) are traditionally said to be taking things that have not been given, committing violence against the law, and having sex with another man's wife. [*8*] A man experiences in his mind-and-heart the good or bad effects of past actions committed in his mind-and-heart, in his speech what he has committed in his speech, and in his body what he has committed with his body. [*9*] A man becomes a stationary object as a result of the faults that are the effects of past actions of the body, a bird or wild animal from those of speech, and a member of one of the lowest castes from those of the mind-and-heart. [*10*] A man is said to have a 'triple rod' if he has established in his consciousness the rod that enforces the mind-and-heart, the rod that enforces speech, and the rod that enforces the body. [*11*] The man who wields this triple rod among all living beings and thoroughly suppresses his lust and anger thereby achieves success.

[*12*] They say that the one who causes this (physical) self to act is the knower of the field, but intelligent men say that the one who actually performs the actions is the elemental self. [*13*]

Another internal self that is born with all who have bodies is called the living soul, through which (the knower of the field) knows all happiness and unhappiness in (successive) births. [14] These two, the great one and the knower of the field, endure, thoroughly intermingled with the elements and pervading the one who endures in high and low living beings. [15] Innumerable physical forms go forth out of his body and constantly set high and low living beings in motion.

[16] After the death of men who have done bad deeds, another solid body, designed to be tortured, is born out of the five elements. [17] When (the living souls) here have suffered with that body the tortures given by Yama, (the bodies) dissolve, each part distributed into its own basic element. [18] And after he has suffered for the faults that are born of attachment to the sensory objects and that result in unhappiness, his stains are erased and he approaches the two who have great energy. [19] Those two together tirelessly watch his religious merit and his evil, for it is through being thoroughly intermingled with that pair that he attains happiness or unhappiness here on earth and after death. [20] If he mostly does right [dharma] and only a little wrong [adharma], he is enveloped in those very elements and experiences happiness in heaven. [21] But if he mostly indulges in wrong and only a little in right, he is abandoned by those elements and experiences the tortures given by Yama. [22] And after the living soul has suffered the tortures given by Yama and his stains are erased, he enters those same five elements again, each part distributed (into its own element). [23] Seeing with his very own intellect these levels of existence of the living soul that result from right and from wrong, a man should always set his mind-and-heart on what is right.

[24] Know that lucidity, energy, and darkness are the three qualities of the self, through which the great one pervades and endures in all these existences, without exception. [25] Whenever one of these qualities entirely prevails in a body, it makes the particular quality predominant in the embodied (soul). [26] Lucidity is traditionally regarded as knowledge, darkness as ignorance, and energy as passion and hate; this is their form, that enters and pervades all living beings. [27] Among these (three), a person should recognize as lucidity whatever he perceives in his self as full of joy, something of pure light which

seems to be entirely at peace. [28] But he should recognize as energy whatever is full of unhappiness and gives his self no joy, something which is hard to oppose and constantly seduces embodied creatures. [29] And he should recognize as darkness whatever is full of confusion, undifferentiated, whatever is sensual and cannot be understood through reason or intelligence.

[30] Now I will also explain, leaving nothing out, the highest, middle, and hindmost fruits that result from these three qualities.

[31] The recitation of the Veda, inner heat, knowledge, purification, suppression of the sensory powers, the rites of duty, and meditation on the soul are the mark of the quality of goodness. [32] Delight in enterprises, instability, persistence in doing what should not be done, and continual indulgence in the sensory objects are the mark of the quality of energy. [33] Greed, sleep, incontinence, cruelty, atheism, losing jobs, habitually asking for hand-outs, and carelessness are the mark of the quality of darkness.

[34] The following should be regarded as the marks of the qualities in a nutshell, in order, as each of these three qualities occurs in the three (time periods). [35] When someone who has done, or is doing, or is going to do an act feels ashamed, a learned man should realize that that whole act has the mark of the quality of darkness. [36] When someone hopes to achieve great fame in this world by a certain act, but does not feel sorry if it fails, that should be known as (an act with the quality of) energy. [37] But when he longs with his all to know something and is not ashamed when he does it, and his self is satisfied by it, that (act) has the mark of the quality of lucidity. [38] Pleasure is the mark of darkness, profit is said to be the mark of energy, and religion the mark of lucidity, and each is better than the one before it.

[39] Now I will tell you, in a nutshell and in order, the transmigrations in this whole (universe) that one achieves by each of these qualities: [40] people of lucidity become gods, people of energy become humans, and people of darkness always become animals; this is the three-fold level of existence. [41] But it should be realized that this three-fold level of existence, which is dependent on the qualities, is itself three-fold: lowest, middle, and highest, according to the specific act and learning (of the actor).

[42] Stationary objects, worms and bugs, fish, snakes, turtles, livestock, and wild animals are the hindmost level of existence to which darkness leads. [43] Elephants, horses, servants, despised barbarians, lions, tigers, and boars are the middle level of existence to which darkness leads. [44] Strolling actors, birds, deceiving men, ogres, and ghouls are the highest level of existence to which darkness leads.

[45] Pugilists, wrestlers, dancers, arms-dealers, and addicted gamblers and drunks are the lowest level of existence to which energy leads. [46] Kings, rulers, the personal priests of kings, and those obsessed with the battle of words are the middle level of existence to which energy leads. [47] Centaurs, gnomes, genies, servants of the gods, and celestial nymphs are the whole of the highest level of existence to which energy leads.

[48] Ascetics, renouncers, priests, the hosts of gods who fly about on celestial chariots, the constellations, and the anti-gods are the first level of existence to which lucidity leads. [49] Sacrificers, sages, gods, the Vedas, the celestial lights, the years, the ancestors, and the Amenables are the second level of existence to which lucidity leads. [50] Wise men say that Brahmā, the creators of the whole universe, religion, the great one, and the unmanifest are the highest level of existence to which lucidity leads.

[51] All that results from the three sorts of action has thus been explained, the entire system of transmigration for all living beings, which is divided into three types, each of which is further subdivided into three. [52] Because of their addiction to their sensory powers and their failure to uphold religion, the worst of men, who have learned nothing, undergo evil transmigrations. [53] Learn, now, in full and in order, what particular womb this living soul enters in this world as a result of each particular action here.

[54] Those who commit major crimes spend a great many years in terrible hells, and when that is over they experience the following transmigrations:

[55] A priest-killer gets the womb of a dog, a pig, a donkey, a camel, a cow, a goat, a sheep, a wild animal, a bird, a 'Fierce' Untouchable, or a 'Tribal'. [56] A priest who drinks liquor enters (the womb) of a worm, bug, or moth, of birds who eat excrement, and of violent creatures. [57] A priest who is a thief (is reborn) thousands of times in spiders, snakes, and lizards, aquatic animals, and violent ghouls. [58] A man who violates his guru's marriage-bed (is reborn) hundreds of times in grasses, shrubs, and vines, in (beasts) that are carnivorous or that have fangs, and (in people) who engage in cruel actions. [59] Violent men become carnivorous (beasts); people who eat impure things become worms; thieves (become animals that) devour one another; and men who have sex with women of the lowest castes become ghosts. [60] A man who has associated with fallen men or has had sex with the wife of another man or has stolen the property of a priest becomes a priest-ogre. [61] A man who out of greed has stolen jewels, pearls, or coral, or the various gems, is born among goldsmiths.

[62] For stealing grain, a man becomes a rat; for brass, a goose; for water, an aquatic bird; for honey, a stinging insect; for milk, a crow; for spices, a dog; for clarified butter, a mongoose; [63] for meat, a vulture; for marrow, a cormorant; for sesame oil, an 'oil-drinker'; for salt, a cricket; and for yogurt, a crane; [64] for stealing silk, a partridge; for linen, a frog; for cotton cloth, a curlew; for a cow, an iguana; for molasses, a bat; [65] for fine perfumes, a muskrat; for leafy vegetables, a peacock; for various kinds of cooked foods, a porcupine, and for uncooked food, a hedgehog. [66] For stealing fire he becomes a heron; for household articles, a house-builder wasp; for stealing dyed clothes, he becomes a pheasant; [67] for a deer or an elephant, a wolf; for a horse, a tiger; for fruit and roots, a monkey; for a woman, a bear; for water, a sparrow; for vehicles, a camel; for livestock, a goat.

[68] Whenever a man has forcibly taken away another man's property, or has eaten an oblation when it has not been offered into the fire, he inevitably becomes an animal. [69] Women, too, who steal in this way incur guilt; they become the wives of those very same creatures. [70] But those classes who slip from their own innate activites when they are not in extremity pass through evil transmigrations and then became the menial servants of aliens. [71] A priest who has slipped from his own duty becomes a 'cometmouth' ghost who eats vomit; a ruler becomes a 'false-stinking' ghost who eats impure things and corpses. [72] A commoner who has slipped from his own duty becomes a ghost 'who sees by an eye in his anus', eating pus; a servant becomes a 'moth-eater' (ghost).

[73] The more that sensual men indulge in the sensory objects, the more their weakness for them grows. [74] Through the repetition of their evil actions, men of little intelligence experience miseries in womb after womb in this world: [75] they are rolled about in dreaded hells like the hell of 'Darkness', and are tied up and chopped up in hells like the 'Forest of Sword Leaves'; [76] they suffer various tortures; they are eaten by crows and owls, burnt by scorching sand, and boiled in pots, which is horrible; [77] they are reborn in bad wombs, which causes constant and overwhelming unhappiness, and are assailed with cold and heat and various terrors; [78] over and over they dwell in wombs and undergo birth, which is horrible; wretched chains are theirs, and they are the menial servants of other men; [79] they are separated from their relatives and dear ones and live with bad people; they make money and lose it, and they make friends and enemies; [80] then comes old age, that cannot be held back, and the suffering brought by diseases, and various troubles; and finally death, that cannot be conquered. [81] But a man reaps the appropriate fruit of any act in a body that has the qualities of the frame of mind in which he committed that act.

[82] All the fruits that are the consequences of actions have thus been pointed out to you; now learn the activity that brings about the supreme good for a priest.

[83] The recitation of the Veda, inner heat, knowledge, the repression of the sensory powers, non-violence, and serving the guru bring about the supreme good. [84] But of all these auspicious activities here on earth, is one activity said to be best able to bring about the supreme good for a man? [85] The knowledge of the self is traditionally regarded as the ultimate of all of these; it is the first of all forms of learning because through it immortality is achieved.

[86] But of the six activities listed above, Vedic activity must always be recognized as the best able to bring about the supreme good both here on earth and after death. [87] For all of these (activities), without exception, are encompassed in the performance of Vedic activity, each in a particular rule for a ritual, one by one in order. [88] There are two kinds of Vedic activity: the one that brings about engagement (in worldly action) and the rise of happiness, and the one that brings about disengagement (from worldly action) and the supreme good. [89] The activity of engagement is said to be driven by desire in this world and the world beyond; but the activity of disengagement is said to be free of desire and motivated by knowledge. [90] The man who is thoroughly dedicated to the activity of engagement becomes equal to the gods; but the man who is dedicated to disengagement passes beyond the five elements.

[91] The man who sacrifices to the self, equally seeing the self in all living beings and all living beings in the self, becomes independent. [92] A priest should give up even the activities described above and devote himself diligently to the knowledge of the self, to tranquillity, and to the recitation of the Veda. [93] For that is what makes a birth fruitful, especially for a priest; by attaining that, and in no other way, a twice-born man has done what has to be done.

[94] The Veda is the eternal eye of the ancestors, gods, and humans; the teachings of the Veda are impossible to master and impossible to measure; this is an established fact. [95] All those revealed canons and various evil doctrines that are outside the Veda bear no fruit after death, for they are all traditionally known to be based upon darkness. [96] The (teachings), differing from that (Veda), that spring up and die out bear no fruit and are false, because they are of a modern date. [97] The four classes, the three worlds, the four stages of life, the past, the present, and the future, are all individually explained by the Veda. [98] Sound, touch, form, taste, and smell as the fifth are brought to birth from the Veda alone; they are born in keeping with their qualities and their innate activities. [99] The eternal teachings of the Veda sustain all living beings; therefore I regard it as the ultimate means of this living creature's fulfilment.

[100] The man who knows the teachings of the Veda is worthy of being general of the army, king, dispenser of punishment, and overlord of all the world. [101] Just as a fire that has gained strength burns up even wet trees, so a man who knows the Veda burns up the fault born of his own action. [102] A man who knows the true meaning of the teachings of the Veda becomes fit for union with ultimate reality even while he remains here in this world, no matter what stage of life he is in. [103] Those who read the books are better than those who do not know them; those who remember them are better than those who

read them; those who understand them are better than those who remember them; and those who put them into action are better than those who understand them.

[104] Inner heat and knowledge are the ultimate cause of the supreme good for a priest; through inner heat he destroys his guilt, and through knowledge he achieves immortality. [105] A man who wants to keep his duty clean must know thoroughly the triad (of authorities for knowledge): eye-witness perception, inference, and the teachings found in various sectarian texts. [106] The man who uses reason, which does not contradict the teachings of the Veda, to investigate the sages' (Veda) and the instructions about duty – he alone, and no one else, knows duty.

[107] The activity that brings about the supreme good has thus been declared, leaving nothing out; now the secret of the teachings of Manu will be taught.

[108] If (the question) should arise, 'What about the laws that have not been mentioned?' (the reply is): 'What educated priests say should be the undoubted law.' [109] And those who have studied the Vedas and its appendages in accordance with the law, and who use the revealed canon and eye-witness perception in their argument, should be recognized as educated priests. [110] Whatever law is agreed upon by an assembly of ten people or more, or even three people or more, who persist in their proper occupations, that law should not be disputed. [111] An assembly of ten people or more should consist of three people each of whom knows one of the three Vedas, a logician, a ritual theologian, an etymologist, a man who can recite the law, and three men from (each of) the first three stages of life. [112] An assembly of three people or more, to make decisions in doubtful questions of law, should consist of a man who knows the Ṛg Veda, a man who knows the Yajur Veda, and a man who knows the Sāma Veda. [113] The law that is determined by even a single priest who knows the

Veda should be recognized as the supreme law, but not one that is proclaimed by millions of ignorant men. [114] If thousands of men join together who have not kept their vow, who do not know the Vedic verses, and who merely live off their (high) caste, they do not constitute an assembly. [115] When fools who incarnate darkness and do not know the law teach it to someone, his evil, multiplied a hundred times, rebounds upon those who propound it.

[116] Everything that brings about the supreme good has thus been described to you. A priest who does not slip from this progresses to the ultimate level of existence. [117] Thus did the lord god tell me the whole of this supreme secret of religion, through his desire to do what is good for people.

[118] Concentrating his mind, a man should see everything, including what is real and unreal, in the self, for if he sees everything in the self he will not set his mind on what is wrong. [119] The self alone is all the deities; everything rests upon the self; for the self engenders the performance of the activities of these embodied creatures. [120] He should superimpose the ether on the openings of his body, the wind on his organs of motion and touch, the supreme brilliant energy on his stomach and sight, the waters on his fat, and the earth on his solid parts; [121] the moon on his mind-and-heart, the cardinal directions on his ear, Viṣṇu on his stride, Hara (Śiva) on his strength, Fire on his speech, Mitra on his excretion, and the Lord of Creatures on his organ of procreation.

[122] He should know that the supreme Man is the ruler of them all, smaller even than the smallest atom, bright as gold, perceptible only in sleep. [123] Some say that he is Fire, others that he is Manu, the Lord of Creatures, others Indra, others the vital breath, others the eternal ultimate reality. [124] With the five physical forms he pervades all living beings and through birth, growth, and decay constantly makes them revolve in transmigration like wheels. [125] Whoever thus sees the self through the self in all living beings achieves equanimity towards all of them and reaches the supreme condition, ultimate reality.

[126] A twice-born man who reads this, the teachings of Manu as proclaimed by Bhṛgu, will always act with the proper conduct and will reach the level of existence that he desires.

[109] This verse refers to the three authorities for knowledge mentioned in 12.105: eye-witness perception, revealed canon (religious texts), and argument (inference).

3

Augustine of Hippo, *Confessions*, Book Eight and Book Nine, Chapters 8–10

Introduction

The life of Aurelius Augustinus, or Augustine of Hippo (354–430 CE), marks that fascinating time of transition between the ancient and medieval worlds. In 313 CE Constantine's Edict of Milan legitimated Christianity among the religions of the Roman Empire. But it would not be until 529 that the Christian Emperor Justinian would move to stifle the philosophical schools of Athens. In between, a young, Roman intellectual from North Africa would find his way to Christianity by a curious path – by way of Greek and Roman philosophy. Upon converting to Christianity, however, and becoming one of early Christendom's most formidable minds, Augustine did not leave philosophy behind. Rather, Augustine's work initiates the great synthesis of philosophy and Scripture – of Athens, Rome, Jerusalem, and Mecca – that would become medieval philosophy.

The following selections are drawn from Augustine's autobiographical *Confessions*. They concern the story of two gardens (against the background of a third garden, of course – Eden). In the first garden, the garden of Book Eight, the reader encounters Augustine at home, wrestling with the question of whether he will become a Christian. At the start of the selection Augustine

From Augustine, *Saint Augustine: Confessions*, trans. V. J. Bourke, New York: Fathers of the Church, Inc., 1953, pp. 195–226, 243–53.

reminds us of his having read books by the Platonists (perhaps by authors that today are often called "Neo-Platonists," such as Plotinus – III.6 of the present volume). Later, Augustine recalls that it was Cicero's *Hortensius* that had first set him on the philosophical path. Plato and the Platonists, it seems, convinced the young inquirer that materialism (the doctrine that only material reality exists) is false and that immaterial being is real. Platonism also seems to have convinced Augustine that the intellect must free itself from the senses and the interference of desire in order to apprehend divine reality. Indeed, the second garden of this selection, the garden of Book Nine, shows Augustine recreating the ascending "ladder of loves" Plato describes in his *Symposium* (IV.1). Seated with his mother, Monica, in the Roman port of Ostia, just before her death, Augustine finds himself immersed in a transcendent conversation with a decidedly religious but non-intellectual woman (perhaps not unlike Plato's Diotima). The *logos* of their discourse combined with the *eros* of their desire to reach the divine draws them beyond their bodies and all matter, beyond their corporeal senses and desires, and beyond space and time: "we advanced step by step through all bodily things up to the sky itself, from which the sun, moon, and stars shine out over the earth, and we ascended still farther in our interior cogitation, conversation, and admiration of Thy works and come to our own minds. Then, we transcended them . . ." (Book Nine, Chapter 10). Climbing Plato's ladder, however, the Augustinian philosopher does not finally encounter Platonic "Forms" or the Neo-Platonic "One." Instead, the end of the philosophical journey has become, in Augustine's hand, the Abrahamic god – a substitution that will define medieval thought generally.

Augustine, in these selections, departs from Plato and the Platonists in other ways, as well. In particular, for Plato virtue and understanding are coextensive. That is, for Plato to be good requires knowing reality (including knowing what is good), and knowing reality requires that one be good. Augustine, however, rejected the tidy symmetry of this Platonic doctrine. In developing his concept of "sin," Augustine argues, as Book Eight illustrates, that knowing what is good and true by no means entails doing the right thing or even wanting the right thing. Book Eight depicts a soul divided and set against itself. While Augustine's intellect and a portion of his will (one might say his "practical intellect") understand that Christianity is true and that the good thing to do is convert, other parts of his will resist, even rebel, against this knowledge. Against the laws of logic and reason, Augustine's account pits the "law of sin" ("*lex fomes*" or "*lex peccati*") or the force of habit, bad habit: "the law of sin is the force of habit by which the mind, though unwilling, is dragged and held tightly" (Book Eight, Chapter 5). The habits of sin restrict and even direct the will contrary to the guidance of the intellect; and because of Original Sin, all are born with their wills perverted by the law of sin. So, for Augustine one may know what is good but do what is bad, even do it *because* it is bad.

This is not to say, however, that for Augustine the will is not free. Augustine vigorously defends the doctrine of free will, most notably in *De libero arbitrio* (*On Free Choice*). Like the young man of Book Eight tossed about by the chaotic war within his soul, Augustine maintains that the free will may, despite power of sinful habit, freely struggle against sin. Of course, free will may fail in this and sin prevail – indeed, for Augustine, the force of sin is likely to prevail. Fortunately, God offers humans relief in the form of what has come to be known as "prevenient grace."[1] Augustine, who became known in the medieval church as the "Doctor of Grace," argued that through grace God may intervene in the human soul, not to compel it to do good but to silence or neutralize the law of sin, clearing a space for the will to act freely to the good, if one so chooses. Augustine's own experience of prevenient grace occurs in the garden when, in a famous passage, he responds to a divine voice that instructs him to "Take it, read it!" What he reads, however, is not Platonic philosophy, but Paul's "Letter to the Romans" (13:13–14).

Note

1 Augustine developed this doctrine in the course of his struggles against what became known as the Pelagian heresy, a doctrine named after Pelagius (360–420) that rejected original sin and maintained that human beings could achieve salvation through their free acts alone. Pelagianism was condemned by the Council of Carthage in 418 and the Council of Ephesus in 431.

Augustine, *Confessions*

Book eight

Chapter 1 My God, may I recall and confess Thy mercies to me, in the act of giving thanks to

Thee. Let my bones be bathed with Thy love and let them say: O Lord, 'who is like to Thee?'* 'Thou hast broken my bonds: I will sacrifice to

* Psalms. 34.10. This Book tells the story of Augustine's final religious conversion. In the first decades of the twentieth century, it became fashionable to deny the truth and honesty of Augustine's account of his conversion. Of the many scholars who maintained that he was converted to Neo-Platonism rather than to Catholicism, in 386, the following may be mentioned: H. Becker, *Augustin, Studien zu seiner geistigen Entwicklung* (Leipzig 1908); P. Alfaric, *L'évolution intellectuelle de s. Augustin* (Paris 1918). The best rebuttal is offered by C. Boyer, *Christianisme et néo-platonisme dans la formation de s. Augustin* (Paris 1920); the essential points are well covered, in English, by Sister M. Patricia, *St. Augustine: Christian or Neoplatonist* (Milwaukee 1939).

Thee the sacrifice of praise.'* How Thou hast broken them I shall tell, and all men who worship Thee will say, when they hear these things: Blessed be the Lord in heaven and on earth; great and wonderful is His Name.†

Thy words had clung tightly within the depths of my heart, and I was fenced in on all sides by Thee. I was certain concerning Thy eternal life, though I saw it 'in an obscure manner and as if through a mirror.'‡ However, all doubt had been removed from me, concerning the incorruptible Substance, and that every substance sprang from it. I was desirous, not of greater certainty concerning Thee, but of becoming more steadfast in Thee. All the things in my temporal life were in a condition of uncertainty. My heart had to be cleansed of the 'old leaven.'§ The way itself, the Saviour, was pleasing, yet there was still some repugnance to walking His difficult ways.

Thou didst put the thought in my mind, and it seemed good in my view, to proceed to Simplicianus,** who seemed to me to be a good servant of Thine, for Thy grace shone in him. I had heard, too, that he had lived from his youth in great devotion to Thee. And now, at this time, he had grown old, and he had a great deal of experience in his long life of following Thy way with such good zeal. It appeared to me that he was learned in many things, and truly he was. The desire came to me to discuss my troubles with him, so that he might indicate what was the proper method for a man, disposed as I was, to walk in Thy way.††

(2) I saw the Church with its full membership; one man proceeded in this way, another in that. The worldly activities in which I was engaged were not pleasing to me and had become quite a burden for me, now that my desires were not inflamed, as they had been, by the hope for honor and wealth to support such a heavy servitude. For, now, these things held no delight for me in comparison with Thy sweetness and the 'beauty of Thy house which I loved.'‡‡ But, I was still firmly held in thralldom by woman. Nor was I prohibited by the Apostle§§ from marrying, though he did exhort to a better state, desiring greatly that all men live as he had. But, being weaker, I chose the easier place, and because of this one thing I was at sea in respect of everything else, enfeebled and consumed by exhausting cares, all because, having yielded and bound myself to the conjugal life, I was compelled to conform myself to it, even in some things that I was unwilling to undergo.

I had heard from the mouth of Truth that 'there are eunuchs who have made themselves so for the sake of the kingdom of heaven'; but, as is added, 'let him accept it who can.'*** 'Vain, indeed, are all men in whom there is not the knowledge of God, and who by these good things that are seen could not discover Him that is.'††† But, I was no longer in this condition of vanity. I had risen above it, and by the testimony of the whole of creation I had found Thee, our Creator, and Thy Word who is God along with Thee, and one God with Thee, through which Word Thou hast created all things.

And there is another kind of impious men, those who, 'knowing God, did not glorify Him as God or give thanks.'‡‡‡ I had also fallen into this error, and Thy right hand§§§ took me, and, removing me from it, Thou didst place me where I could regain my health. For, Thou didst say to man: 'Behold, piety is wisdom,'**** and: 'Do not desire to appear wise, for while professing to be wise they have become fools.'†††† And I had already found the 'precious pearl'‡‡‡‡ and I should have bought it, selling all that I had, but I still hesitated.

---

* Psalms 115–16.
† Cf. Psalms 75.2; 8.2.
‡ 1 Corinthians 13.12.
§ 1 Corinthians 5.7.
** Simplicianus was an outstanding priest. At the death of St. Ambrose, in 397, he became Bishop of Milan. Augustine dedicated a special treatise to Simplicianus: *De diversis quaest. ad Simplicianum*; cf. Augustine, *Epistles* 37.
†† Cf. Psalms 127.1.

‡‡ Psalms 25.8.
§§ St. Paul; cf. 1. Corinthians 7.27–35.
*** Matthew 19.12.
††† Wisdom 13.1.
‡‡‡ Romans 1.21.
§§§ Ps. 17.36.
**** Cf. Job 28.28: 'fear of the Lord, that is wisdom' (Vulgate).
†††† Cf. Romans 1.22.
‡‡‡‡ Matthew 13.46.

Chapter 2 (3) So, I went to Simplicianus, the spiritual father of Ambrose,* who was then bishop, in his reception into grace, and loved by Ambrose like a father. I told him the winding course of my error. When I mentioned that I had read some books of the Platonists, which Victorinus† (at one time a rhetorician in the city of Rome, who had, I heard, died a Christian) had translated into Latin, he congratulated me that I had not happened on the writings of other philosophers, filled with errors and deceptions, according to the elements of this world,‡ while in the writings of the Platonists God and His Word are indirectly introduced at every turn.

Then, in order to exhort me to the humility of Christ, which is hidden from the wise but revealed to the little ones,§ he recalled Victorinus himself, whom he had known as a very close friend when he was in Rome. And he told me a story about him, concerning which I shall not keep silent. It offers ample opportunity to praise Thy grace, which must be confessed unto Thee.

This very learned old man, skilled in all the liberal teachings, who had read and criticized so many works of the philosophers, the teacher of so many noble senators, a man who, as a mark of his distinguished career as a teacher, had deserved and received a statue in the Roman Forum (which the citizens of this world regarded as an outstanding honor), up to that time of his life a worshiper of idols and a participant in the sacrilegious mysteries whereby nearly all the Roman nobility were then puffed up, so that they breathed the cult of Osiris into the people,** about 'every kind of god, monsters, and Anubis the barking god,' who at times battled against 'Neptune, Venus and Minerva,'†† and were beaten, but now Rome sought their help – these things the aged Victorinus had defended with the thundering of his frightening eloquence. Yet, he was not ashamed to be a slave of Thy Christ and a baby at Thy font,‡‡ having bent his neck to the yoke of humility and submitted his forehead to the reproach of the Cross.§§

(4) O Lord, Lord, who hast bowed down the heavens and descended, who hast touched the mountains and they gave forth smoke,*** by what means didst Thou work Thyself into that breast?

He read, as Simplicianus said, the holy Scripture and studied all the Christian writings with greatest care, examining them in detail. He used to say to Simplicianus, not openly, but in a private and friendly way: 'Do you know that I am already a Christian?' The latter would reply: 'I will not believe it, or reckon you among the Christians, unless I see you within the Church of Christ.' But, he would smile and say: 'So, do walls make men Christians?' He said this often, that he was already a Christian, and Simplicianus often gave the same reply, and the bantering remark about the walls was often repeated. For, he was afraid of offending his friends, proud worshipers of demons; he thought that their enmity would fall heavily upon him from the peak of their high position in Babylon,††† as from the cedars of Lebanon‡‡‡ which the Lord had not yet broken down. But, afterwards, by reading and

---

* Augustine's possible meaning, in speaking of Simplicianus as the spiritual father of Ambrose, is that Simplicianus assisted at the baptism of Ambrose, who had been a Roman governor in Milan until the year 374. Cf. Altaner, *Patrologia* (1944) 259.

† Gaius Marius Victorinus, born toward the end of the third century in North Africa, went to Rome in 304, where he became a famous professor of rhetoric. At first a pagan and a bitter critic of Christianity, Victorinus became a Catholic after reading the Scriptures with the intention of refuting them. He probably made the first Latin translations of parts of Plotinus' *Enneads*, of some of Porphyry's works, and of the *Categories* of Aristotle. Cf. P. Monceaux, *Histoire littéraire de l'Afrique chrétienne* (Paris 1905) 3.378–422; and, for more recent bibliography and information on the extant works, P. De Labriolle. *Histoire de la littérature latine chrétienne*, 3me éd., rev. par G. Bardy (Paris 1947) 1.330; 375–379.

‡ Colossians 2.8.

§ Cf. Matthew 11.25.

** Reading *spirabat populo Osirim et* (following de Labriolle, who credits this emendation to Ihm); Skutella suggests *spirabat propolis iam et*. The passage is corrupt, even in the earliest Mss.

†† Cf. *Aeneid* 8.698–700.

‡‡ That is, a newly baptized Christian; cf. John 3.5.

§§ Cf. Galatians 5.11.

*** Cf. Psalms 143.5.

††† Babylon is taken to signify Rome with its seven hills (Apocalypse 17.9) and a city of pride (Isaiah 14.4) .

‡‡‡ Ps. 28.5 and Augustine's *Enarr.* on that verse: 'The voice of the Lord breaking down [*conterens*] the cedars; the voice of the Lord humbling the proud, by contrition of heart [*contritione*].'

longing, he gained firmness of mind and became afraid to be denied by Christ before the holy angels, if he were fearful of confessing Him before men.* By being ashamed of the mysteries of the humility of Thy Word and not being ashamed of the sacrilegious mysteries of proud demons which he had accepted as their proud follower, he appeared to himself to be guilty of a great crime. He put aside the shame arising from vanity and took on the shame arising from truth. Suddenly and unexpectedly, he said to Simplicianus (as the latter told the story): 'Let us go into the church; I wish to become a Christian.' The latter, overcome with joy, went along with him. Whereupon, he was introduced into the first mysteries of instruction† and, shortly afterwards, he also gave in his name‡ to be reborn through baptism, to the amazement of Rome and the joy of the Church. Proud men saw and grew angry; they gnashed their teeth and pined away.§ But, the Lord God was his hope, for Thy servant, and he regarded not vanities and lying follies.**

(5) At last, as the hour approached for the profession of faith (which at Rome was customarily uttered, by those who are about to enter into Thy grace, in set words learned and kept in memory,†† and from a prominent place in full view of the crowd of believers),‡‡ an offer was made by the priests to Victorinus – Simplicianus said – to do it privately. It was customary to make this concession to such people as seemed likely to be frightened by embarrassment. However, he preferred to profess his salvation in the sight of the holy congregation. For, what he taught as a rhetorician was not productive of salvation, yet he had professed that in public. How much less, then, had he to fear Thy meek flock when he uttered Thy word, since he was not afraid of the crowds of madmen when uttering his own words?

Thus, when he got up to make his profession, everyone who knew him and all the people murmured his name among themselves, with a resounding exclamation of thanksgiving. Who was there who did not know him? From the mouths of all who shared the common joy, there resounded a moderated shout: 'Victorinus! Victorinus!' Quickly they cried out in exultation at seeing him, and quickly they fell into an intense silence in order to hear him. He proclaimed the true faith with admirable confidence, and all experienced the desire to snatch him to their hearts. This they did with love and joy, for these were the hands by which they caught him up.

Chapter 3 (6) O good God, what is it that goes on in man, that he rejoices more at the salvation of a soul which has been despaired of and which has been delivered from a greater danger, than if hope had always been with it, or if the danger had been less? Thou too, O merciful Father, dost rejoice 'more over one sinner who repents, than over ninety-nine just who have no need of repentance.'§§ And we listen with great joy, when we hear how the straying sheep is carried back on the exultant shoulders of the Shepherd, and how the drachma is returned to Thy treasury, her neighbors sharing in the joy of the woman who found it. And the festal joy of Thy house sheds tears when they read there of that younger son of Thine, that 'he was dead and has come to life again, he was lost and is found.'*** Indeed, Thou dost rejoice in us, and in Thy angels that are holy with a holy love. For, Thou art ever the same, who knowest always, and in the same manner, all things which are not forever in the same manner.

---

* Cf. Luke 12.9.

† When Victorinus became a catechumen, he would be given elementary religious instruction; the sign of the cross made on his forehead, salt placed on his tongue, the imposition of hands – these rites associated with the catechumens are now performed at baptism.

‡ The names of the catechumens were handed in before the start of Lent, and baptism was conferred on the night of Holy Saturday. Cf. L. Duchesne, *Origines du culte chrétien*, 5me éd. (Paris 1925) 310; F. X. Funk first pointed out that there was really no division of the catechumenate into four classes, as had long been maintained (*Theol. Quartalschr.* 65 [1883] 41–77; 71 [1889] 434–443).

§ Cf. Psalms 111.10.

** Cf. Psalms 39.5.

†† The reference is to the public recital of the Creed.

‡‡ Rufinus, a contemporary of Augustine, has left the earliest written record of the Latin text of the *Credo*; he also describes the ceremony of reciting it. *Comment. Symbolum Apostolorum* (PL 21.339).

§§ Luke 15.7ff.

*** Cf. Luke 15.24. See Augustine's sermon on the prodigal son, prompted by the reading of the parable as a Sunday gospel, as edited in *Misc. Agost.* I 256–264.

(7)   And so, what goes on in the soul, when there is more delight that things which it loves have been found or returned, than if it had always possessed them? Many other cases agree in attesting to this and all things are filled with evidence proclaiming: 'It is so.' The victorious commander triumphs, but he would not have conquered unless he had fought; the greater the danger was in battle, the greater is the joy in the triumph. A storm tosses sailors and threatens shipwreck; all grow pale at the thought of impending death:* the sky and sea become peaceful, and, now, their joy knows no limits, for their fear was without limit. A loved one is sick and his pulse indicates the threat of danger; all those who desire to have him well grow sick at heart together with him. He gets better and walks again, though not yet with his former strength; still, there is already joy such as there never was when he walked well and strong before the illness. Men get these pleasures of human life, not just from unexpected and involuntary happenings, but from planned and voluntary hardships. There is no pleasure in eating and drinking unless they are preceded by the hardship of hunger and thirst. Drunkards eat salty foods, by which a disturbing thirst is produced; then a drink removes it and enjoyment is the result. It is an established practice for engaged girls not to be given immediately in marriage,† lest the husband, when she is given, hold her in low esteem because he did not long for her during an extended engagement.

(8)   This is the case in shameful and blameworthy joy, in that which is permitted and legal, in that most honorable uprightness of friendship, in the case of the son who was dead and came back to life again,‡ who was lost and is found: in all cases the greater joy is preceded by the greater hardship.

Why is this so, O Lord my God, since Thou, Thou Thyself, art Thine own eternal joy, and since certain beings§ made by Thee and dwelling near Thee experience everlasting joy – why is it that this our part of creation alternates between decline and progress, between affronts and reconciliations? Is this their mode of being, just what Thou didst grant, when from the highest heavens** to the lowest parts of the earth, from the beginning unto the end of the ages, from the angelic being down to the worm, from the first movement until the last, Thou didst place all the kinds of good things and all Thy just works each in its proper location, and didst accomplish each in its own time? Ah me, how exalted art Thou in Thy heights, how deep in Thy depths! Thou dost never withdraw, yet we return to Thee only with great difficulty.

Chapter 4   (9)   O Lord, arouse us and recall us, enflame us and carry us off, make us ardent, attract us by Thy sweetness: let us love, let us run!†† Do not many men return to Thee from a deeper hell of blindness than Victorinus, approaching and being enlightened by the reception of the light, and, if they receive it, obtain from Thee the power to become Thy sons?‡‡ However, if they are less well known to the people, then, even they who know them rejoice less over them. For, when one rejoices along with many people, then joy is increased in each person,§§ because they warm themselves and are enkindled by each other. Then, too, those who are known to many people are of influence in the salvation of many, and, as they lead the way, many will follow. That is why there is much rejoicing for them even among those who have preceded them, for the rejoicing is not for them alone.

Far from me, of course, be the notion that in Thy tabernacle the rich should be more highly regarded than the poor, or the noble than the less well born,*** since Thou hast rather chosen the weak things of the world, to put to shame the strong, and Thou hast chosen the ignoble things of this world, and the despised things and those

---

* *Aeneid* 4.644: *Dido . . . pallida morte futura.*

† Note that Augustine himself was to have been engaged for two years before marriage; cf. above, 6.13.23.

‡ Cf. Luke 15.32.

§ These creatures near to God are the good angels.

** Cf. Matthew 24.31.

†† Cf. Canticles 1.3: 'we will run after thee to the odor of thy ointments.'

‡‡ Cf. John 1.12.

§§ Note Augustine's awareness of the importance of crowd psychology.

*** Cf. James 2.1–9; here, partiality toward persons is dealt with; the phrase, *acceptio personarum*, is the standard name for this vice of favoritism in later moral theory. Cf. St. Thomas Aquinas, *Summa Theol.* II–II, q. 63, art. 1–4.

which are not, as if they were, to bring to naught the things that are.* Yet this same man, 'the least of Thy apostles,'† by whose tongue Thou didst pronounce these words, when Paul the proconsul,‡ his pride conquered§ through this man's warfare, was sent to pass under the light yoke of Thy Christ to become an ordinary subject of the great King, this man, though previously known as Saul, was desirous of being called Paul, in testimony of so great a victory. For the Enemy is more completely vanquished in the case of a man over whom he holds fuller sway and through whom he holds sway over a larger number of other men. Now, he has greater power over the proud, because of the prestige of nobility, and through the proud over a larger number of other men by means of the authority of the former. When, therefore, Thy sons thought with satisfaction of the heart of Victorinus, which the Devil had occupied as in an impregnable shelter, and of the tongue of Victorinus, which he had used as a great and sharp weapon to slay many, it was right that they should have rejoiced more abundantly because our King had bound the strong man,** and they saw his vessels taken from him to be cleansed and made suitable for Thy honor, and to become 'useful to the Lord for every good work.'††

Chapter 5 (10) When Thy servant, Simplicianus, told me this story about Victorinus, I burned to imitate him. This, of course, was why he had told it. When he added that, in the time of the Emperor Julian,‡‡ when Christians were prohibited by law from teaching literature and public speaking (Victorinus submitted willingly to this law, for he preferred to abandon the school of wordiness rather than Thy Word, by which Thou dost make eloquent the tongues of babes§§), his courage seemed to me not greater than his good fortune, for he thus found the opportunity to devote his time to Thee. This is what I was sighing for, being tied down not by irons outside myself, but by my own iron will. The Enemy had control of the power of my will and from it he had fashioned a chain for me and had bound me in it. For, lust is the product of perverse will, and when one obeys lust habit is produced, and when one offers no resistance to habit necessity is produced. By means, as it were, of these interconnected links – whence the chain I spoke of – I was held in the grip of a harsh bondage. But, the new will, which had begun to be in me, to serve Thee for Thy own sake and to desire to enjoy Thee, O God, the only sure Joyfulness, was not yet capable of overcoming the older will which was strengthened by age. Thus, my two voluntary inclinations,*** one old and the other new, one carnal and the other spiritual, were engaged in mutual combat and were tearing my soul apart in the conflict.

(11) Thus I came to understand by personal experience the text which I had read, how the flesh 'lusts against the spirit and the spirit against the flesh.'††† Of course, I was on both sides, but I was more on the side of what I approved within myself than on the side of what I disapproved within myself. For, I was less identified with this latter side, since in great part I suffered it unwillingly rather than acted willingly. Still, the habit that opposed me with greater vigor had risen out of my very self, since I had willingly reached a state which I found to be against my will. And who could justly protest if a just punishment pursues the sinner? I no longer had the excuse which permitted me to think that the reason why I had not yet given up the world to serve Thee was that my perception of truth was uncertain; for, now, it also was certain. But, still earthbound, I refused to fight under Thy command‡‡‡ and I feared as much to be freed of all my burdens, as one should fear to be hindered by them.

---

* Cf. 1 Corinthians 1.27–29.
† 1 Corinthians 15.9.
‡ Augustine alludes to Acts 13.7, where the proconsul has the name Sergius Paulus. It is in verses 6–12 that the name Paul first appears as that of the Apostle.
§ *debellata superbia*: cf. *Aeneid* 6.853: *parcere subjectis, et debellare superbos.*
** Cf. Matthew 12.29.
†† 2 Timothy 2.21.
‡‡ This happened in the year 362; cf. J. Bidez, *L'Empereur Julien, Oeuvres complètes* (Paris 1924) 46; and *De civ. Dei*, 18.52.

§§ Wisdom 10.21; cf. Matthew 21.16.
*** Literally, 'two wills'; however, the English term, 'will,' has not the bi-valence of the Latin term, *voluntas*, which means both the power and the act of the power. What Augustine intends is: 'two initial tendencies of appetite.'
††† Galatians 5.17.
‡‡‡ Cf. 2 Timothy 2.4.

(12) So, I was agreeably laden with a worldly burden, as in a dream, and the thoughts by which I meditated on Thee were like the endeavors of those who desire to waken themselves, but who sink back, overcome by a deep sleep. Yet, just as there is no one who wants to sleep all the time, and in the sound judgment of all men it is preferable to be awake, many a man nevertheless puts off the act of disrupting his sleep when there is a heavy lethargy in his bodily parts, and, though it is time to get up, he chooses to enjoy the sleep that is indeed not wholly pleasing. So was I sure that it was better to give myself over to Thy charity, rather than to give in to my own cupidity. But, while charity was attractive and was about to win its victory, cupidity was also alluring and held me in its fetters.* There was no answer for me to give to Thee, when Thou didst say to me: 'Awake, sleeper, and arise from among the dead, and Christ will enlighten thee.'† And, as Thou didst manifest from all sides the truth of Thy statements, there was not a thing for me to answer, being already convinced by the truth, but these slow and sleepy words: 'Later, just a bit later; wait a short time.' However, 'later and later' meant more than a bit, and 'wait a short time' lasted a long time. In vain was I delighted with that law of Thine according to the inner man, when the other law in my members was warring against the law of my mind and making me prisoner to the law of sin that was in my members. For, the law of sin is the force of habit by which the mind, though unwilling, is dragged and held tightly; rightly so, for the mind willingly slipped into this habit. Unhappy man that I was! Who should deliver me from the body of this death, except Thy grace through Jesus Christ, our Lord?‡

Chapter 6 (13) I shall tell and confess unto Thy Name,§ O Lord, my Helper and my Redeemer,** how Thou didst release me from the chains of desire for the pleasures of concubinage, by which I was most firmly bound, and from the bondage of worldly affairs.

I was living my usual life with increasing anxiety, sighing for Thee every day, going often to Thy church, whenever my work, under the weight of which I continued to groan, left me free. Alypius was with me, no longer engaged in the work of a legal consultant now that the third session of the assessor's court was over. He was looking for people to whom he could again sell his legal advice, just as I was selling skill in speaking, if this can be furnished by teaching. Nebridius, however, had yielded to the demands of our friendship and was teaching as an assistant to Verecundus,†† a very good friend of us all, a citizen and grammarian of Milan, who had urgently importuned and warmly begged, by virtue of this friendship, the trusted assistance of one of our group, which he greatly needed. Thus, it was not the desire of personal advantage which attracted Nebridius (he could have derived greater gains from his literary skill, had he desired), but, as a result of his courteous good will, this most lovable and gentle friend was unwilling to turn down our request. He worked most prudently at this task, guarding against becoming well known to personages who are important by this world's standards, and avoiding every mental disturbance by these measures, for he wished to keep his mind free and at liberty for as much time as possible, in order to pursue his own studies, to read or to hear something about wisdom.

(14) So, on a certain day (I do not recall the reason why Nebridius was away), a man named Ponticianus‡‡ came to visit myself and Alypius at our home. He was a compatriot of ours, in the sense that he was from Africa, and the holder of an important position at court. I do not know what he desired of us. We sat down together to have a talk. Just by chance, he noticed a book on the games table before us. He picked it up, opened it, and to his surprise, no doubt, discovered that it was the Apostle Paul. He had thought it one of the books which I was wearing myself out in teaching. He looked at me with a smile and expressed his felicitations and surprise at unexpectedly finding this work, and only this work, before my eyes. In fact, he was a Christian and

---

* *sed illud placebat et vincebat, hoc libebat et vinciebat:* the rhetorical form is difficult to put into English.
† Ephesians 5.14.
‡ Romans 7.22–25.
§ Cf. Psalms 53.8.
** Psalms 18.15.

†† Verecundus later permitted Augustine and his friends to use his country home at Cassiciacum as a place of retirement before baptism; cf. below, 9.3.5.
‡‡ A minor government official, Ponticianus is not otherwise known than by this reference.

a faithful one, accustomed to go on his knees before Thee, our God, in frequent and lengthy prayers in church. When I pointed out to him that I was devoting much attention to these writings, he began to tell the story of Anthony,* the Egyptian monk, whose name shone very brilliantly among Thy servants, but was unknown to us up to that time. When he discovered this, he dwelt upon this point in his conversation, giving much information about this man to us who were ignorant, and expressing surprise at this ignorance of ours. We were amazed, of course, to hear of Thy miracles, of such recent memory and almost in our own times, which were well supported by testimony – miracles performed in the right faith and in the Catholic Church. We were all in a condition of wonder: we two, because these things were so important; he, because we had not heard of them.

(15) From this, his conversation turned to the groups in the monasteries, to their manner of living, sweet with Thy odor, and to the populating of the waste spaces of the desert: of all this we knew nothing. There was even a monastery at Milan, outside the city walls, filled with good brothers under the patronage of Ambrose, and we did not know of it. He went right on speaking of his subject, while we remained silent and engrossed. Then, he happened to tell how he and three companions (I do not know at what time, but certainly it was at Trèves†), during the time of the afternoon that the emperor was attending the show in the circus, went out for a walk in the gardens beside the city walls. There, they happened to pair off, he taking one companion with him, and the other two wandering off likewise, but in another direction. This second pair, strolling along, happened upon a hut where were dwelling some of Thy servants who are 'poor in spirit, for of such is the kingdom of Heaven.'‡ There, they

found a book, in which the *Life of Anthony* had been written. One of them began to read it, and to wonder, and to catch the spark. As he read, he thought of embracing such a life and of giving up secular affairs to serve Thee. (They belonged to the group of officials called 'special agents.'§) Then, suddenly filled with a holy love and angry at himself with virtuous shame, he turned his eyes to his friend and said to him: 'Tell me, I beg of you, what goal do we hope to achieve with all these efforts of ours? What are we looking for? What reason have we for engaging in public service? Could our aspiration at the court be anything greater than to become "friends of Caesar"?** And what is not unstable and full of danger in that position? Through how many dangers must one go to reach a greater danger? And when will one reach it? Now, if I wish, I can be a friend of God immediately.'

He said this and, in the throes of giving birth to a new life, he looked again at the text. As he read, he was changed within, in the part which Thou didst see. His mind withdrew from the world, as soon became evident. For, while he read and his heart surged up and down, he groaned at times as he made his decision. He decided in favor of the better, being now Thine, and said to his friend: 'I have just divorced myself from that ambition of ours and have determined to serve God. I shall begin this service from this hour and in this place. If you do not care to do likewise, do not speak in opposition.' The other man replied that he would cleave to his companion for so great a reward and so important a service. The two men then began building their tower for Thee, making the necessary outlay,†† leaving all their possessions and following Thee.

At this point, Ponticianus and his associate were walking in other parts of the garden and searching for the others. Arriving at the same place and finding them, they advised them to return, for the day was now drawing to a close. The others told about their decision and their resolution; how such a desire arose and became firmly

---

* The *Life of St. Anthony* (not yet published in the new critical edition by H. G. Opitz, whose first volume appeared in Berlin in 1934) was written in Greek by St. Athanasius *c.* 357. Translated into Latin before 385, by Evagrius of Antioch (cf. *PG* 26.835–976), it did much to influence the growth of Western monasticism.
† Trèves (Trier) on the Moselle was one of the residences of the Roman emperors in the late Empire. Gibb-Montgomery (*Conf.,* p. 217.7) conjecture that the incident took place in the reign of Emperor Gratian, who spent much time at Trèves.
‡ Matthew 5.3.

§ *agentes in rebus*: a group of imperial functionaries employed in collecting taxes, messenger work, government inspection, and police work; cf. H. M. Gwatkin in *Cambridge Medieval History* I (1936) 36f.
** *amici imperatoris*: members of the immediate Court circle; cf. Epictetus, *Dissertationes* 4.1.42–50.
†† Cf. Luke 14.28.

established in them. They begged them not to offer any opposition, if they refused to join them. These two men* were not changed from their former disposition, yet they wept for themselves (so Ponticianus said) and loyally felicitated the others, commending themselves to their prayers. With their hearts still dragging along on the earth, they went away to the imperial court, while their friends, with hearts fixed on heaven, remained in the hut.

Both men were engaged to be married. When their fiancées heard about this, they also dedicated their virginity to Thee.

Chapter 7 (16) This was Ponticianus' story. Thou indeed, O Lord, didst twist me back upon myself, while his words were being uttered, taking me away from behind my own back, where I had placed myself because I was unwilling to look at myself, and Thou didst set me right in front of my own face so that I might see how ugly I was, how deformed and vile, how defiled and covered with sores. I saw and was filled with horror, yet there was no place to flee from myself. If I attempted to turn my gaze away from myself, he kept on telling his story, and Thou didst again place me before myself, thrusting me up before my eyes, so that I would discover my iniquity and detest it. I recognized it, but pretended not to: I thrust it from my sight and out of my mind.

(17) At this time, the more ardent was my approval of these men (having heard of their salutary inclinations and how they had given themselves entirely to Thee in order to be healed), the more abhorrent was my condemnation of myself in comparison with them. For, many of my years (about twelve) had flowed by since that period in my nineteenth year when, having read the *Hortensius*† of Cicero, I was aroused by the love of wisdom. I continued to put off the rejection of earthly happiness whereby I might have been free to investigate that wisdom, whose mere quest – not to speak of its discovery – should have been preferred to the actual finding of treasures and kingdoms among men, and to being surrounded by corporeal pleasures at my beck and call. Yet, as a youth, I was quite unhappy, unhappy in the beginning of the period of

adolescence. I even begged chastity of Thee, saying: 'Give me chastity and self-restraint, but not just yet.' I was afraid that Thou wouldst quickly heed my prayer, that Thou wouldst quickly cure me from the disease of concupiscence, which I preferred to be appeased rather than to be abolished. And I had walked the crooked ways‡ in sacrilegious superstition, not exactly certain in it, but preferring it in a way to other teaching which I did not search out with sincerity but which I fought against with enmity.

(18) I maintained the opinion that the reason why I was deferring from day to day§ the rejection of worldly ambition, in order to follow Thee alone, was because nothing by which I could direct my course seemed certain to me. But the day had come on which I was laid bare before myself. My conscience uttered this rebuke within me: 'Where is your tongue? Of course, you have been saying that you are unwilling to cast off the burden of vanity because the true is not certain. See, now it is certain, yet this burden still presses down upon you, while they, who have not been worn out in such a search and have not thought over these things for a decade or more, have taken wings on their less burdened shoulders.'**

Thus was I gnawed from within and exceedingly troubled by a fearful shame, while Ponticianus spoke of such things. When he finished his conversation and the business for which he had come, he went his way, and I to myself. What did I not say within me? With what lashes of judgment did I not whip my soul so that it would follow me who yearned to follow Thee? Yet, it balked; it refused and made no effort to be excused. All arguments were used up and refuted. There remained only dumb fear. As if from death, my soul shrank back from being restrained from the flux of habit, in which it was wasting away unto death.

Chapter 8 (19) Then, in that great struggle within my inner abode – which I had forcibly

---

* Ponticianus and his friend.

† Cf. above, 3.4.7; the present passage is important in establishing the chronology of Augustine's early life.

‡ Cf. Ecclisiastes 2.16.

§ Cf. Ecclisiastes 5.8.

** Cf. Augustine's explanation of these 'wings' in *Enarr. in Ps.* 118, sect. 13. Plato (*Phaedrus* 249) says that the soul of the philosopher may take wings much more quickly than the soul of the ordinary man, because he has never lost sight of the divine, which the wings symbolize.

provoked with my soul in that little room of ours, my heart – being disturbed as much in my countenance as in my mind, I rush in upon Alypius and cry out:* 'What is wrong with us? What does this mean, this story you heard? Unlearned men are rising up and storming heaven,† while we with our teachings which have no heart in them, here we are tumbling about in flesh and blood! Is it because they have led the way that we are ashamed to follow, yet are not ashamed of the fact that we are not following?'

I said some such words, and then my mental agitation tore me away from him; while he kept silent, terrified as he looked upon me. Not even my voice sounded as usual. Forehead, cheeks, eyes, complexion, the way I spoke, gave more indication of my mental condition than did the words I uttered.

A little garden belonged to our residence, and we used it as we did the rest of the house, for our host, the landlord, did not live there. The tumult in my breast carried me out there, where no one could hinder the burning struggle which I had entered upon against myself; to what solution, Thou didst know, but I did not. Yet, my madness was healthful and my dying was life-giving; I was aware of the extent of my evil, but I was unaware of the extent of the good I would shortly attain.

So, I withdrew to the garden, and Alypius followed in my footsteps. There was no lack of personal privacy for me when he was present. Moreover, how could he abandon me in such a frame of mind?

We sat down as far away from the building as possible. I was shaken in spirit, angered by a most violent indignation at the fact that I did not enter into an agreement and covenant with Thee, O my God, for all my bones‡ cried out that I should make this step, and extolled it to the heavens with praises. Entry into this agreement did not require boats or chariots or movement of the feet; I did not even have to go as far as we had gone from the house to the place where we were sitting. For, not merely to go, but actually to reach that disposition, meant nothing else than to wish to go – strongly and completely of course, not just a half-wounded wish, turning now

to this and now to that, nor a will threshing about in a struggle wherein, when one part rises up, another part is cast down.

(20)   At last, in these seething fevers of irresolution, I began to make many gesticulations, such as men wish to make at times, yet cannot, either because they have not the members, or because these members are bound in chains, or are undone by illness, or are hindered in some way. If it were a matter of pulling my hair, or striking my forehead, or grasping my knee with clenched fingers, I did it because I wished it. But, I could have wished and yet not done it, if the mobility of my members had not obeyed. Thus, I did so many things, in situations where willing was not identical with the power to act. Yet, I did not do the thing which was incomparably more attractive to me and which I was capable of executing just as soon as I had the will to act, for, as soon as I had willed it, then surely I willed it. In this case, the ability was identical with the will, and the act of willing was itself the performance. Yet, it was not done. It was easier for my body to obey the slightest wish of my soul, moving its members at a mere nod, than for my soul to obey itself for the carrying out, in the will alone, of a great act of will.

Chapter 9   (21)   What is the source of this monstrosity? What purpose does it serve? Let Thy mercy shine forth and let me ask the question, if perchance the mysteries of men's punishments and the darkest griefs of the sons of Adam can answer me. What is the source of this monstrosity? What purpose does it serve? The mind§ commands the body and is immediately obeyed; the mind commands itself and is resisted. The mind commands the hand to be moved and its readiness is so great that command can hardly be distinguished from enslavement. Yet, the mind is the mind, while the hand is the body. The mind commands the mind to will; it is not something else, yet it does not do it. What is the source of this monstrosity? What purpose does it serve? It commands, I say, that the will-act be performed, and it would not issue the command

---

* Augustine is using the historical present for vividness.
† Cf. Matthew 11.12.
‡ Psalms 34.10.

§ Throughout this section, as elsewhere in the *Confessions*, 'mind' translates *animus*. More precisely, *animus* means the rationally conscious soul; cf. *De civ. Dei* 7.23.1, and Gilson, *Introduction à l'étude de s. Augustin* (2me éd.) 56–57.

unless it willed it, yet its command is not carried out.

But, it does not will it completely, and so it does not command it completely.* For, it commands to the extent that it wills; and what it commands it not done, to the extent that it does not will it, since the will commands that there be a will, not another will, but its very self. So, it does not command with its whole being; therefore, its command is not fulfilled. For, if it were whole, it would not command that it be done; it would already be done. Hence, it is not a monstrosity to will something in part and to oppose it in part; it is rather an illness of the mind, which, though lifted up by truth, is also weighed down heavily by habit; so it does not rise up unimpaired. And, thus, there are two voluntary inclinations, neither one of which is complete, and what is present in one is lacking in the other.

Chapter 10 (22) Just as vain talkers and those who seduce the mind perish from before Thy presence,† O God, so let those perish who, noticing the two voluntary tendencies in the process of deliberation, maintain that there are two natures belonging to two minds: the one a good nature; the other, bad.‡ Truly, they themselves are evil when they entertain these bad opinions, and the same men will themselves become good if they form true opinions and give their assent to those that are true. As Thy Apostle says to them: 'You were once darkness, but now you are light in the Lord.'§ For, they wish to be light, not in the Lord but in themselves, being of the opinion that the nature of the soul is what God is. Thus, they have become denser darkness, since they have, with terrifying arrogance, departed farther from Thee – from Thee, the 'true Light which enlightens every man who comes into

the world.'** Give heed to what you say, be ye ashamed and come ye to Him and be enlightened, and your faces shall not be confounded.††

When I was deliberating on the immediate act of becoming a servant of the Lord, my God, as I had intended for a long time, it was I myself who willed it, it was I who willed it not; it was I in both cases. Yet I neither willed it fully, nor refused wholly to will it. So, I struggled with myself and divided myself from myself. And this disintegration went on involuntarily within me, yet it did not demonstrate the nature of an alien mind but punishment‡‡ of my own. Therefore, it was not I who did this work, but the sin that dwelt in me, arising from the punishment of a sin of a freer man,§§ for I was a son of Adam.

(23) Indeed, if there are as many opposed natures as there are voluntary inclinations which offer mutual resistance, then there will be not two wills, but many. If a person deliberates whether he will go to one of their meetings,*** or to the theatre, they cry out: 'See, two natures; the good one draws in this direction, the bad one draws away in that. Otherwise, whence come this hesitation of opposed wills within him?' But, I say they are both bad, both the one which draws the man to them and the one which draws him away to the theatre. But, they will not believe that there is anything but good in that which leads men to them. Suppose, now, one of our people deliberates and hovers within himself between two disputing inclinations of will, whether to go to the theatre or to our church, would they not themselves hesitate in giving an answer? For, either they will admit, against their will, that to go to our church is based on good will, just as they who go to church are initiated into and engaged in its

---

* The problem of the act of moral command (*imperium*) is particularly difficult in a psychology such as Augustine's, where the faculties of the soul are not clearly distinguished. St. Thomas makes the *imperium* an act of intellect, founded on a preceding act of will (*S.T.*, I–II, q. 17, 1, c.) Instead of this, Augustine distinguishes incomplete will-acts of command from complete ones.
† Psalms 67.3.
‡ Augustine has the Manichaean theory of two wills, one good and the other bad, in mind; cf. *De duabus anim. c. Manich.* 1.1.
§ Ephesians 5.8.

** John 1.9.
†† Psalms 33.6.
‡‡ The punishment (*poena*) is that of original sin. In the following sentence Augustine borrows from Romans 7.17.
§§ Adam originally enjoyed *libertas*, in the sense that he was free to will the good and to avoid sinning; after the Fall, man has *liberum arbitrium*, which consists in the ability to choose either good or evil. Fallen man is, then, less free than Adam in the state of original justice, and less free than a blessed soul in heaven which has regained its *libertas*. Cf. *Opus imperf. c. Julian.* 6.11; cf. Gilson, *Introd. à l'étude de s. Augustin* (2ᵐᵉ éd.) 212–213.
*** I.e., of the Manichaeans.

mysteries, or else they will think that two bad natures and two bad minds are struggling within the one man, and their customary statement will then not be true: that there is one good and the other evil. Or else they will be converted to the truth and will not deny that, when a person deliberates, the one soul is agitated by contrary inclinations of will.

(24) So, when they perceive that two wills are in conflict with themselves within one man, let them no longer say that two contrary minds arising from two contrary substances and from two contrary principles are fighting, one being good and the other evil. For, Thou, the truthful God, dost disprove them, dost refute and convict them: for instance, when both wills are bad, and someone deliberates whether to kill a man with poison or with steel; whether to steal this part or another part of another man's land, when he cannot steal both; whether to purchase sensual pleasure at extravagant cost or hoard his money with avarice; whether to go to the circus or the theatre,* if both are having a performance on the same day – or (adding a third possibility) to go instead to rob another's house, the occasion presenting itself, or (with even a fourth) to set out to commit adultery, if at the same time the possibility of doing so presents itself. If all these possibilities come together in one instant of time, and all are simultaneously desired, but cannot be put into effect at the same time, then they tear the mind to pieces within itself by the opposing tendencies of four volitions, or even by a greater number, so numerous the things that can be desired; yet, the Manichees are not accustomed to claim that there is such a plurality of different substances.

The same is true in the case of good inclinations of will. For, I ask them whether it be good to take delight in the reading of the Apostle, and whether it be good to take delight in a solemn psalm, and whether it be good to discourse upon the Gospel. To each question they will answer: 'It is good.' What then? If they are all equally delightful at one and the same time, then are not contrary wills drawing the heart of man in various directions, while deliberation proceeds as to which action we should seize upon first? All these inclinations are good, yet they vie with each other until one action is chosen, whereto may be directed, one and entire, the will which before had been split into several tendencies.

Thus, too, when eternity delights from above and the sensual appeal of a temporal good pulls from below, it is the same soul which wishes the one or the other, but with a will that is not entire, and so the soul is torn apart with the weight of its vexation while truth causes it to prefer the former, but habit does not permit it to put aside the latter.

Chapter 11 (25) So, I was sick at heart and suffered excruciating torture, accusing myself with a bitterness that far exceeded the customary. I twisted and turned in my chains, until they could be completely broken, for I was now held but weakly by them, but still held. And Thou didst urge from within my depths, O Lord, whipping me in the strictness of mercy with double scourges† of fear and shame, lest I should again relapse and fail to break that weak and thin chain which remained, while it would become strong again and bind me more firmly.

Within myself, I kept saying: 'Here, do it now, do it now,' and, as I spoke, I was already progressing to the moment of decision. Now, I was almost ready to do it, yet I did not. I did not fall back into my previous state, but stood quite near and recovered my breath. I tried again and I was almost there – almost – I was practically grasping and holding it. Yet, I was not there; I neither grasped nor held it, hesitating to die unto death and to live unto life. Stronger within me was the accustomed worse than the unaccustomed better. The closer that point in time came, at which I would become a different being, the more terror did it strike within me; it did not force me back or turn me aside, it held me in suspense.

(26) What held me were the trifles of trifles and vanities of vanities,‡ my former mistresses,

---

* Throughout the *City of God*, Augustine misses no opportunity to condemn theatrical performances. His criticism seems to be based on two points: the obscenity of the shows and the association of the show with pagan festivals. Cf. *De cat. rudibus* 16.24.

† Cf. *Aeneid* 5.457: *dextra ingeminans ictus*.
‡ *vanitates vanitantium*: cf. Ecclesiastes 1.2, which has *vanitas vanitatum*. Later in life, Augustine became aware of the latter reading (*Retract.* 1.7.3: in ref. to *De mor. eccles. Cath.*), but he did not (in the *Retractations*) suggest a change in this text of the *Conf.*, which rests on good Ms. authority.

plucking softly at the garment of my flesh and whispering: 'Do you send us away?' and: 'From this moment unto eternity, we shall not be with you, and: 'From this moment unto eternity, this and that will not be permitted you.' What suggestiveness was there in that phrase, 'this and that' – O my God, what suggestiveness! May Thy mercy avert its gaze from the soul of Thy servant! What sordid things, what indecencies, did those words suggest! Yet, I far less half heard them now, for it was not as though they openly opposed me by going straight for me; rather, they murmured from behind me, furtively twitching, as it were, at me, as I moved to depart, so that I would look back. Yet, they did retard me, hesitant as I was to tear myself away and to cut myself off from them, and to make the leap to the position to which I was called, for, all-powerful custom said to me: 'Can you live without these things, do you think?'

(27)   But, it now was saying this very feebly. For, from the direction to which I had turned my face and to which I was afraid to pass, the chaste dignity of continence began to manifest itself: tranquil and joyful, but not in a lascivious way, inviting me in upright fashion to come ahead and not hesitate; stretching forth to receive and embrace me holy hands filled with a multitude of good examples. There, so many boys and girls; there, youth in great number; people of every age; venerable widows; women grown old in virginity – and in them all continence herself was in no way barren, but the fecund mother* of children, of joys coming from espousal with Thee, O Lord.

With mocking encouragement, she† mocked me, as if saying: 'Can you not live as these men and women do? In fact, do these men and women live by their own powers and not by the Lord their God? The Lord their God gave me to them. Why do you stand upon yourself and so have naught to stand on? Throw yourself upon Him, fear not; He will not pull Himself away and let you fall. Throw yourself confidently; He will take you up and heal you.' I was much ashamed, for I still heard the whisperings of those trifles, and hung as one in suspense. Again, she seemed to say: 'Turn a deaf ear to your unclean members on the earth, in order that they may be mortified. They tell you a story

of delights,‡ but not as the Law of the Lord thy God.' This dispute within my heart was simply myself in opposition to myself. But Alypius kept right at my side and waited in silence for the outcome of my unaccustomed emotion.

Chapter 12   (28)   Now, when profound consideration had pulled out from the hidden depth and heaped together the whole of my wretchedness before the gaze of my heart, a mighty storm arose, bringing a mighty rain of tears. And, in order to shed the whole of it, with its accompanying groans, I stood up, away from Alypius (to me solitude seemed more fitting for the business of weeping), and I withdrew to a distance greater than that at which even his presence could be an annoyance to me. That is the way I felt then, and he perceived it; I suppose I said something or other, and my inflection revealed a voice weighted with tears, and so I had risen. Hence, he stayed where we had been sitting and was much astonished. I threw myself down under a fig tree, unconscious of my actions, and loosed the reins on my tears.§ They burst forth in rivers from my eyes, an acceptable sacrifice** unto Thee. Not, indeed, in these words, but with this meaning, I said many things to Thee: 'And Thou, O Lord, how long?†† How long, O Lord, wilt Thou be angry unto the end? Remember not our former iniquities.' For I still felt that I was held by them and I uttered these wretched words: 'How much longer, how much longer? "Tomorrow" and "tomorrow"? Why not right now? Why not the end of my shame at this very hour?'

(29)   I kept saying these things and weeping with the bitterest sorrow of my heart. And, behold, I heard from a nearby house the voice of someone – whether boy or girl I know not – chanting, as it were, and repeating over and over: 'Take it, read it! Take it, read it!' And immediately, with a transformed countenance, I started to think with greatest concentration whether it was the usual thing for children to chant words such as this in any kind of game, and it did not occur to me that I had ever heard anything like it. Having stemmed the flow of my tears, I got up,

* Cf. Psalms 112.9.
† I.e., chaste continence.
‡ Psalms 118.85.
§ *habenas lacrimis*: cf. *Aeneid* 12.499: *irarumque omnes effudit habenas.*
** Cf. Psalms 50.19.
†† Psalms 6.4; 78.5,8.

taking it to mean that nothing else was divinely commanded me than that I should open a book and read the first passage that I should find. For I had heard about Anthony* that he had been admonished from a reading of the Gospel on which he had come by chance, as if what was being read was said for him: 'Go, sell what thou hast, and give to the poor, and thou shalt have treasure in heaven; and come, follow me,'† and by such a revelation he was at once converted to Thee.

And so I went hurriedly back to the place where Alypius was sitting. I had placed there the copy of the Apostle, when I had got up from the place. Snatching it up, I opened it and read in silence the first passage on which my eyes fell: 'Not in revelry and drunkenness, not in debauchery and wantonness, not in strife and jealousy; but put on the Lord Jesus Christ, and as for the flesh, take no thought for its lusts.'‡ No further did I desire to read, nor was there need. Indeed, immediately with the termination of this sentence, all the darknesses of doubt were dispersed, as if by a light of peace flooding into my heart.

(30) Then, having marked it either with my finger or with some other sign, I closed the book and, with a now peaceful face, informed Alypius. Then, he gave an account of what was going on within him, of which I was in ignorance. He asked to see what I had read. I showed him and he paid attention even beyond that part which I had read. I did not know the section which followed. Actually, the continuation read: 'But him who is weak in faith, receive.'§ This, he applied to himself and he disclosed it to me. But he was strengthened by this admonition, in a decision and resolution which was good and most suitable to his moral qualities, in which he had far surpassed me for a long time, and he joined in without any trouble or delay.

After that, we went in to my mother and told her; she rejoiced. We gave her the story of what had happened; she was exultant, triumphant, and she blessed Thee, 'who art able to accomplish far more than we ask or understand.'** She saw

that much more in regard to me had been granted her by Thee than she was wont to ask with her unhappy and tearful laments. For Thou didst turn me unto Thee, so that I sought no wife or any ambition for this world, standing on that rule of faith†† where Thou hadst shown me in the revelation of so many years before. And 'Thou didst turn her mourning into joy,'‡‡ much more abundant than she had desired, and much more fond and pure than she sought from any grandchildren of my flesh.

Book Nine

Chapter 8 (17) Thou, 'Who dost make men of kindred minds to dwell in one house,'§§ didst also bring Evodius,*** a young man from our own town, into our group. He served as a special government agent, was converted to Thee and baptized before us, and, having left worldly service, was girded in Thine. We were together, intending to live together in holy agreement.

We looked for some place which would offer us the opportunity to serve Thee in a more useful way; we were returning together to Africa. While we were at Ostia on the Tiber,††† my mother *died*.

I pass over many things, for I am in a great hurry. Receive my confessions and my thanks, O my God, for numberless things, even when I am silent. But, I shall not pass over whatever my soul brings forth concerning that servant of Thine who brought me forth in the flesh, so that I was born into the light of time – and in the heart, so that I was born into the light of eternity. I would speak not of her gifts, but of Thine in her. For, she had not made herself, nor had she brought herself up. Thou didst create her; neither her father nor her mother knew what kind of person

---

* Cf. 8.6.14. In *Epistles* 55.37 (written about the same time as the *Conf.*) Augustine disapproves chance consultations of the Gospels for guidance in worldly affairs.
† Matthew 19.21.
‡ Romans 13.13.
§ Romans 14.1.
** Ephesians 3.20.
†† Cf. above, 3.11.19.
‡‡ Psalms 29.12.
§§ Psalms 67.7; the revised English version has: 'God who maketh men of one manner to dwell in a house'; this does not bring out the *unanimes* of Augustine's text.
*** Evodius was a man of fine mind and good education. He is one of the chief speakers in Augustine's dialogues *De libero arbitrio* and *De quantitate animae*. Consecrated Bishop of Uzala in 396, he remained a lifelong friend and co-worker of Augustine.
††† Ostia was the port of Rome; cf. *Aeneid* 1.13.

would spring from them. The rod of Thy Christ, the discipline of Thine only Son in a faithful household, a sound member of Thy Church,* instructed her 'in Thy Fear.'†

In regard to her training, she did not commend her mother's carefulness as much as that of a certain elderly maidservant who had carried her father about as a baby, just as little ones are customarily carried on the backs of grown-up girls. Because of this service and on account of her old age and excellent behavior, she was much respected by those in charge of that Christian home. As a result, she also had the care of the daughters of the family and was assiduous in this, restraining them, when necessary, as one stern in her pious severity, and tutoring them with virtuous prudence.

Except at those times when they were fed very temperately at the parental table, she would not permit them to drink even water, although they might be burning with thirst, thus preventing the formation of a bad habit and making this wise statement in addition: 'You now drink water only because you are not in charge of the wine; however, when you are married and become the mistresses of storerooms and wine-cellars, water will lose its appeal, but the habit of drinking will continue.' By this system of giving practical advice and commanding by means of her authority, she reined in the greediness of the younger years and moulded that thirst of the girls according to the measure of virtue, so that, eventually, that which was unfitting was also unpleasing.

(18) Just the same, it developed surreptitiously, as Thy servant [Monica] told the story to me, her son, that the craving for wine grew upon her. When, in the customary way, she, as a sober girl, was told by her parents to draw wine from the cask, and, having dipped the cup through an opening on the top, before pouring the wine into the decanter, she used to take a little sip with the tips of her lips. She could not take more, because she felt a repugnance for it. She did this not from any immoderate craving, but as a result of a certain overflowing of youthful spirits which bubble over into absurd actions and are usually held down in the minds of children by the weight of the authority of older people.

So, by the addition of a little bit each day to the original sip ('for he that contemneth small things falls by little and little'‡), she had fallen into the habit of eagerly gulping down cups almost full of wine.

Where, then, was the wise old woman, and her stern prohibition? Would anything prevail against a hidden disease, unless Thy medicine§ watched over us,** O Lord? In the absence of father and mother, and of nurses, Thou art present, Thou who dost create, who dost call, who dost even work some good for the salvation of souls through men who are in positions of authority.††

What didst Thou do then, O my God? From what source didst Thou provide a cure? From what source didst Thou restore her to health? Didst Thou not bring forth a hard and sharp taunt from another soul, like a healing scalpel from Thy secret repository, and cut off that decayed matter with one slash?

The maid with whom she used to go to the wine cask began to quarrel with her young mistress, and, as a result, when they were alone with each other, she cast up this misdeed, calling her a wine-bibber,‡‡ by way of most bitter insult. Stung to the quick by this goad, she looked upon her own foulness, immediately condemned it, and cast it from her.

Just as friends may pervert by their flattery, so do enemies often correct by their criticism. Thou dost not repay them for what Thou workest through them, but for what they themselves desired. That angry girl desired to vex her young mistress, not to cure her; and it happened in privacy, either because the time and place of the quarrel happened to find them alone, or because she feared lest she herself fall into danger through having delayed her denunciation for so long.

But Thou, O Lord, the Ruler of things heavenly and earthly, who dost twist the depths of the

---

* Monica's family was thoroughly Christian.
† Psalms 5.8.

‡ Ecclisiastes 19.1.
§ I.e., divine grace.
** Cf. Jeremiah 31.28.
†† *per praepositos homines*: the text would seem to be corrupt; Knöll suggests *reprobos* for *praepositos*, but there is no Ms. authority for the emendation.
‡‡ *meribibulam*: the word occurs only in Augustinian terminology, being found also in *Op. imperf. c. Julian.* 1.68, where it appears that some Pelagian critic picked it up from the *Confessions.*

torrent to Thine own use, and the flood of the centuries to regulated violence, dost even make one soul healthy through the unhealthy fury of another, so that no one, noticing this, may attribute to his own power the fact that another is corrected by his words, even though he intends to correct him.

Chapter 9 (19) Brought up in this modest and sober manner, made subject to her parents by Thee rather than to Thee by her parents, given in marriage when she reached a suitable age, she served this man 'as her lord.'* She was eager to win him for Thee,† speaking to him of Thee through her behavior, in which Thou didst make her beautiful, reverently lovable, and wonderful to her husband. Thus, she even put up with wrongs of infidelity, never permitting any dissension with her husband as a result of such a matter. She looked forward to Thy mercy upon him, that he might become chaste as a believer in Thee.

Moreover, though he was outstanding for his kindness, he was also quick to anger. But, she had learned not to oppose an angry husband, either by action or even by word. Eventually, she would observe that his mood had changed and become tranquil, whereupon she would seize the opportune moment to explain her action to him, if, by chance, he had been thoughtlessly disturbed. In short, while many matrons whose husbands were of milder disposition bore the marks of beatings, even in the form of facial disfigurement, and during friendly conversations they criticized the behavior of their husbands, she criticized their talkativeness, seriously reminding them, but as if it were a joke, that from the time that they had heard the reading of those contracts which are called matrimonial, they should have considered them as legal forms by which they had become slaves; accordingly, being mindful of their condition, they ought not to be haughty in relation to their lords. When they expressed amazement, knowing as they did what a bad-tempered husband she put up with, that there had never been any rumor or indication to suggest that Patricius‡ had beaten his wife, or that they had

quarrelsomely disagreed with each other, even for one day, they asked in a friendly manner for an explanation and she told them her way of getting along, which I have noted above. Those who adopted it were grateful as a result of their own experience; those who did not observe it continued to be annoyed at their subjugation.

(20) At first, too, her mother-in-law was stirred up against her by the whisperings of badly disposed servant-girls. But, she persevered in showing marks of respect, and this won her over by patience and gentleness, with the result that her mother-in-law spontaneously revealed to her son the meddling tongues of the servants, by whom the domestic tranquility between herself and her daughter-in-law was disturbed, and she expressed her desire that they be punished. So, after this, acting in obedience to his mother, in consideration of good order in the family and with concern for the harmony of them all, he had the culprits punished by whipping, in accordance with the recommendation of their denouncer. She promised that like reward should be anticipated by anyone who said anything bad to her about her daughter-in-law, in order to incur her favor. After that, no one made another attempt, and they lived together in a remarkably pleasant state of good will.

(21) Thou hast also given to this good bondswoman of Thine, in whose womb Thou didst create me, O my God, my Mercy,§ the great capacity of serving, whenever possible, as a peacemaker between whatever souls were in disagreement and discord. Thus, when she heard from both parties a good many very bitter remarks about each other – the sort of things which bloated and undigested discord usually vomits up when the indigestion of hatred belches forth into sour gossip with a present friend about an absent enemy – she would not reveal anything about one to the other, unless it would be useful in reconciling them.

---

* Cf. Ephesians 5.21.
† Her husband, Patricius, was a pagan for many years.
‡ In a recent work (R. Pottier, *S. Augustin le Berbère* [Paris 1945]), the thesis is maintained that Augustine's family is completely indigenous to North Africa. This

is quite possible; in fact, there is no real evidence for the contention of many biographers that Patricius was of Roman descent. Many Africans took Roman names. However, Pottier's arguments are more the product of ethnic enthusiasm than scholarship. Cf. A. Dyroff's note on Augustine's parentage, in L. Schopp, *Aurelius Augustinus Selbstgespräche* (München 1938) 114–118.
§ Psalms 58.18.

This would seem but a small good, except that I have had sad experience with countless crowds of people who, through some dreadful and very widespread pestilence of sin, not only run to angry enemies with the statements of their angry enemies, but even add things which were not said. On the contrary, it should be little enough of an obligation for the man who is worthy of his species to refrain from starting or increasing animosities among men by evil talk, if, in fact, one does not even strive to extinguish them by good talk.

Such a person was she, under the influence of Thy teaching as an inner Teacher in the school of her breast.*

(22) Eventually, she won her own husband over to Thee, right at the end of his earthly life, and she found no cause for complaint in him when he was now one of the faithful, such as she had borne when he was not yet in the faith. She was also a servant of Thy servants.† Among them, whoever knew her found much reason in her for praising, honoring, and loving Thee, for one felt Thy presence in her heart through the fruitful evidence of her saintly manner of life.‡ She had been the wife of but one man,§ had made some return to her parents, had managed her own household in piety, and possessed a reputation for good works. She had brought up her children, being in labor with them** each time that she saw them wandering away from Thee. Finally, O Lord, she took such care of all of us, whom in Thy bounty Thou dost permit me to call Thy servants – for, before she went to her rest in Thee we were already living in a group after receiving the grace of Thy baptism – that it was almost as if she were a mother to us all, and she served us in such a way that it was as if she were the daughter of us all.

Chapter 10 (23) When the day on which she was to depart from this life was near at hand (Thou knewest the day; we did not), I believe it happened by Thy management, in Thy hidden ways, that she and I were standing alone, leaning on a window†† from which the garden inside the house‡‡ we occupied could be viewed. It was at Ostia on the Tiber, where, far removed from the crowds after the hardship of a long journey,§§ we were resting in preparation for the sea voyage.

We were talking to each other alone,*** very sweetly, 'forgetting what is behind, straining forward to what is before.'††† Between us, 'in the present truth,'‡‡‡ which Thou art, we tried to find out what the eternal life of the saints would be, which 'eye has not seen nor ear heard, nor hast it entered into the heart of man.'§§§ But, we also yearned with the mouth of our heart for the supernal flood from 'Thy Fountain, the Fountain of Life which is with Thee,'**** so that, having been sprinkled from it as much as our capacity would permit, we might think in some way about such a great thing.

(24) When our talk had reached the conclusion that the greatest delight of the bodily senses, in the brightest bodily light, was not capable of comparison with the joy of that life and, moreover, did not seem worthy of being mentioned, then, lifting ourselves up in the yet greater ardor of our feeling toward the Selfsame,†††† we advanced step by step through all bodily things up to the sky itself, from which the sun, moon,

---

* This theme of Christ as the Interior Master is developed thoroughly in the dialogue, *De magistro*.
† Cf. Genesis 9.25.
‡ Monica is recognized as a saint in Catholic tradition; it is clear that she was so regarded by her son. Other examples of Augustine's esteem, which go beyond mere filial piety, are to be found in *De ordine* 2.1 and *De beata vita* 1.10.
§ For the special position of widows in the early Church, cf. 1 Timothy 5.3–16, phrases from which are here quoted.
** Cf. Galatians 4.19.

†† The painting of this scene by Ary Scheffer (Louvre) has often been reproduced.
‡‡ This was a garden in a courtyard, or peristyle.
§§ The overland trip from Milan to Rome was no doubt a fatiguing journey.
*** Ch. 10, nn. 23–26, describes the much discussed ecstasy at Ostia. For a brief analysis of its philosophical implications, cf. Cayré, *Initiation* 170–173; the same author has made one of the best studies of its spiritual significance, in *La contemplation augustinienne* (Paris 1927) 209–212. Cf. also C. Boyer, 'La contemplation d'Ostie,' *Cahiers de la nouv. journée* 18 (Paris 1930) 137–161. With particular reference to the Plotinian source of the language (*Ennead.* 1.6.8–9; 5.1.11), cf. P. Henry, *La vision d'Ostie* (Paris 1938).
††† Phil. 3.13.
‡‡‡ 2 Peter 1.12.
§§§ 1 Cor. 2.9.
**** Ps. 35.10.
†††† *id ipsum*: cf. above, Bk. 9 n. 46.

and stars shine out over the earth, and we ascended still farther in our interior cogitation, conversation, and admiration of Thy works and came to our own minds.

Then, we transcended them, so that we might touch that realm of unfailing abundance in which Thou feedest Israel eternally on the food of truth.* There, life is wisdom, through which all these things come into being, both those which have been and those which will be. Yet, it is not made, but is as it was, and thus it will be forever. Or, rather, to have been in the past, or to be in the future, do not pertain to it, but simply *to be*, for it is eternal. To be in the past, or to be in the future, is not to be eternal.

And, while we are so speaking and panting for it, we did touch† it a little, with an all-out thrust of our hearts. We sighed and left behind 'the first fruits of the spirit'‡ which were bound there, and we came back to the clattering of our mouths, where the spoken word has its beginning and end. How is it like Thy Word, our Lord, 'remaining ageless in Itself and renewing all things'?§

(25)   We were saying then: 'Suppose, for any person, that the tumult of the flesh be silenced – silenced, the images of earth and water and air; silenced, the very heavens; silenced, his very soul unto himself, then, if he pass beyond himself, ceasing to think of himself by means of images** – silenced, his dreams and imaginary apparitions, every tongue and every sign, and whatever comes to be by transition, if he be granted this complete silence (since, if one can hear, all these things are saying: "We did not make ourselves, but He Who endureth forever made us"††) – and if, having said this, they become quiet, once they

have lifted up his ear to Him who made them; then, if He alone speak, not through them, but through Himself, so that we might hear His Word, not through fleshly speech, or through the voice of an angel, or through the crash of thunder, or through the darkness of a similitude,‡‡ but *Himself* whom we love in these things – and if we might hear Him, without these things, just as now we reached out and, with the speed of thought, touched the Eternal Wisdom abiding above all things – and if this could continue, and other visions of a much lower type were taken away, and this one vision were to enrapture, absorb, and enclose its beholder in inner joys, so that life might forever be like that instant of understanding, for which we had sighed, then surely, this is the meaning of: "Enter into the joy of Thy Master"?§§ When will this be? Perhaps, when "we shall all rise but shall not all be changed"?'***

(26)   Such things I was saying, though not in this way, or in these words.††† Nevertheless, O Lord Thou knowest that, on that day when we were conversing on such things, and this world with all its pleasures became, as we were speaking, contemptible to us, she said these words: 'Son, for myself, I find no pleasure, now, in anything in this life. What I am doing here, now, and why I am here, I do not know; my hope for this world is already fufilled. There was but one thing for which I yearned to remain a little longer in this life. That was to see you a Catholic Christian before I died. My God has more abundantly satisfied my desire, inasmuch as I see you now, having spurned earthly felicity, become His servant. What am I doing here?'

---

* Cf. Ezech. 34.13–14; Psalms 77.71.
† *attingimus*: this reading has the strongest Ms. tradition, and it is taken as a historical present.
‡ Romans 8.23.
§ Cf. Wisdom 7.27: 'remaining in herself the same, she [wisdom] renewed all things.'
** Literally: 'by not cogitating on himself.'
†† Psalms 99.3–5.

‡‡ Cf. 1 Corinthians 13.12.
§§ Matthew 25.21–23.
*** 1 Corinthians 15.51.
††† Actually, the words in the reported conversation are at times very similar to passages in the *Enneads* of Plotinus. It is probable that Augustine, who seems to have had a wonderful memory, used the language of Plotinus without being wholly conscious of the fact.

Boethius, *The Consolation of Philosophy*, Book IV, Sections I and V–VII

Introduction

Ancius Boethius (480–524) was one of the most significant intellectual figures in early medieval Europe. Without his Latin translations and commentaries on Greek texts, it has been suggested that philosophy itself might have died out during the so-called "Dark Ages." His many writings on diverse subjects – music, theology, geometry, and so on – were among the relatively few books commonly read during the period. Boethius was once described as "the last of the Roman philosophers, and the first of the scholastic theologians," and certainly, like Augustine of Hippo (IV.3) a century earlier, Boethius represents an intriguing fusion of classical (especially Neo-Platonic) and Christian thought.

Boethius combined a life of scholarship with public service. Born to an aristocratic Christian family at nearly the same time that Benedict of Nursia was born (c. 480) and that Odoacer deposed Romulus Augustulus, the last emperor in the west (476), Boethius hailed from a family that is said to have included a number of popes and emperors. Boethius's father had held the eminent political office of consul, and Boethius himself quickly rose through the political hierarchy to be named consul himself in 510 by the Ostrogoth

From Boethius, *The Consolation of Philosophy*, trans. V. E. Watts, London: Penguin, 1969, pp. 116–17, 132–44 (two poems omitted).

king of Rome, Theodoric. Later Boethius became, in effect, the head of the western empire's civil service.

Philosophically, Boethius devoted himself mostly to translating and elaborating Greek philosophy, making contributions to logical and dialectical thought that were especially remarkable. He wrote influential text books in logic, music, arithmetic, and geometry for students of the liberal arts *quadrivium*. He produced commentaries on Porphyry's *Isagoge* (*Introduction*) and Aristotle's *De interpretatione*; and he translated Aristotle's other logical texts. In fact, Boethius's translations of Aristotle's logic remained the only texts by Aristotle available to western scholars until well into the twelfth century. In a series of theological treatises, Boethius defended Christian trinitarian orthodoxy against the Arianism that had become so influential in the west.[1]

In 523, however, Boethius became the object of Theodoric's ire – perhaps because of undue sympathy for the eastern emperor's stance on a number of issues that divided Rome and Constantinople. He was imprisoned and in 524, after being cruelly tortured, was put to death by beating. It was during this arduous year of imprisonment that Boethius wrote *The Consolation of Philosophy*, one of the most popular books of the Middle Ages, or for that matter any time, and a text admired by, among others, Alfred the Great, Chaucer, and Dante. Even the famously skeptical Edward Gibbon, more than twelve centuries later, declared the book a "golden volume." The

Consolation, a mixture of prose and verse, takes the form of a conversation between Boethius-the-prisoner and Philosophy, in the personified shape of a woman of "awe-inspiring appearance." The governing metaphor of the work is a medical one: "Lady" Philosophy is a "nurse" applying "moral medication," as one commentator calls it, to heal the spiritual "wounds" of the prisoner-patient. Here Boethius is invoking a familiar stoic, or indeed Socratic, conception of philosophy as ministering to the spiritual needs of afflicted souls and as preparing human beings for death.

The *Consolation* is puzzling in this regard, because it appeals not to Christianity but to philosophy as a guide to life, for an explanation of moral goodness, and for consolation in the face of one's mortality. Boethius draws on ideas appearing in a number of Platonic dialogues (including *Gorgias, Timaeus, Phaedo*, and *Republic*), as well as a number of works by Aristotle. Its lack reference to Christianity however, lends, it an "uncertain status as a text by a Christian writer without explicitly Christian doctrines, and with some ideas which seemed distinctly pagan," such as that of reincarnation.[2] Possibly Boethius's misfortunes had undermined his Christian faith; but it is more likely that here, as in his earlier, confessedly Christian works, he saw no fatal incompatibility between his faith and his appeals to "pagan" views. Still, it remains curious that, *in extremis*, Boethius should turn for consolation to the nurse, Philosophy, rather than to the deity, Jesus Christ.

Much of the *Consolation*, including Book IV, is unsurprisingly an exercise in theodicy – in justifying the will and ways of God in the face of seemingly recalcitrant features of the world, above all the apparent presence in it of evil. For "Lady" Philosophy, as for Augustine and Leibniz (IV.3 and IV.13), this is "the greatest of all questions." The particular issue addressed in what follows from Book IV is how to explain the suffering of good people and the prospering of bad people in a world purportedly ordered by a good god. With the help of an important distinc-

tion between "Providence" (God's simple, overall rational plan) and "Fate" (the law-governed but complex, "ever-changing web" of the actual universe), Boethius argues that this issue may be dissolved. "It is [only] because you [ignorant] men are in no position to contemplate this order that everything seems confused and upset," declares Philosophy. Less ignorant creatures would be able to discern, for example, that undeserved distress, like Boethius's own, is an "opportunity . . . to strengthen his wisdom." More generally, if, as Philosophy has argued in Socratic vein in Book III, happiness and goodness are identical, then it must be an illusion, due to ignorance, that evil people can be happy and good people unhappy.

But perhaps the main consolation offered is hinted at in Section VI of the chapter. This is not the consolation of appreciating that the world of Fate must, for all its apparent horrors, be good, but that a person can – through meditation and drawing close to "the steadfast mind of God" – "escape the necessity imposed by Fate." Spiritual health is achieved less through looking at the world through what critics might regard as rose-colored glasses than through self-transformation, by renouncing the world and retreating to "the still point" around which the world revolves.

Notes

1 "Arianism" – named after the theologian, Arius (250–336), denounced at the Council of Nicaea in 325, but popular in the Gothic-Germanic portions of the empire – is the view that Jesus (God the son) is not equal with the God the Father but is, rather, subordinate to the Father, even created by the Father. Arianism was one of the most contentious theological issues to have faced Christendom before the Reformation.

2 J. Marenbon, "Boethius: From Antiquity to the Middle Ages," in J. Marenbon, ed., *Medieval Philosophy*, London: Routledge, 1998, p. 24.

Boethius, *The Consolation of Philosophy*

Book IV

I Philosophy delivered this sweet and gentle song with dignity of countenance and gravity of expression. But I had still not forgotten the grief within me and I cut her short just as she was preparing to say something.

'You,' I said, 'who are my leader towards the true light, all that you have poured forth in speech up to now has been clearly both divine to contemplate and invincibly supported by your arguments. You have spoken of things I had forgotten because of the pain of what I had suffered, but before this they were not entirely unknown to me.

'But the greatest cause of my sadness is really this – the fact that in spite of a good helmsman to guide the world, evil can still exist and even pass unpunished. This fact alone you must surely think of considerable wonder. But there is something even more bewildering. When wickedness rules and flourishes, not only does virtue go unrewarded, it is even trodden underfoot by the wicked and punished in the place of crime. That this can happen in the realm of an omniscient and omnipotent God who wills only good, is beyond perplexity and complaint.'

'It would indeed be a matter of infinite wonder,' she said, 'it would be something more horrible than any outrage, if, as you reckon, in the well-ordered house of so great a father the worthless vessels were looked after at the expense of the precious ones, which grew filthy. But it is not so.

'If your recent conclusions may remain intact, you can learn from the Creator Himself since it is His realm we are speaking of, that the good are always strong and the wicked always humbled and weak. From Him, too, you can learn that sin never goes unpunished or virtue unrewarded, and that what happens to the good is always happy and that what happens to the bad always misfortune. There are many other considerations of this kind which, once your complaints have been stilled, will give you firm and solid strength.

'You have seen the shape of true happiness when I showed it to you just now, and you saw where it is to be found; and when we have run through all that I think we should clear out of the way

beforehand, I will show you the path that will bring you back home. I will give your mind wings on which to lift itself; all disquiet shall be driven away and you will be able to return safely to your homeland. I will be your guide, your path and your conveyance. [. . .]

V Then I said, 'Yes, I can see there is a kind of happiness and misery which are inseparable from the very actions of good and bad men. But I believe that there is both good and bad in the actual fortune of ordinary people. No wise man prefers being in exile, being poor and disgraced to being rich, respected, and powerful, and to remaining at home and flourishing in his own city. For this is the way that wisdom is more clearly and obviously seen to be operating, when somehow or other the happiness of their rulers is communicated to the people they come into contact with, especially if prison and death and all the other sufferings the law imposes by way of punishment are reserved for the wicked citizens for whom they were intended. Why this is all turned upside down, why good men are oppressed by punishments reserved for crime and bad men can snatch the rewards that belong to virtue surprises me very much, and I would like to know from you the reason for this very unjust confusion. I would be less surprised if I could believe that the confusion of things is due to the fortuitous operations of chance. But my wonder is only increased by the knowledge that the ruling power of the universe is God. Sometimes He is pleasant to the good and unpleasant to the bad, and other times He grants the bad their wishes and denies the good. But since He often varies between these two alternatives, what grounds are there for distinguishing between God and the haphazards of chance?'

'It is not surprising,' she said, 'if ignorance of the principle of its order makes people think a thing is unplanned and chaotic. But even if you don't know the reason behind the great plan of the universe, there is no need for you to doubt that a good power rules the world and that everything happens aright.

'If you knew not the stars of Arcturus
Sail near the highest pole of heaven, or why
The Waggoner is late to take his wain
And late to dip his flames into the sea
Although his rising comes again with haste,

The law observed in heaven would leave you
　dazed.
And let the full moon's gleaming horns grow pale
As night extends his bounds across her disc;
Let Phoebe dimmed the confused stars reveal
Which just before her shining light had masked;
Whole nations by the common error moved
Rain frequent blows on pots and pans of brass.
Yet no one wonders when the north west wind
Sweeps in the roaring waves to beat the shore,
Or when the frozen mass of hard-packed snow
Dissolves before the sun's aestival heat.
The causes in this case are clear to view,
But hidden cause confounds the human heart,
Perplexed by things that rarely come to pass,
For unexpected things the people dread.
Then let the clouds of ignorance give way
And these events will no more wondrous seem.'

VI　'It is so,' I said. 'But since it is part of your task to unravel the causes of matters that lie hidden and to unfold reasons veiled in darkness, and since I am very much disturbed by this strange phenomenon, I do beg you to tell me your teaching on this point.'

She paused and smiled a moment before answering.

'You are urging me to the greatest of all questions, a question that can never be exhausted. The subject is of such a kind that when one doubt has been removed, countless others spring up in its place, like the Hydra's heads. The only way to check them is with a really lively intellectual fire. The usual subjects of inquiry concern the oneness of providence, the course of fate, the haphazard nature of the random events of chance, divine knowledge and predestination, and the freedom of the will; you can see for yourself how difficult they are.

'However, as a knowledge of these things, too, is a part of your treatment, we will try to determine something, in spite of the narrow limits in which we are imprisoned by time. And if the enchantments of song delight you, you will have to postpone your pleasure a little while I weave together the close-knit arguments in their proper order.'

'Whatever you wish,' I said.

Then, as if she were starting a fresh argument, she spoke as follows.

'The generation of all things, the whole progress of things subject to change and whatever moves in any way, receive their causes, their due order

and their form from the unchanging mind of God. In the high citadel of its oneness, the mind of God has set up a plan for the multitude of events. When this plan is thought of as in the purity of God's understanding, it is called Providence, and when it is thought of with reference to all things, whose motion and order it controls, it is called by the name the ancients gave it, Fate. If anyone will examine their meaning, it will soon be clear to him that these two aspects are different. Providence is the divine reason itself. It is set at the head of all things and disposes all things. Fate, on the other hand, is the planned order inherent in things subject to change through the medium of which Providence binds everything in its own allotted place. Providence includes all things at the same time, however diverse or infinite, while Fate controls the motion of different individual things in different places and in different times. So this unfolding of the plan in time when brought together as a unified whole in the foresight of God's mind is Providence; and the same unified whole when dissolved and unfolded in the course of time is Fate.

'They are different, but the one depends on the other. The order of Fate is derived from the simplicity of Providence. A craftsman anticipates in his mind the plan of the thing he is going to make, and then sets in motion the execution of the work and carries out in time the construction of what he has seen all at one moment present to his mind's eye. In the same way God in his Providence constructs a single fixed plan of all that is to happen, while it is by means of Fate that all that He has planned is realized in its many individual details in the course of time. So, whether the work of Fate is done with the help of divine spirits of Providence, or whether the chain of Fate is woven by the soul of the universe, or by the obedience of all nature, by the celestial motions of the stars, or by the power of the angels, by the various skills of other spirits, or by some of these, or by all of them, one thing is certainly clear: the simple and unchanging plan of events is Providence, and Fate is the ever-changing web, the disposition in and through time of all the events which God has planned in His simplicity.

'Everything, therefore, which comes under Fate, is also subject to Providence, to which Fate itself is subject, but certain things which come under Providence are above the chain of Fate. These are things which rise above the order of change ruled over by Fate in virtue of the stability of their position close to the supreme Godhead. Imagine a set of revolving concentric circles. The inmost one comes closest to the simplicity of the centre, while forming itself a kind of centre for those set outside it to revolve round. The circle furthest out rotates through a wider orbit and the greater its distance from the indivisible centre point, the greater the space it spreads through. Anything that joins itself to the middle circle is brought close to simplicity, and no longer spreads out widely. In the same way whatever moves any distance from the primary intelligence becomes enmeshed in ever stronger chains of Fate, and everything is the freer from Fate the closer it seeks the centre of things. And if it cleaves to the steadfast mind of God, it is free from movement and so escapes the necessity imposed by Fate. The relationship between the ever-changing course of Fate and the stable simplicity of Providence is like that between reasoning and understanding, between that which is coming into being and that which is, between time and eternity, or between the moving circle and the still point in the middle.

'The course of Fate moves the sky and the stars, governs the relationship between the elements and transforms them through reciprocal variations; it renews all things as they come to birth and die away by like generations of offspring and seed. It holds sway, too, over the acts and fortunes of men through the indissoluble chain of causes; and since it takes its origins from unchanging Providence, it follows that these causes, too, are unchanging. For the best way of controlling the universe is if the simplicity immanent in the divine mind produces an unchanging order of causes to govern by its own incommutability everything that is subject to change, and which will otherwise fluctuate at random.

'It is because you men are in no position to contemplate this order that everything seems confused and upset. But it is no less true that everything has its own position which directs it towards the good and so governs it. There is nothing that can happen because of evil or because engineered by the wicked themselves, and they, as we have most amply demonstrated, are deflected from their search for the good by mistake and error, while the order which issues from the supreme good at the centre of the universe cannot deflect anyone from his beginning.

'No doubt your objection will be that it is impossible for there to be a more unjust confusion than when the fortunes of good men and bad alike continually vary between adversity and prosperity. And I shall ask you if men have such soundness of mind as to be infallible in their judgement of who is good and who is bad. No, human judgements clash in this matter, and some people think the same men deserve reward as others think worthy of punishment.

'Supposing, however, we grant that someone may be able to judge between good and bad, it will hardly enable him to see the inner hidden temperament, to borrow a term from physics, of men's minds. Indeed, your surprise is like that of a man who does not know why in the case of healthy bodies sweet things agree with some and bitter things with others, or why some sick people are helped by gentle remedies, others by sharp ones. But it is no surprise to the doctor who knows the difference between the manner and temper of health and of sickness. Now, we know that in the case of the mind health means goodness and sickness means wickedness. And that the protector of the good and scourge of the wicked is none other than God, the mind's guide and physician. He looks out from the watch-tower of Providence, sees what suits each person, and applies to him whatever He knows is suitable. This, then, is the outstanding wonder of the order of fate; a knowing God acts and ignorant men look on with wonder at his actions.

'Let us glance at a few facts concerning God's profundity, such as human reason can grasp. In the case of someone you consider a model and a great defender of justice, omniscient Providence thinks otherwise. A member of my own household, the poet Lucan, has reminded us in the first book of his *Pharsalia* how in the struggle between Caesar and Pompey the winning cause pleased the Gods, but the losing cause pleased Cato, although he was a model of virtue. Whenever, therefore, you see something happen here different from your expectation, due order is preserved by events, but there is confusion and error in your thinking.

'But let us suppose that there was someone of such moral goodness that in his case the judgement of man and God coincided; he will still be weak in strength of mind. Should adversity befall him, he will perhaps give up practising the innocence which could not ensure his good fortune. And so a wise direction spares the man whom adversity might affect for the worse, to avoid distressing someone who is not fit for it. Another man may be perfect in every virtue, holy and very close to God: Providence judges that it would be outrageous for him to meet with any adversity to such an extent that he is not even allowed to be upset by bodily illness. As was said by someone more excellent than me:

The body of the holy one was built by heaven.

'Often it happens that supreme power is given to good men so that the exuberance of wickedness may be checked. Others receive a mixture of good and bad fortune according to their quality of mind. Providence stings some people to avoid giving them happiness for too long, and others she allows to be vexed by hard fortune to strengthen their virtues of mind by the use and exercise of patience. Some people are excessively afraid of suffering for which they actually have the endurance; others are full of scorn for suffering they cannot in fact bear. Both kinds she brings to self discovery through hardship. Some men at the price of a glorious death have won a fame that generations will venerate; some indomitable in the face of punishment have given others an example that evil cannot defeat virtue. There is no doubt that it is right that these things happen, that they are planned and that they are suited to those to whom they actually happen.

'The fact, too, that the wicked have their ups and downs of fortune is due to the same causes. When they suffer, no one is surprised, because everyone considers they deserve ill; and their punishments both deter others from crime and correct those on whom they are inflicted. And when they prosper, it is a powerful argument to good men about the kind of judgement they should make of such happiness as they often see wait upon the wicked. And here there is something else I believe to be planned. There is perhaps someone of such a headstrong and impulsive nature that poverty could the more easily provoke him to crime. His sickness is relieved by Providence with a dose of wealth as a remedy. Another man may see his conscience blotched with the wickedness of his deeds and compare his desert with the fortune he enjoys. Perhaps he will begin to fear the hardness of losing all the things whose enjoyment is so pleasant, and therefore change his

ways and abandon wickedness in the fear of losing happiness. Others have been thrown headlong into well deserved disaster by using their happiness unworthily: and some were granted the right to punish in order that they might be a source of trial for the good and of punishment for the bad. For just as there is no agreement between good men and bad men, so even the bad cannot agree amongst themselves. It could scarcely be otherwise when with his own vices tearing his conscience in shreds each one is at loggerheads with himself, and they often do things which they later see should never have been done.

'And so sovereign Providence has often produced a remarkable effect – evil men making other evil men good. For some, when they think they suffer injustice at the hands of the worst of men, burn with hatred for evil men, and being eager to be different from those they hate, have reformed and become virtuous. It is only the power of God to which evils may also be good, when by their proper use He elicits some good result. For a certain order embraces all things, and anything which departs from the order planned and assigned to it, only falls back into order, albeit a different order, so as not to allow anything to chance in the realm of Providence.

'But as the *Iliad* [12, 176] puts it,

'Tis hard for me to speak as though a God.

And it is not allowed to man to comprehend in thought all the ways of the divine work or expound them in speech. Let it be enough that we have seen that God, the author of all natures, orders all things and directs them towards goodness. He is quick to hold all that He has created in His own image, and by means of the chain of necessity presided over by Fate banishes all evil from the bounds of His commonwealth. Evil is thought to abound on earth. But if you could see the plan of Providence, you would not think there was evil anywhere. But I see that you have long been bowed down by the weight of this question. You are worn out by the prolixity of the reasoning and have been looking forward to the sweetness of song. So take a draught that will refresh you and make you able to apply your thoughts more closely to further matters.

'If you desire to see and understand
In purity of mind the laws of God,

Your sight must on the highest point of heaven
   rest
Where through the lawful covenant of things
The wandering stars preserve their ancient
   peace:
The sun forth driven by his glittering flames
Stays not the orbit of the gelid moon;
Nor does the Bear who in the highest pole
Of heaven drives her swiftly-turning course
Which never to the western sea descends
Desire to follow other stars that set,
And merge her fire beneath the Atlantic deep:
By equal intervals of time each day
The Evening Star foretells the evening dusk
And comes again as Morning Star at dawn.
So everlasting courses are remade
By mutual love and war's disunion
Is banished from the shores of heaven above.
This concord governs all the elements
With equal measures, that the power of wet
Will yield by turns unto the hostile dry,
And cold will join in amity with hot;
The pendant fire will surge into the air,
And massive weight of earth will sink below.
And for these reasons when the spring grows
   warm
The flower-bearing year will breathe sweet scent,
In summer torrid days will dry the corn,
Ripe autumn will return with fruit endowed,
And falling rains will moisten wintry days.
This mixture brings to birth and nourishes
All things which breathe the breath of life on
   earth;
This mixture seizes, hides, and bears away
All things submerged in death's finality.
Meanwhile there sits on high the Lord of things,
Who rules and guides the reins of all that's
   made,
Their king and lord, their fount and origin,
Their law and judge of what is right and due.
All things that He with motion stirs to go
He holds and when they wander brings them
   back;
Unless He call them home to their true path,
And force them back their orbits to perfect,
Those things which stable order now protects,
Divorced from their true source would fall
   apart.
This is the love of which all things partake,
The end of good their chosen goal and close:
No other way can they expect to last,
Unless with love for love repaid they turn
And seek again the cause that gave them birth.'

VII   'Do you now see what is the consequence
of all that we have said?'
   'No, what is it?'

'All fortune is certainly good.'
   'How can that be?'
   'Listen. All fortune whether pleasant or adverse
is meant either to reward or discipline the good
or to punish or correct the bad. We agree, therefore, on the justice or usefulness of fortune, and
so all fortune is good.'
   'Your argument is very true, and if I were
thinking of the Providence you taught me
about just now and of Fate, your opinion would
be firmly founded. But let us please include it
among those opinions we some time ago called
inconceivable.'
   'Why so?' she asked.
   'Because it is a common expression, frequently
used by some, that people have bad fortune.'
   'Your wish, then, is that we should draw closer
to everyday language to avoid the appearance of
having moved too far from common usage?'
   'Yes, please.'
   'Well, you think of something that is useful as
being good, don't you?'
   'Yes.'
   'Now, such fortune as either disciplines or
corrects is useful, isn't it?'
   'Yes.'
   'And so good?'
   'Yes.'
   'Now this kind of fortune is that of men who
are either already on the path of virtue when
they battle with adversity, or who turn to the path
of virtue after quitting evil.'
   'It is so.'
   'What about the pleasant fortune, then, that is
given to good men as a reward? People don't say
this is bad, do they?'
   'No. They hold it to be extremely good, as it is.'
   'Then what about the last kind of fortune,
which is adverse and curbs the bad with due
punishment; do people think this is good?'
   'No, they don't; they consider it to be the
most miserable thing that can be imagined.'
   'Take care that in following popular opinions we haven't produced something really
inconceivable!'
   'What do you mean?'
   'Well, the result of all that we have agreed
is that whatever the fortune of those who are in
possession of virtue (whether that possession is
perfect, still growing or only incipient), it is
good, while the fortune of all those who rest in
wickedness is utterly bad.'

'This is true, even if no one would dare to admit it.'

'So a wise man ought no more to take it ill when he clashes with fortune than a brave man ought to be upset by the sound of battle. For both of them their very distress is an opportunity, for the one to gain glory and the other to strengthen his wisdom. This is why virtue gets its name, because it is firm in strength and unconquered by adversity.

'For you who are set on the path of increasing virtue have not come so far only to abandon yourself to delights or languish in pleasure. You are engaged in a bitter but spirited struggle against fortune of every kind, to avoid falling victim to her when she is adverse or being corrupted by her when she is favourable. Hold to the middle way with unshakeable strength. Whatever falls short or goes beyond, despises happiness but receives no reward for its toil. It is in your own hands what fortune you wish to shape for yourself, for the only function of adversity apart from discipline and correction, is punishment. [...]

Anselm of Canterbury, The Ontological Argument, *Proslogion*, Chapters I–V

Introduction

It may be an exaggeration to say that Anselm of Canterbury (1033–1109) was the founder of medieval scholastic philosophy, but it is certainly true that Anselm's work helped ignite the intense wave of study, speculation, and rational investigation of philosophical issues that characterized the schools (*scholae*) of medieval Christendom.

Born into a noble family in the Burgundian city of Aosta, nestled in the Italian Alps, Anselm in his mid-twenties rebelled against his repressive father's authority and fled to the Benedictine abbey of Bec in Normandy. Anselm may have been attracted to Bec because of the reputation of its remarkable abbot, Lanfranc, a Burgundian himself who had engaged in important philosophical disputes with leading thinkers like Berengar of Tours (c. 999–1088) and who had also established a dynamic school at the abbey. Rising in popularity and influence, Anselm followed Lanfranc as abbot of Bec in 1063. In 1093, just 27 years after the Norman Conquest (1066), he was installed as Archbishop of Canterbury. Despite his success, however, Anselm ran afoul of both spiritual and secular authorities. He tangled with William II over church lands and the authority of the crown to appoint bishops; and, although he supported the legitimacy of Urban II's disputed papacy, Anselm openly opposed the pontiff's First Crusade in 1095.

The lasting importance of Anselm's life, however, has been philosophical. In some ways, he served a role for medieval Christian philosophy similar to the one played by al-Kindi (805–873) in medieval Islamic and Saadia ben Gaon (c. 882–942) in medieval Jewish thought. That role was to promote the use of rational analysis in the scrutiny of philosophical topics. Doing so was, of course, nothing new. The contestants at Nicea (325) and the Church's other early doctrinal councils had done so, as had Augustine (354–430; see IV.3), Boethius (480–524; see IV.4), and pseudo-Dionysius the Areopagite (fl. late fifth century). Later thinkers like the *falasifah* intellectuals of Baghdad, Johannes Scots Eriugena (c. 815–77), and others had certainly done the same. But in the wake of al-Kindi and Anselm one finds a dramatic intensification of this sort of philosophy. The magnitude of this cultural event can, of course, be attributed to material factors such as improved accessibility to ancient texts as well as changing economic and political conditions. But part of the changes must also be attributed to the sheer intellectual power of these philosophers' work.

Anselm's output in particular exhibits a kind of succinct, clear, and compelling quality that has garnered him legions of readers over the centuries. He explored epistemological issues, especially the nature of absolute truth, in *De veritate*. In his *Monologion*, he advanced quasi-Platonistic arguments for the existence of God. But it has been

From M. J. Charlesworth, ed., *St. Anselm's* Proslogion: with A Reply on Behalf of the Fool *by Gaunilo and* The Author's Reply to Gaunilo, Oxford: Oxford University Press, 1965, pp. 111–21 (odd numbered pages only).

Anselm's short work, *Proslogion* or *Proslogium* (c. 1077), that has attracted the most attention, principally for the compressed proof that appears in the early pages of the work. It's a proof that has come to be known, following Kant's nomenclature (IV.16), as the "ontological argument."

Anselm's original title for the *Proslogion*, it seems, was to be *Faith Seeking Understanding*. And, indeed, Anselm ends the very first chapter with remarks that suggest that for him the possession of genuine faith is a necessary condition for the intellect to apprehend truth. That is, rather than rationally justified knowledge serving as a foundation for faith, faith must serve as a foundation for knowledge. That's because, in a tradition stretching back through Augustine's Platonism, sin is thought to limit and distort the operations of the intellect — unless faith and grace provide a corrective. Anselm writes: "For I do not seek to understand so that I may believe; but I believe so that I may understand [*credo ut intelligam*]. For I believe this also, that 'unless I believe, I shall not understand'."[1]

Nevertheless, Anselm aims the ontological argument at the declared atheist, aiming to show the remarkably contemporary conclusion that not simply is atheism false but that it is conceptually incoherent. Astonishingly, this classic argument turns upon little else than a definition of God. It's a definition, Anselm thinks, that anybody will accept — even an atheistic "fool." In a famous formulation, Anselm holds that God is, if nothing else, "something than which nothing greater can be thought" (*aliquid quo nihil maius cogitari posit*). Now, of course, contrary to later "negative" theologians like Maimonides, this definition implies that some positive knowledge of God is in fact possible (IV.8). But more importantly, Anselm takes it to entail, in conjunction with just a few other premises, God's existence. The key proposition Anselm conjoins to the definition is that it is "greater" to exist in reality independently of the mind (*en re*) than only to exist as an idea in someone's mind (*en mente; solo intellectu*). That is, whether one considers a unicorn, a loved one, a thousand gold coins or God, it is metaphysically superior to exist in the world than merely to exist as someone's thought, fantasy, or memory. What distinguishes God, however, from unicorns, human beings, or gold coins, follows from God's unique definition: It's impossible for God not to

exist, and it's impossible for God to exist in any but the greatest possible way — that is, outside the mind. So, while maintaining the non-existence (or only the mental existence) of a unicorn, a human being, or a thousand gold coins does not contradict their definitions, maintaining God's non-existence (or mere mental existence) does contradict the definition of God. Anyone, therefore, who maintains that "God does not exist" (or that God is just a fictitious being) asserts a contradiction every bit as much as someone who asserts that "triangles do not have three sides." Not only, according to Anselm, does God exist; God cannot even be thought not to exist.

Here one can see the provocative philosophical power of Anselm's proof. The proof does not rely on revelation, or scientific experiment, or any kind of observation. The proof works strictly on the basis of ideas themselves — and apparently indisputable ideas. The argument played not only upon medieval thinkers like Thomas Aquinas (IV.9) and early moderns like Descartes (III.12), Leibniz (IV.13), and Spinoza (III.13). It has also been taken seriously by important recent philosophers like Kurt Gödel, Charles Hartshorne, Alvin Plantinga, and David Lewis.[2]

Notes

1   Isaiah, 7:9.
2   T. Aquinas, *Summa Theologica*, I.a1.Q2; R. Descartes, *Meditations on First Philosophy* V; B. Spinoza, *Ethics* I:7–14; D. Blumenfeld, "Leibniz's Ontological and Cosmological Arguments," in *Cambridge Companion to Leibniz*, ed. N. Jolley, Cambridge: Cambridge University Press, 1995, pp. 353–81; D. Scott, "Gödel's Ontological Proof," in J. Jarvis Thomson, ed., *Being and Saying*, Cambridge, MA: MIT Press, 1987, pp. 256–7, 388; C. Hartshorne, *Anselm's Discovery*, La Salle, IL: Open Court, 1965; A. Plantinga, *God and Other Minds*, Ithaca, NY: Cornell University Press, 1967; D. Lewis, "Anselm and Actuality," *Noûs* 4 (1970): 175–88; P. Millican, "The One Fatal Flaw in Anselm's Argument," *Mind* 113 (2004): 437–76; Graham Oppy, *Ontological Arguments and Belief in God*, New York: Cambridge University Press, 1996.

Anselm of Canterbury, *Proslogion*

Chapter I: A Rousing of the mind to the contemplation of God

Come now, insignificant man, fly for a moment from your affairs, escape for a little while from the tumult of your thoughts. Put aside now your weighty cares and leave your wearisome toils. Abandon yourself for a little to God and rest for a little in Him. Enter into the inner chamber of your soul, shut out everything save God and what can be of help in your quest for Him and having locked the door seek Him out [Matt. vi. 6]. Speak now, my whole heart, speak now to God: 'I seek Your countenance, O Lord, Your countenance I seek' [Ps. xxvi. 8].

Come then, Lord my God, teach my heart where and how to seek You, where and how to find You. Lord, if You are not present here, where, since You are absent, shall I look for You? On the other hand, if You are everywhere why then, since You are present, do I not see You? But surely You dwell in 'light inaccessible' [1 Tim. vi. 16]. And where is this inaccessible light, or how can I approach the inaccessible light? Or who shall lead me and take me into it that I may see You in it? Again, by what signs, under what aspect, shall I seek You? Never have I seen You, Lord my God, I do not know Your face. What shall he do, most high Lord, what shall this exile do, far away from You as he is? What shall Your servant do, tormented by love of You and yet cast off 'far from Your face' [Ps. i. 13]? He yearns to see You and Your countenance is too far away from him. He desires to come close to You, and Your dwelling place is inaccessible; he longs to find You and does not know where You are; he is eager to seek You out and he does not know Your countenance. Lord, You are my God and my Lord, and never have I seen You. You have created me and re-created me and You have given me all the good things I possess, and still I do not know You. In fine, I was made in order to see You, and I have not yet accomplished what I was made for.

How wretched man's lot is when he has lost that for which he was made! Oh how hard and cruel was that Fall! Alas, what has man lost and what has he found? What did he lose and what remains to him? He lost the blessedness for which he was made, and he found the misery for which he was not made. That without which

nothing is happy has gone from him and that which by itself is nothing but misery remains to him. Once 'man ate the bread of angels' [Ps. lxxvii. 25], for which now he hungers; now he eats 'the bread of sorrow' [Ps. cxxvi. 2], which then he knew nothing of. Alas the common grief of mankind, alas the universal lamentation of the children of Adam! He groaned with fullness; we sigh with hunger. He was prosperous; we go begging. He in his happiness had possessions and in his misery abandoned them; we in our unhappiness go without and miserably do we yearn and, alas, we remain empty. Why, since it was easy for him, did he not keep for us that which we lack so much? Why did he deprive us of light and surround us with darkness? Why did he take life away from us and inflict death upon us? Poor wretches that we are, whence have we been expelled and whither are we driven? Whence have we been cast down and whither buried? From our homeland into exile; from the vision of God into our present blindness; from the joy of immortality into the bitterness and horror of death. Oh wretched change from so great a good to so great an evil! What a grievous loss, a grievous sorrow, utterly grievous!

Alas, unfortunate that I am, one of the miserable children of Eve, separated from God. What have I undertaken? What have I actually done? Where was I going? Where have I come to? To what was I aspiring? For what do I yearn? 'I sought goodness' [Ps. cxxi. 9] and, lo, 'there is confusion' [Jer. xiv. 19]. I yearned for God, and I was in my own way. I sought peace within myself and 'I have found tribulation and sadness' in my heart of hearts [Ps. cxiv. 3]. I wished to laugh from out the happiness of my soul, and 'the sobbing of my heart' [Ps. xxxvii. 9] makes me cry out. I hoped for gladness and, lo, my sighs come thick and fast.

And You, 'O Lord, how long' [Ps. vi. 4]? How long, Lord, will You be unmindful of us? 'How long will You turn Your countenance' from us [Ps. xii. 1]? When will You look upon us and hear us [Ps. xii. 4]? When will You enlighten our eyes and show 'Your countenance' to us [Ps. lxxix. 4]? When will You give Yourself again to us? Look upon us, Lord; hear us, enlighten us, show Yourself to us. Give Yourself to us that it may be well with us, for without You it goes so ill for us. Have pity upon our efforts and our strivings towards You, for we can avail nothing without You. You call to us, 'so help us' [Ps. lxxviii. 9]. I beseech You, Lord, let me not go sighing hopelessly, but make me breathe hopefully again. My heart is made bitter by its desolation; I beseech You, Lord, sweeten it by Your consolation. I set out hungry to look for You; I beseech You, Lord, do not let me depart from You fasting. I came to You as one famished; do not let me go without food. Poor, I have come to one who is rich. Unfortunate, I have come to one who is merciful. Do not let me return scorned and empty-handed. And if now I sigh before I eat [Job iii. 4], give me to eat after my sighs. Lord, bowed down as I am, I can only look downwards; raise me up that I may look upwards. 'My sins are heaped up over my head'; they cover me over and 'like a heavy load' crush me down [Ps. xxxvii. 5]. Save me, disburden me, 'lest their pit close its mouth over me' [Ps. lxviii. 16]. Let me discern Your light whether it be from afar or from the depths. Teach me to seek You, and reveal Yourself to me as I seek, because I can neither seek You if You do not teach me how, nor find You unless You reveal Yourself. Let me seek You in desiring You; let me desire You in seeking You; let me find You in loving You; let me love You in finding You.

I acknowledge, Lord, and I give thanks that You have created Your image in me, so that I may remember You, think of You, love You. But this image is so effaced and worn away by vice, so darkened by the smoke of sin, that it cannot do what it was made to do unless You renew it and reform it. I do not try, Lord, to attain Your lofty heights, because my understanding is in no way equal to it. But I do desire to understand Your truth a little, that truth that my heart believes and loves. For I do not seek to understand so that I may believe; but I believe so that I may understand. For I believe this also, that 'unless I believe, I shall not understand' [Is. vii. 9].

Chapter II: That God truly exists

Well then, Lord, You who give understanding to faith, grant me that I may understand, as much as You see fit, that You exist as we believe You to exist, and that You are what we believe You to be. Now we believe that You are something than which nothing greater can be thought. Or can it be that a thing of such a nature does not exist, since 'the Fool has said in his heart, there is no

God' [Ps. xiii. 1, lii. 1]? But surely, when this same Fool hears what I am speaking about, namely, 'something-than-which-nothing-greater-can-be-thought', he understands what he hears, and what he understands is in his mind, even if he does not understand that it actually exists. For it is one thing for an object to exist in the mind, and another thing to understand that an object actually exists. Thus, when a painter plans beforehand what he is going to execute, he has [the picture] in his mind, but he does not yet think that it actually exists because he has not yet executed it. However, when he has actually painted it, then he both has it in his mind and understands that it exists because he has now made it. Even the Fool, then, is forced to agree that something-than-which-nothing-greater-can-be-thought exists in the mind, since he understands this when he hears it, and whatever is understood is in the mind. And surely that-than-which-a-greater-cannot-be-thought cannot exist in the mind alone. For if it exists solely in the mind even, it can be thought to exist in reality also, which is greater. If then that-than-which-a-greater-cannot-be-thought exists in the mind alone, this same that-than-which-a-greater-*cannot*-be-thought is that-than-which-a-greater-*can*-be-thought. But this is obviously impossible. Therefore there is absolutely no doubt that something-than-which-a-greater-cannot-be-thought exists both in the mind and in reality.

Chapter III: That God cannot be thought not to exist

And certainly this being so truly exists that it cannot be even thought not to exist. For something can be thought to exist that cannot be thought not to exist, and this is greater than that which can be thought not to exist. Hence, if that-than-which-a-greater-cannot-be-thought can be thought not to exist, then that-than-which-a-greater-cannot-be-thought is not the same as that-than-which-a-greater-cannot-be-thought, which is absurd. Something-than-which-a-greater-cannot-be-thought exists so truly then, that it cannot be even thought not to exist.

And You, Lord our God, are this being. You exist so truly, Lord my God, that You cannot even be thought not to exist. And this is as it should be, for if some intelligence could think of something better than You, the creature would be above its creator and would judge its creator – and that is completely absurd. In fact, everything else there is, except You alone, can be thought of as not existing. You alone, then, of all things most truly exist and therefore of all things possess existence to the highest degree; for anything else does not exist as truly, and so possesses existence to a lesser degree. Why then did 'the Fool say in his heart, there is no God' [Ps. xiii. 1, lii. 1] when it is so evident to any rational mind that You of all things exist to the highest degree? Why indeed, unless because he was stupid and a fool?

though he may say these words in his heart either without any [objective] signification or with some peculiar signification. For God is that-than-which-nothing-greater-can-be-thought. Whoever really understands this understands clearly that this same being so exists that not even in thought can it not exist. Thus whoever understands that God exists in such a way cannot think of Him as not existing.

I give thanks, good Lord, I give thanks to You, since what I believed before through Your free gift I now so understand through Your illumination, that if I did not want to *believe* that You existed, I should nevertheless be unable not to *understand* it.

Chapter IV: How 'the Fool said in his heart' what cannot be thought

How indeed has he 'said in his heart' what he could not think; or how could he not think what he 'said in his heart', since to 'say in one's heart' and to 'think' are the same? But if he really (indeed, since he really) both thought because he 'said in his heart' and did not 'say in his heart' because he could not think, there is not only one sense in which something is 'said in one's heart' or thought. For in one sense a thing is thought when the word signifying it is thought; in another sense when the very object which the thing is is understood. In the first sense, then, God can be thought not to exist, but not at all in the second sense. No one, indeed, understanding what God is can think that God does not exist, even

Chapter V: That God is whatever it is better to be than not to be and that, existing through Himself alone, He makes all other beings from nothing

What then are You, Lord God, You than whom nothing greater can be thought? But what are You save that supreme being, existing through Yourself alone, who made everything else from nothing? For whatever is not this is less than that which can be thought of; but this cannot be thought about You. What goodness, then, could be wanting to the supreme good, through which every good exists? Thus You are just, truthful, happy, and whatever it is better to be than not to be – for it is better to be just rather than unjust, and happy rather than unhappy.

6

Al-Ghazālī, "On Causality and Miracles"

Introduction

In the Islamic world, al-Ghazālī (Algazel) — arguably the most influential of its thinkers, after Muhammad himself — is often referred to as "the proof of Islam." This title is applied to him in virtue, above all, of his having been the person who, as a modern commentator puts it, "effectively sealed the fate of Greek thought in Islam."[1] For "the philosophers" whose "incoherence" it was al-Ghazālī's aim to expose in his famous polemical work, The Incoherence of the Philosophers (Tahafut al-falasifah), were those, like Ibn Sīnā (Avicenna; III.8), who had attempted to reconcile the teachings of the Qurʿan with a philosophy drawn from Aristotle and Neo-Platonism. What made his book so intellectually effective was that its case against the falasifah did not rest, primarily, on appeals to scripture or authority, but on the deployment of philosophical argument. An especially clear instance of this use of rationality in the cause of deflating the pretensions of reason is furnished by the chapter — on causality and miracles — that we have selected.

Abū Hāmid Muhammad ibn Muhammad al-Ghazālī was born in Tus, in Persia, in 1058, and was educated in the Ashʿarite tradition of

From Al-Ghazālī, *The Incoherence of the Philosophers*, trans. Michael E. Marmura, Provo, UT: Brigham Young University Press, 2000, pp. 166–77 (notes omitted).

theology that was already at odds with the Greek influenced "rational theology" of the Muʿtazalites. It was during his time as a teacher in Baghdad that al-Ghazālī wrote The Incoherence and several related works. In 1095, he seems to have undergone something of a spiritual crisis from which he emerged, after several years of ascetic solitude, as a champion of Sūfi mysticism, defending it against charges of heresy. He died in 1111.[2]

Heresy is precisely what al-Ghazālī had accused some of the doctrines of the falasifah of committing. These included the claim that the world is eternal, hence not created ex nihilo by God, and the denial of bodily resurrection at the day of judgment. For espousing such "irreligious" doctrines, he insisted, their protagonists deserved the death penalty. This is because, in his view, the effect of such doctrines — while they may not quite constitute atheism — is to diminish the power and majesty of God, reducing Allah, in effect, to a distant "prime mover" or "First Principle," remote from the God of the Qurʿan who is a being that exercises will and is intimately engaged in the workings of the world and the affairs of human beings, a being deserving of worship, of submission.

The falasifahs' doctrine with which al-Ghazālī takes issue in his "seventeenth discussion" is one that Ibn Sīnā, following Aristotle, espoused, to the effect that everything that occurs in the world — since it is a rational and intelligible order — does so by causal necessity. For al-Ghazālī, this is, from a religious perspective, a pernicious doctrine, for it not only implies that miracles are impossible, but that God has no active role at all in the course of worldly and human events. Ironically, his argument against Ibn Sīnā anticipates the religious sceptic, David Hume's, account of causality in terms of the mere "constant conjunction" of types of event (II.10). Between the cause and its effect, there is no necessary connection, asserts al-Ghazālī: it is simply that there is a "continuous habit of their occurrence repeatedly, one time after another," which "fixes unshakably in our minds the belief in their occurrence according to past habit."

The use to which the Muslim theologian puts this analysis of causality is, however, quite different from anything in Hume. For al-Ghazālī, the analysis removes all obstacles in the way of accepting the possibility of miracles (cf. IV.15). More important still – in a move that anticipates the so-called "occasionalism" of Christian philosophers like Nicolas Malebranche (1638–1715) – the analysis renders plausible the thought that the real cause of every event is God's will. If there is nothing about the fire itself that necessitates the burning of the cotton that comes into contact with it, then how can we explain the connection between fire and burning except by appeal to a God who maintains this connection?

Much of al-Ghazālī's discussion consists in showing that his account of causality does not have the unwelcome consequences that critics imagine. It's not true, for example, that accepting the merely contingent connection between causes and effects should create total skepticism about the course of future events. Nor should the claim that

God may conjoin events according to His will be taken to mean that He is capable of the logically impossible or the unintelligible, such as turning a color into a cooking pot.

Whether or not al-Ghazālī's position on causality, and on the other 19 "problems" addressed in *The Incoherence*, was really convincing, he certainly succeeded in convincing the leading guardians of the Islamic faith. One "curious consequence," as the historian of medieval thought, Étienne Gilson, remarked – when describing the immense impact of Arab thought on medieval Europe – was that the great Christian theologians, like Thomas Aquinas (III.10), were "pupils," not of Muslim theologians, notably al-Ghazālī, but of the Aristotelian philosophers, such as Ibn Sīnā, whose views these theologians had denounced as heresy.[3]

Notes

1 A. S. Akbar, *Postmodernism and Islam: Predicament and Promise*, London: Routledge, 1992, p. 85.

2 For a useful sketch of al-Ghazālī's life and work, see the chapter on him by Massimo Campanini in Seyyed Hossein Nasr and Oliver Leaman, eds, *History of Islamic Philosophy*, Part I, London: Routledge, 1996, pp. 258–74.

3 E. Gilson, *History of Christian Philosophy in the Middle Ages*, London: Sheed & Ward, 1955, p. 183.

Al-Ghazālī, *On Causality and Miracles*

(1) The connection between what is habitually believed to be a cause and what is habitually believed to be an effect is not necessary, according to us. But [with] any two things, where "this" is not "that" and "that" is not "this" and where neither the affirmation of the one entails the affirmation of the other nor the negation of the one entails negation of the other, it is not a necessity of the existence of the one that the other should exist, and it is not a necessity of the nonexistence of the one that the other should not exist – for example, the quenching of thirst and

drinking, satiety and eating, burning and contact with fire, light and the appearance of the sun, death and decapitation, healing and the drinking of medicine, the purging of the bowels and the using of a purgative, and so on to [include] all [that is] observable among connected things in medicine, astronomy, arts, and crafts. Their connection is due to the prior decree of God, who creates them side by side, not to its being necessary in itself, incapable of separation. On the contrary, it is within [divine] power to create satiety without eating, to create death without decapitation, to continue life after decapitation, and so on to all connected things. The philosophers denied the possibility of [this] and claimed it to be impossible.

(2) To examine these matters that are beyond enumeration will take a long time. Let us, then, take a specific example – namely, the burning of cotton, for instance, when in contact with fire. For we allow the possibility of the occurrence of the contact without the burning, and we allow as possible the occurrence of the cotton's transformation into burnt ashes without contact with the fire. [The philosophers], however, deny the possibility of this.

(3) The discussion of this question involves three positions.[1]

(4) The first position is for the opponent to claim that the agent of the burning is the fire alone, it being an agent by nature [and] not by choice – hence, incapable of refraining from [acting according to] what is in its nature after contacting a substratum receptive of it. And this is one of the things we deny. On the contrary, we say:

(5) The one who enacts the burning by creating blackness in the cotton, [causing] separation in its parts, and making it cinder or ashes is God, either through the mediation of His angels or without mediation. As for fire, which is inanimate, it has no action. For what proof is there that it is the agent? They have no proof other than observing the occurrence of the burning at the [juncture of] contact with the fire. Observation, however, [only] shows the occurrence [of burning] at [the time of the contact with the fire] but does not show the occurrence [of burning] by [the fire] and [the fact] that there is no other cause for it. For there is no disagreement [with the philosophers] that the infusion of spirit and of the apprehending and motive powers into the animal sperm is not engendered by the natures confined in heat, cold, moistness, and dryness; that the father does not produce his son by placing the sperm in the womb; and that he does not produce his life, sight, hearing, and the rest of the [powers] in him. It is known that these [come to] exist *with* [the placing of the sperm], but no one says that they [come to] exist *by* it. Rather, they exist from the direction of the First, either directly or through the mediation of the angels entrusted with temporal things. This is what the philosophers who uphold the existence of the creator uphold in a conclusive manner, [our] discourse being [at this point in agreement] with them.[2]

(6) It has thus become clear that [something's] existence *with* a thing does not prove that it exists *by* [that thing]. Indeed, we will show this

by an example. If a person, blind from birth, who has a film on his eyes and who has never heard from people the difference between night and day, were to have the film cleared from his eyes in daytime, [then] open his eyelids and see colors, [such a person] would believe that the agent [causing] the apprehension of the forms of the colors in his eyes is the opening of his sight and that, as long as his sight is sound, [his eyes] opened, the film removed, and the individual in front of him having color, it follows necessarily that he would see, it being incomprehensible that he would not see. When, however, the sun sets and the atmosphere becomes dark, he would then know that it is sunlight that is the cause for the imprinting of the colors in his sight.

(7) Whence can the opponent safeguard himself against there being among the principles of existence grounds and causes from which these [observable] events emanate when a contact between them takes place – [admitting] that [these principles], however, are permanent, never ceasing to exist; that they are not moving bodies that would set; that, were they either to cease to exist or to set, we would apprehend the dissociation [between the temporal events] and would understand that there is a cause beyond what we observe? This [conclusion] is inescapable in accordance with the reasoning based on [the philosophers' own] principle.

(8) It is because of this that the exacting among them have agreed that these accidents and events that occur when the contact between bodies takes place – and, in general, when the relationships between them change – emanate from the bestower of forms, who is one of the angels, so that they have said: "The imprinting of the form of color in the eye comes from the bestower of forms, the sun's appearance, the healthy pupil and the colored body being only 'readiers' and preparers for the receptacle's acceptance of these forms." They have made this the case with all temporal events. With this, the claim of those who proclaim that it is fire that enacts the burning, that it is bread that enacts satiety, that it is medicine that produces health, and so on, becomes false.

(9) The second position belongs to those who admit that these temporal events emanate from the principles of temporal events but that the preparation for the reception of the forms comes about through these present, observed causes – except that these principles are also [such that]

things proceed from them necessarily and by nature, not by way of deliberation and choice, in the way [that] light proceeds from the sun, receptacles differing in their reception because of the differences [of] disposition. For the shiny body receives the sun's ray and reflects it, whereby another place is illuminated by it, whereas mud does not; air does not prevent the penetration of light, whereas stone does; some things are softened by the sun, some hardened; some [are] whitened, as with the bleacher's garment, [and] some blackened, as with his face. [In all this, they maintain that] the principle is one but [that] the effects differ because of the differences of the dispositions in the receptacle. Similarly, the principles of existence are ever inundating with what proceeds from them, having neither restraint from granting nor stinginess: the short-coming is only due to the receptacles. This being the case [they argue] then as long as we suppose a fire having the quality [proper to it] and we suppose two similar pieces of cotton that come into contact with it in the same way, how would it be conceivable that one should burn and not the other, when there is no choice [on the part of the agent]? Based on this notion, they denied the falling of Abraham in the fire without the burning taking place, the fire remaining fire, and claimed that this is only possible by taking the heat out of the fire – which makes it no longer fire – or by changing the essence and body of Abraham into a stone or something over which fire has no effect. But neither is this [latter] pos-sible, nor is that [former] possible.

(10) The answer [to this] has two approaches.

(11) The first is to say: "We do not concede that the principles do not act by choice and that God does not act voluntarily." We have finished with refuting their claim concerning this in the question of the world's creation. If, then, it is established that the Agent creates the burning through His will when the piece of cotton comes into contact with the fire, it becomes rationally possible [for God] not to create [the burning] with the existence of the contact.

(12) [To this] it may be said:

(13) This leads to the commission of re-pugnant contradictions. For if one denies that the effects follow necessarily from their causes and relates them to the will of their Creator, the will having no specific designated course but [a course that] can vary and change in kind, then

let each of us allow the possibility of there being in front of him ferocious beasts, raging fires, high mountains, or enemies ready with their weapons [to kill him], but [also the possibility] that he does not see them because God does not create for him [vision of them]. And if someone leaves a book in the house, let him allow as possible its change on his returning home into a beardless slave boy – intelligent, busy with his tasks – or into an animal; or if he leaves a boy in his house, let him allow the possibility of his changing into a dog; or [again] if he leaves ashes, [let him allow] the possibility of its change into musk; and let him allow the possibility of stone changing into gold and gold into stone. If asked about any of this, he ought to say: "I do not know what is at the house at present. All I know is that I have left a book in the house, which is perhaps now a horse that has defiled the library with its urine and its dung, and that I have left in the house a jar of water, which may well have turned into an apple tree. For God is capable of everything, and it is not necessary for the horse to be created from the sperm nor the tree to be created from the seed – indeed, it is not necessary for either of the two to be created from anything. Perhaps [God] has created things that did not exist previously." Indeed, if [such a person] looks at a human being he has seen only now and is asked whether such a human is a creature that was born, let him hesitate and let him say that it is not impossible that some fruit in the marketplace has changed into a human – namely, this human – for God has power over every possible thing, and this thing is possible; hence, one must hesitate in [this matter]. This is a mode wide open in scope for [numerous] illustrations, but this much is sufficient.

(14) [Our] answer [to this] is to say:

(15) If it is established that the possible is such that there cannot be created for man knowledge of its nonbeing, these impossibilities would nec-essarily follow. We are not, however, rendered skeptical by the illustrations you have given because God created for us the knowledge that He did not enact these possibilities. We did not claim that these things are necessary. On the contrary, they are possibilities that may or may not occur. But the continuous habit of their occurrence repeatedly, one time after another, fixes unshakably in our minds the belief in their occurrence according to past habit.

(16) Indeed, it is possible for one of the prophets to know through the ways [the philosophers] have mentioned that a certain individual will not arrive from his journey tomorrow when his arrival is possible, the prophet [knowing, however,] the nonoccurrence of this possible thing. Nay, this is just as when one looks at a common man and knows that he neither knows the occult in any manner whatsoever nor apprehends the intelligibles without instruction; and yet, with all that, one does not deny that the soul and intuition [of this ordinary man] may become stronger so as to apprehend what the prophets apprehend, in accordance with what [the philosophers] acknowledge – although they know that such a possibility has not taken place.

(17) If, then, God disrupts the habitual [course of nature] by making [the miracle] occur at the time in which disruptions of habitual [events] take place, these cognitions [of the nonoccurrence of such unusual possibilities] slip away from [people's] hearts, and [God] does not create them. There is, therefore, nothing to prevent a thing being possible, within the capabilities of God, [but] that by His prior knowledge He knew that He would not do it at certain times, despite its possibility, and that He creates for us the knowledge that He will not create it at that time. Hence, in [all] this talk [of theirs], there is nothing but sheer vilification.

(18) The second approach, with which there is deliverance from these vilifications, is for us to admit that fire is created in such a way that, if two similar pieces of cotton come into contact with it, it would burn both, making no distinction between them if they are similar in all respects.[3] With all this, however, we allow as possible that a prophet may be cast into the fire without being burned, either by changing the quality of the fire or by changing the quality of the prophet. Thus, there would come about either from God or from the angels a quality in the fire which restricts its heat to its own body so as not to transcend it (its heat would thus remain with it, and it would [still] have the form and true nature of fire, its heat and influence, however, not going beyond it), or else there will occur in the body of the prophet a quality which will not change him from being flesh and bone [but] which will resist the influence of the fire. For we see [that] a person who covers himself with talc and sits in a fiery furnace is not affected by it. The one who has not witnessed this will deny it. Hence, the opponent's denial that [divine] power includes the ability to establish a certain quality either in the fire or in the human body that would prevent burning is like the denial of one who has never seen talc and its influence. Among the objects lying within God's power there are strange and wondrous things, not all of which we have seen. Why, then, should we deny their possibility and judge them to be impossible?

(19) Similarly, the raising of the dead and the changing of the staff into a snake are possible in this way – namely, that matter is receptive of all things. Thus, earth and the rest of the elements change into plants, plants – when eaten by animals – into blood, blood then changing into sperm. Sperm is then poured into the womb and develops in stages as an animal; this, in accordance with habit, takes place in a lengthy period of time. Why, then, should the opponent deem it impossible that it lies within God's power to cycle matter through these stages in a time shorter than has been known? And if this is possible within a shorter time, there is no restriction to its being [yet] shorter. These powers would thus accelerate in their actions, and through [this] there would come about what is a miracle for the prophet.

(20) If it is said, "Does this proceed from the prophet's soul or from some other principle at the suggestion of the prophet?" we say:

(21) [In] what you have admitted regarding the possibility of the coming down of rain [and] of hurricanes and the occurrence of earthquakes through the power of the prophet's soul, do [such events] come about from him or from another principle? Our statement in [answering your question] is the same as your statement in [answering ours]. It is, however, more fitting for both you and us to relate this to God, either directly or through the mediation of the angels. The time meriting its appearance, however, is when the prophet's attention is wholly directed to it and the order of the good becomes specifically [dependent] on its appearance so that the order of the revealed law may endure. [All] this gives preponderance to the side of [the] existence [of the miracle], the thing in itself being possible [and] the principle [endowing it being] benevolent and generous. But it does not emanate from Him except when the need for its existence becomes preponderant and the order of the good becomes specified therein. And the order

of the good becomes specified therein only if a prophet needs it to prove his prophethood in order to spread the good.

(22)   All this is consistent with the drift of what they say and a necessary consequence for them as long as they bring up the topic [of the doctrine to which they subscribe – namely,] of the prophet's special endowment with a characteristic contrary to what is customary with people. For the possible amounts of such special [prophetic qualities] are not encompassed by the mind. Why, then, with [all] this, must one disbelieve that whose transmission has been corroborated by innumerable reports, and belief in which is enjoined by the religious law?

(23)   [To proceed] in general, since only the sperm is receptive of the animal form, the animal powers emanating to it from the angels who, according [to the philosophers], are principles of being, [it follows that] from the human sperm only a human is created and from the sperm of the horse only a horse, since [to take the latter case] its realization from the horse is the more necessitating of preponderance because of the greater appropriateness of the equine form over all other forms. In this way, it thus accepts only the preponderant form. For this reason, wheat has never sprouted from barley and apples never from the seed of pears.

(24)   Moreover, we have seen genera of animals that are [spontaneously] generated from earth and are never procreated – as, for example, worms – and others like the mouse, the snake, and the scorpion that are both [spontaneously] generated and procreated, their generation being from the earth. Their dispositions to receive forms differ due to things unknown to us, it being beyond human power to know them, since, according to [the philosophers], forms do not emanate from the angels by whim or haphazardly. On the contrary, there emanates to each receptacle only that to which its reception is specified by being in itself disposed to receive [that thing]. [Now,] dispositions vary, their principles, according to them, being the configuration of the stars and the differing relations of the heavenly bodies in their movements.

(25)   From this it has become clear that the principles of dispositions include strange and wondrous things – so much so that the masters of the talismanic art have arrived, through their knowledge of the special properties of mineral substances and knowledge of the stars, [at the ability] to combine the heavenly powers and the special properties of minerals. They have thus taken certain forms of the terrestrial [properties] and sought for them a specific horoscope, bringing about through them strange things in the world. Thus, they have at times repelled from [one] town the snake and the scorpion, from [another] town the bedbug, and so on to matters known in the talismanic art. If, then, the principles of dispositions are beyond enumeration, the depth of their nature beyond our ken, there being no way for us to ascertain them, how can we know that it is impossible for a disposition to occur in some bodies that allows their transformation in phase of development in the shortest time so that they become prepared for receiving a form they were never prepared for receiving previously, and that this should not come about as a miracle? The denial of this is only due to our lack of capacity to understand, [our lack of] familiarity with exalted beings, and our unawareness of the secrets of God, praised be He, in creation and nature. Whoever studies [inductively] the wonders of the sciences will not deem remote from the power of God, in any manner whatsoever, what has been related of the miracles of the prophets.

(26)   [It may be] said:

(27)   We help you by maintaining that every possible thing is within the power of God, while you help us by maintaining that whatever is impossible is not within [divine] power. There are things whose impossibility is known and there are things whose possibility is known, while there are things the mind confronts undecided, judging them neither to be impossible nor possible. Now, then, what, according to you, is the definition of the impossible? If it reduces to the combining of negation and affirmation in the one thing, then [go on and] say, "In the case of two things, where 'this' is not 'that' and 'that' is not 'this,' the existence of the one does not require the existence of the other," and say that God can create a will without knowledge of the object willed and can create knowledge without life; that He can move a dead man's hand, seating him and with the hand writing volumes and engaging in crafts, the man being all the while open-eyed, staring ahead of him, but not seeing and having no life and no power over [what is being done] – all these ordered acts being created by God together with the moving of [the man's]

hand, the moving coming from the direction of God. By allowing the possibility of this, there ends the distinction between the voluntary movement and the tremor. The well-designed act would no longer prove either the knowledge or the power of the agent. [God] ought then to be able to change genera. He would thus change substance into accident, knowledge into power, blackness into whiteness, sound into smell, just as He had been able to change the inanimate into the animate and stone into gold, and there would follow as necessary consequences impossibilities beyond enumeration.

(28)   [We] answer:

(29)   The impossible is not within the power [of being enacted]. The impossible consists in affirming a thing conjointly with denying it, affirming the more specific while denying the more general, or affirming two things while negating one [of them]. What does not reduce to this is not impossible, and what is not impossible is within [divine] power.

(30)   As for combining blackness and whiteness, this is impossible. For by the affirmation of the form of blackness in the receptacle we understand [(a)] the negation of the appearance of whiteness and [(b) the affirmation of] the existence of blackness. Once the negation of whiteness becomes understood from the affirmation of blackness, then the affirmation of whiteness, together with its negation, becomes impossible.

(31)   It is [further] impossible for the individual to be in two places, because we understand by his being in the house [for example] his not being in [a place] other than the house. Hence, it is impossible to suppose him in [a place] other than the house together with his being in the house, [his being in the house] signifying the denial of [his being] elsewhere other than the house.

(32)   Similarly, we understand by the will the seeking after something known [to the willer]. If, then, a quest is supposed without knowledge, there would be no will. This entails the denial of what we have understood [by will].

(33)   It is impossible, moreover, to create knowledge in inanimate matter. For we understand by the inanimate that which does not apprehend. If apprehension is created in it, then to call it inanimate in the sense we have understood becomes impossible. And if it does not apprehend,

then to call what has been created "knowledge" when its receptacle does not apprehend anything is [also] impossible. This, then, is the way in which this is impossible.

(34)   As for the changing of genera, some of the Islamic dialectical theologians have said that it is within God's capacity [to enact]. We, however, say:

(35)   A thing's becoming something else is unintelligible. For if blackness changes into a cooking pot, does the blackness continue to exist or not? If it ceases to exist, it does not change [into something else]; rather, the thing ceases to exist and something else comes into existence. If it [continues to] exist with the cooking pot, then it did not change, but something was added to it. If [on the other hand] the blackness remains while the cooking pot is nonexistent, then the former did not change, but remained as it had been. [Again,] if we say that blood has changed into sperm, we mean by this that that matter itself took off one form and put on another.[4] This, then, amounts to the fact that one form has ceased to exist and one has come into existence, there being a subsistent matter over which the two forms passed in succession. And when we say that water through heating has changed into air, we mean that the matter receptive of the form of water took off this form and received another form. Matter is thus common, while the quality changes. The same holds when we say that the staff has changed into a serpent and earth into animal.

(36)   Between accident and substance, there is no common matter – nor between blackness and the cooking pot. And there is no common matter between the rest of the genera. It is in this respect, then, that [the transformation of different genera one into another] is impossible.

(37)   As for God's moving the hand of the dead man, setting him up in the form of a living person who is seated and writes so that through the movement of his hand ordered writing ensues, [this] in itself is not impossible as long as we turn over [the enactment of] temporal events to the will of a choosing being. It is only disavowed because of the continuous habit of its opposite occurring. Your statement that, with this, the well-designed act ceases to indicate the [existence of] the knowledge of the agent is not true. For the agent now is God, who is the performer of the well-designed act and [the] knower of it.

(38) As for your statement that there would be no difference between the tremor and the voluntary movement, we say:

(39) We apprehend [this difference] in ourselves. For we have perceived in ourselves a necessary distinction between the two states and have given expression to this difference by the term "power." We thus know that what takes place in the two possible alternatives [is two things], one of them [occurring] in one state, the other in [another] state – namely, the bringing to existence of a motion with the power over it in the one state, and the bringing of motion into existence without the power in the other state. If, however, we look at another person and see many ordered motions, there occurs to us knowledge of their being within his power. For these are cognitions which God creates according to the habitual course [of events], by which we know the existence of one of the two possible alternatives [but] by which the impossibility of the other alternative is not shown, as has been previously said.

Notes

1   In fact, he only discusses *two* positions.

2   This discussion illustrates a familiar strategy of al-Ghazālī's, that of identifying a concession made by his opponents and arguing that consistency requires a much larger concession. In the present instance, if they concede, in certain cases, that x's coexisting with y does not entail x exists through or "by" y, they should concede this in all cases.

3   The translator points out in his Introduction (p. xxiv) that, here, al-Ghazālī is rehearsing a second, "modified Aristotelian" theory of causation and arguing that, even on this theory, miracles remain possible. The translator goes on to point out that, in other writings, al-Ghazālī makes unambiguous his commitment to the first, "occasionalist" approach – according to which God alone is the direct cause of every event.

4   An implication of the point being made here is that, strictly speaking, Jesus could not have performed the miracle of changing water into wine. Nor, presumably, could his blood literally become wine.

7

Ibn Rushd (Averroës), *The Decisive Treatise* (selections)

Introduction

Abu al-Walid Muhammad Ibn Ahmad Ibn Rushd (1126–98), known to medieval Latin philosophers as Averroës, was one of the leading Muslim philosophers of the middle ages and one of the most important conduits for transmitting ancient Greek philosophy to Europe. He also served as a judge in Seville as well as a physician and educator in Marrakech.

Like Maimonides (Moses ben Maimon; IV.8), who was 12 years his junior, Averroës enjoyed the good fortune of living in the relatively open and syncretistic culture of Umayyad al-Andalus (Andalusia) in what is today Spain. Ibn Rushd's access to ancient Greek philosophy was made possible four centuries earlier by the preservation of Greek texts and their translation into Arabic by Baghdad's House of Wisdom under the Abbasid caliphate. But access to texts and the liberties offered by a tolerant, diverse society were not by themselves sufficient to produce the sort of serious engagement with Greek philosophy we find in Ibn Rushd. The importance of Greek philosophy to the Islamic intellectual world, like the Christian, had to be established; and that importance had to be defended against those who regarded Greek philosophy as either irrelevant or

even hostile to Abrahamic culture. The task of that defense was undertaken in the Abbasid world by the Mu'tazili theologians as well as by philosophers (*falsafa*) of the ninth and tenth centuries like al-Kindi (801–73; Alkindus) and the Persians al-Razi (865–925; Rhazes) and al-Farabi (Farabi; 870–c. 950).

When from Baghdad the center of Muslim medieval philosophy shifted westward to the Iberian Peninsula and the vigorous city-states of Andalusia, a new dynamic took hold. Great libraries were amassed by city-states like Toledo and Cordoba, and an active intellectual culture that drew from ancient Greek sources was cultivated – well before something similar emerged in Italian city-states like Florence. Perhaps most importantly, detailed commentaries and translations were painstakingly produced by Andalusian philosophers like Ibn Rushd and Moses ben Maimon. These resources, along with those that would wash into Europe from Byzantium and the Venetian Empire, became the larders from which Christian philosophers of northern Europe collected the ideas that would drive the philosophical thought of the high middle ages and the Renaissance. So important, in fact, were Averroës's Latin commentaries on Aristotle that medieval Christian philosophers like Aquinas referred to him simply as, "The Commentator" (Aristotle was known, correspondingly, as "The Philosopher").[1]

Philosophically, Averroism is most commonly identified with the doctrine that the immortal soul (both the "active" and the "passive" intellect)[2] is not individual and is instead part of a larger

From Averroës, *The Book of the Decisive Treatise Determining the Connection between the Law and Wisdom,* trans. C. E. Butterworth, Provo, UT: Brigham Young University Press, 2001, pp. 1–23 (notes omitted).

universal soul – a position that places him in a family of thinkers including the neo-Platonist Plotinus (III.6) and the early modern Spinoza (III.13). The selection here presents part of Ibn Rushd's defense of ancient Greek philosophy, in this case against the influential critique advanced by al-Ghazālī (1058–1111) and other Ash'arite theologians, as well as his distinctive doctrine that religion and philosophy, while not incompatible, represent two different and separate discourses concerned with a single truth.[3]

Since demonstrative, syllogistic inquiries, following Aristotle, are concerned with the truths of existent reality, they are not only permissible for Muslims, argues Averroës; they are obligatory. Truth as expressed by philosophical reasoning *appears* to differ, however, from the claims of scripture because of the peculiarities of each discourse. Philosophical discourse apprehends truth in a literal, rational, and abstract way. But as this mode of apprehension is extremely difficult for the human mind, only an elite few are capable of undertaking it. Those without the intellectual capacity for philosophical reflection may only approach the truths of God and reality, to the extent they may approach them at all, through the "figurative" language of scripture – a form of language, which, whether understood clearly or not, at least serves to direct people in morally proper ways.

Because, however, scripture's form of expression is figurative, poetic, and didactic, it presents truth in an "apparent" sense that may seem to contradict the truths established by philosophical science. When scripture or religious discourse does so, philosophical science offers a way to "inter-pret" it in such a way as to lay bare its true meaning, its "inner" sense – the true sense in which it does not contradict philosophy. Indeed, the truth of scripture cannot contradict the truth established by science, since again there is only one truth. Because scripture without the interpretive framework of rational philosophy remains opaque,[4] philosophy in Averroës's rendering becomes an interpretive and clarifying device. Perhaps on the other hand, more radically, Averroës is subtly arguing that philosophy determines truth and that scripture merely offers an engaging discourse to keep the masses in line. Perhaps it was suspicion of just this agenda that led Ibn Rushd's work to be suppressed and forced him to flee to North Africa, where he died, after the less tolerant Almohads conquered al-Andalus.

Notes

1 Averroës produced commentaries on nearly all of Aristotle's work, as well as on Plato's *Republic*.

2 For more on this distinction, its history and importance, see Aquinas, II.6, in this volume.

3 Abu Hāmed Mohammad ibn Mohammad al-Ghazālī ("al-Gazali" or "Algazel") presents his critique principally in his *Tahafut al-falasifah* (*The Incoherence of the Philosophers*); see IV.6. Ibn Rushd's most extensive response appears in his *Tahafut al-tahafut* (*The Incoherence of the Incoherence*).

4 O. Leaman, *Averroës and His Philosophy*, London: Routledge, 1997.

Ibn Rushd (Averroës), *The Decisive Treatise*

In the name of God, the Merciful and the Compassionate. May God be prayed to for Muḥammad and his family, and may they be accorded peace.

[I. Introduction]

(1) The jurist, imam, judge, and uniquely learned Abū al-Walīd Muḥammad ibn Aḥmad ibn Rushd (may God be pleased with him) said:

Praise be to God with all praises, and a prayer for Muḥammad, His chosen servant and messenger. Now, the goal of this statement is for us to investigate, from the perspective of Law-based reflection, whether reflection upon philosophy and the sciences of logic is permitted, prohibited, or commanded – and this as a recommendation or as an obligation – by the Law.

[II. That philosophy and logic are obligatory]

[A. *That philosophy is obligatory*] (2) So we say: If the activity of philosophy is nothing more than reflection upon existing things and consideration of them insofar as they are an indication of the Artisan – I mean insofar as they are artifacts, for existing things indicate the Artisan only through cognizance of the art in them, and the more complete cognizance of the art in them is, the more complete is cognizance of the Artisan – and if the Law has recommended and urged consideration of existing things, then it is evident that what this name indicates is either obligatory or recommended by the Law.

That the Law calls for consideration of existing things by means of the intellect and for pursuing cognizance of them by means of it is evident from various verses in the Book of God (may He be blessed and exalted). There is His statement (may He be exalted), "Consider, you who have sight" [59:2]; this is a text for the obligation of using both intellectual and Law-based syllogistic reasoning. And there is His statement (may He be exalted), "Have they not reflected upon the kingdoms of the heavens and the earth and what things God has created?" [7:185]; this is a text urging reflection upon all existing things. And God (may He be exalted) has made it known that one of those whom He selected and venerated by means of this knowledge was Abraham (peace upon him); thus, He (may He be exalted) said, "And in this way we made Abraham see the kingdoms of the heavens and the earth, that he might be . . ." [and so on to the end of] the verse [6:75]. And He (may He be exalted) said, "Do they not reflect upon the camels, how they have been created, and upon the heaven, how it has been raised up?" [88:17]. And He said, "And they ponder the creation of the heavens and the earth" [3:191] – and so on, in innumerable other verses.

[B. *The case for syllogistic reasoning*] (3) Since it has been determined that the Law makes it obligatory to reflect upon existing things by means of the intellect, and to consider them; and consideration is nothing more than inferring and drawing out the unknown from the known; and this is syllogistic reasoning or by means of syllogistic reasoning, therefore, it is obligatory that we go about reflecting upon the existing things by means of intellectual syllogistic reasoning. And it is evident that this manner of reflection the Law calls for and urges is the most complete kind of reflection by means of the most complete

kind of syllogistic reasoning and is the one called "demonstration."

(4) Since the Law has urged cognizance of God (may He be exalted) and of all of the things existing through Him by means of demonstration; and it is preferable – or even necessary – that anyone who wants to know God (may He be blessed and exalted) and all of the existing things by means of demonstration set out first to know the kinds of demonstrations, their conditions, and in what [way] demonstrative syllogistic reasoning differs from dialectical, rhetorical, and sophistical syllogistic reasoning; and that is not possible unless, prior to that, he sets out to become cognizant of what unqualified syllogistic reasoning is, how many kinds of it there are, and which of them is syllogistic reasoning and which not; and that is not possible either unless, prior to that, he sets out to become cognizant of the parts of which syllogistic reasoning is composed – I mean, the premises and their kinds – therefore, the one who has faith in the Law and follows its command to reflect upon existing things perhaps comes under the obligation to set out, before reflecting, to become cognizant of these things whose status with respect to reflection is that of tools to work.

For just as the jurist infers from the command to obtain juridical understanding of the statutes the obligation to become cognizant of the kinds of juridical syllogistic reasoning and which of them is syllogistic reasoning and which not, so, too, is it obligatory for the one cognizant [of God] to infer from the command to reflect upon the beings the obligation to become cognizant of intellectual syllogistic reasoning and its kinds. Nay, it is even more fitting that he do so; for if the jurist infers from His statement (may He be exalted), "Consider, you who have sight" [59:2], the obligation to become cognizant of juridical syllogistic reasoning, then how much more fitting is it that the one cognizant of God infer from that the obligation to become cognizant of intellectual syllogistic reasoning.

It is not for someone to say, "Now, this kind of reflection about intellectual syllogistic reasoning is a heretical innovation, since it did not exist in the earliest days [of Islam]." For reflection upon juridical syllogistic reasoning and its kinds is also something inferred after the earliest days, yet it is not opined to be a heretical innovation. So it is obligatory to believe the same about reflection upon intellectual syllogistic reasoning

– and for this there is a reason, but this is not the place to mention it. Moreover, most of the adherents to this religion support intellectual syllogistic reasoning, except for a small group of strict literalists, and they are refuted by the texts [of the Qur'ān].

(5) Since it has been determined that the Law makes reflection upon intellectual syllogistic reasoning and its kinds obligatory, just as it makes reflection upon juridical syllogistic reasoning obligatory, therefore, it is evident that, if someone prior to us has not set out to investigate intellectual syllogistic reasoning and its kinds, it is obligatory for us to begin to investigate it and for the one who comes after to rely upon the one who preceded, so that cognizance of it might be perfected. For it is difficult or impossible for one person to grasp all that he needs of this by himself and from the beginning, just as it is difficult for one person to infer all he needs to be cognizant of concerning the kinds of juridical syllogistic reasoning. Nay, this is even more the case with being cognizant of intellectual syllogistic reasoning.

(6) If someone other than us has already investigated that, it is evidently obligatory for us to rely on what the one who has preceded us says about what we are pursuing, regardless of whether that other person shares our religion or not. For when a valid sacrifice is performed by means of a tool, no consideration is given, with respect to the validity of the sacrifice, as to whether the tool belongs to someone who shares in our religion or not, so long as it fulfills the conditions for validity. And by "not sharing [in our religion]," I mean those Ancients who reflected upon these things before the religion of Islam.

(7) Since this is the case – and all that is needed with respect to reflection about the matter of intellectual syllogistic reasonings has been investigated by the Ancients in the most complete manner – therefore, we ought perhaps to seize their books in our hands and reflect upon what they have said about that. And if it is all correct, we will accept it from them; whereas, if there is anything not correct in it, we will alert [people] to it.

(8) Since we have finished with this type of reflection and have acquired the tools by which we are able to consider existing things and the indication of artfulness in them – for one who is not cognizant of the artfulness is not cognizant of what has been artfully made, and one who is not cognizant of what has been artfully made is not cognizant of the Artisan – therefore, it is perhaps obligatory that we start investigating existing things according to the order and manner we have gained from the art of becoming cognizant about demonstrative syllogisms. It is evident, moreover, that this goal is completed for us with respect to existing things only when they are investigated successively by one person after another and when, in doing so, the one coming after makes use of the one having preceded – along the lines of what occurs in the mathematical sciences.

For if we were to assume the art of geometry and, likewise, the art of astronomy to be non-existent in this time of ours, and if a single man wished to discern on his own the sizes of the heavenly bodies, their shapes, and their distances from one another, that would not be possible for him – for example, to become cognizant of the size of the sun with respect to the earth and of other things about the sizes of the planets – not even if he were by nature the most intelligent person, unless it were by means of revelation or something resembling revelation. Indeed, if it were said to him that the sun is about 150 or 160 times greater than the earth, he would count this statement as madness on the part of the one who makes it. And this is something for which a demonstration has been brought forth in astronomy and which no one adept in that science doubts.

There is hardly any need to use an example from the art of mathematics, for reflection upon this art of the roots of jurisprudence, and jurisprudence itself, has been perfected only over a long period of time. If someone today wished to grasp on his own all of the proofs inferred by those in the legal schools who reflect upon the controversial questions debated in most Islamic countries, even excepting the Maghrib, he would deserve to be laughed at, because that would be impossible for him – in addition to having already been done. This is a self-evident matter, not only with respect to the scientific arts, but also with respect to the practical ones. For there is not an art among them that a single person can bring about on his own. So how can this be done with the art of arts – namely, wisdom?

(9) Since this is so, if we find that our predecessors in former nations have reflected upon

existing things and considered them according to what is required by the conditions of demonstration, it is perhaps obligatory for us to reflect upon what they say about that and upon what they establish in their books. Thus, we will accept, rejoice in, and thank them for whatever agrees with the truth; and we will alert to, warn against, and excuse them for whatever does not agree with the truth.

(10)   From this it has become evident that reflection upon the books of the Ancients is obligatory according to the Law, for their aim and intention in their books is the very intention to which the Law urges us. And [it has become evident] that whoever forbids reflection upon them by anyone suited to reflect upon them – namely, anyone who unites two qualities, the first being innate intelligence and the second Law-based justice and moral virtue – surely bars people from the door through which the Law calls them to cognizance of God – namely, the door of reflection leading to true cognizance of Him. That is extreme ignorance and estrangement from God (may He be exalted).

If someone goes astray in reflection and stumbles – due either to a deficiency in his innate disposition, poor ordering of his reflection, being overwhelmed by his passions, not finding a teacher to guide him to an understanding of what is in them, or because of a combination of all or more than one of these reasons – it does not follow that they are to be forbidden to the one who is suited to reflect upon them. For this manner of harm coming about due to them is something that attaches to them by accident, not by essence. It is not obligatory to renounce something useful in its nature and essence because of something harmful existing in it by accident. That is why he [that is, the Prophet] (peace upon him) said to the one who complained about having been ordered to give his brother honey to drink for his diarrhea – because the diarrhea increased when he was given the honey to drink – "God spoke the truth, whereas your brother's stomach lied."

Indeed, we say that anyone who prevents someone suited to reflect upon the books of wisdom from doing so on the grounds that it is supposed some vicious people became perplexed due to reflecting upon them is like one who prevents thirsty people from drinking cool, fresh water until they die of thirst because some

people choked on it and died. For dying by choking on water is an accidental matter, whereas [dying] by thirst is an essential, necessary matter. And what occurred through this art is something accidental, [occurring] through the rest of the arts. To how many jurists has jurisprudence been a cause of diminished devoutness and immersion in this world! Indeed, we find most jurists to be like this, yet what their art requires in essence is practical virtue. Therefore, it is not strange that there occurs, with respect to the art requiring scientific virtue, what occurs with respect to the art requiring practical virtue.

[III.   That demonstration accords with the Law]

[A.   The Law calls to humans by three methods]
(11)   Since all of this has been determined and we, the Muslim community, believe that this divine Law of ours is true and is the one alerting to and calling for this happiness – which is cognizance of God (Mighty and Magnificent) and of His creation – therefore, that is determined for every Muslim in accordance with the method of assent his temperament and nature require.

That is because people's natures vary in excellence with respect to assent. Thus, some assent by means of demonstration; some assent by means of dialectical statements in the same way the one adhering to demonstration assents by means of demonstration, there being nothing greater in their natures; and some assent by means of rhetorical statements, just as the one adhering to demonstration assents by means of demonstrative statements.

That is because, when this divine Law of ours called to people by means of these three methods, assent to it was extended to every human being – except to the one who denies it obstinately in speech or for whom no methods have been determined in it for summoning to God (may He be exalted) due to his own neglect of that. Therefore, he [that is, the Prophet] (peace upon him) was selected to be sent to "the red and the black" – I mean, because of his Law containing [different] methods of calling to God (may He be exalted). And that is manifest in His statement, "Call to the path of your Lord by wisdom, fine preaching, and arguing with them by means of what is finest" [16:125].

[B. *Demonstration does not differ from the Law*]

(12) Since this Law is true and calls to the reflection leading to cognizance of the truth, we, the Muslim community, know firmly that demonstrative reflection does not lead to differing with what is set down in the Law. For truth does not oppose truth; rather, it agrees with and bears witness to it.

(13) Since this is so, if demonstrative reflection leads to any manner of cognizance about any existing thing, that existing thing cannot escape either being passed over in silence in the Law or being made cognizable in it. If it is passed over in silence, there is no contradiction here; it has the status of the statutes passed over in silence that the jurist infers by means of Law-based syllogistic reasoning. If the Law does pronounce about it, the apparent sense of the pronouncement cannot escape either being in agreement with what demonstration leads to, or being different from it. If it is in agreement, there is no argument here. And, if it is different, that is where an interpretation is pursued. The meaning of interpretation is: drawing out the figurative significance of an utterance from its true significance without violating the custom of the Arabic language with respect to figurative speech in doing so – such as calling a thing by what resembles it, its cause, its consequence, what compares to it, or another of the things enumerated in making the sorts of figurative discourse cognizable.

(14) Since the jurist does this with respect to many of the Law-based statutes, how much more fitting is it for the one adhering to demonstrative science to do so. The jurist has only a syllogism based on supposition, whereas the one who is cognizant has a syllogism based on certainty. And we firmly affirm that, whenever demonstration leads to something differing from the apparent sense of the Law, that apparent sense admits of interpretation according to the rule of interpretation in Arabic.

No Muslim doubts this proposition, nor is any faithful person suspicious of it. Its certainty has been greatly increased for anyone who has pursued this idea, tested it, and has as an intention this reconciling of what is intellected with what is transmitted. Indeed, we say that whenever the apparent sense of a pronouncement about something in the Law differs from what demonstration leads to, if the Law is considered and all of its parts scrutinized, there will invariably be found in the utterances of the Law something whose apparent sense bears witness, or comes close to bearing witness, to that interpretation.

Because of this idea, Muslims have formed a consensus that it is not obligatory for all the utterances of the Law to be taken in their apparent sense, nor for all of them to be drawn out from their apparent sense by means of interpretation, though they disagree about which ones are to be interpreted and which not interpreted. The Ash'arites, for example, interpret the verse about God's directing Himself [2:29] and the Tradition about His descent, whereas the Ḥanbalites take them in their apparent sense.

The reason an apparent and an inner sense are set down in the Law is the difference in people's innate dispositions and the variance in their innate capacities for assent. The reason contradictory apparent senses are set down in it is to alert "those well grounded in science" to the interpretation that reconciles them. This idea is pointed to in His statement (may He be exalted), "He it is who has sent down to you the Book; in it, there are fixed verses . . ." on to His statement, "and those well grounded in science" [3:7].

(15) If someone were to say: "Muslims have formed a consensus that in the Law are things to be taken in their apparent sense and things to be interpreted, and there are things about which they disagree. So, is it permissible for demonstration to lead to interpreting what they have formed a consensus to take in its apparent sense, or to taking in its apparent sense what they have formed a consensus to interpret?" we would say: "If the consensus were established by a method of certainty, it would not be valid [to do so]; but if the consensus about them were suppositional, then it would be valid [to do so]." That is why Abū Ḥāmid [al-Ghazālī], Abū al-Ma'ālī, and others from among the leading thinkers said that unbelief is to be affirmed of no one for going against consensus by interpreting things like these.

What may indicate to you that consensus is not to be determined with certainty about theoretical matters, as it is possible for it to be determined about practical matters, is that it is not possible for consensus to be determined about a particular question at a particular epoch unless: that epoch is delimited by us; all the learned men existing in that epoch are known to us, I mean, known as individuals and in their total number;

the doctrine of each one of them on the question is transmitted to us by means of an uninterrupted transmission; and, in addition to all this, it has been certified to us that the learned men existing at that time agreed that there is not an apparent and an inner sense to the Law, that it is obligatory that knowledge of every question be concealed from no one, and that there is only one method for people to know the Law.

It has been transmitted that many in the earliest days [of Islam] used to be of the opinion that the Law has both an apparent and an inner sense and that it is not obligatory for someone to know about the inner sense if he is not an adept in knowledge of it nor capable of understanding it. There is, for example, what al-Bukhārī relates about ʿAlī ibn Abū Ṭālib (may God be pleased with him), saying, "Speak to the people concerning what they are cognizant of. Do you want God and His messenger to be accused of lying?" And there is, for example, what is related of that about a group of the early followers [of Islam]. So how is it possible to conceive of consensus about a single theoretical question being transmitted to us when we firmly know that no single epoch has escaped having learned men who are of the opinion that there are things in the Law not all of the people ought to know in their true sense? That differs from what occurs with practical matters, for everybody is of the opinion that they are to be disclosed to all people alike; and, for consensus about them to be reached, we deem it sufficient that the question be widely diffused and that no difference [of opinion] about it be transmitted to us. Now, this is sufficient for reaching consensus about practical matters; but the case with scientific matters is different.

[c. *Whether the philosophers are guilty of unbelief*] (16) If you were to say: "If it is not obligatory to charge with unbelief one who goes against consensus with respect to interpretation, since consensus with respect to that is not conceivable, what do you say about the philosophers among the adherents of Islam like Abū Naṣr [al-Fārābī] and Ibn Sīnā [Avicenna]? For in his book known as *The Incoherence [of the Philosophers]*, Abū Ḥāmid [al-Ghazālī] has firmly charged both of them as unbelievers with respect to three questions: the argument about the eternity of the world, that the Exalted does not know

particulars – may He be exalted above that – and the interpretation of what is set forth about the resurrection of bodies and the way things are in the next life," we would say: "The apparent sense of what he says about that is that he does not firmly charge them with unbelief about that, for he has declared in the book *The Distinction* that charging someone with unbelief for going against consensus is tentative. And it has become evident from our argument that it is not possible for consensus to be determined with respect to questions like these because of what is related about many of the first followers [of Islam], as well as others, holding that there are interpretations that it is not obligatory to expound except to those adept in interpretation."

These are "those well grounded in science" – for we choose to place the stop after His statement (may He be exalted), "and those well grounded in science" [3:7]. Now, if those adept in science did not know the interpretation, there would be nothing superior in their assent obliging them to a faith in Him not found among those not adept in science. Yet God has already described them as those who have faith in Him, and this refers only to faith coming about from demonstration. And it comes about only along with the science of interpretation.

Those faithful not adept in science are people whose faith in them is not based on demonstration. So, if this faith by which God has described the learned is particular to them, then it is obligatory that it come about by means of demonstration. And if it is by means of demonstration, then it comes about only along with the science of interpretation. For God (may He be exalted) has already announced that there is an interpretation of them that is the truth, and demonstration is only of the truth. Since that is the case, it is not possible for an exhaustive consensus to be determined with respect to the interpretations by which God particularly characterized the learned. This is self-evident to anyone who is fair-minded.

(17) In addition to all of this, we are of the opinion that Abū Ḥāmid [al-Ghazālī] was mistaken about the Peripatetic sages when he accused them of saying that He (Holy and Exalted) does not know particulars at all. Rather, they are of the opinion that He knows them (may He be exalted) by means of a knowledge that is not of the same kind as our knowledge of

them. That is because our knowledge of them is an effect of what is known, so that it is generated when the known thing is generated and changes when it changes. And the knowledge God (glorious is He) has of existence is the opposite of this: it is the cause of the thing known, which is the existing thing.

So, whoever likens the two kinds of knowledge to one another sets down two opposite essences and their particular characteristics as being one, and that is the extreme of ignorance. If the name "knowledge" is said of knowledge that is generated and of knowledge that is eternal, it is said purely as a name that is shared, just as many names are said of opposite things – for example, *al-jalal*, said of great and small, and *al-ṣarīm*, said of light and darkness. Thus, there is no definition embracing both kinds of knowledge, as the dialectical theologians of our time fancy.

Prompted by one of our friends, we have devoted a statement to this question. How is it to be fancied that the Peripatetics would say that He (glorious is He) does not know particulars with eternal knowledge, when they are of the opinion that true dream-visions contain premonitions of particular things that are to be generated in the future and that this premonitional knowledge reaches human beings in sleep due to the everlasting knowledge governing the whole and having mastery over it? Moreover, it is not only particulars that they are of the opinion He does not know in the way we know them, but universals as well. For, the universals known to us are also effects of the nature of the existing thing, whereas, with that knowledge [of His], it is the reverse. Therefore, that knowledge [of His] has been demonstrated to transcend description as "universal" or "particular." So there is no reason for disagreement about this question – I mean, about charging them with unbelief or not charging them with unbelief.

(18)   As for the question whether the world is eternal or has been generated, the disagreement between the Ash'arite dialectical theologians and the ancient sages almost comes back, in my view, to a disagreement about naming, especially with respect to some of the Ancients. That is because they agree that there are three sorts of existing things: two extremes and one intermediate between the extremes. And they agree about naming the two extremes but disagree about the intermediate.

One extreme is an existent thing that exists from something other than itself and by something – I mean, by an agent cause and from matter. And time precedes it – I mean, its existence. This is the case of bodies whose coming into being is apprehended by sense perception – for example, the coming into being of water, air, earth, animals, plants, and so forth. The Ancients and the Ash'arites both agree in naming this sort of existing things "generated."

The extreme opposed to this is an existent thing that has not come into existence from something or by something and that time does not precede. About this, too, both factions agree in naming it "eternal." This existent thing is apprehended by demonstration: it is God (may He be blessed and exalted) who is the Agent of the whole, its Giver of Existence, and its Sustainer (glorious is He, and may His might be exalted).

The sort of being between these two extremes is an existent thing that has not come into existence from something and that time does not precede, but that does come into existence by something – I mean, by an agent. This is the world as a whole.

Now, all of them agree on the existence of these three attributes with respect to the world. For, the dialectical theologians admit that time does not precede it – or, rather, that is a consequence of their holding that time is something joined to motions and bodies. They also agree with the Ancients about future time being infinite and, likewise, future existence. And they disagree only about past time and past existence. For the dialectical theologians are of the opinion that it is limited, which is the doctrine of Plato and his sect, while Aristotle and his faction are of the opinion that it is infinite, as is the case with the future.

(19)   So it is evident that this latter existent thing has been taken as resembling the existing thing that truly comes into being and the eternally existing thing. Those overwhelmed by its resemblance to the eternal rather than to what is generated name it "eternal," and those overwhelmed by its resemblance to what is generated name it "generated." But, in truth, it is not truly generated, nor is it truly eternal. For what is truly generated is necessarily corruptible, and what is truly eternal has no cause. Among them are those who name it "everlastingly generated" – namely, Plato and his sect, because time according to them is finite with respect to the past.

(20) Thus, the doctrines about the world are not all so far apart from one another that some of them should be charged as unbelief and others not. Indeed, for opinions to be such that this should happen, it is obligatory that they be excessively far apart – I mean, that they be opposites of each other, as the dialectical theologians suppose they are with respect to this question – that is, that the name "eternity" and that of "generated" with respect to the world as a whole are opposites of each other. And it has already become evident from our statement that the matter is not like that.

(21) In addition to all this, these opinions about the world do not conform to the apparent sense of the Law. For if the apparent sense of the Law is scrutinized, it will become apparent from the verses comprising a communication about the coming into existence of the world that, in truth, its form is generated, whereas being itself and time extend continuously at both extremes – I mean, without interruption. That is because His statement (may He be exalted), "And He is the one Who created the heavens and the earth in six days, and His throne was on the water" [11:7], requires, in its apparent sense, an existence before this existence – namely, the throne and water – and a time before this time, I mean, the one joined to the form of this existence, which is the number of the movement of the heavenly sphere. And His statement (may He be exalted), "On the day the earth shall be changed into other than earth, and the heavens also" [14:48], in its apparent sense also requires a second existence after this existence. And His statement (may He be exalted), "Then He directed Himself toward the heaven, and it was smoke" [41:11], requires in its apparent sense that the heavens were created from something.

(22) Nor do the dialectical theologians conform to the apparent sense of the Law in what they say about the world, but interpret it. For it is not [said] in the Law that God was existing along with sheer nothingness; no text whatever to this effect is to be found. So how is it to be conceived that the dialectical theologians' interpretation of these verses would meet with consensus when the apparent sense of the Law with respect to the existence of the world, which we have stated, has already been stated by a faction among the sages?

(23) It seems that those who disagree about the interpretation of these recondite questions have either hit the mark and are to be rewarded or have erred and are to be excused. For assent to something due to an indication arising in the soul is compulsory, not voluntary – I mean that it is not up to us not to assent or to assent as it is up to us to stand up or not to stand up. Since a condition of responsibility is having choice, the one who assents to error because of vagueness occurring in it is excused if he is an adept of science. Therefore, he [that is, the Prophet] said (peace upon him), "If the judge hits the mark after exerting himself, he will be rewarded twofold; and if he errs, he will have a single reward."

Now what judge is greater than the one who makes judgments about existence, as to whether it is thus or not thus? These judges are the learned ones whom God has selected for interpretation, and this error that is forgiven according to the Law is only the error occasioned by learned men when they reflect upon the recondite things that the Law makes them responsible for reflecting upon.

(24) The error occasioned by any other sort of people is sheer sin, whether it is an error about theoretical or practical matters. Just as the judge who is ignorant of Tradition is not excused when he errs about a judgment, neither is the judge about existing things in whom the conditions for judgment do not exist excused; indeed, he is either a sinner or an unbeliever. And if it is stipulated, with respect to the judge about what is allowed and what is proscribed, that he combine within himself the reasons for exercising personal judgment – namely, cognizance of the roots and cognizance of what is inferred from these roots by means of syllogistic reasoning – then how much more fitting is it for this to be stipulated with respect to the one who is to judge about existing things, I mean, that he be cognizant of the primary intellectual notions and how to infer from them.

(25) In general, error with respect to the Law is of two types:

There is error that is excused for one who is adept in reflection about that thing concerning which error occurs, just as the skillful physician is excused if he errs with respect to the art of medicine and the skillful judge if he errs with respect to a judgment. But one who is not adept in that concern is not excused.

And there is error that is not excused for anyone whosoever. Rather, it is unbelief if it occurs with respect to the principles of the Law and heretical innovation if it occurs with respect to what is subordinate to the principles.

(26) This error is the very one that comes about concerning the things that all the sorts of methods of indications steer to cognizance of. Thus, cognizance of that thing is, in this manner, possible for everyone. Such, for example, is affirmation of [the existence of] God (may He be blessed and exalted); of the prophetic missions; and of happiness in the hereafter and misery in the hereafter. That is because the three sorts of indications due to which no one is exempted from assenting to what he is responsible for being cognizant of – I mean, the rhetorical, dialectical, and demonstrative indications – lead to these three roots.

So the one who denies things like these, when they are one of the roots of the Law, is an unbeliever who resists obstinately with his tongue but not his heart, or [who resists obstinately] due to his neglecting to expose himself to cognizance of what indicates them. For if he is an adept of demonstration, a path to assenting to them has been placed before him by demonstration; and if he is an adept of dialectic, then by dialectic; and if he is an adept of preaching, then by preaching. Therefore, he [the Prophet] (peace upon him) said, "I was ordered to combat people until they say, 'There is no god but God,' and have faith in me" – he means by whatever one of the three methods of bringing about faith that suits them.

(27) Concerning the things that are known only by demonstration due to their being hidden, God has been gracious to His servants for whom there is no path by means of demonstration – either due to their innate dispositions, their habits, or their lack of facilities for education – by coining for them likenesses and similarities of these [hidden things] and calling them to assent by means of those likenesses, since it is possible for assent to those likenesses to come about by means of the indications shared by all – I mean, the dialectical and the rhetorical. This is the reason for the Law being divided into an apparent sense and an inner sense. For the apparent sense is those likenesses coined for those meanings, and the inner sense is those meanings that reveal themselves only to those adept in demonstration. These [likenesses and meanings] are the four or five sorts of existing things that Abū Hāmid [al-Ghazāī] mentioned in the book *The Distinction.*

(28) If it happens, as we have said, that we know something in itself by means of the three methods, there is no need for us to coin a likeness for it; and, as long as it is in its apparent sense, it does not admit of interpretation. If this manner of apparent sense refers to the roots [of the Law], the one who interprets it would be an unbeliever – like someone believing that there is no happiness or misery in the hereafter and that such a statement is intended only to safeguard people from one another in what pertains to their bodies and physical senses, that it is a stratagem, and that a human being has no end other than sensual existence.

(29) If this has been determined for you, then it is apparent to you from our statement that there is an apparent sense of the Law that it is not permissible to interpret. To interpret it is unbelief when it has to do with principles and heretical innovation when it has to do with what is subordinate to principles. There is also an apparent sense that it is obligatory for those adept in demonstration to interpret, it being unbelief for them to take it in its apparent sense. Yet for those not adept in demonstration to interpret it and draw it away from its apparent sense is unbelief or heretical innovation on their part.

(30) Of this sort is the verse about God's directing Himself [2:29] and the Tradition about His descent. Therefore, he [the Prophet] said (peace upon him) with respect to the black woman, when she announced that God was in heaven: "Set her free, for she is one of the faithful." For she was not one of those adept in demonstration. The reason for that is that for the sort of people who come to assent only due to the imagination – I mean, those who assent to something only insofar as they can imagine it – it is difficult to come to assent to an existing thing that is not linked with something imaginable.

This also applies to those who understand the link only as [God having] a place – they are the ones who in their reflection have moved somewhat beyond the rank of the first sort's belief in corporeality. Therefore, the answer to these people about verses and Traditions like these is that they pertain to the verses that resemble one another and that the stop is at His saying (may He be exalted), "None knows their interpretation but God" [3:7]. Even though there is consensus among the people of demonstration that this sort admits of interpretation, they disagree about its interpretation. And that is according to each one's rank with respect to cognizance of demonstration.

(31)   There is a third sort [of verses and Traditions] with respect to the Law, one wavering between these [other] two sorts and about which there is doubt. One group of those who occupy themselves with reflection attach this sort to the apparent sense that it is not permissible to interpret, and others attach it to the inner sense that it is not permissible for the learned to take according to its apparent sense. That is because this sort [of verses and Traditions] is recondite and abstruse. One who commits an error with respect to this is to be excused – I mean, one of the learned.

(32)   If it were said, "Since it has become evident that, in this respect, there are three ranks in the Law, then in which of these three ranks, according to you, belongs what is set forth with respect to descriptions of the next life and its conditions?" we would say, "With respect to this question, it is an evident matter that they belong to the sort about which there is disagreement." That is because we see a group who pretend to demonstration, saying that it is obligatory to take these descriptions in their apparent sense since there is no demonstration rendering that apparent sense preposterous; and this is the method of the Ash'arites. Yet another group, who also occupy themselves with demonstration, interpret these descriptions; and they disagree greatly among themselves in their interpretation. Among this sort are to be counted Abū Ḥāmid [al-Ghazālī] and many of the Sufis. And some combine both interpretations, as Abū Ḥāmid [al-Ghazālī] does in some of his books.

(33)   It seems that the learned person who commits an error with respect to this question is to be excused and the one who hits the mark is to be thanked or rewarded – that is, if he acknowledges the existence [of the next life] and gives a manner of interpretation of it not leading to the disavowal of its existence. With respect to this [question], denying its existence is what is unbelief, because it is one of the roots of the Law and something to which assent comes about by the three methods shared by "the red and the black."

(34)   For anyone not adept in science, it is obligatory to take them [the descriptions of the next life] in their apparent sense; for him, it is unbelief

to interpret them because it leads to unbelief. That is why we are of the opinion that, for anyone among the people whose duty it is to have faith in the apparent sense, interpretation is unbelief because it leads to unbelief. Anyone adept in interpretation who divulges that to him calls him to unbelief; and the one who calls to unbelief is an unbeliever.

(35)   This is why it is obligatory that interpretations be established only in books using demonstrations. For if they are in books using demonstrations, no one but those adept in demonstration will get at them. Whereas, if they are established in other than demonstrative books with poetical and rhetorical or dialectical methods used in them, as Abū Ḥāmid [al-Ghazālī] does, that is an error against the Law and against wisdom.

Yet the man intended only good. That is, he wished thereby to make those adept in science more numerous. But he actually made those adept in wickedness more numerous, yet not without some increase among those adept in science. In that way, one group came to slander wisdom, another group to slander the Law, and another group to reconcile the two. It seems that this was one of the intentions of his books.

An indication that he wished thereby to alert people's minds is that he adhered to no single doctrine in his books. Rather, with the Ash'arites he was an Ash'arite, with the Sufis a Sufi, and with the philosophers a philosopher – so that he was, as it is said:

> One day a Yamanī, if I meet a man from
>   Yaman,
> And if I meet a Ma'addī, then I'm of Adnān.

(36)   What is obligatory for the imams of the Muslims is that they ban those of his books that contain science from all but those adept in science, just as it is obligatory upon them to ban demonstrative books from those not adept in them. Yet the harm befalling people from demonstrative books is lighter, because for the most part only those with superior innate dispositions take up demonstrative books. And this sort [of people] is misled only through a lack of practical virtue, reading in a disorderly manner, and turning to them without a teacher.

Still, totally forbidding demonstrative books bars from what the Law calls to, because it is a wrong to the best sort of people and to the best sort of existing things. For justice with respect to the best sort of existing things is for them to be cognized to their utmost degree by those prepared to be cognizant of them to their utmost degree, and these are the best sort of people. Indeed, the greater the worth of the existing thing, the greater is the injustice with respect to it – namely, ignorance of it. Therefore, He said (may He be exalted), "Associating [other gods with God] is surely a major wrong" [31:13].

[IV. Summary]

(37)   So this is what we were of the opinion we should establish with respect to this type of reflection – I mean, the discussion between the Law and wisdom and the statutes for interpreting the Law. If it were not for this being so widespread among people and these questions we have mentioned being so widespread, we would not have deemed it permissible to write a single letter about it; nor would we have to excuse ourselves to those adept in interpretation for doing so, because these questions are such as to be mentioned in demonstrative books. God is the Guide to and the Successful Giver of what is correct!

[V.   On what is intended by the Law and its methods]

[A.   *What is intended by the Law*]   (38)   You ought to know that what is intended by the Law is only to teach true science and true practice. True science is cognizance of God (may He be blessed and exalted) and of all the existing things as they are, especially the venerable ones among them; and cognizance of happiness in the hereafter and of misery in the hereafter. True practice is to follow the actions that promote happiness and to avoid the actions that promote misery; and cognizance of these actions is what is called "practical science."

Moses ben Maimon (Maimonides) *The Guide for the Perplexed* (selections)

Introduction

Known alternatively as "Maimonides" among Christian schoolmen, "Moses ben Maimon" or "Rambam" among Jews, and "Musa ibn Maimun" among Muslims, Maimonides (1138–1204) was, like Ibn Rushd (IV.7 above), born in that multi-cultural melting pot of Cordoba in al-Andalus (Andalusia), where under Umayyad rule scholarly culture drew deeply from all three Abrahamic intellectual traditions, as well as from those of Greek philosophy.[1] After traveling in Egypt and North Africa and training as a physician, Maimonides produced what would become his greatest philosophical work, the *Guide for the Perplexed* (or *Dalālat alḥā'irīn*). The text of the *Guide* makes the omnivorous syncretism of Cordoba manifest, not only in its very language (written in Arabic by a Jewish hand) but also in its drawing heartily from such diverse sources as the Talmud, the Torah, Muslim, and Christian philosophy, as well as Greek philosophers, especially Aristotle. Maimonides marshals elements from this panoply of sources towards the end of building arguments that reconcile philosophical science with Abrahamic religion.[2]

The following selection presents the heart of what has come to be known as Maimonides' "negative

From Moses Maimonides, *The Guide for the Perplexed*, trans. M. Friedländer, 2nd edition, New York: Dover Publications, 1956, pp. 68–91.

theology." Impressed with both the absolute unity and the absolute transcendence of God, Maimonides rejected the idea that God can be understood using the conventional ideas of "substance," "attribute," and "quality" that found their root in Aristotelian metaphysics. Because God is absolutely unitary, there can be no plurality of the sort that exists between a substance and its qualities or accidents; and because no predication or attributions of quality can be made of God, no definition of God can be formulated. Because God is utterly transcendent, beyond time and space, one cannot speak meaningfully of the relations that exist between God and God's creations, even relations of similarity or comparison: "there is no relation whatever between him and any other being" (Chapter LII); "the terms Wisdom, Power, Will, and Life are applied to God and to other beings by way of perfect homonymity, admitting of no comparison whatever" (Chapter LVI). In a similar way God cannot be named in any way that denotes his essence. Like Aquinas (III.10), Maimonides saw in Exodus metaphysical suggestions that the naming of God (e.g. in the Tetragrammaton, Exodus 20:7, "*yhwh*" or "*Yaweh*", and in the "*Ehyeh asher ehyeh*" of Exodus 3:14) indicates only pure existence without qualification. Indeed, Maimonides' analysis throws the idea that one can say anything positive or affirmative at all about God into profound question – a question that would perplex many medieval philosophers. "In the contemplation of His essence, our comprehension and knowledge prove insufficient; in the examination of His works, how they necessarily result from His will, our knowledge proves to be ignorance, and in the endeavour to extol him in words, all our efforts in speech are mere weakness and failure!"

In what sense is theology at all, then, possible? Instead of opting for a non-rational mysticism characteristic of Orthodox Christianity and Western mystics like Hildegard of Bingen (1098–1179) and Meister Eckhart (c. 1260–1328), Maimonides argues that one can minimally reason about God by reasoning about God's acts, or at least the effects of God's acts, as these indicate something of God's perfection (Chapter LII). But since God's acts are not God, they do nothing to determine God's essence or nature or character with any positive content.[3] While creatures like us, whose cognitive powers are limited to imagination and discursive conceptualization, can at best read scripture poetically and didactically (Chapter LIV), philosophers can acquire something more, namely actual knowledge of God, through a kind of "negative" labor – that is, by establishing what God is not.[4] This negative march of knowledge differs, however, in Maimonides' view, from the formalization of mere ignorance, perhaps because knowing "what X is not" somehow entails real knowledge about "what X is." As he puts it: "for in the same way as by each additional attribute an object is more specified, and is brought nearer to the apprehension of the observer, so by each negative attribute you advance toward the knowledge of God, and you are nearer to it than he who does not negative, in reference to God, those qualities which you are convinced by proof must be negatived" (Chapter LIX). According to Maimonides, even those who have received knowledge about God's commandments or God's creation through revelation, like Moses, remain incapable of grasping God's essence (Chapter LIV).

Notes

1 M. R. Menocal, *The Ornament of the World*, New York: Little, Brown, & Co., 2002.

2 H. Davidson, *Moses Maimonides*, Oxford: Oxford University Press, 2005.

3 In the controversy between medieval philosophers, who held that the world was created, and ancient philosophers, who held that the world has always existed, Maimonides maintains that neither conclusion can be proven but that the creation thesis is less absurd and less vulnerable to objection than the eternity thesis.

4 Compare Hegel's *Phenomenology of Spirit* (III.18) for a different but not unrelated way in which negativity is used to acquire a grasp of absolute reality.

Maimonides, *The Guide for the Perplexed*

Chapter LI

There are many things whose existence is manifest and obvious; some of these are innate notions or objects of sensation, others are nearly so; and in fact they would require no proof if man had been left in his primitive state. Such are the existence of motion, of man's free will, of phases of production and destruction, and of the natural properties perceived by the senses, e.g., the heat of fire, the coldness of water, and many other similar things. False notions, however, may be spread either by a person labouring under error, or by one who has some particular end in view, and who establishes theories contrary to the real nature of things, by denying the existence of things perceived by the senses, or by affirming the existence of what does not exist. Philosophers are thus required to establish by proof things which are self-evident, and to disprove the existence of things which only exist in man's imagination. Thus Aristotle gives a proof for the existence of motion, because it had been denied; he disproves the reality of atoms, because it had been asserted.

To the same class belongs the rejection of essential attributes in reference to God. For it is a self-evident truth that the attribute is not inherent in the object to which it is ascribed, but it is superadded to its essence, and is consequently an *accident*; if the attribute denoted the essence [τὸ τί ἦν εἶναι] of the object, it would be either mere tautology, as if, e.g., one would say "man is man," or the explanation of a name, as, e.g., "man is a speaking animal"; for the words "speaking animal" include the true essence of man, and there is no third element besides life and speech in the definition of man; when he, therefore, is described by the attributes of life and speech, these are nothing but an explanation of the name "man," that is to say, that the thing which is called man, consists of life and speech. It will now be clear that the attribute must be one of two things, either the essence of the object described – in that case it is a mere explanation of a name, and on that account we might admit the attribute in reference to God, but we reject it from another cause as will be shown – or the attribute is something different from the object described, some extraneous superadded element; in that case the attribute would be an accident, and he who merely rejects the appellation "accidents" in reference to the attributes of God, does not thereby alter their character; for everything superadded to the essence of an object joins it without forming part of its essential properties, and that constitutes an accident. Add to this the logical consequence of admitting many attributes, viz., the existence of many eternal beings. There cannot be any belief in the unity of God except by admitting that He is one simple substance, without any composition or plurality of elements; one from whatever side you view it, and by whatever test you examine it; not divisible into two parts in any way and by any cause, nor capable of any form of plurality either objectively or subjectively, as will be proved in this treatise.

Some thinkers have gone so far as to say that the attributes of God are neither His essence nor anything extraneous to His essence. This is like the assertion of some theorists, that the ideals, i.e., the *universalia*, are neither existing nor non-existent, and like the views of others, that the atom does not fill a definite place, but keeps an atom of space occupied; that man has no freedom of action at all, but has acquirement. Such things are only said; they exist only in words, not in thought, much less in reality. But as you know, and as all know who do not delude themselves, these theories are preserved by a multitude of words, by misleading similes sustained by declamation and invective, and by numerous methods borrowed both from dialectics and sophistry. If after uttering them and supporting them by such words, a man were to examine for himself his own belief on this subject, he would see nothing but confusion and stupidity in an endeavour to

prove the existence of things which do not exist, or to find a mean between two opposites that have no mean. Or is there a mean between existence and non-existence, or between the identity and non-identity of two things? But, as we said, to such absurdities men were forced by the great licence given to the imagination, and by the fact that every existing material thing is necessarily imagined as a certain substance possessing several attributes; for nothing has ever been found that consists of one simple substance without any attribute. Guided by such imaginations, men thought that God was also composed of many different elements, viz., of His essence and of the attributes superadded to His essence. Following up this comparison, some believed that God was corporeal, and that He possessed attributes; others, abandoning this theory, denied the corporeality, but retained the attributes. The adherence to the literal sense of the text of Holy Writ is the source of all this error, as I shall show in some of the chapters devoted to this theme.

Chapter LII

Every description of an object by an affirmative attribute, which includes the assertion that an object is of a certain kind, must be made in one of the following five ways: –

First. The object is described by its *definition*, as e.g., man is described as a being that lives and has reason; such a description, containing the true essence of the object, is, as we have already shown, nothing else but the explanation of a name. All agree that this kind of description cannot be given of God; for there are no previous causes to His existence, by which He could be defined: and on that account it is a well-known principle, received by all the philosophers, who are precise in their statements, that no definition can be given of God.

Secondly. An object is described by *part of its definition*, as when, e.g., man is described as a living being or as a rational being. This kind of description includes the necessary connection [of the two ideas]; for when we say that every man is rational we mean by it that every being which has the characteristics of man must also have reason. All agree that this kind of description is inappropriate in reference to God; for if we were to speak of a portion of His essence, we should consider His essence to be a compound. The inappropriateness of this kind of description in reference to God is the same as that of the preceding kind.

Thirdly. An object is described by something different from its true essence, by something that does not complement or establish the essence of the object. The description, therefore, relates to a *quality*; but quality, in its most general sense, is an accident. If God could be described in this way, He would be the substratum of accidents: a sufficient reason for rejecting the idea that He possesses quality, since it diverges from the true conception of His essence. It is surprising how those who admit the application of attributes to God can reject, in reference to Him, comparison and qualification. For when they say "He cannot be qualified," they can only mean that He possesses no quality; and yet every positive essential attribute of an object either constitutes its essence, – and in that case it is identical with the essence, – or it contains a quality of the object.

There are, as you know, four kinds of quality; I will give you instances of attributes of each kind, in order to show you that this class of attributes cannot possibly be applied to God. (*a*) A man is described by any of his intellectual or moral qualities, or by any of the dispositions appertaining to him as an animate being, when, e.g., we speak of a person who is a carpenter, or who shrinks from sin, or who is ill. It makes no difference whether we say, a carpenter, or a sage, or a physician; by all these we represent certain physical dispositions; nor does it make any difference whether we say "sin-fearing" or "merciful." Every trade, every profession, and every settled habit of man are certain physical dispositions. All this is clear to those who have occupied themselves with the study of Logic. (*b*) A thing is described by some physical quality it possesses, or by the absence of the same, e.g., as being soft or hard. It makes no difference whether we say "soft or hard," or "strong or weak"; in both cases we speak of physical conditions. (*c*) A man is described by his passive qualities, or by his emotions; we speak, e.g., of a person who is passionate, irritable, timid, merciful, without implying that these conditions have become permanent. The description of a thing by its colour, taste, heat, cold, dryness, and moisture, belongs also to this class of attributes. (*d*) A thing is described by any of its qualities resulting from quantity as such; we

speak, e.g., of a thing which is long, short, curved, straight, etc.

Consider all these and similar attributes, and you will find that they cannot be employed in reference to God. He is not a magnitude that any quality resulting from quantity as such could be possessed by Him; He is not affected by external influences, and therefore does not possess any quality resulting from emotion. He is not subject to physical conditions, and therefore does not possess strength or similar qualities; He is not an animate being, that He should have a certain disposition of the soul, or acquire certain properties, as meekness, modesty, etc., or be in a state to which animate beings as such are subject, as, e.g., in that of health or of illness. Hence it follows that no attribute coming under the head of quality in its widest sense, can be predicated of God. Consequently, these three classes of attributes, describing the essence of a thing, or part of the essence, or a quality of it, are clearly inadmissible in reference to God, for they imply composition, which, as we shall prove, is out of question as regards the Creator. We say, with regard to this latter point, that He is absolutely One.

Fourthly. A thing is described by its *relation* to another thing, e.g., to time, to space, or to a different individual; thus we say, Zaid, the father of A, or the partner of B, or who dwells at a certain place, or who lived at a stated time. This kind of attribute does not necessarily imply plurality or change in the essence of the object described; for the same Zaid, to whom reference is made, is the partner of Amru, the father of Becr, the master of Khalid, the friend of Zaid, dwells in a certain house, and was born in a certain year. Such relations are not the essence of a thing, nor are they so intimately connected with it as qualities. At first thought, it would seem that they may be employed in reference to God, but after careful and thorough consideration we are convinced of their inadmissibility. It is quite clear that there is no relation between God and time or space. For time is an accident connected with motion, in so far as the latter includes the relation of anteriority and posteriority, and is expressed by number, as is explained in books devoted to this subject; and since motion is one of the conditions to which only material bodies are subject, and God is immaterial, there can be no relation between Him and time. Similarly there is no relation between Him and space. But what we have to investigate and to examine is this: whether some real relation exists between God and any of the substances created by Him, by which He could be described? That there is no correlation between Him and any of His creatures can easily be seen; for the characteristic of two objects correlative to each other is the equality of their reciprocal relation. Now, as God has absolute existence, while all other beings have only possible existence, as we shall show, there consequently cannot be any correlation [between God and His creatures]. That a certain kind of relation does exist between them is by some considered possible, but wrongly. It is impossible to imagine a relation between intellect and sight, although, as we believe, the same kind of existence is common to both; how, then, could a relation be imagined between any creature and God, who has nothing in common with any other being; for even the term existence is applied to Him and other things, according to our opinion, only by way of pure homonymity. Consequently there is no relation whatever between Him and any other being. For whenever we speak of a relation between two things, these belong to the same kind; but when two things belong to different kinds though of the same class, there is no relation between them. We therefore do not say, this red compared with that green, is more, or less, or equally intense, although both belong to the same class – colour; when they belong to two different classes, there does not appear to exist any relation between them, not even to a man of ordinary intellect, although the two things belong to the same category; e.g., between a hundred cubits and the heat of pepper there is no relation, the one being a quality, the other a quantity; or between wisdom and sweetness, between meekness and bitterness, although all these come under the head of quality in its more general signification. How, then, could there be any relation between God and His creatures, considering the important difference between them in respect to true existence, the greatest of all differences. Besides, if any relation existed between them, God would be subject to the accident of relation; and although that would not be an accident to the essence of God, it would still be, to some extent, a kind of accident. You would, therefore, be wrong if you applied affirmative attributes in their literal sense to God, though they contained only relations; these, however, are the most appropriate of all attributes, to be employed, in a less

strict sense, in reference to God, because they do not imply that a plurality of eternal things exists, or that any change takes place in the essence of God, when those things change to which God is in relation.

Fifthly. A thing is described by its *actions*; I do not mean by "its actions" the inherent capacity for a certain work, as is expressed in "carpenter," "painter," or "smith" – for these belong to the class of qualities which have been mentioned above – but I mean the action the latter has performed – we speak, e.g., of Zaid, who made this door, built that wall, wove that garment. This kind of attributes is separate from the essences of the thing described, and, therefore, appropriate to be employed in describing the Creator, especially since we know that these different actions do not imply that different elements must be contained in the substance of the agent, by which the different actions are produced, as will be explained. On the contrary, all the actions of God emanate from His essence, not from any extraneous thing superadded to His essence, as we have shown.

What we have explained in the present chapter is this: that God is one in every respect, containing no plurality or any element superadded to His essence: and that the many attributes of different significations applied in Scripture to God, originate in the multitude of His actions, not in a plurality existing in His essence, and are partly employed with the object of conveying to us some notion of His perfection, in accordance with what we consider perfection, as has been explained by us. The possibility of one simple substance excluding plurality, though accomplishing different actions, will be illustrated by examples in the next chapter.

Chapter LIII

The circumstance which caused men to believe in the existence of divine attributes is similar to that which caused others to believe in the corporeality of God. The latter have not arrived at that belief by speculation, but by following the literal sense of certain passages in the Bible. The same is the case with the attributes; when in the books of the Prophets and of the Law, God is described by attributes, such passages are taken in their literal sense, and it is then believed that God possesses attributes; as if He were to be exalted above corporeality, and not above things connected with corporeality, i.e., the accidents, I mean psychical dispositions, all of which are qualities [and connected with corporeality]. Every attribute which the followers of this doctrine assume to be essential to the Creator, you will find to express, although they do not distinctly say so, a quality similar to those which they are accustomed to notice in the bodies of all living beings. We apply to all such passages the principle, "The Torah speaketh in the language of man," and say that the object of all these terms is to describe God as the most perfect being, not as possessing those qualities which are only perfections in relation to created living beings. Many of the attributes express different acts of God, but that difference does not necessitate any difference as regards Him from whom the acts proceed. This fact, viz., that from one agency different effects may result, although that agency has not free will, and much more so if it has free will, I will illustrate by an instance taken from our own sphere. Fire melts certain things and makes others hard, it boils and burns, it bleaches and blackens. If we described the fire as bleaching, blackening, burning, boiling, hardening and melting, we should be correct, and yet he who does not know the nature of fire, would think that it included six different elements, one by which it blackens, another by which it bleaches, a third by which it boils, a fourth by which it consumes, a fifth by which it melts, a sixth by which it hardens things – actions which are opposed to one another, and of which each has its peculiar property. He, however, who knows the nature of fire, will know that by virtue of one quality in action, namely, by heat, it produces all these effects. If this is the case with that which is done by nature, how much more is it the case with regard to beings that act by free will, and still more with regard to God, who is above all description. If we, therefore, perceive in God certain relations of various kinds – for wisdom in us is different from power, and power from will – it does by no means follow that different elements are really contained in Him, that He contains one element by which He knows, another by which He wills, and another by which He exercises power, as is, in fact, the signification of the attributes of God] according to the Attributists. Some of them express it plainly, and enumerate the attributes as elements added to the essence. Others, however, are more reserved

with regard to this matter, but indicate their opinion, though they do not express it in distinct and intelligible words. Thus, e.g., some of them say: "God is omnipotent by His essence, wise by His essence, living by His essence, and endowed with a will by His essence." (I will mention to you, as an instance, man's reason, which being one faculty and implying no plurality, enables him to know many arts and sciences; by the same faculty man is able to sow, to do carpenter's work, to weave, to build, to study, to acquire a knowledge of geometry, and to govern a state. These various acts resulting from one simple faculty, which involves no plurality, are very numerous; their number, that is, the number of the actions originating in man's reason, is almost infinite. It is therefore intelligible how in reference to God, those different actions can be caused by one simple substance, that does not include any plurality or any additional element. The attributes found in Holy Scripture are either qualifications of His actions, without any reference to His essence, or indicate absolute perfection, but do not imply that the essence of God is a compound of various elements.) For in not admitting the *term* "compound," they do not reject the *idea* of a compound when they admit a substance with attributes.

There still remains one difficulty which led them to that error, and which I am now going to mention. Those who assert the existence of the attributes do not found their opinion on the variety of God's actions; they say it is true that one substance can be the source of various effects, but His essential attributes cannot be qualifications of His actions, because it is impossible to imagine that the Creator created Himself. They vary with regard to the so-called essential attributes – I mean as regards their number – according to the text of the Scripture which each of them follows. I will enumerate those on which all agree, and the knowledge of which they believe that they have derived from reasoning, not from some words of the Prophets, namely, the following four: – life, power, wisdom, and will. They believe that these are four different things, and such perfections as cannot possibly be absent from the Creator, and that these cannot be qualifications of His actions. This is their opinion. But you must know that wisdom and life in reference to God are not different from each other; for in every being that is conscious of itself, life and wisdom are the same thing, that is to say, if by wisdom we understand the consciousness of self. Besides, the subject and the object of that consciousness are undoubtedly identical [as regards God]; for according to our opinion, He is not composed of an element that apprehends, and another that does not apprehend; He is not like man, who is a combination of a conscious soul and an unconscious body. If, therefore, by "wisdom" we mean the faculty of self-consciousness, wisdom and life are one and the same thing. They, however, do not speak of wisdom in this sense, but of His power to apprehend His creatures. There is also no doubt that power and will do not exist in God in reference to Himself; for He cannot have power or will as regards Himself; we cannot imagine such a thing. They take these attributes as different relations between God and His creatures, signifying that He has power in creating things, will in giving to things existence as He desires, and wisdom in knowing what He created. Consequently, these attributes do not refer to the essence of God, but express relations between Him and His creatures.

Therefore we, who truly believe in the Unity of God, declare, that as we do not believe that some element is included in His essence by which He created the heavens, another by which He created the [four] elements, a third by which He created the ideals, in the same way we reject the idea that His essence contains an element by which He has power, another element by which He has will, and a third by which He has a knowledge of His creatures. On the contrary, He is a simple essence, without any additional element whatever; He created the universe, and knows it, but not by any extraneous force. There is no difference whether these various attributes refer to His actions or to relations between Him and His works; in fact, these relations, as we have also shown, exist only in the thoughts of men. This is what we must believe concerning the attributes occurring in the books of the Prophets; some may also be taken as expressive of the perfection of God by way of comparison with what we consider as perfections in us, as we shall explain.

Chapter LIV

The wisest man, our Teacher Moses, asked two things of God, and received a reply respecting both.

The one thing he asked was, that God should let him know His true essence; the other, which in fact he asked first, that God should let him know His attributes. In answer to both these petitions God promised that He would let him know all His attributes, and that these were nothing but His actions. He also told him that His true essence could not be perceived, and pointed out a method by which he could obtain the utmost knowledge of God possible for man to acquire. The knowledge obtained by Moses has not been possessed by any human being before him or after him. His petition to know the attributes of God is contained in the following words: "Show me now thy way, that I may know thee, that I may find grace in thy sight" (Exod. xxxiii. 13). Consider how many excellent ideas found expression in the words, "Show me thy way, that I may know thee." We learn from them that God is known by His attributes, for Moses believed that he knew Him, when he was shown the way of God. The words "That I may find grace in thy sight," imply that he who knows God finds grace in His eyes. Not only is he acceptable and welcome to God who fasts and prays, but everyone who knows Him. He who has no knowledge of God is the object of His wrath and displeasure. The pleasure and the displeasure of God, the approach to Him and the withdrawal from Him are proportional to the amount of man's knowledge or ignorance concerning the Creator. We have already gone too far away from our subject, let us now return to it.

Moses prayed to God to grant him knowledge of His attributes, and also pardon for His people; when the latter had been granted, he continued to pray for the knowledge of God's essence in the words, "Show me thy glory" (*ib.* 18), and then received, respecting his first request, "Show me thy way," the following favourable reply, "I will make all my goodness to pass before thee" (*ib.* 19); as regards the second request, however, he was told, "Thou canst not see my face" (*ib.* 20). The words "all my goodness" imply that God promised to show him the whole creation, concerning which it has been stated, "And God saw everything that he had made, and, behold, it was very good" (Gen. i. 31); when I say "to show him the whole creation," I mean to imply that God promised to make him comprehend the nature of all things, their relation to each other, and the way they are governed by God both in reference to the universe as a whole and to each creature in particular. This knowledge is referred to when we are told of Moses, "he is firmly established in all mine house" (Num. xii. 7); that is, "his knowledge of all the creatures in My universe is correct and firmly established"; for false opinions are not firmly established. Consequently the knowledge of the works of God is the knowledge of His attributes, by which He can be known. The fact that God promised Moses to give him a knowledge of His works, may be inferred from the circumstance that God taught him such attributes as refer exclusively to His works, viz., "merciful and gracious, longsuffering and abundant in goodness," etc., (Exod. xxxiv. 6). It is therefore clear that the ways which Moses wished to know, and which God taught him, are the actions emanating from God. Our Sages call them *mid-dot* (qualities), and speak of the thirteen *middoth* of God (Talm. B. Rosh ha-shanah, p. 17b); they used the term also in reference to man; comp. "there are four different *middoth* (characters) among those who go to the house of learning"; "There are four different *middoth* (characters) among those who give charity" (Mishnah *Abot*, v. 13, 14). They do not mean to say that God really possesses *middot* (qualities), but that He performs actions similar to such of our actions as originate in certain qualities, i.e., in certain psychical dispositions; not that God has really such dispositions. Although Moses was shown "all His goodness," i.e., all His works, only the thirteen *middot* are mentioned, because they include those acts of God which refer to the creation and the government of mankind, and to know these acts was the principal object of the prayer of Moses. This is shown by the conclusion of his prayer, "that I may know thee, that I may find grace in thy sight, and consider that this nation is thy people" (Exod. xxxiii. 16), that is to say, the people whom I have to rule by certain acts in the performance of which I must be guided by Thy own acts in governing them. We have thus shown that "the ways" used in the Bible, and "*mid-dot*" used in the Mishnah, are identical, denoting the acts emanating from God in reference to the universe.

Whenever any one of His actions is perceived by us, we ascribe to God that emotion which is the source of the act when performed by ourselves, and call Him by an epithet which is formed from the verb expressing that emotion. We see, e.g., how well He provides for the life of the embryo of living beings; how He endows with certain faculties both the embryo itself and those who have to rear it after its birth, in order that it may be protected from death and destruction, guarded against all harm, and assisted in the performance of all that is required [for its development]. Similar acts, when performed by us, are due to a certain emotion and tenderness called mercy and pity. God is, therefore, said to be merciful; e.g., "Like as a father is merciful to his children, so the Lord is merciful to them that fear Him" (Ps. ciii. 13); "And I will spare them, as a man spareth (*yaḥamol*) his own son that serveth him" (Mai. iii. 17). Such instances do not imply that God is influenced by a feeling of mercy, but that acts similar to those which a father performs for his son, out of pity, mercy and real affection, emanate from God solely for the benefit of His pious men, and are by no means the result of any impression or change – [produced in God]. – When we give something to a person who has no claim upon us, we perform an act of grace; e.g., "Grant them graciously unto us" (Judges xxi. 22). [The same term is used in reference to God, e.g.] "which God hath graciously given" (Gen. xxxiii. 5); "Because God hath dealt graciously with me" (*ib.* 11). Instances of this kind are numerous. God creates and guides beings who have no claim upon Him to be created and guided by Him; He is therefore called gracious (*ḥannun*). – His actions towards mankind also include great calamities, which overtake individuals and bring death to them, or affect whole families and even entire regions, spread death, destroy generation after generation, and spare nothing whatsoever. Hence there occur inundations, earthquakes, destructive storms, expeditions of one nation against the other for the sake of destroying it with the sword and blotting out its memory, and many other evils of the same kind. Whenever such evils are caused by us to any person, they originate in great anger, violent jealousy, or a desire for revenge. God is therefore called, because of these acts, "jealous," "revengeful," "wrathful," and "keeping anger" (Nah. i. 2); that is to say, He performs acts similar to those which, when performed by us, originate in certain psychical dispositions, in jealousy, desire for retaliation, revenge, or anger; they are in accordance with the guilt of those who are to be punished, and not the result of any emotion; for He is above all defect! The same is the case with all divine acts; though resembling those acts which emanate from our passions and psychical dispositions, they are not due to anything superadded to His essence. – The governor of a country, if he is a prophet, should conform to these attributes. Acts [of punishment] must be performed by him moderately and in accordance with justice, not merely as an outlet of his passion. He must not let loose his anger, nor allow his passion to overcome him; for all passions are bad, and they must be guarded against as far as it lies in man's power. At times and towards some persons he must be merciful and gracious, not only from motives of mercy and compassion, but according to their merits; at other times and towards other persons he must evince anger, revenge, and wrath in proportion to their guilt, but not from motives of passion. He must be able to condemn a person to death by fire without anger, passion, or loathing against him, and must exclusively be guided by what he perceives of the guilt of the person, and by a sense of the great benefit which a large number will derive from such a sentence. You have, no doubt, noticed in the Torah how the commandment to annihilate the seven nations, and "to save alive nothing that breatheth" (Deut. xx. 16) is followed immediately by the words, "That they teach you not to do after all their abominations, which they have done unto their gods; so should you sin against the Lord your God" (*ib.* 18); that is to say, you shall not think that this commandment implies an act of cruelty or of retaliation; it is an act demanded by the tendency of man to remove everything that might turn him away from the right path, and to clear away all obstacles in the road to perfection, that is, to the knowledge of God. Nevertheless, acts of mercy, pardon, pity, and grace should more frequently be performed by the governor of a country than acts of punishment; seeing that all the thirteen *middoth* of God are attributes of mercy with only one exception, namely, "visiting the iniquity of the fathers upon the children" (Exod. xxxiv. 7); for the meaning of the preceding attribute (in the original *ve-nakkeh lo yenakkeh*) is "and he will not utterly destroy"; (and not "He will by no means clear the guilty"); comp. "And she will be utterly destroyed (*ve-nikketah*), she shall sit upon the ground" (Isa. iii. 26). When it is said that God is visiting the iniquity of the fathers upon the children, this refers exclusively to the sin of idolatry, and to no other sin. That this is the case may be inferred from what is said in the ten commandments, "upon the third and fourth generation of my enemies" (Exod. xx. 5), none except idolaters being called "enemy"; comp. Also "every abomination to the Lord, which he hateth" (Deut. xii. 31). It was, however, considered sufficient to extend the punishment to the fourth generation, because the fourth generation is the utmost a man can see of his posterity; and when, therefore, the idolaters of a place are destroyed, the old man worshipping idols is killed, his son, his grandson, and his great-grandson, that is, the fourth generation. By the mention of this attribute we are, as it were, told that His commandments, undoubtedly in harmony with His acts, include the death even of the little children of idolaters because of the sin of their fathers and grandfathers. This principle we find frequently applied in the Law, as, e.g., we read concerning the city that has been led astray to idolatry, "destroy it utterly, and all that is therein" (Deut. xiii. 15). All this has been ordained in order that every vestige of that which would lead to great injury should be blotted out, as we have explained.

We have gone too far away from the subject of this chapter, but we have shown why it has been considered sufficient to mention only these (thirteen) out of all His acts; namely, because they are required for the good government of a country; for the chief aim of man should be to make himself, as far as possible, similar to God: that is to say, to make his acts similar to the acts of God, or as our Sages expressed it in explaining the verse, "Ye shall be holy" (Lev. xxi. 2): "He is gracious, so be you also gracious; He is merciful, so be you also merciful."

The principal object of this chapter was to show that all attributes ascribed to God are attributes of His acts, and do not imply that God has any qualities.

Chapter LV

We have already, on several occasions, shown in this treatise that everything that implies corporeality or passiveness, is to be negatived in reference to God, for all passiveness implies change; and the agent producing that state is undoubtedly different from the object affected by it; and if God could be affected in any way whatever, another being beside Him would act on Him and cause change in Him. All kinds of non-existence must likewise be negatived in reference to Him; no perfection whatever can therefore be imagined to be at one time absent from Him, and at another present in Him: for if this were the case, He would [at a certain time] only be potentially perfect. Potentiality always implies non-existence, and when anything has to pass from potentiality into reality, another thing that exists in reality is required to effect that transition. Hence it follows that all perfections must really exist in God, and none of them must in any way be a mere potentiality. Another thing likewise to be denied in reference to God, is similarity to any existing being. This has been generally accepted, and is also mentioned in the books of the Prophets; e.g., "To whom, then, will you liken me?" (Isa. xl. 25); "To whom, then, will you liken God?" (*ib.* 18); "There is none like unto Thee" (Jer. x. 6). Instances of this kind are frequent. In short, it is necessary to demonstrate by proof that nothing can be predicated of God that implies any of the following four things: corporeality, emotion or change, nonexistence, – e.g., that something would be potential at one time and real at another – and similarity with any of His creatures. In this respect our knowledge of God is aided by the study of Natural Science. For he who is ignorant of the latter cannot understand the defect implied in emotions, the difference between potentiality and reality, the non-existence implied in all potentiality, the inferiority of a thing that exists *in potentiâ* to that which moves in order to cause its transition from potentiality into reality, and the inferiority of that which moves for this purpose compared with its condition when the transition has been effected. He who knows these things, but without their proofs, does not know the details which logically result from these general propositions; and therefore he cannot prove that God exists, or that the [four] things mentioned above are inadmissible in reference to God.

Having premised these remarks, I shall explain in the next chapter the error of those who believe that God has essential attributes; those who have some knowledge of Logic and Natural Science will understand it.

Chapter LVI

Similarity is based on a certain relation between two things; if between two things no relation can be found, there can be no similarity between them, and there is no relation between two things that have no similarity to each other; e.g., we do not say this heat is similar to that colour, or this voice is similar to that sweetness. This is self-evident. Since the existence of a relation between God and man, or between Him and other beings has been denied, similarity must likewise be denied. You must know that two things of the same kind – i.e., whose essential properties are the same, and which are distinguished from each other by greatness and smallness, strength and weakness, etc. – are necessarily similar, though different in this one way; e.g., a grain of mustard and the sphere of the fixed stars are similar as regards the three dimensions, although the one is exceedingly great, the other exceedingly small, the property of having [three] dimensions is the same in both; or the heat of wax melted by the sun and the heat of the element of fire, are similar as regards heat; although the heat is exceedingly great in the one case, and exceedingly small in the other, the existence of that quality (heat) is the same in both. Thus those who believe in the presence of essential attributes in God, viz., Existence, Life, Power, Wisdom, and Will, should know that these attributes, when applied to God, have not the same meaning as when applied to us, and that the difference does not only consist in magnitude, or in the degree of perfection, stability, and durability. It cannot be said, as they practically believe, that His existence is only more stable, His life more permanent, His power greater, His wisdom more perfect, and His will more general than ours, and that the same definition applies to both. This is in no way admissible, for the expression "more than" is used in comparing two things as regards a certain attribute predicated of both of them in exactly the same sense, and consequently implies similarity [between God and His creatures]. When they ascribe to God essential attributes, these so-called essential attributes should not have any similarity to the attributes of other things, and should according to their own opinion not be included in one of the same definition, just as there is no similarity between the essence of God and that of other beings. They do not follow this principle, for they hold that one definition may include them, and that, nevertheless, there is no similarity between them. Those who are familiar with the meaning of similarity will certainly understand that the term existence, when applied to God and to other beings, is perfectly homonymous. In like manner, the terms Wisdom, Power, Will, and Life are applied to God and to other beings by way of perfect homonymity, admitting of no comparison whatever. Nor must you think that these attributes are employed as hybrid terms; for hybrid terms are such as are applied to two things which have a similarity to each other in respect to a certain property which is in both of them an accident, not an essential, constituent element. The attributes of God, however, are not considered as accidental by any intelligent person, while all attributes applied to man are accidents, according to the Mutakallemim. I am therefore at a loss to see how they can find any similarity [between the attributes of God and those of man]; how their definitions can be identical, and their significations the same! This is a decisive proof that there is, in no way or sense, anything common to the attributes predicated of God, and those used in reference to ourselves; they have only the same names, and nothing else is common to them. Such being the case, it is not proper to believe, on account of the use of the same attributes, that there is in God something additional to His essence, in the same way as attributes are joined to our essence. This is most important for those who understand it. Keep it in memory, and study it thoroughly, in order to be well prepared for that which I am going to explain to you.

Chapter LVII

On attributes; remarks more recondite than the preceding. It is known that existence is an accident appertaining to all things, and therefore an element superadded to their essence. This must evidently be the case as regards everything the existence of which is due to some cause; its existence is an element superadded to its essence. But as regards a being whose existence is not due to any cause – God alone is that being, for His existence, as we have said, is absolute – existence and essence are perfectly identical; He is not a substance to which existence is joined as an accident, as an additional element. His existence is always absolute, and has never been a new element or an accident in Him. Consequently God exists without possessing the attribute of existence. Similarly He lives, without possessing the attribute of life; knows, without possessing the attribute of knowledge; is omnipotent without possessing the attribute

of omnipotence; is wise, without possessing the attribute of wisdom; all this reduces itself to one and the same entity; there is no plurality in Him, as will be shown. It is further necessary to consider that unity and plurality are accidents supervening to an object according as it consists of many elements or of one. This is fully explained in the book called Metaphysics. In the same way as number is not the substance of the things numbered, so is unity not the substance of the thing which has the attribute of unity, for unity and plurality are accidents belonging to the category of discrete quantity, and supervening to such objects as are capable of receiving them.

To that being, however, which has truly simple, absolute existence, and in which composition is inconceivable, the accident of unity is as inadmissible as the accident of plurality; that is to say, God's unity is not an element superadded, but He is One without possessing the attribute of unity. The investigation of this subject, which is almost too subtle for our understanding, must not be based on current expressions employed in describing it, for these are the great source of error. It would be extremely difficult for us to find, in any language whatsoever, words adequate to this subject, and we can only employ inadequate language. In our endeavour to show that God does not include a plurality, we can only say "He is one," although "one" and "many" are both terms which serve to distinguish quantity. We therefore make the subject clearer, and show to the understanding the way of truth by saying He is one but does not possess the attribute of unity.

The same is the case when we say God is the First (*Kadmon*), to express that He has not been created; the term "First" is decidedly inaccurate, for it can in its true sense only be applied to a being that is subject to the relation of time; the latter, however, is an accident to motion which again is connected with a body. Besides the attribute "first" is a relative term, being in regard to time the same as the terms "long" and "short" are in regard to a line. Both expressions, "first" and "created," are equally inadmissible in reference to any being to which the attribute of time is not applicable, just as we do not say "crooked" or "straight" in reference to taste, "salted" or "insipid" in reference to the voice. These subjects are not unknown to those who have accustomed themselves to seek a true understanding of the things, and to establish their properties in accordance with the abstract notions which the mind has formed of them, and who are not misled by the inaccuracy of the words employed. All attributes, such as "the First," "the Last," occurring in the Scriptures in reference to God, are as metaphorical as the expressions "ear" and "eye." They simply signify that God is not subject to any change or innovation whatever; they do not imply that God can be described by time, or that there is any comparison between Him and any other being as regards time, and that He is called on that account "the first" and "the last." In short, all similar expressions are borrowed from the language commonly used among the people. In the same way we use "One" in reference to God, to express that there is nothing similar to Him, but we do not mean to say that an attribute of unity is added to His essence.

Chapter LVIII

This chapter is even more recondite than the preceding. Know that the negative attributes of God are the true attributes: they do not include any incorrect notions or any deficiency whatever in reference to God, while positive attributes imply polytheism, and are inadequate, as we have already shown. It is now necessary to explain how negative expressions can in a certain sense be employed as attributes, and how they are distinguished from positive attributes. Then I shall show that we cannot describe the Creator by any means except by negative attributes. An attribute does not exclusively belong to the one object to which it is related; while qualifying one thing, it can also be employed to qualify other things, and is in that case not peculiar to that one thing. E.g., if you see an object from a distance, and on enquiring what it is, are told that it is a living being, you have certainly learnt an attribute of the object seen, and although that attribute does not exclusively belong to the object perceived, it expresses that the object is not a plant or a mineral. Again, if a man is in a certain house, and you know that something is in the house, but not exactly what, you ask what is in that house, and you are told, not a plant nor a mineral. You have thereby obtained some special knowledge of the thing; you have learnt that it is a living being, although you do not yet know what kind of a living being it is. The negative attributes have

this in common with the positive, that they necessarily circumscribe the object to some extent, although such circumscription consists only in the exclusion of what otherwise would not be excluded. In the following point, however, the negative attributes are distinguished from the positive. The positive attributes, although not peculiar to one thing, describe a portion of what we desire to know, either some part of its essence or some of its accidents; the negative attributes, on the other hand, do not, as regards the essence of the thing which we desire to know, in any way tell us what it is, except it be indirectly, as has been shown in the instance given by us.

After this introduction, I would observe that, – as has already been shown – God's existence is absolute, that it includes no composition, as will be proved, and that we comprehend only the fact that He exists, not His essence. Consequently it is a false assumption to hold that He has any positive attribute; for He does not possess existence in addition to His essence; it therefore cannot be said that the one may be described as an attribute [of the other]; much less has He [in addition to His existence] a compound essence, consisting of two constituent elements to which the attribute could refer; still less has He accidents, which could be described by an attribute. Hence it is clear that He has no positive attribute whatever. The negative attributes, however, are those which are necessary to direct the mind to the truths which we must believe concerning God; for, on the one hand, they do not imply any plurality, and, on the other, they convey to man the highest possible knowledge of God; e.g., it has been established by proof that some being must exist besides those things which can be perceived by the senses, or apprehended by the mind; when we say of this being, that it exists, we mean that its non-existence is impossible. We then perceive that such a being is not, for instance, like the four elements, which are inanimate, and we therefore say that it is living, expressing thereby that it is not dead. We call such a being incorporeal, because we notice that it is unlike the heavens, which are living, but material. Seeing that it is also different from the intellect, which, though incorporeal and living, owes its existence to some cause, we say it is the first, expressing thereby that its existence is not due to any cause. We further notice, that the existence, that is the essence, of this being is not limited to its own existence; many existences emanate from it, and its influence is not like that of the fire in producing heat, or that of the sun in sending forth light, but consists in constantly giving them stability and order by well-established rule, as we shall show: we say, on that account, it has power, wisdom, and will, i.e., it is not feeble or ignorant, or hasty, and does not abandon its creatures; when we say that it is not feeble, we mean that its existence is capable of producing the existence of many other things; by saying that it is not ignorant, we mean "it perceives" or "it lives," – for everything that perceives is living – by saying "it is not hasty, and does not abandon its creatures," we mean that all these creatures preserve a certain order and arrangement; they are not left to themselves; they are not produced aimlessly, but whatever condition they receive from that being is given with design and intention. We thus learn that there is no other being like unto God, and we say that He is One, i.e., there are not more Gods than one.

It has thus been shown that every attribute predicated of God either denotes the quality of an action, or – when the attribute is intended to convey some idea of the Divine Being itself, and not of His actions – the negation of the opposite. Even these negative attributes must not be formed and applied to God, except in the way in which, as you know, sometimes an attribute is negatived in reference to a thing, although that attribute can naturally never be applied to it in the same sense, as, e.g., we say, "This wall does not see." Those who read the present work are aware that, notwithstanding all the efforts of the mind, we can obtain no knowledge of the essence of the heavens – a revolving substance which has been measured by us in spans and cubits, and examined even as regards the proportions of the several spheres to each other and respecting most of their motions – although we know that they must consist of matter and form; but the matter not being the same as sublunary matter, we can only describe the heavens in terms expressing negative properties, but not in terms denoting positive qualities. Thus we say that the heavens are not light, not heavy, not passive and therefore not subject to impressions, and that they do not possess the sensations of taste and smell; or we use similar negative attributes. All this we do, because we do not know their substance. What, then, can be the result of our efforts, when we try to obtain a knowledge of a

Being that is free from substance, that is most simple, whose existence is absolute, and not due to any cause, to whose perfect essence nothing can be superadded, and whose perfection consists, as we have shown, in the absence of all defects. All we understand is the fact that He exists, that He is a Being to whom none of His creatures is similar, who has nothing in common with them, who does not include plurality, who is never too feeble to produce other beings, and whose relation to the universe is that of a steersman to a boat; and even this is not a real relation, a real simile, but serves only to convey to us the idea that God rules the universe; that is, that He gives it duration, and preserves its necessary arrangement. This subject will be treated more fully. Praised be He! In the contemplation of His essence, our comprehension and knowledge prove insufficient; in the examination of His works, how they necessarily result from His will, our knowledge proves to be ignorance, and in the endeavour to extol Him in words, all our efforts in speech are mere weakness and failure!

Chapter LIX

The following question might perhaps be asked: Since there is no possibility of obtaining a knowledge of the true essence of God, and since it has also been proved that the only thing that man can apprehend of Him is the fact that He exists, and that all positive attributes are inadmissible, as has been shown; what is the difference among those who have obtained a knowledge of God? Must not the knowledge obtained by our teacher Moses, and by Solomon, be the same as that obtained by any one of the lowest class of philosophers, since there can be no addition to this knowledge? But, on the other hand, it is generally accepted among theologians and also among philosophers, that there can be a great difference between two persons as regards the knowledge of God obtained by them. Know that this is really the case, that those who have obtained a knowledge of God differ greatly from each other; for in the same way as by each additional attribute an object is more specified, and is brought nearer to the true apprehension of the observer, so by each additional negative attribute you advance toward the knowledge of God, and you are nearer to it than he who does not negative, in reference to

God, those qualities which you are convinced by proof must be negatived. There may thus be a man who after having earnestly devoted many years to the pursuit of one science, and to the true understanding of its principles, till he is fully convinced of its truths, has obtained as the sole result of this study the conviction that a certain quality must be negatived in reference to God, and the capacity of demonstrating that it is impossible to apply it to Him. Superficial thinkers will have no proof for this, will doubtfully ask, Is that thing existing in the Creator, or not? And those who are deprived of sight will positively ascribe it to God, although it has been clearly shown that He does not possess it. E.g., while I show that God is incorporeal, another doubts and is not certain whether He is corporeal or incorporeal; others even positively declare that He is corporeal, and appear before the Lord with that belief. Now see how great the difference is between these three men; the first is undoubtedly nearest to the Almighty; the second is remote, and the third still more distant from Him. If there be a fourth person who holds himself convinced by proof that emotions are impossible in God, while the first who rejects the corporeality, is not convinced of that impossibility, that fourth person is undoubtedly nearer the knowledge of God than the first, and so on, so that a person who, convinced by proof, negatives a number of things in reference to God, which according to our belief may possibly be in Him or emanate from Him, is undoubtedly a more perfect man than we are, and would surpass us still more if we positively believed these things to be properties of God. It will now be clear to you, that every time you establish by proof the negation of a thing in reference to God, you become more perfect, while with every additional positive assertion you follow your imagination and recede from the true knowledge of God. Only by such ways must we approach the knowledge of God, and by such researches and studies as would show us the inapplicability of what is inadmissible as regards the Creator, not by such methods as would prove the necessity of ascribing to Him anything extraneous to His essence, or asserting that He has a certain perfection, when we find it to be a perfection in relation to us. The perfections are all to some extent acquired properties, and a property which must be acquired does not exist in everything capable of making such acquisition.

You must bear in mind, that by affirming anything of God, you are removed from Him in two respects; first, whatever you affirm, is only a perfection in relation to us; secondly, He does not possess anything superadded to this essence; His essence includes all His perfections, as we have shown. Since it is a well-known fact that even that knowledge of God which is accessible to man cannot be attained except by negations, and that negations do not convey a true idea of the being to which they refer, all people, both of past and present generations, declared that God cannot be the object of human comprehension, that none but Himself comprehends what He is, and that our knowledge consists in knowing that we are unable truly to comprehend Him. All philosophers say, "He has overpowered us by His grace, and is invisible to us through the intensity of His light," like the sun which cannot be perceived by eyes which are too weak to bear its rays. Much more has been said on this topic, but it is useless to repeat it here. The idea is best expressed in the book of Psalms, "Silence is praise to Thee" (lxv. 2). It is a very expressive remark on this subject; for whatever we utter with the intention of extolling and of praising Him, contains something that cannot be applied to God, and includes derogatory expressions; it is therefore more becoming to be silent, and to be content with intellectual reflection, as has been recommended by men of the highest culture, in the words "Commune with your own heart upon your bed, and be still" (Ps. iv. 4). You must surely know the following celebrated passage in the Talmud – would that all passages in the Talmud were like that! – although it is known to you, I quote it literally, as I wish to point out to you the ideas contained in it: "A certain person, reading prayers in the presence of Rabbi Haninah, said, 'God, the great, the valiant and the tremendous, the powerful, the strong, and the mighty.' – The rabbi said to him, Have you finished all the praises of your Master? The three epithets, 'God, the great, the valiant and the tremendous,' we should not have applied to God, had Moses not mentioned them in the Law, and had not the men of the Great Synagogue come forward subsequently and established their use in the prayer; and you say all this! Let this be illustrated by a parable. There was once an earthly king, possessing millions of gold coin; he was praised for owning millions of silver coin; was this not really dispraise to him?" Thus far the opinion of the pious rabbi. Consider, first, how repulsive and annoying the accumulation of all these positive attributes was to him; next, how he showed that, if we had only to follow our reason, we should never have composed these prayers, and we should not have uttered any of them. It has, however, become necessary to address men in words that should leave some idea in their minds, and, in accordance with the saying of our Sages, "The Torah speaks in the language of men," the Creator has been described to us in terms of our own perfections; but we should not on that account have uttered any other than the three above-mentioned attributes, and we should not have used them as names of God except when meeting with them in reading the Law. Subsequently, the men of the Great Synagogue, who were prophets, introduced these expressions also into the prayer, but we should not on that account use [in our prayers] any other attributes of God. The principal lesson to be derived from this passage is that there are two reasons for our employing those phrases in our prayers: first, they occur in the Pentateuch; secondly, the Prophets introduced them into the prayer. Were it not for the first reason, we should never have uttered them; and were it not for the second reason, we should not have copied them from the Pentateuch to recite them in our prayers; how then could we approve of the use of those numerous attributes! You also learn from this that we ought not to mention and employ in our prayers all the attributes we find applied to God in the books of the Prophets; for he does not say, "Were it not that Moses, our Teacher, said them, we should not have been able to use them"; but he adds another condition – "and had not the men of the Great Synagogue come forward and established their use in the prayer," because only for that reason are we allowed to use them in our prayers. We cannot approve of what those foolish persons do who are extravagant in praise, fluent and prolix in the prayers they compose, and in the hymns they make in the desire to approach the Creator. They describe God in attributes which would be an offence if applied to a human being; for those persons have no knowledge of these great and important principles, which are not accessible to the ordinary intelligence of man. Treating the Creator as a familiar object, they describe Him and speak of Him in any expressions they think proper; they elo-

quently continue to praise Him in that manner, and believe that they can thereby influence Him and produce an effect on Him. If they find some phrase suited to their object in the words of the Prophets they are still more inclined to consider that they are free to make use of such texts – which should at least be explained – to employ them in their literal sense, to derive new expressions from them, to form from them numerous variations, and to found whole compositions on them. This license is frequently met with in the compositions of the singers, preachers, and others who imagine themselves to be able to compose a poem. Such authors write things which partly are real heresy, partly contain such folly and absurdity that they naturally cause those who hear them to laugh, but also to feel grieved at the thought that such things can be uttered in reference to God. Were it not that I pitied the authors for their defects, and did not wish to injure them, I should have cited some passages to show you their mistakes; besides, the fault of their compositions is obvious to all intelligent persons. You must consider it, and think thus: If slander and libel is a great sin, how much greater is the sin of those who speak with looseness of tongue in reference to God, and describe Him by attributes which are far below Him; and I declare that they not only commit an ordinary sin, but unconsciously at least incur the guilt of profanity and blasphemy. This applies both to the multitude that listens to such prayers, and to the foolish man that recites them. Men, however, who understand the fault of such compositions, and, nevertheless, recite them, may be classed, according to my opinion, among those to whom the following words are applied : "And the children of Israel used words that were not right against the Lord their God" (2 Kings xvii. 9); and "utter error against the Lord" (Isa. xxxii. 6). If you are of those who regard the honour of their Creator, do not listen in any way to them, much less utter what they say, and still less compose such prayers. Knowing how great is the offence of one who hurls aspersions against the Supreme Being. There is no necessity at all for you to use positive attributes of God with the view of magnifying Him in your thoughts, or to go beyond the limits which the men of the Great Synagogue have introduced in the prayers and in the blessings, for this is sufficient for all purposes, and even more than sufficient, as Rabbi Haninah said.

Other attributes, such as occur in the books of the Prophets, may be uttered when we meet with them in reading those books; but we must bear in mind what has already been explained, that they are either attributes of God's actions, or expressions implying the negation of the opposite. This likewise should not be divulged to the multitude; but a reflection of this kind is fitted for the few only who believe that the glorification of God does not consist in *uttering* that which is not to be uttered, but in *reflecting* on that on which man should reflect.

We will now conclude our exposition of the wise words of R. Haninah. He does not employ any such simile as: "A king who possesses millions of gold denarii, and is praised as having hundreds"; for this would imply that God's perfections, although more perfect than those ascribed to man are still of the same kind; but this is not the case, as has been proved. The excellence of the simile consists in the words: "who possesses golden denarii, and is praised as having silver denarii"; this implies that these attributes, though perfections as regards ourselves, are not such as regards God; in reference to Him they would all be defects, as is distinctly suggested in the remark, "Is this not an offence to Him?"

I have already told you that all these attributes, whatever perfection they may denote according to your idea, imply defects in reference to God, if applied to Him in the same sense as they are used in reference to ourselves. Solomon has already given us sufficient instruction on this subject by saying, "For God is in heaven, and thou upon earth; therefore let thy words be few" (Eccles. v. 2).

Chapter LX

I will give you in this chapter some illustrations, in order that you may better understand the propriety of forming as many negative attributes as possible, and the impropriety of ascribing to God any positive attributes. A person may know for certain that a "ship" is in existence, but he may not know to what object that name is applied, whether to a substance or to an accident; a second person then learns that the ship is not an accident; a third, that it is not a mineral; a fourth, that it is not a plant growing in the earth; a fifth, that it is not a body whose parts are joined together by nature; a sixth, that it is not a flat object like boards or doors; a seventh, that it is not a sphere; an eighth, that it is not pointed; a ninth, that it is not round-shaped; nor equilateral; a tenth, that it is not solid. It is clear that this tenth person has almost arrived at the correct notion of a "ship" by the foregoing negative attributes, as if he had exactly the same notion as those have who imagine it to be a wooden substance which is hollow, long, and composed of many pieces of wood, that is to say, who know it by positive attributes. Of the other persons in our illustration, each one is more remote from the correct notion of a ship than the next mentioned, so that the first knows nothing about it but the name. In the same manner you will come nearer to the knowledge and comprehension of God by the negative attributes. But you must be careful, in what you negative, to negative by proof, not by mere words, for each time you ascertain by proof that a certain thing, believed to exist in the Creator, must be negatived, you have undoubtedly come one step nearer to the knowledge of God.

It is in this sense that some men come very near to God, and others remain exceedingly remote from Him, not in the sense of those who are deprived of vision, and believe that God occupies a place, which man can physically approach or from which he can recede. Examine this well, know it, and be content with it. The way which will bring you nearer to God has been clearly shown to you; walk in it, if you have the desire. On the other hand, there is a great danger in applying positive attributes to God. For it has been shown that every perfection we could imagine, even if existing in God in accordance with the opinion of those who assert the existence of attributes, would in reality not be of the same kind as that imagined by us, but would only be called by the same name, according to our explanation; it would in fact amount to a negation. Suppose, e.g., you say He has knowledge, and that knowledge, which admits of no change and of no plurality, embraces many changeable things; His knowledge remains unaltered, while new things are constantly formed, and His knowledge of a thing before it exists, while it exists, and when it has ceased to exist, is the same without the least change: you would thereby declare that His knowledge is not like ours; and similarly that His existence is not like ours. You thus necessarily arrive at some negation, without obtaining a true conception of an essential attribute; on the contrary, you are led to assume that there is a plurality in God, and to believe that He, though one essence, has several unknown attributes. For if you intend to affirm them, you cannot compare them with those attributes known by us, and they are consequently not of the same kind. You are, as it were, brought by the belief in the reality of the attributes, to say that God is one subject of which several things are predicated; though the subject is not like ordinary subjects, and the predicates are not like ordinary predicates. This belief would ultimately lead us to associate other things with God, and not to believe that He is One. For of every subject certain things can undoubtedly be predicated, and although in reality subject and predicate are combined in one thing, by the actual definition they consist of two elements, the notion contained in the subject not being the same as that contained in the predicate. In the course of this treatise it will be proved to you that God cannot be a compound, and that He is simple in the strictest sense of the word.

I do not merely declare that he who affirms attributes of God has not sufficient knowlenge concerning the Creator, admits some association with God, or conceives Him to be different from what He is; but I say that he unconsciously loses his belief in God. For he whose knowledge concerning a thing is insufficient, understands one part of it while he is ignorant of the other, as, e.g., a person who knows that man possesses life, but does not know that man possesses understanding; but in reference to God, in whose real existence there is no plurality, it is impossible that one thing should be known, and another unknown. Similarly he who associates an object with [the properties of] another object, conceives a true and correct notion of the one object, and applies that notion also to the other; while those who admit the attributes of God, do not consider them as identical with His essence, but as extraneous elements. Again, he who conceives an incorrect notion of an object, must necessarily have a correct idea of the object to some extent; he, however, who says that taste belongs to the category of quantity has not, according to my opinion, an incorrect notion of taste, but is entirely ignorant of its nature, for he does not know to what object the term "taste" is to be applied. – This is a very difficult subject; consider it well.

According to this explanation you will understand, that those who do not recognize, in reference to God, the negation of things, which others negative by clear proof, are deficient in the knowledge of God, and are remote from comprehending Him. Consequently, the smaller the number of things is which a person can negative in relation to God, the less he knows of Him, as has been explained in the beginning of this chapter; but the man who affirms an attribute of God, knows nothing but the same; for the object to which, in his imagination, he applies that name, does not exist; it is a mere fiction and invention, as if he applied that name to a non-existing being, for there is, in reality, no such object. E.g., some one has heard of the elephant, and knows that it is an animal, and wishes to know its form and nature. A person, who is either misled or misleading, tells him it is an animal with one leg, three wings, lives in the depth of the sea, has a transparent body; its face is wide like that of a man, has the same form and shape, speaks like a man, flies sometimes in the air, and sometimes swims like a fish. I should not say, that he described the elephant incorrectly, or that he has an insufficient knowledge of the elephant, but I would say that the thing thus described is an invention and fiction, and that in reality there exists nothing like it; it is a non-existing being, called by the name of a really existing being, and like the griffin, the centaur, and similar imaginary combinations for which simple and compound names have been borrowed from real things. The present case is analogous; namely, God, praised be His name, exists, and His existence has been proved to be absolute and perfectly simple, as I shall explain. If such a simple, absolutely existing essence were said to have attributes, as has been contended, and were combined with extraneous elements, it would in no way be an existing thing, as has been proved by us; and when we say that that essence, which is called "God," is a substance with many properties by which it can be described, we apply that name to an object which does not at all exist. Consider, therefore, what are the consequences of affirming attributes to God! As to those attributes of God which occur in the Pentateuch, or in the books of the Prophets, we must assume that they are exclusively employed, as has been stated by us, to convey to us some notion of the perfections of the Creator, or to express qualities of actions emanating from Him.

Chapter LXI

It is well known that all the names of God occurring in Scripture are derived from His actions, except one, namely, the Tetragrammaton, which consists of the letters *yod, hé, vau* and *hé*. This name is applied exclusively to God, and is on that account called *Shem ha-meforash*, "The nomen proprium." It is the distinct and exclusive designation of the Divine Being; whilst His other names are common nouns, and are derived from actions, to which some of our own are similar, as we have already explained. Even the name *Adonay*, "Lord," which has been substituted for the Tetragrammaton, is derived from the appellative "lord"; comp. "The man who is the lord (*adone*) of the land spake roughly to us" (Gen. xliii. 30). The difference between *Adoni*, "my lord," (with *ḥirek* under the *nun*), or *Adonay* with *kamez*), is similar to the difference between *Sari*, "my prince," and *Saraï*, Abraham's wife (*ib.* xvi. 1), the latter form denoting majesty and distinction. An angel is also addressed as "*Adonay*"; e.g., "*Adonay* (My lord), pass not away, I pray thee" (*ib.* xviii. 3). I have restricted my explanation to the term *Adonay*, the substitute for the Tetragrammaton, because it is more commonly applied to God than any of the other names which are in frequent use, like *dayyan*, "judge," *shadday*, "almighty," *ẓaddik*, "righteous," *ḥan-nun*, "gracious," *raḥum* "merciful," and *elohim* "chief"; all these terms are unquestionably appellations and derivatives. The derivation of the name, consisting of *yod, hé, vau*, and *hé*, is not positively known, the word having no additional signification. This sacred name, which, as you know, was not pronounced except in the sanctuary by the appointed priests, when they gave the sacerdotal blessing, and by the high priest on the Day of Atonement, undoubtedly denotes something which is peculiar to God, and is not found in any other being. It is possible that in the Hebrew language, of which we have now but a slight knowledge, the Tetragrammaton, in the way it was pronounced, conveyed the meaning of "absolute existence." In short, the majesty of the name and the great dread of uttering it, are connected with the fact that it denotes God Himself, without including in its meaning any names of the things created by Him. Thus our Sages say: "'My name' (Num. vi. 27) means the name which is peculiar to Me." All other names

of God have reference to qualities, and do not signify a simple substance, but a substance with attributes, they being derivatives. On that account it is believed that they imply the presence of a plurality in God, I mean to say, the presence of attributes, that is, of some extraneous element superadded to His essence. Such is the meaning of all derivative names; they imply the presence of some attribute and its substratum, though this be not distinctly named. As, however, it has been proved, that God is not a substratum capable of attributes, we are convinced that those appellatives when employed as names of God, only indicate the relation of certain actions to Him, or they convey to us some notion of His perfection.

Hence R. Haninah would have objected to the expression "the great, the mighty, and the tremendous," had it not been for the two reasons mentioned by him; because such expressions lead men to think that the attributes are essential, i.e., they are perfections actually present in God. The frequent use of names of God derived from actions, led to the belief that He had as many [essential] attributes as there were actions from which the names were derived. The following promise was therefore made, implying that mankind will at a certain future time understand this subject, and be free from the error it involves: "In that day will the Lord be One, and His name One" (Zech. xiv. 9). The meaning of this prophecy is this: He being One, will then be called by one name, which will indicate the essence of God; but it does not mean that His sole name will be a derivative [viz., "One"]. In the *Pirke Rabbi Eliezer* (chap. iii.) occurs the following passage: "Before the universe was created, there was only the Almighty and His name." Observe how clearly the author states that all these appellatives employed as names of God came into existence after the Creation. This is true; for they all refer to actions manifested in the Universe. If, however, you consider His essence as separate and as abstracted from all actions, you will not describe it by an appellative, but by a proper noun, which exclusively indicates that essence. Every other name of God is a derivative, only the Tetragrammaton is a real *nomen proprium*, and must not be considered from any other point of view. You must beware of sharing the error of those who write amulets (*kameot*). Whatever you hear from them, or read in their works, especially in reference to the names which they form by combination, is utterly senseless; they call these combinations *shemot* (names) and believe that their pronunciation demands sanctification and purification, and that by using them they are enabled to work miracles. Rational persons ought not to listen to such men, nor in any way believe their assertions. No other name is called *shem ha-meforash* except this Tetragrammaton, which is written, but is not pronounced according to its letters. The words, "Thus shall ye bless the children of Israel" (Num. vi. 23) are interpreted in Siphri as follows: "'*Thus*,' in the holy language; again '*thus*,' with the *Shem ha-meforash*." The following remark is also found there: "In the sanctuary [the name of God is pronounced] as it is spelt, but elsewhere by its substitutes." In the Talmud, the following passage occurs: "'*Thus*,' i.e., with the *shem ha-meforash*. – You say [that the priests, when blessing the people, had to pronounce] the *shem ha-meforash*; this was perhaps not the case, and they may have used other names instead. – We infer it from the words: 'And they shall put My name' (Num. vi. 27), i.e., My name, which is peculiar to Me." It has thus been shown that the *shem ha-meforash* (the proper name of God) is the Tetragrammaton, and that this is the only name which indicates nothing but His essence, and therefore our Sages in referring to this sacred term said "'*My name*' means the one which is peculiar to Me alone."

Thomas Aquinas, *Summa Theologica*, Part I, Questions II and XIII

Introduction

Thomas Aquinas (1225–74) is arguably the most important figure in the history of Christian philosophical theology. For one thing, it is partly due to his intellectual achievement that rational theology did not suffer the eclipse in medieval Christian Europe that it had in the Islamic world. For another, Aquinas's theology – "Thomism" – remains the "official" position of the Roman Catholic Church. Catholics, it has been said, still "expect to find the answer . . . to almost any question in philosophy or theology" in the pages of Aquinas.[1]

Nicknamed "the dumb ox" in virtue of his physical bulk, reticence, and prodigious industry, Aquinas – himself of aristocratic birth – joined the mendicant order of the Dominican Friars, though most of his life was spent teaching and writing at the courts and universities of Germany, France, and Italy. Although he died at a relatively young age – after hitting his head against a tree while traveling to the Council of Lyons in 1274 – it is unlikely that, had he lived longer, he would have added to his immense output. For a year earlier he had renounced writing, declaring that, in the light of divine revelations made to him, "all . . . I have written seems like straw to me."

From A. Hyman and J. J. Walsh, eds, *Philosophy in the Middle Ages*, 2nd edition, Indianapolis, IN: Hackett, 1974, pp. 523–31.

While it is an exaggeration to describe Thomism as "Aristotelianism baptized," Aquinas's acknowledged debt to Aristotle – "The Philosopher," as Aquinas calls him – is considerable. Not only does he endorse various doctrines of Aristotle, such as that of God as "the prime mover," but he also shares with the Greek both an empiricist temperament and a confidence in the power of rational enquiry (see II.2). While, for Aquinas, there are Christian truths, like that of the doctrine of the Trinity, which are properly sustainable only through faith, he is highly critical both of those who would "abolish the human rights of natural reason" (*ST* II-2.10.10) and appeal to revelation and faith alone, and of those who decry the relevance of ordinary experience to establishing religious truths.

In the following sections from Part I of his gigantic work, the *Summa Theologica*, we find Aquinas addressing, in an admirably succinct manner, three central and related issues: the self-evidence or otherwise of God's existence, how God's existence might be proved, and the meaning of the "divine names" (like "wise" and "good") which are applied to God. The issues are related since, if God's existence is not self-evident, then there is a need for rational demonstration of it; and if this lack of self-evidence is due to our ignorance of God's essential nature, then how are we to understand the terms that purport to describe Him?

Although Anselm (IV.5) is not named in the "First Article" of Question II, this Article should be read, in part, as a qualified rejection of Anselm's "ontological argument." A proposition is self-evident if the predicate is "included" in the subject, as in "Man is an animal." And no doubt, Aquinas thinks, God's existence *is* included in the very concept or essence of God, but the problem is that we, with our limited minds, do not know this essence, so that "to us," "God exists" is not a self-evident proposition (see also III.10). In particular, *pace* Anselm, it is not evident to all of us that "God" means "something than which nothing greater can be thought": and even if it was, it is not evident that this would entail God's actual existence.

It follows that, if we are to have rational confidence in God's existence, it must be demonstrated by argument. In an empiricist spirit, Aquinas holds (Second Article) that demonstration can only take the form of inference to God as a cause from empirically accessible "effects" in the world (perhaps the basic premise of what has come to be known as "natural theology"). There then follows (Third Article) Aquinas's famous "Five Ways" – five arguments for God as a cause of allegedly experienecable features of the world (such as motion and change, or the "purposiveness" of "natural bodies"). One might think that, if Aquinas's arguments are valid, he only needs to spell out one of them to establish that God exists. But this would be to ignore his ambition to demonstrate, not simply that there is a God, but the various, distinct ways in which God acts as a cause of aspects of the world – as a "prime mover," as a designer, as an ideal or "maximum" of perfection to which ordinary goods approximate, and so on.

Since we are ignorant of God's essence, the issue arises (Question XIII) of the status of the terms, like "good" and "wise" that we conventionally apply to God. While Aquinas insists that these terms really do apply to Him – and are not, therefore, being used in a merely figurative way or simply to exclude other terms (like "evil" or "stupid") – he argues that, as applied to God, they do not have the same "univocal" sense they bear when applied to human beings. But nor, he also argues, are they used "equivocally," with quite separate meanings in the two cases. Rather – as with the use of "healthy" to describe such diverse things as bodies, medicines, urine – the terms are employed "analogously," according to a "proportion" that exists between beings as diverse as God and human beings.

All three of the positions advanced by Aquinas in the selected texts have profoundly shaped theological discussion and continue to arouse lively debate.

Note

1 D. Knowles, "The Historical Context of the Philosophical Work of St Thomas Aquinas," in A. Kenny, ed., *Aquinas: A Collection of Critical Essays*, London: Macmillan, 1969, p. 13.

Aquinas, *Summa Theologica*

Part I

Question II.   The Existence of God

FIRST ARTICLE.   *Whether the Existence of God Is Self-Evident?*

We proceed thus to the First Article: –

Objection 1. It seems that the existence of God is self-evident. For those things are said to be self-evident to us the knowledge of which exists naturally in us, as we can see in regard to first principles. But as Damascene says, *the knowledge of God is naturally implanted in all*. Therefore the existence of God is self-evident.

Obj. 2. Further, those things are said to be self-evident which are known as soon as the terms are known, which the Philosopher says is true of the first principles of demonstration. Thus, when the nature of a whole and of a part is known, it is at once recognized that every whole is greater than its part, But as soon as the signification of the name *God* is understood, it is at once seen that God exists. For by this name is signified that thing than which nothing greater can be conceived. But that which exists actually and mentally is greater than that which exists only mentally. Therefore, since as soon as the name *God* is understood it exists mentally, it also follows that it exists actually. Therefore the proposition *God exists* is self-evident.

Obj. 3. Further, the existence of truth is self-evident. For whoever denies the existence of truth grants that truth does not exist: and, if truth does not exist, then the proposition *Truth does not exist* is true: and if there is anything true, there must be truth. But God is truth itself: *I am the way, the truth, and the life* (*Jo.* xiv. 6). Therefore *God exists* is self-evident.

On the contrary, No one can mentally admit the opposite of what is self-evident, as the Philosopher states concerning the first principles of demonstration. But the opposite of the proposition *God is* can be mentally admitted: *The fool said in his heart, There is no God* (*Ps.* lii. 1). Therefore, that God exists is not self-evident.

I answer that, A thing can be self-evident in either of two ways: on the one hand, self-evident in itself, though not to us; on the other, self-evident in itself, and to us. A proposition is self-evident because the predicate is included in the essence of the subject: *e.g., Man is an animal*, for animal is contained in the essence of man. If, therefore, the essence of the predicate and subject be known to all, the proposition will be self-evident to all; as is clear with regard to the first principles of demonstration, the terms of which are certain common notions that no one is ignorant of, such as being and non-being, whole and part, and the like. If, however, there are some to whom the essence of the predicate and subject is unknown, the proposition will be self-evident in itself, but not to those who do not know the meaning of the predicate and subject of the proposition. Therefore, it happens, as Boethius says, that there are some notions of the mind which are common and self-evident only to the learned, as that incorporeal substances are not in space. Therefore I say that this proposition, *God exists*, of itself is self-evident, for the predicate is the same as the subject, because God is His own existence as will be hereafter shown. Now because we do not know the essence of God, the proposition is not self-evident to us, but needs to be demonstrated by things that are more known to us, though less known in their nature – namely, by His effects.

Reply Obj. 1. To know that God exists in a general and confused way is implanted in us by nature, inasmuch as God is man's beatitude. For man naturally desires happiness, and what is naturally desired by man is naturally known by him. This, however, is not to know absolutely that God exists; just as to know that someone is approaching is not the same as to know that Peter is approaching, even though it is Peter who is approaching; for there are many who imagine that man's perfect good, which is happiness, consists in riches, and others in pleasures, and others in something else.

Reply Obj. 2. Perhaps not everyone who hears this name *God* understands it to signify something than which nothing greater can be thought, seeing that some have believed God to be a body. Yet, granted that everyone understands that by this name *God* is signified something than which nothing greater can be thought, nevertheless, it does not therefore follow that he understands that what the name signifies exists actually, but only that it exists mentally. Nor can it be argued that it actually exists, unless it be admitted that there actually exists something than which nothing greater can be thought; and this precisely is not admitted by those who hold that God does not exist.

Reply Obj. 3. The existence of truth in general is self-evident, but the existence of a Primal Truth is not self-evident to us.

SECOND ARTICLE.   *Whether It Can Be Demonstrated that God Exists?*

We proceed thus to the Second Article: –

Objection 1. It seems that the existence of God cannot be demonstrated. For it is an article of faith that God exists. But what is of faith cannot be demonstrated, because a demonstration produces scientific knowledge, whereas faith is of the unseen, as is clear from the Apostle (*Heb.* xi. 1). Therefore it cannot be demonstrated that God exists.

Obj. 2. Further, essence is the middle term of demonstration. But we cannot know in what God's essence consists, but solely in what it does not consist, as Damascene says. Therefore we cannot demonstrate that God exists.

Obj. 3. Further, if the existence of God were demonstrated, this could only be from His effects. But His effects are not proportioned to Him, since He is infinite and His effects are finite, and between the finite and infinite there is no proportion. Therefore, since a cause cannot be demonstrated by an effect not proportioned to it, it seems that the existence of God cannot be demonstrated.

On the contrary, The Apostle says: *The invisible things of Him are clearly seen, being understood by the things that are made* (*Rom.* i. 20). But this would not be unless the existence of God could be demonstrated through the things that are made; for the first thing we must know of anything is, whether it exists.

I answer that, Demonstration can be made in two ways: One is through the cause, and is called *propter quid*, and this is to argue from what is prior absolutely. The other is through the effect, and is called a demonstration *quia*; this is to argue from what is prior relatively only to us. When an effect is better known to us than its cause, from the effect we proceed to the knowledge of the cause. And from every effect the existence of its proper cause can be demonstrated, so long as its effects are better known to us; because, since every effect depends upon its cause, if the effect exists, the cause must pre-exist. Hence the existence of God, in so far as it is not self-evident to us, can be demonstrated from those of His effects which are known to us.

Reply Obj. 1. The existence of God and other like truths about God, which can be known by natural reason, are not articles of faith, but are preambles to the articles; for faith presupposes natural knowledge, even as grace presupposes nature and perfection the perfectible. Nevertheless, there is nothing to prevent a man, who cannot grasp a proof, from accepting, as a matter of faith, something which in itself is capable of being scientifically known and demonstrated.

Reply Obj. 2. When the existence of a cause is demonstrated from an effect, this effect takes the place of the definition of the cause in proving the cause's existence. This is especially the case in regard to God, because, in order to prove the existence of anything, it is necessary to accept as a middle term the meaning of the name, and not its essence, for the question of its essence follows on the question of its existence. Now the names given to God are derived from His effects, as will be later shown. Consequently, in demonstrating the existence of God from His effects, we may take for the middle term the meaning of the name *God*.

Reply Obj. 3. From effects not proportioned to the cause no perfect knowledge of that cause can be obtained. Yet from every effect the existence of the cause can be clearly demonstrated, and so

we can demonstrate the existence of God from His effects; though from them we cannot know God perfectly as He is in His essence.

THIRD ARTICLE.   *Whether God Exists?*

We proceed thus to the Third Article: –

Objection 1. It seems that God does not exist; because if one of two contraries be infinite, the other would be altogether destroyed. But the name *God* means that He is infinite goodness. If, therefore, God existed, there would be no evil discoverable; but there is evil in the world. Therefore God does not exist.

Obj. 2. Further, it is superfluous to suppose that what can be accounted for by a few principles has been produced by many. But it seems that everything we see in the world can be accounted for by other principles, supposing God did not exist. For all natural things can be reduced to one principle, which is nature; and all voluntary things can be reduced to one principle, which is human reason, or will. Therefore there is no need to suppose God's existence.

On the contrary, It is said in the person of God: *I am Who am* (*Exod.* iii. 14).

I answer that, The existence of God can be proved in five ways.

The first and more manifest way is the argument from motion. It is certain, and evident to our senses, that in the world some things are in motion. Now whatever is moved is moved by another, for nothing can be moved except it is in potentiality to that towards which it is moved; whereas a thing moves inasmuch as it is in act. For motion is nothing else than the reduction of something from potentiality to actuality. But nothing can be reduced from potentiality to actuality, except by something in a state of actuality. Thus that which is actually hot, as fire, makes wood, which is potentially hot, to be actually hot, and thereby moves and changes it. Now it is not possible that the same thing should be at once in actuality and potentiality in the same respect, but only in different respects. For what is actually hot cannot simultaneously be potentially hot; but it is simultaneously potentially cold. It is therefore impossible that in the same respect and in the same way a thing should be both mover and moved, *i.e.*, that it should move itself. Therefore, whatever is moved must be moved by another. If that by which it is moved be itself moved, then this also must needs be moved by another, and that by another again. But this cannot go on to infinity, because then there would be no first mover, and, consequently, no other mover, seeing that subsequent movers move only inasmuch as they are moved by the first mover; as the staff moves only because it is moved by the hand. Therefore it is necessary to arrive at a first mover, moved by no other; and this everyone understands to be God.

The second way is from the nature of efficient cause. In the world of sensible things we find there is an order of efficient causes. There is no case known (neither is it, indeed, possible) in which a thing is found to be the efficient cause of itself; for so it would be prior to itself, which is impossible. Now in efficient causes it is not possible to go on to infinity, because in all efficient causes following in order, the first is the cause of the intermediate cause, and the intermediate is the cause of the ultimate cause, whether the intermediate cause be several, or one only. Now to take away the cause is to take away the effect. Therefore, if there be no first cause among efficient causes, there will be no ultimate, nor any intermediate, cause. But if in efficient causes it is possible to go on to infinity, there will be no first efficient cause, neither will there be an ultimate effect, nor any intermediate efficient causes; all of which is plainly false. Therefore it is necessary to admit a first efficient cause, to which everyone gives the name of God.

The third way is taken from possibility and necessity, and runs thus. We find in nature things that are possible to be and not to be, since they are found to be generated, and to be corrupted, and consequently, it is possible for them to be and not to be. But it is impossible for these always to exist, for that which can not-be at some time is not. Therefore, if everything can not-be, then at one time there was nothing in existence. Now if this were true, even now there would be nothing in existence, because that which does not exist begins to exist only through something already existing. Therefore, if at one time nothing was in existence, it would have been impossible for anything to have begun to exist; and thus even now nothing would be in existence – which is absurd. Therefore, not all beings are merely possible, but there must exist something the existence of which is necessary. But every necessary thing either has its necessity caused by another, or not.

Now it is impossible to go on to infinity in necessary things which have their necessity caused by another, as has been already proved in regard to efficient causes. Therefore we cannot but admit the existence of some being having of itself its own necessity, and not receiving it from another, but rather causing in others their necessity. This all men speak of as God.

The fourth way is taken from the gradation to be found in things. Among beings there are some more and some less good, true, noble, and the like. But *more* and *less* are predicated of different things according as they resemble in their different ways something which is the maximum, as a thing is said to be hotter according as it more nearly resembles that which is hottest; so that there is something which is truest, something best, something noblest, and, consequently, something which is most being, for those things that are greatest in truth are greatest in being, as it is written in *Metaph.* ii. Now the maximum in any genus is the cause of all in that genus, as fire, which is the maximum of heat, is the cause of all hot things, as is said in the same book. Therefore there must also be something which is to all beings the cause of their being, goodness, and every other perfection; and this we call God.

The fifth way is taken from the governance of the world. We see that things which lack knowledge, such as natural bodies, act for an end, and this is evident from their acting always, or nearly always, in the same way, so as to obtain the best result. Hence it is plain that they achieve their end, not fortuitously, but designedly. Now whatever lacks knowledge cannot move towards an end, unless it be directed by some being endowed with knowledge and intelligence; as the arrow is directed by the archer. Therefore some intelligent being exists by whom all natural things are directed to their end; and this being we call God.

Reply Obj. 1. As Augustine says: *Since God is the highest good, He would not allow any evil to exist in His works, unless His omnipotence and goodness were such as to bring good even out of evil.* This is part of the infinite goodness of God, that He should allow evil to exist, and out of it produce good.

Reply Obj. 2. Since nature works for a determinate end under the direction of a higher agent, whatever is done by nature must be traced back to God as to its first cause. So likewise whatever is done voluntarily must be traced back to some higher cause other than human reason and will, since these can change and fail; for all things that are changeable and capable of defect must be traced back to an immovable and self-necessary first principle, as has been shown.

Question XIII. The Names of God

SECOND ARTICLE. *Whether Any Name Can Be Applied to God Substantially?*

We proceed thus to the Second Article: –

Objection 1. It seems that no name can be applied to God substantially. For Damascene says: *Everything said of God must not signify His substance, but rather show forth what He is not; or express some relation, or something following from His nature or operation.*

Obj. 2. Further, Dionysius says: *You will find a chorus of holy doctors addressed to the end of distinguishing clearly and praiseworthily the divine processions in the denominations of God.* This means that the names applied by the holy doctors in praising God are distinguished according to the divine processions themselves. But what expresses the procession of anything does not signify anything pertaining to its essence. Therefore the names said of God are not said of Him substantially.

Obj. 3. Further, a thing is named by us according as we understand it. But in this life God is not understood by us in His substance. Therefore neither is any name we can use applied substantially to God.

On the contrary, Augustine says: *For God to be is to be strong or wise, or whatever else we may say of that simplicity whereby His substance is signified.* Therefore all names of this kind signify the divine substance.

I answer that, Names which are said of God negatively or which signify His relation to creatures manifestly do not at all signify His substance, but rather express the distance of the creature from Him, or His relation to something else, or rather, the relation of creatures to Himself.

But as regards names of God said absolutely and affirmatively, as *good, wise,* and the like, various and many opinions have been held. For some have said that all such names, although they are applied to God affirmatively, nevertheless have been brought into use more to remove something

from God than to posit something in Him. Hence they assert that when we say that God lives, we mean that God is not like an inanimate thing; and the same in like manner applies to other names. This was taught by Rabbi Moses. Others say that these names applied to God signify His relationship towards creatures: thus in the words, *God is good,* we mean, God is the cause of goodness in things; and the same interpretation applies to other names.

Both of these opinions, however, seem to be untrue for three reasons. First, because in neither of them could a reason be assigned why some names more than others should be applied to God. For He is assuredly the cause of bodies in the same way as He is the cause of good things; therefore if the words *God is good* signified no more than, *God is the cause of good things,* it might in like manner be said that God is a body, inasmuch as He is the cause of bodies. So also to say that He is a body implies that He is not a mere potentiality, as is primary matter. Secondly, because it would follow that all names applied to God would be said of Him by way of being taken in a secondary sense, as *healthy* is secondarily said of medicine, because it signifies only the cause of health in the animal which primarily is called healthy. Thirdly, because this is against the intention of those who speak of God. For in saying that God lives, they assuredly mean more than to say that He is the cause of our life, or that He differs from inanimate bodies.

Therefore we must hold a different doctrine – viz., that these names signify the divine substance, and are predicated substantially of God, although they fall short of representing Him. Which is proved thus. For these names express God, so far as our intellects know Him. Now since our intellect knows God from creatures, it knows Him as far as creatures represent Him. But it was shown above that God prepossesses in Himself all the perfections of creatures, being Himself absolutely and universally perfect. Hence every creature represents Him, and is like Him, so far as it possesses some perfection: yet not so far as to represent Him as something of the same species or genus, but as the excelling source of whose form the effects fall short, although they derive some kind of likeness thereto, even as the forms of inferior bodies represent the power of the sun. This was explained above in treating of the divine perfection. Therefore, the aforesaid names signify the divine substance, but in an imperfect manner, even as creatures represent it imperfectly. So when we say, *God is good*, the meaning is not, *God is the cause of goodness*, or, *God is not evil*; but the meaning is, *Whatever good we attribute to creatures pre-exists in God*, and in a higher way. Hence it does not follow that God is good because He causes goodness; but rather, on the contrary, He causes goodness in things because He is good. As Augustine says, *Because He is good, we are.*

Reply Obj. 1. Damascene says that these names do not signify what God is because by none of these names is what He is perfectly expressed; but each one signifies Him in an imperfect manner, even as creatures represent Him imperfectly.

Reply Obj. 2. In the signification of names, that from which the name is derived is different sometimes from what it is intended to signify, as for instance this name *stone* [*lapis*] is imposed from the fact that it hurts the *foot* [*lædit pedem*]; yet it is not imposed to signify that which hurts the foot, but rather to signify a certain kind of body; otherwise everything that hurts the foot would be a stone. So we must say that such divine names are imposed from the divine processions; for as according to the diverse processions of their perfections, creatures are the representations of God, although in an imperfect manner, so likewise our intellect knows and names God according to each kind of procession. But nevertheless these names are not imposed to signify the processions themselves, as if when we say *God lives*, the sense were, *life proceeds from Him*, but to signify the principle itself of things, in so far as life pre-exists in Him, although it pre-exists in Him in a more eminent way than is understood or signified.

Reply Obj. 3. In this life, we cannot know the essence of God as it is in itself, but we know it according as it is represented in the perfections of creatures; and it is thus that the names imposed by us signify it.

FIFTH ARTICLE. *Whether What Is Said of God and of Creatures Is Univocally Predicated of Them?*

We proceed thus to the Fifth Article: –

Objection 1. It seems that the things attributed to God and creatures are univocal. For every equivocal term is reduced to the univocal, as many are reduced to one: for if the name *dog* be said equivocally of the barking dog and of the dogfish, it must be said of some univocally – viz., of all barking dogs; otherwise we proceed to infinitude. Now there are some univocal agents which agree with their effects in name and definition, as man generates man; and there are some agents which are equivocal, as the sun which causes heat, although the sun is hot only in an equivocal sense. Therefore it seems that the first agent, to which all other agents are reduced, is a univocal agent: and thus what is said of God and creatures is predicated univocally.

Obj. 2. Further, no likeness is understood through equivocal names. Therefore, as creatures have a certain likeness to God, according to the text of *Genesis* (i. 26), *Let us make man to our image and likeness*, it seems that something can be said of God and creatures univocally.

Obj. 3. Further, measure is homogeneous with the thing measured, as is said in *Metaph.* x. But God is the first measure of all beings. Therefore God is homogeneous with creatures; and thus a name may be applied univocally to God and to creatures.

On the contrary, Whatever is predicated of various things under the same name but not in the same sense is predicated equivocally. But no name belongs to God in the same sense that it belongs to creatures; for instance, wisdom in creatures is a quality, but not in God. Now a change in genus changes an essence, since the genus is part of the definition; and the same applies to other things. Therefore whatever is said of God and of creatures is predicated equivocally.

Further, God is more distant from creatures than any creatures are from each other. But the distance of some creatures makes any univocal predication of them impossible, as in the case of those things which are not in the same genus. Therefore much less can anything be predicated univocally of God and creatures; and so only equivocal predication can be applied to them.

I answer that, Univocal predication is impossible between God and creatures. The reason of this is that every effect which is not a proportioned result of the power of the efficient cause receives the similitude of the agent not in its full degree, but in a measure that falls short; so that what is divided and multiplied in the effects resides in the agent simply, and in an unvaried manner. For example, the sun by the exercise of its one power produces manifold and various forms in these sublunary things. In the same way, as was said above, all perfections existing in creatures divided and multiplied pre-exist in God unitedly. Hence, when any name expressing perfection is applied to a creature, it signifies that perfection as distinct from the others according to the nature of its definition; as, for instance, by this term *wise* applied to a man, we signify some perfection distinct from a man's essence, and distinct from his power and his being, and from all similar things. But when we apply *wise* to God, we do not mean to signify anything distinct from His essence or power or being. And thus when this term *wise* is applied to man, in some degree it circumscribes and comprehends the thing signified; whereas this is not the case when it is applied to God, but it leaves the thing signified as uncomprehended and as exceeding the signification of the name. Hence it is evident that this term *wise* is not applied in the same way to God and to man. The same applies to other terms. Hence, no name is predicated univocally of God and of creatures.

Neither, on the other hand, are names applied to God and creatures in a purely equivocal sense, as some have said. Because if that were so, it follows that from creatures nothing at all could be known or demonstrated about God; for the reasoning would always be exposed to the fallacy of equivocation. Such a view is against the Philosopher, who proves many things about God, and also against what the Apostle says: *The invisible things of God are clearly seen being understood by the things that are made (Rom.* i. 20). Therefore it must be said that these names are said of God and creatures in an *analogous* sense, that is, according to proportion.

This can happen in two ways: either according as many things are proportioned to one (thus, for example *healthy* is predicated of medicine and urine in relation and in proportion to health of body, of which the latter is the sign and the former the cause), or according as one thing is proportioned to another (thus, *healthy* is said of medicine and an animal, since medicine is the cause of health in the animal body). And in this way some things are said of God and creatures

analogically, and not in a purely equivocal nor in a purely univocal sense. For we can name God only from creatures. Hence, whatever is said of God and creatures is said according as there is some relation of the creature to God as to its principle and cause, wherein all the perfections of things pre-exist excellently. Now this mode of community is a mean between pure equivocation and simple univocation. For in analogies the idea is not, as it is in univocals, one and the same; yet it is not totally diverse as in equivocals; but the name which is thus used in a multiple sense signifies various proportions to some one thing: *e.g., healthy,* applied to urine, signifies the sign of animal health; but applied to medicine, it signifies the cause of the same health.

Reply Obj. 1. Although in predications all equivocals must be reduced to univocals, still in actions the non-univocal agent must precede the univocal agent. For the non-univocal agent is the universal cause of the whole species, as the sun is the cause of the generation of all men. But the univocal agent is not the universal efficient cause of the whole species (otherwise it would be the cause of itself, since it is contained in the species), but is a particular cause of this individual which it places under the species by way of participation. Therefore the universal cause of the whole species is not a univocal agent: and the universal cause comes before the particular cause. But this universal agent, while not univocal, nevertheless is not altogether equivocal (otherwise it could not produce its own likeness); but it can be called an analogical agent, just as in predications all univocal names are reduced to one first non-univocal analogical name, which is *being.*

Reply Obj. 2. The likeness of the creature to God is imperfect, for it does not represent the same thing even generically.

Reply Obj. 3. God is not a measure proportioned to the things measured; hence it is not necessary that God and creatures should be in the same genus.

The arguments adduced in the contrary sense prove indeed that these names are not predicated univocally of God and creatures; yet they do not prove that they are predicated equivocally.

10

Duns Scotus, *Ordinatio* I and IV (selections)[1]

Introduction

The "Subtle Doctor," John Duns Scotus (1266–1308), is well known not only for the metaphysical doctrines concerning "transcendentals" and "thisness" we described in Part III of this collection (III.11) but also for advancing a kind of social contract political theory and a "voluntarist" view of God and morality. By the term "voluntarism" philosophers designate a sort of philosophical position that grants primacy or centrality to the "will," usually in relation to the "intellect." The question of voluntarism in a sense finds its root in the question the character of Socrates poses in Plato's dialogue, *Euthyphro* (IV.1): "Is the pious loved by the gods because it is pious, or is it pious because it is loved by the gods?" (10a). Translated into an Abrahamic context, this question might be recast to read: "Are certain things and not others good simply because God wills them to be so; or does God will and command certain things and not others because they are already (in some prior sense) good independently of God's will?" Another way of thinking about the question might be, following Scotus's medieval predecessor Peter Abelard (1079–1142): could God have created the moral universe differently? Could

From Duns Scotus, *Duns Scotus on the Will and Morality*, trans. A. B. Wolter, ed. W. A. Frank, Washington, DC: The Catholic University of America Press, 1997, pp. 183–94.

God, for example, have made the killing of innocent children good? The answer for Scotus is, unsurprisingly, complex – even subtle.

Abelard, in answering this question, developed a kind of "necessitarian" position, not terribly different from the position developed by Leibniz centuries later (III.15; IV.13). Abelard argued that since God is a good, rational, and perfect being, God could not act in any arbitrary way. That is, God cannot act in a way that is not as good and rational as possible. It would be contradictory for a perfectly rational being to act in a way that was not perfectly rational or perfectly and precisely determined by reason; it would be contradictory for a perfectly good being to act in a way that was not perfectly good.[2] Just prior to Scotus's time, leading Christian philosophers like the mystic Hugh of St Victor (1078–1141) and the Cistercian scholar Bernard of Clairveaux (1090–1153) attacked the necessitarian position. Bernard went so far as to challenge Abelard to a public debate on this and other matters at the Council of Sens 1141, after which Abelard was condemned and ordered to retire to Cluny, where he soon afterwards died. The necessitarian doctrine was also condemned by Stephen Tempier, the Bishop of Paris, in 1270 as a theological error inconsistent with Christian truth.

Those who condemned the necessitarian doctrine were concerned that it undermined the contingency of the world and inappropriately constrained God. God, in the orthodox view, is the only necessary being – the only being that need not be caused by something beyond itself, the only being that cannot not be. The created universe, according to this view, is somehow by contrast in its very being "contingent" or not necessary – something that might not exist, that does require an extrinsic cause.[3] Furthermore, as Scotus and others would observe, if among God's creation are beings with free wills – human beings – then the Creator must similarly possess a free will. Freedom, after all, is a kind of perfection, or at least a capacity that renders its possessor superior to non-free beings. So, it would be absurd for created humans to possess a sort of superior capacity absent from God. But defenders of God's freedom had to be careful themselves not to characterize God's acts as somehow arbitrary – as nothing more than whims, without rhyme or reason. Irrational or arbitrary acts, as Abelard understood, would hardly properly describe God either. There is an epistemological implication to all this, as well. If God's acts are arbitrary or in any way less than rational, then they must remain inscrutable to reason, which can only understand conduct by way of postulating reasons for it. Philosophers, then, seem to face a conundrum: if God is to be understood as free, then God becomes inscrutable, irrational, and less than perfect; but if God acts only in a rational and good way, it seems that while God remains apprehensible by reason, God nevertheless cannot be free.

Scotus resolved this conundrum, as philosophers often do, by making a distinction – the distinction between God's "absolute" and "ordained" power (*potentia Dei absoluta et ordinata*). In an "absolute" sense, God is free to do anything that is not logically contradictory, including anything that will not contradict God's nature. So, for example, because God is a necessary being, God cannot by an act of will cease to exist. With regard to the created universe, God faces different possibilities that God may choose or not choose without contradiction. Contrary to what Leibniz would hold, there is not for Scotus one

single possible world that is best and therefore that God must choose. In particular, for example, according to Scotus, God might have without contradiction not created the universe at all; "That things could have been made otherwise is not self-contradictory, neither is the world necessary."

Whatever particular possibilities, however, God does choose to realize, God's actual acts of will must of necessity be "orderly"; for God cannot act in a disordered way. So, while according to Scotus God is both supreme intellect and supreme will, God is also for Scotus an "orderly" will – an "*intelligentissime et ordinatissime volens.*" Or as Allan Wolter has rendered the phrase, God in Scotus's view is a "rational and methodical lover." While perhaps a bit dramatic, Wolter's is an appropriate translation of Scotus's phrase because it emphasizes the way in which the centrality of will in Scotus's thought results in a distinctive characterization of the beatific condition of the afterlife for the blessed. While for Aquinas (IV.9) the content of the heavenly reward is an intellectual apprehension of God, for Scotus the beatific condition is described as a state of perfect love, and in whatever contingent way the created world is ordered the good will must necessarily be ordered to the love of God.

Notes

1 From the Oxford 1300–02 edition of Scotus's *Commentary on the Sentences of Peter Lombard.*
2 P. Abelard, *Theologia Christiana* V. See A. Wolter's introduction to *Duns Scotus on the Will and Morality* (1997), p. 56.
3 Indeed, unless the divine will acts in a contingent way in creating the universe, can the universe itself be contingent? Cf. M. B. Ingham and M. Dreyer, *The Philosophical Vision of John Duns Scotus*, Washington, DC: The Catholic University of America Press, 2004, p. 93ff.

Duns Scotus, *Ordinatio*

Ordinatio IV, dist. 46

Because the forty-sixth distinction [of Bk. IV] treats of how both justice and the mercy of God con-

cur in the punishment of the evildoers, therefore four questions are raised here: first, whether there is justice in God; second, whether there is mercy in God; third, whether in God justice is distinct from mercy; and fourth, whether in his punishment of evildoers justice and mercy concur on God's part.

[Arguments Pro and Con] To the first question it is argued that there is no justice in God:

[Arg. 1] According to Bk. V of the *Ethics*, ch. 6, there is no justice where lord and servant are concerned, because of a lack of equality. All the more so is this true of the God-creature relationship or the creature-God relationship, since what Paul says in 1 Corinthians 4:[7]: "Name something you have not received," could be uttered even more forcefully by God.

[Arg. 2] Furthermore, Bk. X of the *Ethics* [ch. 8] says it is tasteless and injudicious to praise the separate substances [or gods] for acts of virtue, particularly justice. And [Aristotle] confirms this using an analogous argument about why it is meaningless to speak of their temperance and, by the same token, to speak of their justice.

[Arg. 3] Furthermore, justice inclines a person to render others what is their due; but God is a debtor to no one.

To the contrary is that passage from Psalm [48:11]: "Of justice your right hand is full."

[Body of the Question] [Definition of justice] To begin here with a definition of justice: Anselm in his De *veritate* gives the most general notion: "Justice is rectitude of will *served for its own sake*." The Philosopher in V *Ethics* makes this specific with the addition: "it has to do with another."

It is clear that God has justice in both senses: the first, because he has rectitude of will – indeed, a will that cannot be gainsaid, because it is the first rule or norm, and is "served for its own sake." Not that "served" here implies any submission or acceptance on the part of the one ob*serving* it, but rather it is "served for its own sake" in the sense that it is always spontaneously pre*served*. It is clear he also has justice in the second sense, because he is upright to others, and therefore, in all his actions towards others there is rectitude.

[Justice towards another] This second sort of justice is subdivided, because either [a] it is quasi-universal with respect to others, for instance, to the legislator and to the law, insofar as the law is a certain general regulation determined by the legislator, and some call this "legal justice"; or [b] it is particular, for instance, uprightness to another in some specific aspect pertaining to law.

And this second is subdivided, because it can be toward another in an unqualified sense, or to one-self as quasi-other. (This second member of the division is illustrated from what was said about penance, namely, that this sort of punitive justice regards not only others in an unqualified sense, but also oneself as quasi-other, because it is granted to individual persons, as ministers of the judge [God], to punish themselves as guilty.)

Now, the first of these, namely, legal justice, could be postulated of God if there were some other law antecedent to any decision of his will, with which "law and its legislator" as other his own will could rightly agree. Now, there is indeed this law, "God should be loved" – if one ought to call it a "law" rather than a practical principle of law; and in any case it is a practical truth that is prior to any decision on the part of the divine will. As for particular justice, however, it would be the second sort that is in him, namely, that which has to do with oneself as quasi-other, since his will is determined by its very rectitude to will what is becoming to his goodness. And this is a quasi-rendering to himself and his goodness what is due to it as other – if one could call such justice "particular," because it is in some way universal, at least virtually.

And these two kinds of justice, namely, legal justice and particular justice to oneself as quasi-other, are the same thing, as it were, in God, because they are identical with the rectitude of the divine will with respect to his goodness.

[Commutative and distributive justice] If one speaks about the other type of particular justice, which has to do simply with neighbor, this is divided into commutative and distributive; and in this way we distinguish justice in ourselves, as is clear from V *Ethics*. In distributive justice equality of proportion is required; in commutative justice, some require quantitative equality, not only proportional equity. These are explained in that book.

As to whether these are in God, commutative justice properly speaking has to do with punishment and reward, namely, in exchange for merits, as it were, rewards are rendered, and for sins punishments. Distributive justice has to do with natures and their additional perfections, which are bestowed on them, as it were, in proportion to their essential perfection. Just as distributive justice in our republic bestows on persons of various gradated stations in life the goods that pertain to their station, so too in the hierarchy of nature as a whole our princely God distributes to the more noble natures those greater perfections suited to them, whereas the less noble natures receive lesser perfections.

Now, the first of these [i.e., commutative justice] cannot be in God in an unqualified sense where creatures are concerned, since there is no simple equality there, but there can be something akin to it such as obtains between a master and a servant. For a generous or liberal master may fittingly give a greater reward than the servant could merit, and still there could be some proportionality as to what is given in exchange, so that if the servant does what he should, he is rewarded accordingly. In the same way, such a master may punish delinquent servants to a lesser degree than they merit.

But the second [viz., distributive justice] could be present in God in an unqualified sense, because he could give natures the perfections that are their due or are suited to their degree of excellence.

Thus the whole definition of justice, then, insofar as it is applicable to God, could be reduced to two sorts, the first of which would be called rectitude of will with respect to what is due to divine goodness; the other, rectitude of will with respect to what the exigencies of the creature demand. And we find this distinction in Anlsem's *Proslogion*, ch. 10, where he says of God: "When you punish the wicked, it is just, because punishment corresponds to their merits" – so far as the second member goes. He adds immediately: "When you spare the wicked, however, it is just, not because it corresponds to their merits, but because it befits your goodness." This last clause refers to the first member of the division [i.e., what is due to the divine goodness]. And such is the distinction between these two kinds of justice that God cannot operate against or beyond the first justice [viz., what is due to his goodness], but he can go beyond what the second requires, but not in all matters, for he cannot damn the just or the blessed.

[Objections to this view] One may object that in God the first sort of justice cannot be other than the second sort, because then there would be one that is the rule, namely, the first sort of justice, and another that is regulated, namely, the second sort of justice; but in the divine will there cannot be rectitude that is the result of regulation, and this is proved as follows. In us the same virtue inclines us to our proper end and to those things

which are means to that end precisely qua means; therefore, if that virtue which inclines us to our end were simply perfect, it would incline us to the means to that end in a simple unqualified manner, as is clear from the way the virtue of charity functions in the case of the blessed in heaven. Now, the first sort of divine justice is simply perfect; therefore, in the divine will nothing more is required.

However, what is said about the inability of the divine will at times to act against the second sort of justice does not seem probable, for whatever does not include a contradiction, the divine will could do, and therefore could will. But it could not will something that it could not will rightly, because God's will is the first rule or regulation; therefore, whatever does not include a contradiction, God can will and do so rightly, and therefore, he could act contrary to this second justice.

Perhaps some would concede the first of these points, namely, that in God there is not a double justice, but only one, which has, however, two different effects, as it were, namely, insofar as God could will some things as due to his goodness and will other things in accord with the exigencies of the creature.

However, it seems clear that the second argument implies that to whatever the first justice inclines the divine will the second justice does likewise, since it inclines that will definitely after the manner of nature [and hence not freely]; thus it leaves no room for the possibility of the will acting against or beyond what the second justice requires, and so there will be no distinction between those matters where the will could act beyond justice and those where it could not.

[Scotus's own view] Not by way of disparaging these distinctions, I reply with greater brevity to the question that in God there is but one justice, both conceptually and in reality, although by stretching the meaning of "justice" one could say that in addition to the aforesaid justice there is some justice, or rather something just, about the way he deals with creatures.

To explain the first: justice properly speaking represents a habitual state of rectitude of will, and hence as a habit it inclines one in a quasi-natural manner to another or to oneself as quasi-other. Now, the divine will does not have any rectitude that would incline it deterministically to anything other than its own goodness as a quasi-other (recall that the divine will is related to any other object only contingently, so that as will it has the capacity to will either this or its opposite). From this it follows that there is no justice in God except that which inclines him to render to his own goodness what is its due.

Thus there is also but one act, conceptually and in reality, to which this habit of justice inclines this will. Nevertheless this will-act, in terms of what follows from it, has to do with many secondary objects in the same way as we explained (in Bk. I, dist. 35) that the divine intellect, in addition to its one primary object and act, regards a multiplicity of secondary objects. There is a difference, however, between the intellect there and the will here, because the divine intellect of necessity regards these secondary objects, whereas here the will regards its secondary objects only in a contingent manner. And hence not only is it the case that both there and here neither act depends upon its respective secondary objects, but here the will is not necessarily related to its secondary objects in the way the intellect necessarily knows its secondary objects.

But if we wish to distinguish this one real will-act into many conceptually distinct acts, just as there we distinguish one real intellection into many conceptually distinct acts of knowledge insofar as it has to do with a multiplicity of secondary objects, I say that where the will-act is concerned one cannot even speak of conceptually quasi-distinct "justices." In fact we cannot even speak of one justice as regards these multiple secondary objects, howsoever that justice might be distinct or indistinct. The reason is that a habit inclines after the manner of nature and thus limits the respective faculty to but one mode of action, so that it would be repugnant for a potency having such a habit to tend towards the opposite. But there is nothing in the divine will that inclines it specifically to any secondary object in such a way that it would be impossible for it justly to incline towards its opposite. For without contradiction the will could will the opposite, and thus it could justly will such; otherwise it could will something absolutely [i.e., by its absolute power] and not do so justly, which seems incongruous.

And this is what Anselm says in ch. 11 of his *Proslogion*: "Only what you will is just, and only what you do not will is not just." As such, if one postulates in the divine intellect some intellective habit with respect to oneself and to others, one could make a stronger case for a conceptual distinction than in the case at hand, because there the intellect is deterministically inclined to each of the secondary objects, but that is not the case here with the will. Nevertheless, one could say that this single justice, which determinately inclines the divine will to its first act, modifies each of these secondary acts, although not in a necessary manner, as though it could not also modify the opposite of each. Neither does this justice precede the will, as it were, inclining it after the manner of nature to some secondary act; but the will first determines itself in regard to each secondary object. And by this very fact this act is modified by that first justice, because that act is in harmony with the will to which it is conformed as if the rectitude inclining it this way were the first justice itself.

In this second way God is said to do what is right in a creature from the way he makes one created thing correspond to another (just as we say it is just on the part of the creature that fire be hot and water cold, that fire rise and water descend, and so on), because this created nature demands this as something suited to it – just as we could say in politics that while justice exists as such only in the ruler himself, we could still speak of him as being somehow just in the things he ordains, namely, to the extent that he arranges things in such and such a way, since this is something demanded by the things themselves insofar as they are destined by nature for the use of the citizens.

However, the primary justice intrinsic to God does not determine him to be just in this second way in the same manner that it determines him in regard to his first act, because this primary act [of justice towards himself] does not look to any [created] object or secondary act, because insofar as it looks to such his justice does not incline his will in any necessary manner, as was said.

[Objections] against this:

[1] To begin with, justice can only exist in a will if it inclines the will according to some dictate of prudence, which is the conclusion of a practical syllogism; now, the divine intellect does not reason syllogistically, since it does not think step by step.

[2] Also, the divine intellect first knows of a possible action before the will can will it, and the

will cannot disagree with the intellect understanding it; but the intellect apprehends the possible action in a definite way, so that it does
not grasp it as an indefinite either/or; therefore
the will definitely wills this action in such a
way that it cannot will the opposite if it is to will
rightly.

[3] Also, if it is just to save Peter, and God justly
wills this, then it is unjust to damn Peter, and thus
if God can will to do so, he can will something
that is unjust.

[Solutions] To the first, I say that if in us there
can be another moral virtue inclining the will
in accordance with the conclusion of a practical
syllogism, all the more so is there in us a practical appetite which inclines in accord with the
first practical principle, because this principle is
more true, and consequently more correct [than
a conclusion therefrom]. Justice, however, which
in God is one, both conceptually and in reality,
as we said, inclines the will in accord with the
first practical principle, namely, "God ought to be
loved." But if you want to insist that, strictly
speaking, what does not incline in accord with the
conclusion of a practical syllogism is not some
special virtue, I concede that this justice which God
has is only a quasi-universal and root sort of
"virtue," from which all particular sorts of rectitude or justice spring, although not in a necessary manner.

To the second, I say that the intellect grasps or
knows of some possible action before the will can
will it, but it does not apprehend it as something
definite that must be done, as if "to apprehend"
meant "to dictate." Indeed it is offered to the will
as something neutral; after the will makes a
definite decision that this is to be done, the intellect consequently grasps as true that this is to be
done, as was said in the matter about future con-
tingents in Bk I, dist. 39, q. 1.

Granted that before the will wills something,
the intellect apprehends that it should be done
(e.g., "God must be loved") and the will cannot
disagree, it still does not follow, however, that it
is by natural necessity that the will wills this. For
while it cannot disagree about the object, namely,
as regards willing or nilling what is shown to it
as something it ought to will, the way each tends
to that object disagrees, or rather should properly be distinguished. For the intellect tends to it
in its way, namely, naturally, whereas the will tends

in its own way, namely, freely. And these powers
are always in harmony because they always tend
to the same object according to their respective
manner of doing this, just as the imagination
and the intellect do not disagree if the former tends
to the object qua singular and the latter to that
same object qua universal.

To the third, I say the legislator in matters of
state regards something as simply just if it is
right for the public good, whereas he regards
other, partial rights always in the qualified sense
that they do not militate against this unqualified
right of the community at large, and therefore in
certain cases he sees it is right not to observe just
laws concerning these partial rights, namely,
when their observation would be detrimental to
what is just publicly, namely, to what is in the best
interests of the state. In a similar fashion God is
determined to do what is just publicly as something right and becoming to his goodness, and to
do this not for a group that is just an aggregation
of citizens, but rather for a community whose
members are knit together in a far more excellent way. But everything other than what is right
for this community is only a partial right that may
be just in this case but not in that, depending on
how it is ordered to or in harmony with that more
basic right.

I say therefore that God could will that Peter
be damned and be right to will such, because this
particular instance of what is just, viz., "Peter
is saved," is not necessarily required for what is
just for the community in the sense that its
opposite could not also be ordered to that same
end, namely, what is just for the community as
befitting divine goodness. For the attainment of
this end, indeed, no being represents a definitely
necessary requirement.

[Reply to the Initial Arguments] To the first
argument at the beginning I admit there is no
simple equality except in God with respect to
himself, and hence there is no justice in an
unqualified sense except with respect to himself.
Therefore, neither is there any unqualified justice
with respect to himself as quasi-other. As for the
latter, however, there can be a sort of equality such
as obtains between a master and a servant whose
respective stations differ exceedingly.

To the second I grant that no virtues that
imply any imperfection exist there, but only

such as can exist without imperfection. This is clear from the example of temperance, since this requires the nature it tempers to be capable of taking immoderate delight in something, and this represents an imperfection. For that reason one could more properly assume that justice is there, because this does not require some passionate excess or some such imperfection, in the way that temperance does. But it is questionable whether [a] justice as it exists in God is a virtue under this precise aspect that it is something formally distinct from the will that plays a quasi-regulatory function or whether [b] it merely represents the will as determining itself according to some first rule [such as "God should be loved"]. For if the second be the case, then it is easier to answer the argument, because then justice is not present in God precisely as a moral virtue.

To the third, I say that God is no debtor in any unqualified sense save with respect to his own goodness, namely, that he love it. But where creatures are concerned he is debtor rather to his generosity, in the sense that he gives creatures what their nature demands, which exigency in them is set down as something just, a kind of secondary object of this justice, as it were. But in truth nothing outside of God can be said to be definitely just without this added qualification. In an unqualified sense where a creature is concerned, God is just only in relationship to his first justice, namely, because such a creature has been actually willed by the divine will.

Ordinatio I, dist. 44

In this forty-fourth distinction – where the Master [Peter Lombard] asks whether God could have made things better than he did – I raise this question: Could God have made things otherwise than he has ordered them to be made?

[Arguments Pro and Con] It seems not:

For then he could have made things inordinately. The consequent is false, therefore the antecedent is also false.

On the contrary:

That things could have been made otherwise is not self-contradictory, neither is the world necessary; therefore, etc.

[To the Question] I reply:

In every agent acting intelligently and voluntarily that can act in conformity with an upright or just law but does not have to do so of necessity, one can distinguish between its ordained power and its absolute power. The reason is that either it can act in conformity with some right and just law, and then it is acting according to its ordained power (for it is ordained insofar as it is a principle for doing something in conformity with a right or just law), or else it can act beyond or against such a law, and in this case its absolute power exceeds its ordained power. And therefore it is not only in God, but in every free agent that can either act in accord with the dictates of a just law or go beyond or against that law, that one distinguishes between absolute and ordained power; therefore, the jurists say that someone can act *de facto*, that is, according to his absolute power, or *de jure*, that is, according to his ordained legal power.

But when that upright law – according to which an agent must act in order to act ordinately – is not in the power of that agent, then its absolute power cannot exceed its ordained power in regard to any object without it acting disorderly or inordinately. For, as regards such an agent, the law must remain in force, but an action that is not in conformity with this right and just law will be neither right nor ordinate, because the agent is bound to act in accord with that regulation to which it is subject. Hence all who are subject to a divine law, if they do not act according to it, act inordinately.

But whenever the law and its rectitude are in the power of the agent, so that the law is right only because it has been established, then the agent can freely order things otherwise than this right law dictates and still can act orderly, because he can establish another right or just law according to which he may act orderly. In such a case it is not simply necessary that his absolute power exceed his ordered power, because his action might still be ordered according to another law just as it had been earlier, but he would still exceed his ordained power according to the prior law if he acted beyond or against such. This could be illustrated in the case of a ruler and his subjects in regard to a positive law.

Applying this to the issue at hand, I say that there are some general laws, ordering things rightly, that have been set up beforehand by the divine will and not by the divine intellect, as something antecedent to any act of the divine will, as was said in dist. 38. But when the intellect presents such a law to the divine will, for instance, "Everyone to be glorified must first be in a state of grace," if it pleases his free will, then it becomes a right or just law, and so too with other laws.

God, therefore, insofar as he is able to act in accord with those right laws he set up previously, is said to act according to his ordained power; but insofar as he is able to do many things that are not in accord with, but go beyond, these preestablished laws, God is said to act according to his absolute power. For God can do anything that is not self-contradictory or act in any way that does not include a contradiction (and there are many such ways he could act); and then he is said to be acting according to his absolute power.

Hence, I say that many other things can be done orderly; and many things that do not include a contradiction other than those that conform to present laws can occur in an ordained way when the rectitude of such law – according to which one acts rightly and orderly – lies in the power of the agent himself. And therefore such an agent can act otherwise, so that he establishes another upright law, which, if it were set up by God, would be right, because no law is right except insofar as the divine will accepts it as established. And in such a case the absolute power of the agent in regard to something would not extend to anything other than what might happen ordinately if it occurred, not indeed ordainedly with respect to this present order, but ordinately with reference to some other order that the divine will could set up if it were able to act in such a way.

Keep in mind also that what is ordained and happens regularly can occur in two ways:

One way is with reference to a universal order. This would involve common law, like the common law that ordains that "every impenitent sinner must be damned" (as if a king were to establish the law that every murderer is to die). The second way is with reference to a particular order. This involves a particular judgment or decision that does not pertain to a universal law, since a law has to do with cases in general, whereas in a singular case what is involved is not a general law, but rather a decision according to law about something that is against the law (for instance, a decision that this murderer is to die).

I say, therefore, that God can act otherwise than is prescribed not only by a particular order, but also by a universal order or law of justice, and in so doing he could still act ordainedly, because what God could do by his absolute power that is either beyond or runs counter to the present order, he could do ordainedly.

But we speak of ordained power in reference only to an order established by a universal law, and not to that which rightly holds by law for a particular case. This is clear from the fact that it is possible for God to save one whom he does not actually save, a living sinner who will die, however, without repenting and will be damned. Admittedly, however, God could not in the same way save Judas, who is already damned. (But for God's absolute power not even this is impossible, since it does not include a contradiction.) It is impossible, therefore, to save Judas in the same way it is possible to save this other sinner, since it is true that the latter could be saved by God's ordained power, whereas Judas could not. And God could save the sinner not just by a particular order (which is concerned, as it were, with only this specific action and particular operation), but by one that is universal, because if he were to save this sinner, he could still do so within the framework of his preestablished just and right laws about the salvation and damnation of individuals. For the salvation of such a sinner is still consistent with the decree "One who remains evil to the end, will be damned" (which is a preestablished law about those who will be damned). The reason is that this sinner has not yet died in sin, and can still cease to be a sinner (especially while still in this life). By his grace God could prevent him from dying impenitent – like a king who prevents someone from killing, and then if he does not condemn the man, he is not violating his universal law against homicide. But it is not consistent with the particular law he did establish that he could save Judas. God could foresee that Judas could be saved by his ordained power – not what is now his ordained power, for at present Judas could only be saved by God's absolute power; but Judas's salvation could have been accomplished by God's ordained power in another order he might have set up.

The sort of possibility the divine will still retains with regard to particulars and to what has been instituted according to just and right laws, without God actually willing the opposite of what he now wills, is explained in dist. 39.

[Reply to Both Arguments at the Beginning] To the initial argument, it is clear that the implication does not hold, because to make something in another way than is presently ordained is not by that very fact to act inordinately, because other laws could be set up according to which he would be acting ordinately.

To the argument for the opposite I concede that it proves God has absolute power; but if his power were to become a principle or cause of anything, it would by that very fact be ordained, but not according to that same preestablished order he had before.

11

Nicholas Cusanus, *De docta ignorantia*, Book 1, Chapters I–VI, and XXVI; Book 2, Chapter V

Introduction

Each of the Abrahamic philosophical traditions first faced the task of legitimating the use of ancient Greek philosophers. Having succeeded, of course, each tradition also spawned movements critical of Greek philosophy – some reactionary and some progressive.

The progressive thinker Hasdai ben Abraham Crescas (c. 1340–c. 1412) presented to the Jewish philosophical tradition what the reactionary al-Ghazālī (1058–1111; IV.6) had in the Islamic – a trenchant critique of its use of Greek philosophy, especially Aristotelianism. Crescas's philosophical work responds to Jewish predecessors like Maimonides (1135–1204; see IV.8) and Gersonides (1288–1344) who had, in the wake of important Islamic and Christian thinkers, drawn heavily from Aristotle and other Greek philosophers in developing an intellectual structure through which to understand God and the truths of Holy Scripture. Thinkers like Ibn Rushd (1126–98; IV.7) had gone so far as to maintain that scripture and philosophy present two separate discourses, the truths of the former being largely metaphorical and didactic while the precise, scientific truths of metaphysics remain the domain of

From Nicholas of Cusa, *Of Learned Ignorance*, G. Heron, London: Routledge & Kegan Paul, 1954, pp. 7–17, 59–61, 83–6.

the latter. Crescas, by contrast, worked to limit and chasten the pretensions of Greek-centered philosophical thought not merely by condemning it but by exposing its errors and limitations philosophically. Against, for example, the many arguments for the existence of God that depended upon Aristotle's rejection of the existence of "actual infinities" in the created world (for example, arguing that the world must have had a beginning because an infinite chain of causes cannot stretch back into an infinite past; IV.9), Crescas argued that actual infinities are in fact possible.[1] Contrary to Aristotle's contention that a single world has always existed, Crescas argues for the possible existence of many worlds (an idea that would resurface among twentieth-century logicians and metaphysicians);[2] he also argues against Aristotelian ideas about space and the vacuum. Challenging Maimonides most pointedly, Crescas argues that a positive knowledge of God is possible by predicating positive attributes of the deity – for example, that God is omniscient and necessary. Crescas's ideas about God's omniscience and humanity's free will were influential with the early modern Jewish philosopher, Benedictus Spinoza (1632–77; III.13); his cosmological ideas seem to have held import for Pico della Mirandola (1463–94; I.12) as well as, it seems, Giordano Bruno (1548–1600), who was also interested in the plurality of worlds. Crescas's argument that all earthly events, including human conduct, are determined by prior causes has been identified as a harbinger of the modern mechanistic philosophies and compatibilist conceptions of free will.

To represent this progressive critical strain of late medieval and early Renaissance thought, we have selected here, however, work from another important philosopher of the period – Nicolas Cusanus (1401–64; aka "Nicholas of Cusa" or "Nikolaus Krebs"). Born to a merchant family in Kues, Germany, and educated in Padua, Italy, Cusanus became a well-known religious authority and polymath. He served as a papal envoy in the Conciliar Movement (the Roman Catholic Church's effort to reunite with the Greek Orthodox Church) during the tumultuous early years of the fifteenth century, when the Muslim Ottoman Turks were extending their power across the Anatolian peninsula towards Constantinople, which they would conquer in 1453. Cusanus was named a cardinal c. 1448 and made bishop of Brixen in 1450. His speculative rejection of the Aristotelian astronomical claim that celestial entities must move in perfect circles anticipated Johannes Kepler (1571–1630), who referred to Cusanus as "divinely inspired." Cusanus's reflections on "infinity" were influential with later mathematicians; and his political writings became important in limiting the political power of the papacy.[3] Cusanus died in Todi, Umbria; his body was interred in Rome, but his heart was returned to Kues.

The work from which we have selected excerpts here, Cusanus's classic *De docta ignorantia* (*On Learned* Ignorance, 1439–40), advances a critique of Aristotelian rationalism first by appealing to the traditions of supra-rational intuition developed by Platonists and by Christian mystics like Meister Eckhart (1260–1328). But in addition, like Crescas, Cusanus advances his critical work by arguing philosophically for ideas contrary to those of the Aristotelians.[4] Cusanus's text, of course, hearkens back to Socrates' claim in the *Apology* (as well as by later skeptics) that the truly wise are those who acknowledge their ignorance. Curiously, however, Cusanus's acknowledgment of ignorance hinges upon philosophical speculations about God. In a way that seems to anticipate Hegel (III.18), Cusanus emphasizes God's unique standing as a "coincidence of opposites" – an absolute being that transcends or, rather, contains through a special kind of "contraction" all dualisms and oppositions. Because there is an "infinite disproportion" between God and the finite human mind, God can be grasped neither by sensory perception, nor by imagination, nor by the kind of rational knowledge that depends upon binary oppositions and the principle of non-contradiction. Because Cusanus describes God as absolutely comprehensive and transcendent with regard to dualistic oppositions, some have interpreted Cusanus as a pantheist who prefigures Spinoza's conception of "*deus sive natura*" ("God or nature") or the "absolute" of the nineteenth-century German idealists. Cusanus's skeptical epistemology also seems in many ways to prefigure Kant's critique of reason (IV.16). Indeed, along these lines German philosopher Ernest Cassirer goes so far as to call Cusanus "the first modern thinker."[5] Whether the first of the moderns or the last of the medievals, Cusanus presents work whose critical dimensions remain important because they exhibit both the philosophical exhaustion of the Aristotelian paradigm in philosophy characteristic of the fifteenth century as well as one of the first of the many waves of epistemological critique that would preoccupy modern and postmodern thought to come.

Notes

1 Aristotelians commonly contrasted "actual" infinities with "potential" infinities. So, while time (or a chain of causes) might not (and perhaps cannot) be "actually" infinite (actually existing in its infinite entirety), it is "potentially" infinite in the sense that additional moments (or additional causes/effects) can always be added *ad infinitum*. See Aristotle, *Physics* Book I, Chapters 2–4; Book III, Book VI, Chapters 2, 6–7; Book VII, Chapter 1.

2 Consider for example, contemporary ideas about the "multiverse." Cf. G. F. R. Ellis, U. Kirchner, and W. R. Stoeger, "Multiverses and Physical Cosmology," *Monthly Notices of the Royal Astronomical Society* 347 (2004): 921–36.

3 P. E. Sigmunde, *Nicholas of Cusa and Medieval Political Thought*, Cambridge, MA: Harvard University Press, 1963.

4 Meister Eckhart seems to have been especially influential with Cusanus. R. Klibansky, *The Continuity of the Platonic Tradition During the Middle Ages. Outlines of a Corpus Platonicum Medii Aevi*. London: Kraus International

Publications, 1982. W. J. Hoye, "The Meaning of Neoplatonism in the Thought of Nicholas of Cusa," *Downside Review* 104 (1986): 10–18.

5　E. Cassirer, *Individuum und Kosmos in der Philosophie der Renaissance* (Leipzig: Teubner, 1927), p. 10.

Cusanus, *De docta ignorantia*

Book 1

Chapter I   How Knowledge is Ignorance   We see that god has implanted in all things a natural desire to exist with the fullest measure of existence that is compatible with their particular nature. To this end they are endowed with suitable faculties and activities; and by means of these there is in them a discernment that is natural and in keeping with the purpose of their knowledge, which ensures their natural inclination serving its purpose and being able to reach its fulfilment in that object towards which it is attracted by the weight of its own nature. If at times this does not happen, it is necessarily the result of an accident, as when sickness deceives taste or conjecture upsets calculation. That is the explanation of the sound untrammelled intellect's desire for truth, which, by its natural discursive movement, it ceaselessly seeks in all things; and once it takes possession of the object of its natural desire, we say it knows the truth; for, without any hesitation, we call that true, which no sound mind can refuse to embrace. In every enquiry men judge of the uncertain by comparing it with an object presupposed certain, and their judgment is always approximative; every enquiry is, therefore, comparative and uses the method of analogy. When there is comparatively little distance from the object of enquiry back to the object regarded as certain, a judgment is easily formed; when many intermediaries are required, the task becomes difficult. We are familiar enough with this in mathematics, in which the reducing of the first propositions to the well-known first principles is easier, whereas the more remote propositions give rise to more difficulty, because it is only by means of the first propositions that these can be led back to the first principles. Every enquiry, therefore, consists in a relation of comparison that is easy or difficult to draw; for this reason the infinite as infinite is unknown, since it is away and above all comparison. Now, while proportion expresses an agreement in some one thing, it expresses at the same time a distinction, so that it cannot be understood without number. Number, in consequence, includes all things that are capable of comparison. It is not then in quantity only that number produces proportion; it produces it in all things that are capable of agreement and difference in any way at all, whether substantially or accidentally. That is why Pythagoras was so insistent on maintaining that in virtue of numbers all things were understood.

It so far surpasses human reason, however, to know the precision of the combinations in material things and how exactly the known has to be adapted to the unknown that Socrates thought he knew nothing save his own ignorance, whilst Solomon, the Wise, affirmed that in all things there are difficulties which beggar explanation in words; and we have it from another, who was divinely inspired, that wisdom and the locality of the understanding lie hidden from the eyes of all the living. If this is so – and even the most profound Aristotle in his First Philosophy affirms it to be true of the things most evident to us in nature – then in presence of such difficulty we may be compared to owls trying to look at the sun; but since the natural desire in us for knowledge is not without a purpose, its immediate object is our own ignorance. If we can fully realize this desire, we will acquire learned ignorance. Nothing could be more beneficial for even the most zealous searcher for knowledge than his being in fact most learned in that very ignorance which is peculiarly his own; and the better a man will have known his own ignorance, the greater his learning will be. It is in bearing this in mind that I have undertaken the task of writing a few words on learned ignorance.

Chapter II   Preliminary Explanation of all that Follows   As I am about to deal with ignorance as the greatest learning, I consider it necessary to determine the precise meaning of the maximum or greatest. We speak of a thing being the greatest or maximum when nothing greater than it can exist. But to one being alone does plenitude belong, with the result that unity, which is also being, and the maximum are identical; for if such a unity is itself in every way and entirely without restriction then it is clear that there is nothing to be placed in opposition to it, since it is the absolute maximum. Consequently, the absolute maximum is one and it is all; all things are in it because it is the maximum. Moreover, it is in all things for this reason that the minimum at once coincides with it, since there is nothing that can be placed in opposition to it. Because it is absolute, it is in actuality all possible being, limiting all things and receiving no limitation from any. In the First Book I will endeavour to study this maximum, who without any doubt is believed to be the God of all nations. It is a study that is above reason and cannot be conducted on the lines of human comprehension; and for my guide I will take him alone who dwells in light inaccessible.

In the second place, just as we have the absolute maximum, which is the absolute entity by which all things are what they are, so we have from it the universal unity of being which is called the maximum effect of the absolute. In consequence, its existence as the universe is finite, and its unity, which could not be absolute, is the relative unity of a plurality. Though this maximum embraces all things in its universal unity, so that all that comes from the absolute is in it and it in all, yet it could not subsist outside the plurality in which it is contained, for this restriction is inseparably bound up with its existence. Of this maximum, which is the universe, I will have something further to say in the second book.

In the third place, we shall see that there is still one more manner in which to consider the maximum. Since the subsistence in plurality of the universe is necessarily finite, we shall study the plurality itself of things in order to discover the one maximum in which the universe finds especially and most completely its actual and ultimate subsistence. This maximum in the universe is united with the absolute, for the absolute is the ultimate term of all; and as this maximum, which is at once relative and absolute, is the most perfect realization of the purpose of the universe and entirely beyond our reach, my comments on it will be added in accordance with the inspiration of Jesus himself; in fact, this maximum bears the ever blessed name of Jesus.

An understanding of this matter will be attained rather by our rising above the literal sense of the words, than by insisting upon their natural properties, for these natural properties cannot be effectively adapted to such intellectual mysteries. For the reader we must even use drawings as illustrations, but he must rise above these in leaving aside what is sensible in them in order to arrive unimpeded at what is purely intelligible. In pursuing this method I have eagerly tried, by the avoidance of all difficulties of expressions, to make it as clear as possible to the average mind that the foundation for learned ignorance is the fact that absolute truth is beyond our grasp.

Chapter III   Absolute Truth is Beyond our Grasp
From the self-evident fact that there is no gradation from infinite to finite, it is clear that the simple maximum is not to be found where we meet degrees of more and less; for such degrees are finite, whereas the simple maximum is necessarily infinite. It is manifest, therefore, that when anything other than the simple maximum itself is given, it will always be possible to find something greater. Equality, we find, is a matter of degree: with things that are alike one is more equal to this than to that, in-so-far as they belong, or do not belong, to the same genus or species, or in-so-far as they are, or are not, related in time, place or influence. For that reason it is evident that two or more things cannot be so alike and equal that an infinite number of similar objects cannot still be found. No matter, then, how equal the measure and the thing measured are, they will remain for ever different.

A finite intellect, therefore, cannot by means of comparison reach the absolute truth of things. Being by nature indivisible, truth excludes 'more' or 'less', so that nothing but truth itself can be the exact measure of truth: for instance, that which is not a circle cannot be the measure of a circle, for the nature of a circle is one and indivisible. In consequence, our intellect, which is not the truth, never grasps the truth with such precision that it could not be comprehended with infinitely greater precision. The relationship of our intellect to the truth is like that of a polygon to a circle; the resemblance to the circle grows with the multiplication of the angles of the polygon; but apart from its being reduced to identity with the circle, no multiplication, even if it were infinite, of its angles will make the polygon equal the circle.

It is clear, therefore, that all we know of the truth is that the absolute truth, such as it is, is beyond our reach. The truth, which can be neither more nor less than it is, is the most absolute necessity, while, in contrast with it, our intellect is possibility. Therefore, the quiddity of things, which is ontological truth, is unattainable in its entirety; and though it has been the objective of all philosophers, by none has it been found as it really is. The more profoundly we learn this lesson of ignorance, the closer we draw to truth itself.

Chapter IV   The Absolute Maximum is Known but not Understood. Maximum and Minimum are Synonymous   There can be nothing greater in existence than the simple, absolute maximum; and since it is greater than our powers of comprehension – for it is infinite truth – our knowledge of it can never mean that we comprehend it. It is above all that we can conceive, for its nature excludes degrees of 'more' and 'less'. All the things, in fact, that we apprehend by our senses, reason or intellect are so different from one another that there is no precise equality between them. The maximum equality, therefore, in which there is no diversity or difference from any other, is completely beyond our understanding; and for that reason the absolute maximum is in act most perfect, since it is in act all that it can be. Being all that it can be, it is, for one and the same reason, as great as it can be and as small as it can be. By definition the minimum is that which cannot be less than it is; and since that is also true of the maximum, it is evident that the minimum is identified with the maximum.

This becomes clearer when you restrict your considerations to the maximum and the minimum of quantity. The maximum quantity is infinitely great, whilst the minimum is infinitely small. Now, if mentally you lay aside the notions of greatness and smallness, you are left with the maximum and the minimum without quantity, and it becomes clear that the maximum and the minimum are one and the same; in fact, the minimum is as much a superlative as the maximum. The maximum and the minimum, then, are equally predicable of absolute quantity, since in it they are identified.

Distinctions, therefore, are only found to exist among things which are susceptible of 'more' and 'less'; and they exist among these in different ways; in no way do they exist in the absolute maximum, for it is above any form of affirmation and negation. Existence and non-existence can be equally predicated of all that which is conceived to exist; and non-existence cannot to any greater degree than existence be affirmed of all that is conceived not to exist. But the absolute maximum, in consequence, is all things and, whilst being all, it is none of them; in other words, it is at once the maximum and minimum of being. There is, in fact, no difference between these two affirmations: 'God, who is the absolute maximum itself, is light'; and 'God is light at its highest, therefore He is light at its lowest'. It could not be otherwise; for the absolute maximum would not be the realization of all possible perfection, if it were not infinite and if it were not the end to which all things are ordained, whilst it stands subordinate to none. With God's help, we shall explain this in the pages that follow.

This is far and away beyond our understanding, which is fundamentally unable by any rational process to reconcile contradictories. We proceed to truth through the things made known to us by nature; and, as this process falls very far short of the infinite power of the maximum, we are unable to link together by means of it contradictories which are infinitely distant from one another. We know that the absolute maximum is infinite, that it is all things since it is one with the minimum; but this knowledge is away and above any understanding we could reach by discursive reasoning. In this book the terms maximum and minimum are not restricted to quantity of mass or of force; they have here an absolutely transcendent value embracing all things in their absolute simplicity.

Chapter V   Oneness of the Maximum   In what follows we will give a still clearer explanation of what must now be very evident from the foregoing, namely that the absolute maximum is beyond our comprehension yet intelligible, able to be named whilst remaining ineffable. The discursive reason gives names only to those things which are susceptible of 'more' or 'less'; when confronted with the greatest possible or the smallest possible, it is unable to find a name for it. The fact that all things have existence in the best possible way makes it impossible to have plurality of beings without number; for if number is denied then the distinction, hierarchy, relationship, harmony and even plurality of beings must be denied. We would be forced to the same conclusions if the number were infinite, for in that case it would be the maximum in actuality which would be one with the minimum: it is one and the same thing to call a number infinite and to say it is the minimum. If, then, by numerical addition we were to arrive at an actual maximum, since number is finite, we would not have thereby reached the maximum which is the greatest possible, since this would be infinite. Clearly, then, numerical addition is actually finite and will be capable of receiving one more. In the opposite direction the same holds good: just as a higher number is always possible by addition, so no matter how small the given number actually is, a smaller will always be possible by subtraction. If that were not true, number would not be the key to the distinction of thing from thing, nor of the hierarchy of beings; and we could not speak of things in the plural, nor of a 'more' or 'less'; number itself, besides, could not exist. We must in consequence reach a minimum in number which is the smallest possible. Unity is such a minimum; and as there can be nothing less than it, unity will be the simple (absolute) minimum that coincides, as we have just seen, with the maximum.

Being capable of being added to, number can by no means be the simple minimum or maximum; unity cannot, therefore, be a number, though as minimum it is the principle of all number. Therefore absolute unity, where no duality is possible, is the absolute maximum or God Himself. By the fact that it is unity at its absolute perfection, it excludes the possibility of the existence of another such being because it is all that it can be. It cannot therefore, be a number.

Number has led us to the conclusion that absolute unity is a most fitting attribute of God, the ineffable, and that His unity is such that He is actually all that is possible. His is a unity which excludes degrees of 'more' or 'less' and even the possible existence of another being of the same order. God, in consequence, is infinite unity. Nothing could be truer than his own words: 'Hear, O Israel: the Lord our God is one Lord'; and 'For one is your master . . . one is your father, who is in heaven'; nothing could be more

false than the assertion that there is more than one God, for it is nothing short of a denial of God and the entire universe, as we shall prove later. Number, a being of reason, owes its existence to our power of comparing and distinguishing; its reality is limited to the reality it has in my mind; number, therefore, could not exist if it were not taken for granted that it necessarily proceeds from unity. Clearly, too, the multiplicity of beings that proceed from this infinite unity, are so really dependent upon it that without it they could not exist. How could they exist without being? Absolute Unity is infinite being, as we shall see later.

Chapter VI   The Maximum is Absolute Necessity
From what has been said it must now be clear that the absolute maximum alone is infinite and that all else, in reference to it, is finite and limited. Finite, limited being has a beginning and an end, so that there is a being to which it owes existence and in which it will have its end. It would be erroneous to say that that being, finite itself, was greater than any given finite being; equally erroneous would it be to say that we arrive at such a being through an infinite series of greater and greater finite beings; for, in the first place, an actual, infinite series of finites is impossible and, secondly, such a maximum would itself be finite. Therefore, the beginning and end of all finite things is necessarily the Absolute Maximum.

Besides, if the Absolute Maximum did not exist, nothing could be; for all beings less than the Maximum are finite; necessarily they are effects that are produced by another. To say that they produced themselves would be the same as saying that they acted before they existed; to explain them by appealing to an infinite number of principles and causes has been already ruled out. That will be the Absolute Maximum, without which nothing is able to be.

Moreover, supposing the maximum reduced to being, we may say: Nothing is in opposition to the maximum; and for that reason both non-being and minimum being are identical with the maximum. How, then, is it possible to conceive the maximum as incapable of existence, since minimum being is maximum being? Without being we can have no idea that anything exists. But absolute being necessarily is the absolute maximum; therefore, nothing can be conceived to exist independently of the maximum.

Maximum truth, besides, is the absolute maximum. All that we can say or think is exhausted by the following propositions which are the maximum truth on the absolute maximum itself: it is or it is not; it is and it is not; it neither is nor is it not. My point is made no matter which of these you affirm as truth at its maximum, for in the simple maximum I have the maximum truth.

From the foregoing it is clear that 'being' or any other word is not the precise name of the maximum; it is above every name; yet the name 'maximum', must mean that being in the highest, though indescribable, way is predicated of it more than of any being that can be described. For these and a host of similar reasons the ignorance that is learning understands most clearly that the absolute maximum so necessarily exists that it is absolute necessity. Now it has been established that there can be only one absolute maximum; this unity, therefore, of the maximum is the greatest truth.

[. . .]

Chapter XXVI Negative Theology The worship of God, who is to be adored in spirit and truth, necessarily rests on dogmatic assertions about Him; for that reason the cult in every religion is necessarily developed by affirmative theology: God is adored as one and three, as The Most Wise, The Most Good, The Light Inaccessible, The Life, The Truth and so on; and worship always is regulated by a faith which is acquired more surely through learned ignorance. By faith, for example, it is acknowledged that He who is adored as one is one and all; that He who is worshipped as Light Inaccessible, is not light that is material, the opposite of which is darkness, but light absolutely simple and infinite in which darkness is infinite light; that He who is infinite light itself shines always in the darkness of our ignorance, but the darkness cannot comprehend the Light. Negative Theology, in consequence, is so indispensable to affirmative theology that without it God would be adored, not as the Infinite but rather as a creature, which is idolatry, or giving to an image what is due to Truth alone. It will be useful, then, to add a few words on negative theology.

Sacred ignorance has taught us that God is ineffable, because He is infinitely greater than anything that words can express. So true is this that it is by the process of elimination and the use of negative propositions that we come nearer the truth about Him. For that reason the most noble Denis would not have Him called Truth or Intellect or Light or any name that man can utter; and in this he was followed by Rabbi Salomon and all the wise. According to this negative theology, therefore, He is neither Father nor Son nor Holy Ghost; one word alone may be used of Him: Infinite. Infinity, as such, does not engender, is not engendered and does not proceed, – which called from Hilary of Poitiers, whilst distinguishing the Persons, these subtle words: 'In aeterno infinitas, species in imagine, usus in munere.' His meaning is that all we see in eternity is infinity; and, while it is true that infinity is eternity, yet infinity is a negative and for that reason it cannot be conceived as a principle of generation. Eternity, on the other hand, clearly can be so conceived, for eternity is an affirmation of infinite unity or of the infinite present, and is, therefore, a principle that does not proceed from any other. 'Species in imagine' expresses the principle that proceeds from a principle and 'usus in munere' signifies procession from both.

All that is clear enough from what we have already said. We know, in fact, that eternity is infinity, and that both of these belong to the Father in the same way. Yet considered in one way eternity is an attribute of the Father but not of the Son nor of the Holy Ghost, whereas infinity belongs to all the persons equally. Considered from the point of view of unity, infinity is the Father, from the point of view of equality of unity it is the Son, from the point of view of the connection it is the Holy Ghost; but when considered, not from any of these points of view, but absolutely in itself infinity says nothing of Father, Son and Holy Ghost, nor does it say anything of unity or plurality in God. And according to negative theology infinity is all we discover in God. Yet the fact is that infinity, as well as eternity, is each of the Three Persons and conversely each of the Persons is infinity and eternity. As far as negative theology is concerned, then, we must conclude that God cannot be known in this life or in the life to come. God alone knows Himself; He is as incomprehensible to creatures as infinite light is to darkness.

From this it is clear how in theology negative propositions are true and affirmative ones inadequate; and that of the negative ones those are truer which eliminate greater imperfections from the infinitely Perfect. It is truer, for example, to deny that God is a stone than to deny that He is life or intelligence, – truer to deny that He is intemperate than to deny that He is virtuous. In affirmative propositions the contrary holds good: it is truer to assert that God is intelligence and life than to assert that He is earth, stone or anything material.

All these points, which must now be abundantly clear, leave us with the conclusion that, in a way we cannot comprehend, absolute truth enlightens the darkness of our ignorance. That, then, is the learned ignorance for which we have been searching. We have shown how the sole approach to the Maximum – the Triune God of infinite Goodness – passes through the stages of that ignorance which is learning, and how, in consequence, amidst all our gropings, we can always praise Him, the Incomprehensible, for His revelation of Himself to us.

May He be blessed above all for ever.

Book 2

Chapter V Everything in Everything From a keen study of what has already been said we come to understand easily enough, perhaps even more fully than Anaxagoras himself, the depth of the truth he expressed in the words 'everything is everything'. For from the First Book we learned that God is in all things in such a way that all things are in him; in the previous chapter we discovered that God is in all things by the medium, as it were, of the universe; so it follows that all is in all, and each in each. As if by nature's order it was that the most perfect – the universe – came into being before all things, so that anything might be in anything. In fact, in every creature the universe is the creature; consequently each creature receives all, so that in any creature all creatures are found in a relative way. Since all creatures are finite, no creature could be all things in act; but all things are contracted in order to form each creature. If, then, all things are in all, it is clear that all is prior to the individual; and all here does not signify plurality, for prior to the individual there is no plurality. For that reason all without plurality has preceded the individual in the order of nature with

the consequence that in any actual individual there is not more than one: all without plurality is that one.

Only by way of contraction is the universe in things; in fact it is restricted by each actually existing thing to be actually what each thing is. Everything actually existing is in God, for He is the act of all. Act means perfection and the realization of what was possible. Since the universe restricted is in each actually existing individual, then evidently God, Who is in the universe, is in every individual and every individual actually existing is, like the universe, immediately in God. To say that 'everything is in everything' is the same as saying that God, by the intermediary of the universe, is in all things and that the universe, by the intermediary of all things, is in God. How God is without any diversity in all, since everything is everything, and how all is in God, because all is in all, are truths of a very high order which are clearly understood by keen minds. The universe is in each individual in such a way that each individual is in it, with the result that in each individual the universe is by contraction what the particular individual is; and every individual in the universe is the universe, though the universe is in each individual in a different way and each thing is in the universe in a different way.

Here is an example: The infinite line is clearly a line, a triangle, a circle and a sphere; but a finite line receives its existence from the infinite line, and the infinite line is all that the finite line is. All, therefore, that is identified with the infinite line – line, triangle and the others – is also found identified with the finite line. Every figure in the finite line is the line itself; but that does not mean that the triangle or circle or sphere is actually present in it. That everything is in everything does not imply actual presence, for the actual unity of the thing would be destroyed by such a plurality; but the triangle in the line is the line, the circle in the line is the line, and so on. To note that a line can only actually exist in a body – a point to be proved elsewhere – helps you to see this more clearly. No one doubts that in a body with length, breadth and depth all the figures are virtually contained. So in an actual line all the figures are actually the line itself, and in a triangle all are the triangle and so on. In a stone all is stone, in the vegetative soul all is soul, in life all is life, in a sense all is that sense, in sight all is sight, in hearing all is hearing, in the imagination all is imagination, in reason all is reason, in the understanding all is understanding, in God all is God. From that you see how the unity of things or the universe exists in plurality and conversely how plurality exists in unity.

You will also see on closer study how each individual in actual existence is at peace, for all in the individual is the individual and the individual in God is God; and there appears the wonderful unity of things, the admirable equality and the most remarkable connection, by which all is in all. In this we see the one source of the connection and diversity of things. An individual could not be actually all things, for it would be God, and therefore all things would be actualized in it in the way in which they can exist as individual natures. Nor can any two things be absolutely equal, as we proved above when we saw that all things were made in varying degrees of being – like the being which could not possess all at once the perfection of incorruptibility and was made to exist without corruption in temporal succession. Consequently, all things are what they are, because they could not be otherwise nor better.

Without any conflict, therefore, all is in each, because one degree of being cannot exist without another; e.g. in the body one member helps another and all the members are harmoniously united in the body. Since the eye cannot in act

be the hand, foot and all the other members, it is content to be the eye, as the foot is content to be the foot; and all the members help one another, so that each is what it is in the best way possible. The hand is not in the eye, nor is the foot, but in the eye they are the eye, in as much as the eye itself is immediately in man; in this way, too, all the members are in the foot, in-so-far as the foot is immediately in man. The result is that any member through any other is immediately in man; and just as the whole is in its parts – through being in anyone it is in every other – so man, as a whole, is in every member through being in any one.

If you were to think of humanity as an absolute, immutable, illimitable being, and of man as a being in whom absolute humanity exists in an absolute way though contracted by him to the humanity which man is, then you might compare the absolute humanity to God and the contracted to the universe. Absolute humanity is found in man first and foremost and then in each member or part; contracted humanity is the eye in the eye, the heart in the heart and so on of the others, so that by contraction each is in each. Besides supplying us with the comparison of God and the world, our hypothesis is an illustration of all we have dealt with in the last two chapters and of much that is to follow.

Blaise Pascal, "The Wager"

Introduction

It has been said that Pascal's "Wager" vies with
Anselm's Ontological Argument as the most
famous argument in the philosophy of religion.[1] The
argument, originally jotted down on a chaotically
organized sheet of folded paper, belongs to the
series of notes and reflections known as the *Pensées* (thoughts) that Blaise Pascal (1623–62)
wrote during the last few years of his short and
sickly life. Born in the French town of Clermont-
Ferrand, Pascal was a mathematically precocious
child who devoted his working life, much interrupted
by illness, to geometry, mechanics, and – especially
after the spiritual experience famously recorded in
his *Mémorial* in 1654 – to theological reflection.
By this time, he was closely associated, at some
danger to himself, with the Jansenist theology,
partly inspired by Calvin, of the Port-Royal in Paris.

Two important features of Pascal's religious
thinking help to provide a context for the Wager
argument. First, Pascal was a "sceptical fideist,"[2]
who rejected all the standard proofs for the existence of God, claiming that God's existence cannot be a matter of rational knowledge at all. "It
is the heart that feels God, not reason: that is what
faith is' (*Pensées*, p. 157). Second, he paints at

From Blaise Pascal, *Pensées and Other Writings*, trans.
Honor Levi, Oxford: Oxford University Press, 1995,
pp. 153–6 (notes omitted).

least as dark a picture of human existence outside
of a relationship to God as any earlier Christian
thinker, including Augustine. "A human being is
only a reed, the weakest in nature" (p. 72), and
one whose life, if led without religious faith, is one
of "grief and despair." The greatest tragedy, as
Pascal makes clear in his *Mémorial*, is to be "cut
off from" God (p. 178).

Pascal's denial that there can be rational
proofs of God's existence means that, if he is to
argue for religious belief, this must be by appealing to the advantages of holding such a belief,
rather than on the grounds that the belief is true.
And if, as Voltaire and others have charged, it
sounds cynical or mercenary to advocate religious
belief because of the benefits it brings, Pascal's
reply may be that the urgency of persuading
people to live with religious faith more than outweighs scruples about the style of persuasion.
Alternatively, one might with good reason read
Pascal as having advanced the Wager not in
order to justify belief but rather to remove an obstacle to it, namely the concern that faith is contrary
to reason. That is to say, one might interpret the
Wager not as an attempt to demonstrate to unbelievers that the articles of faith are true but rather
as an attempt to show that religious belief, while
itself independent of reason, remains perfectly
consistent with reason and even supported by it.

In any case, Pascal's Wager argument is densely
stated, and in fact there are really two arguments
at work. The first, straightforward one is that the
outcome of wagering on God's existence cannot be

worse, and may – if God really does exist – be significantly better, than the results of wagering that God does not exist. For, if one wagers the latter, and is mistaken, one will be denied the eternal rewards of faith. Pascal, however, seems to appreciate, when replying to an interlocutor who wonders if he isn't "betting too much" on God's existence, that a further argument is needed. This further argument puts the stress on the benefits of truly believing in God being *infinite* – thereby infinitely outweighing any benefits there might be to not wagering on God's existence.

In fact, Pascal adds a third, supplementary argument – one which, ironically, may be more persuasive than the main ones in an age, like our own, when the idea of eternal salvation and damnation is out of fashion. This argument is to the effect that "you will win in this [earthly] life" as well by wagering on God's existence, since this will induce you to live honestly, as a true friend, and so on.

Two worries about the Wager that have been raised would not have disturbed Pascal. One is to the effect that it is impossible to "choose" to believe that God exists (or does not exist). Pascal would reply that this is indeed so, but nothing prevents a person acting in such a way – controlling material desires, for example, or joining in religious ceremonies – that is effective in cultivating religious conviction. Second, it has been charged that Pascal's argument can do nothing to encourage specifically Christian faith since, as Denis Diderot pointed out, an Imam could employ Pascal's reasoning as legitimately as a priest could. But it was never Pascal's intention to provide a case for Christian belief in particular. It is, however, his view that once a person is open to and desirous of faith – which is all that the Wager argument by itself can hope to bring about – then the religion that will most attract him or her, if the playing-field on which it competes with other religions is level, will be Christianity. But this, for Pascal, has to do with the uniquely Christian understanding of sin.

A third objection, however, hinges upon Pascal's having failed to consider the possibilities outside the Abrahamic framework. More specifically, Pascal seems blind to the logical possibility, for example, that belief in the Abrahamic god might actually result in damnation – under the possibility, say, that the deity actually ruling the universe regards belief in the God of Judaism, Christianity, and Islam to be a damnable offense. Considering the many possibilities to which Pascal seems to be blind, one finds that there is simply no more reason to think that faith leads to possible salvation than to think that it leads to possible damnation; and correlatively one finds no more reason to think that disbelief leads to possible damnation than to think that it leads to possible salvation. Why shouldn't the deity (or deities) simply prefer atheists and skeptics to believers, or anyway regard them just as highly? The Christian account, then, to which Pascal seems limited, describes one possible set of outcomes to faith and disbelief; but matrices with contrary outcomes, even contradictory outcomes, are from a logical point of view just as likely.

Notes

1   A. Hájek, "Pascal's Wager," *Stanford Encyclopedia of Philosophy*, http://plato.stanford.edu/entries/pascal-wager. p. 13.
2   See T. Penelhum, "Scepticism and Fideism," in M. Burnyeat, ed., *The Skeptical Tradition*, Berkeley: University of California Press, 1983.

Pascal, "The Wager"

[. . .] If there is a God, he is infinitely beyond our comprehension, since, having neither parts nor limits, he bears no relation to ourselves. We are therefore incapable of knowing either what he is, or if he is. That being so, who will dare to undertake a resolution of this question? It cannot be us, who bear no relationship to him.

Who will then blame the Christians for being unable to provide a rational basis for their belief, they who profess a religion for which they cannot provide a rational basis? They declare that it is a folly, *stultitiam* (1 Cor. 1: 18) in laying it before the world: and then you complain that they do not prove it! If they did prove it, they would not be keeping their word. It is by the lack of proof that they do not lack sense. 'Yes, but although that excuses those who offer their religion as it is, and that takes away the blame from them of producing it without a rational basis, it does not excuse those who accept it.'

Let us therefore examine this point, and say: God is, or is not. But towards which side will we lean? Reason cannot decide anything. There is an infinite chaos separating us. At the far end of this infinite distance a game is being played and the coin will come down heads or tails. How will you wager? Reason cannot make you choose one way or the other, reason cannot make you defend either of the two choices.

So do not accuse those who have made a choice of being wrong, for you know nothing about it! 'No, but I will blame them not for having made this choice, but for having made any choice. For, though the one who chooses heads and the other one are equally wrong, they are both wrong. The right thing is not to wager at all.'

Yes, but you have to wager. It is not up to you, you are already committed. Which then will you choose? Let us see. Since you have to choose, let us see which interests you the least. You have two things to lose: the truth and the good, and two things to stake: your reason and will, your knowledge and beatitude; and your nature has two things to avoid: error and wretchedness. Your reason is not hurt more by choosing one rather than the other, since you do have to make the choice. That is one point disposed of. But your beatitude? Let us weigh up the gain and the loss by calling heads that God exists. Let us assess the two cases: if you win, you win everything; if you lose, you lose nothing. Wager that he exists then, without hesitating! 'This is wonderful. Yes, I must wager. But perhaps I am betting too much.' Let us see. Since there is an equal chance of gain and loss, if you won only two lives instead of one, you could still put on a bet. But if there were three lives to win, you would have to play (since you must necessarily play), and you would be unwise, once forced to play, not to chance your life to win three in a game where there is an equal chance of losing and winning. But there is an eternity of life and happiness. And that being so, even though there were an infinite number of chances of which only one were in your favour, you would still be right to wager one in order to win two, and you would be acting wrongly, since you are obliged to play, by refusing to stake one life against three in a game where out of an infinite number of chances there is one in your favour, if there were an infinitely happy infinity of life to be won. But here there is an infinitely happy infinity of life to be won, one chance of winning against a finite number of chances of losing, and what you are staking is finite. That removes all choice: wherever there is infinity and where there is no infinity of chances of losing against one of winning, there is no scope for wavering, you have to chance everything. And thus, as you are forced to gamble, you have to have discarded reason if you cling on to your life, rather than risk it for the infinite prize which is just as likely to happen as the loss of nothingness.

For it is no good saying that it is uncertain if you will win, that it is certain you are taking a risk, and that the infinite distance between the CERTAINTY of what you are risking and the UNCERTAINTY of whether you win makes the finite good of what you are certainly risking equal to the uncertainty of the infinite. It does not work like that. Every gambler takes a certain risk for an uncertain gain; nevertheless he certainly risks the finite uncertainty in order to win a finite gain, without sinning against reason. There is no infinite distance between this certainty of what is being risked and the uncertainty of what might be gained: that is untrue. There is, indeed, an infinite distance between the certainty of winning and the certainty of losing. But the uncertainty of winning is proportional to the certainty of the risk, according to the chances of winning or losing. And hence, if there are as many chances on one side as on the other, the odds are even, and then the certainty of what you risk is equal to the uncertainty of winning. It is very far from being infinitely distant from it. So our argument is infinitely strong, when the finite is at stake in a game where there are equal chances of winning and losing, and the infinite is to be won.

That is conclusive, and, if human beings are capable of understanding any truth at all, this is the one.

'I confess it, I admit it, but even so . . . Is there no way of seeing underneath the cards?' 'Yes, Scripture and the rest, etc' 'Yes, but my hands are tied and I cannot speak a word. I am being forced to wager and I am not free, they will not let me go. And I am made in such a way that I cannot believe. So what do you want me to do?' 'That is true. But at least realize that your inability to believe, since reason urges you to do so and yet you cannot, arises from your passions. So concentrate not on convincing yourself by increasing the number of proofs of God but on diminishing your passions. You want to find faith and you do not know the way? You want to cure yourself of unbelief and you ask for the remedies? Learn from those who have been bound like you, and who now wager all they have. They are people who know the road you want to follow and have been cured of the affliction of which you want to be cured. Follow the way by which they began: by behaving just as if they believed, taking holy water, having masses said, etc. That will make you believe quite naturally, and according to your animal reactions.' 'But that is what I am afraid of.' 'Why? What do you have to lose? In order to show you that this is where it leads, it is because it diminishes the passions, which are your great stumbling-blocks, etc.

'How these words carry me away, send me into raptures,' etc. If these words please you and seem worthwhile, you should know that they are spoken by a man who knelt both before and afterwards to beg this infinite and indivisible Being, to whom he submits the whole of himself, that you should also submit yourself, for your own good and for his glory, and that strength might thereby be reconciled with this lowliness.

End of this discourse.

But what harm will come to you from taking this course? You will be faithful, honest, humble, grateful, doing good, a sincere and true friend. It is, of course, true; you will not take part in corrupt pleasure, in glory, in the pleasures of high living. But will you not have others?

I tell you that you will win thereby in this life, and that at every step you take along this path, you will see so much certainty of winning and so negligible a risk, that you will realize in the end that you have wagered on something certain and infinite, for which you have paid nothing.

Gottfried Wilhelm von Leibniz, "Principles of Nature and of Grace, Founded on Reason"

Introduction

Gottfried Leibniz (1646–1716) was a polymath, with achievements that included the invention of the differential calculus, who wrote essays and fragments on innumerable philosophical, scientific, and other topics. His only book, however, was the *Theodicy* of 1710, "A Vindication of the Justice of God" – an indication of how seriously Leibniz, the "Rationalist" *par excellence*, regarded the challenge of contemporary figures like Pierre Bayle. These so-called "fideists" argued that faith is required for belief in God's existence, since reason surely speaks *against* the existence of an allegedly benevolent being who created a world that is full of suffering and evil. Four years later, Leibniz wrote a succinct summary of his general metaphysical position and his theodicy for the benefit of Prince Eugene of Savoy. This summary, "Principles of Nature and Grace, Founded on Reason," encapsulates Leibniz's response to challenges like Bayle's.

The first few pages of this essay summarize the doctrines articulated in Leibniz's *Monadology* (see III.15). But in §7 Leibniz turns to the questions of why there is something rather than nothing, and why things exist as they do and not otherwise. Proper answers, he insists, must honor "the principle of sufficient reason," according to which nothing happens without there being a reason which necessitates it. In the following paragraph Leibniz concludes, in a rehearsal of the "cosmological argument" employed by many other theologians, that the reason there is something rather than nothing is God and his creation of the universe – for the cause of events must be sought "outside the series of [merely] contingent things" within the universe. Since God must be perfect, Leibniz is soon able (§10) to provide an answer to his second question. Things are as they are, and not otherwise, because they accord with God's "best possible plan," one that has resulted in a world which combines "the greatest variety together with the greatest order."

An important corollary, for Leibniz, of this "principle of the best" is that God's grace is granted to human beings, not through some interference with or disturbance of the natural order – through, say, miraculous intervention – but in perfect harmony with the natural order. "Grace perfects nature in making use of it."

Arthur Schopenhauer, who thought that ours is the *worst*, not the best, of all possible worlds, wrote that the sole merit of Leibniz's *Theodicy* was that it goaded Voltaire into writing his famous lampoon of Leibniz, *Candide*.[1] Certainly, Leibniz's "optimism" is today better known to readers through Dr Pangloss's advocacy of it in Voltaire's novel than through Leibniz's own writings. Voltaire, inspired

From Gottfried Wilhelm Leibniz, *Philosophical Writings*, ed. G. Parkinson, London: Dent, 1973, pp. 195–204 (some notes omitted).

to write this acerbic satire by the devastating Lisbon earthquake of 1755, is essentially repeating Bayle's point: it is impossible rationally to accept the existence of a benevolent and omnipotent God in the face of massive suffering and evil in a world allegedly created by Him.

Leibniz's critics, however, are guilty of confusion. They confuse the claim that the world is perfect *simpliciter* with the claim – the one Leibniz actually makes – that the world is as perfect as it is *possible* for it to be. Tragedies like the Lisbon earthquake might indeed demonstrate that the world is not perfect but, in Leibniz's view, have no bearing on the doctrine that it is as perfect as possible. He argues, in effect, that "what might seem a fault [e.g. an earthquake] from one perspective, would constitute a [still] greater evil from other points of view."[2] He would add, of course, that we human beings, with our "confused" perception and limited intelligence are incapable of attaining to that perspective from which we could recognize just why each "fault" is necessary for the optimal condition of the world. (The weakest sections in the *Theodicy*, which Schopenhauer castigates as "palpably sophistical," are those where Leibniz actually tries to show how this or that particular fault or evil contributes to the overall good.)

Leibniz is entirely unapologetic to those who accuse of him preaching complacent acceptance while, as it were, Rome burns. Indeed, he criticizes the Stoics for *forcing* themselves patiently to accept things and cultivate tranquility (§18). Anyone who has properly internalized "the principle of the best," he thinks, cannot but be happy about the condition of the world and his or her life in particular. True, we cannot, like God, "completely enjoy" the world, since we lack detailed understanding and appreciation of it. Nevertheless, our "perfect confidence" in God and His plan is bound to produce not only "present contentment" but the assurance of future happiness.

Notes

1   A. Schopenhauer, *The World as Will and Representation*, Vol. II, trans. E. Payne, New York: Dover, 1966, p. 582.
2   G. McDonald Ross, *Leibniz*, Oxford: Oxford University Press, 1984, p. 104.

Leibniz, "Principles of Nature and of Grace, Founded on Reason"

1. *Substance* is a being capable of action. It is simple or compound. *Simple substance* is that which has no parts. *Compound substance* is the combination of simple substances or *monads*. *Monas* is a Greek word which signifies unity or that which is one. Compounds or bodies are pluralities, and simple substances – that is lives, souls, minds – are unities. There must necessarily be simple substances everywhere, because without simple substances there could be no compounds; consequently the whole of nature is full of life.

2. Monads, having no parts, cannot be made or unmade. They can neither begin nor end naturally, and consequently they last as long as the universe, which will be changed but not destroyed. They cannot have shapes, otherwise they would have parts. Therefore one monad, in itself and at a particular moment, can only be distinguished from another by internal qualities and activities, which can be nothing else but its *perceptions* (that is to say, the representations in the simple of the compound or of that which is outside) and its *appetitions* (that is to say, its tendencies to pass from one perception to another), which are the principles of change. For the simplicity of substance does not preclude the possibility of a multiplicity of modifications, which indeed necessarily exist together in the same simple substance, and these modifications must consist in the variety of the relations of the simple substance to things which are outside. Just as in a *centre* or point, in itself perfectly simple, are found an infinity of angles formed by the lines which meet there.

3. All nature is a plenum. Everywhere there are simple substances, effectively separated from one another by actions of their own which are continually altering their relations; and each simple substance or distinct monad, which forms the centre of a compound substance (e.g. of an

animal) and the principle of its oneness, is surrounded by a *mass* composed of an infinity of other monads which constitute the body belonging to this central monad; corresponding to the affections of its body it represents, as in a kind of *centre*, the things which are outside of it. And this *body* is *organic*, when it forms a kind of automaton or natural machine, which is a machine not only as a whole but also in its smallest observable parts. And since because the world is a plenum everything is connected together, and each body acts on every other body more or less according to the distance, and is affected by it by reaction, it follows that every monad is a mirror that is alive or endowed with inner activity, is representative of the universe from its own point of view, and is as much regulated as the universe itself. The perceptions in the monad spring from one another according to the laws of the appetites or the *final causes of good and evil*, which consist in the observable perceptions, regulated or unregulated – in the same way as the changes of bodies and of external phenomena spring from one another according to the laws of *efficient causes*, that is to say of motions. Thus there is a perfect *harmony* between the perceptions of the monad and the motions of the bodies, pre-established at the outset between the system of efficient causes and the system of final causes. Herein consists the concord and the physical union of the soul and the body, which exists without the one being able to change the laws of the other.

4.   Each monad, together with a particular body, makes a living substance. Thus there is not only life everywhere, joined to members or organs, but there are also infinite degrees of it in the monads, some of them more or less dominating over others. But when the monad has its organs adjusted in such a way that by means of them the impressions they receive, and consequently the perceptions which represent them, are distinguished and heightened (as, for example, when by means of the shape of the humours of the eye rays of light are concentrated and act with more force), this may amount to *sensation*, that is to say, to a perception accompanied by *memory* – a perception, to wit, of which a certain echo long remains to make itself heard on occasion. Such a living being is called an *animal*, as its monad is called a *soul*. And when this soul is raised to the level of *reason*, it is something more sublime, and is reckoned as a mind, as will be

explained later. It is true that animals are sometimes in the condition of simple living beings and their souls in the condition of simple monads, to wit, when their perceptions are not sufficiently distinguished to be remembered, as occurs in a deep dreamless sleep or in a swoon. But perceptions which have become entirely confused must necessarily be developed again in animals, for reasons I shall give below (12). Thus it is well to distinguish between *perception*, which is the inner state of the monad representing external things, and *apperception*, which is *consciousness*, or the reflective knowledge of this inner state, and which is not given to all souls, nor at all times to the same soul. It is for want of this distinction that the Cartesians made the mistake of taking no account of perceptions which are not apperceived, as common people take no account of insensible bodies. It is this also which made these same Cartesians believe that minds alone are monads, and that there are no souls in animals, and still less other *principles of life*. And while, in thus denying sensations to animals, they have gone against the common opinion of men too much, so they have, on the other hand, taken too much account of the prejudices of the vulgar, in confusing a *long stupor*, which arises from a great confusion of perceptions, with *actual death*, in which all perception would cease. This teaching of theirs has confirmed the ill-founded belief in the destruction of some souls, and the pernicious view of certain people, self-styled free-thinkers, who have denied the immortality of ours.

5.   There is a connexion between the perceptions of animals, which bears some resemblance to reason: but it is based only on the memory of *facts* or effects, and not at all on the knowledge of *causes*. Thus a dog runs away from the stick with which he has been beaten, because memory represents to him the pain which was caused by that stick. And men, in so far as they are empiricists, that is to say in three-fourths of their actions, only act like brutes. For example, we expect that day will dawn tomorrow, because we have always experienced it to be so; it is only the astonomer who foresees it by reason, and even this prediction will ultimately fail when the cause of daylight, which is not eternal, ceases. But true reasoning depends on necessary or eternal truths (like the truths of logic, numbers, and geometry) which produce the indubitable connexion of ideas, and infallible inferences. Animals in which

such inferences cannot be observed are called *brutes*; but those which know these necessary truths are called *rational animals*, and their souls are called *minds*. These souls are capable of performing acts of reflexion, and of considering what is called self, substance, soul, mind – those things and truths, in short, which are immaterial. It is this which makes us capable of understanding science or demonstrative knowledge.

6. The researches of the moderns have taught us, and it is approved by reason, that the living things whose organs we know, that is to say plants and animals, do not come from putrefaction or chaos as the ancients believed, but from *preformed* seeds, and consequently from the transformation of pre-existing living things. There are little animals in the seeds of the large ones, which by means of conception assume a new vesture, which they appropriate, and which enables them to be nourished and to grow, so as to pass on to a wider stage, and propagate the large animal. It is true that the souls of human spermatic animals are not rational and only become so when through conception these animals are destined for human nature. And as animals are usually not born completely in conception or *generation*, so neither do they perish completely in what we call *death*; for it is reasonable that what does not begin naturally should not come to an end in the order of nature either. Thus, casting off their masks or their rags, they merely return to a more subtle scene, on which, however, they can be as sensible and as well ordered as on the greater one. And what has just been said of large animals occurs also in the generation and death of these spermatic animals themselves; that is to say, they have grown from other smaller spermatic animals, in comparison with which they can be reckoned large; for everything in nature proceeds *ad infinitum*. Thus not only souls but animals also are ingenerable and imperishable: they are only developed, enveloped, re-clad, stripped, transformed; souls never leave the whole of their body, and do not pass from one body to another which is entirely new to them. Thus there is no *metempsychosis*, but there is *metamorphosis*. Animals change, take on and put off parts only: in nutrition this takes place bit by bit, and by small insensible parts, but continually, while in conception and death when much is acquired or lost all at one time the change takes place rarely, but all at once and in a way that can be noticed.

7. Up till now we have spoken as *physicists* merely; now we must rise to *metaphysics*, making use of the *great principle*, commonly but little employed, which holds that *nothing takes place without sufficient reason*, that is to say that nothing happens without its being possible for one who has enough knowledge of things to give a reason sufficient to determine why it is thus and not otherwise. This principle having been laid down, the first question we are entitled to ask will be: *Why is there something rather than nothing?* For 'nothing' is simpler and easier than 'something'. Further, supposing that things must exist, it must be possible to give a reason *why they must exist just as they do* and not otherwise.

8. Now this sufficient reason of the existence of the universe cannot be found in the series of contingent things, that is to say, of bodies and of their representations in souls. For since matter is in itself indifferent to motion or to rest, and to one motion rather than another, it cannot itself contain the reason of motion, still less of a particular motion. And although the present motion which is in matter arises from the one before it, and this in its turn from the one before that, we are no further on however far we go; for the same question always remains. Thus the sufficient reason, which needs no further reason, must be outside this series of contingent things, and must lie in a substance which is the cause of this series, or which is a necessary being, bearing the reason of its existence within itself; otherwise we should still not have a sufficient reason, with which we could stop. And this final reason of things is called *God*.

9. This simple primary substance must include eminently the perfections which are contained in the derivative substances which are its effects. Thus it will have perfect power, knowledge, and will; that is to say, it will have omnipotence, omniscience, and supreme goodness. And as *justice*, taken in a very general sense, is nothing other than goodness in conformity with wisdom, there must clearly also be supreme justice in God. Reason, which has made things exist through Him, makes them also depend on Him in their existence and operation; and they are continually receiving from Him that which endows them with some perfection; but any imperfection which they retain comes from the essential and original limitation of the created thing.

10. It follows from the supreme perfection of God that in producing the universe He chose the best possible plan, containing the greatest variety together with the greatest order; the best arranged situation, place, and time; the greatest effect produced by the simplest means; the most power, the most knowledge, the most happiness and goodness in created things of which the universe admitted. For as all possible things have a claim to existence in the understanding of God in proportion to their perfections, the result of all these claims must be the most perfect actual world which is possible. Otherwise it would not be possible to explain why things have happened as they have rather than otherwise.

11. The supreme wisdom of God has made Him choose especially the *laws of motion* which are the best adjusted and the most fitted to abstract and metaphysical reasons. According to them there is always conserved the same quantity of total and absolute force or activity; the same quantity of relative force or reaction; the same quantity, finally, of force of direction. Moreover the activity is always equal to the reaction, and the whole effect is always equivalent to its full cause. It is surprising that those laws of motion discovered in our day, some of which I have myself discovered, cannot be explained merely by the consideration of *efficient causes* or of matter. For I have found that it is necessary to have recourse to *final causes*, and that these laws do not depend on the *principle of necessity* as do the truths of logic, arithmetic, and geometry, but on the *principle of fitness*, that is to say on the choice of wisdom. And this is one of the most effective and sensible proofs of the existence of God for those who are able to go deeply into these matters.

12. It follows, further, from the perfection of the Supreme Author, that not only is the order of the whole universe the most perfect possible, but also that each living mirror which represents the universe from its own point of view, that is to say each *monad*, each substantial centre, must have its perceptions and appetites regulated in the best way which is compatible with all the rest. From which it follows that *souls*, that is to say the most dominant monads, or rather animals themselves, cannot fail to wake up from the state of stupor in which they may be placed by death or by some other accident.

13. For everything is regulated in things once for all with as much order and agreement as possible, since supreme wisdom and goodness cannot act without perfect harmony: the present is big with the future, what is to come could be read in the past, what is distant is expressed in what is near. The beauty of the universe could be learnt in each soul, could one unravel all its folds which develop perceptibly only with time. But as each distinct perception of the soul includes an infinity of confused perceptions which embrace all the universe, the soul itself does not know the things which it perceives, except in so far as it has perceptions of them which are distinct and heightened: and it has perfection in proportion to its distinct perceptions. Each soul knows the infinite, knows everything, but confusedly. Just as when I am walking along the shore of the sea and hear the great noise it makes, though I hear the separate sounds of each wave of which the total sound is made up, I do not discriminate them one from another; so our confused perceptions are the result of the impressions which the whole universe makes on us. It is the same with each monad. God alone has a distinct knowledge of everything, for he is the source of everything. It has been very well said that he is like a centre which is everywhere; but his circumference is nowhere, since everything is present to him immediately, without being removed from this centre.

14. As regards the rational soul or *mind*, there is in it something more than in monads, or even in simple souls. It is not only a mirror of the universe of created things, but also an image of the Deity. The mind not only has a perception of the works of God, but is even capable of producing something like them, though on a small scale. For, not to mention the wonders of dreams, in which we invent without effort (but also without will) things we could only discover after much thinking when awake, our soul is architectonic in its voluntary activities also, and, discovering the sciences in accordance with which God had regulated things (*pondere, mensura, numero*,* etc.), it imitates in its own sphere, and in the little world in which it is allowed to act, what God performs in the great world.

15. For this reason all minds, whether of men or super-human spirits, entering as they do by virtue of reason and the eternal verities into a kind of society with God, are members of the City of God, that is to say of the most perfect state,

---

* 'by weight, measure, number', etc.

formed and governed by the greatest and best of monarchs: where there is no crime without punishment, no good action without proportionate reward, and finally as much virtue and happiness as is possible; and this, not by any derangement of nature, as if what God has in store for the soul might disturb the laws of the body, but by the actual order of natural things, by virtue of the harmony preestablished from all time between the realms of nature and of grace, between God as Architect and God as Monarch, in such a way that nature itself leads to grace, and grace perfects nature in making use of it.

16. Thus although reason cannot teach us the details of the great future, which are reserved for revelation, we can rest assured by this same reason that things are accomplished in a manner which exceeds our desires. Since, too, God is the most perfect and the most happy and consequently the most lovable of substances, and since *pure true love* consists in the state which causes pleasure to be felt in the perfections and happiness of the beloved, this love ought to give us the greatest pleasure of which a man is capable, when God is the object of it.

17. It is easy to love him as we ought if we know him as I have described. For although God is not sensible to our external senses, he is none the less very lovable and gives great pleasure. We see how much pleasure men derive from honours, although they do not consist of qualities that appear to the external senses. Martyrs and fanatics (although the affection of the latter is ill regulated) show of what the pleasure of the mind is capable: and what is more, even the pleasures of the senses are in the last resort intellectual pleasures, confusedly known. Music charms us although its beauty only consists in the harmony of numbers, and in the account which we do not notice, but which the soul none the less takes, of the beating or vibration of sounding bodies, which meet one another at certain intervals. The pleasures which the eye finds in proportions are of the same kind, and those caused by the other senses amount to much the same thing, although we may not be able to explain it so distinctly.

18. It may even be affirmed that love of God gives us here and now a foretaste of future felicity. And although it is disinterested, it constitutes of itself our greatest good and interest, even though we may not seek them in it, and consider only the pleasure which it gives without regard to the utility it produces; for it gives us a perfect confidence in the goodness of our Author and Master, which produces a true tranquillity of mind, not as in the Stoics, who resolutely force themselves to patience, but by a present contentment, which further assures us a future happiness. And apart from the present pleasure, nothing could be more useful for the future, for the love of God also fulfils our hopes, and leads us in the way of supreme happiness, because in virtue of the perfect order established in the universe, everything is done in the best possible way, as much for the general good as also for the greatest particular good of those who believe in it, and who are satisfied by the Divine government: which cannot fail to be the case with those who know how to love the Source of all good. It is true that supreme happiness (with whatever *beatific vision*, or knowledge of God, it may be accompanied) can never be complete because God, being infinite, cannot be entirely known. Thus our happiness will never consist, and ought not to consist, in a complete enjoyment, in which there would be nothing left to desire, and which would make our mind stupid, but in a perpetual progress to new pleasures and new perfections.

14

Matthew Tindal, *Christianity as Old as the Creation*, Chapters I, II, and VI

Introduction

At the time he was serving as third President of the United States, Thomas Jefferson (1743–1826) was also engaged in a project of scriptural criticism. Taking a blade to the pages of the Bible, Jefferson set about to remove surgically all those passages comprising distortion, superstition, or manipulation. Writing in 1813 to James Madison about the project, Jefferson argued that: "In extracting the pure principles which he [Jesus] taught, we should have to strip off the artificial vestments in which they have been muffled. . . . There will be found remaining the most sublime and benevolent code of morals which has ever been offered to man. I have performed this operation for my own use, by cutting verse by verse out of the printed book, and arranging the matter which is evidently his, and which is as easily distinguishable as diamonds in a dunghill." What remained amounted only to a slim "octavo of forty-six pages, of pure and unsophisticated doctrines."[1] Aside from the questions of whether or not the actual teachings of Jesus are "easily distinguishable" from other contents of the Bible and whether or not those teachings amount to a "sublime and benevolent code," Jefferson's project was not merely academic. It was also an effort

From Matthew Tindal, *Christianity as Old as the Creation*, London: Routledge/Thoemmes Press, 1995, pp. 1–18, 49–57 (notes omitted).

guided by an important current in the philosophy of religion – "deism."

Commonly described as originating in the work of seventeenth-century philosopher Herbert of Cherbury (1583–1648), deism may be more broadly thought of as a variant of the traditions of natural religion that weave through the western and eastern philosophical traditions. Responding to the profound religious conflict of the sixteenth and seventeenth centuries, Herbert searched for a way to reconcile the seemingly irreconcilable claims of religion. Herbert argued in *Tractatus de veritate prout distinguitur a revelatione, a verisimili, a possibili et a falso* (1624) that religious doctrines beyond those that can be verified using the innate ideas and common intuitions of the human mind ought to be ignored. There remain, he maintained, five essential principles common to Christianity and all true religions: (1) that there exists one deity; (2) that the deity should be worshipped; (3) that worshiping the deity entails acting in a morally proper manner; (4) that sin should be avoided and repented; and (5) that the deity will distribute just rewards and punishments. Charles Blount (1654–93) followed Herbert in these, adding to the list a belief in providence.[2]

The advance of deism, then, may be thought of as a series of attempts to pursue this project of rationally distinguishing a true, universal religion from divisive and baseless superstition. By many accounts, the rational project crashed on the shoals of David Hume's criticisms of natural religion, leaving philosophers with the choice of either a non-rational fideistic religion (based on faith alone; IV.18) or no religion at all (IV.20). Nevertheless, deistic gestures persist in those who scour scientific and philosophical theory, not only for ways to render them consistent with religious ideas, but also for intimations that science and rational philosophy actually verify basic elements of religion.[3]

Early modern science, Hobbesian critical materialism (V.10), and Spinoza's historical critique of scripture each influenced deism. John Locke, himself an Anglican rather than a deist, also had a deep impact. Locke's empiricist attack on innate ideas (II.9) was crucial in shifting the deists' methodological focus from a priori arguments lodged in the content and internal relations of ideas to a posteriori arguments grounded in human experience. His *Reasonableness of Christianity* (1695), following the position laid out in *Essay Concerning Human Understanding* (1690), argued that only those revelations that can be established through *a posteriori* methods are acceptable. John Toland followed Locke in this with his *Christianity not Mysterious* (1696). Anthony Collins in *Discourse of Free Thinking* (1713) pursued a similar line but surpassed his predecessors by clearly stating what other deists had circled around more cautiously – namely the idea that what is contrary to reason can be accepted neither as revelation nor as moral; the contradictory and literally immoral dimensions of scripture are at best regarded allegorically.

No deist work, however, achieved the readership of Matthew Tindal's *Christianity as Old as the Creation; or, the Gospel, a Republication of the Religion of Nature* (1730), which became popularly known as the "deist Bible." Oxford-educated Tindal (1657–1733), who had earlier in his life oscillated between Catholicism and Anglicanism, first gained notoriety through his work on the liberty of religion and church-state relations. He deploys in *Christianity as Old as the Creation* a host of arguments, novel and traditional, in defense of deism. According to Tindal, true religion must be eternal (or at least as old as the universe) and universally accessible to all humankind (including the millions who have lived in Asia and elsewhere without exposure to the church). If "God designed all," he writes, "Mankind should at all times know, what he wills them to know, believe, profess, and practice"; God "has given them no other Means for this, but the Use of

Reason." While the truths of Christian scripture, therefore, are not false, they are redundant and unnecessary to the practice of religion.

Since however miracles, responses to prayer, and providential intercessions are arguably contrary to reason, later deists like Tom Paine (V.16) and Ethan Allen increasingly rejected them, as well as scripture *per se*. In his *Age of Reason* (1794), Paine argues that the only true scripture is the "Bible of Creation." "The word of God," Paine writes, "is the creation we behold."[4] Ethan Allen maintains in *Reason, The Only Oracle of Man* (1784) that those "things in nature which we do understand are not miraculous to us, and those things which we do not understand, we cannot with any propriety adjudge to be miraculous."[5] By the time, therefore, deism reaches those like Thomas Jefferson and Ben Franklin, its separation from Christianity and revealed religion is nearly complete.[6]

Notes

1 "The Philosophy of Jesus of Nazareth" (completed in 1804); Jefferson later reworked the text as *The Life and Morals of Jesus of Nazareth* (completed in 1820). Cf. Thomas Jefferson, *The Jefferson Bible: The Life and Morals of Jesus of Nazareth*, Boston, MA: Beacon Press (2001).

2 *Anima mundi* (1679), *Great Is Diana of the Ephesians* (1680), *The Two First Books of Philostratus Concerning the Life of Apollonius Tyaneus*, (1680), *Religio laici* (1683), *Miracles, No Violations of Nature* (1683), and *The Oracles of Reason* (posthumously, 1693).

3 One might, for example, cite persistent investigations into "intelligent design" (cf. IV.18).

4 Thomas Paine, *The Complete Works of Thomas Paine*, ed. P. S. Foner, New York: Citadel Press, 1945, p. 482.

5 Ethan Allen, *Reason, The Only Oracle of Man*, New York: Burt Franklin, 1972, VII, §3, 254. Allen and Paine, like many other deists, also argue that miracles and providential intercessions, which entail God's breaking and interfering with the order of natural law, is inconsistent with God's perfection – since a perfect being would have initially established those laws in a way that they would never need to be broken. If providence operates, for many

deists, it can only be the sort of providence where the deity has so arranged the natural order of things that the proper outcomes are realized without tampering with the clock-work of creation.

6 Franklin (1706–90) himself produced a number of quasi-deistical works, including: *Articles of Belief and Acts of Religion* (1728) and *On the Providence of God in the Government of the World* (1732).

Tindal, *Christianity as Old as the Creation*

Chapter I

That God, at all Times, has given Mankind sufficient Means of knowing what he requires of them; and what those Means are.

A.   THIS early Visit, Sir, gives me hopes it will not be a short one.

B.   I come to talk with you on a Subject, which may, perhaps, keep me longer with you than you desire.

A.   YOUR uncommon Temper and Candor, in debating even the most important Points, will always make your Conversation agreeable, tho' ever so long; but pray, what is to be the Subject of our morning's Discourse?

B.   I was yesterday in company with a great many Clergymen, it being our Bishop's primary Visitation, where the Complaint was general, of the Coldness and Indifference, with which people receiv'd the speculative Points of Christianity, and all its holy Rites; for which formerly they had shewn so great a Zeal. This Coldness they chiefly imputed to those *Low Churchmen*, who lay the main stress on *Natural Religion*; and withall so magnify the Doctrine of *Sincerity*, as in effect to place all Religions on a level, where the Professors are alike sincere. The Promoters of these Notions, as well as these Notions themselves, were expos'd with warmth; how justly, I will not determine, till we have talk'd the matter over with our usual Freedom: For which reason, I have made you this early Visit, and wou'd be glad to know the Sentiments of so good a Judge, on these two important Points; viz. *Sincerity*, and *Natural Religion*.

A.   I thank you for this Favour, and shall freely tell you, I so little agree with those Gentlemen in relation to Sincerity, that I think a sincere

Examination into religious matters can't be too much press'd; this being the only way to discover true Christianity. The Apostles thought themselves oblig'd, in making Proselytes, to recommend an impartial Search; they both desir'd, and requir'd Men *to judge for themselves, to prove all things*, &c. this they thought necessary, in order to renounce a Religion, which the Force of Education had impress'd on their Minds; and embrace another directly contrary to the Notions and Prejudices they had imbib'd. Nay, even those very Men, who most ridicule the Doctrine of Sincerity, never fail on other Occasions to assert, that Infidelity is owing to the want of a sincere Examination; and that whosoever impartially considers Christianity, must be convinc'd of its Truth. And I might add, That could we suppose, a sincere Examination wou'd not always produce this Effect, yet must it always make Men acceptable to God; since that is all God can require; all that it is in their power to do for the Discovery of his Will. These, in short, are my Sentiments as to this point; and as to the other, I think, too great a stress can't be laid on *Natural* Religion; which, as I take it, differs not from *Reveal'd*, but in the manner of its being communicated: The one being the Internal, as the other the External Revelation of the same unchangeable Will of a Being, who is alike at all times infinitely wise and good.

B.   SURELY, Sir, this must be extremely heterodox. Can you believe, that *Natural* and *Reveal'd* Religion differ in nothing, but the Manner of their being convey'd to us?

A.   As heterodox as I may seem at present, I doubt not, but by asking you a few Questions, to let you see, I advance nothing in either of these Points without Reason; and in order to it, I desire to be inform'd, whether God has not, from the Beginning, given Mankind some Rule, or Law for their Conduct? And whether the observing that, did not make 'em acceptable to him?

B.   THERE can be no doubt, but the observing such a Law, must have answered the End for which it was given; and made Men acceptable to God.

A.   WHAT more can any external Revelation do, than render Men acceptable to God? Again, If God, then, from the beginning, gave Men a Religion; I ask, was that Religion imperfect, or perfect?

B.   MOST perfect, without doubt; since no Religion can come from a Being of infinite Wisdom and Perfection, but what is absolutely perfect.

A.   CAN, therefore, a Religion absolutely perfect, admit of any Alteration; or be capable of Addition, or Diminution; and not be as immutable as the Author of it? Can Revelation, I say, add any thing to a Religion thus absolutely perfect, universal and immutable? Besides, if God has given Mankind a Law, he must have given them likewise sufficient means of knowing it; he wou'd, otherwise, have defeated his own Intent in given it; since a Law, as far as it is unintelligible, ceases to be a Law. Shall we say, that God, who had the forming human Understanding, as well as his own Laws, did not know how to adjust the one to the other?

IF God at all times was *willing all Men should come to the knowledge of his Truth*, cou'd not his infinite Wisdom and Power, at all times, find sufficient means, for making Mankind capable of knowing, what his infinite Goodness design'd they shou'd know?

B.   I grant you, that God was always willing, that ALL Men should come to the Knowledge of True Religion; and we say, that the Christian Religion being the Only True, and Absolutely Perfect Religion, was what God, from the Beginning, design'd for all Mankind.

A.   IF so, it follows, That the *Christian* Religion has existed from the Beginning; and that God, both *Then*, and *Ever since*, has continued to give all Mankind sufficient Means to know it; and that 'tis their Duty to know, believe, profess, and practise it: so that *Christianity*, tho' the Name is of a later Date, must be as old, and as extensive, as human Nature; and, as the Law of our Creation, must have been Then implanted in us by God himself.

B.   IT would be too presuming in us poor Mortals, to pretend to account for the Methods Providence takes, in relation to the Discovery of its Will; and therefore, a Person of less Moderation might condemn your Questions, as captious, presumptuous, and founded in Heterodoxy.

A.   IF God never intended Mankind should at any time be without Religion, or have false Religions; and there be but One True Religion, which ALL have been ever bound to believe and profess; I can't see any Heterodoxy in affirming, that the Means to effect this End of infinite Wisdom, must be as universal and extensive as the End itself; or that all Men, at all times, must have had sufficient Means to discover whatever God designed they should know, and practise. I do not mean by this, That All should have equal Knowledge; but that All should have what is sufficient for the Circumstances they are in.

B.   SINCE you have ask'd me Questions, let me, in my turn, demand of you, What are your Sentiments in this matter? Particularly, *What are those Means, which, you suppose, God has, at all times, given the whole Race of Mankind, to enable them to discover what he wills them to know, believe, profess, and practise?*

A.   I ask'd you those few Questions at present, not to determine the Point; but only to let you see, you had no reason to be surpris'd at my saying, *Natural and Revealed Religion only differ as to the Manner of their being communicated.* I shall now readily answer your Questions: And, as I think it my Duty never to disown my religious Sentiments, so I freely declare, that the Use of *those Faculties*, by which Men are distinguish'd from Brutes, is the only Means they have to discern whether there is a God; and whether he concerns himself with human Affairs, or has given them any Laws; and what those Laws are? And as Men have no other Faculties to judge with, so their using these after the best manner they can, must answer the End for which God gave them, and justify their Conduct. For,

IF God will judge Mankind as they are accountable, that is, as they are rational; the Judgment must hold an exact Proportion to the Use they make of their Reason. And it wou'd be in vain to use it, if the due Use of it wou'd not justify them before God: And Men would be in a miserable Condition indeed, if, whether they used it, or not, they should be alike criminal. And if God designed all Mankind shou'd at all times know, what he wills them to know, believe, profess, and practise; and has given them no other Means for this, but the Use of Reason; Reason, human

Reason, must then be that Means: For as God has made us rational Creatures, and Reason tells us, that 'tis his Will, that we act up to the Dignity of our Natures; so 'tis Reason must tell when we do so. What God requires us to know, believe, profess, and practise, must be in itself a reasonable Service; but whether what is offer'd to us as such, be really so, 'tis Reason alone which must judge. As the Eye is the sole Judge of what is visible; the Ear of what is audible; so Reason, of what is reasonable. If then Reason was given to bring them to the Knowledge of God's Will, that must be sufficient to produce its intended Effect, and can never bring Men to take that for his Will, which he designed they, by using their Reason, should avoid as contrary to it.

B.   IF Men, having done all in their power, all that God requires of them, to find out his Will, should fall into opposite Sentiments; must it not be the Will of God that it should be so? Can God will such a previous Examination, and not will what he foreknows must be the necessary Consequence?

A.   THERE is, I think, no way to avoid this Objection, of *God's willing Contrarieties*; but by supposing he requires nothing of Men, but what is founded on the Nature of Things, and the immutable Relations they bear to one another; and what, consequently, they are, as far as concerns 'em, capable of knowing. But this Objection is unanswerable by those who believe the Will of God is not always thus founded; but may contain many merely positive things: since Men may, after having taken all possible care to be in the right, have very opposite Sentiments, and be oblig'd, by the Will of God, to hold and act Contrarieties.

B.   THO' this Subject is attended with the utmost Difficulties, yet I find little or nothing said to solve 'em. I, for my part, know not how to deny Mens being acceptable to God, whatever their Opinions may be, after having used all the Means God has endow'd 'em with for the Discovery of his Will; and yet I don't know how to admit it: For then, what Religion soever Men are of, if they have duly us'd such Means as God ordain'd for the Discovery of his Will; That, I say, how opposite soever to Christianity, must be the Religion God design'd 'em. And, on the other hand, should I own, that the duly using those Means would have caus'd Men to have been all of one Religion; yet I can't see how that cou'd be

the Christian Religion, except it has existed from the Beginning; and all Men, at all times, have had sufficient Means to discover it. For,

IF God was always willing, That *All Men should come to the Knowledge of his Truth*; and there never was a time when God intended Men should have no Religion, or such an imperfect Religion which cou'd not answer the End of its being instituted by an infinitely wise Legislator: This seems, to my *bewilder'd* Reason, to imply, that there was, from the Beginning, but One True Religion, which all Men might know was their Duty to embrace. And if this is true, I can't well conceive how this Character can consist with *Christianity*; without allowing it, at the same time, to be *as old as the Creation*. And yet, notwithstanding all these seeming Difficulties, I am confident the Christian Religion is the Only True Religion. But since these Difficulties are of your raising, I may, in justice, expect that you should solve 'em.

A.   THIS, I must own, is a difficult Point: However, I shall tell you my Sentiments; which I, far from being a *Dogmatizer*, am ready to give up, if you can frame any other *Hypothesis*, not liable to the same Objections, or others equally strong; tho' I may venture to say, that I take mine to be the Only one which can give any tolerable Satisfaction to your present Doubts. And therefore I shall attempt to shew you, That Men, if they sincerely endeavour to discover the Will of God, will perceive, that there's a *Law of Nature*, or *Reason*; which is so call'd as being a Law which is common, or natural, to all rational Creatures; and that this Law, like its Author, is absolutely perfect, eternal, and unchangeable: and that the Design of the Gospel was not to add to, or take from this Law; but to free Men from that Load of Superstition which had been mix'd with it: So that TRUE CHRISTIANITY is not a Religion of Yesterday, but what God, at the Beginning, dictated, and still continues to dictate to Christians, as well as others. If I am so happy as to succeed in this Attempt, I hope not only fully to satisfy your Doubts, but greatly to advance the Honour of *External* Revelation; by shewing the perfect Agreement between *That* and *Internal* Revelation; and by so doing, destroy one of the most successful Attempts that has been made on Religion, by setting the Laws of God at variance.

BUT first I must premise, That in supposing an External Revelation, I take it for granted, that there's sufficient Evidence of the Person's being sent from God who publish'd it: And I further own, that this divine Person, by living up to what he taught, has set us a noble Example; and that as he was highly exalted for so doing, so we, if we use our best Endeavours, may expect a suitable Reward. This, and every thing of the same Nature, I freely own, which is not inconsistent with the Law of God's being the same, whether internally, or externally reveal'd.

B.   YOUR Design, I must own, is highly commendable; but in order to succeed, you are to prove two things. *First*, That the supreme Governour of Mankind has given his Subjects an universal Law, which they, when they come to the Use of their Reason, are capable of knowing. *Secondly*, That the Divine Precepts must be the same, whether internally, or externally reveal'd. If you prove these two Points, you will entirely clear my Doubts; but I almost despair of your doing it, since you seem to me to advance a New *Hypothesis*.

A.   HEAR the Evidence, and then judge. But before I produce it, lest the suppos'd Novelty of this Opinion may prejudice you, I shall put you in mind of what Archbishop *Laud* says upon a like Occasion:*

"That when Errors are grown by Age and Continuance to strength; they who speak for the Truth, tho' far older, are ordinarily challeng'd for bringing in new Opinions: and there's no greater Absurdity stirring this Day in *Christendom*."

NOW, by putting me to prove, that there is a *Law of Nature*, you, I suppose, have a mind to hear what I can say on this Subject. Since none then that believe there's a God, who governs Mankind, but believe he has given them a Law for the governing their Actions; this being imply'd in the very Notion of Governour and

Governed: And since the Law by which he governs Men, and his Government must commence together, and extend alike to all his Subjects; "Is it not," *as Bishop* Tillotson *observes*,†

"a great Mistake, to think that the Obligation of Moral Duties does solely depend upon the Revelation of God's Will made to us in the Holy Scriptures? Is it not plain, that Mankind was always under a *Law*, even before God made an external or extraordinary Revelation? Else, how cou'd God judge the World? How should they, to whom the Word of God never came, be acquitted, or condemned at the last Day? for where there is no Law, there can neither be Obedience, nor Transgression."

IF then, it be absurd to suppose, that Men, tho' they liv'd ever so impiously and immorally, did nothing which God had forbid them; or if ever so piously and virtuously, nothing that God had commanded them; must there not always have been an universal Law so fully promulgated to Mankind, that they could have no just Plea from their Ignorance, not to be tried by it. And cou'd any thing less than its being founded on the Nature of Things, and the Relation Men stand in to God, and one another, visible at all times to all, make it thus universally promulgated? But further to illustrate this Matter; can it be imagined, that if God has been so good to all other Animals, as to give them, not in one Country only, but in all Places whatsoever, sufficient means to act for their own Preservation; that he has had less kindness for the immortal Souls of those made after his own Image, and has not given them, at one time as well as another, and at one place as well as another, sufficient means to provide for their eternal Happiness? Or,

CAN it be suppos'd, an infinitely good and gracious Being, which gives Men notice, by their Senses, what does good or hurt to their Bodies; has had less regard for their immortal Parts, and has not given them at all times, by the Light of their Understanding, sufficient means to discover what makes for the good of their Souls; but

* *Laud*'s Pref. against *Fisher*. [William Laud (1573–1645), Archbishop of Canterbury (1633–45), supporter of Charles I and of the doctrine of the divine right of kings. Accused of treason by the Long Parliament in 1640, he was beheaded on Tower Hill. This quote is taken from the preface of 'An Answer to Mr. Fisher's Relation of a Third Conference . . .' (1624; the conference took place before King James in 1622); cf. *A Relation of the Conference between William Laud, the Late Arch-bishop of Canterbury, and Mr. Fisher the Jesuite, by Command of King James* (1639).]

† Pref to *Wilkins* of *Nat. Relig.* [John Wilkins (1614–72), *Of the Principles and Duties of Natural Religion* (1675). The text was begun by Wilkins but finished by his son in-law, John Tillotson (1630–1694), who became Archbishop of Canterbury and worked to reconcile dissenters with the Church of England.]

has necessitated them, or any of them, to continue from Age to Age in destructive Ignorance or Error? To press this matter further, let me ask you, Whether there is not a clear and distinct Light, that enlightens all Men; and which, the Moment they attend to it, makes them perceive those eternal Truths, which are the Foundation of all our Knowledge? And is it not God himself who illuminates them? What other Reason then can you assign, why infinite Wisdom should act thus; but to give Mankind standing Rules to distinguish Truth from Falshood, especially in matters of the highest consequence to their eternal as well as temporal Happiness?

THERE has, no doubt, been a great number of traditional Religions succeeding one another; and, as far as we know, there is no traditional Religion, which has, except in Name, continu'd the same for any long time; and tho' there are a great number of Sects, who go under the same common Denomination, yet they are almost as much divided among themselves, as if they own'd different Religions; and accordingly charge one another with erring fundamentally; yet all these agree in acknowledging a *Law of Nature*, and that they are indispensably obliged to obey its Dictates: So that this *Light of Nature*, like that of the Sun, is universal; and wou'd, did not Men shut the Eyes of their Understanding, or suffer others to blind them, soon disperse all those Mists and Fogs, which arise either from false Traditions, or false Interpretations of the true Tradition.

Chapter II

That the Religion of Nature consists in observing those Things, which our Reason, by considering the Nature of God and Man, and the Relation we stand in to him and one another, demonstrates to be our Duty; and that those Things are plain; and likewise What they are.

B. THAT we may the better know whether the *Law,* or *Religion of Nature* is universal, and the Gospel a Republication of it, and not a new Religion; I desire you will give a Definition of the *Religion of Nature.*

A. BY *Natural Religion*, I understand the Belief of the Existence of a God, and the Sense and Practice of those Duties which result from the Knowledge we, by our Reason, have of him and his Perfections; and of ourselves, and our own Imperfections; and of the relation we stand in to him and our Fellow-Creatures: so that the *Religion of Nature* takes in every thing that is founded on the Reason and Nature of things. Hence *Grotius* defines the *Law of Nature* to be *Dictatum rectae rationis, indicans actui alicui, ex ejus convenientia aut disconvenientia cum ipsa natura rationali, inesse moralem turpitudinem, aut necessitatem moralem, ac consequenter ab auctore naturae Deo talem actum aut vetari aut preaecipi.**

I suppose you will allow, that 'tis evident by the *Light of Nature,* that there is a God; or, in other words, a Being absolutely perfect, and infinitely happy in himself, who is the Source of all other Beings; and that what Perfections soever the Creatures have, they are wholly deriv'd from him.

B. THIS, no doubt, has been demonstrated over and over; and I must own, that I can't be more certain of my own Existence, than of the Existence of such a Being.

A. SINCE then it is demonstrable there is such a Being, it is equally demonstrable, that the Creatures can neither add to, or take from the Happiness of that Being; and that he cou'd have no Motive in framing his Creatures, or in giving Laws to such of them as he made capable of knowing his Will, but their own Good.

TO imagine he created them at first for his own sake, and has since required things of them for that Reason, is to suppose he was not perfectly happy in himself before the Creation; and that the Creatures, by either observing, or not observing the Rules prescrib'd them, cou'd add to, or take from his Happiness.

IF then a Being infinitely happy in himself, cou'd not command his Creatures any thing for his own Good; nor an all-wise Being things to no end or purpose; nor an all-good Being any thing but for their good: It unavoidably follows, nothing can be a part of the divine Law, but what tends

---

* Lib. I.C.I. par. 10 [Hugo Grotius (Huig de Groot; 1583–1645), *De jure belli ac pacis* (1625), "Natural law is a dictate of right reason indicating that an act, on account of its conformity or lack of conformity with rational nature, has in it a quality of moral turpitude or moral necessity, and that consequently such an act is either commanded or prohibited by God, the author of nature." B. Tierny, *The Idea of Natural Rights* (Grand Rapids: Wm. B. Eerdmans Publishing Co., 1997) pg. 327.]

to promote the common Interest, and mutual Happiness of his rational Creatures; and every thing that does so, must be a part of it.

AS God can require nothing of us, but what makes for our Happiness; so he, who can't envy us any Happiness our Nature is capable of, can forbid us those Things only, which tend to our Hurt; and this we are as certain of, as that there is a God infinitely happy in himself, infinitely good and wise: and as God can design nothing by his Laws but our Good, so by being infinitely powerful, he can bring every thing to pass which he designs for that End.

FROM the Consideration of these Perfections, we cannot but have the highest Veneration, nay, the greatest Adoration and Love for this supreme Being; who, that we may not fail to be as happy as possible for such Creatures to be, has made our acting for our *present*, to be the only Means of obtaining our *future* Happiness; so that we can't sin against him, but by acting against ourselves, *i.e.* our reasonable Natures: These Reflections, which occur to every one who in the least considers, must give us a wonderful and surprizing Sense of the divine Goodness, fill us with Admiration, Transport and Extasy; (of which we daily see among contemplative Persons remarkable Instances): And not only force us to express a never-failing Gratitude in Raptures of the highest Praise and Thanksgiving; but make us strive to imitate him in our extensive Love to our Fellow-Creatures: And thus copying after the Divine Original, and taking God himself for our Precedent, must conform us to his Image, who is all Perfection and all Happiness; and who must have an inexhaustible Love for all, who thus endeavour to imitate him. And here

THE difference between the supreme Being, infinitely happy in himself, and the Creatures who are not so, is, That all his Actions, in relation to his Creatures, flow from a pure disinterested Love; whereas the Spring of all the Actions of the Creatures is their own Good: *We love God, because he first lov'd us*;* and consequently, our Love to him will be in proportion to our Sense of his Goodness to us. Nor can we in the least vary from those Sentiments, which the Consideration of the divine Attributes implant in us, but we must in proportion take off from the Goodness of

God, and from those Motives we have to love him as we ought.

OUR Reason, which gives us a Demonstration of the divine Perfections, affords us the same concerning the Nature of those Duties God requires; not only with relation to himself, but to ourselves, and one another: These we can't but see, if we look into ourselves, consider our own Natures, and the Circumstances God has plac'd us in with relation to our Fellow-Creatures, and what conduces to our mutual Happiness: Our Senses, our Reason, the Experience of others as well as our own, can't fail to give us sufficient Information.

WITH relation to ourselves, we can't but know how we are to act; if we consider, that God has endow'd Man with such a Nature, as makes him necessarily desire his own Good; and, therefore, he may be sure, that God, who has bestow'd this Nature on him, cou'd not require any thing of him in prejudice of it; but on the contrary, that he shou'd do every thing which tends to promote the Good of it. The Health of the Body, and the Vigor of the Mind, being highly conducing to our Good, we must be sensible we offend our Maker, if we indulge our Senses to the prejudice of these: And because not only all irregular Passions, all unfriendly Affections carry their own Torment with them, and endless Inconveniences attend the excess of sensual Delights; and all immoderate Desires (human Nature being able to bear but a certain Proportion) disorder both Mind and Body; we can't but know we ought to use great Moderation with relation to our Passions, or in other Words, govern all our Actions by Reason; That, and our true Interest being inseparable. And in a word, whoever so regulates his natural Appetites, as will conduce most to the exercise of this Reason, the health of his Body, and the pleasure of his Senses, taken and consider'd together, (since herein his Happiness consists) may be certain he can never offend his Maker; who, as he governs all things according to their Natures, can't but expect his rational Creatures shou'd act according to their Natures.

AS to what God expects from Man with relation to each other; every one must know his Duty, who considers that the common Parent of Mankind has the whole Species alike under his protection, and will equally punish him for injuring others, as he would others for injuring him; and consequently, that it is his duty to deal

---

* I John 4.19.

with them, as he expects they should deal with him in the like Circumstances. How much this is his duty, every one must perceive, who considers himself as a weak Creature, not able to subsist without the Assistance of others, who have it in their power to retaliate the Usage he gives them: And that he may expect, if he breaks those Rules which are necessary for Mens mutual Happiness, to be treated like a common Enemy, not only by the Persons injur'd, but by all others; who, by the common Ties of Nature, are oblig'd to defend, and assist each other. And not only a Man's own particular Interest, but that of his Children, his Family, and all that's dear to him, obliges him to promote the common Happiness, and to endeavour to convey the same to Posterity.

ALL *Moralists* agree, that human Nature is so constituted, that Men can't live without Society and mutual Assistance; and that God has endow'd them with Reason, Speech, and other Faculties, evidently fitted to enable them to assist each other in all the Concerns of Life; that, therefore, 'tis the Will of God who gives them this Nature, and endows them with these Faculties, that they should employ them for their common Benefit and mutual Assistance. And the *Philosophers*, who saw that all Society would be dissolv'd, and Men soon become destitute of even the Necessaries of Life, and be a prey to one another, if each Man was only to mind himself, and his own single Interest; and that every thing pointed out the Necessity of mutual Benevolence among Mankind; did therefore rightly judge, that Men were by their Nature fram'd to be useful to one another; *Ad tuendos conservandosque; homines hominem natum esse*, says *Cicero.** Therefore, every Man, for the sake of others as well as himself, is not to disable his Body or Mind by such Irregularities, as may make him less serviceable to them.

IN short, considering the variety of Circumstances Men are under, and these continually changing, as well as being for the most part unforeseen; 'tis impossible to have Rules laid down by any *External* Revelation for every particular Case; and therefore, there must be some standing Rule, discoverable by the *Light of Nature*, to direct us in all such Cases. And we can't be more certain, that 'tis the Will of God,

that those Effects which flow from natural Causes should so flow; than we are, that 'tis the Will of God, that Men shou'd observe, whatever the Nature of Things, and the Relation they have to one another, make fit to be observ'd; or in other Words, we can't but know, if we in the least consider, that, whatever Circumstances Men are plac'd in, by the universal Cause of all things; that 'tis his eternal and immutable Will, by his placing them in these Circumstances, that they act as these require. 'Tis absurd to imagine we are oblig'd to act thus in some Cases, and not in others; when the reason for acting thus in all is the same, This Consideration alone will direct a Man how to act in all Conditions of Life, whether *Father, Son, Husband, Servant, Subject, Master, King,* &c. Thus we see how the reason of things, or the relation they have to each other, teaches us our Duty in all cases whatever. And I may add, that the better to cause Men to observe those Rules, which make for their mutual Benefit, infinite Goodness has sown in their Hearts Seeds of Pity, Humanity and Tenderness, which, without much difficulty, cannot be eradicated; but nothing operates more strongly than that Desire Men have of being in Esteem, Credit, and Reputation with their Fellow-Creatures; not to be obtain'd without acting on the Principles of natural Justice, Equity, Benevolence, &c.

IN a word, as a most beneficent Disposition in the supreme Being is the Source of all his Actions in relation to his Creatures; so he has implanted in Man, whom he has made after his own Image, a Love for his Species; the gratifying of which, in doing Acts of Benevolence, Compassion, and Good Will, produces a Pleasure that never satiates; as on the contrary, Actions of Ill-Nature, Envy, Malice, &c. never fail to produce Shame, Confusion, and everlasting Self-reproach.

AND now let any one say, how 'tis possible God could more fully make known his Will to all intelligent Creatures, than by making every thing within and without them a Declaration of it, and an Argument for observing it.

HAVING thus discovered our Duty, we may be sure it will always be the same; since Inconstancy, as it argues a Defect either of Wisdom or Power, can't belong to a Being infinitely wise and powerful: What unerring Wisdom has once instituted, can have no Defects; and as God is intirely free from all Partiality, his Laws must alike extend to all Times and Places.

---

* De fin[ibus]. 1.3. cap 20. [See I.7.]

FROM these Premises, I think, we may boldly draw this Conclusion, That if Religion consists in the Practice of those Duties, that result from the Relation we stand in to God and Man, our Religion must always be the same. If God is unchangeable, our Duty to him must be so too; if Human Nature continues the same, and Men at all times stand in the same Relation to one another, the Duties which result from thence too, must always be the same: And consequently our Duty both to God and Man must, from the Beginning of the World to the End, remain unalterable; be always alike plain and perspicuous; neither chang'd in Whole, or Part: which demonstrates that no Person, if he comes from God, can teach us any other Religion, or give us any Precepts, but what are founded on those Relations. *Heaven and Earth shall sooner pass away,* than *one Tittle of this* Eternal *Law shall either be abrogated, or alter'd.*

TO sum up all in few words: As Nature teaches Men to unite for their mutual Defence and Happiness, and Government was instituted solely for this End; so to make this more effectual, was Religion, which reaches the Thoughts, wholly ordain'd; it being impossible for God, in governing the World, to propose to himself any other End than the Good of the Governed: and consequently, whoever does his best for the Good of his Fellow-Creatures, does all that either God or Man requires. Thus from the Consideration of our own Imperfections, which we continually feel; and the Perfections of our Creator, which we constantly find in all his Works; we may arrive at the Knowledge of our Duty, both to our Creator and Fellow-Creatures. Hence, I think, we may define, True Religion to consist in a constant Disposition of Mind to do all the Good we can; and thereby render ourselves acceptable to God in answering the End of his Creation.

Chapter VI

That the Religion of Nature is an absolutely perfect Religion; and that external Revelation can neither add to, nor take from its Perfection: and that True Religion, whether internally or externally reveal'd, must be the same.

HAVING prov'd, that God requires nothing for his own sake; I shall now, the way being thus prepar'd, shew you, *That the Religion of Nature is absolutely perfect*; and *that external Revelation can neither add to, nor take from its Perfection:* And in order to it let me ask you, why you believe the Gospel a Law of absolute Perfection, incapable of any Addition, Diminution, or Alteration?

B. BECAUSE 'tis the last Law of God's giving.

A. WAS it not such in itself, That cou'd not make it so; since the Law given to the *Jews* was for many Ages the Only External Law: And yet, I suppose, you grant that this abrogated Law was far from deserving such a Character; but were there anything in this Argument, it makes wholly for the Law of Nature, since That is not only the first, but the last Law of God's giving; if That can be said to be last, which is eternal: A Law, by which God governs his own Actions; and by which he expects all the rational World shou'd govern theirs. And therefore, notwithstanding the Promulgation of the Gospel, he continues daily to implant it in the Minds of all Men, Christians as well as others; and consequently, 'tis as necessary for them as for Others; as necessary since, as before the Coming of Christ: And I may add too, not only necessary to be observ'd in this World, and ten Thousand more, were there so many; but in Heaven itself, and that too for ever.

B. SHOU'D I grant that my Argument, from the Gospel's being the last Law of God's giving, does not fully prove its absolute Perfection; yet it will undeniably follow from the great Agreement there is between That and the Law of Nature, it neither forbidding what that requires, nor requiring what That forbids; and in a Word, containing nothing in it unworthy, but every Thing worthy, of an absolutely-perfect Law-giver.

A. IN saying This, you own the Law of Nature to be the Standard of Perfection; and that by It we must judge antecedently to any traditional Religion what is, or is not a Law absolutely perfect, and worthy of such a Being for its Legislator.

B. INDEED, it must be own'd, that Divines as well as Others, make the same concessions in relation to Natural Religion, which Dr. *Prideaux* does in his celebrated Letter to *Deists* at the End of *Mahomet's* Life:*

---

* P. 127. Edit. 7. 8 vo. [Humphrey Prideaux (1648–1724), *Letter to the Deists* (1696), *Life of Mahomet* (1697).]

"Let what is written in all the Books of the New Testament be try'd by That which is the Touchstone of all Religions; I mean that Religion of Nature and Reason, which God has written in the Hearts of every one of us from the first Creation; and if it varies from it in any one Particular, if it prescribes any one Thing, which may in the minutest Circumstances thereof be contrary to its Righteousness, I will then acknowledge this to be an Argument against us, strong enough to overthrow the whole Cause, and make all Things else that can be said for it totally ineffectual for its Support."

A.   I desire no more than to be allow'd, That there's a Religion of Nature and Reason written in the Hearts of every one of us from the first Creation; by which all Mankind must judge of the Truth of any instituted Religion whatever; and if it varies from the Religion of Nature and Reason in any one Particular, nay, in the minutest Circumstance, That alone is an Argument, which makes all Things else that can be said for its Support totally ineffectual. If so, must not Natural Religion and external Revelation, like two Tallies, exactly answer one another; without any other Difference between them, but as to the Manner of their being deliver'd? And how can it be otherwise? Can Laws be imperfect, where a Legislator is absolutely perfect? Can Time discover any Thing to him, which he did not foresee from Eternity? And as his Wisdom is always the same, so is his Goodness; and consequently from the Consideration of both these, his Laws must always be the same.—Is it not from the infinite Wisdom and Goodness of God, that you suppose the Gospel a most perfect Law, incapable of being repeal'd or alter'd, or of having Additions; and must not you own the Law of Nature as perfect a Law, except you will say, that God did not arrive to the Perfection of Wisdom and Goodness till about seventeen Hundred Years since?

TO plead, That the Gospel is incapable of any Additions, because the Will of God is immutable, and his Law too perfect to need them, is an Argument, was Christianity a new Religion, which destroys itself; since from the Time it commenc'd, you must own God is mutable; and that such Additions have been made to the All-perfect Laws of infinite Wisdom, as constitute a New Religion. The Reason why the Law of Nature is immutable, is, because it is founded on

the unalterable Reason of Things; but if God is an arbitrary Being, and can command Things meerly from Will and Pleasure; some Things to-day, and others to-morrow; there is nothing either in the Nature of God, or in the Things themselves, to hinder him from perpetually changing his Mind. If he once commanded Things without Reason, there can be no Reason why he may not endlessly change such Commands.

I think, no Man has more fully done Justice to the Law of Nature, than a Divine of that Church which requires so many Things contrary to that Law; I mean the celebrated *Charron*, in his *Treatise of Wisdom*,* whose Authority is certainly not the less for being translated by the late Dean of *Canterbury*. He says,

The Law of Nature, by which I mean Universal Reason and Equity, is the Candle of our Maker, lighted up in every Breast, to guide, and shine perpetually. This is the Dictate of God himself, he is the King, and this is the Fundamental Law of the Universe; a Ray and Beam of the divine Nature, which flows from, and has a necessary Connection and Dependance upon that eternal and immutable Law, which the Almighty prescribes to his own Actions. A Man, who proceeds on this Principle, is his own Rule; for he acts in Agreement with the noblest, and most valuable Part of his Nature: This Man's Honesty is essential to, and inseparable from him, not precarious and uncertain, and owing meerly to Chance and Occasion; for this Light and Law is born with, and bred in us; a Piece of our Frame and Constitution; and from thence obtains the Name of Nature, and the Law of Nature: Such a Man, by Consequence, will be a good Man constantly, and at all Times, his Virtue will be uniform, and every Place, every Emergency will find him the same; for this Law of Nature is perpetual, the Obligation of it is lasting and inviolable; the Equity and Reason of it are eternal, written in large and indelible Characters, no Accident can deface them, no Length of Time waste, or wear them out.—These first Principles, which are the Ground of all moral Institutions, admit of no Change, no Increase, no Abatement, no Fits, no Starts, no Ebbings and Flowings—Why then, vain Man, dost thou trouble thyself to

* L.2.C.3. p. 69. [Pierre Charron (1541–1603) *De la sagesse* (1601), a text commonly compared to Michel de Montaigne's *Essais* (1580). The translation Tindal refers to here is probably George Stanhope's *Of Wisdom*, 3 vols. (1697).]

seek abroad for some Law of Rule to Mankind? What can Books, or Masters tell thee, which thou might'st not tell thyself? What can Study, or Travel shew, which, without being at the expence of so much Pains, thou might'st not see at home, by descending into thy own Conscience, and hearkening attentively to its own Admonitions?

To what Purpose is all this Labour and Cost? The toilsome tumbling over of Codes and Institutes?—The two Tables of *Moses*, the twelve Tables of the *Greeks*, the Law written in the Heart of them who had no Law, and in short all the Rules of Equity and good Laws, that have any where been enacted, and obtained in the World, are nothing but Copies and Transcripts produc'd in open Court, and publish'd from that *Original*, which thou keepest close within thee; and yet all the while pretendest to know nothing of the Matter, stifling and suppressing as much as in thee lieth the Brightness of that Light, which shines within thee. As this invisible Fountain within is more exbuberant and plenteous, so it is more lively, pure and strong, than any of the Streams deriv'd from it; of which we need but this single Testimony, That when any Disputes arise about the right Meaning of any positive Law, the constant, and best Method of understanding the Equity and true Intent of it, is by running back to its Head, and observing what is most agreeable to the Law of Nature: This is the Test and Touch, This is the Level, and the Truth, by which the rest are to be judged."

AND in truth, all Laws, whether the law of Nations, or Those of particular Countries, are only the Law of Nature adjusted, and accommodated to circumstances; nor can Religion, even in relation to the Worship of God, as it is a reasonable Service be any thing, but what necessarily flows from the Consideration of God, and the Creatures. 'Twas this made the great Mr. *Selden* say, in an Expression somewhat homely, "That Men look after Religion, as the Butcher did after his Knife, when he had it in his Mouth."*

THE Religion of Nature is so entirely calculated for the Good of human Society, that tho' a Man hurry'd with the Violence of his Passions, breaks it himself, yet he wou'd have all Others most strictly observe it; and accordingly all Legislators punish the Breach of it: Whereas no Man rejects

any positive Institution himself, but is willing that all others shou'd do so too; which plainly shews, Men do not apprehend it to be for the general Good of Mankind. And the contending Parties in Religion, with equal Confidence, cry, "That if our Religion be not true, God must be wanting to Mankind, in what concerns their eternal Happiness; he must be wanting to himself, and to his own Attributes of Goodness, Justice, and Truth: It's repugnant to the very Notion of a God, to let Men be ignorant in a Matter of such Importance without any Help or Remedy." This Reasoning, if true, necessarily infers some universal Law knowable at all Times; and can't be apply'd to any partial Religion unknown to the World for many Ages; and, as not being discoverable by Reason, still unknown to the greatest Part of it.

IN a word, if the highest internal Excellence, the greatest Plainness and Simplicity, Unanimity, Universality, Antiquity, nay, Eternity, can recommend a Law; all These 'tis own'd do, in an eminent Degree, belong to the Law of Nature. A Law, which does not depend on the uncertain Meaning of Words and Phrases in dead Languages, much less on Types, Metaphors, Allegories, Parables, or on the Skill of Honesty of weak or designing Transcribers (not to mention Translators) for many Ages together; but on the immutable Relation of Things always visible to the whole World: And therefore Dr. *Scott* justly says,

"Moral Obligations are not founded like positive ones upon firm and everlasting Reasons, upon Reasons that to all eternity will carry with them the same Force and Necessity as long as we are Creatures of an infinitely perfect Creator, it will be as much our Duty as now to be kind, just, and peaceable in all our Intercourses with them: So that These are such Duties as no Will can dispense with, no Reason abrogate, no Circumstance disannul; but as long as God is what he is, and we are what we are, they must, and will oblige us."†

I could, from many other Considerations, shew you the absolute Perfection of Natural Religion; for instance, must we not, except we speak without any Meaning, or have no true Meaning of the Word *God*, intend by it a Being

---

* Table-Talk. p. 162. [John Selden (1584–1654), author of the *History of Tithes* (1618) was an English jurist and scholar of early English and Jewish law. This quote is from his posthumous *Table-Talk* (1689).]

† *Scott's* Christ. Life, Part 2. Vol. I. Ch. I. p. 66. [John Scott (1639–95), *The Christian Life* (1681).]

of all Perfections, free from all those Defects, which belong even to the most perfect Creatures? And must we not have an Idea of these Perfections, before we can know whether there is any Being who has enjoy'd them from Eternity; and must we not know there is such a Being from our Reason, before we can come to this Question, *Whether he has made any External Revelation?* Nay, Examining into this Question wou'd be to very little Purpose, except we cou'd know whether this Being is bound by his external Word, and had not either at the Time of giving it a secret Will inconsistent with his reveal'd Will, or has not since chang'd his Will? This can't be known from any external Revelation, tho' it express'd itself ever so plainly; because the Question being, *Whether God is obliged to do, as he in it says he will do?* this must be resolv'd antecedently by the Light of Nature, which must discover to us the Veracity of God, and the Immutability of his Will; and the same Reasons which will prove he cou'd not change his Will since he made an external Revelation, will prove his Will was always unchangeable, and at all Times the same; whether internally, or externally reveal'd: Nor cou'd we take a Step towards proving the Veracity of God, or the Immutability of his Will; or indeed, any of his Perfections besides Power, without knowing that the Will of God is always determin'd by the Nature and Reason of Things: Otherwise Falshood and Mutability might be the Will of God, and there cou'd be no such Thing in Nature as Good and Evil, but an arbitrary Will wou'd govern all Things.

WERE we not capable by our Reason of distinguishing Good from Evil, or knowing from the Consideration of the invariable Perfections of God, what the divine Goodness cou'd command, or forbid his Creatures antecedently to any external Revelation, we cou'd not distinguish the true instituted Religion from the many false ones: Or if by Accident we stumbl'd on it, avoid running into many Absurdities in the Interpretation of it, thro' the Difficulties that must attend a Book writ in a dead Language, and so many Ages since; and where, thro' the vast Variety of Readings, we might mistake the true Reading; and tho' we were certain of the Letter, even *the Letter killeth.**

IF Man had not natural Abilities to distinguish between Good and Evil, or to know what is pleasing, or displeasing to God; how cou'd we say he was a moral Agent, or even an accountable Creature?

DID we not allow that Men, by the Light of Nature, are capable of forming a found Judgment in Matters of Religion, they may be so impos'd on by controverted, or mis-interpreted, not to say forg'd Texts, as to admit several Objects of divine Worship in their Practice, while in their Words they own but One; or, in order to advance a supernatural Charity, destroy all natural Humanity; and believe our God may be best shewn by our Hatred to our Fellow-Creatures; and introduce such abominable Notions, as may make Religion, instead of a Benefit, become a Mischief to Mankind.

WHEREAS, if we allow the Light of Nature sufficient to enable us to judge rightly in these Matters, and consequently to distinguish Truth from Falshood, we must own, since there can be no Disagreement in Truth, that there's an exact Conformity between internal and external Revelation, with no other Difference but as to the Manner of their being reveal'd: Or in other Words, that the Gospel, since 'tis impossible to Men at the same time to be under different Obligations, can't command those Things which the Law of Nature forbids, or forbid what That commands; nor can any thing be a Part of Religion by one Law, which by the other is Superstition; nor can External Revelation make That the Will of God, which the Light of Nature continually represents as unworthy of having God for its Author.

THE judicious Writer of the *Rational Catechism* lately reprinted says,†

That one of the most universal Causes of the great Differences among Men in Matters of Religion, is, that they have not examin'd Things to the Bottom; they have fail'd in their Foundation-Work; they have too much sighted that Philosophy which is the Natural Religion of all Men; and which being natural must needs be Universal and Eternal:—They have forsaken the Rule of right Reason, which is only capable to produce true

---

* Corinthians 3:6

† Pref. to Catechism. [William Popple (1638–1708), *The Rational Catechism: Or, An Instructive Conference between Father and Son* (1687)].

Symmetry in their intellectual Buildings; and they have apply'd themselves without any Rule to the Interpretations of Words and Phrases, which being easily susceptible of various Senses have produc'd as many deform'd Irregularities."

THO' all Parties alike pretend to aim at Truth, yet none of them, I think, inform us what Truth is, or wherein it conflicts: Not if Truth in general, implies an Agreement of our Ideas with the Things themselves, Religious Truth, or True Religion must consist in the Agreement of our Ideas with those Things which are the Subjects of our religious Inquiry; *viz.* The Nature of God and Man; and false Religion must consist in having Ideas that are not agreeable to, or do not truly represent those Subjects; and this Agreement which we call Truth in respect to *Theory*, is what we term, in relation to *Action*, fit, just, good or reasonable. Thus God is frequently styl'd in Scripture the *God of Truth*, because his Ideas of Things, and the Things themselves exactly correspond; and all his Actions are agreeable to the Relation Things have to one another: And when our Actions are such we do all that's fit, just, and reasonable, all that God or Man can require; and from hence too it follows, that Iniquity is the same in Action, as Falsity is in Theory.

15

David Hume, "Of Miracles"

Introduction

David Hume (1711–76) concealed his little essay, "Of Miracles," for some time after it was written. But once published in 1748 it quickly became one of his best-known works and the target of countless attacks in North America as well as in Europe. Writing in 1766 to French economist Anne Robert Jacques Turgot (1727–81), Hume remarked that "I cou'd cover the Floor of a large Room with the Books and Pamphlets wrote against me." The clamor issued from quarters beyond the popular press and church pulpits. Academics at Cambridge, Oxford, Aberdeen, and the College of New Jersey (now Princeton), as well as leading clerics, such as John Douglas, later Bishop of Salisbury, inveighed against Hume's essay. There was, however, good reason for the rancor with which the defenders of the faith responded to Hume. Hume's essay presents one of the most devastating, clearest, and most succinct critiques of the rationality of belief in miracles ever produced.

It is important to emphasize at the outset, however, that Hume's argument, like so much of his work, is not what today would typically be called metaphysical – that is, it does not aim to

demonstrate that no miracles have occurred, that miracles are impossible, or that a miracle-working deity does not exist. Many arguments against miracles, for example those of deist Ethan Allen's influential *Reason the Only Oracle of Man* (1784), do labor along such lines.[1] But Hume was no deist; and, indeed, Hume makes it quite clear that his argument is consistent with the possibility that miracles are occurring all around us, every day. Hume's argument is, rather, concerned with belief and the rational justification for belief – in particular, with the rationality of belief in miracles and therefore for the rationality of belief in the accounts of Holy Scripture. His argument advances in two stages, both based on the famous principle of rationality he articulates here: "A wise man . . . proportions his belief to the evidence." If Hume is right, on balance, the naturalistic explanations must always be more rational to adopt over appeals to miracle, even in cases where we don't know what a workable naturalistic explanation might be.

The first stage of Hume's argument might be thought of as an argument from definition, and therefore in a sense an a priori argument. Hume, following common practice, defines a miracle as "a violation of the laws of nature" produced by "a particular volition of the Deity, or by the interposition of some invisible agent." Violations of the laws of nature without cause or resulting from some other cause may be "marvelous," but they are not "miraculous." Miracles themselves may be either "discoverable" by human beings or

From David Hume, *Enquiries Concerning Human Understanding and Concerning the Principles of Morals*, 2nd edition, ed. L. A. Selby-Bigge, Oxford: Oxford University Press, 1902, pp. 109–31.

not. Many events that appear to occur by natural causes may, accordingly, actually be the products of divine agency, even if that agency remains undetectable to us. This definition may seem uncontroversial enough, but within it Hume discerns an explosive charge of enormous proportions. The self-subverting dynamic Hume discerns becomes clear in realizing that *by the very definition of miracles itself* the evidence for them must always be weaker than that for the uniform operations of the laws of nature.

The laws of nature are, according to Hume, matters of fact for which humans possess the highest degree of "proof" (or "probability"),[2] the strongest possible empirical evidence. As *exceptions* to those laws, miracles must be grounded on less, much less, evidence. After all, something can only be an "exception" to a rule when events that follow the rule are more numerous. But in the case of natural laws, the confirming experiences of human beings are not simply more numerous. They are more numerous in the greatest way possible for humans. In *any* contest whatsoever, therefore, where (a) explanations based upon natural laws are balanced against (b) explanations based upon exceptional divine interventions, it is more rational to explain the event by lawful natural causes. And *every possible* observation of a miracle, by definition, presents just such a contest.

If one were, for example, to see the Red Sea part or to hear, along with everyone else on Earth, a voice from the sky announce itself as God, it remains, according to this argument, more rational to believe that there are natural causes for the phenomena, consistent with natural law, than to conclude that those phenomena are miraculous – *even if one doesn't know precisely which laws, which causes, are operant*. That is, it is always, for Hume, more rational to confess that one is ignorant of the probably natural causes of strange events than to posit divine causes. Strikingly,

given the evidence available to human beings, it remains more rational to believe that strange phenomena are the products of natural lawful causes – *even if they actually are miracles*. In Hume's (in)famous remark: "No testimony is sufficient to establish a miracle, unless the testimony be of such a kind, that its falsehood would be more miraculous, than the fact, which it endeavours to establish."

The second stage of Hume's argument aims to show that there is, however, no testimony of this stature, even in Scripture. By examining the poor track record of human testimony and some of the features of human character that lead testimony to err, Hume argues that it is in virtually any case more likely that human testimony is false than that the laws of nature have been violated. So, as difficult as this may be for those who testify to miracles, it must always be more rational to doubt the testimony for miracles – even if, by a miracle, the testimony is true. Testimony for the occurrence of miracles, therefore, can only be accepted either by the irrational or by the rational whose reason has been suspended by a miraculous intercession.[3]

Notes

1 See P. S. Fosl, "Hume, Skepticism, and Early American Deism," *Hume Studies* 25, 1–2 (April–November 1999): 171–92.
2 For more on Hume's distinction between "proof" and "probability," see his *A Treatise of Human Nature* 1.3, "Of Knowledge and Probability."
3 Cf. J. L. Mackie, *The Miracle of Theism*, Oxford: Clarendon Press, 1982; Antony Flew, "The Impossibility of the Miraculous," *Hume's Philosophy of Religion*, Winston-Salem, NC: Wake Forest University Press, 1986.

Hume, "Of Miracles"

Part I

There is, in Dr Tillotson's writings, an argument against the *real presence*, which is as concise, and elegant, and strong as any argument can possibly be supposed against a doctrine, so little worthy

of a serious refutation. It is acknowledged on all hands, says that learned prelate, that the authority, either of the scripture or of tradition, is founded merely in the testimony of the apostles, who were eye-witnesses to those miracles of our Saviour, by which he proved his divine mission. Our evidence, then, for the truth of the *Christian* religion is less than the evidence for the truth of our senses; because, even in the first authors of our religion, it was no greater; and it is evident it must diminish in passing from them to their disciples; nor can any one rest such confidence in their testimony, as in the immediate object of his senses. But a weaker evidence can never destroy a stronger; and therefore, were the doctrine of the real presence ever so clearly revealed in scripture, it were directly contrary to the rules of just reasoning to give our assent to it. It contradicts sense, though both the scripture and tradition, on which it is supposed to be built, carry not such evidence with them as sense; when they are considered merely as external evidences, and are not brought home to every one's breast, by the immediate operation of the Holy Spirit.

Nothing is so convenient as a decisive argument of this kind, which must at least *silence* the most arrogant bigotry and superstition, and free us from their impertinent solicitations. I flatter myself, that I have discovered an argument of a like nature, which, if just, will, with the wise and learned, be an everlasting check to all kinds of superstitious delusion, and consequently, will be useful as long as the world endures. For so long, I presume, will the accounts of miracles and prodigies be found in all history, sacred and profane.

Though experience be our only guide in reasoning concerning matters of fact; it must be acknowledged, that this guide is not altogether infallible, but in some cases is apt to lead us into errors. One, who in our climate, should expect better weather in any week of June than in one of December, would reason justly, and conformably to experience; but it is certain, that he may happen, in the event, to find himself mistaken. However, we may observe, that, in such a case, he would have no cause to complain of experience; because it commonly informs us beforehand of the uncertainty, by that contrariety of events, which we may learn from a diligent observation. All effects follow not with like certainty from their supposed causes. Some events are found, in all countries and all ages, to have been constantly conjoined together: Others are found to have been more variable, and sometimes to disappoint our expectations; so that, in our reasonings concerning matter of fact, there are all imaginable degrees of assurance, from the highest certainty to the lowest species of moral evidence.

A wise man, therefore, proportions his belief to the evidence. In such conclusions as are founded on an infallible experience, he expects the event with the last degree of assurance, and regards his past experience as a full *proof* of the future existence of that event, In other cases, he proceeds with more caution: He weighs the opposite experiments: He considers which side is supported by the greater number of experiments: to that side he inclines, with doubt and hesitation; and when at last he fixes his judgement, the evidence exceeds not what we properly call *probability*. All probability, then, supposes an opposition of experiments and observations, where the one side is found to overbalance the other, and to produce a degree of evidence, proportioned to the superiority. A hundred instances or experiments on one side, and fifty on another, afford a doubtful expectation of any event; though a hundred uniform experiments, with only one that is contradictory, reasonably beget a pretty strong degree of assurance. In all cases, we must balance the opposite experiments, where they are opposite, and deduct the smaller number from the greater, in order to know the exact force of the superior evidence.

To apply these principles to a particular instance; we may observe, that there is no species of reasoning more common, more useful, and even necessary to human life, than that which is derived from the testimony of men, and the reports of eye-witnesses and spectators. This species of reasoning, perhaps, one may deny to be founded on the relation of cause and effect. I shall not dispute about a word. It will be sufficient to observe that our assurance in any argument of this kind is derived from no other principle than our observation of the veracity of human testimony, and of the usual conformity of facts to the reports of witnesses. It being a general maxim, that no objects have any discoverable connexion together, and that all the inferences, which we can draw from one to another, are founded merely on our experience of their constant and regular conjunction; it is evident, that we ought not to make an exception to this maxim in favour of human testimony, whose connexion with any event seems, in itself, as little necessary as any other. Were not the memory tenacious to a certain degree, had not men commonly an inclination to truth and a principle of probity; were they not sensible to shame, when detected in a falsehood: Were not these, I say, discovered by *experience* to be qualities, inherent in human nature, we should never repose the least confidence in human testimony. A man delirious, or noted for falsehood and villany, has no manner of authority with us.

And as the evidence, derived from witnesses and human testimony, is founded on past experience, so it varies with the experience, and is regarded either as a *proof* or a *probability*, according as the conjunction between any particular kind of report and any kind of object has been found to be constant or variable. There are a number of circumstances to be taken into consideration in all judgements of this kind and the ultimate standard, by which we determine all disputes, that may arise concerning them, is always derived from experience and observation. Where this experience is not entirely uniform on any side, it is attended with an unavoidable contrariety in our judgements, and with the same opposition and mutual destruction of argument as in every other kind of evidence. We frequently hesitate concerning the reports of others. We balance the opposite circumstances, which cause any doubt or uncertainty; and when we discover a superiority on any side, we incline to it; but still with a diminution of assurance, in proportion to the force of its antagonist.

This contrariety of evidence, in the present case, may be derived from several different causes; from the opposition of contrary testimony; from the character or number of the witnesses; from the manner of their delivering their testimony; or from the union of all these circumstances. We entertain a suspicion concerning any matter of fact, when the witnesses contradict each other; when they are but few, or of a doubtful character; when they have an interest in what they affirm; when they deliver their testimony with hesitation, or on the contrary, with too violent asseverations. There are many other particulars of the same kind, which may diminish or destroy the force of any argument, derived from human testimony.

Suppose, for instance, that the fact, which the testimony endeavours to establish, partakes of the extraordinary and the marvellous; in that case, the evidence, resulting from the testimony, admits of a diminution, greater or less, in proportion as the fact is more or less unusual. The reason why we place any credit in witnesses and historians, is not derived from any *connexion*, which we perceive a priori, between testimony and reality, but because we are accustomed to find a conformity between them. But when the fact

attested is such a one as has seldom fallen under our observation, here is a contest of two opposite experiences; of which the one destroys the other, as far as its force goes, and the superior can only operate on the mind by the force, which remains. The very same principle of experience, which gives us a certain degree of assurance in the testimony of witnesses, gives us also, in this case, another degree of assurance against the fact, which they endeavour to establish; from which contradition there necessarily arises a counterpoize, and mutual destruction of belief and authority.

I should not believe such a story were it told me by Cato, was a proverbial saying in Rome, even during the lifetime of that philosophical patriot.* The incredibility of a fact, it was allowed, might invalidate so great an authority.

The Indian prince, who refused to believe the first relations concerning the effects of frost, reasoned justly; and it naturally required very strong testimony to engage his assent to facts, that arose from a state of nature, with which he was unacquainted, and which bore so little analogy to those events, of which he had had constant and uniform experience. Though they were not contrary to his experience, they were not conformable to it.†

* Plutarch, in Vita Catonis. [*Life of Cato*]
† No Indian, it is evident, could have experience that water did not freeze in cold climates. This is placing nature in a situation quite unknown to him; and it is impossible for him to tell *a priori* what will result from it. It is making a new experiment, the consequence of which is always uncertain. One may sometimes conjecture from analogy what will follow; but still this is but conjecture. And it must be confessed, that, in the present case of freezing, the event follows contrary to the rules of analogy, and is such as a rational Indian would not look for. The operations of cold upon water are not gradual, according to the degrees of cold; but whenever it comes to the freezing point, the water passes in a moment, from the utmost liquidity to perfect hardness. Such an event, therefore, may be denominated *extraordinary*, and requires a pretty strong testimony, to render it credible to people in a warm climate: But still it is not *miraculous*, nor contrary to uniform experience of the course of nature in cases where all the circumstances are the same. The inhabitants of Sumatra have always seen water fluid in their own climate, and the freezing of their rivers ought to be deemed a prodigy: But they never saw water in Muscovy during the winter; and therefore they cannot reasonably be positive what would there be the consequence.

But in order to encrease the probability against the testimony of witnesses, let us suppose, that the fact, which they affirm, instead of being only marvellous, is really miraculous; and suppose also, that the testimony considered apart and in itself, amounts to an entire proof; in that case, there is proof against proof, of which the strongest must prevail, but still with a diminution of its force, in proportion to that of its antagonist.

A miracle is a violation of the laws of nature; and as a firm and unalterable experience has established these laws, the proof against a miracle, from the very nature of the fact, is as entire as any argument from experience can possibly be imagined. Why is it more than probable, that all men must die; that lead cannot, of itself, remain suspended in the air; that fire consumes wood, and is extinguished by water; unless it be, that these events are found agreeable to the laws of nature, and there is required a violation of these laws, or in other words, a miracle to prevent them? Nothing is esteemed a miracle, if it ever happen in the common course of nature. It is no miracle that a man, seemingly in good health, should die on a sudden: because such a kind of death, though more unusual than any other, has yet been frequently observed to happen. But it is a miracle, that a dead man should come to life; because that has never been observed in any age or country. There must, therefore, be a uniform experience against every miraculous event, otherwise the event would not merit that appellation. And as a uniform experience amounts to a proof, there is here a direct and full *proof*, from the nature of the fact, against the existence of any miracle; nor can such a proof be destroyed, or the miracle rendered credible, but by an opposite proof, which is superior.*

The plain consequence is (and it is a general maxim worthy of our attention), 'That no testimony is sufficient to establish a miracle, unless the testimony be of such a kind, that its falsehood would be more miraculous, than the fact, which it endeavours to establish; and even in that case there is a mutual destruction of arguments, and the superior only gives us an assurance suitable to that degree of force, which remains, after deducting the inferior.' When anyone tells me, that he saw a dead man restored to life, I immediately consider with myself, whether it be more probable, that this person should either deceive or be deceived, or that the fact, which he relates, should really have happened. I weigh the one miracle against the other; and according to the superiority, which I discover, I pronounce my decision, and always reject the greater miracle, If the falsehood of his testimony would be more miraculous, than the event which he relates; then, and not till then, can he pretend to command my belief or opinion.

Part II

In the foregoing reasoning we have supposed, that the testimony, upon which a miracle is founded, may possibly amount to an entire proof, and that the falsehood of that testimony would be a real prodigy: But it is easy to shew, that we have been a great deal too liberal in our concession, and that there never was a miraculous event established on so full an evidence.

For *first*, there is not to be found, in all history, any miracle attested by a sufficient number of men, of such unquestioned good-sense, education, and learning, as to secure us against all delusion

---

* Sometimes an event may not, *in itself*, *seem* to be contrary to the laws of nature, and yet, if it were real, it might, by reason of some circumstances, be denominated a miracle; because, in *fact*, it is contrary to these laws. Thus if a person, claiming a divine authority, should command a sick person to be well, a healthful man to fall down dead, the clouds to pour rain, the winds to blow, in short, should order many natural events, which immediately follow upon his command; these might justly be esteemed miracles, because they are really, in this case, contrary to the laws of nature. For if any suspicion remain, that the event and command concurred by accident, there is no miracle and no transgression of the laws of nature. If this suspicion be removed, there is evidently a miracle, and a transgression of these laws; because nothing can be more contrary to nature than that the voice or command of a man should have such an influence. A miracle may be accurately defined, *a transgression of a law of nature by a particular volition of the Deity, or by the interposition of some invisible agent*. A miracle may either be discoverable by men or not. This alters not its nature and essence. The raising of a house or ship into the air is a visible miracle. The raising of a feather, when the wind wants ever so little of a force requisite for that purpose, is as real a miracle, though not so sensible with regard to us.

in themselves; of such undoubted integrity, as to place them beyond all suspicion of any design to deceive others; of such credit and reputation in the eyes of mankind, as to have a great deal to lose in case of their being detected in any falsehood; and at the same time, attesting facts performed in such a public manner and in so celebrated a part of the world, as to render the detection unavoidable: All which circumstances are requisite to give us a full assurance in the testimony of men.

Secondly. We may observe in human nature a principle which, if strictly examined, will be found to diminish extremely the assurance, which we might, from human testimony, have, in any kind of prodigy. The maxim, by which we commonly conduct ourselves in our reasonings, is, that the objects, of which we have no experience, resembles those, of which we have; that what we have found to be most usual is always most probable; and that where there is an opposition of arguments, we ought to give the preference to such as are founded on the greatest number of past observations. But though, in proceeding by this rule, we readily reject any fact which is unusual and incredible in an ordinary degree; yet in advancing farther, the mind observes not always the same rule; but when anything is affirmed utterly absurd and miraculous, it rather the more readily admits of such a fact, upon account of that very circumstance, which ought to destroy all its authority. The passion of *surprise* and *wonder*, arising from miracles, being an agreeable emotion, gives a sensible tendency towards the belief of those events, from which it is derived. And this goes so far, that even those who cannot enjoy this pleasure immediately, nor can believe those miraculous events, of which they are informed, yet love to partake of the satisfaction at second-hand or by rebound, and place a pride and delight in exciting the admiration of others.

With what greediness are the miraculous accounts of travellers received, their descriptions of sea and land monsters, their relations of wonderful adventures, strange men, and uncouth manners? But if the spirit of religion join itself to the love of wonder, there is an end of common sense; and human testimony, in these circumstances, loses all pretensions to authority. A religionist may be an enthusiast, and imagine he sees what has no reality: he may know his narrative to be false, and yet persevere in it, with

the best intentions in the world, for the sake of promoting so holy a cause: or even where this delusion has not place, vanity, excited by so strong a temptation, operates on him more powerfully than on the rest of mankind in any other circumstances; and self-interest with equal force. His auditors may not have, and commonly have not, sufficient judgement to canvass his evidence: what judgement they have, they renounce by principle, in these sublime and mysterious subjects: or if they were ever so willing to employ it, passion and a heated imagination disturb the regularity of its operations. Their credulity increases his impudence: and his impudence overpowers their credulity.

Eloquence, when at its highest pitch, leaves little room for reason or reflection; but addressing itself entirely to the fancy or the affections, captivates the willing hearers, and subdues their understanding. Happily, this pitch it seldom attains. But what a Tully or a Demosthenes could scarcely effect over a Roman or Athenian audience, every *Capuchin*, every itinerant or stationary teacher can perform over the generality of mankind, and in a higher degree, by touching such gross and vulgar passions.

The many instances of forged miracles, and prophecies, and supernatural events, which, in all ages, have either been detected by contrary evidence, or which detect themselves by their absurdity, prove sufficiently the strong propensity of mankind to the extraordinary and the marvellous, and ought reasonably to beget a suspicion against all relations of this kind. This is our natural way of thinking, even with regard to the most common and most credible events. For instance: There is no kind of report which rises so easily, and spreads so quickly, especially in country places and provincial towns, as those concerning marriages; insomuch that two young persons of equal condition never see each other twice, but the whole neighbourhood immediately join them together. The pleasure of telling a piece of news so interesting, of propagating it, and of being the first reporters of it, spreads the intelligence. And this is so well known, that no man of sense gives attention to these reports, till he find them confirmed by some greater evidence. Do not the same passions, and others still stronger, incline the generality of mankind to believe and report, with the greatest vehemence and assurance, all religious miracles?

Thirdly. It forms a strong presumption against all supernatural and miraculous relations, that they are observed chiefly to abound among ignorant and barbarous nations; or if a civilized people has ever given admission to any of them, that people will be found to have received them from ignorant and barbarous ancestors, who transmitted them with that inviolable sanction and authority, which always attend received opinions. When we peruse the first histories of all nations, we are apt to imagine ourselves transported into some new world; where the whole frame of nature is disjointed, and every element performs its operations in a different manner, from what it does at present. Battles, revolutions, pestilence, famine and death, are never the effect of those natural causes, which we experience. Prodigies, omens, oracles, judgements, quite obscure the few natural events, that are intermingled with them. But as the former grow thinner every page, in proportion as we advance nearer the enlightened ages, we soon learn, that there is nothing mysterious or supernatural in the case, but that all proceeds from the usual propensity of mankind towards the marvellous, and that, though this inclination may at intervals receive a check from sense and learning, it can never be thoroughly extirpated from human nature.

It is strange, a judicious reader is apt to say, upon the perusal of these wonderful historians, *that such prodigious events never happen in our days*. But it is nothing strange, I hope, that men should lie in all ages. You must surely have seen instances enough of that frailty. You have yourself heard many such marvellous relations started, which, being treated with scorn by all the wise and judicious, have at last been abandoned even by the vulgar. Be assured, that those renowned lies, which have spread and flourished to such a monstrous height, arose from like beginnings; but being sown in a more proper soil, shot up at last into prodigies almost equal to those which they relate.

It was a wise policy in that false prophet, Alexander, who though now forgotten, was once so famous, to lay the first scene of his impostures in Paphlagonia, where, as Lucian tells us, the people were extremely ignorant and stupid, and ready to swallow even the grossest delusion. People at a distance, who are weak enough to think the matter at all worth enquiry, have no opportunity of receiving better information. The stories come magnified to them by a hundred circumstances. Fools are industrious in propagating the imposture; while the wise and learned are contented, in general, to deride its absurdity, without informing themselves of the particular facts, by which it may be distinctly refuted. And thus the impostor above mentioned was enabled to proceed, from his ignorant Paphlagonians, to the enlisting of votaries, even among the Grecian philosophers, and men of the most eminent rank and distinction in Rome: nay, could engage the attention of that sage emperor Marcus Aurelius; so far as to make him trust the success of a military expedition to his delusive prophecies.

The advantages are so great, of starting an imposture among an ignorant people, that, even though the delusion should be too gross to impose on the generality of them (*which, though seldom, is sometimes the case*) it has a much better chance for succeeding in remote countries, than if the first scene had been laid in a city renowned for arts and knowledge. The most ignorant and barbarous of these barbarians carry the report abroad. None of their countrymen have a large correspondence, or sufficient credit and authority to contradict and beat down the delusion. Men's inclination to the marvellous has full opportunity to display itself. And thus a story, which is universally exploded in the place where it was first started, shall pass for certain at a thousand miles distance. But had Alexander fixed his residence at Athens, the philosophers of that renowned mart of learning had immediately spread, throughout the whole Roman empire, their sense of the matter; which, being supported by so great authority, and displayed by all the force of reason and eloquence, had entirely opened the eyes of mankind. It is true; Lucian, passing by chance through Paphlagonia, had an opportunity of performing this good office. But, though much to be wished, it does not always happen, that every Alexander meets with a Lucian, ready to expose and detect his impostures.

I may add as a *fourth* reason, which diminishes the authority of prodigies, that there is no testimony for any, even those which have not been expressly detected, that is not opposed by an infinite number of witnesses; so that not only the miracle destroys the credit of testimony, but the testimony destroys itself. To make this the better understood, let us consider, that, in matters of religion, whatever is different is contrary; and that it is impossible the religions of ancient Rome, of Turkey, of Siam, and of China should, all of them, be established on any solid foundation. Every miracle, therefore, pretended to have been wrought in any of these religions (and all of them abound in miracles), as its direct scope is to establish the particular system to which it is attributed; so has it the same force, though more indirectly, to overthrow every other system. In destroying a rival system, it likewise destroys the credit of those miracles, on which that system was established; so that all the prodigies of different religions are to be regarded as contrary facts, and the evidences of these prodigies, whether weak or strong, as opposite to each other. According to this method of reasoning, when we believe any miracle of Mahomet or his successors, we have for our warrant the testimony of a few barbarous Arabians: And on the other hand, we are to regard the authority of Titus Livius, Plutarch, Tacitus, and, in short, of all the authors and witnesses, Grecian, Chinese, and Roman Catholic, who have related any miracle in their particular religion; I say, we are to regard their testimony in the same light as if they had mentioned that Mahometan miracle, and had in express terms contradicted it, with the same certainty as they have for the miracle they relate. This argument may appear over subtile and refined; but is not in reality different from the reasoning of a judge, who supposes, that the credit of two witnesses, maintaining a crime against any one, is destroyed by the testimony of two others, who affirm him to have been two hundred leagues distant, at the same instant when the crime is said to have been committed.

One of the best attested miracles in all profane history, is that which Tacitus reports of Vespasian, who cured a blind man in Alexandria, by means of his spittle, and a lame man by the mere touch of his foot; in obedience to a vision of the god Serapis, who had enjoined them to have recourse to the Emperor, for these miraculous cures. The story may be seen in that fine historian;* where every circumstance seems to add weight to the testimony, and might be displayed at large with all the force of argument and eloquence, if any one were now concerned to enforce the evidence of that exploded and idolatrous superstition.

* Hist. lib. iv. cap. 81. Suetonius gives nearly the same account *in vita* Vesp.

The gravity, solidity, age, and probity of so great an emperor, who, through the whole course of his life, conversed in a familiar manner with his friends and courtiers, and never affected those extraordinary airs of divinity assumed by Alexander and Demetrius. The historian, a cotemporary writer, noted for candour and veracity, and withal, the greatest and most penetrating genius, perhaps, of all antiquity; and so free from any tendency to credulity, that he even lies under the contrary imputation, of atheism and profaneness: The persons, from whose authority he related the miracle, of established character for judgement and veracity, as we may well presume; eye-witnesses of the fact, and confirming their testimony, after the Flavian family was despoiled of the empire, and could no longer give any reward, as the price of a lie. *Utrumque, qui interfuere, nunc quoque memorant, postquam nullum mendacio pretium.* To which if we add the public nature of the facts, as related, it will appear, that no evidence can well be supposed stronger for so gross and so palpable a falsehood.

There is also a memorable story related by Cardinal de Retz, which may well deserve our consideration. When that intriguing politician fled into Spain, to avoid the persecution of his enemies, he passed through Saragossa, the capital of Arragon, where he was shewn, in the cathedral, a man, who had served seven years as a doorkeeper, and was well known to every body in town, that had ever paid his devotions at that church. He had been seen, for so long a time, wanting a leg; but recovered that limb by the rubbing of holy oil upon the stump; and the cardinal assures us that he saw him with two legs. This miracle was vouched by all the canons of the church; and the whole company in town were appealed to for a confirmation of the fact; whom the cardinal found, by their zealous devotion, to be thorough believers of the miracle. Here the relater was also cotemporary to the supposed prodigy, of an incredulous and libertine character, as well as of great genius; the miracle of so *singular* a nature as could scarcely admit of a counterfeit, and the witnesses very numerous, and all of them, in a manner, spectators of the fact, to which they gave their testimony. And what adds mightily to the force of the evidence, and may double our surprise on this occasion, is, that the cardinal himself, who relates the story, seems not to give any credit to it, and consequently cannot be suspected of any concurrence in the holy fraud. He considered justly, that it was not requisite, in order to reject a fact of this nature, to be able accurately to disprove the testimony, and to trace its falsehood, through all the circumstances of knavery and credulity which produced it. He knew, that, as this was commonly altogether impossible at any small distance of time and place; so was it extremely difficult, even where one was immediately present, by reason of the bigotry, ignorance, cunning, and roguery of a great part of mankind. He therefore concluded, like a just reasoner, that such an evidence carried falsehood upon the very face of it, and that a miracle, supported by any human testimony, was more properly a subject of derision than of argument.

There surely never was a greater number of miracles ascribed to one person, than those, which were lately said to have been wrought in France upon the tomb of Abbé Paris, the famous Jansenist, with whose sanctity the people were so long deluded. The curing of the sick, giving hearing to the deaf, and sight to the blind, were every where talked of as the usual effects of that holy sepulchre. But what is more extraordinary; many of the miracles were immediately proved upon the spot, before judges of unquestioned integrity, attested by witnesses of credit and distinction, in a learned age, and on the most eminent theatre that is now in the world. Nor is this all: a relation of them was published and dispersed every where; nor were the *Jesuits*, though a learned body, supported by the civil magistrate, and determined enemies to those opinions, in whose favour the miracles were said to have been wrought, ever able distinctly to refute or detect them. Where shall we find such a number of circumstances, agreeing to the corroboration of one fact? And what have we to oppose to such a cloud of witnesses, but the absolute impossibility or miraculous nature of the events, which they relate? And this surely, in the eyes of all reasonable people, will alone be regarded as a sufficient refutation.

Is the consequence just, because some human testimony has the utmost force and authority in some cases, when it relates the battle of Philippi or Pharsalia for instance; that therefore all kinds of testimony must, in all cases, have equal force and authority? Suppose that the Cæsarean and Pompeian factions had, each of them, claimed the victory in these battles, and that the historians of each party had uniformly ascribed the advantage to their own side; how could mankind, at this distance, have been able to determine between them? The contrariety is equally strong between the miracles related by Herodotus or Plutarch, and those delivered by Mariana, Bede, or any monkish historian.

The wise lend a very academic faith to every report which favours the passion of the reporter; whether it magnifies his country, his family, or himself, or in any other way strikes in with his natural inclinations and propensities. But what greater temptation than to appear a missionary, a prophet, an ambassador from heaven? Who would not encounter many dangers and difficulties, in order to attain so sublime a character? Or if, by the help of vanity and a heated imagination, a man has first made a convert of himself, and entered seriously into the delusion; who ever scruples to make use of pious frauds, in support of so holy and meritorious a cause?

The smallest spark may here kindle into the greatest flame; because the materials are always prepared for it. The *avidum genus auricularum,** the gazing populace, receive greedily, without examination, whatever sooths superstition, and promotes wonder.

How many stories of this nature have, in all ages, been detected and exploded in their infancy? How many more have been celebrated for a time, and have afterwards sunk into neglect and oblivion? Where such reports, therefore, fly about, the solution of the phenomenon is obvious; and we judge in conformity to regular experience and observation, when we account for it by the known and natural principles of credulity and delusion. And shall we, rather than have a recourse to so natural a solution, allow of a miraculous violation of the most established laws of nature?

I need not mention the difficulty of detecting a falsehood in any private or even public history, at the place, where it is said to happen; much more when the scene is removed to ever so small a distance. Even a court of judicature, with all the authority, accuracy, and judgement, which they can employ, find themselves often at a loss to distinguish between truth and falsehood in the most recent actions. But the matter never comes to any issue, if trusted to the common method

* Lucret [Lucretius].

of altercations and debate and flying rumours; especially when men's passions have taken part on either side.

In the infancy of new religions, the wise and learned commonly esteem the matter too inconsiderable to deserve their attention or regard. And when afterwards they would willingly detect the cheat, in order to undeceive the deluded multitude, the season is now past, and the records and witnesses, which might clear up the matter, have perished beyond recovery.

No means of detection remain, but those which must be drawn from the very testimony itself of the reporters: and these, though always sufficient with the judicious and knowing, are commonly too fine to fall under the comprehension of the vulgar.

Upon the whole, then, it appears, that no testimony for any kind of miracle has ever amounted to a probability, much less to a proof; and that, even supposing it amounted to a proof, it would be opposed by another proof; derived from the very nature of the fact, which it would endeavour to establish. It is experience only, which gives authority to human testimony; and it is the same experience, which assures us of the laws of nature. When, therefore, these two kinds of experience are contrary, we have nothing to do but substract the one from the other, and embrace an opinion, either on one side or the other, with that assurance which arises from the remainder. But according to the principle here explained, this substraction, with regard to all popular religions, amounts to an entire annihilation; and therefore we may establish it as a maxim, that no human testimony can have such force as to prove a miracle, and make it a just foundation for any such system of religion.

I beg the limitations here made may be remarked, when I say, that a miracle can never be proved, so as to be the foundation of a system of religion. For I own, that otherwise, there may possibly be miracles, or violations of the usual course of nature, of such a kind as to admit of proof from human testimony; though, perhaps, it will be impossible to find any such in all the records of history. Thus, suppose, all authors, in all languages, agree, that, from the first of January 1600, there was a total darkness over the whole earth for eight days: suppose that the tradition of this extraordinary event is still strong and lively among the people: that all travellers, who return from foreign countries, bring us accounts of the same tradition, without the least variation or contradiction: it is evident, that our present philosophers, instead of doubting the fact, ought to receive it as certain, and ought to search for the causes whence it might be derived. The decay, corruption, and dissolution of nature, is an event rendered probable by so many analogies, that any phenomenon, which seems to have a tendency towards that catastrophe, comes within the reach of human testimony, if that testimony be very extensive and uniform.

But suppose, that all the historians who treat of England, should agree, that, on the first of January 1600, Queen Elizabeth died; that both before and after her death she was seen by her physicians and the whole court, as is usual with persons of her rank; that her successor was acknowledged and proclaimed by the parliament; and that, after being interred a month, she again appeared, resumed the throne, and governed England for three years: I must confess that I should be surprised at the concurrence of so many odd circumstances, but should not have the least inclination to believe so miraculous an event. I should not doubt of her pretended death, and of those other public circumstances that followed it: I should only assert it to have been pretended, and that it neither was, nor possibly could be real. You would in vain object to me the difficulty, and almost impossibility of deceiving the world in an affair of such consequence; the wisdom and solid judgement of that renowned queen; with the little or no advantage which she could reap from so poor an artifice: All this might astonish me; but I would still reply, that the knavery and folly of men are such common phenomena, that I should rather believe the most extraordinary events to arise from their concurrence, than admit of so signal a violation of the laws of nature.

But should this miracle be ascribed to any new system of religion; men, in all ages, have been so much imposed on by ridiculous stories of that kind, that this very circumstance would be a full proof of a cheat, and sufficient, with all men of sense, not only to make them reject the fact, but even reject it without farther examination. Though the Being to whom the miracle is ascribed, be, in this case, Almighty, it does not, upon that account, become a whit more probable; since it is impossible for us to know the attributes or actions of such a Being, otherwise than from the experience which we have of his productions, in the usual course of nature. This still reduces us to past observation, and obliges us to compare the instances of the violation of truth in the testimony of men, with those of the violation of the laws of nature by miracles, in order to judge which of them is most likely and probable. As the violations of truth are more common in the testimony concerning religious miracles, than in that concerning any other matter of fact; this must diminish very much the authority of the former testimony, and make us form a general resolution, never to lend any attention to it, with whatever specious pretence it may be covered.

Lord Bacon seems to have embraced the same principles of reasoning. 'We ought,' says he, 'to make a collection or particular history of all monsters and prodigious births or productions, and in a word of every thing new, rare, and extraordinary in nature. But this must be done with the most severe scrutiny, lest we depart from truth. Above all, every relation must be considered as suspicious, which depends in any degree upon religion, as the prodigies of Livy: And no less so, every thing that is to be found in the writers of natural magic or alchimy, or such authors, who seem, all of them, to have an unconquerable appetite for falsehood and fable.'*

I am the better pleased with the method of reasoning here delivered, as I think it may serve to confound those dangerous friends or disguised enemies to the *Christian Religion*, who have undertaken to defend it by the principles of human reason. Our most holy religion is founded on *Faith*, not on reason; and it is a sure method of exposing it to put it to such a trial as it is, by no means, fitted to endure. To make this more evident, let us examine those miracles, related in scripture; and not to lose ourselves in too wide a field, let us confine ourselves to such as we find in the *Pentateuch*, which we shall examine, according to the principles of these pretended Christians, not as the word or testimony

of God himself, but as the production of a mere human writer and historian. Here then we are first to consider a book, presented to us by a barbarous and ignorant people, written in an age when they were still more barbarous, and in all probability long after the facts which it relates, corroborated by no concurring testimony, and resembling those fabulous accounts, which every nation gives of its origin. Upon reading this book, we find it full of prodigies and miracles. It gives an account of a state of the world and of human nature entirely different from the present: Of our fall from that state: Of the age of man, extended to near a thousand years: Of the destruction of the world by a deluge: Of the arbitrary choice of one people, as the favourites of heaven; and that people the countrymen of the author: Of their deliverance from bondage by prodigies the most astonishing imaginable: I desire any one to lay his hand upon his heart, and after a serious consideration declare, whether he thinks that the falsehood of such a book, supported by such a testimony, would be more extraordinary and miraculous than all the miracles it relates; which is, however, necessary to make it be received, according to the measures of probability above established.

What we have said of miracles may be applied, without any variation, to prophecies; and indeed, all prophecies are real miracles, and as such only, can be admitted as proofs of any revelation. If it did not exceed the capacity of human nature to foretell future events, it would be absurd to employ any prophecy as an argument for a divine mission or authority from heaven. So that, upon the whole, we may conclude, that the *Christian Religion* not only was at first attended with miracles, but even at this day cannot be believed by any reasonable person without one. Mere reason is insufficient to convince us of its veracity: And whoever is moved by *Faith* to assent to it, is conscious of a continued miracle in his own person, which subverts all the principles of his understanding, and gives him a determination to believe what is most contrary to custom and experience.

* Nov. Org. lib. ii. aph. 29. [cf. II.7 in this volume]

Immanuel Kant, from *Critique of Pure Reason* I.2: "The Transcendental Dialectic" II, Chapter III, Sections 4–5[1]

Introduction

Born to a German craftsman in Königsberg, then the capital of East Prussia (today Kaliningrad, Russia), Immanuel Kant (1724–1804) came to philosophical maturity relatively late in life. Having been weaned on thinkers like Gottfried Leibniz (III.15) and Christian Wolff (1679–1754), as well as on Newtonian physics, Kant's early work was largely devoted to developing themes of German rationalism. In 1772, however, two years after having been appointed Professor of Logic and Metaphysics at the University of Königsberg, Kant wrote to a student of having been awoken from a "dogmatic slumber" by the work of David Hume (II.10). This awakening would precipitate a profound change of direction in Kant's thought and, indeed, alter the course of western philosophical thought generally. Kant's reassessment of rationalism and skepticism over a long period of silence finally resulted in the publication of a series of three great "critiques" assessing the human mind's capacities as well as the possibilities of metaphysics, natural science, mathematics, theology, morality, and esthetics.

Kant's first critique, *The Critique of Pure Reason* (1781) both honors Hume's skeptical impulse and rebukes it. His investigations lead Kant to the

From Immanuel Kant, *Critique of Pure Reason*, trans. N. Kemp Smith, London: Macmillan, 1968, pp. 500–18 (some notes omitted).

recognition of severe limitations on the extent to which reason can achieve metaphysical knowledge of reality as it is "in itself" while simultaneously explaining how natural science and mathematics can nevertheless still determine knowledge about the world – if only as human beings "experience" it. The destructive import for theology and speculative metaphysics of these limits earned Kant from the German poet Heinrich Heine (1791–1856) the label, the "Great Destroyer."

Among the most famous targets of Kant's destructive enterprise was the "ontological argument." In various forms the argument has been deployed by, among others, Anselm (IV.5) in his c. 1077 *Proslogion* and Descartes in "Meditation V" of his 1641 *Meditations on First Philosophy* (II.8).[2] This a priori argument, curiously, turns upon nothing more than the concept of God. It makes no reference to the causal order, the beauty and complexity of nature, or to revealed truth. Tersely, the argument may be rendered this way: by definition God is a necessary being, a being whose non-existence is impossible; therefore the statement, "God does not exist," is self-contradictory and necessarily false in the same way that "Triangles do not have three sides" is necessarily false. Just as the concept of "triangle" contains the idea of having three sides, so, the argument goes, the concept of "God" (or the "*ens realissimum*," the realest or greatest being) contains the idea of existing. Kant's attack on this argument is two-pronged.

He argues first that even if the concept of God did contain the idea of existence, it would remain possible to assert God's non-existence by refusing to posit God in the first place: "To posit a triangle, and yet to reject its three angles, is self-contradictory; but there is no contradiction in rejecting the triangle together with its three angles. The same is true of an absolutely necessary being. If its existence is rejected, we reject the thing itself with all its predicates; and no question of contradiction can then arise."

Second, however, and more importantly, Kant rejects the idea that existence is a predicate at all – that either the concept of "God" or any other concept for that matter can contain the idea of existence. Just as conceiving 100 gold coins as either existing or as not existing has no effect on the conception of "100 gold coins," so "existence" adds nothing to the conception of God. "By whatever and by however many predicates," Kant writes, "we may think a thing . . . we do not make the least addition to the thing when we further declare that this thing *is*. Otherwise, it would not be exactly the same thing that exists, but something more than we had thought in the concept; and we could not, therefore, say that the exact object of my concept exists."

Turning to the "cosmological argument" Kant presents a rendering substantially different from the one advanced by Descartes in "Meditation III" but similar to the third of Aquinas's "Five Ways" (IV.9). In a move characteristic of much of his criticism of speculative metaphysics, Kant argues that it is the nature of reason itself and not the nature of reality that leads us to infer the existence of a necessary being from the existence of contingent beings.[3] Along these lines, as Kant writes in the very first sentence of the first Critique, "Human reason has this peculiar fate, that in one species of its knowledge it is burdened by questions which, as prescribed by the very nature of reason itself, it is not able to ignore, but which, as transcending all its powers, it is also not able to answer" (Avii). Among, then, the questions that reason by its very nature cannot ignore but cannot answer are questions concerning the existence of God.[4]

This is not to say that reason has no role to play at all in the philosophy of religion. In the first place,

reason may use the idea of a supreme being as a "regulative" ideal that can guide human inquiry by allowing us to examine the world "as if" (*als ob*) it were the production of divine being. In this way, without "constitutively" positing the actual existence of God we may effectively seek out a systematic, lawful, and necessary unity in the natural order. (In Kant's second Critique, *The Critique of Practical Reason* [1788], he will speak of "postulating," but not proving, the existence of God in order to render morality intelligible.) Reason can also serve a negative, "corrective" function by eliminating incoherent and unintelligible conceptions of God. Or, in Kant's own words: "But although reason, in its merely speculative employment, is very far from being equal to so great an undertaking, namely, to demonstrate the existence of a supreme being, it is yet of very great utility in *correcting* any knowledge of this being which may be derived from other sources, in making it consistent with itself and with every point of view from which intelligible objects may be regarded, and in freeing it from everything incompatible with the concept of an original being and from all admixture of empirical limitations" (A640=B668).

Notes

1. "The Impossibility of an Ontological Proof of the Existence of God" and "The Impossibility of a Cosmological Proof of the Existence of God," *The Critique of Pure Reason* I, Second Part, Second Division, Book II, Chapter III, Sections 4 and 5.

2. Leibniz and Spinoza present versions of the argument, as well. See Leibniz's "That the Most Perfect Being Exists" (1676) and "To the Editor of the Journal de Trévoux" (1701); see Spinoza's *Ethics* (1677): Part I, Proposition XI.

3. See G. E. Michalson, *Kant and the Problem of God*, Oxford: Blackwell, 1999.

4. See M. Grier, *Kant's Doctrine of Transcendental Illusion*, Cambridge: Cambridge University Press, 2001.

Kant, *Critique of Pure Reason*

The Impossibility of an Ontological Proof of the Existence of God

It is evident, from what has been said, that the concept of an absolutely necessary being is a concept of pure reason, that is, a mere idea the objective reality of which is very far from being proved by the fact that reason requires it. For the idea instructs us only in regard to a certain unattainable completeness, and so serves rather to limit the understanding than to extend it to new objects. But we are here faced by what is indeed strange and perplexing, namely, that while the inference from a given existence in general to some absolutely necessary being seems to be both imperative and legitimate, all those conditions under which alone the understanding can form a concept of such a necessity are so many obstacles in the way of our doing so.

In all ages men have spoken of an *absolutely necessary* being, and in so doing have endeavoured, not so much to understand whether and how a thing of this kind allows even of being thought, but rather to prove its existence. There is, of course, no difficulty in giving a verbal definition of the concept, namely, that it is something the non-existence of which is impossible. But this yields no insight into the conditions which make it necessary to regard the non-existence of a thing as absolutely unthinkable. It is precisely these conditions that we desire to know, in order that we may determine whether or not, in resorting to this concept, we are thinking anything at all. The expedient of removing all those conditions which the understanding indispensably requires in order to regard something as necessary, simply through the introduction of the word *unconditioned*, is very far from sufficing to show whether I am still thinking anything in the concept of the unconditionally necessary, or perhaps rather nothing at all.

Nay more, this concept, at first ventured upon blindly, and now become so completely familiar, has been supposed to have its meaning exhibited in a number of examples; and on this account all further enquiry into its intelligibility has seemed to be quite needless. Thus the fact that every geometrical proposition, as, for instance, that a triangle has three angles, is absolutely necessary, has been taken as justifying us in speaking of an object which lies entirely outside the sphere of our understanding as if we understood perfectly what it is that we intend to convey by the concept of that object.

All the alleged examples are, without exception, taken from *judgments*, not from *things* and their existence. But the unconditioned necessity of judgments is not the same as an absolute necessity of things. The absolute necessity of the judgment is only a conditioned necessity of the thing, or of the predicate in the judgment. The above proposition does not declare that three angles are absolutely necessary, but that, under the condition that there is a triangle (that is, that a triangle is given), three angles will necessarily be found in it. So great, indeed, is the deluding influence exercised by this logical necessity that, by the simple device of forming an *a priori* concept of a thing in such a manner as to include existence within the scope of its meaning, we have supposed ourselves to have justified the conclusion that because existence necessarily belongs to the object of this concept – always under the condition that we posit the thing as given (as existing) – we are also of necessity, in accordance with the law of identity, required to posit the existence of its object, and that this being is therefore itself absolutely necessary – and this, to repeat, for the reason that the existence of this being has already been thought in a concept which is assumed arbitrarily and on condition that we posit its object.

If, in an identical proposition, I reject the predicate while retaining the subject, contradiction results; and I therefore say that the former belongs necessarily to the latter. But if we reject subject and predicate alike, there is no contradiction; for nothing is then left that can be contradicted. To posit a triangle, and yet to reject its three angles, is self-contradictory; but there is no contradiction in rejecting the triangle together with its three angles. The same holds true of the concept of an absolutely necessary being. If its existence is rejected, we reject the thing itself with all its predicates; and no question of contradiction can then arise. There is nothing outside it that would then be contradicted, since the necessity of the thing is not supposed to be derived from anything external; nor is there anything internal that would be contradicted, since in rejecting the thing itself we have at the same time rejected all its internal properties. 'God is omnipotent' is a necessary judgment. The omnipotence cannot be rejected if we posit a Deity, that is, an infinite being; for the two concepts are identical. But if we say, 'There is no God', neither the omnipotence nor any other of its predicates is given; they are one and all rejected together with the subject, and there is therefore not the least contradiction in such a judgment.

We have thus seen that if the predicate of a judgment is rejected together with the subject, no internal contradiction can result, and that this holds no matter what the predicate may be. The only way of evading this conclusion is to argue that there are subjects which cannot be removed, and must always remain. That, however, would only be another way of saying that there are absolutely necessary subjects; and that is the very assumption which I have called in question, and the possibility of which the above argument professes to establish. For I cannot form the least concept of a thing which, should it be rejected with all its predicates, leaves behind a contradiction; and in the absence of contradiction I have, through pure *a priori* concepts alone, no criterion of impossibility.

Notwithstanding all these general considerations, in which every one must concur, we may be challenged with a case which is brought forward as proof that in actual fact the contrary holds, namely, that there is one concept, and indeed only one, in reference to which the not-being or rejection of its object is in itself contradictory, namely, the concept of the *ens realissimum*. It is declared that it possesses all reality, and that we are justified in assuming that such a being is possible (the fact that a concept does not contradict itself by no means proves the possibility of its object: but the contrary assertion I am for the moment willing to allow).* Now [the argument proceeds] 'all reality' includes existence; existence is therefore contained in the concept of a thing that is possible. If, then, this thing is rejected, the internal possibility of the thing is rejected – which is self-contradictory.

My answer is as follows. There is already a contradiction in introducing the concept of existence – no matter under what title it may be disguised – into the concept of a thing which we profess to be thinking solely in reference to its possibility. If that be allowed as legitimate, a seeming victory has been won; but in actual fact nothing at all is said: the assertion is a mere tautology. We must ask: Is the proposition that *this or that thing* (which, whatever it may be, is allowed as possible) *exists*, an analytic or a synthetic proposition? If it is analytic, the assertion of the existence of the thing adds nothing to the thought of the thing; but in that case either the thought, which is in us, is the thing itself, or we have presupposed an existence as belonging to the realm of the possible, and have then, on that pretext, inferred its existence from its internal possibility – which is nothing but a miserable tautology. The word 'reality', which in the concept of the thing sounds other than the word 'existence' in the concept of the predicate, is of no avail in meeting this objection. For if all positing (no matter what it may be that is posited) is entitled reality, the thing with all its predicates is already posited in the concept of the subject, and is assumed as actual; and in the predicate this is merely repeated. But if, on the other hand, we admit, as every reasonable person must, that all existential propositions are synthetic, how can we profess to maintain that the predicate of existence cannot be rejected without contradiction? This is a feature which is found only in analytic propositions, and is indeed precisely what constitutes their analytic character.

I should have hoped to put an end to these idle and fruitless disputations in a direct manner, by an accurate determination of the concept of existence, had I not found that the illusion which is caused by the confusion of a logical with a real predicate (that is, with a predicate which determines a thing) is almost beyond correction. Anything we please can be made to serve as a logical predicate; the subject can even be predicated of itself; for logic abstracts from all content. But a *determining* predicate is a predicate which is added to the concept of the subject and enlarges

---

* A concept is always possible if it is not self-contradictory. This is the logical criterion of possibility, and by it the object of the concept is distinguishable from the *nihil negativum*. But it may none the less be an empty concept, unless the objective reality of the synthesis through which the concept is generated has been specifically proved; and such proof, as we have shown above, rests on principles of possible experience, and not on the principle of analysis (the law of contradiction). This is a warning against arguing directly from the logical possibility of concepts to the real possibility of things.

it. Consequently, it must not be already contained in the concept.

'*Being*' is obviously not a real predicate; that is, it is not a concept of something which could be added to the concept of a thing. It is merely the positing of a thing, or of certain determinations, as existing in themselves. Logically, it is merely the copula of a judgment. The proposition, 'God is omnipotent', contains two concepts, each of which has its object – God and omnipotence. The small word 'is' adds no new predicate, but only serves to posit the predicate *in its relation* to the subject. If, now, we take the subject (God) with all its predicates (among which is omnipotence), and say 'God is', or 'There is a God', we attach no new predicate to the concept of God, but only posit the subject in itself with all its predicates, and indeed posit it as being an *object* that stands in relation to my *concept*. The content of both must be one and the same; nothing can have been added to the concept, which expresses merely what is possible, by my thinking its object (through the expression 'it is') as given absolutely. Otherwise stated, the real contains no more than the merely possible. A hundred real thalers do not contain the least coin more than a hundred possible thalers. For as the latter signify the concept, and the former the object and the positing of the object, should the former contain more than the latter, my concept would not, in that case, express the whole object, and would not therefore be an adequate concept of it. My financial position is, however, affected very differently by a hundred real thalers than it is by the mere concept of them (that is, of their possibility). For the object, as it actually exists, is not analytically contained in my concept, but is added to my concept (which is a determination of my state) synthetically; and yet the conceived hundred thalers are not themselves in the least increased through thus acquiring existence outside my concept.

By whatever and by however many predicates we may think a thing – even if we completely determine it – we do not make the least addition to the thing when we further declare that this thing *is*. Otherwise, it would not be exactly the same thing that exists, but something more than we had thought in the concept; and we could not, therefore, say that the exact object of my concept exists. If we think in a thing every feature of reality except one, the missing reality is not added

by my saying that this defective thing exists. On the contrary, it exists with the same defect with which I have thought it, since otherwise what exists would be something different from what I thought. When, therefore, I think a being as the supreme reality, without any defect, the question still remains whether it exists or not. For though, in my concept, nothing may be lacking of the possible real content of a thing in general, something is still lacking in its relation to my whole state of thought, namely, [in so far as I am unable to assert] that knowledge of this object is also possible *a posteriori*. And here we find the source of our present difficulty. Were we dealing with an object of the senses, we could not confound the existence of the thing with the mere concept of it. For through the concept the object is thought only as conforming to the *universal conditions* of possible empirical knowledge in general, whereas through its existence it is thought as belonging to the context of experience as a whole. In being thus connected with the *content* of experience as a whole, the concept of the object is not, however, in the least enlarged; all that has happened is that our thought has thereby obtained an additional possible perception. It is not, therefore, surprising that, if we attempt to think existence through the pure category alone, we cannot specify a single mark distinguishing it from mere possibility.

Whatever, therefore, and however much, our concept of an object may contain, we must go outside it, if we are to ascribe existence to the object. In the case of objects of the senses, this takes place through their connection with some one of our perceptions, in accordance with empirical laws. But in dealing with objects of pure thought, we have no means whatsoever of knowing their existence, since it would have to be known in a completely *a priori* manner. Our consciousness of all existence (whether immediately through perception, or mediately through inferences which connect something with perception) belongs exclusively to the unity of experience; any [alleged] existence outside this field, while not indeed such as we can declare to be absolutely impossible, is of the nature of an assumption which we can never be in a position to justify.

The concept of a supreme being is in many respects a very useful idea; but just because it is a mere idea, it is altogether incapable, by itself alone, of enlarging our knowledge in regard to what exists. It is not even competent to enlighten us as to the *possibility* of any existence beyond that which is known in and through experience. The analytic criterion of possibility, as consisting in the principle that bare positives (realities) give rise to no contradiction, cannot be denied to it. But since the realities are not given to us in their specific characters; since even if they were, we should still not be in a position to pass judgment; since the criterion of the possibility of synthetic knowledge is never to be looked for save in experience, to which the object of an idea cannot belong, the connection of all real properties in a thing is a synthesis, the possibility of which we are unable to determine *a priori*. And thus the celebrated Leibniz is far from having succeeded in what he plumed himself on achieving – the comprehension *a priori* of the possibility of this sublime ideal being.

The attempt to establish the existence of a supreme being by means of the famous ontological argument of Descartes is therefore merely so much labour and effort lost; we can no more extend our stock of [theoretical] insight by mere ideas, than a merchant can better his position by adding a few noughts to his cash account.

The Impossibility of a Cosmological Proof of the Existence of God

To attempt to extract from a purely arbitrary idea the existence of an object corresponding to it is a quite unnatural procedure and a mere innovation of scholastic subtlety. Such an attempt would never have been made if there had not been antecedently, on the part of our reason, the need to assume as a basis of existence in general something necessary (in which our regress may terminate); and if, since this necessity must be unconditioned and certain *a priori*, reason had not, in consequence, been forced to seek a concept which would satisfy, if possible, such a demand, and enable us to know an existence in a completely *a priori* manner. Such a concept was supposed to have been found in the idea of an *ens realissimum*; and that idea was therefore used only for the more definite knowledge of that necessary being, of the necessary existence of which we were already convinced, or persuaded, on other grounds. This natural procedure of reason was, however, concealed from view, and instead of ending with this concept, the attempt was made to begin with it,

and so to deduce from it that necessity of existence which it was only fitted to supplement. Thus arose the unfortunate ontological proof, which yields satisfaction neither to the natural and healthy understanding nor to the more academic demands of strict proof.

The *cosmological proof*, which we are now about to examine, retains the connection of absolute necessity with the highest reality, but instead of reasoning, like the former proof, from the highest reality to necessity of existence, it reasons from the previously given unconditioned necessity of some being to the unlimited reality of that being. It thus enters upon a course of reasoning which, whether rational or only pseudorational, is at any rate natural, and the most convincing not only for common sense but even for speculative understanding. It also sketches the first outline of all the proofs in natural theology, an outline which has always been and always will be followed, however much embellished and disguised by superfluous additions. This proof, termed by Leibniz the proof *a contingentia mundi*, we shall now proceed to expound and examine.

It runs thus: If anything exists, an absolutely necessary being must also exist. Now I, at least, exist. Therefore an absolutely necessary being exists. The minor premiss contains an experience, the major premiss the inference from there being any experience at all to the existence of the necessary.* The proof therefore really begins with experience, and is not wholly *a priori* or ontological. For this reason, and because the object of all possible experience is called the world, it is entitled the *cosmological* proof. Since, in dealing with the objects of experience, the proof abstracts from all special properties through which this world may differ from any other possible world, the title also serves to distinguish it from the physico-theological proof, which is based upon observations of the particular properties of the world disclosed to us by our senses.

The proof then proceeds as follows: The necessary being can be determined in one way only, that

---

* This inference is too well known to require detailed statement. It depends on the supposedly transcendental law of natural causality: that everything contingent has a cause, which, if itself contingent, must likewise have a cause, till the series of subordinate causes ends with an absolutely necessary cause, without which it would have no completeness.

is, by one out of each possible pair of opposed predicates. It must therefore be *completely* determined through its own concept. Now there is only one possible concept which determines a thing completely *a priori*, namely, the concept of the *ens realissimum*. The concept of the *ens realissimum* is therefore the only concept through which a necessary being can be thought. In other words, a supreme being necessarily exists.

In this cosmological argument there are combined so many pseudo-rational principles that speculative reason seems in this case to have brought to bear all the resources of its dialectical skill to produce the greatest possible transcendental illusion. The testing of the argument may meantime be postponed while we detail in order the various devices whereby an old argument is disguised as a new one, and by which appeal is made to the agreement of two witnesses, the one with credentials of pure reason and the other with those of experience. In reality the only witness is that which speaks in the name of pure reason; in the endeavour to pass as a second witness it merely changes its dress and voice. In order to lay a secure foundation for itself, this proof takes its stand on experience, and thereby makes profession of being distinct from the ontological proof, which puts its entire trust in pure *a priori* concepts. But the cosmological proof uses this experience only for a single step in the argument, namely, to conclude the existence of a necessary being. What properties this being may have, the empirical premiss cannot tell us. Reason therefore abandons experience altogether, and endeavours to discover from mere concepts what properties an absolutely necessary being must have, that is, which among all possible things contains in itself the conditions (*requisita*) essential to absolute necessity. Now these, it is supposed, are nowhere to be found save in the concept of an *ens realissimum*; and the conclusion is therefore drawn, that the *ens realissimum* is the absolutely necessary being. But it is evident that we are here presupposing that the concept of the highest reality is completely adequate to the concept of absolute necessity of existence; that is, that the latter can be inferred from the former. Now this is the proposition maintained by the ontological proof; it is here being assumed in the cosmological proof, and indeed made the basis of the proof; and yet it is an assumption with which this latter proof has professed to dispense. For absolute

necessity is an existence determined from mere concepts. If I say, the concept of the *ens realissimum* is a concept, and indeed the only concept, which is appropriate and adequate to necessary existence, I must also admit that necessary existence can be inferred from this concept. Thus the so-called cosmological proof really owes any cogency which it may have to the ontological proof from mere concepts. The appeal to experience is quite superfluous; experience may perhaps lead us to the concept of absolute necessity, but is unable to demonstrate this necessity as belonging to any determinate thing. For immediately we endeavour to do so, we must abandon all experience and search among pure concepts to discover whether any one of them contains the conditions of the possibility of an absolutely necessary being. If in this way we can determine the possibility of a necessary being, we likewise establish its existence. For what we are then saying is this: that of all possible beings there is one which carries with it absolute necessity, that is, that this being exists with absolute necessity.

Fallacious and misleading arguments are most easily detected if set out in correct syllogistic form. This we now proceed to do in the instance under discussion.

If the proposition, that every absolutely necessary being is likewise the most real of all beings, is correct (and this is the *nervus probandi* of the cosmological proof), it must, like all affirmative judgments, be convertible, at least *per accidens*. It therefore follows that some *entia realissima* are likewise absolutely necessary beings. But one *ens realissimum* is in no respect different from another, and what is true of *some* under this concept is true also of *all*. In this case, therefore, I can convert the proposition *simpliciter*, not only *per accidens*, and say that every *ens realissimum* is a necessary being. But since this proposition is determined from its *a priori* concepts alone, the mere concept of the *ens realissimum* must carry with it the absolute necessity of that being; and this is precisely what the ontological proof has asserted and what the cosmological proof has refused to admit, although the conclusions of the latter are indeed covertly based on it.

Thus the second path upon which speculative reason enters in its attempt to prove the existence of a supreme being is not only as deceptive as the first, but has this additional defect, that it is guilty of an *ignoratio elenchi.* It professes to lead us by a new path, but after a short circuit brings us back to the very path which we had deserted at its bidding.

I have stated that in this cosmological argument there lies hidden a whole nest of dialectical assumptions, which the transcendental critique can easily detect and destroy. These deceptive principles I shall merely enumerate, leaving to the reader, who by this time will be sufficiently expert in these matters, the task of investigating them further, and of refuting them.

We find, for instance, (1) the transcendental principle whereby from the contingent we infer a cause. This principle is applicable only in the sensible world; outside that world it has no meaning whatsoever. For the mere intellectual concept of the contingent cannot give rise to any synthetic proposition, such as that of causality. The principle of causality has no meaning and no criterion for its application save only in the sensible world. But in the cosmological proof it is precisely in order to enable us to advance beyond the sensible world that it is employed. (2) The inference to a first cause, from the impossibility of an infinite series of causes, given one after the other, in the sensible world. The principles of the employment of reason do not justify this conclusion even within the world of experience, still less beyond this world in a realm into which this series can never be extended. (3) The unjustified self-satisfaction of reason in respect of the completion of this series. The removal of all the conditions without which no concept of necessity is possible is taken by reason to be a completion of the concept of the series, on the ground that we can then conceive nothing further. (4) The confusion between the logical possibility of a concept of all reality united into one (without inner contradiction) and the transcendental possibility of such a reality. In the case of the latter there is needed a principle to establish the practicability of such a synthesis, a principle which itself, however, can apply only to the field of possible experiences – etc.

The procedure of the cosmological proof is artfully designed to enable us to escape having to prove the existence of a necessary being *a priori* through mere concepts. Such proof would require to be carried out in the ontological manner, and that is an enterprise for which we feel ourselves to be altogether incompetent.

Accordingly, we take as the starting-point of our inference an actual existence (an experience in general), and advance, in such manner as we can, to some absolutely necessary condition of this existence. We have then no need to show the possibility of this condition. For if it has been proved to exist, the question as to its possibility is entirely superfluous. If now we want to determine more fully the nature of this necessary being, we do not endeavour to do so in the manner that would be really adequate, namely, by discovering from its concept the necessity of its existence. For could we do that, we should be in no need of an empirical starting-point. No, all we seek is the negative condition (*conditio sine qua non*), without which a being would not be absolutely necessary. And in all other kinds of reasoning from a given consequence to its ground this would be legitimate; but in the present case it unfortunately happens that the condition which is needed for absolute necessity is only to be found in one single being. This being must therefore contain in its concept all that is required for absolute necessity, and consequently it enables me to infer this absolute necessity *a priori.* I must therefore be able also to reverse the inference, and to say: Anything to which this concept (of supreme reality) applies is absolutely necessary. If I cannot make this inference (as I must concede, if I am to avoid admitting the ontological proof), I have come to grief in the new way that I have been following, and am back again at my starting-point. The concept of the supreme being satisfies all questions *a priori* which can be raised regarding the inner determinations of a thing, and is therefore an ideal that is quite unique, in that the concept, while universal, also at the same time designates an individual as being among the things that are possible. But it does not give satisfaction concerning the question of its own existence – though this is the real purpose of our enquiries – and if anyone admitted the existence of a necessary being but wanted to know which among all [existing] things is to be identified with that being, we could not answer: "This, not that, is the necessary being."

We may indeed be allowed to *postulate* the existence of an all-sufficient being, as the cause of all possible effects, with a view to lightening the task of reason in its search for the unity of the grounds of explanation. But in presuming so far as to say that such a being *necessarily exists,* we are no longer giving modest expression to an admissible hypothesis, but are confidently laying claim to apodeictic certainty. For the knowledge of what we profess to know as absolutely necessary must itself carry with it absolute necessity.

The whole problem of the transcendental ideal amounts to this: either, given absolute necessity, to find a concept which possesses it, or, given the concept of something, to find that something to be absolutely necessary. If either task be possible, so must the other; for reason recognises that only as absolutely necessary which follows of necessity from its concept. But both tasks are quite beyond our utmost efforts to *satisfy* our understanding in this matter; and equally unavailing are all attempts to induce it to acquiesce in its incapacity.

Unconditioned necessity, which we so indispensably require as the last bearer of all things, is for human reason the veritable abyss. Eternity itself, in all its terrible sublimity, as depicted by a Haller, is far from making the same overwhelming impression on the mind; for it only *measures* the duration of things, it does not *support* them. We cannot put aside, and yet also cannot endure the thought, that a being, which we represent to ourselves as supreme amongst all possible beings, should, as it were, say to itself: 'I am from eternity to eternity, and outside me there is nothing save what is through my will, *but whence then am I?*' All support here fails us; and the *greatest* perfection, no less than the *least* perfection, is unsubstantial and baseless for the merely speculative reason, which makes not the least effort to retain either the one or the other, and feels indeed no loss in allowing them to vanish entirely.

Many forces in nature, which manifest their existence through certain effects, remain for us inscrutable; for we cannot track them sufficiently far by observation. Also, the transcendental object lying at the basis of appearances (and with it the reason why our sensibility is subject to certain supreme conditions rather than to others) is and remains for us inscrutable. The thing itself is indeed given, but we can have no insight into its nature. But it is quite otherwise with an ideal of pure reason; it can never be said to be inscrutable. For since it is not required to give any credentials of its reality save only the need on the part of reason to complete all synthetic unity by means of it; and since, therefore, it is in no wise

given as thinkable *object*, it cannot be inscrutable in the manner in which an object is. On the contrary it must, as a mere idea, find its place and its solution in the nature of reason, and must therefore allow of investigation. For it is of the very essence of reason that we should be able to give an account of all our concepts, opinions, and assertions, either upon objective or, in the case of mere illusion, upon subjective grounds.

Discovery and Explanation of the Dialectical Illusion in all Transcendental Proofs of the Existence of a Necessary Being

Both the above proofs were transcendental, that is, were attempted independently of empirical principles. For although the cosmological proof presupposes an experience in general, it is not based on any particular property of this experience but on pure principles of reason, as applied to an existence given through empirical consciousness in general. Further, it soon abandons this guidance and relies on pure concepts alone. What, then, in these transcendental proofs is the cause of the dialectical but natural illusion which connects the concepts of necessity and supreme reality, and which realises and hypostatises what can be an idea only? Why are we constrained to assume that some one among existing things is in itself necessary, and yet at the same time to shrink back from the existence of such a being as from an abyss? And how are we to secure that reason may come to an agreement with itself in this matter, and that from the wavering condition of a diffident approval, ever again withdrawn, it may arrive at settled insight?

There is something very strange in the fact, that once we assume something to exist we cannot avoid inferring that something exists necessarily. The cosmological argument rests on this quite natural (although not therefore certain) inference. On the other hand, if I take the concept of anything, no matter what, I find that the existence of this thing can never be represented by me as absolutely necessary, and that, whatever it may be that exists, nothing prevents me from thinking its nonexistence. Thus while I may indeed be obliged to assume something necessary as a condition of the existent in general, I cannot think any particular thing as in itself necessary. In other words, I can never *complete* the regress to the conditions of existence save by assuming a necessary being, and yet am never in a position to *begin* with such a being.

If I am constrained to think something necessary as a condition of existing things, but am unable to think any particular thing as in itself necessary, it inevitably follows that necessity and contingency do not concern the things themselves; otherwise there would be a contradiction. Consequently, neither of these two principles can be objective. They may, however, be regarded as subjective principles of reason. The one calls upon us to seek something necessary as a condition of all that is given as existent, that is, to stop nowhere until we have arrived at an explanation which is complete *a priori*; the other forbids us ever to hope for this completion, that is, forbids us to treat anything empirical as unconditioned and to exempt ourselves thereby from the toil of its further derivation. Viewed in this manner, the two principles, as merely heuristic and *regulative*, and as concerning only the formal interest of reason, can very well stand side by side. The one prescribes that we are to philosophise about nature as if there were a necessary first ground for all that belongs to existence – solely, however, for the purpose of bringing systematic unity into our knowledge, by always pursuing such an idea, as an imagined ultimate ground. The other warns us not to regard any determination whatsoever of existing things as such an ultimate ground, that is, as absolutely necessary, but to keep the way always open for further derivation, and so to treat each and every determination as always conditioned by something else. But if everything which is perceived in things must necessarily be treated by us as conditioned, nothing that allows of being empirically given can be regarded as absolutely necessary.

Since, therefore, the absolutely necessary is only intended to serve as a principle for obtaining the greatest possible unity among appearances, as being their ultimate ground; and since – inasmuch as the second rule commands us always to regard all empirical causes of unity as themselves derived – we can never reach this unity within the world, it follows that we must regard the absolutely necessary as being *outside* the world.

While the philosophers of antiquity regard all form in nature as contingent, they follow the judgment of the common man in their view of matter as original and necessary. But if, instead of regarding matter relatively, as *substratum* of appearances, they had considered it *in itself*, and as regards its existence, the idea of absolute necessity would at once have disappeared. For there is nothing which absolutely binds reason to accept such an existence; on the contrary it can always annihilate it in thought, without contradiction; absolute necessity is a necessity that is to be found in thought alone. This belief must therefore have been due to a certain regulative principle. In fact extension and impenetrability (which between them make up the concept of matter) constitute the supreme empirical principle of the unity of appearances; and this principle, so far as it is empirically unconditioned, has the character of a regulative principle. Nevertheless, since every determination of the matter which constitutes what is real in appearances, including impenetrability, is an effect (action) which must have its cause and which is therefore always derivative in character, matter is not compatible with the idea of a necessary being as a principle of all derived unity. (For its real properties, being derivative, are one and all only conditionally necessary, and so allow of being removed – wherewith the whole existence of matter would be removed.) If this were not the case, we should have reached the ultimate ground of unity by empirical means – which is forbidden by the second regulative principle. It therefore follows that matter, and in general whatever belongs to the world, is not compatible with the idea of a necessary original being, even when the latter is regarded simply as a principle of the greatest empirical unity. That being or principle must be set outside the world, leaving us free to derive the appearances of the world and their existence from other appearances, with unfailing confidence, just as if there were no necessary being, while yet we are also free to strive unceasingly towards the completeness of that derivation, just as if such a being were presupposed as an ultimate ground.

As follows from these considerations, the ideal of the supreme being is nothing but a *regulative principle* of reason, which directs us to look upon all connection in the world *as if* it originated from an all-sufficient necessary cause. We can base upon the ideal the rule of a systematic and, in accordance with universal laws, necessary unity in the explanation of that connection; but the ideal is not an assertion of an existence necessary in itself. At the same time we cannot avoid the transcendental subreption, by which this formal principle is represented as constitutive, and by which this unity is hypostatised. We proceed here just as we do in the case of space. Space is only a principle of sensibility, but since it is the primary source and condition of all shapes, which are only so many limitations of itself, it is taken as something absolutely necessary, existing in its own right, and as an object given *a priori* in itself. In the same way, since the systematic unity of nature cannot be prescribed as a principle for the empirical employment of our reason, except in so far as we presuppose the idea of an

ens realissimum as the supreme cause, it is quite natural that this latter idea should be represented as an actual object, which, in its character of supreme condition, is also necessary – thus changing a *regulative* into a *constitutive* principle. That such a substitution has been made becomes evident, when we consider this supreme being, which relatively to the world is absolutely (unconditionally) necessary, as a thing in and by itself. For we are then unable to conceive what can be meant by its necessity. The concept of necessity is only to be found in our reason, as a formal condition of thought; it does not allow of being hypostatised as a material condition of existence.

William Paley, "The Argument from Design"

Introduction

Looking back over the history of philosophy today, William Paley's *Natural Theology, or Evidences of the Existence and Attributes of the Deity Collected from the Appearances of Nature* (1805) seems a rather untimely work. Its publication takes place after both the devastating – and for many conclusive – critique of natural theology advanced by David Hume's *Dialogues Concerning Natural Religion* (1779) and Immanuel Kant's *Critique of Pure Reason* (1781), as well as Kant's analysis in the *Critique of Judgment* (1790) of teleological judgment as apprehending nature as "purposive," though without actual purpose. But one must remember that at that time Hume's fame as philosopher was limited, and in Paley's England Hume was far better known as an essayist and historian. Kant's critique had in Paley's day penetrated very little the world of English letters, let alone the intellectual circles of divines.

Paley was born in Peterborough, England, and educated at Christ's College, Cambridge, where he became a fellow and then a tutor. A highly regarded lecturer, Paley's liberal political views – including his call for the abolition of slavery and his latitudinarianism – seem to have limited his rise in the Church of England. Nevertheless, his

From William Paley, *Natural Theology: Selections*, ed. F. Ferré, Indianapolis, IN: Bobbs-Merrill, 1963, pp. 3–12, 32–3, 45–9, 82–6.

treatise in political theory, *The Principles of Moral and Political Philosophy* (1785), proved very popular and earned him a leading place among utilitarian thinkers of the day.

The following selection presents Paley's rendering of the argument for which Paley is, however, today best known – the "argument from design" or "teleological argument." The argument possesses a long and diverse history, appearing among pre-Socratics like Anaxagoras,[1] in Plato,[2] among the ancient Stoics,[3] in the work of various medieval philosophers including Thomas Aquinas (IV.9),[4] and among early modern deists such as Matthew Tindal (IV.14). Its persistence, despite severe criticism, is itself remarkable and possibly suggests that there is something especially natural or easy about the inference upon which it turns. Today the argument survives among a sizeable number of religious philosophers and among proponents of "intelligent design" critiques of natural selection and naturalistic evolutionary theory.[5]

By argument from "design" or "teleological" argument, scholars mean a class of inference common to "natural" theology. "Revealed" theology presents a sort of top-down model for the acquisition of knowledge of things divine and transcendent. Just as Yaweh is said to have presented the Decalogue to Moses (Exodus 20), as God is said to have instructed Joseph to flee to Egypt in a dream (Matthew 2:13), revelation involves the communication of knowledge from the divine to the human mind. "Natural" theology, by contrast, comprises a more bottom-up process. Through the exercise of the intellect or the natural capacity for reason, the mind infers truths about the divine on the basis of nothing more than observations of the natural universe naturally acquired.

In the case of the design or teleological argument, various features of the natural universe are held to exhibit signs of design or intent – that is, to have been organized for some purpose or "end" (Gk: *telos*, pl. *telē*). To make this point, Paley draws the now famous analogy between the natural world, in particular the human body, and a watch. If one were to stumble upon a pocket watch on the ground in the middle of a forest, one would clearly be able to infer that the watch was produced through purposeful action – design.[6] We know this, says Paley, because the parts of the watch work together with such remarkable order and precision to make the watch mechanisms function.[7] Because like the watch the parts of the human body fit together in such an orderly way to support the functions of the human organism – as for example they do in the human eye – the human body, like so much of the natural world, must have been the product of design, as well. Today, many design arguments focus on the complexity rather than the order of the natural world. In the regard of "intelligent design" theorists, many aspects of the natural world exhibit what they call an "irreducible" complexity – a complexity that cannot be explained by the combination of simple elements in the absence of intent or design.

For Paley, the design argument not only fortifies explanations of the origin of the natural world (as having been created), it even proves its point if we take the world to be eternal and uncreated. That is, even if the world is without temporal origin and human beings have always existed the quality of organization of parts in the human body by itself testifies to the operation of intent and design. On the basis of this apparent design, Paley goes on to infer various attributes of God, including "wisdom," "unity," "omnipotence," "omniscience," and "infinity." Paley characterizes these predicates, however, in a guarded way, as at least rhetorical superlatives, if not exactly literal truths.

Notes

1 Anaxagoras: "[15] All things which have life, both the greater and the less, are ruled by Mind [*noûs*]. . . . And the things that were mixed together, and separated off, and divided, were all understood by [*noûs*]. And whatever they were going to be, and whatever things were then in existence that are not now, and all things that now exist and whatever shall exist – all were arranged by Mind [*noûs*]." *Ancient Philosophy*, 5th edition, ed. F. E. Baird and W. Kaufmann, Upper Saddle River, NJ: Prentice Hall, 2008, p. 38.

2 *Phaedo* 96a–98b, *Timaeus* 27dff.

3 Cicero, *Academica* II.xxxix.121–3; *De natura deorum* I.viii–ix; I.xiv; and II.vi.

4 Augustine, *Confessions* X.6. See also the famous "five ways" of Thomas Aquinas: *Summa Theologica*, I.Q2.a3.

5 M. J. Behe, "The Modern Intelligent Design Hypothesis: Breaking Rules," in *God and Design: The Teleological Argument and Modern Science* , ed. N. Manson, London: Routledge, 2003, pp. 277–91; and *Darwin's Black Box: The Biochemical Challenge to Evolution*, New York: The Free Press, 1996. See also R. Collins, "A Scientific Argument for the Existence of God: The Fine-Tuning Design Argument," in M. J. Murray, ed., *Reason for the Hope Within*, Grand Rapids, MI: Eerdmans, 1999, pp. 47–75.

6 While Paley is commonly credited with the "watch" analogy, he seems to have drawn it from Dutch philosopher Bernard Nieuwentyt (1654–1718), *The Existence of God, Shown by the Wonders of Nature* (1715); F. Ferré, *Natural Theology*, xiii.

7 Hume would counter that humans would know the watch was designed only because they have observed the crafting of watches and things like watches. No one, however, says Hume in the *Dialogues*, has observed the intentional production of worlds or of organisms – except, of course, in the natural way.

Paley, "The Argument from Design"

Chapter one: State of the Argument

In crossing a heath, suppose I pitched my foot against a *stone* and were asked how the stone came to be there, I might possibly answer that for anything I knew to the contrary it had lain there forever; nor would it, perhaps, be very easy to show the absurdity of this answer. But suppose I had found a *watch* upon the ground, and it should be inquired how the watch happened to be in that place, I should hardly think of the answer which I had before given, that for anything I knew the watch might have always been there. Yet why should not this answer serve for the watch as well as for the stone; why is it not as admissible in the second case as in the first? For this reason, and for no other, namely, that when we come to inspect the watch, we perceive – what we could not discover in the stone – that its several parts are framed and put together for a purpose, e.g., that they are so formed and adjusted as to produce motion, and that motion so regulated as to point out the hour of the day; that if the different parts had been differently shaped from what they are, or placed after any other manner or in any other order than that in which they are placed, either no motion at all would have been carried on in the machine, or none which would have answered the use that is now served by it. To reckon up a few of the plainest of these parts and of their offices, all tending to one result: we see a cylindrical box containing a coiled elastic spring, which, by its endeavor to relax itself, turns round the box. We next observe a flexible chain – artificially wrought for the sake of flexure – communicating the action of the spring from the box to the fusee. We then find a series of wheels, the teeth of which catch in and apply to each other, conducting the motion from the fusee to the balance and from the balance to the pointer, and at the same time, by the size and shape of those wheels, so regulating that motion as to terminate in causing an index, by an equable and measured progression, to pass over a given space in a given time. We take notice that the wheels are made of brass, in order to keep them from rust; the springs of steel, no other metal being so elastic; that over the face of the watch there is placed a glass, a material employed in no other part of the work, but in the room of which, if there

had been any other than a transparent substance, the hour could not be seen without opening the case. This mechanism being observed – it requires indeed an examination of the instrument, and perhaps some previous knowledge of the subject, to perceive and understand it; but being once, as we have said, observed and understood – the inference we think is inevitable, that the watch must have had a maker – that there must have existed, at some time and at some place or other, an artificer or artificers who formed it for the purpose which we find it actually to answer, who completely comprehended its construction and designed its use.

I. Nor would it, I apprehend, weaken the conclusion, that we had never seen a watch made – that we had never known an artist capable of making one – that we were altogether incapable of executing such a piece of workmanship ourselves, or of understanding in what manner it was performed; all this being no more than what is true of some exquisite remains of ancient art, of some lost arts, and, to the generality of mankind, of the more curious productions of modern manufacture. Does one man in a million know how oval frames are turned? Ignorance of this kind exalts our opinion of the unseen and unknown artist's skill, if he be unseen and unknown, but raises no doubt in our minds of the existence and agency of such an artist, at some former time and in some place or other. Nor can I perceive that it varies at all the inference, whether the question arise concerning a human agent or concerning an agent of a different species, or an agent possessing in some respects a different nature.

II. Neither, secondly, would it invalidate our conclusion, that the watch sometimes went wrong or that it seldom went exactly right. The purpose of the machinery, the design, and the designer might be evident, and in the case supposed, would be evident, in whatever way we accounted for the irregularity of the movement, or whether we could account for it or not. It is not necessary that a machine be perfect in order to show with what design it was made: still less necessary, where the only question is whether it were made with any design at all.

III. Nor, thirdly, would it bring any uncertainty into the argument, if there were a few parts of the watch, concerning which we could not discover or had not yet discovered in what manner they conduced to the general effect; or even some parts, concerning which we could not ascertain whether they conduced to that effect in any manner whatever. For, as to the first branch of the case, if by the loss, or disorder, or decay of the parts in question, the movement of the watch were found in fact to be stopped, or disturbed, or retarded, no doubt would remain in our minds as to the utility or intention of these parts, although we should be unable to investigate the manner according to which, or the connection by which, the ultimate effect depended upon their action or assistance; and the more complex the machine, the more likely is this obscurity to arise. Then, as to the second thing supposed, namely, that there were parts which might be spared without prejudice to the movement of the watch, and that we had proved this by experiment, these superfluous parts, even if we were completely assured that they were such, would not vacate the reasoning which we had instituted concerning other parts. The indication of contrivance remained, with respect to them, nearly as it was before.

IV.   Nor, fourthly, would any man in his senses think the existence of the watch with its various machinery accounted for, by being told that it was one out of possible combinations of material forms; that whatever he had found in the place where he found the watch, must have contained some internal configuration or other; and that this configuration might be the structure now exhibited, namely, of the works of a watch, as well as a different structure.

V.   Nor, fifthly, would it yield his inquiry more satisfaction, to be answered that there existed in things a principle of order, which had disposed the parts of the watch into their present form and situation. He never knew a watch made by the principle of order; nor can he even form to himself an idea of what is meant by a principle of order distinct from the intelligence of the watchmaker.

VI.   Sixthly, he would be surprised to hear that the mechanism of the watch was no proof of contrivance, only a motive to induce the mind to think so:

VII.   And not less surprised to be informed that the watch in his hand was nothing more than the result of the laws of *metallic* nature. It is a perversion of language to assign any law as the efficient, operative cause of any thing. A law presupposes an agent, for it is only the mode according to which an agent proceeds: it implies a power, for it is the order according to which that power acts. Without this agent, without this power, which are both distinct from itself, the *law* does nothing, is nothing. The expression, "the law of metallic nature," may sound strange and harsh to a philosophical ear; but it seems quite as justifiable as some others which are more familiar to him, such as "the law of vegetable nature," "the law of animal nature," or, indeed, as "the law of nature" in general, when assigned as the cause of phenomena, in exclusion of agency and power, or when it is substituted into the place of these.

VIII.   Neither, lastly, would our observer be driven out of his conclusion or from his confidence in its truth by being told that he knew nothing at all about the matter. He knows enough for his argument; he knows the utility of the end; he knows the subserviency and adaptation of the means to the end. These points being known, his ignorance of other points, his doubts concerning other points affect not the certainty of his reasoning. The consciousness of knowing little need not beget a distrust of that which he does know.

Chapter two: State of the Argument Continued

Suppose, in the next place, that the person who found the watch should after some time discover that, in addition to all the properties which he had hitherto observed in it, it possessed the unexpected property of producing in the course of its movement another watch like itself – the thing is conceivable; that it contained within it a mechanism, a system of parts – a mold, for instance, or a complex adjustment of lathes, files, and other tools – evidently and separately calculated for this purpose; let us inquire what effect ought such a discovery to have upon his former conclusion.

I.   The first effect would be to increase his admiration of the contrivance, and his conviction of the consummate skill of the contriver. Whether he regarded the object of the contrivance, the distinct apparatus, the intricate, yet in many parts intelligible mechanism by which it was carried on, he would perceive in this new observation nothing but an additional reason for doing what he had already done – for referring the construction of the watch to design and to supreme art. If that construction *without* this property, or, which is the same thing, before this property had been noticed, proved intention and art to have been employed about it, still more strong would the proof appear when he came to the knowledge of this further property, the crown and perfection of all the rest.

II. He would reflect that, though the watch before him were *in some sense* the maker of the watch which was fabricated in the course of its movements, yet it was in a very different sense from that in which a carpenter, for instance, is the maker of a chair – the author of its contrivance, the cause of the relation of its parts to their use. With respect to these, the first watch was no cause at all to the second; in no such sense as this was it the author of the constitution and order, either of the parts which the new watch contained, or of the parts by the aid and instrumentality of which it was produced. We might possibly say, but with great latitude of expression, that a stream of water ground corn; but no latitude of expression would allow us to say, no stretch of conjecture could lead us to think that the stream of water built the mill, though it were too ancient for us to know who the builder was. What the stream of water does in the affair is neither more nor less than this: by the application of an unintelligent impulse to a mechanism previously arranged, arranged independently of it and arranged by intelligence, an effect is produced, namely, the corn is ground. But the effect results from the arrangement. The force of the stream cannot be said to be the cause or the author of the effect, still less of the arrangement. Understanding and plan in the formation of the mill were not the less necessary for any share which the water has in grinding the corn; yet is this share the same as that which the watch would have contributed to the production of the new watch, upon the supposition assumed in the last section. Therefore,

III. Though it be now no longer probable that the individual watch which our observer had found was made immediately by the hand of an artificer, yet this alteration does not in anywise affect the inference that an artificer had been originally employed and concerned in the production. The argument from design remains as it was. Marks of design and contrivance are no more accounted for now than they were before.

In the same thing, we may ask for the cause of different properties. We may ask for the cause of the color of a body, of its hardness, of its heat; and these causes may be all different. We are now asking for the cause of that subserviency to a use, that relation to an end, which we have remarked in the watch before us. No answer is given to this question by telling us that a preceding watch produced it. There cannot be design without a designer; contrivance without a contriver; order without choice; arrangement without anything capable of arranging; subserviency and relation to a purpose without that which could intend a purpose; means suitable to an end, and executing their office in accomplishing that end, without the end ever having been contemplated or the means accommodated to it. Arrangement, disposition of parts, subserviency of means to an end, relation of instruments to a use imply the presence of intelligence and mind. No one, therefore, can rationally believe that the insensible, inanimate watch, from which the watch before us issued, was the proper cause of the mechanism we so much admire in it – could be truly said to have constructed the instrument, disposed its parts, assigned their office, determined their order, action, and mutual dependency, combined their several motions into one result, and that also a result connected with the utilities of other beings. All these properties, therefore, are as much unaccounted for as they were before.

IV. Nor is anything gained by running the difficulty farther back, that is, by supposing the watch before us to have been produced from another watch, that from a former, and so on indefinitely. Our going back ever so far brings us no nearer to the least degree of satisfaction upon the subject. Contrivance is still unaccounted for. We still want a contriver. A designing mind is neither supplied by this supposition nor dispensed with. If the difficulty were diminished the farther we went back, by going back indefinitely we might exhaust it. And this is the only case to which this sort of reasoning applies. Where there is a tendency, or, as we increase the number of terms, a continual approach toward a limit, *there*, by supposing the number of terms to be what is called infinite, we may conceive the limit to be attained; but where there is no such tendency or approach, nothing is effected by lengthening the series. There is no difference as to the point in question, whatever there may be as to many points, between one series and another – between a series which is finite and a series which is infinite. A chain composed of an infinite number of links can no more support itself than a chain composed of a finite number of links. And of this we are assured, though we never *can* have tried the experiment; because, by increasing the number of links, from ten, for instance, to a hundred, from a hundred to a thousand, etc., we make not the smallest approach, we observe not the smallest tendency toward self-support. There is no difference in this respect – yet there may be a great difference in several respects – between a chain of a greater or less length, between one chain and another, between one that is finite and one that is infinite. This very much resembles the case before us. The machine which we are inspecting demonstrates, by its construction, contrivance and design. Contrivance must have had a contriver, design a designer, whether the machine immediately proceeded from another machine or not. That circumstance alters not the case. That other machine may, in like manner, have proceeded from a former machine: nor does that alter the case; the contrivance must have had a contriver. That former one from one preceding it: no alteration still; a contriver is still necessary. No tendency is perceived, no approach toward a diminution of this necessity. It is the same with any and every succession of these machines – a succession of ten, of a hundred, of a thousand; with one series, as with another – a series which is finite, as with a series which is infinite. In whatever other respects they may differ, in this they do not. In all equally, contrivance and design are unaccounted for.

The question is not simply, how came the first watch into existence? – which question, it may be pretended, is done away by supposing the series of watches thus produced from one another to have been infinite, and consequently to have had no such *first* for which it was necessary to provide a cause. This, perhaps, would have been nearly the state of the question, if nothing had been before us but an unorganized, unmechanized substance, without mark or indication of contrivance. It might be difficult to show that such substance could not have existed from eternity, either in succession – if it were possible, which I think it is not, for unorganized bodies to spring from one another – or by individual perpetuity. But that is not the question now. To suppose it

to be so is to suppose that it made no difference whether he had found a watch or a stone. As it is, the metaphysics of that question have no place; for, in the watch which we are examining are seen contrivance, design, an end, a purpose, means for the end, adaptation to the purpose. And the question which irresistibly presses upon our thoughts is, whence this contrivance and design? The thing required is the intending mind, the adapted hand, the intelligence by which that hand was directed. This question, this demand is not shaken off by increasing a number or succession of substances destitute of these properties; nor the more, by increasing that number to infinity. If it be said that, upon the supposition of one watch being produced from another in the course of that other's movements and by means of the mechanism within it, we have a cause for the watch in my hand, namely, the watch from which it proceeded; I deny that for the design, the contrivance, the suitableness of means to an end, the adaptation of instruments to a use, all of which we discover in the watch, we have any cause whatever. It is in vain, therefore, to assign a series of such causes or to allege that a series may be carried back to infinity; for I do not admit that we have yet any cause at all for the phenomena, still less any series of causes either finite or infinite. Here is contrivance but no contriver; proofs of design, but no designer.

V.   Our observer would further also reflect that the maker of the watch before him was in truth and reality the maker of every watch produced from it: there being no difference, except that the latter manifests a more exquisite skill, between the making of another watch with his own hands, by the mediation of files, lathes, chisels, etc., and the disposing, fixing, and inserting of these instruments, or of others equivalent to them, in the body of the watch already made, in such a manner as to form a new watch in the course of the movements which he had given to the old one. It is only working by one set of tools instead of another.

The conclusion which the *first* examination of the watch, of its works, construction, and movement, suggested, was that it must have had, for cause and author of that construction, an artificer who understood its mechanism and designed its use. This conclusion is invincible. A *second* examination presents us with a new discovery. The watch is found, in the course of its movement, to produce another watch similar to itself; and not only so, but we perceive in it a system or organization separately calculated for that purpose. What effect would this discovery have or ought it to have upon our former inference? What, as has already been said, but to increase beyond measure our admiration of the skill which had been employed in the formation of such a machine? Or shall it, instead of this, all at once turn us round to an opposite conclusion, namely, that no art or skill whatever has been concerned in the business, although all other evidences of art and skill remain as they were, and this last and supreme piece of art be now added to the rest? Can this be maintained without absurdity? Yet this is atheism.

[...]

Chapter six: The Argument Cumulative

Were there no example in the world of contrivance except that of the *eye*, it would be alone sufficient to support the conclusion which we draw from it, as to the necessity of an intelligent Creator. It could never be got rid of, because it could not be accounted for by any other supposition which did not contradict all the principles we possess of knowledge – the principles according to which things do, as often as they can be brought to the test of experience, turn out to be true or false. Its coats and humors, constructed as the lenses of a telescope are constructed, for the refraction of rays of light to a point, which forms the proper action of the organ; the provision in its muscular tendons for turning its pupil to the object, similar to that which is given to the telescope by screws, and upon which power of direction in the eye the exercise of its office as an optical instrument depends; the further provision for its defense, for its constant lubricity and moisture, which we see in its socket and its lids, in its glands for the secretion of the matter of tears, its outlet or communication with the nose for carrying off the liquid after the eye is washed with it; these provisions compose altogether an apparatus, a system of parts, a preparation of means, so manifest in their design, so exquisite in their contrivance, so successful in their issue, so precious, and so infinitely beneficial in their use, as, in my opinion, to bear down all doubt that can be raised upon the subject. And what I wish,

under the title of the present chapter, to observe is that, if other parts of nature were inaccessible to our inquiries, or even if other parts of nature presented nothing to our examination but disorder and confusion, the validity of this example would remain the same. If there were but one watch in the world, it would not be less certain that it had a maker. If we had never in our lives seen any but one single kind of hydraulic machine, yet if of that one kind we understood the mechanism and use, we should be as perfectly assured that it proceeded from the hand and thought and skill of a workman, as if we visited a museum of the arts and saw collected there twenty different kinds of machines for drawing water, or a thousand different kinds for other purposes. Of this point each machine is a proof independently of all the rest. So it is with the evidences of a divine agency. The proof is not a conclusion which lies at the end of a chain of reasoning, of which chain each instance of contrivance is only a link, and of which, if one link fail, the whole fails; but it is an argument separately supplied by every separate example. An error in stating an example affects only that example. The argument is cumulative in the fullest sense of that term. The eye proves it without the ear; the ear without the eye. The proof in each example is complete; for when the design of the part and the conduciveness of its structure to that design is shown, the mind may set itself at rest; no future consideration can detract anything from the force of the example.

[...]

Chapter twenty-four: Of the Natural Attributes of the Deity

It is an immense conclusion that there is a God – a perceiving, intelligent, designing Being, at the head of creation, and from whose will it proceeded. The *attributes* of such a Being, suppose his reality to be proved, must be adequate to the magnitude, extent, and multiplicity of his operations, which are not only vast beyond comparison with those performed by any other power, but so far as respects our conceptions of them, infinite, because they are unlimited on all sides.

Yet the contemplation of a nature so exalted, however surely we arrive at the proof of its existence, overwhelms our faculties. The mind feels its powers sink under the subject. One consequence of which is that from painful abstraction the thoughts seek relief in sensible images, whence may be deduced the ancient and almost universal propensity to idolatrous substitutions. They are the resources of a laboring imagination. False religions usually fall in with the natural propensity; true religions, or such as have derived themselves from the true, resist it.

It is one of the advantages of the revelations which we acknowledge, that while they reject idolatry with its many pernicious accompaniments, they introduce the Deity to human apprehension under an idea more personal, more determinate, more within its compass, than the theology of nature can do. And this they do by representing him exclusively under the relation in which he stands to ourselves; and for the most part, under some precise character, resulting from that relation or from the history of his providences; which method suits the span of our intellects much better than the universality which enters into the idea of God, as deduced from the views of nature. When, therefore, these representations are well founded in point of authority – for all depends upon that – they afford a condescension to the state of our faculties, of which they who have most reflected on the subject will be the first to acknowledge the want and the value.

Nevertheless, if we be careful to imitate the documents of our religion by confining our explanations to what concerns ourselves, and do not affect more precision in our ideas than the subject allows of, the several terms which are employed to denote the attributes of the Deity may be made, even in natural religion, to bear a sense consistent with truth and reason and not surpassing our comprehension.

These terms are omnipotence, omniscience, omnipresence, eternity, self-existence, necessary existence, spirituality.

"Omnipotence," "omniscience," "infinite" power, "infinite" knowledge are *superlatives* expressing our conception of these attributes in the strongest and most elevated terms which language supplies. We ascribe power to the Deity under the name of "omnipotence," the strict and correct conclusion being that a power which could create such a world as this is must be, beyond all comparison, greater than any which we experience in ourselves, than any which we

observe in other visible agents, greater also than any which we can want, for our individual protection and preservation, in the Being upon whom we depend. It is a power likewise to which we are not authorized, by our observation or knowledge, to assign any limits of space or duration.

Very much of the same sort of remark is applicable to the term "omniscience" – infinite knowledge, or infinite wisdom. In strictness of language, there is a difference between knowledge and wisdom, wisdom always supposing action and action directed by it. With respect to the first, namely, *knowledge*, the Creator must know intimately the constitution and properties of the things which he created, which seems also to imply a foreknowledge of their action upon one another and of their changes; at least, so far as the same result from trains of physical and necessary causes. His omniscience also, as far as respects things present, is deducible from his nature, as an intelligent being, joined with the extent, or rather the universality of his operations. Where he acts, he is; and where he is, he perceives. The *wisdom* of the Deity, as testified in the works of creation, surpasses all idea we have of wisdom drawn from the highest intellectual operations of the highest class of intelligent beings with whom we are acquainted; and, which is of the chief importance to us, whatever be its compass or extent which it is evidently impossible that we should be able to determine, it must be adequate to the conduct of that order of things under which we live. And this is enough. It is of very inferior consequence by what terms we express our notion, or rather our admiration of this attribute. The terms which the piety and the usage of language have rendered habitual to us may be as proper as any other. We can trace this attribute much beyond what is necessary for any conclusion to which we have occasion to apply it. The degree of knowledge and power requisite for the formation of created nature cannot, with respect to us, be distinguished from infinite.

The divine "omnipresence" stands, in natural theology, upon this foundation: in every part and place of the universe with which we are acquainted we perceive the exertion of a power which we believe, mediately or immediately, to proceed from the Deity. For instance, in what part or point of space that has ever been explored do we not discover attraction? In what regions do we not find light? In what accessible portion of our globe do we not meet with gravity, magnetism, electricity, together with the properties also and powers of organized substances, of vegetable, or of animated nature? Nay, further, we may ask, what kingdom is there of nature, what corner of space, in which there is anything that can be examined by us, where we do not fall upon contrivance and design? The only reflection perhaps which arises in our minds from this view of the world around us is that the laws of nature everywhere prevail, that they are uniform and universal. But what do you mean by the laws of nature or by any law? Effects are produced by power not by laws. A law cannot execute itself. A law refers us to an agent. Now, an agency so general as that we cannot discover its absence, or assign the place in which some effect of its continued energy is not found, may, in popular language at least, and perhaps without much deviation from philosophical strictness, be called universal; and with not quite the same but with no inconsiderable propriety the person or being in whom that power resides or from whom it is derived may be taken to be omnipresent. He who upholds all things by his power may be said to be everywhere present.

This is called a virtual presence. There is also what metaphysicians denominate an essential ubiquity, and which idea the language of Scripture seems to favor; but the former, I think, goes as far as natural theology carries us.

"Eternity" is a negative idea clothed with a positive name. It supposes, in that to which it is applied, a present existence, and is the negation of a beginning or an end of that existence. As applied to the Deity, it has not been controverted by those who acknowledge a Deity at all. Most assuredly, there never was a time in which nothing existed, because that condition must

have continued. The universal *blank* must have remained; nothing could rise up out of it, nothing could ever have existed since, nothing could exist now. In strictness, however, we have no concern with duration prior to that of the visible world. Upon this article, therefore, of theology it is sufficient to know that the contriver necessarily existed before the contrivance.

"Self-existence" is another negative idea, namely, the negation of a preceding cause, as of a progenitor, a maker, an author, a creator.

"Necessary existence" means demonstrable existence.

"Spirituality" expresses an idea made up of a negative part and of a positive part. The negative part consists in the exclusion of some of the known properties of matter, especially of solidity, of the *vis inertiae*, and of gravitation. The positive part comprises perception, thought, will, power, *action*; by which last term is meant the origination of motion, the quality, perhaps, in which resides the essential superiority of spirit over matter, "which cannot move, unless it be moved; and cannot but move, when impelled by another."* I apprehend that there can be no difficulty in applying to the Deity both parts of this idea.

---

* Bishop Wilkins' *Principles of Natural Religion*, p. 106. John Wilkins (1614–72), Bishop of Chester, was a man of liberal views and the author of works in various fields, his most important book being *An Essay Towards a Real Character and a Philosophical Language* (London, 1668). The work here referred to by Paley is *On the Principles and Duties of Natural Religion* (London, 1678), with a preface by John Tillotson (1630–94), Archbishop of Canterbury. In this work aspects of Joseph Butler's *Analogy* (1736) are anticipated.

18

Søren Kierkegaard, *Fear and Trembling*, Problema II

Introduction

The two most widely read works by the Danish philosopher and theologian, Søren Kierkegaard (1813–55), are *Either/Or* and *Fear and Trembling*. The second book is something of a sequel to the first, for it develops the theme only briefly introduced at the end of the earlier book – the relationship between religious faith and ethics. The discussion revolves around the Genesis story of Abraham's willingness, at the request of God, to sacrifice his only son. Such a deed, Kierkegaard argues, would by any reasonable standard have been an unethical one.[1] Hence, if Abraham is properly to be admired, there must be something "higher" than ethical demands, in virtue of which there may be a "suspension" of the ethical, as Kierkegaard puts in Problema I of *Fear and Trembling* (see I.17 of this volume). Since this "something" must, for Kierkegaard, be related to Abraham's religious faith – to his being a "knight of faith" – the question of whether it is ever legitimate to "suspend" the ethical leads on to the Problema II question, "Is there an absolute duty to God?"

The main critical target in Problema II is the view, espoused by Hegel, for example, that while there are indeed duties to God, these are deriva-

From Søren Kierkegaard, *Fear and Trembling: Dialectical Lyric by Johannes* de Silentio, trans. A. Hannay, Harmondsworth: Penguin, 1985, pp. 96–108 (notes and several lines omitted).

tive from ethical duties. If God is understood in a merely "abstract" way – as the being who endorses and sanctions the moral law – then it becomes a tautology that we have duties to him. But on this view, Kierkegaard shows, Abraham is "done for": since his deed would have been unethical, he would not have been doing his duty to God either. What he insists is that it is always an open question whether what God requests is ethically right, and vice versa. (Readers will note the relevance of Kierkegaard's discussion to those of Plato in his *Euthyphro* (IV.1) and Duns Scotus (IV.10).) The Abraham story indicates that a person's duty may sometimes be that of "single individual to the absolute" (i.e. God), unmediated by ethical obligations. And in Kierkegaard's view, the New Testament indicates this too: for instance, Luke 14.26 which calls on Christ's disciples to "hate," if need be, those who are close to them, such as their sons. Kierkegaard is maintaining, in effect, that there are duties of faith – quite possibly in conflict with moral principles – that someone has in virtue of a particular personal relationship to God. For the purely ethical person, God is always a "He"; for the knight of faith, God is a "Thou." (See the selection from Martin Buber, IV.21.)

Problema II is important for other reasons. It provides, for a start, Kierkegaard's clearest discussion of the distinction between the knight of faith and the "tragic hero," whose predicament is superficially similar. King Agamemnon must choose between his daughter and his people, but it is a choice between conflicting ethical demands, those of fatherhood and kingship, and not, like Abraham's, a choice between the ethical and the divine. Second, Kierkegaard emphazises what might be called the existential loneliness of the knight of faith who breaks with the ethical. Unlike the tragic hero, he cannot take comfort in the thought that his decision accords with a rational moral principle: indeed, he cannot make his decision intelligible to other people at all. He "winds a lonely path, narrow and steep"; in "cosmic isolation," his responsibility is a "dreadful" one.

Finally, Kierkegaard's discussion perfectly illustrates his harsh and extremely serious conception of what religious faith, especially Christianity, involves. To be a true Christian, one must not try to explain away passages like Luke 14:26 in some anodyne way: one must take them literally, and as asserting "paradoxes," "absurdities," that are inaccessible to rational thought, but which we must nevertheless embrace. Kierkegaard's greatest scorn is reserved for those, like Hegel and, as he sees it, most contemporary spokesmen for Christianity, who distort a dispensation that is at once infinitely demanding and beyond the scope of our rational understanding.

Note

1 Since *Fear and Trembling*, like *Either/Or*, was published under a pseudonym, there is a danger in identifying Kierkegaard's own position with that of his pseudonymous author. For a detailed account of *Fear and Trembling* which gives due recognition to this and other problems concerning Kierkegaard's "indirect communication," see J. Lippitt, *Kierkegaard and* Fear and Trembling, London: Routledge, 2003.

Kierkegaard, *Fear and Trembling*

Problema II: *Is there an absolute duty to God?*

The ethical is the universal and as such, in turn, the divine. It is therefore correct to say that all duty is ultimately duty to God; but if one cannot say more one says in effect that really I have no duty to God. The duty becomes duty to God by being referred to God, but I do not enter into relation with God in the duty itself. Thus it is a duty to love one's neighbour; it is a duty in so far as it is referred to God; yet it is not God that I come in relation to in the duty but the neighbour I love. If, in this connection, I then say that it is my duty to love God, I in fact only utter a tautology, in so far as 'God' is understood in an altogether abstract sense as the divine: i.e. the universal, i.e. duty. The whole of human existence is in that case entirely self-enclosed, as a sphere, and the ethical is at once the limit and completion. God becomes an invisible, vanishing point, an impotent thought, and his power is to be found only in the ethical, which fills all existence. So if it should occur to someone to want to love God in some other sense than that mentioned, he is merely being extravagant and loves a phantom which, if it only had the strength to speak, would say to him: 'Stay where you belong, I don't ask for your love.' If it should occur to someone to want to love God in another way, this love would be suspect, like the love referred to by Rousseau when he talks of a person's loving the Kaffirs instead of his neighbour.

Now if all this is correct, if there is nothing incommensurable in a human life, but any incommensurability were due only to some chance from which nothing followed so far as existence is looked at in light of the Idea, then Hegel would be right. But where he is wrong is in talking about faith or in letting Abraham be looked on as its father; for in this latter he has passed sentence both on Abraham and on faith. In the Hegelian philosophy *das Äussere (die Entäusserung)* [the outer, the externalization] is higher than *das Innere* [the inner]. This is often illustrated by an example. The child is *das Innere*, the man *das Äussere*; which is why the child is determined precisely by the outer, and conversely the man as *das Äussere* by the inner. Faith, on the contrary, is this paradox, that interiority is higher than exteriority, or to recall again an expression we used above, that the odd number is higher than the even.

In the ethical view of life, then, it is the individual's task to divest himself of the determinant of interiority and give it an expression in the exterior. Whenever the individual shrinks from doing so, whenever he wants to stay inside, or slip back into, the inner determinant of feeling, mood, etc., he commits an offence, he is in a state of temptation. The paradox of faith is this, that there is an interiority that is incommensurable with the exterior, an interiority which, it should be stressed, is not identical with the first [that of the child], but is a new interiority. This must not be overlooked. Recent philosophy has allowed itself without further ado to substitute the immediate for 'faith'. If one does that it is ridiculous to deny that faith has existed through all ages. Faith in such a case keeps fairly ordinary company, it belongs with feeling, mood, idiosyncrasy, hysteria and the rest. So far philosophy is right to say one should not stop at that. But there is nothing to warrant philosophy's speaking in this manner. Prior to faith there is a movement of infinity, and only then enters faith, *nec opinate* [unexpectedly], on the strength of the absurd. This I am very well able to understand, without claiming thereby to have faith. If faith is no more than what philosophy passes it off as then Socrates himself already went further, much further, rather than the converse, that he didn't come that far. He made the movement of infinity intellectually. His ignorance is the infinite resignation. That task is in itself a match for human strength, even if people nowadays scorn it; yet it is only when this has been done, only when the individual has exhausted himself in the infinite, that he reaches the point where faith can emerge.

Then faith's paradox is this, that the single individual is higher than the universal, that the single individual (to recall a theological distinction less in vogue these days) determines his relation to the universal through his relation to the absolute, not his relation to the absolute through his relation to the universal. The paradox can also be put by saying that there is an absolute duty to God; for in this tie of obligation the individual relates himself absolutely, as the single individual, to the absolute. When people now say that it is a duty to love God, it is in a sense quite different from the above; for if this duty is absolute the ethical is reduced to the relative. It doesn't follow, nevertheless, that [the ethical] is to be done away with. Only that it gets a quite different expression, the paradoxical expression, so that, e.g., love of God can cause the knight of faith to give his love of his neighbour

the opposite expression to that which is his duty ethically speaking.

Unless this is how it is, faith has no place in existence; and faith is then a temptation, and Abraham is done for, since he gave in to it.

This paradox does not allow of mediation; for it rests precisely on the single individual's being only the single individual. As soon as this individual wants to express his absolute duty in the universal, becomes conscious of it in the latter, he knows he is in a state of temptation, and then, even if he otherwise resists the temptation, he does not come to fulfil that so-called absolute duty, and if he does not resist it he sins even if *realiter* [independently of his inclination, wishes, state of mind] his act is the one that was his absolute duty. Thus what could Abraham have done? If he had wanted to say to someone: 'I love Isaac more than everything in the world, and that's why it is so hard for me to sacrifice him', the person would surely have shaken his head and said: 'Then why sacrifice him?', or if he was a perceptive fellow perhaps he might even have seen through Abraham, realized that he was betraying feelings which stood in flagrant contradiction with his deed.

In the story of Abraham we find just such a paradox. Ethically speaking his relation to Isaac is this, that the father is to love the son. This ethical relationship is reduced to the relative as against the absolute relation to God. To the question, why?, Abraham has no other answer than that it is a trial and a temptation, which, as remarked above, is what makes it a unity of being for both God's sake and his own. These two are also correlative in ordinary usage. Thus when we see someone do something that doesn't conform with the universal, we say, 'He can hardly be doing that for the sake of God', meaning by this that he did it for his own sake. The paradox of faith has lost the intermediate term, i.e. the universal. On the one hand it contains the expression of extreme egoism (doing this dreadful deed for his own sake) and on the other the expression of the most absolute devotion (doing it for God's sake). Faith itself cannot be mediated into the universal, for in that case it would be cancelled. Faith is this paradox, and the single individual is quite unable to make himself intelligible to anyone. One might suppose the single individual could make himself understood to another individual who is in the same situation. Such a view would be unthinkable were it not that nowadays people try in so many ways to sneak their way into greatness. The one knight of faith simply cannot help the other. Either the single individual becomes a knight of faith himself by putting on the paradox, or he never becomes one. Partnership in these regions is quite unthinkable. If there is any more precise explanation of the idea behind the sacrifice of Isaac, it is one that the individual can only give to himself. And supposing one could settle, even with some exactitude, in universal terms, how to understand the case of Isaac (which would in any case be the most absurd self-contradiction, namely that the single individual who stands precisely outside the universal be brought in under universal categories, when he is expressly to act as the single individual outside the universal), the individual could still never be assured of [the truth of] this explanation by others, but only by himself as the single individual. So even if someone were so cowardly and base as to want to be a knight of faith on someone else's responsibility, he would never become one; for only the single individual becomes one, as the single individual, and this is the knight's greatness, as I can well understand without being party to it, since I lack courage; though also his terror, as I can understand even better.

As everyone knows, Luke 14.26 presents a remarkable teaching on the absolute duty to God: 'If any man come to me, and hate not his father, and mother, and wife, and children, and brethren, and sisters, yea, and his own life also, he cannot be my disciple.' This is a hard saying, who can bear to hear it? And for that reason it is heard very seldom. Yet this silence is only a futile evasion. The student of theology learns, however, that these words occur in the New Testament, and in one or another exegetical aid he finds the information that *misein* [to hate], both here and in some other passages, is used *per meiosin* [by adopting a weaker sense] to mean: *minus diligo* [love less], *posthabeo* [give less priority to], *non colo* [show no respect to], *nihil facio* [make nothing of]. The context in which these words occur seems, however, not to corroborate this tasteful explanation. For in the next verse [but one] there is a story about someone who plans to erect a tower but first makes some estimate of his capacity to do so, lest he be the object of ridicule later. The close link between this story and the

verse quoted seems to suggest precisely that the words are to be taken in as terrifying a sense as possible in order that everyone should examine his own ability to erect the building.

If this pious and tender-minded exegete, who thinks he can smuggle Christianity into the world by haggling in this way, should succeed in convincing anyone that grammatically, linguistically, and *kata analogian* [by analogy] this was the meaning of the passage, then it is to be hoped that in so doing he also manages to convince the same person that Christianity is one of the most miserable things in the world. For the teaching which in one of its most lyrical outpourings, where the sense of its eternal validity swells up most strongly, has nothing to offer but a sounding phrase that signifies nothing and suggests only that one is to be less kind, less attentive, more indifferent; the teaching which, just as it seems to want to tell us something terrible, ends up in drivel rather than terror – that teaching is certainly not worth standing up for.

The words are terrible, but I feel sure they can be understood without the person who understands them necessarily having the courage to do as they say. And yet there must be honesty enough to admit what is there, to confess to its greatness even if one lacks the courage oneself. Anyone who manages that will not exclude himself from a share in the beautiful story, for in a way it contains a kind of comfort for the man who lacks courage to begin building the tower. But he must be honest and not pass off this lack of courage as humility, since on the contrary it is pride, while the courage of faith is the only humble courage.

One now sees readily that if the passage is to have any sense, it must be understood literally. It is God who demands absolute love. Anyone who, in demanding a person's love, thinks this must be proved by the latter's becoming lukewarm towards all that was hitherto dear to him, is not simply an egoist but a fool, and anyone demanding such a love would simultaneously sign his own death-warrant in so far as his life is bound up in this love he craves. A husband requires his wife to leave her father and mother, but were he to regard it as proof of her special love for him that for his sake she became a lukewarm, indolent daughter, etc., then he would be an idiot among idiots. Had he any notion of what love was, he would want to discover – and should he discover it see in this an assurance that his wife loved him more than any other in the kingdom – that she was perfect in her love as daughter and sister. So what would be considered a sign of egoism and stupidity in a person, one is supposed with the help of an exegete to regard as a worthy conception of the deity.

But how then *hate* them? I shall not take up the human love/hate distinction here, not because I have so much against it, since at least it is a passionate distinction, but it is egoistic and so does not fit here. If I regard the requirement as a paradox, on the other hand, then I understand it, i.e. understand it in the way one can understand a paradox. The absolute duty can then lead to what ethics would forbid, but it can by no means make the knight of faith have done with loving. This is shown by Abraham. The moment he is ready to sacrifice Isaac, the ethical expression for what he does is this: he hates Isaac. But if he actually hates Isaac he can be certain that God does not require this of him; for Cain and Abraham are not the same. Isaac he must love with all his soul. When God asks for Isaac, Abraham must if possible love him even more, and only then can he *sacrifice* him; for it is indeed this love of Isaac that in its paradoxical opposition to his love of God makes his act a sacrifice. But the distress and anguish in the paradox is that, humanly speaking, he is quite incapable of making himself understood. Only in the moment when his act is in absolute contradiction with his feeling, only then does he sacrifice Isaac, but the reality of his act is that in virtue of which he belongs to the universal, and there he is and remains a murderer.

Furthermore, the passage in Luke must be understood in such a way that one grasps that the knight of faith has no higher expression whatever of the universal (as the ethical) which can save him. Thus if we imagine the Church were to demand this sacrifice of one of its members, then all we have is a tragic hero. For qualitatively the idea of the Church is no different from that of the State, inasmuch as the individual can enter it by common mediation, and in so far as the individual has entered the paradox he does not arrive at the idea of the Church; he doesn't get out of the paradox either, but must find either his blessedness or his damnation inside it. An ecclesiastical hero expresses the universal in his deed, and no one in the Church, not even his father or mother, etc., will fail to understand him. But he is not the knight of faith, and has also a different answer from Abraham's; he doesn't say it is a trial or a temptation in which he is being tested.

One as a rule refrains from citing texts like the one in Luke. There is a fear of letting people loose, a fear that the worst will happen once the individual enjoys carrying on like an individual. Moreover living as the individual is thought to be the easiest thing of all, and it is the universal that people must be coerced into becoming. I can share neither this fear nor this opinion, and for the same reason. No person who has learned that to exist as the individual is the most terrifying thing of all will be afraid of saying it is the greatest. But then he mustn't say it in a way that makes his words a pitfall for somebody on the loose, but rather in a way that helps that person into the universal, even though his words can make some small allowance for greatness. The person who dares not mention such passages dares not mention Abraham either, and to think that existing as the individual is an easy enough matter implies a very dubious indirect admission with regard to oneself; for someone who really respects himself and is concerned for his own soul is assured of the fact that a person living under his own supervision in the world at large lives in greater austerity and seclusion than a maiden in her lady's bower. That there may be some who need coercion, who if given free rein would riot in selfish pleasure like unbridled beasts, is no doubt true, but one should show precisely by the fact that one knows how to speak with fear and trembling that one is not of their number. And out of respect for greatness one should indeed speak, lest it be forgotten for fear of the harm which surely won't arise if one speaks as one who knows it is the great, knows its terrors, and if one doesn't know these one doesn't know its greatness either.

Let us then consider more closely the distress and fear in the paradox of faith. The tragic hero renounces himself in order to express the universal; the knight of faith renounces the universal in order to be the particular. As mentioned, it all depends on how one is placed. Someone who believes it is a simple enough matter to be the individual can always be certain that he is not the knight of faith; for stragglers and vagrant geniuses are not men of faith. Faith's knight knows on the contrary that it is glorious to belong to the universal. He knows it is beautiful and benign to be the particular who translates himself into the universal, the one who so to speak makes a clear and elegant edition of himself, as immaculate as possible, and readable for all; he knows it is refreshing to become intelligible to oneself in the universal, so that he understands the universal and everyone who understands him understands the universal through him in turn, and both rejoice in the security of the universal. He knows it is beautiful to be born as the particular with the universal as his home, his friendly abode, which receives him straightaway with open arms when he wishes to stay there. But he also knows that higher up there winds a lonely path, narrow and steep; he knows it is terrible to be born in solitude outside the universal, to walk without meeting a single traveller. He knows very well where he is, and how he is related to men. Humanly speaking he is insane and cannot make himself understood to anyone. And yet 'insane' is the mildest expression for him. If he isn't viewed thus, he is a hypocrite and the higher up the path he climbs, the more dreadful a hypocrite he becomes.

The knight of faith knows it gives inspiration to surrender oneself to the universal, that it takes courage to do so, but also that there is a certain security in it, just because it is for the universal; he knows it is glorious to be understood by every noble mind, and in such a way that even the beholder is thereby ennobled. This he knows and he feels as though bound, he could wish this was the task he had been set. Thus surely Abraham must have now and then wished that the task was to love Isaac in a way meet and fitting for a father, as all would understand and as would be remembered for all time; he must have wished his task was to sacrifice Isaac for the universal, so as to inspire fathers to illustrious deeds – and he must have been well nigh horrified by the thought that for him such wishes were merely temptations and must be treated as such; for he knew it was a solitary path he trod, and that he was doing nothing for the universal but only being tested and tried himself. Or what was it Abraham did for the universal? Let me speak humanly about it, really humanly! It takes him seventy years to get the son of his old age. What others get soon enough and have long joy of takes him seventy years. And why? Because he is being tested and tried. Is that not insanity? But Abraham believed, and only Sarah wavered and got him to take Hagar as his concubine – but for that reason he also had to drive Hagar away. He gets Isaac and now he is to be tried once again. He knew it was glorious to express the universal, glorious to live with Isaac. But this is not the task. He knew it would have been a kingly deed to sacrifice such a son for the universal, he himself would have found repose in that, and everyone would have 'reposed' in their praise of his deed, just as the vowel 'reposes' in its quiescent letter; but this is not the task – he is being tried. That Roman general famous under the name of Cunctator halted the enemy by his delaying tactics, yet what kind of delayer is Abraham by comparison? But he isn't saving the State. This is the sum of one hundred and thirty years. Who can bear it? Should his contemporaries – if they can be called that – not say: 'There is an eternal procrastinating with Abraham; when he finally gets a son – and that took long enough – he wants to sacrifice him; he must be demented; and if only he could explain why he wanted to do that, but no, it's always a "trial"'? Nor could Abraham offer any further explanation, for his life is like a book put under divine seizure and which will never become *publici juris* [public property].

This is what is terrible. Anyone who doesn't see this can always be quite certain he is no knight of faith; but anyone who does see it will not deny that the step of even the most tried tragic hero goes like a dance compared with the slow and creeping progress of the knight of faith. And having seen it and realized he does not have the courage to understand it, he must at least have some idea of the wonderful glory achieved by that knight in becoming God's confidant, the Lord's friend, and – to speak really humanly – in addressing God in heaven as 'Thou', while even the tragic hero only addresses him in the third person.

The tragic hero is soon finished, his struggle is soon at an end; he makes the infinite movement and is now safe in the universal. But the knight of faith is kept awake, for he is under constant trial and can turn back in repentance to the universal at any moment, and this possibility can just as well be a temptation as the truth. Enlightenment as to which is something he can get from no one; otherwise he would be outside the paradox.

The knight of faith has therefore, first and foremost, the passion to concentrate the whole of the ethical that he violates in one single thing;

he can be sure that he really loves Isaac with all his soul.* If he cannot be that, he is in a state of temptation. Next, he has the passion to evoke this certainty intact in a twinkling and in as fully valid a way as in the first instance. If he cannot do this he doesn't get started, for then he must constantly start again from the beginning. The tragic hero, too, concentrates in one single thing the ethical that he teleologically violates, but in this thing he has resort to the universal. The knight of faith has only himself, and it is there the terrible lies. Most people let their ethical obligations last a day at a time, but then they never reach this passionate concentration, this energetic awareness. The tragic hero can in a sense be helped by the universal in acquiring these, but the knight of faith is alone about everything. The tragic hero acts and finds his point of rest in the universal, the knight of faith is kept in constant tension. Agamemnon gives up his claim to Iphigenia, thereby finds his point of rest in the universal, and now proceeds to give her in sacrifice. If Agamemnon had not made the movement, if in the decisive moment, instead of a passionate concentration, his soul had been lost in common chatter about his having several daughters, and *vielleicht das Ausserordentliche* [perhaps something extraordinary] could happen

– then naturally he would not be a hero but a case for charity. Abraham has the hero's concentration too, even though in him it is much more difficult since he has no resort at all to the universal, but he makes one movement more through which he concentrates his soul back upon the marvel. If Abraham hadn't done that he would only have been an Agamemnon, provided it can be explained how his willingness to sacrifice Isaac can be justified other than by its benefiting the universal.

Whether the individual is now really in a state of temptation or a knight of faith, only the individual can decide. Still, it is possible on the basis of the paradox to construct certain criteria which even someone not in it can understand. The true knight of faith is always absolute isolation, the false knight is sectarian. The latter involves an attempt to leap off the narrow path of the paradox in order to become a tragic hero on the cheap. The tragic hero expresses the universal and sacrifices himself for it. [. . .] The knight of faith, on the other hand, is the paradox, he is the individual, absolutely nothing but the individual, without connections and complications. This is the terror that the puny sectarian cannot endure. Instead of learning from this that he is incapable of greatness and plainly admitting it, something I cannot but approve since it is what I myself do, the poor wretch thinks he will achieve it by joining company with other poor wretches. But it won't at all work, no cheating is tolerated in the world of spirit. A dozen sectarians link arms, they know nothing at all of the lonely temptations in store for the knight of faith and which he dare not shun just because it would be more terrible still were he presumptuously to force his way forward. The sectarians deafen each other with their clang and clatter, hold dread at bay with their shrieks, and a whooping Sunday-outing like this thinks it is storming heaven, believes it is following the same path as the knight of faith who, in cosmic isolation, hears never a voice but walks alone with his dreadful responsibility.

As for the knight of faith, he is assigned to himself alone, he has the pain of being unable to make himself intelligible to others but feels no vain desire to show others the way. The pain is the assurance, vain desires are unknown to him, his mind is too serious for that. The false knight readily betrays himself by this instantly acquired proficiency; he just doesn't grasp the point that if another

---

* I will explain once more the difference in the collision as between the tragic hero and the knight of faith. The tragic hero assures himself that the ethical obligation [to his son, daughter, etc.] is totally present in him by virtue of the fact that he transforms it into a wish. Thus Agamemnon can say: this is my proof that I am not violating my paternal obligation, that my duty [to Iphigenia] is my only wish. Here, then, wish and duty match one another. Happy my lot in life if my wish coincides with my duty, and conversely; and most people's task in life is exactly to stay under their obligation, and by their enthusiasm to transform it into their wish. The tragic hero renounces what he wishes in order to accomplish his duty. For the knight of faith, wish and duty are also identical, but the knight of faith is required to give up both. So when renouncing in resignation what he wishes he finds no repose; for it is after all his duty [that he is giving up]. If he stays under his obligation and keeps his wish he will not become the knight of faith; for the absolute duty requires precisely that he give up [the duty that is identical with the wish]. The tragic hero acquires a higher expression of duty, but not an absolute duty.

individual is to walk the same path he has to be just as much the individual and is therefore in no need of guidance, least of all from one anxious to press his services on others. Here again, people unable to bear the martyrdom of unintelligibility jump off the path, and choose instead, conveniently enough, the world's admiration of their proficiency. The true knight of faith is a witness, never a teacher, and in this lies the deep humanity in him which is more worth than this foolish concern for others' weal and woe which is honoured under the name of sympathy, but which is really nothing but vanity. A person who wants only to be a witness confesses thereby that no one, not even the least, needs another person's sympathy, or is to be put down so another can raise himself up. But because what he himself won he did not win on the cheap, so neither does he sell it on the cheap; he is not so pitiable as to accept people's admiration and pay for it with silent contempt; he knows that whatever truly is great is available equally for all.

So either there is an absolute duty to God, and if so then it is the paradox described, that the single individual as the particular is higher than the universal and as the particular stands in an absolute relation to the absolute – or else faith has never existed because it has existed always; or else Abraham is done for; or else one must explain the passage in Luke 14 in the way that tasteful exegete did, and explain the corresponding passages likewise, and similar ones.

19

William James, "Mysticism"

Introduction

During 1901–02, the prestigious Gifford Lectures on Natural Religion at the University of Edinburgh were delivered by the Harvard Professor, William James (1842–1910), the most famous American philosopher and psychologist of the time. One of the two founding fathers, alongside C. S. Peirce, of American Pragmatism, James had been profoundly engaged, both academically and personally, with issues of religious belief and experience since suffering a severe depression and existential crisis in 1870 when, as he later wrote, he was assailed by a "horrible fear of my own existence."[1] The Gifford Lectures were published as a book, *The Varieties of Religious Experience*, which remains a century after its publication a seminal work for psychologists and philosophers of religion.

Of especially abiding influence is James's discussion of mysticism in Lectures XVI–XVII. For one thing, the Lectures provided later students with a veritable treasury of testimonies by mystics from a wide variety of religious and metaphysical persuasions – pantheism, Sufism, Vedanta, Catholicism, and so on. For another thing, the Lectures offer an attractive classification of the many

From William James, *The Varieties of Religious Experience*, Lectures XVI–XVII, New York and London: Longmans, Green & Co., 1923, pp. 379–82, 415–16, 422–8 (some passages and James's footnotes omitted).

varieties of mysticism, together with balanced and informed judgments on the psychological, physiological, and neurological factors that are conducive to the various types of mystical experience. Of greater philosophical interest, however, are the sections included in our selections: the early ones which provide a succinct characterization of mystical experience in any of its various forms; and the closing ones that sympathetically discuss the possible validity of the religious claims that mystics make on the basis of their experiences.

A mystical experience, for James, is distinguished from all other kinds of experience by being at once "ineffable," like a feeling that cannot be communicated, yet, for those whose experience it is, a genuine "state of knowledge," an "insight" into truth. Typically, as well, it is an experience that is both "transient" and "passive," so that it is "as if [one] were grasped and held by a superior power."

It may seem surprising that James – who described his Pragmatism as a "radical empiricism," who constantly emphasized the need for ideas and beliefs to be "expedient" and have a practical "pay-off," and who confesses his own incapacity for mystical experiences – should be as sympathetic to the truth-claims of mystics as he was. Admittedly, such experiences can only be "absolutely authoritative" over the people who actually have them, but the rest of us should concede that they "open out the possibility of other orders of truth" than those recognized by "rationalism" and science. But this initial surprise should evaporate when we recall that Pragmatism, for James, ought to be "completely genial" – wide open, that is, to taking seriously *anything* that, in virtue of its beneficial bearing on the conduct of human life, might be "better for us to believe." After all, his main point in his famous essay "The Will to Believe" – one akin to Pascal's (IV.12 above) – was that one should cultivate religious belief if, as he himself thought, this would encourage a better relationship to the world and to one another.[2]

Three more particular points help to explain James's sympathy for mystical claims. First, it would ill become a "radical empiricist," whose final appeal is always to experience, pre-emptively to restrict the term "experience" to ordinary sense-experience in the manner that, unfortunately, "Positivists" do. Prejudice aside, the mystic's beliefs are no less evidentially and experientially based than the rational scientist's. Second, mystical states do not, generally, "contradict . . . anything that our [ordinary] senses" testify to. Rather they "add a supersensuous meaning,"

manifest a "new expressiveness" and purport to "make a new connection with our active life." And from this it follows, third, that the mystic's claims are no different in status from those of, say, the scientist. In both cases, as James puts it in Lecture III of the book, "unreasoned and immediate assurance is the deep thing in us" – an assurance that goes beyond anything rationally demanded by the data of experience themselves. Once the "rationalist" conceit that beliefs can ever be "inferences logically drawn" from "definite facts of sensation" has been abandoned, we are free to entertain whatever "meanings," "expressions," or "connections" to which we "vitally respond," in particular those gestured at in utterances of the great mystics.

Notes

1 *The Writings of William James,* Chicago: University of Chicago Press, 1977, p. 6.
2 Ibid., p. 733.

James, "Mysticism"

Lectures XVI and XVII: Mysticism

Over and over again in these lectures I have raised points and left them open and unfinished until we should have come to the subject of Mysticism. Some of you, I fear, may have smiled as you noted my reiterated postponements. But now the hour has come when mysticism must be faced in good earnest, and those broken threads wound up together. One may say truly, I think, that personal religious experience has its root and centre in mystical states of consciousness; so for us, who in these lectures are treating personal experience as the exclusive subject of our study, such states of consciousness ought to form the vital chapter from which the other chapters get their light. Whether my treatment of mystical states will shed more light or darkness, I do not know, for my own constitution shuts me out from their enjoyment almost entirely, and I can speak of them only at second hand. But though forced to look upon the subject so externally, I will be as objective and receptive as I can; and I think I shall at

least succeed in convincing you of the reality of the states in question, and of the paramount importance of their function.

First of all, then, I ask, What does the expression 'mystical states of consciousness' mean? How do we part off mystical states from other states?

The words 'mysticism' and 'mystical' are often used as terms of mere reproach, to throw at any opinion which we regard as vague and vast and sentimental, and without a base in either facts or logic. For some writers a 'mystic' is any person who believes in thought-transference, or spirit-return. Employed in this way the word has little value: there are too many less ambiguous synonyms. So, to keep it useful by restricting it, I will do what I did in the case of the word 'religion,' and simply propose to you four marks which, when an experience has them, may justify us in calling it mystical for the purpose of the present lectures. In this way we shall save verbal disputation, and the recriminations that generally go therewith.

1. *Ineffability.* – The handiest of the marks by which I classify a state of mind as mystical is negative. The subject of it immediately says that

it defies expression, that no adequate report of its contents can be given in words. It follows from this that its quality must be directly experienced; it cannot be imparted or transferred to others. In this peculiarity mystical states are more like states of feeling than like states of intellect. No one can make clear to another who has never had a certain feeling, in what the quality or worth of it consists. One must have musical ears to know the value of a symphony; one must have been in love one's self to understand a lover's state of mind. Lacking the heart or ear, we cannot interpret the musician or the lover justly, and are even likely to consider him weak-minded or absurd. The mystic finds that most of us accord to his experiences an equally incompetent treatment.

2. *Noetic quality.*[1] – Although so similar to states of feeling, mystical states seem to those who experience them to be also states of knowledge. They are states of insight into depths of truth unplumbed by the discursive intellect. They are illuminations, revelations, full of significance and importance, all inarticulate though they remain; and as a rule they carry with them a curious sense of authority for after-time.

These two characters will entitle any state to be called mystical, in the sense in which I use the word. Two other qualities are less sharply marked, but are usually found. These are: –

3. *Transiency.* – Mystical states cannot be sustained for long. Except in rare instances, half an hour, or at most an hour or two, seems to be the limit beyond which they fade into the light of common day. Often, when faded, their quality can but imperfectly be reproduced in memory; but when they recur it is recognized; and from one recurrence to another it is susceptible of continuous development in what is felt as inner richness and importance.

4. *Passivity.* – Although the oncoming of mystical states may be facilitated by preliminary voluntary operations, as by fixing the attention, or going through certain bodily performances, or in other ways which manuals of mysticism prescribe; yet when the characteristic sort of consciousness once has set in, the mystic feels as if his own will were in abeyance, and indeed sometimes as if he were grasped and held by a superior power. This latter peculiarity connects mystical states with, certain definite phenomena of secondary or alternative personality, such as prophetic speech, automatic writing, or the mediumistic trance. When these latter conditions are well pronounced, however, there may be no recollection whatever of the phenomenon, and it may have no significance for the subject's usual inner life, to which, as it were, it makes a mere interruption. Mystical states, strictly so called, are never merely interruptive. Some memory of their content always remains, and a profound sense of their importance. They modify the inner life of the subject between the times of their recurrence. Sharp divisions in this region are, however, difficult to make, and we find all sorts of gradations and mixtures.

These four characteristics are sufficient to mark out a group of states of consciousness peculiar enough to deserve a special name and to call for careful study. Let it then be called the mystical group.

[. . .]

Mystical conditions may, therefore, render the soul more energetic in the lines which their inspiration favors. But this could be reckoned an advantage only in case the inspiration were a true one. If the inspiration were erroneous, the energy would be all the more mistaken and misbegotten. So we stand once more before that problem of truth which confronted us at the end of the lectures on saintliness. You will remember that we turned to mysticism precisely to get some light on truth. Do mystical states establish the truth of those theological affections in which the saintly life has its root?

In spite of their repudiation of articulate self-description, mystical states in general assert a pretty distinct theoretic drift. It is possible to give the outcome of the majority of them in terms that point in definite philosophical directions. One of these directions is optimism, and the other is monism. We pass into mystical states from out of ordinary consciousness as from a less into a more, as from a smallness into a vastness, and at the same time as from an unrest to a rest. We feel them as reconciling, unifying states. They appeal to the yes-function more than to the no-function in us. In them the unlimited absorbs the limits and peacefully closes the account. Their very denial of every adjective you may propose as applicable to the ultimate truth, – He, the Self, the Atman, is to be described by 'No! no!' only, say the Upanishads,[2] – though it seems on the surface to be a no-function, is a denial made on behalf of a deeper yes. Whoso calls the Absolute anything in particular, or says that it is *this*, seems implicitly to shut it off from being *that* – it is as if he lessened it. So we deny the 'this,' negating the negation which it seems to us to imply, in the interests of the higher affirmative attitude by which we are possessed. [. . .]

I have now sketched with extreme brevity and insufficiency, but as fairly as I am able in the time allowed, the general traits of the mystic range of consciousness. *It is on the whole pantheistic and optimistic, or at least the opposite of pessimistic. It is anti-naturalistic, and harmonizes best with twice-bornness and so-called other-worldly states of mind.*[3]

My next task is to inquire whether we can invoke it as authoritative. Does it furnish any *warrant for the truth* of the twice-bornness and supernaturality and pantheism which it favors? I must give my answer to this question as concisely as I can.

In brief my answer is this, – and I will divide it into three parts: –

(1) Mystical states, when well developed, usually are, and have the right to be, absolutely authoritative over the individuals to whom they come.

(2) No authority emanates from them which should make it a duty for those who stand outside of them to accept their revelations uncritically.

(3) They break down the authority of the non-mystical or rationalistic consciousness, based upon the understanding and the senses alone. They show it to be only one kind of consciousness. They open out the possibility of other orders of truth, in which, so far as anything in us vitally responds to them, we may freely continue to have faith.

I will take up these points one by one.

1. As a matter of psychological fact, mystical states of a well-pronounced and emphatic sort *are* usually authoritative over those who have them. They have been 'there,' and know. It is vain for rationalism to grumble about this. If the mystical truth that comes to a man proves to be a force that he can live by, what mandate have we of the majority to order him to live in another way? We can throw him into a prison or a madhouse, but we cannot change his mind – we commonly

attach it only the more stubbornly to its beliefs. It mocks our utmost efforts, as a matter of fact, and in point of logic it absolutely escapes our jurisdiction. Our own more 'rational' beliefs are based on evidence exactly similar in nature to that which mystics quote for theirs. Our senses, namely, have assured us of certain states of fact; but mystical experiences are as direct perceptions of fact for those who have them as any sensations ever were for us. The records show that even though the five senses be in abeyance in them, they are absolutely sensational in their epistemological quality, if I may be pardoned the barbarous expression, – that is, they are face to face presentations of what seems immediately to exist.

The mystic is, in short, *invulnerable*, and must be left, whether we relish it or not, in undisturbed enjoyment of his creed. Faith, says Tolstoy, is that by which men live. And faith-state and mystic state are practically convertible terms.

2. But I now proceed to add that mystics have no right to claim that we ought to accept the deliverance of their peculiar experiences, if we are ourselves outsiders and feel no private call thereto. The utmost they can ever ask of us in this life is to admit that they establish a presumption. They form a consensus and have an unequivocal outcome; and it would be odd, mystics might say, if such a unanimous type of experience should prove to be altogether wrong. At bottom, however, this would only be an appeal to numbers, like the appeal of rationalism the other way; and the appeal to numbers has no logical force. If we acknowledge it, it is for 'suggestive,' not for logical reasons: we follow the majority because to do so suits our life.

But even this presumption from the unanimity of mystics is far from being strong. In characterizing mystic states as pantheistic, optimistic, etc., I am afraid I over-simplified the truth. I did so for expository reasons, and to keep the closer to the classic mystical tradition. The classic religious mysticism, it now must be confessed, is only a 'privileged case.' It is an *extract*, kept true to type by the selection of the fittest specimens and their preservation in 'schools.' It is carved out from a much larger mass; and if we take the larger mass as seriously as religious mysticism has historically taken itself, we find that the supposed unanimity largely disappears. To begin with, even religious mysticism itself, the kind that accumulates traditions and makes schools, is much less unanimous than I have allowed. It has been both ascetic and antinomianly self-indulgent within the Christian church. It is dualistic in Sankhya, and monistic in Vedanta philosophy. I called it pantheistic; but the great Spanish mystics are anything but pantheists. They are with few exceptions non-metaphysical minds, for whom 'the category of personality' is absolute. The 'union' of man with God is for them much more like an occasional miracle than like an original identity. How different again, apart from the happiness common to all, is the mysticism of Walt Whitman, Edward Carpenter, Richard Jefferies, and other naturalistic pantheists, from the more distinctively Christian sort. The fact is that the mystical feeling of enlargement, union, and emancipation has no specific intellectual content whatever of its own. It is capable of forming matrimonial alliances with material furnished by the most diverse philosophies and theologies, provided only they can find a place in their framework for its peculiar emotional mood. We have no right, therefore, to invoke its prestige as distinctively in favor of any special belief, such as that in absolute idealism, or in the absolute monistic identity, or in the absolute goodness, of the world. It is only relatively in favor of all these things – it passes out of common human consciousness in the direction in which they lie.

So much for religious mysticism proper. But more remains to be told, for religious mysticism is only one half of mysticism. The other half has no accumulated traditions except those which the text-books on insanity supply. Open any one of these, and you will find abundant cases in which 'mystical ideas' are cited as characteristic symptoms of enfeebled or deluded states of mind. In delusional insanity, paranoia, as they sometimes call it, we may have a *diabolical* mysticism, a sort of religious mysticism turned upside down. The same sense of ineffable importance in the smallest events, the same texts and words coming with new meanings, the same voices and visions and leadings and missions, the same controlling by extraneous powers; only this time the emotion is pessimistic: instead of consolations we have desolations; the meanings are dreadful; and the powers are enemies to life. It is evident that from the point of view of their psychological mechanism, the classic mysticism and these lower mysticisms spring from the same mental level, from that great subliminal or transmarginal region of which science is beginning to admit the existence, but of which so little is really known. That region contains every kind of matter: 'seraph and snake' abide there side by side. To come from thence is no infallible credential. What comes must be sifted and tested, and run the gauntlet of confrontation with the total context of experience, just like what comes from the outer world of sense. Its value must be ascertained by empirical methods, so long as we are not mystics ourselves.

Once more, then, I repeat that non-mystics are under no obligation to acknowledge in mystical states a superior authority conferred on them by their intrinsic nature.

3. Yet, I repeat once more, the existence of mystical states absolutely overthrows the pretension of non-mystical states to be the sole and ultimate dictators of what we may believe. As a rule, mystical states merely add a supersensuous meaning to the ordinary outward data of consciousness. They are excitements like the emotions of love or ambition, gifts to our spirit by means of which facts already objectively before us fall into a new expressiveness and make a new connection with our active life. They do not contradict these facts as such, or deny anything that our senses have immediately seized. It is the rationalistic critic rather who plays the part of denier in the controversy, and his denials have no strength, for there never can be a state of facts to which new meaning may not truthfully be added, provided the mind ascend to a more enveloping point of view. It must always remain an open question whether mystical states may not possibly be such superior points of view, windows through which the mind looks out upon a more extensive and inclusive world. The difference of the views seen from the different mystical windows need not prevent us from entertaining this supposition. The wider world would in that case prove to have a mixed constitution like that of this world, that is all. It would have its celestial and its infernal regions, its tempting and its saving moments, its valid experiences and its counterfeit ones, just as our world has them; but it would be a wider world all the same. We should have to use its experiences by selecting and subordinating and substituting just as is our custom in this ordinary naturalistic world; we should be liable to error just

as we are now; yet the counting in of that wider world of meanings, and the serious dealing with it, might, in spite of all the perplexity, be indispensable stages in our approach to the final fullness of the truth.

In this shape, I think, we have to leave the subject. Mystical states indeed wield no authority due simply to their being mystical states. But the higher ones among them point in directions to which the religious sentiments even of non-mystical men incline. They tell of the supremacy of the ideal, of vastness, of union, of safety, and of rest. They offer us *hypotheses*, hypotheses which we may voluntarily ignore, but which as thinkers we cannot possibly upset. The supernaturalism and optimism to which they would persuade us may, interpreted in one way or another, be after all the truest of insights into the meaning of this life. [. . .]

Notes

1 "Noetic" comes from the Greek word meaning "thought." James's point is that mystical experiences, despite their similarity to feelings, have a cognitive content since, for the mystic, they provide knowledge about reality.

2 The Upanishads are philosophical commentaries from the first millennium BCE on the Indian Vedic texts. James is here referring to a theme prominent in several of these commentaries to the effect that the only possible reply to such questions as "What is Brahman (Absolute Reality)?" is "*Neti! Neti!*" ("Not this! Not this!"). In other words, Brahman and Atman (Self) are ineffable.

3 The state of mind of the "twice-born" religious person, James has explained in Lecture VIII, is that of someone for whom salvation requires renunciation of the natural world in order to discover a "violently contrasted" spiritual truth.

20

Bertrand Russell, "A Free Man's Worship"

Introduction

The author of this essay, published in 1903, was to become the best-known and most influential British philosopher of the twentieth century. A logician of genius, Bertrand Russell's (1872–1970) fame was due less to his technical contributions in logic and metaphysics than to the many essays and books he wrote on issues of greater public interest, including education, marriage, nuclear disarmament, and religion. The expression of his passionate views on such topics required courage: his pacifist position during World War I, for example, cost him his post at Cambridge University and he was arrested, 50 years later, for demonstrating against nuclear weapons.

Russell's urbane, aristocratic bearing masked a soul that was no stranger to "dark nights" and subject to depression.[1] He often articulates, as in "A Free Man's Worship," a bleak vision of a recalcitrant, "evil" world of a kind given voice to in many religions. Russell himself, however, was an atheist, or at any rate – as would befit a philosopher proud to belong to the skeptical tradition of David Hume – an agnostic. The scientific account of the world, which has no place for divine creation or eternal life, is, "if not quite beyond dispute . . . yet . . . nearly certain." Moreover, it

From Bertrand Russell, *Mysticism and Logic: And Other Essays*, London: Allen & Unwin, 1963, pp. 40–7 (note omitted).

is not difficult, Russell thinks, to explain away theistic belief in terms of human yearnings and people's sense of "impotence." Nevertheless, Russell is willing to characterize his own position as "religious," and it is clear that he admired the attitudes associated with some religions. For example, "a form of union of Self and not-Self" – of "the closest constant and most intimate relation with the outer world" – which has been the traditional goal of mystical religion, is, indeed, for Russell, the highest of human goals, albeit one to be pursued through scientific enquiry and philosophy rather than religious practice.[2]

Russell's own "religious" attitude is manifest in the lyrical, much-anthologized essay that follows. The great error of historical religions has been the conviction, in the face of the suffering and evil which confront us, that things *are* in reality how they *ought* to be – a conviction that requires either "slavish" subservience to the will of some imagined gods or the familiar doctrine that God's benevolent plan is too opaque for us to understand the necessary place in it for suffering and evil (see IV.13 above). For Russell, this is a conviction that must be abandoned, in favor of a frank, courageous recognition of an abyss between the way things are and our ideals.

While Christianity, like other religions, is founded on an illusion, it is to be admired, Russell urges, for the emphasis it has placed on the "renunciation" of our "fretful" desires, responsible as these are, not only for much of our suffering, but for a distorted vision of the world.

More generally, the cure for our ills that Russell emphasizes in the 1903 essay is an "internal" one: we must discipline and change ourselves – the economy of our desires, for example – if we are to find happiness in the world. (In later life, Russell's emphasis – as, in his own words, he became less of a "Platonist" – shifted to social and political strategies for happiness.) Above all, we must seek understanding of the world and human life, and indeed of the "eternal" verities of mathematics and philosophy, for in such understanding there resides a kind of "conquest" of the world, and a "freedom" from it. There is a distinct echo, here, of a point that Kant made about the experience of the sublime in his *Critique of Judgment* (1790): in facing up to the vastness and terror of the world, we come to a heightened sense of our own superiority to it. Or, as Russell puts, great as the forces of fate, death, and time may be, "to think of them greatly . . . is greater still."

We should strive as well, Russell continues, to cultivate a sense of the beauty of things, for in the appreciation of beauty there is selflessness, a release from the ego-centered perspective from which the world appears as such a recalcitrant, hostile place. And finally, we should cultivate a compassion for all those other human beings, our "fellow-sufferers," irrespective of their "merits and demerits," who live in the "same darkness" and live out the "same tragedy" as ourselves.

Despite Russell's slighting reference to "Oriental subjection," in which we "bow before the inevitable," readers must surely be struck by the similarities between his position and that of Buddhism (I.9). The rejection of God, the emphasis on compassion as against moral judgment, and the imperative to renounce our fretful desires (our "cravings," as the Buddha called them), indicate an affinity that Russell perhaps did not appreciate between himself and founder of Buddhism.

Notes

1 See R. Monk, *Bertrand Russell: 1872–1920 The Spirit of Solitude*, London: Vintage, 1997.
2 B. Russell, *The Problems of Philosophy*, Oxford: Oxford University Press, 1980, pp. 91ff., and "Mysticism and Logic," in *Mysticism and Logic: And Other Essays*, p. 30.

Russell, "A Free Man's Worship"

To Dr Faustus in his study Mephistopheles told the history of the Creation, saying:

'The endless praises of the choirs of angels had begun to grow wearisome; for, after all, did He not deserve their praise? Had He not given them endless joy? Would it not be more amusing to obtain undeserved praise, to be worshipped by beings whom He tortured? He smiled inwardly, and resolved that the great drama should be performed.

'For countless ages the hot nebula whirled aimlessly through space. At length it began to take shape, the central mass threw off planets, the planets cooled, boiling seas and burning mountains heaved and tossed, from black masses of cloud hot sheets of rain deluged the barely solid crust. And now the first germ of life grew in the depths of the ocean, and developed rapidly in the fructifying warmth into vast forest trees, huge ferns springing from the damp mould, sea monsters breeding, fighting, devouring, and passing away. And from the monsters, as the play unfolded itself, Man was born, with the power of thought, the knowledge of good and evil, and the cruel thirst for worship. And Man saw that all is passing in this mad, monstrous world, that all is struggling to snatch, at any cost, a few brief moments of life before Death's inexorable decree. And Man said: "There is a hidden purpose, could we but fathom it, and the purpose is good; for we must reverence something and in the visible world there is nothing worthy of reverence." And Man stood aside from the struggle, resolving that God intended harmony to come out of chaos by human efforts. And when he followed the instincts which God had transmitted to him from his ancestry of beasts of prey, he called it Sin, and asked God to forgive him. But he doubted whether he could be justly forgiven, until he invented a divine Plan by which God's wrath was to have been appeased. And seeing the present was bad, he made it yet worse, that thereby the future might be better. And he gave God thanks for the strength that enabled him to forgo even the joys that were possible. And God smiled; and when he saw that Man had become perfect in renunciation and worship, he sent another sun through the sky, which crashed into Man's sun; and all returned again to nebula.

' "Yes," he murmured, "it was a good play; I will have it performed again." '

Such, in outline, but even more purposeless, more void of meaning, is the world which Science presents for our belief. Amid such a world, if anywhere, our ideals henceforward must find a home. That Man is the product of causes which had no prevision of the end they were achieving; that his origin, his growth, his hopes and fears, his loves and his beliefs, are but the outcome of accidental collocations of atoms; that no fire, no heroism, no intensity of thought and feeling, can preserve an individual life beyond the grave; that all the labours of the ages, all the devotion, all the inspiration, all the noonday brightness of human genius, are destined to extinction in the vast death of the solar system, and that the whole temple of Man's achievement must inevitably be buried beneath the debris of a universe in ruins – all these things, if not quite beyond dispute, are yet so nearly certain, that no philosophy which rejects them can hope to stand. Only within the scaffolding of these truths, only on the firm foundation of unyielding despair, can the soul's habitation henceforth be safely built.

How, in such an alien and inhuman world, can so powerless a creature as Man preserve his aspirations untarnished? A strange mystery it is that Nature, omnipotent but blind, in the revolutions of her secular hurryings through the abysses of space, has brought forth at last a child, subject still to her power, but gifted with sight, with knowledge of good and evil, with the capacity of judging all the works of his unthinking Mother. In spite of Death, the mark and seal of the parental control, Man is yet free, during his brief years, to examine, to criticize, to know, and in imagination to create. To him alone, in the world with which he is acquainted, this freedom belongs; and in this lies his superiority to the resistless forces that control his outward life.

The savage, like ourselves, feels the oppression of his impotence before the powers of Nature; but having in himself nothing that he respects more than Power, he is willing to prostrate himself before his gods, without inquiring whether they are worthy of his worship. Pathetic and very terrible is the long history of cruelty and torture, of degradation and human sacrifice, endured in the hope of placating the jealous gods: surely, the trembling believer thinks, when what is most precious has been freely given, their lust for blood must be appeased, and more will not be required. The religion of Moloch[1] – as such creeds may be generically called – is in essence the cringing submission of the slave, who dare not, even in his heart, allow the thought that his master deserves no adulation. Since the independence of ideals is not yet acknowledged, Power may be freely worshipped, and receive an unlimited respect, despite its wanton infliction of pain.

But gradually, as morality grows bolder, the claim of the ideal world begins to be felt; and worship, if it is not to cease, must be given to gods of another kind than those created by the savage. Some, though they feel the demands of the ideal, will still consciously reject them, still urging that naked Power is worthy of worship. Such is the attitude inculcated in God's answer to Job out of the whirlwind: the divine power and knowledge are paraded, but of the divine goodness there is no hint. Such also is the attitude of those, who, in our own day, base their morality upon the struggle for survival, maintaining that the survivors are necessarily the fittest. But others, not content with an answer so repugnant to the moral sense, will adopt the position which we have become accustomed to regard as specially religious, maintaining that, in some hidden manner, the world of fact is really harmonious with the world of ideals. Thus Man creates God, all-powerful and all-good, the mystic unity of what is and what should be.

But the world of fact, after all, is not good; and, in submitting our judgment to it, there is an element of slavishness from which our thoughts must be purged. For in all things it is well to exalt the dignity of Man, by freeing him as far as possible from the tyranny of non-human Power. When we have realized that Power is largely bad, that man, with his knowledge of good and evil, is but a helpless atom in a world which has no such knowledge, the choice is again presented to us: Shall we worship Force, or shall we worship Goodness? Shall our God exist and be evil, or shall he be recognized as the creation of our own conscience?

The answer to this question is very momentous, and affects profoundly our whole morality. The worship of Force, to which Carlyle and Nietzsche and the creed of Militarism have accustomed us, is the result of failure to maintain our own ideals against a hostile universe: it is itself a prostrate submission to evil, a sacrifice of our best to Moloch. If strength indeed is to be respected, let us respect rather the strength of those who refuse that false 'recognition of facts' which fails to recognize that facts are often bad. Let us admit that, in the world we know, there are many things that would be better otherwise, and that the ideals to which we do and must adhere are not realized in the realm of matter. Let us preserve our respect for truth, for beauty, for the ideal of perfection which life does not permit us to attain, though none of these things meet with the approval of the unconscious universe. If Power is bad, as it seems to be, let us reject it from our hearts. In this lies Man's true freedom: in determination to worship only the God created by our own love of the good, to respect only the heaven which inspires the insight of our best moments. In action, in desire, we must submit perpetually to the tyranny of outside forces; but in thought, in aspiration, we are free, free from our fellowmen, free from the petty planet on which our bodies impotently crawl, free even, while we live, from the tyranny of death. Let us learn, then, that energy of faith which enables us to live constantly in the vision of the good; and let us descend, in action, into the world of fact, with that vision always before us.

When first the opposition of fact and ideal grows fully visible, a spirit of fiery revolt, of fierce hatred of the gods, seems necessary to the assertion of freedom. To defy with Promethean constancy a hostile universe, to keep its evil always in view, always actively hated, to refuse no pain that the malice of Power can invent, appears to be the duty of all who will not bow before the inevitable. But indignation is still a bondage, for it compels our thoughts to be occupied with an evil world; and in the fierceness of desire from which rebellion springs there is a kind of self-assertion which it is necessary for the wise to overcome. Indignation is a submission of

our thoughts, but not of our desires; the Stoic freedom in which wisdom consists is found in the submission of our desires, but not of our thoughts. From the submission of our desires springs the virtue of resignation; from the freedom of our thoughts springs the whole world of art and philosophy, and the vision of beauty by which, at last, we half reconquer the reluctant world. But the vision of beauty is possible only to unfettered contemplation, to thoughts not weighted by the load of eager wishes; and thus Freedom comes only to those who no longer ask of life that it shall yield them any of those personal goods that are subject to the mutations of Time.

Although the necessity of renunciation is evidence of the existence of evil, yet Christianity, in preaching it, has shown a wisdom exceeding that of the Promethean philosophy of rebellion. It must be admitted that, of the things we desire, some, though they prove impossible, are yet real goods; others, however, as ardently longed for, do not form part of a fully purified ideal. The belief that what must be renounced is bad, though sometimes false, is far less often false than untamed passion supposes; and the creed of religion, by providing a reason for proving that it is never false, has been the means of purifying our hopes by the discovery of many austere truths.

But there is in resignation a further good element: even real goods, when they are unattainable, ought not to be fretfully desired. To every man comes, sooner or later, the great renunciation. For the young, there is nothing unattainable; a good thing desired with the whole force of a passionate will, and yet impossible, is to them not credible. Yet, by death, by illness, by poverty, or by the voice of duty, we must learn, each one of us, that the world was not made for us, and that, however beautiful may be the things we crave, Fate may nevertheless forbid them. It is the part of courage, when misfortune comes, to bear without repining the ruin of our hopes, to turn away our thoughts from vain regrets. This degree of submission to Power is not only just and right: it is the very gate of wisdom.

But passive renunciation is not the whole of wisdom; for not by renunciation alone can we build a temple for the worship of our own ideals. Haunting foreshadowings of the temple appear in the realm of imagination, in music, in architecture, in the untroubled kingdom of reason, and in the golden sunset magic of lyrics, where beauty shines and glows, remote from the touch of sorrow, remote from the fear of change, remote from the failures and disenchantments of the world of fact. In the contemplation of these things the vision of heaven will shape itself in our hearts, giving at once a touchstone to judge the world about us, and an inspiration by which to fashion to our needs whatever is not incapable of serving as a stone in the sacred temple.

Except for those rare spirits that are born without sin, there is a cavern of darkness to be traversed before that temple can be entered. The gate of the cavern is despair, and its floor is paved with the gravestones of abandoned hopes. There Self must die; there the eagerness, the greed of untamed desire must be slain, for only so can the soul be freed from the empire of Fate. But out of the cavern the Gate of Renunciation leads again to the daylight of wisdom, by whose radiance a new insight, a new joy, a new tenderness, shine forth to gladden the pilgrim's heart.

When, without the bitterness of impotent rebellion, we have learnt both to resign ourselves to the outward rule of Fate and to recognize that the non-human world is unworthy of our worship, it becomes possible at last so to transform and refashion the unconscious universe, so to transmute it in the crucible of imagination, that a new image of shining gold replaces the old idol of clay. In all the multiform facts of the world – in the visual shapes of trees and mountains and clouds, in the events of the life of man, even in the very omnipotence of Death – the insight of creative idealism can find the reflection of a beauty which its own thoughts first made. In this way mind asserts its subtle mastery over the thoughtless forces of Nature. The more evil the material with which it deals, the more thwarting to untrained desire, the greater is its achievement in inducing the reluctant rock to yield up its hidden treasures, the prouder its victory in compelling the opposing forces to swell the pageant of its triumph. Of all the arts, Tragedy is the proudest, the most triumphant; for it builds its shining citadel in the very centre of the enemy's country, on the very summit of his highest mountain; from its impregnable watch towers, his camps and arsenals, his columns and forts, are all revealed; within its walls the free life continues, while the legions of Death and Pain and Despair, and all the servile captains of tyrant Fate, afford

the burghers of that dauntless city new spectacles of beauty. Happy those sacred ramparts, thrice happy the dwellers on that all-seeing eminence. Honour to those brave warriors who, through countless ages of warfare, have preserved for us the priceless heritage of liberty, and have kept undefiled by sacrilegious invaders the home of the unsubdued.

But the beauty of Tragedy does but make visible a quality which, in more or less obvious shapes, is present always and everywhere in life. In the spectacle of Death, in the endurance of intolerable pain, and in the irrevocableness of a vanished past, there is a sacredness, an overpowering awe, a feeling of the vastness, the depth, the inexhaustible mystery of existence, in which, as by some strange marriage of pain, the sufferer is bound to the world by bonds of sorrow. In these moments of insight, we lose all eagerness of temporary desire, all struggling and striving for petty ends, all care for the little trivial things that, to a superficial view, make up the common life of day by day; we see, surrounding the narrow raft illumined by the flickering light of human comradeship, the dark ocean on whose rolling waves we toss for a brief hour; from the great night without, a chill blast breaks in upon our refuge; all the loneliness of humanity amid hostile forces is concentrated upon the individual soul, which must struggle alone, with what of courage it can command, against the whole weight of a universe that cares nothing for its hopes and fears. Victory, in this struggle with the powers of darkness, is the true baptism into the glorious company of heroes, the true initiation into the overmastering beauty of human existence. From that awful encounter of the soul with the outer world, enunciation, wisdom, and charity are born; and with their birth a new life begins. To take into the inmost shrine of the soul the irresistible forces whose puppets we seem to be – Death and change, the irrevocableness of the past, and the powerlessness of man before the blind hurry of the universe from vanity to vanity – to feel these things and know them is to conquer them.

This is the reason why the Past has such magical power. The beauty of its motionless and silent pictures is like the enchanted purity of late autumn, when the leaves, though one breath would make them fall, still glow against the sky in golden glory. The Past does not change or strive;

like Duncan, after life's fitful fever it sleeps well;[2] what was eager and grasping, what was petty and transitory, has faded away, the things that were beautiful and eternal shine out of it like stars in the night. Its beauty, to a soul not worthy of it, is unendurable; but to a soul which has conquered Fate it is the key of religion.

The life of Man, viewed outwardly, is but a small thing in comparison with the forces of Nature. The slave is doomed to worship Time and Fate and Death, because they are greater than anything he finds in himself, and because all his thoughts are of things which they devour. But, great as they are, to think of them greatly, to feel their passionless splendour, is greater still. And such thought makes us free men; we no longer bow before the inevitable in Oriental subjection, but we absorb it, and make it a part of ourselves. To abandon the struggle for private happiness, to expel all eagerness of temporary desire, to burn with passion for eternal things – this is emancipation, and this is the free man's worship. And this liberation is effected by a contemplation of Fate; for Fate itself is subdued by the mind which leaves nothing to be purged by the purifying fire of Time.

United with his fellow-men by the strongest of all ties, the tie of a common doom, the free man finds that a new vision is with him always, shedding over every daily task the light of love. The life of Man is a long march through the night, surrounded by invisible foes, tortured by weariness and pain, towards a goal that few can hope to reach, and where none may tarry long. One by one, as they march, our comrades vanish from our sight, seized by the silent orders of omnipotent Death. Very brief is the time in which we can help them, in which their happiness or misery is decided. Be it ours to shed sunshine on their path, to lighten their sorrows by the balm of sympathy, to give them the pure joy of a never-tiring affection, to strengthen failing courage, to instil faith in hours of despair. Let us not weigh in grudging scales their merits and demerits, but let us think only of their need – of the sorrows, the difficulties, perhaps the blindnesses, that make the misery of their lives; let us remember that they are fellow-sufferers in the same darkness, actors in the same tragedy with ourselves. And so, when their day is over, when their good and their evil have become eternal by the immortality of the past, be it ours to feel that, where they suffered, where they failed, no deed of ours was the cause; but wherever a spark of the divine fire kindled in their hearts, we were ready with encouragement, with sympathy, with brave words in which high courage glowed.

Brief and powerless is Man's life; on him and all his race the slow, sure doom falls pitiless and dark. Blind to good and evil, reckless of destruction, omnipotent matter rolls on its relentless way; for Man, condemned today to lose his dearest, tomorrow himself to pass through the gate of darkness, it remains only to cherish, ere yet the blow falls, the lofty thoughts that ennoble his little day; disdaining the coward terrors of the slave of Fate, to worship at the shrine that his own hands have built; undismayed by the empire of chance, to preserve a mind free from the wanton tyranny that rules his outward life; proudly defiant of the irresistible forces that tolerate, for a moment, his knowledge and his condemnation, to sustain alone, a weary but unyielding Atlas, the world that his own ideals have fashioned despite the trampling march of unconscious power.

Notes

1 Moloch was the idol of the Canaanites to which, according to *Leviticus* XVIII, they sacrificed children.
2 See *Macbeth*, Act III, ii.22.

21

Martin Buber, *I and Thou*,
Part III (selections)

Introduction

Published in 1923, *I and Thou* – that "priceless little book," as Gabriel Marcel called it[1] – is the best-known work of the Austrian-born Jewish thinker, Martin Buber (1878–1965), who in old age was to become one of the most revered and influential figures in the newly formed state of Israel. Buber is often described as a "religious existentialist." An acute critic of Jean-Paul Sartre's atheistic existentialism, he was certainly a man of faith: steeped in the Hassidic tradition of his religion, he produced an acclaimed translation of the Bible into German and wrote prolifically on both mysticism and the religious foundation of social ethics.[2] Whether or not he himself is usefully classified as an "existentialist," he certainly shared with Sartre (I.23), Karl Jaspers, and Martin Heidegger (III.24) such characteristically existentialist preoccupations as alienation, the modern sense of living in a meaningless universe, and the possibility of freedom.

The question, Buber once wrote, which "had already accosted me in my youth" and which remained "the innermost question for me," was that of "the possibility and reality of a dialogical relationship between human beings and God."[3] Buber's preferred title for a "dialogical relation-ship" or "meeting" – whether between "man and God," men and women, or people and animals or trees – is "I–Thou relationship." This expression is to be understood in terms of its contrast with "I–It relationship." Something or someone figures for me as an "It" when, roughly speaking, it, he, or she is considered simply as an object of perception and thought, devoid of meaning and replete with properties deemed to exist quite independently of any relation to myself. "I–It" is therefore the mode of relating to things of someone who assumes a "split" between a "ghostly I" and a "ready-made world" – hence a mode of "severance and alienation." This alienated mode of existence has become our default condition, despite the fact that the "I–It" relationship is derivative from a more primordial immersion in the world from which the concepts of a detached "I" and "ready-made," independent objects have been abstracted.

At fleeting, "butterfly" moments – when looking into the eyes of a cat or a lover, for example – this more primordial relationship to the world may be retrieved. At such moments, the sense of standing over against things as subjects to objects evaporates. Instead, the thing, animal, or person "has to do with me": it, he, or she becomes a Thou, ineffably experienced as inextricably related to me in mutual "penetration" and, like myself, as belonging to a whole in and through which we have the identities that we do.

In the third and final part of *I and Thou*, Buber focuses on the "absolute relationship" – the

From Martin Buber, *I and Thou*, trans. R. Gregor Smith, Edinburgh: T. & T. Clark, 1937, pp. 75–81, 95–112.

"I–Thou" relationship between human beings and God. Three themes are prominent in his discussion. First, while Buber eschews standard arguments – whether of an *a priori*, historical, or evidential kind – for God's existence, he proposes that all "I–Thou" experiences are ultimately intelligible only as intimations of a "dialogical relationship" with God. Someone who loves a woman as Thou is, in effect, experiencing "the eternal Thou," since only in a world discerned, however dimly, as imbued with God's presence may anything within it figure for me as Thou. Second, for Buber as for Kierkegaard, it is only through the "I–Thou" relationship with God that I can become a real and not a merely "ghostly" self, and realize my essence as a genuine and free individual. Buber is therefore hostile to mystical talk of a person "dying to self" through "absorption" into the divine "One" – as he also is to Schleiermacher's notion of a person being utterly and non-reciprocally "dependent" on God. ("God needs you," writes Buber, just as "you need God.")

Finally, Buber emphasizes that the "I–Thou" relationship to God is unique in that it can never deteriorate, in the manner of all other "I–Thou" meetings, into an "I–It" one. "The eternal Thou," by its very nature, cannot be perceived, conceptualized, or objectified in the way anything else can: for this presupposes identifying a set of properties, and setting bounds, limits, and measures to objects. In the case of God, no such identification or bounds are possible. To be sure, theologians and philosophers have endlessly tried "making the eternal Thou into It, into some thing," but the very attempt simply registers an incapacity for an authentic sense of God's presence.

Notes

1 "I and Thou," in P. A. Schilpp, ed., *The Philosophy of Martin Buber*, La Salle, IL: Open Court, 1967, p. 41.
2 See IV.8 in this volume for text by Moses ben Maimon (Maimonides), an earlier Jewish thinker.
3 "Autobiographical Fragments," in Schilpp, ed., *op. cit.*, p. 33.

Buber, *I and Thou*

Part III

The extended lines of relations meet in the eternal *Thou*.

Every particular *Thou* is a glimpse through to the eternal *Thou*; by means of every particular *Thou* the primary word addresses the eternal *Thou*. Through this mediation of the *Thou* of all beings fulfilment, and non-fulfilment, of relations comes to them: the inborn *Thou* is realised in each relation and consummated in none. It is consummated only in the direct relation with the *Thou* that by its nature cannot become *It*.

*

Men have addressed their eternal *Thou* with many names. In singing of Him who was thus named they always had the *Thou* in mind: the first myths were hymns of praise. Then the names took refuge in the language of *It*; men were more and more strongly moved to think of and to address their eternal *Thou* as an *It*. But all God's names are hallowed, for in them He is not merely spoken about, but also spoken to.

Many men wish to reject the word God as a legitimate usage, because it is so misused. It is indeed the most heavily laden of all the words used by men. For that very reason it is the most imperishable and most indispensable. What does all mistaken talk about God's being and works (though there has been, and can be, no other talk about these) matter in comparison with the one truth that all men who have addressed God had God Himself in mind? For he who speaks the word God and really has *Thou* in mind (whatever the illusion by which he is held), addresses the true *Thou* of his life, which cannot be limited by another *Thou*, and to which he stands in a relation that gathers up and includes all others.

But when he, too, who abhors the name, and believes himself to be godless, gives his whole being to addressing the *Thou* of his life, as a *Thou* that cannot be limited by another, he addresses God.

*

If we go on our way and meet a man who has advanced towards us and has also gone on *his* way, we know only our part of the way, not his – his we experience only in the meeting.

Of the complete relational event we know, with the knowledge of life lived, our going out to the relation, our part of the way. The other part only comes upon us, we do not know it; it comes upon us in the meeting. But we strain ourselves on it if we speak of it as though it were some thing beyond the meeting.

We have to be concerned, to be troubled, not about the other side but about our own side, not about grace but about will. Grace concerns us in so far as we go out to it and persist in its presence; but it is not our object.

What we know of the way from the life that we have lived, from our life, is not a waiting or a being open.

The *Thou* confronts me. But I step into direct relation with it. Hence the relation means being chosen and choosing, suffering and action in one; just as any action of the whole being which means the suspension of all partial actions, and consequently of all sensations of actions grounded only in their particular limitation, is bound to resemble suffering.

This is the activity of the man who has become a whole being, an activity that has been termed doing nothing: nothing separate or partial stirs in the man any more, thus he makes no intervention in the world; it is the whole man, enclosed and at rest in his wholeness, that is effective – he has become an effective whole. To have won stability in this state is to be able to go out to the supreme meeting.

To this end the world of sense does not need to be laid aside as though it were illusory. There is no illusory world, there is only the world – which appears to us as twofold in accordance with our twofold attitude. Only the barrier of separation has to be destroyed. Further, no "going beyond sense-experience" is necessary; for every experience, even the most spiritual, could yield us only an *It*. Nor is any recourse necessary to a world of ideas and values; for they cannot become presentness for us. None of these things is necessary. Can it be said what really is necessary? – Not in the sense of a precept. For everything that has ever been devised and contrived in the time of the human spirit as precept, alleged preparation, practice, or meditation, has nothing to do with

the primal, simple fact of the meeting. Whatever the advantages in knowledge or the wielding of power for which we have to thank this or that practice, none of this affects the meeting of which we are speaking; it all has its place in the world of *It* and does not lead one step, does not take *the* step, out of it. Going out to the relation cannot be taught in the sense of precepts being given. It can only be indicated by the drawing of a circle which excludes everything that is not this going out. Then the one thing that matters is visible, full acceptance of the present.

To be sure, this acceptance presupposes that the further a man has wandered in separated being the more difficult is the venture and the more elemental the reversal. This does not mean a giving up of, say, the *I*, as mystical writings usually suppose: the *I* is as indispensable to this, the supreme, as to every relation, since relation is only possible between *I* and *Thou*. It is not the *I*, then, that is given up, but that false self-asserting instinct that makes a man flee to the possessing of things before the unreliable, perilous world of relation which has neither density nor duration and cannot be surveyed.

*

Every real relation with a being or life in the world is exclusive. Its *Thou* is freed, steps forth, is single, and confronts you. It fills the heavens. This does not mean that nothing else exists; but all else lives in *its* light. As long as the presence of the relation continues, this its cosmic range is inviolable. But as soon as a *Thou* becomes *It*, the cosmic range of the relation appears as an offence to the world, its exclusiveness as an exclusion of the universe.

In the relation with God unconditional exclusiveness and unconditional inclusiveness are one. He who enters on the absolute relation is concerned with nothing isolated any more, neither things nor beings, neither earth nor heaven; but everything is gathered up in the relation. For to step into pure relation is not to disregard everything but to see everything in the *Thou*, not to renounce the world but to establish it on its true basis. To look away from the world, or to stare at it, does not help a man to reach God; but he who sees the world in Him stands in His presence. "Here world, there God" is the language of *It*; "God in the world" is another language of *It*;

but to eliminate or leave behind nothing at all, to include the whole world in the *Thou*, to give the world its due and its truth, to include nothing beside God but everything in Him – this is full and complete relation.

Men do not find God if they stay in the world. They do not find Him if they leave the world. He who goes out with his whole being to meet his *Thou* and carries to it all being that is in the world, finds Him who cannot be sought.

Of course God is the "wholly Other"; but He is also the wholly Same, the wholly Present. Of course He is the *Mysterium Tremendum* that appears and overthrows; but He is also the mystery of the self-evident, nearer to me than my *I*.

If you explore the life of things and of conditioned being you come to the unfathomable, if you deny the life of things and of conditioned being you stand before nothingness, if you hallow this life you meet the living God.

*

Man's sense of *Thou*, which experiences in the relations with every particular *Thou* the disappointment of the change to *It*, strives out but not away from them all to its eternal *Thou*; but not as something is sought: actually there is no such thing as seeking God, for there is nothing in which He could not be found. How foolish and hopeless would be the man who turned aside from the course of his life in order to seek God; even though he won all the wisdom of solitude and all the power of concentrated being he would miss God. Rather is it as when a man goes his way and simply wishes that it might be the way: in the strength of his wish his striving is expressed. Every relational event is a stage that affords him a glimpse into the consummating event. So in each event he does not partake, but also (for he is waiting) does partake, of the one event. Waiting, not seeking, he goes his way; hence he is composed before all things, and makes contact with them which helps them. But when he has *found*, his heart is not turned from them, though everything now meets him in the one event. He blesses every cell that sheltered him, and every cell into which he will yet turn. For this finding is not the end, but only the eternal middle, of the way.

It is a finding without seeking, a discovering of the primal, of origin. His sense of *Thou*, which

cannot be satiated till he finds the endless *Thou*, had the *Thou* present to it from the beginning; the presence had only to become wholly real to him in the reality of the hallowed life of the world.

God cannot be inferred in anything – in nature, say, as its author, or in history as its master, or in the subject as the self that is thought in it. Something else is not "given" and God then elicited from it; but God is the Being that is directly, most nearly, and lastingly, over against us, that may properly only be addressed, not expressed.

[. . .]

*

Man's religious situation, his *being there* in the Presence, is characterised by its essential and indissoluble antinomy. The nature of its being determines that this antinomy is indissoluble. He who accepts the thesis and rejects the antithesis does injury to the significance of the situation. He who tries to think out a synthesis destroys the significance of the situation. He who strives to make the antinomy into a relative matter abolishes the significance of the situation. He who wishes to carry through the conflict of the antinomy other than with his life transgresses the significance of the situation. The significance of the situation is that it is lived, and nothing but lived, continually, ever anew, without foresight, without forethought, without prescription, in the totality of its antinomy.

Comparison of the religious with the philosophical antinomy will make this clear. Kant may make the philosophical conflict between necessity and freedom into a relative matter by assigning the former to the world of appearances and the latter to the world of being, so that in their two settings they are no longer really opposed, but rather reconciled – just as the worlds for which they are valid are reconciled. But if I consider necessity and freedom not in worlds of thought but in the reality of my standing before God, if I know that "I am given over for disposal" and know at the same time that "It depends on myself", then I cannot try to escape the paradox that has to be lived by assigning the irreconcilable propositions to two separate realms of validity; nor can I be helped to an ideal reconciliation by any theological device: but I am compelled to take both to myself, to be lived together, and in being lived they are one.

*

An animal's eyes have the power to speak a great language. Independently, without needing co-operation of sounds and gestures, most forcibly when they rely wholly on their glance, the eyes express the mystery in its natural prison, the anxiety of becoming. This condition of the mystery is known only by the animal, it alone can disclose it to us – and this condition only lets itself be disclosed, not fully revealed. The language in which it is uttered is what it says – anxiety, the movement of the creature between the realms of vegetable security and spiritual venture. This language is the stammering of nature at the first touch of spirit, before it yields to spirit's cosmic venture that we call man. But no speech will ever repeat what that stammering knows and can proclaim.

Sometimes I look into a cat's eyes. The domesticated animal has not as it were received from us (as we sometimes imagine) the gift of the truly "speaking" glance, but only – at the price of its primitive disinterestedness – the capacity to turn its glance to us prodigious beings. But with this capacity there enters the glance, in its dawn and continuing in its rising, a quality of amazement and of inquiry that is wholly lacking in the original glance with all its anxiety. The beginning of this cat's glance, lighting up under the touch of my glance, indisputably questioned me: "Is it possible that you think of me? Do you really not just want me to have fun? Do I concern you? Do I exist in your sight? Do I really exist? What is it that comes from you? What is it that surrounds me? What is it that comes to me? What is it?" ("I" is here a transcription for a word, that we do not have, denoting self without the ego; and by "it" is to be imagined the streaming human glance in the total reality of its power to enter into relation.) The animal's glance, speech of disquietude, rose in its greatness – and set at once. My own glance was certainly more lasting; but it was no longer the streaming human glance.

The rotation of the world which introduced the relational event had been followed almost immediately by the other which ended it. The world of *It* surrounded the animal and myself, for the space of a glance the world of *Thou* had shone out from the depths, to be at once extinguished and put back into the world of *It*.

I relate this tiny episode, which I have experienced several times, for the sake of the speech of this almost unnoticeable sunrise and sunset of the spirit. In no other speech have I known so profoundly the fleeting nature of actuality in all its relations with being, the exalted melancholy of our fate, the change, heavy with destiny, of every isolated *Thou* into an *It*. For other events possessed between morning and evening their day, even though it might be brief; but here morning and evening flowed pitilessly mingled together, the bright *Thou* appeared and was gone. Had the burden of the world of *It* really been removed for the space of a glance from the animal and from myself? I myself could continue to think about the matter, but the animal had sunk back out of the stammer of its glance into the disquietude where there is no speech and almost no memory.

How powerful is the unbroken world of *It*, and how delicate are the appearances of the *Thou*!

So much can never break through the crust of the condition of things! O fragment of mica, looking on which I once learned, for the first time, that *I* is not something "in me" – with you I was nevertheless only bound up in myself; at that time the event took place only in me, not between me and you. But when one that is alive rises out of things, and becomes a being in relation to me, joined to me by its nearness and its speech, for how inevitably short a time is it nothing to me but *Thou*! It is not the relation that necessarily grows feeble, but the actuality of its immediacy. Love itself cannot persist in the immediacy of relation; love endures, but in the interchange of actual and potential being. Every *Thou* in the world is enjoined by its nature to become a thing for us, or at all events to re-enter continually the condition of things.

Only in one, all-embracing relation is potential still actual being. Only one *Thou* never ceases by its nature to be *Thou* for us. He who knows God knows also very well remoteness from God, and the anguish of barrenness in the tormented heart; but he does not know the absence of God: it is we only who are not always there.

The lover in the *Vita Nuova* rightly and properly says for the most part *Ella* and only at times *Voi*. The spectator of the *Paradiso*, when he says *Colui*, speaks from poetic necessity, and knows it. If God is addressed as He or It, it is always allegorically. But if we say *Thou* to Him, then mortal sense has set the unbroken truth of the world into a word.

*

Every real relation in the world is exclusive, the Other breaks in on it and avenges its exclusion. Only in the relation with God are unconditioned exclusiveness and unconditioned inclusiveness one and the same, in which the whole universe is implied.

Every real relation in the world rests on individuation, this is its joy – for only in this way is mutual knowledge of different beings won – and its limitation – for in this way perfect knowledge and being known are foregone. But in the perfect relation my *Thou* comprehends but is not my Self, my limited knowledge opens out into a state in which I am boundlessly known.

Every real relation in the world is consummated in the interchange of actual and potential being; every isolated *Thou* is bound to enter the chrysalis state of the *It* in order to take wings anew. But in pure relation potential being is simply actual being as it draws breath, and in it the *Thou* remains present. By its nature the eternal *Thou* is eternally *Thou*; only our nature compels us to draw it into the world and the talk of *It*.

*

The world of *It* is set in the context of space and time.

The world of *Thou* is not set in the context of either of these.

Its context is in the Centre, where the extended lines of relations meet – in the eternal *Thou*.

In the great privilege of pure relation the privileges of the world of *It* are abolished. By virtue of this privilege there exists the unbroken world of *Thou*: the isolated moments of relations are bound up in a life of world solidarity. By virtue of this privilege formative power belongs to the world of *Thou*: spirit can penetrate and transform the world of *It*. By virtue of this privilege we are not given up to alienation from the world and the loss of reality by the *I* – to domination by the ghostly. Reversal is the recognition of the Centre and the act of turning again to it. In this act of the being the buried relational power of man

rises again, the wave that carries all the spheres of relation swells in living streams to give new life to our world.

Perhaps not to our world alone. For this double movement, of estrangement from the primal Source, in virtue of which the universe is sustained in the process of becoming, and of turning towards the primal Source, in virtue of which the universe is released in being, may be perceived as the metacosmical primal form that dwells in the world as a whole in its relation to that which is not the world – form whose twofold nature is represented among men by the twofold nature of their attitudes, their primary words, and their aspects of the world. Both parts of this movement develop, fraught with destiny, in time, and are compassed by grace in the timeless creation that is, incomprehensibly, at once emancipation and preservation, release and binding. Our knowledge of twofold nature is silent before the paradox of the primal mystery.

*

The spheres in which the world of relation is built are three.

First, our life with nature, in which the relation clings to the threshold of speech.

Second, our life with men, in which the relation takes on the form of speech.

Third, our life with intelligible forms, where the relation, being without speech, yet begets it.

In every sphere in its own way, through each process of becoming that is present to us, we look out toward the fringe of the eternal *Thou*; in each we are aware of a breath from the eternal *Thou*; in each *Thou* we address the eternal *Thou*.

Every sphere is compassed in the eternal *Thou*, but it is not compassed in them.

Through every sphere shines the one present.

We can, however, remove each sphere from the present.

From our life with nature we can lift out the "physical" world, the world of consistency, from our life with men the "psychical" world, the world of sensibility, and from our life with spiritual beings the "noetic" world, the world of validity. But now their transparency, and with it their meaning, has been taken from them; each sphere has become dull and capable of being used – and remains dull even though we light it up with the names of Cosmos and Eros and Logos. For actually there is a cosmos for man only when the universe becomes his home, with its holy hearth whereon he offers sacrifice; there is Eros for man only when beings become for him pictures of the eternal, and community is revealed along with them; and there is Logos for man only when he addresses the mystery with work and service for the spirit.

Form's silent asking, man's loving speech, the mute proclamation of the creature, are all gates leading into the presence of the Word.

But when the full and complete meeting is to take place, the gates are united in one gateway of real life, and you no longer know through which you have entered.

*

Of the three spheres, one, our life with men, is marked out. Here language is consummated as a sequence, in speech and counter-speech. Here alone does the word that is formed in language meet its response. Only here does the primary word go backwards and forwards in the same form, the word of address and the word of response live in the one language, *I* and *Thou* take their stand not merely in relation, but also in the solid give-and-take of talk. The moments of relation are here, and only here, bound together by means of the element of the speech in which they are immersed. Here what confronts us has blossomed into the full reality of the *Thou*. Here alone, then, as reality that cannot be lost, are gazing and being gazed upon, knowing and being known, loving and being loved.

This is the main portal, into whose opening the two side-gates lead, and in which they are included.

"When a man is together with his wife the longing of the eternal hills blows round about them."

The relation with man is the real simile of the relation with God; in it true address receives true response; except that in God's response everything, the universe, is made manifest as language.

*

– But is not solitude, too, a gate? Is there not at times disclosed, in stillest loneliness, an unsuspected perception? Can concern with oneself not mysteriously be transformed into concern with the mystery? Indeed, is not that man alone who no longer adheres to any being worthy to confront the Being? "Come, lonely One, to him who is alone", cries Simeon, the new theologian, to his God.

– There are two kinds of solitude, according to that from which they have turned. If we call it solitude to free oneself from intercourse of experiencing and using of things, then that is always necessary, in order that the act of relation, and not that of the supreme relation only, may be reached. But if solitude means absence of relation, then he who has been forsaken by the beings to which he spoke the true *Thou* will be raised up by God, but not he who himself forsook the beings. He alone adheres to various ones of these who is greedy to use them; but he who lives in the strength of present realisation can only be bound up in relation with them. And he alone who is so bound is ready for God. For he alone confronts the reality of God with a human reality.

Further, there are two kinds of solitude, according to that towards which they have turned. If solitude is the place of purification, necessary even to the man who is bound in relation, both before he enters the Holy of Holies and in the midst of his ventures between unavoidable failing and the ascent to proving true – to this solitude we are by nature disposed. But if solitude is the stronghold of isolation, where a man conducts a dialogue with himself – not in order to test and master himself for that which awaits him but in the enjoyment of the conformation of his soul – then we have the real fall of the spirit into spirituality. The man can advance to the last abyss, where in his self-delusion he imagines he has God in himself and is speaking with Him. But truly though God surrounds us and dwells in us, we never have Him in us. And we speak with Him only when speech dies within us.

*

A modern philosopher supposes that every man necessarily believes either in God or in "idols", that is, in some sort of finite good – his nation, his art, power, knowledge, the amassing of money, "the ever new subjugation of woman" – which has become for him an absolute value and has set itself up between him and God; it is only necessary to demonstrate to him the conditioned nature of this good, in order to "shatter" the idol, and the diverted religious act will automatically return to the fitting object.

This conception presupposes that man's relation to the finite goods he has "idolized" is of the same nature as his relation to God, and differs only in its object; for only with this presupposition could the mere substitution of the true for the false object save the erring man. But a man's relation to the "special something" that usurps the throne of the supreme value of his life, and supplants eternity, rests always on experiencing and using an *It*, a thing, an object of enjoyment. For this relation alone is able to obstruct the prospect which opens toward God – it is the impenetrable world of *It*; but the relation which involves the saying of the *Thou* opens up this prospect ever anew. He who is dominated by the idol that he wishes to win, to hold, and to keep – possessed by a desire for possession – has no way to God but that of reversal, which is a change not only of goal but also of the nature of his movement. The man who is possessed is saved by being wakened and educated to solidarity of relation, not by being led in his state of possession towards God. If a man remains in this state what does it mean when he calls no longer on the name of a demon or of a being demonically distorted for him, but on the name of God? It means that from now on he blasphemes. It is blasphemy when a man wishes, after the idol has crashed behind the altar, to pile up an unholy sacrifice to God on the desecrated place.

He who loves a woman, and brings her life to present realisation in his, is able to look in the *Thou* of her eyes into a beam of the eternal *Thou*. But he who eagerly desires "ever new subjugation" – do you wish to hold out to his desire a phantom of the Eternal? He who serves his people in the boundlessness of destiny, and is willing to give himself to them, is really thinking of God. But do you suppose that the man to whom the nation is a god, in whose service he would like to enlist everything (for in the nation's he exalts his own image), need only be given a feeling of disgust – and he would see the truth? And what does it mean that a man is said to treat money, embodied non-being, "as if it were God"? What has the lust of grabbing and of laying up treasure in common with the joy in the presence of the Present One? Can the servant of Mammon say *Thou* to his money? And how is he to behave towards God

when he does not understand how to say *Thou*? He cannot serve two masters – not even one after the other: he must first learn to serve *in a different way*.

He who has been converted by this substitution of object now "holds" a phantom that he calls God. But God, the eternal Presence, does not permit Himself to be held. Woe to the man so possessed that he thinks he possesses God!

*

The "religious" man is spoken of as one who does not need to take his stand in any relation to the world and to living beings, since the status of social life, that is defined from outside, is in him surpassed by means of a strength that works only from within. But in this idea of the social life two basically different things are combined – first, the community that is built up out of relation, and second, the collection of human units that do not know relation – modern man's palpable condition of lack of relation. But the bright building of community, to which there is an escape even from the dungeon of "social life", is the achievement of the same power that works in the relation between man and God. This does not mean that this one relation is set beside the others; for it is the universal relation, into which all streams pour, yet without exhausting their waters. Who wishes to make division and define boundaries between sea and streams? There we find only the one flow from *I* to *Thou*, unending, the one boundless flow of the real life. Life cannot be divided between a real relation with God and an unreal relation of *I* and *It* with the world – you cannot both truly pray to God and profit by the world. He who knows the world as something by which he is to profit knows God also in the same way. His prayer is a procedure of exoneration heard by the ear of the void. He – not the "atheist," who addresses the Nameless out of the night and yearning of his garret-window – is the godless man.

It is further said that the "religious" man stands as a single, isolated, separated being before God, since he has also gone beyond the status of the "moral" man, who is still involved in duty and obligation to the world. The latter, it is said, is still burdened with responsibility for the action of those who act, since he is wholly defined by the tension between being and "ought to be", and in grotesque and hopeless sacrificial courage casts his heart piece by piece into the insatiable gulf that lies between them. The "religious" man, on the other hand, has emerged from that tension into the tension between the world and God; there the command reigns that the unrest of responsibility and of demands on oneself be removed; there is no willing of one's own, but only the being joined into what is ordained; every "ought" vanishes in unconditioned being, and the world, though still existing, no longer counts. For in it the "religious" man has to perform his particular duties, but as it were without obligation – beneath the aspect of the nothingness of all action. But that is to suppose that God has created His world as an illusion and man for frenzied being. He who approaches the Face has indeed surpassed duty and obligation – but not because he is now remote from the world; rather because he has truly drawn closer to it. Duty and obligation are rendered only to the stranger; we are drawn to and full of love for the intimate person. The world, lit by eternity, becomes fully present to him who approaches the Face, and to the Being of beings he can in a single response say *Thou*. Then there is no more tension between the world and God, but only the one reality. The man is not freed from responsibility; he has exchanged the torment of the finite, pursuit of effects, for the motive power of the infinite, he has got the mighty responsibility of love for the whole untraceable world-event, for the profound belonging to the world before the Face of God. He has, to be sure, abolished moral judgments for ever; the "evil" man is simply one who is commended to him for greater responsibility, one more needy of love; but he will have to practise, till death itself, decision in the depths of spontaneity, unruffled decision, made ever anew, to right action. Then action is not empty, but purposive, enjoined, needed, part of creation; but this action is no longer imposed upon the world, it grows on it as if it were non-action.

*

What is the eternal, primal phenomenon, present here and now, of that which we term revelation? It is the phenomenon that a man does not pass, from the moment of the supreme meeting, the same being as he entered into it. The moment of meeting is not an "experience" that stirs in the receptive soul and grows to perfect blessedness; rather, in that moment something happens to the man. At times it is like a light breath, at times like a wrestling-bout, but always – it *happens*. The man who emerges from the act of pure relation that so involves his being has now in his being something more that has grown in him, of which he did not know before and whose origin he is not rightly able to indicate. However the source of this new thing is classified in scientific orientation of the world, with its authorised efforts to establish an unbroken causality, we, whose concern is real consideration of the real, cannot have our purpose served with subconsciousness or any other apparatus of the soul. The reality is that we receive what we did not hitherto have, and receive it in such a way that we know it has been given to us. In the language of the Bible, "Those, who wait upon the Lord shall renew their strength". In the language of Nietzsche, who in his account remains loyal to reality, "We take and do not ask who it is there that gives".

Man receives, and he receives not a specific "content" but a Presence, a Presence as power. This Presence and this power include three things, undivided, yet in such a way that we may consider them separately. First, there is the whole fulness of real mutual action, of the being raised and bound up in relation: the man can give no account at all of how the binding in relation is brought about, nor does it in any way lighten his life – it makes life heavier, but heavy with meaning. Secondly, there is the inexpressible confirmation of meaning. Meaning is assured. Nothing can any longer be meaningless. The question about the meaning of life is no longer there. But were it there, it would not have to be answered. You do not know how to exhibit and define the meaning of life, you have no formula or picture for it, and yet it has more certitude for you than the perceptions of your senses. What does the revealed and concealed meaning purpose with us, desire from us? It does not wish to be explained (nor are we able to do that) but only to be done by us. Thirdly, this meaning is not that of "another life", but that of this life of ours, not one of a world "yonder" but that of this world of ours, and it desires its confirmation in this life and in relation with this world. This meaning can be received, but not experienced; it cannot be experienced but it can be done, and this is its purpose with us. The assurance I have of it does not wish to be sealed within me, but it wishes to be born by me into the world. But just as the meaning itself does not permit itself to be transmitted and made into knowledge generally current and admissible, so confirmation of it cannot be transmitted as a valid Ought; it is not prescribed, it is not specified on any tablet, to be raised above all men's heads. The meaning that has been received can be proved true by each man only in the singleness of his being and the singleness of his life. As no prescription can lead us to the meeting, so none leads from it. As only acceptance of the Presence is necessary for the approach to the meeting, so in a new sense is it so when we emerge from it. As we reach the meeting with the simple *Thou* on our lips, so with the *Thou* on our lips we leave it and return to the world.

That before which, in which, out of which, and into which we live, even the mystery, has remained what it was. It has become present to us and in its presentness has proclaimed itself to us as salvation; we have "known" it, but we acquire no knowledge from it which might lessen or moderate its mysteriousness. We have come near to God, but not nearer to unveiling being or solving its riddle. We have felt release, but not discovered a "solution". We cannot approach others with what we have received, and say "You must know this, you must do this".

We can only go, and confirm its truth. And this, too, is no "ought", but we can, we *must*.

This is the eternal revelation that is present here and now. I know of no revelation and believe in none whose primal phenomenon is not precisely this. I do not believe in a self-naming of God, a self-definition of God before men. The Word of revelation is *I am that I am*. That which reveals is that which reveals. That which is *is*, and nothing more. The eternal source of strength streams, the eternal contact persists, the eternal voice sounds forth, and nothing more.

*

The eternal *Thou* can by its nature not become *It*; for by its nature it cannot be established in measure and bounds, not even in the measure of the immeasurable, or the bounds of boundless being; for by its nature it cannot be understood as a sum of qualities, not even as an infinite sum of qualities raised to a transcendental level; for it can be found neither in nor out of the world; for it cannot be experienced, or thought; for we miss Him, Him who is, if we say "I believe that He is" – "He" is also a metaphor, but "Thou" is not.

[. . .]

Sarvepalli Radhakrishnan, "Conflict of Religions: The Hindu Attitude"

Introduction

Sir Sarvepalli Radhakrishnan (1888–1972) was the youngest of a remarkable group of Indian thinkers born toward the end of the nineteenth century and responsible, between them, for a great revival of Hindu thought. As the most "academic" and "professional" of these philosophers, Radhakrishnan never enjoyed the charisma nor commanded the personal following of other members of the group, which included Mahatma Gandhi (see V.20), Sir Rabindranath Tagore (1861–1941), and Aurobindo Ghose (1872–1950). He was, however, a distinguished figure in Indian public life, eventually being elected his country's President in 1962.

Radhakrishnan's own general philosophy, articulated in such works as *Eastern Religions and Western Thought*, eclectically borrowed from Western sources, including Darwin and the American pragmatists, although it remained recognizably within the Advaita Vedanta tradition of Hindu thought (see the selections from Śaṁkara in III.7). He shared however with Gandhi, Tagore, and others the conviction that Western philosophy has much to gain, in return, through attention to Hindu philosophy – not least in the

From Sarvepalli Radhakrishnan, *The Hindu View of Life*, London: George Allen & Unwin, 1927, pp. 26–44 (some passages and notes omitted).

area of philosophy of religion, and especially in connection with the vexed question of whether there exists a "common core" to diverse systems of religious belief.

When the message of what might be called philosophical ecumenicalism – a message not simply of mutual tolerance among religions, but of an underlying unity among them – was proclaimed by the Indian sage, Vivekananda, at the 1893 World Parliament of Religions, it caused as much outrage among many of the delegates as it did enthusiasm among some of the others. This may, in part, have been due to the further message that Hinduism was in a uniquely privileged position to interpret and, as it were, synthesize and distill the teachings of other religions. When Gandhi, a practicing Hindu, famously remarked "I consider myself a Hindu, Christian, Moslem, Jew, Buddhist and Confucian,"[1] he was not announcing an impossible allegiance to the particular doctrines of each of these faiths, but registering the conviction that, as Aurobindo put it, "the Hindu religion is the universal religion which embraces all others."[2]

Radhakrishnan's essay makes clear some of the reasons why Hinduism was, and often still is, viewed as a peculiarly ecumenical dispensation. For one thing, Hinduism was, from the outset, a catholic combination of various religious traditions – animist, Vedic, Dravidian, and so on. Of greater philosophical interest are two other points he makes – points, one may think, which indeed need to be secured if talk of the "oneness" of religions is to be more than pious and, these days, fashionable rhetoric. First, Hinduism in its various forms is imbued with the idea of an ineffable "absolute" (*Brahman*), knowable only through mystical intuition, of which particular gods, such as Śiva or Vishnu, are only manifestations or symbols. It is, perhaps, a short step from here to postulate that the gods of other religions, such as Allah, are similarly only symbolic representations of an impersonal "godhead."

Second, Radhakrishnan locates the essential nature of religion not in a set of metaphysical doctrines, but in a "quest" and a certain style of "righteous living." This is related to a distinctly pragmatist streak in his philosophy. Truth, he writes elsewhere, is what "satisfies our wants . . . and gives peace of mind . . . and contributes to . . . social harmony."[3] To the extent that all the world's great religions contribute in these ways,

they converge on the truth, so understood, and in comparison with this the doctrinal differences between them are of relatively little moment. The only relevant difference to stress between Hinduism and the rest of the world's religions is that the former – with its traditional hospitality toward countless gods and practices – has always implicitly recognized the essential character of religious commitment.

Notes

1 *The Sayings of Mahatma Gandhi*, Singapore: Brash, 1984, p. 10.

2 *The Life Divine*, Pondicherry: Sri Aurobindo Ashram, 1955, p. 153.

3 *Eastern Religions and Western Thought*, Oxford: Clarendon Press, 1939, p. 24.

Radhakrishnan, "Conflict of Religions: The Hindu Attitude"

Students of mysticism are impressed by the universality of the mystic experience, though the differences in the formulations of it are by no means unimportant. The mystics of the world, whether Hindu, Christian or Muslim, belong to the same brotherhood and have a striking family likeness. Miss Evelyn Underhill writes: 'Though mystical theologies of the East and the West differ widely – though the ideal of life which they hold out to the soul differ too – yet in the experience of the saint this conflict is seen to be transcended. When the love of God is reached, divergencies become impossible, for the soul has passed beyond the sphere of the manifold and is immersed in the one Reality. Judged by the characteristic religious experience, St John and St Paul have not any material advantage over Plotinus and Śaṃkara. 'One cannot honestly say,' observes Miss Underhill, 'that there is any wide difference between the Brahmin, the Sufi or the Christian mystics at their best.' A hostile critic of mysticism, Hermann, the German theologian, endorses this view from his own standpoint. Regarding Christian mystics he remarks, 'Whenever the religious feeling in them soars to its highest flights, then

they are torn loose from Christ and float away in precisely the same realm with the non-Christian mystics of all ages.' Again, 'Augustine wrote a work of fifteen books on the Trinity, yet when he stood with his mother at the window of the house at Ostia and sought to express the profound sense he felt of being in the grasp of God, he spoke not of the Trinity, but of the one God in whose presence the soul is lifted above itself and above all words and signs.'

It matters not whether the seer who has the insight has dreamed his way to the truth in the shadow of the temple or the tabernacle, the church or the mosque. Those who have seen the radiant vision of the Divine protest against the exaggerated importance attached to outward forms. They speak a language which unites all worshippers as surely as the dogmas of the doctors divide. The true seer is gifted with a universality of outlook, and a certain sensitiveness to the impulses and emotions which dominate the rich and varied human nature. He whose consciousness is anchored in God cannot deny any expression of life as utterly erroneous. He is convinced of the inexhaustibility of the nature of God and the infinite number of its possible manifestations.

The intellectual representations of the religious mystery are relative and symbolic. As Plato would say, our accounts of God are likely stories, but all the same legendary. Not one of them is full and final. We are like little children on the seashore trying to fill our shells with water from the sea. While we cannot exhaust the waters of the deep by means of our shells, every drop that we attempt to gather into our tiny shells is a part of the authentic waters. Our intellectual representations differ simply because they bring out different facets of the one central reality. From the Ṛṣis, or seers, of the Upaniṣads down to Tagore and Gandhi, the Hindu has acknowledged that truth wears vestures of many colours and speaks in strange tongues. The mystics of other denominations have also testified to this. Boehme says: 'Consider the birds in our forests, they praise God each in his own way, in diverse tones and fashions. Think you God is vexed by this diversity and desires to silence discordant voices? All the forms of being are dear to the infinite Being Himself.' Look at this Sufi utterance in the translation of Professor Browne of Cambridge:

Beaker or flagon, or bowl or jar,
Clumsy or slender, coarse or fine;
However the potter may make or mar,
All were made to contain the wine:
Should we seek this one or that one shun
When the wine which gives them their worth is one?

Bearing in mind this great truth, Hinduism developed an attitude of comprehensive charity instead of a fanatic faith in an inflexible creed. It accepted the multiplicity of aboriginal gods and others which originated, most of them, outside the Aryan tradition, and justified them all. It brought together into one whole all believers in God. Many sects professing many different beliefs live within the Hindu fold. Heresy-hunting, the favourite game of many religions, is singularly absent from Hinduism.

Hinduism is wholly free from the strange obsession of some faiths that the acceptance of a particular religious metaphysic is necessary for salvation, and non-acceptance thereof is a heinous sin meriting eternal punishment in hell. Here and there outbursts of sectarian fanaticism are found recorded in the literature of the Hindus, which indicate the first effects of the conflicts of the different groups brought together into the one fold; but the main note of Hinduism is one of respect and good will for other creeds. When a worshipper of Viṣṇu had a feeling in his heart against a worshipper of Śiva and he bowed before the image of Viṣṇu, the face of the image divided itself in half and Śiva appeared on one side and Viṣṇu on the other, and the two smiling as one face on the bigoted worshipper told him that Viṣṇu and Śiva were one. The story is significant.

In a sense, Hinduism may be regarded as the first example in the world of a missionary religion. Only its missionary spirit is different from that associated with the proselytizing creeds. It did not regard it as its mission to convert humanity to any one opinion. For what counts is conduct and not belief. Worshippers of different gods and followers of different rites were taken into the Hindu fold. Kṛṣṇa, according to the Bhagavadgītā, accepts as his own, not only the oppressed classes, women and Śūdras, but even those of unclean descent (pāpayonayaḥ), like the Kirātas and the Hūṇas.

[. . .]

When in the hour of their triumph the Aryans made up with their dangerous though vanquished rivals, they did not sneer at their relatively crude cults. The native inhabitants of North India clothed the naked forces of nature with the gorgeous drapery of a mythic fancy, and fashioned a train of gods and goddesses, of spirits and elves out of the shifting panorama of nature, and the Vedic Aryans accepted them all and set them side by side with the heavenly host to which they themselves looked with awe and admiration. It was enough for them that those crude objects were regarded by their adherents as sources of the supreme blessings of life and centres of power which can be drawn upon. The gods of the Ṛg Veda and the ghosts of the Atharva Veda melted and coalesced under the powerful solvent of philosophy into the one supreme reality which, according to the qualities with which our imagination invests it, goes by this name or that.

The Epics relate the acceptance or new tribes and their gods into the old family circle. The clash of cults and the contact of cultures do not, as a rule, result in a complete domination of the one by the other. In all true contact there is an interchange of elements, though the foreign elements are given a new significance by those who accept them. The emotional attitudes attached to the old forms are transferred to the new which is fitted into the background of the old. Many tribes and races had mystic animals, and when the tribes entered the Hindu society the animals which followed them were made vehicles and companions of gods. One of them is mounted on the peacock, another on the swan, a third is carried by the bull, and a fourth by the goat. The enlistment of Hanumān, the monkey-general, in the service of Rāma signifies the meeting-point of early nature worship and later theism. The dancing of Kṛṣṇa on Kālīya's head represents the subordination, if not the displacement, of serpent worship. Rāma's breaking of the bow of Śiva signifies the conflict between the Vedic ideal and the cult of Śiva, who soon became the god of the south (Dakṣiṇāmūrti). There are other stories in the Epic literature indicating the reconciliation of the Vedic and the non-Vedic faiths. The heroized ancestors, the local saints, the planetary influences and the tribal gods were admitted into the Hindu pantheon, though they were all subordinated to the one supreme reality of which they were regarded as aspects. The polytheism was organised in a monistic way. Only it was not a rigid monotheism enjoining on its adherents the most complete intolerance for those holding a different view.

It need not be thought that the Aryan was always the superior force. There are occasions when the Aryan yielded to the non-Aryan, and rightly too. The Epics relate the manner in which the different non-Aryan gods asserted their supremacy over the Aryan ones. Kṛṣṇa's struggle with Indra, the prince of the Vedic gods, is one instance. The rise of the cult of Siva is another. When Dakṣa, the protagonist of the sacrificial cult, conceives a violent feud against Śiva, there is disaffection in his own home, for his daughter Sati, who has become the embodiment of womanly piety and devotion, has developed an ardent love for Śiva.

The Vedic culture, which resembles that of the Homeric Greeks or the Celtic Irish at the beginning of the Christian era, or that of the pre-Christian Teutons and Slavs, becomes transformed in the Epics into the Hindu culture through the influence of the Dravidians. The Aryan idea of worship during the earliest period was to call on the Father Sky or some other shining one to look from on high on the sacrificer, and receive from him the offerings of fat or flesh, cakes and drink. But soon pūjā or worship takes the place of homa or sacrifice. Image worship which was a striking feature of the Dravidian faith was accepted by the Aryans. The ideals of vegetarianism and non-violence (ahiṁsā) also developed. The Vedic tradition was dominated by the Āgamic, and today Hindu culture shows the influence of the Āgamas, the sacred scriptures of the Jains, as much as that of the Vedas. The Aryan and the Dravidian do not exist side by side in Hinduism, but are worked up into a distinctive cultural pattern which is more an emergent than a resultant. The history of the Hindu religious development shows occasionally the friction between the two strains of the Vedas and the Āgamas, though they are sufficiently harmonized. When conceived in a large historical spirit, Hinduism becomes a slow growth across the centuries incorporating all the good and true things as well as much that is evil and erroneous, though a constant endeavour, which is not always successful, is kept up to throw out the unsatisfactory elements. Hinduism has the large comprehensive unity of a living organism with a fixed orientation. The Upaniṣad asks us to remember the Real who is One, who is indistinguishable through class or colour, and who by his varied forces provides as is necessary for the needs of each class and of all.

When once the cults are taken into Hinduism, alteration sets in as the result of the influence of the higher thought. The Hindu method of religious reform is essentially democratic. It allows each group to get to the truth through its own tradition by means of discipline of mind and morals. Each group has its own historic tradition, and assimilation of it is the condition of its growth of spirit. Even the savage clings to his superstitions obstinately and faithfully. For him his views are live forces, though they may seem to us no more than childish fancies. To shatter the superstitions of the savage is to destroy his morality, his social code and mental peace. Religious rites and social institutions, whatever they may be, issue out of experiences that may be hundreds of years old. As the Hindu inquirer cast his eyes over the manifold variety of the faiths which prevailed in his world, he saw that they were all conditioned by the social structure in which their followers lived. History has made them what they are, and they cannot be made different all of a sudden. Besides, God's gracious purpose includes the whole of the human race. Every community has inalienable rights which others should respect. No type can come into existence in which God does not live. Robert Burns truly says: 'And yet the light that led astray was light from heaven.' To despise other people's gods is to despise them, for they and their gods are adapted to each other. The Hindu took up the gods of even the savage and the uncivilized and set them on equal thrones to his own.

The right way to refine the crude beliefs of any group is to alter the bias of mind. For the view of God an individual stresses depends on the kind of man he is. The temperament and the training of the individual as well as the influence of the environment determine to a large extent the character of his religious opinions. Any defect in one's nature or onesidedness in one's experience is inevitably reflected in the view the individual adopts with regard to the religious reality. One's knowledge of God is limited by one's capacity to understand him. The aim of the reformer should be to cure the defect and not to criticize the view. When the spiritual life is quickened, the belief is altered automatically. Any change of view to be real must grow from within outwards. Opinions cannot grow unless traditions are altered. The task of the religious teacher is not so much to impose an opinion as to kindle an aspiration. If we open the eyes, the truth will be seen. The Hindu method adopts not force and threats but suggestion and persuasion. Error is only a sign of immaturity. It is not a grievous sin. Given time and patience it will be shaken off. However severe Hinduism may be with the strong in spirit, it is indulgent to the frailties of the weak.

The Hindu method of religious reform helps to bring about a change not in the name but in the content. While we are allowed to retain the same name, we are encouraged to deepen its significance. To take a familiar illustration, the Yahveh of the Pentateuch is a fearsome spirit, again and again flaming up in jealous wrath and commanding the slaughter of man, woman, child and beast, whenever his wrath is roused. The conception of the Holy One who loves mercy rather than sacrifice, who abominates burnt offerings, who reveals himself to those who yearn to know him asserts itself in the writings of Isaiah and Hosea. In the revelation of Jesus we have the conception of God as perfect love. The name 'Yahveh' is the common link which connects these different developments. When a new cult

is accepted by Hinduism, the name is retained though a refinement of the content is effected. To take an example from early Sanskrit literature, it is clear that Kāli in her various shapes is a non-Aryan goddess. But she was gradually identified with the supreme Godhead. Witness the following address to Kāli:

'Thou, O Goddess, O auspicious Remover of the distresses of those who turn to thee for refuge, art not to be known by speech, mind and intellect. None indeed is able to praise thee by words.

'O Goddess, having Brahman as thy personal form, O Mother of the universe, we repeatedly salute thee, full of compassion.

'The work of creation, maintenance and absorption is a mere wave of thy sportive pleasure. Thou art able to create the whole in a moment. Salutation to thee, O all-powerful Goddess! Although devoid of attributes and form, although standing outside of objective existence, although beyond the range of the senses, although one and whole and without a second and all-pervading, yet assuming a form possessed of attributes for the well-being of devotees, thou givest them the highest good. We salute thee, O Goddess, in whom all the three conditions of existence become manifest.'

Similarly Krṣna becomes the highest Godhead in the *Bhagavadgītā* whatever his past origin may have been.

When the pupil approaches his religious teacher for guidance, the teacher asks the pupil about his favourite God, *iṣṭadevata,* for every man has a right to choose that form of belief and worship which most appeals to him. The teacher tells the pupil that his idea is a concrete representation of what is abstract, and leads him gradually to an appreciation of the Absolute intended by it. Suppose a Christian approaches a Hindu teacher for spiritual guidance, he would not ask his Christian pupil to discard his allegiance to Christ but would tell him that his idea of Christ was not adequate, and would lead him to a knowledge of the real Christ, the incorporate Supreme. Every God accepted by Hinduism is elevated and ultimately identified with the central Reality which is one with the deeper self of man. The addition of new gods to the Hindu pantheon does not endanger it. The critic who observes that Hinduism is 'magic tempered by metaphysics' or 'animism transformed by philosophy' is right. There is a distinction between magic tempered by metaphysics and pure magic. Hinduism absorbs everything that enters into it, magic or animism, and raises it to a higher level.

Differences in name become immaterial for the Hindu, since every name, at its best, connotes the same metaphysical and moral perfections. The identity of content signified by the different names is conveyed to the people at large by an identification of the names. Brahmā, Viṣṇu, Śiva, Kṛṣṇa, Kālī, Buddha and other historical names are used indiscriminately for the Absolute Reality. 'May Hari, the ruler of the three worlds worshipped by the Śaivites as Śiva, by the Vedāntins as Brahman, by the Buddhists as Buddha, by the Naiyāyikas as the chief agent, by the Jainas as the liberated, by the ritualists as the principle of law, may he grant our prayers.' Saṁkara, the great philosopher, refers to the one Reality, who, owing to the diversity of intellects (*matibheda*) is conventionally spoken of (*parīkalpya*) in various ways as Brahmā, Viṣṇu and Maheśvara. A south Indian folksong says:

> Into the bosom of the one great sea
> Flow streams that come from hills on every side,
> Their names are various as their springs,
> And thus in every land do men bow down
> To one great God, though known by many names.

The Hindu method of reform enables every group to retain its past associations and preserve its individuality and interest. For as students are proud of their colleges, so are groups of their gods. We need not move students from one college to another, but should do our best to raise the tone of each college, improve its standards and refine its ideals, with the result that each college enables us to attain the same goal. It is a matter of indifference what college we are in, so long as all of them are steeped in the same atmosphere and train us to reach the same ideal. Of course there will be fanatics with narrow patriotism holding up Balliol as the best or Magdalene as modern, but to the impartial spectator the different colleges do not seem to be horizontal levels one higher than the other, but only vertical pathways leading to the same summit. We can be in any college and yet be on the lowest rung of the ladder or be high up in the scale. Where we are does not depend on the college but on ourselves. There are good Christians and bad Christians even as there are good Hindus and bad Hindus.

The Hindu method of reform has been criticized both from the theoretical and the practical points of view. Professor Clement Webb writes: 'With its traditions of periodically repeated incarnations of the deity in the most diverse forms, its ready acceptance of any and every local divinity or founder of a sect or ascetic devotee as a manifestation of God, its tolerance of symbols and legends of all kinds, however repulsive or obscene, by the side of the most exalted flights of world-renouncing mysticism, it could perhaps more easily than any other faith develop, without loss of continuity with its past, into a universal religion which would see in every creed a form, suited to some particular group or individual, of the universal aspiration after one Eternal Reality, to whose true being the infinitely various shapes in which it reveals itself to, or conceals itself from men are all alike indifferent.' While this statement represents the general tendency of the Hindu faith, it is not altogether fair to it when it suggests that for Hinduism there is nothing to choose between one revelation and another. Hinduism does not mistake tolerance for indifference. It affirms that while all revelations refer to reality, they are not equally true to it. Hinduism requires every man to think steadily on life's mystery until he reaches the highest revelation. While the lesser forms are tolerated in the interests of those who cannot suddenly transcend them, there is all through an insistence on the larger idea and the purer worship. Hinduism does not believe in forcing up the pace of development. When we give our higher experiences to those who cannot understand them we are in the position of those who can see and who impart the visual impressions to those born blind. Unless we open their spiritual eyes, they cannot see what the seers relate. So while Hinduism does not interfere with a man's natural way of thinking, which depends on his moral and intellectual gifts, education and environment, it furthers his spiritual growth by lending a sympathetic and helping hand wherever he stands. While Hinduism hates the compulsory conscription of men into the house of truth, it insists on the development of his intellectual conscience and sensibility to truth. Besides, error of judgment is not moral obliquity. Weakness of understanding is not depravity of heart. If a full and perfect understanding of the divine nature is necessary for salvation how many of us can escape the jaws of hell? *Śaktigītā* says: 'There is no limit, O Mother, to thy kindly grace in the case of devotees who are not able to realize thy form consisting of ideal essences, through the defects in the knowledge of principles.' We may not know God, but God certainly knows us.

Hinduism has enough faith in the power of spirit to break the bonds that fetter the growth of the soul. God, the central reality affirmed by all religions, is the continual evolver of the faiths in which men find themselves. Besides, experience proves that attempts at a very rapid progress from one set of rules to a higher one does not lead to advance but abrogation. The mills of the gods grind slowly in the making of history, and zealous reformers meet with defeat if they attempt to save the world in their own generation by forcing on it their favourite programmes. Human nature cannot be hurried. Again, Hinduism does not believe in bringing about a mechanical uniformity of belief and worship by a forcible elimination of all that is not in agreement with a particular creed. It does not believe in any statutory methods of salvation. Its scheme of salvation is not limited to those who hold a particular view of God's nature and worship. Such an exclusive absolutism is inconsistent with an all-loving universal God. It is not fair to God or man to assume that one people are the chosen of God, that their religion occupies a central place in the religious development of mankind, and that all others should borrow from them or suffer spiritual destitution.

After all, what counts is not creed but conduct. By their fruits ye shall know them and not by their beliefs. Religion is not correct belief but righteous living. The truly religious never worry about other people's beliefs. Look at the great saying of Jesus: 'Other sheep I have which are not of this fold.' Jesus was born a Jew and died a Jew. He did not tell the Jewish people among whom he found himself, 'It is wicked to be Jews. Become Christians.' He did his best to rid the Jewish religion of its impurities. He would have done the same with Hinduism had he been born a Hindu. The true reformer purifies and enlarges the heritage of mankind and does not belittle, still less deny it.

Those who love their sects more than truth end by loving themselves more than their sects. We start by claiming that Christianity is the only true religion and then affirm that Protestantism is the only true sect of Christianity, Episcopalianism the only true Protestant Christian religion, and our particular standpoint the only true representation of the High Church view.

The Hindu theory that every human being, every group and every nation has an individuality worthy of reverence is slowly gaining ground. Such a view requires that we should allow absolute freedom to every group to cultivate what is most distinctive and characteristic of it. All peculiarity is unique and incommunicable, and it will be to disregard the nature of reality to assume that what is useful to one will be useful to everyone else to the same extent. The world is wide enough to hold men whose natures are different.

It is argued sometimes that the Hindu plan has not helped its adherents to a freer and larger life. It is difficult to meet such an indefinite charge. Anyway, it is a matter of grave doubt whether Hinduism would have achieved a more effective regeneration if it had displaced by force the old ideas, i.e. if it had adopted the method of conversion and proselytism instead of reform resulting from gradual development. It is quite true that Hinduism did not cut away with an unsparing hand the rank tropical growth of magic and obscurantism. Its method is rather that of sapping the foundations than cutting the growths.

While in the great days of Hinduism there was a great improvement in the general religious life of the Hindus by the exercise of the two principles of respect for man and unbending devotion to truth, there has been a 'failure of nerve' in the Hindu spirit in recent times. There are within Hinduism large numbers who are the victims of superstition, but even in countries where the higher civilization is said to have displaced the lower, the lower still persists. To meet a savage we need not go very far. A great authority in these matters, Sir James Frazer, says: 'Among the ignorant and superstitious classes of modern Europe, it is very much what it was thousands of years ago in Egypt and India, and what it now is among the lowest savages surviving in the remotest corners of the world. Now and then the polite world is startled by a paragraph in a newspaper which tells how in Scotland an image has been found stuck full of pins for the purpose of killing an obnoxious laird or minister, how a woman has been slowly roasted to death as a witch in Ireland, or how a girl has been murdered and chopped up in Russia to make those candles of human tallow by whose light thieves hope to pursue their midnight trade unseen.' Many Christians believe in spells and magic. Habits of human groups are hard to eradicate in proportion to the length of time during which they have existed. Rapid changes are impossible, and even slow changes are exceedingly difficult, for religions tend strongly to revert to type. When primitive tribes whose cults provided them with feminine as well as masculine objects of devotion entered the Buddhist fold they insisted on having in addition to the masculine Buddha the feminine Tārā. When the Græco-Romans worshiping Ashtoreth, Isis and Aphrodite entered the Christian Church, Mariolatry developed. It is related of an Indian Christian convert who attended the church on Sunday and the Kāli temple on Friday, that when the missionary gentleman asked him whether he was not a Christian, he replied, 'Yes, I am, but does it mean that I have changed my religion?' Hindu converts to other faiths frequently turn to Hindu gods in cases of trouble and sickness, presence or dread of death. Outer professions have no roots in inner life. We cannot alter suddenly our subconscious heritage at the bidding of the reformer. The old ideas cannot be rooted out unless we are educated to a higher intellectual and moral level.

The Hindu method has not been altogether a failure. There has been progress all round, though there is still room for considerable improvement. In spite of the fact that Hinduism has no common creed and its worship no fixed form, it has bound together multitudinous sects and devotions into a common scheme. In the Census Report for 1911 Mr Burns observes: 'The general result of my inquiries is that the great majority of Hindus have a firm belief in one supreme God, Bhagavān, Parameśvara, Īśvara, or Nārāyana.' Regarding the spread of Hindu ideas and ideals, Sir Herbert Risley says: 'These ideas are not the monopoly of the learned, they are shared in great measure by the man in the street. If you talk to a fairly intelligent Hindu peasant about the Paramātmā, Karma, Māyā, Mukti, and so forth, you will find as soon as he has got over his surprise at your interest in such matters that the terms are familiar to him, and that he has formed a rough working theory of their bearing on his own future.' There is an inner cohesion among the Hindus from the Himālayas to Cape Comorin.

The work of assimilating the rawest recruits of the hill-tribes and other half-civilized hordes has been a slow one and by no means thorough. Among Hindus are counted many professing crude beliefs and submerged thoughts which the civilization has not had time to eradicate. During the last few centuries Hinduism has not been faithful to its ideals, and the task of the uplift of the uncivilized has been sadly neglected.

Hinduism does not support the sophism that is often alleged that to coerce a man to have the right view is as legitimate as to save one by violence from committing suicide in a fit of delirium. The intolerance of narrow monotheism is written in letters of blood across the history of man from the time when first the tribes of Israel burst into the land of Canaan. The worshippers of the one jealous God are egged on to aggressive wars against people of alien cults. They invoke divine sanction for the cruelties inflicted on the conquered. The spirit of old Israel is inherited by Christianity and Islam, and it might not be unreasonable to suggest that it would have been better for Western civilization if Greece had moulded it on this question rather than Palestine. Wars of religion which are the outcome of fanaticism that prompts and justifies the extermination of aliens of different creeds were practically unknown in Hindu India. Of course, here and there there were outbursts of fanaticism, but Hinduism as a rule never encouraged persecution for unbelief. Its record has been a clean one, relatively speaking. It has been able to hold together in peace many and varied communities of men. Buddhism, which counts among its followers nearly a fifth of the human race, has always respected other faiths and never tried to supplant them by force. One of the earliest Buddhist books relates that Buddha condemned the tendency prevalent among the religious disputants of his day, to make a display of their own doctrines and damn those of others. Buddha asks his followers to avoid all discussions which are likely to stir up discontent among the different sects. Religious toleration is the theme of one of Aśoka's rock edicts, 'The King, beloved of the Gods, honours every form of religious faith, but considers no gift or honour so much as the increase of the substance of religion; whereof this is the root, to reverence one's own faith and never to revile that of others. Whoever acts differently injures his own religion while he wrong's another's.' 'The texts of all forms of religion shall be followed under my protection.' The Hindu and the Buddhist rulers of India acted up to this principle with the result that the persecuted and the refugees of all great religions found shelter in India. The Jews, the Christians, the Parsees were allowed absolute freedom to develop on their own lines. Yuan Chwang reports that at the great festival of Prayāga, King Harṣa dedicated on the first day a statue to the Buddha, another to the sun, the favourite deity of his father, on the second, and to Śiva on the third. The famous Kottayam plates of Sthāṇuravi (ninth century AD) and the Cochin plates of Vijayarāgadeva bear eloquent testimony to the fact that the Hindu kings not only tolerated Christianity but granted special concessions to the professors of that faith. More recently, the Hindu prince of Mysore made a gift to the re-building of the Christian church in his State.

Today the world has become a much smaller place, thanks to the adventures and miracles of science. Foreign nations have become our next-door neighbours. Mingling of populations is bringing about an interchange of thought. We are slowly realizing that the world is a single co-operative group. Other religions have become forces with which we have to reckon, and we are seeking for ways and means by which we can live together in peace and harmony. We cannot have religious unity and peace so long as we assert that we are in possession of the light and all others are groping in the darkness. That very assertion is a challenge to a fight. The political ideal of the world is not so much a single empire with a homogeneous civilization and a single communal will, but a brotherhood of free nations differing profoundly in life and mind, habits and institutions, existing side by side in peace and order, harmony and cooperation, and each contributing to the world its own unique and specific best, which is irreducible to the terms of the others. The cosmopolitanism of the eighteenth century and the nationalism of the nineteenth are combined in our ideal of a world-commonwealth, which allows every branch of the human family to find freedom, security and self-realization in the larger life of mankind. I see no hope for the religious future of the world, if this ideal is not extended to the religious sphere also. When two or three different systems claim that they contain the revelation of the very core and centre of truth and the acceptance of it is the exclusive pathway to heaven, conflicts are inevitable. In such conflicts one religion will not allow others to steal a march over it, and no one can gain ascendancy until the world is reduced to dust and ashes. To obliterate every other religion than one's own is a sort of bolshevism in religion which we must try to prevent. We can do so only if we accept something like the Hindu solution, which seeks the unity of religion not in a common creed but in a common quest. Let us believe in a unity of spirit and not of organization, a unity which secures ample liberty not only for every individual but for every type of organized life which has proved itself effective. For almost all historical forms of life and thought can claim the sanction of experience and so the authority of God. The world would be a much poorer thing if one creed absorbed the rest. God wills a rich harmony and not a colourless uniformity. The comprehensive and synthetic spirit of Hinduism has made it a mighty forest with a thousand waving arms each fulfilling its function and all directed by the spirit of God. Each thing in its place and all associated in the divine concert making with their various voices and even dissonances, as Heraclitus would say, the most exquisite harmony should be our ideal.

That the Hindu solution of the problem of the conflict of religions is likely to be accepted in the future seems to me to be fairly certain. The spirit of democracy with its immense faith in the freedom to choose one's ends and direct one's course in the effort to realize them makes for it. Nothing is good which is not self-chosen; no determination is valuable which is not self-determination. The different religions are slowly learning to hold out hands of friendship to each other in every part of the world. The parliaments of religions and conferences and congresses of liberal thinkers of all creeds promote mutual understanding and harmony. The study of comparative religion is developing a fairer attitude to other religions. It is impressing on us the fundamental unity of all religions by pointing out that the genius of the people, the spirit of the age and the need of the hour determine the emphasis in each religion. We are learning to think clearly about the interrelations of religions. We tend to look upon different religions not as incompatibles but as complementaries, and so indispensable to each other for the realization of the common end. Closer contact with other religions has dispelled the belief that only this or that religion has produced men of courage and patience, self-denying love and creative energy. Every great religion has cured its followers of the swell of passion, the thrust of desire and the blindness of temper. The crudest religion seems to have its place in the cosmic scheme, for gorgeous flowers justify the muddy roots from which they spring. Growing insistence on mysticism is tending to a subordination of dogma. While intellectualism would separate the dissimilar and shut them up in different compartments, higher intuition takes account of the natural differences of things and seeks to combine them in the ample unity of the whole. The half-religious and the irreligious fight about dogmas and not the truly religious. In the biting words of Swift, 'We have enough religion to hate one another but not enough to love one another.' The more religious we grow the more tolerant of diversity shall we become.

23

Reinhold Niebuhr, "The Christian Attitude to Government"

Introduction

When, shortly after his father's death in 1913, 20-year-old K. P. Reinhold Niebuhr (1892–1971) ascended the steps to his father Gustav's pulpit before the small congregation in Lincoln, Illinois, he knew that he was about to assume a more public and prominent role in life. He could not have known, however, that his life would lead him to become, along with his younger brother Richard (1894–1962) and Paul Tillich (IV.24), one of the most important Protestant philosophers of the twentieth century.

Educated at Eden Theological Seminary (then affiliated with the Deutsche Evangelische Synode von Nord-Amerika) and at the divinity school of Yale University, Niebuhr was assigned after his ordination in 1915 to the working-class congregation of Bethel Evangelical Church in Detroit. There Niebuhr observed firsthand the alienating and corrosive effects of American industrial life on the urban poor. His experience led him into the labor and anti-poverty movements, editorializing and preaching on their behalf and frequently inviting union organizers to speak from his pulpit. Repelled by the carnage and mass destruction of World War I, Niebuhr turned to pacifism, and in

From Reinhold Niebuhr, *The Nature and Destiny of Man: A Christian Interpretation* II, New York: Charles Scribner's Sons, 1951, Chapter 9, pp. 269–84 (some notes omitted).

1923 he traveled to Europe to examine the devastation and meet with like-minded clergy. In 1930, he ran as a Socialist Party candidate for the state Senate of New York. His book *Leaves from the Notebook of a Tamed Cynic* (1929) recounts these early stages of his career.

The publication of *Moral Man and Immoral Society* in 1932, however, charts the beginnings of his disaffection with the radical left and his movement toward the more centrist position, often called "Christian realism," for which he would become more widely known. Niebuhr's eloquent publications and his compelling homiletics earned him in 1928 a position on the faculty of Union Theological Seminary in New York City. With the arrival of World War II, Niebuhr became a supporter not only of a politically engaged Christianity but also of the use of military force. Niebuhr's 1940 Gifford Lectures at the University of Edinburgh, published as *The Nature and Destiny of Man* (from which the following selection has been drawn), exemplify the maturation of his views during this period. After the war, he advised the US State Department on the reconstruction of Europe; and he worked with Americans for Democratic Action and other "cold war liberals" in adopting an aggressive posture toward Soviet and Chinese communism abroad while distancing American liberalism from communist and socialist influence at home.[1] In 1951 Niebuhr published the now famous and rather stoic, "Serenity Prayer"; and in 1952, shortly before a debilitating stroke, he saw the release of *The Irony of American History*.

Martin Luther King, Jr, in his 1963 "Letter from a Birmingham Jail" refers favorably to Niebuhr and to his assertion (from *Moral Man and Immoral Society*) that "freedom is never voluntarily given by the oppressor; it must be demanded by the oppressed."[2] Niebuhr himself admired King's work; in 1967 he identified "the two main collective issues of our day" as "the civil-rights movement . . . and opposition to the terrible and mistaken war in Vietnam." More hawkish thinkers, however, have also commonly cited Niebuhr – for example those defending aggressive policies in opposition to the USSR and to radical Islamic militancy.[3] Indeed, Niebuhr appeals to people broadly if not uniformly across the political spectrum. Some reason for this strange diversity among Niebuhr's admirers may be discerned in the distinctive philosophy of the state and political engagement he develops.

Deeply influenced by both Augustine (IV.3) and John Calvin (1509–64), Niebuhr came to adopt what some might call a rather dark view of human nature. Corrupted by sin, fallen human beings are simply not in his view the sort of creatures that can be expected to achieve on their own a thoroughly good, just, and peaceful society: "The final victory over man's disorder is God's and not ours." One implication of this view is that early modern philosophers like Jean-Jacques Rousseau (V.12) and the political movements (e.g. the French Revolution) that would follow them must be seen therefore to suffer from a misplaced faith in human innocence and rationality. And "Anarchic" religious sects (like the Levellers, Diggers, and Quakers), as well as progressive thinkers (like the theologian Walter Rauschenbusch) who embrace more politically engaged ideas of a "Social Gospel," labor vainly under a naively optimistic belief in the perfectibility of human beings. Human beings, in short, cannot according to Niebuhr reason themselves into a better world.

But, unlike many conservative thinkers, Niebuhr does not conclude from this Augustinian/Calvinistic line of thought that one should reject modernity in favor of a romantic traditionalism or adopt a politics of anti-liberal authoritarianism. Yes, those who regard the state as only an institution of oppression or as a usurpation of the authority that is rightfully God's alone fail to appreciate not only the good things that the state can accomplish but also, more importantly, the necessity of government's coercive force to manage the antagonistic contests of power that are intrinsic to social dynamics. Nevertheless, on the other hand, those who follow Paul's "Letter to the Romans" (13:1–3) unquestioning obedience to the state as the instrument of God's authority on Earth remain mired in an "uncritical sanctification of established political authority." Niebuhr writes: "Our idealists are divided into those who would renounce the responsibilities of power for the sake of preserving the purity of our soul and those who are ready to cover every ambiguity of good and evil in our actions by the frantic insistence that any measure taken in a good cause must be unequivocally virtuous." Instead, Niebuhr acknowledges both (a) that political action is by its very nature "morally hazardous" and (b) that political action (including military action) guided by liberal ideals is morally imperative. The ironic destiny of human beings is to live in a world where they are condemned both to pursue goodness politically and to fail to achieve it perfectly. Understanding this realistic truth about the human condition ought to result, in Niebuhr's view, in a humble and chastened form of political action, one that abandons both passivity as well as the fantasy of ridding the world of evil.

Notes

1   Niebuhr, for example, in the ADA's "An Appeal to American Liberals and Progressives," attacked Henry Wallace's 1948 Progressive Party campaign for the US Presidency as backed by communists.

2   Indeed, Niebuhr may be responsible for helping King understand the important difference between "non-resistance" and "non-violent resistance." In *Moral Man and Immoral Society* Niebuhr writes this about Gandhi's tactics: "The emancipation of the Negro race in America probably waits upon the adequate development of this kind of social and political strategy" (London: Continuum, 1960), p. 165.

3   Cf. P. Beinart, *The Good Fight: Why Liberals – and Only Liberals – Can Win the War on Terror and Make America Great Again*, New York: HarperCollins, 2006. Even US President Barack Obama cites Niebuhr as one of his favorite philosophers.

Niebuhr, "The Christian Attitude to Government"

The development of Christian and of modern secular theories of politics is determined by an interplay of one classical and of two Biblical approaches to stuff of the political order. The Bible contains two approaches, which taken together and held in balance, do justice to the moral ambiguities of government. According to the one, government is an ordinance of God and its authority reflects the Divine Majesty. According to the other, the "rulers" and "judges" of the nations are particularly subject to divine judgment and wrath because they oppress the poor and defy the divine majesty. These two approaches do justice to the two aspects of government. It is a principle of order and its power prevents anarchy; but its power is not identical with divine power. It is wielded from a partial and particular locus and it cannot achieve the perfect union of goodness and power which characterizes divine power. The pretension that its power is perfectly virtuous represents its false claim of majesty. This claim elicits alternate moods of reverent obedience and resentful rebellion in history.

The double approach of prophetic criticism and of priestly sanctification of royal or state authority, have armed both conservative and radical schools of Christian thought with plausible proof-texts for their respective positions. Only occasionally is the truth in each position properly appreciated. Unfortunately a single text from St. Paul has done much to destroy the force of the Biblical paradox. St. Paul's very "undialectical" appreciation of government in Romans 13 has had a fateful influence in Christian thought, particularly in the Reformation. But its influence was fortunately never able to extinguish the power of prophetic criticism upon the evils of government in Christian history.

As against these two approaches to the political order in the Bible the classical world thought of politics in simpler and more rational terms. Government was primarily the instrument of man's social nature. Its function of preventing anarchy, so strongly emphasized in Christian thought, and so unduly stressed in the Reformation, was appreciated only indirectly. For Aristotle the purpose of government was fellowship (κοινωνία); and Plato studied the state in his *Republic* as a macrocosm which would reveal all the laws of harmony in larger outline relevant to the microcosm of the individual soul.

In both Aristotle and Plato the harmony of society is practically identified with the constitutional structure, the principles by which it is governed. The approach is, in the parlance of modern philosophy, "non-existential."* They are always looking for forms and principles of justice, for constitutions and arrangements which will bring the rough vitalities of life under the dominion of the *logos*. They do not of course trust the mere force of law to do this. But when they look for the best human agencies to interpret, apply and enforce the principles of law, and try to construct some transcendent vantage point from which government may operate against the conflicts of partial interests (in the case of Aristotle particularly against the conflict between rich and poor) they find it in some class of virtuous and rational men. It is the superior reason of such men or their specialized knowledge in affairs of government, which endows them with the virtue of disinterestedness. Greek political theory believes in other words in an *élite class*. The perils of anarchy according to classical thought arise primarily from the ignorance of common citizens who are unable to comprehend the total needs of the community. Plato seeks to cultivate the disinterestedness of the rulers by semi-ascetic disciplines, as well as by rational excellency. In any case the realm of politics, as a field of vitality and as a contest of power is inadequately

---

* Aristotle declares that "the constitution (πολιτεία) is the life of the *polis*" (*Politics* VI, iv, 11). In Plato's *Laws* the Athenian Stranger declares: "When there has been a contest of power, those who gain the upper hand so entirely monopolize the government as to refuse all share to the defeated party. . . . Now according to our view such governments are not polities at all nor are laws right which are passed for the good of particular classes and not for the good of the whole state. . . . That state in which the law is subject and has no authority, I perceive to be on the highway to ruin; and that state in which the rulers are the inferiors of the law has salvation."

The idea that the practices of states must conform to rules and principles of justice is of course tenable and necessary. But both Plato and Aristotle underestimate the dynamic and vital elements in the political order. They obscure the fact that political life is a contest of power, no matter by what laws it is governed.

comprehended. The Stoic theory, particularly in its distinction between the absolute and the relative natural law, comes closer to the realities of politics. But even the Stoics, and particularly the Roman Stoics, have a too optimistic conception of the political order. Cicero gave a highly moralistic account of politics in general and of Roman imperialism in particular. He regarded the state as a compact of justice, and had little understanding of the power realities which underlie the compact.

The Christian ages, after the dissipation of the eschatological hope and the concomitant political irresponsibility of the early church, worked out a political ethic in which gospel perfectionism and Biblical realism were combined with classical (particularly Stoic) optimism. Augustine was the first to introduce a new and more Pauline note into this field of thought, as he did in so many other fields. Making the criticism of Ciceronian rationalism and optimism his point of departure he denied that the state is a compact of justice, and insisted that "there is not any justice in any commonwealth whatsoever but in that whereof Christ is the founder and ruler."* He regarded the peace of the world as an uneasy armistice between contending social forces. It is "based on strife." It is not so much justice as "the harmonious enjoyment of that which they love" which holds the *civitas* together.† Such a morally neutral definition of political cohesion allows Augustine to compare the harmony of the state with the harmony which thieves maintain among themselves and to suggest that there may be little difference except size, between a state and a robber band.‡

Augustine sees the social life of man as constantly threatened either by conflict between contending forces, held in an uneasy equilibrium, or by the tyranny of the dominant power which "lays a yoke of obedience upon its fellows." This interpretation may not do full justice to the constructive elements of order in either the Roman Empire or in any *res publica* or commonwealth of history. He may have taken the conditions of a declining, rather than a more healthy, Roman Empire as definitive; and he may have sharpened

the contrast too much between the *civitas Dei* and the *civitas terrena,* so as to produce a perfect antithesis between the love of God in the one and the love of self in the other. But despite these errors of overemphasis, the Augustinian conception of the political order gives a much truer picture of both the dynamic and the anarchic elements in political life than classical political theories.

Despite Augustine's great authority, his political realism had only a moderate influence on the course of medieval political theory. The latter incorporated a much larger classical element than is evident in Augustine's thought. Medieval Catholicism succeeded in fact in creating as imposing a synthesis in the realm of political theory as in other fields of thought. The synthesis is still superior to many alternative systems which have developed since the destruction of the synthesis; but it is, of course, subject to the general limitations of its larger principles of synthesis.

Medieval political theory manages to incorporate both strands of Biblical thought with classical perspectives. The prophetic-Biblical criticism upon the injustice and the pride of rulers is never lacking; but unfortunately it becomes the instrument of the papal-ecclesiastical claim of dominion. The Stoic-Christian idea that government is a requirement of the relative, rather than of the absolute, natural law, prevents the inequalities and the coercive necessities of government from being regarded as finally normative. The distinction preserves a minimal note of criticism upon government. There is thus a moderate medieval constitutionalism which makes the ruler subject to both natural law and to civil law.

The authority of the ruler and the idea of necessity of government is upheld at the same time both by Biblical authority and by the Stoic idea of government as a necessity in an imperfect world. The more classical element in medieval political thought is revealed in an essentially rationalistic approach to political problems, tending to obscure the tension of vitalities and interests as a perennial factor in all social life. The peril of tyranny, inherent in the power of the state, is not regarded as arising inevitably from its nature as a centre of power, and from the natural inclination of power, including state power, to become excessive. Instead medieval theory makes moralistic and too absolute and clear-cut distinctions between the justice and tyranny of

---

* *De civ. Dei*, Book II, ch. 21.
† *De civ. Dei*, Book XIX, ch. 24.
‡ *Ibid.*, IV, 4.

rulers.* It does not comprehend that the justice and peace which the power of the state achieves is always subject to some degree of corruption by reason of the inordinate character of this power, and the particular interests of the ruler.

Medieval constitutionalism contains abundant moral justification for resistance to tyranny but the idea is not implemented politically and Lord Acton is therefore slightly extravagant in regarding Aquinas as the fountain of democratic theory.† Medieval theory failed to comprehend the political order as a vast realm of mutually dependent and conflicting powers and interests, and to appreciate the contingent and relative character of any "justice" which might be achieved at a given moment by the power of government and by the specific equilibria of forces existing at that moment. This failure was one cause of its inability to deal realistically with the new forces, and the consequent disbalances introduced into the medieval political economy by rising commerce.

With the decay of the medieval synthesis, the various elements in the compound of political thought took their own more consistent way, as was the case in other realms of thought. Many of the new political theories may be less true, and are certainly less balanced, than the more comprehensive medieval interpretation of the political order. But most of them contain facets of truth which do more justice to the highest possibilities and the darkest realities of the political order than was possible in the medieval synthesis.

The Renaissance in its secular streams of thought developed two fundamental tendencies. The one embodied the rationalistic-optimistic approach to the problem. We cannot trace this tendency in all of its elaborations. It is expressed in the many varieties of the "liberal" approach to politics. In some of them the *laissez-faire*

thesis predominates. It is believed to be a simple matter to achieve a stable equilibrium of social interests if only the inordinate power of government is eliminated. In others the power of government is regarded as a simple rational authority over rational men, which will become more just and more universal as reason is extended.

One contemporary fruit of this stream of Renaissance thought consists in theories of world government, according to which the self-will and moral autonomy of nations could be destroyed by the simple expedient of depriving the sovereignty of nations of its legal sanctity. Other theorists are slightly more realistic and hold that international government must be supported by predominant power. But they would create the central pool of power abstractly by some kind of social contract between the nations, without reference to the organic and vital processes through which equilibria of power and the centralization of power are actually effected in history.

The Renaissance movement, however, developed another stream of thought which appropriated some of the insights of Christian realism and pessimism. It recognized the perils of conflict in the dynamic elements of social existence; but it was prompted by these insights to elaborate absolutistic theories of the state. It failed, in other words, to appropriate any of the prophetic-critical elements in the Christian tradition. To this strain of thought we must, in cursory terms, assign Machiavelli, Thomas Hobbes, Jean Bodin, in some respects Hegel and Bosanquet, and of course a host of other lesser men. Sometimes as in the case of Machiavelli, the political pessimism degenerates into moral cynicism. Marxism has the distinction of being the only pessimistic-realistic school of thought in the modern period which directs its realism against the moral ambiguities of the power of government, rather than upon the perils of social anarchy which government is designed to mitigate.

The strong Biblical basis of sectarian radicalism makes it advisable to consider it in this context in juxtaposition to the orthodox Reformation, rather than in relation to the Renaissance movement. So conceived Protestant Christian theories of politics, in their totality, describe a full arc from the extreme pessimism of the Lutheran Reformation to the extreme optimism of the more radical sects; from the uncritical sanctification of government in Luther to the uncritical

---

* Aquinas defines tyranny as "ruling which is not directed to the common good of the multitude but rather to the private good of the ruler." *De regimine principum.*
† Aquinas did believe that the people had the right to appoint the king and therefore an equal right to depose him (*De regimine principum* I, 6). John of Salisbury even justified regicide as a remedy for tyranny. This critical attitude towards the injustices of government is far superior to modern theories of state absolutism; but it is not democratic in the sense that it provides no constitutional means of resisting the inordinate claims of government or of placing its power under continued popular scrutiny.

rejection of government, as such, in the anarchistic sects; from the uncritical acceptance of inequality as a consequence and remedy for sin in Luther, to the uncritical belief in equality as a simple historical possibility in the communistic sects. In this wide variety of thought the greatest contribution to democratic justice was made by those Protestant groups which came closest to an understanding of both the vice and the necessity of government and both the peril and the necessity of a free interplay of social forces. Among those who came nearest to this understanding were moderate Anglicans who combined Catholic with Renaissance perspectives and whose political theories are most systematically expressed in the thought of Thomas Hooker; semi-sectarian movements like English Independency; and finally the later Calvinists, who rescued Calvinism from its earlier and too consistent pessimism.

This rather sweeping judgment demands historical substantiation, though the limits of this treatise necessarily restrict the analysis of the vast historical material.

Luther's uncritical moral and religious sanctification of the power of government (particularly based upon Romans 13) has been previously considered. It prevented Lutheranism from having any vital relationship with the development of democratic justice in the modern world, with the possible exception of the Scandinavian countries. The development of political theory in modern radical Reformation thought is instructive because Barth is on the whole more Lutheran than Calvinistic in his approach to political questions. He has been Lutheran, at least in his general indifference towards problems of political justice, though he has not quite shared Luther's uncritical acceptance of political authority. His strong emotional reaction to Nazi tyranny has, however, persuaded him to change his emphasis. He now criticizes the Reformation for having regarded government as an ordinance of divine providence without at the same time setting it under the judgment of God. Nevertheless the influence of Reformation perspectives is so powerful in his thought that his doctrinal justification for his opposition to Nazi tyranny is hardly sufficient to explain that opposition.*

As against the uncritical sanctification of established political authority, and the pessimistic acceptance of coercion, inequality and conflict as necessary conditions in a sinful world in Lutheranism, sectarian Protestantism in its many forms manages to express all the various aspects of the critical-prophetic strain of Christian thought.

In the more extreme sects this is done to the point of obscuring the other side of the truth. The perils of government are appreciated, but not its necessity. The contradiction between the majesty of government and the majesty of God is emphasized; but the legitimate majesty of government is not apprehended. Usually the failure to appreciate the necessity of government is derived from perfectionist illusions in regard to human nature and human society. Sometimes government is accepted; but the libertarian emphasis is so strong that all coercive acts of government are morally repudiated.

Sometimes the requirements of the absolute natural law, the ideals of liberty and equality, were rightly restored as principles of criticism and final judgment upon all relative justice and injustice in history; but the inevitability of relative distinctions in history is usually not understood. The eighteenth-century secular theory of equality as a simple "law of nature" is rooted in seventeenth-century sectarian theory. The sect of "Diggers" anticipated, and may have inspired, the Marxist theory of government as primarily a tool of the privileged classes.

---

* Barth defines a just state [*Rechtsstaat*] as follows: "It will realize its own potentialities insofar as it gives the church the freedom [to preach the gospel of justification].... What human justice is cannot be measured by some romantic or liberal conception of natural rights but purely by the concrete right of the freedom which the church must claim for its word, insofar as it is God's word." *Rechtfertigung und Recht*, p. 46. This is a very minimal contribution to the problem of justice in the state. The freedom to preach the gospel of justification means of course that the state would thereby permit the word of divine judgment to be spoken against its pride and pretensions. But none of the intermediate problems of justice are illumined by this final word of judgment.

In his letter to British Christians Barth declares that "it was probably wise of the government to *allow* [*sic*] the British public to discuss peace aims" but he thinks that "British Christians should . . . take as little advantage of this *permission* as possible." *This Christian Cause.*

Though the extremer sects always went too far in challenging either the pessimism of the Reformation or the circumspection of Catholic theories, they did of course provide much of the leaven of modern democratic development. But the more inclusive and comprehensive conceptions of political life were developed by the semisectarian Separatists (Roger Williams), the Independents (John Milton) and by the later Calvinists.

The development of Calvinistic thought from a conservative justification of political authority to a living relation with democratic justice deserves special consideration because, in its final form, Calvinistic theory probably came closest to a full comprehension of all the complexities of political justice.

The earlier Calvin was almost as uncritical as Luther in his sanctification of state authority and in his prohibition of resistance to it. Fortunately he permitted some exceptions to this position. He, himself, extended these to some degree under the stress of history, and later Calvinists developed them into a full-orbed democratic outlook. He allowed disobedience, though not resistance, if the political authority came in conflict with God's demands upon the conscience; and he objected only to private and not official resistance to the authority of the ruler. The "lower magistrates" were not only allowed, but enjoined, to resist the tyranny of kings. It was a simple matter for later Calvinists to think of any elected representatives of the people as lower magistrates, who resisted tyranny officially and not privately.

The later Dutch, French and Scottish Calvinists distinguished between government as an ordinance of God's providence and the particular form of government which might obtain at a given moment. Thus they freed the religious conscience from undue reverence for any particular government and established a critical attitude towards it; while yet preserving religious reverence for the principle of government. They understood, as the proponents of the secular social contract theory of government did not, that it is not within the power of conscious human will to create government. The formation of government and statehood belongs to the slow processes of the ages and its roots are antecedent to any human decision. Government deserves reverence not only because it is necessary but because it is a gift which man did not consciously contrive. But unlike Calvin the later Calvinists did understand the importance of human action in the formation of particular governments and the responsibility of men for the achievement of justice.

Calvin believed that kings had a covenant with God to rule justly and the people had a covenant with God to obey. But he denied that this double covenant implied a contract between the ruler and the people. It was a simple matter for later Calvinists to insist that this covenant was triangular, between the ruler, the people, and God; that it was a covenant of justice; and that if the ruler broke it by injustice, the people were absolved of obedience. Thus justice, rather than mere order and peace, became the criterion for government; and democratic criticism became the instrument of justice. The difference between the democratic temper of later Calvinism and the undue and uncritical reverence for political authority in the early Reformation, both Lutheran and Calvinistic, is well illustrated in John Knox's interpretation of Romans 13. Being asked how he could square his defiance of royal authority with this scriptural injunction in Romans 13, he answered: "The power in that place is not to be understood as the unjust commandment of men but the just power wherewith God hath armed his magistrates and lieutenants to punish sin." Advised that this interpretation implied that subjects could control and judge their rulers, he replied: "And what harm should the commonwealth receive if the corrupt affection of ignorant rulers be moderated and bridled by the wisdom and discretion of Godly subjects so that they would not do violence to any man?"*

Too much must not be claimed for either later Calvinism or Independency in establishing democratic justice in the Anglo-Saxon world. The vindication of the right of self-government and the elaboration of effective constitutional forms for the expression of the right, was the fruit of many secular, as well as religious, movements. But the secular movements were inclined to libertarianism in their reaction to the evils of government; or to base their democratic theories upon the idea of the goodness of human nature; and consequently to underestimate the perils of anarchy, while they directed their attention to the perils of tyranny.

Whatever may be the source of our insights into the problems of the political order, it is import-

* John Knox, *History* II, 282.

ant both to recognize the higher possibilities of justice in every historic situation, and to know that the twin perils of tyranny and anarchy can never be completely overcome in any political achievement. These perils are expressions of the sinful elements of conflict and dominion, standing in contradiction to the ideal of brotherhood on every level of communal organization. There is no possibility of making history completely safe against either occasional conflicts of vital interests (war) or against the misuse of the power which is intended to prevent such conflict of interests (tyranny). To understand this is to labor for higher justice in terms of the experience of justification by faith. Justification by faith in the realm of justice means that we will not regard the pressures and counter pressures, the tensions, the overt and the covert conflicts by which justice is achieved and maintained, as normative in the absolute sense; but neither will we ease our conscience by seeking to escape from involvement in them. We will know that we cannot purge ourselves of the sin and guilt in which we are involved by the moral ambiguities of politics without also disavowing responsibility for the creative possibilities of justice.

24

Paul Tillich, "Courage and Transcendence" (selections)

Introduction

The Courage To Be (1952), despite its difficulty, became something of a best-seller in 1950s America and made its author, who appeared on the cover of *Time* magazine, into a celebrity. Paul Tillich (1886–1965) was educated in Germany where he taught and preached (as a Lutheran minister) until the Nazis came to power in 1933. Tillich then emigrated to the United States, where he taught first at the Union Theological Seminary in New York, then at Harvard, and finally at the University of Chicago.

Described as moving on "the boundaries of psychoanalysis, existentialism and theology,"[1] Tillich's book owed its popularity to its engagement with themes that dominated the post-war intellectual climate – alienation, absurdity, guilt, and the like. Tillich, like Martin Buber, is often classified as an "existentialist theologian," and it is certainly true that he saw in existentialism "the expression of our own situation ... of the anxiety of meaninglessness and of the attempt to take this anxiety into the courage to be as oneself" (*The Courage To Be*, pp. 126, 139). Indeed, by "the courage to be," Tillich means "the ethical act in which man affirms his own being in spite of those elements ... which conflict with his essential

From Paul Tillich, *The Courage To Be*, New Haven, CT, and London: Yale University Press, 2000, pp. 155–67, 171–8.

self-affirmation" (p. 3) or, as he also puts it, "to accept oneself as accepted in spite of being unacceptable" (p. 164). These "elements" are primarily various forms of anxiety – a feeling of guilt, fear of death, trepidation before "fate," but above all a paralyzing sense of the meaninglessness and emptiness of human life and the world at large.

While he admires the existentialists' diagnosis of our present situation, Tillich is nevertheless critical of their solutions to it. For example, Jean-Paul Sartre's doctrine of radical freedom, with its insistence that the self is simply what one makes it to be (see I.23), is in effect a denial of the real existence of the self – and hence a denial of the very possibility of self-affirmation and self-acceptance. Tillich's central claim in the book is that the courage to be, acceptance and affirmation of the self, requires religious faith. It "must be rooted in a power of being that is greater than the power of oneself and the power of one's world." This is a "religious root" since religion is precisely "the state of being grasped by the power of being-itself" (pp. 154–5). The Selections from Chapter 6 that follow explore the character of this religious faith.

Tillich's understanding of religious faith is not a traditional one. Faith, he argues, is not to be found either in the mystic's identification with a transcendental reality beyond the world of appearances, the "veil of Maya," nor in the Protestant Christian's "confidence" in a God revealed in "person-to-person encounter." While faith must incorporate both "confidence" and "participation" in a larger reality, Tillich's point seems to be that

neither mysticism nor theism has sufficiently registered either the sense of utter meaninglessness
in our lives or the corrosive skepticism about
anything we can articulate which constitutes "our
situation," the situation that demands the courage to be. Whatever else an authentic faith may
be, it must incorporate, "paradoxically," a vivid
sense of meaninglessness combined with an experience of our nevertheless being "accepted." This
faith must also involve a recognition that it is without a "concrete content" – for anything "concrete,"
we have come to realize, is liable to doubt.
("Everything defined," he writes, is "dissolved by
doubt and meaninglessness.") This means, in
effect that – as Tillich puts it in the famous closing words of his book – it is only faith in "the God
above the God of theism . . . the God who appears
when God has disappeared in the anxiety of
doubt" which counts as authentic faith.

Remarks like this have, unsurprisingly, attracted
the criticism that Tillich is a closet atheist, subscribing to a notion of God so remote from traditional ones as to amount, in truth, to a rejection
of religious belief. Tillich's own responses to this
criticism are, first, that one victim of the skepticism that is now a fixture of modernity is the
validity of the very distinction between theism and
atheism; second, that "belief" is not the appropriate word for the "ethical act" of "courage"
which he calls for; and, finally, that since what
he is calling for is a surrender to an indefinable
"power of being-itself" then, at least by his own
characterization of religion, it is a genuinely religious act to which he exhorts us.

Note

1 J. Macquarrie, *Existentialism: An Introduction, Guide and Assessment*, Harmondsworth:
Penguin, 1973, p. 260.

Tillich "Courage and Transcendence" [the courage to accept acceptance]

Courage is the self-affirmation of being in spite
of the fact of nonbeing. It is the act of the individual self in taking the anxiety of nonbeing
upon itself by affirming itself either as part of
an embracing whole or in its individual selfhood. Courage always includes a risk, it is always
threatened by nonbeing, whether the risk of
losing oneself and becoming a thing within the
whole of things or of losing one's world in an
empty self-relatedness. Courage needs the power
of being, a power transcending the nonbeing
which is experienced in the anxiety of fate and
death, which is present in the anxiety of emptiness and meaninglessness, which is effective in the
anxiety of guilt and condemnation. The courage
which takes this threefold anxiety into itself
must be rooted in a power of being that is
greater than the power of oneself and the power
of one's world. Neither self-affirmation as a part
nor self-affirmation as oneself is beyond the
manifold threat of nonbeing. Those who are
mentioned as representatives of these forms of
courage try to transcend themselves and the
world in which they participate in order to find
the power of being-itself and a courage to be which
is beyond the threat of nonbeing. There are no
exceptions to this rule; and this means that every
courage to be has an open or hidden religious root.
For religion is the state of being grasped by the
power of being-itself. In some cases the religious
root is carefully covered, in others it is passionately denied; in some it is deeply hidden and in
others superficially. But it is never completely
absent. For everything that is participates in
being-itself, and everybody has some awareness
of this participation, especially in the moments in
which he experiences the threat of nonbeing.
This leads us to a final consideration, the double
question: How is the courage to be rooted in being-
itself, and how must we understand being-itself
in the light of the courage to be? The first question deals with the ground of being as source of
the courage to be, the second with courage to be
as key to the ground of being.

The Power of Being as Source of the Courage to Be

The mystical experience and the courage to be
Since the relation of man to the ground of his
being must be expressed in symbols taken from

the structure of being, the polarity of participation and individualization determines the special character of this relation as it determines the special character of the courage to be. If participation is dominant, the relation to being-itself has a mystical character, if individualization prevails the relation to being-itself has a personal character, if both poles are accepted and transcended the relation to being-itself has the character of faith.

In mysticism the individual self strives for a participation in the ground of being which approaches identification. Our question is not whether this goal can ever be reached by a finite being but whether and how mysticism can be the source of the courage to be. We have referred to the mystical background of Spinoza's system, to his way of deriving the self-affirmation of man from the self-affirmation of the divine substance in which he participates. In a similar way all mystics draw their power of self-affirmation from the experience of the power of being-itself with which they are united. But one may ask, can courage be united with mysticism in any way? It seems that in India, for example, courage is considered the virtue of the *kshatriya* (knight), to be found below the levels of the Brahman or the ascetic saint. Mystical identification transcends the aristocratic virtue of courageous self-sacrifice. It is self-surrender in a higher, more complete, and more radical form. It is the perfect form of self-affirmation. But if this is so, it is courage in the larger though not in the narrower sense of the word. The ascetic and ecstatic mystic affirms his own essential being over against the elements of nonbeing which are present in the finite world, the realm of Maya. It takes tremendous courage to resist the lure of appearances. The power of being which is manifest in such courage is so great that the gods tremble in fear of it. The mystic seeks to penetrate the ground of being, the all-present and all-pervasive power of the Brahman. In doing so he affirms his essential self which is identical with the power of the Brahman, while all those who affirm themselves in the bondage of Maya affirm what is not their true self, be they animals, men, or gods. This elevates the mystic's self-affirmation above the courage as a special virtue possessed by the aristocratic-soldiery. But he is not above courage altogether. That which from the point of view of the finite world appears as self-negation is from the point of view of ultim-

ate being the most perfect self-affirmation, the most radical form of courage.

In the strength of this courage the mystic conquers the anxiety of fate and death. Since being in time and space and under the categories of finitude is ultimately unreal, the vicissitudes arising from it and the final nonbeing ending it are equally unreal. Nonbeing is no threat because finite being is, in the last analysis, nonbeing. Death is the negation of that which is negative and the affirmation of that which is positive. In the same way the anxiety of doubt and meaninglessness is taken into the mystical courage to be. Doubt is directed toward everything that is and that, according to its Maya character, is doubtful. Doubt dissolves the veil of Maya, it undermines the defense of mere opinions against ultimate reality. And this manifestation is not exposed to doubt because it is the presupposition of every act of doubt. Without a consciousness of truth itself doubt of truth would be impossible. The anxiety of meaninglessness is conquered where the ultimate meaning is not something definite but the abyss of every definite meaning. The mystic experiences step after step the lack of meaning in the different levels of reality which he enters, works through, and leaves. As long as he walks ahead on this road the anxieties of guilt and condemnation are also conquered. They are not absent. Guilt can be acquired on every level, partly through a failure to fulfill its intrinsic demands, partly through a failure to proceed beyond the level. But as long as the certainty of final fulfillment is given, the anxiety of guilt does not become anxiety of condemnation. There is automatic punishment according to the law of karma, but there is no condemnation in Asiatic mysticism.

The mystical courage to be lasts as long as the mystical situation. Its limit is the state of emptiness of being and meaning, with its horror and despair, which the mystics have described. In these moments the courage to be is reduced to the acceptance of even this state as a way to prepare through darkness for light, through emptiness for abundance. As long as the absence of the power of being is felt as despair, it is the power of being which makes itself felt through despair. To experience this and to endure it is the courage to be of the mystic in the state of emptiness. Although mysticism in its extreme positive and extreme negative aspects is a comparatively rare event, the basic attitude, the striving for union with ultimate reality, and the corresponding courage to take the nonbeing which is implied in finitude upon oneself are a way of life which is accepted by and has shaped large sections of mankind.

But mysticism is more than a special form of the relation to the ground of being. It is an element of every form of this relation. Since everything that is participates in the power of being, the element of identity on which mysticism is based cannot be absent in any religious experience. There is no self-affirmation of a finite being, and there is no courage to be in which the ground of being and its power of conquering nonbeing is not effective. And the experience of the presence of this power is the mystical element even in the person-to-person encounter with God.

The divine-human encounter and the courage to be
The pole of individualization expresses itself in the religious experience as a personal encounter with God. And the courage derived from it is the courage of confidence in the personal reality which is manifest in the religious experience. In contradistinction to the mystical union one can call this relation a personal communion with the source of courage. Although the two types are in contrast they do not exclude each other. For they are united by the polar interdependence of individualization and participation. The courage of confidence has often, especially in Protestantism, been identified with the courage of faith. But this is not adequate, because confidence is only one element in faith. Faith embraces both mystical participation and personal confidence. Most parts of the Bible describe the religious encounter in strongly personalist terms. Biblicism, notably that of the Reformers, follows this emphasis. Luther directed his attack against the objective, quantitative, and impersonal elements in the Roman system. He fought for an immediate person-to-person relationship between God and man. In him the courage of confidence reached its highest point in the history of Christian thought. Every work of Luther, especially in his earlier years, is filled with such courage. Again and again he uses the word *trotz*, "in spite of." In spite of all the negativities which he had experienced, in spite of the anxiety which dominated that period, he derived the power of self-affirmation from his unshakable confidence in God and from the personal encounter with him. According to

the expressions of anxiety in his period, the negativity his courage had to conquer were symbolized in the figures of death and the devil. It has rightly been said that Albrecht Dürer's engraving, "Knight, Death, and the Devil," is a classic expression of the spirit of the Lutheran Reformation and – it might be added – of Luther's courage of confidence, of his form of the courage to be. A knight in full armor is riding through a valley, accompanied by the figure of death on one side, the devil on the other. Fearlessly, concentrated, confident he looks ahead. He is alone but he is not lonely. In his solitude he participates in the power which gives him the courage to affirm himself in spite of the presence of the negativities of existence. His courage is certainly not the courage to be as a part. The Reformation broke away from the semicollectivism of the Middle Ages. Luther's courage of confidence is personal confidence, derived from a person-to-person encounter with God. Neither popes nor councils could give him this confidence. Therefore he had to reject them just because they relied on a doctrine which blocked off the courage of confidence. They sanctioned a system in which the anxiety of death and guilt never was completely conquered. There were many assurances but no certainty, many supports for the courage of confidence but no unquestionable foundation. The collective offered different ways of resisting anxiety but no way in which the individual could take his anxiety upon himself. He never was certain; he never could affirm his being with unconditional confidence. For he never could encounter the unconditional directly with his total being, in an immediate personal relation. There was, except in mysticism, always mediation through the Church, an indirect and partial meeting between God and the soul. When the Reformation removed the mediation and opened up a direct, total, and personal approach to God, a new nonmystical courage to be was possible. It is manifest in the heroic representatives of fighting Protestantism, in the Calvinist as well as in the Lutheran Reformation, and in Calvinism even more conspicuously. It is not the heroism of risking martyrdom, of resisting the authorities, of transforming the structure of Church and society, but it is the courage of confidence which makes these men heroic and which is the basis of the other expressions of their courage. One could say – and liberal Protestantism often has said – that the courage of the Reformers is the beginning of the individualistic type of the courage to be as oneself. But such an interpretation confuses a possible historical effect with the matter itself. In the courage of the Reformers the courage to be as oneself is both affirmed and transcended. In comparison with the mystical form of courageous self-affirmation the Protestant courage of confidence affirms the individual self as an individual self in its encounter with God as person. This radically distinguishes the personalism of the Reformation from all the later forms of individualism and Existentialism. The courage of the Reformers is not the courage to be oneself – as it is not the courage to be as a part. It transcends and unites both of them. For the courage of confidence is not rooted in confidence about oneself. The Reformation pronounces the opposite: one can become confident about one's existence only after ceasing to base one's confidence on oneself. On the other hand the courage of confidence is in no way based on anything finite besides oneself, not even on the Church. It is based on God and solely on God, who is experienced in a unique and personal encounter. The courage of the Reformation transcends both the courage to be as a part and the courage to be as oneself. It is threatened neither by the loss of oneself nor by the loss of one's world.

Guilt and the courage to accept acceptance In the center of the Protestant courage of confidence stands the courage to accept acceptance in spite of the consciousness of guilt. Luther, and in fact the whole period, experienced the anxiety of guilt and condemnation as the main form of their anxiety. The courage to affirm oneself in spite of this anxiety is the courage which we have called the courage of confidence. It is rooted in the personal, total, and immediate certainty of divine forgiveness. There is belief in forgiveness in all forms of man's courage to be, even in neo-collectivism. But there is no interpretation of human existence in which it is so predominant as in genuine Protestantism. And there is no movement in history in which it is equally profound and equally paradoxical. In the Lutheran formula that "he who is unjust is just" (in the view of the divine forgiveness) or in the more modern phrasing that "he who is unacceptable is accepted" the victory over the anxiety of guilt and condemnation is sharply expressed. One

could say that the courage to be is the courage to accept oneself as accepted in spite of being unacceptable. One does not need to remind the theologians of the fact that this is the genuine meaning of the Pauline-Lutheran doctrine of "justification by faith" (a doctrine which in its original phrasing has become incomprehensible even for students of theology). But one must remind theologians and ministers that in the fight against the anxiety of guilt by psychotherapy the idea of acceptance has received the attention and gained the significance which in the Reformation period was to be seen in phrases like "forgiveness of sins" or "justification through faith." Accepting acceptance though being unacceptable is the basis for the courage of confidence.

Decisive for this self-affirmation is its being independent of any moral, intellectual, or religious precondition: it is not the good or the wise or the pious who are entitled to the courage to accept acceptance but those who are lacking in all these qualities and are aware of being unacceptable. This, however, does not mean acceptance by oneself as oneself. It is not a justification of one's accidental individuality. It is not the Existentialist courage to be as oneself. It is the paradoxical act in which one is accepted by that which infinitely transcends one's individual self. It is in the experience of the Reformers the acceptance of the unacceptable sinner into judging and transforming communion with God.

The courage to be in this respect is the courage to accept the forgiveness of sins, not as an abstract assertion but as the fundamental experience in the encounter with God. Self-affirmation in spite of the anxiety of guilt and condemnation presupposes participation in something which transcends the self. In the communion of healing, for example the psychoanalytic situation, the patient participates in the healing power of the helper by whom he is accepted although he feels himself unacceptable. The healer, in this relationship, does not stand for himself as an individual but represents the objective power of acceptance and self-affirmation. This objective power works through the healer in the patient. Of course, it must be embodied in a person who can realize guilt, who can judge, and who can accept in spite of the judgment. Acceptance by something which is less than personal could never overcome personal self-rejection. A wall to which I confess cannot forgive me. No self-acceptance is possible if one is not accepted in a person-to-person rela-tion. But even if one is personally accepted it needs a self-transcending courage to accept this accept-ance, it needs the courage of confidence. For being accepted does not mean that guilt is denied. The healing helper who tried to convince his patient that he was not really guilty would do him a great disservice. He would prevent him from taking his guilt into his self-affirmation. He may help him to transform displaced, neurotic guilt feelings into genuine ones which are, so to speak, put on the right place, but he cannot tell him that there is no guilt in him. He accepts the patient into his communion without condemning anything and without covering up anything.

Here, however, is the point where the religi-ous "acceptance as being accepted" transcends medical healing. Religion asks for the ultimate source of the power which heals by accepting the unacceptable, it asks for God. The acceptance by God, his forgiving or justifying act, is the only and ultimate source of a courage to be which is able to take the anxiety of guilt and condemnation into itself. For the ultimate power of self-affirmation can only be the power of being-itself. Everything less than this, one's own or anybody else's finite power of being, cannot overcome the radical, infinite threat of nonbeing which is experienced in the despair of self-condemnation. This is why the courage of confidence, as it is expressed in a man like Luther, emphasizes unceasingly exclu-sive trust in God and rejects any other founda-tion for his courage to be, not only as insufficient but as driving him into more guilt and deeper anxiety. The immense liberation brought to the people of the 16th century by the message of the Reformers and the creation of their indomit-able courage to accept acceptance was due to the *sola fide* doctrine, namely to the message that the courage of confidence is conditioned not by anything finite but solely by that which is unconditional itself and which we experience as unconditional in a person-to-person encounter.

[. . .]

Absolute faith and the courage to be We have avoided the concept of faith in our description of the courage to be which is based on mystical union with the ground of being as well as in our description of the courage to be which is based on the personal encounter with God. This is

partly because the concept of faith has lost its gen-uine meaning and has received the connotation of "belief in something unbelievable." But this is not the only reason for the use of terms other than faith. The decisive reason is that I do not think either mystical union or personal encounter fulfills the idea of faith. Certainly there is faith in the elevation of the soul above the finite to the infinite, leading to its union with the ground of being. But more than this is included in the con-cept of faith. And there is faith in the personal encounter with the personal God. But more than this is included in the concept of faith. Faith is the state of being grasped by the power of being-itself. The courage to be is an expression of faith and what "faith" means must be understood through the courage to be. We have defined cour-age as the self-affirmation of being in spite of non-being. The power of this self-affirmation is the power of being which is effective in every act of courage. Faith is the experience of this power.

But it is an experience which has a paradoxi-cal character, the character of accepting acceptance. Being-itself transcends every finite being infinitely; God in the divine-human encounter transcends man unconditionally. Faith bridges this infinite gap by accepting the fact that in spite of it the power of being is present, that he who is sepa-rated is accepted. Faith accepts "in spite of"; and out of the "in spite of" of faith the "in spite of" of courage is born. Faith is not a theoretical affirmation of something uncertain, it is the existential acceptance of something transcending ordinary experience. Faith is not an opinion but a state. It is the state of being grasped by the power of being which transcends everything that is and in which everything that is participates. He who is grasped by this power is able to affirm himself because he knows that he is affirmed by the power of being-itself. In this point mystical experience and personal encounter are identical. In both of them faith is the basis of the courage to be.

This is decisive for a period in which, as in our own, the anxiety of doubt and meaninglessness is dominant. Certainly the anxiety of fate and death is not lacking in our time. The anxiety of fate has increased with the degree to which the schizophrenic split of our world has removed the last remnants of former security. And the anxiety of guilt and condemnation is not lacking either. It is surprising how much anxiety of guilt comes to the surface in psychoanalysis and personal counseling. The centuries of puritan and bourgeois repression of vital strivings have produced almost as many guilt feelings as the preaching of hell and purgatory in the Middle Ages.

But in spite of these restricting considerations one must say that the anxiety which determines our period is the anxiety of doubt and meaninglessness. One is afraid of having lost or of having to lose the meaning of one's existence. The expression of this situation is the Existentialism of today.

Which courage is able to take nonbeing into itself in the form of doubt and meaninglessness? This is the most important and most disturbing question in the quest for the courage to be. For the anxiety of meaninglessness undermines what is still unshaken in the anxiety of fate and death and of guilt and condemnation. In the anxiety of guilt and condemnation doubt has not yet undermined the certainty of an ultimate responsibility. We are threatened but we are not destroyed. If, however, doubt and meaninglessness prevail one experiences an abyss in which the meaning of life and the truth of ultimate responsibility disappear. Both the Stoic who conquers the anxiety of fate with the Socratic courage of wisdom and the Christian who conquers the anxiety of guilt with the Protestant courage of accepting forgiveness are in a different situation. Even in the despair of having to die and the despair of self-condemnation meaning is affirmed and certitude preserved. But in the despair of doubt and meaninglessness both are swallowed by nonbeing.

The question then is this: Is there a courage which can conquer the anxiety of meaninglessness and doubt? Or in other words, can the faith which accepts acceptance resist the power of nonbeing in its most radical form? Can faith resist meaninglessness? Is there a kind of faith which can exist together with doubt and meaninglessness? These questions lead to the last aspect of the problem discussed in these lectures and the one most relevant to our time: How is the courage to be possible if all the ways to create it are barred by the experience of their ultimate insufficiency? If life is as meaningless as death, if guilt is as questionable as perfection, if being is no more meaningful than nonbeing, on what can one base the courage to be?

There is an inclination in some Existentialists to answer these questions by a leap from doubt to dogmatic certitude, from meaninglessness to a set of symbols in which the meaning of a special ecclesiastical or political group is embodied. This leap can be interpreted in different ways. It may be the expression of a desire for safety; it may be as arbitrary as, according to Existentialist principles, every decision is; it may be the feeling that the Christian message is the answer to the questions raised by an analysis of human existence; it may be a genuine conversion, independent of the theoretical situation. In any case it is not a solution of the problem of radical doubt. It gives that courage to be to those who are converted but it does not answer the question as to how such a courage is possible in itself. The answer must accept, as its precondition, the state of meaninglessness. It is not an answer if it demands the removal of this state; for that is just what cannot be done. He who is in the grip of doubt and meaninglessness cannot liberate himself from this grip; but he asks for an answer which is valid within and not outside the situation of his despair. He asks for the ultimate foundation of what we have called the "courage of despair." There is only one possible answer, if one does not try to escape the question: namely that the acceptance of despair is in itself faith and on the boundary line of the courage to be. In this situation the meaning of life is reduced to despair about the meaning of life. But as long as this despair is an act of life it is positive in its negativity. Cynically speaking, one could say that it is true to life to be cynical about it. Religiously speaking, one would say that one accepts oneself as accepted in spite of one's despair about the meaning of this acceptance. The paradox of every radical negativity, as long as it is an active negativity, is that it must affirm itself in order to be able to negate itself. No actual negation can be without an implicit affirmation. The hidden pleasure produced by despair witnesses to the paradoxical character of self-negation. The negative lives from the positive it negates.

The faith which makes the courage of despair possible is the acceptance of the power of being, even in the grip of nonbeing. Even in the despair about meaning being affirms itself through us. The act of accepting meaninglessness is in itself a meaningful act. It is an act of faith. We have seen that he who has the courage to affirm his being in spite of fate and guilt has not removed them. He remains threatened and hit by them. But he accepts his acceptance by the power of being-itself in which he participates and which gives him the courage to take the anxieties of fate and guilt upon himself. The same is true of doubt and meaninglessness. The faith which creates the courage to take them into itself has no special content. It is simply faith, undirected, absolute. It is undefinable, since everything defined is dissolved by doubt and meaninglessness. Nevertheless, even absolute faith is not an eruption of subjective emotions or a mood without objective foundation.

An analysis of the nature of absolute faith reveals the following elements in it. The first is the experience of the power of being which is present even in face of the most radical manifestation of nonbeing. If one says that in this experience vitality resists despair one must add that vitality in man is proportional to intentionality. The vitality that can stand the abyss of meaninglessness is aware of a hidden meaning within the destruction of meaning. The second element in absolute faith is the dependence of the experience of nonbeing on the experience of being and the dependence of the experience of meaninglessness on the experience of meaning. Even in the state of despair one has enough being to make despair possible. There is a third element in absolute faith, the acceptance of being accepted. Of course, in the state of despair there is nobody and nothing that accepts. But there is the power of acceptance itself which is experienced. Meaninglessness, as long as it is experienced, includes an experience of the "power of acceptance." To accept this power of acceptance consciously is the religious answer of absolute faith, of a faith which has been deprived by doubt of any concrete content, which nevertheless is faith and the source of the most paradoxical manifestation of the courage to be.

This faith transcends both the mystical experience and the divine-human encounter. The mystical experience seems to be nearer to absolute faith but it is not. Absolute faith includes an element of skepticism which one cannot find in the mystical experience. Certainly mysticism also transcends all specific contents, but not because it doubts them or has found them meaningless; rather it deems them to be preliminary. Mysticism uses the specific contents as grades, stepping on them after having used them. The experience of meaninglessness, however, denies them (and everything that goes with them) without having used them. The experience of meaninglessness is more radical than mysticism. Therefore it transcends the mystical experience.

Absolute faith also transcends the divine-human encounter. In this encounter the subject-object scheme is valid: a definite subject (man) meets a definite object (God). One can reverse this statement and say that a definite subject (God) meets a definite object (man). But in both cases the attack of doubt undercuts the subject-object structure. The theologians who speak so strongly and with such self-certainty about the divine-human encounter should be aware of a situation in which this encounter is prevented by radical doubt and nothing is left but absolute faith. The acceptance of such a situation as religiously valid has, however, the consequence that the concrete contents of ordinary faith must be subjected to criticism and transformation. The courage to be in its radical form is a key to an idea of God which transcends both mysticism and the person-to-person encounter.

[. . .]

V
Political Philosophy

1

Tao Te Ching (selections)

Introduction

It was with selections from the *Tao Te Ching* that Part III (Metaphysics) of this volume began, and readers are referred to the editors' introduction to those selections for information on the authorship and general philosophical orientation of this work, the most translated and perhaps most popular of all classical Chinese texts. It was pointed out in this introduction that a central claim of Taoism is that human beings should emulate in their lives the "Way" (the *tao* or *dao*) which is the "mother" of all things and, in its mysterious way, disposes over the fate of everything. This is true of no one more than the ruler of a country, state, or empire, for unless the ruler rules in harmony with the Way his or her subjects are bound to suffer the consequences. In the *Tao Te Ching* (or *Daode jing*, "The Way and Its Power (or Virtue)"), the primary emphasis of the work is on proper rule and government. It is important to realize that the work was compiled or significantly modified probably during the fourth century BCE, in the era of Chinese history known as "The Period of the Warring States" – a condition of almost constant civil war between different rulers and warlords. It is unsurprising that the achievement of peace and stability

From Wang Keping, *The Classic of the* Dao: *A New Investigation,* Beijing: Foreign Languages Press, 1998, pp. 221–2, 225, 227–30, 232–4, 236–7, 240–1, 243–7, 250–1, 253–6.

should have been a primary concern of Chinese thinkers, including Confucius and the author(s) of the *Tao Te Ching*.

The political advice given to rulers in this work is typically terse and gnomic, and not always consistent. As a result, the character of this advice has been variously interpreted. At one extreme is the view that the work "functioned as an ideological justification for a ruthless, totalitarian government."[1] This is difficult to reconcile, however, with the many chapters in the work (e.g. 37, 48) that advocate the most distinctive of Taoist virtues, "*wu wei*" – sometimes translated as "non-action," but really a kind of non-assertive, "hands off" and spontaneous style of action. The remarks on *wu wei* have encouraged other commentators to see in the *Tao Te Ching* an "articulation of a democratic approach to the governing of the people," and a defense of a form of "government that refrains from using force and domination."[2] In this sense, *wu wei* seems rather like the liberal principle of non-interference with people's lives.

It is true, certainly, that some chapters of the work condemn violence and war (e.g. 31) and that others (e.g. 38, 57) criticize a society too hemmed in by rites, principles, taboos and laws. It is a sure sign that people have lost the Way – that they are no longer capable of living naturally and spontaneously – when they act according to rules, taboos, and the like. But the liberal-democratic reading of the *Tao Te Ching* is hard to reconcile with passages where the text recommends that the ruler keep his subjects ignorant, limit their desires (e.g. Ch. 3) and treat them like children (e.g. Ch. 49) or "straw-dogs." Perhaps the most plausible interpretation is one that construes the text as, primarily, a Machiavellian one. Certainly there are bits of advice to rulers that the great Florentine writer might almost have copied – enjoining the ruler to keep a low profile, for example, or warning him against showering honors on people lest jealousies are created.

It would, however, be unfair to the author(s) of *Tao Te Ching*, and indeed to Machiavelli (V.9), to suppose that the advice to rulers is given to them solely for their own benefit and survival. There may be some "old-roguish wisdom" in the book, but it is not simply a "brilliantly wicked philosophy of self-protection" in violent times.[3] For while there are indeed passages that make the yielding, gentle, and reticent behavior of the ruler look like a ploy, so that his or her enemies may then more effectively be overcome, there is no reason to

doubt that, for the author(s) of the work, the advice given to the ruler is designed with the good of the people or empire in view. In bloody, warring times – as both Machiavelli and Hobbes (V.10) later recognized – there is often a close correspondence between the interests and survival of the ruler and those of his people.

Notes

1 J. Paper, "'Daoism' and 'Deep Ecology': Fantasy and Potentiality," in N. J. Girardot, J. Miller, and Liu Xiaogan, eds, *Daoism and Ecology*, Cambridge, MA: Harvard University Press, 2001, p. 4.

2 K. Lai, *Learning from Chinese Philosophies*, Aldershot: Ashgate, 2006, pp. 99, 167.

3 Lin Yutang, *My Country and Its People*, London: Heinemann, 1936, p. 112.

Tao Te Ching

Chapter 3

Try not to exalt the worthy,
    So that the people shall not compete.
Try not to value rare treasures,
    So that the people shall not steal.
Try not to display the desirable,
    So that the people's hearts shall not be
        disturbed.
Therefore the sage governs the people by
    Purifying their minds,
    Filling their bellies,
    Weakening their ambitions,
    And strengthening their bones.
He always keeps them innocent of knowledge
    and desires,
    And makes the crafty afraid to run risks.
He conducts affairs on the principle of
    take-no-action,
    And everything will surely fall into order.

[. . .]

Chapter 5

Heaven and Earth are not humane.
They regard all things as straw dogs.[1]

The sage is not humane.
He regards all people as straw dogs. [. . .]

[. . .]

Chapter 13

One is alarmed when in receipt of favor or
    disgrace.
One has great trouble because of one's body
    that he has.
What is meant by being alarmed by favor or
    disgrace?
Favor is regarded as superior, and disgrace as
    inferior.
One is alarmed when one receives them
    And equally alarmed when one loses them.
This is what is meant by being alarmed by favor
    or disgrace.
What is meant by having great trouble because
    of the body?
The reason why I have great trouble is that I
    have a body.
If I had no body,
    What trouble could I have?
Hence he who values the world in the same way
    as he values his body
    Can be entrusted with the world.
He who loves the world in the same way as he
    loves his body
    Can be entrusted with the world.

Chapter 17

The best kind of rulers are those whose existence
    Is merely known by the people below them.
The next-best are those who are loved and
    praised.
The next-best are those who are feared.
The next-best are those who are despised.
If trust in others is not sufficient,
    It will be unrequited.
(The best rulers) are cautious,
    And seldom issue orders.
When tasks are accomplished and affairs
    completed,
    The common people will say,
"We simply follow the way of spontaneity."

Chapter 18

When the great *Dao* is rejected,
    The doctrines of Ren and Yi will arise.
When knowledge and craftiness appear,
    Great hypocrisy will also emerge.
When the six family relations are not in harmony,[2]
    Filial piety and parental affection will be
    advocated.
When a country falls into chaos,
    Loyal ministers will be praised.

Chapter 19

Only when sageness is eliminated and craftiness
    discarded,
    Will people benefit a hundredfold.
Only when humanity is eradicated and
    righteousness abandoned,
    Will people return to filial piety and parental
    affection.
Only when skill is thrown away and profit ignored,
    Will there be no more robbers or thieves.
Yet, these three are inadequate as a doctrine,
We therefore urge the following:
Manifest plainness and embrace simplicity;
    Reduce selfishness and have few desires;
    And get rid of learning and have no worries.

[. . .]

Chapter 22

To yield is yet to be preserved intact.
To be bent is yet to become straight.
To be hollow is yet to become full.

To be worn out is yet to be renewed.
To have little is yet to gain.
To have much is yet to be perplexed.
Therefore the sage holds on to the One
    And thus becomes a model for the world.
He does not cling to his ideas.
Therefore he is able to see things clearly.
He does not claim to be always right.
Therefore he is able to tell right from wrong.
He does not boast of himself.
Therefore he is given credit.
He does not think himself superior.
Therefore he is qualified for leadership.
It is only because he does not compete
    That the world cannot compete with him.
How could such an old saying be false
    As "To yield is yet to be preserved
        intact?"
Truly one will be preserved wholly without
    going to the contrary.
This is a constant and natural precept.

[. . .]

Chapter 28

He who knows the masculine and keeps to the
    feminine
    Will become the ravine of the world.
Being the ravine of the world,
    He will never depart from constant *De*,
    But return to the state of infancy.
He who knows glory but keeps to disgrace
    Will become the valley of the world.
Being the valley of the world,
He will be proficient in constant *De*
    And return to the state of simplicity.
He who knows the white but keeps to the black
    Will become the principle of the world.
Being the principle of the world,
    He will possess constant *De*
    And return to the state of ultimate infinity.
(When simplicity is broken up,
    It is turned into vessels.
By using these vessels,
    The sage becomes the head of officials.
Hence a perfect government is not carved out of
    artificiality.

Chapter 29

I think that one will not succeed
    When he desires to govern the state and act
    upon it.

The state as a sacred vessel should not be acted
upon,
    Nor should it be held on to.
He who acts upon it will harm it.
He who holds on to it will lose it.
Thus the sage takes no action, and therefore
fails in nothing;
He holds on to nothing, and therefore loses
nothing.

Of all the creatures some lead and some follow;
Some breathe and some blow;
Some are strong and some are weak;
Some rise up and some fall down.
Hence the sage discards the extremes,
    The extravagant and the excessive.

Meanwhile, he desires to have no desires.
He does not value rare treasures.
He learns what is unlearned.
He returns to what is missed.
Thus he helps all things in natural development,
    But does not dare to take any action.

Chapter 30

He who assists the ruler with the *Dao*
    Never seeks to dominate the world with
        military force.
The use of force is intrinsically dangerous:
Wherever armies are stationed,
    Briers and thorns grow wild.
As soon as great wars are over,
    Years of famine are sure to afflict the land.
Therefore an adept commander (of a defensive
force) will
    Stop when he has achieved his aim.
He does not use force to dominate the world.
He achieves his aim but does not become arrogant.
He achieves his aim but does not boast about it.
He achieves his aim only because he has no
    other choice.
This is called achieving the aim without using
    force to dominate.
The strong and powerful rob and harm the old
    and weak.
This is called contrary to the *Dao*.
Whatever is contrary to the *Dao* will soon perish.

Chapter 31

Weapons are nothing but instruments of evil.
    They are used only when there is no other
        choice.

Therefore, he who wins a battle is not
    praiseworthy.
If he thinks himself praiseworthy,
    He delights in the victory.
He who delights in the victory,
    Delights in the slaughter of men.
He who delights in the slaughter of men
    Will not succeed under Heaven.
For the multitude killed in the war
    Let us mourn them with sorrow and grief.
For the victory won by force,
    Let us observe the occasion with funeral
        ceremonies.

[. . .]

Chapter 37

The *Dao* invariably takes no action,
    And yet there is nothing left undone.
If kings and lords are able to maintain it,
    All things will submit to them due to self-
        transformation.
If, after submission, they have resurging desires
to act,
    I should subdue them by the nameless
        simplicity.
When they are subdued by the nameless
simplicity,
    They will be free of desires.
Being free of desires, they will be tranquil,
    And the world will of itself be rectified.

Chapter 38

The man of superior *De* is not conscious
    of his *De*,
    And in this way he really possesses *De*.
The man of inferior *De* never loses sight
    of his *De*,
    And in this way he has no true *De*.
The man of superior *De* takes no action
And thus nothing will be left undone.
The man of inferior *De* takes action
And thus something will be left undone.
The man of superior humanity takes action
    And so acts without purpose.

The man of superior righteousness takes action
    And so acts on purpose.
The man of superior propriety takes action,
    And when people do not respond to it,
    He will stretch out his arms and force them
        to comply.

Therefore, only when the *Dao* is lost does *De* disappear.

Only when *De* is lost does humanity appear.

Only when humanity is lost does righteousness appear.

Only when righteousness is lost does propriety appear. [...]

[...]

Chapter 45

What is most perfect seems to be incomplete,
  But its utility cannot be impaired.
What is most full seems to be empty,
  But its utility cannot be exhausted.
The most straight seems to be crooked.
The greatest skill seems to be clumsy.
The greatest eloquence seems to stutter.
The tranquil overcomes the hasty.
The cold overcomes the hot.
By remaining quiet and tranquil,
  One can become a model for all the people.

Chapter 46

When the world has the *Dao*,
  War horses are used in farming.
When the world lacks the *Dao*,
  Even mares in foal have to serve in battle.
There is no guilt greater than lavish desires.
There is no calamity greater than discontentment.
There is no defect greater than covetousness.
Therefore, he who is contented with knowing contentment
  Is always contented indeed.

[...]

Chapter 49

The sage has no fixed mind of his own.
He takes the mind of the people as his mind.
I treat those who are good with goodness
  And I also treat those who are not good with goodness,
  Then everyone will try to become good.
I trust those who are trustworthy
  And I also trust those who are not trustworthy,
  Then everyone will try to become trustworthy.

When the sage governs the world,
  He seeks to put away his personal will
  And to help everyone return to the sphere of simplicity.
While the people all concentrate on their own eyes and ears,
  He renders them back to the sphere of infancy without desires.

[...]

Chapter 53

If I have a little wisdom,
  I will walk along a broad way
  And fear nothing but going astray.
The broad way is very even,
  But the powerful delight in by-paths.
The courts are exceedingly corrupt,
  Whereas the fields are exceedingly weedy
  And the granaries are exceedingly empty.
They are wearing elegant clothes,
  Carrying sharp swords,
  Enjoying exquisite food and drink,
  And owning abundant wealth and treasures.
They can be called robber chieftains.
This is surely against the *Dao*.

[...]

Chapter 57

A state should be governed in a normal way.
An army should be operated in an unusual way.
The world should be administered by doing nothing.
How do I know that it should be so?
Through the following:
The more prohibitive enactments there are in the world,
  The poorer the people will become;
The more sharp weapons men have,
  The more troubled the state will be;
The more crafts and techniques men possess,
  The more vicious things will appear;
The more laws and orders are made prominent,
  The more robbers and thieves will spring up.
Therefore the sage says:
"I take no action and the people of themselves become transformed.
I love tranquility and the people of themselves become righteous.

I disturb nobody and the people of themselves
  become prosperous.
I have no desires and the people of themselves
  become simple."

[...]

Chapter 59

To rule people and to serve Heaven
  Nothing is better than the principle
    of frugality.
Only by frugality can one get ready early.
To get ready early means to accumulate *De*
  continuously.
With the continuous accumulation of *De*,
  One can overcome every difficulty.
If one can overcome every difficulty,
  He will then acquire immeasurable capacity.
With immeasurable capacity,
  He can achieve the *Dao* to govern the
    country.
He who has the *Dao* of the country can
  maintain sovereignty.
This is called the way in which the roots are
  planted deep
  And the stalks are made firm;
  Longevity is achieved and sovereignty is made
    everlasting.

[...]

Chapter 65

In ancient times he who practiced the *Dao* well
  Did not use it to enlighten the people.
Instead he used it to make them simple.
Now the people are difficult to govern
  Because they have too much craftiness.
Thus, governing a country by craftiness is a
  disaster for it.
And not governing it by craftiness is a blessing
  for it.
He who knows these two also knows the
  principle.
It is called profound *De* to always know the
  principle.
Profound *De* is deep and far-reaching;
It returns to the origin with all things,
  And then leads to the great naturalness.

Chapter 66

The great rivers and seas can be kings of the
  mountain streams
  Because they skillfully stay below them.
That is why they can be their kings.
Therefore, in order to be above the people,
  The sage must place himself below them in
    his words.
In order to be ahead of the people,
  He must place himself behind them in
    his person.
In this way, the sage is above the people,
  But they do not feel his weight.
He is ahead of the people,
  But they do not feel his hindrance.
Therefore the whole world delights in
  praising him
  And never gets tired of him.
Simply because he does not compete with
  others,
  Nobody under Heaven can compete
    with him.

[...]

Chapter 75

The people suffer from famine
  Because the ruler levies too much tax-grain.
Thus they suffer from famine.
The people are difficult to rule
  Because the ruler too often takes action.
Thus they are difficult to rule.
The people take life lightly
  Because the ruler longs for life so avidly.
Thus they take life lightly.

[...]

Chapter 78

Nothing in the world is softer and weaker than
  water,
  But no force can compare with it in
    attacking the hard and strong.
For this reason there is no substitute for it.
Everyone in the world knows that
  The soft can overcome the hard,
  And the weak can overcome the strong,
  But none can put it into practice.
Therefore the sage says:
"He who shoulders the disgrace for his nation
  Can be the sovereign of the country;

He who bears the misfortune of his nation
　　Can be the king of the world."
Positive words seem to be their opposite.

[. . .]

Chapter 80

Let there be a small state with few people.
It has various kinds of instruments,
　　But let none of them be used.
Let the people not risk their lives, and not
　　migrate far away.
Although they have boats and carriages,
　　Let there be no occasion to ride in them.
Although they have armor and weapons,
　　Let there be no occasion to display them.
Let the people return to knotting cords and
　　using them.

Let them relish their food,
　　Beautify their clothing,
　　Feel comfortable in their homes
　　And delight in their customs.
Although the neighboring states are within the
　　sight of one another,
　　And the crowing of cocks and barking of dogs
　　On both sides can be heard,
　　Their peoples may die of old age without
　　　　ever meeting each other.

Notes

1　Straw dogs were sacrificial objects that were discarded
　　once they had performed their role. Some com-
　　mentators, incidentally, maintain that the relevant
　　terms should be translated as "straw *and* dogs,"
　　rather than "straw dogs."
2　Father and son, elder and younger brother, and hus-
　　band and wife.

2

Gotama (the Buddha), Selected Sayings on Kingship

Introduction

In some circles, Buddhism still enjoys the image of being an "other-worldly" dispensation, focused not on the betterment of mundane life, but on liberation or release from it. But if there is any truth to this image, it is one that applies only to the concerns of adepts – of monks bent on the goal of nirvanic enlightenment. (In one of the Buddha's *suttas* or "sermons" we have selected, monks are enjoined to be "islands unto yourselves" and "keep to your own preserves.") Certainly Siddhattha Gotama (c. 480–400 BCE), the Buddha, devoted considerable attention to matters of mundane moral concern – to family life and economic affairs, for example, and, more relevantly here, to political conduct. He himself was the son of the ruler of a small principality in Northern India, from which he famously escaped in order to seek and later teach the way to spiritual enlightenment. In fifth-century BCE India, there were emerging urban-based kingdoms, in place of an earlier mosaic of small republics, and Gotama – while himself without political ambitions – was personally acquainted with some of the monarchs and offered advice and reflections on the art of kingship.

From *The Long Discourses of the Buddha: A Translation of the* Dīgha Nikāya, trans. M. Walshe, Boston, MA: Wisdom Publications, 1995, pp. 135–6, 395–401, 413 (notes omitted).

Some of the advice that the Buddha offers is, rather in the style of Machiavelli (V.9), of a fairly pragmatic kind. The sensible king will not, for example, excessively punish troublemakers, since those who escape punishment will seek revenge and threaten the kingdom. But as the term that Gotama applies to his ideal ruler (*cakkavatti* or "wheel-turning monarch") in the longest of the selected *suttas* implies, much of the advice is of a loftier moral character. For, indeed, "turning the wheel" is a standard Buddhist metaphor for setting and preserving in motion the *dhamma* or moral law (cf. IV.2). We read that it is the duty of such a monarch to, *inter alia*, protect both the people and the animals within his kingdom as well as to encourage people to avoid such evils as violence and sexual infatuation.

It is not, however, the king's good sense and moral character which, by themselves, confer authority on him. In §20 of the *Agañña Sutta*, one encounters a brief and very early version of the "social contract" theory of sovereignty that would come to dominate political theorizing in Europe during the seventeenth and eighteenth centuries (V.10–14, 23).[1] Power and wealth are invested by people in a ruler in return for his or protection against those who deserve "censure and banishment." So the ruler's authority is neither raw, ungrounded power, nor something conferred by God, as in the many varieties of "divine right" theories of sovereignty.

The Buddha's version of the social contract is closer in character to that of Thomas Hobbes than to that of John Locke (see V.10 and V.11). Not only does the decision to appoint a king arise in dire, anarchic circumstances akin to Hobbes's "war of all against all," but there is no conception, as there is in Locke, of moral rights that it is the duty of the king to honor as part of the contract whereby he obtains power. (Buddhist moral thought, more generally, seems to have no place for the idea of natural or human rights.) Hence, the argument for what turns out, in both the *Kūtadanta* and the *Cakkavatti Suttas*, to be the primary merit and duty of the king – namely, the alleviation of poverty among his people – rests not on any appeal to a right to a "minimum wage" or to "freedom from want," but on the devastating moral effects of poverty. Almost all social and moral ills – from prostitution to corruption, from violence to incest – are traced back to poverty, in a striking application of the Buddhist doctrine of "conditioned arising" (or genesis).[2]

Gotama's conception of the "wheel-turning monarch" has been immensely influential in Buddhist history. The greatest ruler of ancient India, Aśoka (c. 300–232 BCE), who converted to Buddhism, strove both in practice (his renunciation of war, for instance) and in his famous pillar and rock edicts, to incarnate the virtues of this ideal ruler. To take a much more recent example, the Sri Lankan Jathika Hela Urumaya (National Heritage Party), founded in 2004 and composed of Buddhist monks seeking parliamentary election, purports to re-inject into modern politics the precepts and ideals of *cakkavatti* governance.[3] That these monks do not seem to be heeding the Buddha's exhortation to "keep to your own preserves" has, unsurprisingly, generated heated arguments about their political engagement.

Notes

1 See P. Harvey, *An Introduction to Buddhist Ethics*, Cambridge: Cambridge University Press, 2000, p. 114. Harvey's book provides a useful and broad account of Buddhist social and political thought.

2 See III.5 for texts on "conditioned arising."

3 See Mahinda Deegalle, ed., *Buddhism, Conflict and Violence in Modern Sri Lanka*, London: Routledge, 2006, especially Chapter 15. Several chapters in this book discuss the relevance to contemporary political debate of early Buddhist thought.

Gotama, Selected Sayings on Kingship

5. *Kūtadanta Sutta*: About Kūtadanta, A Bloodless Sacrifice

[The Buddha is here addressing Kūtadanta, a Brahmin (high-caste priest, with special responsibilities for animal sacrifices). The main point of the *sutta* is that true sacrifice does not require the spilling of any creature's blood: but, in the opening sections (10–11) of the address, Gotama speaks more generally about the proper conduct of a king. (Eds)]

10. 'Brahmin, once upon a time there was a king called Mahāvijita. He was rich, of great wealth and resources, with an abundance of gold and silver, of possessions and requisites, of money and money's worth, with a full treasury and granary. And when King Mahāvijita was musing in private, the thought came to him: "I have acquired extensive wealth in human terms, I occupy a wide extent of land which I have conquered. Suppose now I were to make a great sacrifice which would be to my benefit and happiness for a long time?" And calling his minister-chaplain, he told him his thought. "I want to make a big sacrifice. Instruct me, Reverend Sir, how this may be to my lasting benefit and happiness."

11. 'The chaplain replied: "Your Majesty's country is beset by thieves, it is ravaged, villages and towns are being destroyed, the countryside is infested with brigands. If Your Majesty were to tax this region, that would be the wrong thing to do. Suppose Your Majesty were to think: 'I will get rid of this plague of robbers by executions and imprisonment, or by confiscation, threats and banishment', the plague would not be properly ended. Those who survived would later harm Your Majesty's realm. However, with this plan you can completely eliminate the plague. To those in the kingdom who are engaged in cultivating crops and raising cattle, let Your Majesty distribute grain and fodder; to those in trade, give capital;

to those in government service assign proper living wages. Then those people, being intent on their own occupations, will not harm the kingdom. Your Majesty's revenues will be great, the land will be tranquil and not beset by thieves, and the people, with joy in their hearts, will play with their children, and will dwell in open houses."

'And saying: "So be it!", the king accepted the chaplain's advice: he gave grain and fodder, capital to those in trade, . . . proper living wages . . . and the people with joy in their hearts . . . dwelt in open houses.

[. . .]

26. *Cakkavatti-Sīhanāda Sutta*: The Lion's Roar on the Turning of the Wheel

[The Buddha is here addressing his monks on the duties of a "wheel-turning" king whose rule accords with the moral law of the *dhamma*. Sections 15–20 tell, in the form of a fable, of the terrible consequences of failing to alleviate poverty. In section 21, human beings recognize their unbearable condition – akin to a Hobbesian "state of nature" – and subsequent sections tell of their return to their original and happier condition. (Eds)]

1. Thus have I heard. Once the Lord was staying among the Magadhans at Mātulā. Then he said: 'Monks!' 'Lord', they replied, and the Lord said: 'Monks, be islands unto yourselves, be a refuge unto yourselves with no other refuge. Let the Dhamma be your island, let the Dhamma be your refuge, with no other refuge. And how does a monk dwell as an island unto himself, as a refuge unto himself with no other refuge, with the Dhamma as his island, with the Dhamma as his refuge, with no other refuge? Here, a monk abides contemplating body as body, ardent, clearly aware and mindful, having put aside hankering and fretting for the world, he abides contemplating feelings as feelings, . . . he abides contemplating mind as mind, . . . he abides contemplating mind-objects as mind-objects, ardent, clearly aware and mindful, having put aside hankering and fretting for the world.

'Keep to your own preserves, monks, to your ancestral haunts. If you do so, then Māra [the evil one] will find no lodgement, no foothold. It is just by the building-up of wholesome states that this merit increases.

2. 'Once, monks, there was a wheel-turning monarch named Daḷhanemi, a righteous monarch of the law, conqueror of the four quarters, who had established the security of his realm and was possessed of the seven treasures. These are: the Wheel Treasure, the Elephant Treasure, the Horse Treasure, the Jewel Treasure, the Woman Treasure, the Householder Treasurer, and, as seventh, the Counsellor Treasure. He has more than a thousand sons who are heroes, of heroic stature, conquerors of the hostile army. He dwells having conquered this sea-girt land without stick or sword, by the law.

3. 'And, after many hundreds and thousands of years, King Daḷhanemi said to a certain man: "My good man, whenever you see that the sacred Wheel-Treasure has slipped from its position, report it to me." "Yes, sire", the man replied. And after many hundreds and thousands of years the man saw that the sacred Wheel-Treasure had slipped from its position. Seeing this, he reported the fact to the King. Then King Daḷhanemi sent for his eldest son, the crown prince, and said: "My son, the sacred Wheel-Treasure has slipped from its position. And I have heard say that when this happens to a wheel-turning monarch, he has not much longer to live. I have had my fill of human pleasures, now is the time to seek heavenly pleasures. You, my son, take over control of this ocean-bounded land. I will shave off my hair and beard, don yellow robes, and go forth from the household life into homelessness." And, having installed his eldest son in due form as king, King Daḷhanemi shaved off his hair and beard, donned yellow robes, and went forth from the household life into homelessness. And, seven days after the royal sage had gone forth, the sacred Wheel-Treasure vanished.

4. 'Then a certain man came to the anointed Khattiya King and said: "Sire, you should know that the sacred Wheel-Treasure has disappeared." At this the King was grieved and felt sad. He went to the royal sage and told him the news. And the royal sage said to him: "My son, you should not grieve or feel sad at the disappearance of the Wheel-Treasure. The Wheel-Treasure is not an heirloom from your fathers. But now, my son, you must turn yourself into an Ariyan wheel-turner. And then it may come about that, if you perform the duties of an Ariyan wheel-turning monarch,

on the fast-day of the fifteenth, when you have washed your head and gone up to the verandah on top of your palace for the fast-day, the sacred Wheel-Treasure will appear to you, thousand-spoked, complete with felloe, hub and all appurtenances."

5. '"But what, sire, is the duty of an Ariyan wheel-turning monarch?" "It is this, my son: Yourself depending on the Dhamma, honouring it, revering it, cherishing it, doing homage to it and venerating it, having the Dhamma as your badge and banner, acknowledging the Dhamma as your master, you should establish guard, ward and protection according to Dhamma for your own household, your troops, your nobles and vassals, for Brahmins and householders, town and country folk, ascetics and Brahmins, for beasts and birds. Let no crime prevail in your kingdom, and to those who are in need, give property. And whatever ascetics and Brahmins in your kingdom have renounced the life of sensual infatuation and are devoted to forbearance and gentleness, each one taming himself, each one calming himself and each one striving for the end of craving, if from time to time they should come to you and consult you as to what is wholesome and what is unwholesome, what is blameworthy and what is blameless, what is to be followed and what is not to be followed, and what action will in the long run lead to harm and sorrow, and what to welfare and happiness, you should listen, and tell them to avoid evil and do what is good. That, my son, is the duty of an Ariyan wheel-turning monarch."

'"Yes, sire", said the King, and he performed the duties of an Ariyan wheel-turning monarch. And as he did so, on the fast-day of the fifteenth, when he had washed his head and gone up to the verandah on top of his palace for the fast-day, the sacred Wheel-Treasure appeared to him, thousand-spoked, complete with felloe, hub and all appurtenances. Then the King thought: "I have heard that when a duly anointed Khattiya king sees such a wheel on the fast-day of the fifteenth, he will become a wheel-turning monarch. May I become such a monarch!"

6. 'Then, rising from his seat, covering one shoulder with his robe, the King took a gold vessel in his left hand, sprinkled the Wheel with his right hand, and said: "May the noble Wheel-Treasure turn, may the noble Wheel-Treasure conquer!" The Wheel turned to the east, and the King followed it with his fourfold army. And in whatever country the Wheel stopped, the King took up residence with his fourfold army. And those who opposed him in the eastern region came and said: "Come, Your Majesty, welcome! We are yours, Your Majesty. Rule us, Your Majesty." And the King said: "Do not take life. Do not take what is not given. Do not commit sexual misconduct. Do not tell lies. Do not drink strong drink. Be moderate in eating." And those who had opposed him in the eastern region became his subjects.

7. 'Then the Wheel turned south, west, and north . . . (*as verse 6*). Then the Wheel-Treasure, having conquered the lands from sea to sea, returned to the royal capital and stopped before the King's palace as he was trying a case, as if to adorn the royal palace.

8. 'And a second wheel-turning monarch did likewise, and a third, a fourth, a fifth, a sixth, and a seventh king also . . . told a man to see if the Wheel had slipped from its position (*as verse 3*). And seven days after the royal sage had gone forth the Wheel disappeared.

9. 'Then a man came to the King and said: "Sire, you should know that the sacred Wheel-Treasure has disappeared." At this the King was grieved and felt sad. But he did not go to the royal sage and ask him about the duties of a wheel-turning monarch. Instead, he ruled the people according to his own ideas, and, being so ruled, the people did not prosper so well as they had done under the previous kings who had performed the duties of a wheel-turning monarch. Then the ministers, counsellors, treasury officials, guards and doorkeepers, and the chanters of mantras came to the King and said: "Sire, as long as you rule the people according to your own ideas, and differently from the way they were ruled before under previous wheel-turning monarchs, the people do not prosper so well. Sire, there are ministers . . . in your realm, including ourselves, who have preserved the knowledge of how a wheel-turning monarch should rule. Ask us, Your Majesty, and we will tell you!"

10. 'Then the King ordered all the ministers and others to come together, and he consulted them. And they explained to him the duties of a wheel-turning monarch. And, having listened to them, the King established guard and protection, but he did not give property to the needy, and as a result poverty became rife. With the spread of poverty, a man took what was not given, thus

committing what was called theft. They arrested him, and brought him before the King, saying: "Your Majesty, this man took what was not given, which we call theft." The King said to him: "Is it true that you took what was not given – which is called theft?" "It is, Your Majesty." "Why?" "Your Majesty, I have nothing to live on." Then the King gave the man some property, saying: "With this, my good man, you can keep yourself, support your mother and father, keep a wife and children, carry on a business and make gifts to ascetics and Brahmins, which will promote your spiritual welfare and lead to a happy rebirth with pleasant result in the heavenly sphere." "Very good, Your Majesty", replied the man.

11. 'And exactly the same thing happened with another man.

12. 'Then people heard that the King was giving away property to those who took what was not given, and they thought: "Suppose we were to do likewise!" And then another man took what was not given, and they brought him before the King. The King asked him why he had done this, and he replied: "Your Majesty, I have nothing to live on." Then the King thought: "If I give property to everybody who takes what is not given, this theft will increase more and more. I had better make an end of him, finish him off once for all, and cut his head off." So he commanded his men: "Bind this man's arms tightly behind him with a strong rope, shave his head closely, and lead him to the rough sound of a drum through the streets and squares and out through the southern gate, and there finish by inflicting the capital penalty and cutting off his head!" And they did so.

13. 'Hearing about this, people thought: "Now let us get sharp swords made for us, and then we can take from anybody what is not given [which is called theft], we will make an end of them, finish them off once for all and cut off their heads." So, having procured some sharp swords, they launched murderous assaults on villages, towns and cities, and went in for highway-robbery, killing their victims by cutting off their heads.

14. 'Thus, from the not giving of property to the needy, poverty became rife, from the growth of poverty, the taking of what was not given increased, from the increase of theft, the use of weapons increased, from the increased use of weapons, the taking of life increased – and from the increase in the taking of life, people's life-span

decreased, their beauty decreased, and as a result of this decrease of life-span and beauty, the children of those whose life-span had been eighty thousand years lived for only forty thousand.

'And a man of the generation that lived for forty thousand years took what was not given. He was brought before the King, who asked him: "Is it true that you took what was not given – what is called theft?" "No, Your Majesty", he replied, thus telling a deliberate lie.

15. 'Thus, from the not giving of property to the needy, . . . the taking of life increased, and from the taking of life, lying increased, from the increase in lying, people's life-span decreased, their beauty decreased, and as a result, the children of those whose life-span had been forty thousand years lived for only twenty thousand.

'And a man of the generation that lived for twenty thousand years took what was not given. Another man denounced him to the King, saying: "Sire, such-and-such a man has taken what was not given", thus speaking evil of another.

16. 'Thus, from the not giving of property to the needy, . . . the speaking evil of others increased, and in consequence, people's life-span decreased, their beauty decreased, and as a result, the children of those whose life-span had been twenty thousand years lived only for ten thousand.

'And of the generation that lived for ten thousand years, some were beautiful, and some were ugly. And those who were ugly, being envious of those who were beautiful, committed adultery with others' wives.

17. Thus, from the not giving of property to the needy, . . . sexual misconduct increased, and in consequence people's life-span decreased, their beauty decreased, and as a result, the children of those whose life-span had been ten thousand years lived for only five thousand.

'And among the generation whose life-span was five thousand years, two things increased: harsh speech and idle chatter, in consequence of which people's life-span decreased, their beauty decreased, and as a result, the children of those whose life-span had been five thousand years lived, some for two-and-a-half thousand years, and some for only two thousand.

'And among the generation whose life-span was two-and-a-half thousand years, covetousness and hatred increased, and in consequence people's life-span decreased, their beauty decreased, and as a result, the children of those whose life-span had been two-and-a-half thousand years lived for only a thousand.

'Among the generation whose life-span was a thousand years, false opinions increased . . . and as a result, the children of those whose life-span had been a thousand years lived for only five hundred.

'And among the generation whose life-span was five hundred years, three things increased: incest, excessive greed and deviant practices . . . and as a result, the children of those whose life-span had been five hundred years lived, some for two hundred and fifty years, some for only two hundred.

'And among those whose life-span was two hundred and fifty years, these things increased: lack of respect for mother and father, for ascetics and Brahmins, and for the head of the clan.

18. 'Thus, from the not giving of property to the needy, . . . lack of respect for mother and father, for ascetics and Brahmins, and for the head of the clan increased, and in consequence people's life-span and beauty decreased, and the children of those whose life-span had been two-and-a-half centuries lived for only a hundred years.

19. 'Monks, a time will come when the children of these people will have a life-span of ten years. And with them, girls will be marriageable at five years old. And with them, these flavours will disappear: ghee, butter, sesame-oil, molasses and salt. Among them, *kudrūsa*-grain [rye] will be the chief food, just as rice and curry are today. And with them, the ten courses of moral conduct will completely disappear, and the ten courses of evil will prevail exceedingly: for those of a ten-year life-span there will be no word for "moral", so how can there be anyone who acts in a moral way? Those people who have no respect for mother or father, for ascetics and Brahmins, for the head of the clan, will be the ones who enjoy honour and prestige. Just as it is now the people who show respect for mother and father, for ascetics and Brahmins, for the head of the clan, who are praised and honoured, so it will be with those who do the opposite.

20. 'Among those of a ten-year life-span no account will be taken of mother or aunt, of mother's sister-in-law, of teacher's wife or of one's father's wives and so on – all will be promiscuous in the world like goats and sheep, fowl and pigs, dogs and jackals. Among them, fierce enmity will prevail one for another, fierce hatred, fierce anger and thoughts of killing, mother against child and child against mother, father against child and child against father, brother against brother, brother against sister, just as the hunter feels hatred for the beast he stalks . . .

21. 'And for those of a ten-year life-span, there will come to be a "sword-interval" of seven days, during which they will mistake one another for wild beasts. Sharp swords will appear in their hands and, thinking: "There is a wild beast!" they will take each other's lives with those swords. But there will be some beings who will think: "Let us not kill or be killed by anyone! Let us make for some grassy thickets or jungle-recesses or clumps of trees, for rivers hard to ford or inaccessible mountains, and live on roots and fruits of the forest." And this they will do for seven days. Then, at the end of the seven days, they will emerge from their hiding-places and rejoice together of one accord, saying: "Good beings, I see that you are alive!" And then the thought will occur to those beings: "It is only because we became addicted to evil ways that we suffered this loss of our kindred, so let us now do good! What good things can we do? Let us abstain from the taking of life – that will be a good practice." And so they will abstain from the taking of life, and, having undertaken this good thing, will practise it. And through having undertaken such wholesome things, they will increase in life-span and beauty. And the children of those whose life-span was ten years will live for twenty years.

22. 'Then it will occur to those beings: "It is through having taken to wholesome practices that we have increased in life-span and beauty, so let us perform still more wholesome practices. Let us refrain from taking what is not given, from sexual misconduct, from lying speech, from slander, from harsh speech, from idle chatter, from covetousness, from ill-will, from wrong views; let us abstain from three things: incest, excessive greed, and deviant practices; let us respect our mothers and fathers, ascetics and Brahmins, and the head of the clan, and let us persevere in these wholesome actions."

'And so they will do these things, and on account of this they will increase in life-span and in beauty. The children of those whose life-span is twenty years will live to be forty, their children will live to be eighty, their children to be a hundred and sixty, their children to be three hundred and twenty, their children to be six hundred and forty; the children of those whose life-span is six hundred and forty years will live for two thousand years, their children for four thousand, their children for eight thousand, and their children for twenty thousand. The children of those whose life-span is twenty thousand years will live to be forty thousand, and their children will attain to eighty thousand years.

[. . .]

27. Aggañña Sutta:
On Knowledge of Beginnings

[The Buddha is here addressing another Brahmin, Vāsettha. In the context of a fable similar to that in the previous *sutta* (26), Gotama explains the origin of kingship, in contractual terms, but also in subsequent sections the origin of the caste system. In section 21, Mahā-Sammata is the mythical ancestor of the Sakyan clan, to which Gotama belonged; the Khattiyas are the 'warrior-noble' caste; and 'Rāja' is the word for king. (Eds)]

20. 'Then those beings came together and lamented the arising of these evil things among

them: taking what was not given, censuring, lying and punishment. And they thought: "Suppose we were to appoint a certain being who would show anger where anger was due, censure those who deserved it, and banish those who deserved banishment! And in return, we would grant him a share of the rice." So they went to the one among them who was the handsomest, the best-looking, the most pleasant and capable, and asked him to do this for them in return for a share of the rice, and he agreed.

21. '"The People's Choice" is the meaning of Mahā-Sammata, which is the first regular title to be introduced. "Lord Of The Fields" is the meaning of Khattiya, the second such title. And "He Gladdens Others With Dhamma" is the meaning of Rāja, the third title to be introduced. This, then, Vāsettha, is the origin of the class of Khattiyas, in accordance with the ancient titles that were introduced for them. They originated among these very same beings, like ourselves, no different, and in accordance with Dhamma, not otherwise.

Dhamma's the best thing for people
In this life and the next as well. [. . .]

Confucius, *The Analects* (selections)

Introduction

"Confucius" is the Latinized name given to the Chou dynasty teacher, philosopher, and government official, K'ung Fu-tzu (Kǒng Fūzǐ) (c. 551–479 BCE). Several of the classic works of ancient China, including the *I Ching*, were traditionally attributed in part to Confucius, but it is probably only the remarks gathered together by his students in the book known as *The Analects* that may, with some reliability, be attributed to him. Confucius was born in the state of Lu, where he spent much of his life and gained employment as a minor official. His attempts, in Lu and elsewhere, to secure more elevated employment as a Minister failed, and he lived the latter part of his life as the teacher of a small group of students or disciples. Posterity was to more than compensate for the relative neglect of Confucius in his lifetime. During the Han dynasty, 300 years after his death, there was a great revival of interest in his thinking, and Confucian scholarship was to shape the education of the Chinese civil service until the abolition of the examination system only a few years before the collapse of imperial China in 1912.

Despite, or perhaps because of, this unparalleled influence on a political system for two millennia,

From Confucius, *The Analects*, trans. D. C. Lau, Harmondsworth: Penguin, 1979, pp. 59, 63, 65–6, 73–4, 85, 94, 109, 112–16, 118–23, 131, 135 (notes omitted).

Confucianism did not enjoy, among most political philosophers of the twentieth century, a high reputation. And while there has been some resurgence of a more sympathetic interest in Confucius's views, he still retains the reputation of being a dyed-in-the-wool political reactionary. It is true that he greatly admired both the early Chou emperors – mythical as many of their exploits may have been – and the system of "rites" or "propriety" (*li*) that played a decisive part in the society over which they had ruled. But this admiration was not due solely to nostalgia. China had, by the sixth century BCE, descended into a condition of violent chaos, a patchwork of small, warring dukedoms. This descent, in Confucius's judgment, was due to a combination of poor rulers and the atrophy of respect for rites. Rites, as he saw them, were social conventions, tried and tested over time, which not only served as disciplined channels for the exercise of virtue but provided substance to the idea of the Way (*tao* or *dao*) in accordance with which human lives should be led. The Way of which Confucius speaks is not the metaphysical "principle of nature" that it was for Lao Tzu (III.1, V.1), but the path which human beings must follow if there is to be harmony and peace among them. By serving as rules on which members of a society could agree, the rites were an important dimension of this path.

More important still, for Confucius, was the quality of the rulers of a society. "The Confucian ideal of government," it has been said, was to ensure that "the influence and example of men of superior moral qualities is brought to bear upon the population."[1] The state, for Confucius, is not – as it was for Lao Tzu – a necessary evil in times of distress, but the primary agency whereby morally superior persons (*chun-tzu*, "gentlemen" in the translation below) may, primarily through the example they set, educate "the small men."[2]

The primary possession of "the gentleman" is *jen*, translated below as "benevolence" but best understood, perhaps, an inner moral quality that variously manifests itself – in altruism, and in honesty and integrity, for example. An especially significant aspect of *jen* in the case of the ruler or government official is "doing one's best" or "loyalty" with respect to the discharge of one's proper role in society (see Chapter IV, §15). This consideration has prompted a comparison with Plato's notion of the just city (V.4), one in which "everyone does his own job."[3] And one "job" that it is of particular importance for the "gentleman" official loyally to discharge is that of "the rectification of names" (see Chapter XIII, §3).

This is not advocating a pedantic obsession with nomenclature, of a kind with which bureaucrats are sometimes associated, but charging rulers with a moral responsibility for ensuring that how things actually are in society properly corresponds with the names (or, better, the concepts referred to by the names) that, implicitly at least, indicate how things should be – that, for instance, fathers properly perform the duties that are implicit in the very concept of fatherhood. Part of the make up of the Confucian ruler, one might say, is resolute rejection of "spin."

Notes

1   R. Dawson, *Confucius*, Oxford: Oxford University Press, 1981, p. 53.
2   Compare with this view Aristotle's view of the state as necessary for moral development in V.5.
3   Jee Loo Liu, *An Introduction to Chinese Philosophy*, Oxford: Blackwell, 2006, p. 50.

The Analects

Book I

5.   The Master said, 'In guiding a state of a thousand chariots, approach your duties with reverence and be trustworthy in what you say; avoid excesses in expenditure and love your fellow men; employ the labour of the common people only in the right seasons.'

[. . .]

Book II

3.   The Master said, 'Guide them by edicts, keep them in line with punishments, and the common people will stay out of trouble but will have no sense of shame. Guide them by virtue, keep them in line with the rites, and they will, besides having a sense of shame, reform themselves.'

[. . .]

19.   Duke Ai asked, 'What must I do before the common people will look up to me?'

Confucius answered, 'Raise the straight and set them over the crooked and the common people will look up to you. Raise the crooked and set them over the straight and the common people will not look up to you.'

20.   Chi K'ang Tzu asked, 'How can one inculcate in the common people the virtue of reverence, of doing their best and of enthusiasm?'

The Master said, 'Rule over them with dignity and they will be reverent; treat them with kindness and they will do their best; raise the good and instruct those who are backward and they will be imbued with enthusiasm.'

[. . .]

Book IV

11.   The Master said, 'While the gentleman cherishes benign rule, the small man cherishes his native land. While the gentleman cherishes a respect for the law, the small man cherishes generous treatment.'

[. . .]

13. The Master said, 'If a man is able to govern a state by observing the rites and showing deference, what difficulties will he have in public life? If he is unable to govern a state by observing the rites and showing deference, what good are the rites to him?'

14. The Master said, 'Do not worry because you have no official position. Worry about your qualifications. Do not worry because no one appreciates your abilities. Seek to be worthy of appreciation.'

15. The Master said, 'Ts'an! There is one single thread binding my way together.'

Tseng Tzu assented.

After the Master had gone out, the disciples asked, 'What did he mean?'

Tseng Tzu said, 'The way of the Master consists in doing one's best and in using oneself as a measure to gauge others.[1] That is all.'

16. The Master said, 'The gentleman understands what is moral. The small man understands what is profitable.'

[. . .]

Book VI

30. Tzu-kung said, 'If there were a man who gave extensively to the common people and brought help to the multitude, what would you think of him? Could he be called benevolent?'

The Master said, 'It is no longer a matter of benevolence with such a man. If you must describe him, "sage" is, perhaps, the right word. Even Yao and Shun would have found it difficult to accomplish as much.[2] Now, on the other hand, a benevolent man helps others to take their stand in so far as he himself wishes to take his stand, and gets others there in so far as he himself wishes to get there. The ability to take as analogy what is near at hand can be called the method of benevolence.'

[. . .]

Book XII

1. Yen Yüan asked about benevolence. The Master said, 'To return to the observance of the rites through overcoming the self constitutes benevolence. If for a single day a man could return to the observance of the rites through overcoming himself, then the whole Empire would consider benevolence to be his. However, the practice of benevolence depends on oneself alone, and not on others.'

Yen Yüan said, 'I should like you to list the items.' The Master said, 'Do not look unless it is in accordance with the rites; do not listen unless it is in accordance with the rites; do not speak unless it is in accordance with the rites; do not move unless it is in accordance with the rites.'

Yen Yüan said, 'Though I am not quick, I shall direct my efforts towards what you have said.'

2. Chung-kung asked about benevolence. The Master said, 'When abroad behave as though you were receiving an important guest. When employing the services of the common people behave as though you were officiating at an important sacrifice. Do not impose on others what you yourself do not desire. In this way you will be free from ill will whether in a state or in a noble family.'

Chung-kung said, 'Though I am not quick, I shall direct my efforts towards what you have said.'

[. . .]

5. Ssu-ma Niu appeared worried, saying, 'All men have brothers. I alone have none.' Tzu-hsia said, 'I have heard it said: life and death are a matter of Destiny; wealth and honour depend on Heaven. The gentleman is reverent and does nothing amiss, is respectful towards others and observant of the rites, and all within the Four Seas are his brothers. What need is there for the gentleman to worry about not having any brothers?'

[. . .]

7. Tzu-kung asked about government. The Master said, 'Give them enough food, give them enough arms, and the common people will have trust in you.'

Tzu-kung said, 'If one had to give up one of these three, which should one give up first?'

'Give up arms.'

Tzu-kung said,' If one had to give up one of the remaining two, which should one give up first?'

'Give up food. Death has always been with us since the beginning of time, but when there is no trust, the common people will have nothing to stand on.'

[...]

9. Duke Ai asked Yu Juo, 'The harvest is bad, and I have not sufficient to cover expenditure. What should I do?'

Yu Juo answered, 'What about taxing the people one part in ten?'

'I do not have sufficient as it is when I tax them two parts in ten. How could I possibly tax them one part in ten?'

'When the people have sufficient, who is there to share your insufficiency? When the people have insufficient, who is there to share your sufficiency?'

[...]

11. Duke Ching of Ch'i asked Confucius about government. Confucius answered, 'Let the ruler be a ruler, the subject a subject, the father a father, the son a son.' The Duke said, 'Splendid! Truly, if the ruler be not a ruler, the subject not a subject, the father not a father, the son not a son, then even if there be grain, would I get to eat it?'

[...]

13. The Master said, 'In hearing litigation, I am no different from any other man. But if you insist on a difference, it is, perhaps, that I try to get the parties not to resort to litigation in the first place.'

14. Tzu-chang asked about government. The Master said, 'Over daily routine do not show weariness, and when there is action to be taken, give of your best.'

15. The Master said, 'The gentleman widely versed in culture but brought back to essentials by the rites can, I suppose, be relied upon not to turn against what he stood for.'

16. The Master said, 'The gentleman helps others to realize what is good in them; he does not help them to realize what is bad in them. The small man does the opposite.'

17. Chi K'ang Tzu asked Confucius about government. Confucius answered, 'To govern (*cheng*) is to correct (*cheng*). If you set an example by being correct, who would dare to remain incorrect?'

18. The prevalence of thieves was a source of trouble to Chi K'ang Tzu who asked the advice of Confucius. Confucius answered, 'If you yourself were not a man of desires, no one would steal even if stealing carried a reward.'[3]

19. Chi K'ang Tzu asked Confucius about government, saying, 'What would you think if, in order to move closer to those who possess the Way, I were to kill those who do not follow the Way?'

Confucius answered, 'In administering your government, what need is there for you to kill? Just desire the good yourself and the common people will be good. The virtue of the gentleman is like wind; the virtue of the small man is like grass. Let the wind blow over the grass and it is sure to bend.'

Book XIII

1. Tzu-lu asked about government. The Master said, 'Encourage the people to work hard by setting an example yourself.' Tzu-lu asked for more. The Master said, 'Do not allow your efforts to slacken.'

2. While he was steward to the Chi Family, Chung-kung asked about government. The Master said, 'Set an example for your officials to follow; show leniency towards minor offenders; and promote men of talent.'

'How does one recognize men of talent to promote?'

The Master said, 'Promote those you do recognize. Do you suppose others will allow those you fail to recognize to be passed over?'

3. Tzu-lu said, 'If the Lord of Wei left the administration (*cheng*) of his state to you, what would you put first?'

The Master said, 'If something has to be put first, it is, perhaps, the rectification (*cheng*) of names.'

Tzu-lu said, 'Is that so? What a roundabout way you take! Why bring rectification in at all?'

The Master said,' Yu, how boorish you are. Where a gentleman is ignorant, one would expect him not to offer any opinion. When names are not correct, what is said will not sound reasonable; when what is said does not sound reasonable, affairs will not culminate in success; when affairs do not culminate in success, rites and music will not flourish; when rites and music do not flourish, punishments will not fit the crimes; when punishments do not fit the crimes, the common people will not know where to put hand and foot. Thus when the gentleman names something, the name is sure to be usable in speech, and when he says something this is sure to be practicable. The thing about the gentleman is that he is anything but casual where speech is concerned.'

[...]

6. The Master said, 'If a man is correct in his own person, then there will be obedience without orders being given; but if he is not correct in his own person, there will not be obedience even though orders are given.'

[...]

10. The Master said, 'If anyone were to employ me, in a year's time I would have brought things to a satisfactory state, and after three years I should have results to show for it.'

11. The Master said, 'How true is the saying that after a state has been ruled for a hundred years by good men it is possible to get the better of cruelty and to do away with killing.'

12. The Master said, 'Even with a true king it is bound to take a generation for benevolence to become a reality.'

13. The Master said, 'If a man manages to make himself correct, what difficulty will there be for him to take part in government? If he cannot make himself correct, what business has he with making others correct?'

[...]

15. Duke Ting asked, 'Is there such a thing as a single saying that can lead a state to prosperity?'

Confucius answered, 'A saying cannot quite do that. There is a saying amongst men: "It is difficult to be a ruler, and it is not easy to be a subject either." If the ruler understands the difficulty of being a ruler, then is this not almost a case of a saying leading the state to prosperity?'

'Is there such a thing as a saying that can lead the state to ruin?'

Confucius answered, 'A saying cannot quite do that. There is a saying amongst men: "I do not at all enjoy being a ruler, except for the fact that no one goes against what I say." If what he says is good and no one goes against him, good. But if what he says is not good and no one goes against him, then is this not almost a case of a saying leading the state to ruin?'

16. The Governor of She asked about government. The Master said, 'Ensure that those who are near are pleased and those who are far away are attracted.'

17. On becoming prefect of Chü Fu, Tzu-hsia asked about government. The Master said, 'Do not be impatient. Do not see only petty gains. If you are impatient, you will not reach your goal. If you see only petty gains, the great tasks will not be accomplished.'

18. The Governor of She said to Confucius, 'In our village there is a man nicknamed "Straight Body". When his father stole a sheep, he gave evidence against him.' Confucius answered, 'In our village those who are straight are quite different. Fathers cover up for their sons, and sons cover up for their fathers. Straightness is to be found in such behaviour.'

19. Fan Ch'ih asked about benevolence. The Master said, 'While at home hold yourself in a respectful attitude; when serving in an official capacity be reverent; when dealing with others do your best. These are qualities that cannot be put aside, even if you go and live among the barbarians.'

20. Tzu-kung asked, 'What must a man be like before he can be said truly to be a Gentleman?' The Master said, 'A man who has a sense of shame in the way he conducts himself and, when sent abroad, does not disgrace the commission of his lord can be said to be a Gentleman.'

'May I ask about the grade below?'

'Someone praised for being a good son in his clan and for being a respectful young man in the village.'

'And the next?'

'A man who insists on keeping his word and seeing his actions through to the end can, perhaps, qualify to come next, even though he shows a stub-born petty-mindedness.'

'What about men who are in public life in the present day?'

The Master said, 'Oh, they are of such limited capacity that they hardly count.'

[...]

26. The Master said, 'The gentleman is at ease without being arrogant; the small man is arrogant without being at ease.'

27. The Master said, 'Unbending strength, re-soluteness, simplicity and reticence are close to benevolence.'

28. Tzu-lu asked, 'What must a man be like before he deserves to be called a Gentleman?' The Master said, 'One who is, on the one hand, earnest and keen and, on the other, genial deserves to be called a Gentleman – earnest and keen amongst friends and genial amongst brothers.'

29. The Master said, 'After a good man has trained the common people for seven years, they should be ready to take up arms.'

30. The Master said, 'To send the common people to war untrained is to throw them away.'

Book XIV

41. The Master said, 'When those above are given to the observance of the rites, the common people will be easy to command.'

42. Tzu-lu asked about the gentleman. The Master said, 'He cultivates himself and thereby achieves reverence.'

'Is that all?'

'He cultivates himself and thereby brings peace and security to his fellow men.'

'Is that all?'

'He cultivates himself and thereby brings peace and security to the people. Even Yao and Shun would have found the task of bringing peace and security to the people taxing.'

Book XV

18. The Master said, 'The gentleman has moral-ity as his basic stuff and by observing the rites puts it into practice, by being modest gives it expres-sion, and by being trustworthy in word brings it to completion. Such is a gentleman indeed!'

[...]

24. Tzu-kung asked, 'Is there a single word which can be a guide to conduct throughout one's life?' The Master said, 'It is perhaps the word "*shu*". Do not impose on others what you your-self do not desire.'

Notes

1 The word here translated as "using oneself as a mea-sure to gauge others" is *shu*, which is sometimes translated as "empathy". This remark of Con-fucius's should be read alongside XV.24, where he formulates a version of the "golden rule" – "Do not impose on others what you yourself do not desire" – in explaining what is meant by *shu*.

2 Yao and Shun were two ancient and revered sage kings.

3 The point of this remark seems to be that Chi K'ang Tzu, a senior official in Lu, would not be plagued by thieves if he himself were not thieving from the poor.

Plato, *Republic*, Book V, 451c–462e, 471c–480a

Introduction

The son of a powerful aristocratic family, Plato (c. 424–c. 348 BCE) was a descendant of the great Athenian lawgiver, Solon (c. 638–558 BCE). Plato's stepfather, Pyrilampes, was an associate of Pericles, architect of Athenian glory in the fifth century. Two of his uncles – Charmides and Critias – were among the "Thirty Tyrants" that Sparta installed in 404 BCE to rule Athens in the wake of its grinding defeat in the Peloponnesian Wars. It would seem, then, that with such an august pedigree, young Plato was destined for a prominent career in politics. And so he might have been had he not fallen under the spell of the short, wooly-haired, snub-nosed philosophical "midwife" and "gadfly," Socrates (470–399 BCE).

It is unreasonable to believe that the execution of Socrates at the hands of the Athenian democracy, together with the humbling of classical Athens that marked Plato's early years had no effect on his political philosophy, though it is difficult to state precisely the nature of that effect. Plato's political philosophy, like his thought on so many topics, is scattered across a number of dialogues where it is woven cryptically into their framing, setting, and mise-en-scènes, as well as into

From Plato, *The Republic of Plato*, 2nd edition, trans. A. Bloom, New York: Basic Books, 1991, pp. 129–42, 150–61 (notes omitted).

the background, the remarks, and the conduct of characters who may or may not represent Plato's own views. Pre-eminent among Plato's political texts, in any case, is the *Politeia* or *Republic*, and so it is from the *Republic* that the following selections illustrating something of Plato's political philosophy are drawn.

The *Republic* was regarded as one of Plato's relatively subordinate texts through much of ancient times and the Middle Ages. Plato's great metaphysical and seemingly more mystical works – *Timaeus* and *Symposium* – were much more attractive to the minds of religiously oriented philosophers of those times, especially Christian philosophers.[1] Even with the revitalization of wider interest in Plato through the work of the Renaissance humanists like Marsilio Ficino (1433–99), attention to the *Republic* remained rather tepid. As modernity advanced, however, *Republic* became more and more central to the Platonic corpus. By the nineteenth century it had become commonly regarded as his definitive work. The *Republic*'s ideal polity ruled by philosopher-kings, its rebuke of imaginative and poetic claims to wisdom, and its overarching argument that it is better to be a good person thought to be bad than a bad person thought to be good have captivated the minds of generations of readers ever since.

Gathered at the port of Piraeus (the site of Athenian democratic resistance), Socrates in the *Republic* addresses a highly charged group of young men – many of whom (as his readers would have well known) would become important players in the political turmoil that gripped Athens as the fifth century came to a tortuous close, some dying in the course of it. After having been playfully detained by them, Socrates confronts the young upstarts with a series of arguments designed to moderate their ambition, to engender an appreciation for how difficult it is to establish a good society, and to educate them about risks awaiting those who would enter the field of political contest.[2]

Socrates argues for a polity ordered neither for the self-interest of the rulers nor on the whims of the many, but instead around objective principles of goodness discerned by dialectical reasoning (especially temperance, honor, wisdom, and harmony). In fleshing out this vision, Socrates advances "three waves" of argument. First, in order to show that rulers should be selected on the basis only of those traits relevant to leadership, Socrates maintains in one of the earliest of such arguments in the Western philosophical tradition that women should rule, along with men. While he does hold onto the idea that the best women are unlikely to be as capable as the best men, Socrates nevertheless advances the crucial claim that the defining differences between men and women are not relevant to the functions of ruling. "Therefore, my friend, there is no practice of a city's governors which belongs to woman because she's woman, or to man because he's man; but the natures [proper for ruling] are scattered alike among both animals" (455d–456b). It is not only, therefore, natural, according to Socrates in the *Republic*, for women to rule; preventing them from ruling is unnatural (456c).

Second, in order to undermine the discord generated by the competing claims upon rulers to serve both their families' interests and the interests of the society, Socrates argues both that rulers should possess no private property of their own (458c) and that they should hold their spouses and children in common – as if the class of rulers were a single family and its personal wealth coextensive with the commonwealth: "Have we any greater evil for a city than what splits it and makes

it many instead of one? Or a greater good than what binds it together and makes it one?" (462b).

Third, and most famously, Socrates argues that philosophers – or those who are genuinely wisest – should rule. In other words, the best capacity for rule is to be found not simply among those who have disciplined and pleasing characters, or those who command the military power most ably. Rather, those who possess the best and truest understanding of goodness and reality are best able to direct the social order.

Of course, the *Republic*'s vision of an ideal society has seemed less than ideal to many, too. Sir Karl R. Popper (1902–94) famously rooted many of the totalitarian ideologies that have plagued modernity in Plato's hierarchical authoritarian society – a place where a group of intellectuals, believing it knows how other people should live, imposes its philosophical vision upon the rest of society.[3] Indeed, not only does Socrates in *Republic* severely criticize democracy (555b) and describe a natural class hierarchy. In the course of his disquisition, Socrates also advocates eugenics (459aff.), lying to the people for their own good (459d), state censorship and control of the fine arts (377b), and the forced expulsion of recalcitrant elements (540e). Perhaps there is, after all, good reason to read the *Republic*'s political theory with a hermeneutic of suspicion.

Notes

1 Muslim philosophers like al-Farabi (872–950) paid *Republic* more attention.
2 For an elaboration of this view, see Leo Strauss, *The City and Man* (Chicago: University of Chicago Press, 1964) and the interpretive essay accompanying Allan Bloom's edition of *Republic* (see above).
3 K. R. Popper, *The Open Society and Its Enemies*, London: Routledge, 1945. Cf. II.21 of this volume.

Plato, *Republic*

451 c "For human beings born and educated as we described, there is, in my opinion, no right acquisition and use of children and women other than in their following that path along which we first directed them. Presumably we attempted in the argument to establish the men as guardians of a herd."

"Yes."

"So let's follow this up by prescribing the birth and rearing that go along with it and consider whether they suit us or not."

"How?" he said.

"Like this. Do we believe the females of the guardian dogs must guard the things the males guard along with them and hunt with them, and do the rest in common; or must they stay 451 d indoors as though they were incapacitated as a result of bearing and rearing the puppies, while the males work and have all the care of the flock?"

e "Everything in common," he said, "except that we use the female as weaker and the males as stronger."

"Is it possible," I said, "to use any animal for the same things if you don't assign it the same rearing and education?"

"No, it's not possible."

"If, then, we use the women for the same things as the men, they must also be taught the same things."

52 a "Yes."

"Now music and gymnastic were given to the men."

"Yes."

"Then these two arts, and what has to do with war, must be assigned to the women also, and they must be used in the same ways."

"On the basis of what you say," he said, "it's likely."

"Perhaps," I said, "compared to what is habitual, many of the things now being said would look ridiculous if they were to be done as is said."

"Indeed they would," he said.

"What's the most ridiculous thing you see among them?" I said. "Or is it plain that it's the women exercising naked with the men in b the palaestras, not only the young ones, but even the older ones, too, like the old men in the gymnasiums who, when they are wrinkled and not pleasant to the eye, all the same love gymnastic?"

"By Zeus!" he said, "that would look ridiculous in the present state of things."

"Well," I said, "since we've started to speak, we mustn't be afraid of all the jokes – of whatever kind – the wits might make if such a change took c place in gymnastic, in music and, not the least, in the bearing of arms and the riding of horses."

"What you say is right," he said.

"But since we've begun to speak, we must make our way to the rough part of the law, begging these men, not to mind their own business, but to be serious; and reminding them that it is not so long ago that it seemed shameful and ridiculous to the Greeks – as it does now to the many among the barbarians – to see men naked; and that when the Cretans originated the gymnasiums, and then the Lacedaemonians, it was possible for the urbane of the time to make a comedy of all that. Or don't you suppose so?" d

"I do."

"But, I suppose, when it became clear to those who used these practices that to uncover all such things is better than to hide them, then what was ridiculous to the eyes disappeared in the light of what's best as revealed in speeches. And this 452 d showed that he is empty who believes anything is ridiculous other than the bad, and who tries to produce laughter looking to any sight as ridiculous other than the sight of the foolish and the bad; or, again, he who looks seriously to any standard of beauty he sets up other than the e good."

"That's entirely certain," he said.

"Mustn't we then first come to an agreement whether these things are possible or not, and give anyone who wants to dispute – whether it's a man who likes to play or one who is serious – the opportunity to dispute whether female human nature can share in common with the nature of 453 a the male class in all deeds or in none at all, or in some things yes and in others no, particularly with respect to war? Wouldn't one who thus made the finest beginning also be likely to make the finest ending?"

"By far," he said.

"Do you want us," I said, "to carry on the dispute and represent those on the other side ourselves so that the opposing argument won't be besieged without defense?"

"Nothing stands in the way," he said. b

"Then, on their behalf, let's say: 'Socrates and Glaucon, there's no need for others to dispute with you. For at the beginning of the settlement of the city you were founding, you yourselves agreed that each one must mind his own business according to nature.'"

"I suppose we did agree. Of course."

c   "'Can it be that a woman doesn't differ in her nature very much from a man?'"

"But of course she differs."

"'Then isn't it also fitting to prescribe a different work to each according to its nature?'"

"Certainly."

"'How can it be, then, that you aren't making a mistake now and contradicting yourselves, when you assert that the men and the women must do the same things, although they have a nature that is most distinct?' What have you as an apology in the light of this, you surprising man?"

"On the spur of the moment, it's not very easy," he said. "But I shall beg you, and do beg you, to interpret the argument on our behalf too, whatever it may be."

"This, Glaucon, and many other things of the sort," I said, "foreseeing them long ago, is what

d   I was frightened of, and I shrank from touching the law concerning the possession and rearing of the women and children."

453 d   "By Zeus," he said, "it doesn't seem an easy thing."

"It isn't," I said. "However, it is a fact that whether one falls into a little swimming pool or into the middle of the biggest sea, one nevertheless swims all the same."

"Most certainly."

"Then we too must swim and try to save ourselves from the argument, hoping that some dolphin might take us on his back or for some other unusual rescue."

e   "It seems so," he said.

"Come, then," I said, "let's see if we can find the way out. Now we agree that one nature must practice one thing and a different nature must practice a different thing, and that women and men are different. But at present we are asserting that different natures must practice the same things. Is this the accusation against us?"

"Exactly."

454 a   "Oh, Glaucon," I said, "the power of the contradicting art is grand."

"Why so?"

"Because," I said, "in my opinion, many fall into it even unwillingly and suppose they are not quarreling but discussing, because they are unable to consider what's said by separating it out into its forms. They pursue contradiction in the mere name of what's spoken about, using eristic, not dialectic, with one another."

"This is surely what happens to many," he said. "But this doesn't apply to us too at present, does it?"

"It most certainly does," I said. "At least we run the risk of unwillingly dealing in contradiction."

"How?"

"Following the name alone, we courageously, and eristically, insist that a nature that is not the same must not have the same practices. But we didn't make any sort of consideration of what form of different and same nature, and applying to what, we were distinguishing when we assigned different practices to a different nature and the same ones to the same."

"No," he said, "we didn't consider it."

"Accordingly," I said, "it's permissible, as it seems, for us to ask ourselves whether the nature of the bald and the longhaired is the same or opposite. And, when we agree that it is opposite, if bald men are shoemakers, we won't let the longhaired ones be shoemakers, or if the longhaired ones are, then the others can't be."

"That," he said, "would certainly be ridiculous."

"Is it," I said, "ridiculous for any other reason than that we didn't refer to every sense of same and different nature but were guarding only that form of otherness and likeness which applies to 454 the pursuits themselves? For example, we meant that a man and a woman whose souls are suited for the doctor's art have the same nature. Or don't you suppose so?"

"I do."

"But a man doctor and a man carpenter have different ones?"

"Of course, entirely different."

"Then," I said, "if either the class of men or that of women shows its superiority in some art or other practice, then we'll say that that art must be assigned to it. But if they look as though they differ in this alone, that the female bears and the male mounts, we'll assert that it has not thereby yet been proved that a woman differs from a man with respect to what we're talking about; rather, we'll still suppose that our guardians and their women must practice the same things."

"And rightly," he said.

"After that, won't we bid the man who says the opposite to teach us this very thing – with respect
55 *a* to what art or what practice connected with the organization of a city the nature of a woman and a man is not the same, but rather different?"

"At least that's just."

"Well, now, perhaps another man would also say just what you said a little while ago: that it's not easy to answer adequately on the spur of the moment; but upon consideration, it isn't at all hard."

"Yes, he would say that."

"Do you want us then to beg the man who contradicts in this way to follow us and see if we
b can somehow point out to him that there is no practice relevant to the government of a city that is peculiar to woman?"

"Certainly."

" 'Come, now,' we'll say to him, 'answer. Is this what you meant? Did you distinguish between the man who has a good nature for a thing and another who has no nature for it on these grounds: the one learns something connected with that thing easily, the other with difficulty; the one, starting from slight learning, is able to carry discovery far forward in the field he has learned, while the other, having chanced on a lot of learning and practice, can't even preserve what he learned; and the bodily things give adequate service to the thought of the man with the good nature while they oppose the thought of the other man? Are there any other things than these by which you dis-
c tinguished the man who has a good nature for each discipline from the one who hasn't?' "

"No one," he said, "will assert that there are others."

"Do you know of anything that is practiced by human beings in which the class of men doesn't excel that of women in all these respects? Or
455 *c* shall we draw it out at length by speaking of weaving and the care of baked and boiled dishes – just those activities on which the reputation of
d the female sex is based and where its defeat is most ridiculous of all?"

"As you say," he said, "it's true that the one class is quite dominated in virtually everything, so to speak, by the other. However, many women are better than many men in many things. But, as a whole, it is as you say."

"Therefore, my friend, there is no practice of a city's governors which belongs to woman because she's woman, or to man because he's man; but the natures are scattered alike among both animals; and woman participates according to nature in all practices, and man in all, but in all of them woman is weaker than man."   *e*

"Certainly."

"So, shall we assign all of them to men and none to women?"

"How could we?"

"For I suppose there is, as we shall assert, one woman apt at medicine and another not, one woman apt at music and another unmusical by nature."

"Of course."

"And isn't there then also one apt at gymnastic   456 *a*
and at war, and another unwarlike and no lover of gymnastic?"

"I suppose so."

"And what about this? Is there a lover of wisdom and a hater of wisdom? And one who is spirited and another without spirit?"

"Yes, there are these too."

"There is, therefore, one woman fit for guarding and another not. Or wasn't it a nature of this sort we also selected for the men fit for guarding?"

"Certainly, that was it."

"Men and women, therefore, also have the same nature with respect to guarding a city, except insofar as the one is weaker and the other stronger."

"It looks like it."

"Such women, therefore, must also be chosen   *b*
to have and guard with such men, since they are competent and akin to the men in their nature."

"Certainly."

"And mustn't the same practices be assigned to the same natures?"

"The same."

"Then we have come around full circle to where we were before and agree that it's not against nature to assign music and gymnastic to the women guardians."

"That's entirely certain."   456 *b*

"Then we weren't giving laws that are imposs-ible or like prayers, since the law we were setting down is according to nature. Rather, the way   *c*
things are nowadays proves to be, as it seems, against nature."

"So it seems."

"Weren't we considering whether what we say is possible and best?"

"Yes, we were."

"And that it is possible, then, is agreed?"

"Yes."

"But next it must be agreed that it is best?"

"Plainly."

"In making a woman fit for guarding, one education won't produce men for us and another women, will it, especially since it is dealing with *d* the same nature?"

"No, there will be no other."

"What's your opinion about this?"

"What?"

"Conceiving for yourself that one man is better and another worse? Or do you believe them all to be alike?"

"Not at all."

"In the city we were founding, which do you think will turn out to be better men for us – the guardians who get the education we have described or the shoemakers, educated in shoemaking?"

"What you ask is ridiculous," he said.

"I understand," I said. "And what about this? *e* Aren't they the best among the citizens?"

"By far."

"And what about this? Won't these women be the best of the women?"

"That, too, by far," he said.

"Is there anything better for a city than the coming to be in it of the best possible women and men?"

"There is not."

"And music and gymnastic, brought to bear as 457 *a* we have described, will accomplish this?"

"Of course."

"The law we were setting down is therefore not only possible but also best for a city."

"So it is."

"Then the women guardians must strip, since they'll clothe themselves in virtue instead of robes, and they must take common part in war and the rest of the city's guarding, and must not 457 *a* do other things. But lighter parts of these tasks must be given to the women than the men because of the weakness of the class. And the man *b* who laughs at naked women practicing gymnastic for the sake of the best, 'plucks from his wisdom an unripe fruit for ridicule' and doesn't know – as it seems – at what he laughs or what he does. For this is surely the fairest thing that is said and will be said – the beneficial is fair and the harmful ugly."

"That's entirely certain."

"May we then assert that we are escaping one wave, as it were, in telling about the woman's law, so that we aren't entirely swept away when we lay it down that our guardians, men and women, must share all pursuits in common; rather, in a way the argument is in agreement with itself that it says what is both possible and beneficial?"

"And indeed," he said, "it's not a little wave you're escaping."

"You'll say that it's not a big one either," I said, "when you see the next one."

"Tell me, and let me see it," he said.

"The law that follows this one," I said, "and the others that went before is, as I suppose, this."

"What?"

"All these women are to belong to all these men in common, and no woman is to live privately with any man. And the children, in their turn, will be in common, and neither will a parent know his own offspring, nor a child his parent."

"This one is far bigger than the other," he said, "so far as concerns doubt both as to its possibility and its beneficialness."

"As to whether it is beneficial, at least, I don't suppose it would be disputed that the community of women and the community of children are, if possible, the greatest good," I said. "But I suppose that there would arise a great deal of dispute as to whether they are possible or not."

"There could," he said, "very well be dispute *e* about both."

"You mean that there is a conspiracy of arguments against me," I said. "I thought I would run away from the other argument, if in your opinion it were beneficial; then I would have the one about whether it's possible or not left."

"But you didn't run away unnoticed," he said, "so present an argument for both."

"I must submit to the penalty," I said. "Do me this favor, however. Let me take a holiday like the 458 *a* idle men who are accustomed to feast their minds for themselves when they walk along. And such men, you know, before finding out in what way something they desire can exist, put that question 458 *a* aside so they won't grow weary deliberating about what's possible and not. They set down as given the existence of what they want and at once go on to arrange the rest and enjoy giving a full account of the sort of things they'll do when it has come into being, making yet idler a soul that is already idle. I too am by now soft myself, and *b*

I desire to put off and consider later in what way it is possible; and now, having set it down as possible, I'll consider, if you permit me, how the rulers will arrange these things when they come into being and whether their accomplishment would be most advantageous of all for both the city and the guardians. I'll attempt to consider this with you first, and the other later, if you permit."

"I do permit," he said, "so make your consideration."

"Well, then," I said, "I suppose that if the rulers are to be worthy of the name, and their auxiliaries

c likewise, the latter will be willing to do what they are commanded and the former to command. In some of their commands the rulers will in their turn be obeying the laws; in others – all those we leave to their discretion – they will imitate the laws."

"It's likely," he said.

"Well, then," I said, "you, their lawgiver, just as you selected the men, will hand over the women to them, having selected them in the same way too, with natures that are as similar as possible. And all of them will be together, since they have common houses and mess, with no one privately possessing anything of the kind. And, mixed

d together in gymnastic exercise and the rest of the training, they'll be led by an inner natural necessity to sexual mixing with one another, I suppose. Or am I not, in your opinion, speaking of necessities?"

"Not geometrical but erotic necessities," he said, "which are likely to be more stinging than the others when it comes to persuading and attracting the bulk of the people."

"Very much so," I said. "But, next, Glaucon, to have irregular intercourse with one another, or

e to do anything else of the sort, isn't holy in a city of happy men nor will the rulers allow it."

"No," he said, "it's not just."

"Then it's plain that next we'll make marriages sacred in the highest possible degree. And the most beneficial marriages would be sacred."

"That's entirely certain."

459 a "So then, how will they be most beneficial? Tell me this, Glaucon. For I see hunting dogs and quite a throng of noble cocks in your house. Did you, in the name of Zeus, ever notice something about their marriages and procreation?"

"What?" he said.

459 a "First, although they are all noble, aren't there some among them who are and prove to be best?"

"There are."

"Do you breed from all alike, or are you eager to breed from the best as much as possible?"

"From the best."

"And what about this? From the youngest, or b from the oldest, or as much as possible from those in their prime?"

"From those in their prime."

"And if they weren't so bred, do you believe that the species of birds and that of dogs would be far worse for you?"

"I do," he said.

"And what do you think about horses and the other animals?" I said. "Is it in any way different?"

"That would be strange," he said.

"My, my, dear comrade," I said, "how very much we need eminent rulers after all, if it is also the same with the human species."

"Of course it is," he said, "but why does that c affect the rulers?"

"Because it will be a necessity for them to use many drugs," I said. "Presumably we believe that for bodies not needing drugs, but willing to respond to a prescribed course of life, even a common doctor will do. But, of course, when there is also a need to use drugs, we know there is need of the most courageous doctor."

"True, but to what purpose do you say this?"

"To this," I said. "It's likely that our rulers will have to use a throng of lies and deceptions for the benefit of the ruled. And, of course, we d said that everything of this sort is useful as a form of remedy."

"And we were right," he said.

"Now, it seems it is not the least in marriages and procreations, that this 'right' comes into being."

"How so?"

"On the basis of what has been agreed," I said, "there is a need for the best men to have intercourse as often as possible with the best women, and the reverse for the most ordinary men with the most ordinary women; and the offspring of the former must be reared but not that of the others, if the flock is going to be of the most e eminent quality. And all this must come to pass without being noticed by anyone except the rulers themselves if the guardians' herd is to be as free as possible from faction."

"Quite right," he said.

"So then, certain festivals and sacrifices must 459 e be established by law at which we'll bring the brides and grooms together, and our poets must make

460 *a*   hymns suitable to the marriages that take place. The number of the marriages we'll leave to the rulers in order that they may most nearly preserve the same number of men, taking into consideration wars, diseases, and everything else of the sort; and thus our city will, within the limits of the possible, become neither big nor little."

"Right," he said.

"I suppose certain subtle lots must be fabricated so that the ordinary man will blame chance rather than the rulers for each union."

"Quite so," he said.

b   "And, presumably, along with other prizes and rewards, the privilege of more abundant intercourse with the women must be given to those of the young who are good in war or elsewhere, so that under this pretext the most children will also be sown by such men."

"Right."

"And as the offspring are born, won't they be taken over by the officers established for this purpose – men or women, or both, for presumably the offices are common to women and men – and . . ."

"Yes."

c   "So, I think, they will take the offspring of the good and bring them into the pen to certain nurses who live apart in a certain section of the city. And those of the worse, and any of the others born deformed, they will hide away in an unspeakable and unseen place, as is seemly."

"If," he said, "the guardians' species is going to remain pure."

"Won't they also supervise the nursing, leading the mothers to the pen when they are full with

d   milk, inventing every device so that none will recognize her own, and providing others who do have milk if the mothers themselves are insufficient? And won't they supervise the mothers themselves, seeing to it that they suckle only a moderate time and that the wakeful watching and the rest of the labor are handed over to wet nurses and governesses?"

"It's an easy-going kind of child-bearing for the women guardians, as you tell it," he said.

"As is fitting," I said. "Let's go through the next point we proposed. We said, of course, that the offspring must be born of those in their prime."

"True."

e   "Do you share the opinion that a woman's prime lasts, on the average, twenty years and a man's thirty?"

"Which years?" he said.

"A woman," I said, "beginning with her twen- 460 *e* tieth year, bears for the city up to her fortieth; and a man, beginning from the time when he passes his swiftest prime at running, begets for the city up to his fifty-fifth year."

"Of course," he said, "this is the prime of 461 *a* body and prudence for both."

"Then, if a man who is older than this, or younger, engages in reproduction for the commonwealth, we shall say that it's a fault neither holy nor just. For he begets for the city a child that, if it escapes notice, will come into being without being born under the protection of the sacrifices and prayers which priestesses, priests, and the whole city offer at every marriage to the effect that ever better and more beneficial offspring may come from good and beneficial men. This child is born, rather, under cover of darkness in *b* the company of terrible incontinence."

"Right," he said.

"And the same law applies," I said, "when a man still of the age to beget touches a woman of that age if a ruler has not united them. We'll say he's imposing a bastard, an unauthorized and unconsecrated child, on the city."

"Quite right," he said.

"Now I suppose that when the women and the men are beyond the age of procreation, we will, *c* of course, leave them free to have intercourse with whomsoever they wish, except with a daughter, a mother, the children of their daughters and the ancestors of their mother, and, as for the women, except with a son and a father and the descendants of the one and the ancestors of the other; and all this only after they have been told to be especially careful never to let even a single foetus see the light of day, if one should be conceived, and, if one should force its way, to deal with it on the understanding that there's to be no rearing for such a child."

"That is certainly a sensible statement," he said. "But how will they distinguish one another's *d* fathers and daughters and the others you just mentioned?"

"Not at all," I said. "But of all the children born in the tenth month, and in the seventh, from the day a man becomes a bridegroom, he will call the males sons and the females daughters; and they will call him father; and in the same way, he will call their offspring grandchildren, and they in their turn will call his group grandfathers and grandmothers; and those who were born at the same time their mothers and fathers were procreating they will call sisters and brothers. Thus, as we were just saying, they won't touch one another. The law will grant that brothers and sisters live together if the lot falls out that way and the Pythia concurs."

"Quite right," he said.

"So, Glaucon, the community of women and children for the guardians of your city is of this kind. That it is both consistent with the rest of the regime and by far best, must next be assured by the argument. Or what shall we do?"

"That, by Zeus," he said.

"Isn't the first step toward agreement for us to ask ourselves what we can say is the greatest good in the organization of a city – that good aiming at which the legislator must set down the laws – and what the greatest evil; and then to consider whether what we have just described harmonizes with the track of the good for us and not with that of the evil?"

"By all means," he said.

"Have we any greater evil for a city than what splits it and makes it many instead of one? Or a greater good than what binds it together and makes it one?"

"No, we don't."

"Doesn't the community of pleasure and pain bind it together, when to the greatest extent possible all the citizens alike rejoice and are pained at the same comings into being and perishings?"

"That's entirely certain," he said.

"But the privacy of such things dissolves it, when some are overwhelmed and others overjoyed by the same things happening to the city and those within the city?"

"Of course."

"Doesn't that sort of thing happen when they don't utter such phrases as 'my own' and 'not my own' at the same time in the city, and similarly with respect to 'somebody else's'?"

"Entirely so."

"Is, then, that city in which most say 'my own' and 'not my own' about the same thing, and in the same way, the best governed city?"

"By far."

"Then is that city best governed which is most like a single human being? For example, when one of us wounds a finger, presumably the entire community – that community tying the body together with the soul in a single arrangement under the ruler within it – is aware of the fact, and all of it is in pain as a whole along with the afflicted part; and it is in this sense we say that this human being has a pain in his finger. And does the same argument hold for any other part of a human being, both when it is afflicted by pain and when eased by pleasure?"

"Yes, it does," he said. "And, as to what you ask, the city with the best regime is most like such a human being."

"I suppose, then, that when one of its citizens suffers anything at all, either good or bad, such a city will most of all say that the affected part is its own, and all will share in the joy or the pain."

"Necessarily," he said, "if it has good laws."

[. . .]

"It appears to me that just as two different names are used, war and faction, so two things also exist and the names apply to differences in these two. The two things I mean are, on the one hand, what is one's own and akin, and what is alien, and foreign, on the other. Now the name faction is applied to the hatred of one's own, war to the hatred of the alien."

"What you're saying," he said, "is certainly not off the point."

"Now see whether what I say next is also to the point. I assert that the Greek stock is with respect to itself its own and akin, with respect to the barbaric, foreign and alien."

"Yes," he said, "that is fine."

"Then when Greeks fight with barbarians and barbarians with Greeks, we'll assert they are at war and are enemies by nature, and this hatred must be called war; while when Greeks do any such thing to Greeks, we'll say that they are by nature friends, but in this case Greece is sick and factious, and this kind of hatred must be called faction."

"I, for one," he said, "agree to consider it in that way."

"Now observe," I said, "in what is nowadays understood to be faction, that wherever such a thing occurs and a city is split, if each side wastes the fields and burns the houses of the others, it seems that the faction is a wicked thing and that the members of neither side are lovers of their city. For, otherwise, they would never have dared to ravage their nurse and mother. But it seems to be moderate for the victors to take away the harvest of the vanquished, and to have the frame of mind of men who will be reconciled and not always be at war."

"This frame of mind," he said, "belongs to far tamer men than the other."

"Now what about this?" I said. "Won't the city you are founding be Greek?"

470 e   "It must be," he said.

"Then won't they be good and tame?"

"Very much so."

"And won't they be lovers of the Greeks? Won't they consider Greece their own and hold the common holy places along with the other Greeks?"

"Very much so."

471 a   "Won't they consider differences with Greeks – their kin – to be faction and not even use the name war?"

"Of course."

"And they will have their differences like men who, after all, will be reconciled."

"Most certainly."

"Then they'll correct their opponents in a kindly way, not punishing them with a view to slavery or destruction, acting as correctors, not enemies."

"That's what they'll do," he said.

"Therefore, as Greeks, they won't ravage Greece or burn houses, nor will they agree that in any city all are their enemies – men, women, and children – but that there are always a few enemies who are to blame for the differences. And,

b   on all these grounds, they won't be willing to ravage lands or tear down houses, since the many are friendly; and they'll keep up the quarrel until those to blame are compelled to pay the penalty by the blameless ones who are suffering."

"I for one," he said, "agree that our citizens must behave this way toward their opponents; and toward the barbarians they must behave as the Greeks do now toward one another."

"So, shall we also give this law to the guardians

c   – neither waste countryside nor burn houses?"

"Let it be given," he said. "And this and what went before are fine. But, Socrates, I think that if one were to allow you to speak about this sort of thing, you would never remember what you previously set aside in order to say all this. Is it possible for this regime to come into being, and how is it ever possible? I see that, if it should come into being, everything would be good for the city in which it came into being. And I can tell things that you leave out – namely, that they would be

d   best at fighting their enemies too because they

would least desert one another, these men who recognize each other as brothers, fathers, and sons and who call upon each other using these names. And if the females join in the campaign too, either stationed in the line itself, or in the rear, to frighten the enemies and in case there should ever be any need of help – I know that with all this they would be unbeatable. And I see all the   471 good things that they would have at home and are left out in your account. Take it that I agree that there would be all these things and countless others if this regime should come into being, and don't talk any more about it; rather, let's now only try to persuade ourselves that it is possible and how it is possible, dismissing all the rest."

"All of a sudden," I said, "you have, as it were,   472 assaulted my argument, and you have no sympathy for me and my loitering. Perhaps you don't know that when I've hardly escaped the two waves, you're now bringing the biggest and most difficult, the third wave. When you see and hear it, you'll be quite sympathetic, recognizing that it was, after all, fitting for me to hesitate and be afraid to speak and undertake to consider so paradoxical an argument."

"The more you say such things," he said, "the less we'll let you off from telling how it is possible for this regime to come into being. So speak, and don't waste time."

"Then," I said, "first it should be recalled that we got to this point while seeking what justice and injustice are like."

"Yes, it should," he said. "But what of it?"

"Nothing. But if we find out what justice is like, will we also insist that the just man must not differ at all from justice itself but in every way be such as it is? Or will we be content if he is nearest to it and participates in it more than the others?"

"We'll be content with that," he said.

"It was, therefore, for the sake of a pattern," I said, "that we were seeking both for what justice by itself is like, and for the perfectly just man, if he should come into being, and what he would be like once come into being; and, in their turns, for injustice and the most unjust man. Thus, looking off at what their relationships to happiness and its opposite appear to us to be, we would also be compelled to agree in our own cases that the man who is most like them will have the portion most like theirs. We were not seeking them for the sake of proving that it's possible for these things to come into being."

"What you say is true," he said.

"Do you suppose a painter is any less good who draws a pattern of what the fairest human being would be like and renders everything in the picture adequately, but can't prove that it's also possible that such a man come into being?"

"No, by Zeus, I don't," he said.

"Then, what about this? Weren't we, as we assert, also making a pattern in speech of a good *e* city?"

72 e "Certainly."

"Do you suppose that what we say is any less good on account of our not being able to prove that it is possible to found a city the same as the one in speech?"

"Surely not," he said.

"Well, then, that's the truth of it," I said. "But if then to gratify you I must also strive to prove how and under what condition it would be most possible, grant me the same points again for this proof."

"What points?"

73 a "Can anything be done as it is said? Or is it the nature of acting to attain to less truth than speaking, even if someone doesn't think so? Do you agree that it's so or not?"

"I do agree," he said.

"Then don't compel me necessarily to present it as coming into being in every way in deed as we described it in speech. But if we are able to find that a city could be governed in a way most closely approximating what has been said, say that we've found the possibility of these things com- *b* ing into being on which you insist. Or won't you be content if it turns out this way? I, for my part, would be content."

"I would, too," he said.

"So, next, as it seems, we must try to seek out and demonstrate what is badly done in cities today, and thereby keeps them from being governed in this way, and with what smallest change – preferably one, if not, two, and, if not, the fewest in number and the smallest in power – a city would come to this manner of regime."

c "That's entirely certain," he said.

"Well, then," I said, "with one change – not, however, a small or an easy one, but possible – we can, in my opinion, show that it would be transformed."

"What change?" he said.

"Well here I am," I said, "coming to what we likened to the biggest wave. But it shall be said

regardless, even if, exactly like an uproarious wave, it's going to drown me in laughter and ill repute. Consider what I am going to say."

"Speak," he said.

"Unless," I said, "the philosophers rule as kings or those now called kings and chiefs gen- *d* uinely and adequately philosophize, and political power and philosophy coincide in the same place, while the many natures now making their way to either apart from the other are by neces- sity excluded, there is no rest from ills for the cities, my dear Glaucon, nor I think for human kind, nor will the regime we have now described in speech ever come forth from nature, insofar as *473 e* possible, and see the light of the sun. This is what for so long was causing my hesitation to speak: seeing how very paradoxical it would be to say. For it is hard to see that in no other city would there be private or public happiness."

And he said, "Socrates, what a phrase and argument you have let burst out. Now that it's said, you can believe that very many men, and not ordinary ones, will on the spot throw off their *474 a* clothes, and stripped for action, taking hold of whatever weapon falls under the hand of each, run full speed at you to do wonderful deeds. If you don't defend yourself with speech and get away, you'll really pay the penalty in scorn."

"Isn't it you," I said, "that's responsible for this happening to me?"

"And it's a fine thing I'm doing," he said. "But no, I won't betray you, and I'll defend you with what I can. I can provide good will and encour- agement; and perhaps I would answer you more suitably than another. And so, with the assurance *b* of such support, try to show the disbelievers that it is as *you* say."

"It must be tried," I said, "especially since you offer so great an alliance. It's necessary, in my opinion, if we are somehow going to get away from the men you speak of, to distinguish for them whom we mean when we dare to assert the philosophers must rule. Thus, when they have come plainly to light, one will be able to defend oneself, showing that it is by nature fitting for them *c* both to engage in philosophy and to lead a city, and for the rest not to engage in philosophy and to follow the leader."

"It would be high time," he said, "to distinguish them."

"Come, now, follow me here, if we are some- how or other to set it forth adequately."

"Lead," he said.

"Will you need to be reminded," I said, "or do you remember that when we say a man loves something, if it is rightly said of him, he mustn't show a love for one part of it and not for another, but must cherish all of it?"

d "I need reminding, as it seems," he said. "For I scarcely understand."

"It was proper for another, Glaucon, to say what you're saying," I said. "But it's not proper for an erotic man to forget that all boys in the bloom of youth in one way or another put their sting in an erotic lover of boys and arouse him; all seem worthy of attention and delight. Or don't you people behave that way with the fair? You praise the boy with a snub nose by calling him

474 *d* 'cute'; the hook-nose of another you say is 'kingly';
e and the boy between these two is 'well proportioned'; the dark look 'manly'; and the white are 'children of gods.' And as for the 'honey-colored,' do you suppose their very name is the work of anyone other than a lover who renders sallowness endearing and easily puts up with it if it accompanies the bloom of youth? And, in a word, you people take advantage of every excuse and employ any expression so as to reject none of those who

475 *a* glow with the bloom of youth."

"If you want to point to me while you speak about what erotic men do," he said, "I agree for the sake of the argument."

"And what about this?" I said. "Don't you see wine-lovers doing the same thing? Do they delight in every kind of wine, and on every pretext?"

"Indeed, they do."

"And further, I suppose you see that lovers of honor, if they can't become generals, are lieutenants, and if they can't be honored by greater and more august men, are content to be honored

b by lesser and more ordinary men because they are desirers of honor as a whole."

"That's certainly the case."

"Then affirm this or deny it: when we say a man is a desirer of something, will we assert that he desires all of that form, or one part of it and not another?"

"All," he said.

"Won't we also then assert that the philosopher is a desirer of wisdom, not of one part and not another, but of all of it?"

"True."

"We'll deny, therefore, that the one who's finicky about his learning, especially when he's young and doesn't yet have an account of what's *c* useful and not, is a lover of learning or a philosopher, just as we say that the man who's finicky about his food isn't hungry, doesn't desire food, and isn't a lover of food but a bad eater."

"And we'll be right in denying it."

"But the one who is willing to taste every kind of learning with gusto, and who approaches learning with delight, and is insatiable, we shall justly assert to be a philosopher, won't we?"

And Glaucon said, "Then you'll have many strange ones. For all the lovers of sights are in my *d* opinion what they are because they enjoy learning; and the lovers of hearing would be some of the strangest to include among philosophers, those who would never be willing to go voluntarily to a discussion and such occupations but who – just as though they had hired out their ears for hearing – run around to every chorus at the Dionysia, missing none in the cities or the villages. 475 *d* Will we say that all these men and other learners of such things and the petty arts are philosophers?" *e*

"Not at all," I said, "but they are like philosophers."

"Who do you say are the true ones?" he said.

"The lovers of the sight of the truth," I said.

"And that's right," he said. "But how do you mean it?"

"It wouldn't be at all easy to tell someone else. But you, I suppose, will grant me this."

"What?"

"Since fair is the opposite of ugly, they are two."

"Of course." 476 *a*

"Since they are two, isn't each also one?"

"That is so as well."

"The same argument also applies then to justice and injustice, good and bad, and all the forms; each is itself one, but, by showing up everywhere in a community with actions, bodies, and one another, each is an apparitional many."

"What you say," he said, "is right."

"Well, now," I said, "this is how I separate them out. On one side I put those of whom you were just speaking, the lovers of sights, the lovers of arts, and the practical men; on the other, those whom the argument concerns, whom alone one could rightly call philosophers." *b*

"How do you mean?" he said.

"The lovers of hearing and the lovers of sights, on the one hand," I said, "surely delight in fair sounds and colors and shapes and all that craft makes from such things, but their thought is unable to see and delight in the nature of the fair itself."

"That," he said, "is certainly so."

"Wouldn't, on the other hand, those who are able to approach the fair itself and see it by itself be rare?"

c   "Indeed they would."

"Is the man who holds that there are fair things but doesn't hold that there is beauty itself and who, if someone leads him to the knowledge of it, isn't able to follow – is he, in your opinion, living in a dream or is he awake? Consider it. Doesn't dreaming, whether one is asleep or awake, consist in believing a likeness of something to be not a likeness, but rather the thing itself to which it is like?"

"I, at least," he said, "would say that a man who does that dreams."

"And what about the man who, contrary to this, believes that there is something fair itself and is able to catch sight both of it and of what participates in it, and doesn't believe that what participates is it itself, nor that it itself is what participates – is he, in your opinion, living in a dream or is he awake?"

"He's quite awake," he said.

"Wouldn't we be right in saying that this man's thought, because he knows, is knowledge, while the other's is opinion because he opines?"

"Most certainly."

"What if the man of whom we say that he opines but doesn't know, gets harsh with us and disputes the truth of what we say? Will we have some way to soothe and gently persuade him, while hiding from him that he's not healthy?"

"We surely have to have a way, at least," he said.

"Come, then, and consider what we'll say to him. Or do you want us to question him in this way – saying that if he does know something, it's not begrudged him, but that we would be delighted to see he knows something – but tell us this: Does the man who knows, know something or nothing? You answer me on his behalf."

"I'll answer," he said, "that he knows something."

"Is it something that *is* or *is not*?"

"That *is*. How could what *is not* be known at all?"

"So, do we have an adequate grasp of the fact – even if we should consider it in many ways – that what *is* entirely, is entirely knowable; and what in no way *is*, is in every way unknowable?"

"Most adequate."

"All right. Now if there were something such as both to be and not to be, wouldn't it lie between what purely and simply *is* and what in no way *is*?"

"Yes, it would be between."

"Since knowledge depended on what *is* and ignorance necessarily on what *is not*, mustn't we also seek something between ignorance and knowledge that depends on that which is in between, if there is in fact any such thing?"

"Most certainly."

"Do we say opinion is something?"

"Of course."

"A power different from knowledge or the same?"

"Different."

"Then opinion is dependent on one thing and knowledge on another, each according to its own power."

"That's so."

"Doesn't knowledge naturally depend on what *is*, to know of what *is* that it is and how it is? However, in my opinion, it's necessary to make this distinction first."

"What distinction?"

"We will assert that powers are a certain class of beings by means of which we are capable of what we are capable, and also everything else is capable of whatever it is capable. For example, I say sight and hearing are powers, if perchance you understand the form of which I wish to speak."

"I do understand," he said.

"Now listen to how they look to me. In a power I see no color or shape or anything of the sort such as I see in many other things to which I look when I distinguish one thing from another for myself. With a power I look only to this – on what it depends and what it accomplishes; and it is on this basis that I come to call each of the powers a power; and that which depends on the same thing and accomplishes the same thing, I call the same power, and that which depends on something else and accomplishes something else, I call a different power. What about you? What do you do?"

"The same," he said.

"Now, you best of men, come back here to knowledge again. Do you say it's some kind of power, or in what class do you put it?"

"In this one," he said, "as the most vigorous of all powers."

e   "And what about opinion? Is it among the powers, or shall we refer it to some other form?"

"Not at all," he said. "For that by which we are capable of opining is nothing other than opinion."

"But just a little while ago you agreed that knowledge and opinion are not the same."

"How," he said, "could any intelligent man count that which doesn't make mistakes the same as that which does?"

478 *a*   "Fine," I said, "and we plainly agree that opinion is different from knowledge."

"Yes, it is different."

"Since each is capable of something different, are they, therefore, naturally dependent on different things?"

"Necessarily."

"Knowledge is presumably dependent on what *is*, to know of what *is* that it is and how it is?"

"Yes."

"While opinion, we say, opines."

"Yes."

"The same thing that knowledge knows? And will the knowable and the opinable be the same? Or is that impossible?"

"On the basis of what's been agreed to, it's impossible," he said. "If different powers are naturally dependent on different things and both

478 *b*   are powers – opinion and knowledge – and each is, as we say, different, then on this basis it's not admissible that the knowable and the opinable be the same."

"If what *is*, is knowable, then wouldn't something other than that which *is* be opinable?"

"Yes, it would be something other."

"Then does it opine what *is not*? Or is it also impossible to opine what *is not*? Think about it. Doesn't the man who opines refer his opinion to something? Or is it possible to opine, but to opine nothing?"

"No, it's impossible."

"The man who opines, opines some one thing?"

"Yes."

"But further, that which *is not* could not with any correctness be addressed as some one thing

c   but rather nothing at all."

"Certainly."

"To that which *is not*, we were compelled to assign ignorance, and to that which *is*, knowledge."

"Right," he said.

"Opinion, therefore, opines neither that which *is* nor that which *is not*."

"No, it doesn't."

"Opinion, therefore, would be neither ignorance nor knowledge?"

"It doesn't seem so."

"Is it, then, beyond these, surpassing either knowledge in clarity or ignorance in obscurity?"

"No, it is neither."

"Does opinion," I said, "look darker than knowledge to you and brighter than ignorance?"

"Very much so," he said.

"And does it lie within the limits set by these   *d* two?"

"Yes."

"Opinion, therefore, would be between the two."

"That's entirely certain."

"Weren't we saying before that if something should come to light as what *is* and what *is not* at the same time, it lies between that which purely and simply *is* and that which in every way is *not*, and that neither knowledge nor ignorance will depend on it, but that which in its turn comes to light between ignorance and knowledge?"

"Right."

"And now it is just that which we call opinion that has come to light between them."

"Yes, that is what has come to light."

"Hence, as it seems, it would remain for us to   478 *e* find what participates in both – in *to be* and *not to be* – and could not correctly be addressed as either purely and simply, so that, if it comes to light, we can justly address it as the opinable, thus assigning the extremes to the extremes and that which is in between to that which is in between. Isn't that so?"

"Yes, it is."

"Now, with this taken for granted, let him tell me, I shall say, and let him answer – that good   479 *a* man who doesn't believe that there is anything fair in itself and an *idea* of the beautiful itself, which always stays the same in all respects, but does hold that there are many fair things, this lover of sights who can in no way endure it if anyone asserts the fair is one and the just is one and so on with the rest. 'Now, of these many fair things, you best of men,' we'll say, 'is there any that won't also look ugly? And of the just, any that won't look unjust? And of the holy, any that won't look unholy?'"

"No," he said, "but it's necessary that they   *b* look somehow both fair and ugly, and so it is with all the others you ask about."

"And what about the many doubles? Do they look any less half than double?"

"No."

"And, then, the things that we would assert to be big and little, light and heavy – will they be addressed by these names any more than by the opposites of these names?"

"No," he said, "each will always have something of both."

"Then is each of the several manys what one asserts it to be any more than it is not what one asserts it to be?"

c "They are like the ambiguous jokes at feasts," he said, "and the children's riddle about the eunuch, about his hitting the bat – with what and on what he struck it. For the manys are also ambiguous, and it's not possible to think of them fixedly as either being or not being, or as both or neither."

"Can you do anything with them?" I said. "Or could you find a finer place to put them than between being and not to be? For presumably nothing darker than not-being will come to light so that something could *not be* more than it; and nothing brighter than being will come to light so d that something could *be* more than it."

"Very true," he said.

"Then we have found, as it seems, that the many beliefs of the many about what's fair and about the other things roll around somewhere between not-being and being purely and simply."

"Yes, we have found that."

479 d "And we agreed beforehand that, if any such thing should come to light, it must be called opinable but not knowable, the wanderer between, seized by the power between."

"Yes, we did agree."

"And, as for those who look at many fair things   e but don't see the fair itself and aren't even able to follow another who leads them to it, and many just things but not justice itself, and so on with all the rest, we'll assert that they opine all these things but know nothing of what they opine."

"Necessarily," he said.

"And what about those who look at each thing itself – at the things that are always the same in all respects? Won't we say that they know and don't opine?"

"That too is necessary."

"Won't we assert that these men delight in and love that on which knowledge depends, and the others that on which opinion depends? Or   480 a don't we remember that we were saying that they love and look at fair sounds and colors and such things but can't even endure the fact that the fair itself is something?"

"Yes, we do remember."

"So, will we strike a false note in calling them lovers of opinion rather than lovers of wisdom? And will they be very angry with us if we speak this way?"

"No," he said, "that is, if they are persuaded by me. For it's not lawful to be harsh with what's true."

"Must we, therefore, call philosophers rather than lovers of opinion those who delight in each thing that is itself?"

"That's entirely certain."

5

Aristotle, *Politics* I, II: 1–6, VII: 14–15

Introduction

Aristotle of Stagira (384–322 BCE) was not only, of course, Plato's student; he was also one of the Western philosophical traditions' most influential thinkers. In this selection, however, Aristotle argues for a conception of the state that is difficult for many contemporary minds to swallow – namely, that the state or political order is natural to human beings. It is, in fact, only within the political community, according to Aristotle, that human beings can flourish most fully and achieve their highest good. Moreover, Aristotle maintains, in an exquisitely provocative remark, that the state is actually prior to the family – that it is indeed prior to the individual, as well. What on Earth can Aristotle have meant by this perplexing claim?

In the first place, it is important to keep in mind that Aristotle is deeply committed to the idea that human beings possess an abiding nature that defines them "essentially" as "what they are." This essential nature for Aristotle is profoundly social, an idea that would influence later political philosophers as different as David Hume (V.13) and Karl Marx (V.19). Later thinkers Aristotle influenced, however, would likely not follow him in his

From Aristotle, *Politica*, trans. B. Jowett in R. McKeon, ed., *The Basic Works of Aristotle*, New York: Random House, 1941, pp. 1127–58, 1296–1301 (some notes omitted).

explication of that essentially social nature. For Aristotle maintains that individual human beings possess naturally, in addition to material bodies, tripartite immaterial soul-minds (*psychē*) somehow rooted in the immaterial "form" (*ēidos* or *morphos*) of human beings. The most basic part of the human *psychē* Aristotle calls "vegetative," comprising those dimensions devoted simply to maintaining life – e.g. respiration and alimentation. Second, the *psychē* is capable of "appetitive" functions, including sensation, emotion, passion, feeling, and desire. The social nature of the appetitive *psychē* inclines human beings to form and sustain families and kinship networks, as well as small-scale political entities like villages. "A social instinct," says Aristotle, "is implanted in all men by nature" (1253a29).

This view of human nature, of course, has been dramatically rejected by Thomas Hobbes (V.10) and by the more contemporary political philosophers who fancy themselves "realists." Hobbes portrays human beings as naturally asocial (indeed anti-social) beings, for whom social and political association is mere artifice, a technology produced by calculating individuals to serve self-regarding individual desires. But a curious confirmation of Aristotle's view has come from another important stream of modern thinking. Despite the hostility of modern biology to Aristotelian ideas of fixed "forms," genera, and species, Aristotle's theory of natural sociability has found some validation in the recent work of evolutionary theorists who have argued that social inclinations among human beings may have served the evolutionary interests of biological fitness and survival.[1]

John Locke's (V.11) rendering of human existence before the formation of the state also portrays human beings as social creatures existing in familial and small social units. But Locke's political theory departs from Aristotle's in precisely the same manner that modern physics departs from one of the key doctrines of its Aristotelian predecessor – its rejection of the idea of a distinctive *telos* ("final cause" or "final end") for human beings. For thinkers like Locke and those, like Thomas Paine (V.16), who followed him, the state is constructed largely to serve a negative function. That is, the state is created to prevent people from transgressing each other's rights to liberty, property, and personal security. Accordingly, the state's principal function under this view is to prohibit people from doing bad so that on their own, independently of the state, they can achieve something good of their own determination.

For Aristotle, however, the goods of human existence are intimately related to the perfections of human nature. In other words, the realization of those perfections – those excellences, those virtues of human nature – defines the ends or *telē* of human life. And humans are naturally inclined to seek those goods. Crucially for Aristotle, however, human excellences comprise not only the perfections of the second dimension of *psychē* – of human sociability grounded in passion, emotion, and appetite. Human excellence also includes the excellences of the *psychē*'s third dimension, the intellect. This third dimension of *psychē* is, in fact, the most important, because it is the intellect and its perfections that are distinctive to the human essence. That is, it is only through the realization of the perfections of the intellect that human beings can most fully realize their distinctive potential and become most fully what they are.[2]

But here's the rub: for Aristotle, neither the ends of the appetites nor of the intellect can be achieved without the positive support of the political order. The regulations and customs of political society affect the temperament and character of a state's citizens; but more importantly,

the excellences of the intellect are possible only within the framework of law, or reason become policy, and the other institutions a political community underwrites where the human intellect may become active and flourish. Hobbes and Locke may be right that the political community comes into existence in order to secure human goods, but, says Aristotle, its objective is to promote and perfect them.

It is for this reason that Aristotle maintains that "if all communities aim at some good, the state or political community which is the highest of all, and which embraces all the rest, aims at good in a greater degree than any other, and at the highest good" (I.1, 1252a3). Smaller social units, like families and villages, then, may be enough to secure more basic human goods such as those relevant to the body and its passions. Small social units are not sufficient, however, to serve the ultimate perfections of human life. For this task, larger, more sophisticated polities are required. Moreover, because (a) it is the natural ends of the intellect that require the construction of specific social political orders (and not the prior social-political order that constructs the intellect) and because (b) the intellect's ends are more important than those of the passions or of the body, the state for Aristotle is prior to (more fundamental, more deeply connected to what is greatest and most distinctive about human life than) village, family, and individual.[3]

Notes

1 F. Heylighen, "Evolution, Selfishness and Co-operation; Selfish Memes and the Evolution of Cooperation," *Journal of Ideas*, 2.4 (1992), pp. 70–84; E. O. Wilson, *Sociobiology: The New Synthesis*, Cambridge, MA: Belknap Press, 2000, pp. 106–29, 242–55.

2 T. Aquinas, *Commentary on Aristotle's Politics*, trans. R. J. Regan, Indianapolis, IN: Hackett Publishing Co., 2007, pp. 4–19.

3 P. Simpson, *A Philosophical Commentary on the Politics of Aristotle*, Chapel Hill: University of North Carolina Press, 1998.

Aristotle, *Politics*

Book I

1252ᵃ 1 Every state is a community of some kind, and every community is established with a view to some good; for mankind always act in order to obtain that which they think good. But, if all communities aim at some good, the state or political community, which is the highest of all, and which embraces all the rest, aims at good in a greater degree than any other, and at the highest good.

Some people think that the qualifications of a statesman, king, householder, and master are the same, and that they differ, not in kind, but only in the number of their subjects. For example, the ruler over a few is called a master; over more, the manager of a household; over a still larger number, a statesman or king, as if there were no difference between a great household and a small state. The distinction which is made between the king and the statesman is as follows: When the government is personal, the ruler is a king; when, according to the rules of the political science, the citizens rule and are ruled in turn, then he is called a statesman.

But all this is a mistake; for governments differ in kind, as will be evident to any one who considers the matter according to the method which has hitherto guided us. As in other departments of science, so in politics, the compound should always be resolved into the simple elements or least parts of the whole. We must therefore look at the elements of which the state is composed, in order that we may see in what the different kinds of rule differ from one another, and whether any scientific result can be attained about each one of them.

2 He who thus considers things in their first growth and origin, whether a state or anything else, will obtain the clearest view of them. In the first place there must be a union of those who cannot exist without each other; namely, of male and female, that the race may continue (and this is a union which is formed, not of deliberate purpose, but because, in common with other animals and with plants, mankind have a natural desire to leave behind them an image of themselves), and of natural ruler and subject, that both may be preserved. For that which can foresee by the exercise of mind is by nature intended to be lord and master, and that which can with its body give effect to such foresight is a subject, and by nature a slave; hence master and slave have the same interest. Now nature has distinguished between the female and the slave. For she is not niggardly, like the smith who fashions the Delphian knife for many uses; she makes each thing for a single use, and every instrument is best made when intended for one and not for many uses. But among barbarians no distinction is made between women and slaves, because there is no natural ruler among them: they are a community of slaves, male and female. Wherefore the poets say –

'It is meet that Hellenes should rule over barbarians';

as if they thought that the barbarian and the slave were by nature one.

Out of these two relationships between man and woman, master and slave, the first thing to arise is the family, and Hesiod is right when he says –

'First house and wife and an ox for the plough',

for the ox is the poor man's slave. The family is the association establbished by nature for the supply of men's everyday wants, and the members of it are called by Charondas 'companions of the cupboard', and by Epimenides the Cretan, 'companions of the manger.' But when several families are united, and the association aims at something more than the supply of daily needs, the first society to be formed is the village. And the most natural form of the village appears to be that of a colony from the family, composed of the children and grandchildren, who are said to be suckled with the same milk'. And this is the reason why Hellenic states were originally governed by kings; because the Hellenes were under royal rule before they came together, as the barbarians still are. Every family is ruled by the eldest, and therefore in the colonies of the family the kingly form of government prevailed because they were of the same blood. As Homer says:*

'Each one gives law to his children and to his wives.'

For they lived dispersedly, as was the manner in ancient times. Wherefore men say that the Gods

1252ᵇ

---

* *Odyssey* ix. 114, quoted by Plato, *Laws*, 680 B, and in *Nicomachean Ethics* x 1180ᵃ 28.

have a king, because they themselves either are or were in ancient times under the rule of a king. For they imagine, not only the forms of the Gods, but their ways of life to be like their own.

When several villages are united in a single complete community, large enough to be nearly or quite self-sufficing, the state comes into existence, originating in the bare needs of life, and continuing in existence for the sake of a good life. And therefore, if the earlier forms of society are natural, so is the state, for it is the end of them, and the nature of a thing is its end. For what each thing is when fully developed, we call its nature, whether we are speaking of a man, a horse, or a family. Besides, the final cause and end of a thing is the best, and to be self-sufficing is the end and the best.

1253ᵃ

Hence it is evident that the state is a creation of nature, and that man is by nature a political animal. And he who by nature and not by mere accident is without a state, is either a bad man or above humanity; he is like the

'Tribeless, lawless, heartless one,'

whom Homer denounces – the natural outcast is forthwith a lover of war; he may be compared to an isolated piece at draughts.

Now, that man is more of a political animal than bees or any other gregarious animals is evident. Nature, as we often say, makes nothing in vain, and man is the only animal whom she has endowed with the gift of speech. And whereas mere voice is but an indication of pleasure or pain, and is therefore found in other animals (for their nature attains to the perception of pleasure and pain and the intimation of them to one another, and no further), the power of speech is intended to set forth the expedient and inexpedient, and therefore likewise the just and the unjust. And it is a characteristic of man that he alone has any sense of good and evil, of just and unjust, and the like, and the association of living beings who have this sense makes a family and a state.

Further, the state is by nature clearly prior to the family and to the individual, since the whole is of necessity prior to the part; for example, if the whole body be destroyed, there will be no foot or hand, except in an equivocal sense, as we might speak of a stone hand; for when destroyed the hand will be no better than that. But things are defined by their working and power; and we

ought not to say that they are the same when they no longer have their proper quality, but only that they have the same name. The proof that the state is a creation of nature and prior to the individual is that the individual, when isolated, is not self-sufficing; and therefore he is like a part in relation to the whole. But he who is unable to live in society, or who has no need because he is sufficient for himself, must be either a beast or a god: he is no part of a state. A social instinct is implanted in all men by nature, and yet he who first founded the state was the greatest of benefactors. For man, when perfected, is the best of animals, but, when separated from law and justice, he is the worst of all; since armed injustice is the more dangerous, and he is equipped at birth with arms, meant to be used by intelligence and virtue, which he may use for the worst ends. Wherefore, if he have not virtue, he is the most unholy and the most savage of animals, and the most full of lust and gluttony. But justice is the bond of men in states, for the administration of justice, which is the determination of what is just, is the principle of order in political society.

3 Seeing then that the state is made up of households, before speaking of the state we must speak of the management of the household. The parts of household management correspond to the persons who compose the household, and a complete household consists of slaves and freemen. Now we should begin by examining everything in its fewest possible elements; and the first and fewest possible parts of a family are master and slave, husband and wife, father and children. We have therefore to consider what each of these three relations is and ought to be: – I mean the relation of master and servant, the marriage relation (the conjunction of man and wife has no name of its own), and thirdly, the procreative relation (this also has no proper name). And there is another element of a household, the so-called art of getting wealth, which, according to some, is identical with household management, according to others, a principal part of it; the nature of this art will also have to be considered by us.

1253ᵇ

Let us first speak of master and slave, looking to the needs of practical life and also seeking to attain some better theory of their relation than exists at present. For some are of opinion that the rule of a master is a science, and that the management of a household, and the mastership of slaves, and the political and royal rule, as I was saying at the outset, are all the same. Others affirm that the rule of a master over slaves is contrary to nature, and that the distinction between slave and freeman exists by law only, and not by nature; and being an interference with nature is therefore unjust.

4 Property is a part of the household, and the art of acquiring property is a part of the art of managing the household; for no man can live well, or indeed live at all, unless he be provided with necessaries. And as in the arts which have a definite sphere the workers must have their own proper instruments for the accomplishment of their work, so it is in the management of a household. Now instruments are of various sorts; some are living, others lifeless; in the rudder, the pilot of a ship has a lifeless, in the look-out man, a living instrument; for in the arts the servant is a kind of instrument. Thus, too, a possession is an instrument for maintaining life. And so, in the arrangement of the family, a slave is a living possession, and property a number of such instruments; and the servant is himself an instrument which takes precedence of all other instruments. For if every instrument could accomplish its own work, obeying or anticipating the will of others, like the statues of Daedalus, or the tripods of Hephaestus, which, says the poet,

'of their own accord entered the assembly of the Gods';

if, in like manner, the shuttle would weave and the plectrum touch the lyre without a hand to guide them, chief workmen would not want servants, nor masters slaves. Here, however, another distinction must be drawn; the instruments commonly so called are instruments of production, whilst a possession is an instrument of action. The shuttle, for example, is not only of use; but something else is made by it, whereas of a garment or of a bed there is only the use. Further, as production and action are different in kind, and both require instruments, the instruments which they employ must likewise differ in kind. But life is action and not production, and therefore the slave is the minister of action. Again, a possession is spoken of as a part is spoken of; for the part is not only a part of something else, but wholly belongs to it; and this is also true of a possession.

1254ᵃ

The master is only the master of the slave; he does not belong to him, whereas the slave is not only the slave of his master, but wholly belongs to him. Hence we see what is the nature and office of a slave; he who is by nature not his own but another's man, is by nature a slave; and he may be said to be another's man who, being a human being, is also a possession. And a possession may be defined as an instrument of action, separable from the possessor.

5 But is there any one thus intended by nature to be a slave, and for whom such a condition is expedient and right, or rather is not all slavery a violation of nature?

There is no difficulty in answering this question, on grounds both of reason and of fact. For that some should rule and others be ruled is a thing not only necessary, but expedient; from the hour of their birth, some are marked out for subjection, others for rule.

And there are many kinds both of rulers and subjects (and that rule is the better which is exercised over better subjects – for example, to rule over men is better than to rule over wild beasts; for the work is better which is executed by better workmen, and where one man rules and another is ruled, they may be said to have a work); for in all things which form a composite whole and which are made up of parts, whether continuous or discrete, a distinction between the ruling and the subject element comes to light. Such a duality exists in living creatures, but not in them only; it originates in the constitution of the universe; even in things which have no life there is a ruling principle, as in a musical mode. But we are wandering from the subject. We will therefore restrict ourselves to the living creature, which, in the first place, consists of soul and body: and of these two, the one is by nature the ruler, and the other the subject. But then we must look for the intentions of nature in things which retain their nature, and not in things which are corrupted. And therefore we must study the man who is in the most perfect state both of body and soul, for in him we shall see the true relation of the two; although in bad or corrupted natures the body will often appear to rule over 1254ᵇ the soul, because they are in an evil and unnatural condition. At all events we may firstly observe in living creatures both a despotical and a constitutional rule; for the soul rules the body with a despotical rule, whereas the intellect rules the appetites with a constitutional and royal rule. And it is clear that the rule of the soul over the body, and of the mind and the rational element over the passionate, is natural and expedient; whereas the equality of the two or the rule of the inferior is always hurtful. The same holds good of animals in relation to men; for tame animals have a better nature than wild, and all tame animals are better off when they are ruled by man; for then they are preserved. Again, the male is by nature superior, and the female inferior; and the one rules, and the other is ruled; this principle, of necessity, extends to all mankind. Where then there is such a difference as that between soul and body, or between men and animals (as in the case of those whose business is to use their body, and who can do nothing better), the lower sort are by nature slaves, and it is better for them as for all inferiors that they should be under the rule of a master. For he who can be, and therefore is, another's, and he who participates in rational principle enough to apprehend, but not to have, such a principle, is a slave by nature. Whereas the lower animals cannot even apprehend a principle; they obey their instincts. And indeed the use made of slaves and of tame animals is not very different; for both with their bodies minister to the needs of life. Nature would like to distinguish between the bodies of freemen and slaves, making the one strong for servile labour, the other upright, and although useless for such services, useful for political life in the arts both of war and peace. But the opposite often happens – that some have the souls and others have the bodies of freemen. And doubtless if men differed from one another in the mere forms of their bodies as much as the statues of the Gods do from men, all would acknowledge that the inferior class should be slaves of the superior. And if this is true of the body, how much more just that a similar distinction should exist in the soul? but the beauty of the body is seen, whereas the beauty of the soul is not seen. It is clear, then, that some men are by nature free, and others slaves, and that for these latter slavery is both expedient and right.

6 But that those who take the opposite view have in a certain way right on their side, may be easily seen. For the words slavery and slave are used in two senses. There is a slave or slavery by law

as well as by nature. The law of which I speak is a sort of convention – the law by which whatever is taken in war is supposed to belong to the victors. But this right many jurists impeach, as they would an orator who brought forward an unconstitutional measure: they detest the notion that, because one man has the power of doing violence and is superior in brute strength, another shall be his slave and subject. Even among philosophers there is a difference of opinion. The origin of the dispute, and what makes the views invade each other's territory, is as follows: in some sense virtue, when furnished with means, has actually the greatest power of exercising force: and as superior power is only found where there is superior excellence of some kind, power seems to imply virtue, and the dispute to be simply one about justice (for it is due to one party identifying justice with goodwill, while the other identifies it with the mere rule of the stronger). If these views are thus set out separately, the other views have no force or plausibility against the view that the superior in virtue ought to rule, or be master. Others, clinging, as they think, simply to a principle of justice (for law and custom are a sort of justice), assume that slavery in accordance with the custom of war is justified by law, but at the same moment they deny this. For what if the cause of the war be unjust? And again, no one would ever say that he is a slave who is unworthy to be a slave. Were this the case, men of the highest rank would be slaves and the children of slaves if they or their parents chance to have been taken captive and sold. Wherefore Hellenes do not like to call Hellenes slaves, but confine the term to barbarians. Yet, in using this language, they really mean the natural slave of whom we spoke at first;* for it must be admitted that some are slaves everywhere, others nowhere. The same principle applies to nobility. Hellenes regard themselves as noble everywhere, and not only in their own country, but they deem the barbarians noble only when at home, thereby implying that there are two sorts of nobility and freedom, the one absolute, the other relative. The Helen of Theodectes says:

'Who would presume to call me servant who am on both sides sprung from the stem of the Gods?'

1255ᵃ

* Chapter 5.

What does this mean but that they distinguish freedom and slavery, noble and humble birth, by
1255b the two principles of good and evil? They think that as men and animals beget men and animals, so from good men a good man springs. But this is what nature, though she may intend it, cannot always accomplish.

We see then that there is some foundation for this difference of opinion, and that all are not either slaves by nature or freemen by nature, and also that there is in some cases a marked distinction between the two classes, rendering it expedient and right for the one to be slaves and the others to be masters: the one practising obedience, the others exercising the authority and lordship which nature intended them to have. The abuse of this authority is injurious to both; for the interests of part and whole, of body and soul, are the same, and the slave is a part of the master, a living but separated part of his bodily frame. Hence, where the relation of master and slave between them is natural they are friends and have a common interest, but where it rests merely on law and force the reverse is true.

7 The previous remarks are quite enough to show that the rule of a master is not a constitutional rule, and that all the different kinds of rule are not, as some affirm, the same with each other.* For there is one rule exercised over subjects who are by nature free, another over subjects who are by nature slaves. The rule of a household is a monarchy, for every house is under one head: whereas constitutional rule is a government of freemen and equals. The master is not called a master because he has science,† but because he is of a certain character, and the same remark applies to the slave and the freeman. Still there may be a science for the master and a science for the slave. The science of the slave would be such as the man of Syracuse taught, who made money by instructing slaves in their ordinary duties. And such a knowledge may be carried further, so as to include cookery and similar menial arts. For some duties are of the more necessary, others of the more honourable sort; as the proverb says, 'slave before slave, master before master'. But all such branches of knowledge are servile. There is likewise a science of the master, which teaches the use of slaves; for the master as such is concerned, not with the acquisition, but with the use of them. Yet this so-called science is not anything great or wonderful; for the master need only know how to order that which the slave must know how to execute. Hence those who are in a position which places them above toil have stewards who attend to their households while they occupy themselves with philosophy or with politics. But the art of acquiring slaves, I mean of justly acquiring them, differs both from the art of the master and the art of the slave, being a species of hunting or war. Enough of the distinction between master and slave.

8 Let us now inquire into property generally, and 1256a
into the art of getting wealth, in accordance with our usual method,‡ for a slave has been shown§ to be a part of property. The first question is whether the art of getting wealth is the same with the art of managing a household or a part of it, or instrumental to it; and if the last, whether in the way that the art of making shuttles is instrumental to the art of weaving, or in the way that the casting of bronze is instrumental to the art of the statuary, for they are not instrumental in the same way, but the one provides tools and the other material; and by material I mean the substratum out of which any work is made; thus wool is the material of the weaver, bronze of the statuary. Now it is easy to see that the art of household management is not identical with the art of getting wealth, for the one uses the material which the other provides. For the art which uses household stores can be no other than the art of household management. There is, however, a doubt whether the art of getting wealth is a part of household management or a distinct art. If the getter of wealth has to consider whence wealth and property can be procured, but there are many sorts of property and riches, then are husbandry, and the care and provision of food in general, parts of the wealth-getting art or distinct arts? Again, there are many sorts of food, and therefore there are many kinds of lives both of animals and men; they must all have food, and the differences in their food have made differences in their ways of life. For of beasts, some are gregarious, others are solitary; they live in the way which is best

* Plato, *Statesman* 258 E–259 D.

† *Statesman* 259 C, 293 C.

‡ Cf. 1252a 17.

§ Chapter 4.

adapted to sustain them, accordingly as they are carnivorous or herbivorous or omnivorous: and their habits are determined for them by nature in such a manner that they may obtain with greater facility the food of their choice. But, as different species have different tastes, the same things are not naturally pleasant to all of them; and therefore the lives of carnivorous or herbivorous animals further differ among themselves. In the lives of men too there is a great difference. The laziest are shepherds, who lead an idle life, and get their subsistence without trouble from tame animals; their flocks having to wander from place to place in search of pasture, they are compelled to follow them, cultivating a sort of living farm. Others support themselves by hunting, which is of different kinds. Some, for example, are brigands, others, who dwell near lakes or marshes or rivers or a sea in which there are fish, are fishermen, and others live by the pursuit of birds or wild beasts. The greater number obtain a living from the cultivated fruits of the soil. Such are the modes of subsistence which prevail among those whose industry springs up of itself, and whose food is not acquired by exchange and retail trade – there is the shepherd, the husbandman, the brigand, the fisherman, the hunter. Some gain a comfortable maintenance out of two employments, eking out the deficiencies of one of them by another: thus the life of a shepherd may be combined with that of a brigand, the life of a farmer with that of a hunter. Other modes of life are similarly combined in any way which the needs of men may require. Property, in the sense of a bare livelihood, seems to be given by nature herself to all, both when they are first born, and when they are grown up. For some animals bring forth, together with their offspring, so much food as will last until they are able to supply themselves; of this the vermiparous or oviparous animals are an instance; and the viviparous animals have up to a certain time a supply of food for their young in themselves, which is called milk. In like manner we may infer that, after the birth of animals, plants exist for their sake, and that the other animals exist for the sake of man, the tame for use and food, the wild, if not all, at least the greater part of them, for food, and for the provision of clothing and various instruments. Now if nature makes nothing incomplete, and nothing in vain, the inference must be that she has made all animals for the sake of man. And so, in one point of view, the art of

256ᵇ

war is a natural art of acquisition, for the art of acquisition includes hunting, an art which we ought to practise against wild beasts, and against men who, though intended by nature to be governed, will not submit; for war of such a kind is naturally just.

Of the art of acquisition then there is one kind which by nature is a part of the management of a household, in so far as the art of household management must either find ready to hand, or itself provide, such things necessary to life, and useful for the community of the family or state, as can be stored. They are the elements of true riches; for the amount of property which is needed for a good life is not unlimited, although Solon in one of his poems says that

'No bound to riches has been fixed for man'.

But there is a boundary fixed, just as there is in the other arts; for the instruments of any art are never unlimited, either in number or size, and riches may be defined as a number of instruments to be used in a household or in a state. And so we see that there is a natural art of acquisition which is practised by managers of households and by statesmen, and what is the reason of this.

9 There is another variety of the art of acquisition which is commonly and rightly called an art of wealth-getting, and has in fact suggested the notion that riches and property have no limit. Being nearly connected with the preceding, it is often identified with it. But though they are not very different, neither are they the same. The kind already described is given by nature, the other is gained by experience and art.

Let us begin our discussion of the question with the following considerations:

Of everything which we possess there are two uses: both belong to the thing as such, but not in the same manner, for one is the proper, and the other the improper or secondary use of it. For example, a shoe is used for wear, and is used for exchange; both are uses of the shoe. He who gives a shoe in exchange for money or food to him who wants one, does indeed use the shoe as a shoe, but this is not its proper or primary purpose, for a shoe is not made to be an object of barter. The same may be said of all possessions, for the art of exchange extends to all of them, and it arises at first from what is natural, from the circumstance

1257ᵃ

that some have too little, others too much. Hence we may infer that retail trade is not a natural part of the art of getting wealth; had it been so, men would have ceased to exchange when they had enough. In the first community, indeed, which is the family, this art is obviously of no use, but it begins to be useful when the society increases. For the members of the family originally had all things in common; later, when the family divided into parts, the parts shared in many things, and different parts in different things, which they had to give in exchange for what they wanted, a kind of barter which is still practised among barbarous nations who exchange with one another the necessaries of life and nothing more; giving and receiving wine, for example, in exchange for corn, and the like. This sort of barter is not part of the wealth-getting art and is not contrary to nature, but is needed for the satisfaction of men's natural wants. The other or more complex form of exchange grew, as might have been inferred, out of the simpler. When the inhabitants of one country became more dependent on those of another, and they imported what they needed, and exported what they had too much of, money necessarily came into use. For the various necessaries of life are not easily carried about, and hence men agreed to employ in their dealings with each other something which was intrinsically useful and easily applicable to the purposes of life, for example, iron, silver, and the like. Of this the value was at first measured simply by size and weight, but in process of time they put a stamp upon it, to save the trouble of weighing and to mark the value.

1257^{b} When the use of coin had once been discovered, out of the barter of necessary articles arose the other art of wealth-getting, namely, retail trade; which was at first probably a simple matter, but became more complicated as soon as men learned by experience whence and by what exchanges the greatest profit might be made. Originating in the use of coin, the art of getting wealth is generally thought to be chiefly concerned with it, and to be the art which produces riches and wealth; having to consider how they may be accumulated. Indeed, riches is assumed by many to be only a quantity of coin, because the arts of getting wealth and retail trade are concerned with coin. Others maintain that coined money is a mere sham, a thing not natural, but conventional only, because, if the users substitute another commodity for it, it is worthless, and because it is not useful as a means to any of the necessities of life, and, indeed, he who is rich in coin may often be in want of necessary food. But how can that be wealth of which a man may have a great abundance and yet perish with hunger, like Midas in the fable, whose insatiable prayer turned everything that was set before him into gold?

Hence men seek after a better notion of riches and of the art of getting wealth than the mere acquisition of coin, and they are right. For natural riches and the natural art of wealth-getting are a different thing; in their true form they are part of the management of a household; whereas retail trade is the art of producing wealth, not in every way, but by exchange. And it is thought to be concerned with coin; for coin is the unit of exchange and the measure or limit of it. And there is no bound to the riches which spring from this art of wealth-getting. As in the art of medicine there is no limit to the pursuit of health, and as in the other arts there is no limit to the pursuit of their several ends, for they aim at accomplishing their ends to the uttermost (but of the means there is a limit, for the end is always the limit), so, too, in this art of wealth-getting there is no limit of the end, which is riches of the spurious kind, and the acquisition of wealth. But the art of wealth-getting which consists in household management, on the other hand, has a limit; the unlimited acquisition of wealth is not its business. And, therefore, in one point of view, all riches must have a limit; nevertheless, as a matter of fact, we find the opposite to be the case; for all getters of wealth increase their hoard of coin without limit. The source of the confusion is the near connexion between the two kinds of wealth-getting; in either, the instrument is the same, although the use is different, and so they pass into one another; for each is a use of the same property, but with a difference: accumulation is the end in the one case, but there is a further end in the other. Hence some persons are led to believe that getting wealth is the object of household management, and the whole idea of their lives is that they ought either to increase their money without limit, or at any rate not to lose it. The origin of this disposition in men is that they are intent upon living only, and not upon living well; and, as 1258^{a} their desires are unlimited, they also desire that the means of gratifying them should be without limit. Those who do aim at a good life seek the means of obtaining bodily pleasures; and, since the enjoyment of these appears to depend on property, they are absorbed in getting wealth: and so there arises the second species of wealth-getting. For, as their enjoyment is in excess, they seek an art which produces the excess of enjoyment; and, if they are not able to supply their pleasures by the art of getting wealth, they try other arts, using in turn every faculty in a manner contrary to nature. The quality of courage, for example, is not intended to make wealth, but to inspire confidence; neither is this the aim of the general's or of the physician's art; but the one aims at victory and the other at health. Nevertheless, some men turn every quality or art into a means of getting wealth; this they conceive to be the end, and to the promotion of the end they think all things must contribute.

Thus, then, we have considered the art of wealth-getting which is unnecessary, and why men want it; and also the necessary art of wealth-getting, which we have seen to be different from the other, and to be a natural part of the art of managing a household, concerned with the provision of food, not, however, like the former kind, unlimited, but having a limit.

10 And we have found the answer to our original question,* Whether the art of getting wealth is the business of the manager of a household and of the statesman or not their business? – viz. that wealth is presupposed by them. For as political science does not make men, but takes them from nature and uses them, so too nature provides them with earth or sea or the like as a source of food. At this stage begins the duty of the manager of a household, who has to order the things which nature supplies; – he may be compared to the weaver who has not to make but to use wool, and to know, too, what sort of wool is good and serviceable or bad and unserviceable. Were this otherwise, it would be difficult to see why the art of getting wealth is a part of the management of a household and the art of medicine not; for surely the members of a household must have health just as they must have life or any other necessary. The answer is that as from one point of view the master of the house and the ruler of the state have to consider about health, from

another point of view not they but the physician; so in one way the art of household management, in another way the subordinate art, has to consider about wealth. But, strictly speaking, as I have already said, the means of life must be provided beforehand by nature; for the business of nature is to furnish food to that which is born, and the food of the offspring is always what remains over of that from which it is produced. Wherefore the art of getting wealth out of fruits and animals is always natural.

There are two sorts of wealth-getting, as I have said; one is a part of household management, the other is retail trade: the former necessary and honourable, while that which consists in exchange is justly censured; for it is unnatural, and a mode 1258^b by which men gain from one another. The most hated sort, and with the greatest reason, is usury, which makes a gain out of money itself, and not from the natural object of it. For money was intended to be used in exchange, but not to increase at interest. And this term interest, which means the birth of money from money, is applied to the breeding of money because the offspring resembles the parent. Wherefore of all modes of getting wealth this is the most unnatural.

11 Enough has been said about the theory of wealth-getting; we will now proceed to the practical part. The discussion of such matters is not unworthy of philosophy, but to be engaged in them practically is illiberal and irksome. The useful parts of wealth-getting are, first, the knowledge of live-stock – which are most profitable, and where, and how – as, for example, what sort of horses or sheep or oxen or any other animals are most likely to give a return. A man ought to know which of these pay better than others, and which pay best in particular places, for some do better in one place and some in another. Secondly, husbandry, which may be either tillage or planting, and the keeping of bees and of fish, or fowl, or of any animals which may be useful to man. These are the divisions of the true or proper art of wealth-getting and come first. Of the other, which consists in exchange, the first and most important division is commerce (of which there are three kinds – the provision of a ship, the conveyance of goods, exposure for sale – these again differing as they are safer or more profitable), the second is usury, the third, service for hire – of this, one kind is employed in the

* 1256^a 3.

mechanical arts, the other in unskilled and bodily labour. There is still a third sort of wealth-getting intermediate between this and the first or natural mode which is partly natural, but is also concerned with exchange, viz. the industries that make their profit from the earth, and from things growing from the earth which, although they bear no fruit, are nevertheless profitable; for example, the cutting of timber and all mining. The art of mining, by which minerals are obtained, itself has many branches, for there are various kinds of things dug out of the earth. Of the several divisions of wealth-getting I now speak generally; a minute consideration of them might be useful in practice, but it would be tiresome to dwell upon them at greater length now.

Those occupations are most truly arts in which there is the least element of chance; they are the meanest in which the body is most deteriorated, the most servile in which there is the greatest use of the body, and the most illiberal in which there is the least need of excellence.

Works have been written upon these subjects by various persons; for example, by Chares the Parian, and Apollodorus the Lemnian, who have treated of Tillage and Planting, while others have treated of other branches; any one who cares for such matters may refer to their writings. It would be well also to collect the scattered stories of the ways in which individuals have succeeded in amassing a fortune; for all this is useful to persons who value the art of getting wealth. There is the anecdote of Thales the Milesian and his financial device, which involves a principle of universal application, but is attributed to him on account of his reputation for wisdom. He was reproached for his poverty, which was supposed to show that philosophy was of no use. According to the story, he knew by his skill in the stars while it was yet winter that there would be a great harvest of olives in the coming year; so, having a little money, he gave deposits for the use of all the olive-presses in Chios and Miletus, which he hired at a low price because no one bid against him. When the harvest-time came, and many were wanted all at once and of a sudden, he let them out at any rate which he pleased, and made a quantity of money. Thus he showed the world that philosophers can easily be rich if they like, but that their ambition is of another sort. He is supposed to have given a striking proof of his wisdom, but, as I was saying, his device for

1259ª

getting wealth is of universal application, and is nothing but the creation of a monopoly. It is an art often practised by cities when they are in want of money; they make a monopoly of provisions.

There was a man of Sicily, who, having money deposited with him, bought up all the iron from the iron mines; afterwards, when the merchants from their various markets came to buy, he was the only seller, and without much increasing the price he gained 200 per cent. Which when Dionysius heard, he told him that he might take away his money, but that he must not remain at Syracuse, for he thought that the man had discovered a way of making money which was injurious to his own interests. He made the same discovery as Thales; they both contrived to create a monopoly for themselves. And statesmen as well ought to know these things; for a state is often as much in want of money and of such devices for obtaining it as a household, or even more so; hence some public men devote themselves entirely to finance.

12 Of household management we have seen that there are three parts – one is the rule of a master over slaves, which has been discussed already, another of a father, and the third of a husband. A husband and father, we saw, rules over wife and children, both free, but the rule differs, the rule over his children being a royal, over his wife a constitutional rule. For although there may be exceptions to the order of nature, the male is by nature fitter for command than the female, just as the elder and full-grown is superior to the younger and more immature. But in most constitutional states the citizens rule and are ruled by turns, for the idea of a constitutional state implies that the natures of the citizens are equal, and do not differ at all. Nevertheless, when one rules and the other is ruled we endeavour to create a difference of outward forms and names and titles of respect, which may be illustrated by the saying of Amasis about his foot-pan. The relation of the male to the female is of this kind, but there the inequality is permanent. The rule of a father over his children is royal, for he rules by virtue both of love and of the respect due to age, exercising a kind of royal power. And therefore Homer has appropriately called Zeus 'father of Gods and men', because he is the king of them all. For a king is the natural superior of his subjects, but he should be of the same kin or kind

1259ᵇ

with them, and such is the relation of elder and younger, of father and son.

13 Thus it is clear that household management attends more to men than to the acquisition of inanimate things, and to human excellence more than to the excellence of property which we call wealth, and to the virtue of freemen more than to the virtue of slaves. A question may indeed be raised, whether there is any excellence at all in a slave beyond and higher than merely instrumental and ministerial qualities – whether he can have the virtues of temperance, courage, justice, and the like; or whether slaves possess only bodily and ministerial qualities. And, whichever way we answer the question, a difficulty arises; for, if they have virtue, in what will they differ from freemen? On the other hand, since they are men and share in rational principle, it seems absurd to say that they have no virtue. A similar question may be raised about women and children, whether they too have virtues: ought a woman to be temperate and brave and just, and is a child to be called temperate, and intemperate, or not? So in general we may ask about the natural ruler, and the natural subject, whether they have the same or different virtues. For if a noble nature is equally required in both, why should one of them always rule, and the other always be ruled? Nor can we say that this is a question of degree, for the difference between ruler and subject is a difference of kind, which the difference of more and less never is. Yet how strange is the supposition that the one ought, and that the other ought not, to have virtue! For if the ruler is intemperate and unjust, how can he rule well? if the subject, how can he obey well? If he be licentious and cowardly, he will certainly not do his duty. It is evident, therefore, that both of them must have a share of virtue, but varying as natural subjects also vary among themselves. Here the very constitution of the soul has shown us the way; in it one part naturally rules, and the other is subject, and the virtue of the ruler we maintain to be different from that of the subject; – the one being the virtue of the rational, and the other of the irrational part. Now, it is obvious that the same principle applies generally, and therefore almost all things rule and are ruled according to nature. But the kind of rule differs; – the freeman rules over the slave after another manner from that in which the male rules over the female, or the

man over the child; although the parts of the soul are present in all of them, they are present in different degrees. For the slave has no deliberative faculty at all; the woman has, but it is without authority, and the child has, but it is immature. So it must necessarily be supposed to be with the moral virtues also; all should partake of them, but only in such manner and degree as is required by each for the fulfilment of his duty. Hence the ruler ought to have moral virtue in perfection, for his function, taken absolutely, demands a master artificer, and rational principle is such an artificer; the subjects, on the other hand, require only that measure of virtue which is proper to each of them. Clearly, then, moral virtue belongs to all of them; but the temperance of a man and of a woman, or the courage and justice of a man and of a woman, are not, as Socrates maintained,* the same; the courage of a man is shown in commanding, of a woman in obeying. And this holds of all other virtues, as will be more clearly seen if we look at them in detail, for those who say generally that virtue consists in a good disposition of the soul, or in doing rightly, or the like, only deceive themselves. Far better than such definitions is their mode of speaking, who, like Gorgias,† enumerate the virtues. All classes must be deemed to have their special attributes; as the poet says of women,

'Silence is a woman's glory',

but this is not equally the glory of man. The child is imperfect, and therefore obviously his virtue is not relative to himself alone, but to the perfect man and to his teacher, and in like manner the virtue of the slave is relative to a master. Now we determined‡ that a slave is useful for the wants of life, and therefore he will obviously require only so much virtue as will prevent him from failing in his duty through cowardice or lack of self-control. Some one will ask whether, if what we are saying is true, virtue will not be required also in the artisans, for they often fail in their work through the lack of self-control? But is there not a great difference in the two cases? For the slave shares in his master's life; the artisan is less closely connected with him, and only

260ᵃ

---

* Plato, *Meno*, 72 A–73 C.

† *Meno*, 71 E, 72 A.

‡ 1254ᵇ 16–39, Cf. 1259ᵇ 25 sq.

1260^b

attains excellence in proportion as he becomes a slave. The meaner sort of mechanic has a special and separate slavery; and whereas the slave exists by nature, not so the shoemaker or other artisan. It is manifest, then, that the master ought to be the source of such excellence in the slave, and not a mere possessor of the art of mastership which trains the slave in his duties. Wherefore they are mistaken who forbid us to converse with slaves and say that we should employ command only, for slaves stand even more in need of admonition than children.

So much for this subject; the relations of husband and wife, parent and child, their several virtues, what in their intercourse with one another is good, and what is evil, and how we may pursue the good and escape the evil, will have to be discussed when we speak of the different forms of government. For, inasmuch as every family is a part of a state, and these relationships are the parts of a family, and the virtue of the part must have regard to the virtue of the whole, women and children must be trained by education with an eye to the constitution, if the virtues of either of them are supposed to make any difference in the virtues of the state. And they must make a difference: for the children grow up to be citizens, and half the free persons in a state are women.

Book II

1 Our purpose is to consider what form of political community is best of all for those who are most able to realize their ideal of life. We must therefore examine not only this but other constitutions, both such as actually exist in well-governed states, and any theoretical forms which are held in esteem; that what is good and useful may be brought to light. And let no one suppose that in seeking for something beyond them we are anxious to make a sophistical display at any cost; we only undertake this inquiry because all the constitutions with which we are acquainted are faulty.

We will begin with the natural beginning of the subject. Three alternatives are conceivable: The members of a state must either have (1) all things or (2) nothing in common, or (3) some things in common and some not. That they should have nothing in common is clearly impossible, for the

constitution is a community, and must at any rate have a common place – one city will be in one place, and the citizens are those who share in that one city. But should a well-ordered state have all things, as far as may be, in common, or some only and not others? For the citizens might conceivably have wives and children and property in common, as Socrates proposes in the *Republic* of Plato.* Which is better, our present condition, or the proposed new order of society?

2 There are many difficulties in the community of women. And the principle on which Socrates rests the necessity of such an institution evidently is not established by his arguments. Further, as a means to the end which he ascribes to the state, the scheme, taken literally, is impracticable, and how we are to interpret it is nowhere precisely stated. I am speaking of the premiss from which the argument of Socrates proceeds, 'that the greater the unity of the state the better'. Is it not obvious that a state may at length attain such a degree of unity as to be no longer a state? – since the nature of a state is to be a plurality, and in tending to greater unity, from being a state, it becomes a family, and from being a family, an individual; for the family may be said to be more than the state, and the individual than the family. So that we ought not to attain this greatest unity even if we could, for it would be the destruction of the state. Again, a state is not made up only of so many men, but of different kinds of men; for similars do not constitute a state. It is not like a military alliance. The usefulness of the latter depends upon its quantity even where there is no difference in quality (for mutual protection is the end aimed at), just as a greater weight of anything is more useful than a less (in like manner, a state differs from a nation, when the nation has not its population organized in villages, but lives an Arcadian sort of life); but the elements out of which a unity is to be formed differ in kind. Wherefore the principle of compensation, as I have already remarked in the *Ethics*,† is the salvation of states. Even among freemen and equals this is a principle which must be maintained, for they cannot all rule together, but must change at the end of a year or some other period of time or in some order of succession. The result is that upon

1261^a

* *Republic* 423e, 457c, 462b.
† *Nicomachean Ethics* 1132^b 32.

this plan they all govern; just as if shoemakers and carpenters were to exchange their occupations, and the same persons did not always continue shoemakers and carpenters. And since it is better that this should be so in politics as well, it is clear that while there should be continuance of the same persons in power where this is possible, yet where this is not possible by reason of the natural equality of the citizens, and at the same time 61[b] it is just that all should share in the government (whether to govern be a good thing or a bad), an approximation to this is that equals should in turn retire from office and should, apart from official position, be treated alike. Thus the one party rule and the others are ruled in turn, as if they were no longer the same persons. In like manner when they hold office there is a variety in the offices held. Hence it is evident that a city is not by nature one in that sense which some persons affirm; and that what is said to be the greatest good of cities is in reality their destruction; but surely the good of things must be that which preserves them. Again, in another point of view, this extreme unification of the state is clearly not good; for a family is more self-sufficing than an individual, and a city than a family, and a city only comes into being when the community is large enough to be self-sufficing. If then self-sufficiency is to be desired, the lesser degree of unity is more desirable than the greater.

3   But, even supposing that it were best for the community to have the greatest degree of unity, this unity is by no means proved to follow from the fact 'of all men saying "mine" and "not mine" at the same instant of time', which, according to Socrates,* is the sign of perfect unity in a state. For the word 'all' is ambiguous. If the meaning be that every individual says 'mine' and 'not mine' at the same time, then perhaps the result at which Socrates aims may be in some degree accomplished; each man will call the same person his own son and the same person his own wife, and so of his property and of all that falls to his lot. This, however, is not the way in which people would speak who had their wives and children in common; they would say 'all' but not 'each.' In like manner their property would be described as belonging to them, not severally but collectively. There is an obvious fallacy in the term 'all':

* Plato, *Republic* 462c.

like some other words, 'both', 'odd', 'even', it is ambiguous, and even in abstract argument becomes a source of logical puzzles. That all persons call the same thing mine in the sense in which each does so may be a fine thing, but it is impracticable; or if the words are taken in the other sense, such a unity in no way conduces to harmony. And there is another objection to the proposal. For that which is common to the greatest number has the least care bestowed upon it. Every one thinks chiefly of his own, hardly at all of the common interest; and only when he is himself concerned as an individual. For besides other considerations, everybody is more inclined to neglect the duty which he expects another to fulfil; as in families many attendants are often less useful than a few. Each citizen will have a thousand sons who will not be his sons individually, but anybody will be equally the son of 1262[a] anybody, and will therefore be neglected by all alike. Further, upon this principle, every one will use the word 'mine' of one who is prospering or the reverse, however small a fraction he may himself be of the whole number; the same boy will be 'my son', 'so and so's son', the son of each of the thousand, or whatever be the number of the citizens; and even about this he will not be positive; for it is impossible to know who chanced to have a child, or whether, if one came into existence, it has survived. But which is better – for each to say 'mine' in this way, making a man the same relation to two thousand or ten thousand citizens, or to use the word 'mine' in the ordinary and more restricted sense? For usually the same person is called by one man his own son whom another calls his own brother or cousin or kinsman – blood relation or connexion by marriage either of himself or of some relation of his, and yet another his clansman or tribesman; and how much better is it to be the real cousin of somebody than to be a son after Plato's fashion! Nor is there any way of preventing brothers and children and fathers and mothers from sometimes recognizing one another; for children are born like their parents, and they will necessarily be finding indications of their relationship to one another. Geographers declare such to be the fact; they say that in part of Upper Libya, where the women are common, nevertheless the children who are born are assigned to their respective fathers on the ground of their likeness. And some women, like the females of other animals – for example, mares and cows

– have a strong tendency to produce offspring resembling their parents, as was the case with the Pharsalian mare called Honest.

4 Other evils, against which it is not easy for the authors of such a community to guard, will be assaults and homicides, voluntary as well as involuntary, quarrels and slanders, all which are most unholy acts when committed against fathers and mothers and near relations, but not equally unholy when there is no relationship. Moreover, they are much more likely to occur if the relationship is unknown, and, when they have occurred, the customary expiations of them cannot be made. Again, how strange it is that Socrates,* after having made the children common, should hinder lovers from carnal intercourse only, but should permit love and familiarities between father and son or between brother and brother, than which nothing can be more unseemly, since even without them love of this sort is improper. How strange, too, to forbid intercourse for no other reason than the violence of the pleasure, as though the relationship of father and son or of brothers with one another made no difference.

This community of wives and children seems better suited to the husbandmen than to the
1262^b guardians, for if they have wives and children in common, they will be bound to one another by weaker ties, as a subject class should be, and they will remain obedient and not rebel. In a word, the result of such a law would be just the opposite of that which good laws ought to have, and the intention of Socrates in making these regulations about women and children would defeat itself. For friendship we believe to be the greatest good of states and the preservative of them against revolutions; neither is there anything which Socrates so greatly lauds as the unity of the state which he and all the world declare to be created by friendship. But the unity which he commends would be like that of the lovers in the *Symposium*,† who, as Aristophanes says, desire to grow together in the excess of their affection, and from being two to become one, in which case one or both would certainly perish. Whereas in a state having women and children common, love will be watery; and the father will certainly not say 'my son', or the son 'my father'. As a little

sweet wine mingled with a great deal of water is imperceptible in the mixture, so, in this sort of community, the idea of relationship which is based upon these names will be lost; there is no reason why the so-called father should care about the son, or the son about the father, or brothers about one another. Of the two qualities which chiefly inspire regard and affection – that a thing is your own and that it is your only one – neither can exist in such a state as this.

Again, the transfer of children as soon as they are born from the rank of husbandmen or of artisans to that of guardians, and from the rank of guardians into a lower rank,‡ will be very difficult to arrange; the givers or transferrers cannot but know whom they are giving and transferring, and to whom. And the previously mentioned evils, such as assaults, unlawful loves, homicides, will happen more often amongst those who are transferred to the lower classes, or who have a place assigned to them among the guardians; for they will no longer call the members of the class they have left brothers, and children, and fathers, and mothers, and will not, therefore, be afraid of committing any crimes by reason of consanguinity. Touching the community of wives and children, let this be our conclusion.

5 Next let us consider what should be our arrangements about property: should the citizens of the perfect state have their possessions in common or not? This question may be discussed separately from the enactments about women 1263^a and children. Even supposing that the women and children belong to individuals, according to the custom which is at present universal, may there not be an advantage in having and using possessions in common? Three cases are possible: (1) the soil may be appropriated, but the produce may be thrown for consumption into the common stock; and this is the practice of some nations. Or (2), the soil may be common, and may be cultivated in common, but the produce divided among individuals for their private use; this is a form of common property which is said to exist among certain barbarians. Or (3), the soil and the produce may be alike common.

When the husbandmen are not the owners, the case will be different and easier to deal with; but when they till the ground for themselves the

---

* *Republic* 403a–c.
† *Symposium* 191a, 192c.

‡ Plato, *Republic* 415b.

question of ownership will give a world of trouble. If they do not share equally in enjoyments and toils, those who labour much and get little will necessarily complain of those who labour little and receive or consume much. But indeed there is always a difficulty in men living together and having all human relations in common, but especially in their having common property. The partnerships of fellow-travellers are an example to the point; for they generally fall out over everyday matters and quarrel about any trifle which turns up. So with servants: we are most liable to take offense at those with whom we most frequently come into contact in daily life.

These are only some of the disadvantages which attend the community of property; the present arrangement, if improved as it might be by good customs and laws, would be far better, and would have the advantages of both systems. Property should be in a certain sense common, but, as a general rule, private; for, when every one has a distinct interest, men will not complain of one another, and they will make more progress, because every one will be attending to his own business. And yet by reason of goodness, and in respect of use, 'Friends', as the proverb says, 'will have all things common.' Even now there are traces of such a principle, showing that it is not impracticable, but, in well-ordered states, exists already to a certain extent and may be carried further. For, although every man has his own property, some things he will place at the disposal of his friends, while of others he shares the use with them. The Lacedaemonians, for example, use one another's slaves, and horses, and dogs, as if they were their own; and when they lack provisions on a journey, they appropriate what they find in the fields throughout the country. It is clearly better that property should be private, but the use of it common; and the special business of the legislator is to create in men this benevolent disposition. Again, how immeasurably greater is the pleasure, when a man feels a thing to be his own; 263ᵇ for surely the love of self is a feeling implanted by nature and not given in vain, although selfishness is rightly censured; this, however, is not the mere love of self, but the love of self in excess, like the miser's love of money; for all, or almost all, men love money and other such objects in a measure. And further, there is the greatest pleasure in doing a kindness or service to friends or guests or companions, which can only be rendered

when a man has private property. These advantages are lost by excessive unification of the state. The exhibition of two virtues, besides, is visibly annihilated in such a state: first, temperance towards women (for it is an honourable action to abstain from another's wife for temperance sake); secondly, liberality in the matter of property. No one, when men have all things in common, will any longer set an example of liberality or do any liberal action; for liberality consists in the use which is made of property.

Such legislation may have a specious appearance of benevolence; men readily listen to it, and are easily induced to believe that in some wonderful manner everybody will become everybody's friend, especially when some one is heard denouncing the evils now existing in states, suits about contracts, convictions for perjury, flatteries of rich men and the like, which are said to arise out of the possession of private property. These evils, however, are due to a very different cause – the wickedness of human nature. Indeed, we see that there is much more quarrelling among those who have all things in common, though there are not many of them when compared with the vast numbers who have private property.

Again, we ought to reckon, not only the evils from which the citizens will be saved, but also the advantages which they will lose. The life which they are to lead appears to be quite impracticable. The error of Socrates must be attributed to the false notion of unity from which he starts. Unity there should be, both of the family and of the state, but in some respects only. For there is a point at which a state may attain such a degree of unity as to be no longer a state, or at which, without actually ceasing to exist, it will become an inferior state, like harmony passing into unison, or rhythm which has been reduced to a single foot. The state, as I was saying, is a plurality, which should be united and made into a community by education; and it is strange that the author of a system of education which he thinks will make the state virtuous, should expect to improve his citizens by regulations of this sort, and not by philosophy or by customs and laws, like those which prevail at Sparta and Crete respecting common meals, whereby the legislator has made property common. Let us remember that we 1264ᵃ should not disregard the experience of ages; in the multitude of years these things, if they were good, would certainly not have been unknown;

for almost everything has been found out, although sometimes they are not put together; in other cases men do not use the knowledge which they have. Great light would be thrown on this subject if we could see such a form of government in the actual process of construction; for the legislator could not form a state at all without distributing and dividing its constituents into associations for common meals, and into phratries and tribes. But all this legislation ends only in forbidding agriculture to the guardians, a prohibition which the Lacedaemonians try to enforce already.

But, indeed, Socrates has not said, nor is it easy to decide, what in such a community will be the general form of the state. The citizens who are not guardians are the majority, and about them nothing has been determined: are the husbandmen, too, to have their property in common? Or is each individual to have his own? and are the wives and children to be individual or common? If, like the guardians, they are to have all things in common, in what do they differ from them, or what will they gain by submitting to their government? Or, upon what principle would they submit, unless indeed the governing class adopt the ingenious policy of the Cretans, who give their slaves the same institutions as their own, but forbid them gymnastic exercises and the possession of arms. If, on the other hand, the inferior classes are to be like other cities in respect of marriage and property, what will be the form of the community? Must it not contain two states in one, each hostile to the other? He makes the guardians into a mere occupying garrison, while the husbandmen and artisans and the rest are the real citizens. But if so the suits and quarrels, and all the evils which Socrates affirms to exist in other states, will exist equally among them.* He says indeed that, having so good an education, the citizens will not need many laws, for example laws about the city or about the markets; but then he confines his education to the guardians.† Again, he makes the husbandmen owners of the property upon condition of their paying a tribute. But in that case they are likely to be much more unmanageable and conceited than the Helots, or Penestae, or slaves in general.‡ And whether community of wives and property

be necessary for the lower equally with the higher class or not, and the questions akin to this, what will be the education, form of government, laws of the lower class, Socrates has nowhere determined: neither is it easy to discover this, nor is their character of small importance if the common life of the guardians is to be maintained.

Again, if Socrates makes the women common, and retains private property, the men will see to the fields, but who will see to the house? And who will do so if the agricultural class have both their property and their wives in common? Once more: it is absurd to argue, from the analogy of the animals, that men and women should follow the same pursuits, for animals have not to manage a household. The government, too, as constituted by Socrates, contains elements of danger; for he makes the same persons always rule. And if this is often a cause of disturbance among the meaner sort, how much more among high-spirited warriors? But that the persons whom he makes rulers must be the same is evident; for the gold which the God mingles in the souls of men is not at one time given to one, at another time to another, but always to the same: as he says, 'God mingles gold in some, and silver in others, from their very birth; but brass and iron in those who are meant to be artisans and husbandmen.' Again, he deprives the guardians even of happiness, and says that the legislator ought to make the whole state happy.§ But the whole cannot be happy unless most, or all, or some of its parts enjoy happiness. In this respect happiness is not like the even principle in numbers, which may exist only in the whole, but in neither of the parts; not so happiness. And if the guardians are not happy, who are? Surely not the artisans, or the common people. The Republic of which Socrates discourses has all these difficulties, and others quite as great.

6 The same, or nearly the same, objections apply to Plato's later work, the *Laws*, and therefore we had better examine briefly the constitution which is therein described. In the *Republic*, Socrates has definitely settled in all a few questions only; such as the community of women and children; the community of property, and the constitution of the state. The population is divided into two classes – one of husbandmen, and the

126

* *Republic* 464, 465.
† *Republic* iv. 425 D.
‡ *Republic* v. 464 C.

§ *Republic* 419, 420.

other of warriors;* from this latter is taken a third class of counsellors and rulers of the state.† But Socrates has not determined whether the husbandmen and artisans are to have a share in the government, and whether they, too, are to carry arms and share in military service, or not. He certainly thinks‡ that the women ought to share in the education of the guardians, and to fight by their side. The remainder of the work is filled up with digressions foreign to the main subject, and with discussions about the education of the guardians. In the *Laws* there is hardly anything but laws; not much is said about the constitution. This, which he had intended to make more of the ordinary type, he gradually brings round to the other or ideal form. For with the exception of the community of women and property, he supposes everything to be the same in both states; there is to be the same education; the citizens of both are to live free from servile occupations, and there are to be common meals in both. The only difference is that in the *Laws*, the common meals are extended to women,§ and the warriors number 5000, but in the *Republic* only 1000.

The discourses of Socrates are never commonplace; they always exhibit grace and originality and thought; but perfection in everything can hardly be expected. We must not overlook the fact that the number of 5000 citizens, just now mentioned, will require a territory as large as Babylon, or some other huge site, if so many persons are to be supported in idleness, together with their women and attendants, who will be a multitude many times as great. In framing an ideal we may assume what we wish, but should avoid impossibilities.

It is said that the legislator ought to have his eye directed to two points – the people and the country. But neighbouring countries also must not be forgotten by him, firstly because the state for which he legislates is to have a political and not an isolated life. For a state must have such a military force as will be serviceable against her neighbours, and not merely useful at home. Even if the life of action is not admitted to be the best, either for individuals or states; still a city should

be formidable to enemies, whether invading or retreating.

There is another point: Should not the amount of property be defined in some way which differs from this by being clearer? For Socrates says that a man should have so much property as will enable him to live temperately,** which is only a way of saying 'to live well'; this is too general a conception. Further, a man may live temperately and yet miserably. A better definition would be that a man must have so much property as will enable him to live not only temperately but liberally; if the two are parted, liberality will combine with luxury; temperance will be associated with toil. For liberality and temperance are the only eligible qualities which have to do with the use of property. A man cannot use property with mildness or courage, but temperately and liberally he may; and therefore the practice of these virtues is inseparable from property. There is an inconsistency, too, in equalizing the property and not regulating the number of the citizens; the population is to remain unlimited, and he thinks that it will be sufficiently equalized by a certain number of marriages being unfruitful, however many are born to others, because he finds this to be the case in existing states. But greater care will be required than now; for among ourselves, whatever may be the number of citizens, the property is always distributed among them, and therefore no one is in want; but, if the property were incapable of division as in the *Laws*, the supernumeraries, whether few or many, would get nothing. One would have thought that it was even more necessary to limit population than property; and that the limit should be fixed by calculating the chances of mortality in the children, and of sterility in married persons. The neglect of this subject, which in existing states is so common, is a never-failing cause of poverty among the citizens; and poverty is the parent of revolution and crime. Pheidon the Corinthian, who was one of the most ancient legislators, thought that the families and the number of citizens ought to remain the same, although originally all the lots may have been of different sizes: but in the *Laws* the opposite principle is maintained. What in our opinion is the right arrangement will have to be explained hereafter.

265ᵃ

1265ᵇ

---

* *Republic* 373 E.
† *Republic* 412 B.
‡ *Republic* v. 451 E.
§ *Laws*, vi. 780 E.

** *Laws*, v. 737 D.

There is another omission in the *Laws*: Socrates does not tell us how the rulers differ from their subjects; he only says that they should be related as the warp and the woof, which are made out of different wools.* He allows that a man's whole property may be increased fivefold,† but why should not his land also increase to a certain extent? Again, will the good management of a household be promoted by his arrangement of homesteads? for he assigns to each individual two homesteads in separate places, and it is difficult to live in two houses.

The whole system of government tends to be neither democracy nor oligarchy, but something in a mean between them, which is usually called a polity, and is composed of the heavy-armed soldiers. Now, if he intended to frame a constitution which would suit the greatest number of states, he was very likely right, but not if he meant to say that this constitutional form came nearest to his first or ideal state; for many would prefer the Lacedaemonian, or, possibly, some other more aristocratic government. Some, indeed, say that the best constitution is a combination of all existing forms, and they praise the Lacedaemonian because it is made up of oligarchy, monarchy, and democracy, the king forming the monarchy, and the council of elders the oligarchy, while the democratic element is represented by the Ephors; for the Ephors are selected from the people. Others, however, declare the Ephoralty to be a tyranny, and find the element of democracy in the common meals and in the habits of daily life. In the *Laws*‡ it is maintained that the best constitution is made up of democracy and tyranny, which are either not constitutions at all, or are the worst of all. But they are nearer the truth who combine many forms; for the constitution is better which is made up of more numerous elements. The constitution proposed in the *Laws* has no element of monarchy at all; it is nothing but oligarchy and democracy, leaning rather to oligarchy. This is seen in the mode of appointing magistrates;§ for although the appointment of them by lot from among those who have been already selected combines both elements, the way in which the rich are compelled by law to

1266ᵃ

attend the assembly and vote for magistrates or discharge other political duties, while the rest may do as they like, and the endeavour to have the greater number of the magistrates appointed out of the richer classes and the highest officers selected from those who have the greatest incomes, both these are oligarchical features. The oligarchical principle prevails also in the choice of the council, for all are compelled to choose, but the compulsion extends only to the choice out of the first class, and of an equal number out of the second class and out of the third class, but not in this latter case to all the voters but to those of the first three classes; and the selection of candidates out of the fourth class is only compulsory on the first and second. Then, from the persons so chosen, he says that there ought to be an equal number of each class selected. Thus a preponderance will be given to the better sort of people, who have the larger incomes, because many of the lower classes, not being compelled, will not vote. These considerations, and others which will be adduced when the time comes for examining similar polities, tend to show that states like Plato's should not be composed of democracy and monarchy. There is also a danger in electing the magistrates out of a body who are themselves elected;** for, if but a small number choose to combine, the elections will always go as they desire. Such is the constitution which is described in the *Laws*.

[. . .]

Book VII

14 Since every political society is composed of rulers and subjects let us consider whether the relations of one to the other should interchange or be permanent. For the education of the citizens will necessarily vary with the answer given to this question. Now, if some men excelled others in the same degree in which gods and heroes are supposed to excel mankind in general (having in the first place a great advantage even in their bodies, and secondly in their minds), so that the superiority of the governors was undisputed and patent to their subjects, it would clearly be better that once for all the one class should rule and

---

* *Laws*, 734 E, 735 A.
† *Laws*, 744 E.
‡ 693 D, 701 E, iv. 710, vi. 756 E.
§ *Laws*, 756, 763 E, 765.

** *Laws*, 753 D.

the others serve. But since this is unattainable, and kings have no marked superiority over their subjects, such as Scylax affirms to be found among the Indians, it is obviously necessary on many grounds that all the citizens alike should take their turn of governing and being governed. Equality consists in the same treatment of similar persons, and no government can stand which is not founded upon justice. For if the government be unjust every one in the country unites with the governed in the desire to have a revolution, and it is an impossibility that the members of the government can be so numerous as to be stronger than all their enemies put together. Yet that governors should excel their subjects is undeniable. How all this is to be effected, and in what way they will respectively share in the government, the legislator has to consider. The subject has been already mentioned. Nature herself has provided the distinction when she made a difference between old and young within the same species, of whom she fitted the one to govern and the other to be governed. No one takes offence at being governed when he is young, nor does he think himself better than his governors, especially if he will enjoy the same privilege when he reaches the required age.

We conclude that from one point of view governors and governed are identical, and from another different. And therefore their education 333ᵃ must be the same and also different. For he who would learn to command well must, as men say, first of all learn to obey. As I observed in the first part of this treatise, there is one rule which is for the sake of the rulers and another rule which is for the sake of the ruled; the former is a despotic, the latter a free government. Some commands differ not in the thing commanded, but in the intention with which they are imposed. Wherefore, many apparently menial offices are an honour to the free youth by whom they are performed; for actions do not differ as honourable or dishonourable in themselves so much as in the end and intention of them. But since we say that the virtue of the citizen and ruler is the same as that of the good man, and that the same person must first be a subject and then a ruler, the legislator has to see that they become good men, and by what means this may be accomplished, and what is the end of the perfect life.

Now the soul of man is divided into two parts, one of which has a rational principle in itself, and the other, not having a rational principle in itself, is able to obey such a principle. And we call a man in any way good because he has the virtues of these two parts. In which of them the end is more likely to be found is no matter of doubt to those who adopt our division; for in the world both of nature and of art the inferior always exists for the sake of the better or superior, and the better or superior is that which has a rational principle. This principle, too, in our ordinary way of speaking, is divided into two kinds, for there is a practical and a speculative principle. This part, then, must evidently be similarly divided. And there must be a corresponding division of actions; the actions of the naturally better part are to be preferred by those who have it in their power to attain to two out of the three or to all, for that is always to every one the most eligible which is the highest attainable by him. The whole of life is further divided into two parts, business and leisure, war and peace, and of actions some aim at what is necessary and useful, and some at what is honourable. And the preference given to one or the other class of actions must necessarily be like the preference given to one or other part of the soul and its actions over the other; there must be war for the sake of peace, business for the sake of leisure, things useful and necessary for the sake of things honourable. All these points the statesman should keep in view when he frames his laws; he should consider the parts of the soul and their functions, and above all the better and the end; he should also remember the diversities of human lives and actions. For men must be able to engage in business and go to war, but leisure and peace 1333ᵇ are better; they must do what is necessary and indeed what is useful, but what is honourable is better. On such principles children and persons of every age which requires education should be trained. Whereas even the Hellenes of the present day who are reputed to be best governed, and the legislators who gave them their constitutions, do not appear to have framed their governments with a regard to the best end, or to have given them laws and education with a view to all the virtues, but in a vulgar spirit have fallen back on those which promised to be more useful and profitable. Many modern writers have taken a similar view: they commend the Lacedaemonian constitution, and praise the legislator for making conquest and war his sole aim, a doctrine which may be refuted by argument and has long ago been refuted by facts. For most men desire empire in the hope of accumulating the goods of fortune; and on this ground Thibron and all those who have written about the Lacedaemonian constitution have praised their legislator, because the Lacedaemonians, by being trained to meet dangers, gained great power. But surely they are not a happy people now that their empire has passed away, nor was their legislator right. How ridiculous is the result, if, while they are continuing in the observance of his laws and no one interferes with them, they have lost the better part of life! These writers further err about the sort of government which the legislator should approve, for the government of freemen is nobler and implies more virtue than despotic government. Neither is a city to be deemed happy or a legislator to be praised because he trains his citizens to conquer and obtain dominion over their neighbours, for there is great evil in this. On a similar principle any citizen who could, should obviously try to obtain the power in his own state – the crime which the Lacedaemonians accuse king Pausanias of attempting, although he had so great honour already. No such principle and no law having this object is either statesmanlike or useful or right. For the same things are best both for individuals and for states, and these are the things which the legislator ought to implant in the minds of his citizens. Neither should men study war with a view to the enslavement of those who do not deserve to be enslaved; but first of all they should provide against their own enslavement, and in the second place obtain empire for the good of the 1334ᵃ governed, and not for the sake of exercising a general despotism, and in the third place they should seek to be masters only over those who deserve to be slaves. Facts, as well as arguments, prove that the legislator should direct all his military and other measures to the provision of leisure and the establishment of peace. For most of these military states are safe only while they are at war, but fall when they have acquired their empire; like unused iron they lose their temper in time of peace. And for this the legislator is to blame, he never having taught them how to lead the life of peace.

15   Since the end of individuals and of states is the same, the end of the best man and of the best constitution must also be the same; it is therefore evident that there ought to exist in both of them the virtues of leisure; for peace, as has been often repeated, is the end of war, and leisure of toil. But leisure and cultivation may be promoted, not only by those virtues which are practised in leisure, but also by some of those which are useful to business. For many necessaries of life have to be supplied before we can have leisure. Therefore a city must be temperate and brave, and able to endure: for truly, as the proverb says, 'There is no leisure for slaves,' and those who cannot face danger like men are the slaves of any invader. Courage and endurance are required for business and philosophy for leisure, temperance and justice for both, and more especially in times of peace and leisure, for war compels men to be just and temperate, whereas the enjoyment of good fortune and the leisure which comes with peace tend to make them insolent. Those then who seem to be the best-off and to be in the possession of every good, have special need of justice and temperance – for example, those (if such there be, as the poets say) who dwell in the Islands of the Blest; they above all will need philosophy and temperance and justice, and all the more the more leisure they have, living in the midst of abundance. There is no difficulty in seeing why the state that would be happy and good ought to have these virtues. If it be disgraceful in men not to be able to use the goods of life, it is peculiarly disgraceful not to be able to use them in time of leisure – to show excellent qualities in action and war, and when they have peace and leisure to be no better than slaves. Wherefore we should not practise virtue after the manner of the Lacedaemonians. For they, while agreeing with other men in their conception of the highest 1334 goods, differ from the rest of mankind in thinking that they are to be obtained by the practice of a single virtue. And since [they think] these goods and the enjoyment of them greater than the enjoyment derived from the virtues . . . and that [it should be practised] for its own sake, is evident from what has been said; we must now consider how and by what means it is to be attained.

We have already determined that nature and habit and rational principle are required, and, of these, the proper *nature* of the citizens has also been defined by us. But we have still to consider whether the training of early life is to be that of rational principle or habit, for these two must accord, and when in accord they will then form the best of harmonies. The rational principle may be mistaken and fail in attaining the highest ideal of life, and there may be a like evil influence of habit. Thus much is clear in the first place, that, as in all other things, birth implies an antecedent beginning, and that there are beginnings whose end is relative to a further end. Now, in men rational principle and mind are the end towards which nature strives, so that the birth and moral discipline of the citizens ought to be ordered with a view to them. In the second place, as the soul and body are two, we see also that there are two parts of the soul, the rational and the irrational, and two corresponding states – reason and appetite. And as the body is prior in order of generation to the soul, so the irrational is prior to the rational. The proof is that anger and wishing and desire are implanted in children from their very birth, but reason and understanding are developed as they grow older. Wherefore, the care of the body ought to precede that of the soul, and the training of the appetitive part should follow: none the less our care of it must be for the sake of the reason, and our care of the body for the sake of the soul.

Cicero, "The Dream of Scipio" from *De re publica*, VI: IX–XXVI

Introduction

Marcus Tullius Cicero (106–43 BCE) was not of noble birth, having been born instead among the upper middle-class "equestrians." Nevertheless, Cicero quickly ascended the Roman social hierarchy, becoming through spectacular legal victories and spellbinding political rhetoric a "new man" (*novus homo*) in the Senate and one of the most important political figures of the Roman republic – as well as one of Rome's most distinguished philosophers. Cicero was awarded the post of Consul in 63 BCE; but when his political sympathies drew him toward the elitist *optimates* against the more democratic *populares*, he found himself exiled for a year in 58 BCE. As civil war set in between Pompey and Julius Caesar, Cicero, at first neutral, inevitably sided with his friend, Pompey. And upon Caesar's assassination in 44 BCE, Cicero worked feverishly for the restoration of the republic. With, however, the rise of Octavius and Cicero's old adversary Marc Antony, Cicero's fortunes turned for the worse, and he fled to the countryside. Betrayed by one of his own students, Cicero was captured by Antony's soldiers and beheaded on the roadside. His hands, which had

From Cicero, *De re publica* and *De legibus*, Loeb Classical Library XVI, ed. J. Henderson, trans. C. W. Keyes, Cambridge, MA: Harvard University Press, 1928, pp. 261–83 (some notes omitted).

written and gestured so powerfully against Antony, were cut from his body and nailed, along with his head, to the rostra in Rome from which orators spoke – an ornament that would have certainly proven powerful inspiration to other critics of the new regime.[1] Cicero's influence in philosophy, politics, and rhetoric, however, despite the violence of Antony's efforts to silence him, has persisted into modern times.

The selection from Cicero that follows presents a text that had been well known through Macrobius's fifth-century commentary but had itself gone missing for much of the Middle Ages and the modern era. Amazingly, a Vatican librarian rediscovered it only by accident in 1820 in the faint, almost spectral markings of a palimpsest. Appended to the end of Cicero's lengthy, six-book exploration of the political order, *De re publica* [*The Public Thing*], "*Somnium Scipionis*" ["Scipio's Dream"] seems to respond to the dream-like "Myth of Er" with which Plato closes his own *Republic* (V.4). More importantly, however, Cicero's fable also gives us a parable that encapsulates a number of the key themes of Ciceronian political philosophy.

The central task of Plato's *Republic* had been to prove that it is better to be a good person who is nevertheless thought to be bad than a bad person who is thought to be good. In short, Plato aimed to show that virtue is its own reward – that the internal constitution of the soul underwrites true happiness, regardless of harms or benefits one may receive externally. Politically, Plato's story seems to suggest that it is the internal constitution of the political order that determines a society's virtue rather than the state's wealth, power, or reputation in relation to other states.

Plato had, however, perhaps grown excessively disillusioned with politics, having witnessed his friend and teacher, Socrates, put to death unjustly and his dazzling Athens suffer the depredations of the Peloponnesian wars – as well as having his own political ambitions in Syracuse come to nothing. For Plato, individual virtue seems to be the most important task of human life, and he warns his readers of the almost certain corruption to be expected from politics.

Cicero, by contrast, rejects this pessimistic view of the political order. Just as Cicero's catalog of virtues suggests a greater emphasis on social life and political engagement than Aristotle's or Plato's, the endorsement by ancestral and divine figures in "The Dream of Scipio" of public service symbolizes the pre-eminence for Cicero of political excellence and civic virtue. While Cicero does not directly answer the ancient question of whether a good person may come to exist in a bad society (which Plato had answered, with much qualification, in the affirmative), he does indicate that the best people must not only appear in the best societies; they can only become best, he argues, by successfully serving the well-being of those societies.

Aristotle had argued that the state is prior to the individual because it is by means of social institutions that complete individual virtue and the contemplation of divine truth become possible. But in Aristotle's rendering, the functioning of the state remains a means to an end. With the Roman Cicero, just the inverse holds. In the order of importance, it is the well-being of civil society that supersedes whatever excellences are possible for the individual. In fact, individual excellence will require, according to Cicero, the sacrifice of personal interest and sensual pleasures for the sake of civic duty. Like Plato and the Stoics, Cicero advocates training the mind to free itself from the constraints of the body and to apprehend divine truth. But unlike Plato and the Stoics, Cicero maintains that the human end can only be achieved through political excellence. Indeed, read symbolically, one might say that political excellence is the end itself for which Cicero contends:

Do you, therefore, exercise this mind of yours in the best pursuits. And the best pursuits are those which consist in promoting the good of your country. Such employments will speed the flight of your mind to this its proper abode; and its flight will be still more rapid, if, even while it is enclosed in the body, it will look abroad, and disengage itself as much as possible from its bodily dwelling, by the contemplation of things which are external to itself.

This it should do to the utmost of its power. For the minds of those who have given themselves up to the pleasures of the body, paying as it were a servile obedience to their lustful impulses, have violated the laws of God and man; and therefore, when they are separated from their bodies, flutter continually round the earth on which they lived, and are not allowed to return to this celestial region, till they have been purified by the revolution of many ages.

For his parable, Cicero selects the military hero Publius Cornelius Aemilianus Scipio ("Scipio" means "rod") as well as his heroic adoptive father and grandfather as central characters. The three men had been renowned for their military victories against the Carthaginians, as well as for their political leadership. Scipio reluctantly oversaw the final razing of Carthage in 146 BCE, and in this passage he meets with the Numidian prince Massinissa whose support in North Africa would prove crucial to him in that campaign. Scipio, like his grandfather, Scipio Africanus, was also highly praised, however, for his moderation and selflessness. After having taken by surprise the important Carthaginian stronghold at Carthago Nova, in what is today Cartagena, Spain, Scipio the elder is said to have been offered a beautiful captive woman and her dowry as one of the spoils of victory. The victor, however, returned her along with the money to her family, sacrificing his own personal pleasures for the good of Rome – as it should be for a philosopher who advocates political virtue against personal interest.

Note

1   Plutarch, *Parallel Lives*, Chapter 57.

Cicero, "The Dream of Scipio"

IX. *Scipio.* I was military tribune in the Fourth Legion in Africa under the consul Manius Manilius, as you know. When I arrived in that country my greatest desire was to meet King Masinissa, who for excellent reasons was a very close friend of my family. When I came into his presence the aged man embraced me and wept copiously; after a short interval, turning his eyes up to heaven, he uttered these words: "I thank thee, O supreme Sun, and ye other heavenly beings, that, before I depart this life, I see within my kingdom and under my roof Publius Cornelius Scipio, by the mere sound of whose name I am refreshed; so little has the memory of that noble and invincible hero faded from my memory!" Then I questioned him about his kingdom, while he inquired of me about our commonwealth, and we spent the whole day in an extended discussion of both.

X. Later, after I had been entertained with royal hospitality, we continued our conversation far into the night, the aged king talking of nothing but Africanus, and recollecting all his sayings as well as his deeds. When we separated to take our rest, I fell immediately into a deeper sleep than usual, as I was weary from my journey and the hour was late. The following dream came to me, prompted, I suppose, by the subject of our conversation; for it often happens that our thoughts and words have some such effect in our sleep as Ennius describes with reference to Homer, about whom, of course, he frequently used to talk and think in his waking hours. I thought that Africanus stood before me, taking that shape which was familiar to me from his bust rather than from his person. Upon recognizing him I shuddered in terror, but he said:

"Courage, Scipio, have no fear, but imprint my words upon your memory.

XI. "Do you see yonder city, which, though forced by me into obedience to the Roman people, is renewing its former conflicts and cannot be at rest" (and from a lofty place which was bathed in clear starlight, he pointed out Carthage), "that city to which you now come to lay siege, with a rank little above that of a common soldier? Within two years you as consul shall overthrow it, thus winning by your own efforts the surname which till now you have as an inheritance from me. But after destroying Carthage and celebrat-

ing your triumph, you shall hold the censorship; you shall go on missions to Egypt, Syria, Asia and Greece ; you shall be chosen consul a second time in your absence; you shall bring a great war to a successful close; and you shall destroy Numantia. But, after driving in state to the Capitol, you shall find the commonwealth disturbed by the designs of my grandson.

XII. "Then, Africanus, it will be your duty to hold up before the fatherland the light of your character, your ability, and your wisdom. But at that time I see two paths of destiny, as it were, opening before you. For when your age has fulfilled seven times eight returning circuits of the sun, and those two numbers, each of which for a different reason is considered perfect,[*] in Nature's revolving course have reached their destined sum in your life, then the whole State will turn to you and your name alone. The senate, all good citizens, the allies, the Latins, will look to you; you shall be the sole support of the State's security, and, in brief, it will be your duty as dictator to restore order in the commonwealth, if only you escape the wicked hands of your kinsmen."

Laelius cried aloud at this, and the rest groaned deeply, but Scipio said with a gentle smile: Quiet, please; do not wake me from my sleep; listen for a few moments, and hear what followed.

XIII. "But, Africanus, be assured of this, so that you may be even more eager to defend the common wealth: all those who have preserved, aided, or enlarged their fatherland have a special place prepared for them in the heavens, where they may enjoy an eternal life of happiness. For nothing of all that is done on earth is more pleasing to that supreme God who rules the whole universe than the assemblies and gatherings of men associated in justice, which are called States. Their rulers and preservers come from that place, and to that place they return."

XIV. Though I was then thoroughly terrified, more by the thought of treachery among my own kinsmen than by the fear of death, nevertheless I asked him whether he and my father Paulus and the others whom we think of as dead, were really still alive.

"Surely all those are alive," he said, "who have escaped from the bondage of the body as from a

---

[*] τέλεος ἀριθμός; compare Plato, *Timaeus* 39 D. The idea of "perfect numbers" goes back to Pythagoras.

prison; but that life of yours, which men so call, is really death. Do you not see your father Paulus approaching you?"

When I saw him I poured forth a flood of tears, but he embraced and kissed me, and forbade me to weep. XV. As soon as I had restrained my grief and was able to speak, I cried out: "O best and most blameless of fathers, since that is life, as I learn from Africanus, why should I remain longer on earth? Why not hasten thither to you?"

"Not so," he replied, "for unless that God, whose temple is everything that you see, has freed you from the prison of the body, you cannot gain entrance there. For man was given life that he might inhabit that sphere called Earth, which you see in the centre of this temple; and he has been given a soul out of those eternal fires which you call stars and planets, which, being round and globular bodies animated by divine intelligences, circle about in their fixed orbits with marvellous speed. Wherefore you, Publius, and all good men, must leave that soul in the custody of the body, and must not abandon human life except at the behest of him by whom it was given you, lest you appear to have shirked the duty imposed upon man by God. XVI. But, Scipio, imitate your grandfather here; imitate me, your father; love justice and duty, which are indeed strictly due to parents and kinsmen, but most of all to the fatherland. Such a life is the road to the skies, to that gathering of those who have completed their earthly lives and been relieved of the body, and who live in yonder place which you now see" (it was the circle of light which blazed most brightly among the other fires), "and which you on earth, borrowing a Greek term, call the Milky Circle."

When I gazed in every direction from that point, all else appeared wonderfully beautiful. There were stars which we never see from the earth, and they were all larger than we have ever imagined. The smallest of them was that farthest from heaven and nearest the earth which shone with a borrowed light. The starry spheres were much larger than the earth; indeed the earth itself seemed to me so small that I was scornful of our empire, which covers only a single point, as it were, upon its surface.

XVII.   As I gazed still more fixedly at the earth, Africanus said: "How long will your thoughts be fixed upon the lowly earth? Do you not see what lofty regions you have entered? These are the nine circles, or rather spheres, by which the whole is joined. One of them, the outermost, is that of heaven; it contains all the rest, and is itself the supreme God, holding and embracing within itself all the other spheres; in it are fixed the eternal revolving courses of the stars. Beneath it are seven other spheres which revolve in the opposite direction to that of heaven. One of these globes is that light which on earth is called Saturn's. Next comes the star called Jupiter's, which brings fortune and health to mankind. Beneath it is that star, red and terrible to the dwellings of man, which you assign to Mars. Below it and almost mid way of the distance is the Sun, the lord, chief, and ruler of the other lights, the mind and guiding principle of the universe, of such magnitude that he reveals and fills all things with his light. He is accompanied by his companions, as it were – Venus and Mercury in their orbits, and in the lowest sphere revolves the Moon, set on fire by the rays of the Sun. But below the Moon there is nothing except what is mortal and doomed to decay, save only the souls given to the human race by the bounty of the gods, while above the Moon all things are eternal. For the ninth and central sphere, which is the earth, is immovable and the lowest of all, and toward it all ponderable bodies are drawn by their own natural tendency downward."*

XVIII.   After recovering from the astonishment with which I viewed these wonders, I said: "What is this loud and agreeable sound that fills my ears?"†

"That is produced," he replied, "by the onward rush and motion of the spheres themselves; the intervals between them, though unequal, being exactly arranged in a fixed proportion, by an agreeable blending of high and low tones various harmonies are produced; for such mighty motions cannot be carried on so swiftly in silence; and Nature has provided that one extreme shall produce low tones while the other gives forth high. Therefore this uppermost sphere of heaven, which bears the stars, as it revolves more rapidly,

* For the astronomical system see Plato, *Republic* X, 616 B–617 C; *Timaeus* 36 and 38. Most of these ideas appear to go back to the Pythagoreans (especially to Philolaus of Croton, a contemporary of Socrates).

† Compare Plato, *Republic* X 617b; Aristotle, *De Caelo* II, 290b.

produces a high, shrill tone, whereas the lowest revolving sphere, that of the Moon, gives forth the lowest tone; for the earthly sphere, the ninth, remains ever motionless and stationary in its position in the centre of the universe. But the other eight spheres, two of which move with the same velocity, produce seven different sounds, – a number which is the key of almost everything. Learned men, by imitating this harmony on stringed instruments and in song, have gained for themselves a return to this region, as others have obtained the same reward by devoting their brilliant intellects to divine pursuits during their earthly lives. Men's ears, ever filled with this sound, have become deaf to it; for you have no duller sense than that of hearing. We find a similar phenomenon where the Nile rushes down from those lofty mountains at the place called Catadupa; the people who live near by have lost their sense of hearing on account of the loudness of the sound. But this mighty music, produced by the revolution of the whole universe at the highest speed, cannot be perceived by human ears, any more than you can look straight at the Sun, your sense of sight being overpowered by its radiance."

While gazing at these wonders, I was repeatedly turning my eyes back to earth. XIX. Then Africanus resumed:

"I see that you are still directing your gaze upon the habitation and abode of men. If it seems small to you, as it actually is, keep your gaze fixed upon these heavenly things, and scorn the earthly. For what fame can you gain from the speech of men, or what glory that is worth the seeking? You see that the earth is inhabited in only a few portions, and those very small, while vast deserts lie between those inhabited patches, as we may call them; you see that the inhabitants are so widely separated that there can be no communication whatever among the different areas; and that some of the inhabitants live in parts of the earth that are oblique, transverse, and sometimes directly opposite your own; from such you can expect nothing surely that is glory.

XX. "Besides, you will notice that the earth is surrounded and encircled by certain zones, of which the two that are most widely separated, and are supported by the opposite poles of heaven, are held in icy bonds, while the central and broadest zone is scorched by the heat of the sun. Two zones are habitable; of these the southern (the footsteps of whose inhabitants are opposite to yours) has no connection whatever with your zone. Examine this northern zone which you inhabit, and you will see what a small portion of it belongs to you Romans. For that whole territory which you hold, being narrow from North to South, and broader from East to West, is really only a small island surrounded by that sea which you on the earth call the Atlantic, the Great Sea, or the Ocean. Now you see how small it is in spite of its proud name! Do you suppose that your fame or that of any of us could ever go beyond those settled and explored regions by climbing the Caucasus, which you see there, or by swimming the Ganges? What inhabitants of those distant lands of the rising or setting sun, or the extreme North or South, will ever hear your name? Leave out all these and you cannot fail to see what a narrow territory it is over which your glory is so eager to spread. And how long will even those who do talk of us now continue so to do?

XXI. "But even if future generations should wish to hand down to those yet unborn the eulogies of every one of us which they received from their fathers, nevertheless the floods and conflagrations which necessarily happen on the earth at stated intervals would prevent us from gaining a glory which could even be long-enduring, much less eternal. But of what importance is it to you to be talked of by those who are born after you, when you were never mentioned by those who lived before you, [XXII] who were no less numerous and were certainly better men; especially as not one of those who may hear our names can retain any recollection for the space of a single year? For people commonly measure the year by the circuit of the sun, that is, of a single star alone; but when all the stars return to the place from which they at first set forth, and, at long intervals, restore the original configuration of the whole heaven, then that can truly be called a revolving year. I hardly dare to say how many generations of men are contained within such a year; for as once the sun appeared to men to be eclipsed and blotted out, at the time when the soul of Romulus entered these regions, so when the sun shall again be eclipsed at the same point and in the same season, you may believe that all the planets and stars have returned to their original positions, and that a year has actually elapsed. But be sure that a twentieth part of such a year has not yet passed.

XXIII. "Consequently, if you despair of ever returning to this place, where eminent and excellent men find their true reward, of how little value, indeed, is your fame among men, which can hardly endure for the small part of a single year? Therefore, if you will only look on high and contemplate this eternal home and resting place, you will no longer attend to the gossip of the vulgar herd or put your trust in human rewards for your exploits. Virtue herself, by her own charms, should lead you on to true glory. Let what others say of you be their own concern; whatever it is, they will say it in any case. But all their talk is limited to those narrow regions which you look upon, nor will any man's reputation endure very long, for what men say dies with them and is blotted out with the forgetfulness of posterity."

XXIV. When he had spoken thus, I said: "If indeed a path to heaven, as it were, is open to those who have served their country well, henceforth I will redouble my efforts, spurred on by so splendid a reward; though even from my boyhood I have followed in the footsteps of my father and yourself, and have not failed to emulate your glory."

He answered: "Strive on indeed, and be sure that it is not you that is mortal, but only your body. For that man whom your outward form reveals is not yourself; the spirit is the true self, not that physical figure which can be pointed out by the finger. Know, then, that you are a god, if a god is that which lives, feels, remembers, and foresees, and which rules, governs, and moves the body over which it is set, just as the supreme God above us rules this universe. And just as the eternal God moves the universe, which is partly mortal, so an immortal spirit moves the frail body.

XXV. "For that which is always in motion is eternal, but that which communicates motion to something else, but is itself moved by another force, necessarily ceases to live when this motion ends. Therefore only that which moves itself never ceases its motion, because it never abandons itself; nay, it is the source and first cause of motion in all other things that are moved. But this first cause has itself no beginning, for everything originates from the first cause, while it can never originate from anything else; for that would not be a first cause which owed its origin to anything else. And since it never had a beginning, it will never have an end. For if a first cause were destroyed, it could never be reborn from anything else, nor could it bring anything else into being; since everything must originate from a first cause. Thus it follows that motion begins with that which is moved of itself; but this can neither be born nor die, or else all the heavens must fall and all nature perish, possessing no force from which they can receive the first impulse to motion.

XXVI. "Therefore, now that it is clear that what moves of itself is eternal, who can deny that this is the nature of spirits? For whatever is moved by an external impulse is spiritless; but whatever possesses a spirit is moved by an inner impulse of its own; for that is the peculiar nature and property of a spirit. And as a spirit is the only force that moves itself, it surely has no beginning and is immortal.* Use it, therefore, in the best pursuits! And the best tasks are those undertaken in defence of your native land; a spirit occupied and trained in such activities will have a swifter flight to this, its proper home and permanent abode. And this flight will be still more rapid if, while still confined in the body, it looks abroad, and, by contemplating what lies outside itself, detaches itself as much as may be from the body. For the spirits of those who are given over to sensual pleasures and have become their slaves, as it were, and who violate the laws of gods and men at the instigation of those desires which are subservient to pleasure – their spirits, after leaving their bodies, fly about close to the earth, and do not return to this place except after many ages of torture."

He departed, and I awoke from my sleep.

---

* Chapters 25 and 26 are borrowed from Plato, *Phaedrus* 245 c–e. Compare also Cicero, *Tusc. Disp.* I, 53–55.

7

Ibn Tufayl, *The Story of Hayy Ibn Yaqzan* (extracts)

Introduction

The twelfth-century philosophical novel, *Hayy Ibn Yaqzan* ("The Living One, Son of the Vigilant"), has been called "one of the most remarkable books of the Middle Ages."[1] Alongside such books as *The Thousand and One Nights*, it is one of the few Arabic works to have had a marked impact on European literature.[2] Much admired by Leibniz, the novel was a model for the eighteenth-century genre of *contes philosophiques* written by Voltaire, Diderot, Rousseau (V.12), and others. It is said to have inspired Defoe's *Robinson Crusoe* and Goethe's *Bildungsroman*, *Wilhelm Meister*. In telling the story, moreover, of the development of a "feral boy," brought up by animals and in isolation from all human company, *Hayy Ibn Yaqzan* anticipates a whole later style of political philosophizing whose starting point is the human condition in a "state of nature."

The author of this philosophical tale, Abu Bakr Muhammad Ibn Tufayl (c. 1106–85), was a Muslim scientist, physician, poet, and philosopher, who was born in and spent most of his life in what is today southern Spain, an area that had been conquered by Arabs from north Africa some centuries

earlier. Honored for his medical, diplomatic, and other public service, Ibn Tufayl was also known as an important, "rationalist" critic of powerful anti-philosophical tendencies within Islamic theology. As such he had a considerable influence on his younger and more famous contemporary, Averroës (Ibn Rushd). (On the theological debates in which Ibn Tufayl participated see the texts from al-Ghazāli and Ibn Rushd; IV.6 and IV.7).

Hayy Ibn Yaqzan is a supernaturally born child, brought up by a deer. Most of Ibn Tufayl's novel recounts the boy's acquisition of knowledge and understanding of the world around him. By isolating the boy from all human society – hence from inherited beliefs, conventions, prejudices, and so on – the author aims to demonstrate, rather in the manner of Descartes (II.8), what can be known entirely on the basis of one's own individual intellectual effort. Like the Cartesian solitary thinker, Hayy Ibn Yaqzan not only arrives at an understanding of the basic structures and laws of the universe; he also recognizes that this universe – like he himself – must be the product of a perfect creator God. Indeed, the central claim of the novel is to show that knowledge of God's existence and perfection does not require revelation, acquaintance with holy texts, or familiarity with a religious tradition. In a way therefore similar to the work of later deists and Christian rationalists (IV.13–14), Ibn Tufayl sides squarely with the rationalist philosophers of Islam in a defense of "natural religion" against their anti-philosophical rivals.[3]

From *Two Andalusian Philosophers:* The Story of Hayy Ibn Yaqzan *by Abu Bakr Muhammad ibn Tufayl* and The Definitive Statement *by Abu'l Walid Muhammad ibn Rushd*, trans. Jim Colville, London and New York: Kegan Paul International, 1999, pp. 57–65.

The main point of the novel, therefore, is not a political or social one. Indeed, it is only over the last few pages that Hayy Ibn Yaqzan makes the acquaintance of human beings – a visitor to his island, Absal, and then the inhabitants of the neighboring island to which Absal takes him. In these few pages, however, Ibn Tufayl argues for a position that has proved important and controversial, not only within Islamic thought, but in the wider context of reflection on the relationship between politics and religion.

The pious, indeed ecstatically mystical, Hayy Ibn Yaqzan is surprised by the lack of devotion to religious understanding among the islanders and by the amount of energy they devote to acquiring wealth, and he is at first bitterly critical of those – like Absal's former friend and now the island's governor, Salaman – who urge "engagement with society" and condemn ascetic religious practice. He sets out with enthusiasm to reform the islanders, to turn them in the direction of religious contemplation. But he comes to recognize that the great majority of human beings are too stupid, weak, and greedy – too cattle-like – for any such reform to succeed. He comes, eventually, to agree with Salaman, that it is "asking too much" of ordinary people to expect them to do any more than act as reasonably responsible citizens, within a society run according to the "guidelines" of scripture and traditional religious practice. The message of the novel is not that "religion should be kept out of politics," but rather that the religion which enters into politics must be a relatively undemanding "religion of the people" – more a code of decent practice than a repository of theological wisdom. Those few who aspire to something higher – to authentic communion, or even union, with God – must live outside of society. The novel ends with Hayy Ibn Yaqzan and Absal returning to the "sublime station" of the little island on which the former had been raised.

Notes

1 Dalal Malhas Steitieh, "Ibn Tufayl," in J. A. Palmer (ed.), *Fifty Major Thinkers on Education*, London: Routledge, 2001, p. 34.

2 A collection of numerous ancient stories from different sources, *The Thousand and One Nights* seems to have been compiled around 800–900 CE. It appears in Europe first through a French translation in 1704 and then in English in the nineteenth century.

3 For an informed account of Ibn Tufayl's relationship to Islamic philosophy and theology, see L. E. Goodman, "Ibn Tufayl," in S. H. Nasr and O. Leaman, eds, *History of Islamic Philosophy*, Part I, London: Routledge, 1996, pp. 313–29.

Ibn Tufayl, *The Story of Hayy Ibn Yaqzan*

[...] One of the two versions of Hayy ibn Yaqzan's origins mentioned the existence of a neighbouring island and to that island a true faith based upon the teachings of one of the ancient prophets (may God bless them), had come. This religion represented truths by sketching vague outlines in the mind through the use of parables and allegory, as is usual in addressing the masses. It spread steadily throughout the island and flourished to the point where it was adopted by the king who, henceforth, imposed its observance upon the people.

Two sons of the island, young men of goodwill and honour by the names of Absal and Salaman, encountered this faith and embraced it wholeheartedly. Together, they committed themselves to following its teachings and upholding its duties and rituals.[1]

Together, they studied those parts of scripture which described God and His angels, and punishment and reward in the hereafter. Absal was interested in esoteric interpretation and spiritual meaning, while his friend Salaman was concerned with literal meaning and had little time for interpretation, contemplation and independent judgement. Nevertheless, each applied himself to doing good works, examining conscience and controlling desire.

Certain passages of scripture encouraged retreat from the world and solitary meditation, indicating that therein lay salvation and success, while others advocated social engagement and commitment. His contemplative nature, desire for understanding and eagerness for insight into deeper meaning led Absal to advocate the pursuit of solitude and he drew support from verses recommending this. The solitary life, he believed, was the path to the achievement of his aim. Salaman, averse to contemplation and personal choice, urged commitment to society and similarly referred to appropriate passages of scripture for support. Commitment, he believed, was what kept the whisperings of negative thoughts at bay and protected against the temptations of demons.

Their difference of opinion led to the two parting company. Absal knew of the neighbouring island (the one where Hayy ibn Yaqzan was living), its resources, abundance and temperate climate and that solitude was there for whomever so sought it. Deciding to withdraw from society and spend the rest of his life there, he collected what money he had, spent some on the hire of a boat and divided the rest among the poor. He bade farewell to his friend Salaman and set off across the sea. The ship's crew ferried him to the island, set him ashore and sailed away.

Absal stayed on the island to worship and glorify God and contemplate His names and sublime attributes. There was nothing to disturb his mind or cloud his meditation. As need arose, he picked fruit or hunted to satisfy his hunger and, for a time, remained in perfect happiness and communion with his Lord. Daily, he witnessed His goodness, benevolence and grace towards him in easing his quest and sustenance. This gladdened his heart and confirmed his certainty.

Hayy ibn Yaqzan, meanwhile, was totally absorbed at the stations of sublimity. He only left his cave once a week to search for the food he needed. Consequently, Absal did not come across him at first and, although he wandered the length and breadth of the island, he saw no sign of anyone. This increased his sense of communion and joy, since it was the pursuit of solitude that had led him to renounce society. One day, however, it happened that Absal was in the area when Hayy emerged to look for food and they caught sight of one another.

Certain that here was a solitary ascetic, come to the island to withdraw from society as he had himself had done, Absal was afraid to intrude and make Hayy's acquaintance lest he disturb his state of mind and frustrate the fulfilment of his aim. For his part, Hayy had no idea who or what Absal was, never having set eyes on any animal

like him before. He was wearing a kind of loose black tunic made of hair and wool that Hayy thought was his skin. He stood staring at him for a long time, astonished.

Afraid of disturbing him, Absal retreated. Natural inquisitiveness, however, made Hayy follow but, seeing how anxious the other was to avoid him, he kept his distance and himself, out of sight. Believing that Hayy had left the area, Absal began to pray, recite scripture, invoke God's names and prostrate himself in humility in order to calm his mind. Unnoticed to Absal, however, Hayy had crept up close enough to see and hear him in his devotions. He listened to the lovely, rhythmical sound of his voice intoning scripture and watched him humble himself in prayer, something which he had never known any other animal do. He studied his shape and appearance and realised they were the same as his own; and it was obvious that the tunic he wore was not his natural skin but something made, like his.

Appreciating that Absal's prayer, humility and devotion was something good, he became convinced he was an essence that is conscious of the Truth. He wanted to find out what he was up to and what the reason was for his prayer and devotion. He drew closer until, suddenly, Absal became aware of his presence and fled. Hayy gave chase and, with his natural strength and cunning, caught up with Absal and pinned him firmly to the ground.

Absal stared at this man dressed in furs, whose hair had grown so long that most of it reached the ground. He realised that Hayy's speed and physical strength were much greater than his own and tried to appease and placate him in a language that Hayy could not understand – he knew only that it betrayed all the signs of fear. Hayy tried to calm Absal with sounds he had learned from the animals and by patting his head. He stroked his cheeks and smiled at him until, eventually, Absal regained composure and realised that Hayy meant him no harm.

Absal's devotion to scriptural interpretation had led him to learn many languages fluently and he began to ask Hayy questions in every language he knew in an effort to make himself understood but to no avail. Hayy was puzzled by what he heard but had no idea what it meant, except that it seemed to be friendly. Each thought the other so very strange.

Now, Absal still had left a little of the food which he had brought from his own island and he offered this to Hayy. Never having seen anything like it before, Hayy did not know what it was. Absal ate a little and gestured for Hayy to eat as well. Conscious of his dietary rules, Hayy was uncertain whether or not he should accept the offer and, not knowing what it was, refused. However, Absal insisted and was behaving so kindly towards him that Hayy did not want to give offence by continuing to refuse and so he finally accepted. Having tasted and enjoyed the food, he then felt bad about what he had done and regretted breaking his own rules. He wanted to get away and devote himself to the return to his sublime station although it would not be easy. Still, he thought that by remaining with Absal in the material world until he had found out all about him and no longer felt any curiosity towards him, he would then be able to return to his station without distraction. So he decided to stay.

When he discovered that Hayy could not speak, Absal stopped worrying about his faith and resolved to teach him language and instruct him in religious knowledge and practice. Thus would his reward from God be greater. Slowly at first, Absal taught him to speak by pointing at an object and pronouncing its name, repeating it and then having Hayy say the word while pointing at the thing. In this way, he gradually built up his vocabulary until, within a relatively short time, he could speak.

Absal asked Hayy about himself and how he had come to the island. Hayy replied that he knew nothing about his origin and parents, apart from the gazelle who had raised him. He described everything he could about himself and how he had advanced in knowledge and understanding until finally reaching the level of union. He described the truths and the essences, transcendent of the material world, which are conscious of the Divine Essence. He described the Divine Essence, with His attributes of goodness and as much as he could of the rapture of those who had united and the torment of those excluded, he had witnessed when he attained union.

As he listened, Absal had no doubt that everything in scripture about God, His angels, revelation, the prophets, the last day and heaven and hell was an allegory of the things which Hayy ibn Yaqzan had actually witnessed. The perception of

his heart was opened, the fire of his mind was lit and he grasped the conformity between rational understanding and received wisdom. The different paths of scriptural interpretation were reconciled and all the difficulties he had encountered with scripture were resolved. What had before been ambiguous and obscure now became clear and he became a man of understanding. He looked at Hayy ibn Yaqzan with reverence and respect, realising him to be one of those close to God *who have no fear, neither do they grieve*. He undertook to serve and to follow him and be guided by him over any apparent contradictions in the teachings of his faith.

Absal told Hayy all about himself and, in answer to his questions, described conditions on his island, the level of knowledge, how the people had lived before the arrival of religion and the way that they lived now. He told him how scripture described the divine world, heaven, hell, resurrection, judgement and the true path. Hayy understood it all and saw nothing to contradict what he witnessed at the sublime station. He realised that whoever had so described and communicated it, had done so truthfully and was sincere in his claim to be a messenger of God's word. So he declared his belief and testified to the message.

Hayy asked what scripture said about religious duties and the practices of worship. Absal told him about prayer, taxation, the pilgrimage, fasting and other similar, external aspects of the faith. Hayy accepted and undertook to perform these, in line with his belief in the prophet's authenticity. There were, however, two points which surprised him and the wisdom of which eluded him.

First of all, why did this apostle use allegory in most of his descriptions of the divine world and avoid direct disclosure? In consequence, people attribute a great deal of corporeity to the divine world and believe things about the Divine Essence of which it is completely devoid. He had similar misgivings about punishment and reward in the hereafter.

Secondly, why did he circumscribe religious obligations and the duties of worship yet make the acquisition of wealth and excessive consumption permissible? The result is that people occupy themselves in futile ways and turn their backs on truth. He, of course, thought that no-one need eat anything unless it was to keep body and soul together and the concept of money had no meaning for him. He found the regulations of religious law about money, such as the various aspects of taxation, buying and selling, interest and fines all very strange and long-winded.

"If people really understood," he said, "they would avoid these futile things, dispense with them entirely and devote themselves to the truth. No-one needs to be so obsessed with money and property that it has to be begged for, that hands be cut off for stealing or that lives be lost in robbery."

But he had made the mistake of assuming that people are thoughtful, perceptive and resolute. He had no idea of their stupidity, inadequacy, lack of judgement and weak character, of how *they are like cattle, but more lost.*[2]

Hayy developed a deep compassion for humanity and desire to be the cause of mankind's salvation. He became determined to go and explain the truth, in order to enlighten them. He discussed this with Absal and wondered if he could see any way of reaching his island. Absal told him about the people's lack of character and how they had turned from God's will without realising. However, as Hayy remained so attached to his idea, Absal offered encouragement, cherishing the hope that, through him, God might guide an aspiring group of friends who were closer to salvation than the rest. The two decided that, if they remained on the shore day and night, perhaps God would provide them with a way of making the crossing. This they resolved to do and offered prayers to Him for guidance.

By the grace of God, a ship that had been blown off course by the wind and waves was driven within sight of the shore. As it sailed close to land, the crew saw the two men standing on the shore and altered course. They agreed to Absal's request to take Hayy and himself aboard and a fair wind carried the ship to the island in no time at all.

The two disembarked and made their way into the city, where Absal's friends flocked to meet him. He introduced them to Hayy ibn Yaqzan, whom they greeted enthusiastically and treated with much respect and deference. Absal advised Hayy that this was the group closest to understanding and wisdom among the entire population and that, if he was unable to teach them, he would have

even less success in instructing the masses. The island was now governed by Absal's old friend, Salaman, who believed in engagement with society and had argued in favour of outlawing asceticism.

Hayy began to teach and spread the secrets of his wisdom but had progressed only a little beyond the surface forms of things by describing what others had already given them to understand before they started to shut themselves off and shrink from what he had to say. In their hearts they resented him, even if they behaved towards him with courtesy out of consideration for a stranger and proper respect for their old friend, Absal.

Day and night, in public and in private, Hayy tried to win them over and convince them but this only increased their disdain and aversion. They wanted what was good and genuinely desired the truth but, because of their weakness of character, they were not prepared to accept what he said or follow his example by searching for the truth in the way that he had. In fact, they only wanted to learn of the truth by conventional methods. His hopes dashed by their reluctance, he despaired of their reformation.

Hayy then considered the different classes of society and found *each group satisfied with what it had.* They had taken their desires for idols and *their god was their passions.* Desperate to amass the dross of this world, *they are diverted by what they can accumulate, until they reach the grave.* No counsel will avail nor good advice prevail and discussion only serves to entrench them. They have no path to wisdom and no share therein. They are soaked through with ignorance. *What dominates their hearts is the profit they can make. God has laid a veil across their hearts, their ears and eyes and a terrible torment awaits them.*

He knew that a vortex of torment had engulfed them and the darkness of exclusion had descended. All of them, with few exceptions, adhered only to the worldly aspect of their faith. *They have thrown away and sold for a trivial price the good they did, thinking it worthless and slight.* Business and commerce have distracted them from the word of God and *they fear not a day when hearts and minds will be turned upside down.*

Realising this, it became perfectly clear that speaking to people of the path of illumination was impossible and it was asking too much of them to do any more than they already did. Scripture is only of any benefit to the great mass of people as it deals with the material world, to establish the proper framework and bounds of social behaviour. Only the rare exception, *the believer who strives for and devotes himself to the tilth of the hereafter,* will find the happiness of the divine world. *The dwelling of the man who wrongs others and follows the way of the lower life shall be the inferno of hell.*

What is more awful or miserable than the man who, when what he has done from the time he wakes until the time he goes to bed is examined, is seen to have done nothing but spend his day in pursuit of as many sordid sensations as he can, be it amassing wealth, procuring pleasure, gratifying lust, giving vent to rage, winning status, flaunting his piety or saving his own skin? *These are all squalid vices, one on top of another, in a fathomless sea. That there is not one of you who shall not enter hell, is God's absolute decree.*

Now aware of the people's condition and how the majority are just like dumb animals, he understood that it is impossible for all the wisdom, guidance and success of which the prophets spoke and which is contained in scripture, to be any more than it is. There are men for every task and everything is made easy for its purpose. *Thus has God dealt with those who passed before you and there is no change to how He deals.*

So Hayy went to Salaman and his colleagues, apologised for what he had spoken of and retracted it. He told them that he now took their view and would, henceforth, be guided by their example. He advised them to remain within the guidelines of scripture and ritual and not become involved with what does not concern them. He urged them to have faith in and accept the obscure passages of scripture, to uphold tradition and avoid innovation and heresy. He was particularly careful to warn them not to neglect the articles of faith or abandon themselves entirely to worldly matters, as the masses had done.

He and his friend Absal realised that this little group, aspiring but of limited ability, would

only succeed by taking that road. Trying to go beyond, to the plateau of vision and perception, would only disturb and upset them and make it impossible for them to be truly happy. They would waiver and lose their grip, with unfortunate consequences. But by continuing on their present course for the remainder of their lives, they would, in the end, achieve peace and be among those who sit at God's right side.

As for *those who came first for they are the closest to God,* they bade farewell to the group and slipped back to their island to which, by God's grace, they had a safe and easy passage. Hayy ibn Yaqzan set out for his sublime station in the same way as before and found his way back. Absal followed his guidance to the point where he came close to him. And the two of them worshipped God there, on the island, until life's one certainty came to them.

***

This (and may the Spirit of God aid us both) has been the story of Hayy ibn Yaqzan, Absal and Salaman. It has discussed issues not found in books or heard in conventional discourse. It has dealt with a hidden knowledge that those who know God will accept and the deluded will simply ignore. [...]

Notes

1 The religion on the island where Absal and Salaman live is clearly meant to be Islam, and the two men represent opposing tendencies within the Islamic world at the time when Ibn Tufayl was writing. One such conflict, implicitly indicated in the following paragraph, was between those who encouraged and those who criticized individual and independent-minded interpretations of the holy texts.

2 The italicized words are directly taken from the Quran (VII. 179).

8

Marsilius of Padua, *Defensor pacis,* Discourse One, Chapters X and XII; Discourse Two, Chapters VII and VIII

Introduction

Besides those concerned with the origins and nature of the state, investigations into the domain of state power must be ranked among the most important inquiries of political philosophy. Marsilius of Padua (c. 1275–1342) focused his investigations on just this issue; and the result of his labor, the *Defensor pacis* (or *Defender of the Peace,* 1324), marks one of the seminal texts in establishing the theoretical underpinnings of the modern, secular state and the modern concept of sovereignty. In particular, Marsilius advances a series of arguments aimed at establishing the independence of the civil government from ecclesiastical authority, and in fact the civil government's supremacy.

Early Christianity, for example in Paul's "Letter to the Ephesians," had exhibited a decidedly hostile stance to earthly political authority, particularly Rome's.[1] Roman emperors, by contrast, generally ceded little authority to religious classes, often establishing themselves as the supreme religious leader or "Pontifex." So, the acceptance of Roman emperor Constantine of Christianity (in 312) raised profound questions about the relationship of state and imperial power to the Church. In general

From Marsilius of Padua, *Marsilius of Padua: Defender of the Peace,* vol. 2, ed. A. Gewirth, New York: Columbia University Press, 1956, pp. 34–7, 44–9, 152–63 (notes omitted).

practice, the question was settled according to a kind of separate spheres doctrine, commonly known as the doctrine of "two swords" or the "Gelasian Doctrine." By the time of Marsilius, however, this doctrine stood badly in need of revision.

Rooted in a 494 CE letter from Pope Gelasius I to Emperor Anastasius, the Gelasian doctrine maintained that the state and its populace should be subordinate to the Church in spiritual matters, while the officers and members of the Church should submit to civil authorities in matters secular – rendering, as it were, unto Caesar only what is Caesar's (Matthew 22:21) while reserving a large sphere of authority and coercive power to the Church itself.[2]

As consensus on this doctrine began to erode in the century or so preceding Marsilius, assertions and expansions of Church supremacy as well as rebukes to them became increasingly strident. Supporters of Church supremacy and the expansion of its power like Pope Innocent III (1161–1216) argued that the pope possesses "*plentitudo potestatis*" or total power, such that ultimately all authority on Earth flows from God through the papacy. What authority the state or civil authorities may exercise, say supporters of this view, properly belongs to the Church but has been simply delegated to civil rulers for pragmatic reasons. An important group of medieval opponents, including Jean de Paris (c. 1255–1306)[3] and Philippe IV of France (1268–1314), opposed this view. Marsilius's work, then, which may have been completed with the help of Aristotelian scholar Jean de Jandun, may be understood as the zenith of medieval opposition to papal *plentitudo potestatis*. Marsilius, however, aimed not simply to oppose Church supremacy but to invert it.

According to Marsilius, the authority to exercise temporal power, in particular coercive power, flows from God not through the papacy or even through the Church but instead through the people, which he calls the "legislator." Prefiguring democratic theories that would develop more than three centuries later, in particular Rousseau's theory of the "general will" (V.12), Marsilius argues that the civic ruler should rule as an agent, executing laws that are somehow grounded in the "legislator." He writes: "The authority to make the laws belongs, therefore, to the whole body of citizens or to the weightier part thereof" (Bk I, Ch. XII). Echoing Plato's political theory (V.4), Marsilius emphasizes the necessity of this authority remaining unified and not divided (Bk I, Ch. XVII).

The unitary, supreme ruler, however, cannot according to Marsilius be religious for a number of theological reasons – among them God having restricted punishment for sin to the afterlife and prohibited spiritual figures from exercising political power (John 18:36). Indeed, centuries before blasphemy would cease to be a crime in Western Europe, Marsilius argued for a crucial principle of free societies – that rulers should not punish sin, at least not for religious reasons. On the other hand, Marsilius's position entails neither pluralism nor religious tolerance. He requires a Christian ruler and grants that the state may not only prohibit unorthodox religious practices; it may even punish heretics. The state may exert its coercive powers in this way, however, not for theological reasons but only for the sake of secular political stability.

Marsilius's theory, remarkably, not only excises religious institutions from political rule, it subordinates them to the state. Aristotle had maintained that religion is a function of the state (*Politics* VI.8), and extending this position Marsilius argued that the state, through the legislator, possesses the exclusive right to establish churches and their

territory, to appoint priests, to enforce canon law, and even to excommunicate: "the ruler by the authority of the legislator has jurisdiction over all bishops or priests and clergymen, lest the polity be destroyed by having an unordered multiplicity of governments" (Bk I, Ch. VIII). Marsilius seems to have believed that his doctrine updated Aristotle's analysis of revolution (*Politics* V) to a medieval context by showing how excessive Church power may destabilize a polity and how that instability can be prevented.

While Marsilius's theory has been credited with extricating the modern state from theocracy, it also however constructs a theoretical apparatus that prefigures modern, secular totalitarian regimes. Modern liberal political theory demands limited state power, restraining the state's coercive power behind the boundaries established by human rights of non-interference. Its authority is commonly divided among houses of parliament and independent branches of government; and its power is balanced by other institutions of a free society – commercial, familial, intellectual, political, and, yes, religious. Marsilius, by contrast, advocates a total state that concentrates all political power in a single ruler, virtually the secular mirror image of the religious *plentitudo potestatis*.

Notes

1 "The Epistle of Paul the Apostle to the Ephesians," 6:12: "For we wrestle not against flesh and blood, but against principalities, against powers, against the rulers of the darkness of this world, against spiritual wickedness in high places."

2 Gelasius's letter was subsequently combined with texts written by Gregory VII and incorporated into a document known as "*Duo sunt*," part of Gratian's *Decretum* (c. 1140), a compendium that became one of the dominant texts of medieval canon jurisprudence.

3 *De potestate regia et papali* (*On Royal and Papal Powers*; c. 1302).

Marsilius of Padua, *Defensor pacis*

Discourse One

Chapter X: on the distinction of the meanings of the term "law," and on the meaning which is most proper and intended by us   Since we have said that election is the more perfect and better method of establishing governments, we shall do well to inquire as to its efficient cause, wherefrom it has to emerge in its full value; for from this will appear the cause not only of the elected government but also of the other parts of the polity. Now a government has to regulate civil human acts (as we demonstrated in Chapter V of this discourse), and according to a standard (*regulam*) which is and ought to be the form of the ruler, as such. We must, consequently, inquire into this standard, as to whether it exists, what it is, and why. For the efficient cause of this standard is perhaps the same as that of the ruler.

2.   The existence of this standard, which is called a "statute" or "custom" and by the common term "law," we assume as almost self-evident by induction in all perfect communities. We shall show first, then, what law is; next we shall indicate its final cause or necessity; and finally we shall demonstrate by what person or persons and by what kind of action the law should be established; which will be to inquire into its legislator or efficient cause, to whom we think it also pertains to elect the government, as we shall show subsequently by demonstration. From these points there will also appear the matter or subject of the aforesaid standard which we have called law. For this matter is the ruling part, whose function it is to regulate the political or civil acts of men according to the law.

3.   Following this procedure, then, we must first distinguish the meanings or intentions of this term "law," in order that its many senses may not lead to confusion. For in one sense it means a natural sensitive inclination toward some action or passion. This is the way the Apostle used it when he said in the seventh chapter of the epistle to the Romans: "I see another law in my members, fighting against the law of my mind." In another sense this term "law" means any productive habit and in general every form, existing in the mind, of a producible thing, from which as from an exemplar or measure there emerge the forms of things made by art. This is the way in which the

term was used in the forty-third chapter of Ezekiel: "This is the law of the house . . . And these are the measurements of the altar." In a third sense "law" means the standard containing admonitions for voluntary human acts according as these are ordered toward glory or punishment in the future world. In this sense the Mosaic law was in part called a law, just as the evangelical law in its entirety is called a law. Hence the Apostle said of these in his epistle to the Hebrews: "Since the priesthood has been changed, it is necessary that there be a change of the law also." In this sense "law" was also used for the evangelic discipline in the first chapter of James: "He who has looked into the perfect law of liberty, and has continued therein . . . this man shall be blessed in his deeds." In this sense of the term law all religions, such as that of Mohammed or of the Persians, are called laws in whole or in part, although among these only the Mosaic and the evangelic, that is, the Christian, contain the truth. So too Aristotle called religions "laws" when he said, in the second book of his *Philosophy*: "The laws show how great is the power of custom"; and also in the twelfth book of the same work: "The other doctrines were added as myths to persuade men to obey the laws, and for the sake of expediency." In its fourth and most familiar sense, this term "law" means the science or doctrine or universal judgment of matters of civil justice and benefit, and of their opposites.

4.   Taken in this last sense, law may be considered in two ways. In one way it may be considered in itself, as it only shows what is just or unjust, beneficial or harmful; and as such it is called the science or doctrine of right (*juris*). In another way it may be considered according as with regard to its observance there is given a command coercive through punishment or reward to be distributed in the present world, or according as it is handed down by way of such a command; and considered in this way it most properly is called, and is, a law. It was in this sense that Aristotle also defined it in the last book of the *Ethics*, Chapter 8, when he said: "Law has coercive force, for it is discourse emerging from prudence and understanding." Law, then, is a "discourse" or statement "emerging from prudence and" political "understanding," that is, it is an ordinance made by political prudence, concerning matters of justice and benefit and their opposites, and having "coercive force," that is, concerning

whose observance there is given a command which one is compelled to observe, or which is made by way of such a command.

5. Hence not all true cognitions of matters of civil justice and benefit are laws unless a coercive command has been given concerning their observance, or they have been made by way of a command, although such true cognition is necessarily required for a perfect law. Indeed, sometimes false cognitions of the just and the beneficial become laws, when there is given a command to observe them, or they are made by way of a command. An example of this is found in the regions of certain barbarians, who cause it to be observed as just that a murderer be absolved of civil guilt and punishment on payment of a fine. This, however, is absolutely unjust, and consequently the laws of such barbarians are not absolutely perfect. For although they have the proper form, that is, a coercive command of observance, they lack a proper condition, that is, the proper and true ordering of justice.

6. Under this sense of law are included all standards of civil justice and benefit established by human authority, such as customs, statutes, plebiscites, decretals, and all similar rules which are based upon human authority as we have said.

7. We must not overlook, however, that both the evangelical law and the Mosaic, and perhaps the other religions as well, may be considered and compared in different ways in whole or in part, in relation to human acts for the status of the present or the future world. For they sometimes come, or have hitherto come, or will come, under the third sense of law, and sometimes under the last, as will be shown more fully in Chapters VIII and IX of Discourse II. Moreover, some of these laws are true, while others are false fancies and empty promises.

It is now clear, then, that there exists a standard or law of human civil acts, and what this is.

[. . .]

Chapter XII: on the demonstrable efficient cause of human laws, and also on that cause which cannot be proved by demonstration: which is to inquire into the legislator. Whence it appears also that whatever is established by election derives its authority from election alone apart from any other confirmation

We must next discuss that efficient cause of the laws which is capable of demonstration. For I do not intend to deal here with that method of establishing laws which can be effected by the immediate act or oracle of God apart from the human will, or which has been so effected in the past. It was by this latter method, as we have said, that the Mosaic law was established; but I shall not deal with it here even insofar as it contains commands with regard to civil acts for the status of the present world. I shall discuss the establishment of only those laws and governments which emerge immediately from the decision of the human mind.

2. Let us say, to begin with, that it can pertain to any citizen to discover the law taken materially and in its third sense, as the science of civil justice and benefit. Such inquiry, however, can be carried on more appropriately and be completed better by those men who are able to have leisure, who are older and experienced in practical affairs, and who are called "prudent men," than by the mechanics who must bend all their efforts to acquiring the necessities of life. But it must be remembered that the true knowledge or discovery of the just and the beneficial, and of their opposites, is not law taken in its last and most proper sense, whereby it is the measure of human civil acts, unless there is given a coercive command as to its observance, or it is made by way of such a command, by someone through whose authority its transgressors must and can be punished. Hence, we must now say to whom belongs the authority to make such a command and to punish its transgressors. This, indeed, is to inquire into the legislator or the maker of the law.

3. Let us say, then, in accordance with the truth and the counsel of Aristotle in the *Politics*, Book III, Chapter 6, that the legislator, or the primary and proper efficient cause of the law, is the people or the whole body of citizens, or the weightier part thereof, through its election or will expressed by words in the general assembly of the citizens, commanding or determining that something be done or omitted with regard to human civil acts, under a temporal pain or punishment. By the "weightier part" I mean to take into consideration the quantity and the quality of the persons in that community over which the law is made. The aforesaid whole body of citizens or the weightier part thereof is the legislator regardless of whether it makes the law directly by itself or entrusts the making of it to

some person or persons, who are not and cannot be the legislator in the absolute sense, but only in a relative sense and for a particular time and in accordance with the authority of the primary legislator. And I say further that the laws and anything else established through election must receive their necessary approval by that same primary authority and no other, whatever be the case with regard to certain ceremonies or solemnities, which are required not for the being of the matters elected but for their well-being, since the election would be no less valid even if these ceremonies were not performed. Moreover, by the same authority must the laws and other things established through election undergo addition, subtraction, complete change, interpretation, or suspension, insofar as the exigencies of time or place or other circumstances make any such action opportune for the common benefit. And by the same authority, also, must the laws be promulgated or proclaimed after their enactment, so that no citizen or alien who is delinquent in observing them may be excused because of ignorance.

4. A citizen I define in accordance with Aristotle in the *Politics*, Book III, Chapters 1, 3, and 7, as one who participates in the civil community in the government or the deliberative or judicial function according to his rank. By this definition, children, slaves, aliens, and women are distinguished from citizens, although in different ways. For the sons of citizens are citizens in proximate potentiality, lacking only in years. The weightier part of the citizens should be viewed in accordance with the honorable custom of polities, or else it should be determined in accordance with the doctrine of Aristotle in the *Politics*, Book VI, Chapter 2.

5. Having thus defined the citizen and the weightier part of the citizens, let us return to our proposed objective, namely, to demonstrate that the human authority to make laws belongs only to the whole body of the citizens or to the weightier part thereof. Our first proof is as follows. The absolutely primary human authority to make or establish human laws belongs only to those men from whom alone the best laws can emerge. But these are the whole body of the citizens, or the weightier part thereof, which represents that whole body; since it is difficult or impossible for all persons to agree upon one decision, because some men have a deformed nature, disagreeing with the common decision

through singular malice or ignorance. The common benefit should not, however, be impeded or neglected because of the unreasonable protest or opposition of these men. The authority to make or establish laws, therefore, belongs only to the whole body of the citizens or to the weightier part thereof.

The first proposition of this demonstration is very close to self-evident, although its force and its ultimate certainty can be grasped from Chapter V of this discourse. The second proposition, that the best law is made only through the hearing and command of the entire multitude, I prove by assuming with Aristotle in the *Politics*, Book III, Chapter 7, that the best law is that which is made for the common benefit of the citizens. As Aristotle said: "That is presumably right," that is, in the laws, "which is for the common benefit of the state and the citizens." But that this is best achieved only by the whole body of the citizens or by the weightier part thereof, which is assumed to be the same thing, I show as follows: That at which the entire body of the citizens aims intellectually and emotionally is more certainly judged as to its truth and more diligently noted as to its common utility. For a defect in some proposed law can be better noted by the greater number than by any part thereof, since every whole, or at least every corporeal whole, is greater in mass and in virtue than any part of it taken separately. Moreover, the common utility of a law is better noted by the entire multitude, because no one knowingly harms himself. Anyone can look to see whether a proposed law leans toward the benefit of one or a few persons more than of the others or of the community, and can protest against it. Such, however, would not be the case were the law made by one or a few persons, considering their own private benefit rather than that of the community. This position is also supported by the arguments which we advanced in Chapter XI of this discourse with regard to the necessity of having laws.

6. Another argument to the principal conclusion is as follows. The authority to make the law belongs only to those men whose making of it will cause the law to be better observed or observed at all. Only the whole body of the citizens are such men. To them, therefore, belongs the authority to make the law. The first proposition of this demonstration is very close to self-evident, for a law would be useless unless it

were observed. Hence Aristotle said in the *Politics*, Book IV, Chapter 6: "Laws are not well ordered when they are well made but not obeyed." He also said in Book VI, Chapter 5: "Nothing is accomplished by forming opinions about justice and not carrying them out." The second proposition I prove as follows. That law is better observed by every citizen which each one seems to have imposed upon himself. But such is the law which is made through the hearing and command of the entire multitude of the citizens. The first proposition of this prosyllogism is almost self-evident; for since "the state is a community of free men," as is written in the *Politics*, Book III, Chapter 4, every citizen must be free, and not undergo another's despotism, that is, slavish dominion. But this would not be the case if one or a few of the citizens by their own authority made the law over the whole body of citizens. For those who thus made the law would be despots over the others, and hence such a law, however good it was, would be endured only with reluctance, or not at all, by the rest of the citizens, the more ample part. Having suffered contempt, they would protest against it, and not having been called upon to make it, they would not observe it. On the other hand, a law made by the hearing or consent of the whole multitude, even though it were less useful, would be readily observed and endured by every one of the citizens, because then each would seem to have set the law upon himself, and hence would have no protest against it, but would rather tolerate it with equanimity. The second proposition of the first syllogism I also prove in another way, as follows. The power to cause the laws to be observed belongs only to those men to whom belongs coercive force over the transgressors of the laws. But these men are the whole body of citizens or the weightier part thereof. Therefore, to them alone belongs the authority to make the laws.

7. The principal conclusion is also proved as follows. That practical matter whose proper establishment is of greatest importance for the common sufficiency of the citizens in this life, and whose poor establishment threatens harm for the community, must be established only by the whole body of the citizens. But such a matter is the law. Therefore, the establishment of the law pertains only to the whole body of the citizens. The major premise of this demonstration is almost self-evident, and is grounded in the

immediate truths which were set forth in Chapters IV and V of this discourse. For men came together to the civil community in order to attain what was beneficial for sufficiency of life, and to avoid the opposite. Those matters, therefore, which can affect the benefit and harm of all ought to be known and heard by all, in order that they may be able to attain the beneficial and to avoid the opposite. Such matters are the laws, as was assumed in the minor premise. For in the laws being rightly made consists a large part of the whole common sufficiency of men, while under bad laws there arise unbearable slavery, oppression, and misery of the citizens, the final result of which is that the polity is destroyed.

8. Again, and this is an abbreviation and summary of the previous demonstrations: The authority to make laws belongs only to the whole body of the citizens, as we have said, or else it belongs to one or a few men. But it cannot belong to one man alone for the reasons given in Chapter XI and in the first demonstration adduced in the present chapter; for through ignorance or malice or both, this one man could make a bad law, looking more to his own private benefit than to that of the community, so that the law would be tyrannical. For the same reason, the authority to make laws cannot belong to a few; for they too could sin, as above, in making the law for the benefit of a certain few and not for the common benefit, as can be seen in oligarchies. The authority to make the laws belongs, therefore, to the whole body of citizens or to the weightier part thereof, for precisely the opposite reason. For since all the citizens must be measured by the law according to due proportion, and no one knowingly harms or wishes injustice to himself, it follows that all or most wish a law conducing to the common benefit of the citizens.

9. From these same demonstrations it can also be proved, merely by changing the minor term, that the approval, interpretation, and suspension of the laws, and the other matters set forth in paragraph 3 of this chapter, pertain to the authority of the legislator alone. And the same must be thought of everything else which is established by election. For the authority to approve or disapprove rests with those who have the primary authority to elect, or with those to whom they have granted this authority of election. For otherwise, if the part could dissolve by its own authority what had been established by

the whole, the part would be greater than the whole, or at least equal to it.

The method of coming together to make the laws will be described in the following chapter.

[...]

Discourse Two

Chapter VII: summary of the statements made in the preceding chapter, and their clarification and confirmation Let us now summarize what was said concerning the power or authority of the priestly keys which Christ gave to the apostles. In the sinner who is truly penitent, that is, sorrowing for his sin, some things are performed by God alone without any previous ministry on the part of the priest; these are the illumination of the mind, the purging of the guilt or blemish of the sin, and the remitting of eternal damnation. Other things, however, God performs in the same sinner not by himself alone, but through the ministry of the priest, such as, for example, showing in the eyes of the church which persons are to be regarded as being loosed or bound from sins both in this world and in the other world, that is, of which persons God has retained or dismissed the sins. Again, there is something else which God accomplishes with respect to the sinner through the ministry of the priest, namely, the commutation of the penalty of purgatory, which was owed to the sinner for the status of the future life, into some temporal or this-worldly satisfaction. For the penalty is relaxed in whole or in part according to the satisfactions imposed and the condition of the penitent person, all of which must be done by the priest with the key of power in accordance with his discernment. Thus too the priest excludes the contumacious from the communion of the sacraments, and admits those who repent in the manner described near the end of the preceding chapter.

2. This was the view of the Master in Book IV, Distinction 18, Chapter 8, when he said:

With respect to these methods of binding and loosing, it is necessary to understand the sense in which these words are true: "Whatsoever ye shall loose on earth, shall be loosed in heaven; and whatsoever ye shall bind on earth, shall be bound in heaven." For sometimes they [that is, the priests] show persons to be loosed or bound who are not so with God, and sometimes they bind to or loose from the penalty of having to give satisfaction persons who do not deserve it, and they admit the undeserving to the sacraments and exclude the deserving. But their binding and loosing must be understood with respect to those persons whose deserts demand that they be bound or loosed. Therefore, whatever persons they loose or bind while applying the key of discernment to the merits of the parties concerned, these are loosed or bound in the heavens, that is, with God, because the divine judgment approves and confirms the priest's sentence when it proceeds in this manner.

And then the Master said, as it were in epilogue: "This then is the nature and extent of the use of the apostolic keys."

3. To make this even more evident, we shall draw a rather familiar example or comparison to it, which seems closely to fit the words and meaning of Christ and of the saints whose authorities we cited above, and especially Ambrose. For Ambrose said that "the word of God cancels sins, the priest is judge. The priest performs his office, but exercises the rights of no power." Now let us say that in freeing the sinner, the priest, as the turnkey of the heavenly judge, is analogous to the turnkey of the earthly judge. For just as the criminal is condemned to or absolved from civil guilt and punishment by the word or sentence of the judge of this world, namely, the ruler; so by the divine word is a person absolutely bound to or loosed from guilt and the obligation of damnation or punishment for the status of the future world. And just as no one is condemned to or released from civil guilt or punishment by the action of the turnkey of the earthly ruler, but by his action in opening or closing the prison the criminal is merely shown to be released or condemned; so too no one is loosed from or bound to guilt or an obligation of eternal damnation by the action of the priest, but it is shown in the eyes of the church which person is regarded as being loosed or bound by God, when that person receives the priest's benediction and is admitted to the communion of the sacraments, in the manner stated toward the close of the preceding chapter. And hence, while the turnkey of the earthly judge performs his office by opening or closing the prison, he nevertheless exercises the rights of no judiciary power of acquittal or

condemnation; for even though he might in fact open the prison for some criminal whom the earthly judge had not acquitted, and might proclaim to the people that he was acquitted, yet this criminal would not on that account have been released from civil guilt or punishment. And on the other hand, if the turnkey were to refuse to open the prison and were to announce that some person, whom the judge's sentence had really acquitted, was not acquitted but condemned, nevertheless this person would not on that account be liable to civil guilt or punishment. In an analogous way, the priest, the turnkey of the heavenly judge, performs his office by making a verbal announcement of acquittal or condemnation or malediction. But if the priest, from ignorance, malice, or both, were to announce that persons were or would be absolved who really were or would be condemned by the heavenly judge, or the reverse, nevertheless the former would not on that account be absolved nor the latter condemned, since the priest would not have applied with discernment the key or keys to the merits of the persons under trial. And hence he "performs his office," as Ambrose said, but he "exercises the rights of no power," since the priests sometimes announce to the church that persons who are or will be loosed with God, are or will be bound for the future world, and the reverse, as we said above by the authority of the saints and of the Master in Book IV, Distinction 18, Chapter VIII. And therefore the priest does not exercise the rights of power. For if he did, the divine justice and promise might sometimes perish.

4. He alone, therefore, exercises the rights of power in these matters and is the judge having coercive power, who alone cannot be deceived about human thoughts and deeds, for as it is written in Hebrews, Chapter 4: "All things are bare and open to his eyes," and who alone has no vicious desire, for "thou art just, O Lord, and all thy judgments are just, and all thy ways are merciful and true and just," as it is written in Tobias, Chapter 3; and therefore there is only one such judge. Hence in James, Chapter 4, it is written: "There is one lawgiver and judge, that is able to destroy and to deliver"; which James said neither about himself nor about any of the apostles, although he was one of those three "who seemed to be pillars" of the church, as the Apostle said in Galatians, Chapter 2. But such sentences as Christ made or would make in the other world,

he wanted to have announced by the priests by a judgment in the first sense, as it were in prediction, so that by this judgment sinners in this world might be frightened and diverted from crimes and sins to penance, for which purpose the priestly office is much needed and valuable. In this way, if the physician of bodily health, to whom the power to teach and practice the art of medicine has been given by decree of the human judge or legislator, were to promulgate to the people a judgment in accordance with the science of medicine concerning those who were going to be healthy or to die, so that through this judgment men might lead sober lives and be diverted from intemperance in order to maintain or acquire bodily health, then he would also give commands or instructions about such matters, and as physician he would command that they be observed, and would judge that those who observed them would be healthy and those who transgressed them would be ill or would die. These persons, however, would be made healthy or ill not primarily by the physician but by the action of the nature of man, although the physician would be of some service. Nor, again, could the physician by his own authority compel a healthy or a sick person to do certain things no matter how conducive these things might be to bodily health, but he could only exhort, teach, and frighten men by his predictive judgment in the first sense, by making it known to them that health would follow from the observance of certain precepts, and illness or death from their transgression. So too, in an analogous way, the physician of souls, that is, the priest, judges and exhorts about those matters which lead to the soul's eternal health or to its eternal death or temporal punishment for the status of the future world. Yet with reference to these matters the priest neither can nor should compel anyone in this world by a coercive judgment, as we proved by the authority of the Apostle in II Corinthians, Chapter 2, and by the words of Ambrose thereon, together with the explicit statement of Chrysostom which we quoted in Chapter V of this discourse, paragraph 6.

5. For this reason, the priest with respect to his office should not be likened to a judge in the third sense, but rather to a judge in the first sense, that is, to one who has the authority to teach and practice, like the physician, but has no coercive power over anyone. For it was in this way that

Christ called himself a "physician," not a ruler, when in Luke, Chapter 5, he said of himself: "They that are well do not need a physician, but they that are sick"; nor did he say: they need a judge, for he had not come into the world to exercise coercive judgment over litigants, as we showed from Luke, Chapter 12, in Chapter IV of this discourse, paragraph 8. But by such coercive judgment Christ will judge the living and the dead on that day about which the Apostle said in the last chapter of the second epistle to Timothy: "Henceforth there is laid up for me a crown of righteousness, which the Lord, the righteous judge, shall give me at that day." For at that time Christ by coercive judgment will inflict penalties on those who in this world have transgressed the law made immediately by him. And this was the reason why Christ symbolically said to Peter: "I shall give unto thee the keys of the kingdom of heaven"; but he did not say: I shall give unto thee the judgment of the kingdom of heaven. And hence, as we have already said, the turnkey neither of the earthly nor of the heavenly judge has coercive judgment, which we called judgment in the third sense, because neither turnkey exercises the rights of such power, as Ambrose plainly said concerning the priest and as has also been sufficiently shown by the authority of other saints.

And so let this be our conclusion concerning the authority of the priests or bishops, and the power of the apostolic keys which Christ granted to them.

Chapter VIII: on the division of human acts, and how they are related to human law and the judge of this world Every coercive judgment is concerned with human voluntary acts in accordance with some law or custom, and with these acts insofar as they are ordered either toward the end to be attained in this world, that is, sufficiency of worldly life, or toward the end to be attained in the future world, which we call eternal life or glory. Hence, in order to make clearer the distinction between those who judge or ought to judge with regard to each of these ends, and between the laws in accordance with which, the judgments by which, and the manners in which they must respectively judge, let us discuss the differences between the acts themselves. For the determination of these points will be of no little help toward the solution of the earlier questions.

2. Let us say, therefore, that of human acts arising from knowledge and desire, some arise without any control by the mind, and others arise through the control of the human mind. Of the first kind are cognitions, desires, affections, and pleasures which arise from us and in us without any control or command being given about them by the intellect or the appetite; such are the cognitions and emotions which we have when we are aroused from sleep, or which arise in us in other ways without any control by our mind. But these acts are followed by cognitions, feelings, and emotions which are concerned with continuing the prior acts, or with investigating and understanding some of them, as in the action which proceeds through recollection; and these are and are called "controls" or "commands" of the mind, because they are done or elicited by our control, or because certain other acts are elicited by them, such as pursuits and avoidances.

3. But between controlled and uncontrolled acts there is this difference arising from what we have said, that over uncontrolled acts we do not have complete freedom or control as to whether or not they shall be done, but over controlled acts we do have this power, according to the Christian religion. And I have said that we do not have complete power over the former kind of acts, because it is not in our power wholly to prohibit their occurrence, although by acts of the second kind, which are called "controls," and by what follows from them, we may so dispose the soul that it will not easily perform or receive acts of the first kind, that is, when each of us has become accustomed to commanding himself to desire or think about the opposites of these acts.

Of controlled acts some are and are called "immanent," and others "transient." Immanent acts are controlled cognitions, emotions, and the corresponding habits made by the human mind; they are called "immanent" because they do not cross over into any subject other than the agent himself. Transient acts, on the other hand, are all pursuits of things desired, and the omissions thereof, in the manner of privations, and the motions produced by some of the body's external organs, especially of those which are moved in respect of place. Again, of transient acts some exist and are done without harm or injury to any individual, group, or community other than the agent; such are all the kinds of productive activity, and also the giving of money, pilgrimages, castigation of one's own body by scourging or beating or any other way, and other similar acts. Other transient acts, however, exist and are done with the opposite circumstances, that is, with harm or injury to someone other than the agent; such are flogging, theft, robbery, bearing false witness, and many others of various manners and kinds.

4. Now of all these acts which arise from the human mind, especially the controlled ones, there have been discovered certain standards or measures or habits whereby they arise and are done properly and correctly for the attainment of the sufficient life both in this world and in the next. Of these habits or standards there are some in accordance with which the acts of the human mind, both immanent and transient, are guided and regulated in their being done or omitted without any reward or punishment being given to the doer or omitted by someone else through coercive force; such are most of the operative disciplines, both those of action and those of production. But there are other standards in accordance with which such acts are commanded to be done or omitted with reward or punishment being given to the doers or omitters by someone else through coercive force. Of these coercive standards, again, there are some in accordance with which their observers or transgressors are rewarded or punished in and for the status of the present life; such are all human civil laws and customs. But there are other coercive standards in accordance with which doers are rewarded or punished in and for the status of the future life only; such are divine laws for the most part, which are called by the common name "religions," among which, as we said in Chapter VI of Discourse I, only that of the Christians contains the truth and the sufficiency of what must be hoped for the future world.

5. For the sufficient life or living of this world, therefore, there has been laid down a standard of controlled transient human acts which can be done for the benefit or harm, right or wrong, of someone other than the agent; a standard which commands and coerces transgressors by pain or punishment for the status of the present world alone. This standard we called by the common name "human law" in Chapter X of Discourse I; its final necessity and efficient cause we indicated in Chapters XI, XII, and XIII of Discourse I.

On the other hand, for the life or living in this world, but for the status of the future world, a law has been given and laid down by Christ. This law is a standard of controlled human acts, both immanent and transient, which are in the active power of our mind, according as they can be done or omitted rightly or wrongly in this world, but for the status or end of the future world. This law is coercive and distributes punishments or rewards, but inflicts these in the future world, not in the present one, in accordance with the merits or demerits of those who observe or transgress it in the present life.

6. But since these coercive laws, both the divine and the human, lack a soul and a judicial and executive moving principle, they needed to have some animate subject or principle which should command and regulate or judge human acts in accordance with these laws, and which should also execute the judgments and coerce their transgressors. This subject or principle is called a "judge," in what we called the third sense of this term in Chapter II of this discourse. Hence in Book IV of the *Ethics*, the treatise on justice, it is said that "the judge is like an animate justice." It is necessary, then, to have a judge in accordance with human laws, a judge of the kind we have said, having the authority to judge, by a judgment in the third sense, about contentious human acts, to execute the judgments, and to punish by coercive force anyone who transgresses the law. For this judge "is the minister of God," and "a revenger to execute wrath upon him that doeth evil," as the Apostle said in the epistle to the Romans, Chapter 13; he has been sent by God for this purpose, as it is said in the first epistle of Peter, Chapter 2.

7. And the Apostle said: "him that doeth evil," whoever he be, understanding this to apply to all men without differentiation. Consequently, since priests or bishops and generally all ministers of temples, who are called by the common name "clergyman," can do evil by way of commission or omission, and since some (would that it were not most) of them do sometimes in fact harm and wrong other persons, they too are subject to the revenge or jurisdiction of the judges to whom belongs coercive power to punish transgressors of human laws. This was also clearly stated by the Apostle in the epistle to the Romans, Chapter 13: "Let every soul," he said, "be subject to the higher powers," namely,

"to kings, princes, and tribunes," according to the exposition of the saints. For the same proper matter must undergo the action of the same agent which is naturally endowed and ordained to act upon it for the end for which it is apt, as is clear from the second book of the *Physics*. For as it is there written, "each thing is acted upon as it is naturally endowed to be acted upon," and conversely. But the transgressor of the law is the matter or subject upon which the judge or ruler is naturally endowed and ordained to act by bringing it to justice in order to effect due equality or proportion for the purpose of maintaining peace or tranquillity and the living together or association of men, and finally for the sake of the sufficiency of human life. Consequently, wherever such matter or subject is found in a province subject to a judge, this judge must bring him to justice. Since, therefore, the priest can be such proper or essential matter, that is, a transgressor of human law, he must be subject to the judgment of this judge. For to be a priest or non-priest is accidental to the transgressor in his relation to the judge, just as to be a farmer or house-builder; in the same way, to be musical or unmusical is accidental to the healthy or the sick man in his relation to the physician. For that which is essential is not removed or varied by that which is accidental; otherwise there would be infinite species of judges and physicians.

Therefore, any priest or bishop who transgresses human law must be brought to justice and punished by the judge who has coercive power over transgressors of human law in this world. But this judge is the secular ruler as such, not the priest or bishop, as was demonstrated in Chapters XV and XVII of Discourse I, and in Chapters IV and V of this discourse. Therefore, all priests or bishops who transgress human law must be punished by the ruler. And not only must the priest or other minister of the temple be punished for a transgression as the layman is, but he must be punished all the more in proportion as he sins more gravely and unseemingly, since he whose duty it is to be better acquainted with the commands of what must be done and avoided, has greater knowledge and ability to choose; and again, since the sin of the person whose duty it is to teach is more shameful than the sin of the person whose duty it is to be taught. But such is the relation of the priest's sin to that of the non-

priest. Therefore, the priest sins more gravely, and should be punished more.

8.   Nor must the objection be sustained which holds that injuries by word of mouth, or to property or person, and other deeds prohibited by human law, are spiritual actions when inflicted on someone by a priest, and that it does not therefore pertain to the secular ruler to take revenge on the priest for such acts. For such deeds as are prohibited by law, like adultery, beating, homicide, theft, robbery, insult, libel, treason, fraud, heresy, and other similar acts committed by the priest, are carnal and temporal, as is very well known by experience, and as we showed above in Chapter II of this discourse by the words of the Apostle in the first epistle to the Corinthians, Chapters 3 and 9, and in the epistle to the Romans, Chapter 15. And so much the more must these actions be adjudged carnal and temporal, in proportion as the priest or bishop sins by them more gravely and shamefully than do the persons whom he must recall from such actions, for by his vicious example he gives them an opportunity and an excuse for doing wrong.

9.   Therefore, like laymen, every priest or bishop is and ought to be subject to the jurisdiction of the rulers in those matters whose observance is commanded by the human law. The priest neither is himself exempt from the coercive judgment of rulers, nor can he exempt anyone else from it by his own authority. This I demonstrate, in addition to what was said in Chapter XVII of Discourse I, by deducing from its contradictory the greatest evil. For if the Roman bishop or any other priest were thus exempt, so that he would not be subject to the coercive judgment of rulers but would himself be such a coercive judge without the authorization of the human legislator and could separate all ministers of temples, who are called by the common name of "clergymen," from the jurisdiction of rulers, and could subject them to himself, as is done by the Roman pontiffs in modern times, then it would necessarily follow that the jurisdiction of secular rulers would be almost completely annulled. This I believe would be a grave evil of serious import to all rulers and communities; for "the Christian religion deprives no one of his right," as we showed in Chapter V of this discourse from the words of Ambrose on the passage in the epistle to Titus, Chapter 3: "Warn them to be subject to the princes and powers."

The consequence of this evil I show as follows: In divine law one finds that for the priest or bishop to have a wife is not prohibited but rather allowed, especially if he have not more than one, as it is said in the first epistle to Timothy, Chapter 3. But that which is decreed by the human law or constitution can be revoked by the same authority, as such. Therefore, the Roman bishop who makes himself legislator, or who uses his plenitude of power (if one grant that he has this), can allow all priests, deacons, and sub-deacons to have wives, and not only them, but also other persons not ordained in the priesthood or diaconate or otherwise consecrated, who are called "clergy of the simple tonsure"; indeed, he can grant such permission even more fittingly to these latter, as Boniface VIII is seen in fact to have done, in order to increase his secular power. For all who had taken one virgin wife, and who were willing, he enrolled in the company of the clergy, and decreed that they should be so enrolled by his ordinances which are called "decretals"; and not stopping there, these bishops have similarly exempted from human civil laws, duly made, certain laymen who are called "jolly friars" in Italy and Beguins elsewhere; on the same ground they have dealt and can deal at their pleasure with the Knights Templars, the Hospitallers, and many other such orders, like that of Altopascio and so on. But if all such persons are thus exempted from the jurisdiction of rulers in accordance with these decretals, which also grant certain immunities from public or civil burdens to those who are thus exempted, then it seems very likely that the majority of men will slip into these orders, especially since both literate and illiterate persons are accepted indiscriminately. For everyone is prone to pursue his own advantage and to avoid what is disadvantageous. But with the greater number or majority of men slipping into clerical orders, the jurisdiction and coercive power of rulers will become ineffective, and the number of those who have to bear the public burdens will be reduced to almost nothing; which is the gravest evil, and destructive of the polity. For he who enjoys civil honors and advantages, like peace and the protection of the human legislator, must not be exempt from the civil burdens and jurisdiction without the determination of the same legislator. Hence the Apostle said, in the epistle to the Romans, Chapter 13: And for this very reason "pay ye tribute."

To avoid this eventuality it must be granted, in accordance with the truth, that the ruler by authority of the legislator has jurisdiction over all bishops or priests and clergymen, lest the polity be destroyed by having an unordered multiplicity of governments, as was shown in Chapter XVII of Discourse I; and the ruler must determine, in the province subject to him, the definite number of clergymen, as also of the persons in every other part of the polity, lest by their undue increase they be able to resist the ruler's coercive power, or otherwise disturb the polity, or deprive the city or state of its welfare by their insolence and their freedom from necessary tasks, as we showed from the *Politics*, Book V, Chapter 1, in Chapter XV of Discourse I.

Thus, therefore, it is the human law and judge, in the third sense, which have to regulate transient human acts which affect the advantage or disadvantage, right or wrong, of someone other than the agent. To this coercive jurisdiction all men, lay and clergy, must be subject. But there are also certain other judges according to human laws, who have been called judges in the first or the second sense, such as the teachers of these laws; but these judges have no coercive authority, and there is nothing to prevent that in any one community there be many of them, even when they are not subordinate to one another.

[. . .]

9

Niccolò Machiavelli, *The Prince*, Chapters 15 to 18 and 25

Introduction

Like many political tracts written by Renaissance humanists, *The Prince* – composed in 1513 by the erstwhile Florentine diplomat, Niccolò di Bernardo dei Machiavelli (1469–1527) – was a book of advice to a ruler: on this occasion, and in the hope of reviving its author's career, to Lorenzo de Medici, whose family had just been restored to power in Florence after a republican interregnum. This helps to explain the limited scope of the work which, unlike most other classics of political theory, both earlier and later, is virtually silent on such matters as particular laws and political institutions and the justifying grounds for political authority. (It is silent, as well, on the issues that had obsessed medieval writers concerning the relationship between political authority and divine law.) Indeed, Machiavelli makes it clear that his aim is not advice to rulers in general, but specifically to those like Lorenzo who have recently acquired power through 'the arms of others or by good fortune.'

The best known, or most notorious, chapters (XV following) of *The Prince* are those in which Machiavelli adumbrates 'the rules of conduct for a prince towards subjects and friends.' It is these chapters which have not only prompted a host of critics to apply to their author such epithets

From Niccolò Machiavelli, *The Prince*, trans. W. K. Marriott, London: Dent, 1908, pp. 83–100, 139–44 (some lines and notes omitted).

as 'the murderous Machiavel' (Shakespeare) and 'a teacher of evil' (Leo Strauss)[1], but which are also responsible for the coining of the adjective 'Machiavellian' as a term for devious, unprincipled political practice. This is scarcely surprising, given that, in these chapters, one finds Machiavelli advising his prince to engage in, among other things, dissimulation, meanness, and cruelty wherever this is necessary for the achievement of his ends. More generally, 'it is necessary for a prince wishing to hold his own to know how to do wrong . . . according to necessity' (Ch XV).

Despite such remarks, it is not obvious, however, that Machiavelli warrants such labels as a 'teacher of evil' or a political amoralist. To begin with, one needs to stress the phrase 'according to necessity,' for Machiavelli does not maintain that cruelty and other 'vices' are to be permitted when they are unnecessary – in less bellicose and unstable times than his own, for example. Second, he makes it clear that the overriding aim of the prince is not personal, material advantage, but 'the maintenance of the state,' and hence the overall welfare of those living within it. Third, there is no need to doubt the sincerity of Machiavelli's insistence that his 'rules of conduct' are conducive to the principal humanist ideal, derived from such Roman theorists as Cicero (see V.6 above) of *virtú* – defined by one commentator as 'the quality which enables a prince to withstand the blows of Fortune . . . and to rise in consequence to the heights of princely fame, winning honour and glory for himself and security for his government.'[2]

Finally, Machiavelli would argue, in one of two ways, against the charge that he is advocating that princes act viciously or unvirtuously. With respect, for example, to meanness, he argues that this is not really a vice on the ruler's part at all: on the contrary, it is a prince's liberality – resulting in having to raise taxes, and thereby in dissent and perhaps rebellion – that is the true political vice. And with respect to mercy, he argues that, while this is indeed a virtue, earlier humanist theorists have badly misunderstood what it requires. Is it not a tough ruler like Cesare Borgia, willing to administer a short sharp shock, who is more authentically merciful than more squeamish rulers who allow opposition – and hence the prospect of future, large-scale bloodshed – to go undeterred (Ch XVII)?

Machiavelli was scientific in his methodology (analyzing the effect of variations in specific factors of political situations) and pragmatic in his aims – but not, arguably, in the negative sense of being 'Machiavellian.' Rather, Machiavelli is the ancestor of such later approaches in political philosophy as those Michael Oakeshott (V.22), for whom sensible political theorizing must eschew unexamined moral pieties and focus instead on how power can and should actually be exercised in full, rational awareness of the exigencies of the times and circumstances.

Notes

1 See Strauss's *Thoughts on Machiavelli*, Glencoe, IL: University of Chicago Press, 1958.
2 Q. Skinner, *Machiavelli: A Very Short Introduction*, Oxford: Oxford University Press, 2000, p. 40.

Machiavelli, *The Prince*

Fifteenth Chapter: Concerning Things for Which Men, and Especially Princes, Are Praised or Blamed

It remains now to see what ought to be the rules of conduct for a prince towards subjects and friends. And as I know that many have written on this point, I expect I shall be considered presumptuous in mentioning it again, especially as in discussing it I shall depart from the methods of other people. But, it being my intention to write a thing which shall be useful to him who apprehends it, it appears to me more appropriate to follow up the real truth of a matter than the imagination of it; for many have pictured republics and principalities which in fact have never been known or seen, because how one lives is so far distant from how one ought to live, that he who neglects what is done for what ought to be done, sooner effects his ruin than his preservation; for a man who wishes to act entirely up to his professions of virtue soon meets with what destroys him among so much that is evil.

Hence it is necessary for a prince wishing to hold his own to know how to do wrong, and to make use of it or not according to necessity. Therefore, putting on one side imaginary things concerning a prince, and discussing those which are real, I say that all men when they are spoken of, and chiefly princes for being more highly placed, are remarkable for some of those qualities which bring them either blame or praise; and thus it is that one is reputed liberal, another miserly, using a Tuscan term (because an avaricious person in our language is still he who desires to possess by robbery, whilst we call one miserly who deprives himself too much of the use of his own); one is reputed generous, one rapacious; one cruel, one compassionate, one faithless, another faithful; one effeminate and cowardly, another bold and brave; one affable, another haughty; one lascivious, another chaste; one sincere, another cunning; one hard, another easy; one grave, another frivolous; one religious, another unbelieving, and the like. And I know that every one will confess that it would be most praiseworthy in a prince to exhibit all the above qualities that are considered good; but because they can neither be entirely possessed nor observed, for human conditions do not permit it, it is necessary for him to be sufficiently prudent that he may know how to avoid the reproach of those vices which would lose him his state; and also to keep himself, if it be possible, from those which would not lose him it; but this not being possible, he may with less hesitation abandon himself to them. And again, he need not make himself uneasy at incurring a reproach for those vices without which the state can only be saved with difficulty, for if everything is considered carefully, it will be found that something which looks like virtue, if followed, would be his ruin; whilst something else, which looks like vice, yet followed brings him security and prosperity.

Sixteenth Chapter: Concerning Liberality and Meanness

Commencing then with the first of the above-named characteristics, I say that it would be well to be reputed liberal. Nevertheless, liberality exercised in a way that does not bring you the reputation for it, injures you; for if one exercises it honestly and as it should be exercised, it may not become known, and you will not avoid the reproach of its opposite. Therefore, any one wishing to maintain among men the name of liberal is obliged to avoid no attribute or magnificence; so that a prince thus inclined will consume in such acts all his property, and will be compelled in the end, if he wish to maintain the name of liberal, to unduly weigh down his people, and tax them, and do everything he can to get money. This will soon make him odious to his subjects, and becoming poor he will be little valued by any one; thus, with his liberality, having offended many and rewarded few, he is affected by the very first trouble and imperilled by whatever may be the first danger; recognizing this himself, and wishing to draw back from it, he runs at once into the reproach of being miserly.

Therefore, a prince, not being able to exercise this virtue of liberality in such a way that it is recognized, except to his cost, if he is wise he ought not to fear the reputation of being mean, for in time he will come to be more considered than if liberal, seeing that with his economy his revenues are enough, that he can defend himself against all attacks, and is able to engage in enterprises without burdening his people; thus it comes to pass that he exercises liberality towards all from whom he does not take, who are numberless, and meanness towards those to whom he does not give, who are few.

We have not seen great things done in our time except by those who have been considered mean; the rest have failed. Pope Julius II was assisted in reaching the papacy by a reputation for liberality, yet he did not strive afterwards to keep it up, when he made war on the King of France; and he made many wars without imposing any extraordinary tax on his subjects, for he supplied his additional expenses out of his long thriftiness. The present King of Spain would not have undertaken or conquered in so many enterprises if he had been reputed liberal. A prince, therefore, provided that he has not to rob his subjects, that he can defend himself, that he does not become poor and abject, that he is not forced to become rapacious, ought to hold of little account a reputation for being mean, for it is one of those vices which will enable him to govern.

And if any one should say: Caesar obtained empire by liberality, and many others have reached the highest positions by having been liberal, and by being considered so, I answer: Either you are a prince in fact, or in a way to become one. In the first case this liberality is dangerous, in the second it is very necessary to be considered liberal; and Caesar was one of those who wished to become pre-eminent in Rome; but if he had survived after becoming so, and had not moderated his expenses, he would have destroyed his government. And if any one should reply: Many have been princes, and have done great things with armies, who have been considered very liberal, I reply: Either a prince spends that which is his own or his subjects' or else that of others. In the first case he ought to be sparing, in the second he ought not to neglect any opportunity for liberality. And to the prince who goes forth with his army, supporting it by pillage, sack, and extortion, handling that which belongs to others, this liberality is necessary, otherwise he would not be followed by soldiers. And of that which is neither yours nor your subjects' you can be a ready giver, as were Cyrus, Caesar, and Alexander; because it does not take away your reputation if you squander that of others, but adds to it; it is only squandering your own that injures you.

And there is nothing wastes so rapidly as liberality, for even whilst you exercise it you lose the power to do so, and so become either poor or despised, or else, in avoiding poverty, rapacious and hated. And a prince should guard himself, above all things, against being despised and hated; and liberality leads you to both. Therefore it is wiser to have a reputation for meanness which brings reproach without hatred, than to be compelled through seeking a reputation for liberality to incur a name for rapacity which begets reproach with hatred.

Seventeenth Chapter: Concerning Cruelty and Clemency, and Whether it is Better to be Loved than Feared

Coming now to the other qualities mentioned above, I say that every prince ought to desire to be considered clement and not cruel. Nevertheless he ought to take care not to misuse this clemency. Cesare Borgia was considered cruel; notwithstanding, his cruelty reconciled the Romagna, unified it, and restored it to peace and loyalty. And if this be rightly considered, he will be seen to have been much more merciful than the Florentine people, who, to avoid a reputation for cruelty, permitted Pistoia to be destroyed. Therefore a prince, so long as he keeps his subjects united and loyal, ought not to mind the reproach of cruelty; because with a few examples he will be more merciful than those who, through too much mercy, allow disorders to arise, from which follow murders or robberies; for these are wont to injure the whole people, whilst those executions which originate with a prince offend the individual only.

And of all princes, it is impossible for the new prince to avoid the imputation of cruelty, owing to new states being full of dangers. [. . .]

Nevertheless he ought to be slow to believe and to act, nor should he himself show fear, but proceed in a temperate manner with prudence and humanity, so that too much confidence may not make him incautious and too much distrust render him intolerable.

Upon this a question arises: whether it be better to be loved than feared or feared than loved? It may be answered that one should wish to be both, but, because it is difficult to unite them in one person, it is much safer to be feared than loved, when, of the two, either must be dispensed with. Because this is to be asserted in general of men, that they are ungrateful, fickle, false cowardly, covetous, and as long as you, succeed they are yours entirely; they will offer you their blood, property, life, and children, as is said above, when the need is far distant; but when it approaches they turn against you. And that prince who, relying entirely on their promises, has neglected other pre-

cautions, is ruined; because friendships that are obtained by payments, and not by greatness or nobility of mind, may indeed be earned, but they are not secured, and in time of need cannot be relied upon; and men have less scruple in offending one who is beloved than one who is feared, for love is preserved by the link of obligation which, owing to the baseness of men, is broken at every opportunity for their advantage; but fear preserves you by a dread of punishment which never fails.

Nevertheless a prince ought to inspire fear in such a way that, if he does not win love, he avoids hatred; because he can endure very well being feared whilst he is not hated, which will always be as long as he abstains from the property of his citizens and subjects and from their women. But when it is necessary for him to proceed against the life of someone, he must do it on proper justification and for manifest cause, but above all things he must keep his hands off the property of others, because men more quickly forget the death of their father than the loss of their patrimony. Besides, pretexts for taking away the property are never wanting; for he who has once begun to live by robbery will always find pretexts for seizing what belongs to others; but reasons for taking life, on the contrary, are more difficult to find and sooner lapse. But when a prince is with his army, and has under control a multitude of soldiers, then it is quite necessary for him to disregard the reputation of cruelty, for without it he would never hold his army united or disposed to its duties.

Among the wonderful deeds of Hannibal this one is enumerated: that having led an enormous army, composed of many various races of men, to fight in foreign lands, no dissensions arose either among them or against the prince, whether in his bad or in his good fortune. This arose from nothing else than his inhuman cruelty, which, with his boundless valour, made him revered and terrible in the sight of his soldiers, but without that cruelty, his other virtues were not sufficient to produce this effect. And shortsighted writers admire his deeds from one point of view and from another condemn the principal cause of them. That it is true his other virtues would not have been sufficient for him may be proved by the case of Scipio, that most excellent man, not only of his own times but within the memory of man, against whom, nevertheless, his army rebelled in

Spain; this arose from nothing but his too great forbearance, which gave his soldiers more licence than is consistent with military discipline. For this he was upbraided in the senate by Fabius Maximus, and called the corrupter of the Roman soldiery. The Locrians were laid waste by a legate of Scipio, yet they were not avenged by him, nor was the insolence of the legate punished, owing entirely to his easy nature. Insomuch that some-one in the senate, wishing to excuse him, said there were many men who knew much better how not to err than to correct the errors of others. This disposition, if he had been continued in the command, would have destroyed in time the fame and glory of Scipio; but, he being under the control of the senate, this injurious character-istic not only concealed itself, but contributed to his glory.

Returning to the question of being feared or loved, I come to the conclusion that, men loving according to their own will and fearing accord-ing to that of the prince, a wise prince should establish himself on that which is in his own control and not in that of others; he must endeav-our only to avoid hatred, as is noted.

Eighteenth Chapter: Concerning the Way in Which Princes Should Keep Faith

Every one admits how praiseworthy it is in a prince to keep faith, and to live with integrity and not with craft. Nevertheless our experience has been that those princes who have done great things have held good faith of little account, and have known how to circumvent the intellect of men by craft, and in the end have overcome those who have relied on their word. You must know there are two ways of contesting, the one by the law, the other by force; the first method is proper to men, the second to beasts; but because the first is frequently not sufficient, it is necessary to have recourse to the second. Therefore it is necessary for a prince to understand how to avail himself of the beast and the man. This has been figuratively taught to princes by ancient writers, who describe how Achilles and many other princes of old were given to the Centaur Chiron to nurse, who brought them up in his discipline; which means solely that, as they had for a teacher one who was half beast and half man, so it is necessary for a prince to know how to make

use of both natures, and that one without the other is not durable. A prince, therefore, being compelled knowingly to adopt the beast, ought to choose the fox and the lion; because the lion cannot defend himself against snares and the fox cannot defend himself against wolves. Therefore, it is necessary to be a fox to discover the snares and a lion to terrify the wolves. Those who rely simply on the lion do not understand what they are about. Therefore a wise lord cannot, nor ought he to, keep faith when such observance may be turned against him, and when the reasons that caused him to pledge it exist no longer. If men were entirely good this precept would not hold, but because they are bad, and will not keep faith with you, you too are not bound to observe it with them. Nor will there ever be wanting to a prince legitimate reasons to excuse this non-observance. Of this endless modern examples could be given, show-ing how many treaties and engagements have been made void and of no effect through the faith-lessness of princes; and he who has known best how to employ the fox has succeeded best.

But it is necessary to know well how to disguise this characteristic, and to be a great pretender and dissembler; and men are so simple, and so sub-ject to present necessities, that he who seeks to deceive will always find someone who will allow himself to be deceived. One recent example I cannot pass over in silence. Alexander VI did nothing else but deceive men, nor ever thought of doing otherwise, and he always found victims; for there never was a man who had greater power in asserting, or who with greater oaths would affirm a thing, yet would observe it less; never-theless his deceits always succeeded according to his wishes, because he well understood this side of mankind.[2]

Therefore it is unnecessary for a prince to have all the good qualities I have enumerated, but it is very necessary to appear to have them. And I shall dare to say this also, that to have them and always to observe them is injurious, and that to appear to have them is useful; to appear mer-ciful, faithful, humane, religious, upright, and to be so, but with a mind so framed that should you require not to be so, you may be able and know how to change to the opposite.

And you have to understand this, that a prince, especially a new one, cannot observe all those things for which men are esteemed, being often forced, in order to maintain the state, to act contrary to fidelity, friendship, humanity, and religion. Therefore it is necessary for him to have a mind ready to turn itself accordingly as the winds and variations of fortune force it, yet, as I have said above, not to diverge from the good if he can avoid doing so, but, if compelled, then to know how to set about it.

For this reason a prince ought to take care that he never lets anything slip from his lips that is not replete with the above-named five qualities, that he may appear to him who sees and hears him altogether merciful, faithful, humane, upright, and religious. There is nothing more necessary to appear to have than this last quality, inasmuch as men judge generally more by the eye than by the hand, because it belongs to everybody to see you, to few to come in touch with you. Every one sees what you appear to be, few really know what you are, and those few dare not oppose themselves to the opinion of the many, who have the majesty of the state to defend them; and in the actions of all men, and especially of princes, which it is not prudent to challenge, one judges by the result.

For that reason, let a prince have the credit of conquering and holding his state, the means will always be considered honest, and he will be praised by everybody; because the vulgar are always taken by what a thing seems to be and by what comes of it; and in the world there are only the vulgar, for the few find a place there only when the many have no ground to rest on.

One prince[3] of the present time, whom it is not well to name, never preaches anything else but peace and good faith, and to both he is most hostile, and either, if he had kept it, would have deprived him of reputation and kingdom many a time.

[...]

Twenty-Fifth Chapter: What Fortune Can Effect in Human Affairs, and How to Withstand Her

It is not unknown to me how many men have had, and still have, the opinion that the affairs of the world are in such wise governed by Fortune and by God that men with their wisdom cannot direct them and that no one can even help them; and because of this they would have us believe that it is not necessary to labour much in affairs, but

to let chance govern them. This opinion has been more credited in our times because of the great changes in affairs which have been seen, and may still be seen, every day, beyond all human conjecture. Sometimes pondering over this, I am in some degree inclined to their opinion. Nevertheless, not to extinguish our free will, I hold it to be true that Fortune is the arbiter of one-half of our actions, but that she still leaves us to direct the other half, or perhaps a little less.

I compare her to one of those raging rivers, which when in flood overflows the plains, sweeping away trees and buildings, bearing away the soil from place to place; everything flies before it, all yield to its violence, without being able in any way to withstand it; and yet, though its nature be such, it does not follow therefore that men, when the weather becomes fair, shall not make provision, both with defences and barriers, in such a manner that, rising again, the waters may pass away by canal, and their force be neither so unrestrained nor so dangerous. So it happens with Fortune, who shows her power where valour has not prepared to resist her, and thither she turns her forces where she knows that barriers and defences have not been raised to constrain her.

And if you will consider Italy, which is the seat of these changes, and which has given to them their impulse, you will see it to be an open country without barriers and without any defence. For if it had been defended by proper valour, as are Germany, Spain, and France, either this invasion would not have made the great changes it has made or it would not have come at all. And this I consider enough to say concerning resistance to fortune in general.

But confining myself more to the particular, I say that a prince may be seen happy to-day and ruined to-morrow without having shown any change of disposition or character. This, I believe, arises firstly from causes that have already been discussed at length, namely, that the prince who relies entirely upon fortune is lost when it changes. I believe also that he will be successful who directs his actions according to the spirit of the times, and that he whose actions do not accord with the times will not be successful. Because men are seen, in affairs that lead to the end which every man has before him, namely, glory and riches, to get there by various methods; one with caution, another with haste; one by force, another by skill; one by patience, another by its opposite; and each one succeeds in reaching the goal by a different method. One can also see of two cautious men the one attain his end, the other fail; and similarly, two men by different observances are equally successful, the one being cautious, the other impetuous; all this arises from nothing else than whether or not they conform in their methods to the spirit of the times. This follows from what I have said, that two men working differently bring about the same effect, and of two working similarly, one attains his object and the other does not.

Changes in estate also issue from this, for if, to one who governs himself with caution and patience, times and affairs converge in such a way that his administration is successful, his fortune is made; but if times and affairs change, he is ruined if he does not change his course of action. But a man is not often found sufficiently circumspect to know how to accommodate himself to the change, both because he cannot deviate from what nature inclines him to, and also because, having always prospered by acting in one way, he cannot be persuaded that it is well to leave it; and, therefore, the cautious man, when it is time to turn adventurous, does not know how to do it, hence he is ruined; but had he changed his conduct with the times fortune would not have changed.

Pope Julius II went to work impetuously in all his affairs, and found the times and circumstances conform so well to that line of action that he always met with success. Consider his first enterprise against Bologna, Messer Giovanni Bentivogli being still alive. The Venetians were not agreeable to it, nor was the King of Spain, and he had the enterprise still under discussion with the King of France; nevertheless he personally entered upon the expedition with his accustomed boldness and energy, a move which made Spain and the Venetians stand irresolute and passive, the latter from fear, the former from desire to recover all the kingdom of Naples; on the other hand, he drew after him the King of France, because that king, having observed the movement, and desiring to make the pope his

friend so as to humble the Venetians, found it impossible to refuse him soldiers without manifestly offending him. Therefore Julius with his impetuous action accomplished what no other pontiff with simple human wisdom could have done; for if he had waited in Rome until he could get away, with his plans arranged and everything fixed, as any other pontiff would have done, he would never have succeeded. Because the King of France would have made a thousand excuses, and the others would have raised a thousand fears.

I will leave his other actions alone, as they were all alike, and they all succeeded, for the shortness of his life did not let him experience the contrary; but if circumstances had arisen which required him to go cautiously, his ruin would have followed, because he would never have deviated from those ways to which nature inclined him.

I conclude therefore that, fortune being changeful and mankind steadfast in their ways, so long as the two are in agreement men are successful, but unsuccessful when they fall out. For my part I consider that it is better to be adventurous than cautious, because Fortune is a woman, and if you wish to keep her under it is necessary to beat and ill use her; and it is seen that she allows herself to be mastered by the adventurous rather than by those who go to work more coldly. She is, therefore, always, woman-like, a lover of young men, because they are less cautious, more violent, and with more audacity command her.

Notes

1　The reference is to the Florentine authorities' reluctance, with disastrous consequences, to put down the rioting in 1502–03 between rival factions in the nearby town of Pistoia.

2　Alexander VI, "the Borgia Pope," was the father of Cesare Borgia, whom he made Duke of Romagna in 1501. Machiavelli's admiration for the Borgias was a qualified one.

3　King Ferdinand of Spain, the contemporary statesman most admired by Machiavelli.

10

Thomas Hobbes, *Leviathan*, Chapters XIII–XV, XVII, XVIII (selections)

Introduction

In earlier selections – for example, the Buddha's discourse on kingship (V.2) – we have already encountered one of the leading and perennial ideas in political philosophy: that of a "social contract" as the source of legitimate political authority and obligation. But it was not until the seventeenth century that this idea was philosophically elaborated and became the dominant one in European and American political thinking. In the English-speaking world, at least, the decisive first contribution was made by Thomas Hobbes (1588–1679) in his 1651 work, *Leviathan*. Written shortly after the end of the English Civil War – from whose threat Hobbes remarked, without embarrassment, that he "was the first of all who fled" (to Paris, in 1640) – the book plainly reflects the conviction, cemented by the horrors of that conflict, that challenging the authority of the sovereign of a state (in this case, King Charles I) is almost always an evil. Hobbes's conviction, however, hardly needed empirical confirmation, for his argument for virtually absolute obedience to the sovereign has a distinctly *a priori* flavor.

Like other social contract theorists, before and after, Hobbes's version is colored by a depiction

From Thomas Hobbes, *Leviathan Or the Matter, Form and Power of a Commonwealth Ecclesiastical and Civil*, Oxford: Blackwell, 1960, pp. 80–92, 103–5, 109–18.

of a pre-political "state of nature" from which, through a social contract, human beings emerge into a properly social and political condition. Like most other theorists, too, Hobbes does not take it that there has ever actually existed a pristine state of nature, from which some historical act of contract has lifted us. (That said, he thinks that in some "savage" lands, and in circumstances like that of a civil war, people's condition may approximate to a state of nature). Rather, the state of nature is the condition in which people would be living in the absence of any effective political authority, and the contract – to which they implicitly subscribe through obedience to such an authority – is something they would explicitly sign up to, given the alternative, if they were acting rationally.

Hobbes's depiction of the state of nature is famously bleak. It is, potentially at least, a state of "war of every man, against every man," and one in which the life of human beings is "solitary, poor, nasty, brutish, and short." His reasons for supposing that this is how life without political authority would be are rooted in his materialist philosophy and psychological egoism. He himself viewed his political philosophy as logically following from a few mechanical, Galilean premisses extended to human nature. For Hobbes, a human being is simply a physical machine whose so-called "voluntary" behavior is entirely dictated by "appetite and aversion." In particular, an appetite to stay alive and a related aversion to anything that threatens life guarantee that in the absence of constraints on self-interested behavior, everyone will do whatever is necessary – including the killing of others – in order defensively to protect themselves or aggressively to satisfy their appetite. There is, for Hobbes, nothing "wrong" in such behavior, for it is not until the establishment of laws and shared moral norms that talk of right and wrong, good and evil has any purchase.

Even in a state of nature, however, a person will recognize demands of reason such as that, out of self-interest, one "ought to endeavour peace, as far as he has hope of obtaining it." Such demands of reason, Hobbes calls "laws of nature." Since it would be irrational – indeed, psychologically impossible – for a person to renounce his powers unless in return his or her security could be guaranteed, a contract or covenant between the individual and the sovereign becomes rationally sensible. In exchange for security, individuals "transfer" powers and promise obedience to the sovereign. The sovereign, in turn, stands ready to defend members of the contract against one another and against outsiders. After all, as Hobbes puts it, "covenants without the sword, are but words," without binding force. Possessing sufficient power to organize the disparate atoms of desire composing society into an orderly whole, a Leviathan, the sovereign renders would-be contract-breakers averse to violating the rights of others, and he provides each an incentive to abide by the laws of nature universally.

For two reasons, cynical readers may wonder whether, in Hobbes's account, even covenants *with* the sword do anything to establish political authority and obligation. For one thing, critics will question whether a covenant or contract is really doing any work in that account. Isn't it the sword alone that makes lawfulness obligatory – that is, required by rational self-interest – regardless of whether people have entered the contract? (After all, it makes no difference to Hobbes whether the sovereign has been elected or has come to power through military force.) Second, they will ask if, in any genuine sense, it is *obligations* that citizens have to the sovereign. Are they not simply bound, by the mechanism of self-interest, to obey the sovereign, except when their lives are in danger, provided that he or she possesses the power to guarantee peace?

These are questions with which, as we shall see in connection with later texts, like John Locke's (V.11), political thinkers after Hobbes grappled. One thing, though, is apparent. If Hobbes's deduction of the need for a powerful and, if necessary, ruthless sovereign is to be challenged, it must be on the basis of a less dark vision of human nature than Hobbes's own – one which, say, credits human beings with a moral sense distinct from rational self-interest. Observers of the recent fate of Iraq after the removal of one such ruthless sovereign may wonder how inaccurate this vision is.

Hobbes, *Leviathan*

Chapter XIII: Of the Natural Condition of Mankind as Concerning Their Felicity, and Misery

Men by nature equal. NATURE hath made men so equal, in the faculties of the body, and mind; as that though there be found one man sometimes manifestly stronger in body, or of quicker mind than another; yet when all is reckoned together, the difference between man, and man, is not so considerable, as that one man can thereupon claim to himself any benefit, to which another may not pretend, as well as he. For as to the strength of body, the weakest has strength enough to kill the strongest, either by secret machination, or by

confederacy with others, that are in the same danger with himself.

And as to the faculties of the mind, setting aside the arts grounded upon words, and especially that skill of proceeding upon general, and infallible rules, called science; which very few have, and but in few things; as being not a native faculty, born with us; nor attained, as prudence, while we look after somewhat else, I find yet a greater equality amongst men, than that of strength. For prudence, is but experience; which equal time, equally bestows on all men, in those things they equally apply themselves unto. That which may perhaps make such equality incredible, is but a vain conceit of one's own wisdom, which almost all men think they have in a greater degree, than the vulgar; that is, than all men but themselves, and a few others, whom by fame, or for concurring with themselves, they approve. For such is the nature of men, that howsoever they may acknowledge many others to be more witty, or more eloquent, or more learned; yet they will hardly believe there be many so wise as themselves; for they see their own wit at hand, and other men's at a distance. But this proveth rather that men are in that point equal, than unequal. For there is not ordinarily a greater sign of the equal distribution of any thing, than that every man is contented with his share.

From equality proceeds diffidence. From this equality of ability, ariseth equality of hope in the attaining of our ends. And therefore if any two men desire the same thing, which nevertheless they cannot both enjoy, they become enemies; and in the way to their end, which is principally their own conservation, and sometimes their delectation only, endeavour to destroy, or subdue one another. And from hence it comes to pass, that where an invader hath no more to fear, than another man's single power; if one plant, sow, build, or possess a convenient seat, others may probably be expected to come prepared with forces united, to dispossess, and deprive him, not only of the fruit of his labour, but also of his life, or liberty. And the invader again is in the like danger of another.

From diffidence war. And from this diffidence of one another, there is no way for any man to secure himself, so reasonable, as anticipation; that is, by force, or wiles, to master the persons of all men he can, so long, till he see no other power great enough to endanger him: and this is no more than his own conservation requireth, and is generally allowed. Also because there be some, that taking pleasure in contemplating their own power in the acts of conquest, which they pursue farther than their security requires; if others, that otherwise would be glad to be at ease within modest bounds, should not by invasion increase their power, they would not be able, long time, by standing only on their defence, to subsist. And by consequence, such augmentation of dominion over men being necessary to a man's conservation, it ought to be allowed him.

Again, men have no pleasure, but on the contrary a great deal of grief, in keeping company, where there is no power able to over-awe them all. For every man looketh that his companion should value him, at the same rate he sets upon himself: and upon all signs of contempt, or undervaluing, naturally endeavours, as far as he dares, (which amongst them that have no common power to keep them in quiet, is far enough to make them destroy each other), to extort a greater value from his contemners, by damage; and from others, by the example.

So that in the nature of man, we find three principal causes of quarrel. First, competition; secondly, diffidence; thirdly, glory.

The first, maketh men invade for gain; the second, for safety; and the third, for reputation. The first use violence, to make themselves masters of other men's persons, wives, children, and cattle; the second, to defend them; the third, for trifles, as a word, a smile, a different opinion, and any other sign of undervalue, either direct in their persons, or by reflection in their kindred, their friends, their nation, their profession, or their name.

Out of civil states, there is always war of every one against every one. Hereby it is manifest, that during the time men live without a common power to keep them all in awe, they are in that condition which is called war; and such a war, as is of every man, against every man. For WAR, consisteth not in battle only, or the act of fighting; but in a tract of time, wherein the will to contend by battle is sufficiently known: and therefore the notion of *time*, is to be considered in the nature of war; as it is in the nature of weather. For as the nature of foul weather, lieth not in a shower or two of rain; but in an inclination thereto of many days together: so the nature of war, consisteth not in actual fighting; but in the known disposition thereto, during all the time there is no assurance to the contrary. All other time is PEACE.

The incommodities of such a war. Whatsoever therefore is consequent to a time of war, where every man is enemy to every man; the same is consequent to the time, wherein men live without other security, than what their own strength, and their own invention shall furnish them withal. In such condition, there is no place for industry; because the fruit thereof is uncertain: and consequently no culture of the earth; no navigation, nor use of the commodities that may be imported by sea; no commodious building; no instruments of moving, and removing, such things as require much force; no knowledge of the face of the earth; no account of time; no arts; no letters; no society; and which is worst of all, continual fear, and danger of violent death; and the life of man, solitary, poor, nasty, brutish, and short.

It may seem strange to some man, that has not well weighed these things; that nature should thus dissociate, and render men apt to invade, and destroy one another: and he may therefore, not trusting to this inference, made from the passions, desire perhaps to have the same confirmed by experience. Let him therefore consider with himself, when taking a journey, he arms himself, and seeks to go well accompanied; when going to sleep, he locks his doors; when even in his house he locks his chests; and this when he knows there be laws, and public officers, armed, to revenge all injuries shall be done him; what opinion he has of his fellow-subjects, when he rides armed; of his fellow citizens, when he locks his doors; and of his children, and servants, when he locks his chests. Does he not there as much accuse mankind by his actions, as I do by my words? But neither of us accuse man's nature in it. The desires, and other passions of man, are in themselves no sin. No more are the actions, that proceed from those passions, till they know a law that forbids them: which till laws be made they cannot know: nor can any law be made, till they have agreed upon the person that shall make it.

It may peradventure be thought, there was never such a time, nor condition of war as this; and I believe it was never generally so, over all the world: but there are many places, where they live so now. For the savage people in many places of America, except the government of small families, the concord whereof dependeth on natural lust, have no government at all; and live at this day in that brutish manner, as I said before. Howsoever, it may be perceived what manner of life there would be, where there were no common power to fear, by the manner of life, which men that have formerly lived under a peaceful government, use to degenerate into, in a civil war.

But though there had never been any time, wherein particular men were in a condition of war one against another; yet in all times, kings, and persons of sovereign authority, because of their independency, are in continual jealousies, and in the state and posture of gladiators; having their weapons pointing, and their eyes fixed on one another; that is, their forts, garrisons, and guns upon the frontiers of their kingdoms; and continual spies upon their neighbours; which is a posture of war. But because they uphold thereby, the industry of their subjects; there does not follow from it, that misery, which accompanies the liberty of particular men.

In such a war nothing is unjust. To this war of every man, against every man, this also is consequent; that nothing can be unjust. The notions of right and wrong, justice and injustice have there no place. Where there is no common power, there is no law: where no law, no injustice. Force, and fraud, are in war the two cardinal virtues. Justice, and injustice are none of the faculties neither of the body, nor mind. If they were, they might be in a man that were alone in the world, as well as his senses, and passions. They are qualities, that relate to men in society, not in solitude. It is consequent also to the same condition, that there be no propriety, no dominion, no *mine* and *thine* distinct; but only that to be every man's, that he can get: and for so long, as he can keep it. And thus much for the ill condition, which man by mere nature is actually placed in; though with a possibility to come out of it, consisting partly in the passions, partly in his reason.

The passions that incline men to peace. The passions that incline men to peace, are fear of death; desire of such things as are necessary to commodious living; and a hope by their industry to obtain them. And reason suggesteth convenient articles of peace, upon which men may be drawn to agreement. These articles, are they, which otherwise are called the Laws of Nature: whereof I shall speak more particularly, in the two following chapters.

Chapter XIV: Of the First and Second Natural Laws, and of Contracts

Right of nature what. THE RIGHT OF NATURE, which writers commonly call *jus naturale*, is the liberty each man hath, to use his own power, as he will himself, for the preservation of his own nature; that is to say, of his own life; and consequently, of doing any thing, which in his own judgment, and reason, he shall conceive to be the aptest means thereunto.

Liberty what. By LIBERTY, is understood, according to the proper signification of the word, the absence of external impediments:

which impediments, may oft take away part of a man's power to do what he would; but cannot hinder him from using the power left him, according as his judgment, and reason shall dictate to him.

A law of nature what. A LAW OF NATURE, *lex naturalis,* is a precept or general rule, found out by reason, by which a man is forbidden to do that, which is destructive of his life, or taketh away the means of preserving the same; and to omit that, by which he thinketh it may be best preserved. For though they that speak of this subject, use to confound *jus,* and *lex, right* and *law:* yet they ought to be distinguished; *Difference of right and law.* because RIGHT, consisteth in liberty to do, or to forbear: whereas LAW, determineth, and bindeth to one of them: so that law, and right, differ as much, as obligation, and liberty; which in one and the same matter are inconsistent.

Naturally every man has right to every thing. And because the condition of man, as hath been declared in the precedent chapter, is a condition of war of every one against every one; in which case every one is governed by his own reason; and there is nothing he can make use of, that may not be a help unto him, in preserving his life against his enemies; it followeth, that in such a condition, every man has a right to every thing; even to one another's body. And therefore, as long as this natural right of every man to every thing endureth, there can be no security to any man, how strong or wise soever he be, of living out the time, which nature ordinarily alloweth men to live. And consequently it is a precept, or general rule of reason, *that every man, ought to endeavour peace, as far as he has hope of* *The fundamental law of nature.* *obtaining it; and when he cannot* *obtain it, that he may seek, and* *use, all helps, and advantages of war.* The first branch of which rule, containeth the first, and fundamental law of nature; which is, *to seek peace, and follow it.* The second, the sum of the right of nature; which is, *by all means we can, to defend ourselves.*

From this fundamental law of nature, by which men are commanded to endeavour peace, is derived this second law; *that a man be willing, when others are so too, as far-forth, as for peace, and* *defence of himself he shall think it* *The second law of nature.* *necessary, to lay down this right to* *all things; and be contented with so* much liberty against other men, as he would allow other men against himself.* For as long as every man holdeth this right, of doing any thing he liketh; so long are all men in the condition of war. But if other men will not lay down their right, as well as he; then there is no reason for any one, to divest himself of his: for that were to expose himself to prey, which no man is bound to, rather than to dispose himself to peace. This is that law of the Gospel; *whatsoever you require that others should do to you, that do ye to them.* And that law of all men, *quod tibi fieri non vis, alteri ne feceris.*

What it is to lay down a right. To *lay down* a man's *right* to any thing, is to *divest* himself of the *liberty,* of hindering another of the benefit of his own right to the same. For he that renounceth, or passeth away his right, giveth not to any other man a right which he had not before; because there is nothing to which every man had not right by nature: but only standeth out of his way, that he may enjoy his own original right, without hindrance from him; not without hindrance from another. So that the effect which redoundeth to one man, by another man's defect of right, is but so much diminution of impediments to the use of his own right original. *Renouncing a right, what it is.* Right is laid aside, either by simply renouncing it; or by transferring it to another. By *Transferring right what. Obligation.* simply RENOUNCING; when he cares not to whom the benefit thereof redoundeth. By TRANSFERRING; when he intendeth the benefit thereof to some certain person, or persons. And when a man hath in either manner abandoned, or granted away his right; then he is said to be OBLIGED, or BOUND, not to hinder those, to *Duty.* whom such right is granted, or abandoned, from the benefit of it: and that *Injustice.* he *ought,* and it is his DUTY, not to make void that voluntary act of his own: and that such hindrance is INJUSTICE, and INJURY, as being *sine jure;* the right being before renounced, or transferred. So that *injury,* or *injustice,* in the controversies of the world, is somewhat like to that, which in the disputations of scholars is called *absurdity.* For as it is there called an absurdity, to contradict what one maintained in the beginning: so in the world, it is called injustice, and injury, voluntarily to undo that, which from the beginning he had voluntarily done. The way by which a man either simply renounceth, or transferreth his right, is a declaration, or signification, by some voluntary and sufficient sign, or signs, that he doth so renounce, or transfer; or hath so renounced, or transferred the same, to him that accepteth it. And these signs are either words only, or actions only; or, as it happeneth most often, both words, and actions. And the same are the BONDS, by which men are bound, and obliged: bonds, that have their strength, not from their own nature, for nothing is more easily broken than a man's word, but from fear of some evil consequence upon the rupture.

Whensoever a man transferreth his right, or renounceth it; it is either in consideration of some right reciprocally transferred to himself; or for some other good he hopeth for thereby. For it is a voluntary act: and of the voluntary acts of *Not all rights are* every man, the object is some *alienable.* *good to himself.* And therefore there be some rights, which no man can be understood by any words, or other signs, to have abandoned, or transferred. As first a man cannot lay down the right of resisting them, that assault him by force, to take away his life; because he cannot be understood to aim thereby, at any good to himself. The same may be said of wounds, and chains, and imprisonment; both because there is no benefit consequent to such patience; as there is to the patience of suffering another to be wounded, or imprisoned: as also because a man cannot tell, when he seeth men proceed against him by violence whether they intend his death or not. And lastly the motive, and end for which this renouncing, and transferring of right is introduced, is nothing else but the security of a man's person, in his life, and in the means of so preserving life, as not to be weary of it. And therefore if a man by words, or other signs, seem to despoil himself of the end, for which those signs were intended; he is not to be understood as if he meant it, or that it was his will; but that he was ignorant of how such words and actions were to be interpreted.

Contract what. The mutual transferring of right, is that which men call CONTRACT.

There is difference between transferring of right to the thing; and transferring, or tradition, that is delivery of the thing itself. For the thing may be delivered together with the translation of the right; as in buying and selling with ready-money; or exchange of goods, or lands: and it may be delivered some time after.

Again, one of the contractors, may deliver the thing contracted for on his part, and leave the other to perform his part at some determinate time after, and in the mean time be trusted; and then the con-*Covenant what.* tract on his part, is called PACT, or COVENANT: or both parts may contract now, to perform hereafter: in which cases, he that is to perform in time to come, being trusted, his performance is called *keeping of promise*, or faith; and the failing of performance, if it be voluntary, *violation of faith.*

When the transferring of right, is not mutual: but one of the parties transferreth, in hope to gain thereby friendship, or service from another, or from his friends; or in hope to gain the reputation of charity, or magnanimity; or to deliver his mind from the pain of compassion; or in hope of reward in heaven; this is not contract, but *Free-gift.* GIFT, FREE-GIFT, GRACE: which words signify one and the same thing.

Signs of contract Signs of contract, are either *express.* *express*, or *by inference.* Express, are words spoken with understanding of what they signify: and such words are either of the time *present*, or *past*; as, *I give, I grant, I have given, I have granted, I will that this be yours*: or of the future; as, *I will give, I will grant*: *Promise.* which words of the future are called PROMISE.

Signs of cotract Signs by inference, are some-*by inference.* times the consequence of words; sometimes the consequence of silence; sometimes the consequence of actions; sometimes the consequence of forbearing an action: and generally a sign by inference, of any contract, is whatsoever sufficiently argues the will of the contractor.

[. . .]

Covenants of If a covenant be made, wherein *mutual trust,* neither of the parties perform pre-*when invalid.* sently, but trust one another; in the condition of mere nature, which is a condition of war of every man against every man, upon any reasonable suspicion, it is void: but if there be a common power set over them both, with right and force sufficient to compel performance, it is not void. For he that performeth first, has no assurance the other will perform after; because the bonds of words are too weak to bridle men's ambition, avarice, anger, and other passions, without the fear of some coercive power; which in the condition of mere nature, where all men are equal, and judges of the justness of their own fears, cannot possibly be supposed. And therefore he which performeth first, does but betray himself to his enemy; contrary to the right, he can never abandon, of defending his life, and means of living.

But in a civil estate, where there is a power set up to constrain those that would otherwise violate their faith, that fear is no more reasonable; and for that cause, he which by the covenant is to perform first, is obliged so to do.

The cause of fear, which maketh such a covenant invalid, must be always something arising after the covenant made; as some new fact, or other sign of the will not to perform: else it cannot make the covenant void. For that which could not hinder a man from promising, ought not to be admitted as a hindrance of performing.

Right to the end, containeth right to the means. He that transferreth any right, transferreth the means of enjoying it, as far as lieth in his power. As he that selleth land, is understood to transfer the herbage, and whatsoever grows upon it: nor can he that sells a mill turn away the stream that drives it. And they that give to a man the right of government in sovereignty, are understood to give him the right of levying money to maintain soldiers; and of appointing magistrates for the administration of justice.

No covenant with beasts. To make covenants with brute beasts, is impossible; because not understanding our speech, they understand not, nor accept of any translation of right; nor can translate any right to another: and without mutual acceptation, there is no covenant.

Nor with God without special revelation. To make covenant with God, is impossible, but by mediation of such as God speaketh to, either by revelation supernatural, or by his lieutenants that govern under him, and in his name: for otherwise we know not whether our covenants be accepted, or not. And therefore they that vow anything contrary to any law of nature, vow in vain; as being a thing unjust to pay such vow. And if it be a thing commanded by the law of nature, it is not the vow, but the law that binds them.

No covenant, but of possible and future. The matter, or subject of a covenant, is always something that falleth under deliberation; for to covenant, is an act of the will; that is to say, an act, and the last act of deliberation; and is therefore always understood to be something to come; and which is judged possible for him that covenanteth, to perform.

And therefore, to promise that which is known to be impossible, is no covenant. But if that prove impossible afterwards, which before was thought possible, the covenant is valid, and bindeth, though not to the thing itself, yet to the value; or, if that also be impossible, to the unfeigned endeavour of performing as much as is possible: for to more no man can be obliged.

Covenants how made void. Men are freed of their covenants two ways; by performing; or by being forgiven. For performance, is the natural end of obligation; and forgiveness, the restitution of liberty; as being a retransferring of that right, in which the obligation consisted.

Covenants extorted by fear are valid. Covenants entered into by fear, in the condition of mere nature, are obligatory. For example, if I covenant to pay a ransom, or service for my life, to an enemy; I am bound by it: for it is a contract, wherein one receiveth the benefit of life; the other is to receive money, or service for it; and consequently, where no other law, as in the condition of mere nature, forbiddeth the performance, the covenant is valid. Therefore prisoners of war, if trusted with the payment of their ransom, are obliged to pay it: and if a weaker prince, make a disadvantageous peace with a stronger, for fear; he is bound to keep it; unless, as hath been said before, there ariseth some new, and just cause of fear, to renew the war. And even in commonwealths, if I be forced to redeem myself from a thief by promising him money, I am bound to pay it, till the civil law discharge me. For whatsoever I may lawfully do without obligation, the same I may lawfully covenant to do through fear: and what I lawfully covenant, I cannot lawfully break.

The former covenant to one, makes void the later to another. A former covenant, makes void a later. For a man that hath passed away his right to one man to-day, hath it not to pass to-morrow to another: and therefore the later promise passeth no right, but is null.

A man's covenant not to defend himself is void. A covenant not to defend myself from force, by force, is always void. For, as I have showed before, no man can transfer, or lay down his right to save himself from death, wounds, and imprisonment, the avoiding whereof is the only end of laying down any right; and therefore the promise of not resisting force, in no covenant transferreth any right; nor is obliging. For though a man may covenant thus, *unless I do so, or so, kill me*; he cannot covenant thus, *unless I do so, or so, I will not resist you, when you come to kill me*. For man by nature chooseth the lesser evil, which is danger of death in resisting; rather than the greater, which is certain and present death in not resisting. And this is granted to be true by all men, in that they lead criminals to execution, and prison, with armed men, notwithstanding that such criminals have consented to the law, by which they are condemned.

No man obliged to accuse himself. A covenant to accuse oneself, without assurance of pardon, is likewise invalid. For in the condition of nature, where every man is judge, there is no place for accusation: and in the civil state, the accusation is followed with punishment; which being force, a man is not obliged not to resist. The same is also true, of the accusation of those, by whose condemnation a man falls into misery; as of a father, wife, or benefactor. For the testimony of such an accuser, if it be not willingly given, is presumed to be corrupted by nature; and therefore not to be received: and where a man's testimony is not to be credited, he is not bound to give it. Also accusations upon torture, are not to be reputed as testimonies. For torture is to be used but as means of conjecture, and light, in the further examination, and search of truth: and what is in that case confessed, tendeth to the ease of him that is tortured; not to the informing of the torturers: and therefore ought not to have the credit of a sufficient testimony: for whether he deliver himself by true, or false accusation, he does it by the right of preserving his own life.

[. . .]

Chapter XV: Of other Laws of Nature

The laws of nature oblige in conscience always, but in effect then only when there is security. [. . .] The laws of nature oblige *in foro interno*; that is to say, they bind to a desire they should take place: but *in foro externo*; that is, to the putting them in act, not always. For he that should be modest, and tractable, and perform all he promises, in such time, and place, where no man else should do so, should but make himself a prey to others, and procure his own certain ruin, contrary to the ground of all laws of nature, which tend to nature's preservation. And again, he that having sufficient security, that others shall observe the same laws towards him, observes them not himself, seeketh not peace, but war; and consequently the destruction of his nature by violence.

And whatsoever laws bind *in foro interno*, may be broken, not only by a fact contrary to the law, but also by a fact according to it, in case a man think it contrary. For though his action in this case, be according to the law; yet his purpose was against the law; which, where the obligation is *in foro interno*, is a breach.

The laws of nature are eternal. The laws of nature are immutable and eternal; for injustice, ingratitude, arrogance, pride, iniquity, acception of persons, and the rest, can never be made lawful. For it can never be that war shall preserve life, and peace destroy it.

And yet easy. The same laws, because they oblige only to a desire, and endeavour, I mean an unfeigned and constant endeavour, are easy to be observed. For in that they require nothing but endeavour, he that endeavoureth their performance, fulfilleth them; and he that fulfilleth the law, is just.

The science of these laws, is the true moral philosophy. And the science of them, is the true and only moral philosophy. For moral philosophy is nothing else but the science of what is *good*, and *evil*, in the conversation, and society of mankind. *Good*, and *evil*, are names that signify our appetites, and aversions; which in different tempers, customs, and doctrines of men, are different: and divers men, differ not only in their judgment, on the senses of what is pleasant; and unpleasant to the taste, smell, hearing, touch, and sight; but also of what is conformable, or disagreeable to reason, in the actions of common life. Nay, the same man, in divers times, differs from himself; and one time praiseth, that is, calleth good, what another time he dispraiseth, and calleth evil: from whence arise disputes, controversies, and at last war. And therefore so long as a man is in the condition of mere nature, which is a condition of war, as private appetite is the measure of good, and evil: and consequently all men agree on this, that peace is good, and therefore also the way, or means of peace, which, as I have shewed before, are *justice, gratitude, modesty, equity, mercy*, and the rest of the laws of nature, are good; that is to say; *moral virtues*, and their contrary *vices*, evil. Now the science of virtue and vice, is moral philosophy; and therefore the true doctrine of the laws of nature, is the true moral philosophy. But the writers of moral philosophy, though they acknowledge the same virtues and vices; yet not seeing wherein consisted their goodness; nor that they come to be praised, as the means of peaceable, sociable, and comfortable living, place them in a mediocrity of passions: as if not the cause, but the degree of daring, made fortitude; or not the cause, but the quantity of a gift, made liberality.

These dictates of reason, men used to call by the name of laws, but improperly: for they are but conclusions, or theorems concerning what conduceth to the conservation and defence of themselves; whereas law, properly, is the word of him, that by right hath command over others. But yet if we consider the same theorems, as delivered in the word of God, that by right commandeth all things; then are they properly called laws.[1]

Chapter XVII: Of the Causes, Generation, and Definition of a Commonwealth

The end of commonwealth, particular security: The final cause, end, or design of men, who naturally love liberty, and dominion over others, in the introduction of that restraint upon themselves, in which we see them live in commonwealths, is the foresight of their own preservation, and of a more contented life thereby; that is to say, of getting themselves out from that miserable condition of war, which is necessarily consequent, as hath been shown (chapter XIII), to the natural passions of men, when there is no visible power to keep them in awe, and tie them by fear of punishment to the performance of their covenants, and observation of those laws of nature set down in the fourteenth and fifteenth chapters.

Which is not to be had from the law of nature: For the laws of nature, as *justice, equity, modesty, mercy*, and, in sum, *doing to others, as we would be done to*, of themselves, without the terror of some power, to cause them to be observed, are contrary to our natural passions, that carry us to partiality, pride, revenge, and the like. And covenants, without the sword, are but words, and of no strength to secure a man at all. Therefore notwithstanding the laws of nature (which every one hath then kept, when he has the will to keep them, when he can do it safely) if there be no power erected, or not great enough for our security; every man will, and may lawfully rely on his own strength and art, for caution against all other men. And in all places, where men have lived by small families, to rob and spoil one another, has been a trade, and so far from being reputed against the law of nature, that the greater spoils they gained, the greater was their honour; and men observed no other laws therein, but the laws of honour; that is, to abstain from cruelty, leaving to men their lives, and instruments of husbandry. And as small families did then; so now do cities and kingdoms which are but greater families, for their own security, enlarge their dominions, upon all pretences of danger, and fear of invasion, or assistance that may be given to invaders, and endeavour as much as they can, to subdue, or weaken their neighbours, by open force, and secret arts, for want of other caution, justly; and are remembered for it in after ages with honour.

Nor from the conjunction of a few men or families: Nor is it the joining together of a small number of men, that gives them this security; because in small numbers, small additions on the one side or the other, make the advantage of strength so great, as is sufficient to carry the victory; and therefore gives encouragement to an invasion. The multitude sufficient to confide in for our security, is not determined by any certain number, but by comparison with the enemy we fear; and is then sufficient, when the odds of the enemy is not of so visible and conspicuous moment, to determine the event of war, as to move him to attempt.

Nor from a great multitude, unless directed by one judgment: And be there never so great a multitude; yet if their actions be directed according to their particular judgments, and particular appetites, they can expect thereby no defence, nor protection, neither against a common enemy, nor against the injuries of one another. For being distracted in opinions concerning the best use and application of their strength, they do not help but hinder one another; and reduce their strength by mutual opposition to nothing: whereby they are easily, not only subdued by a very few that agree together; but also when there is no common enemy, they make war upon each other, for their particular interests. For if we could suppose a great multitude of men to consent in the observation of justice, and other laws of nature, without a common power to keep them all in awe; we might as well suppose all mankind to do the same; and then there neither would be, nor need to be any civil government, or commonwealth at all; because there would be peace without subjection.

And that continually. Nor is it enough for the security which men desire should last all the time of their life, that they be governed, and directed by one judgment, for a limited time; as in one battle, or one war. For though they obtain a victory by their unanimous endeavour against a foreign enemy; yet afterwards, when either they have no common enemy, or he that by one part is held for an enemy, is by another part held for a friend, they must needs by the difference of their interests dissolve, and fall again into a war amongst themselves.

Why certain creatures without reason, or speech, do nevertheless live in society, without any coercive power. It is true, that certain living creatures, as bees, and ants, live sociably one with another, which are therefore by Aristotle numbered amongst political creatures; and yet have no other direction, than their particular judgments and appetites; nor speech, whereby one of them can signify to another, what he thinks expedient for the common benefit: and therefore some man may perhaps desire to know, why mankind cannot do the same. To which I answer,

First, that men are continually in competition for honour and dignity, which these creatures are not; and consequently amongst men there ariseth on that ground, envy and hatred, and finally war; but amongst these not so.

Secondly, that amongst these creatures, the common good differeth not from the private; and being by nature inclined to their private, they procure thereby the common benefit. But man, whose joy consisteth in comparing himself with other men, can relish nothing but what is eminent.

Thirdly, that these creatures, having not, as man, the use of reason, do not see, nor think they see any fault, in the administration of their common business; whereas amongst men, there are very many, that think themselves wiser, and abler to govern the public, better than the rest; and these strive to reform and innovate, one this way, another that way; and thereby bring it into distraction and civil war.

Fourthly, that these creatures, though they have some use of voice, in making known to one another their desires, and other affections; yet they want that art of words, by which some men can represent to others, that which is good, in the likeness of evil; and evil, in the likeness of good; and augment, or diminish the apparent greatness of good and evil; discontenting men, and troubling their peace at their pleasure.

Fifthly, irrational creatures cannot distinguish between *injury*, and *damage*; and therefore as long as they be at ease, they are not offended with their fellows: whereas man is then most troublesome, when he is most at ease: for then it is that he loves to shew his wisdom, and control the actions of them that govern the commonwealth.

Lastly, the agreement of these creatures is natural; that of men, is by covenant only, which is artificial: and therefore it is no wonder if there be somewhat else required, besides covenant, to make their agreement constant and lasting; which is a common power, to keep them in awe, and to direct their actions to the common benefit.

The generation of a commonwealth. The only way to erect such a common power, as may be able to defend them from the invasion of foreigners, and the injuries of one another, and thereby to secure them in such sort, as that by their own industry, and by the fruits of the earth, they may nourish themselves and live contentedly; is, to confer all their power and strength upon one man, or upon one assembly of men, that may reduce all their wills, by plurality of voices, unto one will: which is as much as to say, to appoint one man, or assembly of men, to bear their person; and every one to own, and acknowledge himself to be author of whatsoever he that so beareth their person, shall act, or cause to be acted, in those things which concern the common peace and safety; and therein to submit their wills, every one to his will, and their judgments, to his judgment. This is more than consent, or concord; it is a real unity of them all, in one and the same person, made by covenant of every man with every man, in such manner, as if every man should say to every man, *I authorize and give up my right of governing myself, to this man, or to this assembly of men, on this condition, that thou give up thy right to him, and authorize all his actions in like manner.* This done, the multitude so united in one person, is called a COMMONWEALTH, in Latin CIVITAS. This is the generation of that great LEVIATHAN, or rather, to speak more reverently, of that *mortal god*, to which we owe under the *immortal God*, our peace and defence. For by this authority, given him by every particular man in the commonwealth, he hath the use of so much power and strength conferred on him, that by terror thereof, he is enabled to form the wills of them all, to peace at home, and mutual aid against their enemies abroad. And in him consisteth the essence of the commonwealth; which, to define it, is *one person, of whose acts a great multitude, by mutual coven-*

The definition of a commonwealth. *ants one with another, have made themselves every one the author, to the end he may use the strength and means of them all, as he shall think expedient, for their peace and common defence.*

Sovereign, and subject, what. And he that carrieth this person, is called SOVEREIGN, and said to have *sovereign power*; and every one besides, his SUBJECT.

The attaining to this sovereign power, is by two ways. One, by natural force; as when a man maketh his children, to submit themselves, and their children to his government, as being able to destroy them if they refuse; or by war subdueth his enemies to his will, giving them their lives on that condition. The other, is when men agree amongst themselves, to submit to some man, or assembly of men, voluntarily, on confidence to be protected by him against all others. This latter, may be called a political commonwealth, or commonwealth by *institution*; and the former, a commonwealth by *acquisition*. And first, I shall speak of a commonwealth by institution.[2]

Chapter XVIII: Of the Rights of Sovereigns by Institution

The act of instituting a commonwealth, what. A *commonwealth* is said to be *instituted*, when a *multitude* of men do agree, and *covenant, every one, with every one,* that to whatsoever *man*, or *assembly of men*, shall be given by the major part, the *right* to *present* the person of them all, that is to say, to be their *representative*; every one, as well he that *voted for it*, as he that *voted against it*, shall *authorize* all the actions and judgments, of that man, or assembly of men, in the same manner, as if they were his own, to the end, to live peaceably amongst themselves, and be protected against other men.

The consequences to such institutions, are: From this institution of a commonwealth are derived all the *rights*, and *faculties* of him, or them, on whom the sovereign power is conferred by the consent of the people assembled,

1. The subjects cannot change the form of government. First, because they covenant, it is to be understood, they are not obliged by former covenant to any thing repugnant hereunto. And consequently they that have already instituted a commonwealth, being thereby bound by covenant, to own the actions, and judgments of one, cannot lawfully make a new covenant, amongst themselves, to be obedient to any other, in any thing whatsoever, without his permission. And therefore, they that are subjects to a monarch, cannot without his leave cast off monarchy, and return to the confusion of a disunited multitude; nor transfer their person from him that beareth it, to another man, or other assembly of men: for they are bound, every man to every man, to own, and be reputed author of all, that he that already is their sovereign, shall do, and judge fit to be done: so that any one man dissenting, all the rest should break their covenant made to that man, which is injustice: and they have also every man given the sovereignty to him that beareth their person; and therefore if they depose him, they take from him that which is his own, and so again it is injustice. Besides, if he that attempteth to depose his sovereign, be killed, or punished by him for such attempt, he is author of his own punishment, as being by the institution, author of all his sovereign shall do: and because it is injustice for a man to do any thing, for which he may be punished by his own authority, he is also upon that title, unjust. And whereas some men have pretended for their disobedience to their sovereign, a new covenant, made, not with men, but with God; this also is unjust: for there is no covenant with God, but by mediation of somebody that representeth God's person; which none doth but God's lieutenant, who hath the sovereignty under God. But this pretence of covenant with

God, is so evident a lie, even in the pretenders' own consciences, that it is not only an act of an unjust, but also of a vile, and unmanly disposition.

2. *Sovereign power cannot be forfeited.* Secondly, because the right of bearing the person of them all, is given to him they make sovereign, by covenant only of one to another, and not of him to any of them; there can happen no breach of covenant on the part of the sovereign; and consequently none of his subjects, by any pretence of forfeiture, can be freed from his subjection. That he which is made sovereign maketh no covenant with his subjects beforehand, is manifest; because either he must make it with the whole multitude, as one party to the covenant; or he must make a several covenant with every man. With the whole, as one party, it is impossible; because as yet they are not one person: and if he make so many several covenants as there be men, those covenants after he hath the sovereignty are void; because what act soever can be pretended by any one of them for breach thereof, is the act both of himself, and of all the rest, because done in the person, and by the right of every one of them in particular. Besides, if any one, or more of them, pretend a breach of the covenant made by the sovereign at his institution; and others, or one other of his subjects, or himself alone, pretend there was no such breach, there is in this case, no judge to decide the controversy; it returns therefore to the sword again; and every man recovereth the right of protecting himself by his own strength, contrary to the design they had in the institution. It is therefore in vain to grant sovereignty by way of precedent covenant. The opinion that any monarch receiveth his power by covenant, that is to say, on condition, proceedeth from want of understanding this easy truth, that covenants being but words and breath, have no force to oblige, contain, constrain, or protect any man, but what it has from the public sword; that is, from the untied hands of that man, or assembly of men that hath the sovereignty, and whose actions are avouched by them all, and performed by the strength of them all, in him united. But when an assembly of men is made sovereign; then no man imagineth any such covenant to have passed in the institution; for no man is so dull as to say, for example, the people of Rome made a covenant with the Romans, to hold the sovereignty on such or such conditions; which not performed, the Romans might lawfully depose the Roman people. That men see not the reason to be alike in a monarchy, and in a popular government, proceedeth from the ambition of some, that are kinder to the government of an assembly, whereof they may hope to participate, than of monarchy, which they despair to enjoy.

3. *No man can without injustice protest against the institution of the sovereign declared by the major part.* Thirdly, because the major part hath by consenting voices declared a sovereign; he that dissented must now consent with the rest; that is, be contented to avow all the actions he shall do, or else justly be destroyed by the rest. For if he voluntarily entered into the congregation of them that were assembled, he sufficiently declared thereby his will, and therefore tacitly covenanted, to stand to what the major part should ordain: and therefore if he refuse to stand thereto, or make protestation against any of their decrees, he does contrary to his covenant, and therefore unjustly. And whether he be of the congregation, or not; and whether his consent be asked, or not, he must either submit to their decrees, or be left in the condition of war he was in before; wherein he might without injustice be destroyed by any man whatsoever.

4. *The sovereign's actions cannot be justly accused by the subject.* Fourthly, because every subject is by this institution author of all the actions, and judgments of the sovereign instituted; it follows, that whatsoever he doth, it can be no injury to any of his subjects; nor ought he to be by any of them accused of injustice. For he that doth anything by authority from another, doth therein no injury to him by whose authority he acteth: but by this institution of a commonwealth, every particular man is author of all the sovereign doth: and consequently he that complaineth of injury from his sovereign, complaineth of that whereof he himself is author; and therefore ought not to accuse any man but himself; no nor himself of injury; because to do injury to one's self, is impossible. It is true that they that have sovereign power may commit iniquity; but not injustice, or injury in the proper signification.

5. *Whatsoever the sovereign doth is unpunishable by the subject.* Fifthly, and consequently to that which was said last, no man that hath sovereign power can justly be put to death, or otherwise in any manner by his subjects punished. For seeing every subject is

author of the actions of his sovereign; he punisheth another for the actions committed by himself.

6. *The sovereign is judge of what is necessary for the peace and defence of his subjects.* And because the end of this institution, is the peace and defence of them all; and whosoever has right to the end, has right to the means; it belongeth of right, to whatsoever man, or assembly that hath the sovereignty, to be judge both of the means of peace and defence, and also of the hindrances, and disturbances of the same; and to do whatsoever he shall think necessary to be done, both beforehand, for the preserving of peace and security, by prevention of discord at home, and hostility from abroad; and, when peace and security are lost, for the recovery of the same. And therefore,

And *judge of what doctrines are fit to be taught them.* Sixthly, it is annexed to the sovereignty, to be judge of what opinions and doctrines are averse, and what conducing to peace; and consequently, on what occasions, how far, and what men are to be trusted withal, in speaking to multitudes of people; and who shall examine the doctrines of all books before they be published. For the actions of men proceed from their opinions; and in the well-governing of opinions, consisteth the well-governing of men's actions, in order to their peace, and concord. And though in matter of doctrine, nothing ought to be regarded but the truth; yet this is not repugnant to regulating the same by peace. For doctrine repugnant to peace, can no more be true, than peace and concord can be against the law of nature. It is true, that in a commonwealth, where by the negligence, or unskilfulness of governors, and teachers, false doctrines are by time generally received; the contrary truths may be generally offensive. Yet the most sudden, and rough busling in of a new truth, that can be, does never break the peace, but only sometimes awake the war. For those men that are so remissly governed, that they dare take up arms to defend, or introduce an opinion, are still in war; and their condition not peace, but only a cessation of arms for fear of one another; and they live, as it were, in the precincts of battle continually. It belongeth therefore to him that hath the sovereign power, to be judge, or constitute all judges of opinions and doctrines, as a thing necessary to peace; thereby to prevent discord and civil war.

7. *The right of making rules; whereby the subjects may every man know what is so his own, as no other subject can without injustice take it from him.* Seventhly, is annexed to the sovereignty, the whole power of prescribing the rules, whereby every man may know, what goods he may enjoy, and what actions he may do, without being molested by any of his fellow-subjects; and this is it men call *propriety*. For before constitution of sovereign power, as hath already been shown, all men had right to all things; which necessarily causeth war: and therefore this propriety, being necessary to peace, and depending on sovereign power, is the act of that power, in order to the public peace. These rules of propriety, or *meum* and *tuum*, and of *good, evil, lawful,* and *unlawful* in the actions of subjects, are the civil laws; that is to say, the laws of each commonwealth in particular; though the name of civil law be now restrained to the ancient civil laws of the city of Rome; which being the head of a great part of the world, her laws at that time were in these parts the civil law.

8. *To him also belongeth the right of judicature and decision of controversy.* Eighthly, is annexed to the sovereignty, the right of judicature; that is to say, of hearing and deciding all controversies, which may arise concerning law, either civil, or natural; or concerning fact. For without the decision of controversies, there is no protection of one subject, against the injuries of another; the laws concerning *meum* and *tuum* are in vain; and to every man remaineth, from the natural and necessary appetite of his own conservation, the right of protecting himself by his private strength, which is the condition of war, and contrary to the end for which every commonwealth is instituted.

9. *And of making war, and peace, as he shall think best.* Ninthly, is annexed to the sovereignty, the right of making war and peace with other nations, and commonwealths; that is to say, of judging when it is for the public good, and how great forces are to be assembled, armed, and paid for that end; and to levy money upon the subjects, to defray the expenses thereof. For the power by which the people are to be defended, consisteth in their armies; and the strength of an army, in the union of their strength under one command; which command the sovereign instituted, therefore hath; because the command of the *militia*, without other institution, maketh him that hath it sovereign. And therefore whosoever is made general of an army, he that hath the sovereign power is always generalissimo. . . .

Notes

1 Here it seems that Hobbes – perhaps disingenuously, given his reputation as an atheist – is trying to inject moral force into the idea of laws of nature. As dictates of reason, they are simply pragmatic guides to enlightened self-interest. But considered as commands issued to his rational creatures by God, they assume the status of moral laws.

2 The distinction between "institution" and "acquisition" turns out not to be especially significant, since as Hobbes explains in Chapter XX, "the rights, and consequences of sovereignty, are the same in both" cases. Provided that the sovereign ensures peace, it is of no consequence if he came to power by less than peaceful means. The King is dead, long live Cromwell!

11

John Locke, "Of Property"

Introduction

John Locke (1632–1704), the most influential
English philosopher of his time, published his
two treatises on government two years after "the
Glorious Revolution" of 1688, which saw the overthrow of the despotic James II and the coronation
of William of Orange and his wife Mary as the
new monarchs, sworn to honor the terms of a
"Declaration of Right." As Locke's Preface, with
its reference to William as "our great restorer,"
makes clear, these were events entirely applauded
by Locke, and it is reasonable to hold that the
two treatises were intended as a justification of
the revolution. The first treatise, after all, is a
demolition of the "divine right of kings" theory,
while the second – "an Essay concerning the true
original, extent and end of civil government" –
famously defends the right of people to overthrow
a ruler who has violated the terms of a social contract to which he or she owed all his authority.
The second treatise, in particular, was to be
invoked in the following century by champions of
both the American and French revolutions.

For Thomas Hobbes (V.10), rebellion was permissible only when, roughly, the sovereign had
already lost the powers effectively to govern and
guarantee peace. That Locke endorses rebellion

From John Locke, *Two Treatises of Government*, ed.
Peter Laslett, New York: New American Library, 1965,
pp. 327–44 (editor's notes omitted).

against a sovereign who still has these powers
indicates important differences between the two
philosophers' conceptions of the social contract
and the state of nature from which the contract
enables a civil society to emerge. The Lockean state
of nature, while it is one of liberty (since there
are as yet no legal sanctions), is "not a state of
licence." Unlike the Hobbesian "war of every man
against every man," Locke's state of nature is a
moral condition, in which people have rights and
obligations that necessarily constrain the kind of
social contract into which people may legitimately
enter. The right on which, with considerable originality, Locke puts most emphasis is the right to
property. Indeed, he writes that the preservation
of property is the "chief end" for which human
beings unite into a commonwealth and "put themselves under Government" (*Second Treatise* §124).

In Chapter 5 of the *Second Treatise of Government*, "Of Property," Locke attempts to provide
a moral justification for the possession of land
and other goods as property. In some of "the most
influential statements he ever made,"[1] Locke
declares that, self-evidently, a human being has
property in his own person and "the labour of his
body," and concludes that through mixing this labor
with something a person thereby removes it from
the state of nature and "makes it his property"
(§27). He is well aware that, left unqualified, this
principle could allow just a few people to own just
about everything, to the detriment of other people.
Locke therefore introduces two constraints designed
to prevent such a situation. The first is that a

person only has a right to acquire further property if "there is enough, and as good left in common for others" (§27). The second is that no one is entitled to more property than he or she can properly use, without it going to waste. Political theorists have ever since debated the adequacy or otherwise of Locke's provisos as safeguards against what would surely be unjust distributions of property.

Locke himself is entirely aware of the complication to his account caused by the introduction of money. After all, a person may possess enormous quantities of gold or silver without it going to waste. Up to this point, Locke has not invoked the idea of consent or contract in the justification of property since, as we saw, the Lockean social contract presupposes the prior legitimate existence of property. Now, however, he invokes "a tacit and voluntary consent" whereby people allow an individual to "possess more land than he himself can use the product of," since he can exchange the surplus produced for money (§50).

Locke has sometimes been derided by thinkers on the Left for offering an apology for private property. But while he clearly did defend private property against the communist radicals of his age, such as the Diggers and Levellers, and while he emphasized the benefits that, in his view, private property brought to civilization, it would be a mistake to think that only an enthusiast for private property needs to provide a justification for property. As Robert Nozick points out, "those believing in collective property" – be they seventeenth-century Levellers or twentieth-century Stalinists – "must also provide a theory of how" the collective's entitlement to own land or "the means of production" arises.[2] The state socialist as much as the capitalist needs to show why not everything belongs, like the air and most of the sea, to a "commons" to which all human beings have access.

Notes

1   P. Laslett, "Introduction" to Locke's *Two Treatises of Government*, p. 114.
2   R. Nozick, *Anarchy, State and Utopia*, Oxford: Blackwell, 1974, p. 178.

Locke, "Of Property"

25.   Whether we consider natural *Reason*, which tells us, that Men, being once born, have a right to their Preservation, and consequently to Meat and Drink, and such other things, as Nature affords for their Subsistence: Or *Revelation*, which gives us an account of those Grants God made of the World to *Adam*, and to *Noah*, and his Sons, 'tis very clear, that God, as King *David* says, *Psal.* CXV. xvi. *has given the Earth to the Children of Men*, given it to Mankind in common. But this being supposed, it seems to some a very great difficulty, how any one should ever come to have a *Property* in any thing: I will not content my self to answer, That if it be difficult to make out *Property*, upon a supposition, that God gave the World to *Adam* and his Posterity in common; it is impossible that any Man, but one universal Monarch, should have any *Property*, upon a supposition, that God gave the World to *Adam*, and his Heirs in Succession, exclusive of all the rest

of his Posterity. But I shall endeavour to shew, how Men might come to have a *property* in several parts of that which God gave to Mankind in common, and that without any express Compact of all the Commoners.

26.   God, who hath given the World to Men in common, hath also given them reason to make use of it to the best advantage of Life, and convenience. The Earth, and all that is therein, is given to Men for the Support and Comfort of their being. And though all the Fruits it naturally produces, and Beasts it feeds, belong to Mankind in common, as they are produced by the spontaneous hand of Nature; and no body has originally a private Dominion, exclusive of the rest of Mankind, in any of them, as they are thus in their natural state: yet being given for the use of Men, there must of necessity be a means *to appropriate* them some way or other before they can be of any use, or at all beneficial to any particular Man. The Fruit, or Venison, which nourishes the wild *Indian*, who knows no Inclosure, and is still

a Tenant in common, must be his, and so his, *i.e.* a part of him, that another can no longer have any right to it, before it can do him any good for the support of his Life.

27. Though the Earth, and all inferior Creatures be common to all Men, yet every Man has a *Property* in his own *Person*. This no Body has any Right to but himself. The *Labour* of his Body, and the *Work* of his Hands, we may say, are properly his. Whatsoever then he removes out of the State that Nature hath provided, and left it in, he hath mixed his *Labour* with, and joyned to it something that is his own, and thereby makes it his *Property*. It being by him removed from the common state Nature placed it in, hath by this *labour* something annexed to it, that excludes the common right of other Men. For this *Labour* being the unquestionable Property of the Labourer, no Man but he can have a right to what that is once joyned to, at least where there is enough, and as good left in common for others.

28. He that is nourished by the Acorns he pickt up under an Oak, or the Apples he gathered from the Trees in the Wood, has certainly appropriated them to himself. No Body can deny but the nourishment is his. I ask then, When did they begin to be his? When he digested? Or when he eat? Or when he boiled? Or when he brought them home? Or when he pickt them up? And 'tis plain, if the first gathering made them not his, nothing else could. That *labour* put a distinction between them and common. That added something to them more than Nature, the common Mother of all, had done; and so they became his private right. And will any one say he had no right to those Acorns or Apples he thus appropriated, because he had not the consent of all Mankind to make them his? Was it a Robbery thus to assume to himself what belonged to all in Common? If such a consent as that was necessary, Man had starved, notwithstanding the Plenty God had given him. We see in *Commons*, which remain so by Compact, that 'tis the taking any part of what is common, and removing it out of the state Nature leaves it in, which *begins the Property*; without which the Common is of no use. And the taking of this or that part, does not depend on the express consent of all the Commoners. Thus the Grass my Horse has bit; the Turfs my Servant has cut; and the Ore I have digg'd in any

place where I have a right to them in common with others, become my *Property*, without the assignation or consent of any body. The *labour* that was mine, removing them out of that common state they were in, hath *fixed* my *Property* in them.

29. By making an explicit consent of every Commoner, necessary to any ones appropriating to himself any part of what is given in common, Children or Servants could not cut the Meat which their Father or Master had provided for them in common, without assigning to every one his peculiar part. Though the Water running in the Fountain be every ones, yet who can doubt, but that in the Pitcher is his only who drew it out? His *labour* hath taken it out of the hands of Nature, where it was common, and belong'd equally to all her Children, and *hath* thereby *appropriated* it to himself.

30. Thus this Law of reason makes the Deer, that *Indian's* who hath killed it; 'tis allowed to be his goods who hath bestowed his labour upon it, though before, it was the common right of every one. And amongst those who are counted the Civiliz'd part of Mankind, who have made and multiplied positive Laws to determine Property, this original Law of Nature for the *beginning of Property*, in what was before common, still takes place; and by vertue thereof, what Fish any one catches in the Ocean, that great and still remaining Common of Mankind; or what Ambergriese any one takes up here, is *by* the *Labour* that removes it out of that common state Nature left it in, *made* his *Property* who takes that pains about it. And even amongst us the Hare that any one is Hunting, is thought his who pursues her during the Chase. For being a Beast that is still looked upon as common, and no Man's private Possession; whoever has imploy'd so much *labour* about any of that kind, as to find and pursue her, has thereby removed her from the state of Nature, wherein she was common, and hath *begun a Property*.

31. It will perhaps be objected to this, That if gathering the Acorns, or other Fruits of the Earth, &c. makes a right to them, then any one may *ingross* as much as he will. To which I Answer, Not so. The same Law of Nature, that does by this means give us Property, does also *bound* that Property too. *God has given us all things richly*, 1 Tim. vi. 17. is the Voice of Reason confirmed by

Inspiration. But how far has he given it us? *To enjoy.* As much as any one can make use of to any advantage of life before it spoils; so much he may by his labour fix a Property in. Whatever is beyond this, is more than his share, and belongs to others. Nothing was made by God for Man to spoil or destroy. And thus considering the plenty of natural Provisions there was a long time in the World, and the few spenders, and to how small a part of that provision the industry of one Man could extend it self, and ingross it to the prejudice of others; especially keeping within the *bounds*, set by reason of what might serve for his *use*; there could be then little room for Quarrels or Contentions about Property so establish'd.

32.   But the *chief matter of Property* being now not the Fruits of the Earth, and the Beasts that subsist on it, but the *Earth it self*; as that which takes in and carries with it all the rest: I think it is plain, that *Property* in that too is acquired as the former. *As much Land* as a Man Tills, Plants, Improves, Cultivates, and can use the Product of, so much is his *Property*. He by his Labour does, as it were, inclose it from the Common. Nor will it invalidate his right to say, Every body else has an equal Title to it; and therefore he cannot appropriate, he cannot inclose, without the Consent of all his Fellow-Commoners, all Mankind. God, when he gave the World in common to all Mankind, commanded Man also to labour, and the penury of his Condition required it of him. God and his Reason commanded him to subdue the Earth, *i.e.* improve it for the benefit of Life, and therein lay out something upon it that was his own, his labour. He that in Obedience to this Command of God, subdued, tilled and sowed any part of it, thereby annexed to it something that was his *Property*, which another had no Title to, nor could without injury take from him.

33.   Nor was this *appropriation* of any parcel of *Land*, by improving it, any prejudice to any other Man, since there was still enough, and as good left; and more than the yet unprovided could use. So that in effect, there was never the less left for others because of his inclosure for himself. For he that leaves as much as another can make use of, does as good as take nothing at all. No Body could think himself injur'd by the drinking of another Man, though he took a good

Draught, who had a whole River of the same Water left him to quench his thirst. And the Case of Land and Water, where there is enough of both, is perfectly the same.

34.   God gave the World to Men in Common; but since he gave it them for their benefit, and the greatest Conveniencies of Life they were capable to draw from it, it cannot be supposed he meant it should always remain common and uncultivated. He gave it to the use of the Industrious and Rational, (and *Labour* was to be *his Title* to it;) not to the Fancy or Covetousness of the Quarrelsom and Contentious. He that had as good left for his Improvement, as was already taken up, needed not complain, ought not to meddle with what was already improved by another's Labour: If he did, 'tis plain he desired the benefit of another's Pains, which he had no right to, and not the Ground which God had given him in common with others to labour on, and whereof there was as good left, as that already possessed, and more than he knew what to do with, or his Industry could reach to.

35.   'Tis true, in *Land* that is *common* in *England*, or any other Country, where there is Plenty of People under Government, who have Money and Commerce, no one can inclose or appropriate any part, without the consent of all his Fellow-Commoners: Because this is left common by Compact, *i.e.* by the Law of the Land, which is not to be violated. And though it be Common, in respect of some Men, it is not so to all Mankind; but is the joint property of this Countrey, or this Parish. Besides, the remainder, after such inclosure, would not be as good to the rest of the Commoners as the whole was, when they could all make use of the whole: whereas in the beginning and first peopling of the great Common of the World, it was quite otherwise. The Law Man was under, was rather for *appropriating*. God Commanded, and his Wants forced him to *labour*. That was his *Property* which could not be taken from him where-ever he had fixed it. And hence subduing or cultivating the Earth, and having Dominion, we see are joyned together. The one gave Title to the other. So that God, by commanding to subdue, gave Authority so far to *appropriate*. And the Condition of Humane Life, which requires Labour and Materials to work on, necessarily introduces *private Possessions*.

36. The measure of Property, Nature has well set, by the Extent of Mens *Labour, and the Conveniency of Life:* No Mans Labour could subdue, or appropriate all: nor could his Enjoyment consume more than a small part; so that it was impossible for any Man, this way, to intrench upon the right of another, or acquire, to himself, a Property, to the Prejudice of his Neighbour, who would still have room, for as good, and as large a Possession (after the other had taken out his) as before it was appropriated. This *measure* did confine every Man's *Possession,* to a very moderate Proportion, and such as he might appropriate to himself, without Injury to any Body in the first Ages of the World, when Men were more in danger to be lost, by wandering from their Company, in the then vast Wilderness of the Earth, than to be straitned for want of room to plant in. And the same *measure* may be allowed still, without prejudice to any Body, as full as the World seems. For supposing a Man, or Family, in the state they were, at first peopling of the World by the Children of *Adam,* or *Noah*; let him plant in some in-land, vacant places of *America,* we shall find that the *Possessions* he could make himself upon the *measures* we have given, would not be very large, nor, even to this day, prejudice the rest of Mankind, or give them reason to complain, or think themselves injured by this Man's Incroachment, though the Race of Men have now spread themselves to all the corners of the World, and do infinitely exceed the small number [which] was at the beginning. Nay, the extent of *Ground* is of so little value, *without labour,* that I have heard it affirmed, that in *Spain* it self, a Man may be permitted to plough, sow, and reap, without being disturbed, upon Land he has no other Title to, but only his making use of it. But, on the contrary, the Inhabitants think themselves beholden to him, who, by his Industry on neglected, and consequently waste Land, has increased the stock of Corn, which they wanted. But be this as it will, which I lay no stress on; This I dare boldly affirm, That the same *Rule of Propriety,* (*viz.*) that every Man should have as much as he could make use of, would hold still in the World, without straitning any body, since there is Land enough in the World to suffice double the Inhabitants had not the *Invention of Money,* and the tacit Agreement of Men to put a value on it, introduced (by Consent) larger Possessions, and a Right to them; which, how

it has done, I shall, by and by, shew more at large.

37. This is certain, That in the beginning, before the desire of having more than Men needed, had altered the intrinsick value of things, which depends only on their usefulness to the Life of Man; or [Men] had *agreed, that a little piece of yellow Metal,* which would keep without wasting or decay, should be worth a great piece of Flesh, or a whole heap of Corn; though Men had a Right to appropriate, by their Labour, each one to himself, as much of the things of Nature, as he could use: Yet this could not be much, nor to the Prejudice of others, where the same plenty was still left, to those who would use the same Industry. To which let me add, that he who appropriates land to himself by his labour, does not lessen but increase the common stock of mankind. For the provisions serving to the support of humane life, produced by one acre of inclosed and cultivated land, are (to speak much within compasse) ten times more, than those, which are yeilded by an acre of Land, of an equal richnesse, lyeing wast in common. And therefor he, that incloses Land and has a greater plenty of the conveniencys of life from ten acres, than he could have from an hundred left to Nature, may truly be said, to give ninety acres to Mankind. For his labour now supplys him with provisions out of ten acres, which were but the product of an hundred lying in common. I have here rated the improved land very low in making its product but as ten to one, when it is much nearer an hundred to one. For I aske whether in the wild woods and uncultivated wast of America left to Nature, without any improvement, tillage or husbandry, a thousand acres will yeild the needy and wretched inhabitants as many conveniencies of life as ten acres of equally fertile land doe in Devonshire where they are well cultivated?

Before the Appropriation of Land, he who gathered as much of the wild Fruit, killed, caught, or tamed, as many of the Beasts as he could; he that so employed his Pains about any of the spontaneous Products of Nature, as any way to alter them, from the state which Nature put them in, *by* placing any of his *Labour* on them, did thereby *acquire a Property in them*: But if they perished, in his Possession, without their due use; if the Fruits rotted, or the Venison putrified, before he could spend it, he offended against the common Law of Nature, and was liable to be punished; he invaded his Neighbour's share, for he had *no Right, farther than his Use* called for any of them, and they might serve to afford him Conveniencies of Life.

38. The same *measures* governed the *Possession of Land* too: Whatsoever he tilled and reaped, laid up and made use of, before it spoiled, that was his peculiar Right; whatsoever he enclosed, and could feed, and make use of, the Cattle and Product was also his. But if either the Grass of his Inclosure rotted on the Ground, or the Fruit of his planting perished without gathering, and laying up, this part of the Earth, notwithstanding his Inclosure, was still to be looked on as Waste, and might be the Possession of any other. Thus, at the beginning, *Cain* might take as much Ground as he could till, and make it his own Land, and yet leave enough to *Abel's* Sheep to feed on; a few Acres would serve for both their Possessions. But as Families increased, and Industry inlarged their Stocks, their *Possessions inlarged* with the need of them; but yet it was commonly *without any fixed property in the ground* they made use of, till they incorporated, settled themselves together, and built Cities, and then, by consent, they came in time, to set out the *bounds of their distinct Territories*, and agree on limits between them and their Neighbours, and by Laws within themselves, settled the *Properties* of those of the same Society. For we see, that in that part of the World which was first inhabited, and therefore like to be best peopled, even as low down as *Abraham's* time, they wandred with their Flocks, and their Herds, which was their substance, freely up and down; and this *Abraham* did, in a Country where he was a Stranger. Whence it is plain, that at least, a great part of the *Land lay in common*; that the Inhabitants valued it not, nor claimed Property in any more than they made use of. But when there was not room enough in the same place, for their Herds to feed together, they, by consent, as *Abraham* and *Lot* did, *Gen.* xiii. 5. separated and inlarged their pasture, where it best liked them. And for the same Reason *Esau* went from his Father, and his Brother, and planted in *Mount Seir, Gen.* xxxvi. 6.

39. And thus, without supposing any private Dominion, and property in *Adam*, over all the World, exclusive of all other Men, which can no

way be proved, nor any ones Property be made out from it; but supposing the *World* given as it was to the Children of Men *in common*, we see how *labour* could make Men distinct titles to several parcels of it, for their private uses; wherein there could be no doubt of Right, no room for quarrel.

40. Nor is it so strange, as perhaps before consideration it may appear, that the *Property of labour* should be able to over-ballance the Community of Land. For 'tis *Labour* indeed that *puts the difference of value* on every thing; and let any one consider, what the difference is between an Acre of Land planted with Tobacco, or Sugar, sown with Wheat or Barley; and an Acre of the same Land lying in common, without any Husbandry upon it, and he will find, that the improvement of *labour makes* the far greater part of *the value*. I think it will be but a very modest Computation to say, that of the *Products* of the Earth useful to the Life of Man $^9/_{10}$ are the *effects of labour*: nay, if we will rightly estimate things as they come to our use, and cast up the several Expenses about them, what in them is purely owing to *Nature*, and what to *labour*, we shall find, that in most of them $^{99}/_{100}$ are wholly to be put on the account of *labour*.

41. There cannot be a clearer demonstration of any thing, than several Nations of the *Americans* are of this, who are rich in Land, and poor in all the Comforts of Life; whom Nature having furnished as liberally as any other people, with the materials of Plenty, *i.e.* a fruitful Soil, apt to produce in abundance, what might serve for food, rayment, and delight; yet for want of improving it by labour, have not one hundredth part of the Conveniencies we enjoy: And a King of a large fruitful Territory there feeds, lodges, and is clad worse than a day Labourer in *England*.

42. To make this a little clearer, let us but trace some of the ordinary provisions of Life, through their several progresses, before they come to our use, and see how much they receive of their *value from Humane Industry*. Bread, Wine and Cloth, are things of daily use, and great plenty, yet notwithstanding, Acorns, Water, and Leaves, or Skins, must be our Bread, Drink and Clothing, did not *labour* furnish us with these more useful Commodities. For whatever *Bread* is more worth

than Acorns, *Wine* than Water, and *Cloth* or *Silk* than Leaves, Skins, or Moss, that is wholly *owing to labour* and industry. The one of these being the Food and Rayment which unassisted Nature furnishes us with; the other provisions which our industry and pains prepare for us, which how much they exceed the other in value, when any one hath computed, he will then see, how much *labour makes the far greatest part of the value* of things, we enjoy in this World: And the ground which produces the materials, is scarce to be reckon'd in, as any, or at most, but a very small, part of it; So little, that even amongst us, Land that is left wholly to Nature, that hath no improvement of Pasturage, Tillage, or Planting, is called, as indeed it is, *wast*; and we shall find the benefit of it amount to little more than nothing. This shews, how much numbers of men are to be preferd to largenesse of dominions, and that the increase of lands and the right imploying of them is the great art of government. And that Prince who shall be so wise and godlike as by established laws of liberty to secure protection and incouragement to the honest industry of Mankind against the oppression of power and narrownesse of Party will quickly be too hard for his neighbours. But this bye the bye. To return to the argument in hand.

43.   An Acre of Land that bears here Twenty Bushels of Wheat, and another in *America*, which, with the same Husbandry, would do the like, are without doubt, of the same natural, intrinsick Value. But yet the Benefit Mankind receives from the one, in a Year, is worth 5 *l.* and from the other possibly not worth a Penny, if all the Profit an *Indian* received from it were to be valued, and sold here; at least, I may truly say, not $^1/_{1000}$. 'Tis *Labour* then which *puts the greatest part of Value upon Land*, without which it would scarcely be worth any thing: 'tis to that we owe the greatest part of all its useful Products: for all that the Straw, Bran, Bread, of that Acre of Wheat, is more worth than the Product of an Acre of as good Land, which lies wast, is all the Effect of Labour. For 'tis not barely the Plough-man's Pains, the Reaper's and Thresher's Toil, and the Bakers Sweat, is to be counted into the *Bread* we eat; the Labour of those who broke the Oxen, who digged and wrought the Iron and Stones, who felled and framed the Timber imployed about the Plough, Mill, Oven, or any other Utensils, which

are a vast Number, requisite to this Corn, from its being seed to be sown to its being made Bread, must all be *charged on* the account of *Labour*, and received as an effect of that: Nature and the Earth furnished only the almost worthless Materials, as in themselves. 'Twould be a strange *Catalogue of things, that Industry provided and made use of, about every Loaf of Bread*, before it came to our use, if we could trace them; Iron, Wood, Leather, Bark, Timber, Stone, Bricks, Coals, Lime, Cloth, Dying-Drugs, Pitch, Tar, Masts, Ropes, and all the Materials made use of in the Ship, that brought any of the Commodities made use of by any of the Workmen, to any part of the Work, all which, 'twould be almost impossible, at least too long, to reckon up.

44.   From all which it is evident, that though the things of Nature are given in common, yet Man (by being Master of himself, and *Proprietor of his own Person*, and the actions or *Labour* of it) had still in himself *the great Foundation of Property*; and that which made up the great part of what he applied to the Support or Comfort of his being, when Invention and Arts had improved the conveniencies of Life, was perfectly his own, and did not belong in common to others.

45.   Thus *Labour*, in the Beginning, *gave a Right of Property*, where-ever any one was pleased to imploy it, upon what was common, which remained, a long while, the far greater part, and is yet more than Mankind makes use of. Men, at first, for the most part, contented themselves with what un-assisted Nature Offered to their Necessities: and though afterwards, in some parts of the World, (where the Increase of People and Stock, with the *Use of Money*) had made Land scarce, and so of some Value, the several *Communities* settled the Bounds of their distinct Territories, and by Laws within themselves, regulated the Properties of the private Men of their Society, and so, *by Compact* and Agreement, *settled the Property* which Labour and Industry began; and the Leagues that have been made between several States and Kingdoms, either expressly or tacitly disowning all Claim and Right to the Land in the others Possession, have, by common Consent, given up their Pretences to their natural common Right, which originally they had to those Countries, and so have, by *positive agreement, settled a Property* amongst

themselves, in distinct Parts and parcels of the Earth: yet there are still *great Tracts of Ground* to be found, which (the Inhabitants thereof not having joyned with the rest of Mankind, in the consent of the Use of their common Money) *lie waste*, and are more than the People, who dwell on it, do, or can make use of, and so still lie in common. Tho' this can scarce happen amongst that part of Mankind, that have consented to the use of Money.

46. The greatest part of *things really useful* to the Life of Man, and such as the necessity of subsisting made the first Commoners of the World look after, as it doth the *Americans* now, *are* generally things *of short duration*; such as, if they are not consumed by use, will decay and perish of themselves: Gold, Silver, and Diamonds, are things, that Fancy or Agreement hath put the Value on, more then real Use, and the necessary Support of Life. Now of those good things which Nature hath provided in common, every one had a Right (as hath been said) to as much as he could use, and had a Property in all that he could affect with his Labour: all that his Industry could extend to, to alter from the State Nature had put it in, was his. He that *gathered* a Hundred Bushels of Acorns or Apples, had thereby a *Property* in them; they were his Goods as soon as gathered. He was only to look that he used them before they spoiled; else he took more then his share, and robb'd others. And indeed it was a foolish thing, as well as dishonest, to hoard up more than he could make use of. If he gave away a part to any body else, so that it perished not uselesly in his Possession, these he also made use of. And if he also bartered away Plumbs that would have rotted in a Week, for Nuts that would last good for his eating a whole Year, he did no injury; he wasted not the common Stock; destroyed no part of the portion of Goods that belonged to others, so long as nothing perished uselesly in his hands. Again, if he would give us Nuts for a piece of Metal, pleased with its colour; or exchanged his Sheep for Shells, or Wool for a sparkling Pebble or a Diamond, and keep those by him all his Life, he invaded not the Right of others, he might heap up as much of these durable things as he pleased; the *exceeding of the bounds of his* just *Property* not lying in the largeness of his Possession, but the perishing of any thing uselesly in it.

47. And thus *came in the use of Money*, some lasting thing that Men might keep without spoiling, and that by mutual consent Men would take in exchange for the truly useful, but perishable Supports of Life.

48. And as different degrees of Industry were apt to give Men Possessions in different Proportions, so this *Invention of Money* gave them the opportunity to continue to enlarge them. For supposing an Island, separated from all possible Commerce with the rest of the World, wherein there were but a hundred Families, but there were Sheep, Horses and Cows, with other useful Animals, wholsome Fruits, and Land enough for Corn for a hundred thousand times as many, but nothing in the Island, either because of its Commonness, or Perishableness, fit to supply the place of *Money*: What reason could any one have there to enlarge his Possessions beyond the use of his Family, and a plentiful supply to its Consumption, either in what their own Industry produced, or they could barter for like perishable, useful Commodities, with others? Where there is not something both lasting and scarce, and so valuable to be hoarded up, there Men will not be apt to enlarge their *Possessions of Land*, were it never so rich, never so free for them to take. For I ask, What would a Man value Ten Thousand, or an Hundred Thousand Acres of excellent *Land*, ready cultivated, and well stocked too with Cattle, in the middle of the in-land Parts of *America*, where he had no hopes of Commerce with other Parts of the World, to draw *Money* to him by the Sale of the Product? It would not be worth the inclosing, and we should see him give up again to the wild Common of Nature, whatever was more than would supply the Conveniencies of Life to be had there for him and his Family.

49. Thus in the beginning all the World was *America*, and more so than that is now; for no such thing as *Money* was any where known. Find out something that hath the *Use and Value of Money* amongst his Neighbours, you shall see the same Man will begin presently to *enlarge* his *Possessions*.

50. But since Gold and Silver, being little useful to the Life of Man in proportion to Food, Rayment, and Carriage, has its *value* only from the consent of Men, whereof Labour yet makes, in great part, *the measure*, it is plain, that Men

have agreed to disproportionate and unequal Possession of the Earth, they having by a tacit and voluntary consent found out a way, how a man may fairly possess more land than he himself can use the product of, by receiving in exchange for the overplus, Gold and Silver, which may be hoarded up without injury to any one, these metalls not spoileing or decaying in the hands of the possessor. This partage of things, in an inequality of private possessions, men have made practicable out of the bounds of Societie, and without compact, only by putting a value on gold and silver and tacitly agreeing in the use of Money. For in Governments the Laws regulate the right of property, and the possession of land is determined by positive constitutions.

51. And thus, I think, it is very easie to conceive without any difficulty, *how Labour could at first begin a title of Property* in the common things of Nature, and how the spending it upon our uses bounded it. So that there could then be no reason of quarrelling about Title, nor any doubt about the largeness of Possession it gave. Right and conveniency went together; for as a Man had a Right to all he could imploy his Labour upon, so he had no temptation to labour for more than he could make use of. This left no room for Controversie about the Title, nor for Incroachment on the Right of others; what Portion a Man carved to himself, was easily seen; and it was useless as well as dishonest to carve himself too much, or take more than he needed.

12

Jean-Jacques Rousseau, *The Social Contract*, Books I and II (selections)

Introduction

Jean-Jacques Rousseau (1712–78) is one of the most influential and intriguing figures of eighteenth-century Europe. A novelist and composer of operas as well as the author of many philosophical works, he also wrote one of the first autobiographies of modern times, *Confessions*, and in his posthumously published *Reveries of a Solitary Walker* (1782) one of the first manifestos of Romanticism. Rousseau's personal life was a complicated and eventful one.[1] Born in Geneva, he was an autodidact who spent many years wandering about Europe before settling in Paris, where he enjoyed an uneasy friendship with the *Encylopédistes*, before being expelled from France and later from his native Switzerland, after the publication of two major works in 1762, *The Social Contract* and his didactic novel *Émile*. Infamously, he abandoned his children. David Hume (1711–76), ignoring the advice that he would be warming a viper in his bosom, played host to the exiled Rousseau, only to be rewarded with ingratitude and animosity from a man now victim to a persecution complex. Rousseau's final years in France were relatively peaceful ones, despite his being subject to arrest for sedition, and he lived

From Jean-Jacques Rousseau, *The Social Contract*, trans. Maurice Cranston, London: Penguin, 2004, pp. 1–9, 12–21, 26–37 (some notes omitted).

long enough to know that he was becoming a hero among young men who, a few years later, would be leading actors in the French Revolution.

Rousseau came to public notice with two Discourses published in the 1750s. In both of these,[2] but especially in *A Discourse on the Origin of Inequality* (1755), he challenges several of the assumptions of Enlightenment thought. Far from there having been "progress" with the emergence of rationally ordered political societies, this emergence has meant a corruption of our original human nature and a substitution of *amour-propre* (vanity, egoism) for the respectable *amour de soi* (concern for self-preservation) found in the state of nature. While Rousseau never called for a "return" to a state of nature, or for emulation of "the noble savage," his hostility to sophisticated, cosmopolitan society was palpable. Certainly there is no celebration of savage innocence in *The Social Contract*. Even the freedom that, according to Rousseau's famous statement early in Book I, man is born to before he becomes enchained, is – it soon emerges – only a "natural independence," a power to do things without obstacles, and not the moral freedom to which one should aspire. Such moral freedom, along with much else one should admire, is achievable only when human beings contract to give up their natural independence and submit to the "direction of the general will."

It is notoriously difficult to know just what Rousseau intends by the idea of a general will, and just how he thinks it can, in practice, ever be identified. Sometimes he gives the impression that the general will is a sort of compromise opinion, what is left over when the views at opposite extremes cancel one another out. But elsewhere he implies that the general will or common interest may be unknown to everyone with the exception, perhaps, of a political genius, "The Lawmaker." Perhaps the best way to understand Rousseau's notion is as follows: the general will of a community is what each individual citizen *would* will if he or she were ideally unselfish and enlightened.

If this is what Rousseau has in mind, it would be consonant with his insistence, throughout his works, on the educative, transformative effect on individuals of membership of a political community. This sort of transformation, arguably, was insufficiently emphasized by earlier writers in the social contract tradition. And it would help, second, to explain some of the features that, in later Books of *The Social Contract*, Rousseau prescribes for a community into which one could rationally contract to enter. It must, for example, be a small community in which people are not strangers. Rousseau's point seems to be that, in such a community, it is much more likely that the "particular wills" of individuals will be harmonized with one another – through discussion, compromise, and so on.

Finally, to understand the general will, to which all citizens must submit, as the will that each of them would have if sufficiently enlightened, helps to take the sting out of some of Rousseau's more sinister remarks – notably his assertion that if a person is forced to obey the dictates of the general will, that person is being "forced to be free." While this is a dangerous assertion, all too liable to misappropriation, perhaps it simply means that no one who opposes the general will can be morally free since, by definition, that person must be in the grip of *amour-propre*, selfish passions, that in enlightened moments he or she must regard as constraints on moral autonomy.

Notes

1 On both his life and his writings, see the magisterial three-volume biography of Rousseau by Maurice Cranston, *Jean-Jacques* (1987), *The Noble Savage* (1991), and *The Solitary Self* (1997).

2 These Discourses are published in Rousseau, *The Social Contract and Discourses*, London: Dent, 1963.

Rousseau, *The Social Contract*

Book I

My purpose is to consider if, in political society, there can be any legitimate and sure principle of government, taking men as they are and laws as they might be. In this inquiry I shall try always to bring together what right permits with what interest prescribes so that justice and utility are in no way divided.

I start without seeking to prove the importance of my subject. I may be asked whether I am a prince or a legislator that I should be writing about politics. I answer no: and indeed that that is my reason for doing so. If I were a prince or a legislator I should not waste my time saying what ought to be done; I should do it or keep silent.

Born as I was the citizen of a free state and a member of its sovereign body, the very right to vote imposes on me the duty to instruct myself

in public affairs, however little influence my voice may have in them. And whenever I reflect upon governments, I am happy to find that my studies always give me fresh reasons for admiring that of my own country.

Chapter I: The subject of Book I   Man was born free, and he is everywhere in chains. Those who think themselves the masters of others are indeed greater slaves than they. How did this transformation come about? I do not know. How can it be made legitimate? That question I believe I can answer.

If I were to consider only force and the effects of force, I should say: 'So long as a people is constrained to obey, and obeys, it does well; but as soon as it can shake off the yoke, and shakes it off, it does better; for since it regains its freedom by the same right as that which removed it, a people is either justified in taking back its freedom, or there is no justifying those who took it away.' But the social order is a sacred right which serves as a basis for all other rights. And as it is not a natural right, it must be one founded on covenants. The problem is to determine what those covenants are. But before we pass on to that question, I must substantiate what I have so far said.

Chapter 2: The First Societies The oldest of all societies, and the only natural one, is that of the family; yet children remain tied to their father by nature only so long as they need him for their preservation. As soon as this need ends, the natural bond is dissolved. Once the children are freed from the obedience they owe their father, and the father is freed from his responsibilities towards them, both parties equally regain their independence. If they continue to remain united, it is no longer nature, but their own choice, which unites them; and the family as such is kept in being only by agreement.

This common liberty is a consequence of man's nature. Man's first law is to watch over his own preservation; his first care he owes to himself; and as soon as he reaches the age of reason, he becomes the only judge of the best means to preserve himself; he becomes his own master.

The family may therefore perhaps be seen as the first model of political societies: the head of the state bears the image of the father, the people the image of his children, and all, being born free and equal, surrender their freedom only when they see advantage in doing so. The only difference is that in the family, a father's love for his children repays him for the care he bestows on them, while in the state, where the ruler can have no such feeling for his people, the pleasure of commanding must take the place of love.

Grotius denies that all human government is established for the benefit of the governed, and he cites the example of slavery.[1] His characteristic method of reasoning is always to offer fact as a proof of right.[*] It is possible to imagine a more logical method, but not one more favourable to tyrants.

According to Grotius, therefore, it is doubtful whether humanity belongs to a hundred men, or whether these hundred men belong to humanity, though he seems throughout his book to lean to the first of these views, which is also that of Hobbes. These authors show us the human race divided into herds of cattle, each with a master who preserves it only in order to devour its members.

Just as a shepherd possesses a nature superior to that of his flock, so do those shepherds of men, their rulers, have a nature superior to that of their people. Or so, we are told by Philo, the Emperor Caligula argued, concluding, reasonably enough on this same analogy, that kings were gods or alternatively that the people were animals.

The reasoning of Caligula coincides with that of Hobbes and Grotius. Indeed Aristotle, before any of them, said that men were not at all equal by nature, since some were born for slavery and others born to be masters.

Aristotle was right; but he mistook the effect for the cause. Anyone born in slavery is born for slavery – nothing is more certain. Slaves, in their bondage, lose everything, even the desire to be free. They love their servitude even as the companions of Ulysses loved their life as brutes.[†] But if there are slaves by nature, it is only because there has been slavery against nature. Force made the first slaves; and their cowardice perpetuates their slavery.

I have said nothing of the King Adam or of the Emperor Noah, father of the three great monarchs who shared out the universe between them, like the children of Saturn, with whom some authors have identified them. I hope my readers will be grateful for this moderation, for since I am directly descended from one of those princes, and perhaps in the eldest line, how do I know that if the deeds were checked, I might not find myself the legitimate king of the human race? However that may be, there is no gainsaying that Adam was the king of the world, as was Robinson Crusoe of his island, precisely because he was the sole inhabitant; and the great advantage of such an empire was that the monarch, secure upon his throne, had no occasion to fear rebellions, wars or conspirators.

---

[*] 'Learned researches on public law are often only the history of ancient abuses, and one is misled when one gives oneself the trouble of studying them too closely.' *Traité manuscrit des intérêts de la France avec ses voisins* by the Marquis d'Argenson.

[†] See a short treatise of Plutarch entitled: *That Animals use Reason.*

Chapter 3: The Right of the Strongest The strongest man is never strong enough to be master all the time, unless he transforms force into right and obedience into duty. Hence 'the right of the strongest' – a 'right' that sounds like something intended ironically, but is actually laid down as a principle. But shall we never have this phrase explained? Force is a physical power; I do not see how its effects could produce morality. To yield to force is an act of necessity, not of will; it is at best an act of prudence. In what sense can it be a moral duty?

Let us grant, for a moment, that this so-called right exists. I suggest it can only produce a tissue of bewildering nonsense; for once might is made to be right, cause and effect are reversed, and every force which overcomes another force inherits the right which belonged to the vanquished. As soon as man can disobey with impunity, his disobedience becomes legitimate; and as the strongest is always right, the only problem is how to become the strongest. But what can be the validity of a right which perishes with the force on which it rests? If force compels obedience, there is no need to invoke a duty to obey, and if force ceases to compel obedience, there is no longer any obligation. Thus the word 'right' adds nothing to what is said by 'force'; it is meaningless.

'Obey those in power.' If this means 'yield to force' the precept is sound, but superfluous; it will never, I suggest, be violated. All power comes from God, I agree; but so does every disease, and no one forbids us to summon a physician. If I am held up by a robber at the edge of a wood, force compels me to hand over my purse. But if I could somehow contrive to keep the purse from him, would I still be obliged in conscience to surrender it? After all, the pistol in the robber's hand is undoubtedly a *power*.

Surely it must be admitted, then, that might does not make right, and that the duty of obedience is owed only to legitimate powers. Thus we are constantly led back to my original question.

Chapter 4: Slavery Since no man has any natural authority over his fellows, and since force alone bestows no right, all legitimate authority among men must be based on covenants.

Grotius says: 'If an individual can alienate his freedom and become the slave of a master, why may not a whole people alienate its freedom and become the subject of a king?' In this remark there are several ambiguous words which call for explanation; but let us confine ourselves to one – to 'alienate'. To alienate is to give or sell. A man who becomes the slave of another does not give himself, he sells himself in return for at least a subsistence. But in return for what could a whole people be said to sell itself? A king, far from nourishing his subjects, draws his nourishment from them; and kings, according to Rabelais, need more than a little nourishment. Do subjects, then, give their persons to the king on condition that he will accept their property as well? If so, I fail to see what they have left to preserve.

It will be said that a despot gives his subjects the assurance of civil tranquillity. Very well, but what does it profit them, if those wars against other powers which result from a despot's ambition, if his insatiable greed, and the oppressive demands of his administration, cause more desolation than civil strife would cause? What do the people gain if their very condition of civil tranquillity is one of their hardships? There is peace in dungeons, but is that enough to make dungeons desirable? The Greeks lived in peace in the cave of Cyclops awaiting their turn to be devoured.

To speak of a man giving himself in return for nothing is to speak of what is absurd, unthinkable; such an action would be illegitimate, void, if only because no one who did it could be in his right mind. To say the same of a whole people is to conjure up a nation of lunatics; and right cannot rest on madness.

Even if each individual could alienate himself, he cannot alienate his children. For they are born men; they are born free; their liberty belongs to them; no one but they themselves has the right to dispose of it. Before they reach the years of discretion, their father may, in their name, make certain rules for their protection and their welfare, but he cannot give away their liberty irrevocably and unconditionally, for such a gift would be contrary to the ends of nature and an abuse of paternal right. Hence, an arbitrary government would be legitimate only if every new generation were able to accept or reject it, and in that case the government would cease to be arbitrary.

To renounce freedom is to renounce one's humanity, one's rights as a man and equally one's duties. There is no possible *quid pro quo* for one who renounces everything; indeed such renunciation is contrary to man's very nature; for if you take away all freedom of the will, you strip a man's actions of all moral significance. Finally, any covenant which stipulated absolute dominion for one party and absolute obedience for the other would be illogical and nugatory. Is it not evident that he who is entitled to demand everything owes nothing? And does not the single fact of there being no reciprocity, no mutual obligation, nullify the act? For what right can my slave have against me? If everything he has belongs to me, his right is *my* right, and it would be nonsense to speak of my having a right *against* myself.

[...]

Chapter 5: That We Must Always Go Back To an Original Covenant   Even if I were to concede all that I have so far refuted, the champions of despotism would be no better off. There will always be a great difference between subduing a multitude and ruling a society. If one man successively enslaved many separate individuals, no matter how numerous, he and they would never bear the aspect of anything but a master and his slaves, not at all that of a people and their ruler; an aggregation, perhaps, but certainly not an association, for they would neither have a common good nor be a body politic. Even if such a man were to enslave half the world, he would remain a private individual, and his interest, always distinct from that of the others, would never be more than a personal interest. When he died, the empire he left would be scattered for lack of any bond of union, even as an oak crumbles and falls into a heap of ashes when fire has consumed it.

'A people,' says Grotius, 'may give itself to a king.' Therefore, according to Grotius a people is *a people* even before the gift to the king is made. The gift itself is a civil act; it presupposes public deliberation. Hence, before considering the act by which a people submits to a king, we ought to scrutinize the act by which people become *a* people, for that act, being necessarily antecedent to the other, is the real foundation of society.

In fact, if there were no earlier agreement, how, unless the election were unanimous, could there be any obligation on the minority to accept the decision of the majority? What right have the hundred who want to have a master to vote on behalf of the ten who do not? The law of majority-voting itself rests on an agreement, and

implies that there has been on at least one occasion unanimity.

Chapter 6: The Social Pact   I assume that men reach a point where the obstacles to their preservation in a state of nature prove greater than the strength that each man has to preserve himself in that state. Beyond this point, the primitive condition cannot endure, for then the human race will perish if it does not change its mode of existence.

Since men cannot create new forces, but merely combine and control those which already exist, the only way in which they can preserve themselves is by uniting their separate powers in a combination strong enough to overcome any resistance, uniting them so that their powers are directed by a single motive and act in concert.

Such a sum of forces can be produced only by the union of separate men, but as each man's own strength and liberty are the chief instruments of his preservation, how can he merge his with others' without putting himself in peril and neglecting the care he owes to himself? This difficulty, in terms of my present subject, may be expressed in these words:

'How to find a form of association which will defend the person and goods of each member with the collective force of all, and under which each individual, while uniting himself with the others, obeys no one but himself, and remains as free as before.' This is the fundamental problem to which the social contract holds the solution.

The articles of this contract are so precisely determined by the nature of the act, that the slightest modification must render them null and void; they are such that, though perhaps never formally stated, they are everywhere the same, everywhere tacitly admitted and recognized; and if ever the social pact is violated, every man regains his original rights and, recovering his natural freedom, loses that civil freedom for which he exchanged it.

These articles of association, rightly understood, are reducible to a single one, namely the total alienation by each associate of himself and all his rights to the whole community. Thus, in the first place, as every individual gives himself absolutely, the conditions are the same for all, and precisely because they are the same for all, it is in no one's interest to make the conditions onerous for others.

Secondly, since the alienation is unconditional, the union is as perfect as it can be, and no individual associate has any longer any rights to claim; for if rights were left to individuals, in the absence of any higher authority to judge between them and the public, each individual, being his own judge in some causes, would soon demand to be his own judge in all; and in this way the state of nature would be kept in being, and the association inevitably become either tyrannical or void.

Finally, since each man gives himself to all, he gives himself to no one; and since there is no associate over whom he does not gain the same rights as others gain over him, each man recovers the equivalent of everything he loses, and in the bargain he acquires more power to preserve what he has.

If, then, we eliminate from the social pact everything that is not essential to it, we find it comes down to this: 'Each one of us puts into the community his person and all his powers under the supreme direction of the general will; and as a body, we incorporate every member as an indivisible part of the whole.'

Immediately, in place of the individual person of each contracting party, this act of association creates an artificial and corporate body composed of as many members as there are voters in the assembly, and by this same act that body acquires its unity, its common *ego*, its life and its will. The public person thus formed by the union of all other persons was once called the *city*, and is now known as the *republic* or the *body politic*. In its passive role it is called the *state*, when it plays an active role it is the *sovereign*; and when it is compared to others of its own kind, it is a *power*. Those who are associated in it take collectively the name of *a people*, and call themselves individually *citizens*, in that they share in the sovereign power, and *subjects*, in that they put themselves under the laws of the state. However, these words are often confused, each being mistaken for another; but the essential thing is to know how to recognize them when they are used in their precise sense.

Chapter 7: The Sovereign   This formula shows that the act of association consists of a reciprocal commitment between society and the individual, so that each person, in making a contract, as it were, with himself, finds himself doubly committed, first, as a member of the sovereign body in relation to individuals, and secondly as a member of the state in relation to the sovereign. Here there can be no invoking the principle of civil law which says that no man is bound by a contract with himself, for there is a great difference between having an obligation to oneself and having an obligation to something of which one is a member.

We must add that a public decision can impose an obligation on all the subjects towards the sovereign, by reason of the two aspects under which each can be seen, while, contrariwise, such decisions cannot impose an obligation on the sovereign towards itself; and hence it would be against the very nature of a political body for the sovereign to set over itself a law which it could not infringe. The sovereign, bearing only one single and identical aspect, is in the position of a private person making a contract with himself, which shows that there neither is, nor can be, any kind of fundamental law binding on the people as a body, not even the social contract itself. This does not mean that the whole body cannot incur obligations to other nations, so long as those obligations do not infringe the contract; for in relation to foreign powers, the body politic is a simple entity, an individual.

However, since the body politic, or sovereign, owes its being to the sanctity of the contract alone, it cannot commit itself, even in treaties with foreign powers, to anything that would derogate from the original act of association; it could not, for example, alienate a part of itself or submit to another sovereign. To violate the act which has given it existence would be to annihilate itself; and what is nothing can produce nothing.

As soon as the multitude is united thus in a single body, no one can injure any one of the members without attacking the whole, still less injure the whole without each member feeling it. Duty and self-interest thus equally oblige the two contracting parties to give each other mutual aid; and the same men should seek to bring together in this dual relationship, all the advantages that flow from it.

Now, as the sovereign is formed entirely of the individuals who compose it, it has not, nor could it have, any interest contrary to theirs; and so the sovereign has no need to give guarantees to the subjects, because it is impossible for a body to wish to hurt all of its members, and, as we shall see, it cannot hurt any particular member. The sovereign by the mere fact that it is, is always all that it ought to be.

But this is not true of the relation of subject to sovereign. Despite their common interest, subjects will not be bound by their commitment unless means are found to guarantee their fidelity.

For every individual as a man may have a private will contrary to, or different from, the general will that he has as a citizen. His private interest may speak with a very different voice from that of the public interest; his absolute and naturally independent existence may make him regard what he owes to the common cause as a gratuitous contribution, the loss of which would be less painful for others than the payment is onerous for him; and fancying that the artificial person which constitutes the state is a mere fictitious entity (since it is not a man), he might seek to enjoy the rights of a citizen without doing the duties of a subject. The growth of this kind of injustice would bring about the ruin of the body politic.

Hence, in order that the social pact shall not be an empty formula, it is tacitly implied in that commitment – which alone can give force to all others – that whoever refuses to obey the general will shall be constrained to do so by the whole body, which means nothing other than that he shall be forced to be free; for this is the necessary condition which, by giving each citizen to the nation, secures him against all personal dependence, it is the condition which shapes both the design and the working of the political machine, and which alone bestows justice on civil contracts – without it, such contracts would be absurd, tyrannical and liable to the grossest abuse.

Chapter 8: Civil Society The passing from the state of nature to the civil society produces a remarkable change in man; it puts justice as a rule of conduct in the place of instinct, and gives his actions the moral quality they previously lacked. It is only then, when the voice of duty has taken the place of physical impulse, and right that of desire, that man, who has hitherto thought only of himself, finds himself compelled to act on other principles, and to consult his reason rather than study his inclinations. And although in civil society man surrenders some of the advantages that belong to the state of nature, he gains in return far greater ones; his faculties are so exercised and developed, his mind is so enlarged, his sentiments

so ennobled, and his whole spirit so elevated that, if the abuse of his new condition did not in many cases lower him to something worse than what he had left, he should constantly bless the happy hour that lifted him for ever from the state of nature and from a stupid, limited animal made a creature of intelligence and a man.

Suppose we draw up a balance sheet, so that the losses and gains may be readily compared. What man loses by the social contract is his natural liberty and the absolute right to anything that tempts him and that he can take; what he gains by the social contract is civil liberty and the legal right of property in what he possesses. If we are to avoid mistakes in weighing the one side against the other, we must clearly distinguish between *natural* liberty, which has no limit but the physical power of the individual concerned, and *civil* liberty, which is limited by the general will; and we must distinguish also between *possession*, which is based only on force or 'the right of the first occupant', and *property*, which must rest on a legal title.

We might also add that man acquires with civil society, moral freedom, which alone makes man the master of himself; for to be governed by appetite alone is slavery, while obedience to a law one prescribes to oneself is freedom. However, I have already said more than enough on this subject, and the philosophical meaning of the word 'freedom' is no part of my subject here.

[. . .]

Book II

Chapter 1: That Sovereignty is Inalienable The first and most important consequence of the principles so far established is that the general will alone can direct the forces of the state in accordance with that end which the state has been established to achieve – the common good; for if conflict between private interests has made the setting up of civil societies necessary, harmony between those same interests has made it possible. It is what is common to those different interests which yields the social bond; if there were no point on which separate interests coincided, then society could not conceivably exist. And it is precisely on the basis of this common interest that society must be governed.

My argument, then, is that sovereignty, being nothing other than the exercise of the general will, can never be alienated; and that the sovereign, which is simply a collective being, cannot be represented by anyone but itself – power may be delegated, but the will cannot be.

For indeed while it is not impossible for a private will to coincide with the general will on some point or other, it is impossible for such a coincidence to be regular and enduring; for the private will inclines by its very nature towards partiality, and the general will towards equality. It is even more inconceivable that there could be a guarantee of harmony between the private and the general will, even if it were to continue always, for such lasting harmony would be the result of chance and not of design. The sovereign might say: 'What I want at present is precisely what this man wants, or at least what he says he wants'; but no sovereign could say: 'What this man is going to want tomorrow I too shall want', for it is absurd that anyone should wish to bind himself for the future, and it is a contradiction in terms to say that any human being should wish to consent to something that is the reverse of his own good. If a people promises simply and solely to obey, it dissolves itself by that very pledge; it ceases to be a people; for once there is a master, there is no longer a sovereign, and the body politic is therefore annihilated.

This is not to say that the commands of leaders may not pass for the general will if the sovereign, while free to oppose them, does not do so. In such a case the silence of the people permits the assumption that the people consents. This will be explained more fully in a later chapter.

Chapter 2: That Sovereignty is Indivisible Just as sovereignty is inalienable, it is for the same reason indivisible; for either the will is general* or it is not; either it is the will of the body of the people, or merely that of a part. In the first case, a declaration of will is an act of sovereignty and constitutes law; in the second case, it is only a declaration of a particular will or an act of administration, it is at best a mere decree.

Nevertheless, our political theorists, unable to divide the principle of sovereignty, divide it

in its purpose; they divide it into power and will, divide it, that is, into executive and legislative, into the rights of levying taxation, administering justice and making war, into domestic jurisdiction and the power to deal with foreign governments. Sometimes our theorists confuse all the parts and sometimes they separate them. They make the sovereign a creature of fantasy, a patchwork of separate pieces, rather as if they were to construct a man of several bodies – one with eyes, one with legs, the other with feet and nothing else. It is said that Japanese mountebanks can cut up a child under the eyes of spectators, throw the different parts into the air, and then make the child come down, alive and all of a piece. This is more or less the trick that our political theorists perform – after dismembering the social body with a sleight of hand worthy of the fairground, they put the pieces together again anyhow.

The mistake comes from having no precise notion of what sovereign authority is, and from taking mere manifestations of authority for parts of the authority itself. For instance, the acts of declaring war and making peace have been regarded as acts of sovereignty, which they are not; for neither of these acts constitutes a *law*, but only an application of law, a particular act which determines how the law shall be interpreted – and all this will be obvious as soon as I have defined the idea which attaches to the word 'law'.

If we were to scrutinize in the same way the other supposed divisions of sovereignty, we should find that whenever we thought that sovereignty was divided, we had been mistaken, for the rights which are taken to be part of that sovereignty prove in fact to be subordinate to it, and presuppose the existence of a supreme will which they merely serve to put into effect.

This want of precision has obfuscated immeasurably the conclusions of our legal theorists when they have come to apply their own principles to determine the respective rights of kings and of peoples. Every reader of the third and fourth chapters of the first book of Grotius can see how that learned man and his translator, Barbeyrac, are trapped in their own sophisms, frightened of saying either too much or alternatively too little (according to their prejudices) and so offending the interests they wish to flatter. Grotius, a refugee in France, discontented with his own country and out to pay court to Louis XIII, to whom his book is dedicated, spares no pains to rob peoples

---

* For the will to be general, it does not always have to be unanimous; but all the votes must be counted. Any formal exclusion destroys its universality.

of all their rights and to invest those rights, by every conceivable artifice, in kings. This would have been very much to the taste of Barbeyrac, who dedicated his translation of Grotius to the King of England, George I. But unfortunately the expulsion of James II – which Barbeyrac calls an 'abdication' – obliged him to speak with a marked reserve, to hesitate and equivocate, so as not to suggest that William III was a usurper. If these two writers had adopted sound principles, all their difficulties would have vanished, and their arguments would have been logical; but then they would, alas for them, have told the truth and paid court only to the people. The truth brings no man a fortune; and it is not the people who hand out embassies, professorships and pensions.

Chapter 3: Whether the General Will Can Err   It follows from what I have argued that the general will is always rightful and always tends to the public good; but it does not follows that the deliberations of the people are always equally right. We always want what is advantageous to us but we do not always discern it. The people is never corrupted, but it is often misled; and only then does it seem to will what is bad.

There is often a great difference between the will of all [what all individuals want] and the general will; the general will studies only the common interest while the will of all studies private interest, and is indeed no more than the sum of individual desires. But if we take away from these same wills, the pluses and minuses which cancel each other out, the balance which remains is the general will.

From the deliberations of a people properly informed, and provided its members do not have any communication among themselves, the great number of small differences will always produce a general will and the decision will always be good. But if groups, sectional associations are formed at the expense of the larger association, the will of each of these groups will become general in relation to its own members and private in relation to the state; we might then say that there are no longer as many votes as there are men but only as many votes as there are groups. The differences become less numerous and yield a result less general. Finally, when one of these groups becomes so large that it can outweigh the rest, the result is no longer the sum of many small differences, but one great divisive difference; then there ceases to be a general will, and the opinion which prevails is no more than a private opinion.

Thus if the general will is to be clearly expressed, it is imperative that there should be no sectional associations in the state, and that every citizen should make up his own mind for himself – such was the unique and sublime invention of the great Lycurgus. But if there are sectional associations, it is wise to multiply their number and to prevent inequality among them, as Solon, Numa and Servius did. These are the only precautions which can ensure that the general will is always enlightened and the people protected from error.

Chapter 4: The Limits of Sovereign Power   If the state, or the nation, is nothing other than an artificial person the life of which consists in the union of its members and if the most important of its cares is its preservation, it needs to have a universal and compelling power to move and dispose of each part in whatever manner is beneficial to the whole. Just as nature gives each man an absolute power over all his own limbs, the social pact gives the body politic an absolute power over all its members; and it is this same power which, directed by the general will, bears, as I have said, the name of sovereignty.

However, we have to consider beside the public person those private persons who compose it, and whose life and liberty are naturally independent of it. Hence we have to distinguish clearly the respective rights of the citizen and of the sovereign,* and distinguish those duties which the citizens owe as subjects from the natural rights which they ought to enjoy as men.

We have agreed that each man alienates by the social pact only that part of his power, his goods and his liberty which is the concern of the community; but it must also be admitted that the sovereign alone is judge of what is of such concern.

Whatever services the citizen can render the state, he owes whenever the sovereign demands them; but the sovereign, on its side, may not impose on the subjects any burden which is not necessary to the community; the sovereign

---

* Please, attentive reader, do not hasten to accuse me of contradiction. I cannot avoid a contradiction of words, because of the poverty of language; but wait.

cannot, indeed, even will such a thing, since according to the law of reason no less than to the law of nature nothing is without a cause.

The commitments which bind us to the social body are obligatory only because they are mutual; and their nature is such that in fulfilling them a man cannot work for others without at the same time working for himself. How should it be that the general will is always rightful and that all men constantly wish the happiness of each but for the fact that there is no one who does not take that word 'each' to pertain to himself and in voting for all think of himself? This proves that the equality of rights and the notion of justice which it produces derive from the predilection which each man has for himself and hence from human nature as such. It also proves that the general will, to be truly what it is, must be general in its purpose as well as in its nature; that it should spring from all for it to apply to all; and that it loses its natural rectitude when it is directed towards any particular and circumscribed object – for in judging what is foreign to us, we have no sound principle of equity to guide us.

For, indeed, whenever we are dealing with a particular fact or right, on a matter which has not been settled by an earlier and general agreement, that question becomes contentious. It is a conflict in which private interests are ranged on one side and the public interest on the other; and I can see neither the law which is to be followed nor the judge who is to arbitrate. It would be absurd in such a dispute to rely on an express decision of the general will; for a decision could only be a conclusion in favour of one of the contending parties, and it would be regarded by the other party as an alien, partial will, a will liable in such circumstances to be unjust and so to fall into error. So we see that even as a private will cannot represent the general will, so too the general will changes its nature if it seeks to deal with an individual case; it cannot as a *general* will give a ruling concerning any one man or any one fact. When the people of Athens, for example, appointed or dismissed its leaders, awarding honours to one, inflicting penalties on another, and by a multitude of particular decrees indiscriminately exercised all the functions of an administration, then the people of Athens no longer had what is correctly understood as a general will and ceased to act as sovereign and acted instead as magistrate. All this may seem at

variance with commonly accepted notions; but I must be given time to expound my own.

It should nevertheless be clear from what I have so far said that the general will derives its generality less from the number of voices than from the common interest which unites them – for the general will is an institution in which each necessarily submits himself to the same conditions which he imposes on others; this admirable harmony of interest and justice gives to social deliberations a quality of equity which disappears at once from the discussion of any individual dispute precisely because in these latter cases there is no common interest to unite and identify the decision of the judge with that of the contending parties.

Whichever way we look at it, we always return to the same conclusion: namely that the social pact establishes equality among the citizens in that they all pledge themselves under the same conditions and must all enjoy the same rights. Hence by the nature of the compact, every act of sovereignty, that is, every authentic act of the general will, binds or favours all the citizens equally, so that the sovereign recognizes only the whole body of the nation and makes no distinction between any of the members who compose it. What then is correctly to be called an act of sovereignty? It is not a covenant between a superior and an inferior, but a covenant of the body with each of its members. It is a legitimate covenant, because its basis is the social contract; an equitable one, because it is common to all; a useful one, because it can have no end but the common good; and it is a durable covenant because it is guaranteed by the armed forces and the supreme power. So long as the subjects submit to such covenants alone, they obey nobody but their own will; and to ask how far the respective rights of the sovereign and the citizen extend is to ask how far these two can pledge themselves together, each to all and all to each.

From this it is clear that the sovereign power, wholly absolute, wholly sacred, wholly inviolable as it is, does not go beyond and cannot go beyond the limits of the general covenants; and thus that every man can do what he pleases with such goods and such freedom as is left to him by these covenants; and from this it follows that the sovereign has never any right to impose greater burdens on one subject than on another, for whenever that happens the matter becomes private and is outside the sovereign's competence.

Granted these distinctions; it becomes manifestly false to assert that individuals make any real renunciation by the social contract; indeed, as a result of the contract they find themselves in a situation preferable in real terms to that which prevailed before; instead of an alienation, they have profitably exchanged an uncertain and precarious life for a better and more secure one; they have exchanged natural independence for freedom, the power to injure others for the enjoyment of their own security; they have exchanged their own strength which others might overcome for a right which the social union makes invincible. Their very lives, which they have pledged to the state, are always protected by it; and even when they risk their lives to defend the state, what more are they doing but giving back what they have received from the state? What are they doing that they would not do more often, and at greater peril, in the state of nature, where every man is inevitably at war and at the risk of his life, defends whatever serves him to maintain life? Assuredly, all must now fight in case of need for their country, but at least no one has any longer to fight for himself. And is there not something to be gained by running, for the sake of the guarantee of safety, a few of those risks we should each have to face alone if we were deprived of that assurance?

[. . .]

Note

1 Hugo Grotius (1583–1645), the great Dutch jurist and theorist of natural law, is a frequent target of Rousseau's criticisms. His main work, and the one Rousseau primarily has in mind, was the hugely influential *De Jure Belli et Pacis*.

13

David Hume, "Of Justice," "Of the Origin of Government," and "Of the Original Contract"

Introduction

In this set of texts, Scottish philosopher David Hume (1711–76) distances himself from the two reigning political philosophies of his day – the social contract theory (liberals and Whigs) and the theory of divine right of kings (Tories). Hume does so not only by dismantling these competing philosophical theories. More radically, he argues that the legitimacy of the state does not and should not derive from philosophical principle. The authority and legitimacy of government, by contrast, he argues finds its root in that pre-philosophical soil of custom and nature he calls, broadly, "common life."[1]

Hume's many other skeptical texts had undercut the idea that people can apprehend any moral or political prescriptions from a transcendent deity, let alone prove such a deity's existence (I.14, II.10, IV.15). People therefore can turn neither to revelation nor to natural moral-political law, implanted by the deity in the natural world, in trying to discern what sort of government human beings should support. In the texts collected here, Hume focuses on the social contract and the idea

From David Hume, *Enquiries Concerning the Human Understanding and Concerning the Principles of Morals*, ed. L. A. Selby-Bigge, 2nd edition, Oxford: Clarendon Press, 1902, pp. 183–204; and David Hume, *Hume's Moral and Political Philosophy*, ed. H. D. Aiken, New York: Hafner Publishing Co., 1948, pp. 311–14, 356–72 (some notes omitted).

that government is legitimated most basically by consent. If governmental authority can be legitimate only through an explicit act of contract, then, Hume observes, almost no governments have been legitimate. Moreover, the practices that are taken to manifest implicit or "tacit" consent are discernible in populations ruled by conquest as well as election.

Instead, Hume maintains in the last essay he would write, "Of the Original Contract" (1774), that government like language develops gradually over time. Just as there was no original contract to give authority to the rules of English grammar, so there was no original contract to form society or even to establish government. Human beings were never born into an a-social "state of nature" postulated by Locke and Rousseau (V.11–12), let alone the sort of "war of all against all" Hobbes had described (V.10). Human beings are now, have always been, and always will live in societies, at least the minimal society of the family. Like the rules of grammar, government's practices of authority originated and then developed in these early societies in an unreflective way. First, language developed, and then grammar was formalized; similarly, first society and political authority was generated, and then political theory explicated it.

If the origin of society and political authority was not rooted in prior philosophical principle, then neither does its legitimacy persist by philosophical principle. Government persists, maintains its legitimacy, and acquires the consent of the governed not by philosophical theory and argument but through the customs and habits of a culture, as well as through the proven usefulness of government in satisfying human wants and needs. The same therefore goes for governments structured around democratic consent (which Hume acknowledges are "the best and most sacred of any") as it goes for heritable monarchies.

Similarly, the rules of justice that govern the control and exchange of property, do not fall from the sky or plop from syllogisms anchored in self-evident truths. Rather, the formal rules of justice are, according to Hume, simply artificial devices invented to help human beings manage very specific social conditions. When goods are either excessively abundant or life-threateningly scarce, the rules of justice are pointless and without use. Social institutions of "justice," instead, arise under conditions of what might be described as those of moderate limitation – that is, where human desires for certain goods exceed their supply, but the supply is not so short as to threaten

widespread loss of life or profound suffering. Under such conditions, human beings invent rules to govern the distribution and possession of goods in order to secure and maintain a peaceful society. Like different languages, human beings in different places and times are likely to develop different rules of justice to achieve these ends; and like the rules of grammar the rules may be revised. But appealing to philosophical speculations of "divine right" or "original contract" in promoting or resisting revision is, according to Hume, not only philosophically specious but also politically dangerous.

Note

1   D. W. Livingston, *Hume's Philosophy of Common Life*, Chicago: University of Chicago Press, 1984.

Hume, "Of Justice"

Part I

145 That Justice is useful to society, and consequently that *part* of its merit, at least, must arise from that consideration, it would be a superfluous undertaking to prove. That public utility is the *sole* origin of justice, and that reflections on the beneficial consequences of this virtue are the *sole* foundation of its merit; this proposition, being more curious and important, will better deserve our examination and enquiry.

Let us suppose that nature has bestowed on the human race such profuse *abundance* of all *external* conveniences, that, without any uncertainty in the event, without any care or industry on our part, every individual finds himself fully provided with whatever his most voracious appetites can want, or luxurious imagination wish or desire. His natural beauty, we shall suppose, surpasses all acquired ornaments: the perpetual clemency of the seasons renders useless all clothes or covering: the raw herbage affords him the most delicious fare; the clear fountain, the richest beverage. No laborious occupation required: no tillage: no navigation. Music, poetry, and con-

templation form his sole business: conversation, mirth, and friendship his sole amusement.

It seems evident that, in such a happy state, every other social virtue would flourish, and receive tenfold increase; but the cautious, jealous virtue of justice would never once have been dreamed of. For what purpose make a partition of goods, where every one has already more than enough? Why give rise to property, where there cannot possibly be any injury? Why call this object *mine*, when upon the seizing of it by another, I need but stretch out my hand to possess myself to what is equally valuable? Justice, in that case, being totally useless, would be an idle ceremonial, and could never possibly have place in the catalogue of virtues.

We see, even in the present necessitous condition of mankind, that, wherever any benefit is bestowed by nature in an unlimited abundance, we leave it always in common among the whole human race, and make no subdivisions of right and property. Water and air, though the most necessary of all objects, are not challenged as the property of individuals; nor can any man commit injustice by the most lavish use and enjoyment of these blessings. In fertile extensive countries, with few inhabitants, land is regarded on the same footing. And no topic is so much insisted on by those, who defend the liberty of the seas, as the unexhausted use of them in navigation. Were the advantages, procured by navigation, as inexhaustible, these reasoners had never had any adversaries to refute; nor had any claims ever been advanced of a separate, exclusive dominion over the ocean.

It may happen, in some countries, at some periods, that there be established a property in water, none in land; if the latter be in greater abundance than can be used by the inhabitants, and the former be found, with difficulty, and in very small quantities.

146   Again; suppose, that, though the necessities of human race continue the same as at present, yet the mind is so enlarged, and so replete with friendship and generosity, that every man has the utmost tenderness for every man, and feels no more concern for his own interest than for that of his fellows; it seems evident, that the use of justice would, in this case, be suspended by such an extensive benevolence, nor would the divisions and barriers of property and obligation have ever been thought of. Why should I bind another, by a deed or promise, to do me any good office, when I know that he is already prompted, by the strongest inclination, to seek my happiness, and would, of himself, perform the desired service; except the hurt, he thereby receives, be greater than the benefit accruing to me? in which case, he knows, that, from my innate humanity and friendship, I should be the first to oppose myself to his imprudent generosity. Why raise landmarks between my neighbour's field and mine, when my heart has made no division between our interests; but shares all his joys and sorrows with the same force and vivacity as if originally my own? Every man, upon this supposition, being a second self to another, would trust all his interests to the discretion of every man; without jealousy, without partition, without distinction. And the whole human race would form only one family; where all would lie in common, and be used freely, without regard to property; but cautiously too, with as entire regard to the necessities of each individual, as if our own interests were most intimately concerned.

In the present disposition of the human heart, it would, perhaps, be difficult to find complete instances of such enlarged affections; but still we may observe, that the case of families approaches

towards it; and the stronger the mutual benevolence is among the individuals, the nearer it approaches; till all distinction of property be, in a great measure, lost and confounded among them. Between married persons, the cement of friendship is by the laws supposed so strong as to abolish all division of possessions; and has often, in reality, the force ascribed to it. And it is observable, that, during the ardour of new enthusiasms, when every principle is inflamed into extravagance, the community of goods has frequently been attempted; and nothing but experience of its inconveniencies, from the returning or disguised selfishness of men, could make the imprudent fanatics adopt anew the ideas of justice and of separate property. So true is it, that this virtue derives its existence entirely from its necessary *use* to the intercourse and social state of mankind.

To make this truth more evident, let us   147 reverse the foregoing suppositions; and carrying everything to the opposite extreme, consider what would be the effect of these new situations. Suppose a society to fall into such want of all common necessaries, that the utmost frugality and industry cannot preserve the greater number from perishing, and the whole from extreme misery; it will readily, I believe, be admitted, that the strict laws of justice are suspended, in such a pressing emergence, and give place to the stronger motives of necessity and self-preservation. Is it any crime, after a shipwreck, to seize whatever means or instrument of safety one can lay hold of, without regard to former limitations of property? Or if a city besieged were perishing with hunger; can we imagine, that men will see any means of preservation before them, and lose their lives, from a scrupulous regard to what, in other situations, would be the rules of equity and justice? The use and tendency of that virtue is to procure happiness and security, by preserving order in society: but where the society is ready to perish from extreme necessity, no greater evil can be dreaded from violence and injustice; and every man may now provide for himself by all the means, which prudence can dictate, or humanity permit. The public, even in less urgent necessities, opens granaries, without the consent of proprietors; as justly supposing, that the authority of magistracy may, consistent with equity, extend so far: but were any number of men to assemble, without the tie of laws or civil jurisdiction; would an equal partition of bread in a famine, though effected by power and even violence, be regarded as criminal or injurious?

148   Suppose likewise, that it should be a virtuous man's fate to fall into the society of ruffians, remote from the protection of laws and government; what conduct must he embrace in that melancholy situation? He sees such a desperate rapaciousness prevail; such a disregard to equity, such contempt of order, such stupid blindness to future consequences, as must immediately have the most tragical conclusion, and must terminate in destruction to the greater number, and in a total dissolution of society to the rest. He, meanwhile, can have no other expedient than to arm himself, to whomever the sword he seizes, or the buckler, may belong: To make provision of all means of defence and security: And his particular regard to justice being no longer of use to his own safety or that of others, he must consult the dictates of self-preservation alone, without concern for those who no longer merit his care and attention.

When any man, even in political society, renders himself by his crimes, obnoxious to the public, he is punished by the laws in his goods and person; that is, the ordinary rules of justice are, with regard to him, suspended for a moment, and it becomes equitable to inflict on him, for the *benefit* of society, what otherwise he could not suffer without wrong or injury.

The rage and violence of public war; what is it but a suspension of justice among the warring parties, who perceive, that this virtue is now no longer of any *use* or advantage to them? The laws of war, which then succeed to those of equity and justice, are rules calculated for the *advantage* and *utility* of that particular state, in which men are now placed. And were a civilized nation engaged with barbarians, who observed no rules even of war, the former must also suspend their observance of them, where they no longer serve to any purpose; and must render every action or encounter as bloody and pernicious as possible to the first aggressors.

149   Thus, the rules of equity or justice depend entirely on the particular state and condition in which men are placed, and owe their origin and existence to that utility, which results to the public from their strict and regular observance. Reverse, in any considerable circumstance, the condition of men: Produce extreme abundance or extreme necessity: Implant in the human breast

perfect moderation and humanity, or perfect rapaciousness and malice: By rendering justice totally *useless*, you thereby totally destroy its essence, and suspend its obligation upon mankind.

The common situation of society is a medium amidst all these extremes. We are naturally partial to ourselves, and to our friends; but are capable of learning the advantage resulting from a more equitable conduct. Few enjoyments are given us from the open and liberal hand of nature; but by art, labour, and industry, we can extract them in great abundance. Hence the ideas of property become necessary in all civil society: Hence justice derives its usefulness to the public: And hence alone arises its merit and moral obligation.

150   These conclusions are so natural and obvious, that they have not escaped even the poets, in their descriptions of the felicity attending the golden age or the reign of Saturn. The seasons, in that first period of nature, were so temperate, if we credit these agreeable fictions, that there was no necessity for men to provide themselves with clothes and houses, as a security against the violence of heat and cold: The rivers flowed with wine and milk: The oaks yielded honey; and nature spontaneously produced her greatest delicacies. Nor were these the chief advantages of that happy age. Tempests were not alone removed from nature; but those more furious tempests were unknown to human breasts, which now cause such uproar, and engender such confusion. Avarice, ambition, cruelty, selfishness, were never heard of: Cordial affection, compassion, sympathy, were the only movements with which the mind was yet acquainted. Even the punctilious distinction of *mine* and *thine* was banished from among that happy race of mortals, and carried with it the very notion of property and obligation, justice and injustice.

151   This *poetical* fiction of the *golden age* is, in some respects, of a piece with the *philosophical* fiction of the *state of nature*; only that the former is represented as the most charming and most peaceable condition, which can possibly be imagined; whereas the latter is painted out as a state of mutual war and violence, attended with the most extreme necessity. On the first origin of mankind, we are told, their ignorance and savage nature were so prevalent, that they could give no mutual trust, but must each depend upon himself and his own force or cunning for protection and security. No law was heard of: No

rule of justice known: No distinction of property regarded: Power was the only measure of right; and a perpetual war of all against all was the result of men's untamed selfishness and barbarity.

Whether such a condition of human nature could ever exist, or if it did, could continue so long as to merit the appellation of a *state*, may justly be doubted. Men are necessarily born in a family-society, at least; and are trained up by their parents to some rule of conduct and behaviour. But this must be admitted, that, if such a state of mutual war and violence was ever real, the suspension of all laws of justice, from their absolute inutility, is a necessary and infallible consequence.

152 The more we vary our views of human life, and the newer and more unusual the lights are in which we survey it, the more shall we be convinced, that the origin here assigned for the virtue of justice is real and satisfactory.

Were there a species of creatures intermingled with men, which, though rational, were possessed of such inferior strength, both of body and mind, that they were incapable of all resistance, and could never, upon the highest provocation, make us feel the effects of their resentment; the necessary consequence, I think, is that we should be bound by the laws of humanity to give gentle usage to these creatures, but should not, properly speaking, lie under any restraint of justice with regard to them, nor could they possess any right or property, exclusive of such arbitrary lords. Our intercourse with them could not be called society, which supposes a degree of equality; but absolute command on the one side, and servile obedience on the other. Whatever we covet, they must instantly resign: Our permission is the only tenure, by which they hold their possessions : Our compassion and kindness the only check, by which they curb our lawless will: And as no inconvenience ever results from the exercise of a power, so firmly established in nature, the restraints of justice and property, being totally *useless*, would never have place in so unequal a confederacy.

This is plainly the situation of men, with regard to animals; and how far these may be said to possess reason, I leave it to others to determine. The great superiority of civilized Europeans above barbarous Indians, tempted us to imagine ourselves on the same footing with regard to them, and made us throw off all restraints of justice, and even of humanity, in our treatment of them. In many nations, the female sex are reduced to like slav-ery, and are rendered incapable of all property, in opposition to their lordly masters. But though the males, when united, have in all countries bodily force sufficient to maintain this severe tyranny, yet such are the insinuation, address, and charms of their fair companions, that women are commonly able to break the confederacy, and share with the other sex in all the rights and privileges of society.

Were the human species so framed by nature 153 as that each individual possessed within himself every faculty, requisite both for his own preservation and for the propagation of his kind: Were all society and intercourse cut off between man and man, by the primary intention of the supreme Creator: It seems evident, that so solitary a being would be as much incapable of justice, as of social discourse and conversation. Where mutual regards and forbearance serve to no manner of purpose, they would never direct the conduct of any reasonable man. The headlong course of the passions would be checked by no reflection on future consequences. And as each man is here supposed to love himself alone, and to depend only on himself and his own activity for safety and happiness, he would, on every occasion, to the utmost of his power, challenge the preference above every other being, to none of which he is bound by any ties, either of nature or of interest.

But suppose the conjunction of the sexes to be established in nature, a family immediately arises; and particular rules being found requisite for its subsistence, these are immediately embraced; though without comprehending the rest of mankind within their prescriptions. Suppose that several families unite together into one society, which is totally disjoined from all others, the rules, which preserve peace and order, enlarge themselves to the utmost extent of that society; but becoming then entirely useless, lose their force when carried one step farther. But again suppose, that several distinct societies maintain a kind of intercourse for mutual convenience and advantage, the boundaries of justice still grow larger, in proportion to the largeness of men's views, and the force of their mutual connexions. History, experience, reason sufficiently instruct us in this natural progress of human sentiments, and in the gradual enlargement of our regards to justice, in proportion as we become acquainted with the extensive utility of that virtue.

Part II

154 If we examine the *particular* laws, by which justice is directed, and property determined; we shall still be presented with the same conclusion. The good of mankind is the only object of all these laws and regulations. Not only it is requisite, for the peace and interest of society, that men's possessions should be separated; but the rules, which we follow, in making the separation, are such as can best be contrived to serve farther the interests of society.

We shall suppose that a creature, possessed of reason, but unacquainted with human nature, deliberates with himself what rules of justice or property would best promote public interest, and establish peace and security among mankind: His most obvious thought would be, to assign the largest possessions to the most extensive virtue, and give every one the power of doing good, proportioned to his inclination. In a perfect theocracy, where a being, infinitely intelligent, governs by particular volitions, this rule would certainly have place, and might serve to the wisest purposes: But were mankind to execute such a law; so great is the uncertainty of merit, both from its natural obscurity, and from the self-conceit of each individual, that no determinate rule of conduct would ever result from it; and the total dissolution of society must be the immediate consequence. Fanatics may suppose, *that dominion is founded on grace,* and *that saints alone inherit the earth;* but the civil magistrate very justly puts these sublime theorists on the same footing with common robbers, and teaches them by the severest discipline, that a rule, which, in speculation, may seem the most advantageous to society, may yet be found, in practice, totally pernicious and destructive.

That there were *religious* fanatics of this kind in England, during the civil wars, we learn from history; though it is probable, that the obvious *tendency* of these principles excited such horror in mankind, as soon obliged the dangerous enthusiasts to renounce, or at least conceal their tenets. Perhaps the *levellers,* who claimed an equal distribution of property, were a kind of *political* fanatics, which arose from the religious species, and more openly avowed their pretensions; as carrying a more plausible appearance, of being practicable in themselves, as well as useful to human society.

It must, indeed, be confessed, that nature is 155 so liberal to mankind, that, were all her presents equally divided among the species, and improved by art and industry, every individual would enjoy all the necessaries, and even most of the comforts of life; nor would ever be liable to any ills, but such as might accidentally arise from the sickly frame and constitution of his body. It must also be confessed, that, wherever we depart from this equality, we rob the poor of more satisfaction than we add to the rich, and that the slight gratification of a frivolous vanity, in one individual, frequently costs more than bread to many families, and even provinces. It may appear withal, that the rule of equality, as it would be highly *useful,* is not altogether *impracticable;* but has taken place, at least in an imperfect degree, in some republics; particularly that of Sparta; where it was attended, it is said, with the most beneficial consequences. Not to mention that the Agrarian laws, so frequently claimed in Rome, and carried into execution in many Greek cities, proceeded, all of them, from a general idea of the utility of this principle.

But historians, and even common sense, may inform us, that, however specious these ideas of *perfect* equality may seem, they are really, at bottom, *impracticable;* and were they not so, would be extremely *pernicious* to human society. Render possessions ever so equal, men's different degrees of art, care, and industry will immediately break that equality. Or if you check these virtues, you reduce society to the most extreme indigence; and instead of preventing want and beggary in a few, render it unavoidable to the whole community. The most rigorous inquisition too is requisite to watch every inequality on its first appearance; and the most severe jurisdiction, to punish and redress it. But besides, that so much authority must soon degenerate into tyranny, and be exerted with great partialities; who can possibly be possessed of it, in such a situation as is here supposed? Perfect equality of possessions, destroying all subordination, weakens extremely the authority of magistracy, and must reduce all power nearly to a level, as well as property.

We may conclude, therefore, that, in order to 156 establish laws for the regulation of property, we must be acquainted with the nature and situation of man; must reject appearances, which may be false, though specious; and must search for those rules, which are, on the whole, most *useful* and *beneficial.* Vulgar sense and slight experience are sufficient for this purpose; where men give not way to too selfish avidity, or too extensive enthusiasm.

Who sees not, for instance, that whatever is produced or improved by a man's art or industry ought, for ever, to be secured to him, in order to give encouragement to such *useful* habits and accomplishments? That the property ought also to descend to children and relations, for the same *useful* purpose? That it may be alienated by consent, in order to beget that commerce and intercourse, which is so *beneficial* to human society? And that all contracts and promises ought carefully to be fulfilled, in order to secure mutual trust and confidence, by which the general *interest* of mankind is so much promoted?

Examine the writers on the laws of nature; and you will always find, that, whatever principles they set out with, they are sure to terminate here at last, and to assign, as the ultimate reason for every rule which they establish, the convenience and necessities of mankind. A concession thus extorted, in opposition to systems, has more authority than if it had been made in prosecution of them.

What other reason, indeed, could writers ever give, why this must be *mine* and that *yours*; since uninstructed nature surely never made any such distinction? The objects which receive those appellations are, of themselves, foreign to us; they are totally disjoined and separated from us; and nothing but the general interests of society can form the connexion.

157 Sometimes the interests of society may require a rule of justice in a particular case; but may not determine any particular rule, among several, which are all equally beneficial. In that case, the slightest *analogies* are laid hold of, in order to prevent that indifference and ambiguity, which would be the source of perpetual dissension. Thus possession alone, and first possession, is supposed to convey property, where no body else has any preceding claim and pretension. Many of the reasonings of lawyers are of this analogical nature, and depend on very slight connexions of the imagination.

Does any one scruple, in extraordinary cases, to violate all regard to the private property of individuals, and sacrifice to public interest a distinction, which had been established for the sake of that interest? The safety of the people is the supreme law: All other particular laws are subordinate to it, and dependent on it: And if, in the *common* course of things, they be followed and regarded; it is only because the public safety and interest *commonly* demand so equal and impartial an administration.

Sometimes both *utility* and *analogy* fail, and leave the laws of justice in total uncertainty. Thus, it is highly requisite, that prescription or long possession should convey property; but what number of days or months or years should be sufficient for that purpose, it is impossible for reason alone to determine. *Civil laws* here supply the place of the natural *code*, and assign different terms for prescription, according to the different *utilities*, proposed by the legislator. Bills of exchange and promissory notes, by the laws of most countries, prescribe sooner than bonds, and mortgages, and contracts of a more formal nature.

In general we may observe that all questions 158 of property are subordinate to the authority of civil laws, which extend, restrain, modify, and alter the rules of natural justice, according to the particular *convenience* of each community. The laws have, or ought to have, a constant reference to the constitution of government, the manners, the climate, the religion, the commerce, the situation of each society. A late author of genius, as well as of learning, has prosecuted this subject at large, and has established, from these principles, a system of political knowledge, which abounds in ingenious and brilliant thoughts, and is not wanting in solidity*.

---

* [Montesquieu] The author of *L'Esprit des Loix.* This illustrious writer, however, sets out with a different theory, and supposes all right to be founded on certain *rapports* or relations; which is a system, that, in my opinion, never will be reconciled with true philosophy. Father Malebranche, as far as I can learn, was the first that started this abstract theory of morals, which was afterwards adopted by Cudworth, Clarke, and others; and as it excludes all sentiment, and pretends to found everything on reason, it has not wanted followers in this philosophic age. See Section I, Appendix I. With regard to justice, the virtue here treated of, the inference against this theory seems short and conclusive. Property is allowed to be dependent on civil laws; civil laws are allowed to have no other object, but the interest of society: This therefore must be allowed to be the sole foundation of property and justice. Not to mention, that our obligation itself to obey the

What is a man's property? Anything which it is lawful for him, and for him alone, to use. *But what rule have we, by which we can distinguish these objects?* Here we must have recourse to statutes, customs, precedents, analogies, and a hundred other circumstances; some of which are constant and inflexible, some variable and arbitrary. But the ultimate point, in which they all professedly terminate, is the interest and happiness of human society. Where this enters not into consideration, nothing can appear more whimsical, unnatural, and even superstitious, than all or most of the laws of justice and of property.

Those who ridicule vulgar superstitions, and expose the folly of particular regards to meats, days, places, postures, apparel, have an easy task; while they consider all the qualities and relations of the objects, and discover no adequate cause for that affection or antipathy, veneration or horror, which have so mighty an influence over a considerable part of mankind. A Syrian would have starved rather than taste pigeon; an Egyptian would not have approached bacon: But if these species of food be examined by the senses of sight, smell, or taste, or scrutinized by the sciences of chemistry, medicine, or physics, no difference is ever found between them and any other species, nor

magistrate and his laws is founded on nothing but the interests of society.

If the ideas of justice, sometimes, do not follow the dispositions of civil law; we shall find, that these cases, instead of objections, are confirmations of the theory delivered above. Where a civil law is so perverse as to cross all the interests of society, it loses all its authority, and men judge by the ideas of natural justice, which are conformable to those interests. Sometimes also civil laws, for useful purposes, require a ceremony or form to any deed; and where that is wanting, their decrees run contrary to the usual tenour of justice; but one who takes advantage of such chicanes, is not commonly regarded as an honest man. Thus, the interests of society require, that contracts be fulfilled; and there is not a more material article either of natural or civil justice: But the omission of a trifling circumstance will often, by law, invalidate a contract, *in foro humano*, but not *in foro conscientiae*, as divines express themselves. In these cases, the magistrate is supposed only to withdraw his power of enforcing the right, not to have altered the right. Where his intention extends to the right, and is conformable to the interests of society; it never fails to alter the right; a clear proof of the origin of justice and of property, as assigned above.

can that precise circumstance be pitched on, which may afford a just foundation for the religious passion. A fowl on Thursday is lawful food; on Friday abominable: Eggs in this house and in this diocese, are permitted during Lent; a hundred paces farther, to eat them is a damnable sin. This earth or building, yesterday was profane; to-day, by the muttering of certain words, it has become holy and sacred. Such reflections as these, in the mouth of a philosopher, one may safely say, are too obvious to have any influence; because they must always, to every man, occur at first sight; and where they prevail not, of themselves, they are surely obstructed by education, prejudice, and passion, not by ignorance or mistake.

It may appear to a careless view, or rather a 159 too abstracted reflection, that there enters a like superstition into all the sentiments of justice; and that, if a man expose its object, or what we call property, to the same scrutiny of sense and science, he will not, by the most accurate enquiry, find any foundation for the difference made by moral sentiment. I may lawfully nourish myself from this tree; but the fruit of another of the same species, ten paces off, it is criminal for me to touch. Had I worn this apparel an hour ago, I had merited the severest punishment; but a man, by pronouncing a few magical syllables, has now rendered it fit for my use and service. Were this house placed in the neighbouring territory, it had been immoral for me to dwell in it; but being built on this side the river, it is subject to a different municipal law, and by its becoming mine I incur no blame or censure. The same species of reasoning it may be thought, which so successfully exposes superstition, is also applicable to justice; nor is it possible, in the one case more than in the other, to point out, in the object, that precise quality or circumstance, which is the foundation of the sentiment.

But there is this material difference between *superstition* and *justice*, that the former is frivolous, useless, and burdensome; the latter is absolutely requisite to the well-being of mankind and existence of society. When we abstract from this circumstance (for it is too apparent ever to be overlooked) it must be confessed, that all regards to right and property, seem entirely without foundation, as much as the grossest and most vulgar superstition. Were the interests of society nowise concerned, it is as unintelligible why another's articulating certain sounds implying consent, should change the nature of my actions with regard to a particular object, as why the reciting of a liturgy by a priest, in a certain habit and posture, should dedicate a heap of brick and timber, and render it, thenceforth and for ever, sacred.*

* It is evident, that the will or consent alone never transfers property, nor causes the obligation of a promise (for the same reasoning extends to both) but the will must be expressed by words or signs, in order to impose a tie upon any man. The expression being once brought in as subservient to the will, soon becomes the principal part of the promise; nor will a man be less bound by his word, though he secretly give a different direction to his intention, and withhold the assent of his mind. But though the expression makes, on most occasions, the whole of the promise, yet it does not always so; and one who should make use of any expression, of which he knows not the meaning, and which he uses without any sense of the consequences, would not certainly be bound by it. Nay, though he know its meaning, yet if he use it in jest only, and with such signs as evidently show, that he has no serious intention of binding himself, he would not lie under any obligation of performance; but it is necessary, that the words be a perfect expression of the will, without any contrary signs. Nay, even this we must not carry so far as to imagine, that one, whom, by our quickness of understanding, we conjecture, from certain signs, to have an intention of deceiving us, is not bound by his expression or verbal promise, if we accept of it; but must limit this conclusion to those cases where the signs are of a different nature from those of deceit. All these contradictions are easily accounted for, if justice arise entirely from its usefulness to society; but will never be explained on any other hypothesis.

It is remarkable, that the moral decisions of the *Jesuits* and other relaxed casuists, were commonly formed in prosecution of some such subtilties of reasoning as are here pointed out, and proceed as much from the habit of scholastic refinement as from any corruption of the heart, if we may follow the authority of Mons. Bayle. See his Dictionary, article LOYOLA. And why has the indignation of mankind risen so high against these casuists; but because every one perceived, that human society could not subsist were such practices authorized, and that morals must always be handled with a view to public interest, more than philosophical regularity? If the secret direction of the intention, said every man of sense, could invalidate a contract; where is our security? And yet a metaphysical schoolman might think, that, where an intention was supposed to be requisite, if that intention really had not place, no consequence ought to follow, and no obligation be imposed. The casuistical subtilties may not be greater

These reflections are far from weakening the obligations of justice, or diminishing anything from the most sacred attention to property. On the contrary, such sentiments must acquire new force from the present reasoning. For what stronger foundation can be desired or conceived for any duty, than to observe, that human society, or even human nature, could not subsist without the establishment of it; and will still arrive at greater degrees of happiness and perfection, the more inviolable the regard is, which is paid to that duty?

The dilemma seems obvious: As justice evidently 160 tends to promote public utility and to support civil society, the sentiment of justice is either derived from our reflecting on that tendency, or like hunger, thirst, and other appetites, resentment, love of life, attachment to offspring, and other passions, arises from a simple original instinct in the human breast, which nature has implanted for like salutary purposes. If the latter be the case, it follows, that property, which is the object of justice, is also distinguished by a simple original instinct, and is not ascertained by any argument or reflection. But who is there that ever heard of such an instinct? Or is this a subject in which new discoveries can be made? We may as well expect to discover, in the body, new senses, which had before escaped the observation of all mankind.

But farther, though it seems a very simple pro- 161 position to say, that nature, by an instinctive sentiment, distinguishes property, yet in reality

than the subtilties of lawyers, hinted at above; but as the former are *pernicious*, and the latter *innocent* and even *necessary*, this is the reason of the very different reception they meet with from the world.

It is a doctrine of the Church of Rome, that the priest, by a secret direction of his intention, can invalidate any sacrament. This position is derived from a strict and regular prosecution of the obvious truth, that empty words alone, without any meaning or intention in the speaker, can never be attended with any effect. If the same conclusion be not admitted in reasonings concerning civil contracts, where the affair is allowed to be of so much less consequence than the eternal salvation of thousands, it proceeds entirely from men's sense of the danger and inconvenience of the doctrine in the former case: And we may thence observe, that however positive, arrogant, and dogmatical any superstition may appear, it never can convey any thorough persuasion of the reality of its objects, or put them, in any degree, on a balance with the common incidents of life, which we learn from daily observation and experimental reasoning.

we shall find, that there are required for that purpose ten thousand different instincts, and these employed about objects of the greatest intricacy and nicest discernment. For when a definition of *property* is required, that relation is found to resolve itself into any possession acquired by occupation, by industry, by prescription, by inheritance, by contract, &c. Can we think that nature, by an original instinct, instructs us in all these methods of acquisition?

These words too, inheritance and contract, stand for ideas infinitely complicated; and to define them exactly, a hundred volumes of laws, and a thousand volumes of commentators, have not been found sufficient. Does nature, whose instincts in men are all simple, embrace such complicated and artificial objects, and create a rational creature, without trusting anything to the operation of his reason?

But even though all this were admitted, it would not be satisfactory. Positive laws can certainly transfer property. It is by another original instinct, that we recognize the authority of kings and senates, and mark all the boundaries of their jurisdiction? Judges too, even though their sentence be erroneous and illegal, must be allowed, for the sake of peace and order, to have decisive authority, and ultimately to determine property. Have we original innate ideas of praetors and chancellors and juries? Who sees not, that all these institutions arise merely from the necessities of human society?

All birds of the same species in every age and country, built their nests alike: In this we see the force of instinct. Men, in different times and places, frame their houses differently: Here we perceive the influence of reason and custom. A like inference may be drawn from comparing the instinct of generation and the institution of property.

How great soever the variety of municipal laws, it must be confessed, that their chief outlines pretty regularly concur; because the purposes, to which they tend, are everywhere exactly similar. In like manner, all houses have a roof and walls, windows and chimneys; though diversified in their shape, figure, and materials. The purposes of the latter, directed to the conveniencies of human life, discover not more plainly their origin from reason and reflection, than do those of the former, which point all to a like end.

I need not mention the variations, which all the rules of property receive from the finer turns and connexions of the imagination, and from the subtilties and abstractions of law-topics and reasonings. There is no possibility of reconciling this observation to the notion of original instincts.

What alone will beget a doubt concerning the 162 theory, on which I insist, is the influence of education and acquired habits, by which we are so accustomed to blame injustice, that we are not, in every instance, conscious of any immediate reflection on the pernicious consequences of it. The views the most familiar to us are apt, for that very reason, to escape us; and what we have very frequently performed from certain motives, we are apt likewise to continue mechanically, without recalling, on every occasion, the reflections, which first determined us. The convenience, or rather necessity, which leads to justice is so universal, and everywhere points so much to the same rules, that the habit takes place in all societies; and it is not without some scrutiny, that we are able to ascertain its true origin. The matter, however, is not so obscure, but that even in common life we have every moment recourse to the principle of public utility, and ask, *What must become of the world, if such practices prevail? How could society subsist under such disorders?* Were the distinction or separation of possessions entirely useless, can any one conceive, that it ever should have obtained in society?

Thus we seem, upon the whole, to have attained 163 a knowledge of the force of that principle here insisted on, and can determine what degree of esteem or moral approbation may result from reflections on public interest and utility. The necessity of justice to the support of society is the sole foundation of that virtue; and since no moral excellence is more highly esteemed, we may conclude that this circumstance of usefulness has, in general, the strongest energy, and most entire command over our sentiments. It must, therefore, be the source of a considerable part of the merit ascribed to humanity, benevolence, friendship, public spirit, and other social virtues of that stamp; as it is the sole source of the moral approbation paid to fidelity, justice, veracity, integrity, and those other estimable and useful qualities and principles. It is entirely agreeable to the rules of philosophy, and even of common reason; where any principle has been found to have a great force and energy in one instance, to ascribe to it a like energy in all similar instances. This indeed is Newton's chief rule of philosophizing.

Hume, "Of the Origin of Government"

Man, born in a family, is compelled to maintain society from necessity, from natural inclination, and from habit. The same creature, in his farther progress, is engaged to establish political society in order to administer justice, without which there can be no peace among them, nor safety, nor mutual intercourse. We are, therefore, to look upon all the vast apparatus of our government as having ultimately no other object or purpose but the distribution of justice, or, in other words, the support of the twelve judges. Kings and parliaments, fleets and armies, officers of the court and revenue, ambassadors, ministers and privy-councillors, are all subordinate in their end to this part of administration. Even the clergy, as their duty leads them to inculcate morality, may justly be thought, so far as regards this world, to have no other useful object of their institution.

All men are sensible of the necessity of justice to maintain peace and order, and all men are sensible of the necessity of peace and order for the maintenance of society. Yet, notwithstanding this strong and obvious necessity, such is the frailty or perverseness of our nature! it is impossible to keep men faithfully and unerringly in the paths of justice. Some extraordinary circumstances may happen in which a man finds his interests to be more promoted by fraud or rapine than hurt by the breach which his injustice makes in the social union. But much more frequently he is seduced from his great and important, but distant, interests, by the allurement of present, though often very frivolous, temptations. This great weakness is incurable in human nature.

Men must, therefore, endeavour to palliate what they cannot cure. They must institute some persons under the appellation of magistrates whose peculiar office it is to point out the decrees of equity, to punish transgressors, to correct fraud and violence, and to oblige men, however reluctant, to consult their own real and permanent interests. In a word, obedience is a new duty which must be invented to support that of justice, and the ties of equity must be corroborated by those of allegiance.

But still, viewing matters in an abstract light, it may be thought that nothing is gained by this alliance, and that the factitious duty of obedience, from its very nature, lays as feeble a hold of the human mind as the primitive and natural duty of justice. Peculiar interests and present temptations may overcome the one as well as the other. They are equally exposed to the same inconvenience, and the man who is inclined to be a bad neighbour must be led by the same motives, well or ill understood, to be a bad citizen or subject. Not to mention that the magistrate himself may often be negligent, or partial, or unjust, in his administration.

Experience, however, proves that there is a great difference between the cases. Order in society, we find, is much better maintained by means of government, and our duty to the magistrate is more strictly guarded by the principles of human nature than our duty to our fellow citizens. The love of dominion is so strong in the breast of man that many not only submit to, but court, all the dangers, and fatigues, and cares of government; and men, once raised to that station, though often led astray by private passions, find in ordinary cases a visible interest in the impartial administration of justice. The persons who first attain this distinction by the consent, tacit or express, of the people must be endowed with superior personal qualities of valour, force, integrity, or prudence, which command respect and confidence; and, after government is established, a regard to birth, rank, and station has a mighty influence over men and enforces the decrees of the magistrate. The prince or leader exclaims against every disorder which disturbs his society. He summons all his partisans and all men of probity to aid him in correcting and redressing it; and he is readily followed by all indifferent persons in the execution of his office. He soon acquires the power of rewarding these services, and, in the progress of society, he establishes subordinate ministers, and often a military force, who find an immediate and a visible interest in supporting his authority. Habit soon consolidates what other principles of human nature had imperfectly founded, and men, once accustomed to obedience, never think of departing from that path in which they and their ancestors have constantly trod, and to which they are confined by so many urgent and visible motives.

But though this progress of human affairs may appear certain and inevitable, and though the support which allegiance brings to justice be founded on obvious principles of human nature, it cannot be expected that men should beforehand be able to discover them or foresee their operation. Government commences more casually and more imperfectly. It is probable that the first ascendant of one man over multitudes begun during a state of war, where the superiority of courage and of genius discovers itself most visibly, where unanimity and concert are most requisite, and where the pernicious effects of disorder are most sensibly felt. The long continuance of that state, an incident common among savage tribes, inured the people to submission; and if the chieftain possessed as much equity as prudence and valour, he became, even during peace, the arbiter of all differences, and could gradually, by a mixture of force and consent, establish his authority. The benefit sensibly felt from his influence made it be cherished by the people, at least by the peaceable and well-disposed among them; and if his son enjoyed the same good qualities, government advanced the sooner to maturity and perfection, but was still in a feeble state, till the farther progress of improvement procured the magistrate a revenue, and enabled him to bestow rewards on the several instruments of his administration, and to inflict punishments on the refractory and disobedient. Before that period, each exertion of his influence must have been particular and founded on the peculiar circumstances of the case. After it, submission was no longer a matter of choice in the bulk of the community, but was rigorously exacted by the authority of the supreme magistrate.

In all governments there is a perpetual intestine struggle, open or secret, between Authority and Liberty, and neither of them can ever absolutely prevail in the contest. A great sacrifice of liberty must necessarily be made in every government, yet even the authority which confines liberty can never and perhaps ought never in any constitution to become quite entire and uncontrollable. The sultan is master of the life and fortune of any individual, but will not be permitted to impose new taxes on his subjects; a French monarch can impose taxes at pleasure, but would find it dangerous to attempt the lives and fortunes of individuals. Religion also, in most countries, is commonly found to be a very intractable principle; and other principles or prejudices frequently resist all the authority of the civil magistrate, whose power, being founded on opinion, can never subvert other opinions equally rooted with that

of his title to dominion. The government which, in common appellation, receives the appellation of "free," is that which admits of a partition of power among several members whose united authority is no less, or is commonly greater, than that of any monarch, but who, in the usual course of administration, must act by general and equal laws that are previously known to all the members and to all their subjects. In this sense it must be owned that liberty is the perfection of civil society, but still authority must be acknowledged essential to its very existence. And in those contests which so often take place between the one and the other, the latter may, on that account, challenge the preference. Unless perhaps one may say – and it may be said with some reason – that a circumstance which is essential to the existence of civil society must always support itself, and needs be guarded with less jealousy than one that contributes only to its perfection, which the indolence of men is so apt to neglect or their ignorance to overlook.

Hume, "Of the Original Contract"

As no party, in the present age, can well support itself without a philosophical or speculative system of principles annexed to its political or practical one, we accordingly find that each of the factions into which this nation is divided has reared up a fabric of the former kind, in order to protect and cover that scheme of actions which it pursues. The people being commonly very rude builders, especially in this speculative way, and more especially still when actuated by party zeal, it is natural to imagine that their workmanship must be a little unshapely, and discover evident marks of that violence and hurry in which it was raised. The one party, by tracing up government to the Deity, endeavour to render it so sacred and inviolate that it must be little less than sacrilege, however tyrannical it may become, to touch or invade it in the smallest article. The other party, by founding government altogether on the consent of the people, suppose that there is a kind of *original contract* by which the subjects have tacitly reserved the power of resisting their sovereign, whenever they find themselves aggrieved by that authority with which they have, for certain purposes, voluntarily entrusted him. These are the speculative principles of the two parties, and these, too, are the practical consequences deduced from them.

I shall venture to affirm *that both these systems of speculative principles are just, though not in the sense intended by the parties,* and *that both the schemes of practical consequences are prudent, though not in the extremes to which each party, in opposition to the other, has commonly endeavoured to carry them.*

That the Deity is the ultimate author of all government will never be denied by any who admit a general providence and allow that all events in the universe are conducted by an uniform plan and directed to wise purposes. As it is impossible for the human race to subsist, at least in any comfortable or secure state, without the protection of government, this institution must certainly have been intended by that beneficent Being who means the good of all his creatures. And as it has universally, in fact, taken place in all countries and all ages, we may conclude, with still greater certainty, that it was intended by that omniscient Being who can never be deceived by any event or operation. But since he gave rise to it, not by any particular or miraculous interposition, but by his concealed and universal efficacy, a sovereign cannot, properly speaking, be called his vicegerent in any other sense than every power or force, being derived from him, may be said to act by his commission. Whatever actually happens is comprehended in the general plan or intention of Providence; nor has the greatest and most lawful prince any more reason, upon that account, to plead a peculiar sacredness or inviolable authority than an inferior magistrate, or even an usurper, or even a robber and a pirate. The same Divine Superintendent who, for wise purposes, invested a Titus or a Trajan with authority, did also, for purposes no doubt equally wise though unknown, bestow power on a Borgia or an Angria. The same causes which gave rise to the sovereign power in every state established likewise every petty jurisdiction in it, and every limited authority. A constable, therefore, no less than a king, acts by a divine commission and possesses an indefeasible right.

When we consider how nearly equal all men are in their bodily force, and even in their mental powers and faculties, till cultivated by education, we must necessarily allow that nothing but their own consent could at first associate them together and subject them to any authority. The

people, if we trace government to its first origin in the woods and deserts, are the source of all power and jurisdiction, and voluntarily, for the sake of peace and order, abandoned their native liberty and received laws from their equal and companion. The conditions upon which they were willing to submit were either expressed or were so clear and obvious that it might well be esteemed superfluous to express them. If this, then, be meant by the *original contract,* it cannot be denied that all government is, at first, founded on a contract, and that the most ancient rude combinations of mankind were formed chiefly by that principle. In vain are we asked in what records this charter of our liberties is registered. It was not written on parchment, nor yet on leaves or barks of trees. It preceded the use of writing, and all the other civilized arts of life. But we trace it plainly in the nature of man, and in the equality, or something approaching equality, which we find in all the individuals of that species. The force which now prevails, and which is founded on fleets and armies, is plainly political, and derived from authority, the effect of established government. A man's natural force consists only in the vigour of his limbs and the firmness of his courage, which could never subject multitudes to the command of one. Nothing but their own consent and their sense of the advantages resulting from peace and order could have had that influence.

Yet even this consent was long very imperfect, and could not be the basis of a regular administration. The chieftain, who had probably acquired his influence during the continuance of war, ruled more by persuasion than command; and till he could employ force to reduce the refractory and disobedient, the society could scarcely be said to have attained a state of civil government. No compact or agreement, it is evident, was expressly formed for general submission, an idea far beyond the comprehension of savages. Each exertion of authority in the chieftain must have been particular, and called forth by the present exigencies of the case. The sensible utility resulting from his interposition made these exertions become daily more frequent; and their frequency gradually produced an habitual and, if you please to call it so, a voluntary and therefore precarious acquiescence in the people.

But philosophers who have embraced a party – if that be not a contradiction in terms – are not contented with these concessions. They assert not only that government in its earliest infancy arose from consent, or rather the voluntary acquiescence of the people, but also that, even at present, when it has attained its full maturity, it rests on no other foundation. They affirm that all men are still born equal, and owe allegiance to no prince or government unless bound by the obligation and sanction of a *promise*. And as no man, without some equivalent, would forego the advantages of his native liberty and subject himself to the will of another, this promise is always understood to be conditional, and imposes on him no obligation, unless he meet with justice and protection from his sovereign. These advantages the sovereign promises him in return; and if he fail in the execution, he has broken on his part the articles of engagement, and has thereby freed his subject from all obligations to allegiance. Such, according to these philosophers, is the foundation of authority in every government, and such the right of resistance possessed by every subject.

But would these reasoners look abroad into the world, they would meet with nothing that in the least corresponds to their ideas, or can warrant so refined and philosophical a system. On the contrary, we find everywhere princes who claim their subjects as their property, and assert their independent right of sovereignty from conquest or succession. We find also everywhere subjects who acknowledge this right in their prince, and suppose themselves born under obligations of obedience to a certain sovereign, as much as under the ties of reverence and duty to certain parents. These connexions are always conceived to be equally independent of our consent, in Persia and China, in France and Spain, and even in Holland and England, wherever the doctrines above mentioned have not been carefully inculcated. Obedience or subjection becomes so familiar that most men never make any inquiry about its origin or cause, more than about the principle of gravity, resistance, or the most universal laws of nature. Or if curiosity ever move them, as soon as they learn that they themselves and their ancestors have, for several ages, or from time immemorial, been subject to such a form of government or such a family, they immediately acquiesce and acknowledge their obligation to allegiance. Were you to preach, in most parts of the world, that political connexions are founded altogether on voluntary consent or a mutual promise, the magistrate would soon imprison you as seditious for loosening the ties of obedience, if your friends did not before shut you up as delirious for advancing such absurdities. It is strange that an act of the mind, which every individual is supposed to have formed, and after he came to the use of reason too, otherwise it could have no authority – that this act, I say, should be so much unknown to all of them that over the face of the whole earth there scarcely remain any traces or memory of it.

But the contract on which government is founded is said to be the *original contract*; and consequently may be supposed too old to fall under the knowledge of the present generation. If the agreement by which savage men first associated and conjoined their force be here meant, this is acknowledged to be real; but being so ancient, and being obliterated by a thousand changes of government and princes, it cannot now be supposed to retain any authority. If we would say anything to the purpose, we must assert that every particular government which is lawful, and which imposes any duty of allegiance on the subject, was at first founded on consent and a voluntary compact. But, besides that this supposes the consent of the fathers to bind the children, even to the most remote generations – which republican writers will never allow – besides this, I say, it is not justified by history or experience in any age or country of the world.

Almost all the governments which exist at present, or of which there remains any record in story, have been founded originally either on usurpation or conquest or both, without any pretence of a fair consent or voluntary subjection of the people. When an artful and bold man is placed at the head of an army or faction, it is often easy for him, by employing sometimes violence, sometimes false pretences, to establish his dominion over a people a hundred times more numerous than his partisans. He allows no such open communication that his enemies can know with certainty their number or force. He gives them no leisure to assemble together in a body to oppose him. Even all those who are the instruments of his usurpation may wish his fall; but their ignorance of each other's intention keeps them in awe, and is the sole cause of his security. By such arts as these many governments have been established; and this is all the *original contract* which they have to boast of.

The face of the earth is continually changing, by the increase of small kingdoms into great empires, by the dissolution of great empires into smaller kingdoms, by the planting of colonies, by the migration of tribes. Is there anything discoverable in all these events but force and violence? Where is the mutual agreement or voluntary association so much talked of?

Even the smoothest way by which a nation may receive a foreign master, by marriage or a will, is not extremely honourable for the people, but supposes them to be disposed of like a dowry or a legacy, according to the pleasure or interest of their rulers.

But where no force interposes, and election takes place, what is this election so highly vaunted? It is either the combination of a few great men, who decide for the whole and will allow of no opposition; or it is the fury of a multitude that follow a seditious ringleader who is not known, perhaps, to a dozen among them, and who owes his advancement merely to his own impudence or to the momentary caprice of his fellows.

Are these disorderly elections, which are rare too, of such mighty authority as to be the only lawful foundation of all government and allegiance?

In reality there is not a more terrible event than a total dissolution of government; which gives liberty to the multitude, and makes the determination or choice of a new establishment depend upon a number which nearly approaches to that of the body of the people. For it never comes entirely to the whole body of them. Every wise man, then, wishes to see at the head of a powerful and obedient army a general who may speedily seize the prize, and give to the people a master which they are so unfit to choose for themselves – so little correspondent is fact and reality to those philosophical notions.

Let not the establishment at the Revolution deceive us, or make us so much in love with a philosophical origin to government as to imagine all others monstrous and irregular. Even that event was far from corresponding to these refined ideas. It was only the succession, and that only in the regal part of the government, which was then changed. And it was only the majority of seven hundred who determined that change for near ten millions. I doubt not, indeed, but the bulk of those ten millions acquiesced willingly in the determination. But was the matter left in the least to their choice? Was it not justly supposed

to be from that moment decided, and every man punished who refused to submit to the new sovereign? How otherwise could the matter have ever been brought to any issue or conclusion?

The republic of Athens was, I believe, the most extensive democracy that we read of in history. Yet if we make the requisite allowances for the women, the slaves, and the strangers, we shall find that that establishment was not at first made, nor any law ever voted, by a tenth part of those who were bound to pay obedience to it; not to mention the islands and foreign dominions which the Athenians claimed as theirs by right of conquest. And as it is well known that popular assemblies in that city were always full of license and disorder, notwithstanding the institutions and laws by which they were checked, how much more disorderly must they prove where they form not the established constitution, but meet tumultuously on the dissolution of the ancient government in order to give rise to a new one? How chimerical must it be to talk of a choice in such circumstances?

The Achæans enjoyed the freest and most perfect democracy of all antiquity; yet they employed force to oblige some cities to enter into their league, as we learn from Polybius.

Harry IV and Harry VII of England had really no title to the throne but a parliamentary election; yet they never would acknowledge it, lest they should thereby weaken their authority. Strange, if the only real foundation of all authority be consent and promise.

It is in vain to say that all governments are or should be at first founded on popular consent, as much as the necessity of human affairs will admit. This favours entirely my pretension. I maintain that human affairs will never admit of this consent, seldom of the appearance of it; but that conquest or usurpation, that is, in plain terms, force, by dissolving the ancient governments, is the origin of almost all the new ones which were ever established in the world. And that in the few cases where consent may seem to have taken place, it was commonly so irregular, so confined, or so much intermixed either with fraud or violence that it cannot have any great authority.

My intention here is not to exclude the consent of the people from being one just foundation of government. Where it has place, it is surely the best and most sacred of any. I only contend that it has very seldom had place in any degree, and never almost in its full extent; and that, therefore, some other foundation of government must also be admitted.

Were all men possessed of so inflexible a regard to justice that of themselves they would totally abstain from the properties of others, they had for ever remained in a state of absolute liberty, without subjection to any magistrate or political society. But this is a state of perfection of which human nature is justly deemed incapable. Again, were all men possessed of so perfect an understanding as always to know their own interests, no form of government had ever been submitted to but what was established on consent, and was fully canvassed by every member of the society. But this state of perfection is likewise much superior to human nature. Reason, history, and experience show us that all political societies have had an origin much less accurate and regular; and were one to choose a period of time when the people's consent was the least regarded in public transactions, it would be precisely on the establishment of a new government. In a settled constitution their inclinations are often consulted; but during the fury of revolutions, conquests, and public convulsions, military force or political craft usually decides the controversy.

When a new government is established, by whatever means, the people are commonly dissatisfied with it, and pay obedience more from fear and necessity than from any idea of allegiance or of moral obligation. The prince is watchful and jealous, and must carefully guard against every beginning or appearance of insurrection. Time, by degrees, removes all these difficulties, and accustoms the nation to regard as their lawful or native princes that family which at first they considered as usurpers or foreign conquerors. In order to found this opinion, they have no recourse to any notion of voluntary consent or promise which, they know, never was in this case either expected or demanded. The original establishment was formed by violence and submitted to from necessity. The subsequent administration is also supported by power, and acquiesced in by the people, not as a matter of choice, but of obligation. They imagine not that their consent gives their prince a title. But they willingly consent, because they think that, from long possession, he has acquired a title independent of their choice or inclination.

Should it be said that, by living under the dominion of a prince which one might leave, every individual has given a *tacit* consent to his authority and promised him obedience, it may be answered that such an implied consent can only have place where a man imagines that the matter depends on his choice. But where he thinks – as all mankind do who are born under established governments – that by his birth he owes allegiance to a certain prince or certain form of government, it would be absurd to infer a consent or choice, which he expressly in this case renounces and disclaims.

Can we seriously say that a poor peasant or artisan has a free choice to leave his country, when he knows no foreign language or manners, and lives from day to day by the small wages which he acquires? We may as well assert that a man, by remaining in a vessel, freely consents to the dominion of the master, though he was carried on board while asleep, and must leap into the ocean and perish the moment he leaves her.

What if the prince forbid his subjects to quit his dominions, as in Tiberius' time it was regarded as a crime in a Roman knight that he had attempted to fly to the Parthians, in order to escape the tyranny of that emperor? Or as the ancient Muscovites prohibited all travelling under pain of death? And did a prince observe that many of his subjects were seized with the frenzy of migrating to foreign countries, he would, doubtless, with great reason and justice restrain them in order to prevent the depopulation of his own kingdom. Would he forfeit the allegiance of all his subjects by so wise and reasonable a law? Yet the freedom of their choice is surely, in that case, ravished from them.

A company of men, who should leave their native country in order to people some uninhabited region, might dream of recovering their native freedom, but they would soon find that their prince still laid claim to them, and called them his subjects even in their new settlement. And in this he would but act conformably to the common ideas of mankind.

The truest *tacit* consent of this kind that is ever observed is when a foreigner settles in any country, and is beforehand acquainted with the prince, and government, and laws, to which he must submit; yet is his allegiance, though more voluntary, much less expected or depended on than that of a natural-born subject. On the contrary, his native prince still asserts a claim to him. And if he punish not the renegade when he seizes him in war with his new prince's commission, this clemency is not founded on the municipal law, which in all countries condemns the prisoner, but on the consent of princes, who have agreed to this indulgence in order to prevent reprisals.

Did one generation of men go off the stage at once, and another succeed, as is the case with silk worms and butterflies, the new race, if they had sense enough to choose their government, which surely is never the case with men, might voluntarily and by general consent establish their own form of civil polity without any regard to the laws or precedents which prevailed among their ancestors. But as human society is in perpetual flux, one man every hour going out of the world, another coming into it, it is necessary in order to preserve stability in government that the new brood should conform themselves to the established constitution, and nearly follow the path which their fathers, treading in the footsteps of theirs, had marked out to them. Some innovations must necessarily have place in every human institution; and it is happy where the enlightened genius of the age give these a direction to the side of reason, liberty, and justice. But violent innovations no individual is entitled to make. They are even dangerous to be attempted by the legislature. More ill than good is ever to be expected from them. And if history affords examples to the contrary, they are not to be drawn into precedent, and are only to be regarded as proofs that the science of politics affords few rules which will not admit of some exception, and which may not sometimes be controlled by fortune and accident. The violent innovations in the reign of Henry VIII proceeded from an imperious monarch, seconded by the appearance of legislative authority; those in the reign of Charles I were derived from faction and fanaticism; and both of them have proved happy in the issue. But even the former were long the source of many disorders, and still more dangers; and if the measures of allegiance were to be taken from the latter, a total anarchy must have place in human society, and a final period at once be put to every government.

Suppose that an usurper, after having banished his lawful prince and royal family, should establish his dominion for ten or a dozen years in any country, and should preserve so exact a discipline in his troops and so regular a disposition in his garrisons that no insurrection had ever been raised or even murmur heard against his administration. Can it be asserted that the people, who in their hearts abhor his treason, have tacitly consented to his authority and promised him allegiance, merely because, from necessity, they live under his dominion? Suppose again their native prince restored by means of an army which he levies in foreign countries. They receive him with joy and exultation, and show plainly with what reluctance they had submitted to any other yoke. I may now ask upon what foundation the prince's title stands? Not on popular consent surely; for though the people willingly acquiesce in his authority, they never imagine that their consent made him sovereign. They consent because they apprehend him to be already, by birth, their lawful sovereign. And as to tacit consent, which may now be inferred from their living under his dominion, this is no more than what they formerly gave to the tyrant and usurper.

When we assert that all lawful government arises from the consent of the people, we certainly do them a great deal more honour than they deserve, or even expect and desire from us. After the Roman dominions became too unwieldy for the republic to govern them, the people over the whole known world were extremely grateful to Augustus for that authority which, by violence, he had established over them; and they showed an equal disposition to submit to the successor whom he left them by his last will and testament. It was afterwards their misfortune that there never was, in one family, any long regular succession, but that their line of princes was continually broken either by private assassinations or public rebellions. The *prœtorian* bands, on the failure of every family, set up one emperor, the legions in the East a second, those in Germany, perhaps, a third; and the sword alone could decide the controversy. The condition of the people in that mighty monarchy was to be lamented, not because the choice of the emperor was never left to them, for that was impracticable, but because they never fell under any succession of masters who might regularly follow each other. As to the violence and wars and bloodshed occasioned by every new settlement, these were not blamable, because they were inevitable.

The house of Lancaster ruled in this island about sixty years; yet the partisans of the white rose seemed daily to multiply in England. The present establishment has taken place during a still longer period. Have all views of right in another family been utterly extinguished, even though scarce any man now alive had arrived at the years of discretion when it was expelled, or could have consented to its dominion, or have promised it allegiance? – a sufficient indication, surely, of the general sentiment of mankind on this head. For we blame not the partisans of the abdicated family merely on account of the long time during which they have preserved their imaginary loyalty. We blame them for adhering to a family which we affirm has been justly expelled, and which from the moment the new settlement took place had forfeited all title to authority.

But would we have a more regular, at least a more philosophical, refutation of this principle of an original contract or popular consent, perhaps the following observations may suffice.

All *moral* duties may be divided into two kinds. The *first* are those to which men are impelled by a natural instinct or immediate propensity which operates on them, independent of all ideas of obligation and of all views either to public or private utility. Of this nature are love of children, gratitude to benefactors, pity to the unfortunate. When we reflect on the advantage which results to society from such humane instincts, we pay them the just tribute of moral approbation and esteem. But the person actuated by them feels their power and influence antecedent to any such reflection.

The *second* kind of moral duties are such as are not supported by any original instinct of nature, but are performed entirely from a sense of obligation, when we consider the necessities of human society and the impossibility of supporting it if these duties were neglected. It is thus *justice*, or a regard to the property of others, *fidelity*, or the observance of promises, become obligatory and acquire an authority over mankind. For as it is evident that every man loves himself better than any other person, he is naturally impelled to extend his acquisitions as much as possible; and nothing can restrain him in this propensity but reflection and experience, by which he learns the pernicious effects of that license and the total dissolution of society which must ensue from it. His original inclination, therefore, or instinct, is here checked and restrained by a subsequent judgment or observation.

The case is precisely the same with the political or civil duty of *allegiance* as with the natural duties of justice and fidelity. Our primary instincts lead us either to indulge ourselves in unlimited freedom, or to seek dominion over others; and it is reflection only which engages us to sacrifice such strong passions to the interests of peace and public order. A small degree of experience and observation suffices to teach us that society cannot possibly be maintained without the authority of magistrates, and that this authority must soon fall into contempt where exact obedience is not paid to it. The observation of these general and obvious interests is the source of all allegiance and of that moral obligation which we attribute to it.

What necessity, therefore, is there to found the duty of *allegiance*, or obedience to magistrates, on that of *fidelity*, or a regard to promises, and to suppose that it is the consent of each individual which subjects him to government, when it appears that both allegiance and fidelity stand precisely on the same foundation and are both submitted to by mankind on account of the apparent interests and necessities of human society? We are bound to obey our sovereign, it is said, because we have given a tacit promise to that purpose. But why are we bound to observe our promise? It must here be asserted that the commerce and intercourse of mankind, which are of such mighty advantage, can have no security where men pay no regard to their engagements. In like manner may it be said that men could not live at all in society, at least in a civilized society, without laws and magistrates and judges to prevent the encroachments of the strong upon the weak, of the violent upon the just and equitable. The obligation to allegiance being of like force and authority with the obligation to fidelity, we gain nothing by resolving the one into the other. The general interests or necessities of society are sufficient to establish both.

If the reason be asked of that obedience which we are bound to pay to government, I readily answer, *because society could not otherwise subsist*; and this answer is clear and intelligible to all mankind. Your answer is, *because we should keep our word.* But besides that nobody, till trained in a philosophical system, can either comprehend or relish this answer – besides this, I say, you find yourself embarrassed when it is asked, *why we are bound to keep our word?* Nor can you give any answer but what would immediately, without any circuit, have accounted for our obligation to allegiance.

But *to whom is allegiance due, and who is our lawful sovereign?* This question is often the most difficult of any, and liable to infinite discussions. When people are so happy that they can answer, *our present sovereign, who inherits, in a direct line, from ancestors that have governed us for many ages,* this answer admits of no reply, even though historians in tracing up to the remotest antiquity the origin of that royal family may find, as commonly happens, that its first authority was derived from usurpation and violence. It is confessed that private justice, or the abstinence from the properties of others, is a most cardinal virtue. Yet reason tells us that there is no property in durable objects such as land or houses, when carefully examined in passing from hand to hand, but must in some period have been founded on fraud and injustice. The necessities of human society, neither in private nor public life, will allow of such an accurate inquiry; and there is no virtue or moral duty but what may with facility be refined away, if we indulge a false philosophy in sifting and scrutinizing it, by every captious rule of logic, in every light or position in which it may be placed.

The questions with regard to private property have filled infinite volumes of law and philosophy, if in both we add the commentators to the original text; and in the end we may safely pronounce that many of the rules there established are uncertain, ambiguous, and arbitrary. The like opinion may be formed with regard to the succession and rights of princes and forms of government. Several cases no doubt occur, especially in the infancy of any constitution, which admit of no determination from the laws of justice and equity; and our historian Rapin pretends that the controversy between Edward the Third and Philip de Valois was of this nature, and could be decided only by an appeal to heaven, that is, by war and violence.

Who shall tell me whether Germanicus or Drusus ought to have succeeded to Tiberius, had he died while they were both alive without naming any of them for his successor? Ought the right of adoption to be received as equivalent to that of blood in a nation where it had the same effect in private families, and had already, in two instances, taken place in the public? Ought Germanicus to be esteemed the elder son because he was born before Drusus, or the younger, because he was adopted after the birth of his brother? Ought the right of the elder to be regarded in a nation where he had no advantage in the succession of private families? Ought the Roman empire at that time to be deemed hereditary, because of two examples; or ought it, even so early, to be regarded as belonging to the stronger or to the present possessor, as being founded on so recent an usurpation?

Commodus mounted the throne after a pretty long succession of excellent emperors, who had acquired their title, not by birth or public election, but by the fictitious rite of adoption. The bloody debauche being murdered by a conspiracy suddenly formed between his wench and her gallant, who happened at that time to be *Prætorian Præfect*, these immediately deliberated about choosing a master to human kind, to speak in the style of those ages, and they cast their eyes on Pertinax. Before the tyrant's death was known, the *Præfect* went secretly to that senator who, on the appearance of the soldiers, imagined that his execution had been ordered by Commodus. He was immediately saluted emperor by the officer and his attendants, cheerfully proclaimed by the populace, unwillingly submitted to by the guards, formally recognized by the senate, and passively received by the provinces and armies of the empire.

The discontent of the *Prætorian* bands broke out in a sudden sedition, which occasioned the murder of that excellent prince; and the world being now without a master and without government, the guards thought proper to set the empire formally to sale. Julian, the purchaser, was proclaimed by the soldiers, recognized by the senate, and submitted to by the people; and must also have been submitted to by the provinces, had not the envy of the legions begotten opposition and resistance. Pescennius Niger in Syria elected himself emperor, gained the tumultuary consent of his army, and was attended with the secret good will of the senate and people of Rome. Albinus in Britain found an equal right to set up his claim; but Severus, who governed Pannonia, prevailed in the end above both of them. That able politician and warrior, finding his own birth and dignity too much inferior to the imperial crown, professed at first an intention only of revenging the death of Pertinax. He marched as general into Italy, defeated

Julian, and, without our being able to fix any precise commencement even of the soldiers' consent, he was from necessity acknowledged emperor by the senate and people, and fully established in his violent authority by subduing Niger and Albinus.

It is to be remarked that Gordian was a boy of fourteen years of age. [*Inter hæc Gordianus Cæsar*," says Capitolinus, speaking of another period, "*sublatus a militibus. Imperator est appellatus, quia non erat alius in præsenti.*]

Frequent instances of a like nature occur in the history of the emperors, in that of Alexander's successors, and of many other countries. Nor can anything be more unhappy than a despotic government of this kind, where the succession is disjointed and irregular and must be determined on every vacancy by force or election. In a free government, the matter is often unavoidable, and is also much less dangerous. The interests of liberty may there frequently lead the people, in their own defence, to alter the succession of the crown. And the constitution, being compounded of parts, may still maintain a sufficient stability by resting on the aristocratical or democratical members, though the monarchical be altered, from time to time, in order to accommodate it to the former.

In an absolute government, when there is no legal prince who has a title to the throne, it may safely be determined to belong to the first occupant. Instances of this kind are but too frequent, especially in the eastern monarchies. When any race of princes expires, the will or destination of the last sovereign will be regarded as a title. Thus the edict of Louis XIV, who called the bastard princes to the succession in case of the failure of all the legitimate princes, would, in such an event, have some authority. Thus the will of Charles the Second disposed of the whole Spanish monarchy. The cession of the ancient proprietor, especially when joined to conquest, is likewise deemed a good title. The general obligation which binds us to government is the interest and necessities of society; and this obligation is very strong. The determination of it to this or that particular prince or form of government is frequently more uncertain and dubious. Present possession has considerable authority in

these cases, and greater than in private property, because of the disorders which attend all revolutions and changes of government.

We shall only observe before we conclude that though an appeal to general opinion may justly, in the speculative sciences of metaphysics, natural philosophy, or astronomy, be deemed unfair and inconclusive, yet in all questions with regard to morals, as well as criticism, there is really no other standard by which any controversy can ever be decided. And nothing is a clearer proof that a theory of this kind is erroneous than to find that it leads to paradoxes repugnant to the common sentiments of mankind, and to the practice and opinion of all nations and all ages. The doctrine which founds all lawful government on an *original contract*, or consent of the people, is plainly of this kind; nor has the most noted of its partisans, in prosecution of it, scrupled to affirm *that absolute monarchy is inconsistent with civil society, and so can be no form of civil government at all,** and *that the supreme power in a state cannot take from any man by taxes and impositions any part of his property, without his own consent or that of his representatives.*† What authority any moral reasoning can have, which leads into opinions so wide of the general practice of mankind in every place but this single kingdom, it is easy to determine.

The only passage I meet with in antiquity where the obligation of obedience to government is ascribed to a promise is in Plato's *Crito*, where Socrates refuses to escape from prison because he had tacitly promised to obey the laws. Thus he builds a *Tory* consequence of passive obedience on a *Whig* foundation of the original contract.

New discoveries are not to be expected in these matters. If scarce any man, till very lately, ever imagined that government was founded on compact, it is certain that it cannot in general have any such foundation.

The crime of rebellion among the ancients was commonly expressed by the terms νεωτερίζειν (*novas res moliri*).

---

* See Locke *On Government*, chap. vii. § 90.

† Locke *On Government*, chap. xi. § 138, 139, 140.

14

Immanuel Kant, *Perpetual Peace: A Philosophical Sketch* (selections)

Introduction

Immanuel Kant's (1724–1804) three *Critiques* – of Pure Reason, Practical Reason, and the Power of Judgment – have been, arguably, the most influential works of modern philosophy in the areas of metaphysics, ethics, and aesthetics respectively. Kant never wrote a work of comparable scale in the area of political philosophy and until recently his name was not frequently invoked in this area, perhaps because of a sense that his views on such staple topics as sovereignty, political freedom, rights, and equality were insufficiently distinct from those of Jean-Jacques Rousseau (V.12), whom the German philosopher greatly admired.

Recent developments on the international stage – ranging from the expansion of the European Union to the globalization of trade, from international terrorism to illegal immigration – have, however, inspired a closer examination of Kant's 1796 work, *Perpetual Peace*. In this 40-page essay, inspired, it is said, by the Treaty of Basel in 1795, which brought a temporary halt to the French Revolutionary Wars, Kant has things to say that are germane to all of the developments mentioned, and to many other ethically charged issues of international politics, such as colonialism. Kant's essay, in fact, is one of the very few con-

From *Kant: Political Writings*, ed. Hans Reiss, trans. H. B. Nisbet, Cambridge: Cambridge University Press, 1991, pp. 93–109, 112–14 (some notes omitted).

tributions to the theory of international politics made by a philosopher of the first rank.

The point is sometimes made that Thomas Hobbes's (V.10) description of "the state of nature" as a state of war of all against all, though intended as an account of how individuals would relate to one another in the absence of a powerful sovereign, more accurately applies to the relationship actually obtaining among independent sovereign states. It is Kant's view, certainly, that in the absence of a "formally instituted" system of international right, nations exist in a state of nature vis-à-vis one another, and that this is a state of war, in the sense that there persists the constant threat of hostilities breaking out among them. Unlike Hegel, a few years later, Kant is entirely without any romantic vision of war as something that might "cleanse" a people or strengthen a nation's moral fiber. As he had put in 1786, "the greatest evils which oppress civilised nations are the result of war," both of actual wars and of "the unremitting . . . *preparation* for war in the future."[1]

The main issue addressed in the essay, therefore, is how to ensure "perpetual peace," by which Kant means, not a "truce" or mere cessation of hostilities, but a condition in which reasons to go to war are "nullified." The ideal solution would be a world state, but this is one which, given linguistic, religious, and other differences, Kant recognizes not to be feasible. What is feasible, however, is a "league" or "pacific federation of nations," in which the freedom and integrity of each member nation is guaranteed under a system of "international right." Scarcely less important, for Kant, is the cultivation of an ethos of "cosmopolitan right," the primary aspect of which is a sense of "universal hospitality" which recognizes that "no-one originally has any greater right than anyone else to occupy any particular portion of the globe" and is, in consequence, receptive to each person's claim to a "right of resort" in any country.

Kant is optimistic that the pacific federation he envisages will indeed be established. For while the argument in favor of such a federation is an *a priori* moral one, such a development is also favored by enlightened self-interest. In particular, increasing trade or commerce between nations fosters a "spirit" that promotes "the noble cause of peace," albeit from non-moral motives.

Perpetual Peace is not confined to the theory of international relations. The essay also contains one of the clearest statements of Kant's "republicanism." By this term, Kant does not mean, as we tend to these days, a non-monarchical form of rule, but a set of principles in accordance with which any legitimate government (including a monarchy) should rule. The main principles indicated by Kant are those of freedom (understood as the "warrant to obey no external laws except those to which I . . . consent"), the rule of law, equality of persons before the law, and the separation of legislative from executive power. Kant's discussion of a republican constitution is not a digression from the main theme of the essay, since it his view that having such a constitution makes it less likely that a country will go to war. A republican country can only go to war with the freely given consent of its people. Too optimistically, perhaps, Kant thinks that a people is much less likely to give this consent than is a ruler – not responsible to, or representative of, the people – to embark on a war, possibly for his own amusement.

Note

1   *Conjectures on the Beginning of Human History*, in *Kant: Political Writings*, pp. 231–2.

Kant, *Perpetual Peace: A Philosophical Sketch*

'The Perpetual Peace'

A Dutch innkeeper once put this satirical inscription on his signboard, along with the picture of a graveyard. We shall not trouble to ask whether it applies to men in general, or particularly to heads of state (who can never have enough of war), or only to the philosophers who blissfully dream of perpetual peace. The author of the present essay does, however, make one reservation in advance. The practical politician tends to look down with great complacency upon the political theorist as a mere academic. The theorist's abstract ideas, the practitioner believes, cannot endanger the state, since the state must be founded upon principles of experience; it thus seems safe to let him fire off his whole broadside, and the *worldly-wise* statesman need not turn a hair. It thus follows that if the practical politician is to be consistent, he must not claim, in the event of a dispute with the theorist, to scent any danger to the state in the opinions which the theorist has randomly uttered in public. By this saving clause, the author of this essay will consider himself expressly safeguarded, in correct and proper style, against all malicious interpretation.

First section: Which Contains the Preliminary Articles of a Perpetual Peace Between States
1. 'No conclusion of peace shall be considered valid as such if it was made with a secret reservation of the material for a future war.'

For if this were the case, it would be a mere truce, a suspension of hostilities, not a *peace*. Peace means an end to all hostilities, and to attach the adjective 'perpetual' to it is already suspiciously close to pleonasm. A conclusion of peace nullifies all existing reasons for a future war, even if these are not yet known to the contracting parties, and no matter how acutely and carefully they may later be pieced together out of old documents. It is possible that either party may make a mental reservation with a view to reviving its old pretensions in the future. Such reservations will not be mentioned explicitly, since both parties may simply be too exhausted to continue the war, although they may nonetheless possess sufficient ill will to seize the first favourable opportunity of attaining their end. But if we consider such reservations in themselves, they soon appear as Jesuitical casuistry; they are beneath the dignity of a ruler, just as it is beneath the dignity of a minister of state to comply with any reasoning of this kind.

But if, in accordance with 'enlightened' notions of political expediency, we believe that the true glory of a state consists in the constant increase of its power by any means whatsoever, the above judgement will certainly appear academic and pedantic.

2. 'No independently existing state, whether it be large or small, may be acquired by another state by inheritance, exchange, purchase or gift.'

For a state, unlike the ground on which it is based, is not a possession (*patrimonium*). It is a society of men, which no-one other than itself can command or dispose of. Like a tree, it has its own roots, and to graft it on to another state as if it were a shoot is to terminate its existence as a moral personality and make it into a commodity. This contradicts the idea of the original contract, without which the rights of a people are unthinkable. Everyone knows what danger the supposed right of acquiring states in this way, even in our own times, has brought upon Europe (for this practice is unknown in other continents). It has been thought that states can marry one another, and this has provided a new kind of industry by which power can be increased through family alliances, without expenditure of energy, while landed property can be extended at the same time. It is the same thing when the troops of one state are hired to another to fight an enemy who is not common to both; for the subjects are thereby used and misused as objects to be manipulated at will.

3. 'Standing armies (*miles perpetuus*) will gradually be abolished altogether.'

For they constantly threaten other states with war by the very fact that they are always prepared for it. They spur on the states to outdo one another in arming unlimited numbers of soldiers, and since the resultant costs eventually make peace more oppressive than a short war, the armies are themselves the cause of wars of aggression which set out to end burdensome military expenditure. Furthermore, the hiring of men to kill or to be killed seems to mean using them as mere machines and instruments in the hands of someone else (the state), which cannot easily be reconciled with the rights of man in one's own person. It is quite a different matter if the citizens undertake voluntary military training from time to time in order to secure themselves and their fatherland against attacks from outside. But it would be just the same if wealth rather than soldiers were accumulated, for it would be seen by other states as a military threat; it might compel them to mount preventive attacks, for of the three powers within a state – the *power of the army*, the *power of alliance* and the *power of money* – the third is probably the most reliable instrument of war. It would lead more often to wars if it were not so difficult to discover the amount of wealth which another state possesses.

4. 'No national debt shall be contracted in connection with the external affairs of the state.'

There is no cause for suspicion if help for the national economy is sought inside or outside the state (e.g. for improvements to roads, new settlements, storage of foodstuffs for years of famine, etc.). But a credit system, if used by the powers as an instrument of aggression against one another, shows the power of money in its most dangerous form. For while the debts thereby incurred are always secure against present demands (because not all the creditors will demand payment at the same time), these debts go on growing indefinitely. This ingenious system, invented by a commercial people [the British] in the present century, provides a military fund which may exceed the resources of all the other states put together. It can only be exhausted by an eventual tax-deficit, which may be postponed for a considerable time by the commercial stimulus which industry and trade receive through the credit system. This ease in making war, coupled with the warlike inclination of those in power (which seems to be an integral feature of human nature), is thus a great obstacle in the way of perpetual peace. Foreign debts must therefore be prohibited by a preliminary article of such a peace, otherwise national bankruptcy, inevitable in the long run, would necessarily involve various other states in the resultant loss without their having deserved it, thus inflicting upon them a public injury. Other states are therefore justified in allying themselves against such a state and its pretensions.

5. 'No state shall forcibly interfere in the constitution and government of another state.'

For what could justify such interference? Surely not any sense of scandal or offence which a state arouses in the subjects of another state. It should rather serve as a warning to others, as an example of the great evils which a people has incurred by its lawlessness. And a bad example which one free person gives to another (as a *scandalum acceptum*) is not the same as an injury to the latter. But it would be a different matter if a state, through internal discord, were to split into two parts, each of which set itself up as a separate state and claimed authority over the whole. For it could not be reckoned as interference in another state's constitution if an external state were to lend support to one of them, because their condition is one of anarchy. But as long as this internal conflict is not yet decided, the interference of external powers would be a violation of the rights of an independent people which is merely struggling with its internal ills. Such interference would be an active offence and would make the autonomy of all other states insecure.

6. 'No state at war with another shall permit such acts of hostility as would make mutual confidence impossible during a future time of peace. Such acts would include the employment of *assassins* (*percussores*) or poisoners (*venefici*), breach of agreements, the instigation of treason (*perduellio*) within the enemy state, etc.'

These are dishonourable stratagems. For it must still remain possible, even in wartime, to have some sort of trust in the attitude of the enemy, otherwise peace could not be concluded and the hostilities would turn into a war of extermination (*bellum internecinum*). After all, war is only a regrettable expedient for asserting one's rights by force within a state of nature, where no court of justice is available to judge with legal authority. In such cases, neither party can be declared an unjust enemy, for this would already presuppose a judge's decision; only the *outcome* of the conflict, as in the case of a so-called 'judgement of God', can decide who is in the right. A war of punishment (*bellum punitivum*) between states is inconceivable, since there can be no relationship of superior to inferior among them. It thus follows that a war of extermination, in which both parties and right itself might all be simultaneously annihilated, would allow perpetual peace only on the vast graveyard of the human race. A war of this kind and the employment of all means which might bring it about must thus be absolutely prohibited. But the means listed above would inevitably lead to such a war, because these diabolical arts, besides being intrinsically despicable, would not long be confined to war alone if they were brought into use. This applies, for example, to the employment of spies (*uti exploratoribus*), for it exploits only the dishonesty of others (which can never be completely eliminated). Such practices will be carried over into peacetime and will thus completely vitiate its purpose.

All of the articles listed above, when regarded objectively or in relation to the intentions of those in power, are *prohibitive laws* (*leges prohibitivae*). Yet some of them are of the *strictest* sort (*leges strictae*), being valid irrespective of differing circumstances, and they require that the abuses they prohibit should be abolished *immediately* (Nos. 1, 5, and 6). Others (Nos. 2, 3, and 4), although they are not exceptions to the rule of justice, allow some *subjective* latitude according to the circumstances in which they are applied (*leges latae*). The latter need not necessarily be executed at once, so long as their ultimate purpose (e.g. the *restoration* of freedom to certain states in accordance with the second article) is not lost sight of. But their execution may not be *put off* to a non-existent date (*ad calendas graecas*, as Augustus used to promise), for any delay is permitted only as a means of avoiding a premature implementation which might frustrate the whole purpose of the article. For in the case of the second article, the prohibition relates only to the *mode of acquisition*, which is to be forbidden hereforth, but not to the present *state of political possessions*. For although this present state is not backed up by the requisite legal authority, it was considered lawful in the public opinion of every state at the time of the putative acquisition.

Second Section: Which Contains the Definitive Articles of a Perpetual Peace Between States A state of peace among men living together is not the same as the state of nature, which is rather a state of war. For even if it does not involve active hostilities, it involves a constant threat of their breaking out. Thus the state of peace must *be formally instituted,* for a suspension of hostilities is not in itself a guarantee of peace. And unless one neighbour gives a guarantee to the other at his request (which can happen only in a *lawful* state), the latter may treat him as an enemy.*

First Definitive Article of a Perpetual Peace:
The Civil Constitution of Every State
shall be Republican

A *republican constitution* is founded upon three principles: firstly, the principle of *freedom* for all members of a society (as men); secondly, the principle of the *dependence* of everyone upon a single common legislation (as subjects); and thirdly, the principle of legal *equality* for everyone (as citizens).† It is the only constitution which can be derived from the idea of an original contract, upon which all rightful legislation of a people must be founded. Thus as far as right is concerned, republicanism is in itself the original basis of every kind of civil constitution, and it only remains to ask whether it is the only constitution which can lead to a perpetual peace.

The republican constitution is not only pure in its origin (since it springs from the pure concept of right); it also offers a prospect of attaining the desired result, i.e. a perpetual peace, and the reason for this is as follows. – If, as is inevitably the case under this constitution, the consent of the citizens is required to decide whether or not war is to be declared, it is very natural that they will have great hesitation in embarking on so dangerous an enterprise. For this would mean calling down on themselves all the miseries of war, such as doing

---

* It is usually assumed that one cannot take hostile action against anyone unless one has already been actively *injured* by them. This is perfectly correct if both parties are living in a *legal civil state*. For the fact that the one has entered such a state gives the required guarantee to the other, since both are subject to the same authority. But man (or an individual people) in a mere state of nature robs me of any such security and injures me by virtue of this very state in which he coexists with me. He may not have injured me actively (*facto*), but he does injure me by the very lawlessness of his state (*statu iniusto*), for he is a permanent threat to me, and I can require him either to enter into a common lawful state along with me or to move away from my vicinity. Thus the postulate on which all the following articles are based is that all men who can at all influence one another must adhere to some kind of civil constitution. But any legal constitution, as far as the persons who live under it are concerned, will conform to one of the three following types:

(1)   a constitution based on the *civil right* of individuals within a nation (*ius civitatis*).
(2)   a constitution based on the *international right* of states in their relationships with one another (*ius gentium*).
(3)   a constitution based on *cosmopolitan right*, in so far as individuals and states, coexisting in an external relationship of mutual influences, may be regarded as citizens of a universal state of mankind (*ius cosmopoliticum*). This classification, with respect to the idea of a perpetual peace, is not arbitrary, but necessary. For if even one of the parties were able to influence the others physically and yet itself remained in a state of nature, there would be a risk of war, which it is precisely the aim of the above articles to prevent.

† *Rightful* (*i.e. external*) *freedom* cannot, as is usually thought, be defined as a warrant to do whatever one wishes unless it means doing injustice to others. For what is meant by a *warrant?* It means a possibility of acting in a certain way so long as this action does not do any injustice to others. Thus the definition would run as follows: freedom is the possibility of acting in ways which do no injustice to others. That is, we do no injustice to others (no matter what we may actually do) if we do no injustice to others. Thus the definition is an empty tautology. In fact, my external and rightful *freedom* should be defined as a warrant to obey no external laws except those to which I have been able to give my own consent. Similarly, external and rightful *equality* within a state is that relationship among the citizens whereby no-one can put anyone else under a legal obligation without submitting simultaneously to a law which requires that he can himself be put under the same kind of obligation by the other person. (And we do not need to define the principle of *legal* dependence, since it is always implied in the concept of a political constitution.) The validity of these innate and inalienable rights, the necessary property of mankind, is confirmed and enhanced by the principle that man may have lawful relations even with higher beings (if he believes in the latter). For he may consider himself as a citizen of a transcendental world, to which the same principles apply. And as regards my freedom, I am not under any obligation even to divine laws (which I can recognise by reason alone), except in so far as I have been able to give my own consent to them; for I can form a conception of the divine will only in terms of the law of freedom of my own reason. [. . .]

the fighting themselves, supplying the costs of the war from their own resources, painfully making good the ensuing devastation, and, as the crowning evil, having to take upon themselves a burden of debt which will embitter peace itself and which can never be paid off on account of the constant threat of new wars. But under a constitution where the subject is not a citizen, and which is therefore not republican, it is the simplest thing in the world to go to war. For the head of state is not a fellow citizen, but the owner of the state, and a war will not force him to make the slightest sacrifice so far as his banquets, hunts, pleasure palaces and court festivals are concerned. He can thus decide on war, without any significant reason, as a kind of amusement, and unconcernedly leave it to the diplomatic corps (who are always ready for such purposes) to justify the war for the sake of propriety.

The following remarks are necessary to prevent the republican constitution from being confused with the democratic one, as commonly happens. The various forms of state (*civitas*) may be classified either according to the different persons who exercise supreme authority, or according to the way in which the nation is governed by its ruler, whoever he may be. The first classification goes by the form of sovereignty (*forma imperii*), and only three such forms are possible, depending on whether the ruling power is in the hands of an *individual,* of *several persons* in association, or of *all* those who together constitute civil society (i.e. *autocracy, aristocracy* and *democracy* – the power of a prince, the power of a nobility, and the power of the people). The second classification depends on the form of government (*forma regiminis*), and relates to the way in which the state, setting out from its constitution (i.e. an act of the general will whereby the mass becomes a people), makes use of its plenary power. The form of government, in this case, will be either *republican* or *despotic. Republicanism* is that political principle whereby the executive power (the government) is separated from the legislative power. Despotism prevails in a state if the laws are made and arbitrarily executed by one and the same power, and it reflects the will of the people only in so far as the ruler treats the will of the people as his own private will. Of the three forms of sovereignty, *democracy*, in the truest sense of the word, is necessarily a *despotism*, because it establishes an

executive power through which all the citizens may make decisions about (and indeed against) the single individual without his consent, so that decisions are made by all the people and yet not by all the people; and this means that the general will is in contradiction with itself, and thus also with freedom.

For any form of government which is not *representative* is essentially an *anomaly*, because one and the same person cannot at the same time be both the legislator and the executor of his own will, just as the general proposition in logical reasoning cannot at the same time be a secondary proposition subsuming the particular within the general. And even if the other two political constitutions (i.e. autocracy and aristocracy) are always defective in as much as they leave room for a despotic form of government, it is at least possible that they will be associated with a form of government which accords with the *spirit* of a representative system. Thus Frederick II [the Great] at least *said* that he was merely the highest servant of the state,* while a democratic constitution makes this attitude impossible, because everyone under it wants to be a ruler. We can therefore say that the smaller the number of ruling persons in a state and the greater their powers of representation, the more the constitution will approximate to its republican potentiality, which it may hope to realise eventually by gradual reforms. For this reason, it is more difficult in an aristocracy than in a monarchy to reach this one and only perfectly lawful kind of constitution, while it is possible in a democracy only by means of violent revolution. But the people are immensely more concerned with the mode of government than with the form of the constitution, although a great deal also depends on the degree

---

* Many have criticised the high-sounding appellations which are often bestowed on a ruler (e.g. 'the divine anointed', or 'the executor and representative of the divine will on earth') as gross and extravagant flatteries, but it seems to me without reason. Far from making the ruler of the land arrogant, they ought rather to fill his soul with humility. For if he is a man of understanding (which we must certainly assume), he will reflect that he has taken over an office which is too great for a human being, namely that of administering God's most sacred institution on earth, the rights of man; he will always live in fear of having in any way injured God's most valued possession.

to which the constitution fits the purpose of the government. But if the mode of government is to accord with the concept of right, it must be based on the representative system. This system alone makes possible a republican state, and without it, despotism and violence will result, no matter what kind of constitution is in force. None of the so-called 'republics' of antiquity employed such a system, and they thus inevitably ended in despotism, although this is still relatively bearable under the rule of a single individual.

Second Definitive Article of a Perpetual Peace:
The Right of Nations shall be based on
a Federation of Free States

Peoples who have grouped themselves into nation states may be judged in the same way as individual men living in a state of nature, independent of external laws; for they are a standing offence to one another by the very fact that they are neighbours. Each nation, for the sake of its own security, can and ought to demand of the others that they should enter along with it into a constitution, similar to the civil one, within which the rights of each could be secured. This would mean establishing a *federation of peoples*. But a federation of this sort would not be the same thing as an international state. For the idea of an international state is contradictory, since every state involves a relationship between a superior (the legislator) and an inferior (the people obeying the laws), whereas a number of nations forming one state would constitute a single nation. And this contradicts our initial assumption, as we are here considering the right of nations in relation to one another in so far as they are a group of separate states which are not to be welded together as a unit.

We look with profound contempt upon the way in which savages cling to their lawless freedom. They would rather engage in incessant strife than submit to a legal constraint which they might impose upon themselves, for they prefer the freedom of folly to the freedom of reason. We regard this as barbarism, coarseness, and brutish debasement of humanity. We might thus expect that civilised peoples, each united within itself as a state, would hasten to abandon so degrading a condition as soon as possible. But instead of doing so, each *state* sees its own majesty (for it would be absurd to speak of the majesty of a *people*) precisely in not having to submit to any external

legal constraint, and the glory of its ruler consists in his power to order thousands of people to immolate themselves for a cause which does not truly concern them, while he need not himself incur any danger whatsoever.* And the main difference between the savage nations of Europe and those of America is that while some American tribes have been entirely eaten up by their enemies, the Europeans know how to make better use of those they have defeated than merely by making a meal of them. They would rather use them to increase the number of their own subjects, thereby augmenting their stock of instruments for conducting even more extensive wars.

Although it is largely concealed by governmental constraints in law-governed civil society, the depravity of human nature is displayed without disguise in the unrestricted relations which obtain between the various nations. It is therefore to be wondered at that the word *right* has not been completely banished from military politics as superfluous pedantry, and that no state has been bold enough to declare itself publicly in favour of doing so. For Hugo Grotius, Pufendorf, Vattel and the rest (sorry comforters as they are) are still dutifully quoted in *justification* of military aggression, although their philosophically or diplomatically formulated codes do not and cannot have the slightest *legal* force, since states as such are not subject to a common external constraint.[1] Yet there is no instance of a state ever having been moved to desist from its purpose by arguments supported by the testimonies of such notable men. This homage which every state pays (in words at least) to the concept of right proves that man possesses a greater moral capacity, still dormant at present, to overcome eventually the evil principle within him (for he cannot deny that it exists), and to hope that others will do likewise. Otherwise the word *right* would never be used by states which intend to make war on one another, unless in a derisory sense, as when a certain Gallic prince declared: 'Nature has given to the strong the prerogative of making the weak obey them.' The way in which

---

* Thus a Bulgarian prince, replying to the Greek Emperor who had kindly offered to settle his dispute with him by a duel, declared: 'A smith who possesses tongs will not lift the glowing iron out of the coals with his own hands.'

states seek their rights can only be by war, since there is no external tribunal to put their claims to trial. But rights cannot be decided by military victory, and a *peace treaty* may put an end to the current war, but not to that general warlike condition within which pretexts can always be found for a new war. And indeed, such a state of affairs cannot be pronounced completely unjust, since it allows each party to act as judge in its own cause. Yet while natural right allows us to say of men living in a lawless condition that they ought to abandon it, the right of nations does not allow us to say the same of states. For as states, they already have a lawful internal constitution, and have thus outgrown the coercive right of others to subject them to a wider legal constitution in accordance with their conception of right. On the other hand, reason, as the highest legislative moral power, absolutely condemns war as a test of rights and sets up peace as an immediate duty. But peace can neither be inaugurated nor secured without a general agreement between the nations; thus a particular kind of league, which we might call a *pacific federation* (*foedus pacificum*), is required. It would differ from a *peace treaty* (*pactum pacis*) in that the latter terminates *one* war, whereas the former would seek to end *all* wars for good. This federation does not aim to acquire any power like that of a state, but merely to preserve and secure the *freedom* of each state in itself, along with that of the other confederated states, although this does not mean that they need to submit to public laws and to a coercive power which enforces them, as do men in a state of nature. It can be shown that this idea of *federalism*, extending gradually to encompass all states and thus leading to perpetual peace, is practicable and has objective reality. For if by good fortune one powerful and enlightened nation can form a republic (which is by its nature inclined to seek perpetual peace), this will provide a focal point for federal association among other states. These will join up with the first one, thus securing the freedom of each state in accordance with the idea of international right, and the whole will gradually spread further and further by a series of alliances of this kind.

It would be understandable for a people to say: 'There shall be no war among us; for we will form ourselves into a state, appointing for ourselves a supreme legislative, executive and juridical power to resolve our conflicts by peaceful means.' But if this state says: 'There shall be no war between myself and other states, although I do not recognise any supreme legislative power which could secure my rights and whose rights I should in turn secure', it is impossible to understand what justification I can have for placing any confidence in my rights, unless I can rely on some substitute for the union of civil society, i.e. on a free federation. If the concept of international right is to retain any meaning at all, reason must necessarily couple it with a federation of this kind.

The concept of international right becomes meaningless if interpreted as a right to go to war. For this would make it a right to determine what is lawful not by means of universally valid external laws, but by means of one-sided maxims backed up by physical force. It could be taken to mean that it is perfectly just for men who adopt this attitude to destroy one another, and thus to find perpetual peace in the vast grave where all the horrors of violence and those responsible for them would be buried. There is only one rational way in which states coexisting with other states can emerge from the lawless condition of pure warfare. Just like individual men, they must renounce their savage and lawless freedom, adapt themselves to public coercive laws, and thus form an *international state* (*civitas gentium*), which would necessarily continue to grow until it embraced all the peoples of the earth. But since this is not the will of the nations, according to their present conception of international right (so that they reject *in hypothesi* what is true *in thesi*), the positive idea of a *world republic* cannot be realised. If all is not to be lost, this can at best find a negative substitute in the shape of an enduring and gradually expanding *federation* likely to prevent war. The latter may check the current of man's inclination to defy the law and antagonise his fellows, although there will always be a risk of it bursting forth anew. *Furor impius intus – fremit horridus ore cruento* (Virgil).*[2]

---

* At the end of a war, when peace is concluded, it would not be inappropriate for a people to appoint a day of atonement after the festival of thanksgiving. Heaven would be invoked in the name of the state to forgive the human race for the great sin of which it continues to be guilty, since it will not accommodate itself to a lawful constitution in international relations.

Third Definitive Article of a Perpetual Peace:
Cosmopolitan Right shall be limited to
Conditions of Universal Hospitality

As in the foregoing articles, we are here concerned not with philanthropy, but with *right*. In this context, *hospitality* means the right of a stranger not to be treated with hostility when he arrives on someone else's territory. He can indeed be turned away, if this can be done without causing his death, but he must not be treated with hostility, so long as he behaves in a peaceable manner in the place he happens to be in. The stranger cannot claim the *right of a guest* to be entertained, for this would require a special friendly agreement whereby he might become a member of the native household for a certain time. He may only claim a *right of resort*, for all men are entitled to present themselves in the society of others by virtue of their right to communal possession of the earth's surface. Since the earth is a globe, they cannot disperse over an infinite area, but must necessarily tolerate one another's company. And no-one originally has any greater right than anyone else to occupy any particular portion of the earth. The community of man is divided by uninhabitable parts of the earth's surface such as oceans and deserts, but even then, the *ship* or the *camel* (the ship of the desert) make it possible for them to approach their fellows over these ownerless tracts, and to utilise as a means of social intercourse that *right to the earth's surface* which the human race shares in common. The inhospitable behaviour of coastal dwellers (as on the Barbary coast) in plundering ships on the adjoining seas or enslaving stranded seafarers, or that of inhabitants of the desert (as with the Arab Bedouins), who regard their proximity to nomadic tribes as a justification for plundering them, is contrary to natural right. But this natural right of hospitality, i.e. the right of strangers, does not extend beyond those conditions which make it possible for them to *attempt* to enter into relations with the native inhabitants. In this way, continents distant from each other can enter into peaceful mutual relations which may eventually be regulated by public laws, thus bringing the human race nearer and nearer to a cosmopolitan constitution.

If we compare with this ultimate end the *inhospitable* conduct of the civilised states of our continent, especially the commercial states, the injustice which they display in *visiting* foreign countries and peoples (which in their case is the same as *conquering* them) seems appallingly great. America, the negro countries, the Spice Islands, the Cape, etc. were looked upon at the time of their discovery as ownerless territories; for the native inhabitants were counted as nothing. In East India (Hindustan), foreign troops were brought in under the pretext of merely setting up trading posts. This led to oppression of the natives, incitement of the various Indian states to widespread wars, famine, insurrection, treachery and the whole litany of evils which can afflict the human race.

China and Japan (Nippon), having had experience of such guests, have wisely placed restrictions on them. China permits contact with her territories, but not entrance into them, while Japan only allows contact with a single European people, the Dutch, although they are still segregated from the native community like prisoners. The worst (or from the point of view of moral judgements, the best) thing about all this is that the commercial states do not even benefit by their violence, for all their trading companies are on the point of collapse. The Sugar Islands, that stronghold of the cruellest and most calculated slavery, do not yield any real profit; they serve only the indirect (and not entirely laudable) purpose of training sailors for warships, thereby aiding the prosecution of wars in Europe. And all this is the work of powers who make endless ado about their piety, and who wish to be considered as chosen believers while they live on the fruits of iniquity.

The peoples of the earth have thus entered in varying degrees into a universal community, and it has developed to the point where a violation of rights in *one* part of the world is felt *everywhere*. The idea of a cosmopolitan right is therefore not fantastic and overstrained; it is a necessary complement to the unwritten code of political and international right, transforming it into a universal right of humanity. Only under this condition can we flatter ourselves that we are continually advancing towards a perpetual peace.

First Supplement: On the Guarantee of
a Perpetual Peace

Perpetual peace is *guaranteed* by no less an authority than the great artist Nature herself (*natura daedala rerum*). The mechanical process of nature visibly exhibits the purposive plan of producing concord among men, even against their will and indeed by means of their very discord. This design, if we regard it as a compelling cause whose laws of operation are unknown to us, is called *fate*. But if we consider its purposive function within the world's development, whereby it appears as the underlying wisdom of a higher cause, showing the way towards the objective goal of the human race and predetermining the world's evolution, we call it *providence*. We cannot actually observe such an agency in the artifices of nature, nor can we even *infer* its existence from them. But as with all relations between the form of things and their ultimate purposes, we can and must *supply it mentally* in order to conceive of its possibility by analogy with human artifices. Its relationship to and conformity with the end which reason directly prescribes to us (i.e. the end of morality) can only be conceived of as an idea. Yet while this idea is indeed far-fetched in *theory*, it does possess dogmatic validity and has a very real foundation in *practice*, as with the concept of *perpetual peace*, which makes it our duty to promote it by using the natural mechanism described above. But in contexts such as this, where we are concerned purely with theory and not with religion, we should also note that it is more in keeping with the limitations of human reason to speak of *nature* and not of *providence*, for reason, in dealing with cause and effect relationships, must keep within the bounds of possible experience. *Modesty* forbids us to speak of providence as something we can recognise, for this would mean donning the wings of Icarus and presuming to approach the mystery of its inscrutable intentions.

[. . .]

We now come to the essential question regarding the prospect of perpetual peace. What does nature do in relation to the end which man's own reason prescribes to him as a duty, i.e. how does nature help to promote his *moral purpose*? And how does nature guarantee that what man *ought* to do by the laws of his freedom (but does not do) will in fact be done through nature's compulsion, without prejudice to the free agency of man? This question arises, moreover, in all three areas of public right – in *political, international* and *cosmopolitan right*. For if I say that nature *wills* that this or that should happen, this does not mean that nature imposes on us a *duty* to do it, for duties can only be imposed by practical reason, acting without any external constraint. On the contrary,

nature does it herself, whether we are willing or not: *fata volentem ducunt, nolentem trahunt*.

1. Even if people were not compelled by internal dissent to submit to the coercion of public laws, war would produce the same effect from outside. For in accordance with the natural arrangement described above, each people would find itself confronted by another neighbouring people pressing in upon it, thus forcing it to form itself internally into a *state* in order to encounter the other as an armed *power*. Now the *republican* constitution is the only one which does complete justice to the rights of man. But it is also the most difficult to establish, and even more so to preserve, so that many maintain that it would only be possible within a state of *angels*, since men, with their self-seeking inclinations, would be incapable of adhering to a constitution of so sublime a nature. But in fact, nature comes to the aid of the universal and rational human will, so admirable in itself but so impotent in practice, and makes use of precisely those self-seeking inclinations in order to do so. It only remains for men to create a good organisation for the state, a task which is well within their capability, and to arrange it in such a way that their self-seeking energies are opposed to one another, each thereby neutralising or eliminating the destructive effects of the rest. And as far as reason is concerned, the result is the same as if man's selfish tendencies were non-existent, so that man, even if he is not morally good in himself, is nevertheless compelled to be a good citizen. As hard as it may sound, the problem of setting up a state can be solved even by a nation of devils (so long as they possess understanding). It may be stated as follows: 'In order to organise a group of rational beings who together require universal laws for their survival, but of whom each separate individual is secretly inclined to exempt himself from them, the constitution must be so designed that, although the citizens are opposed to one another in their private attitudes, these opposing views may inhibit one another in such a way that the public conduct of the citizens will be the same as if they did not have such evil attitudes.' A problem of this kind must be soluble. For such a task does not involve the moral improvement of man; it only means finding out how the mechanism of nature can be applied to men in such a manner that the antagonism of their hostile attitudes will make them compel one another to submit to coercive laws, thereby producing a condition of peace

within which the laws can be enforced. We can even see this principle at work among the actually existing (although as yet very imperfectly organised) states. For in their external relations, they have already approached what the idea of right prescribes, although the reason for this is certainly not their internal moral attitudes. In the same way, we cannot expect their moral attitudes to produce a good political constitution; on the contrary, it is only through the latter that the people can be expected to attain a good level of moral culture. Thus that mechanism of nature by which selfish inclinations are naturally opposed to one another in their external relations can be used by reason to facilitate the attainment of its own end, the reign of established right. Internal and external peace are thereby furthered and assured, so far as it lies within the power of the state itself to do so. We may therefore say that nature *irresistibly wills* that right should eventually gain the upper hand. What men have neglected to do will ultimately happen of its own accord, albeit with much inconvenience.

[. . .]

2. The idea of international right presupposes the separate existence of many independent adjoining states. And such a state of affairs is essentially a state of war, unless there is a federal union to prevent hostilities breaking out. But in the light of the idea of reason, this state is still to be preferred to an amalgamation of the separate nations under a single power which has overruled the rest and created a universal monarchy. For the laws progressively lose their impact as the government increases its range, and a soulless despotism, after crushing the germs of goodness, will finally lapse into anarchy. It is nonetheless the desire of every state (or its ruler) to achieve lasting peace by thus dominating the whole world, if at all possible. But *nature* wills it otherwise, and uses two means to separate the nations and prevent them from intermingling – *linguistic* and *religious** differences. These may certainly occasion mutual hatred and provide pretexts for wars, but as

culture grows and men gradually move towards greater agreement over their principles, they lead to mutual understanding and peace. And unlike that universal despotism which saps all man's energies and ends in the graveyard of freedom, this peace is created and guaranteed by an equilibrium of forces and a most vigorous rivalry.

3. Thus nature wisely separates the nations, although the will of each individual state, even basing its arguments on international right, would gladly unite them under its own sway by force or by cunning. On the other hand, nature also unites nations which the concept of cosmopolitan right would not have protected from violence and war, and does so by means of their mutual self-interest. For the *spirit of commerce* sooner or later takes hold of every people, and it cannot exist side by side with war. And of all the powers (or means) at the disposal of the power of the state, *financial power* can probably be relied on most. Thus states find themselves compelled to promote the noble cause of peace, though not exactly from motives of morality. And wherever in the world there is a threat of war breaking out, they will try to prevent it by mediation, just as if they had entered into a permanent league for this purpose; for by the very nature of things, large military alliances can only rarely be formed, and will even more rarely be successful.

In this way, nature guarantees perpetual peace by the actual mechanism of human inclinations. And while the likelihood of its being attained is not sufficient to enable us to *prophesy* the future theoretically, it is enough for practical purposes. It makes it our duty to work our way towards this goal, which is more than an empty chimera.

[. . .]

Notes

1 Hugo Grotius (1583–1645), Samuel von Pufendorf (1632–94), and Emmerich von Vattel (1714–67) were all influential jurists.
2 "Wicked frenzy rages savagely with blood-stained mouth," *Aeneid* I, 294–6.

---

* *Religious differences* – an odd expression! As if we were to speak of different *moralities*. There may certainly be different historical *confessions*, although these have nothing to do with religion itself but only with changes in the means used to further religion, and are thus the province of historical research. And there may be just as many different religious *books* (the Zend-Avesta, the Vedas, the Koran, etc.). But there can only be *one religion* which is valid for all men and at all times. Thus the different confessions can scarcely be more than the vehicles of religion; these are fortuitous, and may vary with differences in time or place.

Edmund Burke, *Reflections on the Revolution in France* (selections)

Introduction

Edmund Burke (1730–90) was born in Dublin, Ireland, to a prominent attorney and educated at Dublin's Trinity College, an Anglican institution. After emigrating to London to study law at the Middle Temple, Burke began producing philosophical work. His earliest essay, *A Vindication of Natural Society: A View of the Miseries and Evils Arising to Mankind* (1756), presents an apparent *reductio ad absurdum* argument aimed at mocking Tory Lord Bolingbroke's deism by showing how consistent application of the idea of social equality would lead to a primitive anarchy. Satirical *reductio* or not, the essay was taken seriously by later anarchists such as William Godwin (1756–1836), as well as other leftists. The year after the *Vindication* appeared Burke published a treatise on aesthetics, *A Philosophical Enquiry into the Origin of Our Ideas of the Sublime and Beautiful* (1757), which described how art was rooted in natural human sentiments as well as how it cultivated them. In 1765 Burke became secretary to the liberal Whig Prime Minister, the Marquis of Rockingham, and won a seat in Parliament representing Wendover. He would remain an MP for the next 29 years.

From Edmund Burke, *Reflections on the Revolution in France*, ed. W. B. Todd, New York: Holt, Rinehart and Winston, 1959, pp. 64–75, 91–6.

A political Whig and a defender of the North American colonies in their struggle for independence from British rule, Burke has nevertheless come to be seen as one of the grounding figures of modern political conservatism. It is a characterization that is both justifiable and misleading. Reading Burke as a conservative is misleading because Burke never wavered in his support for Parliamentary power or for the liberal reform of society.[1] Burke's reputation as a conservative, however, is justly rooted in the text from which the following selections have been culled, *Reflections on the Revolution in France* (1790). In the *Reflections* Burke advances a series of critical arguments and rhetorical blasts aimed squarely at the liberal political philosophy that underwrote the French Revolution. The essay also develops keen social-psychological analyses of the revolutionary political mind, drawing out and undermining not simply the theoretical apparatus of revolution but also the way revolutionary ideas play out in the "gross and complicated mass of human passions and concerns" characteristic of actual "common life."

Among the most important of Burke's criticisms is his assault on what might be called the "politics of abstract principle." Having set up a social ideal through theoretical reasoning that purportedly claims transcendent independence from common life, abstract political philosophy cuts itself loose from the limiting forces of politics rooted in the customs and traditions of a people. In the absence of these limiting factors, abstract political philosophy becomes unbridled and given to "enthusiasm" or extremism. In fact, it must tend toward extremism – extreme demands and extreme measures – because it requires a kind of absolute logical purity. Hence a government that in actual practice functions reasonably well is judged a "usurpation" and a "mockery" because it fails to live up to the rigorous demands of perfect democratic representation. And states that fail to live up to the impossible standards of abstract theory are required by the most merciless logic to be, therefore, overthrown.

Just as Descartes (II.8), in his quest for a rationally pure and absolutely true science prescribed totally razing the edifice of all prior thoughts and opinions to the ground, so too does the logic of revolution justify clearing out everything in its way on the road to achieving an utterly cleansed and renewed society. Burke writes: "They have 'the rights of men'. Against these there can be no prescription; against these no agreement is binding; these admit no temperament, and no compromise: anything withheld from the full demand is so much of fraud and injustice." In fact, not only do the detached principles of abstract political philosophy legitimate the most extreme violence, they compel people to produce it: "Something they must destroy, or they seem to themselves to exist for no purpose." In these analyses Burke turned out to be horribly prescient, anticipating the Terror of the French Revolution and the purges of Soviet Communism before they were engineered.

If Burke argues against revolutions of principle, more positively he argues for an organic civil society deeply rooted in tradition and composed of a variety of balancing and limiting institutions – religious and philosophical, sentimental and rational. Just as grammar did not precede language, human societies are not based on theoretical plans. Instead, they develop organically and gradually, overlaying and interweaving countless practices for countless reasons. They are woven, however, not just by reason but also by the complexities of sentiment and feeling.

As Burke understood it, therefore, the customs and practices of civil society that have matured over the course of centuries embody the distilled wisdom of generations. Because of the vast extent and deep complexity of the myriad of relations composing the social order, anyone who would make changes faces an information problem not unlike the sort that economist Friedrich Hayek (1899–1992) contended undermines the efficiency of centrally planned economies.[2] The effects of minor alterations, to which Burke does not object, are themselves uncertain, and even social practices that at first seem wrong may have less obvious beneficent effects: "the real effects of moral causes are not always immediate; but that which in the first instance is prejudicial may be excellent in its remoter operation." The effects of wholesale revolution, on the other hand, to the extent they are predictable at all, are generally destructive. It is, therefore, "with infinite caution that any man ought to venture upon pulling down an edifice which has answered in any tolerable degree for ages the common purposes of society."

Accordingly, Burke, notably more than Hume (V.13), places a great deal of stock in the customs and traditional institutions of society, including those of the monarchy and the Church. To his critics, Burke's support for the *status quo* is excessive. To his supporters Burke's thought offers a much-needed vaccine against the terrors and other extremes of policy characteristic of modern revolutionary thought.

Notes

1   See Burke's *Appeal from the New to the Old Whigs* (1791).
2   F. Hayek, *The Road to Serfdom* (1944).

Burke, *Reflections on the Revolution in France*

The present time differs from any other only by the circumstance of what is doing in France. If the example of that nation is to have an influence on this, I can easily conceive why some of their proceedings which have an unpleasant aspect, and are not quite reconcileable to humanity, generosity, good faith, and justice, are palliated with so much milky good-nature towards the actors, and borne with so much heroic fortitude towards the sufferers. It is certainly not prudent to discredit the authority of an example we mean to follow. But allowing this, we are led to a very natural question; – What is that cause of liberty, and what are those exertions in its favour, to which the example of France is so singularly auspicious? Is our monarchy to be annihilated, with all the laws, all the tribunals, and all the antient corporations of the kingdom? Is every land-mark of the country to be done away in favour of a geometrical and arithmetical constitution? Is the house of lords to be voted useless? Is episcopacy to be abolished? Are the church lands to be sold to Jews and jobbers; or given to bribe new-invented municipal republics into a participation in sacrilege? Are all the taxes to be voted grievances, and the revenue reduced to a patriotic contribution, or patriotic presents? Are silver shoe-buckles to be substituted in the place of the land tax and the malt tax, for the support of the naval strength of this kingdom? Are all orders, ranks, and distinctions to be confounded, that out of universal anarchy, joined to national bankruptcy, three or four thousand democracies should be formed into eighty-three, and that they may all, by some sort of unknown attractive power, be organized into one? For this great end, is the army to be seduced from its discipline and its fidelity, first, by every kind of debauchery, and then by the terrible precedent of a donative in the encrease of pay? Are the curates to be seduced from their bishops, by holding out to them the delusive hope of a dole out of the spoils of their own order? Are the citizens of London to be drawn from their allegiance, by feeding them at the expence of their fellow-subjects? Is a compulsory paper currency to be substituted in the place of the legal coin of this kingdom? Is what remains of the plundered stock of public revenue to be employed in the wild project of maintaining two armies to watch over and to fight with each other? – If these are the ends and means of the Revolution Society, I admit they are well assorted; and France may furnish them for both with precedents in point.

I see that your example is held out to shame us. I know that we are supposed a dull sluggish race, rendered passive by finding our situation tolerable; and prevented by a mediocrity of freedom from ever attaining to its full perfection. Your leaders in France began by affecting to admire, almost to adore, the British constitution; but as they advanced they came to look upon it with a sovereign contempt. The friends of your National Assembly amongst us have full as mean an opinion of what was formerly thought the glory of their country. The Revolution Society has discovered that the English nation is not free. They are convinced that the inequality in our representation is a "defect in our constitution so *gross and palpable*, as to make it excellent chiefly in *form* and *theory*."* That a representation in the legislature of a kingdom is not only the basis of all constitutional liberty in it, but of "*all legitimate government*; that without it a *government* is nothing but an *usurpation*;" – that "when the representation is *partial*, the kingdom possesses liberty only *partially*; and if extremely partial it gives only a *semblance*; and if not only extremely partial, but corruptly chosen, it becomes a *nuisance*." Dr. Price considers this inadequacy of representation as our *fundamental grievance*; and though, as to the corruption of this semblance of representation, he hopes it is not yet arrived to its full perfection of depravity; he fears that "nothing will be done towards gaining for us this *essential blessing*, until some *great abuse of power* again provokes our resentment, or some *great calamity* again alarms our fears, or perhaps till the acquisition of a *pure and equal representation by other countries*, whilst we are *mocked* with the *shadow*, kindles our shame." To this he subjoins a note in these words. "A representation, chosen chiefly by the Treasury, and a *few* thousands of the *dregs* of the people, who are generally paid for their votes."

You will smile here at the consistency of those democratists, who, when they are not on their guard, treat the humbler part of the community with the greatest contempt, whilst, at the same time, they pretend to make them the depositories of all power. It would require a long discourse to point out to you the many fallacies that lurk in the generality and equivocal nature of the terms "inadequate representation." I shall only say here, in justice to that old-fashioned constitution, under which we have long prospered, that our representation has been found perfectly adequate to all the purposes for which a representation of the people can be desired or devised. I defy the enemies of our constitution to shew the contrary. To detail the particulars in which it is found so well to promote its ends, would demand a

* Discourse on the Love of our Country, 3d edit. p. 39.

treatise on our practical constitution. I state here the doctrine of the Revolutionists, only that you and others may see, what an opinion these gentlemen entertain of the constitution of their country, and why they seem to think that some great abuse of power, or some great calamity, as giving a chance for the blessing of a constitution according to their ideas, would be much palliated to their feelings; you see *why they* are so much enamoured of your fair and equal representation, which being once obtained, the same effects might follow. You see they consider our house of commons as only "a semblance," "a form," "a theory," "a shadow," "a mockery," perhaps "a nuisance."

These gentlemen value themselves on being systematic; and not without reason. They must therefore look on this gross and palpable defect of representation, this fundamental grievance (so they call it) as a thing not only vicious in itself, but as rendering our whole government absolutely *illegitimate*, and not at all better than a downright *usurpation*. Another revolution, to get rid of this illegitimate and usurped government, would of course be perfectly justifiable, if not absolutely necessary. Indeed their principle, if you observe it with any attention, goes much further than to an alteration in the election of the house of commons; for, if popular representation, or choice, is necessary to the *legitimacy* of all government, the house of lords is, at one stroke, bastardized and corrupted in blood. That house is no representative of the people at all, even in "semblance or in form." The case of the crown is altogether as bad. In vain the crown may endeavour to screen itself against these gentlemen by the authority of the establishment made on the Revolution. The Revolution which is resorted to for a title, on their system, wants a title itself. The Revolution is built, according to their theory, upon a basis not more solid than our present formalities, as it was made by an house of lords not representing any one but themselves; and by an house of commons exactly such as the present, that is, as they term it, by a mere "shadow and mockery" of representation.

Something they must destroy, or they seem to themselves to exist for no purpose. One set is for destroying the civil power through the ecclesiastical; another for demolishing the ecclesiastick through the civil. They are aware that the worst consequences might happen to the public in accomplishing this double ruin of church and state;

but they are so heated with their theories, that they give more than hints, that this ruin, with all the mischiefs that must lead to it and attend it, and which to themselves appear quite certain, would not be unacceptable to them, or very remote from their wishes. A man amongst them of great authority, and certainly of great talents, speaking of a supposed alliance between church and state, says, "perhaps *we must wait for the fall of the civil powers* before this most unnatural alliance be broken. Calamitous no doubt will that time be. But what convulsion in the political world ought to be a subject of lamentation, if it be attended with so desirable an effect?" You see with what a steady eye these gentlemen are prepared to view the greatest calamities which can befall their country!

It is no wonder therefore, that with these ideas of every thing in their constitution and government at home, either in church or state, as illegitimate and usurped, or, at best as a vain mockery, they look abroad with an eager and passionate enthusiasm. Whilst they are possessed by these notions, it is vain to talk to them of the practice of their ancestors, the fundamental laws of their country, the fixed form of a constitution, whose merits are confirmed by the solid test of long experience, and an increasing public strength and national prosperity. They despise experience as the wisdom of unlettered men; and as for the rest, they have wrought under-ground a mine that will blow up at one grand explosion all examples of antiquity, all precedents, charters, and acts of parliament. They have "the rights of men." Against these there can be no prescription; against these no agreement is binding: these admit no temperament, and no compromise: any thing withheld from their full demand is so much of fraud and injustice. Against these their rights of men let no government look for security in the length of its continuance, or in the justice and lenity of its administration. The objections of these speculatists, if its forms do not quadrate with their theories, are as valid against such an old and beneficent government as against the most violent tyranny, or the greenest usurpation. They are always at issue with governments, not on a question of abuse, but a question of competency, and a question of title. I have nothing to say to the clumsy subtilty of their political metaphysics. Let them be their amusement in the schools – "*Illa se jactet in aula*

– *Aeolus, et clauso ventorum carcere regnet.*"[1] – But let them not break prison to burst like a *Levanter*, to sweep the earth with their hurricane, and to break up the fountains of the great deep to overwhelm us.

Far am I from denying in theory; full as far is my heart from withholding in practice (if I were of power to give or to withhold) the *real* rights of men. In denying their false claims of right, I do not mean to injure those which are real, and are such as their pretended rights would totally destroy. If civil society be made for the advantage of man, all the advantages for which it is made become his right. It is an institution of beneficence; and law itself is only beneficence acting by a rule. Men have a right to live by that rule; they have a right to justice; as between their fellows, whether their fellows are in politic function or in ordinary occupation. They have a right to the fruits of their industry; and to the means of making their industry fruitful. They have a right to the acquisitions of their parents; to the nourishment and improvement of their offspring; to instruction in life, and to consolation in death. Whatever each man can separately do, without trespassing upon others, he has a right to do for himself; and he has a right to a fair portion of all which society, with all its combinations of skill and force, can do in his favour. In this partnership all men have equal rights; but not to equal things. He that has but five shillings in the partnership, has as good a right to it, as he that has five hundred pound has to his larger proportion. But he has not a right to an equal dividend in the product of the joint stock; and as to the share of power, authority, and direction which each individual ought to have in the management of the state, that I must deny to be amongst the direct original rights of man in civil society; for I have in my contemplation the civil social man, and no other. It is a thing to be settled by convention.

If civil society be the offspring of convention, that convention must be its law. That convention must limit and modify all the descriptions of constitution which are formed under it. Every sort of legislative, judicial, or executory power are its creatures. They can have no being in any other state of things; and how can any man claim, under the conventions of civil society, rights which do not so much as suppose its existence? Rights which are absolutely repugnant to it? One of the first motives to civil society, and which

becomes one of its fundamental rules, is, *that no man should be judge in his own cause*. By this each person has at once divested himself of the first fundamental right of uncovenanted man, that is, to judge for himself, and to assert his own cause. He abdicates all right to be his own governor. He inclusively, in a great measure, abandons the right of self-defence, the first law of nature. Men cannot enjoy the rights of an uncivil and of a civil state together. That he may obtain justice he gives up his right of determining what it is in points the most essential to him. That he may secure some liberty, he makes a surrender in trust of the whole of it.

Government is not made in virtue of natural rights, which may and do exist in total independence of it; and exist in much greater clearness, and in a much greater degree of abstract perfection: but their abstract perfection is their practical defect. By having a right to every thing they want every thing. Government is a contrivance of human wisdom to provide for human *wants*. Men have a right that these wants should be provided for by this wisdom. Among these wants is to be reckoned the want, out of civil society, of a sufficient restraint upon their passions. Society requires not only that the passions of individuals should be subjected, but that even in the mass and body as well as in the individuals, the inclinations of men should frequently be thwarted, their will controlled, and their passions brought into subjection. This can only be done *by a power out of themselves*; and not, in the exercise of its function, subject to that will and to those passions which it is its office to bridle and subdue. In this sense the restraints on men, as well as their liberties, are to be reckoned among their rights. But as the liberties and the restrictions vary with times and circumstances, and admit of infinite modifications, they cannot be settled upon any abstract rule; and nothing is so foolish as to discuss them upon that principle.

The moment you abate any thing from the full rights of men, each to govern himself, and suffer any artificial positive limitation upon those rights, from that moment the whole organization of government becomes a consideration of convenience. This it is which makes the constitution of a state, and the due distribution of its powers, a matter of the most delicate and complicated skill. It requires a deep knowledge of human nature and human necessities, and of the things which facilitate or obstruct the various ends which are to be pursued by the mechanism of civil institutions. The state is to have recruits to its strength, and remedies to its distempers. What is the use of discussing a man's abstract right to food or to medicine? The question is upon the method of procuring and administering them. In that deliberation I shall always advise to call in the aid of the farmer and the physician, rather than the professor of metaphysics.

The science of constructing a commonwealth, or renovating it, or reforming it, is, like every other experimental science, not to be taught *à priori*. Nor is it a short experience that can instruct us in that practical science; because the real effects of moral causes are not always immediate; but that which in the first instance is prejudicial may be excellent in its remoter operation; and its excellence may arise even from the ill effects it produces in the beginning. The reverse also happens; and very plausible schemes, with very pleasing commencements, have often shameful and lamentable conclusions. In states there are often some obscure and almost latent causes, things which appear at first view of little moment, on which a very great part of its prosperity or adversity may most essentially depend. The science of government being therefore so practical in itself, and intended for such practical purposes, a matter which requires experience, and even more experience than any person can gain in his whole life, however sagacious and observing he may be, it is with infinite caution that any man ought to venture upon pulling down an edifice which has answered in any tolerable degree for ages the common purposes of society, or on building it up again, without having models and patterns of approved utility before his eyes.

These metaphysic rights entering into common life, like rays of light which pierce into a dense medium, are, by the laws of nature, refracted from their straight line. Indeed in the gross and complicated mass of human passions and concerns, the primitive rights of men undergo such a variety of refractions and reflections, that it becomes absurd to talk of them as if they continued in the simplicity of their original direction. The nature of man is intricate; the objects of society are of the greatest possible complexity; and therefore no simple disposition or direction of power can be suitable either to man's nature, or to the quality of his affairs. When I hear the

simplicity of contrivance aimed at and boasted of in any new political constitutions, I am at no loss to decide that the artificers are grossly ignorant of their trade, or totally negligent of their duty. The simple governments are fundamentally defective, to say no worse of them. If you were to contemplate society in but one point of view, all these simple modes of polity are infinitely captivating. In effect each would answer its single end much more perfectly than the more complex is able to attain all its complex purposes. But it is better that the whole should be imperfectly and anomalously answered, than that, while some parts are provided for with great exactness, others might be totally neglected, or perhaps materially injured, by the over-care of a favourite member.

The pretended rights of these theorists are all extremes; and in proportion as they are metaphysically true, they are morally and politically false. The rights of men are in a sort of *middle*, incapable of definition, but not impossible to be discerned. The rights of men in governments are their advantages; and these are often in balances between differences of good; in compromises sometimes between good and evil, and sometimes, between evil and evil. Political reason is a computing principle; adding, subtracting, multiplying, and dividing, morally and not metaphysically or mathematically, true moral denominations.

By these theorists the right of the people is almost always sophistically confounded with their power. The body of the community, whenever it can come to act, can meet with no effectual resistance; but till power and right are the same, the whole body of them has no right inconsistent with virtue, and the first of all virtues, prudence. Men have no right to what is not reasonable, and to what is not for their benefit; for though a pleasant writer said, *Liceat perire poetis*, when one of them, in cold blood, is said to have leaped into the flames of a volcanic revolution, *Ardentem frigiduss Ætnam insiluit,*[2] I consider such a frolic rather as an unjustifiable poetic licence, than as one of the franchises of Parnassus; and whether he were poet or divine, or politician that chose to exercise this kind of right, I think that more wise, because more charitable thoughts would urge me rather to save the man, than to preserve his brazen slippers as the monuments of his folly.

The kind of anniversary sermons, to which a great part of what I write refers, if men are not shamed out of their present course, in commemorating the fact, will cheat many out of the principles, and deprive them of the benefits of the Revolution they commemorate. I confess to you, Sir, I never liked this continual talk of resistance and revolution, or the practice of making the extreme medicine of the constitution its daily bread. It renders the habit of society dangerously valetudinary: it is taking periodical doses of mercury sublimate, and swallowing down repeated provocatives of cantharides to our love of liberty.

[. . .]

It is now sixteen or seventeen years since I saw the queen of France, then the dauphiness, at Versailles; and surely never lighted on this orb, which she hardly seemed to touch, a more delightful vision. I saw her just above the horizon, decorating and cheering the elevated sphere she just began to move in, – glittering like the morning-star, full of life, and splendor, and joy. Oh! what a revolution! and what an heart must I have, to contemplate without emotion that elevation and that fall! Little did I dream when she added titles of veneration to those of enthusiastic, distant, respectful love, that she should ever be obliged to carry the sharp antidote against disgrace concealed in that bosom; little did I dream that I should have lived to see such disasters fallen upon her in a nation of gallant men, in a nation of men of honour and of cavaliers. I thought ten thousand swords must have leaped from their scabbards to avenge even a look that threatened her with insult. – But the age of chivalry is gone. – That of sophisters, oeconomists, and calculators, has succeeded; and the glory of Europe is extinguished for ever. Never, never more, shall we behold that generous loyalty to rank and sex, that proud submission, that dignified obedience, that subordination of the heart, which kept alive, even in servitude itself, the spirit of an exalted freedom. The unbought grace of life, the cheap defence of nations, the nurse of manly sentiment and heroic enterprize is gone! It is gone, that sensibility of principle, that chastity of honour, which felt a stain like a wound, which inspired courage whilst it mitigated ferocity, which ennobled whatever it touched, and under which vice itself lost half its evil, by losing all its grossness.

This mixed system of opinion and sentiment had its origin in the antient chivalry; and the principle, though varied in its appearance by the varying state of human affairs, subsisted and influenced through a long succession of generations, even to the time we live in. If it should ever be totally extinguished, the loss I fear will be great. It is this which has given its character to modern Europe. It is this which has distinguished it under all its forms of government, and distinguished it to its advantage, from the states of Asia, and possibly from those states which flourished in the most brilliant periods of the antique world. It was this, which, without confounding ranks, had produced a noble equality, and handed it down through all the gradations of social life. It was this opinion which mitigated kings into companions, and raised private men to be fellows with kings. Without force, or opposition, it subdued the fierceness of pride and power; it obliged sovereigns to submit to the soft collar of social esteem, compelled stern authority to submit to elegance, and gave a domination vanquisher of laws, to be subdued by manners.

But now all is to be changed. All the pleasing illusions, which made power gentle, and obedience liberal, which harmonized the different shades of life, and which, by a bland assimilation, incorporated into politics the sentiments which beautify and soften private society, are to be dissolved by this new conquering empire of light and reason. All the decent drapery of life is to be rudely torn off. All the super-added ideas, furnished from the wardrobe of a moral imagination, which the heart owns, and the understanding ratifies, as necessary to cover the defects of our naked shivering nature, and to raise it to dignity in our own estimation, are to be exploded as a ridiculous, absurd, and antiquated fashion.

On this scheme of things, a king is but a man; a queen is but a woman; a woman is but an animal; and an animal not of the highest order. All homage paid to the sex in general as such, and without distinct views, is to be regarded as romance and folly. Regicide, and parricide, and sacrilege, are but fictions of superstition, corrupting jurisprudence by destroying its simplicity. The murder of a king, or a queen, or a bishop, or a father, are only common homicide; and if the people are by any chance, or in any way gainers by it, a sort of homicide much the most pardonable, and into which we ought not to make too severe a scrutiny.

On the scheme of this barbarous philosophy, which is the offspring of cold hearts and muddy understandings, and which is as void of solid wisdom, as it is destitute of all taste and elegance, laws are to be supported only by their own terrors, and by the concern, which each individual may find in them, from his own private speculations, or can spare to them from his own private interests. In the groves of *their* academy, at the end of every visto, you see nothing but the gallows. Nothing is left which engages the affections on the part of the commonwealth. On the principles of this mechanic philosophy, our institutions can never be embodied, if I may use the expression, in persons; so as to create in us love, veneration, admiration, or attachment. But that sort of reason which banishes the affections is incapable of filling their place. These public affections, combined with manners, are required sometimes as supplements, sometimes as correctives, always as aids to law. The precept given by a wise man, as well as a great critic, for the construction of poems, is equally true as to states. *Non satis est pulchra esse poemata, dulcia sunto.*[3] There ought to be a system of manners in every nation which a well-formed mind would be disposed to relish. To make us love our country, our country ought to be lovely.

But power, of some kind or other, will survive the shock in which manners and opinions perish; and it will find other and worse means for its support. The usurpation which, in order to subvert antient institutions, has destroyed antient principles, will hold power by arts similar to those by which it has acquired it. When the old feudal and chivalrous spirit of *Fealty*, which, by freeing kings from fear, freed both kings and subjects from the precautions of tyranny, shall be extinct in the minds of men, plots and assassinations will be anticipated by preventive murder and preventive confiscation, and that long roll of grim and bloody maxims, which form the political code of all power, not standing on its own honour, and the honour of those who are to obey it. Kings will be tyrants from policy when subjects are rebels from principle.

When antient opinions and rules of life are taken away, the loss cannot possibly be estimated. From that moment we have no compass to govern us; nor can we know distinctly to what port we steer. Europe undoubtedly, taken in a mass, was in a flourishing condition the day on which your Revolution was compleated. How much of that prosperous state was owing to the spirit of our old manners and opinions is not easy to say; but as such causes cannot be indifferent in their operation, we must presume, that, on the whole, their operation was beneficial.

We are but too apt to consider things in the state in which we find them, without sufficiently adverting to the causes by which they have been produced, and possibly may be upheld. Nothing is more certain, than that our manners, our civilization, and all the good things which are connected with manners, and with civilization, have, in this European world of ours, depended for ages upon two principles; and were indeed the result of both combined; I mean the spirit of a gentleman, and the spirit of religion. The nobility and the clergy, the one by profession, the other by patronage, kept learning in existence, even in the midst of arms and confusions, and whilst governments were rather in their causes than formed. Learning paid back what it received to nobility and to priesthood; and paid it with usury, by enlarging their ideas, and by furnishing their minds. Happy if they had all continued to know their indissoluble union, and their proper place! Happy if learning, not debauched by ambition, had been satisfied to continue the instructor, and not aspired to be the master! Along with its natural protectors and guardians, learning will be cast into the mire, and trodden down under the hoofs of a swinish multitude.*

If, as I suspect, modern letters owe more than they are always willing to own to antient manners, so do other interests which we value full as much as they are worth. Even commerce, and trade, and manufacture, the gods of our oeconomical politicians, are themselves perhaps but creatures; are themselves but effects, which, as first causes, we choose to worship. They certainly grew under the same shade in which learning flourished. They too may decay with their natural protecting principles. With you, for the present at least, they all threaten to disappear together. Where trade and manufactures are wanting to a people, and the spirit of nobility and religion remains, sentiment supplies, and not always ill supplies their place; but if commerce

---

* See the fate of Bailly and Condorcet, supposed to be here particularly alluded to. Compare the circumstances of the trial, and execution of the former with this prediction. [1803]

and the arts should be lost in an experiment to try how well a state may stand without these old fundamental principles, what sort of a thing must be a nation of gross, stupid, ferocious, and at the same time, poor and sordid barbarians, destitute of religion, honour, or manly pride, possessing nothing at present, and hoping for nothing hereafter?

I wish you may not be going fast, and by the shortest cut, to that horrible and disgustful situation. Already there appears a poverty of conception, a coarseness and vulgarity in all the proceedings of the assembly and of all their instructors. Their liberty is not liberal. Their science is presumptuous ignorance. Their humanity is savage and brutal.

Notes

1 'In that palace, let Aeolus [a god of the winds] boast and reign in the prison of the wind' Virgil, *Aeneid*, 1.40.
2 'Let the poets perish . . . [Empedocles] coolly leapt into volcanic [Mount] Etna' Horace, *Ars Poetica*, 465–66.
3 'Its not enough that poetry is beautiful: it must also inspire affection' Horace, *Ars Poetica*, 99.

16

(A)   Thomas Paine, *The Rights of Man* (selections)
(B)   Mary Wollstonecraft, *A Vindication of the Rights of Woman* (selections)

Introduction

One of the most important figures in advancing the idea of human rights, Thomas or "Tom" Paine (1737–1809) was born in Thetford, Norfolk, to a poor Quaker corset maker. After unsuccessfully plying his father's trade, as well as a few others, his fortunes changed when in 1774 he met Benjamin Franklin (1706–90) who convinced him to emigrate to Philadelphia. There Paine worked as an inventor and journalist. Among his articles for *The Pennsylvania Magazine* was one remarkable piece in which Paine argued for the abolition of slavery.

Paine's first forays into political writing had in fact taken place in England, but his work remained little known until the 1776 American publication of his pro-independence essay *Common Sense*. The success of *Common Sense* was both instantaneous and spectacular. Selling about half a million copies, the tract was read by nearly every literate person in the North American colonies (many of the illiterate had it read to them); and it became, with little competition, the best-selling

(A) *From* Thomas Paine, *The Life and Works of Thomas Paine*, ed. W. M. Van der Weyde, New Rochelle, NY: Thomas Paine National Historical Association, 1925, pp. 91–4, 255–9, 263–74. (B) *From* Mary Wollstonecraft, *A Vindication of the Rights of Woman*, and John Stuart Mill, *The Subjection of Women*, ed. M. Warnock, London: Charles E. Tuttle Co., Inc., 1992, pp. 58–85, 154–64.

publication of eighteenth-century America. *Common Sense* influenced the content of the *Declaration of Independence* and gave what would become the new nation its name, "The United States of America." With the outbreak of war, Paine penned *The American Crisis* papers and joined the military effort himself, fighting under General George Washington. While Paine could have become extraordinarily wealthy from the sale of his publications, he channeled nearly all of the money they generated back into the revolutionary cause. Paine remained a fierce advocate for the American republic and traveled to France in 1781 to raise funds for its support. Paine's growing awareness, however, that the revolution had become organized too far in service of the interests of the propertied classes dimmed his devotion.

In 1787 Paine returned to England where he continued his work as a political essayist. After the 1790 publication of Edmund Burke's critical *Reflections on the Revolution in France* (V.15), Paine wrote in response his great apologetic work, *The Rights of Man* (1791–2), from which the following selections are taken. Arguing for a bundle of liberal political policies, including the extension of suffrage to all males over 21 years of age, progressive taxation, public assistance to the poor, and an end to monarchy, *The Rights of Man* was banned by the British government, which feared it might help the French convulsion breach the Channel into the Kingdom of Great Britain. The book nevertheless sold well over a million copies.

Paine, who continued to refuse royalties and made the text available for publication free of charge, was forced to flee the country in order to avoid prosecution for seditious libel. In 1792 he was made a French citizen and elected to the National Assembly. Opposing the execution of Louis XVI, Paine was himself arrested in 1793 and threatened with execution. Initially slow to come to his aid, the US government, through the efforts of James Monroe, finally secured his liberty about a year later. Upon his release, Paine remained in France and published another controversial work, *The Age of Reason* (1793–4), which advanced deistic arguments against revealed religion and its political influence. The book was followed a year later by *Agrarian Justice* (1795) which argued for redistribution of landed wealth for the sake of equality. Paine returned to the United States in 1802, his reputation diminished by his attack on religion. He died in New York City in 1809.

Philosophically, *The Rights of Man* attacks monarchical rule both on grounds of legitimacy and utility. As a matter of legitimacy, monarchy represents a species of conquest. It violates a set of rights to self-determination people possess naturally, intrinsically, and universally rather than as a matter of social artifice or as privileges distributed by the state that can be rescinded when the state finds it convenient to do so. "All hereditary government," Paine writes, "is in its nature tyranny." In this critique Paine aims to restore society to a condition consistent with what he takes to be natural, original, and normative. That is to say, monarchical, hereditary, and aristocratic society is, according to Paine, an invention that has corrupted the good social order prescribed by nature and nature's law. Naturally, people enjoy the liberty to determine the course of their own lives, and whatever social inequities arise can be justified only on the basis of merit.

Monarchy and hereditary inequalities, on the other hand, structure society in an arbitrary and irrational way – conferring power and rank upon the ignorant as readily (more readily) as upon the wise and cultivating practices that serve the interests of the monarch or the ruling class rather than the nation as a collective whole. It is only democratic or representative republican government, in Paine's view, that can truly serve the public interest – the interest of *res publica* – and make possible a rational and peaceful state: "Every government

that does not act on the principle of a *republic* ... is not a good government." Moreover, the system of republican representation makes it possible to extend democratic government over the larger territories characteristic of modern nation states – in contrast to ancient direct democracies like Athens, which were by necessity small.

Mary Wollstonecraft (1759–97) also wrote against Burke's *Reflections* in defense of the French Revolution. Born in Spitalfields, London, to a financially unstable family, Wollstonecraft became a sort of defender of the women in her family against her father's rages and against the oppressive terms of early modern marriage. Supporting herself as an educator, governess, translator, and – remarkably for the time – author, she found access to the world of letters through the liberal *Analytical Review*. Her interest in women's and children's education led to her writing *Thoughts on the Education of Daughters* (1787) and *Original Stories from Real Life* (1788). Burke's *Reflections* provoked her *Vindication of the Rights of Men* (1790), which gained her widespread attention. It was her second vindication, however, her *Vindication of the Rights of Woman* (1792), that earned Wollstonecraft enduring significance.

Like Paine and Rousseau (V.12), Wollstonecraft argues for the restructuring of society in such a manner as to remove the stultifying forces that distort humanity and inhibit the flowering of its natural goodness. Her work is notable for being among the first in the modern liberal tradition to focus on the way social arrangements inhibit the flourishing of women in particular, not simply in the public sphere of government and commerce but in private life, as well. Wollstonecraft does not deny that men and women are properly suited to different spheres of human life. But she advocates (a), contrary to Rousseau, a robust equalizing program of women's education as well as (b) a rejection of norms of femininity that shape women into frivolous, sentimental, and ornamental creatures. Wollstonecraft argues that women must be educated and raised so that they become rational, strong, and independent beings. Only in this way can women achieve their proper place as partners with men in the business of sustaining a free, equal, and just society.

In 1797 Wollstonecraft married left-wing political philosopher William Godwin (1756–1836). She died shortly after giving birth to their daughter, Mary (her second child), who would grow up to become Mary Shelley, the author of *Frankenstein* (1818), a story critical of the attempt to re-engineer human beings and perhaps, therefore, critical of the sort of social engineering to which her parents were devoted. The irregularities of Wollstonecraft's private life, including her having born her first child out of wedlock, led to her thought being suppressed through much of the nineteenth century. In the wake of US women's suffrage in 1920 and the rise of the modern feminist movement, Wollstonecraft's work has again, however, become widely acknowledged.

(A) Paine, *The Rights of Man*

[From Part I]

The French Constitution says, *there shall be no titles*; and of consequence, all that class of equivocal generation, which in some countries is called "*aristocracy*," and in others "*nobility*," is done away, and the *peer* is exalted into *man*.

Titles are but nicknames, and every nickname is a title. The thing is perfectly harmless in itself, but it marks a sort of foppery in the human character which degrades it. It renders man diminutive in things which are great, and the counterfeit of woman in things which are little. It talks about its fine blue *riband* like a girl, and shows its new *garter* like a child. A certain writer, of some antiquity, says, "When I was a child, I thought as a child: but when I became a man, I put away childish things."

It is, properly, from the elevated mind of France, that the folly of titles has been abolished. It has outgrown the babyclothes of *count* and *duke*, and breeched itself in manhood. France has not levelled, it has exalted. It has put down the dwarf to set up the man. The insignificance of a senseless word like *duke, count*, or *earl*, has ceased to please. Even those who possessed them, have disowned the gibberish, and, as they outgrew the rickets, have despised the rattle.

The genuine mind of man, thirsting for its native home, society, contemns the gewgaws that separate him from it. Titles are like circles drawn by the magician's wand, to contract the sphere of man's felicity. He lives immured within the Bastille of a word, and surveys at a distance the envied life of man.

Is it then any wonder that titles should fall in France? Is it not a greater wonder they should be kept up anywhere? What are they? What is their worth, and "what is their amount?" When we think or speak of a *judge* or a *general*, we associate with it the ideas of office and character; we think of gravity in the one, and bravery in the other; but when we use a word merely as a title, no ideas associate with it.

Through all the vocabulary of Adam, there is no such an animal as a duke or a count; neither can we connect any idea to the words. Whether they mean strength or weakness, wisdom or folly, a child or a man, or a rider or a horse, is all equivocal. What respect then can be paid to that which describes nothing, and which means nothing? Imagination has given figure and character to centaurs, satyrs, and down to all the fairy tribe; but titles baffle even the powers of fancy, and are a chimerical nondescript.

But this is not all. If a whole country is disposed to hold them in contempt, all their value is gone, and none will own them. It is common opinion only that makes them any thing or nothing, or worse than nothing. There is no occasion to take titles away, for they take themselves away when society concurs to ridicule them. This species of imaginary consequence has visibly declined in every part of Europe, and it hastens to its exit as the world of reason continues to rise.

There was a time when the lowest class of what are called nobility, was more thought of than the highest is now, and when a man in armor riding through Christendom in search of adventure was more stared at than a modern duke. The world has seen this folly fall, and it has fallen by being laughed at, and the farce of titles will follow its fate.

The patriots of France have discovered in good time, that rank and dignity in society must take a new ground. The old one has fallen through. It must now take the substantial ground of character, instead of the chimerical ground of titles; and they have brought their titles to the altar, and made of them a burnt-offering to Reason.

[From Part II]

Chapter III: On the Old and New Systems of Government Nothing can appear more contradictory than the principles on which the old governments began, and the condition to which society, civilization and commerce, are capable of carrying mankind. Government on the old system is an assumption of power, for the aggrandizement of itself; on the new, a delegation of power, for the common benefit of society. The former supports itself by keeping up a system of war; the latter promotes a system of peace, as the true means of enriching a nation. The one encourages national prejudices; the other promotes universal society, as the means of universal commerce. The one measures its prosperity, by the quantity of revenue it extorts; the other proves its excellence, by the small quantity of taxes it requires.

[. . .]

Though it might be proved that the system of government now called the NEW, is the most ancient in principle of all that have existed, being founded on the original inherent Rights of Man: yet, as tyranny and the sword have suspended the exercise of those rights for many centuries past, it serves better the purpose of distinction to call it a *new*, than to claim the right of calling it the old.

The first general distinction between those two systems is, that the one now called the old is *hereditary*, either in whole or in part; and the new is entirely *representative*. It rejects all hereditary government:

First, as being an imposition on mankind.

Secondly, as being inadequate to the purposes for which government is necessary.

With respect to the first of these heads. It cannot be proved by what right hereditary government could begin: neither does there exist within the compass of mortal power a right to establish it. Man has no authority over posterity in matters of personal right; and therefore, no man, or body of men, had, or can have, a right to set up hereditary government. Were even ourselves to come again into existence, instead of being succeeded by posterity, we have not now the right of taking from ourselves the rights which would then be ours. On what ground, then, do we pretend to take them from others?

All hereditary government is in its nature tyranny. An heritable crown, or an heritable throne, or by what other fanciful name such things may be called, have no other significant explanation than that mankind are heritable property. To inherit a government, is to inherit the people, as if they were flocks and herds.

With respect to the second head, that of being inadequate to the purposes for which government is necessary, we have only to consider what government essentially is, and compare it with the circumstances to which hereditary succession is subject. Government ought to be a thing always in maturity. It ought to be so constructed as to be superior to all the accidents to which individual man is subject; and therefore, hereditary succession, by being *subject to them all*, is the most irregular and imperfect of all the systems of government.

We have heard the Rights of Man called a *levelling* system; but the only system to which the word *levelling* is truly applicable, is the hereditary monarchical system. It is a system of *mental levelling*. It indiscriminately admits every species of character to the same authority. Vice and virtue, ignorance and wisdom, in short, every quality, good or bad, is put on the same level. Kings succeed each other, not as rationals, but as animals. It signifies not what their mental or moral characters are.

Can we then be surprised at the abject state of the human mind in monarchical countries, when the government itself is formed on such an abject levelling system? It has no fixed character. To-day it is one thing; to-morrow it is something else. It changes with the temper of every succeeding individual, and is subject to all the varieties of each. It is government through the medium of passions and accidents.

It appears under all the various characters of childhood, decrepitude, dotage, a thing at nurse, in leading-strings, or on crutches. It reverses the wholesome order of nature. It occasionally puts children over men, and the conceits of non-age over wisdom and experience. In short, we cannot conceive a more ridiculous figure of government than hereditary succession, in all its cases, presents.

Could it be made a decree in nature, or an edict registered in heaven, and man could know it, that virtue and wisdom should invariably appertain to hereditary succession, the objections to it would be removed; but when we see that nature acts as if she disowned and sported with the hereditary system; that the mental characters of successors, in all countries, are below the average of human understanding; that one is a tyrant, another an idiot, a third insane, and some all three together, it is impossible to attach confidence to it, when reason in man has power to act.

[. . .]

Having thus glanced at a few of the defects of the old, or hereditary system of government, let us compare it with the new, or representative system.

The representative system takes society and civilization for its basis; nature, reason, and experience for its guide.

Experience, in all ages, and in all countries, has demonstrated, that it is impossible to control Nature in her distribution of mental powers. She gives them as she pleases. Whatever is the rule by which she, apparently to us, scatters them among mankind, that rule remains a secret to man. It would be as ridiculous to attempt to fix the hereditaryship of human beauty, as of wisdom.

Whatever wisdom constituently is, it is like a seedless plant; it may be reared when it appears, but it cannot be voluntarily produced. There is always a sufficiency somewhere in the general mass of society for all purposes; but with respect to the parts of society, it is continually changing its place. It rises in one to-day, in another to-morrow, and has most probably visited in rotation every family of the earth, and again withdrawn.

As this is the order of nature, the order of government must necessarily follow it, or government will, as we see it does, degenerate into ignorance. The hereditary system, therefore, is as repugnant to human wisdom, as to human rights, and is as absurd, as it is unjust.

As the republic of letters brings forward the best literary productions, by giving to genius a fair and universal chance; so the representative system of government is calculated to produce the wisest laws, by collecting wisdom where it can be found. I smile to myself when I contemplate the ridiculous insignificance into which literature and all the sciences would sink, were they made hereditary; and I carry the same idea into governments. An hereditary governor is as inconsistent as an hereditary author. I know not whether Homer or Euclid had sons; but I will venture an opinion, that if they had, and had left their works unfinished, those sons could not have completed them.

Do we need a stronger evidence of the absurdity of hereditary government, than is seen in the descendants of those men, in any line of life, who once were famous? Is there scarcely an instance in which there is not a total reverse of character? It appears as if the tide of mental faculties flowed as far as it could in certain channels, and then forsook its course, and arose in others. How irrational then is the hereditary system which establishes channels of power, in company with which wisdom refuses to flow! By continuing this absurdity, man is perpetually in contradiction with himself; he accepts, for a king, or a chief magistrate, or a legislator, a person whom he would not elect for a constable.

It appears to general observation, that revolutions create genius and talents; but those events do no more than bring them forward. There is existing in man, a mass of sense lying in a dormant state, and which, unless something excites it to action, will descend with him, in that condition, to the grave. As it is to the advantage of society that the whole of its faculties should be employed, the construction of government ought to be such as to bring forward, by a quiet and regular operation, all that extent of capacity which never fails to appear in revolutions.

This cannot take place in the insipid state of hereditary government, not only because it prevents, but because it operates to benumb. When the mind of a nation is bowed down by any political superstition in its government, such as hereditary succession is, it loses a considerable portion of its powers on all other subjects and objects.

Hereditary succession requires the same obedience to ignorance, as to wisdom; and when once the mind can bring itself to pay this indiscriminate reverence, it descends below the stature of mental manhood. It is fit to be great only in little things. It acts a treachery upon itself, and suffocates the sensations that urge to detection.

Though the ancient governments present to us a miserable picture of the condition of man, there is one which above all others exempts itself from the general description. I mean the democracy of the Athenians. We see more to admire, and less to condemn, in that great, extraordinary people, than in any thing which history affords.

Mr. Burke is so little acquainted with constituent principles of government, that he confounds democracy and representation together. Representation was a thing unknown in the ancient democracies. In those the mass of the people met and enacted laws (grammatically speaking) in the first person.

Simple democracy was no other than the common hall of the ancients. It signifies the *form*, as well as the public principle of the government. As these democracies increased in population, and the territory extended, the simple democratical form became unwieldy and impracticable; and as the system of representation was not known, the consequence was, they either degenerated convulsively into monarchies, or became absorbed into such as then existed.

Had the system of representation been then understood, as it now is, there is no reason to believe that those forms of government, now called monarchical and aristrocratical, would ever have taken place. It was the want of some method to consolidate the parts of society, after it became too populous, and too extensive for the simple democratical form, and also the lax and solitary condition of shepherds and herdsmen in other parts of the world, that afforded opportunities to those unnatural modes of government to begin.

As it is necessary to clear away the rubbish of errors, into which the subject of government has been thrown, I shall proceed to remark on some others.

It has always been the political craft of courtiers and court-governments, to abuse something which they called republicanism; but what republicanism was, or is, they never attempt to explain. Let us examine a little into this case.

The only forms of government are, the democratical, the aristocratical, the monarchical, and what is now called the representative.

What is called a *republic*, is not any *particular form* of government. It is wholly characteristical of the purport, matter, or object for which government ought to be instituted, and on which it is to be employed, *res-publica*, the public affairs, or the public good; or, literally translated, the *public thing*.

It is a word of a good original, referring to what ought to be the character and business of government; and in this sense it is naturally opposed to the word *monarchy*, which has a base original signification. It means arbitrary power in an individual person; in the exercise of which, *himself*, and not the *res-publica*, is the object.

Every government that does not act on the principle of a *republic*, or in other words, that does not make the *res-publica* its whole and sole object, is not a good government. Republican government is no other than government established and conducted for the interest of the public, as well individually as collectively. It is not necessarily connected with any particular form, but it most naturally associates with the representative form, as being best calculated to secure the end for which a nation is at the expense of supporting it.

[. . .]

Those who have said that a republic is not a *form* of government calculated for countries of great extent, mistook, in the first place, the *business* of a government for a *form* of government; for the *res-publica* equally appertains to every extent of territory and population. And, in the second place, if they meant any thing with respect to *form*, it was the simple democratical form, such as was the mode of government in the ancient democracies, in which there was no representation. The case therefore, is not, that a republic cannot be extensive, but that it cannot be extensive on the simple democratical form; and the question naturally presents itself, *What is the best form of government for conducting the* RES-PUBLICA, *or the* PUBLIC BUSINESS *of a nation, after it becomes too extensive and populous for the simple democratical form?*

It cannot be monarchy, because monarchy is subject to an objection of the same amount to which the simple democratical form was subject.

It is possible that an individual may lay down a system of principles, on which government shall be constitutionally established to any extent of territory. This is no more than an operation of the mind, acting by its own powers. But the practise upon those principles, as applying to the various and numerous circumstances of a nation, its agriculture, manufacture, trade, commerce, etc., requires a knowledge of a different kind, and which can be had only from the various parts of society.

It is an assemblage of practical knowledge, which no one individual can possess; and therefore the monarchical form is as much limited, in useful practise, from the incompetency of knowledge, as was the democratical form, from the multiplying of population. The one degenerates, by extension, into confusion; the other, into ignorance and incapacity, of which all the great monarchies are an evidence. The monarchical form, therefore, could not be a substitute for the democratical, because it has equal inconveniences.

Much less could it when made hereditary. This is the most effectual of all forms to preclude knowledge. Neither could the high democratical mind have voluntarily yielded itself to be governed by children and idiots, and all the motley insignificance of character, which attends such a mere animal system, the disgrace and the reproach of reason and of man.

As to the aristocratical form, it has the same vices and defects with the monarchical, except that the chance of abilities is better from the proportion of numbers, but there is still no security for the right use and application of them.

Referring, then, to the original simple democracy, it affords the true data from which government on a large scale can begin. It is incapable of extension, not from its principle, but from the inconvenience of its form; and monarchy and aristocracy, from their incapacity. Retaining, then, democracy as the ground, and rejecting the corrupt systems of monarchy and aristocracy, the representative system naturally presents itself; remedying at once the defects of the simple democracy as to form, and the incapacity of the other two with respect to knowledge.

Simple democracy was society governing itself without the aid of secondary means. By ingrafting representation upon democracy, we arrive at a system of government capable of embracing and confederating all the various interests and every extent of territory and population; and that also with advantages as much superior to hereditary government, as the republic of letters is to hereditary literature.

It is on this system that the American government is founded. It is representation ingrafted upon democracy. It has fixed the form by a scale parallel in all cases to the extent of the principle. What Athens was in miniature, America will be in magnitude. The one was the wonder of the ancient world; the other is becoming the admiration and model of the present. It is the easiest of all the forms of government to be understood, and the most eligible in practise; and excludes at once the ignorance and insecurity of the hereditary mode, and the inconvenience of the simple democracy.

It is impossible to conceive a system of government capable of acting over such an extent of territory, and such a circle of interests, as is immediately produced by the operation of representation. France, great and popular as it is, is but a spot in the capaciousness of the system. It adapts itself to all possible cases. It is preferable to simple democracy even in small territories. Athens, by representation, would have outrivalled her own democracy.

That which is called government, or rather that which we ought to conceive government to be, is no more than some common center, in which all the parts of society unite. This cannot be accomplished by any method so conducive to the various interests of the community, as by the representative system.

It concentrates the knowledge necessary to the interests of the parts, and of the whole. It places government in a state of constant maturity. It is, as has been already observed, never young, never old. It is subject neither to nonage, nor dotage. It is never in the cradle, nor on crutches. It admits not of a separation between knowledge and power, and is superior, as government always ought to be, to all the accidents of individual man, and is therefore superior to what is called monarchy.

A nation is not a body, the figure of which is to be represented by the human body; but is like a body contained within a circle, having a common center, in which every radius meets; and that center is formed by representation. To connect representation with what is called monarchy is eccentric government. Representation is of itself the delegated monarchy of a nation, and cannot debase itself by dividing it with another.

(B)   Wollstonecraft, *A Vindication of the Rights of Woman*

Chapter IV: Observations on the State of Degradation to which Woman is Reduced by Various Causes

That woman is naturally weak, or degraded by a concurrence of circumstances, is, I think, clear. But this position I shall simply contrast with a conclusion, which I have frequently heard fall from sensible men in favour of an aristocracy: that the mass of mankind cannot be anything, or the obsequious slaves, who patiently allow themselves to be driven forward, would feel their own consequence, and spurn their chains. Men, they further observe, submit everywhere to oppression, when they have only to lift up their heads to throw off the yoke; yet, instead of asserting their birthright, they quietly lick the dust, and say, "Let us eat and drink, for to-morrow we die." Women, I argue from analogy, are degraded by the same propensity to enjoy the present moment, and at last despise the freedom which they have not sufficient virtue to struggle to attain. But I must be more explicit.

With respect to the culture of the heart, it is unanimously allowed that sex is out of the question; but the line of subordination in the mental powers is never to be passed over.* Only "absolute in loveliness," the portion of rationality granted to woman is, indeed, very scanty; for denying her genius and judgment, it is scarcely possible to divine what remains to characterise intellect.

The stamen of immortality, if I may be allowed the phrase, is the perfectibility of human reason; for, were man created perfect, or did a flood of knowledge break in upon him, when he arrived at maturity, that precluded error, I should doubt whether his existence would be continued after the dissolution of the body. But, in the present state of things, every difficulty in morals that escapes from human discussion, and equally baffles the investigation of profound thinking, and the lightning glance of genius, is an argument on which I build my belief of the immortality of the soul. Reason is, consequentially, the simple power of improvement; or, more properly speaking, of discerning truth. Every

individual is in this respect a world in itself. More or less may be conspicuous in one being than another; but the nature of reason must be the same in all, if it be an emanation of divinity, the tie that connects the creature with the Creator; for, can that soul be stamped with the heavenly image, that is not perfected by the exercise of its own reason?† Yet outwardly ornamented with elaborate care, and so adorned to delight man, "that with honour he may love,"‡ the soul of woman is not allowed to have this distinction, and man, ever placed between her and reason, she is always represented as only created to see through a gross medium, and to take things on trust. But dismissing these fanciful theories, and considering woman as a whole, let it be what it will, instead of a part of man, the inquiry is whether she have reason or not. If she have, which, for a moment, I will take for granted, she was not created merely to be the solace of man, and the sexual should not destroy the human character.

Into this error men have, probably, been led by viewing education in a false light; not considering it as the first step to form a being advancing gradually towards perfection;§ but only as a preparation for life. On this sensual error, for I must call it so, has the false system of female manners been reared, which robs the whole sex of its dignity, and classes the brown and fair with the smiling flowers that only adorn the land. This has ever been the language of men, and the fear of departing from a supposed sexual character, has made even women of superior sense adopt the same sentiments.** Thus understanding, strictly

---

* Into what inconsistencies do men fall when they argue without the compass of principles. Women, weak women, are compared with angels; yet, a superior order of beings should be supposed to possess more intellect than man; or, in what does their superiority consist? In the same strain, to drop the sneer, they are allowed to possess more goodness of heart; piety, and benevolence. I doubt the fact, though it be courteously brought forward, unless ignorance be allowed to be the mother of devotion; for I am firmly persuaded that, on an average, the proportion between virtue and knowledge, is more upon a par than is commonly granted.

† "The brutes," says Lord Monboddo, "remain in the state in which nature has placed them, except in so far as their natural instinct is improved by the culture *we* bestow upon them."
‡ *Vide* Milton.
§ This word is not strictly just, but I cannot find a better.
** "Pleasure's the portion of th' *inferior* kind;
But glory, virtue, Heaven for *man* designed."

After writing these lines, how could Mrs. Barbauld write the following ignoble comparison?

"To a Lady with some Painted Flowers
"Flowers to the fair: to you these flowers I bring,
And strive to greet you with an earlier spring.
Flowers, sweet, *and gay, and* delicate like you;
Emblems of innocence, and beauty too
With flowers the Graces bind their yellow hair
And flowery wreaths consenting lovers wear.

speaking, has been denied to woman; and instinct, sublimated into wit and cunning, for the purposes of life, has been substituted in its stead.

The power of generalising ideas, of drawing comprehensive conclusions from individual observations, is the only acquirement, for an immortal being, that really deserves the name of knowledge. Merely to observe, without endeavouring to account for anything, may (in a very incomplete manner) serve as the common sense of life; but where is the store laid up that is to clothe the soul when it leaves the body?

This power has not only been denied to women; but writers have insisted that it is inconsistent, with a few exceptions, with their sexual character. Let men prove this, and I shall grant that woman only exists for man. I must, however, previously remark, that the power of generalising ideas, to any great extent, is not very common amongst men or women. But this exercise is the true cultivation of the understanding; and everything conspires to render the cultivation of the understanding more difficult in the female than the male world.

I am naturally led by this assertion to the main subject of the present chapter, and shall now attempt to point out some of the causes that degrade the sex, and prevent women from generalising their observations.

I shall not go back to the remote annals of antiquity to trace the history of woman; it is sufficient to allow that she has always been either a slave or a despot, and to remark that each of these situations equally retards the progress of reason. The grand source of female folly and vice has ever appeared to me to arise from narrowness of mind; and the very constitution of civil governments

> Flowers, the sole luxury which Nature knew,
> In Eden's pure and guiltless garden grew.
> *To loftier forms are rougher tasks assign'd;*
> *The sheltering oak resists the stormy wind,*
> *The tougher yew repels invading foes,*
> *And the tall pine for future navies grows;*
> *But this soft family, to cares unknown.*
> *Were born for pleasure and delights* ALONE.
> Gay without toil, and lovely without art,
> *They spring to* CHEER *the sense, and* GLAD *the heart.*
> Nor blush, my fair, to own you copy these;
> *Your* BEST, *your* SWEETEST *empire is* – to PLEASE."

So the men tell us; but virtue, says reason, must be acquired by *rough* toils, and useful struggles with worldly *cares.*

has put almost insuperable obstacles in the way to prevent the cultivation of the female understanding; yet virtue can be built on no other foundation. The same obstacles are thrown in the way of the rich, and the same consequences ensue.

Necessity has been proverbially termed the mother of invention; the aphorism may be extended to virtue. It is an acquirement, and an acquirement to which pleasure must be sacrificed; and who sacrifices pleasure when it is within the grasp, whose mind has not been opened and strengthened by adversity, or the pursuit of knowledge goaded on by necessity? Happy is it when people have the cares of life to struggle with, for these struggles prevent their becoming a prey to enervating vices, merely from idleness. But if from their birth men and women be placed in a torrid zone, with the meridian sun of pleasure darting directly upon them, how can they sufficiently brace their minds to discharge the duties of life, or even to relish the affections that carry them out of themselves?

Pleasure is the business of woman's life, according to the present modification of society; and while it continues to be so, little can be expected from such weak beings. Inheriting in a lineal descent from the first fair defect in nature – the sovereignty of beauty – they have, to maintain their power, resigned the natural rights which the exercise of reason might have procured them, and chosen rather to be short-lived queens than labour to obtain the sober pleasures that arise from equality. Exalted by their inferiority (this sounds like a contradiction), they constantly demand homage as women, though experience should teach them that the men who pride themselves upon paying this arbitrary insolent respect to the sex, with the most scrupulous exactness, are most inclined to tyrannise over, and despise the very weakness they cherish. Often do they repeat Mr Hume's sentiments, when, comparing the French and Athenian character, he alludes to women, – "But what is more singular in this whimsical nation, say I to the Athenians, is, that a frolic of yours during the saturnalia, when the slaves are served by their masters, is seriously continued by them through the whole year, and through the whole course of their lives, accompanied, too, with some circumstances, which still further augment the absurdity and ridicule. Your sport only elevates for a few days those whom fortune has thrown down, and whom she too, in sport, may really elevate for ever above you. But this nation gravely exalts those whom nature has subjected to them, and whose inferiority and infirmities are absolutely incurable. The women, though without virtue, are their masters and sovereigns."

Ah! why do women – I write with affectionate solicitude – condescend to receive a degree of attention and respect from strangers different from that reciprocation of civility which the dictates of humanity and the politeness of civilisation authorise between man and man? And why do they not discover, when "in the noon of beauty's power," that they are treated like queens only to be deluded by hollow respect, till they are led to resign, or not assume, their natural prerogatives? Confined, then, in cages like the feathered race, they have nothing to do but to plume themselves, and stalk with mock majesty from perch to perch. It is true they are provided with food and raiment, for which they neither toil nor spin; but health, liberty, and virtue are given in exchange. But where, amongst mankind, has been found sufficient strength of mind to enable a being to resign these adventitious prerogatives – one who, rising with the calm dignity of reason above opinion, dared to be proud of the privileges inherent in man? And it is vain to expect it whilst hereditary power chokes the affections, and nips reason in the bud.

The passions of men have thus placed women on thrones, and till mankind become more reasonable, it is to be feared that women will avail themselves of the power which they attain with the least exertion, and which is the most indisputable. They will smile – yes, they will smile, though told that:

> In beauty's empire is no mean,
> And woman, either slave or queen,
> Is quickly scorned when not adored.

But the adoration comes first, and the scorn is not anticipated.

Louis XIV, in particular, spread factitious manners, and caught, in a specious way, the whole nation in his toils; for, establishing an artful chain of despotism, he made it the interest of the people at large individually to respect his station, and support his power. And women, whom he flattered by a puerile attention to the whole sex,

obtained in his reign that prince-like distinction so fatal to reason and virtue.

A king is always a king, and a woman always a woman.* His authority and her sex ever stand between them and rational converse. With a lover, I grant, she should be so, and her sensibility will naturally lead her to endeavour to excite emotion, not to gratify her vanity, but her heart. This I do not allow to be coquetry; it is the artless impulse of nature. I only exclaim against the sexual desire of conquest when the heart is out of the question.

This desire is not confined to women. "I have endeavoured," says Lord Chesterfield, "to gain the hearts of twenty women, whose persons I would not have given a fig for." The libertine who, in a gust of passion, takes advantage of unsuspecting tenderness, is a saint when compared with this cold-hearted rascal – for I like to use significant words. Yet only taught to please, women are always on the watch to please, and with true heroic ardour endeavour to gain hearts merely to resign or spurn them when the victory is decided and conspicuous.

I must descend to the minutiæ of the subject.

I lament that women are systematically degraded by receiving the trivial attentions which men think it manly to pay to the sex, when in fact, they are insultingly supporting their own superiority. It is not condescension to bow to an inferior. So ludicrous, in fact, do these ceremonies appear to me that I scarcely am able to govern my muscles when I see a man start with eager and serious solicitude to lift a handkerchief or shut a door, when the *lady* could have done it herself, had she only moved a pace or two.

A wild wish has just flown from my heart to my head, and I will not stifle it, though it may excite a horse-laugh. I do earnestly wish to see the distinction of sex confounded in society, unless where love animates the behaviour. For this distinction is, I am firmly persuaded, the foundation of the weakness of character ascribed to woman; is the cause why the understanding is neglected, whilst accomplishments are acquired with sedulous care; and the same cause accounts for their preferring the graceful before the heroic virtues.

---

* And a wit always a wit, might be added, for the vain fooleries of wits and beauties to obtain attention, and make conquests, are much upon a par.

Mankind, including every description, wish to be loved and respected by *something*, and the common herd will always take the nearest road to the completion of their wishes. The respect paid to wealth and beauty is the most certain and unequivocal, and, of course, will always attract the vulgar eye of common minds. Abilities and virtues are absolutely necessary to raise men from the middle rank of life into notice, and the natural consequence is notorious – the middle rank contains most virtue and abilities. Men have thus, in one station at least, an opportunity of exerting themselves with dignity, and of rising by the exertions which really improve a rational creature; but the whole female sex are, till their character is formed, in the same condition as the rich, for they are born – I now speak of a state of civilisation – with certain sexual privileges; and whilst they are gratuitously granted them, few will ever think of works of supererogation to obtain the esteem of a small number of superior people.

When do we hear of women who, starting out of obscurity, boldly claim respect on account of their great abilities or daring virtues? Where are they to be found? "To be observed, to be attended to, to be taken notice of with sympathy, complacency, and approbation, are all the advantages which they seek." True! my male readers will probably exclaim; but let them, before they draw any conclusion, recollect that this was not written originally as descriptive of women, but of the rich. In Dr Smith's *Theory of Moral Sentiments* I have found a general character of people of rank and fortune, that, in my opinion, might with the greatest propriety be applied to the female sex. I refer the sagacious reader to the whole comparison, but must be allowed to quote a passage to enforce an argument that I mean to insist on, as the one most conclusive against a sexual character. For if, excepting warriors, no great men of any denomination have ever appeared amongst the nobility, may it not be fairly inferred that their local situation swallowed up the man, and produced a character similar to that of women, who are *localised* – if I may be allowed the word – by the rank they are placed in by *courtesy*? Women, commonly called ladies, are not to be contradicted in company, are not allowed to exert any manual strength; and from them the negative virtues only are expected, when any virtues are expected – patience, docility, good humour, and flexibility – virtues incompatible with any vigorous exertion

of intellect. Besides, by living more with each other, and being seldom absolutely alone, they are more under the influence of sentiments than passions. Solitude and reflection are necessary to give to wishes the force of passions, and to enable the imagination to enlarge the object, and make it the most desirable. The same may be said of the rich; they do not sufficiently deal in general ideas, collected by impassioned thinking or calm investigation, to acquire that strength of character on which great resolves are built. But hear what an acute observer says of the great:

"Do the great seem insensible of the easy price at which they may acquire the public admiration; or do they seem to imagine that to them, as to other men, it must be the purchase either of sweat or of blood? By what important accomplishments is the young nobleman instructed to support the dignity of his rank, and to render himself worthy of that superiority over his fellow-citizens, to which the virtue of his ancestors had raised them? Is it by knowledge, by industry, by patience, by self-denial, or by virtue of any kind. As all his words, as all his motions are attended to, he learns an habitual regard to every circumstance of ordinary behaviour, and studies to perform all those small duties with the most exact propriety. As he is conscious how much he is observed, and how much mankind are disposed to favour all his inclinations, he acts, upon the most indifferent occasions, with that freedom and elevation which the thought of this naturally inspires. His air, his manner, his deportment, all mark that elegant and graceful sense of his own superiority, which those who are born to inferior station can hardly ever arrive at. These are the arts by which he proposes to make mankind more easily submit to his authority, and to govern their inclinations according to his own pleasure; and in this he is seldom disappointed. These arts, supported by rank and pre-eminence, are, upon ordinary occasions, sufficient to govern the world. Louis XIV during the greater part of his reign, was regarded, not only in France, but over all Europe, as the most perfect model of a great prince. But what were the talents and virtues by which he acquired this great reputation? Was it by the scrupulous and inflexible justice of all his undertakings, by the immense dangers and difficulties with which they were attended, or by the unwearied and unrelenting application with which he pursued them? Was it by his extensive knowledge, by his exquisite judgment, or by his heroic valour? It was by none of these qualities. But he was, first of all, the most powerful prince in Europe, and consequently held the highest rank among kings; and then, says his historian, 'he surpassed all his courtiers in the gracefulness of his shape, and the majestic beauty of his features. The sound of his voice, noble and affecting, gained those hearts which his presence intimidated. He had a step and a deportment which could suit only him and his rank, and which would have been ridiculous in any other person. The embarrassment which he occasioned to those who spoke to him, flattered that secret satisfaction with which he felt his own superiority.' These frivolous accomplishments, supported by his rank, and, no doubt too, by a degree of other talents and virtues, which seems, however, not to have been much above mediocrity, established this prince in the esteem of his own age, and have drawn, even from posterity, a good deal of respect for his memory. Compared with these, in his own times, and in his own presence, no other virtue, it seems, appeared to have any merit. Knowledge, industry, valour, and beneficence trembled, were abashed, and lost all dignity before them."

Woman also thus "in herself complete," by possessing all these *frivolous* accomplishments, so changes the nature of things:

> That what she wills to do or say'
> Seems wisest, virtuousest, discreetest, best;
> All higher knowledge in *her presence* falls
> Degraded. Wisdom in discourse with her
> Loses discountenanced, and, like folly shows;
> Authority and reason on her wait.

And all this is built on her loveliness!

In the middle rank of life, to continue the comparison, men, in their youth, are prepared for professions, and marriage is not considered as the grand feature in their lives; whilst women, on the contrary, have no other scheme to sharpen their faculties. It is not business, extensive plans, or any of the excursive flights of ambition, that engross their attention; no, their thoughts are not employed in rearing such noble structures. To rise in the world, and have the liberty of running from pleasure to pleasure, they must marry advantageously, and to this object their time is sacrificed, and their persons often legally prostituted. A man when he enters any profession has

his eye steadily fixed on some future advantage (and the mind gains great strength by having all its efforts directed to one point), and, full of his business, pleasure is considered as mere relaxation; whilst women seek for pleasure as the main purpose of existence. In fact, from the education, which they receive from society, the love of pleasure may be said to govern them all; but does this prove that there is a sex in souls? It would be just as rational to declare that the courtiers in France, when a destructive system of despotism had formed their character, were not men, because liberty, virtue, and humanity, were sacrificed to pleasure and vanity. Fatal passions, which have ever domineered over the *whole* race!

The same love of pleasure, fostered by the whole tendency of their education, gives a trifling turn to the conduct of women in most circumstances; for instance, they are ever anxious about secondary things; and on the watch for adventures instead of being occupied by duties.

A man, when he undertakes a journey, has, in general, the end in view; a woman thinks more of the incidental occurrences, the strange things that may possibly occur on the road; the impression that she may make on her fellow-travellers; and, above all, she is anxiously intent on the care of the finery that she carries with her, which is more than ever a part of herself, when going to figure on a new scene; when, to use an apt French turn of expression, she is going to produce a sensation. Can dignity of mind exist with such trivial cares?

In short, women, in general, as well as the rich of both sexes, have acquired all the follies and vices of civilisation, and missed the useful fruit. It is not necessary for me always to premise, that I speak of the condition of the whole sex, leaving exceptions out of the question. Their senses are inflamed, and their understandings neglected, consequently they become the prey of their senses, delicately termed sensibility, and are blown about by every momentary gust of feeling. Civilised women are, therefore, so weakened by false refinement, that, respecting morals, their condition is much below what it would be were they left in a state nearer to nature. Ever restless and anxious, their over-exercised sensibility not only renders them uncomfortable themselves, but troublesome, to use a soft phrase, to others. All their thoughts turn on things calculated to excite emotion and feeling, when they should reason, their conduct is unstable, and their opinions are wavering – not the wavering produced by deliberation or progressive views, but by contradictory emotions. By fits and starts they are warm in many pursuits; yet this warmth, never concentrated into perseverance, soon exhausts itself; exhaled by its own heat, or meeting with some other fleeting passion, to which reason has never given any specific gravity, neutrality ensues. Miserable, indeed, must be that being whose cultivation of mind has only tended to inflame its passions! A distinction should be made between inflaming and strengthening them. The passions thus pampered, whilst the judgment is left unformed, what can be expected to ensue? Undoubtedly, a mixture of madness and folly!

This observation should not be confined to the *fair* sex; however, at present, I only mean to apply it to them.

Novels, music, poetry, and gallantry, all tend to make women the creatures of sensation, and their character is thus formed in the mould of folly during the time they are acquiring accomplishments, the only improvement they are excited, by their station in society, to acquire. This overstretched sensibility naturally relaxes the other powers of the mind, and prevents intellect from attaining that sovereignty which it ought to attain to render a rational creature useful to others, and content with its own station; for the exercise of the understanding, as life advances, is the only method pointed out by nature to calm the passions.

Satiety has a very different effect, and I have often been forcibly struck by an emphatical description of damnation; when the spirit is represented as continually hovering with abortive eagerness round the defiled body, unable to enjoy anything without the organs of sense. Yet, to their senses, are women made slaves, because it is by their sensibility that they obtain present power.

And will moralists pretend to assert that this is the condition in which one-half of the human race should be encouraged to remain with listless inactivity and stupid acquiescence? Kind instructors! what were we created for? To remain, it may be said, innocent; they mean in a state of childhood. We might as well never have been born, unless it were necessary that we should be created to enable man to acquire the noble privilege of reason, the power of discerning good from evil, whilst we lie down in the dust from whence we were taken, never to rise again.

It would be an endless task to trace the variety of meannesses, cares, and sorrows, into which women are plunged by the prevailing opinion, that they were created rather to feel than reason, and that all the power they obtain must be obtained by their charms and weakness:

Fine by defect, and amiably weak!

And, made by this amiable weakness entirely dependent, excepting what they gain by illicit sway, on man, not only for protection, but advice, is it surprising that, neglecting the duties that reason alone points out, and shrinking from trials calculated to strengthen their minds, they only exert themselves to give their defects a graceful covering, which may serve to heighten their charms in the eye of the voluptuary, though it sink them below the scale of moral excellence.

Fragile in every sense of the word, they are obliged to look up to man for every comfort. In the most trifling danger they cling to their support, with parasitical tenacity, piteously demanding succour; and their *natural* protector extends his arm, or lifts up his voice, to guard the lovely trembler – from what? Perhaps the frown of an old cow, or the jump of a mouse; a rat would be a serious danger. In the name of reason, and even common sense, what can save such beings from contempt; even though they be soft and fair.

These fears, when not affected, may produce some pretty attitudes; but they show a degree of imbecility which degrades a rational creature in a way women are not aware of – for love and esteem are very distinct things.

I am fully persuaded that we should hear of none of these infantine airs, if girls were allowed to take sufficient exercise, and not confined in close rooms till their muscles are relaxed, and their powers of digestion destroyed. To carry the remark still further, if fear in girls, instead of being cherished, perhaps, created, were treated in the same manner as cowardice in boys, we should quickly see women with more dignified aspects. It is true, they could not then with equal propriety be termed the sweet flowers that smile in the walk of man; but they would be more respectable members of society, and discharge the important duties of life by the light of their own reason. "Educate women like men," says Rousseau, "and the more they resemble our sex the less power will they have over us." This is the very point I aim at. I do not wish them to have power over men; but over themselves.

In the same strain have I heard men argue against instructing the poor; for many are the forms that aristocracy assumes. "Teach them to read and write," say they, "and you take them out of the station assigned them by nature." An eloquent Frenchman has answered them, I will borrow his sentiments. "But they know not, when they make man a brute, that they may expect every instant to see him transformed into a ferocious beast. Without knowledge there can be no morality."

Ignorance is frail base for virtue! Yet, that it is the condition for which woman was organised, has been insisted upon by the writers who have most vehemently argued in favour of the superiority of man; a superiority not in degree, but offence; though, to soften the argument, they have laboured to prove, with chivalrous generosity, that the sexes ought not to be compared; man was made to reason, woman to feel: and that together, flesh and spirit, they make the most perfect whole, by blending happily reason and sensibility into one character.

And what is sensibility? "Quickness of sensation, quickness of perception, delicacy." Thus is it defined by Dr Johnson; and the definition gives me no other idea than of the most exquisitely polished instinct. I discern not a trace of the image of God in either sensation or matter. Refined seventy times seven they are still material; intellect dwells not there; nor will fire ever make lead gold!

I come round to my old argument: if woman be allowed to have an immortal soul, she must have, as the employment of life, an understanding to improve. And when, to render the present state more complete, though everything proves it to be but a fraction of a mighty sum, she is incited by present gratification to forget her grand destination, nature is counteracted, or she was born only to procreate and rot. Or, granting brutes of every description a soul, though not a reasonable one, the exercise of instinct and sensibility may be the step which they are to take, in this life, towards the attainment of reason in the next; so that through all eternity they will lag behind man, who, why we cannot tell, had the power given him of attaining reason in his first mode of existence.

When I treat of the peculiar duties of women, as I should treat of the peculiar duties of a citizen or father, it will be found that I do not mean to insinuate that they should be taken out of their families, speaking of the majority. "He that hath wife and children," says Lord Bacon, "hath given hostages to fortune; for they are impediments to great enterprises, either of virtue or mischief. Certainly the best works, and of greatest merit for the public, have proceeded from the unmarried or childless men." I say the same of women. But the welfare of society is not built on extraordinary exertions; and were it more reasonably organised, there would be still less need of great abilities, or heroic virtues.

In the regulation of a family, in the education of children, understanding, in an unsophisticated sense, is particularly required – strength both of body and mind; yet the men who, by their writings, have most earnestly laboured to domesticate women, have endeavoured, by arguments dictated by a gross appetite, which satiety had rendered fastidious, to weaken their bodies and cramp their minds. But, if even by these sinister methods they really *persuaded* women, by working on their feelings, to stay at home, and fulfil the duties of a mother and mistress of a family, I should cautiously oppose opinions that led women to right conduct, by prevailing on them to make the discharge of such important duties the main business of life, though reason were insulted. Yet, and I appeal to experience, if by neglecting the understanding they be as much, nay, more detached from these domestic employments, than they could be by the most serious intellectual pursuit, though it may be observed, that the mass of mankind will never vigorously pursue an intellectual object,* I may be allowed to infer that reason is absolutely necessary to enable a woman to perform any duty properly, and I must again repeat, that sensibility is not reason.

The comparison with the rich still occurs to me; for, when men neglect the duties of humanity, women will follow their example; a common stream hurries them both along with thoughtless celerity. Riches and honours prevent a man from enlarging his understanding, and enervate all his powers by reversing the order of nature, which has ever made true pleasure the reward of labour. Pleasure – enervating pleasure – is, likewise, within women's reach without earning it. But, till hereditary possessions are spread abroad, how

---

* The mass of mankind are rather the slaves of their appetites than of their passions.

can we expect men to be proud of virtue? And, till they are, women will govern them by the most direct means, neglecting their dull domestic duties to catch the pleasure that sits lightly on the wing of time.

"The power of the woman," says some author, "is her sensibility"; and men, not aware of the consequence, do all they can to make this power swallow up every other. Those who constantly employ their sensibility will have most; for example, poets, painters, and composers.* Yet, when the sensibility is thus increased at the expense of reason, and even the imagination, why do philosophical men complain of their fickleness? The sexual attention of man particularly acts on female sensibility, and this sympathy has been exercised from their youth up. A husband cannot long pay those attentions with the passion necessary to excite lively emotions, and the heart, accustomed to lively emotions, turns to a new lover, or pines in secret, the prey of virtue or prudence. I mean when the heart has really been rendered susceptible, and the taste formed; for I am apt to conclude, from what I have seen in fashionable life, that vanity is oftener fostered than sensibility by the mode of education, and the intercourse between the sexes, which I have reprobated; and that coquetry more frequently proceeds from vanity than from that inconstancy which overstrained sensibility naturally produces.

Another argument that has had great weight with me must, I think, have some force with every considerate benevolent heart. Girls who have been thus weakly educated are often cruelly left by their parents without any provision, and, of course, are dependent on not only the reason, but the bounty of their brothers. These brothers are, to view the fairest side of the question, good sort of men, and give as a favour what children of the same parents had an equal right to. In this equivocal humiliating situation a docile female may remain some time with a tolerable degree of comfort. But when the brother marries – a probable circumstance – from being considered as the mistress of the family, she is viewed with averted looks as an intruder, an unnecessary burden on the benevolence of the master of the house and his new partner.

Who can recount the misery which many unfortunate beings, whose minds and bodies are equally weak, suffer in such situations – unable to work, and ashamed to beg? The wife, a cold-hearted, narrow-minded woman – and this is not an unfair supposition, for the present mode of education does not tend to enlarge the heart any more than the understanding – is jealous of the little kindness which her husband shows to his relations; and her sensibility not rising to humanity, she is displeased at seeing the property of *her* children lavished on an helpless sister.

These are matters of fact, which have come under my eye again and again. The consequence is obvious; the wife has recourse to cunning to undermine the habitual affection which she is afraid openly to oppose; and neither tears nor caresses are spared till the spy is worked out of her home, and thrown on the world, unprepared for its difficulties; or sent, as a great effort of generosity, or from some regard to propriety, with a small stipend, and an uncultivated mind, into joyless solitude.

These two women may be much upon a par with respect to reason and humanity, and, changing situations, might have acted just the same selfish part; but had they been differently educated, the case would also have been very different. The wife would not have had that sensibility, of which self is the centre, and reason might have taught her not to expect, and not even to be flattered by, the affection of her husband, if it led him to violate prior duties. She would wish not to love him merely because he loved her, but on account of his virtues; and the sister might have been able to struggle for herself instead of eating the bitter bread of dependence.

I am, indeed, persuaded that the heart, as well as the understanding, is opened by cultivation, and by – which may not appear so clear – strengthening the organs. I am not now talking of momentary flashes of sensibility, but of affections. And, perhaps, in the education of both sexes, the most difficult task is so to adjust instruction as not to narrow the understanding, whilst the heart is warmed by the generous juices of spring, just raised by the electric fermentation of the season; nor to dry up the feelings by employing the mind in investigations remote from life.

* Men of these descriptions pour sensibility into their compositions, to amalgamate the gross materials; and, moulding them with passion, give to the inert body a soul; but, in woman's imagination, love alone concentrates these ethereal beams.

With respect to women, when they receive a careful education, they are either made fine ladies, brimful of sensibility, and teeming with capricious fancies, or mere notable women. The latter are often friendly, honest creatures, and have a shrewd kind of good sense, joined with worldly prudence, that often render them more useful members of society than the fine sentimental lady, though they possess neither greatness of mind nor taste. The intellectual world is shut against them. Take them out of their family or neighbourhood, and they stand still; the mind finding no employment, for literature affords a fund of amusement which they have never sought to relish, but frequently to despise. The sentiments and taste of more cultivated minds appear ridiculous, even in those whom chance and family connections have led them to love; but in mere acquaintance they think it all affectation.

A man of sense can only love such a woman on account of her sex, and respect her because she is a trusty servant. He lets her, to preserve his own peace, scold the servants, and go to church in clothes made of the very best materials. A man of her own size of understanding would probably not agree so well with her, for he might wish to encroach on her prerogative, and manage some domestic concerns himself; yet women, whose minds are not enlarged by cultivation, or the natural selfishness of sensibility by reflection, are very unfit to manage a family, for, by an undue stretch of power, they are always tyrannising to support a superiority that only rests on the arbitrary distinction of fortune. The evil is sometimes more serious, and domestics are deprived of innocent indulgences, and made to work beyond their strength, in order to enable the notable woman to keep a better table, and outshine her neighbours in finery and parade. If she attend to her children, it is in general to dress them in a costly manner; and whether this attention arise from vanity or fondness, it is equally pernicious.

Besides, how many women of this description pass their days, or at least their evenings, discontentedly. Their husbands acknowledge that they are good managers and chaste wives, but leave home to seek for more agreeable – may I be allowed to use a significant French word – *piquant* society; and the patient drudge, who fulfils her task like a blind horse in a mill, is defrauded of her just reward, for the wages due to her are

the caresses of her husband; and women who have so few resources in themselves, do not very patiently bear this privation of a natural right.

A fine lady, on the contrary, has been taught to look down with contempt on the vulgar employments of life, though she has only been incited to acquire accomplishments that rise a degree above sense; for even corporeal accomplishments cannot be acquired with any degree of precision unless the understanding has been strengthened by exercise. Without a foundation of principles taste is superficial; grace must arise from something deeper than imitation. The imagination, however, is heated, and the feelings rendered fastidious, if not sophisticated, or a counterpoise of judgment is not acquired when the heart still remains artless, though it becomes too tender.

These women are often amiable, and their hearts are really more sensible to general benevolence, more alive to the sentiments that civilise life, than the square-elbowed family drudge; but, wanting a due proportion of reflection and self-government, they only inspire love, and are the mistresses of their husbands, whilst they have any hold on their affections, and the Platonic friends of his male acquaintance. These are the fair defects in Nature; the women who appear to be created not to enjoy the fellowship of man, but to save him from sinking into absolute brutality, by rubbing off the rough angles of his character, and by playful dalliance to give some dignity to the appetite that draws him to them. Gracious Creator of the whole human race! hast Thou created such a being as woman, who can trace Thy wisdom in Thy works, and feel that Thou alone art by Thy nature exalted above her, for no better purpose? Can she believe that she was only made to submit to man, her equal – a being who, like her, was sent into the world to acquire virtue? Can she consent to be occupied merely to please him – merely to adorn the earth – when her soul is capable of rising to Thee? And can she rest supinely dependent on man for reason, when she ought to mount with him the arduous steeps of knowledge?

Yet if love be the supreme good, let woman be only educated to inspire it, and let every charm be polished to intoxicate the senses; but if they be moral beings, let them have a chance to become intelligent; and let love to man be only a part of that glowing flame of universal love, which, after encircling humanity, mounts in grateful incense to God.

To fulfil domestic duties much resolution is necessary, and a serious kind of perseverance that requires a more firm support than emotions, however lively and true to nature. To give an example of order, the soul of virtue, some austerity of behaviour must be adopted, scarcely to be expected from a being who, from its infancy, has been made the weathercock of its own sensations. Whoever rationally means to be useful must have a plan of conduct; and in the discharge of the simplest duty, we are often obliged to act contrary to the present impulse of tenderness or compassion. Severity is frequently the most certain as well as the most sublime proof of affection; and the want of this power over the feelings, and of that lofty, dignified affection which makes a person prefer the future good of the beloved object to a present gratification, is the reason why so many fond mothers spoil their children, and has made it questionable whether negligence or indulgence be most hurtful; but I am inclined to think that the latter has done most harm.

Mankind seem to agree that children should be left under the management of women during their childhood. Now, from all the observation that I have been able to make, women of sensibility are the most unfit for this task, because they will infallibly, carried away by their feelings, spoil a child's temper. The management of the temper, the first, and most important branch of education, requires the sober steady eye of reason; a plan of conduct equally distant from tyranny and indulgence: yet these are the extremes that people of sensibility alternately fall into; always shooting beyond the mark. I have followed this train of reasoning much further, till I have concluded, that a person of genius is the most improper person to be employed in education, public or private. Minds of this rare species see things too much in masses, and seldom, if ever, have a good temper. That habitual cheerfulness, termed good humour, is perhaps, as seldom united with great mental powers, as with strong feelings. And those people who follow, with interest and admiration, the flights of genius; or, with cooler approbation suck in the instruction which has been elaborately prepared for them by the profound thinker, ought not to be disgusted, if they find the former choleric, and the latter

morose; because liveliness of fancy, and a tenacious comprehension of mind, are scarcely compatible with that pliant urbanity which leads a man, at least, to bend to the opinions and prejudices of others, instead of roughly confronting them.

But, treating of education or manners, minds of a superior class are not to be considered, they may be left to chance; it is the multitude, with moderate abilities, who call for instruction, and catch the colour of the atmosphere they breathe. This respectable concourse, I contend, men and women, should not have their sensations heightened in the hot-bed of luxurious indolence, at the expense of their understanding; for, unless there be a ballast of understanding, they will never become either virtuous or free: an aristocracy, founded on property or sterling talents, will ever sweep before it the alternately timid and ferocious slaves of feeling.

Numberless are the arguments, to take another view of the subject, brought forward with a show of reason, because supposed to be deduced from nature that men have used morally and physically, to degrade the sex. I must notice a few.

The female understanding has often been spoken of with contempt, as arriving sooner at maturity than the male. I shall not answer this argument by alluding to the early proofs of reason, as well as genius, in Cowley, Milton, and Pope,* but only appeal to experience to decide whether young men, who are early introduced into company (and examples now abound), do not acquire the same precocity. So notorious is this fact, that the bare mentioning of it must bring before people, who at all mix in the world, the idea of a number of swaggering apes of men, whose understandings are narrowed by being brought into the society of men when they ought to have been spinning a top or twirling a hoop.

It has also been asserted, by some naturalists, that men do not attain their full growth and strength till thirty; but that women arrive at maturity by twenty. I apprehend that they reason on false ground, led astray by the male prejudice, which deems beauty the perfection of woman – mere beauty of features and complexion, the vulgar acceptation of the word, whilst male beauty is allowed to have some connection with the mind. Strength of body, and that character of countenance which the French term a *physionomie*, women

* Many other names might be added.

do not acquire before thirty, any more than men. The little artless tricks of children, it is true, are particularly pleasing and attractive; yet, when the pretty freshness of youth is worn off, these artless graces become studied airs, and disgust every person of taste. In the countenance of girls we only look for vivacity and bashful modesty; but, the springtide of life over, we look for soberer sense in the face, and for traces of passion, instead of the dimples of animal spirits; expecting to see individuality of character, the only fastener of the affections.* We then wish to converse, not to fondle; to give scope to our imaginations as well as to the sensations of our hearts.

At twenty the beauty of both sexes is equal; but the libertinism of man leads him to make the distinction, and superannuated coquettes are commonly of the same opinion; for when they can no longer inspire love, they pay for the vigour and vivacity of youth. The French, who admit more of mind into their notions of beauty, give the preference to women of thirty. I mean to say that they allow women to be in their most perfect state, when vivacity gives place to reason, and to that majestic seriousness of character, which marks maturity or the resting point. In youth, till twenty, the body shoots out, till thirty, the solids are attaining a degree of density; and the flexible muscles, growing daily more rigid, give character to the countenance; that is, they trace the operations of the mind with the iron pen of fate, and tell us not only what powers are within, but how they have been employed.

It is proper to observe, that animals who arrive slowly at maturity, are the longest lived, and of the noblest species. Men cannot, however, claim any natural superiority from the grandeur of longevity; for in this respect nature has not distinguished the male.

Polygamy is another physical degradation; and a plausible argument for a custom, that blasts every domestic virtue, is drawn from the well-attested fact, that in the countries where it is established, more females are born than males. This appears to be an indication of nature, and to nature, apparently reasonable speculations must yield. A further conclusion obviously presented itself; if

polygamy be necessary, woman must be inferior to man, and made for him.

With respect to the formation of the fetus in the womb, we are very ignorant; but it appears to me probable, that an accidental physical cause may account for this phenomenon, and prove it not to be a law of nature. I have met with some pertinent observations on the subject in Foster's *Account of the Isles of the South Sea*, that will explain my meaning. After observing that of the two sexes amongst animals, the most vigorous and hottest constitution always prevails, and produces its kind; he adds, – "If this be applied to the inhabitants of Africa, it is evident that the men there, accustomed to polygamy, are enervated by the use of so many women, and therefore less vigorous; the women, on the contrary, are of a hotter constitution, not only on account of their more irritable nerves, more sensible organisation, and more lively fancy; but likewise because they are deprived in their matrimony of that share of physical love which, in a monogamous condition, would all be theirs; and thus, for the above reasons, the generality of the children are born females.

"In the greater part of Europe it has been proved by the most accurate lists of mortality, that the proportion of men to women is nearly equal, or, if any difference takes place, the males born are more numerous, in the proportion of 105 to 100."

The necessity of polygamy, therefore, does not appear; yet when a man seduces a woman, it should, I think, be termed a *left-handed* marriage, and the man should be *legally* obliged to maintain the woman and her children, unless adultery, a natural divorcement, abrogated the law. And this law should remain in force as long as the weakness of women caused the word seduction to be used as an excuse for their frailty and want of principle; nay, while they depend on man for a subsistence, instead of earning it by the exertion of their own hands or heads. But these women should not, in the full meaning of the relationship, be termed wives, or the very purpose of marriage would be subverted, and all those endearing charities that flow from personal fidelity, and give a sanctity to the tie, when neither love nor friendship unites the hearts, would melt into selfishness. The woman who is faithful to the father of her children demands respect, and should not be treated like a prostitute; though I

---

* The strength of an affection is, generally, in the same proportion as the character of the species in the object beloved, lost in that of the individual.

readily grant that if it be necessary for a man and woman to live together in order to bring up their offspring, nature never intended that a man should have more than one wife.

Still, highly as I respect marriage, as the foundation of almost every social virtue, I cannot avoid feeling the most lively compassion for those unfortunate females who are broken off from society, and by one error torn from all those affections and relationships that improve the heart and mind. It does not frequently even deserve the name of error; for many innocent girls become the dupes of a sincere, affectionate heart, and still more are, as it may emphatically be termed, *ruined* before they know the difference between virtue and vice, and thus prepared by their education for infamy, they become infamous. Asylums and Magdalens are not the proper remedies for these abuses. It is justice, not charity, that is wanting in the world!

A woman who has lost her honour imagines that she cannot fall lower, and as for recovering her former station, it is impossible; no exertion can wash this stain away. Losing thus every spur, and having no other means of support, prostitution becomes her only refuge, and the character is quickly depraved by circumstances over which the poor wretch has little power, unless she possesses an uncommon portion of sense and loftiness of spirit. Necessity never makes prostitution the business of men's lives; though numberless are the women who are thus rendered systematically vicious. This, however, arises in a great degree from the state of idleness in which women are educated, who are always taught to look up to man for a maintenance, and to consider their persons as the proper return for his exertions to support them. Meretricious airs, and the whole science of wantonness, have then a more powerful stimulus than either appetite or vanity; and this remark gives force to the prevailing opinion, that with chastity all is lost that is respectable in woman. Her character depends on the observance of one virtue, though the only passion fostered in her heart is love. Nay, the honour of a woman is not made even to depend on her will.

When Richardson* makes Clarissa tell Lovelace that he had robbed her of her honour, he must

have had strange notions of honour and virtue. For, miserable beyond all names of misery is the condition of a being, who could be degraded without its own consent! This excess of strictness I have heard vindicated as a salutary error. I shall answer in the words of Leibnitz – "Errors are often useful; but it is commonly to remedy other errors."

Most of the evils of life arise from a desire of present enjoyment that outruns itself. The obedience required of women in the marriage state comes under this description; the mind, naturally weakened by depending on authority, never exerts its own powers, and the obedient wife is thus rendered a weak indolent mother. Or, supposing that this is not always the consequence, a future state of existence is scarcely taken into the reckoning when only negative virtues are cultivated. For, in treating of morals, particularly when women are alluded to, writers have too often considered virtue in a very limited sense, and made the foundation of it *solely* worldly utility; nay, a still more fragile base has been given to this stupendous fabric, and the wayward fluctuating feelings of men have been made the standard of virtue. Yes, virtue as well as religion has been subjected to the decisions of taste.

It would almost provoke a smile of contempt, if the vain absurdities of man did not strike us on all sides, to observe how eager men are to degrade the sex from whom they pretend to receive the chief pleasure of life; and I have frequently with full conviction retorted Pope's sarcasm on them; or, to speak explicitly, it has appeared to me applicable to the whole human race. A love of pleasure or sway seems to divide mankind, and the husband who lords it in his little harem thinks only of his pleasure or his convenience. To such lengths, indeed, does an intemperate love of pleasure carry some prudent men, or wornout libertines, who marry to have a safe bedfellow, that they seduce their own wives. Hymen banishes modesty, and chaste love takes its flight.

Love, considered as an animal appetite, cannot long feed on itself without expiring. And this extinction in its own flame may be termed the violent death of love. But the wife, who has thus been rendered licentious, will probably endeavour to fill the void left by the loss of her husband's attentions; for she cannot contentedly become merely an upper servant after having been treated like a goddess. She is still handsome, and, instead

---

* Dr Young supports the same opinion, in his plays, when he talks of the misfortune that shunned the light of day.

of transferring her fondness to her children, she only dreams of enjoying the sunshine of life. Besides, there are many husbands so devoid of sense and parental affection that, during the first effervescence of voluptuous fondness, they refuse to let their wives suckle their children. They are only to dress and live to please them, and love, even innocent love, soon sinks into lasciviousness when the exercise of a duty is sacrificed to its indulgence.

Personal attachment is a very happy foundation for friendship; yet, when even two virtuous young people marry, it would perhaps be happy if some circumstances checked their passion; if the recollection of some prior attachment, or disappointed affection, made it on one side, at least, rather a match founded on esteem. In that case they would look beyond the present moment, and try to render the whole of life respectable, by forming a plan to regulate a friendship which one death ought to dissolve.

Friendship is a serious affection; the most sublime of all affections, because it is founded on principle, and cemented by time. The very reverse may be said of love. In a great degree, love and friendship cannot subsist in the same bosom; even when inspired by different objects they weaken or destroy each other, and for the same object can only be felt in succession. The vain fears and fond jealousies, the winds which fan the flame of love, when judiciously or artfully tempered, are both incompatible with the tender confidence and sincere respect of friendship.

Love, such as the glowing pen of genius has traced, exists not on earth, or only resides in those exalted, fervid imaginations that have sketched such dangerous pictures. Dangerous, because they not only afford a plausible excuse to the voluptuary, who disguises sheer sensuality under a sentimental veil; but as they spread affectation, and take from the dignity of virtue. Virtue, as the very word imports, should have an appearance of seriousness, if not of austerity; and to endeavour to trick her out in the garb of pleasure, because the epithet has been used as another name for beauty, is to exalt her on a quicksand; a most insidious attempt to hasten her fall by apparent respect. Virtue and pleasure are not, in fact, so nearly allied in this life as some eloquent writers have laboured to prove. Pleasure prepares the fading wreath, and mixes the intoxicating cup; but the fruit which virtue gives is the recompense of toil, and, gradually seen as it ripens, only affords calm satisfaction; nay, appearing to be the result of the natural tendency of things, it is scarcely observed. Bread, the common food of life, seldom thought of as a blessing, supports the constitution and preserves health; still feasts delight the heart of man, though disease and even death lurk in the cup or dainty that elevates the spirits or tickles the palate. The lively heated imagination likewise, to apply the comparison, draws the picture of love, as it draws every other picture, with those glowing colours, which the daring hand will steal from the rainbow, that is directed by a mind, condemned in a world like this, to prove its noble origin by panting after unattainable perfection, ever pursuing what it acknowledges to be a fleeting dream. An imagination of this vigorous cast can give existence to insubstantial forms, and stability to the shadowy reveries which the mind naturally falls into when realities are found vapid. It can then depict love with celestial charms, and dote on the grand ideal object – it can imagine a degree of mutual affection that shall refine the soul, and not expire when it has served as a "scale to heavenly"; and, like devotion, make it absorb every meaner affection and desire. In each other's arms, as in a temple, with its summit lost in the clouds, the world is to be shut out, and every thought and wish that do not nurture pure affection and permanent virtue. Permanent virtue! alas! Rousseau, respectable visionary! thy paradise would soon be violated by the entrance of some unexpected guest. Like Milton's it would only contain angels, or men sunk below the dignity of rational creatures. Happiness is not material, it cannot be seen or felt! Yet the eager pursuit of the good, which everyone shapes to his own fancy, proclaims man the lord of this lower world, and to be an intelligential creature, who is not to receive but acquire happiness. They, therefore, who complain of the delusions of passion, do not recollect that they are exclaiming against a strong proof of the immortality of the soul.

But leaving superior minds to correct themselves, and pay dearly for their experience, it is necessary to observe, that it is not against strong, persevering passions, but romantic wavering feelings, that I wish to guard the female heart by exercising the understanding: for these paradisiacal reveries are oftener the effect of idleness than of a lively fancy.

Women have seldom sufficient serious employment to silence their feelings; a round of little cares, or vain pursuits frittering away all strength of mind and organs, they become naturally only objects of sense. In short, the whole tenor of female education (the education of society) tends to render the best disposed romantic and inconstant; and the remainder vain and mean. In the present state of society this evil can scarcely be remedied, I am afraid, in the slightest degree; should a more laudable ambition ever gain ground they may be brought nearer to nature and reason, and become more virtuous and useful as they grow more respectable.

But, I will venture to assert that their reason will never acquire sufficient strength to enable it to regulate their conduct, whilst the making an appearance in the world is the first wish of the majority of mankind. To this weak wish the natural affections, and the most useful virtues are sacrificed. Girls marry merely to *better themselves*, to borrow a significant vulgar phrase, and have such perfect power over their hearts as not to permit themselves to *fall in love* till a man with a superior fortune offers. On this subject I mean to enlarge in a future chapter; it is only necessary to drop a hint at present, because women are so often degraded by suffering the selfish prudence of age to chill the ardour of youth.

From the same source flows an opinion that young girls ought to dedicate great part of their time to needlework; yet, this employment contracts their faculties more than any other that could have been chosen for them, by confining their thoughts to their persons. Men order their clothes to be made, and have done with the subject; women make their own clothes, necessary or ornamental, and are continually talking about them; and their thoughts follow their hands. It is not indeed the making of necessaries that weakens the mind; but the frippery of dress. For when a woman in the lower rank of life makes her husband's and children's clothes, she does her duty, this is her part of the family business; but when women work only to dress better than they could otherwise afford, it is worse than sheer loss of time. To render the poor virtuous they must be employed, and women in the middle rank of life, did they not ape the fashions of the nobility, without catching their éase, might employ them, whilst they themselves managed their families, instructed their children, and exercised their own minds.

Gardening, experimental philosophy, and literature, would afford them subjects to think of and matter for conversation, that in some degree would exercise their understandings. The conversation of Frenchwomen, who are not so rigidly nailed to their chairs to twist lappets, and knot ribands, is frequently superficial; but, I contend, that it is not half so insipid as that of those Englishwomen whose time is spent in making caps, bonnets, and the whole mischief of trimmings, not to mention shopping, bargain-hunting, etc., etc.; and it is the decent, prudent women, who are most degraded by these practices; for their motive is simply vanity. The wanton who exercises her taste to render her passion alluring, has something more in view.

These observations all branch out of a general one, which I have before made, and which cannot be too often insisted upon, for, speaking of men, women, or professions, it will be found that the employment of the thoughts shapes the character both generally and individually. The thoughts of women ever hover round their persons, and is it surprising that their persons are reckoned most valuable? Yet some degree of liberty of mind is necessary even to form the person; and this may be one reason why some gentle wives have so few attractions beside that of sex. Add to this, sedentary employments render the majority of women sickly – and false notions of female excellence make them proud of this delicacy, though it be another fetter, that by calling the attention continually to the body, cramps the activity of the mind.

Women of quality seldom do any of the manual part of their dress, consequently only their taste is exercised, and they acquire, by thinking less of the finery, when the business of their toilet is over, that ease, which seldom appears in the deportment of women, who dress merely for the sake of dressing. In fact, the observation with respect to the middle rank, the one in which talents thrive best, extends not to women; for those of the superior class, by catching, at least, a smattering of literature, and conversing more with men, on general topics, acquire more knowledge than the women who ape their fashions and faults without sharing their advantages. With respect to virtue, to use the word in a comprehensive sense, I have seen most in low life. Many poor women maintain their children by the sweat of their brow, and keep together families that the vices of the fathers would have scattered abroad; but gentlewomen are too indolent to be actively virtuous, and are softened rather than refined by civilisation. Indeed, the good sense which I have met with, among the poor women who have had few advantages of education, and yet have acted heroically, strongly confirmed me in the opinion that trifling employments have rendered woman a trifler. Man, taking her* body, the mind is left to rust; so that while physical love enervates man, as being his favourite recreation, he will endeavour to enslave woman: – and, who can tell, how many generations may be necessary to give vigour to the virtue and talents of the freed posterity of abject slaves?†

In tracing the causes that, in my opinion, have degraded woman, I have confined my observations to such as universally act upon the morals and manners of the whole sex, and to me it appears clear that they all spring from want of understanding. Whether this arise from a physical or accidental weakness of faculties, time alone can determine; for I shall not lay any great stress on the example of a few women‡ who, from having received a masculine education, have acquired courage and resolution; I only contend that the men who have been placed in similar situations, have acquired a similar character – I speak of bodies of men, and that men of genius and talents have started out of a class, in which women have never yet been placed.

Chapter IX: Of the Pernicious Effects which Arise from the Unnatural Distinctions Established in Society

From the respect paid to property flow, as from a poisoned fountain, most of the evils and vices which render this world such a dreary scene to the contemplative mind. For it is in the most polished society that noisome reptiles and venomous serpents lurk under the rank herbage;

* "I take her body," says Ranger.
† Supposing that women are voluntary slaves – slavery of any kind is unfavourable to human happiness and improvement." – KNOX's *Essays*.
‡ Sappho, Eloisa, Mrs Macaulay, the Empress of Russia, Madame d'Eon, etc. These, and many more, may be reckoned exceptions; and, are not all heroes, as well as heroines, exceptions to general rules? I wish to see women neither heroines nor brutes; but reasonable creatures.

and there is voluptuousness pampered by the still sultry air, which relaxes every good disposition before it ripens into virtue.

One class presses on another, for all are aiming to procure respect on account of their property; and property once gained will procure the respect due only to talents and virtue. Men neglect the duties incumbent on man, yet are treated like demigods. Religion is also separated from morality by a ceremonial veil, yet men wonder that the world is almost, literally speaking, a den of sharpers or oppressors.

There is a homely proverb, which speaks a shrewd truth, that whoever the devil finds idle he will employ. And what but habitual idleness can hereditary wealth and titles produce? For man is so constituted that he can only attain a proper use of his faculties by exercising them, and will not exercise them unless necessity of some kind first set the wheels in motion. Virtue likewise can only be acquired by the discharge of relative duties; but the importance of these sacred duties will scarcely be felt by the being who is cajoled out of his humanity by the flattery of sycophants. There must be more equality established in society, or morality will never gain ground, and this virtuous equality will not rest firmly even when founded on a rock, if one-half of mankind be chained to its bottom by fate, for they will be continually undermining it through ignorance or pride.

It is vain to expect virtue from women till they are in some degree independent of men; nay, it is vain to expect that strength of natural affection which would make them good wives and mothers. Whilst they are absolutely dependent on their husbands they will be cunning, mean, and selfish; and the men who can be gratified by the fawning fondness of spaniel-like affection have not much delicacy, for love is not to be bought; in any sense of the words, its silken wings are instantly shrivelled up when anything beside a return in kind is sought. Yet whilst wealth enervates men, and women live, as it were, by their personal charms, how can we expect them to discharge those ennobling duties which equally require exertion and self-denial? Hereditary property sophisticates the mind, and the unfortunate victims to it – if I may so express myself – swathed from their birth, seldom exert the locomotive faculty of body or mind, and thus viewing everything through one medium, and that a false one, they are unable to discern in what true merit and happiness consist. False, indeed, must be the light when the drapery of situation hides the man, and makes him stalk in masquerade, dragging from one scene of dissipation to another the nerveless limbs that hang with stupid listlessness, and rolling round the vacant eye, which plainly tells us that there is no mind at home.

I mean therefore to infer that the society is not properly organised which does not compel men and women to discharge their respective duties by making it the only way to acquire that countenance from their fellow-creatures, which every human being wishes some way to attain. The respect consequently which is paid to wealth and mere personal charms is a true north-east blast that blights the tender blossoms of affection and virtue. Nature has wisely attached affections to duties to sweeten toil, and to give that vigour to the exertions of reason which only the heart can give. But the affections which is put on merely because it is the appropriated insignia of a certain character, when its duties are not fulfilled, is one of the empty compliments which vice and folly are obliged to pay to virtue and the real nature of things.

To illustrate my opinion, I need only observe that when a woman is admired for her beauty, and suffers herself to be so far intoxicated by the admiration she receives as to neglect to discharge the indispensable duty of a mother, she sins against herself by neglecting to cultivate an affection that would equally tend to make her useful and happy. True happiness – I mean all the contentment and virtuous satisfaction that can be snatched in this imperfect state – must arise from well-regulated affections, and an affection includes a duty. Men are not aware of the misery they cause, and the vicious weakness they cherish, by only inciting women to render themselves pleasing; they do not consider that they thus make natural and artificial duties clash by sacrificing the comfort and respectability of a woman's life to voluptuous notions of beauty, when in nature they all harmonise.

Cold would be the heart of a husband, were he not rendered unnatural by early debauchery, who did not feel more delight at seeing his child suckled by its mother than the most artful wanton tricks could ever raise, yet this natural way of cementing the matrimonial tie, and twisting esteem with fonder recollections, wealth leads women to spurn. To preserve their beauty, and wear the flowery crown of the day, which gives them a kind of right to reign for a short time over the sex, they neglect to stamp impressions on their husbands' hearts that would be remembered with more tenderness when the snow on the head began to chill the bosom than even their virgin charms. The maternal solicitude of a reasonable affectionate woman is very interesting, and the chastened dignity with which a mother returns the caresses that she and her child receive from a father who has been fulfilling the serious duties of his station is not only a respectable, but a beautiful sight. So singular, indeed, are my feelings – and I have endeavoured not to catch factitious ones – that after having been fatigued with the sight of insipid grandeur and the slavish ceremonies that with cumbrous pomp supplied the place of domestic affections, I have turned to some other scene to relieve my eye by resting it on the refreshing green everywhere scattered by Nature. I have then viewed with pleasure a woman nursing her children, and discharging the duties of her station with perhaps merely a servant-maid to take off her hands the servile part of the household business. I have seen her prepare herself and children, with only the luxury of cleanliness, to receive her husband, who, returning weary home in the evening, found smiling babes and a clean hearth. My heart has loitered in the midst of the group, and has even throbbed with sympathetic emotion when the scraping of the well-known foot has raised a pleasing tumult.

Whilst my benevolence has been gratified by contemplating this artless picture, I have thought that a couple of this description, equally necessary and independent of each other, because each fulfilled the respective duties of their station, possessed all that life could give. Raised sufficiently above abject poverty not to be obliged to weigh the consequence of every farthing they spend, and having sufficient to prevent their attending to a frigid system of economy which narrows both heart and mind, I declare, so vulgar are my conceptions, that I know not what is wanted to render this the happiest as well as the most respectable situation in the world, but a taste for literature, to throw a little variety and interest into social converse, and some superfluous money to give to the needy and to buy books. For it is not pleasant when the heart is opened by compassion, and the head active in arranging plans of usefulness, to have a prim urchin continually twitching back the elbow to prevent the hand from drawing out an almost empty purse, whispering at the same time some prudential maxim about the priority of justice.

Destructive, however, as riches and inherited honours are to the human character, women are more debased and cramped, if possible, by them than men, because men may still in some degree unfold their faculties by becoming soldiers and statesmen.

As soldiers, I grant they can now only gather for the most part vain-glorious laurels, whilst they adjust to a hair the European balance, taking especial care that no bleak northern nook or sound incline the beam. But the days of true heroism are over, when a citizen fought for his country like a Fabricius or a Washington, and then returned to his farm to let his virtuous fervour run in a more placid, but not a less salutary, stream. No, our British heroes are oftener sent from the gaming-table than from the plough; and their passions have been rather inflamed by hanging with dumb suspense on the turn of a die, than sublimated by panting after the adventurous march of virtue in the historic page.

The statesman, it is true, might with more propriety quit the faro bank, or card-table, to guide the helm, for he has still but to shuffle and trick – the whole system of British politics, if system it may courteously be called, consisting in multiplying dependents and contriving taxes which grind the poor to pamper the rich. Thus a war, or any wild-goose chase, is, as the vulgar use the phrase, a lucky turn-up of patronage for the minister, whose chief merit is the art of keeping himself in place. It is not necessary then that he should have bowels for the poor, so he can secure for his family the odd trick. Or should some show of respect, for what is termed with ignorant ostentation an Englishman's birthright, be expedient to bubble the gruff mastiff that he has to lead by the nose, he can make an empty show, very safely, by giving his single voice, and suffering his light squadron to file off to the other side. And when a question of humanity is agitated, he may dip a sop in the milk of human kindness to silence Cerberus, and talk of the interest which his heart takes in an attempt to make the earth no longer cry for vengeance as it sucks in its children's blood, though his cold hand may at the very moment rivet their chains, by sanctioning the abominable traffic. A minister is no longer a minister, than while he can carry a point, which he is determined to carry. Yet it is not necessary that a minister should feel like a man, when a bold push might shake his seat.

But, to have done with these episodical observations, let me return to the more specious slavery which chains the very soul of woman, keeping her for ever under the bondage of ignorance.

The preposterous distinctions of rank, which render civilisation a curse, by dividing the world between voluptuous tyrants and cunning envious dependents, corrupt, almost equally, every class of people, because respectability is not attached to the discharge of the relative duties of life, but to the station, and when the duties are not fulfilled the affections cannot gain sufficient strength to fortify the virtue of which they are the natural reward. Still there are some loop-holes out of which a man may creep, and dare to think and act for himself; but for a woman it is an herculean task, because she has difficulties peculiar to her sex to overcome, which require almost superhuman powers.

A truly benevolent legislator always endeavours to make it the interest of each individual to be virtuous; and thus private virtue becoming the cement of public happiness, an orderly whole is consolidated by the tendency of all the parts towards a common centre. But the private or public virtue of woman is very problematical, for Rousseau, and a numerous list of male writers, insist that she should all her life be subjected to a severe restraint, that of propriety. Why subject her to propriety – blind propriety – if she be capable of acting from a nobler spring, if she be an heir of immortality? Is sugar always to be produced by vital blood? Is one half of the human species, like the poor African slaves, to be subject to prejudices that brutalise them, when principles would be a surer guard, only to sweeten the cup of man? Is not this indirectly to deny woman reason? for a gift is a mockery, if it be unfit for use.

Women are, in common with men, rendered weak and luxurious by the relaxing pleasures which wealth procures; but added to this they are made slaves to their persons, and must render them alluring that man may lend them his reason to guide their tottering steps aright. Or should they be ambitious, they must govern their tyrants by sinister tricks, for without rights there cannot be any incumbent duties. The laws respecting woman, which I mean to discuss in a future part, make an absurd unit of a man and his wife; and then, by the easy transition of only considering him as responsible, she is reduced to a mere cipher.

The being who discharges the duties of its station is independent, and, speaking of women at large, their first duty is to themselves as rational creatures, and the next, in point of importance, as citizens, is that, which includes so many, of a mother. The rank in life which dispenses with their fulfilling this duty, necessarily degrades them by making them mere dolls. Or should they turn to something more important than merely fitting drapery upon a smooth block, their minds are only occupied by some soft platonic attachment; or the actual management of an intrigue may keep their thoughts in motion; for when they neglect domestic duties, they have it not in their power to take the field and march and counter-march like soldiers, or wrangle in the senate to keep their faculties from rusting.

I know that, as a proof of the inferiority of the sex, Rousseau has exultingly exclaimed, How can they leave the nursery for the camp! And the camp has by some moralists been proved the school of the most heroic virtues; though I think it would puzzle a keen casuist to prove the reasonableness of the greater number of wars that have dubbed heroes. I do not mean to consider this question critically; because, having frequently viewed these freaks of ambition as the first natural mode of civilisation, when the ground must be torn up, and the woods cleared by fire and sword, I do not choose to call them pests; but surely the present system of war has little connection with virtue of any denomination, being rather the school of *finesse* and effeminacy than of fortitude.

Yet, if defensive war, the only justifiable war, in the present advanced state of society, where virtue can show its face and ripen amidst the rigours which purify the air on the mountain's top, were alone to be adopted as just and glorious, the true heroism of antiquity might again animate female bosoms. But fair and softly, gentle reader, male or female, do not alarm thyself, for though I have compared the character of a modern soldier with that of a civilised woman, I am not going to advise them to turn their distaff into a musket, though I sincerely wish to see the bayonet converted into a pruning-hook. I only re-created an imagination, fatigued by contemplating the vices

and follies which all proceed from a feculent stream of wealth that has muddied the pure rills of natural affection, by supposing that society will some time or other be so constituted, that man must necessarily fulfil the duties of a citizen, or be despised, and that while he was employed in any of the departments of civil life, his wife, also an active citizen, should be equally intent to manage her family, educate her children, and assist her neighbours.

But to render her really virtuous and useful, she must not, if she discharge her civil duties, want individually the protection of civil laws; she must not be dependent on her husband's bounty for her subsistence during his life, or support after his death; for how can a being be generous who has nothing of its own? or virtuous who is not free? The wife, in the present state of things, who is faithful to her husband, and neither suckles nor educates her children, scarcely deserves the name of a wife, and has no right to that of a citizen. But take away natural rights, and duties become null.

Women then must be considered as only the wanton solace of men, when they become so weak in mind and body that they cannot exert themselves unless to pursue some frothy pleasure, or to invent some frivolous fashion. What can be a more melancholy sight to a thinking mind, than to look into the numerous carriages that drive helter-skelter about this metropolis in a morning full of pale-faced creatures who are flying from themselves! I have often wished, with Dr. Johnson, to place some of them in a little shop with half a dozen children looking up to their languid countenances for support. I am much mistaken, if some latent vigour would not soon give health and spirit to their eyes, and some lines drawn by the exercise of reason on the blank cheeks, which before were only undulated by dimples, might restore lost dignity to the character, or rather enable it to attain the true dignity of its nature. Virtue is not to be acquired even by speculation, much less by the negative supineness that wealth naturally generates.

Besides, when poverty is more disgraceful than even vice, is not morality cut to the quick? Still to avoid misconstruction, though I consider that women in the common walks of life are called to fulfil the duties of wives and mothers, by religion and reason, I cannot help lamenting that women of a superior cast have not a road open by which they can pursue more extensive plans of usefulness and independence. I may excite laughter, by dropping an hint, which I mean to pursue, some future time, for I really think that women ought to have representatives, instead of being arbitrarily governed without having any direct share allowed them in the deliberations of government.

But, as the whole system of representation is now, in this country, only a convenient handle for despotism, they need not complain, for they are as well represented as a numerous class of hard-working mechanics, who pay for the support of royalty when they can scarcely stop their children's mouths with bread. How are they represented whose very sweat supports the splendid stud of an heir-apparent, or varnishes the chariot of some female favourite who looks down on shame? Taxes on the very necessaries of life, enable an endless tribe of idle princes and princesses to pass with stupid pomp before a gaping crowd, who almost worship the very parade which costs them so dear. This is mere gothic grandeur, something like the barbarous useless parade of having sentinels on horseback at Whitehall, which I could never view without a mixture of contempt and indignation.

How strangely must the mind be sophisticated when this sort of state impresses it! But, till these monuments of folly are levelled by virtue, similar follies will leaven the whole mass. For the same character, in some degree, will prevail in the aggregate of society; and the refinements of luxury, or the vicious repinings of envious poverty, will equally banish virtue from society, considered as the characteristic of that society, or only allow it to appear as one of the stripes of the harlequin coat, worn by the civilised man.

In the superior ranks of life, every duty is done by deputies, as if duties could ever be waived, and the vain pleasures which consequent idleness forces the rich to pursue, appear so enticing to the next rank, that the numerous scramblers for wealth sacrifice everything to tread on their heels. The most sacred trusts are then considered as sinecures, because they were procured by interest, and only sought to enable a man to keep *good company*. Women, in particular, all want to be ladies. Which is simply to have nothing to do, but listlessly to go they scarcely care where, for they cannot tell what.

But what have women to do in society? I may be asked, but to loiter with easy grace; surely you would not condemn them all to suckle fools and chronicle small beer! No. Women might certainly study the art of healing, and be physicians as well as nurses. And midwifery, decency seems to allot to them, though I am afraid, the word midwife, in our dictionaries, will soon give place to *accoucheur*, and one proof of the former delicacy of the sex be effaced from the language.

They might also study politics, and settle their benevolence on the broadest basis; for the reading of history will scarcely be more useful than the perusal of romances, if read as mere biography; if the character of the times, the political improvements, arts, etc., be not observed. In short, if it be not considered as the history of man; and not of particular men, who filled a niche in the temple of fame, and dropped into the black rolling stream of time, that silently sweeps all before it into the shapeless void called – eternity. – For shape, can it be called, "that shape hath none"?

Business of various kinds, they might likewise pursue, if they were educated in a more orderly manner, which might save many from common and legal prostitution. Women would not then marry for a support, as men accept of places under Government, and neglect the implied duties; nor would an attempt to earn their own subsistence, a most laudable one! sink them almost to the level of those poor abandoned creatures who live by prostitution. For are not milliners and mantua-makers reckoned the next class? The few employments open to women, so far, from being liberal, are menial; and when a superior education enables them to take charge of the education of children as governesses, they are not treated like the tutors of sons, though even clerical tutors are not always treated in a manner calculated to render them respectable in the eyes of their pupils, to say nothing of the private comfort of the individual. But as women educated like gentlewomen, are never designed for the humiliating situation which necessity sometimes forces them to fill; these situations are considered in the light of a degradation; and they know little of the human heart, who need to be told, that nothing so painfully sharpens sensibility as such a fall in life.

Some of these women might be restrained from marrying by a proper spirit of delicacy, and others may not have had it in their power to escape in this pitiful way from servitude; is not that Government then very defective, and very unmindful of the happiness of one-half of its members, that does not provide for honest, independent women, by encouraging them to fill respectable stations? But in order to render their private virtue a public benefit, they must have a civil existence in the State, married or single; else we shall continually see some worthy woman, whose sensibility has been rendered painfully acute by undeserved contempt, droop like "the lily broken down by a plowshare."

It is a melancholy truth; yet such is the blessed effect of civilisation! the most respectable women are the most oppressed; and, unless they have understandings far superior to the common run of understandings, taking in both sexes, they must, from being treated like contemptible beings, become contemptible. How many women thus waste life away the prey of discontent, who might have practised as physicians, regulated a farm, managed a shop, and stood erect, supported by their own industry, instead of hanging their heads surcharged with the dew of sensibility, that consumes the beauty to which it at first gave lustre; nay, I doubt whether pity and love are so near akin as poets feign, for I have seldom seen much compassion excited by the helplessness of females, unless they were fair; then, perhaps, pity was the soft handmaid of love, or the harbinger of lust.

How much more respectable is the woman who earns her own bread by fulfilling any duty, than the most accomplished beauty! – beauty did I say! – so sensible am I of the beauty of moral loveliness, or the harmonious propriety that attunes the passions of a well-regulated mind, that I blush at making the comparison; yet I sigh to think how few women aim at attaining this respectability by withdrawing from the giddy whirl of pleasure, or the indolent calm that stupefies the good sort of women it sucks in.

Proud of their weakness, however, they must always be protected, guarded from care, and all the rough toils that dignify the mind. If this be the fiat of fate, if they will make themselves insignificant and contemptible, sweetly to waste "life away," let them not expect to be valued when their beauty fades, for it is the fate of the fairest flowers to be admired and pulled to pieces by the careless hand that plucked them. In how many ways do I wish, from the purest benevolence, to impress this truth on my sex; yet I fear that they will not listen to a truth that dear bought experience has brought home to many an agitated bosom, nor willingly resign the privileges of rank and sex for the privileges of humanity, to which those have no claim who do not discharge its duties.

Those writers are particularly useful, in my opinion, who make man feel for man, independent of the station he fills, or the drapery of factitious sentiments. I then would fain convince reasonable men of the importance of some of my remarks; and prevail on them to weigh dispassionately the whole tenor of my observations. I appeal to their understandings; and, as a fellow-creature, claim, in the name of my sex, some interest in their hearts. I entreat them to assist to emancipate their companion, to make her a *helpmeet* for them.

Would men but generously snap our chains, and be content with rational fellowship instead of slavish obedience, they would find us more observant daughters, more affectionate sisters, more faithful wives, more reasonable mothers – in a word, better citizens. We should then love them with true affection, because we should learn to respect ourselves; and the peace of mind of a worthy man would not be interrupted by the idle vanity of his wife, nor the babes sent to nestle in a strange bosom, having never found a home in their mother's.

G. W. F. Hegel, *Philosophy of Right,*
Part III, Section iii

Introduction

In 1821, the most renowned German philosopher of his time, G. W. F. Hegel (1770–1831), published a "text-book" to accompany his Berlin lectures on political philosophy.[1] The last section of this book, "The State," presents Hegel's most detailed discussion, not only of his conception of the "essential" nature of the State, but of the concrete constitutional form that, in his view, the State should take. His remarks on the State have proved extremely controversial. For some commentators, like Sir Karl Popper (1902–94; II.21), they are expressions of a thoroughly fascist view of the State, of a form of "State-worship;" for others, they show that Hegel was a "reform-minded liberal who based his political philosophy on the . . . fulfilment of individual human freedom."[2] Certainly there are lines which seem to support the former interpretation: "the State is the march of God through history," something to "worship," and something to which the individual must entirely subordinate himself, especially at a time of war, which is itself described as "preserving" the "ethical health" of a nation. It is important, however, to look more closely at his account and not to be overly swayed by Hegel's admittedly misleading rhetoric.[3]

From Hegel: Selections, ed. and trans. J. Loewenberg, New York: Charles Scribner's Sons, 1929, pp. 443–68 (some notes omitted).

To begin with, there is nothing faintly fascist in the kind of constitution Hegel proposes for the State. This constitution – very close, in effect, to that of the Prussia in which he was then living – is a constitutional monarchy, with a legislature elected through a limited, indirect franchise, and in which, by the standards of his day, considerable individual freedom and freedom of expression is allowed under the law. It is Hegel's conviction that such arrangements help to promote among the citizens of the country a sense of their close unity as members of a whole. Thus the monarch, whose powers are severely limited, is essentially a symbol of this unity: if, in a metaphorical sense, the State is a "person," it is best represented by a person in the literal sense. More generally, and to switch to another of Hegel's favorite metaphors, if the State is, as it should be, an "organism" – a unified whole – then its constitution must, in various ways, encourage a feeling among its "parts" of belonging to such a whole.

Second, there is no doubt that Hegel believed the rational State to be a precondition of the realization of human freedom, and thereby of the realization of that "world-spirit" (*Geist*) of which, according to his metaphysics, human beings are the "vehicles." (See the Preface to his *Phenomenology of Spirit* in III.18 of this volume.) "God," it is worth noting, is for Hegel often a synonym for *Geist*: so that references to the State as "the actual God" may be construed as meaning that Spirit or Reason is manifested in the State.

But does the "freedom" of which Hegel speaks have much to do with what people today usually have in mind in political discussion? It helps one understand Hegel's conception to consider his remark that the State is "the unification of the family principle with that of civil society."[4] By a "civil society" he means a society of the type envisaged by social contract theorists – an association of self-interested individuals come together to promote those interests. For Hegel, not only is such a society inherently unstable, since people whose self-interest is not being served will turn against it; but it is not, either, a community of free persons, for each of them regards its laws as constraints and necessary evils to be grudgingly obeyed. What is required, in addition to the rights and liberties conferred in civil society, is the kind of loyalty and emotional commitment to a community that is found, in miniature, in family life. Only when people are "patriotic" and hence emotionally bound to one another and to the whole of which they are parts do they become free. For then, and only then, "the contradiction between liberty and necessity vanishes" (*Philosophy of History*). The laws of the "essential" State are no longer perceived as external constraints, but more like the customs and traditions that members of a family willingly follow and recognize as crucial to their constituting a genuine family unit.

Notes

1 The title of Hegel's book, *Grundlinien der Philosophie des Rechts*, is sometimes translated as *Philosophy of Law*. The present text is a substantial selection, by its translator, of passages from Part III §iii ("The State") of this work.

2 For Popper's account, see his *The Open Society and Its Enemies*, Vol. 2, London: Routledge & Kegan Paul, 1945. The quotation is from Kenneth Westphal, "The basic context and structure of Hegel's *Philosophy of Right*," in F. Beiser, ed., *The Cambridge Companion to Hegel*, Cambridge: Cambridge University Press, 1993, p. 234.

3 See R. B. Pippin and O. Höffe, eds, *Hegel on Ethics and Politics*, Cambridge: Cambridge University Press, 2004.

4 Cf. R. Dien Winfield, *The Just State: Rethinking Self-Government*, Amherst, NY: Humanity Books, 2005.

Hegel, *Philosophy of Right*

The State

Idea and Aim of the State The State is the realization of the ethical idea. It is the ethical spirit as revealed, self-conscious, substantial will. It is the will which thinks and knows itself, and carries out what it knows, and in so far as it knows. The unreflected existence of the State rests on custom, and its reflected existence on the self-consciousness of the individual, on his knowledge and activity. The individual, in return, has his substantial freedom in the State, as the essence, purpose, and product of his activity.

The true State is the ethical whole and the realization of freedom. It is the absolute purpose of reason that freedom should be realized. The State is the spirit, which lives in the world and there realizes itself consciously; while in nature it is actual only as its own other or as dormant spirit. Only

as present in consciousness, knowing itself as an existing object, is it the State. The State is the march of God through the world, its ground is the power of reason realizing itself as will. The idea of the State should not denote any particular State, or particular institution; one must rather consider the Idea only, this actual God, by itself. Because it is more easy to find defects than to grasp the positive meaning, one readily falls into the mistake of emphasizing so much the particular nature of the State as to overlook its inner organic essence. The State is no work of art. It exists in the world, and thus in the realm of caprice, accident, and error. Evil behavior toward it may disfigure it on many sides. But the ugliest man, the criminal, the invalid, and the cripple, are still living human beings. The affirmative, life, persists in spite of defects, and it is this affirmative which alone is here in question.

In the State, everything depends upon the unity of the universal and the particular. In the ancient States the subjective purpose was absolutely one with the will of the State. In modern times, on the contrary, we demand an individual opinion, an individual will and conscience. The ancients had none of these in the modern sense; the final thing for them was the will of the State. While in Asiatic despotisms the individual had no inner self and no self-justification, in the modern world man demands to be honored for the sake of his subjective individuality.

The union of duty and right has the twofold aspect that what the State demands as duty should directly be the right of the individual, since the State is nothing but the organization of the concept of freedom. The determinations of the individual will are given by the State objectivity, and it is through the State alone that they attain truth and realization. The State is the sole condition of the attainment of the particular end and good.

Political disposition, called patriotism – the assurance resting in truth and the will which has become a custom – is simply the result of the institutions subsisting in the State, institutions in which reason is actually present.

Under patriotism one frequently understands a mere willingness to perform extraordinary acts and sacrifices. But patriotism is essentially the sentiment of regarding, in the ordinary circumstances and ways of life, the weal of the community as the substantial basis and the final end. It is upon this consciousness, present in the ordinary course of life and under all circumstances, that the disposition to heroic effort is founded. But as people are often rather magnanimous than just, they easily persuade themselves that they possess the heroic kind of patriotism, in order to save themselves the trouble of having the truly patriotic sentiment, or to excuse the lack of it.

Political sentiment, as appearance, must be distinguished from what people truly will. What they at bottom will is the real cause, but they cling to particular interests and delight in the vain contemplation of improvements. The conviction of the necessary stability of the State in which alone the particular interests can be realized, people indeed possess, but custom makes invisible that upon which our whole existence rests; it does not occur to any one, when he safely passes through the streets at night, that it could be otherwise. The habit of safety has become a second nature, and

we do not reflect that it is the result of the activity of special institutions. It is through force – this is frequently the superficial opinion – that the State coheres, but what alone holds it together is the fundamental sense of order, which is possessed by all.

The State is an organism or the development of the idea into its differences. These different sides are the different powers of the State with their functions and activities, by means of which the universal is constantly and necessarily producing itself, and, being presupposed in its own productive function, it is thus always actively present. This organism is the political constitution. It eternally springs from the State, just as the State in turn maintains itself through the constitution. If these two things fall asunder, if both different sides become independent of each other, then the unity which the constitution produces is no longer operative; the fable of the stomach and the other organs may be applied to it. It is the nature of an organism that all its parts must constitute a certain unity; if one part asserts its independence the other parts must go to destruction. No predicates, principles, and the like suffice to express the nature of the State; it must be comprehended as an organism.

The State is real, and its reality consists in the interest of the whole being realized in particular ends. Actuality is always the unity of universality and particularity, and the differentiation of the universal into particular ends. These particular ends seem independent, though they are borne and sustained by the whole only. In so far as this unity is absent, no thing is real, though it may exist. A bad State is one which merely exists. A sick body also exists, but it has no true reality. A hand, which is cut off, still looks like a hand and exists, but it has no reality. True reality is necessity. What is real is eternally necessary.

To the complete State belongs, essentially, consciousness and thought. The State knows thus what it wills, and it knows it under the form of thought.

The essential difference between the State and religion consists in that the commands of the State have the form of legal duty, irrespective of the feelings accompanying their performance; the sphere of religion, on the other hand, is in the inner life. Just as the State, were it to frame its commands as religion does, would endanger the right of the inner life, so the church, if it acts as a State and imposes punishment, degenerates into a tyrannical religion.

In the State one must want nothing which is not an expression of rationality. The State is the world which the spirit has made for itself; it has therefore a determinate and self-conscious course. One often speaks of the wisdom of God in nature, but one must not believe that the physical world of nature is higher than the world of spirit. Just as spirit is superior to nature, so is the State superior to the physical life. We must therefore worship the State as the manifestation of the divine on earth, and consider that, if it is difficult to comprehend nature, it is infinitely harder to grasp the essence of the State. It is an important fact that we, in modern times, have attained definite insight into the State in general and are much engaged in discussing and making constitutions; but that does not advance the problem much. It is necessary to treat a rational matter in the light of reason, in order to learn its essential nature and to know that the obvious does not always constitute the essential.

When we speak of the different functions of the powers of the State, we must not fall into the enormous error of supposing each power to have an abstract, independent existence, since the powers are rather to be differentiated as elements in the conception of the State. Were the powers to be in abstract independence, however, it is clear that two independent things could never constitute a unity, but must produce war, and the result would be destruction of the whole or restoration of unity by force. Thus, in the French Revolution, at one time the legislative power had swallowed up the executive, at another time the executive had usurped the legislative power.

The Constitution   The constitution is rational, in so far as the State defines and differentiates its functions according to the nature of its concept.

Who shall make the constitution? This question seems intelligible, yet on closer examination reveals itself as meaningless, for it presupposes the existence of no constitution, but only a mere mass of atomic individuals. How a mass of individuals is to come by a constitution, whether by its own efforts or by those of others, whether by goodness, thought, or force, it must decide for itself, for with a disorganized mob the concept of the State has nothing to do. But if the question does presuppose an already existing constitu-

tion, then to make a constitution means only to change it. The presupposition of a constitution implies, however, at once, that any modification in it must take place constitutionally. It is absolutely essential that the constitution, though having a temporal origin, should not be regarded as made. It (the principle of constitution) is rather to be conceived as absolutely perpetual and rational, and therefore as divine, substantial, and above and beyond the sphere of what is made.

Subjective freedom is the principle of the whole modern world – the principle that all essential aspects of the spiritual totality should develop and attain their right. From this point of view one can hardly raise the idle question as to which form is the better, monarchy or democracy. One can but say that the forms of all constitutions are one-sided that are not able to tolerate the principle of free subjectivity and that do not know how to conform to the fully developed reason.

Since spirit is real only in what it knows itself to be, and since the State, as the nation's spirit, is the law permeating all its affairs, its ethical code, and the consciousness of its individuals, the constitution of a people chiefly depends upon the kind and the character of its self-consciousness. In it lies both its subjective freedom and the reality of the constitution.

To think of giving people a constitution *a priori*, though according to its content a more or less rational one – such a whim would precisely overlook that element which renders a constitution more than a mere abstract object. Every nation, therefore, has the constitution which is appropriate to it and belongs to it.

The State must, in its constitution, permeate all situations. A constitution is not a thing just made; it is the work of centuries, the idea and the consciousness of what is rational, in so far as it is developed in a people. No constitution, therefore, is merely created by the subjects of the State. The nation must feel that its constitution embodies its right and its status, otherwise the constitution may exist externally, but has no meaning or value. The need and the longing for a better constitution may often indeed be present in individuals, but that is quite different from the whole multitude being permeated with such an idea – that comes much later. The principle of morality, the inwardness of Socrates originated necessarily in his day, but it took time before it could pass into general self-consciousness.

The Power of the Prince   Because sovereignty contains in ideal all special privileges, the common misconception is quite natural, which takes it to be mere force, empty caprice, and synonymous with despotism. But despotism means a state of lawlessness, in which the particular will as such, whether that of monarch or people (*ochlocracy*), is the law, or rather instead of the law. Sovereignty, on the contrary, constitutes the element of ideality of particular spheres and functions under lawful and constitutional conditions.

The sovereignty of the people, conceived in opposition to the sovereignty residing in the monarch, stands for the common view of democracy, which has come to prevail in modern times. The idea of the sovereignty of the people, taken in this opposition, belongs to a confused idea of what is commonly and crudely understood by "the people." The people without its monarch and without that whole organization necessarily and directly connected with him is a formless mass, which is no longer a State. In a people, not conceived in a lawless and unorganized condition, but as a self-developed and truly organic totality – in such a people sovereignty is the personality of the whole, and this is represented in reality by the person of the monarch.

The State must be regarded as a great architectonic edifice, a hieroglyph of reason, manifesting itself in reality. Everything referring merely to utility, externality, and the like, must be excluded from its philosophic treatment. That the State is the self-determining and the completely sovereign will, the final decision being necessarily referred to it – that is easy to comprehend. The difficulty lies in grasping this "I will" as a person. By this it is not meant that the monarch can act arbitrarily. He is bound, in truth, by the concrete content of the deliberations of his council, and, when the constitution is stable, he has often nothing more to do than sign his name – but this name is important; it is the point than which there is nothing higher.

It may be said that an organic State has already existed in the beautiful democracy of Athens. The Greeks, however, derived the final decision from entirely external phenomena, from oracles, entrails of sacrificed animals, and from the flight of birds. Nature they considered as a power which in this wise made known and gave expression to what was good for the people. Self-consciousness had at that time not yet attained to the abstraction of subjectivity; it had not yet come to the realization that an "I will" must be pronounced by man himself concerning the decisions of the State. This "I will" constitutes the great difference between the ancient and the modern world, and must therefore have its peculiar place in the great edifice of the State. Unfortunately this modern characteristic is regarded as merely external and arbitrary.

It is often maintained against the monarch that he may be ill-educated or unworthy to stand at the helm chance. It is therefore absurd to assume the rationality of the institution of the monarch. The presupposition, however, that the fortunes of the State depend upon the particular character of the monarch is false. In the perfect organization of the State the important thing is only the finality of formal decision and the stability against passion. One must not therefore demand objective qualification of the monarch; he has but to say "yes" and to put the dot upon the "i." The crown shall be of such a nature that the particular character of its bearer is of no significance. Beyond his function of administering the final decision, the monarch is a particular being who is of no concern. Situations may indeed arise in which his particularity alone asserts itself, but in that case the State is not yet fully developed, or else is ill constructed. In a well-ordered monarchy the law alone has objective power to which the monarch has but to affix the subjective "I will."

Monarchs do not excel in bodily strength or intellect, and yet millions permit themselves to be ruled by them. To say that the people permit themselves to be governed contrary to their interests, aims, and intentions is preposterous, for people are not so stupid. It is their need, it is the inner power of the idea, which, in opposition to their apparent consciousness, urges them to this situation and retains them therein.

Out of the sovereignty of the monarch flows the prerogative of pardoning criminals. Only to the sovereignty belongs the spiritual power to undo what has been done and to cancel the crime by forgiving and forgetting.

Pardon is the remission of punishment, but does not abolish right. Right remains, and the pardoned is a criminal as he was before the pardon. The act of mercy does not mean that no crime has been committed. This remission of punishment may be effected in religion, for by and in spirit what has been done can be made undone. But in so far as remission occurs in the world, it has its place only in majesty and is due only to its arbitrary decision.

The Executive The main point upon which the function of the government depends is the division of labor. This division is concerned with the transition from the universal to the particular and the individual; and the business is to be divided according to the different branches. The difficulty lies in harmonizing the superior and the inferior functions. For some time past the main effort has been spent in organizing from above, the lower and bulky part of the whole being left more or less unorganized; yet it is highly important that it should become organic, for only thus is it a power and a force; otherwise it is but a heap or mass of scattered atoms. Authoritative power resides only in the organic state of the particular spheres.

The State cannot count on service which is capricious and voluntary (the administration of justice by knights-errant, for instance), precisely because it *is* capricious and voluntary. Such service presupposes acting according to subjective opinion, and also the possibility of neglect and of the realization of private ends. The opposite extreme to the knight-errant in reference to public service would be the State-servant who was attached to his task solely by want, without genuine duty and right.

The efficiency of the State depends upon individuals, who, however, are not entitled to carry on the business of the State through natural [or untutored] fitness, but according to their objective qualifications. Ability, skill, character, belong to the particular nature of the individual; for a particular office, however, he must be specially educated and trained. An office in the State can, therefore, be neither sold nor bequeathed.

Public service demands the sacrifice of independent self-satisfaction, and the giving up of the pursuit of private ends, but grants the right of finding these in dutiful service, and in it only. Herein lies the unity of the universal and the particular interests which constitutes the concept and the inner stability of the State.

The members of the executive and the officials of the State form the main part of the middle class which represents the educated intelligence and the consciousness of right of the mass of a people. This middle class is prevented by the institutions of sovereignty from above and the rights of corporation from below, from assuming the exclusive position of an aristocracy and making education and intelligence the means for caprice and despotism. Thus the administration of justice, whose object is the proper interest of all individuals, had at one time been perverted into an instrument of gain and despotism, owing to the fact that the knowledge of the law was hidden under a learned and foreign language, and the knowledge of legal procedure under an involved formalism.

In the middle class, to which the State officials belong, resides the consciousness of the State and the most conspicuous cultivation; the middle class constitutes therefore the ground pillar of the State in regard to uprightness and intelligence. The State in which there is no middle class stands as yet on no high level.

The Legislature The legislature is concerned with the interpretation of the laws and with the internal affairs of the State, in so far as they have a universal content. This function is itself a part of the constitution and thus presupposes it. Being presupposed, the constitution lies, to that degree, outside the direct province of the legislature, but in the forward development of the laws and the progressive character of the universal affairs of government, the constitution receives its development also.

The constitution must alone be the firm ground on which the legislature stands; hence it must not be created for purposes of legislation. But the constitution not only *is*, its essence is also to *become* – that is, it progresses with the advance of civilization. This progress is an alteration which is imperceptible, but has not the form of an alteration. Thus, for example, the emperor was formerly judge, and went about the empire administering justice. Through the merely apparent advance of civilization it has become practically necessary that the emperor should gradually yield his judicial function to others, and thus came about the transition of the judicial function from the person of the prince to a body of judges; thus the progress of any condition is an apparently calm and imperceptible one. In this way and after a lapse of time a constitution attains a character quite different from what it had before.

In the legislative power as a whole are operative both the monarchical element and the executive. To the former belongs the final decision; the latter as advisory element possesses concrete knowledge, perspective over the whole in all its ramifications, and acquaintance with the objective principles and wants of the power of the State. Finally, in the legislature the different classes or estates are also active. These classes or estates represent in the legislature the element of subjective formal freedom, the public consciousness, the empirical totality of the views and thought of the many.

The expression "The Many" (οἱ πολλοί) characterizes the empirical totality more correctly than the customary word "All." Though one may reply that, from this "all," children, women, etc., are obviously meant to be excluded, yet it is more obvious that the definite expression "all" should not be used when something quite indefinite is in question.

There are, in general, current among the public so unspeakably many distorted and false notions and phrases about the people, the constitution, and the classes, that it would be a vain task to mention, explain, and correct them. The prevalent idea concerning the necessity and utility of an assembly of estates amounts to the assumption that the people's deputies, nay, the people itself, best understand what would promote the common weal, and that they have indubitably the good will to promote it. As for the first point, the case is just the reverse. The people, in so far as this term signifies a special part of the citizens, stands precisely for the part that does not know what it wills. To know what one wills, and, what is more difficult, to know what the absolute will, viz., reason, wills, is the fruit of deep knowledge and insight; and that is obviously not a possession of the people. As for the especially good will, which the classes are supposed to have for the common good, the usual point of view of the masses is the negative one of suspecting the government of a will which is evil or of little good.

The attitude of the government toward the classes must not be essentially a hostile one. Belief in the necessity of this hostile relation is a sad mistake. The government is not one part in opposition to another, so that both are engaged in wrestling something from each other. When the State is in such a situation it is a misfortune and not a mark of health. Furthermore, the taxes, for which the classes vote, are not to be looked upon as gifts, but are consented to for the best interests of those consenting. What constitutes the true meaning of the classes is this – that through them the State enters into the subjective consciousness of the people and thus the people begin to share in the State.

In despotic countries, where there are only princes and people, the people assert themselves, whenever they act, as a destructive force directed against the organization, but the masses, when they become organically related to the State, obtain their interests in a lawful and orderly way. When this organic relation is lacking, the self-expression of the masses is always violent; in despotic States the despot shows, therefore, indulgence for his people, and his rage is always felt by those surrounding him. Moreover, the people of a despotic State pay light taxes, which in a constitutional State are increased through the very consciousness of the people. In no other country are taxes so heavy as they are in England.

There exists a current notion to the effect that, since the private class is raised in the legislature to a participation in the universal cause, it must appear in the form of individuals – either that representatives are chosen for the function, or that every individual exercises a vote. This abstract atomic view prevails neither in the family nor in civic society, in both of which the individual appears only as a member of a universal. The State, however, is in essence an organization of members, and these members are themselves spheres; in it no element shall show itself as an unorganized mass. The many, as individuals, whom one chooses to call the people, are indeed a collection, but only as a multitude, a formless mass, whose movement and action would be elemental, irrational, savage, and terrible.

The concrete State is the whole, organized into its particular spheres, and the member of the State is a member of such a particular class. Only in this objective determination can the individual find recognition in the State. Only in his coöperative capacity, as member of the community and the like, can the individual first find a real and vital place in the universal. It remains, of course, open to him to rise through his skill to any class for which he can qualify himself, including even the universal class.

It is a matter of great advantage to have among the delegates representatives of every special branch of society, such as trade, manufacture, etc. – individuals thoroughly familiar with their branch and belonging to it. In the notion of a loose and indefinite election this important matter is left to accident; every branch, however, has the same right to be represented as every other. To view the delegates as representatives has, then, an organic and rational meaning only if they are not representatives of mere individuals, of the mere multitude, but of one of the essential spheres of society and of its large interests. Representation thus no longer means substitution of one person by another, but it means, rather, that the interest itself is actually present in the representative.

Of the elections by many separate individuals it may be observed that there is necessarily an indifference, especially in large States, about using one's vote, since one vote is of such slight importance; and those who have the right to vote will not do so, no matter how much one may extol the privilege of voting. Hence this institution turns into the opposite of what it stands for. The election becomes the business of a few, of a single party, of a special interest, which should, in fact, be neutralized.

Through the publicity of the assembly of classes public opinion first acquires true thoughts and an insight into the condition and the notion of the State and its affairs, and thus develops the capacity of judging more rationally concerning them; it learns, furthermore, to know and respect the routine, talents, virtues, and skill of the authorities and officers of the State. While publicity stimulates these talents in their further development and incites their honorable display, it is also an antidote for the pride of individuals and of the multitude, and is one of the greatest opportunities for their education.

It is a widespread popular notion that everybody already knows what is good for the State, and that it is this common knowledge which finds expression in the assembly. Here, in the assembly, are developed virtues, talents, skill, which have to serve as examples. To be sure, the ministers may find these assemblies onerous, for ministers must possess large resources of wit and eloquence to resist the attacks which are hurled against them. Nevertheless, publicity is one of the best means of instruction in the interests of the State generally, for where publicity is found the people manifest an entirely different regard for the State than in those places where there are no assemblies or where they are not public. Only through the publication of every one of their proceedings are the chambers related to the larger public opinion; and it is shown that what one imagines at home with his wife and friends is one thing, and what happens in a great assembly, where one feat of eloquence wrecks another, is quite a different thing.

Public Opinion Public opinion is the unorganized way in which what a people wants and thinks is promulgated. That which is actually effective in the State must be so in an organic fashion. In the constitution this is the case. But at all times public opinion has been a great power, and it is particularly so in our time, when the principle of subjective freedom has such importance and significance. What shall now prevail, prevails no longer through force, little through use and custom, but rather through insight and reasons.

Public opinion contains, therefore, the eternal substantial principles of justice, the true content, and the result of the whole constitution, legislation, and the universal condition in general. The form underlying public opinion is sound common sense, which is a fundamental ethical principle winding its way through everything, in spite of prepossessions. But when this inner character is formulated in the shape of general propositions, partly for their own sake, partly for the purpose of actual reasoning about events, institutions, relations, and the recognized wants of the State, there appears also the whole character of accidental opinion, with its ignorance and perversity, its false knowledge and incorrect judgment.

It is therefore not to be regarded as merely a difference in subjective opinion when it is asserted on the one hand –

"Vox populi, vox dei";
and on the other (in Ariosto, for instance) –
"Che'l Volgare ignorante ogn' un riprenda
E parli più di quel che meno intenda."[1]

Both sides co-exist in public opinion. Since truth and endless error are so directly united in it, neither one nor the other side is truly in earnest. Which one is in earnest, is difficult to decide – difficult, indeed, if one confines oneself to the direct expression of public opinion. But as the substantial principle is the inner character of public opinion, this alone is its truly earnest aspect; yet this insight cannot be obtained from public opinion itself, for a substantial principle can only be apprehended apart from public opinion and by a consideration of its own nature. No matter with what passion an opinion is invested, no matter with what earnestness a view is asserted, attacked, and defended, this is no criterion of its real essence. And least of all could public opinion be made to see that its seriousness is nothing serious at all.

A great mind has publicly raised the question whether it is permissible to deceive a people. The answer is that a people will not permit itself to be deceived concerning its substantial basis, the essence, and the definite character of its spirit, but it deceives *itself* about the way in which it knows this, and according to which it judges of its acts, events, etc.

Public opinion deserves, therefore, to be esteemed as much as to be despised; to be despised for its concrete consciousness and expression, to be esteemed for its essential fundamental principle, which only shines, more or less dimly, through its concrete expression. Since public opinion possesses within itself no standard of discrimination, no capacity to rise to a recognition of the substantial, independence of it is the first formal condition of any great and rational enterprise (in actuality as well as in science). Anything great and rational is eventually sure to please public opinion, to be espoused by it, and to be made one of its prepossessions.

In public opinion all is false and true, but to discover the truth in it is the business of the great man. The great man of his time is he who expresses the will and the meaning of that time, and then brings it to completion; he acts according to the inner spirit and essence of his time, which he realizes. And he who does not understand how to despise public opinion, as it makes itself heard here and there, will never accomplish anything great.

Freedom of the Press The freedom of public utterance (of which the press is one means, having advantage over speech in its more extended reach, though inferior to it in vivacity), the gratification of that prickling impulse to express and to have expressed one's opinion, is directly controlled by the police and State laws and regulations, which partly hinder and partly punish its excesses. The indirect guarantee lies in its innocuousness, and this again is mainly based on the rationality of the constitution, the stability of the government, and also on the publicity given to the assemblies of the classes. Another security is offered by the indifference and contempt with which insipid and malicious words are, as a rule, quickly met.

The definition of the freedom of the press as freedom to say and write what one pleases, is parallel to the one of freedom in general, viz., as freedom to do what one pleases. Such view belongs to the uneducated crudity and superficiality of naïve thinking. The press, with its infinite variety of content and expression, represents what is most transient, particular, and accidental in human opinion. Beyond the direct incitation to theft, murder, revolt, etc., lies the art of cultivating the expression which in itself seems general and indefinite enough, but which, in a measure, conceals a perfectly definite meaning. Such expressions are partly responsible for consequences of which, since they are not actually expressed, one is never sure how far they are contained in the utterances and really follow from them. It is this indefiniteness of the content and form of the press which prevents the laws governing it from assuming that precision which one demands of laws. Thus the extreme subjectivity of the wrong, injury, and crime committed by the press, causes the decision and sentence to be equally subjective. The laws are not only indefinite, but the press can, by the skill and subtlety of its expressions, evade them, or criticise the judgment of the court as wholly arbitrary. Furthermore, if the utterance of the press is treated as an offensive deed, one may retort that it is not a deed at all, but only an opinion, a thought, a mere saying. Consequently, impunity is expected for opinions and words, because they are merely subjective, trivial, and insignificant, and, in the same breath, great respect and esteem is demanded for these opinions and words – for the opinions, because they are mine and my mental property, and for the words, because they are the free expression and use of that property. And yet the basic principle remains that injury to the honor of individuals generally, abuse, libel, contemptuous caricaturing of the government, its officers and officials, especially the person of the prince, defiance of the laws, incitement to revolt, etc., are all offenses and crimes of different grades.

However, the peculiar and dangerous effect of these acts for the individuals, the community, and the State depends upon the nature of the soil on which they are committed, just as a spark, if thrown upon a heap of gunpowder, has a much more dangerous result than if thrown on the mere ground, where it vanishes and leaves no trace. But, on the whole, a good many such acts, though punishable by law, may come under a certain kind of Nemesis which internal impotence is forced to bring about. In entering upon opposition to the superior talents and virtues, by which impotence feels oppressed, it comes to a realization of its inferiority and to a consciousness of its own nothingness, and the Nemesis, even when bad and odious, is, by treating it with contempt, rendered ineffectual. Like the public, which forms a circle for such activity, it is confined to a harmless malicious joy, and to a condemnation which reflects upon itself.

Meaning of War[2] There is an ethical element in war. It must not be regarded as an absolute ill, or as merely an external calamity which is accidentally based upon the passions of despotic individuals or nations, upon acts of injustice, and, in general, upon what ought not to be. The recognition of the finite, such as property and life, as accidental, is necessary. This necessity is at first wont to appear under the form of a force of nature, for all things finite are mortal and transient. In the ethical order, in the State, however, nature is robbed of its force, and the necessity is exalted to a work of freedom, to an ethical law. The transient and negative nature of all things is transformed in the State into an expression of the ethical will. War, often painted by edifying speech as a state in which the vanity of temporal things is demonstrated, now becomes an element whereby the ideal character of the particular receives its right and reality. War has the deep meaning that by it the ethical health of the nations is preserved and their finite aims uprooted. And as the winds which sweep over the ocean prevent the decay that would result from its perpetual calm, so war protects the people from the corruption which an everlasting peace would bring upon it. History shows phases which illustrate how successful wars have checked internal unrest and have strengthened the entire stability of the State.

In peace, civic life becomes more extended, every sphere is hedged in and grows immobile, and at last all men stagnate, their particular nature becoming more and more hardened and ossified.

Only in the unity of a body is health, and, where the organs become still, there is death. Eternal peace is often demanded as an ideal toward which mankind should move. Thus Kant proposed an alliance of princes, which should settle the controversies of States, and the Holy Alliance probably aspired to be an institution of this kind. The State, however, is individual, and in individuality negation is essentially contained. A number of States may constitute themselves into a family, but this confederation, as an individuality, must create an opposition and so beget an enemy. Not only do nations issue forth invigorated from their wars, but those nations torn by internal strife win peace at home as a result of war abroad. War indeed causes insecurity in property, but this real insecurity is only a necessary commotion. From the pulpits much is preached concerning the insecurity, vanity, and instability of temporal things, and yet every one, though he may be touched by his own words, thinks that he, at least, will manage to hold on to his possessions. Let the insecurity finally come, in the form of Hussars with glistening sabres, and show its earnest activity, and that touching edification which foresaw all this now turns upon the enemy with curses. In spite of this, wars will break out whenever necessity demands them; but the seeds spring up anew, and speech is silenced before the grave repetitions of history.

The military class is the class of universality. The defense of the State is its privilege, and its duty is to realize the ideality contained in it, which consists in self-sacrifice. There are different kinds of bravery. The courage of the animal, or the robber, the bravery which arises from a sense of honor, the chivalrous bravery, are not yet the true forms of bravery. In civilized nations true bravery consists in the readiness to give oneself wholly to the service of the State, so that the individual counts but as one among many. Not personal valor alone is significant; the important aspect of it lies in self-subordination to the universal cause.

To risk one's life is indeed something more than mere fear of death, but this is only negative; only a positive character – an aim and content – gives meaning to bravery. Robbers and murderers in the pursuit of crime, adventurers in the search of their fanciful objects, etc., also possess courage, and do not fear death. The principle of the modern world – the power of thought and of the universal – has given to bravery a higher form; the higher form causes the expression of bravery to appear more mechanical. The brave deeds are not the deeds of any particular person, but those of the members of a whole. And, again, since hostility is directed, not against separate individuals, but against a hostile whole, personal valor appears as impersonal. This principle it is which has caused the invention of the gun; it is not a chance invention that has brought about the change of the mere personal form of bravery into the more abstract.

International Relations Just as the individual is not a real person unless related to other persons, so the State is no real individuality unless related to other States. The legitimate power of a State, and more especially its princely power, is, from the point of view of its foreign relations, a wholly internal affair. A State shall, therefore, not interfere with the internal affairs of another State. On the other hand, for a complete State, it is essential that it be recognized by others; but this recognition demands as a guarantee that it shall recognize those States which recognize it, and shall respect their independence. Hence its internal affairs cannot be a matter of indifference to them.

When Napoleon, before the peace of Campoformio, said, "The French Republic requires recognition as little as the sun needs to be recognized," his words suggest nothing but the strength of existence, which already carries with it the guarantee of recognition, without needing to be expressed.

When the particular wills of the State can come to no agreement their controversy can be decided only by war. What offense shall be regarded as a breach of treaty, or as a violation of respect and honor, must remain indefinite, since many and various injuries can easily accrue from the wide range of the interests of the States and from the complex relations of their citizens. The State may identify its infinitude and honor with every one of its single aspects. And if a State, as a strong individuality, has experienced an unduly protracted internal rest, it will naturally be more inclined to irritability, in order to find an occasion and field for intense activity.

The nations of Europe form a family according to the universal principle of their legislation, their ethical code, and their civilization. But the relation among States fluctuates, and no judge exists to adjust their differences. The higher judge is the universal and absolute Spirit alone – the World-Spirit.

The relation of one particular State to another presents, on the largest possible scale, the most shifting play of individual passions, interests, aims, talents, virtues, power, injustice, vice, and mere external chance. It is a play in which even the ethical whole, the independence of the State, is exposed to accident. The principles which control the many national spirits are limited. Each nation as an existing individuality is guided by its particular principles, and only as a particular individuality can each national spirit win objectivity and self-consciousness; but the fortunes and deeds of States in their relation to one another reveal the dialectic of the finite nature of these spirits. Out of this dialectic rises the universal Spirit, the unlimited World-Spirit, pronouncing its judgment – and its judgment is the highest – upon the finite nations of the world's history; for the history of the world is the world's court of justice.

NOTES

1 "The voice of the people [is] the voice of God"; "The ignorant vulgar reproaches everybody and speaks most of what it understands least."

2 Hegel has been accused of glorifying war in this section. He would surely reply that he is simply being realistic and reminding readers of some undeniable truths, unpalatable as these may be. Fighting a war may have beneficial results for a nation, ranging from stamping out of corruption to promoting social camaraderie; and nothing is more effective in cultivating a people's sense of unity and identity than its corresponding sense of another people as a hostile "Other."

John Stuart Mill, *On Liberty*, Chapter 1

Introduction

John Stuart Mill's (1806–73) *On Liberty* (1859) has become the most famous of all philosophical defenses of human freedoms, and the best known of his many writings on subjects ranging from logic and epistemology to the emancipation of women and the condition of India. It is a reasonable bet, in modern democratic societies, that people outraged by what they perceive as illegitimate interference with a freedom – by compulsory seat-belts, a ban on fox-hunting, censorship, or whatever – will, often indiscriminately, cite remarks from this book in their support. In particular, they will invoke the "very simple principle," articulated in Chapter 1, to the effect that interference with a person's liberty of action may be justified only in terms of "self-protection" and the prevention of "harm to others." That people disapprove of my actions or opinions, or are offended by them, is never in itself a sufficient reason to interfere with the way I live my life and express my views.

Despite its fame and popularity, *On Liberty* is frequently misunderstood by those who invoke it. For one thing, the work is not, as often imagined, primarily concerned with the limits of the author-ity of the state. In the opening pages, Mill makes it clear that in democratic societies the main

From John Stuart Mill, *Three Essays*, Oxford: Oxford University Press, 1975, pp. 5–20 (final paragraph omitted).

threats to individual liberty come not from gov-ernments, but from "the tyranny of the majority" – from the tendency of a typically anonymous "public" and its spokesmen to suppress views and behavior that fail to conform to its predilec-tions.[1] (Had Mill been writing today, one suspects, he would have been equally concerned by the "tyranny" of some minorities – religious ones, in particular – that threaten violence unless books, plays, cartoons, or whatever which they find "deeply offensive" are banned.)

Second, Mill is often construed as an early champion of "human rights" – of what used to be called "natural" or "abstract" rights. Mill is, it is true, less dismissive of this notion than his godfather, Jeremy Bentham ("the father of utili-tarianism"; c. 1748–1832), who described talk of such rights as "nonsense on stilts." But it is also true that Mill explicitly rejects "any advantage which could be derived to my argument from the idea of abstract right, as a thing independent of utility." His case for individual liberty is, officially at least, entirely grounded in an appeal to utility – to the principle of "the greatest happiness of the greatest number." It is not people's right to indulge their personal tastes, say, which makes it wrong to prevent them from doing so. Rather, it is partly the fact that such indulgence does not genuinely harm other people, and partly the fact that employment of a "moral police" to control people's "self-regarding" behavior almost certainly will cause harm. The "strongest" argument, writes Mill, against interference with "purely personal conduct" is that it is likely to be misguided and "in the wrong place." Individuals, after all, are likely to be better judges of what conduces to their own happiness than are "the moral police" and their employers.

While Mill's defense of liberty is "officially" a purely utilitarian one, there are however also many places in his writings – including Chapter 3 ("Of Individuality") of *On Liberty* and *The Subjection of Women* – that powerfully convey the impression that, for Mill, individuality is valuable in itself, irrespective of its contribution to general happiness. Thus, in the latter work, Mill writes that, while restraint on freedom is undesirable because it may well dry "up the principal fountain of human happiness," it is also so because it tends to impoverish "all that makes life valuable to the individual."[2] The creative, unconstrained individual, who is not guilty of "ape-like imitation," one discovers in *On Liberty*, is not only "valuable to others" but also, equally important, "more valuable to himself."

If *On Liberty* remains undiminished in its impact on modern political and social debate, it remains controversial too among political philosophers. Critical debate has especially focused on the viability of Mill's crucial distinction between "self-regarding" actions ("purely personal conduct"), which should be immune to interference, and "other-regarding actions," which should not. Don't all tastes, opinions and behavior, however "personal" – so critics complain – have repercussions for others? But whether or not a reasonably precise distinction may be drawn between the two classes of action, there is no gainsaying the importance – especially in our present times, perhaps – of Mill's insistence that the "harm" caused to some people by opinions and speech that they try to suppress is a function of their own intolerance and fanaticism.

Notes

1 This concept was first elaborated by Alexis de Tocqueville in his *Democracy in America*, the first volume of which Mill had enthusiastically reviewed the year it appeared (1835).

2 *The Subjection of Women*, Indianapolis, IN: Hackett, 1988, p. 109. This rousing work was significantly inspired by the views of Mill's "most valued friend," and later wife, Harriet Taylor, who under Mill's name, wrote *The Enfranchisement of Women* and seems to have contributed to the re-writing of *On Liberty*. In an 1854 letter to Taylor, Mill remarked: "I shall never be satisfied unless you allow our best book, the book which is to come [perhaps *On Liberty* – eds], to have our two names on the title page. It ought to be so with everything I publish, for the better half of it all is yours."

Mill, *On Liberty*

CHAPTER I

Introductory The subject of this Essay is not the so-called Liberty of the Will, so unfortunately opposed to the misnamed doctrine of Philosophical Necessity; but Civil, or Social Liberty: the nature and limits of the power which can be legitimately exercised by society over the individual. A question seldom stated, and hardly ever discussed, in general terms, but which profoundly influences the practical controversies of the age by its latent presence, and is likely soon to make itself recognized as the vital question of the future. It is so far from being new, that, in a certain sense, it has divided mankind, almost from the remotest ages; but in the stage of progress into which the more civilized portions of the species have now entered, it presents itself under new conditions, and requires a different and more fundamental treatment.

The struggle between Liberty and Authority is the most conspicuous feature in the portions of history with which we are earliest familiar, particularly in that of Greece, Rome, and England. But in old times this contest was between subjects, or some classes of subjects, and the Government. By liberty, was meant protection against the tyranny of the political rulers. The rulers were conceived (except in some of the popular governments of Greece) as in a necessarily antagonistic position to the people whom they ruled. They consisted of a governing One, or a governing tribe or caste, who derived their authority from inheritance or conquest, who, at all events, did not hold it at the pleasure of the governed, and whose supremacy men did not venture, perhaps did not desire, to contest, whatever precautions might be taken against its oppressive exercise. Their power was regarded as necessary, but also as highly dangerous; as a weapon which they would attempt to use against their subjects, no less than against external enemies. To prevent the weaker members of the community from being preyed upon by innumerable vultures, it was needful that there should be an animal of prey stronger than the rest, commissioned to keep them down. But as the king of the vultures would be no less bent upon preying on the flock than any of the minor harpies, it was indispensable to be in a perpetual attitude of defence against his beak and claws. The aim, therefore, of patriots was to set limits to the power which the ruler should be suffered to exercise over the community; and this limitation was what they meant by liberty. It was attempted in two ways. First, by obtaining a recognition of certain immunities, called political liberties or rights, which it was to be regarded as a breach of duty in the ruler to infringe, and which, if he did infringe, specific resistance, or general rebellion, was held to be justifiable. A second, and generally a later expedient, was the establishment of constitutional checks, by which the consent of the community, or of a body of some sort, supposed to represent its interests, was made a necessary condition to some of the more important acts of the governing power. To the first of these modes of limitation, the ruling power, in most European countries, was compelled, more or less, to submit. It was not so with the second; and, to attain this, or when already in some degree possessed, to attain it more completely, became everywhere the principal object of the lovers of liberty. And so long as mankind were content to combat one enemy by another, and to be ruled by a master, on condition of being guaranteed more or less efficaciously against his tyranny, they did not carry their aspirations beyond this point.

A time, however, came, in the progress of human affairs, when men ceased to think it a necessity of nature that their governors should be an independent power, opposed in interest to themselves. It appeared to them much better that the various magistrates of the State should be their tenants or delegates, revocable at their pleasure. In that way alone, it seemed, could they have complete security that the powers of government would never be abused to their disadvantage. By degrees this new demand for elective and temporary rulers became the prominent object of the exertions of the popular party, wherever any such party existed; and superseded, to a considerable extent, the previous efforts to limit the power of rulers. As the struggle proceeded for making the ruling power emanate from the periodical choice of the ruled, some persons began to think that too much importance had been attached to the limitation of the power itself. *That* (it might seem) was a resource against rulers whose interests were habitually opposed to those of the people. What was now wanted was, that the rulers should be identified with the people; that their interest and will should be the interest and will of the nation. The nation did not need to be protected against its own will. There was no fear of its tyrannizing over itself. Let the rulers be effectually responsible to it, promptly removable by it, and it could afford to trust them with power of which it could itself dictate the use to be made. Their power was but the nation's own power, concentrated, and in a form convenient for exercise. This mode of thought, or rather perhaps of feeling, was common among the last generation of European liberalism, in the Continental section of which it still apparently predominates. Those who admit any limit to what a government may do, except in the case of such governments as they think ought not to exist, stand out as brilliant exceptions among the political thinkers of the Continent. A similar tone of sentiment might by this time have been prevalent in our own country, if the circumstances which for a time encouraged it, had continued unaltered.

But, in political and philosophical theories, as well as in persons, success discloses faults and infirmities which failure might have concealed from observation. The notion, that the people have no need to limit their power over themselves, might seem axiomatic, when popular government was a thing only dreamed about, or read of as having existed at some distant period of the past. Neither was that notion necessarily disturbed by such temporary aberrations as those of the

French Revolution, the worst of which were the work of an usurping few, and which, in any case, belonged, not to the permanent working of popular institutions, but to a sudden and convulsive outbreak against monarchical and aristocratic despotism. In time, however, a democratic republic came to occupy a large portion of the earth's surface, and made itself felt as one of the most powerful members of the community of nations; and elective and responsible government became subject to the observations and criticisms which wait upon a great existing fact. It was now perceived that such phrases as 'self-government', and 'the power of the people over themselves', do not express the true state of the case. The 'people' who exercise the power are not always the same people with those over whom it is exercised; and the 'self-government' spoken of is not the government of each by himself, but of each by all the rest. The will of the people, moreover, practically means the will of the most numerous or the most active *part* of the people; the majority, or those who succeed in making themselves accepted as the majority; the people, consequently, *may* desire to oppress a part of their number; and precautions are as much needed against this as against any other abuse of power. The limitation, therefore, of the power of government over individuals loses none of its importance when the holders of power are regularly accountable to the community, that is, to the strongest party therein. This view of things, recommending itself equally to the intelligence of thinkers and to the inclination of those important classes in European society to whose real or supposed interests democracy is adverse, has had no difficulty in establishing itself; and in political speculations 'the tyranny of the majority' is now generally included among the evils against which society requires to be on its guard.

Like other tyrannies, the tyranny of the majority was at first, and is still vulgarly, held in dread, chiefly as operating through the acts of the public authorities. But reflecting persons perceived that when society is itself the tyrant – society collectively, over the separate individuals who compose it – its means of tyrannizing are not restricted to the acts which it may do by the hands of its political functionaries. Society can and does execute its own mandates: and if it issues wrong mandates instead of right, or any mandates at all in things with which it ought not to meddle, it practises a social tyranny more formidable than many kinds of political oppression, since, though not usually upheld by such extreme penalties, it leaves fewer means of escape, penetrating much more deeply into the details of life, and enslaving the soul itself. Protection, therefore, against the tyranny of the magistrate is not enough: there needs protection also against the tyranny of the prevailing opinion and feeling; against the tendency of society to impose, by other means than civil penalties, its own ideas and practices as rules of conduct on those who dissent from them; to fetter the development, and, if possible, prevent the formation, of any individuality not in harmony with its ways, and compel all characters to fashion themselves upon the model of its own. There is a limit to the legitimate interference of collective opinion with individual independence: and to find that limit, and maintain it against encroachment, is as indispensable to a good condition of human affairs, as protection against political despotism.

But though this proposition is not likely to be contested in general terms, the practical question, where to place the limit – how to make the fitting adjustment between individual independence and social control – is a subject on which nearly everything remains to be done. All that makes existence valuable to any one, depends on the enforcement of restraints upon the actions of other people. Some rules of conduct, therefore, must be imposed, by law in the first place, and by opinion on many things which are not fit subjects for the operation of law. What these rules should be, is the principal question in human affairs; but if we except a few of the most obvious cases, it is one of those which least progress has been made in resolving. No two ages, and scarcely any two countries, have decided it alike; and the decision of one age or country is a wonder to another. Yet the people of any given age and country no more suspect any difficulty in it, than if it were a subject on which mankind had always been agreed. The rules which obtain among themselves appear to them self-evident and self-justifying. This all but universal illusion is one of the examples of the magical influence of custom, which is not only, as the proverb says, a second nature, but is continually mistaken for the first. The effect of custom, in preventing any misgiving respecting the rules of conduct which mankind impose on one another, is all the more complete because the subject is one on which it is not generally considered necessary that reasons should be given, either by one person to others, or by each to himself. People are accustomed to believe, and have been encouraged in the belief by some who aspire to the character of philosophers, that their feelings, on subjects of this nature, are better than reasons, and render reasons unnecessary. The practical principle which guides them to their opinions on the regulation of human conduct, is the feeling in each person's mind that everybody should be required to act as he, and those with whom he sympathizes, would like them to act. No one, indeed, acknowledges to himself that his standard of judgement is his own liking; but an opinion on a point of conduct, not supported by reasons, can only count as one person's preference; and if the reasons, when given, are a mere appeal to a similar preference felt by other people, it is still only many people's liking instead of one. To an ordinary man, however, his own preference, thus supported, is not only a perfectly satisfactory reason, but the only one he generally has for any of his notions of morality, taste, or propriety, which are not expressly written in his religious creed; and his chief guide in the interpretation even of that. Men's opinions, accordingly, on what is laudable or blameable, are affected by all the multifarious causes which influence their wishes in regard to the conduct of others, and which are as numerous as those which determine their wishes on any other subject. Sometimes their reason – at other times their prejudices or superstitions: often their social affections, not seldom their antisocial ones, their envy or jealousy, their arrogance or contemptuousness: but most commonly, their desires or fears for themselves – their legitimate or illegitimate self-interest. Wherever there is an ascendant class, a large portion of the morality of the country emanates from its class interests, and its feelings of class superiority. The morality between Spartans and Helots, between planters and negroes, between princes and subjects, between nobles and roturiers [commoners], between men and women, has been for the most part the creation of these class interests and feelings: and the sentiments thus generated, react in turn upon the moral feelings of the members of the ascendant class, in their relations among themselves. Where, on the other hand, a class, formerly ascendant, has lost its ascendancy, or where its

ascendancy is unpopular, the prevailing moral sentiments frequently bear the impress of an impatient dislike of superiority. Another grand determining principle of the rules of conduct, both in act and forbearance, which have been enforced by law or opinion, has been the servility of mankind towards the supposed preferences or aversions of their temporal masters, or of their gods. This servility, though essentially selfish, is not hypocrisy; it gives rise to perfectly genuine sentiments of abhorrence; it made men burn magicians and heretics. Among so many baser influences, the general and obvious interests of society have of course had a share, and a large one, in the direction of the moral sentiments: less, however, as a matter of reason, and on their own account, than as a consequence of the sympathies and antipathies which grew out of them: and sympathies and antipathies which had little or nothing to do with the interests of society, have made themselves felt in the establishment of moralities with quite as great force.

The likings and dislikings of society, or of some powerful portion of it, are thus the main thing which has practically determined the rules laid down for general observance, under the penalties of law or opinion. And in general, those who have been in advance of society in thought and feeling, have left this condition of things unassailed in principle, however they may have come into conflict with it in some of its details. They have occupied themselves rather in inquiring what things society ought to like or dislike, than in questioning whether its likings or dislikings should be a law to individuals. They preferred endeavouring to alter the feelings of mankind on the particular points on which they were themselves heretical, rather than make common cause in defence of freedom, with heretics generally. The only case in which the higher ground has been taken on principle and maintained with consistency, by any but an individual here and there, is that of religious belief: a case instructive in many ways, and not least so as forming a most striking instance of the fallibility of what is called the moral sense: for the *odium theologicum*, in a sincere bigot, is one of the most unequivocal cases of moral feeling. Those who first broke the yoke of what called itself the Universal [ie, Catholic] Church, were in general as little willing to permit difference of religious opinion as that church itself. But when the heat of the conflict was over, without giving a complete victory to any party, and each church or sect was reduced to limit its hopes to retaining possession of the ground it already occupied; minorities, seeing that they had no chance of becoming majorities, were under the necessity of pleading to those whom they could not convert, for permission to differ. It is accordingly on this battle-field, almost solely, that the rights of the individual against society have been asserted on broad grounds of principle, and the claim of society to exercise authority over dissentients, openly controverted. The great writers to whom the world owes what religious liberty it possesses, have mostly asserted freedom of conscience as an indefeasible right, and denied absolutely that a human being is accountable to others for his religious belief. Yet so natural to mankind is intolerance in whatever they really care about, that religious freedom has hardly anywhere been practically realized, except where religious indifference, which dislikes to have its peace disturbed by theological quarrels, has added its weight to the scale. In the minds of almost all religious persons, even in the most tolerant countries, the duty of toleration is admitted with tacit reserves. One person will bear with dissent in matters of church government, but not of dogma; another can tolerate everybody, short of a Papist or a Unitarian; another, every one who believes in revealed religion; a few extend their charity a little further, but stop at the belief in a God and in a future state. Wherever the sentiment of the majority is still genuine and intense, it is found to have abated little of its claim to be obeyed.

In England, from the peculiar circumstances of our political history, though the yoke of opinion is perhaps heavier, that of law is lighter, than in most other countries of Europe; and there is considerable jealousy of direct interference, by the legislative or the executive power, with private conduct; not so much from any just regard for the independence of the individual, as from the still subsisting habit of looking on the government as representing an opposite interest to the public. The majority have not yet learnt to feel the power of the government their power, or its opinions their opinions. When they do so, individual liberty will probably be as much exposed to invasion from the government, as it already is from public opinion. But, as yet, there is a considerable amount of feeling ready to be called forth against any attempt of the law to control individuals in things in which they have not hitherto been accustomed to be controlled by it; and this with very little discrimination as to whether the matter is, or is not, within the legitimate sphere of legal control; insomuch that the feeling, highly salutary on the whole, is perhaps quite as often misplaced as well grounded in the particular instances of its application. There is, in fact, no recognized principle by which the propriety or impropriety of government interference is customarily tested. People decide according to their personal preferences. Some, whenever they see any good to be done, or evil to be remedied, would willingly instigate the government to undertake the business; while others prefer to bear almost any amount of social evil, rather than add one to the departments of human interests amenable to governmental control. And men range themselves on one or the other side in any particular case, according to this general direction of their sentiments; or according to the degree of interest which they feel in the particular thing which it is proposed that the government should do, or according to the belief they entertain that the government would, or would not, do it in the manner they prefer; but very rarely on account of any opinion to which they consistently adhere, as to what things are fit to be done by a government. And it seems to me that in consequence of this absence of rule or principle, one side is at present as often wrong as the other; the interference of government is, with about equal frequency, improperly invoked and improperly condemned.

The object of this Essay is to assert one very simple principle, as entitled to govern absolutely the dealings of society with the individual in the way of compulsion and control, whether the means used be physical force in the form of legal penalties, or the moral coercion of public opinion. That principle is, that the sole end for which mankind are warranted, individually or collectively, in interfering with the liberty of action of any of their number, is self-protection. That the only purpose for which power can be rightfully exercised over any member of a civilized community, against his will, is to prevent harm to others. His own good, either physical or moral, is not a sufficient warrant. He cannot rightfully be compelled to do or forbear because it will be better for him to do so, because it will make him happier, because, in the opinions of others, to do so would be wise, or even right. These are good reasons for remonstrating with him, or reasoning with him, or persuading him, or entreating him, but not for compelling him, or visiting him with any evil in case he do otherwise. To justify that, the conduct from which it is desired to deter him, must be calculated to produce evil to some one else. The only part of the conduct of any one, for which he is amenable to society, is that which concerns others. In the part which merely concerns himself, his independence is, of right, absolute. Over himself, over his own body and mind, the individual is sovereign.

It is, perhaps, hardly necessary to say that this doctrine is meant to apply only to human beings in the maturity of their faculties. We are not speaking of children, or of young persons below the age which the law may fix as that of manhood or womanhood. Those who are still in a state to require being taken care of by others, must be protected against their own actions as well as against external injury. For the same reason, we may leave out of consideration those backward states of society in which the race itself may be considered as in its nonage. The early difficulties in the way of spontaneous progress are so great, that there is seldom any choice of means for overcoming them; and a ruler full of the spirit of improvement is warranted in the use of any expedients that will attain an end, perhaps otherwise unattainable. Despotism is a legitimate mode of government in dealing with barbarians, provided the end be their improvement, and the means justified by actually effecting that end. Liberty, as a principle, has no application to any state of things anterior to the time when mankind have become capable of being improved by free and equal discussion. Until then, there is nothing for them but implicit obedience to an Akbar or a Charlemagne, if they are so fortunate as to find one. But as soon as mankind have attained the capacity of being guided to their own improvement by conviction or persuasion (a period long since reached in all nations with whom we need here concern ourselves), compulsion, either in the direct form or in that of pains and penalties for non-compliance, is no longer admissible as a means to their own good, and justifiable only for the security of others.

It is proper to state that I forgo any advantage which could be derived to my argument from the idea of abstract right, as a thing independent of utility. I regard utility as the ultimate appeal on all ethical questions; but it must be utility in the largest sense, grounded on the permanent interests of man as a progressive being. Those interests, I contend, authorize the subjection of individual spontaneity to external control, only in respect to those actions of each, which concern the interest of other people. If any one does an act hurtful to others, there is a prima facie case for punishing him, by law, or, where legal penalties are not safely applicable, by general disapprobation. There are also many positive acts for the benefit of others, which he may rightfully be compelled to perform; such as, to give evidence in a court of justice; to bear his fair share in the common defence, or in any other joint work necessary to the interest of the society of which he enjoys the protection; and to perform certain acts of individual beneficence, such as saving a fellow creature's life, or interposing to protect the defenceless against ill-usage, things which whenever it is obviously a man's duty to do, he may rightfully be made responsible to society for not doing. A person may cause evil to others not only by his actions but by his inaction, and in either case he is justly accountable to them for the injury. The latter case, it is true, requires a much more cautious exercise of compulsion than the former. To make any one answerable for doing evil to others, is the rule; to make him answerable for not preventing evil, is, comparatively speaking, the exception. Yet there are many cases clear enough and grave enough to justify that exception. In all things which regard the external relations of the individual, he is *de jure* amenable to those whose interests are concerned, and if need be, to society as their protector. There are often good reasons for not holding him to the responsibility; but these reasons must arise from the special expediencies of the case: either because it is a kind of case in which he is on the whole likely to act better, when left to his own discretion, than when controlled in any way in which society have it in their power to control him; or because the attempt to exercise control would produce other evils, greater than those which it would prevent. When such reasons as these preclude the enforcement of responsibility, the conscience of the agent himself should step into the vacant judgement-seat, and protect those interests of others which have no external protection;

judging himself all the more rigidly, because the case does not admit of his being made accountable to the judgement of his fellow creatures.

But there is a sphere of action in which society, as distinguished from the individual, has, if any, only an indirect interest; comprehending all that portion of a person's life and conduct which affects only himself, or if it also affects others, only with their free, voluntary, and undeceived consent and participation. When I say only himself, I mean directly, and in the first instance: for whatever affects himself, may affect others through himself; and the objection which may be grounded on this contingency will receive consideration in the sequel. This, then, is the appropriate region of human liberty. It comprises, first, the inward domain of consciousness; demanding liberty of conscience, in the most comprehensive sense; liberty of thought and feeling; absolute freedom of opinion and sentiment on all subjects, practical or speculative, scientific, moral, or theological. The liberty of expressing and publishing opinions may seem to fall under a different principle, since it belongs to that part of the conduct of an individual which concerns other people; but, being almost of as much importance as the liberty of thought itself, and resting in great part on the same reasons, is practically inseparable from it. Secondly, the principle requires liberty of tastes and pursuits; of framing the plan of our life to suit our own character; of doing as we like, subject to such consequences as may follow: without impediment from our fellow creatures, so long as what we do does not harm them, even though they should think our conduct foolish, perverse, or wrong. Thirdly, from this liberty of each individual, follows the liberty, within the same limits, of combination among individuals; freedom to unite, for any purpose not involving harm to others: the persons combining being supposed to be of full age, and not forced or deceived.

No society in which these liberties are not, on the whole, respected, is free, whatever may be its form of government; and none is completely free in which they do not exist absolute and unqualified. The only freedom which deserves the name, is that of pursuing our own good in our own way, so long as we do not attempt to deprive others of theirs, or impede their efforts to obtain it. Each is the proper guardian of his own health, whether bodily, or mental and spiritual. Mankind are greater gainers by suffering each other to live as seems good to themselves, than by compelling each to live as seems good to the rest.

Though this doctrine is anything but new, and, to some persons, may have the air of a truism, there is no doctrine which stands more directly opposed to the general tendency of existing opinion and practice. Society has expended fully as much effort in the attempt (according to its lights) to compel people to conform to its notions of personal, as of social excellence. The ancient commonwealths thought themselves entitled to practise, and the ancient philosophers countenanced, the regulation of every part of private conduct by public authority, on the ground that the State had a deep interest in the whole bodily and mental discipline of every one of its citizens; a mode of thinking which may have been admissible in small republics surrounded by powerful enemies, in constant peril of being subverted by foreign attack or internal commotion, and to which even a short interval of relaxed energy and self-command might so easily be fatal, that they could not afford to wait for the salutary permanent effects of freedom. In the modern world, the greater size of political communities, and, above all, the separation between spiritual and temporal authority (which placed the direction of men's consciences in other hands than those which controlled their worldly affairs), prevented so great an interference by law in the details of private life; but the engines of moral repression have been wielded more strenuously against divergence from the reigning opinion in self-regarding, than even in social matters; religion, the most powerful of the elements which have entered into the formation of moral feeling, having almost always been governed either by the ambition of a hierarchy, seeking control over every department of human conduct, or by the spirit of Puritanism. And some of those modern reformers who have placed themselves in strongest opposition to the religions of the past, have been no way behind either churches or sects in their assertion of the right of spiritual domination: M. Comte, in particular, whose social system, as unfolded in his *Système de Politique Positive*, aims at establishing (though by moral more than by legal appliances) a despotism of society over the individual, surpassing anything contemplated in the political ideal of the most rigid disciplinarian among the ancient philosophers.[1]

Apart from the peculiar tenets of individual thinkers, there is also in the world at large an increasing inclination to stretch unduly the powers of society over the individual, both by the force of opinion and even by that of legislation: and as the tendency of all the changes taking place in the world is to strengthen society, and diminish the power of the individual, this encroachment is not one of the evils which tend spontaneously to disappear, but, on the contrary, to grow more and more formidable. The disposition of mankind, whether as rulers or as fellow citizens, to impose their own opinions and inclinations as a rule of conduct on others, is so energetically supported by some of the best and by some of the worst feel-ings incident to human nature, that it is hardly ever kept under restraint by anything but want of power; and as the power is not declining, but growing, unless a strong barrier of moral conviction can be raised against the mischief, we must expect, in the present circumstances of the world, to see it increase.

[...]

Note

1 Auguste Comte (1798–1857), often described as the founder of sociology, advocated a "religion of humanity," solidly grounded in allegedly rational and empirically tested principles, to which the feelings and moral views of individuals should conform.

19

(A) Karl Marx, *Manifesto of the Communist Party* (Sections I and II) and "Theses on Feuerbach"
(B) Vladimir Lenin, *State and Revolution* from Chapters I, II, and III

Introduction

"The Communist Manifesto," as it is popularly known, was commissioned by the Second Congress of the Communist League and published in 1848, the year of revolutions – mainly failed – across continental Europe. Its author was the young and relatively obscure Karl Marx (1818–83). It was to be a long time – until after Marx's death, in fact – that the Manifesto was to exert widespread influence. But when it eventually did so, its compact statement of the principal tenets of Marxism made it the most popular of all texts read by the communist revolutionaries of the twentieth century.[1]

The Manifesto represents an interesting juncture in both the life and thought of Karl Marx. Already in trouble with German authorities for his radical pamphlets, the former law student with a doctorate in philosophy on ancient atomism (I.3) was forced after the publication of the fiery Manifesto into exile in London, where he spent most of the remainder of his life. In London, Marx and his family lived in straitened circumstances, albeit considerably alleviated by the generosity of the

(A) *From The Portable Karl Marx*, ed. Eugene Kamenka, London: Penguin, 1983, pp. 203–28 (some passages omitted) and Lawrence H. Simon, ed., *Karl Marx: Selected Writings*, trans. L. D. Easton and K. H. Guddat, Indianapolis, IN: Hackett Publishing, Co., Inc., 1994, pp. 99–101. (B) *From* Vladimir Ilich Lenin, *State and Revolution*, New York: International Publishers, 1943, pp. 7–20, 29–31, 35–9 (some notes omitted).

well-off Friedrich Engels (1820–95). Prior to the Manifesto, most of Marx's writings had been philosophical in character – reflecting an admiration for the dialectic of G. W. F. Hegel (III.18, V.17) while, at the same time, criticizing Hegel for what Marx saw as the excessively "idealist" character of the dialectic. As Marx saw it, Hegel had placed the dialectic of history "standing on its head"; to understand the world it "must be turned right side up again."[2] In Marx's view the dialectical process of history is driven not primarily not by "ideas" but instead by material or economic dynamics. Several of Marx's early writings, including the posthumously published *Economico-Philosophical Manuscripts*, are devoted to this task of righting Hegel and exploring the implications of this correction for the proper understanding of such central Hegelian notions as that of "alienation." After 1848, Marx wrote little of a philosophical type, focusing instead on his massive tome of economics, *Capital*, and on political pamphleteering. In the Manifesto, one finds both resumés of the earlier philosophical reflections and anticipations of the theories of economics and history that occupied Marx in later years.[3]

In Section I of the Manifesto, there is a succinct account of Marx's "dialectical materialist" story of history. The primary determinant of human life, at any given time, is the "mode of production of material life," for it is this which shapes social relations – notably the economic class relations – between people, relations which, in their turn, are the main determinants of the forms taken by political, cultural, legal, and other dimensions of life. Marx does not have much in the Manifesto explicitly to say about politics and the state, but what he does say neatly encapsulates his considered views, ones that were to be inherited by generations of Marxists after his death.

First, Marx records his view that the political state is principally an instrument for class domination, so that, in his own day, the state is but a "committee" for managing the affairs of the bourgeoisie. Second, Marx draws a significant implication from this perception of the state as "merely the organized power of one class for oppressing another" – namely that, with the communist revolution, and the subsequent abolition of all property (and hence of classes), there will be no need for the state. As Engels was famously to put it in the *Anti-Dühring* (1877), the state will "wither away." Each of these two points reflects a third and wider one – that politics, both organizationally and as a system of ideas and ideals, belongs at a relatively superficial level of social reality. Politics, like religion, law, and literature, is part of the "ideological superstructure" of society – its character shaped by underlying social relations and modes of material production. As Marx explains in Section II of the Manifesto, such contemporary political ideals as those of freedom and the right to property are not, as their champions pretend, eternal moral imperatives, but merely "bourgeois notions" designed to serve the interests of the capitalist class. Marx provided much longer, and less digestible, defenses of his position than the Manifesto. But for clarity and rhetorical force, nothing else he wrote contains the same appeal and power. The final words of the Manifesto – "The proletarians have nothing to lose but their chains. They have a world to win. Working men of all countries, unite!" – are perhaps the most memorable and effective that Marx ever composed.

We include here, in addition to the Manifesto, a selection of one of Marx's most important followers, Vladimir Illyich Ulyanov – aka V. I. Lenin (1870–1924), the leader of the October Revolution and the first head of state of the USSR. Born in the Volga river city of Simbirsk, the second son of a government official, Lenin was radicalized when in 1887 his brother was executed and his sister arrested for conspiring to assassinate Tsar Alexander III. Deciding to "follow a different path" from the populist ideas current at the time, Lenin eventually immersed himself in Marxist

political philosophy. His uncompromising commitment to revolutionary ideals powerfully expressed in Lenin's 1903 pamphlet, *What Is to Be Done?*, helped precipitate the Bolshevik–Menshevik split of the Russian Social Democratic party. His more abstract 1909 *Materialism and Empirico-criticism* argued for an empirically grounded social-political science. Lenin's estrangement from social democratic movements became irreparable when, with the outbreak of World War I, Europe's social democratic parties abandoned international unity in favor of national war efforts. Moving to neutral Switzerland Lenin analyzed the war and the prospects for future revolution in what became his 1916 *Imperialism, the Highest Stage of Capitalism*. After the February Revolution of 1917, Lenin concluded that revolution was imminent in Russia, and he agreed to be transported across hostile Germany in a sealed railroad car, arriving famously on April 16 at St Petersburg's Finland Station amid cheering throngs. It was during that anxious summer between the February and October revolts when Lenin completed the book from which the following selection has been culled. In *State and Revolution* Lenin not only refines Marx's indictment of the capitalist state, he also advances a distinctive argument against anti-statist anarchists for not only the necessity of violent revolution but also of a worker's state, a "dictatorship of the proletariat," to defend the revolution and to nurture it until conditions are right for the state's ultimate evaporation.

Notes

1   See L. Kolakowski, *Main Currents of Marxism*, Vol. I, Oxford: Oxford University Press, 1981, for an account of the historical context and aftermath of the publication of the Manifesto.

2   *Das Kapital*, Afterword to the second German edition (1873).

3   Latter-day Marxists are split on the question of whether the shift of focus away from philosophy to economics was something to welcome. Contrast, for example, Louis Althusser's impatience with the "early," "humanistic" Marx in his *For Marx* (London: Penguin, 1990) with Herbert Marcuse's attempt, in *Reason and Revolution* (New York: Humanities, 1955), to inspire interest in precisely those early views.

(A) Marx, *Manifesto of the Communist Party*

I   Bourgeois and Proletarians

The history of all hitherto existing society is the history of class struggles.

Freeman and slave, patrician and plebeian, lord and serf, guild-master and journeyman, in a word, oppressor and oppressed, stood in constant opposition to one another, carried on an uninterrupted, now hidden, now open fight, a fight that each time ended, either in a revolutionary reconstitution of society at large, or in the common ruin of the contending classes.

In the earlier epochs of history, we find almost everywhere a complicated arrangement of society into various orders, a manifold gradation of social rank. In ancient Rome we have patricians, knights, plebeians, slaves; in the Middle Ages, feudal lords, vassals, guild-masters, journeymen, apprentices, serfs; in almost all of these classes, again, subordinate gradations.

The modern bourgeois society that has sprouted from the ruins of feudal society has not done away with class antagonisms. It has but established new classes, new conditions of oppression, new forms of struggle in place of the old ones.

Our epoch, the epoch of the bourgeoisie, possesses, however, this distinctive feature: It has simplified the class antagonisms. Society as a whole is more and more splitting up into two great hostile camps, into two great classes directly facing each other – bourgeoisie and proletariat.

From the serfs of the Middle Ages sprang the chartered burghers of the earliest towns. From these burgesses the first elements of the bourgeoisie were developed.

The discovery of America, the rounding of the Cape, opened up fresh ground for the rising bourgeoisie. The East-Indian and Chinese markets, the colonisation of America, trade with the colonies, the increase in the means of exchange and in commodities generally, gave to commerce, to navigation, to industry, an impulse never before known, and thereby, to the revolutionary element in the tottering feudal society, a rapid development.

The feudal system of industry, in which industrial production was monopolised by closed guilds, now no longer sufficed for the growing wants of the new markets. The manufacturing system took its place. The guild-masters were pushed aside by the manufacturing middle class; division of labour between the different corporate guilds vanished in the face of division of labour in each single workshop.

Meantime the markets kept ever growing, the demand ever rising. Even manufacture no longer sufficed. Thereupon, steam and machinery revolutionised industrial production. The place of manufacture was taken by the giant, modern industry, the place of the industrial middle class by industrial millionaires, the leaders of whole industrial armies, the modern bourgeois.

Modern industry has established the world market, for which the discovery of America paved the way. This market has given an immense development to commerce, to navigation, to communication by land. This development has, in its turn, reacted on the extension of industry; and in proportion as industry, commerce, navigation, railways extended, in the same proportion the bourgeoisie developed, increased its capital, and pushed into the background every class handed down from the Middle Ages.

We see, therefore, how the modern bourgeoisie is itself the product of a long course of development, of a series of revolutions in the modes of production and of exchange.

Each step in the development of the bourgeoisie was accompanied by a corresponding political advance of that class. An oppressed class under the sway of the feudal nobility, an armed and self-governing association in the medieval commune; here independent urban republic (as in Italy and Germany), there taxable "third estate" of the monarchy (as in France); afterwards, in the period of manufacture proper, serving either the semi-feudal or the absolute monarchy as a counterpoise against the nobility, and, in fact, cornerstone of the great monarchies in general – the bourgeoisie has at last, since the establishment of modern industry and of the world market, conquered for itself, in the modern representative state, exclusive political sway. The executive of the modern state is but a committee for managing the common affairs of the whole bourgeoisie.

The bourgeoisie, historically, has played a most revolutionary part.

The bourgeoisie, wherever it has got the upper hand, has put an end to all feudal, patriarchal, idyllic relations. It has pitilessly torn asunder the motley feudal ties that bound man to his "natural superiors," and has left no other nexus between man and man than naked self-interest, than callous "cash payment." It has drowned the most heavenly ecstasies of religious fervour, of chivalrous enthusiasm, of philistine sentimentalism, in the icy water of egotistical calculation. It has resolved personal worth into exchange value, and in place of the numberless indefeasible chartered freedoms, has set up that single, unconscionable freedom – Free Trade. In one word, for exploitation, veiled by religious and political illusions, it has substituted naked, shameless, direct, brutal exploitation.

The bourgeoisie has stripped of its halo every occupation hitherto honoured and looked up to with reverent awe. It has converted the physician, the lawyer, the priest, the poet, the man of science, into its paid wage labourers.

The bourgeoisie has torn away from the family its sentimental veil, and has reduced the family relation to a mere money relation.

The bourgeoisie has disclosed how it came to pass that the brutal display of vigour in the Middle Ages, which reactionaries so much admire, found its fitting complement in the most slothful indolence. It has been the first to show what man's activity can bring about. It has accomplished wonders far surpassing Egyptian pyramids, Roman aqueducts, and Gothic cathedrals; it has conducted expeditions that put in the shade all former exoduses of nations and crusades.

The bourgeoisie cannot exist without constantly revolutionising the instruments of production, and thereby the relations of production, and with them the whole relations of society. Conservation of the old modes of production in unaltered form was, on the contrary, the first condition of existence for all earlier industrial classes. Constant revolutionising of production, uninterrupted disturbance of all social conditions, everlasting uncertainty and agitation distinguish the bourgeois epoch from all earlier ones. All fixed, fast frozen relations, with their train of ancient and venerable prejudices and opinions, are swept away, all new-formed ones become antiquated before they can ossify. All that is solid melts into air, all that is holy is profaned, and man is at last compelled to face with sober senses his real conditions of life and his relations with his kind.

The need of a constantly expanding market for its products chases the bourgeoisie over the whole surface of the globe. It must nestle everywhere, settle everywhere, establish connections everywhere.

The bourgeoisie has through its exploitation of the world market given a cosmopolitan character to production and consumption in every country. To the great chagrin of reactionaries, it had drawn from under the feet of industry the national ground on which it stood. All old-established national industries have been destroyed or are daily being destroyed. They are dislodged by new industries, whose introduction becomes a life and death question for all civilised nations, by industries that no longer work up indigenous raw material, but raw material drawn from the remotest zones; industries whose products are consumed, not only at home, but in every quarter of the globe. In place of the old wants, satisfied by the production of the country, we find new wants, requiring for their satisfaction the products of distant lands and climes. In place of the old local and national seclusion and self-sufficiency, we have intercourse in every direction, universal inter-dependence of nations. And as in material, so also in intellectual production. The intellectual creations of individual nations become common property. National one-sidedness and narrow-mindedness become more and more impossible, and from the numerous national and local literatures there arises a world literature.

The bourgeoisie, by the rapid improvement of all instruments of production, by the immensely facilitated means of communication, draws all, even the most barbarian, nations into civilisation. The cheap prices of its commodities are the heavy artillery with which it batters down all Chinese walls, with which it forces the barbarians' intensely obstinate hatred of foreigners to capitulate. It compels all nations, on pain of extinction, to adopt the bourgeois mode of production; it compels them to introduce what it calls civilisation into their midst, i.e., to become bourgeois themselves. In one word, it creates a world after its own image.

The bourgeoisie has subjected the country to the rule of the towns. It has created enormous cities, has greatly increased the urban population as compared with the rural, and has thus rescued a considerable part of the population from the idiocy of rural life. Just as it has made the country dependent on the towns, so it has made barbarian and semi-barbarian countries dependent on the civilised ones nations of peasants on nations of bourgeois, the East on the West.

The bourgeoisie keeps more and more doing away with the scattered state of the population, of the means of production, and of property. It has agglomerated population, centralised means of production, and has concentrated property in a few hands. The necessary consequence of this was political centralisation. Independent, or but loosely connected provinces, with separate interests, laws, governments, and systems of taxation, became lumped together into one nation, with one government, one code of laws, one national class interest, one frontier and one customs tariff.

The bourgeoisie, during its rule of scarce one hundred years, has created more massive and more colossal productive forces than have all preceding generations together. Subjection of nature's forces to man, machinery, application of chemistry to industry and agriculture, steam navigation, railways, electric telegraphs, clearing of whole continents for cultivation, canalisation of rivers, whole populations conjured out of the ground – what earlier century had even a presentiment that such productive forces slumbered in the lap of social labour?

We see then: the means of production and of exchange, on whose foundation the bourgeoisie built itself up, were generated in feudal society. At a certain stage in the development of these means of production and of exchange, the conditions under which feudal society produced and exchanged, the feudal organisation of agriculture and manufacturing industry, in one word, the feudal relations of property became no longer compatible with the already developed productive forces; they became so many fetters. They had to be burst asunder; they were burst asunder.

Into their place stepped free competition, accompanied by a social and political constitution adapted to it, and by the economic and political sway of the bourgeois class.

A similar movement is going on before our own eyes. Modern bourgeois society with its relations of production, of exchange and of property, a society that has conjured up such gigantic means of production and of exchange, is like the sorcerer who is no longer able to control the powers of the nether world whom he has called up by his spells.

For many a decade past the history of industry and commerce is but the history of the revolt of modern productive forces against modern conditions of production, against the property relations that are the conditions for the existence of the bourgeoisie and of its rule. It is enough to mention the commercial crises that by their periodical return put the existence of the entire bourgeois society on its trial, each time more threateningly. In these crises a great part not only of the existing products, but also of the previously created productive forces, are periodically destroyed. In these crises there breaks out an epidemic that, in all earlier epochs, would have seemed an absurdity – the epidemic of over-production. Society suddenly finds itself put back into a state of momentary barbarism; it appears as if a famine, a universal war of devastation had cut off the supply of every means of subsistence; industry and commerce seem to be destroyed. And why? Because there is too much civilisation, too much means of subsistence, too much industry, too much commerce. The productive forces at the disposal of society no longer tend to further the development of the conditions of bourgeois property; on the contrary, they have become too powerful for these conditions, by which they are fettered, and so soon as they overcome these fetters, they bring disorder into the whole of bourgeois society, endanger the existence of bourgeois property. The conditions of bourgeois society are too narrow to comprise the wealth created by them. And how does the bourgeoisie get over these crises? On the one hand, by enforced destruction of a mass of productive forces; on the other, by the conquest of new markets, and by the more thorough exploitation of the old ones. That is to say, by paving the way for more extensive and more destructive crises, and by diminishing the means whereby crises are prevented.

The weapons with which the bourgeoisie felled feudalism to the ground are now turned against the bourgeoisie itself.

But not only has the bourgeoisie forged the weapons that bring death to itself; it has also called into existence the men who are to wield those weapons – the modern working class – the proletarians.

In proportion as the bourgeoisie, i.e., capital, is developed, in the same proportion is the proletariat, the modern working class, developed – a class of labourers, who live only so long as they find work, and who find work only so long as their labour increases capital. These labourers, who must sell themselves piecemeal, are a commodity, like every other article of commerce, and are consequently exposed to all the vicissitudes of competition, to all the fluctuations of the market.

Owing to the extensive use of machinery and to division of labour, the work of the proletarians has lost all individual character, and, consequently, all charm for the workman. He becomes an appendage of the machine, and it is only the most simple, most monotonous, and most easily acquired knack, that is required of him. Hence, the cost of production of a workman is restricted, almost entirely, to the means of subsistence that he requires for his maintenance, and for the propagation of his race. But the price of a commodity, and therefore also of labour, is equal to its cost of production. In proportion, therefore, as the repulsiveness of the work increases, the wage decreases. Nay more, in proportion as the use of machinery and division of labour increases, in the same proportion the burden of toil also increases, whether by prolongation of the working hours, by increase of the work exacted in a given time, or by increased speed of the machinery, etc.

Modern industry has converted the little workshop of the patriarchal master into the great factory of the industrial capitalist. Masses of labourers, crowded into the factory, are organised like soldiers. As privates of the industrial army they are placed under the command of a perfect hierarchy of officers and sergeants. Not only are they slaves of the bourgeois class, and of the bourgeois state; they are daily and hourly enslaved by the machine, by the overseer, and, above all, by the individual bourgeois manufacturer himself. The more openly this despotism proclaims gain to be its end and aim, the more petty, the more hateful and the more embittering it is.

The less the skill and exertion of strength implied in manual labour, in other words, the more modern industry becomes developed, the more is the labour of men superseded by that of women. Differences of age and sex have no longer any distinctive social validity for the working class. All are instruments of labour, more or less expensive to use, according to their age and sex.

No sooner is the exploitation of the labourer by the manufacturer, so far at an end, that he receives his wages in cash, than he is set upon by the other portions of the bourgeoisie, the landlord, the shopkeeper, the pawnbroker, etc.

The lower strata of the middle class – the small tradespeople, shopkeepers, and retired tradesmen generally, the handicraftsmen and peasants – all these sink gradually into the proletariat, partly because their diminutive capital does not suffice for the scale on which modern industry is carried on, and is swamped in the competition with the large capitalists, partly because their specialised skill is rendered worthless by new methods of production. Thus the proletariat is recruited from all classes of the population.

The proletariat goes through various stages of development. With its birth begins its struggle with the bourgeoisie. At first the contest is carried on by individual labourers, then by the work people of a factory, then by the operatives of one trade, in one locality, against the individual bourgeois who directly exploits them. They direct their attacks not against the bourgeois conditions of production, but against the instruments of production themselves; they destroy imported wares that compete with their labour, they smash to pieces machinery, they set factories ablaze, they seek to restore by force the vanished status of the workman of the Middle Ages.

At this stage the labourers still form an incoherent mass scattered over the whole country, and broken up by their mutual competition. If anywhere they unite to form more compact bodies, this is not yet the consequence of their own active union, but of the union of the bourgeoisie, which class, in order to attain its own political ends, is compelled to set the whole proletariat in motion, and is moreover yet, for a time, able to do so. At this stage, therefore, the proletarians do not fight their enemies, but the enemies of their enemies, the remnants of absolute monarchy, the landowners, the non-industrial bourgeois, the petty bourgeoisie. Thus the whole historical movement is concentrated in the hands of the bourgeoisie; every victory so obtained is a victory for the bourgeoisie.

But with the development of industry the proletariat not only increases in number; it becomes concentrated in greater masses, its strength grows, and it feels that strength more. The various interests and conditions of life within the ranks of the proletariat are more and more equalised, in proportion as machinery obliterates all distinctions of labour, and nearly everywhere reduces wages to the same low level. The growing competition among the bourgeois, and the resulting commercial crises, make the wages of the workers ever more fluctuating. The unceasing improvement of machinery, ever more rapidly developing, makes their livelihood more and more precarious; the collisions between individual workmen and individual bourgeois take more and more the character of collisions between two classes. Thereupon the workers begin to form combinations (trade unions) against the bourgeois; they club together in order to keep up the rate of wages; they found permanent associations in order to make provision beforehand for these occasional revolts. Here and there the contest breaks out into riots.

Now and then the workers are victorious, but only for a time. The real fruit of their battle lies, not in the immediate result, but in the ever expanding union of the workers. This union is helped on by the improved means of communication that are created by modern industry, and that place the workers of different localities in contact with one another. It was just this contact that was needed to centralise the numerous local struggles, all of the same character, into one national struggle between classes. But every class struggle is a political struggle. And that union, to attain which the burghers of the Middle Ages, with their miserable highways, required centuries, the modern proletarians, thanks to railways, achieve in a few years.

This organisation of the proletarians into a class, and consequently into a political party, is continually being upset again by the competition between the workers themselves. But it ever rises up again, stronger, firmer, mightier. It compels legislative recognition of particular interests of the workers, by taking advantage of the divisions among the bourgeoisie itself. Thus the Ten-Hours Bill in England was carried.

Altogether, collisions between the classes of the old society further in many ways the course of development of the proletariat. The bourgeoisie finds itself involved in a constant battle. At first with the aristocracy; later on, with those portions of the bourgeoisie itself, whose interests have become antagonistic to the progress of industry; at all times with the bourgeoisie of foreign countries. In all these battles it sees itself compelled to appeal to the proletariat, to ask for its help, and thus, to drag it into the political arena.

The bourgeoisie itself, therefore, supplies the proletariat with its own elements of political and general education, in other words, it furnishes the proletariat with weapons for fighting the bourgeoisie.

Further, as we have already seen, entire sections of the ruling classes are, by the advance of industry, precipitated into the proletariat, or are at least threatened in their conditions of existence. These also supply the proletariat with fresh elements of enlightenment and progress.

Finally, in times when the class struggle nears the decisive hour, the process of dissolution going on within the ruling class, in fact within the whole range of old society, assumes such a violent, glaring character, that a small section of the ruling class cuts itself adrift, and joins the revolutionary class, the class that holds the future in its hands. Just as, therefore, at an earlier period, a section of the nobility went over to the bourgeoisie, so now a portion of the bourgeoisie goes over to the proletariat, and in particular, a portion of the bourgeois ideologists, who have raised themselves to the level of comprehending theoretically the historical movement as a whole.

Of all the classes that stand face to face with the bourgeoisie to-day, the proletariat alone is a really revolutionary class. The other classes decay and finally disappear in the face of modern industry; the proletariat is its special and essential product.

The lower middle class, the small manufacturer, the shopkeeper, the artisan, the peasant, all these fight against the bourgeoisie, to save from extinction their existence as fractions of the middle class. They are therefore not revolutionary, but conservative. Nay, more, they are reactionary, for they try to roll back the wheel of history. If by chance they are revolutionary, they are so only in view of their impending transfer into the proletariat; they thus defend not their present, but their future interests; they desert their own standpoint to place themselves at that of the proletariat.

The "dangerous class," the social scum, that passively rotting mass thrown off by the lowest layers of old society, may, here and there, be swept into the movement by a proletarian revolution; its conditions of life, however, prepare it far more for the part of a bribed tool of reactionary intrigue.

In the conditions of the proletariat, those of old society at large are already virtually swamped. The proletarian is without property; his relation to his wife and children has no longer anything in common with the bourgeois family relations; modern industrial labour, modern subjection to capital, the same in England as in France, in America as in Germany, has stripped him of every trace of national character. Law, morality, religion, are to him so many bourgeois prejudices, behind which lurk in ambush just as many bourgeois interests.

All the preceding classes that got the upper hand, sought to fortify their already acquired status by subjecting society at large to their conditions of appropriation. The proletarians cannot become masters of the productive forces of society, except by abolishing their own previous mode of appropriation, and thereby also every other previous mode of appropriation. They have nothing of their own to secure and to fortify; their mission is to destroy all previous securities for, and insurances of, individual property.

All previous historical movements were movements of minorities, or in the interest of minorities. The proletarian movement is the self-conscious, independent movement of the immense majority, in the interest of the immense majority. The proletariat, the lowest stratum of our present society, cannot stir, cannot raise itself up, without the whole superincumbent strata of official society being blown to pieces.

Though not in substance, yet in form, the struggle of the proletariat with the bourgeoisie is at first a national struggle. The proletariat of each country must, of course, first of all settle matters with its own bourgeoisie.

In depicting the most general phases of the development of the proletariat, we traced the more or less veiled civil war, raging within existing society, up to the point where that war breaks out into open revolution, and where the violent overthrow of the bourgeoisie lays the foundation for the sway of the proletariat.

Hitherto, every form of society has been based, as we have already seen, on the antagonism of oppressing and oppressed classes. But in order to oppress a class, certain conditions must be assured to it under which it can, at least, continue its slavish existence. The serf, in the period of serfdom, raised himself to membership in the commune, just as the petty bourgeois, under the yoke of feudal absolutism, managed to develop into a bourgeois. The modern labourer, on the contrary, instead of rising with the progress of industry, sinks deeper and deeper below the conditions of existence of his own class. He becomes a pauper, and pauperism develops more rapidly than population and wealth. And here it becomes evident that the bourgeoisie is unfit any longer to be the ruling class in society, and to impose its conditions of existence upon society as an overriding law. It is unfit to rule because it is incompetent to assure an existence to its slave within his slavery, because it cannot help letting him sink into such a state, that it has to feed him, instead of being fed by him. Society can no longer live under this bourgeoisie, in other words, its existence is no longer compatible with society.

The essential condition for the existence and for the sway of the bourgeois class, is the formation and augmentation of capital; the condition for capital is wage labour. Wage labour rests exclusively on competition between the labourers. The advance of industry, whose involuntary promoter is the bourgeoisie, replaces the isolation of the labourers, due to competition, by their revolutionary combination, due to association. The development of modern industry, therefore, cuts from under its feet the very foundation on which the bourgeoisie produces and appropriates products. What the bourgeoisie therefore produces, above all, are its own grave-diggers. Its fall and the victory of the proletariat are equally inevitable.

II Proletarians and Communists

In what relation do the Communists stand to the proletarians as a whole?

The Communists do not form a separate party opposed to other working-class parties.

They have no interests separate and apart from those of the proletariat as a whole.

They do not set up any sectarian principles of their own, by which to shape and mould the proletarian movement.

The Communists are distinguished from the other working-class parties by this only: (1) In the national struggles of the proletarians of the different countries, they point out and bring to the front the common interests of the entire proletariat, independently of all nationality. (2) In the various stages of development which the struggle of the working class against the bourgeoisie has to pass through, they always and everywhere represent the interests of the movement as a whole.

The Communists, therefore, are on the one hand, practically, the most advanced and resolute section of the working-class parties of every country, that section which pushes forward all others; on the other hand, theoretically, they have over the great mass of the proletariat the advantage of clearly understanding the lines of march, the conditions, and the ultimate general results of the proletarian movement.

The immediate aim of the Communists is the same as that of all other proletarian parties: Formation of the proletariat into a class, overthrow of the bourgeois supremacy, conquest of political power by the proletariat.

The theoretical conclusions of the Communists are in no way based on ideas or principles that have been invented, or discovered, by this or that would-be universal reformer.

They merely express, in general terms, actual relations springing from an existing class struggle, from a historical movement going on under our very eyes. The abolition of existing property relations is not at all a distinctive feature of communism.

All property relations in the past have continually been subject to historical change consequent upon the change in historical conditions.

The French Revolution, for example, abolished feudal property in favour of bourgeois property.

The distinguishing feature of communism is not the abolition of property generally, but the abolition of bourgeois property. But modern bourgeois private property is the final and most complete expression of the system of producing and appropriating products that is based on class antagonisms, on the exploitation of the many by the few.

In this sense, the theory of the Communists may be summed up in the single sentence: Abolition of private property.

We Communists have been reproached with the desire of abolishing the right of personally acquiring property as the fruit of a man's own labour, which property is alleged to be the groundwork of all personal freedom, activity and independence.

Hard-won, self-acquired, self-earned property! Do you mean the property of the petty artisan and of the small peasant, a form of property that preceded the bourgeois form? There is no need to abolish that; the development of industry has to a great extent already destroyed it, and is still destroying it daily.

Or do you mean modern bourgeois private property?

But does wage labour create any property for the labourer? Not a bit. It creates capital, i.e., that kind of property which exploits wage labour, and which cannot increase except upon conditions of begetting a new supply of wage labour for fresh exploitation. Property, in its present form, is based on the antagonism of capital and wage labour. Let us examine both sides of this antagonism.

To be a capitalist is to have not only a purely personal, but a social, *status* in production. Capital is a collective product, and only by the united action of many members, nay, in the last resort, only by the united action of all members of society, can it be set in motion.

Capital is therefore not a personal, it is a social power.

When, therefore, capital is converted into common property, into the property of all members of society, personal property is not thereby transformed into social property. It is only the social character of the property that is changed. It loses its class character.

Let us now take wage labour.

The average price of wage labour is the minimum wage, i.e., that quantum of the means of subsistence which is absolutely requisite to keep the labourer in bare existence as a labourer. What, therefore, the wage labourer appropriates by means of his labour merely suffices to prolong and reproduce a bare existence. We by no means intend to abolish this personal appropriation of the products of labour, an appropriation that is made for the maintenance and reproduction of human life, and that leaves no surplus wherewith to command the labour of others. All that we want to do away with is the miserable character of this appropriation, under which the labourer lives merely to increase capital, and is allowed to live only in so far as the interest of the ruling class requires it.

In bourgeois society, living labour is but a means to increase accumulated labour. In communist society, accumulated labour is but a means to widen, to enrich, to promote the existence of the labourer.

In bourgeois society, therefore, the past dominates the present; in communist society, the present dominates the past. In bourgeois society capital is independent and has individuality, while the living person is dependent and has no individuality.

And the abolition of this state of things is called by the bourgeois abolition of individuality and freedom! And rightly so. The abolition of bourgeois individuality, bourgeois independence, and bourgeois freedom is undoubtedly aimed at.

By freedom is meant, under the present bourgeois conditions of production, free trade, free selling and buying.

But if selling and buying disappears, free selling and buying disappears also. This talk about free selling and buying, and all the other "brave words" of our bourgeoisie about freedom in general, have a meaning, if any, only in contrast with restricted selling and buying, with the fettered traders of the Middle Ages, but have no meaning when opposed to the communist abolition of buying and selling, of the bourgeois conditions of production, and of the bourgeoisie itself.

You are horrified at our intending to do away with private property. But in your existing society, private property is already done away with for nine-tenths of the population; its existence for the few is solely due to its non-existence in the hands of those nine-tenths. You reproach us, therefore, with intending to do away with a form of property, the necessary condition for whose existence is the non-existence of any property for the immense majority of society.

In one word, you reproach us with intending to do away with your property. Precisely so; that is just what we intend.

From the moment when labour can no longer be converted into capital, money or rent, into a social power capable of being monopolised, i.e., from the moment when individual property can no longer be transformed into bourgeois property, into capital, from that moment, you say, individuality vanishes.

You must, therefore, confess that by "individual" you mean no other person than the bourgeois, than the middle-class owner of property. This person must, indeed, be swept out of the way, and made impossible.

Communism deprives no man of the power to appropriate the products of society; all that it does is to deprive him of the power to subjugate the labour of others by means of such appropriation.

It has been objected, that upon the abolition of private property all work will cease, and universal laziness will overtake us.

According to this, bourgeois society ought long ago to have gone to the dogs through sheer idleness; for those of its members who work, acquire nothing, and those who acquire anything, do not work. The whole of this objection is but another expression of the tautology: There can no longer be any wage labour when there is no longer any capital.

All objections urged against the communistic mode of producing and appropriating material products, have, in the same way, been urged against the communistic modes of producing and appropriating intellectual products. Just as to the bourgeois, the disappearance of class property is the disappearance of production itself, so the disappearance of class culture is to him identical with the disappearance of all culture.

That culture, the loss of which he laments, is, for the enormous majority, a mere training to act as a machine.

But don't wrangle with us so long as you apply, to our intended abolition of bourgeois property, the standard of your bourgeois notions of freedom, culture, law, etc. Your very ideas are but the outgrowth of the conditions of your bourgeois production and bourgeois property, just as your jurisprudence is but the will of your class made into a law for all, a will whose essential character and direction are determined by the economical conditions of existence of your class.

The selfish misconception that induces you to transform into eternal laws of nature and of reason the social forms springing from your present mode of production and form of property – historical relations that rise and disappear in the progress of production – this misconception you share with every ruling class that has preceded you. What you see clearly in the case of ancient property, what you admit in the case of feudal property, you are of course forbidden to admit in the case of your own bourgeois form of property.

[. . .]

The Communists are further reproached with desiring to abolish countries and nationality.

The working men have no country. We cannot take from them what they have not got. Since the proletariat must first of all acquire political supremacy, must rise to be the leading class of the nation, must constitute itself *the* nation, it is, so far, itself national, though not in the bourgeois sense of the word.

National differences and antagonism between peoples are daily more and more vanishing, owing to the development of the bourgeoisie, to freedom of commerce, to the world market, to uniformity in the mode of production and in the conditions of life corresponding thereto.

The supremacy of the proletariat will cause them to vanish still faster. United action of the leading civilised countries at least, is one of the first conditions for the emancipation of the proletariat.

In proportion as the exploitation of one individual by another is put an end to, the exploitation of one nation by another will also be put an end to. In proportion as the antagonism between classes within the nation vanishes, the hostility of one nation to another will come to an end.

The charges against communism made from a religious, a philosophical and, generally, from an ideological standpoint, are not deserving of serious examination.

Does it require deep intuition to comprehend that man's ideas, views, and conceptions, in one word, man's consciousness, change with every change in the conditions of his material existence, in his social relations and in his social life?

What else does the history of ideas prove, than that intellectual production changes its character in proportion as material production is changed? The ruling ideas of each age have ever been the ideas of its ruling class.

When people speak of ideas that revolutionise society, they do but express the fact that within the old society the elements of a new one have been created, and that the dissolution of the old ideas keeps even pace with the dissolution of the old conditions of existence.

When the ancient world was in its last throes, the ancient religions were overcome by Christianity. When Christian ideas succumbed in the eighteenth century to rationalist ideas, feudal society fought its death battle with the then revolutionary bourgeoisie. The ideas of religious liberty and freedom of conscience merely gave expression to the sway of free competition within the domain of knowledge.

"Undoubtedly," it will be said, "religious, moral, philosophical and juridical ideas have been modified in the course of historical development. But religion, morality, philosophy, political science, and law, constantly survived this change."

"There are, besides, eternal truths, such as Freedom, Justice, etc., that are common to all states of society. But communism abolishes eternal truths, it abolishes all religion, and all morality, instead of constituting them on a new basis; it therefore acts in contradiction to all past historical experience."

What does this accusation reduce itself to? The history of all past society has consisted in the development of class antagonisms, antagonisms that assumed different forms at different epochs.

But whatever form they may have taken, one fact is common to all past ages, viz., the exploitation of one part of society by the other. No wonder, then, that the social consciousness of past ages, despite all the multiplicity and variety it displays, moves within certain common forms, or general ideas, which cannot completely vanish except with the total disappearance of class antagonisms.

The communist revolution is the most radical rupture with traditional relations; no wonder that its development involves the most radical rupture with traditional ideas.

But let us have done with the bourgeois objections to communism.

We have seen above that the first step in the revolution by the working class is to raise the proletariat to the position of ruling class to win the battle of democracy.

The proletariat will use its political supremacy to wrest, by degrees, all capital from the bourgeoisie, to centralise all instruments of production in the hands of the state, i.e., of the proletariat organised as the ruling class; and to increase the total of productive forces as rapidly as possible.

Of course, in the beginning, this cannot be effected except by means of despotic inroads on the rights of property, and on the conditions of bourgeois production; by means of measures, therefore, which appear economically insufficient and untenable, but which, in the course of the movement, outstrip themselves, necessitate further inroads upon the old social order, and are unavoidable as a means of entirely revolutionising the mode of production.

These measures will of course be different in different countries.

Nevertheless, in the most advanced countries, the following will be pretty generally applicable.

1. Abolition of property in land and application of all rents of land to public purposes.

2. A heavy progressive or graduated income tax.

3. Abolition of all right of inheritance.

4. Confiscation of the property of all emigrants and rebels.

5. Centralisation of credit in the hands of the state, by means of a national bank with state capital and an exclusive monopoly.

6. Centralisation of the means of communication and transport in the hands of the state.

7. Extension of factories and instruments of production owned by the state; the bringing into cultivation of waste lands, and the improvement of the soil generally in accordance with a common plan.

8. Equal obligation of all to work. Establishment of industrial armies, especially for agriculture.

9. Combination of agriculture with manufacturing industries; gradual abolition of all the distinction between town and country by a more equable distribution of the population over the country.

10. Free education for all children in public schools. Abolition of children's factory labour in its present form. Combination of education with industrial production, etc.

When, in the course of development, class distinctions have disappeared, and all production has been concentrated in the hands of a vast association of the whole nation, the public power will lose its political character. Political power, properly so called, is merely the organised power of one class for oppressing another. If the proletariat during its contest with the bourgeoisie is compelled, by the force of circumstances, to organise itself as a class; if, by means of a revolution, it makes itself the ruling class, and, as such, sweeps away by force the old conditions of production, then it will, along with these conditions, have swept away the conditions for the existence of class antagonisms and of classes generally, and will thereby have abolished its own supremacy as a class.

In place of the old bourgeois society, with its classes and class antagonisms, we shall have an association in which the free development of each is the condition for the free development of all.

Marx, 'Theses on Feuerbach'

(1)

The chief defect of all previous materialism (including Feuerbach's) is that the object, actuality, sensuousness is conceived only in the form of the *object or perception* [*Anschauung*], but not as *sensuous human activity, practice* [*Praxis*], not subjectively. Hence in opposition to materialism the *active* side was developed by idealism – but only abstractly since idealism naturally does not know actual, sensuous activity as such. Feuerbach wants sensuous objects actually different from thought objects: but he does not comprehend human activity itself as *objective*. Hence in *The Essence of Christianity* he regards only the theoretical attitude as the truly human attitude, while practice is understood and fixed only in its dirtily Jewish form of appearance. Consequently he does not comprehend the significance of "revolutionary," of "practical-critical" activity.

(2)

The question whether human thinking can reach objective truth – is not a question of theory but a *practical* question. In practice man must prove the truth, that is, actuality and power, thissidedness of his thinking. The dispute about the actuality or non-actuality of thinking – thinking isolated from practice – is a purely *scholastic* question.

(3)

The materialistic doctrine concerning the change of circumstances and education forgets that circumstances are changed by men and that the educator must himself be educated. Hence this doctrine must divide society into two parts – one of which towers above [as in Robert Owen, Engels added].

The coincidence of the change of circumstances and of human activity or self-change can be comprehended and rationally understood only as *revolutionary practice*.

(4)

Feuerbach starts out from the fact of religious self-alienation, the duplication of the world into a religious and secular world. His work consists in resolving the religious world into its secular basis. But the fact that the secular basis becomes separate from itself and establishes an independent realm in the clouds can only be explained by the cleavage and self-contradictoriness of the secular basis. Thus the latter must itself be both understood in its contradiction and revolutionized in practice. For instance, after the earthly family is found to be the secret of the holy family, the former must then be theoretically and practically nullified.

(5)

Feuerbach, not satisfied with *abstract thinking*, wants *perception*; but he does not comprehend sensuousness as *practical*, human-sensuous activity.

(6)

Feuerbach resolves the religious essence into the *human* essence. But the essence of man is no abstraction inhering in each single individual. In its actuality it is the ensemble of social relationships.

Feuerbach, who does not go into the criticism of this actual essence, is hence compelled

1. to abstract from the historical process and to establish religious feeling as something self-contained, and to presuppose an abstract – *isolated* – human individual;

2. to view the essence of man merely as "species," as the inner, dumb generality which unites the many individuals *naturally*.

(7)

Feuerbach does not see, consequently, that "religious feeling" is itself a social product and that the abstract individual he analyzes belongs to a particular form of society.

(8)

All social life is essentially *practical*. All mysteries which lead theory to mysticism find their rational solution in human practice and the comprehension of this practice.

(9)

The highest point attained by perceptual materialism, that is, materialism that does not com-

prehend sensuousness as practical activity, is the view of separate individuals and civil society.

(10)

The standpoint of the old materialism is civil society; the standpoint of the new is human society or socialized humanity.

(11)

The philosophers have only *interpreted* the world in various ways; the point is, to *change* it.

(B) Lenin, *State and Revolution*

Chapter I: Class Society and the State

1 The State as the Product of the Irreconcilability of Class Antagonisms What is now happening to Marx's doctrine has, in the course of history, often happened to the doctrines of other revolutionary thinkers and leaders of oppressed classes struggling for emancipation. During the lifetime of great revolutionaries, the oppressing classes have visited relentless persecution on them and received their teaching with the most savage hostility, the most furious hatred, the most ruthless campaign of lies and slanders. After their death, attempts are made to turn them into harmless icons, canonise them, and surround their *names* with a certain halo for the "consolation" of the oppressed classes and with the object of duping them, while at the same time emasculating and vulgarising the *real essence* of their revolutionary theories and blunting their revolutionary edge. At the present time, the bourgeoisie and the opportunists within the labour movement are co-operating in this work of adulterating Marxism. They omit, obliterate, and distort the revolutionary side of its teaching, its revolutionary soul. They push to the foreground and extol what is, or seems, acceptable to the bourgeoisie. All the social-chauvinists are now "Marxists" – joking aside! And more and more do German bourgeois professors, erstwhile specialists in the demolition of Marx, speak now of the "national-German" Marx, who, they aver, has educated the labour unions which are so splendidly organised for conducting the present predatory war!

In such circumstances, the distortion of Marxism being so widespread, it is our first task to *resuscitate* the real teachings of Marx on the state. For this purpose it will be necessary to quote at length from the works of Marx and Engels themselves. Of course, long quotations will make the text cumbersome and in no way help to make it popular reading, but we cannot possibly avoid them. All, or at any rate, all the most essential passages in the works of Marx and Engels on the subject of the state must necessarily be given as fully as possible, in order that the reader may form an independent opinion of all the views of the founders of scientific Socialism and of the development of those views, and in order that their distortions by the present predominant "Kautskyism" may be proved in black and white and rendered plain to all.

Let us begin with the most popular of Engels' works, *Der Ursprung der Familie, des Privateigentums und des Staats*,* the sixth edition of which was published in Stuttgart as far back as 1894. We must translate the quotations from the German originals, as the Russian translations, although very numerous, are for the most part either incomplete or very unsatisfactory.

Summarising his historical analysis Engels says:

> The state is therefore by no means a power imposed on society from the outside; just as little is it "the reality of the moral idea," "the image and reality of reason," as Hegel asserted. Rather, it is a product of society at a certain stage of development; it is the admission that this society has become entangled in an insoluble contradiction with itself, that it is cleft into irreconcilable antagonisms which it is powerless to dispel. But in order that these antagonisms, classes with conflicting economic interests, may not consume themselves and society in sterile struggle, a power apparently standing above society becomes necessary, whose purpose is to moderate the conflict and keep it within the bounds of "order"; and this power arising out of society, but placing itself above it, and increasingly separating itself from it, is the state.†

Here we have, expressed in all its clearness, the basic idea of Marxism on the question of the historical rôle and meaning of the state. The state

is the product and the manifestation of the *irreconcilability* of class antagonisms. The state arises when, where, and to the extent that the class antagonisms *cannot* be objectively reconciled. And, conversely, the existence of the state proves that the class antagonisms *are* irreconcilable.

It is precisely on this most important and fundamental point that distortions of Marxism arise along two main lines.

On the one hand, the bourgeois, and particularly the petty-bourgeois, ideologists, compelled under the pressure of indisputable historical facts to admit that the state only exists where there are class antagonisms and the class struggle, "correct" Marx in such a way as to make it appear that the state is an organ for *reconciling* the classes. According to Marx, the state could neither arise nor maintain itself if a reconciliation of classes were possible. But with the petty-bourgeois and philistine professors and publicists, the state – and this frequently on the strength of benevolent references to Marx! – becomes a conciliator of the classes. According to Marx, the state is an organ of class *domination*, an organ of *oppression* of one class by another; its aim is the creation of "order" which legalises and perpetuates this oppression by moderating the collisions between the classes. But in the opinion of the petty-bourgeois politicians, order means reconciliation of the classes, and not oppression of one class by another; to moderate collisions does not mean, they say, to deprive the oppressed classes of certain definite means and methods of struggle for overthrowing the oppressors, but to practice reconciliation.

For instance, when, in the Revolution of 1917, the question of the real meaning and rôle of the state arose in all its vastness as a practical question demanding immediate action on a wide mass scale, all the Socialist-Revolutionaries and Mensheviks suddenly and completely sank to the petty-bourgeois theory of "reconciliation" of the classes by the "state." Innumerable resolutions and articles by politicians of both these parties are saturated through and through with this purely petty-bourgeois and philistine theory of "reconciliation." That the state is an organ of domination of a definite class which *cannot* be reconciled with its antipode (the class opposed to it) – this petty-bourgeois democracy is never able to understand. Its attitude towards the state is one of the most telling proofs that our Socialist-Revolutionaries and Mensheviks are not Socialists

---

* Friedrich Engels, *The Origin of the Family, Private Property, and the State*, London and New York, 1933.
† *Ibid.*

at all (which we Bolsheviks have always maintained), but petty-bourgeois democrats with a near-Socialist phraseology.

On the other hand, the "Kautskyist" distortion of Marx is far more subtle. "Theoretically," there is no denying that the state is the organ of class domination, or that class antagonisms are irreconcilable. But what is forgotten or glossed over is this: if the state is the product of the irreconcilable character of class antagonisms, if it is a force standing *above* society and "increasingly separating itself from it," then it is clear that the liberation of the oppressed class is impossible not only without a violent revolution, *but also without the destruction* of the apparatus of state power, which was created by the ruling class and in which this "separation" is embodied. As we shall see later, Marx drew this theoretically self-evident conclusion from a concrete historical analysis of the problems of revolution. And it is exactly this conclusion which Kautsky – as we shall show fully in our subsequent remarks – has "forgotten" and distorted.

2 Special Bodies of Armed Men, Prisons, Etc.
Engels continues:

> In contrast with the ancient organisation of the *gens*, the first distinguishing characteristic of the state is the grouping of the subjects of the state *on a territorial basis*. . . .

Such a grouping seems "natural" to us, but it came after a prolonged and costly struggle against the old form of tribal or gentilic society.

> . . . The second is the establishment of a *public force*, which is no longer absolutely identical with the population organising itself as an armed power. This special public force is necessary, because a self-acting armed organisation of the population has become impossible since the cleavage of society into classes. . . . This public force exists in every state; it consists not merely of armed men, but of material appendages, prisons and repressive institutions of all kinds, of which gentilic society knew nothing. . . .*

Engels develops the conception of that "power" which is termed the state – a power arising from society, but placing itself above it and becoming

---

* *Ibid.*

more and more separated from it. What does this power mainly consist of? It consists of special bodies of armed men who have at their disposal prisons, etc.

We are justified in speaking of special bodies of armed men, because the public power peculiar to every state is not "absolutely identical" with the armed population, with its "self-acting armed organisation."

Like all the great revolutionary thinkers, Engels tries to draw the attention of the class-conscious workers to that very fact which to prevailing philistinism appears least of all worthy of attention, most common and sanctified by solid, indeed, one might say, petrified prejudices. A standing army and police are the chief instruments of state power. But can this be otherwise?

From the point of view of the vast majority of Europeans at the end of the nineteenth century whom Engels was addressing, and who had neither lived through nor closely observed a single great revolution, this cannot be otherwise. They cannot understand at all what this "self-acting armed organisation of the population" means. To the question, whence arose the need for special bodies of armed men, standing above society and becoming separated from it (police and standing army), the Western European and Russian philistines are inclined to answer with a few phrases borrowed from Spencer or Mikhailovsky, by reference to the complexity of social life, the differentiation of functions, and so forth.

Such a reference seems "scientific" and effectively dulls the senses of the average man, obscuring the most important and basic fact, namely, the break-up of society into irreconcilably antagonistic classes.

Without such a break-up, the "self-acting armed organisation of the population" might have differed from the primitive organisation of a herd of monkeys grasping sticks, or of primitive men, or men united in a tribal form of society, by its complexity, its high technique, and so forth, but would still have been possible.

It is impossible now, because society, in the period of civilisation, is broken up into antagonistic and, indeed, irreconcilably antagonistic classes, which, if armed in a "self-acting" manner, would come into armed struggle with each other. A state is formed, a special power is created in the form of special bodies of armed men, and every revolution, by shattering the state apparatus, demonstrates to us how the ruling class aims at the restoration of the special bodies of armed men at *its* service, and how the oppressed class tries to create a new organisation of this kind, capable of serving not the exploiters, but the exploited.

In the above observation, Engels raises theoretically the very same question which every great revolution raises practically, palpably, and on a mass scale of action, namely, the question of the relation between special bodies of armed men and the "self-acting armed organisation of the population." We shall see how this is concretely illustrated by the experience of the European and Russian revolutions.

But let us return to Engels' discourse.

He points out that sometimes, for instance, here and there in North America, this public power is weak (he has in mind an exception that is rare in capitalist society, and he speaks about parts of North America in its pre-imperialist days, where the free colonist predominated), but that in general it tends to become stronger:

It [the public power] grows stronger, however, in proportion as the class antagonisms within the state grow sharper, and with the growth in size and population of the adjacent states. We have only to look at our present-day Europe, where class struggle and rivalry in conquest have screwed up the public power to such a pitch that it threatens to devour the whole of society and even the state itself.*

This was written as early as the beginning of the 'nineties of last century, Engels' last preface being dated June 16, 1891. The turn towards imperialism, understood to mean complete domination of the trusts, full sway of the large banks, and a colonial policy on a grand scale, and so forth, was only just beginning in France, and was even weaker in North America and in Germany. Since then the "rivalry in conquest" has made gigantic progress – especially as, by the beginning of the second decade of the twentieth century, the whole world had been finally divided up between these "rivals in conquest," *i.e.*, between the great predatory powers. Military and naval armaments since then have grown to monstrous proportions, and the predatory war of 1914–1917 for the

domination of the world by England or Germany, for the division of the spoils, has brought the "swallowing up" of all the forces of society by the rapacious state power nearer to a complete catastrophe.

As early as 1891 Engels was able to point to "rivalry in conquest" as one of the most important features of the foreign policy of the great powers, but in 1914–1917, when this rivalry, many times intensified, has given birth to an imperialist war, the rascally social-chauvinists cover up their defence of the predatory policy of "their" capitalist classes by phrases about the "defence of the fatherland," or the "defence of the republic and the revolution," etc.!

3 *The State as an Instrument for the Exploitation of the Oppressed Class* For the maintenance of a special public force standing above society, taxes and state loans are needed.

Having at their disposal the public force and the right to exact taxes, the officials now stand as organs of society *above* society. The free, voluntary respect which was accorded to the organs of the gentilic form of government does not satisfy them, even if they could have it. . . .

Special laws are enacted regarding the sanctity and the inviolability of the officials. "The shabbiest police servant . . . has more authority" than the representative of the clan, but even the head of the military power of a civilised state "may well envy the least among the chiefs of the clan the unconstrained and uncontested respect which is paid to him."†

Here the question regarding the privileged position of the officials as organs of state power is clearly stated. The main point is indicated as follows: what is it that places them *above* society? We shall see how this theoretical problem was solved in practice by the Paris Commune in 1871 and how it was slurred over in a reactionary manner by Kautsky in 1912.

As the state arose out of the need to hold class antagonisms in check; but as it, at the same time, arose in the midst of the conflict of these classes, it is, as a rule, the state of the most powerful, economically dominant class, which by virtue

* *Ibid.*

† *Ibid.*

thereof becomes also the dominant class politically, and thus acquires new means of holding down and exploiting the oppressed class. . . .

Not only the ancient and feudal states were organs of exploitation of the slaves and serfs, but

the modern representative state is the instrument of the exploitation of wage-labour by capital. By way of exception, however, there are periods when the warring classes so nearly attain equilibrium that the state power, ostensibly appearing as a mediator, assumes for the moment a certain independence in relation to both. . . .*

Such were, for instance, the absolute monarchies of the seventeenth and eighteenth centuries, the Bonapartism of the First and Second Empires in France, and the Bismarck régime in Germany.

Such, we may add, is now the Kerensky government in republican Russia after its shift to persecuting the revolutionary proletariat, at a moment when the Soviets, thanks to the leadership of the petty-bourgeois democrats, have *already* become impotent, while the bourgeoisie is *not yet* strong enough to disperse them outright.

In a democratic republic, Engels continues, "wealth wields its power indirectly, but all the more effectively," first, by means of "direct corruption of the officials" (America); second, by means of "the alliance of the government with the stock exchange" (France and America).

At the present time, imperialism and the domination of the banks have "developed" to an unusually fine art both these methods of defending and asserting the omnipotence of wealth in democratic republics of all descriptions. If, for instance, in the very first months of the Russian democratic republic, one might say during the honeymoon of the union of the "Socialists" – Socialist-Revolutionaries and Mensheviks – with the bourgeoisie, Mr Palchinsky obstructed every measure in the coalition cabinet, restraining the capitalists and their war profiteering, their plundering of the public treasury by means of army contracts; and if, after his resignation, Mr Palchinsky (replaced, of course, by an exactly similar Palchinsky) was "rewarded" by the capitalists with a "soft" job carrying a salary of 120,000 rubles per annum, what was this? Direct or indi-

rect bribery? A league of the government with the capitalist syndicates, or "only" friendly relations? What is the rôle played by the Chernovs, Tseretelis, Avksentyevs and Skobelevs? Are they the "direct" or only the indirect allies of the millionaire treasury looters?

The omnipotence of "wealth" is thus more *secure* in a democratic republic, since it does not depend on the poor political shell of capitalism. A democratic republic is the best possible political shell for capitalism, and therefore, once capital has gained control (through the Palchinskys, Chernovs, Tseretelis and Co.) of this very best shell, it establishes its power so securely, so firmly that *no* change, either of persons, or institutions, or parties in the bourgeois republic can shake it.

We must also note that Engels quite definitely regards universal suffrage as a means of bourgeois domination. Universal suffrage, he says, obviously summing up the long experience of German Social-Democracy, is "an index of the maturity of the working class; it cannot, and never will, be anything else but that in the modern state."

The petty-bourgeois democrats, such as our Socialist-Revolutionaries and Mensheviks, and also their twin brothers, the social-chauvinists and opportunists of Western Europe, all expect "more" from universal suffrage. They themselves share, and instil into the minds of the people, the wrong idea that universal suffrage "in the *modern* state" is really capable of expressing the will of the majority of the toilers and of assuring its realisation.

We can here only note this wrong idea, only point out that this perfectly clear, exact and concrete statement by Engels is distorted at every step in the propaganda and agitation of the "official" (*i.e.*, opportunist) Socialist parties. A detailed analysis of all the falseness of this idea, which Engels brushes aside, is given in our further account of the views of Marx and Engels on the "modern" state.

A general summary of his views is given by Engels in the most popular of his works in the following words:

The state, therefore, has not existed from all eternity. There have been societies which managed without it, which had no conception of the state and state power. At a certain stage of economic development, which was necessarily bound up with the cleavage of society into classes, the state

* *Ibid.*

became a necessity owing to this cleavage. We are now rapidly approaching a stage in the development of production at which the existence of these classes has not only ceased to be a necessity, but is becoming a positive hindrance to production. They will disappear as inevitably as they arose at an earlier stage. Along with them, the state will inevitably disappear. The society that organises production anew on the basis of a free and equal association of the producers will put the whole state machine where it will then belong: in the museum of antiquities, side by side with the spinning wheel and the bronze axe.*

It is not often that we find this passage quoted in the propaganda and agitation literature of contemporary Social-Democracy. But even when we do come across it, it is generally quoted in the same manner as one bows before an icon, *i.e.*, it is done merely to show official respect for Engels, without any attempt to gauge the breadth and depth of revolutionary action presupposed by this relegating of "the whole state machine . . . to the museum of antiquities." In most cases we do not even find an understanding of what Engels calls the state machine.

4 The "Withering Away" of the State and Violent Revolution Engels' words regarding the "withering away" of the state enjoy such popularity, they are so often quoted, and they show so clearly the essence of the usual adulteration by means of which Marxism is made to look like opportunism, that we must dwell on them in detail. Let us quote the whole passage from which they are taken.

The proletariat seizes state power, and then transforms the means of production into state property. But in doing this, it puts an end to itself as the proletariat, it puts an end to all class differences and class antagonisms, it puts an end also to the state as the state. Former society, moving in class antagonisms, had need of the state, that is, an organisation of the exploiting class at each period for the maintenance of its external conditions of production; therefore, in particular, for the forcible holding down of the exploited class in the conditions of oppression (slavery, bondage or serfdom, wage-labour) determined by the existing mode of production. The state was the official representative of society as a whole, its embodiment in a visible corporate body; but it was this only in so far as it was the state of that class which itself, in its epoch, represented society as a whole: in ancient times, the state of the slave-owning citizens; in the Middle Ages, of the feudal nobility; in our epoch, of the bourgeoisie. When ultimately it becomes really representative of society as a whole, it makes itself superfluous. As soon as there is no longer any class of society to be held in subjection; as soon as, along with class domination and the struggle for individual existence based on the former anarchy of production, the collisions and excesses arising from these have also been abolished, there is nothing more to be repressed, and a special repressive force, a state, is no longer necessary. The first act in which the state really comes forward as the representative of society as a whole – the seizure of the means of production in the name of society – is at the same time its last independent act as a state. The interference of a state power in social relations becomes superfluous in one sphere after another, and then becomes dormant of itself. Government over persons is replaced by the administration of things and the direction of the processes of production. The state is not "abolished," *it withers away*. It is from this standpoint that we must appraise the phrase "people's free state" – both its justification at times for agitational purposes, and its ultimate scientific inadequacy – and also the demand of the so-called Anarchists that the state should be abolished overnight.†

Without fear of committing an error, it may be said that of this argument by Engels so singularly rich in ideas, only one point has become an integral part of Socialist thought among modern Socialist parties, namely, that, unlike the Anarchist doctrine of the "abolition" of the state, according to Marx the state "withers away." To emasculate Marxism in such a manner is to reduce it to opportunism, for such an "interpretation" only leaves the hazy conception of a slow, even, gradual change, free from leaps and storms, free from revolution. The current popular conception, if one may say so, of the "withering away" of the state undoubtedly means a slurring over, if not a negation, of revolution.

Yet, such an "interpretation" is the crudest distortion of Marxism, which is advantageous only to the bourgeoisie; in point of theory, it is

* *Ibid.*

† Friedrich Engels, *Anti-Dühring*, London and New York, 1933.

based on a disregard for the most important circumstances and considerations pointed out in the very passage summarising Engels' ideas, which we have just quoted in full.

In the first place, Engels at the very outset of his argument says that, in assuming state power, the proletariat by that very act "puts an end to the state as the state." One is "not accustomed" to reflect on what this really means. Generally, it is either ignored altogether, or it is considered as a piece of "Hegelian weakness" on Engels' part. As a matter of fact, however, these words express succinctly the experience of one of the greatest proletarian revolutions – the Paris Commune of 1871, of which we shall speak in greater detail in its proper place. As a matter of fact, Engels speaks here of the destruction of the bourgeois state by the proletarian revolution, while the words about its withering away refer to the remains of *proletarian* statehood *after* the Socialist revolution. The bourgeois state does not "wither away," according to Engels, but is "put an end to" by the proletariat in the course of the revolution. What withers away after the revolution is the proletarian state or semistate.

Secondly, the state is a "special repressive force." This splendid and extremely profound definition of Engels' is given by him here with complete lucidity. It follows from this that the "special repressive force" of the bourgeoisie for the suppression of the proletariat, of the millions of workers by a handful of the rich, must be replaced by a "special repressive force" of the proletariat for the suppression of the bourgeoisie (the dictatorship of the proletariat). It is just this that constitutes the destruction of "the state as the state." It is just this that constitutes the "act" of "the seizure of the means of production in the name of society." And it is obvious that such a substitution of one (proletarian) "special repressive force" for another (bourgeois) "special repressive force" can in no way take place in the form of a "withering away."

Thirdly, as to the "withering away" or, more expressively and colourfully, as to the state "becoming dormant," Engels refers quite clearly and definitely to the period *after* "the seizure of the means of production [by the state] in the name of society," that is, *after* the Socialist revolution. We all know that the political form of the "state" at that time is complete democracy. But it never enters the head of any of the opportunists who shamelessly distort Marx that when Engels speaks here of the state "withering away," or "becoming dormant," he speaks of *democracy*. At first sight this seems very strange. But it is "unintelligible" only to one who has not reflected on the fact that democracy is *also* a state and that, consequently, democracy will *also* disappear when the state disappears. The bourgeois state can only be "put an end to" by a revolution. The state in general, *i.e.*, most complete democracy, can only "wither away."

Fourthly, having formulated his famous proposition that "the state withers away," Engels at once explains concretely that this proposition is directed equally against the opportunists and the Anarchists. In doing this, however, Engels puts in the first place that conclusion from his proposition about the "withering away" of the state which is directed against the opportunists.

One can wager that out of every 10,000 persons who have read or heard about the "withering away" of the state, 9,990 do not know at all, or do not remember, that Engels did not direct his conclusions from this proposition against the Anarchists *alone*. And out of the remaining ten, probably nine do not know the meaning of a "people's free state" nor the reason why an attack on this watchword contains an attack on the opportunists. This is how history is written! This is how a great revolutionary doctrine is imperceptibly adulterated and adapted to current philistinism! The conclusion drawn against the Anarchists has been repeated thousands of times, vulgarised, harangued about in the crudest fashion possible until it has acquired the strength of a prejudice, whereas the conclusion drawn against the opportunists has been hushed up and "forgotten"!

The "people's free state" was a demand in the programme of the German Social-Democrats and their current slogan in the 'seventies. There is no political substance in this slogan other than a pompous middle-class circumlocution of the idea of democracy. In so far as it referred in a lawful manner to a democratic republic, Engels was prepared to "justify" its use "at times" from a propaganda point of view. But this slogan was opportunist, for it not only expressed an exaggerated view of the attractiveness of bourgeois democracy, but also a lack of understanding of the Socialist criticism of every state in general. We are in favour of a democratic republic as the best form of the state for the proletariat under capitalism, but we have no right to forget that wage slavery is the lot of the people even in the most democratic bourgeois republic. Furthermore, every state is a "special repressive force" for the suppression of the oppressed class. Consequently, *no* state is either "free" or a "people's state." Marx and Engels explained this repeatedly to their party comrades in the 'seventies.

Fifthly, in the same work of Engels, from which every one remembers his argument on the "withering away" of the state, there is also a disquisition on the significance of a violent revolution. The historical analysis of its rôle becomes, with Engels, a veritable panegyric on violent revolution. This, of course, "no one remembers"; to talk or even to think of the importance of this idea is not considered good form by contemporary Socialist parties, and in the daily propaganda and agitation among the masses it plays no part whatever. Yet it is indissolubly bound up with the "withering away" of the state in one harmonious whole.

Here is Engels' argument:

> ... That force, however, plays another rôle (other than that of a diabolical power) in history, a revolutionary rôle; that, in the words of Marx, it is the midwife of every old society which is pregnant with the new; that it is the instrument with whose aid social movement forces its way through and shatters the dead, fossilised political forms – of this there is not a word in Herr Dühring. It is only with sighs and groans that he admits the possibility that force will perhaps be necessary for the overthrow of the economic system of exploitation – unfortunately! because all use of force, forsooth, demoralises the person who uses it. And this in spite of the immense moral and spiritual impetus which has resulted from every victorious revolution! And this in Germany, where a violent collision – which indeed may be forced on the people – would at least have the advantage of wiping out the servility which has permeated the national consciousness as a result of the humiliation of the Thirty Years' War. And this parson's mode of thought – lifeless, insipid and impotent – claims to impose itself on the most revolutionary party which history has known?*

How can this panegyric on violent revolution, which Engels insistently brought to the attention of the German Social-Democrats between 1878

and 1894, *i.e.*, right to the time of his death, be combined with the theory of the "withering away" of the state to form one doctrine?

Usually the two views are combined by means of eclecticism, by an unprincipled, sophistic, arbitrary selection (to oblige the powers that be) of either one or the other argument, and in ninety-nine cases out of a hundred (if not more often), it is the idea of the "withering away" that is specially emphasised. Eclecticism is substituted for dialectics – this is the most usual, the most widespread phenomenon to be met with in the official Social-Democratic literature of our day in relation to Marxism. Such a substitution is, of course, nothing new; it may be observed even in the history of classic Greek philosophy. When Marxism is adulterated to become opportunism, the substitution of eclecticism for dialectics is the best method of deceiving the masses; it gives an illusory satisfaction; it seems to take into account all sides of the process, all the tendencies of development, all the contradictory factors and so forth, whereas in reality it offers no consistent and revolutionary view of the process of social development at all.

We have already said above and shall show more fully later that the teaching of Marx and Engels regarding the inevitability of a violent revolution refers to the bourgeois state. It *cannot* be replaced by the proletarian state (the dictatorship of the proletariat) through "withering away," but, as a general rule, only through a violent revolution. The panegyric sung in its honour by Engels and fully corresponding to the repeated declarations of Marx (remember the concluding passages of the *Poverty of Philosophy* and the *Communist Manifesto*, with its proud and open declaration of the inevitability of a violent revolution; remember Marx's *Critique of the Gotha Programme* of 1875 in which, almost thirty years later, he mercilessly castigates the opportunist character of that programme) – this praise is by no means a mere "impulse," a mere declamation, or a polemical sally. The necessity of systematically fostering among the masses *this* and just this point of view about violent revolution lies at the root of the *whole* of Marx's and Engels' teaching. The neglect of such propaganda and agitation by both the present predominant social-chauvinist and the Kautskyist currents brings their betrayal of Marx's and Engels' teaching into prominent relief.

* *Ibid.*

The replacement of the bourgeois by the proletarian state is impossible without a violent revolution. The abolition of the proletarian state, *i.e.*, of all states, is only possible through "withering away."

Marx and Engels gave a full and concrete exposition of these views in studying each revolutionary situation separately, in analysing the lessons of the experience of each individual revolution. We now pass to this, undoubtedly the most important part of their work.

[...]

Chapter II: The Experiences of 1848–1851

3   The Formulation of the Question by Marx in 1852   In 1907 Mehring published in the magazine *Neue Zeit* (Vol. XXV 2, p. 164) extracts from a letter by Marx to Weydemeyer dated March 5, 1852. In this letter, among other things, is the following noteworthy observation:

As far as I am concerned, the honour does not belong to me for having discovered the existence either of classes in modern society or of the struggle between the classes. Bourgeois historians a long time before me expounded the historical development of this class struggle, and bourgeois economists, the economic anatomy of classes. What was new on my part, was to prove the following: (1) that the existence of classes is connected only with certain historical struggles which arise out of the development of production [*historische Entwicklungskämpfe der Produktion*]; (2) that class struggle necessarily leads to the dictatorship of the proletariat; (3) that this dictatorship is itself only a transition to the abolition of all classes and to a classless society.

In these words Marx has succeeded in expressing with striking clearness, first, the chief and concrete differences between his teachings and those of the most advanced and profound thinkers of the bourgeoisie, and second, the essence of his teachings concerning the state.

The main point in the teaching of Marx is the class struggle. This has very often been said and written. But this is not true. Out of this error, here and there, springs an opportunist distortion of Marxism, such a falsification of it as to make it acceptable to the bourgeoisie. The theory of the class struggle was *not* created by Marx, but by the bourgeoisie *before* Marx and is, generally speaking, *acceptable* to the bourgeoisie. He who recognises *only* the class struggle is not yet a Marxist; he may be found not to have gone beyond the boundaries of bourgeois reasoning and politics. To limit Marxism to the teaching of the class struggle means to curtail Marxism – to distort it, to reduce it to something which is acceptable to the bourgeoisie. A Marxist is one who *extends* the acceptance of class struggle to the acceptance of the *dictatorship of the proletariat*. Herein lies the deepest difference between a Marxist and an ordinary petty or big bourgeois. On this touchstone it is necessary to test a *real* understanding and acceptance of Marxism. And it is not astonishing that, when the history of Europe put before the working class this question in a practical way, not only all opportunists and reformists but all Kautskyists (people who vacillate between reformism and Marxism) turned out to be miserable philistines and petty-bourgeois democrats, *denying* the dictatorship of the proletariat. Kautsky's pamphlet, *Dictatorship of the Proletariat*, published in August, 1918, *i.e.*, long after the first edition of this book, is an example of petty-bourgeois distortion of Marxism and base renunciation of it *in practice*, while hypocritically recognising it *in words* (see my pamphlet, *The Proletarian Revolution and the Renegade Kautsky*, Petrograd and Moscow, 1918).

The present-day opportunism in the person of its main representative, the former Marxist, K. Kautsky, comes wholly under Marx's characterisation of the *bourgeois* position as quoted above, for this opportunism limits the field of recognition of the class struggle to the realm of bourgeois relationships. (Within this realm, inside of its framework, not a single educated liberal will refuse to recognise the class struggle "in principle"!) Opportunism *does not lead* the recognition of class struggle up to the main point, up to the period of *transition* from capitalism to Communism, up to the period of *overthrowing* and completely abolishing the bourgeoisie. In reality, this period inevitably becomes a period of unusually violent class struggles in their sharpest possible forms and, therefore, the state during this period inevitably must be a state that is democratic *in a new way* (for the proletariat and the poor in general) and dictatorial *in a new way* (against the bourgeoisie).

Further, the substance of the teachings of Marx about the state is assimilated only by one who understands that the dictatorship of a *single* class is necessary not only for any class society generally, not only for the *proletariat* which has overthrown the bourgeoisie, but for the entire *historic period* which separates capitalism from "classless society," from Communism. The forms of bourgeois states are exceedingly variegated, but their essence is the same: in one way or another, all these states are in the last analysis inevitably a *dictatorship of the bourgeoisie*. The transition from capitalism to Communism will certainly bring a great variety and abundance of political forms, but the essence will inevitably be only one: *the dictatorship of the proletariat*.

[...]

Chapter III: Experience of the Paris Commune of 1871: Marx's Analysis

2 What Is to Replace the Shattered State Machinery? In 1847, in the *Communist Manifesto*, Marx answered this question still in a purely abstract manner, stating the problems rather than the methods of solving them. To replace this machinery by "the proletariat organised as the ruling class," by "establishing democracy" – such was the answer of the *Communist Manifesto*.

Without resorting to Utopias, Marx waited for the *experience* of a mass movement to produce the answer to the problem as to the exact forms which this organisation of the proletariat as the ruling class will assume and as to the exact manner in which this organisation will be combined with the most complete, most consistent "establishment of democracy."

The experiment of the Commune, meagre as it was, was subjected by Marx to the most careful analysis in his *The Civil War in France*. Let us quote the most important passages of this work.

There developed in the nineteenth century, he says, originating from the days of absolute monarchy, "the centralised state power, with its ubiquitous organs of standing army, police, bureaucracy, clergy and judicature." With the development of class antagonism between capital and labour, "the state power assumed more and more the character of the national power of capital over labour, of a public force organised for social enslavement, of an engine of class despotism. After every revolution marking a progressive phase in the class struggle, the purely repressive character of the state power stands out in bolder and bolder relief." The state power, after the revolution of 1848–1849 became "the national war engine of capital against labour." The Second Empire consolidated this.

"The direct antithesis of the Empire was the Commune," says Marx. It was the "positive form" of "a republic that was not only to supersede the monarchical form of class rule, but class rule itself."

What was this "positive" form of the proletarian, the Socialist republic? What was the state it was beginning to create?

"The first decree of the Commune ... was the suppression of the standing army, and the substitution for it of the armed people," says Marx.*

This demand now figures in the programme of every party calling itself Socialist. But the value of their programmes is best shown by the behaviour of our Socialist-Revolutionaries and Mensheviks, who, even after the revolution of March 12, 1917, refused to carry out this demand in practice!

The Commune was formed of municipal councillors, chosen by universal suffrage in various wards of the town, responsible and revocable at short terms. The majority of its members were naturally working men, or acknowledged representatives of the working class.... Instead of continuing to be the agent of the Central Government, the police was at once stripped of its political attributes, and turned into the responsible and at all times revocable agent of the Commune. So were the officials of all other branches of the administration. From the members of the Commune downwards, the public service had to be done at *workmen's wages*. The vested interests and the representation allowances of the high dignitaries of state disappeared along with the high dignitaries themselves....

Having once got rid of the standing army and the police, the physical force elements of the old government, the Commune was anxious to break the spiritual force of repression, the "parson power." ...

---

* Karl Marx, *The Civil War in France*, London and New York, 1933.

The judicial functionaries were to be divested of [their] sham independence. . . . Like the rest of public servants, magistrates and judges were to be elective, responsible and revocable.*

Thus the Commune would appear to have replaced the shattered state machinery "only" by fuller democracy: abolition of the standing army; all officials to be fully elective and subject to recall. But, as a matter of fact this "only" signifies a gigantic replacement of one type of institution by others of a fundamentally different order. Here we observe a case of "transformation of quantity into quality": democracy, introduced as fully and consistently as is generally thinkable, is transformed from capitalist democracy into proletarian democracy; from the state (*i.e.*, a special force for the suppression of a particular class) into something which is no longer really the state in the accepted sense of the word.

It is still necessary to suppress the bourgeoisie and crush its resistance. This was particularly necessary for the Commune; and one of the reasons of its defeat was that it did not do this with sufficient determination. But the organ of suppression is now the majority of the population, and not a minority, as was always the case under slavery, serfdom, and wage labour. And, once the majority of the people *itself* suppresses its oppressors, a "special force" for suppression is *no longer necessary*. In this sense the state *begins to wither away*. Instead of the special institutions of a privileged minority (privileged officialdom, heads of a standing army), the majority can itself directly fulfil all these functions; and the more the discharge of the functions of state power devolves upon the people generally, the less need is there for the existence of this power.

In this connection the Commune's measure emphasised by Marx, particularly worthy of note, is: the abolition of all representation allowances, and of all money privileges in the case of officials, the reduction of the remuneration of *all* servants of the state to "*workingmen's wages.*" Here is shown, more clearly than anywhere else, the *break* from a bourgeois democracy to a proletarian democracy, from the democracy of the oppressors to the democracy of the oppressed classes, from the state as a "special force for suppression" of a given class to the suppression of

the oppressors by the *whole force* of the majority of the people – the workers and the peasants. And it is precisely on this most striking point, perhaps the most important as far as the problem of the state is concerned, that the teachings of Marx have been entirely forgotten! In popular commentaries, whose number is legion, this is not mentioned. It is "proper" to keep silent about it as if it were a piece of old-fashioned "naïveté," just as the Christians, after Christianity had attained the position of a state religion, "forgot" the "naïvetés" of primitive Christianity with its democratic-revolutionary spirit.

The reduction of the remuneration of the highest state officials seems "simply" a demand of naïve, primitive democracy. One of the "founders" of modern opportunism, the former Social-Democrat, Eduard Bernstein, has more than once exercised his talents in repeating the vulgar bourgeois jeers at "primitive" democracy. Like all opportunists, including the present Kautskyists, he fails completely to understand that, first of all, the transition from capitalism to Socialism is *impossible* without "return," in a measure, to "primitive" democracy (how can one otherwise pass on to the discharge of all the state functions by the majority of the population and by every individual of the population?); and, secondly, he forgets that "primitive democracy" on the basis of capitalism and capitalist culture is not the same primitive democracy as in prehistoric or pre-capitalist times. Capitalist culture has *created* large-scale production, factories, railways, the postal service, telephones, etc., and *on this basis* the great majority of functions of the old "state power" have become so simplified and can be reduced to such simple operations of registration, filing and checking that they will be quite within the reach of every literate person, and it will be possible to perform them for "workingmen's wages," which circumstance can (and must) strip those functions of every shadow of privilege, of every appearance of "official grandeur."

All officials, without exception, elected and subject to recall *at any time*, their salaries reduced to "workingmen's wages" – these simple and "self-evident" democratic measures, which, completely uniting the interests of the workers and the majority of peasants, at the same time serve as a bridge leading from capitalism to Socialism. These measures refer to the state, to the purely

* *Ibid.*

political reconstruction of society; but, of course, they acquire their full meaning and significance only in connection with the "expropriation of the expropriators," either accomplished or in preparation, *i.e.*, with the turning of capitalist private ownership of the means of production into social ownership. Marx wrote:

> The Commune made that catchword of bourgeois revolutions, cheap government, a reality by destroying the two greatest sources of expenditure – the standing army and state functionarism.*

* *Ibid.*

From the peasantry, as from other sections of the petty bourgeoisie, only an insignificant few "rise to the top," occupy "a place in the sun" in the bourgeois sense, *i.e.*, become either well-to-do people or secure and privileged officials. The great majority of peasants in every capitalist country where the peasantry exists (and the majority of capitalist countries are of this kind) is oppressed by the government and longs for its overthrow, longs for "cheap" government. This can be realised *only* by the proletariat; and by realising it, the proletariat makes at the same time a step forward towards the Socialist reconstruction of the state.

20

M. K. Gandhi,
on *Satyagraha* (selections)

Introduction

Mohandas Gandhi (1869–1948) – dubbed "Mahatma" ("The Great Soul") by his friend, the poet-philosopher Rabindranath Tagore (1861–1941) – wrote voluminously on the many political campaigns and movements in which he was a leading figure. His political involvement both reflected and in turn helped to shape a systematic philosophy that combined religious, epistemological, and ethical themes. This reciprocal influence is especially apparent in the most central and influential doctrine of Gandhi's political thought – that of *satyagraha*, which he adumbrates in many places, including the four short texts we have selected, mostly from around 1920.

Gandhi was born in Porbander in the west of India. Between 1888 and 1891 he studied for the Bar in London and then went to work as a lawyer in South Africa, where he lived until returning to India in 1914. Building on his experience of peaceful and civil disobedience in the face of the unjust laws under which South Africa's Indian community suffered, Gandhi soon introduced similar tactics in India, protesting against, for example, unjust tax laws imposed by the colonial government. By 1940, through his non-violent protest Gandhi was calling for nothing less than the end

From Mahatma Gandhi, *Selected Political Writings*, ed. D. Dalton, Indianapolis, IN: Hackett, 1996, pp. 50–7, 60–4, 81–3 (notes omitted).

of British rule in India. He only lived, however, for a few months after the independence of his nation, an event overshadowed for him by the rending partition of the newborn state by warring Hindus and Muslims at the cost of over a million lives. Gandhi himself was assassinated by a Hindu zealot frustrated by the Mahatma's sympathy for Muslims.

"Those who say that religion has nothing to do with politics," wrote Gandhi in his autobiography, "do not know what religion means."[1] The leading concept in Gandhi's political thinking, *satyagraha*, testifies to the religious or spiritual dimension of his politics. The term was coined by joining words meaning "truth" and "adherence" or "insistence." As Bhikhu Parekh explains, "when the two terms are combined there is a beautiful duality of meaning, implying both insistence *on* and *for* truth."[2] The political activist must not only demand the truth, act on what he or she takes to be true, but also gear this action to the acquisition and furtherance of truth.

Gandhi was always keen to distinguish *satyagraha* from the "passive resistance," of many of the British suffragettes, for example, with which commentators tended to equate it. To begin with, he insists, it is something thoroughly "active," belonging to an endeavor to change human behavior and institutions, rather than a passive refusal to accept certain laws. (One imagines that Gandhi would have welcomed as *satyagraha* the goals of the truth and reconciliation process in post-apartheid South Africa.) Second, the *satyagrahi*, unlike the merely passive resister, is absolutely and on principle committed to non-violence and non-harm (*ahimsa*).

Gandhi's reasons for insisting on *ahimsa* as an essential element in *satyagraha* are rooted in his views on religion and the nature of knowledge. As Parekh, once more, puts it, Gandhi's theory of *satyagraha* is "a theory of both knowledge and action, and much misunderstood when seen as either alone."[3] First, Gandhi maintains, somewhat in the manner of J. S. Mill (V.18), truth will only emerge and be identified through the open, rational dialogue of democratic politics. Second, and more crucially, as he explained to the Disorders Inquiry Committee before which he was hauled in 1919, all claims to truth are fallible: one can never be sure enough of the rightness of one's own views to impose them by force on other people. Indeed, as he explains elsewhere, truth is perspectival. None of us possess a grasp of the complete truth on matters of moment, which is why we must be entirely tolerant of, and indeed draw upon, rival views. This is the point of Gandhi's famous remark that he considered himself a Hindu, Christian, Muslim, Jew, Buddhist, and Confucian.

The success in India of Gandhi's style of politics guaranteed that many social and political movements – from anti-nuclear protest groups, to the US civil rights movement, to anti-globalization organizations – would be inspired by, and would emulate, his tactics. Nevertheless, *satyagraha* has often been criticized for being utopian. The most common criticism, perhaps – to the effect that *ahimsa* can only succeed against relatively "civilized rulers," as Gandhi calls them, who won't indiscriminately massacre protesters – is one that he anticipated and to which he replies. "Even a heart of flint will melt in the fire kindled by the power of the soul. Even a Nero becomes a lamb when he faces love." This is a reply that might confirm the legitimacy of the charge of utopianism in the minds of those familiar with such very flint-hearted rulers as Stalin and Pol Pot.

Notes

1 *An Autobiography or The Story of My Experiments with Truth*, Ahmedabad, India: Navajivan, 1927, p. 420.
2 *Gandhi's Political Philosophy: A Critical Examination*, London: Macmillan, 1989, p. 143.
3 *Ibid*.

Gandhi, on *Satyagraha*

Satyagraha, Civil Disobedience, Passive Resistance, Non-Co-Operation

Satyagraha, then, is literally holding on to Truth and it means, therefore, Truth-force. Truth is soul or spirit. It is, therefore, known as soul-force. It excludes the use of violence because man is not capable of knowing the absolute truth and, therefore, not competent to punish. The word was coined in South Africa [in 1908] to distinguish the non-violent resistance of the Indians of South Africa from the contemporary "passive resistance" of the suffragettes and others. It is not conceived as a weapon of the weak.

Passive resistance is used in the orthodox English sense and covers the suffragette movement as well as the resistance of the nonconformists. Passive resistance has been conceived and is regarded as a weapon of the weak. Whilst it avoids violence, being not open to the weak, it does not exclude its use if, in the opinion of a passive resister, the occasion demands it. However, it has always been distinguished from armed resistance and its application was at one time confined to Christian martyrs.

Civil disobedience is civil breach of unmoral statutory enactments. The expression was, so far as I am aware, coined by Thoreau to signify his own resistance to the laws of a slave state. He has left a masterly treatise on the duty of civil disobedience. But Thoreau was not perhaps an out-and-out champion of non-violence. Probably, also, Thoreau limited his breach of statutory laws to the revenue law, i.e., payment of taxes, whereas the term "civil disobedience" as practiced in 1919 covered a breach of any statutory and unmoral law. It signified the resister's outlawry in a civil, i.e., non-violent manner. He invoked the sanctions of the law and cheerfully suffered imprisonment. It is a branch of satyagraha.

Non-co-operation predominantly implies withdrawing of co-operation from the state that in the non-co-operator's view has become corrupt and excludes civil disobedience of the fierce type described above. By its very nature, non-co-operation is even open to children of understanding and can be safely practiced by the masses. Civil disobedience presupposes the habit of willing obedience to laws without fear of their sanctions. It can therefore be practiced only as a last resort and by a select few in the first instance at any rate. Non-co-operation, too, like civil disobedience is a branch of satyagraha which includes all non-violent resistance for the vindication of Truth.

Satyagraha – Not Passive Resistance

The force denoted by the term "passive resistance" and translated into Hindi as *nishkriya pratirodha* is not very accurately described either by the original English phrase or by its Hindi rendering. Its correct description is "satyagraha." Satyagraha was born in South Africa in 1908. There was no word in any Indian language denoting the power which our countrymen in South Africa invoked for the redress of their grievances. There was an English equivalent, namely, "passive resistance," and we carried on with it. However, the need for a word to describe this unique power came to be increasingly felt, and it was decided to award a prize to anyone who could think of an appropriate term. A Gujarati-speaking gentleman submitted the word "satyagraha," and it was adjudged the best.

"Passive resistance" conveyed the idea of the Suffragette Movement in England. Burning of houses by these women was called "passive resistance" and so also their fasting in prison. All such acts might very well be "passive resistance" but they were not "satyagraha." It is said of "passive resistance" that it is the weapon of the weak, but the power which is the subject of this article can be used only by the strong. This power is not "passive" resistance; indeed it calls for intense activity. The movement in South Africa was not passive but active. The Indians of South Africa believed that Truth was their object, that Truth ever triumphs, and with this definiteness of purpose they persistently held on to Truth. They put up with all the suffering that this persistence implied. With the conviction that Truth is not to be renounced even unto death, they shed the fear of death. In the cause of Truth, the prison was a palace to them and its doors the gateway to freedom.

Satyagraha is not physical force. A satyagrahi does not inflict pain on the adversary; he does not seek his destruction. A satyagrahi never resorts to firearms. In the use of satyagraha, there is no ill-will whatever.

Satyagraha is pure soul-force. Truth is the very substance of the soul. That is why this force is called satyagraha. The soul is informed with knowledge. In it burns the flame of love. If someone gives us pain through ignorance, we shall win him through love. "Non-violence is the supreme dharma" is the proof of this power of love. Non-violence is a dormant state. In the waking state, it is love. Ruled by love, the world goes on. In English there is a saying, "Might is Right." Then there is the doctrine of the survival of the fittest. Both of these ideas are contradictory to the above principle. Neither is wholly true. If ill-will were the chief motive-force, the world would have been destroyed long ago; and neither would I have had the opportunity to write this article nor would the hopes of the readers be fulfilled. We are alive solely because of love. We are ourselves the proof of this. Deluded by modern western civilization, we have forgotten our ancient civilization and worship the might of arms.

We forget the principle of non-violence, which is the essence of all religions. The doctrine of arms stands for irreligion. It is due to the sway of that doctrine that a sanguinary war is raging in Europe.

[...] [A] satyagrahi does not fear for his body, he does not give up what he thinks is Truth; the word "defeat" is not to be found in his dictionary, he does not wish for the destruction of his antagonist, he does not vent anger on him; but has only compassion for him.

A satyagrahi does not wait for others, but throws himself into the fray, relying entirely on his own resources. He trusts that when the time comes, others will do likewise. His practice is his precept. Like air, satyagraha is all-pervading. It is infectious, which means that all people – big and small, men and women – can become satyagrahis. No one is kept out from the army of satyagrahis. A satyagrahi cannot perpetrate tyranny on anyone; he is not subdued through application of physical force; he does not strike at anyone. Just as anyone can resort to satyagraha, it can be resorted to in almost any situation.

People demand historical evidence in support of satyagraha. History is for the most part a record of armed activities. Natural activities find very little mention in it. Only uncommon activities strike us with wonder. Satyagraha has been used always and in all situations. The father and the son, the man and the wife are perpetually resorting to satyagraha, one towards the other. When a father gets angry and punishes the son, the son does not hit back with a weapon, he conquers his father's anger by submitting to him. The son refuses to be subdued by the unjust rule of his father but he puts up with the punishment that he may incur through disobeying the unjust father. We can similarly free ourselves of the unjust rule of the Government by defying the unjust rule and accepting the punishments that go with it. We do not bear malice towards the Government. When we set its fears at rest, when we do not desire to make armed assaults on the administrators, nor to unseat them from power, but only to get rid of their injustice, they will at once be subdued to our will.

The question is asked why we should call any rule unjust. In saying so, we ourselves assume the function of a judge. It is true. But in this world, we always have to act as judges for ourselves. That is why the satyagrahi does not strike his adversary with arms. If he has Truth on his side, he will win, and if his thought is faulty, he will suffer the consequences of his fault.

What is the good, they ask, of only one person opposing injustice; for he will be punished and destroyed, he will languish in prison or meet an untimely end through hanging. The objection is not valid. History shows that all reforms have begun with one person. Fruit is hard to come by without *tapasya* [self-sacrifice]. The suffering that has to be undergone in satyagraha is *tapasya* in its purest form. Only when the *tapasya* is capable of bearing fruit, do we have the fruit. This establishes the fact that when there is insufficient *tapasya*, the fruit is delayed. The *tapasya* of Jesus Christ, boundless though it was, was not sufficient for Europe's need. Europe has disapproved Christ. Through ignorance, it has disregarded Christ's pure way of life. Many Christs will have to offer themselves as sacrifice at the terrible altar of Europe, and only then will real-ization dawn on that continent. But Jesus will always be the first among these. He has been the sower of the seeds and his will therefore be the credit for raising the harvest.

It is said that it is a very difficult, if not an altogether impossible, task to educate ignorant peasants in satyagraha and that it is full of perils, for it is a very arduous business to transform unlettered ignorant people from one condition into another. Both the arguments are just silly. The people of India are perfectly fit to receive the training of satyagraha. India has knowledge of dharma [religious duty], and where there is knowledge of dharma, satyagraha is a very simple matter. The people of India have drunk of the nectar of devotion. This great people overflows with faith. It is no difficult matter to lead such a people on the right path of satyagraha. Some have a fear that once people get involved in satyagraha, they may at a later stage take to arms. This fear is illusory. From the path of satyagraha [clinging to Truth], a transition to the path of a-satyagraha [clinging to untruth] is impossible. It is possible of course that some people who believe in armed activity may mislead the satya-grahis by infiltrating into their ranks and later making them take to arms. This is possible in all enterprises. But as compared to other activities, it is less likely to happen in satyagraha, for their motives soon get exposed and when the people are not ready to take up arms, it becomes almost impossible to lead them on to that terrible path. The might of arms is directly opposed to the might of satyagraha. Just as darkness does not abide in light, soulless armed activity cannot enter the sunlike radiance of soul-force. Many Pathans took part in satyagraha in South Africa abiding by all the rules of satyagraha.

Then it is said that much suffering is involved in being a satyagrahi and that the entire people will not be willing to put up with this suffering. The objection is not valid. People in general always follow in the footsteps of the noble. There is no doubt that it is difficult to produce a satyagrahi leader. Our experience is that a satya-grahi needs many more virtues like self-control, fearlessness, etc., than are requisite for one who believes in armed action. The greatness of the man bearing arms does not lie in the superiority of the arms, nor does it lie in his physical prowess. It lies in his determination and fearlessness in face of death. . . . The strength of a warrior is not measured by reference to his weapons but by his firmness of mind. A satyagrahi needs millions of times more of such firmness than does a bearer of arms. The birth of such a man can bring about the salvation of India in no time. Not only India but the whole world awaits the advent of such a man. We may in the meanwhile prepare the ground as much as we can through satyagraha. . . .

For swaraj, satyagraha is the unfailing weapon. Satyagraha means that what we want is truth, that we deserve it and that we will work for it even unto death. . . .

Truth alone triumphs. There is no dharma [religion] higher than Truth. Truth always wins. We pray to God that in this sacred land we may bring about the reign of dharma by following satyagraha and that thus our country may become an example for all to follow.

There are two methods of attaining one's goal. Satyagraha and *duragraha*. In our scriptures, they have been described, respectively, as divine and devilish modes of action. In satyagraha, there is always unflinching adherence to truth. It is never to be forsaken on any account. Even for the sake of one's country, it does not permit resort to falsehood. It proceeds on the assumption of the ultimate triumph of truth. A satyagrahi does not abandon his path, even though at times it seems impenetrable and beset with difficulties and dangers, and a slight departure from that straight path may appear full of promise. Even in these circumstances, his faith shines resplendent like the midday sun and he does not despond. With truth for his sword, he needs neither a steel sword nor gunpowder. Even an inveterate enemy he conquers by the force of the soul, which is love. Love for a friend is not put to the test. There is nothing surprising in a friend loving a friend; there is no merit in it and it costs no effort. When love is bestowed on the so-called enemy, it is tested, it becomes a virtue and requires an effort, and hence it is an act of manliness and real bravery. We can cultivate such an attitude even towards the Government and, doing so, we shall be able to appreciate their beneficial activities and, as for their errors, rather than feel bitter on their account, point them out in love and so get them rectified. Love does not act through fear. Weakness there certainly cannot be. A coward is incapable of bearing love, it is the prerogative of the brave. Looking at everything with love, we shall not regard the Government with suspicion, nor believe that all their actions are inspired with bad motives. And our examination of their actions, being directed by love, will be unerring and is bound, therefore, to carry conviction with them.

Love can fight; often it is obliged to. In the intoxication of power, man fails to see his error. When that happens, a satyagrahi does not sit still. He suffers. He disobeys the ruler's orders and his laws in a civil manner, and willingly submits to the penalties of such disobedience, for instance, imprisonment and gallows. Thus is the soul disciplined. In this, one never finds that one's time has been wasted and, if it is subsequently realized that such respectful disobedience was an error, the consequences are suffered merely by the satyagrahi and his co-workers. In the event, no bitterness develops between the satyagrahi and those in power; the latter, on the contrary, willingly yield to him. *They discover that they cannot command the satyagrahi's obedience. They cannot make him do anything against his will. And this is the consummation of swaraj, because it means complete independence.* It need not be assumed that such resistance is possible only against civilized rulers. Even a heart of flint will melt in the fire kindled by the power of the soul. Even a Nero becomes a lamb when he faces love. This is no exaggeration. It is as true as an algebraic equation. This satyagraha is India's distinctive weapon. It has had others but satyagraha has been in greater use. It is an unfailing source of strength, and is capable of being used at all times and under all circumstances. It requires no stamp of approval from the Congress or any other body. He who knows its power cannot but use it. Even as the eyelashes automatically protect the eyes, so does satyagraha, when kindled, automatically protect the freedom of the soul.

But *duragraha* is a force with the opposite attributes. . . . The man who follows the path of *duragraha* becomes impatient and wants to kill the so-called enemy. There can be but one result of this. Hatred increases. The defeated party vows vengeance and simply bides its time. The spirit of revenge thus descends from father to son. It is much to be wished that India never give predominance to this spirit of *duragraha*. If the members of this assembly deliberately accept satyagraha and chalk out its program accordingly, they will reach their goal all the more easily for doing so. They may have to face disappointment in the initial stages. They may not see results for a time. But satyagraha will triumph in the end. The *duragrahi*, like the oilman's ox, moves in a circle. His movement is only motion but it is not progress. The satyagrahi is ever moving forward. . . .

The right thing to hope from India is that this great and holy Aryan land will ever give the predominant place to the divine force and employ the weapon of satyagraha, that it will never accept the supremacy of armed strength. India will never respect the principle of might being right. She will ever reserve her allegiance to the principle: "Truth alone triumphs."

On reflection, we find that we can employ satyagraha even for social reform. We can rid ourselves of the many defects of our caste system. We can resolve Hindu-Muslim differences and we can solve political problems. It is all right that, for the sake of convenience, we speak of these things as separate subjects. But it should never be forgotten that they are all closely inter-related. It is not true to say that neither religion nor social reform has anything to do with politics.

Evidence Before Disorders
Inquiry Committee[1]

Mr Gandhi, we have been informed that you are the author of the satyagraha movement?

Yes, sir.

I would like to give you an explanation of what that movement is.

It is a movement intended to replace methods of violence. It is a movement based entirely on truth. It is, as I have conceived it, an extension of the domestic law on the political field, and my own experience has led me to the conclusion that that movement and that movement alone can rid India of the possibilities of violence spreading throughout the length and breadth of the land for the redress of grievances, supposed or real. . . .

For the past thirty years I have been preaching and practicing satyagraha. The principles of satyagraha, as I know it today, constitute a gradual evolution.

Satyagraha differs from passive resistance as North Pole from South. The latter has been conceived as a weapon of the weak and does not exclude the use of physical force or violence for the purpose of gaining one's end, whereas the former has been conceived as a weapon of the strongest and excludes the use of violence in any shape or form.

The term satyagraha was coined by me in South Africa to express the force that the Indians there used for a full eight years and it was coined in order to distinguish it from the movement then going on in the United Kingdom and South Africa under the name of passive resistance.

Its root meaning is holding on to truth, hence truth-force. I have also called it love-force or soul-force. In the application of satyagraha, I discovered in the earliest stages that pursuit of truth did not admit of violence being inflicted on one's opponent but that he must be weaned from error by patience and sympathy. For what appears to be truth to the one may appear to be error to the other. And patience means self-suffering. So the doctrine came to mean vindication of truth, not by infliction of suffering on the opponent, but on one's self.

But on the political field, the struggle on behalf of the people mostly consists in opposing error in the shape of unjust laws. When you have failed to bring the error home to the law-giver by way of petitions and the like, the only remedy open to you, if you do not wish to submit to error, is to compel him by physical force to yield to you or by suffering in your own person by inviting the penalty for the breach of the law. Hence satyagraha largely appears to the public as civil disobedience or civil resistance. It is civil in the sense that it is not criminal.

The law-breaker breaks the law surreptitiously and tries to avoid the penalty; not so the civil resister. He ever obeys the laws of the State to which he belongs not out of fear of the sanctions but because he considers them to be good for the welfare of society. But there come occasions, generally rare, when he considers certain laws to be so unjust as to render obedience to them a dishonor. He then openly and civilly breaks them and quietly suffers the penalty for their breach. And in order to register his protest against the action of the law-givers, it is open to him to withdraw his co-operation from the State by disobeying such other laws whose breach does not involve moral turpitude.

In my opinion, the beauty and efficacy of satyagraha are so great and the doctrine so simple that it can be preached even to children. It was preached by me to thousands of men, women and children commonly called indentured Indians, with excellent results.

When the Rowlatt Bills were published I felt that they were so restrictive of human liberty that they must be resisted to the utmost. I observed too that the opposition to them was universal among Indians. I submit that no State however despotic has the right to enact laws which are repugnant to the whole body of the people, much less a government guided by constitutional usage and precedent such as the Indian Government. I felt too that the oncoming agitation needed a definite direction if it was neither to collapse nor to run into violent channels.

I ventured therefore to present satyagraha to the country emphasizing its civil resistance aspect. And as it is purely an inward and purifying movement, I suggested the observance of fast, prayer and suspension of all work for one day – the 6th of April [1919]. There was a magnificent response throughout the length and breadth of India, even in little villages, although there was no organization and no great previous preparation. The idea was given to the public as soon as it was conceived. On the 6th April there was no violence used by the people and no collision with the police worth naming. The hartal [strike] was purely voluntary and spontaneous. . . .

Was it your intention to enlist as many satyagrahis as possible?

Yes, consistently with the carrying on of the movement in a proper way, that is to say, if I found a million men who were capable of understanding the truth and adhering by it and never using violence, I would certainly be glad to have the million men. . . .

I suppose it is the case in India as elsewhere that people differ as to the justice or injustice of particular laws?

Yes; and that is the reason, the main reason, why violence is eliminated here. The satyagrahi gives his opponent the same right of independence and feeling of truth that he reserves to himself, seeing that [if] he wants to fight for truth he will do so by inviting injury upon his own person. . . .

Is not refusing to obey that or any other law you choose to select a rather drastic way of attempting to do that?

I respectfully differ. When I find that even my father has imposed upon me a law which is repugnant to my conscience, I think it is the least drastic course that I adopt by respectfully telling him, "Father, I cannot obey this." I do nothing but justice to my father when I do that. If I may say so without any disrespect to the Committee, I have simply followed that in my own domestic circle, and I found I had done so with the greatest advantage. I have placed that before Indians and everybody for acceptance. Rather than feel angry with my father, I would respectfully tell him, "I cannot obey this law." I see nothing wrong in that. If it is not wrong for me to say so to my father, there is nothing wrong for me to say so to a friend or to a Government. . . .

Do you not create a condition of very great danger to peace and order?

On the contrary, I promote peace. And I have done it myself on the 6th of April, because I was there in Bombay, and there was some fear of people themselves offering violence. And I am here to tell you that no violence, no real violence was offered by the people, because people were being told the true nature of satyagraha. It was an amazing sight for me to see thousands of people behaving in a perfectly peaceful manner. That would not have been the case if the satyagraha doctrine had not been preached in the right key. . . .

In Ahmedabad . . . your arrest seems to have created a great resentment on their part, and very unfortunately again, on the part of the mob. . . .

I consider that the action of this mob, whether in Ahmedabad or in Viramgam, was totally unjustified, and I have thought that it was a very sad thing that they lost self-control. I do not wish to offer the slightest defense for the acts of the mob, but at the same time I would like to say that the people amongst whom, rightly or wrongly, I was popular were put to such severe stress by Government who should have known better. I think the Government committed an unpardonable error of judgment and the mob committed a similar unpardonable error, but more unpardonable on the part of the mob than on the part of the Government. I wish to say that also as a satyagrahi, I cannot find a single thing done by the mob which I can defend or justify. No amount of provocation, however great, could justify people from doing as they have done. It has been suggested to me that all those who did it were not satyagrahis. That is true. But they chose to take part in the satyagraha movement and came under the satyagraha discipline. These were the terms in which I have spoken to the people; and it gives me the greatest pleasure and also pain to declare my settled conviction before this Committee also.

With regard to your satyagraha doctrine, as far as I am able to understand it, it involves a pursuit of truth?

Yes.

Now in that doctrine, who is to determine the truth? That individual himself?

Yes, that individual himself.

So each one that adopts this doctrine has to determine for himself what is the truth that he will pursue?

Most decidedly.

And in doing that different individuals will take very different views as to what is the truth to be pursued?

Certainly.

It might, on that footing, cause considerable confusion?

I won't accept that. It need not lead to any confusion if you accept the proposition that a man is honestly in search after truth and that he will never inflict violence upon him who holds to truth. Then there is no possibility of confusion.

A man may honestly strive after truth, but however honestly a man may strive, his notions of truth will be quite different from the notions of truth of some other people or his intellectual equipment may be of such a character that his conclusion as regards truth may be entirely opposite to the conclusion of somebody else?

That was precisely the reason why in answer to Lord Hunter I suggested that non-violence was the necessary corollary to the acceptance of satyagraha doctrine.

Some Rules of Satyagraha

Satyagraha literally means insistence on truth. This insistence arms the votary with matchless power. This power or force is connected by the word satyagraha. Satyagraha, to be genuine, may be offered against parents, against one's wife or one's children, against rulers, against fellow-citizens, even against the whole world.

Such a universal force necessarily makes no distinction between kinsmen and strangers, young and old, man and woman, friend and foe. The force to be so applied can never be physical. There is in it no room for violence. The only force of universal application can, therefore, be that of ahimsa or love. In other words it is soul force.

Love does not burn others, it burns itself. Therefore, a satyagrahi, i.e., a civil resister will joyfully suffer even unto death.

It follows, therefore, that a civil resister, whilst he will strain every nerve to compass the end of the existing rule, will do no intentional injury in thought, word or deed to the person of a single Englishman. This necessarily brief explanation of satyagraha will perhaps enable the reader to understand and appreciate the following rules:

As an Individual

1. A satyagrahi, i.e., a civil resister will harbour no anger.
2. He will suffer the anger of the opponent.
3. In so doing he will put up with assaults from the opponent, never retaliate; but he will not submit, out of fear of punishment or the like, to any order given in anger.
4. When any person in authority seeks to arrest a civil resister, he will voluntarily submit to the arrest, and he will not resist the attachment or removal of his own property, if any, when it is sought to be confiscated by authorities.
5. If a civil resister has any property in his possession as a trustee, he will refuse to surrender it, even though in defending it he might lose his life. He will, however, never retaliate.
6. Non-retaliation excludes swearing and cursing.
7. Therefore a civil resister will never insult his opponent, and therefore also not take part in many of the newly coined cries which are contrary to the spirit of ahimsa.
8. A civil resister will not salute the Union Jack, nor will he insult it or officials, English or Indian.
9. In the course of the struggle if anyone insults an official or commits an assault upon

him, a civil resister will protect such official or officials from the insult or attack even at the risk of his life.

As a Prisoner

10. As a prisoner, a civil resister will behave courteously towards prison officials, and will observe all such discipline of the prison as is not contrary to self-respect; as for instance, whilst he will salaam officials in the usual manner, he will not perform any humiliating gyrations and [will] refuse to shout "Victory to Sarkar" [Government] or the like. He will take cleanly cooked and cleanly served food, which is not contrary to his religion, and will refuse to take food insultingly served or served in unclean vessels.

11. A civil resister will make no distinction between an ordinary prisoner and himself, will in no way regard himself as superior to the rest, nor will he ask for any conveniences that may not be necessary for keeping his body in good health and condition. He is entitled to ask for such conveniences as may be required for his physical or spiritual well-being.

12. A civil resister may not fast for want of conveniences whose deprivation does not involve any injury to one's self-respect.

As a Unit

13. A civil resister will joyfully obey all the orders issued by the leader of the corps, whether they please him or not.

14. He will carry out orders in the first instance even though they appear to him insulting, inimical or foolish, and then appeal to higher authority. He is free before joining to determine the fitness of the corps to satisfy him, but after he has joined it, it becomes a duty to submit to its discipline irksome or otherwise. If the sum total of the energy of the corps appears to a member to be improper or immoral, he has a right to sever his connection, but being with it, he has no right to commit a breach of its discipline.

15. No civil resister is to expect maintenance for his dependents. It would be an accident if any such provision is made. A civil resister entrusts his dependents to the care of God. Even in ordinary warfare wherein hundreds of thousands give themselves up to it, they are able to make no previous provision. How much more, then should be the case in satyagraha? It is the universal experience that in such times hardly anybody is left to starve.

In Communal Fights

16. No civil resister will intentionally become a cause of communal [religious] quarrels.

17. In the event of any such outbreak, he will not take sides, but he will assist only that party which is demonstrably in the right. Being a Hindu he will be generous towards Mussalmans and others, and will sacrifice himself in the attempt to save non-Hindus from a Hindu attack. And if the attack is from the other side, he will not participate in any retaliation but will give his life in protecting Hindus.

18. He will, to the best of his ability, avoid every occasion that may give rise to communal quarrels.

19. If there is a procession of satyagrahis they will do nothing that would wound the religious susceptibilities of any community, and they will not take part in any other processions that are likely to wound such susceptibilities.

Note

1   This Committee, presided over by Lord Hunter, was convened in 1919 to investigate the first nation-wide *satyagraha* action organized by Gandhi – a mass strike or *hartal* in protest against the Rowlatt Bills, which authorized the government to imprison suspected dissidents without trial. Among those who gave evidence to the Committee was the notorious General Dyer, the officer whose order to shoot strikers resulted in the "Amritsar Massacre" of April 1919 – an event that proved decisive in shaping Gandhi's attitude towards colonial rule.

Max Horkheimer and Theodor Adorno, "The Concept of Enlightenment"

Introduction

One of the most influential works of social criticism of the twentieth century, *Dialectic of Enlightenment*, was completed in 1944 while its authors, in exile from Hitler's Germany, were living in California. The book is not a work of political philosophy in any narrow sense. As one writer puts it, Adorno and Horkheimer – both of them steeped in the writings of Friedrich Engels and Karl Marx (V.19) – "replaced the critique of political economy with a critique of technological civilization."[1] Nevertheless, many sections of their book – including the first half of the opening chapter we have selected – attest to the political relevance of this critique. It is clear, for example, that the authors discern a close link between "technological civilization" and totalitarian politics. In forging this link, Adorno and Horkheimer draw upon the work of sociologist Max Weber (1864–1920) and psychologist Sigmund Freud (1856–1939) to break loose of the economic reductionism of Marxian analyses and produce a more expansive cultural critique. Totalitarianism, Horkheimer and Adorno find, is more than the superstructure expressed by more basic economic

From Max Horkheimer and Theodor Adorno, *Dialectic of Enlightenment: Philosophical Fragments*, trans. E. Jephcott, Stanford, CA: Stanford University Press, 2002, pp. 1–12 (notes omitted).

forces; it is the result of cultural factors that move according to their own dynamics.

Theodor Adorno (1903–69) – a musicologist and composer as well as a social philosopher – and his older contemporary Max Horkheimer (1895–1973) were leading members of the famous "Frankfurt School" associated with the Institute of Social Research, of which Horkheimer was the first director and whose journal, *Zeitschrift für Sozialforschung* he edited. But it was not until the 1940s when the two men, both of Jewish descent, found themselves refugees in the USA, that they collaborated, producing what became the best-known work of the "Critical Theory" that it was the ambition of the Frankfurt School to articulate. After World War II, the two thinkers returned to Frankfurt where they continued their productive careers. Both men, to their chagrin, were spurned or insulted, during the "student revolt" of 1968, by ultra-radical students, some of whose ideas, ironically, had been inspired by *Dialectic of Enlightenment*.

The central component of Critical Theory was a distinction between "objective" reason and what members of the Frankfurt School alternatively referred to as "subjective," "instrumental," or "technological" reason.[2] This is a distinction between, roughly, the employment of reason to examine and assess the ultimate truths, values, and aims that human beings seek to live by, and its employment simply as a means to help achieve purposes already accepted by "the political-cultural regime" that currently enjoys social-political "hegemony." The main historical claim of Horkheimer and Adorno's book is that, despite the intentions of Enlightenment thinkers to open the way to free, critical thought, the effect of the Enlightenment was to establish the sovereignty of instrumental reason. The primary reason for this legacy was the myopic focus, already marked in the writings of pre-Enlightenment figures like Sir Francis Bacon (II.7), on reason or knowledge as *power*, as something that it is important to exercise or acquire essentially for the purpose of controlling and exploiting nature.

The Enlightenment's legacy has, according to Adorno and Horkheimer, been devastating: "the wholly enlightened earth is radiant with triumphant calamity." The "calamity" consists, in practice, of various "leveling" effects caused by the sovereignty of instrumental reason. To begin with, ideas and theories other than the scientific ones favored by instrumental reason all get leveled down to the status of mere "beliefs" or "literature." From the point of view of instrumental reason, there is nothing to choose between democratic, fascist, and theocratic regimes provided that they are equally "efficient." Second, with critical debate on values and ends, including aesthetic and cultural ones, closed off, a "positivist" cult of "factual," "useful" information flourishes, so that people find themselves "stultified" by a combination of information overload and a "candy-floss entertainment" industry. Finally, the reductionist tendency of the sciences to treat everything as composed of "repeatable," identical components extends to the treatment of human beings. "Under the leveling rule of abstraction . . . and of industry . . . the liberated finally themselves become the 'herd'."

Human individuality is itself erased, so that the emergence of the "herd" – already observed by Hegel and Nietzsche – was indeed "the outcome of enlightenment."

As the authors recall in their 1969 Preface, *Dialectic of Enlightenment* was slow to find readers – but once these were found, the book's influence became considerable and enduring. It has, for example, become something of a sacred text for those "green" activists who identify the roots of the global environmental crisis in precisely the tendencies of instrumental reason, and the equation of knowledge with power, that the book exposes. A more questionable impact, and one that is not warranted by a careful reading of the book, has been upon those "postmodernist" writers who cheerfully rubbish the principles and ambitions of Enlightenment thought. As Adorno and Horkheimer explain, however, it is the collapse of Enlightenment into a "mythology" captured by the technological enterprise and not the Enlightenment's guiding aim of "liberating human beings from fear" that is the proper object of their critique.

Notes

1   R. Eckersley, *Environmentalism and Political Theory*, London: UCL Press, 1992, p. 101.
2   Other important champions of Critical Theory included Walter Benjamin and Herbert Marcuse. Since 1960, the most distinguished exponent of Critical Theory has been Jürgen Habermas: see, especially, his *The Philosophical Discourse of Modernity*, trans. F. Lawrence, Cambridge: Polity Press, 1987.

Horkheimer and Adorno, "The Concept of Enlightenment"

Enlightenment, understood in the widest sense as the advance of thought, has always aimed at liberating human beings from fear and installing them as masters. Yet the wholly enlightened earth is radiant with triumphant calamity. Enlightenment's program was the disenchantment of the world. It wanted to dispel myths, to overthrow fantasy with knowledge. Bacon, "the father of experimental philosophy,"[1] brought these motifs

together. He despised the exponents of tradition, who substituted belief for knowledge and were as unwilling to doubt as they were reckless in supplying answers. All this, he said, stood in the way of "the happy match between the mind of man and the nature of things," with the result that humanity was unable to use its knowledge for the betterment of its condition. Such inventions as had been made – Bacon cites printing, artillery, and the compass – had been arrived at more by chance than by systematic enquiry into nature. Knowledge obtained through such enquiry would not only be exempt from the influence of wealth and power but would establish man as the master of nature:

> Therefore, no doubt, the sovereignty of man lieth hid in knowledge; wherein many things are reserved, which kings with their treasure cannot buy, nor with their force command; their spials and intelligencers can give no news of them, their seamen and discoverers cannot sail where they grow: now we govern nature in opinions, but we are thrall unto her in necessity: but if we would be led by her in invention, we should command her by action.

Although not a mathematician, Bacon well understood the scientific temper which was to come after him. The "happy match" between human understanding and the nature of things that he envisaged is a patriarchal one: the mind, conquering superstition, is to rule over disenchanted nature. Knowledge, which is power, knows no limits, either in its enslavement of creation or in its deference to worldly masters. Just as it serves all the purposes of the bourgeois economy both in factories and on the battlefield, it is at the disposal of entrepreneurs regardless of their origins. Kings control technology no more directly than do merchants: it is as democratic as the economic system with which it evolved. Technology is the essence of this knowledge. It aims to produce neither concepts nor images, nor the joy of understanding, but method, exploitation of the labor of others, capital. The "many things" which, according to Bacon, knowledge still held in store are themselves mere instruments: the radio as a sublimated printing press, the dive bomber as a more effective form of artillery, remote control as a more reliable compass. What human beings seek to learn from nature is how to use it to dominate wholly both it and human beings. Nothing else counts. Ruthless toward itself, the Enlightenment has eradicated the last remnant of its own self-awareness. Only thought which does violence to itself is hard enough to shatter myths. Faced by the present triumph of the factual mentality, Bacon's nominalist credo would have smacked of metaphysics and would have been convicted of the same vanity for which he criticized scholasticism. Power and knowledge are synonymous. For Bacon as for Luther, "knowledge that tendeth but to satisfaction, is but as a courtesan, which is for pleasure, and not for fruit or generation." Its concern is not "satisfaction, which men call truth," but "operation," the

effective procedure. The "true end, scope or office of knowledge" does not consist in "any plausible, delectable, reverend or admired discourse, or any satisfactory arguments, but in effecting and working, and in discovery of particulars not revealed before, for the better endowment and help of man's life." There shall be neither mystery nor any desire to reveal mystery.

The disenchantment of the world means the extirpation of animism. Xenophanes mocked the multiplicity of gods because they resembled their creators, men, in all their idiosyncrasies and faults, and the latest logic denounces the words of language, which bear the stamp of impressions, as counterfeit coin that would be better replaced by neutral counters. The world becomes chaos, and synthesis salvation. No difference is said to exist between the totemic animal, the dreams of the spirit-seer, and the absolute Idea. On their way toward modern science human beings have discarded meaning. The concept is replaced by the formula, the cause by rules and probability. Causality was only the last philosophical concept on which scientific criticism tested its strength, because it alone of the old ideas still stood in the way of such criticism, the latest secular form of the creative principle. To define substance and quality, activity and suffering, being and existence in terms appropriate to the time has been a concern of philosophy since Bacon; but science could manage without such categories. They were left behind as *idola theatri* of the old metaphysics and even in their time were monuments to entities and powers from prehistory. In that distant time life and death had been interpreted and interwoven in myths. The categories by which Western philosophy defined its timeless order of nature marked out the positions which had once been occupied by Ocnus and Persephone, Ariadne and Nereus. The moment of transition is recorded in the pre-Socratic cosmologies. The moist, the undivided, the air and fire which they take to be the primal stuff of nature are early rationalizations precipitated from the mythical vision. Just as the images of generation from water and earth, that had come to the Greeks from the Nile, were converted by these cosmologies into Hylozoic principles and elements, the whole ambiguous profusion of mythical demons was intellectualized to become the pure form of ontological entities. Even the patriarchal gods of Olympus were finally assimilated by the philosophical *logos* as the Platonic Forms. But the Enlightenment discerned the old powers in the Platonic and Aristotelian heritage of metaphysics and suppressed the universal categories' claims to truth as superstition. In the authority of universal concepts the Enlightenment detected a fear of the demons through whose effigies human beings had tried to influence nature in magic rituals. From now on matter was finally to be controlled without the illusion of immanent powers or hidden properties. For enlightenment, anything which does not conform to the standard of calculability and utility must be viewed with suspicion. Once the movement is able to develop unhampered by external oppression, there is no holding it back. Its own ideas of human rights then fare no better than the older universals. Any intellectual resistance it encounters merely increases its strength. The reason is that enlightenment also recognizes itself in the old myths. No matter which myths are invoked against it, by being used as arguments they are made to acknowledge the very principle of corrosive rationality of which enlightenment stands accused. Enlightenment is totalitarian.

Enlightenment has always regarded anthropomorphism, the projection of subjective properties onto nature, as the basis of myth. The supernatural, spirits and demons, are taken to be reflections of human beings who allow themselves to be frightened by natural phenomena. According to enlightened thinking, the multiplicity of mythical figures can be reduced to a single common denominator, the subject. Oedipus's answer to the riddle of the Sphinx – "That being is man" – is repeated indiscriminately as enlightenment's stereotyped message, whether in response to a piece of objective meaning, a schematic order, a fear of evil powers, or a hope of salvation. For the Enlightenment, only what can be encompassed by unity has the status of an existent or an event; its ideal is the system from which everything and anything follows. Its rationalist and empiricist versions do not differ on that point. Although the various schools may have interpreted its axioms differently, the structure of unitary science has always been the same. Despite the pluralism of the different fields of research, Bacon's postulate of *una scientia universalis* is as hostile to anything which cannot be connected as Leibniz's *mathesis universalis* is to discontinuity. The multiplicity of forms is reduced to position and arrangement, history to fact, things to matter. For Bacon, too, there was a clear logical connection, through degrees of generality, linking the highest principles to propositions based on observation. De Maistre mocks him for harboring this "idolized ladder."[2] Formal logic was the high school of unification. It offered Enlightenment thinkers a schema for making the world calculable. The mythologizing equation of Forms with numbers in Plato's last writings expresses the longing of all demythologizing: number became enlightenment's canon. The same equations govern bourgeois justice and commodity exchange. "Is not the rule, '*Si inaequalibus aequalia addas, omnia erunt inaequalia*,' [If you add like to unlike you will always end up with unlike] an axiom of justice as well as of mathematics? And is there not a true coincidence between commutative and distributive justice, and arithmetical and geometrical proportion?" Bourgeois society is ruled by equivalence. It makes dissimilar things comparable by reducing them to abstract quantities. For the Enlightenment, anything which cannot be resolved into numbers, and ultimately into one, is illusion; modern positivism consigns it to poetry. Unity remains the watchword from Parmenides to Russell. All gods and qualities must be destroyed.

But the myths which fell victim to the Enlightenment were themselves its products. The scientific calculation of events annuls the account of them which thought had once given in myth. Myth sought to report, to name, to tell of origins – but therefore also to narrate, record, explain. This tendency was reinforced by the recording and collecting of myths. From a record, they soon became a teaching. Each ritual contains a representation of how things happen and of the specific process which is to be influenced by magic. In the earliest popular epics this theoretical element of ritual became autonomous. The myths which the tragic dramatists drew on were already marked by the discipline and power which Bacon celebrated as the goal. The local spirits and demons had been replaced by heaven and its hierarchy, the incantatory practices of the magician by the carefully graduated sacrifice and the labor of enslaved men mediated by command. The Olympian deities are no longer directly identical with elements, but signify them. In Homer Zeus controls the daytime sky, Apollo guides the sun; Helios and Eos are already passing over into allegory. The gods detach themselves from substances to become their quintessence.

From now on, being is split between *logos* – which, with the advance of philosophy, contracts to a monad, a mere reference point – and the mass of things and creatures in the external world. The single distinction between man's own existence and reality swallows up all others. Without regard for differences, the world is made subject to man. In this the Jewish story of creation and the Olympian religion are at one: "... and let them have dominion over the fish of the sea, and over the fowl of the air, and over the cattle, and over all the earth, and over every creeping thing that creepeth upon the earth." [Genesis I. 26] "O Zeus, Father Zeus, yours is the dominion of the heavens; you oversee the works of men, both the wicked and the just, and the unruly animals, you who uphold righteousness." [Archilochos] "It is so ordained that one atones at once, another later; but even should one escape the doom threatened by the gods, it will surely come to pass one day, and innocents shall expiate his deed, whether his children or a later generation." [Solon] Only those who subject themselves utterly pass muster with the gods. The awakening of the subject is bought with the recognition of power as the principle of all relationships. In face of the unity of such reason the distinction between God and man is reduced to an irrelevance, as reason has steadfastly indicated since the earliest critique of Homer. In their mastery of nature, the creative God and the ordering mind are alike. Man's likeness to God consists in sovereignty over existence, in the lordly gaze, in the command.

Myth becomes enlightenment and nature mere objectivity. Human beings purchase the increase in their power with estrangement from that over which it is exerted. Enlightenment stands in the same relationship to things as the dictator to human beings. He knows them to the extent that he can manipulate them. The man of science knows things to the extent that he can make them. Their "in-itself" becomes "for him." In their transformation the essence of things is revealed as always the same, a substrate of domination. This identity constitutes the unity of nature. Neither it nor the unity of the subject was presupposed by magical incantation. The rites of the shaman were directed at the wind, the rain, the snake outside or the demon inside the sick person, not at materials or specimens. The spirit which practiced magic was not single or identical; it changed with the cult masks which represented the multiplicity of spirits. Magic is bloody untruth, but in it domination is not yet disclaimed by transforming itself into a pure truth underlying the world which it enslaves. The magician imitates demons; to frighten or placate them he makes intimidating or appeasing gestures. Although his task was impersonation he did not claim to be made in the image of the invisible power, as does civilized man, whose modest hunting ground then shrinks to the unified cosmos, in which nothing exists but prey. Only when made in such an image does man attain the identity of the self which cannot be lost in identification with the other but takes possession of itself once and for all as an impenetrable mask. It is the identity of mind and its correlative, the unity of nature, which subdues the abundance of qualities. Nature, stripped of qualities, becomes the chaotic stuff of mere classification, and the all-powerful self becomes a mere having, an abstract identity. Magic implies specific representation. What is done to the spear, the hair, the name of the enemy, is also to befall his person; the sacrificial animal is slain in place of the god. The substitution which takes place in sacrifice marks a step toward discursive logic. Even though the hind which was offered up for the daughter, the lamb for the firstborn, necessarily still had qualities of its own, it already represented the genus. It manifested the arbitrariness of the specimen. But the sanctity of the *hic et nunc*, the uniqueness of the chosen victim which coincides with its representative status, distinguishes it radically, makes it non-exchangeable even in the exchange. Science puts an end to this. In it there is no specific representation: something which is a sacrificial animal cannot be a god. Representation gives way to universal fungibility. An atom is smashed not as a representative but as a specimen of matter, and the rabbit suffering the torment of the laboratory is seen not as a representative but, mistakenly, as a mere exemplar. Because in functional science the differences are so fluid that everything is submerged in one and the same matter, the scientific object is petrified, whereas the rigid ritual of former times appears supple in its substitution of one thing for another. The world of magic still retained differences whose traces have vanished even in linguistic forms. The manifold affinities between existing things are supplanted by the single relationship between the subject who confers meaning and the meaningless object, between rational significance and its accidental bearer. At the magical stage dream and image were not regarded as mere signs of things but were linked to them by resemblance or name. The relationship was not one of intention but of kinship. Magic like science is concerned with ends, but it pursues them through mimesis, not through an increasing distance from the object. It certainly is not founded on the "omnipotence of thought," which the primitive is supposed to impute to himself like the neurotic; there can be no "over-valuation of psychical acts" in relation to reality where thought and reality are not radically distinguished. The "unshakable confidence in the possibility of controlling the world"[3] which Freud anachronistically attributes to magic applies only to the more realistic form of world domination achieved by the greater astuteness of science. The autonomy of thought in relation to objects, as manifested in the reality-adequacy of the Ego, was a prerequisite for the replacement of the localized practices of the medicine man by all-embracing industrial technology.

As a totality set out in language and laying claim to a truth which suppressed the older mythical faith of popular religion, the solar, patriarchal myth was itself an enlightenment, fully comparable on that level to the philosophical one. But now it paid the price. Mythology itself set in motion the endless process of enlightenment by which, with ineluctable necessity, every definite theoretical view is subjected to the annihilating criticism that it is only a belief, until even the concepts of mind, truth, and, indeed, enlightenment itself have been reduced to animistic magic. The principle of the fated necessity which caused the downfall of the mythical hero, and finally evolved as the logical conclusion from the oracular utterance, not only predominates, refined to the cogency of formal logic, in every rationalistic system of Western philosophy but also presides over the succession of systems which begins with the hierarchy of the gods and, in a permanent twilight of the idols, hands down a single identical content: wrath against those of insufficient righteousness. Just as myths already entail enlightenment, with every step enlightenment entangles itself more deeply in mythology. Receiving all its subject matter from myths, in order to destroy them, it falls as judge under the spell of myth. It seeks to escape the trial of fate and retribution by itself exacting retribution on

that trial. In myths, everything that happens must atone for the fact of having happened. It is no different in enlightenment: no sooner has a fact been established than it is rendered insignificant. The doctrine that action equals reaction continued to maintain the power of repetition over existence long after humankind had shed the illusion that, by repetition, it could identify itself with repeated existence and so escape its power. But the more the illusion of magic vanishes, the more implacably repetition, in the guise of regularity, imprisons human beings in the cycle now objectified in the laws of nature, to which they believe they owe their security as free subjects. The principle of immanence, the explanation of every event as repetition, which enlightenment upholds against mythical imagination, is that of myth itself. The arid wisdom which acknowledges nothing new under the sun, because all the pieces in the meaningless game have been played out, all the great thoughts have been thought, all possible discoveries can be construed in advance, and human beings are defined by self-preservation through adaptation – this barren wisdom merely reproduces the fantastic doctrine it rejects: the sanction of fate which, through retribution, incessantly reinstates what always was. Whatever might be different is made the same. That is the verdict which critically sets the boundaries to possible experience. The identity of everything with everything is bought at the cost that nothing can at the same time be identical to itself. Enlightenment dissolves away the injustice of the old inequality of unmediated mastery, but at the same time perpetuates it in universal mediation, by relating every existing thing to every other. It brings about the situation for which Kierkegaard praised his Protestant ethic and which, in the legend-cycle of Hercules, constitutes one of the primal images of mythical violence: it amputates the incommensurable. Not merely are qualities dissolved in thought, but human beings are forced into real conformity. The blessing that the market does not ask about birth is paid for in the exchange society by the fact that the possibilities conferred by birth are molded to fit the production of goods that can be bought on the market. Each human being has been endowed with a self of his or her own, different from all others, so that it could all the more surely be made the same. But because that self never quite fitted the mold, enlightenment throughout the liberalistic period has always sympathized with social coercion. The unity of the manipulated collective consists in the negation of each individual and in the scorn poured on the type of society which could make people into individuals. The horde, a term which doubtless is to be found in the Hitler Youth organization, is not a relapse into the old barbarism but the triumph of repressive *égalité*, the degeneration of the equality of rights into the wrong inflicted by equals. The fake myth of fascism reveals itself as the genuine myth of prehistory, in that the genuine myth beheld retribution while the false one wreaks it blindly on its victims. Any attempt to break the compulsion of nature by breaking nature only succumbs more deeply to that compulsion. That has been the trajectory of European civilization. Abstraction, the instrument of enlightenment, stands in the same relationship to its objects as fate, whose concept it eradicates: as liquidation. Under the leveling rule of abstraction, which makes everything in nature repeatable, and of industry, for which abstraction prepared the way, the liberated finally themselves become the "herd" (*Trupp*), which Hegel identified as the outcome of enlightenment.

The distance of subject from object, the presupposition of abstraction, is founded on the distance from things which the ruler attains by means of the ruled. The songs of Homer and the hymns of the *Rig Veda* date from the time of territorial dominion and its strongholds, when a warlike race of overlords imposed itself on the defeated indigenous population. The supreme god among gods came into being with this civil world in which the king, as leader of the arms-bearing nobility, tied the subjugated people to the land while doctors, soothsayers, artisans, and traders took care of circulation. With the end of nomadism the social order is established on the basis of fixed property. Power and labor diverge. A property owner like Odysseus "controls from a distance a numerous, finely graded personnel of ox herds, shepherds, swineherds, and servants. In the evening, having looked out from his castle to see the countryside lit up by a thousand fires, he can go to his rest in peace. He knows that his loyal servants are watching to keep away wild animals and to drive away thieves from the enclosures which they are there to protect. The generality of the ideas developed by discursive logic, power in the sphere of the concept, is built on the foundation of power in reality. The

superseding of the old diffuse notions of the magical heritage by conceptual unity expresses a condition of life defined by the freeborn citizen and articulated by command. The self which learned about order and subordination through the subjugation of the world soon equated truth in general with classifying thought, without whose fixed distinctions it cannot exist. Along with mimetic magic it tabooed the knowledge which really apprehends the object. Its hatred is directed at the image of the vanquished primeval world and its imaginary happiness. The dark, chthonic gods of the original inhabitants are banished to the hell into which the earth is transformed under the religions of Indra and Zeus, with their worship of sun and light.

But heaven and hell were linked. The name Zeus was applied both to a god of the underworld and to a god of light in cults which did not exclude each other, and the Olympian gods maintained all kinds of commerce with the chthonic deities. In the same way, the good and evil powers, the holy and the unholy, were not unambiguously distinguished. They were bound together like genesis and decline, life and death, summer and winter. The murky, undivided entity worshipped as the principle of *mana* at the earliest known stages of humanity lived on in the bright world of the Greek religion. Primal and undifferentiated, it is everything unknown and alien; it is that which transcends the bounds of experience, the part of things which is more than their immediately perceived existence. What the primitive experiences as supernatural is not a spiritual substance in contradistinction to the material world but the complex concatenation of nature in contrast to its individual link. The cry of terror called forth by the unfamiliar becomes its name. It fixes the transcendence of the unknown in relation to the known, permanently linking horror to holiness. The doubling of nature into appearance and essence, effect and force, made possible by myth no less than by science, springs from human fear, the expression of which becomes its explanation. This does not mean that the soul is transposed into nature, as psychologism would have us believe; *mana*, the moving spirit, is not a projection but the echo of the real preponderance of nature in the weak psyches of primitive people. The split between animate and inanimate, the assigning of demons and deities to certain specific places, arises from this preanimism. Even the division of subject and object is prefigured in it. If the tree is addressed no longer as simply a tree but as evidence of something else, a location of *mana*, language expresses the contradiction that it is at the same time itself and something other than itself, identical and not identical. Through the deity speech is transformed from tautology into language. The concept, usually defined as the unity of the features of what it subsumes, was rather, from the first, a product of dialectical thinking, in which each thing is what it is only by becoming what it is not. This was the primal form of the objectifying definition, in which concept and thing became separate, the same definition which was already far advanced in the Homeric epic and trips over its own excesses in modern positive science. But this dialectic remains powerless as long as it emerges from the cry of terror, which is the doubling, the mere tautology of terror itself. The gods cannot take away fear from human beings, the petrified cries of whom they bear as their names. Humans believe themselves free of fear when there is no longer anything unknown. This has determined the path of demythologization, of enlightenment, which equates the living with the nonliving as myth had equated the nonliving with the living. Enlightenment is mythical fear radicalized. The pure immanence of positivism, its ultimate product, is nothing other than a form of universal taboo. Nothing is allowed to remain outside, since the mere idea of the "outside" is the real source of fear. If the revenge of primitive people for a murder committed on a member of their family could sometimes be assuaged by admitting the murderer into that family, both the murder and its remedy mean the absorption of alien blood into one's own, the establishment of immanence. The mythical dualism does not lead outside the circle of existence. The world controlled by *mana*, and even the worlds of Indian and Greek myth, are issueless and eternally the same. All birth is paid for with death, all fortune with misfortune. While men and gods may attempt in their short span to assess their fates by a measure other than blind destiny, existence triumphs over them in the end. Even their justice, wrested from calamity, bears its features; it corresponds to the way in which human beings,

primitives no less than Greeks and barbarians, looked upon their world from within a society of oppression and poverty. Hence, for both mythical and enlightened justice, guilt and atonement, happiness and misfortune, are seen as the two sides of an equation. Justice gives way to law. The shaman wards off a danger with its likeness. Equivalence is his instrument; and equivalence regulates punishment and reward within civilization. The imagery of myths, too, can be traced back without exception to natural conditions. Just as the constellation Gemini, like all the other symbols of duality, refers to the inescapable cycle of nature; just as this cycle itself has its primeval sign in the symbol of the egg from which those later symbols are sprung, the Scales (Libra) held by Zeus, which symbolize the justice of the entire patriarchal world, point back to mere nature. The step from chaos to civilization, in which natural conditions exert their power no longer directly but through the consciousness of human beings, changed nothing in the principle of equivalence. Indeed, human beings atoned for this very step by worshipping that to which previously, like all other creatures, they had been merely subjected. Earlier, fetishes had been subject to the law of equivalence. Now equivalence itself becomes a fetish. The blindfold over the eyes of Justitia means not only that justice brooks no interference but that it does not originate in freedom.

[...]

Notes

1   Sir Francis Bacon (1561–1626) was an early and prescient advocate of the capacity of the natural sciences to facilitate control over nature. The works of his from which Adorno and Horkheimer quote include "In Praise of Human Knowledge" and *The New Organon*.

2   Joseph de Maistre (1755–1821), conservative and Catholic political theorist. His charge, in *Les Soirées de Saint-Pétersbourg*, that Bacon makes an "idol" out of scale or hierarchy (*échelle*) contains irony, since "idol" was Bacon's own name for various intellectual perversions that "beset men's minds". (See II. 7 in this volume.)

3   The passages cited here are from Sigmund Freud's *Totem and Taboo*.

Michael Oakeshott, "Political Education"

Introduction

Despite, or perhaps partly because of, the urbane, elegant erudition of Michael Oakeshott's (1901–92) writings on politics, these did not attract during his career the degree of attention that, in the view of students of a later generation, they deserved. That Oakeshott was a political conservative, during decades when academic fashion in the UK favored thinkers on the Left, also helps to explain the relative neglect of his writings. Until 1946, when he wrote his now famous introduction to Thomas Hobbes's *Leviathan* (V.10), Oakeshott had been best known for his 1933 book *Experience and Its Modes* in which he argued for a position that was later to inform his writings on politics and education. The book's claim was that we can aspire to no knowledge – whether of the world or of moral conduct – which is not intimated in the tried and tested traditions and practices of human societies. His constant target throughout his career was therefore what Oakeshott called "rationalism" – the idea that we can, independently of acquaintance with such traditions and practices, arrive at truths about the world and ourselves.[1]

"Political Education" was Oakeshott's inaugural lecture as Professor of Political Science at the London School of Economics in 1951. Despite the

From Michael Oakeshott, *Rationalism in Politics and Other Essays*, London: Methuen, 1962, pp. 112–33 (some passages and notes omitted).

title, the concern of the lecture is not with the teaching and study of politics in universities or schools, but with "the kind of knowledge" required in order to engage in politics intelligently. This kind of knowledge cannot, on the one hand, consist simply in piecemeal, pragmatic knowledge of how to satisfy this or that need, want, or interest that people demand or express. But nor, on the other hand, can it consist, as the champions of "rationalism in politics" urge, in knowledge of "political ideology" – of principles and values that can be established "in advance of the activity of attending to the arrangements of a society." The victory in the twentieth century of political rationalism – in the form, for example, of Marxist ideology (V.19) – is a depressing sign that "we no longer understand the place in politics of traditional and tacit knowledge, believing [instead] that whatever is important can be codified."[2]

It would be wrong to suppose that Oakeshott's emphasis on tradition and implicit knowledge of established practices excludes the possibility of criticism of existing political arrangements or progress within them. While it is indeed fruitless to judge political arrangements from an ideological standpoint remote from those arrangements, it remains nevertheless perfectly legitimate, Oakeshott argues, to "pursue the intimations" implicit in those very arrangements. To take his own example, it is both legitimate and desirable to develop the commitment to improving the status of women in society that was already implicit in their enfranchisement, in countries like England, during the nineteenth and early twentieth centuries. As this example suggests, Oakeshott is entirely hostile to the rhetoric of "human rights" or "rights of man" (see, for example, V.16) – at any rate, when these are "insulated" from actual practices and arrangements and taken to be matters of *a priori* moral insight. He writes of freedom, for instance, that it is "not an 'ideal' which we premeditate independently of our political experience, it is what is already intimated in that experience."

It is remarks like these that indicate a further reason for the relative neglect of Oakeshott's writings until very late in his life. It is not simply that his political conservatism was unfashionable. In addition, his philosophical tone – anti-rationalistic, skeptical, anti-systematic – clashed with the prevailing one of the period. It is difficult, for example, to imagine a wider gap than that between John Rawls's approach (V.23) – with

its complex apparatus of principles established by *a priori* moral argument – and that of Michael Oakeshott. In a climate in which political theorists saw their main task to be that of assessing "grand theories" like those of Rawls and Robert Nozick, Oakeshott's appeal to us to get away from theory and to return to a civilized "conversation" was unlikely to be given much air. It is a sign of a change in the philosophical climate that his essays are now paid much greater attention.

Notes

1 For a sympathetic general account of Oakeshott's philosophy, see Robert Grant, *Oakeshott*, London: Claridge, 1990.
2 A. O'Hear, "Michael Oakeshott," in J. Palmer (ed.), *Fifty Modern Thinkers on Education*, London: Routledge, 2001, p. 45.

Oakeshott, "Political Education"

1

The expression 'political education' has fallen on evil days; in the wilful and disingenuous corruption of language which is characteristic of our time it has acquired a sinister meaning. In places other than this, it is associated with that softening of the mind, by force, by alarm, or by the hypnotism of the endless repetition of what was scarcely worth saying once, by means of which whole populations have been reduced to submission. It is, therefore, an enterprise worth undertaking to consider again, in a quiet moment, how we should understand this expression, which joins together two laudable activities, and in doing so play a small part in rescuing it from abuse.

Politics I take to be the activity of attending to the general arrangements of a set of people whom chance or choice have brought together. In this sense, familices, clubs, and learned societies have their 'polities'. But the communities in which this manner of activity is pre-eminent are the hereditary co-operative groups, many of them of ancient lineage, all of them aware of a past, a present, and a future, which we call 'states'. For most people, political activity is a secondary

activity – that is to say, they have something else to do besides attending to these arrangements. But, as we have come to understand it, the activity is one in which every member of the group who is neither a child nor a lunatic has some part and some responsibility. With us it is, at one level or another, a universal activity.

I speak of this activity as 'attending to arrangements', rather than as 'making arrangements', because in these hereditary co-operative groups the activity is never offered the blank sheet of infinite possibility. In any generation, even the most revolutionary, the arrangements which are enjoyed always far exceed those which are recognized to stand in need of attention, and those which are being prepared for enjoyment are few in comparison with those which receive amendment: the new is an insignificant proportion of the whole. There are some people, of course, who allow themselves to speak

As if arrangements were intended
For nothing else but to be mended,

but, for most of us, our determination to improve our conduct does not prevent us from recognizing that the greater part of what we have is not a burden to be carried or an incubus to be thrown off, but an inheritance to be enjoyed. And a certain degree of shabbiness is joined with every real convenience.

Now, attending to the arrangements of a society is an activity which, like every other, has to be learned. Politics make a call upon knowledge. Consequently, it is not irrelevant to inquire into the kind of knowledge which is involved, and to investigate the nature of political education. I do not, however, propose to ask what information we should equip ourselves with before we begin to be politically active, or what we need to know in order to be successful politicians, but to inquire into the kind of knowledge we unavoidably call upon whenever we are engaged in political activity and to get from this an understanding of the nature of political education.

Our thoughts on political education, then, might be supposed to spring from our understanding of political activity and the kind of knowledge it involves. And it would appear that what is wanted at this point is a definition of political activity from which to draw some conclusions. But this, I think, would be a mistaken way of going about our business. What we require is not so much a definition of politics from which to deduce the character of political education, as an understanding of political activity which includes a recognition of the sort of education it involves. For, to understand an activity is to know it as a concrete whole; it is to recognize the activity as having the source of its movement within itself. An understanding which leaves the activity in debt to something outside itself is, for that reason, an inadequate understanding. And if political activity is impossible without a certain kind of knowledge and a certain sort of education, then this knowledge and education are not mere appendages to the activity but are part of the activity itself and must be incorporated in our understanding of it. We should not, therefore, seek a definition of politics in order to deduce from it the character of political knowledge and education, but rather observe the kind of knowledge and education which is inherent in any understanding of political activity, and use this observation as a means of improving our understanding of politics.

My proposal, then, is to consider the adequacy of two current understandings of politics, together with the sort of knowledge and kind of education they imply, and by improving upon them to reach what may perhaps be a more adequate understanding at once of political activity itself and the knowledge and education which belongs to it.

2

In the understanding of some people, politics are what may be called an empirical activity. Attending to the arrangements of a society is waking up each morning and considering, 'What would I like to do?' or 'What would somebody else (whom I desire to please) like to see done?', and doing it. This understanding of political activity may be called politics without a policy. On the briefest inspection it will appear a concept of politics difficult to substantiate; it does not look like a possible manner of activity at all. But a near approach to it is, perhaps, to be detected in the politics of the proverbial oriental despot, or in the politics of the wall-scribbler and the vote-catcher. And the result may be supposed to be chaos modified by whatever consistency is allowed to creep into caprice. They are the politics attributed to the first Lord Liverpool, of whom Acton said, 'The secret of his policy was that he had none', and of whom a Frenchman remarked that if he had been present at the creation of the world he would have said, '*Mon Dieu, conservons le chaos*'. It seems, then, that a concrete activity, which may be described as an approximation to empirical politics, is possible. But it is clear that, although knowledge of a sort belongs to this style of political activity (knowledge, as the French say, not of ourselves but only of our appetites), the only kind of education appropriate to it would be an education in lunacy – learning to be ruled solely by passing desires. And this reveals the important point; namely, that to understand politics as a purely empirical activity is to misunderstand it, because empiricism by itself is not a concrete manner of activity at all, and can become a partner in a concrete manner of activity only when it is joined with something else – in science, for example, when it is joined with hypothesis. What is significant about this understanding of politics is not that some sort of approach to it can appear, but that it mistakes for a concrete, self-moved manner of activity what is never more than an abstract moment in any manner of being active. Of course, politics are the pursuit of what is desired and of what is desired at the moment; but precisely because they are this, they can never be the pursuit of merely what recommends itself from moment to moment. The activity of desiring does not take this course; caprice is never absolute. From a practical point of view, then, we may decry the *style* of politics which approximates to pure empiricism because we can observe in it an approach to lunacy. But from a theoretical point of view, purely empirical politics are not something difficult to achieve or proper to be avoided, they are merely impossible; the product of a misunderstanding.

3

The understanding of politics as an empirical activity is, then, inadequate because it fails to reveal a concrete manner of activity at all. And it has the incidental defect of seeming to encourage the thoughtless to pursue a *style* of attending to the arrangements of their society which is likely to have unfortunate results; to try to do something which is inherently impossible is always a corrupting enterprise. We must, if we can, improve upon it. And the impulse to improve may be given a direction by asking, 'What is it that this understanding of politics has neglected to observe?' What (to put it crudely) has it left out which, if added in, would compose an understanding in which politics are revealed as a self-moved (or concrete) manner of activity? And the answer to the question is, or seems to be, available as soon as the question is formulated. It would appear that what this understanding of politics lacks is something to set empiricism to work, something to correspond with specific hypothesis in science, an end to be pursued more extensive than a merely instant desire. And this, it should be observed, is not merely a good companion for empiricism; it is something without which empiricism in action is impossible. Let us explore this suggestion, and in order to bring it to a point I will state it in the form of a proposition: that politics appear as a self-moved manner of activity when empiricism is preceded and guided by an ideological activity. I am not concerned with the so-called ideological *style* of politics as a desirable or undesirable manner of attending to the arrangements of a society; I am concerned only with the contention that when to the ineluctable element of empiricism (doing what one wants to do) is added a political ideology, a self-moved manner of activity appears, and that consequently this may be regarded in principle as an adequate understanding of political activity.

As I understand it, a political ideology purports to be an abstract principle, or set of related abstract principles, which has been independently premeditated. It supplies in advance of the activity of attending to the arrangements of a society a formulated end to be pursued, and in so doing it provides a means of distinguishing between those desires which ought to be encouraged and those which ought to be suppressed or redirected.

The simplest sort of political ideology is a single abstract idea, such as Freedom, Equality, Maximum Productivity, Racial Purity, or Happiness. And in that case political activity is understood as the enterprise of seeing that the arrangements of a society conform to or reflect the chosen abstract idea. It is usual, however, to recognize the need for a complex scheme of related ideas, rather than a single idea, and the examples pointed to will be such systems of ideas as: 'the principles of 1789', 'Liberalism', 'Democracy', 'Marxism', or the Atlantic Charter. These principles need not be considered absolute or immune from change (though they are frequently so considered), but their value lies in their having been premeditated. They compose an understanding of *what* is to be pursued independent of *how* it is to be pursued. A political ideology purports to supply in advance knowledge of what 'Freedom' or 'Democracy' or 'Justice' is, and in this manner sets empiricism to work. Such a set of principles is, of course, capable of being argued about and reflected upon; it is something that men compose for themselves, and they may later remember it or write it down. But the condition upon which it can perform the service assigned to it is that it owes nothing to the activity it controls. 'To know the true good of the community is what constitutes the science of legislation,' said Bentham; 'the art consists in finding the means to realize that good.' The contention we have before us, then, is that empiricism can be set to work (and a concrete, self-moved manner of activity appear) when there is added to it a guide of this sort: desire and something not generated by desire.

Now, there is no doubt about the sort of knowledge which political activity, understood in this manner, calls upon. What is required, in the first place, is knowledge of the chosen political ideology – a knowledge of the ends to be pursued, a knowledge of what we want to do. Of course, if we are to be successful in pursuing these ends we shall need knowledge of another sort also – a knowledge, shall we say, of economics and psychology. But the common characteristic of all the kinds of knowledge required is that they may be, and should be, gathered in advance of the activity of attending to the arrangements of a society. Moreover, the appropriate sort of education will be an education in which the chosen political ideology is taught and learned, in which the techniques necessary for success are acquired, and (if we are so unfortunate as to find ourselves empty-handed in the matter of an ideology) an education in the skill of abstract thought and premeditation necessary to compose one for ourselves. The education we shall need is one which enables us to expound, defend, implement, and possibly invent a political ideology.

In casting around for some convincing demonstration that this understanding of politics reveals a self-moved manner of activity, we should no doubt consider ourselves rewarded if we could find an example of politics being conducted precisely in this manner. This at least would constitute a sign that we were on the right track. The defect, it will be remembered, of the understanding of politics as a purely empirical activity was that it revealed, not a manner of activity at all, but an abstraction; and this defect made itself manifest in our inability to find a *style* of politics which was anything more than an approximation to it. How does the understanding of politics as empiricism joined with an ideology fare in this respect? And without being over-confident, we may perhaps think that this is where we wade ashore. For we would appear to be in no difficulty whatever in finding an example of political activity which corresponds to this understanding of it: half the world, at a conservative estimate, seems to conduct its affairs in precisely this manner. And further, is it not so manifestly a possible style of politics that, even if we disagree with a particular ideology, we find nothing technically absurd in the writings of those who urge it upon us as an admirable style of politics? At least its advocates seem to know what they are talking about:

they understand not only the manner of the activity but also the sort of knowledge and the kind of education it involves. 'Every schoolboy in Russia,' wrote Sir Norman Angel, 'is familiar with the doctrine of Marx and can recite its catechism. How many British schoolboys have any corresponding knowledge of the principles enunciated by Mill in his incomparable essay on Liberty?' 'Few people,' says Mr E. H. Carr, 'any longer contest the thesis that the child should be educated *in* the official ideology of his country.' In short, if we are looking for a sign to indicate that the understanding of politics as empirical activity preceded by ideological activity is an adequate understanding, we can scarcely be mistaken in supposing that we have it to hand.

And yet there is perhaps room for doubt: doubt first of all whether in principle this understanding of politics reveals a self-moved manner of activity; and doubt, consequentially, whether what have been identified as examples of a *style* of politics corresponding exactly to this understanding have been properly identified.

The contention we are investigating is that attending to the arrangements of a society can begin with a premeditated ideology, can begin with independently acquired knowledge of the ends to be pursued.* It is supposed that a political ideology is the product of intellectual premeditation and that, because it is a body of principles not itself in debt to the activity of attending to the arrangements of a society, it is able to determine and guide the direction of that activity. If, however, we consider more closely the character of a political ideology, we find at once that this supposition is falsified. So far from a political ideology being the quasi-divine parent of political activity, it turns out to be its earthly stepchild. Instead of an independently premeditated scheme of ends to be pursued, it is a system of ideas abstracted from the manner in which people have been accustomed to go about the business of attending to the arrangements of their societies. The pedigree of every political ideology shows it to be the creature, not of premeditation in advance of political activity, but of meditation upon a manner of politics. In short, political activity comes first and a political ideology follows after;

---

* This is the case, for example, with Natural Law; whether it is taken to be an explanation of political activity or (improperly) as a guide to political conduct.

and the understanding of politics we are investigating has the disadvantage of being, in the strict
sense, preposterous.

Let us consider the matter first in relation
to scientific hypothesis, which I have taken to
play a role in scientific activity in some respects
similar to that of an ideology in politics. If a
scientific hypothesis were a self-generated bright
idea which owed nothing to scientific activity,
then empiricism governed by hypothesis could be
considered to compose a self-contained manner
of activity; but this certainly is not its character.
The truth is that only a man who is already a
scientist can formulate a scientific hypothesis;
that is, an hypothesis is not an independent
invention capable of guiding scientific inquiry,
but a dependent supposition which arises as an
abstraction from within already existing scientific
activity. Moreover, even when the specific hypothesis has in this manner been formulated, it
is inoperative as a guide to research without constant reference to the traditions of scientific
inquiry from which it was abstracted. The concrete situation does not appear until the specific
hypothesis, which is the occasion of empiricism being set to work, is recognized as itself the
creature of knowing how to conduct a scientific
inquiry.

Or consider the example of cookery. It might
be supposed that an ignorant man, some edible
materials, and a cookery book compose together
the necessities of a self-moved (or concrete) activity called cooking. But nothing is further from
the truth. The cookery book is not an independently generated beginning from which cooking
can spring; it is nothing more than an abstract
of somebody's knowledge of how to cook: it is
the stepchild, not the parent of the activity. The
book, in its turn, may help to set a man on to
dressing a dinner, but if it were his sole guide
he could never, in fact, begin: the book speaks
only to those who know already the kind of
thing to expect from it and consequently how
to interpret it.

Now, just as a cookery book presupposes
somebody who knows how to cook, and its
use presupposes somebody who already knows
how to use it, and just as a scientific hypothesis
springs from a knowledge of how to conduct a
scientific investigation and separated from that
knowledge is powerless to set empiricism profitably to work, so a political ideology must be

understood, not as an independently premeditated
beginning for political activity, but as knowledge
(abstract and generalized) of a concrete manner
of attending to the arrangements of a society.
The catechism which sets out the purposes to be
pursued merely abridges a concrete manner of
behaviour in which those purposes are already
hidden. It does not exist in advance of political
activity, and by itself it is always an insufficient
guide. Political enterprises, the ends to be pursued,
the arrangements to be established (all the normal ingredients of a political ideology), cannot be
premeditated in advance of a manner of attending to the arrangements of a society; *what* we
do, and moreover what we want to do, is the
creature of *how* we are accustomed to conduct our
affairs. Indeed, it often reflects no more than a
discovered ability to do something which is then
translated into an authority to do it.

On August 4, 1789, for the complex and
bankrupt social and political system of France
was substituted the Rights of Man. Reading this
document we come to the conclusion that somebody has done some thinking. Here, displayed in
a few sentences, is a political ideology: a system
of rights and duties, a scheme of ends – justice,
freedom, equality, security, property, and the
rest – ready and waiting to be put into practice
for the first time. 'For the first time?' Not a bit
of it. This ideology no more existed in advance
of political practice than a cookery book exists
in advance of knowing how to cook. Certainly it
was the product of somebody's reflection, but
it was not the product of reflection in advance of
political activity. For here, in fact, are disclosed,
abstracted and abridged, the common law rights
of Englishmen, the gift not of independent premeditation or divine munificence, but of centuries
of the day-to-day attending to the arrangements
of an historic society. Or consider Locke's *Second
Treatise of Civil Government*, read in America and
in France in the eighteenth century as a statement
of abstract principles to be put into practice,
regarded there as a preface to political activity. But
so far from being a preface, it has all the marks
of a postscript, and its power to guide derived from
its roots in actual political experience. Here, set
down in abstract terms, is a brief conspectus of
the manner in which Englishmen were accustomed to go about the business of attending to
their arrangements – a brilliant abridgment of the
political habits of Englishmen. Or consider this

passage from a contemporary continental writer: 'Freedom keeps Europeans in unrest and movement. They wish to have freedom, and at the same time they know they have not got it. They know also that freedom belongs to man as a human right.' And having established the end to be pursued, political activity is represented as the realization of this end. But the 'freedom' which can be pursued is not an independently premeditated 'ideal' or a dream; like scientific hypothesis, it is something which is already intimated in a concrete manner of behaving. Freedom, like a recipe for game pie, is not a bright idea; it is not a 'human right' to be deduced from some speculative concept of human nature. The freedom which we enjoy is nothing more than arrangements, procedures of a certain kind: the freedom of an Englishman is not something exemplified in the procedure of *habeas corpus*, it *is*, at that point, the availability of that procedure. And the freedom which we wish to enjoy is not an 'ideal' which we premeditate independently of our political experience, it is what is already intimated in that experience.

On this reading, then, the systems of abstract ideas we call 'ideologies' are abstracts of some kind of concrete activity. Most political ideologies, and certainly the most useful of them (because they unquestionably have their use), are abstracts of the political traditions of some society. But it sometimes happens that an ideology is offered as a guide to politics which is an abstract, not of political experience, but of some other manner of activity – war, religion, or the conduct of industry, for example. And here the model we are shown is not only abstract, but is also inappropriate on account of the irrelevance of the activity from which it has been abstracted. This, I think, is one of the defects of the model provided by the Marxist ideology. But the important point is that, at most, an ideology is an abbreviation of some manner of concrete activity.

We are now, perhaps, in a position to perceive more accurately the character of what may be called the ideological *style* of politics, and to observe that its existence offers no ground for supposing that the understanding of political activity as empiricism guided solely by an ideology is an adequate understanding. The ideological style of politics is a confused style. Properly speaking, it is a traditional manner of attending

to the arrangements of a society which has been abridged into a doctrine of ends to be pursued, the abridgment (together with the necessary technical knowledge) being erroneously regarded as the sole guide relied upon. In certain circumstances an abridgment of this kind may be valuable; it gives sharpness of outline and precision to a political tradition which the occasion may make seem appropriate. When a manner of attending to arrangements is to be transplanted from the society in which it has grown up into another society (always a questionable enterprise), the simplification of an ideology may appear as an asset. If, for example, the English manner of politics is to be planted elsewhere in the world, it is perhaps appropriate that it should first be abridged into something called 'democracy' before it is packed up and shipped abroad. There is, of course, an alternative method: the method by which what is exported is the detail and not the abridgment of the tradition and the workmen travel with the tools – the method which made the British Empire. But it is a slow and costly method. And, particularly with men in a hurry, *l'homme à programme* with his abridgment wins every time; his slogans enchant, while the resident magistrate is seen only as a sign of servility. But whatever the apparent appropriateness on occasion of the ideological style of politics, the defect of the explanation of political activity connected with it becomes apparent when we consider the sort of knowledge and the kind of education it encourages us to believe is sufficient for understanding the activity of attending to the arrangements of a society. For it suggests that a knowledge of the chosen political ideology can take the place of understanding a tradition of political behaviour. The wand and the book come to be regarded as themselves potent, and not merely the symbols of potency. The arrangements of a society are made to appear, not as manners of behaviour, but as pieces of machinery to be transported about the world indiscriminately. The complexities of the tradition which have been squeezed out in the process of abridgment are taken to be unimportant: the 'rights of man' are understood to exist insulated from a manner of attending to arrangements. And because, in practice, the abridgment is never by itself a sufficient guide, we are encouraged to fill it out, not with our suspect political experience, but with experience drawn from other (often irrelevant) concretely understood activities, such as war, the conduct of industry, or Trade Union negotiation.

4

The understanding of politics as the activity of attending to the arrangements of a society under the guidance of an independently premeditated ideology is, then, no less a misunderstanding than the understanding of it as a purely empirical activity. Wherever else politics may begin, they cannot begin in ideological activity. And in an attempt to improve upon this understanding of politics, we have already observed in principle what needs to be recognized in order to have an intelligible concept. Just as scientific hypothesis cannot appear, and is impossible to operate, except within an already existing tradition of scientific investigation, so a scheme of ends for political activity appears within, and can be evaluated only when it is related to, an already existing tradition of how to attend to our arrangements. In politics, the only concrete manner of activity detectable is one in which empiricism and the ends to be pursued are recognized as dependent, alike for their existence and their operation, upon a traditional manner of behaviour.

Politics is the activity of attending to the general arrangements of a collection of people who, in respect of their common recognition of a manner of attending to its arrangements, compose a single community. To suppose a collection of people without recognized traditions of behaviour, or one which enjoyed arrangements which intimated no direction for change and needed no attention, is to suppose a people incapable of politics. This activity, then, springs neither from instant desires, nor from general principles, but from the existing traditions of behaviour themselves. And the form it takes, because it can take no other, is the amendment of existing arrangements by exploring and pursuing what is intimated in them. The arrangements which constitute a society capable of political activity, whether they are customs or institutions or laws or diplomatic decisions, are at once coherent and incoherent; they compose a pattern and at the same time they intimate a sympathy for what does not fully appear. Political activity is the exploration of that sympathy; and consequently, relevant political reasoning will be the convincing exposure of

a sympathy, present but not yet followed up, and the convincing demonstration that now is the appropriate moment for recognizing it. For example, the legal status of women in our society was for a long time (and perhaps still is) in comparative confusion, because the rights and duties which composed it intimated rights and duties which were nevertheless not recognized. And, on the view of things I am suggesting, the only cogent reason to be advanced for the technical 'enfranchisement' of women was that in all or most other important respects they had already been enfranchised. Arguments drawn from abstract natural right, from 'justice', or from some general concept of feminine personality, must be regarded as either irrelevant, or as unfortunately disguised forms of the one valid argument; namely, that there was an incoherence in the arrangements of the society which pressed convincingly for remedy. In politics, then, every enterprise is a consequential enterprise, the pursuit, not of a dream, or of a general principle, but of an intimation. What we have to do with is something less imposing than logical implications or necessary consequences: but if the intimations of a tradition of behaviour are less dignified or more elusive than these, they are not on that account less important. Of course, there is no piece of mistake-proof apparatus by means of which we can elicit the intimation most worth while pursuing; and not only do we often make gross errors of judgment in this matter, but also the total effect of a desire satisfied is so little to be forecast, that our activity of amendment is often found to lead us where we would not go. Moreover, the whole enterprise is liable at any moment to be perverted by the incursion of an approximation to empiricism in the pursuit of power. These are features which can never be eliminated; they belong to the character of political activity. But it may be believed that our mistakes of understanding will be less frequent and less disastrous if we escape the illusion that politics is ever anything more than the pursuit of intimations; a conversation, not an argument.

Now, every society which is intellectually alive is liable, from time to time, to abridge its tradition of behaviour into a scheme of abstract ideas; and on occasion political discussion will be concerned, not (like the debates in the *Iliad*) with isolated transactions, nor (like the speeches in Thucydides) with policies and traditions of activity, but with general principles. And in this there is no harm; perhaps even some positive benefit. It is possible that the distorting mirror of an ideology will reveal important hidden passages in the tradition, as a caricature reveals the potentialities of a face; and if this is so, the intellectual enterprise of seeing what a tradition looks like when it is reduced to an ideology will be a useful part of political education. But to make use of abridgment as a technique for exploring the intimations of a political tradition, to use it, that is, as a scientist uses hypothesis, is one thing; it is something different, and something inappropriate, to understand political activity itself as the activity of amending the arrangements of a society so as to make them agree with the provisions of an ideology. For then a character has been attributed to an ideology which it is unable to sustain, and we may find ourselves, in practice, directed by a false and a misleading guide: false, because in the abridgment, however skilfully it has been performed, a single intimation is apt to be exaggerated and proposed for unconditional pursuit and the benefit to be had from observing what the distortion reveals is lost when the distortion itself is given the office of a criterion; misleading, because the abridgment itself never, in fact, provides the whole of the knowledge used in political activity.

There will be some people who, though in general agreement with this understanding of political activity, will suspect that it confuses what is, perhaps, normal with what is necessary, and that important exceptions (of great contemporary relevance) have been lost in a hazy generality. It is all very well, it may be said, to observe in politics the activity of exploring and pursuing the intimations of a tradition of behaviour, but what light does this throw upon a political crisis such as the Norman Conquest of England, or the establishment of the Soviet *régime* in Russia? It would be foolish, of course, to deny the possibility of serious political crisis. But if we exclude (as we must) a genuine cataclysm which for the time being made an end of politics by altogether obliterating a current tradition of behaviour (which is *not* what happened in Anglo-Saxon England or in Russia),* there

is little to support the view that even the most serious political upheaval carries us outside this understanding of politics. A tradition of behaviour is not a fixed and inflexible manner of doing things; it is a flow of sympathy. It may be temporarily disrupted by the incursion of a foreign influence, it may be diverted, restricted, arrested, or become dried-up, and it may reveal so deep-seated an incoherence that (even without foreign assistance) a crisis appears. And if, in order to meet these crises, there were some steady, unchanging, independent guide to which a society might resort, it would no doubt be well advised to do so. But no such guide exists; we have no resources outside the fragments, the vestiges, the relics of its own tradition of behaviour which the crisis has left untouched. For even the help we may get from the traditions of another society (or from a tradition of a vaguer sort which is shared by a number of societies) is conditional upon our being able to assimilate them to our own arrangements and our own manner of attending to our arrangements. The hungry and helpless man is mistaken if he supposes that he overcomes the crisis by means of a tin-opener: what saves him is somebody else's knowledge of how to cook, which he can make use of only because he is not himself entirely ignorant. In short, political crisis (even when it seems to be imposed upon a society by changes beyond its control) always appears *within* a tradition of political activity; and 'salvation' comes from the unimpaired resources of the tradition itself. Those societies which retain, in changing circumstances, a lively sense of their own identity and continuity (which are without that hatred of their own experience which makes them desire to efface it) are to be counted fortunate, not because they possess what others lack, but because they have already mobilized what none is without and all, in fact, rely upon.

In political activity, then, men sail a boundless and bottomless sea; there is neither harbour for shelter nor floor for anchorage, neither starting-place nor appointed destination. The enterprise is to keep afloat on an even keel; the sea is both friend and enemy; and the seamanship consists in using the resources of a traditional manner of

---

* The Russian Revolution (what actually happened in Russia) was not the implementation of an abstract design worked out by Lenin and others in Switzerland: it was a modification of *Russian* circumstances. And the French Revolution was far more closely connected with the *ancien régime* than with Locke or America.

behaviour in order to make a friend of every hostile occasion.

A depressing doctrine, it will be said – even by those who do not make the mistake of adding in an element of crude determinism which, in fact, it has no place for. A tradition of behaviour is not a groove within which we are destined to grind out our helpless and unsatisfying lives. [. . .] But in the main the depression springs from the exclusion of hopes that were false and the discovery that guides, reputed to be of superhuman wisdom and skill, are, in fact, of a somewhat different character. If the doctrine deprives us of a model laid up in heaven to which we should approximate our behaviour, at least is does not lead us into a morass where every choice is equally good or equally to be deplored. [. . .]

5

The sin of the academic is that he takes so long in coming to the point. Nevertheless, there is some virtue in his dilatoriness; what he has to offer may, in the end, be no great matter, but at least it is not unripe fruit, and to pluck it is the work of a moment. We set out to consider the kind of knowledge involved in political activity and the appropriate sort of education. And if the understanding of politics I have recommended is not a misunderstanding, there is little doubt about the kind of knowledge and the sort of education which belongs to it. It is knowledge, as profound as we can make it, of our tradition of political behaviour. Other knowledge, certainly, is desirable in addition; but this is the knowledge without which we cannot make use of whatever else we may have learned.

Now, a tradition of behaviour is a tricky thing to get to know. Indeed, it may even appear to be essentially unintelligible. It is neither fixed nor finished; it has no changeless centre to which understanding can anchor itself; there is no sovereign purpose to be perceived or invariable direction to be detected; there is no model to be copied, idea to be realized, or rule to be followed. Some parts of it may change more slowly than others, but none is immune from change. Everything is temporary. Nevertheless, though a tradition of behaviour is flimsy and elusive, it is not without identity, and what makes it a possible object of knowledge is the fact that all its

parts do not change at the same time and that the changes it undergoes are potential within it. Its principle is a principle of *continuity*: authority is diffused between past, present, and future; between the old, the new, and what is to come. It is steady because, though it moves, it is never wholly in motion; and though it is tranquil, it is never wholly at rest.* Nothing that ever belonged to it is completely lost; we are always swerving back to recover and make something topical out of even its remotest moments: and nothing for long remains unmodified. Everything is temporary, but nothing is arbitrary. Everything figures by comparison, not with what stands next to it, but with the whole. And since a tradition of behaviour is not susceptible of the distinction between essence and accident, knowledge of it is unavoidably knowledge of its detail: to know only the gist is to know nothing. What has to be learned is not an abstract idea, or a set of tricks, not even a ritual, but a concrete, coherent manner of living in all its intricateness.

It is clear, then, that we must not entertain the hope of acquiring this difficult understanding by easy methods. Though the knowledge we seek is municipal, not universal, there is no short cut to it. Moreover, political education is not merely a matter of coming to understand a tradition, it is learning how to participate in a conversation: it is at once initiation into an inheritance in which we have a life interest, and the exploration of its intimations. There will always remain something of a mystery about how a tradition of political behaviour is learned, and perhaps the only certainty is that there is no point at which learning it can properly be said to begin. The politics of a community are not less individual (and not more so) than its language, and they are learned and practised in the same manner. We do not begin to learn our native language by learning the alphabet, or by learning its grammar; we do not begin by learning words, but words in use; we do not begin (as we begin in reading) with what

---

* The critic who found 'some mystical qualities' in this passage leaves me puzzled: it seems to me an exceedingly matter-of-fact description of the characteristics of any tradition – the Common Law of England, for example, the so-called British Constitution, the Christian religion, modern physics, the game of cricket, shipbuilding.

is easy and go on to what is more difficult; we do not begin at school, but in the cradle; and what we say springs always from our manner of speaking. And this is true also of our political education; it begins in the enjoyment of a tradition, in the observation and imitation of the behaviour of our elders, and there is little or nothing in the world which comes before us as we open our eyes which does not contribute to it. We are aware of a past and a future as soon as we are aware of a present. Long before we are of an age to take interest in a book about our politics we are acquiring that complex and intricate knowledge of our political tradition without which we could not make sense of a book when we come to open it. And the projects we entertain are the creatures of our tradition. The greater part, then – perhaps the most important part – of our political education we acquire haphazard in finding our way about the natural-artificial world into which we are born, and there is no other way of acquiring it. There will, of course, be more to acquire, and it will be more readily acquired, if we have the good fortune to be born into a rich and lively political tradition and among those who are well educated politically; the lineaments of *political* activity will earlier become distinct: but even the most needy society and the most cramped surroundings have some political education to offer, and we take what we can get.

[...]

The fruits of a political education will appear in the manner in which we think and speak about politics and perhaps in the manner in which we conduct our political activity. To select items from this prospective harvest must always be hazardous, and opinions will differ about what is most important. But for myself I should hope for two things. The more profound our understanding of political activity, the less we shall be at the mercy of plausible but mistaken analogy, the less we shall be tempted by a false or irrelevant model. And the more thoroughly we understand our own political tradition, the more readily its whole resources are available to us, the less likely we shall be to embrace the illusions which wait for the ignorant and the unwary: the illusion that in politics we can get on without a tradition of behaviour, the illusion that the abridgment of a tradition is itself a sufficient guide, and the illusion that in politics there is anywhere a safe harbour, a destination to be reached or even a detectable strand of progress. 'The world is the best of all possible worlds, and *everything* in it is a necessary evil.'

23

John Rawls, *A Theory of Justice,* Chapter I, Sections 1–4

Introduction

No other work of political philosophy in the second half of the twentieth century had the impact of *A Theory of Justice*, first published in 1971 by the then 50-year-old Professor of Political Philosophy at Harvard, John Rawls (1921–2002). Not only did the book galvanize the discipline, at a time when articles with titles like "Is Political Philosophy dead?" were appearing, but it also quickly exerted an influence on liberal or left-leaning political leaders. As one of those leaders, Bill Clinton, remarked when presenting Rawls with a National Humanities Medal that Rawls's book had helped a whole generation of Americans to "revive their faith in democracy."[1] This does not mean, however, that the book has been immune to criticism. Indeed, it is fair to say that most of the major contributions to political philosophy by Anglo-American writers over the last 30 years have been critical responses to Rawls's work – responses that have elicited from Rawls amendments to and elaborations of his original claims.[2]

Rawls's 600-page work belongs in the venerable tradition of social contract theory, and he acknowledges his debt to, among others, Locke and Rousseau (V.11 and V.12). The main question he addresses, however, is different from the one

From John Rawls, *A Theory of Justice*, Oxford: Oxford University Press, 1971, pp. 3–22 (notes omitted).

asked by those earlier writers. Rawls is concerned, not with establishing the legitimate grounds for, and limits to, a sovereign's power, but with identifying what is the most rationally acceptable conception of justice, that "most important virtue of institutions." This, according to Rawls, is equivalent to establishing what principles should determine the assigning of "rights and duties in the basic institutions of society" and "the appropriate distribution of the benefits and burdens of social cooperation." The proper principles of justice must be "fair" in the sense of being those that human beings, choosing under conditions of fairness, would agree to live by. Those conditions, Rawls argues, are found in his version of "the state of nature," which he calls "the original position of equality." This is the position, roughly, that choosers would be in if they were ignorant of any facts about themselves – including, especially, their likely place or status in society, but also their religious beliefs (if any) and their particular "conceptions of the good" – that might cause them to opt for principles that would favor themselves.

If people were to choose from behind this "veil of ignorance," as Rawls calls it, what principles would they settle upon? Not, he argues, the classical principles of utilitarianism, for these permit the sacrifice of some individuals' interests if this is necessary for maximizing overall utility. This is not something a person in the "original position" could rationally opt for, since it might be his or her interests that get sacrificed. According to Rawls, two primary principles would be fixed upon, which he calls "the liberty principle" and "the difference principle." The first enjoins assigning to people the maximum amount of liberty compatible with each and every one possessing equal liberty. The second requires that "primary goods," including wealth, be equally distributed *unless* inequality benefits everyone, including especially the worst-off. For Rawls, the rational chooser follows the so-called "maximin" strategy of reasoning, where the priority is the "precautionary" one of guaranteeing that one's worst actual outcome is the best it could be.

Rawls provides a preliminary sketch of these claims in the introductory chapter from which we have selected the text that follows. In Section 4, he also introduces the much-discussed idea of the "reflective equilibrium" between principles and everyday intuitions about justice at which, he holds, deliberators must arrived if principles like those he advances are to be rationally acceptable. Despite his confidence that his principles are indeed rationally acceptable, his proposals have, as noted, prompted many criticisms. These include the charge that the cautious "maximin" strategy, with its endorsement of only limited inequalities, would be found much too cautious by many people, who do not regard it as irrational to take risks for large potential rewards. More fundamental is the complaint that the liberal principles that

Rawls purports to derive from reflection on the "original position" are, in effect, built into it from the start. In particular, the insistence that choosers must be ignorant of their own individual conceptions of the good reflects, rather than supports, the characteristically liberal thesis that "the good life for man . . . ought not to be decided from the public standpoint," but is a matter solely of personal choice.[3] Arguments concerning the validity of such criticisms show no sign of disappearing 40 years after the publication of Rawls's magnum opus.

Notes

1 See the article on Rawls in Wikipedia, http://en.wikipedia.org/wiki/John_Rawls, p. 1.

2 Those major contributions include R. Nozick's *Anarchy, State and Utopia*, Oxford: Blackwell, 1974, and M. Sandel's *Liberalism and the Limits of Justice*, Cambridge: Cambridge University Press, 1982. For Rawls's later views, see his *Justice as Fairness: A Restatement*, Cambridge, MA: Belknap Press, 2001.

3 A. Brown, *Modern Political Theory: Theories of the Just Society*, London: Penguin, 1986, p. 71: chapter 3 succinctly summarizes a host of criticisms that Rawls's book has attracted.

Rawls, *A Theory of Justice*

Chapter I: Justice as Fairness

[. . .]

1 The Role of Justice Justice is the first virtue of social institutions, as truth is of systems of thought. A theory however elegant and economical must be rejected or revised if it is untrue; likewise laws and institutions no matter how efficient and well-arranged must be reformed or abolished if they are unjust. Each person possesses an inviolability founded on justice that even the welfare of society as a whole cannot override. For this reason justice denies that the loss of freedom for some is made right by a greater good shared by others. It does not allow that the sacrifices imposed on a few are outweighed by the larger

sum of advantages enjoyed by many. Therefore in a just society the liberties of equal citizenship are taken as settled; the rights secured by justice are not subject to political bargaining or to the calculus of social interests. The only thing that permits us to acquiesce in an erroneous theory is the lack of a better one; analogously, an injustice is tolerable only when it is necessary to avoid an even greater injustice. Being first virtues of human activities, truth and justice are uncompromising.

These propositions seem to express our intuitive conviction of the primacy of justice. No doubt they are expressed too strongly. In any event I wish to inquire whether these contentions or others similar to them are sound, and if so how they can be accounted for. To this end it is necessary to work out a theory of justice in the light of which these assertions can be interpreted and assessed. I shall begin by considering the role of the principles of justice. Let us assume, to fix ideas, that a society is a more or less self-sufficient association of persons who in their relations to one another recognize certain rules of conduct as binding and who for the most part act in accordance with them. Suppose further that these rules specify a system of cooperation designed to advance the good of those taking part in it. Then, although a society is a cooperative venture for mutual advantage, it is typically marked by a conflict as well as by an identity of interests. There is an identity of interests since social cooperation makes possible a better life for all than any would have if each were to live solely by his own efforts. There is a conflict of interests since persons are not indifferent as to how the greater benefits produced by their collaboration are distributed, for in order to pursue their ends they each prefer a larger to a lesser share. A set of principles is required for choosing among the various social arrangements which determine this division of advantages and for underwriting an agreement on the proper distributive shares. These principles are the principles of social justice: they provide a way of assigning rights and duties in the basic institutions of society and they define the appropriate distribution of the benefits and burdens of social cooperation.

Now let us say that a society is well-ordered when it is not only designed to advance the good of its members but when it is also effectively regulated by a public conception of justice. That is, it is a society in which (1) everyone accepts and knows that the others accept the same principles of justice, and (2) the basic social institutions generally satisfy and are generally known to satisfy these principles. In this case while men may put forth excessive demands on one another, they nevertheless acknowledge a common point of view from which their claims may be adjudicated. If men's inclination to self-interest makes their vigilance against one another necessary, their public sense of justice makes their secure association together possible. Among individuals with disparate aims and purposes a shared conception of justice establishes the bonds of civic friendship; the general desire for justice limits the pursuit of other ends. One may think of a public conception of justice as constituting the fundamental charter of a well-ordered human association.

Existing societies are of course seldom well-ordered in this sense, for what is just and unjust is usually in dispute. Men disagree about which principles should define the basic terms of their association. Yet we may still say, despite this disagreement, that they each have a conception of justice. That is, they understand the need for, and they are prepared to affirm, a characteristic set of principles for assigning basic rights and duties and for determining what they take to be the proper distribution of the benefits and burdens of social cooperation. Thus it seems natural to think of the concept of justice as distinct from the various conceptions of justice and as being specified by the role which these different sets of principles, these different conceptions, have in common. Those who hold different conceptions of justice can, then, still agree that institutions are just when no arbitrary distinctions are made between persons in the assigning of basic rights and duties and when the rules determine a proper balance between competing claims to the advantages of social life. Men can agree to this description of just institutions since the notions of an arbitrary distinction and of a proper balance, which are included in the concept of justice, are left open for each to interpret according to the principles of justice that he accepts. These principles single out which similarities and differences among persons are relevant in determining rights and duties and they specify which division of advantages is appropriate. Clearly this distinction between the concept and the various conceptions of justice settles no important questions. It simply helps to identify the role of the principles of social justice.

Some measure of agreement in conceptions of justice is, however, not the only prerequisite for a viable human community. There are other fundamental social problems, in particular those of coordination, efficiency, and stability. Thus the plans of individuals need to be fitted together so that their activities are compatible with one another and they can all be carried through without anyone's legitimate expectations being severely disappointed. Moreover, the execution of these plans should lead to the achievement of social ends in ways that are efficient and consistent with justice. And finally, the scheme of social cooperation must be stable: it must be more or less regularly complied with and its basic rules willingly acted upon; and when infractions occur, stabilizing forces should exist that prevent further violations and tend to restore the arrangement.

Now it is evident that these three problems are connected with that of justice. In the absence of a certain measure of agreement on what is just and unjust, it is clearly more difficult for individuals to coordinate their plans efficiently in order to insure that mutually beneficial arrangements are maintained. Distrust and resentment corrode the ties of civility, and suspicion and hostility tempt men to act in ways they would otherwise avoid. So while the distinctive role of conceptions of justice is to specify basic rights and duties and to determine the appropriate distributive shares, the way in which a conception does this is bound to affect the problems of efficiency, coordination, and stability. We cannot, in general, assess a conception of justice by its distributive role alone, however useful this role may be in identifying the concept of justice. We must take into account its wider connections; for even though justice has a certain priority, being the most important virtue of institutions, it is still true that, other things equal, one conception of justice is preferable to another when its broader consequences are more desirable.

2   *The Subject of Justice*   Many different kinds of things are said to be just and unjust: not only laws, institutions, and social systems, but also particular actions of many kinds, including decisions, judgments, and imputations. We also call the attitudes and dispositions of persons, and persons themselves, just and unjust. Our topic, however, is that of social justice. For us the primary subject of justice is the basic structure of society, or more exactly, the way in which the major social institutions distribute fundamental rights and duties and determine the division of advantages from social cooperation. By major institutions I understand the political constitution and the principal economic and social arrangements. Thus the legal protection of freedom of thought and liberty of conscience, competitive markets, private property in the means of production, and the monogamous family are examples of major social institutions. Taken together as one scheme, the major institutions define men's rights and duties and influence their life-prospects, what they can expect to be and how well they can hope to do. The basic structure is the primary subject of justice because its effects are so profound and present from the start. The intuitive notion here is that this structure contains various social positions and that men born into different positions have different expectations of life determined, in part, by the political system as well as by economic and social circumstances. In this way the institutions of society favor certain starting places over others. These are especially deep inequalities. Not only are they pervasive, but they affect men's initial chances in life; yet they cannot possibly be justified by an appeal to the notions of merit or desert. It is these inequalities, presumably inevitable in the basic structure of any society, to which the principles of social justice must in the first instance apply. These principles, then, regulate the choice of a political constitution and the main elements of the economic and social system. The justice of a social scheme depends essentially on how fundamental rights and duties are assigned and on the economic opportunities and social conditions in the various sectors of society.

The scope of our inquiry is limited in two ways. First of all, I am concerned with a special case of the problem of justice. I shall not consider the justice of institutions and social practices generally, nor except in passing the justice of the law of nations and of relations between states (§57). Therefore, if one supposes that the concept of justice applies whenever there is an allotment of something rationally regarded as advantageous or disadvantageous, then we are interested in only one instance of its application. There is no reason to suppose ahead of time that the principles satisfactory for the basic structure hold for all cases. These principles may not work for the rules and practices of private associations or for those of less comprehensive social groups. They may be irrelevant for the various informal conventions and customs of everyday life; they may not elucidate the justice, or perhaps better, the fairness of voluntary cooperative arrangements or procedures for making contractual agreements. The conditions for the law of nations may require different principles arrived at in a somewhat different way. I shall be satisfied if it is possible to formulate a reasonable conception of justice for the basic structure of society conceived for the time being as a closed system isolated from other societies. The significance of this special case is obvious and needs no explanation. It is natural to conjecture that once we have a sound theory for this case, the remaining problems of justice will prove more tractable in the light of it. With suitable modifications such a theory should provide the key for some of these other questions.

The other limitation on our discussion is that for the most part I examine the principles of justice that would regulate a well-ordered society. Everyone is presumed to act justly and to do his part in upholding just institutions. Though justice may be, as Hume remarked, the cautious, jealous virtue, we can still ask what a perfectly just society would be like. Thus I consider primarily what I call strict compliance as opposed to partial compliance theory (§§25, 39). The latter studies the principles that govern how we are to deal with injustice. It comprises such topics as the theory of punishment, the doctrine of just war, and the justification of the various ways of opposing unjust regimes, ranging from civil disobedience and militant resistance to revolution and rebellion. Also included here are questions of compensatory justice and of weighing one form of institutional injustice against another. Obviously the problems of partial compliance theory are the pressing and urgent matters. These are the things that we are faced with in everyday life. The reason for beginning with ideal theory is that it provides, I believe, the only basis for the systematic grasp of these more pressing problems. The discussion of civil disobedience, for example, depends upon it (§§54–59). At least, I shall assume that a deeper understanding can be gained in no other way, and that the nature and aims of a perfectly just society is the fundamental part of the theory of justice.

Now admittedly the concept of the basic structure is somewhat vague. It is not always clear which institutions or features thereof should be included. But it would be premature to worry about this matter here. I shall proceed by discussing principles which do apply to what is certainly a part of the basic structure as intuitively understood; I shall then try to extend the application of these principles so that they cover what would appear to be the main elements of this structure. Perhaps these principles will turn out to be perfectly general, although this is unlikely. It is sufficient that they apply to the most important cases of social justice. The point to keep in mind is that a conception of justice for the basic structure is worth having for its own sake. It should not be dismissed because its principles are not everywhere satisfactory.

A conception of social justice, then, is to be regarded as providing in the first instance a standard whereby the distributive aspects of the basic structure of society are to be assessed. This standard, however, is not to be confused with the principles defining the other virtues, for the basic structure, and social arrangements generally, may be efficient or inefficient, liberal or illiberal, and many other things, as well as just or unjust. A complete conception defining principles for all the virtues of the basic structure, together with their respective weights when they conflict, is more than a conception of justice; it is a social ideal. The principles of justice are but a part, although perhaps the most important part, of such a conception. A social ideal in turn is connected with a conception of society, a vision of the way in which the aims and purposes of social cooperation are to be understood. The various conceptions of justice are the outgrowth of different notions of society against the background of opposing views of the natural necessities and opportunities of human life. Fully to understand a conception of justice we must make explicit the conception of social cooperation from which it derives. But in doing this we should not lose sight of the special role of the principles of justice or of the primary subject to which they apply.

In these preliminary remarks I have distinguished the concept of justice as meaning a proper balance between competing claims from a conception of justice as a set of related principles for identifying the relevant considerations which determine this balance. I have also characterized justice as but one part of a social ideal, although the theory I shall propose no doubt extends its everyday sense. This theory is not offered as a description of ordinary meanings but as an account of certain distributive principles for the basic structure of society. I assume that any reasonably complete ethical theory must include principles for this fundamental problem and that these principles, whatever they are, constitute its doctrine of justice. The concept of justice I take to be defined, then, by the role of its principles in assigning rights and duties and in defining the appropriate division of social advantages. A conception of justice is an interpretation of this role.

Now this approach may not seem to tally with tradition. I believe, though, that it does. The more specific sense that Aristotle gives to justice, and from which the most familiar formulations derive, is that of refraining from *pleonexia*, that is, from gaining some advantage for oneself by seizing what belongs to another, his property, his reward, his office, and the like, or by denying a person that which is due to him, the fulfillment of a promise, the repayment of a debt, the showing of proper respect, and so on. It is evident that this definition is framed to apply to actions, and persons are thought to be just insofar as they have, as one of the permanent elements of their character, a steady and effective desire to act justly. Aristotle's definition clearly presupposes, however, an account of what properly belongs to a person and of what is due to him. Now such entitlements are, I believe, very often derived from social institutions and the legitimate expectations to which they give rise. There is no reason to think that Aristotle would disagree with this, and certainly he has a conception of social justice to account for these claims. The definition I adopt is designed to apply directly to the most important case, the justice of the basic structure. There is no conflict with the traditional notion.

3 *The Main Idea of the Theory of Justice* My aim is to present a conception of justice which generalizes and carries to a higher level of abstraction the familiar theory of the social contract as found, say, in Locke, Rousseau, and Kant. In order to do this we are not to think of the original contract as one to enter a particular society or to set up a particular form of government. Rather, the guiding idea is that the principles of justice for the basic structure of society are the object of the original agreement. They are the principles that free and rational persons concerned to further their own interests would accept in an initial position of equality as defining the fundamental terms of their association. These principles are to regulate all further agreements; they specify the kinds of social cooperation that can be entered into and the forms of government that can be established. This way of regarding the principles of justice I shall call justice as fairness.

Thus we are to imagine that those who engage in social cooperation choose together, in one joint act, the principles which are to assign basic rights and duties and to determine the division of social benefits. Men are to decide in advance how they are to regulate their claims against one another and what is to be the foundation

charter of their society. Just as each person must decide by rational reflection what constitutes his good, that is, the system of ends which it is rational for him to pursue, so a group of persons must decide once and for all what is to count among them as just and unjust. The choice which rational men would make in this hypothetical situation of equal liberty, assuming for the present that this choice problem has a solution, determines the principles of justice.

In justice as fairness the original position of equality corresponds to the state of nature in the traditional theory of the social contract. This original position is not, of course, thought of as an actual historical state of affairs, much less as a primitive condition of culture. It is understood as a purely hypothetical situation characterized so as to lead to a certain conception of justice. Among the essential features of this situation is that no one knows his place in society, his class position or social status, nor does any one know his fortune in the distribution of natural assets and abilities, his intelligence, strength, and the like. I shall even assume that the parties do not know their conceptions of the good or their special psychological propensities. The principles of justice are chosen behind a veil of ignorance. This ensures that no one is advantaged or disadvantaged in the choice of principles by the outcome of natural chance or the contingency of social circumstances. Since all are similarly situated and no one is able to design principles to favor his particular condition, the principles of justice are the result of a fair agreement or bargain. For given the circumstances of the original position, the symmetry of everyone's relations to each other, this initial situation is fair between individuals as moral persons, that is, as rational beings with their own ends and capable, I shall assume, of a sense of justice. The original position is, one might say, the appropriate initial status quo, and thus the fundamental agreements reached in it are fair. This explains the propriety of the name "justice as fairness": it conveys the idea that the principles of justice are agreed to in an initial situation that is fair. The name does not mean that the concepts of justice and fairness are the same, any more than the phrase "poetry as metaphor" means that the concepts of poetry and metaphor are the same.

Justice as fairness begins, as I have said, with one of the most general of all choices which persons might make together, namely, with the choice of the first principles of a conception of justice which is to regulate all subsequent criticism and reform of institutions. Then, having chosen a conception of justice, we can suppose that they are to choose a constitution and a legislature to enact laws, and so on, all in accordance with the principles of justice initially agreed upon. Our social situation is just if it is such that by this sequence of hypothetical agreements we would have contracted into the general system of rules which defines it. Moreover, assuming that the original position does determine a set of principles (that is, that a particular conception of justice would be chosen), it will then be true that whenever social institutions satisfy these principles those engaged in them can say to one another that they are cooperating on terms to which they would agree if they were free and equal persons whose relations with respect to one another were fair. They could all view their arrangements as meeting the stipulations which they would acknowledge in an initial situation that embodies widely accepted and reasonable constraints on the choice of principles. The general recognition of this fact would provide the basis for a public acceptance of the corresponding principles of justice. No society can, of course, be a scheme of cooperation which men enter voluntarily in a literal sense; each person finds himself placed at birth in some particular position in some particular society, and the nature of this position materially affects his life prospects. Yet a society satisfying the principles of justice as fairness comes as close as a society can to being a voluntary scheme, for it meets the principles which free and equal persons would assent to under circumstances that are fair. In this sense its members are autonomous and the obligations they recognize self-imposed.

One feature of justice as fairness is to think of the parties in the initial situation as rational and mutually disinterested. This does not mean that the parties are egoists, that is, individuals with only certain kinds of interests, say in wealth, prestige, and domination. But they are conceived as not taking an interest in one another's interests. They are to presume that even their spiritual aims may be opposed, in the way that the aims of those of different religions may be opposed. Moreover, the concept of rationality must be interpreted as far as possible in the narrow sense, standard in economic theory, of taking the most effective means to given ends. I shall modify this concept to some extent, as explained later (§25), but one must try to avoid introducing into it any controversial ethical elements. The initial situation must be characterized by stipulations that are widely accepted.

In working out the conception of justice as fairness one main task clearly is to determine which principles of justice would be chosen in the original position. To do this we must describe this situation in some detail and formulate with care the problem of choice which it presents. These matters I shall take up in the immediately succeeding chapters. It may be observed, however, that once the principles of justice are thought of as arising from an original agreement in a situation of equality, it is an open question whether the principle of utility would be acknowledged. Offhand it hardly seems likely that persons who view themselves as equals, entitled to press their claims upon one another, would agree to a principle which may require lesser life prospects for some simply for the sake of a greater sum of advantages enjoyed by others. Since each desires to protect his interests, his capacity to advance his conception of the good, no one has a reason to acquiesce in an enduring loss for himself in order to bring about a greater net balance of satisfaction. In the absence of strong and lasting benevolent impulses, a rational man would not accept a basic structure merely because it maximized the algebraic sum of advantages irrespective of its permanent effects on his own basic rights and interests. Thus it seems that the principle of utility is incompatible with the conception of social cooperation among equals for mutual advantage. It appears to be inconsistent with the idea of reciprocity implicit in the notion of a well-ordered society. Or, at any rate, so I shall argue.

I shall maintain instead that the persons in the initial situation would choose two rather different principles: the first requires equality in the assignment of basic rights and duties, while the second holds that social and economic inequalities, for example inequalities of wealth and authority, are just only if they result in compensating benefits for everyone, and in particular for the least advantaged members of society. These principles rule out justifying institutions on the grounds that the hardships of some are offset by a greater good in the aggregate. It may be expedient but it is not just that some should have less in order that others may prosper. But there is no injustice in the greater benefits earned by a few provided that the situation of persons not so fortunate is thereby improved. The intuitive idea is that since everyone's well-being depends upon a scheme of cooperation without which no one could have a satisfactory life, the division of advantages should be such as to draw forth the willing cooperation of everyone taking part in it, including those less well situated. Yet this can be expected only if reasonable terms are proposed. The two principles mentioned seem to be a fair agreement on the basis of which those better endowed, or more fortunate in their social position, neither of which we can be said to deserve, could expect the willing cooperation of others when some workable scheme is a necessary condition of the welfare of all. Once we decide to look for a conception of justice that nullifies the accidents of natural endowment and the contingencies of social circumstance as counters in quest for political and economic advantage, we are led to these principles. They express the result of leaving aside those aspects of the social world that seem arbitrary from a moral point of view.

The problem of the choice of principles, however, is extremely difficult. I do not expect the answer I shall suggest to be convincing to everyone. It is, therefore, worth noting from the outset that justice as fairness, like other contract views, consists of two parts: (1) an interpretation of the initial situation and of the problem of choice posed there, and (2) a set of principles which, it is argued, would be agreed to. One may accept the first part of the theory (or some variant thereof), but not the other, and conversely. The concept of the initial contractual situation may seem reasonable although the particular principles proposed are rejected. To be sure, I want to maintain that the most appropriate conception of this situation does lead to principles of justice contrary to utilitarianism and perfectionism, and therefore that the contract doctrine provides an alternative to these views. Still, one may dispute this contention even though one grants that the contractarian method is a useful way of studying ethical theories and of setting forth their underlying assumptions.

Justice as fairness is an example of what I have called a contract theory. Now there may be an objection to the term "contract" and related expressions, but I think it will serve reasonably well. Many words have misleading connotations which at first are likely to confuse. The terms "utility" and "utilitarianism" are surely no exception. They too have unfortunate suggestions which hostile critics have been willing to exploit; yet they are clear enough for those prepared to study utilitarian doctrine. The same should be true of the term "contract" applied to moral theories. As I have mentioned, to understand it one has to keep in mind that it implies a certain level of abstraction. In particular, the content of the relevant agreement is not to enter a given society or to adopt a given form of government, but to accept certain moral principles. Moreover, the undertakings referred to are purely hypothetical: a contract view holds that certain principles would be accepted in a well-defined initial situation.

The merit of the contract terminology is that it conveys the idea that principles of justice may be conceived as principles that would be chosen by rational persons, and that in this way conceptions of justice may be explained and justified. The theory of justice is a part, perhaps the most significant part, of the theory of rational choice. Furthermore, principles of justice deal with conflicting claims upon the advantages won by social cooperation; they apply to the relations among several persons or groups. The word "contract" suggests this plurality as well as the condition that the appropriate division of advantages must be in accordance with principles acceptable to all parties. The condition of publicity for principles of justice is also connoted by the contract phraseology. Thus, if these principles are the outcome of an agreement, citizens have a knowledge of the principles that others follow. It is characteristic of contract theories to stress the public nature of political principles. Finally there is the long tradition of the contract doctrine. Expressing the tie with this line of thought helps to define ideas and accords with natural piety. There are then several advantages in the use of the term "contract." With due precautions taken, it should not be misleading.

A final remark. Justice as fairness is not a complete contract theory. For it is clear that the contractarian idea can be extended to the choice of more or less an entire ethical system, that is, to a system including principles for all the virtues and not only for justice. Now for the most part I shall consider only principles of justice and others closely related to them; I make no attempt to discuss the virtues in a systematic way. Obviously if justice as fairness succeeds reasonably well, a next step would be to study the more general view suggested by the name "rightness as fairness." But even this wider theory fails to embrace all moral relationships, since it would seem to include only our relations with other persons and to leave out of account how we are to conduct ourselves toward animals and the rest of nature. I do not contend that the contract notion offers a way to approach these questions which are certainly of the first importance; and I shall have to put them aside. We must recognize the limited scope of justice as fairness and of the general type of view that it exemplifies. How far its conclusions must be revised once these other matters are understood cannot be decided in advance.

4 The Original Position and Justification I have said that the original position is the appropriate initial status quo which insures that the fundamental agreements reached in it are fair. This fact yields the name "justice as fairness." It is clear, then, that I want to say that one conception of justice is more reasonable than another, or justifiable with respect to it, if rational persons in the initial situation would choose its principles over those of the other for the role of justice. Conceptions of justice are to be ranked by their acceptability to persons so circumstanced. Understood in this way the question of justification is settled by working out a problem of deliberation: we have to ascertain which principles it would be rational to adopt given the contractual situation. This connects the theory of justice with the theory of rational choice.

If this view of the problem of justification is to succeed, we must, of course, describe in some detail the nature of this choice problem. A problem of rational decision has a definite answer only if we know the beliefs and interests of the parties, their relations with respect to one another, the alternatives between which they are to choose, the procedure whereby they make up their minds, and so on. As the circumstances are presented in different ways, correspondingly different principles are accepted. The concept of the original position, as I shall refer to it, is that of the most philosophically favored interpretation of this initial

choice situation for the purposes of a theory of justice.

But how are we to decide what is the most favored interpretation? I assume, for one thing, that there is a broad measure of agreement that principles of justice should be chosen under certain conditions. To justify a particular description of the initial situation one shows that it incorporates these commonly shared presumptions. One argues from widely accepted but weak premises to more specific conclusions. Each of the presumptions should by itself be natural and plausible; some of them may seem innocuous or even trivial. The aim of the contract approach is to establish that taken together they impose significant bounds on acceptable principles of justice. The ideal outcome would be that these conditions determine a unique set of principles; but I shall be satisfied if they suffice to rank the main traditional conceptions of social justice.

One should not be misled, then, by the somewhat unusual conditions which characterize the original position. The idea here is simply to make vivid to ourselves the restrictions that it seems reasonable to impose on arguments for principles of justice, and therefore on these principles themselves. Thus it seems reasonable and generally acceptable that no one should be advantaged or disadvantaged by natural fortune or social circumstances in the choice of principles. It also seems widely agreed that it should be impossible to tailor principles to the circumstances of one's own case. We should insure further that particular inclinations and aspirations, and persons' conceptions of their good do not affect the principles adopted. The aim is to rule out those principles that it would be rational to propose for acceptance, however little the chance of success, only if one knew certain things that are irrelevant from the standpoint of justice. For example, if a man knew that he was wealthy, he might find it rational to advance the principle that various taxes for welfare measures be counted unjust; if he knew that he was poor, he would most likely propose the contrary principle. To represent the desired restrictions one imagines a situation in which everyone is deprived of this sort of information. One excludes the knowledge of those contingencies which sets men at odds and allows them to be guided by their prejudices. In this manner the veil of ignorance is arrived at in a natural way. This concept should cause no difficulty if we keep in mind the constraints on arguments that it is meant to express. At any time we can enter the original position, so to speak, simply by following a certain procedure, namely, by arguing for principles of justice in accordance with these restrictions.

It seems reasonable to suppose that the parties in the original position are equal. That is, all have the same rights in the procedure for choosing principles; each can make proposals, submit reasons for their acceptance, and so on. Obviously the purpose of these conditions is to represent equality between human beings as moral persons, as creatures having a conception of their good and capable of a sense of justice. The basis of equality is taken to be similarity in these two respects. Systems of ends are not ranked in value; and each man is presumed to have the requisite ability to understand and to act upon whatever principles are adopted. Together with the veil of ignorance, these conditions define the principles of justice as those which rational persons concerned to advance their interests would consent to as equals when none are known to be advantaged or disadvantaged by social and natural contingencies.

There is, however, another side to justifying a particular description of the original position. This is to see if the principles which would be chosen match our considered convictions of justice or extend them in an acceptable way. We can note whether applying these principles would lead us to make the same judgments about the basic structure of society which we now make intuitively and in which we have the greatest confidence; or whether, in cases where our present judgments are in doubt and given with hesitation, these principles offer a resolution which we can affirm on reflection. There are questions which we feel sure must be answered in a certain way. For example, we are confident that religious intolerance and racial discrimination are unjust. We think that we have examined these things with care and have reached what we believe is an impartial judgment not likely to be distorted by an excessive attention to our own interests. These convictions are provisional fixed points which we presume any conception of justice must fit. But we have much less assurance as to what is the correct distribution of wealth and authority. Here we may be looking for a way to remove our doubts. We can check an interpretation of the initial situation, then, by the capacity of its principles to accommodate our firmest convictions and to provide guidance where guidance is needed.

In searching for the most favored description of this situation we work from both ends. We begin by describing it so that it represents generally shared and preferably weak conditions. We then see if these conditions are strong enough to yield a significant set of principles. If not, we look for further premises equally reasonable. But if so, and these principles match our considered convictions of justice, then so far well and good. But presumably there will be discrepancies. In this case we have a choice. We can either modify the account of the initial situation or we can revise our existing judgments, for even the judgments we take provisionally as fixed points are liable to revision. By going back and forth, sometimes altering the conditions of the contractual circumstances, at others withdrawing our judgments and conforming them to principle, I assume that eventually we shall find a description of the initial situation that both expresses reasonable conditions and yields principles which match our considered judgments duly pruned and adjusted. This state of affairs I refer to as reflective equilibrium. It is an equilibrium because at last our principles and judgments coincide; and it is reflective since we know to what principles our judgments conform and the premises of their derivation. At the moment everything is in order. But this equilibrium is not necessarily stable. It is liable to be upset by further examination of the conditions which should be imposed on the contractual situation and by particular cases which may lead us to revise our judgments. Yet for the time being we have done what we can to render coherent and to justify our convictions of social justice. We have reached a conception of the original position.

I shall not, of course, actually work through this process. Still, we may think of the interpretation of the original position that I shall present as the result of such a hypothetical course of reflection. It represents the attempt to accommodate within one scheme both reasonable philosophical conditions on principles as well as our considered judgments of justice. In arriving at the favored interpretation of the initial situation there is no point at which an appeal is made to self-evidence in the traditional sense either of general conceptions or particular convictions. I do not claim for the principles of justice proposed that they are necessary truths or derivable from such truths. A conception of justice cannot be deduced from self-evident premises or conditions on principles; instead, its justification is a matter of the mutual support of many considerations, of everything fitting together into one coherent view.

A final comment. We shall want to say that certain principles of justice are justified because they would be agreed to in an initial situation of equality. I have emphasized that this original position is purely hypothetical. It is natural to ask why, if this agreement is never actually entered into, we should take any interest in these principles, moral or otherwise. The answer is that the conditions embodied in the description of the original position are ones that we do in fact accept. Or if we do not, then perhaps we can be persuaded to do so by philosophical reflection. Each aspect of the contractual situation can be given supporting grounds. Thus what we shall do is to collect together into one conception a number of conditions on principles that we are ready upon due consideration to recognize as reasonable. These constraints express what we are prepared to regard as limits on fair terms of social cooperation. One way to look at the idea of the original position, therefore, is to see it as an expository device which sums up the meaning of these conditions and helps us to extract their consequences. On the other hand, this conception is also an intuitive notion that suggests its own elaboration, so that led on by it we are drawn to define more clearly the standpoint from which we can best interpret moral relationships. We need a conception that enables us to envision our objective from afar: the intuitive notion of the original position is to do this for us. [. . .]

Date Due
